W9-AEB-925

Dictionary of New Testament Background

Editors:

Craig A. Evans

Stanley E. Porter

Project Manager:

Ginny Evans

InterVarsity Press
Downers Grove, Illinois
Leicester, England

InterVarsity Press, USA
P.O. Box 1400, Downers Grove, IL 60515-1426, USA
World Wide Web: www.ivpress.com
E-mail: mail@ivpress.com

Inter-VarsityPress,England
38 De Montfort Street, Leicester LE1 7GP, England

©2000 by InterVarsity Christian Fellowship/USA®

All rights reserved. No part of this publication may be reproduced, stored in a retrieval system or transmitted in any form or by any means, electronic, mechanical, photocopying, recording or otherwise, without the prior permission of InterVarsity Press.

InterVarsity Press®, U.S.A., is the book-publishing division of InterVarsity Christian Fellowship/USA®, a student movement active on campus at hundreds of universities, colleges and schools of nursing in the United States of America, and a member movement of the International Fellowship of Evangelical Students. For information about local and regional activities, write Public Relations Dept., InterVarsity Christian Fellowship/USA, 6400 Schroeder Rd., P.O. Box 7895, Madison, WI 53707-7895.

Inter-Varsity Press, England, is the book-publishing division of the Universities and Colleges Christian Fellowship (formerly the Inter-Varsity Fellowship), a student movement linking Christian Unions in universities and colleges throughout the United Kingdom and the Republic of Ireland, and a member movement of the International Fellowship of Evangelical Students. For information about local and national activities write to UCCF, 38 De Montfort Street, Leicester LE1 7GP.

All Scripture quotations, unless otherwise indicated, are the authors' own tranlations. Those identified NIV are taken from the Holy Bible, New International Version®. NIV®. *Copyright © 1973, 1978, 1984 by International Bible Society. Used by permission of Zondervan Publishing House. Distributed in the U.K. by permission of Hodder and Stoughton Ltd. "NIV" is a registered trademark of International Bible society. UK trademark number 1448790. Those identified RSV are from the* Revised Standard Version of the Bible, *copyright 1946, 1952, 1971 by the Division of Christian Education of the National Council of the Churches of Christ in the U.S.A., and used by permission. Those identified NRSV are from the* New Revised Standard Version of the Bible, *copyright 1989 by the Division of Christian Education of the National Council of the Churches of Christ in the U.S.A., and used by permission.*

Cover illustration: Erich Lessing/Art Resource, NY

USA ISBN 0-8308-1780-8

UK ISBN 0-85111-980-8

Printed in the United States of America ∞

Library of Congress Cataloging-in-Publication Data

Dictionary of New Testament background : a compendium of contemporary biblical scholarship / editors, Craig A. Evans & Stanley E. Porter.
p. cm.
Includes bibliographical references.
ISBN 0-8308-1780-8 (hardcover : alk. paper)
1. Bible. N.T.—Dictionaries. I. Evans, Craig A. II. Porter, Stanley E., 1956-

BS2312 .D53 2000
225.9'5'03—dc21

00-057544

British Library Cataloguing in Publication Data

A catalogue record for this book is available from the British Library.

26 25 24 23 22 21 29 19 18 17 16 15 14 13 12 11 10 9 8 7 6 5 4 3 2 1
22 21 20 19 18 17 16 15 14 13 12 11 10 09 08 07 06 05 04 03 02 01 00

InterVarsity Press

Project Staff

Reference Book Editor/Project Editor
Daniel G. Reid

Assistant Editors
Drew Blankman
David Zimmerman

Copyeditor
Linda Triemstra

Design
Kathy Burrows

Design Assistant
Mark Smith

Typesetters
Gail Munroe
Marjorie Sire
Audrey Smith

Proofreaders
Bob Buller
Allison Rieck

Editorial Intern
Angela Chang

Technical Support
Tricia Koning
Andy Shermer

InterVarsity Press

Publisher

Robert Fryling

Editorial Director

Andrew T. Le Peau

Associate Editorial Director

James Hoover

Production Manager

Anne Gerth

Contents

Preface _____ *ix*

How to Use This Dictionary _____ *xi*

Abbreviations _____ *xii*

Transliterations _____ *xxx*

List of Contributors _____ *xxxi*

Dictionary Articles _____ *1*

Scripture Index _____ *1304*

Subject Index _____ *1316*

Articles Index _____ *1324*

Preface

The first three dictionaries in this series are dedicated to the principal components of the New Testament: Jesus and the Gospels, Paul and his letters, and the later New Testament writings. These volumes survey well the contents and theological contributions of the New Testament and its principal figures, along with the various critical methods that have been developed to assist interpreters in their work. The present volume hopes to supplement these earlier works in strategic ways.

This, the fourth reference volume, takes a completely different approach. It attempts to situate the New Testament and early Christianity in its literary, historical, social and religious context. This volume is concerned with archaeology, geography, numismatics, related writings, various historical figures, political institutions, historical events, peoples and culture. It is not tied to specific writings of the New Testament, as is the case with the three previous dictionaries.

There are several related books that could be mentioned. C. K. Barrett's *The New Testament Background* (rev. ed., 1987) provides a key selection of primary texts, along with helpful annotations. C. A. Evans's *Noncanonical Writings and New Testament Interpretation* (1992) offers thumbnail descriptions of much primary literature that has bearing on the writings of the New Testament. S. E. Porter's edited volume, *Handbook to Exegesis of the New Testament* (1997), contains a variety of lengthier essays on select background-related topics as they bear on exegesis. Other works take a commentary approach. S. T. Lachs's *A Rabbinic Commentary on the New Testament* (1987) provides useful commentary, but is limited to the Synoptic Gospels and is focused primarily on rabbinic parallels. The *Hellenistic Commentary to the New Testament*, edited by M. E. Boring, K. Berger, and C. Colpe (1995), covers the whole New Testament but only offers parallels from the world of Hellenism (though broadly defined). B. J. Malina's and R. L. Rohrbaugh's *Social-Science Commentary on the Synoptic Gospels* (1992) takes a thematic approach, bringing social, economic and cultural issues to bear, but it is limited to the Synoptic Gospels and discussion is brief. The most comprehensive of these works is C. S. Keener's *The IVP Bible Background Commentary* on the New Testament (1993), which brings relevant data to bear on all of the New Testament writings, passage by passage. However, its treatment—though based on the primary literature—is aimed at a popular audience and so does not include references to the ancient sources.

In contrast to these related and important studies, the present volume limits itself to some 300 topics judged to be relevant to our understanding of the world, or "background," of the New Testament. It may be admitted that *background* is not necessarily the best word. Some will argue that *context, setting, world* or some other word would have been better. Perhaps. But "background" will be widely and immediately understood and will have to do, for the other alternatives pose difficulties of their own. The purpose of the present volume is to clarify the world of thought and experience in the light of which the New Testament should be read and the early Christian church understood.

Readers will find discussion of most of the Dead Sea Scrolls, the Greek papyri and various inscriptions, the writings that make up the Apocrypha and pseudepigrapha, and the biblical languages. Recent archaeological finds are presented, including regional overviews. Important figures are featured—such as Caiaphas, Hillel, Shammai, Simon ben Kosibah and the Roman governors of Palestine—as well as exotic ones, such as Apollonius of Tyana, Jesus ben Ananias or Jewish holy men. Articles focus on major Jewish, Greek and Roman institutions, important cities in Israel and the Roman Empire, as well as on cults, commerce, geographical perspectives and much more. Some two hundred scholars who possess expertise in the various topics treated have contributed to this volume. Many of the contributors are well-known veterans, while others have completed their doctorates in recent years in technical fields that are breaking forth in new avenues of discovery.

The length of the respective articles has been determined on the basis of their relevance to New Testament research or the complexity and vastness of the subject. Several articles are only 500 words; most of the others range from 1,000 to 7,500 words, with some exceeding 10,000 words. All include bibliography, guiding readers to additional literature that treats aspects of the topic in greater depth. Each article attempts to bring the reader up to date, to trace briefly the scholarly discussion and then present the very latest research. Some articles discuss texts that were not available only a few years ago. In some cases, such as archaeology, the material that is discussed has come to light only in the year or so prior to publication. The editors and publisher hope that this collective labor will benefit significantly those who wish to interpret the writings of the New Testament and the early church in full context and as accurately and completely as possible.

The editors wish to express their appreciation to the many scholars who contributed articles—in some cases several articles—to this dictionary. Some contributors came to the rescue on short notice, and for this the editors are very grateful. Reference book editor Daniel G. Reid is to be thanked for guiding the work from beginning to end and for taking an enthusiastic interest in it. A debt of gratitude is also owed to the editorial and production staff of InterVarsity Press for their careful and timely labor. Finally, the editors wish to thank Ginny Evans, who served as project manager, handling the many hundreds of letters, phone calls, e-mail notes and countless other details that such a major and complicated work as this entails. Without her consistent and faithful labor, the project would not have reached completion.

Craig A. Evans
Stanley E. Porter

How to Use This Dictionary

Abbreviations

Comprehensive tables of abbreviations for general matters as well as for scholarly, biblical and ancient literature may be found on pages xii-xxix.

Authorship of Articles

The authors of articles are indicated by their first initials and last name at the end of each article. In cases of articles that are composite in authorship, where possible the contribution of each author are found in brackets at the end of each section of an author's contribution. A full list of contributors may be found on pages xxxi-xxxiv, in alphabetical order of their last name. The contribution of each author is listed alphabetically following their identification.

Bibliographies

A bibliography will be found at the end of each article. The bibliographies include works cited in the articles and other significant related works. Bibliographical entries are listed in alphabetical order by the author's name, and where an author has more than one work cited, they are listed alphabetically by title. In some types of articles, the bibliographies are divided into labeled categories (e.g., "Texts and Editions" and "Studies").

Cross-References

This *Dictionary* has been extensively cross-referenced in order to aid readers in making the most of material appearing throughout the volume. Five types of cross-referencing will be found:

1. One-line entries appearing in alphabetical order throughout the *Dictionary* direct readers to articles where a topic is discussed:

AMULETS. *See* DEMONOLOGY.

2. An asterisk before a single word in the body of an article indicates that an article by that title appears in the *Dictionary*. For example "*Philo" directs the reader to an article entitled **PHILO**.
3. A cross-reference appearing within parentheses in the body of an article directs the reader to an article by that title. For example, (*see* Scholarship, Greek and Roman) directs the reader to an article by that title.
4. Cross-references have been appended to the end of articles, immediately preceding the bibliography, to direct readers to articles significantly related to the subject:

See also ALEXANDRIAN LIBRARY; ALEXANDRIAN SCHOLARSHIP; HELLENISTIC EGYPT.

5. Where appropriate, references are made to articles in the companion volumes, the *Dictionary of Jesus and the Gospels (DJG)*, the *Dictionary of Paul and His Letters (DPL)* and the *Dictionary of the Later New Testament and Its Developments (DLNTD)*. These references are found within the body of the text of articles. For example, a reference such as (*see DJG*, Gentiles) refers to the article on "Gentiles" in the *Dictionary of Jesus and the Gospels*, and a reference such as (see *DLNTD*, Apocalyptic, Apocalypticism §1) refers to a specific section within the article on "Apocalyptic, Apocalypticism" in the *Dictionary of the Later New Testament and Its Developments*.

Indexes

Since most of the *Dictionary* articles cover broad topics in some depth, the *Subject Index* is intended to assist readers in finding relevant information on narrower topics that might, for instance, appear in a standard Bible dictionary. For example, while there is no article entitled "Afterlife," the subject index might direct the reader to pages where the afterlife is discussed in the articles on "Eschatologies of Late Antiquity," "Resurrection" or elsewhere.

A *Scripture Index* is provided to assist readers in gaining quick access to Scripture texts referred to throughout the *Dictionary*.

An *Articles Index* found at the end of the *Dictionary* allows readers quickly to review the breadth of topics covered and select the ones most apt to serve their interests or needs. For those who wish to identify the articles written by specific contributors, they are listed with the name of the contributors in the list of contributors. A *Classified Index of Articles* groups articles according to broad topical fields, such as Languages or Dead Sea Scrolls, is available on the IVP website: www.ivpress.com.

Transliteration

Hebrew, Aramaic and Greek words have been transliterated according to a system set out on page xxx. Greek verbs generally appear in their lexical form (rather than infinitive) in order to assist those with little or no knowledge of the language in using other reference works.

Abbreviations

General Abbreviations

2d ed.	second edition
3d ed.	third edition
A	Codex Alexandrinus
B	Codex Vaticanus
C	Codex Ephraemi Syri
c.	circa, about (with dates); column
cent.	century
cf.	*confer*, compare
chap(s).	chapter(s)
D	Codex Bezae
DSS	Dead Sea Scrolls
e.g.	*exempli gratia*, for example
ed.	edition; editor(s), edited by
esp.	especially
ET	English translation
EVV	English versions of the Bible
exp.	expanded (edition)
fl.	*floruit*, flourished
frag.	fragment (of document)
Gk	Greek
Heb	Hebrew
i.e.	*id est*, that is
km.	kilometer
lit.	literally
LXX	Septuagint (Greek translation of the Old Testament)
mg.	margin
MS or MSS	manuscript or manuscripts
MT	Masoretic Text (standard Hebrew text of the Old Testament)
n.d.	no date
n.s.	new series
NT	New Testament
Olim	formerly
o.s.	old series
OT	Old Testament
p. or pp.	page or pages
pace	with due respect to, but differing from
par.	parallel passage in another/other Gospel(s)
passim	throughout, frequently
pl.	plural
repr.	reprint
rev.	revised (edition)
Sy	Syriac
Tg.	Targum
v. or vv.	verse or verses
v.l.	*vario lectio* ("variant reading")
VL	Vetus Latina
vol.	volume
x	times (2x = two times, etc.)
§ or §§	section or paragraph number(s) (usually indicating Loeb Classical Library numbering system for Josephus)
א	Codex Sinaiticus

Translations of the Bible

AV	Authorized Version (or KJV)
JB	Jerusalem Bible
KJV	King James Version (or AV)
NASB	New American Standard Bible
NEB	New English Bible
NIV	New International Version
NRSV	New Revised Standard Version

Books of the Bible

Old Testament	1-2 Kings	Is	Mic	Mk	1-2 Thess
Gen	1-2 Chron	Jer	Nahum	Lk	1-2 Tim
Ex	Ezra	Lam	Hab	Jn	Tit
Lev	Neh	Ezek	Zeph	Acts	Philem
Num	Esther	Dan	Hag	Rom	Heb
Deut	Job	Hos	Zech	1-2 Cor	Jas
Josh	Ps	Joel	Mal	Gal	1-2 Pet
Judg	Prov	Amos		Eph	1-2-3 Jn
Ruth	Eccles	Obad	*New Testament*	Phil	Jude
1-2 Sam	Song	Jon	Mt	Col	Rev

The Apocrypha and Septuagint

1-2-3-4 Kgdms	1-2-3-4 Kingdoms	Jdt	Judith	Sir	Sirach (or Ecclesiasticus)
Add Esth	Additions to Esther	Ep Jer	Epistle of Jeremiah	Sus	Susanna
Bar	Baruch	1-2-3-4 Macc	1-2-3-4 Maccabees	Tob	Tobit
Bel	Bel and the Dragon	Pr Azar	Prayer of Azariah	Wis	Wisdom of Solomon
1-2 Esdr	1-2 Esdras	Pr Man	Prayer of Manasseh		

The Old Testament Pseudepigrapha

Adam and Eve	*Life of Adam and Eve*
Ahiq.	*Ahiqar*
Apoc. Abr.	*Apocalypse of Abraham*
2 Bar.	2 Baruch (Syriac Apocalypse)
3 Bar.	*3 Baruch (Greek Apocalypse)*
4 Bar.	*4 Baruch (Paraleipomena Jeremiou)*
Apoc. Mos.	*Apocalypse of Moses*
Apoc. Elijah	*Apocalypse of Elijah*
Apoc. Zeph.	*Apocalypse of Zephaniah*
As. Mos.	*Assumption of Moses* (or *Testament of Moses*)
Bib. Ant.	*Biblical Antiquities* of Pseudo-Philo
1-2-3 Enoch	Ethiopic, Slavonic, Hebrew *Enoch*
Ep. Arist.	*Epistle of Aristeas*
Exag.	*Exagoge* of Ezekiel the Tragedian
4 Ezra	4 Ezra
Jos. and As.	*Joseph and Asenath*
Jub.	*Jubilees*
Liv. Proph.	*Lives of the Prophets*
Mart. Isa.	*Martyrdom of Isaiah*
Pss. Sol.	*Psalms of Solomon*
Pseud.-Phoc.	*Pseudo-Phocylides*
Sent. Syr. Men	*Sentences of the Syriac Menander*
Sib. Or.	*Sibylline Oracles*
Syr. Men. Epit.	*Syriac Menander Epitome*
Testaments of the Twelve Patriarchs	
T. Reub.	*Testament of Reuben*
T. Sim.	*Testament of Simeon*
T. Levi	*Testament of Levi*
T. Jud.	*Testament of Judah*
T. Iss.	*Testament of Issachar*
T. Zeb.	*Testament of Zebulon*
T. Dan.	*Testament of Dan*
T. Naph.	*Testament of Naphthali*
T. Gad.	*Testament of Gad*
T. Asher	*Testament of Asher*
T. Jos.	*Testament of Joseph*
T. Benj	*Testament of Benjamin*
T. Abr	*Testament of Abraham*
T. Job	*Testament of Job*
T. Mos.	*Testament of Moses* (or *Assumption of Moses*)
T. Sol.	*Testament of Solomon*
Tr. Shem.	*Treatise of Shem*

Early Christian Literature

Acts, Apocryphal	
Acts Apoll.	*Acts of Apollonius*
Acts Jn.	*Acts of John*
Acts Pil.	*Acts of Pilate*
Acts Paul & Thec.	*Acts of Paul and Thecla*
Acts Thom.	*Acts of Thomas*
Ambrose	
Abr.	*De Abrahamo*
Ep.	*Epistula*
Exp. Ev. Luc.	*Expositio Evangelii Secundum Lucam*
Off.	*De Officiis Ministrorum*
Ps.	*In Psalmos*
Virg.	*De Virginibus*
Amphilochius of Iconium	
Iamb. ad Sel.	*Iambi ad Seleucum*
Ap. Jas.	*Apocryphon of James*
Aphrahat (or Aphraates)	
Dem.	*Demonstrations*
Apocalypses, Apocryphal	
Apoc. Paul	*Apocalypse of Paul*
Apoc. Peter	*Apocalypse of Peter*
Apoc. Sedr.	*Apocalypse of Sedrach*
Aristides	
Apol.	*Apologia*
Asc. Isa.	*Ascension of Isaiah*
Athanasius	
Ar.	*Adversus Arianos*
Ep. Fest.	*Epistulae Festales*
Fug.	*Apologia pro Fuga Sua*
Athenagoras	
Leg.	*Legatio pro Christianis/at Graecos*
Res.	*De Resurrectione*
Augustine	
Civ. D.	*De Civitate Dei*
Conf.	*Confessiones*
De Cons.	*De Consensu Evangelistarum*
Doctr. Christ.	*De Doctrina Christiana*
Ep.	*Epistulae*
Haer.	*De Haeresibus*
Hom.	*Homilia*
Quaest. Evan.	*Quaestiones Evangeliorum*
Serm.	*Sermones*
Trin.	*De Trinitate*
Barn.	*Barnabas*

BG	Berlin Gnostic Codex
CG	Nag Hammadi Gnostic Codices
Chrysostom	
Adv. Jud.	*Adversus Judaeos*
Gen Hom.	*In Genesin Homiliae*
Hom. Act.	*Homiliae in Acta Apostolorum*
Hom. Mt.	*Homiliae in Matthaeum*
Pan. Ign.	*Panegyrics of Saint Ignatius*
Regno	*De Regno*
Clement of Alexandria	
Ecl. Proph.	*Eclogae Propheticae*
Excerpta	*Excerpta ex Theodoto* (*Letter to Theodore*)
Frag. Adum.	*Fragmente in Adumbrationes*
Paed.	*Paedagogus*
Protr.	*Protreptikos*
Quis Div.	*Quis Dives Salvetur*
Strom.	*Stromateis*
Theod.	*Letter to Theodore*
Clement of Rome	
1 Clem.	*1 Clement*
2 Clem.	*2 Clement*
Cyprian	
Dom. Or.	*De Dominica Oratione*
Ep.	*Epistulae*
Laps.	*De Lapsis*
Cyril of Jerusalem	
Cat.	*Catechesis*
Did.	*Didache*
Diogn.	*Epistle to Diognetus*
Apos Ep.	*Epistola Apostolorum*
Epiphanius	
Anac.	*Anacephalaiosis*
Haer.	*Haereses* (or *Panarion*)
Men. Pond.	*De Mensuris et Ponderibus*
Pan.	*Panarion* (also referred to as *Haereses*)
Eusebius	
Chron.	*Chronicon*
Eccl. Theol.	*De Ecclesiastica Theologia*
Hist. Eccl.	*Historia Ecclesiastica*
Dem. Ev.	*Demonstratio Evangelica*
In Ps	*Commentary on the Psalms*
Praep. Ev.	*Praeparatio Evangelica*
Gelasius	
Hist. Eccl.	*Historia Ecclesastica*
Gospels, Apocryphal	
Gos. Bar.	*Gospel of Bartholomew*
Gos. Eb.	*Gospel of the Ebionites*
Gos. Eg.	*Gospel of the Egyptians*
Gos. Heb.	*Gospel of the Hebrews*
Gos. Naass.	*Gospel of the Naassenes*
Gos. Phil.	*Gospel of Philip*
Gos. Pet.	*Gospel of Peter*
Gos. Thom.	*Gospel of Thomas*
Gregory of Nazianzus	
Carm.	*Carmina*
Or.	*Oratio*
Hilary of Poitiers	
Trin.	*De trinitate*
Hippolytus	
Apos. Trad.	*Apostolic Tradition*
Comm. Dan.	*Commentarium in Danielem*
Dem. Chr.	*Demonstratio de Christo et Antichristo*
Haer.	*De Haeresibus*
Refut.	*Refutation of All Heresies*
Ignatius	
Ign. *Eph.*	*Letter to the Ephesians*
Ign. *Magn.*	*Letter to the Magnesians*
Ign. *Phld.*	*Letter to the Philadelphians*
Ign. *Pol.*	*Letter to Polycarp*
Ign. *Rom.*	*Letter to the Romans*
Ign. *Smyrn.*	*Letter to the Smyrneans*
Ign. *Trall.*	*Letter to the Trallians*
Irenaeus	
Haer.	*Adversus Haereses*
Jerome	
Ep.	*Epistulae*
Comm. Ezek.	*Commentariorum in Ezechielem*
Comm. Isa.	*Commentariorum in Isaiam*
In Philem.	*Commentariorum in Epistulam ad Philemonem liber*
Vir.	*De Viris Illustribus*
Ruf.	*Adversus Rufinum*
Justin Martyr	
Apol. I,II	*Apology I,II*
Cohor. Graec.	*Cohortatio ad Graecos*
Dial. Tryph.	*Dialogus cum Tryphone Judaeo*
Resurrec.	*On the Resurrection*
Lactantius	
Div. Inst.	*Divinae Institutiones*
Let. Chur. Lyons Vien.	*Letter of the Churches of Lyons and Vienne*
Mart. Justin	*The Martyrdom of Justin and Companions*
Mart. Pol.	*Martyrdom of Polycarp*
Mur. Frag.	*Muratorian Fragment*
Odes Sol.	*Odes of Solomon*
Origen	
Comm. Joh.	*In Johannem Commentarius*
Comm. Mt.	*In Matthaeum Commentarius*
Cont. Cels.	*Contra Celsum*
De Princ.	*De Principiis* (*Peri Archo4n*)
Exhort. Mart.	*Exhortatio ad Martyrium*
Hom. Luc.	*Homiliae in Lucam*
Pass. Perp. Fel.	*Passion of Perpetua and Felicitas*
Peri Arch.	*Peri Archōn*
Selec. Ps.	*Selecta in Psalmos*
PG	*Patrologia Graeca*, ed. J. P. Migne
Philostorgius	
Hist. Eccl.	*Historia Ecclesiastica*
Photius	
Bibl.	*Bibliotheca*
Polycarp	
Pol. *Phil.*	*Letter to the Philippians*
Protev. Jas.	*Protevangelium of James*
Pseudo-Clementines	
Hom.	*Homilies*

Recogn.	*Recognitions*
Rufinus	
Hist. Eccl.	*Historia Ecclesiastica*
Shepherd of Hermas	
Herm. Man.	*Hermas, Mandate(s)*
Herm. Sim.	*Hermas, Similitude(s)*
Herm. Vis.	*Hermas, Vision(s)*
Socrates Scholasticus	
Hist. Eccl.	*Historia Ecclesiastica*
Sozomen	
Hist. Eccl.	*Historia Ecclesiastica*
Tatian	
Or. Graec.	*Oratio ad Graecos*
Tertullian	
Ad Mart.	*Ad Martyras*
Ad Nat.	*Ad Nationes*
Ad Ux.	*Ad Uxorem*
Adv. Jud.	*Adversus Judaeos*
Adv. Valent.	*Adversus Valentinianos*
Apol.	*Apologeticus*
De An.	*De Anima*
De Bapt.	*De Baptismo*
De Carn.	*De Carne Christi*
De Cor.	*De Corona*
De Cult. Fem.	*De Cultu Feminarum*
De Idol.	*De Idololatria*
De Jejun.	*De Jejunio Adversus Psychicos*
De Orat.	*De Oratione*
De Pat.	*De Patientia*
De Praescr.	*De Praescriptione Haereticorum*
De Pud.	*De Pudicitia*
De Resur.	*De Resurrectione Carnis*
De Spect.	*De Spectaculis*
Marc.	*Adversus Marcionem*
Pud.	*De Pudicitia*
Prax.	*Adversus Praxeas*
Scorp.	*Scorpiace*
Test.	*De Testimonio Animae*
Theophilus of Antioch	
Autol.	*Ad Autolycum*
Victorinus	
Comm. in Apoc.	*Commentary on the Apocalypse*

Classical and Hellenistic Writers and Sources

Achilles Tatius	
Leuc.	*Leucippe and Cleitophon*
Aelian	
De Nat. Anim.	*De Natura Animalum*
V.H.	*Varia Historia*
Aeschylus	
Ag.	*Agamemnon*
Ch.	*Choephoroe*
Pers.	*Persae*
Prom.	*Prometheus Vinctus*
Sept. c. Theb.	*Septem contra Thebas*
Suppl.	*Supplices*
Alexander of Aphrodisias	
Fat.	*De Fato*
Ammonius	
Adfin. Vocab.	*Diff. De Adfinium Vocabulorum Differentia*
Anacharsis	
Ep.	*Epistle to Tereus*
Anacr.	*Anacreontea*
Anth. Gr.	*Greek Anthology*
Antipater	
Anth. Pal.	*Anthologia Palatina*
Appian	
Civ. W.	*Civil Wars*
Mith. W.	*Mithridatic Wars*
Pun.	*Libukē*
Rom. Hist.	*Roman History*
Apollodorus	
Bib.	*Bibliotheca*
Apollonius of Rhodes	
Arg.	*Argonautica*
Apollonius of Tyana	
Ep.	*Epistle*
Apuleius	
Met.	*Metamorphoses*
Aratus	
Phaen.	*Phaenomena*
Aristides	
Or.	*Orationes*
Aristophanes	
Acharn.	*Acharnenses*
Av.	*Aves*
Eq.	*Equites*
Lysis.	*Lysistrata*
Nub.	*Nubes*
Pax	*Pax*
Plut.	*Plutus*
Thes.	*Thesmophorizousai*
Aristotle	
Cael.	*De Caelo*
Eth. Eud.	*Ethica Eudemia*
Eth. Nic.	*Ethica Nicomachea*
Int.	*De Interpretatione*
Poet.	*Poetica*
Pol.	*Politica*
Prob.	*Problemata*
Rhet.	*Rhetorica*
Soph. Elench.	*Sophistici Elenchi*
Arrian	
Alex.	*Alexandri Anabasis* (= *Anab.*)
Anab.	*Anabasis*
Epict. Diss.	*Epicteti dissertationes*
Ind.	*Indike*
Artemidorus	
Oneir.	*Oneirocriticon*
Athenaeus	
Deipn.	*Deipnophistae*
Augustus	
Res Gest.	*Res Gestae Divi Augusti*
Aulus Gellius	
Noc. Att.	*Noctes Atticae*

Caesar
- *B. Civ.* — *Bellum Civile*
- *B. Gall.* — *Bellum Gallicum*

Callimachus
- *Epigr.* — *Epigrammata*

Cato
- *Agr.* — *De Agricultura*
- *Orig.* — *Origines*

Chariton
- *Chaer.* — *De Chaerea et Callirhoe*

Cicero
- *Acad.* — *Academica Quaestiones*
- *Arch.* — *Pro Archia*
- *Att.* — *Epistulae ad Atticum*
- *Balb.* — *Pro Balbo*
- *Caec.* — *Pro Caecina*
- *De Amic.* — *De Amicitia*
- *De Div.* — *De Divinatione*
- *De Fin. Bon. et Mal.* — *De Finibus bonorum et malorum*
- *De Imp. Cn. Pomp.* — *De Imperio Cn. Pompeii*
- *De Inv.* — *De Inventione Rhetorica*
- *De Leg.* — *De Legibus*
- *De Offic.* — *De Officiis*
- *De Orat.* — *De Oratore*
- *De Rep.* — *De Republica*
- *Deiot.* — *Pro Rege Deiotaro*
- *Div. in Caecil.* — *Divinatio in Caecilium*
- *Fam.* — *Epistulae ad Familiares*
- *Flac.* — *Pro Flacco*
- *Nat. Deor.* — *De Natura Deorum*
- *Parad.* — *Paradoxa Stoicorum*
- *Phil.* — *Orationes Philippicae*
- *Q. Fr.* — *Epistulae ad Quintum Fratrem*
- *Quinct.* — *Pro Quinctio*
- *Rab. Perd.* — *Rabirio Perduellionis*
- *Rosc. Am.* — *Pro Sexto Roscio Amerino*
- *Somn.* — *Somnium Scipionis*
- *Tusc.* — *Tusculanae Disputationes*
- *Verr.* — *In Verrem*

Cod. Just. — *Codex Justinianus*

Cod. Theod. — *Codex Theodosianus*

Columella
- *Rust.* — *De Re Rustica*

Cornelius Nepos
- *Vir. Illus.* — *De Viris Illustribus*

Cornutus
- *Theol. Graec.* — *Epidomē tōn kata tēn Hellēnikēn Theologian paradedomenōn*

Corp. Herm. — *Corpus Hermeticum*

Crates
- *Ep.* — *Epistula*
- *Cyr.* — *Cyranides*

Demetrius
- *Eloc.* — *De Elocutione*

Demosthenes
- *Arist.* — *In Aristogitonem*
- *Aristoc.* — *In Aristocratem*
- *Conon* — *In Cononem*
- *De Cor.* — *De Corona*
- *Lacrit.* — *Contra Lacritum*
- *Lep.* — *Adversus Leptinem*
- *Meid.* — *Against Meidias*
- *Neaer.* — *In Neaeram*
- *Olymp.* — *In Olympiodorum*
- *Orat.* — *Orations*
- *Pant.* — *Contra Pantaenetum*
- *Tim.* — *Contra Timotheum*

Dig. Just. — *Digest of Justinian*

Dio Cassius
- *Epit.* — *Epitome*
- *Hist.* — *Roman History*

Dio Chrysostom
- *De Homero* — *De Homero et Socrate*
- *Disc.* — *Discourses*
- *Or.* — *Orationes*

Diodorus Siculus
- *Bib. Hist.* — *Bibliotheca Historica*

Diogenes
- *Ep.* — *Epistula*

Diogenes Laertius
- *Vit.* — *Vitae*

Dionysius of Halicarnassus
- *Ant. Or.* — *De Antiquis Oratoribus*
- *Ant. Rom.* — *Antiquitates Romanae*
- *Comp.* — *De Compositione Verborum*
- *Thuc.* — *De Thucydide*

Dioscorides
- *Mat. Med.* — *De Materia Medica*

Ennius, Quintus
- *Ann.* — *Annales*

Epictetus
- *Disc.* — *Discourses*
- *Diss.* — *Dissertationes*
- *Ench.* — *Enchiridion*

Euripides
- *Alc.* — *Alcestis*
- *Androm.* — *Andromache*
- *Bacch.* — *Bacchae*
- *Cycl.* — *Cyclops*
- *El.* — *Electra*
- *Hec.* — *Hecuba*
- *Heracl.* — *Heraclidae*
- *Hipp.* — *Hippolytus*
- *Iph. Aul.* — *Iphigenia Aulidensis*
- *Iph. Taur.* — *Iphigenia Taurica*
- *Med.* — *Medea*
- *Or.* — *Orestes*
- *Phoen.* — *Phoenissae*
- *Tro.* — *Troades*

Euxistheus
- *Ad Eub.* — *Ad Eubulides*

Firmicus Maternus
- *De Errore Prof. Rel.* — *De Errore Profanarum Religionum*

Gaius
- *Inst.* — *Institutiones*

Galen
- *Ant. Lib.* — *De Antidotis Libri*
- *De Placitis* — *De Placitis Hippocratis et Platonis*
- *Epid.* — *Epidemics*
- *Hypomn. Hippoc.* — *Hypomnema on Hippocrates*

Grk. Anth. — *Greek Anthology*

Heracleitus
- *Frag.* — *Fragment*

Herodian (Aelius Herodianus)
- *Schem. Hom.* — *Schematismi Homerici*

Herodian
- *Hist* — *History of the Empire after Marcus*

Herodotus
- *Hist.* — *Historiae*

Hesiod
- *Astron.* — *Fragmenta Astronomica*
- *Op.* — *Opera et Dies*
- *Cat.* — *Catalogus Mulierum*
- *Theog.* — *Theogonia*

Hippocrates
- *Nat. Hom.* — *De Natura Hominis*

Homer
- *Il.* — *Iliad*
- *Odys.* — *Odyssey*

Horace
- *Ars Poet.* — *Ars Poetica*
- *Carm.* — *Carmina, or Odes*
- *Ep.* — *Epistulae*
- *Odes* — *Odes, or Carmina*
- *Sat.* — *Satirae*

Iamblichus
- *De Myst.* — *De Mysteriis*

Isocrates
- *Ad Nic.* — *Ad Nicoclem*
- *Dem.* — *Ad Demonicum*
- *Or.* — *Orations*
- *Panath.* — *Panathenaicus*
- *Paneg.* — *Panegyricus*
- *Soph.* — *In Sophistas*

Josephus
- *Ant.* — *Antiquities of the Jews*
- *J.W.* — *Jewish Wars*
- *Vit.* — *Vita*
- *Ag. Ap.* — *Against Apion*

Julian
- *Or.* — *Orationes*

Justinian
- *Cod.* — *Codex*
- *Dig.* — *Digesta*, or *Pandectae*
- *Inst.* — *Institutiones*

Juvenal
- *Sat.* — *Satirae*

Lactantius
- *Div. Inst.* — *Divinarum Institutionum Libri*

Livy
- *Epit.* — *Epitome*
- *Hist.* — *History of Rome*
- *Per.* — *Periochae*

Longinus
- *Subl.* — *De Sublimitate*, or *Peri Hypsous*

Longus
- *Daphn. Chl.* — *Daphnis and Chloe*

Lucan
- *Civ. W.* — *Civil War* (or *Pharsalia*)

Lucian of Samosata
- *Alex.* — *Alexander the False Prophet*
- *Anach.* — *Anacharsis*
- *Bis Acc.* — *Bis Accusatus*
- *Cat.* — *Cataplus*
- *Demon.* — *Demonax*
- *Deor. Conc.* — *Deorum Concilium*
- *Dial. Deor.* — *Dialogi Deorum*
- *Dial. Meretr.* — *Dialogi Meretricii*
- *Dial. Mort.* — *Dialogi Mortuorum*
- *Gall.* — *Gallus*
- *Herm.* — *Hermotimus*
- *Herod.* — *Herodotus*
- *Hist. Conscr.* — *Quomodo Historia Conscribenda Sit*
- *Icar.* — *Icaromenippus*
- *Im.* — *Pro Imagines*
- *Ind.* — *Adversus Indoctum*
- *J. Conf.* — *Juppiter Confutatus*
- *J. Tr.* — *Juppiter Tragoedus*
- *Luct.* — *De Luctu*
- *Merc. Cond.* — *De Mercede Conductis*
- *Nav.* — *Navigium*
- *Nigr.* — *Nigrinus*
- *Par.* — *De Parasito*
- *Peregr.* — *De Morte Peregrini*
- *Phal.* — *Phalaris*
- *Phars.* — *Pharsalia*
- *Philops.* — *Philopseudes*
- *Sacr.* — *De Sacrificiis*
- *Salt.* — *De Saltatione*
- *Sat.* — *Saturnalia*
- *Scyth.* — *Scytha*
- *Symp.* — *Symposium*
- *Tim.* — *Timon*
- *Tox.* — *Toxaris*
- *Ver. Hist.* — *Verae Historia*

Lucretius
- *Nat.* — *De Rerum Natura*

Lydus
- *Mag.* — *De Magistratibus*

Marcus Aurelius
- *Med.* — *Meditations*

Martial
- *Epigr.* — *Epigrams*

Maximus of Tyre
- *Or.* — *Oratio*

Menander
- *Frag.* — *Fragments*

Minucius Felix
- *Oct.* — *Octavius*

Nicolaus of Damascus
- *Vit. Caes.* — *Vita Caesaris*

Orosius
- *Hist.* — *Historiarum Adversus Paganos Libri VII*

Orph. Frag. — *Orphic Fragments*

Ovid
- *Ars Am.* — *Ars Amatoria*
- *Met.* — *Metamorphoses*
- *Tr.* — *Tristia*

Parthenius
- *Amat. Nar.* — *Narrationum Amatoriarum Libellus*

Paulus — Iulius Paulus
Sent. — *Sententiae*
Pausanius
Descr. — *Graeciae Description*
Test. — *Testimonium*
Persius
Sat. — *Satirae*
Petronius
Sat. — *Satyricon*
Philo
Abr. — *De Abrahamo*
Aet. Mund. — *De Aeternitate Mundi*
Agric. — *De Agricultura*
Anim. — *De Animalibus*
Arith. — *De Arithmis*
Cher. — *De Cherubim*
Conf. Ling. — *De Confusione Linguarum*
Congr. — *De Congressu Eruditionis Gratia*
Decal. — *De Decalogo*
Det. Pot. Ins. — *Quod Deterius Potiori Insidiari Soleat*
Deus Imm. — *Quod Deus Sit Immutabilis*
Ebr. — *De Ebrietate*
Exsecr. — *De Exsecrationibus*
Flacc. — *In Flaccum*
Fug. — *De Fuga et Inventione*
Gig. — *De Gigantibus*
Hypoth. — *Hypothetica*
Jos. — *De Josepho*
Leg. All. — *Legum Allegoriae*
Leg. Gai. — *Legatio ad Gaium*
Migr. Abr. — *De Migratione Abrahami*
Mut. Nom. — *De Mutatione Nominum*
Omn. Prob. Lib. — *Quod Omnis Probus Liber Sit*
Op. Mund. — *De Opificio Mundi*
Plant. — *De Plantatione*
Poster. C. — *De Posteritate Caini*
Praem. Poen. — *De Praemiis et Poenis*
Prov. — *De Providentia*
Quaest. in Ex. — *Quaestiones in Exodum*
Quaest. in Gen. — *Quaestiones in Genesin*
Rer. Div. Her. — *Quis Rerum Divinarum Heres Sit.*
Sacr. — *De Sacrificiis Abelis et Caini*
Sobr. — *De Sobrietate*
Som. — *De Somnis*
Spec. Leg. — *De Specialibus Legibus*
Virt. — *De Virtibus*
Vit. Cont. — *De Vita Contemplativa*
Vit. Mos. — *De Vita Mosis*
Philostratus
Vit. Ap. — *Vita Apollonii*
Vit. Soph. — *Vitae Sophistarum*
Photius
Bibl. — *Bibliotheca*
Pindar
Isth. — *Isthmionikai*
Plato
Alc. — *Alcibiades*
Apol. — *Apologia*
Charm. — *Charmides*
Crat. — *Cratylus*
Cri. — *Crite*
Ethyd. — *Euthydemus*
Gorg. — *Gorgias*
Hipparch. — *Hipparchus*
Ion — *Ion*
Leg. — *Leges*
Parm. — *Parmenides*
Phaed. — *Phaedo*
Phaedr. — *Phaedrus*
Phileb. — *Philebus*
Protag. — *Protagoras*
Rep. — *Respublica*
Soph. — *Sophista*
Symp. — *Symposium*
Thaeat. — *Theaetetus*
Tim. — *Timaeus*
Plautus
Cas. — *Casina*
Cist. — *Cistellaria*
Mostell. — *Mostellaria*
Poen. — *Poenulus*
Pliny (the elder)
Nat. Hist. — *Naturalis Historia*
Pliny (the younger)
Ep. — *Epistolae*
Panegyr. — *Panegyricus*
Plutarch
Adulat. — *De Adulatore et Amico*
Aem. — *Aemilius Paulus (Vitae Parallelae)*
Ages. — *Agesilaus (Vitae Parallelae)*
Alex. — *De Alexandro (Vitae Parallelae)*
Anton. — *De Antonius (Vitae Parallelae)*
Bride — *Advice to Bride and Groom*
Caes. — *Caesar (Vitae Parallelae)*
Cam. — *Camillus (Vitae Parallelae)*
Cic. — *Cicero (Vitae Parallelae)*
Cleom. — *Cleomenes (Vitae Parallelae)*
Comp. Lyc. Num. — *Comparatio Lycurgi et Numae*
Comp. Thes. Rom. — *Comparatio Thesei et Romuli*
Conv. — *Quaestiones Conviviales*
Def. Orac. — *De Defectu Oraculorum*
Demetr. — *Demetrius (Vitae Parallelae)*
E Delph — *De E apud Delphos*
Fac. Lun. — *De Facie in Orbe Lunae*
Fort. Rom. — *De Fortuna Romanorum*
Gen. Socr. — *De Genio Socratis*
Is. Os. — *De Iside et Osiride*
Lib. Educ. — *De Liberis Educandis*
Luc. — *Lucullus (Vitae Parallelae)*
Lyc. — *Lycurgus*
Mor. — *Moralia*
Nic. — *Nicias (Vitae Parallelae)*
Non Posse Suav. — *Non Posse Suaviter Vivi Secundum Epicuram*
Pel. — *Pelopidas (Vitae Parallelae)*
Per. — *Pericles (Vitae Parallelae)*
Pomp. — *Pompeius (Vitae Parallelae)*
Quaest. Graec. — *Quaestiones Graecae*
Quaest. Rom. — *Quaestiones Romanae*
Reg. Imp. Apophth. — *Regum et Imperatorum Apophthegmata*

Rom.	*Romulus (Vitae Parallelae)*
Ser. Num. Pun.	*De Iis Qui Sero a Numine Puniuntur*
Stoic. Repugn.	*De Stoicorum Repugnantiis*
Thes.	*Theseus (Vitae Parallelae)*
Pollux	
Onom.	*Onomasticon*
Polybius	
Hist.	*Histories*
Proclus	
In Tim.	*In Platonis Timaeum Commentarius*
Propertius	
Eleg.	*Elegia*
Pseudo-Apollodorus	
Bib.	*Bibliotheca*
Pseudo-Cicero	
Rhet. Ad Herenn	*Rhetorica ad Herennium*
Pseudo-Demosthenes	
Neaer.	*In Neaeram*
Quintilian	
Inst. Orat.	*Institutio Oratoria*
Res. Gest.	*Res Gestae Divi Augusti*
Sallust	
Catil.	*Bellum Catilinae* or *De Catilinae coniuratione*
Iug.	*Bellum Iugurthinum*
Seneca (the Elder)	
Contr.	*Controversiae*
Suas.	*Suasoriae*
Seneca (the Younger)	
Apocol.	*Apocolocyntosis*
Ben.	*De Beneficiis*
Brev. Vit.	*De Brevitate Vitae*
Clem.	*De Clementia*
Const.	*De Constantia Sapientis*
Dial.	*Dialogi*
Ep.	*Epistulae*
Ep. Lucil.	*Epistles to Lucilius*
Ep. Mor.	*Epistulae Morales*
Ira	*De Ira*
Marc.	*Ad Marciam*
Nat. Quaest.	*Naturales Quaestiones*
Prov.	*De Providentia*
Vit. Beat.	*De Vita Beata*
Sextus Empiricus	
Pyr.	*Pyrrhoniae Hypotyposes*
SHA	*Scriptores Historiae Augustae*
Hadr.	*Hadrian*
Silius Italicus	
Pun.	*Punica*
Sophocles	
Antig.	*Antigone*
Elec.	*Electra*
Oed. Col.	*Oedipus Coloneus*
Oed. Tyr.	*Oedipus Tyrannus*
Trach.	*Trachiniae*
Stobaeus	
Anth.	*Anthologion*
Ecl.	*Ecloge*
Strabo	
Geog.	*Geographica*
Suda	*Suda/Suidas* (Greek Lexicon)
Suetonius	
Augustus	*(The Twelve Caesars)*
Caligula	*(The Twelve Caesars)*
Claudius	*(The Twelve Caesars)*
Domitian	*(The Twelve Caesars)*
Galba	*(The Twelve Caesars)*
Gram.	*De Grammaticis*
Julius	*(The Twelve Caesars)*
Nero	*(The Twelve Caesars)*
Rhet.	*De Rhetoribus*
Tiberius	*(The Twelve Caesars)*
Titus	*(The Twelve Caesars)*
Vespasian	*(The Twelve Caesars)*
Vit. Ter.	*Vita Terentius*
Tacitus	
Agric.	*Agricola*
Ann.	*Annales ab Excessu Divi Augusti*
Germ.	*Germania*
Hist.	*Historiae*
Terence	
And.	*Andria*
Haut.	*Hauton Timorumenos*
Theocritus	
Id.	*Idylls*
Theon	
Progymn.	*Progymnasmata*
Theophrastus	
Char.	*Characteres*
Thucydides	
Hist.	*History of the Peloponnesian War*
Valerius Maximus	
Fact. ac Dict.	*Factorum ac Dictorum Memorabilium Libri*
Varro	
Ling.	*De Lingua Latina*
Vegetius Renatus	
Epit. Rei Milit.	*Epitoma Rei Militaris*
Virgil	
Aen.	*Aeneid*
Ecl.	*Eclogues*
Geor.	*Georgics*
Vitruvius	
De Arch.	*De Architectura*
Xenophon	
Anab.	*Anabasis*
Cyn.	*Cynegeticus*
Cyr.	*Cyropaedia*
Eq. Mag.	*De Equitum Magistro*
Hell.	*Hellenica*
Hist. Gr.	*History of the Greeks (Hellenica)*
Laced.	*Respublica Lacedaemoniorum*
Mem.	*Memorabilia Socratis*
Oec.	*Oeconomicus*
Symp.	*Symposium*

Papyri

P.Amh.	*The Amherst Papyri,* B. P. Grenfell and A. S. Hunt (London, 1900-)
P.Ant.	*The Antinoopolis Papyri,* C. H. Roberts, J. W. B. Barns and H. Zilliacus (London, 1950 -)
P.Barc.	Barcelona Papyri, Fundación Sant Lucas Evangelista
P.Berol.	Papyrus Berolinensis
P.Bour.	*Les Papyrus Bouriant,* P. Collart (Paris, 1926)
P.Cair.	*Papyrus Cairensis*
P.Cair.Zen.	*Zenon Papyri,* ed. C. C. Edgar (4 vols.; Le Caire, 1925-31; Catalogue générale des antiquités égyptiennes du Musée du Caire).
P.Columb.	Columbia Papyri
P.Eg.	Egerton Papyrus, British Museum, London, England.
P.Eleph.	Elephantine Papyri
P.Fay.	*Fayum Towns and their Papyri,* B.P. Grenfell, A.S. Hunt and D.G. Hogarth (London 1900)
P.Fouad	*Les Papyrus Fouad,* A. Bataille et al. (Cairo, 1939)
P.Gen.	*Les Papyrus de Genève*
PGM	*Papyri-Graecae Magicae: Die griechischen Zauberpapyri,* G. Preisendanz et al (2 vols.; 1973-1974)
P.Hal.	*Dikaiomata: Auszuge aus alexandrinischen Gesetzen und Verordnungen in einem Papyrus des Philologischen Seminars der Universität Halle mit einem Anhang weiterer Papyri derselben Sammlung* (Berlin 1913)
P.Harr.	*The Rendel Harris Papri of Woodbrooke College, Birmingham,* J. E. Powell, (Cambridge, U. K., 1936); *Studia Amstelodamensia ad Epigraphicam, Ius Antiquum et Papyrologiam Pertinentia,* J. A. Ankum et al. (Zutphen, 1985)
P.Heid.Siegmann	*Literarische griechische Texte der Heidelberger Papyrussammlung,* ed. E. Siegmann (Heidelberg 1956)
P.Iand.	*Papyri Iandanae,* E. Schaefer et al. (Leipzig-Berlin, 1897-)
P.Köln	*Kölner Papyri,* B. Kramer, R. Hübner, et al. (Opladen, 1976-)
P.Lond.	*Catalogue of the Literary Papyri in the British Museum,* H. J. M. Milne (London, 1927-)
P.Mert.	*A Descriptive Catalogue of the Greek Papyri in the Collection of Wilfred Merton, F. S. A.,* H. I. Bell et al. (London, 1948-)
P.Mich.	Papyri in the collection of the General Library of the University of Michigan, Ann Arbor
P.Mur.	*Les grottes de Murabbaʾat,* P. Benoit, J. T. Milik and R. de Vaux (DJD 2; Oxford, 1961)
P.Oxy.	*The Oxyrhynchus Papyri,* B. P. Grenfell, A. S. Hunt, et al. (London, 1898-)
P.Par.	*Les Papyrus grecs du Musée du Louvre*
P.Rain.	Papyri in the "Papyrus Erzherzog Rainer" collection of the Nationalbibliothek, Vienna
P.Ryl.	*Catalogue of the Greek Papyri in the John Rylands Library at Manchester*
PSI	*Papiri Greci e Latini, Pubblicazioni della Società italiana per la ricerca dei papiri greci e latini in Egitto* (1912-)
P.Tebt.	*The Tebtunis Papyri* (1902-1976)
P.Vindob.	*Mittheilungen aus der Sammlung der Papyrus Erzh. Rainier* (1887)

Dead Sea Scrolls and Related Texts

CD	Cairo (Genizah text of the) *Damascus Document/Rule*
QD	*Damascus Document,* Qumran copies (4Q267, 4Q270, 5Q12, 6Q15
1Q, 3Q, 4Q etc.	Numbered caves of Qumran, followed by abbreviation or number of document
1QapGen	*Genesis Apocryphon* (1Q20)
1QDM	*Words of Moses* (1Q22)
1QH^{a-b}	*Hodayot,* or *Thanksgiving Hymns*
1QIsa$^{a, b}$	First and second copy of Isaiah
1QJN ar	*New Jerusalem* text (1Q32)
1QM	*Milhamah,* or *War Scroll*

1QMyst	*Mysteries* (1Q27)
1QpHab	*Pesher on Habakkuk*
1QpMic	*Pesher on Micah* (1Q14)
1QpPs	*Pesher on Psalms* (1Q16)
1QpZeph	*Pesher on Zephaniah* (1Q15)
1QS	*Serek hayyaad* or *Rule of the Community, Manual of Discipline*
1QSa	Appendix A, *Messianic Rule,* to 1QS
1QSb	Appendix B, *Rule of Benediction/Book of Blessings,* to 1QS
1QTongues of Fire	*Apocryphon of Moses* (1Q29)
2QJN ar	*New Jerusalem* text (2Q24)
3QCopper Scroll	*Copper Scroll* (3Q15)
4Q'Amram[a-f]	*Visions of Amram* (4Q543-548)
4QAJo ar	*Apocrypon of Joseph* (4Q408)
4QapocrJer C	*Apocryphon of Jeremiah,* or *Pseudo-Prophets* (4Q385b)
4QapocrJoseph[a-c]	*Apocryphon of Joseph* (4Q371-373)
4QapocrMoses A-C	*Apocryphon of Moses* (4Q374-377)
4QAramaic Apocalypse	*"Son of God" Text* (4Q246)
4QBar[e]ki Naphsi[a-e]	"Bless, Oh my Soul" fragments (4Q434, 436, 427-439)
4QBeat	*Beatitudes Text* (4Q525)
4QBenediction	*Benediction,* or *Vineyard Text* (4Q500)
4QBr ar	*Brontologion,* or *Thunder Text* (4Q318)
4QCatena[a-b]	*Catena* (4Q177, 4Q182)
4QCryptic	Magical text
4QDibHam[a-c]	*Words of the Luminaries* (4Q504-506)
4QEn[a-g] ar	*1 Enoch* fragments (4Q201-202, 204-207, 212)
4QEnastr[a-g]	*1 Enoch* fragments from Astronomical Book (4Q208-211)
4QEnGiants	*1 Enoch* fragments from Book of Giants (4Q203)
4QFlor	*Florilegium,* or *Eschatological Midrashim* (4Q174)
4QHoroscope	Astrological text (4Q186)
4QMess ar	*Elect of God,* or *Birth of the Chosen One* (4Q534)
4QMessianic Apocalypse	*Messianic Apocalypse* (4Q521)
4QMez[a-g]	*Mezuzah* (4Q149-155)
4QMMT[a-f]	*Miqṣat Ma'aśeh ha-Torah* (4Q394-399)
4QNarrative	*Narrative A* (4Q458)
4QNJ[a-b] ar	*New Jerusalem* texts(4Q232[?], 4Q554, 4Q555)
4QOrd[a-c]	*Ordinances* and *Purification Texts* (4Q159, 4Q513-514)
4QPEnosh	*Prayer of Enosh* (4Q369)
4QpHos	*Pesher on Hosea* (4Q166-167)
4QPhyl[a-u]	*Phylacteries* (4Q128-148)
4QpIsa	*Pesher on Isaiah* (4Q161-165)
4QpNah	*Pesher on Nahum* (4Q169 + 4Q458)
4QpPs[a-b]	*Pesher on Psalms* (4Q171, 4Q173)
4QPrNab ar	*Prayer of Nabonidus* (4Q242)
4QProto-Esther[a-f]	*Tale of Bagasraw* (Pseudo-Esther) (4Q550[a-f])
4QpsDan[a-c] ar	*Pseudo-Danielic Writings* (4Q243-245)
4QpsEz[a-g]	*Pseudo-Ezekiel* (4Q385-388, 4Q391)
4QPsJosua[a-b]	*Psalms of Joshua* (4Q378-379)
4QpZeph	*Pesher on Zephaniah* (4Q170)
4QRitual of Purification	*Purification Text* (4Q512)
4QSapiential Work	*Secret of Existence* (4Q412-413, 4Q415-421)
4QShirShabb	*Songs of Sabbath Sacrifice,* or *Angelic Liturgy* (4Q400-407; also 11Q17, Mas 1 k)
4QTanh	*Tanhumim,* or *Consolations* (4Q176)
4QTest	*Testimonia* (4Q175)
4QtgJob	*Targum of Job* (4Q157)
4QtgLev	*Targum of Leviticus* (4Q156)
4QTohorotA-G	*Purification Texts* (4Q274-279, 281-284)
4QTQahat ar	*Testament of Qahat* (4Q542)
4QZodiac	Magical text (4Q)
5QNJ ar	*New Jerusalem* text (5Q15)
11QJN ar	*New Jerusalem* text(11Q18)
11QMelch	*Melchizedek* (11Q13)

11QpaleoLev	Copy of Leviticus in paleo-Hebrew script (11Q1)
11QPs[a]	*Psalms Scroll* (11Q5)
11QTemple[a-b]	*Temple Scroll* (11Q19, 11Q20)
11QtgJob	*Targum of Job* (11Q10)

Targumic Material

Tg. Onq.	*Targum Onqelos*	*Tg. Neof.*	*Targum Neofiti I*
Tg. Neb.	*Targum of the Prophets*	*Tg. Ps.-J.*	*Targum Pseudo-Jonathan*
Tg. Ket.	*Targum of the Writings*	*Tg. Yer. I*	*Targum YeruÜalmi I*
Frg. Tg.	*Fragmentary Targum*	*Tg. Yer. II*	*Targum YeruÜalmi II*
Sam. Tg.	*Samaritan Targum*	*Yem. Tg.*	*Yemenite Targum*
Tg. Isa	*Targum of Isaiah*	*Tg. Esth I, II*	*First or Second Targum of Esther*

Order and Tractates in the Mishnah, Tosefta and Talmud

Same-named tractates in the Mishnah, Tosefta, Babylonian Talmud and Jerusalem Talmud are distinguished by ***m.***, ***t.***, ***b.*** and *y.* respectively.

ʿAbod. Zar.	*ʿAboda Zara*	*Maʿaś Š.*	*Maʿaśer Šeni*	*Qod.*	*Qodašim*
ʾAbot	*ʾAbot*	*Mak.*	*Makkot*	*Roš Haš.*	*Roš Haššanah*
ʿArak.	*ʿArakin*	*Makš.*	*Makširin*	*Sanh.*	*Sanhedrin*
B. Bat.	*Baba Batra*	*Meg.*	*Megilla*	*Šabb.*	*Šabbat*
B. Meṣ.	*Baba Meṣiʿa*	*Meʿil.*	*Meʿilah*	*Šeb.*	*Šebiʿit*
B. Qam.	*Baba Qamma*	*Menaḥ.*	*Menaḥot*	*Šebu.*	*Šebuʿot*
Bek.	*Bekorot*	*Mid.*	*Middot*	*Seder*	*Seder*
Ber.	*Berakot*	*Miqw.*	*Miqwaʾot*	*Šeqal.*	*Šeqalim*
Beṣa	*Beṣa* (= *Yom Ṭob*)	*Moʾed*	*Moʾed*	*Soṭa*	*Soṭa*
Bik.	*Bikkurim*	*Moʾed Qaṭ.*	*Moʾed Qaṭan*	*Sukk.*	*Sukkah*
Dem.	*Demai*	*Naš*	*Našim*	*Taʿan.*	*Taʿanit*
ʿErub.	*ʿErubin*	*Nazir*	*Nazir*	*Tamid*	*Tamid*
ʿEd.	*ʿEduyyot*	*Ned.*	*Nedarim*	*Tem.*	*Temura*
Giṭ.	*Giṭin*	*Neg.*	*Negaʿim*	*Ter.*	*Terumot*
Ḥag.	*Ḥagiga*	*Nez.*	*Neziqin*	*Ṭehar.*	*Ṭeharot*
Ḥal.	*Ḥalla*	*Nid.*	*Niddah*	*Ṭ. Yom*	*Ṭebul Yom*
Hor.	*Horayot*	*ʾOhal.*	*ʾOhalot*	*ʿUq.*	*ʿUqṣin*
Ḥul.	*Ḥullin*	*ʿOr.*	*ʿOrlah*	*Yad.*	*Yadayim*
Kelim	*Kelim*	*Parah*	*Parah*	*Yebam.*	*Yebamot*
Ker.	*Keritot*	*Peʾah*	*Peʾah*	*Yoma*	*Yoma* (= *Kippurim*)
Ketub.	*Ketubbot*	*Pesaḥ.*	*Pesaḥim*	*Zabim*	*Zabim*
Kil.	*Kilʾayim*	*Qinnim*	*Qinnim*	*Zebaḥ.*	*Zebaḥim*
Ma ʿaś.	*Maʿaśerot*	*Qidd.*	*Qiddušin*	*Zera.*	*Zeraʿim*

Other Rabbinic Works

ʿAbad.	*ʿAbadim*	*Mek.*	*Mekilta*
ʾAbot R. Nat.	*ʾAbot de Rabbi Nathan*	*Mez.*	*Mezuzah*
ʾAg. Ber.	*ʾAggadat Berešit*	*Midr.*	*Midraš* (cited with abbreviation for biblical book; but *Midr. Qoh.* = *Midraš Qohelet*)
ARN	(*see* *ʾAbot R. Nat.*)		
Bab.	*Babylonian*		
Bar.	*Baraita*	*Pal.*	*Palestinian*
Der. Er. Rab.	*Derek Ereṣ Rabba*	*pq.*	*pereq* (chapter of *Sipra*)
Der. Er. Zuṭ.	*Derek Ereṣ Zuṭa*	*Pesiq. Rab.*	*Pesiqta Rabbati*
Gem.	*Gemara*	*Pesiq. Rab Kah.*	*Pesiqta de Rab Kahana*
Kalla	*Kalla*	*Pirqe R. El.*	*Pirqe Rabbi Eliezer*
Kalla Rab.	*Kalla Rabbati*	*Rab.*	*Rabbah* (following abbreviation for biblical book: *Gen. Rab.* =
Mas. Qeṭ	*Massektot Qeṭannot*		

	Genesis Rabbah)	*Ṣiṣit*	*Ṣiṣit*
Sem.	*Semaḥot*	*Sop.*	*Soperim*
Sep. Torah	*Seper Torah*	*S. ʿOlam Rab.*	*Seder ʿOlam Rabbah*
Sipra	*Sipra* (on Leviticus)	*Tanḥ.*	*Tanḥuma*
Sipre	*Sipre* (on Numbers, on Deuteronomy	*Tep.*	*Tepillin*
		Yal.	*Yalquṭ*

Nag Hammadi Tractates

Acts Pet. 12 Apost.	*The Acts of Peter and the Twelve Apostles*	*Melch.*	*Melchizedek*
Allogenes	*Allogenes*	*Norea*	*The Thought of Norea*
Ap. Jas.	*The Apocryphon of James*	*On Anoint.*	*On the Anointing*
Ap. John	*The Apocryphon of John*	*On Bapt. A*	*On Baptism A*
Apoc. Adam	*The Apocalypse of Adam*	*On Bapt. B*	*On Baptism B*
1 Apoc. Jas.	*The (First) Apocalypse of James*	*On Bapt. C*	*On Baptism C*
2 Apoc. Jas.	*The (Second) Apocalypse of James*	*On Euch. A*	*On the Eucharist A*
Apoc. Paul	*The Apocalypse of Paul*	*On Euch. B*	*On the Eucharist B*
Apoc. Peter	*Apocalypse of Peter*	*Orig. World*	*On the Origin of the World*
Asclepius	*Asclepius 21-29*	*Paraph. Shem*	*The Paraphrase of Shem*
Auth. Teach.	*Authoritative Teaching*	*Pr. Paul*	*The Prayer of the Apostle Paul*
Dial. Sav.	*The Dialogue of the Savior*	*Pr. Thanks.*	*The Prayer of Thanksgiving*
Disc. 8-9	*The Discourse on the Eighth and Ninth*	*Sent. Sextus*	*The Sentences of Sextus*
Ep. Pet. Phil.	*The Letter of Peter to Philip*	*Soph. Jes. Chr.*	*The Sophia of Jesus Christ*
Eugnostos	*Eugnostos the Blessed*	*Steles Seth*	*The Three Steles of Seth*
Exeg. Soul	*The Exegesis on the Soul*	*Teach. Silv.*	*The Teachings of Silvanus*
Gos. Eg.	*The Gospel of the Egyptians*	*Testim. Truth*	*The Testimony of Truth*
Gos. Phil.	*The Gospel of Philip*	*Thom. Cont.*	*The Book of Thomas the Contender*
Gos. Thom.	*The Gospel of Thomas*	*Thund.*	*The Thunder: Perfect Mind*
Gos. Truth	*The Gospel of Truth*	*Treat. Res.*	*The Treatise on the Resurrection*
Great Pow.	*The Concept of Our Great Power*	*Treat. Seth.*	*The Second Treatise of the Great Seth*
Hyp. Arch.	*The Hypostasis of the Archons*	*Tri. Trac.*	*The Tripartite Tractate*
Hypsiph.	*Hypsiphrone*	*Trim. Prot.*	*Trimorphic Protennoia*
Interp. Know.	*The Interpretation of Knowledge*	*Val. Exp.*	*A Valentinian Exposition*
Marsanes	*Marsanes*	*Zost.*	*Zostrianos*

Periodicals, Reference Works and Serials

AAA	American Anthropological Association	*AJAH*	*American Journal of Ancient History*
AARAS	American Academy of Religion Academy Series	*AJBI*	*Annual of the Japanese Biblical Institute*
AARSR	American Academy of Religion Studies in Religion	*AJP*	*American Journal of Philology*
AB	Anchor Bible	*AJT*	*American Journal of Theology*
ABQ	*American Baptist Quarterly*	AK	Arbeiten zur Kirchengeschichte
ABR	*Australian Biblical Review*	ALGHJ	Arbeiten zur Literatur und Geschichte des hellenistischen Judentums
ABRev	*American Benedictine Review*	ALUOS	Annual of Leeds University Oriental Society
ABRL	Anchor Bible Reference Library	*AnBib*	*Analecta Biblica*
AbrN	*Abr-Nahrain*	*AnBoll*	*Analecta Bollandiana*
ACS	American Classical Studies	*ANET*	*Ancient Near Eastern Texts Relating to the Old Testament*, ed. J. B. Pritchard (3d ed.; Princeton, 1969)
ACW	Ancient Christian Writers	*ANF*	*Ante-Nicene Fathers*, ed. A. Roberts and J. Donaldson (10 vols.; 1951 [c. 1890])
AE	*Anée épigraphique* published in *Revue Archéologique* and separately *(1888-)*	*ANRW*	*Aufstieg und Niedergang der römischen Welt*, ed. H. Temporini and W. Haase (Berlin, 1972-)
AER	*American Ecclesiastical Review*	ANYAS	Annals of the New York Academy of Sciences
AGJU	Arbeiten zur Geschichte des antiken Judentums und des Urchristentums	*APAT*	*Die Apokryphen und Pseudepigraphen des Alten Testaments*, trans. and ed. E. Kautzsch
AGSU	Arbeiten zur Geschichte des Spätjudentums und Urchristentums		
AHR	*American Historical Review*		
AJA	*American Journal of Archaeology*		

(2 vols., 1900)
APB Archiv für Papyrusforschung Beiheft
AOS American Oriental Series
APOT *The Apocrypha and Pseudepigrapha of the Old Testament in English,* ed. R. H. Charles (2 vols., 1913)
ArBib The Aramaic Bible
Arch *Archaeology*
ARWAW Abhandlungen der RheinischWestfälischen Akademie der Wissenschaften
AS *Ancient Society*
ASNU Acta seminarii neotestamentici upsaliensis
ASTHL Amsterdam Studies in the Theory and History of Linguistics
ASTI *Annual of the Swedish Theological Institute*
ATANT Abhandllungen zur Theologie des Alten und Neuen Testaments
ATLABibS ATLA Bibliography Series
ATR *Anglican Theological Review*
AusBR *Australian Biblical Review*
AUSS *Andrews University Seminary Studies*
AW *Ancient World*
BA *Biblical Archaeologist*
BAFCS The Book of Acts in Its First Century Setting
BAGD W. Bauer, W. F. Arndt, F. W. Gingrich and F. W. Danker, *Greek-English Lexicon of the New Testament*
BAR *Biblical Archaelogy Review*
BARSup British Archaeological Reports Supplements
BASOR *Bulletin of the American School of Oriental Research*
BASPSup Bulletin of the American Society of Papyrologists: Supplement
BBB Bonner biblische Beiträge
BBR *Bulletin for Biblical Research*
BCJ Brown Classics in Judaica
BDB Brown, Driver and Briggs, *Hebrew and English Lexicon of the Old Testament*
BCP Bristol Classical Paperbacks
BDF F. Blass, A. Debrunner and R. W. Funk, *A Greek Grammar of the New Testament and Other Early Christian Literature*
BECNT Baker Exegetical Commentary on the New Testament
BEFAR Bibliothèque des écoles françaises d'Athènes et de Rome
BET Beitrage zur evangelischen Theologie
BETL Bibliotheca ephemeridum theologicarum lovaniensium
BF Beiträge zur Forschung
BG Berlin Gnostic Codex
BGU *Ägyptische Urkunden aus den Museen zu Berlin: Griech. Urkunden* (15 vols., 1895-1983)
BHT Beiträge zur historischen Theologie
BI *Biblical Interpretation*
Bib *Biblica*
BibO Biblica et Orientica
BibRes *Biblical Research*
BibS(F) *Biblische Studien* (Freiburg, 1895-)
BibS(N) *Biblische Studien* (Neukirchen, 1951-)
BibTh *Biblical Theology*
BIOSCS *Bulletin for International Organization for Septuagint and Cognate Studies*
BIS Biblical Interpretation Series
BJRL *Bulletin of the John Rylands University Library of Manchester*
BJS Brown Judaic Studies
BMI The Bible and its Modern Interpreters
BP Bibliothèque de la Pléiade
BR *Biblical Research*
BRev *Bible Review*
BS Bollingen Series
BSac *Bibliotheca Sacra*
BSBA Baker Studies in Biblical Archaeology
Bsem The Biblical Seminar
BSh *Beth Seʿarim,* vol. 2: *The Greek Inscriptions,* ed. M. Schwabe and B. Lifshitz (New Brunswick, NJ: Rutgers University Press, 1974)
BSJS Brill Series in Jewish Studies
BT *The Bible Translator*
BTB *Biblical Theology Bulletin*
BTS *BiblischTheologische Studien*
BTZ *Berliner Theologicsche Zeitschrift*
BU Biblische Untersuchungen
BUS Brown University Studies
BWANT Beiträge zur Wissenschaft vom Alten (und Neuen) Testament
BZ Biblische Zeitschrift
BZAW Beihefte zur Zeitschrift für die alttestamentliche Wissenschaft
BZNW Beihefte zur Zeitschrift für die Neutestamentliche Wissenschaft
CAH *Cambridge Ancient History*
CALP The Comprehensive Aramaic Lexicon Project
CB *Classical Bulletin*
CBC Cambridge Bible Commentary
CBET Contributions to Biblical Exegesis and Theology
CBQ *Catholic Biblical Quarterly*
CBQMS Catholic Biblical Quarterly Monograph Series
CCSA Corpus Christianorum: Series Apocryphorum
CCWJCW Cambridge Commentaries on Writings of the Jewish and Christian World 200 B.C. to A.D. 200
CD *Church Dogmatics,* Karl Barth
CEB Commentaire Evangélique de la Bible
CEL Collection d'Etudes Latines
CERGR Centre d'Études Romaines et Gallo-Romaines
CGTC *Cambridge Greek Testament Commentary*
CH *Church History*
CIG *Corpus Inscriptionum Graecarum I-IV,* ed. A. Boeckh (4 vols.; Berlin, 1828-1877)
CIJ *Corpus inscriptionum Judaicarum I-II,* ed. J.

	B. Frey ((2 vols.; Rome, 1936-1952)
CIL	*Corpus Inscriptionum Latinarum*
CJ	*Classical Journal*
CJA	Christianity and Judaism in Antiquity
CJT	*Canadian Journal of Theology*
CJZC	*Corpus jüdischer Zeugnisse aus der Cyrenaika,* ed. G. Lüderitz (Wiesbaden, 1983)
CNS	*Cristianesimo nella storia*
CNT	Commentaire du Nouveau Testament
CNTC	Calvin's New Testament Commentaries
COHP	Contributions to Oriental History and Philology
ConB	Coniectanea biblica
ConBNT	Coniectanea biblica Neotestamentica
ConJ	*Concordia Journal*
COQG	Christian Origins and the Question of God
CP	*Classical Philology*
CPG	*Clavis Patrum Graecorum,* ed. M. Geerard, 5 vols. (Turnhout, 1974-1987)
CPJ	*Corpus Papyrorum Judaicarum,* ed. V. Tcherikover, A. Fulks and M. Stern (3 vols.; Cambridge, MA (1957-1964)
CPSSV	Cambridge Philological Society, Supplementary Volume
CQ	Classical Quarterly
CQR	*Church Quarterly Review*
CRB	Cahiers de la Revue Biblique
CRHPR	Cahiers de la Revue d'histoire et de philosophie religieuses
CRINT	Compendia rerum iudaicarum ad novum testamentum
CSCO	Corpus Scriptorum Christianorum Orientalium
CSCT	Columbia Series in the Classical Tradition
CSEL	Corpus Scriptorum Ecclesiasticorum Latinorum
CSHJ	Chicago Studies in the History of Judaism
CTJ	*Calvin Theological Journal*
CTM	*Concordia Theological Monthly*
CTR	*Criswell Theological Review*
CurR	*Currents in Research*
CV	*Communio Viatorum*
DAWB	Deusche Akademie der Wissenschaften zu Berlin
DBAT	*Dielheimer Blätter zum Alten Testament und seiner Rezeption in der Alten Kirche*
DCB	*Dictionary of Christian Biography,* ed. W. Smith and H. Wace
DGRA	*A Dictionary of Greek and Roman Antiquities,* ed. W. Smith, W. Wayte and G. E. Marindin
DJBP	*Dictionary of Judaism in the Biblical Period: 450 B.C.E.–600 C.E.* , ed. J. Neusner and W. S. Green
DJD	Discoveries in the Judaean Desert
DJG	*Dictionary of Jesus and the Gospels*
DLNTD	*Dictionary of the Later New Testament and Its Developments*
DMAHA	Dutch Monographs on Ancient History and Archaeology
DPL	*Dictionary of Paul and His Letters*
DRev	*Downside Review*
DSB	Daily Study Bible
DSD	*Dead Sea Discoveries*
DSSE	*The Dead Sea Scrolls in English,* G. Vermes
DTT	*Dansk teologisk tidsskrift*
DUJ	*Durham University Journal*
EB	*Études bibliques*
EBC	The Expositor's Bible Commentary
EBT	*Encyclopedia of Biblical Theology,* ed. J. B. Bauer
EDNT	*Exegetical Dictionary of the New Testament,* ed. H. Balz and G. Schneider
EGT	Expositor's Greek Testament
EH	Europäische Hochschulschriften
EJL	Early Judaism and Its Literature
EKK	Evangelisch-katholischer Kommentar zum Neuen Testament
ELS	*Enchiridion Locorum Sanctorum. Documenta S. Evangelii Loca Respicientia*
EncJud	*Encyclopaedia Judaica*
EP	*Études de papyrologie*
EPROER	Etudes préliminaires aux religions orientales dans l'empire romain
ER	*The Encyclopedia of Religion,* ed. M. Eliade
ErIs	*Eretz-Israel*
Erev	*Ecumenical Review*
ESH	Exeter Studies in History
ESW	Ecumenical Studies in Worship
ETS	Erfurter Theologische Schriften
EvJ	*Evangelical Journal*
EvQ	*Evangelical Quarterly*
EvT	*Evangelische Theologie*
Exp	*Expositor*
ExpT	*Expository Times*
FAT	Forschungen zum Alten Testament
FB	Facet Books
FCCGRW	First-Century Christians in the GrecoRoman World
FF	Foundations and Facets
FHG	Fragmenta Historicorum Graecorum, C. Müller (Paris, 1841-1970)
FIOTL	Formation and Interpretation of Old Testament Literature
FIRA	Fontes Iuris Romani Antejustiniani
FJ	The Foundation of Judaism
FKD	Forschungen zur Kirchen- und Dogmengeschichte
FN	*Filologia Neotestamentaria*
FRLANT	Forschungen zur Religion und Literature des Alten und Neuen Testaments
GAP	Guides to the Apocrypha and Pseudepigrapha
GBL	*Das Große Bibellexikon*
GBS	Guides to Biblical Scholarship
GG	Grammatici Graeci
GLS	Grove Liturgical Studies
GNS	Good News Studies
GNTE	Guides to New Testament Exegesis
GR	*Greece and Rome*
GRBS	*Greek, Roman, and Byzantine Studies*
GRBSMS	Greek, Roman, and Byzantine Studies Monograph Series

GTJ — *Grace Theological Journal*
HBC — *Harper's Bible Commentary*
HBD — *Harper's Bible Dictionary*
HBT — *Horizons in Biblical Theology*
HCS — Hellenistic Culture and Society
HDB — *A Dictionary of the Bible,* ed. J. Hastings
HDR — Harvard Dissertations in Religion
Herm — Hermeneia
HeyJ — *The Heythrop Journal*
HNT — Handbuch zum Neuen Testament
HNTC — Harper's New Testament Commentaries
HO — Handbuch der Orientalistik
HOS — Handbook of Oriental Studies
HR — *History of Religions*
HSMM — Harvard Semitic Museum Monographs
HSMS — Harvard Semitic Monograph Series
HSS — Harvard Semitic Studies
HTKNT — Herders theologischer Kommentar zum Neuen Testament
HTS — Harvard Theological Studies
HUCA — *Hebrew Union College Annual*
HUCAS — Hebrew Union College Annual Supplement
HUT — Hermeneutische Untersuchungen zur Theologie
HZ — *Historische Zeitschrift*
IBC — *Irish Biblical Studies*
IBD — *Illustrated Bible Dictionary*
IBS — *Irish Biblical Studies*
ICA — Initiations au Christianisme ancien
ICC — International Critical Commentary
IDB — *Interpreter's Dictionary of the Bible*
IDBSup — *Interpreter's Dictionary of the Bible, Supplementary Volume*
IE — *Die Inschriften von Ephesos,* ed. H. Wankel (8 vols.)
IEJ — *Israel Exploration Journal*
IG — *Inscriptiones Graecae, Editio minor (Berlin, 1924-)*
IGRR — *Inscriptioines Graecae ad Res Romanas Pertinentes (1906-)*
ILS — *Inscriptiones Latinae Selectae,* ed. H. Dessau (Berlin, 1892-1916)
INJ — *Israel Numismatic Journal*
Inscr. Cos — *The Inscriptions of Cos,* ed. W. R. Paton and E. L. Hicks (1891)
Int — *Interpretation*
IntC — Interpretation Commentaries
IR:GR — Iconography of Religions: Greece and Rome
IRT — Issues in Religion and Theology
ISBE — *International Standard Bible Encyclopedia* (rev. ed.)
IVPNTC — InterVarsity Press New Testament Commentary
JAC — *Jahrbuch für Antike und Christentum*
JAL — Jewish Apocryphal Literature Series
JBLMS — Journal of Biblical Literature Monograph Series
JAOS — *Journal of the American Oriental Society*
JBL — *Journal of Biblical Literature*
JBR — *Journal of Bible and Religion*
JCBRF — *Journal of the Christian Brethren Research Fellowship*
JCSR — *Journal of Comparative Sociology and Religion*
JE — *Jewish Encyclopedia,* ed. I. Singer (12 vols., 1925)
JECS — *Journal of Early Christian Studies*
JEH — *Journal of Ecclesiastical History*
JES — *Journal of Ecumenical Studies*
JETS — *Journal of the Evangelical Theological Society*
JFSR — *Journal of Feminist Studies in Religion*
JGRCJ — *Journal of Greco-Roman Christianity and Judaism*
JHS — *Journal of Hellenic Studies*
JIGRE — *Jewish Inscriptions of Graeco-Roman Egypt,* ed. W. Horbury and D. Noy (Cambridge 1992)
JIWE — *Jewish Inscriptions of Western Europe,* ed. D. Noy (2 vols.; Cambridge, 1993, 1995)
JJS — *Journal of Jewish Studies*
JLA — Judaism in Late Antiquity
JNES — *Journal of Near Eastern Studies*
JNSL — *Journal of Northwest Semitic Languages*
JPOS — *Journal of Palestine Oriental Society*
JPT — *Journal of Pentecostal Theology*
JQR — *Jewish Quarterly Review*
JR — *Journal of Religion*
JRE — *Journal of Religious Ethics*
JRH — *Journal of Religious History*
JRS — *Journal of Roman Studies*
JSHRZ — *Jüdische Schriften aus hellenistisch-römisher Zeit*
JSJ — *Journal for the Study of Judaism in the Persian, Hellenistic and Roman Period*
JSNT — *Journal for the Study of the New Testament*
JSNTSup — Journal for the Study of the New Testament Supplement Series
JSOT — *Journal for the Study of the Old Testament*
JSOTSup — Journal for the Study of the Old Testament Supplement Series
JSP — *Journal for the Study of the Pseudepigrapha and Related Literature*
JSPSup — Journal for the Study of the Pseudepigrapha and Related Literature Supplement Series
JSS — *Journal of Semitic Studies*
JSS Sup — Journal of Semitic Studies Supplement Series
JTC — *Journal for Theology and the Church*
JTS — *Journal of Theological Studies*
JTS(n.s.) — *Journal of Theological Studies (new series)*
JTSA — *Journal of Theology for Southern Africa*
KAV — Kommentar zu den Apostolischen Vätern
KNT — Kommentar zum Neuen Testament
KP — *Der Kleine Pauly,* ed. K. Ziegler
KTAH — Key Themes in Ancient History
LAE — *Light from the Ancient East,* A. Deissmann
LB — *Linguistica Biblica*
LBS — Library of Biblical Studies
LCC — Library of Christian Classics
LCL — Loeb Classical Library

LD	Lectio divina
LDSS	The Literature of the Dead Sea Scrolls
LEC	Library of Early Christianity
Louw-Nida	J. P. Louw and E. A. Nida, ed., *Greek-English Lexicon*
LR	The Library of Religion
LSJ	Liddell-Scott-Jones, *Greek-English Lexicon*
LTJ	*Lutheran Theological Journal*
LTK[3]	*Lexicon für Theologie und Kirche* (3d ed., 1999)
LW	*Luther's Works,* ed. J. Pelikan and H. T. Lehmann
MAPS	*Memoirs of the American Philosophical Society*
MBCB	Mnemosyne: Bibliotheca Classica Batava
MBPAR	Münchener Beiträge zur Papyrusforschung und Antiken Rechtsgeschichte
MBTh	Münsterische Beiträge zur Theologie
MCL	Martin Classical Lectures
MeyerK	Meyer Kommentar
MFC	Message of the Fathers of the Church
MHUS	Monographs of Hebrew Union College
MM	J. H. Moulton and G. Milligan, *The Vocabulary of the Greek Testament, Illustrated from the Papyri and Other Non-Literary Sources* (1930)
MNTC	Moffatt New Testament Commentary
MNTS	McMaster New Testament Studies
MPAT	*A Manual of Palestinian Aramaic Texts*
MPER	*Mittheilungen aus der Sammlung der Papyrus Erzherzog Rainer,* ed. J. Karabacek (Vienna)
MPI	Monographs of the Peshitta Institute
MSB	Monographic Series of Benedictina
MTh	*Melita Theologica*
MTS	Münchener theologische Studien
Mus	*Le Muséon*
NA26	Nestle-Aland *Novum Testamentum Graece* (26th ed.)
NABPRSS	National Association of Baptist Professors of Religion Special Studies
NAC	The New American Commentary
NAWG	Nachrichten der Akademie der Wissenschaften in Göttingen
NCB	New Century Bible
NClB	New Clarendon Bible
NedTTs	*Nederlands theologisch tijdschrift*
Neot	*Neotestamentica*
NewDocs	*New Documents Illustrating Early Christianity,* ed. G. H. R. Horsley
NGS	New Gospel Studies
NIB	New Interpreter's Bible
NIBC	The New International Biblical Commentary
NICNT	The New International Commentary on the New Testament
NIDNTT	*New International Dictionary of New Testament Theology*
NIGTC	New International Greek Testament Commentary
NLC	New London Commentary
NOHM	The New Oxford History of Music
NovT	*Novum Testamentum*
NovTSup	Supplement to Novum Testamentum
NRT	*La nouvelle revue théologique*
NTAbh	Neutestamentliche Abhandlungen
NTC	TPI New Testament Commentaries
NTCom	New Testament Commentary (Baker)
NTD	Das Neue Testament Deutsch
NTG	New Testament Guides
NTL	New Testament Library
NTOA	Novum Testamentum et Orbis Antiquus
NTP	New Testament Profiles
NTR	New Theology Review
NTS	New Testament Studies
NTTS	New Testament Tools and Studies
NumSup	Numen Supplements
NVBS	New Voices in Biblical Studies
OBO	Orbis Biblicus et Orientalis
OBT	Overtures to Biblical Theology
OCA	Orientalia Christiana analecta
OCD	*Oxford Classical Dictionary*
OCM	Oxford Classical Monographs
OGIS	*Orientis Graeci Inscriptiones Selectae*
OPTAT	*Occasional Papers in Translation and Textlinguistics*
OTM	Old Testament Message
OTP	*The Old Testament Pseudepigrapha,* ed. J. H. Charlesworth
OtSt	*Oudtestamentische Studiën*
PAM	Palestine Archaeological Museum
PB	Papyrological Bruxellensia
PBSR	Papers of the British School at Rome
PC	Proclamation Commentaries
PEQ	*Palestine Exploration Quarterly*
PG	*Patrologiae Graeca,* ed. J.-P. Migne (162 vols.)
PGL	*Patristic Greek Lexicon,* ed. G. W. H. Lampe
PHP	Papyrology and Historical Perspectives
PL	*Patrologia Latina,* ed. J.-P. Migne. (217 vols.)
PNTC	Pillar New Testament Commentary
PQ	*Philological Quarterly*
PRS	*Perspectives in Religious Studies*
PSB	*Princeton Seminary Bulletin*
PSBFMi	Publications of the Studium Biblicum Franciscanum. Collectio minor
PsVTG	Pseudepigrapha Veteris Testamenti Graece
PTMS	Pittsburgh Theological Monograph Series
PTSDSS	Princeton Theological Seminary Dead Sea Scrolls Project
QD	Quaestiones Disputatae
RA	Revealing Antiquity
RAC	*Reallexikon für Antike und Christentum*
RAr	*Revue archéologique*
RB	*Revue biblique*
RC:SS	The Records of Civilization: Sources and Studies
RE	*Real-Encyclopädie der classischen Altertumswissenschaft, ed. Pauly-Wissowa*
RechBib	Recherches bibliques
RelSRev	*Religious Studies Review*
RevExp	*Review and Expositor*

RevQ	*Revue de Qumran*
RGG	*Religion in Geschichte und Gegenwart*
RGRW	Religions in the Graeco-Roman World
RHE	*Revue d'Histoire Ecclésiastique*
RHPR	*Revue d'histoire et de philosophie religieuses*
RHR	*Revue de l'histoire des religions*
RICP	*Revue de l'Institut Catholique de Paris*
RILP	Roehampton Institute London Papers
RLC	Roman Literature and Its Contexts
RMP	Rheinisches Museum für Philologie
RQ	Restoration Quarterly
RSR	*Recherches des science religieuse*
RST	Regensburger Studien zur Theologie
RTL	*Revue théologique de Louvain*
RTR	*Reformed Theological Review*
SA	Studia Antiqua
SAAA	Studies in the Apocryphal Acts of the Apostles
SAC	Studies in Antiquity and Christianity
SacP	Sacra Pagina
SAJ	Studies in Ancient Judaism
SAM	Studies in Ancient Medicine
SANT	Studien zum Alten und Neuen Testament
SASI	Slavery and Abolition Special Issue
SB	Sources bibliques
SB	*Sammelbuch griechischer Urkunden aus Ägypten,* ed. F. Preisigke et al. (1915-)
SBB	Stuttgarter biblische Beiträge
SBEC	Studies in the Bible and Early Christianity
SBFLA	*Studii biblici franciscani liber annuus*
SBLASP	Society of Biblical Literature Abstracts and Seminar Papers
SBLDS	SBL Dissertation Series
SBLEJL	Society of Biblical Literature Early Judaism and Its Literature
SBLMS	SBL Monograph Series
SBLRBS	SBL Resources for Biblical Studies
SBLSBS	SBL Sources for Biblical Study
SBLSCS	Society of Biblical Literature Septuagint and Cognate Studies
SBLSP	SBL Seminar Papers
SBLSS	SBL Supplement Series
SBLSymS	SBL Symposium Series
SBLTT	Society of Biblical Literature Texts and Translations
SBS	Stuttgart Bibelstudien
SBT	Studies in Biblical Theology
SC	Sources chrétiennes
SCBO	Scriptorum Classicorum Bibliotheca Oxoniensis
SCL	Sather Classical Lectures
ScrHier	*Scripta hierosolymitana*
SCJ	Studies in Christianity and Judaism
SCS	Septuagint and Cognate Studies
Schürer	E. Schürer, *The History of the Jewish People in the Age of Jesus Chjrist (175 B.C.-A.D. 135),* rev. and ed. G. Vermes et al. (3 vols.; Edinburgh, 1973-87)
SD	Studies and Documents
SDSSRL	Studies in the Dead Sea Scrolls and *Related Literature*
SE	*Studia Evangelica*
SEÅ	*Svensk Exegetisk Årsbok*
SecCent	*Second Century*
SEG	Supplementum Epigraphicum Graecum (Leiden, 1923-)
Sem	*Semitica*
SESJ	Suomen Ekseegeettisen Seuran Julkaisuja
SFSHJ	South Florida Studies in the History of Judaism
SFSMD	Studia Francisci Scholten memoriae dicata
SH	Studia Hellenistica
SHC	Studies in Hellenistic Civilization
SHJ	Studying the Historical Jesus
SHL	Studies in the History of Linguistics
SHLS	Studies in the History of the Language Sciences
SHT	Studies in Historical Theology
SIG[3]	*Sylloge Inscriptionum Graecarum* (3d ed.; Leipzig, 1915-1924)
SJ	Studia Judaica
SJLA	Studies in Judaism in Late Antiquity
SJSJ	Supplements to the Journal for the Study of Judaism
SJT	*Scottish Journal of Theology*
SJTOP	Scottish Journal of Theology Occasional Papers
SKKNT	Stuttgarter kleiner Kommentar, Neues Testament
SL	*Studia Liturgica*
SM	*Sacramentum Mundi*
SNTW	Studies in the New Testament in Its World
SNTSMS	Society for New Testament Studies Monograph Series
SNTU	*Studien zum Neuen Testament und seiner Umwelt*
SO	*Symbolae osloenses*
SOTBT	Studies in Old Testament Biblical Theology
SP	Studia Patristica
SPB	Studia Post-Biblica
SPP	Studien zur Palaeographie und Papyruskunde
SR	Studies in Religion
SS	Symposium Series
SSEJC	Studies in Scripture in Early Judaism and Christianity
SSLL	Studies in Semitic Languages and Linguistics
SSRH	Sociological Studies in Roman History
ST	*Studia theologica*
StBT	*Studia Biblica et Theologica*
STDJ	Studies on the Texts of the Desert of Judah
STL	Studia theologica Lundensia
STR	Sewanee Theological Review
Str-B	Strack and Billerbeck, *Kommentar zum Neuen Testament*
StudLit	*Studia Liturgica*
StudNeot	*Studia Neotestamentica*
SubBi	Subsidia biblica
SUNT	Studien zur Umwelt des Neuen Testaments
SUNYSCS	SUNY Series in Classical Studies

SupJSJ	Supplements to the Journal for the Study of Judaism
SV	*Stoicorum veterum fragmenta* (4 vols.; Leipzig, 1903-1924)
Syllog.	*Sylloge Inscriptionum Graecorum,* ed. W. Dittenberger (1915-1924)
SVTP	Studia in Veteris Testamenti Pseudepigrapha
SWJT	*Southwestern Journal of Theology*
TAPA	*Transactions of the American Philological Association*
TAVO	*Tübinger Atlas des Vorderen Orients*
TB	Theologische Bücherei
TBC	Torch Bible Commentaries
TBl	*Theologische Blätter*
TBT	*The Bible Today*
TC	Theological Collections
TD	*Theology Digest*
TDGR	Translated Documents of Greece and Rome, ed. R. K. Sherk
TDNT	*Theological Dictionary of the New Testament,* ed. G. Kittel and G. Friedrich
TECC	Textos y Estudios "Cardenal Cisneros"
TEH	Theologische Existenz heute, new series
Text	*Textus*
Them	*Themelios*
THKNT	Theologische Handkommentar zum Neuen Testament
TI	*Theological Inquiries*
TJ (n.s.)	*Trinity Journal (new series)*
TLZ	*Theologische Literaturzeitung*
TNTC	Tyndale New Testament Commentary
TOP	Theology Occasional Papers
TPG	The Presence of God
TPINTC	Trinity Press International New Testament Commentaries
TQ	*Theologische Quartalschrift*
TRE	*Theologische Realenzydlopädie*
TRu	*Theologische Rundschau*
TS	*Theological Studies*
TSAJ	Texte und Studium zum antiken Judentum
TSFBul	*TSF Bulletin*
TS	Texts and Studies
Ttoday	*Theology Today*
TU	Texte und Untersuchungen
TWOT	*Theological Wordbook of the Old Testament*
TynB	*Tyndale Bulletin*
TZ	*Theologische Zeitschrift*
UBSGNT	United Bible Societies Greek New Testament
UCOP	University of Cambridge Oriental Publications
UCPCS	University of California Publications in Classical Studies
UNDSPR	University of Notre Dame Studies in Philosophy of Religion
USFSHJ	University of South Florida Studies in the History of Judaism
USQR	*Union Seminary Quarterly Review*
UT	*Ugaritic Textbook,* C. H. Gordon (1965)
VC	Vigiliae Christianae
VCSup	Supplements to Vigiliae Christianae
VoxEv	*Vox Evangelica*
VT	*Vetus Testamentum*
VTSup	Vetus Testamentum Supplements
WA	Weimar Ausgabe
WBC	Word Biblical Commentary
WEC	Wycliffe Exegetical Commentary
WF	Wege der Forschung
WTJ	*Wesleyan Theological Journal*
WMANT	Wissenschaftliche Monographien zum Alten und Neuen Testament
WS	Women's Studies
WTJ	*Westminster Theological Journal*
WUNT	Wissenschaftliche Untersuchungen zum Neuen Testament
YCS	Yale Classical Studies
ZBNT	Züricher Bibelkommentare: Neues Testament
ZDMG	*Zeitschrift der deutschen morgenländischen Gesellschaft*
ZKG	*Zeitschrift fur Kirchengeschicte*
ZLTK	*Zeitschrift für lutherische Theologie und Kirche*
ZMW	*Zeitschrift für die Musikologie Wissenschaft*
ZNW	*Zeitschrift für die neutestamentliche Wissenschaft*
ZNWB	*Zeitschrift für die neutestamentliche Wissenschaft Beihefte*
ZPE	*Zeitschrift für Papyrologie und Epigraphik*
ZPEB	*Zondervan Pictorial Encyclopedia of the Bible,* ed. M. C. Tenney
ZRG	*Zeitschrift für Religions- und Geistesgeschichte*
ZS: NT	Zacchaeus Studies: New Testament
ZSTh	*Zeitschrift für Systematische Theologie*
ZTK	*Zeitschrift für Theologie und Kirche*
ZWT	*Zeitschrift für wissenschaftliche Theologie*

Transliteration of Hebrew and Greek

HEBREW

Consonants

- א = ʾ
- ב = b
- ג = g
- ד = d
- ה = h
- ו = w
- ז = z
- ח = ḥ
- ט = ṭ
- י = y
- כ = k
- ל = l
- מ = m
- נ = n
- ס = s
- ע = ʿ
- פ = p
- צ = ṣ
- ק = q
- ר = r
- שׂ = ś
- שׁ = š
- ת = t

Long Vowels

- (ה)ָ = â
- ֵי = ê
- ִי = î
- וּ = û
- ָ = ā
- ֵ = ē
- ֹ = ō

Short Vowels

- ַ = a
- ֶ = e
- ִ = i
- ָ = o
- ֻ = u

Very Short Vowels

- ֲ = ^{a}
- ֱ = ^{e}
- ְ = ^{e} (if vocal)
- ֳ = ^{o}

GREEK

- Α = A
- α = a
- Β = B
- β = b
- Γ = G
- γ = g
- Δ = D
- δ = d
- Ε = E
- ε = e
- Ζ = Z
- ζ = z
- Η = Ē
- η = ē
- Θ = Th
- θ = th
- Ι = I
- ι = I
- Κ = K
- κ = k
- Λ = L
- λ = l
- Μ = M
- μ = m
- Ν = N
- ν = n
- Ξ = X
- ξ = x
- Ο = O
- ο = o
- Π = P
- π = p
- Ρ = R
- ρ = r
- Σ = S
- σ/ς = s
- Τ = T
- τ = t
- Υ = U
- υ = u
- Φ = Ph
- φ = ph
- Χ = Ch
- χ = ch
- Ψ = Ps
- ψ = ps
- Ω = Ō
- ω = ō
- ῾Ρ = Rh
- ῥ = rh
- ῾ = h
- γξ = nx
- γγ = ng
- αυ = au
- ευ = eu
- ου = ou
- υι = yi

Contributors

Abegg, Martin G. Jr., Ph.D. Associate Professor of Religious Studies, Trinity Western University, Langley, British Columbia, Canada: **Apocrypha of Moses (1Q29, 4Q374-377, 4Q408); Calendars, Jewish; Hebrew Language; Liturgy: Qumran; Miqṣat Maʿaśey ha-Torah (4QMMT); Pseudo-Prophets (4Q385-388, 390-391); War Scroll (1QM) and Related Texts.**

Anderson, Robert T., Ph.D. Professor Religious Studies, Michigan State University, East Lansing, Michigan: **Samaritan Literature.**

Arbel, V. Daphna, Ph.D. Assistant Professor of Religious Studies, Department of Classical, Near Eastern and Religious Studies, University of British Columbia, Vancouver, British Columbia, Canada: **Liturgy: Rabbinic.**

Arnold, Clinton E., Ph.D. Professor of New Testament, Talbot School of Theology, La Mirada, California: **Magical Papyri.**

Aune, David E., Ph.D. Professor of New Testament and Christian Origins, Loyola University, Chicago, Illinois: **Apocalypticism; Religion, Greco-Roman.**

Barton, Stephen C., Ph.D. Senior Lecturer in New Testament, University of Durham, Durham, England: **Social Values and Structures.**

Basser, Herbert W., Ph.D. Professor of Religious Studies, Queen's Theological College, Kingston, Ontario, Canada: **Priests and Priesthood, Jewish.**

Batey, Richard A., Ph.D. W. J. Millard Professor of Religious Studies, Rhodes College, Memphis, Tennessee: **Jerusalem.**

Bauckham, Richard J., Ph.D. Professor of New Testament Studies, University of St. Andrews, St. Andrews, Scotland, U.K.: **Apocryphal Gospels.**

Beall, Todd S., Ph.D. Chairman, Department of Old Testament Literature and Exegesis Capital Bible Seminary, Lanham, Maryland: **Essenes.**

Bowley, James E., Ph.D. Associate Professor of Religion, King College, Bristol, Tennessee: **Heroes; Pax Romana; Purification Texts (4Q274-279, 281-284, 512-514).**

Brooke, George J., Ph.D. Rylands Professor of Biblical Criticism and Exegesis, University of Manchester, Manchester, England: **Florilegium (4Q174); Pesharim; Testimonia (4Q175).**

Buchanan, Paul, M.A. Chair, Department of English, Biola University, La Mirada, California. **Poetry, Hellenistic.**

Burridge, Richard A., Ph.D. The Dean, King's College London, London, England: **Biography, Ancient.**

Buth, Randall J., Ph.D. Chair, Hebrew Bible and Semitic Languages, Jerusalem University College, Jerusalem, Israel: **Aramaic Language; Aramaic Targumim: Qumran.**

Caragounis, Chrys C., Th.D. Associate Professor of New Testament Exegesis, Lund University, Lund, Sweden: **Aristeas, Epistle of; Scholarship, Greek and Roman.**

Carson, D. A., Ph.D. Research Professor of New Testament, Trinity Evangelical Divinity School, Deerfield, Illinois: **Pseudonymity and Pseudepigraphy.**

Charles, J. Daryl, Ph.D. Associate Professor of Religion, Philosophy and Ethics, Taylor University, Upland, Indiana: **Pagan Sources in the New Testament; Vice and Virtue Lists.**

Charlesworth, James H., Ph.D. George L. Collard Professor of New Testament, Princeton Theological Seminary, Princeton, New Jersey: **Odes of Solomon; Treatise of Shem.**

Chilton, Bruce, Ph.D. Bernard Iddings Bell Professor of Religion, Bard College, Annandale, New York: **Festivals and Holy Days: Jewish; Judaism and the New Testament; Purity; Rabbinic Literature: Targumim; Rabbis; Synagogues; Temple, Jewish.**

Ciampa, Roy E., Ph.D. Professor of Biblical Studies, College of Evangelical Theological Education, Santo Antão do Tojal, Portugal: **Decapolis.**

Clarke, Andrew D., Ph.D. Lecturer in New Testament, University of Aberdeen, Aberdeen, U.K.: **Alexandria; Alexandrian Library; Alexandrian Scholarship.**

Clarke, Kent D., Ph.D. candidate. Lecturer, Trinity Western University, Langley, British Columbia, Canada: **Pseudo-Phocylides.**

Collins, John J., Ph. D. Holmes Professor of Old Testament, Yale University, New Haven, Connecticut: **Apocalyptic Literature; Enoch, Books of; Eschatologies of Late Antiquity; Sibylline Oracles.**

Comfort, Philip W., Ph.D., D. Litt. Et Phil. Senior Editor, Tyndale House Publishers, Wheaton, Illinois: **Temple.**

Cook, Rosalie R. E., Ph.D. Research Fellow, Macquarie University, Sydney, Australia: **Zenon Papyri.**

Cousland, J. R. C., Ph.D. Assistant Professor of Religious Studies, University of British Columbia, Vancouver, British Columbia, Canada: **Athletics; Temples, Greco-Roman; Theaters; Prophets and Prophecy.**

Cross, Anthony R., Ph.D. Research Fellow, Centre for Advanced Theological Research, University of Surrey Roehampton, London, England: **Genres of the New Testament.**

Croy, N. Clayton, Ph.D. Assistant Professor of New Testament, Trinity Lutheran Seminary, Columbus, Ohio: **Epicureanism; Neo-Pythagoreanism; Religion, Personal.**

Davids, Peter H., Ph.D. Theological advisor/educational missionary, International Teams, Innsbruck, Austria: **Homily, Ancient.**

De Roo, Jacqueline C. R., Ph.D. candidate. Teaching Fellow in New Testament, University of Aberdeen, Aberdeen, Scotland, U.K.: **Beatitudes Text (4Q525).**

deSilva, David A., Ph.D. Associate Professor of New Testament and Greek, Ashland Theological Seminary, Ashland, Ohio: **Apocrypha and Pseudepigrapha; Honor and Shame; 3 & 4 Maccabees; Patronage; Ruler Cult; Sirach; Testament of Moses; Wisdom of Solomon; Writing and Literature: Jewish.**

Dillon, John M., Ph.D. Regius Professor of Greek, Trinity College, Dublin, Ireland: **Philosophy; Plato, Platonism.**

Edwards, Ruth B., Ph.D. Honorary Senior Lecturer in New Testament in the Department of Divinity and Religious Studies, University of Aberdeen, Aberdeen, Scotland, U.K.: **Rome.**

Elgvin, Torleif, Ph.D. Associate Professor, Lutheran Theological Seminary, Oslo, Norway: **Belial, Beliar, Devil, Satan.**

Enns, Peter, Ph.D. Associate Professor of Old Testament, Westminster Theological Seminary, Philadelphia, Pennsylvania: **Biblical Interpretation, Jewish.**

Evans, Craig A., Ph.D. Professor of Biblical Studies, Trinity Western University, Langley, British Columbia, Canada:

Apocalypticism, Apollonius of Tyana; Caiaphas Ossuary; Cave 7 Fragments (Qumran); Hebrew Matthew; Hillel, House of; Holy Men, Jewish; Jesus ben Ananias; Messianic Apocalypse (4Q521); Messianism; Narrative A (4Q458); Pilate Inscription; Prayer of Enosh (4Q369, 4Q458); Shammai, House of; Simon ben Kosiba; Son of God Text (4Q246); Therapeutae; Vineyard Text (4Q500).

Falk, Daniel K., Ph.D. Assistant Professor of Biblical Studies and Judaism, University of Oregon, Eugene, Oregon: **Testament of Qahat (4Q542); Visions of Amram (4Q543-548); Words of Moses (1Q22).**

Feldman, Louis H., Ph.D. Professor of Classics, Yeshiva University, New York, New York: **Josephus: Interpretive Methods and Tendencies.**

Fiore, Benjamin, Ph.D. Professor of Religious Studies, Canisius College, Buffalo, New York: **Cynic Epistles; Cynicism and Skepticism.**

Fisk, Bruce N., Ph.D. Assistant Professor of New Testament, Westmont College, Santa Barbara, California: **Genesis Apocryphon (1QapGen); Rewritten Bible in Pseudepigrapha and Qumran.**

Fitzgerald, John T., Ph.D. Associate Professor of Religious Studies, University of Miami, Coral Gables, Florida: **Affliction Lists; Hospitality.**

Flint, Peter W., Ph.D. Associate Professor of Religious Studies, Trinity Western University, Langley, British Columbia, Canada: **Habakkuk Commentary (1QpHab); Prayer of Nabonidus (4Q242) and Pseudo-Daniel (4Q243-245); Psalms and Hymns of Qumran.**

Forbes, Christopher B., Ph.D. Lecturer in Ancient History, Macquarie University, Sydney, New South Wales, Australia: **Epictetus.**

Gamble, Harry Y., Ph.D. Professor of Religious Studies, University of Virginia, Charlotte, Virginia: **Canonical Formation of the New Testament; Literacy and Book Culture.**

Geddert, Timothy J., Ph.D. Associate Professor of New Testament, Mennonite Brethren Biblical Seminary, Fresno, California: **Apocalypticism.**

Gibson, Jeffrey B., D.Phil. Lecturer in New Testament, Loyola Institute for Pastoral Studies, Loyola University, Chicago, Illinois: **Testing and Trial in Secular Greek Thought.**

Gill, David William John, D.Phil., F.S.A. Senior Lecturer in Ancient History and Sub-Dean for the Faculty of Arts and Social Studies, University of Wales Swansea, Swansea, Wales, U.K.: **Roman Political System; Seleucids and Antiochids; Taxation, Greco-Roman.**

Grabbe, Lester L., Ph.D. Professor of Theology, University of Hull, Hull, England: **Jewish History: Greek Period; Jewish History: Persian Period; Jewish History: Roman Period; Jewish Wars with Rome; 1 & 2 Maccabees.**

Greenspoon, Leonard J., Ph.D. Klutznick Chair in Jewish Civilization, Creighton University, Omaha, Nebraska: **Old Testament Versions, Ancient.**

Grossfeld, Bernard, Ph.D. Professor of Hebrew and Aramaic, Spertus College of Judaica, Chicago, Illinois: **Torah.**

Guelich, Robert A., D.Theol. Late Professor of New Testament, Fuller Theological Seminary, Pasadena, California: **Destruction of Jerusalem.**

Habinek, Thomas N., Ph.D. Professor of Classics, University of Southern California, Los Angeles, California: **Seneca.**

Hachlili, Rachel, Ph.D. Professor, Chair of Department of Archaeology, University of Haifa, Haifa, Israel: **Art and Architecture: Jewish.**

Hafemann, Scott, Dr. Theol. Gerald F. Hawthorne Professor of New Testament Greek and Exegesis, Wheaton College, Wheaton, Illinois: **Roman Triumph.**

Hare, Douglas R. A., Th.D. Emeritus William F. Orr Professor of New Testament, Pittsburgh Theological Seminary, Pittsburgh, Pennsylvania: **Lives of the Prophets.**

Harrill, J. Albert, Ph.D. Assistant Professor of Religious Studies, DePaul University, Chicago, Illinois: **Asia Minor; Slavery.**

Harrington, Daniel J., Ph.D. Professor of New Testament, Weston Jesuit School of Theology, Cambridge, Massachusetts: **Pseudo-Philo.**

Hartin, Patrick J., D.Th. Professor of Religious Studies, Gonzaga University, Spokane, Washington: **Apocryphal and Pseudepigraphical Sources in the New Testament.**

Hatina, Thomas R., Ph.D. Assistant Professor, Trinity Western University, Langley, British Columbia, Canada: **Consolations/Tanhumim (4Q176); Exile.**

Heard, Warren J. Jr., Ph.D. Associate Professor of Biblical Studies, Judson College, Elgin, Illinois: **Revolutionary Movements, Jewish.**

Helyer, Larry R., Ph.D. Professor of Biblical Studies, Taylor University, Upland, Indiana: **Judith; Tobit.**

Hershbell, Jackson P., Ph.D. Professor, Classical and Near Eastern Studies, University of Minnesota, Minneapolis, Minnesota: **Plutarch.**

Hock, Ronald F., Ph.D. Professor of Religion, University of Southern California, Los Angeles, California: **Romances/Novels, Ancient.**

Hoehner, Harold W., Ph.D. Professor of New Testament Studies, Dallas Theological Seminary, Dallas, Texas: **Herodian Dynasty.**

Horst, Pieter W. van der, Ph.D. Professor of New Testament and Early Judaism, Utrecht University, Utrecht, The Netherlands: **Bibliomancy; Jewish Literature: Historians and Poets; Maria the Jewish Alchemist.**

Hvalvik, Reidar, Dr. Theol. Associate Professsor of New Testament, Norwegian Lutheran School of Theology, Oslo, Norway: **Prayer of Manasseh.**

Jarick, John, Ph.D. Senior Lecturer in Biblical Studies, University of Surrey, Roehampton, London, England: **Daniel, Esther and Jeremiah, Additions to.**

Jervis, L. Ann, Th.D. Associate Professor, Wycliffe College, Toronto School of Theology, Toronto, Ontario, Canada: **Law/Nomos in Greco-Roman World.**

Johnson, Dianne B., Ph.D. candidate. Minneapolis, Minnesota: **Art and Architecture: Greco-Roman.**

Johnson, Timothy S., Ph.D. Assistant Professor of Classics, University of Florida, Gainesville, Florida: **Cicero; Roman Emperors.**

Kampen, John I., Ph.D. Vice President and Dean of Academic Affairs, Bluffton College, Bluffton, Ohio: **Barki Nafshi (4Q434, 436, 437-439); Wisdom Literature at Qumran.**

Kee, Howard C., Ph.D. Professor of New Testament (Emeritus), Boston University, Boston, Massachusetts; Visiting Professor, University of Pennsylvania, Philadelphia, Pennsylvania: **Hippocratic Letters; Testaments of the Twelve Patriarchs.**

Keener, Craig S., Ph.D. Professor of New Testament, Eastern Seminary, Wynnewood, Pennsylvania: **Adultery, Divorce; Family and Household; Friendship; Head Coverings; Kissing; Marriage; Milk.**

Klassen, William, Ph.D. Professor of New Testament (Retired), Research Professor, École Biblique, Jerusalem, Israel: **Joseph and Aseneth; Musonius Rufus.**

Knight, Jonathan M., Ph.D. Priest-in-Charge, Holywell-cum-Needingworth, [Diocese of Ely] and Honorary Lecturer in Theology, University of Kent, England: **Ascension of Isaiah; Testament of Abraham.**

Kotansky, Roy D., Ph.D. Malibu, California: **Demonology.**

Kreitzer, Larry J., Ph.D. Fellow, Regent's Park College, Oxford; Tutor of New Testament, Oriel College, Oxford; Research Lecturer, Theology Faculty, Oxford University: **Coinage: Greco-Roman.**

Kroeger, Catherine C., Ph.D. Adjunct Associate Professor of Classical and Ministry Studies, Gordon-Conwell Theological Seminary, South Hamilton, Massachusetts: **Women in Greco-Roman World and Judaism.**

Kruse, Colin G., Ph.D. Lecturer in New Testament, Bible College of Victoria, Melbourne, Victoria, Australia: **Persecution.**

Kugler, Robert A., Ph.D. Associate Professor of Religious Studies, Gonzaga University, Spokane, Washington: **Qumran: Place and History.**

Laansma, Jon C., Ph.D. Assistant Professor of Bible, Moody Bible Institute, Chicago, Illinois: **Mysticism.**

Lalleman, Pieter J., Ph.D. Tutor of New Testament, Spurgeon's College, London, England: **Apocryphal Acts and Epistles.**

Lattke, Michael, D. Litt. Professor, University of Queensland, Brisbane, Queensland, Australia: **Psalms of Solomon.**

Levison, John R., Ph.D. Associate Professor of the Practice of Biblical Interpretation, The Divinity School, Duke University, Durham, North Carolina: **Adam & Eve, Literature Concerning; Holy Spirit.**

Lund, Jerome A., Ph.D. Senior Research Associate, Comprehensive Aramaic Lexicon, Hebrew Union College, Cincinnati, Ohio: **Ahiqar; Syriac Bible.**

Maccoby, Hyam, D., Ph.D. Professor of Jewish Studies, Centre for Jewish Studies, University of Leeds, Leeds, U.K.: **Rabbinic Literature: Talmud.**

Mason, Steve, Ph.D. Professor of Humanities, York University, Toronto, Ontario, Canada: **Josephus: Value for New Testament Study; Pharisees; Theologies and Sects, Jewish.**

McCane, Byron R., Ph.D. Associate Professor of Religion, Converse College, Spartansburg, South Carolina: **Burial Practices, Jewish.**

McDonald, Lee Martin, Ph.D. Principal and Professor of Biblical Studies, Acadia Divinity College, Acadia University, Wolfville, Nova Scotia, Canada: **Antioch (Syria); Colossae; Ephesus; Philippi.**

McKnight, Scot, Ph.D. Karl A. Olsson Professor in Religious Studies, North Park University Chicago, Illinois: **Proselytism and Godfearers.**

McRay, John R., Ph.D. Professor of New Testament and Archaeology, Wheaton College, Wheaton, Illinois: **Archaeology and the New Testament; Athens; Caesarea Maritima; Caesarea Philippi; Corinth; Thessalonica; Tiberias.**

Metso, Sarianna, D.Theol. Assistant Professor of Religious Studies, Albion College, Albion, Michigan: **Rule of the Community/Manual of Discipline (1QS).**

Meyer, Marvin W., Ph.D. Professor of Religion and Chair of Department of Religion, Chapman College, Orange, California: **Mysteries.**

Murphy-O'Connor, Jerome, Ph.D. Professor of New Testament, École Biblique et Archéologique Française, Jerusalem, Israel: **Damascus Document (CD and QD).**

Neusner, Jacob, Ph D. Research Professor of Religion and Theology, Bard College, Annandale-on-Hudson, New York: **Rabbinic Literature: Mishnah and Tosefta.**

Newman, Robert C., Ph.D. Professor of New Testament, Biblical Theological Seminary, Hatfield, Pennsylvania: **Rabbinic Parables.**

Newsom, Carol A., Ph.D. Professor of Old Testament/Hebrew Bible, Emory University, Atlanta, Georgia. **Apocrypha of Moses (1Q29, 4Q374-377, 4Q408); Apocryphon of Joshua (4Q378-379); Songs of the Sabbath Sacrifice (4Q400-407, 11Q17, Mas1k).**

Noy, David, Ph.D. Lecturer, Department of Classics, University of Wales Lampeter, U.K.: **Inscriptions and Papyri: Jewish.**

Oakman, Douglas E., Ph.D. Associate Professor of Religion, Pacific Lutheran University, Tacoma, Washington: **Economics of Palestine.**

Olbricht, Thomas H., Ph.D. Distinguished Professor of Religion Emeritus, Pepperdine University, Malibu, California: **Apostolic Fathers; Aristotle, Aristotelianism.**

Ortiz, Steven M., Ph.D. Assistant Professor of Biblical Archaeology, New Orleans Baptist Theological Seminary, New Orleans, Louisiana: **Archaeology of the Land of Israel.**

Osborne, Grant R., Ph.D. Professor of New Testament, Trinity Evangelical Divinity School, Deerfield, Illinois: **Resurrection.**

Palmer, Darryl W., Th.M. Senior Fellow, University of Melbourne, Melbourne, Victoria, Australia: **Pliny the Elder; Pliny the Younger; Suetonius; Tacitus.**

Pearson, Brook W. R., Ph.D. Lecturer in Biblical Studies, University of Surrey Roehampton, London, U.K.: **Alexander the Great; Antioch (Pisidia); Aristobulus; Associations; Civic Cults; Cumanus; Demetrius; Domestic Religion and Practices; Gymnasia and Baths; Hermeticism; Idolatry, Jewish Conceptions of; Polytheism, Greco-Roman; Pompey.**

Phillips, Elaine A., Ph.D. Professor of Biblical and Theological Studies, Gordon College, Wenham, Massachusetts: **Rabbinic Proverbs.**

Porter, Stanley E., Ph.D. Research Professor in New Testament, University of Surrey Roehampton, London, U.K.: **Chronology, New Testament; Diatribe; Festivals and Holy Days: Greco-Roman; Grammarians, Hellenistic Greek; Inscriptions and Papyri: Greco-Roman; Latin Language; Greek of the New Testament; Manuscripts, Greek New Testament; Manuscripts, Greek Old Testament; New Testament Versions, Ancient; Papyri, Palestinian; Septuagint/Greek Old Testament; Textual Criticism.**

Porter, Wendy J., Ph.D. candidate. Research Fellow, Centre for Advanced Theological Research University of Surrey Roehampton, London, U.K.: **Creeds and Hymns; Music.**

Porton, Gary G., Ph.D. Charles and Sarah Drobny Professor of Talmudic Studies and Judaism, University of Illinois at Urbana-Champaign, Urbana, Illinois: **Rabbinic Literature: Midrashim; Sadducees.**

Pucci, Michael S., Ph.D. Lecturer in History and Humanities, Overseas Family College, Singapore, and Occasional Lecturer, The Biblical Graduate School of Theology, Singapore: **Arenas; Circuses and Games.**

Rapske, Brian M., Ph.D. Assistant Professor of New Testament, Northwest Baptist Seminary and ACTS Seminaries, Langley, British Columbia, Canada: **Citizenship, Roman; Prison, Prisoner; Roman Governors of Palestine; Travel and Trade.**

Reasoner, Mark P., Ph.D. Associate Professor of Biblical Studies, Bethel College, St. Paul, Minnesota: **Rome.**

Reid, Daniel G., Ph.D. Senior Editor, InterVarsity Press, Downers Grove, Illinois: **Sacrifice and Temple Service.**

Robinson, Stephen E., Ph.D. Professor of Ancient Scripture, Brigham Young University, Provo, Utah: **Apocalypse of Abraham; Apocalypse of Zephaniah.**

Sandy, D. Brent, Ph.D. Professor of Biblical Studies, Chair of Department of Biblical Studies, Grace College, Winona Lake, Indiana: **Hellenistic Egypt; Ptolemies.**

Schiffman, Lawrence H., Ph.D. Edelman Professor of Hebrew and Judaic Studies, Chair of Skirball Department of Hebrew and Judaic Studies, New York University, New York, New York: **Israel, Land of; Legal Texts at Qumran**.

Schmidt, Thomas E., Ph.D. Santa Barbara, California: **Taxation, Jewish**.

Schniedewind, William M., Ph.D. Associate Professor of Biblical Studies, University of California Los Angeles, Los Angeles, California: **Melchizedek, Traditions of (11QMelch); Rule of the Congregation/Messianic Rule (1QSa)**.

Scholer, David M., Th.D. Professor of New Testament and Associate Dean, Center for Advanced Theological Studies, School of Theology, Fuller Theological Seminary, Pasadena, California: **Writing and Literature: Greco-Roman**.

Schuller, Eileen M., Ph.D. Professor, Department of Religious Studies, McMaster University, Hamilton, Ontario, Canada: **Apocryphon of Joseph (4Q371-373, 539); Thanksgiving Hymns (1QH)**.

Scott, James M., Dr. Theol. Professor of Religious Studies, Trinity Western University, Langley, British Columbia, Canada: **Galatia, Galatians; Geographical Perspectives in Late Antiquity; Heavenly Ascent in Jewish and Pagan Traditions**.

Seeman, Chris J. Ph.D. candidate. University of California/ Graduate Theological Union Berkeley, California: **Judea**.

Sievers, Joseph, Ph.D. Associate Professor of Jewish History and Literature of the Hellenistic Period, Pontifical Biblical Institute, Rome, Italy: **Hasmoneans**.

Spittler, Russell P., Ph.D. Professor of New Testament, Fuller Theological Seminary, Pasadena, California: **Testament of Job**.

Stamps, D. L., Ph.D. Principal of the West Midlands Ministerial Training Course, The Queens Foundation for Ecumenical Theological Education, Birmingham, England: **Children in Late Antiquity; Rhetoric**.

Stanton, Greg R., Ph.D. Associate Professor in Classics and Ancient History, University of New England, Armidale, New South Wales, Australia: **Hellenism**.

Sterling, Gregory E., Ph.D. Associate Professor of Theology, University of Notre Dame, Notre Dame, Indiana: **Historians, Hellenistic; Philo**.

Stoops, Robert F. Jr., Ph.D. Professor, Department of Liberal Studies, Western Washington University, Bellingham, Washington: **Coinage: Jewish**.

Strange, James F., Ph.D. Professor of Religious Studies, University of South Florida, Tampa, Florida: **Galilee**.

Stuckenbruck, Loren T., Ph.D. Reader in New Testament and Early Judaism, University of Durham, Durham, England: **Angels of the Nations**.

Swanson, Cara A., Ph.D. candidate, University of California–Los Angeles, Los Angeles, California: **Birth of the Chosen One (4Q534); Book of Blessings (1QSb)**.

Talshir, Zipora, Ph.D. Senior Lecturer, Department of Bible and Ancient East, Ben Gurion University of the Negev, Beer Sheva, Israel: **1 Esdras.**

Thom, Johan C., Ph.D. Professor of Classics, University of Stellenbosch, Stellenbosch, South Africa: **Stoicism**.

Thompson, Glen L., Ph.D. Director, Multi-Ethnic Preseminary Program Martin Luther College, New Ulm, Minnesota: **Diadochi; Roman Administration; Roman East; Roman Military**.

Trebilco, Paul R, Ph.D. Associate Professor and Head of Department of Theology and Religious Studies, University of Otago, Dunedin, New Zealand: **Diaspora Judaism; Jewish Communities in Asia Minor**.

Twelftree, Graham H., Ph.D. Senior Pastor, North Eastern Vineyard Church, Adelaide, Australia: **Sanhedrin; Scribes**.

Ulrich, Eugene, Ph.D. J. A. O'Brien Professor of Hebrew Scriptures, University of Notre Dame, Notre Dame, Indiana: **Hebrew Bible; Isaiah Scrolls (1QIsaiah$^{a,\ b}$)**.

VanderKam, James C., Ph.D. John A. O'Brien Professor of Theology, University of Notre Dame, Notre Dame, Indiana: **Jubilees**.

Wagner, J. Ross, Ph.D. Assistant Professor of New Testament, Princeton Theological Seminary, Princeton, New Jersey: **Piety, Jewish**.

Walker, Donald D., Ph.D. Assistant Director of Development, University of Chicago Library, Chicago, Illinois: **Benefactor; Lucian of Samosata**.

Wall, Robert W., Th.D. Professor of the Christian Scriptures, Seattle Pacific University, Seattle, Washington: **Intertextuality, Biblical**.

Wansink, Craig, Ph.D. Associate Professor of Religious Studies, Virginia Wesleyan College, Norfolk, Virginia: **Roman Law and Legal System**.

Watson, Duane F., Ph.D., Professor of New Testament Studies, Malone College, Canton, Ohio: **Cities, Greco-Roman; Education: Jewish and Greco-Roman; Greece and Macedon; Roman Empire; Roman Social Classes**.

Weima, Jeffrey A. D., Ph.D. Professor of New Testament, Calvin Theological Seminary, Grand Rapids, Michigan: **Epistolary Theory; Letters, Greco-Roman**.

Westerholm, Stephen, D.Th. Associate Professor of Biblical Studies, McMaster University, Hamilton, Ontario, Canada: **Sabbath**.

Wilcox, Max, Ph.D. Adjunct Professor of Ancient History, Macquarie University, Sydney, New South Wales, Australia: **Semitic Influence on the New Testament**.

Williams, Tyler F., Ph.D. candidate. Assistant Professor of Old Testament/Hebrew Bible, North American Baptist College/ Edmonton Baptist Seminary, Edmonton, Alberta, Canada: **Catena (4Q177)**.

Williamson, H. G. M., D.D. Regius Professor of Hebrew, The Oriental Institute, University of Oxford, Oxford, England: **Samaritans**.

Willis, Wendell L., Ph.D. Associate Professor, Abilene Christian University, Abilene, Texas: **Banquets**.

Wilson, Walter T., Ph.D. Assistant Professor of New Testament, Candler School of Theology, Emory University, Atlanta, Georgia: **Hellenistic Judaism**.

Wise, Michael O., Ph.D. Scholar-in-Residence, Professor of Bible and History, Northwestern College, St. Paul, Minnesota: **Dead Sea Scrolls: General Introduction; New Jerusalem Texts; Secret of Existence (4Q412-413, 415-421); Tale of Bagasraw (Pseudo-Esther) (4Q550$^{a\text{-}f}$); Temple Scroll (11QTemple); Thunder Text (4Q318)**.

Wolters, Al, Ph.D. Professor of Biblical Studies, Redeemer University College, Ancaster, Ontario, Canada: **Copper Scroll (3Q15)**.

Wright, J. Edward, Ph.D. Associate Professor, Near Eastern Studies; Director, Judaic Studies, University of Arizona, Tucson, Arizona: **Baruch, Books of; Esdras, Books of.**

Yamauchi, Edwin M., Ph.D. Professor of History, Miami University, Oxford, Ohio: **Gnosticism; Synagogues**.

ABBA ḤILQIAH. *See* HOLY MEN, JEWISH.

ABRAHAM. *See* APOCALYPSE OF ABRAHAM; HEROES; TESTAMENT OF ABRAHAM.

ADAM AND EVE, LITERATURE CONCERNING

Diverse literary corpora attest to the significance of Adam and Eve for both Christians and Jews during the Greco-Roman era. These corpora include the NT, early Jewish literature that contains references and allusions to Genesis 1—3 and ancient books that focus on the figure of Adam and Eve.

1. Adam and Eve in the New Testament
2. Ancient Jewish References to Adam and Eve
3. Ancient Adam Books

1. Adam and Eve in the New Testament.

Adam functions in a range of ways, from a component in straightforward genealogical lists (Lk 3:38; Jude 14) to an antitype of Christ's resurrection (1 Cor 15:45-49).

1.1. **Imago Dei.** According to Genesis 1:26-27 male and female were created in the image and likeness of God. The author of the letter of James refers to this image to proscribe cursing other human beings "who are made in the likeness of God" (Jas 3:9). Paul, however, tends to interpret the bearer of that image not now as Adam but as Christ, to whom believers are to be conformed (Rom 8:29; 2 Cor 4:4; cf. Phil 2:5-11; Col 1:15-20; 3:9-10; Eph 4:22-24).

1.2. Sin. The dominant association in the NT is between the primeval pair and the origin of sin. The lengthy description of human sin in Romans 1:18-32, which is peppered with allusions to Genesis 1—3, is epitomized in Romans 3:23 in a summary description of the plight of Adam—"all have sinned and fall short of the glory of God"—and interpreted anew in the ascription to Adam of the origin of sin and spread of death in Romans 5:12-21 (cf. Rom 7:7-25). Similarly Paul contrasts Adam and Christ in 1 Corinthians 15:20-22 and their respective bodies (based upon exegesis of Gen 2:7) in 1 Corinthians 15:45-49. The author of the Pastoral Epistles attributes sin to Eve, for "Adam was not deceived, but the woman was deceived and became a transgressor" (1 Tim 2:13-14).

1.3. Transformation. Allusions to Genesis 1—3 in 2 Corinthians 3:4—4:6 suggest how integrally Paul interprets the creation narratives in an effort to describe the transforming power of Christ. He draws the parallel, for instance, between creation and conversion: "For it is the God who said, 'Let light shine out of darkness,' who has shone in our hearts to give the light of the knowledge of the glory of God in the face of Jesus Christ" (2 Cor 4:6). Indeed, many portions of the NT are characterized by contrasts, all of which may be informed by the conception of life "in Adam" over against life "in Christ." (These contrasts play upon the ability to translate the Hebrew word *ʾādām* either as "human" or "Adam.") The believer is said to be a "new creation" (Gal 6:15; 2 Cor 5:17); accordingly the old human (Adamic life) is to be supplanted by the new human (Rom 6:6), which is renewed according to the image and likeness of God (Col 3:9-10; Eph 4:22-24). This new human can also be understood corporately as a reconciliation of Jew and Gentile (Eph 2:13-18).

1.4. Eschatology. As physical corruption characterizes the present age, according to Paul, so will resurrected, *eschatological existence bring in its train the obviation of sin and death and the restoration of Edenic paradise. The world, which is now subject to decay (Rom 8:19-22), will be transformed at the future appearance of Jesus (Rom 8:18; cf. Eph 1:9-10; Col 3:1-4).

1.5. Marriage. The statement of *marriage in Genesis 2:24 reappears in the NT—in the Gospels in conjunction with Genesis 1:27 as Jesus' affirmation of the inviolability of marriage (Mk 10:6-9; Mt 19:4-6), in 1 Corinthians 6:16 to prove that sexual union with a prostitute is the uniting of two into one flesh, and in Ephesians 5:31 to bolster the analogy drawn between human marriage and Christ's love for the church. Further, the creation of woman from man functions in two thorny passages, 1 Corinthians 11:2-10 and 1 Timothy 2:11-15, to suggest the priority and headship of husband over wife—though Paul's argument reflects at least a high level of ambivalence toward this assessment of marriage (e.g., 1 Cor 11:11; *see DPL*, Adam and Christ).

2. Ancient Jewish References to Adam and Eve. These substantial and diverse NT references to Adam, Eve and paradise comprise but a portion of ancient reflection on Genesis 1—3. During the same era, several authors representing the spectrum of Jewish thought incorporated and concomitantly transformed much from the earliest chapters of Genesis.

2.1. Wisdom Tradition. Authors of the wisdom tradition tend to shift their focus from the particular figure of Adam to elements of Genesis 1—3 that characterize human existence in general. Ben Sira (*see* Sirach), although referring once each to the glory of Adam (Sir 49:16) and to the wisdom the first man lacked (Sir 24:28), tends otherwise to employ aspects of the creation narratives that emphasize the mortality of humankind rather than the particular first human (Sir 15:9—18:14; 33:7-13; 40:1-11, 27). The author of the *Wisdom of Solomon refers to the "earthborn protoplast," of whom Solomon, in his shared mortality with all humans, is the descendant (Wis 7:1-6). This anonymous figure functions primarily as a type of the just person whom wisdom aids both to avoid sin (Wis 10:1-2) and to have dominion (Wis 9:1-3). God's inbreathing (Gen 2:7) is universalized as well; it is the implantation of an immortal soul into all human beings (Wis 2:23-24).

2.2. Philo Judaeus. *Philo Judaeus devotes lengthy discussions to Adam and Eve. In *De Opificio Mundi* 24-25, 64-88, 134-50 and 151-69, he interprets Genesis 1—3 seriatim but not uncreatively. He interprets, for example, Adam, Eve and the serpent according to a complex but consistent allegory of the soul. The detail that the woman ate first leads Philo to the interpretation: "Pleasure does not venture to bring her wiles and deceptions to bear on the man, but on the woman, and by her means on him. . . . For in us mind corresponds to man, the senses to woman; and pleasure encounters and holds parley with the senses first, and through them cheats with her quackeries the sovereign mind itself" (Philo *Op. Mund.* 165). In *Legum Allegoriae* 1.31-42, 2.4, Philo addresses the *crux interpretatum* of two creation accounts (Gen 1:26-27; 2:7). He explains that the heavenly man of Genesis 1 represents both the superior mind (i.e., as an anthropological component) as well as the person who lives by reason (i.e., as an ethical category); the earthly man of Genesis 2 represents both the mortal mind, which may succumb to the flesh, and the person who has the capacity for either virtue or vice. In *Quaestiones in Genesin,* Philo responds in a similar vein—with responses both literal and allegorical—to questions raised by Genesis (cf. *Vit. Mos.* 2.59-65). In *De Virtutibus* 199-205, Philo interprets the deluge as a new creation and Noah as a second Adam.

2.3. Rewritten Bible. Attention is also paid to Adam in *rewritten versions of Genesis, such as **Jubilees* and *Liber Antiquitatum Biblicarum* (*Pseudo-Philo). The author of the book of *Jubilees* presents Adam as a virtuous ancestor of Israel, and Eden as a most holy place, perhaps the holy of holies (*Jub.* 2:1—3:32). Adam accordingly offered incense in front of Eden only after covering his nudity, not out of shame but as an act of propriety such as Exodus 28:42-43 demands of priests. By portraying Adam as a properly clad *priest, this author indicts the Jewish priests of his own day (second century B.C.) for neglecting their priestly duties in order to rush into the Greek gymnasia, where they wrestled naked (*see* Athletics; Education).

While *Jubilees* characterizes Adam in a positive light as a priestly patriarch, the author of *Liber Antiquitatum Biblicarum* presents Adam whom the earth gave at God's command (*Bib. Ant.* 16.2) primarily in a negative light by denying him priestly prerogatives: his transgression led to the loss of the fertility that would be assured later by the cult (*Bib. Ant.* 13.8-9) and to the loss of the precious light-giving gems of paradise, which would be restored by the light of Torah and by the priestly garments (*Bib. Ant.* 26.6). If Adam has any positive character, it is that Israel, which came from his rib, offered incense (*Bib. Ant.* 32.15) and that the thorns that arose due to his transgression became the means of revelation to *Moses (*Bib. Ant.* 37.3).

2.4. Josephus. *Josephus recasts Genesis 1—3 (Josephus *Ant.* 1.1.1-4 §§32-51, 1.2.2-3 §§66-72) into conformity with the salient theme of his *Antiquities:* "God, as the universal Father and Lord who beholds all things, grants to such as follow him a life of bliss but involves in dire calamities those who step outside the path of virtue" (Josephus *Ant.* Pref. §20). To this end, Josephus inserts these words into God's mouth in the context of their punishment: "Nay, I had decreed for you to live a life of bliss" (*Ant.* 1.1.4 §46). Adam becomes in Josephus's version a tragic figure who once lived in a luxurious, earthly garden and who forfeited bliss (not immortality) because he sinned. His fall is from bliss to catastrophe, just as all who disobey God fall from bliss into dire calamities.

2.5. Apocalypses. The *apocalyptic authors of 4 Ezra (3:4-11, 20-27; 4:26-32; 6:45-59; 7:11-14, 62-74, 116-31) and *2 Baruch* (4:1-7; 14:17-19; 17:1—18:2; 19:8; 23:4-5; 48:42-47; 54:13-19; 56:6-10), in the wake of the destruction of *Jerusalem, maximize the effects of Adam's sin by reckoning Adam—and Eve in *2 Baruch*—as the inaugurator of the present evil age. Fourth Ezra begins, "And you laid upon him [Adam] one commandment of yours; but he transgressed it, and immediately you appointed death for him and for his descendants" (4 Ezra 3:7). According to *2 Baruch* 56:6, Adam brought an ominous cloud to humanity: "For when he transgressed, untimely death came into being, mourning was mentioned, affliction was prepared, illness was created."

These apocalyptic authors are not content to explore the effect of Adam's sin on the present evil age. They also resolve to discover whether Adam's sin caused not only human suffering but also original sin, not only physical horrors but also moral depravity. The author of 4 Ezra appears to blame Adam: "O Adam, what have you done? For though it was you who sinned, the fall was not yours alone, but ours also who are your descendants. For what good is it to us, if an eternal age has been promised to us, but we have done deeds that bring death? And what good is it that an everlasting hope has been promised us, but we have miserably failed?" (4 Ezra 7:117-20). Despite this indictment, the author does not finally blame Adam for human sin. The *angel responds instead, "This is the meaning of the contest which every person who is born on earth shall wage, that if he is defeated he shall suffer what you have said, but if he is victorious he shall receive what I have said [i.e., glory]" (4 Ezra 7:127-28). The author of *2 Baruch* raises a similar question: "O Adam, what did you do to all who were born after you?" (*2 Bar.* 48:42). His answer, too, is that, while Adam brought physical death to the present evil age, individuals possess the ability to decide their own destiny in the age to come: "For, although Adam sinned first and has brought death upon all who were not in his own time, yet each of them who has been born from him has prepared for himself [or herself] the coming torment" (*2 Bar.* 54:15).

2.6. Miscellaneous. There are in addition many less detailed references to Adam and Eve or allusions to Genesis 1—3 in early Jewish literature. A prayer on the wedding night in Tobit 8:6 cites Genesis 2:24 (*see* Tobit). In *1 Enoch* 32:6, Raphael identifies for Enoch a marvelous tree of wisdom "from which your old father and mother . . . ate and came to know wisdom; and [consequently] their eyes were opened and they realized they were naked and [so] they were expelled from the garden." Adam and Eve are included in the allegory of the animals in *1 Enoch* 85:3-10, 90:37-38 (*see* Enoch, Books of). The Jewish sibyl declares that it is God "who fashioned Adam, of four letters, the first-formed man, fulfilling by his name east and west and south and north" (*Sib. Or.* 3:24-26; *see* Sibylline Oracles).

In other texts the eschatological dimension is evident. In the *Dead Sea Scrolls, reference is made to the eschatological restoration of "all the glory of Adam/humanity"—it is not clear whether human glory or Adam's glory will be restored, since *ʾādām* could refer to either (1QS 4:23; 1QH 17:15; CD 3:20; cf. 4QPs37 3:1-2). According to *Testament of Levi* 18:10-11 (which may be either Jewish or Christian in origin), the messianic deliverer will "open the gates of paradise; he shall remove the sword that has threatened since Adam, and he will grant to the saints to eat of the tree of life" (*see* Testaments of the Twelve Patriarchs).

In addition to innumerable references and allusions in the corpora of *rabbinic literature and the targums, other references to Genesis 1—3 occur in texts that may postdate the period of the NT: *1 Enoch* 37:1; 60:8; 69:9-11; *2 Enoch* (recension J) 30:8—32:2; 41:1; (both J and A)

58:1-3; *Testament of Abraham* (recension A) 8:9; 11:1-12; (recension B) 8:1-16; **Apocalypse of Abraham* 23:1-14; *Sibylline Oracles* 1:5-64; 5:229-30, 244-45; *Testament of Isaac* 3:15; 4:31-32; 6:34; *3 Baruch* 4:8; 9:7; *History of the Rechabites* 7.7-10; 12.1-9; *Apocalypse of Sedrach* 1.21; 4.1—7.13.

3. Ancient Adam Books.
The preceding references and allusions do not exhaust the sort of attention Adam and Eve drew in antiquity. Several literary texts had their foci in these mysterious protoplasts.

3.1. Ancient Testimonies. Several of these ancient Adam books, most of which are probably no longer extant, are cited in the voluminous literature of the bibliographer J. A. Fabricius (1668-1736), the *Apostolic Constitutions* 6.16.3 (fourth century), the Byzantine *List of Sixty Books* (possibly sixth century), the Gelasian Decree (fourth to sixth centuries) and the *Chronicle* of the world, from creation to Diocletian, composed by the Byzantine author George Syncellus (eighth or ninth century).

3.2. Ancient Books. Other ancient books give important traditions that relate to Adam and Eve. Although many of these are Christian in origin or present form, they may preserve ancient, originally Jewish interpretations of Genesis 1—5. The *Discourse on Abbatôn,* the angel of death, is a homily, recorded in Coptic, that is ascribed to Timothy, archbishop of *Alexandria (c. A.D. 380). In this homily, the creation, disobedience and expulsion of Adam and Eve are considered in the context of the salvation of Jesus Christ. The Syriac *Testament of Adam* is divided into three sections: an Horarium, listing the hours of day and night; a Prophecy, given in testamentary form from Adam to Seth; and a Hierarchy, a list of the nine orders of angels and their functions. The Syriac *Cave of Treasures* is a reinterpretation of biblical events from the creation of Adam until the coming of Christ, including traditions that are found as well in the Latin version of the *Life of Adam and Eve,* such as *Satan's refusal to worship Adam. The Ethiopic *Struggle of Adam and Eve with Satan* (also in Arabic), which may be of composite origin, contains three sections: the struggle of Adam and Eve with Satan during the 223 days between their expulsion from paradise and their marriage; history from Cain and Abel to Melchizedek; and a short history of the world from the death of Shem to Jesus Christ. The first section is particularly rich with traditions that are similar to the *Life of Adam and Eve.* Finally, the Coptic *Apocalypse of Adam,* from Nag Hammadi (*see* Gnosticism), found in a codex dating about A.D. 350 and containing earlier traditions, is presented as a revelation given to Seth by Adam in the seven hundredth year; it details, among other traditions, Adam and Eve's loss of glory and knowledge.

***3.3. The* Life of Adam and Eve.** A few decades ago the common consensus was that this text was Jewish in origin, probably written in the first century A.D., and extant in two versions, the Latin and Greek. These points of agreement are now matters of contention (see de Jonge and Tromp). Whether it is of Jewish or Christian origin, the *Life* no doubt contains a rich and relatively early collection of traditions about Adam and Eve. The narrative appears in several versions, including Greek, Latin, Armenian, Georgian and Slavonic; although these versions have much in common, they also exhibit distinctive features that distinguish them from one another. The Greek version, moreover, exists in more than two dozen manuscripts that have correctly been subdivided into three distinct text forms.

In the first Greek text form (e.g., manuscripts DSV), which M. de Jonge and J. Tromp (34) suggest represents the earliest form of the *Life,* the story begins with Eve's realization that Cain has murdered Abel (*Adam and Eve* 1—5). In the ensuing episode, Adam becomes ill and gathers his children; Adam commissions Seth and Eve to set off to paradise to procure for him the healing oil of life (*Adam and Eve* 5—13). Upon their return and the failure to alleviate Adam's pain, Eve tells the story of their lives in the garden (where they each tended a separate portion of paradise), their successive experiences of being deceived and their being cursed (*Adam and Eve* 14—30). When she has completed this reminiscence, Adam's death draws near. He dies, and his soul ascends to paradise while his body is prepared for burial; Eve confesses her sin and then, with Seth, observes the pardoning of Adam (31—43).

The second Greek text form (manuscripts R and M) is similar, with one notable addition. At the end of Eve's testament and prior to the pardoning of Adam, Eve retells her experience of a second temptation and act of disobedience (*Adam and Eve* 29:7-13). Adam and Eve stand in separate rivers, fasting and repenting. Satan, disguised as an angel, comes to the river's edge to tell Eve that God has forgiven her. She leaves the river, only to see that she has been deceived a second time. The inclusion of this story at this point in the *Life* is characteristic as well of the Slavonic version, which is part of a tradition represented by this second Greek text form.

The third Greek text form (e.g., manuscripts NIK) is characterized by an alternative, lengthier introduction to Eve's testament (*Adam and Eve* 14:3—16:3) and by a reordering of the curses following disobedience. In the other versions, Adam is cursed first, then Eve, then the serpent, while in this text form the serpent is cursed before Eve (*Adam and Eve* 24—26).

The Latin, Armenian and Georgian versions begin with an expanded version of Eve's second experience of deception by Satan rather than placing it after Eve's account of the fall, as do the second text form and the Slavonic version. In these versions, the narrative begins not with the death of Abel or Adam's sickness but with the need for physical nourishment following Adam and Eve's expulsion from paradise. Their respective acts of penitence, according to these versions, has the expressed purpose of obtaining nourishment now that they no longer live in paradise. In this context, these versions relate Satan's envy of Adam, his refusal to worship Adam and his consequent expulsion from heaven, as well as the story of the birth of Seth. The Latin version also contains a revelation in which Adam tells Seth of his journey to paradise to speak with God (*Adam and Eve* 25—29).

The *Life of Adam and Eve* is not merely a single, coherent narrative but a collection of versions that comprise a rich repository of traditions about Adam and Eve that were preserved by Christians for centuries. Although its first-century, Jewish origin is no longer an assumption of scholarship, the *Life,* which provides a sustained and detailed narrative of Adam and Eve, probably contains many traditions that circulated among Jews during the Greco-Roman era. Many of the elements that illuminate early Christian literature figure in the *Life of Adam and Eve,* such as the *imago dei* (Greek 10—12; Latin 10—17); the loss of primeval glory (Greek 21—22); the loss of dominion over the animal world (Greek 10—12); the advent of physical pain (Greek 5—14; 31); exclusion from paradise (Greek 27—29) and a detailed depiction of the primeval transgression (Greek 7—8; 16—21; 30).

See also REWRITTEN BIBLE IN PSEUDEPIGRAPHA AND QUMRAN.

BIBLIOGRAPHY. G. A. Anderson, "Adam and Eve in the 'Life of Adam and Eve,'" in *Biblical Figures Outside the Bible,* ed. M. E. Stone and T. A. Bergren (Harrisburg, PA: Trinity Press International, 1998) 7-32; G. A. Anderson and M. E. Stone, eds., *A Synopsis of the Books of Adam and Eve* (2d ed.; SBLEJL 17; Atlanta: Scholars Press, 1999); G. A. Anderson, M. E. Stone and J. Tromp, *Literature on Adam and Eve* (SVTP 15; Leiden: E. J. Brill, 2000); D. A. Bertrand, *La Vie Grecque d'Adam et Ève* (Recherches Intertestamentaires 1; Paris: Maisonneuve, 1987); J. B. Frey, "Adam (Livres Apocryphes sous son Nom)," *Dictionnaire de la Bible: Supplément* (Paris: Letouzey et Ané, 1928) 1:101-34; J. Frishman and L. Van Rompay, eds., *The Book of Genesis in Jewish and Oriental Christian Interpretation* (Traditio Exegetica Graeca 5; Louvain: Peeters, 1997); M. D. Johnson, "Life of Adam and Eve," in *The Old Testament Pseudepigrapha,* ed. J. H. Charlesworth (2 vols.; Garden City, NY: Doubleday, 1983, 1985) 2:249-95; M. de Jonge and J. Tromp, *The Life of Adam and Eve and Related Literature* (GAP; Sheffield: Sheffield Academic Press, 1997); J. R. Levison, "The Exoneration of Eve in the Apocalypse of Moses 15—30," *JSJ* 20 (1989) 135-50; idem, *Portraits of Adam in Early Judaism: From Sirach to 2 Baruch* (JSPSup 1; Sheffield: Sheffield Academic Press, 1988); idem, *Texts in Transition: The Greek Life of Adam and Eve* (SBLEJL; Atlanta: Scholars Press, forthcoming); J. P. Mahé, "Le Livre d'Adam Géorgien," in *Studies in Gnosticism and Hellenistic Religions,* ed. R. van den Broek and M. J. Vermaseren (ẸPROER 91; Leiden: E. J. Brill, 1981) 227-60; O. Merk and M. Meiser, *Das Leben Adams und Evas* (JSHRZ 2.5; Gütersloh: Gütersloher Verlagshaus, 1998); W. Meyer, "Vita Adae et Evae," *Abhandlungen der königlich Bayerischen Akademie der Wissenschaften, philosophisch-philologische Klasse* 14.3 (Munich: Verlag der königlich bayerischen Akademie der Wissenschaften, 1878) 187-250; M. Nagel, *La Vie d'Adam et d'Eve (Apocalypse de Moïse)* (3 vols.; diss., Strasbourg; Lille: Service de Réproduction, Université de Lille III, 1974); M. E. Stone, *Armenian Apocrypha Relating to the Patriarchs and Prophets* (Jerusalem: Israel Academy of Sciences and Humanities, 1982); idem, *A History of the Literature of Adam and Eve* (SBLEJL 3; Atlanta: Scholars Press, 1992); E. Turdeanu, "La Vie d'Adam et d'Eve en Slave et en Roumain," in *Apocryphes*

Slaves et Roumains de l'Ancien Testament (SVTP 5; Leiden: E. J. Brill, 1981) 75-144, 437-38; L. S. A. Wells, "The Books of Adam and Eve," in *The Apocrypha and Pseudepigrapha of the Old Testament*, ed. R. H. Charles (2 vols.; Oxford: Clarendon Press, 1913) 2:123-54. J. R. Levison

ADMINISTRATION, ROMAN. *See* ROMAN ADMINISTRATION.

ADULTERY, DIVORCE

This article covers in turn divorce, adultery and other irregular sexual unions that contemporary Christian ethicists and (in most cases) ancient Jews and Christians would have classed as deviations from the marital ideal (*see* Marriage).

1. Divorce
2. Adultery
3. Other Irregular Unions

1. Divorce.

Divorce was common in the Roman world (Carcopino, 95-100), and under Roman law, children normally remained with their fathers (Pomeroy, 158, 169). Although the early republic probably granted divorces only under the most extreme circumstances (Plutarch *Rom.* 22.3), by the first century some writers said that only a coward would fail to divorce a troublesome wife (Plutarch *Virtue and Vice* 2, *Mor.* 100E). Probably as late as the middle republic women could still not divorce their husbands (McDonnell), but by the imperial period a Roman woman could get a divorce as easily as her husband could (Verner, 40). Either party could unilaterally terminate a marriage; because Roman law deemed private consent essential to the marriage union, it accepted lack of mutual consent in favor of continuing the marriage as sufficient grounds to dissolve it (O'Rourke, 181). Such divorces involved no stigma; dying or divorcing husbands sometimes even arranged new marriages for their ex-wives (Pomeroy, 64).

Diaspora Judaism often followed local customs, and wealthy Jewish aristocrats often followed Greek custom (Josephus *Ant.* 20.7.2 §143; 20.7.3 §§146-47). But in most of Palestinian Judaism only the husband could initiate the divorce, except under extreme circumstances in which a court would require him to terminate the marriage at his wife's demand. Since a divorced woman might bear some social stigmas in Palestinian Jewish society (Safrai, 791), women probably did not seek divorce frequently.

Palestinian Jewish husbands could divorce for virtually any reason (e.g., Josephus *Ant.* 4.8.23 §253, though this is not to imply that the average husband was looking for excuses to divorce his wife). They could divorce their wives for disobedience (Sir 25:26; Josephus *Life* 76 §426; *m. Ketub.* 7:6; *'Abot R. Nat.* 1A) or for burning the bread (*m. Giṭ.* 9:10; *Sipre Deut.* 269.1.1). The agreement of a variety of sources on this matter suggests that the school of Shammai, which accepted only unfaithfulness as valid grounds for divorce—a standard charge in the dissolution of marriages—held the minority opinion in Palestinian Jewish culture at this point, although they were generally the dominant *Pharisaic school in Jesus' day. Further, even Shammaites accepted as legally valid those divorces enacted for reasons with which they disagreed (see Keener, 39-40). The exception clause to Jesus' divorce saying in Matthew 5:32 and 19:9 probably accepts but radicalizes the Shammaite position (Keener, 38-40; *see DJG*, Divorce).

Because the very term for legal divorce meant freedom to remarry, it was understood that without a valid certificate of divorce a woman was not free to remarry (e.g., Josephus *Ant.* 4.8.23 §253; *m. Giṭ.* 2:1). The basic element of the Jewish divorce contract was the phrase "you are free," permitting the wife's remarriage (*m. Giṭ.* 9:3; *CPJ*, 2:10-12 §144); Paul employs the same formula for believers abandoned by unbelieving spouses (1 Cor 7:15; *see DPL*, Marriage and Divorce, Adultery and Incest).

In the imperial period remarriage was the usual practice after divorce or widowhood (*see* Marriage). It was thought that in ancient times widows did not remarry (Pausanius *Descr.* 2.21.7), but this was no longer common in the empire. Failure to remarry could demonstrate exceptional commitment: dying Alcestis begs her husband not to remarry (Euripides *Alc.* 305-25); Isis vowed never to marry after Osiris's death (Diodorus Siculus *Bib. Hist.* 1.22.1). Objections to the remarriage of widowers would have been fewer in the imperial period (Gardner, 82; O'Rourke, 180; *y. Ketub.* 9:8 §4; after widowhood it remained an ideal in some circles [cf. Walcot]), though some opposed remarriage after becoming a widower because stepmothers were considered unhealthy for the children (Diodorus Siculus *Bib. Hist.* 12.14.2-3).

"Husband of one wife" (lit., "one-woman man") in 1 Timothy 3:2 does not likely address monogamy per se (*see* Marriage). But neither may it exclude a divorced or widowed man who has remarried, because the former wife is no longer considered his wife (fidelity to the current wife is most likely in view). A document can prohibit the husband from intercourse with another woman while his wife lives (*P. Tebt.* 104.18-19) yet recognize that she can be divorced and hence no longer count as his wife (*P. Tebt.* 104.27-30; *P. Eleph.* 1.6-7). Likewise, a one-husband wife was one so faithful that her husband lacked reason to ever divorce her (e.g., in Horsley §8, pp. 33-34; Keener, 87-95; for far more detail and fuller documentation from the ancient sources concerning divorce in general, see Keener).

2. Adultery.

Here we survey some ancient Mediterranean views concerning adultery, pagan attributions of such activity to deities, reports about punishment of adultery by human agents and reports about its punishment by divine agents.

2.1. Ancient Mediterranean Views on Adultery. The various sources on adultery in the Roman Empire provide different portraits regarding the frequency and treatment of adultery: laws varied from one ruler to another; historians and biographers often provided deliberate models of feminine virtue; satirists recycled gossip and political propaganda (see especially Richlin). Taken together, however, these diverse sources can provide us a general picture of feelings toward adultery in the ancient Mediterranean world.

A wide range of Jewish sources strongly condemned adultery (e.g., *Sent. Syr. Men.* 45-46; *Tr. Shem* 7:15; 9:9; 10:16; *Asc. Isa.* 2:5; *Num. Rab.* 9:11) and could epitomize evil deeds especially by adultery (Pseudo-Philo *Bib. Ant.* 2.8). But while Jewish people often proved skeptical of Gentiles' fidelity to their marriages (Wis 14:24; *Sib. Or.* 3.594-95), most Greeks and Romans strongly condemned adultery as well (e.g., Athenaeus *Deipn.* 4.167e). The charge of adultery represented a serious insult against another man's morality (Pseudo-Cicero *Invective Against Sallust* 5.15—6.16; Cornelius Nepos 15 [Epaminondas], 5.5). Mediterranean societies viewed a wife as her husband's exclusive property in terms of her sexuality. Hence any other man's use of that property was wife stealing (Artemidorus *Oneir.* 3.11; Epictetus *Disc.* 1.18.11; *Pseud.-Phoc.* 3; *Sib. Or.* 1.178; 3.38, 204; 5.430).

Adultery was shameful (e.g., Diodorus Siculus *Bib. Hist.* 12.21.2; Seneca *Dial.* 2.18.2), even for kings (Alexander 3 in Plutarch *Reg. Imp. Apophth. Mor.* 179E). A minority of philosophers regarded it as acceptable in some situations (Diogenes Laertius *Vit.* 2.99). Most philosophers, however, regarded adultery as wrong (e.g., Epictetus *Disc.* 2.4; 2.10.18; 2.18.15), though they might not seek to prevent it (Epictetus *Disc.* 1.18.12; 3.3.12) or punish those who practiced it (Epictetus *Disc.* 1.18.5-6). Dramatists complained about the shamefulness of wives' adultery (Euripides *Hippol.* 403-18) and warned that they must fear exposure to their husbands (Euripides *Hipp.* 415-18). The behavior also brought shame on the wronged husband (e.g., *2 Enoch* 71:6-11; cf. Gilmore, 4), as is the case in some Middle Eastern societies today (Delaney, 40).

The jibes of satirists like Horace (*Sat.* 1.2.38, 49, 64-110; 2.7.46-47; *Ep.* 1.2.25-26; *Odes* 1.15.19-20), Martial (*Epigr.* 2.47, 49; 6.45.4; 9.2) and Juvenal (*Sat.* 1.77-78; 2.27-29, 68; 6.133-35, 231-41) indicate that public sentiment was against such behavior. Such insults could be harsh: Martial charges that the wife of Candidus is common property of the Roman people (*Epigr.* 3.26.6); Zoilus will not get caught solely because he is impotent (*Epigr.* 6.91). Sallust complains that Sempronia viewed nothing as cheaply as sexual restraint (*Catil.* 25.3-4). Some writers would not have limited their objection against relational infidelity to heterosexual unions; one male character in a novel could complain when another male character seduces the first character's younger boyfriend (Petronius *Sat.* 79).

Nevertheless, adultery seems to have been quite common; following hyperbolic conventions of societal critique, some authors complained that it characterized most women (Seneca *Dial.* 12.16.3; Plutarch *Bride* 46, *Mor.* 144E-F) or that chastity had left the earth (Juvenal *Sat.* 4.1-20). The Greek philosopher Bias reportedly said that one who married a beautiful woman would have to share her (Aulus Gellius *Noc. Att.* 5.11.2). Exaggerating to underline his point, Seneca complains that those who do not commit adultery make themselves conspicuous, that adultery has become the favorite means of betrothal, that it is difficult to find a woman so ugly that she must settle for only two illicit partners a day, and that the only value of husbands to most wives is to provoke the wives' illicit partners (Seneca *Ben.* 1.9.4; 3.16.3). Dio Cassius reports with favor the witty retort of a British captive mocked for alleged polyandry: we mate openly with the best men, but you Roman women sleep around in private with the worst (Dio Cassius *Hist.* 77.16.5). The evidence does not suggest that many aristocratic men were caught in the act, however (see Rawson, 33).

Women were to avoid undue contact with men other than their husbands (*see* Head Coverings §1); even today in some traditional Middle Eastern societies, if a man is alone with a woman for more than twenty minutes people assume they have shared intercourse (Delaney, 41). *Josephus considered women by nature prone to unfaithfulness (*War* 2.8.2 §121), and this view was probably held more widely in the Mediterranean world (Diodorus Siculus *Bib. Hist.* 1.59.3-4), though the resistance of virtuous women to adultery was also recognized (Dionysius of Halicarnassus *Ant. Rom.* 4.66.2—4.67.1). Jewish men also were to avoid the company of women, which could lead to desire or the appearance of it (Sir 9:9; 42:12; *m. Abot* 1:5; *'Abot R. Nat.* 14 §35B; *b. Ber.* 43b, *Bar.; y. Soṭa.* 7:1 §2; *Gen. Rab.* 48:20; 63:7).

2.2. Divine Examples of Adultery. Prominent members of the Greek and Roman pantheon failed to set an example of sexual morality. Though even the gods were supposed to obey the laws about adultery, the god of lust inflamed Zeus to break them (Apuleius *Met.* 6.22). Zeus's adulteries with mortals pervade Greek and Roman mythology (Sophocles *The Searchers* frag. 212-15; Euripides *Antiope* 69-71; *Pirithous* frag. 22-24), though occasionally a mortal woman outwitted him and escaped (Apollonius of Rhodes *Arg.* 2.946-54). Hera did not cooperate willingly with his activities; she quit going to bed with Zeus for a year because of his infidelities (Homeric Hymn 3, to Pythian Apollo 343-44). After Zeus raped a nymph (Ovid *Met.* 2.434-37), Hera punished the nymph for adultery (Ovid *Met.* 2.477-88), just as she punished willing partners (Ovid *Met.* 3.261-72; Appian *Rom. Hist.* 12.15.101) and sometimes their relatives (Ovid *Met.* 4.416-530). Zeus had to hide Dionysus from Hera until his birth (Euripides *Bacch.* 94-98).

Pagan deities seduced (Ovid *Met.* 2.714-47; 3.260-61) and were prepared to rape mortals when they encountered resistance to their sexual advances (Ovid *Met.* 3.1-2; 14.765-77); some even raped and abducted young girls (Ovid *Met.* 5.391-408) or boys (Virgil *Aen.* 1.28; Ovid *Met.* 10.155-219) and might punish a nymph who protested such injustice (Ovid *Met.* 5.409-37). (On occasion nymphs also raped boys—Apollonius of Rhodes *Arg.* 1.1226-39; Ovid *Met.* 4.368-79.) Apollo got Leucippus killed so he could sleep with Daphne (Parthenius *Amat. Nar.* 15.3); he slew one of his human mistresses for sleeping with a man (Ovid *Met.* 2.603-11). Nevertheless, many ancient thinkers regarded such portraits of divine immorality as ridiculous (Seneca *Dial.* 7.26.6; Pliny *Nat. Hist.* 2.5.17); early Christian apologists made much of such stories (Athenagoras 20-22; Theophilus *Autol.* 1.9; Pseudo-Clementines 15.1—19.3). The behavior of deities sometimes set precedent for human culture (Diodorus Siculus *Bib. Hist.* 1.27.1; Achilles Tatius *Leuc.* 1.5.5-7), so it is hardly surprising that Jewish writers sometimes connected Gentiles' worship of these deities with Gentile men's own sexual behavior (Josephus *Ag. Ap.* 2.35 §§244-46, 275; Rom 1:23-25).

2.3. Human Punishments for Adultery. Shame was a common penalty in the ancient world (e.g., Plutarch *Quaest. Graec.* 2, *Mor.* 291F), but the Romans punished adulterers with banishment or yet more severe penalties (Seneca *Ben.* 6.32.1; Quintilian *Inst. Orat.* 7.1.7; Richlin, 228); Augustus banished his own daughter for her public adultery (Seneca *Ben.* 6.32.1). In some stories, a hero might slay a married woman who made sexual advances toward him (Euripides *Stheneboea* frag.); a landowner might also demand an adulterer's imprisonment (Achilles Tatius *Leuc.* 6.5.3-4). Moralist historians eagerly recounted the story of an honorable Roman matron who chose to slay herself if forced to violate her marriage covenant (Diodorus Siculus *Bib. Hist.* 10.19.3; Dionysius of Halicarnassus *Ant. Rom.* 4.66.2—4.67.1; Livy *Hist.* 1.58.1-12; Dio Cassius *Hist.* 2.11.16-19); a woman might go to great lengths to disprove the charge of adultery (Appian *Rom. Hist.* 7.9.56). Harsh punishments for female adultery are also not uncommon in traditional societies (Mbiti, 193, 275; Barnouw, 23; Firth, 119, 475-77; Nukunya, 70-71).

The deadly anger of a husband against an adulterer was by this time proverbial (Prov 5:20, 23; 6:26-35; 7:22-27; 22:14; Phaedrus *Fables* 3.10.27-28; *b. Ned.* 91b). In classical *Athens, a husband might do whatever he wished to an adulterer caught in the act, as long as he did not use a knife (Demosthenes *Against Neaera* 66, *Or.* 59; Plutarch *Solon* 23.1; Diogenes Laertius *Vit.* 6.1.4; Xenophon *Hiero.* 3.3), and people could treat an adulterous woman as they wished short of death (Demosthenes *Neaer.* 86; *Orat.* 59). A Roman man who caught his wife and her illicit partner in the act could slay them immediately, though only if he found the adulterer in his house (Quintilian *Inst. Orat.* 7.1.7; Paulus *Opinions* 2.26). Augustus's legislation forbade the father killing the adulterer without also killing the daughter, which probably meant that in most cases neither would die; but such restrictions did not apply to the husband (Gardner, 7; O'Rourke, 181-82). Augustus made adultery a matter of civil law because he regarded the health of families as essential to that of the larger society (see Treggiari).

Nevertheless, the aggrieved husband might choose to divorce his wife (Apuleius *Met.* 9.27-28). He might accept a monetary payment in exchange for the adulterer's life (Aulus Gellius *Noc. Att.* 17.18); some reportedly practiced mutilation (Martial *Epigr.* 2.60, 83; 3.85). Jewish and Roman law alike required a husband who learned of his wife's affair to divorce her immediately (Gardner, 89; Safrai, 762); if he failed to do so, Roman law allowed him to be prosecuted for the offense of *lenocinium*—pimping (Justinian *Dig.* 48.5.1; Gardner, 131-32; Richlin, 227; Rawson, 33-34). In practice, however, a romance suggests that a man deeply in love with his wife on learning of her adultery might wish his own death (Chariton *Chaer.* 1.4.7), though in a fit of rage he might also assault his wife (Chariton *Chaer.* 1.4.11-12).

Like Romans, at least some Jews regarded tolerance of adultery as pimping (*Pseud.-Phoc.* 177). Pharisees of the Shammaite persuasion reportedly permitted divorce if the husband caught his wife in adultery, but the more liberal Hillelites allowed it if the husband merely suspected it (*p. Soṭa.* 1:1 §2). Although rarely implemented in this period, biblical law mandated death for adultery (Deut 22:22; Lev 10:10; *Jub.* 30:8-9; Pseudo-Philo *Bib. Ant.* 25.10; Josephus *Ag. Ap.* 2.201, 215; *Sipra Qed. pq.* 10.208.2.4; for actual punishments for adultery see Ilan 1996, 135-41), as had other ancient legal collections (e.g., Hammurabi 129).

A double standard regarding gender existed. In old Rome husbands could kill wives found in adultery without a trial, but the wife could not do the same to her husband (Aulus Gellius *Noc. Att.* 10.23.4-5). Under the *lex Julia* the wife could not charge her husband with adultery (Justinian *Cod.* 9.1). Honorable Roman men could sleep with unmarried women provided they were not of honorable lineage, but aristocratic Roman women could sleep only with their husbands (Pomeroy, 160).

The double standard also applied to the way historians evaluated their traditions; although monogamy was the norm (*see* Marriage), a man's multiple sexual relations with unmarried women were seen as far less serious than a married woman's infidelities because adultery was specifically a matter of stealing the wife's affections. Thus the empress Messalina, wife of Claudius, perhaps rendered arrogant by honors early in her husband's reign (see Wood), became a notable and negative public example of adultery; by contrast, a biographer might excuse the legendary Romulus, because unlike Theseus he did not rape women (Plutarch *Comp. Thes. and Rom.* 6).

Although Zeus slept with numerous mortals (e.g., Euripides *Pirithous* frag. 22-24), he terribly destroyed a mortal who boasted that he had slept with Hera (Euripides *Pirithous* frag. 1-13). At the same time, a philosophical tradition might warn that husbands unfaithful to their wives would be tortured in the realm of the dead (Diogenes Laertius *Vit.* 8.1.21), and a moral tradition had long condemned unfaithfulness to one's wife (Isocrates *Nicocles/Cyprians* 40, *Or.* 3.35).

The double standard also existed in traditional Jewish sources (Swidler, 148-54; Wegner, 50-54), although it was sometimes qualified (*Sent. Syr. Men.* 246-47). It may be such a double standard that a biblical author addressed by juxtaposing the story of Judah and Tamar with that of Joseph and Potiphar's wife (Gen 38—39). Joseph became a familiar Jewish model for resisting adultery (e.g., *Jub.* 39:5-9).

2.4. Divine Punishments Against Adulterers. Most peoples believed in divine punishments against adulterers, often in addition to human ones. Thus those slain for adultery were consigned to Tartarus, the part of the realm of the dead that included torture (Virgil *Aen.* 6.612). Suitors courted Penelope while Odysseus remained alive because they feared neither the gods nor human wrath (Homer *Odys.* 22.39-40). As Clytemnestra slew Agamemnon through her adultery (Euripides *El.* 479-81), so the immortals would slay her (Euripides *El.* 482-83). Many traditional societies expect divine punishment for adultery (Mbiti, 268-69).

Jewish sources promised divine punishment against adulterers (e.g., Jer 7:9-14; 23:14-15; Hos 4:2-3; Mal 3:5; *Pss. Sol.* 8:8-10; *Sib. Or.* 3.764-66; cf. *Acts Jn.* 35). Sages could warn that God would openly punish the secret adulterer (Sir 23:21). By the first century at least some Jewish writers understood the biblical ordeal of bitter waters (Num 6:12-15) as causing a slow death to the adulteress (Josephus *Ant.* 3.11.6 §273). Many came to believe that the offspring of an adulterous union would betray the evil act because the child would look like the father (*Pseudo.-Phoc.* 178; *t. Sanh.* 8:6; *Pesiq. Rab Kah.* 11:6; *Lev. Rab.* 23:12; *Num. Rab.* 9:1; Probably Wis 4:6; see also some pagan sources: Aristotle *Pol.* 2.1.13, 1262a; Juvenal *Sat.* 6.595-601). Jewish novels could report the death of adulterers or fornicators in response to the prayers of the righteous (*T. Abr.* 10A; 12B). Paul also believed that God would avenge adultery (1 Thess 4:6).

3. Other Irregular Unions.

Many behaviors would have been distinguished from adultery throughout the Greco-Roman world yet appeared related to it in early Jewish and Christian *vice lists or would be classified by modern Jewish and Christian thinkers as adultery. The broader Greek term for immorality *(porneia)* encompassed adultery, prostitution and, for Jews, any sexual behavior deviating from the biblical norm. Premarital intercourse with a person other than one's future spouse constituted a form of adultery against one's future spouse (Deut 22:20-22; cf. Belkin, 258-59). Although these other examples are not adultery per se, they shed further light on it by providing a broader context for understanding the sexual mores of the Greco-Roman world and those of early Judaism and Christianity.

3.1. Premarital Intercourse. Jewish people often expected sexual immorality from Gentiles (*m. 'Abod. Zar.* 2:1); later teachers held that one could trust a proselyte woman's virginity only if she were converted before the age of three years and one day (*b. Yebam.* 60b). (Even later rabbis would not deny, however, that Jewish people also could be tempted in this area; e.g., *Song Rab.* 7:8 §1.) It was not uncommon for peoples to characterize their rivals as sexually immoral (Euripides *Androm.* 595-604). But Greeks also sometimes recognized that it was difficult to keep young men from women if the latter were available (Euripides *Alc.* 1052-54), and Greek men generally did not demand the same moral standard that Jewish tradition did. Thus, for example, no one seems to have objected when the mythical Argonauts impregnated the Lemnian women and departed after enjoying their time there (Apollonius of Rhodes *Arg.* 1.842-909).

Still, Gentiles recognized some differences and limitations; aristocratic Roman men could sleep with prostitutes or take lower-class concubines, but to sleep with one of high rank invited severe punishment (O'Rourke, 182; Gardner, 124; Rawson, 34). Even in classical Athens, other sexual relations were not on the same level as those employed for producing legitimate heirs (Demosthenes *Mantitheus Against Boeotus* 2.8-10).

Whereas Gentile men might pursue premarital sex in socially accepted manners, they expected women to guard their purity (e.g., Homer *Odys.* 6.287-88). Thus some young virgins, raped and unable to endure this shame, killed themselves (Diodorus Siculus *Bib. Hist.* 15.54.3; *Contest of Homer and Hesiod* 323). Stories circulated of fathers who slew daughters suspected of immorality (Ovid *Met.* 4.237-40, in which she was innocent) or might slay them to prevent their rape and hence protect their honor (Diodorus Siculus *Bib. Hist.* 12.24.3-4; Livy *Hist.* 3.44.4—3.48.9). Rape was universally condemned (e.g., *Pseud.-Phoc.* 198) and constituted a capital charge both in Roman law and the stricter Jewish interpretations (*Jub.* 30:1-6; Gardner, 118-19; cf. *Laws of Eshnunna* 26). Jewish people regarded a woman's premarital sexual activity as equivalent to prostitution (*Sipra Qed. pq.* 7.204.1.1-2).

Jews regarded sexual immorality in general as a terrible sin (CD 7.1), a work of Satan (*see* Belial) or fallen *angels (*1 Enoch* 8:1-2; *Asc. Isa.* 2:5) that banished God's presence (*Sipre Deut.* 258.2.3) and otherwise invited judgment, corporately (*t. Sanh.* 13:8; *y. Sanh.* 6:7 §2; *y. Ta'an.* 4:5 §13) or individually (*Num. Rab.* 13:15). With idolatry and murder, it was one of the most serious of sins (*y. Sanh.* 3:5 §2). Although it was not enforced in this period (Josephus *War* 2.8.1 §117; Matt 1:19), the penalty for sex with a person to whom one was not married was for most cases death (Deut 22:20-24; *Jub.* 20:4; 33:20; Pseudo-Philo *Bib. Ant.* 25.10; Josephus *Ag. Ap.* 2.25 §201; *Sipre Deut.* 242.1.6).

Some couples lived together before marriage until they could afford the economic transaction—a recognized union that could be formalized by a written contract (*P. Ryl.* 154.4, A.D. 66). This custom is also attested for some Jewish couples (the early second century Babatha archive; see Ilan 1993). Nevertheless, many pious Jews warned that a truly godly man would not sleep with his fiancée before the wedding (*Jos. and As.* 21:1/20:8).

Ancients often recognized that customs varied from one location to another. Arrian reports the probably fictitious tradition that Indian women were normally quite chaste but considered it honorable to have intercourse with any man in exchange for an elephant (*Ind.* 17.3). Ancients were aware of various other practices that many would have regarded as aberrant, such as intercourse with a corpse (Parthenius *L.R.* 31.2). Intercourse with animals was known but apparently rarely discussed (Apuleius *Met.* 10.19-22; Lucian *Lucius* 50-51; Artemidorus *Oneir.* 1.80; perhaps Aulus Gellius *Noc. Att.* 6.8); some Jews suspected Gentile males in general of bestiality (*Sib. Or.* 5.393; *m. 'Abod. Zar.* 2:1).

3.2. Prostitution. Many people considered prostitution shameful (Diodorus Siculus *Bib. Hist.* 12.21.2; Artemidorus *Oneir.* 1.78; Aulus Gellius *Noc. Att.* 9.5.8; 15.12.2-3), a disgracefully wasteful excess (Livy *Hist.* 23.18.12) or exploitation (Dio Chrysostom *Or.* 7.133), and exhorted against it (Prov 23:27; Sir 9:6; 19:2; 41:20; Cato collection of distichs 25). Thus Catiline reportedly seduced young men to follow him by securing prostitutes for their use (Sallust *Catil.* 14.6). Plutarch admonished that one could have intercourse for free at home (Plutarch *Lib. Educ.* 7, *Mor.* 5C) and that even single men should avoid prostitutes and concubines to avoid producing lowborn children (Plutarch *Lib. Educ.* 2, *Mor.* 1AB).

Nevertheless, prostitution was legal. The Roman government received substantial tax revenues from this industry (McGinn; Lewis, 145, 171-72). Some people regarded prostitution as a deterrent to adultery (*Grk. Anth.* 7.403). By contrast, Jews generally regarded prostitution as evil (*Sib. Or.* 5.388; *Ex. Rab.* 43:7; *Num. Rab.* 9:24; 20:7), a terrible abuse of nature, degrading the body (Josephus *Ant.* 4.8.9 §206); Philo regards it as a capital offense (Belkin, 256). The *Dead Sea Scrolls condemn "prostitution" (1QS 4:10; CD 4:17; 8:5), although the language could apply to other kinds of sexual immorality or to spiritual infidelity. God would reward those who resisted prostitution for the honor of his name (*b. Menaḥ.* 44a). Nevertheless it remains clear that prostitution existed even in Jewish Palestine (Mt 21:31-32; Goodman, 60; Gibson; Ilan 1996, 214-21).

Laws prohibited prostitutes from being married as long as they continued their practice (Propertius *Elegies* 2.7.7); a prostitute's activity was considered adultery only if she had retired and married (Gardner, 133), and a man could not be considered adulterous if he slept with a promiscuous woman who charged money for her activity (Justinian *Cod.* 9.22, if this custom is early enough). Inns in the Roman world usually doubled as brothels, so that those staying upstairs could send for a maid downstairs for a fee (Casson, 206-7, 211, 215; Pomeroy, 201). Barmaids and waitresses were typically prostitutes (Gardner, 32), but it was illegal for the free owner of the inn to engage in such practices (Justinian *Cod.* 9.29).

Some well-to-do prostitutes could command considerable prestige (Athenaeus *Deipn.* 13.596b; Aulus Gellius *Noc. Att.* 7.7.5-7; *Sipre Num.* 115.5.7). The activity of prostitutes in ancient Near Eastern temples is well documented (Deut 23:17; MacLachlan), but scholars debate the reasons for their presence in temples. (Jewish people believed that prostitution defiled their temple; 2 Macc 6:4.) Yet poverty was probably the primary motivation for most women who entered prostitution (Terence *And.* 73-79); thus when a "public prostitute" was murdered, the woman's destitute mother petitioned the state to force the murderer to provide for the mother's support, claiming she had given her daughter to a brothelkeeper to provide needed funds (BGU 1024.7 in Lewis, 146). Different prostitutes brought different wages, presumably depending on their age, attractiveness and sexual prowess (*CIL* 4.1679 in Sherk, 210-11).

More often, prostitutes were female *slaves forced to provide income to their masters by the exploitation of their bodies. Exposed female infants were often taken in and raised as slaves, normally for the sex trade; infants could be sold into prostitution (Martial *Epigr.* 9.6.7; 9.8). Captured female slaves might be used for the same purpose (Apuleius *Met.* 7.9; *'Abot R. Nat.* 8A). Those slaves found to be freeborn were freed from this life; such a dramatic reversal of apparently lowborn persons being discovered to be highborn reflects a common story line (e.g., Longus *Daphn. Chl.* 4.36), particularly for Terence *(Self-Tormentor; Eunuch; Lady of Andros; Lady of Perinthos)*.

Urban centers naturally provided more opportunities for prostitution. Old *Corinth was notorious for its many temple prostitutes (Strabo *Geog.* 8.6.20; Aulus Gellius *Noc. Att.* 1.8.4; Athenaeus *Deipn.* 13.573cd), even if the reports may be exaggerated (e.g., Saffrey); in classical Athens the phrase "play the Corinthian" denoted sexual promiscuity (Aristophanes *Lysis.* 91). Given its location on the isthmus and consequent regular passage of visitors, Corinth may have revived its reputation for prostitution in the Roman period (see Pausanius *Descr.* 2.4.6; 2.5.1; Martial *Epigr.* 10.70.11-12; Grant, 24; also sources in Murphy-O'Connor, 48, 105-6, 127-28). Rabbis in the southeastern Mediterranean, perhaps reflecting the Greek disdain for Egyptians or their own distrust of Hellenized Alexandrian Jewry, recognized *Alexandria as a center for prostitution (*'Abot R.* Nat. 48 §132B).

3.3. Sexual Use of Slaves. Many considered the sexual use of slave women shameful (Aulus Gellius *Noc. Att.* 15.12.2-3), and some honorably abstained (Homer *Odys.* 1.428-33). Jewish people in particular warned against intercourse with slaves, both those of others (Sir 41:22) and one's own (*Sent. Syr. Men.* 347-53); later traditions promise severe judgment for this practice (*Num. Rab.* 10:1). In contrast to the later Islamic practice, Jewish and Christian tradition warned against the sexual exploitation of slaves (Gordon, 83).

Nevertheless, the sexual exploitation of female slaves was standard practice in the Roman world (Achilles Tatius *Leuc.* 6.20; Artemidorus *Oneir.* 1.78; Martial *Epigr.* 1.84; 3.33; Muson. Ruf. frag. 12; Babrius 10.1-5; *Pesiq. Rab Kah.* 20:6). Many of the texts that warn against it assume that it is common (*m. 'Abot* 2:7). Ancient Greek tradition assumed that women captured in war could be used as concubines (Sophocles *Ajax* 485-91; Arrian *Anab.* 4.19.5). Newly acquired slave women sometimes faced cruel or jealous mistresses (Apollonius of Rhodes *Arg.* 4.35-39); Greek tradition also assumed masters' right to punish cruelly female slaves guilty of promiscuity (Homer *Odys.* 22.465-73).

In the early empire, many female slaves were purchased for breeding (Gardner, 206-9). Jewish sages assumed that slave women and freedwomen were not virgins (*m. Yebam.* 6:5; *t. Hor.* 2:11; *y. Hor.* 3:5 §1). Among the Romans it was legal for slaveholders of some classes to free female slaves for the purpose of marrying them (Gaius *Inst.* 1.19); some Jewish teachers, however, objected if it were thought that the man had been unduly familiar with her before her freedom (Cohen, 149). A Roman, who did not think of intercourse the way Jewish tradition did, might free a slave mistress and provide for her marriage to another (Appian *Civ. W.* 4.4.24).

Mistresses may have occasionally used male slaves sexually (anonymous *Adulteress* in *Select Papyri* [LCL] 3:350-61; Gen 39:7), but it was not the norm, and if this behavior were exposed, it would have brought severe retaliation from the free male arbiters of societal power. Some writers instructed landowners to give their overseers female companions to avoid these servants' intimacy with women of the house (Columella *Rust.* 1.8.5).

3.4. Concubinage. Roman law forbade holding a concubine in addition to a wife (Paulus *Opinions* 2; Gardner, 56-57); Greeks sometimes attributed the practice especially to other peoples (Athenaeus *Deipn.* 13.556b-57e). But the laws against it attest its existence, and evidence suggests that in this period concubinage was widely practiced in the Mediterranean world.

Concubinage was especially common in the military (Gaius *Inst.* 1.57; Gardner, 58, 143; O'Rourke, 182; *OGIS* 674 in Lewis, 141), since soldiers could not legally marry until the term of military service had been fulfilled, a period lasting more than twenty years. Because of the length of time, officials often forgave romances (Fabius Maximus 4, in Plutarch *Sayings of Romans, Mor.* 195EF), though it was best to avoid them (cf. Scipio the Elder 2, in Plutarch *Sayings of Romans, Mor.* 196B). Some military discharge documents from the first century favor the soldiers with the legalization of their prior unions as marriages but add the single stipulation that they should have only one apiece (*ILS* 1986/*CIL* 16.1, from A.D. 52; so also *CIL* 16.42 in A.D. 98). *Pseudo-Phocylides* 181 warns against having intercourse with the concubines—plural—of one's father.

3.5. Incest. Modern discussion of incest usually focuses on those relationships where an adult coerces a younger partner; most ancient references to incest focus on consenting adult partners. The kind of incest involving an innocent partner did, however, occur. In one court case from the early second century a father took his daughter from her husband because the husband threatened to charge him with incest; the husband pleaded that his wife still loved him. In this case, the court ruled that she could decide herself with whom she would live (P. Oxy. 237.7.19-29).

Although exceptions exist, the vast majority of cultures in history have had various forms of the incest taboo, and most have believed that incest merited punishment. For example, old Hawaiian culture prohibited incest on pain of death, except for chiefs (Radcliffe-Brown, 50); some Native Americans believed brother-sister incest led to insanity (Kaplan and Johnson, 211); the Nuer believed it led to death if committed with the closest kin (Evens, 126); traditional Ashanti punished it with death (Fortes, 257). A few cultures, however, have regarded it negatively but without emphasizing punishment (see, e.g., Willner, 152).

Jewish people prohibited incest (Lev 18:6-18; 20:11-21; *y. Ta'an.* 4:5 §8) and believed that it invited divine judgment (Lev 20:10-23; *Jub.* 16:8-9; 33:10-14; *T. Reub.* 1:7-10; *t. Pe'ah* 1:2; *b. 'Arak.* 16a; *Gen. Rab.* 52:3). Although banishment was the penalty for incest (Paulus *Opinions* 2.26; Gardner, 127), *Cicero believed that incest should be punished with death (*De Leg.* 2.9.22). Incest proved to be a serious charge (Tacitus *Ann.* 16.8), and satirists mocked those thought guilty of the crime (Juvenal *Sat.* 2.32-33; 4.8-9).

Jewish law strictly prohibited intercourse between son and mother or father's wife (Lev 18:8; 20:11; Josephus *Ant.* 3.12.1 §274; Philo *Spec. Leg.* 3.3 §19; *b. Ber.* 56b; *y. Ned.* 2:1 §4; Gr. Ezra 4:24). Paul recognized that Gentiles as well as Jews prohibited incest in the line of descent (1 Cor 5:1). Romans defined unions with former mothers-in-law or stepmothers as incestuous (Gaius *Inst.* 1.63). Various stories invoke divine punishments against those who violated the incest taboos: a drunk father's raping his daughter was an impious act that could invite mortal judgment from the gods (Plutarch *Parallel Stories* 19, *Mor.* 310B-C); stories in which daughters seek intercourse with drunk fathers (Gen 19:30-38; Ovid *Met.* 10.314-476) paint them negatively. A son thought to have slept with his father's wife during the father's lifetime might invite a curse, hence swift death (Euripides *Hipp.* 885-90); a man living in open sin with his daughter invited judgment from a deity (Philostratus *Vit. Ap.* 1.10). When Poseidon's sons went insane and raped their mother, Poseidon punished them by burying them alive (Diodorus Siculus *Bib. Hist.* 5.55.6-7). On learning that he had been sleeping with his mother, Periander went insane (Parthenius *L.R.* 17.1-7). Arrian reports only with skepticism the account that Heracles slept with his seven-year-old daughter because he could find no one else worthy of her (Arrian *Ind.* 9.2-3).

One of the most commonly recounted Greek stories was that of Oedipus, who married his mother Iocaste (allusions appear regularly in later literature, e.g., Epictetus *Disc.* 1.24.16; Martial *Epigr.* 10.4.1; Herodian *Hist.* 4.9.3; Justin Martyr *Apol. 1* 27). In its earliest form the story does not make clear that Oedipus acted in ignorance (although his mother did; Homer *Odys.* 11.271-280), but the tragic dramatists played heavily on his ignorance. Oedipus acted in ignorance yet suffered judgment (Sophocles *Oed. Col.* 525-28; *Oed. Tyr.* 1237-79; Euripides *Phoen.* 869-71), as did the offspring of the union (Sophocles *Antig.* 863-66; *Oedipus at Colonus* 1670-72).

Despite such stories, people in power ignored the inevitable hostile gossip and had relations as they pleased. Clymenus consorted with his daughter publicly, though she hated it (Parthenius *L.R.* 13.1-4); Monobazus impregnated his sister Helena (Josephus *Ant.* 20.2.1 §18). Claudius married his niece Agrippina (Suetonius *Claudius* 39; Tacitus *Ann.* 12.5; Dio Cassius *Hist.* 61.31.6). Hostile rumormongers also attributed sibling incest to Gaius Caligula (Suetonius *Caligula* 24) and incest with his mother to Nero (Suetonius *Nero* 34).

Some customs varied geographically, just as definitions of forbidden degrees of kinship vary from one culture to another in more recent times (e.g., Farber). Unlike Jews (Lev 20:11-12; 2 Sam 16:22; 20:3; Amos 2:7; cf. the debate in *Sipre Deut.* 246.1.2), Greeks might not consider it incestuous for a son to sleep with a woman with whom his father had earlier slept (Sophocles *Trach.* 1221-29). Romans could not marry "near relatives" (Plutarch *Rom.* 108, *Mor.* 289D); but whereas he could not marry sisters or aunts, a Roman could marry his brother's daughter (BGU 5.23.70-72; Gaius *Inst.* 1.62). A Seleucid ruler was reported to have given his wife to his son, her stepson, as a wife (Appian *Rom. Hist.*

11.10.61); many thought that Persians permitted mother-son unions (Sextus Empiricus *Pyr.* 1.152; 3.205; Philo *Spec. Leg.* 3.3, §13; Tertullian *Apol.* 9.16; Tatian *Or. Graec.* 28) and that some philosophers found it unobjectionable (Diogenes Laertius *Vit.* 7.7.188; Sextus Empiricus *Pyr.* 1.160).

Brother-sister unions were more commonly known than parent-children unions. In Greek myth, Aeolus married his sons and daughters to each other (Parthenius *L.R.* 2.2; Homer *Odys.* 10.7). Athenian men could marry paternal half-sisters (Achilles Tatius *Leuc.* 1.3.1-2; Cornelius Nepos *Pref.* 4; *Generals* 5 [Cimon], 1.2), which may have also been the custom of the people Abraham addressed in Genesis 20:12 (*Gen. Rab.* 52:11).

More strikingly, Egyptian men could marry full sisters (Paus. 1.7.1; papyri in Lewis, 43-44), a custom that may have also been practiced in ancient Nubia (Adams, 260) but was offensive to Greeks (Herodotus *Hist.* 3.31). This Egyptian custom retroactively illegitimated many unions when Rome conferred citizenship on its people in 212 (see Gardner, 36). Egyptians recounted the sexual union of sibling deities Isis and Osiris (Plutarch *Isis* 12, *Mor.* 356A), and some believed this was the basis for the Egyptian custom (Diodorus Siculus *Bib. Hist.* 1.27.1).

Greeks and Romans also recognized divine sibling unions (e.g., Virgil *Aen.* 1.45-46) without drawing the same inference, but some Jews charged that such stories contributed to pagan immorality (Josephus *Ag. Ap.* 2.38 §275). Some Jewish teachers suggested that Moses' prohibition of brother-sister unions shocked the Israelites recently freed from Egypt (*Sipre Num.* 90.1.1); later rabbis argued that God permitted sibling unions only early in biblical history (*y. Sanh.* 5:1 §4) and assumed that Gentiles sometimes married their siblings (*Gen. Rab.* 18:5).

Romans rejected all marriages with siblings, and Greeks rejected all except with paternal half-siblings (Diodorus Siculus *Bib. Hist.* 10.31.1). Stories of lust for siblings appear (Parthenius *L.R.* 5.2-3; 11.1-3), but such desire was unholy (Ovid *Met.* 9.454-665) and shameful (Parthenius *L.R.* 31.1). Jews condemned all marriages with sisters, including with half-sisters (Lev 18:9, 11; 20:17; Deut 27:22; Josephus *Ant.* 7.8.1 §168).

Clan endogamy was not incestuous (Tob 6:15). Many Jews believed that Gentiles practiced incest (*Ep. Arist.* 152; *Sib. Or.* 5.390-91) but also believed that they knew better and were morally responsible (*Gen. Rab.* 18:5; Cohen, 281). Many believed that God had a lower standard of incest regulations for Gentiles (*Sipra Qed. par.* 4.206.1.2; *y. Qidd.* 1:1 §4), and some appear to have believed he had a lower standard for slaves as well (*y. Yebam.* 11:2 §3).

3.6. Homosexual Intercourse. Ancient Judaism regarded homosexual activity and bestiality as subcategories of the larger issue of sexual immorality (*Sipra Qed. pq.* 10.208.2.12). Despite an exceptional occasion like Nero's marriage to boys (which others regarded as unnatural—Martial *Epigr.* 11.6; Suetonius *Nero* 28-29; Tacitus *Ann.* 15.37) and some Jewish diatribes against Gentile immorality (*Sipra Aharé Mot par.* 8.193.1.7), homosexual love lay outside the confines of marriage and family. Greek myth portrayed deities like Zeus as being particularly adulterous with women (see 2.2 above), but also he raped the boy Ganymede, who fared better than the women (Homer *Il.* 20.232-35; Virgil *Aen.* 1.28; Ovid *Met.* 10.155-61; Achilles Tatius *Leuc.* 2.36.3-4); other deities (Ovid *Met.* 10.162-219) and supernatural creatures (Euripides *Cycl.* 583-87; Athenaeus *Deipn.* 1.23d) might also exhibit homosexual desire.

Male homosexual affection was common and appears often both in biographies (Arrian *Anab.* 4.13.3; 4.13.7; Cornelius Nepos 4 [Pausanias] 4.1; 7 [Alcibiades] 2.2-3) and in fiction (Virgil *Ecl.* 2.17, 45; 8.80-84; Ovid *Met.* 3.353-55; Longus *Daphn. Chl.* 4.12, 16; Petronius *Sat.* 9, 11, 85-86, 92), sometimes even as the focus of the romance (Parthenius *L.R.* 7.1-3; 24). Various thinkers debated whether cross-gender or same-gender sexual love was superior (e.g., Plutarch *Dial. on Love* 5, *Mor.* 751E-752B; Achilles Tatius *Leuc.* 2.35.2-3; Plato *Symp.* 222C). Lesbian affection (e.g., *PGM* 32.1-19) was also known though less widely accepted (Ovid *Met.* 9.720-63; Martial *Epigr.* 1.90). Male prostitutes appear in the writings of Petronius (*Sat.* 8, 21, 23, 28) and Martial (*Epigr.* 3.82).

Homoerotic pleasure was associated particularly with Greeks (Athenaeus *Deipn.* 13.603ab), but it was never limited to them. Roman custom disapproved the practice (Sextus Empiricus *Pyr.* 1.152, 159; 3.199-200; Horace *Sat.* 1.4.27; Quintilian *Inst. Orat.* 2.2.14; Suetonius *Caligula* 16, 36), and some traditional Romans (Cicero *Invective Against Sallust* 6.18; Livy *Hist.* 39.42.8-12) and some philosophers (Seneca *Ep. Lucil.* 47.7; Marcus Aurelius *Med.* 1.16) had resisted the practice. By the first century, however, it had become widespread especially among upper-class Romans who imbibed considerable Greek culture, such as Nero (Dio Cassius *Hist.* 62.13.1) or Tiberius (Suetonius *Tiberiaus* 43-44), and appeared especially at parties (Petronius *Sat.* 41, 79-80). Some could view rejection by women (Propertius *Elegies* 2.4.17-18; Philostratus *Vit. Ap.* 3.38) or loss of a wife (Ovid *Met.* 10.83-85) as causes for male homosexuality.

Jewish people usually viewed homosexual behavior as a pervasively and uniquely Gentile sin (*Ep. Arist.* 152; *Sib. Or.* 3.185-86, 596-600; 5.166, 387; *y. Qidd.* 4.11 §6); they regarded homosexual behavior as meriting death (Josephus *Ant.* 3.12.1 §275; *Ag. Ap.* 2.25. §§199, 215) or punishment by God in the afterlife (*2 Enoch* 10:4). Like some other people (Diodorus Siculus *Bib. Hist.* 32.10.9; cf. Diogenes Laertius *Vit.* 6.2.65; Artemidorus *Oneir.* 1.80), some Jewish people regarded homosexual intercourse as unnatural (Josephus *Ag. Ap.* 2.38 §§273, 275; *Pseud.-Phoc.* 190-91; *T. Naph.* 3:4-5), probably in part because it could not contribute to procreation (Aristotle *Pol.* 1.1.4, 1252a).

See also FAMILY AND HOUSEHOLD; MARRIAGE.

BIBLIOGRAPHY. W. Y. Adams, *Nubia: Corridor to Africa* (Princeton, NJ: Princeton University Press, 1977); V. Barnouw, "Eastern Nepalese Marriage Customs and Kinship Organization," *SWJA* 11 (spring 1955) 15-30; S. Belkin, *Philo and the Oral Law: The Philonic Interpretation of Biblical Law in Relation to the Palestinian Halakah* (HSS 11; Cambridge, MA: Harvard University Press, 1940); J. Car-copino, *Daily Life in Ancient Rome: The People and the City at the Height of the Empire,* ed. H. T. Rowell (New Haven, CT: Yale University Press, 1940); L. Casson, *Travel in the Ancient World* (London: George Allen & Unwin, 1974); B. Cohen, *Jewish and Roman Law: A Comparative Study* (2 vols.; New York: Jewish Theological Seminary of America, 1966); C. Delaney, "Seeds of Honor, Fields of Shame," in *Honor and Shame and the Unity of the Mediterranean,* ed. D. Gilmore (AAA 22; Washington, DC: American Anthropological Association, 1987) 35-48; T. M. S. Evens, "Mind, Logic, and the Efficacy of the Nuer Incest Prohibition," *Man* 18 (March 1983) 111-33; B. Farber, *Comparative Kinship Systems: A Method of Analysis* (New York: John Wiley & Sons, 1968); R. Firth, *We, the Tikopia: A Sociological Study of Kinship in Primitive Polynesia* (2d ed.; Boston: Beacon, 1963); M. Fortes, "Kinship and Marriage among the Ashanti," in *African Systems of Kinship and Marriage,* ed. A. R. Radcliffe-Brown and D. Forde (New York : Oxford University Press, 1950) 252-84; J. F. Gardner, *Women in Roman Law and Society* (Bloomington: Indiana University Press, 1986); J. Gibson, "Hoi Telōnai kai hai Pornai," *JTS* 32 (1981) 429-33; D. D. Gilmore, "Introduction: The Shame of Dishonor," in *Honor and Shame and the Unity of the Mediterranean,* ed. D. Gil-more (AAA 22; Washington, DC: American Anthropological Association, 1987) 2-21; M. Goodman, *State and Society in Roman Galilee, A.D. 132-212,* Oxford Center for Postgraduate Hebrew Studies (Totowa, NJ: Rowman & Allanfield, 1983); M. Gordon, *Slavery in the Arab World* (New York: New Amsterdam, 1989); R. M. Grant, *Gods and the One God* (LEC 1; Philadelphia: Westminster, 1986); G. H. R. Horsley, *New Documents Illustrating Early Christianity: A Review of the Greek Inscriptions and Papyri Published in 1978* (North Ryde, N.S.W.: Ancient History Documentary Research Center, Macquarie University, 1983) vol. 3; T. Ilan, *Jewish Women in Greco-Roman Palestine* (Tübingen: Mohr Siebeck; Peabody, MA: Hendrickson, 1996); idem, "Premarital Cohabitation in Ancient Judea: The Evidence of the Babatha Archive and the Mishnah (*Ketubbot* 1.4)," *HTR* 86 (1993) 247-64; B. Kaplan and D. Johnson, "The Social Meaning of Navaho Psychopathology and Psychotherapy," in *Magic, Faith and Healing: Studies in Primitive Psychiatry Today,* ed. A. Kiev (New York: Free Press, 1964) 203-29; C. S. Keener, . . . *And Marries Another: Divorce and Remarriage in the Teaching of the New Testament* (Peabody, MA: Hendrickson; 1991); N. Lewis, *Life in Egypt Under Roman Rule* (Oxford: Clarendon Press, 1983); B. MacLachlan, "Sacred Prostitution and Aphrodite," *Studies in Religion/Sciences Religieuses* 21 (1992) 145-62; J. S. Mbiti, *African Religions and Philosophies* (Garden City, NY: Doubleday, 1970); M. McDonnell, "Divorce Initiated by Women in Rome: The Evidence of Plautus," *AJAH* 8 (1983) 54-80; T. A. J. McGinn, "The Taxation of Roman Prostitutes," *Helios* 16 (1989) 79-110; J. Murphy-O'Connor, *St. Paul's Corinth: Texts and Archaeology* (GNS 6; Wilmington, DE: Michael Glazier, 1983); G. K. Nukunya, *Kinship and Marriage Among the Anlo Ewe* (London School of Economics Monographs on Social Anthropology 37; New York: Humanities Press, 1969); J. J. O'Rourke, "Roman Law and the Early

Church," in *The Catacombs and the Colosseum: The Roman Empire as the Setting of Primitive Christianity,* ed. S. Benko and J. J. O'Rourke (Valley Forge, PA: Judson, 1971) 165-86; S. B. Pomeroy, *Goddesses, Whores, Wives and Slaves: Women in Classical Antiquity* (New York: Schocken, 1975); A. R. Radcliffe-Brown, "Taboo," in *Reader in Comparative Religion: An Anthropological Approach,* ed. W. A. Lessa and E. Z. Vogt (4th ed.; New York: Harper & Row, 1979) 46-56; B. Rawson, "The Roman Family," in *The Family in Ancient Rome: New Perspectives,* ed. B. Rawson (Ithaca, NY: Cornell University Press, 1986) 1-57; A. Richlin, "Approaches to the Sources of Adultery at Rome," *Women's Studies* 8 (1981) 225-50 [= *Reflections of Women in Antiquity,* ed. H. P. Foley (New York: Gordon & Breach Science Publishers, 1981 379-404]; H. D. Saffrey, "Aphrodite à Corínthe: Réflexions sur une idée reçue," *RB* 92 (1985) 359-74; S. Safrai, "Home and Family," in *The Jewish People in the First Century: Historical Geography, Political History, Social, Cultural and Religious Life and Institutions,* ed. S. Safrai and M. Stern (2 vols.; CRINT Assen: Van Gorcum; Philadelphia: Fortress, 1974, 1976) 728-92; R. K. Sherk, ed., *The Roman Empire: Augustus to Hadrian* TDGR 6; New York: Cambridge University Press, 1988); L. Swidler, *Women in Judaism: The Status of Women in Formative Judaism* (Metuchen, NJ: Scarecrow, 1976); S. Treggiari, "*Leges sine moribus,*" *Ancient History Bulletin* 8 (1994) 86-98; D. C. Verner, *The Household of God: The Social World of the Pastoral Epistles* (SBLDS 71; Chico, CA: Scholars Press, 1983); P. Walcot, "On Widows and their Reputation in Antiquity," *Symbolae Osloenses* 66 (1991) 5-26; J. R. Wegner, *Chattel or Person? The Status of Women in the Mishnah* (New York: Oxford University Press, 1988); D. Willner, "Definition and Violation: Incest and the Incest Taboos," *Man* 18 (March 1983) 134-59; S. Wood, "Messalina, Wife of Claudius: Propaganda Successes and Failures of His Reign," *Journal of Roman Archaeology* 5 (1992) 219-34.

C. S. Keener

AFFLICTION LISTS

Writings from the ancient Mediterranean world contain many lists of afflictions, hardships and tribulations. There are at least seven different types of these lists, which occur in a wide variety of Greek, Roman and Jewish authors, including astrologers, *apocalyptists, writers of *testaments, *novelists, *historians, *letter writers and *philosophers. The following survey contains a brief discussion of the terminology used to describe such lists, an enumeration of the basic types of hardship lists and a discussion of some of their functions.

1. Terminology
2. Types of Affliction Lists
3. Functions

1. Terminology.

In modern scholarly literature these lists are known as peristasis catalogs (German *Peristasenkataloge*). *Peristasis* (plural *peristaseis*) is the Greek term for "circumstance" and can indicate either a pleasant or an unpleasant situation, though the latter is the more common (Epictetus *Diss.* 2.6.16-17). A peristasis catalog is thus a catalog of circumstances, whether positive or negative or both. The most comprehensive lists presuppose a fluctuation in life from one circumstance to another and thus mention both good (e.g., fame and good reputation) and bad (e.g., infamy and obscurity) circumstances; such a list is a catalog of vicissitudes (e.g., Phil 4:12; 2 Cor 6:8). More common are lists of adverse circumstances, commonly called catalogs of hardships (Fitzgerald 1988), tribulation lists (Hodgson) or affliction lists (e.g., 1 Cor 4:9-13).

2. Types of Affliction Lists.

Adversity is a common human experience, so it is not surprising that *peristaseis* formed one of the *topoi* or commonplaces of Greco-Roman literature. The subject could be treated generally in a lecture or treatise (e.g., Maximus of Tyre *Or.* 36; Teles frag. 6) or specifically through narratives and lists (Fitzgerald 1997). The seven most prominent types of lists are (1) catalogs of hardships that specify the ills that humans as humans suffer (Seneca *Marc.* 18.8; Epictetus *Diss.* 3.24.28-29; Dio Chrysostom *Or.* 16.3; Philo *Virt.* 5); (2) lists that delineate the hardships suffered by various nations (Cicero *Tusc.* 2.14.34; Seneca *Prov.* 4.14-15; Dio Chrysostom *Or.* 25.3); (3) catalogs of the hardships encountered by various occupations, such as those faced by the gladiator, whose oath of allegiance took the form of a hardship list (Petronius *Sat.* 117); (4) lists of the punishments, including apocalyptic tribulations, that are inflicted on both the wicked (Sir 39:29-30; *Jub.* 23:13; Seneca *Ep.* 24.3; *Ira* 3.19.1) and the righteous (Plato *Rep.* 361E-362A; Cicero *De Rep.* 3.17.27); (5) the toils and afflictions that are the result of the passions, such as anger (Seneca *Ira* 2.36.5); (6) the vicissitudes of particular individuals, such as Philip of Macedon (Demosthenes *De Cor.* 67), Augustus (Pliny *Nat. Hist.* 7.45.147-50), and others (Chariton *Chaer.* 3.8.9; 4.4.10; 5.5.2; 6.6.4; Achilles Tatius *Leuc.* 5.18.3-6); and (7) the hardships of various human types, such as the orphan (Homer *Il.* 22.487-99) and the wanderer (Homer *Il.* 24.531-33).

Of the various types, the most important for comparison with the NT is the ideal wise man or *sophos,* whose hardships were depicted in numerous peristasis catalogs (Horace *Carm.* 3.3.1-8; *Sat.* 2.7.83-87; Seneca *Const.* 8.3; 15.1; *Ep.* 24.15, 17; 41.4-5; 59.8; 66.21; 76.18; 85.26-27; 91.7-8; *Prov.* 6.6; Dio Chrysostom *Or.* 8.15-16; 9.11-12; Epictetus *Diss.* 1.1.22-25; 1.18.21-23; 1.29.5-6; 2.1.34-35; 2.16.42-43; 2.19.24; 3.5.9; 3.6.5-7; 3.15.10-12; 3.22.45-49; 3.24.113; 4.7.13-15; Plutarch *Mor.* 1057D-E; Philo *Det. Pot. Ins.* 34). For Hellenistic philosophers, the sage was the perfect embodiment of reason and virtue (*see* Vice and Virtue Lists), and both of these qualities were evident in his triumph over adversity. Because discussions of the sage played a central role in both the propaganda and pedagogy of philosophy, he was a well-recognized figure in Greco-Roman culture. As is increasingly recognized by modern scholars, Paul drew on Hellenistic depictions of the *sophos* to depict himself (Malherbe), and in his peristasis catalogs he combined these Hellenistic traditions with Jewish ones about the afflicted righteous man (Kleinknecht) and suffering prophet (*see DPL,* Afflictions, Trials, Hardships). Consequently, the portrait that he gives of the suffering apostle is analogous in many respects to the philosophers' sketch of the suffering sage (Fitzgerald 1988).

3. Functions.

It was axiomatic in the ancient world that adversity is the litmus test of character. A person's attitude and actions while under duress reveal what kind of individual he or she is. "Prosperity," Isocrates says, "helps to hide the baseness even of inferior men, but adversity speedily reveals every man as he really is" (*Archidamus* 101-2, trans. LCL; see also Ovid *Tr.* 4.3.79-80). Calamity is thus virtue's opportunity (Seneca *Prov.* 4.6), for true greatness becomes conspicuous in adverse circumstances. The latter are a test, says Epictetus (*Diss.* 3.10.11), that "show the man" (*Diss.* 1.24.1; see also Proclus in *SVF* 3.49.30-34). Endurance is the proof of virtue (Seneca *Brev. Vit.* 18.1; *Prov.* 4.12; Dio Chrysostom *Or.* 3.3), and the greater the adversity overcome, the greater the proof of an individual's integrity.

In keeping with this widespread view of adversity, philosophers used peristasis catalogs to depict and demonstrate a person's fundamental moral integrity as well as a host of virtues and noble traits, such as endurance (2 Cor 6:4), serenity in the face of hardship (2 Cor 4:8-9), austerity, courage, self-discipline, self-sufficiency (Phil 4:11-12), wisdom, rationality and acceptance of the divine will (2 Cor 12:10). As a traditional means of demonstrating the triumph of virtue in all circumstances of life and over all adversity (Rom 8:35-39), these lists were also used in conjunction with lists of virtues (*2 Enoch* 66:6; 2 Cor 6:6-7; Fitzgerald *β*). Consequently, they functioned to distinguish the genuine sage from those who either falsely or prematurely laid claim to wisdom (Epictetus *Diss.* 2.19.18, 24). In addition, they were used by philosophers to admonish young and immature students who arrogantly thought that they had already attained perfection. In this case, the true philosopher's hardships were set over against the exaggerated claims of the novice, to the latter's embarrassment (Epictetus *Diss.* 4.8.27-31; 1 Cor 4:6-13). Finally, peristasis catalogs were used not only to vilify opponents by compiling a list of the sufferings they inflicted but also ironically to bestow mock praise for endurance of adversity (Josephus *J.W.* 4.3.10 §§165, 171, 174; 2 Cor 11:19-20).

Paul used peristasis catalogs in 1 and 2 Corinthians in much the same manner as did the philosophers, employing them to present himself as a person of integrity, to distinguish himself from false apostles and to admonish the Corinthians for their spiritual arrogance. But whereas philosophers typically used the lists to emphasize the power of a person's mind or will, Paul used them to demonstrate the power of the divine in his life (2 Cor 4:7; see also *T. Jos.* 1:3-7; Seneca *Ep.* 41.4-5).

See also VICE AND VIRTUE LISTS.

BIBLIOGRAPHY. M. Ebner, *Leidenslisten und Apostelbrief: Untersuchungen zu Form, Motivik und Funktion der Peristasenkataloge bei Paulus* (FB 66; Würzburg: Echter, 1991); J. T. Fitzgerald, "The Catalogue in Ancient Greek Literature," in *The Rhetorical Analysis of Scripture: Essays from the 1995 London Conference,* ed. S. E. Porter and T. H. Olbricht (JSNTSup 146; Sheffield: Sheffield Academic Press, 1997) 275-93; idem, *Cracks in an Earthen Vessel: An Examination of the Catalogues of Hardships in the Corinthian Correspondence* (SBLDS 99; Atlanta: Scholars Press, 1988); idem, "Virtue/Vice Lists," *ABD* 6:857-59; R. Hodgson, "Paul the Apostle and First Century Tribulation Lists," *ZNW* 74 (1983) 59-80; K. T. Kleinknecht, *Der leidende Gerechtfertigte: Die altestamentlich-jüdische Tradition vom "leidenden Gerechten" und ihre Rezeption bei Paulus* (WUNT 2.13; Tübingen: Mohr Siebeck, 1984); A. J. Malherbe, "'Gentle as a Nurse': The Cynic Background to 1 Thessalonians 2," in *Paul and the Popular Philosophers* (Minneapolis: Fortress, 1989) 35-48; M. Schiefer Ferrari, *Die Sprache des Leids in den paulinischen Peristasenkatalogen* (SBB 23; Stuttgart: Katholisches Bibelwerk, 1991). J. T. Fitzgerald

AFTERLIFE. *See* BURIAL PRACTICES, JEWISH; ESCHATOLOGIES OF LATE ANTIQUITY; HEAVENLY ASCENT IN JEWISH AND PAGAN TRADITIONS; RELIGION, PERSONAL; RESURRECTION.

AHIQAR

The story of *Ahiqar* is an intriguing folk tale of a wise and skillful scribe who gave counsel to all of Assyria and who imparted wisdom to a young and naive nephew through proverbs, parables and maxims.

1. The Story and Its Versions
2. *Ahiqar* and the New Testament

1. The Story and Its Versions.

The tale enjoyed wide circulation in antiquity with respect both to time and to location. The earliest known text, coming from Elephantine in Egypt, is written in Imperial Aramaic and dates to the fifth century B.C. Later extant versions of the story, all dating from the Christian era, circulated in Syriac, Arabic, Armenian, Ethiopic and Slavonic. The Syriac and Armenian versions stand closest to the Aramaic, while the Arabic version has been thoroughly monotheized. It may have been known, at least in part, to the Greeks. The author of *Tobit, a Jew living in the Persian Empire in the late fourth century B.C., assumes a detailed knowledge of the story on the part of his readers (*see* Jewish History: Persian Period). The texts of Tobit found at *Qumran demonstrate that Jews in Palestine knew of at least the person of Ahiqar around the time of Jesus.

The language of *Ahiqar's* original composition was probably Aramaic (note, for example, the word play *ḥṭ* ["arrow"] and *ḥṭʾ* ["sin"] in saying 41 of the Imperial Aramaic text), though some scholars think it to be Akkadian. Since Ahiqar served both Sennacherib (reigned 704-681 B.C.) and Esarhaddon (reigned 681-669 B.C.), the tale was composed no earlier than the seventh century B.C. Some of the later versions erroneously invert this historical sequence, making Esarhaddon the father of Sennacherib. It is probable that the proverbs were first gathered separately and later integrated into the story, since the two sections reflect slightly different dialects of Aramaic. References to the gods and to the god Shamash indicate that the tale was of non-Jewish origin, even though in the version known to the author of Tobit (presently nonextant), Ahiqar was a Jew (Tob 1:21-22).

The Syriac text offers a complete story, while the Imperial Aramaic text is fragmentary. The major elements of the story are as follows: an introduction describing the greatness of Ahiqar and his adoption of his nephew Nadin (or Nadan); maxims used by Ahiqar in the education of Nadin; Nadin's treachery against Ahiqar; Ahiqar's deliverance through Nabusumiskun (Akkadian *Nabû-šum-iškun*; "Nabu has established a name," i.e., by giving a son; corrupted in one Syriac tradition to *Yabusemakh Meskin*); the episode in which Ahiqar bests Pharaoh and gains great wealth for the king of Assyria; and maxims used by Ahiqar in his chastisement of Nadin.

The story is set in the Assyrian royal court, where Ahiqar was bearer of the seal of the king and counselor of all Assyria. According to Tobit, Ahiqar was second to Esarhaddon in authority (4Q196, frag. 2, line 8 = Tob 1:22). Ahiqar became a wealthy man but lacked a son, even though he had married sixty wives. Ahiqar prayed to God that he might have a son, and God answered by giving him his sister's young son Nadin by adoption. The king expressed his concern that he should have a successor to Ahiqar who might serve in his court. Ahiqar assured the king that his nephew Nadin was that person because he himself had instructed Nadin in all wisdom. Ahiqar then recounts a long series of proverbs by which he has instructed Nadin.

Despite Ahiqar's diligence in instructing Nadin, Nadin failed to heed the instruction. He turned against Ahiqar and plotted his demise. He even convinced the king that Ahiqar was plotting treason and so had him condemned to death. But wise Ahiqar survived by convincing his executioner Nabusumiskun that he should spare him and keep him in hiding until the king would regret his hasty action and want Ahiqar back. Many years earlier, Ahiqar had delivered Nabusumiskun by hiding him when he was in a similar situation.

After hearing that Ahiqar had died, Pharaoh king of Egypt asked the king of Assyria to send him the wisest sage in his land to assist him in building a magnificent castle stretching from earth to heaven. In exchange, Pharaoh promised him three years' tribute from Egypt. But if he failed, the king of Assyria would have to pay Pharaoh the same amount. The king of Assyria was sad, because only Ahiqar could do such a thing, and he thought him dead. Nabusumiskun now told the king of Assyria that he had spared Ahiqar. The king of Assyria reinstated Ahiqar and sent him to Egypt. Ahiqar accomplished his task, outwitting Pharaoh, and brought back three years of tribute for the king of Assyria. While he was in Egypt, clever Ahiqar had bested Pharaoh when challenged with his riddles and seemingly unsolvable problems.

The king of Assyria restored Ahiqar fully and delivered Nadin into his hand for whatever Ahiqar wished. Ahiqar bound Nadin and then reproved him with a lengthy series of proverbs.

When Ahiqar finishes with the statement that God would judge between Nadin and him, Nadin immediately swells up and dies. The narrator concludes that whoever does good will be recompensed good, but whoever does evil will be recompensed evil.

2. *Ahiqar* and the New Testament.

The NT and *Ahiqar* share a number of common literary devices and motifs, although no direct influence of *Ahiqar* on the NT can be established. The most striking parallel is that of the proverbial washed sow who wallows in the mud (2 Pet 2:22; Syriac *Ahiqar* 8:18; Armenian *Ahiqar* 8:24a; Arabic *Ahiqar* 8:15). Other common motifs include the feeding of pigs as a despised task (Lk 15:15; Syriac *Ahiqar* 8:34); the wolf as the enemy of the sheep (Mt 7:15; 10:16; Lk 10:3; Acts 20:29; Arabic *Ahiqar* 2:30); unfruitful trees that should be destroyed (Lk 13:6-9; Syriac *Ahiqar* 8:35; Armenian *Ahiqar* 8:25; Arabic *Ahiqar* 8:30); untrustworthy stewards who abuse subordinates and revel in drunkenness (Mt 24:48-51; Lk 12:45-46; Syriac *Ahiqar* 4:15); and getting rid of an ineffective or offensive bodily part like a hand or an eye (Mt 5:29-30; Mk 9:43, 47; Syriac *Ahiqar* 8:20).

See also TOBIT.

BIBLIOGRAPHY. R. H. Charles, ed., *The Apocrypha and Pseudepigrapha of the Old Testament in English Translation,* 2: *Pseudepigrapha* (Oxford: Clarendon Press, 1913) 715-84 (contains the translations of J. R. Harris of the Syriac, A. S. Lewis of the Arabic and F. C. Conybeare of the Armenian in parallel columns); F. C. Conybeare, J. R. Harris and A. S. Lewis, *The Story of Aḥiḳar from the Aramaic, Syriac, Arabic, Armenian, Ethiopic, Old Turkish, Greek and Slavonic Versions* (2d ed.; Cambridge: Cambridge University Press, 1913); A. Cowley, *Aramaic Papyri of the Fifth Century* B.C. (Oxford: Clarendon Press, 1923; Osna-brück: Otto Zeller, 1967 repr.); H. L. Ginsberg, "The Words of Ahiqar," *ANET* 427-30; J. C. Greenfield, "Ahiqar in the Book of Tobit," in *De la Tôrah au Messie,* ed. M. Carrez, J. Doré and P. Grelot (Paris: Desclée, 1981) 329-36; idem, "The Dialects of Early Aramaic," *JNES* 37 (1978) 93-99, esp. 97; P. Grelot, *Documents Araméens d'Égyptes* (Paris: Éditions du Cerf, 1972) 427-52; I. Kottsieper, *Die Sprache der Ahiqarsprüche* (BZAW 194; Berlin and New York: Walter de Gruyter, 1990); M. Küchler, *Frühjüdische Weisheitstraditionen* (OBO 26; Göttingen: Vandenhoeck & Ruprecht, 1979) 319-413; J. M. Lindenberger, "Ahiqar (Seventh to Sixth Century B.C.): A New Translation and Introduction," in *The Old Testament Pseudepigrapha,* ed. J. H. Charlesworth (2 vols.; Garden City, NY: Doubleday, 1985) 2:479-507; idem, *The Aramaic Proverbs of Ahiqar* (Baltimore and London: Johns Hopkins University Press, 1983); "Histoire et Sagesse d'Aḥikar, d'après le Manuscrit de Berlin 'Sachau 162,'" *Revue de l'Orient Chrétien* 21 (1918-19) 148-160; idem,f F. Nau, "Documents Relatifs à Aḥikar," *Revue de l'Orient Chrétien* 21 (1918-19) 274-307, 356-400; B. Porten and A. Yardeni, *Textbook of Aramaic Documents from Ancient Egypt,* 3: *Literature, Accounts, Lists* (Jerusalem: Hebrew University, 1993) 22-57; A. Schmitt, *Wende des Lebens* (BZAW 237; Berlin and New York: Walter de Gruyter, 1996) 146-83.

J. A. Lund

ALCHEMY. *See* MARIA THE JEWISH ALCHEMIST.

ALEXANDER THE GREAT

The conquest of the Achaemenid (Persian) empire by Alexander III of Macedon in the late fourth century B.C. marked the beginning of a new era. Important in itself, his conquest was especially significant in light of its ongoing legacy of Greek rule, culture and language in the eastern Mediterranean area. The figure of Alexander himself would likewise provide the impetus for the development and implementation of ruler worship in both the Hellenistic successor kingdoms and in the later Roman principate.

1. The Man
2. Alexander's Achievements
3. Alexander and the Jews

1. The Man.

1.1 Early Life and Education. Alexander, born in July 356 B.C., was one of several sons of the monarch of *Macedon, Philip II, by his first wife Olympias, a princess of neighboring Epuria. Tutored in *philosophy, science and culture by the Greek philosopher *Aristotle, among others, and trained in the martial arts in his father's army, Alexander was able to glean for himself the best that the Greek world had to offer. During his youth, his father carried out a campaign of Greek unification and military expansion, playing the largest role in the establishment of the Corinthian League, of which he became the head. Alexander was heavily involved in his father's military campaigning and served as his regent in 340 B.C. During his days at court in Pella, Alexander was able to interact with the finest Greeks and Macedonians alive at the time, from poets and philosophers to actors and engineers, all of whose skills he would eventually put to use for his own formidable causes.

1.2. Succession to the Throne of Macedon. Philip II's assassination in 336 B.C. took place a year after he had put Olympias aside for the younger Macedonian princess, Cleopatra. As a result, both Alexander's contemporaries and later scholars have been very interested in the role that Alexander and his mother may have played in Philip's death. Whatever his involvement or lack thereof, Alexander managed to gain the support of some of Philip's more important generals and secured the succession as king of Macedon for himself. The right of succession of Philip's status as leader (*hēgemōn*) of the Corinthian League had also been granted to his offspring, but Alexander was not able to step so neatly into his father's shoes, for Philip's assassination had left Alexander in a precarious political position. The fragile alliance of Greek city-states that Philip had held together with an iron grip threatened to disintegrate, with the orators and politicians of Athens being by far the most critical of Alexander and the non-Athenian leadership of the coalition. Alexander, however, managed to overcome this opposition, and with the vicious exemplary subjugation and destruction of rebellious Thebes (for which Alexander would later be vilified by Athenian poets and statesmen) he was able to hold together his father's alliance.

2. Alexander's Achievements.

2.1. The Conquest. Alexander's conquest of the Achaemenid Empire by the age of twenty-four was an accomplishment without parallel in the ancient world. He took his father's political mantle upon himself completely and in 334 B.C. set out to wrest control from the Persians of the various areas in *Asia Minor inhabited by Greek-speaking peoples. The famous battles of the Granicus and the Issus (at which the Persian king, Darius II, personally led the Persian troops) set the tone for many spectacular victories over the next several years. These initial victories were decisive harbingers of many to follow, as Alexander first established control over Asia Minor and then began a systematic siege of each Persian-controlled or -sympathetic port along the eastern coast of the Mediterranean, through Phoenicia, Palestine and Egypt. Because he lacked any real navy (and did not trust the loyalty of the small navy supplied by the Corinthian League), after he defeated the Persian land forces at the battle of Issus, his primary objective was to cut the Persian navy off from its land bases. His handling of resistant cities was thorough and savage, killing and/or enslaving the entire population of such cities as Tyre and Gaza. Militarily, Alexander's use of his core Macedonian troops, but especially his Thracian auxiliaries, together with troops from the Corinthian League and other mercenaries, was inspired.

It is, however, this latter coastal conquest that makes Alexander's overall purpose difficult to discern. His military purpose in this coastal conquest can be seen as a defensive one, for the naval power of the Persians would have been an ongoing problem for the newly freed Greek cities along the coast of Asia Minor, as well as within Greece and Macedon. However, it may be that this coastal conquest shows that Alexander was thinking of a much wider conquest from the beginning. On this reading of the evidence, rather than a defensive action, the coastal conquest was his way of decisively protecting his weak rear flank while he went on to conquer the rest of the empire. His rejection of a suit for peace from Darius after the battle of Issus suggests that his objective was always more than simply freeing the Greek cities of Asia Minor. In any case, at the moment he completed this initial conquest and turned his eyes eastward again, his desire for further conquest became evident.

Alexander's campaigning drew to a close in the Indus River region, where his men, tired of conquest and weary of foreign climes, convinced him to stop and return. It was in Babylon, soon after the cessation of his campaigning, that he died. The circumstances of his death are unclear, and hence conspiracy theories abound, but it is probable that he died of natural causes related to heavy drinking, old wounds and possibly malaria, contracted during his campaigning in India.

2.2. Characteristics of Alexander's Conquests and Rule. It is difficult to tell whether the mythological language (following in the tracks of Heracles and Dionysus, who were both thought to have traveled to India) and the rhetoric of scientific quest (for the great Ocean Sea, thought to lie east of India) that surrounded Alexander's eastward conquest were blinds to allow him to continue his conquests with impunity or were the driving forces behind his desire for further campaigning. It seems that beneath the surface of Alexander's military and diplomatic genius was a man driven by devotion to the myths of the Greeks and an overwhelming curiosity for new places and peoples.

One of the most consistent factors throughout Alexander's career was this devotion to myth. At an early age, his tutor Lysimachus gave him the nickname Achilles—the hero of Homer's *Iliad*—and his mother could supposedly trace ancestry to the Homeric figures of both Achilles and Helen of Troy. Likewise, Heracles was seen as the ancestor of the Macedonian kings, and Perseus also found a place within Alexander's lineage. In addition, after her divorce from Philip, Alexander's mother seems to have spread a story that Alexander's paternity was actually divine. Olympias was notorious for her lavish devotion to religion and cult, and it may be that the special relationship Alexander had with his mother was the source of his own religio-mythical devotion. In light of these various emotional and familial ties to the Greek myths and their heroes, some of the stranger things about Alexander's various activities fit (for example, his naked processional around the tomb of Achilles upon arrival in Asia Minor at Troy in 334 B.C., his journey to the famous Oracle at Siwah after his conquest of Egypt in 332 B.C., his identification of himself as the son of Zeus-Ammon [which would have fit well with his mother's claims] and the extent of his eastward conquest [where, at its eastward-most limit, he found Nyssa, the mythic sanctuary of Dionysus, Fox, 340-41]).

There is good evidence to suggest that as his campaigns in Persia and India wore on, Alexander's Macedonian soldiers began to feel that he was becoming a tyrant, that they found his rejection of his own father in favor of Zeus-Ammon unacceptable, that he was taking on far too many oriental characteristics, practices and retainers and that his conquests were going too far and too long. Alexander did occupy a difficult position once he had finally conquered Darius II in Media in 330 B.C. He had set out on his conquest of Asia Minor under the banner of his father's motto of freedom for Greek cities but had ended up conquering not only the Persians in Asia Minor but also the Persian king, and he would go on to conquer the rest of the former Achaemenid territories.

As the new king of Persia, as well as the king of Macedon and leader of the Corinthian League, the line that Alexander was forced to tread was an exceedingly fine one. That there were problems encountered by Alexander from all of these quarters is manifest—at home, there was continued Athenian polemics and ill will toward their Macedonian overlord; in the field, at least two assassination plots were foiled; and, as he moved further eastward into the Persian homelands, the Persians were less and less happy with his presence. It is difficult, however, to make much of the charge that Alexander did become tyrannical, for the evidence does not bear it out. The loyalty of his men and their following of him beyond all previous knowledge of Greek civilization is testimony that he remained, until the end, the popular leader that he always had been. The evidence for his orientalizing tendencies and divine self-image is at best inconclusive (on the latter, see Plutarch *Isis and Osiris* 360D). Given his early death, it is impossible to tell how he would have reigned—as a Macedonian conqueror, as the rightful successor by conquest of the Persian throne or perhaps as both.

2.3. The Spread of Hellenism. Alexander's conquests were significant not only in light of their legacy of Macedonian and Greek political, economic and military domination over much of the Near East but also because of the impact of Greek culture and language on the various peoples under Macedonian/Greek domination. This bipartite influence, coupled with the openness on the part of the Greeks to incorporating Eastern religions, ideas and wisdom into their beliefs, is often called *Hellenism. This phenomenon of Hellenism was to be Alexander's greatest legacy to the world of the NT. On a purely practical level, the widespread use of the Greek language provided a common means of communication; and the unifying force of Greek culture, together with the willingness on the part of the Greeks to amalgamate native religious cults and beliefs with their own, allowed for much cross-fertilization and the spread of both Greek and non-Greek ideas in a way that was not previously possible.

Alexander's direct involvement in the spread of Hellenism is debatable. He established Greek cities (many of which were named Alexandria) throughout his newly conquered territories, peopled them with veterans and loyal retainers and in effect set up both garrisons and Hellenistic centers throughout the former Achaemenid Empire, from Egypt to India. However, the common characterization of Alexander as a missionary of Greek culture is overstated. Alexander's spreading of Greek language and culture was tightly tied to his program of conquest—much as the Romans would later follow a strict policy of Romanization of their territories before incorporation into the empire as provinces, so too Alexander used language and culture to his own ends. The end effect was a saturation of Greek culture at various levels of native societies, and, for the study of the NT, the extent and character of this saturation for both the Jewish and non-Jewish peoples affected by the early Christian movement is an item of much discussion and debate.

3. Alexander and the Jews.

Because Alexander's campaigns took him through the region of Palestine, there is quite a bit of discussion regarding his involvement with Jews and Jewish culture. There are several stories about Alexander recorded in rabbinic literature (*b. Tamid* 31b-32b; *Tg. Ps.-J.* 2:5, 8c; *Gen. Rab.* 61:7), but the most significant Jewish tradition about Alexander is found in *Antiquities* 11.8.1-7 §§304-47, where Josephus records a story that has Alexander thoroughly embroiled in Jewish-Samaritan politics and credits him both with the foundation of the Samaritan sanctuary on Mt. Gerizim and with the reception of a vision telling of his eventual defeat of the Persian king, after which he sacrificed to the God of the Jews in *Jerusalem and granted them extensive rights. This story is repeated in a somewhat different version in *b. Yoma* 69a but is at best improbable in either form. It probably does reflect, however, the beginning of an ascendancy of the Jews over the Samaritans as the result of Alexander's extreme displeasure with the Samaritans after they rebelled while he was in Egypt. At any rate, when compared with a passage such as Daniel 11:2-4, it seems that the Jews were treated somewhat ambivalently by Alexander. This would change over the next two centuries as Alexander's successors (the **Diadochi*) waged the five Syrian wars and implemented a series of differing policies toward the Jews—some positive, some negative. At this initial stage, though, it seems that Alexander's conquests leveled the political playing field for the Jews to a certain extent, in that previously strong neighbors (Samaritans, Phoenicians) were humbled, and at least their first new overlord rulers (Alexander for a short time, and then, after a brief period of Seleucid control, Ptolemy I) were well-disposed toward them.

For the Jews and the early Christians, Alexander's significance after his death was also important—his body, embalmed in Babylon and intended for burial in the northern Seleucid kingdom, was transported in a large funeral chariot that amounted to a moving temple, complete with road builders to smooth the way. Ptolemy I hijacked the funeral caravan, however, taking the body to *Alexandria, where it was housed in a permanent temple, and Alexander was worshiped as either a demigod or a god until the third century A.D. The influence and effects of this cult on Alexandrian Jews and

Christians is not to be underestimated and would have resonated well with such a passage as Isaiah 40:3 (Porter and Pearson). Beyond this, Alexander left the Greco-Roman world as a whole with a personal legacy of mystery and romance. Many Hellenistic and Roman rulers would later try to cash in on this mystique—not least, for the Jews, the young son of the Roman governor of Idumea, *Herod, and their first Roman conquerer, *Pompey.

See also DIADOCHI; GREECE AND MACEDON; HELLENISM; JEWISH HISTORY: GREEK PERIOD; PTOLEMIES; SELEUCIDS AND ANTIOCHIDS.

BIBLIOGRAPHY. **Texts** (chronological order). Diodorus Siculus book 17 (Augustan period); Curtius Rufus (first century); Plutarch *Life of Alexander* (end of first century); Trogus, *Philippic History* (Augustan era, extant only in an abridgment by Justin); Arrian, *Anabasis* (mid-late second century). **Studies.** R. L. Fox, *Alexander the Great* (London: Dial, 1974); P. Green, *Alexander to Actium: The Historical Evolution of the Hellenistic Age* (Berkeley and Los Angeles: University of California Press, 1990); S. E. Porter and B. W. R. Pearson, "Isaiah Through Greek Eyes: The LXX of Isaiah," in *Writing and Reading the Isaiah Scroll: Studies of an Interpretive Tradition*, ed. C. C. Broyles and C. A. Evans (2 vols.; VTSup 70; FIOTL 1; Leiden: E. J. Brill, 1997) 2:531-46; C. B. Welles, *Alexander and the Hellenistic World* (Toronto: Hakkert, 1970); U. Wilcken, *Alexander the Great* (London: Norton, 1967).

B. W. R. Pearson

ALEXANDRIA

During the NT period Alexandria was one of the chief cities of the Roman Empire. A center of shipping and trade, culture and scholarship, and the home of a large Jewish community, it was eventually to become an important center of Christianity.

1. Location
2. History
3. Topography
4. Jewish Community
5. Christian Community

1. Location.

The city of Alexandria is situated on a narrow ridge of limestone between the Mediterranean coast of Egypt to the north and Lake Mareotis to the south, with the Nile Delta to the east. It was built on the site of an earlier Egyptian town called Rhakotis and was named after *Alexander the Great, who authorized its foundation in 331 B.C. but was never to see the city.

The physical site had numerous natural advantages. It was sheltered from the open Mediterranean and the prevailing northerly winds by a narrow strip of rock called Pharos running parallel to the coast, 1.5 kilometers offshore. The center of this island was joined to the mainland by a causeway (*Heptastadion*), thus marking out two deep, protected sea harbors, one on either side of the causeway. A canal led from the western harbor (*Eunostos*) to the freshwater Lake Mareotis. This lake provided an inland harbor for the city together with access by means of a network of canals as far as the great artery of the Nile itself and ultimately to the Red Sea (Dio Chrysostom *Disc.* 32.36).

2. History.

The new city quickly rose to prominence and remained influential both economically and culturally for more than a millennium, under three successive powers: Ptolemaic, Roman and Byzantine.

Following the death of Alexander in 323 B.C., Egypt was ruled by a succession of Ptolemaic kings (*see* Hellenistic Egypt). Under their jurisdiction, Alexandria replaced Memphis as the capital city and principal administrative center of the new kingdom. Nonetheless, no doubt because of its *Hellenistic foundation, the city remained distinct from Egypt proper and had partial autonomy over its own affairs. In outlook it inclined more toward Greece and the Mediterranean than toward Egypt.

During the Ptolemaic period, Alexandria enjoyed considerable prosperity. The city capitalized on the advantages provided by its location and developed a significant commercial reputation, especially in the manufacturing industries of papyrus, glass and linen. From early days it attracted a cosmopolitan population.

Rome annexed Egypt in 30 B.C. Under the emperor Augustus (*see* Roman Emperors), the Alexandrians experienced the humiliation of having their senate abolished (it was not restored until A.D. 200); the Ptolemaic army was disbanded, and Egypt was occupied by Roman forces. Nonetheless, Alexandria continued to enjoy considerable privilege under Roman rule; it became the administrative capital of the Roman province of Egypt (*see* Roman Administration), the cultural center of the eastern empire and the second city in the empire (with a population possibly in excess of 500,000 by the mid-first century A.D.).

3. Topography.

Our principal source of description regarding the topography of Alexandria is provided by the first-century writer Strabo (Strabo *Geog.* 17.1.6-10; *see* Historians and Geographers, Hellenistic). The site was rectangular in shape running parallel to the Mediterranean coastline. Deinokrates of Rhodes is widely cited as the architect of the new city. He adopted a gridded street plan in which the main colonnaded east-west street (33 m wide and 5.5 km long) was called the Canopus Street. This was intersected by a major north-south street (1.5 km long) called the Soma Street. Cleomenes of Naukratis was charged with finding funds for the construction of the city and was appointed its first governor.

The city was divided into ethnic regions. The Egyptian district, in the southwest of the city, corresponded to and was named after the original village Rhakotis. This was the poorest district. Ptolemy III Euergetes (246-221 B.C.) rebuilt the Serapaeum, or Temple of Serapis, in this Egyptian quarter and incorporated within it the daughter library of the great library. Under the Romans, the Serapaeum became one of the great centers of pagan worship in Egypt.

The Greek quarter was called the Brucheion and included the extensive royal palace. Strabo suggests that the palace occupied between a third and a quarter of the city's area (Strabo *Geog.* 17.1.8). Within this district there were many official buildings, including the Soma (the mausoleum of Alexander's body) and the museum.

Philo (*Flacc.* 55) lists five districts named after the first five letters of the Greek alphabet. He suggests that the Jews were concentrated in two of these districts. It is clear from Josephus (*J.W.* 2.18.8 §495) that district Delta (in the northeast) was one of these.

The famous 120-meter-high lighthouse, one of the seven wonders of the ancient world, was built on the eastern end of the island of Pharos in the time of the early Ptolemies and survived until it was destroyed by an earthquake in the thirteenth century. This is the earliest known lighthouse and became known as Pharos. It consisted of three stories: the first was square, the second octagonal, the third cylindrical, at the top of which was a statue to Zeus Soter. A fire burned inside the lighthouse, and its light was reflected through a mirror mechanism such that it could be seen over a considerable distance (Josephus *J.W.* 4.10.5 §613 suggests more than 50 km).

The lighthouse served a number of uses. It provided a landmark to draw attention to Alexandria near the flat alluvial plain of the Nile Delta; it warned sailors of the series of limestone reefs offshore; and, as one of a series of watchtowers along the coast, it was a vantage point from which to gain early warning of attack. In recent years archaeologists have discovered what are considered to be remains of this wonder of the ancient world.

4. Jewish Community.

The city of Alexandria had a cosmopolitan population, including Egyptians, Greeks and Jews, albeit thoroughly Hellenized with Greek as the official administrative language (*see* Hellenistic Judaism). Although there was a general policy of mutual tolerance, this mix of nationalities and cultures inevitably brought periodic tensions. Many Jews sought to balance being pro-Greek and yet maintaining loyalty to their Jewish heritage.

Large numbers of Palestinian Jews emigrated to Alexandria from its earliest times. Josephus (*J.W.* 2.18.7 §487; *Ag. Ap.* 2.4 §§35, 37) records that Alexander himself encouraged Jews to settle in the new city "on terms of equality with the Greeks." They were encouraged to stay there by the Ptolemies and were accorded considerable freedom. (There is early Ptolemaic archaeological and epigraphic evidence of Jews in the city.) This freedom continued under the early days of the *Roman Empire, but then conditions for the Jews deteriorated until the community was virtually annihilated in the early second century A.D.

The Jews organized into their own civic group known as a *politeuma* (*Ep. Arist.* 310) and were encouraged to maintain their cultural and religious customs. There was a significant Jewish synagogue situated along the main thoroughfare, the Canopus Street (recorded in the Talmud, *t. Sukk.* 4:6).

By the first century A.D. the population of Jews in the city may well have been considerable, and this community came to be one of the most influential in the Jewish Diaspora. *Philo, himself an Alexandrian Jew, reports that at this time the number of Jews within Egypt as a whole may have been as much as a million (Philo *Flacc.* 43). Delia and Sly argue that a third of the Alexandrian population may have been Jewish (on the basis of two out of the five Alexandrian districts being predominantly Jewish [Philo *Flacc.* 55]) and therefore possibly amounting to as many as 180,000 Jews.

Periodically, considerable antagonism arose between the Greek and Jewish communities. During the imperial rule of Gaius, an Egyptian prefect called Flaccus was put in an insecure position when the Jewish king Agrippa visited the city in A.D. 38. The situation resulted in nothing less than riot and much violence against the Jews. Flaccus's reaction was to remove many of the privileges that the Jews had been accorded, and they were treated as foreigners and aliens (Philo *Flacc.* 54). The situation improved somewhat under the emperor Claudius, until tension resurfaced again in 66, when another riot was put down directly by the force of the Roman army (*see* Roman Military) under Philo's apostate nephew, Tiberius Julius Alexander. Josephus records significant casualties (Josephus *J.W.* 2.18.7-8 §§487-98). In A.D. 115-117, there was a still greater Jewish uprising in Alexandria and the surrounding region (Eusebius *Hist. Eccl.* 4.2) that led to an exodus of Jews. This marked the end of significant Jewish influence in Egypt.

5. Christian Community.

Primary sources report nothing explicit regarding the origins of Christianity in Alexandria. The NT includes a number of references to Alexandria, but none suggests a successful mission there. There is reference to an Alexandrian Jew who was converted to Christianity and traveled widely (Acts 18:24-25; 1 Cor 1:12; 3:4-6, 22; 16:12; one variant reading of Acts 18:25 records that Apollos "had been instructed in the word in his home country"); some from Egypt were present at Peter's speech at Pentecost (Acts 2:10); and some from Alexandria are recorded as disputing with Stephen (Acts 6:5). Eusebius, the church historian, records a tradition that Mark the Evangelist brought Christianity to Alexandria in about A.D. 40 and that he was later martyred there (Eusebius *Hist. Eccl.* 2.16), but it is unclear whether this tradition is reliable. By the second century, however, Christianity had become more established in Alexandria with the founding of a catechetical school. By the third century, the city had become a significant center of the Christian church (*see DLNTD*, Alexandria, Alexandrian Christianity).

See also ALEXANDRIAN LIBRARY; ALEXANDRIAN SCHOLARSHIP; HELLENISTIC EGYPT.

BIBLIOGRAPHY. J. M. G. Barclay, *Jews in the Mediterranean Diaspora: From Alexander to Trajan (323 B.C.E.—117 C.E.)* (Edinburgh: T & T Clark, 1996); A. K. Bowman, *Egypt After the Pharaohs: 332 B.C.-A.D. 642: From Alexander to the Arab Conquest* (2d ed.; London: British Museum Publications, 1996); A. K. Bowman, ed., *The Augustan Empire, 43 B.C.-A.D. 69* (2d ed.; *CAH* 10; Cambridge: Cambridge University Press, 1996); P. A. Clayton, "The Pharos at Alexandria," in *The Seven Wonders of the Ancient World,* ed. P. A. Clayton and M. J. Price (London: Routledge, 1988); J. A. Crook, ed., *The Last Age of the Roman Republic, 146-43 B.C.* (2d ed.; *CAH* 9; Cambridge: Cambridge University Press, 1994); D. Delia, *Alexandrian Citizenship During the Roman Principate* (Atlanta: Scholars Press, 1991); M. S. El-Din, *Alexandria: The Site and the History* (New York: New York University Press, 1993); P. M. Fraser, *Ptolemaic Alexandria* (3 vols.; Oxford: Oxford University Press, 1972); A. Kasher, *The Jews in Hellenistic and Roman Egypt* (TSAJ 7; Tübingen: Mohr Siebeck, 1985); J. Marlowe, *The Golden Age of Alexandria: From Its Foundation by Alexander the Great in 331 B.C. to Its Capture by the Arabs in 642 A.D.* (London: Victor Gollancz, 1971); J. M. Modrzejewski, *The Jews of Egypt: From Rameses II to Emperor Hadrian* (Edinburgh: T & T Clark, 1995); B. A. Pearson and J. E. Goehring, eds., *The Roots of Egyptian Christianity* (SAC; Philadelphia: Fortress, 1986); D. I. Sly, *Philo's Alexandria* (London: Routledge, 1996); M. True and K. Hamma, eds., *Alexandria and Alexandrianism: Papers Delivered at a Symposium Organized by the J. Paul Getty Museum and the Getty Center for the History of Art and the Humanities and Held at the Museum, April 22-25, 1993* (Malibu, CA: J. Paul Getty Museum, 1996); F. W. Walbank, *The Hellenistic World* (2d ed.; *CAH* 7; Cambridge: Cambridge University Press, 1984). A. D. Clarke

ALEXANDRIAN LIBRARY

The great library of Alexandria contributed significantly to Alexandria's reputation of being paramount among cities. In a climate of intense rivalry, the Ptolemies of Egypt, the Seleucids of Syria and the Attalids of Pergamum all endeavored to establish world-class libraries. The Alexandrian library became the largest and most famous in antiquity (*see* Literacy and Book Culture).

1. Foundation
2. Holdings
3. Location and Destruction

1. Foundation.
Early references to the foundation of the library are lacking, and no archaeological remains survive. The consensus is that Demetrius of Phaleron, a scholar exiled from his native *Athens, was the force behind the establishment of a research institute, the museum, and library under the patronage of Ptolemy I Soter (c. 295 B.C.). The library then greatly expanded under the aegis of Ptolemy II Philadelphus and his successors. Ptolemy III Euergetes built the Serapaeum as a branch or daughter library in order to accommodate the developing collection. The combined library and museum were influential in attracting great scholars to the city. In the Roman period, both the library and the museum became public institutions of the Roman province.

2. Holdings.
The overarching goal behind the establishment of the library was to collect all books in the world. In order to enhance the holdings, manuscripts were acquired by both honest and dishonest means. It is said that Ptolemy III Euergetes confiscated manuscripts from passengers who sailed into Alexandria, had them copied, and kept the originals but returned the copies.

Primary sources provide various estimates as to the number of scrolls the library possessed—ranging from 400,000 to 700,000 in the first century B.C. Antony is then said to have presented the library with 200,000 parchment volumes from the Pergamum library. Callimachus (d. 235 B.C.) compiled a selected classification of the library's holdings, a catalog that amounted to some 120 scrolls entitled "Catalogs of the authors eminent in various disciplines." The catalog was arranged according to subject, within which particularly distinguished authors were listed alphabetically together with brief biographical detail and a critique of their work.

3. Location and Destruction.
Considerable debate surrounds both the location of the library and what became of it. The extant Ptolemaic sources never describe both the museum and the library together. Did the term *library,* then, denote a separate building or merely a collection of scrolls (perhaps housed in the museum)?

The traditional view has been that the library was a distinct building situated near the museum. Plutarch (*Caes.* 49) reports that the "great library" *(megalēn bibliothēkēn)* was destroyed in a fire that spread from the port during the Alexandrian war of Julius Caesar (48-47 B.C.). From this it is assumed that the library building was located near the port and, together with its contents, was destroyed by the fire.

Alternative primary sources propound no such destruction. Strabo in his topographical study of the city (Strabo *Geog.* 17.8) does not explicitly refer to a distinct building described as the library. Suetonius (*Claudius* 42.5), supported by papyrological evidence, suggests that the museum suffered no loss of scrolls during Caesar's campaign, thus implying that the library was a collection of scrolls housed within the museum and not destroyed by fire. It is assumed that another and much smaller (possibly only 40,000) collection of scrolls was destroyed in the fire.

The palace quarter of Alexandria was burned down in the third century A.D. The museum was destroyed at this stage, and it may be assumed that the library suffered also. A project was started in the 1980s to rebuild a new great library of Alexandria on the supposed ancient site of the museum.

See also ALEXANDRIA; ALEXANDRIAN SCHOLARSHIP; SCHOLARSHIP, GREEK AND ROMAN.

BIBLIOGRAPHY. B. L. Canfora, *The Vanished Library* (London: Hutchinson Radius, 1987); D. Delia, "From Romance to Rhetoric: The Alexandrian Library in Classical and Islamic Traditions," *AHR* 97 (1992) 1449-67; M. El-Abbadi, *The Life and Fate of the Ancient Library of Alexandria* (Paris: Unesco/UNDP, 1990); M. S. El-Din, *Alexandria: The Site and the History* (New York: New York University Press, 1993); J. H. Ellens, "The Ancient Library of Alexandria: The West's Most Important Repository of Learning," *BRev* 13 (1997) 18-29, 46; A. Erskine, "Culture and Power in Ptolemaic Egypt: The Museum and Library of Alexandria," *GR* 42 (1995) 38; P. M. Fraser, *Ptolemaic Alexandria* (3 vols.; Oxford: Oxford University Press, 1972); E. A. Parsons, *The Alexandrian Library: Glory of the Hellenic World—Its Rise, Antiquities and Destructions* (London: Cleaver-Hume, 1952).

A. D. Clarke

ALEXANDRIAN SCHOLARSHIP

Throughout the Ptolemaic, Roman and Byzantine periods, Alexandria was one of the great centers of scholarship and learning and attracted the most distinguished scholars of the time. This climate of research was engendered from the city's earliest times through the direct patronage of the *Ptolemaic kings (*see* Hellenistic Egypt).

1. Museum
2. Literature
3. Science
4. Philosophy
5. Christian Scholarship

1. Museum.

Central to the intellectual life of the city were its museum and library. The museum was a residential research institute. It was partially modeled on the *Aristotelian Lyceum and the Academy of *Plato and was dedicated to the Muses, who were believed to inspire mortals with artistic gifts. Unlike its Greek predecessors, however, it was principally a research, rather than a teaching, institute. Under the Ptolemies, scholars came to the museum by royal invitation and were offered stipends, free accommodation and meals, together with immunity from some taxation. The museum and the extensive resources of its associated library stimulated a significant intellectual climate.

Alexandrian scholarship embraced a number of different spheres of learning, including literary criticism, scientific endeavor and philosophical reflection. It can be argued that in this city a truly scientific approach to scholarly research was first developed, and the abiding reputation of Alexandrian scholarship is one of method and detail.

2. Literature.

The library fostered an extensive project of collating, editing, commenting on and, where necessary, translating into Greek large portions of literature. Some of the earlier endeavors included the production of definitive critical editions of many of the classical Greek literary texts, including Homer's *Odyssey* and *Iliad.* Textual-critical work like this was overseen by successive librarians in the library, and a scientific approach to producing "best editions" of significant Greek literary works was developed. In the light of this textual work, it was also possible to make considerable advances in lexicography. Aristophanes of Byzantium, one of the librarians under the reign of Ptolemy IV Philopator, established a method of categorizing words according to their meaning in a given period.

The overall flavor of this literary scholarship was patently Greek. Notwithstanding this there were also endeavors to incorporate literature and scholarship of other cultures. The *Epistle of *Aristeas* recounts how Ptolemy II Philadelphus sent for seventy scholars from Jerusalem to Alexandria in order to translate the Pentateuch into Greek for the library. Much of the account is considered fictional, but the importance of Alexandria in this project is certain (*see* Septuagint/Greek Old Testament). Similarly, Manetho, an Egyptian priest, is credited with having written three volumes on the history and religion of Egypt—although they were written in Greek.

Notwithstanding this scientific approach to literary criticism, Alexandria also was home to much creative literature in its own right. The city became especially well-known for its influence in poetry from the third to first centuries B.C.

3. Science.

Different branches of scholarship blossomed during different periods in Alexandria's history. Under the Ptolemies study of the scientific disciplines advanced considerably, most notably in the fields of mathematics, mechanics, physics, geography and medicine.

The third century B.C. was a particularly prolific period for scientific research. Euclid was a significant Alexandrian figure in the field of geometry and produced definitive works on the subject, including his *Elementa Mathematica,* which was presented to Ptolemy I Soter. Archimedes is here renowned for his invention of the helical screw. Eratosthenes, a true polymath, spanned both literary and geographical studies but is most well-known for his experiment in measuring the circumference of the earth (deducing that the world was indeed round by comparing the shadows cast by the sun at midday on the summer solstice in two different locations). In medical research, the Alexandrians enjoyed a significant heritage from their forebears in the Pharaonic era. Herophilus instigated a new investigation into the anatomy of the human body. By studying the human nervous system, he drew the conclusion that the brain, and not the heart, was the seat of intelligence. The well-known medical scholar Galen, from the second century A.D., built on this Alexandrian tradition.

4. Philosophy.
After the Ptolemaic period, both literary and scientific pursuits grew comparatively less prominent in Alexandria. There was, however, increased interest during the early Roman and Christian periods in the study of *philosophy, although it should be noted that Alexandrian philosophy never matched that in *Athens. The character of Alexandria as a center for the cross-fertilization of ideas inevitably led to a strongly syncretistic approach to philosophy. It was here that Platonic thought in particular had a profound influence on both Jewish and Christian theology. *Philo, Origen and Plotinus are the most significant philosophical figures in Alexandria in Jewish, Christian and secular thought respectively during this Roman period.

The intellectual climate of Alexandria greatly influenced the Jewish community of the city (*see* Hellenistic Judaism). The philosopher and aristocratic Alexandrian, Philo, bridged between Jewish and Greek aspects of thought. As a thoroughly Hellenized Jew, he applied Platonic and Stoic philosophy to his interpretation of the OT and sought to demonstrate that the ancient Jewish traditions could be acceptable also to his Greek contemporaries. He appears to have been significantly dependent on the Alexandrian translation of the Bible called the *Septuagint, and he identified the Hebrew personification of Wisdom with the Greek notion of the *Logos*. This philosophical background also contributed to Philo's extensive use of allegory in his interpretation of the Bible. Partly as a result of this Philonic influence, Jewish scholarship continued to be prominent in the city long after most Jews had fled the city in the early second century A.D.

Plotinus (third century A.D.), together with his student Porphyry, were widely recognized philosophers of Greek thought. They were heavily dependent on the earlier traditions of *Plato, and they drew together disparate religious and philosophical perspectives. Much of this syncretistic approach to scholarship influenced also the study of Christian theology in Alexandria.

5. Christian Scholarship.
As Alexandria had witnessed the decline of the Jewish community in the city, during the second century A.D. it also saw the emergence of a developing Christian scholarship. This academic approach to Christian thought was enhanced by the long-standing scholarly reputation of the city.

In time Alexandria became one of the four principal Christian centers in the Roman Empire, including one of the centers of theological dispute in the ecclesiastical creedal formulations. Within Christian circles, the city became famous for its Christian school (*Didaskaleon*), which may have been founded as early as the first century, although it did not develop a significant reputation until the late second and early third centuries. The church historian Eusebius, who describes the institution as a "school of sacred learning" and a catechetical school (Eusebius *Hist. Eccl.* 5.10.1; 6.3.3), is our principal primary source of information regarding its foundation and ongoing influence, although many scholars question the historicity of his account.

This emerging Alexandrian school has been a key element in the subsequent history of theology. It was the seedbed for what may be regarded as a typically Alexandrian scientific approach to the study of theology that is noted for the clear rapprochement between Greek philosophy and Christian culture. The link with Philo is also apparent in that the Christian school became a leading center advancing the allegorical method of interpretation of biblical texts. It would appear that the school was also a well-stocked scholarly resource, and it is argued that we may be in debt to this Christian library for many of the extant Philonic works.

The school had a distinguished list of senior figures associated with it: notably Pantaenus, Clement and Origen. All three were steeped in Hellenistic philosophy, including *Stoicism, *Platonism and *Aristotelianism. We know relatively little of Pantaenus. His most famous pupil was Clement, to whom we are indebted for his use of and dependence upon Philo. Of these three scholars, most is known of Origen, a pupil of Clement. In the best Alexandrian traditions, Origen applied a scientific approach of textual criticism to his study of the Bible. He carried out a detailed comparison of four Greek translations of the Bible with the Hebrew version. He also adopted a strongly allegorical approach to his interpretation of the Bible.

This syncretistic tendency may be significant

in the fact that *Gnosticism also flourished in Alexandria and wider Egypt during the early Christian period. The city was home to both Basilides and Valentinus, renowned gnostic teachers of the second century A.D.

See also ALEXANDRIA; ALEXANDRIAN LIBRARY; SCHOLARSHIP, GREEK AND ROMAN; HELLENISTIC EGYPT; PHILO.

BIBLIOGRAPHY. A. K. Bowman, *Egypt After the Pharaohs: 332 B.C.-A.D. 642: From Alexander to the Arab Conquest* (2d ed.; London: British Museum Publications, 1986); D. Dawson, *Allegorical Readers and Cultural Revision in Ancient Alexandria* (Berkeley and Los Angeles: University of California Press, 1992); M. El-Abbadi, *The Life and Fate of the Ancient Library of Alexandria* (Paris: Unesco/UNDP, 1990); J. H. Ellens, "The Ancient Library of Alexandria: The West's Most Important Repository of Learning," *BRev* 13 (1997) 18-29, 46; P. M. Fraser, *Ptolemaic Alexandria* (3 vols.; Oxford: Oxford University Press, 1972); A. van den Hoek, "The 'Catechetical' School of Early Christian Alexandria and Its Philonic Heritage," *HTR* 90 (1997) 59-87; B. L. Mack, "Philo Judaeus and Exegetical Traditions in Alexandria," *ANRW* 2.21.1 (1984) 227-71; J. Marlowe, *The Golden Age of Alexandria: From Its Foundation by Alexander the Great in 331 B.C. to Its Capture by the Arabs in 642 A.D.* (London: Victor Gollancz, 1971); B. A. Pearson and J. E. Goehring, eds., *The Roots of Egyptian Christianity* (SAC; Philadelphia: Fortress, 1986); R. Pfeiffer, *History of Classical Scholarship: From the Beginnings to the End of the Hellenistic Age* (Oxford: Clarendon Press, 1968); D. T. Runia, *Exegesis and Philosophy: Studies on Philo of Alexandria* (Collected Studies 332; Aldershot, U.K: Variorum, 1990); idem, *Philo in Early Christian Literature: A Survey* (CRINT 3.2; Assen: Van Gorcum, 1993); F. W. Walbank, ed., *The Hellenistic World* (2d ed.; *CAH* 7; Cambridge: Cambridge University Press, 1984); R. L. Wilken, "Alexandria: A School for Training in Virtue," in *Schools of Thought in the Christian Tradition,* ed. P. Henry (Philadelphia: Fortress, 1984) 15-30.

A. D. Clarke

AMRAM, VISIONS OF. *See* VISIONS OF AMRAM (4Q543-548).

AMULETS. *See* DEMONOLOGY.

ANCESTORS. *See* HEROES; TESTAMENTS OF THE TWELVE PATRIARCHS.

ANGELIC LITURGY. *See* SONGS OF THE SABBATH SACRIFICE (4Q400-407, 11Q17, MAS1K)

ANGELS OF THE NATIONS

Early Jewish understandings of the spiritual world included the notion of particular angels in authority over the nations. This basic understanding, though variously conceived, finds its roots in the Jewish Scriptures.

1. Jewish Scriptures
2. Early Jewish and Rabbinic Literature
3. New Testament

1. Jewish Scriptures.

The particularity of God's election of *Israel was not easily reconciled with the notion that all nations of the world are accountable to the rule of Israel's God. An attempt to hold these ideas together is reflected in some passages among the Hebrew Scriptures that place Yahweh at the pinnacle of an assembly of deities called "sons of God" (see Pss 29:1; 89:7: *bny ʾlym*; 82:6: *ʾlhym, bny ʿlywn*; LXX Deut 32:8 and 4QDeut = 4Q44: *angeloi theou/bny ʾlhym*; LXX Job 2:1: *angeloi theou/bny ʾlhym*; LXX Dan 3:92 to MT 3:25: *angelou theou/br ʾlhyn*). In Deuteronomy 32:8 the nations are assigned to the "sons of *'El*"/"angels of God," while the privileged people of Israel come under the sole jurisdiction of Yahweh as his "portion" and "inheritance." In Psalm 82 this arrangement of the pantheon is further elaborated. The assemblage of deities is, as members of the divine council, responsible for the rule over and the dispensation of justice among the nations. The psalmist has God accuse these deities for failing to ensure that justice is properly administered, and as a result they are to be punished by death (Ps 82:7).

2. Early Jewish and Rabbinic Literature.

In the later Jewish literature, these ideas are picked up and variously developed. In one exegetical tradition, preserved in some of the *rabbinic writings, the special relationship between God and his people is illustrated by the stories about how God was chosen by Israel while the nations were merely content to associate themselves with angels. Thus according to the *midrashic interpretation of Song of Solomon 3:24 in relation to the Shema in Deuteronomy 6:4, the *Deuteronomy Rabbah* 2:34 likens the election of Israel to the reception of a king and his entourage into a city. While some citizens have chosen the king's officials to be their *patrons, the smart one (Israel) has settled for nothing less than the king himself. The tradition is anchored within the context of the giving of the Torah at Mt. Sinai, to which God and the angels were believed to have descended.

By contrast, the medieval Hebrew *Testament of Naphtali* 8—9 applies this tradition to the situation of Abraham. Whereas "each and every nation chose an angel [seventy in number], and none of them remembered the Holy One, blessed be he . . . Abraham answered, 'I choose and I select only the one who spoke and the world came into being, who formed me within the inside of my mother's womb . . . him I will select and to him I will cleave, I and my seed forever.'" These angels function as advocates on behalf of the nations before God (*T. Naph.* 9:4).

Another strand of the tradition is anchored in the dispersion of the peoples after the tower of Babel. Drawing on Deuteronomy 32:8-9, *Philo of Alexandria (first century A.D.) declared that God "set boundaries of nations according to the number of the angels of God," while "Israel became the lot of his inheritance" (Philo *Poster. C.* 89, 91—92; cf. further *Tg. Onq.* to Gen 11:8). In the much earlier Sirach 17:11-18 (second century B.C.; *see* Sirach), the special status of Israel as God's "portion" is declared over against the assignment of celestial beings to rule over the Gentile peoples. Here the sovereign will of God is emphasized.

In addition to generally underlining Israel's privileged status, all these texts presuppose a function of angels as guardians of or advocates for the Gentile nations, which is analogous to the role ascribed to many national deities in the ancient Near East. This analogy between pagan deities and angels of the nations may underlie many rabbinic passages that engage in a polemic against the worship of angels by associating this with idolatry (so esp. *Mek. Rabbi Ishmael, BaHodeš* 6 to Exod 20:4-5; *t. Ḥul.* 2:18; *b. Ḥul.* 40a; cf. *y. Ber.* 9:13a-b; *b. Sanh.* 38b; *Exod. Rab.* 32:4).

As in Deuteronomy 32:8 the documents just cited do not characterize the nations' angelic rulers as either good or bad. In other early Jewish compositions, however, these angelic beings are absorbed into a dualistic cosmology in which (as Ps 82:7) they are held accountable for evil attributed to the impious nations. According to *Jubilees* 15:30-32 (mid-second century B.C.), Israel's election as God's people is contrasted with the appointment over the nations of spirits or angels who "lead them astray" from following God (see also *Jub.* 48:9, 16-17). The author presupposes that these celestial rulers such as Mastema (*Jub.* 48:9, 12) are not always under God's control, whereas the angels who remain strictly obedient to God act on behalf of Israel (cf. *Jub.* 48:13; Jude 5 may identify Christ = *kyrios* with the angel of the Lord who delivers the Israelites from Egypt).

In the Book of Dreams of *1 Enoch,* which is roughly contemporary to *Jubilees,* the nations correspond to seventy angelic "shepherds" who, in their respective eras, are given the task of carrying out divine punishment against the faithless of Israel (*1 Enoch* 89:59—90:19; *see* Enoch, Books of). However, the shepherds become disobedient when of their own accord they exceed the limits set by God on the assignment. The angelic being appointed to monitor the shepherd's treatment of Israel seems to presuppose a tradition that aligns the people of God with an angel. Here the coordination of Israel's position among the Gentiles with a myth about a conflict between bad and good angels surfaces in an incipient form.

The belief that religious-political conflicts mirror a struggle among angels in the sphere of heaven is attested during the second-century B.C. compositions of Daniel, the *Testament of Levi* (*see* Testaments of the Twelve Patriarchs) and the **War Scroll* preserved in Qumran Caves 1 and 4.

In Daniel 10—11 the Persian and Greek empires are each represented by an angelic prince (Dan 10:13, 20) opposed by the angel appearing to Daniel and Michael the prince (Dan 10:13, 20-21; 11:1) and "great captain, who stands guard over" the faithful (Dan 12:1). In a similar way, the *eschatological struggle between "the sons of light" and "the sons of darkness" in the *War Scroll* is described as a conflict between forces led, respectively, by Michael (probably the one designated "the prince of light") and *Belial (1QM 13:9-13; 17:5-8; cf. 1QS 3:20-25).

A conflict among angels may be implied in *Testament of Levi* 5:3-6: the interpreting angel, who assists Levi in avenging the defilement of Dinah against the sons of Hamor, identifies himself as one "who makes intercession for the nation of Israel, that they might not be beaten." The threat posed against Israel by the Parthians and the Medes in the Similitudes of *1 Enoch* is attributed to the work of angels who have stirred the kings of these nations to unrest (*1 Enoch* 56:5-6).

The conflict between Jacob and Esau in *Jubilees* 35:17 is also portrayed in terms of a contest between angels: Jacob's guardian "is greater and mightier and more honored" than the guardian of Esau. Despite the impression that the text seems concerned with angelic guardians of individuals (e.g., *2 Bar.* 12:3; 13:1; *2 Enoch* 19:4; *Adam and Eve* 33; *T. Jos.* 6:7; Mt 18:10; Acts 12:15), Jacob and Esau ultimately function as symbols of their progeny. The representation of the faithful by an angel instead of God directly (as in texts discussed above) is to be understood against an increasing emphasis on divine transcendence during the Second Temple period. Rather than denoting distance, however, the good angels functioned to guarantee the presence of God's effective activity in the world on behalf of his people (e.g., Tob 3:17; 11:14-15; 12:11-22; 2 Macc 10:29-30) while the notion of distance from God may only be presupposed with regard to the nations' angels.

3. New Testament.

Though the angels of the nations motif does not surface explicitly in the NT, several passages have arguably been influenced by the tradition.

3.1. Revelation 12:7-9. In a heavenly battle, Michael and Satan (the dragon), along with their respective armies of angels, engage in a conflict in which the latter group is defeated and thrown to the earth. There they stir up trouble for faithful Christians, eventually in the form of beasts representing Rome (Rev 12:13—13:18). The author, who dispenses with a heaven-earth correspondence between bad angels and the enemies of the faithful (both are on earth), is careful to emphasize the mythical dimension of this story in order to underscore for his readers the defeated nature of Satan's existence.

3.2. Revelation 2:1—3:22. Given that a human being can mediate God's communication to wayward angels in apocalyptic tradition (*1 Enoch* 12:1—15:7; 4Q203 frag. 8; 4Q530 2:21-23 to 3:4-11), the possibility is strengthened that the seven messages to the churches of Asia Minor take the form of a literary fiction that addresses celestial beings. In this instance, there is a one-to-one correspondence between the angels and the congregations. Though there are no exact parallels for this in early Jewish and Christian literature (cf. the similar, yet distinct, ideas in *Asc. Isa.* 3:15 and *Herm. Sim.* 5:5-6), it is likely that the author has adapted the motif of the nations' patron angels. Formally, with only few exceptions, the angels and not the churches are addressed in the messages, and, as the angelic rulers over the Gentiles in Jewish tradition, they are potentially disobedient. Variously praised and reprimanded, they are apprised of the consequences for their faithfulness or disloyalty to Christ.

3.3. Revelation 16:12-16. The demonic powers who assemble the kings from beyond the Euphrates River may well refer to angels who are expected to rouse nations to war in the end time (cf. *1 Enoch* 56:5-6).

3.4. Acts 16:9. an angelic figure, appearing as a "man" in Paul's vision, acts as a representative of Macedonia sent by God to plead that Paul and his associates introduce the gospel there.

See also BELIAL, BELIAR, DEVIL, SATAN.

BIBLIOGRAPHY. H. Bietenhard, *Die himmlische Welt im Urchristentum und Spätjudentum* (WUNT 2; Tübingen: Mohr Siebeck, 1951); M. J. Davidson, *Angels at Qumran: A Comparative Study of 1 Enoch 1—36, 72—108 and Sectarian Writings from Qumran* (JSPSup 11; Sheffield: Sheffield Academic Press, 1992); M. Mach, *Entwicklungsstadien des jüdischen Engelglaubens in vorrabbinischer Zeit* (TSAJ 34; Tübingen: Mohr Siebeck, 1992); J. Michl, "Engel I-IX," in *RAC* 5, cols. 53-258; P. Schäfer, *Rivalität zwischen Engeln und Menschen: Untersuchungen zur rabbinischen Engelvorstellung* (SJ 8; Berlin: Walter de Gruyter, 1975); A. Segal, *Two Powers in Heaven: Early Rabbinic Reports About Christianity and Gnosticism* (SJLA 25; Leiden: E. J. Brill, 1977); L. T. Stuckenbruck, *Angel Veneration and Christology* (WUNT 2.70; Tübingen: Mohr Siebeck, 1995).

L. T. Stuckenbruck

ANTIOCH (PISIDIA)

Antioch, commonly known as Pisidian Antioch, did not become part of the province of Pisidia until A.D. 295. It is located on the southeastern bank of the Anthios River in central Asia Minor, just northeast of Lake Limnai and modern Yalvaç (modern lake Egirdir), and was founded either by one of the early Antiochids of the *Seleucid kingdom or by Seleucus himself sometime in the late fourth or early third century B.C. Rediscovered in modern times by F. V. J. Arundell in the first half of the nineteenth century and preliminarily excavated by W. M. Ramsay in the early twentieth century, it was more fully excavated by Ramsay and an American archaeological team from the University of Michigan in the 1920s, under the leadership of D. M. Robinson. Excavation continues under the direction of M. Taslialan (see Mitchell and Waelkens, 19-35).

1. History of the City
2. Pisidian Antioch in the New Testament

1. History of the City.
Before the establishment of Antioch as a Greek city, it appears that both the site of Antioch and the surrounding areas were under the jurisdiction of a *hieron,* a local holy place dedicated to the Anatolian god Mên (see Strabo *Geog.* 12.3.3; 12.8.14). Ramsay (247, 292-93) is credulous of Strabo's evidence on this point. However, Strabo's grammar is in line with Ramsay's interpretation that the region was controlled by the priesthood of Mên and that the eventual site of Antioch was not necessarily the center of this priesthood—Strabo even suggests that there were several holy places dedicated to Mên in the region (cf. Mitchell and Waelkens, 37-90).

When the Seleucids founded Antioch, it was essentially as a garrison town whose purpose was both to guard against the fearsome Pisidian mountain tribe, the Homanades, and to control the major east-west trading route through the region. As such, Antioch was a strategically important site. Epigraphic (*EGI* 933, where "Magnesian of Phrygia" is an equivalent of "Antiochene") and literary (Strabo *Geog.* 12.8.14) evidence suggests that the original settlers were Greeks from Magnesia, as well as Jews, probably Babylonian (Ramsay, 247-60; cf. 2 Macc 8:20 and Goldstein, 331, for the Seleucid use of Jewish mercenaries, the likely source of Seleucid-era Jewish settlers in Asia Minor; also Josephus *Ant.* 11.8.5 §338; 12.3.4 §§147-53).

Little is known of Hellenistic Antioch, and few archaeological remains are extant from this period. We do, however, know that, after the removal of Seleucid power from the region of *Asia Minor in 189 B.C., Antioch was declared a free city by the Romans (Strabo *Geog.* 12.8.14). We hear little about it again until the last half of the first century B.C., when, in 39 B.C., it was given by Antony to the last king of Galatia, Amyntas, who later fought on Antony's side at the battle of Actium in 31 B.C. Upon Amyntas's death in 25 B.C. (he was killed while fighting the Homanades, Strabo *Geog.* 12.6.3-4), he bequeathed Antioch and the rest of his kingdom to Augustus (*see* Roman Emperors), a transfer of loyalties that seems very similar to that undertaken by *Herod the Great in Judea. The territory then became the Roman province of Galatia. At that point, the city was refounded as a Roman colony (*colonia*)—Colonia Caesareia Antiocheia—whose *citizens (*coloni*) were, as in all Roman *coloniae,* legally of equal status with the citizens and inhabitants of *Rome. As such, after 25 B.C. the city became somewhat of a miniature Rome—it was organized into *vici,* instead of the traditional Hellenistic tribes (with the *vici* perhaps reflecting the twelve *vici* of Rome itself), used an entirely Roman administrative language and structure and became progressively more Roman than its surrounding cities, which retained more of their Hellenistic character (*see* Roman Administration). The settlers of this new Roman *colonia* were largely veteran soldiers of the Legions V and VII (Ramsay, 234; Levick, 103-20; *see* Roman Military) and would have enjoyed a higher status than any of the original inhabitants (*incolae*) of the city, although these in turn would have had a higher status than their neighbors as a result of their city's new status as a *colonia.*

Roman Antioch in the mid-first century was a wonder to behold—its sculptures and architecture were on an even par with those of Rome itself (Robinson 1926a, 6), and its monuments to Augustus would have been breathtaking. Chief among these would have been the temple dedicated to Augustus in its colonnaded square, the colonnaded *Tiberia Platea* (Tiberius Street) connected to the colonnaded *Augusta Platea* by a triple-arched *Propylaea* (gate, completed in A.D. 50) in honor of Augustus's three triumphs. All of these were festooned with sculptures and *inscriptions honoring Augustus and his successors (see Robinson 1926a for discussion and plates). Even today, though ruined and stripped of its decoration, the *Augusta Platea* remains an important site (see Mitchell and Waelkens, 113-73).

2. Pisidian Antioch in the New Testament.
Such was the situation when the city was visited by Paul and Barnabas on their first missionary journey (Acts 13:13-52). Taking place sometime in the late 40s (perhaps A.D. 47), Antioch was the first real stop (except for the port of Perga in Pamphylia, where they were deserted by John

Mark) for Paul and Barnabas in Asia Minor. Their missionary activity was to continue the pattern they had initiated in their evangelization of Cyprus, beginning with the *synagogue. H. Dessau (1910; see also Mitchell 1980, 1074) suggested that Paul and Barnabas's decision to begin their activities in Asia Minor at Antioch may have been influenced by their recent convert on Cyprus, Sergius Paulus, as he was from Antioch, and his family owned large estates in the region (Mitchell 1993, 1:151; Breytenbach, 38-45). Dessau's suggestion that Paul may have changed his name to Paul from Saul as a result of taking Sergius Paulus as a patron is a distinct possibility and would figure well within the overall sociological picture of earliest Christianity (see *Associations). If this is the case, it would seem that Paul and Barnabas, in the face of Jewish resentment, were unable to establish much of a base here, although Acts 14:21 does record that they went to Antioch on the return half of their journey, "strengthening the souls of the disciples, exhorting them to remain in the faith, and that it was necessary for us to pass through much trouble for the sake of the kingdom of God."

Paul's two further trips through the area (Acts 16:1-6; 18:23) may have brought him into Antioch, although this should not be assumed, as neither passage records an explicit itinerary for Paul's journeying through the region, and it may very well be that not all of the original Pauline foundations continued to exist, even within the lifetime of Paul. We know of no explicit literary reference to Christianity in Antioch after the NT, except for the apocryphal second-century work *The Acts of Paul and Thecla*. The writer of Acts purpose(s) for not recording the Pauline itineraries in these two passages, if he knew them, may be linked to his overarching rhetorical strategy in the book of Acts, which continually leaves out details and/or focuses in on smaller incidents that, when taken as a whole, give us a selective picture of the activities of Paul. However, the existence in Antioch of an early (and very large) Byzantine Basilica of St. Paul suggests either a continuing Christian presence in the city or, at the least, a rediscovery of the Christian connection with it. The Basilica, excavated by Ramsay and Robinson in turn, is the current focus of much interest, and has recently yielded not only an early baptistry but also the promise of even more mosaic flooring than originally discovered by Robinson (see Mitchell and Walkens, 210-17).

That Paul's speech in the synagogue of Antioch is one of the longest missionary speeches in the book of Acts is perhaps significant in light of the place it occupies at the outset of Paul's preaching activity, as well as the place it has in the narrative at the beginning of the journey that takes place just before the council of Jerusalem (Acts 15). Paul's strategy in the speech is interesting, in that he seems to play on the tension between *Diaspora Jews and their fellows in Jerusalem (Acts 13:26-29, 40-41), inviting these Asian Jews to show themselves superior to the Palestinian Jews who had rejected, condemned and killed Jesus. The incredible interest that both Jewish (presumably, it was not merely the Gentile Godfearers and their friends who found this message interesting, even if the author of Acts does leave us with that impression in Acts 13:45) and Gentile Antiochians had toward Paul and Barnabas's message makes this response impossible, however, and the Jews reject and contradict the message (Acts 13:45), while the Gentiles—or at least as many as had been destined to do so (Acts 13:48)—accept the message and become believers.

The same thing then happens in Iconium, but this time the author of Acts differentiates between believing and unbelieving Jews (Acts 14:1-2), making it even more likely that the story of Antioch is meant to function as a paradigm, which is then repeated in Iconium, Lystra and Derbe. This paradigm of unbelieving Jews causing trouble for the beset apostles is further suggested by the "strengthening" nature of the message of the apostles as they pass back through the region (Acts 14:21), all of which paints an extremely convenient picture of the Pauline mission to the Gentiles with which to begin the story of the council of Jerusalem. In essence, then, we have no way of knowing the actual success of the Antiochian church nor whether it managed to survive those first few troublesome years prior to and just after the Jerusalem council. Paul's letter to the Galatians would suggest that some, if not many, turned away from the Pauline gospel (Gal 1:6-9) or perhaps fell away altogether, although the difference between these two in Paul's eyes may have been debatable.

See also ANTIOCH (SYRIA); ASIA MINOR; GALATIA, GALATIANS.

Bibliography. C. Breytenbach, *Paulus und Barnabas in der Provinz Galatien: Studien zu Apostelgeschichte 13f.; 16:6; 18:23 und den Adressaten des Galaterbriefes* (AGJU 38; Leiden: E. J. Brill, 1996); H. Dessau, "Der Name des Apostels Paulus," *Hermes* 44 (1910) 347-68; J. A. Goldstein, *2 Maccabees* (AB 41A; Garden City, NY: Doubleday, 1983); F. W. Kelsey, "Where Paul and Barnabas Labored: The Second Michigan Expedition to the Near East, IV," *The Michigan Alumnus* 31 (1925) 699ff.; B. M. Levick, *Roman Colonies of Southern Asia Minor* (Oxford: Oxford University Press, 1967); S. Mitchell, *Anatolia* (2 vols.; Oxford: Oxford University Press, 1993); idem, "Population and the Land in Roman Galatia," *ANRW* 2.7.2 (1980) 1053-81; S. Mitchell and M. Waelkens, *Pisidian Antioch: The Site and Its Monuments* (London: Duckworth with the Classical Press of Wales, 1998); W. M. Ramsay, *The Cities of St. Paul* (London: Hodder & Stoughton, 1907); D. M. Robinson, "Head of Augustus from Pisidian Antioch," *AJA* 30 (1926b) 130-36; idem, "A Preliminary Report on the Excavations at Pisidian Antioch and at Sizma," *AJA* 28 (1924) 435-44; idem, "Roman Sculptures from Colonia Caesarea (Pisidian Antioch)," *Art Bulletin* 9.1 (1926a) 5-69.

B. W. R. Pearson

ANTIOCH (SYRIA)

Antioch, the capital of ancient Seleucid* Syria and later capital of the Roman province of Syria, was situated on the edge of a large and fertile plain on the south bank of the Orontes River fifteen miles from the Mediterranean coast.

1. History Before the First Century
2. Christianity in Antioch
3. Later History

1. History Before the First Century.

Antioch was founded about 300 B.C. by Seleucus I Nicanor, one of *Alexander the Great's generals and the son of Antiochus. Like sixteen other cities, Antioch was named after Antiochus. Among the well-known cities by this name in the New Testament era is *Antioch of Pisidia (Acts 13:14-52). Antioch in Syria was originally built at the foot of Mt. Silpius as a convenience city between the king's home in Anatolia and his eastern possessions, but the city eventually became considerably more important. Seleucus transferred fifty-three hundred residents from *Athens and Macedonia to settle the new city. Its closest harbor, Seleucia, was twelve miles west at the mouth of the Orontes and functioned as the gateway to the city. It always had a mixed population of Greeks, Macedonians, local Syrians, Jews and, after 64 B.C., when it fell to Pompey, many Romans.

After Antioch was annexed by Rome, it became the capital of the province of Syria and was the military headquarters of Rome in the east (*see* Roman Administration; Roman Military). The city was allowed to govern itself from the time Julius Caesar visited the city in 47 B.C. It even had its own calendar, called the Antiochene Era, that began on October 1, 49 B.C., the presumed date of the beginning of Julius Caesar's reign.

Under Augustus and Tiberius the city was enlarged, and according to *Josephus, this expansion was significantly aided by Herod the Great, who built a long (c. 2.5 miles) colonnaded street made of polished marble with a "cloister of the same length," that is, with thirty-two hundred columns and porticoes on each side of the street with broad walkways (Josephus *J.W.* 1.21.11 §425; *Ant.* 16.5.3 §148). The colonnade may have been installed by Tiberius, but possibly also by Herod. There were many clashes between the Jews and other citizens of Antioch, and at one point the Jews were in danger of annihilation (Josephus *J.W.* 7.3.3-4 §§46-62). After the fall of *Jerusalem in A.D. 70, Titus led a triumphal entry into Antioch and brought treasures of the *temple with him, placing them at the Daphne Gate, where most of the Jews lived, in order to humiliate them (Josephus *J.W.* 7.5.1-2 §§96-111).

By the first century A.D. the city may have been third in size in the *Roman Empire behind Rome and *Alexandria. Its strategic location on the great commercial road from Asia to the Mediterranean and its many natural resources, including wine and olive oil produced nearby, contributed to its enormous wealth and prosperity. Estimates of its population vary depending on the sources and range from two hundred thousand (Chrysostom *Pan. Ign.* 4) to three hundred thousand (Strabo *Geog.* 16.2.5) to six hundred thousand (Pliny *Nat. Hist.* 6.122). It may be that the population was just above one hundred thousand, but if the slaves were counted and also the larger geographic area that the city served, then its numbers could well have been much higher.

Antioch had a Jewish population of about

twenty-five thousand to sixty-five thousand (Josephus *J.W.* 7.3.3 §43) that enjoyed the privileges of a political state (a *politeuma*), including the right to keep the sabbath and other Jewish religious practices and exclusion from obligatory military service (Josephus *Ag. Ap.* 2.4 §39; *Ant.* 12.3.1 §119; *J.W.* 7.3.3 §43). These privileges may date to the founding of the city. According to 2 Maccabees 4:33-38, a former Jewish high priest named Onias II lived in the vicinity of Antioch, and some of the temple treasures that were stolen from Jerusalem in the days of Antiochus IV Epiphanes (175-163 B.C.) were taken there. For Jews it ranked in importance with Alexandria in Egypt and Seleucia on the Tigris.

2. Christianity in Antioch.

The book of Acts claims that here the followers of Jesus were first called Christians (Acts 11:26) and that the Christians there were the first to be helpful in caring for the needs of the church in Jerusalem during a famine (Acts 11:27-30). Nicholas, a "proselyte of Antioch," was one of seven leaders of *Hellenists in Jerusalem chosen to do ministries for the church (Acts 6:7). Most importantly, however, Acts names the church at Antioch as the church that initiated the first intentional Gentile mission through Barnabas and Paul. They had ministered in Antioch for a year (Acts 11:19-26), and the church sent Barnabas, Paul and John Mark on its first Jewish and Gentile missionary enterprise (Acts 13:1-3). Later, because of conflict between Paul and Barnabas, that work was expanded to two missionary teams (Acts 15:36-41). Although Peter is the first to have a Gentile mission, to the household of Cornelius (Acts 10), the church at Antioch gave special attention to this ministry. Paul returned here after his first and second journeys (Acts 14:26-28; 18:22) and made this community his base of operations between his journeys (Acts 15:22-36). He alone reports a firsthand activity at Antioch in which he describes a confrontation with Peter, who had come to Antioch from Jerusalem (Gal 2:11-14). The importance of Antioch in the establishment of Gentile Christianity cannot be underestimated (*see DPL, DLNTD,* Antioch on the Orontes).

While Antioch generally was a place where Jewish Christianity flourished, especially after the death of Paul, it is not as certain as some scholars suppose that Paul's message was largely ignored here during his lifetime. Eusebius claims, for instance, that Ignatius, who followed the apostle Peter and Evodius as bishop of Antioch (Eusebius *Hist. Eccl.* 3.22.1; 3.36.2-3), agreed with many of Paul's views, especially regarding the judaizing in the churches that Paul also condemned (Ign. *Magn.* 8.1; 10.3; Ign. *Phld.* 6.1). Ignatius also opposed the gnosticizing heresies of his day that denied the full humanity of Jesus (Ign. *Trall.* 10.1; Ign. *Smyrn.* 2.1—4.2), but after him a number of gnostic Christians were connected with the church at Antioch: Menander, Saturninus, Cerdon, Tatian, Axionicus; (Justin Martyr *Apol. I* 26; Irenaeus *Haer.* 1.22; Eusebius *Hist. Eccl.* 4.10—5.2; Epiphanius *Anac.* 46.1; Tertullian *Adv. Valent.* 4.3). The city itself, though supporting a Gentile mission, did not reject its Jewish heritage but rather was involved in a Jewish and Gentile Christian mission. This is not unlike Paul, whose habit of ministry included "the Jew first and also the Greek" (Rom 1:17).

While no NT writer claims any Christian literature was produced at Antioch, it is possible that the Gospel of Matthew (A.D. 75-90) and Paul's letter to the Galatians originated here. It may also be that the Gospel of Luke was composed here and, as some scholars argue, that Luke used a written Antiochene source in his production of the book of Acts. These are possibilities, but as yet they have not been demonstrated.

3. Later History.

The famous story of the Maccabean martyrs (2 Macc 7-8 and all of 4 Macc) that has been preserved mostly in Christian literature (*Passio ss. Machabaeorum*) is associated with the city of Antioch of Syria before the existence of the church in that area (Acts 11:19-26). The story emerged from Antioch in the pre-Christian era and had a powerful influence upon the fourth-century church and following. A church/martyrium was built at Antioch on what was believed was the site of their martyrdom and the location of their graves. Their story became an inspiration to Christian martyrs in the fourth century, and it has been variously celebrated in the church ever since.

While the date and provenance of *4 Maccabees are not certain (possibly written as early as A.D. 19-54 or as late as the early second century A.D. and possibly also at Antioch of Syria or even Alexandria), the tradition of the place of the martyrdom of the priest Eleazar, the mother and her seven sons is believed by many to have taken place in Antioch of Syria, the headquarters of Antiochus IV Epiphanes, at the beginning of the Antiochus's conflicts with the Maccabean family and the Jews in Palestine. The story and philosophical treatise in 4 Maccabees draws on the story of these martyrdoms and calls for divine reason in the face of *persecution. It may originally have been an address given at the site of the martyrdoms and burial sites (4 Macc 1:10; 3:19), but that is not certain.

By the fourth century A.D., many in the Christian community seem to have commemorated this event and even built a martyrium/church over the martyrdom and burial site in Antioch. A tradition claims that a synagogue was located there before the church, but that is uncertain (Jewish concern for ritual purity may have precluded the building of a synagogue on a burial site). Antioch may have been the first place where a Christian martyrium was built and the death of martyrs celebrated within the church. The story associated with Antioch of Syria is mentioned in many church fathers, including Origen (*Exhort. Mart.* 23-27), Hippolytus (*Comm. Dan.* 2.21, 35), Eusebius (*Hist. Eccl.* 5.1.55), Gregory of Nazianzus (*Or.* 15.1-8), John Chrysostom (*Fourth Homily*), Ambrose (*Off.* 1.41.212; *Ep.* 40.16), and Augustine (*Serm.* 300.2). The supposed bones and relics of the martyrs were moved from Istanbul (Byzantium) in the sixth century to Milan, and finally to Cologne in 1164. Another tradition has the relics and bones moved from Antioch to the Church of San Pietro in Vincoli, Italy.

By the sixth century A.D., celebrations of the Maccabean martyrs were commonplace throughout Christendom. How they came to be included in Christian martyrologies (collections of stories about martyrs) is not clear, but 4 Maccabees came to be accepted by many Christians as a "Christian" book because these Jewish martyrs were looked upon as protomartyrs. Augustine (*Ciiv. D.* 18.36) claims that it was because of the extreme suffering of these martyrs that the books of the Maccabees were welcomed into the church and preserved by the church.

Antioch of Syria was an important city not only in the first century but until the beginning of the seventh century. It was long known for its rhetoricians, historians and later for its theologians. Among the latter is the famous Antiochene School that could speak of such members as Basil the Great, John Chrysostom, Theodore of Mopsuestia and Theodoret of Cyrrhus. Evagrius Scholasticus, in the tradition of Eusebius of Caesarea, came from Antioch. It was a royal city from its beginning, and even though its population had greatly decreased to six to eight thousand residents in the late fourth century A.D., it was strategically important until its capture by the Arabs in the seventh century following a lengthy Persian occupation. In its prime, the city had many beautiful buildings, eight pagan temples and eventually several churches. Most important to the Roman Empire, however, was its strategic location for launching military campaigns in the east. The city survived the persecutions of Decius, Diocletian and Licinius and became a favored city of Constantine. By A.D. 390, Antioch had become almost completely Christian with a few pagans and a large number of Jews, mostly at Daphne, three miles away (Chrysostom *Adv. Jud.* 1.4; *PG* 48, 849). Until the Persian invasion and occupation of the area (A.D. 610-628), Antioch was the military administrative center of the eastern empire, and a large army was stationed there.

As an important religious center, the patriarchate of Antioch was second in importance in the east only to Alexandria, but because of the changes that came with the expansion of the patriarchate of Constantinople, the newly created patriarchate at Jerusalem was given jurisdiction over the Palestinian dioceses (formerly under Antioch). As a result of decisions made at the Council of Chalcedon (A.D. 451) and also because of the emergence of Nestorianism and Monophysitism at Antioch, its value as a Christian center declined significantly near the end of the fifth century.

Several other factors led to the gradual demise of the city as a center for Christian mission, including earthquakes in the sixth century (A.D. 528, 529, 551, 577) that killed 250,000 or more residents; the capture and sacking of the city in A.D. 528 by el-Mundhir the Lakhmidian, a Persian ally; a similar plundering by the Persians in A.D. 540; and a severe plague that lasted from A.D. 542 to 573. After these calamities, Antioch's one-time splendor was over, even though Justinian I (A.D. 483-565) tried to rebuild the city, renaming it Theopolis ("divine city" or "city of God"). The debris of the former destructions, however, was never fully carried away, and its former grandeur was never recaptured. The great marble road of Herod, for instance, was covered over by basalt. The city was captured by the Crusaders in A.D. 1098, by the Mamelukes in A.D. 1268 and by the Turks in A.D. 1516. The modern city of Antakya, Turkey, home to eighty thousand people, occupies the ancient site, and only limited excavations have been undertaken at the site.

See also ALEXANDRIA; ANTIOCH (PISIDIA); CITIES, GRECO-ROMAN; CORINTH; EPHESUS; JERUSALEM; ROME.

BIBLIOGRAPHY. H. A. Anderson, "4 Maccabees," in *OTP* 2:532-43; R. E. Brown, *An Introduction to the New Testament* (ABRL; Garden City, NY: Doubleday, 1997); R. E. Brown and J. P. Meier, *Antioch and Rome: New Testament Cradles of Catholic Christianity* (New York: Paulist, 1983); L. DeVries, *Cities of the Biblical World* (Peabody, MA: Hendrickson, 1997); G. Downey, *A History of Antioch in Syria* (Princeton, NJ: Princeton University Press, 1961); M. Hengel and A. M. Schwemer, *Paul Between Damascus and Antioch: The Unknown Years* (Louisville, KY: Westminster John Knox, 1997); H. W. G. Liebeschütz, *Antioch: City and Imperial Administration in the Later Roman Empire* (Oxford: Clarendon Press, 1972); W. Meeks and R. Wilken, *Jews and Christians in Antioch in the First Four Centuries of the Common Era* (SBLSBS 13; Missoula, MT: Scholars Press, 1978); F. W. Norris, "Antioch," *ABD* 1:265-69; O. Pasquato, "Antioch," in *Encyclopedia of the Early Church*, ed. A. Di Berardino (2 vols.; New York: Oxford University Press, 1992) 1:47-48, 51; L. V. Rutgers, "The Importance of Scripture in the Conflict Between Jews and Christians: The Example of Antioch," in *The Use of Sacred Books in the Ancient World*, ed. L. V. Rutgers et al. (CBET 22; Leuven: Peeters, 1998) 287-303; G. Tate, "Antioch on Orontes," in *Oxford Encyclopedia of Archaeology in the Near East*, ed. E. M. Meyers (New York: Oxford University Press, 1997) 1:144-45; D. S. Wallace-Hadrill, *Christian Antioch: A Study of Early Christian Thought in the East* (Cambridge: Cambridge University Press, 1982).

L. M. McDonald

ANTIOCHIDS. *See* SELEUCIDS AND ANTIOCHIDS.

ANTIPAS. *See* HERODIAN DYNASTY.

APOCALYPSE OF ABRAHAM

The *Apocalypse of Abraham* is a *pseudepigraphon written in two separate genres. The first eight chapters offer a narrative account of the conversion of the patriarch Abraham from paganism to the worship of the one true God. This narrative is followed by an *apocalyptic vision purportedly given to Abraham that expands at great length upon the vision of the patriarch recorded in Genesis 15 and adds to it a wealth of theological, cosmological and *eschatological details.

1. Provenance, Date and Composition
2. Content

1. Provenance, Date and Composition. *Apocalypse of Abraham* is generally believed to be a Jewish composition containing Christian interpolations. However, no convincing argument has yet been proposed why it could not have been written by a Christian familiar with Jewish traditions. At any rate, the nature of the Christianity that may have influenced or perhaps even created *Apocalypse of Abraham* is problematic. This was not mainstream Christianity, and it has been suggested that the Christian elements are the work of Bogomils, a heterodox medieval sect with strong dualist or even *gnostic affinities who influenced much of the apocryphal literature preserved in Slavonic.

The date of composition for *Apocalypse of Abraham* cannot be established with certainty, but the work is probably a rough contemporary of the NT. The author of *Apocalypse of Abraham* was aware of the destruction of the Jewish *temple in A.D. 70, an indication that the work cannot have been written before that time. However, *Apocalypse of Abraham* shares many features with other Jewish and Christian literature composed during the first two centuries of the present era. The contents of *Apocalypse of Abraham* do not match as well the concerns of either Judaism or Christianity at a later period. Moreover, a passage devoted to Abraham in the early-third-century *Clementine Recognitions* (1.32) is likely an allusion to *Apocalypse of Abraham.* In this passage the conversion and apocalyptic vision of Abraham are joined together exactly as in *Apocalypse of Abraham,* complete with the angelic mentor/guide and the revelation of Israel's future. The evidence suggests a date for *Apocalypse of Abraham* sometime after the fall of Jerusalem but before the end of the second century.

It has been suggested that the two separate sections of this text, the narrative and the apocalyptic, were separate compositions about Abraham that have subsequently become joined.

However, in the present text of *Apocalypse of Abraham* the two sections appear intentionally intertwined. Also, the passage from the *Recognitions,* even if it is not a direct reference to *Apocalypse of Abraham,* demonstrates at the least that the narrative account of Abraham's conversion from idolatry and his apocalyptic vision were already complementary parts of a single tradition at that time. If the narrative and apocalyptic portions of *Apocalypse of Abraham* have been fused together from separate sources, then that event likely occurred before the *Recognitions* were composed in the early third century. Since *Apocalypse of Abraham* was surely written after A.D. 70, and probably sometime in the second century, this does not leave much time for a fusion of separate narrative accounts. Economy of theory would argue for positing both narrative and apocalyptic elements in the original work.

Apocalypse of Abraham is found today only in Slavonic versions. The manuscript evidence is very late, dating between the fourteenth and seventeenth centuries. The work appears to have been translated into Slavonic from Greek, perhaps as early as 900. However, the large number of Semitisms preserved in the Slavonic text provides some evidence for a Hebrew or an Aramaic original.

2. Content.
The story of *Apocalypse of Abraham* begins with Abraham's conversion to the worship of the one God (*Apoc. Abr.* 1—8). While tending to his father's business as a carver of idols, Abraham perceives the helplessness of these human artifacts. Stone gods break; wooden gods burn; either may be sunk in the waters of a river or be smashed in a fall. Abraham realizes that rather than being gods to his father, Terah, the idols are his father's creatures. It is Terah who functions as a god in creating the idols. As Abraham ponders the helplessness of his father's idols, he hears the voice of the Mighty One coming to him from heaven and commanding him to leave his father's house. This he does just in time to avoid destruction.

The apocalyptic portion of *Apocalypse of Abraham* begins in chapter 9 with the voice of God coming to the patriarch. Abraham is overcome by this, and God sends the angel Iaoel to raise, strengthen and comfort him (*Apoc. Abr.* 10—11). Fasting for forty days, the two figures make their way to Horeb, where Abraham offers prescribed sacrifices (*Apoc. Abr.* 12). Abraham is confronted by Azazel, the fallen angel who opposed God and revealed heavenly secrets to humans, but Iaoel teaches Abraham how to overcome this evil one and assures the patriarch that Azazel's former heavenly garment is now reserved for Abraham (*Apoc. Abr.* 13—14).

Abraham then ascends into the heavens (*see* Heavenly Ascent) with the angel Iaoel (*Apoc. Abr.* 15—18), where the Holy One approaches him upon the great *merkabah* (or chariot) throne (described in terms borrowed from Ezek 1). Abraham looks down and sees the seven firmaments beneath him, each with its different class of angels carrying out their duties in the administration of the cosmos (*Apoc. Abr.* 19). Abraham also sees the history of the world, both past and future, depicted upon the firmament of heaven (*Apoc. Abr.* 20). He views the creation of the universe, Eden and Adam and Eve. He sees the Fall, the history of nations, the destruction of the Jerusalem temple, the checkered future of his own posterity and, finally, the end of the world with its plagues and judgments upon the wicked and the heathen (*Apoc. Abr.* 21—32).

In the midst of Abraham's panoramic vision of the world and its history, *Apocalypse of Abraham* 29 constitutes a clear Christian interpolation. Here Abraham sees Christ, who is contradictorily described as both "going out from the heathen" and "from your [Abraham's] tribe." Many heathen "will trust in him," and those of Abraham's seed who worship Christ will be delivered from oppression when the present "age of impiety" is succeeded by the coming "age of justice."

See also APOCALYPTIC LITERATURE; TESTAMENT OF ABRAHAM.

BIBLIOGRAPHY. G. H. Box and J. I. Landsman, *The Apocalypse of Abraham* (London: SPCK, 1918); J. H. Charlesworth, "The Jewish Roots of Christology: The Discovery of the Hypostatic Voice," *SJT* 39 (1986) 19-41; idem, *The Pseudepigrapha and Modern Research with a Supplement* (SCS 7; Missoula, MT: Scholars Press, 1981) 68-69; A.-M. Denis, *Introduction aux pseudépigraphes grecs d'Ancien Testament* (SVTP 1; Leiden: E. J. Brill, 1970) 37-38; R. G. Hall, "The 'Christian Interpolation' in the Apocalypse of Abraham," *JBL* 107 (1987) 107-12; G. W. E. Nickelsburg, *Jewish Literature Between the Bible and the Mishnah* (Philadelphia: Fortress, 1981) 294-99; A. Pennington, "The Apocalypse of Abraham," in *The*

Apocryphal Old Testament, ed. H. F. D. Sparks (Oxford: Clarendon Press, 1984) 363-91; R. Rubinkiewicz and H. G. Lunt, "The Apocalypse of Abraham," in *The Old Testament Pseudepigrapha,* ed. J. H. Charlesworth (2 vols.; Garden City, NY: Doubleday, 1983, 1985) 1:681-705; M. E. Stone, "Apocalyptic Literature," in *Jewish Writings of the Second Temple Period, ed. M. E. Stone* (CRINT 2,2; Assen: Van Gorcum; Philadelphia: Fortress, 1984) 415-18; E. Turdeanu, "L'Apocalypse d'Abraham in slave," *JSJ* 3 (1972) 153-80; idem, *Apocryphes slaves et roumains de l'Ancien Testament* (Leiden: E. J. Brill, 1981). S. E. Robinson

APOCALYPSE OF ZEPHANIAH

The document known as the *Apocalypse of Zephaniah* purports to record revelation received by the OT prophet Zephaniah beyond what is now found in his canonical book of the Bible. It instead expresses the views of a Hellenistic Jewish writer from approximately the time of Hillel and Jesus (roughly between 100 B.C. and A.D. 100) who associated the name of the OT prophet with his own work, perhaps in an attempt to bolster its credibility. There is some evidence of subsequent Christian influence upon the text.

Apocalypse of Zephaniah is a pseudepigraphon of the OT that has been preserved incompletely, and it is possible, as argued by Steindorff, that the material now extant represents more than a single original work. Two partial manuscripts in Coptic and a passage explicitly attributed to Zephaniah in the writings of Clement of Alexandria (Clement *Strom.* 5.11.77) allow reconstruction of perhaps one-fourth of the ancient material. The earlier of these two Coptic manuscripts dates from before A.D. 400. However, the citation in Clement must be dated to around A.D. 175, thus providing an upward limit for date of composition. Further, in order for the Christian Clement to cite *Apocalypse of Zephaniah* as a genuine document possessing some normative authority, as he seems to do, some time must be allowed for prior circulation of the work—hence an upward estimate of sometime in the first century A.D. At the other extreme, the earliest possible date of composition is provided by a reference in *Apocalypse of Zephaniah* to the story of Susanna and the wicked elders (*Apoc. Zeph.* 6:10), for the apocryphal story of Susanna would not have circulated widely in Diaspora Judaism as part of the Greek *Septuagint until the first century B.C. (*see* Daniel, Esther and Jeremiah, Additions to).

It is likely that *Apocalypse of Zephaniah* was written in Egypt, and probably in *Alexandria, since it is preserved only in Coptic manuscripts and cited only by the Alexandrian Clement. Moreover, mention of a celestial boat (*Apoc. Zeph.* 8:1) and of a divine judgment that consists of weighing good and evil in a balance also indicates Egyptian influence. The original language of *Apocalypse of Zephaniah* appears to have been Greek, since there is evidence in the text that the author was unfamiliar with Hebrew or Aramaic. A later Christian document, the *Apocalypse of Paul* or *Visio Pauli,* is dependent upon *Apocalypse of Zephaniah.*

Apocalypse of Zephaniah is a textbook example of Jewish *apocalyptic literature. In the passage from Clement, the seer Zephaniah has been caught up into the fifth heaven and observes the nature and activities of the *angels there (cf. 2 Cor 12:1-4). Other elements of this cosmic journey are recorded in the Coptic fragments. There the seer is accompanied by a glorious angel who guides him from scene to scene and answers his many questions. He witnesses the torments of the wicked dead in Hades by terrible angels, and he also sees the bliss of the righteous dead. Zephaniah views the earth and his own city with its inhabitants, both good and evil, from the perspective of heaven (*Apoc. Zeph.* 2). He pleads for compassion upon the wicked who suffer in Hades (*Apoc. Zeph.* 2:8-9) and is himself confronted by "the Accuser" there, escaping with the help of his angelic companion and through his own purity (*Apoc. Zeph.* 4; 6).

As Zephaniah nears the end of his cosmic journey, he exchanges his mortal garb for an angelic garment (*Apoc. Zeph.* 8:3); he is informed that his name is recorded in the Book of the Living (*Apoc. Zeph.* 9:2); and he hears the angelic trumpets announce the judgments of God upon the earth (*Apoc. Zeph.* 9—12), although he is not allowed to witness the events of the end time (*Apoc. Zeph.* 12:4-5).

While the fragmentary nature of the extant material makes firm conclusions difficult concerning the theology and worldview of *Apocalypse of Zephaniah,* there are several intriguing elements. Human beings seem to be judged by God on two different occasions, once at death and once again at the end time, with the apparent possibility of postmortem repentance and the extension of divine mercy before or at the final judgment (*Apoc. Zeph.* 10:10-11). To this end the patriarchs and all the saints in heaven daily offer intercessory *prayers to God on behalf of the sinners in Hades (*Apoc. Zeph.* 11:1-6).

Several passages from *Apocalypse of Zephaniah* relate directly to the NT. Perhaps the strongest connection between *Apocalypse of Zephaniah* and the NT comes at 2:2-4, where, as Zephaniah views his own city, he sees "two men walking together on one road," then "two women grinding together at a mill," and finally "two upon a bed." The similarities to Jesus' words in Luke 17:34-36 and Matthew 24:40-41 are striking and undeniable. It would appear that both *Apocalypse of Zephaniah* and Jesus are citing a cautionary proverb of the day in which death, in a seemingly arbitrary manner, snatches one of two individuals engaged in identical pursuits.

Apocalypse of Zephaniah also shows strong affinities with the NT book of Revelation. When Zephaniah first sees the angel Eremiel, he mistakes him for the Lord God and falls upon his face to worship. Eremiel stops this immediately by identifying himself as an angel (*Apoc. Zeph.* 6:14-15). This same scenario is played out twice in the book of Revelation between the seer and his angelic visitor (Rev 19:10; 22:8). Moreover the angel Eremiel here and Son of Man in Revelation are described in unmistakably similar terms as having golden girdles about their breasts and feet like bronze melted in a fire or furnace (*Apoc. Zeph.* 6:11-12; Rev 1:13-15). Also related to the NT book of Revelation are the motifs of finding one's name written—or not written—in "the book of the living" (*Apoc. Zeph.* 3:7; 9:2; cf. Rev 3:5; 13:8; 20:12; 21:27; 22:19) and of individual revelations or acts of God being preceded by blasts on angelic trumpets (*Apoc. Zeph.* 9:1; 10:1; 12:1; cf. Rev 8—11). Zephaniah is also described as seeing a lake of fire and brimstone (*Apoc. Zeph.* 6:1-2) into which the wicked dead are thrown as in judgment scenes in Revelation (*Apoc. Zeph.* 10:3-9; cf. Rev 19:20; 20:14). Perhaps it is not surprising that *Apocalypse of Zephaniah* would have affinities with the Revelation of John, since both compositions are of the same literary genre (apocalypse) and were written during the same general period of time.

See also APOCALYPTIC LITERATURE.

BIBLIOGRAPHY. U. Bouriant, "Les papyrus d'Akhmim," in *Mémoires publiées par les membres de la mission archéologique Française au Caire,* 1.2 (Paris: 1885) 242-304, esp. 260-79; J. H. Charlesworth, *The Pseudepigrapha and Modern Research* (SCS 7; Missoula, MT: Scholars Press, 1981) 220-23; A.-M. Denis, *Introduction aux pseudépigraphes Grecs d'Ancien Testament* (SVTP 1; Leiden: E. J. Brill, 1970) 192-93; M. R. James, *The Lost Apocrypha of the Old Testament* (London: Oxford University Press, 1920) 72-74; K. H. Kuhn, "The Apocalypse of Zephaniah and an Anonymous Apocalypse," in *The Apocryphal Old Testament,* ed. H. F. D. Sparks (Oxford: Clarendon Press, 1984) 915-25; C. Schmidt, "Der Kolophon des Ms. Orient. 7594 des Britischen Museums; eine Untersuchung zur Elias-Apokalypse," in *Sitzungberichte der Preussischen Akademie der Wissenschaften* (Phil.-Hist. Klasse; Berlin: 1925) 312-21; G. Steindorff, *Die Apokalypse des Elias, eine unbekannte Apokalypse und Bruchstücke der Sophonias-Apokalypse* (TU 17.3a; Leipzig: 1899); O. S. Wintermute, "Apocalypse of Zephaniah," in *The Old Testament Pseudepigrapha,* ed. J. H. Charlesworth (2 vols.; Garden City, NY: Doubleday, 1983. 1985) 1:497-515.

S. E. Robinson

APOCALYPTIC LITERATURE

Apocalyptic literature first emerges in Judaism in the centuries immediately before the rise of Christianity. It is represented in the OT only in the book of Daniel. It was extremely important for the thought-world in which Christianity originated, and it has continued to fascinate Christians (and some Jews) for two millennia.

1. Terminology
2. Historical Apocalypses
3. The Apocalyptic Worldview
4. Apocalypses from the Late First Century
5. The Otherworldly Journeys
6. Conclusion

1. Terminology.

1.1. Ancient Usage. Apocalyptic literature takes its name from the last book of the NT, the book of Revelation, or the Apocalypse of John, which is usually dated to the last decade of the first century A.D. In that book John reports a series of supernatural revelations, mostly in the form of visions. These concern impending upheavals that culminate in the end of this world and a new creation. The word *apocalypse* (Gk *apokalypsis*) means "revelation." From the second century A.D. it is used with increasing frequency in the titles of books, as a virtual *genre label (Smith). So, for example, the Cologne Mani Codex says that each of the forefathers showed his own *apokalypsis* to the elect and goes on to mention apocalypses of Adam, Sethel, Enosh, Shem and Enoch. Whether all of these alleged apocalypses existed as books is uncertain. They are primarily concerned with ascents to heaven (*see* Heavenly Ascent), and this is true of many of the texts that are called apocalypses in the ancient manuscripts.

*1.2. **Modern Usage.*** Modern discussions of apocalyptic literature, however, have been primarily concerned with the antecedents of Revelation rather than with what came after it. The publication of the Ethiopic *Book of Enoch (1 Enoch; see* Enoch, Books of) early in the nineteenth century led to the realization that there was a whole genre of literature similar to Revelation in ancient Judaism, even though in antiquity it lacked a clear genre label. The writings in question included the biblical book of Daniel and the apocryphal 2 Esdras (also known as 4 Ezra; *see* Esdras, Books of). The rediscovery of several other *pseudepigraphic writings in the course of the nineteenth century filled out the corpus. These included *2 Enoch, 2 Baruch, 3 Baruch* (*see* Baruch, Books of) and the **Apocalypse of Abraham.*

In the 1970s a systematic analysis of apocalyptic and related literature was undertaken under the auspices of the Society of Biblical Literature. This project surveyed Jewish and Christian writings that could plausibly be dated before A.D. 250, and it also took account of Gnostic, Greco-Roman and Persian writings. The analysis yielded the following definition of the genre:

> An apocalypse is a genre of revelatory literature with a narrative framework, in which a revelation is mediated by an otherworldly being to a human recipient, disclosing a transcendent reality which is both temporal, insofar as it envisages eschatological salvation, and spatial, insofar as it involves another, supernatural world. (J. J. Collins 1979, 9)

Within the spectrum of material covered by this fairly broad definition two types of apocalypses were distinguished, the historical and the mystical. The historical type, familiar from the biblical book of Daniel, gives an overview of a large sweep of history, often divided into periods. This overview is presented in the guise of a prediction, much of which is prophesied after the fact but which invariably concludes with a real prediction of the end of history and a final judgment. This kind of apocalypticism is often called millennarianism, from the expectation of a millennium, or thousand-year reign, in the book of Revelation. The mystical type of apocalypse describes the ascent of the visionary through the heavens. In some apocalypses of the Christian era the heavens are numbered. Eventually the idea of seven heavens became standard. Some scholars view these two types of apocalypses as two distinct genres, but several writings mix elements of both types. Both attach great importance to the heavenly world and anticipate the judgment not only of nations on earth but also of the individual dead.

2. Historical Apocalypses.

The historical type of apocalypse has roots both in biblical and in Zoroastrian traditions.

*2.1. **Persian Apocalypticism.*** The relationship between Persian apocalypticism and its Jewish counterpart is notoriously problematic. The main Persian apocalyptic texts are preserved in Pahlavi writings from the ninth century A.D. Scholars are divided as to how far older traditions can be reconstructed from this literature. N. Cohn has argued that Zoroaster, whom he dates to the second millennium B.C., should be credited with first developing the linear view of history that is characteristic of apocalypticism. Other scholars, however, argue that Persian apocalypticism is a late development.

The most fully developed Persian apocalyptic writing, the *Bahman Yasht,* is a Pahlavi writing, which is quite late in its present form. It is a commentary on a lost work of the Avesta, however, and some of the material it preserves may be quite old. In the first chapter Zoroaster has a vision of a tree with four branches, one of gold, one of silver, one of steel and one of mixed iron. Ahura Mazda (the high god of Zoroastrianism) explains the vision, saying that the four branches were four kingdoms of which the last is ruled by the "divs who have disheveled hair." Many scholars have taken this as a reference to the Greeks. Their kingdom is supposed to come when the tenth century, or millennium, of Zoroaster is at an end. If the reference is to the Greeks, this would suggest that the vision dates to the early *Hellenistic period and that the well-known motif of four kingdoms may have been of Persian origin. The similarity between this vision and Daniel 2 is striking, although it is not possible to show that one author depended directly on the other.

The periodization of history, however, is more broadly typical of Persian thought than it is of Jewish. The Zoroastrian view of history also included upheavals and disturbances at the end of an era and looked forward to the resurrection of the dead. Only the Bahman Yasht, however, combines the typically apocalyptic form of revelation (a vision interpreted by a god) with the periodization of history and *eschatology. Like many of the Pahlavi writings, the *Bahman Yasht* is a compendium of materials, although it bears closer resemblance to the historical apocalypses than does any other Persian work. Because of the difficulty of dating the Persian materials, their role in the development of apocalypticism is likely to remain controversial.

2.2. Biblical Prophecy. There is obvious continuity between the Jewish and Christian apocalypses and the Hebrew prophets, in their concern with history and expectation of divine intervention and judgment. In antiquity both Daniel and John of Patmos were often regarded as prophets. It is possible to trace the evolution of some literary forms from prophecy to apocalypticism. For example, the role of the interpreting *angel, the supernatural mediator, appears first in Zechariah, in the late sixth century B.C. P. Hanson has argued that "the dawn of apocalyptic" should be located in the prophetic texts of the early postexilic period, especially in Isaiah 56—66, which speak already of "a new heaven and a new earth." The new earth envisioned in Isaiah 65—66, however, may be understood as differing from the world as we know it only in degree, with life on earth still subject to mortality, although people live longer and have fewer problems. The apocalypses of the Hellenistic period, in contrast, anticipate life with the angels in heaven. While there is continuity between postexilic prophecy and apocalypticism, the novelty of the later literature should not be underestimated.

2.3. Enoch and Daniel. In the Jewish context, the books of Enoch and Daniel mark the emergence of a new kind of literature, usually dated by modern scholarship to the early second century B.C. (*1 Enoch* is a collection of at least five distinct books; *see* Enoch, Books of). Daniel uses the literary form of the vision, which can be seen as a development of prophetic visions, especially those of Zechariah. The revelations of Enoch purport to relate what he had seen on his heavenly journey. Under a second-century dating, both Enoch and Daniel are of course pseudonyms. Enoch is a biblical figure from before the flood, but none of the writings attributed to him can be older than the third century B.C. Daniel is the hero of miraculous stories set in the Babylonian exile (Dan 1—6), but his visions focus without exception on the persecution of the Jews by Antiochus IV Epiphanes in the second century B.C. Pseudonymity was a widespread device in the literature of the Hellenistic period and was not peculiar to the apocalyptic genre. Within Judaism we also have a wisdom book attributed to Solomon, although it is well informed in Greek philosophy, and *Psalms of Solomon,* a work that reflects events in the Roman period. Greek authors similarly produced new works in the name of Plato, Heraclitus or the sibyl. While the psychology of pseudonymity remains obscure to us, we should not dismiss it as a form of deception, and it should not detract from the moral seriousness of the works in question (*see* Pseudonymity and Pseudepigraphy).

Both Enoch and Daniel are credited with lengthy revelations of the course of history, much of which were clearly written after the fact. To a degree, this device was a byproduct of pseudonymity. If Enoch supposedly lived before the flood, he had to "predict" the course of history before he could get to the events of the actual author's time. But the device of prophecy after the fact also conveyed a sense that history was predetermined, since it could be predicted so long in advance.

3. The Apocalyptic Worldview.

3.1. The Heavenly World. The main novelty of Enoch and Daniel, however, was not a matter of literary form but of worldview. Angels and demonic forces (*see* Belial, Beliar, Devil, Satan) figure in this literature to a far greater degree than is the case in the older biblical books. In Daniel 10, human conflicts on earth are reflections of the struggles between the patron *angels of the nations. The success of the Jewish people depends on the victory of the archangel Michael. In *1 Enoch,* the defilement of the earth is due to the sin of the fallen angels. Enoch adds a cosmological dimension to the revelation by claiming to have seen the ends of the earth, the abodes of the dead and the place prepared for the coming judgment. The theme of judgment looms large in these writings. In Daniel it is imminent; this is the only ancient apocalypse that attempts to calculate the number of days until the end. Some of the Enochic writings also suggest that the last period of history has been reached. The judgment will ensure the victory of the righteous. In these books the righteous are not coterminous with the Jewish people but are conceived rather as a remnant within it. Daniel speaks of a kingdom that will be given to the people of the holy ones, and the Enochic writings also expect some reversal of social roles on earth.

The real focus of these books, however, is on salvation after death. Daniel is the first book in the Hebrew Bible to speak unambiguously of *resurrection. But the resurrected do not return to life on earth. The martyrs, at least, are elevated to shine like the stars (Dan 12:2). The meaning of this analogy is made clear by a parallel in *1 Enoch:* "you will shine like the lights of heaven and will be seen, and the gates of heaven will be opened to you. . . . Be hopeful and do not abandon your hope, for you will have great joy like the angels of heaven . . . for you shall be associates of the host of heaven" (*1 Enoch* 104:2, 4, 6). The expectation of life with the angels after death entailed a radical shift in the worldview of ancient Judaism. In most of the Hebrew Bible, human life and its rewards were conceived in strictly earthly terms. The hope was to see one's children and one's children's children and to enjoy the fertility of the land. If the goal of life was fellowship with the angels, however, different values might follow, and a more otherworldly kind of spirituality became possible (*see* Afterlife).

3.2. The Dead Sea Scrolls. This new apocalyptic worldview could be expressed in other literary genres besides the apocalypse. The Dead Sea sect, whose writings were found near *Qumran, preserved multiple copies of the apocalypses of Daniel and Enoch but produced few if any new apocalypses of their own (*see* Dead Sea Scrolls). Yet the worldview of the sect is apocalyptic. In the **Rule of the Community,* the human condition is explained by the fact that God created two spirits, one of Light and one of Darkness, and humanity is divided between them. (This idea was adapted from Zoroastrian dualism.) These forces contend with each other throughout the periods of history, but God has appointed an end to wickedness. The War Rule (*see* War Scroll) describes the final war between the two forces, each of which operates at both the angelic and the human levels. The archangel Michael leads the Sons of Light while *Belial is the leader of the Sons of Darkness. The scrolls say little about the kind of society that will follow this war, although they speak frequently of both a royal and a priestly *messiah. More important was the prospect of eternal life for the righteous and eternal damnation for their enemies.

The most distinctive feature of the eschatology of Qumran, however, was the idea that the community could attain in the present the fellowship with the angels that was promised to the righteous after death in Daniel and Enoch. For that reason, the scrolls seldom speak of resurrection. The essential transition to eternal life was made within the community itself. All of this was guaranteed by revelation. The mode of revelation, however, was not the vision such as we find in the apocalypses but the inspired exegesis of Scripture, practiced by the Teacher of Righteousness and his successors.

3.3. The New Testament. The NT contains only one apocalypse, the book of Revelation, but here again we may speak of an apocalyptic worldview that is much more widespread. According to the Synoptic Gospels, Jesus predicted imminent upheavals that would be followed by the coming of the Son of Man on the clouds of heaven (Mk 13 and par.). Scholars dispute whether or how far such predictions should be attributed to Jesus himself or were composed by his followers after his death. It seems reasonable to suppose that the teachings of the early church must have been continuous with the teachings of Jesus. He must have provided some basis for the apocalyptic teachings of his followers. The message that the kingdom of God was at hand lent itself readily to an apocalyptic interpretation. Paul explains the resurrection in an apocalyptic context. Christ is the firstfruits of the general resurrection, and if there is no general resurrection of the dead, then Christ has not been raised (1 Cor 15). Paul believed that the time was short and that not all of his generation would die. Those who were left alive would be caught up to meet the Lord in the air. This expectation of an imminent end of history and final judgment gave early Christianity much of its urgency.

4. Apocalypses from the Late First Century.

4.1. The Book of Revelation. Written toward the end of the first century, the Apocalypse draws heavily on the imagery of Ezekiel and Daniel. The persecution of Christians is due to the fact that Satan has been cast down from heaven, and his time is short. The *Roman Empire is likened to the beasts that came up out of the sea (Dan 7), and Rome is compared with a great harlot. The book concludes with a vision of Christ coming as a warrior from heaven. This is followed by a thousand-year reign on earth for the martyrs who had lost their lives and finally by the general resurrection and new creation. The book of Revelation was controversial for a long time in early Christianity, and its canonicity was disputed. Eventually it was accepted as part of Scripture (*see* Canonical Formation of the New Testament), and it continues to have profound influence.

4.2. Later Jewish Apocalypses. The last great Jewish apocalypses of the historical type were produced in the aftermath of the destruction of *Jerusalem. Representing a theological tradition quite different from that of *Enoch* are 4 Ezra and *2 Baruch.* They attach less importance to the heavenly world and more to the observance of the law. Some scholars have suggested that they were composed in the circles of the *Pharisees, but this is far from certain. These apocalypses are essentially reflections on the problem of theodicy, or the justice of God, who allowed Babylon (Rome) to prosper while Jerusalem was destroyed. They respond to this problem in different ways; *2 Baruch* reassures the reader that the real Jerusalem is still intact in heaven. For both authors, however, the ultimate vindication of divine justice is expected in a future judgment.

5. The Otherworldly Journeys.

5.1. A Widespread Phenomenon. The ascent of visionaries to heaven and descent to the netherworld is attested in many cultures and is often associated with shamanism (Culianu). Homer reports the descent of Odysseus to Hades. There is an Assyrian report of a dream of a prince named Kumarbi in which he descends to the netherworld (Kvanvig). There is an elaborate Persian story of an ascent, the *Book of Arda Viraf,* from the early medieval period, but the tradition may be old. There are older Persian accounts of the ascent of the soul after death. In Greco-Roman literature, Plato's Myth of Er, in book 10 of the *Republic,* describes the experience of a man who died on the battlefield and later revived. This story was enormously influential. Other noteworthy examples of otherworldly journeys include the descent of Aeneas to the netherworld in *Aeneid* book 6 and *Cicero's *Dream of Scipio.* (For an inventory of Greco-Roman texts see Attridge.)

5.2. Jewish Ascent Literature. In the Jewish context, the prototypical ascent was that of Enoch. According to the Bible, Enoch walked with *elohim* (Gen 5:22, 24), which may mean either angels or God. In the apocalypses, this was interpreted to mean that he was returned to earth to reveal what he had seen before being taken up permanently. The Book of the Watchers (*1 Enoch* 1—36) describes his ascent to the divine throne, followed by a tour in which he is shown the garden of Eden and the abodes of the dead. All the books of Enoch presuppose this ascent, including the Similitudes of Enoch, which is heavily indebted to the book of Daniel for the imagery of the Son of Man.

The most elaborate ascent texts from ancient Judaism are found in *2 Enoch* and *3 Baruch.* Significantly, these books are ascribed to the Egyptian Diaspora. The date of *2 Enoch* is uncertain; *3 Baruch* is clearly a meditation on the destruction of the temple. Neither of these books pays much attention to history or the kind of public eschatology found in the historical apocalypses. Instead they describe the ascent of the visionary through a numbered series of heavens, and *2 Enoch* has seven heavens. Baruch's ascent seems to be aborted after five heavens, and scholars dispute whether this was the original form of the text. This kind of apocalypse is developed in later Judaism in the form of *Hekalot* *mysticism (Gruenwald). The *hekal* was the temple or palace of God; the name implies that the mystic ascends through several heavenly temples. The **Songs of Sabbath Sacrifice* (4Q400-407) from Qumran, which do not describe an ascent but describe the heavenly liturgy, may already presuppose a form of *Hekalot* mysticism. One of the more important later examples is *Seper Hekalot,* also known as *3 Enoch.*

5.3. Christian Ascent Literature. The ascent of the visionary became the most popular form of apocalypse in early Christianity after the first century (A. Y. Collins 1979). Among the most important early apocalypses of this type are the

Apocalypse of Peter and *Apocalypse of Paul.* There are also some examples of the genre in the Coptic Gnostic library from Nag Hammadi (*see* Gnosticism). Perhaps the greatest literary influence of this genre was achieved in the Middle Ages: Dante's *Inferno.*

6. Conclusion.

*Rabbinic Judaism generally turned away from apocalypticism, but the tradition never died out, and it reappears periodically down to modern times (Collins, McGinn and Stein). Many of the church fathers also viewed it with distrust, but again the tradition persisted. It erupted forcefully in the Middle Ages, notably in the preaching of Joachim of Fiore, and there have been numerous apocalyptic and millennarian movements in modern times, many of them in North America (see especially Boyer on the Millerites). Apocalypticism has also been an important component in Islam.

Apocalyptic visions are products infused by the imagination rather than rational discourse. They derive some of their force from the use of traditional images, many of which can be traced back for millennia. They explicitly rely on revelation and admit of verification only when they predict specific events at specific times. When they do, they are almost invariably proven wrong. The attempt of the Millerites in the nineteenth century to predict the end of the world is probably the most famous example of a case when prophecy failed, but there have been numerous such cases throughout history. Yet the appeal of apocalypticism to many people is not diminished. Ultimately this appeal does not depend on any specific prediction but on the conviction that this world is not the end and on the hope for a higher form of life beyond death. These convictions lie at the core of Christianity and also of some forms of Judaism and Islam.

See also APOCALYPSE OF ABRAHAM; APOCALYPSE OF ZEPHANIAH; APOCALYPTICISM; BARUCH, BOOKS OF; ENOCH, BOOKS OF; ESCHATOLOGIES OF LATE ANTIQUITY; ESDRAS, BOOKS OF; HEAVENLY ASCENT IN JEWISH AND PAGAN TRADITIONS.

BIBLIOGRAPHY. H. W. Attridge, "Greek and Latin Apocalypses," *Semeia* 14 (1979) 159-86; P. Boyer, *When Time Shall Be No More: Prophecy Belief in Modern American Culture* (Cambridge, MA: Harvard University Press, 1992); N. Cohn, *Cosmos, Chaos and the World to Come: The Ancient Roots of Apocalyptic Faith* (New Haven, CT: Yale University Press, 1993); A. Y. Collins, *Cosmology and Eschatology in Jewish and Christian Apocalypticism* (Leiden: E. J. Brill, 1996); idem, "The Early Christian Apocalypses," *Semeia* 14 (1979) 61-121; J. J. Collins, *The Apocalyptic Imagination* (2d ed.; Grand Rapids, MI: Eerdmans, 1998); idem, *Apocalypticism in the Dead Sea Scrolls* (London: Routledge, 1997); J. J. Collins, ed., *Apocalypse: The Morphology of a Genre* (*Semeia* 14; Missoula, MT: Scholars Press, 1979); J. J. Collins, B. McGinn and S. Stein, eds., *The Encyclopedia of Apocalypticism* (3 vols.; New York: Continuum, 1998); I. Culianu, *Psychanodia I: A Survey of the Evidence Concerning the Ascension of the Soul and Its Relevance* (Leiden: E. J. Brill, 1983); I. Gruenwald, *Apocalyptic and Merkavah Mysticism* (Leiden: E. J. Brill, 1980); P. D. Hanson, *The Dawn of Apocalyptic* (Philadelphia: Fortress, 1975); D. Hellholm, ed., *Apocalypticism in the Mediterranean World and the Near East* (Tübingen: Mohr Siebeck, 1983); M. Himmelfarb, *Ascent to Heaven in Jewish and Christian Apocalypses* (New York: Oxford University Press, 1993); A. Hultgård, "Persian Apocalypticism," in *The Encyclopedia of Apocalypticism,* ed. J. J. Collins, B. McGinn and S. Stein (3 vols.; New York: Continuum, 1998) 1:39-83; H. S. Kvanvig, *Roots of Apocalyptic: The Mesopotamian Background of the Enoch Figure and of the Son of Man* (Neukirchen-Vluyn: Neukirchener Verlag, 1988); C. Rowland, *The Open Heaven: A Study of Apocalyptic in Judaism and Early Christianity* (New York: Crossroad, 1982); M. Smith, "On the History of *Apokalypto* and *Apokalypsis,*" in *Apocalypticism in the Mediterranean World and the Near East,* ed. D. Hellholm (Tübingen: Mohr Siebeck, 1983) 9-20.

J. J. Collins

APOCALYPTICISM

The term *apocalypticism* is a transliterated form of the Greek term *apokalypsis,* which means "disclosure," "revelation." The author of the NT Apocalypse, or Revelation of John, was the first Jewish or Christian author to use the term *apokalypsis* in describing the content of his book, which is essentially a narrative of a series of revelatory visions that disclose the events surrounding the imminent end of the present age: "[This is] the revelation [*apokalypsis*] of John, which God gave to him, to show to his servants what must soon take place" (Rev 1:1). Following Revelation 1:1, the term *apocalypse* has been used since the early nineteenth century, when it was popularized by the German NT scholar F. Luecke (1791-1854), as a generic term to describe documents with a content and structure similar to the Revelation of John.

1. Defining Apocalypticism
2. The Origins of Apocalypticism
3. Characteristics of Apocalypticism
4. Jesus and Apocalypticism
5. Paul and Apocalypticism
6. Later New Testament Writings and Apocalypticism

1. Defining Apocalypticism.

The term *apocalypticism* is a modern designation widely used to refer to a worldview which characterized segments of early Judaism from c. 200 B.C. to A.D. 200, and which centered on the expectation of God's imminent intervention into human history in a decisive manner to save his people and punish their enemies by destroying the existing fallen cosmic order and by restoring or recreating the cosmos in its original pristine perfection. Knowledge of cosmic secrets (one of the contributions of the wisdom tradition to apocalypticism) and the imminent eschatological plans of God were revealed to apocalyptists through dreams and visions, and the apocalypses they wrote were primarily narratives of the visions they had received and which were explained to them by an interpreting angel. All extant Jewish apocalypses are believed to be *pseudonymous, that is, written under the names of prominent ancient Israelite or Jewish figures such as Adam, Enoch, Moses, Daniel, Ezra and Baruch. Only the earliest Christian apocalypses, the Revelation of John and the *Shepherd of Hermas*, were written under the names of the actual authors. The most likely reason for the phenomenon of apocalyptic pseudonymity is that it was a strategy to provide credentials and thereby assure the acceptance of these revelatory writings at a point in Israelite history when the reputation of prophets had sunk to an extremely low point. *Apocalypticism* is therefore a term used to describe the particular type of eschatological expectation characteristic of early Jewish and early Christian apocalypses. The Jewish religious compositions which are generally regarded as apocalypses include Daniel 7—12 (the only OT apocalypse), the five documents which comprise *1 Enoch* (1—36, the Book of Watchers; 37—71, the Similitudes of Enoch; 72—82, the Book of Heavenly Luminaries; 83—90, the Animal Apocalypse; 92—104, the Epistle of Enoch), *2 Enoch*, 4 Ezra, *2 Baruch*, *3 Baruch* and the *Apocalypse of Abraham*. Early Christian apocalypses include the Revelation of John (the only NT apocalypse) and the *Shepherd of Hermas* (*see* Apocalyptic Literature).

There are four aspects of apocalypticism that need to be distinguished:

(1) *Apocalyptic eschatology*, a type of eschatology that is found in apocalypses or is similar to the eschatology of apocalypses, characterized by the tendency to view reality from the perspective of divine sovereignty (e.g., the eschatologies of the *Qumran community, Jesus and Paul)

(2) *Apocalypticism* or *millennialism*, a form of collective behavior based on those beliefs (e.g., the movement led by John the Baptist, and the revolts of Theudas reported in Acts 5:36 and Josephus *Ant.* 20.5.1 §§97-98, and the unnamed Egyptian reported in Acts 21:38; Josephus *Ant.* 20.8.6 §§169-72; *J.W.* 2.13.5 §§261-63; *see* Revolutionary Movements)

(3) *Apocalypse*, a type of literature in which those beliefs occur in their most basic and complete form, and which centers on the revelation of cosmic lore and the end of the age

(4) *Apocalyptic imagery*, the various constituent themes and motifs of apocalyptic eschatology used in various ways in early Jewish and early Christian literature

The focus in this article will be on Jewish apocalyptic eschatology and the ways in which Jesus and NT authors adapted some of the basic themes and structures of apocalyptic eschatology into their own theological thought.

2. The Origins of Apocalypticism.

A number of proposals have been made regarding the origins of apocalypticism, and these proposals have often reflected the positive or negative attitude which scholars have had toward the phenomenon of apocalypticism. Following the lead of F. Luecke in the mid-nineteenth century, many scholars have viewed apocalypticism favorably as a development of OT prophecy, perhaps as a result of the disillusionment of the postexilic period, which included subjection to foreign nations and tension within the Jewish community. Other scholars who discerned a sharp break between OT prophecy and later apocalypticism proposed that many of the basic features of apocalypticism originated in ancient Iran and had penetrated

Jewish thought during the Hellenistic period (c. 400-200 B.C.) or more generally from the syncretistic tendencies during the Hellenistic period when there was a blending of religious ideas from both West and East.

2.1. The Setting of Apocalypticism. The fact that most apocalypses are pseudonymous has made it difficult to reconstruct the social situations within which they were written and to which they responded. There is nevertheless wide agreement that Jewish apocalypses were written or revised during times of social or political crisis, though such crises may run the spectrum from real to perceived. Focusing his attention on the period 400-200 B.C., Ploeger discerned a split in the postexilic Jewish community into two sharp divisions, the theocratic party (the ruling priestly aristocrats), which interpreted prophetic eschatology in terms of the Jewish state, and the eschatological party (forerunners of the apocalyptists), which awaited the fulfillment of the eschatological predictions of the prophets. More recently, P. D. Hanson has argued that apocalypticism is a natural development of Israelite prophecy originating in the intramural struggle between visionary prophets and hierocratic (Zadokite) priests which took place from the sixth through the fourth centuries B.C.

2.2. Eschatology and Apocalypticism. A distinction has generally been made between *eschatology and apocalypticism. *Eschatology* is a term which began to be used in the nineteenth century as a label for that aspect of systematic theology which dealt with topics relating to the future of the individual (death, resurrection, judgment, eternal life, heaven and hell) and topics relating to corporate or national eschatology, that is, the future of the Christian church or the Jewish people (e.g., the coming of the Messiah, the great tribulation, resurrection, judgment, the Second Coming of Christ, the temporary messianic kingdom, the re-creation of the universe). A distinction has often been made between prophetic eschatology and apocalyptic eschatology, which serves the useful function of emphasizing the continuities as well as the changes in Israelite-Jewish eschatological expectation. Following this model, prophetic eschatology was an optimistic perspective which anticipated that God would eventually restore the originally idyllic and pristine conditions by acting through historical processes. The Israelite prophet proclaimed God's plans for Israel to both king and people in terms of actual historical and political events and processes. Prophecy sees the future as arising out of the present, while apocalyptic eschatology regards the future as breaking into the present; the former is essentially optimistic, while the latter is pessimistic.

2.3. Prophecy and Apocalypticism. The problem of the relationship between prophecy and apocalypticism is one aspect of the problem of the degree of continuity or discontinuity thought to exist between Jewish apocalypticism and earlier Israelite religious and political traditions. It is important to recognize that prophecy and apocalypticism exhibit both elements of continuity and discontinuity. The sharp contrasts often thought to exist between prophecy and apocalypticism are somewhat mitigated by the recognition that prophecy itself underwent many changes and that there are numerous striking similarities between late prophecy and early apocalyptic (Hanson). Late prophetic books which exhibit tendencies that were later to emerge more fully developed in Jewish apocalyptic literature include the visions of Zechariah 1—6 (with the presence of an angelic interpreter), Isaiah 24—27, 56—66, Joel and Zechariah 9—14.

2.4. Wisdom and Apocalypticism. Many scholars have argued that there was a fundamental break between prophecy and apocalypticism. G. von Rad, for example, rejected the view that the primary roots of apocalypticism were to be found in Israelite prophecy. Von Rad described apocalypticism as consisting in a clear-cut dualism, radical transcendence, esotericism and gnosticism, and proposed that apocalypticism arose out of the wisdom literature of the OT. Themes common to wisdom and apocalyptic literature, and which suggest the connection between the two types of literature, include the following: (1) both sages and apocalyptists are referred to as "the wise," and preserved their teaching in written form often emphasizing their special "knowledge" and its antiquity; (2) both exhibit individualistic and universalistic tendencies; (3) both are concerned with the mysteries of nature from a celestial perspective; and (4) both reflect a deterministic view of history.

The proposal that Israelite wisdom, not Israelite prophecy, was the mother of Jewish apocalypticism has found little scholarly support in the form in which it was proposed by von Rad.

Yet there are undeniably links between wisdom and apocalyptic (Wis 7:27; Sir 24:33), both of which are *scribal* phenomena. The wisdom tradition in Israel was certainly one of the many influences upon the development of Jewish apocalypticism. Nevertheless it is important to distinguish between two types of wisdom: *proverbial wisdom* and *mantic wisdom*. The latter type is related to the role of the "wise" in interpreting dreams as reflected in the biblical traditions concerning Joseph and Daniel, both of whom were able to explain the meaning of ambiguous revelatory dreams through divine wisdom (Gen 40:8; 41:25, 39; Dan 2:19-23, 30, 45; 5:11-12). The figure of the *angelus interpres* ("interpreting angel") occurs frequently in Jewish apocalypses where he plays the analogous role of a supernatural revealer who is able to reveal the deeper significance of the dreams and visions experienced by the apocalyptist (Dan 7—12; Zech 1—6; 4 Ezra).

2.5. Pharisaism and Apocalypticism. The monumental three-volume work on Judaism by G. F. Moore was based on the assumption that "normative" Judaism of the first few centuries of the Christian era, "the age of the Tannaim," did not include Jewish apocalypticism. Similarly, A. Schweitzer sharply distinguished the teaching of the apocalyptists (and therefore Jesus) from the teaching of the rabbis. However, the pharisaic emphases on the resurrection, the age to come and the *Messiah make it difficult to distinguish sharply the religious and political concerns of apocalyptists from the *Pharisees, even though Pharisees appear to have become disenchanted with many aspects of apocalypticism in the aftermath of the disastrous first revolt against Rome (A.D. 66-73). W. D. Davies has argued that there are several links between apocalypticism and Pharisaism: (1) both share a similar piety and attitude toward the Torah; (2) both share similar views on such eschatological topics as the travail of the messianic era, the gathering of exiles, the days of the Messiah, the New Jerusalem, the judgment and Gehenna; (3) both have populist and scholastic tendencies.

3. Characteristics of Apocalypticism.

3.1. Major Aspects of Apocalypticism. There are a number of features of apocalyptic eschatology upon which there is some scholarly agreement:

(1) the temporal dualism of the two ages

(2) the radical discontinuity between this age and the next coupled with pessimism regarding the existing order and otherworldly hope directed toward the future order

(3) the division of history into segments (four, seven, twelve) reflecting a predetermined plan of history

(4) the expectation of the imminent arrival of the reign of God as an act of God and spelling the doom of existing earthly conditions

(5) a cosmic perspective in which the primary location of an individual is no longer within a collective entity such as Israel or the people of God, and the impending crisis is not local but cosmic in scope

(6) the cataclysmic intervention of God will result in salvation for the righteous, conceived as the regaining of Edenic conditions

(7) the introduction of angels and demons to explain historical and eschatological events

(8) the introduction of a new mediator with royal functions

These characteristics are not exhaustive, but they serve the useful purpose of focusing on some of the distinctive features of the apocalyptic worldview.

3.2. The Apocalyptic Scenarios. Since narratives that describe the events attending the close of the present era and the inauguration of the future era are essentially a type of folklore, there are many divergent descriptions of expected future events with little consistency between them. In producing a synthesis of the great variety of apocalyptic scenarios found in apocalyptic literature, therefore, the emphasis must be on the more typical features found in such descriptions. Apocalypticism or apocalyptic eschatology centers on the belief that the present world order, which is both evil and oppressive, is under the temporary control of Satan and his human accomplices. This present evil world order will shortly be destroyed by God and replaced with a new and perfect order corresponding to Eden. During the present evil age, the people of God are an oppressed minority who fervently await the intervention of God or his specially chosen agent, the Messiah. The transition between the old and the new ages, the end of the old age and the beginning of the new, will be introduced by a final series of battles fought by the people of God against the human allies of Satan. The outcome is never in question, however, for the enemies of God are predestined to be defeated and destroyed. The inauguration of the new age will begin with the arrival of God or his accredited agent to judge the wicked and reward the righteous and will be concluded by the re-creation or transformation of the universe.

3.3. Limited Dualism. One of the basic features of apocalypticism is the conviction that the cosmos is divided under two opposing supernatural forces, God and Satan, who represent the moral qualities of good and evil (cosmological dualism). However, the Jewish conviction that God is absolutely sovereign implies that he is the originator of evil and that the resultant dualism of good and evil is neither eternal nor absolute (like the dualism of ancient Iranian religion), but limited. This essentially limited cosmological dualism was understood in various different but related types of dualistic thought in early Jewish apocalypticism: (1) *Temporal or eschatological dualism* makes a sharp distinction between the present age and the age to come. (2) *Ethical dualism* is based on a moral distinction between good and evil and sees humanity divided into two groups, the righteous and the wicked, in a way that corresponds to good and evil supernatural powers. (3) *Psychological or microcosmic dualism* is the internalization of the two-age schema that sees the forces of good and evil struggling for supremacy within each individual.

3.3.1. Temporal or Eschatological Dualism. The belief in two successive ages, or worlds, developed only gradually in Judaism. The earliest occurrence of the rabbinic phrase "the world to come" is found in *1 Enoch* 71:15 (c. 200 B.C.). The doctrine of two ages is fully developed by c. A.D. 90, for according to 4 Ezra 7:50, "The Most High has not made one Age but two" (see 4 Ezra 8:1). The day of judgment is considered the dividing point between the two ages (4 Ezra 7:113): the "day of judgment will be the end of this age and beginning of the immortal age to come."

3.3.2. Ethical Dualism. Daniel 12:10 distinguishes between the "wicked" and the "wise"; **Jubilees* distinguishes between Israelites who are "the righteous nation" (*Jub.* 24:29), "a righteous generation" (*Jub.* 25:3) and the Gentiles who are sinners (*Jub.* 23:24; 24:28); the Qumran **War Scroll* similarly distinguishes between the people of God and the Kittim (1QM 1:6; 18:2-3); and the *Testament of Asher* contrasts "good and single-faced people" (*T. Asher* 4:1) with "people of two faces" (*T. Asher* 3:1).

3.3.3. Psychological or Microcosmic Dualism. In this type of dualism the antithetical supernatural cosmic powers, conceived of in the moral categories of good and evil, have an analogous correspondence to the struggle between good and evil experienced by individuals. In some strands of Jewish apocalyptic thought, notably the Qumran community and the circles which produced the **Testaments of the Twelve Patriarchs,* it was believed that God created two spirits, the spirit of truth and the spirit of error (i.e., the evil spirit called *Belial, 1QS 1:18-24; *T. Jud.* 20:1-5; see Jn 14:17; 15:26; 16:13; 1 Jn 4:6), and humans may live in accordance with one or the other; the Prince of Lights controls the lives of the children of righteousness, while the Angel of Darkness has dominion over the children of falsehood (1QS 3:17—4:1; 4:2-11; 1QM 13:9-12). However, even the sins of the children of righteousness are ultimately caused by the spirit of error, for both spirits strive for supremacy within the heart of the individual (1QS 4:23-26; *T. Asher* 1:3-5). The dominion of the spirit of error is temporally limited, however, for God will ultimately destroy it (1QS 4:18-19). The doctrine that the spirit of truth and the spirit of error strive for supremacy in the heart of each person is similar to the rabbinic doctrine of the good and evil impulses.

3.4. Messianic Expectation. *Messianism was not an invariable feature of all the various eschatological schemes that made up Jewish apocalypticism. During the Second Temple period there were at least two main types of Jewish messianism, restorative and utopian messianism. Restorative messianism anticipated the restoration of the Davidic monarchy and centered on an expectation of the improvement and perfection of the present world through natural development (*Pss. Sol.* 17) and modeled on an idealized historical period; the memory of the past is projected into the future. Utopian messianism anticipated a future era which would surpass everything previously known. Jewish messianism tended to focus, not on the restoration of a dynasty, but on a single messianic king sent by God to restore the fortunes of Israel. However, as a theocratic symbol, the Messiah is dispensable, since a Messiah is not invariably part of all Jewish eschatological expectation. No such figure, for example, plays a role in the eschatological scenarios of Joel, Isaiah 24—27, Daniel, Sirach, *Jubilees*, the *Testament of Moses*, Tobit, 1 and 2 Maccabees, Wisdom, *1 Enoch* 1—36 (the Book of Watchers), 90—104 (the Epistle of Enoch), *2 Enoch*.

3.5. The Temporary Messianic Kingdom. There is little consistency in Jewish apocalyptic regarding the arrival of the kingdom of God. It was conceptualized by some as the arrival of an eternal kingdom, but by others as a temporary messianic kingdom which would be succeeded by an eternal kingdom (see 1 Cor 15:24). The conception of a temporary messianic kingdom which would function as a transition between the present evil age and the age to come, between monarchy and theocracy, solved the problem of how the transition from the Messiah to the eternal reign of God (where such a conception is present) might be conceived. In Jewish apocalyptic thought generally, the kingdom of God is more centrally important than the figure of a Messiah. A messianic interregnum, therefore, functions as an anticipation of the perfect and eternal theocratic state which will exist when primordial conditions are reinstated forever. This interim kingdom was expected to be transitional since it is depicted as combining some of the characteristics of this age with those of the age to come. In Christian apocalypticism this anticipation of a temporary messianic kingdom is clearly reflected in Revelation 20:4-6, and according to some scholars is also reflected in 1 Corinthians 15:20-28. The expectation of a future temporary messianic kingdom is found in only three early Jewish apocalypses, the Apocalypse of Weeks, or *1 Enoch* 91:12-17, 93:1-10; (written between 175 and 167 B.C.), 4 Ezra 7:26-44; 12:31-34 (written c. A.D. 90), and *2 Baruch* 29:3—30:1; 40:1-4; 72:2—74:3 (written c. A.D. 110). Though some have claimed that the conception of a temporary messianic kingdom is found in *2 Enoch* 32:2—33:1 and *Jubilees* 1:27-29; 23:26-31, the evidence is not compelling.

3.5.1. Apocalypse of Weeks. In *1 Enoch* 91:12-17 and 93:1-10, an earlier apocalypse inserted into the Epistle of Enoch (*1 Enoch* 91—104), history is divided into ten weeks (i.e., ten ages), with a non-messianic temporary kingdom appearing in the eighth week and an eternal kingdom arriving in the tenth week (*1 Enoch* 91:12-17).

3.5.2. Fourth Ezra. According to 4 Ezra 7:26-30, the Messiah will appear in the last days and live with the righteous for four hundred years. The Messiah, together with all other people on earth, will then die and the world will return to seven days of primeval silence. After this the resurrection will occur (4 Ezra 7:32), and the Most High will take his place on the seat of judgment and will execute judgment on all nations (4 Ezra 7:36-43). In 4 Ezra 12:31-34, on the other hand, the Davidic Messiah will sit on the seat of judgment and, after reproving the ungodly and the wicked, will destroy them (4 Ezra 12:32). This judgment exercised by the Messiah is preliminary to the final judgment which will be exercised by God after the arrival of the end (4 Ezra 12:34). Nowhere in 4 Ezra, however, does the Messiah play a role in the eternal theocratic kingdom which is inaugurated with the resurrection.

3.5.3. Second Baruch. After twelve periods of tribulation (*2 Bar.* 27:1-5), the messianic kingdom is depicted as a period of phenomenal abundance inaugurated by the appearance of the Messiah (*2 Bar.* 29:3) and concluded by his return to glory (*2 Bar.* 30:1). The elect who lived during the messianic kingdom will then be joined by the resurrected righteous, but the souls of the wicked will fear judgment (*2 Bar.* 30:1-5). The author assumes rather than clearly states the fact that those who lived during the messianic kingdom will experience a transformation into a resurrection mode of existence like the resurrected righteous. In *2 Bar.* 39—40 the predicted fall of the fourth kingdom (Rome) will be followed by the revelation of the Messiah (*2 Bar.* 39:7), who will destroy the armies of the final wicked ruler, who will be brought bound to Zion, where he will be judged and executed by the Messiah (*2 Bar.* 40:1-2). The kingdom of the Messiah will last "forever," that is, until the world of corruption has ended, which means that this kingdom is temporary but of unspecified duration. Finally, in *2 Baruch* 72:2—74:3, the warrior Messiah will summon all nations together, sparing some and executing others (*2 Bar.* 72:2-6). Following this period of judgment will be an era in which Edenic conditions will be restored to the earth (*2 Bar.* 73:1-7). As in 4 Ezra, the Messiah plays no role in the eternal kingdom which is inaugurated after he is taken up into heaven.

3.6. The Eschatological Antagonist. In Jewish apocalyptic literature there are two traditions of a wicked eschatological figure who functions as an agent of Satan, or Beliar, in leading astray, opposing and persecuting the people of God; both traditions represent historicizations of the ancient combat myth (*see* Belial). One tradition focuses on a godless tyrannical ruler who will arise in the last generation to become the primary adversary of God or the Messiah. This satanic agent was expected to lead the forces of evil in the final battle between the forces of evil and the people of God (1QM 18:1; 1QS 4:18-18; *T. Dan* 5:10-11; *T. Mos.* 8).

The historicization of the combat myth is already found in the OT where the chaos monsters Rahab and Leviathan are sometimes used to symbolize foreign oppressors like Egypt (Ps 74:14; 87:4; Is 30:7; Ezek 29:3; 32:2-4). Several OT traditions provided the basis for the later apocalyptic conception of the eschatological antagonist, including the figure of Gog, the ruler of Magog in the Gog and Magog oracle in Ezekiel 38—39 (see Rev 20:8; *3 Enoch* 45:5), the references to a vague "enemy from the north" found in several OT prophecies (Ezek 38:6, 15; 39:2; Jer 1:13-15; 3:18; 4:6; 6:1, 22), and the depicting of Antiochus IV Epiphanes, the "little horn" in Daniel 7—8 as the oppressor of the people of God. The career of the Greco-Syrian king Antiochus IV Epiphanes (175-164 B.C.), whose actions against the Jewish people are described in 1 Maccabees 1:20-61 and 2 Maccabees 5:11—6:11, is presented as a mythologized apocalyptic figure in Daniel 11:36-39, claiming to be God or to be equal with God (Dan 11:36-37; *Sib. Or.* 5:33-34; *Asc. Isa.* 4:6; *2 Enoch* [Rec. J] 29:4).

Later the characteristics of the eschatological adversary were augmented and embellished by traditions about the *Roman emperors Caligula and Nero, both of whom had divine pretensions which their Roman contemporaries considered tacky and which outraged the Jews. The other tradition concerns the false prophet who performs signs and wonders to legitimate his false teaching (cf. Deut 13:2-6). Occasionally Satan and the eschatological antagonist are identified as the same person, as in *Sibylline Oracles* 3:63-74 and *Ascension of Isaiah* 7:1-7, where Nero (= the eschatological antagonist) is regarded as Beliar (= Satan) incarnate.

*3.7. **The Re-creation or Transformation of the Cosmos.*** In Isaiah 65:17 and 66:22 the creation of a new heavens and a new earth is predicted. The theme of the re-creation or renewal of creation was taken up into apocalyptic literature as the final eschatological act. Essentially the expectation of a new creation or a renewed creation is a particular application of the two-age schema in which the first creation is identified with the present evil age (or world) and the new or renewed creation is identified with the age (or world) to come. While there are many references to the new creation in Jewish apocalyptic literature, it is not always clear whether the present order of creation is reduced to chaos before the act of re-creation (*1 Enoch* 72:1; 91:16; *Sib. Or.* 5:212; *Jub.* 1:29; 4:26; *Bib. Ant.* 3:10; *Apoc. Elijah* 5:38; 2 Pet 3:13; Rev 21:1, 5; see 2 Cor 5:17; Gal 6:15), or whether the renewal or transformation of the existing world is in view (*1 Enoch* 45:4-5; *2 Bar.* 32:6; 44:12; 49:3; 57:2; *Bib. Ant.* 32:17; 4 Ezra 7:30-31, 75; see Rom 8:21). In many of these passages the pattern for the new or transformed creation is based on the Edenic conditions thought to have existed on the earth before the fall of Adam and Eve. [D. E. Aune]

4. Jesus and Apocalypticism.
During the nineteenth century biblical scholars attempted to defend Jesus against the charge that he was an apocalyptic dreamer who wrongly predicted an early and cataclysmic end to the existing world order. Some defended Jesus by claiming that Jesus did not intend to predict literal future events for the world, but was speaking spiritually. The apocalyptic predictions, it was argued, all had been spiritually fulfilled.

Others defended Jesus by charging the early church and the Gospel writers with error. One view is that chapters like Mark 13 did not derive from anything Jesus really said. Rather an early Jewish apocalypse was taken up by the Gospel writers and erroneously credited to Jesus. This "little apocalypse" theory, first advanced by T. Colani, has been defended by an array of scholars ever since.

Many nineteenth-century scholars portrayed Jesus as a gentle teacher who taught the nearness of God. Unfortunately, they lamented, Jesus has been misrepresented in the Gospels as a fanatical preacher of coming judgment.

At the turn of the century J. Weiss and A. Schweitzer overturned that consensus by reconstructing a historical Jesus who was thoroughly apocalyptic in outlook, indeed more so than those who had preserved the traditions about him. Under this new reckoning, Jesus believed that the expected divine intervention which would inaugurate the new age would occur at some time during his ministry. His expectations were disappointed more than once, and he finally went to his death imagining that by so doing he would surely spur God to act. The early church was left with the challenge of giving Jesus a more respectable image, covering up his errors and presenting his teaching in a way which served the needs of a community that knew the end (and the kingdom of God) had not come as predicted, but that still believed it would come soon.

This view in its various forms, generally known as "consistent eschatology," has been influential during the twentieth century. Some, like R. Bultmann, have been unconcerned with defending Jesus' apocalyptic perspective or even attempting to reconstruct a portrait of the historical Jesus. Bultmann's famous program of demythologizing the NT did not attempt to strip Jesus of his mythological trappings (as did many nineteenth-century interpreters) but to reinterpret those mythical elements in terms of their existential meaning. Understood from this perspective, the mythology inherent in Jesus' apocalyptic teaching was a means of addressing men and women with the need to be open to God's future—a future near at hand for each individual. Others scholars, such as R. H. Hiers, do not find it troubling to think of Jesus as someone who had mistaken expectations and made inaccurate predictions.

Not all twentieth-century interpreters have been persuaded that Jesus was an apocalyptic preacher who predicted an imminent end to the world. C. H. Dodd and others have insisted on a realized eschatology, maintaining that Jesus fulfilled OT prophetic hopes and preached a kingdom that was inaugurated in his own ministry. Those passages which suggested a future fulfillment were either intended to be interpreted in this light or were the creation of the early church.

Both consistent and realized eschatology seem problematic. Many conservative scholars such as G. E. Ladd, E. E. Ellis and I. H. Marshall have adopted a compromise position first defended by W. G. Kümmel. The kingdom is paradoxically "present" and "still to come." Jesus' mission was to inaugurate the kingdom, but he taught that it would be consummated at a future coming.

The Gospel writers faithfully preserve this paradoxical position. They use apocalyptic imagery to report and interpret events in Jesus' earthly life (e.g., Mt 27:51-53; 28:2-4), and they also use apocalyptic imagery to refer to events predicted for the future (God's final act of judgment and salvation at the coming of the Son of Man; cf. Mt 25:31-46; Mk 13:24-27).

This already/not yet approach may be open to the charge that it is very convenient (unfalsifiable and therefore indefensible, some would say), but unless some such paradoxical interpretation is adopted, neither Jesus' view nor any of the Gospel writers' views can be understood adequately. [T. J. Geddert]

5. Paul and Apocalypticism.

5.1. Sources and Problems. Critical scholarship regards the seven generally acknowledged Pauline letters as providing a firm basis for analyzing Pauline theology. These letters include Romans, 1 and 2 Corinthians, Galatians, Philippians, 1 Thessalonians and Philemon. Letters whose authenticity remains in some doubt (2 Thessalonians; Colossians) or whose Pauline authorship is generally rejected (Ephesians; 1 and 2 Timothy; Titus) are used only to supplement data found in the basic corpus of seven letters. The book of Acts is another important source for our knowledge of Paul's life, but this work too must be used only as a supplement to the core of genuine letters.

One of the major problems in the study of Paul's life and thought is that of determining the extent to which it is appropriate to label Pauline thought as "apocalyptic." There is widespread agreement that Paul was influenced by apocalyptic eschatology, but the extent to which he modified apocalypticism in light of his faith in Christ remains a central problem. Baumgarten holds that Paul demythologizes apocalyptic traditions by consistently applying them to the present life of the community.

Another problem centers on the issue of the origin of Paul's apocalyptic thought. Baumgarten (43-53) has suggested that apocalyptic traditions came to Paul through the Hellenists at *Antioch.

5.2. The Center or Structure of Pauline Thought. The complexity of Paul's theological thought is exacerbated by the fact that the primary evidence for his views is found in occasional letters written in a variety of specific contexts for the purpose of addressing particular problems and issues; they are historically contingent pastoral communications. Further, the basic seven-letter corpus can hardly be regarded as a representative sample of Pauline thought. Despite the difficulties, many attempts have been made to understand the coherence of Paul's thought and on that basis to identify the core or center of his thought. Some scholars have doubted whether Paul himself thought in terms of such a "core" or whether the evidence from seven occasional letters is adequate for such a task. Some of the more important suggestions for identifying the central message of Paul's thought include: (1) the gospel, (2) christology, (3) the death and resurrection of Jesus, (4) the theme "in Christ" (participatory categories), (5) ecclesiology, (6) justification by faith (the traditional Lutheran view) and (7) anthropology (F. C. Baur; R. Bultmann). It is evident, however, that many of these topics are closely related to others, so that the choice of a core for Pauline thought becomes a matter of nuance. It is clear, for example, that Paul's polemical doctrine of justification by faith is an aspect of his christology and that the topics of anthropology and ecclesiology are two ways of looking at individual Christians who at the same time hold membership in the people of God.

Other scholars have proposed that it is more important to identify the structure of Paul's thought. Two of the most important proposals include: (1) salvation history, that is, God, who is the central actor in history, has had an ultimate salvific goal for humanity from the beginning, which originally centered on Israel and ultimately on all who believe in Christ, a structure particularly evident in Romans 9—11; and (2) apocalyptic eschatology. However, salvation history and apocalyptic eschatology must not be considered antithetical, since the latter is simply a more specific and particular version of the former. Further, it is a matter of continuing debate whether these suggestions constitute the horizon or kernel of Paul's thought.

5.3. Paul as a Visionary and Mystic. The authors of apocalypses, though they usually concealed their true identities behind pseudonyms, received divine revelations through visions and for that reason they structured the apocalypses they wrote as narratives of the visions they had actually received or pretended to receive. There was a close relationship between Jewish *merkabah* *mysticism (based on Ezek 1; *see* Heavenly Ascent) and apocalypticism (Gruenwald), though out-of-body visions were more common in the former and bodily ascensions to heaven more common in the latter. While there is no evidence that Paul himself wrote an apocalypse, he claims to have been the recipient of revelatory visions or ecstatic experiences (Gal 1:11-17; 1 Cor 9:1; 15:8; see Acts 9:1-9; 16:9; 18:9-10; 22:6-11, 17-21; 26:12-18; 27:23-24). In Galatians 1:12 he speaks of his Damascus Road experience as an *apokalypsis* ("revelation") from Jesus Christ, and in 2 Corinthians 12:1 he speaks of "visions and revelations [*apokalypseis*] of the Lord," which are presumably descriptions of his own experience. It is likely that Paul is the man of whom he speaks, who experienced a journey to the third heaven, where he heard unspeakable things (2 Cor 12:1-10).

5.4. Apocalyptic Scenarios. There are four relatively extensive apocalyptic scenarios in the Pauline letters, three of which center on the Parousia of Jesus (1 Thess 4:13-18; 2 Thess 1:5-12; 1 Cor 15:51-57), and the so-called "Pauline apocalypse," which centers on the coming of the eschatological antagonist (2 Thess 2:1-12). There are also a number of shorter scenarios which appear to be formulaic in character and therefore of pre-Pauline or extra-Pauline origin (1 Thess 1:9-10; 3:13; 5:23).

5.5. Limited Dualism. The Pauline view of the sovereignty of God (Rom 9—11) makes it apparent that he shares the basic dualistic convictions of Jewish apocalypticism during the late Second Temple period.

5.5.1. Temporal or Eschatological Dualism. In continuity with the temporal dualistic thought of Jewish apocalypticism, Paul also contrasted the present evil age with the coming age of salvation (Gal 1:4; Rom 8:18; 1 Cor 1:26; see Eph 5:16) and believed that he was living at the end of the ages (1 Cor 10:11). Yet Paul considerably modified the sharp distinction usually made in apocalyptic thought between these two ages. Paul understood the death and resurrection of Jesus in the past as cosmic eschatological events that separated "this age" (Rom 12:2; 1 Cor 1:20; 2:6), or "this present evil age" (Gal 1:4), from "the age to come." This present age is dominated by rulers, demonic powers who are doomed to pass away (1 Cor 2:6-7).

Paul's belief in the resurrection of Jesus the Messiah convinced him that eschatological events had begun to take place within history and that the resurrection of Jesus was part of the traditional Jewish expectation of the resurrection of the righteous (1 Cor 15:20-23). For Paul the present is a temporary period between the death and resurrection of Christ and his return in glory in which those who believe in the gospel share in the salvific benefits of the age to come (Gal 1:4; 2 Cor 5:17). This temporary period is characterized by the eschatological gift of the Spirit of God, who is experienced as present within the Christian community in general as well as within particular believers who are members of the Christian community (Rom 8:9-11; 1 Cor 6:19; 12:4-11; 1 Thess 4:8). While Paul did not explicitly use the phrase "the age to come" in 2 Corinthians 5:17 and Galatians 6:15, he uses the phrase "new creation," a phrase with apocalyptic associations (Is 65:17; 66:22; Rev 21:1). Though the final consummation still lay in the future, for Christians the new age was present because the Messiah had come.

The basic salvation-history framework of Paul's thought incorporates within it the apocalyptic notion of the two successive ages. This is evident in Romans 5:12-21, where Paul schematizes history in terms of the two realms of Adam and Christ, which are both made part of present experience. Paul therefore made an "already"/ "not yet" distinction indicated by his use of the indicative and imperative in passages such as Galatians 5:25: "If we live [indicative] in the Spirit, let us also walk [imperative] in the Spirit." While the flesh has been crucified with Christ (Gal 2:20; 3:24; 6:14; Rom 6:2, 6-7, 22; 8:13), the desires of the flesh still pose temptations for Christians (Gal 5:16-18; Rom 6:12-14; 8:5-8). The daily obedience of the Christian provides the continual and necessary authentication of the original act of believing in Christ until the future redemption of creation and the freedom of the children of God becomes a reality (Rom 8:19-20).

5.5.2. Spatial Dualism. Ancient Israelite cosmology conceived of a cosmos in three levels: heaven, earth and Sheol. This same conception of the universe was transmitted to early Judaism, though the emphasis on the transcendence of God which characterized late Second Temple Judaism presupposed a sharper distinction between the heavenly world and the earthly world. This spatial dualism (heaven as the dwelling place of God and his angels; earth as the dwelling place of humanity) coincided with temporal or eschatological dualism in the sense that the kingdom of God, or the age to come, was a heavenly reality which would eventually displace the earthly reality of the present evil age. For Paul, "the things that are seen are transient, but the things that are not seen are eternal" (2 Cor 4:18; see Phil 3:20; 2 Cor 5:1-5). There are therefore three cosmic realms: heaven, earth and the region below the earth (Phil 2:10), though the normal focus is on the two primary cosmic realms: heaven and earth (1 Cor 8:5; 15:47-50; see Col 1:16, 20; Eph 1:10; 3:15). Heaven is where God and his angels dwell (Rom 1:18; 10:6; Gal 1:8; see Eph 6:9) and is the place where Christ is now seated at the right hand of God, a tradition based on the pre-Pauline Christian interpretation of Psalm 110:1 (Rom 8:34; Col 3:1). Heaven is the place from which Jesus will return in the near future as both savior and judge (1 Thess 1:10; 4:16; Phil 3:20; see 2 Thess 1:7).

5.5.3. Ethical Dualism. For Paul the two antithetical cosmic powers were God and Satan, who respectively represent the moral qualities of good and evil. God is the ultimate source of love (Rom 5:5; 8:39; 2 Cor 13:14). It is God who has expressed love toward humanity by sending his Son to die an atoning death for them (Rom 5:8). The influence of the Spirit of God, that is, God's active presence in the world, is reflected in such ethical virtues as love, patience, kindness and self-control (Gal 5:22-23). There is an essential similarity between the lists in 1QS 4:2-6, 9-11, in which the virtues encouraged by the spirit of truth are contrasted with the vices promoted by the spirit of error, and the lists in Galatians 5:16-24, where vices are the products of the flesh, while virtues are the products of the Spirit. Satan is frequently mentioned as the supernatural opponent of God and Christians and as the source of evil in the world (Rom 16:20; 1 Cor 7:5; 2 Cor 2:11; 11:14; 12:7; 1 Thess 2:18).

5.5.4. Psychological or Microcosmic Dualism. Assuming that the structure of Paul's theology is in part the product of his adaptation of Jewish apocalypticism as the framework for understanding the significance of the death and resurrection of Jesus the Messiah, that same apocalyptic framework had a profound effect on the way in which he understood the effects of salvation on individual Christians. The basic structure of Jewish apocalypticism consisted of a temporal or eschatological dualism consisting of two ages, the present era (a period of oppression by the wicked), which will be succeeded by a blissful future era. While Jewish apocalypticism had a largely future orientation, Paul's recognition of the fact that Jesus was the Messiah who was a figure of the past as well as the present and future, led him to introduce some significant modifications. The most significant modification is the softening of the distinction between this age and the age to come with his emphasis on the hidden presence of the age to come within the present age.

Paul exhibits a tendency to conceptualize human nature and existence as a microcosmic version of a Christianized form of apocalyptic eschatology. In other words, the apocalyptic structure of history was considered paradigmatic for understanding human nature. In effect the Christian person is situated at the center of history in the sense that in him or her the opposing powers which dominate the cosmos are engaged in a struggle. Just as Paul's Christian form of apocalyptic thought is characterized by a historical or eschatological dualism consisting in the juxtaposition of the old and new ages, so his view of human nature reflected a similarly homologous dualistic structure. This is evident in 2 Corinthians 5:17 (NRSV): "So if anyone is in Christ, there is a new creation: everything old has passed away; see, everything has become new!" Here Paul uses the basic apocalyptic expectation of the renewal of creation (i.e., the inauguration of the age to come) following the destruction of the present evil age as a paradigm for the transformation experienced by the individual Christian who has moved from unbelief to belief. Thus the apocalyptic expectation of an impending cosmic change from the present evil age to the future age of salvation has become paradigmatic for the transformation of the individual believer.

Since this apocalyptic transformation affects only those "in Christ," the external world and its inhabitants remain under the sway of the old age. The new age is thus concealed in the old age. The phrase "new creation" refers to the renewal or re-creation of heaven and earth following the destruction of the old cosmos (Is 65:17; 66:22; *1 Enoch* 91:16; 72:1; *2 Bar.* 32:6; 44:12; 49:3; 57:2; *Bib. Ant.* 3:10; 2 Pet 3:11-13; Rev 21:1). Bultmann's existentialist understanding of Pauline anthropological terms (i.e., the human person as a free agent responsible for his or her own decisions), and E. Käsemann's apocalyptic or cosmological understanding of Paul's anthropology (i.e., the human person is a victim of supernatural cosmic forces) are not mutually exclusive categories. Paul also conceives of the struggle within each Christian as the conflict between the Spirit and the flesh, as in Galatians 5:16: "Walk in the Spirit and you will not fulfill the desires of the flesh."

5.6. Jesus the Messiah. One of the major obstacles impeding Jewish belief in Jesus as the Messiah of Jewish expectation was the fact of the crucifixion (1 Cor 1:18-25; Gal 5:11; see Heb 12:2). One of the unsolved problems in the investigation of early Christianity is the reason why early Christians recognized the messianic status of Jesus despite the fact that he fulfilled none of the central functions which the Jewish people expected of the figure of the Davidic Messiah, including his role as an eschatological high priest, a paradigmatic benevolent and all-powerful king, a judge and destroyer of the wicked, a deliverer of the people of God (*Pss. Sol.* 17; 4 Ezra 12; *2 Bar.* 40).

In the seven undisputed letters of Paul the term *Christos,* meaning "Anointed One," "Christ" or "Messiah," occurs 266 times, usually as a proper name for Jesus (e.g., "Jesus Christ"), often with some residual titular quality (evident in the name "Christ Jesus)," and occasionally as a name for a specific Messiah, Jesus (Rom 9:5), but never as a general term for an eschatological deliverer within Judaism. In the seven core Pauline letters *Christos* is never used as a predicate (e.g., "Jesus is the Christ"), *Christos* is never given a definite article following the name "Jesus" (e.g., "Jesus the Christ"), and *Christos* is never accompanied by a noun in the genitive (e.g., "the Christ of God"). It is safe to conclude that the messianic status of Jesus was not a matter of dispute or concern to Paul. Paul assumes but does not argue that Jesus is the Messiah.

5.7. The Parousia and Judgment. The later OT prophets frequently referred to the day of the Lord as the occasion when God would judge the world (Amos 5:18-20; Zeph 1:14-16; Joel 2:2). In Jewish apocalyptic literature the inauguration of the eschaton occurs with the coming of God or of an accredited agent of God, the Messiah, to bring both salvation and judgment. While Paul can speak of "the day of the Lord" (1 Thess 5:2) and God's role as eschatological judge (Rom 3:6), the center of his eschatological hope has shifted from God to Christ, so that he can speak both of the impending day of the Lord (1 Thess 5:2) but claim that on that day God will judge the secrets of humans by Christ Jesus (Rom 2:16; see 2 Tim 4:1). The Parousia is referred to by Paul both as "the revelation [*apokalypsis*] of our Lord Jesus Christ" (1 Cor 1:6) and (on the analogy of the OT expression "the day of the Lord") as "the day of Jesus Christ" (1 Cor 1:8; Phil 1:6; 3:12-21; Rom 14:7-12, 17-18; 2 Cor 5:10; 1 Thess 4:13-18; 1 Cor 15:20-28, 50-58).

5.8. The Resurrection. For Paul the resurrection of Jesus was not an isolated miraculous event but rather the first stage of the general resurrection of the righteous dead (1 Cor 15:20-23). As an eschatological event, Paul expects that the resurrection of the righteous will occur when Christ returns (Phil 3:20; 1 Thess 4:13-18; 1 Cor 15:51-53). Those who are raised from the dead will be transformed into a new mode of existence (1 Cor 15:51-53; Phil 3:20-21). A similar expectation occurs in Jewish apocalyptic literature (Dan 12:3; *1 Enoch* 39:4-5; 62:15; *2 Enoch* 65:10; *2 Bar.* 49:3). But the resurrection of Jesus, which guarantees the resurrection of believers, is not simply a past event with future consequences. Nor is the death of Jesus simply a historical fact. For Christians, baptism represents a real identification with Christ in both his death and resurrection, signaling death to the old life and resurrection to the new (Rom 6:1-14; 8:10-11; see Col 3:1-3; Eph 2:1-10).

5.9. The Eschatological Antagonist. The Christian doctrine of the incarnation of Christ made it all but inevitable that a satanic counterpart to Christ would be incorporated into early Christian apocalyptic expectation. In the Synoptic apocalypse the appearance of false messiahs and false prophets at the end of the age is predicted (Mk 13:21-22; Mt 24:23-24). This figure is called the antichrist in Johannine literature (1 Jn 2:18, 22; 4:3; 2 Jn 7). In Revelation the two major antichrist traditions, the godless, tyrannical ruler and the false, seductive prophet, are kept separate. The evil ruler is called the Beast from the Sea (Rev 13:1-10; 16:13; 19:20), while the false prophet is called the Beast from the Land, or the False Prophet (Rev 13:11-18; 16:13; 19:20). There is a single extended discussion of the coming of the eschatological antagonist in the Pauline letters (2 Thess 2:1-12), though strangely there are no allusions to this figure elsewhere in the Pauline letters. There Paul combines into a single figure the two major eschatological antagonist traditions, that of the godless, tyrannical ruler and that of the false, seductive prophet. This person is called both the "man of lawlessness" and the "son of perdition" (2 Thess 2:3; see Dan 11:36-37; *Sib. Or.* 5:33-34; *Asc. Isa.* 4:6; *2 Enoch* [Rec. J] 29:4), who will install himself in the temple of God, proclaim himself to be God (2 Thess 2:4) and perform miracles to legitimate his claims (2 Thess 2:9; see Mk 13:22; Mt 24:24; Rev 13:13-14). This eschatological antagonist has not yet appeared because someone or something is restraining him or it (2 Thess 2:7), though there is no agreement regarding whether this restraining force is Satan, the Roman Empire, the Roman emperor or perhaps some supernatural force. This eschatological antagonist will be slain by the Lord Jesus when he returns in judgment (2 Thess 2:8).

5.10. The Problem of a Temporary Messianic Kingdom. The relevance of 1 Corinthians 15:20-28 to the early Jewish and early Christian view of a temporary intermediate messianic kingdom is disputed, though the general view is that there is no clean and convincing evidence that Paul, like the author of Revelation (Rev 20:1-6), expected a messianic interregnum.

A. Schweitzer summarized Paul's apocalyptic beliefs in this way: (1) the sudden and unexpected return of Jesus (1 Thess 5:1-4); (2) the resurrection of deceased believers and the transformation of living believers, all of whom meet the returning Jesus in mid-air (1 Thess 4:16-17); (3) the messianic judgment presided over either by Christ (2 Cor 5:10) or God (Rom 14:10); (4) the inauguration of the messianic kingdom (not described by Paul, but hinted at in 1 Cor 15:25; Gal 4:26); (5) the transformation of all nature from mortality to immortality during the messianic kingdom (Rom 8:19-22) and the struggle with angelic powers (Rom 16:20) until death itself is conquered (1 Cor 15:23-28); (6) the conclusion of the messianic kingdom (Paul does not mention its duration); (7) the general resurrection at the conclusion of the messianic kingdom (1 Cor 6:3); (8) the judgment upon all humanity and defeated angels. According to Schweitzer, Paul introduced two resurrections although Jewish eschatology before him knew only a single resurrection, either at the beginning or the end of the messianic kingdom. This modification was motivated by Paul's belief in the death and resurrection of Jesus the Messiah. The first resurrection enables believers who have died as well as living Christians to participate in the messianic kingdom, all enjoying a resurrection mode of existence.

Schweitzer's reconstruction of Pauline eschatology is subject to several criticisms. (1) There is no evidence in 1 Thessalonians 4:13-18 or 1 Corinthians 15:20-28 that Paul expected an intermediate messianic kingdom (Wilcke). (2) There is no evidence to indicate that Paul expected a general resurrection of both the righteous and the wicked dead.

There are a number of reasons for thinking that it is more probable that 1 Corinthians 15:20-28 indicates that the Parousia will shortly be followed by the resurrection and judgment, which together will usher in the final consummation of history (Davies 1970, 295-97): (1) For Paul the kingdom of God is an unending kingdom (1 Thess 2:12; Gal 5:21; 1 Cor 6:9-10; 15:50; see 2 Thess 1:4-5; Col 4:11). (2) The only text which mentions the "kingdom of Christ" (Col 1:12-13) understands it as a present fact. (3) Paul connects the Parousia with the judgment of the world (1 Cor 1:7-8; 2 Cor 1:14; Phil 1:6, 10; 2:16). It is probable that Paul has essentially historicized the apocalyptic conception of a temporary messianic kingdom in terms of a temporary period between the crucifixion and resurrection of Jesus and his Parousia. [D. E. Aune]

6. Later New Testament Writings and Apocalypticism.

In later NT writings the expectation of the Parousia is enriched by anticipations of a renewed heaven and earth, including a renewed Jerusalem. 2 Peter 3:10-14 speaks of cosmic transformation, wherein the "the day of the Lord will come like a thief, and then the heavens will pass away with a loud noise, and the elements will be dissolved with fire, and the earth and the works that are upon it will be burned up" (2 Pet 3:10 RSV). Hebrews 12:18-24 and 13:14 speak of a new Jerusalem, a theme envisioned in several scrolls from Qumran (e.g., 1Q32, 2Q24, 4Q554-555, 5Q15, 11Q18; *see* New Jerusalem Texts) and ultimately inspired by the visions of Ezekiel. This theme is treated in the NT in the greatest detail in Revelation 21—22. According to the seer: "Then I saw a new heaven and a new earth; for the first heaven and the first earth had passed away, and the sea was no more. And I saw the holy city, new Jerusalem, coming down out of heaven from God, prepared as a bride adorned for her husband; and I heard a loud voice from the throne saying, 'Behold, the dwelling of God is with men. He will dwell with them, and they shall be his people, and God himself will be with them; he will wipe away every tear from their eyes, and death shall be no more, neither shall there be mourning nor crying nor pain any more, for the former things have passed away' " (Rev 21:1-4 RSV). The description of this new Jerusalem, which emphasizes the number twelve, blends together Jewish apocalyptic with Christian emphasis on Jesus, God's "lamb," whose return is eagerly awaited. [C. A. Evans]

See also APOCALYPSE OF ABRAHAM; APOCALYPSE OF ZEPHANIAH; APOCALYPTIC LITERATURE; BARUCH, BOOKS OF; BELIAL, BELIAR, DEVIL, SATAN; DEAD SEA SCROLLS: GENERAL INTRODUCTION; ENOCH, BOOKS OF; ESCHATOLOGIES OF LATE ANTIQUITY; ESDRAS, BOOKS OF; HEAVENLY ASCENT IN JEWISH AND PAGAN TRADITIONS; MESSIANISM; MYSTICISM; NEW JERUSALEM TEXTS; REVOLUTIONARY MOVEMENTS; SIBYLLINE ORACLES; TESTAMENT OF MOSES; TESTAMENTS OF THE TWELVE PATRIARCHS; WAR SCROLL (11QM) AND RELATED TEXTS.

BIBLIOGRAPHY. D. C. Allison, *The End of the Ages Has Come* (Philadelphia: Fortress, 1985); J. Baumgarten, *Paulus und die Apokalyptik* (Neukirchen-Vluyn: Neukirchener Verlag, 1975); G. R. Beasley-Murray, *Jesus and the Future* (London: Macmillan, 1954); idem, *Jesus and the Kingdom of God* (Grand Rapids, MI: Eerdmans, 1986); J. Becker, "Erwägungen zur apokalyptischen Tradition in der paulinischen Theologie," *EvT* 30 (1970) 593-609; J. C. Beker, *Paul the Apostle* (Philadelphia: Fortress, 1980); idem, *Paul's Apocalyptic Gospel: The Coming Triumph of God* (Philadelphia: Fortress, 1982); H. D. Betz, "On the Problem of the Religio-Historical Understanding of Apocalypticism," *JTC* 6 (1969) 134-56; V. P. Branick, "Apocalyptic Paul?" *CBQ* 47 (1985) 664-75; J. J. Collins, ed., *Apocalypse: The Morphology of a Genre* (Semeia 14; Missoula, MT: Scholars Press, 1979); idem, *Apocalypticism in the Dead Sea Scrolls* (London: Routledge, 1997); W. D. Davies, "Apocalyptic and Pharisaism," in *Christian Origins and Judaism* (Philadelphia: Westminster, 1962) 19-30; idem, *Paul and Rabbinic Judaism* (3d ed.; London: SPCK, 1970); I. Gruenwald, *Apocalyptic and Merkavah Mysticism* (Leiden: E. J. Brill, 1980); P. D. Hanson, *The Dawn of Apocalyptic* (Philadelphia: Fortress, 1975); R. H. Hiers, *Jesus and the Future* (Atlanta: John Knox, 1981); E. Käsemann, "On the Subject of Primitive Christian Apocalyptic," in *New Testament Questions of Today* (Philadelphia: Fortress, 1969) 108-37; K. Koch, *The*

Rediscovery of Apocalyptic (SBT 2.22; Naperville, IL: Allenson, 1970); L. J. Kreitzer, *Jesus and God in Paul's Eschatology* (Sheffield: JSOT, 1987); H. P. Mueller, "Mantische Weisheit und Apokalyptik," in *Congress Volume* (VTSup 22; Leiden: E. J. Brill, 1972) 268-93; O. Ploeger, *Theocracy and Eschatology* (Richmond: John Knox, 1959); G. von Rad, *Old Testament Theology* (2 vols.; New York: Harper & Row, 1962-65); C. C. Rowland, *The Open Heaven: A Study of Apocalyptic in Judaism and Early Christianity* (New York: Crossroad, 1982); D. S. Russell, *The Method and Message of Jewish Apocalyptic* (Philadelphia: Fortress, 1964); A. Schweitzer, *The Mysticism of Paul the Apostle* (New York: Holt, 1931); M. Smith, "On the History of *Apokalypto* and *Apokalypsis*," in *Apocalypticism in the Mediterranean World and the Near East*, ed. D. Hellholm (Tübingen: Mohr Siebeck, 1983) 9-20; H.-A. Wilcke, *Das Problem eines messianischen Zwischenreichs bei Paulus* (ATANT 51; Zurich: Zwingli, 1967).

D. E. Aune, T. J. Geddert and C. A. Evans

APOCRYPHA AND PSEUDEPIGRAPHA

The term *Apocrypha* is applied by Protestant Christians to the books included in the OT by the Roman Catholic, Coptic and Eastern Orthodox churches but which are not found in the Jewish or Protestant canon. The term *Pseudepigrapha* refers to a much larger body of texts, most of which share the literary device of being written under the pseudonym of a great or an ancient figure in Israel's heritage (Roman Catholic and Orthodox writers usually refer to this body as Apocrypha). These collections preserve important voices that witness to the thought, *piety and conversations within the Judaisms of the Second Temple period and that provide essential background for the theology, cosmology, ethics, history and culture of the authors of the NT and shapers of the early church, many of whom knew, valued and drew upon the traditions preserved in these texts.

1. Definitions of Terms
2. Contents and Leading Ideas
3. Significance

1. Definitions of Terms.

1.1. Apocrypha. The word *apocrypha* (Gk "hidden things") was originally an honorable title for books containing a special, esoteric wisdom that was "too sacred or profound to be disclosed to any save the initiated" (Charles). Some scholars locate the origin of this term in 4 Ezra 14:44-47 (= 2 Esdr 14:44-47; *see* Esdras, Books of), which speaks of "hidden books" containing divine wisdom for the "wise among the people" and which are distinct from the canonical collection that contains divine wisdom for the unworthy and the wise alike (Rowley; Fritsch). In the wake of controversies in the early church and again in the aftermath of the Reformation, the term took on negative connotations, signifying books that were withheld on account of their "secondary or questionable" value (Charles) and that were potentially "false, spurious, or heretical" (Charles; Rowley).

The term is now used in Protestant circles to designate thirteen to eighteen texts included as part of the OT that include historical works (1 and 2 *Maccabees, 1 *Esdras), tales (*Tobit, *Judith, 3 Maccabees, an expanded Esther, additional tales about Daniel), wisdom literature (*Wisdom of Solomon, Wisdom of Ben *Sira), pseudepigraphical prophetic literature (*Baruch, Letter of Jeremiah), liturgical texts (*Prayer of Manasseh, Psalm 151, Prayer of Azariah and the Song of the Three Young Men; *see* Daniel, Esther and Jeremiah, Additions to), an *apocalypse (2 Esdras) and a philosophical encomium (4 Maccabees). These books are found, with the exceptions of 4 Ezra and Prayer of Manasseh, in numerous manuscripts of the *Septuagint and were clearly prized by the early church and read as Scripture. Recent discoveries at Qumran show that such works were not only preserved among Christian circles—Ben Sira, Tobit and Letter of Jeremiah were all found among the *Dead Sea Scrolls, together with numerous pseudepigrapha (*1 Enoch* [*see* Enoch, Books of], **Jubilees* and other pseudepigraphic works not previously known; Stone).

The lack of consensus concerning what books belong in the Apocrypha bears witness to the variety in OT canon among Christian churches. All of these books are considered by some Christian communions as canonical. J. H. Charlesworth calls for a uniform and exclusive delineation of Apocrypha, following the lists of the majority of LXX manuscripts rather than the Vulgate. He would exclude 3 and 4 Maccabees, Prayer of Manasseh and 2 Esdras (2 Esdras 3—14 = 4 Ezra) from the Apocrypha and include them among the Pseudepigrapha. The more recent study Bibles (Meeks; Metzger and Murphy) opt for a more inclusive collection of Apocrypha (all eighteen). In LXX manuscripts 3 and 4 Maccabees have in their favor a strong presence, commanding great respect in the Greek Orthodox church. C. A. Evans rightly notes that the line between Apocrypha and Pseudepigrapha is not clearly drawn and is blurred even further as one considers the relationship between Jude and *1 Enoch* and **Assumption of Moses* (Evans 22 Russell 1993). We may never arrive at the consensus for which Charlesworth calls.

The books contained in the Apocrypha have had a spotted history of reception in the church, and not all eighteen (or thirteen) have fared equally well in that history (see Fritsch for a fuller discussion). Paul clearly knew and used Wisdom of Solomon, and echoes of Ben Sira appear in the sayings of Jesus. The apostolic fathers (Polycarp, Clement, Pseudo-Barnabas) quote from or allude to Wisdom of Solomon, Tobit and Ben Sira as authoritative writings, and numerous allusions to other Apocrypha appear as well. Some leading figures in the church, like Jerome and Origen, recognized the difference between the collection of OT Scriptures used by the church and the Hebrew canon, and Jerome especially calls for a practical distinction to be made between the "canonical" texts and "ecclesiastical" texts, which are useful and edifying but not of the same order. Other figures, such as Clement of Alexandria and Augustine, embrace the larger collection as of uniform inspiration and value.

Only the Protestant Reformation forced a decision. Martin Luther decisively separated the books or parts of books (e.g., the Additions to Esther and Daniel) that were not included in the Hebrew canon from his OT as "books which cannot be reckoned with the canonical books and yet are useful and good for reading" (quoted by Rowley). The rest of the Protestant Reformers followed his practice. The apocryphal books continued to be printed and recommended as edifying material, but they were not to be used as a basis for doctrine or ethics apart from the canonical books. The Roman Catholic church responded at the Council of Trent (1546) by declaring these books (excluding 1 and 2 Esdras, Prayer of Manasseh and 3 and 4 Maccabees) to be fully canonical.

The opinion of many Protestants concerning the Apocrypha has fallen considerably from Luther's estimation. Emphasis on "Scripture alone" and the "sufficiency of Scripture," fueled by centuries of tension between Catholic and Protestant churches, has rendered the Apocrypha more suspected than respected, and lack of acquaintance with the texts among most Protestants has reinforced this aversion. Nevertheless, the collection of texts included in the Apocrypha merits careful attention not only on the basis of its testimony to the currents and developments within Judaism during the intertestamental period but also on the basis of the influence these texts exercised on the church during its formative centuries.

1.2. Pseudepigrapha. The term *pseudepigrapha* (Gk, "things bearing a false ascription") highlights primarily a literary characteristic of many writings from the Hellenistic and Greco-Roman periods, that is, writing under the assumed name of a great figure from the distant past. The term does not in itself distinguish the body of texts to which it refers from canonical writings, as numerous scholars have maintained that pseudepigrapha are present within the canon (e.g., Daniel, Song of Songs, Deutero-Isaiah, numerous psalms). Study of the larger phenomenon of pseudepigraphy among Jewish and Greco-Roman writings of the period might, however, help students assess the implications of canonical pseudepigraphy (Evans; *see* Pseudonymity and Pseudepigraphy).

This term, like "apocrypha," has acquired negative connotations. Charlesworth's survey of several dictionary articles shows that in common parlance the term denotes "spurious works" that are "not considered canonical or inspired." These dictionaries, Charlesworth correctly avers, perpetuate a misleading equation of pseudepigraphy with illegitimacy. Moreover, he rightly asks for clarification concerning the question of canonicity and inspiration. A number of these books are cited as authentic and authoritative texts. We must beware, then, of attaching modern value judgments on an ancient literary practice.

The term is used by scholars to refer to the "rest of the 'outside books'" (Rowley) or to "literature similar to the Apocrypha which is not in the Apocrypha" (Stone 1984). The turn of the twentieth century witnessed the publication of two important collections of pseudepigrapha (Kau-tzsch and Charles), although these were "reductional" collections of only a dozen or so texts (Charlesworth). Charlesworth and his team sought a broader delineation of this body of literature, including sixty-three texts that matched the general description proposed for the corpus. These texts (1) were almost exclusively Jewish or Christian; (2) were often attributed to ideal figures in Israel's past; (3) customarily claimed to contain God's word or message; (4) built on narratives or ideas in the OT; (5) were written between 200 B.C. and A.D. 200 (or, if they were written later, appeared to preserve substantially earlier traditions). Charlesworth asserts that these criteria are meant to describe a collection, not present hard-and-fast criteria for what constitute Pseudepigrapha.

Major bodies of texts are not grouped among the Pseudepigrapha (*see* Writing and Literature: Jewish). *Philo and *Josephus have left voluminous materials, but, as the authorial attestation is not pseudepigraphic, their works stand outside of this category. The *Dead Sea Scrolls contain many pseudepigraphic texts, but, since the "channel of transmission" (Stone) is so well defined, these are treated as a separate corpus. Finally, there are the targums (*see* Rabbinic Literature: Targumim) and other rewritings of biblical texts (*see* Rewritten Bible) that share much in common with books like *Jubilees* but are not included in the Pseudepigrapha.

The phenomenon of pseudepigraphy is complex. R. H. Charles sought the origin of the practice in the rise of a monolithic Jewish orthodoxy based on a closed canon of Law and Prophets, which would not permit authors to claim inspiration in their own name. The image of a normative Judaism before A.D. 70 has largely been refuted. Perhaps more useful is S. Cohen's suggestion that Jews in the Second Temple period perceived themselves as living in a postclassical age: this awareness led authors to connect their work with some figure from the classical (preexilic or exilic) period. In the case of apocalypses, the phenomenon may be even more complex, with authors identifying, in some ecstatic experience, with the figure of the past and giving new voice to the ancient worthy. The choice of pseudonym may indicate a conscious attempt to link one's own work with the "received tradition of teaching" related to that name (Stone). Evans echoes this view with approval, extending it into the period after the apostolic age, during which authority was mediated only through the classical figures of the church's first generation and pseudepigraphy again became a common phenomenon.

Scholars have noted the limitations of both terms. First, *apocrypha* and *pseudepigrapha* are not equal terms. One derives from canonical debates and usage; the other from a peculiar literary characteristic. *Apocrypha* is an especially problematic term for the historical study of these documents, since decisions about canon are much later than the period in which the texts were produced and often come only centuries after a document has been in use and exercising an important influence (cf. Charlesworth; Nickelsburg). By using *pseudepigrapha* to refer to a body of texts outside the Protestant canon and the Apocrypha, we obscure the pseudepigraphic nature of many texts within these bodies of literature (Nickelsburg; Russell). C. T. Fritsch adds rightly that some pseudepigrapha are anonymous rather than pseudonymous (e.g., 3 and 4 Macc), and that, even where the label is correct, it "unduly emphasizes a feature of minor importance."

Problems with both terms lead many scholars to treat Jewish literature not by these often value-laden or anachronistic categories but by genre, geographic derivation or period (Newsome, Nickelsburg, Schürer, Kraft and Nickelsburg, Stone). Apocrypha and Pseudepigrapha appear side by side under the categories of wisdom literature, historical writings, liturgical pieces, and the like. Fritsch and Russell advocate using the term *apocrypha* to cover all Protestant noncanonical texts, following the usage of the modern synagogue ("exterior books"), although this suggestion, too, betrays a certain canonical bias.

Despite these difficulties, there is some value in retaining the terms (Charlesworth). The consideration of the Apocrypha as a collection bears witness to the early church's selection of certain Jewish writings that, although they did not belong to the Hebrew canon, were nevertheless held to be of special value and inspiration and exercised an important influence on the church from its inception. As long as one recognizes that these categories could remain somewhat fluid (witnessed by Jude's use of *1 Enoch* and *As. Mos.* and the inclusion of 3 and 4 Macc in many LXX codices), the terms remain valuable as a prioritizing of the vast wealth of Jewish literature that has come down to us.

2. Contents and Leading Ideas.

Although there is significant overlap between

the two collections, this article will survey them separately for the sake of clarity and definition.

2.1. Apocrypha. The two historical books, 1 and 2 Maccabees, provide essential information about a series of events that shaped Jewish consciousness during the later Second Temple period. The forced *hellenization program of the high *priests Jason and Menelaus (175-164 B.C.), the rise of the *Hasmonean family as the saviors of Israel and the combining of the high priesthood and kingship under that one dynasty had long-lasting ramifications for the period. The ethos of the later Zealot movement (*see* Revolutionary Movements), the notion of a military messiah (*see* Messianism) and the aversion toward lowering the boundaries between Jew and Gentile (e.g., Jewish resistance to Paul's mission) all have strong roots in this period. It was also during this period that the major sects within Judaism took shape—frequently in reaction against (e.g., Qumran *Essenes, *Pharisees) or in support of (*Sadducees) the Hasmonean administration of the *temple. Second Maccabees also provides an important early witness to the belief in the *resurrection of the righteous and to a growing angelology.

The Wisdom of Ben *Sira, written in *Jerusalem in about 180 B.C., supports commitment to Torah as the only path to honor and as the way of true wisdom. It contains instruction on a wide array of topics, but its teachings on *prayer, forgiveness, almsgiving and the right use of wealth have left an indelible impression on later Jewish ethical instructions and on the early church. *Wisdom of Solomon, a product of Egyptian Judaism from the turn of the era, also promotes the Jewish way of life, emphasizing the eternal importance of God's verdict on one's life, the rewards and nature of wisdom and the actions of God on behalf of God's people, Israel. The author takes the personification of Wisdom to its highest level, and this became very influential for the early church's reflection on the divinity and preexistence of Jesus. Wisdom of Solomon helps Jews remain dedicated to Torah also through a demonstration of the folly of Gentile religion, much of which is paralleled in Paul's attacks on Gentile depravity and on idolatry. Here we might mention also the Letter of Jeremiah, which reinforces Jews' conviction that idols are nothing and that Gentiles are alienated from true religion (*see* Daniel, Esther and Jeremiah, Additions to).

Although it is not properly a wisdom book, 4 *Maccabees also promotes adherence to Judaism, assuring Jewish readers through a philosophical demonstration that strict obedience to Torah trains one in all the cardinal virtues so highly prized and regarded by the Greco-Roman culture (*see* Vice and Virtue Lists). Indeed, Jews trained by Torah surpass all others in the exercise of virtue, as the courage and endurance of the martyrs of the hellenization crisis (the subjects of the author's praise) show (*see* Hellenism). Particularly those commandments that separate Jews from people of other races—those laws that frequently occasion the contempt of non-Jews—are shown to lead to virtue and honor.

The Apocrypha also contains numerous edifying tales that provide useful windows into the *piety of the period. Hebrew Esther was expanded to bring direct references to God and expressions of piety (prayer, dietary *purity) into the story (*see* Daniel, Esther and Jeremiah, Additions to). *Tobit, a story from the Diaspora and perhaps the oldest book in the Apocrypha, tells a tale of God's providence, the activity of angels and *demons, the efficacy of prayer, and exorcism. The story promotes almsgiving and acts of charity within the Jewish community, as well as the value of kinship and endogamy (*see* Family and Household). *Judith, possibly a Palestinian work from the Maccabean period, tells of a heroine who used her charm to trap and kill a Gentile oppressor. The story affirms the importance of prayer, dietary purity, the virtue of chastity and God's care for God's people in times of adversity.

Third *Maccabees may also be classified as an edifying legend that provides a saga for *Diaspora Judaism that parallels the story of 2 Maccabees. It affirms God's special care and closeness to Jews living in the Diaspora and separated from the Promised Land, and it attests to the tensions between faithful Jews, apostate Jews and the dominant Gentile culture. First *Esdras may be counted among this group, although it is more a rewriting of biblical books (2 Chron 35:1—36:23; Ezra; Neh 7:38—8:12). The only original portion of this book is a courtly tale about the wisdom of Zerubbabel (1 Esdr 3:1—5:6). Two tales featuring the hero Daniel (originally independent tales) appear in the expanded, Greek version of that book (*see* Daniel, Esther and Jeremiah, Additions to). The first, Susanna, like 1 Esdras 3:1—5:6, celebrates the wisdom of a Jewish leader. The second, Bel and the Dragon, demonstrates the folly of idolatry in Daniel's undermining of the credibility of an image of Bel and a living serpent as gods.

A number of liturgical texts are included among the Apocrypha. Psalm 151 recalls God's choice of David and David's triumph over the Philistine giant—surely a potent image for the place of Israel among the giant Gentile kingdoms that held sway over Israel throughout this period save for the time of the Hasmonean dynasty. Jewish poets were watchful for points in the biblical story that called for a prayer or a psalm but did not record them. Two additions to Daniel and the *Prayer of Manasseh supply what the narratives lack: a prayer of repentance and call for help in the fiery furnace (Prayer of Azariah), a psalm of deliverance (Song of the Three Young Men) and another penitential prayer (Prayer of Manasseh) that affirms that no sinner is beyond God's mercy and power to forgive. Although essentially a pseudepigraphic prophetic book, *Baruch also contains much liturgical material. The opening chapters (Bar 1:1—3:8) present penitential prayers affirming God's justice in bringing upon Israel and Judah the curses of Deuteronomy but also open the door to the hope of return as God is remembered and obeyed afresh in the land of exile. There follows a wisdom psalm, identifying wisdom wholly and exclusively with the Torah of Moses in a manner reminiscent of Ben Sira (Bar 3:9—4:4). The final sections take on a more prophetic cast, introducing oracles promising the gathering of the Diaspora Jews, the judgment of the cities that oppressed the Jews and the exaltation of Zion.

Finally, the collection includes an apocalypse, 2 Esdras (or 4 Ezra). The author writes in response to the destruction of Jerusalem in A.D. 70, and even more directly in response to God's slowness in punishing Rome, the instrument of destruction. In its negation of hope for this age, its hope for reward in the age to come, its visions of the many-headed eagle and the man from the sea, this text provides an important window into Jewish apocalypticism that offers instructive parallels for NT apocalyptic material.

Throughout this corpus, one notices the prominence of the covenant theology of Deuteronomy—the conviction, rooted in the blessings and curses of Deuteronomy 28—32, that the nation and the individuals who follow Torah will be rewarded, and the nation or individual who departs from Torah will be punished. During this tumultuous period, this view was frequently altered to seek that reward or punishment in the *afterlife (whether by resurrection, as in 2 Macc, or in the immortality of the soul, as in Wis), but it was never abandoned. Much of the literature is vitally concerned with God's care for God's people, what it means to live as a faithful and obedient people and how to respond to the pressures that threaten that loyalty.

*2.2. **Pseudepigrapha.*** Among the Pseudepigrapha are found samples of a wide variety of genres: apocalypses, testaments, expansions of biblical narratives, wisdom literature, philosophical literature, liturgical texts, historical works, poetry and drama all have their representatives.

Many of the Pseudepigrapha fall into the genre of apocalypse. Of these the most important and accessible may be *1 *Enoch* and *2 *Baruch.* The oldest strata of *1 Enoch,* which is a composite work, may date from the third century B.C. This work presents a journey to the places prepared for the punishment of the wicked and reward of the righteous, an advanced angelology based on the story of the "Watchers" (cf. Gen 6:1-4; *see* Angels of the Nations) and a scheme of history placing the recipients near the time of God's breaking into the fabric of history to execute judgment. The Similitudes (*1 Enoch* 37—71), composed perhaps during the first century A.D., bear witness to developments of the figure of the Son of Man and thus provide relevant material for the study of that title in the Gospels. The work as a whole left its mark on Jude (which quotes *1 Enoch* 1:9) and especially Revelation. Like 4 Ezra, *2 Baruch* is an apocalyptic response to the destruction of Jerusalem. It also counsels renewed commitment to Torah as the path to God's vindication of the chastised nation, assuring readers of the nearness of God's deliverance and the certainty of the chastisement of Rome. Other apocalypses of note include *2 Enoch,* the **Sibylline Oracles,* the *Apocryphon of Ezekiel,* the **Apocalypse of Abraham* and the **Treatise of Shem.*

Closely related to apocalypses are the texts that fall within the genre of testament. These are typically deathbed speeches by great figures of Israel's past, and they present a narrative review of the figure's life (often as a model for virtuous living), ethical exhortations and frequently eschatological predictions, closing with the death and burial of the hero. The most important of these are the **Testaments of the Twelve Patriarchs,* which preserve important examples of developments in angelology, demonology, the priestly and regal functions of the Messiah and ethics. The **Testament of Job* highlights once again the folly of idolatry but also provides important material for the development of the figure of Satan (*see* Belial). The **Testament of Moses,* essentially an expansion of Deuteronomy 31—34, attests to the regard shown *Moses as prophet, mediator and perpetual intercessor, thus providing useful background for NT reflections on Moses. The stance of nonviolent resistance advocated by this book stands in stark contrast to more militaristic ideologies of the period, and the idea of a day of repentance that precedes the coming of God's kingdom parallels Jesus' summons to repentance as a preparation for God's coming (cf. Mk 1:14-15).

Of the expansions of biblical narratives, the most important are **Jubilees* and *Martyrdom of Isaiah* (*see* Ascension of Isaiah). Dating from the late second century B.C., *Jubilees* rewrites the stories of Genesis and Exodus and is of great value for its witness to the development of a theology of Torah. The law revealed to Moses is presented as an eternal law, written on heavenly tablets and obeyed even by archangels. The patriarchal narratives are retold to emphasize their obedience to the Torah, particularly ritual and liturgical observances. The book also reinforces strong boundaries between Jew and Gentile (especially Idumeans) and locates the origin of evil in the activity of Satan and his angels rather than in Adam's weakness. The author looks forward to an imminent renewal of obedience to Torah that will result in a return to primeval longevity. *Martyrdom of Isaiah* tells of the apostasy of Manasseh and the arrest and execution of Isaiah (he was sawn in two; cf. Heb 11:37) at the instigation of a false prophet, Belkira, a demon working to lead Jerusalem astray. In its present form, the *Martyrdom* has been thoroughly Christianized, presenting Isaiah as an explicit witness to Jesus and the history of the early church (*Mart. Isa.* 3:13-31).

Within this category we might also consider the **Letter of Aristeas,* written in Greek near the end of the second century B.C. This work is not directly based on a biblical narrative or character but is more of an edifying tale in defense of the *Septuagint, the Greek translation of the Hebrew Scriptures, and the rational character of a life lived according to Torah. It tells of the wisdom of the Jewish scholars who translated the Torah into Greek and the compatibility of obedience to Torah with the best traditions of Greek ethical philosophy, and it upholds the reliability of the LXX. Other notable expansions of biblical narratives include **Joseph and Asenath, *Life of Adam and Eve* and the *Liber Antiquitatum Biblicarum,* otherwise known as *Pseudo-Philo.

Among the Pseudepigrapha are also found *liturgical texts. The collection of the eighteen **Psalms of Solomon* reflects upon the corruption of the Hasmonean house in its final decades, the intervention of Pompey the Great (who besieged Jerusalem at the request of a claimant for the Hasmonean throne and entered the holy place of the temple) and the death of Pompey in Egypt. All these events are seen as demonstrating the principle of Deuteronomy that departure from the law brings punishment, but also that the Gentile instrument of punishment will not go free. The psalms speak of God's generous provision for all creation, promote the way of life of the righteous person, critique hypocrisy and pride, affirm the value of God's correction and depict the advent of the messianic age under the leadership of a Son of David, the Lord Messiah. Of special interest also are the Hellenistic Synagogal Prayers, which show the blending of Jewish and Christian piety in the early church and which, stripped of their Christian additions, provide a unique view into the piety of the synagogue. Among these poetical texts may also be found several additional psalms of David and the **Odes of Solomon,* a Christian collection with close affinities to the Fourth Gospel.

A number of wisdom texts, often showing the degree to which Jews could adapt and use Greek philosophy, maxims and ethics, are also included in the collection, as well as literary works (poetry and drama), which again frequently show conscious imitation of Greek forms. Finally, the collection includes fragments of historians, which probe the early history of the Jews in a manner reminiscent of *Josephus's *Antiquities* (*see* Jewish Literature: Historians and Poets).

3. Significance.

The period between the Testaments is not a silent age. The texts contained in the Apocrypha and Pseudepigrapha introduce the modern reader to many important and influential voices from the Hellenistic and Roman periods (*see* Jewish History: Greek Period; Jewish History: Roman Period). Without these texts our picture of the Judaism within which the church was born would be most incomplete. These voices demonstrate the diversity within Judaism during the Second Temple period, a view that has replaced early twentieth-century views about a "normative" (legalistic) Judaism before A.D. 70 (Charlesworth vs. Charles). It was a dynamic period of "ferment" within Judaism (Russell 1993), of wrestling with Jewish identity and covenant loyalty amid great social pressures and political upheavals.

The study of these texts leads to a deeper understanding of the Judaism and range of Jewish traditions that shape the proclamation of Jesus and the early church, and this is not the Judaism of the Hebrew Scriptures alone. The intertestamental voices highlight parts of the OT tradition that remained especially important but also attest to new developments, emphases and lines of interpretation that were not original to, but rather were assumed by, the early church. The cosmology, angelology, eschatology, christology and ethics of the early church owe much to the developments of this vibrant period. Some of these texts shed light on the ideology of those who opposed the Jesus movement or the Pauline mission. Many others were the conversation partners of founding figures within the church, and our full appreciation of the work of the latter depends on our acquaintance with the former.

See also APOCALYPTIC LITERATURE; DEAD SEA SCROLLS; JEWISH LITERATURE: HISTORIANS AND POETS; PSEUDONYMITY AND PSEUDEPIGRAPHY; RABBINIC LITERATURE; REWRITTEN BIBLE IN PSEUDEPIGRAPHA AND QUMRAN.

BIBLIOGRAPHY. R. H. Charles, ed., *The Apocrypha and Pseudepigrapha of the Old Testament in English* (2 vols.; Oxford: Clarendon Press, 1913); J. H. Charlesworth, *The Pseudepigrapha and Modern Research, with a Supplement* (SCS 7; Chico, CA: Scholars Press, 1981); idem, "The Renaissance of Pseudepigrapha Studies: The SBL Pseudepigrapha Project," *JSJ* 2 (1971) 107-14; J. H. Charlesworth, ed., *The Old Testament Pseudepigrapha* (2 vols.; Garden City, NY: Doubleday, 1985); S. Cohen, *From the Maccabees to the Mishnah* (Philadelphia: Westminster, 1987); C. A. Evans, *Noncanon-ical Writings and New Testament Interpretation* (Peabody, MA: Hendrickson, 1992); C. T. Fritsch, "Apocrypha," *IDB* 1:161-66; idem, "Pseudepigrapha," *IDB* 3:960-64; E. Kautzsch, ed., *Die Apokryphen und Pseudepigraphen des Alten Testaments* (2 vols.; Hildesheim: Georg Olms, 1962 [1900]); R. A. Kraft and G. W. E. Nickelsburg, eds., *Early Judaism and Its Modern Interpreters* (Philadelphia: Fortress; Atlanta: Scholars Press, 1986); W. A. Meeks, ed., *The HarperCollins Study Bible* (New York: HarperCollins, 1993); B. M. Metzger, *An Introduction to the Apocrypha* (Oxford: Oxford University Press, 1957); B. M. Metzger and R. E. Murphy, *The New Oxford Annotated Bible with the Apocrypha* (New York: Oxford University Press, 1991); J. D. Newsome, *Greeks, Romans, Jews* (Philadelphia: Trinity Press International, 1992); G. W. E. Nickelsburg, *Jewish Literature Between the Bible and the Mishnah* (Philadelphia: Fortress, 1981); H. H. Rowley, *The Relevance of Apocalyptic* (London: Athlone, 1944); D. S. Russell, *Between the Testaments* (London: SCM, 1960); idem, "Pseudepigrapha," in *The Oxford Companion to the Bible,* ed. B. M. Metzger and M. D. Coogan (Oxford: Oxford University Press, 1993) 629-31; E. Schürer, *The History of the Jewish People in the Age of Jesus Christ (175 B.C.-A.D. 135),* rev. and ed. G. Vermes, F. Millar and M. Goodman (3 vols., Edinburgh: T & T Clark, 1986) 3.1; M. E. Stone, "The Dead Sea Scrolls and the Pseudepigrapha," *Dead Sea Discoveries* 3 (1996) 270-95; idem, "Pseudepigrapha," *IDBSup* 710-12; M. E. Stone, ed., *Jewish Writings of the Second Temple Period* (CRINT 2.2; Assen: Van Gorcum; Philadelphia: Fortress, 1984). D. A. deSilva

APOCRYPHA OF MOSES (1Q29, 4Q374-377, 4Q408)

During the late Second Temple period many writings were composed that claimed Mosaic authorship: **Jubilees,* the **Temple Scroll,* the *Words of Moses* and several fragmentary texts. Except for *Jubilees,* all of these writings are known only from the *Dead Sea Scrolls, though they do not appear to be compositions of the *Qumran sectarian community. While these texts contain narrative, admonitions and prayers, they also often invoke the authority of Moses in support of halakic or other religious practices the author of the apocryphon wishes to establish.

1. Prophets and High Priests (1Q29, 4Q375, 376, 4Q408)
2. The Figure of Moses (4Q374, 377)

1. Prophets and High Priests (1Q29, 4Q375, 376, 4Q408).

Originally entitled "Three Tongues of Fire," 1Q29 was published in 1955. As the Cave 4 materials became available, overlapping text between 1Q29 and 4Q376, and the similar context and genre of 4Q375, suggested a broader work which appears to be a reworking of sections of the Pentateuch. The publication of 4Q408 (originally *Sapiential Work*) has also revealed common text with 1Q29 and 4Q376. This composition uses the Tetragrammaton when referring to God, a fact that some researchers have concluded resists the categorization of the composition as a Qumran sectarian work. However, sectarian language (e.g., "Prince of the congregation," 4Q376 frag. 1 iii 1) present in the text suggests otherwise. The oldest manuscript (4Q376) was copied in about 50 B.C.

Fragment 1 of 4Q375 rehearses the test of a prophet found in Deuteronomy 13:1-5. Following this passage, the Qumran text poses a question not found in the biblical discussion: what if the tribe to which the prophet belongs comes forth and claims, "He must not be executed, for he is a righteous man, he is a [trus]tworthy prophet" (4Q375 frag. 1 i 6-7)? In answer, the prophet is taken before the anointed high priest, who conducts a ritual similar to that performed on the Day of Atonement. The text specifies that the high priest is to consult laws contained in the ark and to return to the assembly, presumably to announce his judgment.

The role of the high priest in an oracular decision is described in 1Q29 and 4Q376. The oracle is given by means of the Urim and Thummim, which, according to this text, were attached to the high priest's breastplate and referred to as "the left-hand stone" and "the right-hand stone." The shining of one or the other stone indicated the will of God. Although the text is badly damaged, one section appears to concern the authentication of a prophet, another a decision about military strategy. *Josephus (Josephus *Ant.* 3.8.9 §§214-18) gives a similar account of the oracular shining of the stones on the high priest's shoulders.

This description of the Urim and Thummim is also supported by a reading of Exodus 28:30, which is preserved in the LXX. English translations, following a contrasting exegetical tradition, read, "You shall put the Urim and the Thummim *in* [Heb. *ʾel*] the breastplate of judgment." This interpretation supports the picture of sacred dice—perhaps jewels or stones—that were examined to give a positive or negative answer to the question posed by the priest. The LXX understood the Hebrew to mean that the Urim and Thummim were placed *on* (Greek *epi*) the breastplate. In addition to 1Q29 and 4Q376, this interpretation is also echoed by 4Q164 (pesher Isaiah[d]) in its commentary on Isaiah 54:12a: "'*I shall make all your pinnacles as rubies.*' This refers to the twelve [priests . . .] who make the Urim and the Thummim shine in judgment [. . .]."

It is possible that these four documents, along with the *Words of Moses* (1Q22), are all copies of the same composition. All share a similar pseudo-Deuteronomistic style, with Moses speaking in the first person, and 1Q29, 4Q375 and 4Q376 share a common interest in the high priest as medium of God's will in situations of uncertainty and conflict, in particular the authentication of prophets. Part of the ultimate purpose of the composition may have been to identify the eschatological prophet. In 4Q376, the fragmentary column following the test of the prophet begins: "And if the Prince of the whole congregation is in the camp or i[f ...]." "Prince of the congregation" is an acknowledged messianic appellation in the Qumran corpus (CD 7:20, 1QSb 5:20; 4Q285 frag. 7 4). Perhaps the *Apocryphon* is more accurately an eschatological work and the recognition of the prophet is the key to recognizing the end of the age (1QS 9:10-11). If this is so, discussions of Deuteronomy 18:15-22 and 34:10 likely followed the surviving portions.

2. The Figure of Moses (4Q374, 377).

Two other fragmentary compositions refer to Moses but have a rather different style. In 4Q374 the speaker recalls the deliverance from Egypt. Moses' role is described as like "God" to the leaders of the Egyptians and "mediator" for the Israelites. The references to Moses appear to be in the third person, but it is not clear who the speaker is. Similarly in 4Q377 a speaker exhorts the Israelites to obey the commandments "spoken by Moses," through whose mouth God would speak "as though he were an angel." Both of these texts glorify the figure of Moses, but they do not appear to present direct speech by Moses, as do the texts discussed above. Their narrative settings are not clear, but if they are recollections of Moses after his death, then they might be part of a rewritten and expanded version of the book of Joshua (*see* Apocryphon of Joshua).

See also APOCRYPHON OF JOSEPH (4Q371-372, 539); APOCRYPHON OF JOSHUA (4Q378-379); TESTAMENT OF MOSES; WORDS OF MOSES (1Q22).

BIBLIOGRAPHY. G. Brin, "The Laws of the Prophets in the Sect of the Judean Desert: Studies in 4Q375," in *Studies in Biblical Law* (JSOTSup 176; Sheffield: Sheffield Academic Press, 1994) 128-64; C. A. Newsom, "374: 4QDiscourse on the Exodus/Conquest Tradition," in *Qumran Cave 4.14: Parabiblical Texts, Part 2,* ed. M. Broshi et al. (DJD 19; Oxford: Clarendon Press, 1995) 99-110 and plate xiii; A. Steudel, "408: 4QApocryphon of Moses[c]?" in *Qumran Cave 4:26: Cryptic Texts and Miscellanea, Part 1,* ed. P. Alexander et al. (DJD 36; Oxford: Clarendon Press, 2000) 298-315; J. Strugnell, "375: 4QApocryphon of Moses[a]" and "376: 4QApocryphon of Moses[b]," in *Qumran Cave 4:14: Parabiblical Texts, Part 2,* ed. M. Broshi et al. (DJD 19; Oxford: Clarendon Press, 1995) 111-36 and plates xiv-xv.

C. A. Newsom and M. G. Abegg Jr.

APOCRYPHAL ACTS AND EPISTLES

The group of NT *apocrypha is not a fixed corpus, but the books included in it differ among scholars (*see* Apocryphal Gospels; for the apocalyptic and prophetic texts, *see DLNTD,* Apocryphal and Pseudepigraphical Writings). The texts are now readily accessible in modern editions (Elliott, Schneemelcher). The present article offers a definition of its own. The discussion will then naturally include the relationship of these books to the nascent NT. It will become evident that the apocryphal books are far from homogeneous as a group.

1. Definition
2. Motives for Writing
3. Epistles
4. Acts

1. Definition.

The large number of early Christian writings has never been satisfactorily divided into categories. Even the well-known term "apostolic fathers" is not without its problems. The label *apocryphal,* however, suggests some intended relationship to books of the NT. The presence of this relationship should decide the inclusion or exclusion of a book. The connection can express itself in the fact that a book in the category of NT apocrypha covers ground also covered in a NT document, in its ascription to an apostle or another important biblical character and/or in the imitation of one of the genres that are represented in the NT, namely, Gospel, acts, epistle and apocalypse. At the time of the origin of most apocrypha, the NT was not yet a fixed entity (*see* Canonical Formation of the New Testament).

Because texts like the epistles of Ignatius and *The Shepherd of Hermas* lack this conscious anchoring to one or more books of the NT, they are not to be included among the apocrypha. The same holds for the epistle ascribed to Barnabas, because it is a kind of tract that does not include his name and was only later ascribed to him (*see* Apostolic Fathers).

It is also disputed whether relevant texts from the library of Nag Hammadi, found in 1947 (*see* Gnosticism), should be included among the NT apocrypha (Schneemelcher does so, Elliott does not). In view of the great diversity of outlooks among the books and tracts that make up this collection, there is no compelling reason to keep them separate from other early Christian literature (see 3.6 and 4.8 below).

Among the NT apocrypha that fall within the genres of epistles and acts, not a single text seriously claims an origin before 125 A.D.; in this respect the situation here differs from that with the apocryphal Gospels. This means that the texts discussed below were not in existence when the NT documents were written. Rather the apocrypha reflect the reception of the books that were later canonized. As such, they can help the interpreter understand the world into which the canonical writings were launched and the way in which they were used or sometimes not used. The apocryphal acts largely reflect popular forms of Christianity and are valuable sources for students of the early church.

With the exception of the *Epistle to the Laodiceans,* the Western church never even considered the inclusion of these writings into the canon. Their textual history therefore stands apart from that of the NT, and many of them, especially the acts, have suffered badly in transmission.

2. Motives for Writing.

The texts under consideration differ so much that a general reason for their writing cannot be given. As they are nearly all anonymous or *pseudonymous, only the texts themselves can give us a clue. Because by definition we include only pseudonymous epistles among the apocrypha, all examples of this genre involve a kind of pious fraud. Some authors of apocrypha wanted to supplement an existing text (the *Acts of Peter* and *Acts of Paul* supplement Acts of the Apostles) or to replace lost information (the *Epistle to the Laodiceans).* In other cases a doctrinal bias *(Acts of John* and *Acts of Thomas)* is clearly visible. Many later acts largely satisfy the curiosity of the believers concerning the fate of those apostles not dealt with in the canonical Acts of the Apostles.

3. Epistles.

The apocryphal epistles have little in common. In general they were written by one hand and transmitted without much later alteration. The number of apocryphal epistles is limited because at an early stage the church had its canon of epistles closed; consequently, creative activity turned to the writing of acts. Modern scholarship so far pays little attention to these epistles.

3.1. ***Epistles by Abgar and Christ.*** These two brief letters have been preserved by the historian Eusebius. Though it is old, nobody seriously believes that the correspondence is authentic. In it, King Abgar of Edessa in Syria asks Jesus to visit him in order to heal him. Jesus answers that after his departure one of his apostles will come to Abgar's country.

3.2. ***Third Corinthians.*** This alleged letter of Paul once belonged to the canon of the Armenian church. It is preceded by a letter from Corinthian elders to Paul, to which *3 Corinthians* claims to form the answer. Both brief letters exist as parts of the *Acts of Paul* (see 4.4 below) and also independently, as in one of the Bodmer papyri. Originally they were composed independently of the *Acts of Paul.* Their tendency is anti-Gnostic and forms a defense of the bodily resurrection of Christ (see Luttikhuizen in Bremmer 1996).

3.3. ***Laodiceans.*** In Colossians 4:16 Paul states that he has written an epistle to the believers in Laodicea. This letter evidently disappeared very early; the present *Epistle to the Laodiceans* intends to replace it. It is a brief pastiche of Pauline phrases that has been preserved only in Latin.

3.4. ***Epistles of Paul and Seneca.*** This fictitious correspondence originated as an effort to make Christianity more acceptable to educated pagans. It consists of fourteen short letters in Latin, the last two of which were added after the time of Jerome.

3.5. ***Epistle of the Apostles.*** This second-century document has the form of an epistle, whereas its contents form a dialogue between Jesus and his disciples that deals mainly with future events. Some scholars prefer to classify this text as a kind of gospel. Unknown until 1895, it has mainly been preserved in Coptic and Ethiopic. The tendency is anti-Gnostic.

3.6. ***Epistle of Peter to Philip*** *(NHC VIII.2).* This is a composite work, of which the letter forms only the brief first part. The main part contains several revelations of Christ to his apostles and a sermon by Peter. This text makes Jesus portray the *gnostic faith as the higher form of Christianity. The author makes ample but critical use of the NT Gospels and Acts. The date could be about A.D. 200 .

3.7. ***Epistle of Titus.*** This relatively long letter is in bad Latin and forms a plea for ascetic life. Its unknown author often quotes the NT and the other apocrypha, which shows that the text is rather late, probably from fifth-century Spain.

4. Acts.

The five major apocryphal acts, those of Peter, Paul, Andrew, Thomas and John, have been transmitted as a corpus attributed to a certain Leucius. Modern research has established that Leucius was a fictive person, but with certain scholars he has been replaced by the no less fictitious figures of female authors. Although the books in question pay relatively much attention to *women and to renunciation of *marriage and love, the case for female authorship is weak. The major acts mentioned above have as many differences as they have things in common, so that they must be studied individually. These five differ from the other acts mentioned below because they were the earliest to be written. The value of even the earliest apocryphal acts for our knowledge of the first century, however, nearly equals zero. Generically, these writings draw close to the ancient pagan novels, which deal mainly with love and travels. Except in the *Acts of John,* a lot of attention is paid to the martyrdom of the eponymous apostle.

The production of books concerning apostles and the rewriting of earlier books of the kind continued into the Middle Ages. Sometimes a critical eye was needed to distinguish the older texts from the later versions. Nowadays most later texts can be dated by their familiarity with contemporary developments such as doctrinal reflection, meetings of councils and the establishment of ecclesiastical offices.

4.1. Acts of John. This is the earliest of the apocryphal acts, having been written in *Asia Minor not later than 150 A.D. The beginning and several episodes have been lost. Influence of Acts of the Apostles is visible in the imitation of its unique "we" form, which occurs at irregular intervals in the *Acts of John,* without identification of the "I" and without change of narrative perspective. The text has a docetic Christology, and it has been interpolated with a gnostic piece that forms an interpretation of the suffering of Christ. This part of the text directly contradicts the words of the Fourth Gospel. The *Acts of John* was known to the authors of the following three acts.

4.2. Acts of Andrew. This is the worst preserved of the five major acts. It is disputed whether its peculiar ideology is gnostic. In any case the text rejects marriage in a straightforward manner. Its origin is probably second-century Asia Minor. At the end of the sixth century, Gregory of Tours wrote a kind of summary of this text from which he omitted all heretical elements.

4.3. Acts of Peter. This book testifies to a simple, popular form of Christianity, which is unconscious of the fact that ideologically it falls far below the level of contemporary texts. Although the anonymous author knew the Roman *regula fidei,* in places where he was influenced by the *Acts of John* he turns quasi-Gnostic. The narrative focuses on a contest in *Rome between Peter and Simon Magus (cf. Acts 8). This Simon, assumed to have been a Gnostic, is also a main character in other early Christian writings.

4.4. Acts of Paul. R. J. Bauckham has shown that this text was intended to report the events that took place after Acts 28. Large parts of the book have been lost. Important among the preserved elements are the romantic story concerning Paul and the pious virgin Thecla and *Third Corinthians* (see 3.2). The description of Paul's appearance in the Thecla episode is based on a physiognomic reading of 2 Corinthians 10—13 (see Bóllok in Bremmer). Tertullian (*De Bapt.* 17.5) refers to the *Acts of Paul* as a product of second-century Asia Minor.

4.5. Acts of Thomas. This writing is the only one of the acts to have been written in Syriac and also the only one that has been preserved as a whole. It includes a famous hymn that has been called the most beautiful piece of early Christian literature, the Hymn of the Pearl. It has Thomas travel to India and preach the cessation of marriage and procreation. Its tendency is ascetic and probably gnostic.

4.6. Acts of Philip. A fourth- or fifth-century text, these acts were influenced by the major five mentioned above. The tendency is encratic but not heretical. Of the fifteen separate and heterogeneous acts of which it consisted, thirteen and a half have been preserved in the original Greek.

4.7. Acts of Andrew and Matthias. Although by the time of Gregory of Tours (see 4.2 above) this text was part of the *Acts of Andrew,* it is much later, probably fifth century (contra D. R. MacDonald). It lacks the philosophic and gnosticizing tendencies as well as the speeches and the theme of sexual abstinence that characterize the *Acts of Andrew.*

4.8. Acts of Peter and the Twelve Apostles (NHC VI.1). This brief Nag Hammadi text is not specifically gnostic and can be dated in the second or third century. It consists of three or four originally separate episodes, some concentrating on Peter and some on the eleven apostles (the title is not original). Part of the text has Peter narrate in the first person. Jesus is called Lithargoel. Like the other tracts from Nag Hammadi, the present Coptic text is a translation of a Greek original.

See also APOCRYPHA AND PSEUDEPIGRAPHA; APOCRYPHAL GOSPELS; APOSTOLIC FATHERS; CANONICAL FORMATION OF THE NEW TESTAMENT; GNOSTICISM.

BIBLIOGRAPHY. F. Amsler, F. Bovon and B. Bouvier, *Actes de l'apôtre Philippe* (Collection de poche de l'AELAC 8; Turnhout: Brepols, 1996); R. J. Bauckham, "The *Acts of Paul* as a Sequel to Acts," in *The Book of Acts in Its Ancient Literary Setting,* ed. B. W. Winter and A. D. Clarke (BAFCS 1; Grand Rapids, MI: Eerdmans, 1993) 105-52; M. Bonnet, *Acta Apostolorum Apocrypha* (Hildesheim: Georg Olms, 1959 repr.); F. Bovon et al., *Les Actes apocryphes des apôtres* (Geneva: Labor et Fides, 1981); J. N. Bremmer, ed., *The Apocryphal Acts of John* (SAAA 1; Kampen: Kok Pharos, 1995); idem, ed., *The Apocryphal Acts of Paul and Thecla* (SAAA 2; Kampen: Kok Pharos, 1996); idem, ed., *The Apocryphal Acts of Peter: Magic, Miracles and Gnosticism* (SAAA 3; Louvain: Peeters, 1998); idem, ed., *The Apocryphal Acts of Andrew*

(SAAA 5; Louvain: Peeters, 2000); J. K. Elliott, ed., *The Apocryphal New Testament* (Oxford: Clarendon Press, 1993); E. Junod and J.-D. Kaestli, *Acta Iohannis* (2 vols.; CCSA 1-2; Turnhout: Brepols: 1983); A. F. J. Klijn, *The Acts of Thomas* (NovTSup 5; Leiden: E. J. Brill, 1962); P. J. Lalleman, *The Acts of John: A Two-Stage Initiation into Johannine Gnosticism* (SAAA 4; Louvain: Peeters, 1998); D. R. MacDonald, *The Acts of Andrew and the Acts of Andrew and Matthias in the City of the Cannibals* (Atlanta: Scholars Press, 1990); M. W. Meyer, *The Letter of Peter to Philip* (SBLDS 53; Chico, CA: Scholars Press, 1981); E. Plümacher, "Apokryphe Apostelakten" in *Paulys Realencyclopedie der classischen Altertumswissenschaft* Supplementband 15 (1978) 11-70; J.-M. Prieur, *Acta Andreae* (CCSA 5-6; Turnhout: Brepols, 1989); J. M. Robinson, ed., *The Nag Hammadi Library in English* (3d ed.; Leiden: E. J. Brill, 1988); W. Schneemelcher, ed., *New Testament Apocrypha* (2 vols.; rev. ed.; Louisville, KY: Westminster John Knox, 1991-92); Ph. Vielhauer, *Geschichte der urchristlichen Literatur: Einleitung in das Neue Testament, die Apokryphen und die Apostolischen Väter* (Berlin: Walter de Gruyter, 1975). The Journal *Apocrypha* is devoted to this literature.

P. J. Lalleman

APOCRYPHAL AND PSEUDEPIGRAPHICAL SOURCES IN THE NEW TESTAMENT

This study examines the possible NT usage of the OT *apocryphal and pseudepigraphal writings. Attention will be restricted to the more significant allusions.

1. The Apocrypha and the New Testament
2. The Pseudepigrapha and the New Testament

1. The Apocrypha and the New Testament. The term "Old Testament Apocrypha" refers to a group of thirteen works (Epistle of Jeremiah, *Tobit, *Judith, *1 Esdras, Additions to Esther, Prayer of Azariah and the Song of the Three Young Men, Susanna, Bel and the Dragon, *Baruch, *Sirach, *Wisdom of Solomon, and 1 and 2 *Maccabees; *see* Daniel, Esther and Jeremiah, Additions to) found in the Codex Vaticanus, Codex Sinaiticus and the Codex Alexandrinus. These writings, with the exception of 1 Esdras, are accepted by Roman Catholics as canonical, while Protestants and Jews exclude these writings as belonging to the *Biblia Hebraica*.

Although the NT writings do not quote them directly, their influence permeates the NT. The following are among the more significant connections between the *Apocrypha and the NT.

Belief in an *afterlife emerged during the intertestamental period and became a central tenet of the NT writings. The seeds of this belief occur in the Wisdom of Solomon and 2 Maccabees and developed further in the *pseudepigraphical writings of the **Psalms of Solomon* and *1 Enoch (see* Enoch, Books of).

Belief in *angels and *demons also began to flourish in this intertestamental period. Apocryphal writings such as Tobit, 2 Maccabees and the pseudepigraphical writings of *1 Enoch* and other *apocalyptic writings show a growing reflection on the world of angels and of demons.

NT parallels and allusions to the Apocrypha are also noteworthy. Scholars adopt different assessments in this regard. Some support a literary connection, while others see them coming from the common linguistic matrix of the society.

In the Gospels and the apocryphal writings there are a few similarities between the teaching of Jesus and the book of Sirach. "Come to me, all you that are weary and are carrying heavy burdens, and I will give you rest" (Mt 11:28-30, NRSV; compare with Sir 51:23, 26, 27). A further close parallel is Jesus' parable of the rich fool who lays up treasure in his own achievements, then dies and leaves his wealth behind (cf. Lk 12:16-21 with Sir 11:18-19). Other similarities can be observed in Jesus' saying: "When you are praying, do not heap up empty phrases as the Gentiles do; for they think that they will be heard because of their many words" (Mt 6:7, NRSV; compare with Sir 7:14).

The letters of Paul show a number of allusions to the book of Wisdom (cf. Rom 1:20-22 with Wis 13:1-8 and Rom 1:26, 29 with Wis 14:24-27). The line of thought is distinctive: humanity can come to an understanding of God by reflecting upon creation. However, humanity rejected this and replaced God with the worship of idols. Further allusions to the book of Wisdom can be seen in comparing Romans 9:20-22 with Wisdom 12:12 and 12:20. Noteworthy in these texts is the thought of the impossibility of resisting God's power. (See Metzger 158-63, for a detailed comparison of these and the following texts.)

The letter to the Ephesians also shows some allusions to the book of Wisdom: Ephesians 1:17 and Wisdom 7:7 both speak about praying for a spirit of wisdom and understanding. In Ephesians 6:13-17 and Wisdom 5:17-20 the imagery of the armor of God and the breastplate of righteousness seems to call for a common source.

Hebrews 11 appears to reflect the hymn in Sirach 44 honoring *Israel's founding fathers.

The letter of James bears a number of close allusions to the vocabulary and thought of Sirach: "You must understand this, my beloved: let everyone be quick to listen, slow to speak, slow to anger" (Jas 1:19 NRSV). "Be quick to hear, but deliberate in answering" (Sir 5:11 NRSV). James's lament on the tongue (Jas 3:1-12) also reflects a theme common in Sirach, namely, the misuse of speech and the tongue (Sir 20:5-7, 18-19; 28:13-26). The strange image of gold and silver rusting occurs also only in James 5:3 and Sirach 29:9-10.

The book of Revelation shows some similarities with Sirach: the image of God seated on the throne is one that opens Sirach (1:8) and frequently occurs in the book of Revelation (Rev 4:2, 9; 5:1, 7, 13; 6:16; 7:10, 15; 19:4; 21:5).

One cannot prove conclusively that these different NT writers used these apocryphal writings because in no instance is there an exact quotation. Nevertheless, the similarities do show a common thought and vocabulary reflective of the world of first-century Judaism.

2. The Pseudepigrapha and the New Testament. The term *pseudepigrapha* refers to Jewish writings coming from the intertestamental period and beyond.

First Enoch was undoubtedly the most influential of these writings for the NT. The epistle of Jude 14-15 quotes *1 Enoch* 1:9 directly. Noteworthy is not simply Jude's usage of this writing but the way in which he introduces the quotation: "Enoch . . . prophesied." R. J. Bauckham (96) notes that by using this verb *(proephēteusen)* "Jude regarded the prophecies in *1 Enoch* as inspired by God, [but] it need not imply that he regarded the book as canonical Scripture."

Jude 9 contains a further quotation that scholars have identified as coming from the **Assumption of Moses*, a work that has since been lost (see the index of allusions at the end of K. Aland et al., 910). Bauckham (65-76) has recently argued that Jude 9 quotes a lost ending to the work **Testament of Moses*. While this suggestion has prompted much discussion, it has not received general support. J. H. Charlesworth has provided an insightful discussion and rejection of this proposal: "the amount of traditions and documents written with Moses in mind, or attributed to Moses, leaves me unconvinced that Jude quoted from the lost ending of the Testament of Moses. I have learned never to discount the knowledge of Origen; and he attributed Jude's quotation to a document entitled 'the Ascension of Moses'" (Charlesworth 1987, 77).

Hebrews 11 also contains allusions to a number of pseudepigraphical writings. For example, Hebrews 11:37 speaks about those who had suffered martyrdom in that "they were sawn in two." This verb *(epristhēsan)* is found only here in the NT. It refers to the martyrdom of Isaiah as it is narrated in the **Martyrdom of Isaiah:* "Because of these visions, therefore, Beliar was angry with Isaiah, and he dwelt in the heart of Manasseh, and he sawed Isaiah in half with a wood saw" (*Mart. Isa.* 5:1, translation by M. A. Knibb, "Martyrdom and Ascension of Isaiah," in Charlesworth 1985, 2:163; *see* Belial). Hebrews 11:5 refers to Enoch being taken up by God. Genesis 5:24 also refers to this event, but given the importance of the traditions related to Enoch in Second Temple Judaism it is possible that this is a further allusion to *1 Enoch.*

Other possible connections to *1 Enoch* occur in many common terms and images; for example, the use of the term "Son of Man" in *1 Enoch* 37—71. The meaning and origin of this term "Son of Man" is one of the most widely discussed issues in NT scholarship, and undoubtedly its usage in *1 Enoch* helps to throw light upon its usage in the Gospels (*see DJG,* Son of Man).

Further, the book of Revelation speaks of the bottomless pit as the place of punishment for the fallen angels and demons (Rev 9:1). This image is also found in *1 Enoch* 18:11-16.

The *Psalms of Solomon* 17:21-35 (a writing from the middle of the first century B.C.) gives a lucid description of the understanding and role of the Messiah that illustrates the meaning and use of this term at the time of the birth of the NT.

NT allusions to these writings do not necessarily mean that the writers considered them to be inspired or canonical. They also quote from Greek sources that they did not consider canonical or sacred. For example, in 1 Corinthians 15:33 Paul quotes from the play *Thais* (218) by Menander; in Paul's sermon to the Athenians in

Acts 17:28 Luke makes use of two quotations: from *Phaenomena* (5) by Aratus and from the *Hymn to Zeus* by the *Stoic Cleanthes; and the author of Titus 1:12 quotes a saying attributed to Epimenides (*De Oraculis*) about the Cretans (*see* Pagan Sources in the New Testament).

The focus has been on illustrating possible parallels and allusions within the extracanonical material. However, the value of these writings for the NT also lies in providing a cultural, social and religious environment that helps to understand more fully the matrix out of which the NT emerged. While common terms might not directly indicate use of a particular source, nevertheless they demonstrate that these images and words belong to a common heritage.

See also APOCRYPHA AND PSEUDEPIGRAPHA; PAGAN SOURCES IN THE NEW TESTAMENT.

BIBLIOGRAPHY. K. Aland et al., "Index of Allusions and Verbal Parallels," in *The Greek New Testament* (3d ed. corrected; Stuttgart: United Bible Societies, 1983); R. J. Bauckham, *Jude, 2 Peter* (WBC 50; Waco: Word, 1983); J. H. Charlesworth, *The Old Testament Pseudepigrapha and the New Testament* (SNTSMS 54; Cambridge: Cambridge University Press, 1987); J. H. Charlesworth, ed., *The Old Testament Pseudepigrapha* (2 vols.; Garden City, NY: Doubleday, 1983, 1985); idem, *The Pseudepigrapha and Modern Research with a Supplement* (Ann Arbor, MI: Scholars Press, 1981); B. M. Metzger, *An Introduction to the Apocrypha* (New York: Oxford University Press, 1957); G. W. E. Nickelsburg, *Jewish Literature Between the Bible and the Mishnah* (Philadelphia: Fortress, 1981); idem, "Riches, the Rich and God's Judgment in *1 Enoch* 92-105 and the Gospel According to Luke," *NTS* 25 (1979) 324-44.

P. J. Hartin

APOCRYPHAL GOSPELS

Many Gospels or narrative accounts of all or part of Jesus' earthly life and teaching, including his appearances on earth between the resurrection and the ascension, were written in the early centuries of Christianity, besides the four Gospels that became canonical. Most of these noncanonical, or apocryphal, Gospels do not resemble the canonical Gospels in *genre. Some works that were entitled Gospels, such as the *Gospel of Truth,* the *Gospel of Philip,* the Coptic *Gospel of the Egyptians* and the *Gospel of Eve,* do not conform to the definition of providing narrative accounts of the life or teaching of Jesus. Many extracanonical traditions about the life and teaching of Jesus, some of great importance for the study of the NT and its background, are not found in Gospels as such but in other early Christian literature.

1. Fragments of Unknown Gospels
2. *Gospel of Thomas*
3. *Gospel of Peter*
4. Jewish-Christian Gospels
5. *Gospel of the Egyptians*
6. *Secret Gospel of Mark*
7. Birth and Infancy Gospels
8. *Gospel of Nicodemus*
9. Postresurrection Revelations

1. Fragments of Unknown Gospels.

Most of the fragments (on papyrus or parchment) of unknown Gospels resemble the canonical Gospels in distinct ways, often by recounting an episode similar to one found in the canonical Gospels or by using the language of these Gospels. Although several of these may be versions of canonical Gospels, it is more likely that they are parts of documents that cannot be identified as belonging to any known Gospel. The following are the most important.

1.1. P. Egerton 2. This manuscript, dating from around A.D. 150, is one of the two earliest extant Christian manuscripts (along with the fragment of the Gospel of John in P.Ryl. Greek 457 [P^{52}], although some have argued that a set of fragments with the Gospels of Matthew and Luke [Paris, Bibl. Nat., Suppl. Gr. 1120 (P^{4}), Oxford Magdalen Coll. Gr. 17 (P^{64}) and P.Barc. 1 (P^{67}) and a fragment of Hebrews [P.Vindob. G 42417], may date to the late first century). It contains fragments of four pericopes. The first gives the conclusion of a controversy between Jesus and the Jewish leaders, in which Jesus has been accused of breaking the law and at the conclusion of which he escapes an attempt to stone him. There is close verbal relationship with several parts of John's Gospel. The second pericope concerns the healing of a leper, the third contains a version of the question about the tribute money, and the fourth contains an otherwise unknown miracle story. The second and third resemble Synoptic material. Recently an additional four lines of this text have been published as P.Köln 255.

The relationship of this unknown Gospel to the canonical Gospels is disputed. Some scholars have argued that it is independent of all four, shares common tradition with them or was even a source used by Mark and John. If this were accepted, the distinctively Johannine material in the first pericope would be important for the study of the sources of John's Gospel. But it seems more probable on the basis of the mix of materials that this unknown Gospel draws on tradition, either oral or written, that had been substantially influenced by the canonical Gospels.

1.2. P.Oxy. 840. This fourth- or fifth-century manuscript contains the conclusion of a discourse by Jesus, followed by a visit to the *temple in which Jesus engages in a discussion about ritual purification with a *Pharisaic chief *priest named Levi. Some scholars have defended the historicity of the account.

1.3. P.Oxy. 1081. This small fragment from the third or fourth century contains a conversation between Jesus and his disciples. The text appears to be *gnostic, and some scholars have thought that it is from the *Sophia of Jesus Christ* (see 9 below).

1.4. P.Oxy. 1224. The legible parts of this fourth-century manuscript contain parallels to three Synoptic sayings of Jesus and one otherwise unknown saying whose authenticity was defended by J. Jeremias. This fragment could be from an early Gospel independent of the Synoptics, but is too brief for any firm conclusions to be drawn.

1.5. P.Oxy. 210. This fragment from a third-century codex, often neglected in studies of the apocryphal Gospels (see Porter forthcoming), combines passages that apparently come from Matthew 1:24 and 7:17-19 (par. Lk 6:43-44), along with Philippians 2:6 and possibly Colossians 1:15. It was earlier thought that this might be a fragment from the *Gospel of the Egyptians* (see 5 below), but this is no longer held.

1.6. P.Vindob. G 2325 (Fayyum Fragment). This third-century fragment from a scroll, the first apocryphal Gospel fragment found from the sands of Egypt and published (1885), parallels Mark 14:26-30 and Matthew 26:30-34. It is too brief for its relationship to the canonical Gospels to be ascertainable. The name of Peter (written as a *nomen sacrum*) is in red ink, an unusual feature for these fragments.

1.7. P.Cair. 10735. This sixth- to seventh-century fragmentary manuscript includes passages similar to Matthew 2:13 and Luke 1:36, with Joseph being told to take Mary to Egypt and the *angel telling Mary of Elizabeth's pregnancy.

1.8. P.Berol. 11710. These two leaves of a small codex from the sixth century may originally have been an amulet. The text is based on John 1:49, with Nathanael addressing Jesus as rabbi.

1.9. P.Mert. II 51. This fragmentary manuscript from the third century has language from Luke 7 and Luke 6:45 (par. Mt 12:35).

1.10. Strasbourg Coptic Fragment. Unlike the preceding fragments, which are all in Greek, this fifth- or sixth-century fragment is in Coptic. "We, the apostles" are the speakers, but this phrase could be consistent with attribution to a particular apostle (cf. *Gos. Pet.* 14.59). The contents are a prayer of Jesus, a conversation with the disciples and a revelation of his glory to them, all in the context of bidding them farewell, most probably before the passion but possibly before the ascension. There are close contacts with both Synoptic and Johannine material, on which this unknown Gospel is probably dependent.

2. *Gospel of Thomas.*

The Coptic version of the *Gospel of Thomas* was discovered in 1945 among the Nag Hammadi codices. Since then it has received more scholarly attention than any other noncanonical Gospel, mainly because of the claim that it preserves early Gospel traditions independently of the canonical Gospels. It is more important for the study of Jesus and the canonical Gospels than any other noncanonical Gospel of which we have a complete text, although its importance might not be greater than that of some of the fragmentary Gospels noted above, such as P. Egerton 2. As well as the Coptic version of the whole *Gospel of Thomas,* there are three fragments in Greek, which were discovered among the Oxyrhynchus *papyri and published in 1897 and 1904 (P.Oxy. 1, 654, 655) but not recognized as fragments of the *Gospel of Thomas* until the Coptic version became known. Before then, they were often referred to as logia of Jesus. Though there are significant differences between the Greek fragments, which are from three distinct copies of the work, and the Coptic text, they are recognizably from the same work, which must therefore have existed in at least two redactions. The original language was probably Greek, though some have argued for a Semitic original.

The earliest of the Greek fragments (P.Oxy. 1) was probably written no later than A.D. 200 and provides the only firm terminus ad quem for the writing of the Gospel. Hippolytus, writing between A.D. 222 and 235, provides the earliest reference to it by name. The Gospel has been dated as early as A.D. 50 to 70 and as late as the end of the second century. Since parallels to its more explicitly gnostic concepts and terminology date from the second century, it is probably no older than the end of the first century. The attribution of the Gospel to Didymus Judas Thomas (prologue) shows that it derives from the East Syrian Christian tradition, centered in Edessa (*see DLNTD,* Syria, Syrian Christianity). Only in this tradition, from which come also the *Book of Thomas* and the *Acts of Thomas,* was the apostle Thomas known as Judas Thomas and regarded as a kind of spiritual twin brother of Jesus. Thomas was thought, perhaps correctly, to have been in some sense responsible for the founding of the church in this area, and it is probable that the oral Gospel traditions of this church were transmitted under the name of Thomas and that the *Gospel of Thomas* drew on these oral traditions. Its points of contact with other literature from this area and especially its probable use by the *Acts of Thomas* (end of second or early third century) confirm this hypothesis.

The *Gospel of Thomas* is a collection of sayings of Jesus, numbered as 114 sayings (logia) by modern scholars. There are no narratives and only minimal narrative contexts provided for a few sayings (*Gos. Thom.* 22, 60, 100). The few narrative contexts are important for showing that *Thomas* does not, as do most of the gnostic Gospels (see 9 below), have a postresurrection setting. As a sayings collection, *Thomas* has often been compared with the hypothetical Gospel source Q and with the many ancient collections of sayings of the wise. The genre is consistent with the theology of *Thomas,* which presents Jesus as a revealer of the secret wisdom by which the elect may recognize their true spiritual identity and recover their heavenly origin. Some scholars deny that *Thomas* is properly gnostic and locate it instead in the tradition of Jewish wisdom theology or in the encratite tradition characteristic of East Syrian Christianity. Although there are contacts with both these traditions, some of the sayings most distinctive of *Thomas* express a distinctively gnostic theology (e.g., *Gos. Thom.* 18, 29, 50, 83, 84).

The tradition of the sayings of Jesus on which *Thomas* draws was probably Jewish-Christian in origin (see especially saying 12 on James the Just) but had developed in a gnosticizing direction. Some sayings of clearly gnostic origin had entered the tradition, and the editor of *Thomas* selected from the tradition sayings that were compatible with his gnostic theology. The apostle Thomas has become the authority for an esoteric interpretation of the tradition of the sayings of Jesus (cf. *Gos. Thom.* 1, 13).

The majority of the sayings in the *Gospel of Thomas* have parallels in the Synoptic Gospels (including the triple tradition, the Q material and matter peculiar to Matthew and to Luke), but whether *Thomas* is dependent on the canonical Gospels is still debated. Arguments for dependence try to show both that *Thomas* reflects the specifically Matthean and Lukan redactions of Gospel traditions and that its differences from the Synoptics are deliberate redactional changes expressing a gnostic interpretation. Neither of these points has been conclusively established. The order of the sayings in *Thomas* almost never corresponds to that of the Synoptics, while the association of sayings by catchword connections—one of the few reasons that can be discerned for the order in *Thomas*—is characteristic of oral tradition. It has been argued on form-critical grounds that *Thomas* sometimes preserves sayings, especially parables, in a more primitive form than do the Synoptics. Finally, since a significant number of the sayings in *Thomas* that do not have parallels in the canonical Gospels are also attested in other noncanonical sources, it is impossible to argue that the canonical Gospels were the only source of Gospel traditions used by *Thomas.* It follows that even if the editor of *Thomas* knew the canonical Gospels, a parallel to them need not derive from them.

A commonly held opinion is that *Thomas* is dependent on a tradition substantially independent of the canonical Gospels, though influence from the canonical Gospels cannot be ruled out—whether during the oral transmission of the tradition or at the stage of editing or at the stage of translation into Coptic. *Thomas,* according to this view, can therefore provide useful evidence for the study of the origins and development of the traditions behind the canonical Gospels, provided that due allowance is made for its greater distance both theologically and probably chronologically from the historical Jesus, which may account for some of its Johannine elements. Some scholars have argued that a few of the sayings in *Thomas* that have no parallels in the canonical Gospels (such as the parables in *Gos. Thom.* 97 and 98) are authentic sayings of Jesus (*see DLNTD,* Thomas, Gospel of).

3. *Gospel of Peter.*

A substantial fragment of the *Gospel of Peter,* in a manuscript of the eighth or ninth century, was discovered in 1887 in a coffin at Akhmim, Egypt (P. Cair 10759). It contains a narrative that begins at the end of the trial of Jesus, includes the crucifixion, burial and resurrection of Jesus and breaks off in the course of a story that probably described a resurrection appearance to a group of the disciples. The words "I, Simon Peter" (*Gos. Pet.* 14.60) identify the text as part of the Gospel attributed to Peter to which some writers of the early church refer. We have only two other indications of the rest of its contents. The Syriac *Didascalia* (early third century), which used the *Gospel of Peter,* refers briefly (chap. 21) to the resurrection appearance in the house of Levi that probably followed the end of the Akhmim fragment. According to Origen (*Comm. Mt.* 10.17), the *Gospel of Peter* supplied evidence that the brothers of the Lord were sons of Joseph by his first marriage. This may indicate that the Gospel began with a birth narrative. In addition to the Akhmim fragment, there is another fragmentary Greek manuscript of the *Gospel of Peter* (*P. Oxy.* 2949) from the late second or early third century. The textual differences between readings in this manuscript and the Akhmim text suggest that the latter cannot be relied on to preserve the text of the original Gospel very accurately. It has also been posited that *P. Oxy.* 4009, from the second century, is a fragment of the *Gospel of Peter,* although it does not overlap with any of the Akhmim text.

The quite probable use of the *Gospel of Peter* by Justin and very probable use of it by Melito of Sardis (*see DLNTD,* Melito of Sardis) suggest that it must date from before the middle of the second century. At the end of the second century, bishop Serapion of Antioch heard of a dispute over its use in the church of Rhossus. When he discovered it was being used to support docetic heresy and that a few passages in it were suspect from this point of view, he disallowed its use (Eusebius *Hist. Eccl.* 6.12). Recent scholarship has concluded that, on the evidence of the Akhmim fragment, the Gospel itself cannot be considered docetic, though there are phrases that Docetists could interpret in their support. This conclusion is confirmed by its probable use by Justin, Melito and the Syriac *Didascalia,* which suggests that it was quite widely read in early Christian circles.

The Gospel is distinguished, in the text we have, by its interest in the fulfillment of prophecy in the passion narrative, its strongly anti-Jewish bias that emphasizes the sole responsibility of the Jews for the death of Jesus, its heightening of the miraculous, its high christology as indicated by its use of titles for Jesus and its apologetic interest in supplying evidence for the resurrection. Distinctive features include *Herod's participation in the trial of Jesus and ordering of the crucifixion to be carried out by Jews, and the account (which has a close parallel in *Asc. Isa.* 3:16-17) of the exit from the tomb of the risen Christ, escorted by angels.

The Gospel's relationship to the canonical Gospels is disputed. There are parallels to all four canonical Gospels but remarkably few verbal parallels, perhaps not surprising considering the lateness of the manuscript being compared. There are three major positions on the *Gospel of Peter* and its relation to the canonical Gospels. The traditional view, held since soon after discovery of the Akhmim fragment, is that it is dependent on all four canonical Gospels. This position is maintained on the basis of what appear to be instances of clear usage of the canonical Gospels, including John. The resulting relative lateness of the document is confirmed by such other features as historical inaccuracies even in the part of the *Gospel of Peter* purported to be the earliest, a secondhand familiarity with Judaism that seems to be post-A.D. 70, an apologetic streak that runs throughout the text, a high christology and confessional elements as part of the account.

Some scholars have thought, however, that the *Gospel of Peter* is independent of the canonical Gospels. J. D. Crossan has argued that although sections dependent on the canonical Gospels have been secondarily added to the text, the greater part of the Akhmim text is not only independent of the canonical Gospels but a source used by all four canonical Gospels. He calls this the *Cross Gospel* and claims that it is the single extant source for the passion and resurrection narratives in the canonical Gospels. The numerous features noted above have resulted in few apart from Crossan and a handful of others holding to such a position.

A mediating view builds on the observation that the major parallels of the *Gospel of Peter* are with special Matthean material (M) and with Markan material; close verbal parallels are largely limited to the passages parallel to Markan material, which are closer to the text of Mark itself than to Matthew's redaction of Mark; and Matthew and the *Gospel of Peter* show different connections between Markan and M passages. By this view, the *Gospel of Peter* drew primarily on Mark's Gospel and on Matthew's special source independently of Matthew's Gospel. Whereas Matthew gave priority to the Markan narrative and augmented it from his special source, the *Gospel of Peter* gave priority to the narrative of M and augmented it from Mark. M was probably the oral tradition of the church of *Antioch and its neighboring churches, which acquired written form in the *Gospel of Peter* no doubt some decades after Matthew had used it. If this view is correct, the *Gospel of Peter* would be valuable evidence for the study of Matthew's use of his sources but not of the earliest tradition.

4. Jewish-Christian Gospels.

The Gospels used by specifically Jewish-Christian groups in the early church—whether, like the *Ebionites, they were heretical in the eyes of the catholic church, or, like the Nazarenes, they were orthodox but separate from the predominantly Gentile catholic church—have unfortunately survived only in quotations by the Fathers, along with some untrustworthy evidence from the Middle Ages. The titles that the Fathers use for these Gospels and the manner in which they refer to them leave it unclear how many such Gospels there were and from which the surviving quotations are derived. Recent scholarly consensus distinguishes three, all of which seem to have resembled the Synoptic Gospels in genre.

4.1. ***Gospel of the Hebrews.*** The most recent investigation by A. F. J. Klijn assigns seven quotations to this Gospel. These show no sign of dependence on the canonical Gospels. One saying also appears in the *Gospel of Thomas* (2). Otherwise the traditions are distinctive to this Gospel, including the account of the risen Christ's appearance to his brother James the Just, who was highly revered in Jewish-Christian tradition. The Gospel was written in Greek before the middle of the second century. It may have originated in Egypt, where its title would have designated it the Gospel of the Greek-speaking Jewish-Christian community and distinguished it from the *Gospel of the Egyptians* (see 5 below), used by the Gentile-Christian community in Egypt.

4.2. ***Gospel of the Nazarenes.*** Klijn assigns twenty-two quotations definitely to this Gospel, but many of these are passages where only a few words differ from the text of Matthew's Gospel. Others are more substantial additions to or variations from Matthew. Thus this Gospel was evidently a free translation (in *targumic style) of Matthew into *Aramaic or Syriac. The view of Jerome and others that it was the Semitic original from which our Greek Matthew was translated cannot be maintained. In Jerome's time it was used by the Nazarene community in Berea in Syria and may have originated among them in the second century.

4.3. ***Gospel of the Ebionites.*** Epiphanius preserves seven quotations of this Gospel, which was composed in Greek and based on all three Synoptic Gospels. With Matthew as its principal authority, it also drew on Mark and Luke in order to combine the three in a harmonized narrative. It is thus an example of the apparently rather common second-century tendency to produce harmonies of the various Gospel texts, of which Tatian's *Diatessaron* is the most famous example.

Ebionite theology is evident in the quotations. Since the Ebionites rejected the virginal conception and held an adoptionist christology, the Gospel began with the baptism of Jesus. The Ebionite prohibition on eating meat and their opposition to the temple cult are also reflected (*see DLNTD*, Ebionites).

5. ***Gospel of the Egyptians.***

This Gospel appears to have been the one predominantly used by Gentile Christians in Egypt until it was superseded by the canonical Gospels in orthodox circles. Unfortunately little is known of it. The only clear information comes from Clement of Alexandria, who refers to a conversation it contained between Jesus and Salome (a woman disciple of Jesus who is prominent in apocryphal, especially gnostic, Gospel traditions). This contained sayings, also known from the *Gospel of Thomas* (22, 37; see also *2 Clem.* 12.1-2), about the rejection of sexuality, which reflect an encratite view of salvation as the restoration of the original condition of humanity without sexual differentiation. Whether the Gospel was not merely encratite but gnostic is unknown. The Sethian gnostic work from Nag Hammadi, which is also known as the *Gospel of the Egyptians* (CG III, 2 and IV, 2), is a different work.

6. *Secret Gospel of Mark.*
M. Smith discovered in 1958 but did not publish until 1973 a previously unknown letter of Clement of Alexandria copied into the back of a seventeenth-century edition of the letters of Ignatius of Antioch. The majority of scholars have provisionally accepted Smith's case for the authenticity of the letter, though not all rule out the possibilities that it is an ancient *pseudepigraphon, in which case its witness to the *Secret Gospel of Mark* could still be of value, or even a modern forgery.

In the letter Clement claims to know three versions of Mark's Gospel: the Gospel used publicly in the church (our canonical Mark), which Mark wrote first; the *Secret Gospel,* which Mark wrote later in *Alexandria, by adding to his earlier text certain secret traditions that are revealed only to initiates; the version used by the Carpocratian Gnostics, who made their own additions to the *Secret Gospel.* Clement gives no more than two words of the material peculiar to the Carpocratian version but quotes the two passages that the *Secret Gospel* adds to the canonical Gospel. After Mark 10:34, the *Secret Gospel* had a story set in Bethany that is clearly related to the Johannine account of the raising of Lazarus but told in Markan rather than Johannine language. Six days after Jesus raised the young man (who is anonymous in the *Secret Gospel*) from the dead, he came to Jesus at night, wearing only a linen cloth, and Jesus taught him the mystery of the kingdom of God. The reference must be to some kind of initiation, most likely involving baptism. The *Secret Gospel's* second addition to Mark occurs in 10:46: it is an oddly brief reference to Jesus' refusal to receive the young man's sister and his mother and Salome.

Smith argued that the additional material is so characteristically Markan that it must derive from the same body of tradition as canonical Mark. Some scholars have argued that canonical Mark is a later, expurgated version of the *Secret Gospel.* Others regard the material in the *Secret Gospel* as late interpolations, deliberately imitative of Markan style and content. So far the evidence remains subject to differing interpretations (*see DLNTD, Mark, Secret Gospel of*).

7. Birth and Infancy Gospels.
From the second century onward, interest in the family background and early life of Jesus produced many works devoted solely to this theme. Two second-century works on this theme proved extraordinarily popular for many centuries, and all later Gospels of this kind were indebted to one or both of them.

7.1. **Protevangelium of James.** This tells of the miraculous birth of Mary to her childless parents Joachim and Anna, who dedicate her to the temple where she lives until entrusted to Joseph. The story from the annunciation to the massacre of the innocents (concluding with the martyrdom at that time of Zechariah the father of John the Baptist) makes free use of the narratives of both Matthew and Luke, laying special emphasis on the virginity of Mary. The birth of Jesus in a cave is miraculous, preserving Mary's virginal state. Her perpetual virginity is implied, since the brothers of Jesus are considered sons of Joseph by a previous marriage. The work is attributed to one of them, James, though he does not appear in the narrative. The main purpose of the work is clearly the glorification of the figure of Mary as a virgin, though an apologetic defense of her virginity against Jewish anti-Christian polemic may also have influenced its composition. It has been called *midrashic (according to the loose use of that term in some NT scholarship) because of its creative use of OT texts in developing the narrative. It probably originated in second-century Syria, where its ideas about the virginity of Mary can be paralleled from other texts.

7.2. **Infancy Gospel of Thomas.** This work consists solely of a series of stories of miracles performed by the child Jesus up to his twelfth year. For example, Jesus makes sparrows out of clay and brings them to life, a story that later found its way into the Qur'an. He heals the injured, raises the dead, curses his enemies so that they die and proves superior in knowledge to all his schoolteachers. The general effect is to manifest his superhuman nature to all who encounter him. In its original form this work must date from the second century, but from the extant texts in many versions it is difficult to establish the original text.

7.3. Later Gospels. The *Coptic History of Joseph* does for Joseph what the *Protevangelium of James* did for Mary. The *Latin Infancy Gospel of Matthew* (often called Pseudo-Matthew) transmitted much of the content of the *Protevangelium of James* and the *Infancy Gospel of Thomas,* along with further legends of its own, to the medieval West. The medieval *Latin Infancy Gospel* (British Library Arundel 404) published by M. R. James in 1927 is important for one of its sources, otherwise unknown, which may reflect second-century Greek docetic thought. Many other late birth and infancy Gospels in many languages are extant.

8. *Gospel of Nicodemus.*

This title is given to a work combining two distinct parts: the *Acts of Pilate* and the *Descensus ad Inferos* (descent to Hades). The *Acts of Pilate* is an account of the trial and crucifixion of Jesus and of an investigation by the Sanhedrin that receives evidence of the resurrection of Jesus. The work is notable for its anti-Jewish and apologetic tendencies. *Descensus ad Inferos* is the fullest account from the early church of Christ's activity in the realm of the dead between his death and his resurrection: his victory over the powers of Hades and his liberation of Adam and the righteous dead. The *Gospel of Nicodemus* in its present form is generally assigned to the fifth century but undoubtedly draws on earlier sources.

9. Postresurrection Revelations.

Those wishing to amplify the known teaching of Jesus or to trace to Jesus secret revelations handed down in esoteric tradition found the most suitable literary vehicle to be an account of Jesus teaching his disciples in the period between his resurrection and ascension. Often such accounts take the form of a dialogue, in which Jesus is questioned by his disciples about subjects left unclear by his teaching before his death. Gospels of this kind sometimes draw on traditions of the sayings of Jesus in order to interpret and develop them further, but often the contents are unrelated to Gospel traditions. Though the apocalyptic discourse of Jesus in the Synoptics (Mt 24 par.) was sometimes a model for such works, their genre is often as close to that of the *apocalypses as to other kinds of Gospels, and so several of these works are entitled apocalypses.

Though this kind of Gospel proved especially useful to and popular among Gnostics, it did not originate with nor was it confined to Gnostics. Significant for the Gospel traditions they contain are the orthodox examples from the early second century of the *Apocalypse of Peter* and the *Epistle of the Apostles,* the latter for the way in which it seems to draw on the canonical Gospels, including John, within a continuing oral tradition. The Freer Logion (added to Mark 16:14 in one manuscript) is not a complete work but illustrates the second-century tendency to ascribe additional revelations to the risen Christ. Later non-gnostic works of this type, from the third century or later, are the *Questions of Bartholomew,* the Syriac *Testament of Our Lord* and the Ethiopic *Testament of Our Lord in Galilee.* Gnostic works of this type include the *Apocryphon of James* (CG I, 2), the *Book of Thomas* (CG II, 7), the *Sophia of Jesus Christ* (CG III, 4 and BG 8502, 3), the *Dialogue of the Savior* (CG III, 5), the *First Apocalypse of James* (CG V, 3), the Coptic *Apocalypse of Peter* (CG VII, 3), the *Gospel of Mary* (BG 8502, 1), the *Pistis Sophia* and the *Books of Jeu.*

See also APOCRYPHAL ACTS AND EPISTLES; BIOGRAPHY, ANCIENT; GENRES OF THE NEW TESTAMENT.

BIBLIOGRAPHY. R. E. Brown, "The Gospel of Peter and Canonical Gospel Priority," *NTS* 33 (1987) 321-43; J. H. Charlesworth and C. A. Evans, "Jesus in the Agrapha and Apocryphal Gospels," in *Studying the Historical Jesus,* ed. B. Chilton and C. A. Evans (NTTS 19; Leiden: E. J. Brill, 1994) 479-533; J. H. Charlesworth and J. R. Mueller, *The New Testament Apocrypha and Pseudepigrapha: A Guide to Publications* (ATLABibS 17; Metuchen, NJ: American Theological Library Association and Scarecrow Press, 1987); J. D. Crossan, *The Cross That Spoke* (San Francisco: Harper & Row, 1988); idem, *Four Other Gospels* (Minneapolis: Winston, 1985); J. K. Elliott, ed., *The Apocryphal New Testament* (Oxford: Clarendon Press, 1993); F. T. Fallon and R. Cameron, "The Gospel of Thomas: A Forschungsbericht and Analysis," *ANRW* 2.25.6 (1988) 4195-4251; S. Gero, "Apocryphal Gospels: A Survey of Textual and Literary Problems," *ANRW* 2.25.5 (1988) 3969-96; E. Hennecke et al., eds., *New Testament Apocrypha* (2 vols.; London: SCM, 1963) vol. 1; G. Howard, "The Gospel of the Ebionites, *ANRW* 2.25.5 (1988) 4034-53; A. F. J. Klijn, "Das Hebräer- und das Nazoräerevangelium," *ANRW* 2.25.5 (1988) 3997-4033; H. Koester, *Ancient Christian Gospels: Their History and Development*

(Philadelphia: Trinity Press International, 1990); P. Perkins, *The Gnostic Dialogue* (New York: Paulist, 1980); S. E. Porter, "The Greek Apocryphal Gospels Papyri: The Need for a Critical Edition," in *Akten des 21. Internationalen Papyrologenkongresses, Berlin 1995,* ed. B. Kramer et al. (2 vols.; APB 3; Stuttgart: Teubner, 1997) 795-803; idem, "POxy II 210 as an Apocryphal Gospel and the Development of Egyptian Christianity," in *Atti del XXII Congresso Internazionale di Papirologica, Firenze (23-29 agosto 1998),* ed. G. Bastianini et al. (Florence: Istituto Papirologico G. Vitelli, forthcoming); D. R. Schwartz, "Viewing the Holy Utensils (P. Ox. V, 840)," *NTS* 32 (1986) 153-59; M. Smith, "Clement of Alexandria and Secret Mark: The Score at the End of the First Decade," *HTR* 75 (1982) 449-61; idem, *The Secret Gospel* (New York: Harper & Row, 1973); C. Tuckett, *Nag Hammadi and the Gospel Tradition* (Edinburgh: T & T Clark, 1986); D. Wenham, ed., *Gospel Perspectives 5: The Jesus Tradition Outside the Gospels* (Sheffield: JSOT, 1985): D. F. Wright, "Papyrus Egerton 2 (the Unknown Gospel)—Part of the Gospel of Peter?" *SecCent* 5 (1985-86) 129-50.

R. J. Bauckham and S. E. Porter

APOCRYPHON OF JEREMIAH. *See* PSEUDO-PROPHETS (4Q385-388, 390-391)

APOCRYPHON OF JOSEPH (4Q371-372, 539)

Apocryphon of Joseph is the title that has been given to a Second Temple work that treats the biblical figure of Joseph, son of Jacob. The copies preserved in the *Dead Sea Scrolls have only been studied in a preliminary manner, and there are still many unresolved questions about this work.

The text is found in two fragmentary but overlapping manuscripts of the Dead Sea Scrolls, 4Q371 and 4Q372. One large fragment of 4Q372 contains a narrative about Joseph (lines 1-16) followed by a psalm spoken by Joseph (lines 16-32), and on the basis of this fragment the name was given to the document. However, there are about thirty smaller fragments in these two manuscripts, and they cover a wide variety of subjects, including mention of Zimri (Num 25:14) and the five kings of Midian (Num 31:8), Jubilee and even a weasel (perhaps as an example of an unclean animal; cf. Lev 11:29). Since the title *Apocryphon of Joseph* does not reflect the nature of the work as a whole, the more generic title *Narrative and Psalmic Work* will be used in the official publication. To further complicate matters, there is some evidence that 4Q373 and 2Q22 may also belong to this work; these are fragments of an autobiographical psalm in which an unnamed figure (David or *Moses) praises God for his victory over a giant (Goliath or Og).

The text about Joseph in 4Q371 and 4Q372 is not a retelling of the Joseph story of Genesis 37—50; rather Joseph seems to be a designation for the northern tribes (cf. Ps 78:67; Amos 5:6; Ezek 35:15-23; Zech 10:6-10). The narrative section talks of a time of destruction and conflict and opposition to "the tent of Zion," though the text is so fragmentary that it is very difficult to know what is being described. "In all this" (4Q371 10, 14), Joseph "was cast into lands he did not know" and "into the hands of foreigners." In his distress "he called to God to save him from their hands." The psalm that Joseph speaks is a plea for deliverance and a praise of God's kindness. There may be an anti-Samaritan polemic behind this text, that is, a denial of the Samaritan claim to be the descendants of Joseph (cf. Josephus *Ant.* 9.10.14. §291) since the "true Joseph" is far off in exile, praying and relying on God for deliverance. Nothing in the text indicates that the composition was sectarian or written by the *Essenes. The manuscripts date to the latter part of the first century B.C., but the text may have been composed somewhat earlier.

One of the most interesting features of the psalm of Joseph is its opening invocation, "My father and my God." It has often been noted that God is not addressed directly as father in a prayer context in the Hebrew Bible. There are a few examples in Greek texts (3 Macc 6:3; Wis 14:3; perhaps in Sir 23:1, 4 in the Greek translation); in rabbinic *prayer the address to God as "our father" is well attested, but it is very difficult to say how early these prayers developed since our copies are only from much later. 4Q372 provides clear evidence that at least in some Jewish prayer of the first century B.C. God was addressed as "my father" (*ʾabi*). This passage has been of considerable interest for NT scholars in the study of those texts where Jesus and the early church address God as father (*ʾabba,* or "our father").

In addition to the manuscripts discussed above, there is an Aramaic manuscript, 4Q539, that has sometimes also been given the title *Apocryphon of Joseph* because two small fragments have some similiarity to material in the Greek *Testament of Joseph* (15:1—17:2) in the **Testaments of the Twelve Patriarchs*. The Aramaic work may have been a source used by the author of the Greek testament.

See also APOCRYPHON OF JOSHUA (4Q378-379); APOCRYPHON OF MOSES (4Q374-377).

BIBLIOGRAPHY. E. M. Schuller, "4Q372 1: A Text About Joseph," *RevQ* 14 (1990) 349-76; idem, "A Preliminary Study of 4Q373 and Some Related (?) Fragments," in *The Madrid Qumran Congress: Proceedings of the International Congress on the Dead Sea Scrolls, Madrid, March 18-21, 1991,* ed. J. Trebolle Barrera and L. Vegas Montaner (STDJ 11.2; Leiden: E. J. Brill, 1992) 515-30; idem, "The Psalm of 4Q372 1 Within the Context of Second Temple Prayer," *CBQ* 54 (1992) 67-79.

E. M. Schuller

APOCRYPHON OF JOSHUA (4Q378-379)

Apocryphon of Joshua (4Q378-379), also known as the *Psalms of Joshua,* is an example of the literary phenomenon referred to as the *rewritten Bible. In this type of literature, popular in the late Second Temple period, the story of a biblical book was retold and embellished with narrative detail, speeches, prayers and so forth (see, e.g., **Jubilees,* *Pseudo-Philo, **Genesis Apocryphon*). Since both of the manuscripts of the *Apocryphon of Joshua* are very fragmentary, it is not possible to say whether it covered the same narrative scope as did the canonical book of Joshua, but certain fragments from 4Q378 suggest that it may have begun somewhat differently. Those fragments preserve an account of the Israelites' mourning for *Moses after his death, an account of Joshua's accession to leadership (paralleling Josh 1) and a long speech by Joshua to the people, modeled after Moses' speech in Deuteronomy (especially Deut 1—3 and 28—31). One of the fragments contains a *prayer that refers to both Moses and Joshua in the third person. The name of the speaker is lost, however. Material from a slightly later part of the composition is preserved in 4Q379. One fragment makes reference to the crossing of the Jordan (parallel to Josh 3); another cites and expands the curse on the rebuilder of Jericho from Joshua 6:26. In both manuscripts the majority of fragments contain admonitory speeches, prayers, songs or other rhetorical forms rather than simple narration.

Apart from the rough indication of date from paleographical analysis (4Q379 is written in a Hasmonean semicursive, 4Q378 in a Herodian formal hand), only a few details suggest the time or social group in which the *Apocryphon of Joshua* was produced. 4Q379 12 calculates the date of the entry of the people into the land as occurring in a Jubilee year, a date that correlates with the information in *Jubilees* 50:4. The development of the curse against the rebuilder of Jericho into a highly polemical denunciation of this figure as a "man of Belial" (4Q379 22 ii; *see* Belial) is apparently a topical reference to the Hasmonean ruler John Hyrcanus. Not only did he conduct extensive building activity in Jericho, but also his sons, Antigonus and Aristobolus I, died in 103 B.C., within a year of their father's death. The expanded curse in the *Apocryphon of Joshua* was excerpted in the Qumran **Testimonia* document (4Q175), where it follows three other biblical citations that were understood to foretell the eschatological prophet, the Davidic *messiah and the priestly messiah. Since Hyrcanus claimed to combine the offices of ruler, high priest and prophet, the citation of the curse from the *Apocryphon of Joshua* apparently serves as a criticism of Hyrcanus's pretensions.

Despite its citation in the Qumran *Testimonia,* the *Apocryphon of Joshua* was probably not composed at *Qumran. Both the orthographic practices of 4Q379 and the usage of the tetragrammaton and other terms for God differ from the scribal practices at Qumran, although the younger manuscript, 4Q378, is consistent with Qumran orthography. Thus the *Apocryphon of Joshua* was most likely produced around the beginning of the first century B.C. in the same intellectual circle responsible for *Jubilees.* Like *Jubilees,* it was preserved, read and copied by the Qumran community. It is possible that other fragmentary texts from Qumran and Masada may preserve more pseudo-Joshua material, though whether these are parts of the same composition or different ones is uncertain (*see* Apocryphon of Moses [4Q374-377]).

See also APOCRYPHON OF JOSEPH (4Q371-372, 539); APOCRYPHON OF MOSES (4Q374-377); REWRITTEN BIBLE IN PSEUDEPIGRAPHA AND QUMRAN; TESTIMONIA (4Q175).

BIBLIOGRAPHY. H. Eshel, "The Historical Background of the Pesher Interpreting Joshua's Curse on the Rebuilder of Jericho," *RevQ* 15 (1992) 409-20; C. A. Newsom, "378-379. 4QApocryphon of Joshua^{a-b}," in *Qumran Cave 4. XVII: Parabiblical Texts, Part 3,* ed. G. Brook et al. (DJD 22; Oxford: Clarendon Press, 1996) 263-88 and plates xxi-xxv; E. Qimron, "About the 'Deeds of Joshua' from Qumran" (Hebrew), *Tarbiz* 63 (1994) 503-8; S. Talmon, "Fragments of a Joshua Apocryphon—Masada 1039-1211 (final photo 5254)," *JJS* 47 (1996) 128-39.

C. A. Newsom

APOLLONIUS OF TYANA

In the early third century A.D., Philostratus of Athens wrote a work entitled *The Life of Apollonius of Tyana* (*Vita Apollonii*). The author's goal was to defend the legendary first-century sage from recent attacks. Some years later Hierocles wrote a work entitled *Lover of Truth,* in which he made comparison between Jesus and Apollonius, one of the more colorful of the late Pythagorean *philosophers. The early church historian Eusebius wrote a treatise against this work entitled *Against the Life of Apollonius of Tyana.*

Apollonius is said to have performed miracles and even to have been resurrected. The point that Hierocles wished to make is that the miracles of Jesus, no more numerous or significant than those performed by Apollonius, hardly justified the Christians' excessive claim that Jesus was God. Against these claims Eusebius tries to impress upon his readers the significant differences between Jesus and his contemporary Apollonius.

The teachings and activities of Apollonius of Tyana have been of interest to scholars concerned with research about Jesus. It has often been suggested, in the past especially, that early Christians and later the Evangelists embellished the Jesus tradition along the lines of Hellenistic wonderworkers such as Apollonius. M. Dibelius (70-103) and R. Bultmann (218-44) made form-critical comparisons between the miracles of Jesus and those attributed to Apollonius. On the basis of these comparisons Dibelius and Bultmann were convinced that most of the miracle stories neither derived from the historical Jesus nor originated in Palestine; rather, they originated in Hellenism. Dibelius (102) averred: "The Tale-tellers have taken over foreign traits or actions and have Christianized them." Bultmann (240-41) adds: "the *Hellenistic* origin of [most of] the miracle stories is overwhelmingly the more probable" and "in Mark and most of all in his miracle stories Hellenism has made a vital contribution."

Apart from the questionable dichotomy between Palestinian and Hellenistic, the value of the parallels between Jesus and Apollonius has in the estimation of some been exaggerated (e.g., Twelftree, Koskenniemi, Evans). Better parallels are seen in the *rabbinic traditions, as well as in the OT and in some of the *pseudepigrapha. The principal miracles attributed to Apollonius that have often been compared with the miracles of Jesus are the following.

(1) Healing the Lame Man (Philostratus *Vit. Ap.* 3.39). By massaging a man's hip, Apollonius cures a man from his lameness.

(2) Healing the Blind Man (Philostratus *Vit. Ap.* 3.39). Not described.

(3) Healing the Paralytic (Philostratus *Vit. Ap.* 3.39). Not described.

(4) Healing the Woman (Philostratus *Vit. Ap.* 3.39). In order to assist a woman who had had severe trouble in childbirth, Apollonius tells her husband to carry a hare into the wife's chamber as she was about to give birth, circle the bed and then release the hare. If the hare were not driven out of the chamber, then the womb itself would extrude together with the newborn.

(5) Exorcism of the Demon from the Youth (Philostratus *Vit. Ap.* 4.20). The gaze of Apollonius terrifies the demon within the possessed youth, which then obediently exits and tips over a statue as it departs to prove that it has left. The youth recovered; abandoning his effeminate garb and his hedonistic way of life, he adopted the lifestyle of the philosophers and "donned their cloak" to follow Apollonius.

(6) Raising the Dead Girl (Philostratus *Vit. Ap.* 4.45). Intercepting a funeral in progress, Apollonius touches a girl who had died the very day she was to be wed and speaks her name. She awakens fully recovered. Relatives wish to bestow on Apollonius an enormous sum of money, which he said he would give to the bride as a dowry. Apollonius does admit that he had detected a spark of life in the girl, having perceived a "vapor that went up from her face."

(7) Miraculous Transports (Philostratus *Vit. Ap.* 4.10; 8.12). Stories are told how Apollonius seemingly could be at two places at once, or leave one place and be present at another instantly (e.g., from Smyrna to Ephesus).

(8) Ascension of Apollonius (Philostratus *Vit. Ap.* 8.30). Near the time of his death, Apollonius entered a temple whose doors opened for him and then closed behind him, and a voice was

heard, "Hasten thou from earth, hasten thou to heaven, hasten."

(9) Postmortem Appearance (Philostratus *Vit. Ap.* 8.31). The spirit of Apollonius is said to have spoken to a young man who doubted the former's immortality.

At first blush many of the miracles attributed to Apollonius find parallels in the ministry of Jesus. Jesus heals the lame (Mt 11:5 par. Lk 7:22; Mt 15:30-31), blind (Mk 8:22-26; Mt 9:27-31 par. Mk 10:46-52 and Lk 18:35-43), paralyzed (Mt 9:1-8 par. Mk 2:1-12 and Lk 5:17-26; Mt 12:9-14 par. Mk 3:1-6 and Lk 6:6-11), demonized (Mk 1:21-28 par. Lk 4:31-37; Mt 17:14-29 par. Mk 9:14-29 and Lk 9:37-43) and even raises the dead (Mt 9:18-19, 23-26 par. Mk 5:21-24, 35-43 and Lk 8:40-42, 49-56; Lk 7:11-17; Jn 11). Jesus is also said to have ascended (Lk 24:51; Acts 1:9). But there are no miraculous transports from one city to another (but cf. Jn 6:21, which is probably not a miraculous transport). Jesus touches people, even makes clay of spittle, but he does not massage disabled limbs, nor does he make use of animals or fetishes.

There are many features of the miracles and wonders attributed to Apollonius that find no parallel in the stories of Jesus. We encounter elements of gimmickry and trickery on the part of Apollonius, such as removing and replacing his foot in leg irons while in prison (*Vit. Ap.* 7.38). We find other bizarre elements, such as scaring off an evil spirit by writing a threatening letter (*Vit. Ap.* 3.38) or by making tripods walk and performing other telekinetic acts (*Vit. Ap.* 3.17; cf. Eusebius *Against the Life of Apollonius of Tyana* 18). There are some interesting parallels, but Apollonius comes across as a wizard (of which he is frequently accused). Many of his sayings and actions, moreover, are ostentatious. When the circumstances require, Apollonius does not hesitate to imply that he is a god. Some of his statements, including his apology before Emperor Domitian, smack of conceit and self-importance.

There is also serious question about the credibility of the sources utilized by Philostratus. B. F. Harris has concluded that the life of Apollonius is heavily seasoned with imagination and exaggeration. E. L. Bowie agrees and has criticized scholars for too readily giving credence to the stories attributed to Apollonius of Tyana.

See also HOLY MEN, JEWISH; NEO-PYTHAGOREANISM.

BIBLIOGRAPHY. E. L. Bowie, "Apollonius of Tyana: Tradition and Reality," *ANRW* 2.16.2 (1978) 1652-99; R. Bultmann, *The History of the Synoptic Tradition* (Oxford: Blackwell, 1968) 218-44; D. R. Cartlidge and D. L. Dungan, *Documents for the Study of the Gospels* (London and New York: William Collins; Philadelphia: Fortress, 1980) 205-42; F. C. Conybeare, *Philostratus: The Life of Apollonius of Tyana* (2 vols.; LCL 16-17; Cambridge, MA: Harvard University Press, 1912); M. Dibelius, *From Tradition to Gospel* (London: James Clarke, 1971) 70-103; C. A. Evans, "Jesus and Apollonius of Tyana," in *Jesus and His Contemporaries: Comparative Studies* (AGJU 25; Leiden: E. J. Brill, 1995) 245-50; M. Hadas and M. Smith, *Heroes and Gods: Spiritual Biographies in Antiquity* (London: Routledge & Kegan Paul, 1965) 196-258; B. F. Harris, "Apollonius of Tyana: Fact or Fiction?" *JRH* 5 (1969) 189-99; E. Koskenniemi, *Apollonius von Tyana in der neutestamentlichen Exegese* (WUNT 2.61; Tübingen: Mohr Siebeck, 1994); M. Smith, *Jesus the Magician* (New York: Harper & Row, 1979) esp. 87-93; G. H. Twelftree, *Jesus the Exorcist: A Contribution to the Study of the Historical Jesus* (WUNT 2.54; Tübingen: Mohr Siebeck, 1993; repr. Peabody, MA: Hendrickson, 1993) esp. 23-27.

C. A. Evans

APOSTOLIC FATHERS

"The apostolic fathers" has been a designation for a collection of early church documents for at least three hundred years. These individual manuscripts began to appear together in later centuries, so that the collection and terminology are post-Reformation. These discourses were written late in the first century or in the second century. They were called apostolic fathers because it was presumed that the authors had direct contact with the apostles. It is likely that in 1672 J. B. Cotelier, a French patristics scholar, first conceived of these early documents as special in that the writers presumably either knew one of the twelve apostles or at least were taught by someone who knew them. Cotelier's list was the *Epistle of Barnabas,* the letters of Ignatius, Polycarp's *Letter to the Philippians,* the *Martyrdom of Polycarp, 1 Clement, 2 Clement* and the *Shepherd of Hermas.* In 1875 a Parisian scholar, A. Gallandi, added the *Epistle to Diognetus,* the *Apology* of Quadratus and fragments of Papias. Later printed collections included the *Epistle to Diognetus* but not Quadratus or Papias (*see DLNTD,* Apostolic Fathers).

1. *Epistle of Barnabas*
2. *Didache*
3. Letters of Ignatius
4. Polycarp's *Letter to the Philippians*
5. *Martyrdom of Polycarp*
6. *First Clement*
7. *Second Clement*
8. *Shepherd of Hermas*
9. *Epistle to Diognetus*

1. *Epistle of Barnabas.*
The *Epistle of Barnabas* was written at the end of the NT period. Some of the early churchmen held the letter to be inspired and were disposed toward including it in the canon of the NT (*see* Canonical Formation of the New Testament). *Barnabas* is found in the Codex Sinaiticus, placed after OT and NT texts along with the *Shepherd of Hermas*. Clement of Alexandria cited *Barnabas* as though it were Scripture, and both Jerome and Clement declared it to be authored by the traveling companion of Paul, who in Acts was designated an apostle (Acts 14:14). Authorship by Barnabas, however, seems doubtful. It seems more likely that the name *Barnabas* was attached to the document in order to give it apostolic status. The *Epistle of Barnabas* was likely written A.D. 96-100, possibly in *Alexandria of Egypt (see Barnard).

The main contribution of the *Epistle of Barnabas* to the NT exegete is the manner in which it draws upon the OT and how its rhetoric and hermeneutic compares and contrasts with Hebrews and to a lesser extent with the writings of Paul. The document is more a discourse than a letter, much like Hebrews. The author recommends hope, righteousness according to judgment and the love of joy in an evil time. He declares that the OT prophets (by which he means from Moses on) heralded these latter times and disclosed the means of combating the malfeasance. He ends with the two-way teaching of embracing either light or darkness, life or death. Unlike Hebrews, which sustains a closely reasoned theological argument, *Barnabas* is a discursive marshaling of prophetic utterances.

Barnabas has no specific reference to contemporary Judaism. He believes that Israel failed in its response to God but that more importantly, the real message of the OT prophets anticipates the followers of Jesus. Like the writers of the NT Epistles, the author rarely references or quotes words and deeds of Jesus. By his time, Christians, as evidenced in the production of the canonical Gospels, relished the words and works of Jesus but still cited the OT as the authentic word from God. With some frequency *Barnabas* explicates extended allegorical meaning in texts, for example, in regard to the Numbers 18 offering of a heifer (*Barn* 8.1). The sacrifice clearly points ahead to Christ's sacrificial death. Though *Barnabas* employs allegorical interpretation, the application is more practical and theological than philosophical in a Philonic sense.

2. *Didache.*
The full title of the document now designated the *Didache* was *Teaching of the Twelve Apostles*. A subheading identified it as "the teaching of the Lord through the twelve apostles to the nations." The *Didache* was highly regarded in the fourth-century church and was believed in some quarters to have been composed by or in behalf of the original twelve disciples of Jesus, a conclusion that no scholar now embraces. It is thought to have been written between 80 and 120, probably in *Antioch of Syria and most likely by a Jewish Christian. The work bears comparison with the Pauline Pastoral Epistles and indicates how some NT injunctions are later fleshed out.

In this short work the author contrasts the way of life, which entails love and keeping God's commandments, with the way of death, which is filled with lust and other undesirable traits denounced in Scripture. Thereupon follow instructions in regard to foods, baptism, fasting, prayer, sound teaching, the roles of apostles and prophets, wandering Christians, bishops and deacons, monetary assistance, assembly, correction and warnings.

These instructions are grounded first in the OT, especially in regard to violations that lead to death. The instructions for the believing community incorporate many echoes from the Gospels and some from the Epistles, though some of these may be from common sources rather than directly from the NT writings. In terms of clear dependence, more allusions may be found to the Gospel of Matthew than to the other three. References tend to be short phrases and allusions rather than direct quotations. Their applications tend to be more literal rather than metaphorical or allegorical. In this manner the bringing in of biblical materials reflects a different hermeneutic than that of the *Epistle of Barnabas*. Almost no effort is directed toward showing how the OT was fulfilled in Christ.

3. Letters of Ignatius.

Ignatius (c. 35-107) was reputed to be the second bishop of (Syrian) *Antioch. He was singled out for martyrdom and traveled from Antioch to Rome accompanied by ten soldiers. Little is known about his life otherwise. On the journey across Asia Minor Ignatius wrote seven letters, probably during the years 105-110. These letters reflect what he considered the most pressing matters for the believers as he anticipated death. He made stops in Smyrna, where he was honored by Polycarp, and Troas. The letters from Smyrna were to Tralles, Magnesia, Ephesus and Rome. From Troas letters were sent to Philadelphia, Smyrna and Polycarp.

These letters are important to the exegete in regard to comparisons and contrasts with the canonical epistles. The purview of Ignatius's letters is somewhat more narrowly conceived, but they are worth consulting in regard to epistolary style and rhetorical features. The tendencies are less metaphorical and allegorical than, for example, are the works of Clement of Alexandria. In regard to topics they are especially helpful in respect to polity. Evidences of an early monoepiscopacy may be found in the letters, though the full meaning and implications are to a degree problematic. Another topic worthy of pursuit is the creedal material embedded in the letters. These may be compared and contrasted with creedal statements in the NT and with other early creeds such as the Apostolic Creed in its various versions. Perspectives on servanthood and martyrdom are also worthy of perusal. It should also be noted that Ignatius eschews heresy but is not too specific in regard to the sorts of heresy he has in mind. The most obvious seems to be some version of Docetism. He also highlights Christian OT foundations over the Jewish, but this is not a major concern. Other topics less developed include perspectives on the baptism of Jesus, the ramifications of the cross, the Lord's Supper, unity and Onesimus.

4. Polycarp's *Letter to the Philippians*.

Polycarp was a respected leader (bishop or elder) of the church in Smyrna. He was martyred in Smyrna, probably on February 23, 155. He wrote an epistle to the church in Philippi in conjunction with efforts of Irenaeus and at their request. The letter that has survived may be the conflating of two of his letters. The letter of Polycarp is of interest because of the manner in which he cites NT Epistles. In contrast with *Barnabas,* he refers little to the OT. He infrequently cites the Gospels but on occasion refers to Matthew. His use of statements from the Epistles is mostly straightforward with little metaphorical implication. He cites epistles not so much by way of shoring up his points but as a manner of amplification.

The epistle sets out a profile of righteousness. Polycarp mostly provides exterior specifics rather than theological or psychological ramifications, in contrast to Paul's theological reflection upon God, the cross and the Parousia. Polycarp also rejects a docetic christology, perhaps with Marcion in mind, but this is not certain. Comparison and contrast with the Johannine epistles will be of value. In addition, he emphasizes the unity of the church and the need to respect church leaders.

5. *Martyrdom of Polycarp*.

The *Martyrdom of Polycarp* was apparently written by a witness to Polycarp's martyrdom not long after it occurred, February 23, 155. The author clearly parallels the death of Polycarp with that of Jesus. The *Martyrdom* assumes an epistolary form, but aside from the introduction and conclusion it may best be described as a discourse on martyrdom. Little reference is made to Scripture, but a knowledge of the death of Christ in a Gospel or the Gospels is presupposed.

The *Martyrdom of Polycarp* is the first in a catalog of Christian martyrdoms, unless one includes Paul's reflections on death for Christ's sake or certain comments in Revelation. In order to explicate NT depictions, a foray into the martyrdom literature is of value. In the *Martyrdom of Polycarp* Christians are dissuaded from seeking out martyrdom but are not to resist it if no other avenue is available. The grounds for standing firm according to conviction is expressed in this document. Especially of concern are the previous actions of Christ and the confidence that God will give life anew to those who have witnessed unto death.

6. *First Clement*.

1 Clement is normally accepted as an authentic

letter from Clement of Rome to the church in Corinth sometime between 81-96. If so, it is among the earliest of the noncanonical Christian materials. The situation assumes rifts in the church at Corinth. It is interesting, however, that the causes are not addressed directly as, for example, in Paul's first letter to the Corinthians. The form is epistolary, but it incorporates elements of Greek diatribe and synagogue homiletic style. A number of references are made to the OT with occasional quotations, especially from Genesis. The biblical examples are incorporated so as to illustrate the results of jealousy and division. The references to the Gospels are largely from Matthew. Some of the letters of Paul were apparently familiar to Clement, as was the epistle of James. Little allegorical or metaphorical use is found. *1 Clement* was often alluded to by Clement of Alexandria (150-215), and he adduces evidence that various early churchmen considered it inspired and belonging in the canon.

1 Clement focuses on the fractures that appeared in the Corinthian community. The ideal church situation exhibits order or peace. The case for peace is expounded not so much from the ramifications of the cross, as in 1 Corinthians, but through the advancement of OT examples, which by contrast display the deleterious consequences of jealousy and strife (though Clement does emphasize the humility of Christ). Repentance and obedience are the solution. Order, Clement argues, is endemic in nature, almost as in Stoic thought, and all aspects of creation demonstrate obedience. Perennial incidents of revived nature likewise establish sufficient grounds for affirming the resurrection of Christ, as does the legend of the Phoenix metaphorically.

7. *Second Clement*.
On the grounds of internal style and the absence of external evidence, *2 Clement* has been assigned to an unknown author who postdates Clement of Rome. Clement of Alexandria did not seem to know of *2 Clement,* and the early church historian Eusebius questioned its authenticity. The style is that of a tractate or an early homily rather than an epistle. Some have supposed that it is a letter addressed to the Corinthian church at a later date, and since it was stored with *1 Clement,* have presumed it to be by the same author. The document should probably be dated between 120 and 140. It includes many references to Isaiah, and its allusions to the NT are more numerous than those found in *1 Clement.* The author obviously knew the canonical Epistles as well as the Synoptic Gospels, particularly Matthew and Luke.

The author affirms the God relationship of Christ and the salvation that he alone provided. Believers therefore need to respond in service and obedience. The Christian life is one of righteousness and holiness, and the wayward are exhorted to heed the call for repentance. The author for the most part addresses general problems rather than situations explicitly located in the Corinthian church.

8. *Shepherd of Hermas*.
The *Shepherd of Hermas* is of particular value for the study of the *apocalyptic genre of biblical materials, but also for legal and parabolic materials. It reflects both similarities and differences. The setting for the document is ostensibly Rome during a time of persecution. The date is less certain, and if the work is in two parts the first (1—24) is from about 90-110, and the second (25—114) is from about 100-150. The work falls into three parts: *Visions* (1—25), *Commandments* (26—49) and *Parables* (50—113). The *Shepherd* was highly respected and sometimes regarded as canonical. Jerome and Origen argued that the author was the Hermas of Romans 16:14. In the second vision (*Herm.* 8.3) Clement is mentioned, and some scholars argue he is the author of *1 Clement.*

Since the author is reporting original visions, he makes no appeal to the Scriptures so as to authenticate his statements. Few quotations from the OT or the NT may be found, but allusions to both are present, especially the Gospels and James. The allusions are not as clear or as frequent, however, as are those to the OT in the canonical Revelation. Scriptures are employed in much the same manner as in Revelation, that is, to amplify with canonical language specific statements. The intentional metaphorical use of Scripture is minimal. The visions and parables, however, depend on highly metaphorical or symbolic entities in regard to the church and heavenly powers. The visions in their narrativity look forward more to John Bunyan's *Pilgrim's Progress* rather than back to prior biblical materials. Key topics in the *Shepherd of Hermas* have to do with repentance, purity, the church and loyalty to it, the characteristics of the Spirit and christology. The author is especially interested in whether forgiveness is possible after having been baptized, arguing that it is, but only once.

9. *Epistle to Diognetus.*

The author of *Diognetus* is unknown but most likely is a non-Jewish Christian who wrote toward the end of the second century. Scholars have suggested various dates between 117 and 310. The consensus view is that the document consists of two separately circulated parts later joined. The first (1—10) is in the form of a letter. The second (11—12) is a treatise or a homily. Though the document is not a narrative history of Christianity as is Acts, a comparison of the apologetic outlook of each is rewarding.

The author speaks of Christianity as a new way of worship, neither pagan nor Jewish. Christianity is a third way. Pagans, he charges, worship objects made from stone, wood and metal, using arguments similar to those of Isaiah 44. It is not certain, however, that he is drawing on Isaiah. The Jews in contrast with the pagans have rules with respect to the sabbath and other celebrations that impede human welfare and become idolatrous. Christians live as all others in outward appearance but are pilgrims in the world, a third race. They do not expose their children (i.e., abandon infants), and they love all persons. Christians constitute the soul of the people of the world, just as the individual soul sustains the body. Christians are imprisoned in the world and thereby support the world. The last section of the epistle extols the committed life, and such believers are destined to enjoy the fruits that God has provided. Allusions to Scripture mostly borrow biblical language and ideas.

See also APOCRYPHAL ACTS AND EPISTLES; APOCRYPHAL GOSPELS; CANONICAL FORMATION OF THE NEW TESTAMENT.

BIBLIOGRAPHY. **Texts and Translations.** E. J. Goodspeed, *The Apostolic Fathers: An American Translation* (New York: Harper & Brothers, 1950); R. M. Grant, ed., *The Apostolic Fathers: A New Translation and Commentary* (6 vols.; New York.: Thomas Nelson, 1964-68); K. Lake, *The Apostolic Fathers* (2 vols.; LCL 24/25; Cambridge, MA: Harvard University Press, 1977); J. B. Lightfoot and J. R. Harmer, *The Apostolic Fathers,* rev. and ed. M. W. Holmes (2d ed.; Grand Rapids, MI: Baker, 1992). **Studies.** B. Altaner, *Patrology* (Freiburg: Herder, 1960); R. E. Brown and J. P. Meier, *Antioch and Rome: New Testament Cradles of Christianity* (New York: Paulist, 1983); L. W. Barnard, "The Problem of the *Epistle of Barnabas,*" *CQR* 159 (1958) 211-30; V. Corwin, *St. Ignatius and Christianity in Antioch* (Yale University Publications in Religion 1; New Haven, CT: Yale University Press, 1960); F. L. Cross, *The Early Christian Fathers* (London: Gerald Duckworth, 1960); K. P. Donfried, *The Setting of Second Clement in Early Christianity* (NovTSup 38; Leiden: E. J. Brill, 1974); E. Ferguson, ed., *Encyclopedia of Early Christianity* (New York: Garland, 1990); W. H. C. Frend, *Martyrdom and Persecution in the Early Church* (Oxford: Oxford University Press, 1965) 268-302; idem, *The Rise of Christianity* (Philadelphia: Fortress, 1985); R. M. Grant, *Greek Apologists of the Second Century* (Philadelphia: Westminster, 1988); D. A. Hagner, *The Use of the Old and New Testaments in Clement of Rome* (NovTSup 34; Leiden: E. J. Brill, 1973); P. N. Harrison, *Polycarp's Two Epistles to the Philippians* (Cambridge: Cambridge University Press, 1936); C. N. Jefford, *Reading the Apostolic Fathers: An Introduction* (Peabody, MA: Hendrickson, 1996); H. Koester, *Introduction to the New Testament* (2 vols.; Philadelphia: Fortress, 1982); R. A. Kraft, *Barnabas and the Didache* (The Apostolic Fathers 3; New York: Thomas Nelson, 1965); H. G. Meecham, *The Epistle to Diognetus* (Manchester: Manchester University, 1949); C. Osiek, *Rich and Poor in the Shepherd of Hermas: An Exegetical-Social Investigation* (CBQMS 15; Washington, DC: Catholic Biblical Association, 1983); J. Quasten, *Patrology* (Westminster, MD: Christian Classics, 1990) vols. 1-4; J. A. Robinson, *Barnabas, Hermas and the Didache* (New York: Macmillan, 1920); T. A. Robinson, *The Early Church: An Annotated Bibliography of Literature in English* (Metuchen, NJ: Scarecrow, 1993); W. F. Schoedel, *Ignatius of Antioch: A Commentary on the Letters of Ignatius of Antioch* (Philadelphia: Fortress, 1985); idem, *Polycarp, Martyrdom of Polycarp, Fragments of Papias* (The Apostolic Fathers 5; New York: Thomas Nelson, 1965) 3-49; J. C. Wilson, *Toward a Reassessment of the Shepherd of Hermas: Its Date and Its Pneumatology* (Lewiston, NY: Edwin Mellen Press, 1993).

T. H. Olbricht

APOTHEOSIS. *See* HEAVENLY ASCENT IN JEWISH AND PAGAN TRADITIONS.

AQUILA. *See* SEPTUAGINT/GREEK OLD TESTAMENT.

ARAMAIC LANGUAGE

Aramaic was one of the major languages of the ancient Middle East. Along with Canaanite (Phoenician, Hebrew, Moabite, Edomite) and Ugaritic, it belongs to the Northwest group of Semitic languages. Aramaic is distinguished within the Northwest Semitic languages by having an article *the* marked at the end of a noun and by the lack of a verb pattern with prefix "*n*" (the Niphal in Hebrew). Characteristic syntax, vocabulary and sound changes also distinguish the language at various time periods.

1. History
2. The Names *Aramaic* and *Syrian*, or *Syriac*
3. Dialects of Aramaic and the New Testament
4. Written and/or Spoken Aramaic: Dialect Models for First-Century Aramaic
5. Aramaic or Hebrew Style in the Gospels?
6. The Language of Jesus' Teaching
7. The Origin and Importance of the Aramaic Targums

1. History.

Already in the ninth century B.C. we find Aramaic being used for royal *inscriptions, as evidenced by the recently discovered Tel Dan inscription. For such inscriptions, the kingdom of Sam'al (Zincirli, near the present border between Turkey and Syria) switched from Phoenician in the ninth century to a local Aramaic dialect and then to a more standard Old Aramaic dialect within three generations. The Assyrian Empire started to use the Aramaic language for official documents and inscriptions by the eighth century B.C. A bilingual text from Tel Fakhariye in Akkadian and Aramaic makes this clear. The biblical account of the siege of Jerusalem in 701 B.C. (Is 36:11) gives further testimony to the widespread use of Aramaic as a diplomatic language.

Aramaic attained its most prestigious position as a world language under the Persian Empire (*see* Jewish History: Persian Period). During the period of the Persian Empire it was the preeminent international, legal and administrative language throughout the ancient Near East. Its status was upset by the conquests of *Alexander the Great (d. 323 B.C.) and the rapid spread of *Hellenism and Greek culture in the following century. Affairs of state were conducted in Greek. The power of the Greek city-state and its role in spreading Greek literature and culture made Greek the dominant political and administrative language for much of the Near East from that time throughout the Roman and Byzantine periods, right up to the Arabic conquests in the seventh century A.D.

Along with *Greek and *Hebrew, Aramaic was one of the three languages in most common use in the land of Israel during the first century of this era. It is the language most commonly mentioned in NT scholarship as providing the Semitic background for the teaching of Jesus.

Aramaic retained considerable importance as a language for daily affairs, commerce, legal formulas and religious traditions, and its influence continued for over a millennium after Alexander's conquest. Aramaic dialects continued to be spoken and used from the East Mediterranean Sea to Central Asia to the Indian Ocean. Aramaic loanwords appear in the Qur'an and classical Arabic. Much of the postmishnaic *rabbinic literature and the literature of Eastern Christianity was written in later Aramaic dialects. Isolated pockets of modern Aramaic dialects have survived to the present. A Western Aramaic descendent is spoken in Ma`lula (50 km northeast of Damascus, Syria) and descendants of Central-Eastern dialects are still spoken in some communities in Turkey, Azerbaijan, Iran and Iraq.

2. The Names *Aramaic* and *Syrian*, or *Syriac.*

The Aramaic language developed in the area of present-day Syria, a region whose ancient name from the end of the second millennium B.C. was Aram (Aramu). Already in the ninth century its name appeared in Assyrian as *'armitu* ("language of Aram"; cf. *'ărāmît* in Is 36:11), and that remained its standard name in the ancient Near East (cf. *'ărāmît* in Dan 2:4; Ezra 4:7).

With the spread of Greek culture and language a new name for Aramaic developed. The Greeks used the name Syria for the old area of Aram. In Greek the name of the Aramaic language became *syriakē glōssa* ("Syrian language") and as an adverb *syristi* ("in Syrian"). For example, the *Septuagint translates *'ărāmît* as *Syristi.* In addition, an appendix to the Septuagint of Job 42:17 mentions translating the book "from the Syrian language" (*ek tēs Syriakēs*), evidently referring to using an Aramaic translation of Job.

In the *Letter of Aristeas* (*see* Aristeas, Epistle of), paragraph 11, we read "They [Jews] are assumed to use Aramaic (*Syriakē*) [for their Scriptures], but it isn't, it is a different manner of language [i.e., the Bible is Hebrew]."

In the land of Israel and among rabbis the Greek name was taken over into Hebrew as *sursi:* "Rabbi Yonatan of Bet Guvrin [late third century A.D.] said, 'there are four languages useful in the world, Greek for song, Latin for war, Sursi [Aramaic] for mourning and Hebrew for speech'" (*y. Soṭa* 7.2). Also Rabbi Shmuel bar Nahman (c. A.D. 300) said in the name of Rabbi Yochanan (third century A.D.), "Don't treat the Sursi language as insignificant. It is used in the Torah, Prophets and Writings" (*y. Soṭa* 7.2) [Gen 31:47; Jer 10:11; Dan 2:4b—7:28; Ezra 4:8—6:18; 7:12-26]. Aramaic is not specifically named in the NT. At Acts 1:19 "in their language" is used for an Aramaic name "Blood Field," *ḥ^{a}qēl dāmā*ʾ.

Many scholars think that when Hebrew is mentioned in the NT (Jn 5:2; 19:13, 17, 20; 20:16; Acts 21:40; 22:2; 26:14 [Rev 9:11; 16:16]) it refers usually to Aramaic. However, the proof for such a usage is weak and limited to proper names, where the etymology of the names is technically Aramaic (Jn 5:2; 19:13, 17). Names are a special category of language and can be adopted into a language. For example, in America Ian is a British name that means "beloved," though etymologically it is Hebrew. Similarly, calling names Hebrew that were etymologically Aramaic should not be taken to mean that "Hebrew" meant "Aramaic."

In John 20:16 *rabbouni* is correctly called Hebrew. The dialectical form *rabbûni* ("my teacher") is found in Mishnaic Hebrew at *Taʿanit* 3:8 in Codex Kaufman, the most reliable manuscript of the Mishnah. (The standard form in *Targum Onqelos* and also later Hebrew is *ribbôn,* which apparently reflects a Babylonian vocalization tradition. The older Hebrew vocalization *rabbûni* could also occur in Aramaic. It has been found in at least one vocalized genizah manuscript of the Palestinian targum tradition at Genesis 44:18).

3. Dialects of Aramaic and the New Testament. The most important dialects for NT background span a period from the sixth century B.C. to the tenth century A.D. The earlier phases of the language in this period are Official Aramaic and Middle Aramaic. By the Late Aramaic phase (third century A.D. to tenth century), there are three distinct dialectic areas: Western Late Aramaic (Galilean, Samaritan and Christian Palestinian Aramaic) Central Late Aramaic, (Syriac) and Eastern Late Aramaic (Babylonian Talmudic Aramaic and Mandean).

Official Aramaic (700-200 B.C.) became the standard written language of the Persian Empire (sixth to fourth centuries). This is the dialect of the Biblical Aramaic (BA) texts in Ezra and Daniel, with some allowance made for spelling changes.

Middle Aramaic is a name given to the various dialects attested from 200 B.C. to A.D. 200 (Fitzmyer 1979, 57-84). During this period there appears to have been a dialect continuum from Nabatean to Judean/Qumran (QA) to Palmyran to Syriac and Hatran (Cook 1992). The Official dialect no longer dominated written Aramaic, and local dialect features more and more penetrated into the written language. The dialects from this period are only sparsely attested except for the documents found in the Dead Sea area. Late Aramaic dialects (post-A.D. 200) show more diversity and are better attested.

The *targums of *Onqelos* to the Torah and *Jonathan* to the Prophets (TO/J) raise special questions as to their dialect. Many scholars attribute the basic consonantal text of these targums to Judea from the first or second centuries A.D. while acknowledging that the tradition was revised and vocalized in Babylonia beginning with the third century. However, they may represent a written dialect whose origin is more Central than the Western Late Aramaic dialects (see Cook 1994).

Galilean Aramaic (GA) is the name often given to the Jewish Palestinian Aramaic dialect found in parts of the Jerusalem *Talmud and midrashim. These reflect the period of A.D. 300 to 600. Inscriptions in Judea show that this dialect was influential beyond Galilee.

The dialect of Palestinian Targumic Aramaic (PTrA) consists of fragments from the Cairo Genizah, Codex Neofiti and the *Fragmentary Targum.* It is close to that of Galilean Aramaic, but it appears to be a separate and slightly earlier dialect, perhaps from the second century A.D., and perhaps from Judea (see Tal 1979, 1986).

Samaritan Aramaic is roughly contemporary to Galilean Aramaic and Christian Palestinian Aramaic and has been preserved in the religious literature of the Samaritan community. It is important for tracing the development of Western Late Aramaic.

Christian Palestinian Aramaic (CPA) is mainly

preserved in church lectionaries of the Bible. This Western Late Aramaic dialect is from the sixth to the eighth centuries A.D. and represents the continuation of Judean Aramaic from the first half of the first millennium A.D.

Syriac is a major literary language whose dialectical origin was centered in Edessa. It is our most widely documented Late Aramaic dialect. It is useful for NT studies from many perspectives. Textually, it preserves ancient translations and textual traditions of the NT. Historically, it preserves the teachings, records and literature of the Aramaic-speaking churches. Along with its importance, a caveat must be sounded for the NT student: Syriac is not a Palestinian Aramaic dialect, and it does not directly preserve first-century Aramaic traditions. The Old Syriac Gospels and the Syriac Peshitta versions are translations from Greek. On the positive side, they do show how the Greek NT was interpreted in the second to the fifth centuries A.D. by bilingual speakers.

4. Written and/or Spoken Aramaic: Dialect Models for First-Century Aramaic.

The question of a distinct written dialect over against a colloquial dialect has been debated in evaluating the nature of the Aramaic material. The Palestinian targum(s), and even more so Galilean Aramaic, are distinct from the Qumran Aramaic texts. How is this difference to be explained? Two broad approaches have been taken.

One school of thought attributes the main differences between Qumran Aramaic and Palestinian Targumic Aramaic to time and somewhat to geography. The Palestinian targums are close to Galilean Aramaic but they lack some forms with final-*nun* that are so prominent in Galilean Aramaic. This makes these Palestinian Targumic Aramaic forms parallel both to earlier Qumran Aramaic and later Christian Palestinian Aramaic forms. Palestinian Targumic Aramaic also uses a separated object pronoun like Christian Palestinian Aramaic. This hints at a Judean origin of the Palestinian Targum. But the difference of the Palestinian Targum from Qumran Aramaic and its closeness to Galilean Aramaic would point to a later time than Qumran Aramaic and an earlier time than Galilean Aramaic or Christian Palestinian Aramaic. The Palestinian Targum may represent a Galilean development of a second-century A.D. Judean tradition. The Bar Kokhba disaster (A.D. 135) would be the obvious historical catalyst for the process (Tal 1986).

Another school of thought views the Palestinian targums and Talmud (grouped together) as being closer to the spoken dialects and closer to colloquial first-century Aramaic. The Aramaic of Qumran is viewed as literary and not a good example of spoken Aramaic. In this approach the documents of Qumran Aramaic are literary and Palestinian Targumic Aramaic/Galilean Aramaic are colloquial, and Palestinian Targumic Aramaic is claimed to be contemporary in origin to Qumran Aramaic.

Two lines of argument support the viewpoint that time is the more predominant factor over against the literary/colloquial explanation for the dialect distinctions.

First and foremost, all of the texts in question were written. Qumran, the Palestinian Targum and later Galilean texts are all written texts. It is especially problematic to take later religious, liturgical texts like the Palestinian Targum and pose them as pure colloquial texts.

Second, there appears to have been an Aramaic "dialect continuum" in existence in Middle Aramaic. There was not a dominating, standard literary dialect. A dialect continuum implies colloquial contact throughout the region, and this was reflected to some degree in the writing, since the dialect continuum is only observed in writing. Thus the literary nature of the Judean desert documents should not be overemphasized (*see* Dead Sea Scrolls). A careful comparison of Qumran Aramaic shows that it was already accepting colloquial and dialectical changes. Qumran Aramaic was no longer under a tight model of the Official Aramaic of the Persian Empire or any standardized Aramaic.

The Qumran texts are contemporary to the NT and therefore are the best examples of what written Aramaic would look like from the first century and are probably the best examples of what colloquial Aramaic would have looked like when written down.

5. Aramaic or Hebrew Style in the Gospels?

The Gospels of Matthew, Mark, Luke and John all appear to have been written in Greek, though they all show varying degrees and kinds of Semitic influence (*see* Semitic Influence on the New Testament). Written Greek sources that go back to Semitic sources for some or much of their material remains probable. Is it possible to tell whether the Semitic sources would have been more probably in Hebrew or Aramaic?

First-century and Middle Aramaic narratives from Qumran show a particular style with a narrative conjunction *edayin,* "then." This shows up in unstylized Greek translation as *tote,* "then" (Buth 1990). Mark and Luke both reflect Semitic style, yet both clearly lack a narrative conjunction *tote.* This combination of evidence that is positive toward Semitic influence yet negative for Aramaic narrative would point directly to Hebrew as the more likely source for Semitic material behind Mark and Luke.

Matthew writes Greek with an Aramaic style, especially in his using *tote* ("then, next") as a narrative conjunction. Comparison with the other Gospels makes it unlikely that Matthew's style was representative of some kind of Jewish-Greek dialect. Comparison with the other Gospels also makes it unlikely that this style represents a source. The narrative conjunction "then" occurs in triple tradition, material shared only with Mark, double tradition with Luke, and Matthew's own material. Matthew's Greek is best described as a distinctive idiolect. If Matthew is working from Mark, then his Aramaizing Greek style is almost certainly his own and not reflecting a source.

At the same time, the existence of such an Aramaizing Greek style by Matthew adds to our understanding of first-century Aramaic. It reinforces the picture that our Qumran Aramaic narrative texts accurately reflect first-century Aramaic style and strengthens the claim that the Semitic sources behind Mark and Luke were Hebrew, not Aramaic.

6. The Language of Jesus' Teaching.

Especially since H. Birkeland's monograph in 1954, the question of the language in which Jesus taught has been continually debated (*see* Greek of the New Testament). A few scholars have argued Greek as a major teaching language, though Jesus' interaction with first-century Jewish culture and rabbinic idiom throughout the Gospels make that improbable. The majority of those who have dealt with the issue have argued for Aramaic as the primary language of teaching. Evidence of inscriptions, Aramaic words in the NT, Aramaic papyri, Aramaic in the Jerusalem Talmud and the existence of the targums (but see below) are brought forward to show that Aramaic was probably the most common spoken language in the Galilee and thus arguably the most appropriate and probable as Jesus' language.

The Aramaic quotations in Mark 5:41, Mark 7:34 (understanding *ephphatha* not as Hebrew but as a dialectical form of Aramaic *ʾetpataḥ)* and Mark 15:34, are more enigmatic than helpful in revealing the language in which Jesus taught. (Mark 15:34 is too complex textually and synoptically to treat in this article. Matthew's phrase is better, while Mark may be hinting at a midrashic interpretation or a divine voice.) The words in Mark 5:41 and Mark 7:34 are "insipid" and do not contribute any insight into Jesus' teaching in the way that modern readers might expect from the trouble of quoting foreign material. Of all of Jesus' words, why quote these? Their purpose may have been to provide a Roman audience with a sense of mystery and awe to some healing accounts. If Mark's language switch implies that Jesus switched languages, then the words would imply that Jesus did not normally teach in Aramaic.

Another approach to the sociolinguistic problem is to investigate the language used commonly in the first century by the Jewish teachers and miracle workers. Who communicated with the people, who won their hearts and respect? What language did those teachers use? The rabbinic literature paints a fairly uniform picture up into the second century A.D. Such a picture is reinforced by the *Dead Sea Scrolls, in which Hebrew was still alive in the first century and Second Temple period. From the evidence we have, one would expect that Hebrew would most probably be used for parables (*see* Rabbinic Parables), *prayers, scriptural exposition, sermons and the oral "publication" of a teaching—in short, for much of the oral material in our Gospels. On balance this would argue strongly for Hebrew as Jesus' teaching language, and such a view would fit with the Hebraic color of written source material to the Gospels (see 5 above).

We must remember that the Jewish society was highly multilingual. One needs to be careful with claims of unique Aramaisms because most are also found in Mishnaic Hebrew, and vice versa. For example, Hebrew *rabbûni,* mentioned above, is often cited as only a colloquial Aramaic word. Words like *korban (qorbān),* abba *(ʾabbāʾ)* and *raka (rêqā)* were both Mishnaic Hebrew and Aramaic. Rabbinic idioms like "kingdom of heaven," "bind and loose," "establish this Scripture," "debt" (for sin) and "sons of the bride-chamber" are in Hebrew in sayings from Tannaim (Jewish teachers before A.D. 200) and in both Hebrew and Aramaic in sayings from Amoraim (teachers after 200). Even in the later Talmudic age, up through the sixth century, Jewish children were expected to understand Hebrew in the Galilee, though the children sometimes had trouble doing so (Fraade 1992).

7. The Origin and Importance of the Aramaic Targums.

The Jewish community preserved various Aramaic translations of the Bible that raise many important issues for NT studies (*see* Rabbinic Literature: Targumim). The Aramaic translations include much material that reflects some of the interpretation current at their time of composition.

Most scholars working after the discovery of the Dead Sea Scrolls have argued or assumed that the texts of *Onqelos* and *Jonathan* started out in Judea and were taken to Babylon. Recently, E. M. Cook has made a good case for suggesting that they are not Judean but early Central/Syrian (Cook 1994).

Perhaps equally important is the question of when these targumic traditions started. *Onqelos* and *Jonathan* are missing from Qumran. (The only clear evidence of any targum at Qumran are two copies of Job, a unique work in the Hebrew Bible. There is also a piece of an Aramaic document related to Leviticus 16; *see* Aramaic Targums: Qumran.) This silence is quite loud in comparison to the many Aramaic texts found at Qumran and would suggest that the origins of *Onqelos* and *Jonathan* are more probably to be dated after A.D. 70 than before. But they probably arrived in Babylon before 200.

The Palestinian Targum traditions complicate this picture. They are distinct from Qumran Aramaic yet have ties to Judean Aramaic and are also close to later Galilean Aramaic. Their dialect would testify to the late second century A.D. or early third century as the most likely period of formation. Thus the time of origin of both *Onqelos/Jonathan* and the Palestinian Targum may overlap in the second century. The Palestinian Targum is likely to have been written down from A.D. 150 to 250 and *Onqelos/Jonathan* sometime between A.D. 70 and 200.

The Palestinian Targum contains considerably more midrashic, interpretative material than *Onqelos/Jonathan*. The *Onqelos/Jonathan* tradition may represent a stripped-down targumic style that was more appropriate in Bablyon, where more of a need for the simple explanation of the Hebrew text was felt. The *Onqelos/Jonathan* targum chose a more Central Aramaic dialect and a more conservative translation style than the Palestinian. In contrast, the Palestinian Targum clearly uses a local Western dialect and includes much interpretive material. It provided a rabbinic spin to the reading of the Bible.

The Aramaic targums are especially important as a depository of traditional interpretations. For example the targum to the Psalms 118:22 mentions that the "stone" is *talya*, "the child." The targum reads: "the child that the builders left behind was the descendants of Jesse and qualified to be appointed to reign." This would seem to preserve an old pluralistic/collective messianic interpretation based on the Hebrew midrashic development of the wordplay *ʾeben*, "stone," and *ben*, "son." Of additional interest is the fact that *Midrash Tehillim* does not record this tradition for this verse. The Aramaic targum is our only source.

The biggest problem with the targumic literature for the NT is one of dating. One must carefully compare Qumran, intertestamental, rabbinic and targumic traditions before concluding whether material was or was not a part of the first-century background to the NT.

Much work remains to be done on all of the above areas of investigation. The Qumran and rabbinic texts are being published in more accessible and reliable editions. They are also becoming available electronically. A Comprehensive Aramaic Dictionary Project is integrating much of this material. The fields of Aramaic and the linguistic background to the NT are in a positive flux. The new Hebrew and Aramaic texts made available in the last half of the twentieth century are still being carefully sifted and are adding to our knowledge.

See also ARAMAIC TARGUMIM: QUMRAN; GREEK OF THE NEW TESTAMENT; HEBREW LANGUAGE; LATIN LANGUAGE; RABBINIC LITERATURE; SEMITIC INFLUENCE ON THE NEW TESTAMENT.

BIBLIOGRAPHY. K. Beyer, *Die aramäischen Texte vom Toten Meer* (Göttingen: Vandenhoeck & Ruprecht, 1984); idem, *Die aramäischen Texte vom Toten Meer (Ergänzungsband)* (Göttingen: Vandenhoeck & Ruprecht, 1994); H. Birkeland, *The*

Language of Jesus (Avhandlinger Utgitt av det Norske Videnkaps-Akademi i Oslo II. Hist.-Filos. Kl., 1954/1; Oslo: Jacob Dybwad, 1954); R. Buth, "Edayin/Tote—Anatomy of a Semitism in Jewish Greek," *Maarav* 5-6 (1990) 33-48; B. Chilton, "Eight Theses on the Use of Targums in Interpreting the New Testament," in *Judaic Approaches to the Gospels,* ed. B. Chilton (Atlanta: Scholars Press, 1994) 305-15; E. M. Cook, "A New Perspective on the Language of Onkelos and Jonathan," in *The Aramaic Bible: Targums in Their Historical Context,* ed D. R. G. Beattie (Sheffield: JSOT, 1994) 142-56; idem, "Qumran Aramaic and Aramaic Dialectology," in *Studies in Qumran Aramaic,* ed. T. Muraoka (Supplement 3.1-21; Louvain: Peeters, 1992); S. E. Fassberg, *A Grammar of the Palestinian Targum Fragments from the Cairo Geniza* (HSS; Atlanta: Scholars Press, 1979); J. A. Fitzmyer, *A Wandering Aramean: Collected Aramaic Essays* (SBLMS 25; Chico, CA: Scholars Press, 1979); J. A. Fitzmyer and D. J. Harrington, *A Manual of Palestinian Aramaic Texts* (BibO 34; Rome: Biblical Institute, 1978); J. A. Fitzmyer and S. Kaufmann, *An Aramaic Bibliography,* Part 1: *Old, Official and Biblical Aramaic* (CALP; Baltimore, MD: Johns Hopkins University Press, 1992); S. D. Fraade, "Rabbinic Views on the Practice of Targum and Multilingualism in the Jewish Galilee of the Third-Sixth Centuries," in *The Galilee in Late Antiquity,* ed. L. I. Levine (New York: Jewish Theological Seminary of America, 1992) 253-86; S. A. Kaufmann, "Dating the Language of the Palestinian Targums and Their Use in the Study of the First Century CE Texts," in *The Aramaic Bible: Targums in Their Historical Context,* ed. D. R. G. Beattie (Sheffield: JSOT, 1994) 118-41; E. Y. Kutscher, *Studies in Galilean Aramaic* (Ramat-Gan, Israel: Bar-Ilan University Press, 1976); C. Levias, *A Grammar of Galilean Aramaic to the Language of the Jerusalem Talmud and the Midrashim* (Hebrew) (New York: Jewish Theological Seminary of America, 1986); T. Muraoka, "The Aramaic of the Old Targum of Job from Qumran Cave XI," *JJS* 25 (1974) 425-43; Z. Safrai, "The Origins of Reading the Aramaic Targum in Synagogue," *Immanuel* 24-25: *The New Testament and Christian-Jewish Dialogue: Studies in Honor of David Flusser* (1990) 187-93; M. Sokoloff, *A Dictionary of Jewish Palestinian Aramaic of the Byzantine Period* (Ramat-Gan, Israel: Bar-Ilan University Press, 1990); A. Tal, "The Dialects of Jewish Palestinian Aramaic and the Palestinian Targum of the Pentateuch," *Sefarad* 46 (1986) 441-48; idem, "Layers in the Jewish Aramaic of Palestine: The Appended Nun as a Criterion" (Hebrew) *Lešonénu* 43 (1979) 165-84.

R. Buth

ARAMAIC TARGUMIM: QUMRAN

Only three texts of Aramaic translations of the Bible have been discovered in the Qumran vicinity. (An Aramaic translation in a Jewish cultural context is usually referred to as a targum, which is an Aramaic and Hebrew word for "translation.") Yet these three texts give us important, new data on Jewish use of the Bible in the first century. Paradoxically, the general lack of Aramaic biblical translations at Qumran may be as important for our understanding of Jewish practices as the texts that have been discovered.

1. The Texts
2. The Significance of the Qumran Targumim

1. The Texts.

Two Aramaic translations of a biblical text were discovered in 1952 in Cave 4 and were published in 1977.

4Q156 (4QtgLev) comprises two fragments that contain eight verses, Leviticus 16:12-15, 18-21, and have been dated on paleographic grounds to the end of the second century B.C. The translation style is quite literal and close to the Masoretic Hebrew text. It does not exactly match any of the later written targums (*Onqelos, Jonathan, Neofiti, Pseudo-Jonathan*).

4Q157 (4QtgJob), the other Aramaic translation found in Cave 4, contains Job 3:5 and 4:16—5:4. The translation style of this fragment is also literal. Neither of these two Cave 4 texts shows midrashic interpretations characteristic of much Jewish targumic material, though since they are short fragments, such a conclusion may be based on an accidental argument from silence (*see* Rabbinic Literature: Midrashim; Rabbinic Literature: Targumim).

A third Aramaic translation of a biblical text was discovered in Cave 11 in 1956. Significantly, it is also an Aramaic translation of Job. This text of Job, 11QtgJob, was published for the first time in 1971, and the fragments cover parts of Job 17—42.

The dialect of Aramaic represented in this Qumran text is of a literary type that includes a few features that faintly hint at the East, far from Judea. The same features give it a slightly old, formal style. A general audience would appear to be in view, for example, Jews in the Eastern *Diaspora as much as in Judea. We do not know where the translation was originally made, though we can assume that it is from outside the Qumran community. Nothing about it is distinctly Qumranian. The copy of 11QtgJob is from the mid-first century A.D., but on linguistic grounds the original translation can be dated to around 100 B.C. (It is not related textually or linguistically to the Talmudic/post-Talmudic targum to Job that is printed in rabbinic Bibles.)

Job is a unique book in the Hebrew Bible. There are many obscure words, and it is difficult to categorize the Hebrew book with any other known dialect of Hebrew. The Aramaic translation 11QtgJob aims to make the difficult Hebrew text understandable, occasionally at the expense of the poetic structure. However, the translation is still to be classified as literal and does not appear to incorporate the kind of homiletical expansions that are known from the written targum traditions of later times. The strange and difficult nature of the Hebrew text of Job may help to explain why such a book may have been singled out for translation into Aramaic at an early date.

2. The Significance of the Qumran Targumim. These two different texts of a targum to Job, one from Cave 4 and one from Cave 11, suggest that the Qumran community did not follow a supposed *Pharisaic/rabbinic prohibition against a written Aramaic targum. The Qumran community was not alone in this regard, since a targum to Job is fairly widely attested for the first century.

The Mishnah (c. A.D. 200; *see* Rabbinic Literature: Mishnah) stipulates that in the synagogue an oral Aramaic translation of the biblical reading was to be provided without using any written document. This may partially explain why all of our traditional, written targums are relatively late, redacted during and after the Talmudic period. We do not know when, how or where the Mishnaic procedure developed, nor how widely or consistently it was practiced. For example, the NT (cf. Lk 4:14-30; Acts 13:15, 27; 14:11; 15:21; 22:2) is silent on the question. Z. Safrai has shown a confluence of tradition indirectly pointing to the period immediately after A.D. 135 for the establishment of the synagogue practice.

A rabbinic story about Gamaliel (the same person referred to in Acts 5:34; 22:3) mentions a targum to Job (*t. Šabb.* 13:2; *y. Šabb.* 15c). When Gamaliel was shown a targum to Job he rejected it and gave it to some builders to insert in some temple stonework. He may have rejected this book because he did not want to see a written targum circulating.

An additional note in the *Septuagint at Job 42:17 mentions using an Aramaic copy of Job for its Greek translation. There is no correspondence, however, between our Qumran Aramaic texts and the Septuagint Greek text. In almost every case where our Qumran Aramaic text is significantly different from the Masoretic Hebrew text, our Greek Septuagint text sides with the Masoretic Hebrew text.

This coincidence of detail between naming Job in the rabbinic story, an additional note in the Greek Septuagint and finding two Aramaic copies of Job at Qumran may mean that Job was already popular in translation before the first century of this era. Perhaps Job was the first biblical book to be translated into Aramaic and published in a written form.

Finding two copies of Job in the Judean desert raises a larger question: Why are other Aramaic texts of the Bible apparently lacking at Qumran?

The lack of any significant targumic material beyond Job shows that the Qumran community used Hebrew and Hebrew texts for their access to the Bible. They were apparently comfortable with the Hebrew text, though perhaps appreciating popularized texts like 1QIsaiah[a] (the long Isaiah scroll; *see* Isaiah Scroll).

The fragments from Leviticus (4Q156) are from the section on the Day of Atonement and may be part of a work other than a translation of the whole book of Leviticus. (Cf. *m. Yoma* 7:1 for traditions of reading on Yom ha-Kippurim.) Consequently, 4Q156 should not be cited as a confirmation that an Aramaic translation to the whole Torah existed at Qumran.

This lack of a translation of biblical texts in Aramaic comes into better focus when compared with a number of noncanonical Aramaic texts found in the vicinity of Qumran. For example, 4Q196-199 are copies of *Tobit in Aramaic. 4Q213-214 contain an Aramaic work related to Levi (see also 4Q540, 4Q541 and 1Q21). 4Q542 is an Aramaic *Testament of Qahat,* 4Q537 an Aramaic *Apocryphon of Jacob,* 4Q538 an Aramaic *Apocryphon of Judah,* 4Q539 an Aramaic **Apocryphon of Joseph* and 4Q543-548 an Aramaic work now designated as **Visions of Amram*. 4Q201-212 are Aramaic fragments of **Enoch;* 4Q530-533 and 1Q23 relate to another Aramaic work on Enoch, while 4Q242-245 are Aramaic texts dealing with a pseudo-Daniel. All of these works show that the Qumran community was happy to include Aramaic books in their libraries, but their existence and proliferation at Qumran highlights the general lack of a written Aramaic translation to the Hebrew Bible. Their Bible was in Hebrew.

How widely does the Qumran situation reflect practices and attitudes throughout the Judean province? The fact that they had two copies of a targum (Job) that they did not translate themselves shows that they were in contact with wider circles of Jews. It is thus probable that the lack of Aramaic targums reflects the wider Jewish society as well, since one might assume that other targumic texts would be in their library if they were in general circulation. Thus, the Qumranian practice of direct access to biblical texts in Hebrew probably reflects the practice of the wider Jewish society around them.

See also RABBINIC LITERATURE: MIDRASHIM; RABBINIC LITERATURE: TARGUMIM.

BIBLIOGRAPHY. B. Chilton, "Eight Theses on the Use of Targums in Interpreting the New Testament," in *Judaic Approaches to the Gospels*, ed. B. Chilton (Atlanta: Scholars Press, 1994) 305-15; E. M. Cook, "Qumran Aramaic and Aramaic Dialectology," in *Studies in Qumran Aramaic*, ed. T. Muraoka (Supplement 3.1-21; Louvain: Peeters, 1992); J. Fitzmyer, "The Targum of Leviticus from Qumran Cave 4," *Maarav* 1.1 (1978) 5-23; S. D. Fraade, "Rabbinic Views on the Practice of Targum and Multilingualism in the Jewish Galilee of the Third-Sixth Centuries" in *The Galilee in Late Antiquity*, ed. L. I. Levine (New York: Jewish Theological Seminary of America, 1992) 253-86; J. C. Lübbe, "Describing the Translation Process of 11QtgJob: A Question of Method," *RevQ* 13 (1988) 583-93; T. Muraoka, "The Aramaic of the Old Targum of Job from Qumran Cave XI," *JJS* 25 (1974) 425-43; J. P. M. van der Ploeg and A. S. van der Woude, eds., *Le Targum de Job de la Grotte XI de Qumran* (Leiden: E. J. Brill, 1971); Z. Safrai, "The Origins of Reading the Aramaic Targum in Synagogue," in *Immanuel* 24-25: *The New Testament and Christian-Jewish Dialogue: Studies in Honor of David Flusser* (1990) 187-93; M. Sokoloff, *Targum to Job from Qumran Cave XI* (RamatGan, Israel: Bar-Ilan University Press, 1974); A. Tal, "Layers in the Jewish Aramaic of Palestine: The Appended Nun as a Criterion" (Hebrew) *Lešonénu* 43 (1979) 165-84; R. de Vaux and J. T. Milik, *Qumran Grotte 4.2:1 Archeologie; II. Tefillin, mezuzot et targums (4Q128-4Q157)* (DJD 6; Oxford: Clarendon Press, 1977); A. D. York, "The Dating of the Targumic Literature," *JSJ* 5 (1974) 49-62.

R. Buth

ARCHAEOLOGY AND THE NEW TESTAMENT

Archaeology is a science but not an exact or exclusive discipline. It is a method of studying the past that amalgamates many disciplines, including history, geography, language, numismatics, ceramics and even medicine. The word means "a study of antiquity or ancient things." Its contribution to human society is its ability to retrieve the past, or more accurately, significant aspects of the past, which can greatly enhance our understanding of history and culture.

1. Definitions
2. Methodology of Archaeology
3. Important Discoveries Relating to the New Testament
4. Jesus and His World
5. The World of the Early Church
6. Prospects for the Future

1. Definitions.

NT archaeology is not an independent discipline but an application of archaeological methods to the study of the NT and the ancient culture that produced it. As such, it can neither prove nor disprove theological assertions contained in the NT. But it has shed significant light on its cultural history and often provides clarity to enigma, replaces inaccuracy with precision and invigorates skepticism with confidence.

As a scientific discipline, archaeology employs the most recent and highly sophisticated methods of excavation, including subsurface interface radar, photogrammetry, magnetometers, resistivity-measuring instruments, infrared photography, laser-guided and computerized transits, small computers and microfiche systems, neutron-activation analysis and petrographic analysis. All of these are used to analyze and record material that is found in excavations that are conducted according to careful procedures involving surveying, digging, record keeping, and restoring and preserving artifacts.

Some of the archaeologists who work in the area of NT studies are highly trained professionals. However, most of the scholars trained in Greek and Roman archaeology, the period with which the NT is involved, are classical archaeologists and do not deal with the biblical material. Quite often those who work in NT archaeology have been trained in other areas, such as NT, early church history, Greek or theology, and pursue archaeology as an avocation. These people are normally trained pragmatically by participation in various kinds of excavations and then transfer their interest and expertise to NT interests.

2. Methodology of Archaeology.
The usual procedure in modern excavation, whether one is working in OT, classical or NT periods, is first to determine the identity of the site to be excavated. Cities like *Athens, *Rome, *Jerusalem and Jericho have remained occupied through the centuries, and there is no question as to their identity. However, some cities, like Jerusalem and Jericho, have shifted the center of their activity in various periods of their history, and although they remain in the same basic area, the modern city may be a few hundred yards to a few miles apart from the ancient site.

Once the site has been sufficiently identified to warrant the time and expense of excavation, a survey of the area will be conducted to locate any prominent features. Next it will be plotted on a checkerboard graph. Each of the sections or areas will then be numbered for accurate record keeping.

Since an entire city can rarely be excavated, selections of squares will be made, based on potential importance, and assigned to area supervisors. A supervisor and his or her team of ten to twenty diggers will begin the process of clearing the site and then slowly removing the soil that has accumulated through the centuries. As the digging progresses the walls of the square, called balks, are carefully observed and changes in soil texture or content recorded. Balk tags are placed on the walls to identify these changes, and they are recorded in the supervisor's record book as well as drawn on graph paper and photographed.

The digging progresses in this careful, scientific way, utilizing all the methodology listed above in the process. Artifacts discovered are carefully labeled, taken to the tech shed (the field office), washed, analyzed and stored.

When the season is ended, this material will be studied carefully, written up into a brief report for immediate publication in periodicals or on the Internet and then stored with previously dug materials for constant reference and study as the dig progresses from season to season. At the designated end of the project, the materials will be carefully analyzed once more and a final report published by the director of the excavation. Unfortunately these final reports sometimes never are published, and the benefit of the time and money spent on the project is never fully realized.

3. Important Discoveries Relating to the New Testament.
One of the greatest benefits of archaeology for the study of the NT is its contribution in situating a particular portion of the NT (person, city, event) in its historical, cultural and geographical context. This contributes to a more accurate understanding of the text for its readers, both then and now.

Archaeological excavations of the NT period are being conducted extensively in many countries of the Mediterranean world, especially in Egypt, Turkey, Greece, Italy, Jordan, Syria, Lebanon and Israel. For example, in the half century that Israel has been a nation, excavations have been conducted on its soil at an almost unbelievable pace with astonishing results. Almost thirty digs were scheduled for the 1998 season, for both OT and NT periods (*see* Archaeology of the Land of Israel).

Nearly every major site in Israel has either been partially excavated or reexcavated during these fifty years. These sites include, among others, Jerusalem, Herodium, Masada, *Qumran, Jericho, Samaria, Shechem, Megiddo, Beth Shan, Tiberias, Sepphoris, *Caesarea Maritima, *Caesarea Philippi, Capernaum, Bethsaida and Chorazim. Almost one hundred sites where digging has been at least partially done are discussed in *Excavations and Surveys in Israel* (vol. 15, 1996) published by the Israel Antiquities Authority in 1998.

4. Jesus and His World.
The NT states that Jesus was born during the reign of Herod the Great (Mt 2:1). Archaeological evidence of Herod's presence abounds in

the Holy Land. An inscription was found in 1997 at Masada, one of Herod's palace/fortresses near the Dead Sea, which reads "Herod, king of the Jews." Although Herod's name has been found on *coins from the period, this is the first time this title has been found. His palace at Masada has been thoroughly excavated, as have his palaces at Jericho and Herodium. He died in the former and was buried in the latter. Building stones containing a raised boss in the center and a smooth margin around the edges, which are unique to Herod's building programs, have been found in several sites in Israel, including Jerusalem and Hebron. An aqueduct built by Herod has been found at Caesarea Maritima, and a street belonging to his building activity was discovered in 1995 along the west side of the Temple Mount in Jerusalem.

Evidence of this king's love of Rome and things Roman has been found in Athens in two inscriptions discovered on the Acropolis between the Propylaea and the Erechtheum. Josephus wrote in his first-century history of the Jewish wars that Athens and other cities were "filled with Herod's offerings" (Josephus *J.W.* 1.21.11 §425). These inscriptions read as follows:

> The people
> [erect this monument to]
> King Herod, Lover
> of Romans, because of the benefaction
> and good will
> [shown] by him
>
> The people
> [erect this monument to]
> King Herod, Devout
> and a Lover of Caesar, because
> of his virtue and benefaction

Luke says that Pontius Pilate was the governor of Judea when John the Baptist began his ministry and baptized Jesus shortly thereafter (Lk 3:1, 21). The name of Pilate was found carved on a monumental stone near the theater in Caesarea Maritima, where he resided.

In November 1990, a tomb was discovered south of Jerusalem that appears to be the burial cave of the Caiaphas family. The high priest before whom Jesus appeared just before his death was named Caiaphas (Mt 26:3, 57; Lk 3:2; Jn 11:49; 18:13, 14, 24, 28). Later both Simon Peter and John appeared before Caiaphas in Jerusalem (Acts 4:6). The tomb is located in the Peace Forest, south of the Hinnom Valley.

In 1989, while the road along the east end of this Gehenna Valley was being widened, bulldozers uncovered three previously unknown burial caves which had remained undisturbed for almost fifteen hundred years. This discovery produced evidence that has provoked a reexamination of the three other long-known but little-noticed burial caves in this area, and taken together the evidence from these six caves makes the continued identification of this site as Akeldama implausible. Akeldama, the "field of blood" (Acts 1:19), was the burial site for poor people, but these burials were of wealthy people.

In these caves have been found some of the most superb Herodian tombs ever discovered. There is impressive evidence that one of them may have belonged to the high priest Annas. It is located near the recently discovered family tomb of his son-in-law and successor, Caiaphas. Both men were priests before whom Jesus appeared (Lk 3:2; Jn 18:13-14).

Beneath the floor of the presently standing remains of a Byzantine period synagogue in Capernaum, excavators have discovered the floor of a synagogue dating to the time of Jesus. The first-century synagogue was 60 feet wide by 79 feet long, essentially the same as the later one built above it. Here we have evidence of what may have been the synagogue in which Jesus preached, the one built by a Roman centurion for the Jewish nation he loved (Lk 7:1-5).

The house of Simon Peter may also have been found in Capernaum. Eighty-four feet to the south of the synagogue, an octagonal building with mosaic floors had stood in partial remains for centuries. The octagon itself is like those that Byzantine Christians built to commemorate holy places, such as the one over the birthplace of Jesus in Bethlehem.

Beneath this fifth-century building was found a fourth-century church whose hall was part of an earlier house built in the mid-first century A.D. The walls of this house, unlike those of the synagogue, were narrow and would not support a second story or a masonry roof. The roof would have been made of wooden branches covered with mud, in all probability similar to the one described in Capernaum through which a hole was "dug out" in order to let the paralytic down to Jesus (Mk 2:4). Simon Peter was praying on such a roof belonging to the house of Simon the tanner in Joppa when visitors came from Caesarea (Acts 10:9).

The house in Capernaum was built around two interior courtyards not unlike the other houses found in Capernaum in either size or building material. Sometime in the mid-first century the large (20 x 21 ft.) room in the center of the house was plastered along with its ceiling and floors. During the mid-first century, the pottery used in the room ceased to be typical domestic types, and after that there appear only storage jars and oil lamps. Thus the room must have begun to be used for some purpose other than normal residential living at that time. From then until the fourth century it may have been used as a chapel. More than 150 fragments of inscriptions were scratched on its walls in Greek, Syriac, Hebrew, Aramaic and Latin.

All the evidence presently available suggests the possibility that this chapel was built over a first-century house that had been set apart in the middle of that century for public viewing and continued to be so in subsequent centuries. This evidence has led many scholars to share the view of James Charlesworth that "Peter's house in which Jesus lived when he moved to Capernaum from Nazareth has probably been discovered."

The discovery of the *Dead Sea Scrolls at Qumran has been called "the greatest archaeological discovery of the century" by Hershel Shanks, editor of *Biblical Archaeology Review*. More than eight hundred different manuscripts have been found at Qumran and were appropriately celebrated in a fiftieth anniversary of the first discoveries at Cave 1 in 1947.

These Dead Sea Scrolls are a cache of ancient documents, dating from the first century B.C. to the first century A.D., that were found in eleven caves near the Qumran settlement on the northwest shore of the Dead Sea in Israel. Most scholars have identified this community of Jewish monastic-type religious devotees with the Essenes, the third largest sect of Jews in ancient Israel. However this identification, initially widely accepted, is now being vigorously challenged. Evidence of a significant settlement of Essenes has recently been found on the southern edge of Mt. Zion just above the Hinnom Valley. Part of the foundation of the Essene Gate in this southern wall, some of their ritual baths and some latrines have been found by Bargil Pixner.

A few more scrolls and thousands of fragments were subsequently discovered in ten other caves by both bedouin and archaeologists engaged in an intensive investigation of the area around the settlement during the mid-1950s.

The Dead Sea Scrolls have been of enormous value in the reassessment of Jewish sectarianism in the Second Temple period, which includes the time of the NT. They provide us with interesting background material for the study of the ministry of John the Baptist, who may have been associated with this group at one time. Thus far, however, there is no evidence from Qumran that bears directly on either Jesus of Nazareth or the NT. The many outlandish claims of Christianity's dependence on Qumran published by early sensationalists have been shown, upon more mature investigation of the scrolls, to be without foundation.

In 1998 what may be the foundation walls of the temple of the *Samaritans, probably alluded to in John 4:20, were found on Mt. Gerizim. It may have been patterned on the *temple in Jerusalem, where excavations have revealed more of the walls supporting the Temple Mount extensions during the time of Herod the Great, both on the west and on the east. On the west these include a Herodian street, a drain and portions of the huge stones supporting the western side of the mount. On the east it includes the "pinnacle of the temple" area (Mt 4:5).

Excavations adjacent to the southern wall of the Temple Mount have revealed steps from the time of Jesus that led up into the Double Gates by which entrance was had to the temple courts. Also uncovered were a number of *mikvaoth* (i.e., baptisteries), which were used for ritual immersion of persons like Joseph and Mary, who *purified themselves before going onto the Mount for Mary's purification after giving birth to Jesus (Lk 2:22).

Directly relating to the ministry of Jesus is the discovery of the pool of Bethesda in Jerusalem. It was here that Jesus healed the invalid described in John 5:1-5. This pool is about 100 yards inside the Stephen Gate (ancient Sheep Gate, 5:2) and about 100 yards north of the Temple Mount's northern wall.

The pool of Siloam, where Jesus restored the sight of a man who was born blind (Jn 9:1-12), has been located at the southern end of the 1749-foot-long tunnel of Hezekiah, cut through solid rock about 100 feet below ground.

The site on the east side of the Sea of Galilee, where Jesus cast the demons out of a man and into a herd of swine (Mk 5:1; Mt 8:28; Lk 8:26), has probably been identified by excavations. The history of these texts of the Gospels is problematical, with Matthew placing it in Gadara and Mark and Luke in Gerasa. The problem is in the similarity of spelling in Greek. Ancient scribes probably heard or saw one name in the process of copying a manuscript and thought they heard another.

Gerasa is modern Jerash in Jordan, located 37 miles southeast of the Sea of Galilee. Gadara is modern Umm Qeis, also in Jordan, located 5 miles southeast of the sea. Both of these are impossible to harmonize with the context of the story, which says that the pigs stampeded off a steep bank into the sea and drowned. This is not possible at either of these two sites. However, on geographical and archaeological grounds another variant reading in early manuscripts is undoubtedly the right one. This third site, Gergesa, is modern El Kursi, located in Israel on the east bank of the Sea of Galilee. In the early 1970s a Byzantine church was excavated there. It had been built over a spot considered holy because of some activity of Jesus there, just as were the Church of the Nativity in Bethlehem and the Holy Sepulchre Church in Jerusalem. Rising up on the east behind the church is a hill in which tombs have been found, just as the story describes. And on the west of the church is a steep bank, the only one on the entire eastern shore of the sea, which extended to the water's edge. Archaeologists excavated a memorial tower and chapel between the church and the cemetery that they conclude were built to mark the spot as the place of the miracle.

Archaeological excavations have shed light on some aspects of the burial of Jesus in Jerusalem. About seven hundred tombs of the Second Temple period have been found within 3 miles of Jerusalem. Careful study of these tombs has demonstrated that they are built on a similar pattern. Some of them were built with multiple chambers, and others consisted of two chambers, a burial chamber and an entrance chamber between it and the doorway. Rolling stones sealed the entrance to these tombs. Two of these stones have been found in Jerusalem in the Herod family tomb and in the tomb of Queen Helena of Adiabene. A rolling stone has also been found perfectly preserved in a tomb in Heshbon, Jordan. These, among others, help the modern student of the NT to envision the scene in which an angel "rolled back the stone" (Mt 28:2; Mk 16:3; Lk 24:2) that sealed the entrance to the tomb of Jesus and "sat upon it." Thus, a practice of burial that is foreign to modern society is illuminated by archaeological discovery.

These types of tombs differ from the Garden Tomb at Gordon's Calvary in Jerusalem, which nearby excavations have shown to belong to the Iron Age, the time of David about a thousand years before Christ. It is now known to be part of a cemetery that reaches northward into the courtyard of the French École Biblique. All the tombs excavated there are of the Iron Age. Thus, it could not be the tomb of Jesus.

5. The World of the Early Church.

Archaeology continues to provide illuminating discoveries relevant to the rise and spread of the early church as well as the life of Jesus. Information relating to the activities of the apostle Paul, as described in Acts and his letters, is impressive in both quantity and quality.

In 1997 excavations in Caesarea revealed an inscription in a mosaic floor that has been tentatively identified as belonging to the official Roman bureau for internal security with its praetorium, where Paul appeared before Felix and Festus (Acts 24:27; *see* Roman Administration). The site where it was found includes a large palace, offices, a bathhouse and a courtyard.

The governmental complex is the only seat of Roman government unearthed in Israel and one of the few ever excavated in the ancient Roman world. Roman rule over Palestine was centered in Caesarea, and the praetorium complex there functioned as the seat of Roman government from the first until the middle of the third century (*see* Roman Governors of Palestine).

Interestingly, in 1961 three lines of an inscription were found in the theater in Caesarea that contained the name of Pontius Pilate along with the word *tiberium.* It reads "Tiberium (of the Caesareans?) . . . Pontius Pilate Prefect of Judea . . . has given . . ." The connection, if any, between these inscriptions is yet to be determined, but they clearly testify to the presence of two Roman officials' headquarters in this city, both of whom are mentioned in the NT (*see* Pilate Inscription).

Critics have argued that Luke was wrong in designating officials in Thessalonica before whom Paul's followers appeared as politarchs (Acts 17:6; *see* Roman Political System), because no such office had been found in extant literary records—an argument from silence, which is always precarious at best. Archaeology has been able to contribute significantly to this debate. In 1960 C. Schuler published a list of thirty-two inscriptions containing this term that had been identified by archaeologists. Nineteen of them come from Thessalonica, and three of them date to the first century. Two more inscriptions from nearby Berea and Amphipolis containing this title were published in the 1970s.

Further light has been shed on sites mentioned by Acts in the journeys of Paul in the city of *Corinth. Luke wrote that Paul appeared before the Roman proconsul Gallio here (Acts 18:12-17). The platform or rostrum (Gk *bēma)* on which Gallio stood was discovered in 1935 and identified by O. Broneer in 1937. It is situated in the heart of the marketplace, close to the Bouleuterion (senate chamber). Considerable portions of this huge stone platform are still standing, and it is a major tourist attraction. It was identified by an inscription found nearby in the excavations that reads "He rivetted [i.e., covered] the Bema and paid personally the expense of making all its marble." Luke, writing in Greek, translates the term *rostra* in the Latin inscription as *bēma.*

The discovery of four fragments of an inscription carved in stone at Delphi, across the Corinthian Gulf from Corinth, which contain information about the accession of Gallio, helps us to determine the date of his tenure in office and thus provides a pinpoint for establishing Pauline chronology. The fragments were published in 1905 by E. Bourguet. An account of early publications of the inscription is given by A. Deissmann in *St. Paul: A Study in Social and Religious History.*

The fragments are from a copy of a letter sent from Claudius to the city of Delphi, either to the people of Delphi or to the successor of Gallio, and although it is fragmentary, it contains the name of Gallio, in addition to that of Claudius, with dates for his reign. It reads:

> Tiberius Claudius Caesar Augustus Germanicus (Pontifex Maximus, of tribunican authority for the 12th time, imperator the 26th time, father of the country, consul for the 5th time, honorable, greets the city of the Delphians. Having long been well disposed to the city of the Delphians. . . . I have had success. I have observed the religious ceremonies of the Pythian Apollo . . . now it is said also of the citizens . . .) as Lucius Junius Gallio, my friend, and the proconsul of Achaia wrote. . . . (on this account I accede to you still to have the first . . .).

The letter from Claudius is dated to A.D. 52 by J. Finegan in his *Handbook of Biblical Chronology.* Both Finegan and, more recently, R. Riesner date the beginning of Gallio's term of office to 51. And since Paul had arrived in Corinth eighteen months earlier than his appearance before Gallio (Acts 18:11), he would have entered Corinth in the winter of 49/50, perhaps in January of 50. This would coincide well with the "recent" arrival of Priscilla and Aquila from Claudius's expulsion in 49. This expulsion is also referred to in other ancient sources and can be dated to 49.

An important pinpoint of Pauline chronology is the date when Festus succeeded Felix as procurator of Palestine (Acts 24:27). Most chronologies have assumed a date of 59, as did F. F. Bruce in *Paul, Apostle of the Heart Set Free.* G. Ogg, in *The Chronology of the Life of Paul,* placed it at 61. However, J. Vardaman has found a coin with micrographic writing on it that affirms the date of Festus's accession as 56, which is about three to five years earlier than previous chronologies have allowed. This date has been accepted by Finegan (1981), who in his previous work (1964) had dated the accession to 57. This would mean that Paul stood before Festus (Acts 24:27) in the spring (perhaps May) of 56, and that he had arrived in Jerusalem at the end of his third journey two years earlier (Acts 24:27). Finegan has incorporated Vardaman's work into his chronology in *The Archaeology of the New Testament: The Mediterranean World of the Early Christian Apostles* (14). Vardaman's coin has been ignored, however, by R. Riesner in his recent discussion of chronology (*see* Chronology, New Testament).

Another important discovery at Corinth illuminates the visit of Paul to this city. Paul evidently converted a man named Erastus during the eighteen months he was in Corinth (Acts 18:11). There are 104 inscriptions found in Corinth that date from 44 B.C. to the early second century A.D. Of these, 101 are in Latin and only 3 in Greek. One of the paving stones excavated beside the city's theater contains part of an abbreviated Latin inscription that J. Kent, an excavator and epigrapher at Corinth, reads "Erastus in return for his aedileship laid (the pavement) at his own expense." The Erastus of this inscription is identified by Kent with the Erastus mentioned by Paul in a letter later written from Corinth, in which he said: "Erastus, the city treasurer, salutes you" (Rom 16:23). This identification is also accepted by B. Winter in his study of the social background of ancient cities. This is undoubtedly the same Erastus who later remained in Corinth when Paul was taken to Rome (2 Tim 4:20). He was also with Paul in Ephesus on his third journey (Acts 19:22). This man provides an interesting cross-cultural link in the Corinthian church. The name is an uncommon one in Corinth and is not otherwise found in the literature and inscriptions of the city. However, C. Hemer notes that the cognomen Erastus was not uncommon among prominent people in Ephesus. The pavement on which the name occurs was laid in approximately A.D. 50, the time when Paul arrived in Corinth.

A significant point of contact between Paul and his world has been found in the city of *Ephesus on the west coast of Turkey. It is a theater referred to in Acts 19:29-32. This theater, which would have seated twenty-four thousand people, is the most impressive structure still standing in the city. It was enlarged under Claudius about the time Paul was there. It stood adjacent to the lower commercial market near the harbor where the riot against Paul probably broke out.

Two huge statues of Artemis (called Diana by Romans) have been found in excavations of the town hall adjacent to this theater. These statues were reproduced on a miniature scale by a guild of silversmiths and placed in miniature shrines or altars (Acts 19:24) for sale to worshipers who visited her temple. This was a major source of income for these artisans, and Paul's success in converting people from idolatry was affecting their business. Opposition to Paul's teaching in Ephesus became acute when he began to affect the pocketbooks of the artisans. Demetrius, who was probably the president of the guild, gathered his fellow artisans together in the theater, where public meetings of this kind were normally held, and incited them against Paul. One can stand today on the upper levels of the theater, gaze into the adjacent marketplace and recreate the scene rather vividly. Archaeology has helped to provide the geographical and sociological milieu for the story.

Excavations in Ephesus have also produced what appear to be the foundations of the hall of Tyrannus, in which Paul taught for two years (Acts 19:9). It was identified by an inscription. The structure is located adjacent to the marketplace and across the street from the theater.

Paul traveled the Roman roads of the Mediterranean world on his missionary journeys from city to city. The famous international highway known as the Egnatian Way ran from Apollonia and Dyrrachium on the western coast of Macedonia to Kypsela (modern Maritza) on the east coast, north of the island of Samothrace. Paul would have traveled the portion of that road between Neapolis and Thessalonica. Sections of it have been excavated that show that it was made of large rectangular stones closely fitted together. One section has been discovered running east-west along the north edge of the Roman forum in *Philippi.

When Paul arrived in *Athens he would have gazed in awe at the temple of Athena, the Parthenon, which stood majestically upon the crest of the Acropolis. Although it was badly damaged by an explosion during the Crimean War, the structure still stands as a landmark of the city and undergoes constant efforts at preservation and restoration. It was in clear view when Paul spoke of the idolatry of the Greeks on Mars Hill nearby (Acts 17). Adjacent to its east side was the Temple of Rome and Augustus, evidence of the importance of emperor worship at this time (*see* Roman Emperors). Portions of that temple's remains contain an inscription identifying it.

In the Roman forum below the north side of the Acropolis there still stands a marble clock tower and weathervane called the Tower of the Winds. Paul undoubtedly looked at it when he was in the forum in order to get the time of day. This forum, rather than the nearby Greek agora to the west, was the commercial marketplace of Paul's day. Luke records Paul's presence here in Acts 17:17: "So he argued in the synagogue with the Jews and the devout persons, and in the marketplace every day with those who chanced to be there."

In his letter to the church in Pergamum (Rev 2:12-13), John refers to "the place where Satan's throne is" and the place "where Satan dwells." A magnificent altar of Zeus was found here that is

112 x 118 feet in size and covered in marble. It was disassembled and taken to Berlin, where it has been reconstructed in the Pergamum Museum. Although some scholars have tried to identify it as the throne referred to by John, excavations have not been able to prove that this was what John had in mind, and since John wrote in the context of emperor worship, it is more likely that he had in mind the Temple of Augustus, which was the first provincial temple built to a Roman emperor in Asia Minor. This is an instance in which archaeology whets the appetite and delights the imagination but fails to provide the needed confirmation.

6. Prospects for the Future.
Archaeological investigation will continue to be an important element in the study of antiquity. With the rapidly expanding number of sites being excavated and the growing interest in ancient sites by both scholar and tourist, as well as the explosion in communication resources such as television, video services, computer web sites and e-mail, the almost instantaneous availability of information on recent discoveries promises to bring abundant discoveries into the offices and homes of people everywhere. Archaeological discoveries are no longer the private domain of a few scholars. The recent rescue of the Dead Sea Scrolls from the control of a few scholars and making them available to everyone both in print and on computers represents the beginning of an exciting new era in NT archaeology.

See also ARCHAEOLOGY OF THE LAND OF ISRAEL; ART AND ARCHITECTURE; ASIA MINOR; CITIES, GRECO-ROMAN; COINAGE; INSCRIPTIONS AND PAPYRI; QUMRAN: PLACE AND HISTORY; TEMPLE, JEWISH; TEMPLES, GRECO-ROMAN; THEATERS; TRAVEL AND TRADE.

BIBLIOGRAPHY. F. F. Bruce, *Paul: Apostle of the Heart Set Free* (Grand Rapids, MI: Eerdmans, 1977) 475; J. Charlesworth, *Jesus Within Judaism: New Light from Exciting Archaeological Discoveries* (New York: Doubleday, 1988) 112; A. Deissmann, *St. Paul: A Study in Social and Religious History* (New York: Hodder & Stoughton, 1912) 235-60; J. Finegan, *The Archaeology of the New Testament: The Mediterranean World of the Early Christian Apostles* (Boulder: Westview Press, 1981); idem, *Handbook of Biblical Chronology* (Princeton, NJ: Princeton University Press, 1964) 318, 324; D. Gill, "Erastus the Aedile," *TynB* 40 (November 1989) 293-302; N. Golb, "Khirbet Qumran and the Manuscripts of the Judean Wilderness: Observations on the Logic of Their Investigation," *JNES* 49 (April 1990) 102-14; C. Hemer, *The Book of Acts in the Setting of Hellenistic History* (Tübingen: Mohr Siebeck, 1989) 235; J. Kent, *Corinth: The Inscriptions 1926-1950* (Princeton, NJ: Princeton University Press, American School of Classical Studies in Athens, 1966) vol. 8, pt. 3, #232, p. 99, and plate 21; J. McRay, *Archaeology and the New Testament* (Grand Rapids, MI: Baker, 1991) 294, 331-33; G. Ogg, *The Chronology of the Life of Paul* (London: Epworth, 1968) 200; B. Pixner, "Jerusalem's Essene Gateway: Where the Community Lived in Jesus's Time," *BAR* 23 (May/June 1997) 23-31; R. Riesner, *Paul's Early Period: Chronology, Mission Strategy, Theology* (Grand Rapids, MI: Eerdmans, 1998) 202-11; H. Shanks, *BAR* 23.6 (November/December 1997) 63; G. Theissen, "Social Stratification in the Corinthian Community: A Contribution to the Sociology of Early Hellenistic Christianity," in *The Social Setting of Pauline Christianity* (Philadelphia: Fortress, 1982) 83; B. Winter, *Seek the Welfare of the City: Christians as Benefactors and Citizens* (Grand Rapids, MI: Eerdmans, 1994) 195.

J. R. McRay

ARCHAEOLOGY OF THE LAND OF ISRAEL

Archaeology is a unique discipline in that its research goals, theoretical framework and methodology encompass several disciplines (e.g., history, anthropology, sociology, biblical studies, linguistics). Archaeology is the discipline that studies the material correlates of ancient society; more specifically, the material record as it has been patterned by human behavior. Archaeologists participate with other social scientists in an attempt to reconstruct the past by analyzing the patterns of material culture and historical landscapes and correlating the results with other disciplines.

1. Introduction
2. Settlement Pattern and Sites
3. Architecture
4. Pottery
5. Epigraphy
6. Other Material Culture
7. Summary

1. Introduction.
Archaeological research contributes to the study of NT backgrounds by defining the context in

which the texts were written. Archaeological evidence complements the historical record of political events and the geographical landscape through an analysis of settlement patterns based on archaeological excavations and surveys. The archaeological record also reveals social interaction and cultural systems that are not recorded in the textual record: for example, the relation between rural economic and social systems to urban centers, ethnicity, religious practice and, more specific to the period under discussion, the nature and extent of Hellenism in Palestine and its interaction with the local culture.

1.1. Theoretical Shifts and Emphases. Archaeology in the land of Israel was initially viewed as a subdiscipline of biblical studies utilized to verify events of the Bible. The next phase of development was an attempt by archaeologists working in the southern Levant to separate their research goals from those of the historians, who emphasized textual data. Thus there was an attempt to establish archaeology as a separate discipline from biblical studies with its own agenda and research methodologies. The emphasis became Syro-Palestinian archaeology instead of biblical archaeology. The current trend is to view textual and archaeological records as separate but complementary data sets with their own methods of analysis and interpretation. Each set is valuable to the other in the mutual endeavor to reconstruct the past. The archaeological record is dynamic and constantly being enlarged and changed as ongoing excavations and research allow for the constant reevaluation and interpretation of the past. Hence, archaeological research plays a vital role as a necessary foundation for understanding the background of the NT and reconstructing the context in which the text developed.

Archaeology in the land of Israel has adopted current theoretical and methodological trends in anthropological theory. A major shift occurred in the 1960s and 1970s as the paradigm of processual archaeology ("new archaeology") became a dominant influence. Although this introduced current scientific advances and modern excavation techniques within the methodology of archaeological practice, the main influence was the incorporation of the research questions of archaeological and anthropological theory. Currently, with the natural dialogue between texts and artifacts, Syro-Palestinian archaeology is poised to fully adopt the postprocessual trends of the last decade in the larger field. An underlying paradigm in archaeology is to view history as the *longue durée,* in which the archaeological record is viewed as part of a historical continuum with a multitude of variables that pattern it. Archaeology in the land of Israel now defines ancient Palestine as a small part of a larger region instead of its own isolated entity. Patterns are viewed in the larger world systems of the Mediterranean basin and the Near East.

1.2. Hellenistic Archaeological Research. Only recently has the archaeology of the Hellenistic period in the land of Israel been explicitly defined and analyzed. Research has generally focused on issues relating to the Hebrew Bible or the NT, resulting in an emphasis on the Iron Age or Roman periods. Archaeological research is now focusing on the reconstruction of ancient social systems instead of the confirmation of NT events and places. Due to the quantity of literary material for this period, archaeological research has tended to place an emphasis on interpreting the archaeological data within the context of the textual data.

Although the *Hellenistic period is well documented in the textual record, not much archaeological data was known at the beginning of the twentieth century. At that time, the only known sites with archaeological exploration were Marisa, 'Iraq el-Emir, Samaria and Gezer. This led many scholars to assume that Palestine was not part of the Hellenistic revival. Arav notes that the paucity of data was due to the difficulty in distinguishing this period in the archaeological record from the earlier Iron Age-Persian and the later Roman-Byzantine periods.

Another problem is that the building activity in the following Roman period destroyed most of the Hellenistic remains with deep and extensive building foundations. The archaeology of the Hellenistic period was first defined between the two world wars. As precision in dating of ceramics and coins was established, the first archaeological syntheses of the Hellenistic period were produced—C. Watzinger's 1935 survey of the Hellenistic presence in Palestine *(Denkmaeler Palaestinas),* and W. F. Albright's 1945 synthesis in *The Archaeology of Palestine.* Albright divided the period into two periods ("Lagides," later to be the Ptolemaic, and the "Seleucid"), and he made two observations about the material culture that have set the stage for the current research trends in the archaeology of Palestine during the Hellenistic period. The first observation was that Hellenic influence greatly penetrated into Palestine. Albright demonstrated this through the city plan of Marisa, the monument of the Tobiads at 'Iraq el-Emir, and the coins and Rhodian jars found in large numbers throughout the region. The second observation was that this initial Hellenic influence later receded and there was a reemergence of local styles.

These observations have been expanded as scholars differentiate between Western and Oriental elements in the artifact record and note that the emergence of the *Hasmonean state brought about a local conservatism against the foreign elements that Hellenistic culture brought. Currently these themes are being developed within the wider context of the smaller Palestinian communities interacting with the internationalism of the age.

1.3. Archaeological Periods. Archaeological periods are based on a correlation with historical periods and changes in the material culture. The Hellenistic period is divided into two major archaeological subdivisions, which are further divided each into two subsets based on the history: the Early Hellenistic period (331-150 B.C.), which encompasses the Ptolemaic and Seleucid periods, and the Late Hellenistic period (150-63 B.C.), which correlates with the rise and expansion of the Hasmonean state.

2. Settlement Pattern and Sites.

Palestine had more Hellenized cities per square kilometer than did any other province outside of Greece (Arav). The geopolitical situation greatly affected the settlement patterns of the Holy Land. The Early Hellenistic period coincides with *Alexander the Great's conquest and the subsequent control by the Ptolemaic and Seleucid empires. Evidence of these conquests that are visible in the archaeological record are possible destruction layers at Ashkelon and Dor. The political changes are evident in the construction of new customs houses at Acco and Gaza and the minting of new coins. The settlement and economy of Palestine remained virtually the same as that of the previous Persian period (*see* Jewish History: Persian Period).

Throughout the first half of the second century B.C., the turmoil in Judea remained almost completely contained within that region. In the second half of the century many peoples in Palestine and Phoenicia sought to consolidate their territory, revenues and political power. In the south the Nabateans expanded their dominion in the Negev and southern Transjordan, while in the north the Itureans moved into the Golan. In central Transjordan an ambitious dynast named Zeno Cotylas seized Philadelphia and its environs. Economic independence and its byproducts also allowed for the establishment of new settlements. The most comprehensive archaeological evidence for a population increase during the Late Hellenistic period comes from the Upper Galilee and the adjacent Huleh Valley, areas traditionally included in the hinterland of Tyre. At this time, while most sites outside Judea and Samaria were well fortified, only the central hills show a consistent pattern of destruction (e.g., Beth-Zur, Gezer, Tirat Yehuda), evidence of the Hasmonean colonization efforts throughout Judea and Samaria. The change in settlement patterns is also documented by newly developed sites and abandoned sites (e.g., Tel Dothan). By the late second century B.C. the Itureans expanded from the interior of Lebanon into the northern Golan and Mt. Hermon, where more than one hundred sites, mostly unwalled farmsteads with animal pens, were discovered.

2.1. Northern Coast. The sites along the coast provide the best evidence for the internationalization of the Holy Land. The port cities were the first to experience this impact, and the connections between these coastal communities and the southern Phoenician cities of Tyre and Sidon illustrate the mercantile character of the area. The major sites are Dor, Acco and *Caesarea.

Dora (Dor) is located on the Carmel coast, 14 miles south of Haifa. Excavations have revealed three strata of a well-planned city, built on an orthogonal plan with several residential buildings adjacent to the city wall and a row of shops and workshops abutting the city wall. One of these workshops contained a local dye industry. Excavated public buildings include some of the largest Hellenistic temples and a large ashlar-built public building apparently connected with some sort of administrative-commercial activity in the area. The Roman forum was later built over this building. The building style was Phoenician-ashlar piers with rubble fill and was at least two stories high. Archaeological data reveal that Dor was a pagan Greek city.

Ptolemais (Acco) is located at the northern end of Haifa Bay on a broad plain. Excavations on the mound and at several sections within the modern city have exposed several components of a Hellenistic city. Ptolemais was defended by an extensive fortification system of walls and towers. At least two strata have been excavated from the Hellenistic period and exhibit a well-designed city plan that included a building constructed in the Phoenician technique with ashlar headers and stretchers interspersed with field stones. Residential quarters contained homes with spacious courts with numerous cooking ovens. One public building was a small temple dedicated to Zeus Sotēr on behalf of King Antiochus VII Sidetes. The Hellenistic founders of Ptolemais constructed their port facilities on the open sea.

Strato's Tower (Caesarea) is another coastal city on the northwest corner of the Sharon plain. Although archaeological excavations have revealed an abundance of third- and second-century B.C. pottery, not much architecture can be dated to the Hellenistic period. Most scholars date a series of wall segments with round towers to the late second century B.C. The masonry consists of drafted kurkar (local sandstone) blocks laid alternately as headers and stretchers. The harbor of Strato's Tower is north of the city using a natural bay. A massive wall (preserved for 30 x 5 m) built along the waterline on the contour of the rocky shelf is associated with the quay. It is an ashlar structure built of irregular blocks in the headers technique (see 3.1 below). Two excavated segments of a wall provide evidence of the northern boundary of the harbor.

Various other sites along the coast have been excavated with Hellenistic remains. On the Sharon plain, 'Atlit, Tel Mevorakh, Apollonia (Arsuf) and Tel Zeror have produced finds. Tel Mevorakh and Tel Zeror were agricultural estates. Two forts have been excavated at Shiqmona on the Carmel cape and at Tel Michal at the southern end of the Sharon plain. At Tel Michal, a small fort dating to the Hasmonean period was built.

2.2. North: Galilee and Golan. Recent archaeological research in Galilee shows that the northern regions were thinly populated in the third century B.C. but experienced a population explosion in the second century B.C. Most of the major excavated sites producing Hellenistic remains are in the Huleh and Beth Shean valleys.

Situated at the juncture between the Jezreel and Jordan valleys is Scythopolis (Beth-Shean). It was founded before the middle of the third century B.C. as a polis and played a major role in Hellenistic Palestine. The city expanded off the ancient tel to the crests of the nearby hills and later descended to the low-lying areas. The city center probably moved to the northern bank of the Ḥarod Brook at Tell Iṣṭaba, where remains of Hellenistic buildings were discovered as well as pottery vessels and small objects. Most noteworthy are several hundred amphorae handles with seal impressions.

Along the southwestern end of the Sea of Galilee is Beth Yeraḥ. This site is identified as Hellenistic Philoteria. It was defended by a thick wall built of mudbrick with basalt foundations and had outward-jutting, alternating square and round towers. Part of the town was excavated. The houses, separated by a nine-meter-wide street, were rectangular in shape with the rooms facing rubble-paved courtyards. Some were preserved up to their windows and were decorated with colorful marbles and with plaster imitations of marble, a common fashion in Hellenistic urban sites.

Excavations at Tel Anafa, located in the Huleh Valley, have revealed a rich Hellenized settlement consisting of an acropolis surrounded by an extensive lower town. The wealth of the city is evidenced by the excavation of a large stucco building (c. 38 sq m). The building plan consists of suites of rooms on four sides opening onto a central courtyard (9 x 12 m). This building has a bath complex consisting of three rooms.

At the north of the Huleh Valley at the foot of Mt. Hermon is Tel Dan and Banias. The ancient site of Dan had a high place initially built during the ninth century B.C. It was a large platform built of headers and stretchers. A bilingual Greek-Aramaic dedicatory inscription mentions "to the Gods of Dan," indicating that this high place was also used in the Hellenistic period. At the foot of Mt. Hermon is the Sanctuary of Pan at Banias. This is a natural grotto in which a temple was built. The nature of the Hellenistic sanctuary is unknown; only a few Hellenistic remains were found outside, which suggests that in this period the cult place was confined to the natural cave.

Gamala is the only Hellenistic site in the Golan that has been excavated. The site is surrounded by a thick wall with a round tower. The excavations have uncovered a public house, a ritual bathhouse, streets, a residential quarter and possibly a synagogue. The city was constructed with fine masonry and decorated with frescos and architectural ornamentation.

*2.3. **Philistine Coastal Plain.*** Most of the major Iron Age port cities were occupied in the Hellenistic period. Located at the border of the Sharon and Philistine plains is Joppa (Jaffa). Although Hellenistic remains have been exposed in three areas, the evidence is too fragmentary to give a complete picture of the city. In one area (Area A) part of a square fortress with some type of industrial area was discovered dating to the third century B.C. The fortress was constructed of brick-shaped, ashlar blocks set on their narrow end, and it had a room containing an altar built of field stones. In Area C part of a courtyard of a catacomb was discovered. A fragment containing a dedicatory inscription mentioning Ptolemy IV Philopator suggests the existence of a Hellenistic temple. In Area Y many tombs and various installations were found, as well as the corner of a large building built of ashlar masonry, thought to be the agora.

Various salvage excavations in the Yarkon basin have exposed several buildings and wine presses dating from the Ptolemaic occupation. Several structures along the line of the Yarkon River have been interpreted as the defense line of Alexander Janneus described by *Josephus. They have also been interpreted as watchtowers. It appears that this region had several agricultural estates that reflect an extensive wine industry in the Yarkon basin.

On the southern coast is Azotus (Ashdod). Excavations have revealed a well-planned city with streets separating various buildings. The main building belongs to the city's agora. The main room of this building contained large pottery jars, similar to Rhodian wine jars. An altar constructed of two flat stones with a third laid across was found in a corner of a room, as well as two miniature stone altars, weapons and a lead plaque probably representing a deity with a fish tail. This site was destroyed at the end of the second century B.C. The sister port city was at Tel Mor on the banks of Naḥal Lachish. Stratum I consisted of a large public building located at the eastern slope of the tel and a dye installation located on the northern slope. The dye installation contained several plastered pools connected by pipes, near a cistern that contained thousands of shells and pottery vessels.

Ascalon (Ashkelon) was not as important as Gaza during the Hellenistic period. Although Ascalon had an extensive Persian and Roman occupation, few remains were found that can be accurately attributed to the Hellenistic period. It appears that during the Hellenistic period the major port moved to Gaza.

Textual data indicates that Gaza's importance far exceeded that of Ascalon during the Hellenistic era; however, not much is known of the archaeological remains of the city. Recent excavations have exposed parts of the Hellenistic city's fortifications. Further inland from Gaza at the site of Tell Hesi, residential settlements in two distinct phases from the Middle and Late Hellenistic periods have been found. Located 6 kilometers south of Gaza, on the southern bank of the Besor River, is Tell Jemmeh, where excavations have revealed that the site was primarily occupied by large mudbrick granaries. A total of ten granaries have been excavated. They were entered through two opposite doorways, from which steps descended to a high platform projecting to each side of the structure. The granaries were in use until about 150 B.C. An ostracon bearing a South Arabic monogram suggests that this site may have been connected to the Arabic caravan traffic.

*2.4. **Shephelah and Negev.*** Some of the most extensive Hellenistic remains excavated have been in the Judean Shephelah, most notably at the site of Marisa (Mareshah). Marisa was one of the first Hellenistic sites to be excavated in Palestine, and excavations have shown it to be one of the most impressive Hellenistic settlements, with three major Hellenistic strata. Marisa became the vital city in the Shephelah during the mid-third century B.C. and the following periods. The Hellenistic city was square in plan and was surrounded by a city wall with square and rectangular towers. Public buildings include a marketplace, a caravansary and a building used as the administrative and religious center. Two types of private buildings were found: the complex house and the courtyard house (see below). These houses had remains of hearths, basins and steps leading to second stories and roofs. Finds consist of hundreds of vessels, Rhodian handles, lead figurines, limestone tablets, coins and three Greek dedicatory inscriptions. The site is known for its extensive and rich necropolis. The burial caves contained tombs of several chambers with several elaborate friezes depicting various individuals, musicians, riders, several types of animals and inscriptions. One of the fascinating discoveries of recent excavations is an extensive underground city. Almost every house had access to subterranean complexes: units, workshops and storage rooms interconnected by tunnels. Found underground were forty columbaria used for pigeon raising, sixteen olive presses and more than one hundred cisterns.

Although the capital of the Shephelah was moved from Lachish to Marisa, a temple was built at Lachish during the Hellenistic period, possibly in the Persian period. The sanctuary is oriented on an east-west axis, the inner and innermost parts were elevated, and a limestone altar was found in the court. This temple went out of use during the second century B.C., perhaps as part of the Hasmonean resurgence.

At the site of Gezer at least two Hellenistic strata have been isolated. Stratum III is dated to the third century B.C. and Stratum II to the Hasmonean period (second half of the second century B.C.). The city wall appears to have used the previous Iron Age wall with a rebuilding of the gate. During the Hasmonean period the gate was hastily repaired, the threshold was narrowed, and semicircular bastions were added around the tower. Several fine courtyard houses were partially excavated in Fields II and VII. Also excavated, in an area northeast of the gate, was a private home consisting of a northern wing with several rooms surrounding a courtyard and a southern wing with a later addition of a miqveh. Boundary markers have been found in the fields, and a Greek political graffito was found in the vicinity of the gate, "To blazes with Simon's palace!"

In the Negev two sites have Hellenistic remains, Beersheba and Arad. Beersheba was located at a central point for trade during its long history. During the Hellenistic period the ruined Iron Age strata was leveled by a massive fill. On top of this a fortress containing a temple was built, of which only a few parts remain. Outside the fortress several large courtyards, dwellings and domestic installations served as suburbs. Excavators have found two strata dating to the Hellenistic period, the first dating to the second century B.C. and the second to the first century B.C. A bathhouse was added in the second period. Arad is located 30 kilometers east of Beersheba on the eastern end of the Negev basin. Level IV dates to the Hellenistic period, third-second centuries B.C. A large tower was built in the center of the early Israelite tower on the acropolis. This tower was 12 x 12 meters and stood on a platform 19 x 19 meters. Around this watchtower several rooms were found, possibly the barracks.

2.5. Judea and Samaria. The only early Hellenistic settlements of any size found in the northern central hills are Samaria, Shechem and Mt. Gerizim. This region was used extensively for subsistence agriculture. Several small, stone field towers have been found through surveys of the region. These towers served the agricultural settlements and were used for temporary shelter and storage.

At Samaria the Hellenistic city occupied the acropolis and the lower city. The acropolis was defended by a wall fortified with round towers—one of the most impressive monuments of the Hellenistic period in Palestine. During the Early Hellenistic period, the old walls of the acropolis were still in use and huge round towers were added, one of which is about 20 meters in diameter. In the middle of the second century B.C. a new wall was built around the acropolis. This wall enclosed an area of 230 x 120 meters and measured 4 meters in thickness. The round towers went out of use, and square towers were built at intervals of 40 to 50 meters. The city had been deserted for half a century when it was rebuilt under Gabinius. Part of this city was excavated exposing eight insulae with five streets. Each insulae had four houses and a row of shops; the average dimensions were 28 x 12.5 meters. One house had a paved central court with columns *in antis* on Doric bases. Evidence of plaster, some painted to look like marble, was found in the homes.

Another site in the Samarian hills is Shechem. Although the complete plan of the city is not known, four levels of occupation were defined. In Stratum IV (331-250 B.C.) the Middle Bronze Age (MB) fortifications and the MB eastern gate were reused. In Stratum III (250-190 B.C.) rebuilding of the MB fortification continued along with the rebuilding of the glacis. A wealthy quarter with houses of fine masonry and painted walls was excavated. This stratum was destroyed, and the next level (Stratum II) dates to the Seleucid occupation. In this stratum, the city was rebuilt with only one fortification, a tower erected directly east of the East Gate. An ephemeral Stratum I phase was evidently destroyed by John Hyrcanus (134-104 B.C.). Scholars note that Shechem never took on the shape of a Hellenistic town. At Tel Dothan, 22 kilometers north of Shechem, a rural settlement was found at the top of the mound. The excavation reports are fragmentary and suggest that the few Hellenistic remains are evidence of a planned settlement.

To the west of the site of Shechem is Mt. Gerizim, consisting of two ridges. The upper ridge is Tell el-Râs. During the Hellenistic period a walled city encompassed an area of about 100 acres. The city was divided into four residential quarters and a sacred precinct on the summit. In the western quarter (Area A), excavations revealed a large tripartite structure consisting of a main building, a service building and a western building. Each of the parts contained courtyards, or plazas, paved with stone slabs and several rooms. Stairways and second-story collapse were evidence for the existence of multistory buildings. In the main building one room served as a bathroom, with a stone bathtub and a small plastered washbasin. Several other buildings were excavated in the other quarters. One building in the northern quarter (Area T) contained an oil press, while in another quarter outside the city (Area K) three houses built around a central courtyard were found. These houses were inferior in building construction and finds compared with the houses found inside the city.

Excavations in the 1960s exposed the remains of two temples on the summit. The later temple, built by Hadrian, measures 20 x 14 meters with a staircase on the slope. It stands on a podium that rises above a large stable platform 68.5 x 43 x 7 meters. This temple was erected in the second century B.C. Walls of an earlier building with a half cube of unhewn stones, thought to be the altar, were found under the Roman temple. The excavator identified this earlier building with the Samaritan temple and notes that it was probably destroyed by John Hyrcanus in 128 B.C. Other scholars date this earlier temple to the Roman period.

Much of what we know of Hellenistic *Jerusalem comes from texts. Archaeological finds dating to Herodian Jerusalem (Roman period) are abundant, and it is assumed that this city destroyed most of the earlier Hellenistic remains; fortunately there is enough fragmentary evidence to allow a reconstruction of the Hellenistic city. The city was confined to the Temple Mount and the area of the City of David in the Early Hellenistic period. Occupation expanded to the Western Hill during the Hasmonean period. Sections of the Hasmonean fortifications were found at the City of David, where a fortified gate identified as the Valley Gate was rebuilt. Other Hellenistic fortifications found are Josephus's "First Wall" protecting the upper city and two sections of the city wall in the northwest corner of the Jewish Quarter. One section, discovered in the courtyard of David's Citadel, is still standing 11 meters in height with three projecting towers that form the northwest corner of the wall.

South of Jerusalem is Beth-Zur, on the boundary between Judea and Idumea in the Hebron hills. The site is identified with Khirbet et-Tubeiqah, a natural conical hill that flourished in the Hellenistic period. In the third century B.C. a citadel was built and was subsequently rebuilt throughout the period as the town apparently changed hands. Several houses, including bathing facilities and several shops, were found dating to the reign of Antiochus IV Epiphanes. Under Judas Maccabeus the Middle Bronze Age wall and the citadel were rebuilt and used. The citadel was again rebuilt under Bacchides. By 100 B.C. Beth-Zur was deserted.

In the Jericho region where Wadi Qelt enters the valley from the hills, a Hasmonean winter palace complex was excavated at Tulul Abu el-'Alayiq. The palace was built in stages, expanding from an earlier tower and an artificial mound. The palace consists of a large main building (50 x 50 m) built of mudbricks on a rubble foundation with a swimming pool complex containing two large pools, pavilion and a colonnaded garden surrounded by a spacious court with a fine plastered floor. In the northwest corner of the palace a mikveh complex was found having two pools, one with steps and a pipe connecting them.

The Judean desert contains several forts that have Herodian remains, some possibly dating to the Hasmonean period. Each one of these fortresses has architectural features or finds dating to this period. These fortresses are Alexandrium, Macherus, Masada, Doq, Dagon, Kypros, Threx and Tauros.

At the site of *Qumran, two phases date to the Hellenistic period. In Phase Ia the settlers used the remnants of the Israelite period, adding two new cisterns. In Phase Ib the complex consisted of a main building with a tower, a central courtyard, a large assembly hall and a potter's workshop. Just east of Qumran on the shore of the Dead Sea, a rectangular house and an inner court with surrounding rooms was excavated at 'Ein Feshkha. Part of the building served as an administrative or residential court. Further south at the oasis of En-Gedi, a military fortress was founded in about the fourth century B.C. at the ancient settlement of Tel Goren. The citadel of Stratum III consists of two parts. The western section was built on a trapezoidal plan with a rectangular tower at its western end. The eastern section was a large rectangle with a rectangular tower in the southern part. The total area of the citadel was about 350 square meters. Most of the finds date to the late Hasmonean period, although there were a few coins from the time of the Ptolemies and Seleucids and a few Early Hellenistic potsherds.

2.6. Transjordan. The settlement pattern in Transjordan was similar to the central hill country of Judea and Samaria. In the *Decapolis several cities have been excavated, and monumental Roman remains have been found. Although we know from textual records that several of these cities were established during the Hellenistic period, the archaeological record is limited. Pella, on the western slope of the Gilead across the valley from Scythopolis, produced the only architectural evidence of a Hellenistic city. A modest, rectangular house, constructed of mudbrick and covered with fine white plaster, was exposed. Most of the Hellenistic pottery dates from the second century B.C. At Abila, a limited number of pottery sherds are the only evidence of the Hellenistic city found, along with some tombs in the necropolis. Gerasa and Gadara, both well known from texts, produced only scant ceramic evidence of the Hellenistic cities.

Excavation soundings at Tell es-Sa'idiyeh, located in the Jordan Valley between the Sea of Galilee and the Dead Sea, revealed a Hellenistic structure, 21.2 x 13.3 meters. The building had a spacious hall at the east end from which a corridor, flanked by three rooms on each side, leads toward the west. Ninety-seven circular storage pits and two rectangular mudbrick-lined bins were excavated.

Although Philadelphia (Rabbath-Ammon) had continuous occupation from the Persian through the Roman periods, the Hellenistic remains are minimal. The only excavated remains of the Hellenistic city are walls of the acropolis constructed of polygonal blocks in dry construction (a technique from Greece in the first half of the fourth century B.C.) and a subterranean reservoir at the north end of the acropolis.

The site of 'Iraq el-Emir, between Jericho and Amman, consists of a small mound, two large buildings to the south (Qasr al-'Abd and the Square Building), some water channels, fortification walls and a series of natural and hewn caves in cliffs to the north. The site is identified with the Tyros fortress built by Hyrcanus the Tobiad in the early second century B.C. and is mentioned by Josephus. This identification is validated with inscriptions reading "Tobiah" carved over the entrances of two caves. The building, known as Qasr al-'Abd, was a huge building with monolithic pillars and four monumental relief panels each depicting a large feline identified as either a lion or a leopard. The original plan is uncertain because the building was used during the Byzantine period as a church. Based on the earliest ceramic dates, its original construction is dated to the early second century B.C.

3. Architecture.

3.1. City Planning and Construction Techniques. Although each region demonstrates a different picture of urban life, a careful study of city plans shows that most cities adopted a Hippodamic plan—a grid plan that divides the residential areas into symmetrical blocks separated by right-angle dissecting streets. This plan also divides parts of the town into different functions (i.e., residential, public, cultic). Examples of this Hippodamic plan can be seen at Dor, Shiqmona and Acco.

Construction techniques, especially as seen in fortifications, are of the Phoenician-Greek masonry, which uses header-stretchers (i.e., with one stone laid lengthwise and two widthwise, and fieldstone fill between them). Fortification systems include round and some square towers interspersed along the city wall. Samaria is the best example of this. These new fortification systems were in direct relation to changes in warfare, mainly the introduction of the catapult in the Hellenistic period. Catapult stones are found at several sites. Another noticeable change in construction techniques is the almost complete use of stones for foundations and the superstructure.

3.2. Temples. Two complete temple plans have been discovered (e.g., Lachish, Dor): a long temple composed of three successive areas in which the ritual was conducted mainly in the cella, or inner sanctuary; the broad type with one or more chambers in which the ritual usually took place in an enclosed court in front of the temple building.

3.3. Public Buildings. Several parts of public buildings have been excavated revealing well-planned and monumental construction. Unfortunately, very few have been exposed. It is possible that there may have been some Hellenistic public buildings reused or extensively rebuilt in the Roman period. No complete buildings have been found dating to the Early Hellenistic period. The Hasmonean palace exhibits clear architectural features. The characteristics of Hasmonean palaces include a central court surrounded by rooms. A hall with two columns *in antis* in the southern part of the court led to the triclinium and probably served as a reception hall. This basic plan is characteristic of all the palaces at Masada, as well as the twin palaces at Jericho.

3.4. Private Houses and Estates. Advances in household construction techniques in Palestine were made during the Hellenistic period. The introduction and adaptation of new architectural components, such as the arch and vault, high-quality mortar and the development and use of professional builders and architects were key turning points in private construction in Palestine.

The private house consisted of distinct units (sleeping, bathing, storage, stables, workrooms and even shops). Most dwellings had an upper story used for living and sleeping. This was either an open roof or, in several instances, a complete second-floor structure. The basic architectural unit was the open courtyard in which most of the household's activities and industries took place. It is common to find ovens, vats or storage bins in the courtyard.

A complete synthesis and analysis of private houses and estates has been produced by Hirschfeld. He defines four basic house types from the Hellenistic to Byzantine periods. The *simple house,* the most basic and common dwelling, consists of a one-room structure with an attached open courtyard. The only example from the Hellenistic period was found at Gamala. The second type is a *complex house,* which is similar to the simple house but has been extensively modified with new additions of dwelling units built around the courtyard (e.g., Qasr e-Leja in the region of Samaria). The *courtyard house* is a well-planned dwelling consisting of a central courtyard surrounded on all four sides by the wings of the dwelling structures. This type was used exclusively by wealthy families (e.g., Samaria, Mt. Gerizim, Marisa and Beth Yeraḥ). The fourth type, the *peristyle house,* is rare in Palestine. It originated in Italy in the second century B.C. Its main defining characteristic is a small peristyle courtyard. This type became the model for the classical Roman house of the affluent. One example dating to the Hellenistic period has been excavated at Tel Anafa.

4. Pottery.

Although pottery is the basic building block for archaeology, the pottery of the Hellenistic period has not had synthetic studies and reports as has the pottery of the Bronze and Iron Ages. To date, archaeologists have broadly defined Hellenistic ceramic typology based on early and late Hellenistic assemblages and broad-based regional variations: north, central hills and the coastal region. The variations are based on social and economic factors. In general, the pottery of the region maintains local traditions with Mediterranean fine tablewares and amphorae (locally made and imported). During the Hellenistic period new groups of imported vases appeared: such wares as the "west slope," the "Megarian" and the "Terra Sigillata," as well as many new types of lamps. Undecorated everyday ware also began to appear in the region, such as heavy bowls, cooking pots and the wine amphorae from the eastern Greek islands. The pottery also reflects geographical dynamics.

Archaeologists have defined three assemblages: the northern, the central hills and the coast. It appears that coastal sites used more variety in shapes and decorations for tableware than did the other two regions. They also had two types of cooking pots in contrast to the single globular cooking pot of the north and hill sites. During the third century B.C., Greek-derived fineware appeared in the region. Greek black-gloss wares were derived from imports as well as their local imitations. During the late Hellenistic period pottery assemblages from the northern and coastal sites started to have more vessels in common, while the assemblages from the central hills continued by comparison to be poor in both the quantity and quality. Phoenician influence and manufacture are evident, especially in the northern sites, with several semifine storage and serving vessels, most notably the red-slipped Eastern Sigillata A ware. A Late Hellenistic phase is typified by platters with thickened feet, small floral stamps around the center and small hemispherical footed cups. Several types of cooking vessels were used, including cooking pots, casseroles and baking dishes. Imported Aegean wine amphorae are also commonly found. Some assemblages reflect a regional-ethnic distinctiveness (e.g., Nabatean pottery, Phoenician semifine ware). During the early part of the third century B.C. lamps began to be made in molds. Hellenistic lamps tend to have a round body and a concave disk for the filling hole. The base is flat with an elongated nozzle and a sharp triangle or bow-shaped end.

5. Epigraphy.

Epigraphic data provide a window into the sociocultural dynamics of the Holy Land during the Hellenistic period and provide important information for chronology, trade and glyptic data. From these sources we know that the population was mixed, and the Holy Land became part of the larger international sphere and the multilingual character of the region. The nature and content of the epigraphic data provide evidence that the general population of Hellenistic Palestine was more literate than was previously thought.

5.1. Inscriptions. Several *inscriptions have been found in archaeological excavations and explorations. Evidence of the Seleucid military presence during the Early Hellenistic period is illustrated by the Hefzibah inscription. It is a copy of a series of letters sent by local officials to the Seleucid king pleading for removal of troops from their homes and placing them away from the towns. The Yavne-Yam inscription documents a Sidonian occupation initially established under Antiochus III.

In addition to political-military data, other public inscriptions included temple and city signs. The Zoilus inscription is a bilingual inscription in Greek and Aramaic found in the cult precinct at Tel Dan. It is a flat limestone slab with a four-line dedicatory inscription mentioning Zoilus offering a vow to the god who is in Dan. At Gezer the city limit was marked by several bilingual boundary signs/markers. To date, eleven Gezer boundary stones have been found; nine have the words "Boundary of Gezer" scratched on them in Hebrew, and all but one of these also has "of Alkios" inscribed in Greek.

The well-to-do also adorned their family tombs with decorations and inscriptions. The Mareshah tomb inscription contained a Greek inscription above the tomb of Apollophanes, son of Sesmaios, who is identified as "chief of the Sidonians at Marisa." This tomb contained some of the most extraordinary and elaborate wall decorations depicting humans and animals. Jason's Tomb was another tomb with an inscription illustrating the wealth of the Jewish aristocracy in Jerusalem. This was a family sepulcher excavated in a Jerusalem neighborhood. Carved on the interior walls were several Greek and Aramaic inscriptions, including a three-line Aramaic inscription lamenting Jason.

5.2. Coins. Several *coins contain Greek as well as Hebrew inscriptions. The use of coins expanded during the Hellenistic period. Coins from the Ptolemaics and the Seleucians were common, as well as many city coins belonging to the autonomous polis (e.g., Acco, Dor, Jaffa, Ashkelon, Gaza). Other coins found come from commercial centers such as *Alexandria in Egypt and *Antioch in Syria. During the Hasmonean era, the rulers struck their own coins. A typical hoard would consist of an assortment of the above-mentioned coins demonstrating the rapid growth in international commerce in the Holy Land. Minting of coins became a regular practice in Palestine under Alexander the Great. This continued throughout the Ptolemaic and Seleucid periods. The Hasmonean dynasty also minted its own coins. Common Hasmonean motifs are anchors, stars, palm branches, cornucopiae and pomegranate flowers.

5.3. Pottery. At Khirbet el-Qôm, a small village in the Judean hills, six ostraca were found recording business transactions dating to the late fourth and early third centuries B.C. The longest, containing nine lines, was a loan and receipt in Aramaic and Greek in the sixth year of Ptolemy II (i.e., 277 B.C.). It recorded a loan of thirty-two drachmas from an Idumean shopkeeper/moneylender named Qôs-yada to Nikeratos. A second ostracon was found at Mareshah detailing an Edomite wedding vow between two rich Edomite families. This is the only example of a marriage contract written on a potsherd. Scholars conclude that it is probably an earlier draft or a copy. The groom, QWSRM, requests that the bride, Arsinoe, be given to him and that the couple's sons will inherit their property. The last lines provide the value of the property. Stamped ceramics provide evidence for government administration and trade, for example, the YHD stamped handles as well as the numerous imported Rhodian stamped amphora handles.

6. Other Material Culture.

6.1. Weights. The Greek standard was introduced during the Persian period and became dominant in the Hellenistic period. The Greek weights were made of lead and shaped as rectangular disks that depicted some numbers and the names of the officials or cities responsible for their accuracy.

6.2. Figurines. The Hellenistic as well as the earlier Persian period experienced an explosion of figurines due to private cult practice and the adoption of moldmade figurines. The terra cotta figurines constitute a heterogeneous group exhibiting stylistic influences from Phoenicia, Persia, Egypt, Cyprus, Rhodes and Greece. In general, figurines can be divided between earlier Eastern and later Western types. Attic-style figurines made their first appearance and became the models for local types copying the Greek technique of hollow and molded figurines.

6.3. Glass. Alexandria was apparently a leading center of glass making in the Hellenistic period, but very few of its products have been found in Palestine. Glass was a luxury item. Glass drinking bowls became fashionable during the second century B.C., and this fashion increased in the first century B.C. With the discovery of glass blowing in the second half of the first century B.C., glass became readily available and glass-making workshops have been found in the Roman period in Palestine.

7. Summary.

Archaeology has only recently matured as an independent discipline apart from the other social sciences. Archaeological research and inquiry are ongoing and continue to provide new data, allowing constant reevaluation of current historical reconstructions and interpretations. The archaeological record complements the textual record, more so during the Hellenistic and later Roman periods, which have an abundance of texts compared with earlier periods. The systematic study of the material culture of ancient Palestine contributes to an understanding of the background of the NT by broadening our knowledge of the sociopolitical and cultural landscape.

See also ARCHAEOLOGY AND THE NEW TESTAMENT; ART AND ARCHITECTURE; CITIES, GRECO-ROMAN; HELLENISM; INSCRIPTIONS AND PAPYRI; JEWISH HISTORY; QUMRAN: PLACE AND HISTORY; SYNAGOGUES; TEMPLE, JEWISH; TRAVEL AND TRADE.

BIBLIOGRAPHY. S. Applebaum, *Judea in Hellenistic and Roman Times: Historical and Archaeological Essays* (Leiden: E. J. Brill, 1989); R. Arav, *Hellenistic Palestine: Settlement Patterns and City Planning, 337-31 B.C.E.* (BAR International Series 485; Oxford: BAR, 1989); A. M. Berlin, "Between Large Forces: Palestine in the Hellenistic Period," *BA* 60 (1997) 2-51; idem, "From Monarchy to Markets: The Phoenicians in Hellenistic Palestine," *BASOR* 306 (1997) 75-88; J. Betlyon, "Archaeological Evidence of Military Operations in Southern Judah During the Early Hellenistic Period," *BA* 54 (1991) 36-43; J. Elam, M. Glascock and K. Slane, "A Reexamination of the Provenance of Eastern Sigillata A," in *Proceedings of the 26th International Symposium on Archaeometry, Toronto, 1988,* ed. R. M. Farquhar (Toronto: University of Toronto Press, 1989) 179-83; D. Grose, "The Syro-Palestinian Glass Industry in the Later Hellenistic Period," *Muse* 13 (1979) 54-65; J. Gunneweg, I. Perlman and J. Yellin, *The Provenience, Typology and Chronology of Eastern Terra Sigillata* (Jerusalem: Hebrew University Institute of Archaeology, 1983); R. Harrison, "Hellenization in Syria-Palestine: The Case of Judea in the Third Century BCE," *BA* 57 (1994) 98-108; Y. Hirschfeld, *The Palestinian Dwelling in the Roman-Byzantine Period* (Jerusalem: Franciscan Printing Press, 1995); A. Kasher, *Jews and Hellenistic Cities in Eretz-Israel* (TSAJ 21; Tübingen: Mohr Siebeck, 1990); A. Kasher, U. Rappaport and G. Fuks, eds., *Greece and Rome in Eretz Israel: Collected Essays* (Jerusalem: Israel Exploration Society, 1990); E. Netzer, "The Hasmonean Palaces in Eretz-Israel," in *Biblical Archaeology Today 1990,* ed. A. Biran and J. Aviram (Jerusalem: Israel Exploration Society, 1993); U. Rappaport, "The Birth of the Hasmonean State," in *Recent Archaeology in the Land of Israel,* ed. H. Shanks and B. Mazar (Jerusalem: Israel Exploration Society, 1984); E. Stern, "Between Persia and Greece: Trade, Administration and Warfare in the Persian and Hellenistic Periods (539-63 B.C.)," in *The Archaeology of Society in the Holy Land,* ed. T. Levy (New York: Facts on File, 1995) 432-45. S. M. Ortiz

ARCHELAUS. *See* HERODIAN DYNASTY.

ARENAS

The arena serves as a vivid microcosm of the ancient Roman world and its values. It instantiated in a physical setting the tensions of *honor and ignominy and order and cruelty that characterized the Roman regime and society. Its pull at the popular as well as political levels and the ambivalence of moral esteem and shame associated with this institution have troubled historians of Roman society for centuries. It is apparent then as now that whatever sense one made of the phenomenon, it could not be ignored; all eyes were drawn to the arena.

1. Definition and Description
2. Arena Shows
3. The Role of the Arena in Greco-Roman Life
4. Arenas and Execution
5. Arenas and the New Testament

1. Definition and Description.

The arena (Latin for "sand") was the venue for public spectacle in the Roman world that from the time of Augustus came to develop permanent sites to replace the more temporary wooden edifices hastily thrown together in the forum. Because of the expense and time involved in the construction of permanent large-scale public buildings, this development coincided with the establishment of a permanent wealth and power base, concentrated in the household of Caesar (*Domus Caesaris*), in contrast to the system of annually elected colleges of magistrates operating during the Roman republic.

1.1. At Rome. The largest and most famous of these arenas was the Colosseum (*Amphitheatrum Flavium*) at Rome. It was an elliptical amphitheater built by Vespasian (A.D. 69-79) and formally inaugurated by Titus in the heart of Rome (June 80). It measured 156 x 128 x 50 meters with an arena measuring 86 x 54 meters and could hold a capacity of at least forty to fifty thousand people seated and five thousand standing. It became the architectural model for amphitheaters and the benchmark for grand-scale public buildings in general throughout the *Roman Empire and European history.

1.2. Outside of Rome. The arena or amphitheater was the most visible and practical way for a provincial city to participate in *Romanitas* (Romanness) and to communicate its loyalty to Rome. Even Herod had an amphitheater built in cities outside of Judea proper, despite the fact that earlier opposition to such *Hellenizing had sparked the *Hasmonean revolt. Estimates suggest there were as many as 272 stone amphitheaters throughout the empire, not to mention the many earthenwork amphitheaters that were common in northwest Europe. Many Greek cities had the advantage of already-existing buildings suitable for public spectacle that were transformed to function as an arena (e.g., the stadium at Ephesus). Others tried to cut corners with cheaply constructed sites and paid the consequences when they collapsed and killed thousands of people, as at Fidenae in A.D. 27 (Tacitus *Ann.* 4.63).

2. Arena Shows.

The amphitheater became the permanent building used for *venationes,* staged wild-beast hunts (*see* Circuses and Games 1.2), occasionally *naumachiae* (naval battles made possible by a system of drains that allowed flooding of certain arenas) and *munera gladiatoria* (gladiatorial contests). The day's events usually followed the above order with wild-beast hunts in the morning, naval battles around midday and gladiatorial combats reserved for the afternoon. From at least c. A.D. 61 on the scheduled midday break was filled with the execution of criminals.

The earliest gladiatorial contests (from c. 264 B.C.), in which a few combatants engaged in single combat to the death at the funeral of a respected citizen, were private spectacles to be distinguished from the traditional public religious festivals (*ludi*) of the circus and the processional games of the triumph (*see* Roman Triumph). Unlike the *ludi,* which were state-funded, the *munera* continued to be largely privately funded. Even those put on by the emperors were done in a quasi-private capacity in their familial role as Caesar rather than as *Princeps*.

The gladiatorial contest developed from its origins as a funeral rite put on by a private citizen to honor a dead relative into a gift that was owed by a wealthy citizen not only to his ancestors but also to the community. The Roman spirit of civic competition and valuation of military virtue (*virtus*) gave the contest increasing status as a demonstration of the wealth and social importance of the deceased and his family. In the late republic the *munera* became useful political tools in the campaign for office for those who capitalized on the popularity of the events and the efficacy of what was communicated by them (Suetonius *Julius* 39).

This prestige was later monopolized during the principate by the emperors, who put on the grandest shows, imposed limits on the number (2) per year and size (maximum 120 pairs) of *munera* put on by civic magistrates, and they came to control the supply and training of gladiators as well. After Domitian (A.D. 81-96), only emperors gave gladiatorial contests at Rome, and only those with imperial approval were put on elsewhere in the empire. They became a widespread demonstration of imperial control at the popular level.

3. The Role of the Arena in Greco-Roman Life. *Munera* were infrequent compared with other public spectacles and so punctuated Roman life with the excitement of an anticipated special event. These became the focus of culture, the place to be and to be seen (Tertullian *De Spect.* 25). There was also the added incentive of prizes, vouchers of gifts from the *editor* (the host putting on the show) catapulted into the crowd. Betting was part of the event and served as a factor of social integration as both rich and poor, noble and commoner could share in this point of contact.

3.1. Economics of the Arena. Arenas represented a vast industry largely controlled by and benefitting the emperor. In the provinces the trainers (*lanistae*) provided many of the gladiators at the expense of the *editor,* who did not want to be seen as stingy. There was also an imperial hand in the expensive provision of exotic beasts. A decree of A.D. 177 preserves a record of scaled prices (salary caps) for the different grades of gladiator, and there was an imperial surtax of 33 percent on the whole show as well. Because top gladiators could be worth as much as twelve thousand sesterces, their value to their trainer as well as their popularity, especially if they were free citizens, often kept them alive to fight another day.

3.2. Sociological Function of the Arena. The sociological approach has contributed much to the question of the appeal and purpose of combat sports in Roman society. It has enabled scholars to look beyond the undeniable brutality of the killing in the arena to cultural aspects of the events in their context. The gladiatorial contest served as a way to keep alive the memory of the deceased by a vivid reminder of death and by the embodiment of the struggle of life and death as a combat. The arena was the place where the honor of fighting and facing death and the shame of running away and ignobly flinching at death was broadcast and even experienced vicariously by the audience. The crowds were symbolically empowered to control these forces as the decision of life or death (the *editor*'s) was often influenced by the people. The glorification of abasement and the belief that one was empowered in the voluntariness of one's submission to death contributed to a widespread ethos that drew all of society into the amphitheater and members of every level of society down into the shame and glory of the arena itself.

The concentration of gladiatorial games at the end of the year also suggests that these games of death were a way of coming to terms with the annual cycles of death and rebirth in nature. The event also enacted in a controlled environment the more specific threat faced by Rome as an empire, namely, war. This might explain why the growth in popularity of the *munera* paralleled Roman military expansion.

3.3. Arena as Social Exchange. There was also a sense in which what took place in the arena was reciprocal. The *editor* was expected to give enthusiastically the gift of the contests to the community (Suetonius *Augustus* 45), but unless the community was also expected to receive the gift, there could be no social exchange. The act of the citizen in attending reinforced a fundamental social relationship in Roman society. It expressed the client's gratitude toward and acknowledgment of the great patron of the community, or in the case of the caesar himself, patron of the empire. Hence the indignation shown toward a public figure who failed to provide *munera* was equaled by that shown toward one who refused to participate in the communal exchange of the arena shows. Overt nonparticipation was a provocative demonstration of alienness for philosophers (e.g., Stoics) and Christians alike. The seating in the amphitheater also reinforced traditional social relationships as it reflected and reinforced the class and gender structures in Roman society.

4. Arenas and Execution.

The arena was a public execution ground for criminals and enemies of the state, who were sometimes forced to kill each other. The gladiatorial contests and public executions can be seen as the symbolic subjugation of barbarism by Roman society. Alien and threatening people were conquered in the arena (on dressing Christians in animal skins before executing them, see Tacitus *Ann.* 15.44). Representations of dangerous enemies were at once figuratively integrated into and actually expelled from society by their death. These roles were extended so far as to include the staging of executions as mythological reenactments in which the deaths of the criminals played out the tortures and deaths of the mythical characters.

4.1. The Civic Nature of Execution. Capital punishment as well was made public in the arena, not merely as a deterrent but as an assurance of order to the people. Squeamishness at the sight of public punishment of criminals was a sign of moral weakness and would have signified an undue sympathy toward the disorderly elements of the Roman world or an unwillingness to exercise one's right as a citizen to participate in the maintenance of civic law. At the martyrdom of Perpetua and Felicity in Carthage (c. 203), the crowd demanded to see the bodies of the criminals "so that their eyes could participate in the killing as the sword entered their flesh" (*The Passion of Perpetua and Felicity* 21.7).

4.2. Kinds of Death. The punishments in the Roman world varied according to one's citizenship and status. Death by the sword was reserved for criminal Roman citizens, who could at least die with dignity. Some criminals were condemned to spend five years in a gladiatorial school (*Gregarii condemnati ad ludos*), the equivalent and one of the few possible sites of imprisonment besides the mines (*ad metalla*). Their entertainment worth doubled if they managed to survive their first encounter, usually against a trained gladiator. Some, especially captured barbarians or rebel enemies, were killed en masse in the arena by the sword (*noxii ad gladium damnati*). Noncitizen criminals might be condemned *ad bestias.* They were worthy only to be thrown to the beasts, a punishment at least as base as crucifixion (*ad crucem*) or being burned at the stake (*ad flammas*) but a much more exotic and costly performance. Such execution provided the lightweight entertainment of the midday break, the prelude to the day's main events.

4.3. Christians and the Arena. That Christians were considered criminals is undisputed, but there is controversy as to the reasons why they were so perceived by the Romans. Perhaps some light is shed on the question by the fact that the public executions were punishments thought appropriate for temple robbers, parricides and arsonists. Since Christians believed in a coming judgment of fire, they may have been thought guilty of inciting to arson merely by being Christians. This may be the legal reasoning employed by Fabius Sabinus, the urban prefect during the reign of Nero, who laid the blame for Rome's burning (64) on Christians generically (Tacitus *Ann.* 15.44; Suetonius *Nero* 16). Christian martyrdom in the arena was a public event demonstrated within the context of the civic community. The act of opting out of the pagan world in some sense should have taken place right in the heart of that world, the arena. Early Christian self-identification by antagonism with the world and participation in the sufferings of Christ could have had no more literal instantiation than death in the arena.

5. Arenas and the New Testament.

The apostle Paul himself may have experienced the arena if one interprets the passage in 2 Timothy 4:17, "and I was delivered from the lion's mouth" (*kai errysthēn ek stomatos leontos*) as a description of a deliverance from an actual lion. The line "At my first answer" (*en tē prōtē mou apologia,* 2 Tim 4:16) suggests a setting not unlike that attested by other accounts of martyrdom trials in the arena. Moreover, the first part of the verse referring to one of the reasons for this ordeal, namely, "that all the nations might hear" his preaching, tends to support the theory that it was a public event with a crowd. However, he could be using the lion's mouth as symbolic of death in general, which he has escaped. Or more specifically, he could be referring to the fact that he was spared that particular punishment *(ad bestias)*. This explanation is compatible with other incidents (Acts 25:10-11) in which Paul was delivered from worse punishment on account of his citizen status and appeal to Caesar *(petitio principii)* and also concurs with early traditions that relate his initial acquittal and later execution by the sword.

Paul is at least familiar enough with the arena to employ it in his writings. He refers to fighting wild beasts *(ethēriomachēsa)* as a metaphor of dealing with his enemies in Ephesus (1 Cor 15:32). In 1 Corinthians 4:9 Paul says that God has ordained death for the apostles. They are to be a spectacle for the world, angels and humanity. Here God is like an *editor* (cf. Tertullian *Ad Mart.* 3), and their deaths become *munera* (public offerings to the community; cf. Cyprian *Ep.* 10.5). In addition, the conflation of the images of soldier and gladiator in classical literature (e.g., Seneca *Prov.* 4.4) often translated into cross-fertilization of the metaphors of soldier and gladiator in the NT. For some the gladiator was the only "soldier" familiar to them. This may suggest a reexamination of NT metaphors of the soldier (e.g., Eph 6:10-17) with the arena in mind (cf. Seneca *Vit. Beat.* 15.5; Cyprian *Ep.* 58.8).

See also CIRCUSES AND GAMES; PERSECUTION; ROMAN TRIUMPH.

BIBLIOGRAPHY. R. Auguet, *Cruelty and Civilization: The Roman Games* (London: Routledge, 1994); C. A. Barton, *The Sorrows of the Ancient Romans: The Gladiator and the Monster* (Princeton, NJ: Princeton University Press, 1993); K. M. Coleman, "Fatal Charades: Roman Executions Staged as Mythical Enactments," *JRS* 80 (1990) 44-73; A. Futrell, *Blood in the Arena: The Spectacle of Roman Power* (Austin: University of Texas Press, 1997); J.-C. Golvin, *L'Amphitheatre Romain: Essai sur la Theorisation de sa Forme et de ses Fonctions* (2 vols.; Paris: Publications du Centre Pierre, 1988); E. Gunderson, "The Ideology of the Arena," *Classical Antiquity* 15 (1996) 113-51; K. Hopkins, "Murderous Games," in *Death and Renewal* (SSRH; Cambridge: Cambridge University Press, 1983) vol. 2; W. Meeks, *The First Urban Christians: The Social World of the Apostle Paul* (New Haven, CT: Yale University Press, 1984); J. Pearson, *Arena* (London: Thames & Hudson, 1973); J. S. Pobee, *Persecution and Martyrdom in the Theology of Paul* (Sheffield: Sheffield Academic Press, 1985); L. Robert, *Les Gladiateurs dans L'orient Grec* (Paris: Champion, 1940); T. E. J. Wiedemann, *Emperors and Gladiators* (London: Routledge, 1995); idem, "Single Combat and Being Roman," *Ancient Society* 27 (1996) 91-103; M. Wistrand, *Entertainment and Violence in Ancient Rome: The Attitudes of Roman Writers of the First Century* A.D. (Västervik, Sweden: Ekblads, 1992).

M. Pucci

ARISTEAS, EPISTLE OF

The *Epistle* (a *diēgēsis,* "Narrative") *of Aristeas* purports to be an eyewitness account by a Gentile official at the court of Ptolemy II Philadelphus of the circumstances that led to the translation of the *Septuagint. The story of the translation, however, is peripheral, the bulk of the book being concerned with a panegyric on the Jewish people and the superiority of their religion, ethics and wisdom to those of the Gentiles.

1. The Contents of the Book
2. The Historical Background
3. The Character of the Book
4. The Reception of *Aristeas* by Later Jewish and Christian Authors
5. The Date
6. The Purpose

1. The Contents of the Book.

The book falls naturally into three main parts, with a proem and an epilogue.

In the proem (*Ep. Arist.* 1-8) Aristeas dedicates his book to his brother (*Ep. Arist.* 7, 120) Philocrates and announces its theme: the translation of the Jewish law (*Ep. Arist.* 3).

In the first major section (*Ep. Arist.* 9-34a) Demetrius of Phalerum, the librarian, reports to King Ptolemy II Philadelphus that he had already collected more than two hundred thousand books, his aim being soon to bring their number to five hundred thousand, and informs the king of the desirability to include the Jewish law, which needed to be translated (*Ep. Arist.* 9-11). Aristeas, a Gentile at court (*Ep. Arist.* 16, 40, 43), petitions the release of about one hundred thousand Jewish captives as a goodwill gesture to the Jewish high priest Eleazar, ostensibly to dispose him to provide the translators (*Ep. Arist.* 12-18). Following the report of Demetrius (*Ep. Arist.* 28-32), the king consents not only to the liberation of the captives but also to sending sumptuous gifts to Eleazar with a letter in his name (*Ep. Arist.* 19-34a).

This section (*Ep. Arist.* 34b-300) constitutes the bulk of the epistle and is concerned with the king's letter to Eleazar requesting six scholars from each tribe (*Ep. Arist.* 35-40) and Eleazar's complying reply (*Ep. Arist.* 41-46) naming the seventy-two scholars (*Ep. Arist.* 47-50). The author then indulges in a long description of the king's presents to Eleazar (*Ep. Arist.* 51-82), *Jerusalem (*Ep. Arist.* 83-120), the *temple (*Ep. Arist.* 84-91), the priestly offices and the temple sacrifices (*Ep. Arist.* 92-95), the high-priestly vestments (*Ep. Arist.* 96-99), the citadel (*Ep. Arist.* 100-104), the city and its environs (*Ep. Arist.* 105-11) and trade (*Ep. Arist.* 112-20). He continues with Eleazar's farewell to the translators (*Ep. Arist.* 121-27), a long exposé by Eleazar of the superiority of the Jewish law and criticism of Gentile idolatry and immorality (*Ep. Arist.* 128-69), Eleazar's sacrifices and the departure of the scholars (*Ep. Arist.* 172). The section ends with the honorable reception of the translators by the king (*Ep. Arist.* 173-86) and the seven-day feast that the king holds in their honor during which, asked very hard questions on politics, royal behavior, and so on, each of the scholars distinguishes himself by giving answers that amazed not only Aristeas but also the Gentile philosophers present (*Ep. Arist.* 187-300).

Having been feasted, the translators are taken to a building specially prepared, and they apply themselves to their task (*Ep. Arist.* 301). The translation is arrived at in session during which they compared their views (*Ep. Arist.* 302: "They proceeded in such a way that agreement among them was reached on every point by comparison" [lit., "confrontation"]). The work proceeded from morning to 3 o'clock in the afternoon and was completed in seventy-two days (*Ep. Arist.* 307). The translation is read to the Jews of *Alexandria, who ratify it and pronounce curses on anyone who might change anything in it (*Ep. Arist.* 308-11), after which the king hears it read and is delighted, and he charges Demetrius to take good care of it (*Ep. Arist.* 312-17). The translators are sent back to Judea with gifts (*Ep. Arist.* 318-21).

In the epilogue (*Ep. Arist.* 322) Aristeas charges Philocrates to avoid reading myths and concentrate instead only on true stories like his own.

2. The Historical Background.
Aristeas's claim that the translation of the LXX (only the Law) took place during the reign of Ptolemy II Philadelphus (coregent with his father, Ptolemy I Soter since 285 B.C., sole king 282-246 B.C.) while Demetrius of Phalerum (350?-283/2 B.C., see Diogenes Laertius *Vit.* 5.75-83) was the librarian and the philosopher Menedemos of Eretria (339/8-265 B.C., see Diogenes Laertius *Vit.* 2.125-44) was at the Alexandrian court, is unhistorical. Demetrius, who was invited to Egypt by Ptolemy Soter in 297 B.C., was the founder of the museum and in all probability of the library but apparently never served as librarian, especially under Philadelphus (*see* Alexandrian Library). He was banished by Philadelphus at the death of his father, Soter, for having advised against his succession to the throne, and shortly thereafter he died. The first librarian was Zenodotos (see P. Oxy. 1241 for a list of librarians), who entered his office in 285 (-270 B.C.) being succeeded by Apollonios Rhodios (270-245 B.C.). Furthermore Menedemos, who once did visit Cyprus, is not known to have visited Alexandria. The apocryphal stories about the divine punishment of Theopompos (c. 378-300 B.C.), who during his Alexandrian visit in 305 B.C. was almost put to death by Soter for being a busybody (*polypragmōn,* which may well explain the legend), and Theodectes (c. 375-334 B.C.; *Ep. Arist.* 314-16) are otherwise unknown.

3. The Character of the Book.
The unhistorical framework is surpassed by the fantastic presentation of the main characters of the story—all Gentiles—as though they were devout converts to Judaism. Thus, not only Aristeas, a Gentile, intercedes repeatedly for the captive Jews (*Ep. Arist.* 12-19) and speaks with excessive admiration for the Jewish people and their law, but also Demetrius knows that "the law is august and of divine origin, and that God punished busybodies" (*Ep. Arist.* 313).

The fantasy of *Aristeas* runs riot with Ptolemy's behavior. Ptolemy is presented as addressing a humble request to his vassal Eleazar as to an equal at the fabulous expense of 200-300 talents of gold (*Ep. Arist.* 33, 319-20), 170 talents of silver (*Ep. Arist.* 33, 40), precious stones five times the value of the gold (*Ep. Arist.* 82), granting, moreover, the return of more than one hundred thousand Jews—almost a second exodus—at 400 talents manumission costs (*Ep. Arist.* 20, 37), and finally giving the unredeemable promise of the release of all Jews in the world now and in the future (*Ep. Arist.* 38). It is utterly incredible that this behavior should come from one of those kings who had given orders to confiscate any books found on ships visiting egypt, and who had borrowed from athens the standard edition of the three great tragedians (aeschylus, sophocles, euripides) in order to have them copied, giving 15 talents as guarantee for their return, but who, afterward, kept the original and sent back a copy (*Historia tou Hellenikou Ethnous*, 2:278-79; see also Galen, *In Hippokratis lib. 3 epid. comm.*, 607-8). But there is more.

Contrary to custom, according to which Ptolemy let royal ambassadors wait for thirty days before being admitted to his presence, the translators gain immediate admittance (*Ep. Arist.* 174-76). At the showing of the parchments the king, like a pious Jew, makes his devout sevenfold obeisance before the law (*Ep. Arist.* 177) and thanks God for his oracles (*Ep. Arist.* 177). Eleazar praises the king's "piety toward our God" (*Ep. Arist.* 42). At the banquet the king dismisses his own priests and requests the oldest of the translators to offer prayers (*Ep. Arist.* 184). At the reading of the completed translation the king is astonished that such wonderful writings were not mentioned by any Greek historians (*Ep. Arist.* 312), bows devoutly before them and commits them to Demetrius's safekeeping (*Ep. Arist.* 317). At the end, in typically *pseudepigraphical fashion Aristeas protests his truthfulness: "I have related the story just as it happened, keeping myself pure from all blame" (*Ep. Arist.* 297), and then distinguishes himself from "mythologists" (*Ep. Arist.* 322).

The apologetic nature of *Aristeas* is so transparent that Bentley (in 1699) called it "a clumsie cheat." It may therefore appear all the more surprising that the character of the book does not seem to have been exposed before L. Vives (in 1522), J. J. Scalinger (1609) and especially H. Hody (in 1684) (see Jellicoe, 31-32). This has its explanation not in any supposed credulity on the part of Christian Greek authors, but in the circumstance that they found in this work a convenient account that sanctioned the equation of the LXX with the Hebrew text. Thus Aristeas not only escaped their censure but also his account was embellished by some of them.

In spite of its unhistorical character in details, the *Epistle of Aristeas* contains a core of historical truth: the Hebrew law book was translated sometime in the third century B.C.; the translation was executed by Alexandrian Jewry; it was a group effort; and by the second century B.C. it had not yet been accorded equality with the Masoretic Text.

4. The Reception of *Aristeas* by Later Jewish and Christian Authors.

In spite of *Aristeas*'s extravagances in propagating the Jewish cause, its account of the translation of the LXX is fairly restrained, and herein lies its value. The translators arrived at the adopted text after discussion and comparison of their several proposals. This realistic procedure is later exchanged for a miraculous one. The earliest author showing knowledge of the contents of *Aristeas* is the Jewish author Aristobulus (180-145 B.C.), who argued that Greek philosophy derived from the OT, which had been translated into Greek before the translation executed under Philadelphus (Eusebius *Praep. Ev.* 13.12.1-2; cf. Gooding, passim).

With *Philo (*Vit. Mos.* 2.6-7) the translators have become inspired "prophets" and write "not each one different things, but the same word for word, as though each one was tutored by an invisible prompter." It is a moot question whether Philo reflects *Aristeas* or has knowledge of the story independently (the same goes for Aristobulus). *Josephus, however, is the first author to refer explicitly to *Aristeas* and reproduce a large part of it (Josephus *Ant.* 12.2 §§1-118).

The first Christian author to mention *Aristeas* is Justin Martyr, who, however, has Philadelphus address not Eleazar but King Herod (Justin Martyr *Apol. I* 31). The miraculous line struck out by Philo is followed by Irenaeus. He (in *Haer.* 3.21.2, in Eusebius *Hist. Eccl.* 5.8.11-15) has Ptolemy Soter rather than Philadelphus address the Jerusalemites rather than Eleazar. Once in Alexandria, the king separated the translators to avoid any secret agreement among them but found, to his surprise, that "they all had translated the same things with the same words." A similar story is related by Clement of Alexandria (*Strom.* 1.22). Extended quotations of *Aristeas* occur in Eusebius (*Praep. Ev.* 8.2-5, 9).

5. The Date.

There is no consensus on the date of *Aristeas*. The proposed dates range between 200 B.C. and A.D. 33. The first century A.D. may be dismissed as too improbable for such a letter to be written at a time when the LXX was well established. In general, scholars have held to 200-170 B.C. (e.g., Schürer, Orlinsky, Tramontano, Pelletier, Jellicoe, Shutt), 150-100 (e.g., Andrews, Bickermann, Kahle, Hadas, Würthwein) and the first century B.C. (e.g., Wendland, Thackeray, Riessler). The internal evidence of *Aristeas* is indecisive. If we could be certain that Aristobulus quoted *Aristeas* (Eusebius *Praep. Ev.* 13.12; cf. Fraser 1:694), then the work ought to have been written before 150 B.C. However, the use of Aristobulus by *Aristeas* cannot be ruled out, and it is not improbable that both drew from an earlier work.

The peaceful and prosperous conditions in Palestine (*Ep. Arist.* 84-171) might reflect an idyllic view of the circumstances before the Seleucid conquest of Judea (c. 198 B.C.). The citadel of Jerusalem (*Ep. Arist.* 100), which should be distinguished from the later Syrian fortress (cf., e.g., 1 Macc 1:33; 13:49-52; Josephus *Ant.* 12.4.4 §252; *J.W.* 5.4.1 §§136-41), is probably that mentioned by Nehemiah 2:8; 7:2 (see also 2 Macc 4:12, 27; 5:5; Josephus *Ant.* 12.3.3 §§133, 138) and later rebuilt as Antonia, thus reflecting an earlier date. An earlier date is also suggested by the depiction of the high priest as a theocratic leader and of the priests as performing spontaneously their duties (*Ep. Arist.* 92-96), both of whom, somewhat later, had come under the spell of Hellenism. The knowledge by *Aristeas* of Egyptian protocol implies a Jew in high office, something that was possible under Ptolemy VI Philometor (180-145 B.C.). Jellicoe's suggestion, following Klijn's lead, that it was written to vindicate the claims of the LXX and of the Jerusalem *temple over against those of the new Jewish center, Onias's temple at Leontopolis (c. 160 B.C.; cf. Josephus *Ant.* 12.7 §§387-88; 13.3.1-3 §§62-73; 13.4 §§283-87; *J.W.* 7.10.2-3 §§421-36), and its supposed rival version, would explain the bulk of the book. However, in the absence of any evidence for the existence of such a version, this view is incapable of proof. By contrast, Orlinsky has used the absence of any reference in *Aristeas* to the temple of Leontopolis to support an earlier date. At present the best option is to date *Aristeas* at about 200 or at the latest 170 B.C. (but see Fraser 1:696; 2:970-71).

6. The Purpose.

Like the date, the purpose of the book has defied solution. The ostensible reason for *Aristeas* was to describe the origin of the LXX translation, though in reality it was to promote the Jewish faith. The question is whether *Aristeas* is addressed to Gentile or to Jewish readers. At a time when the Greek language, literature and culture were making a strong impact upon the Jews, in particular Diaspora Jews, who, severed from their fatherland, from the temple and its sacrifices—the symbols and rallying point of their particularistic religion—were in danger of distancing themselves from their ancestors' faith, it was quite natural that an idyllic account of Judaism and the esteem it had enjoyed with Greek monarchs and philosophers were felt to be the needed antidote. *Aristeas* was not written for Greek readers: its simplistic narrative and historical blunders could not but alienate them and thus defeat its purpose. It was written for Jewish consumption outside Palestine, in particular Alexandria.

See also ALEXANDRIA; HELLENISTIC JUDAISM; SEPTUAGINT/GREEK OLD TESTAMENT.

BIBLIOGRAPHY. (See the excellent bibliographies in Jellicoe and Schürer.) **Texts and Translations:** M. Hadas, ed., *Aristeas to Philocrates* [*Letter of Aristeas,* reproducing the text of Thackeray] (New York: Harper, 1951); A. Pelletier, *Lettre d'Aristée a Philocrate* (SC 89; Paris: Editions du Cerf, 1962); H. St. J. Thackeray, "The Letter of Aristeas," in *An Introduction to the Old Testament in Greek,* ed. H. B. Swete (Cambridge: Cambridge University Press, 1914). **Studies:** H. Andrews, "The Letter of Aristeas," in *The Apocrypha and Pseudepigrapha of the Old Testament in English,* ed. R. H. Charles (2 vols.; Oxford: Clarendon Press, 1913) 2:94-122; E. J. Bickermann, "Zur Datierung des Pseudo-Aristeas," *ZNW* 29 (1930) 280-98; P. M. Fraser, *Ptolemaic Alexandria* (3 vols.; Oxford: Clarendon Press, 1972) 1:687-716; 2:957-1000; Galen, *In Hippokratis librum 3 epidemiarum commentarii,* ed. C. G. Kühn (22 vols.; Hildesheim: Georg Olms, 1964-65 [1821-33]; D. W. Gooding, "Aristeas and Septuagint Origins: A Survey of Recent Studies," *VT* 13 (1963) 357-79; *Historia tou Hellenikou Ethnous* (15 [16] vols.; Athens: Ekdotike Athēnon, 1972-78); G. E. Howard, "The *Letter of Aristeas* and Diaspora Judaism," *JTS* 22 (1971) 337-48; S. Jellicoe, *The Septuagint and Modern Study* (Oxford: Clarendon Press, 1968); P. E. Kahle, *The Cairo Geniza* (2d ed.; London: Blackwell, 1959) esp. 209-14; J. J. Lewis, "The Table-Talk Section in the Letter of Aristeas," *NTS* 13 (1966) 53-56; O. Murray, "Aristeas and Ptolemaic Kingship," *JTS* 18 (1967)

337-71; H. M. Orlinsky, "The Septuagint as Holy Writ and the Philosophy of the Translators," *HUCA* 46 (1975) 89-114; E. Schürer, *The History of the Jewish People in the Age of Jesus Christ (175 B.C.-A.D. 135)*, rev. G. Vermes, F. Millar, M. Goodman (3 vols.; Edinburgh: T & T Clark, 1973-87) 3:1: 474-93, esp. 677-87; R. J. H. Shutt, "Letter of Aristeas," in *OTP* 2:7-34; G. Zuntz, "Aristeas Studies I: 'The Seven Banquets,'" *JSS* 4 (1959) 109-26. C. C. Caragounis

ARISTOBULUS

The five fragments of works by the second-century Jewish author Aristobulus are preserved in Eusebius's two works, *Historia Ecclesiastica* (7.32.16-18 = frag. 1, a citation of a citation of Aristobulus) and *Praeparatio Evangelica* (8.10 and 13.12 = frags. 2-5). Clement of Alexandria's *Stromata* (1; 5; 6) also has parallels to fragments 2-5 but in a less reliable form than in Eusebius.

1. Date
2. The Author and His Work
3. Outline of Contents

1. Date.

Although both Eusebius and Clement seem to think that Aristobulus addressed his work to Ptolemy VI Philometer (181–145 B.C.), Eusebius's quotation of Anatolius *On the Passover* in fragment 1 seems to suggest that there is an earlier date, during the reign of Ptolemy II Philadelphus (283–246 B.C.). There is also the related matter of the attribution by the writer of 2 Maccabees (*see* 1 and 2 Maccabees) of a letter addressed to Aristobulus and the Jews of *Alexandria from Judas Maccabeus (2 Macc 1:10, claiming to have been written shortly after the end of 164), which would place him within the reign of Ptolemy VI. Given that the letter in 2 Maccabees is most likely a forgery, it is difficult to know how to take its suggestion that Aristobulus was the teacher of the king, but, if this can be taken seriously, then it may be that Aristobulus could be dated as early as 176 to 170 B.C., when Ptolemy VI was younger and would have needed a teacher. If the evidence in 2 Maccabees is to be seen as fabrication, then a date nearer the end of Philometer's reign would seem more likely (c. 150 B.C.).

2. The Author and His Work.

Aristobulus has been called the first Jewish *philosopher (Hengel, 1:163), and his extant work would indeed support such a title. Although in the introduction to fragment 1, Anatolius suggests that Aristobulus was one of the seventy translators of the *Septuagint, it is more likely that Aristobulus was an *Alexandrian Jew of the early to mid-second century. Fragments 2 and 3 suggest that Aristobulus was schooled in *Aristotelian philosophy (in conjunction with "that of his ancestors," frag. 2), and his extant work revolves around a desire to promote Mosaic law as a true philosophy. He thus argues for the dependence of early Greek philosophers (Pythagoras, Socrates, *Plato) on a translation of the Pentateuch earlier than the LXX (frags. 3 and 4). It seems clear that his work was done in Greek, and he displays a deep knowledge and interaction with various aspects of Greek culture and philosophy (*see* Hellenism).

Although A. Y. Collins (833) suggests that "it is somewhat unlikely that a Jew would have been a teacher of a Ptolemy" during the second century B.C., there is no reason to think that this is the case—Aristobulus's clear facility with a variety of Greek philosophers and schools may have made him the ideal candidate to be a teacher of the young Ptolemy, regardless of his racial or religious background. It is possible that the arguments Aristobulus made concerning the dependence of Greek philosophy on the Mosaic law were taken seriously by his contemporaries—given the Greek insecurity with regard to the relative youth of their culture in comparison with the Eastern cultures, such claims would hit a particularly weak spot for the Greeks. If this is the case, it would have been appropriate for Aristobulus to present these arguments to the king as a teacher. The relationship between the two halves of Aristobulus's dual Jewish and Greek thought world is in need of further investigation, but it is clear that he stands early in a tradition that would find its Jewish climax in *Philo of Alexandria and continue in importance for the Christian tradition through the NT (one has only to think of Apollos) and the early church.

3. Outline of Contents.

Fragment 1 is a detailed astronomical discussion of the date of the Passover. Fragment 2 is a discussion of anthropomorphisms in the Mosaic law with regard to the nature of God. Fragment 3 discusses the way in which Plato and Pythagoras were dependent on an early translation of the Pentateuch and connects the translation of the LXX with the activities of Demetrius of Phalerus, supporting the chronology for the translation given by the *Letter of Aristeas* (*see* Aristeas, Epistle of). Fragment 4 combines the arguments from fragments 2 and 3, adding several quotations of pagan authors (Orpheus, Aratus—some verses of which are also known from independent sources) to prove his point that, on the one hand, Greek authors have been dependent on the Mosaic law, and on the other hand, if Greek philosophy undergirds Greek culture and is similar to Moses' philosophy, then the Mosaic law, on account of its anteriority, should be seen as superior, or at least accepted as a viable alternative. Fragment 5 follows directly on from fragment 4 in Eusebius's text and is a discussion of the *sabbath and a panegyric on wisdom as the first principle of creation (seen as preexistent) and the light of all people. Fragment 5 cites Hesiod's *Works and Days,* some unknown Homeric material and a verse attributed to Linus, a singer from Greek myth. Fragment 5 is largely taken up by an extended discussion of the number seven and its significance in creation, a theme probably drawn from Pythagoras.

See also ALEXANDRIA; HELLENISTIC JUDAISM; PHILOSOPHY.

BIBLIOGRAPHY. A. Y. Collins, "Aristobulus," in *The Old Testament Pseudepigrapha,* ed. J. H. Charlesworth (2 vols.; Garden City, NY: Doubleday, 1983, 1985) 2:831-42; M. Hengel, *Judaism and Hellenism* (2 vols.; London: SCM, 1974) 1:163-69, 2:105-10; N. Walter, *Der Thoraausleger Aristobulus* (TU 86; Berlin: Akademie Verlag, 1964).

B. W. R. Pearson

ARISTOTLE, ARISTOTELIANISM

Standard reference works on the NT give short notice to Aristotle (384-322 B.C.) and Aristotelianism. For example, Helmut Koester wrote: "Aristotle himself and his philosophy cannot be discussed here. For several centuries very little effect of Aristotle's philosophy can be detected" (*Introduction to the New Testament,* 1:144). It has been widely assumed that Plato (427-347 B.C.) and Platonism had much greater influence on emerging Christendom. But with new interest in *rhetorical analysis as well as ethics and morals, along with the attendant moral lists (*Haustafeln; see* Family and Household), a reconsideration of the importance of Aristotle is of merit. The future course of Christianity was much influenced by the Aristotelian corpus beginning with Boethius (c. 480-c. 524) but especially with Thomas Aquinas (c. 1225-1274). Aristotle's work—which encompassed the sciences, arts and humanities—exerted great influence on Christianity, Judaism and Islam until the 1700s.

1. Life and Works
2. Influence

1. Life and Works.

Aristotle was born in the village of Stagira on the peninsula of Macedonia, in northern Greece. His father, Nicomachus, was court physician to Amyntas, father of Philip II and grandfather of *Alexander the Great (356-323 B.C.). The medical culture of Aristotle's childhood no doubt encouraged his interest in biology and the sciences, along with an interest in intellectual rigor and logic. Upon the death of his father Aristotle was sent in 367 B.C. to the Academy of Plato (427-347) at *Athens and remained there for twenty years. With the death of Plato in 347 Aristotle left the academy, spent three years in Asia Minor and then returned to Macedonia and became tutor to Alexander the Great. When Alexander became king in 336, Aristotle again took up residence in Athens and founded the Lyceum as a rival to Plato's Academy. He lectured for twelve years, often while walking the grounds and under a portico, thereby gaining the appellation *peripatetic* (from *peripatoi,* "walks"). With the rise of anti-Macedonian sentiment at the death of Alexander, Aristotle felt forced to leave Athens. He died a year later.

The works of Aristotle include six treatises on logic, three on natural science, five on zoology, two on psychology, one on metaphysics, two on ethics, two on political science and one each on rhetoric and poetics. The discourse on metaphysics includes Aristotle's theology, in which he posits a first or unmoved mover. This unmoved mover is neither creator nor interested in the affairs of other beings but is the fountainhead of all motion. He is purely intellectual, and his highest form of activity is self-contemplation. Aristotle's approach to ethics is teleological; ends are endemic in nature but not created by deity. At stake are not so much moral absolutes but guidelines whereby humans can secure the greatest good and thereby insure their happiness, defined as an activity of the soul in accordance with virtue. Attainment of virtue in humans comes about through reasoned action, resulting in honorific habits, and just as in God, the highest form of human activity is intellectual contemplation.

The successors of Aristotle at the Lyceum, especially his immediate academic heir, Theophrastus (c. 370-c. 285), maintained a genuine Aristotelian perspective. For a time after Theophrastus, apparently many of Aristotle's manuscripts were hidden or stored. Known for the most part in the pre-Christian era were his more popular literary essays, several of which were written in dialogues in the fashion of Plato. The dialogues have been lost, but in their time they influenced the Stoic philosopher Panaetius (180-109 B.C.) as well as Latin discourse beginning with *Cicero (106-43 B.C.).

The scientific, literary and philosophical treatises of Aristotle were little consulted in the pre-Christian and Christian century. They pose a conundrum in respect to their composition in that they are redundant and choppy, and the flow of thought is often interrupted by what appear to be insertions. Three main explanations have been offered: these treatises result from the editing of student notes; these are Aristotle's own lecture notes; and the original manuscripts were recovered in a deteriorated condition. It seems best to conclude with Wheelwright (xix-xxv) that the extant treatises represent Aristotle's own efforts to preserve his ideas as his career was winding down, and they include his own interpolations as he revised for subsequent lectures. Multiple manuscripts of the treatises were copied and later collated in the first century B.C. What we have then are the ideas of Aristotle essentially in his own manner of expression.

2. Influence.

The influence of Aristotle has been a continuing one in Greece, the Roman Empire* and the West. It was not until the fifth century A.D. that his influence on Christian theology became obvious. But with Porphyry (c. 232-c. 303) and Pseudo-Dionysius (c. 500) the influence of the elementary study of Aristotelian logic and the categories emerged. One reason for early suspicion of Aristotle was that he posited a naturalistic explanation of the cosmos, unlike Plato, who in the *Timaeus* presented God as creator through a demiurge. Aristotle departed from Plato's view that perfect forms (ideas) exist only in suprasensible reality (philosophical realism) by arguing that forms exist only in discrete entities (moderate realism). For Plato, the empirical (i.e., sensible world) was inferior reality, whereas for Aristotle it was the only reality. For that reason the Platonic vision appealed much more to the early church fathers.

Two ways in which the works of Aristotle may have influenced NT documents more than has previously been thought are in respect to moral forms and lists and rhetorical features.

2.1. Moral Lists. Aristotle's reflections regarding moral philosophy are found in the *Politics (peri politikē)* and the *Nicomachean Ethics (ethos).* The *Politics* was probably written c. 338 B.C., when Aristotle was in Macedonia, and the *Nicomachean Ethics* in the later Athenian period, or about 330 B.C. In these documents Aristotle discussed "household management" *(peri oikonomias)* and indicated how these patterns also influenced the state. David Balch in *Let Wives Be Submissive* (n. 2), writes:

> Aristotle gave the philosophical discussion of "household management" *(peri oikonomias)* a particular outline that does not occur elsewhere, for example, not in the Hebrew Bible, not in Plato, and not among the Stoics. He observed that a "house" includes three relationships, "master and slave, husband and wife, father and children" (Pol I 1253b 1-14; see NE V 1134b 9-18). Authority and subordination are, he argued, natural to these relationships (Pol I 1254a 22-24 and 1260a 9-14). A household provides models for the various forms of constitution in the state, and democracy occurs in households in which there is no master (NE VIII 1160b 23-1161a 10). Freedom given to women is detrimental to the state (Pol II 1269b 12-1270a 15).

While one cannot argue that the *Haustafeln* in Colossians 3:18—4:1 and Ephesians 5:21—6:4 are directly dependent upon a reading of Aristotle, the structure may ultimately be traced to an Aristotelian source.

2.2. Rhetorical Forms. *The Rhetoric* (*texnē rhetorikē*) of Aristotle was probably completed about 335 B.C., just before Aristotle returned to Athens to found the Lyceum. He had commenced lecturing on *rhetoric in Plato's Academy about 355 B.C. The five classical divisions of rhetoric, especially in the Roman period, were invention, so called by later writers; arrangement; style; delivery; and memory. Of these, Aristotle discussed three, set forth here in the order of the space to which he assigned them: invention, or in Aristotle's terminology, "proofs" *(pisteis);* then style *(leksis);* and finally arrangement *(taksis).* In another important observation, Aristotle declared that there are three rhetorical genres *(tria genē)* corresponding to three types of hearers: deliberative *(symbouleutikon),* forensic or juridical *(dikanikon)* and epideictic, or demonstrative *(deiktikon).*

The means of persuasion *(pisteis)* were divided in nonartistic *(atechnoi)* and artistic *(entechnoi).* The former consisted of what in the courtroom are called exhibits such as objects, contracts and witnesses. Speakers or writers invent artistic proofs; that is, they select these means by which they hope to persuade their specific audience. There are three types of artistic proofs: the speaker's character *(ēthos),* logical argument and evidence *(logos)* and emotive appeal *(pathos).* In popular speeches arguments take the form of enthymemes *(enthymēmata).* These have their power because they commence from premises accepted by the auditors. Biblical critics have employed various of Aristotle's categories and observations to analyze the documents of both the OT and NT. Aristotle did not write *The Rhetoric* for critics but for rhetorical practitioners, which means that rhetorical critics are forced to extrapolate a method of criticism from *The Rhetoric.*

In recent years rhetorical analysis of the Scriptures has come to the forefront in NT studies. Various rhetorical criticisms, both ancient and modern, have been employed, and many of these are dependent upon Aristotle. Some of the early proponents of rhetorical criticism in the 1950s and 1960s were J. Muilenburg (in OT), H.-D. Betz and G. A. Kennedy. Several international conferences have been held on the rhetorical analysis of the Scriptures: Heidelberg (1992), Pretoria (1994), London (1995), Malibu (1996) and Florence (1998). The proceedings of each of these conferences have been published by the Sheffield Press and edited by S. E. Porter and T. H. Olbricht, and the later two by S. E. Porter and D. L. Stamps.

The question remains as to whether Aristotle and his rhetoric may have influenced the writers of the NT. It is extremely doubtful that any of the writers of the NT were acquainted at first hand with *The Rhetoric.* However, it is conceivable that certain ones may have been influenced by rhetorical handbooks that drew upon Aristotle. Many features of Aristotelian rhetoric may be found in the NT, but since Aristotle was making universal observations about discourse of the public arena, any document should exhibit these characteristics. It would be surprising if first-century persons having been immersed in Hellenistic culture were not indebted to Aristotle.

See also FAMILY AND HOUSEHOLD; PLATO, PLATONISM; RHETORIC; STOICISM.

BIBLIOGRAPHY. J. L. Ackrill, *Aristotle the Philosopher* (Oxford: Oxford University Press, 1981); L. Arnhart, *Aristotle on Political Reasoning* (DeKalb: Northern Illinois University Press, 1981); H. F. A. von Arnim, *Die Entstehung der Gotteslehre des Aristoteles* (Vienna: Holder, Pichler-Tempsky, 1931); D. L. Balch, *Let Wives be Submissive: The Domestic Code in 1 Peter* (Chico, CA: Scholars Press, 1981); J. Barnes, ed. *The Complete Works of Aristotle: The Revised Oxford Translation* (Princeton, NJ: Princeton University Press, 1984); R. Brachet, *L'ame Religieuse du Jeune Aristotle* (Paris: Editions Saint-Paul, 1990); E. Gilson, *History of Christian Philosophy in the Middle Ages* (New York: Random House, 1955); G. A. Kennedy, *Aristotle, On Rhetoric: A Theory of Civic Discourse* (New York: Oxford University Press, 1991); T. H. Olbricht, "An Aristotelian Rhetorical Analysis of 1 Thessalonians," *Greeks, Romans and Christians: Essays in Honor of Abraham J. Malherbe,* ed. D. L. Balch, E. Ferguson, W. A. Meeks (Minneapolis: Fortress, 1990); S. E. Porter, ed., *Handbook of Classical Rhetoric in the Hellenistic Period 330 B.C.-A.D. 400* (Leiden: E. J. Brill, 1997); J. H. Randall Jr., *Aristotle* (New York: Columbia University Press, 1962); J. L. Stocks, *Aristotelianism* (Bristol: Thoemme's Press, 1993 [1925]); D. F. Watson and A. J. Hauser, *Rhetorical Criticism of the Bible: A Comprehensive Bibliography with Notes on History and Method* (Leiden: E. J. Brill, 1994); P. Wheelwright, *Aristotle* (New York: Odyssey Press, 1951).

T. H. Olbricht

ARMY, ROMAN. *See* ROMAN MILITARY.

ART AND ARCHITECTURE: GRECO-ROMAN

Both art and architecture reached a state of perfection in the Greco-Roman world and give us avenues for understanding both its cultural ideals and aspects of everyday life.

1. Sculpture
2. Painting
3. Mosaics
4. Frescoes

5. Minor Art Forms
6. Architecture

1. Sculpture.
Roman sculpture was primarily Greek in inspiration, and the finest pieces are often remarkable reproductions of earlier works. The Greeks in turn had taken their direction from the Egyptians, who had created a rather wooden prototype of the human body. From the archaic to the *Hellenistic period the Greek concern was to recreate the human form in as lifelike a manner as possible. The stiff figure with clenched fists was replaced with graceful forms caught in natural poses, bared limbs displaying muscles and veins beneath the flesh. One of the crowning glories of Greek sculpture was the representation of the draped female. Especially admired was the wet look of clothing pressed against the flesh as though the subject had just emerged from bathing. Where arms or legs were exposed, muscles and veins could be seen beneath the skin in marvelous detail.

While Greek art exhibited astounding innovation and development of technique, the Roman represents imitation in its highest form, borrowing heavily from the cultures encompassed by the empire (*see* Roman Empire). This is especially true of the statuary that can still be seen in abundance in museums and at ancient ruins and archaeological excavation sites. Statues were erected for decoration and adoration on public streets, in temples, courtyards, marketplaces, baths, gardens and even butcher shops. This proliferation of statues dedicated to the gods apparently drew the ire of the apostle Paul at *Athens (Acts 17:16). Cruder statuary, produced from molds, was available cheaply for religious veneration or votive offerings, an example being the silver figurines of Artemis of *Ephesus (Acts 19:24).

The Roman genius was by no means confined to imitation, however. Brilliant creativity is manifested especially in the representation of various animals and in pieces of whimsy and caricature. There was as well a desire for realism that sometimes transcended that of the Greeks. Masterpieces, both carved and painted, were subjects of lively discussion among the literati (e.g., Philostratus *Imagines;* Achilles Tatius *Leuc.* 1); and they would have understood the statement that Christ was the "express image" of God (Heb 1:3). In many instances, several Roman copies remain even when the original statue has been lost. Thus the magnificent works of Praxiteles and Phidias are known through presumably faithful reproductions. Some, however, are of inferior workmanship and give us disappointing and somewhat clumsy impressions of what the original must have been.

While Greek artists had usually chosen gods and mythological heroes for their subjects, the Romans, consummate politicians, saw propagandistic value in the productions of the sculptor. Once again they returned to Greece and ultimately to Egypt to create their political and religious statuary. From a workshop in *Alexandria emerged a new and utilitarian form, the head of which could be removed and replaced with the likeness of a person in power or with that of a current religious leader. As was often the case with Greco-Roman art, communication of a religious or political message led to diminished artistic value. The clean, classical lines of Greek sculpture grew more encumbered and voluminously ornate. Worship of the Roman emperors (*see* Ruler Cult) had created a need for a distinctive iconography. Thus, in the Holy Land, after the fall of *Jerusalem, there are portraits of emperors and eventually Jesus and the Buddha, all wearing the same draped garment. This mobility of portrait heads might be of particular value in a volatile situation. At one point, in the carving of a bas relief of the imperial family, the artist found it diplomatic to change the features of different individuals several times during the execution of the piece. Death, divorce, exile, disgrace and new marriages all needed to be reckoned with in the representation of the family.

Works that were originally intended as political statements might be reproduced in other contexts. A relief molded at Cyzicus on a temple pillar apparently celebrated the victory of Kings Eumenes II and Attalos II over the Gauls. The motif was transposed into a freestanding piece of group statuary at Rhodes by Apollonius and Tauriscos of Caria in *Asia Minor. Another enlarged reproduction, the Farnese Bull, is the largest piece of group statuary known from the Roman world and now towers in the Naples Museum. The emphasis is no longer upon military deliverance but upon a mystic salvation indicated by a multitude of decorative symbols understood only by those initiated into the cult of Dionysus. Since the highly popular *mystery religions were based upon secret lore, it is not always possible to ascertain the meaning or even the extent of mystic symbolism.

2. Painting.
In the Greek world, great advances were made in painting during the fifth century B.C. The flat color of earlier artists was replaced by the light-and-shadow technique of Apollodorus, who was said to "render surface naturalistically" (Pliny *Nat. Hist.* 35.60; Plutarch *De Gloria Atheniensium* 2 [*Mor.* 346a]). His was a mastery not only of perspective but also of shading and blending colors, a tradition continued by Zeuxis. The four primary colors of the fifth century—red, white, black and yellow—had been replaced with a full spectrum that yielded a realistic painting (Plato *Crat.* 434a-b). Sharply contrasting patches of colors could be juxtaposed in optical fusion to produce stunning effects, a "true view" from a distance (cf. Wis 15:4; Plato *Leg.* 663c). Roman painting would put more emphasis upon light than upon accuracy of form.

In classical Athens, vase painting had flourished as a consummate art. Vessels with a variety of shapes and uses were handsomely decorated, with distinct schools of potters and artists. Tens of thousands of fine pieces remain, the earliest in black on red vases and later the red on black. Geometric patterns gave way to scenes of life and legend. Vase paintings sometimes provide information about the social world and everyday life that is not available elsewhere. The themes varied according to the uses for which the pottery was intended. The linear figures developed into subjects displaying emotional depth, sometimes in the midst of high drama. One of the most affective is a representation of the Amazon Penthesilea at the moment of her death. As Achilles plunges the sword into her breast, he views her face and at that moment, struck by her beauty, too late falls in love with her. This mingling of emotion vests Greek vase painting with extraordinary power.

3. Mosaics.
Elegant private houses as well as public buildings boasted fine floors made of small pieces of colored marble. In these mosaics, the four seasons, the zodiac, agricultural and marine themes are well represented, but fertility, religious and mythological subjects are frequently a unifying component. Many fine mosaics may still be seen at excavation sites throughout the Roman world, and especially in the museums of Antakya and Tunisia. Although most of the ancient paintings have vanished, the delicately shaded pieces of mosaic bespeak the skill of the ancient painter. A mosaic found at Pompeii (buried by a volcanic eruption in A.D. 79) re-creates a famous painting of the late fourth or early third century B.C. The original was probably the one commissioned by Cassander, *Alexander's successor as king of *Macedonia. The painting had been executed by Philoxenus of Eritrea, whose work was "surpassed by none" (Pliny *Nat. Hist.* 35.110). The scene is an intricate depiction of Alexander the Great's victory over Darius, with Alexander riding recklessly on horseback while the Persian flees in his chariot, their eyes meeting for a moment. Around them rages the battle, but the critical point is in the eye contact. Here indeed is the artist's skill in representing "characteristic expressions and emotions" (Pliny *Nat. Hist.* 35.98).

4. Frescoes.
Walls of dwellings and tombs were decorated with fine paintings while the plaster was still wet. The resulting frescoes reveal a high degree of artistry and religious imagination. This is especially true of the masterpieces recovered in situ at Pompeii and Herculaneum, some still brilliantly colored. One of the finest sets decorates the Villa of the Mysteries just outside the walls of Pompeii. It is valuable to historians of religion because of its representation of initiation into the Dionysiac mysteries. Many frescoes, however, are repetitive of others in style and subject, suggesting that collections of reproductions were available for less creative artists to copy.

Tomb paintings have sometimes proven an invaluable source of information involving Roman beliefs about the *afterlife. What the ancients dared not tell was sometimes embodied in the art within their graves. Even the *Gnostics decorated their tombs with distinctive symbols, a mute testimony to their theological perspectives. Within ancient graves, vases and small figurines were more likely to have survived intact and represent consolation messages more explicitly than do the surviving texts. Frescoes appeared early in the catacombs and afford us a glimpse of the worship and attitudes of early Christians. At first of inferior quality, these paintings advanced in artistic merit and in the ability to portray spiritual fervor and passion. The face of the

Donna Velata in the Catacomb of St. Priscilla is considered one of the most expressive pieces of early Christian art. Conventional pagan symbols reappeared with new significance as artists groped their way toward distinctive symbols and expressions of their faith.

5. Minor Art Forms.

Bas reliefs on the stone coffins known as sarcophagi are sometimes brilliantly executed and highly informative about the religious aspirations of both pagans and Christians. Commonplace emblems were frequently carved in advance, with the facial features of the deceased being added at the time of death. Other decorated objects included lamps, vases, cups, bottles, furniture, pins, jewelry, intaglios, cameos, mirrors, combs, jewel boxes and ossuary caskets (*see* Burial Practices, Jewish). Of necessity, these were the possessions of those who could afford the work of an artist, whether highly skilled or mediocre. Glimpses into the viewpoints of common people can be gained through graffiti and other sorts of crude sketches. One of the most interesting to Christians is that of the crucifixion of a donkey-headed man. The inscription beside it reads "Marcus worships his God."

Of some art forms, only the written description remains. This is especially true of the needle and loom work of women. The finest embroidered pieces narrated a story (Ovid *Met.* 6.5-145) and excited enormous admiration. Beside the literary descriptions in such as that of Achilles' shield in the *Iliad* and of Aeneas in the *Aeneid,* a few pieces of fine metalwork remain. Decorative helmets worn by gladiators have been recovered at Pompeii and elsewhere (*see* Circuses and Games).

Ordinary Romans viewed certain forms of art as magical, some as apotropaic, to be used in warding off the evil eye. Erotic elements, especially the male phallus, occur repeatedly throughout Greco-Roman art, not only as a decorative feature but also as a representation of sexual and divine power. Obscenity was valued not only for its ribald aspect but also as an appropriate means for the promotion of fertility.

6. Architecture.

Roman architecture, too, though originally based on Greek and Etruscan prototypes, developed in new directions. It was the Roman genius, however that developed the basilica, the use of high-grade concrete and the barrel-vaulted arch. These inventions made possible the construction of enormous edifices, such as the giant amphitheater known as the Colosseum. The use of the arch enabled the construction of buildings not dependent upon the flat lintel that is used so effectively in Greek architecture to support doorways, ceilings and windows. The new technology, along with new wealth derived from the Roman conquests, made possible construction on a level previously unimagined. An abundance of *slaves provided cheap manpower for the most ambitious of public works. Palaces, public baths (*see* Gymnasia and Baths), administrative buildings, *temples, *theaters, fortresses and market complexes rose not only in *Rome but also in major cities throughout the empire (*see* Cities, Greco-Roman). Three- and four-story tenements afforded cheap public housing and commercial space as well. The structure enclosed a city block, with shops lining the street level and apartments rising above. The interior of the block, known as an island, was given over to the gardens and dwellings of the well-to-do.

The direction for temples came both from the Greeks and from the Etruscans. A typical, Etruscan-inspired temple was considered to be tripartite, with large flanks of steps and three cellas (for the three gods Minerva, Venus and Jupiter). Temples were made of mud brick covered in plaster with deep porches and colonnades only in front. Far from being a dazzling display of white marble, both Greek and Roman temples were brightly painted, sometimes in what would by modern tastes be considered garish colors. Unlike the lofty marble temples of the Greeks, which were large and surrounded by huge colonnades, early Roman temples at times assumed the shape of the primitive houses. After the conquest of Greece, more ambitious buildings arose with similar patterns. Nevertheless, the typical temple, though sometimes of awe-inspiring proportions, was not constructed to hold a large number of worshipers at the same time. The inner chamber was built to house the statue of the deity to whom the shrine was erected. There might be treasury chambers, storage rooms and lodging facilities for the cult personnel, but the pattern was not useful for Christian purposes.

At first Christians had often gathered in private homes, sometimes altered to enlarge the meeting room or to add a baptistry. Occasionally a warehouse or public hall was pressed into service. The basilica, originally designed for the conduct of public business (government administration, courthouses, markets and promenades), became serviceable as a design for churches. The normative model was delineated by the first-century B.C. architect Vitruvius (*De Arch.* 5.1-4; 6.3-9), but the multiple needs that could be filled in Roman society led to increasing versatility of construction. The basic plan provided a front portico and a long central nave with two or more side aisles. These aisles were divided from the central hall by a series of pillars and arches. Light was admitted through openings close to the ceiling. At the far end opposite the porch was a rounded area, covered with a vaulted dome. This plan, whether simple or increasingly complex, was adopted by the emperor Constantine in the construction of three major fourth-century churches: those of St. Paul's, outside the Walls, the old St. Peter's and St. John of the Lateran. The NT writers evinced considerable interest in matters of architecture and building (1 Cor 3:9-17; 2 Cor 6:16; Eph 2:20-22; 1 Pet 2:4-8). They clearly understood the toil and expense involved in construction (Lk 14:28-30), but they envisioned temples of the spirit and pictures of eternal splendor.

See also ART AND ARCHITECTURE: JEWISH; CITIES, GRECO-ROMAN; GYMNASIA AND BATHS; TEMPLES, GRECO-ROMAN.

BIBLIOGRAPHY. T. H. Carpenter, *Art and Myth in Ancient Greece: A Handbook* (London: Thames & Hudson, 1991); P. Finney, *The Invisible God: The Earliest Christians on Art* (New York: Oxford University Press, 1994); G. M. A. Hanfman, *Roman Art: A Modern Survey of the Art of Imperial Rome* (New York: Norton, 1975); E. C. Keuls, *Poet and Painter in Ancient Greece: Iconography and the Literary Arts* (Stuttgart and Leipzig: Teubner, 1997); Philostratus the Elder, the Younger, *Imagines;* Calistratus *Descriptions* (LCL; Cambridge, MA: Harvard University Press, 1969); D. S. Robertson, *Greek and Roman Architecture* (Cambridge: Cambridge University Press, 1943); L. M. White, *Building God's House in the Roman World: Architectural Adaptation Among Pagans, Jews and Christians* (Baltimore: Johns Hopkins University Press, 1990). D. B. Johnson

ART AND ARCHITECTURE: JEWISH

Jewish art and architecture of the Second Temple period (Hellenistic to early Roman, second century B.C. to first century A.D.) begins with the remains of the *Hasmonean sites that were later reconstructed or renewed by the Herodian architectural projects, which left a more enduring impression upon the art and architecture of the period.

Hasmonean architecture survives mostly in remains of fortifications, desert fortresses, water systems and the recently excavated Hasmonean palace at Jericho. The palace's characteristic features consist of a central court surrounded by rooms; a hall with two columns *in antis* in the southern part of the court, which led to the triclinium and probably served as a reception hall. This basic plan, inspired by Hellenistic architecture, characterizes the Hasmonean palaces at Masada, as well as the twin palaces at Jericho.

1. Architecture
2. Art

1. Architecture.

1.1. Herodian Architecture. The sources related to the construction projects undertaken during Herod's reign (37-4 B.C.) are literary and archaeological. The major literary sources are the works of *Josephus, particularly *Antiquities* 15—17 and *Jewish War* 1, 2 and 5. Josephus mentions thirty-three building projects, twenty of which were within the borders of Herod's kingdom and thirteen of which were in other countries. These Herodian architectural projects include the construction, reconstruction and extension of towns, fortifications, palaces and fortresses, as well as the *temple in *Jerusalem and the Royal Stoa—the largest single structure, the largest palace at Herodium and one of the largest harbors ever constructed in antiquity—at *Caesarea Maritima. Many of these monumental structures have survived and have been extensively excavated in the last few decades.

Most of these structures were built during Herod's reign, but renovations and reconstructions were undertaken during the first century A.D. until the destruction of Jerusalem and the Second Temple in A.D. 70. Herod built three new towns: Antipatris, Caesarea, with its magnificent harbor, and Sebaste (Samaria), with its temple of Augustus. In the newly established towns, Herod built temples, palaces, theaters, stadia, fortifications and harbors. Within the Jewish kingdom Herod carried out several projects. He built extensively in Jerusalem, particularly its temple, a palace and town fortifications and towers, as well as many public buildings and institutions, private buildings and villas. In the Judean desert Herod constructed or renovated several splendid palace-fortresses and the winter palaces at Jericho, which combined luxurious, leisurely living with the need for security. Herod's most prominent and important of these projects was the Jerusalem temple.

1.1.1. The Temple in Jerusalem. Herod's *temple in Jerusalem is the largest known temple in antiquity, one of the architectural wonders of the ancient world and a unique structure. The temple was the focal point for the Jewish nation, the center for worship and the place where political, economic and spiritual affairs of world Jewry could be discussed and determined. It was also the destination for pilgrims during the feasts (*see* Festivals and Holy Days), and therefore it needed to accommodate thousands of people who gathered there to celebrate. The architectural excavations carried out during the last decades (1968-1978; 1994-1997) have resulted in important data being disclosed concerning the areas of the Temple Mount gates, the areas outside the retaining walls, streets, squares and monumental passageways.

1.1.2. Herodian Palaces. King Herod concerned himself especially with building palaces that could be used for both administrative and recreational purposes. The typical features of the Herodian palaces followed the common plans of the Roman *domus* and *villa* (town and country house respectively). A Herodian palace was usually an elaborate building with several wings: the main wing, which contained a triclinium, a peristyle court and an inner garden; a bath house and dwelling rooms. The extended palace complex usually also included entertainment facilities: pools for swimming and sailing boats; elaborate gardens, such as the sunken garden at Jericho, palace III. Water installations, such as aqueducts and channels, brought water to the pools and gardens, as well as to the residential wings.

1.1.3. Fortresses. Seven fortresses in the Judean desert—Masada, Herodium, Cypros, Hyrcania, Alexandrium, Machaerus and Doq—constitute an important component of Herodian architecture. Built on mountaintops, isolated and autonomous, these structures were strongly fortified and have extensive systems for the entrapment and storage of water. These fortresses functioned primarily as military bases for defense but also as places of refuge for political and spiritual reasons, as shelters in times of violent confrontation and upheaval. They served as administrative centers for important routes, agricultural and royal farm areas and palaces; they were also used for guarding borders. They even served as burial places for the Hasmoneans and for Herod. Elaborate palaces were constructed on their premises. Masada was the most spacious of all and had several palaces on its summit that served as leisure resorts. The fortresses sometimes extended into the lower areas of their mountains; Herodium had buildings and installations built below the mount.

The characteristic features of Herodian architecture were high-level planning of complexes with focal points and with a variety of functional purposes. The techniques of building included the use of stone and sun-dried bricks, white plastering, opus quadratum, opus reticulatum and barrel vaulting. Herod named cities, as well as public and private structures, for relatives and Roman patrons.

1.2. Funerary Architecture and Jewish Burial Practices. Two cemeteries of the Second Temple period in Jerusalem and Jericho constitute our data for funerary architecture, art and burial customs (*see* Burial Practices, Jewish). These cemeteries were located outside the town limits, in accordance with Jewish law (*m. B. Bat.* 2:9), and two basic tomb plans exist, the loculi type *(kokhim)* and the arcosolia type, which is chronologically later. Each serves as a family tomb but with provision for separate burial of each individual.

The loculi tomb consists of a square burial chamber, often with a pit dug into its floor to enable a man to stand upright, and three or four benches on each side of the tomb. From one to three arched loculi *(kokhim)* are hewn into the walls. The tomb is sealed by a rectangular blocking stone or by mudbricks and small stones. Loculi tombs sometimes consist of a monumental tomb that has a memorial or *nephesh* standing next to or above it. The origin of the plan for the rock-cut loculi tomb of the Second Temple period in Judea is to be sought in Egypt, particularly in Leontopolis, from as early as Has-monean times.

The arcosolia type, in use at the end of the Second Temple period, is a benchlike aperture with an arched ceiling hewn into the length of the wall.

In the Jerusalem necropolis both loculi and arcosolia tombs are found; the Jericho cemetery consists of loculi tombs only. The monumental tombs of Jerusalem are characterized by a partly rock-hewn and partly built free-standing monument either above or next to the chamber and loculi tomb. The monument usually has a pyramid or tholus surmounting a cube-shaped base. A group of monumental tombs, located in the Kidron Valley (dated to the first century B.C. to first century A.D.), consists of the Tomb of Zachariah, the Bene Hezir tomb and the Absalom tomb with its adjacent Tomb of Jehoshaphat. Another tomb that belongs to this group is Jason's Tomb in the western part of modern Jerusalem. Several Jerusalem rock-hewn tombs portray ornamented facades or gables, consisting of a combination of features that characterize Jewish funerary art in Jerusalem.

Two distinctly different types of loculi tomb burials, primary and secondary, were discovered during the excavations in the Jericho cemetery. They can be classified typologically, chronologically and stratigraphically into primary burials in chestlike wooden coffins, which is the earliest type of burial in the Jericho cemetery, and secondary burials of collected bones that were either placed in individual ossuaries or piled in heaps. Bodies were prepared for secondary burial by a primary burial that allowed the flesh to decay until only the bones remained. The evidence from Jericho proves that loculi tombs were first designed and used for primary burial in coffins. The same tomb plan continued to be used in the case of ossuary burials.

Ossuaries, often decorated, were hewn from one large block of limestone, usually in the shape of a rectangular box resting on four low legs, with a flat, slightly curved or gabled lid. The inscriptions, sometimes incised on ossuaries, usually included the name of the interred and the person's family relation, place of origin, age or status.

Dates for the burial customs are still the subject of debate. Primary burials in coffins can be dated to the mid-first century B.C. to about A.D. 10, and secondary burials in ossuaries immediately followed, dating to about A.D. 10-68. L. Y. Rahmani, however, dates the practice of secondary burials in ossuaries in Jerusalem to 30/20 B.C. to A.D. 70, continuing sporadically until about A.D. 135 or the beginning of the third century.

Jewish burial practices of the late Second Temple period reveal a corresponding importance on both the individual and the family. This is reflected in the plan of the loculi tomb, which provided for individual burial of coffins or ossuaries in separate loculi while at the same time allowing a family to be buried together in the same tomb.

What is most extraordinary in the Jewish burial customs of the Second Temple period is the fact that within a comparatively short space of time burial practices, usually among the most conservative customs in a society, underwent rapid changes. Loculi tombs appear with primary coffin burials, and within a century secondary burials in ossuaries in similar loculi tombs becomes the prevalent custom, a practice that lacks parallels with any other contemporary neighboring culture. At the same time, these customs were short-lived and show little affinity to either the earlier Israelite customs or the later Jewish rituals of late antiquity, which contain only traces of these Second Temple period customs. Archaeological investigation has been unable, moreover, to uncover the causes for these ossuary burial innovations. It may be conjectured that the Jews blamed their loss of independence and their state, in A.D. 6 (*see* Jewish History: Roman Period), on their sinful behavior; the custom of secondary burial of the bones in ossuaries, after the flesh had decayed, became a way to expiate sins.

1.3. Second Temple Period Synagogues. Several public structures of the Second Temple period that have been discovered in the last decades are considered to be *synagogues: at Masada, Herodium, Gamla, a recently uncovered structure at Capernaum, under the later synagogue, and another synagogue, now lost, reported at Chorazin. The excavated structures are assumed by scholars to be synagogues because of the circumstantial evidence of similarity to each other in architectural plan and therefore in function, even though no proof has been uncovered.

Upon the evidence of the structures themselves, it should be noted that they differ from later synagogues in plan, function and decoration. First, from the architectural point of view no new conceptions in construction have been discerned, but the impression is rather one of local extemporization. Second, these structures existed only for a short time in the first century A.D. and were never built again, except for Capernaum. Third, these assembly halls lack the most important feature of the later synagogue: the Torah shrine. Finally, during the first century the temple in Jerusalem was still the center for worship and ritual for the entire Jewish community in Judea and the Diaspora. At the temple they could participate in the ceremonies and in the teaching of the Law conducted in the temple courtyards. They could also settle administrative questions in the temple courts.

The assembly structures at the fortresses of Masada, Herodium and Gamla probably served as local assembly halls during the years of the revolt against Rome, a time during which it was extremely difficult for the congregations to travel to Jerusalem in order to participate in temple worship (*see* Jewish Wars with Rome). At the same time as these structures were serving as small community centers, worship presumably was also being conducted in them, although no convincing proof of this supposition has been found. With the destruction of the temple, local structures began to flourish. Of necessity they replaced the national center and became local worship and community centers. In these halls reading of the Torah was emphasized, and thus the distinctive feature of the later synagogues, the Torah shrine, emerges.

2. Art.

Second Temple period Jewish art is a purely decorative art characterized by a mixture of native traditions and Hellenistic-Roman features. However, resistance to the intrusive culture was strong because of the force and vitality of the Jewish religion, which controlled the community's activities. Judaism also conceptually dominated its decorative art so that neither figurative nor symbolic representations were depicted.

The various ornamental devices and the repertoire of motifs were part of the general stream of Roman art, especially its provincial and eastern tributaries. The style of Jewish art followed the basic oriental elements of the endless patterns, *horror vacui,* by plasticity of carving and by symmetrical stylization. Decoration of buildings, palaces, houses and bath houses of the Second Temple period mainly focused on the use of wall paintings, stucco-plaster moldings, stone carving and ornamental floor pavements. Mosaics decorated the floors of Second Temple Herodian palaces and private homes of the upper-class Jerusalemites. These mosaics consisted of geometric and floral designs with no symbolic or iconic patterns. The decorative elements, motifs and designs are characterized by a lack of animate motifs and symbolic emblems. This stems from the reluctance of all Jews, including the ruling families, to decorate any building or tomb with religious or iconic symbols. Consequently, it can be stated that the Jews of the Second Temple period honored the biblical injunctions by refraining from representations of humans and animals in their art.

During the Second Temple period the land of Israel was a Jewish state having a central temple in Jerusalem. The art of the period shows connections with the neighboring Greco-Roman culture. However, at the same time Jewish art withstood foreign influences by evolving strictly aniconic features; it is characterized together with the other arts of the period by highly skilled indigenous stonework and by predominant oriental elements.

Jewish art and architecture of the Second Temple period concentrate on extensive architectural projects consisting of large complexes and structures, not only in Jerusalem, where the temple itself was rebuilt, but also throughout the country in major winter and summer palace complexes, in a magnificent harbor and other architectural installations. The art includes the ornamentation and embellishment of buildings, tombs, sarcophagi and ossuaries. The strictly aniconic and nonsymbolic art characterizing the Second Temple period is the outcome of Judaism's struggle against paganism and idolatry. By the strict observance of the prohibition against animate images, the Jews retained their own identity and distinctiveness.

See also ARCHAEOLOGY OF THE LAND OF ISRAEL; ART AND ARCHITECTURE: GRECO-ROMAN; BURIAL PRACTICES, JEWISH; CAESAREA MARITIMA; HELLENISM; HERODIAN DYNASTY; JERUSALEM; SYNAGOGUES; TEMPLE, JEWISH; THEATERS.

BIBLIOGRAPHY. N. Avigad, *Ancient Monuments in the Kidron Valley* (Jerusalem: The Bialik Institute, 1954; Hebrew); idem, *Discovering Jerusalem* (Nashville: Nelson, 1983); M. Avi-Yonah, *Oriental Art in Roman Palestine* (Rome: Centro di Studi Semitici, 1961); M. Ben Dov, *The Dig at the Temple Mount* (Jerusalem: Keter, 1983); J. M. Chiat, "First-Century Synagogue Architecture: Methodological Problems," in *Ancient Synagogues, the State of Research,* ed. J. Gutmann (Chico, CA: Scholars Press, 1981); G. Foerster, *Masada VI*

(Jerusalem: Israel Exploration Society, 1995); R. Hachlili, *Ancient Jewish Art and Archaeology in the Land of Israel* (Leiden: E. J. Brill, 1988); R. Hachlili and A. Killebrew, "Jewish Funerary Customs During the Second Temple Period in Light of the Excavations at the Jericho Necropolis," *PEQ* 115 (1983) 109-39; N. Netzer, *Greater Herodium, Qeden 13* (Jerusalem: Institute of Archaeology, Hebrew University, 1981); idem, "The Hasmonean and Herodian Winter Palace at Jericho," *IEJ* 25 (1975) 89-100; idem, "Herod's Building Projects: State Necessity or Personal Need? A Symposium," *The Jerusalem Cathedra* 1 (1981) 48-80; idem, *Masada III* (Jerusalem: Israel Exploration Society, 1991); L. Y. Rahmani, *A Catalogue of Jewish Ossuaries in the Collections of the State of Israel* (Jerusalem: Israel Antiquities Authority, 1994); Y. Yadin, *Masada* (New York: Random House, 1966); Y. Yadin, ed. *Jerusalem Revealed* (Jerusalem: Israel Exploration Society, 1975). R. Hachlili

ARTAPANUS. *See* JEWISH LITERATURE: HISTORIANS AND POETS.

ASCENSION OF ISAIAH

The *Ascension of Isaiah* is an early Christian *apocalypse of considerable importance for the light that it sheds on the development of Christianity in the immediate postapostolic period. The text incorporates an angelomorphic christology and offers a rudimentary trinitarianism that illuminates such enigmatic passages as Matthew 28:19. In order to understand the value of the *Ascension of Isaiah,* we must briefly consider the textual problems that bedevil all serious study of this apocalypse.

1. Text and Date
2. Theological Considerations
3. View of Prophecy
4. Social Setting

1. Text and Date.

The text was written almost certainly in Greek, but only a fragmentary Greek text has survived. The apocalypse is found in full only in an Ethiopic translation, which was probably made in the fourth or fifth century A.D. The major but not the only critical question is whether an existing Semitic document called the *Martyrdom of Isaiah* was incorporated in the present and undeniably Christian apocalypse. This view was popular in the first half of the twentieth century, but it was challenged by the Italian scholar M. Pesce in his own contribution to his 1983 edited collection (itself the proceedings of a 1981 conference on the *Ascension of Isaiah*). Pesce argued that the author of the apocalypse was a creative individual who worked with various strands of Jewish tradition but not with any written document as such.

So far as the date is concerned, no one would now agree with R. H. Charles that it was compiled in the late second or early third century A.D., although Charles conceded that the putative constituents were earlier. R. J. Bauckham has argued for a date of about A.D. 70 to 80; J. M. Knight, during the Trajanic persecution in the second decade of the second century. The criteria used in the identification of these dates are respectively the possibility that *Ascension of Isaiah* 4:13 alludes to living eyewitnesses of Jesus himself and the question of whether the vivid description of martyrdom does not of itself suggest that *persecution was a recent feature of the author's own experience.

2. Theological Considerations.

The *Ascension of Isaiah* is an important text for discerning the origins of what has come to be called belief in the heavenly preexistence of Jesus. It incorporates a motif whereby the Beloved One, as the heavenly Christ is often called in the apocalypse, descends to earth and appears as Jesus of Nazareth. Although it has been questioned by D. D. Hannah whether this represents a docetic christology as such, the motif does appear to come from Jewish angelology and to have parallels in a work such as *Tobit, in which the archangel Raphael appears on earth as a human person. The christology may thus be called an angelomorphic one. This is not to say that the Beloved One in the *Ascension of Isaiah* is an angel but that motifs drawn from Jewish angelology resourced the way this author chose to describe the Beloved One and his saving activity. An angelomorphic christology is a feature of some NT literature, including the Synoptic transfiguration narrative and the description of the heavenly Christ in Revelation 1:12-15.

The *Ascension of Isaiah* has an ambiguous trinitarianism in which the *Holy Spirit is specifically said to be an angel (*Asc. Isa.* 9:38-40) and in which equality between the three divine beings is expressed in terms of their reception of worship alone (*Asc. Isa.* 8:18). The *Ascension of*

Isaiah shows such rudimentary trinitarianism powerfully emergent, in company with other postapostolic literature. This is a significant thing given the relative silence of the NT on the matter. The Spirit's function in the apocalypse is primarily the inspiration of classical and contemporary prophecy (*see* Prophets and Prophecy).

The first half of the *Ascension of Isaiah* contains a historical review of the kind familiar from other apocalypses (*Asc. Isa.* 3—4). In the construction of this material, it seems likely that *Ascension of Isaiah* 3:13-18 (traditions about Jesus) and 4:1-13 (material about Nero) were taken over from an existing source or sources.

3. View of Prophecy.

This leaves *Ascension of Isaiah* 3:21-31 as very probably the author's own creation. In this section, the demise of prophecy in the author's own time is lamented. While all due interpretive caution is called for, it does seem that this material discloses something of the author's understanding of his contemporary situation. He reveals himself as a person sympathetic to the prophets who regretted the fact that their ministry was passing from the church at large. Such prophecy certainly included the exegesis of the *Hebrew Bible and contemporary oracles, but the description of Isaiah's mystical ascension in *Ascension of Isaiah* 6—11 suggests that it also had a mystical or ecstatic element (*see* Mysticism). This again is significant for understanding the historical development of Christianity in the later first century, especially when we consider that a mystical experience was enjoyed by Paul (2 Cor 12).

4. Social Setting.

Recent research on apocalypticism has done much to expose its social setting. Although we should beware of the assumption that all apocalypses necessarily came from marginalized people, the *Ascension of Isaiah* contains evidence to indicate that its authors felt threatened on more than one front. There is implied antipathy toward contemporary Judaism (*Asc. Isa.* 3:8-10), the Roman administration in Syria (*Asc. Isa.* 4:1-13) and even the hierarchy of Christian leadership (*Asc. Isa.* 3:21-31). Part of the purpose of the apocalypse seems to have been the attempt to encourage readers by reminding them of the truth that the Beloved One had defeated *Beliar when he descended from the seventh heaven to appear as Jesus, together with the promise that a new world order was impending on the Beloved One's return to earth (*Asc. Isa.* 4:14-18). This reading of the text shows that a soteriology underlies the *Ascension of Isaiah,* as it does almost every representative of the Jewish and Christian apocalyptic tradition.

The *Ascension of Isaiah* contains a richness and diversity of material to which a short article can hardly do justice. It must be emphasized in conclusion that the *Ascension of Isaiah,* despite its relative neglect in the past, is a significant text for the study of early Christianity. It must be restored to its rightful position alongside *1 Clement, Barnabas* and the *Shepherd of Hermas* as postapostolic literature of the greatest importance (*see DLNTD,* Apostolic Fathers).

See also APOCALYPTIC LITERATURE; APOCALYPTICISM.

BIBLIOGRAPHY. A. Acerbi, *L'Ascensione di Isaia: Cristologia e profetismo in Siria nei primi decenni del II secolo* (Milan: Vita e Pensiero, 1989); idem, *Serra lignea: Studi sulla fortuna della Ascensione di Isaia* (Rome: Editrice A.V.E., 1984); R. Bauckham, *The Fate of the Dead* (Leiden: E. J. Brill, 1998) 363-90; P. Bettiolo et al., *Ascensio Isaiae: Textus* (CCSA 7; Turnhout: Brepols, 1995); P. C. Bori, "L'estasi del profeta: 'Ascensio Isaiae' 6 e l'antico profetismo cristiano," *CNS* 1 (1980) 367-89; R. H. Charles, *The Ascension of Isaiah* (London: Black, 1900); R. G. Hall, "The *Ascension of Isaiah:* Community Situation, Date, and Place in Early Christianity," *JBL* 109 (1990) 289-306; D. D. Hannah, "Isaiah's Vision in the Ascension of Isaiah and the Early Church," *JTS* 50 (1999) 80-101; J. M. Knight, *The Ascension of Isaiah* (GAP 2; Sheffield: Sheffield Academic Press, 1995); idem, *Disciples of the Beloved One: Studies in the Christology, Social Setting and Theological Context of the Ascension of Isaiah* (JSPSup 18; Sheffield: Sheffield Academic Press, 1996); E. Norelli, Ascension du prophète Isaïe (Turnhout: Brepols, 1993); idem *Ascensio Isaiae: Commentarius* (CCSA 8; Turnhout: Brepols, 1995); idem, L'Ascensione di Isaia: Studi su un apocrifo al crocevia dei cristianesimo (Bologna: Centro editoriale dehoniano, 1994); M. Pesce, ed., *Isaia, il diletto e la Chiesa* (Brescia: Paideia, 1983). J. M. Knight

ASIA MINOR

Asia Minor is the westernmost peninsula of Asia, stretching over ancient Anatolia (modern Turkey) from the Aegean and the Black Sea to the Euphrates River and the Syrian desert. Classical geography gave the name *Asia* to both a continent (the whole of Anatolia) and a country (on the Aegean coast forming a Roman province). The continent had an all-embracing network of roads and a permanent military presence. The Roman government concentrated its hegemony over cities and borders, leaving whole geographic regions surrounded by its forces but otherwise largely untouched by its institutions (*see* Roman Administration). The interior was an outback of mountains and upland plateau where indigenous Anatolian culture endured well into the Byzantine age. There were many Greek and then Roman colonies along the coast. The main Roman provinces were Asia, Lycia and Pamphylia, Cilicia, Galatia, Pontus and Bithynia, and Cappadocia, although provincial administration shifted and changed more boundaries in Anatolia than in almost any other part of the empire.

1. Aegean and Mediterranean Coastal Areas
2. Anatolian Interior
3. Black Sea and Frontier Regions

1. Aegean and Mediterranean Coastal Areas.

1.1. Asia. The Roman consular province of Asia extended along the western coast of the Anatolian peninsula, bounded in the north by Bithynia, in the east by Galatia and in the south by Lycia. It came into Rome's possession in 133 B.C. after the death of the Hellenistic monarch Attalus III of Pergamum, who had bequeathed his kingdom to the Romans. *Provincia Asia* enjoyed commercial prosperity from agriculture and especially its many textile industries, which produced even luxury goods (e.g., the businesswoman Lydia, a "dealer in purple cloth" [Acts 16:14]). Its rich natural resources and many rivers were chief factors in the success of its economic and cultural life. The province contained three major inland districts: Mysia on the north, Lydia in the center and Caria on the south; the narrow strips of plain that stretched along the Aegean seaboard took their names from the three branches of early Greek settlers: Aeolis, Ionia and Doris. The major cities were Pergamum, *Ephesus, Smyrna and Sardis.

1.1.1. Pergamum. Called the Athens of Asia, the city of Pergamum ranked among the most spectacular in the ancient world. The monumental architecture of its terraced, fan-shaped upper acropolis, a legacy of the Attalid kings who had beautified the city into a Hellenistic cultural capital, included a royal palace, famed sacred buildings and the majestic library of Eumenes II (the library had two hundred thousand volumes when Mark Antony offered it to Cleopatra). Eumenes II (d. 158 B.C.), an Attalid king, is famous for inventing parchment (Gk *Pergamēnē;* Lat *Pergamena*), when papyrus from Egypt was in short supply.

One of the temples housed the Great Altar of Zeus, a masterpiece of the Pergamene school of Greek sculpture. Another was the sanctuary of Asclepius, god of healing, which the famous rhetorician Aelius Aristides (b. A.D. 118) visited frequently to seek curative treatments. The city was the birthplace of Galen (b. A.D. 129), one of the most illustrious physicians of the ancient world. Pergamum was also the first Asian city to receive an imperial cult center for worship of the goddess Roma and of the Roman emperor, a titular honor known as Temple Warden *(Neokoros)*. In response, some early Christians came to lament this city as a place "where Satan's throne is" (Rev 2:13).

1.1.2. Ephesus. Ephesus was the leading city in Asia. With a population of two hundred thousand in Roman times, it rivaled *Antioch in Syria as the third largest metropolis in the ancient Mediterranean world, behind only *Alexandria in Egypt and *Rome itself. Under the early empire, the city eclipsed Pergamum as the provincial capital, the seat of the Roman governor, and as a major commercial port. The ancient geographer Strabo writes that Ephesus "grows daily and is the largest emporium in Asia this side of the Taurus Mountains" (Strabo *Geog.* 14.1.24). Ephesus figures prominently in ancient literature, serving as the center of two ancient novels: *An Ephesian Tale of Anthia and Habrocomes,* by Xenophon of Ephesus, and *The Adventures of Leukippe and Kleitophon,* by Achilles Tatius (*see* Romances/Novels).

*Archaeology attests to the ancient city's grandeur and beauty; in 1995 the Austrian Archaeological Institute in Vienna celebrated its centenary year of excavations at Ephesus. The ruins include an impressive theater (with a seating capacity of twenty-four thousand), the Prytaneion (town hall), an agora (commercial market), a complex of baths and gymnasiums, a stadium (for the Artemisia, Ephesia and other regional athletic contests) and a medical school (of Rufus and Soranus, two important ancient doctors). The most prominent structure, however, is the Great Artemision, the Ionic-style temple to the Greek goddess Artemis (Roman Diana), one of the seven wonders of the ancient world. Knowledge of the Ephesian Artemis cult is critical for the interpretation of Acts 19, where crowds shout "Great is Artemis of the Ephesians!" (Acts 19:28).

There was a substantial Jewish population in the city, which gained citizenship rights and exemption from military service.

1.1.3. Smyrna. Smyrna (modern Izmir) appears in inscriptions and coins as the "Glory of Ionia," "the First of Asia in beauty and greatness" and the legendary birthplace of the Greek poet Homer. One of the three great Ionian ports (the other two being Ephesus and Miletus), it lay at the end of a long gulf that took its name from the city, about 45 miles north of Ephesus. "The division of the streets," writes Strabo, "is exceptionally good, in straight lines as far as possible; and the streets are paved with stone; and there are large quadrangular porticoes, with both lower and upper stories" (Strabo *Geog.* 14.1.37). Because of its international renown and wealth, the emperor Tiberius (A.D. 14-37) selected Smyrna as a Temple Warden of the imperial cult in Asia. Famed for its devotion to science, medicine and education, it was a major center of the *rhetorical and literary movement known as the Second Sophistic. Aelius Aristides, Smyrnean and rhetorician, persuaded the emperor Marcus Aurelius to rebuild the city after earthquakes in 178 and 180.

Early Christians in the city experienced local, sporadic persecutions (Rev 2:8-11), although by the second century they enjoyed relative wealth and power as vigorous communities. The martyrdom narrative of an early, famous bishop, Polycarp, survives (*see* Apostolic Fathers).

1.1.4. Sardis. Inland, on the Hermus River basin, the most fertile of all Asia Minor, stood the city of Sardis (Sardeis). It held strategic position under a fortified, precipitous hill of white marble; the difficulty of capturing its acropolis became proverbial. Because the city was the western highway station on the Royal Road (described by Herodotus *Persian Wars* 5.52-54) connecting Asian coastal cities to inner Anatolia, the city was important for ancient travel. It was the old capital of the Lydian kingdom whose last king, Croesus (560-546 B.C.), entered legend for amassing local river gold dust, which Strabo reports by Roman times had "given out" (Strabo *Geog.* 13.4.5). After the reign of Croesus, the city served as headquarters of the principal Persian satrapy and then as one of many royal capitals of the *Seleucid Empire. Under Roman rule it continued to be politically and commercially dominant as chief city of Lydia, Roman Asia's eastern district (not to be confused with Lycia; see 1.2.1 below).

Sardis enjoyed a prosperous economy. The textile industry there was the most important in Asia and perhaps its most ancient center. Sardian carpets, finely wrought, covered the palace floors of Persian kings, and its purple couch covers were known in *Athens as early as 400 B.C. Ancient tradition, albeit apocryphal, claimed that Sardian artisans invented the dyeing process. The city's perfumes were famous, excelled only by those produced at Ephesus. Sardis was the place for travelers to find luxury goods.

The population included a significant number of Jews; inscriptions list Jews as goldsmiths, marble sculptors, shopkeepers, dyers, mosaic workers and members of the city's council. Archaeological excavation has unearthed the synagogue of Sardis, the largest extant from antiquity. A famous early Christian bishop, Melito of Sardis (d. A.D. 190), expressed vehement hostility toward the city's Jewish people, perhaps out of envy of this highly favored synagogue and of the community's prominence.

1.2. Lycia and Pamphylia. In southwest Asia Minor, bordering the Mediterranean Sea, the Roman province of Lycia and Pamphylia was created by the emperor Claudius in A.D. 43, when he took the southern portion of Galatia and added lands once governed by the Lycian league of cities.

1.2.1. Lycia. A great mountain range dominates the landscape of Lycia. The range is an extension of the Taurus, shaped like a horseshoe ringing the center of the district. "The scene of the myth of Chimaera," writes Strabo, "is laid in the neighborhood of these mountains" (Strabo *Geog.* 14.3.5). There was a Lycian ravine called Chimera, named after the mythic monster, site of an unusual natural phenomenon: the periodic venting of highly flammable gas from a small rock-face niche, the burning jets of which ancients called the everlasting fire. This phenomenon caused wonder in antiquity as well as today.

The ancient people of Lycia drew their commerce principally from the mountainous resources. The forests provided shipbuilding timber. Goats' hair was manufactured into robes. A local species of thorny shrub was prized as the source of a famous medicinal elixir. A chalk mine operated in the area. Off the coast, especially among the islands, there were valuable fisheries; the sponges from Lycia were savored as a delicacy. As a whole, however, because of the shortage of good land and the relatively limited population, the economy of Lycia never reached the level of that in the neighboring districts of Pamphylia, Pisidia and Caria.

The mountains made transportation and urban development difficult, and at times they isolated Lycia from outside influence. Indigenous Lycian culture and language (belonging to the Anatolian branch of the Indo-European linguistic family) survived into the classical era. As one might expect, most of the Greco-Roman *cities were along the coast, where the sea or the main highway that ran parallel to it facilitated travel. While these cities were small compared with the metropolises of Asia, they nonetheless had an unusual capacity for collaboration and federation.

1.2.2. Pamphylia. Pamphylia is Greek for "land of all tribes." Inspired by classical tradition, the name expresses the belief that the land was supposedly founded by the mixed multitude of Greeks who wandered across Asia Minor after the Trojan War. The inhabitants of one city, Aspendus, claimed kinship with the Mycenean civilization of the Argives. While this claim is highly unlikely, local Greek dialects nonetheless exhibited affinities with Cypriot and Arcadian as well as traditional Anatolian languages.

Unlike mountainous Lycia to the west, Pamphylia was a coastal plain, along southern Anatolia. In this plain, five great cities arose: Attaleia (modern Antalya), Perge, Sillyum, Aspendus and Side. These cities clustered along a short, forty-mile stretch and formed an arc of a circle, dense with urbanization by ancient standards.

Attaleia was the newest, founded by Attalus II of Pergamum (220-138 B.C.) to focus Attalid political power in southern Asia Minor. It served as the chief port of the southern littoral. Under the Roman early empire, Augustus settled the lands with Italian legionary veterans. Perge, which Acts reports Paul visited (Acts 13:13; 14:24-25), was famous for the native cult of Pergean Artemis, a Greco-Anatolian goddess whose likeness appeared on the city's coins. It was the birthplace of the mathematician Apollonius (fl. 200 B.C.), whose work in ancient geometry (specifically, conics) was as foundational as that of Euclid. Perge vied with its neighboring city Side for the rank of first city in Pamphylia. The competition came in part from Side's excellent harbor, an international hub of sea connections to Syria, Egypt, Cyprus and Rhodes. These and other Pamphylians, according to Strabo, shared "much of the traits of the Cilician stock of people" and did "not wholly abstain from the business of piracy" (Strabo *Geog.* 12.7.2; see also 14.3.2). Municipal magistrates routinely cooperated with Cilician pirates, allowing dockage in the harbor and subsequent selling of kidnapped captives. In this way, Side earned its place in the history of the Roman *slave trade.

1.3. Cilicia. The Greeks and Romans applied the name *Cilicia* to various southern Asia Minor regions in different periods, but by the time of the NT it came to designate a Roman province in the eastern half of the southern coast. Roman Cilicia is perhaps the best example of what the Latin word *provincia* originally meant—not a bounded geography under uniform administration but a sphere of military duties (called *imperium*) granted a Roman magistrate overseas. In this way, modern maps of the Roman Empire can mislead. The first Roman command *(imperium)* there, under the praetor Marcus Antonius (d. 87 B.C.; grandfather of the triumvir Mark Antony), was little more than an authorization to patrol the southern Anatolian coast against pirates.

Roman Cilicia was not a territorial unity, being two dissimilar countries. Tracheia ("Rugged") Cilicia in the west afforded, according to Strabo, "a poor livelihood" because of its rough, mountainous terrain and the very little level ground on its narrow coastline. The eastern country of Pedias ("Level") Cilicia "consists for the most part of plains and fertile land" (Strabo *Geog.* 14.5.1). Pedias was one of the most abundant producers of flax, vines, olives and barley in Asia Minor; its rich supply of ship timber proved valuable to local pirates.

Long before early Christians made it famous as the home of the apostle Paul (Acts 22:3) and an ancient center of Christian activity (Acts 9:30; 11:25), Cilicia had obtained its international reputation (more precisely, infamy) in classical antiquity as the home of pirates. Yet piracy in the ancient world should not be thought of in its modern sense of individual, renegade outlaws working independently of any governmental sponsorship. As we saw in the case of ancient Side, Cilician pirates enjoyed the support of monarchs and magnates in ports all along the Anatolian coastline. The economies of many ancient cities depended on the success of piracy, and Rome was no exception. Only when pirates threatened the Egyptian corn supply to the city of Rome did the Senate finally take action, commissioning the task to *Pompey the Great (67 B.C.). In only a few months, and in an uncomplicated naval exercise, Pompey ended one hundred years of infestation by Cilician pirates of the eastern Mediterranean. In the western seaboard of Greece and Asia Minor, however, piracy continued. Cilician pirate fleets of the next generation (38-36 B.C.) fought in the Roman Republican civil wars (ironically under the command of Pompey's son, Sextus Pompeius) to oppose the forces of young Octavian, the future emperor Augustus.

2. Anatolian Interior.

Barely touched by Greek, much less Roman, influence before the first century B.C., the vast interior of Anatolia was among the wildest in the ancient world. The highlands were invaded in 278 B.C. by northern European Celtic (Gallic) tribes who migrated across the Hellespont into Asia. Also known as Gauls (hence the geographic name *Galatia*), these tribes became the most dominant influence in central Anatolian society, culture and religion. This was the outback of Asia Minor and included the lands of Phrygia and Galatia.

2.1. Phrygia. Although it was not a formal province of Rome—the land was divided between the provinces of Asia and Galatia—ancient Phrygia nonetheless had its own national identity. The Phrygian language, known from inscriptions at both an early (Old Phrygian) and a later (New Phrygian) stage, continued to be spoken well into the third century A.D.; New Phrygian simply adopted the Greek alphabet. The Phrygian religion also endured and practiced cultic worship of Agdistis, the Phrygian mother goddess, her youthful consort Attis and other Anatolian deities associated with righteousness, vengeance and justice. This native religious life enjoyed a strict moral code of behavior, and it was responsive to ancient Judaism and early Christianity. Christian communities flourished there in the second and third centuries, including the controversial Montantist church with its prophecy of the heavenly Jerusalem descending on two Phrygian villages, Pepuza and Tymion. Phrygian Jews are reported in the narrative of Acts (Acts 2:10), and the excavated synagogue (dating to the reign of Nero) in the Phrygian city of Acmonia has produced the only Hebrew inscriptions found in the interior of Asia Minor outside Sardis; other Jewish inscriptions are in Greek. To the Greeks, Phrygians were barbarians; to the Romans, recalcitrant savages suitable only as slaves (Appian *Civ. W.* 2.74.308).

2.2. Galatia. The term *Galatia,* or *Gallo-Graecia,* denoted both central Asia Minor generally and the province of Rome by that name in particular (Galatia proper). The Roman province, formed in 25 B.C. from the former kingdom of the Galatian tetrarch Amyntas, comprised much of eastern Phrygia, Lycaonia (Acts 14:11, for the language), the Taurus Mountain region of Isauria, Pisidia (Acts 13:14) and northern Pamphylia (Acts 14:24), and within the next eighty or so years Rome added to it regions in Paphlagonia and Pontus. Knowledge of the continuous shifting of borders of an already ill-defined territory makes understandable the debate in NT scholarship over whether Paul's letter was addressed to the inhabitants in Roman Galatia proper (the so-called North Galatian theory) or the inhabitants of the southern cities of Pisidian Antioch, Iconium, Lystra and Derbe (the so-called South Galatian theory; *see DPL,* Galatians, Letter to the).

The Romans never successfully pacified the Galatians, and the province required military intervention from the outset. The emperor Augustus (63 B.C.-A.D. 14) stationed an army legion (Legio VII) in the south and veteran settlements throughout the area. The intransigent natives nonetheless maintained their Gallic character fiercely; Celtic continued to be a living language in rural districts as late as Byzantine rule.

Galatian social structure was tribal—the Tolistobogii in the west, the Tectosages around Ancyra (modern Ankara) and the Trocmi in the east (Strabo *Geog.* 12.5.1). To the Romans, the Galatians lived on the margin of civilization, plundering temples, sacking cities and inspiring fear throughout the Asian countryside. They often fought naked with rhythmic chanting.

Traditional Greco-Roman polytheism made

little headway into Galatian tribal religion, a syncretism of Celtic and Anatolian. Chieftains were notorious for Druid-style ritualized human sacrifice, a practice similar to that noted by Julius Caesar among the Celts in Gaul. In sacred groves, devotees worshiped the Great Mother goddess of Anatolia, Cybele, and her Phrygian persona Agdistis (plus Attis), along with other indigenous mountain deities. Anatolian priests (named *Galli*) were eunuchs, and their self-induced castration in drunken frenzy was "madness" to Greco-Roman sensibility (Epictetus *Disc.* 2.20.17). Interpretation of Paul's letter, particularly the apostle's censure of circumcision practices, should include consideration of the Anatolian cultic context in which the original, Galatian recipients would have heard those words.

3. Black Sea and Frontier Regions.

The northern districts of Asia Minor held importance for their Black (Euxine) Sea maritime commerce and their highways to Syria and the eastern frontiers.

3.1. Pontus and Bithynia. Bithynia became in name a Roman province in 75 B.C. through the bequest of its Hellenistic king, Nicomedes III. At that time, however, neighboring Pontus was Rome's most dangerous enemy. Its monarch, Mithridates IV, had already fought two wars against Rome and was unwilling to allow Roman control over Bithynia and its entrance to the Black Sea. The outbreak became known as the Third Mithridatic War (74-63 B.C.). Mithridates lost. The conflict made Pompey the Great master of Asia, and he subsequently redrew the map of Anatolia into a continuous line of Roman provinces around the coast. Bithynia was extended to embrace the western part of Pontus, dividing administrative control among eleven cities. Thus the province got its paired name Bithynia and Pontus.

The Bithynians were a mixture of Greek, Roman and Thracian ethnicities. The population in Pontus was oriental in outlook, the Mithridatic royal house being descended from Persian nobles. We know more about daily life in this Roman province Bithynia and Pontus than any other in the empire, because of the famous correspondence (A.D. 110) between its governor, Pliny the Younger, and the emperor Trajan. This correspondence gives rare insight not only into Roman provincial administration but also into early Christian experience. It is the earliest external account of early Christian worship and the fullest statement of the reasons Roman magistrates found cause to imprison and execute Christians (Pliny *Ep.* 10.96).

3.2. Cappadocia. To the south of Pontus and east of Galatia lay the frontier region of Cappadocia, extending to the Euphrates River and the border of Armenia. Topographically it was rolling plateau, almost treeless in the western portions, with volcanism in the central mountain ranges. Historically it had cultural ties to Persia, which had divided it into two satrapies, Cappadocia Pontus (which the Romans later joined to Bithynia) and Greater Cappadocia (the Roman province by that name, near the Taurus Mountains). The country was isolated from both the Mediterranean world and the Mesopotamian lowlands. The economy depended on timber, the production of cereals and fruits and the operation of many mines (quartz, salt, cinnabar and silver).

Roman Cappadocia was chiefly a region of large senatorial estates and imperial properties. Different from other provinces in Asia Minor, it was administered, like Egypt, through the domains and estates, not the cities. Pasturelands made the grazing of horses popular, and since much of the land was the personal property of the Roman emperor, the emperors kept studs of racehorses there.

Jews resided in the region (Acts 2:9), as did early Christians (1 Pet 1:1). In the fourth century an important school of Christian theology took its name from the province, under Gregory of Nazianzus with the brothers Gregory of Nyssa and Basil the Great, the so-called Cappadocian church fathers. They worked, among other places, in *Caesarea, the Cappadocian capital city.

See also ANTIOCH (PISIDIA); CITIES, GRECO-ROMAN; COLOSSAE; EPHESUS; GALATIA, GALATIANS; GEOGRAPHICAL PERSPECTIVES IN LATE ANTIQUITY; GREECE AND MACEDON; JEWISH COMMUNITIES IN ASIA MINOR; ROMAN EMPIRE.

BIBLIOGRAPHY. R. E. Allen, *The Attalid Kingdom: A Constitutional History* (Oxford: Clarendon Press, 1983); H. Brewster, *Classical Anatolia: The Glory of Hellenism* (London: I. B. Tauris, 1993); S. M. Elliott, "Choose Your Mother, Choose Your Master: Galatians 4:21—5:1 in the Shadow of the Anatolian Mother of the Gods," *JBL* 118 (1999) 661-83; A. Farrington, *The Roman Baths of*

Lycia: An Architectural Study (British Institute of Archaeology at Ankara Monograph 20; London: British Institute of Archaeology at Ankara, 1995); D. H. French, "The Roman Road-System of Asia Minor," *ANRW* 2.7.2 (1980) 698-729; D. H. French, ed., *Studies in the History and Topography of Lycia and Pisidia: In Memoriam A. S. Hall* (British Institute of Archaeology at Ankara Monograph 19; London: British Institute of Archaeology at Ankara, 1994); G. W. A. Hanfmann, *Sardis from Prehistoric to Roman Times: Results of the Archaeological Exploration of Sardis 1958-1975* (Cambridge, MA: Harvard University Press, 1983); B. F. Harris, "Bithynia: Roman Sovereignty and the Survival of Hellenism," *ANRW* 2.7.2 (1980) 857-901; H. Koester, ed., *Ephesos: Metropolis of Asia: An Interdisciplinary Approach to Its Archaeology, Religion and Culture* (HTS 41; Valley Forge, PA: Trinity Press International, 1995); idem, ed., *Pergamon: Citadel of the Gods* (HTS 46; Valley Forge, PA: Trinity Press International, 1998); B. Levick, *Roman Colonies in Southern Asia Minor* (Oxford: Clarendon Press, 1967); S. Lloyd, *Ancient Turkey: A Traveler's History of Anatolia* (Berkeley and Los Angeles: University of California Press, 1989); A. D. Macro, "The Cities of Asia Minor Under Roman Imperium," *ANRW* 2.7.2 (1980) 658-97; D. Magie, *Roman Rule in Asia Minor: To the End of the Third Century After Christ* (2 vols.; Princeton, NJ: Princeton University Press, 1950); S. Mitchell, *Anatolia: Land, Men and Gods in Asia Minor* (2 vols.; Oxford: Clarendon Press, 1993); idem, "Population and Land in Roman Galatia," *ANRW* 2.7.2 (1980) 1053-81; T. B. Mitford, "Roman Rough Cilicia," *ANRW* 2.7.2 (1980) 1230-61; S. R. F. Price, *Rituals and Power: The Roman Imperial Cult in Asia Minor* (Cambridge: Cambridge University Press, 1984); R. Syme, *Anatolica: Studies in Strabo,* ed. Anthony Birley (Oxford: Clarendon Press, 1995); P. R. Trebilco, *Jewish Communities in Asia Minor* (SNTSMS 69; Cambridge: Cambridge University Press, 1991); E. M. Yamauchi, *The Archaeology of New Testament Cities in Western Asia Minor* (BSBA; Grand Rapids, MI: Baker, 1980). J. A. Harrill

ASSOCIATIONS

During the *Hellenistic era, voluntary associations of various types began to flourish. In Greek, such organizations are typically referred to as *orgeones, thiastoi* or *eranistai,* while the typical Latin designation is *collegia.* Lists of known associations in the Hellenistic era amount to at least twelve hundred (Poland), and, during the early principate, at around twenty-five hundred (Waltzing). Primarily these associations fall into three kinds, divided on account of their membership bases: "those associated with the household, those formed around a common trade (and civic locale), and those formed around the cult of a deity" (Kloppenborg, 26). Whereas previous research on associations has suggested that they existed primarily as *collegia tenuiorum* or *collegia funeraticia* (to provide their members with proper *burials), recent research has suggested that this was a secondary function of associations that may have come to the fore only during Hadrian's time, if even then (Kloppenborg, 20-23, contra Stambaugh and Balch, 125-26).

1. Associations in the Greco-Roman World
2. Associations and Second Temple Judaism
3. Associations and the New Testament

1. Associations in the Greco-Roman World. The phenomenon of the voluntary association, whether primarily as a professional, religious or social grouping, came about in the wake of the destabilizing effects of the conquests of *Alexander the Great and the subsequent political, social and cultural changes in the wars of succession. Membership of voluntary associations was largely if not exclusively made up of the lower classes—*slaves, freedmen and the disenfranchised—for the *polis* and state (from whose membership the lower classes were excluded) provided the necessary social cohesion for the upper classes which voluntary associations were designed to replace. These associations, then, provided a way for the disenfranchised to enfranchise themselves. It may be this single reason (rather than political influence or activity on the part of associations, both of which are difficult to demonstrate) that caused both senatorial and imperial displeasure with them at various points up until the reign of Hadrian. If so, whatever their specifics, we can see in the associations a broad sociological phenomenon that worked against—or was feared to work against—the interests of the privileged few who controlled Greco-Roman society.

It seems that the most frequent activity of associations, whatever their particular stripe, was social gathering. From the tendency towards hierarchalization (more so in Roman than Hellenistic associations) and title-giving, to the frequent common meals and the responsibility for funereal rites, the association was the Greco-Roman *polis* writ small. In this context it appears likely that the association figured as both a means of enfranchisement (as above) as well as a means of social control. Especially those associations that met within a given household would have come under the watchful eye of the patron, who would likely also have been related to members of the association in a more formal way (i.e., as master or employer). Likewise, the dearth of evidence of more than local membership in any given association suggests that broader organization and independence from localized control was not encouraged.

Membership was often limited, with vacancies opening only as members died or new family members were added. Inclusion or exclusion revolved around the promise to abide by the rules of the society (of which we have many epigraphic and a few papyrological examples; see Tod, 71-93) and the payment of the appropriate entry dues and maintenance fees, as well as any fines the member may have incurred as a result of infringement of the rules of the society.

2. Associations and Second Temple Judaism. The role of the association in the Greco-Roman world was not limited to merely pagan associations, nor does it seem that pagan associations had exclusively pagan membership. Recent research (Richardson) has suggested that the early *synagogue can be seen as falling under the phenomenon of the *collegium,* both legally and functionally, and T. Seland (1996) has demonstrated that *Philo and other *Alexandrian Jews were involved on some basis in pagan associations. In addition, some work has suggested, on the basis of the **Rule of the Community* from *Qumran, that the Qumranites or perhaps the *Essenes as a whole were of the same legal status as a typical Hellenistic association (Bardtke; Schneider; see also Hengel, 1:244-45).

In some ways, it may be possible to see the association, at least in Hellenistic times, as a lower-class cognate to the *gymnasium, the central social, *educational and political institution of the Greek *polis.* If so, then the overlap between the association and the synagogue, which also displays features analogous to the gymnasium, becomes even clearer.

The widespread Hellenistic phenomenon of the association may have been the impetus toward the foundation of various groupings within *Judaism as a whole in the Second Temple period. The widespread social unrest and reordering that came about as a result of the Macedonian conquest of the East led to a variety of social and political redefinitions. Whereas the city-state had been the central focus of allegiance in the Greek world, this gave way to more centralized power in the form of the Hellenistic kingdoms, which was in turn somewhat weakened by the increased mobility and intermixture of both peoples and cultures in this period. For those, like the Jews, formerly under Persian domination (*see* Jewish History: Persian Period), there was the added feature of a certain loss of identity—where before they had been Jews either resistant to or involved in Persian culture, this force was all but removed in the wake of the Macedonian conquest. With the amount of time that had elapsed between the exile, the various returns and the eventual removal of Achaemenid control, Jewish culture was in a state of almost total disrepair.

It should then be unsurprising that the Jewish cultural and religious redefinition in the wake of Macedonian conquest should draw many of its organizational features from the Greek world. As such, the association provided an excellent model upon which to build this newly defined Judaism and Jewish self-identity. Jews in both *Diaspora and Palestinian settings would be able to go about daily life in social structures that, while perhaps differing in content, were cognate to social structures in the world in which they lived. It may be that *Josephus's descriptions of the various *haireseis* in Second Temple Judaism (Josephus *Life* 1.1.2 §§9-12; *Ant.* 13.4.9 §§171-73; 18.1.2-6 §§11-25; *J.W.* 2.8.2-14 §§119-66; *see* Theologies and Sects, Jewish), rather than distorted pictures of Jewish life as a result of Josephus's concern to make Jews intelligible to his non-Jewish readers, are good representations of the various kinds of Greco-Roman Jewish religious associations. These would have fulfilled all of the roles that usual associations filled and seem to have fallen largely along socioeconomic lines, with the highest level of Jewish society probably not playing much of a role, much as with other Greco-Roman associations.

3. Associations and the New Testament. In the wider Greco-Roman world, the association had a firm societal place, if one that on occasion met with disapproval from the Roman government. Into this world the early church both spread and had its initial existence. The first churches probably met in people's homes (Rom 16:5; Col 4:15; Philem 2), and, as in the case of pagan associations, the homeowner would often be a patron of the association. Where the Pauline churches seem to differ somewhat is in the assumption that the patron was also intricately involved in the association itself rather than being a distant patron, as seems to have been the usual case (hence the letter to Philemon is to Philemon and the church that meets in his house but switches to the second person singular pronoun for the bulk of the letter). It would make a great deal of sense for Paul's missionary strategy if he were, in the first place, to involve himself in the local synagogue (or *collegium Judaicari,* to coin a term) and then establish his fledgling churches along lines familiar both to himself and to his new converts—the voluntary association under the patronage of one or more wealthy patrons. That Paul himself was involved in the *patronage system has long been suggested by his name change from Saul to Paul, in light of his meeting and conversion of Sergius Paulus on Cyprus (Dessau; *see* Antioch [Pisidia]), and it may have been that this pattern of patronage continued throughout the rest of his missionary activity (see Garnsey and Saller).

It is probable that members of the new Christian churches continued to various degrees in their previous associations—many of the troubles that churches such as those at *Corinth and *Rome had could be explained by the continued meeting of Christians with their former associations (e.g., 1 Cor 8 and Rom 14 with regard to meat offered to idols; 1 Cor 11, where the conduct of the "Lord's Supper" seems to recall the riotous feasting that typified the associations' meals; see also Eph 5:18). It is even possible that the author of Acts presents the various typical features of the early church (regular meetings, common meals, remembrance of a significant figure) in a way that would be reminiscent for his readers of the way in which they had themselves been involved in various associations, or that he gives us a picture of the way the early church was, which was like other associations of the period.

The importance of the associations for the study of the world of the NT is commensurate with the amount of material available on them—*inscriptions, *papyri and classical authors all provide us with invaluable evidence for the reconstruction of both the membership of these associations and their role within society.

See also FAMILY AND HOUSEHOLD; GYMNASIA AND BATHS; PATRONAGE; SOCIAL VALUES AND STRUCTURES; SYNAGOGUES.

BIBLIOGRAPHY. H. Bardtke, "Die Rechsstellung der Qumran-Gemeinde," *TLZ* 86 (1961) 93-104; H. Dessau, "Der Name des Apostels Paulus," *Hermes* 44 (1910) 347-68; P. Garnsey and R. Saller, "Patronal Power Relations," *Paul and Empire: Religion and Power in Roman Imperial Society,* ed. R. A. Horsley (Harrisburg, PA: Trinity Press International, 1997) 96-103; M. Hengel, *Judaism and Hellenism: Studies in Their Encounter in Palestine During the Early Hellenistic Period* (2 vols.; London: SCM, 1974); J. L. Kloppenborg, "Collegia and *Thiasoi:* Issues in Function, Taxonomy and Membership," in *Voluntary Associations in the Greco-Roman World,* ed. J. L. Kloppenborg and S. G. Wilson (London and New York: Routledge, 1996) 16-30; J. L. Kloppenborg and S. G. Wilson, eds., *Voluntary Associations in the Greco-Roman World* (London and New York: Routledge, 1996); F. Poland, *Geschichte des greichischen Vereinswesens* (Leipzig: Zentral-Antiquariat der Deutschen Demokratischen Republik, 1967 [1909]); P. Richardson, "Early Synagogues as Collegia in the Diaspora and Palestine," in *Voluntary Associations in the Greco-Roman World,* ed. J. L. Kloppenborg and S. G. Wilson (London and New York: Routledge, 1996) 90-109; C. Schneider, "Zur Problematik des Hellenistischen in den Qumrantexten," in *Qumranprobleme: Vorträge des Leipziger Symposions über Qumranprobleme von 9.-14. 10. 1961,* ed. H. Bardtke (Schriften der Sektion Alterumskunde 2; Berlin: Deutsche Akademie der Wissenschaften in Berlin, 1963) 299-314; T. Seland, "Philo and the Clubs and Associations of Alexandria," in *Voluntary Associations in the Greco-Roman World,* ed. J. L. Kloppenborg and S. G. Wilson (London and New York: Routledge, 1996) 110-27; J. E. Stambaugh and D. L. Balch, *The New Testament in Its Social Environment* (LEC 2; Philadelphia: Westminster, 1986); M. N. Tod, *Ancient Inscriptions: Sidelights on Greek History* (Chicago: Ares, 1974 repr.); J. P. Waltzing, *Étude Historique sur les Corporations Professionelles chez les Romains Depuis les Origines Jusqu' à la Chute de l'Empire d'Occident* (4 vols.; Louvain: Peeters, 1895–1900; Hildesheim: Georg Olms, 1970).

B. W. R. Pearson

ASSUMPTION OF MOSES. *See* TESTAMENT OF MOSES.

ASTROLOGY. *See* RELIGION, PERSONAL.

ASTROLOGY, JEWISH. *See* THUNDER TEXT (4Q318); TREATISE OF SHEM.

ATHENS

Athens was named for the Greek goddess Athena, whose world-renowned temple, the Parthenon, stood on top of the Acropolis in the heart of town. The Acropolis is located 4 miles east of Piraeus, the port of Athens in the southern province of Greece known as Achaia. Although the Piraeus harbor was destroyed in 86 B.C. it was restored and functioning when Paul was in Athens. Apollonius of Tyana, a contemporary of Paul, and Pausanias, an author in the second century, both seem to have entered Athens from this harbor.

1. Athens in Historical Perspective
2. Paul in Athens

1. Athens in Historical Perspective.

Athens was known as the center of classical studies in philosophy and literature in the ancient world. It typified the *Hellenistic culture that permeated the world after the time of *Alexander the Great in the fourth century B.C. Poets, philosophers, authors, sculptors and architects gave Greece its renown. Paul the apostle, a Jew from Tarsus, which also was a famous educational center, knew Greek poets and quoted them in his address to Athenian officials on Mars Hill (Acts 17:28).

However, by the time of the NT, Athens, unlike the great cities of the time such as *Antioch of Syria, *Ephesus, *Alexandria, *Rome and even *Corinth, could only be described as a provincial backwater, a small university town of about twenty-five thousand people, more concerned with ideas than commerce and living in the memories of its glorious history.

2. Paul in Athens.

Paul's visit to Athens during the reign of the emperor Claudius (A.D. 41-54) came during a brief resurgence of building activity comparable to that earlier under the reign of Augustus (27 B.C.-A.D. 14) and later under the emperor Hadrian (A.D. 117-138; *see* Roman Emperors).

We can only assume that Paul and his companions went to the top of the Acropolis; if so, they would have climbed the marble staircase built by Claudius in A.D. 42, about seven years before their arrival. Walking through the porch at the top of the stairway, they would have stepped into an open area where forty steps in front of them they gazed upon a colossal bronze statue of Athena, sculpted in 458 B.C. by Phidias. Looking around them they saw several pagan temples. The Parthenon stood imposingly on the southern side of the Acropolis. The Erechtheion, another temple of Athena, with its Porch of Maidens, stood opposite the Parthenon on the northern side.

Less well known but more significant for Paul and his "new religion" was the temple of Rome and Augustus, only a few yards east of the Parthenon. It was built soon after 27 B.C. and is identified through a dedicatory inscription on the structure. This temple, dedicated to the goddess Roma and the emperor Augustus, emphasizes the importance of emperor worship in the NT period, reflected especially in the book of Revelation.

Everywhere he looked Paul would have seen statues to Greek and Roman deities as well as to the deified emperors Augustus and Claudius. Thirteen small altars dedicated to Augustus have been found in the lower city.

Although we must assume that Paul visited the Acropolis, it is explicitly recorded that he carried on discussions daily in the agora (Acts 17:17), a Greek word for marketplace. There were both a Greek agora and a Roman forum in Athens when Paul visited the city.

The western, Greek market lay due north of the Areopagus (Mars Hill) and contained the prominent temple of Hephaestus and the reconstructed Stoa (Colonnaded Porch) of Attalos, where poet and philosopher met to promenade and talk. The square was kept free of public and private buildings for almost five hundred years, being reserved for political purposes, but beginning with the arrival of the Romans in the reign of Augustus the entire public square had begun to be filled with buildings and monuments. There was almost no political activity in the Greek market after the death of Augustus, so Paul probably spent most of his time in the commercial Roman market to the east.

The western market had become a virtual museum by the mid-first century, when Paul strolled its walkways. It contained such a repository of altars, statues and temples that Petronius, the Roman satirist, remarked "it was easier to find a god than a man in Athens" (Petronius *Sat.* 17).

Paul was impressed that among so many objects of pagan superstition there should be an altar dedicated to an "unknown god" (Acts 17:23). Although this altar no longer exists, Pausanias, who visited Athens between 143 and 159, saw such altars. Describing his trip from the harbor to Athens he wrote: "The Temple of Athene Skiras is also here, and one of Zeus further off, and altars of the 'Unknown gods'. . ." (Pausanius *Descr.* 1.1.4.). Apollonius of Tyana spoke of Athens as the place where there are "altars of unknown gods" (Philostratus *Vit. Ap.* 6.3). Oecumenius also wrote of altars dedicated to unknown gods (comments on Acts 17:23, in *PG* 118:238), as did Diogenes Laertius (Diogenes Laertius *Vit.* 1.110).

By contrast, the eastern sector of the agora named for Caesar and Augustus would have been alive with everyday commercial activity. Here Paul would more likely have found a hearing among the ordinary citizens of Athens. This eastern market is 360 feet square, about the same size as the Forum of Julius Caesar in Rome.

This eastern area contains one of the best preserved ancient monuments in Greece, a tall octagonal marble tower containing sculptured images of the eight winds around the top of its eight sides, and popularly called the Tower of the Winds. It was a huge water clock, sundial and weathervane, and it served as a public timepiece for the city. We can well imagine Paul checking the time of day by this clock while he carried on his teaching in this forum.

While preaching to Godfearers in this agora, Paul was arrested and taken before the Areopagus (Acts 17:17), which in the decades preceding his arrival in Athens had seemingly begun to act as a municipal senate. By the time of Paul's visit, the council of the Areopagus had become prominent among the three corporations of Athenian government. Since Paul had been speaking about "foreign divinities" (Acts 17:18), he fell under the jurisdiction of the Areopagus, which had surveillance over the introduction of foreign divinities.

The location of the meeting place of the Areopagus at this time is not certain. It met in various locations in the classical period, but Mars Hill, on the west side of the Acropolis, was the traditional location for its meetings. Evidence from Lucian, a contemporary of Paul, seems to indicate that jury panels were assigned to hear trials from this point. While there is no certainty that the council was meeting here when Paul stood before it, neither is there any compelling reason to deny that it was. The eastern part of Mars Hill, now a barren limestone hilltop, was undoubtedly covered in marble in Paul's day.

See also ARCHAEOLOGY AND THE NEW TESTAMENT; CORINTH; GREECE AND MACEDON.

BIBLIOGRAPHY. R. Barber, *Blue Guide, Greece* (New York: Norton, 1988) 74-186; J. Camp, *The Athenian Agora* (London: Thames & Hudson, 1986); D. J. Geagan, "Roman Athens, Some Aspects of Life and Culture, 1: 86 B.C.-A.D. 267," *ANRW* 2.7.1 (1979) 371-437; H. L. Hammond, *Atlas of the Greek and Roman World in Antiquity* (Park Ridge, NJ: Noyes, 1981); J. McRay, *Archaeology and the New Testament* (Grand Rapids, MI: Baker, 1991); T. L. Shear Jr., "Athens: From City State to Provincial Town," *Hesperia* 50 (1981) 372; J. Travlos, *Pictorial Dictionary of Ancient Athens* (New York: Praeger, 1971) 494. J. R. McRay

ATHLETICS

To the ancient world athletics were synonymous with Greek culture. Greek athletic festivals commemorated Greek deities, and athletic training was an integral part of Greek education. Beginning as Pan-Hellenic phenomena, athletics eventually spread throughout the Hellenistic and Roman world. While some Jews were hostile to athletics because of their pagan associations, others, particularly in the *Diaspora, were more accepting of the advantages that athletics conferred. Given their prevalence, athletics also came to be appropriated as a metaphor for philosophical training.

1. Festivals
2. Athletics and Education
3. Judaism and Athletics
4. Metaphorical Usage

1. Festivals.

The word *athletics* is derived from *athleō* (Gk meaning "to contend for a prize"). Such contests were characteristically Greek, and they are attested early and most famously in book 23 of the *Iliad.* They appear to have originated as funerary rites for notables or as commemorative rituals for heroes that evolved into regular festivals. The four most notable became Pan-Hellenic contests *(agōnes):* the Olympian Games, traditionally founded 776 B.C.; the Pythian Games, made Pan-Hellenic 582 B.C.; the Isthmian Games, c. 582 B.C.; and the Nemean Games, c. 573 B.C. Each of these was held periodically (i.e., at two- or four-year intervals) in honor of its presiding deity. Both the Olympian and Nemean games were held in honor of Zeus, while the Pythian Games were dedicated to Apollo and the Isthmian Games to Poseidon. These dedications attest to the intimate association between Greek athletics and religion: "sports were definitely placed under the patronage of the gods, and the victorious athlete felt that he was well-pleasing to the gods and owed his success to them. It was to religion that Greek athletics and athletic festivals owed their vitality" (Gardiner, 33).

While the contests varied from festival to festival and became more elaborate over time, the main sporting events typically included competitions in chariot racing, running, long jumping, discus and javelin throwing, boxing, wrestling and the pancratium (a form of all-in wrestling). Participants would assemble from throughout the Greek world to compete, and the victors were honored with wreaths. Victory meant fame, as the *Odes* of Pindar attest, and often valuable civic awards by the victor's hometown or city.

These periodic games formed the nucleus of the contests that spread throughout the Mediterranean world in the Hellenistic period and later, under the Roman principate. As sacred games they spawned many festivals named and modeled after them, particularly in the East. These games continued to be dedicated to deities or in some instances to divinized rulers. Even Rome, which had once been largely indifferent to Greek athletic institutions (favoring *circus spectacles instead; *see* Arenas), began to adopt the practices. The emperors Tiberius and Nero, for instance, both participated in the Olympian Games.

2. Athletics and Education.

In Greece, athletics were a constituent element of the educational process (*paideia*) designed to instill in youths an ideal balance between mind and body. The chief locus for this *paideia* was the *gymnasium (latterly, a building complex including a sports ground or palaestra), where youths would be schooled in athletics as well as in the liberal arts. The training process was calculated to form the consummate Greek gentleman and prepare youths for citizenship within their *polis*. The alumni of this process, "those from the gymnasium," would often comprise a select and influential body within Greek and Hellenistic society. For these reasons, entrance into the gymnasium was much prized.

3. Judaism and Athletics.

*Alexander the Great's conquest of Palestine (332 B.C.) brought Greek athletics in its wake: "wherever Hellenism took root, gymnasiums and stadiums and all the rest of the paraphernalia appeared" (Marrou, 116). *Jerusalem was no exception. During the rule of Antiochus IV Epiphanes (175-164 B.C.), a gymnasium was constructed beneath the Temple Mount, and even the temple priests reportedly participated in the competitions (1 Macc 1:14; 2 Macc 4:9-15). Presumably because of the strong associations between athletics and pagan ritual, 2 Maccabees categorically condemns the practice, accusing the participants of failing to reverence the divine laws (2 Macc 4:17). Not surprisingly, therefore, athletics were evidently proscribed under Maccabean rule, only to reemerge under Herod the Great. He established periodic athletic contests in honor of Augustus and endowed them with lucrative prizes to attract contestants. He also built a theater in Jerusalem, an amphitheater (perhaps a hippodrome?) "in the plain" (Josephus *Ant.* 15.8.1 §268) and similar structures elsewhere. They became commonplace within Palestine, especially in the Hellenized centers (*see* Hellenistic Judaism).

H. A. Harris (96) has argued that, in spite of their pagan associations, athletic events were popular among the Jewish populace of Palestine. There is little support for his argument, however. *Josephus remarks that Herod's structures were "foreign to Jewish custom" (*Ant.* 15.8.1 §268), and later rabbinic writings reinforce this impression by condemning Jewish involvement with athletics *(m. ʿAbod. Zar.* 1:7; *t. ʿAbod. Zar.* 2:7; *Sipra ʿAḥarê Mot* 13:10; though cf. *m. Šabb.* 22:6). *Jubilees'* (3:31) proscription of being "uncovered as the Gentiles are uncovered" may also be a rejection of the Greek custom of exercising in the nude.

If athletics were suspect in Palestine, a different situation appears to have pertained in the Diaspora. Philo was likely a frequenter of games (Philo *Omn. Prob. Lib.* 26; Harris, 51-95), while the letter of Claudius to the Alexandrians (*CPJ* 153) implies that Jewish Alexandrians were seeking to secure citizenship for their sons by enrolling them in gymnasia. Similar examples can be adduced from throughout the Diaspora (Barclay; Trebilco, passim). A qualified acceptance of athletics, therefore, was likely the prevailing Jewish attitude (cf. Safrai and Stern, 447-49, against Hegermann, 162).

4. Metaphorical Usage.

Given the popularity of sports in the ancient world, athletic terminology soon came to be adopted by philosophers, especially *Cynics and *Stoics. Rejecting athletics as largely beneath notice (cf. Philo *Agric.* 113-19), they nevertheless used the notion of athletic training *(askēsis)* as a metaphor for a virtuous and disciplined mode of life. Epictetus famously describes those who live a virtuous philosophical existence as "Olympic victors" (*Disc.* 1.24.2), and Paul appropriates and employs this metaphorical use of athletic imagery in his epistles (e.g., 1 Cor 9:24-27; 4 Macc 17:11-16).

See also GYMNASIA AND BATHS.

BIBLIOGRAPHY. J. Barclay, *Jews in the Mediterranean Diaspora: From Alexander to Trajan (323 BCE - 117 CE)* (Edinburgh: T & T Clark, 1996); E. N. Gardiner, *Athletics of the Ancient World* (Oxford: Clarendon Press, 1930); M. Golden, *Sport and Society in Ancient Greece* (Cambridge: Cambridge University Press, 1998); J. Goldstein, "Jewish Acceptance and Rejection of Hellenism," in *Jewish and Christian Self-Definition,* ed. E. P. Sanders et al. (3 vols.; Philadelphia: Fortress, 1981) 2:64-88; H. A. Harris, *Greek Athletics and the Jews* (Cardiff: University of Wales Press, 1976); H. Hegermann, "The Diaspora in the Hellenistic Age" in *The Cambridge History of Judaism,* 2: *The Hellenistic Age,* ed. W. D. Davies and L. Finkelstein (2 vols.; Cambridge: Cambridge University Press, 1989) 115-66; D. G. Kyle, "Games, Prizes, and Athletes in Greek Sport: Patterns and Perspectives (1975-1997)," *CB* 74 (1998) 103-27; H.-I. Marrou, *A History of Education in Antiquity* (London: Sheed & Ward, 1956); S. G. Miller, *Arete: Greek Sports from Ancient Sources* (2d ed.; Berkeley and Los Angeles: University of California Press, 1991); V. Pfitzner, *Paul and the Agon Motif* (NovTSup 16; Leiden: E. J. Brill, 1967); M. Poliakoff, "Jacob, Job and Other Wrestlers: Reception of Greek Athletics by Jews and Christians in Antiquity," *Journal of Sport History* 11 (1984) 48-65; S. Safrai and M. Stern, eds., *The Jewish People in the First Century* (2 vols.; CRINT 1; Assen: Van Gorrum; Philadelphia: Fortress, 1974-76) vol. 1; P. Trebilco, *Jewish Communities in Asia Minor* (SNTSMS 69; Cambridge: Cambridge University Press, 1991).

J. R. C. Couslan

AUXILIARIES. *See* ROMAN MILITARY.

B

BABATHA ARCHIVE. *See* INSCRIPTIONS AND PAPYRI: JEWISH; PAPYRI, PALESTINIAN.

BAGASRAW, TALE OF. *See* TALE OF BAGASRAW (PSEUDO-ESTHER) (4Q550[a-f])

BANQUETS

In most ancient societies banquets were the favored and expected occasions for social entertainment and enjoyment. This simple truth is easily overlooked in modern Western societies that view banquets very differently. For one thing, because our societies have so many opportunities and platforms for social entertainment we too easily assume that ancients did as well. Another way in which their expectations about banquets differed greatly from those of modern societies is that, being accustomed to having plenty to eat, we have great difficulty appreciating that for most persons in antiquity the banquet was a rare opportunity to have food that was both desirable and bountiful.

In antiquity virtually all banquets and common family meals were to some degree religious. Most meals that had meat, whether at homes or dining halls or temples, were connected with sacrifice. All major religions of antiquity employed the sacrifice ritual as a basic component. Sacrifices were of two types: bloodless (bread, wine, oil, milk, flowers) and blood (animal). Space forbids an investigation into the origins and nature of sacrifice in the Greco-Roman world. Suffice it to say that even the earliest authors regarded sacrifice to have originated in the dim shadows of the beginnings of humanity. Homer regards it as ancient practice. Thus while there was an active critique of sacrifice both in *Judaism and *Hellenism before the time of Christianity, no one doubted that sacrifice was part and parcel of religious life. The same sources assume that following sacrifice there is normally a meal. This meal included a portion of meat from the sacrificed animal for the worshipers—the sacrifice was not just for the god's benefit.

While sacrifice and meat meals did not occur weekly or even monthly, neither were they matters of great rarity. There were a wide variety of sacrificial occasions: public religious *festivals, state festivals, private associations and familial associations. For understanding early Christianity the most important interpretive question is what was the significance of this religious association—what did it mean to the participants?

1. Banquets Described in Jewish Sources
2. Banquets Described in Greco-Roman Sources
3. Meanings Proposed for Religious Meals
4. Banquets Described in the New Testament

1. Banquets Described in Jewish Sources.

1.1. History of Meal Customs. Most often in considering Jewish dining practices the focus is upon the dietary (kosher) laws described in the Bible and extended in common practices of Second Temple Judaism (*see* Purity). In the present investigation, however, the kosher laws will be considered only in relationship to how they may affect banquet meals.

1.2. Opportunities for Banquets. Paul alludes in 1 Corinthians 10:18 to a Jewish fellowship of the altar that involves *sacrifice. In 1 Corinthians 9:13 he mentions that the priests eat from the sacrifices of the altar. This description of meal sacrifice is also witnessed in the OT (Ex 24:4-11; Deut 12:4-28). Thus Paul can say that those "who eat" are "partners" or "fellowshipers" with the sacrificial altar.

Just as in Hellenism, in Judaism it was common for a banquet to follow animal sacrifice. This is not to say that all animal food was associated with *sacrifice (fish were not, for example), but the killing of mammals for sacrifice was commonly followed by a meal except in the unusual case of a "whole offering." Even when they were not offered in sacrifice, animals slain for food were killed in the same manner as was done in sacrifice. The best-known Jewish sacrificial event, Passover, is openly and specifically connected to a communal meal that follows (*see* Festivals).

In the annual Passover observance, with its stipulated menu, there is a clear instruction that this is to be a communal meal. Thus if one does not have a family large enough to consume a lamb, the meal should be planned to share with others. In a similar way, this meal was to emphasize social acceptance, since the stranger and alien should be invited to share the meal.

Other banquet associations of Judaism were the "meal fellowship" known among the *Pharisees. Some contemporary scholars regard the Pharisees as essentially a dining fellowship, and even many who do not share this assessment of pre-Christian Phariseeism acknowledge that Pharisees sought to apply the norms for eating at the *temple to the whole of life, including daily meals, thereby sanctifying all eating before God (Neusner).

1.3. Eschatological Banquet. Finally, in evaluating the Jewish banquet practice and rationale, one must consider the common use in the OT of the image of the messianic banquet. Among the *eschatological images often found in Judaism, the image of a great banquet was often employed to depict both the abundance of the hoped for future and the ultimate association of those chosen by God. Perhaps the classic picture is given in Isaiah 25:6-8 (see also Joel 2:24-28; *1 Enoch* 62:12-14). This imagery is continued in the NT (Mt 22:1-10 = Lk 14:16-24; Mt 8:11-12 = Lk 13:28-29), most powerfully in Revelation 19:9-17. The eschatological hopes associated with the great banquet may also be alluded to in Jesus feeding the multitudes.

2. Banquets Described in Greco-Roman Sources.

2.1. Familial Settings. In family life banquets were rare for all people except the uppermost segment of society. For the average person there were neither the financial resources nor the private space for a real banquet. This may be one reason why associations outside the home had such importance and attraction as is indicated in 1 Corinthians 8 and 10.

2.2. Religious Festivals. These were largely public events recurring on established times. Most were observed regionally, perhaps the most famous being the Panathenea in Athens. But there were also occasions based upon state events such as the emperor's birthday, or upon some military victory. These varied occasions have been described as a combination of fair, sporting event, religious occasion and banquet. M. Nilsson said that such meals took place in some sacred precinct, were dedicated to some god and were accompanied by sacrifice.

The Roman *lectisternium* festival was an annual religious and social event that stressed *friendliness and *hospitality. It resembled a city-wide open house in which people opened their homes and placed varied kinds of food for any and all passers-by to enjoy.

2.3. Voluntary Associations. There were a large variety of voluntary *associations in the Greco-Roman world. Some were based on family or clan, others on occupations or geographical place of origin. There were associations of military people, of *philosophical interests, voluntary fire departments, *athletics and perhaps even clubs organized to assure a proper *burial. As a focal point of their gatherings all these shared meals and all were, broadly speaking, religious associations. Their meetings were under the aegis of a patron deity, and there was commonly sacrifice offered.

People in the Greco-Roman world loved clubs, and all these were in some way connected with religion and featured dining together. The earliest forms seem to have been tribal, but in the Hellenistic period they were often focused upon a common interest. Many people would be a member of more than one group. It is anachronistic and artificial to divide them into secular and religious associations, for all were nominally religious—but all were also marked by festivity rather than solemnity. *Aristotle says that "some associations appear to be formed for the sake of pleasure, for example religious guilds and dining clubs which are unions for sacrifice and social intercourse" (Aristotle *Eth. Nic.* 8.9.5). It has been suggested that they might be compared with modern Freemasons.

2.4. Mystery Religions. The most intriguing meal occasions in antiquity were those associated with the *mystery religions. While directly involving only a minority of persons, the mystery religions because of their uniqueness were of great interest in antiquity, as they are today. The prototype mystery was that of Eleusis, the shrine of Demeter and Kore about 14 miles west of *Athens. Equally prominent and more widespread was the cult of Dionysius (or Bacchus), prominent in poetry and art for its wild naturalism. Finally, the cult of Mithras, which originated in Persia, was spreading westward contemporary with Christianity and also featured mysteries to see and a banquet to be shared.

In all these mystery religions, and others that are less well-known, a meal shared by the worshipers is an important event. The great difficulty is knowing how those who shared the banquet understood what they were doing and what motivated them to share the meal. This has been the area of greatest speculation, although many have appealed to the mystery religions as a major influence on early Christian eucharistic theology without acknowledging this speculation.

A number of invitations to banquets have survived from Hellenistic Egypt. These are associated with the god Serapis, who had been thoroughly Hellenized by this time, and are issued either in his name (rarely) or to his shrine. These are all very brief and thus susceptible to a variety of interpretations. The reasons for the banquet are not usually given, but a few mention a birthday or coming-of-age party for a child. The assessment offered by the foremost authorities on these meals says that they are basically secular in meaning.

Also surviving from antiquity are *inscriptions that give regulations for the meals of various cultic associations—some clearly religious, others perhaps only nominally so. The regulations stipulate the equitable sharing of the meal and give rules for good behavior at the banquets. Thus there are fines for those who start fights or try to take the seat assigned another. One inscription forbids the bringing up of any business matter at the meal, lest it distract from the joy of the occasion.

The picture of occasions for social conviviality that these rules create is supported from references in ancient literary sources that describe these banquets. *Philo, the Alexandrian Jew, complains that the pagan religious meals are really drinking bouts and bawdy parties. This assessment is given, though lampooned, in Greek comedy. In Aristophanes' comedies (late fifth century B.C.) cult festivals are characterized by drunkenness, and men are depicted as stealing food from the sacrifices on the table of the gods.

3. Meanings Proposed for Religious Meals.

3.1. Sacramental. Almost a century ago, at the height of the so-called *religonsgeschichtliche Schule* (history-of-religions school) with its interpretation of Christianity as derived from and dependent upon Hellenism, the common assumption was that the Christian sacrament of the Lord's Supper was modeled upon a prior sacramental meal in Greek religions (especially the mystery religions). This interpretation held that at the cultic meal following sacrifice the worshipers believed they were ingesting, either actually or symbolically, the god. Drawing upon a particular understanding of pagan mystery religions, the religious meal thus was interpreted as a medium by which one partook of the god. Very often Paul was held to be the source of this Hellenistic sacramentalism being brought into Christianity. In particular 1 Corinthians 10:16-22 often has been alleged to prove that Paul equated the Christian sacramental meal with that of paganism. On this view, the sacramental meaning of pagan meals has influenced and been adopted by Christians. But the point of comparison in 1 Corinthians 10 is not sacramentalism but that meals define group identity and mutual obligations.

In part this sacramentalist interpretation of pagan meals may well initially have been derived from medieval Christian eucharistic thought. The later development of Christian sacramental theology moved toward a mystical presence of the Lord in the Eucharist (to the doctrine of the "real presence" in medieval Catholic thought). It may well be that this Christian belief has led modern scholars to interpret those pagan meals contemporary with early Christianity through the eyes of later Christian sacramental theology.

3.2. Communal. In this interpretation the meal is regarded as shared with the deity who came as a guest to the banquet. The portion for the god was placed on a table reserved for him, and the worshipers who ate felt a sense of common fellowship with the god. The presence and participation of the god at the meal makes it sacred—the diners are his guests. This is obviously a lesser claim than the mystical-sacramental interpretation, and it has a wide currency today. Still, even this reconstruction too may be read back into Hellenistic cult banquets through a lens provided by later Christian (especially Reformation) sacramental thought. The argument in the Reformation era was the "how" of the presence of the Lord, but that he is present was everywhere granted—both by Catholics and Reformers.

3.3. Social. Just as there are real but subtle differences between the first and second interpretations so also there are between the second and the third. The difference may be stated that in the communal view the meal is an occasion of conscious worship, in which the meal is sacred because the deity shares the meal with the worshipers; in the social view, while the deity was given regard and a portion allotted him, the focus is on the relationship that the meal established among the diners. The sharing of the dinner defined who was in the group and how the members of the group were to regard each other (and others not in the group).

4. Banquets Described in the New Testament. The social and religious significance of meals, especially banquets, in antiquity sheds light on the meals described in the NT, both in Jesus' ministry and in the early church.

4.1. Jesus' Ministry. Although Jesus' ministry often includes special meals, only the Last Supper is explicitly related to a sacrifice (Passover). But in both his word and deed Jesus presumes upon and uses common ideas about dining. Banquet imagery is used to present the kingdom of God in Luke 14:15-24, and Jesus' dining companions both illustrate the nature of repentance and create a scandal among the righteous (Lk 5:27-32; cf. Lk 7:36-50). Jesus draws upon the social etiquette of the day as a means of teaching humility (Lk 14:7-14). A banquet is presented as the image of the final bliss (Lk 13:29; 14:15; Mt 8:11 and esp. 22:1-10; Rev 19:9) recalling OT expectations such as Isaiah 25:6. In both Luke 24:30-31 and John 21:9-14 it is at a shared meal that the resurrected Lord is recognized and confessed (and perhaps Luke understands the Emmaus supper to anticipate the Christian communion).

4.2. Early Church. Within the history of the early church, the shared table is a sign of the shared faith. While these meals may not qualify as banquets, it is clear that in Acts the common image of the church assembled is for a meal (Acts 2:42-47; 20:7), and if this community meal is disrupted it calls into question the reality of faith (Gal 2:11-14; cf. 1 Cor 11:17-34). This shared meal experientially embodies the church, so that the refusal of the church to share a meal with a person is serious punishment for a sin (1 Cor 5:11).

See also CIVIC CULTS; FESTIVALS AND HOLY DAYS: JEWISH; HOSPITALITY; RELIGION, GRECO-ROMAN; TEMPLE, JEWISH; TEMPLES, GRECO-ROMAN.

BIBLIOGRAPHY. H.-J. Klauck, *Herrenmahl und hellenistischer Kult: Eine religions-geschichtliche Untersuchung z. ersten Korintherbrief* (NTAbh n.s. 15; Münster: Aschendorff, 1975); J. Neusner, *From Politics to Piety* (Englewood Cliffs, NJ: Prentice-Hall, 1973); D. E. Smith, "Messianic Banquet," *ABD* 4:788-91; idem, "Table Fellowship as a Literary Motif in the Gospel of Luke," *JBL* 106 (1987) 613-38; W. L. Willis, *Idol Meat in Corinth* (SBLDS 68; Chico, CA: Scholars Press, 1985); H. C. Youtie, "The Kline of Sarapis," *HTR* 41 (1948) 9-29. W. L. Willis

BAR KOKHBA LETTERS. *See* INSCRIPTIONS AND PAPYRI: JEWISH; PAPYRI, PALESTINIAN; SIMON BEN KOSIBA.

BARKI NAFSHI (4Q434, 436, 437-439)

This group of texts gets its name from the phrase *barkî napšî ʾet ʾadōnay* ("Bless the Lord, O my soul"), also known from Psalms 103 and 104. Whether the preponderance of these fragments are all copies of one text or fragments of the same copy is hard to establish. The six sets of fragments were originally sorted according to scribal hand and similarities in leather. The majority of them represent a collection of hymns devoted to the praise of God's goodness. The functional role of hymns in the *Qumran sect has not yet been established; that is, were they used in communal worship, as a substitute for *temple ritual or to accompany *sacrificial rites?

1. Characteristics of the Texts
2. Analysis of the Texts

1. Characteristics of the Texts. Among the fragments originally ascribed to 4Q434 are fragments of a composition that do not share all of the hymnic features common to the remainder of this material. Designated as 4Q434a, they have been published by M. Weinfeld and are thought to constitute a blessing after a meal in the house of a mourner (Weinfeld). Since, however, they appear to be from the same piece of leather as 4Q434 1 and since the traces of the word *barkî* are evident in line 11, we may have evidence of the more complicated nature of the original text rather than of an independent composition. The identification of this text means that the column numbers for fragment 1 of 4Q434 require readjustment (Wacholder and Abegg, 309-11; Wise, Abegg and Cook, 394-96; Cook, 14-15; but see García Martínez, 436-37, 439).

4Q439 appears to be from a different composition than do 4Q434-438. Whether that composition resembled the text of these fragments or was closer to the *Hodayot* texts (*see* Thanksgiving Hymns) bears further analysis (Seely, 205-6).

2. Analysis of the Texts.

4Q434 comprises the largest block of material and hence is the starting point of any analysis. It begins, "Bless the Lord, O my soul, for all his wondrous deeds forever." Then the text begins to recount what those deeds are: "For he has delivered the life of the poor" (*ʾebyôn*). Others listed as the recipients of God's grace in the next few lines are the *ʿānāw* ("afflicted") and the *dal* ("needy"), the latter being listed twice. It is then the afflicted who are graced by the abundance of God's mercy, whose eyes are opened to see his ways and ears to hear his teaching. They are the ones delivered because of his *ḥesed* ("steadfast love") and whose feet "he has established on the way." What God has done for these people continues to be itemized in the remainder of the column.

While biblical allusions such as Jeremiah 20:13 and Psalm 22:25 are evident in these citations, so is the corresponding material in Qumran texts such as $1QH^a$ 13 (*olim* 5):13 and 18. Whether these allusions are to a defined group that sees itself as oppressed is an issue for further study. While *ʾebyôn* and *ʿānāw* are terms familiar to us from Qumran texts (e.g., 1QH) containing evidence of sectarian identification, the *dallîm* receive almost no mention in these texts (Seely, 198-99, 211-13). Scholars have recognized the extreme difficulties involved in establishing a sectarian provenance for liturgical and hymnic texts, particularly those preserved only in fragments. The present state of research does not permit us to determine whether the *Barki Nafshi* texts were sectarian compositions or whether their content proved compatible with the worldview of this movement and were adopted by its adherents at some unknown point in its development.

4Q435 consists of only a few fragments, the largest of which overlaps with the fragments of other *Barki Nafshi* texts.

We find in the opening line of 4Q436 frag. 1 the reference "to comfort the needy [*dallîm*] in the time of their distress," the same problem they have in 4Q434 frag. 1 i 2. This column is notable in its stated desire "to establish the hands of the fallen to become vessels of knowledge; to give knowledge to the wise, to increase learning for the upright." This employment of wisdom terminology, continued throughout this text, is integrated with themes of law and covenant. This abundant use of wisdom terminology in texts that would not be defined as wisdom texts on the basis of either form or content is also known to us from other compositions such as the **Rule of the Community* (1QS), the **Damascus Document* (CD) and the **Thanksgiving Hymns* (*Hodayot*).

In both 4Q436 and 437 God is addressed in the second person, rather than the third person as in 4Q434. This difference is also evident in Psalm 103 (third) and Psalm 104 (second). One fragment of 4Q437 parallels 4Q434 frag. 1 i. Other fragments of this text are small but can be formed into partial lines with intelligible phrases. The themes parallel those found in the previous texts. 4Q438 is very fragmentary.

It can be argued that 4Q434-438 are different portions of the same text (Seely, 206-10). This can be demonstrated on textual, thematic and terminological grounds.

See also LITURGY: QUMRAN; THANKSGIVING HYMNS (1QH).

BIBLIOGRAPHY. E. M. Cook, "A Thanksgiving for God's Help," in *Prayer from Alexander to Constantine: A Critical Anthology,* ed. M. Kiley et al. (London: Routledge, 1997) 14-17; F. García Martínez, *The Dead Sea Scrolls Translated: The Qumran Texts in English* (Leiden: E. J. Brill, 1994) 435-37, 439; S. A. Reed, "What Is a Fragment?" *JJS* 45 (1994) 123-25; D. R. Seely, "The Barki Nafshi Texts (4Q434-439)," in *Current Research and Technological Developments on the Dead Sea Scrolls: Conference on the Texts from the Judean Desert, Jerusalem, 30 April 1995,* ed. D. W. Parry and S. D. Ricks (STDJ 20; Leiden: E. J. Brill, 1996) 194-214; G. Vermes, *The Dead Sea Scrolls in English* (4th ed.; London: Penguin, 1995) 280-81; B. Z. Wacholder and M. G. Abegg Jr., *A Preliminary Edition of the Unpublished Dead Sea Scrolls: The Hebrew and Aramaic Texts from Cave Four* (3 vols.; Washington, DC: Biblical Archaeology Society, 1995) 3:309-28; M. Weinfeld, "Grace After Meals in Qumran," *JBL* 111 (1992) 427-40; M. O. Wise, M. G. Abegg Jr. and E. M. Cook, *The Dead Sea Scrolls: A New Translation* (San Francisco: HarperCollins, 1996) 394-97.

J. I. Kampen

BARUCH, BOOKS OF

Baruch ben Neriah was a scribe who lived during the days when Judah was under Neo-Babylonian domination. Although he was a relatively obscure character in the Bible, he became larger than life in postbiblical Jewish and Christian tradition. Not only were the few stories about him in the Bible creatively expanded, but several new books were pseudepigraphically attributed to him.

1. Baruch in the Bible
2. The Book of Baruch
3. *Second* (Syriac *Apocalypse of*) *Baruch*
4. *Third* (Greek *Apocalypse of*) *Baruch*

1. Baruch in the Bible.

Baruch ben Neriah was the prophet Jeremiah's loyal scribe, but in the postbiblical literature ascribed to him he came to be depicted as a learned sage and *apocalyptic seer. Baruch lived in Jerusalem during the tumultuous days leading up to and following the Babylonian destruction of Judah in 587/6 B.C. Baruch appears only in the book of Jeremiah and that in only four passages (Jer 32:12-16; 36; 43:1-7; 45). He was a scribe—a prominent social position in sixth-century Judah—whose service to the prophet went beyond what was traditionally expected of a scribe. Not only did Baruch assist Jeremiah by certifying land transactions and writing down his revelations, but Baruch also, at great personal and professional risk, read some of these revelations to King Jehoiakim, who summarily destroyed the material. Because of this involvement in writing Jeremiah's revelations and sermons, some scholars have suggested that Baruch was responsible for editing at least some portions of the biblical book of Jeremiah as we now have it. For some reason, however, Baruch became more than a scribe in the religious imagination of ancient Jews and Christians. There developed a wealth of extrabiblical traditions about Baruch that can now be found in the books *pseudepigraphically attributed to Baruch. The term *pseudepigrapha* designates a vast amorphous collection of extrabiblical Jewish and Christian texts that were attributed to but not written by various biblical figures.

That Baruch was regarded as a special person was suggested initially in the Greek translation of the book of Jeremiah in the *Septuagint. This Greek version of the book of Jeremiah has roughly the same contents as the Hebrew version, but several of the chapters are presented in a different order. In the Greek version of Jeremiah the penultimate chapter of the book (Jer 51 LXX) contains a divine oracle directed to Baruch (Hebrew/English Jer 45). Apparently Baruch had complained about his personal sufferings because of his service to God and to Jeremiah during the fall of Jerusalem. Although God told Baruch not to expect "great things" for himself, God did promise him that he would escape the coming tragedy. The fact that Baruch is the last person addressed by God in the Greek version of Jeremiah suggests that its editors regarded Baruch as Jeremiah's successor: God spoke to him last and assured him that he would be kept alive through the coming disasters.

2. The Book of Baruch.

The LXX contains several books that are not found in the Hebrew Bible. These books are typically designated the *Apocrypha. The LXX's reorganized version of the book of Jeremiah (see Daniel, Esther and Jeremiah, Additions to) is immediately followed by the *Book of Baruch,* one of these apocryphal books. This book is a collection of several independent texts that themselves do not explicitly mention Baruch. These independent units were brought together, and once the introduction that mentions Baruch was added, the entire book became associated with Baruch. The *Book of Baruch* was so closely associated with the Greek version of the book of Jeremiah that it was not known separately as the *Book of Baruch* until as late as the eighth century A.D. in some Christian circles. The *Book of Baruch,* therefore, was regarded as the final part of the Greek version of the book of Jeremiah in some Jewish and Christian circles for many centuries, thereby indicating that there was no universal agreement on the exact structure of the Greek version of the book of Jeremiah. Although the *Book of Baruch* was originally composed in Hebrew as early as the mid-second century B.C., it must be noted that in the ancient biblical manuscripts that have come down to us, the *Book of Baruch* was appended only to the Greek version of Jeremiah, the version that hinted that Baruch would be Jeremiah's successor. This early and intimate connection between Greek Jeremiah and the *Book of Baruch* suggests an ancient belief in Baruch as a recipient of divine revelations and leader of the people.

The *Book of Baruch* opens with Baruch residing with the Jewish exiles in Babylon (*Bar* 1:1-14). The introduction presents this *Book of Baruch* as a book that Baruch wrote and then read to a gathering of exiles who followed him as their leader. This introduction presents Baruch as a leader who, much like Ezekiel or Jeremiah, had people gather around him to hear divine revelations (cf. Jer 25:1-2; 26:7; Ezek 8:1; 33:30-32). The introduction is followed by a long prayer (*Bar* 1:15—3:8) that consists of several quotations from the prayer in Daniel 9. This prayer makes Baruch look like one of those pious people who led the exiles and who dutifully prayed for the restoration of Jerusalem.

The next section of the book (*Bar* 3:9—4:4) is a poem in praise of wisdom that recalls the depiction of wisdom in Job 28 and 38 and in Proverbs 1—9. Here wisdom is characterized as obedience to the divine commandments: a wise person is one who obeys God's commandments. Wisdom is not simply knowing ancient lore or being skilled in scribal activities, but it is living in obedience to God's commandments. This poem presents Baruch as the type of leader who models fidelity to the traditional religious and cultural teachings honored by the Jewish community. If one wishes to know how to behave while living in exile, Baruch would be a perfect example to follow.

The book closes with a poem designed to inspire the exiles to remain faithful to God in spite of their sufferings (*Bar* 4:5—5:9). Their hope is inspired by their belief that God will restore them to their land once they repent and begin obeying his commandments (*Bar* 4:21-23, 29-30, 36-37; 5:5-9). By associating this unit with Baruch, the editor of this book depicts Baruch as a leader who, again like Jeremiah (cf. Jer 29—31), encouraged the exiles to remain faithful to God as they awaited their return to Jerusalem. All these features portray Baruch as a great spiritual leader and indicate the community's interest in promoting obedience to God's commandments as the way to achieve wisdom while awaiting the restoration of Jerusalem.

3. *Second* (Syriac *Apocalypse of*) *Baruch*.
Another text pseudepigraphically attributed to Baruch ben Neriah is *2 Baruch*. The text of *2 Baruch* has been preserved only in Syriac, although a few Greek fragments have also been discovered. It appears that *2 Baruch* was composed in Hebrew or Aramaic, translated into Greek and ultimately translated from Greek into Syriac. This process seems complicated, but many early Jewish extrabiblical texts were highly esteemed by Christian communities who translated these texts into their native languages. Because these communities did not read Hebrew and Aramaic, they preserved and transmitted only the translations they had made for themselves. As a result, in order to study what was originally a Jewish text composed in Hebrew, Aramaic or perhaps Greek, one must learn the languages of the Christian communities who valued and preserved these texts (e.g., Armenian, Coptic, Ethiopic, Greek, Latin, Old Church Slavonic, Syriac). Although the narrative setting of *2 Baruch* is the Babylonian destruction of the first Jerusalem temple in 587/6 B.C., the text was composed sometime after the Roman destruction of the Second Temple in A.D. 70 (*see* Jewish Wars with Rome). If, as some assume, the author of *2 Baruch* used the seven-vision structure of 4 Ezra as a model, then this dependence would set the date of this apocalypse no earlier than the early second century A.D.

As an apocalypse, *2 Baruch* narrates a divine revelation given to a human that contains information that is beyond normal human ken: apart from the revelation granted to Baruch by God, none of the information transmitted here could have been known. An *apocalypse, then, is a form of literature in which God reveals to humans otherwise unknowable information that has either a temporal (eschatological) or spatial (otherworldly) focus. Readers of the NT are most familiar with this literary form in the book of Revelation. *Second Baruch*, therefore, presents Baruch as an apocalypticist who has had visions from God that reveal some of the secrets of the cosmos and of human history and destiny. This text, much like 4 Ezra (i.e., 2 Esd 3—14; *see* Esdras, Books of), consists of seven visions in which Baruch and God debate over issues centering on the problem of theodicy: how can God be just if the righteous suffer and the wicked prosper? The debates in *2 Baruch*, however, lack the emotional fever pitch of those in 4 Ezra. The overall goal of *2 Baruch* is to promote obedience to God's commandments as the way to survive in difficult times. In many ways like some of the themes in the book of Hebrews, *2 Baruch* maintains that Jews can thrive in spite of the destruction of the temple in Jerusalem if they only remain obedient to the commandments in the Torah.

In this apocalypse Baruch is a pseudonym for the person who wrote this text. The intriguing passages of this text are those that recount the interactions between Baruch and the people. These passages suggest that Baruch was viewed as their divinely sent, inspired leader and biblical interpreter. Behind the pseudepigraphic veil of this text, it seems that these passages reflect the attitudes of a community toward their leader(s). Their leaders are those people on whom they depend to give their lives meaning and structure. In this way the text reinforces the authority of the writer of this text, who presents himself as the transmitter of Baruch's teachings and visions. The author intended that the readers view him as a divinely inspired seer like Baruch and view his teachings and especially this text as divinely inspired.

4. *Third* (Greek *Apocalypse of*) *Baruch*.
When we turn to *3 Baruch* we find that Baruch is here depicted as an apocalyptic seer who has taken a guided tour of the heavenly realms (*see* Heavenly Ascent in Jewish and Pagan Traditions). Although once again set in the days of the destruction of Jerusalem in 587/6 B.C., *3 Baruch* was likely written in the second or third century A.D., long after the destruction of Jerusalem by the Romans. The heavenly tour in *3 Baruch* comes in response to Baruch's turmoil over the destruction of Jerusalem. The angel Phamael led Baruch through five heavens, where he learned all manner of cosmological secrets and of God's control of history. As a result of his ascent to heaven, Baruch was comforted over the destruction of Jerusalem. His debates with God taught him that although his present circumstances seemed hopeless, nonetheless God remains in control and listens intently to the *prayers of his people.

Third Baruch recounts Baruch's tour through five heavens. Many have suggested that this five-heaven scheme results from an abbreviation of an original account that had a seven-heaven schema. However, since the questions Baruch had in chapter 1 are answered in the course of the ascent to heaven as Baruch learned that God controls history and attends to human prayers, it seems that *3 Baruch* is a complete text that has not suffered purposed or accidental abbreviation. There were many different models of the cosmos in antiquity, and *3 Baruch* may attest a five-heaven model. Or *3 Baruch* may assume the common but not universal seven-heaven model, and the fact that Baruch ascended to the fifth heaven may indicate that its author did not think it appropriate for humans to ascend into God's presence in the highest heaven.

The ascent theme became popular in Jewish literature during the Greco-Roman period. This growing prominence suggests a shift among some Jews regarding the nature and means of authority. The ascent as a means of claiming religious authority was promoted neither in the biblical materials nor in the subsequent rabbinic materials. Apart from Enoch (Gen 5:21-24) and Elijah (2 Kings 2), the biblical materials suggest that the ancient Israelites did not believe that people could ascend into the heavenly realm. In fact, Deuteronomy 30:11-14 indicates that the divine teachings—that is, everything humans need to know to live rightly—are not secreted in heaven, where one need ascend to learn them; rather they are immediately at hand in the Torah (cf. Deut 29:29). While Moses (Ex 24:1-2, 9-11), Michaiah ben Imlah (1 Kings 22), Isaiah (Is 6) and Ezekiel (Ezek 1) may have caught glimpses of the divine presence, their feet never left the earth. These are accounts of visions of the divine presence, not of journeys into the divine presence.

All this changed during the Persian and Greco-Roman eras. Both the Greeks and the Persians developed beliefs in the heavenly origin and ultimate destiny of the soul. While every soul undertook a postmortem journey, some exceptional people were granted heavenly tours while they were alive. These ascents to heaven appear in many Greek, Roman, Jewish and Christian texts. One feature that they all have in common is that while in the other realm the seer is granted insight into what awaits people after death. Such knowledge then serves as a powerful tool in persuading people to adopt a course of life that will ensure that their postmortem fate is pleasant. Moreover, these heavenly ascents grant people knowledge that enables them to face the trials and tribulations of life. It gives meaning and purpose to their lives. In *3 Baruch,* for example, Baruch learned many things about the functioning of the cosmos, the history of humanity and the cultic activities going on in heaven, but the most important thing for him was learning that God daily attends to the prayers of the saints and that his angels are working on behalf of the saints. This belief then comforts Baruch in his agony over the sufferings of Jerusalem. The apostle Paul also claimed to have ascended into the "third heaven," where he learned divine secrets so profound that he could not repeat them to anyone (2 Cor 12:1-4). For Paul, the ascent to heaven served to legitimate his appointment by God to be an apostle of the gospel of Jesus Christ.

Baruch ben Neriah was a popular figure in the religious imaginations of ancient Jews and Christians, and many books were pseudepigraphically attributed to him. This popularity in the use of Baruch as the pseudonymous author of several texts is due not to his presence in the Hebrew Bible alone but to the developments in how he was being depicted in the course of the Persian, Greek and Roman periods.

See also APOCRYPHA AND PSEUDEPIGRAPHA; DANIEL, ESTHER AND JEREMIAH, ADDITIONS TO; HEAVENLY ASCENT IN JEWISH AND PAGAN TRADITIONS.

BIBLIOGRAPHY. P.-M. Bogaert, "Le Nom de Baruch dans la Littérature Pseudépigraphique: L'apocalypse Syriaque et le Livre Deutérocanonique," in *La Littérature Juive entre Tenach et Mischna: Quelques Problèmes,* ed. W. C. Van Unnik (Recherches Bibliques 9; Leiden: E. J. Brill, 1974) 56-72; J. H. Charlesworth, ed., *The Old Testament Pseudepigrapha* (2 vols.; Garden City, NY: Doubleday, 1983-85); J. J. Collins, *The Apocalyptic Imagination* (New York: Crossroad, 1984); J. J. Collins, ed., *Apocalypse: The Morphology of a Genre* (*Semeia* 14; Missoula, MT: Scholars Press, 1979); D. C. Harlow, *The Greek Apocalypse of Baruch (3 Baruch) in Hellenistic Judaism and Early Christianity* (SVTP 12; Leiden: E. J. Brill, 1996); M. Himmelfarb, *Ascent to Heaven in Jewish and Christian Apocalypses* (New York: Oxford University Press, 1993); J. R. Lundbom, "Baruch, Seraiah and Expanded Colophons in the Book of Jeremiah," *JSOT* 36 (1986) 89-114; J. Muilenburg, "Baruch the Scribe," in *Proclamation and Presence,* ed. J. I. Durham and J. R. Porter (Richmond: John Knox, 1970) 232-38; F. J. Murphy, *The Structure and Meaning of Second Baruch* (Atlanta: Scholars Press, 1985); G. B. Sayler, *Have the Promises Failed? A Literary Analysis of 2 Baruch* (SBLDS 72; Chico, CA: Scholars Press, 1984); M. E. Stone, ed., *Jewish Writings of the Second Temple Period* (CRINT 2.2; Assen: Van Gorcum; Philadelphia: Fortress, 1984); J. D. Tabor, *Things Unutterable: Paul's Ascent to Paradise in Its Greco-Roman, Judaic and Early Christian Contexts* (Lanham, MD: University Press of America, 1986); E. Tov, *The Septuagint Translation of Jeremiah and Baruch: A Discussion of an Early Revision of Jeremiah 29—52 and Baruch 1:1—3:8* (HSM 8; Missoula, MT: Scholars Press, 1976); J. E. Wright, "Baruch: His Evolution from Scribe to Apocalyptic Seer," in *Biblical Figures Outside the Bible,* ed. M. E. Stone and T. A. Bergren (Harrisburg, PA: Trinity Press International, 1998) 264-89; idem, "The Social Setting of the Syriac Apocalypse of Baruch," *JSP* 16 (1997) 83-98.

J. E. Wright

BEATITUDES TEXT (4Q525)

The text of 4Q525, also known as 4QBeatitudes, offers several interesting features. For NT scholars this *Dead Sea Scroll is especially important in light of its series of makarisms, or beatitudes.

1. Description
2. Relation to Wisdom Literature

1. Description.

The *Beatitudes Text* 4Q525 is written in an elegant and refined hand (see PAM 40.611, 40.614, 40.617, 40.969, 41.412, 41.520, 41.678, 41.788, 41.866, 41.917, 41.949, 42.441, 42.511, 42.908, 43.595, 43.596, 43.600). The script looks like early Herodian (Puech has reached this conclusion; 1991, 83). The series of five beatitudes found in fragment 2, column ii, catch immediately the reader's attention. They recall the famous collections of beatitudes in Matthew 5:3-10 and Luke 6:20-23 (*see DJG,* Sermon on the Mount). However, unlike the NT makarisms, the *Qumran beatitudes do not tell us why the person in question is blessed (Viviano 1992, 53-54). The Qumran beatitudes remind us even more of those found in Sirach 14:20-27 and in Proverbs 3:13 and 8:32, 34, which, unlike the NT makarisms, also have "the pursuit of wisdom [*ḥwkmh*]" as a theme. "Blessed is the man who attains wisdom and walks in the law of the Most High" (frag. 2 ii 3-4; cf. Viviano 1993, 76).

2. Relation to Wisdom Literature.

2.1. Style and Content. Both the style and the content of 4Q525 remind us of traditional Jewish wisdom books, in particular Proverbs and

*Sirach. Several parallels will be mentioned.

When we read the opening section of 4Q525 we immediately notice a striking resemblance to Jewish wisdom literature already known to us. In fragment 1 someone is said to have spoken "in the wisdom God gave him." The words that follow, "to know wisdom and discipline, to understand," recall the beginning of Proverbs 1 (Puech 1991, 83).

As in Proverbs and Sirach, "the pursuit of wisdom" is a main emphasis in 4Q525. "Blessed is the man who attains wisdom" (frag. 2 ii 2; cf. in particular Prov 3:13; Sir 14:20, but also Prov 4:5, 7; 8:11; 15:33; Sir 1:14; 25:10; 45:26).

The preeminence of wisdom over gold, silver and precious jewels is stressed both in 4Q525 and in Proverbs (compare 4Q525, frag. 2 iii 1-7 with Prov 3:13-15).

The contrast between sincerity and deceitfulness occurs in 4Q525 as well as in Proverbs and Sirach (cf. frag. 2 ii 1-3 with Prov 12:5, 17, 20; 14:8; Sir 1:28-29).

As in Proverbs and in Sirach, folly (*ʾwlh*) is contrasted with wisdom and understanding in 4Q525 (compare frag. 2 ii 2 with Prov 14:18, 29; Sir 8:15; 47:23).

The idea of a wholesome tongue versus a perverse tongue and the tendency of a person to sin with the tongue is present in Proverbs and Sirach as well as in 4Q525 (compare frag. 2 ii 1; frag. 14 ii 18-28 with Prov 10:20, 31; 12:18-19; 15:2, 4; 17:20; 18:21; 31:26; Sir 5:13; 6:5; 19:6, 16; 20:18; 22:27; 28:26; 51:2-6).

Humility (*ʿnwh*) is viewed as a quality that goes hand in hand with wisdom and fearing God in Proverbs, Sirach and 4Q525 (compare frag. 2 ii 6 with Prov 15:33; 18:12; 22:4; Sir 2:17).

2.2. Qumran Elements. It must also be observed, however, that 4Q525 contains elements that are not found in traditional Jewish wisdom literature, because it is a typical Qumran sectarian document. In fragment 14 the speaker tells "the discerning one" to listen (l. 18) and warns him not to use his tongue unwisely by complaining too soon (l. 23) or by offending someone (l. 26). Related to this is the interesting paradox we find in fragment 16: not those who lack understanding but "the discerning ones" are led astray (l. 3). In traditional Jewish wisdom literature it is always the naive or the foolish who are misguided by the wicked. They are among the ones who are told to listen and who receive a warning (see Prov 7:7-22; 8:5-6; Wis 14:11). On this point 4Q525 surely deviates from traditional Jewish wisdom literature but not from Qumran sectarian literature, as these quotes demonstrate:

And now, *listen, all you who know righteousness,* and understand the works of God. (CD 1:1)

Listen, *O wise men* [*ḥkmym*], meditate upon knowledge. . . . Be of steadfast mind [. . .] Increase prudence. *O righteous men* [*ṣdyqym*], put away iniquity! Hold fast [to the Covenant], *all you perfect of way* [*wkwl tmymy drk*]. (1QH 9:35-36)

The paradox in the last quotation should be observed. Why would righteous people need to put away iniquity? In order to be able to answer the question we need to determine who the wise, the righteous and the perfect of way are. These three expressions may all refer to the same group of people, that is, to the people of God's lot, the Qumran community. First, CD 6:2-5 speaks of "the discerning ones [*nbwnym*] from Aaron" and "the wise [*ḥkmym*] from Israel" who "dug the well." The well symbolizes the Law, and the diggers are "the converts of Israel who went out of the land of Judah to sojourn in the land of Damascus." In the **Damascus Document* the name *Damascus* is used as a symbol for Qumran (Schiffman, 93-94). So "the wise" and "the discerning ones" represent the Qumran community. Second, in 1QS 2:2 it is "the men of the lot of God" who are characterized as those "who walk perfectly in all his ways [*hhwlkym tmym bkwl drkyw*]." Third, those who belong to the lot of God are described as "the sons of righteousness [*bny ṣdq*]" (1QS 3:20-22). "All the sons of righteousness" are led astray by "the Angel of Darkness" (1QS 3:22). This explains why "the righteous men" in 1QH 9:36 are told to "put away iniquity." It also clarifies why "the discerning men" in 4Q525, fragment 16, line 3 are led astray. They belong to the Qumran community.

The use of vocabulary in 4Q525 strongly suggests that it is a Qumran sectarian document. Several words are employed in this work that have a Qumranian flavor. They are not necessarily unique to Qumran, but they occur with lesser frequency in the OT. Moreover, several of them are key words in Qumran theology. The terms *ʿwlh* ("injustice," frag. 2 ii 7; frag. 4 i 10; frag. 10 i 4), *ʿnwh* ("humility," frag. 2 ii 6; frags. 8-9 i 4; frag. 14 ii 20; frag. 26 i 2), *snʿ* ("to be humble," frag. 4 i 10), *hlk tmym* ("to walk perfectly," frag. 4 i 10), *twkhh* ("chastisement," frag. 4 i 9), *hmt tnynym* ("poison of snakes," frag. 15 i 4) and

ʾbny ḥpṣ ("stones of desire," frag. 2 iii 3), which we find in 4Q525, all occur with more frequency in the Qumran sectarian literature than they do in the OT. Also, the particular phrase *drk(y) ʿwlh* ("the way[s] of injustice," frag. 2 ii 2) and the idiomatic expression *b ʿnwt npšw* ("in the humility of his soul," frag. 2 ii 6) are not used in the OT, but they do occur in 4Q525 as well as in the Qumran sectarian documents.

See also WISDOM LITERATURE AT QUMRAN.

BIBLIOGRAPHY. C. A. Evans, *Jesus and His Contemporaries: Comparative Studies* (Leiden: E. J. Brill, 1995) 141-48; J. A. Fitzmyer, "A Palestinian Collection of Beatitudes," in *The Four Gospels: Festschrift Frans Neirynck,* ed. F. Van Segbroeck et al. (4 vols.; BETL 100; Louvain: Louvain University Press, 1992) 2:509-15; É. Puech, "4Q525 et les Péricopes des Béatitudes en Ben Sira et Matthieu," *RB* 98 (1991) 80-106; idem, "Un Hymne Essénien en Partie Retrouvé et les Béatitudes," *RevQ* 13 (1988) 59-88; J. C. R. de Roo, "Is 4Q525 a Qumran Sectarian Document?" in *The Scrolls and the Scriptures,* ed. S. E. Porter and C. A. Evans (Sheffield: Sheffield Academic Press, 1997) 338-67; L. H. Schiffman, *Reclaiming the Dead Sea Scrolls* (New York: Doubleday, 1995); B. T. Viviano, "Eight Beatitudes at Qumran in Matthew?" *SEÅ* 58 (1993) 71-84; idem, "Beatitudes Found Among Dead Sea Scrolls," *BAR* 18 (November/December 1992) 55, 66; B. Z. Wacholder and M. G. Abegg Jr., *A Preliminary Edition of the Unpublished Dead Sea Scrolls: The Hebrew and Aramaic Texts from Cave Four* (Washington, DC: Biblical Archaeology Society, 1992) 2:185-203; M. O. Wise, M. G. Abegg Jr. and E. M. Cook, *The Dead Sea Scrolls: A New Translation* (San Francisco: HarperCollins, 1996) 423-26. J. C. R. de Roo

BELIAL, BELIAR, DEVIL, SATAN

The NT concepts of Satan and his host are closely related to ideas that develop in the intertestamental period and are found in early Jewish literature. In their interpretation of OT passages, various books among the *Pseudepigrapha and *Qumran literature give different explanations to the presence of evil in the world. Some writings describe the struggle between good and evil as a cosmic-spiritual struggle and anticipate the ultimate annihilation of evil and the evil powers. In some texts, the evil powers have an *angelic leader named Semihaza, Mastema, Belial or the Prince of Darkness.

1. The Old Testament Background
2. The Wicked Kingdom and Its Angelic Leader
3. Conclusion

1. The Old Testament Background.

Some biblical passages are important for later interpreters who relate them to the evil forces in the world. Genesis 6:1-5 describe how the "sons of God" mingled with the daughters of men. This passage is often interpreted as referring to a fall among the angels. In some late texts we encounter an odd or accusing member of God's heavenly court, subordinate to the sovereign Yahweh: in 1 Kings 22 (a sixth-century text describing a ninth-century event) a spirit gets God's permission to deceive the *prophets of *Samaria. In Job 1—2, one of "God's sons," *haśśaṭan* ("the accuser"), gets permission from the Lord to test Job and inflict trials upon him (cf. Zech 3:1-2). As a proper name, "Satan" occurs only in 1 Chronicles 21:1. Some isolated references to figures easily interpreted as demons (*see DJG,* Demon, Devil, Satan) do not play a significant role in intertestamental interpretation.

Biblical texts refer to Gentile peoples antagonistic to Yaweh, his anointed and his people (Ps 2, 46, 110). Isaiah 14, Ezekiel 28 and Ezekiel 32 portray the evil king and the oppressive empire in mythological tones. Further, the prophetic tradition knows that God will judge the empires on earth. These ideas would be combined by the *apocalyptists: empires and their rulers symbolize cosmic evil forces who will be judged by God. The cosmic judgment and renewal is described by the so-called Isaianic apocalypse (Is 24—27). This textual unit uses mythological language when it proclaims that after the downfall of the oppressive city (Babylon?; Is 24:7-13; 25:1-6; 26:5-6; 27:10-11) God will swallow up death forever (Is 25:8; cf. Is 26:19-20), punish Leviathan and slay the sea dragon (Is 27:1). Powers antagonistic to God ("the heavenly host above and the kings on the earth below") will be punished and shut up (Is 24:21-23).

2. The Wicked Kingdom and Its Angelic Leader.

2.1. In Daniel and Early Pseudepigrapha. The idea of heavenly forces antagonistic to God becomes commonplace in Israelite tradition of the second century B.C. This motif is found in a number of pseudepigraphic writings represented in the Qumran caves (some of these were known before the discovery of the *Dead

Sea Scrolls). These writings were probably written before the emergence of the *yaḥad,* the community reflected in the Qumran scrolls. They were known by the *yaḥad* and were influential in the framing of the theology of this community.

The earliest postbiblical source that elaborates on evil angelic forces is probably the Enochic Book of Watchers (*1 Enoch* 6—16; 17—36), which should be dated around 200 B.C. These chapters interpret Genesis 6:1-5: the angelic watchers cohabit with earthly women and bring *magic, sin and violence to the earth. Enoch is shown the coming judgment on the angels, who in vain ask him to intercede for them. Their leader is Semihaza, but he is not portrayed as a cosmic opponent to God or the elect. *1 Enoch* 10:4 reflects a variant tradition, in which Azazel is the leading angel. The watchers are bound until the final judgment (*1 Enoch* 10:11-12), while the offspring of the illegitimate union between angels and women become evil spirits who spread sin and destruction on earth (*1 Enoch* 15:8—16:1). The archangels participate on God's side in the spiritual struggle.

The biblical book of Daniel may be discussed here, since Daniel 7—12 was written 167 to 164 B.C. and thus belongs to this same period. The four beasts of Daniel 7 symbolize earthly kings and kingdoms. However, these kingdoms are portrayed in a way that point to cosmic significance; behind them one can sense superhuman spiritual powers. According to Daniel 7—12, the struggle between the *Seleucids and faithful Jews reflects a cosmic spiritual battle in which angelic forces are involved. The Jews are supported by an unnamed angelic leader (Dan 10:4—11:2) and their guardian angel, "the great prince" Michael (Dan 10:13, 20; 12:1). These two are engaged in battle against the evil forces, including the angelic Prince of Persia and Prince of Greece, probably referring to the national gods of the Gentiles. Ultimately the people of God and their angelic supporters will triumph (Dan 7:13-27; 12:1-3).

To the early Maccabean period belongs the Enochic Animal Apocalypse (*1 Enoch* 85—90) and probably also the Apocalypse of Weeks (*1 Enoch* 91:11-17; 93:1-10). Cosmic history and the history of Israel are described in symbolic terms: the angels fall down from heaven and interfere with humanity, and they are bound by the archangels (*1 Enoch* 86—88). During the history of Israel, God gives the people into the power of evil shepherds (*1 Enoch* 89—90). These shepherds symbolize Gentile kingdoms and the angelic powers behind them, who inflict evil upon Israel and will be annihilated together with the watchers at the judgment (*see* Angels of the Nations). Both apocalypses expect the ultimate judgment upon evil in the world and the fallen angels (*1 Enoch* 90:18-27; 91:12-15).

In the middle of the second century B.C. 4QPseudo-Moses (4Q386-390) portrays the history of Israel in similar terms. Israel is subject to the "angels of *mastemot* [destruction]," demonic angels symbolizing the rule of the *Diadochian kings and the ungodly high priests Jason, Menelaus and Alcimus (174-160 B.C.): "I will remove that man (i.e., *Alexander the Great) [and] abandon the land into the hands of the angels of destruction [and they will cause the people(?)] to worship other god[s . . .] like abominations [. . . and there will rise] three [priests] that will rul[e in the land . . . and they will defile the h[oly of holie]s" (4Q388 frag. 1 ii 6-9). A Gentile kingdom (that of Alexander the Great or Antiochus IV Epiphanes) is probably designated "that [evil k]ingdom" (*mamleket hariš'ah hahi',* 4Q387 frag. 3 ii 9).

The book of *Jubilees* was probably written in the early Maccabean period (*see* Jubilees) and perhaps belongs to circles antecedent of the *yaḥad. Jubilees,* which pretends to be angelic revelation to Moses on Mt. Sinai, is dependent on the Book of Watchers: the fallen angels are bound before the deluge, but their offspring, the evil spirits, lead the children of Noah to sin. Also the spirits are bound, but their leader Mastema (Destruction) gets God's permission for one tenth of the spirits to stay on earth under his command, so that he can execute his dominion over humankind, corrupt people and lead them astray (*Jub.* 5; 10). Prince Mastema is a figure close to Satan of the NT. He is the leader of the demonic hosts; he rules the spirits of men and women and opposes God's plans for his people.

These ideas recur in the writings of the *yaḥad* and *Testament of Reuben* 2—4 (it is presupposed here that the apocalyptic and dualistic passages in the *Testaments of the Twelve Patriarchs* were formed in Jewish circles between the mid-second and mid-first century B.C.). *Jubilees* contains other terms relevant to our subject. Moses prays that the "spirit of belial" should not rule over Israel (*Jub.* 1:20). In this text "spirit of belial" probably means "spirit of nought," so "belial" is not a personal name. According to the eschatological poem in *Jubilees* 23, Israel shall enjoy a time of blessing without any "satan" (antagonist) or "destroyer" (*Jub.* 23:29; also in the Qumran scrolls "satan" is not used as a proper name, cf. 11QPs[a] Plea 15-16, "Let not a satan rule over me, nor an unclean spirit. Neither let pain nor evil inclination have control over my bones"; 4Q213a [Levi[b]] 1-2 17, "let not any satan have power over me"). Perhaps Mark 8:33 and the parallels should be translated "Get behind me, satan!" (i.e., in this you are an antagonist to the will of God).

Some pre-*yaḥad* writings preserved in the Qumran caves mention cosmic evil forces. Similar to the Book of Watchers and *Jubilees*, 1Q/4QMysteries (*see* Book of Mysteries) reflects a dualistic worldview and refers to cosmic antagonists of God. This work mentions "the mysteries of wickedness" (1Q27 1 i 2, 7), "the wisdom of evil cunning and the de[vices of nought(?)]" (4Q299 frag. 3a ii 5) and "migh[ty mysteries of light and the ways of dark]ness" (4Q299 frag. 5 2; cf. the first-century B.C. 1QapGen 1:2 "the wrath of the mystery of evil"; *see* Genesis Apocryphon). It looks forward to the time "when the begotten of unrighteousness are delivered up, and wickedness is removed from before righteousness, as darkness is removed from before light. Then, just as smoke wholly ceases and is no more, so shall wickedness cease forever, and righteousness shall be revealed as the sun (throughout) the full measure of the world. And all the adherents of the mysteries of wickedness are to be no more" (1Q27 frag . 1 i 5-7).

An eschatological passage in 4QInstruction describes the end-time judgment on the powers antagonistic to God: "In heaven he will judge the work of iniquity . . . [the] kingd[om of iniquity(?)] will tremble, the water and the depths will fear. . . . And all iniquity shall be consumed" (4Q416 frag. 1 10-13/4Q418 frag. 212 1). If it is correctly reconstructed, this passage refers to the "kingdom of iniquity," which trembles at God's judgment, as did the watchers in *1 Enoch* 13. The presectarian 4QVisions of Amram (*see* Visions of Amram) refers to two angelic princes in strife over the dominion of men, who are divided into the sons of light and the sons of darkness (4Q548 1). The ruler of darkness is called King of Wickedness (Melchiresha, 4Q544 frag. 2 3, this name also occurs in 4Q280 [4QBerakot[f]] 1 2 "Cursed be you Melchiresha . . . may God set you trembling at the hand of the avengers!"). M. Philonenko has suggested that the name Melchiresha represents an interpretation of "Bera King of Sodom" and "Birsha King of Gomorrah" in Genesis 14:2 (*Tg. Ps.-J.* and *Gen. Rab.* read Bera as "son of evil," Birsha as "son of wickedness").

Early interpreters thus saw evil powers behind Abram's adversaries and found in the same chapter *Melchizedek—King of Righteousness—as their positive antitype. 4Q544 probably referred to Melchizedek as leader of the angelic host (in 11QMelch, written in the *yaḥad*, Melchizedek is the angelic leader who will overcome Belial and his spirits). *Testament of Dan* 6 testifies to the same apocalyptic tradition: "the kingdom of the enemy" belongs to Satan and his spirits and is the cause of "Israel's period of lawlessness," but finally "the enemy's kingdom will be brought to an end" (here the name *Satan* probably represents Christian editing of an earlier Jewish text). The faithful are supported by the "angel of peace," who intercedes for them, so that they might not submit to Beliar, the spirit of deceit (*T. Levi* 5; *T. Benj.* 6). The later *Birkat haminim*, the curse on the infidels in the daily prayers, is based on an earlier prayer that asked God to subdue the kingdom of evil.

2.2. In the Writings of the Yaḥad. The *yaḥad* was founded in the second half of the second century and was probably an elite group within a wider *Essene movement. The library of *Qumran was related to the *yaḥad*, although only a few dozen of its books were authored within the community. The *yaḥad* drew inspiration from a number of dualistic-*apocalyptic works, including the books of **1 Enoch* and **Jubilees* (the latter was considered an authoritative book by the community), when they described the cosmic realities that encountered their "community of latter-days saints." From their predecessors and literary heritage they learned about the cosmic struggle between light and darkness and the spiritual forces that oppose the sons of light.

A developed philosophical dualism is found in the Two-Spirit Treatise (1QS 3:13—4:26; *see* Rule of the Community), which was included in the copy of the community's manual found in Cave 1 (the treatise is not represented among the Cave 4 fragments; its theology was not necessarily shared by everyone in the community). God has created two opposing spirits, the spirit of truth (the Prince of Light) and the spirit of deceit (the Angel of Darkness). As he allotted each man his portion, he ordained for him to walk with one of these spirits until the judgment, when he will make an end to all evil. There is eternal enmity between these spirits and those who follow them, between the sons of light and the sons of deceit. According to the last part of the discourse (perhaps a later explanation), every man has been allotted a portion of both spirits (the balance between them will vary from one man to another), who fight their battle in the human heart (*T. Jud.* 20 and *T. Asher* 1—6 present similar doctrines).

Other texts of the *yaḥad* also reflect a cosmic dualism that is experienced existentially by the sons of light. According to the **War Scroll*, there is an ongoing struggle between the heavenly powers, lead by Michael, Prince of Light, and Belial, Prince of Darkness. The community considers itself in fellowship with the angels and partakes with them in the battle and the *eschatological war, which has its scene both in heaven and on earth. Unfaithful Israel is identified as sons of darkness and the army of Belial. However, Belial is subordinate to God, "who made Belial to corrupt, an angel of hatred" (1QM 13:11). God has ordained a day "to annihilate the sons of darkness, (when there will be) rejoicing for al[l the sons of light]" (1QM 13:16).

According to the **Damascus Document*, the watchers of heaven fell as they did not follow the precepts of God (CD 2:18). This Qumranic work attributes the rising of Moses and Aaron to the Prince of Light and their adversaries to Belial: "For in ancient times, during the first deliverance of Israel, there arose Moses and Aaron, by the hand of the Prince of Lights; and Belial, with his cunning, raised up Jannes and his brothers" (CD 5:18-19). In the present time Israel at large is subject to the dominion of Belial (CD 4:12-19). The first part of the *Rule of the Community*, prescribes a covenant ceremony to be conducted by the community "for all the days of Belial's dominion" (1QS 1:18; 2:19)—the present age is "Belial's dominion" on earth (cf. Jn 12:31; 14:30; 16:11, "the prince of the world"). The liturgy has the sons of light pronounce curses against the sons of darkness, "the men of Belial's lot" (1QS 2:4-5).

In the writings of the *yaḥad* Belial is a proper name, derived from the word *b^eliya'al* ("nought") in the Bible, and later usage such as "the spirit of belial." The sons of light have their angelic partner in Michael (or, in the case of 11QMelch: Melchizedek), who will implement the judgment on Belial and the fallen angels.

2.3. Other Texts. A highly developed doctrine of Satan is found in the **Testament of Job*, written in Greek, perhaps in Egypt around the turn of the era. Humans are objects of Satan's attacks and deceiving schemes. He is designated Satan, the devil, the evil one, the antagonist. But also here, Satan derives his limited authority from God. An elaborate account of the fall of Satan occurs in *Life of Adam and Eve* (see Adam and Eve), perhaps written around the end of the first century A.D. An influential verse is Wisdom 2:24: "through the devil's envy death entered the world, and those who belong to his company experience it."

3. Conclusion.

The NT relates to widespread Jewish ideas on the evil one and the presence of evil in the world when it describes the Jesus event, the role of the end-time community and the conditions that meet both humanity in general and the disciple in particular. A particular NT emphasis is the central role of Jesus in the cosmic-spiritual struggle (Rev 12:7-9 perhaps preserves an earlier tradition, in which Michael fights and overcomes Satan).

See also ANGELS OF THE NATIONS; APOCALYPTICISM; DEMONOLOGY; MELCHIZEDEK, TRADITIONS OF; WAR SCROLL (1QM) AND RELATED TEXTS.

BIBLIOGRAPHY. A. Y. Collins, *The Combat Myth in the Book of Revelation* (HDR 9; Missoula, MT: Scholars Press, 1976); J. J. Collins, *Apocalypticism in the Dead Sea Scrolls* (The Literature of the Dead Sea Scrolls; London: Routledge, 1997); J. R. Davila, "Melchizedek, Michael and War in Heaven," SBLSP 35 (1996) 259-72; D. Dimant, "Qumran Sectarian Literature," *Jewish Writings of the Second Temple Period: Apocrypha, Pseudepigrapha, Qumran Sectarian Writings, Philo, Josephus*, ed. M. E. Stone (CRINT 2.2.; Assen: Van Gorcum; Philadelphia: Fortress, 1984) 483-550; T. Elgvin, *Wisdom and Apocalyptic in 4QInstruction* (STDJ; Leiden: E. J. Brill, 2000); idem, "Wisdom and Apocalypticism at Qumran," in *The Bible and the Dead Sea Scrolls*, ed. J. H. Charlesworth (5 vols.; Minneapolis: Fortress, forthcoming) vol. 3; P. J. Kobelski, *Melchizedek and Melchiresa* (CBQMS

10; Washington, DC: Catholic Biblical Association, 1981); M. T. Milik, "*Milkî-ṣedeq et Milkî-rešaʿ* dans les anciens écrits juifs et chrétiens," *JJS* 23 (1972) 95-144; P. von der Osten-Sacken, *Gott und Belial* (SUNT 6; Göttingen: Vandenhoeck & Ruprecht, 1969); M. Philonenko, "Melkiresa et Melkira: Note sur les 'Visions de Amram,'" *Sem* 41-42 (1993) 159-62; P. Sacchi, *Jewish Apocalyptic and Its History* (JSPSup 20; Sheffield: Sheffield Academic Press, 1997).

T. Elgvin

BENEFACTOR

Life in Greco-Roman society depended greatly on the wealthy individual who provided for others, that is, a benefactor *(euergetēs),* whose gifts were called *euergesiai.* Recognition as an *euergetēs* was a great honor, even appearing among royal titles. When granting freedom or disaster relief, the benefactor was further hailed as a savior (*sōtēr;* cf. Acts 4:9; 10:38). Benefactions given for festivals and warfare in the discharge of civic (which included religious) offices were called liturgies *(leitourgiai).* Although these were mandated by law, providing more than required transformed them into *euergesiai,* and greater honor *(timē)* accrued to the giver. When civic needs arose not covered by regular offices, special subscriptions *(epidoseis)* were enacted to solicit gifts. In Latin a benefactor was called a patron *(patronus)* and a dependent, a client *(cliens;* no Greek equivalent, but "the flatterer" and "parasite" offer degraded parallels). A civic patron could be recognized officially as such by popular election *(cooptare).*

1. The Principle of Reciprocity
2. Political Structures and Benefaction
3. Jewish and New Testament Concepts of Benefaction

1. The Principle of Reciprocity.

Benefaction was one manifestation of the reciprocity that permeated ancient culture. In law this appeared as retaliation, in ethics as the return of injury to enemies and help to friends, in justice as yielding to others their due and in friendship as gift exchange. In benefaction social elites expressed their superiority, and recipients affirmed that standing, perhaps by applause, honorary decrees or public office. Such gifts were gratuitous in that they could not be repaid, serving to emphasize the greatness of the giver; yet they came with strings attached, as an appropriate response (e.g., gratitude and honors) was expected from recipients. Such giving is not disinterested but flows from *philotimia,* ambition and public spirit. Thus largesse allowed benefactors to express their status and care for the civic body while accumulating *honor and goodwill *(eunoia),* thereby increasing their influence (i.e., authority). Thus generosity and gratitude provided the means by which civic relationships were initiated, solidified, reaffirmed and articulated.

2. Political Structures and Benefaction.

Political structures shaped the particular expression of this general pattern, yielding variety in the characteristics of benefaction. In classical *Athens, wealthy people provided liturgies, sacrifices and *banquets to the citizen body and *hospitality to visitors. The equal status of citizens, their freedom of speech and election by lot, however, made it difficult for any one person to dominate the city by dint of benefactions. In the Hellenistic kingdoms, rulers held absolute power and could make benefactions that citizens of a Greek city-state could not (e.g., tax relief, amnesties, rights of asylum, jurisdictional privileges and immunities). Such beneficent gestures became formalized into standard measures (called *philanthrōpa*), which sought to elicit subjects' goodwill. Hellenistic kings further spread their greatness by funding buildings in both subject and free cities, especially in Pan-Hellenic sanctuaries.

Still different dynamics existed between patron and client in the Roman republic. More formality appears in the co-opting of patrons and in the relationship between freed *slaves and former masters. Moreover, benefits were given to clients, and thus not to formal equals and not to the citizen body. Building a clientele expressed one's greatness and could help in the competition for honors. As private control of armies and the wealth amassed by conquest allowed some notables to eclipse their peers, one man, Octavian, eventually succeeded in dominating *Rome. As his burial inscription suggests, much of Augustus's clout rested on his position as universal patron. To generosity in Rome he added foreign benefactions, which helped to build the empire (*see* Roman Empire). Augustus did not eliminate other patrons, but he formed the center of patronage networks extending across the empire. These included family members, client kings (e.g., Herod the Great), friends, dynastic families, imperial freedmen, displaced Italians, priests of the imperial cult and the newly rich. Such networks were vital for governing his widespread empire, particularly in view of its minimal bureaucracy (*see* Roman Administration). These networks grew and became interconnected by means of letters of recommendation, hospitality, protégés and gifts of freedom or *citizenship. The cult of Roma and Augustus provided a way to express loyalty to Rome and gratitude for benefits received (*see* Civic Cults).

Though the emperor eclipsed all other benefactors, the wealthy citizens of each city remained important, opening their own purses or using their connections to open Rome's (*see* Roman Emperors). In fact, throughout the Roman Empire public offices, which included priesthoods, were synonymous with public philanthropy. Benefactors financed civic life, paying for entertainments, festivals, public buildings (e.g., *temples, *theaters, *baths, *gymnasia, stoas, markets) and public-works projects (e.g., city walls, aqueducts, fountains, sewers, roads, harbors). They also served as ambassadors. The honors elicited by their generosity included statues, inscriptions, crowns, favored seating, prayers, ritualized greetings and, for the truly great, heroization after death.

Benefactions could take a more personal form. Ransoming captives, financing marriages and funerals, paying for education and offering legal representation were typical. The grain dole in Rome and relief elsewhere for famines, fires and earthquakes reflect attempts to alleviate human suffering. Patrons also sponsored cultural life. Poets, artists and philosophers often turned to wealthy people (friends or otherwise) to find support for their enterprises (cf. Lk 1:3; Acts 1:1). By admitting them into their entourage, patrons enlivened their dinners, gained advisors and received honorific poems.

The outline of benefaction offered so far is idealized. Social pressure was typical in benefaction and at times was explicit. Some benefactors gave only because of compulsion and/or provided only the barest minimum; others refused to give. Expressions of gratitude, meanwhile, sought to elicit future gifts. Moreover, benefactions did not always win over the crowds. Herod, for example, failed to win the Jews' goodwill—*Josephus even claims falsely that Herod built nothing for the Jews (Josephus *Ant.* 19.7.3 §329). Luke 22:24-27 objects to the politics of lionizing the powerful as benefactors, perhaps recognizing the freedom of the wealthy and powerful to inflict indignities on their lessers and disavowing the status that wealth accrued. The transience of public honors appeared clearly when despised rulers died: their memory was condemned and their public monuments were erased (e.g., Nero and Domitian). This suggests that social networks responded to political and military power. Patronage, however, offered a friendlier face, provided a moral vocabulary and supplied legitimacy (cf. the perspective of slave owners in 1 Tim 6:2). Political theorists viewed philanthropy as basic to acceptable rule.

3. Jewish and New Testament Concepts of Benefaction.

Benefactors were part of Jewish life. Josephus was hailed as a benefactor and savior (Josephus *Life* 244 §47; 259 §50). Herod used gifts to rally popular support. Synagogues also depended on benefactors, who received the honorific title *synagogue leader (archisynagōgēs)*. Specifically, however, almsgiving differed from Greco-Roman benefaction: not only wealthy, socially important people offered alms; individuals received alms, not the body politic; almsgiving had a religious ideology and motivation.

Ideas of benefaction are fundamental to the assumptions of NT authors. F. W. Danker has emphasized these in Luke-Acts, particularly in connection with salvation. The widow's mite and the secrecy of giving criticize euergetism (Lk 21:1-4; Mt 6:2-4). The idea that receiving a gift entails gratitude and obligation underlies Paul's ethical thinking (Rom 1:21; 12:1; 1 Cor 4:7; 6:19-20; 2 Cor 8:8-9; Gal 2:21). The role of benefactor offers important background to Romans 16:1-2: to label Phoebe a deacon not only misrepresents *diakonos* but overlooks her leadership as patroness (*prostatis;* cf. 1 Thess 5:12). Benefaction also indicates how over the early centuries the church's care of widows and orphans, the burial of the dead and the ransoming of captives helped it to win a leading role within its culture, while after Constantine the building and furnishing of churches became another public expression of Christian benefaction. The language of eschatological reward, however, supplanted that of public-spiritedness.

See also CIRCUSES AND GAMES; CITIES, GRECO-ROMAN; CIVIC CULTS; HONOR AND SHAME; PA-

TRONAGE; SOCIAL VALUES AND STRUCTURES.

BIBLIOGRAPHY. F. W. Danker, *Benefactor: Epigraphic Study of a Greco-Roman and New Testament Semantic Field* (St. Louis: Clayton, 1982); A. R. Hands, *Charities and Social Aid in Greece and Rome* (Ithaca, NY: Cornell University Press, 1968); S. C. Mott, "The Power of Giving and Receiving: Reciprocity in Hellenistic Benevolence," in *Current Issues in Biblical and Patristic Interpretation,* ed. G. F. Hawthorne (Grand Rapids, MI: Eerdmans, 1975) 60-72; A. D. Nock, "*Sotēr* and *Euergetēs,*" in *The Joy of Study: Papers on New Testament and Related Subjects to Honor Frederick Clifton Grant,* ed. S. L. Johnson (New York: Macmillan, 1951) 127-48, reprinted in *Essays on Religion and the Ancient World,* ed. Z. Stewart (2 vols.; Cambridge, MA: Harvard University Press, 1972) 2:720-35; S. R. R. Price, *Rituals and Power: The Roman Imperial Cult in Asia Minor* (Cambridge: Cambridge University Press, 1984); T. Rajak and D. Noy, "*Archisynagogoi:* Office, Title and Social Status in the Greco-Jewish Synagogue," *JRS* 83 (1993) 75-93; R. P. Saller, *Personal Patronage Under the Early Empire* (Cambridge: Cambridge University Press, 1982); P. Veyne, *Bread and Circuses: Historical Sociology and Political Pluralism* (New York: Allen Lane/Penguin, 1990); A. Wallace-Hadrill, ed., *Patronage in Ancient Society* (New York: Routledge, 1989); B. Winter, *Seek the Welfare of the City: Christians as Benefactors and Citizens* (FCCGRW Grand Rapids, MI: Eerdmans, 1994). D. D. Walker

BETROTHAL. *See* MARRIAGE.

BIBLICAL INTERPRETATION, JEWISH

Interaction with the OT was a regular and pervasive component of the NT writers' attempts to explicate the gospel to the first-century audience. By a conservative count, there are roughly 300 NT passages that explicitly cite a specific OT passage and roughly 250 separate OT passages that find their way into the pages of the NT. In addition, there are in the NT a host of allusions to the OT (e.g., Revelation) not to mention the ubiquitous development of various OT themes (e.g., temple, kingship, messiah, covenant).

The mere fact of the presence of the OT in the NT is a truism. The issue that generates lively discussion, however, is the manner in which the NT authors make use of the OT. NT authors often call upon the OT in curious and unexpected ways in support of an argument or to illustrate a particular point. Even a comparison in an English Bible between a NT author's use of an OT passage and the OT context in which that passage was originally situated shows, to say the least, that the NT authors do not always seem to reproduce the original sense of that passage. So the question arises, Why do the NT writers handle the OT the way they do? Attempts to answer this question have generated a fairly steady stream of scholarly activity in modern times. Opinions to account for this phenomenon are varied, and the discussion will continue for the foreseeable future.

One particular issue that is of central importance for understanding the manner in which the NT authors used the OT is Jewish biblical interpretation during what is commonly referred to as the Second Temple period (from the return from Babylonian captivity and the building of the second temple in 516 B.C. to its destruction in A.D. 70). Throughout this period, *Judaism was engaged in an extensive, vibrant, even intense, interaction with its Scriptures. The centuries leading up to the NT period were anything but a hermeneutical dark age. Rather, this period displays a sophisticated and intricate approach to biblical interpretation. By the time the NT authors began their literary activity, there already preceded several hundred years of significant interaction with the OT, evidence of which is seen in the wealth of documents that make up the literature of the Second Temple period. It stands to reason, therefore, that a proper understanding of the NT's use of the OT must include an understanding of the Jewish hermeneutical background that not only preceded it but also was active during the time in which it was being written.

1. Diverse Data: The Variety of Second Temple Literature
2. Broad Contours of Second Temple Biblical Interpretation
3. The Nature of the New Testament's Use of the Old Testament in Its Second Temple Context

1. Diverse Data: The Variety of Second Temple Literature.

What makes the discussion of Jewish biblical interpretation so daunting is that it requires one to gain a familiarity with, if not mastery of, a broad range of literature. We have first of all the OT itself. Regardless of the diversity of opinions on this issue, the OT was written over a considerable period of time. Some of the books were written during the Second Temple period, obvious examples being Chronicles, Ezra, Nehemiah and various psalms, with a fair number of other books, either in whole or in part, that are up for debate. It is important that the OT itself not be ignored in the discussion, since within its pages the trajectories for later Jewish interpretation are already set. Authors of exilic and postexilic biblical books were already engaged in interaction with previously written material. One need only turn to the Chronicler's distinctive, creative handling of the Deuteronomistic History (Joshua, Judges, Samuel, Kings) or Daniel's interpretation of Jeremiah's "seventy weeks" (Dan 9:1-27) to see that biblical interpretation was happening during this period. The years following the Babylonian exile were not a period of literary inactivity. Rather, from the point of view of biblical interpretation, it is when such activity got started in earnest. Whatever the state of biblical interpretation may have been at an earlier point, it began to flourish during and after the exile. This interpretive activity is already seen in those biblical books that were either written or received their final form during this period. This trajectory is carried through to the Second Temple period as a whole.

The centuries that followed the return from exile evinced a flurry of literary activity, all of which is directly relevant to the question at hand. Perhaps the most diverse collection of these works are commonly referred to as Pseudepigrapha and Apocrypha (*see* Apocrypha and Pseudepigrapha). OT Pseudepigrapha is the general term referring to texts written during the Second Temple period that make some claim of inspiration and authority but remain extracanonical. The Apocrypha are those works that have remained outside the traditional Jewish and Protestant canon but have received canonical recognition in other traditions, namely, Roman Catholicism and Greek Orthodoxy. Labels are a necessity, but they can also be misleading. One should not conclude that the works conveniently subsumed under these labels are in any way uniform, any more than are those contained under the rubrics Old Testament or New Testament. Each boasts a variety of genres like those found in the traditional Jewish and Protestant canons, for example, *letters, wisdom (itself a diverse genre), psalms, historical books, *apocalyptic, and others. What they have in common, however, besides their essential Second Temple date and questionable canonical status is that they all engage the OT on some level. Some of these works include extensive retellings or expansion of portions of the OT (e.g., **Jubilees* and *Book of Biblical Antiquities* [*see* Pseudo-Philo; Rewritten Bible]), which are particularly important for forming a well-rounded understanding of early Jewish interpretation, since this genre especially is involved in sustained interaction with the OT.

In addition to their inestimable value for text-critical and related matters, the *Dead Sea Scrolls have also greatly enhanced our picture of Second Temple biblical interpretation. These scrolls contain not only copies of biblical books and a number of strictly sectarian works but also commentaries on OT books, perhaps the most famous of which is the commentary on chapters 1 and 2 of Habakkuk (*see* Habakkuk Commentary). Although the sectarian nature of this community would suggest caution in drawing general conclusions from its writings, no one disputes the importance of these documents for our understanding of Second Temple biblical interpretation in general and NT backgrounds in particular. The Dead Sea Scrolls have proved to be an invaluable and unprecedented source of information for biblical interpretation for about a three-hundred-year span beginning in the second century B.C., and they have redirected many currents of scholarly debate.

Another important body of literature is the works of *Philo, who lived around the turn of the first century A.D. Philo's writings clearly exhibit influences from the philosophical currents of his time, and he continues to be studied as an embodiment of the interface of Greek and Jewish cultures. But the importance of Philo's works extend beyond philosophy. Many of his works are expositions of the OT. What is of particular interest for our topic is not only his well-known allegorical handling of the OT but the fact that some of his own particular interpretations are also found in other Second Temple texts, some of which antedate his own writings. In other words, it seems that his understanding of Scripture is at times dependent, either consciously or unconsciously, upon previously existing exegetical activity. The same can be said of *Josephus. In his *Antiquities of the Jews,* Josephus recounts Israel's history, but in doing so he often reports incidents that are not found in the OT itself but are found in other Second Temple sources. He, like Philo, seems to be conversant with and even reliant on interpretive traditions that preceded him.

Two other bodies of literature should not be neglected. The first of these is the translations, particularly the *targums and the *Septuagint. These translations are not simply important for the light they shed on the nature and state of the Hebrew text in Second Temple times. As translations they are also interpretations; at many points they diverge from the Masoretic Text, not because they represent a different textual tradition but because the translators are attempting to clarify some element in the text. In fact, the targums, especially those in the Palestinian tradition (e.g., *Targum Pseudo-Jonathan*), reproduce rather lengthy and seemingly superfluous interpretive traditions by incorporating them into their translations, some of which are found in other Second Temple texts, including the NT.

Finally, mention must be made of *rabbinic literature. The scope of this literature is formidable, and in the past its relevance to NT studies has been overstated. Strictly speaking, rabbinic literature is post-NT (and therefore not Second Temple), so its bearing on the question of Jewish biblical interpretation as background for the NT would seem minimal. It has been correctly emphasized that great caution and nuance must be exercised when suggesting parallels, for example, between exegetical techniques in the Talmud and in Paul. Still, it is also an overstatement to dismiss the rabbinic material as wholly irrelevant. Not only do we find a number of rabbinic interpretive techniques already anticipated in Paul's writings, for example, but in rabbinic literature we find specific interpretations that are also found, in whole or in part, in earlier literature, including the NT. This phenomenon stands to reason, since, although written after the destruction of the Second Temple, rabbinic literature did not arise out of a vacuum. Its antecedents are well at home in Second Temple Jewish literature, and hence the relevance of rabbinic literature should not be dismissed out of hand.

2. Broad Contours of Second Temple Biblical Interpretation.

The variety of Second Temple literature, only outlined above, is sufficient to demonstrate that conclusions concerning the nature of Second Temple biblical interpretation cannot be drawn hastily. There are mountains of material, any of which is worthy of a lifetime of study. It goes without saying, then, that the full scope of Second Temple literature cannot even be adequately outlined, let alone explored, in this context. But it is within our means, even here, to get a general feel for how interpreters during this time handled Scripture. The temptation to catalog the manifold interpretive methods exhibited in the literature will be avoided. Not only are these methods too diverse to lend themselves to such an approach, but their categorization might yield the false conclusion that the phenomenon of Second Temple biblical interpretation is thus understood. Rather, Second Temple interpretive activity will be distilled into two broad categories. These categories approach the subject from two very different angles and thus give us a broader perspective from which to view the nature of Jewish biblical interpretation as a whole. Moreover, both categories are clearly present in the NT, and although the first has received its share of attention, the second does not always receive the prominence it deserves. The two categories are (1) conscious, deliberate interaction with the biblical material and (2) incorporation of previously existing interpretations. These are broad categories, especially the first, but they are sound points of departure for subsequent discussion.

2.1. Deliberate Exegesis of Old Testament Passages. It goes without saying that biblical interpreters during the Second Temple period looked upon Scripture with high reverence as a divine gift and therefore authoritative. This reverence for Scripture is reflected in their own writings. In fact, interaction with the Bible defines the essence of these works. They exist and have been perpetuated because of their close affinity with Scripture. This affinity may be seen, in the case of many, in their mimicry of biblical style or claim to authorship by some biblical figure.

The motives for which Scripture is adduced in these works is manifold. Some of the works of this period call upon scriptural passages and broad themes for particularly apologetic purposes, to defend, for example, a specific view of the cultic calendar (*Jubilees*). Similarly, others attempt to reconcile Scripture with prevailing views of their age (political, philosophical) and hence are engaged in a defense of the faith in general (**Wisdom of Solomon*, Philo, Josephus). The *Qumran material is especially known for exhibiting an apologetic tendency. The Habakkuk commentary, for example, is a defense of the Qumran community and its leader on the basis of a creative handling of the prophetic book.

The motives for the interpreters' engagement of Scripture are diverse, and so are the methods they employed to do so. For some, their purpose was served by alluding generally to a biblical story or theme. At the other extreme, we find a precise, word-by-word, line-by-line exegesis of a passage that at times even seems to be cognizant of varying textual traditions and to exploit this phenomenon with ample dexterity (Qumran's *pesher style). On the one hand, the methods these writers employed and their reasons for doing so are worthy of systematic treatment, particularly since some of these motives and methods are found in the NT (e.g., Paul's apologetic use of the Abraham story to defend the primacy of faith over works in Rom 4; the author of Hebrews' pesher-like handling of Ps 95 in Heb 3:7—4:13). Yet a systematic and even exhaustive categorization (if such a thing is even possible) may not get at the heart of the manner in which the interpreters handled Scripture.

Despite the great variety of motives and methods evinced in this vast body of material, one principle seems to underlie the practical results of the interpretive activity of this period. These interpreters shared a general attitude: biblical interpretation meant bringing the Scriptures to bear on their present circumstances. Whether these circumstances included *persecution, self-definition amid the influence of *Hellenism, support for separatist or *revolutionary agendas or some other setting, these interpreters all sought to see themselves and their audience in light of Scripture. They were no mere academics, playing with Scripture for the sake of it. They were engaged in their work for particular purposes that had serious religious significance for them and for those to whom they were writing.

To put it another way, what constituted proper interpretation for these ancient interpreters was not determined by the same set of criteria that dominates the modern hermeneutical landscape. To interpret the Bible properly was not merely a matter of objectively getting at the meaning the biblical text may have had in some bygone era, such as that of the original author, without imposing one's own subjective views into the text. Rather, any interpretation worthy of the name occurred only when that past message was called upon to define present circumstances. The goal, in other words, was to understand themselves in light of Scripture, and conversely to understand Scripture in such a way to bring meaning to their situation. The particular methods an interpreter may have called upon to serve this purpose are, in this respect, not the point. The methods are varied, but what they all have in common is that they are subservient to the general goal the interpreter wishes to attain, which is to have Scripture speak to his or her situation. This is what binds together, for example, the highly exegetical Habakkuk pesher from Qumran and Ben Sira's roll call of famous biblical figures (Sir 44—50). It is perhaps a great irony that the reverence for Scripture that drove these interpreters to look to the text for a sense of self-definition also often led them to handle the text in ways that at times have little, if anything, to do with the original meaning of that text. But such is the nature of early Jewish interpretation. The irony is something to be observed and respected, although by modern standards it is something that may be difficult to understand or justify.

2.2. Incorporation of Previously Existing Interpretations. There is a further irony to be observed. If we wish to understand the nature of biblical interpretation during the Second Temple period, we must look beyond the way in which these interpreters handled Scripture. Another factor, more subtle but no less important, adds an important dimension to the discussion. The nature of Jewish biblical interpretation is seen not only in how individual interpreters consciously engaged the Bible but in how they did not. In the course of their expositions of Scripture, we see embedded a number of expansions or embellishments of biblical material, unexpected twists and turns that seem to have little justification in the biblical material itself. The existence of these phenomena is interesting in and of itself, but with respect to the nature of early Jewish biblical interpretation, their real importance lies in the fact that the same or similar interpretive anomalies appear in a variety of works. On the whole, it is virtually impossible to locate the point of origin for these traditions, but the fact remains that they are found in works of differing agendas and purposes and that, in some cases, span a considerable period of time. How is it that such a thing occurs? How is it that ancient interpreters—who lived in different places and at different times and wrote to different audiences for different reasons—could reproduce similar, apparently quirky notions about a particular OT passage?

It is best to illustrate this phenomenon with a brief example or two. According to Exodus 12:35-36, the Israelites upon leaving Egypt are said to "plunder" (*nāṣal*) the Egyptians. There are a number of early interpreters, however, who put a different spin on this incident, one of them being the author of the apocryphal book the Wisdom of Solomon. The Israelites did not actually plunder the Egyptians. Rather, "She rewarded holy ones for their labors" (Wis 10:17). This interpreter understands the plunder to be a *reward* (*misthon*), a just recompense for the labors (*kophōn*) the Israelites endured for their years of slavery. They left Egypt with no mere plunder, such as brigands might take, but payment for services rendered. It is likely that the inspiration for this interpretation was apologetic: it was an attempt to justify Israel's seemingly less than sanctified behavior, particularly in the face of anti-Semitic polemics during the Second Temple period. Exodus 12:35-36 was handled in such a way as to relieve the tension between the world of the text and the world of the Jews the writer was addressing. Thus the writer's audience would maintain their connection with the past by making it speak meaningfully to their present.

But more to the point is the fact that this same interpretation of Exodus 12:35-36 is also found in a number of other works of the period: *Jubilees* 48:18; Philo (*Vit. Mos.* 1.141); Ezekiel the Tragedian's *Exagoge* 162-66. The earliest of these is likely *Jubilees* (early second century B.C.), although *Exagoge* is roughly contemporaneous. This raises the question of dependence. It is far too simplistic to argue that later authors, such as the author of Wisdom, are getting this interpretation directly and consciously from earlier sources, as if the author of Wisdom had in front of him a copy of *Jubilees* and thought to incorporate the earlier interpretation into his own. It is far more likely that all the sources mentioned above had already accepted a more or less common understanding of Exodus 12:35-36 and were reproducing it in their own works without needing to rely on any one specific previous work.

A second example will help to reinforce the point. In Wisdom 10:21, the author is commenting on the Song at the Sea (Ex 15), and he mentions a curious fact, that the "tongues of infants" were made "clear" (*tranas*) in order to be able to join in the singing. The specific reasons that gave rise to this comment will not detain us here. What is important to note is not only that this particular author has infants joining in the singing after the crossing of the Red Sea, but a number of other sources do as well (*Ex. Rab.* 1.12 and 23.8; *Tg. Ps.-J.* to Exodus 15:2; *t. Soṭa* 11b; *Pirqe R. El.* 42; *Pesiq. Rab Kah.* 17.6; *b. Soṭa* 30b; *Tg. Ezek.* 16). One is immediately impressed by how far-reaching this tradition is, spanning the first several hundred years of the first millennium A.D. It is highly unlikely that even the earliest rabbinic examples of this tradition were in any way directly dependent on the Wisdom of Solomon. For one thing, the rabbinic examples are more extended comments on infants singing at the sea whereas Wisdom has but a passing allusion to this tradition. It is hard to imagine that Wisdom's brief, almost matter-of-fact reference to infants singing at the sea would have been the point of origin for the rich tradition of the rabbis. And it goes without saying that Wisdom 10:21, written before the middle of the first century A.D., would not have had access to rabbinic literature several hundred years before it was written. It is more likely that the brief allusion to infants in Wisdom 10:21 and the extended rabbinic examples are evidence of an interpretive tradition that preceded both of them. Moreover, Wisdom's terse reference to the tradition suggests that by his time this tradition of singing infants had already become widely known.

It should be stressed that these are only two examples of this phenomenon. The literature of the Second Temple period can offer countless others. The point to be made is that biblical interpretation was an active exercise in the centuries following the return from Babylon. Furthermore, it is not only the case that many of the writings of this period exhibited similar motives and methods in their engagement of Scripture but also that specific interpretations themselves have been reproduced in a variety of interpretive works, many of which have little else in common with each other. By the time the NT was written, there already preceded an extensive network of detailed and widespread interpretive activity that centered around the Hebrew Scriptures. This Jewish background must come firmly to the foreground when investigating the nature of the NT's use of the OT.

3. The Nature of the New Testament's Use of the Old Testament in Its Second Temple Context.

The foregoing discussion helps provide the broad contours within which to investigate the uses of the OT by the NT authors. The manner in which the NT authors handled the OT is firmly at home in the hermeneutical world of Second Temple literature.

Like other literature of the Second Temple period, the NT is actively engaged in interpreting the OT. To isolate an example or two would almost serve to dampen one's impression of how pervasive this phenomenon is. There are, as mentioned above, hundreds of OT passages that are either explicitly cited or alluded to. The methods employed by the NT writers are by no means uniform. We have, for example, the commentary on Psalm 95 in Hebrews 3:7—4:13 that approaches in style the line-by-line pesher found in some of the Qumran material. Paul's use of the OT promise to Abraham and his curious understanding of "seed" to refer to one specific offspring in Galatians 3:15-29 is reminiscent of interpretive techniques found in a variety of works. In fact, at least one rabbinic text handles "seed" in a similar way (*b. Sanh.* 59b). Other examples exist where a NT author seems to change or augment an OT passage in order to appropriate that text more fully. We have, for example, Romans 11:26, which speaks of the deliverer to come *from* Zion rather than *to* (or *on behalf of*) Zion, as Isaiah 59:20 has it. Even allowing for the fact that the precise state of the Hebrew and Greek OT texts were not settled and that the NT itself witnesses to this variety, there are numerous examples in the NT where an author's citation of the OT differs from the OT not for text-critical reasons but for theological reasons. Also, Paul's use of Isaiah 59:20 in Romans 11:26 appears not to be his own creative handling of the OT but seems to reflect a Jewish messianic understanding of Isaiah 59:20, evidence of which is found in the Talmud.

A parade example of the manner in which the NT uses the OT is found in Matthew's use of Hosea 11:1 (Mt 2:15). It is clear, despite occasional attempts to argue the contrary, that Matthew was not interested in reproducing the meaning that Hosea 11:1 might have had for the prophet or his audience. It is not the case that Matthew read Hosea and arrived at the objective conclusion that this passage is speaking of Christ. Rather, like other interpreters of his era, Matthew began with the assumption that Scripture speaks to his situation. In other words, he understood Christ to be the proper goal of interpretation. With this proper goal in mind, he set out to interpret the OT in such a way as to bring this goal to the forefront. In doing so, Matthew is reflecting what we see throughout the NT as a whole. Although the exegetical methods that are employed by individual NT writers might differ, their motive for interpretation is essentially one, to interpret the OT in light of the coming of Christ. The methods of interpretation are subservient to the goal. The NT writers' experience of the risen Christ drove them back to the pages of the OT and caused them to understand its message afresh: the OT speaks of Christ, and proper, responsible, biblical interpretation will draw this out.

In addition to how the NT authors handled the OT directly, we have also the second phenomenon addressed above. A good deal of what the NT authors say about the OT reflects not their own conscious deliberations but the deliberations of others. In the pages of the NT are found a number of interpretive traditions that did not originate with the NT authors themselves but with interpreters who preceded them, a factor that indicates that the NT authors shared with these interpreters at some level a similar understanding of that particular portion of the OT. Some examples of this phenomenon include 1 Corinthians 10:4, where Paul's matter-of-fact reference to "the rock that followed them" seems dependent on a tradition of a "moveable well" (*Bib. Ant.* 10:7; 11:15; 20:8; *t. Sukk.* 3.11; *Tg. Onq.* to Num 21:16-20). In addition, Paul (Gal 3:19), Luke (Acts 7:53) and apparently the author of Hebrews (Heb 2:2) seem to assign *angelic activity to the mediation of the law given to *Moses. Although this is not found in the OT, it is a tradition documented as far back as *Jubilees* 1:27—2:1 and Philo (*Som.* 1.141-43). A third example, 2 Timothy 3:8, explicitly refers to Jannes and Jambres, the magicians who opposed Moses in Egypt. These characters are not mentioned in the OT but are mentioned frequently in a variety of ancient sources as early as the **Damascus Document* 5:17-19. In 2 Peter 2:5

Noah is called a "preacher of righteousness," a description found only outside of the OT (e.g., Josephus *Ant.* 1.3.1-2 §§73-75; *Sib. Or.* 1.125-31, 149-51). In Jude 9 we find the extrabiblical tradition of the archangel Michael's dispute with the devil over Moses' body *(As. Mos.),* and Jude 14-15 cites a portion of a prophecy supposedly uttered by Enoch *(1 Enoch 1:9).* Stephen in Acts 7:22 makes a point of mentioning Moses' education in Egypt, which is not in the OT but is a favorite topic especially in Hellenistic sources (e.g., Philo *Vit. Mos.* 1.21-24).

Again, these are not isolated examples, and mentioning in passing just a few runs the danger of deflecting the full force of the presence of these traditions in the NT. Many complex issues surround this topic, but the evidence presents a fairly consistent picture. The NT's use of the OT is a phenomenon that cannot be treated in isolation from the hermeneutical milieu of Second Temple biblical interpretation. Despite the undeniably distinctive elements of the NT's use of the OT (e.g., the decidedly christological focus; lack of protracted, systematic commentary such as we find at Qumran; virtual absence of allegory [but see Gal 4:21-31?]), those differences can only be properly understood from the vantage point of the similarities that the NT and Second Temple literature share at their core: the Hebrew Scriptures, because they are from God, are meant to speak to them. Exegetical methods, therefore, were not objective tools, as modern Westerners sometimes think of them, but a means of realizing a grander purpose. Jewish biblical interpretation during the Second Temple period constitutes the interpretive milieu for a proper understanding of the ways in which the OT appear in the NT. A strong familiarity with the literature of the time is a vital component to advancing significant discussion on the topic.

See also HABAKKUK COMMENTARY (1QPHAB); HEBREW BIBLE; INTERTEXTUALITY, BIBLICAL; PESHARIM; RABBINIC LITERATURE: MIDRASHIM; RABBINIC LITERATURE: TALMUD; RABBINIC LITERATURE: TARGUMIM; REWRITTEN BIBLE IN PSEUDEPIGRAPHA AND QUMRAN.

BIBLIOGRAPHY. R. Bloch, "Midrash," *IDBSup* 5, reprinted in *Theory and Practice: Approaches to Ancient Judaism,* ed. W. S. Green (Missoula, MT: Scholars Press, 1978) 1:29-50; J. H. Charlesworth, ed., *The Old Testament Pseudepigrapha* (2 vols.; Garden City, NY: Doubleday, 1983); J. H. Charlesworth and C. A. Evans, eds., *The Pseudepigrapha and Early Biblical Interpretation* (JSPSup 14; Sheffield: JSOT, 1993); P. Enns, *Exodus Retold: Ancient Exegesis of the Departure from Egypt in Wisdom 10:15-21 and 19:1-9* (HSMM 57; Atlanta: Scholars Press, 1997); idem, "The 'Moveable Well' in 1 Corinthians 10:4: An Extrabiblical Tradition in an Apostolic Text," *BBR* 6 (1996) 23-38; C. A. Evans and W. F. Stinespring, eds., *Early Jewish and Christian Exegesis: Studies in Memory of William Hugh Brownlee* (Atlanta: Scholars Press, 1987); M. Fishbane, *Biblical Interpretation in Ancient Israel* (Oxford: Clarendon Press, 1985); idem, "From Scribalism to Rabbinism: Perspectives on the Emergence of Classical Judaism," in *The Sage in Israel and the Ancient Near East,* ed. J. G. Gammie and L. G. Perdue (Winona Lake, IN: Eisenbrauns, 1990) 439-56; D. Instone Brewer, *Techniques and Assumptions in Jewish Exegesis Before 70 C.E.* (TSAJ 30; Tübingen: Mohr Siebeck, 1992); J. L. Kugel, "The Bible's Earliest Interpreters," *Prooftexts* 7 (1987) 269-83; idem, *In Potiphar's House: The Interpretive Life of Biblical Texts* (San Francisco: HarperCollins, 1990); idem, *Traditions of the Bible: A Guide to the Bible as It Was at the Start of the Common Era* (Cambridge, MA: Harvard University Press, 1998); "Two Introductions to Midrash," *Prooftexts* 3 (1983) 131-55, reprinted in *Midrash and Literature,* ed. G. H. Hartman and S. Budick (New Haven, CT: Yale University Press, 1986) 77-103; J. L. Kugel and R. A. Greer, *Early Biblical Interpretation* (Philadelphia: Westminster, 1986); D. McCartney, "The New Testament's Use of the Old Testament," in *Inerrancy and Hermeneutic: A Tradition, A Challenge, A Debate,* ed. H. M. Conn (Grand Rapids, MI: Baker, 1988) 101-16; M. P. Miller, "Targum, Midrash and the Use of the Old Testament in the New Testament," *JSJ* 1-2 (1970-71) 29-82; J. M. Mulder, ed., *Mikra: Reading, Translation and Interpretation of the Hebrew Bible in Ancient Judaism and Early Christianity* (CRINT 2.1; Assen: Van Gorcum; Philadelphia: Fortress, 1990); D. Patte, *Early Jewish Hermeneutic in Palestine* (SBLDS 22; Missoula, MT: Scholars Press, 1975); M. E. Stone, ed., *Jewish Writings of the Second Temple Period* (CRINT 2.2; Assen: Van Gorcum; Philadelphia: Fortress, 1984); G. Vermes, *Scripture and Tradition in Judaism* (SPB 4; 2d ed.; Leiden: E. J. Brill, 1973).

P. Enns

BIBLIOMANCY

In the Hellenistic and Roman periods one can observe in various religious milieus the phenomenon that books that have gained canonical status and are regarded as divinely inspired are used as lot oracles. The Greeks do so with Homer, the Romans with Virgil, and Jews and Christians with the Bible. The procedure is often simple: The holy book is opened at random, and the first passage that strikes the eye is regarded as the message of God or the gods to the petitioner.

1. Jewish and Christian Examples
2. Pagan Practices and Influence

1. Jewish and Christian Examples.
The earliest Jewish instances are the passages in 1 Maccabees 3:48 and 2 Maccabees 8:23, where before a decisive battle between the Jewish and the *Seleucid armies the Jews unroll the Torah scroll at random in the hope that the first line their eyes hit upon will instruct them about what God has in store for them or expects them to do. In *rabbinic literature this random way of consulting the oracular Scriptures usually takes the form of cledonomancy (i.e., the art of prognostication by means of auditive omens): biblical verses rehearsed by schoolchildren and inquired after or overheard by rabbis tip the balance in all kinds of decision-making processes (e.g., *b. Ḥag.* 15a-b; *b. Ḥul.* 95b). The underlying idea is that Holy Scripture, being the depository of God's own wisdom, contains all available knowledge, not only of the past but also of the present and the future, and that God himself guides the process of consultation.

Many instances of this practice are known from early Christian literature, the most famous of them being the conversion of Augustine to an ascetic lifestyle in the *tolle lege* scene in Milan (*Conf.* 8.12, 28-29): By random opening the epistle to the Romans, his eyes hit upon Romans 13:13-14, and this changes his life for good. Sulpicius Severus tells in his *Vita Martini* (9.5-7) that the people want Martin to become the bishop of Tours, but another bishop called Defensor is against it. When Martin is on his way to the church, the reader, whose duty it was to read the Scriptures that day, fails to appear. Then one of the bystanders lays hold of the Psalter and seizes upon the first verse that presents itself to him and that says "thou mightest destroy the enemy and the avenger [*defensor*]." It was believed that this psalm was chosen by divine ordination, so that Defensor would be confounded. Churchly authorities, however, in the decrees of their councils and synods, often condemned bibliomantic practices as pagan.

2. Pagan Practices and Influence.
We see this practice flourishing in pagan circles where the poetry of "the divine Homer" was held in as high esteem as the Bible among Jews and Christians and was used for oracular purposes. Dio Cassius (*Hist.* 79.8.6 and 40.3) says that in Syrian Apamea there was an oracular site of Zeus Belos that delivered its oracles in the form of verses from Homer, and Pseudo-Plutarch (*On Homer* 2.218.4) remarks that several people use Homer's poems for mantic purposes "as if they are the oracles of a god." From the same period (third century A.D.) we also have a papyrus with a so-called *Homeromanteion,* consisting of a list of 148 oracular answers in the form of 216 Homeric verses in an apparently random order but preceded by three numbers (running from 1-1-1 to 6-6-6). The petitioner who consulted the oracle had to roll three dice, and the resulting numbers referred to the Homeric line on the papyrus at the start of which these three numbers were found. That line contained the answer to the question of the petitioner. Probably the oraclemonger was supposed to provide some exegesis if necessary. In Latin-speaking circles the prestige of Virgil quickly rose to the same height as that of Homer, and the *Historia Augusta* provides us with many examples of emperors consulting the *sortes Vergilianae* in order to be informed about their future (*see* Roman Emperors).

We can observe the same phenomenon in specially prepared copies of the Bible, in particular the Gospels, that Christians consulted to learn their fortunes. In one of the most famous biblical manuscripts, the Codex Bezae (fifth century A.D.), a later hand added at the foot of the pages containing the first ten chapters of the Gospel of Mark a list of sixty-nine short sentences, all of them preceded by the word *proshermēneia,* which are responses to oracular questions.

It is hard to say whether the Jewish practice of bibliomancy has been influenced by the Greek one—both may have arisen independently—but it seems quite sure that Christian bibliomancy came into being under the influence of both Jewish and Greco-Roman practice.

The thesis that bibliomancy was also practiced by Jesus in view of his handling the Isaiah text in Luke 4:17 is weak, since it seems far more probable that Jesus followed some kind of lectionary system.

See also LITERACY AND BOOK CULTURE; MAGICAL PAPYRI.

BIBLIOGRAPHY. F. Boehm, "Los, Losbücher," *Handwörterbuch des deutschen Aberglaubens* (Berlin: Walter de Gruyter, 1933) 5:1351-1401; G. Björck, "Heidnische und christliche Orakel mit fertigen Antworten," *Symbolae Osloenses* 19 (1939) 86-98; P. Courcelle, "L'enfant et les Sorts Bibliques," *VC* 7 (1953) 194-220; V. I. J. Flint, *The Rise of Magic in Early Medieval Europe* (Oxford: Oxford University Press, 1991) 220-23, 273-83; H. Y. Gamble, *Books and Readers in the Early Church* (New Haven, CT: Yale University Press, 1995) 237-41; M. Gaster, "Divination (Jewish)," *Encyclopedia of Religion and Ethics*, ed. J. Hastings (12 vols.; Edinburgh: T & T Clark, 1911) 4:806-14; P. W. van der Horst, "*Sortes:* Sacred Books as Instant Oracles in Late Antiquity," in *The Use of Sacred Books in the Ancient World*, ed. L. V. Rutgers et al. (Louvain: Peeters, 1998) 143-74; idem, "Ancient Jewish Bibliomancy," *JGRCJ* 1 (2000) 9-17; Y. de Kisch, "Les *Sortes Vergilianae* dans l'Histoire Auguste," *Mélanges d'archéologie et d'histoire de l'Ecole Française de Rome* 82 (1970) 321-62.

P. W. van der Horst

BIOGRAPHY, ANCIENT

Ancient biography is an important subject for the study of the NT background because of its relationship to the *genre of the Gospels. Debate about whether the Gospels are biographies or not has gone in a full circle over the last century of critical scholarship. Modern literary theory is clear that genre is a key convention guiding both the composition and the interpretation of all communication, including written texts. Genre forms a kind of contract or agreement, often unspoken or unwritten, or even unconscious, between an author and a reader, by which the author writes according to a set of expectations and conventions and the reader agrees to read or to interpret the work using the same conventions.

Ancient literary critics were also interested in genre, with the later *grammarians attempting to describe and classify the main features of key genres such as tragedy and *history. However, these were never rigid rules, and it is best to look at examples of each genre. This is particularly important in the case of ancient biography. The word *biographia* itself does not occur until the ninth century A.D., with works prior to that called simply "lives" *(bioi* or *vitae).* Ancient writers sometimes tried to distinguish *bioi* from other genres, such as history, as in Plutarch's introduction to his *Alexander* 1.1-3. However, this probably only reflects the fact that he cannot include all the historical material available in his shorter life of *Alexander. In fact, as Pelling's analysis of Plutarch has shown, some ancient biographies are quite historical, while others include features of *philosophy, *rhetoric, *romance, religious or political works. Therefore, we must study the works themselves for a full picture.

1. The Development of Ancient Biography
2. Classification
3. Generic Features
4. The Gospels and Ancient Biography
5. Conclusion

1. The Development of Ancient Biography.

1.1. Jewish Biography. Although there is biographical material in the OT about people like Moses, David and Elijah, it is significant that the ancient Jews never wrote any biographies, even within the later *rabbinical tradition, probably because the central focus was always on the law and its interpretation and traditions rather than on any one person (see Alexander, 40-41). Momigliano (35-36) points out that the nearest examples are autobiographical books like Nehemiah written in the service of the Persian king (*see* Jewish History: Persian Period).

1.2. Greek Biography. The origins of Greek biography also lie in the Persian period with the travel writings of Skylax of Caryanda (c. 480 B.C.) and Ion of Chios (c. 440). The first surviving works to concentrate on a person's life are encomia, laudatory speeches, such as Isocrates' *Evagoras* and Xenophon's *Agesilaus* (370-360 B.C.). The other key factor came from the philosophical schools of the fourth century with works about Socrates and other philosophers. The third century was dominated by the house of Macedon, so Hellenistic accounts of Philip and Alexander the Great were composed. Meanwhile vast amounts of material were amassed for the libraries (*see* Alexandrian Library) at *Alexandria, leading to the production of books like Satyrus's *Lives of the Tragedians,* of which only parts of his *Euripides* survive. When Philo later writes his *Life of Moses* (c. A.D. 25-30), it is consciously modeled on this Greek biographical tradition.

*1.3. **Roman Biography.*** Concern for the ancestors and for precedent led the Romans naturally toward biography. In the middle of the first century B.C., Varro and Cornelius Nepos wrote accounts of famous leaders and generals, philosophers and writers, while political leaders like Caesar and *Cicero published their memoirs. The first century A.D. provided opportunities for propagandistic accounts of early emperors like Augustus (*see* Roman Emperors), as well as of political opponents like Cato the Younger. The period around A.D. 100 saw a flowering of biography with *Tacitus's *Life of Agricola,* his father-in-law and governor of Britain from A.D. 77 to 84, Plutarch's *Parallel Lives,* comparing famous Greeks with Romans, and *Suetonius's *Lives of the Caesars,* full of scandal and gossip. The second-century philosophical satirist Lucian composed lively accounts of various people. The third century saw Diogenes Laertius's compendium of *Lives of the Philosophers,* while Philostratus described the travels, teaching and miracles of *Apollonius of Tyana.* Biography then became an important tool in pagan-Christian debates around 300 with Iamblichus's *Pythagoras,* Porphyry's *Plotinus* and Eusebius's *Origen.* Political, philosophical and religious biography continued beyond the Roman Empire and into the early Middle Ages with lives of emperors, kings and saints.

2. Classification.
Attempts to classify this wide range of ancient biographies with their different subjects and approaches have produced much debate among classical scholars. F. Leo's great analysis of Greco-Roman biography attempted to distinguish two main groups: the Plutarchian, arranged chronologically for generals and politicians, and the Suetonian, more systematically ordered for literary men. Although Leo argued that the former came from the early philosophical schools and the latter from Alexandria, more recent work, particularly by A. Momigliano and J. Geiger, has shown that this distinction cannot be sustained. C. H. Talbert (1977, 93-98) proposed a fivefold classification of ancient biographies according to their social functions; however, most ancient lives had several purposes and cut across Talbert's categories. Instead, it is better to view ancient biography as a highly flexible genre, adapting to various cultures and growing through the centuries. It seems to occur naturally among those following or interested in particular people, such as leaders, teachers or writers, and it often functions within a context of didactic or philosophical debate and conflict.

3. Generic Features.
Instead of such categorization, an alternative approach is to compare different works from different authors to illustrate the nature of the genre. R. A. Burridge has analyzed a diverse group of ancient biographies of all types ranging from the fourth century B.C. to the third century A.D. Despite such lives comprising a flexible genre, there is recognizable family resemblance in both form and content.

From the formal or structural perspective, biographies are written in continuous prose narrative, between ten thousand and twenty thousand words—the amount on a typical scroll of about thirty to thirty-five feet in length. Unlike modern biographies, Greco-Roman lives do not cover a person's whole life in chronological sequence, and they have no psychological analysis of the subject's character. As regards content, they may begin with a brief mention of the hero's ancestry, family or city, his birth and an occasional anecdote about his upbringing; usually the narrative moves rapidly on to his public debut later in life. Accounts of generals, politicians or statesmen are more chronologically ordered, recounting their great deeds and virtues, while lives of philosophers, writers or thinkers tend to be more anecdotal, arranged topically around collections of material to display their ideas and teachings. While the author may claim to provide information about his subject (and we note that no ancient lives are written by women), often his underlying aims may include apologetic (to defend the subject's memory against others' attacks), polemic (to attack his rivals) or didactic (to teach his followers about him). Many ancient biographies cover the subject's death in great detail, since here he reveals his true character, gives his definitive teaching or does his greatest deed.

Finally, detailed analysis of the verbal structure of ancient biographies reveals another generic feature. While most narratives have a wide variety of subjects, it is a peculiar characteristic of biography that the attention stays focused on one particular person. Burridge's analysis has demonstrated that it is quite common in ancient biography for a quarter or a third of the verbs to be dominated by the subject, while another 15 percent to 30 percent of the verbs can occur in sayings, speeches or quotations from the person (Burridge, 261-74).

4. The Gospels and Ancient Biography.

4.1. History of the Debate. Traditionally the Gospels were viewed as biographies of Jesus. Over the course of the nineteenth century, biographies began to explain the character of great persons by considering their upbringing, formative years, schooling, psychological development and so on. During the 1920s, form critics rejected the notion that the Gospels were biographies: they have no interest in Jesus' personality or appearance, nor do they tell us anything about the rest of his life, other than his brief public ministry and an extended concentration on his death. Instead, the Gospels were seen as popular folk literature, collections of stories handed down orally over time, and as such they were unique (see Bultmann, 371-74). However, the rise of redaction criticism and the development of new literary approaches viewed the writers of the Gospels as both theologians and conscious literary artists. This reopened the question of the genre of the Gospels and their place within the context of first-century literature, with scholars like Talbert and Aune beginning to treat the Gospels as biographies (*see DJG,* Gospel [Genre]).

4.2. The Biographical Features of the Gospels. Like other ancient biographies, the Gospels are continuous prose narratives of the length of a single scroll, composed of stories, anecdotes, sayings and speeches. Their concentration on Jesus' public ministry, from his baptism to death, and on his teaching and great deeds is not very different from the content of other ancient biographies. Similarly, the amount of space given to the last week of Jesus' life, his death and the resurrection reflects the space given to the subject's death and subsequent events in works by Plutarch, Tacitus, Nepos and Philostratus. Verbal analysis demonstrates that Jesus is the subject of a quarter of the verbs in Mark's Gospel, with a further fifth spoken by him in his teaching and parables. About half of the verbs in the other Gospels either have Jesus as the subject or are on his lips; Jesus' deeds and words are of vital importance for the Evangelists as they paint their different portraits of Jesus. Therefore marked similarities of form and content can be demonstrated between the Gospels and ancient biographies.

5. Conclusion.

Consideration of ancient biography can contribute much to New Testament study. Although the genre is diverse and flexible, it still has a clear family resemblance, which the Gospels also share. The Evangelists' move from the Jewish concentration upon the law and traditions, seen in rabbinical anecdotes, to describing the life, death and resurrection of one particular person in the form of a Greco-Roman biography is a crucial christological claim. Therefore we must study the Gospels with the same biographical concentration upon their subject to see the particular way each author portrays his understanding of Jesus. Furthermore, additional study of ancient biography will help illuminate the social functions of the Gospels within their first-century context in the early Christian communities.

See also GENRES OF THE NEW TESTAMENT; SUETONIUS; TACITUS.

BIBLIOGRAPHY. P. S. Alexander, "Rabbinic Biography and the Biography of Jesus: A Survey of the Evidence," in *Synoptic Studies: The Ampleforth Conferences of 1982 and 1983,* ed. C. M. Tuckett (JSNTSup 7; Sheffield: JSOT, 1984) 19-50; D. E. Aune, *The New Testament in Its Literary Environment* (LEC 8; Philadelphia: Westminster, 1987); R. Bultmann, *The History of the Synoptic Tradition* (rev. ed.; Oxford: Blackwell, 1972); R. A. Burridge, *What Are the Gospels? A Comparison with Greco-Roman Biography* (SNTSMS 70; Cambridge: Cambridge University Press, 1992; 1995); P. Cox, *Biography in Late Antiquity: A Quest for the Holy Man* (Berkeley and Los Angeles: University of California Press, 1983); A. Dihle, *Studien zur griechische Biographie* (2d ed.; Göttingen: Vandenhoeck & Ruprecht, 1970); J. Geiger, *Cornelius Nepos and Ancient Political Biography* (Historia Einzelschriften 47; Stuttgart: Franz Steiner, 1985); F. Leo, *Die griechisch-römische Biographie nach ihrer literarischen Form* (Leipzig: Teubner, 1901); A. Momigliano, *The Development of Greek Biography* (Cambridge, MA: Harvard University Press, 1971; exp. ed., 1993); C. B. R. Pelling, "Plutarch's Adaptation of His Source Material," *JHS* 100 (1980) 127-40; idem, "Plutarch's Method of

Work in the Roman Lives," *JHS* 99 (1979) 74-96; D. R. Stuart, *Epochs of Greek and Roman Biography* (Berkeley and Los Angeles: University of California Press, 1928); C. H. Talbert, "Once Again: Gospel Genre," *Semeia* 43 (1988) 53-73; idem, *What Is a Gospel? The Genre of the Canonical Gospels* (Philadelphia: Fortress, 1977).

R. A. Burridge

BIRTH OF THE CHOSEN ONE (4Q534)

The Birth of the Chosen One is one of the names that has been given to the Aramaic document designated 4Q534 found in Cave 4 at *Qumran. The fragmentary nature of this document, along with its interesting and unusual content, has sparked much debate among scholars of the NT and Jewish *messianism. The text contains a reference to *bḥyr ʾlhʾ*, "chosen of God," which has caused many scholars to associate the text with the NT reference to Jesus in John 1:34, "I myself have seen it and have borne witness that this is God's Chosen One." However, many scholars now prefer to see this text as part of the parabiblical literature of Qumran that uses the Bible as its starting point and elaborates on a passage, expanding the text with other traditions. Rather than being viewed as a description of the birth of a messianic figure, this text can be seen as an embellished account of the birth of one of Israel's heroes of old.

1. Description and Content
2. Relationship to the New Testament

1. Description and Content.
There have been several treatments of this problematic text. J. Starcky (1964) was the first to publish its contents, and since then others have added to his insights and contested his conclusions. Starcky noticed the connection with John 1:34 and quickly labeled the text messianic. By contrast, J. A. Fitzmyer, despite the charged phrase, did not see the same messianic overtones that Starcky detected and contested this identification. Fitzmyer instead interpreted the *Birth of the Chosen One* as a reference to Noah and the miraculous nature of his birth. He proposed that the text is a further example of the fascination associated with the birth of Noah in intertestamental literature. He submits examples throughout Qumran literature to demonstrate this awe Noah inspired (*1 Enoch* 106—108; *Jub.* 4—10; *Genesis Aprocryphon;* Josephus *Ant.*). He also points to the document's shared vocabulary with *1 Enoch* 106—108 (i.e., "secrets," "books," "sin," "destruction" and "waters"), implying that this similarity may point to shared content or ideas. However, he does admit that nowhere in biblical literature or otherwise is Noah referred to as the elect of God.

The text is fragmentary, which makes a clear translation impossible. F. García Martínez's translation for the most part agrees with that of Fitzmyer and Starcky. The text consists of two columns, each between eighteen and nineteen lines in length. The second column contains many lacunae and is the more broken of the two columns.

Fitzmyer sees an unusual reference to "barley and lentils" in the description of the newborn child (4Q534 1:2). He suggests that this may refer to moles or birthmarks that would mark the child as unique. Column 1 continues to describe the childhood of the "youth" who "does not know any[thing until] the time when he shall become skilled in the three books" (4Q534 1:4, 5). The three books mentioned in line 5 do not likely refer to the three books of the OT, the *Torah, Nevi'im* and *Ketubim* (Starcky, Fitzmyer). Since the literature often referred to in intertestmental material is sectarian and *apocalyptic, the three books referred to in the *Birth of the Chosen One* are probably also sectarian and apocalyptic. According to the text, the youth's training in these three books will lead him to wisdom, counsel and prudence.

The phrase *bḥyr ʾlhʾ* ("the Chosen One of God") is at the center of much of the debate over the messianic nature of this document. In the Hebrew Bible the term *bᵉḥîrî*, "my chosen one," occurs in various places. It is used of Moses (Ps 106:23), of David (Ps 89:4), of the Servant of Yahweh (Is 42:1) and in a collective sense of Israel (Is 43:20; 45:4). In addition to *Birth of the Chosen One,* this term occurs in a plural form in a Qumran Hebrew text (1QpHab; *see* Habakkuk Commentary), and it is applied to the Qumran community. The problem with assigning messianic meaning to this phrase in *Birth of the Chosen One* involves relating it to a similar term used in *1 Enoch* (*see* Enoch, Books of). The term is found in the Parables of Enoch, which uses the phrase "the Elect One" interchangeably with "Son of Man" and "his Anointed," clearly messianic references. However, the passages in which these phrases occur are not among the parts of *1 Enoch* that have been found at Qumran, so the connection is tenuous (Fitzmyer).

2. Relationship to the New Testament.
The text is of great interest to students of the NT and early Christian literature for it provides an earlier example of a birth announcement and worthwhile comparison to the birth descriptions of both Jesus and John the Baptist in the Gospels. If it is viewed as an elaboration of a biblical passage dealing with Noah, then it is an interesting example of how Scripture was treated by the sect at Qumran as opposed to how it is used in the NT. If it is viewed as having messianic overtones, then it allows for a greater understanding of some of the religious concerns that would erupt during the time of the NT.

See also MESSIANISM; QUMRAN: PLACE AND HISTORY; SON OF GOD TEXT (4Q246).

BIBLIOGRAPHY. J. A. Fitzmyer, "The Aramaic 'Elect of God' Text from Qumran Cave IV," in *Essays on the Semitic Background of the New Testament,* ed. J. A. Fitzmyer (London: Chapman, 1974) 127-60; F. García Martínez, *The Dead Sea Scrolls Translated: The Qumran Texts in English* (Leiden: E. J. Brill, 1994); J. Starcky, "Un texte messianique araméen de la grotte 4 de Qumrân" (Ecole des langues orientales anciennes de l'Institut Catholique de Paris 10; Paris: Bloud et Gay, 1964) 51-66. C. A. Swanson

BOETHUSIANS. *See* SADDUCEES.

BOOK CULTURE. *See* LITERACY AND BOOK CULTURE.

BOOK OF BLESSINGS (1QSb)

The *Book of Blessings* (1QSb [1Q28b])is part of the corpus of sectarian literature found at *Qumran. This document is significant not only for understanding the Qumran community but also for analysis and study of early Jewish *bᵉrākôt* ("blessings") and other *prayer formulas used in the Bible. The study of this document is beneficial in many ways. First, because of its liturgical nature, it sheds light on the practices of the sect at Qumran (*see* Liturgy: Qumran). Even more than that it allows us insight into the different positions within the community and gives us more information to use in comparison to other known Jewish sects of the Second Temple period. Furthermore, the liturgical content and *eschatological concerns in the *Book of Blessings* make for interesting comparison to similar topics seen in the NT.

1. Description
2. Content
3. Relationship to the New Testament

1. Description.
The *Book of Blessings* contains a series of blessings that were pronounced over various members of the community at Qumran. Many scholars speak of the *Book of Blessings* in conjunction with two other sectarian documents, the **Rule of the Community/Manual of Discipline* and the **Rule of the Congregation,* because all three documents were originally copied on the same leather scroll. Although these works were probably not penned by the same hand (but see Carmignac), they share common concerns and contain reference to members of the same title in the community. The first and earliest document of the three works, the *Manual of Discipline,* defines the guidelines by which the members of the community were to live. The second, the *Rule of the Congregation,* describes the community at the end of the age. The third, the *Book of Blessings,* is thought to have been prescribed for use in a ceremony during the final times of the end of the age. Paleographically the Hebrew writing can be dated to around the same time: from about 100 to 75 B.C. Because of their early date, the study of these three texts can give us insight into the life of the community at Qumran in its formative years.

2. Content.
The *Book of Blessings* contains five columns, each of which in present form are of varying length. All five columns contain broken text, but the first column is the most fragmentary. Even with the fragmentary nature of the text, three distinct introductions can be distinguished. One is directed to "those who fear God," another to the "sons of Zadok, the priests" and another to the "prince of the congregation." Each introduction begins its section by proclaiming "the words of blessing of the Instructor [the *Maśkîl*] to bless." The blessings that follow provide information regarding the different stations of members of the community and also some of the theological concerns of the sect.

2.1. Theology. The first benediction is directed to those who fear God. Those who fear

God are those "who remain held fast in his holy covenant and walk with perfection [on the paths of] his truth" but also those "he has chosen for an eternal covenant which endures forever" (1QSb 1:2-3). This benediction evidences the strong role that the doctrine of election played in the community and recalls similar passages in the NT that also show a strong adherence to the doctrine of election (Rom 8:29-30; Eph 1:4-5; 1 Pet 1:2).

The next benediction, directed to the priests, describes these members as those "God has chosen to strengthen the covenant, [forever, to dis]tribute all his judgments in the midst of his people, to instruct them in accordance with his commandment" (1QSb 3:23-24). Again, the sect's strong adherence to the doctrine of election is clear in this blessing, but also clear is a sense of division that existed in priestly circles. This benediction is directed to the Zadokite priests who keep the covenant, as contrasted to the priests who did not keep the covenant (Charlesworth and Stuckenbruck, 120). The blessing also asks God to "[r]enew the covenant of [eternal] priesthood" (1QSb 3:26), perhaps suggesting that the office of priest within the community was a station that required a covenant renewal ceremony.

The third benediction that can be distinguished is addressed to the prince of the congregation, who "will establish the kingdom of his people forever" (1QSb 5:21). This blessing asks that God would raise the prince "to an everlasting height" (1QSb 5:23). This section of the benedictions gives evidence for the oft-observed hierarchy present in the sectarian literature. It also illustrates the messianic concerns at Qumran.

*2.2. **Suggested Reconstructions.*** The content and amount of fragmented text between the introductions suggest that other groups, whose names were not preserved, received a blessing from the instructor. For this reason scholars have posited various reconstructions. J. T. Milik suggests that originally four categories were addressed, each representing a separate and distinct group within the community. In this reconstruction, one is directed to the "Faithful," one to the "High Priest," one to the "Priests" and one to the "Prince of the Congregation" (Milik). Milik's has been one of the simpler reconstructions; most are more complex. For example, J. Licht contests Milik's reconstruction, insisting instead that the benedictions show a more logical order. Licht believes that the blessings are arranged from the least to the most important members of the community. In this arrangement the blessings begin by addressing "those who fear God" and end with the "Prince of the Congregation." Yet another reconstruction, that of J. Carmignac, agrees with Licht's logical arrangement but breaks up the text so that more members of the community are addressed. Charlesworth and Stuckenbruck suggest yet another breakdown:

1:1—2:21	Blessing of the Faithful
2:22-28	Blessing of a Part (perhaps an individual) of the Sect
3:1-16	Blessing of an Officiating Priest
3:17-21	Blessing of Another Part of the Sect
3:22—4:21	Blessing of the Sons of Zadok
4:22-28	Blessing of the Zadokite High Priest
5:1-19	Blessing of an Unidentifiable Part of the Sect
5:20-29	Blessing of the Prince of the Congregation

The content and structure of the text make it clear that the missing sections include members other than the three mentioned in the introductions preserved. It seems best to assume a logical order to the blessings (following Licht; Carmignac; Charlesworth and Stuckenbruck).

*2.3. **Relationship to Other Material from Qumran.*** Already the relationship of the *Book of Blessings* to the *Manual of Discipline* and to the *Rule of the Congregation* has been established, but there is other literature to which comparison can be made. Because of its ritualistic nature, the *Book of Blessings* should also be studied with other liturgical texts such as the **Songs of the Sabbath Sacrifice* or the other **Blessings* texts (4Q280, 4Q286-290) to determine more about the religious practices of the Qumran sect.

3. Relationship to the New Testament.

The *Book of Blessings* provides interesting parallels to NT literature. The NT also contains benedictions (Heb 13:20-21; 1 Jn 2:12-14; Eph 1:17-19; 3:16-19), some of which are eschatological in scope and therefore make for fruitful comparison with those found in the *Book of Blessings.* In addition, the theology displayed within the benedictions is similar to the theological concerns with election and unity that are seen in the NT. The *Book of Blessings,* however, is unique in its particular vocabulary and in its blessing of the members of the community according to their position. Although the NT mentions different stations within the Christian community, never is there a strict demarcation of blessings given such as the one we see in the *Book of Blessings*. Continued study of the *Book of Blessings* and other sectarian literature will add to our knowledge of the historical setting of the NT by giving us a window through which to view this formative time period (*See DPL*, Benediction, Blessing, Doxology, Thanksgiving; *DLNTD*, Blessing).

See also BLESSINGS (4Q280, 286-290); LITURGY: QUMRAN; RULE OF THE COMMUNITY/MANUAL OF DISCIPLINE (1QS); RULE OF THE CONGREGATION/MESSIANIC RULE (1QSA).

BIBLIOGRAPHY. J. Carmignac, "Quelques détails de lecture dans la 'Règle de la Congrégation,' le 'Recueil des Bénédictions' et les 'Dires de Moise,'" *RevQ* 13 (1963) 83-96; J. H. Charlesworth and L. T. Stuckenbruck, "Blessings (1QSb)," in *The Dead Sea Scrolls: Rule of the Community*, ed. J. H. Charlesworth et al. (Louisville, KY: Westminster John Knox, 1996); J. Licht, "The Benedictions (*Recueil des Bénédictions*, 1QSb)," in *The Rule Scroll—A Scroll from the Wilderness of Judea: 1QS, 1QSa, 1QSb—Text, Introduction and Commentary* (Jerusalem, Bialik 1965) 273-89; J. T. Milik, "Recueil des Bénédictions (1QSb)," in *Qumran Cave 1*, ed. D. Barthélemy and J. T. Milik (DJD 1; Oxford: Carendon Press, 1955) 118-30; L. Schiffman, "The Rule of the Benedictions and Its Place in the Rule Scroll," in *The Eschatological Community of the Dead Sea Scrolls: A Study of the Rule of the Congregation* (SBLMS 38; Atlanta: Scholars Press, 1989) 72-76; S. Talmon, "The 'Manual of Benedictions' of the Sect of the Judean Desert," *RevQ* 8 (1960) 475-500.

C. A. Swanson

BOOK OF MYSTERIES (4Q299-301 & 1Q27). *See* DEAD SEA SCROLLS: GENERAL INTRODUCTION.

BRONTOLOGION. *See* THUNDER TEXT (4Q318).

BURIAL PRACTICES, JEWISH

Rituals and beliefs of Jewish people during the first century A.D. regarding death and the dead included ceremonies for disposal of the human corpse, burial techniques, rites of mourning and theological beliefs about the dead and the afterlife. In the NT period, Jewish burial practices both preserved ancient traditions going back to the time before the kingdom of Israel and made use of more recent developments brought on by the rising influence of Greek culture.

1. Background
2. Burial
3. Mourning
4. Theological Beliefs About the Dead and the Afterlife
5. Conclusion

1. Background.

1.1. Israelite Background. The contribution of ancient Israel to first-century Jewish burial practices is most evident in the fact that first-century Jews continued to follow the traditional Israelite practice of secondary burial, that is, the reburial of human bones after the flesh had decayed. Like their Israelite forebears, Jews in the NT period reburied bones by family groups in underground chambers. Burial practices of this sort had deep local roots in Syro-Palestine, going back as far as the Middle Bronze Age (c. 2000-1500 B.C.), when circular underground chambers were first used for the burials of many individuals, most likely members of the same clan or family group. In these tombs, bones were piled together on one side of the chamber, along with miscellaneous grave goods such as jewelry, pots, jars and juglets.

By the Late Bronze Age (c. 1500-1200 B.C.), architectural improvements such as plastered surfaces on the walls and floor were beginning to appear in these chambers, but it was during the Iron Age (especially Iron II, c. 925-586 B.C.) that these rather simple underground chambers developed into the characteristic Israelite bench tomb. A bench tomb was a square cave with waist-high benches around three of the four sides; the fourth side usually held the entrance, which typically featured a stairway leading down from a small doorway. Often the area under one of the benches was hollowed out as a repository for human bones. Corpses were laid on the benches to decompose, and when desiccation was complete, the bones were gathered into the repository underneath the bench. Over time, the repository came to hold the bones of a family's ancestors, so that the recurrent biblical idiom "to be gathered to one's fathers" (e.g., 2 Kings 22:20) vividly captures the way in which ancient Israelites practiced secondary burial.

1.2. Hellenistic Background. By the NT period, significant changes had appeared in these burial practices, changes that were largely due to the rising influence of Greek culture (*see* Hellenism) after the conquest of Palestine by *Alexander the Great in 332 B.C. In particular, Jews no longer employed the characteristic Israelite bench tomb but began to carve niches into the walls of their underground tombs and to place bodies in these niches. Two kinds of niche, both of which originated in the Greek world, began to appear in Jewish tombs during the Hellenistic period (332-63 B.C.) and had become common by the first century A.D.: the *loculus*, or *koḥ*, a deep, narrow niche carved into the wall of the tomb, large enough to hold one body; and the *arcosolium*, a broad, arch-shaped niche carved along the wall of the tomb, creating a shelf on which a body could be laid (*see* Art and Architecture: Jewish).

A typical loculus tomb could contain as many as ten or twelve such niches, three or four in each wall, while an arcosolium tomb could usually hold only three niches, one along each wall (except for the entrance wall). Still later, during the Roman period (esp. the Early Roman Period, 63 B.C.-A.D. 135) Jews also began to use some types of Roman burial containers, such as stone sarcophagi (i.e., containers carved from single blocks of limestone, large enough to hold a single body) and wooden coffins (i.e., containers constructed from wood, large enough to hold a single body). Even though these Hellenistic and Roman influences had found their way into Jewish burial practices by the time of Jesus, important differences between Jews and pagans remained. Roman sarcophagi, for example, typically featured pictorial representations of humans, flora and fauna, but Jewish sarcophagi from the NT period were generally decorated only with geometric and occasionally floral patterns.

2. Burial.

2.1. Burial Rituals. Jews of the NT period buried their dead promptly, as soon as possible after death and almost always on the same day. Preparations began at the moment of death: the eyes of the deceased were closed, the corpse was washed with perfumes and ointments (Acts 9:37), its bodily orifices were stopped and strips of cloth were wound tightly around the body—binding the jaw closed, the feet together and the hands to the sides of the body (Jn 11:44). The corpse was then placed on a bier and carried in a procession to the family tomb (Lk 7:12). Eulogies were spoken, and the corpse was placed inside the tomb, along with items of jewelry or other personal effects. The funeral was thus conducted without delay, and most bodies were interred by sunset on the day of death. But Jewish burial rituals did not conclude with this first, or primary, burial. A year after the death, members of the immediate family returned to the tomb for a private ceremony in which the bones were reburied after the body had decayed.

2.2. Burial Techniques. By far the most common Jewish burial technique in Palestine during the NT period was secondary burial in limestone chests known as ossuaries. An ossuary was constructed by hollowing out a single block of limestone, with the size of the ossuary being determined by the size and length of the large bones in the body (i.e., skull, femur). At primary burial, the corpse was laid in a loculus or in an arcosolium, and when decomposition was complete the bones were collected and placed in an ossuary. Inscribed with the name of the deceased, the ossuary might then be placed virtually anywhere within the tomb: in a loculus, in an arcosolium, on a shelf or on a bench along the side of the tomb or even on the floor.

The use of ossuaries was especially common in and around the city of Jerusalem during the first century A.D., so much so that L. Y. Rahmani has attempted to characterize them as a "uniquely Jerusalemite" burial technique. Since ossuaries have also been found at locations in Palestine far from Jerusalem, however (e.g., Horvat Tilla), this view is probably not correct. Ossuaries were simply the burial technique that was most popular among Jews in and around Jerusalem during the first century A.D.. Even in Jerusalem, though, ossuaries were not always used; bones have been found gathered directly into niches (without any burial container), piled in a corner of the tomb or even collected in a separate chamber of the tomb (i.e., a charnel room). In the *Diaspora, Jews did not use ossuaries but buried their dead in underground tombs, or catacombs, depositing bodies in niches, sarcophagi and coffins.

3. Mourning.

During the time between primary and secondary burial, members of a Jewish family were in a state of mourning and abstained from full participation in the normal course of ordinary life. *Rabbinic sources describe a series of mourning rituals that unfolded in three stages. For the first seven days after a death in a Jewish family, the nearest relatives of the deceased would remain at home, grieving and receiving the condolences of extended family and friends (Jn 11:19). During this time, relatives would usually leave home only to visit the tomb (Jn 11:31). After seven days of intense grieving, there followed a thirty-day period of less acute mourning, during which the immediate family was expected not to attend festive social gatherings or to leave town. After thirty days, most aspects of normal life resumed, except in the case of a parent's death: when one's parents died, mourning for them lasted until the day of secondary burial (Mt 8:21-22).

4. Theological Beliefs About the Dead and the Afterlife.
Israelite religion handed down to Jews the belief that human corpses were impure and that even incidental or indirect contact with a corpse rendered one ritually unclean (Num 19:11-22). During the NT period, then, Jews in Palestine generally avoided unnecessary contact with the dead. Tombs were usually located well outside of towns and cities and were marked with whitewash during the Passover season to warn unwary pilgrims of their potential danger. Several NT texts evoke this Jewish avoidance of contact with the dead (e.g., Mt 23:27-28; Lk 10:31-32; 11:44). This theological belief had a social impact; unlike some cultures in which ancestors retain a significant place in the society of the living, Jewish culture gave the dead no ongoing role in society. Jewish beliefs about the afterlife were, as most human conceptions of the afterlife tend to be, rather vague and fluid, but one concept was clearly defined: resurrection of the body. As part of a general *apocalyptic worldview, many Jews during the NT period, including Jesus and Paul, expected that the dead would be raised bodily on the last day. Secondary burial in ossuaries, a burial technique that preserved the individual identity of the deceased, may have been at least partially motivated by this belief.

5. Conclusion.
Anthropologists have found that human death rituals typically celebrate the life values of a culture (Metcalf and Huntington). Jewish burial practices during the NT period drew upon both ancient Israelite traditions and more recent Hellenistic developments in order to bury the dead in a way that celebrated distinctively Jewish cultural ideals. Secondary burial, underground tombs, mourning, corpse impurity and resurrection of the body all cohered in a set of burial practices that symbolically valorized the Jewish ideal of life in relationship with God and family.

See also ART AND ARCHITECTURE: JEWISH; RESURRECTION.

BIBLIOGRAPHY. E. Bloch-Smith, *Judahite Burial Practices and Beliefs about the Dead* (JSOTSup 123; Sheffield: JSOT, 1992); P. Figueras, *Decorated Jewish Ossuaries* (Leiden: E. J. Brill, 1983); B. R. McCane, "Let the Dead Bury Their Own Dead: Secondary Burial and Matthew 8:21-22," *HTR* 83 (1990) 31-43; P. Metcalf and R. Huntington, *Celebrations of Death: The Anthropology of Mortuary Ritual* (2d ed.; New York: Cambridge University Press, 1992); E. M. Meyers, "Secondary Burials in Palestine," *BA* 33 (1970) 2-29; L. Y. Rahmani, "Ancient Jerusalem's Funerary Customs and Tombs," *BA* 44 (1981) 171-77, 229-35; 45 (1982) 43-53, 109-19; idem, *A Catalogue of Jewish Ossuaries* (Jerusalem: Israel Antiquities Authority, 1994); R. H. Smith, "An Early Roman Sarcophagus of Palestine and Its School," *PEQ* 103 (1973) 71-82.

B. R. McCane

C

CAESAREA MARITIMA

Two cities in Israel bear the name *Caesarea* in the NT. One is *Caesarea Philippi, built by Herod the Great, 25 miles north of the Sea of Galilee and later enlarged by his son Herod Philip, who then named it for himself and Augustus Caesar (*see* Roman Emperors). The other is Caesarea Maritima, a city of about 165 acres, which is located on the Mediterranean coast of Israel about midway between Haifa and Tel Aviv.

1. Herodian Construction
2. Political Volatility

1. Herodian Construction.

Prior to the construction of the city of Caesarea, this site had been occupied by a "town on the coast" called Strato's Tower, which *Josephus said was dilapidated. It was built by Herod the Great over a period of about twelve years (22-c. 10/9 B.C.; Josephus *Ant.* 15.9.6 §341; ten years is the time given in *Ant.* 16.5.1 §136). This town Herod "entirely rebuilt with white stone, and adorned with the most magnificent palaces, displaying here, as nowhere else, the innate grandeur of his character" (Josephus *Ant.* 1.21.5 §208).

One of these palaces has been found in recent excavations at Caesarea by E. Netzer, who has demonstrated the probability that Herod's palace was the Promontory Palace whose remains lie south of the harbor and west of the theater. According to Netzer, "the palace had become the *praetorium,* or official residence of the Roman governor" (Burrell, Gleason and Netzer 1993, 56). The buildings and pools found here were reused after Herod's time as a large bathhouse (Burrell, Gleason and Netzer 1994, 75).

Herod's engineers built the city on the format of major Roman *cities with an orthogonal, or checkerboard, system of paved streets, sophisticated water and sewer systems, a theater, bathhouse, palaces, temples and an impressive harbor. For many years a number of different teams have excavated in Caesarea, and the results of their labors are impressive.

In addition to his palace, Herod built a harbor to provide a major link between Palestine and the Western world. Josephus described this harbor as being bigger than the impressive harbor for *Athens at Piraeus (Josephus *J.W.* 1.21.5 §410). Excavations, both on land and under the water, have confirmed this description. Palestine had only one natural harbor, at Haifa, and the one at Caesarea was the first artificial harbor constructed in the ancient world. One of the underwater excavators, R. Hohlfelder (800), has shown that this harbor, called Sebastos, consisted of four harbors joined together. The inner harbor extended well inside the modern shoreline to a series of storage vaults running north and south, above which stood the temple of Augustus and Roma, a spectacular sight to ships entering the outer harbor.

The temple area above the harbor has been under excavation since 1989 by the Caesarea Land Excavation Project, under the direction of K. Holum. That work has demonstrated that the temple was an impressive structure, centrally located and adjacent to the inner harbor area. This proximity of the religious and the commercial in the ancient world is well established and widespread.

To provide the city with water, Herod built an aqueduct from an underground spring in the mountains east of Caesarea to the coast, where it turned south and emptied in the city. The distance is 13 miles. This high-level aqueduct reached an elevation of 20 feet along the coast, and a well-preserved section of it is still standing just north of the harbor. It is built on standard

Roman arches with remains of channels on the top that held sections of clay pipes. Some of these pipes can best be seen in a preserved portion of the aqueduct on the east side of the modern Haifa-Tel Aviv highway. A second aqueduct was eventually built on the west side of this one in about A.D. 130. Sections of it still stand beside the Herodian one. An inscription on the side of the aqueduct mentions the second and tenth Roman legions, which were stationed here in the time of the emperor Hadrian (117-138). In ancient Rome, the legions did construction work as well as carrying on military campaigns (*see* Roman Military).

Josephus mentions a *theater built by Herod (Josephus *J.W.* 1.21.8 §415; *Ant.* 15.9.6 §341). The theater, south of the harbor, still stands partially preserved. The orchestra (floor) of the theater has been repaired or rebuilt numerous times since excavations in 1962 found thirteen floors superimposed on one another. The floors were covered with plaster, not marble, and had to be replaced frequently due to wear. Much of the theater seen today is later reconstruction and stands almost adjacent to the palace of Herod identified by Netzer. According to Josephus, Herod Agrippa I entered the theater at daybreak one day to address an admiring crowd of people. He was dressed "in a garment woven completely of silver," and the crowd was so awed that they said, "We agree that you are more than mortal in your being." Herod did not reject this religious expression, and he was immediately stricken with "pain in his heart and . . . an ache in his stomach." He died five days later (Josephus *Ant.* 19.8.2 §§343-50). This event is documented in the NT (Acts 18:20-23), which attributes his death to his being smitten by an angel of the Lord.

2. Political Volatility.

The Jews and Syrians in Caesarea were quarreling and killing each other over the issue of equal civic rights (Levey), and the situation had deteriorated to the point that Felix hired assassins to kill Jonathan, the Jewish ex-high priest who had initially urged the appointment of Felix as procurator (Josephus *Ant.* 20.8.1 §§162-63). When Paul stood before Felix, the procurator was clearly confronted with a serious problem. He had no desire to agitate the already volatile Jewish situation with which he continually wrestled, as did his successor, Festus (Acts 25:9).

Ten years later, however, these hostilities reached a climax, when in A.D. 66 the Syrians massacred about twenty thousand Jews in Caesarea and sent the remainder to the galleys. Josephus says the city was thus "completely emptied of Jews" at that time (Josephus *J.W.* 2.18.1 §457). This precipitated the war with Rome that resulted in the destruction of the Jerusalem temple in A.D. 70 (*see* Jewish Wars with Rome).

An inscription discovered in 1997 by Y. Porath has been tentatively identified as belonging to the official Roman bureau for internal security, where Paul appeared before Felix and Festus (Acts 24:27). The building complex where it was found is 15,000 square meters in size and includes a large palace, administrative offices, a bathhouse and a courtyard, according to Porath, who is in charge of Israel Antiquities Authority excavations there. It is located between the palace of Herod on the coast and the hippodrome to the east.

According to Porath, this governmental complex is the only seat of Roman government unearthed in Israel and one of the few ever excavated in the ancient Roman world (*see* Roman Administration). Further exploration is necessary for clarification of its purpose. Since Roman rule over Palestine was centered in Caesarea, the praetorium complex there functioned as the seat of Roman government from the first until the middle of the third century. A mosaic inscription on one of the floors reads "I came to this office—I shall be secure."

See also CAESAREA PHILIPPI; HERODIAN DYNASTY.

BIBLIOGRAPHY. B. Burrell, K. Gleason and E. Netzer, "Caesarea, the Promontory Palace," in *Excavations and Surveys in Israel* (Jerusalem: Israel Antiquities Authority, 1994) 14:75; idem, "Uncovering Herod's Seaside Palace" *BAR* 19 (May/June 1993) 56; D. Goldberg, ed., *Caesarea: Queen of the Coast* (Ramat Gan, Israel: Israel National Parks Authority, 1996); R. L. Hohlfelder, "Caesarea," *ABD* 1:798-803; K. G. Holum et al., *King Herod's Dream: Caesarea on the Sea* (New York: Norton, 1988); I. Levey, "Caesarea and the Jews," in *The Joint Expedition to Caesarea Maritima,* 1: *Studies in the History of Caesarea Maritima,* ed. D. N. Freedman (*BASOR* Supplemental Studies 19; Missoula, MT: Scholars Press, 1975) 43-78; J. McRay, "Caesarea Maritima," in *Archaeology and the New Testament* (Grand Rapids, MI: Baker, 1991) 139-45.

J. R. McRay

CAESAREA PHILIPPI

One of two cities in Israel that are named Caesarea (the other is *Caesarea Maritima), Caesarea Philippi was built by Herod the Great and enlarged by his son Philip (*see* Herods). Caesarea Philippi flourished during the time of Herod Agrippa II.

1. Name and Location
2. Early History

1. Name and Location.

Caesarea Philippi was a city located 25 miles north of the Sea of Galilee and east of Dan, at the easternmost of three headwaters of the Jordan River. An underground stream of cold, fresh water surfaces here at the foot of Mount Hermon and is known as the Nahal Hermon (River Hermon) and also as the Wadi Banias (*wadi,* in Arabic, means "riverbed"). The site is also called Banias today, a term derived from the long-standing Greek name *Paneas,* which was used to designate a cave in the mountain dedicated to a Greek god of nature, Pan (the *p* in Paneas is pronounced like a *b*). *Josephus refers to the town and district as Paneas and to the sanctuary of Pan as the Paneion (Josephus *Ant.* 15.10.3 §§360-61, 363-64; *J.W.* 1.21.3 §§404-5; see Smith, 474).

In 20 B.C. Augustus Caesar (*see* Roman Emperors) granted Herod the Great control of the Huleh River basin along with other portions of northern *Galilee. This included the Paneas sanctuary, where, Josephus says, "Herod . . . dedicated to him [Augustus] a temple of white marble near the sources of the Jordan, at a place called Paneion" (Josephus *J.W.* 1.21.3 §404; *Ant.* 15.10.3 §363). This temple is probably the one depicted on a coin struck by Philip in A.D. 1, which has the head of Augustus on one side and a tetrastyle (four-columned) facade of a temple on the other (see Meshorer, 76, coin #76 on plate 10; *see* Coinage: Jewish).

Remains of this temple have been excavated. Two parallel walls, 10.5 meters apart, were found below a cave in the cliff above the springs of fresh water. The western wall was originally lined with marble plaques and contained alternating semicircular and rectangular niches along its length. The particular kind of masonry construction used in the temple, opus quadratum, is found also in the sunken garden of another palace of Herod in Jericho (*see* Art and Architecture: Jewish).

2. Early History.

When Herod died, his son Philip was made tetrarch of the districts of Iturea and Trachonitis (Lk 3:1), which included Paneas. Josephus lists the site of Paneas along with the districts of Gaulonitis, Trachonitis and Batanea as part of the tetrarchy assigned to Philip in the will of Herod the Great (Josephus *Ant.* 17.8.1 §189).

Philip then enlarged the city and named it Caesarea (Josephus *Ant.* 18.2.1 §28; *J.W.* 2.9.1 §168) in honor of Augustus Caesar. Either Philip (Wilson and Tsaferis, 57) or others later in the first century A.D. (Kutsko, 803) added his name to that of Caesar, calling the city Caesarea Philippi.

Philip ruled from 4 B.C. until his death in A.D. 41, at which time his nephew Agrippa I inherited this territory. His reign lasted only three years, and at his death in A.D. 44 the city was placed under the control of the Roman governor of Syria for almost a decade (*see* Roman Administration).

In A.D. 53, Herod Agrippa II was given control of the city with the territories belonging to it and ruled it for forty years, until 93. V. Tsaferis, the director of the ongoing excavations here, has found the remains of a large and elaborate structure that he identifies as the royal palace of Agrippa II on the basis of the historical evidence recorded in Josephus (Josephus *Ant.* 1.21.3 §404-6), the numismatic evidence, the ceramic evidence and the style of the building construction.

The excavators, Tsaferis and J. Wilson, believe the palace was erected after the 66-70 Jewish revolt against Rome (*see* Jewish Wars with Rome) was crushed, and construction possibly was financed by the Roman emperor in gratitude for Agrippa's loyalty to Rome during the revolt. Agrippa reigned for almost a half century with such political diplomacy that he was given the title of king. During this time Agrippa kept Caesarea Philippi as his capital, enlarging it and making appropriate renovations.

The palace must have been impressive. Remains discovered on a lower level include a large basilica (an elongated rectangular building that had a central room with side aisles), fountains and pools, towers and passageways. A row of vaulted rooms were found along the eastern side of the upper level.

After the Jewish revolt was subdued, Josephus wrote that the Roman general Titus brought his troops to the city for recuperation and "exhibited all kinds of spectacles" for them (Josephus *J.W.* 7.2.1 §23), including combat between both humans and animals and burning (*see* Arenas). More than twenty-five hundred Jews taken captive in the revolt were brought here and destroyed in this way (Josephus *J.W.* 7.3.1 §38).

After the death of Agrippa, Caesarea Philippi became a politically insignificant town on the fringes of the province of Syria, and his beautiful palace was converted into a public bathhouse that attracted tourists. A portion of it has been preserved.

See also ARCHAEOLOGY OF THE LAND OF ISRAEL; CAESAREA MARITIMA.

BIBLIOGRAPHY. J. Kutsko, "Caesarea Philippi," *ABD* 1:803; Y. Meshorer, *Jewish Coins of the Second Temple Period* (Tel Aviv: Am Hassefer, 1967); G. A. Smith, *Historical Geography of the Holy Land* (New York: Hodder & Stoughton, 1896); Z. Uri-Ma'oz, "Banias," in *The New Encyclopedia of Archaeological Excavations in the Holy Land*, ed. Ephraim Stern (New York: Simon & Schuster, 1993) 1:136-43; J. Wilson and V. Tsaferis, "Banias Dig Reveals Kings' Palace," *BAR* 24 (January-February 1998) 54-61.

J. R. McRay

CAESAR'S HOUSEHOLD. *See* ROMAN SOCIAL CLASSES.

CAIAPHAS OSSUARY

The high *priest Caiaphas, who condemned Jesus and handed him over to Pontius Pilate, prefect of Judea (*see* Roman Governors of Palestine), was appointed by Valerius Gratus in A.D. 18 to succeed Simeon ben Qimḥit. Caiaphas was removed from office shortly after Pilate's dismissal in late 36 or early 37. The immediate cause for Pilate's removal was the governor's violent action taken against the *Samaritans who had gathered at the foot of Mt. Gerizim in hopes of finding the lost vessels of the Samaritan temple, which had been destroyed by the *Hasmoneans some 150 years earlier. Caiaphas may have been removed by Vitellius for having advised Pilate to act as he did, but that is only supposition.

The "house of Caiaphas" is apparently mentioned in rabbinic literature: "I hearby give testimony concerning . . . the house of Qaipha [*byt qyp*ʾ] . . . from them have been chosen high priests" (*t. Yebam.* 1:10); "Menahem, son of Maxima, the brother of Jonathan Qaipha [*qyp*ʾ]" (*y. Maʿaś.* 52a). *Josephus makes specific reference to the high priest "Joseph Caiaphas" and "Joseph called (or nicknamed) Caiaphas" (Josephus *Ant.* 18.2.2 §35; 18.4.3 §95). The *Mishnah (*m. Parah.* 3:5) speaks of a high priest named Elihôʿēynai ben ha-Qayyaph (*hqyyp*, the Hebrew form of the Aramaic *qyp*ʾ, though some MSS read *hqwp*, which could be vocalized *ha-Qôph* or *ha-Qûph*), who may have been the son of Joseph Caiaphas. The NT refers to the high priest simply as Caiaphas (Mt 26:3, 57; Lk 3:2; Jn 11:49; 18:13, 14, 24, 28; Acts 4:6).

The recent discovery of an ossuary, on which the name of Caiaphas may have been inscribed, has generated interest and disagreement. In November 1990 workers in Jerusalem's Peace Forest, about 1 mile south of the Old City, accidentally uncovered an ancient burial cave in which one dozen ossuaries were found. Six of these ossuaries had lain undisturbed for two millennia; the other six had been ransacked by grave robbers. Two of the untouched ossuaries bear the name *qyp*ʾ. One of these ossuaries, which contained the skeletons of two infants, a toddler, a teenager, a young adult female and a man in his sixties (see Zias), bears the fuller names, as transcribed by R. Reich (1991, 1992): *yhwsp br qp*ʾ (on the plain end) and *yhwsp br qyp*ʾ (on the plain side). Vocalized, these may be the names Yehoseph bar Qaphaʾ and Yehoseph bar Qayaphaʾ, which are probably variant spellings of one man's name. These names, as well as others, are crudely inscribed, perhaps with the two iron nails found in the tomb. Reich (1991, 1992), Z. Greenhut, W. R. Domeris and S. M. Long, among others, have concluded that this person in all probability should be identified with the Joseph Caiaphas mentioned by Josephus and the NT.

The ornate and well-preserved Caiaphas ossuary is housed in the Israel National Museum in Jerusalem. The skeletal remains have been interred on the Mt. of Olives. In the nearby Akeldama field and ravine, the tomb of Annas (Lk 3:2; Jn 18:13, 24; Acts 4:6; cf. Josephus *Ant.* 20.9.1 §§197-98), the high-priestly father-in-law of Caiaphas, may also have been identified (Ritmeyer and Ritmeyer; on possible identification of the family house, see Rupprecht).

W. Horbury and E. Puech disagree with the Caiaphas identification, arguing that the Qayaphaʾ reading is difficult and improbable. Rather, they think the name is probably Qôphaʾ, Qûphaʾ or even Qēphaʾ. The consonants inscribed on the ossuary favor a two-syllable name (e.g., Qôpha'), not a three-syllable name (e.g., Qayapha'), which would be required to make the identification with the Greek Caiaphas found in Josephus and the NT. Perhaps, but Greek forms of Jewish names often expand and so add another syllable. The name Qatros or Qadros may offer a pertinent example, for this high-priestly figure, whose name appears as Qadrôs in *t. Menaḥot* 13:19, 21 and as Qatrôs on a stone weight in the ruins of the Burnt House in the Old City, may be the Cantheras (*Kanthēras*) mentioned in Josephus (*Ant.* 20.1.3 §16; Reich 1991). If so, we have a clear example of how a shorter Semitic form of a name transliterates into a longer form in Greek. Part of the difficulty is the relative rarity of the Qayapha' name, which results in inadequate data for comparative analysis, as well as the poor quality of the ossuary inscriptions themselves, making certain identification of the *yod* (so Reich et al.), as opposed to the *waw* (so Horbury and Puech), very difficult.

See also BURIAL PRACTICES, JEWISH.

BIBLIOGRAPHY. W. R. Domeris and S. M. Long, "The Recently Excavated Tomb of Joseph Bar Caipha and the Biblical Caiaphas," *JTSA* 89 (1994) 50-58; Z. Greenhut, "Burial Cave of the Caiaphas Family," *BAR* 18 (September/October 1992) 28-36, 76; W. Horbury, "The 'Caiaphas' Ossuaries and Joseph Caiaphas," *PEQ* 126 (1994) 32-48; A. Kloner, "A Tomb with Inscribed Ossuaries in East Talpiyot, Jerusalem," *ʿAtiqot* 29 (1996) 15-22; E. Puech, "A-t-on redécouvert le tombeau du grand-prêtre Caïphe?" *Le monde de la Bible* 80 (1993) 42-47; idem, *La croyance des Esséniens en la vie future,* vol. 1 (EB 21; Paris: Gabalda, 1993) 193-95; R. Reich, "Caiaphas Name Inscribed on Bone Boxes," *BAR* 18 (September/October 1992) 38-44, 76; idem, "Ossuary Inscriptions from the 'Caiaphas' Tomb," *ʿAtiqot* 21 (1992) 72-77; idem, "Ossuary Inscriptions from the 'Caiaphas Tomb," *Jerusalem Perspective* 4 (1991) 13-21; R. Riesner, "Wurde das Familiengrab des Hohenpriesters Kajaphas entdeckt?" *Bibel und Kirche* 46 (1991) 82-84; L. Ritmeyer and K. Ritmeyer, "Akeldama: Potter's Field or High Priest's Tomb?" *BAR* 20.6 (1994) 22-35, 76; A. Rupprecht, "The House of Annas-Caiaphas," *Archaeology in the Biblical World* 1 (1991) 4-17; J. Zias, "Human Skeletal Remains from the 'Caiaphas' Tomb," *ʿAtiqot* 21 (1992) 78-80.

C. A. Evans

CALENDARS, JEWISH

The reckoning of time and seasons is important for any culture, and for Judaism the calendar carried the burden of correctly identifying the festivals and holy days assigned by Yahweh for Israel's observation. In Second Temple Judaism, particularly in the *Dead Sea Scrolls, we find evidence of a calendar at variance with that of the Hebrew Bible.

1. The Calendar of the Hebrew Bible
2. The Competing Calendars of Second Temple Judaism

1. The Calendar of the Hebrew Bible.

1.1. The Month. Month names in the biblical record reflect variously Canaanite (Abib: Ex 13:4; Ziv: 1 Kings 6:1; Ethanim: 1 Kings 8:2; Bul: 1 Kings 6:38) and Babylonian nomenclature (Nisan: Neh 2:1; Sivan: Esther 8:9; Elul: Neh 6:15; Chislev: Neh 1:1; Tebet: Esther 2:16; Shebat: Zech 1:7; Adar: Ezra 6:15), but most reflect frequently a system that used ordinals (first month, Ex 12:2; second month, Gen. 7:11; and so forth). The fact that every ordinal between first and twelfth is used, but none higher, indicates clearly that there were but twelve months in the year (see 1 Kings 4:7–19). It has been held that Genesis 7:24 and 8:3 (150 days is given as the periods that the flood prevailed and then decreased) indicate a 30-day month, but this fact is never indicated explicitly and must remain doubtful. The Babylonian calendar that was in use by the time of the exile (6th century B.C.) has twelve months, alternating between 29 and 30 days.

1.2. The Year. Neither is there any explicit reference to the length of the year in the biblical record. Even the evidence concerning when the year began is conflicting. The classic rabbinic solution is that there were four New Years: the first of Nisan for kings and feasts; the first of Elul for the tithe of cattle, the first of Tishri for the years of (foreign) kings, the years of Release, Jubilee years, for the planting (of trees), and for vegetables; and the first of Shebat for (fruit) trees (*m. Roš Haš.* 1:1). By the exile, the increased frequency in the use of Babylonian month names suggests that the year was reckoned at 354 days and began in the spring (Nisan). The evidence from the papyri from Elephantine (5th century B.C.) and Wadi ed-Daliyeh Papyri (4th century B.C.) corroborate.

2. The Competing Calendars of Second Temple Judaism.

That there were competing calendar reckonings among the Jews of late antiquity became clear in the nineteenth century when the books of **Jubilees* and **1 Enoch* became available to Western scholars. Both of these works revealed a "solar" calendar of 364 days comprised of four quarters of 91 days, which stood in clear opposition to the 354-day Babylonian model of normative Judaism. The Dead Sea Scrolls have revealed the same 364-day calendar detailed in *Jubilees* and *1 Enoch*. It has also become evident from the polemical nature of the scroll discussions (1QpHab 11:2-8; 1QS 1:11-15) that the calendar was an element of contention leading to the separation of the Qumran sect from the *Judaism of the Second Temple period.

2.1. The Cycles of the Qumran Calendar. The 364-day calendar is best understood by its characteristic cyclical patterns, which range from the 7-day week to the 294-year cycle of six Jubilees.

2.1.1. Seven-Day Week. The most basic cycle is not natural, but theological: "And on the seventh day God finished the work that he had done" (Gen 2:2). As in the Hebrew Bible, the week began on "Sunday" and ended on the sabbath. The weeks were then designated by the names of the twenty-four priestly courses (1 Chron 24:7-18) which began their temple service on the sabbath (*see* Sacrifice and Temple Service). Zechariah, of the priestly division of Abijah, was serving his rotation when the angel appeared and announced the birth of his son, John the Baptist (Lk 1:5-23).

2.1.2. Twenty-nine-/Thirty-Day Lunar Month. The most curious feature of the Qumran calendar cycles is the inclusion of an alternating 29-/30-day lunar month. Although several of the calendars chart the full moon, the first crescent, and in some cases even its phases, it is everywhere subordinate to the solar month and regulates no liturgical matters.

2.1.3. Thirty-/Thirty-One-Day Solar Month. The sequence of numbered solar months follows the pattern of 30-30-31 days. This follows no natural phenomenon but is rather based on the seven-day week. Each quarter is exactly thirteen weeks.

2.1.4. The 364-Day Year. The year always began on a Wednesday, when, according to Genesis 1:14, God made the sun, moon and stars "for signs, and for seasons, and for days and years." This 364-day year becomes a repeated polemic in the scroll corpus. 4Q252, *Commentary on Genesis,* recasts the flood story as a proof of the 364-day sectarian calendar. Exactly one year following the beginning of the flood (II/17 according to commentator), Noah left the ark. The *Psalms Scroll* from Cave 11 attests to 364 songs that David composed for the daily *sacrifice, thus associating the great king of Israel with the correct position in the debate over the calendar.

2.1.5. Three-Year Lunar Cycle. As in the Babylonian calendar, lunar months alternate between twenty-nine and thirty days, the first period reckoned at twenty-nine. Thirty-six lunar months total 1,062 days, thirty days short of a like number of months in the 364-day calendar (1,092 days). Hence, at the end of this thirty-six lunar-month period, instead of a twenty-nine-day month that the normal alternation requires, a thirty-day "leap month" is added to bring the sun and moon into accord once again. This phenomenon again emphasizes the theological nature of the calendar, as lunar-solar conjunctions on the first day of every third year do not occur naturally.

2.1.6. Six-Year Priestly Cycle. The twenty-four priestly courses recorded in 1 Chronicles 24:7-18 took turns serving in the temple. As a full year accounted for two and one-sixth full rotations of the priestly divisions, six years were required before first course (Gamul) was again serving at the beginning of the year. This six-year cycle enabled the scroll writers to refer to particular years, months or weeks according to the course that was serving in the temple.

2.1.7. Forty-Nine-Year Jubilee. For the scroll writers the Jubilee period was the forty-nine-year interval marked off by two Jubilee years. 4Q319, *Otot,* or "signs," is dependent on this cycle.

2.1.8. 294-Year Cycle of Six Jubilees. This period is defined by the number of forty-nine-year cycles necessary before the first priestly division (Gamul) was once again serving in the temple in the first week of a new Jubilee.

2.2. The Festival Calendar. The calendar polemic in the scrolls most frequently concerns the proper time for the festival days (*see* Festivals and Holy Days). Competing calendars would have meant that the proper day to celebrate a festival would have been disputed (1QS 1:11-15). Also of interest are the additions and subtractions from the biblical list. The following table records the biblical festivals and the month/day on which they were celebrated.

Passover/Unleavened Bread	I/14 (evening)-21
Omer/Firstfruits of the Barley	I/26
Weeks/Firstfruits of the Wheat	III/15
Day of Remembrance	VII/1
Day of Atonement	VII/10
Feast of Booths	VII/15-22

2.2.1. Date of the Feast of Weeks. The biblical instruction for the dating of the Feast of Weeks (Lev 23:15–20) touched off a long-standing controversy within Jewish circles. The Qumran sectarians understood the word *sabbath* (Lev 23:15) to refer to the seventh day of the week and started counting the required fifty days on the first Sunday after the feast of Unleavened Bread. The rabbis took *sabbath* to mean the day after the first day of Unleavened Bread and dated Weeks to III/6 (*m. Menaḥ.* 10:3). In the Qumran calendars the count is made inclusive from the day that the Omer was waved (I/26) to the fiftieth day on III/15. This festival, called Pentecost (fifty) in Greek, marked the coming of the Holy Spirit and the birth of the church according to Acts 2:1-13.

2.2.2. Three Extrabiblical Festivals. The following three extrabiblical festivals—firstfruit offerings of new wine and oil, and the wood offering—are additions to the biblical list.

Firstfruits of the Wine	V/3
Firstfruits of the Oil	VI/22
Wood Offering	VI/23-27, 29

2.2.2.1. Firstfruit of the Wine. On the pattern of the count to the Feast of Weeks another inclusive count of fifty is begun on III/15, determining V/3 as the Feast of Wine. The addition of this and the following Feast of Oil are never justified in the Qumran texts but were likely to have been felt implicit in the triad of the firstfruits of God's blessing: grain, wine and oil (see 11QTemple 43:3-10; Num 18:12; Deut 7:13).

2.2.2.2. Firstfruit of the Oil. Again following the pattern of the pentacontad count beginning on V/3, the Festival of the Oil is established on VI/22. This then is the fourth and last of a series of firstfruit festivals begun with the Waving of the Omer on 1/26.

2.2.2.3. Wood Offering. Nehemiah 10:34-35 and 13:31 record that members of the Jerusalem community volunteered the regular supply of wood for the temple "for the wood offering." The *Temple Scroll* directs the twelve tribes—two tribes a day for six days—to present the contributions associated with the Wood Offering. The date of the wood offering is somewhat doubtful but probably began the second day of the week following the Festival of the Oil.

2.3. Esther. The fact that the Feast of Purim (Esther 9:26-32) is not recorded in the calendars, coupled with the lack of Esther among the biblical manuscripts from Qumran, suggests that the Qumran sectarians might not have considered the book authoritative.

2.4. Intercalation. A 364-day calendar raises the question of intercalation to account for the 1¼-day differential with the true solar year. Although theories have been proposed (Glessmer), the explicit theological basis for the calendar tends to argue against any such intercalation. The calendar is clearly founded on the principle of the seven-day week and forty-nine-year Jubilee; these are theological, not observational phenomena. Even the moon is unrealistically harnessed to this theological construct and forced into conjunction with the sun every three years. Given this evident theological structure, it is more likely that the calendar was considered ideal and biblical. The lack of observational reality was likely explained by the evil nature of the time, a factor that God would make right at the end of the age when righteousness reigned.

2.5. The Hebrew Bible and the 364-Day Calendar. Despite the rather difficult biblical data, A. Jaubert has suggested a pattern among the disparate details (Jaubert). Beginning with the 364-day calendar of *Jubilees* and the supposition of a special Israelite attitude toward the sabbath, Jaubert was able to reconstruct the framework of the "Qumran" calendar before a description of the scroll manuscripts had been published. When this calendar was compared to the dates recorded in the Bible it was discovered that among the sixty dated events, with only two exceptions (Esther 9:15 and 2 Chron 3:2), the biblical dating favored activities on Sunday, Wednesday and Friday, while at the same time avoiding the sabbath. If this is purposeful, those who promulgated a 364-day calendar during the late Second Temple period might be considered conservative (biblical) rather than innovative in their calendar views.

2.6. The Passion Week and the 364-Day Calendar. Jaubert has also theorized that the presence of two Jewish calendars might explain the discrepancy between the Synoptic Gospels and John regarding the events of the passion week (Jaubert). The Synoptics date the Last Supper (Passover Meal) to I/14 and the crucifixion to I/15, while John dates the crucifixion to I/14, before Jesus' captors had celebrated the Passover. According to Jaubert, the Synoptics used the 364-day calendar, whereas John reflected the "official" 354-day calendar. The Last Supper would have then been on Tuesday evening and the crucifixion on Friday, a result that is problematic to most NT scholars.

See also FESTIVALS AND HOLY DAYS: JEWISH.

BIBLIOGRAPHY. M. G. Abegg Jr., "The Calendar at Qumran," in *The Judaism of Qumran: A Systematic Reading of the Dead Sea Scrolls,* ed. B. Chilton, A. Avery-Peck and J. Neusner (JLA 5; Leiden: E. J. Brill, 2000); J. Finegan, "The Principles of the Calendar and the Problems of Biblical Chronology," in *Light from the Ancient Past* (vol. 2; 2d ed.; Princeton, NJ: Princeton University Press, 1959) 552–98; U. Glessmer, "Calendars in the Qumran Scrolls," in *The Dead Sea Scrolls After Fifty Years: A Comprehensive Assessment,* ed. P. Flint and J. VanderKam (Leiden: E. J. Brill, 1999) 213-78; A. Jaubert, *The Date of the Last Supper* (New York: Alba House, 1965); J. VanderKam, *Calendars in the Dead Sea Scrolls: Measuring Time,* ed. G. Brooke (LDSS; London and New York: Routledge, 1998); S. Talmon, U. Glessmer, and S. Pfann, *Qumran Cave 4.16: Calendrical Texts* (DJD 21, Oxford: Clarendon Press, forthcoming); B. Z. Wacholder and S. Wacholder, "Patterns of Biblical Dates and Qumran's Calendar: The Fallacy of Jaubert's Hypothesis," *HUCA* 66 (1995) 1-40.

M. G. Abegg Jr.

CALENDARS, ROMAN. *See* FESTIVALS AND HOLY DAYS, GRECO-ROMAN.

CANONICAL FORMATION OF THE NEW TESTAMENT

The NT canon, a fixed and closed collection of twenty-seven documents, was the outcome of a process spanning the first through the fifth centuries. This process was characterized by two movements: the growth of Christian writings and their rise to scriptural status, which transpired mainly in the first two centuries; and the limitation of those writings that were to be regarded as Scripture, read in the church and considered authoritative for its faith and life, which occurred mainly in the fourth and fifth centuries. These two movements were not entirely separate and sequential, and the development of the canon was not purely linear. The process of canonical formation was also complex, being indebted to a variety of factors, including the composition and dissemination of Christian writings, the history of their use and interpretation, theological conflicts in early Christianity, judgments of scholars, promulgations of bishops and councils and even the technology of book production. Nevertheless, the canon of Scripture that finally emerged corresponded closely to those writings that had been most widely valued and used in the church of the first three centuries.

1. Scripture and Canon
2. The Growth of Christian Scripture and the Formation of Early Small Collections
3. The Shaping of the Canon

1. Scripture and Canon.

Differing conceptions of the history of the NT canon have turned largely upon definitions of terms. Until fairly recently, no sharp distinction was made between the terms *Scripture* and *canon.* If a writing was cited as authoritative by early witnesses, designated as Scripture *(graphē)* or quoted with a citation formula such as "it is written" *(gegraptai),* then it was commonly claimed that the document in question was at least functionally canonical. But the view that increasingly prevails rests upon a clear distinction between the terms *Scripture* and *canon.* Scripture *(graphē)* designates religiously authoritative literature, without regard to its scope or limits. The use or citation of a document as authoritative says nothing, however, about its canonical status. Canon, by contrast, signifies a definitive and closed list of religiously authoritative writings and thus explicitly addresses the question of their scope and limits (Sundberg). Although the Greek word *kanōn* means "measuring rod" and, by extension, a norm or rule, in its earliest application to Christian writings it signified a list, specifically the list of Christian writings that were permitted to be read in the church, that is, publicly in the liturgical assembly. Once such a list was drawn up, the writings within it were held to be exclusively authoritative canonical Scriptures. Thus the formation of the canon presupposes the availability of Scriptures, but the existence of religious Scriptures does not of itself imply or require the formation of a canon.

Although the recent emphasis on this distinction has tended to represent the fourth and fifth centuries as the critical period of canonical formation, this should not be permitted to obscure the early beginnings of the attribution of authority to Christian writings or the relatively rapid rise of certain Christian writings to scriptural status and use during the first three centuries. By the middle of the second century several Gospels and the Pauline letters, as well as a few other documents, had attained broad use and high authority in Christianity. The subsequent formation of the NT canon was therefore not a matter of conferring authority upon selected Christian writings but of clearly delineating the scope of those writings that had, at least for the most part, already acquired broad recognition as authoritative Christian Scripture and thus also of excluding others.

2. The Growth of Christian Scripture and the Formation of Early Small Collections.
The Scriptures of earliest Christianity were those it inherited from Judaism (*see* Hebrew Bible). These included the Torah, the prophetic books and a variety of other writings, though these had not yet come to constitute a canon in Judaism. Nevertheless, the Scriptures of Judaism were fundamental to early Christianity, being read in worship and used as resources of Christian preaching, teaching and practice. No distinctively Christian writings were available in the first decades of Christianity, and only gradually did they come into being. The earliest extant Christian writings are the letters of Paul, composed between A.D. 48 and 58. Other early Christian writings—Gospels, letters, apocalypses and Acts—were composed in the last several decades of the first century, and the production of Christian literature continued apace in the second century (*see* Genres of the New Testament). None of these early Christian writings was composed as Scripture or initially regarded as such. Yet through their dissemination and use, especially the reading of them in services of worship alongside the Scriptures of Judaism, many of them soon acquired a similar religious authority and came to be considered Scripture.

2.1. The Growth of Early Small Collections. It can readily be seen that the NT canon is largely made up of three smaller collections: the four Gospels, the letters of Paul and the General, or Catholic, Epistles. Each of these collections had a prehistory distinct from the formation of the canon as a whole, yet the emergence of these collections is a part of the larger history of the canon.

2.1.1. The Fourfold Gospel. A great variety of Gospel-type writings were produced in the late first and early second centuries, though many of these are now known only fragmentarily or merely secondhand. Beyond Mark, Matthew, Luke and John, we must reckon also with the Synoptic Sayings Source (Q), *Gospel of Thomas, Gospel of Peter, Gospel of the Hebrews,* the "Unknown Gospel" (P. Eg. 2), *Dialogue of the Savior* and *Apocryphon of James,* among others (Koester). All such documents were partial redactions of a rich fund of oral traditions about Jesus that persisted for a time alongside written Gospels and sometimes was preferred to them, until it was finally displaced toward the middle of the second century. Thus the authority that belonged inherently to the words and deeds of Jesus in early Christianity gradually passed from oral tradition to written codifications of it. The various written Gospels were not only collections but also interpretations of the traditions about Jesus, and each has a distinctive character. Each Gospel writer apparently intended his composition to be a self-sufficient, if not exhaustive, representation of the tradition.

As written Gospels came into being, they circulated individually, and it was probably typical at first for any given Christian community to know and use only one. But with the ever wider dissemination of such documents during the second century, Christian communities became acquainted with multiple Gospels, which were then variously compared, criticized and defended. Early in the second century Papias (Eusebius *Hist. Eccl.* 3.39.15-16) knew the Gospel of Mark and possibly the Gospel of Matthew, and he defended Mark against some objections, though he expressed a preference, if not for oral tradition then for firsthand information.

The first Christian writer to show a clear knowledge and appreciation of written Gospels is Justin, who was active in Rome near the middle of the second century. Justin refers to Gospels as "memoirs" *(apomnēmoneumata)* of the apostles and those who followed them (Justin Martyr *Apol. I* 66.3; 67.3; *Dial. Tryph.* 100.4; 101.3; etc.). He apparently knew at least the Gospels of Matthew, Mark and Luke, but he also cited traditions not found in these, and so he was acquainted with a wider body of materials. It is uncertain whether Justin knew the Gospel of John, but he seems not to have used it (Sanders; Hillmer). The Gospel of John was especially favored in the second century by gnostic Christians and Montanists, which may have inhibited its use by others. But reservations about this Gospel must have rested mainly on its far-reaching differences from other, more popular Gospels, and it was easier to neglect or reject it than to account for the discrepancies.

2.1.2. Multiple Gospels. The availability of multiple Gospels was problematic on two counts. First, from the beginning, Christians had used the term *gospel* to designate the fundamental Christian message, which was singular and unitary. When the term began to be applied also to written accounts about Jesus (a development attested by Justin), it was natural to think that there should be only one. Second, Christians regarded the written Gospels as historical records, and therefore the considerable discrepancies among them were found troublesome. These problems made it difficult to acknowledge or to use multiple Gospels.

The desire for a single, self-consistent and theologically adequate Gospel produced two conflicting tendencies in the history of Gospel literature: on the one hand, toward a continuing proliferation of Gospels, and on the other toward a reduction of their number, whether by preferring one to the exclusion of all others or by conflating several into one (Cullmann, Merkel). The signal but not the sole instance of the latter tendency was the *Diatessaron* of Tatian (c. A.D. 170), who wove together the texts of Matthew, Mark, Luke and John and drew also on some additional materials in order to create a single Gospel in place of many. The production of the *Diatessaron* also shows that, although the contents of written Gospels were valued, their texts could still be freely altered. Indeed, the larger manuscript tradition of the Gospels reveals that various additions to and harmonizations among the Gospels were made during the second century (Petersen), so that their texts were scarcely firmly fixed, much less considered sacrosanct.

2.1.3. Limited Gospel Collections. The problem of multiple and to some extent discordant Gospel writings was resolved in another way toward the end of the second century by the creation of a limited collection of Gospels. The first witness to such a collection is Irenaeus, bishop of Lyons in Gaul (c. A.D. 180). He sharply criticized Christian groups that made use of only one Gospel (Irenaeus *Haer.* 3.11.7) and insisted, with the aid of elaborate allegorical warrants, that there could be neither more nor fewer than four Gospels, namely, John, Luke, Matthew and Mark (Irenaeus *Haer.* 3.11.8-9). Irenaeus speaks of the gospel as given "under four aspects" that are mutually complementary, or as having a "fourfold form."

This solution, which was ingenious in preserving the idea of the unity of the gospel while allowing a certain multiplicity through distributive authorship, seems to have arisen in the last decades of the second century (but cf. Skeat). It had not gained any strong foothold in the East, for about the same time in Egypt Clement of Alexandria made frequent appeal to the *Gospel of the Hebrews* and *Gospel of the Egyptians,* while in Syria the *Gospel of Peter* was still in use (Eusebius *Hist. Eccl.* 6.12.2), and Tatian's *Diatessaron* gained broad popularity. Even in Rome the Gospel of John could be drawn into question in the early third century (Epiphanius *Haer.* 51.3ff.). Nevertheless, just such a collection is represented in an early manuscript, P^{46}, dating from the early third century and containing the four Gospels and Acts, and during the third century the fourfold Gospel came into broad use and ultimately displaced all competitors.

2.2. The Pauline Letters. The letters of Paul are not only the earliest extant items of Christian literature but also the earliest Christian literature to be circulated and collected. One or more collections of Paul's letters must have come into being about the end of the first century, for by the early second century Ignatius, Polycarp and the author of 2 Peter were all acquainted with multiple letters of Paul, presumably in collections of some sort. But the early history of Paul's letters can only be inferred on the basis of editions of the Pauline corpus that were current in the second century and later.

2.2.1. Marcion's Edition. The first witness to a full-blown edition of the Pauline corpus is Marcion, about A.D. 140. His edition consisted of ten letters, in this order: Galatians, 1 and 2 Corinthians, Romans, 1 and 2 Thessalonians, Laodiceans (= Ephesians), Colossians, (Philemon?) and Philippians. It has become increasingly clear, however, that Marcion's Pauline corpus was textually and structurally derivative from another (Frede; Dahl; Clabeaux). Notably, with the exception of Galatians, Marcion's order of the letters follows the principle of decreasing length, with letters to the same communities being counted together. But since the principle of decreasing length was not consistently followed by Marcion and had no real importance for him, his edition must have depended upon another for which this principle was constitutive. This earlier and probably original edition of Paul's letters was consistently ordered by decreasing length, counted together letters to the same community, and likewise had ten letters, but in this order: 1 and 2 Corinthians, Romans, Ephesians, 1 and 2 Thessalonians, Galatians, Philippians, Colossians and Philemon. Such an edition of the letters throws emphasis on the number of communities to which Paul wrote, namely, seven churches. This edition must go back to near the beginning of the second century and has a good claim to being the earliest form of the Pauline collection. Several observations support this claim.

2.2.2. A Seven-Churches Edition. An edition of Paul's letters as "letters to seven churches" was responsive to a problem that the early church saw in Paul's letters, namely, their particularity. Since Paul wrote to individual churches about issues of local and immediate interest, it was a question whether and how such letters could be relevant and useful to other churches. It can be seen from the manuscript tradition that early on, probably in the first century, the problem of the particularity of Paul's letters was met by textual emendations that generalized the addressees of some letters (1 Cor 1:2; Rom 1:1, 7; Eph 1:1).

An edition that presented the letters as written to precisely seven churches and thus (since the number seven symbolized universality) to Christendom at large met the same issue but more effectively (Dahl). It may be that a seven-churches edition of Paul's letters is reflected in the otherwise peculiar fact that in the late first and early second century we find two other groups of letters similarly addressed to seven churches: the letters of the Apocalypse (Rev 2:1—3:22) and the letters of Ignatius of Antioch.

2.2.3. Other Forms of Pauline Letter Collections. During the second century other forms of the Pauline letter collection arose. Apart from his own textual revisions, Marcion's edition was probably not of his making. An order like his, placing Galatians at the head, must have antedated him and was perhaps an effort to adapt an order by decreasing length toward a chronological order (Frede). That this arrangement is also presupposed by the so-called Marcionite prologues, which are not Marcionite, indicates that the edition beginning with Galatians was a catholic product, not a Marcionite innovation (Dahl). Far more widespread, however, was a form of the collection presenting the same ten letters of Paul but ordering them individually by decreasing length, thus producing this arrangement: Romans, 1 Corinthians, 2 Corinthians, Ephesians, Galatians, Philippians, Colossians, 1 Thessalonians, 2 Thessalonians, Philemon. The earliest manuscript evidence of this edition is P^{46}, dating to about A.D. 200, in which, however, Hebrews is included after Romans. The epistle to the Hebrews was not an original element of this edition, and in the first several centuries was current mainly in the East (see also below).

2.2.4. The Pastoral Epistles. Like Hebrews, the Pastoral Epistles (1-2 Tim, Tit) do not appear to have belonged to any of the identifiably early editions of the *corpus Paulinum,* and they found no place even in P^{46}. It could be and apparently was objected that because they were addressed to individuals they lacked catholic relevance even more obviously than did Paul's letters to particular churches. Nevertheless, by the early third century they were made an addendum to the community letters and were valued not only for their ostensibly apostolic teaching but also for their practical administrative directives.

2.2.5. Theories About Circulation of Paul's Letters. How Paul's letters to specific churches initially entered into general circulation, became widely authoritative, were collected and edited is largely obscure, and several theories have been offered in explanation of this (Lovering). These theories depend partly on evidence about the shape and substance of second-century editions, partly on the internal evidence of the corpus and partly on general considerations.

A traditional view is that from the outset Paul's letters were highly valued by the communities that had received them, soon came to be exchanged among Paul's churches and then were made available to still other churches. In this way small partial collections could have emerged in different churches of the Pauline mission field until, by a natural process of accretion, all of Paul's letters would finally have been brought together and published as a group. It is problematic for this view that some of Paul's letters were apparently lost (1 Cor 5:9; 2 Cor 2:4) or perhaps fragmentarily preserved. Since the letters were concerned with issues of local and immediate relevance, it cannot be taken for granted that their original recipients would have thought them permanently valuable or that other communities would have taken much interest in them. It can also be objected that the author of Acts evinces no knowledge of Paul's letters, which would be strange if the letters had early entered general circulation.

For these reasons, E. J. Goodspeed proposed that Paul's letters held only immediate and passing interest even for their original recipients, were soon neglected and were rescued from obscurity only by the publication of Acts, which stimulated some admirer of Paul to search out his letters among the churches mentioned in Acts and then to publish them as a collection. This collector, moreover, was thought to have written Ephesians as a summation of Paul's thought and a frontispiece to the collection, which thus consisted of nine authentic letters plus Ephesians. For all its ingenuity, this theory falters on many fronts: that Paul's letters were soon forgotten is no less an assumption than that they quickly gained notoriety; it is unlikely that their retrieval was occasioned by Acts since Acts does not mention the letters; and Ephesians is not a summary of Pauline thought, nor is there any evidence that it ever stood at the head of the collection.

Yet another theory was advanced by W. Schmithals, who proposed that the Pauline letters as we have them are editorial composites of diverse fragments, reworked to incorporate anti-Gnostic polemic and consolidated in a collection of precisely seven letters (1 and 2 Corinthians, Galatians, Philippians, 1 and 2 Thessalonians, Romans) in order to signify Paul's ecumenical relevance. The larger aim of this effort was to provide the church with a powerful weapon in its struggle against Gnosticism by representing Paul as a sternly anti-Gnostic apostle. This theory furnishes a context and motive for the extensive editorial conflations that Schmithals discovers in the Pauline corpus, but few would agree that most or all of the Pauline letters are redactional products, and little patristic or manuscript evidence supports the idea that the initial collection consisted of precisely seven letters.

A far more plausible theory is that the collection of Paul's letters was produced by a Pauline school, a group of persons who acknowledged Paul's authority, valued his teaching and sought to perpetuate, interpret and extend his influence after his death (Schenke). It is argued that such a school may have had roots in the circle of Paul's historical associates and coworkers, who would have taken up Paul's mantle after his death. Its activity would explain why the Pauline corpus shows evidence of some editorial revision in the authentic letters and also contains arguably *pseudonymous letters that are indebted to the authentic letters but seek to interpret and elaborate Paul's teaching in view of post-Pauline circumstances and issues (*see DLNTD*, Pauline Legacy and School).

From the end of the first century onward, Paul's letters commanded wide recognition and use (Rensberger; Lindemann) among Christian communities within and beyond Paul's original missionary field. They were valued not only for their substance, but also because few other writings were available that were certifiably from apostolic figures.

2.3. The General (Catholic) Epistles. The third major component collection of the NT canon comprises the seven letters: 1 and 2 Peter, James, Jude and 1, 2 and 3 John. Eusebius, early in the fourth century, is the first to refer to them as a collection (Eusebius *Hist. Eccl.* 2.23.25, "the seven called catholic"), though Eusebius himself reckoned all the General Epistles except 1 Peter and 1 John as "disputed" (Eusebius *Hist. Eccl.* 2.25.3). In fact only these two appear to have been widely known and used in the second and third centuries (Eusebius *Hist. Eccl.* 3.3.1; 3.39.17; 4.14.9).

During that time the other General Epistles were largely neglected. The earliest use of Jude was made by the author of 2 Peter (2 Pet 2:1-22, incorporating much of Jude 4-16), and it was sparingly cited by Clement of Alexandria, Origen and Tertullian. The first explicit mention of 2 Peter is provided by Origen (*Comm. Joh.* 5.3, disputing its authenticity). Irenaeus quotes from 1 and 2 John (Irenaeus *Haer.* 3.16.5, 8); Clement of Alexandria speaks of 1 John as the "larger epistle," thus implying at least a knowledge of 2 John (Clement of Alexandria *Strom.* 2.15.66);

and Origen apparently knew 2 and 3 John but considered them of doubtful genuineness (Eusebius *Hist. Eccl.* 6.25.10). Little else is heard of 2 and 3 John in the second or third centuries. The collection of seven General Epistles appears to have arisen only in the late third century. It was conceivably formed to document teaching ascribed to primitive apostles, perhaps principally the "pillar apostles" James, Peter and John (cf. Gal 2:9; Luhrmann), and to provide a broader apostolic witness than was offered by the letters of Paul.

2.4. Other Writings. Aside from these three groups, the canon of the NT came to include only two other writings, the Acts of the Apostles and Revelation, each of which had its individual history of reception and use.

2.4.1. Acts. Acts was originally the companion piece of the Gospel of Luke, both being parts of a continuous two-volume work (Acts 1:1), but its separation from Luke occurred early, when Luke was treated as one Gospel among others and eventually incorporated into the fourfold Gospel. The early history of Acts as a separate work is obscure. A knowledge of it seems to be shown by Justin (Justin Martyr *Apol. II* 50.12), but the first clear use of it was made late in the second century by Irenaeus (Irenaeus *Haer.* 3.12.1-15), who appealed to it in proof of the consensus of the apostles and their teaching, and it was cited also by Clement of Alexandria and Tertullian. While its early neglect can perhaps be accounted for by reason of its peculiar literary type, its depiction of the apostolic unity of the early church made it a valuable resource in the struggle against heterodox groups in the late second century.

2.4.2. Revelation. Revelation had an uneven history in the ancient church, even though it makes some of the most explicitly authoritative claims of all early Christian writings. Composed around A.D. 96, it was first clearly mentioned by Justin half a century later (Justin Martyr *Dial. Tryph.* 81.15). Nearer the end of the second century Irenaeus, himself a chiliast, mentioned it frequently. It was apparently well-known in Gaul (Eusebius *Hist. Eccl.* 5.1), and Tertullian knew and used it in North Africa. Thereafter it was widely received and used in the West, although it came under temporary dispute, along with the Gospel of John, because of the appeals made to these writings by Montanists.

In the East, however, Revelation fared less well. Though it was variously used by Melito of Sardis, Theophilus of Antioch and Clement of Alexandria in the late second century, and also by Origen, Revelation was drawn into question about the middle of the third century. A certain Nepos wrote a treatise, "Refutation of the Allegorists," rejecting the allegorical interpretation of Revelation (practiced by Origen, among others) and insisting on a literalist approach in support of a millenarian view. Dionysius, bishop of Alexandria, responded with a treatise "On Promises" (excerpted in Eusebius *Hist. Eccl.* 7.25), in which he persuasively questioned the apostolic origin of Revelation, and thereafter Eastern Christian writers generally rejected it.

2.4.3. Hebrews. Although it was eventually drawn into the orbit of the Pauline epistles, the epistle to the Hebrews had a fate in the West that was in some respects comparable to that of the Apocalypse in the East. Hebrews had been known to Clement of Rome, and possibly to Hermas and to Irenaeus, but otherwise it was neglected in the West until the fourth century. The reason was probably its teaching against the possibility of any repentance after baptism (Heb 6:4-8; 10:26-31; 12:14-17), a view that appealed to moral rigorists like the Montanists and Tertullian but ran counter to the penitential ideas and practices developing in the Western church. In addition, Hebrews had no strong tradition of apostolic authorship even in the East, though there it was variously attributed to Paul (Eusebius *Hist. Eccl.* 6.25.11-14). Thus only in the late fourth century did Hebrews acquire general use and authority in the Western church.

2.4.4. Other Writings. Apart from these writings, many others that were not ultimately reckoned canonical nevertheless attained scriptural or nearly scriptural status in the first several centuries. Among these *1 Clement* was prominent. Irenaeus spoke highly of it (Irenaeus *Haer.* 3.3.3), and Clement of Alexandria called it "a writing of the apostle Clement" (Clement of Alexandria *Strom.* 4.17). Eusebius underlines its persistent popularity by remarking that it "was publicly read in the common assembly in many churches in the old days and in our own time" (Eusebius *Hist. Eccl.* 3.16).

Similarly, the *Epistle of Barnabas* early gained authority, especially in the East. Clement regarded it as a letter of the apostle Barnabas (Clement of Alexandria *Strom.* 2.6; 7.5). The *Shepherd of Hermas,* composed in Rome in the first half of the second century, claimed to be an inspired revelation and was fully acknowledged as Scripture by Irenaeus (Irenaeus *Haer.* 4.20.2), Clement of Alexandria (Clement of Alexandria *Strom.* 1.17.29; 2.1.9, 12) and Tertullian (Tertullian *De Orat.* 16). It was appreciated for its teaching of the possibility of postbaptismal repentance (cf. Hebrews) and came into wide use in the East as well as the West (*see* Apostolic Fathers).

Other writings that gained a good measure of authority and bid fair for recognition as Scripture included the *Apocalypse of Peter, Didache, Gospel of the Hebrews, Gospel of Peter* and *Acts of Paul.* Indeed, some of these writings appear in canon lists of the fourth and fifth centuries and even in some early manuscripts of the Bible.

In sum, a considerable number of early Christian writings, even beyond those mentioned here, were widely reckoned as Scripture in the ancient church and were used as such. Others still had a more limited local or regional currency, and some undoubtedly are no longer known to us. Among all these writings, those that came to be most broadly known and used as Scripture were our four Gospels and the letters of Paul, but they were only foremost among many valued documents.

3. The Shaping of the Canon.

Strictly speaking, the canonical formation of the NT occurred with the creation of closed lists of authoritative writings. Such catalogs apparently began to be drawn up only in the fourth and fifth centuries. While it has been commonly supposed that one such list, the Muratorian Fragment, was created in Rome in the late second or early third century, it is increasingly acknowledged that this list had a fourth-century, Eastern origin (Sundberg; Hahneman). Hence there is a widespread reluctance to use the terms *canon* and *canonical* in reference to the preceding period. At the same time, it has to be recognized that by the beginning of the third century not only had many Christian writings acquired the status of Scripture but also some had been shaped into smaller collections that were effectively closed and definitive, namely, the fourfold Gospel and the Pauline corpus.

3.1. Early Canon Lists. Numerous canon lists survive from the ancient church, only some of which can be mentioned here. Although they are broadly similar, these lists do not all have the same form. Some merely list accepted or recognized writings (sometimes individually, sometimes as groups) without elaborative comments, while others provide descriptions and explanations, and some work, explicitly or implicitly, with more than two categories. And the lists vary in stipulating what writings are canonical.

3.1.1. Eusebius. The earliest discussion of authoritative books that approaches the form of a catalog is provided by Eusebius, bishop of Caesarea, in his *Church History* (Eusebius *Hist. Eccl.* 3.25.1-7), written in the first quarter of the fourth century. Here Eusebius allocates into three categories those early Christian writings known to him that had been variously in use up to his time: (1) the "acknowledged" books (*homologoumena*): the four Gospels, Acts, the letters of Paul (presumably including Hebrews), 1 John, 1 Peter and, "if it seems desirable," Revelation; (2) the "disputed" (*antilegomena*) and "spurious" (*notha*) books: James, Jude, 2 Peter, 2 and 3 John, *Acts of Paul, Shepherd of Hermas, Apocalypse of Peter, Epistle of Barnabas, Didache,* and, "if this view prevail," Revelation and the *Gospel of the Hebrews;* and (3) the "fabrications of heretics," namely, the *Gospels of Peter, Thomas* and *Matthias* and *Acts of Andrew and John.*

This catalog is not clear-cut: there is a manifest uncertainty about Revelation, and the use of the subcategory *spurious* under the "disputed" books likewise indicates a certain fluidity of regard. It was apparently not possible in the time of Eusebius to make a simple division between acknowledged and disputed books. Moreover, the variety of categories and the admitted differences of opinion about which writings belong to them suggest that the use of such categories was relatively new in Eusebius's day and that on many books judgments diverged. Hence with Eusebius the effort to define a fixed list or canon of Christian Scriptures was in its early stages.

3.1.2. Codex Claromontanus. Another important early list is preserved in the Codex Claromontanus, a bilingual (Greek/Latin) manuscript of the sixth century, though the list itself seems to have a fourth-century and Eastern origin. It stipulates as comprising "the holy scriptures" the four Gospels, ten letters of Paul, the seven General Epistles, *Barnabas,* Revelation, Acts, the *Shepherd of Hermas, Acts of Paul* and *Apocalypse of Peter.* The omission of Philippians and 1 and 2 Thessalonians is almost certainly accidental, so that originally this list proposed a canon of thirty writings (or possibly thirty-one, if Hebrews was also accidentally overlooked). However, a scribal mark stands before *Barnabas,* the *Shepherd, Acts of Paul* and *Apocalypse of Peter,* which probably indicates some hesitation about these items by the writer or a later copyist.

3.1.3. Cheltenham Canon. The so-called Cheltenham (or Mommsen) Canon, a stichometric catalog that originated in North Africa about A.D. 360, proposes a canon of twenty-four books (with appeal to the twenty-four elders of Rev 4:10): the four Gospels, thirteen unnamed letters of Paul, Acts, Revelation, three Johannine letters and two letters ascribed to Peter. The addition of the phrase *una sola* ("one only") after the Johannine and the Petrine letters suggests a preference for only 1 John and 1 Peter, and thus it echoes the early tendency to acknowledge only these two among the General Epistles.

3.1.4. Cyril of Jerusalem. Cyril, bishop of Jerusalem (A.D. 315-386), in the fourth of his *Catechetical Lectures* (c. A.D. 350), warns against the use of "apocryphal" or "disputed" writings and provides a catalog of writings that should be read as Scripture. His list includes the four Gospels, Acts, seven General Epistles and fourteen epistles of Paul, for a total of twenty-six books. Notable in this Eastern list is the absence of Revelation. Cyril relegates all others to "a secondary rank" and thus makes a clear distinction between what is read in the churches and what is not.

3.1.5. Athanasius. Importance has traditionally been attached to the canon list set forth by Athanasius, bishop of Alexandria, in his Thirty-ninth Festal (Easter) Letter, issued in 367. Seeking to regularize Egyptian usages and forestall heretical ones, he provided a list of those writings "handed on by tradition and believed to be divine," and his list is the first to name as exclusively authoritative precisely the twenty-seven books that belong to our NT. Athanasius mentions other books that, though not to be read in church, might yet be used by catechumens, namely, the *Didache* and the *Shepherd,* two works that were widely popular in the earlier period. Athanasius's list appears not to have been fully decisive even for Egypt (Brakke), let alone for other regions, and it should be regarded not as the final result but only as an anticipation of the final shape of a still-developing canon.

3.1.6. Epiphanius. Epiphanius, bishop of Salamis in Cyprus (c. A.D. 315-403), provided a catalog of Christian writings in his antiheretical treatise *Haereses* (or *Panarion*) 76.5. Here he stipulates the four Gospels, Acts, fourteen letters of Paul, James, 1 Peter, 1 John, Jude and Revelation. While omitting 2 Peter, 2 and 3 John, this list is remarkable because it includes Revelation, which was unusual in Eastern lists, and because it lists among Christian books the *Wisdom of Solomon and *Sirach, and thus it reckons twenty-six writings as canonical.

3.1.7. Muratorian Canon. The Muratorian Canon, which probably belongs to the same period and was originally composed in Greek, is fragmentary at the beginning, where Luke is mentioned as "the third Gospel book." It must have discussed Matthew and Mark first. In addition to the four Gospels, it lists Acts, thirteen letters of Paul, Jude, 1 and 2 John, Wisdom of Solomon, Revelation and *Apocalypse of Peter,* for a total of twenty-four books, though it is noted that some do not wish the *Apocalypse of Peter* to be read in the church. Explicitly rejected are an epistle of Paul to the Laodiceans and certain unnamed books of heretics. The *Shepherd* is named as suitable for reading, but not in the church. The Muratorian Canon is distinguished from other catalogs by its labored warrants for the various books it approves. The careless Latin translation in which we have it cautions against assuming that the original document is represented with full accuracy.

3.1.8. Gregory of Nazianzus. Two catalogs of canonical books have been transmitted under the name of Gregory of Nazianzus (A.D. 329-389). The first (Gregory of Nazianzus *Carm.* 12.30-39), doubtless written by him, lists the four Gospels, Acts, fourteen letters of Paul and seven General Epistles. Revelation is omitted in the Eastern custom. The second list is not from Gregory but from his contemporary Amphilochius of Iconium (fl. A.D. 380). In his list of "the canon of inspired scriptures" (Amphilochius of Iconium *Iamb. ad Sel.* 7.289-331), he included the four Gospels, Acts and fourteen letters of Paul. Otherwise he allowed that "of the catholic epistles, some maintain we ought to accept seven, and others three only, one of James, one of Peter, and one of John," and that Revelation "some reckon among the scriptures, but the majority say it is spurious." A considerable uncertainty is apparent, and beyond the Gospels, Acts and the Pauline letters, only James, 1 Peter and 1 John belong to consensus.

3.1.9. Church Councils. Catalogs of the NT were also drawn up by church councils of the fourth and fifth centuries. One of the earliest of these was adopted by the Council of Laodicea (A.D. 363), which specified "only the canonical books" as suitable for reading in church. It enumerated twenty-six of these, precisely those in our NT, save that Revelation was excluded. We also have records of two North African councils of the late fourth century that promulgated lists of authoritative books. The Council of Hippo (A.D. 393) and the Council of Carthage (A.D. 397) both named the twenty-seven books of our NT, but, in accordance with the Western disposition toward Hebrews, they speak of "thirteen letters of the Apostle Paul" and "of the same, one to the Hebrews."

3.1.10. Early Manuscripts. Although they are not catalogs, the contents of the earliest complete manuscripts of the NT are instructive about the state of the canon in the fourth and fifth centuries. Codex Sinaiticus, a fourth-century manuscript, contains all twenty-seven writings of our NT, but these were followed by the *Epistle of Barnabas,* the *Shepherd of Hermas* and perhaps some other writings (the end of the manuscript is lost). Codex Alexandrinus, written in the fifth century, also contains all twenty-seven writings of our NT, but after them it has also *1 Clement, 2 Clement* and the *Psalms of Solomon.*

The frequent appearance of catalogs of scriptural books during the fourth century, and their absence before that time, indicates that the question of the precise limits of Scripture, and hence the notion of a canon, arose in this period, just as the variations in the terminology, categories and contents of these various catalogs show that the situation was still somewhat indeterminate and that some points were resolved only at a late date. The recognition of Revelation in the East and of Hebrews in the West was finally negotiated in this period, and hesitations about some of the General Epistles (Jude, 2 Peter, 2 and 3 John) were overcome. But the four Gospels, the letters of Paul and Acts are staple items of all such lists, and this indicates that they had become so firmly established in use and esteem from an early time that no question could arise about their place. Hence by the end of the fourth century there was a very broad, if not absolute, unanimity within the Christian community about the substance and shape of its canon of authoritative Scripture. This is remarkable insofar as there was never any official, ecumenically binding action of the ancient church that formalized this canon.

3.2. Forces in the Formation of the Canon. Because the canonical formation of the NT was only a dimension of the larger life of the ancient church, many forces contributed to it in one way or another. But their significance has been diversely estimated, and often it is hard to determine their particular consequences.

3.2.1. Conflicts with Heterodoxy. It has commonly been claimed, especially by those who regard the second century as the decisive period in the history of the canon (Harnack; von Campenhausen), that the chief forces in the formation of the canon are to be sought in conflicts with heterodox movements, especially Marcionism, Gnosticism and Montanism. Marcion is often represented as the prime mover, compelling the church to create a more comprehensive canon of its own as a counter to his and providing the basic structure of Gospel and apostle, such that the NT canon is seen as "an anti-Marcionite creation on a Marcionite basis" (Harnack). It has been suggested that the Gnostics, who both produced writings of their own and appealed to unwritten, esoteric traditions of apostolic teaching, stimulated the church to create a canon that excluded gnostic writings and furnished instead a broad-based and accessible collection of apostolic writings embodying catholic teaching. And it has been argued that the Montanists, by invoking charismatic authority and offering new revelations, motivated the church to close its canon and limit authoritative revelation to traditional authoritative documents.

But none of these claims is persuasive. The Pauline letters had been collected and were widely valued prior to Marcion, and the dual authority of "the Lord and the apostles" was already well established. Gnostic groups appear to have valued most of the same literature as Christians at large but brought to them different hermeneutical assumptions and methods and so warranted their systems at the level of interpretation. And in response to Montanism the church did not deny continuing manifestations of the Spirit or confine revelation to a fixed number of books. While each of these movements accentuated questions about the appropriate resources, authorities and limits of Christian teaching, there is no good evidence that they had significant, much less decisive, consequences for the development of Christian Scriptures, for the much later definition of the canon of those Scriptures, or for the structure or content of the NT canon.

3.2.2. Use in the Church. To the contrary, in the larger history of the NT canon the primary force was the developing pattern of the use of Christian writings in the early church, and principally their use in the liturgical assembly as resources of preaching and instruction. In drawing up his list of acknowledged books, Eusebius appealed almost exclusively to the traditional usage of those writings in the churches from an early time or to their use by prominent Christian writers such as Irenaeus, Clement of Alexandria and Origen.

In the nature of the case, the force of traditional usage could not come explicitly into play until the third and fourth centuries, by which time the church had some retrospect on its customary practices. Yet it is possible to see that the books that were held in highest regard in the fourth century were those that had been longest and most widely in use during the first three centuries. Statistical studies of the frequency of citation (relative to length) of early Christian writings demonstrates that from the second century onward, the Gospels and the principal Pauline letters were cited with very high frequency, that the other books eventually included in the canon were much less often called into service, and that books ultimately excluded from the canon were used very little (Stuhlhofer).

Thus the NT canon that finally took shape appears fairly to reflect which writings had in the earlier period consistently claimed the attention of the church and proven most useful in sustaining and nurturing the faith and life of Christian communities. To this extent the canonization of early Christian writings did not so much confer authority on them as recognize or ratify an authority that they had long enjoyed, making regulative what had previously been customary. The catalogs of the fourth and fifth centuries are for the most part articulations of a consensus of usage that had arisen through the practices of the preceding centuries, and they aimed to exclude rather than to include.

3.2.3. Other Influences. In relation to some writings, however, the pattern of usage was either unclear or regionally inconsistent, and in these cases other forces came into play. The judgments of prominent Christian thinkers were often influential on the fate of individual books. Athanasius's favorable regard for Revelation was undoubtedly important in repristinating its standing in the East, which had suffered from the criticisms of Dionysius. Similarly, the eventual acceptance of Hebrews in the West, where it had had little currency, depended heavily on its acknowledgment by such figures as Hilary, Ambrose and Jerome.

Moreover, what was at stake in the history of the canon was not merely texts but equally the way they were understood, so that the history of interpretation also played a role. For example, Revelation finally found acceptance in the East only on the presupposition of its allegorical exegesis; earlier the Gospel of John was capable of being accommodated to the other Gospels on the premise that it was a "spiritual Gospel" and not a straightforward historical account; and even Paul's letters had to be read and understood as having catholic relevance, in spite of their particularity.

On a broader level, the literal-historical type of interpretation characteristic of Antiochene Christianity tended to favor a smaller body of authoritative writings, while the allegorical approach that typified Alexandrian Christianity allowed a much larger scope to Scripture. The canon that eventually took shape represents to some extent a compromise among regional usages, including more books than were traditionally recognized in Syria (e.g., all the General Epistles) but fewer than in Egypt (e.g., *Gospel of the Hebrews, 1 Clement, Barnabas, Shepherd*).

Nor are certain events and circumstances in the life of the early church without relevance to the development of the canon. Early on, the relative paucity of Christian writings, especially in small and provincial communities, may have encouraged the use of almost anything that came to hand. In larger Christian centers, the rapid diffusion and local accumulation of Christian writings must have posed questions about which books ought to be used, and how. The experience of persecution sometimes entailed the confiscation and destruction of Christian books by Roman authorities, most notably in the Great Persecution (A.D. 303-305) under Diocletian. The requirement that Christian books be surrendered probably provoked pressing questions in the church about which books were sacred and should by no means be handed over and others which might be given up to imperial agents.

Even the technology of book production had some bearing on the canonical formation of the NT. Early codices were not capacious, normally running to a maximum of about two hundred leaves, and most were much smaller. Christian Scriptures could not be collected and provided together in one volume, and early codices usually contained only one or two documents or a discrete collection. Not until the fourth century was it possible to manufacture codices that could contain many writings, and even then it was rare that whole Bibles (pandects) were produced. In their absence, the importance of lists or catalogs of Christian Scriptures is obvious. Still, any effort to produce a whole Bible or even a whole NT raised the practical issue of what should be included in it. All of these considerations belong, with varying importance, to the formation of the NT canon, but none of them had the fundamental and decisive consequence that followed from traditional use.

3.3. ***Criteria of Canonicity.*** Beyond the historical forces that were at work in the formation of the canon, certain theoretical considerations were also adduced, especially in the fourth and fifth centuries, by way of judging the suitability of writings for inclusion in the canon, most especially of writings about which there was some uncertainty. These so-called criteria of canonicity were mainly traditional use, apostolicity, catholicity and orthodoxy (Ohlig).

3.3.1. Traditional Use. As previously indicated, the primary basis for the inclusion of any document in the canon of the NT was its longstanding, widespread and well-established use among Christian communities. Such traditional usage was a matter of fact before the church began to reflect on its historic practice and made it an explicit criterion for canonical standing. Certain writings, including the Gospels and Paul's letters, had been used so widely and so long that there could be no question about their place in the canon. But if customary use was a clear prerequisite, it was not in every case sufficient by itself. Some documents that adequately met this standard were not finally included in the canon (e.g., *Shepherd of Hermas, Didache* and *1 Clement*). Other criteria were of a more theoretical sort.

3.3.2. Apostolicity. From an early time Christians considered their Scriptures to be apostolic. This did not necessarily mean that authoritative documents must have been written by apostles, though from an early time apostolic authorship was valued. This is shown not only by the general authority that quickly accrued to Paul's letters but also by the development of traditions attributing certain anonymous Gospels (Matthew and John) to apostolic authors or at least to apostolic sources (Mark and Luke) by the use of apostolic *pseudonymity (e.g., 2 Peter, the Pastoral Epistles, *Barnabas*), and by the disuse that affected some writings by reason of doubts raised about their apostolic authorship (Revelation, Hebrews). Yet some documents explicitly claiming apostolic authorship either failed to gain canonical standing (e.g., *Didache, Barnabas, Gospel of Peter, Apocalypse of Peter*) or gained it only with difficulty (e.g., 2 Peter, Jude). Thus the criterion of apostolicity in the narrow sense of authorship was hardly decisive. In fact, the conception of apostolicity was elastic and might refer, beyond direct authorship, to indirect authorship, derivation from the apostolic period or conformity of content with what was generally understood as apostolic teaching.

3.3.3. Catholicity. Catholicity was another consideration: in order to be authoritative a document had to be relevant to the church as a whole and even intended to be so by its author. Writings addressed to only small groups or having a narrow purpose were accordingly devalued. Most of the writings that became canonical were originally intended for limited constituencies, and some even for individuals. Hence they failed to meet this criterion, but this was not so obvious to the ancient church or was counterbalanced by other factors. What is at work in the ideal of catholicity is a preference for broad accessibility and general usefulness, as against private, idiosyncratic or esoteric resources.

3.3.4. Orthodoxy. It was a largely tacit judgment that for a writing to be authoritative, let alone canonical, it must be orthodox; that is, its content had to correspond with the faith and practice of the church as that was generally understood. Such a judgment presupposes that what the church took to be its proper teaching was somehow available independently of Scripture, namely, in the rule of faith (*regula fidei*), a terse, traditional summary statement of principal convictions (cf. Irenaeus *Haer.* 3.4.1-2; Tertullian *De Praescr.* 8-12). Since the rule of faith was itself understood to be a summary of apostolic teaching derived through apostolic tradition, there could scarcely be discord between it and Scriptures that were also taken to be apostolic.

These criteria were variously applied in the history of the canon, but rarely with systematic rigor. The *Gospel of Peter* was removed from use in Rhossus by Serapion, bishop of Antioch, because of doubts about its orthodoxy (Eusebius *Hist. Eccl.* 6.12.2-6), in spite of its putative apostolic origins. The *Shepherd of Hermas,* though catholic, orthodox and widely used, suffered because it did not derive from the time of the apostles (Muratorian Canon, ll. 73-80). The epistle to the Hebrews was ultimately accepted as canonical in the West in spite of persistent uncertainty about its authorship. Once established in general use, the catholic status of Paul's letters was taken for granted in spite of their particularity.

Such examples indicate that the more theoretical criteria of apostolicity, catholicity and orthodoxy were selectively used. Although they may be distinguished in respect of their specific foci, these criteria are closely related. The ancient church assumed that whatever was apostolic, even in the broadest sense, was also catholic and orthodox, and although what was orthodox and catholic might not be apostolic in the strictest (authorial) sense, it conformed by definition to a tradition that was considered apostolic in substance. While they were important as traditional warrants, such criteria were rarely the effective reasons for the positive canonical recognition of any writing. Rather they were employed mainly either to disqualify the authority of certain writings or to warrant the standing that others had attained by reason of established use.

See also APOCRYPHA AND PSEUDEPIGRAPHA; HEBREW BIBLE; LITERACY AND BOOK CULTURE; SEPTUAGINT/GREEK OLD TESTAMENT.

BIBLIOGRAPHY. J. Barton, *Holy Writings, Sacred Texts: The Canon in Early Christianity* (Louisville, KY: Westminster John Knox, 1997); D. Brakke, "Canon Formation and Social Conflict in Fourth-Century Egypt: Athanasius of Alexandria's Thirty-Ninth Festal Letter," *HTR* 87 (1994) 395-419; F. F. Bruce, *The Canon of Scripture* (Downers Grove, IL: InterVarsity Press, 1988); H. von Campenhausen, *The Formation of the Christian Bible* (Philadelphia: Fortress, 1972); J. J. Clabeaux, *A Lost Edition of the Letters of Paul: A Reassessment of the Text of the Pauline Corpus Used by Marcion* (CBQMS 21; Washington, DC: Catholic Biblical Association, 1989); O. Cullmann, "The Plurality of the Gospels as a Theological Problem in Antiquity," in *The Early Church* (Philadelphia: Westminster, 1956); N. A. Dahl, "The Origin of the Earliest Prologues to the Pauline Letters," *Semeia* 12 (1978) 233-77; idem, "The Particularity of the Pauline Epistles as a Problem in the Ancient Church," in *Neotestamentica et Patristica* (NovTSup 6; Leiden: E. J. Brill, 1962); H. J. Frede, "Die Ordnung der Paulusbriefe," *Vetus Latina* 24.2 (Freiburg: Herder, 1969); E. J. Goodspeed, *New Solutions to New Testament Problems* (Chicago: University of Chicago Press, 1927); G. M. Hahneman, *The Muratorian Fragment and the Development of the Canon* (Oxford: Clarendon Press, 1992); A. von Harnack, *The Origin of the New Testament and the Most Important Consequences of the New Creation* (London: Williams & Norgate, 1925); M. R. Hillmer, "The Gospel of John in the Second Century" (Ph.D. diss., Harvard University, 1966); H. Koester, *Ancient Christian Gospels: Their History and Development* (Philadelphia: Trinity Press International, 1990); A. Lindemann, *Paulus im altesten Christentum* (BHT 58; Tübingen: Mohr Siebeck, 1979); E. Lovering, "The Collection, Redaction and Early Circulation of the Corpus Paulinum" (Ph.D. diss., Southern Methodist University, 1988); D. Luhrmann, "Gal. 2:9 und die katholischen Briefe," *ZNW* 72 (1981) 65-87; L. M. McDonald, *The Formation of the Christian Biblical Canon* (rev. ed.; Peabody, MA: Hendrickson, 1995); H. Merkel, *Die Pluralitat der Evangelien als theologisches und exegetisches Problem in der alten Kirche* (Bern: Peter Lang, 1978); B. M. Metzger, *The Canon of the New Testament: Its Origin, Development and Significance* (Oxford: Clarendon Press, 1987); K.-H. Ohlig, *Die theologische Begrundung des neutestamentlichen Kanons in der alten Kirche* (Dusseldorf: Patmos, 1972); W. L. Petersen, ed., *Gospel Traditions in the Second Century* (Notre Dame, IN: University of Notre Dame Press, 1989); D. Rensberger, "As the Apostle Teaches: The Development and Use of Paul's Letters in Second Century Christianity" (Ph. D. diss., Yale University, 1981); J. N. Sanders, *The Fourth Gospel in the Early Church* (Cambridge: Cambridge University Press, 1943); H.-M. Schenke, "Das Weiterwirkung des Paulus und die Pflege seines Erbs durch die Paulusschule," *NTS* 21 (1975) 505-18; W. Schmithals, *Paul and the Gnostics* (Nashville: Abingdon, 1972); T. C. Skeat, "Irenaeus and the Four-Gospel Canon," *NovT* 34 (1992) 194-99; F. Stuhlhofer, *Der*

Gebrauch der Bibel von Jesus bis Euseb: Eine statistische Untersuchung zur Kanongeschichte (Wuppertal: Brockhaus, 1988); A. C. Sundberg, "Canon Muratori: A Fourth-Century List," *HTR* 66 (1973) 1-41; idem, "Toward a Revised History of the New Testament Canon," *SE* 4 (1968) 452-61; D. Trobisch, *Die Endredaktion des Neuen Testament: Eine Untersuchung zur Enstehung der christlichen Bibel* (NTOA 31; Göttingen: Vandenhoeck & Ruprecht, 1996); T. Zahn, *Geschichte des neutestamentlichen Kanons* (2 vols.; Erlangen: Deichert, 1888-92).

H. Gamble

CATENA (4Q177)

This composition, 4QCatena[a] (4Q177), is an eschatological commentary on Psalms 6—17 and a number of prophetic texts. It is dated paleographically to the first half of the first century B.C. and consists of more than thirty nonadjacent fragments, making the material reconstruction of the scroll extremely difficult and tentative. While the editor of the principal edition did not attempt a reconstruction (Allegro, 67-74, pl. XXIV-XXV[a]), this was remedied by J. Strugnell, who offered a partial reconstruction and corrected a number of misreadings in the original publication (236-48, 260-61). The most thorough material reconstruction has been recently proposed by A. Steudel (1992, 1994), who argues on the basis of similar content and style that 4QCatena and *4QFlorilegium (4Q174) make up two different copies of the same literary work, identifying it as 4QMidrEschat[a.b], "A Midrash on Eschatology." While this is possible, the lack of any overlap between the manuscripts remains problematic. (For an English translation roughly following Steudel's reconstruction see García Martínez, 209-11, and for Strugnell's reconstruction see Wise, Abegg and Cook, 233-37.)

The manuscript consists of a series of quotations from Psalms 6—17 followed by their interpretation, hence the original title "Catena" (i.e., a string of interpretations). More properly the composition is a thematic midrash with some parallels with earlier *pesharim (Steudel 1994, 190-92; 1992, 538). The verses from Psalms are cited or alluded to in consecutive order according to the MT Psalter, with possibly two exceptions (Pss 11; 12; 5(?); 13; 16; 17; 6 according to Steudel [1994, 129]; but Pss 6; 11; 12; 5(?); 13; 16; 17 according to Strugnell [236, 245]). The commentary on the psalms is typically introduced by a pesher formula ("its interpretation is"), while quotations from prophetic books, which figure prominently in the interpretation, are typically introduced by the phrase "it is written" (*ktwb*).

The composition itself concerns the last days (*ʾḥryt hymym*), the time of persecution and testing of the righteous before the final judgment when the wicked will be destroyed and the just will be delivered. This period before the end is characterized by the distress and suffering of the children of light on account of *Belial and his agents. As with other "sectarian" writings from *Qumran, the enemies are described as "the community of those seeking easy interpretations" (*ʿdt dwršy ḥlqwt*; cf. **Damascus Document;* **Thanksgiving Hymns;* 4QpNah; etc.). They will rise up and seek to destroy the community (*yaḥad*), but the righteous will be protected and delivered by God's angel of truth. Ultimately good will triumph and evil will perish at the final reckoning. The composition also mentions the coming of the "Interpreter of the Torah" (*dwrš htwrh*). This eschatological figure is also mentioned in 4QFlorilegium and other Qumran writings and may refer to the anointed *priest (or possibly prophet) who will usher in the new and just reign of God.

While the fragmentary state of this work does not allow much elaboration, the general eschatological expectation of the Qumran community as reflected in this document has some affinities to the perspective found in the NT, such as the emphasis on the end times. Moreover, the emphasis on the psalms and their prophetic interpretation is similar to what is found in the NT.

See also FLORILEGIUM (4Q174); PESHARIM.

BIBLIOGRAPHY. J. M. Allegro, ed., *Qumran Cave 4.I (4Q158-4Q186)* (DJD 5; Oxford: Clarendon Press, 1968); F. García Martínez, *The Dead Sea Scrolls Translated: The Qumran Texts in English* (Leiden: E. J. Brill, 1994); A. Steudel "4QMidrEschat: 'A Midrash on Eschatology' (4Q174 + 4Q177)," in *The Madrid Qumran Congress: Proceedings of the International Congress on the Dead Sea Scrolls: Madrid 18-21 March, 1991,* ed. J. T. Barrera and L. V. Montaner (STDJ 11.1; Leiden: E. J. Brill, 1992) 531-41; idem, "Eschatological Interpretation of Scripture in 4Q177 (4Q Catena[a])," *RevQ* 14 (1990) 473-81; idem, *Der Midrasch zur Eschatologie aus der Qumrangemeinde (4QMidrEschat[a,b])* (STDJ 13; Leiden: E. J. Brill, 1994); J. Strugnell, "Notes en marge du volume V des 'Discoveries in the Judean Desert of Jordan,'" *RevQ* 7 (1969-71) 163-276; M. O. Wise, M. G. Abegg Jr., and E. M. Cook, *The Dead Sea Scrolls: A New Translation* (New York: HarperCollins, 1996). T. F. Williams

CAVE 7 FRAGMENTS (QUMRAN)

Unlike the other ten caves, Qumran's seventh cave contained several Greek manuscripts. A sensation was created when it was claimed that some of these Greek fragments were of NT writings. Among these fragments, 7Q1 has been identified as Exodus 28:4-7. 7Q2 has been identified as Epistle of Jeremiah 43—44. In *DJD* 3 (Baillet, Milik and De Vaux) 7Q3-5 are cited as "biblical texts(?)." 7Q6-18, which comprise only tiny fragments, yielding only one complete word among them (the definite article in the masculine dative singular), are described simply as "various fragments."

A decade after the publication of the *editio princeps,* J. O'Callaghan began publishing studies in which he identified several of these fragments as belonging to various NT writings. His identifications are as follows:

7Q4	= 1 Tim 3:16; 4:1, 3
7Q5	= Mark 6:52-53
7Q6.1	= Mark 4:28
7Q6.2	= Acts 27:38
7Q7	= Mark 12:17
7Q8	= Jas 1:23-24
7Q9	= Rom 5:11-12
7Q10	= 2 Pet 1:15
7Q15	= Mark 6:48

O'Callaghan regards the identifications of 7Q4—6.1 and 7Q8 as "certain," the identifications of 7Q6.2, 7Q7 and 7Q9 as "probable" but 7Q10 and 7Q15 as only "possible."

Most scholars have rejected O'Callaghan's identifications, but a few have accepted some of them. His identification of 7Q5 as Mark 6:52-53 has been accepted by F. Rohrhirsch (1990) and C. P. Thiede. However, C. Focant, R. H. Gundry and papyrologists S. R. Pickering and R. R. E. Cook believe these identifications are highly improbable, if not impossible. The identification of 7Q5 is an interesting case in point, for this fragment is larger than the others and the chances of identification are somewhat better.

M. Baillet restores 7Q5 as follows: [2]] . *tōi a* . [. . . [3]]*ē kai tō*[. . . [4] *ege*]*nnēs*[*en* . . . [5]]*thēes*[. The only complete, extant word is *kai* ("and"), while the one restored word is *egennēsen* ("he begat"). O'Callaghan restores it differently: [2] *a*]*utōn ē* [*kardia* . . . [3]]*ē kai ti*[*aperasantes* . . . [4] *Ge*]*nnēs*[*aret* . . . [5] *prosōrmis*]*thēsa*[*n* = "their heart . . . and crossing over . . . Gennesaret . . . they moored (the boat)." This reconstruction is problematical at four points: (1) The letter *ēta* in line 2, which O'Callaghan thinks is the definite article, is more probably an *alpha.* (2) The letter that O'Callaghan thinks is a *nu* in line 2, in order to restore *autōn* ("their"), is almost certainly an *iota* and not a *nu* (so Gundry and others). (3) O'Callaghan must assume that the prepositional phrase *epi tēn gēn* ("to the land"), which in almost all manuscripts of Mark occurs after the participle "crossing over," was not present in 7Q5. (4) O'Callaghan must assume that the letter *tau,* instead of the expected *delta,* was used in the spelling of *ti[aperasantes]* ("crossing over"). The first two problems virtually rule out the identification with Mark 6:52-53, with the second two only lending additional weight to this misidentification.

More recently scholars have identified some of the Greek fragments with the pseudepigraphal work known as *1 Enoch* (*see* Enoch, Books of). E. A. Muro has identified 7Q4.1, 7Q8 and 7Q12 as belonging to *1 Enoch* 103:3-8. E. Puech has identified 7Q4.2 as either *1 Enoch* 98:11 or *1 Enoch* 105:17, 7Q11 as *1 Enoch* 100:12, and 7Q13 as *1 Enoch* 103:15. It is probable that the other Greek fragments are either portions of Greek *Enoch* or other Greek *pseudepigraphal texts. This view is supported by the presence of several *Enoch* fragments found in other Qumran caves.

See also PAPYRI, PALESTINIAN; TEXTUAL CRITICISM.

BIBLIOGRAPHY. M. Baillet, J. T. Milik and R. de Vaux, *Les "Petites Grottes" de Qumrân* (DJD 3; Oxford: Clarendon Press, 1962); G. D. Fee, "Some Dissenting Notes on 7Q5 = Mark 6:52-53," *JBL* 92 (1973) 109-12; C. Focant, "Un fragment du second évangile à Qumran: 7Q5 = Mc 6,52-53?" *RTL* 16 (1985) 447-54; R. H. Gundry, "No *NU* in Line 2 of 7Q5: A Final Disidentification of 7Q5 with Mark 6:52-53," *JBL* 118 (1999) 698-707; C. J. Hemer, "New Testament Fragments at Qumran?" *TynB* 23 (1972) 125-28; E. A Muro, "The Greek Fragments of Enoch from Qumran Cave 7," *RevQ* 18 (1997) 307-12; W. Nebe, "7Q4—Möglichkeit und Grenze einer Identifikation," *RevQ* 13 (1988) 49-52; J. O'Callaghan, "¿Papiros neotestamentarios en la cueva 7 de Qumrân?" *Bib* 53 (1972) 91-100; S. R. Pickering and R. R. E. Cook, *Has a Greek Fragment of the Gospel of Mark Been Found at Qumran?* (PHP 1; Sydney: Macquarie University Press, 1989); E. Puech, "Notes sur les Fragments Grecs du Manuscrit 7Q4 = 1 Hénoch 103 et 105," *RB* 103 (1996) 592-600; C. H. Roberts, "On Some Presumed Papyrus Fragments of the New Testament from Qumran," *JTS* 23 (1972) 446-47; F. Rohrhirsch, *Markus in Qumran? Eine Auseinandersetzung mit den Argumenten für und gegen das Fragment 7Q5 mit Hilfe des methodischen Fallibilismusprinzips* (Wuppertal and Zurich: Brockhaus, 1990); idem, "Das Qumranfragment 7Q5," *NovT* 30 (1988) 97-99; C. P. Thiede, "7 Q—Eine Rückkehr zu den neutestamentlichen Papyrusfragmenten in der siebten Höhle von Qumran," *Bib* 65 (1984) 538-59.

C. A. Evans

CELIBACY. *See* MARRIAGE.

CENSUS. *See* TAXATION, GRECO-ROMAN.

CENTURION. *See* ROMAN MILITARY.

CHILDBEARING. *See* FAMILY AND HOUSEHOLD; MARRIAGE.

CHILDREN IN LATE ANTIQUITY

The life and experience of children in the world of the NT compared with the experience of being a child in the world of the twenty-first century clearly illustrates the difference between the two worlds. The modern understanding of a child and childhood as a special class of society with distinctive cultural worth and values stems from the Renaissance onward. When the word *child* is read in the NT, the understanding is quite different. The focus of this discussion is a brief survey of the role and place of children in late antiquity, second century B.C. to second century A.D., using the following divisions:

1. Children in Greco-Roman Culture and Society
2. Children in Jewish Culture and Society
3. Children in the Life of the Early Church
4. Relevance for the Study of the New Testament

1. Children in Greco-Roman Culture and Society.

There is little direct writing about children in the literature associated with Greco-Roman antiquity. Insights must be gleaned from comments made in the context of another subject. Most of the ancient texts are written by males and by the upper socioeconomic groups. One wonders if the flavor and content of such comments would have been different if they were written by women (mothers) and by the common or poor social groups.

1.1. Role or Place of Children in Greco-Roman Society. It is difficult to articulate the place children held in Greco-Roman society. Their role was defined through the social and economic system. Children were seen as part of the kinship tradition who carried on the family name and business and who provided care for the elderly parents. In religious contexts, children were regarded as innocent, chaste and naive, thus channels or intermediaries for the gods. Children were perceived as unformed adults who lacked reason and thereby required training, which included beating. Plato stated: "Of all the wild beasts, the child is the most intractable; for insofar as it, above all others, possesses a fount of reason that is as yet uncurbed, it is a treacherous, sly and most insolent creature. Wherefore the child must be strapped up, as it were, with many bridles" (Plato *Leg.*, 808D). Children were also valued as individuals, and the many grave epitaphs reveal genuine parental love and affection.

Children were born into households (*see* Family and Household). It was in relation to this social network that children gained their primary identity. Boys were trained to take over headship, and girls were trained to take on the domestic responsibilities. The household would have included the parents, children, possibly extended family members, adopted children, paid servants and slaves. The household would have been presided over by the *paterfamilias,* the eldest surviving male ascendant. At one time the father of the Roman household had absolute rule, even over the life or death of a family member, especially the children, but this ultimate authority was curbed by law in the first century A.D. The father's authority was usually executed and mediated through a family council.

It was a Roman custom to place a newborn on the ground in front of the father for him to inspect. When the father lifted the child it symbolized the child's acceptance into the family (the Latin verb *suscipere,* "to lift up," came to mean "survival"). Weak, handicapped, unwanted girls, or another unwanted mouth to feed, would be left on the ground with the implication that the child should be exposed. Exposure was the practice of leaving an unwanted child at a site, usually a garbage dump or dung heap, where the child either died or was taken by a stranger to be raised, usually as a slave. Such infanticide practices were never sanctioned but never condemned by Roman law (*see* Roman Law and Legal System). Exposure had a long history and was advocated by the philosophers (Plato *Rep.* 460 C; Plutarch *Lyc.* 16.1; cf. Philo *Spec. Leg.* 3.110-119, who condemns the practice).

The next step for the child was the naming ceremony, for boys on the ninth day, for girls on the eighth day. The delay is attributed to the high mortality rate of infants. Many newborns never survived the first week, less than half survived to their fifth year, and only 40 percent lived to their twentieth birthday (Wiedemann, 15-16). Those who lived the first week were ceremonially washed, sacrifices were offered on their behalf, and a name was given. The ritual was called *dies lustricus*, "day of purification."

In the early years, the child was often cared for by a wet nurse. Swaddling was perceived as an important part of training a young child. Weaning usually occurred at 18-24 months and was regarded as the time when children were old enough to receive blows and threats as instruction. When the child was mobile, he or she would be put into the care of a male childminder, a *paedagogus*, often a Greek slave specifically secured for this task. Eventually the minder would take the child to school and stay with the child in order to discipline the child. Though the role of the *paedagogi* was not educational, the child would have learned much from their care, often including facility in the Greek language. Childhood would have included play, with toys like balls, board games, kites, models of people and animals, hoops, wooden swords, and with games like "knucklebone," a game like jacks with bones, and "Troy," a game of one person resisting the pack who tried to drag you across a line. The girls also played with rag dolls and dolls of wax or clay made to look like young women.

1.2. Education of Children in Greco-Roman Society. For centuries *education had two forms; at around age six or seven the Greeks sent children to organized schools with trained teachers, and the Romans based education in the home and assigned the primary task to the parents. In the first century B.C., the Greek practice was adopted throughout the Roman Empire. Among the wealthy, at around the age of seven the male children and a few female children began their formal education, learning writing, reading and basic arithmetic, often combined with physical education. The school day was long, beginning early and lasting into the evening with a break for a midday meal. Flogging was a common practice and was perceived as an important practice to instill discipline. At age twelve those who could afford it, and only males, moved to the second stage; girls continued their education at home learning the expected duties of a female in a household. Under the *grammaticus*, *language, *literature, *music, *philosophy and basic *rhetoric were taught (Cicero, *De Orat.*, 1.187). The next stage began around age sixteen and the teacher was known as the *rhetor*. During this time the rhetorical school would build upon earlier studies, focusing particularly on literature, language and rhetorical skills in order to develop polished public speakers. The very elite finished formal study around age eighteen by studying at a foreign academy. In his work *Institutio Oratoria*, Quintilian, a former teacher (first cent. A.D.), describes this practice of education and calls for the reform of putting the needs of the child as foremost. Other forms of education included apprenticeships in practical skills and crafts, and military training.

More controversial is the education of males at the *gymnasium, which included sports, usually in the nude, and the pederasty which often went with it. The sexual relationship between an adult male and a boy was a Greek practice designed for military training; it later carried over to the gymnasium and then to the teacher and pupil relationship. The practice was not universal and opinions varied about its value, but it was commonplace enough to feature in the childhood experience of many young boys. Corollary to this was the experience of many slave girls and boys who served as child prostitutes.

1.3. Transition into Adulthood. For boys, usually between the age of fourteen and sixteen, the father would take the son to be registered on the list of citizens. This was the first stage in taking on adult responsibilities. Around the same time, at the feast of the *Liberalia* on March 17, a young man and his friends would ceremoniously exchange their *toga praetexta* (white with purple hem) for the *toga pura* (all white), which was a public sign of adulthood. Sometimes this transition period included shaving the boy's first beard and keeping the shavings in a shrine (*depositio barbae*).

Marriage was the primary transition. Legally, girls could marry at twelve, boys at fourteen. But among the wealthy most girls married in their late teens with boys in their twenties; among the more common social classes, marriage was often earlier. Marriage included the ritual of taking off and storing the *bulla*, the good-luck amulet worn around the neck as a child. A girl also would dedicate her dolls to Venus as part of the marriage process. With marriage, for both girls and boys, childhood ended.

2. Children in Jewish Culture and Society.

Sources for understanding the role and place of children in Jewish culture are not numerous. The Bible and other Jewish religious writings give hints of family and social structures, but little direct or extended information. Equally, Judaism was not monolithic, so some social constructs and practices may have varied with different Jewish communities. In addition, differences between life in Palestine and life in *Diaspora Judaism probably affected the experience of children.

2.1. The Role and Place of Children in Jewish Society. The understanding of children must be placed within the context of Jewish identity. The perception of Jewish people as people of a "holy race" (Ezra 9:2), a covenant people, a people of the *Torah, defined community life and shaped the social boundaries. Within this community ethos, children were perceived as a blessing (Ps 127:3-5) and insurance of the nation's perpetuity. Conversely, a woman who was childless was considered barren and shamed (1 Sam 1:10-11; Lk 1:25). The expectation of maintaining the race through procreation was written into the law (Gen 1:28; 12:3). It was the obligation of the parents and the community to teach and pass on the faith to the children (Deut 4:9; 6:7; 11:19; 31:1-13; also Josephus *Ag. Ap.* 2.25 §204). In this context, it is not surprising that infanticide, abortion (Ex 21:22-25) and birth control (Gen 38:8-10) were not practiced and were often condemned (Philo *Spec. Leg.* 3.110-19; Tacitus *Hist.* 5.5).

Once again, the home and family were the primary social structure where children gained their identity. Sons, especially the firstborn, were the guarantee of lineage and the promise of maintaining the family holdings. Levirate law (Deut 25:5-10) ensured that a man's name would continue if he died without children, as the brother was obliged to marry his sister-in-law, with any children of this union regarded as heirs of the dead kinsman. The emphasis on sons and the role of the father reveals the patriarchy of the Jewish culture (cf. Mt 14:21; 15:38).

The Jewish ritual of male circumcision occurred after eight days. It is possible in the first century A.D. that this practice included naming the child (Lk 1:59; 2:21), a practice probably adopted from Greco-Roman culture. Naming the child was an important cultural practice, whether for a girl or boy, and in Jewish culture the practice was to draw upon the family names with the mother selecting but with the father having the final say (Gen 35:18; Lk 1:58-64). Other rituals included presenting the firstborn sons to the Lord and the rite of purification for the woman following childbirth (Ex 13:2, 20; 34:20; Lev 12:6-8; Lk 2:22-24).

Perhaps the key social rule which dominated a Jewish child's perspective was the law, "honor your father and your mother" (Ex 20:12; Deut 27:16). Disobedient or dishonoring children could receive the most severe punishment (Deut 21:18-21). In this light, the training and discipline of children is an important topic in wisdom literature (Prov 13:24; 22:15; Sir 30:1-13). It included beating; in fact, the OT verb "to educate" is *yāsar* which originally meant, "to flog or chastise."

Children also played an important part in the religious life of the home as part of their training. Exodus 13:8 instigated the practice of children asking key questions in the home rituals for the Passover (*m. Pesaḥ.* 10:4). This practice probably carried over into other key festivals and the weekly sabbath. Other home religious practices included citing the *Shema* (Deut 6:4-5) and Deuteronomy 33:4, "Moses commanded us a law, as a possession for the assembly of Jacob."

2.2. Education of Jewish Children. For centuries education was based in the home and was centered around the religious tradition and passing on the family trade. A girl was prepared for marriage, so it was important that her virginity be preserved (Sir 42:9-14) and that she be trained as a competent manager of the household (Prov 31:10-31).

For boys, education was primarily religious education centered on the study of Torah. This began with learning biblical *Hebrew, then reading and memorizing large portions of the Scriptures. Writing was not a required part of this education and generally was learned, if learned, in the apprenticeship of a trade. The next stage was learning the comments and explanations of the Torah by the ancestral teachers of the law. According to the *Talmud, this education began passing from the home to formal schools (*Beth-Sepher*, "the house of the book") in the first century B.C. according to the instruction of Simeon ben Shetah, but was firmly established by Joshua ben Gamla in the first century A.D. It is possible that formal schooling was available at an earlier period (and continued in various forms) at local *synagogues. Boys began this formal schooling at age six or seven. These Jewish schools were probably both a counter to and imitation of the Greco-Roman education system. As such they preserved the cultural distinctive and made possible the description of Paul's Diaspora Jewish upbringing in Philippians 3:5. Nonetheless, many Jewish children received a "Greek" education as well, as is evident in the writings of Paul, *Josephus and *Philo.

2.3. Transition to Adulthood. One of the major rituals for adulthood for boys occurred at age thirteen when they took on the "yoke of the Torah." This signaled the completion of an education process and the assumption of responsibility for further study and observance of the Torah. *Marriage, generally perceived as an obligation, concluded childhood for both girls and boys. It was arranged early and most often occurred in the mid-teens for girls and late teens for boys ("at eighteen a man is fit for the bridal chamber" [*m. ʾAbot* 5:21].

3. Children in the Life of the Early Church.

Evidence of the life of children in the NT is scant. Two aspects dominated the life of children in the early church. First, they continued to live within the cultural patriarchy and the general social structure of the household. Second, they were accepted as part of the Christian community.

In the NT children are generally placed in relationship to the parents in line with the conventional social structures of the day, for instance as in the household codes (Eph 6:1-4; Col 3:20-21; 1 Tim 5:4). Similarly the parental responsibility for the discipline and instruction of children is reinforced (1 Tim 3:4, 12; Tit 1:6; *1 Clem.* 26.6, 8; *Did.* 4.9; Pol. *Phil.* 4.2). The positive regard for children as in the Jewish perspective is also evident in the NT. Paul indicates that children of Christian parents are "holy" (1 Cor 7:14). The value of children as a blessing is continued in later Christian literature, which condemns the practice of infanticide (*Did.* 2.2; Justin Martyr *Apol. I* 27).

What is more surprising is the assumed presence and participation of children in the Christian faith (Acts 2:39) and early Christian gatherings. The record of the growth of Christianity in Acts includes households (Acts 11:14; 16:15, 31, 34; 18:8) and children (Acts 20:9, 12; 21:5). The fact that the epistles to the Ephesians and Colossians includes instructions to children assumes their presence at such gatherings. Since the early church gathered in homes, it may have been natural to include children. Matthew 14:21 (cf. Mt 15:38), "some five thousand men shared in this meal, not counting women and children," a record of the feeding of the five thousand, may be a redactional indication of Matthew's view that the community of faith included women and children; this compares favorably with Paul's comment on children as "holy" (1 Cor 7:14).

4. Relevance for the New Testament.

A survey of children in antiquity provides several insights for the study of the NT (more detailed discussions can be found in *DJG*, Child, Children; *DPL*, Households and Household Codes; *DLNTD*, Household, Family; Sonship, Child, Children). First, it contributes to the overall understanding of the social and cultural milieu as the backdrop against which the NT was written and in which the writers of the NT lived. Second, it provides insight into the instruction regarding children found in the teachings of Jesus and in the epistles, with particular relevance to the household codes. Third, understanding the role and nature of childhood clarifies the use of the words "child," "infant" and related words and ideas as a metaphor for Christian growth or discipleship. In the epistles there is the general perspective that a child represents a stage of development that one is to grow out of (i.e., immaturity) or a state of being that is unrealized potential (1 Cor 13:11; 14:20; Jas 1:6; Heb 5:13; 1 Pet 2:2). In the Gospels children represent an identity to which disciples should aspire and from which disciples should learn (Mt 18:1-5; Mk 9:33-37; 10:13-16). The difference between Jesus' teaching and the epistles is an interesting point of theological and historical reflection. A corollary use is the way Paul (1 Cor 4:14-15; Gal 4:19; 1 Thess 2:11) and the writer of the Johannine epistles (1 Jn 2:1, 18, 28; 3:7, 18; 5:21; 3 Jn 4) portray their relationship with the recipients as father to children, implicitly and explicitly.

See also EDUCATION: JEWISH AND GRECO-ROMAN; FAMILY AND HOUSEHOLD; MARRIAGE.

BIBLIOGRAPHY. S. C. Barton, *The Family in Theological Perspective* (Edinburgh: T & T Clark, 1996); L. deMause, ed., *The History of Childhood* (London: Souvenir Press, 1974); A. Oepke, "παῖς κτλ," *TDNT* 5:636-54; C. Osiek and D. L. Balch, *Families in the New Testament World: Households and House Churches* (Louisville: Westminster John Knox, 1997); H. S. Pyper, ed., *The Christian Family: A Concept in Crisis* (Norwich: Canterbury Press, 1996); B. Rawson, ed., *The Family in Ancient Rome: New Perspectives* (Ithaca, NY: Cornell University Press, 1986); W. A. Strange, *Children in the Early Church: Children in The Ancient World, the New Testament and the Early Church* (Carlisle: Paternoster, 1996); D. C. Verner, *The Household of God: The Social World of the Pastoral Epistles* (SBLDS 71; Chico, CA: Scholars Press, 1983); H.-R. Weber, *Jesus and the Children: Biblical Resources for Study and Preaching* (Geneva: World Council of Churches, 1979); T. Wiedemann, *Adults and Children in the Roman Empire* (London and New York: Routledge, 1989). D. L. Stamps

CHRONOLOGY, NEW TESTAMENT

The study of chronology in the ancient world is highly complex. The major limitations are in terms of the amount of data and evidence available, the relatively few fixed points by which other dates can be set, and the facts that the ancients were not concerned in the same way with calculating and recording time as moderns are and that the means used to record dates are not always clear or easy to use. With few fixed and agreed upon dates to utilize, any attempt to set a chronology requires cautious weighing of a range of evidence, much of it coming from outside of the biblical documents and requiring knowledge of background material. This is the case for the two major sets of dates for the NT, events in the life of Jesus and in the life of Paul (see Porter, forthcoming, on which the following discussion depends).

1. Events in the Life of Jesus
2. Events in the Life of Paul
3. Conclusion

1. Events in the Life of Jesus.

The four major events in the life of Jesus are his birth, the beginning of his ministry, the duration of that ministry and his death. Each of them presents problems for establishing a chronology, much of it related to how the biblical events relate to extrabiblical data (the data are for the most part presented in Donfried; *see DJG*, Chronology).

1.1. Jesus' Birth. The birth of Jesus is inextricably intertwined with three other major events: the death of *Herod the Great, the Lukan/Palestinian census and the visit of the magi. Each of these dates is problematic and must be examined within its larger context of the world of the NT.

The NT says that Jesus was born during Herod's reign over Judea (Mt 2:1; Lk 1:5) and that Herod died while Jesus was less than two years old (Mt 2:15, 19-20). In determining the date of Herod's death, the Jewish *historian *Josephus proves crucial, though not without his own problems. Josephus states that Herod died thirty-four years after putting to death Antigonus (37 B.C.) and thirty-seven years after being appointed king by the Romans (Josephus *Ant.* 17.8.1 §§190-91; *J.W.* 1.33.8 §665). The date of Herod's death would be 4 B.C., if one calculates from 40 B.C. as the date of his regnal appointment (this date is determined through calculations dependent on Roman history, such as the reign of Augustus [*see* Roman Emperors]). Josephus also states that there was an eclipse of the moon the year Herod died (Josephus *Ant.* 17.6.4 §167), calculated for March 12 or 13, 4 B.C. Josephus also says that the Passover (*see* Festivals and Holy Days) that year occurred soon after Herod's son Archelaus assumed the kingship (Josephus *Ant.* 17.9.3 §213; *J.W.* 2.1.3 §10). In 4 B.C., the Passover would have occurred on April 17. Thus, by these calculations (nevertheless, some recent scholarship has argued for a date of 4/3 B.C. for Herod's death; see Kushnir-Stein), Jesus was born before April in 4 B.C.

Other references in the NT make this dating not as straightforward as it appears to be, however. Notoriously problematic is the Lukan/Palestinian census (see Pearson, who marshals and discusses the relevant data below). Luke 2:1-5 states that Augustus took a census before Jesus was born and that Jesus' parents traveled to their hometown, Bethlehem, to be counted. However, no Roman historian mentions a census in around 4 B.C. Luke 2 reports the census as occurring under the governorship of Quirinius, who became governor of Syria in A.D. 6 and took a census then (see Josephus *Ant.* 17.13.5 §355; 18.1.1 §§1-2; *see* Roman Governors of Palestine). In the light of the tension between these two dates, many, if not most, scholars hold that Luke has made an error in his chronology. He may have made several possible errors, including incorrectly identifying the governor of Syria as Quirinius, giving Quirinius the wrong title or fabricating an earlier census that never occurred. Late in the nineteenth century, W. M. Ramsay (227-28) thought that an inscription from Tivoli, now housed in the Vatican Museum, may have identified someone as twice governor of Syria. But the inscription may have been mistranslated, and in any event it does not identify this person, to say nothing of identifying him as Quirinius.

In a situation in which there are clear difficulties in establishing a chronology, one must carefully sift the evidence available. A number of extrabiblical factors not at first apparently germane may help to clarify the biblical references. On the basis of the *papyri from Egypt, it is now recognized that the Romans undertook periodic censuses throughout their empire (*see* Roman Empire). In Roman Egypt, from A.D. 33/34 until 257/258 censuses were taken at fourteen-year intervals. This evidence has been known for a number of years but seems to work against the Lukan account. However, some recently discussed evidence indicates that Egyptian censuses were taken at seven-year intervals during the reign of Augustus and can be established with indirect and direct evidence for the years of 11/10 B.C., 4/3 B.C., A.D. 4/5 and A.D. 11/12 (see Bagnall and Frier).

At the close of Herod's reign, due in no small part to his paranoia over real and/or imagined threats to his power from within his family and strained relations between him and *Rome (leading to his sons not succeeding him as king), there was considerable turmoil in Palestine (see Josephus *Ant.* 16.10.1—11.8 §§300-404; *J.W.* 1.26.2—27.6 §§516-51). Herod's being a client king, and the inevitable difficulties with transition of power in such a context, might well have led Augustus to extend the Egyptian census of 4/3 B.C. or perform one something like it in Judea. The reference in Luke 2:1 would then be the only reference to this census from antiquity. In A.D. 104 Vibius Maximus issued an edict that states that it is essential for all people to return to their homes for the census (P. Lond. III 904.18-27, repr. in LCL *Select Papyri* II 220), thus indicating at least the plausibility of the trip to Bethlehem recorded in the Gospels. B. W. R. Pearson argues that Luke 2:2 (in Greek) may be saying that this was "the previous census, before Quirinius was governor of Syria." In this case, Luke may be using Quirinius's governorship and his census as a reference point. Quirinius's census in A.D. 6 marked Judea's becoming part of Syria, which was traumatic for the Jews, since it indicated the formal end of even the pretense of self-rule. Since much historical study depends upon plausible reconstructions of events, the above factors might well be seen to provide further support for a date of around 4 B.C. for Jesus' birth.

Further difficulty attends the coming of the magi (or astrologers) recorded in Matthew 2:1-12, often introduced in calculations regarding Jesus' birth. They came searching for Jesus, since they had seen a star in the east. This star has been dismissed as a literary artifice in the Gospel account, but a number of scholars have attempted to correlate the literary with the historiographical evidence (see Donfried and Hoehner for suggestions). Halley's comet, which can be seen every 76 years, and would have been visible in 12/11 B.C., seems too early to be taken into account. There is no firm evidence for the positing of some form of exploding star or supernova around 5/4 B.C. The closest one can come to finding a firm phenomenon is the astronomer Kepler's calculation in 1606 that there had been a conjunction of the planets of Mars, Jupiter and Saturn in 7 B.C., which happens every 805 years. Astrology was widespread in the ancient Near East, with special events often seen to accompany the births of significant people (e.g., *Alexander the Great and Julius Caesar). That Herod is reported in the Gospels to have killed children of two years and younger may be related to the difference between when the magi saw the star (possibly in 7 B.C.) and when they appeared in Judea (5/4 B.C.), or it may reflect the paranoia that typified Herod at the end of his life (he had his own sons executed on very slender evidence). The story of the magi, therefore, adds little to estimating the date of Jesus' birth (*see DJG,* Birth of Jesus).

All of this evidence indicates that Jesus was born at the latest in April 4 B.C. and possibly a short while before that, in 5/4 B.C. In the sixth century A.D. a mistake in calculating dates was made by Dionysius Exiguus; this error has not been corrected, thus accounting for the fact that Jesus was not born in the year "0" (there is no year 0 in our B.C./A.D. scheme, which goes from 1 B.C. to A.D. 1).

1.2. The Beginning of Jesus' Ministry. The second significant chronological point in Jesus' life is the beginning of his ministry. This event revolves around three temporal points, each of which presents its own chronological difficulties in the light of extrabiblical evidence: the ministry of John the Baptist, a statement in the Gospels about Jesus' age, and the building of the *temple. Jesus' appearing in the temple when he was twelve years of age (Lk 2:41-51) provides no solid chronological evidence, due to the vagueness of the reference, to say nothing of dispute over the historicity of the event.

In Luke 3:1-2, the beginning of John the Baptist's ministry is directly linked to the fifteenth year of the reign of the emperor Tiberius. Regnal years are important for establishing ancient chronology; however, their calculation is often difficult. In this instance, if the newly instituted Julian calendar is used, the date would be A.D. 29; if the regnal years beginning with Tiberius's own regency are used (the most likely method of calculation), the date would be A.D. 28/29; if the regnal years beginning with Tiberius's co-rule with Augustus are used (11/12), the date would be A.D. 25/26 (this co-regency is disputed). These three schemes assume that Luke calculated dates according to these methods, something that cannot be taken for granted. According to most scholars, the last date, A.D. 25/26, would be too early, although for others the first two dates would be too late. Furthermore, the NT gives no indication regarding the amount of time between the beginning of John's ministry and Jesus' baptism by him. Failing to find a consensus, one can probably accept that the date of around A.D. 28/29 is likely for the beginning of John the Baptist's ministry, with Jesus' ministry beginning at about the same time or very soon thereafter.

A second strand of evidence considers a direct statement in the Gospels about Jesus' age. Luke 3:23 says that Jesus was "about thirty years of age" when he began his ministry. The word translated "about" (*hōsei*) indicates that the figure "thirty" is being used approximately. Reckoning from the date of Jesus' birth in about 4 B.C. would indicate that he began his ministry around A.D. 27, or later since the figure is approximate.

A last indicator of the beginning of Jesus' ministry is found in John 2:13—3:21. While conversing with the Jews in *Jerusalem at Passover (*see* Festivals and Holy Days), Jesus is told that the temple had already taken forty-six years to build (it was not fully completed when the Romans destroyed it in A.D. 70). Josephus says that Herod's rebuilding of the temple began in the eighteenth year of his reign (Josephus *Ant.* 15.11.1 §380; in *J.W.* 1.21.1 §401, however, Josephus dates it to the fifteenth year), the same year that Augustus arrived in Syria (*Ant.* 15.10.3 §354). According to information from Dio Cassius (*Hist.* 54.7.4) Augustus's arrival in Syria can be calculated to 20 B.C. Herod's eighteenth year would thus have been 20/19 B.C., and forty-six years from beginning the temple project would make the year approximately A.D. 28.

These several strands of evidence converge to indicate that Jesus probably began his ministry sometime around A.D. 28/29, when he was about thirty-one or thirty-two years old.

1.3. The Duration of Jesus' Ministry. This is one of the most controversial aspects in establishing the chronology of Jesus' life, in this instance since the Synoptic Gospels and John's Gospel appear to be at odds. The Synoptic Gospels mention one Passover (Mt 26:17; Mk 14:1; Lk 22:1), while John's Gospel mentions three (Jn 2:13, 23; 6:4 [some church fathers may not have had this reference]; 11:55). This apparent discrepancy in the sources has led to various proposals for the length of Jesus' ministry ranging from one to four years in length. Many of the church fathers held to a one-year ministry. Some of them argued this on the basis of John's Gospel, with John 2:13 and 11:55 marking the beginning and ending of Jesus' ministry with Passovers. Those who argue for a three-to four-year ministry for Jesus also base this upon John's Gospel, some advocating an unmentioned fourth Passover between John 2:13 and 6:4.

Much criticism has been leveled against those

who base a chronological reconstruction upon John's Gospel, due to his theological tendencies, which in this view means that he cannot be an accurate historical narrator. Attempts to eliminate any historically based chronology in John's Gospel and explain every reference to Passover in strictly theological terms is, at least in this instance, difficult to accept. The Synoptic Gospels emphasize that Jesus, from the beginning of his ministry, is heading toward Jerusalem. It is understandable that they would not mention more than one Passover so that Jesus' path to the cross is seen to be without diversion. Therefore, it is more likely that Jesus had a three- or four-year ministry, as John's Gospel indicates.

1.4. Jesus' Death. The death of Jesus involves consideration of two important temporal factors: the day of his death and the year. Neither of them is without problems in determining the chronology involved. Again, extrabiblical evidence comes into play in the calculations (see Hoehner).

All four Gospels agree that Jesus was crucified on a Friday (Mt 27:62; Mk 15:42; Lk 23:54; Jn 19:31, 42), before the beginning of the *sabbath, and that it was the time of the Passover, which occurs on Nisan 15 (they also agree that Jesus was resurrected on the third day, that is, Sunday). Furthermore, the Synoptic Gospels depict Jesus as eating a Passover-like meal (the Last Supper) with his disciples on the night before he was crucified (Mt 26:17-35; Mk 14:12-25; Lk 22:7-38). There is some question whether the Synoptics may consider the day of unleavened bread as the day before the Passover (Mt 27:62; Mk 14:12; Lk 23:54). In the Synoptics, Jesus' arrest, trial and crucifixion apparently take place on Passover (Nisan 15), the day before the sabbath. John's Gospel, however, portrays the situation differently, with Jesus eating the Last Supper on the day before the Passover (Jn 19:14, 16), that is, the day of preparation (Nisan 14), the same day on which he was killed, and also the day before the sabbath.

Numerous attempts have been made to reconcile these apparent discrepancies between the Synoptic Gospels and John's Gospel. Of the proposals with some likelihood of being correct, the following merit mention. Some scholars have proposed that Mark, who was followed by Matthew and Luke, made a mistake in linking the Last Supper with the Passover meal. Others contend that there was a private pre-Passover meal celebrated by Jesus and his disciples. Still others believe that the Passover was celebrated on several successive days because of the large numbers of animals to be slaughtered. It has been proposed that there were two different calendars in operation, according to region or religious association. The *Qumran community may have followed a solar calendar, rather than the lunar calendar followed by other Jews. There is no evidence, however, that Jesus and his followers used the Qumran calendar, which is required for this theory. Lastly, some have proposed that what constituted a day was calculated differently, with some calculating from sunrise to sunrise (in this instance, the Synoptic Gospels, Galileans and *Pharisees) and others from evening to evening (John's Gospel, Judeans and *Sadducees). This last proposal provides a means of harmonizing the Gospel accounts. On the basis of John's Gospel and possible ambiguity in the Synoptics, many scholars contend that Jesus was crucified on Friday, Nisan 14, the day before the Passover. There is no scholarly consensus on this issue, however.

Not only the day but also the year of Jesus' death is the subject of disagreement. Determining the year of Jesus' death is also dependent upon what one determines for the day of his death, since the factors to consider are years when Nisan 14 falls on a Friday and the time when the people involved in Jesus' death were in office. Although Herod Antipas, tetrarch of Galilee and Perea from 4 B.C. to A.D. 39 (Lk 23:6-12; Josephus *Ant.* 18.7.1-2 §§240-56; 19.8.2 §351), and Caiaphas, high *priest from A.D. 18 to 37 (Mt 26:3, 57; Jn 11:49-53; 18:13-14; Josephus *Ant.* 18.2.2 §35; 18.4.3 §§90-95), are important people in terms of Jesus' death, the most important is Pontius Pilate, prefect of Judea from A.D. 26 to 36 (Mt 27:2-6; Mk 15:1-15; Lk 23:1-25; Jn 18:28-19:16; Acts 3:13; 4:27; 13:28; Josephus *Ant.* 18.4.2 §89). The years of A.D. 27, 30, 33 and 36 are theoretical possibilities for Nisan 14 falling on a Friday during Pilate's tenure. However, A.D. 27 is too early and A.D. 36 is too late for Jesus' death, according to the calculations above. Scholars who argue for a shorter ministry of Jesus tend to believe that Jesus was killed in A.D. 30, while scholars who argue for a longer ministry of Jesus favor his being killed in A.D. 33.

2. Events in the Life of Paul.

Determining the chronology of the life of Paul

involves examination of three major sets of data: the book of Acts, Paul's letters and extrabiblical people and events (*see DPL,* Chronology of Paul). Since Acts may well have been written by someone closely associated with the early Christian missionary movement and who may have known and even traveled with Paul, and since Paul's letters were not written with historical chronology in mind, the distinction often made between Acts as a secondary source and Paul's letters as primary sources is overdrawn. All of the available data must be seriously weighed (the data are presented in Donfried and esp. *DPL,* Chronology of Paul).

*2.1. **The Book of Acts.*** Acts provides the following sequentially listed information regarding the chronology of the early church. First are the stoning of Stephen, at which Paul is a "young man" (Acts 7:58; possibly indicating birth in A.D. 5 to 15); Paul's conversion, stay in Damascus and dramatic escape (Acts 9:1-25; cf. 22:5; 26:12); Paul's first trip to Jerusalem and then to Tarsus and *Antioch (Acts 9:26-30; 11:25-26); his second trip to Jerusalem, bringing famine relief from Antioch (Acts 11:27-30; 12:25). Next are Paul's and Barnabas's first missionary journey, from Antioch to Cyprus to Perga to *Pisidian Antioch to Iconium to Lystra to Derbe and back through the cities of Roman *Galatia to Antioch (Acts 13:1—14:28) and Paul's third trip to Jerusalem, for the so-called Jerusalem council, and then back to Antioch (Acts 15:1-35).

Then comes Paul's second missionary journey, from Antioch to Syria and Cilicia, passing through Phrygia and Galatia, to Troas to *Philippi to *Thessalonica to Berea to *Athens to *Corinth to *Ephesus to *Caesarea (then probably to Jerusalem) to Antioch (Acts 15:35—18:22; some scholars put the events of Acts 18:18—19:20 together; however, in Acts Antioch marks the point of termination and beginning for the Pauline journeys; see Porter 1999). Next in sequence are Paul's third missionary journey from Antioch through Galatia and Phrygia to Ephesus to *Macedonia to *Greece to Macedonia (Philippi) to Troas to Miletus to Tyre to Caesarea (Acts 18:23—21:16) and Paul's final (either his fourth or fifth) trip to Jerusalem, with a visit to the temple, arrest, hearing before the Sanhedrin (Acts 21:17—23:10). Paul then is imprisoned for two years in Caesarea under Felix and Festus, a time that includes his hearing before Festus and Agrippa (Acts 23:12—26:32). Finally Paul journeys to Rome and is imprisoned there for two years (Acts 27:1—28:31).

Despite what appears to be a well-ordered chronology, it is extremely difficult to establish the amounts of time that each event in Acts took, since the book of Acts has only infrequent references to durations of time (see Acts 11:26; 14:3, 28; 18:11; 19:8, 10, 22; 20:3; 24:2, 7; 28:30; see Alexander, 119).

*2.2. **Paul's Letters.*** Paul's letters, especially Galatians 1—2, provide the following chronology. Since these events are reconstructed from the individual letters, there is substantial disagreement by scholars. These events include Paul's conversion (Gal 1:12-16), his stay in Arabia and his return to Damascus (Gal 1:17). "Then after three years" from either his conversion or his return to Damascus (these events may have been close in time), Paul first travels to Jerusalem for fifteen days (Gal 1:18-20) and stays in Syria and Cilicia (Gal 1:21-24). "Then through the interval of fourteen years" from either his conversion or his stay in Syria and Cilicia (in other words, fourteen years total or fourteen years added to the first three), he travels again to Jerusalem to confer with Peter (Gal 2:1-10), and there is the incident at Antioch with Peter (Gal 2:11-14), although some scholars think this occurred before the second trip to Jerusalem.

There are hints of a first missionary journey to Macedonia and Achaia (Greece), involving visits to Philippi, Thessalonica and Athens (1 Thess 1:8; 3:1; cf. Phil 4:15-16); Paul's stay in Ephesus, where he suffered some affliction (2 Cor 1:8-11), before his going to Troas and then to Macedonia (1 Cor 16:8-9; 2 Cor 2:12-13); and a clear reference to what was probably a later Macedonian (Philippian) and Achaian (Greece) missionary journey, with the intention of gathering a collection to take to Jerusalem before heading to Spain by way of Rome (1 Cor 16:1-9; 2 Cor 8—9; Rom 15:19-32).

Apart from the two references in Galatians (Gal 1:18; 2:1), there are no specific temporal indicators in Paul's letters. Thus the above list offers a likely chronological arrangement of the events. It is possible that the hinted-at first missionary journey occurred before the second trip to Jerusalem, however, since 1 Thessalonians does not mention the Jerusalem visit. The sequencing of Galatians 1—2 makes this unlikely, however.

*2.3. **Extrabiblical People and Events.*** There are

at least eight extrabiblical points of chronological reference that scholars cite as having possible bearing on the Pauline chronology. However, each one of these has debatable interpretations, which can only be mentioned in passing (see Alexander, 120; Ogg; and Jewett on most of these).

The first concerns when Aretas was king of Damascus. In 2 Corinthians 11:32-33, Paul mentions that the ethnarch of Aretas was guarding Damascus. There are several critical questions regarding this incident, however. One is a dispute over the date of Aretas's death, with the range being somewhere between A.D. 38 and 40; another is the date at which Aretas took control of Damascus, with this possibly occurring as late as A.D. 37 on the accession of the emperor Caligula; and a third is whether this passage requires that Aretas was in control of Damascus at the time. This event may indicate that Paul's escape took place between A.D. 37 and 38-40, although it may indicate that it took place before A.D. 38-40 (see Riesner, 75-89).

The second concerns Agabus. Acts 11:28 says that a prophet named Agabus foretold a great famine, which took place during the reign of the emperor Claudius (A.D. 41 to 54). Scholars have discussed a number of possible dates for this famine, ranging from A.D. 45, 46 or 48 to after 51. Others have disputed that there was a famine, and certainly that there was a worldwide one (see Suetonius *Claudius* 18; Tacitus *Ann.* 12.43). A further difficulty with this account providing information for the time of the second Jerusalem trip is that the prophecy may have been given well in advance of the famine.

The third point of reference is Acts 12:20-23 and the death of Herod Agrippa I in 44 (see Josephus *Ant.* 19.9.5 §§343-52). Acts places this event between the story of Peter in Acts 12:1-19 and the summative statement of Acts 12:24 and resumption of Paul's story in Acts 12:25. It is difficult to establish the exact chronological relation of these events, although it is likely that the sequence is correct, with the first missionary journey being after Herod Agrippa's death.

The fourth event is the proconsulship of Cyprus by Sergius Paulus in Acts 13:7. Several inscriptions link a Sergius Paulus with Cyprus (Ogg, 60-65), but information regarding the identification of this Sergius Paulus and his dates is lacking (see Riesner, 137-46).

The fifth significant event is the expulsion of the Jews from Rome. Acts 18:2 refers to the emperor Claudius having commanded all the Jews to leave Rome, and Suetonius (*Claudius* 25.4), the second-century Roman historian, describes the expulsion of Jews from Rome who were causing disturbances at the instigation of a certain *Chrestus* (it is not certain that this is a reference to Christ). In neither case is a date given for the expulsion. The traditional date ascribed is A.D. 49, which is established on the basis of a statement by the fifth-century church historian Orosius (7.6.15), linking the expulsion to the ninth year of Claudius's reign (49). Dio Cassius states (*Hist.* 60.6.6) that, because of their large numbers, expulsion of the Jews was not possible during Jewish uprisings in A.D. 41. Nevertheless, the alternative date of A.D. 41 has been proposed due to the questionable reliability of Orosius's information and the possibility of harmonizing Dio Cassius's statement with Acts, with the expulsion involving only some Jews (e.g., Lüdemann, 164-71; Slingerland; contra Riesner, 157-201).

There are several consequential effects of shifting the date of the expulsion of the Jews from A.D. 49 to 41. The earlier date suggests an early date for Paul's first visit to Corinth but would also require a second visit to Corinth during the time of Gallio's proconsulship (discussed below), possibly either just before or just after the Jerusalem council. Acts 18 also provides some evidence of conflation of accounts, because Acts 18:8 refers to Crispus and Acts 18:17 to Sosthenes as the ruler of the synagogue. The later date, still probably the best estimation, suggests that Acts 18 records a single visit to Corinth during the time of Gallio.

Gallio's proconsulship is the sixth event to note. According to Acts 18:12, Paul was dragged by Jews in front of Gallio, the proconsul of Achaia. The fragmentary Gallio inscription, found at Delphi, records an edict by Claudius referring to Gallio as proconsul (*see* Inscriptions and Papyri: Greco-Roman). On the basis of this inscription and other inscriptions that establish the date of this one (see Ogg, 104-11), as well as the fact that proconsuls served one-year terms (except under unusual circumstances), it is possible to date Gallio's term of office to A.D. 51/52. Some scholars have recently doubted the certainty of this date, but they have not provided plausible alternatives. Whether Paul was in Corinth for the first time or not, it appears that he had arrived there by A.D. 51 or 52 (see Riesner, 202-11).

The seventh event is Paul's appearance before Ananias the high priest in Acts 23:2 and 24:1. Appointed in A.D. 47, Ananias was sent to Rome in A.D. 52 as the result of a dispute between the Jews and *Samaritans, but he was probably restored to power when Claudius ruled in favor of the Jews. He continued in that office until he was replaced, probably in A.D. 59 (see Josephus *Ant.* 20.6.2-3 §§128-36; *J.W.* 2.12.6 §§241-44), thus overlapping with Paul's imprisonment first in Jerusalem and then in Caesarea.

The final episode involves Paul's being in Roman custody (Acts 23:24—26:32). Paul was in the procurator Felix's custody for two years (Acts 24:27), before the procurator Festus succeeded him. Within a matter of days after his arrival in Palestine, so Acts says, Festus was persuaded in Jerusalem to put Paul on trial, whereby Paul appealed to Caesar. Then, a few days later, when King Herod Agrippa II visited Caesarea, Paul appeared before him. Josephus indicates that Felix took up his procuratorship in A.D. 52 or 53 (*J. W.* 2.12.8 §247; *Ant.* 20.7.1 §137). There is some dispute over when his term came to an end, however. Many biblical scholars argue for a date around A.D. 55, but classical scholars tend to argue for a later date. The early date is based on the notion that Felix's brother, Pallas, the wealthy and highly influential treasurer of Claudius (see Suetonius *Claudius* 28), when he fell out of favor with Nero in A.D. 55, must have immediately lost his power and with it his ability to keep Felix in power. However, there is also evidence (e.g., Tacitus *Ann.* 13-14) that Pallas retained much power, until he was poisoned by Nero in A.D. 62. This scenario is compatible with Josephus's account, in which it appears that Felix remained in power and quite active under Nero (Josephus *J.W.* 2.13.1-7 §§250-70). The exact date for Festus's succeeding Felix, however, is still disputed. Estimates range from A.D. 56 on the basis of the Latin translation of Eusebius's *Chronicle* (2.155) to A.D. 58 to 61. It is plausible that Festus assumed his position as procurator sometime around A.D. 59.

2.4. Creating a Plausible Pauline Chronology. Several different plausible and justifiable Pauline chronologies can be created on the basis of the evidence presented above. Alternative timelines can be found in other scholarly sources (see the bibliography), but the following is one plausible reconstruction. What is significant from my standpoint is that the scenarios from Acts and the Pauline letters have a surprisingly high degree of harmony. Nevertheless, not all of the data fit equally well, as the several disputed items treated above indicate.

Paul was probably converted in A.D. 33 or 34, after which he stayed for three years in Arabia and Damascus, before visiting Jerusalem in A.D. 37 for the first time. After approximately ten more years (Gal 2:1 probably indicates fourteen years after his conversion), Paul made his famine visit to Jerusalem (Acts 11:28-30; probably to be equated with Gal 2:1-10). The first missionary journey was then from A.D. 47 to 48, and the Jerusalem council of Acts 15 in A.D. 49. This order, which follows Acts, is not incompatible with the Pauline chronology established by his letters. The second missionary journey (first Macedonian and Achaian visit noted above) lasted from A.D. 49 to 52 and the third (second Macedonian and Achaian visit noted above) from A.D. 53 to 57. Paul was arrested in Jerusalem and imprisoned in Caesarea from A.D. 57 to 59. In A.D. 59, after Festus became proconsul, he was sent to Rome, where he was imprisoned until A.D. 62, and he may well have died there.

At this point, Acts states nothing further about a Pauline chronology. The Pastoral Epistles, as well as evidence from the church fathers, suggest that Paul may have been released in A.D. 62, traveled for two years in the Mediterranean, possibly went west to Spain, and then was arrested and killed in Rome in A.D. 64 or 65 under the persecution of Nero.

3. Conclusion.

Like few other areas of NT study, the establishment of a NT chronology is directly dependent on a range of extrabiblical evidence (see Bickerman). However, in this case, the extrabiblical evidence is in many instances as problematic and subject to interpretation as is the evidence from the NT. Nevertheless, for those interested in historical questions, including establishing the background against which the NT was written, establishing a plausible and workable NT chronology is an important and necessary task. The result is that a careful process of weighing all of the available evidence and reconstructing and evaluating the various plausible scenarios is a vital task of the NT interpreter. Even if the resulting chronology is tentative at many points and subject to further evaluation on the basis of either new evidence or reassessment of the existing evidence, it provides a useful framework for much interpretation of the rest of the NT account.

See also INSCRIPTIONS AND PAPYRI: GRECO-ROMAN; JEWISH HISTORY: ROMAN PERIOD; JOSEPHUS: VALUE FOR NEW TESTAMENT STUDY; ROMAN GOVERNORS OF PALESTINE.

BIBLIOGRAPHY. L. C. A. Alexander, "Chronology of Paul," *DPL* 115-23; R. S. Bagnall and B. W. Frier, *The Demography of Roman Egypt* (Cambridge: Cambridge University Press, 1994); E. J. Bickerman, *Chronology of the Ancient World* (2d ed.; Ithaca, NY: Cornell University Press, 1980); K. P. Donfried, "Chronology: New Testament," *ABD* 1:1011-22; H. W. Hoehner, "Chronology," *DJG* 118-22; R. Jewett, *Dating Paul's Life* (London: SCM, 1979); A. Kushnir-Stein, "Another Look at Josephus' Evidence for the Date of Herod's Death," *Scripta Classica Israelica* 14 (1995) 73-86; G. Lüdemann, *Paul, Apostle to the Gentiles: Studies in Chronology* (Philadelphia: Fortress, 1984); G. Ogg, *The Chronology of the Life of Paul* (London: Epworth, 1968); B. W. R. Pearson, "The Lukan Censuses, Revisited," *CBQ* 61 (1999) 262-82; S. E. Porter, "New Testament Chronology," in *Eerdmans Dictionary of the Bible,* ed. D. N. Freedman (Grand Rapids, MI: Eerdmans, forthcoming); idem, *The Paul of Acts: Essays in Literary Criticism, Rhetoric, and Theology* (WUNT 115; Tübingen: Mohr Siebeck, 1999); W. M. Ramsay, *Was Christ Born in Bethlehem?* (Minneapolis: James Family Publishing, 1978 [1898]); R. Riesner, *Paul's Early Period: Chronology, Mission Strategy, Theology* (Grand Rapids, MI: Eerdmans, 1998); H. D. Slingerland, *Claudian Policymaking and the Early Imperial Repression of Judaism at Rome* (Atlanta: Scholars Press, 1997).

S. E. Porter

CICERO

Marcus Tullius Cicero (106-43 B.C.) was the dominant statesman of the Roman republic in the turbulent years of the first century, which witnessed the demise of the traditional constitution and the transition to imperial dictatorship.

1. Political Career
2. Works and Influence
3. On the Jews

1. Political Career.

Although he was a *novus homo* ("new man," not of the nobility) from Arpinum, Cicero won election to the consulship (63 B.C.) mostly through *auctoritas,* gained by his eloquence in the courts (Cicero *Quinct.; Rosc. Am; Div. in Caecil; Verr*). As consul, he exposed the conspiracy led by Cataline, and after compelling Cataline to leave Rome, he executed the conspirators without trial. This victory, which earned him the title *pater patriae* ("father of the fatherland"), resulted ironically in his exile instigated by his enemy Publius Clodius (58 B.C.). Upon his recall a year later, he led the opposition to Caesar, and after the dictator's death (44 B.C.) Cicero vehemently opposed Mark Antony (Plutarch *Cic.* 1.1-12). Often criticized as necessarily pragmatic in the temporary alliances he formed with Caesar, Pompey and Octavian (*see* Roman Emperors), Cicero remained the staunchest guardian of senatorial authority until the vengeful Antony ordered his head and hands nailed to the rostra (Plutarch *Cic.* 48—49; Seneca *Contr.* 7.2; Seneca *Suas.* 17).

2. Works and Influence.

The Ciceronian legacy is political, but more so literary. He delivered more than 150 speeches (58 extant), wrote 800 letters and authored more than 25 titles on philosophy, rhetoric and religion. The breadth, excellence and profundity of his work are the mark of a keen intellect and a mind of boundless energy. The quantity alone necessitates that most histories on the late Republic are dependant on Cicero, and he has greatly influenced the NT environment, especially its *rhetoric and *philosophy. Ciceronian rhetoric is persuasion based foremost on *ethos,* the character of the *bonus orator* (Cicero *De Orat.* 2.182-84). There is a moral position that can and should be defended, and this is the prevalent voice of the Gospels and Pauline letters (*see* Rhetoric), as well as the church fathers, most notably Augustine, Jerome and Ambrose.

3. On the Jews.

One year before his exile (59 B.C.), Cicero defended Valerius Flaccus against the charge, among others, of stealing gold that the Jews in his Asian province (62/61 B.C.) were sending to the *temple in Jerusalem. Cicero denied the theft: all the gold, although some was refused shipment, could be accounted for. This was not, however, Cicero's main defense; in typical fashion he contrasted the *auctoritas* of his defendant with the unreliability of the complainants. Whereas Flaccus was following a precedent of the Senate and was acting for the Republic, the Jews, whose notorious *superstitio* often contradicted Rome, were known to band together for political attacks (Cicero *Flac.* 66-69). Although Cicero's caricature may well have been overstated for effect (as was the preceding description of the Greeks), its success relied on the common assumptions held by the jury, and it is evidence that already by the first century Jews, specifically their religious practices and the cohesiveness of their culture, were considered hostile to Rome. Cicero concludes, as Roman religion demands, that Jerusalem's capture and subjugation signaled the gods' rejection of the Jewish nation. Flaccus was acquitted.

See also JEWISH HISTORY: ROMAN PERIOD; PHILOSOPHY; RHETORIC.

BIBLIOGRAPHY. D. R. S. Bailey, *Cicero* (London: Gerald Duckworth, 1971); S. F. Bonner, *Roman Declamation in the Late Republic and Early Empire* (Liverpool: University of Liverpool, 1969); M. L. Clarke, *Rhetoric at Rome: A Historical Survey* (London: Cohen and West, 1953); W. K. A. Drumann (rev. P. Groebe), *Geschichte Roms in seiner Ubergange von der republikanischen zur monarchischen Verfassung oder Pompejus, Caesar, Cicero und ihre Zeitgenossen nach Geschlectern und genealogischen Tabellen* (Berlin: Gebruder Borntrager, 1929); E. Fantham, *Roman Literary Culture from Cicero to Apuleius* (Baltimore: Johns Hopkins University Press, 1996); A. M. Fiske, "Hieronymus Ciceronianus," *TAPA* 96 (1965) 119-38; M. Gelzer, "M. Tullius Cicero (als Politiker)," *RE* 7A (1939) 827-1091; W. L. Grant, "Vir Bonus," *CJ* 38 (1941-42) 472-78; C. Habicht, *Cicero the Politician* (Baltimore: Johns Hopkins University Press, 1990); G. A. Kennedy, *New Testament Interpretation Through Rhetorical Criticism* (Chapel Hill: University of North Carolina Press, 1984); H. J. Leon, *The Jews of Ancient Rome* (Philadelphia: Jewish Publication Society of America, 1960); P. MacKendrick, *The Philosophical Books of Cicero* (New York: St. Martin's, 1989); J. May, *Trials of Character: The Eloquence of Ciceronian Ethos* (Chapel Hill: University of North Carolina Press, 1988); P. Schäfer, *Judeophobia: Attitudes to the Jews in the Ancient World* (Cambridge, MA: Harvard University Press, 1997); R. Syme, *The Roman Revolution* (Oxford: Oxford University Press, 1939).

T. S. Johnson

CIRCUSES AND GAMES

The festivals, races and games of the circus held a place of prominence in Greco-Roman life. The social, religious and political functions of the place and its events formed an integral and often central part of the culture and context into which the New Testament authors communicated the Christian faith.

1. Definitions and Description
2. Games and Worship
3. Games and New Testament Analogies

1. Definitions and Description.

Circus is the Latin word referring to the oval-shaped grounds designed and sanctified for public festivals and for hosting chariot races. The typical circus consisted of a narrow, elongated racing track encircled with seating for spectators and enclosed at one end by stables and at the other by a semicircular stadium for additional seating. Any definition for games in the Greco-Roman world at the turn of the Christian era should take into account the two traditions in which the events participated, namely, the Greek *athletic games and the Roman festivals. The Roman religious festivals (*ludi,* frequently translated as "games") were events regularly given in the circus by magistrates and funded by the state treasury. The number of such festivals filling the Roman calendar year increased in the first centuries B.C., and by the time of Augustus (*see* Roman Emperors) seven annual state *ludi* took up sixty-five days (thirteen for chariot racing and forty-eight for theatrical festivals). In addition to the regular games, votive games, following a triumph (*see* Roman Triumph), were given as a thank offering to the gods for a recent military victory.

1.1. Locations. The grandest circus was the Circus Maximus, allegedly founded by the Roman king Tarquinius Priscus (616-579 B.C.) (Livy *Hist.* 1.35) and restored by Julius Caesar (Pliny *Nat. Hist.* 36.102). It was situated just south of the center of *Rome and could seat more than two hundred thousand people. Due to the enormous expense of chariot racing and games as well as the building costs, only the major cities in the provinces could afford circuses. There were famous sites at *Antioch, *Alexandria, Merida and Urso in Spain, and later at Constantinople. Often a combination of private and public funds was required to finance the smaller-scale shows in the provincial cities.

1.2. Events. Chariot racing was developed in the Greek world as a nonviolent form of competition between aristocrats and their cities. Along with other elements of Greek elite culture, it was introduced to Rome by the so-called Etruscan kings. These events consisted of normally four teams of from two to ten horses running multiple laps (usually seven) around a center set of rails. Under the emperors these teams became permanent institutions distinguished by color (Greens and Whites versus Blues and Reds). Teams drew the backing of ardent supporters, some with a loyalty to their color faction equal to and typical of any modern sports fan. The chariot race was a powerful force for vertical social integration, encouraging the participation (by cheering or betting) of everyone in Roman society from slave to emperor.

Circuses also hosted the athletic competitions *(agōnes),* the games of skill, speed and endurance that we have come to associate with the Olympic Games. These competitions of Greek origin often included footraces, jumping, boxing and wrestling as well as the more overtly military skills such as archery or javelin throwing. It is perhaps better to understand the stadium (*stadion*), the Greek running track, as inclusive of circuses rather than vice versa. The Roman festivals and chariot races were held throughout the empire (see Roman Empire), whereas the Greek games were disparaged and not celebrated in Rome itself until the institution of the Capitoline Games during the reign of Domitian (A.D. 81-96). The Romans adopted the custom from the Greek games of awarding perishable crowns as symbolic rewards, but perhaps symbolic of the cultural difference, the Romans traditionally awarded these crowns for valor rather than athletic competition. Before the construction of permanent amphitheaters, circuses also hosted gladiatorial combats (*see* Arenas).

Unlike other events, which had precedents in the Hellenistic world, the staged wild-beast hunt (*venatio*) was a peculiarly Roman event. Exotic animals were brought from the furthest reaches of the empire to be displayed, pitted against one another or hunted in the circus. Hence these hunts can be seen as not only a show of prowess but also a symbolic demonstration of the extent of Roman rule. The more infamous uses of these beasts were as tools of torture, as circuses were also one of the sites used for public execution of condemned criminals (*see* Arenas; Persecution).

2. Games and Worship.

The circus was sacred ground, the property of the gods, in essence a *temple. The Roman *ludi* as well as the Greek games served as a community offering to the gods.

In the provinces annual *ludi* were associated with honoring Rome and the *emperor. Hence the festival games became a visible symbol of loyalty to the Roman state, its power and its culture. These took place in whatever stadium the municipality could offer. It was not incongruent in polytheism for *ludi* honoring the emperor to be compatible with and even simultaneously expressed with games held in honor of traditional gods. Increasingly provincials in the East and West competed to integrate imperial worship into their own local cults (see Civic Cults). Herod (c. 73-4 B.C.) distinguished himself both by being the patron *(agōnothetēs)* of the Olympic games (12 B.C.) and by instituting the Roman games in honor of Augustus in the city he built for the same purpose, *Kaisareia Sebaste* (Josephus *J.W.* 1.12 §426-28; *Ant.* 15.8.1 §§268-76; 16.5.1 §§136-41). So while the calendar of games honoring the Olympic deities continued to have a large influence over which festivals were celebrated, both the control and the honor of the games were increasingly shared by the Roman emperor. The burden of religious responsibility also fell to the emperor, whose magisterial duty it was to ensure that such honors as were due the gods were performed. They believed the welfare of the state depended on the peace of the gods (*pax deorum*), which was achieved by dutifully and publicly performing acts of homage, including the games.

3. Games and New Testament Analogies.

The apostle Paul was familiar with athletic competitions; his letters are peppered with allusions to *agōnes.* This fact communicates much about the assumptions he makes regarding his audience. Like the many allusions in classical literature (Pindar is especially important in contributing to the athletic ideal), Paul assumes the games will be familiar, even commonplace, to his Hellenistic audience and to the Jews as well, albeit unpopular (see 1 Macc 1:14; 4:12-13), and he consequently utilizes them as analogies of the Christian life.

3.1. Analogy of Spiritual Struggle. The *agōn* signified the setting where the games were held or the assembly of spectators. It could also refer generically to the contests, races, combats or conflicts themselves. In Hebrews 12:1-2 the author writes, "Wherefore seeing we have encircling us [*echontes perikeimenon hēmin*] so great a cloud of witnesses, let us put off all bulk weight, and the loosely fitting sin [Greek athletes competed in the nude], and let us run with patience the race [*agōna*] that is set before us. Looking unto Jesus, the leader [*archēgon*] and finisher [*teleiōtēn*] of the faith." This passage treats of both the contest and the setting of the spiritual struggle in the games. The stadium/circus crowd of saints and prophets encircles the athletes competing in their contest, and the runner is made the model of Christian endurance. For the author of Hebrews the Christian faith is metaphorically the *agōn.*

Christ ran and finished the race before us, and yet he is also in some sense above the games, governing them, and the one in whose honor and by whose beneficence the competition of faith is held, like many of the great provincial or city magistrates who served as *agōnothetēs*. The meanings of *archēgos* as "magistrate or ruler" and "first or initiator" are compatible and offer a double meaning in the context of the games. Not only does Jesus start the runner on his course, but also he demonstrated how the race was won. Christ himself endured his *agōn* to win joy and the victor's place of honor at the right hand of God, perhaps specifying even more clearly the metaphor of triumphal games.

3.2. Analogy of Moral Integrity. In 2 Timothy 2:5 Paul uses the games to teach a moral lesson. He writes, "And if a man competes in the games, he is not crowned unless he competes according to the rules" (*Ean de [kai] athlē tis, ou stephanoutai, ean mē nomimōs athlēsē).* As in the strictly judged and monitored Greek games, the Christian contest cannot be won by cheating.

3.3. Analogy of Discipline. Paul also uses the character of a winning athlete as a model for success in the Christian life. He writes, "Do you not know that those running in a race-course [*en stadiō*] all run indeed, but one attains the prize. Run thus, that you may win. Everyone who contends [*agōnizomenos*] is self-disciplined in everything, that they indeed might win a perishable victor's crown [cf. Gal 2:2; Lucian *Anach.* 9—14], but we an imperishable. Therefore I run thus, not as if uncertainly; I box [*pukteuō*] thus, not as if shadow-boxing [cf. Plato *Laws* 830a-c]; but I punch [*hypōiazō*] my body and I treat it harshly [like beating a slave, *doulagōgō),* lest perhaps having proclaimed to others, I myself should become a failure [*adokimos*]" (1 Cor 9:24-27). Here the two commonplace analogies from the games, a race and a boxing match, underscore the severity of the Christian struggle. Paul warns against running to run instead of to win, and reminds the church at Corinth of the commitment and self-control required of the Christian. Paul himself is as merciless to his fleshly appetites as a boxer is to his opponent because he knows that as in the games, if he were to fail the test of valor against his opponent, he too would be eliminated from the spiritual contest. The Christian faith has an excellence modeled well and immediately by athletics to the Corinthians, who celebrated the Ithsmian Games, and for whom like the rest of the Hellenized world the concepts of discipline and education were bound to athletics.

3.4. Analogy of Spiritual Victory. The conclusion of athletic contests also provides parallels with the anticipated closure of the successful Christian's struggle. In Philippians 3:12 Paul writes, "Not as though I had already attained victory, or was already finished; but I strive (*diōkō*), if indeed I may win that for which I am won of Christ Jesus. Brethren, I count not myself to have won, but this one thing I do, forgetting those things which are behind, and stretching forward for those things which are before, I strive toward the goal for the prize of the high summons of God in Jesus Christ" (cf. Lucian *On Slander* 12). Here Paul does not say that he is finished, but he says that he is still in the race and focused on finishing and winning while remembering that he himself is the prize Christ won. Later, Paul exhorts Timothy to "compete a good contest of faith" *(agōnizou ton kalon agōna tēs pisteōs)* (1 Tim 6:12; cf. 1 Tim 1:20), which requires exertion expended toward the goal. Finally, in 2 Timothy 4:7 Paul is able to say "I have competed a good contest, I have finished the race, I have kept the faith: Henceforth there is laid up for me a victor's crown of righteousness" *(ton agōna ton kalon ēgōnismai, ton dromon teteleka, tēn pistin tetērēka: loipon apokeitai moi ho tēs dikaiosynēs stephanos).* The analogy, like the games themselves, seeks the closure, the consummation of struggle not just in completion of the race but in the promised reward, the victor's crown.

See also ARENAS; ATHLETICS; THEATERS.

BIBLIOGRAPHY. A. Cameron, *Circus Factions: Blues and Greens at Rome and Byzantium* (Oxford: Clarendon Press, 1976); J. Humphrey, *Roman Circuses: Arenas for Chariot Racing* (Berkeley and Los Angeles: University of California Press, 1986); G. Johnston, "Christ as Archegos," *NTS* 27 (1981) 381-85; S. G. Miller, ed., *Arete: Greek Sports from Ancient Sources* (Berkeley and Los Angeles: University of California Press, 1991); V. C. Pfitzner, *Paul and the Agon Motif: Traditional Athletic Imagery in Pauline Literature* (Leiden: E. J. Brill, 1967); M. Poliakoff, *Combat Sports in the Ancient World* (New Haven, CT: Yale University Press, 1987); W. Raschke, ed., *The Archaeology of the Olympics: The Olympics and Other Festivals in Antiquity* (Madison: University of Wisconsin Press, 1988); E. Rawson, "Chariot-Racing in the Roman Republic," *Papers of the British School at Rome* 49 (1981) 1-16; D. Sansone, *Greek Athletics and the Genesis of Sport* (Berkeley and Los Angeles: University of California Press, 1988); V. Tcherikover, *Hellenistic Civilization and the Jews* (New York: Atheneum, 1977); B. Witherington III, *Conflict and Community in Corinth: A Socio-Rhetorical Commentary on 1 and 2 Corinthians* (Grand Rapids, MI: Eerdmans, 1995). M. Pucci

CITIES, GRECO-ROMAN

While ancient Greek and Roman cities clearly had their unique features, they were remarkably similar. These cities, found throughout the ancient Mediterranean, were modeled on the *polis* (city) of classical Greece. The *polis* was adapted for empire building by *Alexander the Great and his generals in the Hellenistic era and later by the Romans. The Greek *polis* was the cradle of democracy and Greek civilization. Alexander the Great used the city as a vehicle of stability and cultural influence in his new empire. The Romans also discovered the value of colonial cities for military and economic stability in their new empire (*see* Roman Empire), imitating the Greeks in founding new and refounding old cities.

Ancient cities of Greece and Rome were founded on well-traveled roads, along rivers and near natural harbors. These cities were often walled for security, with gates that were opened during the day and closed at night. In the first century A.D., *Rome and *Alexandria had approximately five hundred thousand inhabitants. More typical was Pompeii with twenty thousand inhabitants.

1. The Classical Greek *Polis*
2. The Hellenistic *Polis*
3. The Roman City

1. The Classical Greek *Polis*.

This form of the city emerged in Greece and its colonies by at least the seventh century B.C. as a walled, fortified city. The *polis* was a politically and economically independent city that governed the surrounding countryside. The inhabitants of the *polis* were the aristocracy, the official citizens and resident foreigners. The *polis* ranged in size from fewer than one thousand to more than two hundred thousand people, the latter being the case for *Athens in the fifth and fourth centuries B.C.

The *polis* was governed by a constitution that defined its form of government as oligarchic or democratic, and it was governed by a *boulē*, *dēmas* and a group of magistrates. The *boulē* was a council made up of aristocratic families that generated legislation. The assembly was the official citizens of the city, which discussed the legislation of the *boulē*. The magistrates were usually appointed or elected for one year and administered the city and its civic religion. They maintained public buildings, streets, roads and the water works.

The *polis* funded public works by various means. The aristocracy funded larger projects, such as outfitting a warship or paying for a religious festival. The *polis* owned farms and imposed *taxes and tolls on resident aliens that provided income for other expenses. Agriculture was the mainstay of the economy of the *polis*. People within the city walls often derived their income from farms they owned outside the walls. In addition to agriculture, the work of the various craftsmen and artisans contributed to the ideal of the self-sufficient *polis*.

The portion of the *polis* within the city walls was called the *asty*. Its pattern and buildings were distinctive and became the defining features of a Greco-Roman city. City planners from the fifth century B.C. preferred the orthogonal, or grid, plan developed by Hippodamos of Miletus. The grid was formed by laying down three or four parallel avenues of considerable width and then constructing streets intersecting the avenues at right angles. Colonnades often covered the sidewalks along the main streets for the convenience of conversation and business. In older cities the grid often did not extend beyond the public spaces to the residential areas, for the latter were organized earlier on an organic plan following the contours of the land and previous settlement.

One of the main avenues led from the gate to the *agora,* or market, located in the heart of the city. The *agora* was the center of commerce as well as a public meeting place or civic center. Many public buildings were located near the *agora.* The *bouleuterion,* or council house, was an enclosed building for meetings of the *boulē.* Large, open steps were constructed for the meetings of the citizen assembly. The *prytaneion* was a meeting house for the magistrates that housed the sacred hearth of the city—the symbol of security—and statues of gods and heroes. The *agora* was graced with stoas, roofed colonnades for walking while conducting teaching, business or law. Throughout the city one would find temples to various gods, springs, fountains and statues.

The **gymnasium* was the educational and physical training facility for the young men and the continuing education and exercise facility for the older men (e.g., the Academy of Athens). To provide room for the needs of *athletics, the *gymnasium* was located outside the city walls. Other public facilities included a *stadion* for athletic contests and a *theater descending a hillside with seating surrounding a circular staging area at the bottom.

Houses were positioned on the side streets with their backs to the street and the door facing the street. They were either built around a center courtyard or faced a garden in the rear. Construction was of adobe brick with flat roofs. Wealthy homes were of multiple stories, built around a courtyard and decorated with mosaic floors. They might even have been connected to the city water supply if it was available.

With such warm and dry weather, the majority of the population spent its time outdoors in public places. A quarter of each city was devoted to public areas, with private areas being densely packed. Daily conversation and business were conducted in the streets. These public places were spectacular because cities strove to outdo others in the grandeur of their public buildings and receive the greater honor.

2. The Hellenistic *Polis.*

Alexander the Great founded cities throughout his new eastern empire to solidify his power and advance the influence of Greek culture. He modeled these cities on the Greek *polis* as he built cities in *Asia Minor, Syria, Palestine, Egypt and Mesopotamia. These cities provided the models for future cities built by Alexander's generals and their successors. These cities served as royal capitals, military posts and trading centers. Alexandria in Egypt and Antioch in Syria were built as royal capitals. These cities had a rich mix of peoples and cultures. Typically inhabitants included Greek settlers, native peoples, Jews and immigrant merchants and craftsmen. For example, Antioch was founded in 300 B.C. with a mixture of Greeks, Syrians and Jews.

Royal cities were financed largely by the kings themselves. Local aristocracy often funded major building projects to increase their favor with the king and honor with the people. For example, Herod the Great (*see* Herods) paved in marble one of the main streets of Antioch of Syria in honor of Augustus (*see* Roman Emperors). Traditional means of financing from agriculture, taxes and tolls continued in the smaller cities. Cities prospered depending upon their proximity to good harbors and trade routes and concentration of coveted industry.

Hellenistic cities looked like the classical cities of Greece except that the buildings were larger and more heavily decorated. The traditional public buildings remained the same with the addition of large estates for the aristocracy and palaces in royal cities for the kings. The temple of the guardian deity was also a dominant building in the oriental city.

Old cities often experienced Hellenistic makeovers. Buildings were remodeled and Greek institutions added. Antiochus IV Epiphanes tried to make Jerusalem into a *polis* with a *boulē* and temple priests into magistrates. Herod the Great rebuilt Samaria in Hellenistic style, added a roofed stadium and renamed it Sebaste (Gk for Augusta, after Caesar Augustus). He rebuilt much of *Jerusalem, especially the *temple, in Hellenistic style and added a theater and stadium. Herod built *Caesarea Maritima (25-13 B.C.), which included an artificial harbor, colonnaded streets, forum, baths, aqueduct, theater, amphitheater, hippodrome and stadium (*see* Archaeology of the Land of Israel).

3. The Roman City.

As Rome began its expansion in Italy in the fourth and third centuries B.C. it built cities in its colonies and inhabited them with Roman citizens, and it built Latin cities and inhabited them with Latin peoples. These cities were laid out in the orthogonal pattern of the Greek *polis*. In the expansion of Rome outside the Italian peninsula in the first century B.C., Roman generals founded similar towns and rebuilt conquered towns in this image. The colonial cities were governed by councils of decurions and administered by committees of magistrates elected yearly by all the inhabitants (*see* Roman Administration). During the Roman period Hellenistic cities were governed more on the oligarchic than the democratic model. Being ruled by an aristocracy themselves, the Romans were more comfortable utilizing the aristocracy of the areas they conquered to establish regional government.

The Roman city was walled, with the majority of the population living in small houses on the individual farms surrounding it. Whereas the Greek city had three or four parallel streets, the Roman city was laid out around the intersection of main streets running north-south *(cardo)* and east-west *(decamus)*. Ideally these streets intersected at the *forum*, the commercial and political hub of the city. Streets ran through the *forum*, whereas in the *agora* they did not. The *forum* contained a temple to Jupiter in imitation of the temple to Jupiter on the Capitoline Hill in Rome, a *curia* for meetings of the town council, a *basilica* for conducting law and business, statues, temples, public baths, theaters and amphitheaters for gladiatorial games (*see* Arenas).

The two main intersecting streets determined the layout of the city as well as the surrounding farmland that radiated from it. The most important buildings would run down one of the two main streets. Unlike Greek cities, specific public and residential areas were more carefully distinguished in Roman cities. In Rome the wealthy lived in villas outside the city and in apartments in the city. Many city dwellers lived in small apartments within large, multistoried apartment buildings. Housing reflected the more rigid social stratification within the Roman society.

The Roman cities copied many buildings found in Rome, including the statues, arches and temples. Peculiar to Roman architecture was the widespread use of concrete in construction; the commemorative arch; the basilica, a hall near the forum for conducting business and law; the amphitheater; public baths (*see* Gymnasia and Baths) for exercise, bathing and lectures; and aqueducts. In the first century A.D. construction in Greek cities also used concrete, and cities were retrofitted with some of the innovative Roman buildings. Culture was shared, for styles of glassware, pottery, furniture, and wall and floor coverings were similar throughout the empire.

Agriculture provided the mainstay of the economy. Similar businesses clustered together in the city, so that there would be streets of jewelers, cobblers and booksellers, among many others. Those in the same business often formed trade *associations to pursue not economic advantage but honor for the group. Some occupations, like traders, drovers and porters, gathered near the city gates, while others less suited to an urban environment, like smithies and tanners, were relegated outside the city gates.

See also ARENAS; ART AND ARCHITECTURE: GRECO-ROMAN; CIRCUSES AND GAMES; CITIZENSHIP, ROMAN; CIVIC CULTS; FAMILY AND HOUSEHOLD; GYMNASIA AND BATHS; THEATERS; TRAVEL AND TRADE.

BIBLIOGRAPHY. F. Castagnoli, *Orthogonal Town Planning in Antiquity* (Cambridge, MA: MIT Press, 1971); P. M. Fraser, *Cities of Alexander the Great* (Oxford: Clarendon Press, 1996); G. Glotz, *The Greek City and Its Institutions* (New York: Barnes & Noble, 1929); P. Grimal, *Roman Cities* (Madison: University of Wisconsin Press, 1983); A. H. M. Jones, *The Cities of the Eastern Roman Provinces* (2d ed.; London: Oxford University Press, 1971); idem, *The Greek City from Alexander to Justinian* (Oxford: Clarendon Press, 1940); W. L. MacDonald, *Architecture of the Roman Empire,* 2: *An Urban Appraisal* (New Haven, CT: Yale University Press, 1986); R. MacMullen, *Roman Social Relations* (New Haven, CT: Yale University Press, 1974); W. A. Meeks, *The First Urban Christians: The Social World of the Apostle Paul* (New Haven, CT: Yale University Press, 1983); O. F. Robinson, *Ancient Rome: City Planning and Administration* (New York: Routledge & Kegan Paul, 1992); D. Sperber, *The City in Roman Palestine* (Oxford: Oxford University Press, 1997); J. E. Stambaugh, *The Ancient Roman City* (Baltimore: John Hopkins University Press, 1988); J. E. Stambaugh and D. L. Ralch, *The New Testament in Its Social Environment* (LEC 5; Philadelphia: Westminster, 1986) 107-37; R. Stillwell, W. L. MacDonald and M. H. McAllister, eds., *The Princeton Encyclopedia of Classical Sites* (Princeton, NJ: Princeton University Press, 1976); J. B. Ward-Perkins, *Cities of Ancient Greece and Italy: Planning in Classical Antiquity* (New York: George Braziller, 1974); R. E. Wycherley, *How the Greeks Built Cities* (2d ed.; London: Macmillan, 1962).

D. F. Watson

CITIZENSHIP, ROMAN

Possession of Roman citizenship in its various shades was one of the significant markers of personal identity. While increasingly more extensive grants of citizenship throughout the empire into the second century A.D. were perceived by some to have cheapened the value of the franchise (Tacitus *Ann.* 3.40.2), the eagerness of many to obtain it was undiminished for the advantages it conferred.

1. Citizenship and Privilege
2. Obtaining Citizenship
3. Citizenship and Trouble

1. Citizenship and Privilege.

Citizenship was attended by distinctions and entitlements that affected every area of life. In the realms of business (holding property, making contracts and paying taxes), domestic affairs (getting married, having legitimate children and making wills) and litigation (courts, custody and punishments), the citizen was accorded better treatment than was the imperial subject who did not possess the franchise. Admittedly, other markers (e.g., family heritage, offices held, honors received, wealth, gentility, and such) did cut across the distinction between citizens and aliens and did figure prominently in the process of coming to one's rights (Ulpian *Digest of Justinian* 48.3.1; cf. Garnsey, Kelly). But Roman citizens, particularly those living or traveling among extern populations as did Paul and Silas, possessed significant advantages if they chose to make a disclosure.

2. Obtaining Citizenship.

2.1. Dual Citizenship. It was not possible in the time of the Republic actively to maintain dual or multiple citizenship because of what some have called the rule of incompatibility, which asserted that change of soil meant change of state (Sherwin-White 1974, 46; cf. Cicero *Balb.* 28-30; Cicero *Caec.* 100; Cicero *De Leg.* 2.2.5). The principle stood behind the practices of exile *(exilium)* and return *(postliminium),* which implied loss of and reinstatement to citizenship respectively. This either-or arrangement posed obvious difficulties when the franchise began to be extended as a reward to loyal allies. The disadvantages were at first mitigated by extending a limited type of Roman citizenship. However, as the pressures of disadvantage became more acute, the principle was relaxed.

By the time of Claudius (*see* Roman Emperors), the principle of dual citizenship was thoroughly established. The fact that the apostle Paul claims Roman and Tarsian citizenship (Acts 16:37-38; 21:39; 22:25) cannot be contested. That he claims to be citizen born, however, calls for precedents at least as early as the turn of the first century A.D. and possibly earlier. Legal precedents dating to the reign of Augustus can be found (FIRA 1:55, 68), so the probability for Paul's claim is high.

2.2. Citizenship and Judaism. Bringing together a serious Judaism with Roman citizenship created significant tensions. *Roman military service, one means of obtaining citizenship, was scarcely an option for religious Jews because it called for involvement in the *ruler cult, the consecrated standards and the *auguria*. It also called for *sabbath breaking. The Romans realized the impracticability of pressing normal expectations upon religious Jews. *Josephus's record of three consular edicts by Lucius Cornelius Lentulus Crus (Josephus *Ant.* 14.10.13 §§228-29; 14.10.16 §234; 14.10.19 §§237-40) and the letters of Mark Antony (Josephus *Ant.* 14.10.17 §235), Titus Ampius Balbus (Josephus *Ant.* 14.10.13 §230) and the Syrian governor Publius Cornelius Dolabella (Josephus *Ant.* 14.10.12 §§225-27) confirm the simultaneous possession of strong Jewish religious sensibilities and citizenship. The documents grant exemption from military conscription to "Jews who are Roman citizens" and "Jewish citizens of ours."

Roman citizenship also called for inclusion in a tribe *(gens),* but this was not significantly problematic. Outside Rome, one's inclusion in a *gens* was a political and legal fiction requiring no religious bond; in Rome and especially for those who wished to vote or hold office, however, there would be religious implications.

Religious Jews would not sacrifice to the *emperor. But Jews did offer sacrifices for him twice a day in the Jerusalem *temple and more often on special days. They prayed for him throughout the *Diaspora and showed their devotion to him through various dedicatory symbols and actions (sources in Scramuzza, 5:284). Inscriptional evidence also shows citizen Jews holding formal offices in Diaspora communities and *synagogues (sources in Schürer, 2:435; 3.1:61, 133; *NewDocs.* 4:111; Trebilco, passim). While Paul's declarations of an ardent *Pharisaism (Acts 23:6; Phil 3:5) and his simultaneous status as a Roman citizen might create tensions, they were not seriously incompatible.

2.3. How Citizenship Was Obtained. The franchise could be obtained in one of a number of ways. One might be born to citizen parents *(ingenuus).* A *slave might receive citizenship by manumission (*manumissio;* Pliny *Ep.* 10.104-5). Auxiliary soldiers who had completed the required military service were extended the grant (*ARS* 131, 179, 184, 186, 189). Citizenship might be the reward for some valuable service rendered to the Roman state (*ARS* 60; Cicero *Balb.* 8.19). It could be granted en bloc through colonization or promotion to Latin rights (Strabo *Geog.* 5.1.6; Suetonius *Julius* 28). Finally, preferment in the grant of citizenship was available at times for financial consideration (Cicero *Phil.* 2.92; 5.11-12; Dio Cassius *Hist.* 60.17.5-6; Tacitus *Ann.* 14.50.1).

Paul obtained his citizenship by the first means (Acts 22:28; cf. 22:3). How Paul's parents received the citizenship, however, is unclear. The later theory (Jerome *In Philem.* 23; *Vir.* 5) that Paul and his parents were taken from Gischala to Tarsus as prisoners of war, receiving the grant thereafter, contradicts the NT record at several points (Acts 22:3, 28). The notion that Paul's father was a nonobservant Jew serving in the Roman army as a leather worker is questionable in light of Acts 22:3 and 23:6.

Favorable relations between the city of Tarsus, where Paul was born, and Pompey, Julius Caesar, Mark Antony and Augustus, who had the power of conferral, allow that Paul might have been born Cn. Pompeius Paulus, C. Julius Paulus or M. Antonius Paulus (Hemer, 179). The chiliarch Claudius Lysias's purchase of citizenship at great expense matches well what we know of the earlier period of Claudius's reign (Dio Cassius *Hist.* 60.17.5-6). Of Silas (Acts 16:37-38), we know nothing.

2.4. Proof of Citizenship. In the regular course of life it was expected that one's citizen status would be disclosed and its advantages seized.

2.4.1. Roman Names. Citizens had three names *(tria nomina):* a personal or individual name *(praenomen),* a name that associated one with the largest number of relatives (*nomen* or *nomen gentilicium)* and a *cognomen* by which one normally was known. We have only the names *Saul* and *Paul* by which to evaluate the apostle. The context of Acts 13:9 suggests that "Paul" is the apostle's Roman *cognomen* and "Saul" his unofficial Jewish name (*signum* or *supernomen).* As *cognomina* go, "Paulus" would sound most respectable to Roman ears and suggest citizenship (Judge, 13, 36 n. 20). Paul would hardly have risked making two disclosures of citizenship and an appeal to Caesar unless he could legitimately use the *tria nomina.* There were severe penalties for the false use of Roman names (Suetonius *Claudius* 25.3; Arrian *Epict. Diss.* 3.24.41; cf. Paulus *Sent.* 5.25.11). Even an unsatisfactory claim could result in prosecution or death (Cicero *Arch.* 4.7; Cicero *Verr.* 2.5.169). These indications suggest citizenship for Paul.

2.4.2. Documents. F. F. Bruce (39-40) notes that legislation at the turn of the first century A.D. called for a legitimately born child of Roman citizens to be registered within thirty days of birth. Children born in the provinces would be legally acknowledged *(professio)* before the Roman provincial authority at the public record office *(tabularium publicum).* The *professio* was then entered in the register *(album professionum).* We do not know if Paul's birth was before or after this legislation, but some such formal procedure had to have been in effect earlier. At regular intervals a citizen's name, age, status and property holdings would thereafter be recorded by census.

Near home, most citizens would have no problem proving their citizenship. Away from home, a certified private copy of the *professio*—called a *testatio*—might be carried in which the letters *c.r.e.,* representing *c(iuem) r(omanam/um) e(xscripsi/t),* clearly indicated citizenship (Sanders, 410; Schulz 1943, 56). Pensioned auxiliary soldiers received a document in bronze (*diploma militaris* or *instrumentum)* that was more serviceable for travel, and there is record of civilian citizen documents under the name *diploma* (Suetonius *Nero* 12). Magistrates might give such documents credit, but they were not bound by law to do so. In Tarsus or Jerusalem Paul's claim of citizenship might be confirmed with little difficulty; on missions, the presumptive proof would rest on verbal declarations, documentary support and the circumstances of their employment.

3. Citizenship and Trouble.

When persons stood in a Roman court of law, it was expected that they would disclose their full legal identity and claim its entitlements for the most favorable possible consideration. Among the privileges was the right to appeal for protection from the capital jurisdiction or violent discipline of magistrates. Successive laws were passed over time to revive these protections, perhaps owing to the growing population of citizen travelers and of externs newly granted the franchise. There are examples of consideration to citizen status (Josephus *J.W.* 1.32.5 §640; 1.33.7 §664; *Ant.* 18.6.6 §§189-90; Tacitus *Ann.* 16.10; Pliny *Ep.* 6.31; 10.96; Lucian *Tox.* 17; *Let. Chur. Lyons Vien.* 1.44). In other cases, however, magistrates and communities discounted or disregarded citizenship (Suetonius *Galba* 9.1; Josephus *J.W.* 2.14.9 §308; Dio Cassius *Hist.* 54.7.6; 57.24.6; 60.24.2; 64.2.3; Tacitus *Hist.* 3.12; Pliny *Ep.* 2.11; FIRA 1:103). A citizenship unadorned by sufficient additional upper-class markers might not garner magisterial or public consideration.

In *Philippi (Acts 16), Paul's and Silas's failure to make a claim of citizenship against abusive treatment at the "Roman" (i.e., the earliest possible) time has been the cause of much modern skepticism regarding Paul's possession of citizenship. Given the fact that they are accused as trouble-making Jews by Roman citizens, a claim of citizenship would be tantamount to a denial of their fulfilled Judaism (= Christianity) and their gospel message. Moreover, the fledgling Philippian church might wonder whether only those suitably enfranchised could afford to be believers. Silently submitting to official action preserved the apostles' religious and missionary integrity at the expense of giving a false public impression concerning their legal identity as Romans.

The apostles' disclosure of their true legal identity and the sit-down strike the next day in the prison are late from a Roman perspective, but they have an ancient logic to them. Paul protests the outrage of a public humiliation and a private release for Romans (Acts 16:37; cf. 1 Thess 2:2). He insists upon a status transfer to restore a measure of dignity—it calls for the magistrates to lift up the apostles by humbling themselves in providing a public escort out of the prison (Acts 16:39). Paul's intent beyond this may have been to protect the Philippian congregation from further troubles.

The priorities underlying Paul's conduct at Philippi are also evident in Jerusalem (Acts 22). Paul will not trade away his heritage in and connections with fulfilled Judaism by resort to a well-timed (i.e., Roman) citizenship declaration before his countrymen. Rather, it occurs late and in the sole presence of the Roman military. Moreover, far from protesting, pleading or declaring the right, Paul insinuates his citizenship by a hypothetical, second-person query (Acts 22:25). Paul is fully prepared to suffer if needs be (Acts 9:15-16). This, coupled with a citizenship superior to that of the prosecuting authority, which subsequent comparison reveals (Acts 22:27-29; cf. Suetonius *Julius* 17.2), bears remarkable fruit in a lightened custody and substantial official assistance.

Exactly what principle in Roman law underlies Paul's appeal to Caesar before Festus (Acts 25:10-12) has been extensively debated. Discussion early focused upon whether it was a case of *provocatio* (to the people and against the magistrate's verdict) or *appellatio* (to a superior magistrate against a colleague or a subordinate before or after a verdict). Some have spoken of a special case of *provocatio,* that is, appeal before the verdict. P. D. A. Garnsey has argued that Paul invokes the principle of *reiectio* whereby a defendant rejects a judge, plan or tribunal as hostile or unjust. More recently, A. W. Lintott has offered that *appellatio* and *provocatio* are not strictly defined and that Paul's may be an example of one form of recourse to the tribune's help *(auxilium).* Whatever the specific underlying principle in law, it is clear that Paul's appeal was unusual. It is equally clear from Festus's recourse to counsel before final decision (Acts 25:12) that he was not bound or compelled to grant referral, though Roman law counseled strongly that he do so.

Questioning the accuracy of the record in Acts, based upon the Pauline epistles' silence regarding Paul's citizenship and their eloquence concerning his troubles (esp. 2 Cor 6:4-10; 11:23-25), hardly seems legitimate. We have seen that Paul's citizenship disclosures in Acts are rather consistently untimely and allusive. Moreover, it is as a citizen that Paul has profound troubles. The disclosures in Acts, far from being naïve Lukan romancing, rather reflect a strategy governed by ministry priorities—namely, that Paul's religious identity, the integrity of his message, the most favorable hearing of his listeners and the faith of his converts should never be compromised in the interest of personal dignity, comfort or safety. Ministry priorities define the parameters within which the apostle permits the Roman franchise to serve him. Simply put, Paul is a Christian charged with a mission first; he is a Roman citizen second.

See also ROMAN LAW AND LEGAL SYSTEM; ROMAN MILITARY; ROMAN SOCIAL CLASSES.

BIBLIOGRAPHY. S. Applebaum, "The Legal Status of the Jewish Communities in the Diaspora," in *The Jewish People in the First Century,* ed. S. Safrai et al. (2 vols.; CRINT 1; Assen: Van Gorcum; Philadelphia: Fortress, 1974) 420-63; F. F. Bruce, *Paul: Apostle of the Heart Set Free* (Grand Rapids, MI: Eerdmans, 1977); P. D. A. Garnsey, "The Criminal Jurisdiction of Governors," *JRS* 58 (1966) 51-59; idem, "The *Lex Julia* and Appeal Under the Empire," *JRS* 56 (1960) 167-89; idem, *Social Status and Legal Privilege in the Roman Empire* (Oxford: Clarendon Press, 1970); C. J. Hemer, "The Name of Paul," *TynB* 36 (1985) 179-83; E. A. Judge, *Rank and Status in the World of the Caesars and St. Paul* (Broadhead Memorial Lecture 1981/UCP 29; Christchurch, NZ: University of Canterbury, 1982); J. M. Kelly, *Roman Litigation* (Oxford: Clarendon Press, 1966); A. W. Lintott, "Provocatio: From the Struggle of the Orders to the Principate," *ANRW* 1.2 (1972) 226-67; A. Nobbs, "Cyprus," in *The Book of Acts in Its Greco-Roman Setting,* ed. D. W. J. Gill and C. Gempf (BAFCS 2; Grand Rapids, MI: Eerdmans, 1994) 279-89; A. M. Rabello, "The Legal Condition of the Jews in the Roman Empire," *ANRW* 2.13 (1980) 662-762; B. M. Rapske, *The Book of Acts and Paul in Roman Custody* (BAFCS 3; Grand Rapids, MI: Eerdmans, 1994); H. A. Sanders, "The Birth Certificate of a Roman Citizen," *CP* 22 (1927) 409-13; F. Schulz, "Roman Registers of Births and Birth Certificates," *JRS* 32 (1942) 78-91; 33 (1943) 55-64; E. Schürer, *The History of the Jewish People in the Age of Jesus Christ (175 B.C.-A.D. 135),* rev. and ed. G. Vermes et al. (3 vols.; Edinburgh: T & T Clark, 1973-87); V. M. Scramuzza, "The Policy of the Early Roman Emperors Towards Judaism," in *The Beginnings of Christianity—The Acts of the Apostles,* ed. F. J. Foakes Jackson and K. Lake (Grand Rapids, MI: Baker, 1979 [1932]) 5:277-97; A. N. Sherwin-White, "The Roman Citizenship: A Survey of Its Development into a World Franchise," *ANRW* 1.2 (1974) 23-58; idem, *Roman Society and Roman Law in the New Testament* (Sarum Lectures 1961/62; Oxford: Clarendon Press, 1963); R. D. Sullivan, "The Dynasty of Judea in the First Century," *ANRW* 2.8 (1977) 296-354; P. R. Trebilco, *Jewish Communities in Asia Minor* (SNTSMS 69; Cambridge: Cambridge University Press, 1991).

B. M. Rapske

CIVIC CULTS

Civic cults, usually dedicated to a specific deity, were sponsored by local cities or city governments. Early Christian mission, which encountered some of these civic cults, sometimes found them to be a source of opposition.

1. The Role of Cities' Foundational Myths
2. Civic Cults and the Jews
3. Civic Cults and the New Testament

1. The Role of Cities' Foundational Myths.

Throughout the Mediterranean world prior to the conquests of Alexander the Great, the city (Gk *polis*), in a reciprocal relationship with surrounding countryside, was the basic form of government and administration. Such "cities" were typically small civic centers and would generally be dedicated to the worship of a particular god or goddess, whose cult was often centered either in the city itself or nearby (for instance, *Jerusalem, dedicated to Yahweh; Memphis, dedicated to the Attis bull; *Ephesus, in which the great temple to Artemis was located). This is perhaps a simplistic presentation, but it is generally correct for all areas throughout the Mediterranean world.

However, in the new world of widespread *Hellenistic culture in the wake of *Alexander's conquests, the life of each individual *polis* and its position within the wider Greco-Roman world depended partially upon the connection of these local cults and their foundation myths with acceptable Greek mythology. As a result, many local deities of non-Greek extraction often became associated with some aspect of Greek mythology. As Wallace and Williams point out, "this could be done by fabricating foundation stories and associating local cults with the myths of the Olympian gods" (Wallace and Williams, 97). There were some convenient ways of doing this. In Greek mythology, heroes such as Perseus, the demigod Herakles and the god Dionysus were reputed to have traveled widely. This allowed cities such as Tarsus in Cilicia (the home city of Paul, which claimed to have a connection to Argo via Perseus [Strabo *Geog.* 14.5.12.673c; cf. Wallace and Williams, 99]) and Tyre (which Alexander the Great was convinced contained an altar to his "ancestor" Herakles, but was actually an altar to the Tyrian god, Melkarth; Fox, 181) to claim truly Hellenistic roots. Another manner of accomplishing this "connection" was to claim that the city had been founded by settlers from a Greek city. In some areas this was, of course, true (for instance, the Magnesians who had been convinced by either Antiochus I or II to settle *Antioch-next-to-Pisidia), but was often a concoction (Sparta was a favorite place of origin for several cities in Asia Minor; cf. Jones, 50).

One of the most important ways of establishing priority via a foundation myth, however, was the association of a local cult with the city. Wallace and Williams (100) point out the interesting example of the oracle of Apollo at Klaros, in the territory of the rather minor city of Kolophon (just north of Ephesus). In a sense, the inhabitants of Kolophon parleyed this rather insignificant shrine into a major first-century religious "theme park," complete with temple, underground passages, mysteries into which one could be initiated and, of course, the oracle, but an oracle which delivered its messages in complex variations of sung metrical verse.

Even in places where there was no such internationally famous shrine, the civic cult was an important source of social integration and order within the life of the *polis*. Regular *festivals were generally held by the city in honor of its deity, and it is not uncommon to find the deity's picture on a city's coinage. Processions in honor of the deity were not uncommon, and lavish amounts of money were often dedicated to their worship and veneration. Although a city such as Corinth or Ephesus might contain a plethora of different shrines and other cult centers, the typical practice was for one deity in particular to be the favored one and for that god or goddess to then be seen as that city's protector. Important temples in a city, such as that of Artemis in Ephesus, would bring enormous prestige to the city. In the case of Ephesus, the city was known as *neōkoros*, "warden of the temple" (e.g., *IE* II:236; IV:1238) or, once the imperial cult became established in the city, *dis neōkoros* "*twice* temple-keeper" (cf. Friesen, 52-56; van Tilborg, 197-201). This title is used as an honorific in inscriptions relating to the city and its activities.

2. Civic Cults and the Jews.

The idea of a civic cult is often discussed strictly in connection with cities and peoples who saw themselves as fitting within the Hellenistic or Greco-Roman world. We are not surprised to see *Corinth, *Rome, *Ephesus, *Athens, etc. appearing in such discussions. However, the *Interpretatio Graeca*—that way of seeing all things as reflections of the Greek myths or culture—caused many cities which may not have formerly cast their own traditions in such a light to feel the need to do so now. Hengel's (1:255-309) sustained treatment of the *Interpretatio Graeca* of Judaism in light of the later attempt of Hellenistic reform in (and possibly refoundation of) Jerusalem itself in the mid-second century B.C. is a good example of this (cf. 1 Macc 1:11-15; 2 Macc 4:7-20). As Hengel (1:278) states, to advance the causes of the pro-Hellenistic faction within Jewish life and leadership, "these aims could be most easily achieved by the *transformation of Jerusalem*—and thus of the whole Jewish ethnos in Judea—*into a Greek 'polis'*." There were other attempts to show the superior nature of the Jewish people and cult: for example, the Jewish philosopher *Aristobulus tries to show that the Greek philosophers had taken their ideas from *Moses; and within the Maccabean literature, there is evidence that there was an attempt to show the Jewish origin of the Spartan people (1 Macc 12:5-23; cf. Josephus *Ant.* 12.4.10 §§225-27; 13.5.8 §§166-70). It may also be that the way in which Philo treats Moses, whom he typically calls the "Lawgiver," is in keeping with a further aspect of some foundation myths: the existence of an early lawgiver or leader who provided the essential elements of the constitution of a given *polis* (e.g., Solon of Athens; cf. Wallace and Williams, 97-98).

3. Civic Cults and the New Testament.

There are some very obvious examples of civic cults that show up in the NT. Paul's predicament in Ephesus at the hands of Demetrius the Silversmith (Acts 19:23-41) is, according to the author, the result of a perceived threat to the smith's trade providing votive statuettes for the worship of Artemis. The multiple difficulties experienced by the earliest Christians in Jerusalem also fit within this rubric—the conflict between this new religion or sect of Christianity with the older, more established Jewish cult centered in Jerusalem. On the other hand, there are less obvious examples than these. The way in which, for instance, Jesus Christ is portrayed by Paul in the letter to the Philippians (esp. Phil 2) may very well be meant by Paul as a distinct contrast to the way in which the Roman emperor was portrayed. In the setting of the Roman *colonia* of *Philippi, this would be a direct attack on the increasingly important pan-Roman civic cult: emperor worship (*see* Ruler Cult). It may also be that the Lycaonians' "mistaking" of Paul and Barnabas as Zeus and Hermes (Acts 17) is less an example of extreme credulity on the part of the Lycaonians than of their attempt to place these two messengers of the gods into a context more in keeping with their syncretistic religious understanding, possibly linked with their local cult.

As Christianity developed into a religion in its own right, there was an increasing concern that the single-minded devotion of its adherents was a threat to the overall fabric of Roman religion. As the famous correspondence of *Pliny and Trajan shows, "the spread of Christianity in Bithynia had alarmed [Pliny], for temples had become deserted and rites suspended" (Bowersock, 184; cf. Pliny *Ep.* 10). Trajan's *rescriptum* (Pliny *Ep.* 10.97) would provide the basis for Roman legal treatment of Christians until the time of Hadrian (approximately A.D. 122), when Hadrian made it clear, in a response to the proconsul of Asia, that he had no desire to see anyone punished in a way that was out of keeping with the crime they had committed (Eusebius *Hist. Eccl.* 4.3). On the other hand, if Golan's hypothesis with regard to the foundation of Aelia Capitolina on the former site of the Jerusalem temple is correct (Golan, 226-39), Hadrian's desire to combat the growing influence of the Christian movement may have been far more excessive than that of his predecessor Trajan. A threat to civic religion was a threat to the warp and weft of Roman society and Roman life.

See also CITIES, GRECO-ROMAN; HEROES; RELIGION, GRECO-ROMAN; RELIGION, PERSONAL; RULER CULT; TEMPLES, GRECO-ROMAN.

BIBLIOGRAPHY. G. W. Bowersock, "Greek Intellectuals and the Imperial Cult in the Second Century A.D.," *Fondation-Hardt* 19 (1973) 184-91; R. L. Fox, *Alexander the Great* (London: Allen Lane, 1973); S. J. Friesen, *Twice Neokoros: Ephesus, Asia and the Cult of the Flavian Imperial Family* (RGRW 116; Leiden: E. J. Brill, 1993); D. Golan, "Hadrian's Decision to Supplant 'Jerusalem' by 'Aelia Capitolina,'" *Historia* 35.2 (1986) 226-39; M. Hengel, *Judaism and Hellenism: Studies in their Encounter in Palestine During the Early Hellenistic Period* (2 vols.; London: SCM, 1974); A. H. M. Jones, *The Greek City* (Oxford: Sandpiper, 1998 [1940]); S. van Tilborg, *Reading John in Ephesus* (NovTSup 83; Leiden: E. J. Brill, 1996); R. Wallace and W. Williams, *The Three Worlds of Paul of Tarsus* (London and New York: Routledge, 1998).

B. W. R. Pearson

CLEODEMUS-MALCHUS. *See* JEWISH LITERATURE: HISTORIANS AND POETS

COINAGE: GRECO-ROMAN

The contribution that ancient coins make to our understanding of the Greco-Roman world has been largely focused on their role in dating archaeological sites. Although coins have an invaluable contribution to make in terms of addressing such matters as historical dating, they also can enhance our understanding of the NT in several other ways. As a primary resource of antiquity, coins stand as one window through which we can catch glimpses of the first-century world in which the events described within the NT took place and were recorded for posterity. In this respect, coins, together with the various surviving inscriptions, statues and paintings of the first-century world, are direct evidence of the NT world. Coins are legitimate historical sources, even if they are infrequently called upon to give their evidence within relevant scholarly investigations into the background of the NT documents. Yet a number of recent NT studies have begun to give consideration to the contribution of numismatics for our understanding of the background of the NT (see Kraybill, Kreitzer and Scott, to name but a few examples).

1. Portraiture of Historical Figures
2. Indicators of Places, Events and Dates
3. Evidences of First-Century Life

1. Portraiture of Historical Figures.

It is universally agreed that the NT story takes place against the backdrop of the early years of the *Roman Empire. In the NT we are introduced to many people who helped to shape the course of history. Through the agency of coins we are able to see what some of these key players in the drama of human history looked like. For example, the NT mentions or alludes to several *Roman emperors, including Augustus, Tiberius, Claudius and Nero, all of whom are well represented on coin issues of the Roman mints. We can see the idealized portraiture of Augustus, styled after the image of the demigod Julius Caesar; we can inspect the no-nonsense, grim-faced Tiberius of "tribute-penny" fame; we can examine the visage of the scholarly Claudius, who drove the Jews and Christians from Rome in A.D. 49; we can gaze at the bull-necked emperor Nero and recall that to this man Paul made his "appeal to Caesar" (Acts 26:32).

In addition, within the NT we have mention of other political figures, such as the Jewish leaders Herod Philip II (Lk 3:1), Herod Agrippa I (Acts 12:1-3, 21-23) and Herod Agrippa II (Acts 25:13; 26:2, 28). Each of these men has his portrait preserved on coins of the time. At the same time, other NT figures can also be brought to life through the agency of coins. Thus we feel that people such as Pontius Pilate (Mt 27:2; Lk 3:1; Acts 4:27; 1 Tim 6:13) and Antonius Felix (see Acts 23:23—24:27), although not visible to us in the form of coin portraits, are nonetheless made a bit more real through the bronze coins that bear both their names and their inscriptions and emblems.

2. Indicators of Places, Events and Dates. Coins serve as valuable indirect evidence of some of the historical events that helped to shape the NT world. Within the ancient world coinage functioned much as postage stamps do in the modern world, with the various themes, concerns and topics of the issuing authority in evidence within the artistry of the coin types. Thus there is a sense in which Greco-Roman coinage could be described as a medium of political propaganda. Here the interests of the imperial mints are proudly set forth for all to see, particularly on the coins that serve as the basis for trade and monetary exchange. One of the most important examples of this is the so-called Jewish revolt of A.D. 66-70, which culminated in the destruction of the city of Jerusalem by the Romans (*see* Jewish Wars with Rome). The city of Rome awarded a triumph for the emperor Vespasian and his son Titus, who commanded the Roman legions at the destruction of the city. Scenes of this military triumph, including a portrayal of a personification of a female Judea figure being conquered and overshadowed by a Roman soldier, are among the most common reverse types on imperial coins of the Flavian period (coins of Vespasian, Titus and Domitian depict the subjugation of the Jewish nation in some fashion). Such coins also provide useful background for the triumph imagery that is contained in 2 Corinthians 2:14-16 and Colossians 2:15 (*see* Roman Triumph).

Other examples of imperial coinage also reflect the circumstances of the day. Thus we may find an indication of the tension between Paul the apostle and the religiopolitical authorities in *Ephesus (Acts 19:23-41) surfacing in Roman coinage. The emperor Claudius issued a series of silver cistophorii in A.D. 50-51 to celebrate his marriage to Agrippina the Younger. These coins depict on their reverse evocative portrayals of the temple of Diana in Ephesus, including the cultic statue of the goddess, which appears to have been at the heart of Paul's confrontation with Demetrius and the silversmiths.

It is sometimes suggested that the Matthean account of the so-called temple tax (Mt 17:24-27, and unique in his Gospel) reflects the situation of A.D. 70-96, in which the tax was being levied by the Romans for the reconstruction of the temple of Jupiter Capitolinus following the Jewish revolt. Such a scenario has radical implications for the dating of the Gospel of Matthew as a whole, shifting the arena of conflict between Christians and Jews from one based in Jesus' own life to that of the Matthean community following the destruction of the *temple in A.D. 70.

Much of our discussion has concentrated on coinage of the Greco-Roman world, and within the NT period this means our focus falls upon coins that are issued under the auspices of the Roman state, which to a large degree controlled the production of money. However, individual cities of the ancient world often issued their own coins, proudly proclaiming on these the images and sites associated with their locality. One of the best examples of how this numismatic evidence can be used within NT studies concerns the seven churches of Revelation 2—3. Through the various coins issued by these cities of *Asia Minor we gain a better understanding of local religious beliefs and practices within the province, and through that we arrive at a more balanced interpretation of the meaning of the Apocalypse as a whole.

By means of coins we are able to glimpse some of the sights that would have been seen by the early Christians as they traveled around the Roman Empire in the course of their missionary journeys. For example, we see on the reverse of a sestertius from the reign of Nero a depiction of the harbor at Ostia, which Paul may have visited during his final captivity in Rome. We have on another sestertius a fine depiction of Vespasian's Colosseum, according to legend the site at which many early Christians were martyred for their faith.

3. Evidences of First-Century Life.

One of the most intriguing ways in which coinage can lift the veil on the NT world is by its revelation of the details of everyday life. One could argue that the kinds or denominations of coins mentioned within the various Gospel accounts serve as an indicator of the relative wealth of the community concerned. (Does the fact that Matthew uses coin designations that seem to indicate a familiarity with wealth suggest his congregation is richer than that of Luke?) In short, it seems reasonable that the sociological profiles of the various churches of the NT be plotted against their engagement with wealth.

All sorts of images are portrayed in coinage. Everything from the kinds of sacrificial implements employed in making an offering to the gods, to snapshots of sacrificial ceremonies in which we see the wild-eyed bull whose life is to be offered, to images of taxes being gathered for the Roman state, to depictions of the kinds of boats that are used in travel, to the wide variety of women's hairstyles, and much more, are there for the attentive observer.

In conclusion, the study of numismatics may be likened to a new continent waiting to be explored as far as NT studies is concerned. Careful study of numismatics offers not only the possibility of new explanations of some passages long deemed difficult and troublesome but also the chance discovery of unimagined answers to problems that have hitherto proved insoluble for interpreters of the NT.

See also COINAGE: JEWISH; TAXATION, GRECO-ROMAN; TAXATION, JEWISH.

BIBLIOGRAPHY. C. J. Hemer, *The Letters to the Seven Churches of Asia in Their Local Setting* (JSNTSup 11; Sheffield: Sheffield Academic Press, 1986); J. N. Kraybill, *Imperial Cult and Commerce in John's Apocalypse* (JSNTSup 132; Sheffield: Sheffield Academic Press, 1996); L. J. Kreitzer, *Striking New Images: Roman Imperial Coinage and the New Testament World* (JSNTSup 134; Sheffield: Sheffield Academic Press, 1996); R. Oster, "Numismatic Windows into the Social World of Early Christianity: A Methodological Inquiry," *JBL* 101 (1982) 195-223; J. J. Rousseau and R. Arav, *Jesus and His World: An Archaeological and Cultural Dictionary* (London: SCM, 1996) 55-68; J. M. Scott, "The Triumph of God in 2 Cor 2.14: Additional Evidence of Merkabah Mysticism in Paul," *NTS* 42 (1996) 260-81.

L. J. Kreitzer

COINAGE: JEWISH

Ancient coins produced by or for Jews have been studied since the Renaissance for insights into political, economic and religious history. Coins were introduced into biblical lands through trade with neighboring nations perhaps as early as the sixth century B.C. Coins were rare in Israel until the last part of the fifth century B.C. References to money or silver in earlier periods indicate payments in raw metal, measured by weight. Transactions in coined money became common by the second half of the fourth century, but they never completely displaced bartering.

1. Coins from the Persian Period
2. Coins from the Hellenistic Period
3. Hasmonean Coins
4. Coins from the Roman Period

1. Coins from the Persian Period.

Under Persian rule (*see* Jewish History: Persian Period), small silver coins intended for local use were minted in or near Jerusalem beginning in the early fourth century B.C. These coins are known as the Yehud series because the Aramaic form of Judea *(YHD)* appears on many of them. The designs imitate those of Greek coins.

Prior to E. L. Sukenik's study, the inscription on a unique, larger specimen was incorrectly read as *YAHU*, the divine name. Therefore the coin's depiction of a deity seated on a wheeled and winged throne was associated with the visions of Ezekiel 1. This coin was probably issued by Persian rather than Jewish authorities, but the interpretation of the image is still debated.

Late in the Yehud series, the legends "Hezekiah" and "Hezekiah the Governor" suggest that Judea enjoyed a limited degree of autonomy within the Persian Empire. A few coins of similar design bear the legend "Yohanan the Priest."

2. Coins from the Hellenistic Period.

The Yehud coins continue into the Hellenistic period (*see* Jewish History: Greek Period), and some may date to the reign of *Alexander the Great. Regional coins minted under the early Ptolemies employ the Hebrew form of Judea *(YHDH)*. Their imagery, which derives from royal issues, includes portraits of Ptolemy I and Queen Berenice produced under Ptolemy II. Later Ptolemaic rulers standardized their coinage, eliminating regional varieties.

The *Seleucid kings continued direct supervision of mints in the region. One coin type belonging to Antiochus VII Sidetes and dated to 132-130 B.C. is found frequently near Jerusalem. A mint was probably opened there after the Syrians reasserted control of Judea in 134 B.C.

3. Hasmonean Coins.

The *Hasmoneans were the first Jewish rulers to issue coins on their own authority. Apart from one rare type in lead, their coins are bronze issues meant for local use. Foreign mints, especially Tyre and Sidon, still supplied silver and gold coins. Most Hasmonean coins employ symbols made familiar on Seleucid coins: anchor, star, lily, palm branch and double cornucopia with a pomegranate. However, no portraits appear; often an inscription surrounded by a wreath identifies the minting authority.

Debate continues on the question of which Hasmonean first produced coins. Some scholars believe that John Hyrcanus I (135/4-109 B.C.) issued coins in his own name. It is more likely that Alexander Jannaeus (103-76 B.C.), who assumed the title of king as well as high priest, produced the first Hasmonean coins.

One of Jannaeus's designs has a lily surrounded by "Yehonatan the King" in Hebrew on the obverse. The reverse bears an anchor and the legend "Alexander the King" in Greek. His most common type has a similar reverse, but its obverse displays an eight-rayed star surrounded by a royal diadem. Between the rays of the star an inscription in Hebrew or Aramaic reads "Yehonatan the King." Some of these coins are dated to the twenty-fifth year of his reign. A third type pairs the inscription "Yehonatan the High Priest and the Community of the Jews" within a wreath on the obverse with a double cornucopia and pomegranate on the reverse. This combination was often imitated by later Hasmoneans.

Many of Jannaeus's coins were overstruck to replace "Yehonatan the King" with "Yonatan the High Priest and the Community of the Jews," eliminating both the royal title and the combination of letters *YHW*, which could be read as the name of God. The restriking was probably done after Jannaeus's death, during the reign of Queen Salome Alexandra (76-67 B.C.).

The power struggle between Salome's sons is reflected in the numismatic record. Judah Aristobolus II, who held the high priesthood from 67 to 63 B.C., inscribed his coins with "Yehudah the High Priest and the Community of the Jews" in Hebrew within a wreath. The reverse carries the double cornucopia with pomegranate. The first coins of John Hyrcanus II (67, 63-40 B.C.) are similar but bear the legend "Yehohanan the High Priest and the Community of the Jews." The change to "Yehohanan the High Priest, Head of the Community of the Jews" reflects the grant of the title *ethnarch* from Julius Caesar in 47 B.C. The monogram A or AP on many of Hyrcanus's coins indicates that the mint was supervised by Antipater, Hyrcanus's Idumean advisor and father of Herod the Great. Hyrcanus II issued coins in several other varieties and denominations.

The last Hasmonean, Mattathias Antigonus, spent his entire reign (40-37 B.C.) fighting Herod for control of the country. His initial designs were similar to those of his predecessors except that he restored the claim to kingship and the use of Greek along with Hebrew. Shortly before his defeat, he introduced a new type, which displayed temple furnishings, the showbread table and the menorah, for the first time.

4. Coins from the Roman Period.

Under Roman rule (*see* Jewish History: Roman Period), numerous local and foreign coin types were used in Judea.

Herod the Great and his successors minted bronze coins with Greek (rarely Latin) inscriptions. The designs are typical of the Roman provincial mints. Later Herodians, whose coins were intended for mixed or predominantly Gentile populations, employed portraits of Roman emperors and occasionally themselves.

Some Roman officials in Judea also minted small bronze coins, the equivalent of a peruta or quadrans, for local use. They generally avoided imperial portraits, used Hebrew characters and chose symbols that had Jewish associations. Only Pilate, who was unusually insensitive to Jewish opinion, portrayed distinctively Roman cult implements on his coins. The temple tax was probably paid with a Roman silver denarius. The "widow's mite" of Mark 12:42 would have been a Greek *lepton*, a tiny bronze coin weighing just over half a gram.

During the first Jewish revolt (A.D. 66-70) both silver and bronze coins were minted in Jerusalem (*see* Jewish Wars with Rome). The production of large silver coins was a clear assertion of autonomy. The silver coins are identified by denomination: shekel of Israel, half-shekel or quarter-shekel. The inscription surrounds a chalice. The reverse bears a pomegranate and the legend "Jerusalem the Holy" or "Holy Jerusalem," perhaps in imitation of the legend "Tyre, Holy and Inviolate" found on the Tyrian coins they were meant to replace.

Bronze coins were issued in the second and third years of the revolt with the inscription "For the Freedom of Zion." In the fourth year the slogan was changed to "For the Redemption of Zion." No bronze coins are dated to either the first or last year of the revolt. The bronzes employ a greater variety of symbols associated with the land or temple: a palm tree or branch, a grapevine or pomegranate, the etrog and lulav, an amphora or a chalice.

Roman authorities celebrated their victory in the Jewish War with an extensive series of Judea Capta coins (*see* Coinage: Greco-Roman).

The coins of the second revolt (A.D. 132-35) were all made by restriking coins already in circulation. The process replaced offensive, mostly Roman, images with the religious and political propaganda of the rebels on the only mass medium known to the ancient world. The Bar Kokhba coins are dated "Year one of the Redemption of Israel" and "Year two of the Freedom of Israel." Coins from the third and fourth years carry only the slogan "For the Freedom of Jerusalem." Since none of the Bar Kokhba coins have been found in Jerusalem, it appears that the rebels never captured the city.

The silver shekels bore an image of the temple, which the rebels hoped to rebuild. Between the central pillars the ark appears in a form that resembles a torah shrine. The word *Jerusalem* surrounds the temple on the early types; it was replaced by "Simon" during the second year. The reverse bears the date or slogan and a lulav, usually accompanied by an etrog.

During the second year, a pair of crossed lines was added above the temple facade. On later dies, the lines become a rosette, a design that frequently represents a star in ancient architectural decoration. The star may allude to Simon, since the rosette first appears on the dies that introduce his name. Because the appellation "Bar Kokhba" does not appear in contemporary documents, it is more likely that the star suggests divine, perhaps angelic, power protecting or returning to a restored temple. The wavy line above the cornice of the temple on late coins probably represents the gigantic, golden grapevine that had adorned the front of the second temple.

The smaller silver coins carry symbols associated with the land and temple: palm branches, grape clusters, vessels and musical instruments. The most common obverse has Simon's name within a wreath, but sometimes the name flanks one of the symbols. The phrase "Eleazar the Priest" appears on some early coins.

The bronze coins were grouped into three denominations according to size. In the first year some were issued under the name of Eleazar the priest. Later that name was replaced by "Jerusalem," "Simon" or "Simon, Prince of Israel." In addition to the symbols found on the denarius, a seven-branched palm tree was particularly popular.

With the defeat of Bar Kokhba, the coins lost their status as legal tender, but many were saved and worn as amulets by later generations, in spite of rabbinic objections.

Early in the third century, the alliance between the mostly Jewish citizens of Sepphoris and the people of Rome was commemorated on the last ancient coins that might be considered Jewish.

See also COINAGE: GRECO-ROMAN; TAXATION: JEWISH.

BIBLIOGRAPHY. D. Barag, "Some Notes on a Silver Coin of Johanan the High Priest," *BA* 48 (1985) 166-68; D. Barag and S. Qedar, "The Beginning of the Hasmonean Coinage," *Israel Numismatic Journal* 4 (1980) 8-21; A. Ben-David, "When Did the Maccabees Begin to Strike Their First Coins?" *PEQ* 104 (1972) 93-103; J. W. Betlyon, "Coinage," *ABD* 1:1076-89; idem, "The Provincial Government of Persian Period Judea and the Yehud Coins," *JBL* 105 (1986) 633-42; D. Hendin, *Guide to Ancient Jewish Coins* (New York: Attic Books, 1976); Y. Meshorer, *Ancient Jewish Coinage* (2 vols.; Dix Hills, NY: Amphora Books, 1982); idem, "Jewish Numismatics," in *Early Judaism and Its Modern Interpreters,* ed. R. A. Kraft and

G. W. E. Nickelsburg (Atlanta: Scholars Press, 1986) 211-20; idem, "Sepphoris and Rome," in *Greek Numismatics and Archaeology: Essays in Honor of Margaret Thompson,* ed. O. Morkholm and N. Waggoner (Wettern, Belgium: Editions NR, 1979) 159-71; L. Mildenberg, *The Coinage of the Bar Kokhba War,* ed. P. Mottahedeh (Typos Monographien zur antiken Numismatic 6; Aarau, Switzerland: Sauerländer, 1984); idem, "Yehud: A Preliminary Study of the Provincial Coinage of Judea," in *Greek Numismatics and Archaeology: Essays in Honor of Margaret Thompson,* ed. O. Morkholm and N. Waggoner (Wettern, Belgium: Editions NR, 1979) 183-96; U. Rappaport, "Numismatics," in *The Cambridge History of Judaism,* ed. W. D. Davies and L. Finkelstein (Cambridge: Cambridge University Press, 1984) 1:25-59; S. Schwartz, "On the Autonomy of Judea in the Fourth and Third Centuries B.C.," *JJS* 45 (1994) 157-68; L. Sporty, "Identifying the Curving Line on the Bar-Kokhba Temple Coin," *BA* 46 (1983) 121-23; E. L. Sukenik, "The Oldest Coins of Judea," *JPOS* 14 (1934) 178-84.

R. F. Stoops

COLOSSAE

Colossae was a small town in the first century A.D. located on the southern bank of the Lycus River at the foot of Mt. Cadmus (elevation, 8,435 feet) 11 miles east of Laodicea and about 15 miles south southeast of Hierapolis (Pamukkale). It was located near a major highway running through the territory of Phrygia in the Roman province of Asia (*see* Asia Minor). The closest town is Honaz Dagi, which is on the slopes of Mt. Cadmus in western central Turkey.

1. History
2. The Church and Doctrinal Questions

1. History.

According to Herodotus (*Hist.* 7.30), the city was the largest in the Lycus Valley in the five centuries before the Christian era. Xenophon (*Anab.* 1.2.6) described it as a large and prosperous city in about 400 B.C., but by the first century B.C. it had declined considerably in size and importance and was overshadowed by its closest neighbor, Laodicea. Numerous *coins have been found in the area that point to the worship of the Ephesian Artemis, the Laodicean Zeus, Men, Selene, Demeter, Hygieia, Helios, Athena, Tyche, Boule and the Egyptian deities Isis and Serapis (*see* Religion, Greco-Roman). The make-up of the population is not certain, but *Cicero indicated that in the three cities of Hierapolis, Laodicea and Colossae there were some ten thousand Jewish males (Cicero *Flac.* 68). By the middle of the first century A.D., the Jews of this area were so plentiful that the Roman governor, in order to finance many projects in the region, would not allow them to send money outside of the province to pay their Jerusalem temple *tax. The Jewish influence in this region can also be seen in the references in the letter to the Colossians to circumcision (Col 2:11), keeping the *sabbath (Col 2:16) and the differences between Jews and Gentiles (Col 1:27; 3:11).

By the first century A.D. Colossae was overshadowed by Laodicea and was described as a smaller city by Strabo (*Geog.* 12.8.13). The days of its former wealth were apparently over. After a major earthquake in the Lycus Valley that destroyed Colossae and Laodicea (c. A.D. 60-64; Tacitus *Ann.* 14.27), Colossae was never fully rebuilt, and by the eighth century it was abandoned. The site has not yet been excavated.

2. The Church and Doctrinal Questions.

While it is possible that Paul may have visited this area on his way to Ephesus by way of the Lycus and Maeander valleys (Acts 18:23; 19:1) and that he may have founded this church, few scholars draw the latter conclusion. Most agree that Epaphras, the companion of Paul, started the church at Colossae (Col 1:7), most likely in the home of Philemon, whose famous runaway *slave, Onesimus, became a companion of Paul's in ministry (Philem 2, 10, 22; 2 Tim 3:20; Col 4:9). Paul's awareness of the church was probably due to the reports from Epaphras (Col 4:7-17; Philem). Colossians 2:1 suggests that he had not been there when he wrote the letter, but later he made plans to visit Colossae (Philem 22).

When that church faced a significant doctrinal threat, Paul, the likely author of the letter to the Colossians, addressed a number of doctrinal issues that were surfacing in the city. Primary among these issues was the identity of Jesus Christ, which Paul dealt with by citing a hymn of the early church (Col 1:15-20), but also Jewish legalistic concerns (Col 2:8-14) and behavioral issues (Col 3:1-17). A strange and imprecise syncretism or mixture of elements found in Hellenistic *mysticism and *Hellenistic Judaism appears to have influenced or concerned the small church at Colossae. This syncretistic milieu included the worship of angels, understanding the identity of Jesus and matters of ethical behavior. While these issues were a part of the so-called Colossian heresy that Paul confronted, the precise nature of these religious concerns is still not clear. It is unlikely that what is later called *Gnosticism was current during the time when Paul wrote, but early strands of that philosophy were likely present in that community. Nothing in the first century, however, can clearly be equated with the Gnosticism of the second century.

See also ASIA MINOR; EPHESUS.

BIBLIOGRAPHY. C. E. Arnold, "Colossae," *ABD* 1:1089-90; idem, *The Colossian Syncretism: The Interface Between Christianity and Folk Belief at Colossae* (WUNT 2.77; Tübingen: Mohr Siebeck, 1995); E. C. Blake, *Biblical Sites in Turkey* (Istanbul: Redhouse Press, 1977, 1990); R. E. Brown, *An Introduction to the New Testament* (ABRL; New York: Doubleday, 1997); E. F. Ferguson, *Backgrounds of Early Christianity* (2d ed.; Grand Rapids, MI: Eerdmans, 1993); F. O. Francis and W. A. Meeks, eds., *Conflict at Colossae* (2d ed.; SBLSBS 4; Missoula, MT: Scholars Press, 1975); E. Lohse, *Colossians and Philemon* (Herm; Philadelphia: Fortress, 1971); J. McRay, "Colossae, Colossians," *Encyclopedia of Early Christianity* (2 vols.; 2d ed.; New York: Garland, 1997) 1:269-70.

L. M. McDonald

COMMERCE. *See* TRAVEL AND TRADE.

CONCUBINAGE. *See* ADULTERY, DIVORCE.

CONSOLATIONS/TANḤUMIN (4Q176)

The *Qumran document known as 4Q176Tanḥumim was originally published by J. M. Allegro as a collection of fifty-seven fragments. Of these, only fragments 1-11 and 19-21 are of sufficient size for identification. Fragments 19-21, the more tenuous of the two sets, have been identified as the text of *Jubilees* 23:21-23, 30-31. These fragments are of great value for evaluating the accuracy of extant Latin and Ethiopic translations that currently preserve the book of *Jubilees* (*see* Jubilees). In their translation of the scrolls, M. O. Wise, M. G. Abegg and E. M. Cook claim that fragments 19-20 do not belong to 4Q176 but to a different document (some suggest 4QJub^{f}; but see the studies by M. Kister and G.-W. Nebe).

Fragments 1-11 are of greater value for NT studies. They are a fairly well preserved anthology of biblical texts. Except for the possible reference to Psalm 79:2-3 at the beginning of the first fragment, all of the quotations are taken from what is today called Second Isaiah, namely, Isaiah 40:1-5; 41:8-10; 43:1-7; 49:7, 13-18; 51:22-23b; 51:23c—52:3; 54:4-10a. The quotations are arranged sequentially and preserved accurately, which suggests that the compiler read progressively through Isaiah 40—55 and recorded certain texts. While the fragmentary condition of the document prevents us from understanding the broader significance that the quotations once had for the Qumran community, an informed inference can be made on the basis of a common theme running through the quotations. In every quotation Yahweh offers words of consolation or comfort—the meaning of the Hebrew word Tanḥumim in the title given the scroll—to his people Israel by assuring them that he is a faithful and loving God who will soon bring restoration to those in despair. Although Second Isaiah was originally concerned with the release of the Israelites from Babylonian exile, the Qumran community interpreted these texts as prophecies relevant for their own day.

4Q176 is important for NT studies in at least two ways. First, it sheds light on the use of written texts by ancient readers. This type of note taking may have provided the basis for the inclusion of select biblical quotations in early Christian writings. But, unlike the long-standing proposal that early Christian writers relied on a common thematic collection of quotations from various sources (as we see in 4Q175), 4Q176 raises the possibility that individual writers compiled their own collections of important texts in the course of their reading. C. D. Stanley argues that this explanation best accounts for the close integration of many biblical quotations into Paul's arguments. Second, the *eschatological interpretation of these select passages from Second Isaiah may illumine their function in early Christian writings. Of particular importance is Isaiah 40:3, since it is quoted in all four Gospels. Like the Qumran community, the early Christians found in this text the prophetic announcement of imminent restoration and deliverance from exile, albeit in spiritual terms through the work of Christ.

See also DEAD SEA SCROLLS: GENERAL INTRODUCTION; JUBILEES.

BIBLIOGRAPHY. J. M. Allegro, *Qumran Cave 4. 1 (4Q158-4Q186)* (DJD 5; Oxford: Clarendon Press, 1968) 60-67; M. Kister, "Newly Identified Fragments of the Book of Jubilees: Jub 23:21-23, 30-31," *RevQ* 12 (1987) 529-36; G.-W. Nebe, "Ergänzende Bemerkung zu 4Q176, Jubiläen 23, 21," *RevQ* 14 (1989) 129-30; C. D. Stanley, "The Importance of 4QTanhumim (4Q176)," *RevQ* 15 (1992) 569-82; M. O. Wise, M. G. Abegg Jr. and E. M. Cook, *The Dead Sea Scrolls: A New Translation* (New York: HarperCollins, 1996) 231-33.

T. R. Hatina

COPPER SCROLL (3Q15)

One of the most enigmatic of the *Dead Sea Scrolls, the *Copper Scroll* is a list of buried treasure inscribed in Hebrew on three copper sheets, originally riveted together to form a single metal scroll. When it was discovered in 1952 in Cave 3 (2 km north of *Qumran), the copper was completely oxidized, and the scroll could not be unrolled. In 1956 it was finally coated with adhesive and then cut open for reading. It proved to contain a text that consists of sixty-four sections, each describing a treasure (usually various amounts of gold and silver) and indicating where the treasure is hidden (usually in places in or near the *temple in Jerusalem). Although some scholars have doubted the authenticity of the document or dated it later than the other Dead Sea Scrolls, most accept it as a genuine first-century record of real treasure, originally belonging either to the Qumran covenanters or more probably to the temple in Jerusalem. Thus the treasure may well represent part of the vast wealth of the temple, hidden before the destruction of Jerusalem by the Romans in A.D. 70 (*see* Jewish Wars with Rome).

Apart from this probable connection with the temple in Jerusalem, the *Copper Scroll* is relevant for the study of the NT in two ways: in demonstrating that *Hebrew was a living language in first-century Palestine and in helping to recover the name of the pool in Jerusalem where Jesus healed an invalid (Jn 5:2).

The *Copper Scroll* is written in a kind of Hebrew that is quite different from the classical literary Hebrew of the other Hebrew Dead Sea Scrolls. In fact, it represents an early form of Mishnaic Hebrew, marked for example by the use of the preposition *šel* and the masculine plural ending *-in*, and thus reflects the spoken form of the language as it had developed from biblical Hebrew. This provides decisive evidence against the view that Hebrew was no longer a living language in the first century and that Jesus is therefore unlikely to have spoken it.

In column 11, line 12 of the *Copper Scroll* one of the hiding places is described as follows: "In Beth Eshdatain, in the reservoir [or pool]." This is probably a reference to the place described in John 5:2 as "a pool, which in Aramaic [or Hebrew] is called Bethesda." The Greek manuscripts of this verse vary between "Bethzatha," "Bethsaida," "Bethesda," and other readings, but the evidence of the *Copper Scroll* seems to clinch the correctness of the reading *Bethesda*.

See also DEAD SEA SCROLLS: GENERAL INTRODUCTION.

BIBLIOGRAPHY. J. K. Lefkovits, *The Copper Scroll—3Q15—a Reevaluation: A New Reading, Translation and Commentary* (Leiden: E. J. Brill, 1999); J. T. Milik, "Le rouleau de cuivre provenant de la grotte 3Q (3Q15)," in *Les "petites Grottes" de Qumrân*, ed. M. Baillet et al. (DJD 3; Oxford: Clarendon Press, 1962) 200-302; A. Wolters, *The Copper Scroll: Overview, Text and Translation* (Sheffield: Sheffield Academic Press, 1996); idem, "The Copper Scroll," in *The Dead Sea Scrolls After Fifty Years*, ed. P. W. Flint and J. C. VanderKam (Leiden: E. J. Brill, 1998) 302-23.

A. Wolters

COPTIC NEW TESTAMENT. *See* NEW TESTAMENT VERSIONS, ANCIENT.

CORINTH

Corinth was named from the currant, a type of grape that grew in abundance in the vicinity. The city is situated about 50 miles west of *Athens on the northern side of the Peloponnesus. Three locations named Corinth exist in proximity. A modern village called Old Corinth, which was partially destroyed by an earthquake in 1858, contains the ruins of ancient Corinth (the Corinth of Paul's time). The devastation wrought by the earthquake allowed excavations in search of the ancient city to begin in 1886, and they continue today. New Corinth, the modern commercial city, was rebuilt in recent times 3.5 miles northeast of the old city, on the coast of the Gulf of Corinth, 1.5 miles west of the Corinthian canal.

1. Location and Description
2. Religious Structures in Corinth
3. Prominent Converts in Corinth

4. Opposition to Paul in Corinth
5. Paul and Gallio
6. Roman Influence in Corinth
7. Jewish Influence in Corinth

1. Location and Description.
Unlike Athens, Corinth was an international crossroads of commerce and travel. Since it was situated southwest of the Corinthian Gulf and northwest of the Saronic Gulf it was served by harbors on these two gulfs (Strabo *Geog.* 8.6.22). Ships sailed from Asia and Egypt into the eastern Saronic harbor at Cenchrea and from Europe into the western Corinthian harbor at Lechaeum. Corinth was thus a gateway between Asia and Europe. All the vices and crimes of such a melting pot must have characterized this city. It would undoubtedly have been the last city of all those through which Paul traveled that he might have expected to be receptive to the gospel.

The city was situated between the northern slopes of the Acrocorinth (elevation 1,886 feet) and the Gulf of Corinth, 4 miles to the north. It had a population far exceeding that of Athens, and although no scientific calculation has been definitively made, estimates run from 150,000 (Wiseman) to 300,000 or more (Barber), plus 460,000 *slaves, according to Athenaeus, who lived in the first century B.C. The walls are now known to have extended for 6 miles around the city.

Corinth was one of the largest and most important commercial cities in the Roman Empire, ranked by some after *Rome and *Alexandria (Fee, 2 n. 5). Strabo wrote that "the city of the Corinthians was always great and wealthy" (Strabo *Geog.* 8.6.23). Isthmia, near Corinth, was one of four permanent sites for the Pan-Hellenic Games, which resembled the modern Olympics (*see* Athletics; Circuses and Games). Mentioned by Strabo (*Geog.* 8.6.20), Plutarch (*Conv.* 5.3.1-3; 8.4.1) and Pausanias (*Descr.* 2.2), these games must have provided enormous income for the city. The superintendent of these games had his office in the south stoa of the forum at Corinth.

There was a large forum in Corinth around which were located a number of commercial and civic buildings, as well as fountains, shops and public toilets. The forum was entered from the north by means of a gravel road, later paved, originating in the harbor of Lechaeum on the Gulf of Corinth. On the south it could be entered on a road coming from Cenchrea, a route Paul would have walked when he left Corinth at the end of his second journey (Acts 18:18).

2. Religious Structures in Corinth.
In A.D. 49, during his second missionary journey, Paul, being unable or unwilling to wait for the return of Timothy and Silas from Thessalonica, left Athens and went on to Corinth. He probably entered the city from the north on the Lechaeum road. Architecture everywhere reflected the transition from a half millennium of Greek culture to a Roman colony—religious, commercial, civic and athletic—a shift the apostle had recently seen in the Roman colony of *Philippi.

Pagan sanctuaries abounded in Corinth. Just inside the northern city wall, on the west side of the road, was the sanctuary of Asclepius, where medicine was practiced in the context of pagan idolatry. Nearer the forum was the temple of Athena. It is one of the oldest in Greece and had been restored by the time Paul arrived. Its earlier identification as the temple of Apollo is derived almost entirely from the imprecise account of Pausanius (*Descr.* 2.3.6.). Fragments of an inscription found on Temple Hill, where this temple is located, suggest Athena as a better possibility (Williams, 26-37; Wiseman 1979, 475, 530 and footnotes). Nearby, on the west end of the forum there was a huge temple that was probably built during the reign of the emperor Tiberius (A.D. 14-37; *see* Roman Emperors) or possibly earlier to house the imperial cult. The temple testifies to the shift in emphasis in the first century from worship of the Olympian gods to that of the emperor (*see* Ruler Cult). Adjacent to the temple of the imperial cult, another small temple stood on the northeast corner of its temenos, and the identity of this temple is uncertain.

The sanctuary of Demeter and Persephone, on the slopes of the Acrocorinth, had been remodeled, and one of its buildings served as the temple, while ritual dining was done outside in tents. In addition, several other smaller temples were standing at the western end of the forum.

According to Strabo, the temple of Aphrodite, located on the Acrocorinth, once "owned a thousand temple-slaves, prostitutes, whom both men and women had dedicated to the goddess," and because of these temple slaves, he maintained, "the city was crowded with people and grew rich." The accuracy of this statement has been challenged by J. Murphy-O'Connor (1984, 152), who calls it "pure fabrication" (*ABD* 1:1136). But there can be little question that Corinth had a history of being an exceptionally immoral city, and it was still filled with immorality in Paul's day. Paul speaks of the "prevalent immorality" in the city (1 Cor 7:1).

The existence of the temple of Aphrodite in the time of Paul is clearly indicatd by Strabo, who used the present tense when he said "Now the summit [of the Acrocorinth] has a small temple of Aphrodite" (Strabo *Geog.* 8.6.21). C. Blegen, who did some limited excavation on the Acrocorinth and found evidence of the temple's foundations, estimated its size to have been no larger than 33 feet by 52 feet, which agreed with Strabo's description of it as small. Furthermore, Corinthian coins show the temple of Aphrodite as restored on the Acrocorinth (Williams).

3. Prominent Converts in Corinth.

During the eighteen months he was in Corinth (Acts 18:11) Paul evidently converted a man named Erastus, who provides an interesting cross-cultural link in the Corinthian church. One of the most imposing structures in Corinth was the fourteen-thousand-seat *theater, located northwest of the forum and renovated about five years before Paul arrived. About this time (c. 50, during the reign of Claudius) a large stone plaza was also laid at the northeast corner of the theater area. There an inscription was found that contained part of an abbreviated Latin statement: "Erastus in return for his aedileship laid [the pavement] at his own expense." The Erastus of this inscription is identified by the excavators with the Erastus mentioned by Paul in a letter later written from Corinth to Rome, in which he said: "Erastus, the city treasurer, salutes you" (Rom 16:23). This is undoubtedly the same Erastus who later remained in Corinth when Paul was taken to Rome (2 Tim 4:20). He was also with Paul in *Ephesus on his third journey (Acts 19:22). Although this name is found among prominent people in Ephesus, it is an uncommon one in Corinth, not otherwise found in the literature and inscriptions of the city.

People who held Erastus's position possessed both wealth (Kent, 100) and high civic status (Meeks, 59). Those who held office by the permission of Roman authority (*see* Roman Administration) found it expedient to express appreciation by donating some work of art or architecture to the city. It is obvious that Paul did not limit his ministry to the poor. Another inscription was found on a monument erected earlier by Cnaeus Babbius Philinus, who was a city treasurer in the reign of Augustus. This inscription says Babbius erected the monument at his own expense.

Another example of the sociological level of Paul's churches includes a couple who were also somewhat prosperous. In Corinth, Paul met Priscilla and her husband, Aquila (Acts 18:2), who had recently arrived from Rome because the emperor Claudius had expelled the Jews (c. 49). Like Paul, they were tentmakers, or leatherworkers (Acts 18:2-3), but apparently they had done well in their business. They were prosperous enough either to have a home in which Christians could meet, presumably in Corinth, certainly later in Ephesus (1 Cor 16:19) and even later in Rome (Rom 16:5), or possibly they rented a vaulted shop with a high ceiling, and, as was customary, built a wooden platform halfway up to the top to divide the room into two levels. The upper room was often used as living quarters for the shopkeepers. These rooms were usually 8 to 14 feet wide and 12 to 24 feet deep. Such a room could accommodate ten to twenty persons. In large cities only prosperous people could afford a private home, called a *domus*, or a villa, some of which have been found in Corinth just northwest of the forum. The poorer classes lived in high-rise apartment houses.

The fact that Priscilla's name is mentioned before that of her husband, once by Paul (Rom 16:3, but not in 1 Cor 16:19) and twice by Luke (Acts 18:18, 26, but not in 18:2), may suggest that she had a higher status than he (Meeks, 59). And the fact that she, as well as her husband, was involved in teaching the eloquent and learned Apollos (Acts 18:24-26), her name even being mentioned first on this occasion, underscores her stature.

In Corinth, Paul "argued in the synagogue every sabbath, and persuaded Jews and Greeks" (Acts 18:4). The typical reaction of Jewish opposition and reviling of his message caused Paul to "shake out his garments" and "go to the Gentiles" (Acts 18:6). He was subsequently hosted by a Godfearer, Titius Justus, who "lived next door to the synagogue" (Acts 18:7). The use of the word *synagogue* in this context indicates a building, not just a group of people. The ruler of this synagogue, Crispus, also believed, together with all his house (Acts 18:8). Titius Justus was among Paul's "first converts in Achaia" (cf. 1 Cor 16:15 with 1:15-16), and since he was Paul's host in Corinth, he may be otherwise known as Gaius, whom Paul also says was host to him in Corinth and to all the church (Rom 16:23). If so, his Roman name would have been Gaius Titius Justus. Paul specifically remembered baptizing Gaius, as well as Crispus and the house of Stephanas. "Beyond that I do not know whether I baptized anyone else," he said (1 Cor 1:15-16). Timothy and Silas probably did most of the baptizing for Paul, since they arrived soon after Paul arrived in Corinth (Bruce, 252).

4. Opposition to Paul in Corinth.
Even though Corinth was different from any other city where Paul had ministered, he did not become discouraged by his rejection and leave Corinth as he did at Athens (Acts 17:33—18:1). Nor did he feel the need to flee the city as he had at Iconium (Acts 14:6). Neither was he driven out by irate synagogue members and civic leaders as he had been in some cities of Galatia and Macedonia (Acts 13:50; 14:19; 16:39). Nor did the new converts send him away for his own safety as they had previously done in Thessalonica (Acts 17:10) and Berea (Acts 17:14). Why? Luke writes that in Corinth "the Lord said to Paul one night in a vision, 'Do not be afraid, but speak and do not be silent; for I am with you, and no man shall attack you to harm you; for I have many people in this city'" (Acts 18:9-10).

After a year and a half, the Jews made a united attack on Paul, presumably because of the inauguration of a new proconsul named Gallio in May or June of 51 (Acts 18:12). This man was the brother of *Seneca, a Greek *Stoic philosopher who would become an adviser to the emperor Nero and perhaps influence the favorable outcome of Paul's first arrest in Rome. Gallio found no violation of Roman law or custom by Paul, no "wrongdoing or vicious" crime (Acts 18:14). Refusing to be a judge of Jewish law, Gallio drove Paul's accusers from the "tribunal" (Acts 18:16-17).

5. Paul and Gallio.
One of the most important discoveries at Corinth relating to the NT is this very tribunal (Gk *bēma),* or speaker's platform, from which official proclamations might be read and citizens might appear before appropriate officials. Here Paul stood before Gallio. The structure was identified by several pieces of an inscription found nearby and dated to the period between A.D. 25 and 50, just prior to Paul's arrival in the city (Scranton).

Since Gallio became proconsul in A.D. 51, the year in which the Pan-Hellenic Games were being held at Isthmia, he may have been en route to the games and stopped by Corinth, where the office of the superintendent of the games was located in the forum.

6. Roman Influence in Corinth.
The extent to which the rebuilt Greek city of Corinth had become Roman, after the commissioning of the colony in 44 B.C., is seen in the fact that after this date Latin predominated its inscriptions. Of 104 inscriptions prior to the reign of Hadrian in the early second century, 101 are in Latin and only 3 in Greek (Kent, 19). The structure and administration of Corinth was Roman, but Paul wrote to the church there in Greek, which indicates that the unofficial language was still Greek. By the time of Hadrian and the visit of Pausanias, Greek had established itself once again as the official language. Corinth was a Roman colony, like Philippi, and exhibited evidence of its Roman base through these Latin inscriptions. Eight of the surviving seventeen names of Corinthian Christians are Latin: Aquila (Acts 18:1), Fortunatus (1 Cor 16:17), Gaius (Rom 16:23), Lucius (Rom 16:21), Priscilla (Acts 18:1, or Prisca, Rom 16:3), Quartus (Rom 16:23), Tertius (Rom 16:22) and Titius Justus (Acts 18:7). The other names are Greek: Achaicus (1 Cor 16:17), Erastus (Acts 19:22; Rom 16:23; 2 Tim 4:20), Jason (Acts 17:5, 6, 7, 9; Rom 16:21), Crispus (Acts 18:8; 1 Cor 1:14), Phoebe (Rom 16:1), Sosipater (Rom 16:21), Sosthenes (Acts 18:17; 1 Cor 1:1), Stephanas (1 Cor 1:16; 16:15, 17) and Chloe (1 Cor 1:11).

7. Jewish Influence in Corinth.
Corinth contained a sizable Jewish population. There were Jews in Corinth as early as the reign of Caligula (A.D. 37-41; Philo *Leg. Gai.* 281), and others came during the expulsion of Jews from Rome under Claudius (Acts 18:2; Suetonius *Claudius* 25.4; Orosius *Hist.* 7.6.15). Jewish inscriptions have appeared in the recent publication of inscriptions that were found piecemeal in the area of Corinth from 1951 to 1976. Most

of these are funerary inscriptions of the Christian period, and one of them (#29) is bilingual, in Hebrew and Greek (Pallas and Dautis, 61ff.; Blegen, VIII. Part I, 111, 115, Part III, 214).

See also ATHENS; GREECE AND MACEDON.

BIBLIOGRAPHY. R. Barber, *Greece, Blue Guide* (5th ed.; New York: Norton, 1987) 261; C. Blegen, "Excavations at the Summit," in *Corinth,* vol. 3, pt. 1: *Acrocorinth* (Cambridge, MA: Harvard University Press, 1930) 20; B. Blue, "Acts and the House Church," in *The Book of Acts in Its Greco-Roman Setting,* ed. D. W. J. Gill and C. Gempf (BAFCS 2; Grand Rapids, MI: Eerdmans, 1994) 119-222; idem, "In Public and in Private: The Role of the House Church in Early Christianity" (Ph.D. diss., University of Aberdeen, 1989); F. F. Bruce, *Paul: Apostle of the Heart Set Free* (Grand Rapids, MI: Eerdmans, 1977); G. D. Fee, *The First Epistle to the Corinthians* (NICNT; Grand Rapids, MI: Eerdmans, 1987); R. Jewett, "Tenement Churches and Communal Meals in the Early Church," *BibRes* 38 (1993) 23-43; J. Kent, *The Inscriptions 1926-1960,* vol. 8, pt. 3: *Corinth* (Princeton, NJ: American School of Classical Studies in Athens, 1966); J. McRay, *Archaeology and the New Testament* (Grand Rapids, MI: Baker, 1991); W. A. Meeks, *The First Urban Christians: The Social World of the Apostle Paul* (New Haven, CT: Yale University Press, 1983); J. Murphy-O'Connor, "The Corinth that Saint Paul Saw," *BA* 47 (1984) 147-59; idem, *St. Paul's Corinth: Texts and Archaeology* (Wilmington, DE: Michael Glazier, 1983); idem, "Corinth," *ABD* 1:1134-39; D. I. Pallas and S. P. Dautis, "Epigraphes apo tē Korinthon," *AE* (1977) 61-83; R. Scranton, *Corinth: Monuments in the Lower Agora and North of the Archaic Temple* (Princeton, NJ: American School of Classical Studies, 1951) vol. 1, pt. 3; C. K. Williams, "The Refounding of Corinth: Some Roman Religious Attitudes," in *Roman Architecture in the Greek World,* ed. S. Macready and F. H. Thompson (London: Society of Antiquaries, 1987) 26ff.; J. Wiseman, "Corinth and Rome I: 228 B.C.-A.D. 267," *ANRW* 2.7.1 (1979) 438-548; idem, *The Land of the Ancient Corinthians* (Studies in Mediterranean Archaeology; Goteborg: Aström, 1978) vol. L.

J. R. McRay

CREEDS AND HYMNS

Hymnic and creedal statements are thought to have played a significant role in the development of the Christian church. Fragments of these and references to others are thought to be found in the NT and merit further discussion.

1. Definition of Terms
2. Approaches to the Material
3. A Closer Look at Some Hymns and Creeds
4. Other References to Hymns and Creeds

1. Definition of Terms.

The writing of hymns has a long history. For instance, the Greek word *hymnos* ("hymn") was used for many centuries in Greek classical culture before Christianity's inception. At least since the time of Homer, a hymn was a song of adoration to a god (Allen and Sikes). Performance of a hymn addressed to a god was also the focus of competitions in the ancient world, which probably includes the second-century B.C. paean to Apollo, known as the First Delphic Hymn (Henderson, 363; see also West, 14-21). Later examples include Cleanthes' *Hymn to Zeus* (*SVF* I, no. 537).

Biblical psalms that are considered hymns are those that express adoration to God (Cumming, 18), and the language of some NT hymnic passages is reminiscent of hymns found either in the *Hebrew Bible or in the Greek *Septuagint. However, the kind of language found in OT psalms/hymns is common also to some Assyrian and Sumerian hymns (see, e.g., Cumming; Vanderburgh). The Christian hymn from the third century after Christ (*P. Oxy.* 1786 in Grenfell and Hunt) also shows a use of language similar to that of these various predecessors.

Sometimes the context distinguishes NT hymns from pagan hymns, and sometimes it is the language, such as the use of terms like "the God of Israel" and certainly references to Christ. Many NT hymns and creedal statements are also distinct from those found in the OT in that they are christological (although see Hengel, 86, who refers to Psalm 110 as christological).

The earliest Christians' perspective on the hymn seems to be fairly broad. E. Werner writes that "early Christianity frequently referred indiscriminately to all sung praises as hymns" (1959, 1:207) and that the "difficulty lies chiefly in the ambiguous term *hymnos,* since Biblical pieces like the canticles, as well as post-Biblical spontaneous utterances and Apocryphal compositions were all termed hymns" (1947, 434). Augustine's often cited definition is "Hymns are praises of God with song. . . . If there be praise, and it is not of God, it is not a hymn; if there be praise, and praise of God, and it is not sung, it is not a hymn. If it is to be a hymn, therefore, it must have three things: praise, and that of God, and song" (McKinnon 1987, no. 360).

Since the early part of the twentieth century there have been increasing numbers of studies on hymns and creeds in the NT, although the distinctions between the two are often a matter for debate (Meeks, 144). Hymnic or creedal passages are often formally identified, for instance, on the basis of heightened poetical language or structure, uncharacteristic vocabulary or the formulaic use of introductory phrases such as *pistos ho logos* ("this is a faithful saying," e.g., 2 Tim 2:11-13) or *homologoumenōs* ("undeniably," e.g., 1 Tim 3:16), a relative pronoun, such as *hos* ("who," e.g., Phil 2:6-11; Col 1:15-20) or the connective *hoti* ("that," e.g., Rom 10:9; 1 Cor 15:3-5). E. Norden mixes content and form when he distinguishes three basic kinds of hymn, one addressed to God, one about God and one based on the relative clause or participle that introduces it (Norden, 143-76). R. P. Martin tends toward the criterion of content when he says that scholars look for passages that have "a lyrical quality and rhythmic style, an unusual vocabulary. . . , some distinctive piece of Christian doctrine" (Martin 1978, 48). Frequently the definitions used are fairly general and mixed, although each hymnic passage is usually thought to have a poetic quality that contributes to its distinctiveness within the larger context (*see DPL*, Hymns, Hymn Fragments, Songs, Spiritual Songs; *DLNTD*, Hymns, Songs).

The threefold reference in the NT to "psalms, hymns and spiritual songs" (Eph 5:19; Col 3:16) has raised the obvious question as to what distinctions there are between these three terms. Most scholars think there is none. However, E. Wellesz's view should perhaps be reconsidered. He musically differentiated psalms as referring to psalmody or the cantillation of Jewish psalms (combining some features of speaking as well as of singing), hymns as more syllabic songs of praise, and spiritual songs as jubilant or ecstatic chants and alleluias (Wellesz 1955, 2; 1998, 33-34). Other NT references to hymns include the parallel verses in Matthew 26:30 and Mark 14:26 ("when they had sung a hymn"; commonly thought to refer to the *Hallel*, Psalms 113—18), the hymns that Paul and Silas were singing at midnight in prison (Acts 16:25) and the kind of hymn a Corinthian brings "when you come together" (1 Cor 14:26).

Creedal formulas are statements that succinctly sum up the basic beliefs of the Christian faith (Leith; *see DPL*, Creed; *DLNTD*, Creeds, Confessional Forms). It has long been thought that the earliest and most essential statement of Christian belief is found in the brief creedal statement "Jesus is Lord" (Rom 10:9). Creedal formulas are frequently associated with baptism; however, while several NT creeds are clearly derived from the context of baptism, the liturgical context of others is unknown. Creedal phrases or related concepts include the following categories: "Jesus is the Christ/the Christ is Jesus" (Mk 8:29; Acts 17:3; 18:5; 1 Jn 5:1); "Jesus the Son of God" (Acts 9:20); "Jesus (Christ) is Lord" (Acts 10:36; 11:20; Rom 10:9); "Jesus Christ our Lord" (Rom 1:3-4); "Jesus is the Son of God" (1 Jn 4:15); "Jesus Christ has come in the flesh" (1 Jn 4:2); the significance of the death of Christ (1 Jn 2:2); the oneness of God (Jas 2:19); formal doxology (Rom 16:25-27; Jude 24-25); creedal formula centered on the resurrection of Christ (1 Cor 15:3-5); observing the Lord's Supper as proclaiming Christ's death (1 Cor 11:26); two-article affirmation of "one God, the Father . . . one Lord, Jesus Christ" (1 Cor 8:6); three-article affirmation of Father, Son and Holy Spirit (Mt 28:19; 2 Cor 13:13); creedlike phrases (1 Tim 1:17; 6:15-16); statements opening with "faithful is the saying" (Knight; 1 Tim 1:15); anti-docetic creedal formulation (Phil 2:5-11, but generally regarded as a hymn). A later creedal formula is found in the well known acronym ΙΧΘΥΣ (*ichthys*: "Jesus Christ, Son of God, Savior," Ι *Iēsous* = Jesus; Χ *Christos* = Christ; Θ *Theou* = (of) God; Υ *Huios* = Son; Σ *Sōtēr* = Savior).

Categorizing the passages, as has already been noted, is not without its difficulties. Basic distinctions have been made, but frequently texts will fall in more than one category, and there are numerous differences of opinion regarding categorization. Some hymns are direct quotations from the *Hebrew Bible/OT (e.g., 1 Pet 2:6-8), while others are based more on the Greek OT, the *Septuagint (such as Lk 1:46-55). Some of the texts are highly poetic (e.g., 1 Tim 3:16), while some are basic creedal statements (e.g., Mk 8:29; Rom 10:9). Some are thought to be baptismal (e.g., Tit 3:4-7). Some are doxological in nature (e.g., 1 Tim 6:15-16; Rev 4:8) and some are christological (e.g., Phil 2:5-11; Col

1:15-20). Some have binary parallel structures (e.g., 1 Cor 8:6), and some have ternary parallel structures (e.g., Eph 5:14).

Passages that may be hymnic or creedal include Matthew 28:19; Mark 8:29; Luke 1:46-55, 68-79; 2:14, 29-32; John 1:1-16; Acts 4:24-30 (or 24-26); 5:42; 9:20, 22; 10:36; 11:20; 17:3; 18:5, 28; 22:6; Romans 1:3-4; 3:13-18, 24-26; 9:33; 10:9-10; 11:33-36; 16:25-27; 1 Corinthians 5:4; 8:6; 11:26; 12:3; 13:1-4; 15:3-5; 2 Corinthians 1:3-4; 5:18-21; 11:12-15; 13:13; Ephesians 1:3-14; 2:12-19 (or 14-16); 4:4-9/10; 5:14; Philippians 2:(5)6-11; Colossians 1:15-20 (12-14); 2:8, 9-15 (or 13-15); 1 Timothy 1:15, 17; 3:16; 6:12, 15-16; 2 Timothy 1:8-10; 2:11-13; Titus 3:4-7; Hebrews 1:3; James 2:19; 4:12; 1 Peter 1:3-5 (or 3-12); 1:18-21 (or 1:20); 2:6-7/8 (or 4-8); 2:21-25 (or 21-22); 3:18-22 (or 18); 1 John 2:2, 22; 4:2, 10, 15; 5:1, 5; Jude 24-25; Revelation 1:4-8; 4:8, 11; 5:9-10, 12, 13; 7:10, 12; 11:15, 17-18; 12:10-12; 14:3; 15:3-4; 16:5-7; 19:1-2, 3, 5; 19:6-8; 22:17 (or seven antiphonal units: 4:8-11; 5:9-14; 7:9-12; 11:15-18; 16:5-7; 19:1-4, 5-8 [Aune, 315]).

2. Approaches to the Material.

2.1. Source-Critical Studies. The beginning of source-critical studies of these passages began especially with the form-critical work of Norden that pointed to certain passages originating in earlier sources. Norden noticed that there was a higher level of writing in certain brief passages and suggested that this may be because the verses came from a source other than that particular writer. Source-critical studies have often focused on the Jewish backgrounds to these passages. The structure of the passages themselves is thought to give indications of their original language, giving rise to the notion of translating them back into their original language (for example, *Aramaic) for the purpose of study. Some of the hymnic passages, such as the canticles found in Luke, are obviously paraphrased from or rendered in the style of the Hebrew or Greek OT. It has also been suggested that the Greek sources of some passages were written and used by the earliest church gatherings, for example, the church at Antioch (Gundry 1970, 221-22). Some scholars have more recently included the possibility of the biblical author writing these passages, though perhaps in an elevated style (e.g., Wright).

2.2. Form-Critical Studies. Related to source-critical studies, as noted above, features of these passages have been important in attempts to distinguish different forms. For instance, what may seem at first like a simple question—whether 1 Timothy 3:16 consists of two groups of three lines or three groups of two lines—has been the subject of a long debate that has not reached a consensus (Gundry 1970). Each passage has a history of its own regarding the scholarly view of its structure and form. Passages of high contention also include Colossians 1:15-20 and Philippians 2:5-11.

2.3. Functionalist Studies. A fundamental issue that has been the subject of more recent discussion is how these passages function within the NT contexts. S. E. Fowl concentrates this approach on several supposed hymns in Paul's writings (Phil 2:5-11; Col 1:15-20; 1 Tim 3:16). Fowl suggests that isolating the definition, source and form of a hymn may be of less importance than how it functions in its present NT context. The fact that Paul does not call these passages hymns suggests that it is an unimportant distinction for his purpose, which is to develop his point or to present his case.

2.4. Musical and Liturgical Studies. In attempting to reconstruct the musical and liturgical world of the NT and the early church, scholars are dependent on isolated and fragmentary references to musical and liturgical practice. Some scholars contend that the early church took over the practices of the Jewish *synagogue, while others believe that psalmody, for instance, was not widely used in early Christian liturgy. Nonetheless, there is a steadily increasing body of knowledge about the sacred music and the liturgy of the early Christian church, with ongoing attempts to find more clues as to its earliest history (see, e.g., Bradshaw; Holleman; Jeffery; McKinnon 1986; Quasten; J. A. Smith; W. S. Smith; Werner 1984).

3. A Closer Look at Some Hymns and Creeds.

3.1. Luke 1:46-55. The Magnificat, which begins "My soul magnifies the Lord," is thought to be in the line of traditional Jewish psalmody (Farris, 116). J. A. Fitzmyer considers it to be much like other "'hymns of praise' among the canonical psalms," such as Psalm 136 (Fitzmyer, 359). The language of the Magnificat, or Mary's song, seems to rely on the Greek Septuagint, however, with little evidence of the song having existed previously in Hebrew or Aramaic. Fitzmyer calls it "a mosaic of OT expressions drawn from the LXX" (Fitzmyer, 359). The Jewish thought, rather than Christian, suggests an author other than the Lukan author (Marshall 1978, 79). Some textual variants have the name Elizabeth instead of Mary, although the attribution to Mary is generally upheld; whether this means that she wrote the song is debatable. A text that has some similarities to Mary's song is 1 Samuel 2:1-10, the song of Hannah, thought by many scholars to be the main influence on the Lukan passage. S. Farris writes that the hymn "displays . . . the characteristic structure of the declarative psalm of praise," which means that it begins with praise and then gives the reasons for that praise (Farris, 114). He thinks that attempts to divide the hymn into strophes, which have variously resulted in two, three and four strophes, are unnecessary and contends that the hymn fits within the "consistent promise-fulfilment-praise progression in Luke 1—2" (112), thereby fulfilling the function of Luke's narrative to show this progression (*see DJG*, Mary's Song).

3.2. John 1:1-18 (or 1:1-16). Scholars are not agreed on whether the prologue to John's Gospel, "In the beginning was the Word," is a hymn. Those who say it is point out the uses of parallelism and chiasm, for instance, that elevate the language from prose to poetry. Some split the passage into sections of verses that may represent an earlier hymn, with authorial insertions of polemical and explanatory prose (Dunn 1977, 137). However, D. A. Carson suggests that the prologue to the Fourth Gospel may not be drawn from a source but that it was written in its entirety by the author, an opinion he bases on the similarity of the writing style of the prologue to that of the rest of the Gospel, as well as the close correspondence of the material to the rest of the book (Carson, 112). This relates to its function as well, for Carson notes that the prologue is essential and integral to the rest of the book. Musically, C. K. Kraeling and L. Mowry believe that this passage suggests a combination of Jewish and Greek musical characteristics (Kraeling and Mowry, 309).

3.3. Romans 10:9. This creedal statement, "That if you confess with your mouth, 'Jesus is Lord,' and believe in your heart that God raised him from the dead, you will be saved," is thought by many to contain the earliest baptismal confession of faith: "Jesus is Lord." J. D. G. Dunn writes that it "is clearly a public confession of a solemn nature" and that Paul is citing a creedal formula that is well established (Dunn 1988, 606). Discussions about the use of the word *Lord* attempt to determine whether this word would have been perceived with Jewish overtones because of its common use in the Septuagint, where it is frequently used to replace the Hebrew, Yahweh, or understood in its contemporary usage in the Greco-Roman world.

3.4. 1 Corinthians 15:3-5. First Corinthians 15:3-5 is one of the main NT creedal statements (see Schweizer's comparison with 1 Tim 3:16), the essence of which is Christ died, was buried, was raised and was seen. R. P. Martin clearly sees the characteristics of a "credal formulary" in these verses: "The four-fold 'that' introduces each member of the creed. . . . The vocabulary is unusual, containing some rare terms and expressions which Paul never employs again. The preface to the section informs us that Paul 'received' what follows in his next sentences as part of his instruction . . . now in turn, he transmits . . . to the Corinthian Church what he has received as a sacred tradition" (Martin 1963, 57-58). Although there are many arguments for a Semitic source and the passage shows dependence on Isaiah 53, the form in the NT is a Greek composition (Conzelmann). H. Conzelmann says the passage is clearly two double statements: in the first statement, "he died, he was buried," and in the second, "he was raised, he appeared." Others find an essentially three-part statement: Christ died, was buried and was raised from the dead.

3.5. Ephesians 5:14. This hymnic fragment reads "Therefore, it is said, 'Wake up, O sleeper, rise from the dead, and Christ will shine upon you.'" The rhythm of the language and the two introductory phrases both indicate the distinctiveness of the passage. Whether it is an early Christian hymn or one written by Paul himself, two OT references that seem to have influenced the passage are Isaiah 26:19 and 60:1, 2. From the first passage there is the influence of the rhythmic pattern and the use of the three concepts rise, waken and the dead. From the second comes the contrast of light and darkness (O'Brien 1999). Some consider the form of this hymn to be ternary, although the first two are a couplet of parallel imperative statements, while the third is a responding statement. The function of this hymn seems to be calling the nonbeliever to believe and is thought to have been used in a baptismal context.

*3.6. **Philippians 2:6-11.*** This passage is widely acknowledged as an early Christian hymn (but see Fee, 30). Fowl states that "in calling these passages hymns we are using a term that is the construction of a later, critical community, and not a straightforward translation of *hymnos* in either its specific or generic sense" (Fowl, 33). Nevertheless, most would agree that the writing style of these six verses is distinctly different from the preceding and following verses. As a result, many scholars think that this passage is a quotation by Paul of a work written earlier than the writing of the epistle (Martin 1997, xxxiv). However, Pauline authorship is gaining ground (Fee; Gundry 1994, 288; Silva, 105; Martin 1997, 42-62; Wright, 352). The Philippian hymn may stand at the forefront of christological hymns of the Christian church, providing a template for Christian theology and hymn writing that reflects a ternary pattern: Christ's preexistence, his incarnation and death on a cross, and his resurrection and ultimate exaltation (contra Dunn 1989, 114-25).

Fowl's discussion of hymns as exemplars suggests that Paul uses it to offer a solution to the Christian community that was being persecuted (Fowl, 93). Musically speaking, Kraeling and Mowry think the hymn exemplifies a mixture of features: "As read in the original Greek the lyric . . . has a regularity of construction hardly to be imitated in translation. . . . The absence of parallelism, the brevity and equality of the lines and the stanza-form shows that we are dealing here with a composition even more remote from Jewish psalmody. The lyric is in fact a hymn to Christ as *Kyrios* or Lord, and hence quite out of keeping with Jewish tradition. Yet the rhythm is not quantitative but accentual, with three beats to the line, which suggests that it must have been sung in oriental fashion and not in one of the Greek modes" (Kraeling and Mowry, 309).

*3.7. **Colossians 1:15-20.*** This christological passage, which begins "he is the image of the invisible God," uses exalted language to declare the supremacy of Christ in creation and in redemption. The use of an introductory relative clause *hos estin* ("who is"), a style that suggests a strophic arrangement, the use of rhetorical devices and distinct language are all considered indications that this is a traditional hymn (O'Brien 1982), and the majority of NT scholars see this as clearly a pre-Pauline hymn (see discussion in Cannon). Various proposals as to sources or influences on this passage include Jewish circles influenced by Greek ideas, *Gnosticism, *rabbinic Judaism and *Hellenistic Judaism. P. J. Achtemeier (1990) and others maintain that claims that the hymn is non-Pauline do not hold up, however, and that it is much more likely that Paul wrote the hymn, whether prior to the writing of the epistle or at the time, for the passage is central to the work, not a disjunctive leap. As to its form, many scholars agree that the passage consists of two strophes but disagree as to where the second strophe begins. The hymn may have been used against the Colossian heresy by emphasizing that even the cosmic powers are subject to Christ: Christ was first in creation; now through his resurrection, he is first in everything. E. Käsemann, however, discusses it in terms of a primitive Christian baptismal liturgy (Käsemann, 149-61).

*3.8. **1 Timothy 3:16.*** Traditionally Paul the apostle has been thought to be the author of 1 Timothy, although many scholars now think that the letter is *pseudepigraphal and was written later than the time of Paul, with proposals ranging from the end of the first century to as late as mid-second century (Guthrie 1970, 623-24; *see DPL*, Pastoral Letters). There is a similar lack of consensus regarding who wrote the specific passage found in 1 Timothy 3:16. Since the beginning of the twentieth century, the view that has found increasing acceptance is that the writer of 1 Timothy quotes an early Christian hymn or creed (Norden, 250-63; cf. Fowl, 37-45). The use of *homologoumenōs* ("undeniably") in the introductory phrase is thought to be an indicator of this hymnic passage, as is the use of *hos* ("who"; but see Marshall 1999, 523).

In Martin's outline of the characteristics of a creed compared with those that define a hymn (Martin 1963, 14-17), 1 Timothy 3:16 fits with some of his criteria of a creed, but in more cases with those of a hymn. The verse uses a different style of writing that sets it apart from the rest of the letter. The writing is compact—a total of eighteen words in six lines. The content, however, of these six lines is expansive, summarizing six events in which Christ is central. The use of the six verbs in the passive voice is a means by which Christ is understood to be the grammatical subject of each clause. The fact that this hymn was placed within the letter provides an insight into the author's view of the story of

Christ, as well as how he saw it functioning within the larger context of the letter. In its bold christology, the hymn addresses asceticism in the church (Fowl), as well as negative speech among its members (Guthrie 1990, 42-43). The succinct and poetical nature of the words of the hymn is particularly apparent in its parallel Greek form with its six passive verbs, a factor that suggests musical and liturgical use.

3.9. 1 Peter 3:18-22. The beginning of this creedal hymn states "For Christ died for our sins once for all, the righteous for the unrighteous, to bring you to God. He was put to death in the body but made alive by the Spirit." Of the full passage, L. Goppelt says that "nowhere else are so many aspects of the second article of the Apostles' Creed found in a preliminary stage of development" (Goppelt, 247). But, although both traditional creedal and hymnic elements are used, P. H. Davids writes that "arguments for a hymnic structure in part or all of this passage are not yet convincing" (Davids, 134-35). Achtemeier suggests that failed attempts to reconstruct an original hymn or creedal statement are because this passage only alludes to familiar traditions without taking over their original form (Achtemeier 1996). He identifies some of the more important linguistic features that point to the use of earlier traditions or materials as the use of *hoti* ("that"), *hina* ("so that"), *hos* ("who"), parallel phrases, reference to the exaltation of Christ, a threefold statement that Christ died, was made alive and ascended into heaven, and the use of *hapax legomena.* It is thought that the context for this passage is a baptismal setting, but F. L. Cross proposed that it is baptism within the paschal liturgy, noting that "as far back as our evidence takes us, the Paschal Liturgy has been for Christians a regular occasion for baptism" (Cross, 28).

3.10. Revelation 4:8. The hymn found in this verse "Holy, holy, holy, Lord God Almighty, who was, and is, and is to come" bears a resemblance to Isaiah 6:3: "Holy, holy, holy is the Lord Almighty; the whole earth is full of his glory" (the latter is known as the *Tersanctus,* "Thrice Holy," found in the Hebrew liturgy). The first name of God in Revelation 4:8 is "Lord God Almighty," which seems to be used because of its frequent use in the Septuagint, while the second name of God, the one "who was, and is, and is to come," has been thought to be drawn from the Hebrew OT and Jewish exegetical tradition (Beale, 332). It is also, however, a familiar description found in Greco-Roman literature (e.g., Plato *Tim.* 37E; see Aune). D. E. Aune contends that John depended on two main influences in writing the hymns found in Revelation: Jewish traditions regarding the heavenly liturgy and the court ceremonial practices of Hellenists and Romans to sing hymns and shout acclamations to the emperor (Aune, 316). The context of this verse has been thought to be directly related to the liturgy of the early church or Jewish synagogue. G. J. Beale argues that the passage does not indicate what the liturgical patterns were but is meant to be the pattern after which the church shapes its worship.

3.11. Revelation 5:12. This doxological hymn, rather than describing attributes of God, lists those things that the Lamb is worthy to receive: "Worthy is the Lamb, who was slain, to receive power and wealth and wisdom and strength and honor and glory and praise." These are of the highest order and by rights belong only to God, but it is clearly shown that now they are also transferred to Christ, the Lamb. Lists similar to the one found here can be found in 1 Chronicles 29:11 and in the Greek version of Daniel 2:37 but also in writings such as *Philo (*Ebr.* 75).

4. Other References to Hymns and Creeds.
There are hymnic or creedal passages and references to others in contemporary literature outside the NT, but only brief reference can be made to them here. Early references to hymns are found in the well-known letters of Pliny the Younger to the emperor Trajan (written c. A.D. 107–115; for some discussion, see van Beeck), and mention of primitive Greek hymns is found in the *Apostolic Constitutions* (fourth century), examples of which are appended to Codex Alexandrinus (fifth century) and are expanded forms of the greater doxology, "Glory to God in the highest." The lesser doxology, *Doxa Patri* (identical with the Latin *Gloria Patri*) "Glory be to the Father, and to the Son, and to the Holy Spirit: as it was in the beginning, is now, and ever shall be, world without end. Amen," was in use in Rome already by the time of Clement, about A.D. 91 (Bichsel).

See also MUSIC; PSALMS AND HYMNS OF QUMRAN.

BIBLIOGRAPHY. P. J. Achtemeier, *1 Peter: A Commentary on First Peter* (Hermeneia; Minneapolis: Fortress, 1996); idem, "*Omne Verbum Sonat*:

The New Testament and the Oral Environment of Late Western Antiquity," *JBL* 109 (1990) 3-27; T. W. Allen and E. E. Sikes, *The Homeric Hymns* (London: Macmillan, 1904); D. E. Aune, *Revelation 1—5* (WBC 52A; Dallas: Word, 1997); C. K. Barrett, *A Commentary on the First Epistle to the Corinthians* (2d ed.; BNTC; London: Adam & Charles Black, 1971); G. J. Beale, *The Book of Revelation* (NIGTC; Grand Rapids, MI: Eerdmans, 1999); F. J. van Beeck, "The Worship of Christians in Pliny's Letter," *SL* 18 (1988) 121-31; M. A. Bichsel, "Hymns, Early Christian," *ABD* 3:350-51; P. F. Bradshaw, *The Search for the Origins of Christian Worship: Sources and Methods for the Study of Early Liturgy* (Oxford: Oxford University Press, 1992); G. E. Cannon, *The Use of Traditional Materials in Colossians* (Macon, GA: Mercer University Press, 1983) 19-37; D. A. Carson, *The Gospel According to John* (Leicester: InterVarsity Press, 1991); H. Conzelmann, *1 Corinthians* (Hermeneia; Philadelphia: Fortress, 1975); C. E. B. Cranfield, *A Critical and Exegetical Commentary on the Epistle to the Romans,* vol. 2, *Commentary on Romans IX—XV and Essays* (ICC; Edinburgh: T & T Clark, 1979); F. L. Cross, *1 Peter: A Paschal Liturgy* (New York: Morehouse-Gorham, 1954); C. G. Cumming, *The Assyrian and Hebrew Hymns of Praise* New York: AMS Press, 1966 [1934]); P. H. Davids, *The First Epistle of Peter* (NICNT; Grand Rapids, MI: Eerdmans, 1990); R. Deichgräber, *Gotteshymnus und Christushymnus in der frühen Christenheit* (SUNT 5; Göttingen: Vandenhoeck & Ruprecht, 1967); G. Dix, *The Shape of the Liturgy* (Westminster: Dacre, 1954); J. D. G. Dunn, *Christology in the Making: A New Testament Inquiry into the Origins of the Doctrine of the Incarnation* (2d ed.; Grand Rapids, MI: Eerdmans, 1989); idem, *Romans 9—16* (WBC 38B; Dallas: Word, 1988); idem, *Unity and Diversity in the New Testament: An Inquiry into the Character of Earliest Christianity* (Philadelphia: Westminster, 1977); S. Farris, *The Hymns of Luke's Infancy Narratives: Their Origin, Meaning and Significance* (JSNTSup 9; Sheffield: Sheffield Academic Press, 1985); G. D. Fee, "Philippians 2:5-11: Hymn or Exalted Pauline Prose?" *BBR* 2 (1992) 29-46; J. A. Fitzmyer, *The Gospel According to Luke I—IX* (AB 28; Garden City, NY: Doubleday, 1981); S. E. Fowl, *The Story of Christ in the Ethics of Paul: An Analysis of the Function of the Hymnic Material in the Pauline Corpus* (JSNTSup 36; Sheffield: JSOT, 1990); L. Goppelt, *A Commentary on 1 Peter* (Grand Rapids, MI: Eerdmans, 1993); B. P. Grenfell and A. S. Hunt, "Christian Hymn with Musical Notation," in *The Oxyrhynchus Papyri,* XV (Egypt Exploration Society Greco-Roman Memoirs; London: Egypt Exploration Society, 1922), no. 1786, 21-25; R. H. Gundry, "The Form, Meaning and Background of the Hymn Quoted in 1 Timothy 3:16," in *Apostolic History and the Gospel: Biblical and Historical Essays Presented to F. F. Bruce,* ed. W. W. Gasque and R. P. Martin (Exeter: Paternoster, 1970) 203-22; idem, "Style and Substance in 'The Myth of God Incarnate' According to Philippians 2:6-11," in *Crossing the Boundaries: Essays in Biblical Interpretation in Honour of Michael D. Goulder,* ed. S. E. Porter, P. Joyce and D. E. Orton (Leiden: E. J. Brill, 1994) 271-93; D. Guthrie, *New Testament Introduction* (rev. ed.; Downers Grove, IL: InterVarsity Press, 1970); idem, *The Pastoral Epistles: An Introduction and Commentary* (TNTC; rev. ed.; Grand Rapids, MI: Eerdmans, 1990) 224-40; C. Hannick, "Christian Church, Music of the Early," in *New Grove Dictionary of Music and Musicians,* ed. S. Sadie (20 vols.; London: Macmillan, 1980) 4:363-71; I. Henderson, "Ancient Greek Music," in *Ancient and Oriental Music,* ed. E. Wellesz (NOHM 1; London: Oxford University Press, 1966 [1957]) 336-403; M. Hengel, "Hymns and Christology," in *Between Jesus and Paul: Studies in the Earliest History of Christianity* (Philadelphia: Fortress, 1983) 78-96; A. W. J. Holleman, "Early Christian Liturgical Music," *SL* 8 (1971) 185-92; P. Jeffery, "The Earliest Christian Chant Repertory Recovered: The Georgian Witnesses to Jerusalem Chant," *Journal of the American Musicological Society* 67 (1994) 1-38; E. Käsemann, "A Primitive Christian Baptismal Liturgy," in *Essays on New Testament Themes* (Philadelphia: Fortress, 1964) 149-61; G. W. Knight III, *The Faithful Sayings in the Pastoral Letters* (Kampen: Kok Pharos, 1968); C. K. Kraeling and L. Mowry, "Music in the Bible," in *Ancient and Oriental Music,* ed. E. Wellesz (NOHM 1; London: Oxford University Press, 1966 [1957]) 283-312; J. H. Leith, "Creeds, Early Christian," *ABD* 1:203-6; I. H. Marshall, *The Gospel of Luke* (NIGTC 3; Grand Rapids, MI: Eerdmans, 1978); idem, *The Pastoral Epistles* (ICC; Edinburgh: T & T Clark, 1999); R. P. Martin, "Aspects of Worship in the New Testament Church," *VoxEv* 2 (1963) 6-32; idem, *Carmen Christi: Philippians 2:5-11 in Recent Interpretation and in the Setting of Early Christian Worship* (SNTSMS 4; Cambridge: Cambridge University Press, 1967; Grand Rapids, MI: Eerdmans, 1983) 42-62 [= *A Hymn of Christ: Philippians 2:5-11 in*

Recent Interpretation and in the Setting of Early Christian Worship (Downers Grove, IL: InterVarsity Press, 1997) 42-62]; idem, "Some Reflections on New Testament Hymns," in *Christ the Lord,* ed. H. H. Rowden (Downers Grove, IL: InterVarsity Press, 1982) 37-49; idem, *Worship in the Early Church* (2d ed.; Grand Rapids, MI: Eerdmans, 1978); J. McKinnon, "The Exclusion of Musical Instruments from the Ancient Synagogue," *Proceedings of the Royal Musical Association* 106 (1979–80) 77-87;idem, "On the Question of Psalmody in the Ancient Synagogue," in *Early Music History: Studies in Medieval and Early Modern Music,* ed. I. Fenlon (Cambridge: Cambridge University Press, 1986) 6:159-91; J. McKinnon, ed., *Music in Early Christian Literature* (Cambridge Studies in the Literature of Music; Cambridge: Cambridge University Press, 1987); W. A. Meeks, *The First Urban Christians: The Social World of the Apostle Paul* (New Haven, CT: Yale University Press, 1983); L. Mowry, "Revelation 4—5 and Early Christian Liturgical Usage," *JBL* 71 (1952) 75-84; E. Norden, *Agnostos Theos: Untersuchungen zur Formengeschichte religiöser Rede* (Darmstadt: Wissenschaftliche Buchgesellschaft, 1956 [1913]); P. T. O'Brien, *Colossians, Philemon* (WBC 44; Waco: Word, 1982); idem, *The Letter to the Ephesians* (PNTC; Grand Rapids, MI: Eerdmans, 1999); W. J. Porter, "Misguided Missals: Is Early Christian Music Jewish or Is It Graeco-Roman?" in *Christian-Jewish Relations Through the Centuries,* ed. S. E. Porter and B. W. R. Pearson (RILP 6; JSNTSup; Sheffield: Sheffield Academic Press, forthcoming 2000); J. Quasten, *Music and Worship in Pagan and Christian Antiquity* (Washington, DC: National Association of Pastoral Musicians, 1980); J. T. Sanders, *The New Testament Christological Hymns* (SNTSMS 15; Cambridge: Cambridge University Press, 1971); G. Schille, *Frühchristliche Hymnen* (Berlin: Evangelische Verlagsanstalt, 1965); E. Schweizer, "Two New Testament Creeds Compared," in *Issues in New Testament Interpretation: Essays in Honor of Otto A. Piper,* ed. W. Klassen and G. F. Snyder (London: SCM, 1962) 166-77; J. E. Scott, "Roman Music," in *Ancient and Oriental Music,* ed. E. Wellesz (NOHM 1; London: Oxford University Press, 1966 [1957]) 404-20; M. Silva, *Philippians* (WEC; Chicago: Moody, 1988); J. A. Smith, "First-Century Christian Singing and Its Relationship to Contemporary Jewish Religious Song," *Music & Letters* 75 (1994) 1-15; W. S. Smith, *Musical Aspects of the New Testament* (Amsterdam: W. Ten Have, 1962); F. A. Vanderburgh, *Sumerian Hymns: From Cuneiform Texts in the British Museum* (COHP 1; New York: AMS Press, 1966 [1908]); E. Wellesz, "Early Christian Music," in *Early Medieval Music up to 1300,* ed. A. Hughes (NOHM 2; London: Oxford University Press, 1954; rev. ed., 1955) 1-13; idem, *A History of Byzantine Music and Hymnography* (2d ed.; Oxford: Clarendon Press, 1961; repr. Sandpiper Books, 1998); E. Werner, "The Conflict Between Hellenism and Judaism in the Music of the Early Christian Church," *HUCA* 20 (1947) 407-70; idem, "'If I Speak in the Tongues of Men . . . ': St. Paul's Attitude to Music," *Journal of the American Musicological Society* 13 (1960) 18-23; idem, *The Sacred Bridge: The Interdependence of Liturgy and Music in Synagogue and Church During the First Millenium* (vol. 1: New York: Columbia University Press, 1959; vol. 2: New York: Ktav, 1984); M. L. West, *Ancient Greek Music* (Oxford: Clarendon Press, 1992); N. T. Wright, "ἁρπαγμός and the Meaning of Philippians 2:5-11," *JTS* n.s. 37 (1986) 321-52 [repr. in revised form as "Jesus Christ Is Lord: Philippians 2:5-11," in *The Climax of the Covenant: Christ and the Law in Pauline Theology* (Edinburgh: T & T Clark, 1991) 56-98].

W. J. Porter

CUMAEAN SIBYL. *See* PROPHETS AND PROPHECY.

CUMANUS, VENTIDIUS

Ventidius Cumanus was the Roman procurator of Judea from A.D. 48 to 52 (*see* Roman Governors of Palestine). *Josephus and *Tacitus are the only extant ancient sources on Cumanus's career, although Tacitus's account is more concerned with Antonius Felix, the procurator mentioned in Acts 24 (who was also the less discerning brother of Pallas, the ex-slave who rose to power as financial secretary under Claudius; see Tacitus *Ann.* 12.53; Suetonius *Claudius* 28).

Josephus tells two stories that precede Tacitus's account. The first (Josephus *J.W.* 2.12.1 §§223-27 = *Ant.* 20.5.2-3 §§103-12) relates that Cumanus was the successor to Tiberius Alexander as procurator of Judea. He goes on to tell of an incident during Passover where a soldier, on duty on the roof of the *temple portico, showed his backside (Josephus *J.W.* 2.12.1 §224) or genitals (Josephus *Ant.* 20.5.3 §108) to the people in the temple yard. In response, some people in the crowd began throwing stones at the soldier. Cumanus, instead of disciplining the soldier, began pouring in reinforcements, and between ten thousand and thirty thousand people were purportedly trampled to death (there is a discrepancy between the number in *J.W.* and *Ant.*, as well as a text-critical problem in some of the manuscripts of *J.W.*). The second event (Josephus *J.W.* 2.12.2 §§228-31 = *Ant.* 20.5.4 §§113-17) was the attack by brigands on one Stephen, slave of the emperor, who robbed him of his baggage. In response to this, Cumanus sent troops to round up prominent men from neighboring villages. One of these troops, finding a copy of the Torah, ripped it up and threw the pieces into a fire, which enraged the Jews in the area. They demanded the death of the soldier, to which Cumanus acquiesced, apparently having learned caution from his earlier mishandling of Jewish religious sentiment.

The end of Cumanus's career followed on his mishandling of an armed conflict between the Galileans and the Samaritans (Josephus *J.W.* 2.12.3-7 §§232-46 = *Ant.* 20.6.1-3 §§118-36; Tacitus *Ann.* 12.53). The problem started when several *Samaritans set upon and killed some Galilean Jews attempting to go through Samaritan territory to get to Jerusalem at *festival time. Cumanus refused to avenge the deaths, as he was in the pay of the Samaritans (Josephus *Ant.* 20.6.1 §118). As a result, several Galileans, angered by Cumanus's failure to act, sought vengeance under the leadership of Eleazar Ben Dinai, known elsewhere as a very violent zealot (see *Song Rab.* 2:18 and *m. Sota* 9:9). They massacred the inhabitants of several villages and were deterred from further violence only by the intervention of Cumanus and his troops and by the entreaties of several leaders from Jerusalem. In the aftermath, the Samaritans sent an embassy to Ummidius Quadratus, the governor of Syria, presenting their grievances, not as an offense against themselves but as an offense against Rome. The Jewish counterembassy focused instead on Cumanus's corruption. Quadratus's investigation showed that the Samaritans had been responsible for the disorder and, by extension, that Cumanus was to blame for its escalation. Cumanus was subsequently tried either by Claudius in Rome (Josephus *J.W.* 2.12.7 §§245-46 = *Ant.* 20.6.3 §§134-36) or by Quadratus in Judea (Tacitus *Ann.* 12.53), where he was found to be culpable and banished. Tacitus adds that Felix was governor of Samaria at the same time and that both governors were responsible. According to Tacitus, because of Felix's link with Pallas, Cumanus was made to take the blame for both of them—a sequence of events which seems to fit with the political climate of that (or any) period.

See also ROMAN GOVERNORS OF PALESTINE; ROMAN POLITICAL SYSTEM.

BIBLIOGRAPHY. D. W. J. Gill, "Acts and Roman Policy in Judea," in *The Book of Acts in Its Palestinian Setting*, ed. R. Bauckham (BAFCS 4; Grand Rapids, MI: Eerdmans, 1995) 15-26; E. Schürer, *The History of the Jewish People in the Age of Jesus Christ (175 B.C.-A.D. 135)*, rev. and ed. G. Vermes, F. Millar and M. Goodman (3 vols.; Edinburgh: T & T Clark, 1973-87) vol. 1; E. M. Smallwood, *The Jews Under Roman Rule* (Leiden: E. J. Brill, 1976); S. Safrai and M. Stern, eds., *The Jewish People in the First Century* (CRINT 1.1; Assen: Van Gorcum; Philadelphia: Fortress, 1974).

B. W. R. Pearson

CYNIC EPISTLES

*Cynicism, as a *philosophical movement, rested on the lived example of its proponents rather than on a body of doctrine systematically elaborated. Some Cynics produced a literary output in traditional forms such as tragedy, dialogue and poetry, but the countercultural stance of the philosophy led its teachers to bend these forms toward parody and burlesque. More characteristically, however, Cynics tended toward satire and smaller forms such as the *chreia* or anecdote and the *letter.

Although many of the letters date from the Augustan Age, there is a considerable range in the date of composition among them. The bulk of the letters in the collection are ascribed to prominent Cynics of the past such as Diogenes, Antisthenes and Crates. Others bear the names of non-Cynics as well, such as Anacharsis, Heraclitus, Hippocrates, Socrates and his followers. The Cynic views advanced in the letters represent Cynicism as it experienced a revival after a two-century lapse into obscurity. The letters range from Cynic propaganda to a discussion of issues that were being debated within Cynicism at the time.

1. The Epistles of Anacharsis
2. The Epistles of Crates
3. The Epistles of Diogenes
4. The Epistles of Heraclitus
5. The Epistles of Socrates and the Socratics

1. The Epistles of Anacharsis.
Ten letters are attributed to Anacharsis, a sixth-century B.C. Scythian prince who visited *Greece to find wisdom. This "noble savage" came to be characterized as one who despised all Greeks but the Spartans. His critical attitude and more natural way of life suited him well to be connected with Cynic philosophy. F. H. Reuters places all but *Epistle* 10 in the third century B.C., thus expanding U. von Wilamowitz-Moellendorff's view that *Epistle* 5 dates to the third century B.C. Reuters's argument rests on the fact that the letters are written in Koine Greek with words not used before the third century; the absence of Atticism, a second-century movement; and vocabulary that predates 250 B.C. Thus a date of 300 to 250 B.C. seems most likely.

The Cynic critique of culture in the letters is attributed to Anacharsis, uncultured by Greek standards. To A. J. Malherbe they represent a rare witness to Cynicism in the third century B.C., a time when the movement was long claimed to have died out until its revival in the early empire. *Epistle* 10 is circulated only by Diogenes Laertius and is in Ionic with no traces of Koine and seems to be by a different author from *Epistles* 1-9. It probably dates to the fifth or fourth centuries B.C. Topics in the letters include the value of content over dialect and pronunciation; wisdom even among non-Greeks; sobriety; envy; the good ruler; kindness; possessiveness.

2. The Epistles of Crates.
The thirty-six letters in this collection have long been recognized to be different from those that Diogenes Laertius (*Vit.* 6.98) ascribed to Crates of Thebes, pupil of Diogenes and prominent Cynic philosopher in the fourth to third centuries B.C. With the exception of letters 24 and 25, all the letters relate in content and/or language with the letters ascribed to Diogenes and are believed to be literarily dependent on them but from a different author. The letters of Crates, later than those of Diogenes, date no earlier than the first or second centuries B.C.

Within the collection, *Epistle* 35 has been found to be more *Stoic than Cynic and *Epistles* 27 and 32 are very similar to *Epistles* 26 and 30. Thus one hypothesizes that 27 and 32 served as rhetorical exercises based on 26 and 30. W. Capelle finds three authors for the collection: I for *Epistles* 1-26, 28, (29?), 30, 31, 33, (34?) and (36?); II for *Epistles* 27 and 32: III for *Epistle* 35, while A. Olivieri suggests up to six authors. The letters are generally paraenetic except for *Epistles* 20 and 24 (narrative) and *Epistles* 7, 24 and 25 (invective). Topics in the collection include the philosophical (Cynic) life; praise of Diogenes; virtue's adornment; temperance; asceticism; friends; women philosophers; slave and free.

3. The Epistles of Diogenes.
A now lost collection of letters was ascribed by Epictetus (*Ench.* 4.1.29-31, 156) and Julian (*Or.* 7.212D) to Diogenes of Sinope (fourth century B.C.) and were known to Sotion (200 B.C.) and Diogenes Laertius (*Vit.* 6.80). The fifty-one letters in the collection of Cynic Epistles come from a later period.

Diversity in style, content and point of view indicate multiple authors to W. Capelle, who hypothesizes four groups of letters. The first group is *Epistles* 8, 30, 31, 33 and 35-38, which share an anecdotal and nonrhetorical style. Perhaps also included in this group are *Epistles* 3, 9-12, (26), 44, 47 and (34). References to the Olympiad and one of its victors in *Epistle* 31 date that letter to the first century B.C. and thus also all the other letters in the group. The second group is *Epistles* 1, 2 and 4-7. The third group is *Epistles* 13-18, 20, (21), 22-25, 27, 32, 41-43, 46 and 48-51. *Epistle* 16 was known to Diogenes Laertius (*Vit.* 6.23) and so the group might well be dated to the late second or early third century A.D. *Epistles* 19, 28, 29, 39, 40 (43, 45) are from a variety of authors and over a long period of time; that is, from shortly after 28 B.C. for *Epistle* 19 to the fourth century B.C. for *Epistle* 39, which reflects a decline in Cynicism and the rise of *Platonism. Most were probably written as Cynic propaganda.

K. von Fritz, who focuses on form rather than content, notes that *Epistles* 28-40 seem to belong together because of their length. Furthermore, *Epistles* 31, 33 and 35-39 exhibit Socratic influence. *Epistles* 29-40 focus on philosophical formation in a Socratic mode.

V. E. Emeljanow agrees that *Epistles* 30-40 share Socratic interest and a late Hellenistic vocabulary and characterize Diogenes as a wandering Cynic. He finds that *Epistles* 1-29 are simpler, shorter, explain less and depict their characters differently from *Epistles* 30-40. The fact that some manuscripts have only these letters suggests that *Epistles* 1-29 are an earlier collection (first century B.C. or earlier). *Epistles* 30-40 (c. second century A.D.) were written with

Epistles 1-29 in mind but were published separately. *Epistles* 41-51 are like *Epistles* 30-40 with their Socratic references, but they lack contexts for the anecdotes, which are themselves more abrupt and pointed. They might constitute a separate collection.

All told, Malherbe finds that three or even four authors were at work on the collection that they wrote to provide a positive picture of Cynicism in answer to critiques such as that in *Lucian. In doing this they presented a picture of diversity over the course of development in Cynicism. Topics include Cynic simplicity; subduing passions; begging and *beneficence; rough path to virtue; indifference; hospitality; honor.

4. The Epistles of Heraclitus.

The nine-letter corpus contains two (*Ep.* 1 and 3) under the name of the Persian king Darius and seven attributed to Heraclitus (sixth to fifth century B.C.). Text-critical studies, especially of PGen 271, establish their date to the middle of the second century A.D. They were probably written by members of the same school. H. W. Attridge separates *Epistles* 1 and 2 from the others; places together *Epistles* 3, 4, 7 and 8, which deal with Hermadorus's exile; and joins them with *Epistle* 9 on the same topic. The latter is always first in the manuscripts that contain it, as an introduction to the collection. *Epistles* 5 and 6 treat Heraclitus's attitude toward medicine but share particular details with the letters on Hermadorus's exile, such as piety and the setting up of altars. They were either written along with those letters or added to conform to them. Attridge showed the letters, especially 4 and 7, to reflect a Cynic-Stoic orientation and not Jewish, as J. Bernays hypothesized. Topics include satisfaction with little; gods; healing; law and justice; virtue.

5. The Epistles of Socrates and the Socratics.

Codex Vaticanus Graecus 64 (1969-70) preserves this collection of thirty-five letters, and all other manuscripts depend on it. *Epistle* 28, from Speusippus to Philip, might be genuine, while *Epistle* 35 seems to belong with Pythagorean literature in view of the exclusivity of the philosophical enterprise described there. The other letters, deemed pseudepigraphical since R. Bentley in the seventeenth century, include those of Socrates, *Epistles* 1-7, and those of his disciples, *Epistles* 8-27 and 29-34. Different authors for these groups have been detected from their content, language and style.

Epistles 1-7 are didactic and use Socrates as an ethical paradigm. Cynic thought is preferred, and historical details are not given great attention. *Epistles* 1 and 6 are a diatribe in letter form. Mention of these letters in a third-century A.D. papyrus establishes their date as earlier, perhaps even to the first century.

The letters of the Socratics are less didactic and show more historical interest. The individual characters conform to their depiction in the biographical tradition, but the author papers over the differences among the members of the Socratic circle, save for the opposition between Antisthenes and Aristippus. Rigorous Cynicism is not in favor with this author, whose sympathy is with Aristippus. The author knows rhetorical theory and quotes a rule on the use of a tone appropriate to the situation of the letter writer, which *Cicero also refers to (Cicero *Fam.* 2.4.1). He also seems to use *Plutarch and possibly the epistles of Diogenes and Crates. These letters are mentioned by Stobaeus (fifth century A.D.), who refers to no author later than the fourth century. This leads Malherbe to date them to the early third century. The author might have known the letters of Socrates and most likely had contacts with Platonists from the knowledge and esteem for Plato that he expresses. The effort to mediate between rigorous and hedonistic Cynicism in these letters is readily apparent. Their characterization of these two trends provides valuable insight into the course of development in the Cynic movement. Topics include true and false teachers; Cynic virtues; friendship; rulers; memoirs of Socrates and his followers.

See also PHILOSOPHY; CYNICISM AND SKEPTICISM.

BIBLIOGRAPHY. H. W. Attridge, *First Century Cynicism in the Epistles of Heraclitus* (Missoula, MT: Scholars Press, 1976); R. Bentley, *A Dissertation upon the Epistles of Phalaris, Themistocles, Socrates, Euripedes and upon the Fables of Aesop* (London, 1699; Berlin, 1874); J. Bernays, *Die Heraklitischen Briefe* (Berlin: Hertz, 1869); W. Capelle, "De Cynicorum Epistulis" (Ph.D. diss., Göttingen, 1896); V. E. Emeljanow, "The Letters of Diogenes" (Ph.D. diss., Stanford University, 1964); K. von Fritz, "Quellenuntersuchungen zu Leben und Philosophie des Diogenes von Sinope," *Philologus*, Supp. 18 (1926) 67ff.; O.

Gigon, "Kynikerbriefe," in *Lexikon der alten Welt* (Zurich and Stuttgart: Artemis, 1965) 1658-59; R. Hercher, *Epistolographi Graeci* (Paris, 1873; repr. 1965); A. J. Malherbe, *The Cynic Epistles: A Study Edition* (Missoula, MT: Scholars Press, 1977); A. Olivieri, "Le epistole del Pseudo-Cratete," *Rivista di filologia* 27 (1899) 406-21; F. H. Reuters, "De Anacharsis epistulis" (Diss., Bonn, 1957); J. Sykutris, "Epistolographie," in *Pauly-Wissowa Realencyclopaedie* Supp.5 (1931) 210-11; U. von Wilamowitz-Moellendorff, *Commentariolum Grammaticum III* (Göttingen, 1889). B. Fiore

CYNICISM AND SKEPTICISM

In contemporary New Testament studies, cynicism is sometimes appealed to as a philosophical movement that illuminates our understanding of Jesus and his followers as well as of Paul. In discussing Cynicism it is useful to begin with ancient Skepticism.

1. Skepticism
2. Cynicism

1. Skepticism.

Skeptics commonly believed that true happiness could be found only apart from existing reality and from the attempt to derive knowledge from its interpretation. Doubt affected scientific and dogmatic knowledge, and this led Skeptics to view probability as a satisfactory foundation for moral action. What resulted from this was eclecticism. Guided by one's own judgment or experience of usefulness, one could accept or reject any opinion or insight of a *philosophical school without the need to adhere to an entire system or even to think it through.

Skepticism started with the question of whether it is possible to gain objective knowledge and then to give any results completely and unmistakably. At the same time, the Skeptics criticized the reliability of sense perception. The resulting doubt ultimately led to the criticism of ethical decisions and norms. *Cicero, who learned modified Skepticism from Academician Philo of Larissa, held that action is superior to theoretical knowledge and thus that ethics is the primary subject of *philosophy.

Heraclitus is said to have delivered many Skeptical pronouncements such as "the majority understand Logos not at all." Socrates showed Skeptic tendencies in his mistrust of the absolute value of truth claims and the Sophists' ethical valuations. He seems to have understood knowledge (*epistēmē*) to be the knowledge of things acquired through practical activity.

After Socrates, three groups of Skeptics can be identified. First is the school of Pyrrho of Elis (360-271 B.C.) and Timon of Phlius (320-230 B.C.). Pyrrho is the recognized founder of Skepticism. His Skepticism rests on the view that value judgments rely on human convention (*ethei kai nomoi*) for their confirmation or denial. He also rejected nature (*physis*), as opposed to convention (*nomos*) as an absolute criterion. He thereby challenged not just the value of things but even their knowability. Pyrrho preferred to suspend judgment (*epochē*) about value and existence, for each statement is as well-founded as its equally persuasive counterpart (*isostheneia tōn logōn*). As a result people should be undisturbed (*ataraxia*) by external occurrences that are unavoidable (*adiaphora*).

With Timon, his disciple, Pyrrhonism dissolved and was carried forward through Arcesilaus of Pitane (d. c. 242 B.C.) and the Middle Academy. Their appeal to satiric verses and Homeric parodies led Xenophanes to produce parodies on philosophical questions (*silloi*) that approached Cynic wit and sharply critical polemic.

The second group was the younger Skeptic school of Aenesidemus of Cnossos (fl. 40 B.C.) and Sextus Empiricus, to whom we are indebted for nearly all of what we know of Skepticism. Taught by Herodotus of Tarsus (fl. end first century A.D.), Sextus wrote from A.D. 180 to 200 and brought Pyrrhonic Skepticism's arguments to bear on all areas of knowledge. His works constitute a negative encyclopedia of knowledge. The Pyrrhonic Hypotheses opposed the dogmatists and the mathematicians. Aenesidemus taught in *Alexandria, and his *Eight Books of Pyrrhonic Sayings* reestablished Pyrrhonic Skepticism, prematurely declared dead by Cicero (*De Orat.* 3; *De Offic.* 1.6).

The third group comprised the Academics in *Athens in their Skeptic phase from Arcesilaus to Philo of Larissa. Carneades of Cyrene (219-129 B.C.) restored the Skeptical foundations of Arcesilaus by disputing the reliability of the senses and the Stoic teaching of *kataleptikē phantasia* (Cicero *Acad.* 1.64-90). While he promoted suspension of judgment (*epochē*), he left open the possibility of practical decisions on the basis of what appears to be true, that is, the probable (*to pithanon*). His pupils and heirs are Clitomachus of Carthage (187/6-110/9 B.C.), Zeno of Alexandria, Hagnon of Tarsus, Metrodorus of Stratonicea and Philo of Larissa (160/59-80 B.C.). The latter, pupil and successor to Clitomachus as head of the Academy, in 88 B.C. went to *Rome, where he influenced Cicero. He later moved away from Skepticism and claimed that things could be known on the basis of their nature (*physis*).

2. Cynicism.

Cynicism is a fourth-century B.C. popular philosophical movement whose aim was to extricate people from a life of vice and set them on the road of virtue. Since it stressed example as its primary teaching tool Cynicism is commonly thought to have been an oral rather than a literary movement. Nonetheless, literary remains give evidence of a wide range of literary activity among Cynics.

Diogenes Laertius (*Vit.* 6.2-15) suggests that Antisthenes of Athens (455-360 B.C.) gave lessons in the *gymnasium at Cynosarges and was the first to achieve the Cynic ideals of indifference (*apatheia*), self-control (*enkrateia*) and patient endurance (*karteria*), thus founding the Cynic doctrine and name. But Diogenes of Sinope (414-323 B.C.), his pupil and continuator according to Diogenes Laertius, came to Athens after Antisthenes' death. Despite Diogenes Laertius's views, it seems that later tradition (only in the third century is he linked to the folded mantle) appropriated Antisthenes to Cynicism. Some scholars even suggest that Cynicism was not a Socratic derivation but rather stemmed from mendicant Pythagorean sectarians from Sicily who were resident in fourth-century Athens. Diodorus of Asperidus, for example, was said (Diogenes Laertius *Vit.* 6.13) to have been the first to double his mantle, let his beard grow and carry a staff and knapsack, all later Cynic signatures.

Diogenes of Sinope would then be the sect's originator and provided a model of life for other Cynics, including Bion of Borysthenes (325-255 B.C.), Teles of Megara (fl. 235 B.C.), Cercidas of Megalopolis (290-220 B.C.) and Onesicritus of Astypalaea. The sect's name would then derive not from Cynosarges but from the shameless, doglike life of the early Cynics.

Cynics' criticism of the folly (*anoia*) of popular opinion led to their reputation as irreligious (*atheoi*). They saw the requirements and cultic practices of traditional religion and popular fears of the caprices of the god Fortune (*Tychē*) and of death and punishment as naïve and obstacles to self-sufficiency (*autarkeia*) and indifference (*apatheia*). Religion, as part of convention (*nomos*), held no interest for Cynics, as they pursued life according to the role assigned by nature (*physis*). Antisthenes is quoted as expressing the Cynic ideal as leading a pious and just life (*eusebos kai dikaios zēn*).

Bion of Borysthenes' diatribes on religious problems, Diogenes' anecdotes and chreiai on religious topics and Menippus's spiritual letters in the name of divine personages represent some of the diverse and original forms of literary productions of Cynics. These smaller forms, at the margins of classical literature, consisted in prose of burlesques, parodies on myths, proverbs, wills, diaries, diatribes, satires and epistles. In poetry they expressed their views in iambics, elegiacs, hexameters and in the new meter meliambus. The new forms served the Cynics' critique of conventional thought and literary genres.

Diogenes' chreiai and anecdotes, rhetorical puns, parodies and symbolic gestures (e.g., his choice of a *pithos,* or large wine jar, in which to dwell in the marketplace at Athens) were applications of *rhetoric to immediate circumstances. This expressed Cynic rejection of high theory and elaborated doctrine in a systematic body of abstract argument as irrelevant to practice and instructive example. Diogenes (Diogenes Laertius *Vit.* 6.38) saw himself as a character in a tragedy: without a city, a house or a fatherland, a beggar, a wanderer, with bread for a single day. The Cynics held freedom high among their values and practiced freedom of speech (*parrēsia*) and playful satire (*spoudogeloion*) to challenge conventional thought and opinion.

Cynics claimed attachment to no city, for a city was against nature, but were citizens of the world. They belonged to the community of wise persons and expected a commonality (*koinōnia*) of all goods as humanity's common patrimony. Their effort to teach, lead, oversee, cure, save and benefit people constituted a deep philanthropy. Cynic life had three aspects: itinerant begging with knapsack, cloak and staff; the slogan "be countercultural" (*paracharattein to nomisma*); the Cynic literary genres such as Bion's diatribes and playful satire of Monimus, Crates, Metrocles and Menippus.

Cynics did not establish a school as such but

comprised a small circle of disciples who practiced Diogenes' ascetical way of life. *Plato is said to have called Diogenes "Socrates gone mad" (Diogenes Laertius *Vit.* 6.54) in that he pushed the chief features of a wise man to extremes: frugality to asceticism, oblique reference (*eironeia*) to frank criticism (*parrēsia*), moderation (*sōphrosynē*) to indifference (*apatheia*), disregard of opinion to shamelessness. His followers included Hegesias of Sinope, Philiscus of Aegina, Menander, Monimus of Syracuse, Pasiphon and Androsthenes. They fashioned their own versions of the Cynic life. Crates of Thebes (d. c. 290 B.C.) was known for *philanthrōpia* (versus Diogenes' reputation for *autarkeia*) and criticized his friends for their own improvement but did not beg. He wed Hipparchia, the "female philosopher," and wore Cynic garb. Bion of Borysthenes left memoirs, sayings and diatribes and was court philosopher to Alexander Gonatas at Pella. Menippus of Gadara (first half of the third century B.C.) adapted the dialog for comic and satiric purposes (*to spoudogeloion*).

The Cynics lost prominence after 200 B.C. until the revival in the first century A.D. Romans preferred *gravitas* as suited to well-bred Romans, and they lauded their own countercultural heroes such as Cato and Cincinnatus. Demetrius is the first Cynic name to appear (mid-first century) after two centuries of obscurity. The Cynics were banished from Rome along with the Stoics, with whom they were confused, from 75 to 71 B.C. for teaching doctrines inappropriate to the age and for thereby corrupting people (Dio Cassius *Hist.* 65.12). From the reign of Vespasian to that of Marcus Aurelius Cynicism grew stronger, and Cynics were the butt of uncomplimentary references in literature, especially in Alexandria. Cynics tended to stay in the East, where the climate favored their mendicant ways, and they avoided large urban centers in favor of the countryside and towns. *Slaves and artisans found in Cynicism an alternative to their oppressive and monotonous lives, and many used Cynicism to find escape from the restraints of ordered society. It might be called the philosophy of the proletariat.

From the first century A.D. on Cynicism was characterized by significant diversity. Contrary to their original distance from philosophical considerations, Cynics became more open to philosophy, and prominent Cynics favored those doctrines that they viewed as contributing to progress in virtue. Evidence from the pseudonymous *Cynic Epistles under the name of the Socratic philosophers indicates a leaning toward philosophy generally. Other features of diversity can also be detected in the movement, despite idealized characterizations of Cynics by *Epictetus, *Lucian of Samosata, Maximus of Tyre and the emperor Julian.

The Cynic Epistles express the contrasting tendencies of austere or rigorous and mild or hedonistic Cynicism. The pseudonymous epistles of Crates and Diogenes, as well as those of Simon the Shoemaker and Antisthenes, express the ideals and practices of austere Cynicism. These include wearing Cynic garb and battling against moral softness, common opinion and appearances by their example of simplicity and direct rebuke. The rigorous Cynics had a generally pessimistic view of the moral prospects of the mass of people. To counteract the depravity and intransigence of the corrupt human condition, they resorted to scathing criticism (*parrēsia*) and blunt, shameless gestures to force a spiritual cure (see the Cynic Epistles of Crates, Heraclitus, Diogenes and Hippocrates). This earned them the reputation of misanthropy.

Less pessimistic and dismissive of popular culture were the mild or hedonistic Cynics. These are represented in the Cynic letters of Plato and Aristippus, which stress the benefit of their approachable lifestyle and behavior. These maintained Cynic simplicity of life and dress and gave scant attention to conventional calculations of virtue and vice but proved warm toward education and culture while avoiding shamelessness and off-putting ascetical extremes. Lucian of Samosata identifies this diversity in the presentation of his Cynic characters; that is, Peregrinus for austere Cynicism and Demonax for the milder variety.

See also CYNIC EPISTLES; PHILOSOPHY.

BIBLIOGRAPHY. J. D. Crossan, *The Historical Jesus: The Life of a Mediterranean Jewish Peasant* (San Francisco: Harper SanFrancisco, 1991); F. G. Downing, *Cynics and Christian Origins* (Edinburgh: T & T Clark, 1992); D. R. Dudley, *A History of Cynicism from Diogenes to the Sixth Century A.D.* (Chicago: Ares, 1980 [1937]); P. R. Eddy, "Jesus as Diogenes? Reflections on the Cynic Jesus Thesis," *JBL* 115 (1996) 449-69; M.-O. Goulet-Cazé, *Le Cynisme Ancien et ses prolonguements* (Paris: Presses Universitaires de France, 1993); A. J. Malherbe, "Self-Definition Among Epicureans and Cynics," in *Jewish and Christian Self-Definition: Self-Definition in the Greco-Roman World,* ed. B. F. Meyer and E. P. Sanders (3 vols.; Philadelphia: Fortress, 1982) vol. 2; K. Ziegler and W. Sontheimer, *Der Kleine Pauly: Lexikon der Antike in fuenf Baenden* (Munich: Deutsche Taschenbuch Verlag, 1979).

B. Fiore

D

DAILY PRAYERS (4Q503). *See* LITURGY: QUMRAN.

DAMASCUS DOCUMENT (CD AND QD)

The *Damascus Document* is one of the Dead Sea Scrolls containing an admonition and a series of laws. The "C" in the abbreviation CD stands for Cairo, where the first copies of the text were found in the genizah of the Quaraite Ezra Synagogue in 1896. The community that produced the document could not be identified. It was attributed to an unknown Jewish sect until publication of the *Dead Sea Scrolls made it probable that its authors came from the same group. This hypothesis became a certitude when fragments of CD were discovered in Caves 4, 5 and 6 at *Qumran. The inhabitants of Qumran were *Essenes (Fitzmyer 1995).

"Damascus" appears in the title because the document focuses on those who entered a "new covenant in the land of Damascus" (CD 6:19; 8:21; 19:34; 20:12). S. Schechter, its discoverer and first editor, called it *Fragments of a Zadokite Work* (1910) because of its references to "Zadok" (CD 4:1, 3; 5:5). This was retained by R. H. Charles in his influential *Apocrypha and Pseudepigrapha of the Old Testament in English* (1913). C. Rabin preferred *The Zadokite Documents* as the title of his critical edition (1954). *Zadokite Fragments* is still found occasionally (e.g., *ABD* 6:1036) but has been supplanted by *Damascus Document.* German scholars started to use this title immediately after the First World War (e.g., Bertholet), and its neutrality won it growing popularity. In addition it came to be recognized that "Zadokite" was misleading in that it was also applicable to the *Sadducees, the sworn enemies of the Essenes. In modern usage the abbreviation CD is supplemented by QD to designate the copies of the *Damascus Document* found at Qumran.

1. Manuscripts
2. What QD Adds to CD
3. The Admonition
4. The Laws
5. History
6. The *Damascus Document* and the New Testament

1. Manuscripts.

Schechter recovered two manuscripts from the genizah. Manuscript A contains eight leaves written on both sides and numbered 1—16. It is dated to the tenth century A.D. The twelfth-century A.D. Manuscript B is represented by only one leaf written on both sides and numbered 19 and 20, to make it clear that it belonged to a different document. The best published photographs of these manuscripts are to be found in M. Broshi, where the transcription of the text is by E. Qimron. Broshi's volume also contains a bibliography (1970-1989) by F. García Martínez. J. M. Baumgarten (9-16) and D. R. Schwartz (1-8, 19-20) have published a critical edition and translation.

The fragments of QD found in Caves 5 and 6 at Qumran, first published by M. Baillet and J. T. Milik, have been republished by Baumgarten with M. T. Davis. The one fragment from Cave 5 (5Q12) contains five lines corresponding to CD 9:7-10 in the legal section. Four fragments from Cave 6 contain minute sections of the admonition. The fifth fragment of 6Q15 contains very few words and has no parallel in the genizah manuscripts but corresponds to a passage in 4Q270.

Eight copies of QD were found in Cave 4 at Qumran. All are to be dated in the century following 70 B.C., the oldest belonging to the period 70 to 50 B.C. (Milik, 58). With the exception of the sections dealing with skin disease (Baumgarten with Davis, 64-75) the official critical edition has not yet been published, but an English translation has been made available by García Martínez (47-70). Together the Cave 4 fragments yield 689 lines of text, of which 144 parallel the admonition and 182 parallel the laws. The 363 additional lines, however, make it clear that the genizah material represents a truncated version of the *Damascus Document* in use at Qumran (Baumgarten with Davis, 59).

2. What QD Adds to CD.

Material from every page of the admonition in CD, with the exception of 19, is found in at least one of the QD fragments, some in as many as four. There is no evidence of different recensions. The QD fragments, however, reveal that CD lacks the equivalent of two pages at the beginning of the admonition. The first page is represented by 4Q267 fragment 1 and the second by 4Q267 fragment 2 = 4Q266 frag. 1, both of which continue with CD 1:1ff. (García Martínez, 47-48). The new material is an exhortation addressed to the Sons of Light to depart from the paths of wickedness and heed the voice of *Moses.

With respect to the laws, Milik's deduction (151) from the content that CD 15—16 should come before CD 9 is confirmed by 4Q267 fragment 17, column ii (García Martínez, 54). CD 15, however, is preceded by much new material, whose content the editors (Baumgarten and Schwartz, 5; Baumgarten with Davis, 60-61) summarize, with slight inconsistency regarding the order, thus: (1) introduction to the laws; (2) the role of priests; (3) the ordeal of the suspected adulteress; (4) diagnosis of skin diseases; (5) impurity resulting from fluxes and childbirth; (6) the law of fraud applied to the arrangement of marriages; (7) agricultural laws; (8) impurity of metals used in pagan cults. Then follows the legislation of CD 15—16, 9—14, which is brought to a conclusion by a penal code for infractions of community discipline and a ritual for the expulsion of those who fail to conform. The last line of the ordinances is "And so, then, all this is with regard to the last interpretation of [the law]" (4Q270 frag. 11 col ii, 14-15; García Martínez, 67), which is followed by six blank lines before the bottom margin.

3. The Admonition.

The admonition lacks a coherent structure. There is no clear line of development. The infidelity of Israel past and present, the lessons of history, the imminence of a final judgment, the renewal of the covenant by a privileged few, the inspired role of the Teacher, the revelation of hidden things, the need for perfect observance of the exact interpretation of the law—all these fundamental themes weave around each other surfacing and fading only to reappear in a slightly different guise. The result is a vigorous summons to the members of the sect to be faithful to their covenant commitment. To this extent one may speak of the admonition as "essentially a unity" (Knibb 1994, 155).

Schechter's impression that the admonition was made up of "extracts from a larger work" (x) put the question of its literary unity on the academic agenda from the beginning. Many responded to the challenge. Their hypotheses are explained and criticized by P. R. Davies (1983, 5-47). He maintains that the original admonition contained only 1:1—7:9 + 20:27-34. After the return to Palestine 7:9—8:19 was added. A number of interpolations were inserted by a redactor at Qumran who added 19:33—20:27. The complexity of Davies's suggestion does more justice to the problems of the admonition than hypotheses of one basic source broken up by later insertions, but it does not adequately account for all facets of the text.

Recognizing that very different situations are implied by the various parts of the text, J. Murphy-O'Connor (1972, 562-63; 1985, 232; see Knibb 1987, 14, 27, 50, 67, 71) considers the admonition to be made up of four originally independent source documents: (1) a missionary document (CD 2:14—6:11) designed to win converts to the Essene reform; (2) a memorandum (CD 6:11—8:2) whose purpose was to recall members of the community to more faithful observance; (3) a document (CD 8:3-19) criticizing the ruling class in Judea for its lack of support for the Essene movement and (4) a document (the source behind CD 19:33—20:22) written as part of an effort to stem a rising tide of disaffection within the community.

These sources, which for Murphy-O'Connor antedate the move of some Essenes to Qumran, were combined into the present admonition at Qumran, where an editor added the QD material mentioned in section 2 above + CD 1:1—2:13, and two series of interpolations, one to enhance the hortatory effect by adapting it to a Qumran perspective, the other to identify a particular individual as the focus of opposition to the community (QD 4:19; 8:13).

The admonition was compiled within forty years of the death of the Unique Teacher (CD 20:1, 14-15; Fitzmyer 1992). This personage is to be identified with the Teacher of Righteousness (CD 1:11; 20:32), who was a mature adult in the middle of the second century B.C. (Murphy-O'Connor *ABD*). Hence the compilation can be dated around 100 B.C., which harmonizes perfectly with the date of the oldest manuscript (see 1 above).

4. The Laws.

Nothing in the admonition demands that it be understood as a hortatory preface to the laws. Part of the beginning may be missing, but 20:22-34 is a formal conclusion (Knibb 1987, 76). It is a literary whole, capable of independent existence. Equally a legal corpus can stand by itself. Moreover, the two are very different in tone. The polemical edge of the admonition is absent in the laws (Knibb 1994, 153). An organic relationship between the admonition and the laws has been presumed simply because of the format of Schechter's publication. However, the handwriting and number of lines of CD 1—8 differ from those of CD 9—16; the two do not belong to the same manuscript. Admonition and laws, however, are found together in 4Q267 (Stegemann in Knibb 1994, 160), and some relation can no longer be denied (against Stegemann 1990).

Certain elements in the admonition presuppose the laws, which may explain why the two documents were copied together. The reminder "observe the sabbath day in its exact detail" (CD 6:18; *see* Sabbath) is pointless unless highly specific legislation is provided elsewhere. This is precisely what we find in CD 10:14—11:18 and nowhere else in the Qumran literature (Schiffman 1975, 77-133). Similarly the "hidden things" (CD 4:14) must be spelled out somewhere. The laws, therefore, antedate the sources of the admonition. They governed the lives of the Essenes prior to the advent of the Teacher of Righteousness (CD 1:7-11). They were "the first ordinances," which are distinguished from "the last ordinances" laid down by the Teacher of Righteousness (CD 20:8, 31-32). Their permanent validity for the group at Qumran is asserted by 1QS 9:10 and confirmed by the number of copies of QD, the latest dated in the early first century A.D. (Baumgarten with Davis, 60).

The laws give a rather clear picture of the group they governed. The head of the whole movement (CD 14:8-12) supervised communities with a minimum membership of ten each with its own overseer, who should be a priest if possible (CD 13:1-4). He was responsible for instructing the community (CD 13:7-10), examining and admitting new members (CD 9:17-22). Legal matters were the province of ten judges, four priests and six laymen aged between twenty-five and sixty (CD 10:4-10). At meetings all sat in order, priests, Levites, laymen and proselytes (CD 14:3-4). The membership comprised men, women and children (CD 7:7; 15:5; 16:10-12; 4Q268 frag. 1 i 12-14). Whether women were full members is debated (Schuller). The members had private incomes from which they had to contribute at least two days' wages a month to the common fund to meet charitable needs, which included subsidies to unmarried women (CD 14:13-16).

Since Genesis 1:28 was understood as a commandment, it must be assumed that all male Essenes were married. According to *Josephus (*J.W.* 2.8.13 §§160-61), however, they married very young women who had menstruated only three times (reading *trimenoi* ["three months"] for the impossible *trietia* ["three years"]; Beall, 112). These were expected to have a child every year, because procreation was the only justification for *marriage. Inevitably many women died prematurely, and their husbands could not marry again (CD 4:20-21; see 6 below). Hence, the false impression of their contemporaries (*Philo in Eusebius *Praep. Ev.* 8.11.14; Josephus *J.W.* 2.8.2 §120; *Ant.* 18.1.5 §21) that there were two branches of the Essenes, married and unmarried (Stegemann 1993, 269-71). Qumran, therefore, was not a celibate community, and the legislation of CD remained relevant.

According to L. H. Schiffman (1983b, 14-17), the laws were produced by inspired exegesis of Scripture. Regular study sessions (1QS 6:6-8) were the medium through which God made known the hidden things. Since these sessions continued throughout the whole life of the sect one must assume that the laws were accumulated gradually over many years as problems were perceived and dealt with.

An unusual feature of the laws is the high proportion of ordinances dealing with relations with Gentiles (Schiffman 1983a). They concern trade, *slave labor, lodging, food, sabbath rest and the need to maintain good public relations with the majority (CD 11:14-15; 12:6-11). Such laws reflect a time when the community lived in "a foreign, non-Judean environment" (Iwry, 85). This excludes both the hypothesis that the laws were the legislation of the pre-Qumran Hasideans (1 Macc 2:42; Stegemann 1990, 428) and the common view that the laws were written for Essenes living outside Qumran in the towns and villages of Palestine (Knibb 1987, 15). No matter how Hellenized Judea was it could not be considered a Gentile environment at any stage.

5. History.

According to CD, the Interpreter of the Law (CD 6:7) brought the sect into being during the exile in Babylon, which it called "Damascus" (CD 6:19; 8:21; 19:34; 20:12; Davies 1990 against Knibb 1994, 159). This is an appropriate Gentile context for the laws. Some members of the sect returned to Palestine (CD 1:5-8), 390 years later, in 172 B.C. (Puech, 506 n. 29). They strove to win converts to their interpretation of the law (CD 2:14—6:11) but got no support from the religious establishment in Judea (CD 8:3-18). In consequence, morale in the group began to deteriorate (CD 6:11—8:3).

About twenty years later the Teacher of Righteousness joined them (CD 1:10-11). A senior Zadokite, who had been acting high priest until displaced by Jonathan in 152 B.C., he was the conduit by which Judean ideas and works entered the sect's bloodstream (Murphy-O'Connor 1985, 239-40). His assumption of the title and role of the expected "Teacher of Righteousness at the end of days" (CD 6:11; Davies 1983, 123) led to a split in the group (CD 19:33-34), for which the followers of the Teacher blamed the Man of Mockery (CD 1:15; 4:19) also called the Man of Lies (CD 8:13), even though it was the Teacher's group that moved out to Qumran. The new legislation for the small foundation at Qumran in CD 20:1-8 shows it to be secure in its faith and confident in its organization. The death of the Teacher (CD 20:1, 14-15) must have been traumatic. Subsequently there was an influx of Jewish converts (CD 20:22), probably refugee *Pharisees seeking safety around 100 B.C. (Milik 88). The admonition was written in order to rekindle the idealism of the enlarged community.

6. The *Damascus Document* and the New Testament.

When taken literally CD 4:19—5:2 permits only one wife in a man's lifetime (Davies 1987, 73-85). It is commonly interpreted as a prohibition of polygamy and remarriage after divorce (amounting to a prohibition of divorce, which is the right of remarriage: "you are free to marry any man," *m. Giṭ* 9:3) by invoking 11QTemple 57:17-19, which forbids polygamy and divorce, for the king but authorizes him to take a second wife after the death of the first. The legitimacy of such an extension to all of a royal prerogative is debatable; what is forbidden to the king is forbidden to all, but not vice versa. If the limiting interpretation is accepted, CD 4:19-20 forbids divorce and affords a historical background for the question on divorce addressed to Jesus in Mark 10:2-12 and the parallels, to which he gives the Essene answer.

CD 5:8-11 classifies as *zenut* ("unchastity") all marriages within the forbidden degrees of kinship, not just those explicitly excluded by Leviticus 18:6-18. Since *porneia* ("unchastity") is the normal Greek translation of *zenut,* this text confirms the interpretation of the exceptive clauses in Matthew 5:32 and 19:9 based on the technical use of "unchastity" in Acts 15:20, 29 to refer to the forms of sexual relations condemned by Leviticus 18:6-18 (Fitzmyer 1976). Matthew, in other words, excluded from the dominical prohibition of divorce those marriages that Jewish law considered invalid. To break up such marriages would not have been a divorce.

CD 9:2-8 demands the same series of three steps as Matthew 18:15-17 in dealing with a member who has committed a fault. First the offender must be reproved privately (CD 7:2-3). Then the reproof must be uttered before witnesses. Finally the individual is brought before the assembly or its representatives. Despite the structural identity of the procedure, the differences are profound (Carmody). In the laws the first reproof is motivated by the accuser's intention to avoid complicity. The second is to ensure that there are the witnesses required by law. Finally the judges must apply the prescribed penalty. In Matthew's community, on the contrary, there is no such legalism. The concern at each stage is for the reformation of sinners. Even if they remain intransigent before the assembly no punishment is assigned, only the recognition that the sinners have removed themselves from the community.

See also DEAD SEA SCROLLS: GENERAL INTRODUCTION; ESSENES; RULE OF THE COMMUNITY/ MANUAL OF DISCIPLINE (1QS); RULE OF THE

CONGREGATION/MESSIANIC RULE (1QSA).

BIBLIOGRAPHY. M. Baillet, J. T. Milik and R. de Vaux, *Les "Petites Grottes" de Qumran* (DJD 3; Oxford: Clarendon Press, 1962); J. M. Baumgarten and D. R. Schwartz, "Damascus Document (CD)," in *The Dead Sea Scrolls: Hebrew, Aramaic and Greek Texts with English Translations, 2: Damascus Document, War Scroll and Related Documents,* ed. J. H. Charlesworth (Tübingen: Mohr Siebeck Louisville, KY: Westminster John Knox, 1995) 4-57; J. M. Baumgarten with M. T. Davis, "Cave IV, V, VI Fragments Related to the Damascus Document (4Q266-73 = 4QD^{a-h}, 5Q12 = 5QD, 6Q15 = 6QD)," in *The Dead Sea Scrolls: Hebrew, Aramaic and Greek Texts with English Translations,* 2: *Damascus Document, War Scroll and Related Documents,* ed. J. H. Charlesworth (Tübingen: Mohr Siebeck Louisville, KY: Westminster John Knox, 1995) 59-79; T. S. Beall, *Josephus's Description of the Essenes Illustrated by the Dead Sea Scrolls* (SNTSMS 58; Cambridge: Cambridge University Press, 1988); A. Bertholet, "Zur Datierung der Damaskus-Schrift," *Beiträge zur ZAT* 34 (1920) 31-37; M. Broshi, *The Damascus Document Reconsidered* (Jerusalem: Israel Exploration Society, 1992); T. R. Carmody, "Matthew 18:15-17 in Relation to Three Texts from Qumran Literature (CD 9:2-8, 16-22; 1QS 5:24—6:1)," in *To Touch the Text: Biblical and Related Studies in Honor of Joseph A. Fitzmyer, S.J.,* ed. M. P. Horgan and P. J. Kobelski (New York: Crossroad, 1989) 141-59; P. R. Davies, *Behind the Essenes: History and Ideology in the Dead Sea Scrolls* (BJS 94; Atlanta; Scholars Press, 1987); idem, "The Birthplace of the Essenes: Where Is 'Damascus'?" *RevQ* 14 (1990) 503-19; idem, *The Damascus Covenant: An Interpretation of the "Damascus Document"* (JSOTSup 25; Sheffield: JSOT, 1983); J. A. Fitzmyer, "The Gathering In of the Community's Teacher," *Maarav* 8 (1992) 223-28; idem, "The Matthean Divorce Texts and Some New Palestinian Evidence," *TS* 37 (1976) 197-226; idem, "The Qumran Community: Essene or Sadducean?" *HeyJ* 36 (1995) 467-76; F. García Martínez with W. G. E. Watson, *The Dead Sea Scrolls Translated: The Qumran Texts in English* (Leiden: E. J. Brill, 1994); S. Iwry, "Was There a Migration to Damascus? The Problem of *sby ysr'l,*" in *Eretz Israel* 10 (W. F. Albright Volume; Jerusalem: Israel Exploration Society, 1969) 80-88; M. A. Knibb, "The Place of the Damascus Document," in *Methods of Investigation of the Dead Sea Scrolls and the Khirbet Qumran Site: Present Realities and Future Prospects,* ed. M. O. Wise et al. (Annals of the New York Academy of Sciences 722; New York: New York Academy of Sciences, 1994) 149-62; idem, *The Qumran Community* (CWJCW; Cambridge: Cambridge University Press, 1987) 13-76; J. T. Milik, *Ten Years of Discovery in the Wilderness of Judea* (SBT 26; London: SCM, 1959); J. Murphy-O'Connor, "The *Damascus Document* Reconsidered," *RB* 92 (1985) 223-46; idem, "A Literary Analysis of Damascus Document 19:33—20:34," *RB* 79 (1972) 544-64; idem, "Teacher of Righteousness," *ABD* 6:340-41; E. Puech, *La Croyance des Esséniens en la Vie Future: Immortalité, Résurrection, Vie Éternelle?* (EB n.s. 22; Paris: Gabalda, 1993); S. Schechter, *Documents of Jewish Sectaries: Vol. 1: Fragments of a Zadokite Work* (Cambridge: Cambridge University Press, 1910); L. H. Schiffman, *The Halakhah at Qumran* (SJLA 16; Leiden: E. J. Brill, 1975); idem, "Legislation Concerning Relations with Non-Jews in the *Zadokite Fragments* and in Tannaitic Literature," *RevQ* 11 (1983a) 379-89; idem, *Sectarian Law in the Dead Sea Scrolls: Courts, Testimony and the Penal Code* (BJS 33; Chico, CA: Scholars Press, 1983b); E. M. Schuller, "Women in the Dead Sea Scrolls," in *Methods of Investigation of the Dead Sea Scrolls and the Khirbet Qumran Site: Present Realities and Future Prospects,* ed. M. O. Wise et al. (Annals of the New York Academy of Sciences 722; New York: New York Academy of Sciences, 1994) 115-27; H. Stegemann, *Die Essener, Qumran, Johannes der Täufer und Jesus* (Freiburg: Herder, 1993); idem, "Das Gesetzkorpus der 'Damaskusschrift' (CD ix-xvi)," *RevQ* 14 (1990) 409-34.

J. Murphy-O'Connor

DANIEL, ESTHER AND JEREMIAH, ADDITIONS TO

The Greek translation of the OT, the *Septuagint, or LXX, includes in three biblical books some extra material that is not present in the *Hebrew Bible. LXX Daniel contains an additional 172 verses and LXX Esther a further 107 that have no counterpart in the traditional Masoretic Text, and LXX Jeremiah has appended to it two further compositions comprising 213 verses unknown in Hebrew.

1. Additions to Daniel
2. Additions to Esther
3. Additions to Jeremiah
4. Possible New Testament Resonances

1. Additions to Daniel.

LXX Daniel includes extra material at two

places. The first comes after Daniel 3:23, where Daniel's three Judean compatriots have been thrown into a furnace of blazing fire by the Babylonians. The Greek text provides a prayer on the lips of one of the men (Azariah, also known as Abednego) and a hymn of praise to the Lord on the lips of all three men; accordingly, this addition is known as the Prayer of Azariah and the Song of the Three Young Men (LXX Dan 3:24-90). The second block of extra material comes after Daniel 12:13, where the Hebrew book ends but the Greek version continues with further stories illustrating Daniel's wisdom and zeal: Susanna (LXX Dan 13), in which he establishes the innocence of a woman accused of *adultery; and Bel and the Dragon (LXX Dan 14), in which he establishes the falseness of two gods worshiped by the Babylonians.

2. Additions to Esther.
LXX Esther includes extra material at five places, although it is all grouped together at the end of the book in the Vulgate and thus also in some English versions. The first comes before Esther 1:1 and introduces the hero Mordecai by means of a dream he has and a plot against the king that he foils (LXX Esther A:1-17 [Vulgate 11:2—12:6]). After Esther 2:13 the Greek version presents the text of the king's first letter (B:1-7 [13:1-7]); after Esther 4:17 it presents prayers by Mordecai and Esther (C:1-30 [13:8—14:19]) and describes Esther's approach to the king (D:1-16 [15:1-16]); and after Esther 8:12 it presents the text of the king's second letter (E:1-24 [16:1-24]). Finally, after Esther 10:3, where the Hebrew book ends, the Greek version rounds matters off with Mordecai's account of the fulfillment of his dream and a short postscript on the transmission and translation of the book (F:1-11 [10:4—11:1]).

3. Additions to Jeremiah.
After the book of Jeremiah, the Greek Bible includes two further Jeremianic works in addition to the book of Lamentations, which it also places in this category. The first is the book of *Baruch, sometimes called 1 Baruch to distinguish it from other compositions associated with the name of Jeremiah's secretary. It comprises an introduction on the purpose of the book (Bar 1:1-14), a prayer of confession (Bar 1:15—3:8), a poem in praise of wisdom (Bar 3:9—4:4) and a psalm of encouragement and hope (Bar 4:5—5:9). The other addition is the brief Epistle of Jeremiah (73 verses, presented as Baruch 6 in the Vulgate and thus also in some English versions). It calls upon the Judean exiles in Babylon not to become involved in the worship of the Babylonian gods.

4. Possible New Testament Resonances.
Although it is reasonable to suppose that these additions were a seamless part of the Greek Bible familiar to the early Christians, no clear citation of or allusion to them appears in the NT. The additions may, however, have made a modest contribution to some of the ideas expressed by NT writers.

Dragons are uncommon and inconsequential in the canonical OT, but they appear with significance in the additions to Daniel (14:23-27) and Esther (A:5 [11:6]; F:4 [10:7]), where they play the part of a false god in Daniel's clash with idolatry and portend a mighty battle in Mordecai's vision of the struggle between the people of God and their enemies. The figure of a dragon who stands opposed to God is deployed also in a NT vision (Rev 12—13), but there is no place in John's imagery for Mordecai's corresponding good dragon. The dream of Esther's guardian utilizes other images too that become familiar in eschatological discourse (cf. Esther A:7-8 [11:8-9] with Mk 13), though these are not unique within the OT writings.

Baruch presents some possible affinities with certain NT texts. Wisdom appearing on earth and living with humankind (Bar 3:37) may be echoed in the Word becoming flesh and living among us (Jn 1:14). Perhaps too Baruch's rhetorical point that no one has ascended into heaven (*see* Heavenly Ascent) to bring wisdom down (Bar 3:29) but that God has given her to his loved ones (Bar 3:36) is reflected in John's assertion that no one has ascended into heaven except the Son of Man (Jn 3:13), whom God has given to the world out of love (Jn 3:16). Paul's disparaging reference to making sacrifices to demons rather than God (1 Cor 10:20) is matched by the same language in Baruch 4:7—but both writers probably derived their image from Deuteronomy 32:17 (*see* Demonology).

A final example of a NT writer's thought apparently echoing an expression in one of the additions is the claim in James 2:23 that Abraham was called "the friend of God." Abraham is not so called in Genesis, but he is in the prayer of Azariah (at Dan 3:35 [Azariah v. 12]), though the choice of Greek words is different in the LXX and NT occurrences (forms of *agapaō* and *phileō* respectively). However, the expression found in Azariah's prayer also appears elsewhere in the OT (in Is 41:8 and 2 Chron 20:7), so once again we are left with no clear instance of a NT writer making use of an addition to Daniel, Esther or Jeremiah.

See also APOCRYPHA AND PSEUDEPIGRAPHA; SEPTUAGINT/GREEK OLD TESTAMENT.

BIBLIOGRAPHY. **Texts.** Critical Greek editions have been published in the Göttingen Septuagint series (*Septuaginta: Vetus Testamentum Graecum* [Göttingen: Vandenhoeck & Ruprecht]): Daniel (vol. 16.2, ed. J. Ziegler, 1954); Esther (vol. 8.3, ed. R. Hanhart, 1966); Jeremiah (vol. 15, ed. J. Ziegler, 1957, 2d ed., 1976). For English translations, consult editions of the Bible that include the apocryphal/deuterocanonical books or see Moore below. **Studies.** D. J. A. Clines, *The Esther Scroll: The Story of the Story* (JSOTSup 30; Sheffield: JSOT, 1984); W. H. Daubney, *The Three Additions to Daniel: A Study* (Cambridge: Deighton Bell & Co., 1906); L. Day, *Three Faces of a Queen: Characterization in the Books of Esther* (JSOTSup 186; Sheffield: Sheffield Academic Press, 1995); C. A. Moore, *Daniel, Esther and Jeremiah: The Additions* (AB 44; Garden City, NY: Doubleday, 1977); E. Tov, *The Book of Baruch Also Called 1 Baruch* (SBLTT 8; Missoula, MT: Scholars Press, 1975); idem, *The Septuagint Translation of Jeremiah and Baruch* (HSM 8; Missoula, MT: Scholars Press, 1976). J. Jarick

DEAD SEA SCROLLS: GENERAL INTRODUCTION

In late 1946 or early 1947 a Bedouin shepherd, Muhammed edh-Dhib, followed a stray into a cave along the shores of the Dead Sea and so chanced upon the first of a group of ancient manuscripts that have since revolutionized biblical studies and the study of ancient *Judaism. Seven substantial scrolls emerged from that cave, copies of biblical and extrabiblical writings alike. They were only the beginning. Following the initial discovery, Bedouin and scholars competed to explore the caves of the region in hopes of new manuscript finds. After a search of hundreds of caves, eleven eventually yielded literary texts, now known as the Dead Sea Scrolls (DSS). Approximately 875 (generally fragmentary) manuscripts came to light in the course of these explorations. The nearby site of *Qumran, hitherto regarded as an ancient fortress, was also excavated during five campaigns between 1952-1956, for scholars suspected that the site was connected to the caves and the scrolls.

Publication of the discoveries was comparatively rapid at first. Six of the seven major scrolls from the site of the first discovery, now known as Cave 1, were completely published within seven years. The sixth, the **Genesis Apocryphon*, appeared in a partial edition in 1956 (and much more of the work has since been deciphered and published in preliminary form). The great bulk of the discoveries were early consigned to an international editorial team of seven scholars from Europe and the United States. This team succeeded in sorting most of the fragments and published some of the DSS in a series of volumes, *Discoveries in the Judaean Desert* (DJD; "*of Jordan*" appears on some volumes). Five volumes of DJD appeared in the decade spanning the late 1950s to the late 1960s. In the decades that followed, however, even with occasional preliminary editions, the rate of publication slowed to a crawl. Volume 6 of the series appeared in 1977, nine years after volume 5; volume 7 had to wait another five years, and volume 8 seven more, only appearing in 1989. By 1991, estimates of the percentage of material that remained unpublished ranged between 40 and 60 percent. The reasons for failure to publish so much vital material after forty years were various, some legitimate (the fragmentary condition of the scrolls; deaths of original team members; the demands of academic responsibilities), but others suggesting scandalous scholarly conduct. The late 1980s, in particular, were marred by growing scholarly wrangling over the slow pace of publication and rights of access to the unpublished materials.

In December 1991, pressured by bootleg editions of the scrolls that had begun to appear and the Huntington Library's decision to open its virtually complete collection of photographs of the unpublished texts to all qualified scholars, the Israel Antiquities Authority (IAA) decided to lift restrictions. Henceforth it would allow people to study the unpublished manuscripts and, within certain limits, publish the results of their research. At about the same time, the IAA and the new editor-in-chief of the publication project, E. Tov, moved to expand the number of scholars working on the texts for official publication in the DJD series. Over sixty scholars were now assigned texts. The augmented team soon began to publish the scrolls at a pace much faster than ever before in the history of the project. Some twenty additional volumes of DJD appeared between 1994 and early 2000. As a result of these changes, what had been a stagnant field of research from 1968-1990 became a swirl of scholarly activity.

1. Description of Contents
2. Interpretation of the Finds
3. The Dead Sea Scrolls and the New Testament

1. Description of Contents.

1.1. Biblical Materials. The biblical scrolls recovered from the caves number about 225. They include copies of every book of the Hebrew Bible, with the exception of the book of Esther. The most frequently attested books are Genesis, Exodus, Deuteronomy, Isaiah and Psalms—this last book numbering some thirty-five copies.

The biblical scrolls from Qumran have had a tremendous impact on the study of the Hebrew Bible, both with regard to textual criticism and with regard to what was once known as higher criticism. Their importance for textual criticism is obvious when one considers that prior to their discovery the oldest complete manuscripts of the Hebrew Bible dated from the tenth century A.D. The DSS lifted the curtain to a period over a millennium earlier in the formation of the text (*see* Hebrew Bible).

With regard to matters of higher criticism, perhaps a discussion of the manuscript known as 11QPs^{a} can serve as a typical example of the rich applications the scrolls make possible (*see* Psalms and Hymns of Qumran). It contains forty-one of the biblical psalms as well as apocryphal Psalms 151, 154 and 155. 11QPs^{a} also embraces three hitherto unknown psalms, a portion of Ecclesiasticus chapter 51, and a ten-line prose supplement enumerating the total of David's writings (given as 3,600). The date of composition for the three unknown psalms is disputed by scholars, but is probably the late Persian or early Hellenistic period. The scroll's text of Ecclesiasticus 51 differs markedly from the form previously familiar from the *Septuagint and other early versions. Its presence in a collection attributed entirely to David is instructive, serving as a premier example of the tendency in Second Temple Judaism to ascribe poetic writings of unknown authorship to David. Concomitantly, its inclusion in 11QPs^{a} appears to confirm the long-held suspicion that Jesus ben Sirach did not write the fifty-first chapter of Ecclesiasticus (*see* Sirach).

But this manuscript of the book of Psalms raises much broader issues. The order of the psalms in 11QPs^{a} differs significantly from the order in the traditional or Masoretic Text. At least once (Ps 145), the Qumran scroll evidences a different form of a canonical psalm. Certain groupings of psalms, such as the Songs of Ascent and the Passover Hallel—viewed as units by the Masoretic Text—appear scattered throughout the Qumran text. And 11QPs^{a} is not an isolated example. Half a dozen other non-Masoretic psalters are included among the DSS. These facts suggest that the Psalter as we know it was only one variant in use among the Jews at the time of Jesus. Taken together with other similar evidence, 11QPs^{a} tends to suggest that the third division of the canon, the Writings, was still in flux at the time. Indeed, the Qumran biblical scrolls have reopened study of the formative process of the entire canon. Variant literary editions of Exodus, Numbers, Jeremiah, Psalms and numerous other books seem to show that the writings we consider canonical grew and assumed new forms for a considerable period after the traditional time of their composition. Other writings that did not become part of the canon for later Judaism or Christianity quite likely were such for some groups of Second Temple Jews.

1.2. Nonbiblical Materials. The vast majority of manuscripts from the caves near Qumran are nonbiblical texts. Many of these writings were entirely unknown prior to the discoveries. Others were familiar to scholars only by name or through short quotations in ancient literature. Since the diversity of the scrolls does not lend itself to a single classificatory scheme, what follows is organized according to these broad categories: major (i.e., lengthy) texts, interpretive texts, apocryphal and pseudepigraphic texts, liturgical texts, legal texts, and "magical" and calendrical texts.

1.2.1. Major Texts.

Damascus Document (CD). This work, once known as the Zadokite Fragments, first came to light long before the discovery of the Qumran texts. At the end of the nineteenth century, S. Schechter discovered two fragmentary exemplars deposited in the genizah of a Karaite synagogue in Fustat, the old city of Cairo. To these medieval manuscripts the DSS have added extensive fragments of eight copies of the **Damascus Document* from Qumran Cave 4 (4Q266-273) and tiny fragments of two other copies of the work from caves 5 and 6.

Taken as a whole, the twelve copies represent two versions, or recensions, conventionally designated A and B. Recension A is by far the better attested. When dealing with either recension, scholars usually subdivide the work into two approximate halves according to content: the Admonition and the Laws. The term "Admonition" is something of a misnomer, for one can isolate at least four separate addresses or "sermons" within this section. The Admonition encompasses stylized historical summaries that prefer ciphers to actual names when designating the actors in the drama. So one finds mention of a "Teacher of Righteousness," a "Spouter of Lies" and an "Interpreter of the Law." An enemy group, the "Seekers After Smooth Things," is also prominent. The thrust of the Admonition is to compare two periods of God's wrath: the first at the time of Nebuchadnezzar (586 B.C.; *see* Jewish History: Persian Period), and the second at the time of the Roman invasion of Palestine (63 B.C.; *see* Jewish History: Roman Period). The point of the comparison is to proclaim a typological parallel: just as apostasy in the first instance led to destruction and *exile for Israel, so, too, in the Roman period disaster of an even greater magnitude lies ahead—unless the people repent and embrace the text's legal perspectives.

These perspectives, the laws, constitute halakic regulations for a communal life lived out in "camps," but their contents differ somewhat from manuscript to manuscript. No single, "canonical" form of the *Damascus Document* ever developed. Rather, different leaders of the movement evidently modified a central core to fit their own needs. Most telling in this regard is the substantial overlap between the legal portions of the *Damascus Document* and the *Rule of the Community* (*see* Rule of the Community [1QS]). In some instances manuscripts of these two works contain identical laws, suggesting that one and the same sectarian group used both. This inference gains additional support from the fact that other Qumran writings also overlap similarly (e.g., *Halakha A* [4Q251], *Serekh-Damascus* [4Q265] and *4QMMT* [4Q394-399] all overlap one another). The oft-repeated hypothesis that a stricter branch of the sect lived at *Qumran and followed the *Rule of the Community,* while a less disciplined, broader movement living throughout Palestine was regulated by the *Damascus Document,* no longer seems viable.

The Rule of the Community (1QS). Among the initial discoveries from Cave 1 was a virtually complete copy of the writing variously termed the **Rule of the Community, Discipline Scroll,* or *Manual of Discipline.* The *Rule of the Community* (its actual, ancient Hebrew designation, found inscribed on a scroll tab) describes sundry regulations for the communal life of a group calling itself the *Yahad.* They are to share all meals, pool their property and follow a very strict regimen of ritual *purity. Scholars early recognized that this is a work whose form, as with the *Damascus Document,* is the result of a process of editing and redaction. Recent publication of the fragments of eleven copies of the *Rule of the Community* from Cave 4 (4Q255-264a) have confirmed this understanding and afford insight into the redactional process by which the work grew. In turn, recognition of the literary growth-pattern carries historical implications. It now appears that the movement behind the text was organized at first in semidemocratic fashion. "The Many" (*hārabbîm*), or general membership, had much of the power to make decisions about policy and finances. At a certain juncture a group called the Sons of Zadok (presumably related, whether actually or mythically, to the Zadokite priesthood) usurped this power. The Many was thereafter governed by a priestly oligarchy. Why and when this change took place is unknown. The Cave 4 copies also show that, as with the *Damascus Document,* no canonical version of the *Rule of the Community* ever displaced all rivals. Instead, earlier versions continued to be recopied even after more developed ones had come on the scene. Presumably the unavailability of developed forms at the time a copy was needed explains the scribal decision to recopy older ones. Such scarcity was common in book cultures of Greco-Roman times (*see* Literacy and Book Culture).

In addition to the principal text, the Cave 1 manuscript included two so-called appendices. The first, known as the *Rule of the Congregation* or *Serekh ha-edah* (1QSa/1Q28a), is two columns long and deals with the "last days" (*see* Rule of the Congregation/Messianic Rule [1QSa]). The work's actual connection with the principal text is unclear, for although it originally belonged to the same scroll, it was written by another scribe and differs both in concept and terminology. The *Rule of the Congregation* legislates for the education of children raised in the community, the stages of progression within the movement according to age and ability, and procedures for the communal meal presided over by *priests and a so-called "messiah of Israel." Recently five additional copies of the *Rule of the Congregation* have been identified, written in a cryptic script on papyrus (4Q249a-249e). The second appendix, the *Rule of Benediction* (1QSb/1Q28b; *see* Book of Blessings [1QSb]), is very poorly preserved. Several blessings pronounced by the *maśkîl* ("wise leader") over the community, the priests and the prince make up its content. As with the *Rule of the Congregation,* this second appendix has a very pronounced eschatological setting (*see* Messianism).

The War Scroll (1QM). This scroll consists of nineteen badly deteriorated columns. It was originally somewhat longer, but how much is now impossible to determine. The work is ostensibly a manual to guide the self-styled "Sons of Light" in a final eschatological war, in which they are to face, and eventually vanquish, the "Sons of Darkness." Nevertheless, the text is essentially a theological, not a military, composition.

Among the topics the **War Scroll* treats are: preliminary preparations for the war; rules for the sounding and inscription of trumpets used to guide the course of the battle; the dimensions and inscriptions of shields and standards used; the battle array, including who may and may not participate in the conflict; the role of the priests and Levites; and the ebb and flow of the final battle against the *Kittim* (probably the Romans).

Most scholars agree that the weapons and tactics that the scroll describes suggest Roman rather than Greek military strategy. If so, these descriptions enable the dating of the text *in the form we have it* to be narrowed to the later decades of the first century B.C. But literary analysis further suggests that the text as we now have it is considerably expanded and reworked from an earlier version or versions, perhaps utilizing as its kernel a work based on Daniel 11:40—12:3. This literary hypothesis finds some support in fragments of six exemplars of the *War Scroll* discovered in Cave 4. Some of these fragments reveal a much shorter version of the work and otherwise differ markedly from the Cave 1 manuscript.

A work intimately related to the *War Scroll,* even perhaps part of one recension of it, is *Sefer ha-Milhamah.* Two copies have survived, 4Q285 and 11Q14 (*see* War Scroll [11QM] and Related Texts). One fragment of this writing has been interpreted to say that a messianic figure known from several of the DSS, the "Prince of the Congregation," will be put to death by his enemies. He would then be a sort of dying messiah. A more probable interpretation of the ambiguous Hebrew phrase in question is that the Prince of the Congregation himself puts an enemy king to death.

The Hymns (1QH^a). The composition known as the *Hymns,* or 1QHodayot (*see* Thanksgiving Hymns [1QH]), comprises in the *editio princeps* eighteen partial columns and sixty-six numbered fragments. Subsequent to that original edition scholars identified two additional fragments. Because none of the columns is complete, students of the text have proposed differing divisions and, consequently, competing reckonings as to the number of hymns 1QH^a contains. Six manuscripts from Cave 4 further complicate the situation. While these copies fill in lacunae in the manuscript from Cave 1, they also prove that the order of hymns was somewhat variable. Indeed, the Cave 4 copies tend to support literary analysis arguing that more than one version of the work existed. At the core, and originally circulating as a self-contained book, were some eight columns of hymns authored by the Teacher of Righteousness. These were the so-called *Teacher Hymns.* Subsequent leaders of the movement added hymns fore and aft, sometimes deriving these added hymns from sources that have also come down to us separately. The added hymns are conventionally known as *Community Hymns.*

Most of the hymns begin either "I thank Thee, Lord," or "Blessed Art Thou, O Lord." Many scholars have tried to fit them into a model known to biblical form critics as "psalms of individual thanksgiving." Deviations from the biblical patterns, however, are sufficient to make the genre of these compositions a moot point. Many of the hymns have nothing to do with thanksgiving, or even lament, but are more like a discourse. Also debated is the question of what function(s) the writings served within the movement(s) that produced or employed them. Another important aspect of the hymns is their midway position between the psalmic literature of the Hebrew Bible and that of later Judaism, including the NT.

One of the hymns added to the core of the *Teacher Hymns* (at 1QH^{a} 25:35—26:10) survived only in fragmentary form but has recently been the subject of considerable research. The Cave 4 materials make it possible to reconstruct about half of the hymn. The writer portrays a remarkable figure who asks, "Who is like me among the angels?" (Heb *ʾēlîm,* lit. "gods"), echoing in daring fashion the biblical question addressed to God, "Who is like you among the angels?" He also asks, "Who is like me for lack of evil? Does any compare to me?" and (alluding to the Servant Songs of Isaiah) "Who has been contemptuously despised like me?" Though much research remains to be done on this "Hymn of the Exalted One," it bears obvious comparison to NT statements about Jesus and to the NT use of divine language from the OT to describe him. Moreover, the figure is, like the Jesus of Hebrews, seated on a throne at the right hand of God.

The Temple Scroll. Known in three copies from Cave 11 and one or two from Cave 4, the principal copy of the *Temple Scroll* (11QTemple; also 11QTorah; *see* Temple Scroll [11QTemple]) is the longest of the surviving DSS. Unwound, this copy of the scroll is twenty-eight feet from beginning to end. The *Temple Scroll* is a melange of biblical and extrabiblical ordinances and descriptions concerned with a *temple, its services and its *festivals. The first well-preserved columns describe the temple building with its key installations. From there the text proceeds to detail various festivals, *sacrifices and procedures, the temple courtyards and laws of impurity (*see* Purity), finishing with extracts from the Deuteronomic Code (Deut 12—26). Among the most striking literary features of the scroll is the change of all biblical quotations attributed to Moses from third to first person. This well-calculated change has the effect of making Moses seem at once the author and addressee of the text, thus imbuing its contents with Mosaic authority.

The New Jerusalem Text. Although not well enough preserved to be considered "major," a text that is related to the *Temple Scroll* may conveniently be brought into the discussion here (*see* New Jerusalem Texts). This is the Aramaic writing designated the *New Jerusalem,* which is attested by copies from caves 1, 2, 4, 5 and 11. The author presents the work as a vision in which he ("Ezekiel"?) is led about a future Jerusalem by an angel and shown various buildings, streets and gates; in each case measurements both in cubits and reeds are provided. The description is very schematic, and many measurements are unrealistically large. Evidently inspired by Ezekiel 48:16-17, the city described is approximately 18 by 13 miles in size. Numerous measurements for features of the city and its temple are identical to those of the *Temple Scroll,* suggesting that the *New Jerusalem* was a source for that work.

The Copper Scroll (3Q15). Perhaps no DSS has occasioned greater difficulties in its reading and interpretation than the *Copper Scroll* (*see* Copper Scroll [3Q15]). This is the only work inscribed on copper, and unlike all but a few it was composed in early Mishnaic *Hebrew rather than in archaizing Late Biblical Hebrew. The twelve columns consist of a series of sixty-four or sixty-five topographic descriptions, or toponymns, often followed by the instruction to dig a given depth. Then follows a specified weight of bullion or amount of money, precious vessels or the like. The *Copper Scroll,* in other words, is a list of treasure trove and a guide to the hiding places. At first glance the amounts of treasure seem incredible; estimates in terms of modern value exceed one hundred million dollars.

Interpretations of this document include the original editor Milik's theses that it represents either a "folkloristic treasure trove" or the work of a madman, in either case having no connection to the Qumran movement. For Milik the *Copper Scroll* was only coincidentally found along with the group's materials in Cave 3, being removed somewhat from the other deposits of that cave. His approach requires two independent deposits. The first deposit in Cave 3 occurred about A.D. 70, when all the other DSS were hidden in the caves. The *Copper Scroll,* on the other hand, belonged to a putative second deposit made around A.D. 100. Although popular in the 1950s and 1960s, Milik's views can claim no significant support today. Most scholars now believe that the scroll was placed in the cave at the same time as all the others. They further deny that the scroll is a work of imagination; its genre is documentary, that of "list," a common genre in Greco-Roman times. The contents described in the scroll are therefore of an actual treasure, probably associated with the Jerusalem temple. Only the connection with a major institution of Jewish society can explain the vast sum of treasure. Some argue that the treasure was taken *from* Herod's temple, others that it was intended *for* Herod's temple. Accordingly, the *Copper Scroll* occupies a central position in arguments about who wrote the Dead Sea Scrolls.

1.2.2. Interpretive Texts.

Pesharim. Among the most fascinating of the Hebrew texts discovered in the caves are those known as the *pesharim (*p^e^šārîm*, pl. of *pešer*, meaning "solution" or "interpretation"). These are usually grouped into two categories—thematic and continuous. Thematic pesharim consist of selected portions of the Bible with interpretive comments and are organized around a central theme or idea. In contrast, continuous pesharim comment *seriatim* on a portion of the Bible, usually the prophets, but sometimes so-called prophetic psalms. At least fifteen, perhaps eighteen, texts belonging to this latter category have been identified.

The pesharim purport to be mysterious explications of divine truth from Scripture, a truth revealed only to the author and his group. None of these commentaries is concerned with the literal sense of the text; instead, they use metaphor, paronomasia and development of key words or phrases to unmask the hidden significance of a given biblical portion. The most complete of the pesharim is the commentary on Habakkuk (*see* Habakkuk Commentary [1QpHab]). This pesher preserves thirteen almost complete columns, providing the text of Habakkuk along with commentary. The form of the book of Habakkuk to which it witnesses is often different from that of the Masoretic Text.

Also relatively complete is the pesher designated 4Q171, which preserves the text of Psalms 37:7-40; 45:1-2 and possibly 60:8-9. Psalm 37 is a psalm of personal tribulation, offering the righteous hope in spite of the evident prosperity of the wicked. It thus fits perfectly the literary requirements for the author of the pesher, who interprets the tribulation in terms of his community's own troubles, their enemies and approaching eschatological justification.

From a historical vantagepoint, the pesher on Nahum (4Q169) is the most important of the pesharim. Eschewing ciphers at certain junctures, this author mentions a "Demetrius, King of Greece," and refers to a Jewish ruler who crucified great numbers of his opponents. Apparent references to these same persons and events appear in the writings of *Josephus, leading most scholars to identify Demetrius as Demetrius III Eucaerus (95-87 B.C.) and the Jewish ruler as Alexander Janneus (103-76 B.C.). The crucifixion mentioned equates, most think, with Janneus's known execution of eight hundred of his opponents in the wake of a failed *coup d'état.* That event occurred in 88 B.C.

Of the thematic pesharim, none has aroused more profound interest than 11QMelchizedek (*see* Melchizedek, Traditions of). Fourteen fragments preserve the remains of three columns of this manuscript. The author comments on isolated OT texts (in particular Lev 25:9, 10, 13; Deut 15:2; and Is 61:1), but Daniel 9:24-27 structures his commentary. The events connected with these biblical texts are portrayed as taking place in "the end of days," which is further identified as the "tenth Jubilee" and the "Day of Atonement." Melchizedek will free those who belong to his "inheritance" and (if suggested restorations are followed) "atone for their iniquities." He will further exact God's vengeance upon *Belial and those of his "lot." The text presents a conception of Melchizedek that is both approximately contemporary with and comparable to that of Hebrews 7: connecting him with divine judgment, a Day of Atonement and a primary role among God's *angels. A second figure in the pesher, the "Herald," may be identified with the Teacher of Righteousness, but this point remains controversial.

Three additional thematic pesharim are important. The first of these is known as 4QOrdinances, which exists in three copies (4Q159, 513-514). This halakic pesher interprets Exodus 30:11-16 (the scriptural basis for the temple tax traditionally required of all male Jews annually) as referring not to annual taxes, but instead to a one-time payment. Leviticus 25:39-46, which prohibits the purchase of fellow Israelites as slaves, is here understood to ban also the sale of a Jew to Gentiles.

The second thematic pesher is 4QFlorilegium (*see* Florilegium [4Q174]). Here four large fragments have been joined to form two columns, leaving twenty-three extra, unjoined sections. The author combines quotations from 2 Samuel 7:10-14; Exodus 15:17-18; Amos 9:11; Psalm 1:1; Isaiah 8:11; Ezekiel 37:23 (uncertain) and Psalm 2:1 with interpretive comments. All of these verses are related to the "end of days," when God will order that a new "temple of Adam" be built. Therein men will perform sacrifices and the "deeds of the Torah," free from outside harassment or impurity. Prominent in the text are references to the "Shoot of David" and the "Interpreter of the Law," eschatological figures familiar from other Qumran texts.

The third thematic pesher, 4QTestimonia, has (perhaps falsely) furnished many scholars with the basic substance of Qumran messianic expectation (*see* Testimonia [4Q175]). The text is a catena of quotations from Deuteronomy 5:28-29; 18:18-19; Numbers 24:15-17; Deuteronomy 33:8-11; Joshua 6:26 and an extrabiblical work also found among the scrolls, 4QPsalms of Joshua (*see* Apocryphon of Joshua [4Q378-379]). The body of the text arranges these quotations into four groups, each group set off by a scribal device and so, inferentially, concerning separate topics. One reason this text is important is because it furnishes explicit evidence for the existence, long posited, of *testimonia,* or *florilegia* (collections of proof-texts), in pre-Christian Judaism.

Targumim. Three Aramaic targumim (*targûmîm,* plural of *targûm,* meaning "translation" or "interpretation" of the Hebrew Bible; *see* Aramaic Targums: Qumran) number among the DSS. Much the longest and most complete of these is the Job targum from Cave 11 (*see* Targum of Job [11Q10 & 4QtgLev, 4QtgJob]). This text represents the only incontestably pre-Christian targum of any appreciable length. Surviving portions include Job 17—42, with the last six chapters the least damaged. On the whole, despite slight additions, subtractions and dislocations, the Hebrew text behind the Aramaic translation seems to have been essentially the Masoretic Text. Even the supposedly disordered third cycle of debates (22:1—31:40) and the Hymn to Wisdom (28:1—28:28, often regarded as an interpolation) are here and in the same problematic order as in the Masoretic Text.

The other two targumim are extremely fragmentary. The first (4Q156) contains an Aramaic rendering of Leviticus 16:12-15, 18-21, but whether these fragments were part of a targum at all is uncertain. Equally conceivable is that they come from a liturgical work that quoted these verses. If, nevertheless, they do represent portions of a targum, then we have for the first time a pre-Christian targum to a book of the Pentateuch. The translation of the Hebrew is literal (unexpanded). Finally, 4Q157 preserves portions of Job 3:5-9 and 4:16—5:4, reflecting a text virtually identical to the Masoretic Text.

1.2.3. Apocryphal and Pseudepigraphic Texts. Included among the DSS are manuscripts of nonbiblical books that were known in some form even before the discoveries at the caves. Apocryphal writings attested include *Tobit (in both Hebrew and Aramaic) and Ecclesiasticus (also known as *Sirach). Pseudepigraphic works include the *Testament of Levi* (in Aramaic), a portion of the *Testament of Naphtali* (in Hebrew; *see* Testaments of the Twelve Patriarchs), **Enoch* and **Jubilees. Jubilees* was especially popular, to judge by the fourteen or fifteen manuscripts thus far identified from caves 2, 3, 4 and 11. Not surprisingly, previously unknown texts that can now be classified as pseudepigraphic were also unearthed. Among these are testaments of Jacob, Judah, Joseph and Kohath, the *Psalms of Joshua* mentioned above and a Daniel cycle.

1 Enoch. In 1976, Milik published his long-awaited book on the fragments of *Enoch* discovered in Cave 4. Milik's book contains most (but not all) of the Qumran *Enoch* manuscripts, all in Aramaic, and attests parts of every subdivision of *1 Enoch* except for one. Thus it includes seven fragmentary manuscripts (4QEn^{a-g}) that together preserve some of the Book of Watchers, the Book of Dreams and the Epistle of Enoch. Also included in the book are four other manuscripts (4QEnastr^{a-d}) that point to a much longer recension of what is known in *1 Enoch* as the Astronomical Book. Additionally, portions of a literature clearly related to *1 Enoch,* but previously unknown, are included under the title, Book of Giants (4QEnGiants^{a-e}). Significant by its absence from the Qumran fragments is the so-called Book of Parables, which uses the term "son of man," an important self-designation of Jesus. Scholars are divided on the reason for this absence. Milik himself thought that the Book of Parables must be a Christian writing, but most scholars today reject that view. The Book of Parables was probably, at least in an early form, pre-Christian, but was not included among the Qumran deposits either fortuitously or because some of its ideas were unacceptable.

Genesis Apocryphon. One of the pseudepigraphic texts that surfaced among the DSS was the otherwise unknown **Genesis Apocryphon*

(1QapGen). Dated around the turn of the eras, this Aramaic writing presents the patriarchs of Genesis telling their own stories. In so doing it adheres closely to the biblical stories, but with frequent expansions derived from unknown midrashic sources (including, it seems, a Testament of Noah). Columns 1 through 5 mostly concern the birth of Noah; 6 through 17 deal with the flood and the postdiluvian division of the earth among Noah's sons; 18 through 22 (where the text breaks off) concern Abram according to Genesis 11—15.

Most scholars, while recognizing features more akin to the known *targumim, regard the *Genesis Apocryphon* as a *midrashic composition. It is thus related to intertestamental works such as *Jubilees,* which are often called *"rewritten Bible." Perhaps the primary importance of the text lies in its language. Because it is one of the longest Aramaic texts from Qumran, the *Genesis Apocryphon* is of special significance in the effort to recover the varieties of Palestinian *Aramaic used by the Jews at the time of Jesus. In general its language is of a form transitional between the book of Daniel and the targumim, antedating as well the materials from the Wadi Murabbaʿat, Wadi Seiyal and Wadi Ḥabra.

Prayer of Nabonidus. Fragments of an Aramaic pseudepigraphon known as the *Prayer of Nabonidus* were found in Cave 4 (*see* Prayer of Nabonidus and Pseudo-Daniel [4Q242-245]). The fragments make up two incomplete columns, including the beginning of column 1. As the name suggests, the text is ostensibly a prayer delivered by the last king of Babylon, Nabonidus, telling the story of the king's seven-year period of illness—a time when he prayed to "the gods of silver and gold" for a cure. At length, a Jewish "exorcist" delivered him, and in gratitude the king wrote this prayer. The parallels with the fourth chapter of Daniel and the story of Nebuchadnezzar's madness are patent, leading many scholars to conclude that in this text we have remnants of the popular traditions from which the Aramaic portions of Daniel derived.

The Daniel Cycle. The prayer of Nabonidus is just one part of a "Daniel cycle" that apparently included at least five additional works. Three of these (4QpsDan^{a-c} [4Q243-245]) contain one or more apocalyptic overviews of Jewish history narrated by or involving Daniel. The fourth writing (4Q552-553) recounts a dream in which four trees (or their "angels") speak to the author. Each tree represents a kingdom (compare Daniel 2 and 7), the first of which is identified as Babylon and the second as Persia. This work has a bearing on the interpretation (or history of interpretation) of the fourth kingdom mentioned in Daniel 2 and 7. Another text from this Daniel cycle is known as 4QpsDanA^{a} (*see* Son of God Text [4Q246]). This fragmentary but striking work preserves the phrases "son of God" and "son of the Most High," as well as phraseology reminiscent of Luke 1:32 and 1:35. One additional writing, 4Q248, the *Acts of a King,* is related to the contents of Daniel but of disputed interpretation. According to one view, it relates events from the time of Ptolemy I Soter, about 300 B.C.; according to the other, it records episodes of the reign of Antiochus IV Epiphanes, about 170 B.C.

Words of Moses. The **Words of Moses* (1Q22) is a sort of apocryphon to Deuteronomy. God speaks to Moses, who in turn relays the commands to the people, evidently via Eleazar and Joshua. At one point the text requires the appointment of officials (perhaps priests), "to clarify . . . all these words of the Torah." Another example of interpretive explanation occurs in the third column (3:8-10), where the date of the Day of Atonement is explained by reason that "your fathers were wandering in the desert until the tenth day of the month."

Book of Mysteries. Another tantalizing pseudepigraphon is the **Book of Mysteries,* known in three or four copies (1Q27, 4Q299-300; 4Q301 is disputed). The work derives its name from the recurrent and prominent term *raz,* "mystery, secret." Some of the work is cast as poetic oracles, while the eloquent prose that follows each poetic section provides "signs" by which the truth of the oracles is to be proved. The most extensive run of continuous text, in 1Q27 column 1, delivers an indictment against those who neither meditate upon the "former things" nor recognize the significance of the "mystery of existence" (*raz nihyeh; see* Secret of Existence [4Q412-413, 415-421]). Of particular interest is the appearance in 1Q27 of the phrase *razê pešaʿ*. This phrase is probably the Hebrew equivalent of the Greek *mystērion tēs anomias* of 2 Thessalonians 2:7.

Other Pseudepigraphic Writings. The Cave 4 materials include a wealth of material that is difficult to classify using the scholarly categories familiar from the past. For many of these works the term now being used is *parabiblical.* They relate to the biblical corpus and to the authors of the Hebrew Bible in varied, even uncertain ways, yet the relation is incontestable. Such works include *Reworked Pentateuch* (4Q158, 364-367; *see* Rewritten Bible), which comprises a running commentary on the Pentateuch with exegetical additions and omissions. Some of the additions are of significant size. Other parabiblical writings new to scholarship include: 4Q369, the **Prayer of Enosh*; 4Q382, *Parakings* (or *Paraphrase of Kings*); and 4Q422, a paraphrase of Genesis and Exodus. *Commentaries on Genesis* (or *Genesis Pesher*), including both straightforward and sectarian exegesis of the biblical text, are found in 4Q252-254a. Also parabiblical is 4Q473, *The Two Ways,* a work related to Deuteronomy but also bearing comparison with early Christian writings using this motif, such as *Didache* 1—6. Numerous additional, very fragmentary parabiblical works, most having no evident sectarian characteristics, have also come to light. Among these are 4Q559, *Biblical Chronology,* an Aramaic chronograph whose surviving portions treat the length of the Egyptian sojourn, the time of Israel's wandering in the wilderness and the period of the early judges.

1.2.4. Liturgical Texts. Among the texts from Qumran many are either clearly liturgical or plausibly so construed (*see* Liturgy: Qumran). Of these writings perhaps the most interesting is the *Angelic Liturgy*, or **Songs of the Sabbath Sacrifice.* The composition is partially preserved in eight manuscripts from Cave 4 (4Q400-407), as well as in fragments from Cave 11 (11Q17) and Masada (Mas1k). The author portrays heaven as a complicated temple consisting of seven sanctuaries attended by seven chief prince-priests, their deputies and seven angelic priesthoods. Also detailed are the praise offerings that the *angels offer up on the *sabbath. Altogether the work comprises thirteen separate compositions, one for each of the first thirteen sabbaths of the year. The *Songs of the Sabbath Sacrifice* is important for the study of angelology, Second Temple liturgical song and early Jewish *mysticism. A striking phrase in the first hymn avers that the angelic priests, by their heavenly cultus, "atone for those who turn from sin." One may understand this statement to mean that the earthly temple cultus is really not essential. Here, then, is an important witness to a conception of Judaism that is not temple-centered (at least in a physical sense). Such ideas, of course, were starting points both for Christianity and rabbinic Judaism.

A second noteworthy liturgical opus is the *Words of the Luminaries* (4Q504-506). Fragmentary remaining headings show that the compositions contained in this manuscript were meant to be recited on given days of the week. With one exception, the mood of these compositions is penitential; hence, they may appropriately be classed *taḥ^{a}nûnîm* (confessional prayers reflecting such biblical passages as Dan 9:4-19). The instructions evidence that these *taḥ^{a}nûnîm* were used liturgically, as in later Judaism. The single evident exception to the somber tone of the *Words of the Luminaries* is a composition for the sabbath. This prayer is full of praise rather than contrition, reflecting the traditional Jewish understanding of the sabbath as a time of joy.

Among many that might be singled out, two further liturgically oriented works can be mentioned here. One is 4QApocryphal Lamentations A (4Q179). The text is comprised of five fragments, the order of which is still uncertain. As the name implies, it is a lament or series of laments over the city of Jerusalem, whose imagery is achieved chiefly by allusion to Lamentations, Isaiah and Jeremiah. Possibly the work was occasioned by a destruction of Jerusalem at the time of Antiochus IV Epiphanes (compare 1 Macc 1:29-32), or by another destruction at Roman hands in 63 B.C. Alternatively, 4Q179 may be no more than a poetic reminiscence of the famous razing by the forces of Nebuchadnezzar in 586 B.C.

The second text contains vocabulary strikingly similar to that of the *Rule of the Community* and the *Rule of Benediction,* and is known as *Berachot* (4Q286-290) (*see* Blessings [4Q280, 286-290]). The writing depicts a covenant ceremony incorporating numerous blessings and curses. The blessings are recited by all heavenly and earthly creatures faithful to the laws of creation and by the members of the movement who are faithful to the Law. The curses descend upon *Belial and the evil angels who are his lot.

Another group of manuscripts from Qumran that are broadly related to liturgy and worship are the phylacteries or *t^{e}pillîn.* A number have surfaced from caves 1, 4, 5, 8 and an unidentified cave, "Cave X." They are instructive regarding the content and order of the portions of Scripture they contain and also witness to noteworthy textual variants. Four *t^e^pillîn* were discovered in their capsules, enabling scholars to investigate technical points that are treated extensively in rabbinic literature—such matters as the shape of the capsule, the nature of the leather for scriptural portions, and the type of thread with which the capsules are tied.

Moreover, the order of the scriptural portions in the *t^e^pillîn* has been a matter of heated controversy in the history of Judaism. The most famous controversy on this subject occurred in the early medieval period between Rashi and Rabbenu Tam. As a whole, the Qumran *t^e^pillîn* are not strictly in the order for which either man argued. The fact that some from Cave 8 are arranged according to Rashi's system, while others from the approximately contemporary finds at Murabbaʿat accord with the position of Rabbenu Tam, suggests that first-century Jews used both systems concurrently. The contents of the *t^e^pillîn* published so far often add verses to the classical portion of Scripture, but the verses added differ among the various examples. No clear rationale has been adduced to explain this fact. Notably, 1Q13, 4Qa (4Q128) and XQPhyl. 3 all contain the Decalogue (Deut 5:1-21), which is never included in rabbinic phylacteries. Thus the phylacteries from Qumran raise many questions about the laws governing their production and do not seem to fall into a single "sectarian" categorization.

1.2.5. Legal Texts. Many of the writings already discussed have a significant legal component, especially the *Rule of the Community,* the *Rule of the Congregation, Damascus Document, Temple Scroll* and 4QOrdinances. Another writing of great importance for understanding the types and functions of religious law in Second Temple Judaism is 4QMMT, short for **Miqṣat Maʿaśey ha-Torah,* "some rulings concerning the Law." Published in the DJD series in 1994, 4QMMT includes a list of some twenty-three legal controversies concerning which the authors find fault with current practice in the Jerusalem temple. The work appears to be addressed to someone in position to change those practices, presumably the reigning high priest (although some have argued that the work is intrasectarian). In at least two instances, the laws of 4QMMT are identical to those of opponents to the Pharisees in rabbinic writings, making clear once again (for there are many other indicators) that the Qumran movement was in its essence antipharisaic. The laws of 4QMMT also demonstrate, if further demonstration were needed, the priestly character of the movement: the laws favor the priests when compared with rabbinic legislation. Such is true of the entire Qumran legal corpus. 4QMMT seems to prove that the Qumran movement split with greater Judaism primarily over legal issues, not matters of philosophy or the legitimacy of the high priest, as often suggested. Indeed, the publication of this writing has spurred—and coincided with—a much greater attention to the importance of religious law for an understanding not only of the culture, but also of the history, of the NT period. Different movements in Second Temple Judaism, including Christianity, *were different* in large part because of different ideas about the law.

A variety of other legal works among the scrolls have added impetus to this research (*see* Legal Texts at Qumran; Torah). These writings include *Halakhah A* (4Q251), which tabulates a variety of laws on subjects such as the sabbath, firstfruits, the selling of ancestral lands and the slaughter of pregnant animals. *Tohorot A* (4Q274) legislates for the type of impurity produced by leprosy. *Tohorot B^b* and *Tohorot B^c* (4Q276-277) deal with the ritual preparation of the red heifer—the only means for purification from impurity of the dead—as stipulated by Numbers 19. 4QLeqet (4Q284a) provides laws to regulate gleaning; unlike the Bible, it requires gleaners to be ritually pure. The work entitled *Rebukes by the Overseer* (4Q477) lists by name several members of the Qumran movement whom the Overseer has publicly rebuked for breach of the group's laws. The movement required the overseer to record all such rebukes in writing. Several of the legal causes for rebuke are unknown from other Qumran writings. *Serekh Damascus* (4Q265) regulates the paschal sacrifice, procedures for the novitiate, group life (with a penal code largely but not entirely identical to that known from the *Damascus Document* and the *Rule of the Community*), and the parturient.

1.2.6. "Magical" and Calendrical Texts. Calendar and "magic" were not entirely separate concerns in the ancient world, for magic often—and the calendar always—involved study of the heavenly bodies. Thus one magical work from Qumran combines a peculiar calendar (see below), the earliest known Jewish naming of the signs of the zodiac, and divination by thunder (4Q318; *see* Thunder Text). 4QHoroscope

(4Q186) is an encoded series of horoscopes whose scribe mixes the ordinary Jewish script with the alphabets of Paleo-Hebrew, Greek and Cryptic Script A (one of three secret alphabets found among the scrolls); he further inscribes his text, *à la* Leonardo da Vinci's notebooks, in mirror writing. The surviving fragments describe three people in reference to their astrological birth signs, deriving therefrom each person's physical and spiritual qualities. 4QHoroscope possesses notable terminological parallels with the *Rule of the Community.* These writings show that astrological ideas had been assimilated deeply by the Jews, in spite of the apparent biblical condemnations (for example, Is 47:13-14; Jer 10:1-3). Interest in such matters may be related to the story of the magi in Matthew's Gospel. An Aramaic work similar in method to 4QHoroscope, but lacking the sectarian terminology, is 4Q561.

Another scroll known as the *Elect of God* (4Q534) has been termed a "messianic horoscope." This very poorly preserved Aramaic text contains the phrase *bḥyr ʾlh),* the equivalent of the Greek *ho eklektos tou theou* ("the elect of God") witnessed by some manuscripts of John 1:34. It is uncertain, however, that the Aramaic phrase carries a messianic connotation. The words occur as part of the description of an unborn child who will possess wisdom and precocious intellect. He is to have a long life, and the success of his plans is assured by his position as the "elect of God." Since the text lacks astrological terminology, it might better be considered an example of physiognomic literature rather than as a horoscope. Moreover, as some scholars maintain, the *Elect of God* may describe the birth of Noah, not a messiah (cf. *1 Enoch* 106).

A work hesitantly identified by the original team as a collection of proverbs, 4Q560, has now been shown to be an apotropaic incantation or exorcism, the earliest ever known from Palestine (*see* Magical Papyri). The preserved portions of the formula adjure various spirits by name, evidently employing the sacred name of Yahweh. The concerns are those of similar texts elsewhere in the ancient Near East: childbirth, diseases, sleep or dreams, and (perhaps) safety of possessions. One of the demons, the Fever-demon, may illuminate the Synoptic story of Peter's sick mother-in-law. Matthew 8:15 and Mark 1:31 report the event as a simple healing by Jesus, but Luke 4:39 can be translated, "Then he stood over her and rebuked the Fever-demon, and it left her."

Perhaps the one element that more than any other binds the DSS into an ideological unity is the type of calendar they insist upon. Unlike the 354-day luni-solar calendar of the Pharisees and rabbinic Judaism (which is essentially the modern Jewish calendar), the calendar of the scrolls is a solar device. Each year comprises 364 days, and each quarter of the year has 91 days; months are either thirty or thirty-one days long. The regularity of this system is such that all festivals occur on the same day from year to year, and never on the sabbath. Avoiding having a festival fall on the sabbath solved all sorts of halakic problems. This "Qumran calendar" was actually a very old priestly mechanism antedating the rise of the Qumran movement. Forms of this calendar date to at least the third century B.C. Evidence of its use is clear from the Septuagint—even, some scholars believe, from the Hebrew Bible. And its later advocacy was not limited to Qumran circles. The texts found at Masada include at least two writings embracing or probably embracing the solar calendar (Mas1j, 1k), and *Josephus's narrative describing the *sicarii* at Masada (Josephus *J.W.* 4.7.2 §§402-5) further suggests that this priestly group followed a calendar different from their contemporaries at En Gedi. In fact, for at least three centuries a kind of calendar war raged among the Jews of Palestine, finally being settled only by the destruction of one party to the dispute in the First Revolt against Rome (A.D. 66-73/74). The DSS are a strong witness to the views of the losing priestly party.

The 364-day calendar underlies or is explicit in all of the major Qumran writings: the *Rule of the Community,* the *Damascus Document,* the *War Scroll,* the *Temple Scroll,* the *Hymns,* the pesharim, 4QMMT. Likewise, it underlies or is explicit in many of the lesser works. Hundreds of the DSS attest to this calendar. (On the other hand, not a single Qumran writing favors the pharisaic version.) A significant number of calendrical works—that is, writings whose sole purpose is to explain certain details of the calendar—have also emerged from the caves. Such works include 4Q320-321a, synchronistic calendars that tabulate a form of the luni-solar calendar over against the 364-day instrument. Other calendar writings explain the timing of priestly service in the temple by sabbaths, months and seasons, according to a six-year cycle: 4Q325, 4Q326, 4Q328, 4Q329, 4Q329a and 4Q334. An especially interesting calendrical writing, sometimes called the *Annalistic Calendar,* is extant in six fragmentary copies (4Q322-324c). Similar to certain modern calendars that mention "President's Day" or "Independence Day" on the appropriate day of the year, the *Annalistic Calendar* refers to historical events on given days, and uses actual names of the Hasmonean period. The names of John Hyrcanus I, John Hyrcanus II, Aristobulus II and Shelamzion or Alexandra all appear in the work. These were rulers of the Jews between 134-63 B.C. The name "Aemilius" also appears, doubtless a reference to M. Aemilius Scaurus, one of Pompey's leading generals when the Romans invaded Palestine and ended Jewish independence in 63 B.C. This writing, in particular, is very important in the attempt to discover who wrote the scrolls and when.

2. Interpretation of the Finds.
The majority of scholars identify the DSS as the products of the ancient Jewish sect known as the *Essenes. For this identification scholars rely on a combination of "external" and "internal" evidence.

The "external" evidence combines a passage from *Pliny the Elder with the archaeology of the site of Qumran (*see* Qumran: Place and History). In the course of a late first-century travelogue, Pliny describes the Essenes as living along the shores of the Dead Sea, with En Gedi "below" or "south" of them (the Latin preposition *infra* is ambiguous; "below" means topometrically lower, as the bottom of a hill is below the top). This description could fit Qumran. Archaeology further indicates that the site was in use during the time Pliny describes. Structures found at Qumran have been identified as functional for such a community and include what have been understood as a potter's shop and a communal dining hall. Three inkwells and other materials construed as evidence of scribal activity suggest to some scholars that the scrolls found in the nearby caves were written on the site. Recent analysis of the graveyard near Qumran by J. Zias indicates that only men were buried there in ancient times; the few graves of women seem to be much later, early-modern Bedouin intrusions. If so, then the graveyard suggests a celibate male community, just what Pliny describes for the Essenes.

"Internal" evidence consists of a comparison between passages describing the Essenes in *Philo and Josephus, on the one hand, with the contents of texts such as 1QS and CD on the other. All these sources agree in describing or presupposing a communal organization. Similarities include novitiate periods, communal regulations, strict observance of the sabbath vis-à-vis rabbinic law, and certain legal positions such as the transmission of ritual impurity by oil.

Neither the external nor the internal evidence is without problems. N. Golb in postulating his "Jerusalem hypothesis" has pointed out many of them. As the name suggests, Golb argues that the DSS derive from Jerusalem and various libraries there. To date, however, Golb and his fellow advocates remain a minority in scholarship on the scrolls. One point on which he has persuaded many scholars is that of provenance. While most would reject his view that the DSS are not, as a whole, Essene products, the modified notion that many of the scrolls were produced *by Essenes* elsewhere than at the site, perhaps in Jerusalem, has proved attractive.

If such a view were correct, then the potential significance of the scrolls for an understanding of Judaism at the time of Jesus is substantially greater than the 1950s view of provenance would imply. For on this interpretation, the DSS represent the product of a wider portion of society than the hypothesis of their production at Qumran stipulates. The ancillary question of how much wider remains to be addressed by further research.

3. The Dead Sea Scrolls and the New Testament.
On the whole, NT scholarship in relation to the DSS is best described as outdated. For example, no book is more often quoted in this regard than the volume edited by K. Stendahl in 1957, *The Scrolls and the New Testament.* It is paradigmatic that rather than produce a new series of essays on relations between Qumran studies and the NT, the book simply continues to be reprinted. Similarly, the excellent two-volume work by H. Braun, *Qumran und das Neue Testament,* is now outdated. Both of these works still contain useful material, but because so much has happened in DSS studies since they were written, one must use them very cautiously.

An illustration of the potential for new understandings may be found in the work alluded to above, 4QMMT. As noted, this text lists over twenty legal topics upon which the text's authors and the temple authorities disagree. In this fact alone its significance for NT studies is enormous, for previously we really had no factual statement about what was going on in the temple just before Jesus' day. Josephus's descriptions of the temple cultus are difficult to use with confidence, because he often describes things the way they ought to have been (that is, as he understood the relevant OT texts) rather than the way they really were. This fact becomes apparent when comparing the theoretical descriptions of his *Antiquities* with the historical narratives of his *War* and *Vita;* not infrequently they disagree. The tannaitic legal discussions are likewise often idealizing (*see* Rabbinic Literature). With 4QMMT, we can discover what was really happening, at least with regard to the topics upon which it touches. For example, the authors oppose allowing Gentiles to make offerings on the grounds that such promotes idolatry. The assumption was that, regardless of outward procedures, in their hearts Gentiles would be honoring their own gods, not the God of Israel. It will be recalled that the First Revolt with Rome was partly fueled by just such sentiments, as Eleazar bar Ananias seized control of the temple and refused to allow any more sacrifices on behalf of Gentiles (*see* Jewish Wars with Rome).

Another insight from 4QMMT consists in the manner of its halakic argument. Repeatedly its authors precede their legal positions with the phrases *ʾᵃnaḥnû ḥôšbîm ʾᵃnaḥnû ʾômrîm,* "we believe, we say." The formal identity with Matthew's depiction of Jesus' legal arguments in the Sermon on the Mount ("You have heard . . . but *I say*") is patent. Presumably, therefore, Matthew has preserved a common first-century rhetorical structure heretofore unparalleled in early Jewish materials.

Moving to more general considerations, perhaps the most interesting relationship between the DSS and the NT concerns their principal personages. The NT focuses, of course, on Jesus of Nazareth; correspondingly, a group of the DSS focus on the enigmatic figure of the Teacher of Righteousness, (*môrēh haṣṣedeq*). One can examine the Teacher's writings, the *Teacher Hymns,* to extract his ideas about himself. To do so fully, one must in every case compare what he writes with the hundreds of OT portions that he cites or to which he alludes. Understanding the original literary context of his quotations is essential. Also, the Hebrew words his hymns do not actually quote, but that surround those quotes in the original OT context, are assumed to be in the minds of his audience. Analyzing the implied ideas these portions might communicate is very important, too. By this method of "deep reading" one can reconstruct aspects of the Teacher's theology or ideology, and then compare other DSS to round out the picture. It emerges that, like Jesus, the Teacher considered himself a prophet, and more than a prophet. Like Jesus, the Teacher proclaimed a completed law of Moses, perfected by his own direct revelation from God. Like Jesus, the Teacher spoke of charity, the poor and love of one's fellows; forbade *divorce; and proclaimed the imminent coming of the kingdom of God. And, like Jesus, the Teacher was received as a *messiah by his followers and founded an apocalyptic Jewish movement that within a century numbered in the thousands. Many other parallels exist, inviting much further research, just as is true of the DSS and the NT generally.

It has been said that Christianity is an apocalyptic Judaism that survived. The DSS are in many regards our best analogy, for this movement, too, was an apocalyptic Judaism. It did not survive, but thanks to the discovery of many of its writings in the Judean Desert, it lives again.

See also APOCRYPHA OF MOSES (1Q29, 4Q374-377, 4Q408); APOCRYPHON OF JOSEPH (4Q371-372, 539); APOCRYPHON OF JOSHUA (4Q 378-379); ARAMAIC TARGUMS: QUMRAN; BARKI NAFSHI (4Q434, 436, 437-439); BEATITUDES TEXT (4Q525); BIRTH OF THE CHOSEN ONE (4Q534); BOOK OF BLESSINGS (1QSB); CATENA (4Q177); CONSOLATIONS/TANHUMIM (4Q176); COPPER SCROLL (3Q15); DAMASCUS DOCUMENT (CD AND QD); FLORILEGIUM (4Q174); GENESIS APOCRYPHON (1QAPGEN); HABAKKUK COMMENTARY (1QPHAB); ISAIAH SCROLLS (1QISAIAH[A, B]); MELCHIZEDEK, TRADITIONS OF; MIQṢAT MAʿAŚEY HA-TORAH (4QMMT); NEW JERUSALEM TEXTS; PRAYER OF ENOSH (4Q369 + 4Q458); PRAYER OF NABONIDUS AND PSEUDO-DANIEL (4Q242-245); PROPHETIC APOCRYPHON (4Q384-390, 2Q21, 2Q22); PSALMS AND HYMNS OF QUMRAN; PURIFICATION TEXTS (4Q274-279, 281-284, 512-514); QUMRAN: PLACE AND HISTORY; REWRITTEN BIBLE IN PSEUDEPIGRAPHA AND QUMRAN; RULE OF THE COMMUNITY/MANUAL OF DISCIPLINE (1QS);

RULE OF THE CONGREGATION/MESSIANIC RULE (1QSA); SECRET OF EXISTENCE (4Q412-413, 415-421); SON OF GOD TEXT (4Q246); SONGS OF THE SABBATH SACRIFICE (4Q400-407, 11Q17, MAS1K); TALE OF BAGASRAW (PSEUDO-ESTHER) (4Q550^{A-F}); TEMPLE SCROLL (11QTEMPLE); TESTAMENT OF QAHAT (4Q542); TESTIMONIA (4Q175); THANKSGIVING HYMNS (1QH); THUNDER TEXT (4Q318); VINEYARD TEXT (4Q500); VISIONS OF AMRAM (4Q543-548); WAR SCROLL (1QM) AND RELATED TEXTS; WORDS OF MOSES (1Q22).

BIBLIOGRAPHY. **Texts and Translations.** M. Abegg Jr., P. Flint and E. Ulrich, *The Dead Sea Scrolls Bible* (San Francisco: HarperSanFrancisco, 1999); P. Alexander and G. Vermes, *Qumran Cave 4.19: 4QSerekh Ha-Yahad and Two Related Texts* (DJD 26; Oxford: Clarendon Press, 1998); J. M. Allegro, *Qumrân Cave 4.1 (4Q158-4Q186)* (DJD 5; Oxford: Clarendon Press, 1968); H. Attridge et al., *Qumran Cave 4.8: Parabiblical Texts, Part 1* (DJD 13; Oxford: Clarendon Press, 1994); N. Avigad and Y. Yadin, *A Genesis Apocryphon: A Scroll from the Wilderness of Judaea* (Jerusalem: Magnes Press and Heikhal Ha-Sefer, 1956); M. Baillet, *Qumrân grotte 4.3 (4Q482-4Q520)* (DJD 7; Oxford: Clarendon Press, 1982); M. Baillet, J. T. Milik and R. de Vaux, *Les "petites grottes" de Qumrân: Exploration de la falaise, les grottes 2Q, 3Q, 5Q, 6Q, 7Q à 10Q, le rouleau de cuivre* (DJDJ 3; Oxford: Clarendon Press, 1962); D. Barthélemy and J. T. Milik, *Qumran Cave I* (DJD 1; Oxford: Clarendon Press, 1955); J. Baumgarten, *Qumran Cave 4.13: The Damascus Document (4Q266-273)* (DJD 18; Oxford: Clarendon Press, 1996); G. Brooke et al., *Qumran Cave 4.17: Parabiblical Texts, Part 3* (DJD 22; Oxford: Clarendon Press, 1996); M. Broshi, *The Damascus Document Reconsidered* (Jerusalem: Israel Exploration Society, 1992); M. Broshi et al., *Qumran Cave 4.14: Parabiblical Texts, Part 2* (DJD 19; Oxford: Clarendon Press, 1995); E. Chazon et al., *Qumran Cave 4.20: Poetical and Liturgical Texts, Part 2* (DJD 29; Oxford: Clarendon Press, 1999); F. M. Cross, *Qumran Cave 4.12: Samuel* (DJD 17; Oxford: Clarendon Press, forthcoming); F. M. Cross et al., *Scrolls from Qumrân Cave I: The Great Isaiah Scroll, the Order of the Community, the Pesher to Habakkuk* (Jerusalem: Albright Institute and Shrine of the Book, 1972); D. Dimant, *Qumran Cave 4.21: Parabiblical Texts, Part 4* (DJD 30; Oxford: Clarendon Press, forthcoming); R. Eisenman and M.O. Wise, *The Dead Sea Scrolls Uncovered* (Shaftesbury, Dorset: Element, 1992); T. Elgvin et al., *Qumran Cave 4.15: Sapiential Texts, Part 1* (DJD 20; Oxford: Clarendon Press, 1997); E. Eshel et al., *Qumran Cave 4.6: Poetical and Liturgical Texts, Part 1* (DJD 11; Oxford: Clarendon Press, 1999); F. García Martínez, *The Dead Sea Scrolls Translated: The Qumran Texts in English* (2d ed.; Leiden: E. J. Brill/Grand Rapids, MI: Eerdmans, 1996); F. García Martínez, E. J. C. Tigchelaar and A. S. van der Woude, *Qumran Cave 11 (11Q2-18, 11Q20-30)* (DJD 23: Oxford: Clarendon Press, 1997); U. Glessmer, S. Pfann and S. Talmon, *Qumran Cave 4.16: Calendrical Texts* (DJD 21; Oxford: Clarendon Press, forthcoming); J. T. Milik, *The Books of Enoch* (Oxford: Clarendon Press, 1976); C. Newsom, *Songs of the Sabbath Sacrifice: A Critical Edition* (HSS 27; Atlanta: Scholars Press, 1985); J. P. van der Ploeg and A. S. van der Woude, *Le targum de Job de la grotte XI de Qumran* (Leiden: E. J. Brill, 1971); D. L. Penney and M. O. Wise, "By the Power of Beelzebub: An Aramaic Incantation Formula from Qumran (4Q560)," *JBL* 113 (1994) 627-50; É. Puech, *Qumran Cave 4.18: Textes Hébreux (4Q521-4Q528, 4Q576-4Q579)* (DJD 25; Oxford: Clarendon Press, 1998); idem, *Qumran Cave 4.17: Textes en Araméen, tome I: 4Q529-549)* (DJD 31; Oxford: Clarendon Press, forthcoming); E. Qimron and J. Strugnell, *Qumran Cave 4.5: Miqsat Ma ʿase Ha-Torah* (DJD 10; Oxford: Clarendon Press, 1994); J. A. Sanders, *The Psalms Scroll from Qumran Cave 11 (11QPs^a)* (DJDJ 4; Oxford: Clarendon Press, 1965); E. Schuller, *Non-Canonical Psalms from Qumran: A Pseudepigraphic Collection* (HSS 28; Atlanta: Scholars Press, 1986); P. Skehan, E. Ulrich and J. E. Sanderson, *Qumran Cave 4.4: Palaeo-Hebrew and Greek Biblical Manuscripts* (DJD 9; Oxford: Clarendon Press, 1995 [1992]); J. Strugnell, D. J. Harrington and T. Elgvin, *Qumran Cave 4.24: 4QInstruction (Musar le-Mevin): 4Q415ff* (DJD 34; Oxford: Clarendon Press, 2000); S. Talmon and Y. Yadin, *Masada VI: Yigael Yadin Excavations 1963-1965 Final Reports: Hebrew Fragments from Masada; The Ben Sira Scroll from Masada* (Jerusalem: Israel Exploration Society, 1999); E. Tov, *The Greek Minor Prophets Scroll from Nahal Hever (8HevXIIgr): The Seiyâl Collection, I* (DJD 8; Oxford: Clarendon Press, 1989); E. Ulrich, *Qumran Cave 4.10: The Prophets* (DJD 15; Oxford: Clarendon Press, 1997); idem, *Qumran Cave 4.11: Psalms to Chronicles* (DJD 16; Oxford: Clarendon Press, 1999); idem, *Qumran Cave 4.9: Deuteronomy, Joshua, Judges, Kings* (DJD 14; Oxford: Clarendon Press, 1995); E. Ulrich and F. M.

Cross, *Qumran Cave 4.7: Genesis to Numbers* (DJD 12; Oxford: Clarendon Press, 1994); E. Ulrich, P. Flint and M. Abegg, *Qumran Cave 1.2: The Isaiah Texts* (DJD 32; Oxford: Clarendon Press, forthcoming); R. de Vaux and J. T. Milik, *Qumrân grotte 4.2: I. Archéologie, II. Tefillin, Mezuzot et Targums (4Q128-4Q157)* (DJD 6; Oxford: Clarendon Press, 1977); G. Vermes, *The Complete Dead Sea Scrolls in English* (New York: Penguin, 1998); B. Z. Wacholder and M. G. Abegg, *A Preliminary Edition of the Unpublished Dead Sea Scrolls* (4 vols.; Washington, DC: Biblical Archaeology Society, 1991-95); M. O. Wise, *A Critical Study of the Temple Scroll from Qumran Cave 11* (Chicago: Oriental Institute, 1990); idem, "To Know the Times and the Seasons: A Study of the Aramaic Chronograph 4Q559," *JSP* 15 (1997) 3-51; M. Wise, M. Abegg Jr. and E. Cook, *The Dead Sea Scrolls: A New Translation* (San Francisco: HarperSanFrancisco, 1996); Y. Yadin, *The Temple Scroll* (3 vols. plus supplementary plates; Jerusalem: Israel Exploration Society, 1983). **Studies.** E. Cook, *Solving the Mysteries of the Dead Sea Scrolls* (Grand Rapids, MI: Zondervan, 1994); F. M. Cross, *The Ancient Library of Qumran and Modern Biblical Studies* (rev. ed.; New York: Doubleday, 1961); P. Flint, *Dead Sea Psalms Scrolls and the Book of Psalms* (STDJ 17; Leiden: E. J. Brill, 1997); N. Golb, *Who Wrote the Dead Sea Scrolls? The Search for the Secret of Qumran* (New York: Scribners, 1994); L. H. Schiffman, *Reclaiming the Dead Sea Scrolls* (New York: Jewish Publication Society of America, 1994); L. H. Schiffman and J. C. VanderKam, eds., *Encyclopedia of the Dead Sea Scrolls* (3 vols.; New York: Oxford University Press, 2000); E. Ulrich, *The Dead Sea Scrolls and the Origins of the Bible* (Grand Rapids, MI: Eerdmans, 1999); J. C. VanderKam, *Calendars in the Dead Sea Scrolls: Measuring Time* (New York: Routledge, 1998); idem, *The Dead Sea Scrolls Today* (Grand Rapids, MI: Eerdmans, 1994); M. O. Wise, *The First Messiah: Investigating the Savior Before Christ* (San Francisco: HarperSanFrancisco, 1999); idem, "*Mylab ynwmk ym*: A Study of 4Q491c, 4Q471b, 4Q427 7 and 1QHa 25:35-26:10," *DSD* 7 (2000) forthcoming; idem, "*Primo Annales Fuere:* An Annalistic Calendar from Qumran," *Thunder in Gemini* (JSPSS 15; Sheffield: JSOT, 1994) 186-221; idem, "Thunder in Gemini: An Aramaic Brontologion (4Q318) from Qumran," *Thunder in Gemini* (JSPSS 15; Sheffield: JSOT Press, 1994) 1-50.

M. O. Wise

DECAPOLIS

Literally "ten cities," the term *Decapolis* refers to a region in southern Syria and northeastern Palestine that was composed of a number of *Hellenistic cities with the surrounding countryside pertaining to each. During the first century A.D. the territory was an administrative unit attached to Syria. Jesus' visits to the territory anticipate the church's ministry among Gentiles and reveal the boundless nature of his messianic authority.

1. Cities of the Decapolis
2. Nature of the Decapolis
3. History of the Decapolis
4. Jews and the Decapolis
5. New Testament and the Decapolis

1. Cities of the Decapolis.

In Pliny's *Natural History* (5.18.74) he admits that the known lists of the cities of the Decapolis were not in agreement, but he suggests that most lists included the following: Damascus, Philadelphia, Raphana, Scythopolis (the only member situated west of the Jordan River), Gadara, Hypos, Dion, Pella, Galasa (Gerasa), and Canatha. Since Josephus (*J.W.* 3.9.7 §446) tells us that Scythopolis was the largest city of the Decapolis, it has been doubted whether he considered Damascus to be a part of the Decapolis. A certain "good-messenger—Abila of the Decapolis" is mentioned in a Greek inscription from A.D. 134 found in the region of Palmyra in Syria (Parker, 128; Rey-Coquais, 116) and suggests that Abila was counted as a city of the Decapolis. Ptolemy, the second-century A.D. geographer, provides a list of the cities of the Decapolis and Coele-Syria, which includes all of Pliny's cities except Raphana, and adds nine more cities of southern Syria. Stephen of Byzantium indicates that the Decapolis consisted of as many as fourteen cities at one point (Parker, 128). It seems that for part of the history the number ten may have been more traditional than it was precise.

2. Nature of the Decapolis.

Although there is no evidence that the cities ever formed a league or confederation, as was suggested in the past, they all shared a commitment to Hellenistic culture that distinguished them from their neighbors. A Greek inscription from the late first century mentions a Roman prefect or procurator of the Decapolis indicating that at the time it was a Roman administrative unit attached to the province of Syria (Isaac, 70-71; *see* Roman Administration).

3. History of the Decapolis.

3.1. Hellenistic Period. Although most Decapolis sites show signs of occupation since the preclassical period, the majority of the cities claimed to be founded by *Alexander the Great or one of his successors (Parker, 128; Rey-Coquais, 117-18).

In his conquest of Syria, southern Phoenicia and Palestine in 200 B.C. Antiochus III (the Great) brought the Decapolis region under *Seleucid rule. At the end of the second century and the beginning of the first century the Jewish and Nabatean kingdoms took advantage of the weakening of the Seleucid empire. The *Hasmonean king Alexander Janneus took the cities of Scythopolis, Gadara, Abila, Dion and Pella (Josephus *Ant.* 13.15.3-4 §§393-97), and the Nabateans gained possession of Philadelphia (Josephus *J.W.* 1.6.3 §129; *see* Jewish History: Greek Period).

3.2. Roman Period. When Pompey established Roman authority over the region in 63 B.C. the Decapolis cities were given their freedom (municipal autonomy) and were attached to the province of Syria (Josephus *Ant.* 14.4.4 §§74-76; *J.W.* 1.7.7 §§155-57).

Augustus (*see* Roman Emperors) gave *Herod part of the area north of Hauran after 23 B.C. In 30 B.C. he added Gadara and Hippos to Herod's kingdom (Josephus *Ant.* 15.7.3 §217). Upon Herod's death in 4 B.C., Gadara and Hippos regained their autonomy and were reattached to the province of Syria (Josephus *Ant.* 17.11.4 §320), while the area north of Hauran, including Canatha and Raphana, was passed on to the tetrarch Philip and then to king Agrippa I. After a period under Syrian administration, the kingdom went to Agrippa II until his death in A.D. 93.

The emperor Trajan brought the end to any political entity known as the Decapolis in A.D. 106, when he established the province of Arabia and divided the cities of the Decapolis among the provinces of Syria, Arabia and Palestine.

4. Jews and the Decapolis.

Between the second century B.C. and the first century A.D. there was constant tension regarding Jewish authority over, or ambitions regarding, the region. The territory had at one time been incorporated into the Davidic kingdom (2 Sam 8:5-15; Josephus *Ant.* 7.5.3 §104), and David's empire may have come to set the standard for Jewish hopes and expectations (Hengel and Schwemer, 55). When the Hasmonean king Alexander Janneus retook much of the territory, he forced its inhabitants to accept the Jewish religion (Josephus *Ant.* 13.15.3-4 §§393-97; cf. 13.11.3 §318). The cities' liberation by Pompey was the key theme of their *coins. Although there were significant Jewish communities within the cities of the Decapolis in the first century A.D., there is also evidence of a strong hostility toward them on the part of their Gentile neighbors (Josephus *J.W.* 2.18.2, 5 §§461, 478; 7.8.7 §367; 1.4.3 §88; see also Kasher). At the outbreak of the Jewish revolt in A.D. 66, the Jews attacked a number of the cities of the Decapolis. Most of the cities retaliated by slaughtering their Jewish citizens (*see* Jewish Wars with Rome).

5. New Testament and the Decapolis.

5.1. Jesus and the Decapolis. The Decapolis passages in the Gospels are Matthew 4:24-25; 8:28-34; Mark 5:1-20; 7:31-37; and Luke 8:26-39. The two key themes emphasized to different degrees by the Gospel writers in their references to the Decapolis or its territory are mission and christology. A third issue to be considered is the geographical accuracy of the references made to the region of Gadara or Gerasa in the Synoptic Gospels.

5.1.1. Mission. The references to Jesus' presence in the Decapolis or its regions are intended to emphasize that Jesus has crossed into Gentile territory. It is generally agreed that in such passages we find an affirmation of Jesus' ministry to Gentiles in Gentile territory that anticipates and affirms the church's outreach to the broader Gentile world. Although the fear and distrust of the people in the region of Gerasa or Gadara are consistent with the history of resistance to any show of Jewish power in the region, in the Gospel narratives (perhaps especially in Luke) we can see that the scene anticipates not only the future ministry of the church to the Gentile world but also the opposition that the gospel will encounter there (Green).

5.1.2. Christology. The attraction of large crowds from these territories (Mt 4:24-25; 8:34; Mk 5:14; Lk 8:35-36) and the exercise of Jesus' power over Gentiles (and demons) and the acclamation of that power by Gentiles in Gentile territory (Mk 5:20; 7:37; Lk 8:39) all serve to reinforce Jesus' limitless authority and his messianic credentials. Through the demoniac(s), Jesus' messianic identity and authority are recognized even in Gentile territory (Mt 8:29; Mk 5:7; Lk 8:28).

The list of places mentioned in Matthew 4:24-25 echoes the earlier quotation (Mt 4:15-16) from Isaiah 9:1-2 and may be intended to symbolically represent "the whole of Israel" (Hagner). The fact that Jesus draws followers from such a vast area suggests his charismatic power and perhaps a subtle hint that like David's power and influence, his is also felt throughout the larger territory that was once the whole of Israel.

5.1.3. Geography. The fact that the Gospels of Mark and Luke indicate the encounter with the demoniac takes place in Gerasa and that Matthew indicates it was in the region of Gadara has been a problem for commentators, as has the fact that Gadara was located about 6 miles southeast of the Sea of Galilee while Gerasa was located about 33 miles southeast of it. Some manuscripts read "Gergesa" for each text, and that reading has been adopted by some commentators for both Mark and Luke. It has been suggested that Gergesa was located at modern Kursi, a village on the shore of the Sea of Galilee just outside the Decapolis but in Gentile territory. The event may have occurred at Gergesa, but the better manuscripts seem to support Gerasa (for Mark and Luke) and Gadara (for Matthew). It is not necessary to suppose that the Gospel writers had vague or inaccurate knowledge of the area, as has often been suggested. It may be a question of each author choosing to mention the nearest geographical reference point that he thinks his particular readers are likely to recognize given the fact that their knowledge of the area is sketchy (Bock).

5.2. Paul and the Decapolis. Even if Damascus is not counted as one of the cities of the Decapolis, Paul would have passed through that region on his way to Arabia and then on his return trip to Damascus (Gal 1:17). The Hellenistic Jewish communities there with their God-fearing Gentile associates would have been attractive contexts for his ministry (Hengel and Schwemer).

5.3. The Early Church and the Decapolis. Eusebius (*Hist. Eccl.* 3.5.5) informs us that the Christians of Jerusalem fled to the countryside of Pella before the fall of Jerusalem in 70 (*see DLNTD*, Pella, Flight to).

See also ARCHAEOLOGY OF THE LAND OF ISRAEL; GALILEE; JEWISH HISTORY: GREEK PERIOD.

BIBLIOGRAPHY. H. Bietenhard, "Die syrische Dekapolis von Pompeius bis Trajan," *ANRW* 2.8 (1977) 220-61; D. L. Bock, *Luke* (BECNT; Grand Rapids, MI: Baker, 1994); M. Goodman, "Jews in the Decapolis," *ARAM Periodical* 4 (1992) 49-56 (vol. 4.1 of *ARAM Periodical* is dedicated to the topic of the Decapolis); D. Graf, "Hellenization and the Decapolis," *ARAM Periodical* 4 (1992) 1-48; J. B. Green, *The Gospel of Luke* (NICNT; Grand Rapids, MI: Eerdmans, 1997); D. A. Hagner, *Matthew 1—13* (WBC 33a; Dallas: Word, 1993); M. Hengel and A. M. Schwemer, *Paul Between Damascus and Antioch: The Unknown Years* (London: SCM, 1997); B. Isaac, "The Decapolis in Syria: A Neglected Inscription," *Zeitschrift für Papyrologie und Epigraphik* 44 (1981) 67-74; A. Kasher, *Jews and Hellenistic Cities in Eretz-Israel: Relations of the Jews in Eretz-Israel with the Hellenistic Cities During the Second Temple Period (332 B.C.E.-70 C.E.)* (TSAJ 21; Tübingen: Mohr Siebeck, 1990); S. T. Parker, "Decapolis," in *The Oxford Encyclopedia of Archaeology in the Near East*, ed. E. M. Meyers (5 vols.; Oxford: Oxford University Press, 1997) 2:127-30; J.-P. Rey-Coquais, "Decapolis," *ABD* 2:116-21. R. E. Ciampa

DECURIONS. *See* ROMAN SOCIAL CLASSES.

DELPHIC ORACLE. *See* PROPHETS AND PROPHECY.

DEMETRIUS

Of the six fragments usually attributed to Demetrius, only four bear his name (frags. 2-4). The first five of these fragments are preserved in Eusebius (*Praep. Ev.* 9) and the sixth in Clement of Alexandria (*Strom.* 1.141.1-2). The five fragments from Eusebius are quotations of Alexander Polyhistor *(On the Jews)*, which quotes from Demetrius's work. If Clement is to be trusted, the title of this work was *On the Kings in Judea.* There is some question as to whether or not fragments 1 and 4 are by Demetrius, as fragment 1 is anonymous and fragment 4 is very brief. Certainty in either case is difficult. Difficult to date with any certainty, the sixth fragment (from Clement) suggests that the reign of Ptolemy IV Philopator (221–204 B.C.) is a *terminus ante quem* for Demetrius's work.

The extant work of Demetrius revolves

chiefly around the chronology of the biblical accounts as found in Genesis. Because Demetrius's work is similar in content to books such as **Jubilees,* the rabbinic *Seder ʿOlam Rabbah* and the **Genesis Apocryphon* from Cave 4 at *Qumran, B. Z. Wacholder (1964, 56) has suggested that these writings fall into three different schools of interpretation of biblical history, with Demetrius on the most developed end and the rabbinic *Seder ʿOlam Rabbah* on the most conservative, with the sectarian *Jubilees* and *Genesis Apocryphon* closer in approach to Demetrius and other writings such as [pseudo]-Eupolemus and Artapanus. In fragment 2, Demetrius precisely calculates the dates of the various figures in Genesis starting with Jacob and ending with Moses. Fragment 3 picks up the story with Moses' murder of the Egyptian overseer and ends with a discussion of the genealogy of Zipporah, explaining the difficulty of Moses' and Zipporah's marriage (Ex 2:16 LXX), since they seem to come at mutually exclusive points in the lineage from Abraham. Fragment 4 is a conflation of unknown ratio of both the OT and Demetrius's chronographic work, dealing with the short story in Exodus 15:22-27 of the bitter fountain turned sweet after the appropriate wood is thrown in, and the oasis at Elim. Fragment 5 explains the possession by the Israelites of weapons (Ex 17:8-13), when they supposedly only went out to pray for three days, and suggests that the arms were salvaged from the drowned Egyptians. Fragment 6, taken from Clement of Alexandria, is a brief chronology of the time from the fall of the northern kingdom of Israel until the accession of Ptolemy IV. There is apparently some corruption in this last fragment, leading to chronological problems, for which various emendations have been suggested.

Demetrius is obviously concerned to deal with lacunae and contradictions found in the biblical writings, especially with regard to chronology, but also, apparently, with regard to other thorny details, such as the possession of weapons by the Israelites when they had merely gone out to pray. So little of Demetrius's work survives that it is difficult to determine its exact nature—it is entirely possible that the chronographic sections that make up the bulk of the surviving Demetrius were only a small part of the whole, which his title (if we are to trust Clement), *On the Kings of Judea,* would suggest might have been wider in scope.

See also JOSEPHUS; REWRITTEN BIBLE IN PSEUDEPIGRAPHA AND QUMRAN; WRITING AND LITERATURE: JEWISH.

BIBLIOGRAPHY. H. W. Attridge, "Historiography," in *Jewish Writings in the Second Temple Period: Apocrypha, Pseudepigrapha, Qumran Sectarian Writings, Philo, Josephus,* ed. M. E. Stone (CRINT 2.2; Assen: Van Gorcum; Philadelphia: Fortress, 1984) 161-62; E. J. Bickerman, "The Jewish Historian Demetrios," in *Christianity, Judaism and Other Greco-Roman Cults,* ed. J. Neusner (SJLA 12.3; Leiden: E. J. Brill, 1975) 72-84; J. Freudenthal, *Alexander Polyhistor und die von ihm erhaltenen Reste jüdischer und samaritanischer Geshichtswerke* (Hellenistische Studien 1, 2; Breslau: von Grass, Barth & Comp., 1874–75) 35-82, 205-7, 219-23; J. Hanson, "Demetrius the Chronographer," in *The Old Testament Pseudepigrapha,* ed. J. H. Charlesworth (2 vols.; Garden City, NY: Doubleday, 1983, 1985) 2:843-54; B. Z. Wacholder, *Eupolemus: A Study of Judeo-Greek Literature* (Cincinnati: Hebrew Union College Press, 1974) 98-104, 280-82; idem, "How Long Did Abram Stay in Egypt? A Study in Hellenistic, Qumran and Rabbinic Chronography," *HUCA* 35 (1964) 43-56.

B. W. R. Pearson

DEMONOLOGY

Demonology is the study of the influence of supernatural entities, usually malevolent and invisible, upon human life and society. Epigraphic, papyrological and literary sources for the study of demonology are widespread. Since amulets and *magical texts have been undervalued as a source of comparative material, they will be highlighted here, along with the material from Qumran.

1. Semitic Terms for Demons
2. Greek Terms for Demons
3. Demonic Attacks and Diseases
4. Therapy
5. Conclusion

1. Semitic Terms for Demons.

1.1. Old Testament and Ancient Near Eastern Texts. The distinctive terms for "evil spirits," *šēdîm* ("demons"; Deut 32:17; Ps 106:37) and *śᵉʿîrîm* ("hairy demons," "satyrs"; Lev 17:7: 2 Chron 11:15; Is 13:21; 34:14), occur in the plural only. General references to natural phenomena as demons and to theriomorphic demons (Lilith, Azazel etc.; cf. Kuemmerlin-McLean, 139), although important, are rare in the OT and do not seem to have influenced later concepts. More important is the classical reference in 1 Samuel 16:14-23; 18:10 to an "evil spirit" *(rûaḥ-rāʿāh)* said to come from God (Yahweh/ Elohim) that both "startles" *(bʿt)* Saul and either "rushes to" or actually "enters into" him (*ṣlḥ . . . el*), causing him to "rave in a prophetic trance" (Hitpael of *nbʾ*). This spirit would "depart" (*srh*) whenever young David played his harp. The notion, despite the pejorative "evil" spirit, is akin to the Greek concept of *enthousiasmos*, the divine prophetic indwelling of a spirit. This early concept of David as exorcist recurs in the DSS.

1.2. Dead Sea Scrolls and Intertestamental Period. The DSS notion of a conflict of "Sons of Light" versus "Sons of Darkness" is widely known. More importantly, the **Genesis Apocryphon* (1Q20) is remarkable for its retention of the notion of an "evil spirit" sent by God to protect Abraham's wife from Pharaoh. In *Genesis Apocryphon* 20:16-30 God sends a "pestilential spirit" (*rwḥ mkdš*), or "evil spirit" *(rwḥ bʾšʾ)*, that "afflicts" (*ktšʾ*) Pharaoh, his household and all the magicians sent to heal him (cf. too 4Q213[a] Levi).

Equally important is the famous exorcistic passage in the fragments of Tobit from the DSS, already known from the LXX. There Michael describes how the innards of a fish smoked before one possessed by a demon or spirit will exorcize it (4Q196 frag. 13 = Tob 6:7-8; frag. 14 i = Tob 6:14-15, 16-18).

More traditional biblical nomenclature is found in the exorcistic poems in the Songs of the Sage, where, for example, the Master proclaims God's majesty in order "to frighten and terrify all the spirits of the bastards, the demons, Lilith, the howlers (?) and [the yelpers]" (4Q510 5; trans. Vermes, *DSSE*, 420). More specific demonology occurs in the *Damascus Document*, which speaks of potential members "ruled" *(mšl)* by the "spirits of Belial" *(rwḥwt blyʿl)* who preach apostasy (CD 23:2-3 A). Belial is the principal "satanic" figure throughout the DSS (1QH; 4Q286 = Berakhot[a], frag. 7, etc.; cf. 2 Cor 6:14—7:1). Another, a kind of counterpart to *Melchizedek, is the satanic Melkireshaʿ (= "My king is wickedness," 4Q280 = 4QBenedictions[f], 4Q545 frag. 2 = Test Amram). Azazel, as a demonic figure, occurs in connection with the scapegoat ritual (*Temple Scroll*, 11QTemple 26:3-13; cf. Lev 16). In the same class belongs the so-called Plea for Deliverance (11Q5 19:1-18), a non-Masoretic psalm whose lines 15-16 read, "Let not Satan rule over me, nor an unclean spirit *[rwḥ ṭmʾh];* neither let pain *[mkʾwb]* nor the evil / inclination [*yṣr rʿ*] take possession of my bones" (trans. J. A. Sanders, in Charlesworth, 195). The "unclean spirit" is the exact equivalent of the Gospels' *pneuma akatharton*, and the concept of the possession within the bones is mirrored in the later amulets (see 3.1 below).

More specifically, the text known as "David's Compositions" (11Q5 27:2-11) mentions in an inventory four "songs for the stricken" (lines 9-10) whose very texts seem to have been preserved in fragmentary condition in 11QApPs[a] = 11Q11 ("A Liturgy for Healing the Stricken"). This document preserves four incantatory "psalms" addressed specifically to the exorcism of demons: Psalm I (frags. A-B-C) mentions an "adjuration" (*šbwʿh*, frag. A, 2; *mšb*[*yʿ*], frag. A, 6); "the demons" (*hšydm*, frag. A, 9); Psalm II (cols. 1.1—4.3) contains a Solomonic adjuration of "spirits and demons" (1:2-3), "Belial" (1:5), an "adjuring of all angels" (2:5), including Raphael (4:3); Psalm III (cols. 4.4—5.3) preserves an "incantation in the name of YHWH" (4.4), apparently against Belial and Satan; and Psalm IV (5:3-14) contains the text of Ps. 91, famous in later antiquity as an amuletic prayer. In a word, these texts are all early amuletic compositions, perhaps even pre-Qumranic (see Sanders, 216, with refs.). In this respect they belong in the same class as 4Q560, an actual amulet against evil spirits that cause fever, chills and other afflictions: (1) an "evil visitant" (*pqr bʾyš*, 1:2); (2) a "demon" (*š*[*yd*]); and perhaps (3) a male and female "wasting demon" (?) or "poison" (*ḥlḥlyʾ*, 1:3); (4) a "shrine-spirit" (*prk*); and (5) a "breacher" demon (reading unsure). All but the first are conjectural. The genre of the text clearly belongs to that of the later amulets, discussed below. Particularly important, too, is the notion of the spirit entering the flesh of the possessed (*ʿʿl bšbrʾ*, 1:3).

In the intertestamental period, the "pseudepigraphic" fame of Solomon and of Raphael the archangel as exorcists are particularly noteworthy. Raphael's role has been alluded to above (cf. 11Q11; Tob), and Solomon's fame as an exorcist of demons is most famously known from the *Testament of Solomon* (of uncertain date) and from numerous Greek amulets of a Jewish sort

(Kotansky 1995; Jordan and Kotansky 1997).

1.3. Palestinian Jewish Amulets. The corpus of amulets published by Naveh and Shaked (cited here by amulet #) provides an important source for contemporary beliefs. Even though most texts postdate the NT period, they are to be classed with the earlier exorcistic "amulets" of the DSS. The following are the types of demons named:

(1) "(evil) spirit" (*rwḥtʾ/h / rwḥh byšth*: A 1:20, 21; 2:9; 3:4; 4:15; 7:6, [12]; 9:1; 12:1, 12, 32; 13:7, 11; 14:[3]; 15:25; 18:1, 8; 19:3, 24, 26; 21:4; 23:3; 24:20 [*rwḥ rʿh*]; 25:5; 26:10, 14; 27:12, 15, 19, 29; 29:7);

(2) "demon/demoness" (*šd/šydh:* A 2:8; 7:6, 12; 7b:3; 13:7; A 21:5; 24:20; 29:7; cf. Deut 32:17; Ps 106:37; Assyr. *šēdu*; JPAram *šēd / šēdāʾh*);

(3) "shadow demon" (*tlnyth*: A 4:15; 7:6, 13; 7b:3; 11:8; 13:8; 22:3; 24:2, 12 ["male or female"], 20);

(4) "harmer" (*mzqh/mzyqʾ:* A 7:13: 7b:2; 11:8; 13:5, 9; A 27:5-6 ["evil"]; [noun from the verb *nzq*, "injury," "harm"; cf. *nizeq*, "accident," "harm," "injury," from *zqq*, "touch"; "junction"]);

(5) "destroyer" (*mḥblh*: A 7:13; 7b:2 [from *ḥbl*, "to injure," "ruin," "destroy"]);

(6) "blast demon" (*zyqʾ:* A 11:8 and bowls);

(7) "pebble spirit" (*ḥwmrʾ*: magic bowls B 1:5; 13:17, 22, etc.);

(8) "vision" (*ḥzwʾ*: A 20:3 [cf. Gk *phantasma*, "apparition"]);

(9) "evil assailant" (*sʿyʾbyšʾ*: A 27:5).

2. Greek Terms for Demons.

In the Greek papyri the demonic "entity" is called a *daimōn* (or *daimonion*); a "spirit" (*pneuma*, lit. "wind/breath") and can be qualified as "bad" (*kakon*), "impure/unclean" (*akatharton*) or "foul" (*phaulon*); a "shadow" (*skia*, viz. a "shade" of the dead, SM I.13). Literary sources also use *eidōlon* ("phantom/ghost"; from *eidos*, "what is seen," "image"); *phantasma* ("apparition," "ghost," Plutarch *Dion* 2; *phantasmation* in Plutarch *Dion* 2.766b) for visual appearances (see, in general, Johnston; Kotansky 1995, 246-47). Common to magical texts is the *nekydaimōn*, "spirit-of-a-corpse" (viz. "ghost"), although this (with *daimōn*) is commonly found in curses and love-spells that adjure (*exorkizō*) subterranean spirits to work magic on the practitioner's behalf (Kotanksy 1995, 250-51, 260). The concept of a demonology of the dead may owe considerably more to the general anthropology of NT demonic possession than to anything else (see the insights of Bolt).

3. Demonic Attacks and Diseases.

3.1. Semitic Evidence. In the Jewish Aramaic amulets, the demonic affliction itself is described with a rich array of expressions. In A 1:21-22, a demon is referred to as the "spirit of the bones" (*rwḥ grmyh*) that "walks within the tendons and bones of Quzma, son of Salmina." Similarly, a cache of silver amulets found in the synagogue of Nirim includes one (A 11) that expels demons causing *kplrgyʾ*—clearly the exact equivalent of Greek *kephalargia*, "headache," a term common in Greek magic.

In A 26 we have an unusual "encounter" (see below) of a demon that "rushes" upon its victim, taking the form of "either a male or female, a Gentile or Israelite" and "any likeness by which you appear to people." Here we may have an instance of a spirit of the dead invoked to harm the living.

The presence of the demon is felt to be the universal cause of the medical complaint, most often fever, an acute malady particularly life-threatening in antiquity. Female demons *(šydth)* and spirits *(rwḥth)* are judged responsible for the "fever-and-shivering" of Yaʾitha on an amulet from Ḥorvat Kanaf in Galilee (A 2); on a copper amulet from the same site (A 3) we find that a "bad, evil-causing demon" causes pain and fever to Rabbi Eleazar; similarly, on another amulet the "shadow spirit, whether male or female" is said to be the cause of Qaduma's "fever and shiver" (A 24:11-12); a "shadow spirit" and other fever-causing demons need to be "shaken" from the 248 limbs of Aqemu, daughter of Em-Rabban (A 4 [Aleppo]); an amulet from Oxyrhynchus exorcizes "the spirit called fever-shivering" from the 248 limbs of Marian, daughter of Esther (A 9); a bronze amulet from Ḥorvat Kannah (biblical Cana?) removes sundry fevers from Simon son of Kattia (A 19) by invoking divine and angelic names, among which is a *Yšr-ṭmnwʾl* "who sits on the river whence all evil spirits emerge" (A 19:35-37).

A handful of amulets were written, too, to protect mothers and their unborn children from malignant, abortifacient demons (A 12, A 24, A 28, A 30). One of these appears, as well, to have been written for dystocia or amenorrhea (A 24:13-14).

3.2. Greek Evidence. A common term for the

demonic attack uses the language of "encounter" *(synantēma/apantēma)* or "occurrence" (*synkyrēma* [Jordan and Kotansky 1996]) or "the thing that comes" *(ton erchomenon* [SM I 13:9, 22]). In magical amulets various diseases (esp. fever) are said to "possess" *(synechein)* or "hold" (*echein*; SM I 14:3) the victim.

As with the Semitic evidence, diseases are explained as demonic attacks. The preponderance of fever complaints far outweighs any other medical complaints in the papyrological and epigraphic literature.

4. Therapy.

4.1. Semitic Evidence. A number of mechanisms, using various forms of prayers, threats and incantations, are employed to eradicate a demon. The use of the adjuration *(šbʿ)* against demons is common in the Aramaic/Hebrew amulets (A 18:1; 19:10, 30, 34; 26:1, 9, 14; 27:14), but the most important "exorcistic" verb, as shown below, is *gʿr,* "to shout" or "to rebuke," which is usually rendered "to drive away"/"to expel"/"to exorcize" (A 2:8 [comm.], 11; 9:2, 4; 14:9; 18:2; 19:1, 24; 20:3; 22:4; 25:5; 27:12, 15, 16, 18).

Additional verbs addressed to demons are the following: "to be extinguished" (Itp. of *kly,* "to terminate; extinguish," A 7 [Turkey]); "to be moved away and expelled" *(tzwʿ wtgʿr)*; "to be chased away" (*rdp,* A 22:4) by God; "to move away from" *(zwʿ),* "to be expelled" *(gʿr)* and "to keep far from" *(rḥq)* the client; "to uproot/eradicate" (*ʿqr,* A 11, A 17).

More prophylactic terminology is expressed in the verb "to heal" (cf. *ʾswth,* "healing" in A 21:3 [left]; 22:3). The imperfect form *yʾsʾ* (cf. A 1:13) makes plausible a wordplay on Jesus as healer (both Greek *iaomai* "heal"—cf. *iatros,* "physician"—and *therapeia,* "cure," to be compared with Aramaic *trpyh,* "may you heal him/her," in A 22:3), if we suppose a Semitic background to such passages as Mark 1:34; 3:10, 15; 5:29, etc.

"Sealing" as a mode of protection seems also to be a distinctly Semitic phenomenon (A 18:6), early on associated with the activity of Solomon. So also "to guard" *(ntr)* someone from demons (A 19:7; 25:9; 27:22; 29:3, 6, 8; 31:7).

4.2. Greek Evidence. Magical texts employ a combination of ritual and amulet to ward off demons, including a "passive" language of prevention (protection, warding off, banishing, containment) and a more "active" vocabulary of exorcism and expulsion (Kotansky 1991). The popular mindset also presumes the use of some divine agency (a deity, set of angels, powerful names, syllables, magic "symbols" [*charaktēres*], or string of vowels) to cure disease.

The most common verb for guarding against demonic attack is *diaphylassō,* "to protect (from)," although a number of special verbs are employed: for example, "check and annihilate" (*kataschēson kai katargēson,* as in SM I 13:7-8).

A standard and perhaps very old formula in Greek magic is the "flee"-formula (Greek *pheugō*), as well as that of "chasing away" (*apodiōkein*) and "driving off" (*apelaunein*) the entity (Kotansky 1991).

Magic texts also employ the language of "exorcism" ([*ex*]*orkizō,* "adjure"; [*ex*]*orkismos,* "adjuration"), whose original sense was that of employing a "solemn oath" (*ex-,* "utterly" + *horkos,* "oath") to call up a spirit of the dead; however, in exorcistic contexts the verb has come to refer to the "oathing out" (*ex-*) of a demon from a person (hence, "to exorcize" = "to adjure [the demon] out" [Kotansky 1995]). This concept is probably Jewish in origin (Kotansky 1995) and is reflected in the Hebrew and Aramaic of the Dead Sea Scrolls.

5. Conclusion.

The use of *gʿr* has important implications for the study of NT demonology. The verb means "to shout, rebuke," viz. "to shout (a demon) out" (hence, "to expell/exorcize" it), and this is precisely the equivalent found in the NT (Twelftree, 44-47, who seems unaware of Greenfield 1980 and Naveh 1983).

It has been observed that *epitimaō* in Greek is a suitable equivalent of the exorcistic *gʿr* in Semitic. When Jesus "rebukes" Peter's disapproval of the Son of Man's prediction of death in Mark 8:31-33 (par.), referring to him as "Satan," he is in effect performing an exorcism: he is "expelling by rebuke" *(gʿr)* the "Satan" in Peter. This is mirrored in a fragmentary sentence of A 14 that reads, "exorcize Satan from" *(gʿwr sṭn mn,* line 9). It is also possible that *gʿr* preserves a root (viz. *gʿ*; cf. *gʿh/gʿʿ,* "to roar, scream"; *gʿš,* "to rumble(?), belch") that lies at the heart of a classical Greek term for "sorcerer"/"magician," the *goēs* (cf. *goēteia,* "sorcery" or "magic"). Part of the itinerant magician's repertory included "wailing" (cf. *goētēs* in Aeschylus *Ch.* 822; the Greek verb *goaō* means "to groan, wail"; cf.

Johnston, 112).

The idea that spirits may be exorcized from the body of a person is Semitic. Greek spells that preserve the notion have a thoroughly Jewish ring about them. This is borne out in the vocabulary of the amulets, for the Aramaic pieces often refer to spirits being driven "from the body" (*mn gwph*) of the afflicted. This accords with the Semitic disposition of seeing demons as largely (unseen) spirits that enter the body. Exorcism, per se, is a Semitic concept (Kotansky 1995).

See also BELIAL, BELIAR, DEVIL, SATAN; BIBLIOMANCY; HOLY SPIRIT; MAGICAL PAPYRI.

BIBLIOGRAPHY. H. D. Betz, ed., *The Greek Magical Papyri in Translation, Including the Demotic Spells* (2d ed.; Chicago: University of Chicago Press, 1992); P. G. Bolt, "Jesus, the Daimons, and the Dead," in *The Unseen World: Reflections on Angels, Demons, and the Heavenly Realm,* ed. A. N. S. Lane (Grand Rapids, MI: Baker, 1996) 75-102; J. G. Charlesworth, The Dead Sea Scrolls: Hebrew, Aramaic, and Greek Texts with English Translations 4A:Pseudepigraphic and Non-Masoretic Psalms and Prayers (Louisville, KY: Westminster John Knox, 1998); R. W. Daniel and F. Maltomini, eds. *Supplementum Magicum I-II* (Abhandlungen der Nordrhein- Westfälischen Akademie der Wissenschaften. Sonderreihe Papyrologica Coloniensia 16.1-2; Opladen: Westdeutscher Verlag, 1990, 1992) [= SM]; J. A. Fitzmyer, *The Genesis Apocryphon of Qumran Cave I* (BibO 18A; Rome: Biblical Institute, 1971); J. Greenfield, "The Genesis Apocryphon—Observations on Some Words and Phrases," in *Studies in Hebrew and Semitic Languages,* ed. G. B. Sarfati, (Ramat Gan, Israel, 1980) xxxii-ix; S. I. Johnston, *Restless Dead: Encounters between the Living and the Dead in Ancient Greece* (Berkeley and Los Angeles: University of California Press, 1999); D. R. Jordan and R. D. Kotansky, "IV. Magisches. 338. A Solomonic Exorcism," in *Kölner Papyri (P. Köln),* ed. M. Gronewald, K. Maresch, and C. Römer (Papyrologica Coloniensia, vol. 7.8; Abhandlungen der Nordrhein-Westfälischen Akademie der Wissenschaften; Opladen: Westdeutscher Verlag, 1997) 53-69; D. R. Jordan and R. D. Kotansky, "Two Phylacteries from Xanthos," *RAr* (1996) 161-74; D. R. Jordan, M. Jameson and R. Kotansky, *A Lex Sacra from Selinous* (GRBSMS 11; Durham, NC: Duke University Press, 1993); R. Kotansky, "Greek Exorcistic Amulets," in *Ancient Magic & Ritual Power,* ed. M. Meyer and P. Mirecki (RGRW 129; Leiden: E. J. Brill, 1995) 243-77; idem, *Greek Magical Amulets: The Inscribed Gold, Silver, Copper, and Bronze Lamellae.* Pt. I: *Published Texts of Known Provenance* (Abhandlungen der Nordrhein-Westfälischen Akademie der Wissenschaften. Sonderreihe Papyrologica Coloniensia 17.1; Opladen: Westdeutscher Verlag, 1994); idem, "Incantations and Prayers for Salvation on Inscribed Magical Amulets," in *Magika Hiera: Ancient Greek Magic and Religion,* ed. D. Obbink and C. A. Faraone (Oxford: Oxford University Press, 1991) 107-37; idem, "An Inscribed Copper Amulet from ʿEvron," *'Atiqot* 20 (1991) 81-87; idem, "Two Inscribed Jewish-Aramaic Amulets from Syria," *IEJ* 41 (1991) 267-81; R. Kotansky, J. Naveh and S. Shaked, "A Greek-Aramaic Silver Amulet from Egypt in the Ashmolean Museum," *Le Muséon* 105 (1992) 5-24; J. K. Kuemmerlin-McLean, "Demons," *ABD* 2:138-40; J. Naveh, "Fragments of an Aramaic Magical Book from Qumran," *IEJ* 48 (1998) 252-61; idem, "A Recently Discovered Palestinian Jewish Aramaic Amulet," in *Arameans and Aramaic Literary Tradition,* ed. M. Sokoloff (Ramat Gan, Israel, 1983) 81-88; J. Naveh and S. Shaked, *Amulets and Magic Bowls: Aramaic Incantations from Late Antiquity* (Jerusalem: Magnes; Leiden: E. J. Brill, 1985); J. Naveh and S. Shaked, *Magic Spells and Formulae: Aramaic Incantations from Late Antiquity* (Jerusalem: Magnes, 1993); D. L. Penney and M. O. Wise, "By the Power of Beelzebub: An Aramaic Incantation Formula from Qumran (4Q560)," *JBL* 113 (1994) 627-50; J. A. Sanders, "A Liturgy for Healing the Stricken (11QPsAp^a = 11Q11)," in *The Dead Sea Scrolls. Hebrew, Aramaic, and Greek Texts with English Translations,* 4A: *Pseudepigraphic and Non-Masoretic Psalms and Prayers,* ed. J. H. Charlesworth (Tübingen: Mohr Siebeck; Louisville: Westminster John Knox, 1997) 216-33; G. H. Twelftree, *Jesus the Exorcist* (WUNT 54; Tübingen: Mohr Siebeck, 1993).

R. Kotansky

DESTRUCTION OF JERUSALEM

1. The Jewish War
2. The Destruction of Jerusalem
3. The Destruction of Jerusalem in Jewish Literature
4. The Destruction of Jerusalem in the Gospels

1. The Jewish War.

The destruction of Jerusalem in A.D. 70 brought

to a climax a war between the Romans and the Jews of Palestine (*see* Jewish Wars with Rome). The war has become known as the Jewish War, following the lead of the first-century Jewish historian Flavius *Josephus, who referred to his seven-volume history of events leading up to the fall of the Jerusalem as *peri tou Ioudaikou polemou* ("concerning the Jewish War," *Life* 74 §412).

1.1. Events Precipitating the War. After many years of tension under Roman rule, several crucial events directly led to the outbreak of the war. On the one hand, the policies and cruelty of the Roman procurator Florus (A.D. 64-66) set the stage for the war (Josephus *Ant.* 20.11.1 §257; Tacitus *Hist.* 5.10.1). First, he antagonized the Jews by siding with the Greeks in several incidents during A.D. 66 in a long-standing civil-rights conflict between the Jews and Greeks of *Caesarea. Then in the summer of A.D. 66 Florus took seventeen talents from the sacrosanct *temple treasury to allay governmental expenses (Josephus *J.W.* 2.14.6 §293) and compounded the offense by having Roman troops sack part of the city and scourge and crucify prisoners in reaction to the resulting public protest (Josephus *J.W.* 2.14.6-8 §§296-308). When he later moved two cohorts (c. 1200 men) to Jerusalem, crowds prevented them from reaching the Roman garrison at the Antonia in a confrontation that resulted in a stampede that left many dead (Josephus *J.W.* 2.15.5 §§325-28).

On the other hand, in response to Florus's activities, the Jews laid the "foundation for the war" by stopping *sacrifices for Gentiles and thus the twice-daily sacrifices for the emperor's welfare (Josephus *J.W.* 2.17.2 §409). This was an act of rebellion. The sacrifices represented a special concession from the Romans to the Jews in lieu of their participating in the rituals of emperor worship (Josephus *J.W.* 2.17.3 §§415-16; *see* Ruler Cult). Florus's activities in Jerusalem gave rise to a group of insurgents in Jerusalem (*see* Revolutionary Movements) who captured the Antonia and massacred the Roman garrison there in August of A.D. 66. Later they attacked Herod's palace and the camp of Florus's cohort and massacred the Roman forces after they had agreed to surrender in exchange for safe passage (Josephus *J.W.* 2.17.7-8 §§430-40). With the Roman fortress of Masada having already fallen to a rebel force (Josephus *J.W.* 2.17.2 §408), the revolt spread to other attacks against the Romans and the taking of the Herodian fortresses of Cypros near Jericho and Machaeros in Perea (Josephus *J.W.* 2.18.6 §§484-86).

1.2. The Course of the War. After the Jews' successful attack and massacre of the Roman forces in Jerusalem, the capture of the surrounding fortresses in early fall of A.D. 66 and the outbreaks of violence in Caesarea, the Decapolis and Syrian cities (Josephus *J.W.* 2.18.1-5 §§457-80), it was time for *Rome's intervention. Cestius Gallus, the Syrian legate, assembled an army of 30,000 and moved on the province on Rome's behalf. He took control of *Galilee with little resistance (Josephus *J.W.* 2.18.11 §§510-12) and then marched on Jerusalem, eventually making his camp a mile to the north on Mt. Scopus in November of A.D. 66 (Josephus *J.W.* 2.19.4 §§527-28). Though victory was in his grasp, Cestius for some inexplicable reason abandoned the siege after about a week (Josephus *J.W.* 2.19.6-7 §§538-40). Withdrawing his forces in retreat, he suffered nearly 5,000 casualties and the loss of valuable military supplies to the Jews (Josephus *J.W.* 2.19.7-9 §§540-55).

During the winter months of A.D. 66/67 the Jews made preparation for the inevitable attack by Rome in the spring by setting up a revolutionary government throughout the province. The peace party led by the high priests, having greater influence on the populace than the rebel leaders, initially took control and selected the ex-high priest Ananus as commander of the forces (Josephus *J.W.* 2.20.3 §§562-64). The revolutionary government divided the territory into six districts (Idurea, Perea, Jericho, western Judea, northeastern Judea, Galilee) and set up military governors to establish civil administration and prepare for war (Josephus *J.W.* 2.20.3-4 §§562-68). Josephus was made the military governor of Galilee (Josephus *J.W.* 2.20.4 §568; *Life* 7 §29). Many distinguished inhabitants, however, took the occasion to leave Jerusalem as if it were a "sinking ship" (Josephus *J.W.* 2.20.1 §556).

In the spring of A.D. 67 the Roman general Vespasian, sent by Nero, and his son Titus arrived with an army of nearly 60,000 men (Josephus *J.W.* 3.4.2 §69). Using friendly Sepphoris as a base in Galilee, Vespasian encountered little resistance in that district except from the fortified places where most of the resistance had moved. His first sustained opposition came from the hilltop fortress Jotapata under Josephus's command. After a seven-week siege it fell in July

A.D. 67 (Josephus *J.W.* 3.7.5-31 §§150-288; 3.7.33-36 §§316-39). Josephus surrendered and was taken prisoner (Josephus *J.W.* 3.8.8 §392; cf. 4.10.7 §§622-29). Then the Roman forces took the port of Joppa (Josephus *J.W.* 3.9.7-8 §§445-61) in late July to protect the supply routes, Tiberias in August (Josephus *J.W.* 3.9.2-4 §§414-31), Tarichaeae in September (Josephus *J.W.* 3.10.1-5 §§462-502), the fortress of Gamala in October after a four-week siege (Josephus *J.W.* 4.1.3-7 §§11-53; 4.1.9-10 §§62-83) and finally Gischala. There the rebel leader, John of Gischala, escaped with his band of followers for Jerusalem (Josephus *J.W.* 4.2.1-5 §§84-120). Having subdued the district of Galilee, Vespasian set up garrisons throughout the area during the winter months to maintain control.

Military activities resumed in the spring of A.D. 68. In March Vespasian took the district of Perea, except for the fortress Machaeros, when the wealthy surrendered the capital Gadara (Josephus *J.W.* 4.8.3 §413). He then moved through western Judea with little resistance and took Idumea (Josephus *J.W.* 4.8.2 §§443-48). Jericho capitulated on his arrival in June (Josephus *J.W.* 4.8.1-2 §§450-51), leaving him with control of almost all the province of Judea. He then set up strategic military camps to prepare for the attack on Jerusalem (Josephus *J.W.* 4.9.1 §§486-90).

The actual siege of Jerusalem, however, was delayed for nearly two years. First came the news of Nero's death in June A.D. 68. Since a military command terminated with the death of the emperor who had given it, Vespasian waited for word from the new emperor (Josephus *J.W.* 4.9.2 §§497-98). But no word came out of the ensuing political turmoil in Rome, with Galba's accession and assassination in January A.D. 69, then Otho's accession and assassination in April A.D. 69, followed by Vitellius's struggle for power. In June of A.D. 69, still having received no official word, Vespasian resumed military action on his own and consolidated his gains in Judea, only to break off the activities in July when he was proclaimed emperor by the Roman forces in the East (Josephus *J.W.* 4.10.4, 6 §601, §§616-20). After consolidating his strength in the East in the spring of A.D. 70 he left *Alexandria, Egypt, for Rome and placed Titus in charge of taking Jerusalem (Josephus *J.W.* 4.11.5 §658).

2. The Destruction of Jerusalem.

Josephus, our primary source of information about the war, describes the isolation, surrounding, siege and fall of Jerusalem in *Jewish War*, books 4—6. It is a period of political turmoil in Rome, a change of Roman command in Judea and a disastrous civil war among the Jews within the walls of Jerusalem. The city eventually fell to the Romans but more a result of Jewish self-destruction than Roman military power.

2.1. Civil War. The city was torn by internal power struggles almost from the beginning of the war. On the one hand, the political forces were divided between extremists and moderates, a war party and a peace party. On the other hand, the extremists themselves were divided not only from the moderates but among themselves.

Initially, after the successful rout of Cestius, the moderates had gained control of Jerusalem under the leadership of the ex-high priest Ananus. By the end of A.D. 67, however, the war party led by Eleazar son of Simon, who had distinguished himself in the attack on the retreating Cestius, and a group around him which Josephus called the "Zealots" (Josephus *J.W.* 2.8.13 §§160-61) gained strength from numerous other extremists and brigands who had moved to Jerusalem after Vespasian's invasion of Galilee (Josephus *J.W.* 4.3.3 §§135-36).

Joined by these extremist forces Eleazar and his band began terrorizing the moderates and attacking the authority of the high priests (Josephus *J.W.* 4.3.4-6 §§138-50). They seized the temple and replaced the high priest with a priest chosen by lot (Josephus *J.W.* 4.3.6 §§147-50). Ananus, supported by a public aroused by the sacrilege, regained the outer courts and pinned Eleazar and the Zealots inside (Josephus *J.W.* 4.3.11-12 §§193-207). The Zealots, however, were encouraged by John of Gischala, who had come to Jerusalem after being routed from Gischala by Titus (Josephus *J.W.* 4.2.4 §106; 4.3.1-3 §§121-28, 135-37) and was supposedly on the side of Ananus and the moderates, to seek help from the Idumeans (Josephus *J.W.* 4.4.1 §§224-32). Eventually a large Idumean force entered the city under cover of a severe storm (Josephus *J.W.* 4.4.6-7 §§288-304) and linked up with the Zealots by retaking the outer courts and killing the ex-high priest Ananus (Josephus *J.W.* 4.5.1-2 §§305-17). The Zealots then went on such a brutal rampage, attacking supporters of the moderates, that the majority of the Idumean force broke with Eleazar and returned home. Others went over to John of Gischala and his band (Josephus *J.W.* 4.5.5—6.1 §§345-65). The extremists had gained control of the city.

The Zealots under Eleazar, however, soon split with John of Gischala because of his desire for absolute power (Josephus *J.W.* 4.7.1 §§389-90; 5.1.2 §§5-8). In the spring of A.D. 69 these two rival groups were joined by a third led by Simon bar Giora from Gerasa. Simon had first moved to Masada after losing his command in northeastern Judea in A.D. 67 (Josephus *J.W.* 4.9.3 §§503-8). When he learned about Ananus's death, he gathered a force from the refugees of the Zealot's brutal campaign in Jerusalem, along with some Idumeans, and pitched camp outside Jerusalem (Josephus *J.W.* 4.9.8 §§538-44). From there he was admitted into the city by the remainder of the moderates and a populace wearied of the brutality of John and the Zealots (Josephus *J.W.* 4.9.11 §§573-76).

In the struggle that followed, Simon became the "master of Jerusalem" (Josephus *J.W.* 4.9.12 §577), with an army of nearly 15,000 that controlled most of the city. John occupied the outer courts of the temple and part of the Lower City of Jerusalem with 6,000 men. The Zealots held the inner temple with 2,400 (Josephus *J.W.* 5.6.1 §§248-51). During Titus's siege of Jerusalem in the spring of A.D. 70, John used the opening of the temple during the Passover to storm the inner courts and force the Zealots to join him against Simon (Josephus *J.W.* 5.3.1 §§98-105). Only as Titus was about to breach the walls did he reluctantly agree to recognize and work with Simon in defense of the city (Josephus *J.W.* 5.7.4 §§278-79). Meanwhile the civil war had not only cost unity and hundreds of lives, but the vital stores of grain had been destroyed by fire during the internal conflict (Josephus *J.W.* 5.1.4-5 §§22-28). According to Josephus the ensuing famine alone cost over 600,000 lives (Josephus *J.W.* 5.13.7 §569).

*2.2. **The Fall of Jerusalem.*** In the spring of A.D. 70 Titus took command of the Roman forces. During Passover of A.D. 70 he moved his troops closer to the city walls and began his assault from the north. In May he breached Agrippa's wall after nearly two weeks of attack (Josephus *J.W.* 5.6.4—7.2 §§275-302).

When the Jewish resistance appeared to slow the preparations for the siege of the second north wall and the Antonia, Titus threw up a four-mile circumvallation around the city with troops stationed at posts along the wall to prevent provisions from reaching the famine-starved inhabitants (Josephus *J.W.* 5.12.2 §§502-11). On more than one occasion Josephus noted the impossibility of escape from the city, a condition that existed even prior to the building of the Roman wall around it (Josephus *J.W.* 4.9.1 §490). Attempted escape from the city meant death either from the rebels on the inside or from the Romans on the outside (Josephus *J.W.* 4.9.10 §§564-65; 5.13.4 §551; 6.6.2 §323).

In July Titus broke through the second north wall and the Antonia and moved his forces into position to attack the north and west temple fortifications. He managed to get control of the outer courts on the ninth of August and took the inner courts on the tenth, plundering the temple, setting it on fire and slaughtering thousands (Josephus *J.W.* 6.4.7—5.2 §§260-85). John's troops, who had held the temple and the Lower City, escaped to the Upper City (Josephus *J.W.* 6.5.1 §277). In celebration the Romans desecrated the Jewish sanctuary by offering a sacrifice to their standards in the outer court (Josephus *J.W.* 6.6.1 §316).

In September Titus ordered the burning and sacking of the city (Josephus *J.W.* 6.6.3 §354). After taking the Lower City, his forces took the Upper City, breaching it in less than a day and gaining control of Herod's palace and towers (Josephus *J.W.* 6.8.4 §§392-99). John, who along with Simon, had escaped into underground passages, eventually surrendered (Josephus *J.W.* 6.9.5 §433). Simon was captured attempting to tunnel his way out (Josephus *J.W.* 7.2.1 §§26-33). Titus then had the temple and city walls razed "to the ground" except for Herod's three towers and a part of the west wall, which he left standing to show the "character and strength" of the city (Josephus *J.W.* 6.9.1 §413; 7.1.1 §§1-4). Since it was too late in the year to sail to Rome, he waited until the spring to return with his spoils from the temple and nearly 100,000 prisoners, including Simon and John, to join Vespasian in a triumphal march in Rome in A.D. 71 (Josephus *J.W.* 7.5.3-6 §§121-57; *see* Roman Triumph).

The fall and destruction of Jerusalem effectively ended the Jewish War. The only resistance remained in the fortresses of Herodian, Machaeros and Masada. Their reductions followed in A.D. 71-73, with Masada, commanded by Eleazar son of Jair (Josephus *J.W.* 7.8.1 §253), the last to fall (Josephus *J.W.* 7.8.5—9.2 §§304-406). [R. A. Guelich]

3. The Destruction of Jerusalem in Jewish Literature.
The destruction of Jerusalem in A.D. 70 stimulated a great deal of theological meditation in the Jewish community. Some of this literature attempts to discover why God allowed the tragedy. Some literature claims that the destruction was in fact foreseen.

3.1. Explanation of the Destruction. In the guise of reflection on the first destruction of the city and temple at the hands of the Babylonians in 586 B.C., some literature portrays the priests as admitting their corruption and unworthiness to be the stewards of God's house (cf. 4 Ezra 10; *2 Bar.* 1:1-5; *3 Bar.* 1:1-7; *4 Bar.* 1—4; *b. Ta*ʿ*an. 29a;* Lev. Rab. 19:6 [on Lev 15:25]). Much of this literature goes on to reassure readers that the city's destruction was but one more step in the divine plan that will eventually lead to Israel's redemption.

3.2. Predictions of Destruction. There is significant evidence that the destruction of Jerusalem and the temple were predicted by various persons and literary traditions. According to *Testament of Levi* 10:3, "the curtain of the temple will be torn." The destruction of a corrupt priesthood is foretold in *Testament of Levi* 15:3 (cf. 16:1-5), while siege, destruction, fire and captivity are forecast in *Testament of Judah* 23:1-5. Jerusalem's siege appears to be predicted in *Sibylline Oracles* 3:665. The men of the Renewed Covenant at *Qumran anticipate the destruction of the Jerusalem *priestly establishment (1QpHab 9:2-7; 12:3-5; 4QpNah 1:1-3). The author of the *Lives of the Prophets* also foretells the destruction of Jerusalem and the temple (*Jonah* 10—11; *Habakkuk* 11). Josephus says he predicted the city's doom (Josephus *J.W.* 3.8.3 §§351-52; 6.2.1 §109; 6.5.4 §311). Josephus also tells us of one *Jesus ben Ananias who, alluding to Jeremiah 34, foretold the doom of the city and the temple (Josephus *J.W.* 6.5.3 §300-309). Finally, there are rabbinic traditions that claim that certain *rabbis, most notably Yohanan ben Zakkai and Zadok, predicted the destruction of Jerusalem and the temple (*y. Soṭa* 6:3; *b. Yoma* 39a; *Lam. Rab.* 1:5 §31; *b. Giṭ.* 56a; *ʾAbot R. Nat.* 4). Most of these traditions have been informed by the vocabulary and imagery of Israel's classical prophets who foretold the first destruction of Jerusalem and the temple. [C. A. Evans]

4. The Destruction of Jerusalem in the Gospels.
Apart from the mention of the destruction of a city in the parable of the great supper in Matthew 22:7 (frequently taken as an allusion to the destruction of Jerusalem) and the lament over Jerusalem in Matthew 23:37-38 (par. Lk 13:34-35), only Luke directly alludes to a siege of the city. The lament of Matthew 23:37-38 and its parallel in Luke 13:34-35 speak generally of a coming abandonment and desolation of her "house" in the language of Jeremiah 12:7 and 22:5. By contrast Luke 19:43-44, with the reference to a siege and surrounding of Jerusalem, comes closest to the actual events described by Josephus (19:43-44; cf. Josephus *J.W.* 5.6.2 §262; 5.11.4 §466; 5.12.2 §§508-11), while Luke 21:20 [cf. Mk 13:14]) identifies the city's approaching "desolation" (cf. Dan 12:11 LXX) with the surrounding of the city by troops (cf. Josephus *J.W.* 5.11.6 §§486-90). The frequent reference to Jerusalem's destruction corresponds to the prominent role of Jerusalem for Luke-Acts.

All four Gospels have Jesus making reference to a future destruction of the temple (Mt 24:2; Mk 13:2; Lk 21:6; cf. Mt 26:61; Mk 14:38; Jn 2:19), an event that of necessity would seem to assume the fall of Jerusalem. Furthermore, the warning against the "abomination of desolation" in the Olivet Discourse (Mk 13:14; cf. Dan 12:11) has often been interpreted as referring to the Roman desecrating presence in one form or another in the temple during the war.

Despite those who would attribute these references to the influence of hindsight, nothing in either of the references to the fate of Jerusalem or the temple corresponds so closely to the events as to necessitate the sayings being created in the light of the events of A.D. 66-70. Luke's description of the siege and razing of Jerusalem (Lk 19:43-44; 21:20) reflects the normal strategy for taking a fortified city in the ancient world (e.g., Jer 6:3, 6). Neither reference contains any distinctive feature of the destruction of Jerusalem such as the barricading of the city with a four-mile wall, the disastrous civil war and famine from within, or the fall of the temple. Some elements actually conflict with the information given by Josephus. For example, the Roman presence and wall leaves the warning against entering and the summons to flee the city (Lk 21:20) without a historical reference point. Furthermore, the Roman presence in the temple could hardly have represented the "abomination of desolation" (Mk 13:14). Rome breached the temple at the climax of the war, a fact that again makes the call for those in Judea to flee anachronistic: by that time they had been conquered and under control of Roman forces for nearly two years. The frequent use of OT prophetic imagery in these passages indicates that these sayings were prophecies of pending judgment. The events of A.D. 70 may have given poignancy to Jesus' sayings in Luke 19:43-44 and 21:20, but the underlying prophecy of the coming destruction of Jerusalem and the temple ultimately have their roots in Jesus' ministry. Jesus, as had several in his time, warned of impending judgment. This warning, doubtlessly interpreted by the ruling priests as a threat, was a major factor in the decision to have Jesus arrested. [R. A. Guelich]

See also JERUSALEM; JESUS BEN ANANIAS; JEWISH HISTORY: ROMAN PERIOD; JEWISH WARS WITH ROME; JOSEPHUS: GENERAL; REVOLUTIONARY MOVEMENTS; ROMAN MILITARY; TEMPLE, JEWISH.

BIBLIOGRAPHY. M. Aberbach, *The Roman-Jewish War (66-70 A.D.): Its Origins and Consequences* (London: R. Golub, 1966); P. Bilde, "The Causes of the Jewish War According to Josephus," *JSJ* 10 (1979) 179-202; M. N. A. Bockmuehl, "Why Did Jesus Predict the Destruction of Jerusalem?" *Crux* 25.3 (1989) 11-18; S. G. F. Brandon, *The Fall of Jerusalem and the Christian Church* (London: SPCK, 1951); C. H. Dodd, "The Fall of Jerusalem and the 'Abomination of Desolation,'" *JRS* 37 (1947) 47-54; C. A. Evans, "Predictions of the Destruction of the Herodian Temple in the Pseudepigrapha, Qumran Scrolls, and Related Texts," *JSP* 10 (1992) 89-147; L. Gaston, *No Stone on Another: Studies in the Significance of the Fall of Jerusalem in the Synoptic Gospels* (SNTSMS 23; Leiden: E. J. Brill, 1970); M. Goodman, "The First Jewish Revolt: Social Conflict and the Problem of Debt," *JJS* 33 (1982) 417-27; M. Hengel, *Die Zeloten* (Leiden: E. J. Brill, 1976); R. A. Horsley, "Banditry and the Revolt against Rome AD 66-70," *CBQ* 43 (1981) 409-32; B. Reicke, "Synoptic Prophecies on the Destruction of Jerusalem," in *Studies in New Testament and Early Christian Literature: Essays in Honor of A. P. Wikgren*, ed. D. E. Aune (*SNT* 33; Leiden: E. J. Brill, 1972) 121-34; D. M. Rhoads, *Israel in Revolution 6-74 C.E.* (Philadelphia: Fortress, 1976); E. M. Smallwood, *The Jews Under Roman Rule: From Pompey to Diocletian: A Study in Political Relations* (SJLA 20; Leiden: E. J. Brill, 1981).

R. A. Guelich and C. A. Evans

DEVIL. *See* BELIAL, BELIAR, DEVIL, SATAN.

DIADOCHI

The Greek word *diadochoi* ("successors") has been used since the first century B.C. to refer to the immediate successors of *Alexander the Great. Since there were many important figures of the period, there is no agreed-upon list of *diadochi*. Generally, however, the term is used of the dozen or so Macedonian generals who carved out kingdoms in the eastern Mediterranean during the half-century after Alexander's death. While the period of the *diadochi* clearly begins in 323 B.C., its end is variously put at 301 (death of Antigonus), 286 (defeat of Demetrius), 281 (deaths of Lysimachus and Seleucus) or 276 (Antigonus Gonatas ensconced in Macedon). The most inclusive meaning is used here. Having mentioned the chief sources for the period, we will sketch the complicated political history of the period in a greatly simplified form and conclude with an overview of its major social, religious and cultural developments.

1. Sources
2. Political History
3. Politics and Society
4. Religion and Philosophy
5. Literature, Art and Architecture

1. Sources.

The most helpful ancient literary sources for this period are Diodorus Siculus (especially *Bib. Hist.* bks. 18—22), who reproduces lost contemporary source material, especially the work of Hieronymus of Carda, an intimate of Eumenes, Antigonus and Demetrius, whose history covered our entire period; and Plutarch's lives of Demetrius, Eumenes, Phocion and Pyrrhus. These must be supplemented by the epitome of Pompeius Trogus's work and the appropriate parts of Arrian's *History of Alexander* and Appian's *Syrian History*. Documentary sources include epigraphical, papyrological, numismatic and archaeological evidence of importance.

2. Political History.

2.1. 323-321 B.C. When Alexander died suddenly in 323 at Babylon, not only the kingship of Macedon but also rule over his vast conquests was left vacant. The only close blood ties to the royal house were those of his half-brother Philip III Arrhidaeus (seemingly epileptic and/or mentally unfit) and Alexander IV, Alexander's soon-to-be-born son by his Bactrian wife, Roxane. Alexander's Macedonian generals and advisors opted to divide the empire: Antipater would remain general and regent of Macedon and Greece; Perdiccas would have charge of the royal army in Asia; Craterus was named guardian of the two royal family members. In addition, Ptolemy was given charge of Egypt, Antigonus the One-Eyed of western Anatolia, Lysimachus of Thrace, and Eumenes, the only Greek, of Cappadocia and Paphlagonia, still mostly unconquered.

Alexander's idea of interracial marriages between his Macedonians and the conquered Persian aristocracy was promptly abandoned. Only Seleucus remained married to his Persian wife, and only Eumenes joined him in retaining important roles for his eastern generals and troops. While anti-Macedonian uprisings took place among the Greeks of Bactria, on Rhodes and in Greece, the biggest battles were soon among the *diadochi* themselves. Perdiccas and Craterus were the first victims (321) in what was to become a half-century of jockeying for territory and treasure. A new balance of power was brokered at Triparadeisus in 321, with Seleucus joining the inner ranks as governor of Babylon. Already at this early date little hope remained of keeping the empire united. The coming decades would repeatedly see one of the *diadochi* becoming too successful and the others promptly allying themselves against him until his ambitions were thwarted.

2.2. 321-311 B.C. When Antipater died, he left the regency of Greece and Macedon to Polyperchon, passing over his own son, Cassander. The latter promptly gathered an army and fleet and spent two decades seeking to carve out a kingdom for himself. With the empire hopelessly divided, Alexander's two blood heirs were eliminated (Arrhidaeus in 317, Alexander IV in 310) along with the other remnants of the royal household. Eumenes also failed to find his niche in the new order and was executed in 315. For a time Antigonus's share expanded to include much of Mesopotamia, but he was forced to cede the east to Seleucus in 312, the date the *Seleucids would give to the foundation of their kingdom. By 311 Cassander controlled much of Greece, and Lysimachus much of Thrace, while Ptolemy held Egypt, Antigonus kept *Asia Minor, and Seleucus controlled Mesopotamia.

2.3. 311-301 B.C. Antigonus failed in his continued attempts to recapture eastern territory. Seleucus meanwhile was taking over more and more of Iran, though he had to concede the far eastern empire to the Indian general Chandragupta. Cassander prospered in Macedonia while Polyperchon was confined to governing the Peloponnese until his death (302). The aged Antigonus meanwhile sought continued expansion of his realm through his son, Demetrius Poliorkētēs ("the Besieger of Cities"). Demetrius earned his nickname by taking away Cyprus from Ptolemy (306) but failed in his advance on Egypt. After a second failure, this one against Rhodes (for which the Rhodians in thanksgiving erected the famous Colossus), Demetrius gained a foothold at Athens and organized a new Greek league as a base from which to attack Cassander in Macedon. However, the other players attacked Antigonus's realm from the east, forcing father and son to meet their combined forces at Ipsus in Phrygia (301). Antigonus was killed, but Demetrius escaped. After the great victory over Ptolemy in 306, Antigonus and Demetrius had assumed the title, honors and regalia of kings. They were soon followed by Ptolemy, Seleucus, Lysimachus and Cassander.

2.4. 301-276 B.C. The victors at Ipsus annexed Antigonus's realm, giving Lysimachus much of Asia Minor, Seleucus northern Syria, and Cassander more of Greece. Ptolemy took southern Syria and Palestine for himself. Meanwhile Demetrius, whose kingdom was now reduced to Cyprus, Tyre, Sidon and some Greek cities and islands, used his control of the sea to harass his enemies and build a new power base. His chance in Greece and Macedon came after the death of Cassander (298/297), and he established a firm base there by 294. By his death in 286, however, he had lost his other islands and cities and left his son Antigonus Gonatas with only a foothold in Greece and Thessaly and a claim to Macedonia.

Lysimachus, who started this period in control of Thrace, also experienced initial successes in seizing much of Asia Minor, Thessaly and parts of Macedonia. When Seleucus invaded Asia, however, and penetrated as far as Sardis, the aging Lysimachus's support melted away, hastening his end (281). Seleucus tried to follow up this victory by crossing into Macedon but was assassinated. His son Antiochus I took over his throne but had to be satisfied with a mainly Syrian and Mesopotamian kingdom.

After fighting off a Gallic invasion (277), Antigonus Gonatas firmly established himself in Macedon. Ptolemy continued his rule of Egypt and many of the Mediterranean islands until his death (283/282), and he was succeeded by his son, Ptolemy II Philadelphus, who ruled jointly with him at the end. Thus, though they would continue to feud over borders (Palestine would be caught in the ongoing struggle between Ptolemies and Seleucids), the general lines of the hereditary Hellenistic kingdoms were now established for the coming decades.

3. Politics and Society.
An array of Greek and Macedonian cultural elements were present at the courts of the *diadochi* and in the garrisons and colonies that buttressed their rule. This influence Hellenized the various regions to different degrees and at different paces. The kingdoms sought to increase their external stability with interdynastic marriages, especially after 301. Supplies of loyal soldiers and administrators were ensured by the founding of Greek colonies and garrisons throughout the subject regions. *Antioch-on-the-Orontes and Alexandria Troas are but two of the cities founded by the *diadochi* that were important in the NT world. A king advised by a council *(synedrion)* made up of his Greek and Macedonian advisors or friends *(philoi)* became the administrative model. Local laws usually remained in force and local dynasties were allowed to rule as long as they remained loyal to the larger realm, but the king's decisions were in reality if not in name the final law. International commerce, as well as royal *patronage of literature and the arts, eventually produced commonalities in language (Koine or Hellenistic Greek) and culture (*see* Greek of the New Testament).

4. Religion and Philosophy.
Alexander had not only become the new "Great King" or "King of Kings" (The Title of the defeated persian emperor; see also 1 Tim 6:15; Rev 17:14, 19:16) but had been the recipient of cultic worship (*see* Ruler Cult). While giving divine honors to living men had also occasionally occurred in the Aegean world (e.g., the cults of Lysander, Dionysius of Syracuse and the previous Macedonian kings), the scope changed dramatically when many of the *diadochi* were so honored. Cassander and Lysimachus as well as Antigonus, Seleucus, Ptolemy and their successors all received divine sacrifice and worship. While the form varied from ruler to ruler and from city to city, the main elements were the same: being officially decreed as savior *(sōtēr),* divinity *(theos)* or *benefactor *(euergetēs);* the erection of a divine statue *(agalma),* often in a new public temple and at times with specially appointed priests; regular sacrifices; annual festivals with competitive musical, dramatic and *athletic games *(agōnes);* and often having months or days of the week renamed in their honor. In addition each main dynasty took a distinctive divinity as its patron and protector.

While local gods in the East were often identified with members of the Greek pantheon and some oriental deities in turn were introduced among the Greeks, the traditional gods often took a back seat to the new dynasts, the god-men who affected daily life most and responded most clearly to such worship (*see* Religion, Greco-Roman). The Athenians sang the praises of Demetrius in 290 by saying, "For other gods are either far away, or have no ears, or don't exist, or don't listen to us; but we can see you with our own eyes, not in word or in stone, but truly!" (Austin, #35). While some expressed such sentiments merely to gain political points, others were doubtless sincere.

Meanwhile, the unsettled political world inherited by the *diadochi* gave rise to a new search for peace—inner peace and self-sufficiency *(autarkeia)* rather than a peace based on the *polis* (city-state). Not only did the cult of Fate *(Tychē)* grow rapidly, but also new worldviews and lifestyles deemphasized the city and exalted the individual. While the Golden Age of Greek philosophy had just ended (*Plato, 347; *Aristotle, 322), the founders of Cynicism, Stoicism and Epicureanism (*see* Philosophy) all lived during the period of the *diadochi* and provided their adherents with new philosophical answers—all downplaying the *polis* and the traditional religious pantheon and championing political indifference and personal withdrawal. Zeno, the founder of *Stoicism, emphasized the brotherhood of man and the world as a single state in which each man must play to the fullest his fated role in the cosmic drama. Epicurus preached withdrawal from politics and society.

The good life for him was found in a circle of friends all seeking spiritual peace in mastery of their passions. While the educated had these philosophical options for dealing with fate, the common person was more likely to strike a bargain with an Olympian god (promising an *ex voto* offering in return for help), seek initiation into one of the increasingly popular mystery cults or turn to *magic.

5. Literature, Art and Architecture.

The lack of political interest is seen also in the popularity of the New Comedy at Athens. Menander and his colleagues avoided the political jibes that pervaded Old and Middle Comedy. Instead complicated plots and misunderstandings set the stage for very ordinary stock characters—the grumpy father, the lovesick son, the insolent and scheming slave, the pompous soldier.

Painters like Apelles and sculptors in the tradition of Praxiteles (who died shortly before this period) pushed representational realism to new levels, striving for the ideal representation *(mimēsis)*. Meanwhile Ptolemy I in his final years founded a new scientific and artistic research center, the museum of *Alexandria. Painters, poets (like Aratus, quoted by Paul [Acts 17:28]), literary critics, philosophers, scientists, mathematicians and medical experts were supported in scholarly pursuits amid the tranquility of the museum and its library (*see* Alexandrian Library).

In architecture the energy of the times was shown in projects like the Colossus of Rhodes, the Pharos lighthouse at Alexandria and the vastly expanded temple complexes at Ephesus, Didyma, Sardis and Priene (*see* Temples, Greco-Roman). Thus while the distinctive form of the Greek *polis* had now dotted vast new areas of the East, during the period of the *diadochi* the atmosphere within had changed somewhat. Few of the older cities were as independent as they had been in the classical period, but there were important new religious, philosophical and social breezes blowing that would influence civilizations in the coming millennia.

See also ALEXANDER THE GREAT; ART AND ARCHITECTURE: GRECO-ROMAN; HELLENISM; RULER CULT.

BIBLIOGRAPHY. M. Austin, *The Hellenistic World from Alexander to the Roman Conquest: A Selection of Ancient Sources in Translation* (Cambridge: Cambridge University Press, 1981); R. S. Bagnall and P. Derow, *Greek Historical Documents: The Hellenistic Period* (SBLSBS 16; Chico, CA: Scholars Press, 1981); H. Bengtson, *Die Diadochen: Die Nachfolger Alexanders des Grossen (323-281 v. Chr.)* (Munich: C. H. Beck, 1987); R. A. Billows, *Antigonos the One-Eyed and the Creation of the Hellenistic State* (Berkeley and Los Angeles: University of California Press, 1990); S. M. Burstein, *The Hellenistic Age from the Battle of Ipsos to the Death of Kleopatra VII* (TDGR 3; Cambridge: Cambridge University Press, 1985); R. M. Errington, "Diodorus Siculus and the Chronology of the Early Diadochoi, 320-311 B.C.," *Hermes* 105 (1977) 478-504; idem, "From Babylon to Triparadeisos, 323-320 B.C.," *JHS* 90 (1970) 49-77; J. J. Gabbert, *Antigonus II Gonatas: A Political Biography* (London: Routledge, 1997); P. Green, *Alexander to Actium: The Historical Evolution of the Hellenistic Age* (Berkeley and Los Angeles: University of California Press, 1990); E. S. Gruen, "The Coronation of the Diadochoi," in *The Craft of the Ancient Historian: Essays in Honor of Chester G. Starr*, ed. J. W. Eadie and J. Ober (Lanham, MD: University Press of America, 1985) 253-71; C. Habicht, *Gottmenschentum und griechische Staedte* (2d ed.; Zetemata 14; Munich: C. H. Beck, 1970); P. Harding, *From the Peloponnesian War to the Battle of Ipsus* (TDGR 2; Cambridge: Cambridge University Press, 1985); J. Hornblower, *Hieronymus of Cardia* (Oxford: Oxford University Press, 1981); H. S. Lund, *Lysimachus: A Study in Early Hellenistic Kingship* (London: Routledge, 1992); J. Seibert, *Das Zeitalter der Diadochen* (Darmstadt: Wissenschaftliche Buchgesellschaft, 1983); F. W. Walbank et al., *The Hellenistic World* (2d ed.; *CAH* 7, pt. 1; Cambridge: Cambridge University Press, 1984). G. L. Thompson

DIASPORA JUDAISM

By the first century A.D. Jewish communities had become established in almost every part of the then-civilized world. Our period of investigation will be from the foundation of the various Diaspora communities until the second century A.D., although material relating to later periods will be discussed occasionally.

1. Definitions
2. Sources
3. A Geographical Survey of Diaspora Communities
4. Population
5. Economic Situation

6. The Diaspora Synagogue
7. Community Leadership
8. Diaspora Communities in the Greek City
9. The Assimilation, Acculturation and Accommodation of Diaspora Communities
10. Facets of Jewish Identity in the Diaspora
11. Diaspora as Exile
12. Diaspora in the New Testament
13. Conclusions

1. Definitions.
Scholars of earlier generations categorized *Judaism as either Palestinian Judaism or *Hellenistic Judaism. The former was regarded as "uncontaminated" and "normative" and, as the name suggests, restricted to Palestine. The latter was an adulterated, Hellenized form of Judaism found in the Diaspora. However, recent scholarship has noted how inadequate such a distinction is since strong Hellenizing influences were at work in Palestine, and Diaspora communities continued to regard themselves as Jewish and can in no way be thought of as somehow less genuine.

Therefore, the primary distinction made in the study of Judaism is a geographical one between Judaism in Palestine and that in the Diaspora. Further, it is generally acknowledged that there was much diversity in Judaism in both geographical areas and that the development of Jewish life was influenced by the social and political context of each community.

2. Sources.
Often it is difficult to determine which Jewish texts from our period come from the Diaspora, but the following certainly or almost certainly do: Artapanus, *Aristobulus, *Demetrius, Ezekiel, **Joseph and Aseneth,* *Josephus, the **Epistle of Aristeas,* *3 and 4 Maccabees, *Philo, *Pseudo-Philo, **Pseudo-Phocylides,* the *Septuagint, some of the **Sibylline Oracles,* **Testament of Abraham* and *Wisdom of Solomon. We have a significant number of papyri and inscriptions that shed valuable light on Diaspora Jewish life, although their preservation and discovery is haphazard, and it is often difficult to determine their dating and whether they are Jewish. In addition six Diaspora *synagogues have been excavated. Further information about Diaspora Judaism comes from texts written by non-Jewish authors who provide us with insight into how Jews and Judaism were perceived by others. Overall our evidence is sufficient for us to construct a coherent account of Jewish life in only a very few places.

3. A Geographical Survey of Diaspora Communities.
By the first century A.D. there were significant Jewish communities throughout the Greco-Roman world, so that there were probably few major cities or regions that were without a community of resident Jews (see Philo *Leg. Gai.* 214, 281-83; *Flacc.* 45-46; *Vit. Mos.* 2.232; Josephus *Ant.* 14.7.2 §115; *J.W.* 7.3.3 §43; 1 Macc 15:23-24; *Sib. Or.* 3:271-72; Acts 2:9-11). There were two main reasons for the development of communities in the Diaspora. First, on occasions conquerors forcibly deported Jews; for example, the Babylonians carried numerous Jews to Babylonia, and Pompey took hundreds of Jews to *Rome as prisoners of war. Second, voluntary migration from Palestine to the Diaspora, arising from diverse motives, was highly significant.

The origins of the Jewish communities in Babylonia lie in the exile, since many Jews chose to remain in Babylonia when Cyrus allowed them to return to *Jerusalem (2 Chron 36:22-23; Ezra 1:1-4). Josephus wrote of the size of the Jewish population beyond the Euphrates in his time (Josephus *Ant.* 15.8.2.2 §14; cf. Philo *Leg. Gai.* 216, 282); there were significant Jewish settlements in Nehardea, Nisibis (Josephus *Ant.* 18.9.1 §§311-12) and Seleucia (Josephus *Ant.* 18.9.8-9 §§372-79). Queen Helena of Adiabene and her son Izates were converted to Judaism in the middle of the first century A.D. (Josephus *Ant.* 20.2.1-5 §§17-53). During the Jewish War of A.D. 66-70 Jews in Palestine attempted to arouse hostility against the Romans among their fellow Jews beyond the Euphrates (Josephus *J.W.* 6.6.2 §343). The synagogue in Dura-Europos, which was a modified house, was decorated with the most elaborate frescoes to survive from the ancient Jewish world.

The Jewish community in *Antioch, which was the largest in Syria, probably began in the third century B.C. (Josephus *Ant.* 12.3.1 §119). Under the Romans the Jewish community continued to grow, and Josephus notes its size, wealth and success in gaining sympathizers and proselytes (Josephus *J.W.* 7.3.3 §45). However, Jewish-Gentile tensions grew in the first century A.D., particularly among the lower social classes, and during the Jewish War of A.D. 66-70 the Jewish communities in many Syrian cities suffered on several occasions at the hands of the Gentile majority (Josephus *J.W.* 2.18.1 §§457-60; 2.18.5 §§477-79; 7.3.1-4 §§40-62). After the war the inhabitants of Antioch asked Titus to expel the Jews from the city, but Titus refused to do so and confirmed the Jews' former rights (Josephus *J.W.* 7.5.2 §§100-111). We also know of other Jewish communities in Syria in Apamea, Damascus, Caesarea and elsewhere.

Between 210-205 B.C. Antiochus III transferred two thousand Jewish families from Mesopotamia and Babylonia to Lydia and Phrygia as military settlers; this provides us with the first unambiguous evidence of Jewish communities in Asia Minor (Josephus *Ant.* 12.3.4 §§147-53). In *Pro Flacco* 28.67-68 Cicero writes of significant amounts of temple tax that had been seized in Asia in 62 B.C. by the Roman governor, Flaccus, giving evidence of the size and prosperity of some Jewish communities. A series of probably generally authentic documents preserved by Josephus and to be dated from 49 B.C. to A.D. 2/3 provide evidence for a number of Jewish communities in Asia Minor (Josephus *Ant.* 12.3.2 §§125-28; 14.10.1-26 §§185-267; 16.2.3-5 §§27-61; 16.6.1-8 §§160-78; Philo *Leg. Gai.* 315). They indicate these Jewish communities experienced ongoing tension in their local cities with respect to their social and religious privileges. The evidence suggests the Jewish communities were a significant and influential presence in the cities concerned and some Jews were of social and economic importance, but their limited participation in the main currents of city life led to their being a considerable irritant as far as the local cities were concerned (*see* Jewish Communities in Asia Minor).

By the beginning of the first century A.D., however, hostility toward the Jewish communities seems to have abated. An inscription from Acmonia shows that Julia Severa, a high priestess of the imperial cult in the time of Nero (*see* Ruler Cult), built the Jewish community a synagogue (*CIJ* 766). She was thus a Gentile *benefactor of the local Jewish community, a fact that shows Jews had friends in the highest social circles. Luke indicates that Jews were able to influence the local Gentile population in some places, which suggests that the Jews were respected in their cities (Acts 13:50; 14:2, 5). The presence of Godfearers of some social standing also suggests Jews were a respected group (e.g., Acts 13:16, 48-50; 14:1). Revelation 2:9 and 3:9 suggest that around A.D. 95 the Jewish communities in Smyrna and Philadelphia actively opposed Christians. Asian Christians addressed by Ignatius clearly were tempted to go to the synagogue and adopt Jewish customs (Ign. *Phld.* 6.1-2; Ign. *Magn.* 8.1; 9.1-2; 10.3), a circumstance that points to the impact of some Jewish communities on local Christians.

From the second century A.D. onward it seems clear that some Jewish communities and individuals in Asia played a prominent part in their cities (e.g., *CIJ* 745, 748, 770; *Monumenta Asiae Minoris Antiqua* 6, 335a; Trebilco, 37-103). The size and prominence of the Sardis synagogue points to the social integration and civic prestige of this Jewish community. It seems that at least some of these communities were able to become acculturated and integrated into their cities while remaining faithfully Jewish. They seem to have belonged in their cities, where they were respected and made significant social contributions without compromising their Jewish identity.

We know that Jews lived in at least three towns in the kingdom of Bosporus. An almost certainly Jewish inscription from Gorgippia, dated A.D. 41, refers to the manumission of a female *slave, which was carried out in a synagogue (*CIJ* 690; cf. *CIJ* 683-84, 683a-b from Panticapaeum).

We are best informed about the Jewish communities in Egypt, which were the largest Diaspora communities in our period. At the time of the Babylonian conquest some Jews fled to Egypt (Jer 43:6-7; 44:1; 46:14); Aramaic papyri of the fifth century B.C. give evidence of a Jewish military colony at Elephantine, a colony that included a Jewish temple.

Jewish immigration into Egypt, both forced and voluntary, was significant from the third century B.C., with the result that Jews came to be settled throughout Egypt. The Ptolemaic era was a period when the Jews in Egypt encountered little hostility (although there were some notable exceptions) and came to fill a significant and prominent role in the economic, political, military and social life of Egypt (*see* Hellenistic Egypt). They generally flourished as Jews who retained their ethnic identity while also being strongly attracted to Hellenistic culture. However, their position was also precarious, since they had become alienated from significant sections of the wider populace.

At Leontopolis there was another significant Jewish community, formed by Jewish military settlers around 160 B.C. and including the temple of Onias, which served the needs of the military colony (Tcherikover and Fuks, hereafter *CPJ*, 3:145-63; Josephus *Ant.* 13.3.1-3 §§62-73). In Philo's day Jews lived throughout *Alexandria but were particularly concentrated in two of its five quarters (Philo *Flacc.* 55; Josephus *J.W.* 2.18.8 §495). Synagogues were to be found throughout the city (Philo *Leg. Gai.* 132).

Octavian reaffirmed the privileges of the Jewish community in Egypt when he annexed that country in 30 B.C. The Romans also redefined the various classes of the population and emphasized the distinctions Romans, citizens of Greek cities and "foreigners." The Jews seem to have been relegated en bloc to the same category as the Egyptians and thus were compelled to pay the poll tax (*laographia*); Romans and citizens of Greek cities were exempted from paying this tax or paid at a lower rate. This was not only a financial burden; to be grouped with the native Egyptians was also a grave cultural affront, particularly to the upper classes of the Jewish population. Hence the matter of civic status became an increasingly important one for some Jews. Thus began a period of decline for the Jews in Egypt.

Jewish-Greek tension erupted in A.D. 38, when the Greeks destroyed synagogues or put up images of Gaius inside them. Flaccus, the Roman governor, declared the Jews to be "foreigners and aliens" in Alexandria and ordered them all to live in one section of the city (Philo *Flacc.* 25-57; *Leg. Gai.* 120-35). Murder of Jews and widespread looting also occurred. Flaccus was subsequently dismissed from office, and both sides sent delegations to Caligula, who died in A.D. 41 before giving his decision on the matter of Jewish communal privileges, which Flaccus had annulled.

Further trouble erupted in A.D. 41, which led to hearings before Claudius. He wrote a letter to the city (*CPJ* 153; cf. Josephus *Ant.* 19.5.2 §§280-85) in which he called upon the Alexandrians to allow the Jews to keep their customs and ordered the Jews not to seek any privileges beyond those they had enjoyed for a long period. He also forbade the Jews from participating in the *gymnasium and told them to be satisfied with the benefits they were enjoying in "a city not their own." Both these last factors support the view that the Jews had never possessed *citizenship rights as a body in the city (Smallwood, 235-55). However, it seems clear that some Jews had become citizens individually. Claudius's letter halted the social and cultural integration of such Jews and their children.

The conflict between Jews and Greeks erupted again in A.D. 66 and resulted in the slaughter of a large number of Jews (Josephus *J.W.* 2.18.7-8 §§487-98). After the Jewish War some of the most zealous insurgents escaped to Egypt, where they endeavored to stir up the Jewish population against the Romans, although they met strong opposition from the leaders of the Jewish community (Josephus *J.W.* 7.10.1 §§409-19). In A.D. 115 to 117 Jews in Egypt, Cyrenaica, Cyprus and Mesopotamia attacked their Greek neighbors and launched a revolt. The loss of life was huge, and the Diaspora communities concerned were decimated as a result. Messianic expectation, resentment against the local population and radical social disaffection seem to have been factors behind this revolt.

Jewish settlement in Cyrenaica probably dates from near the beginning of Ptolemaic rule in the area (Josephus *Ag. Ap.* 2.4 §44), with numerous inscriptions testifying to a large Jewish population (see Lüderitz). In Cyrene the Jews formed a well-established and independent body, since Strabo notes that the population of the city was made up of citizens, farmers, resident aliens and Jews (Josephus *Ant.* 14.7.2 §115). Inscriptions show that in the first century A.D. some Jews were taking part in the life of the city and had attained considerable standing politically and culturally. The city also produced the Jewish historian Jason, who wrote a history of the Hasmonean revolt that was abbreviated in 2 Maccabees. He indicates the high cultural level attained by some Jews in Cyrene.

Three inscriptions suggest that some Jews in Berenice had been successful in their social and cultural integration into city life and that other Jews considered this to be legitimate (Lüderitz, nos. 70-72). The community seems to have called a building it owned an amphitheater. We also know of Jewish communities in Teuchira, Apollonia and Ptolemais and in Latin-speaking North Africa.

Philo (*Leg. Gai.* 281-82) gives evidence for a number of Jewish communities in Macedonia and Greece; he lists Thessaly, Boetia, Macedonia, Aetolia, Attica, Argos, Corinth, most of the Peloponnese and the islands of Euboea and Crete. In Paul's time there were Jews in Philippi, Thessalonica, Berea, Athens and Corinth (Acts 16:13; 17:1, 10, 17; 18:4). The Jewish communities in these areas were probably never large, and the epigraphical data for them are limited. One inscription from Corinth, to be dated after the NT period, speaks of a "synagogue of the Hebrews" (*CIJ* 718). An inscription from Stobi (*CIJ* 694) records the grant of part of a private house for use as a synagogue. The Jews of Cyprus participated in the revolt under Trajan; clearly they were numerically strong. We have some information about Jews living on Cos, Rhodes and Samos, and a synagogue, built in the first century B.C., has been discovered on Delos.

A significant number of Jews lived in Rome. We do not know when Jews first settled there, but given the significance of Rome and the contacts between the Romans and Hasmonean Judea, it was probably in the second century B.C. Some Jews were probably expelled from the city in 139 B.C. (see Valerius Maximus 1.3.3; Goodman in Lieu, North and Rajak, 69-70). A number of Jews were brought to Rome as prisoners of war by Pompey in 63 B.C. (Josephus *Ant.* 14.4.4-5 §§70-71, 79), and in 59 B.C. Cicero suggests that they were securely established in the city (*Flac.* 28.66-67). Josephus reports that eight thousand Roman Jews supported an embassy from Judea in 4 B.C. (Josephus *Ant.* 17.11.1 §300). The community flourished in the Augustan era while maintaining its Jewish identity; a number of Roman authors commented on the presence and practices of Jews in Rome in this period (e.g., Horace *Serm.* 1.4.139-43; 1.5.96-104; 1.9.60-78; Ovid *Ars Am.* 1.75-80, 413-16).

In A.D. 19 the Jews were expelled from Rome because of their burgeoning influence (Josephus *Ant.* 18.3.4-5 §§65-84; Tacitus *Ann.* 2.85); however, it is doubtful that all the Jews living in Rome left the city. There was further trouble in the 40s, although the evidence is problematic. Two events probably occurred: first, a prohibition of assemblies in A.D. 41 referred to by Dio Cassius (*Hist.* 60.6.6), and second, an expulsion mentioned by Suetonius (*Claudius* 25.4), Acts 18:2 and Orosius (*Hist.* 7.6.15-16), which the latter dates to A.D. 49. According to *Suetonius, the Jews were expelled since "they were constantly rioting at the instigation of Chrestus." This probably refers to troubles resulting from Jewish Christian missionaries' preaching about Christ among Jews in Rome; it seems likely that only known troublemakers were expelled (e.g., Acts 18:2: Priscilla and Aquila).

For the rest of the first century A.D. the Jews in Rome were in an ambiguous position; they thrived, were able to maintain their identity through faithfulness to their traditions and won admirers and imitators from Romans belonging to a range of social classes. They were also subject to criticism from some quarters, mainly because they were seen as a threat to Roman traditions.

Inscriptions from the Roman Jewish catacombs, mostly to be dated in the second to fourth centuries A.D., show that there was a significant number of Jews spread over several parts of the city in this period. From these inscriptions we learn the names of eleven synagogues in Rome, including "the synagogue of the Hebrews," and synagogues named after Augustus and probably Marcus Agrippa. *1 Clement,* written from Rome in the A.D. 90s (*see* Apostolic Fathers), tells us nothing about Jews in the city.

A synagogue has been discovered in Ostia, the port of Rome. Part of the building was erected toward the end of the first century A.D.; it was expanded in the second and third centuries and received its final form in the fourth century A.D. We also know of Jews in other cities in Italy, including Puteoli, Pompeii, Venosa and Naples.

4. Population.

Although we lack sufficient data to ascertain accurately the number of Jews in the Diaspora, our sources give some information. Some ancient authors emphasize the large numbers of Jews in Egypt and elsewhere (Strabo *Geog.* 16.2.28; Philo *Vit. Mos.* 2.232; *Leg. Gai.* 214, 245; *Flacc.* 43; Josephus *Ant.* 11.5.2 §133; 17.11.1 §300; 18.3.4-5 §§65-84; *J.W.* 7.9.2 §445), and the amount of temple tax seized by Flaccus in four Asian cities suggests a considerable Jewish population in these areas (Cicero *Flac.* 66-69). That the Jews of Egypt, Cyrenaica, Cyprus and Mesopotamia fought a protracted war in the time of Trajan suggests that the total population of the Jews in these areas of the Diaspora was considerable, although again we are unable to give estimates. It does seem clear, however, that the total Jewish population of the Diaspora considerably exceeded the Jewish population in Palestine (Tcherikover, 292-95) and that Diaspora Jews constituted a group of significant size. Scholars often suggest that five to six million Jews were living in the Diaspora in the first century, but such figures can be only speculative.

5. Economic Situation.

Diaspora Jews participated in a variety of branches of economic life. We know, for example, of Jews who were soldiers, land-owning farmers, agricultural laborers, shepherds, artisans, manual workers, traders, merchants, bankers, government officials and slaves. In some Roman writers Jewish poverty was a byword (e.g., Juvenal *Sat.* 3.14-16; 6.542-47), but we also know of some very wealthy Jews (Josephus *Ant.* 20.7.3 §147; *J.W.* 7.11.1-2 §§442-45). Diaspora Jews, then, were found in almost all socioeconomic strata of the period (Safrai and Stern, 701-27).

6. The Diaspora Synagogue.

6.1. Synagogue Buildings. Synagogues have been discovered at Delos, Ostia, Sardis, Dura-Europos, Stobi and Priene. The existence of many others is clear from inscriptions or literary evidence. There would have been more than one synagogue in a large city; eleven are attested for Rome, and Philo says that there were many synagogues in Alexandria (Philo *Leg. Gai.* 132; cf. *Spec. Leg.* 2.62). Acts shows that there were many synagogues throughout the regions where Paul traveled (Acts 9:2; 13:5, 14; 14:1; 17:1, 10, 17; 18:4-7, 19-26; 19:8). Small communities would meet in a house belonging to a member. The earliest synagogue buildings were probably originally private houses modified for use by the community (e.g., Delos and Priene).

The earliest references to a Diaspora synagogue building are dated between 246-221 B.C. and come from Egypt (Horbury and Noy, nos. 22, 117). At first the building seems to have been called a *proseuchē,* or place of prayer (see *CPJ* 129, 134, 138, 432; Horbury and Noy, nos. 9, 13, 22, 25, 27, 125-26; 3 Macc 7:20; Philo *Flacc.* 41, 45, 122; Josephus *Vit.* 280; *CIJ* 682-84, 690, 726); sometimes the congregation that gathered in the building is called *synagōgē,* which means "assembly." However, later the building in which they assembled is more often called the *synagōgē*.

There was no uniform architectural design for Diaspora synagogues, and the very different plans of the six known buildings are clearly influenced by local factors; however, they do share some common features. They generally contain an architectural feature for keeping the biblical scrolls and sometimes had a platform for a reader and benches. Often there were also guest rooms or a dining hall adjoining the assembly room. The Dura-Europos synagogue contains an outstanding set of frescoes that provide our most important evidence for the existence of Jewish figurative art in this period. The Sardis synagogue, which was one part of a complex of buildings including a bathhouse and gymnasium in the center of the city, is the largest synagogue known from antiquity. The synagogue reveals a confident Jewish community that was also integrated to some extent into the wider city (see Kraabel in Urman and Flesher, 95-126).

6.2. The Synagogue as an Institution. The synagogue was the focus of community life for Diaspora Jews and was organized by the community for the community. Not only was it the center of religious life where the sabbath service was held, but also it was the focus for the educational, political, economic, social and judicial life of the community; communal meals were also often held there. It was thus a crucial institution for the maintenance of Jewish identity and played a central role in Jewish life.

Sources describe synagogue services primarily in terms of the reading and study of Scripture (Philo *Vit. Mos.* 2.215-16; Josephus *Ag. Ap.* 2.17 §175). That some of the buildings were called "prayer houses" indicates that prayer was also an important feature.

6.3. Godfearers. A recently discovered inscription from Aphrodisias lists, along with a number of Jews, fifty-four Gentiles who are called *theosebis* or "Godfearers" (see Reynolds and Tannenbaum). Although some scholars argue that the title *Godfearer* here means the Gentiles concerned have simply expressed their support for the Jews as fellow townspeople, it seems much more likely that the term indicates that these Gentiles were linked in some formal way to the Jewish community, without being proselytes. This and other inscriptions, and some literary sources, strongly suggest that there were a number of Gentile "Godfearers" who were formally associated with the Jewish community, were involved in at least some facets of synagogue life and kept some of the commandments without becoming proselytes who joined the community (see Trebilco, 145-66; Juvenal *Sat.* 14.96-99; Josephus *Ant.* 14.7.2 §110; *J.W.* 7.3.3 §45; *see* Proselytism and Godfearers).

Although Diaspora Jews do not seem to have been involved in an organized active mission to convert Gentiles (see Goodman in Lieu, North and Rajak, 53-78), they do seem to have welcomed Gentiles who were attracted to the Jewish community either as Godfearers or proselytes. The role of the Jews here then was passively to bear witness through their existence and life. It also seems likely that at least some Diaspora synagogues were visible and open to outsiders. It is also noteworthy that we know of some proselytes (see Juvenal *Sat.* 14.96-106; Josephus *J.W.* 2.19.2 §520; 2.20.2 §§559-61; Acts 6:5 and some inscriptions), although their numbers are quite small.

We can also note the fairly widespread adoption of some Jewish customs such as lighting of lamps (Josephus *Ag. Ap.* 2.38 §282; Persius *Sat.* 5.179-84) and not working on the sabbath (Ovid *Ars Am.* 1.413-16) by Gentiles who did not come into the more formal category of Godfearers. Clearly Gentiles were attracted to Judaism to varying degrees throughout our period.

7. Community Leadership.
The names and functions of community leaders probably varied from place to place. In the third century B.C. a *gerousia* represented the Jews of the whole city of Alexandria (*Ep. Arist.* 310). At the time of Strabo an *ethnarchēs* stood at the head of the Jews (Josephus *Ant.* 14.7.2 §117 quoting Strabo), but in A.D. 11 Augustus modified the situation by either reintroducing the *gerousia* or giving it the power previously vested in the *ethnarchēs* (Philo *Flacc.* 74, 117).

The position of *archōn* or ruler was widespread among Diaspora Jews, although the title may have meant different things in different places. In some communities the *archontes* were elected, formed the executive committee of the *gerousia* and looked after all the affairs of the community. The title of *presbyteros*, or elder, is found in some places (e.g., *CIJ* 663, 735, 739; *Ep. Arist.* 310). The relation of *archōn* and *presbyteros* is unclear; they may have been alternative titles, or the members of the *gerousia* who were not members of the executive committee (the archons) may have been called *presbyteroi*. In some places a *gerousiarchēs* was head of the gerousia. The *archisynagōgos*, or ruler of the synagogue, had a role in making arrangements for the services of the synagogue (Acts 13:15) and probably also had some responsibility for maintaining Jewish life and teaching (Acts 18:17). They were often wealthy people of influence and standing in the community, who were *benefactors and *patrons.

Other titles found in inscriptions include *phrontistēs* ("overseer"), *grammateus* ("clerk"), *prostatēs* ("patron"), father or mother of the synagogue, rabbi and priest. It is often difficult to determine what these titles meant (see van der Horst, 89-98).

We know of more than twenty women who held titles such as "ruler of the synagogue," "mother of the synagogue," "elder," "leader" or "priestess." If holding the equivalent title involved a man in active leadership (as opposed to being an honorary title), then it seems likely that when a woman held the title she too was involved in active leadership in the synagogue. There is a continuing debate, however, about whether some of these positions were essentially honorific for all holders of the posts, in which case those who held the titles would have benefitted the Jewish community through their munificence or patronage (see Rajak in Lieu, North and Rajak, 22-24). We have no evidence that women were segregated in Diaspora synagogues, and no ancient text calls for segregation.

8. Diaspora Communities in the Greek City.
We do not have any clear evidence that in the Hellenistic and early Roman periods Jews possessed citizenship as a body in any Greek city. Josephus's statements that suggest that they did have citizenship (e.g., Josephus *Ant.* 12.3.1 §119; 12.3.2 §§125-26; *Ag. Ap.* 2.4 §§37-39) are all historically dubious or ambiguous (see Safrai and Stern, 440-81). Clearly, however, some individuals did obtain citizenship in their cities (e.g., Paul in Acts 21:39; Philo *Leg. Gai.* 155-57; Trebilco, 172).

Diaspora Jews generally organized themselves into communities, although the constitutional position of these communities varied from place to place and over time. The position of the Jewish community within any city probably depended on local factors such as when, how and for what purpose the Jewish community became established in that particular locality. In some cities, such as Alexandria, they seem to have formed self-governing groups. It is often suggested that the Jews there were officially recognized as a *politeuma,* that is, a formally constituted, semiautonomous civic body within a city whose members were not citizens but possessed some important rights. However, the term *politeuma* is found only once in Jewish literature from Alexandria (*Ep. Arist.* 310). Since it is unclear to whom it refers there (see Lüderitz in van Henten and van der Horst, 183-225), it is precarious to base far-reaching theories on this one reference. In Berenice we have evidence for a Jewish *politeuma,* but it was probably a kind of council of the Jews of the city rather than an organization for the whole Jewish community. In other cities the position of the Jews is best compared with that of other associations of immigrants who lived as foreign people in a city. The actual form of communal life probably varied from place to place, as is shown by the variety of terms used to express the notion of community, including the terms "the Jews," "the people," *synodos, politeuma, katoikia,* the *ethnos* and the *synagōgē.*

A crucial matter in relations between the Jewish Diaspora communities and the cities in which they lived was being granted certain privileges that enabled them to live as Jews in accordance with their law and maintain their identity as communities. The support of the Roman authorities for these privileges was crucial in the face of periodic challenges from individual cities, with Julius Caesar and Augustus being particularly noteworthy in their support for Jewish privileges. These included being able to meet regularly, organize their own community life and have internal jurisdiction, to own buildings, to have their "ancestral" food, to collect and send the temple tax to Jerusalem and to live according to their customs and laws, such as observing the sabbath. Privileges connected with observing the sabbath included being free from appearing in court on the sabbath and an exemption from serving in the Roman army. That they enjoyed these privileges, without being citizens and participating fully in a city's life and cults, often led to friction between the Jews and the city authorities.

The status of Diaspora Jewish communities was not greatly affected after the revolt of A.D. 66-70, in which Diaspora Jews were little involved. Titus resisted demands for the abolition of Jewish communal privileges in Antioch and Alexandria (Josephus *J.W.* 7.5.2 §§100-11), and generally privileges remained unmodified outside Judea. The diversion of the temple tax to the *fiscus Judaicus* in order to support the temple of Jupiter Capitolinus was the one important change that affected the Diaspora after A.D. 70. Domitian exacted the tax with special severity; Nerva prohibited the accusations to officials that had resulted from Domitian's policy.

9. The Assimilation, Acculturation and Accommodation of Diaspora Communities.

We have noted that the old distinction between "pure" Palestinian Judaism and "Hellenized" Diaspora Judaism is no longer viable. We cannot analyze Diaspora Judaism by simple measurement against Palestinian Judaism; we must find appropriate criteria for the analysis of Diaspora Judaism and in particular the ways Jews reacted to their environment.

In this regard J. M. G. Barclay notes that we can distinguish among different kinds of Hellenization, such as political, social, linguistic, educational, ideological, religious and material Hellenization. Further, engagement with Hellenism could occur to a different degree in each of these areas, which were not all equally significant. Barclay has devised three scales to depict these different kinds of Hellenization (Barclay, 92-102).

First is an assimilation scale, which refers to the level of social integration and concerns social contacts, interaction and practices. Someone at the top of the assimilation scale had abandoned the social distinctives fundamental to Jewish identity; someone at the bottom confined his or her social life entirely to the Jewish community. Second is an acculturation scale, which refers to the linguistic, educational and ideological aspects of a cultural matrix. Someone at the top of the acculturation scale had scholarly expertise in Hellenistic scholarship; someone at the bottom knew no Greek. Third is an accommodation scale, which refers to the use to which acculturation is put. Here Barclay distinguishes between integrative trends, which involved the imitation of Hellenistic culture and its use in reinterpreting the Jewish traditions and could lead to the submersion of Jewish cultural uniqueness, and oppositional trends, which involved the use of Hellenistic weapons in polemic against Hellenism itself and could lead to antagonism to Greco-Roman culture. Thus "acculturation could be used to construct either bridges or fences between Jews and their surrounding cultures" (Barclay, 98). Although our evidence only rarely enables us to plot Diaspora Jews on these three scales, their use allows us to distinguish among the many different ways Diaspora Jews interacted with their environment. (For the following see in particular Barclay, 103-228, 320-80.)

9.1. Assimilation. There was an enormous range in the degree of assimilation of Diaspora Jews into non-Jewish society. Those who were highly assimilated, to the degree of losing their Jewish distinctiveness and abandoning Jewish practices, included Jews who were fully integrated into political and/or religious affairs of state (e.g., Tiberius Julius Alexander [see Barclay, 105-6]; *CIJ* 749; Josephus *J.W.* 7.3.3 §50); those who abandoned some aspects of Jewish customs in order to be socially successful or to gain some other benefit (Philo *Vit. Mos.* 1.31; Josephus *Ant.* 12.4.6 §§186-89; 18.5.4 §141); those who married Gentiles and did not rear their children as Jews (e.g., Philo *Spec. Leg.* 3.29); those who had become critics of their own traditions (Philo *Abr.* 178-93; *Conf. Ling.* 2-13); those whose allegorical interpretations of the law led them to abandon key Jewish practices (Philo *Migr. Abr.* 89-93); and those whose isolated social circumstances necessitated a high level of assimilation (e.g., *CPJ* 7, 148).

The category of medium assimilation includes those who had significant social ties with the non-Jewish environment but who also preserved their Jewish identity. Again, types of assimilation can be discerned. First were those who were well educated and participated in the social and cultural life of a city or had significant social ties to the non-Jewish world but remained faithful to Jewish tradition (e.g., Alexander the Alabarch [Josephus *J.W.* 5.5.3 §205]; the author of the *Epistle to Aristeas;* Philo; Jewish ephebes, city magistrates and citizens [*CIJ* 755; Acts 21:39; citizenship did not necessarily entail loss of Jewish distinctiveness]). Many Jews were well integrated into civic life (e.g., Lüderitz, no. 36; *CIJ* 748), attained influential positions within their cities and adopted many local customs; yet "a degree of integration did not mean the abandonment of an active attention to Jewish tradition or of Jewish distinctiveness. It was as Jews that they were involved in, and a part of, the life of the cities in which they lived" (Trebilco, 187). Second were those who were in various forms of employment with or for non-Jews (e.g., in the Ptolemaic army). Third were those who were associated with non-Jews in legal matters. Fourth were those who gained patrons, supporters or converts among non-Jews, which suggests there was considerable social interaction between these Jews and non-Jews.

Barclay (329) concludes that "the patterns of life we have observed in the Mediterranean Diaspora suggest that Jews were neither socially and culturally isolated nor simply blended into some social amalgam. While their boundaries may have been defined variously in differing circumstances, it was precisely the ability to maintain these boundaries while continuing everyday social contacts with non-Jews that was the peculiar achievement of the successful Diaspora communities."

In the category of low assimilation are Jews whose social contact with non-Jews was minimal. Factors leading to low assimilation include the existence of Jewish residential districts (e.g., *CPJ* 423, 468; Josephus *Ant.* 14.10.24 §§259-61); the isolation of some communities such as the *Therapeutae, a group found throughout Egypt that in some ways resembled the *Essenes (Philo *Vit. Cont.* 2-90); and social conflict with non-Jews (e.g., in Alexandria in A.D. 38), which expressed and encouraged social alienation.

This range in levels from high assimilation to careful preservation of Jewish distinction means that we cannot rule out in advance what was or was not possible for Jews in their assimilation.

9.2. Acculturation and Accommodation. Clearly there was a range in the levels of acculturation of Diaspora Jews, from those authors who expertly utilized different genres of Hellenistic literature to Jews who had no capacity in Greek, although the latter must have been rare, since papyri and inscriptions show us that Greek was used for nearly all communication in virtually all Diaspora communities. In general the involvement of Diaspora Jews in the life, ways and thought forms of the Greek city (*see* Cities, Greco-Roman) helps to explain the flourishing of Diaspora Jewish literature written in Greek in this period (*see* Writing and Literature: Jewish). But what use did Diaspora Jews make of their acculturation? This leads to the question of what sort of accommodation was effected by Diaspora Jews with their social and cultural environments. Barclay (125-228, 336-80) divides the written texts that can be assigned to the Diaspora with some confidence into those that embrace cultural convergence (while normally retaining some form of Jewish distinction) by integrating Jewish practices with the norms and values of their cultural context and those that emphasize cultural antagonism.

9.2.1. Cultural Convergence. A number of texts exhibit cultural convergence and show the ability of Diaspora Jews to express their traditions within a Hellenistic moral, historical, philosophical and theological framework. The following examples are representative. First, Artapanus was self-consciously Jewish while also being supportive of the Hellenized Egyptian culture he clearly appreciated (*see* Jewish Literature: Historians and Poets). Artapanus claims biblical characters brought culture and *philosophy to Egypt, thus claiming national superiority for the Jews; yet his work also has a pro-Egyptian tone, for example, when it is asserted that Moses established the annual flooding of the Nile. In order to boost Moses' and his people's reputation further, Artapanus gives a positive evaluation of Egypt and its religion. Clearly the author is very much at home in Egypt, whose culture, temples, priests and cults he eulogizes. Artapanus represents a cultural synthesis, an Egyptianized Judaism, and shows that some Jews stood for an important measure of synthesis with Egyptian culture, including Egyptian religion. Barclay (132) notes that "he indicates the possibility of being both a proud Egyptian and a self-conscious Jew." He is a clear example of cultural convergence.

Second, Ezekiel the Tragedian (*see* Jewish Literature: Historians and Poets) rewrote the exodus in the form of a Greek tragedy and thus represents a synthesis with Greek literary tradition. He has an enthusiastic appreciation of Greek *education and is another example of acculturation. The drama is thoroughly Jewish in character, but the form and cultural framework of the classical Greek tradition has made it comprehensible and attractive to Greeks. The work seems to be an attempt to align Jews with Greeks in the common environment in Egypt, without weakening Jewish ethnic loyalty. Ezekiel was Greek and Jewish at the same time, being skilled in Greek poetry, literature and history and committed to the Jewish tradition.

Third, *Philo represents the climax of a Jewish philosophical tradition that was deeply engaged with Hellenistic culture. He received a thorough Hellenistic education and participated in *Alexandrian cultural life. He also received an intensive Jewish education and was intimately acquainted with the life and traditions of the Jewish community in Alexandria, to which he was deeply loyal. He does not give any indication of a tension between Greek and Jewish values. As Barclay (91) puts it, Philo was both "Jewish to the core and Hellenized to the same core."

For Philo the most sublime expression of philosophy was found in the Pentateuch. However, his debt to *Plato was just as great, since his thought was structured by Platonic dualism. Philo tried to show the profound philosophical truths found in the Pentateuch by means of allegorical exegesis. An effect of his allegorization was to dehistoricize the text and to shift from the particular to the universal. Hence the exodus was about the escape of the soul from the confines of the body to the virtues (Philo *Som.* 2.255). His philosophy thus led away from Jewish particularity; Jewish laws were of universal significance. In this way he sought to build bridges between his Mosaic text and Hellenistic culture and to understand Judaism in the light of the themes, motifs and intellectual horizons of his Hellenistic environment. However, "ultimately his allegorical reading of Scripture functions not to submerge Moses' authority in the sea of Hellenism or to parallel Moses with Plato as equal sources of truth. Rather the whole gamut of Hellenistic culture is subordinated to Moses, pressed into service to endorse his original achievement. As Dawson observes, Philonic allegory "is an effort to make Greek culture Jewish rather than to dissolve Jewish identity into Greek culture" (in Barclay, 173). Thus Greek culture is subordinated to Jewish cultural and religious identity.

Overall Philo's erudition in Greek ways of thought was used in the service of his Judaism. In his reaction to extreme allegorizers (Philo *Migr. Abr.* 89-93), Philo shows that his identity was ultimately defined by the Jewish community; his leadership of the embassy to Gaius showed that this was where his social and political commitments lay. With Philo the integration of Judaism into Hellenistic culture was exceptionally profound, but he ultimately used that synthesis for the Jewish community and remained loyal to his Jewish heritage.

Other examples of cultural convergence include the *Epistle of Aristeas*, *Aristobulus and **Pseudo-Phocylides*.

9.2.2. Cultural Antagonism. In some other Diaspora texts acculturation is used in the service of a sociocultural stance that is predominantly oppositional and antagonistic to Judaism's social and cultural environment. In these cases acculturation results in a religious and social critique of other peoples and a call to resist the cultural pressures of the wider society. Again, some representative examples can be noted.

First, the author of the Wisdom of Solomon clearly had a thoroughgoing Greek education, and there is a strong universalist strand in the work. However, the predominant theme is social and cultural antagonism between Jews and non-Jews. The author's Greek education and acculturation serve not to integrate his Judaism with his environment but rather to construct a sophisticated attack upon the latter. It is a deeply Hellenized exercise in cultural aggression and a vigorous defense of Jewish particularity.

Second, the author of **Joseph and Aseneth* uses the Hellenistic form of the romance to launch an attack on Hellenistic religion (*see* Religions, Greco-Roman). A sense of cultural antagonism and alienation between Jews and non-Jews is the predominant tone of the book. The work may be thought to show an open attitude to outsiders, but such outsiders can be welcomed only if they have been totally changed by conversion.

Third, **Sibylline Oracles* 3 and 5 speak of the moral and religious superiority of Israel and the author's cultural antagonism toward non-Jews. They also reveal a cultural and social alienation between Jews and non-Jews. The oracles emphasize the Jews' national greatness, centered on *temple and *Torah. The acculturation revealed by the use of the Sibylline genre is thus used to express antagonism toward that culture.

Other examples of cultural antagonism include *3 and 4 Maccabees.

10. Facets of Jewish Identity in the Diaspora. Despite the evident diversity of Diaspora Judaism, we can also identify elements that enabled Jewish communities to endure as coherent entities and that made the difference between a Jew and a non-Jew clear to Jews themselves and to others. We should note that we are looking at Diaspora Judaism as a social as well as a religious and intellectual phenomenon. The following facets were integral to the identity of Diaspora Jews; they were bonds that held Diaspora Jews together and enabled their communities to survive as coherent entities over time (for what follows see in particular Barclay, 399-444; Trebilco, 12-19).

10.1. Ethnicity. At the core of Diaspora Jewish identity was ethnicity or the ethnic bond, that is, the combination of ancestry and customs that could be voluntarily adopted or abandoned. The importance of ethnicity is demonstrated by the following evidence. First, Diaspora literature emphasizes the significance of the "nation," "race" or "people" as the bearer of the Jewish tradition, with Jews being seen as "people of the same race," bound together by a common ethnicity (e.g., Philo *Vit. Mos.* 2.43-44; *Exag.* 12, 35, 43; Noy 1995, no. 240). Second, non-Jewish authors consistently refer to Judaism as an ethnic entity. Thus the Romans allowed the Jews to follow their "ancestral customs," or time-honored ethnic practices, which points to the combination of kinship and custom that defines ethnicity. Third, proselytes who joined the Jewish community underwent a thorough resocialization, so that they acquired a new ethnicity. The conversion process meant that they were transferred to the Jewish nation (Philo *Spec. Leg.* 1.51-52; *Jos. and As.*), which points to the significance of ethnicity. Fourth, the recognition of the importance of endogamy by Diaspora Jews underlines the significance of ethnicity (e.g., Demetrius in Eusebius *Praep. Ev.* 9.29.1; Philo *Spec. Leg.* 3.29). Finally, the emphasis on the training of children in the Jewish way of life was to ensure that Judaism continued as an ethnic phenomenon (e.g., 4 Macc 18:10-19; Philo *Leg. Gai.* 115, 195). The evidence thus suggests that ethnicity constituted the core of Jewish identity.

10.2. The Local Community. A crucial factor in affirming the identity of Diaspora Jews was the life of the local community. As we have indicated, the nature of the local Diaspora Jewish community varied from place to place and over time, with some owning prayer houses or synagogues, others meeting in private houses, some communities having a range of officials, operating their own courts, voting their own decrees and negotiating with civic authorities, while other communities were less institutionalized. Clearly a strong local community of Jews would have provided invaluable support for the retention of Jewish identity by individuals.

Some elements of communal life were particularly important in binding Jews together. First, *festivals and fasts (Passover [*Exag.* 184-92; *CIJ* 777]; Tabernacles [*CPJ* 452a; Lüderitz, no. 71]; the Day of Atonement [*CIJ* 725]; see also Philo *Vit. Mos.* 2.42; Josephus *Ag. Ap.* 2.5 §55) meant Diaspora Jews could express their solidarity with one another. Second, the weekly sabbath gathering at the synagogue was of immense social significance and was a crucial feature of Diaspora Jewish life (Philo *Leg. Gai.* 156-57; *Spec. Leg.* 2.62-63). These gatherings and the instruction that occurred during them bound the community together in loyalty to their distinctive way of life. Third, Diaspora communities generally paid the temple tax (Philo *Spec. Leg.* 1.77-78; *Leg. Gai.* 156-57, 311-16; Josephus *Ant.* 14.10.1-26 §§185-267; 16.6.17 §§162-73; 18.9.1 §§312-13; Cicero *Flac.* 28.67-68); its payment reinforced the individual's sense of belonging to the local community.

10.3. Links with Jerusalem and Other Diaspora Communities. Diaspora Jewish communities were connected with Jerusalem and "the homeland" by payment of the temple tax and other gifts for the temple. Through the tax, Diaspora communities were linked to and participated in the temple's life and worship. Diaspora literature shows a deep respect for the holiness of the temple (*Ep. Arist.* 83-120; Philo *Leg. Gai.* 184-85). Diaspora Jews also went on pilgrimage to the temple, probably in considerable numbers (Philo *Spec. Leg.* 1.69; Josephus *Ant.* 18.9.1 §§310-13; *J.W.* 6.9.3 §425; *CIJ* 1404), indicating that the temple's symbolic power was considerable even if its impact on daily life was less significant. Pilgrimage to Jerusalem probably provided significant contact for the Diaspora communities with developments in Jerusalem and Palestine in general and further consolidated the bond between the Diaspora and Palestine. On pilgrimage and in other ways Diaspora Jews would have come into contact with others from the Diaspora and thus forged important connections.

There were also strong social and political links between the Diaspora and Palestine (e.g., 2 Macc 1:1-9; Josephus *Ant.* 12.3.2 §§125-26; 17.12.1 §§324-31), and some Diaspora literature expresses a strong attachment to the land of Palestine (*see* Israel, Land of) and a sense of solidarity between the Diaspora and Jews in *Judea (Artapanus 27.21; *Sib. Or.* 5:281, 328-32; Wis 12:3, 7; 3 Macc). However, an attachment to Palestine did not necessarily weaken a strong sense of being at home in the Diaspora (Philo *Flacc.* 45-46). In general Palestine retained some significance as the Holy Land, and the continuing relationship between Diaspora communities and Palestine was an important facet of Jewish identity, but the strength of attachment to Palestine probably varied from community to community.

10.4. The Torah. The *Torah was clearly the key text for Diaspora Jews (Josephus *Ag. Ap.* 2.32 §§232-35; *Sib. Or.* 3:584-85, 768-69; 4 Macc 5:16-21). The existence of the *Septuagint, a translation begun in the third century B.C. probably in Alexandria, shows that at this time Egyptian Jews regarded the Torah as their key text. This is also illustrated by synagogue architecture in which some piece of furniture for the law was prominent (e.g., Ostia; see Noy 1993, 22-26). The dependence of Diaspora authors on the Scriptures is clear (e.g., *Pseud.-Phoc.*), and the allegorical method used by Aristobulus and Philo presupposes the supreme authority of the Scriptures. "Whether as legislation, mystery, constitution, philosophy, founding legend or moral guide, the Jewish Scriptures were integral to all the social and intellectual achievements of Diaspora Judaism" (Barclay, 425).

Instruction in the law formed a key element in Diaspora synagogue life and laid the foundation for Jewish identity (Josephus *Ag. Ap.* 2.16-18 §§171-78; Philo *Leg. Gai.* 156-57). Devotion to the law is regularly noted in the inscriptions from Rome (Noy 1995, nos. 103, 212, 281, 576). In general Diaspora Jewish communities preserved the distinctive customs that were laid down in the law. That Jewish communities took the initiative in the defense of their customs in the face of difficulties with the civic authorities in, for example, Asia and Cyrenaica, and the consistency with which the distinctive traits prescribed by the law were noted as characteristics of Diaspora Jews by outsiders indicate the continuing loyalty of Diaspora Jews to the law and their conviction that their way of life should be ruled by God's law.

Moses, as the person most prominent in the Torah, was also a key figure for Jewish identity. He was seen by Diaspora Jews as a skillful lawgiver, a profound philosopher, a noble king, a supreme military commander, miracle worker and priest (e.g., Philo *Vit. Mos.;* Josephus *Ag. Ap.* 2.15 §§151-72).

10.5. Jewish Practices and Beliefs. Four features of Jewish practice and belief visibly marked off Diaspora Jews from their neighbors and thus were key boundary markers of Jewish identity, with great social significance.

First, Diaspora Jews generally worshiped the one God of Israel (3 Macc 5:13; *Jos. and As.* 11:10) and rejected other alien and iconic cults (Wis 13:1—15:17; *Ep. Arist.* 134-39; Josephus *Ant.* 12.3.2 §126; Philo *Conf. Ling.* 168-73). It seems that Jews were generally exempt from the obligation to worship local gods; we have no documentary evidence for this (and it is unlikely that such an exemption was ever officially expressed), but the outrage expressed when the customary exemption was in danger of being suspended suggests it was a privilege with some consistency (Philo *Leg. Gai.* 117, 134).

Second, the evidence suggests that Jewish dietary laws were generally kept in the Diaspora (e.g., 3 Macc 3:3-7; 7:11). These customs and the consequent separatism at meals would have bound the Jewish communities together and created a consistent social distinction between Jews and non-Jews (Philo *Leg. Gai.* 361-62; *Ep. Arist.* 139-42).

Third, although circumcision was practiced by some other groups, it seems to have constituted a strong affirmation of Jewish identity for men (Philo *Migr. Abr.* 89-93; Josephus *Ant.* 1.10.5 §192).

Fourth, sabbath observance was well-known by non-Jews as a characteristic feature that marked off Jewish communal life from that of other peoples (e.g., Horace *Sat.* 1.9.69-70). The evidence suggests that Diaspora Jews generally observed the sabbath and abstained from work on this day (Philo *Som.* 2.123-24; *Leg. Gai.* 158; Josephus *Ant.* 14.10.12 §§225-27; 14.10.25 §§262-64; *CPJ* 10). The vigor with which Asian Jews, for example, defended the sabbath indicates the depth of their commitment to its observance (e.g., Josephus *Ant.* 16.2.3 §27; 16.6.2-4 §§163-68). It was a highly visible sign of their unique identity as a people.

Each of these strands of Jewish identity—ethnicity, the local community, links with Jerusalem and other Diaspora communities, the Torah, and specifically Jewish practices and beliefs—was interwoven with the others. Together they enabled Diaspora communities to survive in very diverse circumstances.

That Diaspora Jewish identity was reinforced by this combination of factors meant that Diaspora Jews could interpret their traditions in many different ways. "It was not necessary, for instance, to interpret the ethnic bond only in terms of 'election' and 'covenant.' Other metaphors, derived from historical (Ezekiel) or political (Aristeas) spheres, could serve equally well so long as they fulfilled the requisite social functions" (Barclay, 443). This led to diversity in interpretations of Judaism in the Diaspora; unanimity was unnecessary, provided the various customs were preserved intact. This meant that Diaspora communities endured and flourished not by being isolated from their environment but by having clearly differentiated boundary markers at key points. This very strength meant Diaspora communities suffered hostility at times, precisely because they were considered a social and political offense as communities that remained unassimilated. [P. R. Trebilco]

11. Diaspora as Exile.

Although *Diaspora* often functions as a merely descriptive, neutral term, in many Jewish religious writings it is associated with *exile, with roots reaching back to the Babylonian captivity itself. The fact that Israel remained a country with free access to its temple and holy city, at times even more or less politically autonomous, until the defeat of *Simon ben Kosiba, means that traditions persist in seeing the scattered state of the Jewish people in negative terms.

This perspective is attested in diverse writings ranging from the Greek to the Roman periods. Jesus ben Sirach prays, "Gather all the tribes of Jacob and give them their inheritance, as at the beginning" (Sir 36:11; cf. 48:10). The righteous Tobit laments, "He has scattered us among them" (Tob 13:3). The author of 2 Maccabees comments, "We have hope in God that he will soon have mercy on us and will gather us from everywhere under heaven into his holy place" (2 Macc 2:18). Writing shortly after the Roman capture of Jerusalem in 63 B.C., the author of the *Psalms of Solomon* prays, "Bring together the dispersed of Israel with mercy and goodness" (*Pss. Sol.* 8:28). He anticipates that God will gather his people: "Sound in Zion the signal trumpet of the sanctuary; announce in Jerusalem the voice of one bringing good news . . . and look at your children, from the east and west assembled together by the Lord" (*Pss. Sol.* 11:1-4). Indeed, the Lord's Messiah "will distribute [the Jewish people] upon the land, according to their tribes" (*Pss. Sol.* 17:28). According to the author of the *Testament of Moses*, "the ten tribes will grow and spread out among the nations during the time of their captivity" (*T. Mos.* 4:9). The author does not have in mind primarily the Babylonian exile, but the ongoing dispersion of the Jewish people at the time of writing (c. A.D. 30).

Philo believes that this exile will come to an end, not by human effort but by divine power: "For even though they dwell in the uttermost parts of the earth, in slavery to those who led them away captive . . . one day will bring liberty to all . . . they will pass from exile to their home" (Philo *Praem. Poen.* 162-63). Following the disaster of A.D. 70, these hopes continue to be expressed. According to the author of *2 Baruch*, the Lord "will assemble all those again who were dispersed" (*2 Bar.* 78:7). The idea that God "will bring near our exiles" is expressed in the Targum, especially with respect to messianic expectation (cf. *Tg. Isa.* 53:8; *Tg. Hos.* 14:8; *Tg. Mic.* 5:1-3).

12. Diaspora in the New Testament.

In the NT the Diaspora is referred to in a more or less neutral sense (as in Jn 7:35 and Jas 1:1). But the Diaspora is also associated with exile, in reference to Israel's subjugation to the nations (particularly Rome), which only Messiah Jesus can remedy.

12.1. Jesus and the Gospels. Jesus says very little about the Diaspora. Nevertheless, two sayings may have important bearing on the question. In a saying found in Q, Jesus says, "I tell you, many will come from east and west and sit at table with Abraham, Isaac and Jacob in the kingdom of heaven" (Mt 8:11; cf. Lk 13:29, which also has "north and south"). Although many commentators have assumed that Jesus is speaking of Gentiles, it is more probable that he is speaking of Jews, as the allusion to Isaiah 43:5 ("I will bring your offspring from the east, and from the west I will gather you"), Zechariah 8:7 ("Behold, I will save my people from the east country and from the west country") and Psalm 107:3 ("gathered in from the lands, from the east and from the west, from the north and from the south") implies. The contrast lies between privileged Jews who live in the land of Israel under the shadow of the temple and have seen and heard Jesus personally (i.e., "sons of the kingdom," Mt 8:12) and less privileged Jews who live outside the Land (Allison).

Jesus' allusion to Isaiah 56:7, during his action in the temple precincts (Mk 11:17), also apparently envisions a regathering of the Jews of the Diaspora, including eunuchs and Gentiles (cf. Is 56:1-8). If the temple fulfills its God-given task, then it will be a place of worship for all, scattered Jews and even Gentiles who respect God (Evans; Hengel; Schnabel).

Finally, Jesus' appointment of the Twelve points to the restoration of the nation of Israel as a whole and to the renewal of the covenant. Implicit in the number twelve is the anticipation of the regathering of all twelve tribes, including the ten "lost" tribes.

12.2. Paul. For Paul, Israel's exile has more to do with spiritual blindness and hardness of heart and little to do with the geographical realities of the Diaspora. Israel is in bondage, not because many Jews are scattered and the Roman Empire dominates the land of Israel, but because the Jewish people attempt to establish their righteousness through the law.

However, Paul's missionary efforts attest to his concern that the gospel be preached to Jews in the Diaspora and not only to the Gentiles. His motto, "to the Jew first, then to the Greek" (Rom 1:16; 2:9-10; cf. Acts 13—18), reflects implicitly a commitment to the Jews of the Diaspora, who must hear the gospel, for "all Israel will be saved" (Rom 11:26).

12.3. General Epistles. James addresses his letter "to the twelve tribes in the Diaspora: Greeting" (Jas 1:1). There is no hint here of exile. But exile is associated with the Diaspora in the address of 1 Peter: "Peter, an apostle of Jesus Christ, To the exiles of the Diaspora in Pontus, Galatia, Cappadocia, Asia and Bithynia" (1 Pet 1:1). The author goes on to exhort Christian believers: "Beloved, I beseech you as aliens and exiles to abstain from the passions of the flesh that wage war against your soul. Maintain good conduct among the Gentiles" (1 Pet 2:11-12). Here we have the traditional Jewish picture: these "exiles" live among Gentiles in the Diaspora, awaiting redemption. [C. A. Evans]

13. Conclusions.

One feature to emerge from recent study of Diaspora Judaism is its diversity. Diversity within and among Diaspora communities is clearly apparent in a number of areas, including social status and conditions, wealth, size, community organization, assimilation, acculturation and accommodation. We must investigate each community and period as well as the particular circumstances of Jewish individuals and communities in each environment. Clearly factors such as when the Jews settled in a given city and under what conditions, how the community developed, ongoing relations with other groups and the number of new Jewish settlers over time were all crucial factors in the development of particular communities and their religious traditions, and these factors led to diversity among communities. This means that there were no typical Diaspora conditions; nor can we speak of a Diaspora Jew or a Diaspora community as typical.

It is also to be noted that Diaspora communities in the imperial period seem to have developed largely outside *rabbinic control and influence, so these communities were not directed by any central authority and should probably be thought of as nonrabbinic (see Rajak in Lieu, North and Rajak, 9-28). Without an authority to impose uniformity, great variety could develop in Diaspora Judaism, which became a complex and variegated phenomenon. We should also note that at least for a time Jewish Christian communities in the Diaspora would have been seen as one more dimension of this diversity.

Some earlier scholars thought that in order to remain as faithful Jews, it was necessary for Diaspora communities to live in social isolation. It is now recognized that although some Diaspora Jews probably did form tightly enclosed communities with relatively closed boundaries, many other Diaspora communities showed a higher degree of openness to their political, social and cultural environment. Yet clearly different Diaspora communities, with different sociocultural stances, continued to regard themselves as Jewish and maintained their identity as Jews over time while often expressing that Judaism in a particular way that varied from the practices of other Jewish communities. Thus we have been able to draw attention to a number of facets of Diaspora Jewish identity that enabled Jewish communities to endure as coherent entities over time and that meant that there was some commonality between different communities. We also have no evidence that Diaspora Jews were significantly involved in syncretism.

Literary and inscriptional sources indicate that some Jewish communities in the Diaspora continued to flourish until the end of antiquity. The presence of local Diaspora Jewish communities was often a real factor in the life of the early Christian churches. [P. R. Trebilco]

See also ALEXANDRIA; EXILE; HELLENISM; HELLENISTIC JUDAISM; INSCRIPTIONS AND PAPYRI: JEWISH; JEWISH LITERATURE: HISTORIANS AND POETS; ISRAEL, LAND OF; JEWISH COMMUNITIES IN ASIA MINOR; JUDAISM AND THE NEW TESTAMENT; PHILO; RULER CULT; SEPTUAGINT/GREEK OLD TESTAMENT; TEMPLE, JEWISH; THERAPEUTAE; WRITING AND LITERATURE: JEWISH.

BIBLIOGRAPHY. D. C. Allison Jr., "Who Will Come from East and West? Observations on Matt 8.11-12/Luke 13.28-29," *IBS* 11 (1989) 158-70; J. M. G. Barclay, *Jews in the Mediterranean Diaspora from Alexander to Trajan (323 BCE-117 CE)* (Edinburgh: T & T Clark, 1996); B. J. Brooten, *Leaders in the Ancient Synagogues: Inscriptional Evidence and Background Issues* (BJS 36; Chico, CA: Scholars Press, 1982); S. J. D. Cohen and E. S. Frerichs, eds., *Diasporas in Antiquity* (BJS 288; Atlanta: Scholars Press, 1993); J. J. Collins, *Between Athens and Jerusalem: Jewish Identity in the Hellenistic Diaspora* (New York: Crossroad, 1986); W. D. Davies, "Paul and the New Exodus," in *The Quest for Context and Meaning: Studies in Biblical Intertextuality in Honor of James A. Sanders*, ed. C. A. Evans and S. Talmon (BIS 28; Leiden: E. J. Brill, 1997) 443-63; C. A. Evans, "Aspects of Exile and Restoration in the Proclamation of Jesus and the Gospels," in *Exile: Old Testament, Jewish, and Christian Conceptions*, ed. J. M. Scott (JSJSup 56; Leiden: E. J. Brill, 1997) 299-328; L. H. Feldman, *Jew and Gentile in the Ancient World: Attitudes and Interactions from Alexander to Justinian* (Princeton, NJ: Princeton University Press, 1993); J. B. Frey, *Corpus Inscriptionum Judaicarum* (2 vols; vol. 1 originally published 1936, rev. B. Lifshitz; New York: Ktav, 1975; vol. 2, Rome: Pontificio Istituto di archaeologia christiana, 1952); S. J. Hafemann, "Paul and the Exile of Israel in Galatians 3—4," in *Exile: Old Testament, Jewish, and Christian Conceptions*, ed. J. M. Scott (JSJSup 56; Leiden: E. J. Brill, 1997) 329-71; M. Hengel, "The Origins of the Christian Mission," in *Between Jesus and Paul: Studies in the Earliest History of Christianity* (Philadelphia: Fortress, 1983) 48-64, 166-79; J. W. van Henten and P. W. van der Horst, eds., *Studies in Early Jewish Epigraphy* (AGJU 21; Leiden: E. J. Brill, 1994); W. Horbury and D. Noy, eds., *Jewish Inscriptions of Graeco-Roman Egypt* (Cambridge: Cambridge University Press, 1992); P. W. van der Horst, *Ancient Jewish Epitaphs* (Kampen: Kok Pharos, 1991); H. J. Leon, *The Jews of Ancient Rome*, introduction by

C. A. Osiek (updated ed.; Peabody, MA: Hendrickson, 1995); I. Levinskaya, *The Book of Acts in its Diaspora Setting* (BAFCS 5; Grand Rapids, MI: Eerdmans, 1996); J. Lieu, J. North and T. Rajak, eds., *The Jews Among Pagans and Christians in the Roman Empire* (London: Routledge, 1992); G. Lüderitz, *Corpus jüdischer Zeugnisse aus der Cyrenaika. Mit einem Anhang von J. M. Reynolds* (Beihefte zum Tübinger Atlas des Vorderen Orients, Reihe B, Nr. 53, Wiesbaden: Reichert, 1983); S. McKnight, *A Light Among the Gentiles: Jewish Missionary Activity in the Second Temple Period* (Minneapolis: Fortress, 1991); J. M. Modrzejewski, *The Jews of Egypt from Rameses II to Emperor Hadrian* (Philadelphia and Jerusalem: Jewish Publication Society of America, 1995); J. Neusner, ed., *Judaism in Late Antiquity: Part One, The Literary and Archaeological Sources; Part Two, Historical Synthesis* (HO 1.16-17; Leiden: E. J. Brill, 1995); D. Noy, *Jewish Inscriptions of Western Europe,* vol. 1: *Italy (Excluding the City of Rome), Spain and Gaul* (Cambridge: Cambridge University Press 1993); vol. 2: *The City of Rome* (Cambridge: Cambridge University Press, 1995); J. A. Overman and R. S. MacLennan, *Diaspora Jews and Judaism: Essays in Honor of, and in Dialogue with, A. Thomas Kraabel* (SFSHJ 41; Atlanta: Scholars Press, 1992); J. Reynolds and R. Tannenbaum, *Jews and Godfearers at Aphrodisias* (CPSSV 12; Cambridge: Cambridge Philological Society, 1987); S. Safrai and M. Stern, eds., *The Jewish People in the First Century* (2 vols.; CRINT 1; Assen: Van Gorcum; Philadelphia: Fortress Press, 1974-76); E. Schnabel, "Jesus and the Beginnings of the Mission to the Gentiles," in *Jesus of Nazareth: Lord and Christ,* ed. J. B. Green and M. Turner (Grand Rapids, MI: Eerdmans, 1994) 37-58; E. Schürer, *The History of the Jewish People in the Age of Jesus Christ (175 B.C.-A.D. 135),* rev. and ed. G. Vermes, F. Millar and M. Goodman (3 vols.; Edinburgh: T & T Clark, 1973-87); E. M. Smallwood, *The Jews Under Roman Rule: From Pompey to Diocletian* (2d ed.; Leiden: E. J. Brill, 1981); M. Stern, *Greek and Latin Authors on Jews and Judaism* (3 vols.; Jerusalem: Israel Academy of Sciences and Humanities, 1974, 1981, 1984); M. E. Stone, ed., *Jewish Writings of the Second Temple Period* (CRINT 2.2; Assen: Van Gorcum; Philadelphia: Fortress, 1984); V. Tcherikover, *Hellenistic Civilization and the Jews* (Philadelphia: Jewish Publication Society of America, 1961); V. Tcherikover and A. Fuks, *Corpus Papyrorum Judaicarum* (3 vols.; vol. 3 with M. Stern and D. M. Lewis; Jerusalem: Magnes; Cambridge, MA: Harvard University Press, 1957, 1960, 1964); P. R. Trebilco, *Jewish Communities in Asia Minor* (SNTSMS 69; Cambridge: Cambridge University Press, 1991); D. Urman and P. V. M. Flesher, *Ancient Synagogues: Historical Analysis and Archaeological Discovery* (2 vols.; SPB 47; Leiden: E. J. Brill, 1995).

P. R. Trebilco and C. A. Evans

DIATESSARON. *See* NEW TESTAMENT VERSIONS, ANCIENT.

DIATRIBE

Diatribe is a dialogical form of teaching in which the teacher proceeds to knowledge by means of question and answer with the students. A number of books in the NT, reflective of the wider use of diatribe in the Greco-Roman world, utilize diatribal literary techniques. The major question in discussion of diatribe with regard to the study of the NT is whether the diatribe constituted a literary form or *genre or whether it represents merely a set of literary conventions.

1. Authors of Diatribes Outside of the New Testament
2. Characteristics of Diatribe
3. Diatribe in the New Testament and Its Interpretive Significance

1. Authors of Diatribes Outside of the New Testament.

The diatribe became a well-known literary form in the Greco-Roman world and is reflected in a number of authors of importance for study of the NT. The diatribe perhaps has its basis in the dialogues of *Plato. Some of these literary constructions were probably based upon dialogues between Socrates and his disciples, but many of them may well have been greatly enhanced literarily by Plato, with some of them almost certainly his own creation. In these dialogues, Socrates engages in discussion with enquirers and leads himself and his discussion partner(s) to knowledge through positing and answering of questions. The process of discovering transpires through Socrates posing questions that lead the respondent either to suggest the answer or to defer to Socrates, at which point Socrates often develops the answer in greater length before moving the dialogue forward.

A number of authors in the Greco-Roman period made use of the techniques of diatribe.

Some of the best known include *Epictetus, Dio Chrysostom, Teles and *Musonius Rufus. Diatribes are also attributed to a number of other authors, especially *Stoic writers, for example, in Diogenes Laertius. The former *slave Epictetus, who became an itinerant *philosopher with a group of followers, has left eight books of his disputations with his followers. They are recorded by Arrian, who also wrote a history of *Alexander's conquest of Persia. They purport to be the record of Epictetus's conversations with his students, and a number of features suggest that they may be genuine. However, a number of features indicate that literary artifice is involved in these dialogues, presumably by Arrian in the course of recording these dialogues. Several of these features include consistent and stylized use of *rhetorical questions, distinctive phrasing by Epictetus and, perhaps most importantly, the feature of Epictetus's inevitable ability to respond appropriately.

2. Characteristics of Diatribe.

A number of features of diatribe are often cited as characterizing this literary form. Once these have been discussed, the question of whether diatribe constitutes a literary genre will be asked.

The major features of the diatribe are, first, its dialogical format. In many diatribes, such as those of Epictetus and Teles, there is what purports to be actual questioning and answering that is recorded, often with the questioner posing short questions that the philosopher-teacher answers. These questions and answers often involve the use of rhetorical questions, that is, questions in which the answer becomes obvious from the way that the dialogue has progressed and the question is posed. These questions also sometimes use the so-called hortatory subjunctive, in which the speaker includes himself in the question being asked, in the form of "should we say . . . ?" or the second person imperative. Often the questions and answers involve parallelism and balance in their construction, so it is obvious that the answer directly addresses the question being asked. This parallelism distinguishes much diatribe. Epictetus, like Paul but unlike most other writers of diatribe (see A. J. Malherbe), uses the phrase translated "may it never be" *(mē genoito)* a number of times as a response to a particularly outlandish suggestion in one of the rhetorical questions, showing the absurdity of such a proposal, which runs contrary to the wisdom of the teacher. In the course of making a moralistic appeal, the philosopher-teacher would often draw upon examples, and these would often involve citing a particular figure, such as an earlier philosopher or wise person, often referred to as an *exemplum*. Often connective words are used that heighten the dialogue (e.g., strong adversatives or contrastive statements).

In the late nineteenth and early twentieth centuries, diatribe was fairly widely recognized as a genre by such scholars as E. Norden and P. Wendland. In his 1910 work on Paul and *Cynic-Stoic diatribe, R. Bultmann took this position in his study. The conclusion at that time was that diatribe constituted a distinct literary form or genre, which was utilized by a number of writers of the ancient world, including some of those in the NT (see 3 below). This consensus did not last, however, with scholars soon afterward beginning to question and then abandon the concept of diatribe as a genre. After World War II, the view emerged that diatribe was to be seen as a literary style or set of techniques, often found in rhetorical philosophical prose.

In the most recent major studies, S. K. Stowers (1981) and T. Schmeller analyze the Pauline writings in terms of the diatribal characteristics rather than in terms of it being a distinct ancient genre. The same kind of debate is paralleled among recent discussion by classicists (see Porter for a survey of research). To a large extent, the debate over whether diatribe constitutes a distinctive genre reflects how the literature of the NT is being viewed by the scholarship of the time. In a period in which the books of the NT are being placed firmly within their Greco-Roman literary milieu or as the product of history of religions research, it is more typical to find advocates of NT diatribe as a genre in its own right. However, when the texts of the NT are being analyzed in terms of their being part of a specifically religious milieu, such as distinctive Jewish or Christian literature, the tendency is to see the diatribe as a set of literary conventions utilized within these other literary genres.

3. Diatribe in the New Testament and Its Interpretive Significance.

Several books within the NT can be characterized as diatribe, or at least as utilizing various features of the diatribe style. These include the book of James and some of Paul's letters, such as Romans and 2 Corinthians, among others. One of the major distinctives of the NT use of diatribe, however, is that the author of the respective book creates a fictive dialogue in which he writes both sides of the debate. This is particularly obvious in the use of rhetorical questions, where the biblical author guides the course of the argument by means of positing questions that he then answers.

The book of Romans provides one of the most instructive NT books for appreciating the features of diatribe. Scholars have seen elements of diatribe in at least Romans 2, 3, 4, 5, 6, 9, 11 and 14, if not others. Some of these features include the following. For example, in Romans 3:1-9 Paul carries on a dialogue with himself, posing rhetorical questions that he then answers in order to get at the issue of God's faithfulness, despite human failing. There are various ways to analyze these questions and answers in terms of which ones are to be put into the mouth of Paul's interlocutor and which ones into his own mouth, but Paul is writing both sides of the discussion (see Stowers 1984).

Paul also uses the rhetorical question with the hortatory subjunctive in such places as Romans 4:1 and 6:1 ("What then shall we say . . . ?"). In Romans 6:1 Paul responds to the absurdity that believers should continue to sin by answering "may it never be" *(mē genoito).* Romans 5 has many more features of diatribe than has often been recognized (see Porter). For example, if the better-attested textual variant is accepted in Romans 5:1, the section can begin with a hortatory subjunctive ("Let us enjoy peace with God"). There is also abundant parallelism throughout the chapter. Romans 5:9-11 makes parallel statements regarding justification, reconciliation and salvation. Romans 5:12-21 is also full of parallelism, in which statements are made of Christ and Adam. The use of Abraham in Romans 4, as well as Christ and Adam in Romans 5, illustrates the use of the *exemplum* (see Stowers 1981, 65-71), in which one person stands as an example for others. Other features in this and other books could be cited, but the above give an idea of how diatribal style is used in some places in Romans.

The interpretive significance of the use of diatribal style is severalfold. First, one can more fully appreciate the literary milieu in which certain books of the NT were written. They were written following recognized literary conventions of the Greco-Roman world, possibly even adapting a recognized literary genre. However, one can more fully appreciate the way in which the biblical author presents and develops his argument. Rather than consisting of the presentation of propositions, biblical books utilizing features of diatribe present their arguments in a progressive way that moves from point to point, often in the course of disputing the opposing views of others. Thus one must exercise caution in how much weight is placed upon any particular statement without considering the larger context in which this part of the argument is developed.

See also GENRES OF THE NEW TESTAMENT; RHETORIC.

BIBLIOGRAPHY. R. Bultmann, *Der Stil der paulinischen Predigt und die kynisch-stoische Diatribe* (FRLANT; Göttingen: Vandenhoeck & Ruprecht, 1984 [1910]); A. J. Malherbe, "ME GENOITO in the Diatribe and Paul," *HTR* 73 (1980) 231-40; E. Norden, *Die Antike Kunstprosa vom VI. Jahrhundert v. Chr. bis in die Zeit der Renaissance* (2 vols.; Darmstadt: Wissenschaftliche Buchgesellschaft, 1958, [1898]); S. E. Porter, "The Argument of Romans 5: Can a Rhetorical Question Make a Difference?" *JBL* 110 (1991) 655-77; T. Schmeller, *Paulus und die "Diatribe": Eine vergleichende Stilinterpretation* (Münster: Aschendorff, 1987); S. K. Stowers, "The Diatribe," in *Greco-Roman Literature and the New Testament,* ed. D. E. Aune (SBLSBS 21; Atlanta: Scholars Press, 1988) 71-83; idem, *The Diatribe and Paul's Letter to the Romans* (SBLDS 57; Chico, CA: Scholars Press, 1981); idem, "Paul's Dialogue with a Fellow Jew in Romans 3:1-9," *CBQ* 46 (1984) 707-22; P. Wendland, *Die hellenistisch-römische Kultur in ihren Beziehung zu Judentum und Christentum* (HNT 2; Tübingen: Mohr Siebeck, 1972 [1907]).

S. E. Porter

DIETARY LAWS, JEWISH. *See* PURITY.

DIONYSIUS OF HALICARNASSUS. *See* HISTORIANS, GRECO-ROMAN.

DIVINATION. *See* RELIGION, PERSONAL.

DIVORCE. *See* ADULTERY, DIVORCE.

DOMESTIC RELIGION AND PRACTICES

Domestic religion, briefly defined, is the practice of religion in the home or in private circumstances. At times this sort of religious expression may have been very public (such as in a wedding or a funeral), while other expressions would have been more closed, such as pouring out libations to gods before a meal or in the consummation of a *marriage. Nevertheless, these sorts of religious expression played a fundamental role in the experience of ancient peoples. This article focuses especially on the Roman period and makes references to domestic religion in the NT.

1. Domestic Religion in the Greco-Roman Period
2. Domestic Religion and the New Testament
3. Addendum on Syncretism

1. Domestic Religion in the Greco-Roman Period.

1.1. Roman Domestic Cult: The Gods of Family Life and the Families of the Great Gods. In a well-known passage, Augustine (*Civ. D.* 6.9.3) mocks the pagan belief in a variety of gods and goddesses related to the everyday aspects of life by cataloguing those deities connected with various aspects of the wedding night: "If there is any modesty among men, though there be none among the gods, when a bridal pair believe that so many gods of both sexes are present and intent on the operation, are they not so affected with shame that he will lose his ardour and she increase her resistance? And surely if the goddess Virginensis is there to undo the virgin's girdle, the god Subigus to subject her to her husband, the goddess Prema to keep her down when subjected so that she will not stir, then what job does the goddess Pertunda have here? Let her blush and go outside, let the husband have something to do!" This is, of course, an outsider's perspective. Nevertheless, this passage gives us an interesting picture of the intricate weaving of religious sensibilities into the daily life of the Roman people.

The chief gods of the home were the Genius (or protective spirit) of the master of the household, the Lar domesticus and the Penates. The center of this cult was the hearth, which "was in primitive times in the atrium, the common room, which it blackened with its smoke. When images of these gods were made, it was here that they were placed. Here too was where the *pater* said the family prayer and where, before the meal, he offered the household gods the first helpings of food and drink from the nearby table" (Dumézil, 2:611-12). The rhythms of family life were reflected in the cadences of domestic cult, and the theology of the Roman cult used this as the basic building block in its understanding of how the gods related one to another. Dumézil's theory concerning the organization of the multiplicity of minor gods suggests that the "catalogs of *indigitamenta* [i.e., lists of gods associated with various aspects of daily life like marriage, agriculture, etc.] are not breeding grounds for the gods" (Dumézil 1:35), as some have suggested, but rather that the "minor entities grouped in one of these lists are as it were the *familia* of a 'great' god" (Dumézil 1:38). This traditional reflexive relationship between Roman society and religion was one of the key aspects underscoring the importance of Roman devotion to the ancestral cult.

1.2. Domestic Religion and Social Upheaval in the Hellenistic Period. In the wake of *Alexander the Great's conquests, the structures of *family and city life, including the traditional, stabilizing roles of *civic cults and domestic religion, were thrown into a degree of flux. Personal mobility—geographical, social, financial, etc.—was possible in a way not previously experienced in the Mediterranean world, and this mobility brought about change to the religious structures of the traditional cultures of the entire Mediterranean basin. The *interpretatio graeca* (the identification of others' gods in Greek terms) is perhaps the best-known element in the new drive toward the conglomeration of religious sensibilities, but too much emphasis can be placed on the syncretistic characteristics of religion in this period (see 3 below). As with modern society, the most conservative unit in society tends to be the family. If one were looking for an area where a reactionary trend might be found, certainly domestic religious practices and sensibilities must represent one such force. (Hence, as with Rome, whose famous concern for societal responsibilities and adherence to tradition marked it as different from surrounding groups, so must the strong reliance on tradition and family within Jewish practice help to explain its ability to resist syncretism in many quarters.)

The marked societal movement which characterized both the Hellenistic period and that of Rome's early expansion into the East (*see* Roman East) often brought with it a concomitant weakening of the traditional building blocks of both Greek and non-Greek society. As the article on voluntary *associations in this dictionary makes clear, Greco-Roman society grew during this period to allow for the enfranchisement of those members of society who, traditionally, would have been so enfranchised through family and *polis*—the voluntary association allowed those who had been left out of the life of the *polis* to find a valid role within an identifiable group. As discussed in that article, it is clear that, without known exception, voluntary associations were religious in character, though to differing degrees. This Greco-Roman social phenomenon must surely, then, likewise be within the rubric of "domestic religion."

2. Domestic Religion and the New Testament. The NT contains comparatively few scenes of daily household life. Various scenes and vignettes from the life of Jesus as represented in the Gospels do allow us glimpses into several Jewish households (e.g., dining with Zacchaeus, Lk 19:1-10; the meal with the disciples in Emmaus, Lk 24:28-35), and, by definition, most of what Jesus does in these instances could be construed to be "religious." This introduces a difficulty in discussing "domestic religion" in the NT, for, as with everything in the Gospels, we are constantly faced with issues of authenticity. In the case of religious or liturgical actions undertaken by Jesus—especially those that are somehow mirrored in the developed Christian cult—the tenets of form criticism suggest that we are in even deeper difficulty than in other instances, for many of these scenes and vignettes are easily lent to interpretations which suggest that their genesis was not in the lifetime of Jesus but rather in the cultic celebrations of the early Christians. Or, perhaps more moderately, one could suggest that their form as represented in the Gospels may reflect *not only* the story of Jesus but *also* the liturgical needs of the early Christian communities.

An excellent example of this is, of course, the representation of the Last Supper (Mt 26:17-30; Mk 14:12-26; Lk 22:7-31; Jn 13:21-36)—an event which, by its very definition, represents not only domestic religion (for how else can the Passover meal be thought of?) but also a defining moment in what would eventually become a very nondomestic event. This reveals a tension that is seemingly inherent in any discussion of domestic religion in the NT: at its inception and for centuries afterwards, *the entire Christian movement could be construed as a domestic cult.* Christian worship took place in homes (*see* Family and Household). There were no public buildings (*see DLNTD,* Architecture, Early Church). Even in Jerusalem, where it appears that Christians were, to some degree, still involved in the *temple cult, the specifically *Christian* element of their religious practice took place elsewhere, and most probably in the homes of its wealthier members (Acts 2:2; cf. Philem 1; Rom 16:3-5).

It is possible to construe the house churches of the earliest Christian communities as representatives of the wider social phenomenon of voluntary associations (*see* Associations for further discussion of this point). The brief discussion of associations above (see 1 above) outlines a means by which we might then characterize—at least in its early days—the whole of Christianity as "domestic religion." In many ways this perspective could allow us new insights into the way in which we try to reconstruct the early Christians' ideas of how their "religion," or perhaps their religious sensibilities, fit into the wider religious makeup of their societies. One danger faced by all who wish to view the NT historically is that gaps in our knowledge about the time of the NT—especially those gaps that are not perceived as such—will be filled in by our own modern understandings. In the case of positioning earliest Christianity within the religious makeup of different Mediterranean societies, this becomes especially difficult after the larger part of two millennia of the church's religious dominance in most Western societies. No matter what our country of origin or residence, we are likely familiar with the idea of a church building and, indeed, with church buildings of great immensity. The ancient cathedrals and churches of Europe and Asia, the crystal cathedrals of North America, the great sites of pilgrimage in South America—these are all locations of Christian public worship, past and present—and they have left an indelible mark on our understanding of the place of Christianity within the religious makeup of society as a whole. This, however, was not the case in the earliest days of the church. As suggested above, we would perhaps do better to construe earliest Christianity as primarily a domestic religion, whose identity is not equivalent to that of modern or even post-Constantinian Christianity.

There are, however, elements of the NT that seem to reflect the more traditional definition of "domestic religion," such as that characterized above (see 1.1 above) by Dumézil. One thinks here especially of the conversion of entire households in the book of Acts (e.g., Acts 16:33, the conversion of the household of the Philippian jailer; and Acts 18:8, the conversion of the household of the *archisynagōgos*, Crispus), and those mentioned by Paul (e.g., 1 Cor 1:16). This sort of action, often discussed in connection with the appropriate *time* of baptism for a Christian (i.e., in infancy, or upon some sort of adult decision), could also play a very important role in determining how the tradition of a domestic religious cult headed by the *paterfamilias* functions in earliest Christianity (Hartman, 135-36, comes close to seeing this). The household baptisms in Acts come at three or four junctures in the book: two at Philippi (the households of the jailer, mentioned above, and of Lydia, Acts 16:14-15) and one at Corinth (the household of Crispus). Likewise, it may be that Peter's baptism of the centurion Cornelius and those in his household represents a similar household baptism, but in this case, it would appear that the audience is somewhat larger than merely the household of Cornelius (cf. Acts 10:24), and the baptism at the end of chapter 10 of those who hear Peter's message does not use the same language as in the three mentioned cases of Paul's baptisms of whole households. This is not the place for an extended discussion of the nature of these passages. Yet, no matter what one makes theologically of the baptism of an entire household, the idea that whole households had now become part of the new religion must have spoken volumes to Roman readers of Acts. These converts were more than merely individuals who were now joining a fringe group, or even (avoiding a value judgment) joining a group whose identity was that of a voluntary association without the same value of traditional Roman religion. In at least these three instances in the book of Acts, the author portrays Christianity as a religion at least partly in the traditional mold.

The above paragraphs are not meant to give the impression that Christianity was simply another voluntary association like all the rest—possibly even trying to capitalize on traditional religious values usurped by other domestic voluntary associations. The Christian groups of the earliest centuries exhibited differences from these standard varieties. Christian local specificity was not, in our opinion, as realized as in most specifically religious voluntary associations (cf. Pearson 46 n. 11 on the local nature of the different groupings of one such cult in the Roman world). The lines of communication between different Christian communities and the interchange of ideas, writings, teachings and controversies so common to the later church seem, at least to some degree, to have distinguished the Christian endeavor from the beginning. Nor was the kind of countercultural message of the earliest Christian church something that could sit entirely comfortably with, or function as an exact replacement for, traditional domestic religious practice.

Instead, we might say that Christianity *functioned* within the vacuum created by the demise of the traditional domestic religious practices of its adherents (or that more amorphous space opened up by the wide-scale social movement within the Greco-Roman world). Yet this does not constitute sufficient evidence to establish its *identity* as a domestic cult (if "domestic cult" could even be construed as an independent category). Its emergence into the light as a tolerated and eventually official religion of the Roman Empire gives us an indication that Christianity, while occupying the above-mentioned space, was nevertheless quite able to expand into the larger stage without much difficulty.

3. Addendum on Syncretism.

Syncretism is difficult to define, for its identity seems to revolve around a resistance to definitions and the blending of categories. In the period of the NT, as mentioned above, there was a tension between a variety of differing religious sensibilities. On the one hand, the Roman Empire was built on the strength of tradition and a strong "Roman" identity. The strict social stratification of Roman society was even represented within the way traditional Roman religion was conceived by its practitioners, and the responsibility of Roman citizens to observe the ancestral cult was keenly felt (cf. Cicero *Flac.* 28; La Piana, 325).

On the other hand, the *interpretatio graeca* represents the attempt in the Hellenistic period to essentially do away with those boundaries. On one level, this was represented by such things as the identification of various ethnic gods as simply different names for the same deity. On a different level, this represented the move to de-localize the worship of various gods, making them into deities whose worship was both transportable and transplantable.

The first of these two levels is clearly demonstrated in Plutarch's discussion of the Egyptian religion, especially the common identification of Osiris with Dionysus (Plutarch *Is. Os.* 356B; 362B; 364E-65B; 377D: "But as for Isis, and the gods associated with her, all peoples own them and are familiar with them, although they have learned not so long ago to call some of them by the names which come from the Egyptians," 377F LCL; cf. also Diodorus Siculus *Bib. Hist.* 1.11.3-4; 1.13.5; 1.22.6-7). Another striking passage in this regard is Diodorus Siculus *Bibliotheca Historica* 1.25.1-2, where he discusses the identification of Sarapis with Dionysus, Zeus, Pluto, Ammon and Pan.

The second level is observable in the spread of nontraditional religions in various forms throughout the Roman world. A striking example of this is in the development of the Phrygian Mother Goddess cult in Rome itself. La Piana (297, cf. 335-37) assesses the Claudian legalization of this cult as follows: "this grant, which was a departure from tradition, could not fail to create a precedent and to mark a turning-point in the religious policies of the government. There were sound motives behind it . . . the oriental cults had gained a firm foothold in Rome and were a real power in the life of the masses. To ignore them officially was to let them develop and spread without public control, a bad policy for a government so suspicious of all associations . . . it seemed better and safer to bring them entirely within the law, rather th[a]n let them live by toleration or privilege." This reflects both the desire to transport and transplant gods and the role that Roman sensibilities played in both blocking and facilitating this ongoing movement of different religious practices throughout the empire.

See also ASSOCIATIONS; FAMILY AND HOUSEHOLD; FESTIVALS AND HOLY DAYS: GRECO-ROMAN; IDOLATRY, JEWISH CONCEPTION OF; RELIGION, GRECO-ROMAN; RELIGION, PERSONAL; RULER CULT; TEMPLES, GRECO-ROMAN.

BIBLIOGRAPHY. G. Dumézil, *Archaic Roman Religion* (2 vols.; Chicago: University of Chicago Press, 1970 [1966]); L. Hartman, *"Into the Name of the Lord Jesus": Baptism in the Early Church* (SNTW; Edinburgh: T & T Clark, 1997); G. La Piana, "Foreign Groups in Ancient Rome During the First Centuries of the Empire," *HTR* 20 (1927) 183-403; A. de Marchi, *Il Culto privato di Roma antica* (2 vols; Milan: U. Hoepli, 1896, 1903); B. W. R. Pearson, "Baptism and Initiation in the Isis and Sarapis Cult," in *Baptism, the New Testament and the Church: Historical and Contemporary Studies in Honour of R. E. O. White*, ed. S. E. Porter and A. R. Cross (JSNTSup 171; Sheffield: Sheffield Academic Press, 1999) 42-61; N. Turchi, *La religione di Roma antica* (Storia di Roma 18; Bologna: L. Cappelli, 1939). B. W. R. Pearson

DOSITHEANS. *See* SAMARITANS.

DOWRY. *See* MARRIAGE.

DREAMS AND DIVINATION. *See* RELIGION, PERSONAL.

DUALISM. *See* APOCALYPTICISM.

E

ECCLESIASTICUS. *See* SIRACH.

ECONOMICS OF PALESTINE

The economic historian Karl Polanyi noted that there have been two senses of the word *economic:* a substantive economics that strives to provide the necessities of life for the individual, family, tribe or society; and a formal economics that refers to rational choices between scarce means in the pursuit of human ends.

While both of these senses are applicable to antiquity, the ancients tended to think consciously about economics primarily in the first sense. For them, economics had essentially to do with the management of the household (Gk *eco/oikos,* "house"; *nomia,* "management"). "Household" could mean the family homestead, the large estate or even the imperial realm (*see* Family and Household). Since the fundament of ancient economics was agriculture, both Greek and Roman literature produced moralistic treatises on this subject (Xenophon, Cato). In NT times, the *Roman Empire was managed by the imperial powers as an extended household. Easy access to the Mediterranean Sea encouraged maritime trade in the Hellenistic-Roman periods, but this was controlled by elites or their agents (Trimalchio in *The Satyricon* of Petronius).

Thus it is equally crucial in considering the economics of Palestine in the biblical periods to keep in mind that social ends were determined by powerful elites, and so ancient economy was political economy. Moreover, in the conservative, traditional agrarian societies of antiquity, individual or even group economic choice was a relatively limited factor in the context of larger ecological and social forces.

1. Palestine as a Region of Mediterranean Ecological Adaptation
2. Agrarian Economy and Society Within the Bible
3. The Economic Values of Jesus
4. Economic Factors in Early Christianity and the Later New Testament Period

1. Palestine as a Region of Mediterranean Ecological Adaptation.

F. Braudel referred to the Mediterranean region as the land around the Mediterranean Sea from the limit of the olive to the north to the appearance of the palm to the south. As a part of the Mediterranean littoral, Palestine has always been characterized by peculiar ecological factors pertinent to a discussion of economics. Geology and climate have unquestionably shaped ecological-economic dynamics and related human adaptations. Since the Cretaceous period, the Mediterranean area has experienced severe faulting and on the south tectonic stresses and repeated encroachments by the sea itself. The geology of Palestine shows these features well in its abrupt transitions between lowlands and mountain; its extensive limestone formations, combined to the north with volcanic features; and its rainfall and weather patterns that produce the typical Mediterranean vegetation pattern of "evergreen thicket-woodland" (Hepper).

The Mediterranean climate of Palestine produces rainfall in the winter and drought in the summer. With as little as 50 meters annually in the Negev increasing to 800 meters or more in Upper Galilee and the Lebanese Mountains, dry-farming methods of agriculture need to prevail. Plowing breaks only the topsoil in order to preserve the subsoil moisture; grains and trees are naturally selected that have quick growing properties or can survive the annual drought. The Bible, therefore, characterizes Canaan as "a land of wheat and barley, of vines and fig trees and pomegranates, a land of olive trees and honey" (Deut 8:8 NRSV). The difficulty of agriculture in ancient Palestine is also acknowledged (Gen 3:17-19). Biblical parables often speak through the imagery of the typical vegetation (Judg 9:8-15) or familiar agricultural operations such as sowing (Mk 4:3), harvesting grain (Mk 4:29) or gathering the vintage (Mt 20:1; see Rev 14:19-20).

The main agricultural objects of production were grain, especially barley and wheat, olives for oil and grapes for wine. Grain, wine and oil were the staples of life (Hos 9:2, 4; Prov 9:5; Neh 5:11). Grain was harvested in late spring and early summer; grapes were gathered and processed in summer, olives in early fall. The early rains of September-October helped to prepare the soil hardened by drought for plowing. Once sown, growing grain had to be weeded and was threatened by many natural predators (Mt 13:26; Mk 4:4-7). The late rains of winter helped the cereals to mature toward harvest in late spring. The average yield was around fivefold, compared with thirty- or fortyfold today (aided by modern fertilizers). Fig and olive trees often appear in the Bible because they, along with the grapevine, can withstand the summer drought. Such trees have wide-spreading or deep root systems to capture water and pass a minimal amount of moisture to the air through their leaves. Fig and olive trees take time to come into bearing years and so are associated in the Bible with peaceful times (1 Kings 4:25; Mic 4:4; 1 Macc 14:12).

Herding played an important role in biblical economy as well. Goat's milk and cheese supplemented the proteins and calories from grain and oil. Sheep appear in biblical parables (2 Sam 12:1-4; Lk 15:3-7). Animals might be *sacrificed for their meat, though ordinary people partook of meat only on important occasions (Lk 15:23). The temple economy depended upon significant numbers of animal offerings per year (Josephus *Ant.* 3.9.1 §§224-32).

Some generalizations can be made about the organization of production and labor, as well as distribution and consumption, in the biblical periods. Preindustrial societies depended mainly upon human and animal energies devoted to producing enough to eat. Such societies have been called agrarian societies because they were made possible by the plow (Lenski). In agrarian societies, a social chasm always existed between the relatively few elite urban and town dwellers whose energies were devoted to politics or religious occupations and the many villagers who tilled the soil. The finite surplus made possible by preindustrial agriculture placed restraints on the absolute size of the elite. The long sweep of ancient Near Eastern history witnessed a succession of world empires whose civilizations were dependent upon collecting the agrarian surpluses of the sedentary agriculturalists. The earliest known writings often have to do with accounting in royal and temple operations. Village economy in such empires was focused on domestic need and agriculture; urban economy was based on taxation of surplus and redistribution for elite ends.

While the Greco-Roman society of the NT period was more complex than that of predecessor societies, especially in the encouragement of Mediterranean commerce, its population was still divided between the majority who labored (around 90 percent) and the elite fraction of the population who did not and whose estates worked by tenants or *slaves supplied the necessities of life (Mt 13:24-30; Lk 12:16-21). Strong rulers could also utilize peasant labor to build aqueducts, temples, palaces and cities (Herod the Great: Sebaste, *Caesarea Maritima, *Jerusalem).

Josephus's claim that "ours is not a maritime country" (Josephus *Ag. Ap.* 1.12 §60) rings true for the biblical literature, except that in special circumstances elites did take advantage of trading opportunities offered by caravans to the east or sea-lanes to the west. Both villager and city dweller sought self-sufficiency, having all of the necessaries stored up or readily available near-by. Commercial ventures and fine imported wines and wares were available only to powerful elites. Pliny relates that frankincense caravan tolls for a trip from Sabota (in Arabia) to Gaza on the Mediterranean coast ran to 688 denarii per camel (Pliny *Nat. Hist.* 12.63-65; a denarius was a day's wage on an estate [Mt 20:2]).

Villagers not only labored to raise agricultural produce but also made their own clothing, sandals, simple tools and even houses. Specialists, usually holding monopolistic power and controlled by powerful families, produced pottery, glass vessels, metal tools and weaponry, fine furniture, and the like. Literate elites nonetheless looked down on all who worked with their hands (Sir 38:25-34). Free markets hardly existed in the ancient world; participants in urban markets, except for small-value exchanges, traded on very unequal terms. Money was essentially an elite tool to facilitate tax collection or to aid elite-sponsored commerce. For the majority of the population, after they had paid their taxes there was barely enough to eat.

Such an ecological adaptation encouraged certain values within biblical culture. Low productivity and social inequities encouraged a notion of limited good, in which the goods of life were believed to have been distributed and could not be increased absolutely (in contrast to modern, postindustrial values in which productivity is ever-increasing). Biblical references to the evil eye are manifestations of limited-good beliefs—evil eye refers to the envious glance that would lead to seizure of what is not rightfully one's own (Prov 23:1-6; 28:22; Mt 20:15).

2. Agrarian Economy and Society Within the Bible.

Economic justice was a constant preoccupation in biblical times. W. Brueggemann has identified a useful paradigm by which to discuss social tensions within Israelite traditions. In discussing the "royal consciousness" exhibited by Pharaoh in Egypt and again by Israelite monarchs like Solomon, Brueggemann analyzes agrarian social dynamics in terms of a politics of oppression, an economics of affluence and a religion of immanence. Just as Rameses II, a god on earth, had conscripted the Israelites as forced labor (Ex 1:11), so Solomon was remembered ambivalently by the Deuteronomistic historians as both wise and oppressive (1 Kings 4:29-31; 5:12 contrasts with 1 Kings 9:15-22). The usurpations of Israelite kings were condemned in traditions like 1 Samuel 8:11-18 or the story of Naboth's vineyard (1 Kings 21). Conversely, Moses and the prophets appear as Yahweh's champions, as critics of a religious ideology that underwrites the royal arrangements. Elite economics is thus organized around the provisioning of the royal estate (1 Kings 4:22-28) as well as the royal temple (1 Kings 6).

Biblical law is concerned with justice in economic arrangements—for instance, regarding slaves (Ex 21:2-11; Deut 15:12-18), property and damages (Ex 22) or the regulation of debt (Deut 15). The classical prophets, with varying emphasis, denounce "immanent religion" and economic injustice (Amos 5:21-24; 8:4-6; Is 1:10-17; Mic 2:1-2). Of special concern are the widow and the orphan (Ex 22:22; Is 1:17). Israelite wisdom too mulls over the plight of the poor and the persistence of the wicked wealthy (Prov 22:16, 22-23; Eccles 4:1-3). Poverty in the Bible means not only powerlessness and physical want but also public disgrace and shame (Malina).

The context of Jesus likewise was afflicted by social disparities and concerns (Lk 16:19-31). In his day, Palestine had been under the control of great world empires since the Babylonian exile. *Hasmonean rule (1 Macc 13:41-42) marked about a century's exception (142-63 B.C.). The house of Herod the Great provided client rule for the Romans at the turn of the eras. Jesus' parables often describe the typical social features of a colonial situation with large estates controlled by absentee landlords: A landlord's departure provides the occasion for moneylending by retainers (Lk 19:12-27). A landlord has to resort to violence to collect the rent (Mk 12:1-9). A tax collector secures the tax with his own body (Mt 18:23-34). Estate stewards (*oikonomoi*, "household managers") and slaves make frequent appearances (Lk 12:42; 16:1-8; Mk 13:34-35).

Many of these social features are common to agrarian or peasant societies. Comparative studies have shown that preindustrial societies often have enormous social disparities and inequities, that economic phenomena are controlled by powerful centralized or urban elites and that injustice is regularly experienced by the majority. The biblical traditions set the stage for a more hopeful type of human relations. Such hopes come into sharp focus in some of the Mosaic traditions, the prophets and especially Jesus of Nazareth.

3. The Economic Values of Jesus.

The recent third quest for the historical Jesus and Galilean studies enhanced by archaeology have reinvigorated the question of the relationship of the historical activity of Jesus of Nazareth to economic dimensions of his contemporary society. While many aspects of this discussion are as yet undecided and debate centers especially around the social character of Jesus' environment and the movement that emerged through his activity, it is clear that Jesus paid careful attention to economic phenomena. These were entwined with the meaning of his work, and understanding those phenomena can enhance our understanding of Jesus.

Central to the vision of Jesus of Nazareth was his conviction that the reign of God (Aram *malkûtha' dišmayā'*) was imminent or even present in his activity. Scholars debate the degree to which Jesus' vision should be construed through wisdom perspectives (God's reign is integral to creation or the natural order [Lk 12:22-31]) or through *apocalyptic Jewish elements, which surely appear in the Gospels (Mk 13:26-27). The question of the meaning of the reign of God for Jesus depends upon such assessments.

There is strong evidence that Jesus associated God's reign with his own activity. It is likely that some aspects of this phrase resonated with the views of Judas the Gaulanite or Galilean (Josephus *Ant.* 18.1.1 §4; 18.6.6 §23), since Jesus gained a following in the vicinity of the Galilean lake. Jesus can refer to God's power at work in his exorcisms (Lk 11:20, alluding to Ex 8:19). He also showed strong interest in Passover, the time for remembrance of God's liberation of the Israelites from Egyptian bondage. The passion narratives link Jesus' understanding of God's reign with Passover (Mk 14:22-25 and par.). There are perhaps echoes of the beginning of the Passover Haggadah in Jesus' Q-Sermon:

Passover Haggadah (Aramaic introduction): This is the bread of poverty which our forefathers ate in the land of Egypt. Let all who are hungry enter and eat; let all who are needy come to our Passover feast. This year we are here; next year may we be in the Land of Israel. This year we are slaves; next year may we be free men (Glatzer).

Passover Haggadah	Q-Beatitudes (Lk 6:20-21)
The bread of poverty	Blessed are you poor
Let all who are hungry	Blessed are the hungry
This year we are here	Blessed are those who mourn

Central in the early Jesus traditions is also a concern for debt and taxation. The politics of oppression familiar to first-century Galileans had to do with the Roman colonial arrangements of client rule. After Judas the Gaulanite and the revolt surrounding the census of A.D. 6, questions about taxation became loaded. Jesus did not speak openly against imperial taxation (Mk 12:17), but he did suggest to his disciples that the "sons are free" of *temple taxation (Mt 17:26; *see DJG*, Taxes).

In the Lord's Prayer (Lk 11:2-4/Mt 6:9-13) God's rule is related directly to release from indebtedness and concomitant taxation. While a complete analysis of the prayer is not possible here, the petitions seem internally integrated by reference to social-systemic problems: Hunger (Lk 11:3/Mt 6:11) is a function of indebtedness to landlord or overlord (Lk 11:4a/Mt 6:12), and the courts enforced debt contracts (Lk 11:4b/Mt 6:13) if the tradition about Hillel's *prosbol* is to be trusted (*m. Šeb.* 10.3-7; *b. Giṭ.* 37a; Murabba'at 18, a mid-first-century debt contract from the Dead Sea area, secures a loan without the *prosbol*). Relations of indebtedness have as their social corollary that the few will have security in more than they need. Jesus carries on a vigorous critique against *mamōnas*, "mammon" (Gk, from an Aramaic word), signifying stored wealth upon which one places trust (Lk 12:16-20; 16:13).

One of Jesus' strategies was to go to the friction point between the Greco-Roman order and the harassed producers. Jesus ate with tax collectors and "sinners" (debtors?) in order to achieve some relief for the indebted (Mk 2:15-16; Lk 18:9-14). The story of Zacchaeus (Lk 19:1-10), however one judges its authenticity, captures the economic import of such associations.

Jesus thus spoke in behalf of a politics of liberation and compassion (Borg). For Jesus, God's rule was a power opposed to the social order established by *Rome. Its arrival offered the poor and lowly a vision of hope and new social possibilities, just as in the first exodus. What did Jesus envision constructively as an expression of that rule? He offers a theology of paradoxical transcendence (*malkûtha'*, "reign") and immanence (*'Abba'*, "Father"). God's rule overthrows the dominant political economy in favor of a fictive family. Political economy is to be transformed into domestic economy, a vision consonant with the traditions of Israel (Deut 15:2; Lev 25:35-46; Neh 5:6-13).

Relations within Jesus' entourage are to be modeled on those of close kin. Exchanges are to take place through arrangements of generalized reciprocity (Lk 6:27-36; 14:12-14; Mt 18:23-34). Generalized reciprocity, unlike the redistributive arrangements of the dominant powers, takes no accounting of exchanges. Seeking the reign of God first will bring carefree economic security and true happiness (Lk 12:22-31; Mk 10:29-30).

Jesus' vision of the reign of God and his concomitant call for human solidarity against injustice through fictive kin relations apparently was rejected by worldly wise villagers. The message made sense to fishers and some alienated peasants, but Jesus' reception in Nazareth seems to have been typical (Mk 6:4). He garnered no large-scale peasant following. No vestiges of Galilean Christianity are apparent in the years after his death. The horizon of most peasants is limited; discontent does not often consolidate into transvillage movements. When Jesus was crucified in Jerusalem as a bandit, a rebel against the Roman order, not only did his popular support vanish, but also he was abandoned for a time even by his close associates. Experience of his resurrection signified a new stage of his cause, and his message would be carried beyond Palestine within a new social stratum.

4. Economic Factors in Early Christianity and the Later New Testament Period.

Jesus' hope for a more humane economic order did not die. The Gospels continued to mediate his economic interests and values to later Christian communities, though interests appropriate to town and urban contexts also come into view. W. A. Meeks gives evidence that a substantial role was played in early Christian communities by freedmen, those former slaves who were now legally free though sometimes still obligated to former patrons. Freedmen tended to be involved in trade and commercial pursuits, a point that seems generally corroborated about leaders in the Christian circles of the eastern Mediterranean by the Acts of the Apostles (e.g., Acts 16:14-15; 18:2-3).

Such interests are already evident in the Pauline literature. Paul indicates that urban Christian groups such as those in *Corinth are comprised of few who could be recognized as elite (1 Cor 1:26; note that birth and power are key social variables, not economics). The Corinthian community is sundered by inequities of social power and wealth (1 Cor 11:22). It is patronized by powerful people like Erastus, the city treasurer (Rom 16:23) but networks with others who have lesser status (Stephanus, 1 Cor 16:15). The Corinthian correspondence well illustrates that early Christian groups were organized around households, with the more powerful and wealthy as sponsors of a fictive-kinship assembly/*ekklēsia* (1 Cor 16:15, 19; Philem 1-2). D. Georgi has argued that Paul's collection (1 Cor 16:1-4; 2 Cor 8—9) was an animating issue in his historical activity, both an expression of solidarity with the Jerusalem church (Gal 2:10) and a statement of conviction about the eschatological ingathering of the Gentiles anticipated in the Israelite prophetic tradition (Is 45:14, 20, 22-25). This collection already represents an anomaly in terms of Jesus' interests, since a collection is a redistributive tax (like the temple tax sent in the first century by Diaspora Jews to Jerusalem).

In the later first century, issues of political economy present recurrent moral difficulties for the developing Christian movement. Revelation states the situation in apocalyptic terms (Rev 13:16-17; 18:3, 9, 11, 15-18). Jesus' loyal followers are those who have no truck with Roman commerce (Rev 2:9; 3:8, 17; 13:16-17). Others, however, are perceived to have been permanently corrupted (Rev 2:14-15, 20; 3:9; probably cryptic references to Christians who compromise with Greco-Roman culture in pursuit of economic interests). Acts provides a more irenic picture of the Christian position under the Roman Empire. Roman justice furthers the interests of the movement (Acts 18:15; 26:31-32). Commerce is not demonized as in Revelation (or *Gos. Thom.* 64). Moreover, economic relations within the early Christian community are viewed in communistic terms (Acts 2:44-45; 4:32, 36-37; see 1QS 6:22).

The paraenesis of James identifies central economic problems for the future. As the Christian movement experienced success, wealth became a divisive issue (Jas 2:1-7), and social injustice emerged clearly as an intra-Christian concern (Jas 2:16; 5:4). James exhorts the wealthy to take stock (Jas 1:9-10; 5:1-6) and to practice the royal law of neighborly love (Jas 2:8; cf. 1:25). With similar moral stress, Acts reports that Jesus "himself said, 'It is more blessed to give than to receive'" (Acts 20:35, the only explicit saying of Jesus in the NT preserved outside the Gospels; see Lk 22:26). The moral standing of wealth becomes a permanent concern of the Christian tradition, leading to later developments such as Clement of Alexandria's treatise *Quis Dives Salvetur?* and the Franciscan movement in medieval Italy or the Anabaptist communities of the Reformation. Jesus' followers are still left perhaps with uneasy consciences in times that celebrate mammon and the successes of industrial and technological capitalism.

See also BENEFACTOR; COINAGE, JEWISH; FAMILY AND HOUSEHOLD; PATRONAGE; SLAVERY; SOCIAL VALUES AND STRUCTURES; TAXATION, GRECO-ROMAN; TAXATION, JEWISH; TRAVEL AND TRADE.

BIBLIOGRAPHY. K. E. Bailey, "Agriculture," "Clothing," "Crafts," "Houses, Furniture, Utensils," "Trade and Transport," in *The Oxford Companion to the Bible,* ed. B. M. Metzger and M. D. Coogan (New York: Oxford University Press, 1993) 18-19, 125-26, 139-40, 293-99, 748-49; M. J. Borg, *Jesus: A New Vision* (San Francisco: Harper & Row, 1987); F. Braudel, *The Mediterranean and the Mediterranean World in the Age of Philip II* (2d ed.; 2 vols.; New York: Harper & Row, 1972-73); W. Brueggemann, *The Prophetic Imagination* (Philadelphia: Fortress, 1978); L. W. Countryman, *The Rich Christian in the Church of the Early Empire: Contradictions and Accommodations* (New York: Edwin Mellen Press, 1980); D. Georgi, *Remembering the Poor: The History of Paul's Collection for Jerusalem* (Nashville: Abingdon, 1992); N. N. Glatzer, *The Passover Haggadah* (3d ed.; New York: Schocken, 1979); K. C. Hanson and D. E. Oakman, *Palestine in the Time of Jesus: Social Structures and Social Conflicts* (Minneapolis: Fortress, 1998); F. N. Hepper, *Baker Encyclopedia of Bible Plants* (Grand Rapids, MI: Baker, 1992); R. A. Horsley, *Archaeology, History and Society in Galilee: The Social Context of Jesus and the Rabbis* (Valley Forge, PA: Trinity Press International, 1996); idem, *Galilee: History, Politics, People* (Valley Forge, PA: Trinity Press International, 1995); idem, *Jesus and the Spiral of Violence: Popular Jewish Resistance in Roman Palestine* (San Francisco: Harper & Row, 1987); J. H. Kautsky, *The Politics of Aristocratic Empires* (Chapel Hill: University of North Carolina Press, 1982); G. E. Lenski, *Power and Privilege: A Theory of Social Stratification* (2d ed.; Chapel Hill: University of North Carolina Press, 1984); B. J. Malina, "Wealth and Poverty in the New Testament and Its World," *Int* 41 (1987) 354-67; V. H. Matthews, *Manners and Customs in the Bible* (rev. ed.; Peabody, MA: Hendrickson, 1991); W. A. Meeks, *The First Urban Christians: The Social World of the Apostle Paul* (New Haven, CT: Yale University Press, 1983); H. Moxnes, *The Economy of the Kingdom: Social Conflict and Economic Relations in Luke's Gospel* (OBT; Philadelphia: Fortress, 1988); D. E. Oakman, "The Ancient Economy," in *The Social Sciences and New Testament Interpretation,* ed. R. L. Rohrbaugh (Peabody, MA: Hendrickson, 1996) 126-43; idem, "The Archaeology of First-Century Galilee and the Social Interpretation of the Historical Jesus," *SBLSP* (1994) 220-51; idem, *Jesus and the Economic Questions of His Day* (SBEC 8; Lewiston, NY: Edwin Mellen Press, 1986); J. J. Pilch and B. J. Malina, *Biblical Social Values and Their Meaning: A Handbook* (Peabody, MA: Hendrickson, 1993); K. Polanyi, *The Livelihood of Man,* ed. H. W. Pearson (Studies in Social Discontinuity; New York: Academic Press, 1977); R. L. Rohrbaugh, *The Biblical Interpreter: An Agrarian Bible in an Industrial Age* (Philadelphia: Fortress, 1978); A. M. Rostovtzeff, *Social and Economic History of the Roman Empire* (2d ed.; 2 vols.; Oxford: Clarendon Press, 1957); J. J. Rousseau and R. Arav, *Jesus and His World: An Archaeological and Cultural Dictionary* (Minneapolis: Fortress, 1995); Z. Safrai, *The Economy of Roman Palestine* (London: Routledge, 1994); G. Theissen, *The Social Setting of Pauline Christianity: Essays on Corinth,* ed., with an introduction by J. H. Schütz (Philadelphia: Fortress, 1982).

D. E. Oakman

EDICT OF CLAUDIUS. *See* INSCRIPTIONS AND PAPYRI: JEWISH.

EDUCATION: JEWISH AND GRECO-ROMAN

In the Greco-Roman world there was no public system of education. Families paid fees for the education of their youth, either at home by tutors or in a teacher's private school. Curriculum was established by convention, and the methods used and the authors studied were rarely changed. Primary education focused on reading and writing skills. Secondary education concerned the seven liberal arts: grammar, *rhetoric, dialectic, arithmetic, music, geometry and astronomy. Study of the professions of medicine and architecture was also available. In Greece *philosophy was the pinnacle of education, while in Rome it was rhetoric, which prepared the student for public life in law and politics. In Greece the seven liberal arts continued to be the core of education, while in Rome grammar and rhetoric became the more narrow focus, with the other liberal arts being subordinate and studied for utilitarian reasons from Greek tutors. The Hellenistic age witnessed the separation of education into the three stages of primary, grammar and rhetoric. Education became specialized, with grammar, rhetoric, mathematics and philosophy being taught in separate schools.

Jewish education was instituted in part as a response to the influence of Hellenism. It was centered on learning to read and memorizing the Torah and the oral tradition. Teachers came from within *Judaism. Education culminated in an apprenticeship for a trade rather than rhetorical instruction. The religious life of the Jews was also an important tool of education.

1. Greco-Roman Education
2. Jewish Education

1. Greco-Roman Education.
Greek education was well established before the Roman conquest. After the Roman conquest of Greece, Greek scholars went to Rome, bringing with them their language, curriculum and teaching methods. It can be said that Roman education was patterned after Greek education. Rome eventually developed its own grammar and rhetoric courses in Latin. However, both Greek and Roman language and literature continued to be studied side by side.

1.1 Primary Education. The Greeks had an established system of primary education in the Hellenistic period. The *gymnasium was the center of *athletics, reading, writing and music. Boys were accompanied to school by a pedagogue *(paidagōgos)* who protected them from physical and moral harm from boyhood to adulthood and often provided the primary education.

In the agrarian society of early Rome of the third century B.C., when their sons were about seven, fathers trained them at home in reading, writing, Roman law and tradition and the use of weapons. Roman tradition was encapsulated in paternal precepts *(praecepta paterna),* which covered practical, social, political and moral subjects, illustrated by the examples of famous individuals from Roman history. There was also some practical instruction in mathematics and weights and measures. If the father died prematurely or in war, the mother or other relatives assumed the role of educator. In wealthy Roman homes, Greek tutors from Greece and Asia Minor were employed to supplement the father's instruction. They taught the Greek language and literature (especially Homer), *poetry, rhetoric, philosophy, sculpting, painting and sports. Girls were educated by tutors in reading, writing and poetry.

Primary schools began to appear in Rome in the late third century B.C. The teachers of the primary schools began as *slaves. They were educated by their masters to enhance their value and/or were reared with the master's sons and accompanied them to school. Upon manumission they founded schools. Instruction was mainly in Latin for the poorer students and in Greek and Latin in the better schools. The curriculum centered on reading, writing and some arithmetic. Reading was taught in progression from letters to short passages with moral content and value for living, often from the poets. Writing, memorization and recitation were next, along with needed grammatical instruction to facilitate writing.

1.2. Secondary Education: Grammar. By the Hellenistic period Greece had a systematic grammar education. In the mid-second century B.C. native Greek tutors came to Rome, either as slaves or freedmen. They became tutors for the wealthy and, not finding any educational system in place in Rome, later opened grammar schools patterned on those of Greece. By the early empire, grammatical instruction was available in Rome in both Greek and Latin. Boys and also some girls attended grammar school from ages twelve to fifteen.

A grammar teacher was known as a *grammatikos* (Gk) or *grammaticus* or *ludi magister* (Lat). He taught reading, grammar, literature, exposition of poetry and mythology, for which the study of poetry was essential. Grammatical instruction focused on speaking and writing correctly. Such instruction was in two parts. The first part was learning the phonetic value of letters and their classifications, syllables and the parts of speech. The second part concerned pronunciation, spelling and syntax, especially to avoid barbarisms (faults in the use of a word) and solecisms (faults in syntax) in both speaking and writing. Dionysius Thrax, a student of Aristarchus, wrote the first systematic grammar textbook, which formed the basis of all subsequent Greek grammars (*see* Grammarians, Hellenistic Greek).

Literary instruction centered on studying the complete texts of the poets. Epic poetry was primary, especially Homer's *Iliad* and *Odyssey* from Greece, and in the first century A.D. the Romans added their own Virgil's *Aeneid.* The teacher would introduce the poetic text, discussing its author, plot and purpose. He would model the reading of the text for imitation, and then students would read and later recite the text from memory. After the reading the teacher commented about the text's tropes, figures of speech and thought, poetic technique, arrangement, characterization, subject matter and mythological and historical background. Commentaries on the poetic texts were also studied.

1.3. Secondary Education: Rhetoric. By the fourth century B.C. there was systematic teaching of rhetoric in *Athens, typically by the Sophists. By the mid-second century B.C., rhetoric instruction was available in Rome by private Greek tutors and a century later by Roman teachers using Latin rhetorical handbooks (e.g., Cicero *De Inventione*). Greek and Latin rhetorical instruction flourished side by side in Rome until the first century A.D., when the latter prevailed. Boys attended rhetoric school from ages fifteen to seventeen.

Rhetorical instruction focused on judicial and deliberative rhetoric in preparation for the legal profession. Both rhetorical theory and practice were taught. Theory included the instruction of Greek and Latin rhetorical handbooks *(technai),* which encapsulated rules learned from practice. Practice included voice training, reciting speeches from law courts and public assemblies and composing and delivering speeches.

A major component of rhetorical instruction was the *progymnasmata.* These were preliminary exercises in composing speeches. They developed in the Hellenistic period and were standardized in the first century B.C. They were graded by order of difficulty and included work with the sayings of famous people *(chreia),* maxims *(sententia),* fables, mythological and historical narrative, development of commonplaces, encomium and denunciation, comparison, speech in character (impersonation), vivid description, thesis and discussion of the advantages or disadvantages of a law. These exercises were illustrated by famous prose works. Students would work each exercise using paraphrase, negation, pro and con, example and comparison. These elements of a full speech were combined with instruction from the rhetorical handbooks, which outlined how to compose and deliver a speech using invention of arguments, arrangement of the parts of the speech, style, memorization and delivery techniques. These were expounded by the teacher and illustrated by famous speeches, with *Cicero's speeches being the favorite in Roman education.

Declamation was one type of practice speech for specific training as a judicial advocate. Declamations were of two types: deliberative *(suasoriae)* and judicial *(controversia).* Deliberative speeches offered counsel to a famous historical or legendary person or group at a moment of crisis. The judicial speeches supported one or the other side of an imaginary court case. Being easier, the deliberative speeches were learned by younger students, while the more difficult judicial speeches were learned by older students. The teachers offered situations for declamations and helped the students isolate the main and subsidiary issues. The students then composed their declamations and delivered them from memory, arguing one or both sides of the issue.

In Rome, when boys took the toga of manhood at fifteen to seventeen years of age, they left the rhetorical school to work a year as apprentices in either the forum if they were interested in the legal and political arenas (*see* Roman Law and Legal System; Roman Political System) or the military life if they were interested in a military career (*see* Roman Military). Sometimes this apprenticeship was followed by the study of philosophy, history, law and more rhetoric, occasionally abroad.

1.4. The Means and Mechanics of Instruction. In Hellenistic Greece education was conducted in public institutions. These included the gymnasia, palaestrae and temples dedicated to the Muses (the Museum). If teachers were not employed in these public institutions, they had to find their own accommodations. In Rome education was not conducted in public institutions. In both Greece and Rome the climate permitted education outdoors. In Rome education took place near the forum, temples, public squares and arcades. Rooms could be rented above the arcades of shops. In the time of Trajan public buildings, like the gymnasium, were extended for instruction.

The teacher sat in a high-backed chair, and his students sat on backless benches in a semicircle around him. There were no desks, so all work was done on the lap. Using a stylus of metal or wood, the students wrote on wooden tablets coated with wax that could be brushed smooth after each use. By the first century A.D. parchment (animal skin) bound in books was in use among those who could afford it.

Class sizes ranged from a handful to two hundred in both the grammar and rhetorical schools. The teacher of larger classes had assistants that he paid out of his own fees. School began at dawn. The morning of instruction was followed by exercise, lunch and a bath, and then an afternoon of more instruction. Homework of composition and memorization was common. Summer break was from June or July to mid-October.

Teachers were paid by the parents for negotiated fees. In Rome primary, grammar and rhetoric teachers were paid in the proportion of one-four-five respectively as indicative of their skill level. In Hellenistic Greece some positions were funded by the public, a wealthy *benefactor or an endowment. In Rome Vespasian was the first to appoint imperial chairs, one for Greek and one for Latin rhetoric.

1.5. The Quadrivium. The quadrivium are the mathematical arts of arithmetic, geometry, astronomy and music. These subjects were being taught in Athens as early as the fifth century B.C. and continued as a standard part of education. In Roman education these remained subordinate to grammar and rhetoric and were learned for utilitarian purposes from Greek tutors, usually philosophers. Some mathematics were included in primary education and were also studied by those going into business. Astronomy was studied for its practical benefit in navigating, planting crops and literary allusions. The standard text was Aratus's *Phaenomena.* Musical instruction was in voice and instruments to enable a citizen to participate in social and religious gatherings.

1.6. Professional Education. Medicine, architecture and teaching were the three learned professions of the ancient world. Teaching did not require formal training beyond secondary education. Medicine emerged as a discipline by the fifth century B.C. in Greece and came to Rome by the close of the third century B.C. The Romans did not develop medical instruction for themselves but left it to the Greeks, and it remained in the Greek language. Students were apprenticed to physicians beginning about age fourteen, when they had finished grammar school. They lived with the physician and studied texts, like the works attributed to Hippocrates and those of Galen, as well as observed the physician on his hospital rounds. Schools of architecture had their own curriculum and standard textbooks. Formal education in law did not develop until the Augustan age. It was a five-year course with a set curriculum as to which categories of laws and which legal works would be studied each year.

1.7. Philosophical Schools. Four philosophical schools began in Athens in the fourth century B.C. *Plato founded the Academy, and *Aristotle founded the Lyceum. Epicurus started a school for the *Epicureans, and Zeno formed a school for the *Stoics. Under Marcus Aurelius the four schools had salaried chairs at Athens. Unlike other students in education, philosophy students usually lived on their master's estate.

The philosophical schools assumed the completion of the grammar education. Curriculum in these schools varied, but the texts of the founder of the school and commentaries on them were central. The teacher gave an introduction to the texts, the students read them, and the teacher expounded upon them. Formal lectures were akin to moral exhortation, almost like a sermon, followed by student question and answer after the Socratic method.

2. Jewish Education.

The study of Jewish education comes mainly from Talmudic sources, particularly Palestinian. The study of the Torah was the main component of all the stages of Jewish education in the Greco-Roman period. The Torah was the basis of the social and legal system and the corporate and individual lives of the Jews.

2.1. Home Instruction. At home it was the father's responsibility to teach the Torah to his sons. There is evidence for Jewish primary schools emerging in *Jerusalem in the first century B.C. and of secondary schools in the second century B.C., partly in response to maintaining Jewish identity in light of the influence of *Hellenism. The primary schools developed a century later than the secondary schools because primary education was considered the father's responsibility. By the first century A.D. many boys were educated in primary and secondary schools. In the second century A.D. virtually all towns in Israel had elementary schools for learning written law *(bet seper)* and secondary schools for oral law *(bet talmud, bet midrash),* which each had its own scribes. Girls did not regularly attend school.

2.2. Primary and Secondary Education. Boys attended primary schools from six to ten years of age. The curriculum was akin to Greco-Roman education, but Hebrew replaced Greek or Latin as the language of study, and the Scriptures replaced the classics like Homer and Virgil. Boys learned the alphabet by writing the letters on a small wax tablet with a stylus. There was little grammar education. Reading was a matter of memorization. The Greco-Roman practice of writing from dictation was absent because of the prohibition of copying Scripture from dictation. Instead of dictation the class read small scrolls with passages of Torah written on them (*megillah*) and eventually entire books. Students began reading portions of Leviticus and then turned to Genesis. They eventually read all the books of Scripture in this order: Torah, Prophets and Writings. Memorization of large portions of the texts read was the desired result. In great distinction from Greco-Roman education, writing was taught separately from reading as a professional skill.

Boys attended secondary school from ten to thirteen years of age to study the oral Torah in the forms of midrash (sustained commentary on the text; *see* Rabbinic Literature: Midrashim) and mishnah (study of the text by topical arrangement; in Gal 1:14 Paul indicates he studied at this level; *see* Rabbinic Literature: Mishnah). The oral law was taught by recitation, usually chanting aloud, until the material was mastered.

No Greek was taught in Jewish schools. Those who needed Greek to administrate or trade within the *Diaspora were taught in Greek schools, both in Israel and elsewhere. These people included the upper classes of *Sadducees and *Pharisees (e.g., Paul knew Greek). The earliest reference to gymnasia in Palestine is one in Jerusalem founded by Jason the high priest in 175 B.C., but Greek education was probably available from Greek tutors before that time. After that time there are references to gymnasia scattered in larger cities of Israel. The sons of the upper class of Jerusalem may have been sent to study rhetoric in *Alexandria or other centers of Hellenistic education. In the Diaspora many Jews of the upper class were anxious for their children to have a Hellenistic education, while others preferred the traditional Jewish education, considering the influence of the polytheistic nature of Greek instruction to be a danger to faith (*see* Hellenistic Judaism).

2.3. Apprenticeship. There was no systematic education for a boy after age thirteen. After this age the father was obligated to teach his son his trade or apprentice him to a craftsman of another trade of the boy's choice. A boy could further study the law with adults who studied in their spare time. If he were gifted he could study with a scholar for several more years. Those preparing to be scribes, teachers, judges or heads of the synagogue continued their study of the Torah, often in small groups or as disciples of a scholar. There was also the study of astronomy and mathematics to calculate time, months and years, and mystical and philosophical studies centered on Genesis 1 (creation) and Ezekiel 1 (chariot vision), also at the instruction of a scholar.

2.4. Means and Mechanics of Instruction. Sometimes schools were attached to the *synagogues and classes held in the prayer hall or a room adjoining the synagogue. Sometimes scribes held class in the courtyard of their homes. Mothers accompanied their sons to school. Classes started early in the morning and went until noon, reconvening in the evening. School was held every day of the week, including the *sabbath. However, on the sabbath no new material was taught; only previously studied material was reviewed. The scribes were paid by the fathers and by taxes levied on the town's inhabitants.

2.5. Other Formal and Informal Education. In addition to public education from the second century B.C. there was the *bet midrash,* which was a school of the scribes or rabbis for study of the written and oral law and for study in the methods of interpretation. These were located in Palestine and the Diaspora. The scribe usually supported himself with a trade and studied the law in his spare time. Their pupils did likewise, so instruction was often in the evening in school, synagogue, town square or market. Some scribes wandered from town to town using the hospitality of individuals for support (cf. Mt 10:9-11). Question and answer was a typical method of instruction.

Informal education was an important part of worship in the synagogue (*see* Liturgy). On the sabbath and other *festivals there was public reading of the targums to the Pentateuch and the Prophets and a sermon based on both. The

Aramaic targumim were translations of the biblical text into Aramaic and explanation by midrashic, legal, and didactic interpretation (*see* Rabbinic Literature: Targumim). The sermon was usually haggadic and brought the developments of the school and public together.

See also ALEXANDRIAN LIBRARY; ALEXANDRIAN SCHOLARSHIP; ATHLETICS; GRAMMARIANS, HELLENISTIC GREEK; GYMNASIA AND BATHS; LITERACY AND BOOK CULTURE; PHILOSOPHY; POETRY, HELLENISTIC; RABBINIC LITERATURE; RABBIS; RHETORIC; SCHOLARSHIP, GREEK AND ROMAN; SYNAGOGUES; WRITING AND LITERATURE: GRECO-ROMAN; WRITING AND LITERATURE: JEWISH.

BIBLIOGRAPHY. S. F. Bonner, *Education in Ancient Rome: From the Elder Cato to the Younger Pliny* (Berkeley and Los Angeles: University of California Press, 1977); D. L. Clark, *Rhetoric in Greco-Roman Education* (New York: Columbia University Press, 1957); M. L. Clarke, *Higher Education in the Ancient World* (London: Routledge & Kegan Paul, 1971); J. L. Crenshaw, *Education in Ancient Israel: Across the Deadening Silence* (New York: Doubleday, 1998); N. H. Drazin, *History of Jewish Education from 515 B.C.E. to 220 C.E.* (John Hopkins University Studies in Education 29; Baltimore: Johns Hopkins University Press, 1940); E. Ebner, *Elementary Education in Ancient Israel During the Tannaitic Period (10-220 C.E.)* (New York: Bloch, 1956); J. J. Eyre, "Roman Education in the Late Republic and Early Empire," *Greece and Rome* 2d ser. 10 (1963) 47-59; B. Gerhardsson, *Memory and Manuscript: Oral Tradition and Written Transmission in Rabbinic Judaism and Early Christianity* (ASNU 22; Lund: C. W. K. Gleerup; Copenhagen: Ejnar Munksgaard, 1961) 56-92; A. Gwynn, *Roman Education: From Cicero to Quintilian* (Classics in Education 29; New York: Columbia Teacher's College Press of Columbia University, 1962 repr.) M. Hengel, *Judaism and Hellenism* (2 vols.; Philadelphia: Fortress, 1974) 1:65-83; R. A. Kaster, "Notes on 'Primary' and 'Secondary' Schools in Late Antiquity," *TAPA* 113 (1983) 323-46; H.-I. Marrou, *A History of Education in Antiquity* (Madison: University of Wisconsin Press, 1982 repr.); M. P. Nilsson, *Die hellenistische Schule* (Munich: C. H. Beck, 1955); E. P. Parks, *The Roman Rhetorical Schools as a Preparation for the Courts Under the Early Empire* (Baltimore: Johns Hopkins University Press, 1945); S. Safrai, "Education and the Study of the Torah," in *The Jewish People in the First Century* (2 vols.; CRINT; Assen: Van Gorcum; Philadelphia: Fortress 1974-76) 945-70; J. T. Townsend, "Ancient Education in the Time of the Early Roman Empire," in *The Catacombs and the Colosseum: The Roman Empire as the Setting of Early Christianity,* ed. S. Benko and J. J. O'Rourke (Valley Forge, PA: Judson, 1971) 139-63; M. Winterbottom, "Schoolroom and Courtroom," in *Rhetoric Revalued,* ed. B. Vickers (Medieval and Renaissance Texts and Studies 19; Binghamton, NY: Center for Medieval and Early Renaissance Studies, 1982) 59-70.

D. F. Watson

EGYPTIAN, THE. *See* REVOLUTIONARY MOVEMENTS, JEWISH.

ELEAZAR THE EXORCIST. *See* HOLY MEN, JEWISH.

ELECT OF GOD (4Q534). *See* BIRTH OF THE CHOSEN ONE (4Q534).

EMPERORS. *See* ROMAN EMPERORS.

ENOCH, BOOKS OF

The name *Enoch* first appears in Genesis 4:17, where we are told that Cain begat Enoch and named a city after him. According to Genesis 5:24, "Enoch walked with God. Then he was no more, for God took him" (the word for "God," *elohim,* could also be interpreted as "angels"). In later tradition this enigmatic verse is taken to mean that Enoch was taken alive up to heaven, where he was shown the tablets of heaven and mysteries hidden from other mortals. Enoch thus resembles the legendary Sumerian king, Enmeduranki, or Enmenduranna, who appears as seventh king in several Mesopotamian lists of antediluvian rulers, and was taken into the council of the gods where he was set on a throne of gold and shown the techniques of divination and the tablet of the gods. The statement that "God took him" also likens Enoch to the Babylonian flood hero Utnapishtim, who was taken to live with the gods at the end of his life. For Jews of the Babylonian exile, Enoch would likely have been viewed as a Jewish counterpart to both the Sumerian hero-king and the Babylonian flood hero. Within Judaism of the Second Temple period there developed a rich tradition of speculation regarding Enoch's ascent to heaven. This continued in the Jewish mystical tradition and is preserved in several extant books of Enoch.

1. *First Enoch*
2. *Second Enoch*
3. *Third Enoch,* or *Seper Hekhalot*
4. The Status of Enochic Writings

1. *First Enoch.*

1.1. The Composite Book. The oldest writings attributed to Enoch are found in the composite book known as *1 Enoch,* which is fully preserved in Ethiopic and was made known to the Western world by the translation of R. Laurence in 1821. Fragments of this book are preserved in Greek, and Aramaic fragments of several sections have been found among the *Dead Sea Scrolls. This book includes at least five distinct compositions: The Book of the Watchers (*1 Enoch* 1—36), the Similitudes (*1 Enoch* 37—71), the Astronomical Book (*1 Enoch* 72—82), the Book of Dreams (*1 Enoch* 83—90) and the Epistle of Enoch (*1 Enoch* 91—105). Within the Book of Dreams, the Apocalypse of Weeks (*1 Enoch* 93:1-10; 91:11-17) stands out as a distinct unit. It is generally believed that fragments of a *Book of Noah* are also preserved in *1 Enoch* (García Martínez; cf. *1 Enoch* 10:1-3; 54:7—55:2; 60:7-10, 24; 106—7). The Similitudes is the only section of the book of which no fragments have been found in the Dead Sea Scrolls.

1.2. The Book of the Watchers. Itself a composite book, this part of *1 Enoch* takes its name from the story of the fallen angels, or Watchers, of Genesis 6, which is retold in expanded form in *1 Enoch* 6—16 (*see* Angels of the Nations). J. T. Milik held that this form of the story was presupposed in Genesis, but most scholars agree that it is more likely to be an expansion of the biblical text. The oldest Aramaic fragments of this work in the Dead Sea Scrolls date from the first half of the second century B.C. The story of the Watchers is presupposed in other sections of *1 Enoch* that can be dated by content to the time of the Maccabean revolt. The Book of the Watchers, then, took shape in the third or early second century B.C.

Chapters 1—5 serve as an introduction to the book. The opening chapter describes a theophany on the day of judgment, but chapters 2—5 have the character of wisdom instruction. Chapters 6—16 tell the story of the Watchers, in which two stories seem to be woven together. In one, the leader of the fallen angels is named Asael (Azazel in the Ethiopic text), and the primary sin is improper revelation; in the other the leader is Shemihazah, and the primary sin is marriage with humans and procreation of giants. These stories can be understood plausibly as an allegory for the impact on the Near East of *Hellenistic culture, with its new attitudes to knowledge and sexuality. But they also constitute a way of explaining the origin of sin and evil as the products of *demonic forces (Sacchi). The Watchers beget giants on earth by their union with human women. Out of these giants come evil spirits that lead humanity astray (*1 Enoch* 15:11-12; this motif is elaborated further in **Jubilees*). In the short term, the crisis of the Watchers is resolved when God sends the flood to cleanse the earth.

Enoch is introduced in chapter 12 as a scribe, whom the Watchers ask to intercede for them. Enoch ascends to heaven on a cloud and comes before the heavenly throne in chapter 14, in a passage that is important for the history of Jewish *mysticism (*see* Heavenly Ascent). His intercession, however, is rejected. The Watchers abandoned heaven for the attraction of the flesh. Enoch represents the opposite tendency: he is a human being who is taken up to heaven to live with the angels.

In chapters 17—36, Enoch is taken on a tour by the angels, to the ends of the earth. He sees cosmological secrets such as the storehouses of the winds and the elements, but much of what he sees has *eschatological import. In chapter 22 he sees the places where the spirits of the dead are kept inside a mountain. This passage is not preserved in Aramaic, and the text is corrupt. The spirits are divided into three compartments: the righteous, the wicked who were not punished on earth, and sinners who were killed. (There are indications that originally four compartments were envisioned.) Chapter 25 describes a fragrant tree that will be given to the righteous when God "comes down to visit the earth for good," and chapters 26—27 describe Gehenna. In chapter 32 Enoch sees the garden of Eden and the tree from which Adam ate. While the Book of the Watchers knows of the sin of Adam, it does not attribute to it any importance comparable to the sin of the Watchers.

1.3. The Astronomical Book. *1 Enoch* 72—82 may be even older than the Book of the Watchers. The oldest Aramaic fragments have been dated to the third century B.C. This book is primarily concerned with the movements of the stars. The astronomical observations are primitive in relation to the contemporary Babylonian and Hellenistic astronomy. The heavens are peopled with angels. Uriel, the leader of the lights of heaven, is said to serve as Enoch's guide. One major purpose of this text is to show that "the year amounts to exactly three hundred and sixty-four days" (*1 Enoch* 72:32). It thus supports a *calendar that was different from the 354-day calendar that came to be accepted by *rabbinic Judaism and was probably already in place in the Second Temple period. The 364-day calendar is also defended by *Jubilees* and is presupposed in the sectarian Dead Sea Scrolls. The Astronomical Book concludes with some eschatological predictions. According to chapter 80, "in the days of the sinners the years will become shorter . . . and many heads of the stars in command will go astray." This will eventually lead to destruction. Chapter 81, which is probably an addition to the Astronomical Book, speaks of the death of the righteous and seems to imply some form of afterlife.

1.4. The Book of Dreams. *1 Enoch* 83—90 consists of two *apocalypses. The first, in chapters 83—84, is a simple vision of cosmic destruction. The second, known as the Animal Apocalypse, is a complex allegory in which people are represented by animals. Adam is a white bull. Cain and Abel are black and red bullocks; Israel are sheep. In the period after the exile, the sheep are given over to seventy shepherds, representing the angelic patrons of the nations. The reign of these shepherds is divided into four periods, which are allotted twelve, twenty-three, twenty-three and twelve shepherds respectively. At the end of the third period we are told that "small lambs were born from these white sheep, and they began to open their eyes" (*1 Enoch* 90:6). This is generally taken to refer to the Hasidim who supported Judas Maccabus. Judas is represented by a great horn that grew on one of the sheep. Eventually God comes down and sets up his throne for judgment. The Watchers and the seventy shepherds are destroyed, but so are the "blind sheep," or apostate Jews. Those that had been destroyed are brought back, presumably by resurrection, and all are transformed into "white bulls"—the condition of Adam and the early patriarchs. This apocalypse was evidently written at the time of the Maccabean revolt by people who supported the Maccabees (*see* Jewish History: Greek Period).

1.5. The Apocalypse of Weeks. *1 Enoch* 93:1-10; 91:11-17 also comes from the Maccabean era. The order of this text was disrupted in the Ethiopic manuscripts, but it is preserved in the Aramaic fragments from *Qumran. The apocalypse reports what Enoch saw in a heavenly vision and understood from the tablets of heaven. The content of revelation concerns the course of history, which is divided into "weeks," presumably weeks of years as in Daniel 9. Ten weeks are specified. These are punctuated by the emergence of righteous figures, for example, Noah in the second week, Abraham in the third. The seventh week is dominated by an apostate generation, but at its end "the chosen righteous from the eternal plant of righteousness" will be selected. The election of this group is the focal point of the text. In the eighth week, sinners are destroyed by the sword. In the ninth, the righteous judgment is revealed to the whole world, and "the world is written down for destruction." In the tenth week "the eternal judgment will be executed on the Watchers." Then the first heaven will pass away, and a new heaven will appear. After this "there will be many weeks without number forever in goodness and righteousness."

In view of the reference to the sword, it is reasonable to conclude that this apocalypse too supported the Maccabean revolt. The group that is here called the chosen righteous is presumably the same as the lambs whose eyes were opened in the Animal Apocalypse. These people probably represent the circles where the early Enoch books were written. Some scholars identify them with the Hasidim.

1.6. The Epistle of Enoch. *1 Enoch* 91—105 differs from the other early Enoch books insofar as it is not a report of revelation but an instruction and exhortation. Enoch asserts his authority by such formulae as "I say to you" or "I swear to you," and he undergirds his authority by claiming that "I have read the tablets of heaven and seen the writing of the holy ones" (*1 Enoch* 103:1-2). The bulk of the epistle is taken up with woes against sinners and exhortations for the righteous. The sinners are condemned mainly for social offenses. They "build their houses with sin" (*1 Enoch* 94:8) and "trample upon the humble through your power" (*1 Enoch* 96:5). The reward of the righteous, however, has ultimately an otherworldly character. They will "shine like the lights of heaven and be associates of the host of heaven" (*1 Enoch* 104:2-6).

They are also promised some more mundane gratification. The wicked will be given into their hands, and they will cut their throats (*1 Enoch* 98:12). Some scholars have dated the epistle to the early first century B.C. (Charles, 171). More recent scholarship, however, favors the view that this text originated about the same time as the other early Enoch books, in the early second century B.C.

1.7. The Similitudes. *1 Enoch* 37—71 constitute the only section of *1 Enoch* that is not found in the Dead Sea Scrolls. The date of the composition is disputed. J. T. Milik suggested that it was a late-third-century A.D. Christian composition (Milik, 89-98), but there are no clear Christian features in this text. The most striking feature of the Similitudes is the repeated reference to a figure called "that Son of Man," who is implicitly identified as the "one like a son of man" of Daniel 7. It is unlikely that a Jewish author would have given such prominence to this figure after the "Son of Man" had become widely identified with Jesus by the early Christians. The closest parallels in the NT are found in Matthew 19:28 and 25:31, which refer to a glorious throne. These Matthean passages may well depend on the Similitudes. The only explicit historical references are the mention of the Parthians and Medes in *1 Enoch* 56:5-7, which point to a date after 40 B.C., and the mention of hot springs in *1 Enoch* 67:5-13, which has been taken as an allusion to Herod's search for a cure in the waters of Callirhoe (Josephus *Ant.* 17.6.5 §§171-73; *J.W.* 1.33.5 §§657-58). None of these references is conclusive for dating, but the most probable date is the early first century A.D., prior to 70. An earlier date would be difficult to justify in view of the absence of the Similitudes from Qumran.

The Similitudes consist of three "parables" (*1 Enoch* 38—44, 45—57 and 58—69) and a double epilogue in *1 Enoch* 70 and 71. The main theme is the coming judgment, "when the Righteous One appears before the chosen righteous whose works are weighed by the Lord of Spirits" (*1 Enoch* 38:2). Then the rulers of the earth will be dumbfounded and humbled. The Righteous One is also called the Chosen One and "that Son of Man" who accompanies the "Head of Days" as in Daniel 7 (*1 Enoch* 46:1-2). We are told that the Son of Man was named "even before the sun and the constellations were created" (*1 Enoch* 48:3), and that "he was chosen and hidden before the world was created" (*1 Enoch* 48:6). There is no suggestion that he has ever appeared on earth. The righteous are those who believe in him or those to whom his existence has been revealed. The kings and the mighty do not believe in him and will be astounded when they see him sitting on his throne of glory (*1 Enoch* 62:5).

In the first epilogue (*1 Enoch* 70:1) we are told that Enoch's name was lifted up to the presence of that Son of Man and to the presence of the Lord of Spirits. In the second epilogue, however, Enoch is greeted by an angel who tells him "you are the Son of Man who was born to righteousness" (*1 Enoch* 71:14). It is very unlikely that Enoch was supposed to be identified with the Son of Man throughout the Similitudes, as there is no reference to his earthly life, and he never recognizes himself. Also Enoch is clearly distinct from the Son of Man in *1 Enoch* 70:1. It is possible that the angel's greeting means only that Enoch is "a son of man who has righteousness" and so is akin to the heavenly righteous one. If he is meant to be identified with the heavenly Son of Man, then we must assume that this is a secondary addition to the Similitudes, possibly intended to preclude the Christian claim that the Son of Man was identical with Jesus.

2. *Second Enoch.*

The Book of the Secrets of Enoch, or *2 Enoch,* is preserved in two Slavonic recensions, one short and one long. The original language was probably Greek. Although Milik claimed that it was a late, Christian work (Milik, 107-16), the consensus is that it was Jewish, because of the importance attached to animal sacrifice. Egypt is the most likely place of composition, because of parallels to Philo and allusions to Egyptian mythology.

Second Enoch provides a far more lengthy account of Enoch's ascent than was found in *1 Enoch* (*2 Enoch* 3—37). Enoch ascends through seven heavens. This may be the earliest instance of the motif of seven heavens in a Jewish or Christian apocalypse. The observations in the first, fourth and sixth heavens are mainly cosmological (e.g., the governance of the stars and the movements of the sun). The second, third and fifth heavens contain the places of reward and punishment. Paradise is located in the third heaven. Enoch writes down all he has seen in 360 books, which he transmits to humanity. Chapters 38—66 of

2 Enoch contain Enoch's instructions to his children after his return to earth. These instructions are remarkably humanistic and are mainly concerned with feeding the hungry, clothing the naked, and so forth. "Whoever offends the face of a man offends the face of God" (*2 Enoch* 44:1; cf. 52:6; 60:1). This ethic is grounded in creation: God made humanity in his own likeness. Moreover, a link between humanity and animals was established at creation, and the souls of animals may accuse humanity at the judgment (*2 Enoch* 58). Unlike the apocalypses in *1 Enoch, 2 Enoch* shows little interest in history, and its revelations may be regarded as wisdom teaching, although the wisdom rests on the authority of heavenly revelation. The story of the birth of Melchizedek is appended to the apocalypse of *2 Enoch* but does not appear to be intrinsically related to it, except insofar as both Enoch and Melchizedek are figures from the dawn of history (*see* Melchizedek, Traditions of).

3. *Third Enoch,* or *Seper Hekhalot.*
The last Enochic writing to be considered here is a Hebrew composition from the fifth or sixth century A.D., which is part of the *Hekhalot* literature, or Jewish mystical tradition. This is not strictly a book of Enoch. It purports to be the account of an ascent to heaven by Rabbi Ishmael. His heavenly guide is a superangel called Metatron, who identifies himself as follows: "I am Enoch, the son of Jared. . . . The Holy One, blessed be he, appointed me in the height as a prince and ruler among the ministering angels" (*3 Enoch* 4). The objections of the angels are overruled by the Most High, who makes for Enoch a throne like the throne of glory, gives him a crown and calls him "the lesser YHWH" (*3 Enoch* 12). At first Metatron sat and judged the heavenly beings, but when *ʾaḥer* (the heretic Elisha ben Abuya) entered paradise, he declared "There are indeed two powers in heaven." Then Metatron was made to stand on his feet and was given sixty lashes of fire (*3 Enoch* 16). Much of the work is taken up with discourses on the hierarchies of the angels and the mysteries of the cosmos. While this book is considerably later than *1 Enoch* and *2 Enoch,* it may in a sense be considered the culmination of the tradition about Enoch's ascent to heaven.

4. The Status of Enochic Writings.
Since multiple copies of several of the component writings of *1 Enoch* were preserved at Qumran, it is quite possible that they were regarded as Scripture by the Dead Sea sect. It was not preserved by *rabbinic Judaism, but it enjoyed high status in some Christian circles. The epistle of Jude in the NT alludes to the story of the Watchers and seems to regard the story as authoritative (*see DLNTD,* Jude). This is also the case in the *Epistle of Barnabas* (*see DLNTD,* Barnabas, Epistle of). *First Enoch* was still cited as authoritative Scripture by Tertullian at the end of the second century A.D. Tertullian addresses the status of *1 Enoch* explicitly. He acknowledged that the authority of Enoch was not acknowledged by all and that some people doubted whether it could have been transmitted from before the flood. Tertullian countered that Enoch was grandfather of Noah and that Noah would have preserved the tradition. Moreover, the Spirit could have restored the book through inspiration (VanderKam 1996, 52). Eventually the Enochic writings were rejected by the Western church and were lost to a great extent. They were preserved, however, in Ethiopia, where they were regarded as sacred Scripture.

See also APOCALYPTIC LITERATURE; APOCRYPHA AND PSEUDEPIGRAPHA; DEAD SEA SCROLLS; HEAVENLY ASCENT IN JEWISH AND PAGAN TRADITIONS.

BIBLIOGRAPHY. P. Alexander, "3 (Hebrew Apocalypse of) Enoch," in *OTP,* 1:223-315; F. I. Andersen, "2 (Slavonic Apocalypse of) Enoch," in *OTP* 1:91-221; M. Black, *The Book of Enoch or 1 Enoch* (Leiden: E. J. Brill, 1985); G. Boccaccini, *Beyond the Essene Hypothesis: The Parting of the Ways Between Qumran and Enochic Judaism* (Grand Rapids, MI: Eerdmans, 1998); C. Böttrich, *Weltweisheit, Menschheitsethik, Urkult: Studien zum slavischen Henochbuch* (Tübingen: Mohr Siebeck, 1992); R. H. Charles, "1 Enoch," in *The Apocrypha and Pseudepigrapha of the Old Testament,* ed. R. H. Charles (2 vols.; Oxford: Clarendon Press, 1913) 163-281; J. J. Collins, *The Apocalyptic Imagination: An Introduction to Jewish Apocalyptic Literature* (2d ed.; Grand Rapids, MI: Eerdmans, 1998) 43-84, 177-93, 243-47; G. García Martínez, "*4QMess Ar* and the *Book of Noah,*" in *Qumran and Apocalyptic* (STDJ 9; Leiden: E. J. Brill, 1992) 1-44; M. A. Knibb, *The Ethiopic Book of Enoch: A New Edition in the Light of the Aramaic Dead Sea Fragments* (Oxford: Clarendon Press, 1978); R. Laurence, *The Book of Enoch the Prophet* (Oxford: Clarendon Press, 1821); J. T. Milik, *The*

Books of Enoch: Aramaic Fragments from Qumran Cave 4 (Oxford: Clarendon Press, 1976); G. W. Nickelsburg, "Enoch, First Book of," *ABD* 2:508-16; P. Sacchi, *Jewish Apocalyptic and Its History* (Sheffield: Sheffield Academic Press, 1997); D. Suter, *Tradition and Composition in the Parables of Enoch* (Missoula, MT: Scholars Press, 1979); P. A. Tiller, *A Commentary on the Animal Apocalypse of 1 Enoch* (Atlanta: Scholars Press, 1993); J. C. VanderKam, *Enoch: A Man for All Generations* (Columbia: University of South Carolina Press, 1995); idem, *Enoch and the Growth of an Apocalyptic Tradition* (Washington, DC: Catholic Biblical Association, 1984); idem, "The Status of Enochic Literature in Early Christianity," in *The Jewish Apocalyptic Heritage in Early Christianity*, ed. J. C. VanderKam and W. Adler (Minneapolis: Fortress, 1996) 33-101. J. J. Collins

ENOSH. *See* PRAYER OF ENOSH (4Q369, 4Q458).

EPHESUS

As the capital of the province of Asia during Roman occupation, Ephesus enjoyed significant prosperity due to its strategic location, banking and commerce. Ancient Ephesus was situated at the mouth of the Cayster River near modern Selçuk on the western coast of Turkey. Its best known history dates from the seventh century B.C. but certainly predates that period, and in the NT era Ephesus was one of the largest and most important cities of the *Roman Empire. In Ephesus Paul ministered some three years (Acts 19:8-10; 20:31). His Corinthian correspondence was produced in Ephesus, and perhaps also several other letters (see discussion below).

1. Early Mythology and History
2. The Classical Period
3. The Ministry of Paul and His Companions
4. Pauline Correspondence Produced at Ephesus
5. The Ministry of John

1. Early Mythology and History.

There is a scarcity of reliable information from antiquity about the city, but both Strabo and Pausanias relate the story of the founding of the city by the legendary Amazons, a mythical race of female warriors, who removed ("pinched out" or "cauterized") the right breast so not to impede their javelin-throwing abilities (Strabo *Geog.* 11.5.1; Apollodorus 2.5.8). The Amazons derived their name from this practice (*maza,* "breast"; *amaza,* "breastless"), and at Ephesus Hippolyte and her Amazons reportedly set up a statue of Artemis and established an annual circular dance with weapons and shields (Callimachus *Hymns* 3.110). The particular Amazon who captured Ephesus was named Smyrna (later Izmir).

The name *Ephesus* is somewhat obscure but may derive from Apis, which means "bee." Some early Ephesian coins had a bee on them; in the ancient mythology of that region this had significance because of the abundance of bees as well as their ability to produce honey and also offer a sting. Pausanias claims that the earliest temple to the Ephesian goddess was begun by Coresus, an aboriginal, and by Ephesus, "who is thought to have been a son of the river Caijster," from whom the city may have received its name (Pausanius *Descr.* 6.2.7). Pausanias himself, however, reported that Androclus of Codrus came to Anatolia by appointment from *Athens primarily because of an oracle from Apollo. In this vision he was told to settle where he found a fish and a boar. As his company landed at the harbor of Ephesus, a boar jumped out of a thicket, and Androclus chased after the boar and killed it. On the site of that killing, he supposedly founded the city of Ephesus. A picture of that story is depicted on a frieze from the temple of Hadrian, which is still visible.

Ephesus may also have acquired its name from the mother goddess known as Artemis Ephesia, whose followers believed her to be a fertile mythological woman from around 7000 B.C. and the mother of everything who also ruled everything. She was the most popular goddess in Anatolia, and her fame and influence spread to Mesopotamia, Egypt, Arabia, Greece, Rome and even Scandinavia. Pausanias claims that even before the Ionians came from Athens to the coastal areas of Anatolia, the "cult of Ephesian Artemis" was already established (Pausanius *Descr.* 6.2.6). Relics from a Mycenean grave at Ephesus suggest that the city may have originated sometime between 1400 and 1300 B.C., but the details of that presence in the area are lacking. Similarly, Hittite cuneiform tablets found at Miletus just south of Ephesus contain the name of a village, Apasas, which some scholars consider an older form of the name *Ephesus.*

2. The Classical Period.

Little of the earliest history of Ephesus is known

for certain, but it appears that before the arrival of the Greeks in Ephesus, the residents there offered sacrifices to the mother goddess Cybele, who later was identified with the Greek goddess Artemis (*see* Religion, Greco-Roman). After the Ionian cites were established on the western coast of Anatolia (c. 750 B.C.), Lydian kings attacked these cities (primarily Ephesus, Miletus, Priene and Didyma) and ruled over them in the seventh and sixth centuries B.C. After Cyrus of Persia defeated Croesus, the last Lydian king, in the sixth century, Ephesus was ruled by the Persians until the time of *Alexander the Great (334 B.C.).

The famous Artemision, or temple of Artemis, commonly identified as one of the seven wonders of the world, was built in her honor in the seventh century B.C. The elaborate marble temple, the first of its kind, was later attacked by the Cimmerians and was demolished. It was rebuilt on a grander scale in the mid-sixth century and was under construction when Croesus captured the city. He aided in the rebuilding of the temple by adding a number of column capitals and reliefs to its construction along with golden statues of calves. One of the column capitals had his name on it. During this period the famous philosopher Heraclitus lived in the city. Hipponax, a sixth-century poet who was expelled from Ephesus in 540 B.C., claimed that a section of Ephesus was called Smyrna. Later, according to Strabo, Smyrneans left Ephesus and resettled near today's Izmir, which is the location of NT Smyrna (Rev 2:8-11; *see* Asia Minor).

Ephesus became a tributary of Athens in 466, but it fell again to the Persians at the beginning of the fourth century B.C. In 356 the Artemision was set on fire and partially destroyed by a madman seeking fame. Alexander the Great took the city without resistance in 334, and the temple had not yet been rebuilt. He offered to help the citizens of the community rebuild the temple, but they implored him not to do the rebuilding since it was inappropriate for a god to do that. Lysimachus, one of Alexander's successor generals (*see* Diadochi), built a 6-mile-long wall around the city of Ephesus, some of which can still be seen. The temple of Artemis was again rebuilt and was recognized as a place of asylum or refuge, though the limits and conditions of the refuge policy often changed without notice and frequently at the expense of those who wrongfully thought that they could find security there. In 289 Lysimachus named the city after his wife, Arsinoe, but soon after his death the name was changed back to Ephesus.

Ephesus was under Greek rule until 133, when it was bequeathed to the Romans by Attalus III of Pergamum. At this time Ephesus replaced Pergamum as the capital of the province of Asia and was one of the most prominent cities of the *Roman Empire throughout the early Christian era. Under Roman rule the worship of Artemis continued uninterrupted, but the residents also erected an alter to honor Augustus (*see* Roman Emperors) in the sacred precinct of the temple. At the end of the first century, a temple was built to honor Domitian, but it was torn down after his death. Later in the second century a temple was built to honor Hadrian. Strabo described Ephesus's place among the league of twelve Ionian cities as "the royal seat of the Ionians" (Strabo *Geog.* 633). By the first century A.D. the city had grown to around 250,000 citizens and was perhaps the third largest city in the east behind *Alexandria and *Antioch on the Orontes (Syria), but its place of prominence was third behind *Rome and Alexandria.

3. The Ministry of Paul and His Companions. There is considerable question about the origins of the Christian community in Ephesus. It appears from Acts 18:18-22 that Paul spoke briefly with the Jews at Ephesus on his first visit to that city, but it is not clear that he started a church at that time. Priscilla and Aquila were left in the city, and they, along with Apollos, may be the founders of the church at Ephesus (Acts 18:24-28) even though its most significant growth came later through Paul's ministry.

After a lengthy stay in *Corinth, Paul returned to Ephesus for three years of ministry (Acts 19:8-10; cf. 20:31). When his ministry in the synagogue began to have a more hostile reception, he met in the lecture hall of Tyrannus for an additional two years. As a result of the effectiveness of Paul's preaching at Ephesus, the sales of religious paraphernalia diminished and fear broke out that worship at the temple of Artemis would be scorned. The enraged residents of the city came to the *theater, which seated twenty-four thousand people, to demand that this be stopped and that those causing the problem be punished (Acts 19:23-41). It may well be that this was the occasion of an arrest and imprisonment of Paul in Ephesus. Paul himself states that his ministry at Ephesus was mixed with danger that included being forced to "fight with wild animals" (or fierce opponents) and "many adversaries" (1 Cor 15:32; 16:9). A careful sifting of his letters and other early traditions about his stay in Ephesus strongly suggests that Paul was imprisoned at Ephesus (1 Cor 16:8-9; 2 Cor 1:8; Rom 16:3-4).

On his return to Jerusalem, Paul was apparently fearful of stopping at Ephesus and chose to meet with the elders of the city while his ship docked at Miletus (Acts 20:14-15). This also fits with the tradition of Paul's imprisonment on the western end of the wall built by Croesus and the numerous Christian pilgrimages to that place in later church history. This story of Paul's lengthy ministry in Ephesus culminates the story of his missionary career in Acts.

The size of the church at Ephesus in the first century is not known, but it is likely that Ephesus was the center for Christian missionary activity in Asia that led to the founding of the churches at Laodicea, *Colossae, Hierapolis and elsewhere (Col 4:13) and perhaps also at Smyrna, Pergamum, Thyatira, Philadelphia, Sardis and elsewhere (Rev 2—3). In most of these cities there were significant numbers of Jews and *synagogues where, according to Paul's practice (Rom 1:16-17; Acts 13:5, 14-16; 14:1; 16:13; 17:1-2, 10-11; 18:4-7, 19-21; 19:8), he frequently launched his ministry. *Josephus tells of the presence of a large Jewish community at Ephesus that petitioned and was granted considerable freedom in the observance of the *sabbath and other of religious practices, as well as their freedom from military service (Josephus *Ant.* 14.10.25 §§262-64). He also observes that similar grants from Rome were given to the Jews at Delos, Laodicea, Pergamum, Halicarnassus and Sardis (Josephus *Ant.* 14.10.11-24 §§223-61).

4. Pauline Correspondence Produced at Ephesus.

Of the several letters written by Paul, the Corinthian correspondence (1 Cor 16:8) was written here shortly after his arrival in Ephesus, probably in the fall of A.D. 52. The letter to the church at Colossae and also the personal letter to Philemon were perhaps written at Ephesus. The fact that Paul sent greetings to the Corinthians from the "churches of Asia" (1 Cor 16:19) further indicates that Ephesus was the location of his writing of this correspondence. It is possible that the letter to the Philippians was written from here, and, if his letter to the Galatians was intended for a north Galatian destination, then it is likely that this letter was written here as well.

Many scholars today do not believe that Romans 16 was an original part of the letter to the Romans, but rather it was added later when the letters of Paul began to be circulated in the churches. H. Koester (122-24) argues that Romans 16 was written by Paul to the church at Ephesus, indicating that the list of twenty-six names is more logically located in Ephesus than any other community with which Paul was associated. This list of names is mentioned in the fourth century by Eusebius (Eusebius *Hist. Eccl.* 3.3.6). If this list of greetings was originally sent to the Ephesian church, it would appear that the composition of the church was largely Gentile. Only six in the list of twenty-six names are clearly Jewish (Maria, Prisca, Aquila, Junia, Andronika and Herodion).

It is likely, whether or not Paul wrote the NT letter, that Ephesians was not sent to the church at Ephesus. The opening designation "in Ephesus" (Eph 1:1) is lacking in the most important ancient manuscripts of this letter (P^{46}, ℵ and B), and there is little in the letter that shows any familiarity with the readers such as one would expect from one who had ministered three years in that church. There is no typical list of greetings at the end such as one would expect from Paul's normal practice. The correspondence to Timothy, whether by Paul or another, presumes that the letters were sent to Ephesus (1 Tim 1:3). Second Timothy presumes that Onesiphorus from Ephesus was also in Rome and was not ashamed of Paul but ministered to him in Rome and in Ephesus (2 Tim 1:16-18). Alexander the coppersmith, about whom Timothy is warned (2 Tim 4:14-15), may be the Alexander of Acts 19:33, but that is not certain. Timothy's connection with the Ephesian church as its first appointed bishop is mentioned by Eusebius (Eusebius *Hist. Eccl.* 3.4.5). Onesimus, who fled his master (Philemon) in Colossae and was allowed to return to Paul in Ephesus (Col 4:9), may eventually have become the bishop in Ephesus at the beginning of the second century (see Ign. *Eph.* 1.3; 6.2), but again, that is not certain.

At the end of the first century, the author of the book of Revelation wrote letters to seven churches of Asia. The first was addressed to the

Ephesians, who were praised for their vigilance for the truth (Rev 2:2-3, 6), though it was at the expense of their love. Their diligence for the truth is also praised later by Ignatius, but so is their love (Ign. *Eph.* 9.1; cf. Acts 20:29-30; 1 Tim 1:3, 18-20; 4:1-4; cf. 1 Cor 15:32; 16:9b; see also Clement of Alexandria *Quis Div.* 42; Irenaeus *Haer.* 3.3.4). Both Acts 19 and the apocryphal *Acts of John* tell of the continuous conflict between the Christians at Ephesus and those who followed the religion of Artemis.

5. The Ministry of John.

There is a strong church tradition but little clear evidence that connects John the apostle with Ephesus in the latter part of the first century. Ignatius of Antioch, for instance, refers to Paul's ministry at Ephesus in his letter but says nothing of John the apostle. Eusebius identifies John the apostle as the author of the Fourth Gospel and 1 John (Eusebius *Hist. Eccl.* 3.24) and tells of John's banishment to the island of Patmos (see also Rev 1:7) during the reign of Domitian, but he may have the prophet or elder John confused with the apostle.

Justin Martyr stayed in Ephesus near the middle of the second century and frequently refers to the Gospels of Matthew and Luke, but he never mentions John or his Gospel (see Justin *Dial. Tryph.* 81.4). The same could be said of Polycarp and Papias. Eusebius's references to two Johns are confusing, and it is not clear which he has in mind, but he may well confuse the two (Eusebius *Hist. Eccl.* 2.22.5; 3.1.1; 3.23.4-5; 3.24-25). After Domitian's death, Eusebius claims, John was released from prison and took up residence in Ephesus. He cites both Clement of Alexandria and Irenaeus as sources for this information (Eusebius *Hist. Eccl.* 3.20.9—3.23.19). In the second century (the date is uncertain) a small church was built over the site of the grave where it is believed that John the apostle was buried. In the sixth century a major reconstructed basilica was built by the emperor Justinian on the same spot, and the supposed burial place was located under the apse of the church.

See also COLOSSAE; RELIGION, GRECO-ROMAN.

BIBLIOGRAPHY. C. E. Arnold, "Ephesus," *DPL* 249-53; A. Bammer, "Ephesus," in *Oxford Encyclopedia of Archaeology in the Near East,* ed. E. M. Meyers (5 vols.; New York: Oxford University Press, 1997) 2:252-55; E. C. Blake and A. G. Edmonds, *Biblical Sites in Turkey* (4th ed.; Istanbul: Redhouse Press, 1990); H. Koester, "Ephesos in Early Christian Literature," in *Ephesos: Metropolis of Asia: An Interdisciplinary Approach to Its Archaeology, Religion and Culture,* ed. H. Koester (HTS 41; Valley Forge, PA: Trinity Press International, 1995) 119-40; V. Limberis, "The Council of Ephesos: The Demise of the See of Ephesos and the Rise of the Cult of the Theotokos," in *Ephesos: Metropolis of Asia: An Interdisciplinary Approach to Its Archaeology, Religion and Culture,* ed. H. Koester (HTS 41; Valley Forge, PA: Trinity Press International, 1995) 321-40; G. McMahon, "Anatolian Mythology," *ABD* 1:236-40; idem, "History of Ancient Anatolia," *ABD* 1:233-36; J. McRay, *Archaeology and the New Testament* (Grand Rapids, MI: Baker, 1991) 250-61; R. E. Oster, *A Bibliography of Ancient Ephesus* (Metuchen, NJ: Scarecrow, 1987); idem, "The Ephesian Artemis as an Opponent of Early Christianity," *JAC* 19 (1976) 27-44; idem, "Ephesus," *ABD* 2:542-49; idem, "Ephesus, Ephesians," in *Encyclopedia of Early Christianity,* ed. E. F. Ferguson (2 vols.; 2d ed.; New York: Garland, 1997) 1:373-76; E. Yamauchi, *Archaeology of New Testament Cities of Western Asia Minor* (Grand Rapids, MI: Baker, 1980) 79-114.

L. M. McDonald

EPICTETUS

The Stoic philosopher Epictetus lived through the reign of Nero and the Flavian Emperors, and on into the second century. He is thus a near-contemporary of the NT writers and one of the earliest non-Christian witnesses to the spread of Christianity into Europe. His acerbic comments on what he saw as the follies of most ordinary life, and the calling of the philosopher to help people reform their lives, provide a crucial window into the moral environment of the NT.

1. Life
2. Sources of Information
3. Teachings
4. Knowledge of Christianity
5. Parallels and Contrasts wµith Early Christian Ideas
6. Later Influence

1. Life.

Epictetus lived in the period A.D. 50-120. Born a slave in Hierapolis (10 km. north of Laodicea) in Phrygia, and like his older contemporary *Seneca in poor health throughout his life, he was also lame (*Disc.* 1.8.14; 1.16.20), possibly due to his master's mistreatment in his youth (Origen *Cont. Cels.* 7.53, though cf. *Suda sv.* Epictetus). His primary philosophical training, while he was still a slave of Epaphroditus, Nero's freedman and official (*Disc.* 1.1.20; 1.9.28) was under *Musonius Rufus, an unconventional Roman Stoic who flourished under Nero and the early Flavians, and whom Epictetus often quotes. We do not know how or when he gained his freedom.

Epictetus taught philosophy in *Rome until philosophers were banished by Domitian in 89 or 92/93 (Aulus Gellius *Noc. Att.* 15.11.5), and eventually he settled in Nicopolis, in Epirus, which seems to have remained his base for the rest of his life. There he taught his students, mostly wealthy young men seeking public careers (though one slave is mentioned by one of his students, writing later). Occasionally he was visited by curious travelers. One such was the Corinthian student of rhetoric to whom he delivers a dressing down in *Discourses* 3.1.1-45. Late in life he is said to have married, in order to bring up an abandoned child.

2. Sources of Information.

We have detailed reports of Epictetus's views only because one of his students, later the noted historian Arrian of Nicomedia, recorded (somewhere before A.D. 113) at least five and possibly eight detailed books of his teachings (frag. 9, Aulus Gellius *Noc. Att.* 19.1.14). Four of these survive, along with a brief outline (the *Enchiridion,* or *Handbook).* They seem to reflect the lecture-room teaching of Epictetus, though the degree of stylistic interference from Arrian is unclear. Epictetus used a vigorous *diatribe, studded with interjections and objections from students and from imagined opponents, and false conclusions stated only to be refuted. Its style is strongly reminiscent of that of Paul, particularly in Romans.

3. Teachings.

3.1. Ethical Focus. We learn little from Epictetus of the study of cosmology or formal logic among the *Stoics, except that he valued and taught those subjects to his students (*Disc.* 1.7.1-33). What he cared about, and what Arrian particularly wanted to record, was his concern for practical ethics. Cosmology and logic, he regularly reminds his students, are worthless when they are studied for their own sakes. What matters is that people apply logic and cosmological premises to the improvement of their own moral will and life (*Disc.* 1.4.1-17; 1.17.13-29; 2.9.13-22; 3.2.1-18).

For one who held up calm *(apatheia)* and serenity *(euroia)* as the best state for humanity, Epictetus gives the impression of being extraordinarily vigorous and mentally robust rather than serene. He held, with the rest of Stoicism, that the only good that humans had within their grasp was the control of their own moral choices. All else—wealth, public office, good health or reputation—was outside human control, and hence morally indifferent. To desire such things was irrational and the cause of all human misery. Freedom and happiness were to be found only in the studied judgment of all impulses to desire or avoid things, and the rejection of those desires, the outcome of which were beyond our control.

3.2. Moral Optimism. Epictetus believed in the rationality of human moral judgment. Wicked people make moral errors, or are deceived, but they do not sin deliberately. They ought to be pitied as blind rather than despised or hated as immoral. He subscribed to the Socratic dictum that no one is deceived willingly. Good and evil lie fully within the realm of human choice (and are the only things that do). Nothing is to be feared except mistakes about the nature of good and evil, because to value irrationally is to make oneself a slave (*doulos, Disc.* 1.25.23). However, some people are naturally better suited to philosophy, and hence to a virtuous life, than are others. The truly rational man, according to Epictetus, cannot be enslaved by his desires or by anything else: Zeus has set him free. "Or do you really think he was likely to let his own son be made a slave?" (*Disc.* 1.19.9; cf. 4.7.17). On true freedom and slavery see the striking formulation in *Discourses* 4.1.175: "Freedom is not acquired by satisfying yourself with what you desire but by destroying your desire." Unlike many earlier Stoics, Epictetus believed in moral progress, particularly by way of the studied development of good habits.

3.3. Religious Views. Stoics generally were critical of many forms of popular religion but not of religion as such. They firmly believed in divine providence and benevolence and tended toward an inclusive monotheism that was equally happy talking about "God" or "the gods." Epictetus not only emphasized divine providence and benevolence but also expressed a profound personal piety. Humans are not just creations of but children of Zeus; their rationality makes them so (*Disc.* 1.3.1-3).

4. Knowledge of Christianity.
Nothing in Epictetus can be shown to demonstrate direct knowledge of the NT. One passage in the *Discourses,* however, demonstrates an awareness of the existence of the early Christian movement. In *Discourses* 4.7.6, arguing that both insanity and habit can produce moral firmness and lack of fear, "as with the Galileans," he goes on to argue that rational demonstrations of the nature of things ought to be able to produce such effects. There is little doubt that the "Galileans" in question are members of a church in Nicopolis, mentioned in passing in Titus 3:12.

A second passage has often been understood to refer to Christians, but the inference is far less likely. In *Discourses* 2.9.19-21 Epictetus describes certain people as "play-acting the Jew, though they are Greek." This could be a misunderstanding of Gentile conversion to Christianity, but it could equally refer to Godfearers or to nonobservant Diaspora Jews. The reference in the same context to "counterfeit baptists" (*parabaptistai,* a term not found in Greek before Epictetus) who have pretensions to the reputation of philosophy may or may not suggest that Christians are meant. The translation *baptists* may be a red herring. *Parabaptistai* may be a dyeing analogy, meaning people whose "colors are false" or "false dyers." But since the term is an emendation in the text, it is best not to put too great a weight on it.

5. Parallels and Contrasts with Early Christian Ideas.
Epictetus's thought exhibits both striking parallels with and contrasts to early Christian language and ideas. Since it is most unlikely that Epictetus has read any of the NT, these parallels and contrasts must reflect the differing uses the various authors make of their common linguistic and cultural background.

5.1. Gospels. *Handbook* 33.5 advises us to avoid oaths as far as possible (though Epictetus gives no reason; cf. Mt 5:33-34). In *Discourses* 3.14.4-6 Epictetus warns the budding philosopher not to do his *asketikos,* his training in self-discipline, so as to be noticed by people (cf. Mt 6:1-4). Likewise in *Discourses* 4.10.25 (cf. *Handbook* 13): "You cannot be continually giving attention to both externals and your own governing principle" suggests Jesus' statement, "No man can serve two masters."

5.2. Letters. In *Discourses* 1.28.25 Epictetus uses the metaphors of the besieging and destruction of cities in warfare to describe what happens to people who accept faulty judgments. Similarly in 2 Corinthians 10:4-5 Paul describes arguments that "demolish [other] arguments and every pretension that sets itself up against the knowledge of God" as being weapons that destroy fortresses in spiritual warfare.

In *Discourses* 2.10.4-5 citizen duties are briefly discussed using the common "parts of the body" metaphor, but with the emphasis on order, subordination and unity more than on unity in diversity, as it is in 1 Corinthians 12:12-26.

In *Discourses* 2.23-29, the various faculties of the human being are described as *charitas theou,* gifts of God's grace, but preeminently so the "ruling faculty" of rational judgment.

On marriage and celibacy as callings see *Discourses* 1.11 and 3.22.67-82. Epictetus here articulates common Greco-Roman attitudes in a manner reminiscent of Paul in 1 Corinthians 7:28-40.

In *Discourses* 3.9.14, like Paul in 2 Corinthians 11:6, Epictetus sees himself as vulnerable to the charge of being an inelegant speaker, but he asserts the superior importance of substance over style. His critique of the carefully groomed young student orator from *Corinth (*Disc.* 3.1.1-45) tells us precisely the sorts of graces Paul was criticized for lacking by the Corinthians (2 Cor 10:10).

Because of his firm belief in divine providence, Epictetus expresses a positive attitude to death and suffering combined with an awareness of the necessity of living to serve God (*Disc.* 1.9.10-17; 2.1.38; cf. Phil 1:20-26). Note his detailed discussion of the life of sufferings of the "missionary Cynic" in *Discourses* 3.22: the *Cynic's life involves being flogged like an ass but loving as a father or brother those who flog him (cf. *Disc.* 3.22.54, 82); Diogenes, the archetypal Cynic, took pride in his many sufferings (or, more precisely, in his attitude to them, *Disc.* 3.22.58-59). All this is tied to the Cynic's role as herald *(keryx)* of the gods (*Disc.* 3.22.69), exercising oversight *(episkopountes)* over humanity (*Disc.* 3.22.77) as worship to Zeus, whom he serves

(*Disc.* 3.22.82). God is to be praised in all circumstances (*Disc.* 1.16.16-21; 4.7.9).

It should be noted here that Epictetus, a Stoic, seems to conceive of the Cynic not as a follower of a separate school but as a true Stoic, a "frontline Stoic." The Cynic must embody what he teaches in a particularly dramatic fashion.

5.3. General Teachings. More broadly, for Epictetus the rational person is a child of God; God is creator, Father and guardian, and human beings are naturally akin *(syngeneis)* to God (*Disc.* 1.9.25). In *Discourses* 2.16.44 being a friend of God and a child of God are linked; friendship with God is also said to be true freedom (*Disc.* 2.17.29).

For Epictetus the role of the philosopher is delineated with several striking metaphors. The philosopher ought to function as a scout *(kataskopos)* for the rest of humanity, sent by God to spy out the "moral territory" (*Disc.* 1.24.3). The philosopher acts as a witness *(martys)* for God (*Disc.* 1.29.46-49; cf. 3.24.112). The Cynic is sent *(apesteltai)* to humanity by Zeus as both messenger *(angelos)* and scout (*kataskopos, Disc.* 3.22.23). Zeus exhibits him *(deiknysi)* to humanity in his poverty, powerlessness and illness, in exile or prison. The parallel with Paul's concept of his apostolic embodiment of the gospel, in its most radical and alienating form (1 Cor 4:9-13), is remarkable.

Epictetus presents four crucial metaphors for humanity's proper role in the world. God is putting on spectacular festival games (*see* Circuses and Games); it is our task to be good spectators and applaud (*Disc.* 4.1.105-6). (For a more standard *athletic metaphor comparable to Paul's in 1 Cor 9:24-27, see *Disc.* 4.4.30-32). God has provided a feast: enjoy what is set before you and do not grumble (*Ench.* 15). Play the game of social life you are part of, but without coveting the implements, as children will play games with potsherds without coveting the sherds themselves (*Disc.* 4.7.5, 20, 30). Merely play your role. Play, like the children, until you can no longer enjoy the game; then leave it (*Disc.* 1.24.20; 1.25.7-8). Play the role you are given like a good actor (*hypocritēs, Handbook* 17, cf. *Disc.* 1.29.44-46).

6. Later Influence.

Epictetus is first mentioned in early Christian literature by Origen *Contra Celsum* 6.2. Thereafter his popularity as a moral writer grows slowly but steadily and remains high into the nineteenth century.

See also ARISTOTLE, ARISTOTELIANISM; CYNICISM AND SKEPTICISM; EPICUREANISM; PHILOSOPHY; PLATO, PLATONISM; STOICISM.

BIBLIOGRAPHY. D. Balch, "1 Cor 7:32-35 and Stoic Debates About Marriage, Anxiety and Distraction," *JBL* 102 (1983) 429-39; S. Benko, "Pagan Criticism of Christianity During the First Two Centuries A.D.," *ANRW* 2.23.2 (1980) 1055-1118 (N.B. 1077-78); P. A. Brunt, "From Epictetus to Arrian," *Athenaeum* 55 (1977) 19-48; A. J. Droge, "Mori Lucrum: Paul and Ancient Theories of Suicide," *NovT* 30 (1988) 263-86; J. P. Hershbell, "The Stoicism of Epictetus: Twentieth-Century Perspectives," *ANRW* 2.36.3 (1989) 2148-63; R. F. Hock, "'By the Gods, It's My One Desire to See an Actual Stoic': Epictetus' Relations with Students and Visitors in His Personal Network," *Semeia* 56 (1992) 121-42; A. J. Malherbe, "Hellenistic Moralists and the New Testament," *ANRW* 2.26.1 (1992) 267-333 (N.B. 313-20); idem, "*Mē Genoito* and the Diatribe of Paul," *HTR* 73 (1980) 231-40; F. Millar, "Epictetus and the Imperial Court," *JRS* 55 (1965) 141-48; P. Oakes, "Epictetus (and the New Testament)," *VoxEv* 23 (1993) 39-56; J. N. Sevenster, "Education or Conversion: Epictetus and the Gospels," *NovT* 8 (1966) 247-62; P. Stadter, *Arrian of Nicomedia* (Chapel Hill: University of North Carolina Press, 1980); W. O. Stephens, "Epictetus on How the Stoic Sage Loves," *Oxford Studies in Ancient Philosophy* 14 (1996) 193ff; S. K. Stowers, *The Diatribe and Paul's Letter to the Romans* (SBLDS 57; Chico, CA: Scholars Press, 1981); B. W. Winter, *Philo and Paul Among the Sophists* (Cambridge: Cambridge University Press, 1997). C. Forbes

EPICUREANISM

Epicureanism refers to the system of moral and natural *philosophy that was founded by Epicurus in the late fourth century B.C. Epicurus promoted pleasure and friendship as ideal values and encouraged withdrawal from civic activities. His philosophy spawned close-knit communities of followers, most famously the Garden in *Athens, and met with both popularity and controversy throughout the *Hellenistic era.

1. Beginnings
2. Other Figures
3. Leading Ideas
4. Epicureanism and the New Testament
5. Evaluation and Comparison

1. Beginnings.

Epicurus was born to Athenian parents on the island of Samos in 341 B.C. He began the study of philosophy as a teenager and came under the influence of Nausiphanes, a follower of the atomism and naturalism of Democritus, the likely source of Epicurus's theory of physics. After establishing schools during brief sojourns in the Aegean cities of Mitylene and Lampsacus, Epicurus moved to Athens in about 306 and bought a house, including a garden that became the headquarters and eponym of his school. Unlike the more famous Academy of *Plato and the Lyceum of *Aristotle, the Garden of Epicurus admitted women and slaves. Followers of Epicurus lived on simple fare, shunning political involvement and enjoying one another's friendship.

Epicurus was a prolific writer; according to one report he composed about three hundred works (Diogenes Laertius *Vit.* 10.26). Only a few of these writings are extant, chiefly three letters and two collections of sayings: the *Letter to Herodotus,* dealing with Epicurus's physics; the *Letter to Pythocles,* on meteorology; the *Letter to Menoeceus,* a summary of Epicurean ethics; the *Kyriai Doxai* or Authoritative Maxims, forty ethical reflections; and the *Vatican Sayings,* a collection of eighty-one similar maxims found in a Vatican manuscript discovered in the late nineteenth century. The first four sources are preserved in the *Lives of Eminent Philosophers* by Diogenes Laertius. In addition to these writings, there are the remains of the library of Philodemus, a first-century B.C. Epicurean, fragments of whose works survived the eruption of Mt. Vesuvius in Herculaneum, entombed but significantly charred by ash and lava.

2. Other Figures.

Unlike most other schools of Hellenistic philosophy, the Garden of Epicurus generated more loyal followers than it did creative and independently minded successors. The essential points of Epicurus's philosophy were dogmatic and remained unchanged in the succeeding centuries. His estate was turned over to trustees; the direction of the school was left to Hermarchus of Mitylene, who was followed by Polystratus. The school's founder was commemorated monthly, and his birthday was celebrated each year. Prominent Epicureans of the second and first centuries B.C. included Demetrius of Lacon, Apollodorus, Phaedrus and Zeno of Sidon. The popularity of the school in the late Roman republic is seen in *Cicero's favorable remarks and especially in the work of Lucretius (c. 95-55), whose *De Rerum Natura,* "On the Nature of Things," is a poetic exposition of Epicurus's atomism and, to a lesser extent, his ethics. Our present-day knowledge of Epicureanism owes much to Lucretius.

3. Leading Ideas.

Atomism, pleasure, *friendship and retirement from public life were among the central ideas of Epicureanism. The basis of Epicurus's physics was atomism, a doctrine for which he was probably indebted to Democritus. Epicurus taught that all matter was composed of indivisible particles called atoms. Atoms existed in space, or the void, and were in constant motion, "falling" as Epicurus put it. But for objects to be formed, atoms had to collide and coalesce; therefore, their motion could not be entirely uniform. Thus, Epicurus introduced the swerve, a random movement of the atoms that permitted the formation of all things and ultimately made possible human free will.

Epicurus was, in the truest sense, a materialist. Matter was eternal, uncreated and without a divinely imputed purpose. Anything that had existence was material; this necessarily included the soul and even the gods. The soul was composed of finer atoms than the body but was still material. The gods likewise had material existence. They had immortal bodies, dwelt apart from the world in supreme happiness and did not interfere in human affairs. This understanding of the soul and the gods was closely related to a second Epicurean idea: pleasure.

Epicurus identified pleasure as the supreme value in life, the goal of philosophy. This was not, however, the kind of immoderate self-indulgence that is commonly associated with the modern term *Epicurean.* Pleasure was understood as the absence of disturbances. Epicurus taught that "whenever we say that pleasure is the goal, we do not mean the pleasures of dissolute persons or the pleasures that are found in sensuality, . . . but rather the absence of pain in the body and of trouble in the soul" (Diogenes Laertius *Vit.* 10.131). External testimony corroborates this; Diocles, a first-century B.C. philosopher, speaks of the Epicureans as "living a very simple and frugal life; at all events they were content with half a pint of thin wine and were, for the rest, thoroughgoing water-drinkers" (Diogenes Laertius *Vit.* 10.11) Thus Epicurus's hedonism was quite temperate. The pleasurable life, Epicurus insisted, must also be a wise and just life (Diogenes Laertius *Vit.* 10.140).

An important concept in Epicureanism was *ataraxia,* or imperturbability, the capacity to live life free of vexation and fear. Epicurus was especially concerned to eradicate the fears that popular religion inflicted on human beings: the fear of death, the gods and punishment in the afterlife. Since the gods were unconcerned with human beings in this life and there was no afterlife (inasmuch as the soul was material and disintegrated at the point of death), there was no need to fear one's demise or the prospect of judgment. Epicurus reasoned that "death is nothing to us since, while we exist, death is not present, and when death arrives, we do not exist" (Diogenes Laertius *Vit.* 10.125).

Two final ideas are closely related: friendship and retirement from public life. In contrast to the schools of Plato and Aristotle, Epicurus discouraged involvement in politics. Civic entanglements were likely to lead to stress; it was better to spend one's life quietly and in relative privacy, living simply and enjoying the company and conversation of friends. In antiquity even the enemies of Epicureanism had to concede that the fellowship and mutual devotion of members of the Garden were attractive.

4. Epicureanism and the New Testament. Epicureans are mentioned together with *Stoic philosophers in Acts 17:18 in connection with Paul's preaching of the gospel in Athens. The crowd's response to Paul, particularly to his mention of the resurrection of the dead, was mixed: some scoffed, but others requested a further audience with him (Acts 17:32). Although the connection is not explicitly made, it is plausible that the Epicurean philosophers were the scoffers and the Stoics were those intrigued enough to suggest a continued conversation (Croy). Epicurean physics and their emphasis on pleasure would have ruled out any notion of resurrection and final judgment, whereas Stoics entertained theories of the soul's at least limited survival of death.

Although Epicureans are not mentioned elsewhere in the NT, it has been suggested that they or some like-minded group are the targets of the polemic in 2 Peter (Neyrey 1980). The author of this epistle combats skepticism about the return of Christ and the judgment that will accompany it. Although doubts about prophecy and the afterlife were by no means limited to Epicureans, the opponents of 2 Peter may have belonged to, or at least been influenced by, this school of thought.

5. Evaluation and Comparison. Epicureans were falsely criticized in antiquity on two accounts: hedonism and atheism. It was noted that Epicurus's advocacy of pleasure was a call not to self-indulgence but to the moderate enjoyment of life's goods and the avoidance of pain. Moreover, Epicurus distinguished between immediate pleasures, which would sometimes be rejected, and long-term or ultimate pleasures that were to be pursued. The atheism of Epicurus was also a false charge. He clearly affirmed the existence of the gods, their immortality and their blessedness (Diogenes Laertius *Vit.* 10.123-24). He did not, however, affirm providence in the sense of divine care and provision for human beings and, in particular, any judicial or punitive role for the gods. Prayer was therefore meaningless, although the contemplation of the gods might serve the purpose of inspiring human beings to a similar happiness. In some of these respects, the Epicureans were remarkably like the Jewish sect of the Sadducees. Of the latter *Josephus wrote, "The Sadducees . . . do away with Fate altogether, and remove God beyond, not merely the commission, but the very sight, of evil. . . . As for the persistence of the soul after death, penalties in the underworld, and rewards, they will have none of them" (Josephus *J.W.* 2.8.14 §§164-65).

Epicureanism clearly differed from early Christianity and non-Sadducean Judaism on a number of points. Resurrection of the body had no place in Epicurean philosophy; neither did divine providence or judgment. Monotheism was never explicitly affirmed, and the Christian notion of divine incarnation would have violated Epicurus's belief in the gods' perfect blessedness. However, the intimate fellowship of Epicureans in the Garden and elsewhere, inclusive of *women and slaves, compares favorably with early Christian groups, which, according to Paul, also relativized distinctions of socioeconomic class and gender (Gal 3:28; 1 Cor 12:13). Finally, one can occasionally see in some of Paul's letters certain Epicurean-like emphases:

the call to a quiet, unobtrusive and responsible life in close community (1 Thess 4:9-12) and the need for personal freedom to be tempered by love and service to others (Gal 5:13).

See also ARISTOTLE, ARISTOTELIANISM; CYNICISM AND SKEPTICISM; EPICTETUS; PHILOSOPHY; PLATO, PLATONISM; STOICISM.

BIBLIOGRAPHY. C. Bailey, ed., *Epicurus: The Extant Remains* (Oxford: Oxford University Press, 1926); F. D. Caizzi, "The Porch and the Garden: Early Hellenistic Images of the Philosophical Life," in *Images and Ideologies: Self-Definition in the Hellenistic World,* ed. A. Bulloch et al. (Berkeley and Los Angeles: University of California Press, 1993) 303-29; D. Clay, *Epicurus and Lucretius* (Ithaca, NY: Cornell University Press, 1983); N. C. Croy, "Hellenistic Philosophies and the Preaching of the Resurrection (Acts 17:18, 32)," *NovT* 39 (1997) 21-39; N. W. Dewitt, *Epicurus and His Philosophy* (Minneapolis: University of Minnesota Press, 1954); B. Farrington, *The Faith of Epicurus* (New York: Basic, 1967); A. J. Festugière, *Epicurus and His Gods* (Oxford: Blackwell, 1955); B. Frischer, *The Sculpted Word: Epicureanism and Philosophical Recruitment in Ancient Greece* (Berkeley and Los Angeles: University of California Press, 1982); R. W. Hibler, *Happiness Through Tranquillity: The School of Epicurus* (Lanham, MD: University Press of America, 1984); A. A. Long and D. N. Sedley, *The Hellenistic Philosophers* (2 vols.; Cambridge: Cambridge University Press, 1987); J. H. Neyrey, "Acts 17, Epicureans and Theodicy: A Study in Stereotypes," in *Greeks, Romans and Christians: Essays in Honor of Abraham J. Malherbe,* ed. D. L. Balch, E. Ferguson and W. A. Meeks (Minneapolis: Fortress, 1990) 118-34; idem, "The Form and Background of the Polemic in 2 Peter," *JBL* 99 (1980) 407-31; D. Obbink, "The Atheism of Epicurus," *GRBS* 30 (1989) 187-223; J. M. Rist, *Epicurus: An Introduction* (Cambridge: Cambridge University Press, 1972); R. W. Sharples, *Stoics, Epicureans and Skeptics: An Introduction to Hellenistic Philosophy* (New York: Routledge, 1996). N. C. Croy

EPIGRAPHY. *See* INSCRIPTIONS AND PAPYRI: GRECO-ROMAN.

EPISTOLARY THEORY

An analysis of epistolary theory in Greco-Roman antiquity is confronted with three sobering realities. First, our knowledge of ancient epistolary theory is limited due to the paucity of available sources as well as the uncertainties surrounding their authorship and date. Second, the few epistolary handbooks and other relevant writings that have survived fail to provide a unified picture of how people viewed a letter in the Greco-Roman world. Third, what little can be learned about ancient epistolary theory does not comport well with the practice of letter writing (*see* Letters, Greco-Roman). Despite these realities, it is important to see what ideals about letter writing can be discerned from the epistolary handbooks, *rhetorical theory and the *educational curriculum.

1. Letter Writing in the Epistolary Handbooks
2. Letter Writing in Rhetorical Theory
3. Letter Writing in the Educational Curriculum
4. Summary

1. Letter Writing in the Epistolary Handbooks. Although it is clear that more epistolary handbooks were in existence in the ancient world, only two such manuals have survived: Pseudo-Demetrius's *Epistolary Types* and Pseudo-Libanius's *Epistolary Styles.*

1.1. Pseudo-Demetrius. The first handbook, *Epistolary Types,* is falsely attributed to Demetrius of Phalerum (commonly referred to as Pseudo-Demetrius). Proposed dates for this work range from 200 B.C. to A.D. 300, and recent investigation has failed to provide any narrower limits for its origin. It is possible that the handbook has undergone a number of revisions before it assumed its present form.

The document is ostensibly addressed to a certain Heraclides whom the author wishes to advise about the various epistolary types *(typoi)* and the proper style of writing. Pseudo-Demetrius stresses that the type of letter chosen must fit the circumstance to which it is addressed and be written as skillfully as possible. He then distinguishes between twenty-one kinds *(genē)* of letters, each named after its primary function: friendly, commendatory, blaming, reproachful, consoling, censorious, admonishing, threatening, vituperative, praising, advisory, supplicatory, inquiring, responding, allegorical, accounting, accusing, apologetic, congratulatory, ironic and thankful. For each of these twenty-one *genē* of letters, Pseudo-Demetrius provides some introductory comments that are followed by a sample letter.

1.2. Pseudo-Libanius. The second surviving

handbook, *Epistolary Styles,* exists in two differing manuscript traditions, one attributing the document to Libanius, the other to Proclus. Although the two versions differ greatly in title, contents and arrangement of material, they both likely originate from a common archetype that was produced by neither named author. Yet because the version attributed to Libanius has greater external support, the handbook is more often associated with his name than with Proclus. No fixed date exists for the work, with proposals ranging from A.D. 300 to 600. Although there are some superficial similarities between the handbooks of Pseudo-Libanius and Pseudo-Demetrius, the differences are so great that there is likely no interdependence between these two documents.

The prologue (1—4) to this epistolary handbook encourages letters to be written with the greatest precision and care. Yet it also recognizes that a letter is a kind of written conversation in which one should speak not too formally but as if in the presence of the absent person. The first major section (5—45) introduces some forty-one kinds (*prosēgoriai*) of letters: paraenetic, blaming, requesting, commending, ironic, thankful, friendly, praying, threatening, denying, commanding, repenting, reproaching, sympathetic, conciliatory, congratulatory, contemptuous, counteraccusing, replying, provoking, consoling, insulting, reporting, angry, diplomatic, praising, didactic, reproving, maligning, censorious, inquiring, encouraging, consulting, declaratory, mocking, submissive, enigmatic, suggestive, grieving, erotic and mixed. The second major section (46—50) contains instructions on various writing styles *(charaktēres)* that can be used, arguing for clarity, unpretentious speech and a length appropriate to the subject matter. The final section (51—92) presents sample letters of each of the forty-one kinds.

1.3. Observations. The focus of concern in the two extant handbooks lies in the body section of letters, as nothing is said about the opening and closing sections (the only exception is Pseudo-Libanius's brief comment that epistolary prescripts should be very plain: "So-and-so to So-and-so, greeting" [51]). Although each manual differs in the number and names of the distinct letter types that are identified, they share the conviction that the type chosen must match the specific situation of the letter. In other words, the letter type must be appropriate to the nature of the relationship that exists between the sender and the recipient as well as to the particular occasion for writing.

The criteria that Pseudo-Demetrius and Pseudo-Libanius use for classifying letters is different from modern typologies for ancient letters. The epistolary theorists were seemingly not concerned with the structural form of a letter or with formulaic expressions but instead categorized letters according to their purpose or historical occasion. Modern epistolographers have preferred instead to classify ancient letters into various forms or genres *(Gattungen).*

The most striking observation about the epistolary handbooks, however, is how few of their sample letters are found in the correspondence of that day. With the exception of the letter of introduction or commendation, the proposed letter types are only sparsely represented among the thousands of ancient letters that have thus far been recovered. The evidence indicates, therefore, that the epistolary theorists were not successful in influencing the practice of letter writing.

2. Letter Writing in Rhetorical Theory.

A second source for ideas about letter writing in the Greco-Roman world is rhetorical theory. Nevertheless, the subject of letter writing is connected with ancient *rhetoric in only a tangential way. The discussion of epistolary theory is absent from the earliest extant rhetorical handbooks and is found merely as an excursus or appendix in later writings on rhetoric.

The most important and extensive treatment of letter writing by a rhetorician is found in the treatise *De Elocutione* ("On Style"), erroneously attributed to Demetrius of Phalerum (the same person who is also wrongly associated with the epistolary handbook). No agreement for the exact date of this document exists, but most proposals range from the second century B.C. to the first century A.D. Demetrius's remarks about letter writing come in an excursus (223-35) on the plain style, the third of the four styles of speaking.

After citing the opinion of Artemon, the editor of Aristotle's correspondence, that the letter ought to be written in the same manner as a conversation, Demetrius argues instead that the style of the letter should be a little more studied than a dialogue, since it is committed to writing and sent to the recipient as a kind of literary gift.

Yet the letter must not be too stilted or long, or else it will only be a treatise with letter headings. Demetrius further advises that the letter must reflect the writer's character such that he "reveals his own soul." In addition to a proper epistolary style, there also are appropriate epistolary topics. Subjects such as natural history or logical subtleties do not belong in letters, while the use of proverbs and old sayings are acceptable as long as they serve merely to augment the expression of one's affections and friendship.

Other rhetoricians also broach the topic of letter writing but in a much more cursory fashion. And while a survey of this material reveals that they repeat a number of the points found in Demetrius, it also exposes the strikingly brief attention given to letter writing. Demetrius discusses this subject in an excursus, *Cicero makes no room for a systematic treatment of it in his works on rhetoric, Quintilian and Theon contain only sporadic references to it, Philostratus of Lemnos *(On Letters)* and Gregory of Nazianzus (*Epistle* 51) address it in brief fashion, and Julius Victor relegates it to an appendix (*Art of Rhetoric* 27). The lack of attention given to letter writing is especially surprising in light of the fact that many who were trained in rhetoric functioned as secretaries in chanceries.

Letter writing and rhetoric, therefore, should not be too quickly linked. Not only do the rhetorical handbooks contain few references to letters, but also the epistolary handbooks similarly fail to relate letter writing to the five traditional aspects of rhetorical practice (invention, arrangement, style, memory and delivery) or to the three traditional species of rhetoric (judicial, deliberative and epideictic). This fact serves as an important caution against the all-too-popular practice of using Greco-Roman rhetoric as a hermeneutical key to interpret NT letters, especially the letters of Paul.

3. Letter Writing in the Educational Curriculum.

A third source for understanding more about ancient epistolary theory is the educational curriculum, since this subject was likely taught in the second stage of education (*see* Education). After completing an elementary training in the grammar and form of letters, it seems that students (now about twelve to fifteen years old) went on to receive instruction in epistolary theory and the subtleties of letter writing.

The epistolary manuals that would have been used to teach letter writing and that would provide clear evidence that this subject was taught in the educational curriculum have not survived (the handbooks of Pseudo-Demetrius and Pseudo-Libanius were probably used in the training of professional letter writers rather than in the regular educational curriculum). Nevertheless, the fact that the overall form of a letter and its constituent epistolary formulas remain so consistent over several centuries is most likely due to the training in letter writing that took place in school. In addition, the grammatical handbooks used in this era (e.g., Dionysius of Alexander [first century A.D.], Apollonius Dyscolus [second century A.D.]) presuppose a basic knowledge of letters—a knowledge that the students had previously been taught in school. There is also the evidence of the bilingual Bologna Papyrus, PBon 5 (third to fourth century A.D.), which appears to be the exercises of a student who was working with a manual on epistolary theory. This manuscript contains eleven examples in Latin and Greek of various types of letters, without any accompanying explanation of each type. But despite compelling evidence that epistolary theory was taught in the education curriculum in the Greco-Roman world, virtually none of the texts used in the schools have survived, thereby providing little information on how the ancients conceived of letters.

4. Summary.

The epistolary handbooks, the rhetorical writings and the educational curriculum reveal a genuine interest in epistolary theory—the ideal characteristics and style of a letter. Nevertheless, the epistolary theorists and rhetoricians did not appear to have much impact on the practice of writing letters, and very little about this subject can be learned from the training received in the schools. A more accurate understanding of letter writing, therefore, requires an analysis of the several thousand letters from antiquity that have survived.

See also EDUCATION: JEWISH AND GRECO-ROMAN; LETTERS, GRECO-ROMAN; RHETORIC.

BIBLIOGRAPHY. D. E. Aune, "Letters in the Ancient World," in *The New Testament in Its Literary Environment* (LEC 8; Philadelphia: Westminster, 1987) 158-82; W. G. Doty, *Letters in Primitive Christianity* (Philadelphia: Fortress, 1973) 1-17; H. Koskenniemi, *Studien zur Idee und Phraseologie des griechischen Briefes bis 400 n. Chrs.* (Helsinki: Akateeminen Kirjakauppa, 1956) 18-53; A. J. Malherbe, *Ancient Epistolary Theorists* (Atlanta: Scholars Press, 1988); S. K. Stowers, *Letter Writing in Greco-Roman Antiquity* (LEC 5; Philadelphia: Westminster, 1986); K. Thraede, *Grundzüge griechish-römischer Brieftopik* (Munich: C. H. Beck, 1970); J. L. White, *Light from Ancient Letters* (Philadelphia: Fortress, 1986) 189-220.

J. A. D. Weima

EQUESTRIAN ORDER. *See* ROMAN SOCIAL CLASSES.

ESCHATOLOGIES OF LATE ANTIQUITY

The word *eschatology* was coined by Protestant theologians in the seventeenth century. It refers to the last things, which may be either the end of the world or the end of the individual and that which follows it. The range of the word has broadened over time to include any kind of teleology. In this article we will distinguish four kinds of eschatology: political eschatology, which envisions a definitive kingdom or other form of society; cosmic eschatology, which envisions the end of this world and a new creation; personal eschatology, which is concerned with forms of afterlife; and realized eschatology, in which the definitive future state is anticipated in the present.

1. Political Eschatology
2. Cosmic Eschatology
3. Personal Eschatology
4. Realized Eschatology

1. Political Eschatology.

1.1. The Hope for Definitive Kingship. The hope for a definitive, lasting political order was widespread in the ancient Near East and was most often associated with ideal kingship. The Babylonian Uruk prophecy from the sixth century B.C. extols a king who "will establish judgments for the land" and restore the shrines of Uruk. The king in question is most probably Nebuchadnezzar. The prophecy continues: "After him his son will arise as king in Uruk and rule the entire world. He will exercise authority and kingship in Uruk and his dynasty will stand forever. The kings of Uruk will exercise authority like the gods" (Hunger and Kaufman). The biblical prophet Isaiah envisions the reign of "a shoot from the stump of Jesse" in utopian terms. The wolf will lie down with the lamb, and the child will play safely by the adder's lair (Is 11). This kind of royal ideology could be used in late antiquity either as an imperial ideology, to vindicate the powerful, or as a revolutionary ideal on the part of peoples who had lost their native kingship.

1.2. The Motif of Four Kingdoms and a Fifth. One widespread formulation of political eschatology that could be adapted to meet different purposes was the schema of four kingdoms followed by a fifth. The Greek *historian Herodotus, writing in the fifth century B.C., had already noted a sequence of empires in Asia: first the Assyrians, then the Medes, then the Persians (Herodotus *Hist.* 1.95, 130). This view became traditional and may be taken to reflect the official Persian view of history, whereby the Persian Empire represented the end of the process. In the *Hellenistic era, however, the sequence of kingdoms was extended. A fragment of an otherwise unknown author Aemilius Sura, preserved by Velleius Paterculus around the turn of the era, says that "the Assyrians were the first of all races to hold power, then the Medes, after them the Persians and then the Macedonians. Then when the two kings, Philip and Antiochus, of Macedonian origin, had been completely conquered, soon after the overthrow of Carthage, the supreme command passed to the Roman people" (Swain, 2). The references to the overthrow of Macedonia and Carthage suggest that Aemilius wrote in the second century B.C., probably about 175 B.C. The same sequence of kingdoms, with Rome as the climactic fifth, is found in Polybius, in the late second century B.C., Dionysius of Halicarnassus around the turn of the era and *Tacitus, about A.D. 100.

A similar sequence, without reference to Rome, is found in several Near Eastern writings. Best known of these is the book of Daniel. Daniel interprets Nebuchadnezzar's dream of a huge statue made of different metals in terms of a sequence of kingdoms, which are easily identified as Babylon, Media, Persia and Greece (Dan 2; J. J. Collins 1993, 166-70). Since Media never ruled over Judea, the sequence is evidently traditional (*see* Jewish History: Persian Period). Daniel departs from the traditional order only insofar as he substitutes Babylon for Assyria as the first kingdom. In Daniel's interpretation, the four kingdoms represented by the statue will be shattered, and then the God of heaven will set up a kingdom that will never pass to another people. The sequence is repeated in Daniel 7, where the kingdoms are represented by beasts rising from the sea and the kingdom is given to the heavenly "one like a son of man" and the holy ones of the Most High.

The traditional order of Assyria, Media, Persia and Greece is found in another Jewish source, the fourth *Sibylline Oracle.* The kingdom of the Macedonians coincides with the tenth generation and the fourth kingdom. In the extant text of the Sibyl, however, the fourth kingdom is followed by the rise of Rome. Rome is not assigned a number and seems to be a late insertion to update the oracle. The original oracle probably dated from the Hellenistic period and implied that Macedonia would fall when the fourth kingdom had exhausted its allotted time (Flusser).

A close parallel to Daniel is found in a Persian source, the *Bahman Yasht,* which is late in its present form but probably reflects the basic structure of a text from the Hellenistic period. Zoroaster is shown "the trunk of a tree on which there were four branches: one of gold, one of silver, one of steel and one of mixed iron." Each branch is interpreted as the reign of a king. That of mixed iron is the evil sovereignty of "the 'divs' having disheveled hair." These latter were probably the Macedonians. The unkempt hair of Alexander and his followers contrasts with the neatly stylized hair of the Persians in ancient portrayals. The implication of the vision is that the course of history will be reversed when the fourth kingdom has run its course (Eddy, 17; Hultgård 1991, 114-34).

The Roman author Aemilius Sura shows that the motif of four kingdoms and a fifth could easily be made to serve as propaganda for an imperial power. Conversely, Daniel 2, the Sibyl and probably also the *Bahman Yasht* show that it could be a medium for revolutionary hope that the sovereignty of the present order is predetermined and limited. The same is true for any idea of a definitive kingdom.

1.3. Imperial Eschatology. The main examples of imperial eschatology from late antiquity are provided by the *Roman Empire. In book 1 of Virgil's *Aeneid,* Jupiter teaches the mother of Aeneas about the secrets of fate and concludes: "For these [the Romans] I set neither bounds nor periods. Dominion without end *(imperium sine fine)* I give to them" (Virgil *Aeneid* 1.278-79).

The Fourth Eclogue similarly claimed that a final age *(ultima aetas)* was at hand when the earth would be transformed. This age would be the confirmation and fulfillment of Roman rule, not its overthrow (see further Cancik).

1.4. Resistance to Hellenistic and Roman Rule. Naturally the peoples of the East who had been subjected by Rome saw things differently. The richest deposit of revolutionary political eschatology is found in Jewish literature, replete with hopes for a kingdom of God or for a messianic reign on earth (*see* Apocalypticism). S. K. Eddy made a sweeping argument that such revolutionary eschatology was widespread throughout the Near East in the Hellenistic and Roman periods. There is some evidence in support of this thesis, but it is limited. The *Bahman Yasht* may have been formulated as an anti-Hellenistic apocalypse (*see* Apocalyptic Literature). Somewhat later (first century B.C.) the *Oracle of Hystaspes* professed hope that a great king would come from heaven to restore the right order. (Whether the *Oracle* can be accepted as an authentic expression of Persian ideas is disputed, but it has been ably defended by Hinnells.)

In Egypt, the *Demotic Chronicle* speaks enigmatically of a man from Herakleopolis who would arise after the Ionians. The least controversial example of an anti-Hellenistic prophecy from the ancient Near East is found in the *Potter's Oracle* from Hellenistic Egypt (second century B.C.). This oracle clearly looks for the destruction of the city by the sea (*Alexandria) and for the coming of a king from the sun—a legitimate Egyptian king (Koenen). It should be noted that several passages in the Jewish **Sibylline Oracles* are of uncertain provenance and could well have been written by Gentiles. A notable example is found in *Sibylline Oracle* 3.350-80, which denounces Rome for its greed and arrogance and prophesies that the wealth will be returned to Asia (see further J. J. Collins 1997a). In all of these texts, the goal is the restoration of a righteous society on earth. This was also the goal of Jewish messianic hope.

1.5. Early Christianity. Early Christian eschatology is ambiguous with respect to the political order. On the one hand, we find scathing denunciations of Rome in the book of Revelation. On the other hand, little is said about the nature of the just society that should ensue when Rome is overthrown. Revelation at least provides for a thousand-year reign on earth; however, its ultimate goal is not the transformation of the political order but the destruction of this world and the emergence of a new creation. We do find a continuing interest in political eschatology in such texts as the *Apocalypse of Elijah* and *Sibylline Oracles* 8 from Egypt in the second to third centuries A.D.

2. Cosmic Eschatology.

2.1. Jewish and Christian Apocalypses. The classic expressions of cosmic eschatology are found in Jewish and Christian apocalypses, culminating in the book of Revelation. The notion of the end of the world had its origin in the hyperbolic metaphors of the Hebrew prophets, who used the language of cosmic destruction to predict the downfall of specific places. Beginning in the early second century B.C. this language comes to be understood more literally. The Apocalypse of Weeks in *1 Enoch* (*see* Enoch, Books of) says that at a fixed point in the future the world will be written down for destruction and the old heaven will be taken away and replaced with a new one (*1 Enoch* 91:15-17). In the *Dead Sea Scrolls we read of fiery floods of *Belial that will consume the earth (1QH 11:29-36). The apocalypse of 4 Ezra, written at the end of the first century A.D., envisions a period of primeval silence between the destruction of the old world and the new creation (4 Ezra 7:30; *see* Esdras, Books of). Revelation also predicts the destruction of this world and a new creation (Rev 21:1).

In the Jewish apocalypses, cosmic eschatology usually complements and completes the traditional political eschatology. In the earlier apocalypses and in the Dead Sea Scrolls, the relationship between the two is often left unclarified. The book of Daniel (Dan 7) still speaks of a kingdom of the people of the holy ones on earth, but the kingdom is given to a figure who comes on the clouds. The holy ones are *angels, and the emphasis in Daniel is on the transformation of righteous humanity to an angelic state. The writings of the first century A.D., however, are increasingly systematic. So, for example, 4 Ezra 7 provides for a four-hundred-year messianic reign in which the promises to *Israel are fulfilled before the new creation. Revelation also provides for a period of earthly fulfillment in the thousand-year reign of Christ. But Christianity in general had less interest than did Judaism in the promises to Israel or in earthly fulfillment. In the Gospels and in the epistles of Paul the focus of eschatology is on the coming of Christ on the clouds, final judgment and afterlife. Although Jesus is called Christ, Messiah, he does not restore the kingdom of Israel but is understood in cosmic terms after the model of Daniel's "one like a son of man."

2.2. Zoroastrianism. Outside of Judaism and Christianity, the main source for cosmic eschatology in the ancient world was Zoroastrianism. Zoroastrian eschatology is complex and is fully developed only in the Pahlavi literature of the early Middle Ages (Hultgård 1998). Already in the Gathas, however, there is a strong belief in the ultimate triumph of righteousness. Plutarch reports a form of Zoroastrian myth that he claims to have derived from Theopompus, who wrote about 300 B.C.

According to this myth, the world is divided between Horomazes (Ahura Mazda) and Areimanius (Ahriman), representing light and darkness respectively. Each is said to dominate the other for three thousand years, and for another three thousand years they will fight and make war, until one smashes up the domain of the other. In the end Hades shall perish, and humanity shall be happy (Plutarch *On Isis and Osiris* 46—47). Centuries later we find a more explicit form of this myth in the *Bundahishn,* a compendium of cosmological material whose final compilation dates to the period after the Arab-Muslim conquest of Iran: "Ohrmazd knew in his omniscience that within these nine thousand years, three thousand years would pass entirely according to the will of Ohrmazd, three thousand years in the period of mixture according to the will of both Ohrmazd and Ahreman, and that in the last battle it would be possible to make the Evil Spirit powerless and that he [Ohrmazd] would [thus] prevent aggression against the created world" (Hultgård 1998, 45-46). This dualistic view of history is adapted in the writings of the Jewish Dead Sea sect (see especially the Treatise on the Two Spirits in 1QS 3—4 and the War Rule; *see* Rule of the Community/Manual of Discipline; War Scroll).

The last three thousand years of this system is subdivided into three millennia, and the end of each millennium is characterized by tribulations and disasters, heralding the coming of a new savior. At the end of the final millennium, those who are still alive will not die, and those who are dead will be raised in a general resurrection. The righteous go to paradise, but the wicked are thrown back to hell for three days and three nights to purify them. Then they are brought back to earth and finally cleansed in streams of fire, as part of the purification of the world. The classic expression of this conflagration is found in the *Bundahishn:*

> Afterwards the fire and halo melt the Shatvairo in the hills and mountains, and it remains on this earth like a river. Then all men will pass into that melted metal and become pure; when one is righteous, then it seems to him just as though he walks continually in warm milk; but when wicked, then it seems to him in such manner as though in the world he walks continually in melted metal. (*Bundahishn* 34; West, 125-26)

A similar account is found in Lactantius (*Divinae Institutiones* 7.21), who most probably derived it from the *Oracle of Hystaspes.* Justin Martyr (*Apol. I* 20.1) also affirms that Hystaspes, like the Sibyl, predicted the destruction of the world by fire. After this conflagration, all things will be made new.

2.3. Greek and Latin Literature. Cosmic eschatology is not prominent in Greek and Latin writings, but there are some relevant ideas. Hesiod portrays world history as a sequence of ages, symbolized by metals, and may imply a doctrine of eternal return. (At the end of the sequence he says "I would not want to sojourn with the fifth, but either die before it or live after it"; Hesiod *Op.* 106-201). *Plato puts in the mouth of an Egyptian speaking to Solon the legend that the world must undergo many destructions, the chief ones being by fire and water (Plato *Tim.* 22b). The periodic destruction of the world, first by water and then by fire, is an important motif in the Jewish and Christian *Sibylline Oracles* and also appears in the *Life of Adam and Eve* 49:3 (*see* Adam and Eve) and in 2 Peter 3. For Plato, however, the world was ultimately made imperishable and immortal (Plato *Politicus* 273b).

The notion of cosmic conflagration *(ekpyrōsis)* held a prominent but controversial place in *Stoic thought (Cancik, 115-16). The *ekpyrōsis* would effect the purification of the cosmos but would not entail a judgment. The Stoics disputed among themselves whether it would be followed by *palingenesia,* renewed birth, and the repetition of all things. *Seneca offered one formulation of Stoic eschatology in his *Consolation to Marcia* (Seneca *Marc.* 26): "When the time comes at which the world extinguishes itself in order to renew itself again, the elements will scatter through their own power, and stars collide with stars, and when all matter burns, what now shines disposed in distinct places will burn with one single fire." Seneca claimed support for these ideas from Berossus, the Babylonian priest who presented Babylonian lore in Hellenistic dress in the early Hellenistic period: "Berossus, who translated Belus, said these things happen in accordance with the course of the stars. He makes the assertion so confidently that he even assigns a time for the conflagration and the flood" (Seneca *Nat. Quaest.* 3.29). There is no basis for such predictions in Babylonian tradition, however (Lambert).

Greek thinkers usually thought of the cosmos as eternal. *Cicero similarly speculates that the world either must be eternal or at least must last a very long time because of nature's providential care (Cicero *Nat. Deor.* 2.85). The Jewish philosopher *Philo similarly allowed that the world may be made immortal by the providence of God (Philo *Decal.* 58) and cites the view of some philosophers that "though by nature destructible it will never be destroyed, being held together by a bond of superior strength, namely the will of its Maker" (Philo *Rer. Div. Her.* 246; cf. Plato's *Tim.* 41A). The *Wisdom of Solomon, which comes from the same *Alexandrian milieu as did Philo, seems to imply a similar view.

2.4. Egyptian Tradition. A rare example of cosmic eschatology in the Egyptian tradition is found in the late *Apocalypse of Asclepius,* which is written in Greek and associated with the *Hermetic corpus. This apocalypse retains some of the essential characteristics of political oracles. An evil age is caused by the invasion of foreigners, and this is followed by a radical transformation of the earth. This apocalypse differs from earlier Egyptian tradition, however, by envisioning a destruction of the world by fire and flood and a restitution of the world to its pristine state (*Asclepius* 24-26; Nock and Festugière, 326-30).

3. Personal Eschatology.

3.1. Egypt. Most peoples in the ancient world believed in the survival of a soul after death, but in many cases this was a weak, shadowy existence. This was true both of the Hebrew idea of the *nepeš* and of the Homeric idea of the *psychē.* Egypt was distinctive in the ancient world for its belief in the judgment of the dead (Griffiths). The *Book of the Two Ways* describes ways that await the deceased, many of them tortuous and fearful. The text was usually inscribed on the inside base of coffins, as a guide for the dead. The deceased must pass through a series of gates, each one defended by a terrifying guardian, which must be overcome by spells. But the main issues that determined the welfare of the person in the hereafter were innocence and purity. In the *Book of the Dead* (125) the deceased is instructed to say: "See I have come to you without sin, without guilt, without evil, without there being any evil in me, without there being a witness against me." Other motifs that are characteristic of Egyptian eschatology are the weighing of the souls of the dead and the association of the right side with salvation and of the left with damnation. Also characteristic is the role of the god Thoth as impartial recorder in the tribunal after death.

3.2. Greece and Rome. In Greek tradition belief in the judgment of the dead is associated especially with the Orphic tradition. New light has been shed on Orphic eschatology by a series of texts inscribed on gold leaves, found in tombs in Italy, Crete and Thessaly (Graf; Cancik, 97-98). Typical of the tradition is the reversal of life and death: "Now you have died and now you have come into being, O thrice happy one, on this same day." The dead are instructed to say to Persephone that "Bacchus himself has freed you" from the sin of the Titans who had killed and eaten the child Dionysus. The dead person awaits transformation into a god and will partake in a symposium of the blessed. Similar ideas informed the mystery cults. Cicero, who was initiated in the Eleusinian mysteries, writes that "we truly have recognized the foundations *(principia)* of life and not only received a reason to live with joy, but also to die with a better hope" (Cicero *De Leg.* 2.14.36). A passage in Plutarch comments on the connection between death and the mysteries:

> Here [on earth] it [the soul] is ignorant, unless it is already at the point of death. Then, however, it has an experience like those who are initiated into the great mysteries; therefore, the word is similar to the word and the thing is similar to the thing: *teleutān—teleisthai,* die—be initiated. First a wandering in error, an arduous running around, a fearful walking in the dark, which finds no goal; then before the end itself, all the monstrosity, shudders, trembling, sweat and astonishment. After this a wonderful light comes to meet [them], pure places and meadows receive them with voices and dances and the celebration of holy sounds and venerable apparitions: amidst this moves the already perfected initiated, having been freed and released. (Plutarch frag. 178, in Stobaeus; see Cancik, 97)

Plato's ideas on the judgment of the dead are generally believed to be derived from Orphic tradition. In the *Gorgias* 253, he tells us that "he who has lived all his life in justice and holiness shall go, when he is dead, to the Islands of the Blessed, and dwell there in perfect happiness out of the reach of evil; but he who has lived unjustly and impiously shall go to the house of vengeance and punishment, which is called Tartarus," and he goes on to describe the judgment in detail. The most influential Platonic discussion of the judgment is found in the Myth of Er in *Republic* 10.614b-621. The Pamphylian Er, who had apparently died on the battlefield, is sent back from the netherworld as a "messenger of the afterlife." He reports the judgment of the dead and the punishment of the wicked and then the choice of lifestyle by the soul and reincarnation. For Plato, the soul was eternal, uncreated and imperishable. Souls must be reincarnated repeatedly for ten thousand years but can be freed earlier from the cycle of reincarnation by the philosophical life or by a life of virtue (Plato *Phaedr.* 248-49).

The motif of the otherworldly journey is used by philosophical authors such as Cicero *(Somn.),* Seneca *(Marc.)* and Plutarch *(Gen. Socr.; Ser. Num. Vind.)* as a way of inculcating beliefs about the afterlife. This motif is ridiculed by the second century A.D. humorist Lucian in his *Icaromenippus.* The motif of the descent to the netherworld is found in Homer's *Odyssey* 11. In Virgil's *Aeneid* 6, the descent of Aeneas to the netherworld provides an occasion for scenes of postmortem judgment and a prophecy about the future of Rome. The descent motif too was parodied by Lucian in his *Nekyomanteia* (see further Attridge). The ascent texts (*see* Heavenly Ascent) sometimes entail the idea of astral immortality. Already in the fifth century B.C. Aristophanes had joked about "what people say, that when we die we straightaway turn to stars" (Aristophanes *Pax* 832-34). The popularity of this belief is attested in epitaphs of the Hellenistic and Roman periods (Cumont, 142-288).

3.3. Persia. The belief in the afterlife of the

soul is well attested in the Gathas, the oldest stratum of Zoroastrian tradition. After death, the soul must cross the Činwad bridge, or the bridge of the accountkeeper or judge. The souls of the deceitful recoil when they reach the bridge. The most elaborate account of the afterlife is provided by the late Pahlavi *Ardā Wirāz Nāmag. Wirāz* is a pious man who is commissioned to go to heaven to verify the utility of the religious ceremonies of his community. He is taken to a fire temple and given a drink of wine mixed with henbane. When he falls asleep, his soul leaves the body and crosses the Činwad bridge. On the seventh day he awakes and gives a report of his journey. He is accompanied by two heavenly figures who function as guides. He visits both the abodes of the righteous and the places of punishment of the damned. (Most of the book is devoted to the latter.) There are references to such otherworldly journeys in other texts. Such journeys are attributed to Zoroaster himself and to Vištāsp, the first king to embrace the teachings of Zoroaster (Hultgård 1998, 62-63).

3.4. Judaism. Traditionally Israelites believed in the survival of the *nepeš*, or shade, in Sheol but rejected the idea of a judgment of the dead. This skeptical view still persists in the book of *Sirach (Sir 41:1-4), written in the early second century B.C., and is stated emphatically by Qoheleth. About this time, however, the belief in a differentiated afterlife was emerging in apocalyptic circles. *1 Enoch* 22 describes three distinct places in which the spirits of the souls of the dead are segregated before judgment. (The original text seems to have envisioned four.) More typical of the early apocalyptic tradition is *1 Enoch* 104, which assures the righteous that they will shine like the lights of heaven and become companions of the host of heaven. Similarly, in Daniel 12 the resurrected wise ones will shine like the stars. The stars were commonly identified with the host of heaven in Semitic traditions. In the case of Daniel, there may also be some overtones of the Hellenistic belief in astral immortality (J. J. Collins 1993, 394-98).

These early apocalypses do not envision bodily resurrection. The book of **Jubilees* says explicitly that "their bodies will rest in the earth and their spirits will have much joy" (*Jub.* 23:22). Resurrection takes on a physical character, however, in the story of the *Maccabean martyrs, in 2 Maccabees 7. Both the idea of a spiritual body and of a physical *resurrection were current in the first century A.D. The issue of the form of the resurrected body is discussed explicitly in *2 Baruch* 50—51, written at the end of the first century A.D. Baruch is assured that the earth will restore bodies just as it received them so that they can be recognized. The righteous, however, "shall be made like the angels and be made equal to the stars; and they shall be changed into whatever form they will" (*2 Bar.* 51:10; *see* Baruch, Books of).

There are few clear references to resurrection in the *Dead Sea Scrolls (J. J. Collins 1997b, 110-29). These are found in the so-called *Messianic Apocalypse* (4Q521) and **Pseudo-Ezekiel* (4Q385 + 4Q376). There is ample evidence in the scrolls, however, for reward and punishment after death. According to the Treatise on the Two Spirits in the *Rule of the Community,* those who walk in the way of light will be rewarded with "eternal enjoyment with endless life, and a crown of glory with majestic raiment in eternal light" (1QS 4:7-8). The wicked will receive "a glut of punishments at the hands of all the angels of destruction, for eternal damnation for the scorching wrath of the God of revenge, for permanent error and shame without end, with the humiliation of destruction by the fire of the dark regions" (1QS 4:12-13; compare *Josephus's account of the eschatology of the *Essenes, in *J.W.* 2.8.11 §§154-56).

The abodes of the blessed and the places of punishment of the damned are explored in greater detail in apocalypses that describe ascents through the heavens *(2 Enoch, 3 Baruch)* or descent to the netherworld *(*Apocalypse of Zephaniah).* While the prototype of such visions was the Enochic Book of the Watchers (*1 Enoch* 1—36), the main examples of this subgenre come from the Hellenistic *Diaspora. Also typical of the Diaspora is the Platonic idea of the immortality of the soul, which is endorsed by the philosopher Philo and the *Wisdom of Solomon.

3.5. Early Christianity. Because of the central role of the resurrection of Jesus, belief in afterlife is ubiquitous in early Christianity. In the Gospels, the resurrection is associated with the stories about the empty tomb. Paul, however, who is probably our earliest witness to the tradition, does not mention the empty tomb in his defense of the resurrection of the dead in 1 Corinthians 15. Instead he argues that "flesh and blood cannot inherit the kingdom of God" (1 Cor

15:50) and that what is raised is "a spiritual body." After the NT period, Christianity increasingly emphasizes the immortality of the soul while retaining the expectation of a final, general resurrection. There is an abundance of early Christian apocalypses, in the names of Peter, Paul, John, Mary and others (A. Y. Collins). These are predominantly otherworldly journeys and are largely concerned with rewards and punishments in the afterlife. Even an apocalypse like the *Apocalypse of Peter,* which does not describe a heavenly journey, contains an extensive account of the places of punishment and a brief vision of paradise. The Christian fascination with the punishment of the damned can be seen in *Sibylline Oracle* 2, in which an older Jewish oracle has been adapted by a Christian interpolator. There is also an extensive corpus of *Gnostic apocalypses from Nag Hammadi, in which the primary concern is with personal eschatology (Fallon).

4. Realized Eschatology.

4.1. John. Finally, we may deal more briefly with the idea of realized eschatology, which claims that the salvation promised to the righteous after death can be experienced proleptically in the present. The classic expression of realized eschatology is found in the Gospel of John, in which Jesus assures his followers that "anyone who hears my word and believes him who sent me has eternal life, and does not come under judgment, but has passed from death to life" (Jn 5:24).

4.2. The Dead Sea Scrolls. A precedent for such an idea of present salvation can be found in the Dead Sea Scrolls, in which the author of the *Hodayot* claims to enjoy in the present the life with the angels that is promised to the righteous after death in the apocalypses of Daniel and *Enoch:* "I thank you, Lord, because you saved my life from the pit, and from Sheol and Abaddon you have lifted me up to an everlasting height, so that I can walk on a boundless plain. . . . The corrupt spirit you have purified from the great sin so that he can take his place with the host of the holy ones, and can enter into communion with the congregation of the sons of heaven" (1QH 11:19-23). This belief explains why there is so little interest in resurrection in the Dead Sea Scrolls. The transition to eternal life was made upon joining the community.

4.3. Gnosticism. The idea of realized eschatology is especially characteristic of the Gnostic writings from Nag Hammadi. At the risk of some overgeneralization, it may be said that gnosis is enlightenment and involves the retrieval of the particles of light from the realm of darkness (Rudolph, 115). This process can be completed only at death, but enlightenment can be experienced in this life. Resurrection is understood as spiritual awakening. So we read in the *Gospel of Philip:* "Those who say: 'First one will die and [then] rise' are wrong. If men do not first experience the resurrection while they are alive, they will not receive anything when they die" (Rudolph, 191).

According to the Letter to Rheginus on the resurrection, the resurrection is "the revelation of those who have [now already] risen. . . . It is not an illusion *[phantasy]* but truth! But rather it is fitting to say that the world *[kosmos]* is more an illusion than the resurrection" (Rudolph, 192). Death is viewed as liberation, followed by the ascent of the soul. This too can be called resurrection: "'The dead shall leap up from the grave,' that is, from their earthly bodies, being regenerated as spiritual men, not carnal" (so the Naassenes according to Hippolytus *Refutatio* 5.8.22-24). The Gnostics could also conceive of an end of the world. For the Valentinians, according to Irenaeus, this would take place "when all that is 'spiritual' *[pneumatic]* is shaped and perfected through knowledge *[gnōsis]*" (Irenaeus *Adv. Haer.* 1.6.1). Some texts speak of an *Apokatastasis,* or restoration of the particles of light, in the Pleroma, in a manner reminiscent of Stoic eschatology (Rudolph, 196). What is envisioned is the dissolution of the material world rather than a new creation. It should be emphasized, however, that the Gnostic texts do not constitute a consistent system and that there is considerable variation among the texts.

See also APOCALYPTIC LITERATURE; APOCALYPTICISM; HEAVENLY ASCENT IN JEWISH AND PAGAN TRADITIONS; RESURRECTION.

BIBLIOGRAPHY. H. W. Attridge, "Greek and Latin Apocalypses," *Semeia* 14 (1979) 162-67; H. Cancik, "The End of the World, of History and of the Individual in Greek and Roman Antiquity," in *The Encyclopedia of Apocalypticism,* ed. J. J. Collins, B. McGinn and S. Stein (3 vols.; New York: Continuum, 1998) 1:84-125; A. Y. Collins, "The Early Christian Apocalypses," *Semeia* 14 (1979) 61-121; J. J. Collins, *The Apocalyptic Imagination* (2d ed.; Grand Rapids, MI: Eerdmans,

1998); idem, *Apocalypticism in the Dead Sea Scrolls* (London: Routledge, 1997b); idem, *Daniel* (Minneapolis: Fortress, 1993); idem, "Jewish Apocalypticism Against Its Hellenistic Near Eastern Environment," in *Seers, Sibyls and Sages in Hellenistic-Roman Judaism* (Leiden: E. J. Brill, 1997a) 59-74; F. Cumont, *Lux Perpetua* (Paris: Geuthner, 1949); S. K. Eddy, *The King Is Dead: Studies in the Near Eastern Resistance to Hellenism 334-331 B.C.* (Lincoln: University of Nebraska Press, 1961); F. Fallon, "The Gnostic Apocalypses," *Semeia* 14 (1979) 123-58; D. Flusser, "The Four Empires in the Fourth Sibyl and in the Book of Daniel," *Israel Oriental Studies* 2 (1972) 148-75; F. Graf, "Dionysian and Orphic Eschatology," in *Masks of Dionysos*, ed. T. H. Carpenter and C. Faraone (Ithaca, NY: Cornell University Press, 1993) 239-58; J. G. Griffiths, *The Divine Verdict: A Study of Divine Judgment in the Ancient Religions* (Leiden: E. J. Brill, 1991); J. R. Hinnells, "The Zoroastrian Doctrine of Salvation in the Roman World: A Study of the Oracle of Hystaspes," in *Man and His Salvation: Studies in Memory of S. G. F. Brandon*, ed. E. J. Sharpe and J. R. Hinnells (Manchester: Manchester University Press, 1973) 125-48; A. Hultgård, "*Bahman Yasht:* A Persian Apocalypse," in *Mysteries and Revelations: Apocalyptic Studies Since the Uppsala Colloquium*, ed. J. J. Collins and J. H. Charlesworth (Sheffield: Sheffield Academic Press, 1991) 114-34; idem, "Persian Apocalypticism," in *The Encyclopedia of Apocalypticism*, ed. J. J. Collins, B. McGinn and S. Stein (3 vols.; New York: Continuum, 1998) 1:39-83; H. Hunger and S. A. Kaufman, "A New Akkadian Prophecy Text," *JAOS* 95 (1975) 371-75; L. Koenen, "The Prophecies of a Potter: A Prophecy of World Renewal Becomes an Apocalypse," in *Proceedings of the Twelfth International Congress of Papyrology*, ed. D. H. Samuel (Toronto: Hakkert, 1970) 249-54; W. Lambert, "History and the Gods: A Review Article," *Orientalia* 39 (1979) 170-77; G. W. E. Nickelsburg, *Resurrection, Immortality and Eternal Life in Intertestamental Judaism* (Cambridge, MA: Harvard University Press, 1972); A. D. Nock and A. J. Festugière, *Corpus Hermeticum*, vol. 2, *Asclepius* (Paris: Les Belles Lettres, 1945); É. Puech, *La croyance des Esséniens en la vie future: immortalité, résurrection vie éternelle?* (Paris: Gabalda, 1993); Rudolph, *Gnosis* (San Francisco: Harper & Row, 1977); J. W. Swain, "The Theory of the Four Monarchies: Opposition History Under the Roman Empire," *CP* 35 (1940) 1-21; E. W. West, *The Sacred Books of the East*, vol. 5, ed. F. Max Mueller (Oxford: Clarendon Press, 1880).

J. J. Collins

ESDRAS, BOOKS OF

Ezra the scribe is remembered in Jewish tradition as one of the central figures in the history of Judaism and the Jewish people. According to the biblical narratives, Ezra led a group of exiled Jews back to Jerusalem in 458 B.C. with the authorization and financial support of the Persian government (*see* Jewish History: Persian Period). Ezra's appointed task was to enforce obedience to Jewish law as understood and applied by the Jewish authorities who had returned from Babylon to Jerusalem. Ezra was ultimately regarded as second only to *Moses as a divinely inspired lawgiver. Because he held such an exalted position in Jewish tradition, numerous extrabiblical texts were *pseudepigraphically attributed to him.

1. Second Esdras
2. Other Ezra Texts

1. Second Esdras.

The book of 2 Esdras is a compilation of three different Ezra texts. The core is the Jewish *apocalypse in 2 Esdras 3—14, commonly known as 4 Ezra. There has been considerable variety in designating the other two Christian texts collected in 2 Esdras. Chapters 1—2 are Christian texts that were prefixed to 4 Ezra (2 Esdr 3—14) and intended to serve as an introduction to the Jewish apocalypse. Second Esdras 1—2 is designated either 2 Ezra or 5 Ezra. Second Esdras 15—16 is a Christian appendix to the apocalypse, and these final two chapters of 2 Esdras are designated either 5 Ezra or 6 Ezra. This inconsistency in how scholars refer to these three texts can be confusing; however, their contents are so distinct that any description immediately clarifies which text is meant.

In 2 Esdras 1—2 (5 Ezra) we read of Ezra's call into ministry, a call that is lacking in the Bible, and of his denunciations of the Jewish people for failing to obey the commandments. The text focuses on God's denunciation of the people for failing to obey his commandments in spite of all the benefits he had bestowed on them throughout their history. Although Jewish texts can take up the theme of Israel's failure to obey the commandments, that this is a Christian composition is clear from two passages. First, we read that God decided to replace *Israel with other people (i.e., the Christians) who would believe and follow the commandments and who though they had not seen the prophets nonetheless follow their morality (2 Esdr 1:35-36). Second, at the end of 2 Esdras 2 we read of people who are lauded and rewarded for having confessed the "Son of God" in the world (2 Esdr 2:45). This Christian text has no explicit link to the Jewish apocalypse in 2 Esdras 3—14 (4 Ezra), but the editors who prefixed it to the apocalypse must have thought that it served as a fitting introduction to the apocalypse. By adding this introduction, the editors were trying to transform the original Jewish text into a Christian one.

Second Esdras 3—14 (4 Ezra) is a Jewish apocalypse in which Ezra and God debate theodicy in a manner that reminds one of Job's debates with his interlocutors. Ezra is dumbfounded as he watches the wicked prosper while the righteous suffer. Moreover, the wicked can even inflict severe sufferings on the righteous. How can this be? Does God not see? Does he not care? The debate is at times biting, and we occasionally blush at the utter boldness of Ezra's challenges to God's sense of justice. How can he speak so impudently with God?

Fourth Ezra was written around A.D. 100 as one response to the sufferings of the Jewish people in the wake of the destruction of the Jerusalem *temple by the Romans in A.D. 70. It seems that this apocalypse is a literary work that reflects the anonymous author's struggles over these painful issues. That is to say, rather than being a theological treatise, this is almost a biography of one person's psychological and theological struggles over the sufferings of his people at the hands of the Romans. It is an intensely personal text. The narrative is presented as seven separate visionary experiences.

In the first three visions (2 Esdr 3:1—9:25), Ezra and God (or his angel) argue in a question-and-answer format. Ezra's difficult questions are never directly answered by God in these visions that all end with God showing Ezra the signs of the end times. These signs are inadequate answers that seem to disregard Ezra's anguished questions.

Then, in the fourth vision (2 Esdr 9:26—10:59), Ezra sees a woman weeping over the loss of a child. Ezra tells her to stop crying for the loss of one child when all Israel is suffering. This woman then suddenly transforms into a city, *Jerusalem. Ezra learns that the advice he gave to the woman is the advice he should heed: stop wailing over your personal pain and consider the travail being suffered by all Israel. The fourth vision is thus Ezra's catharsis. He learns that the traditional theology set forth by God and his angel in the first three visions, the very theology that Ezra had opposed or found inadequate, is the only answer. Ezra converted. Now that he had accepted the traditional theological explanation of things, he has three much more traditional apocalyptic experiences (visions 5-7). In visions 5 and 6 he sees messianic figures coming to rescue Israel (2 Esdr 11—13). The book ends with an account of how Ezra received the revelation of the twenty-four books of the Hebrew Bible and seventy esoteric books (the apocryphal/apocalyptic books). He made known the biblical books but hid the seventy other books that were meant only for the eyes of the elect.

This powerful apocalypse intends to show that the traditional theology—that God decrees and accomplishes all that takes place and yet is not the author of evil—is the only adequate answer to the problem of evil in the world. Humans sin, and God holds them accountable. Sometimes that sin brings harm to others, including the righteous. The first three visions show that apocalypses do not necessarily focus exclusively on *eschatological matters. Here the information God revealed to Ezra in the course of their debate has to do with practical intellectual or theological issues. The fifth and sixth visions focus almost exclusively on eschatological matters and suggest that one day God will send the Messiah to rescue the righteous and destroy the wicked, and this hope inspires God's people to remain steadfast to his teachings and enables them to endure the many tribulations they face.

As typical historical apocalypses focusing on the eschaton, the fifth and sixth visions (2 Esdr 11—13) have many thematic links with Daniel and the book of Revelation. These are historical apocalypses whose focus is on the final, cataclysmic battle between the forces of good and evil when good triumphs and vanquishes all evil. Thus, what one encounters in the book of Revelation, although rather odd when compared with the rest of NT literature, is a typical example of one kind of ancient apocalypse.

Second Esdras 15—16 (6 Ezra) is a Christian

appendix to the Jewish apocalypse that continues the eschatological focus of 2 Esdras 11—13 by cataloging the calamities that mark the onset of the eschaton, a catalog that has thematic affinities with similar descriptions of the end times in the NT (cf. Mt 24; Mk 13; Lk 17:20-37; 21:5-36; 2 Thess 2:1-12; 2 Pet 3:3-13; Rev 4—22). This dark piece nevertheless intends to inspire the faithful because no matter what trials and tribulations they may face, in the end God will rescue them and give them the reward for which they have hoped.

2. Other Ezra Texts.

Ezra is surely one of the most prominent figures in the Bible, but this is not what inspired the wealth of texts *pseudepigraphically attributed to him. Each of the other Ezra texts discussed below in some way depends upon or is inspired by 4 Ezra (2 Esdr 3—14). The fact that they were all indebted to 4 Ezra indicates the popularity of this text. Moreover, 4 Ezra was part of the *Septuagint, or Greek Bible, used by the early Christians. This was the official Bible of most churches, and so 4 Ezra was read as Scripture, as it still is in Roman Catholic and Orthodox churches.

The *Greek Apocalypse of Ezra* is a Christian composition, but precisely when it was composed is not certain. Dates ranging from the second to the tenth centuries A.D. and later have been suggested. This apocalypse, much like 4 Ezra, opens with Ezra praying and fasting in order to induce God to grant him a vision. Unlike 4 Ezra, however, the *Greek Apocalypse of Ezra* is an ascent text (*see* Heavenly Ascent). Here Ezra ascends to heaven and descends into Tartarus in his quest to understand God's justice and to intercede for sinners who suffer postmortem punishments. This text serves as a powerful tool to persuade people to live a righteous life because it describes the bliss enjoyed by the faithful as well as the punishments endured by sinners. Still, Ezra's concern is with the sinners who suffer, and he asks God to have pity on them. Knowing that a good fate awaits the righteous surely induces people to live righteous lives in order not to miss out on postmortem bliss. In the end Ezra realizes that God is just in whatever he does, even though humans might not be able to understand the details of his justice. All persons will be rewarded or punished accordingly when they die.

Visions of heaven and hell became popular in Christianity, culminating in Dante Alighieri's *The Divine Comedy.* Why were these stories of journeys to heaven and hell so popular? They give humans the kinds of information that is otherwise beyond their reach. Everyone wants to know what the realms beyond earth are like and what awaits humans after death. These extraterrestrial travelogs provide just such information. Of course, the authors use these travelogs to promote their own kinds of piety. Thus, a Christian text will promote Christian virtues, although the particulars will differ from community to community, and a Jewish or an Islamic ascent text will promote Jewish or Islamic values. Moreover, these travelogs prove that there is another realm beyond our experience and that admission into the regions of bliss is based on strict requirements. This is then the power of these texts. Everyone wants to go to heaven and enjoy a blissful eternity in the presence of the divine. By defining precisely how one gets into heaven and avoids the punishments of hell, these texts shape behavior and beliefs. The real or pseudepigraphic authors of these texts stand as witnesses to the reality of the other realm and the guidelines for admission.

The *Vision of the Blessed Ezra* is a Christian document composed in Greek sometime between the second and eleventh centuries A.D. This text recounts how Ezra first visited Tartarus to see the excruciating punishments of the wicked and then visited paradise to see the glorious abodes of the righteous. Again, much like the *Greek Apocalypse of Ezra* and later medieval texts such as Dante's *Divine Comedy,* the visions of this text are intended to encourage fidelity to the traditional values of the church. Depictions of the frightening postmortem torments of sinners and the indescribable bliss of the righteous create a striking portrait of the afterlife. God assured Ezra that each person will get the reward he or she deserves. After death everyone faces a test, and only the righteous escape unscathed while the wicked fall irretrievably into punishment.

The *Apocalypse of Sedrach* consists of a Christian sermon on love and what appears to be an originally Jewish ascent text describing Sedrach's tour through the heavenly realm. We associate this text with Ezra because the name *Sedrach* appears to be a corruption of Ezra and does not seem to be the friend of Daniel by this same name (Dan 1:7). The sermon on love praises the value of love to transform and ennoble human life—"O blessed love that bestows all good things" (*Apoc. Sedr.* 1:24). As we have come to expect with Ezra texts, the apocalypse contains a debate between Sedrach and God over the issue of God's justice in condemning sinners. Sedrach learns that sinners are punished because they refuse to repent of their wicked deeds. If people should repent, God is ready to deliver them "in an instant" (*Apoc. Sedr.* 15:2-3). There is thus hope for everyone until the end.

The last two Ezra works discussed here have proven to be very difficult to date, and they may have been composed as late as the early Middle Ages. The *Questions of Ezra* has been preserved only in Armenian and describes what happens to a human's soul after death. As is his custom, Ezra debates with the angel of God over the justice of sentencing people to punishment for having sinned, since all people sin in some way. Ezra's questions focus on the final state of the soul after death, but God's answers highlight the values of righteous living; the two never really come together, again much like the debates in the first three visions in 4 Ezra (2 Esdr 3—14). Ezra learns that after death the righteous will experience great joy while the wicked will suffer unceasing torment. Moreover, the purpose of the postmortem ascent of the soul is to test and purify it before allowing it to enter the realm where God dwells.

The *Revelation of Ezra* differs from all the other Ezra texts in that its interests are strictly astrological. This text claims to predict the nature of the coming year based on the day of the week on which a year begins. For example, if the year begins on Venus Day (i.e., Friday) then "winter will be moderate, summer bad, fall dry; the grain harvest will be worthless, the grape harvest good; eyes will be inflamed; infants will die; there will be an earthquake; kings will be in danger; oil will be abundant, but sheep and bees will die." The *Revelation of Ezra,* therefore, transforms Ezra into an astrologer.

Ezra holds a prominent place in Jewish and Christian tradition. In Jewish tradition he is principally remembered as a lawgiver second only to Moses. In Christian tradition this feature is augmented by the depiction of Ezra as the friend of sinners. In the several texts pseudepigraphically attributed to him, Ezra appears as the one who is willing to argue with God incessantly in order to move God to have mercy on sinners. Ezra saw the many punishments being inflicted on sinners both in the heavenly and the infernal realms, and the sight of these people's sufferings drove him to pity. Although in the end he bows to God's omniscience and omnipotence, his concern was to save sinners from the punishments they unfortunately deserved. The writings attributed to Ezra intend to warn people of the consequences of sin and to inspire them to live holy lives. The changes in how Ezra was being depicted in the early Jewish and Christian communities indicate that when these people mention biblical (i.e., OT) figures, the image they have of them is not strictly limited to what was written about them in the Hebrew Bible. The depictions of biblical figures in later writings shows how the popular understanding of these characters continued to evolve. These changes in depicting these figures indicate how the later authors were updating the images of the ancient, esteemed figures in order to have them speak to the pressing moral, theological or cultural issues of their days.

See also APOCALYPTICISM; APOCALYPTIC LITERATURE; APOCRYPHA AND PSEUDEPIGRAPHA; 1 ESDRAS.

BIBLIOGRAPHY. T. A. Bergren, *Sixth Ezra: The Text and Origin* (New York: Oxford University Press, 1998); J. H. Charlesworth, ed., *The Old Testament Pseudepigrapha* (2 vols.; Garden City, NY: Doubleday, 1983, 1985); J. J. Collins, *The Apocalyptic Imagination* (New York: Crossroad, 1984); J. J. Collins, ed., *Apocalypse: The Morphology of a Genre* (*Semeia* 14; Missoula, MT: Scholars Press, 1979); E. Gardiner, ed., *Visions of Heaven and Hell Before Dante* (New York: Italica Press, 1989); M. Himmelfarb, *Ascent to Heaven in Jewish and Christian Apocalypses* (New York: Oxford University Press, 1993); idem, *Tours of Hell* (Philadelphia: Fortress, 1988); R. A. Kraft, "Ezra Materials in Judaism and Christianity," in *ANRW* 2.19.1 (1979) 119-36; J. M. Myers, *I and II Esdras* (AB 42; Garden City, NY: Doubleday, 1974); G. W. E. Nickelsburg, *Jewish Literature Between the Bible and Mishnah* (Philadelphia: Fortress, 1981); M. E. Stone, *Fourth Ezra: A Commentary on the Book of Fourth Ezra* (Herm; Minneapolis: Augsburg Fortress, 1990); M. E. Stone, ed. *Jewish Writings of the Second Temple Period* (CRINT 2.2; Assen: Van Gorcum; Philadelphia: Fortress, 1984).

J. E. Wright

1 ESDRAS

The book of 1 Esdras has survived in Greek as one of the books of the *Apocrypha, at least as far as the Hebrew canon is concerned. The church, too, has not granted 1 Esdras a definite canonical status, especially because of Jerome's influential position, which relegated the book to an appendix in the Vulgate.

In the main Greek tradition, 1 Esdras is the title of the book, whereas it is called 3 Esdras in the Latin tradition. Thus it is distinguished from the other books named after Ezra, primarily the canonical books of Ezra-Nehemiah, for which there is a continuous, consistent translation in the corpus of the *Septuagint known as 2 Esdras (*see* Esdras, Books of).

1. Contents and Chronology
2. Relationship to Canonical Books

1. Contents and Chronology.

The greater part of 1 Esdras (1 Esdr 1—2; 5—9) is a straightforward translation of 2 Chronicles 35—36, Ezra 1—10 and Nehemiah 8. Only two chapters (1 Esdr 3—4) that tell the Story of the Three Youths have no counterpart in the canonical books. The relationship between 1 Esdras and Chronicles and Ezra-Nehemiah is therefore somewhat similar to the relationship between the canonical books of Daniel and Esther and their expanded Septuagint versions (*see* Daniel, Esther and Jeremiah, Additions to). In our view, the Story of the Three Youths was originally written in Aramaic and interpolated into the Hebrew-Aramaic material that now forms the canonical books. This composite version was then translated into Greek.

The contents of 1 Esdras are similar to its parallel parts in Chronicles and Ezra-Nehemiah, except for the additional story and the ensuing changes in the course of events. It begins with the last part of the kingdom of Judah—from Josiah's Passover through the destruction and exile (1 Esdr 1 = 2 Chron 35—36). It continues with Cyrus's edict permitting the return of the exiles and the building of the temple (*see* Jewish History: Persian Period). It passes abruptly to the complaint sent to Artaxerxes that brought about the interruption of the building of the temple (1 Esdr 2 = Ezra 1; 4:6-24). At this point the Story of the Three Youths is introduced. The story, which takes place in Darius's court, tells about a contest between three of the king's bodyguards. The contest consists of a question: What is the strongest thing of all? The first praises the power of wine, the second advocates the king, and the third, Zerubbabel, argues for women and finally for truth. Zerubbabel wins and is granted permission to return to Jerusalem and resume the building of the temple and the city (1 Esdr 3—4, unparalleled in the OT).

After the list of returnees is provided, Zerubbabel and Jeshua are said to have built the altar and founded the temple. However, the work is interrupted again by adversaries (1 Esdr 5 = Ezra 2:1—4:5). It is resumed by the encouragement of the prophets Haggai and Zechariah at the beginning of Darius's reign. Thus, in the sixth year of Darius, the temple is completed and celebrated (1 Esdr 6—7 = Ezra 5—6). Then the book turns to the story of Ezra, his return, the separation from foreign women and the reading of the Torah and celebration of the Feast of Tabernacles (1 Esdr 8—9 = Ezra 7—10; Neh 8).

The chronology of 1 Esdras is difficult and the course of events is cluttered, passing from Cyrus to Artaxerxes and back to Darius. The confusion comes from the interpolation of the Story of the Three Youths, which provides another version of the rise of Zerubbabel in addition to the one borrowed from the book of Ezra. The two versions exclude one another.

2. Relationship to Canonical Books.

The differences between 1 Esdras and the canonical books may be summed up as follows: the outer limits of the book; the interrelationships among the books of Chronicles, Ezra and Nehemiah; the order of the chapters; above all, the interpolation of the Story of the Three Youths. This story is the raison d'être of the book, and therefore it explains almost all the differences between 1 Esdras and the parallel canonical material.

In 1 Esdras, Ezra 1 directly continues 2 Chronicles 35—36. In our view, the author of 1 Esdras did not initiate the combination of the books of Chronicles and Ezra. Since his obvious goal was to present his version of the return as portrayed in the Story of the Three Youths, he had no reason to combine the last two chapters of Chronicles were it a separate book. Rather, Chronicles and Ezra constituted one cluster in his tradition. This argumentation is also relevant regarding the ongoing debate of whether 1 Esdras originally contained the entire book of Chronicles or whether it opened, as it does, with Josiah's celebration of the Passover. It seems illogical that in order to interpolate the Story of the Youths the author copied the entire book of Chronicles. He rather made his decision to begin with Josiah, the cherished king (see his addition in 1 Esdr 1:21-22), and continue with the return and revival of Judah under Zerubbabel and Ezra.

In 1 Esdras the letter of complaint to Artaxerxes (Ezra 4:6-24 = 1 Esdr 2:15-25) stands immediately after Cyrus's edict (Ezra 1 = 1 Esdr 2:1-14), while the parallel to Ezra 2:1—4:5 shifts to just after the Story of the Three Youths. Undoubtedly the events are reordered to form a reasonable context for the story. That is, since the latter is designed to introduce Zerubbabel, the material that features Zerubbabel (Ezra 2:1—4:5) must be postponed until after the Story of the Three Youths is completed.

In 1 Esdras, Nehemiah 8 directly continues Ezra 10. The fact that the author of 1 Esdras used together with Nehemiah 8 the preceding verse (Neh 7:72), which concludes the former unit, proves that 1 Esdras does not attest an original version in which the reading of the Torah (Neh 8) continued the story of Ezra's activities (Ezra 7—10). Rather, the author of 1 Esdras decided to extract the material concerned with Ezra and place it with the rest of Ezra's activities. In 1 Esdras there is no trace of Nehemiah 1—7; 9—13. It appears that the author of 1 Esdras decided to attribute Nehemiah's achievements to Zerubbabel. Thus the story of the return revolves around Zerubbabel and Ezra.

The outer limits of the current version of 1 Esdras make it difficult to see the book as a self-contained entity. The book begins in the middle of Josiah's reign, and the end, which parallels Nehemiah 8:13, breaks off not only in the middle of the events but also literally in midsentence. The damage most probably took place in the Greek translation, as the translator of 1 Esdras would not perpetuate a defective ending in the original work.

First Esdras is neither a fragment surviving from a book that for the most part has been lost nor strictly a compilation of chosen units from the canonical books. Rather, the author of 1 Esdras deliberately cut a section from the books of Chronicles and Ezra-Nehemiah to form a framework for the Story of the Three Youths. First Esdras seems to be one of the first products of the rich literary activity around the books of the OT that took place in the last centuries B.C.

See also APOCRYPHA AND PSEUDEPIGRAPHA; DANIEL, ESTHER AND JEREMIAH, ADDITIONS TO; ESDRAS, BOOKS OF.

BIBLIOGRAPHY. H. W. Attridge, "Historiography," in *Jewish Writings of the Second Temple Period,* ed. M. E. Stone (CRINT 2.2; Philadelphia: Fortress; Assen: Van Gorcum, 1984) 157-60; D. Böhler, *Die heilige Stadt in Esdras A und Esra-Nehemia* (Göttingen: Vandenhoeck & Ruprecht, 1997); R. J. Coggins and M. A. Knibb, *The First and Second Books of Esdras* (CBC; Cambridge: Cambridge University Press, 1979); S. A. Cook, "I Esdras," in *The Apocrypha and Pseudepigrapha of the Old Testament in English,* ed. R. H. Charles (2 vols.; Oxford: Clarendon Press, 1913) 1:1-58; J. Crenshaw, "The Contest of Darius' Guards," in *Images of Man and God: Old Testament Short Stories in Literary Focus,* ed. B. O. Long (Sheffield: Almond Press, 1981) 74-88; W. R. Goodman, "Esdras, First Book of," *ABD* 2:609-11; R. Hanhart, *Esdrae liber 1* (Septuaginta 8.1; Göttingen: Vandenhoeck & Ruprecht, 1974); idem, *Text und Textgeschichte des 1. Esrabuches* (Göttingen: Vandenhoeck & Ruprecht, 1974); B. M. Metzger, *An Introduction to the Apocrypha* (New York: Oxford University Press, 1957) 11-19; J. M. Myers, *I and II Esdras: Introduction, Translation and Commentary* (AB 42; Garden City, NY: Doubleday, 1974); G. W. E. Nickelsburg, "Stories of Biblical and Early Post-Biblical Times," in *Jewish Writings of the Second Temple Period,* ed. M. E. Stone (CRINT 2.2; Philadelphia: Fortress; Assen: Van Gorcum, 1984) 131-35; K. F. Pohlmann, *Studium zum dritten Esra* (Göttingen: Vandenhoeck & Ruprecht, 1970); E. Schürer, *The History of the Jewish People in the Age of Jesus Christ (175 B.C.-A.D. 135),* ed. G. Vermes, F. Millar, M. Goodman (3 vols.; Edinburgh: T & T Clark, 1973-87) 3:708-17; Z. Talshir, *1 Esdras: From Origin to Translation* (SCS 47; Atlanta: Society of Biblical Literature, 1999); C. C. Torrey, *The Apocryphal Literature* (New Haven, CT: Yale University Press, 1945) 43-54; idem, *Ezra Studies* (Chicago: University of Chicago Press, 1910); F. Zimmerman, "The Story of the Three Guardsmen," *JQR* 54 (1963-64) 179-200.

Z. Talshir

ESSENES

The Essenes were an ancient Jewish sect existing from the second century B.C. to the end of the first century A.D. Various Greek and Latin writers, most notably *Philo, *Josephus and *Pliny, describe the group. Since the discovery of the *Dead Sea Scrolls at *Qumran in 1947, most scholars have regarded the Qumran community as Essene. In the treatment that follows, Essene customs and beliefs according to the classical sources will first be presented, followed by a comparison of this information with the data from Qumran.

1. Sources
2. Essene Customs and Beliefs
3. The Essenes and the Qumran Community
4. The Essenes and the New Testament

1. Sources.

Unlike other Jewish sects such as the *Pharisees or *Sadducees, the Essenes are not mentioned in the NT or in Talmudic literature. The earliest mention of the Essenes is by Philo, in *Quod Omnis Probus Liber Sit* 12-13 §§75-91 and *Hypothetica* 11.1-18, both written prior to A.D. 40. Philo does not seem to have firsthand knowledge of the Essenes, and he presents what appears to be an idealized picture of the group, with frequent favorable comparisons to Greek thought and practice.

A second important reference to the Essenes is given by Pliny the Elder, in his *Natural History* 5.15 §73, completed in A.D. 77. Pliny mentions the Essenes in the context of his description of the topography of Judea. He states that they are located on the west bank of the Dead Sea, with Engedi below them, and Masada even further south. Pliny's account thus puts the Essenes in the same area as Qumran.

The Jewish historian Josephus (c. A.D. 37-100) provides the most detailed ancient description of the Essenes. He mentions the group thirteen times in his writings, with two extensive descriptions in *The Jewish War* (*J.W.* 2.8.2-13 §§119-61), written about A.D. 73, and in *The Antiquities of the Jews* (*Ant.* 18.1.2, 5 §§11, 18-22), written about A.D. 94. While Josephus claims to have spent time with each of the three sects (Pharisees, Sadducees and Essenes) at the age of sixteen, the chronology he presents indicates that he could have spent only a few months with the Essenes (*Life* 1.2 §§10-12). Still, the probability of his having direct contact with the group makes his account all the more important. As with Philo, Josephus's desire to present *Judaism in a favorable manner to his audience undoubtedly resulted in idealization and accommodation to Greek thought in his description of the group.

The Essenes are also mentioned briefly by Hegesippus, a second-century Christian historian. The Roman bishop Hippolytus (c. A.D. 170-236) describes the Essenes in a more lengthy account similar to that of Josephus, an account that may be dependent upon Josephus or derived from a common source (*Refut.* 9.18-28). Hippolytus is the first of many later Christian writers to view the Essenes as a heretical Jewish sect. The later Christian writers provide no new information about the group.

2. Essene Customs and Beliefs.

The classical sources give us information on several facets of Essene customs and beliefs. (For parallels with the Qumran community see 3 below.)

2.1. Name. The name of the sect is rendered variously in the classical sources. The group is generally called *Essēnoi* or *Essaioi* in Greek, while in Latin they are called *Esseni*. Epiphanius mentions both a group called the *Ossēnoi* as well as a different group he calls *Essenoi*.

The etymology of the name is unclear. Philo suggests that it is related to the Greek word *hosiotēs* ("holiness"); elsewhere he calls the group *hosioi* ("holy ones"; *Omn. Prob. Lib.* 12 §75; 13 §91). Similarly, some modern scholars believe the name is derived from the Aramaic *ḥasayyâ* (= Heb *ḥasîdîm*, "pious ones"; so Schürer, Cross). If this is correct, it might suggest that the Essenes are related to the Hasideans (*ḥasîdîm*, Gr *asidaioi*) mentioned in 1 Maccabees 2:42; 7:13 and 2 Maccabees 14:6 (*see* 1 and 2 Maccabees), though the root *ḥsy* does not mean "pious" in the Palestinian dialect.

Some of the many recently suggested etymologies in light of the Qumran material are that the name is taken from the Hebrew word *ʿēṣâ*, which means "council" in Qumran literature (so Dupont-Sommer); that it is from the Hebrew verb *ʿaśâ* ("to do, bear, bring forth"), with the idea that the Essenes are the "doers" of the law who will "bring forth" redemption (so Goranson); or that it is derived from the Aramaic *ʾsyyʾ* ("healers"; so Vermes). But none of these proposals are compelling.

2.2. Location. Philo and Josephus both indicate that the total number of Essenes was more than four thousand and that they lived in many cities in Palestine (Josephus *J.W.* 2.8.4 §124; Philo *Hypoth.* 11.1; though in *Omn. Prob. Lib.* 12 §76 Philo says they avoided the cities). Pliny places them by the Dead Sea, above Engedi. Perhaps there was a major settlement in the Dead Sea area with other, smaller pockets of Essenes scattered around Palestine.

*2.3. **Admission and Organization.*** There was a three-year initiation period to attain full admission. During the first year, the novice followed the Essene way of life but remained outside the community; in the second and third years, he could join in their purificatory baths but could not share the common meals. Finally he was admitted as a full member after taking "awesome oaths" (Josephus *J.W.* 2.8.7 §§137-42). Rigid organization and adherence to authority characterized the group. Obedience to the elders was stressed, with severe offenses resulting in expulsion (Josephus *J.W.* 2.8.6 §134; 2.8.7 §142; 2.8.8-9 §§143-46).

*2.4. **Property.*** Entrants to the sect transferred their property to the order. Even food and clothing were shared. Extreme frugality was practiced. Members elected overseers of the common property (Josephus *J.W.* 2.8.3 §§122-23; 2.8.4 §126; *Ant.* 18 §20; Philo *Hypoth.* 10.4; 11.10-12; *Omn. Prob. Lib.* 12 §77; Pliny *Nat. Hist.* 5.15 §73).

*2.5. **Celibacy.*** Josephus, Philo and Pliny all state that all Essenes were male and did not marry (Josephus *Ant.* 18 §21; *J.W.* 2.8.2 §120; Philo *Hypoth.* 11.14–17; Pliny *Nat. Hist.* 5.15 §73). Josephus later mentions a second group of Essenes who did marry (*J.W.* 2.8.13 §§160-61).

*2.6. **Daily Work.*** While Josephus states that the Essenes worked entirely in agriculture, Philo indicates they were also shepherds, beekeepers and craftsmen (Josephus *Ant.* 1.5 §19; Philo *Hypoth.* 11.8). They did not own slaves or make implements of war (Philo *Omn. Prob. Lib.* 12 §§78-79), though Josephus speaks of John the Essene as leading in war (Josephus *J.W.* 3.2.1 §§9-12). Their daily routine consisted of rising before sunrise, prayer, work until midday, purificatory bath and common meal, work until evening and a second common meal (Josephus *J.W.* 2.8.5 §§128-32).

*2.7. **Rituals.*** Ritual *purity was very important to the Essenes. A daily purificatory bath was taken by all except novices, they dressed in white, and senior Essenes touched by juniors were required to wash (Josephus *J.W.* 2.8.3 §123; 2.8.5 §129; 2.8.10 §150). They treated the common meal as sacred, with the *priest praying before and after the meal, and silence during it (Josephus *J.W.* 2.8.5 §§129-33). Ritual morning prayers were offered before sunrise (Josephus *J.W.* 2.8.5 §128).

With respect to *sacrifices, the evidence is unclear. The Latin version of Josephus indicates that the Essenes did not offer sacrifices, but the Greek text omits the negative. Assuming the Greek text is correct, Josephus indicates that the Essenes offered sacrifices by themselves rather than at the *temple, because of a disagreement over purification rites (Josephus *Ant.* 18.1.5 §19).

*Moses and the law were revered by the Essenes. As part of their devotion to the law, they were very strict in observing the *sabbath, not cooking, moving a vessel or even in relieving themselves (Josephus *J.W.* 2.8.9 §§145, 147; Philo *Omn. Prob. Lib.* 12 §§81-82).

*2.8. **Other Beliefs.*** The Essenes were interested in the study of "the writings of the ancients" (Josephus *J.W.* 2.8.6 §136; 2.8.12 §159; Philo *Omn. Prob. Lib.* 12 §§80-82), including both the biblical books and most likely other books as well, since Josephus notes that the Essenes used these writings to "search out medicinal roots and the properties of stones" (Josephus *J.W.* 2.8.6 §136). They also regarded the "names of the angels" as important (Josephus *J.W.* 2.8.7 §142). They were deterministic, believing that "fate is the ruler of all things" (Josephus *Ant.* 18.1.5 §18; 13.5.9 §§171-72).

Some Essenes apparently were *prophets. Josephus states that "rarely, if ever, do they err in their predictions" (*J.W.* 2.8.12 §159). Elsewhere he gives three examples of Essene prophecies: Judas (*J.W.* 1.3.5 §§78–80 and *Ant.* 13.11.2 §§311-13), Simon (*J.W.* 2.7.3 §§111-13 and *Ant.* 17.13.3 §§346-48); and Menahem (*Ant.* 15.10.4-5 §§371-79).

On the afterlife, Josephus depicts the Essene view as similar to that of the Greeks, with the body considered a prison house of the soul and the soul set free after the body's death (Josephus *J.W.* 2.8.11 §§154-58). Hippolytus states that the Essenes believed in a bodily resurrection (*Refut.* 9.27). Hippolytus may be adding a Christian slant to the Essene beliefs, but it is also possible that his account here is more trustworthy than that of Josephus.

3. The Essenes and the Qumran Community. Ever since the discovery of the Dead Sea Scrolls, many scholars have identified the Qumran community as Essene. This identification rests on the similarities between the ancient accounts of the Essenes and the archaeological and scroll evidence from Qumran.

*3.1. **Chronology.*** The archaeological and paleographic data from Qumran confirm the existence of the Qumran community from the mid-second century B.C. to A.D. 68. Since Josephus first mentions the Essenes during the exploits of Jonathan Maccabeus (c. 145 B.C.; Josephus *Ant.* 13.5.9 §171) and himself claims to have spent time with the group during his youth (c. A.D. 53), the chronology of the Essenes fits that of the Qumran community.

*3.2. **Location.*** Pliny's placement of the Essenes on the west bank of the Dead Sea between Jericho and Engedi is an important piece in the identification of the Essenes with the Qumran community. Pliny states that the Essenes lived among palm trees, fitting the region between Qumran and Ain Feshka, the spring immediately south of the community's farmland. There is no other known site that would match the description given by Pliny. Though Pliny writes about the Essenes in the present tense, even though Qumran would have been destroyed earlier (in A.D. 68), it is probable that he used source material written earlier than the final publication of his work in A.D. 77.

*3.3. **Admission and Organization.*** Admission into the Qumran community is described in detail in the Dead Sea Scroll writing entitled the **Rule of the Community* (1QS 6:13-23). The general process is similar to Josephus's account of the Essenes. Both speak of a period of time spent outside the group followed by a two-year initiation period within the community. The common meal is denied to the novice, and an elaborate oath is made before the applicant is fully accepted.

The Qumran documents also stress the importance of order and obedience to authority. The person of lower rank had to obey those of higher rank, and anyone who murmured against the authority of the community was expelled (1QS 5:2-3, 23; 6:2, 25-26; 7:17).

*3.4. **Property.*** Both the Qumran documents and archaeology of the site confirm the sharing of property that Philo and Josephus mention as a prominent feature of the Essenes. The *Rule of the Community* speaks of new members transferring their property to the community (1QS 1:11-12; 5:1-2; 6:17-22). Elsewhere, however, 1QS 7:8-9 deals with reimbursement to the community for damaged property; and another sectarian writing, the **Damascus Document,* indicates that property could be lost or stolen from its owner (CD 9:10-16). Thus there may have been some personal property each member was allowed to keep.

Archaeology supports pooled possessions at Qumran. Hundreds of coins were found in the administration building, but none in the living quarters. Furthermore, according to F. Cross and E. Eshel, an ostracon found in 1996 at the site records the gift of a man's property (including a slave) to the community, further supporting the practice of transfer of a new member's property to the group (though A. Yardeni disputes the Cross/Eshel reconstruction; see *IEJ* 47 [1997] 17-28, 233-37).

*3.5. **Celibacy.*** Evidence from Qumran is mixed on the matter of celibacy. The *Damascus Document* and the *Rule of the Congregation* speak of *marriage (prohibition of polygamy in CD 4:19—5:2; see also CD 5:6-7; 7:6-7; 12:1-2; 16:10-12; and 1QSa 1:9-12), but the *Rule of the Community* is silent. In the excavation of the site of Qumran, all skeletons excavated in the main, planned part of the cemetery were male, while the outskirts also yielded skeletons of women and children. While this evidence has been used to suggest that there may have been both a celibate group at Qumran as well as a married group nearby, recent findings indicate that the skeletons on the outskirts may be only several hundred years old. Thus the only skeletons that come from the time of the ancient Qumran settlement are male. This supports the statements by Josephus, Philo and Pliny that the Essenes were male.

*3.6. **Daily Work.*** The scrolls do not speak of the daily work of the group at Qumran, but archaeology of the area indicates that they were involved in agriculture and craft work. This matches the statements by Philo and Josephus concerning the Essenes.

*3.7. **Rituals.*** Both the *Rule of the Community* and the *Damascus Document* describe purificatory washings (1QS 5:13-14; CD 11:21-22). In addition, archaeologists have found seven large cisterns with steps that may have been used for washings.

Evidence for the common meal spoken of by Josephus is also present at Qumran. The *Rule of the Community* describes the common meal (1QS 6:2-5; see also 1QS 5:13; 6:16-17, 22, 24-25; 7:19-20; 8:16-18). Archaeological evidence includes a large room with an adjacent pantry containing more than one thousand vessels.

Similar to Josephus's statements on the subject, the matter of sacrifices at Qumran is not clear. Though CD 6:11-13 states that "none of those who have entered the covenant shall enter the temple to kindle his altar in vain," this statement may be speaking of exercising care when offering sacrifices rather than being an outright prohibition (see also CD 6:14; 11:17-22). Probably both Josephus and the Qumran data should be understood as permitting sacrifices that were offered in a ritually pure manner.

The Qumran scrolls also speak often of devotion to the law and strict sabbath observance (see 1QS 1:1-3; 5:8; 8:22; CD 10:14—11:18; 15:8-9, 12-13; 16:2).

3.8. Other Beliefs. The Essene interest in books is abundantly evident at Qumran. In addition to many sectarian works, biblical, deuterocanonical and *pseudepigraphical books are all well attested. As with the Essenes, there is much interest in angels in the Qumran writings (**1 Enoch*, **Hodayot*, **War Scroll* and the **Songs of the Sabbath Sacrifice*). A deterministic outlook is also seen in their writings, especially in the *Hodayot* (1QH 1:7-8; 7:31-32; 15:12-15, 17; see also 1QS 3:15-16; 9:23-24; 1QM 17:5).

The importance of prophecy and prophets is seen both in the large numbers of copies of biblical prophetic books as well as the citations from prophetic books in other Qumran literature. In addition, there are eighteen *pesharim, or commentaries, found at Qumran that reinterpret biblical prophetic texts to find fulfillment in the community's current situation (for example, 1QpHab; *see* Habakkuk Commentary).

On the *afterlife, the scrolls speak of everlasting life (1QS 4:6-8; CD 3:20) and possibly bodily *resurrection (see 1QH 3:10-22; 6:34; 11:12; 1QM 12:1-4).

3.9. Possible Discrepancies. All in all, there is a good correspondence between the Essenes as described by the ancient sources and the Qumran community, even in matters of small detail (see Beall, 123-29). Sometimes our sources concerning the Essenes disagree with themselves (for instance, on the issue of marriage, where Philo states the Essenes are celibate but Josephus acknowledges a group of Essenes who do marry). Sometimes the Qumran scrolls differ from one another (for example, the *Rule of the Community* speaks of joint ownership of property, but the *Damascus Document* describes individual ownership). Here it should be recognized that these documents were almost certainly written during different stages of the community's development, and this may well account for the differences. In general, the classical sources on the Essenes agree more closely with the *Rule of the Community* than with the *Damascus Document.*

Some areas mentioned in the scrolls are not discussed in the classical descriptions of the Essenes: the importance of priests; prominent figures such as the Wicked Priest and the Teacher of Righteousness; the *messianic expectations of the group; and the solar *calendar. Perhaps Josephus and Philo did not consider these matters important to their overall purpose: to present this Jewish sect favorably to Greeks.

In recent years, especially with the publication of **Miqsat Ma'asey ha-Torah* (4QMMT), some scholars have gone back to an earlier suggestion that the Qumran community may be Sadducean rather than Essene. 4QMMT provides agreement with the Sadducees (versus the Pharisees) in a few legal matters, such as the view that a stream of liquid conveys impurity. But 4QMMT does not contradict any known Essene position; in fact, it supports Josephus's statement about the Essene avoidance of oil. In addition, the scrolls speak of the existence of angels and the importance of fate, both contrary to the Sadducean way of thinking as we know it.

In summary, though the precise history of both the Essenes in general and the Qumran community in particular is still hotly debated (see works in the bibliography for further discussion), both the chronology and the location of the Qumran community correspond well with what we know of the Essenes. The numerous parallels in customs and beliefs, as briefly outlined above, all point forcefully to the identification of the Qumran community as an Essene group.

4. The Essenes and the New Testament.

In light of the Dead Sea Scrolls, there has been a resurgence of interest in the question of Essene influence on the NT. The Essenes are not directly mentioned in the NT, as are the Pharisees, Sadducees and *Herodians, but they may have influenced some of the main people and writers of the NT. For the purposes of this section, the identity of the Qumran community as Essene will be assumed, and thus the Qumran data will also be considered here. We will briefly look at four areas: John the Baptist, Jesus, Paul and John.

4.1. The Essenes and John the Baptist. Some scholars have contended that John the Baptist was an Essene. It is true that John began his ministry in the wilderness of Judea, that is, the western shore of the Dead Sea; his father was a priest; his diet and appearance were ascetic; and his baptism for the remission of sins is similar in some respects to the purificatory washings of the Essenes. Yet, while John the Baptist may have had some contact with the Essenes, it is unlikely that he was an Essene. John's ministry was centered north of Qumran at Bethany and Aenon (Jn 1:28; 3:23); John's diet of locusts and honey is not mentioned by the ancient sources or Qumran literature; and most importantly, his baptism was a one-time act performed publicly for anyone who came to him, not a daily washing available only to members of a sect. Still, the testimony concerning the Essenes from the ancient sources and Qumran literature helps to paint a fuller, richer background for the ministry of John the Baptist within first-century Judaism.

4.2. The Essenes and Jesus. A few scholars have suggested that Jesus was an Essene or possibly even the Teacher of Righteousness mentioned in Qumran literature. But these suggestions have less to commend them than the linkage of John the Baptist and the Essenes. Jesus' teachings differed from the Essenes on a number of vital issues: Jesus was not as concerned about the law (sabbath was made for humanity, not humanity for the sabbath); he was not ascetic; there is no emphasis on rituals in Jesus' ministry; and he freely associated with those regarded as unworthy by first-century Jewish standards. As for Jesus being the Teacher of Righteousness, the Teacher preceded the birth of Jesus by more than a hundred years; the Teacher was not regarded as the end-time Messiah; and there is no special significance attached to the Teacher's death (and no resurrection).

4.3. The Essenes and Paul's Writings. There are a number of similarities between Paul's writings and Essene/Qumran writings. These include the utter sinfulness of humanity; dualism, especially the figurative use of light and darkness (see esp. 2 Cor 6:14—7:1, which also contains the name **Belial*, used frequently in Qumran literature); and the concept of mystery, indicating a secret hidden in God and now made manifest. But the idea of the utter sinfulness of humanity is rooted first in the OT, which Paul cites freely in Romans 3; and Paul's solution to the problem of humanity's sinfulness—justification by faith in Christ—is nowhere found in Essene/Qumran theology. As for the light/darkness dualism representing good and evil, this concept too is seen frequently in the OT (e.g., Job 30:26; Is 5:20). And the content of the mystery for Paul is quite different from the Qumran sectarians: for Paul it is the church or salvation in Christ, but for the Qumran sect it is the interpretation of Scripture as given by the Teacher of Righteousness.

A possible reference to Essene thinking may be present in Paul's warnings against false teachers, especially in Ephesians and Colossians. At the least, Paul's opponents in these letters appear to have some of the same tendencies as did the Essenes: excessive observance of external rituals and devotion to angels, to mention but two.

4.4. The Essenes and John's Writings. Finally, similarities may be seen in John's writings and Qumran literature. Chief here are the dualistic concepts of light/darkness and truth/lying. While similar language is sometimes employed in John's writings and the scrolls (e.g., the sons of light, the Spirit of truth), the content of the image is often quite different. For instance, at Qumran the Sons of Light are those who obey the law, while in John the sons of light are those who follow the Light of the world, Jesus. And in the sectarian writings, the spirits appear to be cosmological beings. One important result of a comparison of the Dead Sea Scrolls with John's writings is that there is no longer need to assume a second-century Greek model for the concepts in John, since these parallels also clearly existed within a first-century Palestinian environment.

While direct Essene/Qumran influence upon the people and writings of the NT is difficult to prove, a greater understanding of this ancient Jewish sect significantly enhances our knowledge and appreciation of the first-century Jewish background of the NT.

See also DEAD SEA SCROLLS: GENERAL INTRODUCTION; QUMRAN: PLACE AND HISTORY; THEOLOGIES AND SECTS, JEWISH; THERAPEUTAE.

BIBLIOGRAPHY. A. Adam, *Antike Berichte über die Essener* (2d ed.; Berlin: Walter de Gruyter,

1972); T. Beall, *Josephus's Description of the Essenes Illustrated by the Dead Sea Scrolls* (SNTSMS 58; Cambridge: Cambridge University Press, 1988); M. Black, *The Scrolls and Christian Origins: Studies in the Jewish Background of the New Testament* (London: Nelson, 1961); G. Boccaccini, *Beyond the Essene Hypothesis* (Grand Rapids, MI: Eerdmans, 1998); P. Callaway, *The History of the Qumran Community* (Sheffield: JSOT, 1988); J. Campbell, "Essene-Qumran Origins in the Exile: A Scriptural Basis?" *JJS* 46 (1995) 143-56; J. H. Charlesworth, ed., *Jesus and the Dead Sea Scrolls* (Garden City, NY: Doubleday, 1992); idem, *John and the Dead Sea Scrolls* (New York: Crossroad, 1991); F. M. Cross, *The Ancient Library of Qumran* (3d ed.; Minneapolis: Fortress, 1995); P. R. Davies, "Was There Really a Qumran Community?" *Currents in Research: Biblical Studies* 3 (1995) 9-35; L. Feldman, *Josephus and Modern Scholarship (1937-1980)* (Berlin: Walter de Gruyter, 1984); F. García Martínez and J. T. Barrera, *The People of the Dead Sea Scrolls* (Leiden: E. J. Brill, 1995); J. Murphy-O'Connor, "The Essenes and Their History," *RB* 81 (1974) 215-44; J. Murphy-O'Connor and J. H. Charlesworth, eds., *Paul and the Dead Sea Scrolls* (New York: Crossroad, 1990); E. Schürer, G. Vermes, F. Millar et al., *The History of the Jewish People in the Age of Jesus Christ* (rev. ed.; 3 vols. in 4; Edinburgh: T & T Clark, 1973-87); H. Shanks, ed., *Understanding the Dead Sea Scrolls* (New York: Random House, 1992); G. Stemberger, *Jewish Contemporaries of Jesus: Pharisees, Sadducees, Essenes* (Minneapolis: Fortress, 1995); J. VanderKam, *The Dead Sea Scrolls Today* (Grand Rapids, MI: Eerdmans, 1994); G. Vermes, *The Dead Sea Scrolls: Qumran in Perspective* (Cleveland: Collins & World, 1978); G. Vermes and M. Goodman, *The Essenes According to the Classical Sources* (Sheffield: JSOT, 1989).

T. Beall

ESTHER, ADDITIONS TO. *See* DANIEL, ESTHER AND JEREMIAH, ADDITIONS TO.

ETHNOGRAPHY, ANCIENT. *See* HISTORIANS, GRECO-ROMAN.

EUPOLEMUS. *See* JEWISH LITERATURE: HISTORIANS AND POETS.

EXILE

The term *exile* conjures up social, political and religious images of judgment, captivity, banishment, displacement, uprootedness, alienation and deportation. In the OT exile constitutes a major theme, weaving itself through almost every major account from Genesis to Malachi. It is so pervasive that the OT has on occasion been referred to as the foundational metanarrative of exile. Some of the more well known expressions of exile are found in stories such as *Adam and Eve's banishment from the garden of Eden, Abraham's journey to the land of Canaan, Joseph's deportation to Egypt, *Moses' wandering in the wilderness, David's escape from Saul's paranoia, and the most established of them all: *Israel's exilic experiences in Assyria and Babylon. The theme of exile, however, does not function in isolation. In the two most important expressions for the study of the NT—the stories of Adam and Eve's banishment and the deportation of the Israelites to Babylon—exile, which is always a result of sin, is accompanied by the hope that God will liberate and restore.

1. Exile in Second Temple Judaism
2. Exile in the Teaching and Activities of Jesus
3. Exile in the Gospels
4. Exile in Paul

1. Exile in Second Temple Judaism.

While the biblical accounts of exile serve as an important background for NT studies, the retelling and reexperiencing of these accounts among the Jewish people in the Second Temple period is all the more influential. When the literature of this period is probed to see if a fulfillment of the promises proclaimed by the exilic prophets was realized, one is hard pressed to show a postexilic return in the grandiose manner often predicted. The hope of the prophets, from Isaiah to Zechariah, of a return from exile was not realized. When Persia provided an opportunity for an exodus, the majority of Jews either remained in Babylon or assimilated themselves among their neighbors (*see* Diaspora; Jewish History: Persian Period).

During the Second Temple period, many in Palestine still considered themselves as being in exile because they were under foreign rule, which was an indication to the faithful that Yahweh had not yet returned to Zion (Ezra 9:8-9; Neh 9:36). This perception was continually confirmed by the oppressive regimes of Antiochus IV Epiphanes, *Pompey and Titus (*see* Seleucids and Antiochids; Jewish History: Roman Period). The underlying reason why many Jews saw themselves as still remaining in exile was their assumed perennial state of sinfulness (Bar 1:15—3:8; *1 Enoch* 89:73-75), a concept that is grounded in the "cursing and blessing" motif in Deuteronomy 27—32. The true return from exile was inseparably bound with the forgiveness of sins. And as long as Israel was dominated by foreign oppressors, the sins were not yet forgiven.

Several key examples within this period underscore not only the feeling of exile but also the *eschatological anticipation of God coming to restore his people (Is 40:3-5). One important example that has often been considered is Daniel 9, a text that extends Jeremiah's prophecy (e.g., Jer 25:11-12) of a seventy-year desolation for Jerusalem sevenfold. Recently J. M. Scott, following A. Lacocque and O. H. Steck, has shown how Daniel's *prayer of confession for the transgression of his people parallels the "sin-exile-restoration" theme of Deuteronomy 27—32 and thus brings to the forefront the reason for the belief in a continued exile, namely, covenant unfaithfulness.

Second, the *Dead Sea Scrolls contain a number of references that recall biblical accounts of the Egyptian exodus (e.g., 4Q385 [*see* Pseudo-Ezekiel]), the Assyrian exile (e.g., 4Q372 [*see* Apocryphon of Joseph]) and especially the Babylonian exile (e.g., CD 1:4-11 [*see* Damascus Document]). In some cases the imagery is used in relation to the *Qumran community that is camped in the wilderness outside Jerusalem awaiting the eschatological battle that will bring liberation (e.g., 1QM 1:3 [*see* War Scroll]). The community understands itself as the righteous remnant that is in exile and yet in the process of exodus. In other cases, the imagery is used in relation to the Teacher of Righteousness who is pursued by the Wicked Priest (e.g., 1QpHab 11:4-6 [*see* Habakkuk Commentary]) who seeks to destroy the Teacher and to disperse his followers. Despite the difficulty in trying to establish a consistent exile theology, the exilic imagery plays a significant role in the soteriological understanding of the community at Qumran.

A third example is found in *Josephus's depiction of first-century hope and the idea of exile in the activities of Theudas (Josephus *Ant.* 20.5.1 §§97-98) and the Egyptian Jew (Josephus *J.W.* 2.13.4-5 §§258-63; *Ant.* 20.8.6 §§167-72). Each of the two revolutionaries saw himself as the promised successor to Moses (Deut 18:15, 18-19) who would reenact the exodus and lead the Israelites in a new conquest of the promised land. Though this example expresses a more military tone, it nevertheless conveys the common feeling of exile among the Jews in first-century Palestine.

And fourth, one of the most expressive texts showing the enduring experience of exile is the prophecy of restoration in Tobit 14:5 (*see* Tobit), which reads:

> But God will again have mercy on them, and God will bring them back into the land of Israel; and they will rebuild the temple of God, but not like the first one until the period when the times of fulfillment shall come. After this they all will return from their exile and will rebuild Jerusalem in splendor; and in it the temple of God will be rebuilt, just as the prophets of Israel have said concerning it. (NRSV)

On the whole, the exilic motif is found dispersed throughout literature extending from the Babylonian era well beyond into the tannaitic and early amoraic periods (Sir 36:8; *T. Mos.* 10:1-10; *1 Enoch* 85—90; *T. Levi* 16—18; *Apoc. Abr.* 15—29; *T. Jud.* 24:1-3; *Jub.* 1:15-18, 24; *T. Naph.* 4:2-5; *T. Asher* 7; *T. Benj.* 9; 2 Macc 1:27-29; 1 Esdr 8:73-74; 2 Esdr 9:7).

2. Exile in the Teaching and Activities of Jesus. Biblical exile theology together with its expression in the interpretive traditions in early Judaism constitutes an important background for understanding Jesus and the origins of Christianity. With reference to Jesus, much discussion has taken place about the relationship between Jesus' understanding of his mission and the alleged despair or feeling of exile experienced in popular Jewish *piety, especially among peasants who endured not only Roman occupation and a burdensome tax load, but also the corruption of the *temple establishment.

N. T. Wright's proposal in *Jesus and the Victory of God* has recently captured much of the attention. According to Wright, Jesus understood himself to be the Messiah who had come to liberate Israel from its continuing state of exile ("the present evil age") and bring it into a state of restoration ("the age to come"). He came as a messiah who not only represented the people of Yahweh by taking on himself the suffering of the nation in the tradition of the Jewish martyrs and the wrath of disobedient Israel but also enacted their liberation from exile by intentionally dying in order to achieve victory over Satan, who constituted the true enemy of Israel. The result is a renewal of the covenant, the forgiveness of sins, the coming of the kingdom of God and the fulfillment of Israel's original mission to be a servant people who are a light to the world.

Whereas Wright's approach is broad, other scholars have pointed to specific points of contact between Jewish exile theology and the teaching and actions of Jesus. For example, C. A. Evans argues that at least five features justify a connection: Jesus' appointment of the Twelve, which may suggest the reconstitution of the twelve tribes of Israel; the request for a sign from heaven (Mk 8:11-13), which may reflect the signs promised by *messianic pretenders; Jesus' appeal to Isaiah 56:7 during the demonstration in the temple (Mt 21:12-13 par.), which, when the oracle of Isaiah 56:1-8 is in view, indicates that Jesus chastises the religious leaders for neglecting to live up to the eschatological expectation; Jesus' allusion to Zechariah 2:6 (Heb v. 10) in Mark 13:27, which recalls the gathering of God's people; and Jesus' criticism of the Jewish religious leaders (Mt 11:21-23 par.), which appears to threaten judgment of exile.

3. Exile in the Gospels.

Exile theology has also played an important role for some scholars in understanding the aim of the Evangelists. Though the exile motif emerges in all the Synoptics, perhaps the most concentrated use of the exile-exodus motif is found in recent studies of Mark, which is not surprising given the Evangelist's placement of the quotation of Isaiah 40:3 at the beginning of his narrative. For example, R. E. Watts argues that the exile-exodus motif in Isaiah provides the best integrative paradigm for reading Mark's Gospel as a whole. The internal basis for Watts's schema is the conflation of Scripture texts from Exodus 23:20, Malachi 3:1 and Isaiah 40:3 in Mark 1:2-3, which fuse together two basic thematic contours of the Gospel: the fulfillment of the delayed new exodus promise and the possible judgment due to the lack of preparedness.

In this light, Watts claims that recognized references to Scripture were perceived by the audience as iconic indicators that pointed back not so much to the larger biblical themes of restoration as antitypes but to actual promises that were regarded as fulfilled in the coming of Jesus. In addition to the textual basis, Watts claims that the self-understanding of Mark's original audience was shaped by the ideological paradigm of Israel's hope of restoration since the exile, namely, the prophetic transformation of the first exodus into the future hope of a new one.

Watts's attempt to integrate Markan structure and themes, particularly the function of Isaiah's new exodus motif within a structural paradigm, is a valiant response to approaches that reject theological or literary coherence of Mark's Gospel as a whole. And "the way" or "new exodus" may well be a legitimate theme that aids the reading of Mark's story. The difficulty, however, with this and other similar readings of Mark is that the metanarrative of the Isaianic new exodus threatens to overshadow whatever narrative might be discovered as latent in the Gospel itself as well as the role of Mark's quotations and echoes of other books of Scripture, such as the Psalms, Daniel, Zechariah and the Pentateuch. Metanarratives may be helpful as analogies, but as hermeneutical keys they can distort the originality and integrity of Mark's story and his creative reading of Scripture.

Matthew and Luke also incorporate the exile motif, but it is not as pronounced. In Matthew it often lies in the shadows of more major motifs such as Jesus as a second Moses who comes to bring the new Torah and Jesus as the fulfillment of Scripture. The prominent motifs of exodus and liberation are grounded in an assumption that Israel is in a state of alienation and in need of restoration. The same state of exile undergirds Luke's major theme of salvation, though unlike in Matthew, it also incorporates the Gentiles. What is further unique about Luke is that his Jesus preaches not only a spiritual liberation but a social and economic one as well. Luke's emphasis on the marginalized, oppressed and neglected people of his day (e.g., the poor, *women) suggests that the motif of exile can be extended to the daily realities of life (Lk 6:20-24; 12:16-11; 14:12-14; 16:19-26). One of the ways in which this is strongly conveyed is through Jesus' announcement in Luke 4:16-21 (quoting Is 61:1-2; 58:6), when he proclaims to his fellow Nazarenes at the beginning of his ministry that he has come to bring "good news to the poor," "liberty to the captives," "freedom for the oppressed" and the arrival of the "acceptable year of the Lord."

In the Johannine tradition, the motif of exile is also subtle, often overshadowed by the theme of exodus, expressed in Jesus' activities as a liberator and the prophet like Moses. Several scholars have observed that John is not only influenced by the promise of the prophet in Deuteronomy 18:15-18 but is indebted to the Moses tradition especially for the construction of Jesus' farewell discourse. In addition to the Deuteronomic influence, John presents Jesus as a preexistent messianic figure who comes to rescue his people from this world of darkness, hostility and sin. Those who place their faith in Jesus participate in "eternal life" (Jn 3:16). They are born of the Spirit (Jn 3:5), live in the "light" (Jn 8:12), become the children of God (Jn 1:12), are known and given knowledge (Jn 10:14) and are connected with God through the Son of Man who spans heaven and earth (Jn 1:51). By implication, these images of restoration and exodus suggest that the individual who does not believe in Jesus exists in the realm of darkness, ignorance and death. Since those who do not believe in Jesus are not regarded as the "children of God," they are in a spiritual sense living in exile because they are alienated from God.

4. Exile in Paul.

With regard to Paul, the exilic motif fits well within his large-scale attempt to explain the coherence of the revelation of Jesus with the salvation history of Israel. Although Paul never explicitly mentions the exilic judgment of Israel, his understanding of the "old covenant" that spanned from Abraham to Christ is informed by it. The larger motif of Israel's restoration in light of the coming of Christ is necessarily rooted in Israel's and the world's alienation from the Creator (*see DPL,* Restoration of Israel). For Paul, the coming of Christ brought to an end an era that resulted in judgment against both Israel and the world. Israel's failed mission to be a light to the world, due to its sin, resulted in the world's slavery to sin and "exile" from God (e.g., Gal 1:4; 4:1-11). The new era in Paul's twofold redemptive history brings to fulfillment the mission of Israel in the coming of its representative, Jesus Messiah, whose obedience unto death and vindication in the resurrection constitutes a new Adam and a new Israel (e.g., Rom 5:12-21). This is effective, however, only for those Jews and Gentiles who receive by faith through the Spirit their inheritance as adopted sons and daughters of God (e.g., Rom 8:14-17). Members of this remnant are no longer "in Adam" but "in Christ," for they have been liberated from "slavery" (and thus released from exile) and re-created to be the eschatological people of God (2 Cor 5:17).

See also DIASPORA JUDAISM; ISRAEL, LAND OF; JEWISH HISTORY: PERSIAN PERIOD.

BIBLIOGRAPHY. P. R Ackroyd, *Exile and Restoration: A Study of Hebrew Thought of the Sixth Century B.C.* (OTL; Philadelphia: Westminster, 1968); J. Ashton, *Understanding the Fourth Gospel* (Oxford: Clarendon Press, 1991); C. A. Evans, "Jesus and the Continuing Exile of Israel," in *Jesus and the Restoration of Israel: A Critical Assessment of N. T. Wright's Jesus and the Victory of God,* ed. C. C. Newman (Downers Grove, IL: InterVarsity Press, 1999) 77-100; R. T. France, *Matthew: Evangelist and Teacher* (NTP; Downers Grove, IL: InterVarsity Press, 1989); P. Garnet, *Salvation and Atonement in the Qumran Scrolls* (WUNT 2.3; Tübingen: Mohr Siebeck, 1977); M. Hengel, *The Pre-Christian Paul* (Philadelphia: Trinity Press International, 1991); A. Lacocque, "The Liturgical Prayer in Daniel 9," *HUCA* 47 (1976) 119-42; S. E. Loewenstamm, *The Evolution of the Exodus Tradition* (Jerusalem: Magnes, 1992); I. H. Marshall, *Luke: Historian and Theologian* (3d ed.; NTP; Downers Grove, IL: InterVarsity Press, 1988); W. A. Meeks, *The Prophet-King: Moses Tradition and the Johannine Christology* (NovTSup 14; Leiden: E. J. Brill, 1967); J. Neusner, *Self-Fulfilling Prophecy: Exile and Return in the History of Judaism* (Boston: Beacon, 1987); E. P. Sanders, *Jesus and Judaism* (Philadelphia: Fortress, 1985); idem, *Paul and Palestinian Judaism: A Comparison of Patterns of Religion* (Philadelphia: Fortress, 1977); J. M. Scott, ed., *Exile: Old Testament, Jewish and Christian Conceptions* (SupJSJ 56; Leiden: E. J. Brill, 1997); idem, "Paul's Use of Deuteronomic Tradition," *JBL* 112 (1993) 645-65; O. H. Steck, *Israel und das gewaltsame Geschick der Propheten: Untersuchungen zur Überlieferung des deuteronomistischen Geschichtsbildes im Alten Testament, Spätjudentum und Urchristentum* (WMANT 23; Neukirchen-Vluyn: Neukirchener Verlag, 1967); idem, "Das Problem theologischer Strömungen in nachexilischer Zeit," *EvT* 28 (1968) 445-58; R. E. Watts, *Isaiah's New Exodus and Mark* (WUNT 2.88; Tübingen: Mohr Siebeck, 1997); N. T. Wright, *Jesus and the Victory of God* (COQG 2; Minneapolis: Fortress, 1996); *The New Testament and the People of God* (COQG 1; Minneapolis: Fortress, 1992).

T. R. Hatina

EXORCISM. *See* DEMONOLOGY.

EXPOSURE OF INFANTS. *See* FAMILY AND HOUSEHOLD.

EXTRAMARITAL SEXUAL INTERCOURSE. *See* ADULTERY, DIVORCE.

EZEKIEL THE TRAGEDIAN. *See* JEWISH LITERATURE: HISTORIANS AND POETS

F

FALSE PROPHECY. *See* PROPHETS AND PROPHECY.

FAMILY AND HOUSEHOLD

The vast disparity between the income of rich and poor makes it somewhat difficult to generalize about all ancient households; a wealthy householder had more than seven hundred times the income of a peasant, and the extremely wealthy might have more than fifteen thousand times the income of a peasant (Bastomsky). Although most of the literary remains depict life in fairly well-to-do households that could include *slaves, most of the free inhabitants of the Roman Empire were impoverished peasants whose households differed significantly from this norm. Their houses were overcrowded (sometimes twenty-five to a one-room house; MacMullen, 13-14), helping explain why many peasants abandoned babies on local trash heaps. Nevertheless, extant information on ancient Mediterranean households is abundant and provides numerous insights into first-century home life. Much information from the ancient household relevant to early Christian texts focuses on *marriage; here we focus on other household relationships, especially parent-child and slaveholder-slave relationships.

1. Household Codes and Marriage
2. Children
3. Slaves
4. Conclusion

1. Household Codes and Marriage.

Ancient moralists frequently defined household relationships in terms of the authority relations between the male householder and other respective groups within the aristocratic household: wives, children and slaves.

1.1. Household Codes. *Aristotle developed household codes to advise aristocratic men about the various ways they should rule their wives, children and slaves (Aristotle *Pol.* 1.2.1-2, 1253b; 1.5.3-4, 1259b; 3.4.4, 1278b; see Balch 1981, 1988); these three groups also appear together (with some other groups) not only in Greek (e.g., Artemidorus *Oneir.* 1.24) but also in *rabbinic sources (Swidler, 84, 117). Aristotle and others thought that order in the household would produce order in society as a whole; thus societal norms and household norms affected one another. Although there were differences between them (e.g., Aristotle *Pol.* 1.1.2, 1252a; 1.5.6, 1260a), codes concerning household management could be linked with the broader category of advice on city management, as in the context in Aristotle (Aristotle *Pol.* 1.2.1, 1253b) and some other works (Lührmann; Lycurgus 21 in Plutarch *Sayings of Spartans, Mor.* 228CD).

Household codes probably also affected the formulation of some laws in terms of relationships among children, wives and slaves (Gaius *Inst.* 1.48-51, 108-19). *Josephus's apologetic included an emphasis on biblical law's great virtues (Josephus *Ag. Ap.* 2.42 §§291-96), and it is not surprising that Jewish writers with Greek or Hellenized audiences stressed such codes as a way of identifying Judaism with the prevailing values of the dominant culture (see Balch 1988, 28-31). Citing the three groups that appeared in household codes from Aristotle forward, Paul adapts the content of the codes but retains their structure (Eph 5:21—6:9; Col 3:18—4:1), possibly to help Christians witness within their culture (1 Cor 9:19-23; Tit 2:5, 8; cf. Keener, 133-224).

1.2. Marriage. Although some writers advocated either celibate or promiscuous singleness, marriage was the norm in both Jewish and broader Greco-Roman society. Adultery was widespread but viewed as immoral (*see* Adultery, Divorce); divorce was widespread but usually was viewed as merely unfortunate. Although homosexual relations were common, especially in Greek culture, marriages were heterosexual, a primary purpose of marriage being seen as procreation, and the Greek and Roman norm was monogamy. In Greek society men on average were about a decade older than their wives, perhaps due to a shortage of women stemming from a greater percentage of girl babies being abandoned; among Jews the age disparity was less, but throughout the ancient Mediterranean women usually first married in their teens. Husbands held much higher rank than did wives in the marriage relationship, though the husbands proved more dominating in some societies (e.g., classical *Athens) than in others.

In contrast to Jewish people, most Mediterranean Gentiles, especially those influenced by Greek culture, did not limit male sexual activity to marriage. In Greek culture, where men typically married around age thirty (Hesiod *Op.* 696-98; *see* Marriage), boys could have intercourse with slaves, prostitutes or one another.

1.3. Relations with Stepfamily and Extended Kin. For remarriages, see the article on divorce, but here we comment briefly on typical relations in stepfamilies. The image of the stepmother was often one of cruelty (Lucan *Civ.W.* 4.637-38; Dixon, 49), even a "viper" (Euripides *Alc.* 310), and in a dream constituted a bad omen (Artemidorus *Oneir.* 3.26). Many times stepchildren resented their father's new wife; for example, a man throwing a stone at a dog missed, struck his stepmother instead and concluded that he had done better than expected (Plutarch *Dinner of 7 Wise Men* 2, *Mor.* 147C). Stepmothers could be compared with days of misfortune, as opposed to good days compared with a mother (Hesiod *Op.* 825; Aulus Gellius *Noc. Att.* 17.12.4).

Thus one selecting a new wife might consider a stepmother who would care for the children (e.g., Tacitus *Ann.* 12.2); it was said that one lawgiver even prohibited from office a man who brought home a stepmother over his children, regarding it as a sign of poor administrative skill (Diodorus Siculus *Bib. Hist.* 12.12.1). Sexual desire for a stepson or a stepmother was regarded as terrible (Euripides *Hipp.* 885-90; Appian *Rom. Hist.* 11.10.59; Gaius *Inst.* 1.63-64; *Pseud.-Phoc.* 179-81), though it was known to exist (Apuleius *Met.* 10.3), and some Eastern rulers were thought to allow for this more readily (Appian *Rom. Hist.* 11.10.61).

Extended kin ties were important (see Gardner, 5-6), but inscriptions suggest that the nuclear family was the primary close bond in Roman antiquity (Saller and Shaw), as well as in Roman Palestine (Goodman, 36; cf. Prov 27:10). Male patriarchs held power not only over their children but also over grandchildren and great-grandchildren, if they lived that long (Gardner, 5-6).

Fictive kin ties were also important in ancient Mediterranean society; fictive kinship language was common both among ethnic and religious groups, so that a Jew might thus address fellow Israelites (Tob 5:10; 6:10; 7:3; 2 Macc 1:1; Acts 2:29; 3:22; 9:17). Sibling terminology could likewise extend to fellow rabbis or fellow disciples (*Sipre Deut.* 34.5.3; *b. 'Abod. Zar.* 18a, *Bar.;* cf. Mt 23:8); co-initiates into mysteries (Burkert, 45); alliances (e.g., 1 Macc 10:18; 12:6, 10, 21; 14:40); friendships (Euripides *Iph. Taur.* 497-98; Plutarch *Many Friends* 2, *Mor.* 93E; Marcus Aurelius *Med.* 1.14; *Ahiq.* 49, col. 4); and other commonalities (*CPJ* 3:41 §479; Diodorus Siculus *Bib. Hist.* 1.1.3); in conspicuous hospitality to a stranger (*T. Abr.* 2:5B; see also fictive parental language in Virgil *Aen.* 9.297; Diodorus Siculus *Bib. Hist.* 17.37.6; Rom 16:13).

2. Children.

Both minor and adult children were responsible to honor their parents; adult children were required to care for aged parents.

2.1. Honoring and Obeying Parents. Despite some Jewish suspicions that Gentiles might dishonor or even kill their parents (*Sipre Deut.* 81.4.1-2), Greek moralists stressed honoring one's parents, which could appear with similar exhortations to respect authority in paraenesis (Isocrates *Dem.* 16; *Or.* 1; Solon in Diogenes Laertius *Vit.* 1.60). Greek thinkers sometimes advised that one should behave toward one's parents as one would wish one's children to behave toward oneself (Isocrates *Dem.* 14; *Or.* 1; Hierocles *Fraternal Love* 4.27.20; Thales in Diogenes Laertius *Vit.* 1.37). Jewish wisdom similarly stressed that one's old age would go better if one took care of one's father in his old age (Sir 3:12-15); in Jewish narrative one who dishonored his parents might meet the same fate at the hands of his children (*Jub.* 35:10-11; 37:5, 11).

Jewish tradition emphasized the honor of parents even more heavily than did Greek and Roman tradition (*Jub.* 7:20; 35:1-6; *Ep. Arist.*

238; *Sent. Syr. Men.* 95; *Pseud.-Phoc.* 180; *Gen. Rab.* 36:6; Eph 6:1-3). One should honor one's parents, without whom one would not exist (*ʾAbot R. Nat.* 35 §79). Because one biblical text mentions the mother first (Lev 19:3), rabbis argued that one should honor both parents equally (*Mek. Pisha* 1.28; Bahodesh 8.28-32; *Gen. Rab.* 1:15); one should "honor" and "please" one's mother, given the pregnancy and the pains of birth she endured for her children (Tob 4:3-4; *Sent. Syr. Men.* 96-98). Later rabbis consistently extolled people who honored their parents (*b. Qidd.* 31ab; *Pesiq. Rab.* 23/24:2). Not surprisingly, a Jewish philosopher like *Philo, who draws on both Jewish and Greek thought, strongly emphasizes honoring parents (Philo *Spec. Leg.* 2.42 §§234-36; *Ebr.* 5 §17; *Omn. Prob. Lib.* 12 §87).

Jewish teachers often claimed that one should honor one's parents directly after God (Josephus *Ag. Ap.* 2.27 §206; *Sent. Syr. Men.* 9-10; *Pseud.-Phoc.* 8); many considered honoring parents the greatest commandment in the law (*Ep. Arist.* 228), though they undoubtedly implicitly accepted obedience to God first. Some rabbis held that the honor due one's parents is equivalent to that due God, though ultimately obedience to God came first (*b. B. Meṣ* 32a, *Bar.);* because parents participated in a person's creation, honoring them counted as honoring God (*b. Kid.* 30b, *Bar.; Pesiq Rab.* 23/24:2). For Philo parents are copies of God's power because they also create (Philo *Spec. Leg.* 2.1 §2); as begetter-creators they are midway between human and divine, to their children what God is to the world (Philo *Spec. Leg.* 2.38 §§224-25; cf. *Decal.* 22 §§106-7).

The Jewish understanding of parents as divine representatives probably reflects broader Mediterranean conceptions; philosophers sometimes regarded parents as images of the gods (Hierocles *Toward One's Parents* 4.25.53). On a more popular level, a Gentile could exhort a sibling to honor their mother as one would honor a deity (*Select Papyri* 1:320-21, lines 27-28); deities like Isis also offered such exhortations (Horsley, 1:11, 17 §2); one should not dishonor one's father because Zeus was god of fathers (Epictetus *Disc.* 3.11.5). Philosophers often counseled the highest honor for gods, but among people the highest honor for parents (Pythagoras in Diogenes Laertius *Vit.* 8.1.22-23; *Stoics in Diogenes Laertius *Vit.* 7.1.120; Hierocles *Toward One's Parents* 4.25.53).

Moralists also insisted that one should love one's parents (Dicta Catonis collection of distichs 2; Cato *Distichs* 3.24; *Sent. Syr. Men.* 94); the affection between parents and children could be undermined only by a terrible misdeed (Cicero *Amicitia* 8.27). One item for biographers' praise was gratitude to one's parents (Diogenes Laertius *Vit.* 10.1.9). The harmony of children with parents was highly valued (Menander's maxims 4 in *Select Papyri* 3:260-61). Foolish behavior shamed one's family (Prov 10:1; 17:21, 25; 23:24-25; 28:7; 29:3, 15), and ancients typically understood juvenile delinquency as a problem for the youth's family (Garland).

Anger with one's mother was shameful (Diogenes Laertius *Vit.* 2.29). Striking one's father was very bad (e.g., Aristophanes *Nub.* 1332-33), warranting death in Jewish law (Ex 21:15); Josephus felt that even attempted misbehavior toward parents warrants execution (Josephus *Ag. Ap.* 2.31 §217). Some early writers had predicted that children would stop honoring aged parents in the end time, after which the human race would be quickly destroyed (Hesiod *Op.* 182-85; cf. Mk 13:12; 2 Tim 3:1-2). Abusive language toward an aged father invited divine punishment (Hesiod *Op.* 331-34); dishonoring one's mother invited calamity (Dion. Hal. *Ant. Rom.* 8.53.1). Even a countercultural sage like Diogenes the Cynic reportedly reproved one who despised his father by reminding him that he owed even his ability to act thus to his father.

Early Jewish and Christian sources also warned of divine judgment against those who dishonored their parents (*Sent. Syr. Men.* 20-24; *Sib. Or.* 1.74-75; 2.275-76; Rom 1:30, 32; Ethiopic *Apoc. Peter* 11). Those who honored parents would have long life (Ex 20:12; Deut 5:16; Sir 3:5-6; Pseudo-Philo *Bib. Ant.* 11:9); many taught that this work would also be rewarded in the world to come (*m. Pe'ah* 1:1; *Sipre Deut.* 336.1.1; ARN 40A).

Part of honoring one's parents was obeying them. Although far more texts emphasize honoring parents than obeying them, perhaps because the latter applied in practice most fully to minors still at home, many texts do emphasize children's obedience to their parents. Only children who learned the discipline of obedience would understand how to exercise authority over others (Isocrates *Ad Nic.* 57, *Or.* 3.37). Some qualified the demand by debating whether all a father's commands must be obeyed (Aulus Gellius *Noc. Att.* 2.7; cf. 1 Sam 19:1-6; 20:31-33); an adult son who found it necessary to act contrary to his mother's wishes nevertheless would need to do so very respectfully (Dixon, 180-82, 234). Jewish wisdom emphasized honoring and obeying one's parents (Sir 3:1-4) in deeds as well as words (Sir 3:8), serving them as one's masters (Sir 3:7); positive models in stories also honored and obeyed their parents (*T. Jud.* 1:4-5; *T. Abr.* 5B).

Some philosophers did write that gratitude toward one's parents for conception was unnecessary, since they had procreated for pleasure rather than intentionally (Diogenes *Ep.* 21); true kinship was determined by shared commitment to the good, rather than genetic ties (Diogenes Laertius *Vit.* 7.1.33), just as in Jewish texts God's law took priority over family fidelity (Deut 13:6-9; 4 Macc 2:10). Skeptics like Sextus Empiricus even regarded such norms as parent-honoring as cultural, pointing to Scythians who allegedly slit their parents' throats once they reached the age of sixty (*Pyr.* 3.210, 228). Most, however, counseled that one bear with even an unjust parent (Publilius Syrus 8) and respected a son who did so (Appian *Rom. Hist.* 3.2; *b. Qidd.* 31a).

*2.2. **Providing for Aged Parents.*** Providing for aged parents was essential in ancient ethics (Diogenes Laertius *Vit.* 1.37), and in Jewish tradition it was part of honoring them (*Jub.* 35:11-13). Roman law required children to support aged parents or face imprisonment, an implicit exception obviously being made for minor children (Quintilian *Inst. Orat.* 7.6.5); elsewhere in Mediterranean antiquity a mother could file suit against a daughter who failed to provide for her (*P. Enteuxeis* 26; 220 B.C.). From a Jewish and a Christian standpoint, whoever abandoned parents in old age was like a blasphemer (Sir 3:16) or worse than a typical Gentile (1 Tim 5:8).

Ancient writers viewed this care of parents as repayment for rearing children (1 Tim 5:4). From an early period writers complained that those who died young failed to repay their parents (Homer *Il.* 4.477-78; 17.302). Some early Greek writers declared that children ought to repay aged parents for rearing them but would not do so in the end time (Hesiod *Op.* 188-89). Caring for parents in this manner imitated their care for the children after birth (Hierocles *Toward One's Parents* 4.25.53); however one provides for one's parents, one can expect from one's children (Diogenes Laertius *Vit.* 1.37). Some Jewish sources claim that a son who fails to provide for his parents, so repaying them, must die by stoning (Josephus *Ag. Ap.* 2:28 §206); or that those who fail to repay aged parents, abandoning them, will suffer eternal punishment (*Sib. Or.* 2.273-75, maybe a Christian interpolation). Some other cultures also believe that God punishes those who neglect aging parents (Mbiti, 269); modern Western culture, with its societal safety nets for the aged, is more the exception than the rule in history. Some of these texts may reflect the wider concern for just treatment of widows (Is 1:17; Wis 2:10; Jas 1:27; *Sipre Deut.* 281.1.2; elsewhere in the Mediterranean, e.g., *P. Ryl.* 114.5), incumbent first of all on the heirs (*Gen. Rab.* 100:2).

*2.3. **Stereotypical Parent Images.*** In contrast to stereotypes one might expect from Greek New Comedy, the Roman mother was seen not as a sentimental model of gentleness but as an "unbending moral mentor, guardian of traditional virtue and object of a lifelong respect" (Dixon, 7; cf. 105). She was a figure of authority to her children of both genders, especially for the daughters (Dixon, 227). The most critical point in the mother-daughter bond may have formed especially when the daughter became a young woman starting her own family (Dixon, 211-12). Perhaps in contrast with (or nuancing) this western Mediterranean model, however, eastern Mediterranean Jewish sources portray mothers as more affectionate than fathers, sharing their children's feelings (4 Macc 15:4).

Fathers were expected to provide for their children (Socrates *Ep.* 6; Seneca *Ben.* 3.11.2; *Ep. Arist.* 248; 2 Cor 12:14) and became the ideal model for ancient benefactors (Stevenson). They could be known for their gentleness (Homer *Odys.* 2.47, 234; 1 Cor 4:15, 21; 1 Thess 2:11; Dixon, 28). One could address as "father" an elder brother who functioned more broadly in this role (*P. Par.* 47.1).

Fictive kinship terminology based on active rather than genetic relationship was common (e.g., Phaedrus *Fables* 3.15.18), and "father" was a title of great respect (Homer *Il.* 24.507; Virgil *Aen.* 8.115; 9.735; 11.184, 904; 12.697). Ancients employed such fictive kinship terminology in an honorary manner, sometimes in direct address (e.g., 2 Kings 5:13; 13:14; Diodorus Siculus *Bib. Hist.* 21.12.5). For example, they employed titles like "father of the Jews" (2 Macc 14:37); "fathers of the world" for the first-century schools of Hillel and Shammai (*Gen. Rab.* 12:14); "fathers" for Roman senators (Plutarch *Rom.* 58, *Mor.* 278D; Lucan *Civ. W.* 3.109; Livy *Hist.* 1.8.7; 1.26.5; Sallust *Catil.* 6.6), for other societal leaders or benefactors (Dionysius of Halicarnassus *Ant. Rom.* 12.1.8; Pausanius *Descr.* 8.48.5-6; 8.51.7) and for older mentors (Homer *Odys.* 1.308). "Father" could apply to any respected elders (Acts 7:2; 22:1; 1 Tim 5:1; 1 Jn 2:13; *4 Bar.* 5:28; Homer *Il.* 24.507); thus, for example, the honorary title "father of a synagogue" (e.g., *CIJ* 1:xcv-xcvi; 1:66 §93; 1:250-51 §319); see also "mothers of synagogues" (*CIJ* 1:118 §166; 1:362 §496; 1:384 §523). Age by itself was grounds for respect (*t. Meg.* 3:24; Hom. *Il.* 1.259; 23.616-23), so from the earliest period younger persons could address older men respectfully as fathers (Homer *Il.* 9.607), and older men could address younger men as sons (Homer *Il.* 24.373; *Odys.* 1.308; *4 Bar.* 5:28), as could leaders their followers (e.g., Virgil *Aen.* 1.157). One could address even an older stranger as "father" (Homer *Il.* 24.362, 371; *Odys.* 7.28, 48; 8.145, 408; 17.553; 18.122; 20.199).

Various texts apply father/son language to teachers and their disciples (Epictetus *Disc.* 3.22.82); disciples were called children of their teachers (*4 Bar.* 7:24; *Sipre Deut.* 34.3.1-3, 5; 305.3.4; 3 Jn 4), and their teachers were their fathers (2 Kings 2:12; *4 Bar.* 2:4, 6, 8; 5:5; *t. Sanh.* 7:9; Mt 23:9). Wisdom discourses, which employ the sort of rhetoric one would expect among the early sages, were often addressed to sons (Prov 1:8; *Ahiq.* 96.14A; Sir 2:1; *1 Enoch* 81:5); such wisdom language often occurs in the testamentary *genre and hence requires such language (*Jub.* 21:21; Tob 4:3-12; 1 Macc 2:50, 64; *1 Enoch* 92:1; *T. Job* 1:6; 5:1; 6:1; *T. Reub.* 1:3). Because rabbis sometimes claimed greater respect than parents (*m. B. Meṣ* 2:11; *m. Ker.* 6:9; *Sipre Deut.* 32.5.12), it is not surprising that some early sages used the paternal title *abba* in the same way that most came to use "rabbi" (Sandmel, 106). Thus Jesus calling his disciples "children" (Jn 13:33) would have offered ancients no confusion between the Father and Son roles elsewhere in that Gospel.

*2.4. **Paternal Authority.*** It is not without reason that Paul addresses not parents but fathers in Ephesians 6:4: a father held the primary authority in the household as the *paterfamilias,* the male head of the home addressed in household codes (see 1.1 above). By contrast, despite the authority inherent in their role, mothers held no legal authority over their own children (Gaius *Inst.* 1.104).

A father was expected to govern his household (Marcus Aurelius *Med.* 1.9). Indeed, because the skills necessary to govern a household were also those necessary to govern cities (Euripides *El.* 386-87; Isocrates *Ad Nic.* 19, *Or.* 2; Plutarch *Dinner of Seven Wise Men* 12, *Mor.* 155D) and because it was natural to reason from private to public affairs (Demosthenes *Lep.* 9), many regarded this demonstration as a prerequisite that one could govern in the larger society (Isocrates *Ad. Nic.* 41, *Or.* 3.35; Diodorus Siculus *Bib. Hist.* 12.12.1; Marcus Aurelius *Med.* 1.16.4; Diogenes Laertius *Vit.* 1.70; *Sipre Deut.* 32.5.12; 1 Tim 3:4-5).

Patria potestas, the father's authority of life and death over family members, permeated the fabric of Roman society (Lacey) but had declined in effectiveness by the period of the empire to the extent that in practice fathers could not kill their children (Sextus Empiricus *Pyr.* 3.211; Carcopino, 76-80), though some laws were officially revoked only much later. The father's power of life and death over children was distinctive of Roman law (Gaius *Inst.* 1.55), but Josephus concluded that parents had sufficient authority to function as their children's judges (Josephus *Ant.* 4.260).

Paternal authority remained the standard throughout the Mediterranean world; a writer could describe the father's just rule over his children as a "universal law" (Dionysius of Halicarnassus *Ant. Rom.* 3.23.19). Greek ethical tradition granted a father authority over his children comparable to that of a ruler over his subjects (Aristotle *Eth. Nic.* 8.11.2, 1161a). Children were freed from the Roman father's authority only by his death or loss of Roman citizenship (Gaius *Inst.* 1.127-28). The nature of paternal authority did differ depending on whether the children were minors or adults (Cohen, 174); both household codes (Aristotle *Pol.* 1.5.12, 1260b) and Roman law (Sextus Empiricus *Pyr.* 3.211) recog-nized that boys, unlike wives, matured and became sharers in governing the state. Given the average life expectancy, many adult children no longer had fathers living (Saller, 264), though in theory the older custom of *patria potestas* extended even to grandchildren (Gardner, 5-6).

It is clear, however, that Roman parents loved their children (Dupont, 118-19), as did

Greeks (Aristotle *Eth. Nic.* 8.12.2-3, 1161b). Latin poetry expressed great affection for one's children (Frank, 25); Stoics felt that such love came naturally to good people but not so to bad ones (Diogenes Laertius *Vit.* 7.1.120). Greek ideals suggested ruling one's children lovingly (Agasicles 2, in Plutarch *Sayings of Spartans, Mor.* 208B). Fathers could be severe, but most extant cases of such severity are reported as exceptional (Dixon, 27). A satirist condemns a miser hated even by his wife and children because he values money more than their welfare (Horace *Sat.* 1.1.84-87).

2.5. Parental Instruction and Discipline. The mother apparently constituted the main parental influence on a son until age seven, after which the father assumed primary responsibility (Lincoln, 400); the father's deferred responsibility also appears in other cultures (2 Kings 4:18-19; Mbiti, 169). Some scholars argue that children often appear in Greek texts as objects of instruction rather than as individuals (Lindemann).

Moralists emphasized the need for good *paideia,* *education and discipline (e.g., Plutarch *Educ.* 7, *Mor.* 4C; Epictetus *Disc.* 1.2.6; Wis 3:11; *Ep. Arist.* 248). Such education was the father's responsibility in Palestinian Jewish (Sir 30:2-3; Goodman, 72; Safrai, 770) as well as Greek and Roman (Meeks, 61) circles. Some educators emphasized discerning to what forms of guidance (such as control, fear, appeals to ambition) each boy responded (Quintilian *Inst. Orat.* 1.3.6-7); teachers should be strict in their discipline (Quintilian *Inst. Orat.* 2.2.4). Rigorists naturally preferred harsher treatment even for young children, to condition them to life's hardships (e.g., Crates *Ep.* 33).

Character was particularly developed in youth, though it could be modified later (Gill; Quintilian *Inst. Orat.* 1.1.5, 9); serious learning might begin later, but emotional development occurred in the earliest years (Dixon, 141). Many later rabbis did not regard young children as morally cognizant or responsible (*m. Parah* 3:4; *Gen. Rab.* 26:1), a view shared by most Roman jurists (Gaius *Inst.* 3.208). Rabbis believed that the evil impulse started in infancy (ARN 16A; cf. Crates *Ep.* 12), but knowledge of the law brought moral power (4 Macc 2:23; *Sipre Deut.* 45.1.2; ARN 16A; *b. Qidd.* 30b, *Bar.;* cf. *T. Asher* 3:2). Romans had a coming-of-age ceremony (e.g., Dupont, 229; Gaius *Inst.* 1.196; 2.113); Jewish boys also became young men around puberty (1 Esdr 5:41), and later rabbis attributed the beginning of the good impulse and moral responsibility to this time (*m. 'Abot* 5:21; ARN 16A). Children could not bear legal witness (*t. Sanh.* 9:11).

Disciplining a son with a rod was considered loving behavior for a father (Columbanus, probably Catonian lines, 52; Petronius *Sat.* 4), and even mothers could be exhorted not to spoil their children by encouraging their pleasure (Pseudo-Theano in Malherbe 1986, 83). Like slaves (e.g., Aristophanes *Nub.* 1414), children could be beaten or whipped (Aristophanes *Nub.* 1409-10), but a parent who acts in rage will regret it (Publilius Syrus 514; cf. *Pesiq. Rab Kah.* 15.4). Jewish wisdom also emphasized physical discipline in rearing boys (Sir 7:23; 30:12; *Ahiq.* 81.3; 82.4; see Pilch), regarding beating as loving (Sir 30:1; cf. Prov 13:24; *Pss. Sol.* 13:9-10; Heb 12:6; Rev 3:19). Though one might combine firm discipline with loving gentleness (ARN 31, §67B), some sages felt laughing and playing with one's children were too indulgent (Sir 30:9-10). (One should teach a good son wisdom but pray for a bad son's death and train him for gladiatorial combat, *Sent. Syr. Men.* 27-44.) Jewish custom also permitted rabbis to beat their disciples (Goodman, 78), though the rabbis disapproved of beatings that were dangerously severe (*m. Mak.* 2:2).

Some writers protested against excessive discipline or harshness (*Pseud.-Phoc.* 150, 207; Eph 6:4), but they appear to have been the minority. Quintilian notes that flogging was the standard custom but nevertheless rejects it as useful only for slaves, not pupils (Quintilian *Inst. Orat.* 1.3.13-14); he felt that excessive severity sometimes discouraged a boy from trying (Quintilian *Inst. Orat.* 2.4.10). Other moralists, while not necessarily balking at corporal punishment, advised gentleness before scolding (Plutarch *Flatterer* 28, *Mor.* 69BC).

2.6. Childbearing. Ancient texts, both Jewish (Wis 7:2; 4 Macc 16:7; *Sent. Syr. Men.* 97) and Gentile (Virgil *Ecl.* 4.61; Ovid *Fasti* 1.28-33; Quintilian *Inst. Orat.* 8.3.54; Aulus Gellius *Noc. Att.* 6.1.4; Arrian *Anab.* 7.12.6; *PGM* 101.36-37; Isis aretalogy in Grant 1953, 132), regularly speak of the duration of human pregnancy as ten months; this was the consensus of both physicians and philosophers (Aulus Gellius *Noc. Att.* 3.16). One Epidauros inscription (inscr. 1) does note an exception: a woman named Cleo was pregnant for five years until Asclepius healed her, and on his birth the boy born to her immediately washed himself and began walking around (Grant 1953, 56). It was understood that children normally bore their parents' image (Gen 5:3; 4 Macc 15:4; Pseudo-Philo *Bib. Ant.* 50:7; Chariton *Chaer.* 2.11.2; 3.8.7; *P. Oxy.* 37).

Especially among peasants in impoverished areas like much of Egypt, the childhood mortality rate was extremely high. A disproportionate number died in infancy, and of those who survived into adolescence roughly half reached twenty-five, with the number of survivors continuing to be halved every decade of life, making the average life expectancy for live births around twenty-five or thirty years (N. Lewis, 54; elsewhere in the empire, see Dupont, 222; for other traditional societies, see Mbiti, 153). Skeletal remains in Palestine likewise testify to a very high child mortality rate (see several articles in *'Atiqot* 21 [1992]: 55-80; among ancient Jews in general, survey *CIJ,* e.g., 1:308, §399, though burial inscriptions probably disproportionately report the youngest deaths [Leon, 230]). Even among the well-to-do, children often died tragically young (Plutarch *Consol. to Wife, Mor.* 608C, 609D, 611D), though ancient medical writers attest significant knowledge of medical care for children (Demaitre). (For the importance of childbearing in Mediterranean antiquity, *see* Marriage §§1.3, 1.4).

2.7. Exposure of Unwanted Infants. The father had the right to refuse to rear a newborn, even against the mother's objections (Gardner, 6). Deformed infants were sometimes killed (Den Boer, 98-99, 113, 116; in other cultures, e.g., Dawson, 324), but most babies were abandoned. Even if the percentage of babies abandoned has been overestimated (see Engels 1984, skeptical of the ten percent figure for infanticide), the exposure of children was a widely known custom (Pausanius *Descr.* 2.26.4); abandoned babies figure commonly in legends (Diodorus Siculus *Bib. Hist.* 4.64.1; 8.4.1; 19.2.3-5; Appian *Rom. Hist.* 1.1.2) and novels (Longus *Daphn. Chl.* 1.2, 5).

The high mortality rate among children may have provided one contributing factor for the abandoning of children; at the least it may have reduced the openness to emotional attachment (cf. Dixon, 113; Dupont, 221). Still, ancients were sad when their children died and did not abandon infants out of dislike for them (Golden). Often poverty required exposure or killing (Ovid *Met.* 9.675-84) of infants, but even a rich family might expose a child if they already had too many (Longus *Daphn. Chl.* 4.24; perhaps Suetonius *Tiberius* 47).

For economic reasons (the expense of the dowry), girls appear to have been abandoned more often than boys (*P. Oxy.* 744; Ovid *Met.* 9.675-84, 704-13), resulting in a high age for marriage for Greek males (*see* Marriage). Of the dozens of census declarations from Egypt, only two list more daughters than sons, and even then only one or two more (N. Lewis, 54-55; cf. Tarn, 101). Some scholars object that high rates of female infanticide would decimate the population (Engels 1980), but this ignores substantial concrete evidence (Harris). Moreover, Roman writers do suggest gradual declines in the Greek population, and in any case selective abandonment did not prevent propagation as effectively as widespread infanticide would. Rescued females often became slave prostitutes (*see* Adultery, Divorce).

When women married, they were lost to the family of origin, thus supporting a preference for sons (*Gen. Rab.* 26:4), but for whatever reasons, most families appear to have preferred sons, both among Gentiles (Artemidorus *Oneir.* 1.15; 4.10) and Jews (*Sipre Deut.* 138.2.1; 141.2; *b. Ber.* 5b; *Pesiq. Rab Kah.* 9.2). Nevertheless, daughters were loved, especially by fathers (mothers loved especially sons; Plutarch *Bride* 36, *Mor.* 143B). And though all early Jewish sources portray the birth of a daughter as a relative disappointment, Jewish people did not seek to artificially reduce their numbers as their pagan counterparts did (Ilan, 44-48).

Because Egyptian religion prohibited killing infants, Egyptians often rescued babies exposed by Hellenistic settlers in Egypt's nomes; the rescue is reflected in some children's names (e.g., Kopreus, "off the dunghill" [N. Lewis, 54]). Sometimes those who rescued such infants adopted them as children (Juvenal *Sat.* 6.602-9), but the children more often became *slaves; the Roman government imposed heavy inheritance tax penalties on those who tried to adopt them as children (BGU 1210; N. Lewis, 58). In places like *Ephesus the public bought infants cheaply, whom they then enslaved to Artemis (*I. Eph.* 17-19 in Trebilco, 343). Under Roman law a father who later recognized a child he had abandoned must pay the expenses of his rearing before taking him back (Quintilian *Inst. Orat.* 7.1.14).

Those infants not rescued would have been eaten by dogs and birds (Philo *Spec. Leg.* 3.115).

Like Egyptians and reportedly Germans (Tacitus *Germ.* 19), Jewish people rejected the exposure of infants (Philo *Spec. Leg.* 3.115-17; Josephus *Ag. Ap.* 2.25 §202; *Sib. Or.* 3.765-66; Diodorus Siculus *Bib. Hist.* 40.3.8), just as they abhorred child sacrifice (Lev 20:2-5; Wis 12:5-6; 14:23; Pseudo-Philo *Bib. Ant.* 4:16) and pagan oppressors killing others' infants (Pseudo-Philo *Bib. Ant.* 2:10). It is possible that some Jewish parents in mixed cities may have exposed their infants, but it was far less frequent than among Gentiles (*m. Makš.* 2:7); Jewish and Chinese cultures may have also had a lower incidence of child abuse than did Roman society (see Breiner). Due to their emphasis on procreation Stoics also rejected child abandonment (Malherbe 1986, 99). Child exposure became illegal in A.D. 374 (Gardner, 6), and Justinian in the sixth century regarded all exposed children as free (Rawson 1986a, 172; *see* Marriage).

2.8. Nurses. The milk that sustained infants normally came from human breasts, often from a nurse (e.g., Marcus Aurelius *Med.* 5.4). Sheep and goats' milk usually was pressed into cheeses (Longus *Daphn. Chl.* 1.23; Epictetus *Disc.* 1.16.8) after it was taken to town (Virgil *Priapea* 2.10-11). It was known, however, that one could use animal milk to sustain a child if necessary, though most examples stem from novels, myths and legends (Virgil *Aen.* 11.570-72; Livy *Hist.* 1.4.6; Propertius *Elegies* 4.1.55-56; Longus *Daphn. Chl.* 1.2, 5, 16); adult Scythians' drinking of mares' milk was noteworthy enough to have merited specific mention (e.g., Hesiod *Cat.* 39-40). In 1 Corinthians 3:1-2 Paul, like some of his contemporaries, thus employs the image of nurse or mother.

Roman women of high status often employed nurses (Dixon, 146), but Mediterranean women of high status rarely became nurses unless they were forced by dire financial straits (Demosthenes *Orat.* 57; Euxistheus *Ad Eub.* 35). Nursing contracts stipulating the amount of pay were a standard practice (Horsley, 2:7-8 §1). The nurse could be slave or free. If she were the former (e.g., Chariton *Chaer.* 1.12.9), the slaveholder profited from her labor (*P. Oxy.* 91.16); if the latter, she would agree to nurse the child in her own home for a fixed amount of time: sixteen months (BGU 1107.7), eighteen months (*CPJ* 2:15-19 §146) or two years (the median, N. Lewis, 146; Pseudo-Philo *Bib. Ant.* 51:1). If the child dies, she must nurse another child for the full length of time or lose her pay. She would be paid some money in advance, more in monthly installments of both olive oil (presumably for the infant's skin) and cash (N. Lewis, 146-47). In one case a foundling died, and those who entrusted it to the nurse demanded not merely the advance but also her own child, which they insisted was the foundling; the child looked like her and the judge ruled in her favor (*P. Oxy.* 37). Some contracts prohibit the nurse from intercourse, pregnancy or nursing another child lest she deplete her milk (BGU 1107.13-14; *CPJ* 2:15-19, §146); later rabbis also permitted a husband to spill his seed outside for two years after his wife had given birth to avoid another pregnancy that could interfere with lactation (Safrai, 764). Most often the nurslings in Egypt were abandoned babies whose finders wanted to raise them as slaves (N. Lewis, 146).

The well-to-do sought educated nurses from whom children from infancy would learn correct manners of speech (Plutarch *Lib. Educ.* 5, *Mor.* 3DE; Quintilian *Inst. Orat.* 1.1.4-5). Nurses were thought to love their charges (Epictetus *Disc.* 1.11.22, from a former slave); nursing at the same breast was also thought to nurture fraternal bonds (4 Macc 13:20). After growing to adulthood, a boy who had been nursed might honor his nurse even if she were a slave (Homer *Odys.* 1.435; 19.354; Dixon, 145), and nurses were so fondly recalled that they sometimes became models for teachers (Malherbe 1970, 211-12; Quintilian *Inst. Orat.* 2.4.5-6), an image Paul may employ in 1 Thessalonians 2:7. (Jewish teachers could also compare their teaching with nursing [*Sipre Deut.* 321.8.5].) Such nurses' epitaphs may not reveal how nurses felt about their profession, however, which many may have experienced as demeaning despite the bonds (Bradley 1986, 220-22; cf. Plutarch *Table Talk* 5, *Mor.* 672F-673A; Joshel appeals to more recent historical analogies).

For the sake of the maternal bond, some moralists advised mothers to nurse their own babies if possible (Plutarch *Lib. Educ.* 5, *Mor.* 3CD; Aulus Gellius *Noc. Att.* 12.1), yet few well-to-do Roman mothers appear to have followed this counsel (Treggiari 1976, 87; Dixon, 3), and there is little evidence that bonds between children and nurses prevented the child's bonding with parents (Dixon, 129). Some Jewish teachers felt that a wife could delegate breastfeeding if she brought enough slave help (*m. Ketub.* 5:5; *T. Benj.* 1:3); even a Gentile could nurse an Israelite baby (*m. 'Abod. Zar.* 2:1). In some later rabbinic Haggadah, God miraculously enabled a male to nurse so the child would not starve (*b. Šabb.* 53b, *Bar.; Gen. Rab.* 30:8), or God miraculously enabled Sarah to feed a multitude of Gentile infants (*Gen. Rab.* 53:9).

3. Slaves.

The most basic distinction between persons in Roman law was that between free person and *slave (Gaius *Inst.* 1.9), and among the free, whether they were freeborn or freed (Gaius *Inst.* 1.10). Household slaves were regularly considered as part of the household, under the authority of the *paterfamilias,* or male head of the household.

3.1. Slaves in Relation to Other Members of the Household. The inclusion of slaves in traditional household codes is not surprising; both in the Greek *oikos* and in the Roman *familia,* slaves were members of the household (Rawson 1986b, 7; Dixon, 16; N. Lewis, 57; Barrow, 22-64). The same is true of Jewish households (*CPJ* 1:249-50 §135; *y. Ter.* 8:1); the extended household designation was broad enough for one early sage to include the poor who depended on a charitable householder (*m. ʾAbot* 1:5). Although we do not treat them here, freedpersons were also part of the household (e.g., Cicero *Fam.* 1.3.2).

The portrait of a centurion's household in Acts 10:2 may presuppose slaves (cf. Acts 10:7; Mt 8:6; Lk 7:2). Soldiers enlisted for twenty or more years, during which time they were not officially permitted to marry. Although soldiers often did marry or cohabit with local women (Livy *Hist.* 43.3.2), their offspring were not considered legitimate, preventing soldiers from leaving them any inheritance (BGU 5.34-35). This situation was, however, often remedied by a special grant from the government (BGU 140.10-33; Plutarch *Fabius Maximus* 4, *Sayings of Romans, Mor.* 195EF; Herodian *Hist.* 3.8.5). High officers had more freedom but might refrain for the sake of honor (Plutarch *Scipio the Elder* 2, *Sayings of Romans, Mor.* 196B). In the first century an auxiliary horseman would make about 300 sesterces per year (Speidel); a legionary soldier made roughly three drachmas a day, which if entirely saved in a year would provide enough funds to pay for a modest house or one of the less expensive slaves (N. Lewis, 208; although one would then have to feed and clothe the slave). A centurion received at least fifteen times the pay of a legionary, whereas a *pilus primus,* a senior centurion, could receive four times that amount (sixty times that of a legionary; Jones, 202-3); thus many retired centurions could have acquired servants.

In urban areas, slaves constituted about one-third of the population (based on the report of Galen; Verner, 63). In classical Athens and in the southern United States in slaveholding times, about one-quarter of free families held slaves, and the percentage in Roman Italy would probably not be higher. In Roman Egypt about 10 percent were slaves and about 20 percent of families held slaves, because there were few slaves per household rather than larger plantations as in Italy (Verner, 60; Finley 1980, 80; MacMullen, 103). Slaveholding was more common in the urban centers of Roman Egypt: most Hellenistic citizens in capitals of Egyptian nomes apparently had one or two slaves, and about a quarter of their households had more (N. Lewis, 53). In a major urban center like *Alexandria, a wealthy family might hold one hundred slaves (N. Lewis, 57).

Though making distinctions between the specific roles, Aristotle linked the householder's relationship to his wife with that to his slave (Aristotle *Pol.* 1.1.5-6, 1252b). Josephus compared the character and status of wives and slaves (Josephus *Ant.* 4.219), as did many rabbis (*m. Ḥag.* 1:1; *m. Sukk.* 2:8; Stern, 628). Despite such comparisons, however, many would have distinguished clearly between the household head's guardianship of his wife and his rule over his slaves (Livy *Hist.* 34.7.13).

That slaves were often bought as young children (e.g., *CPJ* 3:73 §490) suggests that slaveholders often broke up slave families, selling off young children (Dixon, 17). Of more than sixty private slave-sale documents, no male slave sold was accompanied by a wife or children; only rarely were children sold alongside women (Finley 1980, 76; for a fuller description of slaves' hardships, see Bradley 1992). Slaves could be divided among children as part of an inheritance (*PSI* 903). Establishing a family life proved particularly difficult if the partners belonged to different households (Rawson 1986b, 24). Even after the decline of slavery in the empire, slave unions did not count as legal marriages wronged by adultery (Justinian *Cod.* 9.23). Nevertheless, many slaves in Egypt remained in the same family for three or four generations and often were then manumitted rather than sold (N. Lewis, 58-59). Further, that slave parents at times found the funds to dedicate a funerary inscription for a deceased child now in another household shows that the bonds of affection ran deep (Dixon, 17-18).

3.2. Sources for Slaves. Various sources existed for slaves (see Buckland, 397-436; Barrow, 1-21; Bartchy, 45-50; Lyall, 29-35), but the most common initial reason was war. Typically prisoners of war were enslaved (Diodorus Siculus *Bib. Hist.* 2.18.5; 14.68.3; 20.105.1; Livy *Hist.* 4.29.4; 26.34.3; 41.11.8), especially the women and children, who were less able to retaliate (Dionysius of Halicarnassus *Ant. Rom.* 10.26.3; Diodorus Siculus *Bib. Hist.* 17.46.4; Pausanius *Descr.* 3.23.4; Herodian *Hist.* 3.9.11); the funds from their sale might be placed in the state treasury (Livy *Hist.* 5.22.1). This practice was viewed as a form of mercy—saving prisoners of war rather than killing them (Justinian *Inst.* 1.3.3). Thus one historian explains that Romans procured slaves "by the most just means," normally from prisoners of war (Dionysius of Halicarnassus *Ant. Rom.* 4.24.2, LCL). At one point up to ten thousand slaves were said to be sold in a day on Delos, the primary slave market, for various prices depending on their skills and utility (Grant 1964, 104).

Recently enslaved children often died, but this offered little trouble to the empire so long as wars provided a fresh supply of slaves. Because wars declined in the first two centuries A.D., however, slaveholders began encouraging the production of slave offspring, so that "homeborn" increasingly appears as a description of slaves in papyri from this period (N. Lewis, 57). Both before (*CPJ* 1:125-27 §4) and during the Roman period a number of Jewish people were slaves (*see* Jewish History: Roman Period).

3.3. Slave Roles. Many slaves in Italy worked the massive agricultural estates, which appear to have proved economically profitable to the owners (Appian *Civ. W.* 1.1.8; Petronius *Sat.* 37-38; Finley 1973, 83-84; Barrow, 65-97); the Greco-Roman world took slavery to a new level and became one of the economies in history most dominated by slavery (Finley 1980, 9, 67; Padgug, 21-22). Agricultural slaves were rarer elsewhere in the empire, however; in Egypt peasants could be exploited far more cheaply (N. Lewis, 57). In most of the empire slavery was primarily an urban phenomenon (Finley 1980, 79).

The most degrading and deadly form of slavery was condemnation to work the mines, usually at isolated outposts, described by W. W. Tarn as "a hell on earth" (Tarn, 104). For this job employers used lower-class convicts and slaves, notably captives from the Jewish revolts and in a later period Christians (N. Lewis, 137-38).

Slaves in wealthy households tended toward specialized roles (see Treggiari 1975; Barrow, 22-64). Some slaves in well-to-do households may have appreciated their positions; a servant on an estate ruled by a benign landowner might well fear the change of masters (Apuleius *Met.* 8.15). A high-ranking slave in the imperial household might wield more power than did free aristocrats (Herodian *Hist.* 1.12.3). Those who slept with slaves were thereby enslaved (Tacitus *Ann.* 12.53), but some could marry into slavery to improve their status. Some people employed slavery as a means of upward mobility (Martin, 30-42). For most slaves, however, their state was degrading and difficult (Euripides *Androm.* 88-90; *Hec.* 332-33); half the female imperial slaves died before thirty (Pomeroy, 194), and in poor homes the ages may have been younger (cf. *ILS* 5215, 7420, 7428 in Sherk, 227-28).

A variety of occupations were open to women servants in wealthy households (Treggiari 1976). Slave women had long functioned as concubines (Sophocles *Ajax* 485-91; Arrian *Anab.* 4.19.5), and slaves continued to be sexually exploited in the Roman period (e.g., Appian *Civ. W.* 4.4.24; Babrius *Fables* 10.1-5; *see* Adultery, Divorce, the section on the sexual use of slaves).

Although slaves in comparable roles held lower social status than did free persons (Livy *Hist.* 4.3.7), roughly the same range of occupations existed among slaves as among the free (Finley 1980, 81-82; Dupont, 56-57). Rural peasants constituted perhaps 90 percent of the empire's free work force, and they, like field slaves but unlike household slaves, had virtually no opportunities for social mobility (Phaedrus *Fables* 1.15); rare is an inscription in which a peasant rose to a local aristocracy (*CIL* 9.3088 in MacMullen, 47). Cato's slaves received more bread than the average Egyptian peasant could eat, and the freer (less dependent on a *patron) a peasant was in some locations, the closer to potential starvation (Finley 1973, 107-8).

3.4. Negative Views About Slaves and Treatment of Slaves as Property. In aristocratic ideology, slaves were of inferior moral character (e.g., Josephus *Ant.* 4.8.15 §219); *Cicero lumps them with the insane and exiles (Cicero *Acad.* 2.47.144). Various sources present them as evil rather than virtuous (Plato *Alc.* 1.135C), as insulting (Seneca *Dial.* 2.11.3); deceptive (Terence *Haut.* 668-78; *And.* 495; Chariton *Chaer.* 2.10.7; 6.5.5) or even a perjurer (Apuleius *Met.* 10.7); lazy (Homer *Odys.* 17.320-21; Sir 33:24-28; *b. Qidd.* 49b); gossipy (Lucian *Lucius* 5); cowardly (Achilles Tatius *Leuc.* 7.10.5); or promiscuous (*m. 'Abot* 2:7; *m. Soṭa* 1:6). One loses half one's worth when one becomes a slave (Homer *Odys.* 17.322-23).

It was thought that one could distinguish one of royal descent by his appearance (Homer *Odys.* 4.63-64), but also a slave (Homer *Odys.* 24.252-53; Arrian *Anab.* 5.19.1; *T. Jos.* 11:2-3); free persons were normally thought more attractive (Chariton *Chaer.* 1.10.7; 2.1.5; 2.2.3; 3.3.10). A free person acting as a slave was shameful (Josephus *Ant.* 4.238), and slavery was a state intolerable to a genuinely free person (Dionysius of Halicarnassus *Ant. Rom.* 19.9.4; Dio Cassius *Hist.* 1.5.12; 8.36.3; Chariton *Chaer.* 1.11.3; Philo *Praem. Poen.* 24 §137; *Omn. Prob. Lib.* 5 §36); calling a free person a "slave" thus constituted a deliberate insult (Demosthenes *Lep.* 132; Epictetus *Disc.* 1.6.30; 1.9.20; Diogenes Laertius *Vit.* 6.2.33, 43).

In some respects law and custom treated slaves as property, in connection with their economic functions (Buckland, 10-38). Thinkers like Aristotle had long before declared the slave to be the master's tool, analogous to the body as the soul's tool (Aristotle *Eth. Eud.* 7.9.2, 1241b; cf. *Pol.* 1.1.4, 1252a; 1.2.3-6, 10, 1253b-54a); as there could be no friendship between a person and an inanimate object, neither could there be friendship between a slaveholder and his slave, a living tool (Aristotle *Eth. Nic.* 8.11.6-7, 1161b). Slaves and animals alike had no purposes for their own lives (Aristotle *Pol.* 3.5.10, 1280a); subordinating and using them was no different from one's use of animals (Aristotle *Pol.* 1.2.8-14, 1254ab).

Such theories translated naturally into economic practice. Thus slaves were regularly sold, both before (P Cair. Zen. 59003) and during (*P. Oxy.* 95; Buckland, 30-72) the Roman period. In the Ptolemaic period as later slaveholders paid taxes on slaves as on other kinds of property (*P. Columb. Inventory* 480); failure to register slaves in a Roman census could lead to their confiscation (BGU 5.60.155), as could exporting slaves in violation of proper tax rules (BGU 5.65-67). Slaves could be branded (Diodorus Siculus *Bib. Hist.* 34/35.2.32); divided as part of the deceased's estate (Horsley, 1:69-70 §24); or at times all executed for the suspected act of one, despite notable public protests (Tacitus *Ann.* 14.42-45).

Slaveholders in the empire officially held the power of life and death over their slaves (Gaius *Inst.* 1.52). Jewish legal interpreters in what probably represented the dominant tradition also understood slaveholders as exercising considerable authority because slaves were technically their property (*m. Giṭ* 1:6); at least one early rabbi even forbade saying a funeral oration over a deceased slave, arguing that this death should be treated merely as lost property (*b. Ber.* 16b, *Bar.*).

Gentler Romans might say that flogging was appropriate not for children but only for slaves (Quintilian *Inst. Orat.* 1.3.13-14). Slaves were also far more likely to receive capital sentences than were more directly guilty free persons (Apuleius *Met.* 10.12), even if the latter were foreigners (Livy *Hist.* 22.33.1-2).

Slaves could be examined under torture under the supposition that this practice increased their truthfulness, both in classical Greek culture (Demosthenes *Pant.* 27; *Olymp.* 18-19; *Tim.* 55-58; *Neaer.* 122) and in the Roman period (*Rhet. Ad Herenn.* 2.7.10; Tacitus *Ann.* 3.67; 4.29; Appian *Civ. W.* 1.3.20; Apuleius *Met.* 10.28; Herodian *Hist.* 4.5.4), though in the latter it was often a final resort (Justinian *Dig.* 48.18.1). So typically was torture the lot of slaves that free persons who suffered this abuse could be compared with slaves (Livy *Hist.* 32.38.8). The custom seems to have generated fewer objections than one might hope: even a novel's hero might torture female servants without any remorse (Chariton *Chaer.* 1.5.1). Many ancients were, however, skeptical of torture's effectiveness in always securing truth (Apuleius *Met.* 10.10); in the law court one would either accept or question such evidence depending on the side for which one was arguing (Aristotle *Rhet.* 1.15.26, 1376b; Quintilian *Inst. Orat.* 5.4.1).

In contrast to Israelite law (Deut 23:15), most legal systems did not look favorably on harboring escaped slaves (e.g., Eshnunna 50; it is a capital offense in Hammurabi 15-19). Roman law prohibited encouraging slaves to run away or harboring them (Justinian *Dig.* 48.15.6.2; Llewelyn with Kearsley, 6:56-57 §7), perhaps explaining Josephus's understanding that God's law mandated punishment for fugitive slaves (Josephus *J.W.* 3.8.5 §373). In the empire methods of locating and capturing such fugitives could prove harsh (Finley 1980, 111-12); if the country from which a slave escaped was on good terms with the country to which the slave escaped, the slave might be extradited (Livy *Hist.* 41.23.1-5). Escaped slaves were sometimes thought to spend money extravagantly (Chariton *Chaer.* 4.5.5).

3.5. Views About Slaves as Persons. In other respects law treated slaves as persons, and popular sentiments generally viewed them in this manner as well, albeit not with a modern egalitarian slant. It was illegal to kill or inflict excessively cruel punishment on a slave (Gaius *Inst.* 1.53); by the late first century slaveholders could not arbitrarily hand over innocent slaves to fight in the wild animal shows (Justinian *Dig.* 48.8.11.2). In the Roman period, slaves were usually considered responsible for their own misdeeds (Llewelyn with Kearsley, 7:188-89 §8); slaves also often proved loyal to slaveholders (Martial *Epigr.* 3.21; Appian *Rom. Hist.* 7.1.2; 8.3.17; *Civ. W.* 4.4.26; *T. Abr.* 15A), although some did not (Herodian *Hist.* 5.2.2). By means of what constituted a legal fiction, slaves could procure and hold money or property (e.g., Apuleius *Met.* 10.13), even at times other slaves (*y. Yebam.* 7:1 §2; on this institution, called the *peculium,* see further Buckland, 187-238; Cohen, 179-278).

Relationships between household slaves and slaveholders usually reflected the reality of persons interacting. Slaves could offer good advice, although slaveholders might disregard it (Aristophanes *Plut.* 1-5; 1 Sam 9:6). Even Aristotle admitted that in practice slaves were human, though different by nature from their masters (Aristotle *Pol.* 1.5.3, 1259b).

Many writers advocated concern for slaves or warned against harsh discipline of them (Seneca *Clem.* 1.18.1; 1.26.1; *Ep. Lucil.* 47.4-5, 18-19; Epictetus *Disc.* 1.13.2), sometimes warning that those who failed to show appropriate care provoked the suffering that resulted (Diodorus Siculus *Bib. Hist.* 34/35/2.32-39; Seneca *Clem.* 1.18.3). *Epicurus warned against harsh discipline of slaves, and they were among members of his school (Diogenes Laertius *Vit.* 10.1.9; 10.118). Beating another person's slaves violated convention (Demosthenes *Conon* 4), but most people seem also to have disapproved of or ridiculed harsh beatings of one's own (Martial *Epigr.* 2.66.1-8; 8.23; cf. 2.82), especially if the beatings risked disfiguring slaves (Achilles Tatius *Leuc.* 5.17.8-9).

Jewish writers could warn against mistreating a slave (*Pseud.-Phoc.* 223-27) and could advocate especially kind treatment for the diligent servant (Sir 7:18, 21; 10:25; *Sent. Syr. Men.* 166-67); rabbinic literature suggests generally friendly relations between slaves and slaveholders (Bonsirven, 147-48), perhaps because the norm appears to have been household slavery on a relatively small scale.

Some moralists could report with approval the notion that honor accrues to merit, not to free birth (Phaedrus *Fables* 2.9.1-4); indeed, some philosophers were slaves (Aulus Gellius *Noc. Att.* 2.18). Many felt that slaves differed from free only by their circumstances, not by their nature (Dionysius of Halicarnassus *Ant. Rom.* 4.23.1; Seneca *Ep. Lucil.* 47.11; Epictetus *Disc.* 1.13.4; Hierocles *Fraternal Love* 4.27.20); they were equal in their humanity (Seneca *Ep. Lucil.* 47.10; Sevenster, 185-89). Thus by serving willingly, a slave can grant a benefaction to the slaveholder (Seneca *Ben.* 7.4.4; 1 Tim 6:2). Some went further. Some philosophers argued that slavery was against nature; people should be judged by virtue rather than class, and hence one should not object to eating with slaves (Heraclitus *Ep.* 9).

Such a position would have disturbed Aristotle, who wrote a few centuries before most of these writers. Aristotle maintained that nature demonstrates the superiority of some over others and that it is to the advantage of both for the superior to rule (Aristotle *Pol.* 1.2.12, 1254b); the equality of those who were not equal was unjust (Aristotle *Pol.* 3.5.8-9, 1280a). Slaves differed by nature from free persons (Aristotle *Pol.* 1.2.7-8, 1254a); unlike free persons, they were physically designed for manual labor, as animals were (Aristotle *Pol.* 1.2.14, 1254b), and differed from free persons not only in body but also in soul (Aristotle *Pol.* 1.2.14-15, 1254b). Barbarians by nature were always fit to be slaves and ruled by Greeks (Aristotle *Pol.* 1.1.4, 1252b; 1.2.18, 1255a). Aristotle warned, however, that a few people thought slavery was *para physin,* "contrary to nature," hence unjust—a view to which Aristotle himself strenuously objected (Aristotle *Pol.* 1.2.3, 1253b).

3.6. Views About Slavery as an Institution. Despite Aristotle's earlier worry, however, most people did not translate the theory of equality into practical abolitionism. When a slave protested to Zeno, founder of the Stoic school, that it was merely his fate to have misbehaved, Zeno allegedly responded, "And also to be beaten" (Diogenes Laertius *Vit.* 7.1.23). Seneca argued not for abolition but for just treatment (Watts). One of the more radical examples is that Pliny dined with his freedpersons by bringing himself to their level (Pliny *Ep.* 2.6.3-4), but these were freedpersons and not slaves, and this is hardly abolition. Seneca urged friendlier association with slaves, allowing for talking and planning together (Seneca *Ep. Lucil.* 47.13). A few went so far as to advocate treating a servant as oneself (Sir 33:30-31; but cf. 33:24-28), even serving them (Eph 6:9 in the light of 6:5-8).

Yet writers could cite more radical models on the fringes of Mediterranean society to challenge the excessive material desire of their culture, even if these models did not prove perfect for their purposes. Some report with approval the lack of slaveholding among Indians (Diodorus Siculus *Bib. Hist.* 2.39.5; Arrian *Ind.* 10.8-9), although sometimes observing with curiosity the caste system (Diodorus Siculus *Bib. Hist.* 2.40.1). Egyptian tradition reportedly punished with death the murder of slave and free alike, regarding slavery as a mere difference in circumstance (Diodorus Siculus *Bib. Hist.* 1.77.6). Tacitus seems impressed by the character of slavery in Germany, where slaves' independence struck him more than their subordination (Tacitus *Germ.* 25), though he reports some sacred slaves drowned in a ritual (Tacitus *Germ.* 40).

Most striking is the model of the *Essenes. Philo claimed that the Therapeutae regarded slaveholding as contrary to nature (Philo *Vit. Cont.* 70) and claimed that the Essenes rejected slaveholding as contrary to nature, which established equality (Philo *Omn. Prob. Lib.* 79; *Hypoth.* 11.4), a good Greek concept. In similar language, Josephus claimed that Essenes avoided slaveholding lest it make them unjust (Josephus *Ant.* 18.21). In contrast to the earlier *Institutes* of Gaius, Justinian, perhaps from Christian or Stoic influence and possibly in conjunction with the economic decline of slavery in late Roman antiquity, also regards slavery as *contra naturam,* "against nature" (Justinian *Inst.* 1.3.2; 1.5 introduction). One wonders, however, the extent to which the image concerning the Essenes is the rhetorical invention of Hellenistic Jewish apologetic; wilderness Essenes possessed neither slaves nor other private property, but some other Essenes may have simply been forbidden to sell their slaves to Gentiles (CD 12:10-11; *see* Damascus Document).

Of those who may have disliked slavery, no one in the first century seemed prepared to try to overthrow it as an institution, nor would such an attempt have been successful. A number of slave revolts did occur in Roman history (Diodorus Siculus *Bib. Hist.* 34/35.2.5-48; 36.4.1—36.11.3; Livy *Hist.* 32.26.4-8; 39.29.8), including the earlier full-scale war led by Spartacus (Lucan *Civ. W.* 2.554; Appian *Rom. Hist.* 12.16.109; *Civ. W.* 1.14.116-20), and various agitators sought to encourage this (Sallust *Iug.* 66.1; Livy *Hist.* 3.15.9). But such revolts were sometimes undermined by other slaves who betrayed them (Livy *Hist.* 4.45.2; 32.26.9, 14). Most slave revolts were small in scale, so that M. I. Finley estimates only four full-scale slave wars in recorded history, of which three occurred in Italy or Sicily from 140-70 B.C.; all were unsuccessful (Finley 1980, 114-15). He admits that the Haitian revolt of the modern period was successful, however; he also seems unaware of several successful major slave revolts against Arab rulers in the medieval period (see B. Lewis, 56-57). But these represent military situations different from that of the Roman Empire at the pinnacle of its power.

Even when slaves sought their own freedom by various means, this does not indicate that they sought to abolish the institution of slavery. Freedpersons themselves acquired slaves whenever possible (*ILS* 7503; Martin, 42), as occasionally happened in North American slavery (Koger). Although some early Christians such as John Chrysostom made a case for emancipation, Augustine's tradition permitting slavery prevailed through most of the church's history until it was repudiated by some nineteenth-century Christian abolitionists (Longenecker, 60-66; Rupprecht; Sunderland).

3.7. Manumission. Emancipation contracts are common fare among ancient business documents (e.g., *P. Oxy.* 722), and the matter was so routine that manumissions were sometimes enacted en route from one location to another (Gaius *Inst.* 1.20). Slaves were sometimes freed for loyal service or special skills (e.g., Aulus Gellius *Noc. Att.* 2.18.9-10), but sometimes they purchased their own freedom (Dionysius of Halicarnassus *Ant. Rom.* 4.24.4; *m. Qidd.* 1:3; see on the *peculium,* §3.5 above). Roman law permitted a slaveholder to free as many slaves as he wished while alive (Gaius *Inst.* 1.44) but set limits on manumission in wills (Gaius *Inst.* 1.41-43; revoked in Justinian *Inst.* 1.6-7). Roman gravestones suggest more freedpersons than freeborn (Finley 1973, 71), but former slaves were more apt to boast in having acquired freedom than slaveholders were apt to provide gravestones for all slaves.

Slaves of citizens meeting specific conditions automatically become Roman citizens on their emancipation (Gaius *Inst.* 1.13-17; Dionysius of Halicarnassus *Ant. Rom.* 4.23.3), providing a higher status than that of provincials. Nevertheless, freed slaves were of lower social rank than were the freeborn citizens (Gaius *Inst.* 1.10); rabbinic sources generally rank them below proselytes and offspring from illegitimate unions (e.g., *Num. Rab.* 6:1). They remained dependents of the person who had freed them, hence his clients (Dupont, 65-66); they could be included as heirs and consequently share responsibilities for debts (*CPJ* 2:20-22, §14).

Because freed slaves continued to be part of a wealthy patron's household, they received a considerable political and economic boost not available to most of the freeborn (see *ILS* 7486, 7558, 7580 in Sherk, 228-29; MacMullen, 124; López Barja de Quiroga). They often possessed significant economic and social power (*CIL* 6.8583 in Sherk, 240), though some of higher rank despised them (Epictetus *Disc.* 1.1.20); reminding one of slave birth could constitute an insult (Martial *Epigr.* 1.81). So rapidly did many freed slaves advance in society that they became targets of aristocratic satirists, sometimes with a hint of envy (Petronius *Sat.* 38, 57). Although first-generation freedpersons were barred from aristocratic status, their children represented a disproportionate percentage of the free population to achieve higher status; in urban centers like Ostia perhaps one-third of the local aristocracy consisted of sons of freed slaves (Finley 1973, 72).

4. Conclusion.

The ancient household included spouse and children, but also other dependents who lived in the household. Among the well-to-do, especially some of the urban free, households often included some slaves. Ancient thinkers most frequently defined household relationships in terms of the male householder's appropriate authority relationships with regard to various groups, especially wives, children or grandchildren and slaves.

See also ADULTERY, DIVORCE; CHILDREN IN LATE ANTIQUITY; MARRIAGE; PATRONAGE; ROMAN SOCIAL CLASSES; SLAVERY; WOMEN IN GRECO-ROMAN WORLD AND JUDAISM.

BIBLIOGRAPHY. D. L. Balch, "Household Codes," in *Greco-Roman Literature and the New Testament: Selected Forms and Genres,* ed. D. E. Aune (SLBSBS 21; Atlanta: Scholars Press, 1988); idem, *Let Wives Be Submissive: The Domestic Code in 1 Peter* (SBLMS 26; Chico, CA: Scholars Press, 1981); R. H. Barrow, *Slavery in the Roman Empire* (New York: Barnes & Noble, 1968); S. S. Bartchy, *MALLON CHRESAI: First-Century Slavery and the Interpretation of 1 Corinthians 7:21* (SBLDS 11; Missoula, MT: Society of Biblical Literature, 1973); S. J. Bastomsky, "Rich and Poor: The Great Divide in Ancient Rome and Victorian England," *GR* 37 (1990) 37-43; J. Bonsirven, *Palestinian Judaism in the Time of Jesus Christ* (New York: Holt, Rinehart & Winston, 1964); K. Bradley, "'The Regular, Daily Traffic in Slaves': Roman History and Contemporary History," *CJ* 87 (1992) 125-38; idem, "Wet Nursing at Rome: A Study in Social Relations," in *The Family in Ancient Rome: New Perspectives,* ed. B. Rawson (Ithaca, NY: Cornell University Press, 1986) 201-29; S. J. Breiner, "Child Abuse Patterns: Comparison of Ancient Western Civilization and Traditional China," *Analytic Psychotherapy and Psychopathology* 2 (1985) 27-50; W. W. Buckland, *The Roman Law of Slavery: The Condition of the Slave in Private Law from Augustus to Justinian* (Cambridge: Cambridge University Press, 1908); W. Burkert, *Ancient Mystery Cults* (Cambridge, MA: Harvard University Press, 1987); J. Carcopino, *Daily Life in Ancient Rome: The People and the City at the Height of the Empire,* ed. H. T. Rowell (New Haven, CT: Yale University Press, 1940); B. Cohen, *Jewish and Roman Law: A Comparative Study* (2 vols.; New York: Jewish Theological Seminary of America, 1966); J. Dawson, "Urbanization and Mental Health in a West African Community," in *Magic, Faith and Healing: Studies in Primitive Psychiatry Today,* ed. A. Kiev (New York: Free Press, 1964) 305-42; L. Demaitre,

"The Idea of Childhood and Child Care in Medical Writings of the Middle Ages," *Journal of Psychohistory* 4 (1977) 461-90; W. Den Boer, *Private Morality in Greece and Rome: Some Historical Aspects* (Leiden: E. J. Brill, 1979); S. Dixon, *The Roman Mother* (Norman: Oklahoma University Press, 1988); F. Dupont, *Daily Life in Ancient Rome* (Oxford: Blackwell, 1992); D. Engels, "The Problem of Female Infanticide in the Greco-Roman World," *CP* 75 (1980) 112-20; idem, "The Use of Historical Demography in Ancient History," *CQ* 34 (1984) 386-93; M. I. Finley, *The Ancient Economy*, (Sather Classical Lectures 43; Berkeley and Los Angeles: University of California Press, 1973); idem, *Ancient Slavery and Modern Ideology* (New York: Viking, 1980); T. Frank, *Aspects of Social Behavior in Ancient Rome* (Cambridge, MA: Harvard University Press, 1932); J. F. Gardner, *Women in Roman Law and Society* (Bloomington: Indiana University Press, 1986); R. Garland, "Juvenile Delinquency in the Greco-Roman World," *History Today* 41 (1991) 12-19; C. Gill, "The Question of Character Development: Plutarch and Tacitus," *CQ* 33 (1983) 469-87; M. Golden, "Did the Ancients Care When Their Children Died?" *GR* 35 (1988) 152-63; M. Goodman, *State and Society in Roman Galilee, A.D. 132-212* (Oxford Center for Postgraduate Hebrew Studies; Totowa, NJ: Rowman & Allanfield, 1983); F. C. Grant, "The Economic Background of the New Testament," in *The Background of the New Testament and Its Eschatology: In Honor of C. H. Dodd*, ed. W. D. Davies and D. Daube (Cambridge: Cambridge University Press, 1964) 96-114; idem, *Hellenistic Religions: The Age of Syncretism* (Indianapolis: Bobbs-Merrill, 1953); W. V. Harris, "The Theoretical Possibility of Extensive Infanticide in the Greco-Roman World," *CQ* 32 (1982) 114-16; G. H. R. Horsley, ed., *New Documents Illustrating Early Christianity* (North Ryde, N.S.W.: Ancient History Documentary Research Center, Macquarie University, 1981-82) vols. 1-2; T. Ilan, *Jewish Women in Greco-Roman Palestine* (Tübingen: Mohr Siebeck; Peabody, MA: Hendrickson, 1996); J. L. Jones, "The Roman Army," in *The Catacombs and the Colosseum: The Roman Empire as the Setting of Primitive Christianity*, ed. S. Benko and J. J. O'Rourke (Valley Forge, PA: Judson, 1971) 187-217; S. R. Joshel, "Nurturing the Master's Child: Slavery and the Roman Child-Nurse," *Signs* 12 (1986) 3-22; C. S. Keener, *Paul, Women and Wives: Marriage and Women's Ministry in the Letters of Paul* (Peabody, MA: Hendrickson, 1992); L. Koger, *Black Slaveowners: Free Black Slavemasters in South Carolina, 1790-1860* (Jefferson, NC: McFarland, 1985); W. K. Lacey, *"Patria Potestas,"* in *The Family in Ancient Rome: New Perspectives*, ed. B. Rawson (Ithaca, NY: Cornell University Press, 1986) 121-44; H. J. Leon, *The Jews of Ancient Rome* (Philadelphia: Jewish Publication Society of America, 1960); B. Lewis, *Race and Slavery in the Middle East: A Historical Inquiry* (New York: Oxford University Press, 1990); N. Lewis, *Life in Egypt Under Roman Rule* (Oxford: Clarendon Press, 1983); A. T. Lincoln, *Ephesians* (WBC 42; Dallas: Word, 1990); A. Lindemann, "Die Kinder und die Gottesherrschaft: Markus 10:13-16 und die Stellung der Kinder in der Späthellenistischen Gesellschaft und im Urchristentum," *Wort und Dienst* 17 (1983) 77-104; S. R. Llewelyn with R. A. Kearsley, *New Documents Illustrating Early Christianity* (North Ryde, N.S.W.: Ancient History Documentary Research Center, Macquarie University, 1992, 1994) vols. 6-7; R. N. Longenecker, *New Testament Social Ethics for Today* (Grand Rapids, MI: Eerdmans, 1984); P. López Barja de Quiroga, "Freedmen's Social Mobility in Roman Italy," *Historia* 44 (1995) 326-48; D. Lührman, "Neutestamentliche Haustafeln und antike Ökonomie," *NTS* 27 (1980) 83-97; F. Lyall, *Slaves, Citizens, Sons: Legal Metaphors in the Epistles* (Grand Rapids, MI: Zondervan, 1984); R. MacMullen, *Roman Social Relations: 50 B.C. to A.D. 284* (New Haven, CT: Yale University Press, 1974); A. J. Malherbe, "'Gentle as a Nurse': The Cynic Background to 1 Thess 2," *NovT* 12 (1970) 203-17; idem, *Moral Exhortation, A Greco-Roman Sourcebook* (LEC 4; Philadelphia: Westminster, 1986); D. B. Martin, *Slavery as Salvation: The Metaphor of Slavery in Pauline Christianity* (New Haven, CT: Yale University Press, 1990); J. S. Mbiti, *African Religions and Philosophies* (Garden City, NY: Doubleday, 1970); W. A. Meeks, *The Moral World of the First Christians* (LEC 6; Philadelphia: Westminster, 1986); R. A. Padgug, "Problems in the Theory of Slavery and Slave Society," *Science and Society* 40 (1976) 3-27; J. J. Pilch, "'Beat His Ribs While He Is Young' (Sir 30:12): A Window on the Mediterranean World," *BTB* 23 (1993) 101-13; S. B. Pomeroy, *Goddesses, Whores, Wives and Slaves: Women in Classical Antiquity* (New York: Schocken, 1975); B. Rawson, "Children in the Roman *Familia*," in *The Family in Ancient Rome: New Perspectives*, ed. B. Rawson (Ithaca, NY: Cornell University Press, 1986a) 170-200; idem, "The Roman Family," in *The*

Family in Ancient Rome: New Perspectives, ed. B. Rawson (Ithaca, NY: Cornell University Press, 1986b) 1-57; A. W. Rupprecht, "Attitudes on Slavery Among the Church Fathers," in *New Dimensions in New Testament Study,* ed. R. N. Longenecker and M. C. Tenney (Grand Rapids, MI: Zondervan, 1974) 261-77; S. Safrai, "Home and Family," in *The Jewish People in the First Century: Historical Geography, Political History, Social, Cultural and Religious Life and Institutions,* ed. S. Safrai and M. Stern (2 vols.; CRINT 1; Assen: Van Gorcum; Philadelphia: Fortress, 1974, 1976) 2:728-92; R. P. Saller, "Review Article," *CP* 83 (1988) 263-69; R. P. Saller and B. D. Shaw, "Tombstones and Roman Family Relations in the Principate: Civilians, Soldiers and Slaves," *JRS* 74 (1984) 124-56; S. Sandmel, *Judaism and Christian Beginnings* (New York: Oxford University Press, 1978); J. N. Sevenster, *Paul and Seneca* (NovTSup 4; Leiden: E. J. Brill, 1961); R. K. Sherk, ed., *The Roman Empire: Augustus to Hadrian* (TDGR 6; New York: Cambridge University Press, 1988); M. A. Speidel, "Roman Army Pay Scales," *JRS* 82 (1992) 87-106; M. Stern, "Aspects of Jewish Society: The Priesthood and Other Classes," in *The Jewish People in the First Century: Historical Geography, Political History, Social, Cultural and Religious Life and Institutions,* ed. S. Safrai and M. Stern (2 vols.; CRINT 1; Assen: Van Gorcum; Philadelphia: Fortress, 1974, 1976) 2:561-630; T. R. Stevenson, "The Ideal Benefactor and the Father Analogy in Greek and Roman Thought," *CQ* 42 (1992) 421-36; L. R. Sunderland, *The Testimony of God Against Slavery* (Boston: Webster & Southard, 1835); L. Swidler, *Women in Judaism: The Status of Women in Formative Judaism* (Metuchen, NJ: Scarecrow, 1976); W. W. Tarn, *Hellenistic Civilization* (3d ed.; New York: New American Library, 1974); P. Trebilco, "Asia," in *The Book of Acts in Its Greco-Roman Setting,* ed. D. W. J. Gill and C. Gempf (Grand Rapids, MI: Eerdmans, 1994) 291-362; S. Treggiari, "Jobs for Women," *AJAH* 1 (1976) 76-104; idem, "Jobs in the Household of Livia," *PBSR* 43 (1975) 48-77; D. C. Verner, *The Household of God: The Social World of the Pastoral Epistles* (SBLDS 71; Chico, CA: Scholars Press, 1983); W. Watts, "Seneca on Slavery," *DRev* 90 (1972) 183-95.

C. S. Keener

FATE. *See* RELIGION, PERSONAL.

FELIX. *See* ROMAN GOVERNORS OF PALESTINE.

FESTIVALS AND HOLY DAYS: GRECO-ROMAN

Festivals and holy days not only were important to the Jews (*see* Festivals and Holy Days: Jewish) but also were widely celebrated by many people throughout the Greco-Roman world. Festivals or holy days as repeated rites, whether yearly or otherwise, and often of great length and elaboration, were widely celebrated during Greco-Roman times for a variety of reasons. Some of these festivals were celebrated for religious purposes, although often the celebrations had been enshrined in the Roman calendar and the exact reasons for them forgotten. There were also celebrations that were related to personal religion that were not part of the official calendar (*see* Religion, Personal). The rural population, which constituted the largest portion of the population in ancient times, also celebrated festivals in ways that did not necessarily coincide with the more institutionalized festivals that occurred in the major cities, such as *Rome. As important as all of these celebrations were, this article focuses on the festivals and holy days recognized throughout the Roman world of the first century A.D.

1. The Origins and Development of Festivals and Holy Days
2. The Roman Calendar and Festivals in Rome
3. Greco-Roman Festivals and Holy Days Outside of Rome

1. The Origins and Development of Festivals and Holy Days.

In antiquity, religion and folklore were not separate, as they are today (Nilsson 1961, 40). The origins of Greek and Roman religious festivals are obscure but seem to be related to the cycle of nature. This relation to nature is found in both the object of worship and the time of worship. Festivals were apparently mostly formed around the celebration of significant times in the cycle of nature, such as spring and harvest, and took place in conjunction with the cycle of the moon, often at full moon. Many of the religious celebrations that grew up around these significant events appear to have predated worship of a specific deity, often were first located in particular places rather than situated in *temples, and reflect the rural and agrarian origins of pagan worship. The objects central to worship and the times of year reflect the life cycle of those in a rural context, who were dependent upon nature for their survival. Only later did these celebrations come to be linked to a particular deity, with stronger deities later pushing out lesser deities to establish themselves as the cultic focus, and centered upon specific sites built for their worship, such as temples.

Other types of celebrations besides worship, which often involved such rituals as *sacrifice, soon became associated with these festive occasions as well, such as *games and markets, which drew people together from the surrounding area (Nilsson, "Festivals," 435). From the outset, therefore, festivals and holy days are also joined to calendrical calculations. Although Roman religion followed similar patterns to that of Greek religion, Roman religion did not have the same background of a heroic age. Hence the Romans inherited much of their religious mythology from others, such as the Greeks (see E. Ferguson, 125). There was also a strong tendency in Roman circles for what were originally religious festivals to lose their religious significance and to take on a mainly social or even highly political character.

2. The Roman Calendar and Festivals in Rome. One of the distinguishing features of Roman religious festivals and holy days is how they are linked to the Roman calendar. The calendar was early on used by the Romans, probably as a means of indicating the times of religious celebration. Although mythology has it that Romulus derived the first calendar, the Roman calendar was probably established in 450 B.C. as part of the Twelve Tables, indicating the days when legal proceedings could not occur due to religious worship. A calendar was later posted on white tablets in the Roman Forum, so Livy (*Hist.* 9.46.5) and *Cicero (*Att.* 6.1.8; *Pro Murena* 25) say, indicating dates for conducting legal business and probably listing the dates for meetings of the assemblies.

It also became fashionable for calendars to be placed on the walls of various buildings, including private residences. They were decorative but also functional for their information, including personal days of remembrance and lucky and unlucky days (the Romans were highly superstitious, especially avoiding odd numbers). This practice seems to have reached its high point in the first century A.D., no doubt because of the need to widely publish the new solar calendar instituted by Julius Caesar (Salzman, 4-7; cf. Ogilvie, 70-72).

The earliest Roman calendar was based on the lunar cycle and had only ten months, with the period following the conclusion of the agricultural year and prior to the beginning of the new one not being indicated. Probably during Etruscan times two more months were added, which encompassed the entire year. This calendar had four months with 31 days each, seven with 29 days and February with 28, totaling 355 days. The calendar became a vital instrument for indicating a variety of information, including a number of fixed festivals as well as a number of festivals whose days varied. One can see that the calendar would soon get out of line, so at periodic intervals a number of days would be added to bring the calendar back into line. Due to a variety of circumstances, including miscalculations but also political manipulation of the calendar, the calendar would often not get adjusted appropriately to bring the months and seasons into calibration. During the time of Julius Caesar, he inaugurated a new solar rather than lunar calendar with months of thirty and thirty-one days, with one day repeated in February every four years (Rose 1948, 50-52; Ogilvie, 70-71).

The month in a Roman calendar had three main days: the Kalends, or day of proclamation, on the new moon of the length of time until the next main day; the Ides, or the time of the full moon; and the Nones the day eight days (nine by Roman counting) before the Ides. Around these three main days all other days were arranged in terms of their being a number of days before or after these named ones. A Roman calendar indicated the status of every day of the year in terms of whether it was a holiday or working day. There were also several different levels of holidays. On the Roman calendar, about one-third of the days qualified as some form of holiday, with some months being predominantly holidays, such as February. The calendar also indicated working days and the days when the assemblies or other legal bodies could meet (Ogilvie, 71-72). Once the calendar was established under Augustus, there were few alterations of the formal structure of the Roman calendar, except for the further addition of public holidays, often in terms of honoring *emperors or worshiping other deities (see below; Reid, 101, in Sandys). However, the Julian calendar was not adopted everywhere in the empire at the same time. In the West it was adopted early on, but in the East it was accepted with local modifications at various times and in conjunction with its acceptance by local rulers. The province of Asia, for example, did not accept the Julian calendar until 9 B.C. on Augustus's birthday of September 23, commemorated in the well-known Priene calendar inscription (see Bickerman, 47-50).

Some months had more festivals and holidays than others (see Ogilvie, 73-99, for discussion of the following festivals and holy days of Rome; cf. Fowler, 172, in Sandys for a chart of the festivals). For example, January 1 was the day in which the consuls made a procession to the Capitol, and white bulls were sacrificed to the god Jupiter to keep the Roman state safe. This was a fixed event, even though the calendar indicates it as a working day, while the Compitalia was a movable festival, celebrating the close of the agricultural year and making remembrance in anticipation of a productive following year. February had two major festivals, Parentalia, a celebration commemorating the dead during which temples were closed and marriages were forbidden, and the Lupercalia, celebrated at the same time, when two rival groups of young men had a feast and engaged in a race at the bottom of the Palatine Hill. March had a number of festivals for Mars, the god of war, including a feast on March 14, and on March 1 the sacred fire was relit in the shrine of the Vesta.

April, with the coming of spring, meant a number of festivals were celebrated, although many of these were more social than religious occasions. Still important, however, were Parilia, Floralia and Feriae Latinae. Parilia on April 21, originally a festival to purify the sheep, became a celebration of the founding of Rome; Floralia on April 28 became a whole week of games in celebration of fertility; and Feriae Latinae was a festival of the unification of the Latin people. May's chief festival was Lemuria on May 9, 11 and 13, which commemorated the dead members of a household who came to haunt their homes. June had a major time of celebration at the shrine of Vesta. From June 7 to 15 a series of celebrations took place, culminating in a thorough cleaning of the shrine. June 13 was also, however, a night of drunken festivities for certain groups. June also had the Fors Fortuna festival on June 24, during which huge numbers of Romans went to offer sacrifices at the shrines of Fortune.

July's festivals were small by comparison, but August had several major festivities: August 12 involved sacrifice to Hercules, who was beloved by Romans; August 13 celebrated the cult of Diana and involved a day off for *slaves (a rare occasion). September had a number of celebrations in conjunction with games; most notably September 13 celebrated the dedication of the temple of Jupiter, the patron god of Rome, with a huge feast.

October marked a shift in emphasis in celebrations, with October 19 becoming a formal marking of the change of seasons; and October 15 a sacrifice of a horse to Mars. November also had a feast of Jupiter similar to the one in September. The year closed with a number of festivals in December. These included the movable feast to Bona Dea (the "good goddess") in a magistrate's house at which men were forbidden; and December 17, the feast of Saturnalia or Cronos, the father of Zeus, involving sacrifice at the temple of Saturn and a public banquet attended by all.

3. Greco-Roman Festivals and Holy Days Outside of Rome.

The preceding festivals and holy days are particularly related to Rome and its environs. It is known that other cities had comparable calendars, although these calendars are not extant in a number of important areas, such as the eastern provinces of the empire and Africa especially for the first century. The assumption is that many of the Roman colonies would have had similar calendars, since keeping track of consuls was also part of the calendrical function (see Sherwin-White, 105). However, much of the information we have about calendrical cycles is furnished by a number of calendars that date to the fourth century A.D., and it is difficult to judge how much they reflect the practice of festivals and holy days in the first century.

Religious cults of the Greco-Roman world had a variety of celebrations and forms of worship of their deity or deities, many of them private celebrations not part of official festivals and holy days. For example, worshipers of the Cabiri or "mother of the gods" of Samothrace grew in numbers during this time in the Greek and Aegean area, until they became a dominant force in such cities as *Thessalonica in the third century. However, despite their importance—we know that they had places where they met and worshiped—we know virtually nothing about their actual forms of worship, except that one could become an initiate at any time of the year. This was more attractive in many ways than the Eleusian cult, which had initiatory rites that occurred twice a year, in February and September, and attracted a number of people throughout the Roman republic and empire from the first century B.C. to the second century A.D. (see E. Ferguson, 199-205).

Two further sets of religious events resulted in festivals and holy days being added to the Roman calendar. The first was the growth of the emperor cult (*see* Ruler Cult). Julius Caesar was the first to have been accorded divinity, followed by Augustus, and in the first century Claudius, Vespasian and Titus. Within the finds of *papyri from Dura-Europos is a small scroll with four columns of Latin writing giving a list of religious festivals. Dating to Severus Alexander (A.D. 224-35), this calendar provides a list of the religious festivals celebrated by those in the Roman auxiliary stationed in this area in the eastern part of the empire. It is reasonable to think, however, that this reflected practice throughout the empire and may well reflect practice from the time of Augustus, who was responsible not only for institutionalizing the calendar on a widespread basis but also for military reform. This calendar indicates that twenty people, including six women, were worshiped as divine figures in the early third century A.D. (see Kreitzer, 72-73, for the above information; cf. J. Ferguson, 95-96, for a list of the divine figures).

The second religious development of this time is the growth in importance of the Egyptian deities, Isis, Osiris and Serapis (*see* Mysteries). Egyptian religion was very popular in the Roman Empire of the first two centuries A.D. Even though these deities originated in the East, they became Hellenized and were integrated into the Roman world of religious belief as well, but without losing their sense of foreignness and the related intrigue that went along with this. Although in the first century B.C. and into the first century A.D. there were attempts to suppress Egyptian religion, by A.D. 38 a temple to Isis had been built in Rome, indicating that full integration into the empire had occurred (note that evidence of the Isis cult can be found throughout the empire; see Witt, 264-65, for a map). The Isis cult had two annual festivals, one in October/November and the other in March, besides daily ceremonies in the Isis temples. Forms of worship of the Isis cult outside of Egypt added practices of the mystery religions patterned after those of the Eleusian cult (see E. Ferguson, 211-21, on the Isis cult). These Isis festivals were integrated into the Roman religious calendar (Reid, 101, in Sandys). Witt argues that Paul's missionary journeys and his letter correspondence are to a large extent directed against various elements of the Isiac cult, found throughout the Roman Empire of the first century A.D. (Witt, esp. 255-68).

See also FESTIVALS AND HOLY DAYS: JEWISH; MYSTERIES; RELIGION, GRECO-ROMAN; RELIGION, PERSONAL; RULER CULT; TEMPLES, GRECO-ROMAN.

BIBLIOGRAPHY. E. J. Bickerman, *Chronology of the Ancient World* (2d ed.; Ithaca, NY: Cornell University Press, 1980); E. Ferguson, *Backgrounds of Early Christianity* (Grand Rapids, MI: Eerdmans, 1987); J. Ferguson, *The Religions of the Roman Empire* (Ithaca, NY: Cornell University Press, 1970); L. J. Kreitzer, *Striking New Images: Roman Imperial Coinage and the New Testament World* (JSNTSup 134; Sheffield: Sheffield Academic Press, 1996); M. P. Nilsson, "Festivals (Greek)," *OCD* (2d ed.), 435; idem, *Greek Folk Religion* (Philadelphia: University of Pennsylvania Press, 1961 [1940]); idem, *A History of Greek Religion* (2d ed.; Oxford: Clarendon Press, 1949); R. M. Ogilvie, *The Romans and Their Gods* (London: Chatto & Windus, 1969); H. J. Rose, *Ancient Greek Religion* (London: Hutchinson, 1946); idem, *Ancient Roman Religion* (London: Hutchinson, 1948); M. R. Salzman, *On Roman Time: The Codex-Calendar of 354 and the Rhythms of Urban Life in Late Antiquity* (Berkeley and Los Angeles: University of California Press, 1990); J. E. Sandys, ed., *A Companion to Latin Studies* (Cambridge: Cambridge University Press, 1910); A. N. Sherwin-White, *Roman Society and Roman Law in the New Testament* (Oxford: Clarendon Press, 1961); R. W. Witt, *Isis in the Ancient World* (Baltimore: Johns Hopkins University Press, 1971).

S. E. Porter

FESTIVALS AND HOLY DAYS: JEWISH

The festivals of *Israel mark a deep involvement with the agricultural rhythm of the land set aside by God for his people. Each festival is at base a week or so of harvest: in the spring, in the summer, in the autumn. Spring brings early grain and is also time to move the flocks on from one pasture to another. Summer sees the larger harvest of grain. Autumn is the last time of gathering for the cycle, and the grapes and olives win more attention than do other crops. Although the *calendar of ancient Israel developed in the depth of its explanations of these festivals and in the addition of other feasts, fasts and commemorative moments, the primacy of agricultural practice and experience needs to be recollected throughout if one is to appreciate the sense of the calendar and the joy involved in the festivals. The fundamental importance of the three great agricultural festivals is signaled by the requirement that every male of Israel appear before the Lord every year at these times (Ex 23:14-17; 34:23; Deut 16:16-17). Even if that is an idealized expectation, it enables us to appreciate how deeply felt was the connection between the rhythm of the fields and the rhythm of God's choice of Israel.

Each of the major festivals has its own character and over time would generate its own explanation in terms of the remembrances that formed the understanding of Israel (the exodus, the covenant, the sojourn in the wilderness that brought Israel to its land; *see DJG,* Judaism). But the fact of harvest in each case gives the festival a communal, celebratory and sacrificial character. The greater and richer the harvest, the more intense and cooperative the work of any agricultural commune in Israel must be. That demands a social structure at the local scale, and the hard labor of harvesting was undertaken by the Israelites themselves: slavery does not appear to have been a major institution until the monarchy, and even then it had more to do with building and service than with agriculture. A primary motivation in this communal work was the urgency of harvest. Once ripe, a crop must be taken in quickly, with as little waste and damage possible, if the full benefit is to be enjoyed. One way to enjoy the crop is to share some of it (indeed, a great deal of it) at the time of harvest itself. That celebration leads naturally to sacrifice, a moment when Israel gathers with Israel's God to consume with pleasure and generosity what God permits to be produced on God's land.

1. The Foundations of Judaic Festivals and Holy Days
2. The Festivals and Holy Days in the New Testament

1. The Foundations of Judaic Festivals and Holy Days.

1.1. Passover. The spring festival as a whole, including the Feast of Unleavened Bread, came to be called Passover, as is attested by the end of the first century by Josephus (Josephus *Ant.* 17 §213; 20 §106; cf. his tendency to distinguish the two in his earlier work, *J.W.* 2 §280; 6 §§423-24). The historical association of the exodus from Egypt is dominant to this day and has been since the *rabbinic period (see *m. Pesaḥ.* 10:5; *see DJG,* Rabbinic Traditions and Writings). But the term *pesaḥ* means "limping" (or "skipping," as some scholars more delicately express the same kind of movement) and referred initially to the limping of the spring lamb, a male yearling, hobbled prior to its being slaughtered, sacrificed and eaten.

It was a regular practice in Israel throughout the year not to eat the sinew on the inside of the hip (see Gen 32:32); the reason for that seems to be that the animal was bound or wounded there before it was killed. The ritual dance of those who took part in the sacrifice could be designated by the term *pesaḥ,* as could the entire festival. Killing a lamb in spring prior to moving on to new pastures produced an early benefit of the extensive organization required to shepherd flocks and provided an occasion for the gathering of Israel, even before Israel possessed its land (*see DJG,* Judaism). It is striking that Jacob, a rich shepherd at this point in Genesis, is given the name *Israel* for struggling with God (Gen 32:28), that he is caused to limp by his wrestling and that his injury is directly connected to the Israelite practice of not eating the sinew on the inside of the hip (Gen 32:24-32). Here we have an image of Israel before the possession of the land: the struggle with God is linked to the consumption from the flock and the blessings that are promised.

The pastoral festival of *pesaḥ* was already an Israelite tradition during the period in Egypt. Indeed, the desire to sacrifice is given by Moses to Pharaoh as the motivation for what at first was to be a brief departure to offer in a way Egyptians would find objectionable (Ex 5:1; 8:8, 25-32). That departure, in a sequence of events remembered as constituting national Israel, proved to be definitive, and the events of Passover and Unleavened Bread in that sense came to dominate over the meaning of the spring festival, at least for those who composed the Scriptures (see Ex 12): now it is God who misses a step when he comes to the houses of the Israelites (Ex 12:23), and the lack of yeast in the bread is a sign of Israel's haste in departing (Ex 12:34).

But the persistent celebration of Passover as households (authorized in Ex 12:3-4), rather than in the central *temple in Jerusalem, reflects the deeper roots of the festival, both in the history of Israel and in the affections of those who kept the practice. Under the reign of Josiah (see 2 Kings 23:21-23; Deut 16:1-8), a determined and largely successful attempt was made to centralize the feast by arranging for the sacrifice of the animals in the temple, prior to their distribution for consumption in Jerusalem alone. The animals at issue now are not only lambs but bulls as well, in keeping with the more elite institution in the wealthier, national Israel that is envisaged. The temple was destroyed soon after Josiah's reform, but the process of canonizing Scriptures (*see* Canonical Formation) favored the tight association between Passover and the temple. As a result, later rabbinic practice, established after the destruction of the temple in A.D. 70, does not include the consumption of lamb and distinguishes itself from "the Passover of Egypt" (see *m. Pesaḥ.* 9:5). Still, the possibility of local observance of the festival as set out in Exodus 12 both before and after the destruction of the temple cannot be excluded, and even the description of Josiah's reform includes the notice that there were priests who did not eat unleavened bread in Jerusalem but preferred to do so locally (2 Kings 23:9).

1.2. Unleavened Bread. Passover in ancient Israel was the prelude to the Feast of Unleavened Bread. During that feast, first grain of the year, especially barley, was consumed without yeast. The removal of yeast, and its eventual replacement with fresh yeast, carried a practical benefit. Yeast acts as an agent in fermentation, and its effects are passed on; that is, yeasted dough, introduced into new dough, will result in leavened bread. But although the process carries on, after many generations the agency of the yeast is weakened owing, it is now taught, to contamination by other strains of yeast or by other microorganisms. So yearly renewal is beneficial, a fresh start with new yeast of proven quality.

By effecting that removal and renewal at the time of the spring wheat, Israel enjoys its first crop of grain without the usual intervention of leavening. Grain unleavened was the only way in which cereal could be offered to God in sacrifice (see Lev 2:11; 6:17), and yeast as such was proscribed in connection with direct offering to God (Ex 23:18; 34:25), so the Feast of Unleavened Bread was a period in which Israel consumed grain in the way that God was held to. Just as the lamb of Passover came to be associated with the exodus, so did the unleavened bread. Rabbinic practice (see *m. Pesaḥ.* 1:1-4) emphasizes the removal of leaven within each household in Israel, and that serves to retain the original, domestic sensibility of Passover and Unleavened Bread. What survives within rabbinic practice is nonsacrificial, in that the destruction of the temple makes legitimate cultic offering impossible but trenchantly domestic, and to that extent it is an interesting reversion to the conception of Exodus 12.

1.3. Weeks/Pentecost. Seven weeks after the close of the entire festival of Passover and Unleavened Bread came the feast called Weeks, or Pentecost (in Greek, referring to the period of fifty days that was involved; see Lev 23:15-22; Deut 16:9-12). The waving of the sheaf before the Lord at the close of Passover anticipated the greater harvest, especially of wheat (see Ex 34:22), which was to follow in the summer, and that is just what Weeks celebrates (Lev 23:10-15).

An especially interesting feature of the range of sacrifices involved in the celebration of Weeks is the specific mention of leavened bread (Lev 23:17). Every major festival occasions a large expenditure of celebratory wealth, but why should mention be made of yeast, which had been so rigorously removed just eight weeks before? That reference enables us to see two features of both Unleavened Bread and Weeks that might otherwise have escaped us. First, the removal of leaven early in the spring is symmetrical with its re-introduction early in the summer; taken together, these festal practices make it clear that the removal of yeast was not intended to be definitive but contributes to Israel's usage of yeast through the year. Second and relatedly, the bread that is specified as leavened is for human consumption. Although the context in which it is presented is sacrificial, this bread is not for divine consumption; it is for waving before God, not for assigning to him in the fire. For that reason, the fact of its being leavened does not abrogate the general requirement that cereal given to God should be unleavened (see 1.2 above). One of the major points of sacrifice generally is that Israel enjoys what is assigned to Israel and that God takes pleasure in what is God's; together, Unleavened Bread and Weeks show us that yeast was Israel's and that the appropriate celebration of the festivals would assure the continuation of that benefit.

The agricultural focus of Weeks was emphatic; there is, as is often noted, no precise connection made within the Bible between that festival and the formation of Israel in a way comparable to Passover and Unleavened Bread. Still, the book of Deuteronomy makes the association between Weeks and remembering that one was a slave in Egypt: that remembrance was to motivate one to observe and perform the statutes (Deut 16:12). By the time of the book of **Jubilees* in the second century B.C., the feast is associated with the covenant and the Torah as mediated by Moses (see *Jub.* 1:1-26), as well as with the covenants with Noah (*Jub.* 6:1, 10-11, 17-19) and Abraham (*Jub.* 15:1-16). At a later stage, certain rabbinic traditions (but by no means all) would make the giving of the law in Exodus 19 the lectionary reading of Weeks (see *b. Meg.* 31a) and would recall that the word of God was split into the seventy languages of the nations (*b. Šabb.* 86b). Although the specific association with the giving of the Torah cannot be established as a controlling sense by the time of the NT, that meaning grew out of the generative connection between Weeks and divine covenant that had been made long before.

*1.4. **Sukkoth.*** The last great harvest, and the last of the three great festivals, is Sukkoth, meaning "Booths," or "Tabernacles." The term *sukkah* can also mean "thicket," such as an animal might lurk in; the point is to refer to a rough, natural shelter of plaited branches that would permit the celebrants to lodge in the fields. Grapes and olives were taken in at this time; they require particular care in handling and storage, and sometimes it is prudent to protect the ripened yield. Camping in the fields was a wise practice.

Sukkoth, in its material and social dimensions, was a feast of particular joy and the principal festival of ancient Israel (it may predate Israel; see Judg 9:27). It could be referred to as "Feast of the Lord," without further specification (see Lev 23:39; Judg 21:19), in view of its prominence. As in the cases of Passover and of Weeks, the festival was also associated with the formation of Israel, and the *sukkoth* were held to be reminiscent of the people's period in the wilderness. But that was a later development, reflected from the time of the Priestly source (see Lev 23:39-43), which also specified the greatest amount of sacrifice for Sukkoth among all the festivals (see Num 29). Deuteronomy also would have the three great festivals, Passover, Weeks and Sukkoth, conceived as feasts of pilgrimage (Deut 16;16-17) that involve travel to the central sanctuary in Jerusalem, although they were in origin and probably remained in practice, under various forms, local, festal celebrations.

The success of the Deuteronomic calendar corresponds to the emergence of the canon and results in the agricultural year becoming the covenantal year: the cycle of exodus, Sinai and wilderness was superimposed on the cycle of barley, wheat and grapes, and the temple (the only place where sacrifice could be offered) became the focus of all three festivals. But it is noteworthy that of the three major feasts of Judaism, Sukkoth has survived best in the rabbinic revision of practice that followed the A.D. 70 destruction of the temple. Sacrifice, of course, is not involved, but the construction of the *sukkah* and associated practices of festivity make this the most joyous occasion of the Jewish year (see *m. Sukk.*).

Yet in ancient Israel, whether on the agricultural or the covenantal explanation, sacrifice was central to all the festivals, and sacrifice on a monumental scale. It is not surprising that Sukkoth is marked as the greatest sacrifice in terms of the quantity and value of offerings, because it came at the time of year when the disposable wealth of produce was at its height. The underlying dynamic of sacrifice is that when Israel enjoys the produce of God's land with God, according to the preparation and timing and consumption that God desires, Israel is blessed. Sacrifice is a holy consumption that carries in itself the promise of further enjoyment. Penance may be involved in sacrifice, but most of the sacrifices of Israel—the festival sacrifices above all—are emphatically understood as occasions of communal, festal joy such as developed countries in our time are for the most part ignorant of. For that reason, the temple itself is a house of joy, and its dedication is crucial. In this context, it is vital to note that even before it was associated with the period in the wilderness, Sukkoth was named as the time that the temple was dedicated by Solomon (see 1 Kings 8:2).

Tishri, during which Sukkoth occurs, is the seventh month, and the temple's dedication then made Sukkoth the time when in a sabbath year the Torah would be read (Deut 31:9-13). That is the basis of the later rabbinic celebration of *Simḥat Torah* ("joy of the law") that closes Sukkoth. The number seven is basic to the entire calendar that coordinates the feasts, each of which was to last a week. (Although that is not specified in the case of Weeks, both its status as a festal convocation [Lev 23:21] and its name make that probable.) The weeks of the year mark the quarters of the lunar month, and each week ends with the *sabbath, which is itself a regular feast. The timing of each major feast in the middle of its month corresponds to the full moon, as is appropriate for a feast of harvest. The sabbath year and the Jubilee year, a sabbath of sabbaths, fit into the scheme that makes seven a basic unit of measurement. So there is a sense in which Tishri marks the new year, as well as Aviv (later called Nisan), the month of the Passover. When the book of Zechariah envisages the establishment of worship for all the nations in Jerusalem in a new, eschatological dispensation, it is natural that the feast concerned should be Sukkoth (Zech 14:16-21).

1.5. Other Notable Days. During the *Maccabean period, the restoration of worship in the temple was accomplished in the ninth month, and the feast that marks it was known as the Dedication, Hanukkah (see 1 Macc 4:36-61). That seems to have been a popular feast as well as an officially sanctioned festival, but it was not as important as Purim, a spring festival one month before Passover, which celebrated victory over people such as the legendary Haman, described as "the Jews' harasser" (Esther 8:1), when the book of Esther was read dramatically and with the enthusiastic participation of the audience. The term *Purim* derives from Babylonian religion, which appears to have provided much of the practice and background of the feast; there was a strong tendency during the Maccabean period to call it the Day of Mordecai, naming it after Esther's uncle, and to assimilate it to the Day of Nicanor, the commemoration of a military triumph (see 2 Macc 14:12—15:36).

The initial dedication of the temple and of the system of the sabbatical cycle at Booths makes it understandable that the principal occasion of repentance, the Day of Atonement, takes place just prior to Booths (see Lev 16). As in the case of other occasions of penitence, the sacrifice takes a distinct form: what was usually consumed by people alongside God's consumption is now offered to God alone. But the national range of the Day of Atonement makes this occasion uniquely important as an act of rededicatory penitence. After the destruction of Solomon's temple, fasts were also developed in the fourth, fifth, seventh and tenth months (see Zech 8:19). These are resisted in the book of Zechariah, but fasting seems to have become an increasingly important aspect of Judaic practice, and it is interesting that what one gives of oneself in penitence (flesh and blood) can be compared with what earlier had been offered on the altar in rabbinic literature (see *b. Ber.* 17a).

2. The Festivals and Holy Days in the New Testament.

The NT does not offer a systematic treatment of the principal festivals and holy days, but it does reflect the deep engagement of the church with the calendar of Judaism. That is easily seen by observing direct references to the festal calendar and other indications of cultic and communal activities associated with that calendar.

2.1. Sukkoth. Jesus' entry into Jerusalem is likely to have occurred at or near the time of Sukkoth, and the leafy branches that were to be used within the procession of Sukkoth are an important symbol within the scene as presented in the Gospels (see Neh 8:14-16 and *m. Sukk.* 3:1-9; 3:12—4:5, together with Mt 21:8; Mk 11:8; Jn 12:13). The focus of Jesus' action on the temple, in his occupation of the outer court as a protest and enactment of the sort of purity he demanded there, comports well with the centrality of the temple at the close of the book of Zechariah. Even his appropriation of property (the foal that he rides into the city; Mt 21:2-3; Mk 11:2-3; Lk 19:30-31) may be seen as an enactment of Zechariah's prophecy, since the book claims that the very horses in Jerusalem will be marked ornamentally with the words "holy to the Lord" (Zech 14:20). All this was to be the case because the identity of the Lord as king was recognized, and in the targum that is taken to refer to the revelation of the kingdom of God (*Tg. Zech.* 14:9; see Mk 11:10; Lk 19:38; Jn 12:13). In all of this, the deep connection to an eschatological understanding of Sukkoth is evident.

2.2. The Dedication and Purim.

2.2.1. The Dedication. The Feast of the Dedication is explicitly mentioned in the Gospel according to John (Jn 10:22). The reference appears in the midst of an extended controversy (ranging over Jn 10) over Jesus' self-designation as "the gate of the sheep" (Jn 10:7) and God's son (Jn 10:15). The controversy over Jesus as the gate is also reflected in the martyrdom of James as presented by Hegesippus, a writer of the second century. Cited by Eusebius (Eusebius *Hist. Eccl.* 2.23.1-18), Hegesippus characterizes James, Jesus' brother, as the person who exercised immediate control of the church in Jerusalem. Although Peter had initially gathered a group of Jesus' followers in Jerusalem, his interests and activities further afield left the way open for James to become the natural head of the community there. That change and political changes in Jerusalem itself made the temple the effective center of the local community of Jesus' followers. James practiced a careful and idiosyncratic purity in the interests of worship in the temple. He abstained from wine and animal flesh, did not cut his hair or beard, forsook oil and bathing and wore only linen garments. According to Hegesippus, those special practices gave him access even to the sanctuary.

In Hegesippus's account, James is interrogated by the authorities as he stands on a parapet of the temple, Tell us: what is the gate of Jesus? James responds with a strong declaration of Jesus as the Son of Man who will come to judge the world. The authorities then push him from the parapet and have James stoned. He is killed by someone with a club, who beats in his head. James's devotion to the temple and his devotion to his brother were coextensive. In each case, the focus was on the throne of God, of which Jesus was the gate and the temple the court. His court on earth was in Jerusalem, where James continued to offer worship and to insist on that purity throughout Jesus' movement that made that worship possible and acceptable to God. The temple was the threshold to God's throne in heaven, much as in the vision of the prophet in Isaiah 6. And in the vision of James, the Son of Man associated with that throne was none other than Jesus, the gateway to heaven itself. Devotion to him and to the temple together constituted the effective worship of God.

Loyalty to Jesus and loyalty to the temple both demanded rigorous attention to the issue of holiness, of what belongs to God in human comportment. John 10, together with Hegesippus's portrayal of James and his martyrdom, provide insight into the worship of what was in its time the most influential and public expression of faith in Jesus. Because the Messiah was traditionally expected to restore true worship in the temple (see Chilton 1982, 86-96), the Feast of the Dedication became for followers of the risen Jesus who worshiped in Jerusalem a powerful occasion of christological reflection and christological controversy.

2.2.2. Purim. Such is the dominance of Passover within the calendar of Christianity that Purim has little echo. Still, Herod Antipas is pictured in Mark (Mk 6:23) as promising up to half his kingdom to Salome, which is what Ahasuerus repeatedly promises Esther (Esther 5:3, 6; 7:2). Of course, the events concerning John the Baptist's beheading are no Purim but a terrible reversal of the heroism of Esther. Salome's famous dance and its result represent an antithesis of the themes of Purim. The elements of the story in aggregate serve to exculpate Antipas from what only Antipas could be responsible for: John's death. There is an obvious analogy with the treatment of Pilate in the Gospels, where he is made to seem the dupe of the system he was in fact in charge of. In any case, it is notable the Luke's Antipas is more vigorous (see Lk 3:19-20; 9:7-9) and makes his decision quite literally without the song and dance: Salome makes no appearance in Luke.

2.3. Passover. The influence of James and his circle is by no means limited to the Feast of the Dedication. The most distinctive appropriation of a Judaic festival within the church was occasioned by Passover. Although the Gospel according to John presents Jesus' death as at the time the paschal lambs were slain (Jn 19:14, 31), the Synoptics' portrayal of the Last Supper evokes a Seder, the meal of Passover (Mt 26:17-20; Mk 14:12-17; Lk 22:7-14). There are several reasons for which this identification is implausible. No mention is made in the account of the supper of the lamb, the bitter herbs, the unleavened bread or the exodus from Egypt, all of which are prescribed in the book of Exodus (Ex 12). Moreover, the cultic authorities are presented as solemnly deciding to act in the case of Jesus before the feast itself (Mt 26:3-5; Mk 14:1-2). It seems clear that Jesus died near the time of Passover (having entered Jerusalem at or near Sukkoth) and that this timing then became coordinated with the Passover itself within the practice of the church (*see DJG,* Last Supper).

Again, the later history of the church permits us to understand the development and the theology of this practice (*see also* DLNTD, Lord's Supper, Love Feast). During the second century, a crisis concerning the calendar divided Christians seriously (see Eusebius *Hist. Eccl.* 5.23-24). Most celebrated Easter on Sunday, the Lord's day, and chose the Sunday following the time of Passover. Others, chiefly in Asia Minor, followed what they said was an ancient tradition and broke the fast prior to Easter only on the fourteenth day of Nisan: the day the lambs of Passover were to be slain and then consumed at evening (the start of the fifteenth day of Nisan). Further, they claimed that this corresponded to the movement of the heavenly bodies, in that Passover fell precisely on the first full moon after the vernal equinox, as Passover was regularly calculated.

Here we have a tradition, according to which Passover was to be kept precisely and that is connected with astronomy. Astronomical and calendrical observance is what Paul attacks in Galatians, as part of the program of the group he considers an artificial judaizing (see Gal 4:9-10; cf. 2:14). Chief among his disputants are followers of James (Gal 2:12). But the principal point of contention between Paul and the Judaizers is the necessity of circumcision (Gal 2:3-10; 5:6-12; 6:12-16). James himself seems not to have required circumcision of all believers; that is, he granted that non-Jews could be baptized and as such were to be acknowledged as saved by Jesus (Acts 15:13-21). But by presenting the last supper as a Seder, James and his circle assured that the leadership of the church would be Judaic in character, because Exodus itself stipulated that only the circumcised, whether Israelites or not, were to eat of the paschal meal (Ex 12:48).

2.4. Weeks/Pentecost. Just as the influence of James and his circle is greatest in connection with Passover, Weeks (Pentecost) is the most notable contribution in calendrical terms of Peter and his circle. The timing of the coming of the Holy Spirit is unequivocal (Acts 2:1-4), and the theme of Moses' dispensing of the Spirit on his elders is reflected (see Num 11:11-29). The association of Weeks with the covenant with Noah may help to explain why the coming of Spirit then was to extend to humanity at large (see Acts 2:5-11). First fruits were celebrated at Weeks (see Num 28:26), and they express the gift of Spirit and resurrection in Paul's theology (Rom 8:23; 11:16; 1 Cor 15:20, 23). We should expect such connections with the Pentecostal theology of Peter in one of Peter's students (see Gal 1:18), as we should expect him to be especially concerned to keep the Feast of Pentecost (see 1 Cor 16:8; Acts 20:16) despite what he said about calendrical observations in Galatians.

2.5. Destruction of the Temple. As the Feast of Purim finds itself inverted in the presentation of Mark, so the destruction of the temple is treated not as an occasion of mourning but as the culmination of *apocalyptic prophecy in Matthew 24—25; Mark 13; Luke 21. In rabbinic Judaism, the destruction of the temple was remembered on the ninth of Av (the fifth month, corresponding mostly to August), an apparent compromise between the recollection of the destruction of the first temple on the seventh of Av (2 Kings 25:8) and of the Second Temple on the tenth of Av after Jeremiah 52:12 (Josephus *J.W.* 6 §250). The compromise was already well advanced in Josephus's mind, who places both destructions on the tenth of Av. That still does not explain why the ninth triumphed as a day of fasting, and H. Schauss plausibly explains it as an agricultural practice, well prior to harvest (Schauss, 295-96).

The destruction of the temple also had a signal impact on the understanding of the Day of Atonement in both Judaism and Christianity. In the Mishnah, tractate *Yoma* (*m. Yoma* 1:1—5:7) rehearses the meticulous preparations for that great occasion, in anticipation that the temple would function again. In the epistle to the Hebrews (Heb 9:1-12), all the elements of sacrifice, temple and priesthood are understood only to have foreshadowed the perfect offering of Christ, once for all.

The appropriation of the Judaic festal and penitential calendar was not merely a matter of replication. Throughout, from Jesus to the author of Hebrews, the evident conviction is reflected that Israel's time, a time of celebrating divine providence in nature and in history, had become final time, the moment of eschatological fulfillment.

See also CALENDARS, JEWISH; SABBATH; TEMPLE; TEMPLE SERVICE AND SACRIFICE.

BIBLIOGRAPHY. B. D. Chilton, *A Feast of Meanings: Eucharistic Theologies from Jesus Through*

Johannine Circles (NovTSup 72; Leiden: E. J. Brill, 1994); idem, *The Glory of Israel: The Theology and Provenience of the Isaiah Targum* (JSOTSup 23; Sheffield: JSOT, 1982); idem, *Pure Kingdom: Jesus' Vision of God,* (SHJ 1; Grand Rapids, MI: Eerdmans, 1996); idem, *The Temple of Jesus: His Sacrificial Program Within a Cultural History of Sacrifice* (University Park: Pennsylvania State University Press, 1992); J. Mann, "The Observance of the Sabbath and the Festivals in the First Two Centuries of the Current Era According to Philo, Josephus, the New Testament and the Rabbinic Sources," *The Jewish Review* 4 (1914) 433-56, 498-532; L. L. Morris, *The New Testament and the Jewish Lectionaries* (London: Tyndale, 1964); F. Rochber-Halton, "Calendars," *ABD* 1:810-14; H. Schauss, *The Jewish Festivals: History and Observance* (New York: Schocken, 1962); R. Y. Stanier et al., *The Microbial World* (Englewood Cliffs, NJ: Prentice-Hall, 1986); J. C. VanderKam, "Calendars, Ancient Israelite and Early Jewish," *ABD* 1:814-20.

B. D. Chilton

FLORILEGIUM (4Q174)

Twenty-six fragments from *Qumran's Cave 4 have been identified as probably belonging to a manuscript that has become widely known as 4QFlorilegium (4Q174). *Florilegium* is the Latin term that corresponds with the Greek "anthology." Commonly florilegia are collections of quotations from a variety of literary sources, and there are many reasons why such collections were made in antiquity. The contents of the principal fragments of 4Q174 contain not only extracts from literary sources, especially the books of Deuteronomy, 2 Samuel and the Psalms, but also an intricate exegetical commentary on those passages, setting their significance in the last days (*see* Eschatologies of Late Antiquity). Because of this many commentators prefer to label the composition more precisely on the basis of its content as an "eschatological *midrash." The composition has similarities to several other texts found at Qumran, notably 4QCatena A, but there are no overlaps between them to prove that they are two copies of the same work.

1. Form
2. Genre
3. Content
4. Comparisons with the New Testament

1. Form.

The most extensive analysis of the principal fragments of this composition (Steudel) has convincingly argued that the fragment containing the extract from Deuteronomy 33 probably preceded those that contain the citations and interpretations of 2 Samuel and the Psalms. Thus it seems as if the scriptural extracts were placed in the order of Law, Prophets and Psalms (cf. 4Q397 14-21 10-11; cf. Lk 24:44), providing the history books were understood to be part of the prophetic corpus at that time. That is then the order that was the basis of the later canonical ordering of the Hebrew Bible.

2. Genre.

The genre of 4Q174 is much debated. Because of the phrase "in the last days" in its several sections, it is widely acknowledged that the selection of passages and their interpretations have been carefully put together thematically. 4Q174 is often cited as a prime example of a thematic *pesher (Carmignac). However, the commentaries in this composition are not all the same. In what survives, only the sequence of quotations from the Psalms are explicitly given commentary that is technically introduced by a formula including the term *pesher;* the remaining sections have commentary of a more general kind. This variation raises the question whether the compiler of 4Q174 considered that the psalms had a different status from the prophetic extracts from the blessing of Levi and from the oracle of Nathan, which are also commented upon in the work, or whether it could be that he used a variety of exegetical sources. In other Qumran compositions pesher is used technically for interpreting unfulfilled or partially fulfilled blessings, curses and prophecies (including the Psalms), but not all such texts always receive pesher in the community's sectarian works.

The section of 4Q174 that contains the interpretation of the psalms is introduced by the formula "a midrash of" (*mdrš mn*). Although this formal use of the word *midrash* might indicate that what follows is "an interpretation" (cf. 1QS 8:15; Lim), it is possible that the term was used somewhat technically. It is very unlikely, however, that the commentary in 4Q174 can be read as a direct precursor of the later *rabbinic midrashim. The term *midrash* has a similar quasi-technical role in the title of another Qumran composition, *Midrash Sepher Moshe* (4Q249), a commentary on the law. The appearance of the terms *midrash* and *pesher* together in just one part of this complex thematic commentary shows how important it is that great care should be exercised before any particular kind of early Jewish or early Christian interpretation is labeled generically.

3. Content.

3.1. The Temples. 4Q174 describes three temples and assumes the existence of a fourth. The interpretation of 2 Samuel 7 contains a reference to the Solomonic temple that was destroyed. There is also mention of a future ideal temple from which non-Israelites will be banned; this probably corresponds with the divinely constructed temple as mentioned in the **Temple Scroll* (11QTemple 29:9; cf. Heb 9:11). While the commentary seems to assume the existence of the Second *Temple, the focus of the contemporary realization of Nathan's oracle is the divine establishment of a "sanctuary of Adam" (*miqdaš ʾādām*). The phrase is deliberately ambiguous, referring both to the community's aspiration for the restoration of Eden as a sanctuary where the glory of Adam would be restored (CD 3:19-20 [*see* Damascus Document]; Wise) and to the human composition of this sanctuary. In other words, the community saw itself as an anticipation of the ultimate divinely built temple (Brooke 1985; Dimant). Since the community, at least at the outset, was priestly in makeup and outlook, this substitution of the community for the temple in *Jerusalem is a striking example of how political and other circumstances can force even a traditional and institutionally oriented group to spiritualize the basis of its self-understanding.

3.2. The Eschatological Figures. Nathan's oracle contains a play on words that is visible even in English. God will establish "a house for David"; the term *house* carries the double meaning of temple building and royal house. The quotation of 2 Samuel 7:11-13 cleverly omits the words that speak directly of David's immediate successor, Solomon. This process of abbreviation makes Nathan's oracle have concern only with the eschatological future. At that time, the interpretation comments a "shoot of David" will arise to save *Israel. This "shoot" is referred to in other community compositions (4QpIsa[a] frags. 7-10 iii 22; 4QCommentary on Genesis A 5:3-4; 4Q285 frag. 5 3, 4); the phrase derives from Jeremiah 23:5, part of what is widely understood as a messianic oracle, and Jeremiah 33:15. This explicit Davidic *messianism would seem to reflect the later thinking of the community (second half of first century B.C.), royal messianism in earlier compositions being represented by the more general designation "Messiah of Israel" (e.g., 1QS 9:11). In 4Q174 it is not clear how the Davidic shoot will save Israel.

The Davidic Messiah is accompanied by the Interpreter of the Law (cf. CD 6:7; 7:18). In some Qumran compositions the Messiah of Israel is accompanied by the Messiah of Aaron, and many commentators have justifiably identified 4Q174's Interpreter of the Law with the priestly Messiah. Such an identification is strengthened by the presence in 4Q174 of an interpretation of the blessing of Levi of Deuteronomy 33, a text that in the earlier 4QTestimonia almost certainly refers to the eschatological priest.

3.3. The Community. Although much in 4Q174 is concerned with the future temple and the figures who will appear in the last days, much in 4Q174 concerns the community itself. Not only is the community identified as a proleptic sanctuary, it also features strikingly in the interpretation of Psalm 2. The interpretation occurs at the bottom of a slightly damaged column, but it seems to be the case that the final consonant of *mšyḥw* is read as a plural suffix, "his anointed ones." Thus, rather than understanding the Psalm to be referring to the Messiah, the interpreter applies the words to "the elect of Israel in the last days." Given the reference to the Davidic Messiah in the previous section of the composition, this corporate understanding of Psalm 2:2 is all the more striking. As in some sections of the NT the concept of messianism is democratized and extended to the faithful community.

The contents of column 2 of the principal group of fragments refer to the community's expected eschatological suffering, a time of trial for the faithful when *Belial holds dominion (cf. Mt 5:11-12).

4. Comparisons with the New Testament.

4.1. The Acts of the Apostles. Psalm 2:1-2 is cited and given interpretation in Acts 4:25-26, but the closest parallel in Acts with 4Q174 is the use of 2 Samuel 7:11-16 as the source of the vocabulary of much of Acts 13:33-37, in which Psalm 2:7 is cited explicitly. The juxtaposition of 2 Samuel 7 and Psalm 2 in both texts need not suggest dependence on a common written source. The two scriptural texts have an intertextual affinity that is independently discernible (Brooke 1998).

In Acts 15:16 the textual form of Amos 9:11 is more in agreement with that represented in 4Q174 1-3 i 12 and CD 7:16 than with any other known witness. This shows that scriptural citations in both the scrolls and the NT need to play an ongoing significant role in the study of the transmission of the biblical text.

4.2. 2 Corinthians 6:14—7:1. Several scholars (see Brooke 1985, 211-17) have argued that 2 Corinthians 6:14—7:1 is an interpolation in Paul's letter, possibly introduced by Paul himself to represent the views he was trying to argue against. Several motifs in the passage are echoed in 4Q174, especially the identification of the community with the temple and the appeal to Ezekiel 37 and 2 Samuel 7:14. Perhaps this material indicates that *Essenism in some form was spread in the Jewish *Diaspora as well as throughout Palestine.

4.3. Hebrews. The linked quotation of Psalm 2:7 and 2 Samuel 7:14 in Hebrews might suggest that the combination was known to the author from some written tradition of the exegesis of the passages taken together as in 4Q174. However, since both passages refer to the "son" in a royal context, it is just as likely that as in Acts 13:33-37 the compilers of 4Q174 and of Hebrews had no common source but worked directly with the inherent *intertextuality that the biblical texts suggest for themselves (Brooke 1998).

See also BIBLICAL INTERPRETATION, JEWISH; PESHARIM; RABBINIC LITERATURE: MIDRASHIM.

BIBLIOGRAPHY. G. J. Brooke, *Exegesis at Qumran: 4QFlorilegium in Its Jewish Context* (JSOTSup 29; Sheffield: JSOT, 1985); idem, "Shared Intertextual Interpretations in the Dead Sea Scrolls and the New Testament," in *Biblical Perspectives: Early Use and Interpretation of the Bible in Light of the Dead Sea Scrolls,* ed. M. E. Stone and E. G. Chazon (STDJ 28; Leiden: E. J. Brill, 1998) 35-57; J. Carmignac, "Le Document de Qumrân sur Melkisédeq," *RevQ* 7 (1969-71) 343-78; D. Dimant, "4QFlorilegium and the Idea of the Community as Temple," in *Hellenica et Judaica: Hommage à Valentin Nikiprowetzky,* ed. A. Caquot, M. Hadas-Lebel and J. Riaud (Louvain: Peeters, 1986) 165-89; T. H. Lim, "Midrash Pesher in the Pauline Letters," in *The Scrolls and the Scriptures: Qumran Fifty Years After,* ed. S. E. Porter and C. A. Evans (JSPSup 26; Sheffield: Sheffield Academic Press, 1997) 280-92; A. Steudel, *Der Midrasch zur Eschatologie aus der Qumrangemeinde (4QMidr-Eschat$^{a.b}$)* (STDJ 13; Leiden: E. J. Brill, 1994); M. O. Wise, *Thunder in Gemini and Other Essays on the History, Language and Literature of Second Temple Palestine* (JSPSup 15; Sheffield: JSOT, 1994) 152-85.

G. J. Brooke

FOURTH PHILOSOPHY. *See* REVOLUTIONARY MOVEMENTS, JEWISH.

FREEDMEN. *See* ROMAN SOCIAL CLASSES.

FRIENDSHIP

Friendship constituted a regular topic of discussion in ancient literature, although specific views on friendship varied in different periods, places and authors. Some of the ideals of friendship impact our understanding of NT passages even where the specific term is unused.

1. Kinds of Friendship in Antiquity
2. Ideals for Friendship in Antiquity
3. Dying for Friends
4. Friendship with God
5. Friendship Contrasted with Servanthood
6. Friendship in the New Testament

1. Kinds of Friendship in Antiquity.

Friendship was a regular ancient topic of discourse (e.g., Epictetus *Disc.* 2.22), the leading subject of numerous essays, for instance, by *Aristotle (*Eth. Eud.* 7.1234b-1246a; *Eth. Nic.* 8—9); Plutarch (*Many Friends, Mor.* 93A-97B); Dio Chrysostom (*Third Discourse on Kingship* 99-100); *Cicero *(De Amic.);* Seneca (*Ep. Lucil.* 3, "On True and False Friendships"; 9, "On Philosophy and Friendship"; see further Sevenster, 172-77); and Theophrastus (according to Aulus Gellius *Noc. Att.* 1.3.10-11). Scholars have produced detailed studies of friendship in *Philo, who develops some *Stoic ideals (see Sterling); on Aristotle (Schroeder, 35-45) and his followers, the Peripatetics (Schroeder, 45-56; for other sources, see especially Fitzgerald 1997b, 7-10). Even before Aristotle, many ideals of friendship circulated that later became pervasive in the Roman world (see Fitzgerald 1997a).

There were a variety of perspectives on and kinds of friendship, not only in the philosophers but also throughout Greco-Roman and Jewish society. Friendship could signify a relationship of dependence or of equality, of impersonal alliances or of personal bonds of affection.

1.1. Political Friendship. We will first survey some political kinds of friendship. The Roman ideal of *amicitia* was less apt to emphasize sentiment and male affection than did the Greek ideal of *philia;* it often represented an alliance of utility characteristic of partisan politics among the Roman elite (Stowers, 29). The claim that Romans "were rather incapable of a heartfelt friendship" (Friedländer, 1:225) is an exaggeration stemming from overdependence on the literature of the elite (and ignoring the abundance of genuine affection, e.g., in Cicero's letters), but it does reflect the recognition of the importance of political connections in urban Roman friendship ideals. But there was considerable interpenetration of Greek and Roman ideals by the early empire (e.g., in Plutarch; see O'Neil), and political uses of friendship did not start with Rome.

Friendship has been said to be largely political in writers such as Cicero (see Fiore) and Dionysius of Halicarnassus (see Balch). One may contrast the older Stoic values of Chrysippus (Diogenes Laertius *Vit.* 7.7.189), but politically based relationships were common even among earlier Greeks. Whereas Aristotle notes friendships based on goodness, pleasure or utility (Aristotle *Eth. Eud.* 7.2.9-13, 1236a; 7.10.10, 1242b; *Eth. Nic.* 8.13.1, 1162ab), he assigns most to utility (Aristotle *Eth. Eud.* 7.2.14, 1236a; for political friendship in Aristotle, see further Schroeder).

One of the most common political uses of "friendship" in our literary sources refers to political dependence on a royal patron. This appears in ancient Israel (e.g., 2 Sam 15:37; 16:16-17; 1 Kings 4:5; 1 Chron 27:33) and applies to tyrants of the classical period (Diogenes Laertius *Vit.* 1.54), to the intimate circle of Alexander of Macedon (Diodorus Siculus *Bib. Hist.* 17.31.6; 17.39.2; 17.100.1) and to those of Cassander (Diodorus Siculus *Bib. Hist.* 18.55.1), to a high office in Hellenistic Syria (Diodorus Siculus *Bib. Hist.* 33.4.4a). This use of royal friendship appears with other rulers as well (Cornelius Nepos *Vir. Illus.* 9, 2.2; 18, 1.6; Chariton *Chaer.* 8.8.10), including in various Jewish sources (1 Macc 10:20; 15:28, 32; 2 Macc 7:24; *Ep. Arist.* 40-41, 44, 190, 208, 225, 228, 318; Josephus *Ant.* 12.366; 13.146, 225; *Life* 131; cf. *Sipre Deut.* 53.1.3). In the Roman imperial period it applies especially to friendship with Caesar (Epictetus *Disc.* 4.1.45-50; Martial *Epigr.* 5.19.15-16; Herodianus 4.3.5; inscriptions in Deissmann, 378), although of Jewish tetrarchs and rulers, apparently only King Agrippa I (Acts 12:1-21) felt secure enough to adopt this title on his coins (Meyshan). John 19:12 probably refers to this position of honor (see e.g., Sherwin-White, 47); John 15:15 might present friendship with Jesus as friendship with a king.

In one of its most common uses in ancient literature, "friendship" could apply to alliances, cooperation or nonaggression treaties among peoples. Epics could use such language for alliances (Homer *Il.* 3.93, 256; 4.17; 16.282; Virgil *Aen.* 11.321), as might orators (Demosthenes *On the Navy Boards* 5; *On the Embassy* 62; *Letters* 3.27; cf. *Rhet. Ad Herenn.* 3.3.4). It also appears in geographers (Strabo *Geog.* 8.5.5) and apologists (Josephus *Ag. Ap.* 1.109; 2.83b). Naturally, this language predominates in biographers and historians. We can attest it abundantly in biographers such as Arrian (*Alex.* 1.28.1; 4.15.2, 5; 4.21.8; 7.15.4); Plutarch (*Comp. Lyc. Num.* 4.6; *Pel.* 5.1; 29.4; also *Epameinondas* 17 in *Reg. Imp. Apophth., Mor.* 193DE); Cornelius Nepos (*Vir. Illus.* 7.4.7; 7.5.3; 7.7.5; 14.8.5; 23.10.2), and others (Josephus *Life* 30, 124). It is if anything more abundant in the historians, such as Polybius (e.g., *Hist.* 14.1); Dionysius of Halicarnassus (e.g., Ant. Rom. 3.28.7; 3.51.1; 5.26.4; 5.50.3); Diodorus Siculus (e.g., *Bib. Hist.* 14.30.4; 14.56.2; 17.39.1); Livy (e.g., *Hist.* 6.2.3; 27.4.6; 43.6.9); and 1 Maccabees (1 Macc 12:1, 3, 8; 14:40).

Ancient writers frequently apply the designation *friendship* to personal or familial relationships undertaken for political expediency (e.g., Achilles Tatius *Leuc.* 4.6.1-3); Plutarch provides abundant examples (e.g., Plutarch *Ages.* 23.6; *Pomp.* 70.4; *Statecraft* 13, *Mor.* 806F-809B; *Philosophers and Men in Power* 1, *Mor.* 776AB; *Whether an Old Man Should Engage in Public Affairs* 6, *Mor.* 787B).

1.2. Patron-Client Friendship. Closely related to other political uses of friendship is the relationship between patrons and clients, often defined as friendship. In the Roman world, people probably often thought of both the royal and the nonroyal political images of friendship in terms of patron-client relationships. Patrons were called the clients' friends (*AE* 1912.171, as cited in Sherk, 235), and even more often clients were called friends of their patron (Martial *Epigr.* 3.36.1-3; 3 Macc 5:26; probably P. Oxy. 2861). This image of dependence could be applied even to a magician dependent on a spirit (*PGM* 1.172, 190-91). Although the patron-client relationship involved fundamental inequality, the fact that ancient Greek ideals of friendship involved equality (see §1.3 below) allowed some clients to exploit this language to challenge some inequities in their patrons' understanding of the relationship (see Konstan). This patron-client usage may have influenced the use of "friendship" to describe the relationship between philosopher and disciple (Diogenes Laertius *Vit.* 6.2.36; Stowers, 39).

1.3. Nonhierarchical Friendship. But not all ancient Mediterranean conceptions of friendship reflected this hierarchical sort of relationship, even though friendship normally anticipated reciprocity. In the eastern Mediterranean, societies of friends could include fellow members of one's guild (Horsley, 4:17-18 §3). Although age-group societies may have declined in the Hellenistic and Roman periods, the classical Greek wealthy image of friendship tended to be companionship based on groupings of the same sex and age, which constituted political parties (Stowers, 28-30, 39, 60; cf. Gould, 143-45). One may perhaps compare the relationship of associates in the Jewish *ḥabûrah* (cf. Oesterley, 172). Among the Greek schools, the *Epicureans in particular emphasized friendship, regarding it as a source of pleasure (Diogenes Laertius *Vit.* 10.120; 148.27-28); the view of the Epicurean Lucretius (*De Rerum Natura* 5.1019-23) even sounds like later social contract theories. Plutarch (*Table Talk* 4. introduction, *Mor.* 660A) advocates befriending only the good while showing goodwill toward all.

Although Roman patronal friendship made at best a vague pretense to equality, this traditional Greek image of friendship, even when related to benefaction, demanded at least the idea of equality. Aristotle cited the earlier proverb, "Friendship is equality" (Aristotle *Eth. Eud.* 7.9.1, 1241b), and is said to have "defined friendship as an equality of reciprocal good-will" (Diogenes Laertius *Vit.* 5.31, as translated in LCL 1:478-79). Of course, what Aristotle meant by "equality" differs considerably from our usage of that concept. Any kind of friendship could exist either between equals or with one as a superior (Aristotle *Eth. Eud.* 7.3.2, 1238b; 7.10.10, 1242b; *Eth. Nic.* 8.7.1, 1158b; 8.13.1, 1162ab); Aristotle further defined "equality" more proportionately than quantitatively (Aristotle *Eth. Nic.* 8.7.2-3, 1158b). In the same way, his teacher *Plato stressed both the friendship held by loving equals and that which stemmed from the poor's need for the rich (Plato *Leg.* 8, 837AB).

Nevertheless, equality remained part of the traditional Greek ideal of friendship. As early as Homer a leader could honor a special friend above his other companions, regarding him as equal to himself (Homer *Il.* 18.81-82). Others could speak of a friend as "another I" (Diogenes Laertius *Vit.* 7.1.23); Neo-Pythagorean tradition stressed friendship as equality (see Thom). Alexandrian Jewish writers also picked up on this; in *Epistle of Aristeas* 228, the highest honor is to be shown to parents but the next honor to one's friends, for a friend is the "equal of one's own soul" (Hadas, 189). This view continued to affect popular thought. Thus one letter recommends a friend *(amicum)* by exhorting the receiver to view him "as if he were me" (*P. Oxy.* 32.5-6, 2d cent. A.D.); this ideal may inform the background of Philemon 17-19.

Whether patronal or among peers, friendship was in general conditional. It normally included "obligations and expectations" (Meeks, 30), whether formally or informally. Friendship appears frequently in private letters, where it often refers to friendship among peers. In such letters it appears "usually in the context of performing services for each other," such as watching over one another's families or taking care of the other's debts in his absence until his return (Evans, 202).

2. Ideals for Friendship in Antiquity.

2.1. Friendship Involving Loyalty. Hellenistic ideals of friendship included a strong emphasis on loyalty. Isocrates argued that good men love their friends always, even when far away, but base men honor friends only when they are present (Isocrates *Dem.* 1, *Or.* 1). Others carried on the criticism of those who were merely friends in name and the lamentation that faithfulness in friends was rare (Phaedrus 3.9.1; cf. Prov 20:6). Jewish works such as (probably) the *Sentences of the Syriac Menander* stress loyalty to friends (*Sent. Syr. Men.* 25). The Jewish writer in Sirach 6:7-10, 14-16 and 12:8 also argues that one knows one's friends only in the hard times, when friends' loyalty is tested.

In narratives, the loyalty of a good friend adds to the delight of the story; for instance, in Chariton's novel *Chaereas and Callirhoe,* Polycharmus leaves his parents to face danger with his friend *(hetairos)* Chaereas (Chariton *Chaer.* 3.5.7-8), because he was his friend (*philos;* Chariton *Chaer.* 3.3.1); at the end of the book, Polycharmus is rewarded for his faithful friendship with Chaereas's sister in marriage (Chariton *Chaer.* 8.8.12-13; on Polycharmus's role see further Hock, 147-57). Readers would recognize the same sort of relationship in the narratives about David and Jonathan in the OT, where Jonathan proves even more loyal to David than to his father.

2.2. Friendship Involving Intimacy and Shared Confidences. Intimacy frequently appears in discussions of friendship (e.g., Theocritus work 12, *The Beloved).* Isocrates advises a careful testing of friends to see if they are worthy of confidence with secrets (Isocrates *Dem.* 24-25, *Or.* 1). Aristotle notes that true friendship requires confidence (*pistis*) in one's friend, which requires standing the test of time (Aristotle *Eth. Eud.* 7.2.40, 1237b).

That true friends are those who can speak openly (with *parrēsia*), rather than only praising a person to his face, became a commonplace among Greek and Roman moralists (Isocrates *Ad Nic.* 28, *Or.* 2; Seneca *Dial.* 10.15.2). Plutarch devotes an essay to the contrast between flatterers and friends, an idea that may inform Paul's defense of his open speech to his churches (1 Thess 2:4-6).

This ideal of friendship proves common in early Jewish sources. *Josephus, writing about Judaism for a Greco-Roman readership, is eager to point out the similar emphasis in Jewish ethics:

> [the Law] allows us to conceal nothing from our friends, for there is no friendship without absolute confidence; in the event of subsequent estrangement, it forbids the disclosure of secrets. (Josephus *Ag. Ap.* 2.28 §207, LCL 1:376-77)

Philo's portrayal of Abraham suggests that friends were recipients of one's confidence and intimacy (Philo *Sobr.* 55). Earlier sages especially expected friends to be able to maintain confidences (Sir 6:9; 22:22; 27:17; cf. 42:1). This kind of intimacy and equality could carry over into talk about God, as in the case of Abraham, with whom God "no longer talked . . . as God with man but as a friend with a familiar" (Philo *Abr.* 273, LCL). It is thus not surprising to read that Jesus shares with his disciples intimate secrets he would not share with servants (Jn 15:15).

2.3. Friendship and Sharing All Resources. Aristotle defines as a friend any who seeks to do for another what he believes to be to the other's benefit (Aristotle *Rhet.* 1.5.16, 1361b). As Plutarch notes, friends share not only secrets but, ideally, everything they possess (e.g., Plutarch *Flatterer* 24, *Mor.* 65AB). That friends shared all things in common becomes a common phrase in the literature of Greco-Roman antiquity, in satirists (Martial *Epigr.* 2.43.1-16; perhaps 8.18.9-10), historians (Herodianus 3.6.1-2; cf. 1 Macc 12:23), biographers (Cornelius Nepos *Vir. Illus.* 15.3.4), and others (perhaps *Pseud.-Phoc.* 30; Euripides *Androm.* 585, but cf. 632-35; Plutarch *Bride* 19, *Mor.* 140D; Longus *Daphn. Chl.* 1.10).

But *Stoics made special use of this idea. Diogenes Laertius describes the Stoic view of friendship: "And by friendship they mean a common use of all that has to do with life, wherein we treat our friends as we should ourselves" (Diogenes Laertius *Vit.* 7.1.124, LCL 2:228-29; cf. Seneca *Ben.* 7.4.1). Although the ideal of friends sharing all things in common was widespread, Cynics and Stoics particularly propagated the syllogism that the wise man was a friend of the gods, the gods owned everything, and therefore everything belongs to the wise man. This reasoning purportedly prevailed as early as Diogenes the Cynic (Diogenes Laertius *Vit.* 6.2.37, 72; cf. Antisthenes in 6.1.11) but became common among Stoics (Diogenes Laertius *Vit.* 7.1.125; cf. Seneca *Dial.* 1.1.5; *Ben.* 7.4.6; Philo *Cher.* 84). Many scholars believe that this reasoning underlies the thought of 1 Corinthians 3:21-23 (e.g., Conzelmann, 80). This may account for the sharing of Jesus' things with the disciples, his friends (Jn 15:15), through the Spirit of truth, just as Jesus had shared the Father's things (Jn 16:14-15), but this context probably emphasizes specifically sharing God's truths (Jn 16:13; 15:15).

3. Dying for Friends.

Loyalty to friends and treating friends as one's own equals, as another self, might require dying for them. Early Jewish sources prohibit sacrificing another to spare one's own life but allowed that one's life takes precedence over another's life (Akiba in Jacobs, 42-44). Nevertheless, though one was not required to love one's neighbor more than oneself, Judaism did praise as heroic those rare persons who would sacrifice their lives on behalf of their friends (Jacobs, 47).

Courageous, heroic and honorable death was an ancient Mediterranean virtue (e.g., Epameinondas 2 in Plutarch *S.K., Mor.* 192C). Greek tradition viewed as noble Iphigeneia's willingness to die to "save" Greece (Euripides *Iph. Aul.* 1420); Roman military oaths also demanded willingness to die on behalf of the state (*IGRR* 3.137; *OGIS* 532; *ILS* 8781, as cited in Sherk, 31); texts portrayed favorably *slaves willing to die for their masters (Appian *Civ. W.* 4.4.26). Josephus likewise portrays favorably those desiring to die nobly for their nation or for fame (e.g., Josephus *J.W.* 1.5 §§43-44, 58); later rabbis praised a Roman senator (probably fictitious) who died to spare the Jews (*Deut. Rab.* 2:24). Self-sacrifice on behalf of another was voluntary and not expected (Euripides *Alc.* 689-90); nevertheless Greeks regarded it highly (Euripides *Alc.* 12-18; *Heracl.* 547-601; *Androm.* 413-15; cf. Hengel, 9). Romans also regarded highly dying on behalf of one's nation (Livy *Hist.* 10.28.12-18; 10.29.1; Lucan *Civ.W.* 2.380-83). Ancients also recognized the occasional value of such sacrifice as "an expiatory sacrifice to assuage the anger of the gods" (Hengel, 19, 27; cf. Euripides *Iph. Aul.* 1394-97, 1553-60; Livy *Hist.* 22.57.6; Plutarch *Greek and Roman Parallel Stories* 35, *Mor.* 314C-D). Thus Greeks or Romans would readily grasp the early Christian concept that Jesus died on their behalf, even if they lacked exposure to atonement in the levitical system.

In the context of such ideas, death on behalf of a friend would provide one of the most concrete expressions of loyalty possible. Perhaps especially because great dangers normally obliterated the closest ties, even those of friendship (Achilles Tatius *Leuc.* 3.3.5), true friends were viewed as those who would share in one's hardships (Isocrates *Dem.* 25, *Or.* 1) and do whatever proved necessary to help one (e.g., P. Oxy. 32.5, 8-14), including in war (Euripides *Or.* 652) or in the law court (Aulus Gellius *Noc. Att.* 1.3.4-8). In this vein, the greatest expression of devoted friendship was regarded as willingness to die for one another (Diodorus Siculus *Bib. Hist.* 10.4.4-6; Epictetus *Disc.* 2.7.3); where this was impossible, they could at least die together (e.g., Euripides *Or.* 1069-74, 1155; *Iph. Taur.* 674-86; Chariton *Chaer.* 4.3.5; 7.1.7; cf. *Sent. Syr. Men.* 406-7; *Syr. Men. Epit.* 22-23).

Yet even in view of this emphasis on such signs of devotion in ancient literature, they proved infrequent in practice. Thus Epicurus reportedly noted that the wise person would "sometimes" die on a friend's behalf (*hyper philou;* Diogenes Laertius *Vit.* 10.120; cf. Rom 5:7). Lucian seems predisposed to satirize or minimize the traditional ideal (see Pervo). Such self-sacrifice was truly the "greatest" act of love one could bestow (Jn 15:13).

Thus in Jesus' discussion of love (Jn 15:9-17; *phileō* and *agapaō* appear roughly interchangeable in this Gospel) he digresses to illustrate his love for his friends by speaking of how he would lay down his life for them (Jn 15:13-15). Likewise, if Jesus' disciple friends (Jn 15:15) love one another as he has loved them (Jn 15:12), they must lay down their lives for one another (Jn 15:13; cf. 1 Jn 3:16). The same Gospel illustrates this principle earlier when Jesus speaks of going to Lazarus, because Lazarus was their "friend" (*philos,* Jn 11:11), whom Jesus "loved" (*phileō,* Jn 11:3) and for whose life Jesus laid down his own (Jn 11:8-16); Thomas literally understands, and the reader symbolically understands, Jesus' "going" in terms of his death (Jn 11:16).

4. Friendship with God.

The supreme example of patronal friendship in ancient sources might be thought to be discovered in passages referring to friendship with God. Surprisingly, however, it is not the patronal but the voluntary, reciprocal elements of the relationship that dominate many of these texts. Some references are too brief for this to be determined, as in some Cynic epistles, where the wise person alone is God's friend (Crates *Ep.* 26, *to the Athenians*; cf. Diogenes *Ep.* 10, *to Metrocles*); one may also compare the fellowship between mortals and deities in the Golden Age (Babrius *Fables prol.* 13).

But *Epictetus addresses the subject more frequently. Heracles had few friends, indeed, no friend closer than God; thus he was an obedient son of God (Epictetus *Disc.* 2.16.44). One who does not care about circumstances is like a free man and can "look up to heaven as a friend of God" (Epictetus *Disc.* 2.17.29, LCL 1:344-45). Loving others is important, but the first responsibility of one who is truly free is to be a friend to the gods (Epictetus *Disc.* 3.24.60). As a free person himself Epictetus was a "friend of God," for he chose to obey him willingly (Epictetus *Disc.* 4.3.9).

Some Diaspora Jewish writers use the phrase in a manner resembling that of Epictetus. In *Wisdom of Solomon, Wisdom enters the righteous, making them God's friends and prophets (Wis 7:27; cf. 7:14; 8:18); in Philo, Virtue makes God a friend of the righteous (Philo *Vit. Cont.* 90, though there is a variant reading here), just as he is a friend to virtue (Philo *Op. Mund.* 81) and to wisdom (Philo *Sobr.* 55). The second-century Tanna Rabbi Meir, whose image of friendship may have been affected by Greco-Roman conceptions to a lesser degree, observed that whoever occupies himself with the Torah for its own sake is called God's friend (*m. 'Abot* 6:1). In *rabbinic parables, Israel is sometimes portrayed as a friend of God the king (e.g., *Sifre Deut.* 53.1.3; *b. Sukk.* 55b). In Justin Martyr's *Dialog with Trypho* 28, God's friend is whoever knows and obeys him; in *Sentences of Sextus* 86ab, self-discipline produces piety, which seeks friendship with God.

Following the OT designation of Abraham as God's friend (Is 41:8; 2 Chron 20:7), early Jewish literature naturally applies the title regularly to Abraham (*Jub.* 19:9), including in Philo (*Abr.* 89, 273; *Sobr.* 55); the rabbis (*Mek. Shir.* 10.54-55; *Gen. Rab.* 65:10; *Ex. Rab.* 27:1; *Lev. Rab.* 11:7); and other early Jewish (*T. Abr.* 1:7; 2:3, 6; 8:2; 9:7; 15:12-14; 16:3A; *Apoc. Abr.* 10:5, no earlier than second century A.D.; *see* Apocalypse of Abraham; *Apoc. Zeph.* 9:4-5; *see* Apocalypse of Zephaniah) and Christian (Jas 2:23; *1 Clem.* 10, 17) sources. Writers applied the title only rarely to postbiblical characters (Rabbi Ishmael in *3 Enoch* 1:8; *see* Enoch, Books of) or biblical characters other than Abraham or *Moses (Levi, in *Jub.* 30:20-21; Isaac and Jacob in CD 3:3-4, *see* Damascus Document; Jacob in some manuscripts of *Jos. and As.* 23:10; cf. *Gen. Rab.* 69:2). Abraham receives this title especially because of his intimate relationship with God, so that God could take Abraham into his confidence, not treating him as a servant (cf. Jn 15:15): Because wisdom was God's friend rather than servant, God also calls Abraham his friend (Philo *Sobr.* 55). Or, it is because of his obedience to God instead of his own spirit's will (CD 3:2; cf. Jn 15:14). This friendship apparently extends even to sharing secrets (a characteristic of friendship noted in §2.2 above); one might compare God sharing his secrets with Abraham in Genesis 18:17-18 and probably *Testament of Abraham* 9:2, recension A.

In Exodus 33:11, Moses is the friend of God; this becomes the basis on which he can appeal to God for a revelation of his glory (Ex 33:13-18). Early Jewish texts repeat this designation for Moses (Philo *Sacr.* 130; Pseudo-Philo *Bib. Ant.* 23:9; 24:3; 25:5; *Sipre Num.* 78.1.1; *Ex. Rab.* 45:2; but *Sib. Or.* 2.245 is probably a Christian interpolation); his special closeness to God also appears in Diaspora magical texts (Gager, 140-45). In tannaitic parables, Moses appears as God's friend four times, Israel three times and a few others, including Abraham, once each (Johnston, 591). This is probably a primary background for the "friends of God" image in John 15:15, especially because in John 1:14-18 the disciples are compared with a new Moses to whom God revealed his glory in Jesus, the embodiment of Torah in flesh (cf. 2 Cor 3:6-18).

5. Friendship Contrasted with Servanthood.

The contrast between friends and servants was familiar enough in Mediterranean antiquity; a Roman, for example, could describe conquered people as "slaves" but allies as "friends" (Sallust *Iug.* 102.6). Writers could also draw a contrast between servants and friends of God. Philo declares that God gives priority to his friends in inheriting virtue rather than to his slaves (Philo *Migr. Abr.* 45). Abraham, like Wisdom, is God's friend and not his servant, and those who are his friends are also his only son (Philo *Sobr.* 55).

Thus John supplements his earlier contrast between servants and children (Jn 8:33-35; cf. Gal 4:7) with a contrast between friends and servants in John 15:15. John's contrast between being Jesus' friends and slaves may also help explicate the context, because only friends share all things in common. Under traditional Jewish law, a slave could not inherit, no matter how many goods were left to him, unless the master's will freed the slave or granted him "all" his master's goods (including himself; *m. Pe'ah* 3:8). There would be no point in Jesus promising to share his words or goods with the disciples, unless they were friends and not slaves.

6. Friendship in the New Testament.

The preceding discussion sheds light on many NT passages; we treat here only some of the possible insights the data provide for early Christian texts not already mentioned. Much of the conventional language of friendship, although not our specific term, recurs in Paul's letters, possibly presupposed in Paul's conflict with the

Corinthians (see Marshall, especially 132-33; Mitchell, 230-31), in his *pathos* section in Galatians 4:12-20 (Mitchell, 227-30) and probably important in his letter to the Philippians (Mitchell, 233-36 and the numerous authors he cites).

Luke-Acts employs a great deal of friendship imagery (see Mitchell, 236-57). The matter of reciprocal obligation may inform some of these texts, for example, in the case of the friend at midnight (Lk 11:5-8). The centurion's friends act as his messengers (Lk 7:6), perhaps performing a favor in return for his benefactions (Lk 7:5) or acting as his clients (cf. Acts 10:7-8). The friends in view in Luke 15:6, 9, 29; 21:16 are one's equals; in Luke 14:12 they could be social peers but possibly clients (cf. Lk 14:10), as also in Acts 10:24, where relatives are likely dependents, given the social status of a Roman officer in the provinces (*see* Family and Household). In Luke 16:9 the friends in the context might be clients in some sense, but the emphasis is on networking with allies bound to one by reciprocal obligation (cf. Lk 16:5-7). Luke 23:12 clearly designates the friendship of political alliance. The accusation in Q that Jesus is friends with sinners (Mt 11:19 par. Lk 7:34) probably stems from Palestinian Jewish ideas about table fellowship (cf. Ps 1:1), but Greco-Roman readers of Luke might recognize how this practice (Lk 5:29; 15:1-2) could be shockingly misinterpreted in terms of a patron endorsing clients or a client sage teaching at banquets of the well-to-do. The Asiarchs may be Paul's patrons in some sense in Acts 19:31.

In Acts 2:44-47, the ancient context of friendship as sharing possessions, as equality and as patronage all provide part of the context. Although Acts 2:44-47 does not employ the term *friendship,* its emphasis on shared possessions would evoke for many Greek readers the ideal of friendship held by various other communities, at the same time challenging the usual expectation of reciprocity in ancient friendship. In contrast to the patronal model of friendship, higher-status members of Luke's audience are to use their possessions to provide benefaction without expecting reciprocation, even in honor (Lk 6:34-35; 14:12-14; Acts 20:35; Mitchell, 237-49; cf. perhaps Acts 27:3). Luke thus pushes the notion of equality in friendship further than traditions of patronage; Paul probably does the same (2 Cor 8:13-14). As in Roman party politics, those who share common allies also share common enemies (Jas 4:4).

The "friend of the bridegroom" in John 3:29 may represent a custom different from what we have discussed; many commentators relate this to the *shoshbin,* the best man of traditional Jewish weddings (e.g., Abrahams, 2:213; Dodd, 386). At least according to our later sources, the *shoshbins* of bride and groom functioned as witnesses in the wedding (*Deut. Rab.* 3:16), normally contributed financially to the wedding (Safrai, 757) and would be intimately concerned with the success of the wedding; thus, for example, the bride's *shoshbin* might have the evidence of her virginity (*Num. Rab.* 18:12). Some have linked the *shoshbin* with the marriage negotiator (Batey, 16-17). This may have been sometimes the case; agents *(šālîaḥîm)* often negotiated betrothals (e.g., *t. Yebam.* 4:4; *b. Qidd.* 43a; Romans also negotiated betrothals through intermediaries [Friedländer, 1:234]), and sometimes these agents were probably significant persons who might also fill a role in the wedding, which might fit the image of John the Baptist in this context (Jn 3:27-29) as one sent by God. (Three of the four tannaitic parables regarding a marriage broker present Moses as the intermediary between God and Israel; Johnston, 589.) But such agents were sometimes servants (e.g., *b. Giṭ* 23a), not likely to become *shoshbins.* When possible, a *shoshbin* of status even higher than that of the groom was preferred (*b. Yebam.* 63a).

We commented on the ideal of friends dying for one another in John 15:13-15 (§3 above), one of the most explicit friendship passages in the NT, and addressed this text in terms of both Greco-Roman and Jewish writers' comments on friendship with God (§4 above). Although the passage may depend partly on the idea of patronal friendship, the ancient ideals of loyalty, intimacy and sharing are more dominant. Jesus intimately shares the secrets of his heart with his disciples, treating them as friends as God treated Abraham and Moses by revealing himself to them. The parallels with John 16:13-15 indicate that the Spirit of truth would continue passing down the revelations from the Father and Jesus to the disciples, just as in Jesus' own ministry (Jn 5:20; 8:26). They are his friends and therefore objects of his self-sacrifice (Jn 15:13), if they do what he commands them (Jn 15:14). The paradoxical image of friends, not slaves, who obey Jesus' commandments is meant to jar the hearer to attention; friendship means not freedom to disobey but an intimate relationship that continues to recognize distinctions in authority. (Authority distinctions remained in patron-client relationships; at the same time Jesus' complete sharing with his disciples resembles the Greek notion of equality in friendships.) Disciples as Jesus' friends might stem from Jesus tradition (Lk 12:4, though stylistically a Lukan preference). It may have become a title for believers (3 Jn 15) as in some philosophical groups.

See also FAMILY AND HOUSEHOLD; MARRIAGE; PATRONAGE.

BIBLIOGRAPHY. I. Abrahams, *Studies in Pharisaism and the Gospels* (2d series; Cambridge: Cambridge University Press, 1924); D. L. Balch, "Political Friendship in the Historian Dionysius of Halicarnassus, *Roman Antiquities*," in *Greco-Roman Perspectives on Friendship*, ed. J. T. Fitzgerald (SBLRBS 34; Atlanta: Scholars Press, 1997) 123-44; R. A. Batey, *New Testament Nuptial Imagery* (Leiden: E. J. Brill, 1971); H. Conzelmann, *1 Corinthians: A Commentary on the First Epistle to the Corinthians*, ed. G. W. MacRae (Philadelphia: Fortress, 1975); A. Deissmann, *Light from the Ancient East* (Grand Rapids, MI: Baker, 1978 repr.); C. H. Dodd, *Historical Tradition in the Fourth Gospel* (Cambridge: Cambridge University Press, 1965); K. G. Evans, "Friendship in Greek Documentary Papyri and Inscriptions: A Survey," in *Greco-Roman Perspectives on Friendship*, ed. J. T. Fitzgerald (SBLRBS 34; Atlanta: Scholars Press, 1997) 181-202; B. Fiore, "The Theory and Practice of Friendship in Cicero," in *Greco-Roman Perspectives on Friendship*, ed. J. T. Fitzgerald (SBLRBS 34; Atlanta: Scholars Press, 1997) 59-76; J. T. Fitzgerald, "Friendship in the Greek World Prior to Aristotle," in *Greco-Roman Perspectives on Friendship*, ed. J. T. Fitzgerald (SBLRBS 34; Atlanta: Scholars Press, 1997a) 13-34; idem, "Introduction," in *Greco-Roman Perspectives on Friendship*, ed. J. T. Fitzgerald (SBLRBS 34; Atlanta: Scholars Press, 1997b) 1-11; L. Friedländer, *Roman Life and Manners Under the Early Empire* (4 vols.; New York: Barnes & Noble; E. P. Dutton & Company, 1907-13); J. G. Gager, *Moses in Greco-Roman Paganism* (SBLMS 16; Nashville: Abingdon for SBL, 1972); T. Gould, *Platonic Love* (London: Routledge & Kegan Paul, 1963); M. Hadas, trans., *Aristeas to Philocrates: Letter of Aristeas* (New York: Harper & Brothers for The Dropsie College for Hebrew and Cognate Learning, 1951); M. Hengel, *The Atonement: The Origins of the Doctrine in the New Testament* (Philadelphia: Fortress, 1981); R. F. Hock, "An Extraordinary Friend in Chariton's *Callirhoe:* The Importance of Friendship in the Greek Romances," in *Greco-Roman Perspectives on Friendship*, ed. J. T. Fitzgerald (SBLRBS 34; Atlanta: Scholars Press, 1997) 145-62; G. H. R. Horsley, *New Documents Illustrating Early Christianity* (North Ryde, N.S.W.: Ancient History Documentary Center, Macquarie University, 1987) 4:17-18, §3; L. Jacobs, "Greater Love Hath No Man . . . The Jewish Point of View of Self-Sacrifice," *Judaism* 6 (1957) 41-47; R. M. Johnston, "Parabolic Interpretations Attributed to Tannaim" (Ph.D. diss., Hartford Seminary Foundation, 1977); D. Konstan, "Patrons and Friends," *CP* 90 (1995) 328-42; P. Marshall, *Enmity in Corinth: Social Conventions in Paul's Relations with the Corinthians* (Tübingen: Mohr Siebeck, 1987); W. A. Meeks, *The First Urban Christians: The Social World of the Apostle Paul* (New Haven, CT: Yale University Press, 1983); J. Meyshan, "Jewish Coins in Ancient Historiography: The Importance of Numismatics for the History of Israel," *PEQ* 96 (1964) 46-52; A. C. Mitchell, "'Greet the Friends by Name': New Testament Evidence for the Greco-Roman *Topos* on Friendship," in *Greco-Roman Perspectives on Friendship*, ed. J. T. Fitzgerald (SBLRBS 34; Atlanta: Scholars Press, 1997) 225-62; W. O. E. Oesterley, *The Jewish Background of the Christian Liturgy* (Oxford: Clarendon Press, 1925); E. N. O'Neil, "Plutarch on Friendship," in *Greco-Roman Perspectives on Friendship*, ed. J. T. Fitzgerald (SBLRBS 34; Atlanta: Scholars Press, 1997) 105-22; R. I. Pervo, "With Lucian: Who Needs Friends? Friendship in the *Toxaris*," in *Greco-Roman Perspectives on Friendship*, ed. J. T. Fitzgerald (SBLRBS 34; Atlanta: Scholars Press, 1997) 163-80; S. Safrai, "Home and Family," in *The Jewish People in the First Century: Historical Geography, Political History, Social, Cultural and Religious Life and Institutions*, ed. S. Safrai and M. Stern (2 vols.; CRINT 1; Assen: Van Gorcum; Philadelphia: Fortress, 1974, 1976) 2:728-92; F. M. Schroeder, "Friendship in Aristotle and Some Peripatetic Philosophers," in *Greco-Roman Perspectives on Friendship*, ed. J. T. Fitzgerald (SBLRBS 34; Atlanta: Scholars Press, 1997) 35-57; J. N. Sevenster, *Paul and Seneca* (NovTSup 4; Leiden: E. J. Brill, 1961); R. K. Sherk, ed., *The Roman Empire: Augustus to Hadrian* (TDGR 6; New York: Cambridge University Press, 1988); A. N. Sherwin-White, *Roman Society and Roman Law in the New Testament* (Grand Rapids, MI: Baker, 1978 repr.); G. E. Sterling, "The Bond of Humanity: Friendship in Philo of Alexandria," in *Greco-Roman Per-*

spectives on Friendship, ed. J. T. Fitzgerald (SBLRBS 34; Atlanta: Scholars Press, 1997) 203-23; S. K. Stowers, *Letter Writing in Greco-Roman Antiquity* (LEC 5; Philadelphia: Westminster, 1986); J. C. Thom, "'Harmonious Equality': The *Topos* of Friendship in Neo-Pythagorean Writings," in *Greco-Roman Perspectives on Friendship,* ed. J. T. Fitzgerald (SBLRBS 34; Atlanta: Scholars Press, 1997) 77-103.

C. S. Keener

G

GALATIA, GALATIANS

Who are the addressees of Paul's letter to the Galatians and where precisely do they live—in North Galatia, in and around Ankara and Pessinus, or in South Galatia, where Paul and Barnabas are said to have established churches in Pisidian *Antioch, Iconium, Lystra and Derbe on the so-called first missionary journey? This question of NT introduction has been practically unresolvable during the past century, and with some exceptions (Breytenbach, Scott, Strobel), there has been little fresh work on the subject in recent years. As a result, NT scholars tend either to repeat older answers to the question, which have hardened into dogmas, or to deny the significance of the question.

At first sight, the question of the addressees of Galatians may seem of merely antiquarian interest for those who specialize in minutiae. Upon closer examination, however, its answer has potentially significant theological ramifications. For if the South Galatian hypothesis is correct, then Galatians may be the earliest Pauline letter, written perhaps soon after the apostolic council. In that case, the remarkable similarities between Galatians and Romans—possibly the latest Pauline letter—would render the supposition of a major development in Paul's theology improbable. If the North Galatian hypothesis is correct, then the similarity between Galatians and Romans may be explained by their having been written within a relatively short period of time of one another, toward the end of Paul's career.

Traditionally, the question of the Galatian addressees has been discussed almost exclusively from the perspective of historical geography, based on Greco-Roman sources. A possible Jewish background has not been considered, despite the fact that Paul's letter to the Galatians is thoroughly Jewish in its argumentation.

1. Greco-Roman Background
2. Jewish Background

1. Greco-Roman Background.

1.1. Hellenistic Galatia. In 278 B.C., three tribes of Gauls from Europe migrated across the Hellespont and eventually settled in central *Asia Minor in a region that was called Galatia, containing tribal capitals in Pessinus, Ancyra and Tavium. The name *Galatians,* or *Gauls, (Galatai)* applied to Celts wherever they happened to live in Europe or Asia Minor.

When Attalus of Pergamum conquered the Galatians in about 230 B.C., they were considered "the most formidable and warlike nation in Asia" (Polybius *Hist.* 18.41.7), known for barbarian lawlessness (Polybius *Hist.* 3.3.5; 21.40.1; *Anth. Gr.* 7.492; *Sib. Or.* 3.599-600). Hence, the Attalids celebrated the containment of the Gauls to central Anatolia as a victory of Hellenic civilization over barbarianism.

Despite this resounding defeat, the Galatians continued to enjoy autonomy and even regained some of their previous formidability in the first century B.C., when they fought on the side of Rome against Mithridates VI of Pontus (95-63). The Romans rewarded the Galatians by adding large tracts of territory to their land (63-36). By the beginning of the *Roman Empire under Augustus (*see* Roman Emperors), the Galatian client king of the Romans, Amyntas, ruled all of central Anatolia, his kingdom reaching even to the Mediterranean.

1.2. Roman Galatia. When Amyntas was killed during a campaign against the Homonades in 25 B.C., most of his kingdom was annexed by Augustus and became the Roman province of Galatia. At this time, the province included not only the original area of Galatian settlement in and around Pessinus, Ancyra and Tavium, but also much of eastern Phrygia, Lycaonia, Isauria, Pisidia and Pamphylia (cf. *TAVO* B V 7). Subsequent additions between 6 B.C. and A.D. 4 included Paphlagonia to the north and the Pontic regions to the northeast.

Regardless of the shifting boundaries of the Roman province, the composite whole was still called Galatia (cf., e.g., *CIG* 3991; *ILS* 9499). It is far less certain, however, whether the name *Galatian* was likewise applied to all inhabitants of the province, including those in South Galatia. That would be a reasonable inference perhaps, but examples of this usage are almost wholly lacking. C. Breytenbach argues, therefore, that the name *Galatian* applies to any and all ethnic Galatians and that documentary evidence shows their presence in the southern portion of the Roman province. On this view, Galatians 3:1 ("you foolish Galatians") is addressed to these ethnic Galatians, despite the fact that such people would have composed only a tiny minority in the mixed population of South Galatia and therefore also only a small part of the churches in Antioch, Iconium, Lystra and Derbe.

We should not be surprised that "Galatian" could be used both in a strict sense and in a more inclusive sense. Recent research on ethnicity has shown the widespread phenomenon of identity switching and situational ethnicity, whereby people can often claim membership in several different ethnic groups according to the relevance of the particular traditions available (cf. Hackstein). This potential variability sometimes leads to difficulties when it comes to describing ethnic groups between the two poles of tribal and state organization.

Future studies of the possible Greco-Roman background of Paul's use of "Galatia" and "Galatians" will also need to consider the vocative in Galatians 3:1 in light of other insults and plural ethnics in the Greek address system (cf. Dickey).

2. Jewish Background.

2.1. Jewish Geography and Ethnography. The fundamental point of departure for Jewish conceptions of *geography and ethnography is Genesis 10 (cf. 1 Chron 1), which gives a list of Noah's descendants who spread abroad on the earth after the flood and established nations (Scott; *see* Geographical Perspectives in Late Antiquity). During the Second Temple period, this tradition was greatly expanded to include, for example, not only a descriptive geography of the world that was divided among the three sons of Noah (*Jub.* 8:11—9:15), but also the contemporary Greco-Roman equivalents for the biblical nations listed in Genesis 10 (Josephus *Ant.* 1.5 §§120-47). As in later *rabbinic literature, Josephus gives these equivalents in terms of Roman provinces.

2.2. Josephus's Identification of Gomer with the Galatians. In his exposition of the biblical table of nations, Josephus explains that the sons of Japheth originally gave their own names to the nations that they founded but that the Greeks changed the names. He illustrates this point beginning with Gomer, the first son of Japheth (Josephus *Ant.* 1.6.1 §§123, 126): "Thus, those whom the Greeks now call Galatians were named Gomarites, having been founded by Gomar. . . . Gomar had three sons, of whom Aschanaxes founded the Aschanaxians, whom the Greeks now call Rheginians, Riphathes the Riphataeans—the modern Paphlagonians—and Thugrames the Thugramaeans, whom the Greeks thought good to call Phyrgians." When Josephus identifies Riphathes (biblical Riphath), the second son of Gomer (Gen 10:3), with the Paphlagonians, he betrays a conception of the extent of Galatia that postdates 6/5 B.C., when Paphlagonia was incorporated into the Roman province. It seems, therefore, that by identifying the Gomerites with the contemporary Galatians (*Galatai*), Josephus refers to all the inhabitants of the Roman province of Galatia as Galatians. If this is correct, then Josephus provides additional support for the South Galatian hypothesis.

See also ASIA MINOR; GEOGRAPHICAL PERSPECTIVES IN LATE ANTIQUITY.

BIBLIOGRAPHY. C. Breytenbach, *Paulus und Barnabas in der Provinz Galatien: Studien zu Apostelgeschichte 13f.; 16,6; 18,23 und den Adressaten des Galaterbriefes* (AGJU 38; Leiden: E. J. Brill, 1996); W. M. Calder and S. Mitchell, "Galatia," *OCD* (3d ed., 1996) 621; E. Dickey, *Greek Forms of Address: From Herodotus to Lucian* (Oxford: Oxford University Press, 1996); K. Hackstein, "Situative Ethnizität und das Kartieren ethnischer Gruppen im Vorderen Orient," in *Von der Quelle zur Karte: Abschlußbuch des Sonderforschungsbereichs "Tübinger Atlas des Vorderen Orients,"* ed. Wolfgang Röllig (Weinheim: VCH/Acta humaniora, 1991) 217-27; G. W. Hansen, "Galatia," in *The Book of Acts in Its Greco-Roman Setting,* ed. D. W. J. Gill and C. Gempf (BAFCS 2; Grand Rapids, MI: Eerdmans, 1994) 377-95; idem, "Galatians, Letter to the," *DPL,* 323-

34; S. Mitchell, *Anatolia: Land, Men and Gods in Asia Minor* (2 vols.; Oxford: Clarendon Press, 1993); idem, "Galatia," *ABD* 2:870-72; idem, "Population and the Land in Roman Galatia," in *ANRW* 2.7.2 (1980) 1053-81; H. D. Rankin, *Celts and the Classical World* (London: Croom Helm, 1987); J. M. Scott, *Geography in Early Judaism and Christianity: The Book of Jubilees* (SNTSMS; Cambridge: Cambridge University Press, forthcoming); idem, *Paul and the Nations: The Old Testament and Jewish Background of Paul's Mission to the Nations with Special Reference to the Destination of Galatians* (WUNT 84; Tübingen: Mohr Siebeck, 1995); R. K. Sherk, "Roman Galatia: The Governors from 25 B.C. to A.D. 114," in *ANRW* 2.7.2 (1980) 954-1052; K. Strobel, *Die Galater: Geschichte und Eigenart der keltischen Staatenbildung auf dem Boden des hellenistischen Kleinasien*, 1: *Untersuchungen zur Geschichte und historischen Geographie des hellenistischen und römischen Kleinasien I* (Berlin: Akademie Verlag, 1996); R. Syme, *Anatolica: Studies in Strabo*, ed. Anthony Birley (Oxford: Clarendon Press, 1995); *TAVO* B V 7, "Östlicher Mittel-meerraum und Mesopotamien: Die Neuordnung des Orients von Pompeius bis Augustus (67 v. Chr.–14 n. Chr.)" (Wiesbaden: Reichert, 1992).

J. M. Scott

GALILEE

We derive the name *Galilee* historically from the Hebrew word for "area" or "region" *(gālîl)*. Specifically Galilee is the northernmost mountain region of Canaan and Israel. It displayed dense and lush vegetation in antiquity, including forests of Mt. Tabor oak, styrax, terebinth, carob, hawthorn, wild olive, wild fig, arbutus, bay laurel, myrtle, caper, sumac and lentisk. Wild game abounded in the Galilee, including the fox, hare, boar, roe deer and a species of chukar.

1. Topography
2. History of Galilee from Herod to the End of the Second Century A.D.
3. Roads
4. Products of Galilee
5. Social Structures and Economics
6. Synagogues and Ritual Purity
7. Sepphoris as Chief City of Galilee

1. Topography.

Topographically Galilee includes upper Galilee and lower Galilee, the northern and southern halves of the area. Upper Galilee reaches upward just short of 4,000 feet above sea level, while lower Galilee extends upward to nearly 2,000 feet above sea level. The boundary between upper and lower Galilee reaches westward from Chorazin to Acco-Ptolemais. Upper Galilee receives in excess of 42 inches of rainfall per year, while lower Galilee gets as much as 36 inches of rainfall in the same period, while the parts of lower Galilee on the western shores of the lake seldom receive 20 inches per year. Upper Galilee is formed of a single mountain, called Jebel Jarmaq in Arabic and Har Meron in Hebrew. We do not know its biblical name. A series of east-west valleys cut between low ridges comprise lower Galilee. Two of the best known of these valleys are the Beit Netopha Valley north of ancient Sepphoris and the Tur'an Valley east of the Beit Netopha with the Horns of Hattin, an extinct volcano, at its eastern end. A single, isolated high hill or mountain dominates the southeast corner of lower Galilee near the Sea of Galilee. This is Mt. Tabor, which is 1,929 feet high. This is the traditional site of the transfiguration.

The natural boundaries of the whole of Galilee are the Mediterranean Sea on the west, the Plain of Jezreel on the south and the Sea of Galilee (also known as Lake Tiberias) on the east. There is no natural boundary to the north until the deep gorge of the River Litani in Lebanon. Its political boundary to the north has varied, but in the NT period it included Lake Huleh in the Huleh Valley, avoiding Roman Cadasa (OT Kedesh), then ran south and west to exclude the coastal territory of Phoenicia. Phoenicia included the coastal cities of Tyre, Ecdippa (OT Akhzib), Acco-Ptolemais, Sycamenum (at Mt. Carmel) and Dor. The Sea of Galilee is 8 miles across and 12.8 miles long. It is the largest freshwater lake in the region and a major landmark as well as the focus of Jesus' ministry.

2. History of Galilee from Herod to the End of the Second Century A.D.

Archaeology demonstrates that Galilee was a favorite place of habitation from earliest times because of its climate favorable to the early agriculture and because of its rich grasses for pasturage. Neanderthal skeletons have appeared in early occupation of caves near Nazareth. The great tell or city-mound of Khirbet Kerak on the southwestern shores of the Sea of Galilee exhibits Canaanite occupation as early as 2600 B.C. But it was the so-called Amorite waves of occupation beginning about 2000 B.C.

that brought the main Canaanite occupants to Galilee. Some of the cities of this time in Galilee included Megiddo, Hazor, Kedesh and Acco. Subsequently, in the fifteenth century B.C., when Pharoah Thut-Mosis II invaded Canaan, he listed fourteen Canaanite cities in Galilee that he subdued.

The Israelite conquest and settlement finds the tribes of Asher, Naphtali, Issachar and Zebulun within the limits of Galilee. Asher occupied the old territory of the Phoenicians. Naphtali to the east included cities such as Kedesh and Chinnereth on the northwest shore of the Sea of Galilee. In the OT more than forty sites of upper and lower Galilee appear in the text. The best-known are Hannathon, Rama, Gath-Hepher and Hazor.

In 733 B.C. Tiglath Pileser III, king of Assyria, conquered all of Judah and Israel, including Galilee. He lists eleven cities of Galilee that he destroyed, including Hazor, Hannathon and finally Megiddo at the western end of the Plain of Jezreel. All of Galilee down to and including the Jezreel Plain became the Assyrian province of Megiddo, named after the city he understood to be the greatest in the district. This almost depopulated province in turn became part of the Babylonian Empire, the successor to the Assyrians.

The sharpest turn for the better came in 539 B.C. when Cyrus, king of Persia, conquered Babylon and took control of the entire Babylonian Empire. According to the Greek *historian Herodotus, all of Palestine *(Palaistinē)* belonged to the Fifth Satrapy of the Persian Empire (Herodotus *Hist.* 3.86).

We hear little of Galilee until the Maccabean period. Simon Maccabeus moved men and materiel into Galilee in order to fight the Gentiles who were threatening to annihilate the Jewish population (1 Macc 4:15, 5:21; *see* 1 and 2 Maccabees). He rescued the Jews of Arbata (Narbate) in lower Galilee and brought them to Jerusalem in 163 B.C. Nineteen years later, in 144 B.C., the Jewish king Jonathan Maccabaeus defeated Demetrius I, the *Seleucid ruler of Palestine, at Hazor in Galilee. Jonathan chased the Syrian Greek army all the way to Cadasa and captured their camp. Jonathan did not rule over Galilee after this feat, for we only read that John Hyrcanus considered Galilee part of the Jewish kingdom before his death in 135 B.C. (*see* Hasmoneans). The Jewish king Aristobulus in 104 to 103 B.C. (his one-year reign) added upper Galilee to the kingdom. His brother Alexander Janneus, who consolidated his hold on the Galilee and on Gaulantis across the Jordan and across the Sea of Galilee, succeeded Aristobulus. This was the Galilee that the Roman forces would know when they entered the land to lay siege to *Jerusalem in 63 B.C.

The boundaries of Roman Galilee or NT Galilee include the Sea of Galilee and Luke Huleh in the east. The boundary extends southwest from Lake Huleh south of Cadasa, then bends back southeast to an east-west line drawn west from just north of Chorazin. This line advances to within 7 miles of the coastline at Acco-Ptolemais, then turns south about 17 miles at a point west of Sepphoris to turn again to the west, crossing Mt. Carmel so as to include Geba in Galilee. The Great Jezreel Plain, called the Esdraelon in Greek, was now separated from Galilee. West of Galilee lay the independent Greek cities of Geba and Acco-Ptolemais, former Phoenician territory.

NT Galilee was 31 miles west to east, including the Sea of Galilee, measuring from the first milestone at the territory of Acco-Ptolemais but not including the latter territory, which was considered to be Phoenician. From north to south Galilee was somewhat larger, extending from the southeastern hills north of Scythopolis-Beth Shean 43 miles to its northernmost point near Cadasa. This oddly shaped region has an area of about 730 square miles.

The Roman administrator Gabinius saw in 55 B.C. that the province of Palestine needed civil administration (*see* Roman Administration). He set up Galilee, with Sepphoris as its chief city, as one of these districts. Gabinius gave an administrative council or a *synedrion* to Sepphoris (Josephus *Ant.* 14.5.4 §91; *J.W.* 1.8.5 §170). *Herod (later known as Herod the Great), the younger son of the procurator Antipater the Idumean, governed Galilee. Herod fled to *Rome during the Parthian invasion of 40 B.C., returning as the appointee of the Roman senate and of Augustus (*see* Roman Emperors) to be king of Judea, an appointment conditioned on his successful prosecution of the civil war and the imposition of order.

Galilee became part of the stage for a bitter civil war waged by Herod against Antigonus, who had accepted appointment as ruler by the Parthians. Herod had adopted Sepphoris as his capital and chief residence in the north, keeping a garrison of soldiers there and an armory for weapons and armor. By 37 B.C. Herod had killed the last rebels at the caves of Arbela north of Tiberias and consolidated his power (Josephus *Ant.* 14.15.4 §414; *J.W.* 1.16.2 §304).

During his long reign Herod administrated the whole of his kingdom in five districts. Galilee was one of these districts. Three or four toparchies formed the civil administration of Galilee under Herod: Tiberias, Tracheae (which was otherwise known as Magdala), Sepphoris and perhaps Araba.

At the death of Herod, Judah ben Hezekiah led some citizens of Sepphoris in revolt, perhaps hoping for independent status after long years as Herod's capital (Josephus *Ant.* 17.10.9 §289; *J.W.* 2.4.1 §56). Instead the Roman governor Varus retaliated with great force, destroying the city and killing the men, selling its women and children as slaves (*see* Roman Governors of Palestine). Herod Antipas, the new tetrarch, ordered the razed city rebuilt as a Roman city, building it as the "ornament of all Galilee," according to Josephus (*Ant.* 18.2.1 §27). Later, when the city had passed to the hegemony of Herod Antipas, the same Judah ben Hezekiah plundered weapons and money from Sepphoris (Josephus *Ant.* 17.10.5 §271; *J.W.* 2.5.1 §68). Herod Antipas ruled Galilee and Perea, two separated parts of his father's kingdom.

Fewer then ten cities and towns of Galilee figure in the ministry of Jesus. Jesus was reared at Nazareth, according to the Gospels. After his baptism at the hands of John he moved his headquarters to Capernaum on the northwest shores of the Sea of Galilee. From that vantage he visited the cities and towns of Cana, perhaps Gennesaret, Nain (in the Jezreel Valley), Gergesa (or Gadara or Garasa, a town on the east shore of the Sea of Galilee) and Bethsaida of Golanitis (the territory of his half-brother Herod Philip) and apparently Chorazin. Notably absent in this list are Sepphoris and Tiberias. At both these cities Herod Antipas ("that fox," according to Jesus) had palaces built, and it is possible that Jesus was staying away from an unnecessary conflict with Antipas. We know of Magdala only as the city of Mary Magdalene in the Gospels.

Galilee apparently played different roles in the two devastating revolts against Rome, the first in A.D. 66 to 70 and the second in A.D. 135 (*see* Jewish Wars with Rome). During the first revolt Galilee formed one military command under the leadership of the general *Josephus, later known as a historian. Vespasian, the Roman commander sent by the emperor Nero, marched south from Tyre to Acco-Ptolemais and set up a headquarters. From there he routed any Jewish defenders in Galilee on his way eastward to Sepphoris. The city fathers of Sepphoris met him in the field and declared their loyalty to Rome and their abhorrence of the revolt, petitioning Vespasian for a garrison to protect them from their more warlike neighbors (Josephus *J.W.* 3.2.4 §§30-34; *Life* 74 §411). Josephus and the few defenders he could gather entered Jotapata in the mountains about 10 miles north of Sepphoris. Vespasian besieged the city for forty-seven days, then took it in a fearsome slaughter. He discovered Josephus, arrested him and saved him for later. After the surrender of Tiberias and the defeat of the Jewish rebels in a pitched battle on the Sea of Galilee, Vespasian had secured Galilee and needed only to march to Jerusalem to prosecute the siege there and finally at Masada. He accomplished both sieges successfully.

After the first revolt the Romans added Galilee to a new independent province, the governor of whom was of senatorial rank and a former praetor. The authorities also stationed the Tenth Legion, the Fretensis ("Ironsides") on the ruins of Jerusalem. Vespasian gave Sepphoris special status because of its peace stance during the revolt by handing over to Sepphoris the toparchy of Araba. Vespasian thereby doubled its city territory.

Galilee scarcely took part in the Bar Kochba revolt of A.D. 131 to 135. Bar Kochba (*see* Simon bar Kosiba) tried to involve the Galileans, but perhaps the memories of A.D. 66 to 70 burned too brightly. Galilee seems to have mainly stayed quiet, although tunnels in which Jews hid during the revolt have been discovered. It was after the revolt, perhaps after A.D. 160, that Sepphoris became known by its Greek name, Diocaesarea.

3. Roads.

There was a highly developed, local trade network in Galilee upon which the citizens of Galilee transported goods and services. Lower Galilee was outlined by (1) a major road that traversed lower Galilee from Acco-Ptolemais to Sepphoris and from there to Tiberias. Nine milestones of the second century A.D. and later are known between Acco-Ptolemais and Tiberias. (2) From Tiberias a Roman road led south on the western shores of the Sea of Galilee and from there to Scythopolis-Beth Shean. Nine milestones are known between Tiberias and Scythopolis-Beth Shean. (3) From Scythopolis-Beth Shean a major road of the second century departs west and a little north to a site called today Khirbet Ladd. At Khirbet Ladd this road turns southwest to Legio-Capercotani in the western Jezreel Valley. This is where the Roman authorities stationed the Sixth Legion in the second century. In this track of about 21 miles there are at least fifteen Roman milestones. (4) A major second-century Roman road leads north and a little west from Legio-Capercotani to Acco-Ptolemais. Seven Roman milestones are known from this road. (5) To the north nearly on the border between upper and lower Galilee there was a Roman road that could be followed from Bethsaida-Julias to Acco-Ptolemais 24 miles to the west.

Other roads inherited from the time of the united monarchy also play their part in Galilean trade. Two of the main roads were on the coast from Jokneam to Acco-Ptolemais, from there to Achzib and Tyre; and in the interior, from Mt. Tabor to Roman Kefar Hittaia or a point nearby, then east to the Sea of Galilee, then north via Chinnereth to the north. In upper Galilee one finds seven "local and lateral roads," most of which run east and west. One of these roads runs from Acco-Ptolemais to Tell Keisan and from there southeast to the west end of the Beit Netopha Valley. This happens to be the course of the major Roman road from Acco to Sepphoris. In other words, the Romans used a venerable track to move men and material in this area.

From the west end of the Beit Netopha Valley one walked a road eastward to Rimmon and thence south and east toward the south end of the Sea of Galilee. About 4 miles east of Rimmon the road also forks north to Kefar Hittaia and east to the lake. Despite this impressive number of Iron Age roads, Iron Age lower Galilee is traversed by fewer roads on the maps than is upper Galilee.

4. Products of Galilee.

The trade network made it possible for villages to specialize in a single product. The villages of Shikhin, Kefar Hananiah and Nahf (to give their modern names) produced pottery vessels. This is both a literary and an archaeological fact. Certain villages were wheat production centers: the plain of Arbela and therefore the town of Arbela and Kefar Hittaia ("Village of Wheat") about 3 miles west and a little south of Arbela, Hukkok 6 miles west of Capernaum, and Chorazin, which is about 2 miles north and a little west of Capernaum. The *Talmud of Jerusalem speaks of the wheat of Sepphoris and the wheat of Tiberias (*y. B. Qam.* 6D), which suggests that Tiberias and Sepphoris were central markets for wheat.

We find archaeological and literary evidence for agricultural products such as figs, pomegranates, olives and oil pressing, flax, barley, fresh, pickled and dried fish, herbs, greens, cattle, and sheep and goat products, but also for finished products made from agricultural products, such as cloth, clothing, dye stuffs, basketry, furniture, breads and perfumes.

Winepresses are to be found on many hilltops in lower Galilee. Wine manufacture, storage and shipment is one of the most important industries of the Galilee. We have the names of at least seven villages and cities that were involved in the wine industry in some fashion: Sepphoris, Tiberias, Kefar Sogane, Sallamin, Acchabaron, Beth Shearim and Gennesaret (Josephus *J.W.* 3.3.3 §45; 3.10.8 §519; *m. Menaḥ.* 8:6; *y. Meg.* 72D; *Eccl. Rab.* 3:3, *m. Kil.* 4:4 [Salmin]; *b. ʿAbod. Zar.* 30A [Acchabaron]). Furthermore the name of the Valley of Beth Ha-Kerem ("House of the Vineyard") and the village of the same name in that valley implies that wine production was its major industry.

A discovery at Hefzibah in the Beth Shean Valley revealed a set of Greek inscriptions recording the correspondence between Antiochus III the Great (223-187 B.C.), the Seleucid Greek ruler, and a certain Ptolemaios, the strategos or local owner and governor of a huge estate near Beth Shean. Ptolemaios was de facto if not de jure a ruler of his estate, which included villages. Such land ownership also in Galilee may be presupposed in Josephus and in the NT. Note that Herod the Great did not favor owners of large estates.

Archaeological surveys of the Galilee confirm that large farmhouses, presumably of wealthy landowners, dot the landscape, but so do small farmhouses. The survey of Khirbet Buraq in *Samaria, which should be comparable to a town of that size in Galilee, has suggested that seventy families farmed 445 acres, which gives us 6.3 acres per family. It is possible that there may be farmers on small farms so small that those plots will not support a family for a full year. If so, then these farmers were the source for agricultural laborers or skilled workers for at least part of the year.

5. Social Structures and Economics.

It is important to know that *women produced many products in their homes and by their own hands. These products included those produced by weaving, dying, sewing and spinning. These would be clothing and cloth stuffs. The most formidable economic activity was that of villages and cities. We can find literary or archaeological evidence for the following productions: pottery (see above), glass vessels, raw glass production, fish, caravans, shipping (on the Sea of Galilee), drying, pickling and salting of fish and other commodities, weaving, fast-food production in cities at taverns, masonry, carpentry, digging of cisterns and tombs, stone vessel production for ritual purity, and clothing. In addition one found shopkeepers, agricultural workers, bakers, courts with judges, bailiffs and guards, bankers and moneychangers, and coin minting in Sepphoris and Tiberias.

There is reason to believe that the social structure was organized more or less by wealth and by position of birth. At the apex of the social structure were to be found the elites (the "rich," or *plousios*, Mk 12:16-21), many of whom were Herod's retainers. We also find absentee landlords (*kyrios*, Mk 12:1-12 par. Mt 21:33-46), owners of estates (*kyrios*, Mt 25:14-30), major importer/exporters or merchants (*emporos*, Mt 13:45-46), a chief tax collector (*architelōnēs*, Lk 19:1-10) and the judge (*kritēs*, Mt 5:25).

In a much larger middle stratum of society one found the following: the professional scribe (*grammateus*, Mt 2:4), the teacher (*didaskalos*, Mt 8:19), the lawyer (*nomikos*, Mt 22:34-40), the hand worker, mason, carpenter or cooper (*tektōn*, Mt 13:55), the shopkeeper, the family farmer, the banker or moneychanger (*trapezitēs*, Mt 25:27), fisherman (*halieus*, Mt 4:18-22), tax collector (*telōnēs*, Lk 18:9-14), foreman (*epitropos*, Mt 20:1-16; the owner of the vineyard calls his *epitropos*, perhaps related to the *oikonomos* of Lk 16:1-8), the money lender (*daneistēs*, Lk 7:41-43), the master of a household (*oikodespotēs*), the manager of a household or steward (*oikonomos*, Lk 12:42-46; 16:1-8), the ironsmith, coppersmith, silversmith or goldsmith. To these one may add from other sources, whose status we do not know, the caravaneer, peddler, charcoal maker, lime maker, tanner, leather worker, soldier, healer, exorcist, physician, herbalist, and actors and entertainers.

At the bottom of the social structure in terms of wealth and birth, as well as in terms of historical circumstances, one found the following: the tenant farmer (*geōrgos*, Mk 12:1 par. Mt 21:33-41), day worker (*misthios*, literally "wage earner" or "hired worker," Lk 15:11-32 [vv. 17, 19, 21]), agricultural worker, reaper (*theristēs*, Mt 13:24-30 only), guard for a prison (*hyperetēs*, Mt 5:25), shepherd for sheep and goats (*poimēn*, Mt 9:36), slave child (*pais*, Lk 12:35-48, Mt 24:45-51, not used in Mark; see Lk 15:11-32, where the elder brother calls one of these to ask what is going on), slave (*doulos*, e.g., Mt 13:24-30), beggar (*prosaitēs*, Jn 9:8), thief (*kleptēs*, Jn 12:6), the sick (*lepros*, leper), the poor (*ptōchos*, jobless [?] Lk 14:16-24; Mt 22:1-14), the prostitute (*pornē*, Mt 21:31-32) and the rebel or bandit (*lēstēs*, Mt 27:38).

6. Synagogues and Ritual Purity.

The old description of Galilee as predominantly Gentile (Is 9:1, "Galilee of the Gentiles") or heterodox Jewish can no longer be sustained. Housing and public structures would resemble those almost anywhere in the empire, but this does not in and of itself imply Gentilization of Galilee. These are owner-built homes of native materials, namely, stone covered with lime and clay plaster.

Public buildings in Sepphoris and Tiberias, not to mention Taricheae-Magdala, stand as metaphors for Roman dominance and the process of *Hellenization. Such buildings would include basilicas, *theaters, amphitheaters or *circuses, hippodromes, city gates, forums or agora, and the like. The Galileans decorated the facades of their buildings in high stone relief with floral and other decorations. The low-relief geometric and floral decorations of the Second Temple did not yet appear in lower Galilee. This bespeaks the Galilean participation in the wider *Roman Empire but does imply that they had become assimilated, to use a modern term, or Hellenized, to use the scholarly term.

As another example, a few buildings in the Galilee have been identified as *synagogues.

These are at Capernaum (beneath the white limestone synagogue) and at Magdala. Outside of Galilee other first-century synagogues are known from Gamala, Masada, Herodium and at Herod's palace at Jericho. In addition there are about twenty synagogue sites in upper and lower Galilee dated from the middle of the third century A.D. These buildings of the first and third centuries have one constant architectural feature, namely, the habit to place a row of columns between the benches against the walls and the central worship space.

Roman custom is to place rows of columns behind the backs of gathered spectators or participants in a *bouleutērion* or in an *ecclēsiastērion,* or even in a theater. Perhaps the synagogue buildings reflect the temple forecourts in Jerusalem. Josephus explains that the inner courts of the temple were adorned with colonnades or cloisters. Thus the Court of Women, the Court of Israel and the Court of the Priests would all present this feature. (Josephus *J.W.* 5.5.2 §200). This feature is omitted in Samaritan synagogues and two Judean broadhouses.

Another ritual installation found in Galilee are Jewish ritual baths beneath the floors of houses or nearby at Sepphoris, Jotapata, Khirbet Shema, Meiron, and other Galilean sites. These commonly are dated by the excavators to the first centuries B.C. and A.D. Ritual baths meet the demand for ritual purity.

Another item of the early Roman Jewish world was a class of soft, white stone vessels that appear in no fewer than sixty-five sites all over ancient Palestine. At least fourteen of these sites are in upper and lower Galilee (Gush Halav, Nabratein, Meiron, Kefar Hananya, Capernaum, Yodfat, Ibelin, Kefar Kenna, Sepphoris, Reina, Nazareth, Bethlehem of Galilee, Migdal Ha-Emeq and Tiberias). A site for the manufacture of these vessels has been found at Reina, about 6 kilometers north of Nazareth.

The design of these vessels meets the requirements of the laws of purity. They seem to be distinctively Jewish, as they only superficially resemble the marble vessels well known in the Roman world. They are both handmade and made by turning on a lathe. They include "measuring cups" with one and sometimes two handles, and a square bowl with ledge handles under the rims. Others, which were turned on a lathe, include large, barrel-shaped vessels with a pedestal base and no handles and small cups or chalices with no handles. The large, lathe-turned vessels play a role in the pericope of the turning of water into wine at Cana of Galilee (Jn 2:6).

Two of the cities of Galilee minted their own *coins, namely, Sepphoris and Tiberias. The city coins of Tiberias honor the emperor Tiberius and feature his portrait nearly from the beginnings of minting coins in that Galilean city. Yet the coins of Herod Antipas, the ethnarch of Galilee and of Perea, and the city coins of Sepphoris and Tiberias minted by Antipas, lack a ruler's portrait on their obverse (Rosenberger, 3:60; Meshorer 1982: 35-41, 242-43, 279, pl. 6; Meshorer 1990-1991: 108, pl. 25).

7. Sepphoris as Chief City of Galilee.

Sepphoris was known as an important walled town from the first year of the reign of Alexander Yannai when Ptolemy Lathrus of Egypt besieged it unsuccessfully on a *sabbath (106 B.C.; Josephus *Ant.* 13.12.5 §338). The fact that Ptolemy made war on a sabbath suggests that he knew the inhabitants were Jewish. Excavation shows that there was an impressive city of the late Hellenistic period at Sepphoris. Housing of the second century B.C. to the first century A.D. reveals ritual baths beneath their floors, attesting to their Jewishness. Fragments of stone vessels (see 6 above) attest to their Jewishness as well. Some of the housing on top of the hill of Sepphoris was in villas, evidently of wealthy landowners or merchants. White mosaic floors appeared in the wealthiest first-century houses.

Excavation in the foundations of the civil basilica on the east side of the city at the intersection of the Cardo Maximus and the Decumanus show that the basilica was built hurriedly on the foundations of a destroyed building. The excavators believe that they have found evidence for Herod Antipas's orders to rebuild Sepphoris—and in a Roman image.

The theater of Sepphoris is surely first-century, though some scholars believe that its builder was an unknown person of the late first century A.D., not Herod Antipas. It could seat four thousand spectators, the same size as the theater in the capital city of *Caesarea. Likewise there is a fortification near the top of the site that bespeaks fortification of the acropolis in the first century. A network of streets paved with crushed limestone carried information and people around the Hippodamian grid of Sepphoris in the first century. Before 134 the city council paved the Cardo and the Decumanus in Roman style, probably in anticipation of the emperor Hadrian.

The water system of Sepphoris is extraordinary, matched only by the one at the city of Abila of the Decapolis across the Jordan. The early Roman aqueduct led water from the spring at the village of Abila of Galilee 3 miles distant. The aqueduct featured a huge underground reservoir and a pool. The pool is typical of Herodian waterworks everywhere. A reference in a late Jewish text speaks of the "wheels of Sepphoris," usually understood to be water wheels (*Eccl. Rab.* 12:6). Even in the first century Sepphoris did not manufacture all its goods. It brought in wine, oil and other agricultural products from its own territory. Some of the farmers of the outlying fields doubtless lived within the walls of Sepphoris.

At the destruction of Jerusalem in A.D. 70 the *priestly family of Jedaiah settled at Sepphoris. Another twenty-three priestly families settled at other Galilean cities and villages, including Nazareth.

Sepphoris minted coins from A.D. 68, before Vespasian was declared emperor. On these coins the city name appears as Irenopolis Neronias Seppho[ris], or *ΕΙΡΗΝΟΠΟΛΙ ΝΕΡΩΝΙΑΣ ΣΕΠΦΩ*. The name of Irenopolis ["City of Peace"] reminded one of the city's peace stance beginning in A.D. 68, during the first revolt. The second name, Neronias, declares the city's continued loyalty to the emperor Nero and to Rome.

On coins minted at Sepphoris during the reign of Trajan (A.D. 98-117) the name of the citizens of the city is given in Greek as the Sepphorean *(ΣΕΠΦΩΡΗΝΩΝ)*. Therefore Sepphoris was spelled *ΣΕΡΦΩΡΙΣ* in Greek, which agrees with the spelling in Josephus. The obverse of the coins declared that Trajan lent one of his titles to the city, namely, Autokratoris, or *ΑΥΤΟΚΡΑΤ-ΩΡΙΣ*. Herod Antipas called the city Autokratoris, according to Josephus (*Ant.* 18.2.1 §27).

After Hadrian the city was renamed Diocaesarea or *ΔΙΟΚΑΙΣΑΡΕΑ*, which also appears on milestones. The full name of the city on coins from the emperor Caracella onward is *ΔΙΟ-ΚΑΙΣΑΡΕΑ (Ι)ΕΡΑ ΑΣΥΛ(ΟΣ) ΚΑΙ ΑΥΤΟΝΟ-ΜΟΣ* or Diocaesarea the Holy, [City of] Refuge and Autonomous. This naming is likely a political act adopted by the council of the city in honor of Hadrian, who took the title Divi or Zeus, which appeared on his coins from A.D. 117 onward. Four other cites share these three titles of Holy City, City of Refuge and Autonomous, namely, the coastal city of Dora, and the three cities of the Decapolis, Abila, Gadara and Capitolias.

Diocaesarea is the name that will appear in Greek literature produced by Romans and by Christians in the later Roman Empire. Interestingly enough it will not survive in the Arabic-language historians, who only know the name Saffuriyeh. This strongly suggests that this local Galilean name among Aramaic speakers continued to be the old name of Sepphoris even when its official name was Diocaesarea.

The Sepphoris of the second century A.D. was a great Jewish intellectual center. It was at Sepphoris that the work of Rab Juda, also known as the Prince, culminated in the compilation of the oral law, or the *Mishnah, at the beginning of the third century of the common era.

See also ARCHAEOLOGY OF THE LAND OF ISRAEL; CAESAREA PHILIPPI; DECAPOLIS; ECONOMICS OF PALESTINE; JUDEA; TIBERIAS.

BIBLIOGRAPHY. D. A. Dorsey, *The Roads and Highways of Ancient Israel* (Baltimore: Johns Hopkins University Press, 1991); D. R. Edwards and C. T. McCollough, eds., *Archaeology and the Galilee: Texts and Contexts in the Greco-Roman and Byzantine Periods* (SFSHJ; Atlanta: Scholars Press, 1997); D. A. Fiensy, *The Social History of Palestine in the Herodian Period: The Land Is Mine* (SBEC 20; Lewiston, NY: Edwin Mellen Press, 1991); S. Freyne, *Galilee from Alexander the Great to Hadrian 323 B.C.E. to 135 C.E.: A Study of Second Temple Judaism* (Edinburgh: T & T Clark, 1998 [1980]); B. Golomb and Y. Kedar, "Ancient Agriculture in the Galilee Mountains," *IEJ* 21 (1971) 136-40; M. Goodman, *State and Society in Roman Galilee, A.D. 132-212* (Totowa, NJ: Rowman & Allanfield, 1983); K. C. Hanson and D. E. Oakman, *Palestine in the Time of Jesus: Social Structures and Social Conflicts* (Minneapolis: Fortress, 1998); R. A. Horsley, *Archaeology, History and Society in Galilee: The Social Context of Jesus and the Rabbis* (Valley Forge, PA: Trinity Press International, 1996); idem, *Galilee: History, Politics, People* (Valley Forge, PA: Trinity Press International, 1995); W. H. Landau, "A Greek Inscription Found Near Hefzibah," *IEJ* 11 (1961) 54-70; L. I. Levine, ed., *The Galilee in Late Antiquity* (New York: Jewish Theological Seminary of America, 1992); R. M. Nagy et al., eds., *Sepphoris in Galilee: Crosscurrents of Culture* (Raleigh, NC: North Carolina Museum of Art, 1996); J. F. Strange, "The Art and Archaeology of Ancient Judaism," in *Judaism in Late Antiquity,* pt. 1: *The Literary and Archaeological Sources* (HOS; Leiden: E. J. Brill, 1995) 64-114, illustrated; idem, "First-Century Galilee from Archaeology and from the Texts," in *Archaeology and the Galilee: Texts and Contexts in the Greco-Roman and Byzantine Periods,* ed. D. R. Edwards and C. T. McCollough (SFSHJ; Atlanta: Scholars Press, 1997) 39-48; idem, "Six Campaigns at Sepphoris: The University of South Florida Excavations, 1983-89," in *The Galilee in Late Antiquity,* ed. L. I. Levine (New York: Jewish Theological Seminary of America, 1992) 339-55; Y. Tsafrir, L. Di Segni and J. Green, *Tabula Imperii Romani: Iudaea, Palestina: Eretz Israel in the Hellenistic, Roman and Byzantine Periods. Maps and Gazetteer* (Union Academique Internationale; Jerusalem: Israel Academy of Sciences and Humanities, 1993). J. F. Strange

GALLIO INSCRIPTION. *See* INSCRIPTIONS AND PAPYRI: GRECO-ROMAN.

GAMES. *See* ATHLETICS; CIRCUSES AND GAMES.

GENDER ROLES. *See* MARRIAGE; WOMEN IN GRECO-ROMAN WORLD AND JUDAISM.

GENESIS APOCRYPHON (1QapGen)

Of the first seven scrolls to be retrieved in 1947 from the Dead Sea caves, the most poorly preserved was an Aramaic rewriting of portions of Genesis, known today as the *Genesis Apocryphon* (1QapGen). Only six of the twenty-two surviving columns are preserved to any great extent: in column 2 (now thought to be column 3) Lamech relates events accompanying the birth of Noah (Gen 5:28-29); column 12 (13), though fragmentary, has Noah describe events after the flood (Gen 9:13-21); columns 19-22 (20-23), the best preserved of all, rewrite and embellish the Abram episodes of Genesis 12:8—15:4. The full length of the original scroll cannot now be determined.

1. Date and Language
2. Genre and Literary Relationships
3. New Testament Parallels
4. Early Jewish Biblical Interpretation

1. Date and Language.

Genesis Apocryphon is generally dated to the first century B.C. or A.D., prior to the destruction of the *Qumran settlement (c. A.D. 68). The work employs a Palestinian dialect of Middle *Aramaic, somewhat later than the Aramaic parts of Daniel and close to *Targum Onqelos* as well as to the Aramaic words preserved in the Greek texts of the NT and *Josephus, making *Genesis Apocryphon* valuable for reconstructing the Aramaic dialect used in Jesus' day. Along with the Qumran targums of Job and Leviticus, *Genesis Apocryphon* confirms that biblical books were already being rendered into Aramaic during the Second Temple period. Biblical citations in *Genesis Apocryphon* witness to a Palestinian text type.

2. Genre and Literary Relationships.

Genesis Apocryphon is commonly classified as a work of *rewritten Bible (along with *Pseudo-Philo's *Biblical Antiquities,* *Josephus's *Antiquities* and **Jubilees*) since it is principally concerned with reshaping, expanding and interpreting, though not replacing, the biblical narrative. *Genesis Apocryphon* does not, however, fit neatly into any single generic category. Up until *Genesis Apocryphon* 21:23, the predominant mode is pseudonymous autobiography, like *1 Enoch* (*see* Enoch, Books of), 4Q160 and the testamentary literature. Later portions (1QapGen 21:23—22:34; cf. 20:1-9, 16-20, 23-26) are composed in the third person and follow the biblical precursor much more closely, resembling the style of later targums (*see* Rabbinic Literature: Targumim). Interpretive traditions and hermeneutical strategies have often been compared with later rabbinic midrash (*see* Rabbinic Literature: Midrashim).

Genesis Apocryphon cannot properly be called sectarian; it contains nothing clearly *Essene in nature, nor does it adopt an *apocalyptic or pesher-style hermeneutic (*see* Pesharim). This may suggest the document was acquired rather than composed by the community, although nonlegal narrative expansions such as *Genesis Apocryphon* are far less likely to reveal sectarian distinctives than are halakic (legal) materials (*see* Legal Texts at Qumran).

Numerous parallels with *Jubilees* as well as *1 Enoch* 106—107 suggest substantial literary dependence, although the direction of influence is debated. If *Genesis Apocryphon* is secondary to Jubilees (Fitzmyer; Nickelsburg), its author appears to have excised sectarian elements (e.g., *calendrical references); if prior (Avigad and Yadin; Vermes), *Jubilees* has abridged its source, introduced its own doctrinal materials and cast the memoirs of the patriarchs as revelations made to *Moses.

3. New Testament Parallels.

3.1. Linguistic and Cultural Parallels. *Genesis Apocryphon* 21:13 (cf. Gen 13:16) contains one of the earliest postbiblical Aramaic uses of the phrase "son of man" (*br ʾnwš*), a phrase found frequently on the lips of Jesus in the Synoptic Gospels (*ho hyios tou anthrōpou*). Unlike *1 Enoch* 46—48 and 4 Ezra 13 (*see* Esdras, Books of), which echo Daniel 7:13, the phrase "son of man" in *Genesis Apocryphon* (with negative *lʾ*) functions like an indefinite pronoun ([no] one, human being). A similar generic usage occurs at 11QtgJob 26:3 and probably 9:9. The fact that the phrase could be used in the Palestinian Aramaic of Jesus' day without any technical or titular force is clearly relevant to discussions of the significance of Son of Man language in the Gospels. Other NT words and phrases finding parallels in *Genesis Apocryphon* include "Lord of heaven and earth" (Mt 11:25; Lk 10:21; 1QapGen 22:16); "spirit of sickness" (Lk 13:11; 1QapGen 20:16); "evil spirit" (Lk 7:21; 8:2; 11:26; Mt 12:45; 1QapGen 20:16-17, 28-29); and "rebuke/banish/subjugate" [a demon] (*gʿr* in 1QapGen 20:28-29; cf. 1QM 14:10; *epitimaō* in Mk 1:25; 9:25; Lk 4:41).

The account of Abram's dealings with Pharaoh affords several cultural parallels to the world of Jesus. At Abram's request, God sent an evil spirit to afflict Pharaoh's household and his healers with a plague (1QapGen 20:12-20), recalling the NT idea that some illnesses are *demon-induced (Mk 1:32-34; 9:14-29; cf. 1 Sam 16:14). The plague is finally lifted through Abram's *prayer, exorcism and laying on of hands (1QapGen 20:21-22, 28-29; cf. Mk 5:23; 6:5; 7:32; 8:32-35; 16:18; Lk 4:40-41; 13:13; Acts 9:12, 17-18; 28:8). And the scroll appears to portray Abram praying "for his enemy" (1QapGen 20:28; cf. Gen 20:17; Mt 5:44; Rom 12:17).

3.2. Possible Parallels to Matthew's Birth Narrative. A comparison of Jesus' birth narrative in Matthew 1:18—2:23 with the scroll's narration of Noah's birth (cols. 2-5) and Abram's descent into Egypt (cols. 19-20) yields numerous striking similarities, though not enough to suggest a literary relationship between the two compositions (see chart on next page).

4. Early Jewish Biblical Interpretation.

4.1. Interpretive Traditions.

4.1.1. Noah and Enoch. Early Jewish literature expressed considerable interest in and speculation about the figure of Noah, in part because Noah's birth is the occasion for a prophecy (Gen 5:29) and because Noah's story (Gen 6:5—10:32) follows on the heels of the episode of the "fallen angels" in Genesis 6:1-4 (*Jub.* 4—10; *1 Enoch* 106—107; Josephus *Ant.* 1.3.1-2 §§72-76; 4QMess ar). *Genesis Apocryphon* calls Noah "righteous" (1QapGen 6:2; Gen 6:9; cf. Heb 11:7; 2 Pet 2:5; *Jub.* 5:19; Josephus *Ant.* 1.3.2 §75) and may attribute to him an eschatologically symbolic role (1QapGen 2—4; cf. Mt 24:37-39; Lk 17:26-27; 1 Pet 3:18-22; *1 Enoch* 10—11; 106:13—107:1).

Genesis Apocryphon also attaches great importance to Enoch, Noah's great-grandfather (Gen 5:18-24), whose dwelling was with the angels (1QapGen 2:20-21), and who alone could confirm that Noah was not the son of an angelic Watcher (1QapGen 5:3-4; cf. *1 Enoch* 107:2). Popular traditions about Enoch's righteousness, bodily ascent and heavenly existence (Sir 49:14; *Jub.* 4:16-19; 10:17; Josephus *Ant.* 1.3.4 §85; Heb 11:5; based on Gen 5:22, 24; cf. 2 Kings 2:1) help explain the high regard for *1 Enoch* among the early Christians (cf. Jude 14-15).

4.1.2. Abram and Sarai. The scroll's account of Abram and Sarai in Egypt (1QapGen 19:10—20:33; cf. Gen 12:8—13:1) is heavily embellished: Sarai willingly cooperates with Abram's plan for her to pose as his sister (1QapGen 19:21-23; 20:9-10); Abram is greatly troubled by Sarai's abduction (1QapGen 20:10-16); while in Pharaoh's house Sarai's chastity is preserved (1QapGen 20:15-18; cf. Josephus *Ant.* 1.8.1 §§162-65; Philo *Abr.* 96-98; *Gen. Rab.* 41:2); Pharaoh suffers plagues because of Abram's prayers (1QapGen 20:12-15); Pharaoh first seeks help from his conjurers before summoning Abram (1QapGen 20:18-21); Hagar is among the gifts Pharaoh gave to Sarai (1QapGen 20:32; cf. *Gen. Rab.* 45:1); and it was Lot who informs Pharaoh's house that Sarai was Abram's wife (1QapGen 20:22-23). Sarai is portrayed as a willing but sorrowful heroine who remains pure and undefiled, and Abram as a righteous seer, dreamer and interpreter of dreams, a fervent and effective prayer warrior, and an exorcist/healer. NT portraits of Abraham and Sarah are noticeably less embellished but are similarly

Noah's Birth in Genesis Apocryphon Lamech observes the unusual appearance of the infant Noah (1QapGen 2:1-2; cf. *1 Enoch* 106:2-4).	*Jesus' Birth in Matthew* Matthew (Mt 1:18; cf. Lk 1:35) describes the miraculous conception of Jesus.
Lamech suspects Noah is not his but was conceived by holy ones or Nephilim (1QapGen 2:1-2).	Joseph discovers Mary is pregnant, knows he is not the father and plans to divorce her secretly (Mt 1:18-19).
Lamech confronts his wife, Bitenosh (1QapGen 2:3-7), who swears passionately that Lamech, not a "son of heaven," is Noah's father (1QapGen 2:8-18).	No record of dialog between Joseph and Mary. In Luke (Lk 1:26-38), Mary responds to the angelic messenger.
Lamech asks father Methuselah to inquire of grandfather Enoch (1QapGen 2:19-25; cf. *1 Enoch* 106:5-12).	No record of Joseph seeking counsel from anyone.
Enoch, whose dwelling was among the angels ("holy ones"), confirms that Noah is Lamech's son (1QapGen cols. 3-5; cf. *1 Enoch* 106:13—107:3).	An angel tells Joseph in a dream not to divorce Mary, because her child was "of the Holy Spirit" (Mt 1:20-21).
Abram's Descent into Egypt in Genesis Apocryphon. Abram journeys to Egypt because of a famine (1QapGen 19:9-12).	*Jesus' Descent into Egypt in Matthew.* Joseph and his family flee to Egypt to escape Herod (Mt 2:14).
Abram has a symbolic dream at the border of Egypt about two trees and tree cutters, representing Abram, Sarai and the threat to Abram's life (1QapGen 19:13-16).	Joseph has a nonsymbolic dream of an angel warning of Herod's murderous plan and telling them to flee (Mt 2:13).
Abram interprets the dream to mean that his life is in danger (1QapGen 19:17-18) and asks Sarai to say she is his sister (1QapGen 19:19-20).	Joseph's dream requires no interpretation; he immediately obeys, taking Mary and Jesus to Egypt (Mt 2:14).

idealized (Lk 16:22-31; Jn 8:53; Acts 7:2-8; Rom 4:1-25; Gal 3:6-9; 4:22-31; Heb 6:13-15; 7:4-10; 11:8-12, 17-19; Jas 2:21-23; 1 Pet 3:6).

4.1.3. Melchizedek. The story of *Melchizedek (1QapGen 22:12-17; cf. Gen 14:18-20), though relatively unembellished, may be helpfully compared with the midrashic homily of Hebrews 7:1-10. Some interpreters have wondered why the author of Hebrews doesn't fortify his Melchizedekan christology with the biblical phrase "Melchizedek . . . brought out bread and wine" (Gen 14:18); indeed, later interpreters (e.g., Ambrosiaster, Clement of Alexandria, Chrysostom, Jerome) could not resist reading this phrase eucharistically. This reticence of Hebrews, however, accords well with *Genesis Apocryphon* 22:14-15, which describes Melchi-zedek bringing out "food and drink" (*mʾkl ûmšth*)—simple nourishment for Abram and his men. In this interpretive tradition, evidently shared by Hebrews (but not by Josephus *Ant.* 1.10.2 §181), the act was clearly distinct from Melchizedek's priestly blessing upon Abram (Gen 14:19-20). Although the Melchizedek of Hebrews 7 enjoys greater status and significance than does his *Genesis Apocryphon* counterpart, neither comes close to the exalted figure portrayed in 11QMelch or *2 Enoch* 71—72 (*see* Melchizedek, Traditions of).

4.2. Hermeneutical Strategies.

4.2.1. Narrative Expansion. As a window on early Jewish Palestinian hermeneutics roughly contemporary with the NT, the value of *Genesis Apocryphon* can scarcely be overstated. The principal interpretive strategy is narrative expansion, the practice of filling the gaps in the notoriously laconic Hebrew narrative. Thus, *Genesis Apocry-*

phon 2—4 provides background for Lamech's oracle at Noah's birth (Gen 5:29); a passing reference to Sarai's beauty (Gen 12:15) expands into eloquent poetry (1QapGen 20:1-8; cf. Philo *Abr.* 19 §93; *Gen. Rab.* 40.5); and the silence of Genesis 13:17-18 regarding Abram's movements before settling down is replaced with a detailed travelog (1QapGen 21:15-19a). Compare also *Genesis Apocryphon* 22:3-5 with Genesis 14:13.

4.2.2. Problem Solving. Sometimes the tradent rewrites to solve problems in the text. Not only does Abram's decision to present Sarai as his sister (Gen 12:13) appear faithless and self-serving, but also there is no record of divine discipline, and Abram profits from the ruse (Gen 12:16). Unlike *Jubilees* (13:10-15), which ignores the episode, and Josephus (*Ant.* 1.8.2 §162), who offers a purely rational explanation, *Genesis Apocryphon* has God give Abram a dream to warn him of the danger and suggest survival tactics (1QapGen 19:13-19). And Pharaoh offers gifts, not because he acquired Sarai (Gen 12:16) but because Abram lifted the plague (1QapGen 20:31-33; cf. Josephus *Ant.* 1.8.1 §165). *Genesis Apocryphon* 21:32-33 solves another sort of problem—the apparent contradiction between Genesis 14:10 and Genesis 14:17, 21—by having only the king of Gomorrah and not the king of Sodom fall into the pits (cf. *Jub.* 13:22; *Gen. Rab.* 42:7).

4.2.3. Intertextuality. A subtle but highly effective interpretive strategy is the appeal to other, ostensibly unrelated biblical passages to shape and explain the primary narrative sequence (*see* Intertextuality). Abram's reason for venturing to Egypt—"I heard that in Egypt there was grain" (1QapGen 19:9-10)—is almost certainly imported from the Joseph cycle (Gen 42:1; cf. Acts 7:12), fueled by verbal parallels between Genesis 12:10 and Genesis 41:54, 56-57; 43:1 and by thematic links between the two stories: both involve a trek into Egypt because of a famine, a Pharaoh, oppression of God's people, plagues on Egypt and miraculous deliverance. Abram functions as a Joseph figure, who learns of the future in a dream and enjoys the gift of interpretation (1QapGen 19:14-19).

Several other embellishments arise under the influence of Genesis 20, including Hyrcanos's dream (1QapGen 20:22), Abram's intercession for Pharaoh (1QapGen 20:28) and the timing of Pharaoh's gifts (1QapGen 20:31-33). Likewise, the Salem = Jerusalem equation (1QapGen 22:13; cf. Gen 14:18) is likely indebted to Psalm 76:2 (cf. Josephus *Ant.* 1.10.2 §180; *Tg. Neof.* Gen 14:18; contrast Heb 7:2 and Philo *Leg. All.* 3.25 §79). Some biblical echoes are less readily identified: Abram's dream of the two trees (1QapGen 19:13-16) may be indebted to other texts (Ezek 31, Dan 4, Judg 9 and perhaps Ps 92:13), and the poetic description of Sarai's beauty likely echoes Song of Solomon 7.

See also BIBLICAL INTERPRETATION, JEWISH; MELCHIZEDEK, TRADITIONS OF (11QMELCH); REWRITTEN BIBLE IN PSEUDEPIGRAPHA AND QUMRAN.

BIBLIOGRAPHY. P. S. Alexander, "Retelling the Old Testament," in *It Is Written: Scripture Citing Scripture,* ed. D. A. Carson and H. G. M. Williamson (Cambridge: Cambridge University Press, 1988) 99-121; N. Avigad and Y. Yadin, *A Genesis Apocryphon, A Scroll from the Wilderness of Judea* (Jerusalem: Magnes, 1956); C. A. Evans, "The Genesis Apocryphon and the Rewritten Bible," *RevQ* 13 (1988) 153-65; M. Fishbane, "Use, Authority and Interpretation of Mikra at Qumran," in *Mikra: Text, Translation, Reading and Interpretation of the Hebrew Bible in Ancient Judaism and Early Christianity,* ed. M. J. Mulder (CRINT 2.1; Assen: Van Gorcum; Minneapolis: Fortress, 1990) 339-77; J. A. Fitzmyer, *The Genesis Apocryphon of Qumran Cave I* (Rome: Biblical Institute, 1966, 1971); idem, *A Wandering Aramean: Collected Aramaic Essays* (Chico, CA: Scholars Press, 1979); M. L. Gevirtz, "Abram's Dream in the Genesis Apocryphon: Its Motifs and Their Function," *Maarav* 8 (1992) 229-43; H. C. Kee, "The Terminology of Mark's Exorcism Stories," *NTS* 14 (1968) 232-46; J. E. Miller, "The Redaction of Tobit and the Genesis Apocryphon," *JSP* 8 (1991) 53-61; G. W. E. Nickelsburg, "The Bible Rewritten and Expanded," in *Jewish Writings of the Second Temple Period,* ed. M. E. Stone (CRINT 2.2; Assen: Van Gorcum; Philadelphia: Fortress, 1984) 104-7; E. Qimron, "Toward a New Edition of the Genesis Apocryphon," *JSP* 10 (1992) 11-18; E. Schürer, *The History of the Jewish People in the Age of Jesus Christ,* rev. and ed. G. Vermes, F. Millar and M. Goodman (3 vols.; Edinburgh: T & T Clark, 1973-87) 3.1:318-25; J. C. VanderKam, "The Poetry of I Q Ap Gen, XX, 2-8a," *RevQ* 10 (1979) 57-66; idem, "Textual Affinities of the Biblical Citations in the Genesis Apocryphon," *JBL* 97 (1978) 45-55; G. Vermes, "The Life of Abraham (2)," in *Scripture and Tradition in Judaism: Haggadic Studies* (rev. ed.; Leiden: E. J. Brill, 1973) 96-126.

B. N. Fisk

GENRES OF THE NEW TESTAMENT

Genre is a term sometimes used to refer to the constituent elements within a larger work, for which the term *form* is also often used, or as the classification of a work in relation to other, similar works. The latter usage is followed in this article, adopting D. E. Aune's definition (1987, 13): "a *literary genre* may be defined as a group of texts that exhibit a coherent and recurring configuration of literary features involving form (including structure and style), content and function." At the macro level genre is concerned with the identification of the book as a whole, while at the micro level it helps us understand the forms, sometimes referred to as subgenres, used within the whole.

Genres are neither universal nor static. Therefore, to avoid anachronism, it is important that a genre is classified within its era and literary milieu. For the NT books, this means placing them properly within the context of the Greco-Roman world of the first century A.D. Identification of a work's genre helps us understand its place within the literary history of both early Christianity and the Greco-Roman world and aids us in its interpretation. This article will review and assess various recent attempts to identify the genres of NT literature.

1. The Gospels
2. John
3. Acts
4. The Letters
5. Revelation

1. The Gospels.

None of the four accounts of Jesus' ministry originally identified itself as a Gospel (*euangelion*). However, there is good reason to concur with M. Hengel (1985, 64-84) in his judgment that (with "a considerable degree of probability") the titles of the Gospels can be traced back to the time of the origin of the four Gospels as a collection circulating among the Christian communities in the period A.D. 69-100, and that the root of the identification lies in Mark's terminology (Mk 1:1). The noun *gospel* and its cognate verb (*euangelizō*, "to preach the gospel") are used extensively in the NT (e.g., Mk 1:14-15; Rom 1:16), and evidently this use in the earliest communities gave rise to the generic title.

In the NT *euangelion* always occurs in the singular and refers to the content of Christian belief, a pattern generally followed in the Fathers. Justin Martyr is the earliest extant author to use it, particularly in the plural, in reference to written documents, a practice that became established over time when it was applied to the canonical Gospels but also to the *apocryphal and *Gnostic Gospels. Justin's description of the Gospels as "memoirs" (*apomnēmoneumata,* e.g., Justin Martyr *Apol. I* 66) paralleled Xenophon's study of Socrates in *Memorabilia,* suggesting that the Gospels are to be understood as historical-biographical writings. This is how they were understood up to the early part of the twentieth century, as is clear in the nineteenth-century writers of lives of Jesus. However, the development of form criticism and its dominance in NT scholarship from the 1920s to 1960s focused on the preliterary Gospel units, denigrating the Evangelists' roles. The Gospels were seen as unsophisticated writings, and the consensus developed of regarding them as *sui generis,* originating in the kerygma of the early church and therefore not fitting into any other literary category (e.g., Kümmel, 37; Gundry 1974; Guthrie, 17-21; see survey by R. Guelich in Stuhlmacher, 186-94).

But this perception changed with the rise of redaction criticism, which rediscovered the Evangelists as theological interpreters of the Jesus tradition (i.e., authors in their own right) and contributors to the literary process (*see DJG,* Gospel [Genre]). Various cultural milieux have been explored in the attempt to discover a genre for the Gospels: Jewish and, more productively, Greco-Roman.

Some scholars have attempted to find parallels to the Gospels in either the OT or *rabbinic literature. M. G. Kline has argued that the longer OT sections that concentrate on one figure offer a close analogy to the Gospels, yet OT historical narratives focus on God's dealings with Israel, not on the teachings of a leader or prophet, which occur within these larger sections. M. D. Goulder believes that the Synoptics were inspired by the OT, specifically the various passages used in synagogue liturgy, thereby accounting for the inherent difficulties of believing that so many details of Jesus' life matched such OT passages by contending that many Gospel stories were midrashically created. Others have attempted to classify the Gospels, particularly Matthew (Gundry 1982), as a form of midrash. Midrash, however, is variously and often imprecisely defined. As a genre, midrash is an exposition of the Hebrew Scriptures (*see* Rabbinic Literature: Midrashim), and none of the Gospels is a simple commentary on a significant extended portion of the OT. As an interpretive method, midrash is clearly not applicable as a generic classification of the Gospels, which tell the story of the life, death and resurrection of Jesus. This is not, however, to deny the presence of midrash at certain points within the Gospels.

Rabbinic material in general has not provided a comparable genre to the Gospels, for, while rabbinic parallels can be found for individual Gospel units (Evans, 227-31), there is nothing like the Gospels as whole works, and in any case the *rabbinic literature comes from a later period.

While some of the evidence for a correlation between the Gospels and Jewish lectionaries is impressive, critics have pointed out that we do not know what first-century Jews read in their synagogues. Even if these readings could be established with confidence, there are no convincing reasons why Christians who stressed the gospel should have based their worship on lectionaries stressing the law. Further, the lectionary view, which presumes an orderly worship, cannot be reconciled with what we know of the charismatic character of much NT worship. As such, lectionary theories build one hypothesis on another (L. L. Morris in France and Wenham 1983, 148-49). While it is likely that the Gospels were originally intended to be used for reading and teaching within Christian worship and later developed a role in the church's liturgy, this is quite different from locating their origin in the church's liturgy.

Arguments that the Gospels and Acts should be classified as legend, novel or historical fiction have accompanied negative assessments of their historicity. M. Hadas and M. Smith contended that the Gospels are a form of aretalogy, an ancient form of biography recording the teaching and miracles of a divine man (*theios anēr*). This view has now been abandoned because the works that were supposed to represent this genre (e.g., Philo's *Life of Moses* and Philostratus's *Life of Apollonius of Tyana*) are not called aretalogies, and aretalogies themselves vary widely in form, function and content (*see DJG*, "Divine Man/Theios Anēr"). Some have proposed that Mark's story of Jesus reflects the general structure of Greek tragedy (e.g., Aristotle's *Poetics*), following the pattern of introduction, rising action, climax/crisis, falling action, catastrophe and denouement (Bilezikian), but most scholars have concluded (Aune 1987, 48-49) that this is coincidental and that Mark follows a pre-Markan Jesus tradition, and in this he was followed by Matthew, Luke and John.

From the 1920s through the 1960s a consensus had developed that the Gospels were not to be identified as Greco-Roman biographies. G. N. Stanton (1974) offered the first notable attempt to criticize this consensus, arguing also that the Gospels were distinct from both Jewish and rabbinic literature and later Christian and Gnostic Gospels. But while maintaining that the Gospels should be considered biographical, he demurred from calling them biographies. C. H. Talbert followed Stanton's criticism of the form-critical view of the Gospels' uniqueness but went further by proposing that they be understood as Greco-Roman biographies. He argued (1977) that such biographies were of an unhistorical type, of which there were many in the ancient world, and that the Gospels shared their mythical structure, originating in cultic legends devoted to the religion's founder and possessing an optimistic worldview. Talbert has been criticized for his interpretation of some classical texts and his scant use of secondary literature (Aune in France and Wenham 1981; and Burridge, 84-86), though his classification of a type of Greco-Roman biography has been taken up in modified form by M. Hengel, D. E. Aune and R. A. Burridge. Hengel challenged the view that the Gospels contained little that was genuinely historical, maintaining that the Gospels should be compared with those forms of ancient biography that provide a "relatively trustworthy historical report" (Hengel 1979, 16, contra, e.g., Shuler, 36-37). In this, Hengel has spoken for an increasing number of scholars.

The strength of the work of Hengel, Aune and Burridge lies in their knowledge of the Greco-Roman world and its literature. This gives their views a greater credibility and historical value, steers them away from careless anachronisms and prevents them from inventing a genre to fit a theory. An example of the latter is P. L. Shuler, who proposed that Matthew be classified as an "encomium biography," failing to recognize that it is doubtful that such a genre ever existed (Burridge, 88). Burridge develops the line of argument suggested by Aune in his criticism of Talbert, using the idea of family resemblance (or group identity; see the essays in Stuhlmacher), focusing on the Gospels' similarities rather than their differences: "each [Gospel] is indeed different, unique and special in its own right, but intimate knowledge of them from the inside and comparison with others outside the family show their shared family features arising from a common ancestry." He concludes that the "increasing tendency among New Testament scholars to refer to the gospels as 'biographical' is vindicated; indeed, the time has come to go on from the use of the adjective 'biographical,' for *the gospels are βίοι* [lives]!" (Burridge, 243). More specifically, they form a subgenre of Gospels, or βίοι Ἰησοῦ (Burridge, 47; *see DJG*, Gospel [Genre], 276, 281-82).

2. John.
In the foregoing discussion it has been assumed that the classification of the Synoptics as a subgenre of the *bioi* genre applies also to John's Gospel (Burridge, 220-39). But is this justified? It should be noted that when titles were given to the Gospels the *kata* construction (*kata Iōannēn,* "according to John") shows that John's Gospel was understood to belong with and to be of the same literary type as the Synoptics.

Burridge supports this conclusion with the following arguments. (1) Like the Synoptics, John lacks any kind of biographical title, but it does begin with a formal prologue after which the subject's name is mentioned—a common feature of *bioi.* (2) Verbal analysis shows Jesus to be the subject of 20 percent of the verbs, a further 33 percent being credited to him, a dominance paralleled in the Synoptics and other *bioi.* Further, the 20 percent of which Jesus is the subject demonstrate that John has not abandoned narrative about Jesus. A similar proportion of space is allocated to the passion and resurrection as in the Synoptics. (3) John shares similar modes of representation, size, structure and scale to the Synoptics and *bioi,* using similar literary units, oral and written, to display Jesus' character through word and deed. (4) The four Gospels share similar internal features of settings, topics and atmospheres with *bioi* (Burridge, 222-39). J. D. G. Dunn (in Stuhlmacher, 322) highlights the "striking fact" that "the Fourth Evangelist obviously felt it necessary to retain the format of a *Gospel.* For all its differences from the Synoptics, John is far closer to them than to any other ancient writing."

3. Acts.
The church has traditionally understood Acts to be a history of the earliest church, but this has been challenged in recent years. It is now common to find Acts variously classified as one of the three primary genres of the Roman world—a novel, biography or history—and it has even been suggested that it is a scientific treatise. Much has depended on a writer's assessment of the historical content and worth of Acts, though this should be a separate matter: "Genre is not a question that can be settled simply on the grounds of how reliable or unreliable the material of a particular work may be" (Pearson and Porter, 143).

That Acts is an ancient historical novel intended to edify and entertain has been argued by R. I. Pervo. He believes that all attempts to characterize Luke as a historian have been mistaken, though the aim to edify and entertain was by no means peculiar to novels (see Lucian's *How to Write History* §53: historians should write "what will interest and instruct" their audience). Pervo believes that Luke's inclusion of exciting episodes, such as supernatural events (dreams and visions), imprisonments, trials and shipwrecks, and his use of literary devices, such as humor, pathos and oratory, means Acts resembles the unquestionably fictional and later apocryphal Acts (e.g., the *Acts of Peter* and *Acts of Paul;* see Bauckham in Winter and Clarke, 105-52), yet comparison of the canonical Acts with these later writings immediately shows their differences, the former lacking the triviality and clearly mythical content of the latter. S. M. Praeder also rejects the history genre and identifies Luke-Acts as an ancient novel, which category she also claims for Matthew, Mark and John. Due to their contents, setting and intention, for her they form a subgenre of Christian "ancient novel" (*see* Romances/Novels, Ancient).

D. E. Aune (1987, 80), however, has rejected Pervo's argument: while writing to entertain, ancient historians did not think this meant sacrificing truth and usefulness; "historical novel" should be used of novels following a historical sequence of events (e.g., Xenophon's *Education of Cyrus*), not for fictional narratives set in the real world; the factual accuracy of Acts is irrelevant to identifying its genre if Luke intended to narrate historical events, and Luke's adoption of historical prefaces and reference to use of sources are features absent from novels; Luke-

Acts is to be treated as a single genre, while Pervo examines Acts alone; many of the episodes and their constituent subjects and motifs can be found in both factual and fictional writings. We need only dissent with Aune on the necessity of the fourth point, as this need not be the case. To these must be added a sixth point: there does not appear to be such a genre as "historical novel" (Pearson and Porter, 145).

While no single figure dominates the narrative of Acts, a number of scholars have contended that Acts is a biography. C. H. Talbert (1974) argued that the two-volume Luke-Acts is a biographical succession narrative, the Gospel recording the life of the founder of Christianity, the Acts being a narrative about his disciples and successors and a summary of the teaching of the school, the church. Talbert cites Diogenes Laertius's *Lives of Philosophers,* written about A.D. 250, as its closest generic example. Again Aune (1987, 78-79) has criticized this view by questioning the existence of such a genre and noting discrepancies between the two works.

Burridge (245-46) has noted that the borders between historiography, historical monograph and biography are blurred and flexible and suggests the possibility that, like the Gospel, Acts belongs to *bios* literature, either as an example of lives of the main subjects or as a *bios* of the church, and that these three literary genres are all reflected in Acts. He qualifies this when he notes that it is possible that the Gospel and Acts belong to distinct though related genres. It seems that while Luke has been influenced by features of the biography genre (cf. Barr and Wentling), this does not necessitate its belonging to a biographical genre (*see DLNTD,* Acts of the Apostles §1.1). Criticism of a biographical genre for Acts is also offered by C. J. Hemer (91-94).

L. C. A. Alexander has adopted a different approach by noting the differences between Luke's preface (Lk 1:1-4) and those of Greek historiographers. Luke's is brief in comparison with the more elaborate Greek historians and lacks a number of characteristic features of the latter, not least its omission of general moral reflections. Such observations lead Alexander to identify the closest analogues to Luke 1:1-4 and Acts 1:1 in the scientific and technical manuals on medicine (such would be consonant with Luke the physician, Hemer, 35), mathematics and engineering. She proposes that Luke's narrative is scientific in the sense that it is concerned to relate the tradition of accumulated teaching on Jesus and the early Christian movement. J. B. Green, for example, notes that the affinities between Luke and the scientific tradition do not negate the identification of Luke-Acts with historiography, adducing that Luke-Acts does not always match the formal features of Greco-Roman historiography because the genre was flexible. Luke, Green argues, has been influenced by OT and Jewish historiography (see also Hall, 171-208), and in describing his work as a "narrative" (Lk 1:1), Luke identifies his project as a long narrative of many events for which the chief discernible prototypes were the histories by Herodotus and Thucydides. Further, the many forms used by Luke (symposia, travel narratives, letters and speeches) provide a positive comparison with Greco-Roman historiography (*see DLNTD,* Acts of the Apostles, §1.1; Alexander is also criticized by Palmer in Winter and Clarke, 21-26).

Many recent studies have reinforced the earlier view of the church that Acts is an example of an ancient historiographical work (Pearson and Porter, 147-48). A variety of historiographical genres have been suggested. Aune (1987, 138-39) places Acts within the larger context of Hellenistic, Israelite and Jewish historiography and concludes that it is therefore a general history. R. Maddox (15-18) takes up the influence of OT and later Jewish histories and proposes the genre of theological history. G. L. Sterling (374) believes Acts is apologetic historiography, but while it may be granted that Acts has an apologetic function, its length, scope, focus and formal features suggest it is a short historical monograph (Palmer in Winter and Clarke, 1-18; see also Hengel 1979, 36; Berger, 1275, 1280-81; *see DLNTD,* Acts of the Apostles, §1.1). This classification, of all those explored, appears to be the one that does Acts the most justice, though a number of scholars, recognizing the strengths of the biographical and historical genres in describing Acts (both being genres concerned with history), nevertheless allow the theological subject matter of Acts to lead them to explore the possibility that Acts belongs to a unique genre (Marshall 1992, 22-23; this possibility was also explored by Hemer, 40-43, who conceded that Acts might be regarded "as in some aspects *sui generis,*" but qualified the term differently "from the way Bult-mann meant it about the Gospels," 42).

A final note needs to be made, recognizing that the question of the genre of Acts is greatly complicated by its relation to Luke's Gospel. Some scholars see the two volumes as generically linked, while others see them as belonging to different genres. Aune (1987, 77) is unwilling to separate the two volumes, which is why he cannot accept Luke as a biography, though there are no necessary reasons why the two volumes cannot belong to different genres without denying "their essential unity and continuity" (Hemer, 33; cf. Palmer in Winter and Clarke, 3; Burridge, 244-47).

4. The Letters.

The twenty-one NT letters have traditionally fallen into two categories: the Pauline letters and the General, or Catholic, letters. A. Deissmann drew the distinction between letters and epistles, contending that only the former were real letters in that they were nonliterary because they were occasional, neither intended for public readership nor for posterity, but only for the person or persons to whom they were addressed. In contrast, epistles were literary works intended for public reading, adopting various forms of rhetoric and intended for posterity (*see* Epistolary Theory).

While some scholars have accepted the usefulness of such classification, others have firmly rejected it (e.g., Aune 1987, 160; Longenecker 1990, ci-ciii; Pearson and Porter, 148-51). Contra Deissmann, it seems more than likely that the NT letter writers had various purposes in mind when they wrote, being situational, adopting forms of *rhetoric (the importance of rhetorical criticism is stressed by Aune 1987, 198-99; Porter 1991; *see DPL* Rhetorical Criticism; *DLNTD,* Rhetoric, Rhetorical Criticism) and intending them for posterity. In light of this, then, the two terms, "letters" and "epistles," will be used synonymously.

Ancient letters (see Stowers; Aune 1987, 158-82; White 1986; White in Aune 1988, 86-105) ranged from brief, intimate and informal notes to friends and family to carefully constructed treatises intended for a public readership. R. N. Longenecker reports that Demetrius listed twenty-one types of letter and Proclus forty-one. While none of the NT letters exactly corresponds to the types mentioned in these handbooks they nevertheless can be classified roughly according to one or other of the types of contemporary letters, recognizing that differences arose out of their differing purpose, mood, style, structure and Christian content and also allowing for the fact that the NT writers were evidently eclectic in their use of other literary traditions that can be found within the letters, for example, rhetoric, liturgical elements, apocalyptic (Longenecker 1990, ciii).

Hellenistic letters followed broad compositional conventions that allowed a considerable degree of flexibility to the author (Aune 1987, 158). The general threefold pattern comprised an opening, a body and a closing (Aune 1987, 183-91; White in Aune 1988, 88-101). The opening/prescript comprised the following elements: the *superscriptio* (sender) to the *adscriptio* (recipient) with *salutatio* (greetings), often accompanied by a wish for good health. The body or text of the letter contained three parts: the body opening, body middle and body closing, and this was followed by the closing or postscript, which frequently included greetings to persons other than the addressees, a final greeting or prayer and sometimes a date. However, some scholars argue for a four-part structure (Weima, 11), in which a thanksgiving section was added between the opening and body, and even five-part letters, in which a paraenetic section was added before the closing (Doty, 27-43; on this debate see Pearson and Porter, 151-52).

The NT letters were constructed along the lines of this broad epistolary pattern and were clearly adapted to meet their authors' requirements, allowing them, at times, to expand elements or omit them and to combine Jewish with Hellenistic features (see Aune 1987, 174-80), such as combining Greek and Jewish salutations ("grace and peace"; *see DPL,* Peace, Reconciliation, §3, for a discussion of this) and expanding paraenetic material. (For examples of how the NT letters do these, see the overviews in *DPL,* Letters, Letters Forms, §2; *DLNTD,* Letter, Letter Form, §§2-3). Aune cautions that the NT letters tend to resist rigid classification in terms of ancient epistolary and rhetorical categories: "Most early Christian letters are multifunctional and have a 'mixed' character, combining elements from two or more epistolary types. In short, each early Christian letter must be analyzed on its own terms" (Aune 1987, 203).

Nearly two decades ago it was suggested that the letters could be classified as either pastoral or tractate letters (Longenecker 1983, 102-6). On this reckoning, the former (1 and 2 Cor, Gal, Phil, Col, Philem, 1 and 2 Thess, 1 and 2 Tim, Tit, 2 Pet, 2 and 3 Jn, Jude) took their form from contemporary conventions and conveyed the apostolic presence, teaching and authority, and as such were to be read within the churches (see Col 4:16; 1 Thess 5:27). The latter (Rom, Eph, Heb, Jas, 1 Pet, 1 Jn), in content and tone, suggest they were intended to be more than strictly pastoral responses to specific situations in the churches of *Rome and *Ephesus. However, such classification lacks the refinement and precision that many scholars seek.

More recently, genre critics have classified letters either functionally or rhetorically. From the former perspective, 1 Thessalonians and 1 and 2 Timothy have been described as paraenetic letters, which seek to exhort to or dissuade from a specific course of action or attitude, often employing antithesis and personal example, while Philemon is seen as a letter of recommendation, as is, perhaps, 3 John. Rhetorical analysis has classified Galatians as a diatribe, or, with Philippians and Hebrews, as a deliberative letter (an attempt to persuade or dissuade from a certain future course of action), Romans and Hebrews as epideictic rhetoric (using praise or blame to argue the adoption of a particular position or set of values) and 2 Corinthians as an apologetic self-commendatory letter (see Blomberg, 43-44; for different classifications see Aune 1987, 204-22).

4.1. The Letters of Paul. There are thirteen Pauline letters, some of which are understood by many scholars to be pseudonymous or written by a member of a Pauline school (*see DLNTD*, Pauline Legacy and School). But if some of the letters (e.g., Ephesians and the Pastorals) are really pseudonymous writings, then this affects their interpretation, as they can no longer be read as genuine letters from the apostles but as literary creations that mimic genuine letters, thus raising ethical questions regarding their content, purpose and canonicity (see Porter 1995, 113-23; Ellis; Pearson and Porter, 136-37; for an alternative view of the Pastorals see Marshall 1996; *see DLNTD*, Pseudepigraphy). Here the whole Pauline corpus is understood as authentically Pauline.

J. L. White believes that "the common letter tradition, though certainly not the only tradition on which Paul depends, is the primary literary *Gattung* to which Paul's letters belong" (White 1972, xii). While we can agree that the Pauline corpus is comprised of letters, scholars are by no means agreed on the more precise classification of the letters, a debate that can only be hinted at here.

Some scholars have proposed genres for which there are no historical examples; therefore caution needs to be taken in the more detailed generic classification of individual letters. For example, it has been claimed that Galatians is an apologetic letter, though no other example of such a genre has been identified and it seems more likely that it is a letter of rebuke and request (Longenecker 1990, ciii-cv) or a deliberative letter (Aune 1987, 206-8).

Romans appears to be an occasional letter (Rom 1:7, cf. the specifics on the recipients in Rom 16:3-16), but is striking for its general and sustained theological argument in Romans 1:16—11:36 with its lack of any allusions to details peculiar to the Roman church, a situation that changes little in Romans 12:1—15:13, suggesting to some that the main body of the letter is a treatise incorporated within an occasional letter. This has led D. J. Moo (14-15) to argue that Romans is a tractate letter, rejecting claims that it is a diatribe, which he believes to have been a style rather than a genre. However, S. E. Porter (1991) has shown that *diatribe was a genre and that Paul has used the diatribe throughout the body of the letter (on the diatribe see Aune 1987, 200-202, and Stowers in Aune 1988, 71-83). Other proposed labels include epideictic, ambassadorial or protreptic letter and even letter essay, but while Romans has similarities to all these, perhaps Dunn's agnosticism about genre is nearer the mark: "The key fact here is that the distinctiveness of the letter far outweighs the significance of its conformity with current literary or rhetorical custom" (Dunn 1988, lix-lx).

Most of Paul's letters were addressed to Christian communities, were intended to be read within their liturgy and were clearly contextual, written to address the particular needs and circumstances of the recipients. At an early date the private letters (e.g., 1 and 2 Tim, Tit and Philem) were circulated and read among the churches, while even the most general of Paul's letters (Rom) includes material of limited interest (e.g., the greetings to individuals, Rom 16:3-16) and was also widely circulated among the churches in the same way as, though perhaps at a later date than, the letters intended for more than one church (e.g., Gal and Col).

4.2. The General Letters. Many features of the General letters have caused scholars to doubt their classification as letters, though with the exception of Hebrews they were known as the "epistles called catholic" by Eusebius in the fourth century (Eusebius *Hist. Eccl.* 2.23.24-25). In contrast to the Pauline letters, which are identified by their recipients, the General letters (excluding Hebrews) are identified by their authors.

For the most part discussion of the genre of the General letters has suggested various epistolary subcategories: 1 Peter an apocalyptic diaspora letter (Michaels 1988, xlvi-xlix; *see DLNTD,* 1 Peter) or a circular letter to several churches; 2 Peter has been classified as both a letter and a testament (Bauckham 1986, 131-35; *see DLNTD,* 2 Peter); 1 John's genre is much debated, suggestions ranging from a general treatise, sermon or encyclical, while 2 John and 3 John are the most obvious letters in the NT; and Jude is a letter, more specifically an "epistolary sermon" (Bauckham 1986, 3). However, the bulk of scholarly interest has focused on Hebrews and James.

Hebrews has been classified as a Jewish Hellenistic and early Christian homily or sermon that has been greatly influenced by classical rhetoric, noting its self-description as a "word of exhortation" (Heb 13:22), but it has also been defined as a written speech of encomium (*see DLNTD,* Letter, Letter Form, §3.1; many of the suggestions are listed by Ellingworth, 60-61 n. 27). Strictly speaking it does not conform to the letter genre, having no formal prescript, though it does have a benediction within its postscript (Heb 13:20-21) and greetings from the sender and his companions (Heb 13:24) followed by a second benediction (Heb 13:25), which has led P. Ellingworth (62) to accept its epistolary character, which displays "both written and (indirectly) oral communication." In the earliest manuscripts Hebrews is always included among the Pauline letters (Lane, lxix-lxx), and this probably explains its traditional classification as a letter. However, the consensus still maintains that Hebrews is a sermon or a homily (see Lane, lxx-lxxiv; *DLNTD,* Hebrews, §5).

Some scholars have argued that James is a sermon or a collection of sermons (for various suggestions see Adamson, 110-13), yet it has a clear prescript (sender, recipients and greeting, Jas 1:1), suggesting it is a circular letter to the numerous churches in the dispersion. Though it has no clear body, James 1:2-27 acts like the opening to a two-part body comprising James 2:1—5:12 and James 5:13-20, the latter replacing a formal postscript. On this basis it is seen as a letter (Martin 1988, xcviii-civ; Adamson, 113-18, believes it is a pastoral epistle, even "the first 'Papal Encyclical'").

5. Revelation.

The most common classifications for the genre of Revelation are an apocalypse, a letter or a prophetic book.

5.1. Revelation as an Apocalypse. The great majority of scholars regard Revelation as an apocalypse, particularly if the Society for Biblical Literature Genre Project's definition is accepted: "a genre of revelatory literature with a narrative framework, in which a revelation is mediated by an otherworldly being to a human recipient, disclosing a transcendent reality which is both temporal, insofar as it envisages eschatological salvation, and spatial, insofar as it involves another, supernatural world" (J. J. Collins, 9; cf. Aune 1997, lxxxi-lxxxii; this definition is not without its critics, e.g., D. Hellholm in A. Y. Collins, 26-27). This definition was subsequently modified, adding that apocalyptic was "intended to interpret present earthly circumstances in light of the supernatural world and of the future, and to influence both the understanding and the behavior of the audience by means of divine authority" (A. Y. Collins, 7).

While much of Revelation's contents comprise a series of visions, the author reports them in the first person (e.g., Rev 1:10; 4:1; 5:1), and since the book is accredited to John, suggestions of its pseudonymity (a characteristic of apocalyptic) are to be rejected because this John is not identified as a Christian worthy of the past. The recipients of the book evidently knew who John was: their "brother and companion in the persecution and kingdom" (Rev 1:9), a "servant of Jesus Christ" and one of the prophets (Rev 22:9).

In classifying Revelation's genre, much depends on whether *apokalypsis* in Revelation 1:1 is transliterated "apocalypse" or translated "revelation." Apocalypses were widely known in Jewish literature of the late centuries B.C. and early centuries A.D. and Christian circles of the postapostolic period; however, the word is used only in Revelation 1:1 as a description of the book, whereas "prophecy" is used in Revelation 1:3, then a further four times (Rev 22:7, 10, 18, 19; possibly a fifth in Rev 19:10). The juxtaposition of apocalypse and revelation in Revelation 1:1, 3 raises the possibility that to John the latter informs the former, and they are perhaps interchangeable, an equation also found in Paul (1 Cor 14:6, which also mentions knowledge and teaching; see also 1 Cor 14:26-33). In this case *apokalypsis* should be translated "revelation" (NIV), which means that the revelation is an oracle of God given to a Christian prophet and that the largest section of the book (Rev 4:1—22:9) comprises an otherworldly journey.

We can conclude, then, that while Revelation fits some definitions of an apocalypse, the author's self-references indicate he wrote as a Christian prophet. Since apocalyptic is widely believed to have developed out of the OT prophetic tradition this need be no surprise.

5.2. Revelation as a Prophecy. Not only is "revelation" a likely translation of Revelation 1:1, but also there is a great deal of internal evidence that supports the view that John was a Christian prophet (Rev 22:9) and a member of a larger group of Christian prophets (Rev 22:16a). If this is accepted, then Revelation is evidence that Christian prophecy adopted features characteristic of Jewish apocalypses at an early stage, a pattern also found in Daniel, Isaiah 25—27, Isaiah 40—55, Ezekiel 38—39 and Zechariah 9—14.

5.3. Revelation as a Letter. Both of the preceding suggestions have to take into account the fact that this apocalyptic prophecy has been set in the framework of a letter. Revelation 1:4-6 is clearly epistolary in form, referring to the sender, John, and the recipients, "the seven churches in the province of Asia" (Rev 1:4a), and is followed by a benediction (Rev 1:4b-5), ending with a brief benediction (Rev 22:21). In Revelation 1:11 John is commanded to write what he sees and send it to the seven churches in Asia, a command that relates to the whole book, not just the letters to the seven churches (Rev 2—3). These seven letters display some forms of ancient letters, but Aune has classified them as ancient royal or imperial edicts, which, as a collection, have no close analogies (Aune 1997, 130). These edicts never existed independently, as each church received the letters to the other churches and would have sent copies of the whole book to churches in other cities in the province (Ephesus being the administrative center of the province; Aune 1997, 130-32; cf. Victorinus *Comm. in Apoc.* 1.7: "what he says to one, he says to all"). The whole book was intended to be read to the gathered congregations (cf. Rev 1:3 and the epilogue in Rev 22:6-21).

If Revelation is a letter, then it is best classified as a general, or catholic, letter (cf. Gal, Col, 1 Pet and Jas), not a personal one, and it was probably a circular letter intended for the seven churches in Asia Minor (Rev 1:4; 2—3). Adoption of first-person style, while compatible with prophetic or apocalyptic literature ("autobiographical form" according to Aune in A. Y. Collins, 86-87), most clearly resembles the style of a letter, though Revelation is a letter with a story line, "apocalyptic in detailing visions mediated by angelic figures and prophetic in exhorting the churches with words of warning and encouragement" (Michaels 1992, 31). However, though the epistolary form of Revelation was known in the early church (Eusebius *Hist. Eccl.* 7.25.9-10), this "was accorded little or no interpretive significance" (Aune 1997, lxxii; see also lxxxii).

There are, then, reasons to classify Revelation as a mixed genre; for example, J. R. Michaels (1987) classifies it as a letter, more specifically a prophetic letter because of the long title prefixed to the letter proper (Rev 1:1-3), or an apocalyptic letter on the basis of its content, noting that if it is a letter, or an apocalypse or a prophecy, then it is unlike any other examples we have of these genres (Michaels 1992, 31-32). R. Bauckham has similarly suggested that three different genres are evident in Revelation (1993, 3-33). However, recognition of the prophetic and epistolary forms within the book does not necessarily overturn the consensus view that Revelation is a Christian apocalypse. Nevertheless, there is perhaps more at work in Revelation on the level of genre than that of apocalypse" (Pearson and Porter, 159).

See also APOCALYPTIC LITERATURE; BIOGRAPHY, ANCIENT; EPISTOLARY THEORY; LETTERS, GRECO-ROMAN; LITERACY AND BOOK CULTURE; WRITING AND LITERATURE: GRECO-ROMAN; WRITING AND LITERATURE: JEWISH.

BIBLIOGRAPHY. J. B. Adamson, *James: The Man and the Message* (Grand Rapids, MI: Eerdmans, 1989); L. C. A. Alexander, *The Preface to Luke's Gospel: Literary Convention and Social Context in Luke 1:1-4 and Acts 1:1* (SNTSMS 78; Cambridge: Cambridge University Press, 1993); D. E.

Aune, *The New Testament in Its Literary Environment* (Philadelphia: Westminster, 1987); idem, *Revelation 1—5* (WBC 52; Dallas: Word, 1997); D. E. Aune, ed., *Greco-Roman Literature and the New Testament: Selected Forms and Genres* (Atlanta: Scholars Press, 1988); D. L. Barr and J. L. Wentling, "The Convention of Classical Biography and the Genre of Luke-Acts: A Preliminary Study," in *Luke-Acts: New Perspectives from the Society of Biblical Literature Seminar,* ed. C. H. Talbert (New York: Crossroad, 1984) 63-88; R. Bauckham, "The Acts of Paul as a Sequel to Acts," in *The Book of Acts in Its Ancient Literary Setting,* ed. B. W. Winter and A. D. Clarke (BAFC 1; Grand Rapids, MI: Eerdmans, 1993); idem, *Jude, 2 Peter* (WBC 50; Waco, TX: Word, 1986); idem, *The Theology of the Book of Revelation* (NTT; Cambridge: Cambridge University Press, 1993); K. Berger, "Hellenistische Gattungen in Neuen Testament," in *ANRW* 2.25.2 (1984) 1031-1432; G. G. Bilezekian, *The Liberated Gospel: A Comparison of the Gospel of Mark and Greek Tragedy* (Grand Rapids, MI: Baker, 1977); C. L. Blomberg, "New Testament Genre Criticism for the 1990s," *Themelios* 15 (1990) 40-49; R. A. Burridge, *What Are the Gospels? A Comparison with Greco-Roman Biography* (SNTSMS 70; Cambridge: Cambridge University Press, 1992); A. Y. Collins, ed., *Early Christian Apocalypticism: Genre and Social Setting, Semeia* 36 (1986); J. J. Collins, ed., *Apocalypse: The Morphology of a Genre, Semeia* 14 (1979) 1-20; A. Deissmann, *Light from the Ancient East* (4th ed.; London: Hodder & Stoughton, 1927) 224-46; W. G. Doty, *Letters in Primitive Christianity* (Philadelphia: Fortress, 1973); J. D. G. Dunn, *Romans 1—8* (WBC 38A; Waco, TX: Word, 1988); P. Ellingworth, *The Epistle to the Hebrews: A Commentary on the Greek Text* (NIGTC; Grand Rapids, MI: Eerdmans, 1991); E. E. Ellis, "Pseudonymity and Canonicity of New Testament Documents," in *Worship, Theology and Ministry in the Early Church: Essays in Honor of R. P. Martin,* ed. M. J. Wilkins and T. Paige (JSNTSup 87; Sheffield: JSOT, 1992) 212-24; C. A. Evans, *Noncanonical Writings and New Testament Interpretation* (Peabody, MA: Hendrickson, 1992); R. T. France and D. Wenham, eds., *Gospel Perspectives: Studies of History and Tradition in the Four Gospels, Vol. 2* (Sheffield: JSOT, 1981); idem, *Gospel Perspectives: Studies in Midrash and Historiography, Vol. 3* (Sheffield: JSOT, 1983); M. D. Goulder, *The Evangelists' Calendar* (London: SPCK, 1978); R. H. Gundry, *Matthew: A Commentary on His Literary and Theological Art* (Grand Rapids, MI: Eerdmans, 1982); idem, "Recent Investigations into the Literary Genre 'Gospel,'" in *New Dimensions in New Testament Study,* ed. R. N. Longenecker and M. C. Tenney (Grand Rapids, MI: Zondervan, 1974) 97-114; D. Guthrie, *New Testament Introduction* (4th ed.; Downers Grove, IL: InterVarsity Press, 1990); M. Hadas and M. Smith, *Heroes and Gods: Spiritual Biographies in Antiquity* (New York: Harper & Row, 1962); R. G. Hall, *Revealed Histories: Techniques for Ancient Jewish and Christian Historiography* (JSPSup 6; Sheffield: Sheffield Academic Press, 1991); C. J. Hemer, *The Book of Acts in the Setting of Hellenistic History* (WUNT 49; Tübingen: Mohr Siebeck, 1989); M. Hengel, *Acts and the History of Earliest Christianity* (London: SCM, 1979); idem, *Studies in the Gospel of Mark* (London: SCM, 1985); M. G. Kline, "The Old Testament Origins of the Gospel Genre," *WTJ* 38 (1975) 1-27; W. G. Kümmel, *Introduction to the New Testament* (17th ed.; Nashville: Abingdon, 1975); W. L. Lane, *Hebrews 1—8* (WBC 47A; Waco, TX: Word, 1991); R. N. Longenecker, *Galatians* (WBC 41; Waco, TX: Word, 1990); idem, "On the Form, Function and Authority of the New Testament Letters" in *Scripture and Truth,* ed. D. A. Carson and J. D. Woodbridge (Leicester: InterVarsity Press, 1983) 101-14; R. Maddox, *The Purpose of Luke-Acts* (SNTW; Edinburgh: T & T Clark, 1982); I. H. Marshall, *The Acts of the Apostles* (NTG; Sheffield: JSOT, 1992); idem, "Prospects for the Pastorals," in *Doing Theology for the People of God: Studies in Honor of J. I. Packer,* ed. D. Lewis and A. E. McGrath (Downers Grove, IL: InterVarsity Press, 1996) 137-55; R. P. Martin, *James* (WBC 48; Waco, TX: Word, 1988); J. R. Michaels, *1 Peter* (WBC 49; Waco, TX: Word, 1988); idem, *Interpreting the Book of Revelation* (GNTE; Grand Rapids, MI: Baker, 1992); idem, "Jewish and Christian Apocalyptic Letters: 1 Peter, Revelation and 2 Baruch 78—87," *SBLSP* 26 (1987) 268-75; D. J. Moo, *The Epistle to the Romans* (NICNT; Grand Rapids: Eerdmans, 1996); B. W. R. Pearson and S. E. Porter, "The Genres of the New Testament," in *Handbook to Exegesis of the New Testament,* ed. S. E. Porter (Leiden: E. J. Brill, 1997) 131-65; R. I. Pervo, *Profit with Delight: The Literary Genre of the Acts of the Apostles* (Philadelphia: Fortress, 1987); S. E. Porter, "The Argument of Romans 5: Can a Rhetorical Question Make a Difference?" *JBL* 110 (1991) 655-77; idem, "Pauline Authorship and the Pastoral Epistles: Implications for Canon," *BBR* 5 (1995)

105-23; S. M. Praeder, "Luke-Acts and the Ancient Novel," *SBLSP* 20 (1981) 269-92; P. L. Shuler, *A Genre for the Gospels: The Biographical Character of Matthew* (Philadelphia: Fortress, 1982); G. N. Stanton, *Jesus of Nazareth in New Testament Preaching* (SNTSMS 27; Cambridge: Cambridge University Press, 1974); G. L. Sterling, *Historiography and Self-Definition: Josephus, Luke-Acts and Apologetic Historiography* (NovTSup 64; Leiden: E. J. Brill, 1992); S. K. Stowers, *Letter Writing in Greco-Roman Antiquity* (LEC 5; Philadelphia: Westminster, 1986); P. Stuhlmacher, ed., *The Gospel and the Gospels* (Grand Rapids, MI: Eerdmans, 1991); C. H. Talbert, *Literary Patterns, Theological Themes and the Genre of Luke-Acts* (SBLMS 20; Missoula, MT: Scholars Press, 1974); idem, *What Is a Gospel? The Genre of the Canonical Gospels* (Philadelphia: Fortress, 1977); D. L. Tiede, "Religious Propaganda and the Gospel Literature of the Early Christian Mission," in *ANRW* 2.25.2 (1984) 1705-29; J. A. D. Weima, *Neglected Endings: The Significance of the Pauline Letter Closings* (JSNTSup 101; Sheffield: JSOT, 1994); J. L. White, *The Form and Function of the Body of the Greek Letter: A Study of the Letter Body in the Nonliterary Papyri and in Paul the Apostle* (SBLDS 5; Missoula, MT: Scholars Press, 1972); idem, *Light from Ancient Letters* (Philadelphia: Fortress, 1986); B. W. Winter and A. D. Clarke, eds., *The Book of Acts in Its Ancient Literary Setting* (BAFCS 1; Grand Rapids, MI: Eerdmans, 1993).

A. R. Cross

GEOGRAPHICAL PERSPECTIVES IN LATE ANTIQUITY

The study of geographical perspectives in late antiquity is fraught with difficulties arising from the nature of the evidence. Very few world maps survive from antiquity that might aid us in directly perceiving these geographical perspectives. The Babylonian world map (c. 700-500 B.C.) is a rare exception (Horowitz). This paucity of artifactual evidence can be explained either as an accident of preservation or as an indication that world maps were uncommon in the ancient world. In any case, we are largely reliant on often obscure textual sources for reconstructing the geographic perspectives of late antiquity. Without the controls of maps, however, we cannot be sure that we are reading the sources correctly rather than foisting distortions, modern or otherwise, onto them.

This problem is compounded by the fact that NT scholars have shown little interest in studying ancient geographical perspectives, despite the fact that the geographic and ethnographic expansion of earliest Christianity from Jerusalem to the ends of the earth (Acts 1:8) could be greatly illuminated by these insights. Most attempts to write the history of early Christianity use the benefit of hindsight and global perspective to trace the larger patterns and developments of which individuals are a part. A classic example of this can be seen in the standard maps of the journeys of the apostle Paul included in most Bible atlases or appended to many modern Bibles. We are so accustomed to using such maps that we hardly stop to consider that the image of the world portrayed on them looks strangely modern in orientation, outline and scale. Thus we unwittingly read back into the biblical text our image of the world, an image that is the product of a centuries-long development (Whitfield).

In order to understand the NT on its own terms and in its own context, we need to engage with the geographical perspectives that were current in that day. Our task will not necessarily be straightforward and simple, for most NT writers moved freely between two worlds—the Greco-Roman and the OT/Jewish. To a certain degree these worlds overlapped, since Judaism had undergone extensive *Hellenization by the time of the NT. As a result, Greek and Roman conceptions of geography often permeate Jewish writings of the Second Temple period, including the NT.

1. Greco-Roman Background
2. Jewish Background

1. Greco-Roman Background.

Perhaps the best way to illustrate the interface between Greco-Roman and Jewish geographic conceptions in NT times is to take a specific example. The epigram of Philip of Thessalonia (*Anth. Gr.* 9.778) praises an artistic tapestry, which was made probably by Kypros, the wife of Agrippa I, the last king of Judea, and offered as a gift to a reigning "great Caesar," in all likelihood to Emperor Gaius (Scott). Woven into the fabric of the tapestry was an image of the world, which probably took the form of a disk-shaped earth encircled by ocean—a common Hellenistic conception (e.g., Homer *Il.* 18.399; *Odys.* 20.65; Herodotus *Hist.* 4.36; Strabo *Geog.* 2.5.17; Cicero *Somn.* 20).

It is probable that Kypros took as the model for her work the famous Agrippa map erected by Emperor Augustus in the Porticus Vipsanius in Rome. It is not impossible, however, that her inspiration was drawn from tapestries and textiles that were associated with the Jerusalem *temple and its priesthood (e.g., Wis 18:24; Josephus *Ant.* 3.7.7 §§183-84). Insofar as both the Agrippa map and the high-priestly vestment were influenced by Hellenistic conceptions of the world, the two possible influences may stem from a common cartographic source. By the same token, Kypros may have blended both Roman and Jewish traditions into her representation of the world, resulting in a novel, hybrid form—an orientalized version of the Agrippa map. In any case, the Kypros map well illustrates both the limitations of our sources and their potential for unlocking the complexities of ancient worldviews. The fascinating interplay between Greco-Roman and Jewish geographical conceptions has only begun to be investigated, and close study may yield rich dividends.

2. Jewish Background.

The so-called table of nations in Genesis 10 (cf. 1 Chron 1:4-23), along with a few other biblical givens, provides the basis for subsequent Jewish tradition that seeks to represent the world and its inhabitants (e.g., *Jub.* 8—9; **Genesis Apocryphon* 12—17; Josephus *Ant.* 1.5 §§120-47; Pseudo-Philo *Bib. Ant.* 4). Among these texts, *Jubilees* 8—9 seems to have had a major influence on early Christian tradition, including the book of Acts, the Jewish-Christian source in the Pseudo-Clementine *Recognitions* 1.27-71, Theophilus of Antioch, Hippolytus of Rome and the highly ramified *Diamerismos* tradition. Hence, we shall focus our attention here on the **Jubilees* text.

Jubilees 8:11—9:15 consists of two interrelated parts that are based on Genesis 10 but go well beyond the biblical text. In the first part (*Jub.* 8:11-30), Noah divides the earth by lot among his three sons, Shem, Ham and Japheth. This is the same order as they are at first listed in Genesis 10:1, that is, the order of their priority and primogeniture. In the second part (*Jub.* 9:1-15), Noah's sons, still in the presence of their father, subdivide their portions among their own sons, according to the order Ham, Shem and Japheth, that is, from south to north. As a result the whole world is covered twice, first by the three major lines of demarcation and then by the smaller subdivisions.

Whereas the original table of nations in Genesis 10 contains merely a list of Noah's descendants in which his grandsons appear directly after listing of each son, *Jubilees* 8—9 contains separate sections for the sons and the grandsons and provides explicit geographical boundaries between them. The procedure in *Jubilees* is thus more akin to the famous geographic work of Dionysius Periegetes of Alexandria, *Geographical Description of the Inhabited World,* written during the reign of Hadrian (A.D. 117-138), which first outlines the world by continents (Africa/ Libya, Europe, Asia [line 9]) and then subdivides the continents by tracing lines according to major geographical landmarks and noting the nations along the way (lines 170-1165). Also otherwise *Jubilees* 8—9 and Dionysius's work have many points in common. It may be, therefore, that *Jubilees* is adapting a Hellenistic method of geographical description at this point.

The first section of the *Jubilees* account begins in 8:11 by setting the scene: "When he [Noah] summoned his children, they came to him—they and their children. He divided the earth into the lots which his three sons would occupy. They reached out their hands and took the book from the bosom of their father Noah." This mention of a book of Noah is important, for the rest of *Jubilees* 8—9 goes on to describe the lots contained in that book. Thus, beginning with Shem, we read: "In the book there emerged as Shem's lot the center of the earth" (*Jub.* 8:12). Unlike the book of Noah to which 1QapGen 5:29 refers, the book in *Jubilees* 8:11, 12 does not record Noah's autobiography but rather a title deed drawn up by Noah for distributing land among his sons that is analogous to the distribution of the promised land among the twelve tribes.

From this book of Noah it becomes clear that Shem receives the most favorable portion in the temperate center of the earth (*Jub.* 8:12-21), with Mt. Zion "in the middle of the navel of the earth" (*Jub.* 8:19; cf. Ezek 5:5; 38:12); Ham receives the hot southern portion (*Jub.* 8:22-24); and Japheth receives the cold northern portion (*Jub.* 8:25-30). The geographical extent of these portions and the natural physical boundaries between them are described in great detail, following a circular path in each case: the descriptions of the territories of Shem and Japheth make a counterclockwise circuit beginning at the source of the Tina River; and the description of Ham's territory makes a clockwise circuit beginning at a place beyond the Gihon River, to the right (south) of the garden of Eden. Each description ends with a formula indicating that the portion allotted to that son became a possession to him and his descendants "forever" (*Jub.* 8:17, 24, 29).

The second section of the *Jubilees* account describes the further subdivision of the earth among the sons of Ham (9:1), Shem (9:2-6) and Japheth (9:7-13). Again, the natural physical boundaries of the portions are set out. At the conclusion of the process, Noah compels his sons and grandsons in *Jubilees* 9:14-15 to "swear by oath to curse each and every one who wanted to occupy the share which did not emerge by his lot. All of them said: 'So be it!' So be it for them and their children until eternity during their generations until the day of judgment on which the Lord God will punish them with the sword and fire because of all the evil of their errors by which they have filled the earth with wickedness, impurity, fornication, and sin." This conclusion gives *Jubilees* 8—9 an *apocalyptic orientation. Here there seems to be a connection between violation of territorial boundaries and the future divine judgment. In that case, world conquerors such as the Macedonians and later the Romans would be particularly subject to the coming judgment.

Jubilees 8—9 helps us appreciate how completely different Jewish geographical conceptions are from our modern Western perspectives. Here we see an orientation on the east rather than the north; a recognition of Jerusalem as the *omphalos,* or navel, of the world; and a tripartite division of the world going back purportedly to the time of Noah. This text forces us to rethink our assumptions as we interpret the NT's view of the geographic and ethnographic expansion of earliest Christianity.

See also ASIA MINOR; GALATIA, GALATIANS; GREECE AND MACEDON.

BIBLIOGRAPHY. L. Alexander, "Narrative Maps: Reflections on the Toponomy of Acts," in *The Bible in Human Society: Essays in Honor of John Rogerson,* ed. M. Daniel et al. (JSOTSup 200; Sheffield: Sheffield Academic Press, 1995) 17-57; P. S. Alexander, "Geography and the Bible (Early Jewish)," *ABD* 2:977-88; idem, "Notes on the 'Imago Mundi' of the Book of Jubilees," *JJS* 33 (1982) 197-213; O. A. W. Dilke, *Greek and Roman Maps* (London: Thames & Hudson, 1985); R. M. Grant, "Early Christian Geography," *VC* 46 (1992) 105-11; J. B. Harley and D. Woodward, eds., *The History of Cartography,* 1: *Cartography in Prehistoric, Ancient and Medieval Europe and the Mediterranean* (Chicago: University of Chicago Press, 1987); W. Horowitz, *Mesopotamian Cosmic Geography* (Mesopotamian Civilizations 8; Winona Lake, IN: Eisenbrauns, 1998); C. Nicolet, *Space, Geography and Politics in the Early Roman Empire* (Jerome Lectures 19; Ann Arbor: University of Michigan Press, 1991); A. V. Podossinov, "Die Orientierung der alten Karten von den ältesten Zeiten bis zum frühen Mittelalter," *Cartographica Helvetica* 7 (1993) 33-43; N. Purcell, "Geography," *OCD* (3d ed., 1996) 632-33; H. A. Redpath, "The Geography of the Septuagint," *AJT* 7 (1903) 289-307; J. S. Romm, *The Edges of the Earth in Ancient Thought: Geography, Exploration and Fiction* (Princeton, NJ: Princeton University Press, 1992); F. Schmidt, "Jewish Representations of the Inhabited Earth During the Hellenistic and Roman Periods," in *Greece and Rome in Eretz Israel: Collected Essays,* ed. A. Kasher et al. (Jerusalem: Yad Izhak Ben-Zvi/Israel Exploration Society, 1990) 119-34; J. M. Scott, *Geography in Early Judaism and Christianity: The Book of Jubilees* (SNTSMS; Cambridge: Cambridge University Press, forthcoming); idem, "Luke's Geographical Horizon," in *The Book of Acts in Its Greco-Roman Setting,* ed. D. W. J. Gill and C. Gempf (BAFCS 2; Grand Rapids, MI: Eerdmans; 1994) 483-544; idem, *Paul and the Nations: The Old Testament and Jewish Background of Paul's Mission to the Nations with Special Reference to the Destination of Galatians* (WUNT 84; Tübingen: Mohr Siebeck, 1995); L. I. J. Stadelmann, *The Hebrew Conception of the World: A Philological and Literary Study* (AnBib 39; Rome: Pontifical Biblical Institute, 1970); R. J. A. Talbert, "Mapping the Classical World: Major Atlases and Map Series 1872-1990," *Journal of Roman Archaeology* 5 (1992) 5-38; S. Talmon, "The 'Navel of the Earth' and the Comparative Method," in *Literary Studies in the Hebrew Bible: Form and Content: Collected Studies* (Jerusalem: Magnes, the Hebrew University; Leiden: E. J. Brill, 1993) 50-75; J. C. VanderKam, "1 Enoch 77:3 and a Babylonian Map of the World," *RevQ* 11 (1983) 271-78; idem, "Putting Them in Their Place: Geography as an Evaluative Tool," in *Pursuing the Text: Studies in Honor of Ben*

Zion Wacholder on the Occasion of his Seventieth Birthday, ed. J. C. Reeves and J. Kampen (JSOTSup 184; Sheffield: Sheffield Academic Press, 1994) 46-69; A. Vasaly, *Representations: Images of the World in Ciceronian Oratory* (Berkeley and Los Angeles: University of California Press, 1993); P. Whitfield, *The Image of the World: Twenty Centuries of World Maps* (London: The British Library, 1994).

J. M. Scott

GNOSTICISM

Gnosticism is a term that designates a variety of religious movements that stressed salvation through *gnōsis*, or "knowledge," that is, of one's origins. Most scholars would identify as an essential of Gnosticism the element of cosmological dualism—an opposition between the spiritual world and the evil, material world.

1. Varieties of Gnosticism
2. Sources
3. Gnostic Doctrines
4. Gnostic Ethics
5. Gnostic Communities
6. Scholarship on Gnosticism

1. Varieties of Gnosticism.

Because of the variegated nature of Gnosticism, it is difficult to fit every gnostic teacher into a common framework. Marcion, who advocated the concept of two gods, the god of the OT and the god of the NT, has many affinities with the Gnostics, yet he lacked their mythology and emphasized faith rather than saving *gnōsis*. A major branch of Gnosticism, which followed the teachings of Valentinus, was heavily influenced by *Platonism. Scholars have recognized another branch of Gnosticism, which has been termed Sethianism, a more mythological system that exalted the OT figure Seth as a key revealer (see Layton).

It should be noted that the ancient sources of these movements and their Christian critics do not use the term *Gnosticism* and rarely used the term *Gnostics*. M. A. Williams has therefore called upon scholars to abandon the term. But it is not likely that his proposed substitution, "biblical demiurgical traditions," will be adopted. But his reminder that "Gnosticism" is a scholarly construct should always be borne in mind.

2. Sources.

Texts that are unambiguously gnostic date from the second century A.D. Those who maintain a pre-Christian Gnosticism assume the early existence of Gnosticism and interpret the NT texts in the light of this assumption. Some of the Nag Hammadi treatises, though late in composition, have been adduced by some scholars as evidence of a pre-Christian Gnosticism.

2.1. Patristic Sources. Until recently scholars were entirely dependent upon the descriptions of the Gnostics found in the church fathers. In some cases the patristic sources preserved extracts of the gnostic writings. Our most important sources include Justin Martyr of Samaria (d. 165), Irenaeus of Lyons (d. c. 225), Clement of Alexandria (d. c. 215), Tertullian of Carthage (d. c. 225), Hippolytus of Rome (d. c. 236), Origen of Alexandria and Caesarea (d. 254) and Epiphanius of Salamis in Cyprus (d. 403) (see Grant).

Especially valuable is Irenaeus's account, which has been preserved in a Latin translation, *Adversus Haereses*. He refers to an *Apocryphon of John*, copies of which were found at Nag Hammadi. The *Philosophoumena* of Hippolytus was identified in 1842. Clement and Origen were in some ways sympathetic to the gnostic emphasis of a spiritual elite. Tertullian railed against Marcion and Valentinus. Though Epiphanius had some firsthand contact with Gnostics in Egypt, his *Panarion*, while comprehensive, is not very reliable.

As one would expect, the earlier sources are the most reliable and the later sources less so. Needless to say, these accounts were highly polemical. Nothing in the recently recovered gnostic sources from Nag Hammadi supports the patristic description of licentious Gnosticism.

2.2. Gnostic Teachers. The church fathers, including the historian Eusebius (fourth century), provide a list of prominent Gnostics and their teachings.

The church fathers were unanimous in regarding Simon of Samaria as the arch-Gnostic, though our earliest source, Acts 8, describes him only as someone who practiced *magic. According to the patristic sources Simon claimed to be divine and taught that his companion, a former prostitute, was the reincarnated Helen of Troy. Those who accept the patristic view of Simon believe that Acts has not given us an accurate portrayal of Simon. Most scholars, however, believe that the church fathers were mistaken (see Filoramo, 148).

According to the church fathers, Simon was followed by a fellow Samaritan, Menander, who taught at *Antioch in Syria toward the end of the first century. He claimed that those who believed in him would not die.

Also teaching in Antioch at the beginning of the second century was Saturninus, who held that the "incorporeal" Christ was the redeemer. That is, he held a docetic view of Christ that denied the incarnation (cf. 1 Jn 4:3). He also taught that *marriage and procreation were from Satan.

Teaching in Asia Minor in the early second century was Cerinthus, who held that Jesus was but a man upon whom Christ descended as a dove at his baptism. As Christ could not suffer, he withdrew from Jesus before the crucifixion.

Another early gnostic teacher was Basilides, to whom we have attributed both a dualistic system by Irenaeus and a monistic system by Hippolytus. Basilides regarded the god of the Jews as an oppressive angel. He held that Christ did not suffer, but that Simon of Cyrene was crucified in his place, while the invisible Christ stood by laughing. Similar docetic concepts are now attested in two Nag Hammadi tractates, the *Second Treatise of the Great Seth* (CG VII,2) and the *Apocalypse of Peter* (CG VII,3).

An important though atypical Gnostic was Marcion of Pontus (northern Turkey), who taught at Rome from 137 to 144. He contrasted the god of the OT with the god of the NT. Marcion drew up the first canon or closed list of NT books, including a truncated Gospel of Luke. Jesus simply appeared; his body was a "phantom." Marcion's followers spread to Egypt, Mesopotamia and Armenia. His docetic teachings were sharply rebuked by Tertullian. A. Harnack hailed Marcion as the church's first great theologian and characterized Gnosticism as the acute *Hellenization of Christianity (see Helleman).

The most famous gnostic teacher was Valentinus, who came from *Alexandria to Rome in 140. He taught that there was a series of divine eons or emanations. He divided humankind into three classes: *hylics,* or unbelievers immersed in nature and the flesh; *psychics,* or common Christians who lived by faith; and *pneumatics* or spiritual Gnostics. The later Valentinians divided into an Italian and an Oriental school over the question of whether Jesus had a psychic or pneumatic body. The many outstanding Valentinian teachers included Ptolemaeus, Theodotus and Marcus. The earliest known commentary on a NT book is Heracleon's on the Gospel of John, passages of which are preserved by Origen in his commentary.

A number of the Nag Hammadi tractates such as *The Gospel of Truth* (CG I,3 and XII,2), *The Treatise on the Resurrection* (CG I,4), *The Tripartite Tractate* (CG I,5), *The Gospel of Philip* (CG II,3) and *A Valentinian Exposition* (CG XI,2) have been identified as Valentinian. Contrary to the earlier impression that the Valentinians were only concerned with the pneumatics, who would be saved by the *gnōsis* of their nature, a study by M. R. Desjardins indicates that they were also concerned about the psychics, who would have to lead sinless lives to be saved.

2.3. Mandaic Sources. The Mandean communities in southern Iraq and southwestern Iran are today the sole surviving remnants of Gnosticism. Their texts, though known only through late (seventeenth- or eighteenth-century) manuscripts, were used by the history-of-religions scholars to reconstruct an alleged pre-Christian Gnosticism. In addition to the manuscripts there are earlier magic bowl texts (A.D. 600) and some magical lead amulets, which may date to as early as the third century A.D. There is no firm evidence to date the origins of Mandeanism earlier than the second century A.D. (see Yamauchi 1970).

2.4. Coptic Sources. Coptic is a late form of Egyptian written mainly in Greek letters. In the nineteenth century two Coptic gnostic codices were published: the Codex Askewianus containing the *Pistis Sophia,* and the Codex Brucianus containing the *Books of Jeu*—both relatively late gnostic compositions. A third work, the Codex Berolinensis (BG 8502), though acquired in the nineteenth century, was not published until 1955. It contains a *Gospel of Mary* (Magdalene), a *Sophia of Jesus, Acts of Peter* and an *Apocryphon of John*—the work mentioned by Irenaeus.

2.5. The Nag Hammadi Library. In 1945 a cache of eleven Coptic codices and fragments of two others were found by peasants near Nag Hammadi in Upper Egypt, 370 miles south of Cairo, where the Nile bends from west to east (*see DLNTD,* Gnosis, Gnosticism). The first translation of a tractate, that of *The Gospel of Truth,* appeared in 1956. Through the efforts of J. M. Robinson and his collaborators, an English translation of the fifty-one treatises was produced in 1977.

The Nag Hammadi Library, as the collection

is now called, contains a variety of texts: non-gnostic, non-Christian gnostic and Christian gnostic. The most famous tractate is *The Gospel of Thomas,* which contains 114 purported sayings of Jesus. In 1897 and in 1904 B. P. Grenfell and A. S. Hunt had discovered at Oxyrhynchus in Egypt noncanonical sayings or the so-called logia of Jesus. We now know that these papyri came from the Greek text that had been translated as the Coptic *Gospel of Thomas* (*see* Gospels, Apocryphal).

2.6. Hermetic Sources. The *Hermetica* are writings ascribed to Hermes Trismegistos ("thrice-great"), the Greek title for Thoth, the Egyptian god of wisdom (*see* Hermeticism). Composed in the second to third century A.D. in Greek in Egypt, they were highly esteemed in medieval times. The Greek *Corpus Hermeticum* was influenced by dualistic Platonism and pantheistic *Stoicism. Hermetic tractates have also been found in the Nag Hammadi Codex VI. Though there are affinities with Gnosticism, the *Hermetica* lack its radical dualism.

2.7. Syriac Sources. Some Syriac texts such as the **Odes of Solomon* and the *Hymn of the Pearl* from the *Acts of Thomas* have been cited by some scholars such as K. Rudolph as early gnostic sources. Other scholars, however, doubt their gnostic character.

2.8. Manichean Sources. Mani (A.D. 216-276) established a remarkably successful gnostic movement, which spread from Mesopotamia to the West, where Augustine became an adherent for nine years, and to the East, where it reached China along the Silk Road. Manicheanism was a highly syncretistic religion that combined materials taken from Judaism, Christianity, Zoroastrianism and Buddhism. The publication of a tiny Greek manuscript in 1970, the Cologne Codex, confirmed that Mani had emerged from a baptistic sect known as the Elchasaites. Manichean texts were written in many languages, including Coptic, Syriac, Persian, Uighur (a Turkish dialect) and Chinese (see Klimkeit).

3. Gnostic Doctrines.

Because there was no central authority or *canon of scriptures, the Gnostics taught a bewildering variety of views. Fundamental to clearly gnostic systems was a dualism that opposed the transcendent God and an ignorant demiurge (often a caricature of the OT Jehovah). In some systems the creation of the world resulted from the presumption of Sophia (Wisdom). The material creation, including the body, was regarded as inherently evil. Sparks of divinity, however, had been encapsuled in the bodies of certain pneumatic or spiritual individuals, who were ignorant of their celestial origins. The transcendent God sent down a redeemer, who brought them salvation in the form of secret *gnōsis.* Gnostics hoped to escape from the prison of their bodies at death and to traverse the planetary spheres of hostile demons to be reunited with God. There was for them, of course, no reason to believe in the *resurrection of the body.

4. Gnostic Ethics.

According to the church fathers, Carpocrates urged his followers to participate in all sins, while his son Epiphanes taught that promiscuity was God's law. The Valentinians held a positive view of marriage, not so much for the sake of procreation but as a symbol of the archetypal unity of the sexes. Most Gnostics took a radically ascetic attitude toward sex and marriage, deeming the creation of woman the source of evil and the procreation of children but the multiplication of souls in bondage to the powers of darkness.

5. Gnostic Communities.

We know very little about the cult and the community of the Gnostics. As a general rule the Gnostics interpreted rites such as *baptism and the Eucharist as spiritual symbols of *gnōsis.* Several of the Nag Hammadi tractates contain violent polemic against water baptism. E. Pagels has argued that gnostic groups gave women a greater position in leadership than the orthodox church fathers such as Irenaeus and Tertullian. But D. Hoffman has shown that women were exploited by Gnostics.

6. Scholarship on Gnosticism.

Prior to the twentieth century scholars had uncritically accepted the patristic description of Gnosticism as a failed Christian heresy. Though S. Pétrement has attempted to defend this traditional view, most scholars now believe that Gnosticism is best understood as an independent religion. Whether it existed prior to the birth of Christianity or was roughly contemporary with its development is still a disputed issue.

The concept of a pre-Christian Gnosticism

was first proposed by W. Anz in 1897 and then forcefully promoted by the *religionsgeschichtliche Schule*, or history-of-religions school, most notably by W. Bousset (d. 1920) and R. Reitzenstein (d. 1931).

Inspired by the history-of-religions scholars as well as by publication of Mandaic texts, in 1925 R. Bultmann outlined a classic model of the pre-Christian gnostic redeemer myth. Bultmann and his influential students interpreted much of the NT on the assumption of a pre-Christian Gnosticism. An extreme application of this viewpoint has been promoted by W. Schmithals, who has interpreted all of Paul's opponents, even those in Galatia, as Gnostics.

With the discovery of the Nag Hammadi corpus, a renewed attempt has been made by J. M. Robinson and others to establish a case for a pre-Christian Gnosticism on the basis of a number of Nag Hammadi tractates.

One clear example of the appropriation of a gnostic text by a Christian editor is the recasting of the non-Christian *Eugnostos* (CG III,3 and V,1) by *The Sophia of Jesus Christ* (CG III,4 and BG 8502). But the alleged non-Christian nature of *Eugnostos* has been disputed as well as its Gnostic character.

Several scholars have contended that *The Apocalypse of Adam* (CG V,5) is a non-Christian work that provides evidence of a pre-Christian redeemer myth. One passage relates thirteen numbered kingdoms that are faulty explanations of the Illuminator. But the alleged non-Christian character of this tractate has been challenged because of a reference to the punishment of the flesh of the Illuminator upon whom the holy spirit came.

The Paraphrase of Shem (CG VII,1) has also been claimed to be evidence of a pre-Christian Gnosticism by F. Wisse, who first published studies on it. But more recent studies have concluded that its sharp polemic against water baptism is best understood as a sectarian protest against the dominant church.

G. (Schenke) Robinson has interpreted the *Trimorphic Protennoia* (CG XIII,1) as containing evidence of a pre-Christian gnostic Logos hymn underlying the prologue of the Gospel of John. Verbal parallels to the prologue, however, convince others that this Coptic text bears evidence of a dependence upon John's prologue.

W. Bauer's seminal work, *Rechtgläubigkeit und Ketzerei im ältesten Christentum,* first published in 1934, was belatedly translated into English as *Orthodoxy and Heresy in Earliest Christianity* in 1971. His provocative thesis was that contrary to the triumphalistic history of Eusebius, earliest Christianity was quite pluralistic. In fact, in Syria, Asia Minor and Egypt the earliest Christians and the most numerous Christians were gnostic rather than orthodox. Orthodoxy was established only much later through the influence of the Roman church. Scholars such as T. A. Robinson have pointed out that many of Bauer's propositions were based on arguments from silence. The evidence of the papyri in Egypt and other texts speak against his revisionist view of early Christian history.

See also HERMETICISM; ODES OF SOLOMON.

BIBLIOGRAPHY. W. Bauer, *Orthodoxy and Heresy in Earliest Christianity,* ed. R. Kraft and G. Krodel (Philadelphia: Fortress, 1971); M. R. Desjardins, *Sin in Valentinianism* (Atlanta: Scholars Press, 1990); G. Filoramo, *A History of Gnosticism* (Oxford: Blackwell, 1992); R. M. Grant, ed., *Gnosticism: A Sourcebook of Heretical Writings from the Early Christian Period* (New York: Harper & Brothers, 1961); W. E. Helleman, ed., *Hellenization Revisited* (Lanham, MD: University Press of America, 1994); D. Hoffman, *The Status of Women and Gnosticism in Irenaeus and Tertullian* (Lewiston, NY: Edwin Mellen Press, 1995); H.-J. Klimkeit, *Gnosis on the Silk Road* (New York: HarperCollins, 1993); B. Layton, ed., *The Rediscovery of Gnosticism* (2 vols.; Leiden: E. J. Brill, 1980-81); E. Pagels, *The Gnostic Gospels* (New York: Random House, 1979); B. A. Pearson, *Gnosticism, Judaism and Egyptian Christianity* (Minneapolis: Fortress, 1990); P. Perkins, *Gnosticism and the New Testament* (Minneapolis: Fortress, 1998); S. Pétrement, *A Separate God: The Christian Origins of Gnosticism* (San Francisco: HarperCollins, 1990); J. M. Robinson, ed., *The Nag Hammadi Library in English* (3d ed.; San Francisco: HarperCollins, 1990); T. A. Robinson, *The Bauer Thesis Examined* (Lewiston, NY: Edwin Mellen Press, 1988); K. Rudolph, *Gnosis* (San Francisco: HarperCollins, 1987); W. Schmithals, *Neues Testament und Gnosis* (Darmstadt: Wissenschaftliche Buchgesellschaft, 1984); J. D. Turner and A. McGuire, eds., *The Nag Hammadi Library After Fifty Years* (Leiden: E. J. Brill, 1997); M. A. Williams, *Rethinking "Gnosticism": An Argument for Dismantling a Dubious Category* (Princeton, NJ: Princeton University Press, 1996); E. M. Yamauchi, *Gnostic Ethics and Mandean Origins* (Cambridge, MA: Harvard University Press, 1970); idem, *Pre-Christian Gnosticism* (2d ed.; Grand Rapids, MI: Baker, 1983).

E. M. Yamauchi

GODFEARERS. *See* PROSELYTISM AND GODFEARERS.

GODS. *See* RELIGION, GRECO-ROMAN; RELIGION, PERSONAL

GOVERNORS. *See* ROMAN GOVERNORS OF PALESTINE.

GRAMMARIANS, HELLENISTIC GREEK

Self-conscious and systematic study of the Greeks' own language came relatively late to their intellectual discourse. Nevertheless, the Greco-Roman period was important for advancements made in understanding of the Greek language, although the comments remain rudimentary by modern linguistic standards.

1. Classical Thought on Greek Grammar
2. The Hellenistic Greek Grammarians
3. Implications for Study of the Greek of the New Testament

1. Classical Thought on Greek Grammar.
Despite the formative influence of such *philosophers as *Plato and *Aristotle on many areas of intellectual investigation, their comments on language remained undeveloped, suggesting but not resolving fundamental issues. This was especially true in the area of formal grammar. In the area of semantics, more productive comments were made, but without systematizing their observations.

There are a number of early, incidental, linguistically sound comments in Greek writers. For example, Heraclitus (B 93) appears to have been the first to distinguish between saying and signifying, recognizing that the two are not synonymous. Some other thinkers who made revealing comments are Protagoras, who distinguishes gender and some types of sentences; Prodicus, who was concerned with usage; Hippias of Elis, who was interested in the power of letters and syllables; and Democritus, who was intrigued by the fact that a single item can have several names and that a word can refer to several different things (Wouters, 33).

Many of these comments reveal a curiosity with individual words and especially names—where they come from and what they might mean. This is an understandable interest in the light of the oral culture out of which Greek thought developed (Sluiter 1997, 155-77). Homer makes the necessary temporal distinction between past, present and future (Homer *Il.* 1.70), as do Euripides (*Tro.* 468 and *El.* frag. 3.15) and Plato (*Rep.* 392D). (In none of these examples are the aorist, present and future tenses used in a way that equates them with past, present and future time.) Several authors also make distinctions in kind of action (e.g., Plato *Thaeat.* 155BC; Aristotle *Eth. Nic.* 1173A34-B4). Despite their obvious fundamental understanding of linear time and kinds of action, however, the Greeks took much longer to formulate a theory of temporality and tense usage (an item of continuing debate regarding Greek language), and much longer still to formulate a grammatical theory.

It was Plato who offered some of the first descriptive categories of language, differentiating between the nominal and verbal components of sentences. Aristotle did likewise, adding a third category of conjunctions. Aristotle first explicitly posited that the verb is "the thing that indicates time" (Aristotle *Int.* 16B; however, some scholars believe that these statements are later additions to Aristotle) and developed the idea of predication. One of the major tensions in classical Greek linguistic thought was that between the perspectives that the correctness of names was because of their inherent nature (*physis*) or because of human convention (*nomos*). Plato's *Cratylus,* arguably the only ancient writing on general linguistic questions, is concerned to show that naming derives from nature rather than convention (see Sluiter 1997). This is consistent with Plato's concern for truth and reality, as opposed to opting for a philosophical and linguistic relativism. At one point, Plato offers this etymology of the word *anthrōpos* ("man"). He says that it comes from the verb *anathērei* ("look up") and *opōpe* ("he has seen"), because only man looks up and has seen. Although this example may sound ridiculous, it reveals his fundamental philosophical orientation being worked out in linguistic thought.

Aristotle's position on the meaning of language, found most fully in *On Interpretation,* which became probably the most discussed ancient work that treats linguistic questions, departs from the view of Plato that links words and things. Without working out a full theory of language but being more concerned with how one makes judgments, Aristotle anticipated much later work by recognizing a functional dimension to language and by expanding the concept of the linguistic sign to encompass its symbolic rather than mimetic value (Sluiter 1997, 109-10).

2. The Hellenistic Greek Grammarians.

In the Hellenistic period, thought concerning language was divided into two branches, with philosophers (*Stoics and *Epicureans) concerned with larger issues and grammarians concerned with philology. The philological issues concern this article.

The only extant manual of Greek grammar, called the *Technē* of Dionysius the Grammarian, is attributed to the Alexandrian scholar Dionysius Thrax, who lived around 120 B.C. Some scholars, however, attribute this work to the third or fourth century A.D., and there is considerable question about the arrangement of the sections of the work, which indicates that the grammar underwent much alteration and editing. This is shown by the fact that Dionysius's grammar exists in several different manuscripts (Uhlig and Hilgard, vol. 1.1:3-101), including papyri from Egypt (Wouters, 33-124), and in several different languages (Syrian and Armenian), with fairly extensive scholia on various points as well (Uhlig and Hilgard, *Dionysii Thracis*, vol. 1.3). Dionysius's grammar is an exercise in classification and division for students, in which he claims to do an empirical study based upon what the poets and writers do. As a result he discusses how writing works, including such things as reading, sound, accentuation and recitation. He also discusses the components of language, such as the letters, syllables (by length) and the word, the smallest unit of syntax.

Under the category of the word, Dionysius distinguishes eight sections. The first is the noun, where he, for example, notes the three genuses and three numbers, besides several categories regarding word formation and declension. He also lists meaning relations, such as homonyms, synonyms and antonyms. The second major category is the verb, where he distinguishes mood, voice, number and time, plus several subsections regarding word formation and declension. Perhaps of most interest and continuing relevance for scholarly discussion is what he says of the times or tenses. He distinguishes three times—present, past and future—and four kinds of past tense, the imperfect, perfect, pluperfect and aorist. Dionysius is perhaps the first ancient author to use the term *aorist* to label a tense form. He also notes three relationships among the tenses: present to imperfect, perfect to pluperfect and aorist to future. His temporal categories do not equate with single tense forms, and although he notes relations between the forms, it is unclear whether these are based on form or function. Dionysius then has sections on the correspondence of certain letters, the participle (which shares characteristics of the noun and verb), the article, pronouns, prepositions, adverbs and conjunctions. Although his grammar is comprehensive, it does not go into detail, being content with classification and division at the level of the word. It was left to later writers to develop the categories further, although Dionysius gives a good idea of the kinds of terms and forms available for discussion.

The second category of grammarians is the Stoics. Although Stoicism itself predates the writings of Dionysius Thrax and there are a number of important comments regarding language that predate him (see for example comments recorded in such authors as Diogenes Laertius *Vit.*, esp. book 7), much of this work was governed more by philosophical interests than by linguistic concerns (see Sluiter 1990, 5-37). For example, the Stoics first differentiated between signifier and signified (Diogenes Laertius *Vit.* 7.62). As a result, the most important Stoic writing on grammar seems to be in response to the work of Dionysius Thrax.

Of the many Stoic grammarians, the later scholiast Stephanus is perhaps the most important. His comments, along with numerous observations of others on Dionysius's work, are found in a thirteenth-century codex now located in the Vatican (see Uhlig and Hilgard, vol. 1.3, 192-292 passim). Beginning with the letters, Stephanus makes comments on most parts of Dionysius's grammar. One of Stephanus's most im-portant set of comments is upon the times or tenses. Although reflecting the Alexandrian terminology, Stephanus works from tense form oppositions and utilizes both temporal distinctions and kind of action. The present form is thus defined as present incomplete and the imperfect form as past incomplete, and these are clearly related to each other on the basis of completion and sound (they are formed around the same stem). For complete action, Stephanus refers to the perfect and pluperfect forms. However, since they both deal with past accomplishment, the same scheme as above does not apply. The aorist is invoked to distinguish between the two: an act represented by the aorist as just occurring becomes the perfect, in the sense of "I just did" becomes "I have done," and an act in the distant past becomes the pluperfect. The aorist is defined as being related to the future on the basis of its indefiniteness. Despite the commendable attempt to reconcile time and kind of action, the Stoic view as represented by Stephanus is flawed by its failure to adequately define the aorist, future and perfect/pluperfect and by his retention of the time-based scheme.

The third category of grammarians is Apollonius Dyscolus, whose work is dated to the second century A.D. (see Sluiter 1990, 39-142). A number of works are ascribed to Apollonius Dyscolus, including several minor works on such topics as pronouns, adverbs and conjunctions (Uhlig and Schneider, vol. 2.1). Even though these are considered among his minor works, they go into far greater detail than those of any previous grammarian whose work is extant. His work moves beyond simple classification and division to include examples from earlier authors, such as Homer. Much of this work is derivative from Dionysius Thrax, however. Apollonius Dyscolus's most well known work, however, is his extensive syntax (see Householder; Blank). This is the only extant treatise of this sort from the ancient world. There is much terminology in common between Apollonius Dyscolus and the Stoic grammarians, for example regarding verbal structure, which commonalty has led to questions of genetic relationship. Some scholars attribute the Stoic position directly to Apollonius Dyscolus, while others differentiate the two. The less systematic nature of Apollonius Dyscolus's treatment, and his greater inclusion of examples, tends to indicate later and derivative thought, in which he has provided examples for others' categories. According to tradition, Apollonius Dyscolus's son was Herodianus, who wrote an extensive treatise on Greek grammar. However, Herodianus's writings have not been preserved and must be reconstructed by compiling later references and quotations (as has been done in Lentz, 3.1 and 3.2).

The fourth and final category of Hellenistic Greek grammarians includes those unnamed grammarians whose fragmentary writings have been discovered, especially in the papyri (see Wouters). Although no complete manual has yet been discovered in these papyri, there are a number of fragments of importance. Several of these fragments are portions of the manuals already known, such as fragments assigned to Dionysius Thrax (P.Hal. 55a; *PSI* 1.18), while others clearly have a relationship to his work (P. Yale 1.25; P.Lit.Lond. 182; P.Mich. 7.429; P.Lit. Lond. 184). Others, however, are unassigned, often having only a column or two of text (P.Heid. Siegmann 197, 198; *PSI*. 505 and 7.761, P.Brooklyn 47.218.36; P.Oslo 2.13; P.Iand. 83a and 5.83; P.Harr. 59; P.Amh. 2.21; P.Ant. 2.68). Nevertheless these fragmentary texts provide suggestive material. For example, they illustrate that there was difference of opinion among the ancient writers of grammatical manuals regarding the number of the parts of speech, their sequence and their definitions. The scope and arrangements of these works, as well as their use of examples, seem to have differed as well. The relationship of these manuals to more scholarly treatises, such as that by Apollonius Dyscolus, is also a matter of scholarly debate (see Wouters, 44-45). Insofar as grammatical treatises are concerned, there are fragments from a number of authors that have been found on papyri. These include Herodianus's work on prosody (P.Ant. 2.67, which according to Wouters provides a resume); several works on noun inflection, including one unknown (P.Oxy. 15.1801) and one a compendium of Herodianus's work (P.Firenze 3005); a number on verbal inflection, including one on participles (P.Rain. 1.19); one on irregular words by Heraclides of Miletus (P.Rain. 3.33A); one on augments (*PSI* 7.849); one on contracted verbs (P.Oxy. 3.469) and one on the perfect tense (P.Iand. 1.5); and a work on the Aeolic dialect (P.Bour. 8).

3. Implications for Study of the Greek of the New Testament.

Several comments can be made with regard to the value of studying the Hellenistic Greek grammarians for understanding the background to the NT. The first is that one gains a clearer picture of the kinds of linguistic questions being asked and the kinds of answers being provided by the ancients regarding the Greek that they used. Rather than idealizing the accomplishments of the ancients or unnecessarily denigrating their failures, we need to realize that linguistic investigation was in its rudimentary forms. One should not be overly critical of their attempts, since every author's work must be seen in the context of its origins. However, despite their efforts, much has been learned since.

A second observation is that the foundational work that Dionysius Thrax and the Stoics performed, and to a lesser extent Apollonius Dyscolus and various unnamed grammarians, has perhaps had too much of a restrictive influence on subsequent thought. To a large extent, many of the categories of subsequent grammatical discussion of Greek and Latin have been formulated on the basis of this work (even up to the twentieth century), and this has had a retarding effect on much investigation. For example, because the Hellenistic Greek grammarians discussed tense forms primarily in terms of time and were unable to clearly formulate what they instinctively recognized about the role of kind of action, temporal categories—though they clearly failed to be explanatory then (and now)—were maintained as determinative (see Porter, 18-22).

The third observation is that the work of the ancients should provide impetus for continuing to gain a better understanding of Greek grammar. The ancients themselves lacked much understanding of their own language, but much has been learned since their work, and much more potentially can be learned in the future.

See also GREEK OF THE NEW TESTAMENT; SCHOLARSHIP, GREEK AND ROMAN.

BIBLIOGRAPHY. D. L. Blank, *Ancient Philosophy and Grammar: The Syntax of Apollonius Dyscolus* (ACS 10; Chico, CA: Scholars Press, 1982); F. Householder, trans., *The Syntax of Apollonius Dyscolus* (ASTHL 3; SHL 23; Amsterdam: Benjamins, 1981); A. Lentz, ed., *Herodiani Technici Reliquiae* (GG 3.1, 2; Leipzig: Teubner, 1867, 1868; Hildesheim: Georg Olms, 1965); R. Pfeiffer, *A History of Classical Scholarship* (Oxford: Clarendon Press, 1968); S. E. Porter, *Verbal Aspect in the Greek of the New Testament, with Reference to Tense and Mood* (SBG 1; New York: Peter Lang, 1989); R. H. Robins, *Ancient and Medieval Grammatical Theory in Europe: With Particular Reference to Modern Linguistic Doctrine* (London: Bell, 1951); idem, *A Short History of Linguistics* (2d ed.; London: Longmans, 1979); R. Schneider, ed., *Apollonii Dyscoli Scripta Minora, Commentarius Criticus et Exegeticus* (GG 2.1; Leipzig: Teubner, 1878; Hildesheim: Georg Olms, 1965); I. Sluiter, *Ancient Grammar in Context: Contributions to the Study of Ancient Linguistic Thought* (Amsterdam: VU University Press, 1990); idem, "The Greek Tradition," in *The Emergence of Semantics in Four Linguistic Traditions: Hebrew, Sanskrit, Greek, Arabic,* W. van Bekkum, J. Houben, I. Sluiter and K. Versteegh (SHLS 82; Amsterdam: Benjamins, 1997) 147-224; G. Uhlig and A. Hilgard, eds., *Dionysii Thracis Ars Grammatica, Scholia in Dionysii Aratem Grammaticam* (GG 1.1, 3; Leipzig: Teubner, 1883, 1901; Hildesheim: Georg Olms, 1965); G. Uhlig and R. Schneider, eds., *Apollonii Dyscoli De Constructione Libri Quattuor, Librorum Apollonii Deperditorum Fragmenta* (GG 2.2, 3; Leipzig: Teubner, 1910; Hildesheim: Georg Olms, 1965); A. Wouters, *The Grammatical Papyri from Greco-Roman Egypt: Contributions to the Study of the "Ars Grammatica" in Antiquity* (Verhandelingen van de Koninklijke Academie voor Wetenschappen, Letteren en Schone Kunsten van Belgie, Klasse der Letteren 92; Brussels: Paleis der Academi'n, 1979).

S. E. Porter

GREECE AND MACEDON

Ancient Greece was located on the southern portion of the Balkan peninsula, occupying much of the same area as it does today. Greek peoples could also be found on the islands of the Aegean, the coast of *Asia Minor, Sicily, Crete and sometimes Cyprus. Greece was a federation of loosely affiliated city-states during much of the biblical period. Macedonia was located on the northern portion of the Balkan peninsula bordering Greece.

1. Settlement Before 2000 B.C.
2. The Minoan Civilization (c. 2000-1400 B.C.)
3. The Mycenean Civilization (c. 1400-1200 B.C.)
4. The Dark Age (c. 1200-800 B.C.)
5. The Archaic Period (c. 800-500 B.C.)
6. The Classical Period (c. 500-338 B.C.)
7. The Hellenistic Period (338-146 B.C.)
8. The Roman Period (146 B.C.-A.D.100)

1. Settlement Before 2000 B.C.

The first written source for the history of Greece is Homer's *Iliad* from about 800 B.C. Any discussion of the earlier period of Greek history must rely on archaeology and philology. Archaeology tells us that the earliest settlers came from Asia Minor in the Early Bronze Age (2600-2000 B.C.). These peoples settled in

Crete, Cyprus and Cyclades, establishing an agricultural and pastoral society of small farming villages. Archaeology indicates that they traded with Babylon and Asia Minor. Many of these immigrants were Greek-speaking, exhibiting different Greek dialects.

2. The Minoan Civilization (c. 2000-1400 B.C.). During the Early Bronze Age the Minoan civilization thrived on Crete. Its chief cities were Knossos and Phaistos. Minoan civilization was highly developed. Homes were two stories with indoor plumbing. The Minoans worked extensively in copper to make tools and weapons and in gold to make jewelry. They were also skilled painters, weavers and workers in ceramics and bronze. Both genders participated in public sports, including the popular bull leaping—jumping over the back of charging bulls. The primary religion was devotion to the Mother Goddess (Demeter to the Greeks), perhaps owing to the influence of Anatolia in Asia Minor. The trading of the Minoans extended as far as Egypt and Syria, and they invented a pictographic writing system, presumably to facilitate this trade. The pictographic system was replaced about 1600 B.C. with a non-Greek, linear script known as Linear A that has never been deciphered. This civilization came to an abrupt end about 1400 B.C.; archaeology reveals that the palaces were destroyed. The causes for the demise of the Minoans are unknown, but invasion by the Myceneans or pirates are strong possibilities.

3. The Mycenean Civilization (c. 1400-1200 B.C.). From 1400 to 1200 B.C. Mycenean civilization dominated parts of the southern Balkan peninsula as well as Crete, where the Myceneans established Knossos as a capital. The Myceneans had arrived as part of the migrations of Greek-speaking peoples beginning about 3000. They were greatly influenced by the Minoan civilization. This can be witnessed in the styling of their pottery, jewelry and religious symbols. In turn the Myceneans had a great influence on what became known as Greek civilization. The Mycenean age was the heroic age of Greek mythology.

The Myceneans were great traders and warriors. Their warriors used horse-drawn chariots. One of their most unusual legacies is the grave circles for the burial of their heroes, some measuring nearly 90 feet in diameter. The heroes within are buried with their weaponry and gold-foil death masks that show the skill of the Myceneans in gold-working. The Myceneans traded extensively with their neighbors, importing silver from Asia Minor, copper from Syria and gold and papyrus from Egypt. They exported timber and foodstuffs. The Myceneans created Linear B, a recognizably Greek language, written on clay tablets. Their language had previously been primarily oral, but as the clay tablets reveal they developed the written form for purposes of administration and trade. Extant tablets indicate that the Myceneans had an extensive bureaucracy for the administration of their peoples. Mycenean religion is difficult to reconstruct, but a tablet from Pylos mentions offerings to seven Greek deities, including Hera, Hermes and Poseidon.

4. The Dark Age (c. 1200-800 B.C.). The Dark Age of Greece designates the period between the collapse of the Mycenean civilization in the twelfth century B.C. and the renaissance of the eighth century B.C. It was a time of great migration of nomadic, Greek-speaking peoples from central Asia Minor and the north, including the Dorians. These peoples destroyed the remnants of Mycenean civilization and its great cities (e.g., Troy and Tarsus) and displaced other Greek peoples (e.g., the Aeolians and Ionians), who themselves traveled to Thrace, Asia Minor and the Greek islands, further destroying Mycenean civilization. The Dorians settled in the southern portion of the Balkan peninsula, the Peloponnesus, and were the founders of Sparta. The Ionians migrated to the east-central Balkan peninsula, Attica, and were the founders of *Athens. They continued east to occupy also the western coast of Asia Minor and the island of Samos. They spoke Ionic, perhaps the oldest Greek dialect, the language of Homer and Hesiod. Homer's *Iliad* describes and preserves the Ionian traditions.

During this Dark Age writing ceased along with all traces of Linear B, but oral epic continued, as Homer's *Iliad* and *Odyssey* attest. Cultural endeavors like painting, carving and masonry ceased as well, but working in iron was discovered for making weapons and plows somewhere around 1100 B.C. This skill perhaps was borrowed from the Near East.

5. The Archaic Period (c. 800-500 B.C.).

The turning point into the Archaic Age is dated around 800 B.C., a time marked by many important changes. Trade was reestablished, as ivory from Syria and Phoenicia found in Crete, Athens and Sparta attests. The Phoenician alphabet was adopted, a verbal system was developed, and writing was reintroduced from the East. Greek literature was flourishing, as the works of Homer and Hesiod attest.

Such changes were made possible by the development of the *polis,* the Greek city-state, which provided stability. These city-states were independent units, often working in leagues with other cities for trade and protection. This was a period of great building. Cities were walled for defense, harbors built for trade and public buildings erected. Along with the *polis* the institutions that define the classical age were also established. These include the gymnasium for bodily and military training (*see* Education), *athletics and organized athletic events and the symposium for instilling values. The beginnings of science, *philosophy and lyric poetry date to this age. In sports, Hippias of Elis dates the first Olympian Games to 776 B.C. These games were one of the few occasions in which the Greeks put aside local interests and worked together to honor the chief god, Zeus.

*Religion was a key element in the new city-states. Families worshiped an assortment of gods and goddesses and were expected to maintain the family shrine. Political groups also had a religious element, worshiping the appropriate deity in their meetings. Individuals and the city as a whole worshiped Hestia, the goddess of the hearth. In the seventh century *temples were built as houses for the gods. By the sixth century mystery religions had arisen with Demeter, Dionysus and Orpheus as their gods and goddesses. Religion was centered at the sanctuaries of Olympia, the home of Zeus the king of the gods; Delphi; Delos; Isthmia; and Nemea. Regions competed for the allegiance of the people to their sanctuary, a competition that often led to war between city-states.

In the beginning the city-states were governed by local, landowning aristocrats, that is, kings, who received their power either from custom, religious sanction or constitution. About the mid-seventh century B.C. the city-states were often governed as tyrannies. Powerful individuals with their followers ruled the city-states, usually limiting freedom and incurring the indignation of the citizenry. Athens and Sparta were exceptions with their democratic process among the free citizens, although there were periods of tyrannical leadership in Athens in the late sixth century under Pisistratus and his sons and in Sparta later in the *Hellenistic period.

Athens was a walled city settled by Ionians displaced by the Dorian migrations. With better ports, Athens developed naval strength. The silver mines of Attica, the territory Athens controlled, helped sustain the Athenian economy. Athens replaced the monarch with first three and then nine archons or magistrates who performed defined functions for the city-state (e.g., military administration). After civil unrest broke out over diminished individual freedoms, Athens chose an aristocrat named Solon to reform its laws. Under Solon's reforms (594 b.c.), Athens abandoned the Draconian code devised by aristocrats and laid the foundation for democracy. Solon created two legislative bodies: the Council of the Areopagus composed of ex-archons, and a new Council of Four Hundred *(boulē)* composed of one hundred members of each of the four main tribes of Athens. For judicial work he also established an assembly whose members were chosen by lot from the citizenry of Athens. These reforms established wealth rather than birth as a criterion for important office. Citizens of low social status could now participate in government.

Sparta was a group of unwalled villages originally settled by Dorians, a Greek tribe, during the Mycenean era. These banded together under one king about 800 B.C. and proceeded to expand. It subjugated its neighbors, Laconia and Messenia, and made its inhabitants its slaves or helots. Sparta stressed military defense, and its army was the strongest in Greece until the Hellenistic period. This military emphasis governed society. Men and women were segregated, even when married. Men left home at age twelve to live and train together, a state in which they lived all their lives, even when married. Homosexuality was common among both genders. Isolationism prevailed, with foreign travel prohibited and foreigners unwelcomed.

Colonization of areas of Greece by Greeks was intensified, including the southern Balkan peninsula, and in the north on the shores of the Black Sea. The Greek city-states set up trading colonies in areas of trade interest. These colonies could be found in Spain, Sicily, Italy and North Africa and were competitors to Phoenician trade. This competitive trade created warfare between mother cities in Greece and between their colonies.

The only outside pressure at this time was from the Persians. Cyrus, king of Persia, controlled the Greek colonies of Ionia and Aeolia in Asia Minor after a war against Lydia, an ally of Sparta, in 546 B.C. Persia continued to expand as an empire. By 510 B.C. Sparta had formed an alliance with its neighbors for the purpose of dealing with Persia, an alliance accepting the leadership of Sparta in military matters. By 500 B.C. Darius I of Persia controlled all Greek territory except the Greek mainland of the Balkan peninsula. In 499 B.C. Ionian city-states in Asia Minor under Persian control revolted and asked Sparta and Athens in turn for support. Sparta refused, and Athens sent part of its fleet but eventually backed down; Persia regained the territory by 493 B.C. In 490 B.C. Darius launched the Persian wars when he sent his army and navy against Athens and the Athenians defeated the Persian army at the battle of Marathon despite Persia's naval capabilities. Anticipating another Persian attack Athens commissioned Themistocles to build a navy of two hundred ships. Athens was also ready in 480-479 B.C. when Xerxes, son of Darius, attacked. After losing many smaller land and sea battles and even seeing the population of Athens evacuated to the island of Salamis and the city burned, the Greeks, including Athenians and Spartans working together, defeated Xerxes and permanently repelled Persian control.

To the north other important developments were taking place. After centuries of dominance by the Phrygians, Perdiccas I founded the Argead dynasty about 650 B.C., a dynasty that lasted in Macedon until *Alexander the Great. Macedon remained relatively untouched during the Persian invasions by collaborating with the Persians, especially supplying the timber for their ships. However, Alexander I of Macedon did secretly supply the Greeks in their war with Xerxes. After the war the Persians allowed Alexander I of Macedon to expand his territory east and west.

6. The Classical Period (c. 500-338 B.C.).
The first major period of the classical age is often described as the Pentekontaetia or "period of fifty years" (480-430 B.C.). It is the period between the last Persian war (479 B.C.) and the Peloponnesian war (431-404 B.C.). Due to conflict with Athens, Sparta withdrew from leadership of the league it had organized. Athens and its allies created the Delian League in 478-477 B.C. for the purpose of mutual protection, fighting piracy and controlling the Aegean for trade. Although an ally with Greece during the Persian wars, Sparta did not participate and grew resentful of Athens's growing influence, especially the influence that its new navy afforded it on the Aegean islands and with the colonies in Asia Minor.

Toward the mid-fifth century B.C., as the Persian threat waned, Athens's influence on the Delian League waned, and it retained power over its allies by force. Athens supported Egypt in its war with Persia, and the Persians destroyed Athens's fleet in 454 B.C. After anticipating conflict, Athens and Persia made peace in 449 B.C.; this peace entailed Athens giving up Cyprus and control of Ionia in Asia Minor. Seeing its weakness Athens's allies revolted shortly thereafter. Tension between Athens and Sparta escalated into the Peloponnesian war of 431-404 B.C. (two parts: 431-421, 416-404) in which Sparta defeated Athens and made it an ally. As the classical period ended, Athens, Sparta and Thebes fought among themselves for dominance. The end of the fifth century and the fourth century saw Greece and its colonies decreasing in power and engaging in repeated civil war as well as war with outside forces.

Athens moved toward full democracy as residual privilege of the aristocracy was eliminated through the efforts of Pericles, majority leader of the assembly in Athens (461 B.C.). Culture flourished after the Persian war in what has become known as the classical period. The great buildings of the Athenian acropolis were built at this time, including the Parthenon (447-438 B.C.), the temple of Athena Nike (427-424 B.C.) and the Erectheion (421-407 B.C.). Great architects, painters, sculptors and potters were active. Literature in such subjects as *history, poetry, comedy and tragedy and philosophy flourished. Pindar wrote lyric poetry. For his history of the Persian wars, which was a first attempt to analyze the forces behind historical events, Herodotus came to be considered the father of history. Thucydides wrote a history of the Peloponnesian war. This was also the height of

Greek theater. The dramatists Aeschylus, Aristophanes, Euripedes, Menander and Sophocles wrote plays, while stone theaters were erected for their performance. The philosophy of Pythagoras, Socrates, *Plato, and later *Aristotle laid the foundation for Western thought. Alexander I of Macedon and his successors in the Argead dynasty were patrons of Greek culture and brought Hellenization to Macedon.

7. The Hellenistic Period (338-146 B.C.). Philip II became king of Macedon in 359 B.C. and created one of the first states where power did not reside in a city. He expanded into a weakened Greece, defeating the Greeks at the battle of Chaeronea in 338 B.C. and ruling the entire Balkan peninsula. He turned his attention to Persia but was assassinated in 336 B.C. by an aristocrat of Macedon. The campaign was carried out by his son and successor, Alexander the Great, who assumed power at the age of twenty. Alexander marched against Persia in 334 B.C., conquering Asia Minor, Syria and Egypt on the way. He eventually conquered Persia and the eastern territories all the way to India. He died in Babylon in 323 B.C. at the age of thirty-two. His most lasting achievement derived from his love of Greek culture instilled in part by his tutor, Aristotle. He built Greek cities and spread Greek culture throughout his conquered territories. This cultural influence has become known as *Hellenism.

After Alexander died having left no legitimate heirs, his successors vied for power throughout the conquered territories. In 276 B.C., after nearly a fifty-year series of rulers and civil war, Antigonus II Gonatas assumed power in Macedon and Greece, establishing the Antigonid dynasty (276-168 B.C.). Seleucus emerged as successor to Alexander in Asia Minor, Syria and Mesopotamia, founding the *Seleucid dynasty. Ptolemy was successor to Alexander in Egypt, founding the Ptolemaic dynasty (*see* Ptolemies). The Seleucids and Ptolemies were rivals throughout the period, often engaging in war in Syria.

Macedon returned to a kingdom similar to the one before Alexander the Great, but it still tried to exert its influence in all of Greece. For the remainder of the fourth and the third centuries Greece was a protectorate of Macedon. Piracy was a constant problem for Greek coastal cities in the third century B.C., and the need to fight off this common enemy drew the Greeks into leagues as in their previous history. These leagues occasionally revolted against Macedon. After coming to the aid of Athens in its struggle with Macedon in 197 B.C., *Rome declared the city-states of Greece independent. Philip V of Macedon supported Hannibal of Carthage in his quest against Rome in the Second Punic War (218-201 B.C.). As a later consequence, Rome, in league with Athens, defeated Perseus, son of Philip V, at the end of the Macedonian war of 171-168 B.C. at the battle of Pydna, ended its royal dynasty, and divided the territory into four republics.

8. The Roman Period (146 B.C.-A.D. 100). After an uprising in Macedon in 148 B.C. by Andriscus, who claimed to be Philip, the son of Perseus, Rome annexed the territory and created the province of Macedonia. The Achean League of Greece arose against Rome, and Rome defeated the league in 146 B.C. and seized direct control of southern Greece, razing *Corinth to serve as an example of the consequences of defying Rome. From that point on Rome governed the affairs of Greece from Macedonia, although Athens and Sparta were permitted to remain free cities. Rome formed the province of Achaia in 46 B.C. During the Roman civil wars, Julius Caesar defeated Pompey in Thessaly (48 B.C.), and Antony and Octavian fought on Greek soil (42 B.C.). Greece supported Brutus in the civil wars, and as a consequence the victor, Octavian, made Greece the province of Achaia in 46 B.C.

In the first century A.D. Greece was composed of two provinces: Macedonia in the north and Achaia in the south. These two provinces were senatorial provinces, that is, their governor was appointed by the senate of Rome (*see* Roman Administration). In A.D. 15 Augustus combined these provinces with the province of Moesia, north of Macedonia, into an imperial province with their governor appointed by the emperor (*see* Roman Emperors). In A.D. 44 Claudius divided the province back into its component three provinces. The book of Acts refers to these two provinces as sites of Paul's ministry (Acts 19:21). Paul refers to these two provinces together as regions of his ministry that supported the collection for the Jerusalem church (Rom 15:26) and as regions evangelized in part by the Thessalonian church (1 Thess 1:7-8).

In the first century a.d., the term Greek referred less to a country and more to those who spoke Greek and accepted Greek culture. The word *Greece (Hellas)* appears only once in the NT, in the context of Paul's last journey to *Jerusalem, where it is used in conjunction with Macedonia to refer to the province of Achaia (Acts 20:1-2). References to Greeks *(Hellēnēs)* are frequent in the NT, meaning those who spoke Greek and accepted Greek culture (Acts 16:1), and are often in contrast to "Jew," meaning "Gentile" (Acts 14:1). References to Greeks can also refer to Hellenized Jews who lived in the *Diaspora (Jn 12:20) or, as Luke calls them, Hellenists (*Hellēnistai,* Acts 6:1; *see* Hellenistic Judaism).

Paul's second and third missionary journeys took him to Macedonia and Achaia (A.D. 50-55; Acts 16:11—20:6; 2 Cor 8:1-6). The Pauline churches of *Philippi, *Thessalonica and Berea were located in Macedonia and those of Athens and Corinth in Achaia. The book of Acts recounts Paul's imprisonment in Philippi, preaching at the Areopagus in Athens and his difficulties prying the Corinthian church away from its pagan worldview. The NT letters of 1 and 2 Thessalonians and Philippians are addressed to churches in Macedonia, and 1 and 2 Corinthians are addressed to Corinth in Achaia.

Although Greece was no longer a political power, its cultural influence—the Hellenization begun by Alexander the Great—was a powerful force molding not only Palestinian culture but Roman as well. Greece continued as a cultural and intellectual center during the Roman period, being the location of choice for upper-class Romans to finish their formal education. The influence of Hellenism upon the church was also marked. The early church used *rhetorical and other facets of a Greek *education in its preaching and teaching, modes of worship and ethical exhortation, among others things. This Greek influence is particularly seen in the fact that the early church used the *Septuagint, a Greek translation of the OT, and wrote the documents of the NT in Greek. This influence continued beyond the first-century church to play a role in interpretation and theological formulations.

See also ATHENS; CORINTH; GREEK OF THE NEW TESTAMENT; HELLENISM; HELLENISTIC JUDAISM; PHILIPPI; THESSALONICA.

BIBLIOGRAPHY. J. Boardman, J. Griffin and O. Murray, eds., *The Oxford History of the Classical World: Greece and the Hellenistic World* (Oxford: Oxford University Press, 1986); J. Boardman et al., eds., *The Expansion of the Greek World, Eighth to Sixth Centuries B.C.* (2d ed.; *CAH* 3.3; Cambridge: Cambridge University Press, 1982); idem, *Persia, Greece and the Western Mediterranean, c. 525 to 479 B.C.* (2d ed.; *CAH* 4; Cambridge: Cambridge University Press, 1988; plates to vol. 4, 2d ed., by J. Boardman); A. R. Burn, *Persia and the Greeks* (2d ed.; London: Duckworth, 1984); P. A. Cartledge and F. D. Harvey, eds., *Crux: Essays in Greek History Presented to G. E. M. de Ste. Croix on His Seventy-fifth Birthday* (London: Duckworth, 1985); J. Chadwick, *The Mycenean World* (Cambridge: Cambridge University Press, 1976); O. Dickinson, *The Aegean Bronze Age* (Cambridge: Cambridge University Press, 1994); R. M. Errington, *A History of Macedonia* (Berkeley and Los Angeles: University of California Press, 1990); P. Green, ed., *Hellenistic History and Culture* (Berkeley and Los Angeles: University of California Press, 1993); N. G. L. Hammond, *A History of Greece to 322 B.C.* (3d ed.; Oxford: Clarendon Press, 1986); idem, *A History of Macedonia,* 1: *Historical Geography and Prehistory* (Oxford: Clarendon Press, 1972); idem, *The Macedonian State: Origins, Institutions and History* (Oxford: Clarendon Press, 1989); N. G. L. Hammond with G. T. Griffith, *A History of Macedonia,* 2: *550-336 B.C.* (Oxford: Clarendon Press, 1979); N. G. L. Hammond with F. W. Walbank, *A History of Macedonia,* 3: *336-167 B.C.* (Oxford: Clarendon Press, 1988); B. Laourdes and C. Makaronas, eds., *Ancient Macedonia* (2 vols.; Thessaloniki: Institute for Balkan Studies, 1977); O. Murray, *Early Greece* (2d ed.; Cambridge, MA: Harvard University Press, 1993); S. B. Pomeroy et al., *Ancient Greece: A Political, Social and Cultural History* (Oxford: Oxford University Press, 1998); M. Rostovzeff, *Social and Economic History of the Hellenistic World* (3 vols.; Oxford: Clarendon Press, 1941); M. B. Sakellariou, ed., *Macedonia: Four Thousand Years of History and Civilization* (Greek Lands in History; Athens: Ekdotike Athēnon, 1983); F. W. Walbank, *The Hellenistic World* (rev. ed.; Cambridge, MA: Harvard University Press, 1993); idem, *A History of Macedonia* (3 vols.; Oxford: Clarendon Press, 1972-88); P. M. Warren, *The Aegean Civilizations* (Oxford: Elsever, 1975).

D. F. Watson

GREEK OF THE NEW TESTAMENT

The NT, apart from a few *Aramaic and/or *Hebrew words and phrases, is written in a form of ancient Greek. This Greek, however, is not the Greek of the classical writers, such as *Plato, Thucydides or the tragedians, but is that of the Greek of the Greco-Roman world of the first century. This Greek is represented by a number of different sources, including not only the NT but also the Greek of the papyri and other authors, such as *Epictetus, Appian and *Josephus.

1. History and Development of the Greek Language
2. The Greek of the New Testament
3. Issues in Recent Study of Greek
4. The Languages of Jesus
5. Conclusion

1. History and Development of the Greek Language.

Greek has a long and interesting history, virtually unparalleled among other languages (see Horrocks; Palmer; and Porter 1997, which is used for what follows). Greek is one of the Indo-European languages. Proto-Indo-European (PIE) is a scholarly reconstruction of the prototypical language from which all of the Indo-European languages descended. One of the branches of PIE developed into Proto-Greek, another hypothetical language that predates the settlement of the Balkan peninsula in the early second millennium B.C. but is the progenitor of nearly three thousand years of unbroken history of the Greek language. The earliest recognizable forms of Greek go back to the Myceneans, who came to occupy what we know as the Greek islands and mainland. Mycenean civilization reached its greatest heights in the late second millennium on Crete and mainland Greece. This great civilization declined or was destroyed by approximately 1200 to 1100 B.C., which led to what has been called a Greek dark age, of which very little is known, especially linguistically. In the nineteenth century, a number of tablets and other inscriptions were found, especially at the remains of the city of Pylos on the Greek mainland. These tablets and inscriptions were written in what is called today Linear B, the written script of the Myceneans. Deciphered in 1952, Linear B is a syllabic form of writing that is recognizably Greek (Chadwick).

In approximately 800 B.C., the Greek islands and mainland emerged out of their dark age, and the extant evidence indicates that a number of different people groups used a number of different dialects of Greek. As a result, this period has been linguistically referred to as the dialect period. The traditional view regarding the rebirth of Greek civilization was that several waves of settlement from outside the area resulted in different regional Greek dialects on the Greek islands and mainland. More recently, the idea has been promoted that the various regional dialects can be attributed to linguistic developments by indigenous people groups, originally perhaps divided into eastern and western Greek language varieties. The distribution of the various dialects, however, makes the settlement theory still seem more likely at this point. The major regional dialects of Greek discussed by scholars and described in different ways by them (see Horrocks, 6-16) are four: Attic-Ionic, in which Attic was a fairly conservative subvariety of Ionic (see below); Arcado-Cypriot; (often separated into two, Arcadian and Cypriot); Doric and other west Greek varieties (such as Boetian); and Aeolic.

A number of different linguistic features distinguish these dialects. These features include differences in vowel length, varying sound changes, whether and how contraction of vowels occurred, differences in declensional endings for both nouns/adjectives and verbs, the use and variety of particles, occasional differences in case relations, and some differing vocabulary. In some instances, the dialects may have been unintelligible to each other due to significant sound changes, but it appears that the written forms of the languages were more easily understood. The early fifth-century B.C. historian Herodotus wrote that the Greeks were of one blood and of one tongue (Herodotus *Hist.* 8.144.2). The Homeric or epic dialect, in which Homer's *Iliad* and *Odyssey* were written, was a literary dialect based upon a form of Ionic but with influence from other dialects. Not a spoken language in the sense that people spoke it to each other, it was a poetic form of language regionally adapted as the poems were recited and later written down.

After the so-called archaic period (ninth to fifth centuries B.C.), there emerged during the fifth century what is called the classical period of Greek civilization. This period describes and reflects the ascendance of the city of *Athens in its military and economic power, culture, *philosophy, literature and the arts. This relatively insignificant city, insofar as location and history would indicate, was transformed by economic prosperity into a city of central importance. Along with its ascendant cultural and economic position came the significance of its language. Widespread and persistent Athenian cultural dominance led to its particular variety of the Ionic dialect of Greek being widely used, especially by significant writers and thinkers, with the result that much of the literature from this period is written in Athenian Ionic Greek. The conservative, and in some ways even archaic, earlier form of Attic gave way to a more progressive form of Greek. This form of language reflected many of the more innovative features of the Ionic dialect. This Greek became the literary and administrative language of Athens and had wider influence and use throughout Greece, especially in the fifth and fourth centuries. This variety of Greek formed the basis of the common written language of the Hellenistic world, or Koine Greek.

The rise to power of the Macedonian conqueror *Alexander III ("the Great") marked a major turning point in the development and dissemination of the Greek language (*see* Hellenism). As noted in the survey above, all languages develop under the influence of a variety of factors. This development is not predetermined, nor does it occur at a set rate. In any case, the influence of Alexander cannot be underestimated on the course and pace of development of Greek. Alexander's love of Greek culture, instilled by his father, Philip II of Macedon, who saw that Alexander was educated by *Aristotle, undoubtedly was more instrumental in the NT being written in Greek than any other single factor. When Macedonia exerted its hegemony over the Greek mainland in the fourth century B.C., it adopted various Greek practices and characteristics, including the Greek language of Athens, which had become the administrative language of the mainland. With an army of fifty thousand Greek soldiers, Alexander's conquests, initially of the Persian Empire but soon extended to include much more, instigated an important linguistic movement at the same time as he inaugurated his military expedition. The result of Alexander's widespread conquests was that the Greek language went with him and was established as the common language of communication. It even came to dominate local and regional indigenous languages as various people groups were conquered and submitted to Alexander's rule.

This Attic-Ionic form of common Greek, which we now call Hellenistic or Koine Greek, was used both as a written and as a spoken language. The process of linguistic change was propelled by a number of factors. These include its widespread dissemination as Greek came into contact with a variety of other languages and as the various dialects of the soldiers and others mixed. As a result, regional peculiarities were leveled and a more universally used and recognized common dialect clearly emerged. There is much debate about the depth of Hellenistic cultural penetration. Undoubtedly in many areas this assimilation was widespread and profound (*see* Hellenistic Egypt; Hellenistic Judaism). Nevertheless, even in places where the cultural elements were nothing more than superficial, the use of Greek seems to have been one of the most consistently far-reaching Hellenistic elements. This pattern of domination in large part through linguistic unification was a pattern developed early and continued after the death of Alexander—the four succeeding Hellenistic kingdoms, including the *Ptolemies and the *Seleucids, and later the Romans, continued the same patterns. Greek thus became the *lingua franca,* or the language of common interaction, throughout the Greco-Roman world.

The result of Alexander and his conquests, and the subsequent political developments around the Mediterranean world, was that Hellenistic Greek became the prestige language of the Greco-Roman world. This remained the case even after *Latin established itself as a significant language of the empire, especially in the East, by the second century A.D. Being the prestige language does not mean that Greek was the first language of everyone, or even that it was the language of first choice. What it means is that Greek was the language that those who enjoyed political, cultural and economic superiority used and that those who wished to attain such status or to carry on effective interaction with such people had to know. The evidence for this status is found in a variety of authors and types of literature. Even though native languages continued to be used in a variety of places throughout the empire, such as in *Asia Minor, the *Roman East and Egypt, Greek was the language of commerce. This is evidenced by the thousands of ephemeral business contracts and receipts found in the documentary papyri from Egypt, as well as the papyri found more recently in the Roman East, such as the Babatha archive (*see* Papyri, Palestinian). These documents, most of which were discovered in the nineteenth century and the early part of the twentieth century, comprise thousands of examples of the use of the Greek language over the span of the Hellenistic and Greco-Roman periods in a variety of contexts, most of which reflect day-to-day life.

Literary authors as well, including many of those writing histories of Rome, such as Dio Cassius and Polybius, also used Greek. Even the Jewish historian *Josephus wrote in, or had rendered into, Greek his history of the Jewish war and his account of his people. This level of usage is also exemplified by a wealth of nonliterary texts, one of the most important of which is the NT.

There were several perhaps understandable and predictable responses to the clear and widespread ascendance of Greek. One was that a number of people maintained the use of indigenous languages. During the classical, Hellenistic and Greco-Roman periods, Asia Minor was particularly rife with indigenous (or epichoric) languages, such as Lycian, Lydian, Sidetian, Carian, Phrygian and Galatian, besides Persian and Aramaic, as well as Greek (Blomqvist). The book of Acts notes that several of these dialects continued, even though Greek was the *lingua franca.* Some scholars have even contended that the result was a number of hybrid dialects of Greek that combined Greek with an indigenous language, such as demotic in Egypt or Aramaic in Palestine. The evidence for the persistence of such creole languages, in which two languages were mixed for temporary communicative purposes, is lacking (see below). Not all were as content with the developments that had occurred within Greek, however. There were two movements that reacted against the use of the Koine As early as the third century B.C., several poets rejected the common form of the Greek language and wrote poetry in forms of earlier Greek dialects.

Similarly, in the third century B.C., there was the rise of what is called Asianism. This was a reaction against the balanced and measured style of the literary form of Hellenistic Greek, such as found in Polybius, and so these writers indulged in a more exuberant and ornate style. Some have thought that the book of 2 Peter reflects this Asianic style (see Watson). Somewhat in reaction to Asianism, a movement called Atticism developed and reached its peak in the second century A.D. Atticistic writers rejected what they perceived to be the corruption or debasing of the Greek language and advocated a return to the standards of vocabulary and style of the best classical writers of Athens. Neither Asianism nor Atticism ever had much influence apart from on certain literary authors, including some later Christian writers.

As a result, one of the noteworthy—and in some ways perhaps surprising—features of the linguistic situation of the first century is the overall consistency and uniformity of Hellenistic Greek across the span of the Greco-Roman world. Even in Phrygia and Lycaonia, in the interior of Asia Minor, where regional dialects did a better job of surviving, Greek was the common language, although perhaps with some regional differences in pronunciation and phonetically based spelling variations (the papyri of Egypt attest to a number of phonetic spellings). L. R. Palmer says of this common language that it "smothered and replaced the ancient local dialects": "Profound linguistic consequences might have been expected from the adoption of what was basically the Attic dialect by users of not merely non-Attic, but non-Greek speech. In fact the changes were remarkably slight" (Palmer 175, 176).

In distinction from earlier forms of Greek, the major linguistic features of Hellenistic Greek include the following (apart from instances of retention or revival of earlier features by Atticists, though rarely in the exact way that the earlier Attic writers used them):

- Regularized features of pronunciation;
- Vowel reduction;
- Declensional endings of nouns/adjectives and verbs regularized and simplified, with regular first aorists replacing irregular second aorist endings;
- Final *nu* used more frequently, especially in instances where the third declension was being formed like the first/second declensions;
- Increased use of certain prepositions;
- Disappearance of some particles;
- *Mi* verbs regularized into *omega* verbs;
- Optative virtually disappearing;
- Dual number, already restricted, being eliminated;
- Middle voice being reduced in importance,

often replaced by the passive;
- Subjunctive with *hina* beginning to replace the infinitive;
- Dative case under pressure as the role of the accusative case was expanded;
- Use of *an* increased;
- Periphrasis in a variety of contexts increased in frequency.

Many of these features are present in the Greek of the NT, as the standard reference grammars make clear (see Blass and Debrunner; Moulton; Robertson; cf. Porter 1989b, 143-56).

2. The Greek of the New Testament.
Despite the preceding evidence, the question of the kind of Greek found in the NT has been a contentious issue, because the complex theological, ethnic and cultural issues related to its composition has clouded linguistic analysis (see Porter 1991; 1996, 75-99). Before the beginning of the twentieth century—in large part because the discoveries of Egyptian papyri had not yet been profitably assessed in terms of the language of the NT (see Deissmann; Moulton)—there was a widespread and persistent belief in some circles that the Greek of the NT constituted a special biblical dialect, possibly even a divinely inspired or Holy Ghost Greek. Without these papyrus documents for reference, significant differences between the Greek of the NT and the Greek of literary writers—for example, the convoluted periodic style of Thucydides or the complex and artificial style of Polybius—seemed otherwise incomprehensible, if one wished to maintain the special qualities of the biblical documents. Similar views were formed regarding the unique vocabulary of the NT.

In the light of assessment of the papyri, however, a number of scholars, led by A. Deissmann and J. H. Moulton, began to recognize the common linguistic features of these ephemeral documents and the Greek of the NT. Important discoveries were made in terms of syntax and vocabulary. A number of features that had been thought to be unparalleled in the Greek of the NT were seen to be commonplace in the Greek of the papyri, and numerous words thought to be unique were found to have parallel senses in the papyri. After the deaths of Moulton, Deissmann, and others who had advocated the importance of the papyri, there was an apparent backlash against their position. The Jewish origins of Christianity made it understandable that numerous scholars should assume that the language of the NT—even though it is Greek—was also Semitic in some ways, perhaps influenced by the *Septuagint or *synagogue worship.

Several different Semitic hypotheses were advanced to explain the Greek of the NT. Some early Semitic-language advocates argued that numerous books in the NT were direct translations from Aramaic (e.g., the Gospels and Acts, as well as Revelation), while a few others have claimed that Hebrew was the original language of composition for some of the books of the NT (e.g., John's Gospel). Most scholars did not go this far, however, making instead the much more modest claim that the Greek of the NT documents reflected the fact that their authors' first language was Aramaic, apart from the words of Jesus, which had been translated at some stage out of Aramaic, and still reflected an Aramaic substratum. This purported confrontation between Aramaic and Greek has led a few scholars once again to posit that the mix of the two languages led to the development of a special dialect of Semitic Greek, either a temporary language created when the two came into initial contact or an independent variety of Semitic Greek that continued to be used in the early church. Those wishing to claim special characteristics of the NT have occasionally welcomed this position, despite the lack of evidence for the creation and certainly the persistence of such a creole language.

The last two decades of the twentieth century saw a return to the Greek hypothesis. M. Silva has shown that the linguistic distinction between *langue* (the language system) and *parole* (a particular writer's use of it) helps to clarify the linguistic situation in Palestine in the first century. Although one's individual *parole* may have had peculiarities brought about through knowledge of a Semitic language, the *langue* in use was clearly Hellenistic Greek. G. Horrocks (92-95) maintains that most features of the Greek of the NT can be paralleled either in the Septuagint, seen as one of the most important examples of Hellenistic vernacular literature, or in low-level Koine (i.e., Hellenistic) Greek texts such as are found in Egypt. The Palestinian linguistic situation was not one of two languages, Aramaic and Greek, competing on an even footing. Greek was the prestige language of Palestine, and anyone wishing to conduct business on any extended scale, including any successful fishermen from the Hellenized region of Galilee and probably any craftsmen or artisans who would have come into contact with Roman customers, would have needed to have known—indeed, would have wanted to know—Greek (see Porter 2000a, 126-80).

3. Issues in Recent Study of Greek.

Despite the fact that Greek has a continuous history of three millennia and it has been studied for centuries, a number of issues regarding the language merit further discussion. These can only be mentioned in passing here (see Porter 1996, 7-20).

3.1. Modern Linguistics and the Tools for Study of the Greek New Testament. One of the major shortcomings in NT studies is the fact that virtually all reference grammars for the study of the Greek of the NT were written before the insights of modern linguistics were applied to analysis of the language. Only within the last twenty or so years has NT study benefitted from what can be considered a modern linguistic approach (see Porter 1989a, for what follows). Modern linguistics is a complex discipline in its own right, with a number of different competing models. There are features of a linguistic investigation that differentiate it from other forms of study. For example, an informed linguistic approach does not involve the ability to speak many languages, nor does it require that one know more languages than the one being studied (e.g., if one is studying Greek, one does not need to know the Semitic languages, unless comparative study is being done); it is not to be equated with historical linguistics or the study of the history of a language and its development (this includes etymologies, genuine or otherwise); it is not classical philology or the studying of a few select literary texts as the benchmark for evaluating other Greek (as do Blass and Debrunner in their grammar); and it is not to be equated with translational ability, a limited tool for showing linguistic knowledge.

A functional approach to the study of language has yielded significant insights in recent investigation of Greek. Functionalism emphasizes the function of various components of a language, treating the language as a system in which the various elements are interconnected and form a coordinated structure. This systematic and structural dimension to language is crucial to understanding the use of language in context and hence its meaning. Description and analysis of the language should begin from empirical data and present these data in an explicit fashion, open to analysis by others. Thus estimation of the function of, for example, participles, is determined on the basis of a complex set of definable factors, such as tense form, case, syntax and especially context. Furthermore, synchronic analysis takes precedence over diachronic analysis, although the two are interrelated. That is, any given synchronic state is the result of diachronic change. For example, the Greek four/five case system (five, if one counts the vocative as an independent case, four if one does not) may earlier have had eight cases, but it is the four/five cases that must be defined in terms of their use in the NT. Diachronic information may be interesting and even informative, but it is not to be equated with or elevated above synchronic description and analysis of the use of the language at hand.

3.2. Written Texts and Literacy. Whereas much of the traditional emphasis of modern linguistic investigation has been upon the spoken forms of language, there is an obvious limitation when approaching an ancient language, where there are no native speakers of that form of the language. Adjustments must be made in linguistic method, especially when it is considered that, at the most, probably only 20 to 30 percent of the men of a classical city were able to read or write (Harris; *see* Literacy and Book Culture). In other words, the instances of linguistic usage come from a highly selective part of the population. Speculation about the relation of these written texts, even those of the papyri, as unselfconscious and lacking in artifice as they are, to the spoken language is limited by the fact that one cannot use a native informant to check the analysis.

Nevertheless, one does not wish to overstate the opposition between written and spoken forms of language. Some recent analysis across a broad spectrum of *genres has shown that there are greater similarities between these broad forms of text than has been realized (see Biber). One of the means of overcoming some of these limitations is by utilizing a greater corpus of material against which to check specific findings and broader generalizations. Corpus linguistics, in which corpora of texts selected for particular purposes and grammatically tagged in a machine-readable way, is providing a conceptual means of advancement. However, the limitation remains of not having an adequately tagged text for even the Greek NT, to say nothing of the language of the surrounding Greco-Roman world (O'Donnell).

3.3. Greek Verbal Structure. Study of Greek verb structure has undergone radical changes in the last almost two hundred years (see Porter 1989b; 1996, 11-17, 21-38). The rationalist period, represented by the influential grammarian G. B. Winer, analyzed Greek verbal structure in terms of a logical framework, in which, for example, tense forms were said to be equated with temporal values. This kind of rigid framework is still found in a number of elementary or teaching grammars. Great advances were made in the study of languages in the nineteenth century, when it was realized that many languages had family resemblances. As a result of this discovery, new categories of thought were applied to analysis of languages ancient and modern. K. Brugmann, who developed the theory of *Aktionsart,* stated that verb structure is related not only or exclusively to temporal categories but also to the kind of action or the way that an event occurs. *Aktionsart* theory stated that a language has various means, including the use of verb tenses, verbal roots, and affixing of prepositions, to express the ways in which action occurs.

This theory made its way into NT study through the work of F. Blass and J. H. Moulton and is still found in A. T. Robertson, C. F. D. Moule and N. Turner. The development of verbal aspect theory, a logical continuation of *Aktionsart* theory, recognizes that verbs are not primarily concerned either with time or with objectified action but with a subjective perspective on action. Major studies include those by B. M. Fanning, K. L. McKay and S. E. Porter (1989b). There is still significant disagreement among these three proponents, however. One of the major points of disagreement is whether the Greek verb carries any denotation of time when it is used in the indicative mood (grammarians of Greek, including that of the NT, already recognized at the beginning of the twentieth century that Greek verbs do not refer to time in the nonindicative moods). Various means of testing such a hypothesis have been tried. In recent discussion the issue of the relationship between verbal aspect and other grammatical choices has been analyzed (i.e., is choice of aspect dependent upon other grammatical choices, such as mood). The argument has been put forward by critics of aspectual theory that verbal aspect is dependent upon the choice of other grammatical categories. Recent research has shown that choice of aspect in virtually all instances is made independent of other grammaticalized constraints (Porter and O'Donnell).

3.4. Register Analysis. Dialect is concerned with the variety of language by various users, especially as this use is reflected in their variations in pronunciation. Register is concerned with variety of language according to its use. Following the work of M. A. K. Halliday (Halliday and Hasan), some recent linguistic analysis of the Greek of the NT has attempted to incorporate the category of register. Register is concerned with various constraints on language usage created by the context of situation in which language is used. These constraints affect three major components of language: its mode, or the textual meaning component (written and spoken forms, the ways in which the text holds together, etc.); its tenor, or the interpersonal meaning component (who is addressing and being addressed in the text); and its field, or the ideational meaning component (who does what to whom about what). Isolating and analyzing these three components, rather than treating all data on the same plane, provides for a more detailed and nuanced analysis of a text and its context of situation.

Register analysis is proving to be a helpful tool with regard to several different areas of investigation of the Greek of the NT. The first is in the area of discussion of the various languages in use in the first century. The term *diglossia,* a subject of considerable discussion in linguistic circles for the last four decades of the twentieth century, has been used as a way of categorizing the uses of language in Palestine and elsewhere, noting that there were at least three languages—Greek, Aramaic and Hebrew—and that these languages were used in various ways on the basis of the speakers and their purposes. Diglossia does not appear to be the correct term to describe this situation, however, in which there are languages that are not the high and low forms of a single language (the sense in which diglossia is probably best used).

Instead, analysis of the various uses of language, including various registers of the use of Greek, has proved useful. Thus one can effectively describe differences in the registers that

Paul is using in his various letters (Porter 2000c). By extension, one can perhaps use register analysis to work from the text back to a plausible context of situation that would have generated a text of this sort. This kind of analysis has been applied to Mark's Gospel (Porter 2000b). One is able to overcome much of the dichotomous thinking regarding Semitic influence on the Greek of the NT through the use of register analysis. Rather than thinking in terms of whether Greek is or is not Semitized, one can consider a variety of contextual factors that may result in shifts of features of register, some of which may involve, for example, drawing upon features of the Greek of the Septuagint. A further extension of this method has recently been introduced in historical-Jesus research to attempt to formulate new criteria for authenticating sayings of Jesus. The various dimensions of register can be analyzed to see if a given discourse of Jesus reveals similar or different variables of register than the surrounding narrative (Porter 2000a, 210-37).

4. The Languages of Jesus.

A related question to the issue of the Greek of the NT is that of which language or languages Jesus spoke (see Fitzmyer). The vast majority of scholars rightly contend that Jesus' primary and first language was probably Aramaic (Casey). Many scholars also entertain the possibility that, at least in a religious context such as that indicated by Luke 4:16-20, Jesus may have spoken Hebrew as well. This linguistic scenario seems well founded. Jesus was born to a Palestinian Jewish family and was apparently well versed in the institutions of the Jewish people, including the use of Aramaic, the language of the Jews since their return under the Persians from exile in Babylon. Not only did Aramaic remain a low-level vernacular in Syria during the time of the Seleucids and after, but also Aramaic continued to be used by Jews during the first century, as is well attested from the *Dead Sea Scrolls finds and other related documents. Jewish worship during this time was often carried on in Aramaic, with an interpretative translation into Aramaic (known as a *targum) of the biblical text being offered.

A more contentious issue in recent scholarship, however, is whether Jesus knew and used Greek and possibly even taught in it on occasion (see Porter 2000a, 126-80 for discussion). Many scholars recognize this possibility in theory but hesitate to specify particular instances where this may have occurred. Jesus came from an area that had been highly influenced by Hellenism. Nazareth was a small village, but it was on the same trade route as an excellent example of a Greek city in Palestine, Sepphoris, where both Greek and Aramaic were spoken, and near the primarily Gentile Decapolis, Hellenistic cities or villages in the region of Galilee. Jesus was involved in a trade where it is reasonable to assume that he would have had contact with others than his townspeople, possibly including Romans or others who spoke Greek. In the course of his itinerant ministry, Jesus also traveled to various parts of Palestine where he may have had contact with Greek speakers. Several of his disciples, including Andrew, Philip, and even possibly Peter, had Greek names, despite being Jewish.

On the basis of the linguistic context of first-century Palestine, as well as Jesus' background, a set of criteria have recently been developed to test whether Jesus spoke in Greek and whether any of the words of Jesus in the Gospels may record his actual words (see Porter 2000a, 126-237). The criteria that have been developed are three: the criterion of Greek language and its context, which determines the likelihood that in a given context Jesus would have spoken Greek; the criterion of Greek textual variance, which determines whether any of the words recorded can be attributable to Jesus; and the criterion of discourse features, which examines features of discourse, analyzing the words and actions of Jesus through the category of register.

This examination has shown that there is a plausibility that in a number of contexts Jesus may well have used Greek in conversing with others: (1) Matthew 8:5-13 par. John 4:46-54: Jesus' conversation with the centurion or commander (but the Johannine account diverges in terms of wording); (2) John 4:4-26: Jesus' conversation with the Samaritan woman; (3) Mark 2:13-14 par. Matthew 9:9; Luke 5:27-28: Jesus' calling of Levi/Matthew; (4) Mark 7:25-30 par. Matthew 15:21-28: Jesus' conversation with the Syrophoenician or Canaanite woman; (5) Mark 12:13-17 par. Matthew 22:16-22; Luke 20:20-26: Jesus' conversation with the *Pharisees and Herodians over the Roman *coin of Caesar; (6) Mark 8:27-30 par. Matthew 16:13-20; Luke 9:18-21: Jesus' conversation with his disciples at

*Caesarea Philippi; (7) Mark 15:2-5 par. Matthew 27:11-14; Luke 23:2-4; John 18:29-38: Jesus' trial before Pilate. Furthermore, on the basis of Greek textual variance, in several of these contexts his actual words may be recorded (Jesus' conversation with the Syrophoenician or Canaanite woman, his conversation with Pharisees and Herodians, his conversation at *Caesarea Philippi and his trial before Pilate).

5. Conclusion.

Despite the long history of discussion of the Greek of the NT, there remain many issues of contention and debate. Nevertheless, despite these areas of continuing disagreement, there have also been many important accomplishments in recent years, as modern linguistic principles have been applied to the study of the Greek NT. These studies have led in a number of different directions, some of them having the potential for shifting into more profitable areas of research what have become longstanding but stagnant positions.

See also ARAMAIC LANGUAGE; GRAMMARIANS, HELLENISTIC GREEK; HEBREW LANGUAGE; LATIN LANGUAGE.

Bibliography. D. Biber, *Variation Across Speech and Writing* (Cambridge: Cambridge University Press, 1988); F. Blass and A. Debrunner, *A Greek Grammar of the New Testament and Other Early Christian Literature* (Chicago: University of Chicago Press, 1961); J. Blomqvist, "Translation Greek in the Trilingual Inscription of Xanthus," *OpAth* 14 (1982) 11-20; M. Casey, *Aramaic Sources of Mark's Gospel* (SNTSMS 102; Cambridge: Cambridge University Press, 1998); J. Chadwick, *Linear B and Related Scripts* (London: British Museum Publications, 1987); A. Deissmann, *Light from the Ancient East* (4th ed.; London: Hodder & Stoughton, 1927); B. M. Fanning, *Verbal Aspect in New Testament Greek* (OTM; Oxford: Clarendon Press, 1990); J. A. Fitzmyer, "The Languages of Palestine in the First Century a.d.," *CBQ* 32 (1970) 501-31; M. A. K. Halliday, *An Introduction to Functional Grammar* (2d ed.; London: Arnold, 1994); M. A. K. Halliday and R. Hasan, *Language, Context and Text: Aspects of Language in a Social-Semiotic Perspective* (Geelong, Victoria, Australia: Deakin University Press, 1985); W. V. Harris, *Ancient Literacy* (Cambridge, MA: Harvard University Press, 1989); G. Horrocks, *Greek: A History of the Language and Its Speakers* (London: Longmans, 1997); K. L. McKay, *A New Syntax of the Verb in New Testament Greek: An Aspectual Approach* (SBG 5; New York: Peter Lang, 1993); C. F. D. Moule, *An Idiom Book of New Testament Greek* (2d ed.; Cambridge: Cambridge University Press, 1959); J. H. Moulton, *A Grammar of the Greek New Testament,* 1: *Prolegomera* (3d ed.; Edinburgh: T & T Clark, 1908); M. B. O'Donnell, "The Use of Annotated Corpora for New Testament Discourse Analysis: A Survey of Current Practice and Future Prospects," in *Discourse Analysis and the New Testament: Approaches and Results,* ed. S. E. Porter and J. T. Reed (JSNTSup 170; SNTG 4; Sheffield: Sheffield Academic Press, 1999) 71-117; L. R. Palmer, *The Greek Language* (London: Duckworth, 1980); S. E. Porter, *The Criteria for Authenticity in Historical-Jesus Research: Previous Discussion and New Proposals* (JSNTSup 191; Sheffield: Sheffield Academic Press, 2000a); idem, "Dialect and Register in the Greek of the New Testament: Theory," and "Register in the Greek of the New Testament: Application with Reference to Mark's Gospel," in *Rethinking Contexts, Rereading Texts: Contributions from the Social Sciences to Biblical Interpretation,* ed. M. D. Carroll R. (JSOTSup 299; Sheffield: Sheffield Academic Press, 2000b); idem, "The Functional Distribution of Koine Greek in First-Century Palestine," in *Diglossia and Other Topics in New Testament Linguistics,* ed. S. E. Porter (JSNTSup 193; SNTG 6; Sheffield: Sheffield Academic Press, 2000c) 53-78; idem, "The Greek Language of the New Testament," in *Handbook to Exegesis of the New Testament,* ed. S. E. Porter (NTTS 25; Leiden: E. J. Brill, 1997) 99-130; idem, ed., *The Language of the New Testament: Classic Essays* (JSNTSup 60; Sheffield: JSOT, 1991); idem, *Studies in the Greek New Testament: Theory and Practice* (SBG 6; New York: Peter Lang, 1996); idem, "Studying Ancient Languages from a Modern Linguistic Perspective: Essential Terms and Terminology," *FN* 2 (1989a) 147-72; idem, *Verbal Aspect in the Greek of the New Testament, with Reference to Tense and Mood* (SBG 1; New York: Peter Lang, 1989b); S. E. Porter and M. B. O'Donnell, "The Greek Verbal Network Viewed from a Probabilistic Standpoint: An Exercise in Hallidayan Linguistics," *FN* (forthcoming); A. T. Robertson, *A Grammar of the Greek New Testament in the Light of Historical Research* (4th ed.; Nashville: Broadman, 1934); M. Silva, "Bilingualism and the Character of New Testament Greek," *Bib* 61 (1978) 198-219; N. Turner, *Syntax,* vol. 3 of *A Grammar of New Testament*

Greek, by J. H. Moulton (Edinburgh: T & T Clark, 1963); D. F. Watson, *Invention, Arrangement and Style: Rhetorical Criticism of Jude and 2 Peter* (SBLDS 104; Atlanta: Scholars Press, 1988); G. B. Winer, *A Treatise on the Grammar of New Testament Greek Regarded as a Sure Basis for New Testament Exegesis* (3d ed.; Edinburgh: T & T Clark, 1882).

S. E. Porter

GREEK OLD TESTAMENT. *See* SEPTUAGINT/GREEK OLD TESTAMENT.

GREEK PAPYRI, PALESTINIAN. *See* PAPYRI, PALESTINIAN.

GYMNASIA AND BATHS

The gymnasium, a Greek institution that seems to have existed as far back as early classical times, went through various changes in its millennium-long history. During Greek and *Hellenistic times, the gymnasium formed the basis for the Greek *polis,* which itself formed the basis for the state. In Hellenistic times, the gymnasium was the center of *education, from primary education in letters through secondary education in Greco-Roman authors (Homer chief among them) to tertiary education in *rhetoric. Along with these intellectual pursuits came a variety of physical undertakings and training in sports and combat, performed in the nude. Attendance of a gymnasium was an essential prerequisite to citizenship in the *polis,* and hence membership was jealously guarded and brought with it heavy responsibilities. The two most important offices of the gymnasium, *gymnasiarch* and *kosmētēs,* both carried with them a financial load. The *gymnasiarch,* or ruler of the gymnasium, was usually elected for a year-long term and was responsible for the supply of the basic needs of the gymnasium—fuel for hot water and oil for anointing and lighting. The *kosmētēs,* or master of order, was also elected for a year and was responsible for the supervision of the procedures and routines through which the *ephēbes,* as students in the gymnasium were called, would pass (Lewis, 46-47).

1. Gymnasia
2. Baths

1. Gymnasia.

1.1. Gymnasia in Greek and Hellenistic Life. The archaeological, inscriptional and papyrological evidence for gymnasia in the Hellenistic era is outstanding and has allowed us much insight into the structure of this important Hellenistic institution (see Delorme for pictures and plans). The essential architectural features of the gymnasium were the *palaistra,* an open court for wrestling, and the *dromos,* a track for running. The *palaistra* was typically surrounded with colonnades, and a variety of other rooms opened off of it (cloakroom, anointing room, oil room, dusting room, ball-playing rooms, room for exercising with the punch ball, the usual rooms of a bathhouse [see below], teaching/conversation rooms and even sometimes lecture theaters [Jones, 220-26]). These various additions accrued over time to the original two-part structure, in varying degrees of complexity. The Attalid kings of Asia Minor are recorded as having built one gymnasium for each of the various levels of education, students moving from one to the other somewhat like the modern Western educational system (Jones, 220 and n. 20 [351]). Some gymnasia are even thought to have kept rather extensive libraries.

1.2. Gymnasia in Roman Life. The gymnasium eventually became part of the Roman world, but with a varying degree of change—in the highly Hellenized Egypt (*see* Hellenistic Egypt), only a certain amount of practical change took place, with the civic function of the gymnasium remaining virtually unchanged (Lewis, 35). In other places the change was so fundamental as to suggest that the gymnasium remained such in name only. On an athletic level, the gymnasium became a place of demonstration rather than involvement—physical training in Rome was confined to the Campus Martius and was essentially aimed at military activity (Bonner, 47). Gymnasia under Roman rule thus became largely educational institutions, and the architectural evidence points toward this change (Delorme; see also Yegul). Differences in Roman society necessitated this—rather than the highest citizenship being that of the *polis* or *metropolis,* Romans looked toward a more centralized *empire, and *citizenship of that empire was of more importance than individual citizenship of the city. City citizenship was still important, but its role had been fundamentally changed, and this change brought a similar change in the role of the gymnasium.

1.3. The Gymnasium and the Jews. First Maccabees 1:13-15 and 2 Maccabees 4 (*see* 1 and 2 Maccabees) record the famous episode of the establishment of a gymnasium in *Jerusalem. Apparently, in about 175 B.C., Jason asked Antiochus IV Epiphanes for two things: the right to refound Jerusalem as a Greek city, named Antioch in his honor, and to establish a gymnasium there. Some important points must be noted with regard to this episode. As A. H. M. Jones (220) has pointed out, "Any barbarian community which aspired to the status of a Greek city must found a gymnasium." Jerusalem was, in the eyes of its Greek overlords, such a barbarian city. However, the institution of a gymnasium could only have taken place, as M. Hengel (73, 244) has pointed out, with much support from his fellow Jerusalemites and at the end of a sufficient amount of Hellenization that would suggest to Antiochus that this would be a suitable city upon which to bestow this honor.

The largest problem with the foundation of such an institution in Jerusalem was the fact that athletic activities in the gymnasium were done in the nude, which was in itself unlawful to Jews. However, 2 Maccabees 4 and Josephus (*Ant.* 12.5.1 §§240-41) suggest that Jews were undergoing operations to undo the effects of circumcision so as to avoid embarrassment, and priests were even neglecting their duties in the temple to partake in the gymnasium activities. We have no way of knowing the veracity of the reports in the Maccabean literature, given its pro-Hasmonean stance (*see* Hasmoneans) and outright vilification of its enemies. We also have no reason to imagine that the gymnasium as an institution fell out of use after the establishment of the Hasmonean state (see Hengel, 76-77). Jason's gymnasium foundation was, however, a flash point in an ever increasing movement toward the Hellenization of Judaism and Palestine. It was indeed a—perhaps *the*—decisive moment in the overt Hellenization of Jewish culture, and it brought with it all kinds of religious, cultural and political implications, so much so that we should not be surprised to see this particular event held up for contempt in the way that it is in the Maccabean literature (*see* Hellenistic Judaism).

Jews in *Alexandria seem to have been more at ease with the gymnasium, as *Philo seems to assume a gymnasium education for upper-class Alexandrian Jews (e.g., Philo *Som.* 69), and the edict of Claudius in A.D. 41 (*CPJ* 2 no. 153) to forbid gymnasium membership and hence citizenship to Jews was received with much consternation, until the so-called revolt of Quietus in A.D. 115 to 117 virtually wiped out the Jewish community in Egypt (Hengel, 68-69).

2. Baths.

The practice of regular bathing was very important in Roman culture. In the Roman period, the bathhouse in many ways took the place of the gymnasium, and it is not uncommon to have the two institutions connected architecturally as well as functionally. We have examples of bathhouses from the core to the furthest extents of the Roman Empire (the famous baths at Bath, England [of first-century origin] or the Herodian bathhouse on Masada [mid-first century B.C.]). The usual construction of a bathhouse included four rooms: the *apoditerium,* for changing; the *frigidarium,* with cold water; the *tepidarium,* with lukewarm water; and the *caldarium,* with hot water. One moved through the various rooms starting with the *caldarium,* and so one was able to progressively cleanse the body with various rubbings and scrapings. Bathhouses were variously segregated and unisex—even where they were formally separated into men's and women's sides, it is probable that these divisions were not always enforced. Depending on the size and relative wealth of a bathhouse, along with the various washings, patrons would have access to assorted other ministrations, such as massage, hairstyling or cosmetics. A bathhouse was not solely for these purposes of hygiene, however. It also formed a central focus for social life in the Roman city, and as such people often spent a great deal of time at the bathhouse, even conducting business in alcoves provided for the purpose (see Yegul).

See also ATHLETICS; CIRCUSES AND GAMES; EDUCATION: JEWISH AND GRECO-ROMAN; HELLENISM; HELLENISTIC JUDAISM; ROMAN SOCIAL CLASSES; THEATERS.

BIBLIOGRAPHY. S. F. Bonner, *Education in Ancient Rome* (London: Methuen, 1977); J. Delorme, *Gymnasium: Étude sur les Monuments Consacrés à l'Éducation en Grèce (des Origines à l'Empire Romain)* (Bibliothèque des Écoles françaises d'Athènes et de Rome 196; Paris: Boccard, 1960); M. Hengel, *Judaism and Hellenism* (2 vols.; London: SCM, 1974) 1:65-83; A. H. M. Jones, *The Greek City* (Oxford: Oxford University Press, 1998 [1940]) 220-26; N. Lewis, *Life in Egypt Under Roman Rule* (Oxford: Oxford University Press, 1983); F. Yegul, *Baths and Bathing in Classical Antiquity* (Architectural History Foundation; Cambridge, MA: M.I.T. Press, 1996 repr.).

B. W. R. Pearson

H

HABAKKUK COMMENTARY (1QpHab)

One of the original Dead Sea Scrolls to be discovered in 1947, *Pesher Habakkuk* (the Commentary on Habakkuk) is of special significance in view of its early publication in 1951 and its relative completeness. This scroll has been the subject of several studies and is regarded as the paradigm by which other example of the pesher genre are to be assessed.

1. Description
2. Facets of the Biblical Text and the Commentary

1. Description.

Copied in the second half of the first century B.C., this prophetic pesher was written in thirteen columns of seventeen lines each and ended with the conclusion of Habakkuk 2 in the middle of the thirteenth column. One interesting feature of this scroll is its presentation of the divine name or Tetragrammaton YHWH in paleo-Hebrew letters, with the rest of the text in the more regular square Hebrew script.

1QpHab may be outlined by its comment on Habakkuk as follows:

Religious strife in Israel [On Hab 1:1-4]
The Man of the Lie, the new covenant, and the last days [On Hab 1:5]
The coming of the cruel and mighty Romans (the "Kittim") [On Hab 1:6-11]
The need to remain faithful to God's law [On Hab 1:12-13]
The Kittim, who sacrifice to their standards [On Hab 1:14-17]
On the Teacher of Righteousness [On Hab 2:1-3a]
Exhortation to remain faithful amidst suffering [On Hab 2:3b-4a]
Escaping the final judgment by remaining loyal to the Teacher [On Hab 2:4b]
On the Wicked Priest [On Hab 2:5-6]
The fate and death of the Wicked Priest [On Hab 2:7-11]
The Man of the Lie or the "Spouter of Lies" [On Hab 2:12-14]
The Wicked Priest persecutes the Teacher of Righteousness [On Hab 2:15]
Further details on the fate of the Wicked Priest [On Hab 2:17]
Condemnation of Gentile idolatry [On Hab 2:18]

2. Facets of the Biblical Text and the Commentary.

The form of this pesher is citation of the biblical text, followed by commentary introduced by a citation formula (either "its meaning is" or "the meaning of the item is with respect to"). On occasion words that were quoted earlier but not commented on are introduced by formulas of secondary quotation ("for this is what it says" or "and as for what it says").

The scriptural text of Habakkuk quoted by *Pesher Habakkuk* is of some text-critical importance since it at times varies from the Masoretic Text. One example is found at Habakkuk 1:5 (1QpHab 2:1), where 1QpHab agrees with the *Septuagint in implying "traitors" (*bôg^{e}dîm*), as opposed to "among the nations" (*baggôyim*) in the Masoretic Text. However, in several instances 1QpHab cites a verse in one form but then comments on an apparently different form. For example, in 1QpHab 9:9-13 the citation of Habakkuk 2:16 reads "also drink (imperative) *and stagger*," whereas the pesher of this verse refers to one "who did not circumcise the foreskin of his heart" (apparently from "*and be uncircumcised*" in the Masoretic Text).

Several exegetical techniques are to be found in *Pesher Habakkuk*. In some cases the base text is simply paraphrased or expanded for purposes of clarity; for example, in interpreting Habakkuk 1:17 ("he shall not have mercy") the commentator quotes Isaiah 13:18 ("they shall not have mercy on the fruit of the womb"). Another device is to make specific terms that are generic or vague in the base text: for example, specifying that the "wicked one" of Habakkuk 1:13 is the Man of the Lie (1QpHab 5:11) and identifying the "arrogant man" of Habakkuk 2:5 as the Wicked Priest (1QpHab 8:8).

In many instances a person or thing specified in the base text is interpreted as a completely different one. For example, the Chal-deans that were mentioned by the prophet Habakkuk are now identified as the Kittim (i.e., the Romans) of the pesher and of the author's own time. A similar approach is adopted by the NT writers, who frequently reinterpret earlier Scriptures, especially prophetic texts, as referring to the life, death or resurrection of Jesus. It is also interesting to note that the term *new covenant* is used in 1QpHab; in 2:3 the "traitors" of Habakkuk 1:5 are associated with "the traitors of the new covenant."

See also BIBLICAL INTERPRETATION, JEWISH; DEAD SEA SCROLLS; PESHARIM.

BIBLIOGRAPHY. M. J. Bernstein, "Introductory Formulas for Citation and Recitation of Biblical Verses in the Qumran Pesherim: Observations on a Pesher Technique, *DSD* 1 (1994) 30-70; G. J. Brooke, "The Pesharim and the Origins of the Dead Sea Scrolls," in *Methods of Investigation of the Dead Sea Scrolls and the Khirbet Qumran Site: Present Realities and Future Prospects*, ed. M. O. Wise et al. (Annals of the New York Academy of Sciences 722; New York: New York Academy of Sciences, 1994) 339-52; W. H. Brownlee, *The Midrash Pesher of Habakkuk: Text, Translation, Exposition with an Introduction* (SBLMS 24; Missoula, MT: Scholars Press, 1979); S. Talmon, "Notes on the Habakkuk Scroll," *VT* 1 (1951) 34-37.

P. W. Flint

HALAKHA A (4Q251). *See* LEGAL TEXTS AT QUMRAN.

ḤANINA BEN DOSA. *See* HOLY MEN, JEWISH.

HARVESTING/LEQET TEXT (4Q284a). *See* LEGAL TEXTS AT QUMRAN.

HASMONEANS

The Hasmoneans were a Jewish family that became instrumental in freeing Judea from *Seleucid rule, beginning in 167 B.C. Several generations served as high *priests, governors and kings, until Roman intervention in 63 B.C. curtailed their role and *Herod the Great ousted the last Hasmonean king in 37 B.C. The origin of the family's name is obscure but is most plausibly related to an otherwise unknown eponymous ancestor by the name of *Hašmônay* (*m. Mid.* 1:6 and elsewhere in *rabbinic literature; *Asamōnaios* in Josephus *J.W.* 1.1.3 §36; cf. Josephus *Ant.* 12.6.1 §265 and passim). Sometimes the term *Hasmonean* is restricted to John Hyrcanus I and his descendants, while here as in Josephus and in rabbinic literature it is used in reference to the preceding generations as well.

1. Background of the Family
2. Rebels and Rulers
3. Other Notable Hasmoneans
4. The Significance of the Hasmoneans

1. Background of the Family.

The family had its home base in Modein, northwest of *Jerusalem, where Simon is said to have built a grandiose family tomb (1 Macc 13:25-30; cf. 2:70; 9:19; Josephus *J.W.* 1.1.3 §36). It claimed to belong to the priestly course of Joarib (1 Macc 2:1; 14:29; cf. 1 Chron 24:7), but its Aaronite descent may not have been beyond doubt (Smith). Between 153/152 and 35 B.C., nine Hasmoneans served as high priests of the Jerusalem *temple. While Judas Maccabeus and his father Mattathias before him held only informal leadership functions, the Hasmonean high priests usually also held civil and military offices. They were gradually recognized as governors or local rulers by different Seleucid kings. A certain independence was proclaimed about 142 B.C. by Simon (1 Macc 13:41-42), but autonomy was not complete until the last decade of the second century (Barag). Beginning with John Hyrcanus I, the Hasmoneans issued their own *coinage, generally bronze coins of small denomination (Meshorer; Barag). By the end of the second cen-tury, they were able to claim the title of king, which they held until Roman intervention in 63 B.C. After that, Hyrcanus II was allowed to continue to hold the office of high priest and *ethnarch* ("ruler over a tribe or people"). The re-newed royal claim of Mattathias Antigonus (40-37 B.C.) quickly gave way to the rule of Herod the Great, who under political pressure named one last Hasmonean high priest for a short time (35 B.C.).

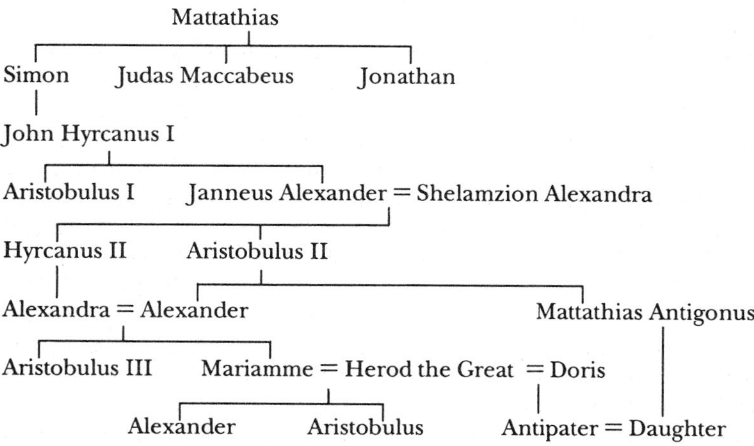

The Hasmoneans

The popularity of the Hasmoneans obviously changed over the years. Judas was considered a hero by people with different outlooks (cf. 1 Macc 3:1-9; 9:20-22; 2 Macc 15:11-17; *1 Enoch* 90:9-16). His successors gradually gathered wider support, but their high priesthood did not remain uncontested. Opposition to it is expressed in a variety of circumstances in different sources (**Habakkuk Commentary* [1QpHab] and elsewhere in the *Dead Sea Scrolls; 1 Macc 10:61; 11:21, 25-26; Josephus *J.W.* 1.2.1 §48; *Ant.* 13.10.5 §291; 13.13.5 §§372-73; *b. Qidd.* 66a). Yet the most severe blow to the Hasmoneans' position seems to have come through the internecine strife between the two sons of Shelamzion Alexandra, which led to Roman intervention. According to Josephus, who prided himself on being descended from the Hasmoneans (Josephus *Ant.* 16.7.1 §187; *Life* 1 §§1-4), even the last high priest from this family, Jonathan Aristobulus III, enjoyed great popularity, in part because of his ancestry (Josephus *Ant.* 15.3.3-4 §§52-57). The quest for dynastic legitimation seems to have played a role in Herod's marriage to Mariamme (Josephus *J.W.* 1.12.3 §§240-41), the granddaughter of Hyrcanus II and Aristobulus II, and in Antipater's marriage to a daughter of King Mattathias Antigonus (Josephus *Ant.* 17.5.2 §92). Herod did not rest until he had eliminated all male descendants of the Hasmoneans (Josephus *Ant.* 15.7.10 §266). Even after his death (4 B.C.), the Hasmonean house remained so popular that someone impersonating a son of Mariamme at least briefly attracted widespread support among *Diaspora Jews (Josephus *J.W.* 2.7.1-2 §§101-10; *Ant.* 17.12.1-2 §§324-38).

2. Rebels and Rulers.

2.1. Mattathias. Mattathias (died c. 166 B.C.) is said to have refused to offer a pagan sacrifice in Modein and thereby to have initiated a revolt against the decree of Antiochus IV that forbade under threat of death the observance of Jewish law (1 Macc 2:1-28; cf. Josephus *J.W.* 1.1.3 §§36-37). He is compared to Phinehas (cf. Num 25:1-15) in his zeal for *Torah observance. The account of his actions in 1 Maccabees 2:1-70 seems to be greatly influenced by later dynastic concerns (Sievers 1990, 29-37).

2.2. Judas Maccabeus. Judas Maccabeus was the third son of Mattathias. His surname may be related to the Hebrew/Aramaic root *mqb* (perhaps "hammerlike"). It gave the title to books about him and his brothers (1-2 Macc). "Maccabees" is sometimes used as a quasi-synonym of "Hasmoneans" (3-4 Macc have no direct relation to him). Judas became the leader of a growing popular revolt against the Seleucid authorities and their Judean supporters. After initial victories, he was able to have the defiled temple of Jerusalem *purified and rededicated (1 Macc 4:36-59; 2 Macc 10:1-8; *Megillat Ta'anit).* This event was and is remembered in the Jewish *feast of Hanukkah ("dedication"; *b. Šabb.* 21b; cf. Jn 10:22). Despite this success and the revocation of Antiochus IV's decree the revolt continued. Judas seems to have sought support even in *Rome, through a formal alliance (1 Macc 8) that was renewed by several of his successors. He was killed in battle after being abandoned by many of his earlier followers (161/160; 1 Macc 9:5-18; differently Bar-Kochva, 48-49, 399).

*2.3. **Jonathan.*** Judas's brother Jonathan took over as leader of the rebellion. After years of relative obscurity, he was courted by several contenders for the Seleucid throne and accepted the high priesthood from King Alexander Balas (153 or 152 B.C.). While maintaining a strong military force, Jonathan achieved more by diplomacy than by warfare, cooperating with Alexander Balas and fostering alliances with Rome and allegedly even with Sparta. He was killed by order of the Seleucid pretender Tryphon, after being captured through a ruse (143/142 B.C.).

*2.4. **Simon.*** Simon, the last surviving brother, took over a leadership position immediately after Jonathan's capture. He too became high priest, although the details of his appointment remain obscure. Only in his third year was he confirmed in office by a popular assembly (1 Macc 14:27-49; Sievers 1990, 119-27). In the meantime he had conquered Gazara (Gezer) and the *Akra* ("citadel"), a fortified quarter of Jerusalem that had remained in the hands of opponents of the Hasmoneans for more than twenty-five years. Like all his brothers, he died a violent death: he was killed by his own son-in-law, who sought in vain to gain power over Judea (spring 135 or 134 B.C.).

*2.5. **John Hyrcanus I.*** John Hyrcanus I (135/134-104 B.C.) succeeded his father, Simon, as high priest. However, the Seleucids still maintained their claim of sovereignty and taxation over Judea. Antiochus VII Sidetes attacked Jerusalem soon after Hyrcanus's accession. After a protracted siege Hyrcanus was able to work out a compromise that included payment of tribute and military support for Antiochus's eastern campaign but that left Jerusalem without a Seleucid garrison. Apparently only during his last years did Hyrcanus conquer additional territory for Judea in Idumea to the south and in *Samaria and lower *Galilee to the north. The destruction of the buildings on Mt. Gerizim, including the Samaritan temple precinct, has recently been confirmed by archaeological excavations. The numismatic evidence there and at other sites points to a conquest by Hyrcanus in 111 B.C. or shortly thereafter (Barag). Toward the end of his life, Hyrcanus had to deal with intra-Judean opposition. Whether this meant a change of his allegiance from the *Pharisees to the *Sadducees, as Josephus reports (Josephus *Ant.* 13.10.5-7 §§288-99), cannot be otherwise confirmed (cf. *b. Qidd.* 66a).

*2.6. **Judas Aristobulus I.*** Judas Aristobulus I (104-103 B.C.) became high priest after his father's death. According to Josephus, he was the first Hasmonean to assume the title of king (Josephus *J.W.* 1.3.1 §70; *Ant.* 13.11.1 §301; 20.10.3 §§240-41). Power struggles within and around the family induced Aristobulus to put his mother and his brother Antigonus to death. He himself fell ill and died shortly thereafter.

*2.7. **Alexander Janneus.*** Alexander Janneus (103-76 B.C.) took over high priesthood and kingship after his brother. He made additional conquests, bringing the Hasmonean kingdom to its largest extent, including much of Galilee and Transjordan and the coastal region from the Carmel mountains to Rhinocorura, south of Gaza. Internal opposition to his rule was strong, especially during his later years. This led to bloody civil war, with the temporary intervention of one of the last Seleucid kings, Demetrius III, in 88 B.C., and repressive action by Janneus. According to Josephus, Janneus had eight hundred of his enemies crucified and their wives and children slain before their eyes (Josephus *J.W.* 1.4.6 §97; *Ant.* 13.14.2 §380). These events are also remembered in 4QpNah 3-4 i 2-8, where the name of Demetrius is partially preserved and Janneus is called "the Lion of Wrath." Another text from Qumran (4Q448) has been interpreted as a prayer for the welfare of Janneus (Eshel, Eshel and Yardeni), but this interpretation is disputed (Main).

*2.8. **Shelamzion Alexandra.*** Shelamzion Alexandra (76-67 B.C.) is probably to be distinguished from Salina or Salome Alexandra, the wife of Aristobulus I (Ilan 1993). She succeeded her husband after his death. Her name is given only as Alexandra by Josephus, but her true Hebrew name, Shelamzion, is now attested at Qumran (4Q322 2:4). Such female succession was nearly unprecedented in the history of Judea but was probably influenced by the practice in neighboring *Ptolemaic Egypt, where it had become quite common. The queen appointed the elder of her two sons, Hyrcanus II, high priest and associated herself with the Pharisees, who had been among the internal enemies persecuted by her husband. She allowed them to take action against her husband's supporters. She was able to maintain external peace, relying on a largely mercenary army. Rabbinic literature generally views her in very favorable light. Josephus, whose work is here partly based on that of Herod's court historian Nicolaus of Damascus, gives contradictory evaluations of her reign (Ilan 1996, 237-42).

2.9. Aristobulus II. Aristobulus II, the younger of the two sons of Shelamzion, supplanted his brother Hyrcanus II, already high priest and designated to become king. Hyrcanus, however, was induced by Antipater, the father of King Herod the Great, to seek reinstatement. With assistance from the Arab king Aretas they defeated Aristobulus and besieged his remaining supporters in Jerusalem. The siege was lifted by the threat of Roman intervention. When later both Hasmoneans asked the Roman proconsul *Pompey, then in Damascus, for his support, a third Judean delegation accused both of them of trying to enslave their people and petitioned that neither of them be king (Josephus *Ant.* 14.3.2 §§41-45; Diodorus Siculus *Bib. Hist.* 40.2 = M. Stern 1974-84, 1:185-87). When Aristobulus did not obey Roman orders and the fights between the brothers continued, Pompey advanced against Jerusalem and conquered it after a three-month siege in the summer of 63 B.C. He now assigned the high priesthood again to Hyrcanus II, while Aristobulus was sent to Rome as a prisoner. After escaping and being recaptured, he was sent by Julius Caesar to fight against Pompey but was poisoned by partisans of Pompey before he could go into action (Josephus *Ant.* 14.7.4 §§123-24).

2.10. Hyrcanus II. Hyrcanus II served as high priest during the reign of his mother, assumed royal power upon her death, was ousted almost immediately by his brother and reinstated as high priest and ethnarch by Pompey in 63 B.C. He is said to have been lacking initiative and to have been entirely under the influence of Antipater, the father of Herod the Great. Yet, Hyrcanus's active involvement in support of Julius Caesar and his allies is evidenced in Roman documents (Josephus *Ant.* 14.10.2-7 §§190-212) and in several Greek historians (Josephus *Ant.* 14.8.3 §§138-39 = M. Stern 1974-84, nos. 76, 79, 107). He was confirmed in office by Caesar in 47 B.C. but was ousted by his nephew Mattathias Antigonus (40 B.C.). The latter not only had him put into Parthian custody but also mutilated his ears, in order to disqualify him from high priestly service (cf. Lev 21:17-21). After being freed by the Parthians Hyrcanus returned to Jerusalem. He was killed by Herod in 30 B.C., because his very existence was seen as a challenge to Herod's claim to royalty (Josephus *J.W.* 1.22.1 §§433-34; *Ant.* 15.6.1-4 §§164-82).

2.11. Mattathias Antigonus. Mattathias Antigonus (40-37 B.C.) briefly served as the last Hasmonean ruler, brought to power by the Parthians. On his coins, his titles are given as high priest (in Hebrew) and king (in Greek). He was besieged in Jerusalem by Herod, who conquered the city through brutal Roman intervention. Antigonus was taken into Roman custody and beheaded in *Antioch, apparently out of fear that his continued popularity might be dangerous to Herod's rule and thus might undermine Roman control (Josephus *J.W.* 1.18.1-3 §§347-57; *Ant.* 14.16.2 §470; 15.1.2 §10).

3. Other Notable Hasmoneans.

Among the Hasmoneans who did not reach official leadership positions, the best known are those who became part of Herod's court, in particular his wife Mariamme and her mother, Alexandra. Herod's sons by Mariamme, Alexander and Aristobulus, also prided themselves on their Hasmonean ancestry. All four were killed by order of Herod, because they too were perceived as a threat to his own dynastic aspirations. The prominence given by Josephus, especially in the *Antiquities,* to the above mentioned and other Hasmonean women is due in part to the biases of his main source for the period, Nicolaus of Damascus (Ilan 1996). Yet, it is clear that several Hasmonean women in addition to Shelamzion Alexandra became active in areas that had been largely male-dominated (Sievers 1989).

4. The Significance of the Hasmoneans.

During the course of more than a century, the Hasmonean family played a central role in the life of Judea and of Judaism. It was the tenacity of the martyrs and the courage of Judas Maccabeus and his companions that saved monotheism for Judaism and thus for humanity (Bickerman). The development of distinct Jewish groups, or Judaisms, in the late Second Temple period occurred partly in response to some of the later Hasmoneans. Thus the influence of the Hasmoneans reaches well beyond their own time.

See also HERODIAN DYNASTY; JEWISH HISTORY:

GREEK PERIOD; JEWISH HISTORY: ROMAN PERIOD; 1 & 2 MACCABEES; PRIESTS AND PRIESTHOOD, JEWISH; SELEUCIDS AND ANTIOCHIDS.

BIBLIOGRAPHY. D. Barag, "New Evidence on the Foreign Policy of John Hyrcanus I," *Israel Numismatic Journal* 12 (1992-93) 1-12; B. Bar-Kochva, *Judas Maccabeus: The Jewish Struggle Against the Seleucids* (Cambridge: Cambridge University Press, 1989); E. Bickerman, *The God of the Maccabees: Studies on the Meaning and Origin of the Maccabean Revolt* (SJLA 32; Leiden: E. J. Brill, 1979 [1937]); E. Eshel, H. Eshel and A. Yardeni, "A Qumran Composition Containing Part of Ps. 154 and a Prayer for the Welfare of King Jonathan and His Kingdom," *IEJ* 42 (1992) 199-229; L. L. Grabbe, *Judaism from Cyrus to Hadrian* (2 vols.; Minneapolis: Fortress, 1992) vol. 1; T. Ilan, "Queen Salamzion Alexandra and Judas Aristobulus I's Widow," *JSJ* 24 (1993) 181-90; idem, "Josephus and Nicolaus on Women," in *Geschichte—Tradition—Reflexion: Festschrift für Martin Hengel,* ed. H. Cancik, H. Lichtenberger and P. Schäfer, 1: *Judentum* (Tübingen: Mohr Siebeck, 1996) 221-62; E. Main, "For King Jonathan or Against? The Use of the Bible in 4Q448," in *Biblical Perspectives: Early Use and Interpretation of the Bible in Light of the Dead Sea Scrolls,* ed. M. Stone and E. G. Chazon (STDJ 28; Leiden: E. J. Brill, 1998) 113-35; D. Mendels, *The Rise and Fall of Jewish Nationalism* (ABRL; New York: Doubleday, 1992); Y. Meshorer, *Ancient Jewish Coinage,* 1: *Persian Period Through Hasmoneans* (Dix Hills, NY: Amphora, 1982); T. Rajak, "The Jews Under Hasmonean Rule," *CAH* (2d ed.) 9:274-309, 777; E. Schürer, *The History of the Jewish People in the Age of Jesus Christ (175 B.C.-A.D. 135),* rev. ed. G. Vermes, F. Millar and M. Goodman (3 vols.; Edinburgh: T & T Clark, 1973-87); D. R. Schwartz, "Josephus on Hyrcanus II," in *Josephus and the History of the Greco-Roman Period: Essays in Memory of Morton Smith,* ed. F. Parente and J. Sievers (SPB 41; Leiden: E. J. Brill, 1994) 210-32; I. Shatzman, *The Armies of the Hasmoneans and Herod* (TSAJ 25; Tübingen: Mohr Siebeck, 1991); J. Sievers, *The Hasmoneans and Their Supporters: From Mattathias to the Death of John Hyrcanus I* (SFSHJ 6; Atlanta: Scholars Press, 1990); idem, "The Role of Women in the Hasmonean Dynasty," in *Josephus, the Bible, and History,* ed. L. H. Feldman and G. Hata (Detroit: Wayne State University Press, 1989) 132-46; M. Smith, "Were the Maccabees Priests?" in *Studies in the Cult of Yahweh,* ed. S. J. D. Cohen (2 vols. RGRW 130; Leiden: E. J. Brill, 1996) 1:320-25; G. Stemberger, "The Maccabees in Rabbinic Tradition," in *The Scriptures and the Scrolls: Studies in Honor of A. S. van der Woude,* ed. F. García Martínez, A. Hilhorst and C. J. Labuschagne (Lei-den: E. J. Brill, 1992) 193-203; E. Stern, ed., *The New Encyclopedia of Archaeological Excavations in the Holy Land* (4 vols.; Jerusalem: Israel Exploration Society; New York: Simon & Schuster, 1993); M. Stern, *Greek and Latin Authors on Jews and Judaism* (3 vols.; Jerusalem: Israel Academy of Sciences and Humanities, 1974-84); idem, *Hasmonaean Judaea in the Hellenistic World* (in Hebrew), ed. D. R. Schwartz (Jerusalem: Zalman Shazar Center, 1995).

J. Sievers

HEAD COVERINGS

Among customs that invite a discussion of NT background, head coverings is one of the most quickly recognized because it is one most foreign to modern Western culture. For the same reason, however, this custom remains one of the more perplexing to many people. This article surveys the frequent assignment of women to the domestic sphere, a broader concept often held to be related to head coverings; various Mediterranean customs about head covering; the gender-specific head covering customs and possible class associations most likely in view in the NT passage that addresses them (1 Cor 11:2-16).

At the outset we should comment on the nature of head coverings probably presupposed in Paul's comments. Some scholars have argued that Paul addressed not genuine head coverings but merely hair piled up on the head (Hurley, 200, 214), but the best evidence for this hairstyle being widespread dates to a generation after Paul (see Balsdon, 24, 27). The arguments against this interpretation of 1 Corinthians 11:2-16 are compelling (Oster, 485-86; Fee, 496, 506-7, 528-29); a woman compelled to cover her head with only her hair was considered particularly destitute (ARN 17A). Rather, Paul presumably refers to the sort of head coverings widely used in the eastern Mediterranean. We should also note that except in Arabia and further east, women normally veiled only their heads, not their faces (MacMullen, 210 n. 4).

1. Women Assigned to the Domestic Sphere
2. Various Reasons for Covering Heads
3. Women's Head Coverings
4. Status and Class Differences
5. Conclusion

1. Women Assigned to the Domestic Sphere. Many husbands expected their wives to cover their heads to preserve their beauty solely for their husbands, a rationale also prominent in the seclusion of women in many societies. In Islamic Middle Eastern villages today, a woman's head covering substitutes for seclusion when the latter ideal proves impractical (see Delaney, 41). Some segments of ancient Mediterranean society seem to have also used head coverings as a substitute for seclusion, inviting comment on the practice of seclusion.

In our earliest Greek sources, a respectable matron was ashamed to go by herself among men (Homer *Odys.* 18.184). Although the case has been overstated, sufficient evidence reveals an even higher degree of separation of genders in classical *Athens (Gould, 47; Dover, 145). Exceptions existed, such as in Greek drama (Foley, 161), but these do not represent the pervasive social custom among urbanites outside the elite.

Although women's relative seclusion diminished over time, it remained the norm; thus second- and first-century B.C. marriage contracts from *Hellenistic Egypt forbade the wife to leave the marital residence without permission (Verner, 38). In the romances, a groom-to-be was sometimes the first man to gaze on a modest virgin's face (Chariton *Chaer.* 1.1.4-6; *Jos. and As.* 15:1-2; 18:6). To force a husband to expose his wife's beauty in public was scandalous, even immoral (Chariton *Chaer.* 5.4.10).

In an earlier period conservative Romans also normally secluded wives (Dionysius of Halicarnassus *Ant. Rom.* 8.39.1) and virgins (Dionysius of Halicarnassus *Ant. Rom.* 3.21.2). Romans associated public appearances of women with sexual license and revolt against their husbands. When aristocratic matrons massed in public to beg for the repeal of the Oppian law in 195 B.C., they were said to ignore modesty and their husbands' orders to remain at home (Livy *Hist.* 34.1.5). Thus Marcus Porcius Cato complained that it was inappropriate for them to be in public speaking with other women's husbands (Livy *Hist.* 34.2.9; 34.4.18), or did they think themselves more attractive to other women's husbands than to their own (Livy *Hist.* 34.2.10)? If they gained their cause, he argued, these women would achieve not only equality but ultimately superiority over their husbands (Livy *Hist.* 34.3.1-3). The opposing speech, however, won, noting some precedents for women appearing in public (Livy *Hist.* 34.5.7-10).

Even in the late first century moralists might maintain that virtuous women stayed at home unless they were in their husbands' company (Plutarch *Bride* 9, *Mor.* 139C; 30-32, 142CD). At least in the western Mediterranean, however, this attitude was always an ideal rather than a custom strictly followed (Hallett, 245). By this later period Roman matrons could enter the front rooms of the house where guests were admitted, but the Greek custom continued to restrict them to the interior of the house (Cornelius Nepos *Preface* 6-7). Men might also refuse to be seen in public, but only for special reasons unrelated to their gender, for example, grief (Chariton *Chaer.* 2.1.1). A degree of gender segregation continues in some Mediterranean cultures, such as the Garrese of Sicily (Giovannini, 67).

*Diaspora Jewish fathers usually preferred to keep their virgin daughters secluded from men, who might prove promiscuous (4 Macc 18:7-8; *Pseud.-Phoc.* 215-16; Sir 26:10; 42:11-12; Philo *Spec. Leg.* 3.169; *Flacc.* 89). Palestinian Jewish women seem to have exercised more freedom in going to the marketplace. The Tannaim seem to make relative seclusion an ideal, to protect the wife's sexuality from the public domain (see Wegner, 18, 148-67), but this was probably difficult to implement in practice (Ilan, 128-29). Yet though they could go out, wives' official roles focused on the home (Goodman, 37).

2. Various Reasons for Covering Heads. People in the ancient Mediterranean covered their heads for various reasons. Mourning, shame and Roman worship were among the most common reasons for covering one's head. We omit discussion of some more restricted customs such as the bridal veil (Lucan *Civ.W.* 2.360, 364) or shaving one's head to fulfill a vow (Num 6:18; Acts 18:18).

2.1. Mourning. People in the ancient Mediterranean world not only tore their hair in mourning (e.g., Euripides *Androm.* 1209-10; *El.* 150; Ovid *Met.* 11.682) but also expressed mourning in other intentionally masochistic manners. Often they would cut their hair in mourning (Homer *Il.* 23.46; Euripides *Alc.* 216, 427, 512; *El.* 241, 335; *Hipp.* 1425-26; Arrian *Alex.* 7.14.4; Herodian *Hist.* 4.8.5; Athenaeus *Deipn.* 12.523b); it was also customary to leave a lock of cut hair at the tomb of the deceased (Sophocles *Elect.*

900-1; Euripides *Alc.* 101-3; *El.* 91, 515, 520; *Or.* 96; Ovid *Met.* 13.427-28).

By contrast, one might let his hair and beard grow long with mourning (Diodorus Siculus *Bib. Hist.* 36.15.2; Lucan *Civ.W.* 2.375-76), also a likely masochistic expression (cf. Lev 21:1-5; Deut 14:1). Plutarch indicated that Roman men covered their heads for mourning and Roman women uncovered their heads and loosed their hair (Plutarch *Quaest. Rom.* 14, *Mor.* 267A), perhaps as self-inflicted suffering by reversing norms of honor. Others also recognized that Roman women had unloosed hair for mourning (Livy *Hist.* 1.13.1; 1.26.2; Ovid *Met.* 6.288-89; Petronius *Sat.* 111); typically this implied also disheveled hair (Hdn. 1.13.1).

But members of both genders often covered their own heads while mourning the deaths of others or their own plight (Virgil *Aen.* 12.312; Plutarch *Rom.* 26, *Mor.* 270D; Chariton *Chaer.* 1.3.6; 1.11.2; 3.3.14; 8.1.7; ARN 1A; *y. Mo'ed Qaṭ.* 3:5 §20). In a much earlier period, David covered his head and walked barefoot when mourning Absalom's revolt (2 Sam 15:30). One who was sick might also cover his head (Petronius *Sat.* 101), and an ancient author might regard as noteworthy a woman going about with her hair hanging loose, signifying the urgency of the moment (3 Macc 1:4).

One's head would be veiled before execution (Livy *Hist.* 1.26.11; 23.10.9). Those about to die often veiled themselves or their head with their robe (Livy *Hist.* 3.49.5; 4.12.11; Appian *Civ.W.* 2.16.117; Dio Cassius *Hist.* 42.4.5), or asked another to cover them thus (Euripides *Hec.* 432-33; *Hipp.* 1458). One might cover the body of a fallen officer (Livy *Hist.* 3.18.9; perhaps 2 Sam 20:12). Perhaps these customs arose to keep others from viewing one's open-eyed corpse (a great shame; see Homer *Odys.* 11.426), but mourning may also be a factor in the custom; a woman might also keep her body covered while dying to guard her modesty and honor (Ovid *Met.* 13.479-80).

2.2. Shame. Shame functioned as a specific form of mourning; ancients recognized them as related emotions (e.g., Aulus Gellius *Noc. Att.* 19.6.1). Greeks sometimes covered their heads for shame (Homer *Odys.* 8.84-85, 92; Euripides *Hipp.* 243-46; *Heracl.* 1198-1201; Epictetus *Disc.* 1.11.27), as did Jewish people (*m. Soṭa* 9:15; ARN 9 §25B; *Gen. Rab.* 17:8). Covered heads may indicate subjugation (2 Macc 4:12), and walking about bareheaded may symbolize respectability (Petronius *Sat.* 57). In Jewish sources one could uncover one's head also to show reverence (*Pesiq. Rab Kah.* 9.5); conversely, Enoch may cover his face to hide it from God's glory (*1 Enoch* 14:24; *see* Enoch, Books of).

2.3. Geography and Religion. Although geographical factors are important in some of the other examples in this article, we mention some general considerations here. In general, the further east one went the more of their skin men expected women to cover. Thus Persian women were completely covered (Diodorus Siculus *Bib. Hist.* 17.35.5). Head coverings were more in vogue in *Asia Minor and other parts of the East than they were in Roman *Corinth (see Thompson, 113). Other veiling customs also varied geographically; for example, men of Chalcedon veiled a cheek whenever they met others they did not know, especially if the other people were of superior rank (Plutarch *Quaest. Graec.* 49, *Mor.* 302E).

The geographical difference is most striking, however, in the area of Greek and Roman *religion; whereas Greeks uncovered their heads for worship, Romans covered their heads (Oster, 494; Moffatt, 149). Greek women typically let down their hair for worship (see Schüssler Fiorenza, 227). More sober Romans might take special note of Greek-style ecstasies; worshipers of Dionysus typically had disheveled hair (Ovid *Met.* 3.726-27; 7.257-58; Livy *Hist.* 39.13.12). Yet whereas in some mysteries a veil was forbidden (*Syllog.* 2.401-11), a Roman writer expects female Isis worshipers in Roman Corinth to have their heads covered (Apuleius *Met.* 11.10). Diaspora Jews could also portray female demons as having disheveled hair (*T. Sol.* 13:1). Even in Greek culture, exceptions existed; thus the priestess of a particular sanctuary must wrap her head with a white veil before entering the sanctuary (Pausanius *Descr.* 6.20.3).

Among Romans, both genders veiled their heads in the presence of the sacred (Ovid *Met.* 1.398), and some Roman priests and priestesses wore head coverings (Oster, 495-96, 503; also Varro *Ling.* 5.29.130); both men (Dionysius of Halicarnassus *Ant. Rom.* 15.9.2) and women (Plutarch *Rom.* 10, *Mor.* 266C) covered their heads for prayer and worship. Some exceptions did exist; Roman women worshiped Saturn and Honor with uncovered heads (Plutarch *Rom.* 11, 13, *Mor.* 266E-67A).

As a Roman colony in Greece, new Corinth included both descendants of original Roman settlers and Greeks who had settled after its foundation. Yet neither Greeks nor Romans segregated this custom by gender, however, probably making the distinction less relevant for interpreting women's head coverings in Roman Corinth (Keener, 28).

3. Women's Head Coverings.

Whereas people in the ancient Mediterranean covered their heads for various reasons, the gender-based coverings mentioned in 1 Corinthians 11:2-16 reflect a more specific custom that existed in Mediterranean antiquity, including in Palestinian *Judaism. Although various reasons may have supported the covering of women's hair, the primary one was to protect the wife's or future wife's beauty for her husband alone.

3.1. Head Coverings in the Greek and Roman World. The customs of women covering their heads were quite ancient in the Mediterranean; thus Penelope always kept a veil before her face when addressing the suitors (Homer *Odys.* 1.332-33; 16.416; 18.210; 21.65). Head coverings for women became a common practice (e.g., Chariton *Chaer.* 1.13.11); exposed hair became rare enough that on one occasion women with exposed hair reportedly threw guards into a panic, because the guards thought them night spirits (Dio Cassius *Hist.* 42.11.2-3).

The evidence that this practice continued in Asia Minor and in Greece includes both literary sources and funerary reliefs (see MacMullen, 209, esp. n. 4), and the practice was probably not limited to the East (see Petronius *Sat.* 14, 16). Plutarch even thinks Roman women were forbidden to cover their heads in earlier times (Plutarch *Rom.* 14, *Mor.* 267BC); by itself his argument might not be compelling, but it is supported by other evidence (Valerius Maximus *Fact. ac Dict.* 5.3.10-12; 6.3.10).

3.2. Jewish Use of Head Coverings. Later rabbis expected women to cover their hair (*Sipre Num.* 11.2.2; ARN 1A), although perhaps making an exception for middle and upper classes (Ilan, 129-32). The public loosing of a woman's hair produced shame (*m. B. Qam.* 8:6; ARN 3A). Jewish sources from the first century (Philo *Spec. Leg.* 3.56; Josephus *Ant.* 3.11.6 §270) through the Amoraic period (*Num. Rab.* 9:16; *Pesiq. Rab.* 26:1/2) attest the tradition of removing a wife's head covering when she was suspected of adultery (Num 5:18), thereby assuming the pervasiveness of the wife's head covering in early Palestinian Judaism and Judaism further to the east.

Head coverings appear at least as early as the story of Susanna, whose face appears to have been covered to conceal her beauty from men's lust (Sus 13:32 = Dan 13:32 LXX). To be sure, *Judith does not appear to have been veiled (Schüssler Fiorenza, 116, correctly cites Jdt 10:7; 11:21), but Judith, unlike Susanna (Sus 1—4), is unmarried (Jdt 8:2-7), and even in Palestine it is not clear that unmarried women were expected to cover their heads, though they were not forbidden to do so.

3.3. Prostitutes and Head Coverings. A loose woman might have her hair cropped (Aristophanes *Lysis.* 89); prostitutes also typically exposed more of their legs as well as their hair (Gardner, 251). As early as the twelfth century B.C., Middle Assyrian laws associated veiling with marriage and prohibited prostitutes from wearing veils (tablet A 40); a third-century A.D. tradition in the eastern Mediterranean also presupposes that prostitutes normally avoid veils (*Gen. Rab.* 85:8). But the issue was not prostitution itself; rather, uncovered hair invited male attention, an attitude that could signify promiscuity whether or not it was connected with official, legal prostitution.

3.4. Head Coverings and Male Lust. A primary reason for head coverings in the ancient Mediterranean world resembles that followed in some traditional parts of the Islamic Middle East today, where hair becomes an object of male lust and must be covered at puberty (Delaney, 42) or after marriage (Eickelman, 165). In some areas women who go about uncovered are considered common sexual property, and a girl who is not covered might be deemed promiscuous and hence forfeit the possibility of marriage (Delaney, 42). This is less true among many peasants (see Eickelman, 165, 194); Greek customs may have also been less strict in rural areas (e.g., the nymphs in Longus *Daphn. Chl.* 1.4; 2.23).

Head coverings, like long hair (1 Cor 11:14-15), might function as a symbolic gender marker. Beards functioned as a male gender marker (Phaedrus *Fables* 4.17.1-5; Aulus Gellius *Noc. Att.* 6.12.5). But a more basic purpose of the gender-based head covering was to shield married women from the gaze of men other than their husbands.

Women who purposely exposed any part of their body to gaze were thought to be intent on seduction. Greek women typically wore long robes (e.g., Homer *Il.* 18.385), and women usually kept their arms and legs concealed (Aulus Gellius *Noc. Att.* 6.12.2). Nevertheless, men lusted after whatever was sometimes uncovered: ankles (Homer *Odys.* 5.333); feet (Euripides *Bacch.* 862-64); arms (Ovid *Met.* 1.501; Chariton *Chaer.* 6.4.5; *T. Jos.* 9:5; cf. the frequent description of Greek women as "white-armed," e.g., Homer *Il.* 1.55, 195, 208; I have counted at least thirty-seven instances in Homer). Roman men might consider especially virtuous a wife who would not want other men to view even her bare arm (Plutarch *Bride* 31, *Mor.* 142CD).

But hair was the prime object of male lust (Apuleius *Met.* 2.8-9). Uncovering and loosing a woman's hair publicly revealed her beauty (Chariton *Chaer.* 1.14.1). Thus later rabbis warned that a woman uncovering her head could lead to a man's seduction (ARN 14 §35; cf. *Num. Rab.* 18:20), and the priests must beware when loosing the hair of a suspected adulteress (*Sipre Num.* 11.2.1-3; *y. Sanh.* 6:4 §1). A wife going in public with loosed hair appears in a list of promiscuous behaviors warranting *divorce without repayment of the marriage settlement (*m. Ketub.* 7:6; even more explicitly in *Num. Rab.* 9:12).

This was why married women in particular were expected to cover their hair. Women normally covered their heads after marriage, so being taken away "unveiled" *(akalyptos)* indicated the loss of their marriage (3 Macc 4:6). The Spartan custom was noteworthy but perhaps represented a more common sentiment: wives went into public veiled, but virgin daughters were unveiled because they needed to find husbands (Charillus 2 in Plutarch *Sayings of Spartans, Mor.* 232C).

4. Status and Class Differences.

Literary sources testify abundantly to women's head coverings in the eastern Mediterranean, but mosaics usually depict women with their heads uncovered. Naturally mosaics and busts, which represent upper-class women, reveal fashionable hairstyles rather than head coverings (see, e.g., photographs in Balsdon); who would pay to have a bust sculpted with her hair covered? Upper-class women, imitating fashion changes dictated by the imperial women and concerned to display their expensive and stylish hair arrangements, probably frequently went uncovered, in contrast to their lower-class counterparts (MacMullen, 217-18; also Kroeger, 37; cf. 1 Tim 2:9). In the Corinthian house churches, where many people of lower status met in more well-to-do homes, such a culture clash could have created tension as it apparently did on other issues such as *rhetoric (1 Cor 1—4), Paul's activity as an artisan (1 Cor 9) and foods offered to idols (1 Cor 8, 10). (For further discussion of Paul's specific arguments in 1 Corinthians 11:2-16, see Keener, 31-46.)

5. Conclusion.

People in the ancient Mediterranean world covered their heads for a variety of reasons. The most important for the NT passage that addresses head coverings is the sort of head coverings worn by married women, especially in the eastern Mediterranean (though not limited to Asia and Judea as a sign of sexual modesty). Women of greater means and status may have disdained the confinement of such coverings, but head coverings appear to have been popular among women of lower social status.

See also WOMEN IN GRECO-ROMAN WORLD AND JUDAISM.

BIBLIOGRAPHY. J. P. V. D. Balsdon, "Women in Imperial Rome," *History Today* 10 (1960) 24-31; C. Delaney, "Seeds of Honor, Fields of Shame," in *Honor and Shame and the Unity of the Mediterranean,* ed. D. D. Gilmore (AAA 22; Washington, DC: American Anthropological Association, 1987) 35-48; K. J. Dover, "Classical Greek Attitudes to Sexual Behavior," in *Women in the Ancient World: The Arethusa Papers,* ed. J. Peradotto and J. P. Sullivan (Albany, NY: State University of New York, 1984) 143-58; D. F. Eickelman, *The Middle East: An Anthropological Approach* (2d ed.; Englewood Cliffs, NJ: Prentice-Hall, 1989); G. D. Fee, *The First Epistle to the Corinthians* (NICNT; Grand Rapids, MI: Eerdmans, 1987); H. P. Foley, "The Conception of Women in Athenian Drama," in *Reflections of Women in Antiquity,* ed. H. P. Foley (New York: Gordon and Breach Science Publishers, 1981) 127-68; J. F. Gardner, *Women in Roman Law and Society* (Bloomington: Indiana University Press, 1986); M. J. Giovannini, "Female Chastity Codes in the Circum-Mediterranean: Comparative Perspectives," in *Honor and Shame and the Unity of the Mediterranean,* ed. D. D. Gilmore (AAA 22; Washington, DC: American Anthropological Association, 1987) 61-74; M. Goodman, *State and Society in Roman Galilee, A.D. 132-212* (Oxford Center for Postgraduate Hebrew Studies; Totowa, NJ: Rowman & Allanfield, 1983); J. Gould, "Law, Custom and Myth: Aspects of the Social Position of Women in Classical Athens," *JHS* 100 (1980) 38-59; J. P. Hallett, "The Role of Women in Roman Elegy: Counter-Cultural Feminism," in *Women in the Ancient World: The Arethusa Papers,* ed. J. Peradotto and J. P. Sullivan (Albany, NY: State University of New York, 1984) 241-62; J. B. Hurley, "Did Paul Require Veils or the Silence of Women? A Consideration of 1 Cor 11:2-16 and 1 Cor 14:33b-36," *WTJ* 35 (1973) 190-220; T. Ilan, *Jewish Women in Greco-Roman Palestine* (Peabody, MA: Hendrickson, 1996); C. S. Keener, *Paul, Women and Wives: Marriage and Women's Ministry in the Letters of Paul* (Peabody, MA: Hendrickson, 1992); C. C. Kroeger, "The Apostle Paul and the Greco-Roman Cults of Women," *JETS* 30 (1987) 25-38; R. MacMullen, "Women in Public in the Roman Empire," *Historia* 29 (1980) 209-18; J. Moffatt, *The First Epistle of Paul to the Corinthians* (MNTC; London: Hodder & Stoughton, 1938); R. E. Oster, "When Men Wore Veils to Worship: The Historical Context of 1 Corinthians 11:4," *NTS* 34 (1988) 481-505; E. Schüssler Fiorenza, *In Memory of Her: A Feminist Theological Reconstruction of Christian Origins* (New York: Crossroad, 1983); C. L. Thompson, "Hairstyles, Head Coverings and St. Paul: Portraits from Roman Corinth," *BA* 51 (1988) 101-15; D. C. Verner, *The Household of God: The Social World of the Pastoral Epistles* (SBLDS 71; Chico, CA: Scholars Press, 1983); J. R. Wegner, *Chattel or Person? The Status of Women in the Mishnah* (New York: Oxford University Press, 1988).

C. S. Keener

HEALING AND HEALING MIRACLES. *See* APOLONIUS OF TYANA; HIPPOCRATIC LETTERS; RELIGION, PERSONAL.

HEAVENLY ASCENT IN JEWISH AND PAGAN TRADITIONS

The NT contains numerous references to heavenly ascent or rapture: for example, the transfiguration (Mk 9:2-8 par.); the ascension (Lk 24:50-3; Acts 1:1-12; cf. 2:34; Jn 3:13-14; 6:62; 20:17; Phil 2:6-11; Eph 4:8-10; Rev 12:5); the rapture of the church to meet the Lord in the air (1 Thess 4:17; cf. 1 Cor 15:51-52); Paul's ascent into third heaven/paradise (2 Cor 12:2-4); Enoch's rapture (Heb 11:5; cf. Gen 5:24). The list grows longer if we include NT texts that presuppose the ascension (e.g., Mk 14:62).

It is possible in this article merely to adumbrate the enormous primary and secondary literature that may be relevant to the various NT texts (see most recently Zwiep). This situation is aggravated by the fact that heavenly ascent is a widespread motif in both Greco-Roman and Jewish sources of many different kinds. Hence the question frequently arises whether the NT references to ascent are to be characterized as Jewish, non-Jewish or a combination of both. A full discussion of the primary source materials, including ancient Near Eastern parallels (e.g., Assmann) and form-critical analysis, remains a desideratum. Additional work is also needed on cosmological assumptions on which the spatial orientation of ascent texts are based (Colpe). What accounts, for example, for the inverted orientation in the *Hekhalot* literature, where one is said to "descend to the Merkabah" (Kuyt; Stroumsa)?

1. Greco-Roman Background
2. Jewish Background

1. Greco-Roman Background.

K. Luck-Huyse's recent study on the dream of flying in antiquity includes ascent texts from the most prominent Greco-Roman sources. It will suffice here to mention only a few categories of this voluminous and diverse material.

1.1. Ascent as Apotheosis. In Greco-Roman sources, the gods are frequently portrayed as ascending into heaven. In the Rhapsodic Theogony, for example, Zeus is said to have been carried into heaven on the back of a goat (West). Euhermeros claimed that gods such as Uranos, Kronos and Zeus were humans who had subsequently been apotheosized (Diododorus Siculus *Bib. Hist.* 13.1—17.2). Deification of a mortal hero or ruler was a common idea in the *Hellenistic world. *Alexander the Great himself was thought to have been granted apotheosis. Later the idea was accepted by *Roman emperors as a posthumous ceremony, although Gaius emphasized his own divinity even before death. The deified emperor was endowed with the title *divus* (divine), and his ascent to heaven was symbolized by various signs, such as an eagle or a chariot (*see* Ruler Cult). The Arch of Titus in Rome, for instance, depicts the emperor being carried into heaven on the back of an eagle (Pfanner).

Apollonius of Tyana, a Neo-Pythagorean holy man who has often been compared to Jesus, led the life of an ascetic wandering teacher, endured persecution under Nero and Domitian, and finally ascended into heaven (Philostratus *Vit. Ap.* 8.29-30). He was the object of a posthumous cult attracting the patronage of the Severan emperors (Koskenniemi).

1.2. Ascent and Shamanism. Shamanism is a widespread phenomenon in the ancient world. The shaman can be described as "a social functionary who, with the help of guardian spirits, attains ecstasy in order to create a rapport with the supernatural world on behalf of his group members" (Hultkrantz). This ecstatic state usually involves the perception that the soul of the shaman is ascending or descending to levels outside of mundane reality. For instance, Parmenides (DK 28 B 1) used shamanistic imagery in his philosophical poem, speaking of a cosmic chariot journey of the will, through the gates of Day and Night, to consult a goddess. The seven stages of the shaman's journey to heaven are represented by seven tiers or notches in a pillar or tree, which stood for an imagined column at the center of the world (Schibli; West).

1.3. Ascent of the Soul After Death. *Cicero's *Somnium Scipionis* regards ascent to the stars as the destiny of the good soul after death (Cicero *De Rep.* 6.9-26; cf. Plato *Tim.* 41d-e).

2. Jewish Background.

In Jewish sources, it is often difficult to ascertain whether an ascent text is the product of mystical experience, exegetical speculation or both. Sometimes an explicitly visionary experience can be described in terms of a bodily ascent (*1 Enoch* 14:8). Occasionally the texts themselves register doubt about whether the ascent is in the body or out of the body (2 Cor 12:2-4; Schäfer 1981, §680). The goal of heavenly ascent varies widely in Jewish sources—anything from apotheosis (see below) to reconnaissance of the inhabited world (*T. Abr.* 9:8) to understanding the inscrutable ways of God (4 Ezra 4:8). Sometimes the individual initiates ascent; at other times God or an angel does so. In the process of ascending, a person may receive priestly vestment (Himmelfarb), or one's body may undergo transformation into a purified angelic form of fire or light (Morray-Jones 1992). Ascension seems to be an exclusively male prerogative among humans.

2.1. Ascent in the Old Testament. Several texts seem to refer to ascension in the OT (Schmitt). In Genesis 5:24, Enoch is said to have "walked with God," which may refer to an ascent prior to his final translation, when "God took him." This is how later Jewish and Christian sources interpreted the account (e.g., Philo *Quaest. in Gen.* 1.86; Wis 4:10-11; *1 Clem.* 9.3; *Tg. Neof.* to Gen 5:24; *1 Enoch* 71:16; 93:8; *2 Enoch* 68:1; Pseudo-Clementine *Recognitions* 1.52.5; *see* Enoch, Books of).

The builders of the tower of Babel wanted to build a tower whose top was in the heavens (Gen 11:4). This was frequently interpreted to mean that the builders wanted to ascend into heaven (e.g., *Jub.* 10:19; *Sib. Or.* 3:100; Josephus *Ant.* 1.4.3 §118).

According to the narrative in Exodus 24, Moses, together with Aaron, Nadab, Abihu and the seventy elders, "went up and they saw the God of Israel" (Ex 24:9-10). Moses was given "the tablets of stone, with the law and the commandment, which I have written for their instruction" (Ex 24:12). In Deuteronomy 30:12, Moses insists that the divine commandment is neither too difficult nor too far away: "It is not in heaven that you should say, 'Who will go up to heaven for us, and get it for us so that we may hear it and observe it?'" When we put these texts together, it is understandable why later Jewish tradition regarded *Moses' ascent to receive the law on Mt. Sinai as an ascent into heaven and an encounter with the Merkabah throne-chariot of God (cf. Ps 68:19 and the tradition based on it; Halperin).

Standing in the line of the greatest prophet Moses, the other Hebrew prophets are frequently said to have had visions of the divine throne, although their ascent into heaven is never described. These visions have a twofold purpose: to establish the authority and legitimacy of the prophet as an intermediary between heaven and earth and to provide revealed information.

Psalm 110:1 can be interpreted to mean that the Davidic king is exalted and enthroned in heaven next to God himself: "The LORD says to my lord, 'Sit at my right hand until I make your enemies your footstool.'" This passage, together with Isaiah 6, Ezekiel 1 and Daniel 7, later gave rise to further mystical speculation about the divine Merkabah, including accounts of individuals who ascended to heaven (e.g., *1 Enoch* 14; *Apoc. Abr.* 17; *Jos. and As.* 17:7-8; *T. Abr.* 11; Rev 4; *2 Enoch* 22; see further 4Q530 2:16-19). Elijah's ascension into heaven and his expected return at the end of time also played a significant role in Jewish tradition (cf. 2 Kings 2:1-18; Mal 3:22-3; *1 Enoch* 89:52; Sir 48:9-12; 1 Macc 2:58).

2.2. Ascent of the Soul After Death. W. Bousset suggested that the ascent of the visionary is an anticipation of the ascent of the soul after death, an idea that is found in many apocalypses of the Christian era (Himmelfarb 1991). The language of 1QH 3:19-20 is suggestive in this regard: "I thank you, Lord, for you have redeemed my life from the pit and from Sheol of the dead; you have raised me up to an eternal height." Possible parallels to the aforementioned Ciceronian passage can be found in Daniel 12:3 and Matthew 13:43. In the first-century Similitudes of Enoch (*1 Enoch* 71:16) and in the second-century, Jewish-Christian source in Pseudo-Clementine *Recognitions* 1.27-71 (1.52.5), Enoch is a model for all those who have pleased God and are similarly translated into heaven and are being preserved for the kingdom of God (see also Philo *Quaest. in Gen.* 1.86).

2.3. Ascent as Apotheosis. The ascension and deification of a mortal is found in the early Jewish literature of both Palestine and the Diaspora (Collins 1995). The Egyptian Diaspora features the apotheosis of Moses in several writings. For example, the *Exagoge* of Ezekiel the Tragedian, written in the second century B.C., describes Moses' ascent to Mt. Sinai and his enthronement in heaven. The figure on the throne on high abdicates his throne and beckons Moses to sit on it (*Exag.* 68-76), thereby conferring upon Moses universal sovereignty (*Exag.* 77-78, 85-89). Philo of Alexandria also describes the apotheosis of Moses (Philo *Vit. Mos.* 1.158; cf. Borgen).

The apotheosis of Moses was evidently known also in Palestine. In a text from *Qumran (4Q491 Frag. 11 i 11-18; cf. Smith; Hengel), the author (not an angel) claims to have ascended into heaven, to have received the "mighty throne in the congregation of the gods" and to have been "reckoned with the gods." J. J. Collins suggests that this text was written by someone who held the office of teacher or interpreter of the law and who understood himself either as a new Moses or a complement of Moses. Like Moses, this teacher in the late first century B.C. saw himself enthroned in the heavens and issuing teachings and rulings of irresistible power. Related materials have been observed in 4Q427, 4Q458 and 4Q471 (cf. Abegg; Schuller).

According to Theophilus of Antioch (*Autol.* 2.24), a second-century, Jewish-Christian apologist who makes extensive use of Jewish traditions, apotheosis was God's original intention for humans. When God created man, he "transferred him out of the earth from which he was made into paradise, giving him an opportunity for progress so that by growing and becoming mature, and furthermore having been declared a god, he might also ascend into heaven (for man was created in an intermediate state, neither entirely mortal nor entirely immortal, but capable of either state), possessing immortality." Perhaps Theophilus viewed Jesus as a second Adam who follows a similar course of exaltation to that of the first (cf. Grant).

From another perspective, however, apotheosis can be seen as a presumptuous invasion of heaven. In Isaiah 14:12-20, the prideful king of Babylon, who wants to ascend to heaven and become like God, is cast down to the underworld (Is 14:11). D. J. Halperin discusses the rabbinic tradition based on this passage (e.g., *b. Ḥag.* 13a). P. Borgen finds the tradition of ascension as invasion of heaven already in Philo of Alexandria.

2.4. Ascent as Legitimation of a Revelatory Mediator. Ascent provides a vehicle for divine revelation and a means by which to legitimate the revelatory mediator. In the Book of Watchers (*1 Enoch* 1—36), for example, the heavenly ascent of Enoch to the divine throne (*1 Enoch* 14) has a revelatory aspect similar to the call visions of the Hebrew prophets. For *1 Enoch* the ascent establishes Enoch's legitimacy and authority as mediator between heaven and earth, as well as providing revealed information. 4QLevi^{b} ar (4Q213a) 2:13-18 describes a vision that Levi received after praying. This vision is not found in the Greek *Testament of Levi* (*see* Testaments of the Twelve Patriarchs). Instead, we find a more extensive ascent account in a dream vision (*T. Levi* 2:5—5:7), which is evidently designed to confirm the priesthood of Levi and to communicate divine revelation. Philo of Alexandria provides an autobiographical account of his own heavenly journey in *De Specialibus Legibus* 3.1-2 (Borgen). This ascent equips Philo not only to read the laws of Moses but also "to peer into each of them and unfold and reveal what is not known to the multitude" (Philo *Spec. Leg.* 3.6). The well-known story of the Four Who Entered Paradise, which is found both in the Talmud and in *Hek-*

halot literature (cf. Morray-Jones), tells how only Rabbi Aqiba was deemed worthy of beholding God's glory behind the curtain. J. R. Davila (1996) has recently suggested that this story is reflected in a Qumran text (1QH[a] 16:4-26).

2.5. Ascent as a Periodization of History. In the *apocalyptic section of the *Apocalypse of Abraham* (9—32), which is a *midrash on Abraham's vision in Genesis 15, the length of time that the elect are expected to suffer under foreign domination is expressed in terms of a cryptic chronology of four "ascents" (*Apoc. Abr.* 28:2-5; cf. 27:3). We may compare the rabbinic interpretation of Jacob's dream in Genesis 28:12 (*Lev. Rab.* 29:2; *Pesiq. Rab Kah.* 23), according to which the angels of God ascending and descending on the ladder to heaven are the guardian angels of the nations of the world who preside over the rise and fall of their respective empires. The number of rungs ascended represents the number of years that each of these empires reigned before their decline. Thus, Jacob saw Babylon ascend 70 rungs; Media, 52 rungs; Greece, 180 rungs; and Edom (Rome), an unknown number of rungs (cf. Kugel; Gafni).

2.6. Communal Aspects of Ascent. J. R. Davila (1994) argues that the later *Hekhalot* literature, which developed in part from traditions found in Second Temple apocalyptic literature, functioned in the context of a community: the shaman intermediary ascended or descended to the Merkabah, in order to create rapport with the supernatural world on behalf of his group. Other evidence suggests perhaps a more direct participation of the community in heavenly ascent or at least contemplation of the Merkabah. Halperin emphasizes that Merkabah speculation was well established in synagogue worship. According to H. Schreckenberg and K. Schubert, the zodiac signs in the synagogues of Hammath Tiberias and Beth Alpha are symbols, as in *Hekhalot* texts, for the ascension of the worshiper through the seven heavenly "palaces" *(hekhalot)* to the throne of God. The **Songs of the Sabbath Sacrifice* from Qumran Caves 4 and 11 have demonstrated that participation in the heavenly liturgy was the goal of worshipers already in the Second Temple period (Newsom).

See also MYSTICISM.

BIBLIOGRAPHY. M. G. Abegg Jr., "Who Ascended to Heaven? 4Q491, 4Q427 and the Teacher of Righteousness," in *Eschatology, Messianism and the Dead Sea Scrolls,* ed. C. A. Evans and P. W. Flint (Grand Rapids, MI: Eerdmans, 1997) 61-73; J. Assmann, "Himmelsaufstieg," *Lexikon der Ägyptologie* 2 (1977) 1205-11; P. Borgen, "Heavenly Ascent in Philo: An Examination of Selected Passages," in *The Pseudepigrapha and Early Biblical Interpretation,* ed. J. H. Charlesworth and C. A. Evans (JSPSup 14; Sheffield: JSOT, 1993) 246-68; A. B. Bosworth, "Alexander, Euripides and Dionysius: The Motivation for Apotheosis," in *Transitions to Empire: Essays in Greco-Roman History, 360-146 B.C., in Honor of E. Badian,* ed. R. W. Wallace and E. M. Harris (Oklahoma Series in Classical Culture 21; Norman: University of Oklahoma Press, 1996) 140-66; W. Bousset, "Die Himmelsreise der Seele," *Archiv für Religionswissenschaft* 4 (1901) 136-69; J. J. Collins, "A Throne in the Heavens," in *The Scepter and the Star: The Messiahs of the Dead Sea Scrolls and Other Ancient Literature* (ABRL; New York: Doubleday, 1995) 138-53; idem, "A Throne in the Heavens: Apotheosis in Pre-Christian Judaism," in *Death, Ecstasy and Other Worldly Journeys,* ed. J. J. Collins and M. Fishbane (Albany, NY: State University of New York Press, 1995) 43-58; C. Colpe, "Himmelfahrt," *RAC* (1991) 212-19; M. J. Edwards, "Flight of the Mind," *OCD* (3d ed., 1996) 601; J. R. Davila, "The Hekhalot Literature and Shamanism," *SBLSP* 33 1994) 767-89; idem, "The Hodayot Hymnist and the Four Who Entered Paradise," *RevQ* 17 (1996) 457-77; C. A. Evans, "Ascending and Descending with a Shout: Psalm 47:6 and 1 Thessalonians 4:16," in *Paul and the Scriptures of Israel,* ed. C. A. Evans and J. A. Sanders (JSNTSup 83; Sheffield: JSOT, 1993) 238-53; idem, "Jesus and the Messianic Texts from Qumran: A Preliminary Assessment of the Recently Published Materials," in *Jesus and His Contemporaries: Comparative Studies* (AGJU 25; Leiden: E. J. Brill, 1995) 83-154; I. Gafni, "Concepts of Periodization and Causality in Talmudic Literature," *Jewish History* 10 (1996) 21-38; A. Goshen-Gottstein, "Four Entered Paradise Revisited," *HTR* 88 (1995) 69-133; R. M. Grant, ed. and trans., *Theophilus of Antioch* (Ad Autolycum; Oxford: Clarendon Press, 1970); N. R. Gulley, "Ascension of Christ," *ABD* 1:472-74; D. J. Halperin, *The Faces of the Chariot: Early Jewish Responses to Ezekiel's Vision* (TSAJ 16; Tübingen: Mohr Siebeck, 1988); W. H. Harris III, *The Descent of Christ: Ephesians 4:7-11 and Traditional Hebrew Imagery* (AGJU 32; Leiden: E. J. Brill, 1996); M. Hengel, " 'Sit at My Right Hand!' The Enthronement of Christ at the Right Hand of God and Psalm 110:1," in *Studies in Early Christology* (Edinburgh: T & T Clark, 1995) 119-225; M. Himmelfarb, *Ascent to Heaven in Jewish and Christian Apocalypses* (New York and Oxford: Oxford University Press, 1993); idem, "The Practice of Ascent in the Ancient Mediterranean World," in *Death, Ecstasy and Other Worldly Journeys,* ed. J. J. Collins and M. Fishbane (Albany, NY: State University of New York Press, 1995) 123-37; idem, "Revelation and Rapture: The Transformation of the Visionary in the Ascent Apocalypses," in *Mysteries and Revelations: Apocalyptic Studies After the Uppsala Colloquium,* ed. J. J. Collins and J. H. Charlesworth (Sheffield: JSOT, 1991) 89-102; A. Hultkrantz, "A Definition of Shamanism," *Temenos* 9 (1973) 25-37; H.-J. Klauck, "Die Himmelfahrt des Paulus (2 Kor 12:2-4) in der koptischen Paulusapokalypse aus Nag Hammadi (NHC V/2)," *SNTU* 10 (1985) 151-90; E. Koskenniemi, *Apollonios von Tyana in der neutestamentlichen Exegese* (WUNT 2.61; Tübingen: Mohr Siebeck, 1994); J. Kugel, "The Ladder of Jacob," *HTR* 88 (1995) 209-27; A. Kuyt, *The "Descent" to the Chariot: Towards a Description of the Terminology, Place, Function and Nature of the Yeridah in Hekhalot Literature* (TSAJ 45; Tübingen: Mohr Siebeck, 1995); K. Luck-Huyse, *Der Traum vom Fliegen in der Antike* (Palingenesia 62; Stuttgart: Franz Steiner, 1997); R. Mondi, "The Ascension of Zeus and the Composition of Hesiod's Theogony," *GRBS* 25 (1984) 325-44; C. R. A. Morray-Jones, "The 'Descent to the Chariot' in Early Jewish Mysticism and Apocalyptic," in *Mapping Invisible Worlds,* ed. G. D. Flood (Cosmos 9; Edinburgh: Edinburgh University Press, 1993) 7-21; idem, "Paradise Revisited (2 Cor 12:1-12): The Jewish Mystical Background of Paul's Apostolate, Part 1: The Jewish Sources," *HTR* 86 (1993) 177-217; idem, "Paradise Revisited (2 Cor 12:1-12): The Jewish Mystical Background of Paul's Apostolate, Part 2: Paul's Heavenly Ascent and Its Significance," *HTR* 86 (1993) 265-92; idem, "Transformational Mysticism in the Apocalyptic-Merkabah Tradition," *JJS* 43 (1992) 1-31; C. Newsom, *Songs of the Sabbath Sacrifice: A Critical Edition* (HSS 27; Atlanta: Scholars Press, 1985); G. C. Nicholson, *Death as Departure: The Johannine Descent-Ascent Schema* (SBLDS 63; Chico, CA: Scholars Press, 1983); M. Pfanner, *Der Titusbogen* (Beiträge zur Ersch-ließung hellenistischer und kaiserlicher Skulptur und Architektur 2; Mainz am Rhein: Philipp von Zabern, 1983); C. Rose, *Die Wolke der Zeugen: Eine exegetisch-traditionsgeschichtliche Untersuchung zu Hebräer 10:32—12:3* (WUNT 2.60; Tübingen: Mohr Siebeck, 1994) 178-91; C. Rowland, "Apocalyptic, Mysticism and the New Testament," in *Geschichte—Tradition—Reflexion: Festschrift für Martin Hengel zum 70, Geburtstag, Bd. I: Judentum,* ed. P. Schäfer (Tübingen: Mohr Siebeck, 1996) 405-30; P. Schäfer, "New Testament and Hekhalot Literature: The Journey into Heaven in Paul and in Merkabah Mysticism," *JJS* 35 (1984) 19-35; idem, *Synopse zur Hekhalot-Literatur* (TSAJ 2; Tübingen: Mohr Siebeck, 1981); H. S. Schibli, *Pherekydes of Syros* (Oxford: Clarendon Press, 1990); A. Schmitt, *Entrückung—Aufnahme—Himmelfahrt: Untersuchungen zu einem Vorstellungsbereich im Alten Testament* (2d ed.; FzB 10; Stuttgart: KBW, 1976); H. Schreckenberg and K. Schubert, *Jewish Historiography and Iconography in Early Medieval Christianity* (CRINT 3.2; Assen: Van Gorcum; Minneapolis: Fortress, 1992) 167-68; E. Schuller, "A Hymn from a Cave Four Hodayot Manuscript: 4Q427 7 i + ii," *JBL* 112 (1993) 605-28; J. M. Scott, "Throne-Chariot Mysticism in Qumran and in Paul," in *Eschatology, Messianism and the Dead Sea Scrolls,* ed. C. A. Evans and P. W. Flint (Grand Rapids, MI: Eerdmans, 1997) 101-19; idem, "The Triumph of God in 2 Cor 2:14: Additional Evidence of Merkabah Mysticism in Paul," *NTS* 42 (1996) 260-81; A. F. Segal, "Heavenly Ascent in Hellenistic Judaism, Early Christianity and the Environment," *ANRW* 2.23.2 (1980) 1333-94; idem, "Paul and the Beginning of Jewish Mysticism," in *Death, Ecstasy and Other Worldly Journeys,* ed. J. J. Collins and M. Fishbane (Albany, NY: State University of New York Press, 1995) 95-122; T. Silverstein and A. Hilhorst, *Apocalypse of Paul: A New Critical Edition of Three Long Latin Versions* (Cahiers d'Orientalisme 21; Geneva: Cramer, 1997); M. Smith, "Ascent to the Heavens and Deification in 4QM^a," in *Archaeology and History in the Dead Sea Scrolls: The New York University Conference in Memory of Yigael Yadin,* ed. L. H. Schiffman (JSPSup 2; Sheffield: JSOT, 1990) 181-88; idem, "Two Ascended to Heaven—Jesus and the Author of 4Q491," in *Jesus and the Dead Sea Scrolls,* ed. J. H. Charlesworth (ABRL; New York: Doubleday, 1992) 290-301; G. G. Stroumsa, "Mystical Descents," in *Death, Ecstasy and Other Worldly Journeys,* ed. J. J Collins and M. Fishbane (Albany, NY: State University of New York Press, 1995) 139-54; J. D. Tabor, "Heaven, Ascent to," *ABD* 3:91-94; idem, *Things Unutterable: Paul's Ascent to Paradise in Its*

Greco-Roman, Judaic and Early Christian Contexts (Studies in Judaism; Lanham, MD: University Press of America, 1986); J. D. Turner, "The Gnostic Threefold Path to Enlightenment: The Ascent of Mind and the Descent of Wisdom," *NovT* 22 (1980) 324-51; M. L. West, *The Orphic Poems* (Oxford: Clarendon Press, 1983); E. R. Wolfson, "Visionary Ascent and Enthronement in Hekhalot Literature," in *Through a Speculum That Shines: Vision and Imagination in Medieval Jewish Mysticism* (Princeton, NJ: Princeton University Press, 1994) 74-124; A. W. Zwiep, *The Ascension of the Messiah in Lukan Christology* (NovTSup 87; Leiden: E. J. Brill, 1997).

J. M. Scott

HEBRAISMS. *See* SEMITIC INFLUENCE ON THE NEW TESTAMENT.

HEBREW BIBLE

The Hebrew Bible, or OT, is the principal resource—together with the effect of experience of Jesus—used by those first-century Jews who followed him as they attempted to understand, categorize and articulate the character and significance of Jesus the Christ. It is the primary source for the religious foundations, vocabulary, concepts, motifs, roles, stories and theology of the NT. After considering the problem of terminology, this article will discuss the character of the text of the Scriptures and the extent of the collection of the Scriptures that were available for use by the NT authors, followed by an impressionistic sketch of the ways the Hebrew Bible was used as a resource in composing the books of the NT.

1. The Problem of Terminology
2. The Text of the Hebrew Bible in the New Testament Era
3. The Canon of the Hebrew Bible in the New Testament Era
4. The Hebrew Bible as a Source for the Composition of the New Testament
5. Summary

1. The Problem of Terminology.

No term for the Hebrew Bible (HB) is entirely satisfactory from all points of view for denoting this corpus of sacred literature. The exact contents of that Bible were not yet established and agreed upon at the time of the origins of Christianity, and so *Scriptures* as a not necessarily fully delimited collection might be a preferable term. The Christians increasingly used the Greek translation of the HB, called the *Septuagint (LXX), and so neither Hebrew nor Bible seems satisfactory. *Tanakh* is the word used in *Judaism for the delimited collection of *Torah* (Pentateuch), *Nevi'im* (Prophets) and *Ketubim* (Writings) as transmitted in the Masoretic Text (MT); but that collection eventually established by the *rabbis was not yet fully delimited and accepted generally by Jews at the time of Jesus.

"Old Testament," in contrast, can be understood to imply that a New Testament is a logical complement to the Old or is even the necessary, inevitable fulfillment of the OT. Though this may be acceptable from the standpoint of Christian faith, it is at odds historically, literarily and religiously with the fact that other groups within Judaism found other complements or logical developments of the Hebrew Scriptures. Foremost among these is rabbinic Judaism, which finds in the *Mishnah and *Talmud the fuller exposition of Tanakh. "Old," paired with "New," also can imply that the "old" has been superseded by the "new" and is no longer necessary or valid; it should not be necessary to point out how dangerous are the consequences of such supersessionist thought or how odious is the anti-Jewish reading of the NT. "First Testament" versus "Second Testament" has also been offered as a solution, but that suggestion has not been accepted widely.

Despite the fact that "Hebrew Bible" is not a fully satisfactory term, it will generally be used here—since no other term is clearly more satisfactory—to denote the somewhat varying collection of books of Scripture, most of which were originally composed in Hebrew (though some with Aramaic portions and a few composed in Greek), whether used in their *Hebrew, *Greek or *Aramaic forms. But occasionally other terms will be used when appropriate for different perspectives. The emphasis throughout will focus on the situation during the period of Jesus and the composition of the NT, that is, the first century A.D.

2. The Text of the Hebrew Bible in the New Testament Era.

What was the character of the text of the Scriptures used by the NT authors? The textual form of the individual books was not always identical to that encountered in Bibles used today. The NT itself adequately demonstrates this, but it is necessary to start from the correct perspective.

*2.1. **Earlier Views.*** Already in the opening chapters of Matthew, it is claimed that a prophetic statement was being fulfilled since Jesus "will be called a Nazorean" (Mt 2:23). This is the last of a set of five prophetic quotations cited to illustrate scenes narrating Jesus' birth, and the first four are readily found in the traditional HB; thus the fifth should also presumably have derived somehow from the HB. There are other quotations in the NT also not to be found in the traditional OT, among them John 7:38; 2 Corinthians 4:6; Ephesians 5:14. Various tortured explanations have been given. The form of the HB found in the MT is often considered to be the sole form of it, and if that is the starting assumption, then the NT will be interpreted as quoting it inaccurately. The *Dead Sea Scrolls, however, demonstrate that the incorrect element is the starting assumption. Rather, the biblical text was pluriform then, the MT preserves only one form of the ancient texts, and the NT generally presents quotations in the textual form that was being used by the author at that time. The most likely explanation of Matthew 2:23 is that the author was using and correctly quoting from a textual form of the prophetic books that did not survive the second century.

*2.2. **The Dead Sea Scrolls.*** A significant breakthrough in the second half of the twentieth century was the realization that the text of the HB had been pluriform in nature and that there had been two phases in the history of the text. The *Qumran scrolls provided the overwhelming evidence for this breakthrough, though clues had been available before that. It is important to note that, though the biblical scrolls were found at Qumran, most were probably copied at Jerusalem or other places in the land and brought to Qumran. They are not "sectarian" or "aberrant" or "vulgar" texts but represent the Scriptures of general Judaism as they existed at the close of the Second Temple period. They are our oldest, best, most authentic witnesses to the texts of the Scriptures in this crucial period. They demonstrate that there had been, prior to the phase of textual uniformity that scholarship has been accustomed to see in the MT, an earlier phase when the books of Scripture were still in their compositional development and thus were pluriform.

Scrolls from the entire spectrum of the Bible show that many of the books were available in variant literary editions at the time—an edition of a book that had been intentionally expanded or developed beyond another earlier but still extant edition of that book. Just as a science textbook might undergo a second edition, and one person might use the earlier edition while another uses the revised and expanded edition, so too was the case for the biblical text. The biblical text was normally transmitted faithfully and accurately, but occasionally a religious leader would creatively re-edit a book in light of changed historical or theological circumstances. Examples would be the postdestruction Priestly edition of the preexilic pentateuchal traditions, and the Matthean re-edition of the Markan traditions. The Qumran scrolls offer many examples of variant literary editions of individual biblical books.

2.2.1. The Pentateuch. For the Torah, one extensively preserved scroll of Exodus (4Qpaleo-Exod^{m}) agrees in the main with the traditional MT form of Exodus, enough to make clear that it is a manuscript of the biblical book. At a number of points, however, it is amplified with verses that prove to be harmonizations, that is, supplementary passages drawn from elsewhere in Exodus or from related passages in Deuteronomy. On closer inspection, it is clear that all of these expansions were long since attested in the Samaritan form of Exodus (*see* Samaritan Literature). The two specifically Samaritan theological variants, however, were not present, and so the scroll represents a variant literary edition of the book of Exodus circulating in Judaism at the turn of the era; though it did not otherwise survive, it was the Jewish form of Exodus adopted by the Samaritans and minimally altered for their version of the Pentateuch. Eventually, an analogous manuscript of Numbers (4QNum^{b}) also emerged, in close agreement with the MT but much closer to the Samaritan Pentateuch except for the specifically Samaritan theological changes. These scrolls are sometimes labeled pre-Samaritan, but more accurate phraseology would be variant literary editions of the Jewish scriptural text also utilized by the Samaritans as the basis of their form of the Torah.

2.2.2. The Prophets. Similar manuscripts were found both for the Former and the Latter Prophets. A scroll of Joshua (4QJosh^{a}) shows an earlier literary version with a significant difference in the sequence of the narrative. This scroll places the site where Joshua built the first altar in the newly entered promised land at Gilgal, immediately after crossing the Jordan (before Josh 5:1). Later theological claims apparently relocated it first at Shechem on Mt. Gerizim (cf. Deut 27:4 Sam.; VL) and then through a Judean counterclaim on Mt. Ebal (Josh 8:30-35 MT; after 9:2 LXX). Parallel to the NT authors using an alternate literary edition of a book, the first-century historian *Josephus must have used a biblical text like 4QJosh[a], for he also places the altar at Gilgal (Josephus *Ant.* 5.1.4 §20), exactly in the same place and in the same sequence as 4QJosh[a].

A fragment of Judges (4QJudg[a]) shows that the MT has secondarily expanded the text of Judges 6 with a Deuteronomistic-sounding passage: Judges 6:7-10 (long suspected as a theological insertion) does not appear in this fragment, which moves smoothly from Judges 6:6 to 6:11.

An extensively preserved manuscript of Samuel (4QSam[a]), again strongly confirmed by Josephus, shows repeatedly that it was a more influential text of that book than was the form transmitted in the MT. It attests the form of Samuel used by the Chronicler in composing 1—2 Chronicles, the form translated by the original LXX and the form used by Josephus when composing his *Jewish Antiquities*.

A scroll of Isaiah (1QIsa[a]), the only scroll that preserves a biblical book in its entirety, displays more than a thousand variants from the MT form of Isaiah. Most are minor, with the preferable reading sometimes in the scroll, sometimes in the MT, sometimes in the LXX. But there are at least ten major variants where the MT adds a verse or even more beyond 1QIsa[a] or the LXX (*see* Isaiah Scroll).

It has long been known that the LXX of Jeremiah transmits a text approximately one-eighth shorter than that of the MT. It is now clear that the edition in the LXX is earlier and that the MT preserves a subsequent edition that has been consistently expanded. A Hebrew fragment of Jeremiah (4QJer[b]) now attests that the LXX was translated faithfully from an earlier Hebrew variant literary edition of the book.

The book of Daniel also shows two literary editions. This time the shorter edition is transmitted in the MT, and the longer edition with "the Additions" is in the LXX (*see* Daniel, Esther and Jeremiah, Additions to). To date, none of the eight Qumran manuscripts of Daniel point toward the longer LXX edition, but it may nevertheless be safely presumed that the Old Greek translation of Daniel (as opposed to the dominant Theodotionic Greek recension) was faithfully translated from a Hebrew-Aramaic text circulating in its day, including the disputed chapters, Daniel 4—6.

2.2.3. The Writings or Poetic and Wisdom Books. It has long been known that the MT forms versus the LXX translations of Job and Proverbs differed in major ways, which we can now attribute to variant Hebrew editions. But the great *Psalms Scroll* (11QPs[a]) best illustrates both the differences in textual forms for this section of the Bible and the gains recently made in understanding the history of the biblical text.

This well-preserved scroll has been the subject of debate since before its publication in 1965. It contains most of the psalms from the last third of the Psalter, but the order is repeatedly quite different from the traditional MT-LXX order. Furthermore, it contains ten compositions not found in MT Psalter, one of which is a prose summary totaling the 4,050 psalms and songs David wrote (*see* Psalms and Hymns of Qumran). Its editor published it as a Psalms scroll, though several major scholars denied its biblical status, considering it a postbiblical liturgical composition or library edition. But each of the reasons marshaled against its biblical status has fallen in the face of mounting evidence from other biblical manuscripts, including the MT.

2.3. Earlier Clues for the Compositional Phase. Clues for the earlier compositional phase of the biblical text had long lay in our sources. The Samaritan Pentateuch, had it been taken more seriously as attesting an ancient Jewish form of the biblical text, and the LXX, had it been studied objectively and not in the context of Jewish-Christian or Protestant-Catholic polemics, offered plenty of evidence for the history of the biblical text, as can be seen above. Similarly, Josephus's *Jewish Antiquities* are a more reliable witness to the form of the biblical text in the first century than is usually thought. Some of the details in his narrative that agree, for example, with 4QSam[a] are judged as unscriptural details because they disagree with the MT, but they were derived from a biblical text circulating in Judaism at the time of the composition of the NT.

2.4. The Compositional Process of the Hebrew

Bible. Thus the new knowledge provided by the Qumran manuscripts attesting the pluriformity of the biblical text and the multiple literary editions for many of the biblical books dovetails perfectly with all our other textual data from the first century and earlier. It also dovetails with the results of the past two centuries of scholarship concerning the dynamic composition of the HB, which shows that the final forms of the biblical texts are the result of a long and complex developmental process of successive literary editions (see 2.2 above). The Qumran manuscripts, together with the Samaritan Pentateuch, the LXX and other sources such as Josephus, all witness to the final stages of that compositional phase of the HB. Sometime after the First Jewish Revolt (A.D. 66-74), and perhaps as late as the Second Revolt (A.D. 132-135; *see* Jewish Wars with Rome), creativity on the Hebrew texts ceased. Only the rabbinic form of Judaism survived under that name, and the rabbis eventually preserved only a single Hebrew form of each book that then became standardized and emerged as the MT collection. But the texts of the Scriptures, as circulating in Judaism at the time of Jesus and as available for NT authors, were pluriform.

3. The Canon of the Hebrew Bible in the New Testament Era.

What was the extent of the collection of books considered as Scripture by the NT authors? Just as the textual form of the individual books was not identical with the received MT, so too the collection of books viewed as Scripture was not entirely coterminous with later Jewish, Protestant or Catholic canons.

3.1. Terminology. The canon is a postbiblical reality, and thus the term is anachronistic in the NT period. Clear evidence of the canon dates from the fourth century, though its existence may predate that somewhat. The term *canon* is a technical term in theology with a long history, but it is sometimes used in a confused manner, vitiating its meaning and purpose. Three points are important.

First, the canon is a result of a reflexive judgment, a postfact confirmatory decision. Certain sacred books had been functioning as authoritative sources governing the community's life; but it was not until questions had been raised, matters considered and debated and official decisions made and generally accepted that selected works and not others were judged henceforth essential to the identity of the community. There were acknowledged authoritative books at an early stage, and there was a long process that led toward canon, but properly canonical decisions probably happened only in the second century for Judaism and in the fourth for Christianity (*see* Canonical Formation of the New Testament).

Secondly, "canon" denotes a final, closed list. It is the result of an explicit decision, involving not only the inclusion of essential books that are in the official collection, but also importantly the exclusion of books that are out (Barr; Metzger; Ulrich; Barton). Thus there can be no open canon, although again there was from an early period a developing collection of authoritative books moving toward what would become the canon.

Thirdly, both in Judaism (until at least the end of the first century) and in Christianity the book, not the textual form of a book, was authoritative and became canonical (*m. Yad.* 3:5; 4:6). Thus, for example, the book of Jeremiah was authoritative, whether in its 4QJer[b]-LXX form or its MT form, as was the book of Psalms, whether in its MT, LXX or 11QPs[a] form.

3.2. The Sacred, Authoritative Books of Judaism. Thus, at the time of Jesus and the composition of the NT, a number of books considered uniquely authoritative and essential were circulating among the diverse groups within Judaism. The most common term was the Law and Prophets. By at least the second century B.C. (see the Prologue to *Sirach) the Law and Prophets were certainly considered especially sacred and authoritative (see also 1QS 1:1-3; Josephus *Ag. Ap.* 1.7-8 §§37-43; and Lk 16:16; Acts 26:22 for Qumranic, *Pharisaic and Christian Judaism), except by the Samaritans and possibly the *Sadducees, who held only the Law in this supreme category. The five books of Moses were undoubtedly included in the Law. But the boundaries of the prophetic collection were still flexible: the major prophetic books were included, but the evidence for certain books invites attention.

3.2.1. The Psalter and Daniel. The Qumran *Psalms Scroll* claims the status of a prophetic book for the Psalter: "all these [David] spoke through prophecy given to him from the Most High" (11QPs[a] 27:11). This is an explicit affirmation of a view that was eventually accepted generally: the Psalter, originally a collection of human hymns addressed to God, became Scripture, God's word addressed to humans through David. Luke 24:44 mentions "the Law of Moses and the Prophets and Psalms." This is sometimes interpreted as hinting at a tripartite canon already. But it is suspicious that such appears nowhere else in the NT. In fact, Luke-Acts usually has "the Law/Moses and the Prophets" (Lk 16:16, 29, 31; 24:27; Acts 26:22; 28:23), and the Psalms are being used in Luke 24:44 manifestly as a prophetic witness to Jesus. Prophetic use of the Psalter is common throughout the NT, especially in the letter to the Hebrews, and also at Qumran, where three *pesharim ("commentaries") on the Psalms occur. Such continuous pesharim were apparently written only on prophetic books.

Daniel seems to have been universally reckoned among the prophets (cf. the **Florilegium* [4Q174 2:3]; Mt 24:15; Josephus *Ant.* 10.11.4, 7 §§249, 266-67). It retained its prophetic status in Christianity (Melito, in Eusebius *Hist. Eccl.* 4.26.14), while the Talmud is the first Jewish source to classify it among the Writings, possibly to deemphasize the prophetic interpretation and emphasize the wisdom aspects of the book.

3.2.2. Books Quoted in the New Testament. Quotations in the NT, just as in the Dead Sea Scrolls, are frequent from the books of the Law and the Prophets (including Psalms and Daniel) but sparse or nonexistent from most of the Writings.

3.2.3. Books Beyond the Law and the Prophets. The Prologue to Sirach three times mentions the books of Scripture in a way that is often interpreted as the traditional tripartite canon (e.g., Beckwith). There are good reasons, however, to reexamine that interpretation. "The Law and the Prophets and the other books of our ancestors" may perhaps better be seen as the Scriptures ("The Law and the Prophets") plus other traditional religious writings that were not, or not yet, in that category. Among the reasons to support this view are the lack of literary attestation that a tripartite canon existed and the lack of use of the Writings in the literary evidence available. No other source in the next two centuries seems to know of a three-part canon; there appears no knowledge or discussion of such prior to the fall of the temple in A.D. 70. Moreover, the Writings (excluding Psalms and Daniel) are not significantly influential in either Jewish or Christian writings.

3.2.4. 1 Enoch, Jubilees, Tobit and Sirach. Other books such as **1 Enoch*, **Jubilees*, *Tobit and *Sirach appear to have been considered by some groups as Scripture. The epistle of Jude 14-15 cites *1 Enoch* 1:9 as Scripture, explicitly saying Enoch "prophesied" (*see* Apocryphal and Pseudepigraphal Sources in the New Testament). Moreover, about twenty copies of the book were collected from Qumran, ranking with the books of the Torah in number found there, and it retained its status as Scripture in the Ethiopian church.

The book of *Jubilees* makes the arresting claim that it is divine revelation from God through an "angel of the presence" to Moses, rehearsing the biblical story from Genesis 1 to Exodus 24. At least fifteen copies were found at Qumran, and the **Damascus Document* cites its lengthy title, *The Book of the Divisions of the Times into Their Jubilees and Weeks* (CD 16:2-3), and gives a quotation from it as an authoritative book (CD 10:8-10).

A number of other works that have retained their status as Scripture in various communities were also found among the fragments in the Judean desert, including the Greek Epistle of Jeremiah, one Hebrew and four Aramaic manuscripts of Tobit and two manuscripts of the Hebrew of Sirach (plus another in the Cairo Genizah as well as the incorporation of the Hebrew poem from Sirach 51 in $11QPs^{a}$).

3.2.5. The Witness of 4 Ezra and Josephus. The passage in 4 Ezra 14:45-48 (*see* Esdras Books of), written toward the end of the first century, speaks of twenty-four books that are to be made available to the public, but interestingly of an additional seventy books presumably of a higher order to be reserved for "the wise." Josephus, writing about the same time, gives "twenty-two" as the number of books of Scripture: five books of Moses, thirteen books of prophetic histories, and four books of hymns and precepts (*Ag. Ap.* 1.7-8 §§37-43). It is important to note that neither his total of twenty-two nor his division between the prophetic and wisdom books match well with those of the traditional MT or LXX.

3.3. The Collection of the Scriptures. Thus the evidence suggests that during the period of the composition of the NT, the decisions concerning the collection of the books of Scripture into the canon as we know it had not yet taken place. There were uniquely authoritative scriptural books, but precisely which books were to be included in that category and which were to be excluded from that essential list had not yet been decided. There is little evidence that such questions were yet being seriously debated, or needed to be. The Law was securely in the canon-to-be. There was also a collection of prophetic books acknowledged widely as divine revelation, but the exact contents of that collection were not yet delimited. And there was an abundant and widely varied assortment of religious writings to which different groups attributed different degrees of importance. It is likely that the disciples and early Christian writers would have found themselves amid these differing groups.

Materially, individual scriptural and other works in the first century would have been copied on discrete scrolls, not collected into a codex (a stack of pages bound together in book form). The Scriptures would have comprised a collection of separate scrolls; no single scroll could have contained the entire Law and the Prophets. Not until the third or fourth century, when the codex became common, was the practical decision required to determine the exact contents of the Bible to be included within the covers of a codex (*see* Literacy and Book Culture).

4. The Hebrew Bible as a Source for the Composition of the New Testament.

The HB is the primary resource used by early disciples of Jesus and early Christian authors for the religious basis, vocabulary, concepts, motifs, roles, stories, beliefs and theology of the NT. Only a brief, selective sketch can be provided here.

4.1. The Dead Sea Scrolls. Just as the biblical scrolls have illumined the text and canon of the HB, so have the scrolls—biblical, parabiblical and nonbiblical—illumined many aspects of the NT and the ways post-Tanakh literature was composed. The **Rule of the Community* (1QS, 4QS^{a-j}, 5QS), for example, is saturated with allusions to and phraseology from the Law and the Prophets, and much of the NT is similarly composed, in matter and in form.

4.2. Theological Themes. The major theological themes of the NT are principally derived from those of the HB: creation, covenant, torah, ethics, election, salvation. Moreover, many distinctly Christian developments in theology are re-adaptations of themes of the HB: new creation, new covenant, new or heavenly Jerusalem, the time of the end (*see* Eschatologies) and resurrection of the dead. Moreover, J. A. Fitzmyer interestingly demonstrates that Paul's doctrine of justification by faith—also clearly based on elements from the HB—finds a transitional phase in the Qumran *Rule of the Community* (1QS) and **Thanksgiving Hymns* (1QH).

4.3. The Life and Portraits of Jesus. Virtually the entire narrative of the life of Jesus is modeled on the HB and its vocabulary drawn from there, from "In the beginning" (Jn 1:1 = Gen 1:1) to "Into your hands I commend my spirit" (Lk 23:46 = Ps 31:5) and even "Sit at my right hand" (Heb 1:13 = Ps 110:1). Moreover, many figures from the HB serve as models or prototypes of Jesus.

4.3.1. Origins and Birth. Just as John's Gospel makes use of creation allusions to express the divine origins of Jesus, the Matthean and Lukan Evangelists form their accounts of his human origins according to the literary form of the HB genealogies: Matthew 1:1-17 through Abraham and David, Luke 3:23-38 back through David and Abraham to Adam. Matthew further develops his birth narrative through five vignettes designed to show that "all this happened to fulfill what had been spoken by God through the prophet[s]" (Mt 1:22; 2:5, 15, 17, 23). Similarly, all the brush strokes in the opening scene painted for Luke's diptych are inspired by the HB: a priest in the temple, who had a "barren" wife and receives a message from a heavenly being, about a birth with Nazirite allusions (cf. Judg 13:2-5, 25; 16:17); and another heavenly messenger, announcing to a virgin who will bear a son to inherit the throne of David and who sings a canticle reminiscent of Hannah's (cf. 1 Sam 1:2, 11; 2:1-10).

4.3.2. Life, Ministry, Teaching, Miracles. The portraits of Jesus painted by the Evangelists and Paul are sketched against the background of the principal figures and roles of the HB. He is the "last Adam" (1 Cor 15:45; cf. 15:21-22; Rom 5:14), the one in whom "the blessing of Abraham passes on to the Gentiles" (Gal 3:14), and is "greater than our ancestor Jacob" (Jn 4:12).

Matthew paints him as the new lawgiver, the new Moses: from the scene of the slaughter of the innocent children (Mt 2:16 = Ex 1:16, 22) and "out of Egypt I have called my son" (Hos 11:1) to the restructuring of Jesus' teaching into five major discourses to symbolize a new Torah. And D. P. Moessner has noted that the composition of Luke 9 is influenced by Deuteronomy in its parallel to the journey, out of Egypt and through the wilderness, of the "prophet like Moses" (Deut 18:15-18), with a strong correspondence in the calling, ministry and destiny of the chosen one who must die in the effort to bring his people to salvation.

Jesus teaches the Torah as the pinnacle of revelation: the greatest commandment (Mk 12:28-31) is selected from Deuteronomy 6:4-5 and the second greatest from Leviticus 19:18. The HB is the acknowledged basis for settling halakic disputes (Mt 15:4; 19:4-8 par. Mk 10:3-9; Mt 22:23-32 par. Mk 12:18-27 par. Lk 20:27-38), though in Paul it eventually yields to the supreme truth incarnate in Jesus Christ (Gal 3:21-26). The same shift is signaled when the saying "I have come not to abolish but to fulfill [the Law]" (Mt 5:17) moves into the revisory formula, "You have heard it said: *x*, but I say to you *y*" (Mt 5:21-22, 27-28, 31-34, 38-39, 43-44). Note also the periodization of salvation history in Luke 16:16: "It was the Law and the Prophets until John; since then it is the good news of the kingdom of God." His rootedness in, but especially his transcending of, the Law and the Prophets, symbolized by the figures of Moses and Elijah, is affirmed in his transfiguration (Mt 17:1-8 par. Mk 9:2-8 par. Lk 9:28-36; see also Heb 1:1-2).

Luke depicts Jesus as the new Elijah. After his inaugural reading from the scroll of Isaiah in the synagogue at Nazareth, where "today you have heard this scripture fulfilled" (Lk 4:16-21), he appeals to the examples of Elijah and Elisha (Lk 4:24-27) regarding his rejection. T. L. Brodie and C. A. Evans demonstrate close parallels to Elijah and Elisha, including several miracles, for example, the raising of the widow's son in Nain (Lk 7:11-17 = 1 Kings 17:17-24; see also Elisha's raising of a woman's son in 2 Kings 4:32-37). The healing of the centurion's slave (Lk 7:1-10; cf. Mt 8:5-13) may also find echoes in the Elijah and Elisha cycles (cf. 1 Kings 17:8-16; 2 Kings 5:1-14).

Like David, Jesus is God's son (Heb 1:2, 5, 8 = Ps 2:7; 2 Sam 7:14) but greater than David (Mt 22:42-45) and "greater than Solomon" (Mt 12:42; Lk 11:31). In addition to his role as king, he is also seen as surpassing the HB leadership roles of priest (Heb 4:14—5:14; 7:1-21) and prophet (Heb 1:1-2; Mk 9:4, 7 par. Mt 17:3, 5 par. Lk 9:30, 35), as well as guarantee of the new covenant (Heb 7:22; 8:8-13).

4.3.3. Death, Resurrection and Glory. Jesus' suffering and death were foretold by Moses and the prophets (Lk 24:25-27). His death was interpreted with overtones of Abraham's sacrifice of Isaac (Gen 22:1-18; Jn 3:16; 1 Jn 4:9-10; Rom 8:32; cf. Heb 11:17-19), the Suffering Servant (Is 52:13—53:12; Acts 8:32-33; 1 Pet 2:21-25) and the Son of Man (Mt 26:64 = Dan 7:13). Psalm 22 provides details (Jn 19:24; Mt 27:39), and Passover regulations are fulfilled (Jn 19:36 = Ex 12:46). His dying utterances quote scriptural texts (Mk 15:34 par. Mt 27:46 = Ps 22:1; Lk 23:46 = Ps 31:5; Jn 19:28; cf. Ps 69:21). After his death he was buried for three days to rise on the third day (Mt 12:40 = Jon 1:17; Lk 24:46). Now glorified, he is "superior to the angels" (Heb 1:4) and sits enthroned as God's Son at his right hand (Heb 1:3-13 = Pss 2:7; 110:1).

5. Summary.

Thus the NT is thoroughly constructed from and saturated with the themes and motifs, the stories and prototypical figures, the terminology and theology of the HB. The Gospels are not retelling the HB but are retelling the Jesus story, but they do so by drawing principally and almost exclusively from the HB. Many minds and voices contributed to the composition of the NT (just as they did for the HB), and they were searching the ancient Scriptures in their attempt to understand and articulate what God was doing in Jesus. They did so from texts and from a collection of sacred books that did not necessarily coincide with the textual forms or the canons in use today. They did so from texts that were still in the pluriform compositional phase of the Scriptures and thus were not necessarily in agreement with our inherited texts, and they did so from a collection of sacred books that would largely, though not entirely, coincide with the later Jewish, Protestant, Catholic, Orthodox or Ethiopic canons.

See also APOCRYPHA AND PSEUDEPIGRAPHA; ARAMAIC TARGUMIM: QUMRAN; BIBLICAL INTERPRETATION, JEWISH; CANONICAL FORMATION OF THE NEW TESTAMENT; DANIEL, ESTHER AND JEREMIAH, ADDITIONS TO; HEBREW LANGUAGE; MANUSCRIPTS, GREEK OLD TESTAMENT; OLD TESTAMENT VERSIONS, ANCIENT; PESHARIM; PSALMS AND HYMNS OF QUMRAN; RABBINIC LITERATURE: MIDRASHIM; RABBINIC LITERATURE: TARGUMIM; REWRITTEN BIBLE IN PSEUDEPIGRAPHA AND QUMRAN; SAMARITAN LITERATURE; SEPTUAGINT/GREEK OLD TESTAMENT; SYRIAC BIBLE; WRITING

AND LITERATURE: JEWISH.

BIBLIOGRAPHY. M. Abegg Jr., P. Flint and E. Ulrich, *The Dead Sea Scrolls Bible: The Oldest Known Bible Translated for the First Time into English* (San Francisco: HarperSanFrancisco, 1999); D. E. Aune, "Qumran and the Book of Revelation," in *The Dead Sea Scrolls After Fifty Years,* ed. P. W. Flint and J. C. VanderKam with A. E. Alvarez (2 vols.; Leiden: E. J. Brill, 1999) 2:622-48; J. Barr, *Holy Scripture: Canon, Authority, Criticism* (Philadelphia: Westminster, 1983); J. Barton, *Holy Writings, Sacred Text: The Canon in Early Christianity* (Louisville: Westminster John Knox, 1997); idem, "The Significance of a Fixed Canon of the Hebrew Bible," in *Hebrew Bible / Old Testament: The History of Its Interpretation,* ed. M. Sæbø (Göttingen: Vandenhoeck & Ruprecht, 1996) 1.1:67-83; R. Beckwith, *The Old Testament Canon of the New Testament Church* (Grand Rapids, MI: Eerdmans, 1985); T. L. Brodie, *Luke the Literary Interpreter: Luke-Acts as a Systematic Rewriting and Updating of the Elijah-Elisha Narrative* (Rome: Pontifical University of St. Thomas Aquinas, 1987); G. J. Brooke, "4Q500 1 and the Use of Scripture in the Parable of the Vineyard," *DSD* 2/3 (1995) 268-94; C. A. Evans, "Jesus and the Dead Sea Scrolls," in *The Dead Sea Scrolls After Fifty Years,* ed. P. W. Flint and J. C. VanderKam with A. E. Alvarez (2 vols.; Leiden: E. J. Brill, 1999) 2:573-98; C. A. Evans and J. A. Sanders, *Luke and Scripture: The Function of Sacred Tradition in Luke-Acts* (Minneapolis: Fortress, 1993); M. Fishbane, *Biblical Interpretation in Ancient Israel* (New York: Oxford University Press, 1985); J. A. Fitzmyer, "Paul and the Dead Sea Scrolls," in *The Dead Sea Scrolls After Fifty Years,* ed. P. W. Flint and J. C. VanderKam with A. E. Alvarez (2 vols.; Leiden: E. J. Brill, 1999) 2:599-621; idem, "The Use of Explicit Old Testament Quotations in Qumran Literature and in the New Testament," *NTS* 7 (1961) 297-333; P. W. Flint, *The Dead Sea Psalms Scrolls and the Book of Psalms* (STDJ 17; Leiden: E. J. Brill, 1997); S. Z. Leiman, *The Canonization of Hebrew Scripture: The Talmudic and Midrashic Evidence* (Hamden, CT: Archon, 1976); B. M. Metzger, *The Canon of the New Testament: Its Origin, Development, and Significance* (Oxford: Clarendon Press, 1987); D. P. Moessner, *Lord of the Banquet* (Minneapolis: Fortress, 1989); J. A. Sanders, "Canon," *ABD* 1:837-52; E. Tov, *Textual Criticism of the Hebrew Bible* (Minneapolis: Fortress, 1992); E. Ulrich, "Canon," in *Encyclopedia of the Dead Sea Scrolls,* ed. L. H. Schiffman and J. C. VanderKam (New York: Oxford University Press, 2000) 117-20; idem, *The Dead Sea Scrolls and the Origins of the Bible* (SDSSRL 2; Grand Rapids, MI: Eerdmans; Leiden: E. J. Brill, 1999); J. C. VanderKam, "Authoritative Literature in the Dead Sea Scrolls," *DSD* 5 (1998) 382-402; idem, *The Dead Sea Scrolls Today* (Grand Rapids, MI: Eerdmans, 1994).

E. Ulrich

HEBREW LANGUAGE

Aside from the Aramaic passages (Jer 10:11; Dan 2:4b—7:28; Ezra 4:8—6:18; 7:12-26) and two words in Genesis 31:47, Hebrew is the language of the OT (98.5 percent). It is a member of the language family known as Semitic (after Noah's son Shem, Gen 5:32), which has been the predominant language group in the Middle East for at least the last five millennia. Semitic languages range from Akkadian, the language of the Babylonians and Assyrians in the Northeast; Arabic and Geʿez in the South; and Hebrew, Aramaic, Phoenician and various other Canaanite dialects in the Northwest. Hebrew is then a Northwest Semitic language.

The Hebrew language has shown a remarkable stability over the past three millennia. A modern Hebrew reader could with little difficulty understand literature ranging from the earliest biblical Hebrew, the Dead Sea Scrolls and medieval midrashim. The evident catalyst for such uniformity has been the Hebrew Bible.

1. Biblical Hebrew
2. Mishnaic Hebrew
3. Dead Sea Scrolls
4. Importance for New Testament Study

1. Biblical Hebrew.

Hebrew grammarians have discerned sufficient differences in the written record to describe Biblical Hebrew (BH), the language of the Hebrew Bible, and Mishnaic Hebrew (MH), the language of the Mishnah and other later rabbinic compositions. The first division is often further subdivided into Classical Biblical Hebrew (CBH; the Pentateuch and Former Prophets) and Late Biblical Hebrew (LBH; Ezra-Nehemiah, Esther, and the nonsynoptic portions of Chronicles). Practically speaking, however, differences used to make this distinction are minor, and due to pressures in antiquity to modernize (Ecclesiastes?) or archaize (Esther) the text, these disagreements are in large part only relative. As

Waltke and O'Connor conclude, "The Hebrew of scripture, though far from uniform, is essentially a single language," and "The bulk of the Hebrew Bible . . . presents a single if changing grammar" (15).

2. Mishnaic Hebrew.
This picture alters to a somewhat greater degree in regard to MH. The Mishnah (c. A.D. 200) is the earliest and best example of this particular Hebrew idiom. Considered by grammarians of the nineteenth century to be an artificial construct rather than a spoken language, most now argue that it does indeed reflect the language of discourse in the third century A.D. and perhaps was even in use as early as the second century B.C. (Rabin). The distinction between BH and MH are clearly more substantial than the relative differences within BH. The following list is a sample of the more important differences between BH and MH.

(1) MH no longer uses the consecutive forms of the verb.

(2) The MH verbal system expresses three *tenses* (time of action), with the participle providing the present. BH verbs largely signify *aspect* (type of action), and the participle is used as a verbal adjective.

(3) MH distinguishes between genders only in the third singular pronoun, whereas BH expresses gender in both second and third persons, singular and plural.

(4) MH introduces relative clauses with *še* while BH regularly uses *ʾašer*.

(5) The common construct relationship of BH is often expressed by the particle *šel* in MH (a combination of the relative particle *še* plus the preposition *l-*).

In addition to these grammatical changes there are noticeable shifts in vocabulary—MH uses many words that are unknown in BH but are common in *Aramaic—and stylistic changes (Segal).

Just when the transition was made from BH (LBH) to MH is one of the Holy Grails of Hebrew language research. That some form of Hebrew was spoken during the Second Temple period is clearly indicated by the ancient writers. According to Nehemiah 13:23-24 half of the Jewish children with mothers from Ashdod, Ammon and Moab could not speak Hebrew. That Nehemiah took steps to rectify this situation witnesses that an ability to speak Hebrew was expected in Jerusalem in the mid-fifth century B.C. In accordance with the Hebrew of the book itself, the language of Nehemiah would be LBH.

3. The Dead Sea Scrolls.
The next piece of evidence has only been known since 1947 and the discovery of the *Dead Sea Scrolls. In the ten years that followed the initial find, more than 900 scrolls were uncovered in eleven caves to the northwest of the Dead Sea. Fully 202 of these are biblical manuscripts. Of the remaining 700 texts, 120 are written in *Aramaic, and 28 in *Greek. The remaining 550 scrolls were written in Hebrew. E. Qimron has determined as the fruit of twenty years of intense personal research that, "Broadly speaking, the language of the Qumran sectarian literature is similar (especially in phraseology and syntax) to the language of those biblical books that were written in the post exilic period" (Qimron and Strugnell). The written language at Qumran thus represents a continuation of LBH.

3.1. The Copper Scroll. There are, however, two literary works from the Qumran caves that evidence MH characteristics. The first of these, the famous **Copper Scroll* (3Q15), is a list of some sixty-five sites where treasure was to be buried (none has been found). This scroll is likely a product of the *temple *priesthood and very possibly a map to temple treasury to be hidden from the approaching Roman armies (c. A.D. 70). The surmise that this unique scroll is probably not a part of the Qumran sectarian collection (which is antitemple), but was only coincidentally hidden in the same vicinity, suggests that it represents the language of Jerusalem in the first century A.D.

3.2. 4QMMT. The second composition is **Miqṣat Maʿaśey ha-Torah* (Some of the Works of the Law), or 4QMMT, very possibly dating to the middle of the second century B.C. This text is a composite of six fragmentary manuscripts and was called 4QMishnaic by its original editor, J. T. Milik, because of MH characteristics. The final editors (Qimron and Strugnell) have concluded that although the "MMT's language appears to be closer to MH than to BH," especially in the way of vocabulary and style, "Its grammar . . . is mainly the grammar of Qumran, one which differs extensively from MH."

3.3. Qumran Hebrew and the Language of Judea. How the character of this text affects our understanding of the nature of Qumran Hebrew

(QH) and how it relates to the language of *Judea at large is dependent on the answer to two questions. First, is Qumran Hebrew antilanguage? In other words, is it a purposed reaction to the language (MH or Aramaic) of the nonsectarian Jews (Schniedewind). There are several indications among the scrolls that this is the case. 1QH[a] 12:16 reports that the people had corrupted the words of the prophets with "stammering speech and a strange tongue" (see also 1QH[a] 10:19). CD 5:11-12 states that the Pharisees had taught the statutes of God's covenant with a "blasphemous language." On the other hand, the Qumran psalmist refers to his own language as the "tongue of one of your disciples" (1QH[a] 15:10).

The second question concerns the identity of the recipient of 4QMMT. The current majority view is that the Jerusalem establishment and perhaps the high priest are the intended recipients (Qimron and Strugnell). Perhaps more defensible is the conclusion that it was a fellow covenanter (and the group he represents) who had fallen under the influence of Pharisaic thought (*see* Miqṣat Maʿaśey ha-Torah [4QMMT]). In either case 4QMMT very likely reflects the spoken language of the recipient.

If QH is an antilanguage, then 4QMMT represents either the spoken vernacular of the Qumran sect (recipient = fellow sectarian) or a concession to the language of the people (recipient = Jerusalem establishment). If QH is not an antilanguage, then 4QMMT represents the spoken language of Qumran and, if its recipient is of the Jerusalem establishment, the language of Jerusalem as well. Aside from these uncertainties of detail, when taken together the *Copper Scroll* and 4QMMT suggest that during the last couple of centuries B.C. and the first century A.D., LBH had begun the transition to the MH of the later rabbinic period. The Qumran sectarians, as is evidenced by the LBH-nature of the vast majority of the Hebrew scrolls and the presence of the MH characteristics in 4QMMT, may have practiced a form of *diglossia*, an upper language (LBH) for formal occasions and writing, and a lower language (with characteristics of MH) that was spoken in everyday life. The inhabitants of Judea and Jerusalem very likely spoke a Hebrew very similar to MH.

4. Importance for New Testament Study.

4.1. Language of Jesus. Having established that the form of Hebrew spoken in the Jewish community of the first century A.D. was characterized by Mishnaic Hebrew (MH) grammar, a second question needs to be addressed: was the language of Jesus MH? That his legal discussions with the various Jewish parties (i.e., *Pharisees, *Sadducees, *scribes) were couched in MH is strongly suggested by 4QMMT and quotations of the early sages (Tannaim) preserved in the Mishnah and Talmuds. However, the multilingual nature of the Qumran manuscripts (79 percent Hebrew, 17 percent Aramaic, 4 percent Greek), in a setting where Hebrew was evidently preferred for theological reasons, warns against a simple solution to the question. There are additional indications that the Jewish community was largely multilingual.

4.1.1. Evidence from Masada. The Masada manuscripts would have been deposited just shortly after those of Qumran (c. A.D. 73-74) and provide the last manuscript evidence until the Second Jewish Revolt (A.D. 132-135; *see* Jewish Wars with Rome). Apart from *Latin and *Greek lists, pay stubs and letters which evidence occupation by the Roman army following the fall of Masada, there exist the remains of seven biblical manuscripts and a substantial portion of a Hebrew copy of Ben Sira (*see* Sirach). Ben Sira, a book exalting the wisdom of Jerusalem, was composed in Hebrew in 132 B.C. and translated into Greek in 117 B.C. by Ben Sira's grandson. Although a Greek version was later included in the Roman Catholic canon, it should be noted that the Hebrew text was preferred by the zealots who carried their copy to Masada. Of the eight remaining nonbiblical manuscripts, seven are Hebrew and one very fragmentary text may be Aramaic.

4.1.2. Evidence from Josephus. An interesting aside by the Jewish historian *Josephus at the end of *Jewish Antiquities* allows a quite different glimpse of the spoken languages of the first century A.D.

> I have also taken a great deal of pains to obtain the learning of the Greeks, and understand the elements of the Greek language, although I have so long accustomed myself to speak our native tongue, that I cannot pronounce Greek with sufficient exactness. For our nation does not encourage those that learn the languages of many nations, and so adorn their discourses with the smoothness of their diction. . . . But they

> give him the testimony of being a wise man who is fully acquainted with our laws and is able to interpret the meaning of the Holy Scriptures. (Josephus *Ant.* 20.11.2 §§263-64)

Josephus suggests that a knowledge of Greek was not much sought after by the Jews, but that facility in Hebrew was a sign of wisdom. As to the identity of his own "native tongue," most scholars have posited Aramaic, as is suggested by the Aramaic forms of religious terminology in the Greek text of his works. This also appears to be the meaning of his introductory statement to *Jewish War*, that he wrote in his "vernacular tongue" for his fellow Jews "beyond the Euphrates and the inhabitants of Adiabene" (Josephus *J.W.* Preface 1 §§3, 6). This region—the upper Tigris—was with little doubt populated by Aramaic-speaking peoples.

4.1.3. Evidence from the Bar Kokhba Caves. The last piece of evidence comes from the caves in Naḥal Ḥever and Wadi Murabbaʿat, hideouts for Jewish rebels in the Second Jewish Revolt. The documents from these caves are of a different character, being contracts, inventories, genealogies and letters rather than the literary works of Qumran and Masada. But they provide a snapshot of the languages being used in the Jewish community of the early second century A.D. Among the fragments from Wadi Murabbaʿat which are large enough to determine language there are 17 Hebrew (16 percent), 16 Aramaic (15 percent), 75 Greek (69 percent) and 1 Nabatean text, an Aramaic dialect. The caves in Naḥal Ḥever reveal the same languages with a slightly different profile: 17 Hebrew (14 percent), 40 Aramaic (33 percent), 51 Greek (41 percent), and 15 Nabatean (12 percent). One of the Greek letters (5/6Ḥev 52) is a request from *Bar Kokhba (or one of his lieutenants) to have provisions set aside for Succoth. In it he writes (dictates), "the letter is written in Greek as we have found no one to write it in Hebrew." Although the word translated "Hebrew" might also refer to Aramaic, the fact that XḤev/Se 30, a letter written to Bar Kokhba, and Mur 43 and 44, letters from Bar Kokhba (Mur 42, 45-52 are likely from him as well) are all in written Hebrew makes the translation sure. It is clear that Bar Kokhba preferred to carry out his communications in Hebrew but turned to Greek when the evidently waning Hebrew literacy demanded (*see* Simon ben Kosiba).

4.1.4. Evidence from the Gospel Accounts. It is in this context that Jesus ministered. The evidence reviewed suggests that the language among the Jews in Jerusalem and Judea in the early first century A.D. was Hebrew, communication with Jews outside of these environs was likely carried on in Aramaic, while business with the Roman government was conducted in Greek. It is of note, then, that some thirty instances of Jesus' Semitic speech in the NT are almost entirely in Aramaic. Most of these occurrences are single words (Passover, sabbath) and do not allow a certain judgment to be made as there was much sharing of vocabulary between Aramaic and MH. Thus two instances of longer verbal expressions are of special interest to scholars. Mark 5:41 records the episode of the healing of a young girl in Capernaum in which Jesus says in Aramaic, *tālîtāʾ qûm*, which translated means, "Little girl, get up." It is probable that the language among the natives of the Galilee and the hill country round about (including Nazareth) was Aramaic. The second instance is Jesus cry from the cross recorded at Matthew 27:46, *ʾēî, ʾēlî, lĕmaʾ šᵉbāqtānî*, "My Lord, My Lord, why have you forsaken me?" Matthew begins in Hebrew (Mark 15:34 with *ʾᵉlāhî, ʾᵉlāhî* is Aramaic) and finishes in Aramaic. The crowds of Jewish pilgrims in Jerusalem for the Passover from regions outside of Judea would have understood the Aramaic translation of Psalm 22:1 more readily than the Hebrew. A third verbal instance pointed out by scholars, *Ephphatha*, "Be opened" (Mark 7:34), is ambiguous and by form more likely Hebrew than Aramaic.

4.1.5. Conclusion. There is little doubt that Jesus spoke Aramaic when the context required. More speculative, but in agreement with the evidence from Qumran, Masada and the Bar Kokhba caves, is the likelihood that he also spoke Hebrew in his interactions with the scribes, Pharisees and Sadducees in and around Jerusalem. His intercourse with Roman officials (i.e., Jn 18:4) was probably carried out in Greek.

4.2. Necessity of Hebrew for New Testament Study. In this age of specialization, the student of the New Testament who also reads Hebrew has become somewhat of a rarity. The recent release of the Dead Sea Scrolls and their wealth of information toward the study of New Testament backgrounds, coupled with a growing realization that Christianity has roots deep within Judaism, should begin to mitigate this trend. Only a mature knowledge of the Hebrew Bible and its subsequent use can provide the necessary context for understanding the ministry of Jesus, the beginnings of Christianity, and the collection of first-century Jewish texts known as the NT.

See also ARAMAIC LANGUAGE; GREEK OF THE NEW TESTAMENT; LATIN LANGUAGE; SEMITIC INFLUENCE ON THE NEW TESTAMENT.

BIBLIOGRAPHY. Z. Ben-Ḥayyim, "Traditions in the Hebrew Language, with Special Reference to the Dead Sea Scrolls," in *Scripta Hierosolymitana IV: Aspects of the Dead Sea Scrolls*, ed. C. Rabin and Y. Yadin (Jerusalem: Magnes, 1958) 200-14; J. Blau, "The Structure of Biblical and Dead Sea Scroll Hebrew in Light of Arabic Diglossia and Middle Arabic," *Lesû* 60 (1997) 21-32; J. Fitzmyer, "Languages of Palestine in the First Century A.D.," in *A Wandering Aramean: Collected Aramaic Essays* (Missoula, MT: Scholars Press, 1979) 29-56; W. Gesenius, *Gesenius' Hebrew Grammar*, ed. E. Kautzsch (Oxford: Oxford University Press, 1980); P. Joüon and T. Muraoka, *A Grammar of Biblical Hebrew* (2 vols.; SubBi 14; Rome: Pontifical Biblical Institute, 1991); E. Kutscher, "Hebrew Language," *EncJud* 16:1560-1662; E. Qimron, *The Hebrew of the Dead Sea Scrolls* (HSS 29; Atlanta: Scholars Press, 1986); idem, "Observations on the History of Early Hebrew (1000 B.C.E.-200 C.E.) in the Light of the Dead Sea Documents," in *The Dead Sea Scrolls: Forty Years of Research*, ed. D. Dimant and U. Rappaport (Leiden: E. J. Brill; Jerusalem: Magnes, 1992) 349-61; E. Qimron and J. Strugnell, *Qumran Cave 4.5: Miqsat Maʿase ha-Torah* (DJD 10; Oxford: Clarendon Press, 1994) 65-108; C. Rabin, "Hebrew and Aramaic in the First Century," in *Jewish People in the First Century*, ed. S. Safrai and M. Stern (2 vols.; CRINT 1; Assen: Van Gorcum; Philadelphia: Fortress, 1976) 2:1007-39; W. Schniedewind, "Qumran Hebrew as an Antilanguage," *JBL* 118 (1999) 235-52; M. H. Segal, *A Grammar of Mishnaic Hebrew* (Oxford: Clarendon Press, 1927); B. Waltke and M. O'Connor, *An Introduction to Biblical Hebrew Syntax* (Winona Lake, IN: Eisenbrauns, 1990); R. J. Williams, *Hebrew Syntax: An Outline* (Toronto: University of Toronto Press, 1976).

M. G. Abegg Jr.

HEBREW MATTHEW

The complete text of a Hebrew Matthew has been preserved in a fourteenth-century Jewish polemical treatise known as the *Even Bohan* ("Touchstone") and authored by the Spanish rabbi Shem-Tob ben Isaac ben Shaprut (also referred to as Ibn Shaprut). G. Howard (1987, 225) believes that this Hebrew text is not a translation of canonical Greek Matthew or a version of one of the Jewish Gospels (viz., the *Gospel of the Hebrews*, the *Gospel of the Nazarenes*, the *Gospel of Ebionites*) but an independent tradition that in its earliest form may reach back to the first century. Howard's text is based on Add no. 26964 (British Library) for Matthew 1:1—23:22 and Ms. 2426 (Jewish Theological Seminary of America) for Matthew 23:23—28:20.

The belief that the Evangelist Matthew produced a Hebrew Gospel was widespread in the early church. Papias remarks that the Evangelist "Matthew collected the oracles [of Jesus] in the Hebrew language [*hebraidi dialektō*], and each interpreted them as best he could" (Eusebius *Hist. Eccl.* 3.39.16). Irenaeus comments that "Matthew also issued a written Gospel among the Hebrews in their own dialect" (Irenaeus *Haer.* 3.1.1). The same opinion is expressed by Origen, who says that Matthew published his Gospel "for those who from Judaism came to believe, composed as it was in Hebrew letters [*grammasin hebraikois*]" (Eusebius *Hist. Eccl.* 6.25.4). Eusebius himself says that "Matthew had first preached to the Hebrews, and when he was on the point of going to others he transmitted in writing in his native language [*patriō glottē*] the Gospel according to himself" (Eusebius *Hist. Eccl.* 3.24.6). Epiphanius also speaks of a Gospel "in Hebrew letters [*hebraikois grammasin*]" (Epiphanius *Pan.* 30.3.7). Finally, Jerome also says Matthew "wrote the Gospel in the Hebrew language" (Jerome *Ep.* 20.5). Howard thinks Shem-Tob's Hebrew Matthew may be this Hebrew text, of which some early Fathers had heard.

Reviews of Howard's book have been mixed. W. L. Petersen has been the most critical, arguing that Shem-Tob's Hebrew Matthew "can only be regarded as a secondary work, based on earlier medieval traditions related to the Vetus Latina and Vetus Syra" (Petersen, 726). W. Horbury has also expressed skepticism, doubting that Shem-Tob's Hebrew Matthew has first-century roots. D. J. Harrington, however, thinks that Howard has succeeded in laying the foundation on which future study of Matthew's Hebrew substratum should build. Indeed, Harrington advises NT *textual critics to take into account the readings of Shem-Tob's Hebrew Matthew.

Significant comparative textual evidence supports the conclusions of Howard and Harrington. Howard (1989, 1992) is able to cite examples where Shem-Tob's Hebrew Matthew agrees with readings found only in Codex Sinaiticus, while in more recent studies R. F. Shedinger (1997) is able to cite many readings where Shem-Tob's text agrees with readings found only in P[45]. Some of these readings include: (1) At Luke 11:13, P[45] reads "good spirit" (instead of "Holy Spirit" or, in the parallel at Mt 7:11, "good things"), which agrees with Shem-Tob's "his good spirit." (2) Only P[45] at Luke 11:33 (par. Mt 5:15) and Shem-Tob omit "under a basket." (3) At Matthew 26:3, P[45] and Shem-Tob omit "and the scribes." (4) The variant word order in P[45] at Matthew 26:23a is in agreement only with Shem-Tob's Hebrew Matthew. Shedinger (1999) also cites a number of agreements between Shem-Tob's Hebrew Matthew and other old Greek texts and ancient versions. He finds some sixty-seven textual variants that agree with neither the Byzantine manuscript tradition nor the Vulgate and Latin tradition. He believes that this evidence "strongly suggests that [Shem-Tob's Hebrew Matthew] has roots going back to a much earlier time" (Shedinger 1999, 689). Some of these variants include: (1) Shem-Tob's omission at Matthew 7:27 of "and the winds blew," which agrees with א* 33; (2) Shem-Tob's omission of Matthew 10:37b-38, which agrees fully with P[19] and partly with B* D; (3) Shem-Tob's plural "they ate" at Matthew 12:4 agrees with א B 481; (4) Shem-Tob at Matthew 15:36 omits "and giving thanks," which agrees with C*; and (5) Shem-Tob's surprising variant at Matthew 25:28, "give it to the one who gained five gold coins," agrees with and explains the reading in D, "give it to the one who has five talents." D's reading is confusing, because no one in the parable of the talents has five gold coins. Shem-Tob's reading makes it clear that the single talent was to be given to the one who had ten (i.e., the one who had "gained five").

See also APOCRYPHAL GOSPELS.

BIBLIOGRAPHY. D. J. Harrington, Review of G. Howard, *The Gospel of Matthew,* in *CBQ* 50 (1988) 717-18; W. Horbury, Review of G. Howard, *The Gospel of Matthew,* in *JTS* 43 (1992) 166-69; G. Howard, *The Gospel of Matthew According to a Primitive Hebrew Text* (Macon, GA: Mercer University Press, 1987; rev., 1995); idem, "A Note on Codex Sinaiticus and Shem-Tob's Hebrew Matthew," *NovT* 34 (1992b) 46-47; idem, "A Note on Shem-Tob's Hebrew Matthew and the Gospel of John," *JSNT* 47 (1992a) 117-26; idem, "A Note on the Short Ending of Matthew," *HTR* 81 (1988) 117-20; idem, "A Primitive Hebrew Gospel of Matthew and the Tol'doth Yeshu," *NTS* 34 (1988) 60-70; idem, "The Pseudo-Clementine Writings and Shem-Tob's Hebrew Matthew," *NTS* 40 (1994) 622-28; idem, "The Textual Nature of an Old Hebrew Version of Matthew," *JBL* 105 (1986) 49-63; idem, "The Textual Nature of Shem-Tob's Hebrew Matthew," *JBL* 108 (1989) 239-57; P. E. Lapide, "Der 'Prüfstein' aus Spanien," *Sefarad* 34 (1974) 227-72; W. L. Petersen, Review of G. Howard, *The Gospel of Matthew,* in *JBL* 108 (1989) 722-26; R. F. Shedinger, "A Further Consideration of the Textual Nature of Shem-Tob's Hebrew Matthew," *CBQ* 61 (1999) 686-94; idem, "The Textual Relationship between P[45] and Shem-Tob's Hebrew Matthew," *NTS* 43 (1997) 58-71.

C. A. Evans

HEKHALOT LITERATURE. *See* HEAVENLY ASCENT IN JEWISH AND PAGAN TRADITIONS; MYSTICISM.

HELLENISM

The term *Hellenism* has become popular since the early nineteenth century. It was then used of Greek civilization in the period after the death of *Alexander the Great (323 B.C.), but it is currently used to refer to the whole span of Greek history or more specifically to a set of values and practices attributed to the ancient Greeks. The Greek word *hellēnismos* is first used of the adoption of or enthusiasm for Greek culture in 2 Maccabees (*see* 1 & 2 Maccabees). Greek ideas and customs penetrated most of the vast area encompassed by Alexander's eastern expedition and can be discerned in Palestine from the third century B.C. on. There was a violent reaction to Greek influence in the Maccabean period, but by the time of Jesus the Palestinian landscape included Greek architecture (*gymnasia, *theaters; *see* Art and Architecture: Greco-Roman) and Greek social institutions. The Gospels mention encounters with people of Greek culture. James the brother of Jesus, and probably Jesus himself, spoke Greek as well as Aramaic (and understood Hebrew). Paul and his companions met Greek civilization not only in Greece and Macedonia but also (often fused with native cultures) in Sicily, *Asia Minor, Cyprus, Syria and Palestine. The Hellenists of Acts were probably not simply members of Greek-speaking synagogue congregations but people favorably inclined toward Greek practices.

1. Meanings of "Hellenism"
2. Historical and Cultural Background
3. Palestine and Greek Influence
4. Who Were the Hellenists?
5. Characteristics of the Hellenic Way of Life

1. Meanings of "Hellenism."

1.1. The Modern Term. The fundamental reference of "Hellenism" is to ancient Greek language and culture. It is used in its broadest sense by A. J. Toynbee, who gave to his Home University Library volume *Hellenism* (London: Oxford University Press, 1959) the subtitle *The History of a Civilization* for a book that embraced the whole period from the late second millennium B.C. to the seventh century of our era; similarly F. E. Peters used the subtitle *A History of the Near East from Alexander the Great to the Triumph of Christianity* for *The Harvest of Hellenism* (London: Allen & Unwin, 1972) to denote a period of eight centuries. However, the German word *Hellenismus* is commonly used in a more restricted sense, of the culture that resulted from Greek penetration into the lands of the Near East, particularly following the expedition of Alexander. J. G. Droysen's *Geschichte des Hellenismus* 1 (Hamburg: Perthes, 1836) gave currency to this focus (for his predecessors see R. Bichler, *"Hellenismus": Geschichte und Problematik eines Epochenbegriffs* [Impulse der Forschung 41; Darmstadt: Wissenschaftliche Buchgesellschaft, 1983] 34-48).

The tension between alluding to Greek culture generally and referring to a specific period has led to a certain fluidity of usage. Thus modern collections of essays such as *Studies in Classics and Jewish Hellenism,* edited by R. Koebner (*ScrHier* 1; Jerusalem: Hebrew University, Magnes Press, 1954) or H.-D. Betz's *Hellenismus und Urchristentum* (Tübingen: Mohr Siebeck, 1990) refer to the content of Greek culture, albeit with a particular emphasis on the Hellenistic (or intertestamental) period.

The English word *Hellenism* can denote a preference, sometimes even an enthusiasm, for the Greek way of life. Matthew Arnold gave this usage a boost by writing of "the simple and attractive ideal which Hellenism holds out before human nature." He contrasted Hellenism, whose governing idea is "spontaneity of consciousness," with Hebraism, in which the governing idea is "strictness of conscience" (*Culture and Anarchy: An Essay in Political and Social Criticism* [London: Smith, Elder, 1869] 147, 151). A recent study by L. C. Dowling of *Hellenism and Homosexuality in Victorian Oxford* (Ithaca, NY: Cornell University Press, 1994) is concerned not only with systematic study in the nineteenth century of the history, literature and philosophy of the ancient Greeks but also with a new ideal of Greek civilization (inter alia, as a means of establishing a transcendent value that forms an alternative to Christian theology). S. Prickett may overstate the case slightly in writing (in *Rediscovering Hellenism: The Hellenic Inheritance and the English Imagination,* ed. G. W. Clarke [Cambridge: Cambridge University Press, 1989], 147), "For the German Hellenists of the late eighteenth and early nineteenth centuries Greece had ceased to be a place and had become a permanent manifestation of the human spirit"; but there has been a wave of enthusiasm in western Europe for what were seen as Greek ideals.

1.2. Greek Vocabulary. The corresponding Greek noun, *hellēnismos,* is derived from the verb *hellēnizein,* which normally means "to speak Greek" (e.g., Dio Chrysostom *Or.* 4.55; 36.9; contrasted with *barbarizein,* "to speak Greek badly," in 36.26), though it can mean "to imitate the Greeks," "to become Greek" (similarly Will and Orrieux, 9-11). The noun was not used by the Greeks of the classical period, as far as the surviving evidence indicates. It can mean "pure Greek [language]," as when Diogenes of Babylon (second century B.C.) defined one of the five excellences of speech, *hellēnismos,* as "language faultless in its grammar and without vernacular usage" (in Diogenes Laertius *Vit.* 7.59). The first attested occurrence with a cultural overtone happens to be in a Jewish context: in 2 Maccabees 4:13 the epitomator of Jason of Cyrene speaks of "a climax in adoption of Greek customs and a rise in adoption of alien practices" (with parallelism between *akmē hellēnismou* and *prosbasis allophylismou*). The process is later referred to as "the change to Greek customs" *(ta Hellēnika)* (2 Macc 11:24).

After the adoption of Christianity as the state cult of the *Roman Empire *hellēnismos* was used by patristic writers to denote paganism, that is, Greek cultic practice. Basil of Caesarea, for example, opens his twenty-fourth *Homily* (*PG* 31.600b) with the statement that Judaism is in conflict with *hellēnismos* and both with Christianity, just as the Egyptians and Assyrians were enemies of each other and of *Israel. In the next century Socrates Scholasticus writes of Julian as emperor (A.D. 361-363) supporting the cause of paganism (*hellēnismos;* Socrates *Hist. Eccl.* 3.11.4 [*PG* 67.409b]). Philostorgius says that Gallus taught his half-brother Julian to lean toward *hellēnismos* in the period when his cousin Constantius II was still emperor (Philostorgius *Hist. Eccl.* 3.27 [*PG* 65.513c]). He reports the sufferings of men, one a bishop, who apostatized and turned to *hellēnismos* (Philostorgius *Hist. Eccl.* 7.13 [*PG* 65.549d-552a]). Sozomen speaks of a governor of Egypt and *Alexandria named Julian, who was especially favorable to paganism and prejudiced against the Christians (Sozomen *Hist. Eccl.* 5.7.9 [*PG* 67.1233c]) and of a city extremely favorable to paganism (Sozomen *Hist. Eccl.* 5.9.7 [*PG* 67.1240a]; *hellēnismos* with *chairein* in both passages).

Similarly, Licinius, when preparing for a battle with Constantine (c. 324), reverted to pagan cult (*hellēnismos*): Sozomen *Hist. Eccl.* 1.7.2 (*PG* 67.873c); the same phrase is used in 3.19.4 (*PG* 67.1097a) of the fear that Constantine, still unbaptized, might revert to paganism. Precisely the same usage can be seen from the pagan side, for Julian in 362 expressed his disappointment that *hellēnismos* (pagan cult) had not yet made the progress that it ought to have (Julian *Letter* 84 Bidez, 429c). (There is a unique instance in Epiphanius [*PG* 41.168a], who labels *hellēnismos* the third epoch, beginning after the tower of Babel with the time of Serug [Gen 11:20-23]; but soon after [168c] the noun refers to pagan thought.)

In a brilliant move, Julian exploited the multivalence of the term in an attempt to prevent Christians who prayed and wrote in Greek from teaching Greek literature and thought; if they repudiated paganism (*hellēnismos* in one sense), they should repudiate Greek culture (*hellēnismos* in another sense). Gregory of Nazianzus responded vigorously by pointing out that the same term has more than one meaning. If Julian means by "Hellenism" cultic worship *(thrēskeia),* he should show where and from which priests Hellenism received its rules, show what victims are to be sacrificed and to which deities. Rather, he refers to a people *(ethnos)* and to those who first discovered the resources of their Greek language (Gregory of Nazianzus *Or.* 4.103 [*PG* 35.637b-640a]; see Bowersock, 6-13, 27-28, 33-35, 72; Smith, 207-8, 212-14, 279 n. 108).

The primary reference of "Hellenism," then, is to a preference for, or at least an acceptance of, Greek culture and Greek practices, including use of the Greek language. The term is not restricted to the characteristics and values of Greek culture, but it may be applied to harking back to an idealized picture of ancient Greek civilization and literature, especially to enthusiasm for Greek culture in the classical period. There is a parallel phenomenon in Neo-Hellenism, whereby western Europeans and Greeks of the nineteenth and twentieth centuries have interacted with ancient Greek myth and literature (Leontis).

2. Historical and Cultural Background.

2.1. The Distant Past. Rhetorically trained writers such as Aelius Aristides, active in the middle of the second century A.D., repeatedly talk about events of the distant past as though they happened yesterday. This orator can, for example, refer the citizens of the leading cities of Asia—Pergamum, Smyrna and *Ephesus—to ancient Greece (since, he says, they are practically all colonists of the Greeks there), and specifically to the unity of purpose shown by the Spartans and Athenians in the face of Xerxes' invasion of 481/480 B.C., in order to promote harmony among the leading cities in his own time (Aristides *Or.* 23.42-48).

Other rhetorically trained writers of the movement known as the second sophistic made Greek culture and speech "the emblems of civilization" and "spent much of their time living in the same composite Greek world of the past" (Swain, 2, 101). The earliest Greek literature was particularly significant for Greeks of the first two centuries. Homer was the Bible of the Greeks in the sense that the educated classes habitually referred to the *Iliad* and the *Odyssey* for precedents and for understanding of the gods and human nature; by the Roman period the text and its interpretation were debated in much the same manner as modern commentaries debate the interpretation of biblical passages (*see* Scholarship, Greek and Roman).

2.2. The Span of Pre-Hellenistic Greek History. Greek history can be traced back to the Bronze Age civilizations of Crete and Mycenae of the second millennium B.C., although the written evidence for them is so limited that they are sometimes regarded as prehistory. Use of the Greek language is known to go back to the late Bronze Age on the Greek mainland and on Crete, thanks to the decipherment in the 1950s of the Linear B script on clay tablets. Writing was subsequently lost to the Aegean world, but when the Phoenician script was adapted to the Greek language the first literature was the Homeric poems, whose substantive composition belongs in the eighth century B.C., and the poems of Hesiod, including *Theogony*.

The period down to the Persian wars is known as the archaic period. The Greeks were involved in colonization in the eighth and seventh centuries. This planting of Greek settlements around the shores of the Mediterranean and Black Seas must have increased the Greeks' sense of what was peculiarly Greek. Subsequently a number of Greek cities *(poleis)* experienced takeovers of their governments by autocrats known as tyrants. A small number of cities had institutions that would later be looked on as democratic; this was true of *Athens in the later sixth century. The Greek *poleis* repelled (in the decade 490-479 B.C.) the raiding party of the Achaemenid king Darius and the full-scale invasion of the Greek mainland by his son and successor Xerxes.

The classical period (fifth and fourth centuries B.C.) saw the flourishing of Greek literature, including Athenian tragedy, comedy and oratory; of Greek art and architecture, including the work of Pheidias at Olympia and elsewhere; and of Greek philosophy, including the dialogues of *Plato. While historians might wish to treat each period of Greek history as valuable in its own right, popular perception today focuses attention on the artistic and literary achievement of Athens, especially in the fifth century B.C., which is taken to be the zenith of Greek culture.

2.3. The Rise of Macedon. Already by the middle of the fourth century, Macedon was starting to assert itself under its king Philip II. He and his son and successor Alexander the Great took over much of the Greek world and proceeded to invade Asia. In the decade 334-325 B.C. Alexander conquered most of the Persian Empire, and though he did not consolidate an empire of his own, he left numerous Greek-speaking settlements in his trail. After his death the massive empire that superficially he had won broke into three parts (*see* Diadochi): apart from his base in Macedonia, the *Seleucid kingdom was established in Syria, with influence extending at various times as far west as the Aegean and as far east as modern Afghanistan, and the Ptolemaic kingdom was established in Egypt (it similarly tried to gain possessions as far northwest as the Greek mainland; *see* Hellenistic Egypt). In the third and second centuries B.C. the Attalid kings carved out a fourth empire from their base at Pergamon (Bergama) in northwestern Turkey.

3. Palestine and Greek Influence.

3.1. The Hellenistic Period. The Hellenistic period is generally considered to begin with the death of Alexander in 323 B.C., but there is some point in dating it back to about 360 B.C. in order to include earlier penetration of the East by Greeks and Macedonians. It can be shown that Greek culture spread to inland areas of Anatolia, for example in Caria, in the fifty years before Alexander (see S. Hornblower, *Mausolus* [Oxford: Clarendon Press, 1982]). In Palestine the period should not be considered to have ended with the death of Cleopatra VII in 30 B.C. but about A.D. 100, with the end of the kingdom of Agrippa II and the Nabateans (so Hengel 1974). That there was an element of deliberate purpose on the part of Roman rulers in the growth of Hellenism is suggested by the Jewish writer *Philo from Alexandria, who speaks of Augustus "Hellenizing the barbarian world in its most important regions" (Philo *Leg. Gai.* 21.147, using a compound of the verb *hellēnizein* [see 1.2 above]; *see* Hellenistic Judaism).

Because of the multiplicity of Eastern languages, cultures and thought, the process of fusion was a complex and varied one. It continued and reached its climax under Roman rule of the East. Later there was a counterrevival by languages such as Syriac and Coptic (Hengel 1989, 1). Judaism similarly was not monolithic: not only were Jews of the Diaspora subject to varied Greek influences, but also there was variation and tension in Palestine itself, although it must be admitted that the evidence for Syria and Palestine in the Hellenistic period is extremely uneven (so F. G. B. Millar in Kuhrt and Sherwin-White).

As E. J. Bickerman (79-80) pointed out, it is hard to evaluate the impact of Greek civilization in third-century Palestine. We cannot draw any conclusions from the Greek borrowings (names of musical instruments) in the Aramaic of the book of Daniel (Dan 3:5, 7, 10, 15). Nor is it clear that banquets in Greek Jerusalem, run on Greek lines, were imitating Athens rather than competing with Damascus or Sidon. But naked athletes and images of naked goddesses must have offended Jews (cf. Gen 3:21; *see* Athletics).

3.2. The Maccabean Revolt. Antiochus IV Epiphanes took over the Seleucid throne in Antioch in 175 B.C. (1 Macc 1:10). The most obvious ways in which Jason, his appointee as high priest, "brought his compatriots over to the Greek way of life" (2 Macc 4:10) were the construction of a gymnasium at the foot of the Temple Mount in Jerusalem and the establishment of a body of aristocratic youth educated as ephebes for citizenship of a Greek polity (1 Macc 1:14; 2 Macc 4:9, 12; *see* Education: Jewish and Greco-Roman). The priests put the highest value on Greek forms of prestige and Greek ways of living (2 Macc 4:15-16). There was also, then or subsequently, refusal to circumcise boys and concealment of circumcision and construction of pagan altars (1 Macc 1:15, 47; 2:45-46). In 169 B.C. Antiochus entered the sanctuary and removed sacred objects and two years later erected a "desolating sacrilege" (NRSV) on the altar of burnt offering (1 Macc 1:20-61; 2 Macc 5:11-23). Under the leadership of Judas Maccabeus and his brother Jonathan, the Jews in 161 B.C. became "friends and allies" of *Rome (1 Macc 8:20; 2 Macc 4:11; renewal in 1 Macc 12:1-4, 16) and later of the Nabateans (1 Macc 9:35) and managed to choose the victor between rival claimants to the Seleucid throne. The Maccabeans continued their efforts to remove the Hellenizers from Jerusalem, but they did not succeed until 141 B.C. (1 Macc 13:49-52), despite the fact that in 150 B.C. Jonathan became provincial governor and one of the First Friends (1 Macc 10:65) of the victor, Alexander Balas. The decree (1 Macc 14:26-27, 48) recognizing Simon as high priest and head of the nation (140 B.C.) was engraved and set up in a distinctly Greek manner (T. Rajak, in *CAH* 9 [2d ed., 1994], 285).

3.3. Palestine After the Maccabean Revolt. Despite the success of the Maccabean revolt against Seleucid control and the boost to national and cult renewal resulting from it, Greek habits remained strong. The Jewish homeland was surrounded by Greek cities, not only on the Phoenician coast but also to the north and east. According to Josephus (*Ant.* 13.11.3 §318) the son and successor of John Hyrcanus, Aristobulus (104-103 B.C.), styled himself Philhellene (*see* Hasmoneans). His brother Alexander Janneus (103-76 B.C.) issued bilingual *coins, as did the latter's grandson Mattathias Antigonus during his war against Herod and the Romans (40-37 B.C.; details in Meshorer, 118-23, 155-59 with plates 4-7, 54-55).

The incorporation of Judea into the Roman Empire following the campaigns of Pompey the Great (64-63 B.C.) increased the degree of Hellenism. Herod the Great is reported to have had stronger connections with the Greeks than the Jews (Josephus *Ant.* 19.7.3 §329; *see* Herods). He fostered the construction of Greek-style buildings (*see* Archaeology of the Land of Israel; Art and Architecture: Jewish), was patron of some distinguished Greek writers, wrote his own memoirs in Greek and staged Greek entertainments. One of his sons, Herod Antipas, in the principate of Tiberius (A.D. 14-37), founded a largely Jewish city in Galilee, Tiberias, with the constitutional machinery typical of a Greek *polis* (*see* Cities, Greco-Roman). His ties with Greek islands in the Aegean and with Athens are attested by inscriptions (*OGIS,* nos. 416-17). By this time not only had Jewish writings, most notably the OT, been translated into Greek (*see* Septuagint), but also original works were being written in Greek, such as those by Ezekiel the Tragedian and *Philo (see esp. Schürer, 3.1-2). While the *Talmud (*m. Soṭah* 9:14) attests attempts to ban the learning of Greek from the beginning of the second century of our era (the war of Quietus, A.D. 117/118; Sevenster, 47-49), earlier Jews read the Homeric poems and studied Greek philosophy. Certainly Greek education was available in Jerusalem (e.g., Josephus *Ant.* 12.4.6 §191; 15.10.5 §373).

4. Who Were the Hellenists?

The tensions within Judaism affected the early church. Groups described as Hellenists appear in the records of the earliest Christian communities: Acts 6:1-6; 9:29; 11:20. One would naturally assume that Hellenists (Gk *Hellēnistai*) are distinct from Greeks *(Hellēnes),* were it not that *Hellēnes* as well as *Hellēnistai* occurs in the manuscript readings of Acts 11:20. But the conclusion can still be drawn that Hellenists are people of non-Greek origin who adopt and promote Greek customs.

Part of the difficulty lies in the fact that the word *Hellēnistēs* is first attested in Greek literature in Acts of the Apostles. A working definition, given its formation from the verb *hellēnizein* (see 1.2 above), is one who uses Greek customs or the Greek language. There have been strong but unjustified statements (e.g., Hengel 1989, 7) that the difference is purely one of language, so that the contrast between the Hellenists and the Hebrews in Acts 6 refers to members of different synagogues, one group holding services in the Greek language and the other in (probably) Aramaic. The word *Hellēnistēs* is not attested after Acts for three hundred years, and then it appears in passages dependent on that book (see Cadbury, 59-60). Little assistance is to be gained from patristic literature, where there is a divergence between John Chrysostom's exegesis of Acts 6:1 (Chrysostom *Hom. Act.* 14.1; *PG* 60.113) and 9:29 (Chrysostom *Hom. Act.* 21.1; *PG* 60.164), interpreting *Hellēnistai* as referring to Greek speakers, and the use of the word to mean "pagan" or "supporter of paganism" (so Philostorgius *Hist. Eccl.* 7.1 [*PG* 65.537a-b] of Julian allowing pagan activists everywhere to torture and kill Christians; Sozomen *Hist. Eccl.* 5.5.7 [*PG* 67.1228c] of Julian favoring like-minded *Hellēnistai*). The latter usage is also seen in Julian (*Letter* 84 Bidez, 430d).

At their first appearance (Acts 6:1) the Hellenists complain in the rapidly growing Christian community in Jerusalem that their widows were being overlooked in the daily distribution of money or food. On the assumption that the men chosen to attend to the problem came largely from the group making the complaint, we may examine the names of the seven chosen. Given that Parmenas is an abbreviation of Parmenides, the names (Acts 6:5) are all standard Greek names, not adaptations of Semitic names. Nicolas, however, is described as a proselyte from *Antioch; since Antioch attracted many immigrants (cf. Acts 11:19; 13:1; Josephus *J.W.* 7.3.3 §45), he could have come from any of several ethnic backgrounds before being attracted to Judaism. By implication the other six were born Jews (see Barrett).

The first man listed, Stephen (*Stephanos*), is introduced in a manner suggesting that he will be important in the ensuing story (as he is). We may note that the people outside the Christian community with whom he debates (Acts 6:9) are Greek speakers, including, one may assume, the ex-slaves whose inclusion is signaled by the Latin loan word *libertinoi.* The Hebrews against whom the Hellenists complain in Acts 6:1 were Aramaic-speaking Jews who were members of the Christian community. I. H. Marshall (278) raised the possibility that Paul's Hebrews could include both Luke's Hebrews and his Hellenists. Recent scholarship (Barrett; C. C. Hill in Witherington; *see DLNTD,* Hellenists) is no doubt right to insist that the Hellenists and the Hebrews are not factions but loose groupings, each containing people with divergent beliefs and practices. Acts 6:1-6; 15:1-35 and Galatians 2:1-14 suggest that there was debate within as well as between the churches in Jerusalem and Antioch.

The Hellenists with whom Saul of Tarsus (Paul) argued in Jerusalem following his conversion cannot have been the same as those in Acts 6 (Simon, 14-15). They are contrasted with "the believers" of Acts 9:30; they were so strongly opposed to the teaching that Jesus was Lord that they attempted to kill Saul (Acts 9:29). At the least they were Jews who belonged to Greek-language synagogues. M. Simon (12-19) may well be right in suggesting that the term *Hellenistai* was used by Greek-speaking Jews, who were themselves in a literal sense Hellenists, to disparage other Greek-speaking Jews who promoted Greek ways. The nuance of the word may be captured by the English epithets *paganizing* or *godless.* The basic verb *hellēnizein* (see 1.2 above) may also be used in a derogatory sense of aping Greek customs (see Mann, 301-2).

We have further information about two of the named Hellenists, Stephen and Philip. Stephen's fresh review of Israelite history (Acts 7) leads to the conclusion that God's presence cannot be localized in one place; his accusers represented it as a constant theme of Stephen's (Acts 6:13-14) that the *temple would be destroyed. He drew the conclusion that the current Jewish leadership was "stiff-necked and uncircumcised in heart and ear" and disobedient to the law, largely (it seems) because they did not recognize the murdered Jesus as the righteous one who was to come (Acts 7:51-53). Philip's message was similar (Acts 8:5, 12), but he showed he was ready to proclaim the good news to unusual audiences. It seems that, apart from their belief that Jesus was the Messiah, these two Hellenists were on the progressive side of Palestinian Judaism. They both participated in practical service to the disadvantaged, spoke bluntly to those who rejected the Christian message and seized unique opportunities to spread the gospel.

It remains to explain the usage in Acts 11:20. There is evidence of either incomprehension or carelessness in both Codex Alexandrinus and the first hand of Codex Sinaiticus that suggests that their testimony at this point should be set aside. The weight of the manuscripts favors "Hellenists" *(Hellēnistai),* and as B. M. Metzger observes (*A Textual Commentary on the Greek New Testament* [London: United Bible Societies, 1971], 388), there was a temptation for editor or scribe to replace the unfamiliar word *Hellēnistai* with the easy and familiar word *Greeks (Hellēnes),* and no countervailing temptation.

In any case *Hellēnes* might well carry the idea of support for Greek culture, for it would have to be admitted that the related term *Hellēnis* (lit. "Greek woman") has cultural overtones when it is immediately followed by an ethnic description: "a *Hellēnis* of Syro-Phoenician origin" (Mk 7:26). In Acts 11:20 the author modifies his report that those scattered by the persecution that took place over Stephen spoke the word of God only to Jews (Acts 11:19) with the statement that some of them, who originated from Cyprus and Cyrene, came to Antioch and spoke also to the Hellenists. The contrast indicates that the Hellenists in question were not Jews, but they can have been people of non-Greek origin who, like the Jewish Hellenists, favored Greek language and customs. We may conclude that the distinction between the Hellenists and the Hebrews does not simply refer to a difference of language use but to a wider cultural divergence. Perhaps the best critique of alternative views is that by E. Ferguson, who takes the primary meaning of "Hellenists" to be "people who follow the Greek manner of life."

5. Characteristics of the Hellenic Way of Life. The constructed environment obviously had an impact on Jews and early Christians, but one needs to ask also whether Greek social conventions exercised significant influence.

5.1. The Architectural Landscape. Jews and Christians in the eastern half of the Roman Empire in the first century were familiar with the buildings of Hellenistic cities: an open space surrounded by shops and public buildings (the *agora),* a council house *(bouleuterion),* a ceremonial headquarters *(prytaneion),* a theater such as the great one at Ephesus, a range of temples and (under Roman influence) baths. Even in Palestine many cities had these features. Thus Herod's buildings at *Caesarea Maritima (previously Strato's Tower) included a theater and an amphitheater (Josephus *Ant.* 15.9.6 §341; *J.W.* 1.21.8 §415) and at Ascalon baths (Josephus *J.W.* 1.21.11 §422). The coastal cities from Ptolemais to Gaza in the first century "functioned publicly as Greek cities" (Millar 357). Inscriptions show that Gerasa had a gymnasium. The theater at Sepphoris, less than 6 kilometers from Nazareth, was probably built by Herod Antipas. Paul's use of athletic imagery (e.g., 1 Cor 9:24-26) strongly suggests he had experience of the gymnasium if not also of the athletic festivals.

5.2. Women. *Women did not have the vote in any of these cities. Officially they needed a male guardian in order to make legal transactions, unless they had three children. But, especially in elite society, they could be very influential (e.g., Herod's wife, Mk 6:17-28; or the women stirred up against Paul and Barnabas in *Pisidian Antioch, Acts 13:50). Wealthier women provided for Jesus and his team in Galilee "out of their own resources" (Lk 8:1-3; Mk 15:40-41). The women who acted as patrons of Paul (e.g., Lydia in *Philippi, Acts 16:13-15, 40; the mother of Rufus, Rom 16:13) had a parallel in Jewish women *benefactors. Benefaction was a means by which wealthy women generally were given public office and honors, at least in Asia Minor, though the offices were largely nominal (see van Bremen). Presumably poorer women were very restricted in freedom of movement and legal activity.

5.3. Slavery. *Slaves performed domestic tasks in many households as well as working in agriculture, the civil service, industry and mining, where slave gangs were often leased. The institution was part of the social fabric in Palestine as well as elsewhere in the Roman Empire. Hence it is not unexpected that Jesus told parables about slaves, including slaves in charge of other slaves or of the whole estate (e.g., Lk 12:41-48). Paul also was a product of his age, using the legal realities of slavery in argument (e.g., Rom 8:15-17; Gal 4:6-7, 21-24; 4:30—5:1) and maintaining a slave while he was a prisoner (Philem 9-13). But while he and other NT writers enjoined submission on slaves (e.g., Eph 6:5-8; Col 3:22-25; 1 Pet 2:18-21), Paul also made statements (e.g., 1 Cor 7:22; Gal 3:28; Eph 6:8-9) that encouraged later Christians to question the institution of slavery.

5.4. Patronage. The system of *patronage

meant that poorer people were able to feed their families on handouts from wealthy or influential patrons. Paul and his companions were beneficiaries of Publius's *hospitality on Malta (Acts 28:7). This might be considered ritualized or guest friendship, but J. H. Neyrey (in Witherington) has argued that Paul be located in the sociological category designated "the retainer class." In *Thessalonica the Jews employed ruffians from the agora to form a mob and create uproar in the city (Acts 17:5). In Jerusalem a violent demonstration was stirred up against Paul (Acts 21:27-30) in a similar manner to the outcry against Jesus (Mk 15:11-15 par.). Faction leaders could also form an alliance, as did Gentiles and Jews at Iconium in an attempt to assault and kill Paul and Barnabas (Acts 14:5-6).

5.5. Education. Greek *education, or *paideia,* was available in Jewish Palestine from at least the second century B.C. (Hengel 1989, 20, cites Meleager of Gadara and others). Already in the fourth century the Athenian orator Isocrates asserted that "Hellenes" designated those who shared in Greek education, whether or not of Greek descent (*Or.* 4 *Paneg.* 50). In the second century after Christ Dio Chrysostom linked Hellenism closely with *paideia,* though he does recognize that non-Greek teachers can have something to offer (see Bowie).*Lucian of Samosata, on the upper Euphrates, tells of his struggle to gain *paideia* (Swain, 308-12).

Some *letters in the NT fit the pattern of contemporary Greek letters (see the formal openings of Jas 1:1; Acts 15:23; 23:26). But many Pauline letters are longer and more complex, though they have some affinities with the short letters in 2 Maccabees 1:1-10a and 2 Maccabees 1:10b—2:18. Attempts to assimilate the Gospels and Acts either to the Hellenistic *biography, especially that of the holy man, or to the romance show that the parallels are far from close. Moreover, making the genre of the Gospels the basis on which every passage must be interpreted is too rigid (see R. A. Burridge, *What Are the Gospels?* [SNTSMS 70; Cambridge: Cambridge University Press, 1992], esp. chaps. 4 and 10; idem, "About People, by People, for People: Gospel Genre and Audiences," in *The Gospels for All Christians: Rethinking the Gospel Audiences*, ed. R. Bauckham [Grand Rapids, MI: Eerdmans, 1998] 113-45).

5.6. Philosophical Schools. Philosophical training must also have been a feature of higher education, though here the evidence for Palestine is weaker. Qoheleth seems aware of currents in Greek philosophy, such as universalism and individuality (e.g., Eccles 2:18-21; 3:19-22; 4:7-11), and the Epicurean philosopher Philodemus came from Gadara and the *Stoic-inclined Platonist Antiochus from Ascalon. The parallels between the Christian communities founded by Paul and the Hellenistic schools of philosophy—moral exhortation, the respect for the founder, the exegesis of canonical texts (see Nock)—are stronger than the parallels with traditional Roman religion or many of the Oriental cults (L. Alexander in Engberg-Pedersen, 60-83). There are also, as E. A. Judge pointed out *(JRH* 1 [1960] 4-15, 125-37), parallels between the "retinue" of Paul and that of traveling sophists (see 2.1 above), but the latter did not leave behind groups like Paul's that in his view required pastoral care.

H. Maccoby claimed (*Paul and Hellenism* [London: SCM, 1991] esp. chap. 3) that Paul derived a central element in his doctrine of salvation—that the death of Jesus was the indispensable means of atonement for human sin—from the mystery religions (e.g., the violent death of Dionysus or Attis). But Maccoby's view minimizes the strong connections of Paul's doctrine with the Hebrew Bible (whether interpreted in a Hellenized way or not) and seems to entail rejection (H. Maccoby, *The Mythmaker: Paul and the Invention of Christianity* [London: Weidenfeld & Nicolson, 1986] esp. chaps. 6 and 15) of Paul's unambiguous claims that he was born a Jew and had a strictly *Pharisaic training.

5.7. Language. *Greek was already spoken in Palestine in the third century B.C. Inscribed sherds (ostraca), *inscriptions on stone and the Zenon *papyri found in Egypt all testify to this. (The Greek language we are talking about is not classical Greek but the common dialect, based largely on the dialect spoken in Athens, which was spread throughout the East in the Hellenistic period. For a recent survey of documents on perishable materials, written predominantly in Greek, from the Roman provinces of Syria, Mesopotamia, Arabia and Judea see Cotton, Cockle, and Miller). Some scholars have sought to minimize the amount of Greek spoken, but the fact that Greek was used even by those who promoted Hebrew for ideological reasons (e.g., Hasmonean moneyers [see 3.3 above], supporters of the Bar Kokhba revolt) is telling. Josephus may have had an accent in speaking Greek and may have had assistants, but he was undeniably a fluent writer of the language, even in *Antiquities* (pace Feldman, 83, 91, 98-99). We may conclude that by the time of Jesus areas such as Galilee and Judea were trilingual, with *Aramaic the language used for many day-to-day activities, Mishnaic *Hebrew used for religious worship and learned discussion and Greek the normal language for commerce, trade and administration. Some synagogues were presumably for Jews who spoke only Greek (these people would be candidates for Hellenists), while others were for the Hebrews who had only a general familiarity with Greek and spoke Aramaic at home.

It remains controversial (see *NewDocs* 5, 19-23; and *DJG*, Languages of Palestine) whether Jesus spoke Greek as well as Aramaic and presumably Hebrew, but there is no evidence against it. If he did not speak Greek, we have to accept an immediate layer of interpretation in the translation of his sayings into Greek in the Gospels. The Gospel narratives assume that Jesus could converse with Pilate or a centurion from Capernaum. Most probably the language of such interchanges was Greek. Jesus may have adapted a Greek proverb to the Semitic form "Blessed it is . . ." (Acts 20:35). James seems to have been bilingual, for his speech in Acts 15:13-21 must have been intelligible to those who spoke only Greek while his exposition of Amos 9:11-12 betrays understanding of the Hebrew text (so R. Bauckham in Witherington, 156-57, 182-84). Greek was probably Paul's first language, with fluency in Aramaic and Hebrew being attained during his education in Palestine. He was exposed to Greek institutions from birth and knew sufficient Greek *poetry to quote it on occasion (Acts 17:28; 1 Cor 15:33; Tit 1:12).

See also ART AND ARCHITECTURE: GRECO-ROMAN; ALEXANDER THE GREAT; ATHENS; CITIES, GRECO-ROMAN; GREECE AND MACEDON; GREEK OF THE NEW TESTAMENT; HELLENISTIC EGYPT; HELLENISTIC JUDAISM; PHILOSOPHY; POETRY, HELLENISTIC; PTOLEMIES; RELIGION, GRECO-ROMAN; SELEUCIDS AND ANTIOCHIDS; SCHOLARSHIP, GREEK AND ROMAN; SEPTUAGINT/GREEK OLD TESTAMENT; WRITING AND LITERATURE: GRECO-ROMAN.

BIBLIOGRAPHY. C. K. Barrett *The Acts of the Apostles* (2 vols.; ICC; Edinburgh: T & T Clark, 1994, 1998); E. J. Bickerman, *The Jews in the Greek Age* (Cambridge, MA: Harvard University Press, 1988); P. Bilde et al., eds., *Religion and Religious Practice in the Seleucid Kingdom* (Studies in Hellenistic Civilization 1; Aarhus: Aarhus University Press, 1990), esp. essays by N. Hyldahl and S. J. D. Cohen; G. W. Bowersock, *Hellenism in Late Antiquity* (Jerome Lectures 18; Ann Arbor: University of Michigan Press, 1990); E. L. Bowie, "Hellenes and Hellenism in Writers of the Early Second Sophistic," in *ʽΕΛΛΗΝΙΣΜΟΣ: Quelques Jalons pour une Histoire de l'Identité Grecque,* ed. S. Saïd (Leiden: E. J. Brill, 1991) 195-99; R. van Bremen, *The Limits of Participation: Women and Civic Life in the Greek East in the Hellenistic and Roman Periods* (DMAHA 15; Amsterdam: Gieben, 1996); H. J. Cadbury, "The Hellenists," in *The Beginnings of Christianity,* ed. F. J. Foakes Jackson and K. Lake (London: Macmillan, 1933) 1.5:59-60; J. J. Collins, *Between Athens and Jerusalem: Jewish Identity in the Hellenistic Diaspora* (New York: Crossroad, 1986); H. M. Cotton, W. E. H. Cockle and F. G. B. Millar, "The Papyrology of the Roman Near East: A Survey," *JRS* 85 (1995) 214-35; T. Engberg-Pedersen, ed., *Paul in His Hellenistic Context* (Minneapolis: Fortress, 1995), esp. essays by A. F. Segal and L. Alexander; L. H. Feldman, "How Much Hellenism in Jewish Palestine?" *HUCA* 57 (1986) 83-111; E. Ferguson, "The Hellenists in the Book of Acts," *RQ* 12 (1969) 159-80; J. A. Goldstein, "Jewish Acceptance and Rejection of Hellenism," in *Jewish and Christian Self-Definition,* 2: *Aspects of Judaism in the Graeco-Roman Period,* ed. E. P. Sanders et al. (Philadelphia: Fortress, 1981) 64-87 = *Semites, Iranians, Greeks and Romans: Studies in Their Interactions* (BJS 217; Atlanta: Scholars Press, 1990) 3-32; F. C. Grant, *Roman Hellenism and the New Testament* (Edinburgh: Oliver & Boyd, 1962); M. Hadas, *Hellenistic Culture: Fusion and Diffusion* (New York: Columbia University Press, 1959); M. Hengel, *The "Hellenization" of Judaea in the First Century After Christ* (London: SCM, 1989); idem, *Judentum und Hellenismus: Studien zu ihrer Begegnung unter besonderer Berücksichtigung Palästinas bis zur Mitte des 2.Jh.s v.Chr.* (2d ed.; WUNT 10; Tübingen: Mohr Siebeck, 1973), ET *Judaism and Hellenism: Studies in Their Encounter in Palestine During the Early Hellenistic Period* (London: SCM, 1974); C. C. Hill, *Hellenists and Hebrews: Reappraising Division Within the Early Church* (Minneapolis: Fortress, 1992); A. Kuhrt and S. M. Sherwin-White, eds., *Hellenism in the East: The Interaction of Greek and Non-Greek Civilizations from Syria to Central Asia After Alexander* (London: Duckworth, 1987), esp. essays by F. G. B. Millar and M. A. R. Colledge; A. Leontis, *Topographies of Hellenism: Mapping the Homeland* (Ithaca, NY: Cornell University Press, 1995); C. S. Mann, "'Hellenists' and 'Hebrews' in Acts 6:1," in J. Munck, *The Acts of the Apostles,* rev. W. F. Albright and C. S. Mann (AB 31; Garden City, NY: Doubleday, 1967), 301-4; I. H. Marshall, "Palestinian and Hellenistic Christianity: Some Critical Comments," *NTS* 19 (1972-73) 271-87; Y. Meshorer, *Ancient Jewish Coinage* (2 vols.; Dix Hills, NY: Amphora, 1982) vol. 1; F. G. B. Millar, *The Roman Near East 31 B.C.—A.D. 337* (Cambridge, MA: Harvard University Press, 1993), esp. chaps. 6, 8, 10, 13; A. D. Momigliano, *Alien Wisdom: The Limits of Hellenization* (Cambridge: Cambridge University Press, 1975); A. D. Nock, *Conversion: The Old and the New in Religion from Alexander the Great to Augustine of Hippo* (Oxford: Oxford University Press, 1933); E. Schürer, *The History of the Jewish People in the Age of Jesus Christ (175 B.C.—A.D. 135),* rev. and ed. G. Vermes, F. Millar and M. Goodman (2d ed.; 3 vols.; Edinburgh: T & T Clark, 1973-87); J. N. Sevenster, *Do You Know Greek? How Much Greek Could the First Jewish Christians Have Known?* (NovTSup 19; Leiden: E. J. Brill, 1968); M. Simon, *St. Stephen and the Hellenists in the Primitive Church* (The Haskell Lectures 1956; London: Longmans, Green, 1958); R. Smith, *Julian's Gods: Religion and Philosophy in the Thought and Action of Julian the Apostate* (London: Routledge, 1995); F. S. Spencer, *The Portrait of Philip in Acts: A Study of Roles and Relations* (JSNTSup 67; Sheffield: Sheffield Academic Press, 1992); S. Swain, *Hellenism and Empire: Language, Classicism and Power in the Greek World A.D. 50-250* (Oxford: Clarendon Press, 1996); E. Will and C. Orrieux, *Ioudaïsmos-Hellènismos: Essai sur le Judaïsme Judéen à l'Époque Hellénistique* (Nancy: Presses Universitaires, 1986); B. Witherington III, ed., *History, Literature and Society in the Book of Acts* (Cambridge: Cambridge University Press, 1996), esp. essays by C. C. Hill, R. Bauckham and J. H. Neyrey.

G. R. Stanton

HELLENISTIC EGYPT

The unopposed incursion of *Alexander the Great and his army into Egypt in 332 B.C. inaugurated a new phase in the history of Egypt. The midpoint of the period was marked by another encroachment: the calculated Roman involvement and assumption of control after the death of Cleopatra in 30 B.C. The period ended with the beginning of the Byzantine age, generally dated to the reign of Diocletian, A.D. 284-305. Hellenistic Egypt divides into two parts, the first ruled by the *Ptolemies, and the second by the *Romans. The designation *Hellenistic* refers to an era of Greek influence after the time of Alexander the Great.

Hellenistic Egypt was a flourishing kingdom with wide-ranging influence in the Mediterranean world, especially under the first three Ptolemies. Given its proximity and similarities to life in Palestine and given the unusual amount of evidence for its culture, Egypt is an important region for comparison with the Jewish homeland: "The condition of Palestine as depicted in the New Testament strikingly recalls that of Ptolemaic Egypt" (Rostovtzeff, 1:350). This classic statement alludes to the value of the better documented Hellenistic Egypt for understanding the less well documented Palestine. The evidence from the papyri largely preserved in the sands of Egypt—but rarely preserved in Palestine—provides valuable background to the NT.

1. People
2. Sources
3. Language
4. Ptolemaic Egypt
5. Roman Egypt

1. People.

Egypt in the Hellenistic period was impacted by the phenomenon affecting all of the eastern Mediterranean civilizations to some degree: the intrusion of Greek culture and politics. Modern scholarship's assessment of the acculturation of this age has sometimes been exaggerated, but for Egypt the extent of the change was significant. Though the impact of the Greeks and their ways had been felt centuries before Alexander the Great marched his armies throughout and beyond the Persian Empire, when the dust settled after Alexander's untimely death, the Greek and Macedonian invaders were there to stay and to rule. In Egypt, that would last for almost three centuries. And on the heels of the Greek rulers, high-ranking governors known as prefects were sent out from *Rome to rule the land for the next several centuries.

These rulers from Greece and Rome were not the only foreigners present. Many immigrants made their way into the lands of opportunity, especially in the decades following Alexander the Great's conquests, attracted primarily to the cities. Egypt had long appealed to the Greeks for its wealth and mystery, which brought the curious and the fortune seekers to the brave new world. The Ptolemies needed soldiers and skilled artisans as well as people of education, so they sent recruiters to various areas around the Mediterranean, promising good wages, land holdings and in some cases royal patronage. The result is evident in the papyri: people were residing in Egypt from more than two hundred places outside Egypt, including Palestine. This mixture of peoples and composite of cultures (Greek plus native) gives this period in the history of the Mediterranean world the title *Hellenistic* (*see* Hellenism). The concept of Hellenization, however, can easily be misunderstood. It was a process that was more incidental than intentional, to the extent that substantial mergers of culture even took place. The notion of the people of the Near East being mesmerized by the wonderful culture from Hellas (i.e., Greece) is a carryover of an earlier prejudice among scholars in favor of the learning and literature of the classical age. While *Hellenization* can be a misleading term, it can also be misleading to subsume these six centuries of life in Egypt under the single heading *Hellenistic.* For there are ample exceptions to a continuity of culture throughout the Greco-Roman period.

2. Sources.

Egypt is the best documented of the Hellenistic kingdoms, and in one sense Ptolemaic and Roman Egypt are better documented than are any of the ancient Mediterranean civilizations. That is attributed to the unique topography and climate that allowed extensive though uneven samples of the day-to-day written records to be preserved in moisture-starved sand. Places where flooding did not occur—such as the edges of the desert on the fringes of the Nile Valley—were especially conducive to the preservation of papyri (*see* Inscriptions and Papyri).

Papyrus was the ancient paper of the Mediterranean world, used everywhere for almost everything that was put in writing—from great works of literature to school exercises, from government records to personal love letters. Judging by the extant papyri, the government created the majority of the paperwork: laws and regulations, tax lists, internal correspondence. In addition the people needed proofs of ownership and records of various transactions. These papyri are called documentary, in contrast to the literary papyri, which contain poetry, history, Scripture, and so on. The documentary papyri are the unofficial and unintentional records of the past that happened to be preserved, usually just small snatches of information about individuals and about specific circumstances—all of which must be painstakingly deciphered and pieced together to get any sense of the whole. But they expose everything from the earthiness of people's personal lives to the often high-handed bureaucracy of the central offices.

It would have been rare for anyone living at that time not to be mentioned somewhere in a written record, except perhaps in the case of a newborn who died before its existence was recorded. The third century B.C., particularly the reigns of Ptolemy II and Ptolemy III, has an unusually large number of extant papyri, partly because of some long government documents (e.g., the revenue laws) and because of the files of *Zenon papyri found at Philadelphia.

Papyrus was the primary writing material but not the only one. Others included wooden tablets, ostraca (pieces of broken pottery), pieces of bone, parchment (carefully prepared animal skins) and stone—the last two generally used for things intended to be more lasting and/or more public. All these written records of the daily lives of the Egyptians do not, however, require a conclusion of a high degree of *literacy. For the majority of people, writing was a secondhand experience—dependent on professional scribes to create the document, in some cases with the author's signature included at the end. Even so, probably every household had some written documents in their possession, whether or not they could read them.

In addition to the papyrological sources, which are largely unique to Egypt, the material remains and archaeological finds have provided much to enhance knowledge of the region, true for the other Hellenistic kingdoms as well. Major museums now house significant Hellenistic artifacts from excavations. Numismatic evidence (*coinage) and epigraphic evidence (*inscriptions) provide important clues to chronology, the economy and the affairs of government. Unfortunately, there are no extant literary sources specifically written as histories of Ptolemaic or Roman Egypt (except for a few fragments). The history of Hellenistic Egypt must be carefully patched together from authors whose works are fragmentary, flawed in method or heavily biased, such as Polybius and Diodorus Siculus and Justin's abridgment of Pompeius Trogus; and Jewish authors, such as *Philo and *Josephus. An interesting exception to this is Callixenus's description of the grand procession of Ptolemy II, quoted in Athenaeus.

3. Language.

Throughout the Hellenistic kingdoms, there were native languages and there was *Greek, the universal language. The same had been true in the Persian Empire, where the communication barrier among disparate cultures was solved by speaking *Aramaic. In the Roman Empire, Greek remained the common language, though Latin was also used, but primarily only in the army and politics. In Egypt, resolving the language barrier was up to the Egyptians: if they wanted to communicate with the government, they needed to learn Greek. But alongside Greek, the Egyptians continued to speak and write their own language. When written it could be in one of three forms: hieroglyphic, hieratic and demotic, the last reflecting the final stage in the shift from a script based on pictograms to one based on an alphabet. In the Hellenistic age, the Egyptians still occasionally used the hieroglyphic script for special circumstances, and in the religious community they often used hieratic, a derivative from hieroglyphic. But the common form of Egyptian in use was demotic. The Rosetta Stone, a trilingual inscription from 196 B.C. with the same text in hieroglyphic, demotic and Greek, provided the key to deciphering the ancient hieroglyphs. Though numerous demotic papyri are extant, the data available on them are only recently being combined with the data from the Greek papyri to give a fuller picture of life in Hellenistic Egypt.

Among the papyri, Greek and demotic are the most common languages, with Greek outnumbering Demotic by a large ratio. But there are others. As a result of a Jewish military colony stationed at Elephantine in Upper Egypt near the close of the Persian period, there is a group of Aramaic papyri. Very few Latin papyri have been found. In the third century, Egyptians began using Coptic, a derivative of demotic but written largely with the Greek alphabet. Until after the Roman period, the only Coptic papyri that have been found are Christian.

4. Ptolemaic Egypt.

From the death of Alexander in 323 B.C. to the death of Cleopatra in 30 B.C., Egypt was under the control of a single dynasty, the Ptolemies (though Ptolemy I did not officially take the title of king until 305 B.C.). Of the Hellenistic kingdoms, Ptolemaic Egypt and Seleucid Asia were the great powers, and both showed evidence of territorial ambitions. Unfortunately for Palestine, the area the two superpowers most often clashed over was Palestine, resulting in six major wars, with most of the battles fought in this quasi-buffer zone between the two kingdoms. For more than a century Egypt maintained control of Palestine, and the papyri that reflect the activities of Egyptian agents there provide important insights into Palestine in the third century B.C.

The Ptolemaic success in maximizing Egypt's natural resources and manpower was achieved with remarkable speed, a still imponderable accomplishment given their recent arrival in a strange land. Within fifty years, the economy in Egypt was strong, the land was producing more-than-ample crops, the army was achieving success, the cities were bustling with activity, intellectual life was expanding—but things were about as good as they would get during the Ptolemaic period. During the second century, things deteriorated rapidly. Between 245 and 50 B.C. there were at least ten native revolts against the government, indicative of internal problems. The quality and numbers of Greek soldiers were declining, making native draftees essential to the protection of the state. Externally, Egypt was losing control of valuable territories, such as the loss of Palestine to the Seleucid kingdom in 200 B.C.

When the Seleucid king Antiochus IV successfully invaded Egypt and set up a governor in Memphis in 168 B.C., the Romans came to Egypt's rescue, though it was largely for their own self-defense. It marked a growing involvement of Rome in affairs in Egypt, from protection to managing financial affairs, even to becoming legal guardian for the young Ptolemy XIII. Cleopatra VII, the last and most capable of the end of the Ptolemaic dynasty, became intricately involved with Julius Caesar and Mark Antony, leading to Octavian's takeover of Egypt after defeating Cleopatra and Antony in a naval battle (*see* Roman Emperors).

Key to the Ptolemaic success, especially of

the early Ptolemies, was the careful management of all aspects of the economy. From banking to agriculture, from imports to exports, from mercenaries to markets, the Ptolemies sought to make the most of Egypt's potential. A carefully monitored but independently operated system of taxation was very effective at generating the revenue the government needed. But the Ptolemies left much of the local culture intact. Separate legal systems—one for the natives and one for the Greeks—encouraged the Egyptians to maintain their identity, though it also gave favored status to the Greeks. The Ptolemies were tolerant and supportive of native religious practices and the temples. In addition to being Greek rulers, the Ptolemaic dynasty portrayed themselves as Egyptian Pharaohs.

One of the remarkable accomplishments of the Ptolemies was the city of *Alexandria. Founded by Alexander the Great, it was not only the capital and principal port of the Ptolemaic kingdom but also quickly became the intellectual capital of the ancient world, with its library and museum (*see* Alexandrian Library; Alexandrian Scholarship). The monumental lighthouse erected at the entrance to the port was considered one of the seven wonders of the world. Within a century of the founding of the city, Alexandria had become the greatest city of all the countries surrounding the Mediterranean. It maintained that position until it was superseded by Rome.

A defining factor of life in Hellenistic Egypt was ethnicity. If you were Greek or Macedonian, you were privileged—in the tax system and socially. With the swelling population of immigrants who were primarily from the Greek world, this privileged class was growing rapidly. If you were Egyptian, you were second-class and likely exploited. There would be no chance for upward mobility except by *marriage or exceptional ability in the Greek language. And the only examples known of intermarriage were of Greek men with Egyptian women. Some of the natives solved this issue of identity by taking on both nationalities. Double grave markers for the same family—one in Greek using Greek names and titles and the other in hieroglyphics using Egyptian names and titles—illustrate the increasing evidence for dual identities (Bagnall 1995, 18-20). A debated issue among scholars is the extent to which the different ethnicities cooperated and interacted with one another. Was it coexistence or coalescence (Lewis 1986, 4)? D. J. Thompson's careful study of Ptolemaic Memphis clearly supports the latter.

5. Roman Egypt.
From the victory of Augustus over Antony and Cleopatra and annexation of Egypt to Roman control, it was clear that the valley of the Nile would become a vital part of the success and prosperity of the early empire (*see* Roman East). The changes the Romans introduced affected many aspects of life. Though some of the terminology and functions of the former Ptolemaic administrative structure were carried over, on the whole the similarities were more superficial than substantial. The new rulers granted full ownership to land that the previous administration had granted use of only in exchange for military service. Thus in the second and third centuries large estates became common, contributing to class distinctions between the aristocracy and the peasants. The more significant cultural division, however, was between the primarily Greek-speaking residents of the cities and the primarily Egyptian-speaking residents of the villages.

Part of the Roman administrative strategy (*see* Roman Administration) to see Egypt achieve its potential was to institute an extensive system of liturgies—public services to supervise agriculture and public works, to maintain dikes, to collect taxes. These liturgies were supposedly voluntary, but in that they were tied to land ownership, they were more often obligatory. The Romans also adapted to Egypt a form of local government common to Hellenistic cities in the eastern provinces, creating town councils to rule local affairs. The liturgies together with the self-governance of the cities had advantages and disadvantages, but in general the papyri reveal a tendency to dissatisfaction in the populace. Nevertheless, Egypt's potential for agricultural productivity reached its optimum in the Roman period, and the arrival of Alexandrian shipments of grain in the port of Rome were essential to the strength of the empire's economy. Whereas under the Ptolemies the revenue generated by the productivity of Egypt largely remained in the country, under Roman rule the fiscal interests of Rome determined what happened in Egypt, and the wealth of Egypt was exploited by the emperor.

One of many problems that surfaced during

the Roman period was the large Jewish population (*see* Diaspora; *see DLNTD,* Diaspora Judaism). Jews had been immigrating into Egypt for centuries, particularly during the Ptolemaic period, making Egypt the largest concentration of Jews living outside their homeland. The best documented place and time period for the Jewish presence is first-century Alexandria, with reportedly two of the five quarters of the city being exclusively Jewish, plus other Jews living throughout the city. Like native Egyptians, Jews were not allowed to be citizens, though they could have their own legal and political systems. For reasons not always clear, the Romans initiated vicious pogroms against the Jewish community, resulting in much loss of life and appeals to the emperor. By the end of the second century the Jewish presence in Alexandria had all but disappeared.

The relationship between the Jewish community and the growing Christian presence beginning in the middle of the first century is largely unknown. Though Christianity in Egypt would later tend to be unorthodox, the evidence suggests that the early Christian community in Egypt was similar to Christians living in other areas around the Mediterranean—characterized by rapid growth, theological diversity and persecution.

In the third century the Roman Empire began to show signs of weakness: the costs of government were exceeding revenues, the gap between upper and lower classes was increasingly wider and the frontiers were more vulnerable. The result was internal splintering complicated by external threats. In the fourth century those problems were less acute, but the era known as Hellenistic Egypt had come to a close.

See also ALEXANDRIA; ALEXANDRIAN LIBRARY; ALEXANDRIAN SCHOLARSHIP; HELLENISM; PTOLEMIES; ROMAN EAST.

BIBLIOGRAPHY. R. S. Bagnall, *Egypt in Late Antiquity* (Princeton, NJ: Princeton University Press, 1993); idem, *Reading Papyri, Writing Ancient History* (New York: Routledge, 1995); R. S. Bagnall and B. W. Frier, *The Demography of Roman Egypt* (Studies in Population, Economy and Society in Past Time 23; Cambridge: Cambridge University Press, 1994); R. S. Bianchi, *Cleopatra's Egypt: Age of the Ptolemies* (New York: Brooklyn Museum, 1988); A. K. Bowman, *Egypt After the Ptolemies: 332 B.C.—A.D. 642 from Alexander to the Arab Conquest* (Berkeley and Los Angeles: University of California Press, 1986); S. M. Burstein, "The Hellenistic Age," in *Ancient History: Recent Work and New Directions* (Publications of the Association of Ancient Historians 5; Claremont, CA: Regina, 1997); P. M. Fraser, *Ptolemaic Alexandria* (Oxford: Clarendon Press, 1972); P. Green, *Alexander to Actium: The Historical Evolution of the Hellenistic Age* (Berkeley and Los Angeles: University of California Press, 1990); A. Kasher, *The Jews in Hellenistic and Roman Egypt: The Struggle for Equal Rights* (Tübingen: Mohr Siebeck, 1985); N. Lewis, *Greeks in Ptolemaic Egypt: Case Studies in the Social History of the Hellenistic World* (Oxford: Clarendon Press, 1986); idem, *Life in Egypt Under Roman Rule* (Oxford: Clarendon Press, 1983); J. M. Modrzejewski, *The Jews of Egypt from Rameses II to Emperor Hadrian* (Philadelphia: Jewish Publication Society of America, 1995); B. A. Pearson, "Earliest Christianity in Egypt: Some Observations," in *The Roots of Egyptian Christianity,* ed. B. A. Pearson and J. E. Goehring (Philadelphia: Fortress, 1986); S. B. Pomeroy, *Women in Hellenistic Egypt: From Alexander to Cleopatra* (New York: Schocken, 1984); D. Rathbone, *Economic Rationalism and Rural Society in Third-Century A.D. Egypt: The Heroninos Archive and the Appianus Estate* (Cambridge: Cambridge University Press, 1991); M. Rostovtzeff, *The Social and Economic History of the Hellenistic World* (3 vols.; Oxford: Clarendon Press, 1941); A. E. Samuel, *From Athens to Alexandria: Hellenism and Social Goals in Ptolemaic Egypt* (SH 26; Louvain, 1983); idem, *The Shifting Sands of History: Interpretations of Ptolemaic Egypt* (Publications of the Association of Ancient Historians 2; Lanham, MD: University Press of America, 1989); D. J. Thompson, *Memphis Under the Ptolemies* (Princeton, NJ: Princeton University Press, 1988).

B. Sandy

HELLENISTIC JUDAISM

"Hellenistic Judaism" is a modern designation for the various forms of ancient Jewish religion and life that can be distinguished in some way by their involvement with the phenomenon of *Hellenism. Hellenism refers to the multiform interactions of Greek civilization with the cultures of innumerable indigenous populations in the eastern Mediterranean basin and the ancient Near East, beginning in the late fourth century B.C. (in the wake of *Alexander the Great's conquests) and extending into the first few centuries of the Christian era, the time of Roman imperial rule throughout the Mediterranean world. As such, over its long history Hellenism showed signs of Greek, Roman and native influence, though it was in fact a dynamic convergence of old and new elements, one that varied from place to place and was constantly developing over time. The terms *Hellenized* and *Hellenization* can be used to describe the different processes by which members of the indigenous populations assimilated to varying degrees the social patterns and practices that emerged from this confluence, including especially the use of the Greek language, or *koine,* and the conventions of *literature, *philosophy, *religion, *art, *education, government and technology associated with the cultural legacy of ancient Greece.

1. Judaism and Hellenism
2. Palestinian Judaism and Hellenistic Judaism
3. Varieties of Hellenization
4. The Status of Jewish Communities in Greco-Roman Society

1. Judaism and Hellenism.
It appears that Jewish people, dispersed as they were throughout the ancient world, were unavoidably caught up in the forces of Hellenism, and, like other populations, their reaction to these forces was complex. The available historical information, taken as a whole, testifies to a wide-ranging and fluid exchange between Hellenism and Judaism during this time; rather than invariably resisting each other in some sort of mutual ideological or cultural antagonism, it seems that Judaism and Hellenism frequently interacted in many different spheres and with many different results.

To be sure, Jewish people shared a number of essential commitments and characteristics that distinguished them from their non-Jewish neighbors: a common religious, ethnic and historical heritage, written and oral traditions preserving that heritage and different institutions embodying that heritage, such as circumcision, *sabbath observance and the *synagogue. No doubt allegiance to this heritage could create certain social boundaries for Jews, certain impediments to full participation in Hellenism, especially since many Hellenistic practices proceeded according to polytheistic religious assumptions that were offensive to Jewish sensibilities.

At the same time, many Jews of the era spoke *Greek and learned the elements of Hellenistic culture, some out of political or economic necessity, some as a means of social mobility and others in the interests of Jewish apologetic. Like other indigenous peoples, Jews could both accept and reject elements of the host culture, all the while preserving their own heritage and identity, exploring ways to be both Jewish and Greek. On the Hellenistic scene, coexistence and mutual influence were the norm for the majority of Jewish people, not self-isolation or confrontation. This would have been in keeping with the spirit of Hellenism, where the distinguishing aspects of one's particular beliefs were for the most part expressed and interpreted in an environment of religious pluralism and innovation.

The example par excellence of this development in Judaism would be *Philo of *Alexandria. An elite, educated, urban Jew of the first century A.D., Philo in his impressive corpus exhibits a mastery of the concepts of Hellenistic philosophy, especially *Platonism, and the methods of Hellenistic literary interpretation, especially allegory. His chief interest, though, was not to promote the achievements of Greek learning but to usurp them, to use them to show how Judaism was "the best philosophy," the purest expression of piety and virtue, conceived in terms comprehensible to any Hellenized person, Jewish or otherwise (Philo *Virt.* 65). Even as he moved with confidence in the highest levels of Greco-Roman society, Philo remained fiercely loyal to the Jewish community and convinced of the Torah's sacred and binding authority. In all this he exemplifies how Hellenistic Jews went about determining their identity as part of a critical dialogue with ideas and methods appropriate to their Greco-Roman context; this is the manner in which they established the plausibility of their traditions, seeking to cultivate both the respect of outsiders and the allegiance of insiders in a changing world.

2. Palestinian Judaism and Hellenistic Judaism.
To the extent that Jews residing in both Palestine and the *Diaspora, especially those in the Mediterranean Diaspora, lived during the Hellenistic era and were part of the Hellenistic world, all were in some sense Hellenistic, though important differences between these two broad geographic areas can be noted. Diaspora Jews,

who belonged to communities dominated by Hellenized Gentiles, were under constant pressure to participate in Hellenistic life, and it stands to reason that our most important evidence for Hellenized interpretations of Judaism originates from Diaspora regions like Egypt and Asia Minor (*see* Jewish Communities in Asia Minor). Palestinian Jews, owing to the different social and political realities of the Jewish homeland, were less exposed to the forces of Hellenism, less likely to interact with Hellenized people, and *Hebrew and *Aramaic functioned as the vernacular for the large majority of the population, which was overwhelmingly Jewish.

These differences, however, should not be overestimated, especially in our assessment of the dynamics of Jewish religious thought during this era. Indeed, the distinction, once commonly drawn by scholars, between Palestinian Judaism (i.e., Hebrew-speaking, *rabbinic or orthodox Judaism) and Hellenistic Judaism (i.e., marginal forms of Judaism corrupted by Greek influence) has lost much of its value in the light of recent reevaluations of Jewish history and literature. There have been at least two important and related reasons for this development.

It is evident that from even early on in the Hellenistic period and on all levels of society Palestine felt the impact of Hellenistic culture and that this impact continued, gradually expanding, under *Ptolemaic, *Seleucid, Hasmonean and Roman rule. The work of M. Hengel in particular has conclusively demonstrated this fact. In his book on the Hellenization of Judea, for instance, Hengel has assembled extensive archaeological, inscriptional and numismatic data pointing to the presence of a multilingual society in Palestine during the first century A.D., where Greek played an important role alongside Hebrew and Aramaic. In connection with this, we know of some thirty Greek cities in Palestine during this time, some (like Gadara) centers of Hellenistic intellectual life, others (like *Caesarea Maritima) with substantial Jewish communities. And even in *Jerusalem and its environs Hengel concludes that "we have to assume an independent Jewish Hellenistic culture," consisting of Jewish families who spoke Greek as their primary language, representing approximately 10 to 20 percent of the total population.

It comes as no surprise, then, that the impact of Greek culture is discernible also in Palestinian Jewish religious literature. The didactic poem *On the Jews,* for example, authored by a certain Jew named Theodotus, was probably written in Palestine during the late second century B.C. (preserved in Eusebius *Praep. Ev.* 9.22). Here we have a biblically inspired epic poem (*see* Poetry, Hellenistic) in Greek hexameters, rendered in a superior Greek style and with apparent knowledge of Greek epics like Homer's *Iliad,* intended for a Jewish audience, justifying Jewish aggression against *Samaria (under John Hyrcanus, a Jewish leader of the Hasmonean era) and urging acceptance of the Jewish law. The text presupposes a reading audience that would appreciate a typical and sophisticated form of Greek literature, even as it serves as an expression of Jewish nationalistic propaganda and insists on the need to uphold distinctively Jewish practices, such as circumcision and the prohibition of exogamy. In this and many other cases, the appropriateness of the distinction (at least as traditionally conceived) between Palestinian Jewish literature and Hellenistic Jewish literature would appear to be suspect.

Furthermore, the forms of Judaism accessible to us are far too diverse ideologically and stylistically and overlap in too many complex ways to be neatly classified according to one of these two categories, Palestinian or Hellenistic. Here it needs to be emphasized that the distinguishing aspects of Jewish identity during this era were never expressed with respect to anything like a normative Judaism. Jews exercised considerable freedom in terms of how they defined their Jewish heritage, how they determined appropriate allegiance to that heritage and how they negotiated the relationship between that heritage and Hellenism. This was possible in part because there was nothing like a generally recognized authority to establish standards of belief and practice for all Jewish communities. As a consequence, there was nothing univocal or monolithic about Jewish thought during this time, something that the simplistic distinction between Hellenistic Judaism and Palestinian Judaism does not adequately address. This diversity was due in no small part to the various ways that Jewish people interacted with the forces of Hellenism.

3. Varieties of Hellenization.

The different manifestations of Hellenization that we discover in ancient Judaism correspond to the different avenues available to Jewish people for manifesting their identity, including literary, religious, political, economic and artistic forms of expression. The Jewish varieties of Hellenization include diverse efforts to reconfigure Judaism according to Hellenistic categories, to capitalize on the resources of Hellenistic civilization for Jewish purposes or to carve out a place for Jewish people in a world in which they were often socially and politically vulnerable. The four examples that follow will give some idea of the various ways in which these efforts could proceed.

3.1. The Septuagint. Among the earliest and most influential projects of Hellenistic Judaism was the *Septuagint, or LXX, the Greek rendering of the Hebrew Bible, compiled mostly in the third and second centuries B.C. Especially for Diaspora Jews, who knew little or no Hebrew, the LXX would have been accorded the same sacred authority for Jewish life and worship as the original; for them, the host of Greek terms, concepts and expressions employed in the LXX were understood as biblical. While the lion's share of the LXX's contents were, naturally enough, translated in the Diaspora, at least a few of its texts (e.g., Esther) may instead be of Palestinian origin. Indeed, according to the legend preserved in the *Epistle of *Aristeas* (a Greek text of the late second century B.C., possibly penned by a Jewish member of the Ptolemaic court), the LXX as a whole was translated by seventy-two fully bilingual Judean elders, working in Alexandria at the behest of Ptolemy II Philadelphus. While the translation on the whole is quite literal, there are numerous points where the LXX appears to diverge from its source (e.g., in Proverbs) or where significant additions have been made (e.g., Daniel). We also discover in the LXX a number of new, *apocryphal books added to the Scriptures, some, like the *Wisdom of Solomon, composed originally in Greek, others, like 1 *Maccabees, translated into Greek from Hebrew originals. All of this suggests something of the fluidity of the biblical canon at this time.

3.2. Herod. The Jewish king Herod the Great (reigned 37-4 B.C.) was a tireless agent of Hellenization whose manner of rule was practically indistinguishable from that of other Hellenistic monarchs, with whom he frequently fostered political and economic ties. Herod used purely Greek inscriptions for Jewish coins and weights and sponsored numerous Hellenistic building projects, including impressive temples to his political patron, the emperor Augustus. Even improvements to the *Temple Mount made during his tenure were in the style of Hellenistic architecture, part of broader efforts to transform Jerusalem into a center of Greco-Roman culture. In the same vein, Herod welcomed Greek intellectuals, politicians and artisans to live at the royal court (most notably the Peripatetic philosopher and historian Nicolaus of Damascus) and encouraged Greek education among the Judean upper classes. All of this Hellenizing activity was tightly bound up with the national and religious identity of Judaism, as a way of advancing Jewish interests on an international stage. These policies were continued under Herod's sons, especially Philip and Herod Antipas (*see* Herods).

3.3. Josephus. In the life and writings of *Josephus we have in a single individual a bridge between the social contexts and conflicting loyalties of a Judean priest of the *Pharisaic party and a privileged, Greek-speaking client of the Roman imperial household. Captured while leading Jewish revolutionary forces in Galilee during the Jewish-Roman War (A.D. 66-70; *see* Jewish Wars with Rome), he defected to the Roman side and assisted his former adversaries during the siege of Jerusalem. He was subsequently granted Roman *citizenship and provided with a pension while residing in his adopted home, the imperial capital. Two of his major works, the *Jewish War* and the *Jewish Antiquities,* both written in Greek, are modeled after the style of Hellenistic historians like Polybius and Dionysius of Halicarnassus. Published for a broad reading public, these writings have mixed aims. Josephus wants to exonerate the Romans from responsibility for the war or for the devastation that it caused in Palestine, especially the destruction of the *temple, arguing that they were simply reluctant instruments of divine providence. Simultaneously he wants to sway Roman opinion in favor of Jewish rights, to elicit sympathy for the plight of the Jewish people and to accommodate Jews to the postwar political situation, in order to abet some kind of reconciliation between the two groups.

3.4. Dura-Europos. In the city of Dura-Europos a major synagogue has been excavated, originally built in the mid-third century A.D. on the Roman frontier with Parthia and decorated with numerous painted and mosaic images. While all the murals on the sanctuary walls contain biblical subject matter of some type and the message of certain pictures even conveys a critique of pagan idolatry, the Jewish community that built and used this structure found fit also to incorporate symbols and motifs derived from pagan religious art, including representations of pagan deities. This fascinating artistic fusion suggests among other things that the second commandment's rejection of iconic cult could be variously interpreted by Hellenistic Jews. While the significance of the Dura synagogue for our understanding of Jewish worship continues to be much debated, the paintings seem to represent a form of religious expression that differs not only from contemporaneous rabbinic Judaism but also from forms known to us from other Hellenized Jewish sources (e.g., Philo *Rer. Div. Her.* 169).

4. The Status of Jewish Communities in Greco-Roman Society.

As with the Jewish response to Hellenism, it is difficult to generalize about the response of pagan, Hellenized society to the Jews and their religion. Anti-Judaism, like Hellenism itself, was largely an urban phenomenon; our main examples for violent anti-Jewish outbreaks, for instance, come from major metropolises like Alexandria and Rome. The refusal of Jewish communities to renounce their own customs and commitments sometimes meant that they could not take their fair share of civic responsibilities or recognize the pagan religious foundations of civic life (*see* Civic Cults). This must have been a source of irritation and resentment among the Gentile majorities, who took these responsibilities and foundations seriously. A corpus of anti-Jewish propaganda developed in the Greco-Roman world, libeling Jews as misanthropic and lazy people with peculiar, superstitious practices and questioning their loyalty to the state (e.g., Tacitus *Hist.* 5.1-13).

At the same time, in many Hellenistic circles the Jews were highly regarded, even being depicted as philosophers preserving a special legacy of wisdom comparable to that of the Greeks (e.g., Josephus *Ag. Ap.* 1.161-212 §22). The monotheism and high moral standards observed by the Jewish community were admired by many non-Jews, especially by educated people, as was the antiquity of their religious traditions. *Moses in particular won respect among Gentiles as a valiant founder figure and virtuous lawgiver (e.g., Diodorus Siculus *Bib. Hist.* 40.3). There is ample evidence for pagan sympathizers and supporters of Judaism during this time, for whom different forms of partial attachment to the Jewish community were available; stories of pagan converts to Judaism are not uncommon either (e.g., Juvenal *Sat.* 14.96-106). Elements of the Jewish way of life (e.g., some manner of sabbath observance) also appear to have enjoyed a degree of popularity in pagan communities (e.g., Josephus *Ag. Ap.* 2.282 §38).

In this context it should be noted that the rights of Jews to follow their "ancestral customs" were generally protected by local and imperial authorities. There is substantial though scattered documentation that in some cities at least (e.g., *Ephesus) Jews could win for themselves certain legal privileges, though these could be subject to subsequent modification or revocation (e.g., Josephus *Ant.* 14.213-264 §§8-25). They might, for example, enjoy exemption from civic religious duties or from military service; they might also have the right to hold communal meetings and meals, to adjudicate internal legal disputes, to own sacred property (officially recognized and protected as such) and to collect, hold and transport financial contributions (e.g., for the annual temple tax). Similarly, some Jews were both Roman citizens and citizens of their own cities. In some places (e.g., Berenice), Jews were granted permission to incorporate as a *politeuma* or something similar, a semiautonomous civic association. All this suggests the extent to which Jews were not only integrated into Hellenistic political culture but also able to play an influential and public role in the civic life of many of the major urban centers of the Hellenistic world.

See also ALEXANDRIA; ARISTEAS, EPISTLE OF; DIASPORA JUDAISM; EDUCATION: JEWISH AND GRECO-ROMAN; HELLENISM; HERODS; JEWISH COMMUNITIES IN ASIA MINOR; JEWISH HISTORY: GREEK PERIOD; JOSEPHUS; PHILO; PROSELYTISM AND GODFEARERS; ROMAN EAST; SEPTUAGINT/GREEK OLD TESTAMENT; WRITING AND LITERATURE: JEWISH.

BIBLIOGRAPHY. R. Arav, *Hellenistic Palestine* (Oxford: BAR, 1989); J. M. G. Barclay, *Jews in the Mediterranean Diaspora* (Edinburgh: T & T Clark, 1996); E. Bickerman, *The Jews in the Greek Age* (Cambridge, MA: Harvard University Press, 1988); G. Boccaccini, *Middle Judaism: Jewish Thought 300 B.C. to 200 C.E.* (Minneapolis: Fortress, 1991); J. J. Collins, *Between Athens and Jerusalem: Jewish Identity in the Hellenistic Diaspora*

(New York: Crossroad, 1986); W. D. Davies and L. Finkelstein, eds., *The Cambridge History of Judaism, 2: The Hellenistic Age* (Cambridge: Cambridge University Press, 1989); L. H. Feldman, *Jew and Gentile in the Ancient World* (Princeton, NJ: Princeton University Press, 1993); E. R. Goodenough, *Jewish Symbols in the Greco-Roman Period* (13 vols.; New York: Pantheon, 1953-68); L. L. Grabbe, *Judaism from Cyrus to Hadrian* (2 vols.; Minneapolis: Fortress, 1992); M. Hengel, *The "Hellenization" of Judea in the First Century After Christ* (London: SCM, 1989); idem, *Judaism and Hellenism* (London: SCM, 1974); A. Kuhrt and S. Sherwin-White, eds., *Hellenism in the East* (London: Duckworth, 1987); A. Momigliano, *Alien Wisdom: The Limits of Hellenization* (Cambridge: Cambridge University Press, 1975); J. Neusner, *Jerusalem and Athens: The Congruity of Talmudic and Classical Philosophy* (Leiden: E. J. Brill, 1997); G. W. E. Nickelsburg, *Jewish Literature Between the Bible and the Mishnah* (Philadelphia: Fortress, 1981); L. V. Rutgers, *The Jews in Late Ancient Rome* (Leiden: E. J. Brill, 1995); E. P. Sanders, ed., *Jewish and Christian Self-Definition, 2: Aspects of Judaism in the Greco-Roman Period* (Philadelphia: Fortress, 1981); E. Schürer, *The History of the Jewish People in the Age of Jesus Christ,* rev. and ed. by G. Vermes, F. Millar and M. Goodman (3 vols.; Edinburgh: T & T Clark, 1973-87); E. M. Smallwood, *The Jews Under Roman Rule* (2d ed.; Leiden: E. J. Brill, 1981); M. E. Stone, ed., *Jewish Writings of the Second Temple Period* (CRINT 2.2; Assen: Van Gorcum; Philadelphia: Fortress, 1984); V. Tcherikover, *Hellenistic Civilization and the Jews* (Philadelphia: Jewish Publication Society, 1961); V. Tcherikover and A. Fuks, eds., *Corpus Papyrorum Judaicarum* (3 vols.; Cambridge, MA: Harvard University Press, 1957-64).

W. T. Wilson

HERMETICISM

Hermeticism is closely associated with the *Hermetica,* or Hermetic literature, preserved in manuscripts of the fourteenth century and later. This literature includes materials that are astrological, magical, philosophical and religious. Scholars think that some of this material may clarify the background of certain themes and writings in the NT.

1. Hermetic Literature
2. Hermeticism, New Testament and Early Christianity
3. Hermetic and Jewish Literature

1. Hermetic Literature.

1.1. Definition and Origins. Hermetic literature is that which claims the authorship of Hermes Trismegistos—Hermes the three-times great, also identified with the Egyptian god Thoth, who in turn is identified with the Greek god Asclepius. Interest in this literature in late antiquity was great and widespread: "The books of Hermes . . . enjoyed wide dissemination in the Roman empire, while their doctrine typified and combined the Roman world's literary and religious orientalism, and its yearning for revealed knowledge" (Fowden, 213); and the appeal of this literature continued to be felt throughout the following centuries, culminating in Hermetic influence in Renaissance thought (see Yates).

The content of this literature is diverse, and its mythological origins complex. In the Byzantine period, when Hermetic scholarship was perhaps at its height, it was thought that "there were two gods named Hermes. The first was Thoth, who originally carved the sacred writings on stelae in hieroglyphics. The second Hermes, named Trismegistus, was the son of Agathodaimon and the father of [the Egyptian god] Tat; after the flood he transferred the carvings to books, which came to be translated from Egyptian to Greek" (Copenhaver, xvi). However, despite this obvious Egyptian connection, the *Hermetica,* for the bulk of the twentieth century, were thought to be of Greek extraction, with "very few Egyptian elements beyond the personnel" (Nock, 1:v). This was largely the result of the immense influence of A.-J. Festugière and A. D. Nock (cf. Festugière 1949-54 and multiple essays in Nock), whose important Budé critical edition and French translation of the *Hermetica* (see below), together with hundreds of essays on the topic, set the tone for scholarship on the *Hermetica* for several decades. The continuing influence and importance of their work (and others who followed the Greek line) is not to be underplayed.

The early theory of Reitzenstein (1904) that, rather than simply *seeming* to have an Egyptian setting, the *Hermetica* were actually of Egyptian origin was dismissed as "Egyptomania" (Zielinski). However, it is now widely thought that the *Hermetica* stem from a Hellenistic- or Greco-Egyptian context. This is in part because of the discovery in codex VI of the Nag Hammadi codices (*see* Gnosticism) of several Hermetic writings, which suddenly put Hermetic writings not only in Egypt at an early date, but also written in *Egyptian*. Coupled with this is the evidence, in Hellenistic Egypt, of devotion to Thoth/Hermes in keeping with the texts which have come down to us as the *Hermetica* (cf. Ray; Copenhaver, xiii-xvi). Although support for the Egyptian hypothesis had been gathering since 1949, it was the Nag Hammadi finds that finally broke the dominance of the Greek hypothesis (see esp. Mahé and now Fowden; see Copenhaver, xiii-xxxii and lvii for further bibliography). The important work by Mahé on the Coptic *Hermetica* has a tendency toward the same sort of extremism that characterized the Greek paradigm, and at several points he argues too exclusively for an Egyptian provenance.

Now, though, much like religion-historical work on early Christianity, this swing from one extreme to the other seems poised at a middle position. The important work of Fowden (1986) and the support that his position has gained in the following decade and a half suggests that "neither of the extreme positions occupied by Festugière or Mahé are likely to be justifiable, since we are dealing with a syncretistic culture whose elements . . . were not easily separable" (Fowden, 68).

1.2. Collections and Texts. The Hermetic literature is available to us today in seven different places: (1) the seventeen Greek treatises of the *Corpus Hermetica* (which, in the individual treatises' current forms, probably date roughly to the second to fourth centuries A.D., but whose origins may be somewhat earlier, cf. Mahé); (2) the probably fourth-century A.D. Latin *Asclepius*; (3) the, at the earliest, fourth-century A.D. Coptic *Hermetica* of Nag Hammadi Codex VI (*The Discourse on the Eighth and Ninth,* VI.6; *The Prayer of Thanksgiving,* VI.7; the *Scribal Note,* VI.7a; and *Asclepius 21-29,* VI.8); (4) the probably sixth-century Armenian *Hermes Trimegistus to Asclepius: Definitions* (though cf. Mahé, who assigns them an early, even first-century B.C. date); (5) the forty early-sixth-century A.D. Hermetic texts and fragments found in the *Anthology* of John of Stobi (or Stobaeus); (6) many of the Greek and demotic magical papyri; and (7) the papyrus fragments of the Vienna collection (PVindob Graecae 29456 recto and 29828 recto, dated at the earliest to the late second century A.D.).

The standard Greek and Latin texts for the *Corpus Hermetica* (*CH*), the *Asclepius* and the Stobaeus excerpts (along with other fragments) is the four-volume Budé edition, compiled and edited by A. D. Nock and A.-J. Festugière from 1946-54 (now in a third edition, Nock and Festugière 1972). This also includes a French translation of these works, but Copenhaver's recent English translation of the *Hermetica* (including *CH* and the *Asclepius*) is now widely available, as are the English translations of the Nag Hammadi codices (Robinson) and the Greek and demotic magical papyri (Betz).

1.3. Theoretical and Technical Hermeticism. One of the chief elements of controversy in the discussion of the *Hermetica* is the division between so-called theoretical, or philosophical, and technical, or popular, Hermeticism. The treatises of the *CH,* as they are now available to us, are largely lacking in magical, astrological, alchemical or generally "occult" features. "They deal instead with theological or, in some loose sense, philosophical issues: they reveal to man knowledge of the origins, nature and moral properties of divine, human and material being so that man can use this knowledge to save himself," and this same "blend of theology, cosmogony, anthropogony, ethics, soteriology and eschatology" also characterizes the rest of the Hermetic literature we have available to us, except the magical papyri (Copenhaver, xxxii-xxxiii). This broad thematic unity has led to the designation *theoretical* Hermeticism, which stands over against a long tradition of Hermetic texts whose interest is primarily in astrology, divination, magic and alchemy (cf. the list in Copenhaver, xxxiii-xxxvi). Once despised as "rubbish" (see Scott) and dismissed as "popular" (Festugière 1967, 30), Fowden's recent analysis suggests that both varieties of Hermetic writing, though taking different approaches, seek to address the same issues. In keeping with this recognition, he prefers the title *technical* Hermeticism to describe this latter genre (Fowden, 1-4, 140-41, 161-213).

2. Hermeticism, New Testament, and Early Christianity.

In 1935 C. H. Dodd published *The Greeks and the Bible,* followed eighteen years later by the publication of *The Interpretation of the Fourth Gospel.* Both of these works give a great deal of attention to the relationship between the *Hermetica* and the Septuagint, other works of *Hellenistic Judaism, and the NT. Others have also pursued this course, but primarily in investigating the influence of Hermeticism on Gnosticism and, in turn, the Christian and Jewish influence on Hermeticism.

3. Hermetic and Jewish Literature.

While it is unlikely that Hermeticism, at least as we have it in the literature now available to us, influenced early Judaism to any noticeable extent, there is something to be gained by a comparison of the two. On the one hand, during the Hellenistic period, Judaism experienced many different challenges as a result of interaction with Hellenistic cultures and kingdoms. These challenges—cultural, economic, military and perhaps most significant in this connection, religious—brought about many different responses. Perhaps the most important body of evidence for uncovering these responses is the Jewish literary works either written in Greek during this period (e.g., the works of *Josephus, *Philo, [Pseudo-]Eupolemus, the **Letter of Aristeas*), or translated into Greek from earlier documents (esp. the *Septuagint, but also many of the OT pseudepigrapha now available only in Greek translation; *see* Apocrypha and Pseudepigrapha), or even in those works not written in Greek, but yet interacting with many of the materials now current in the Hellenistic period in a way hitherto not experienced in Jewish culture (e.g., the *Dead Sea Scrolls).

As a result of the varying levels of interaction with Hellenism in this literature, debate surrounding the influence of Hellenism on Judaism is no new thing. One missing strand in this ongoing area of research, however, is systematic comparison of Judaism of the Hellenistic period with the ways in which *other* oriental cultures interacted with Hellenism. If nothing else, a striking comparison can be drawn between the history of scholarship relating the "background" of Jewish literature and earliest Christianity and the history of scholarship traced above with regard to virtually exclusive Greek or Egyptian origins for the Hermetic literature. The recent realization that it is only in the mixture of the two—a "Hellenistic Egyptianism"—that understanding of the Hermetic literature can be gained has a parallel development in the investigation of early Judaism and, indeed, earliest Christianity.

However, there are more striking comparisons to be drawn. Despite the relative lack of interest among contemporary NT scholars in anything but the Jewish background of earliest Christianity, it is in a complex play of cultures that not only this Judaism of the Hellenistic and Greco-Roman periods developed, but it was also within this complicated cultural milieu that Christianity began and spread. Although there were many religions spread across the Greco-Roman world with which early Christianity must have interacted, the Egyptian cults had a predominance within the Roman Empire and its capital not enjoyed by many other oriental cults. That the Hermetic literature currently available to us is of a somewhat later date by no means undercuts its value as the remains of a cultural intermixture not unlike that of the Judaism out of which Christianity sprang, and it also has links with one of the more important cults in the world into which Christianity spread.

See also GNOSTICISM; MAGICAL PAPYRI; MYSTERIES; PHILOSOPHY; RELIGION, GRECO-ROMAN.

BIBLIOGRAPHY. H. D. Betz, *The Greek Magical Papyri in Translation Including the Demotic Spells. 1: The Texts* (2nd ed.; Chicago: University of Chicago Press, 1992); B. P. Copenhaver, *Hermetica: The Greek Corpus Hermeticum and the Latin Asclepius in a New English Translation, with Notes and Introduction* (Cambridge: Cambridge University Press, 1992); C. H. Dodd, *The Greeks and the Bible* (London: Hodder & Stoughton, 1935); idem, *The Interpretation of the Fourth Gospel* (Cambridge: Cambridge University Press, 1953); A.-J. Festugière, *Hermetisme et mystique paienne* (Paris: Aubier-Montaigne, 1967); idem, *La Révélation d'Hermès Trismégiste* (4 vols.; Paris: Gabalda, 1949-54); G. Fowden, *The Egyptian Hermes: A Historical Approach to the Late Pagan Mind* (Cambridge: Cambridge University Press, 1986); J.-P. Mahé, *Hermes en Haute-Égypte: les textes hermétiques de Nag Hammadi et leurs parallèles grecs et latins* (Bibliothèque copte de Nag Hammadi. Section Textes 3, 7; Quebec: Presses de l'Université Laval, 1978-82); A. D. Nock, *Essays on Religion and the Ancient World* (2 vols.; Oxford: Clarendon Press, 1972); A. D. Nock and A.-J. Festugière, *Corpus hermeticum* (Collection des universites de France; Paris: Les Belles Lettres, 1946-54); J. D. Ray, *The Archive of Hor* (Excavations at North Saqqara: Documentary Series 1; Texts from Excavations 2; London: Egypt Exploration Society, 1976); R. Reitzenstein, *Poimandres: Studien zur griechischägyptischen und frühchristlichen Literatur* (Leipzig: Teubner, 1904);

J. M. Robinson, ed., *The Nag Hammadi Library in English* (3d ed.; Leiden: E. J. Brill, 1988); W. Scott, *Hermetica: The Ancient Greek and Latin Writings Which Contain Religious or Philosophic Teachings Ascribed to Hermes Trismegistos* (Oxford: Clarendon Press, 1924–36); F. A. Yates, *Giordano Bruno and the Hermetic Tradition* (Frances Yates selected works 2; London: Routledge, 1999 [1964]); T. Zielinski, *Hermes und die Hermetik* (Archiv fur Religionswissenschaft 8.3-4; Leipzig: Teubner, 1905–6).

B. W. R. Pearson

HEROD THE GREAT. *See* HERODIAN DYNASTY.

HERODIAN DYNASTY

The Herodian family ruled over the Palestinian area from 40 B.C. until around A.D. 100. In order to understand the political and social setting of Jesus' ministry, it is important to understand the story of the Herods up through the first four decades of the first century A.D.

1. Herod the Great (47-4 B.C.)
2. Archelaus (4 B.C.-A.D. 6)
3. Philip the Tetrarch (4 B.C.-A.D. 34)
4. Herod Antipas (4 B.C.-A.D. 39)
5. The Herodians

1. Herod the Great (47-4 B.C.).

1.1. Herod's Family Origins. The demise of the *Hasmonean dynasty, the transference of Syria and Palestine to Roman rule, and the civil wars that marked the decay of the nation all created confusion, which opened the way for the Herodian family to come into prominence. Upon her death Alexandra Salome's eldest son, Hyrcanus II, succeeded as king and high priest (*see* Priests and Priesthood) in 67 B.C. only to be displaced three months later by his aggressive brother, Aristobulus II.

Antipater II, father of Herod the Great, was an Idumean (Josephus *J.W.* 1.6.2 §123; cf. also *Ant.* 14.1.3 §9; Justin Martyr *Dial. Tryph.* 52.3; Eusebius *Hist. Eccl.* 1.6.2; 7.11; *b. B. Bat.* 3b-4a; *b. Qidd.* 70a). He realized he would not be able to be king and high priest, but he knew he could become the power behind the throne, and thus he sided with the weak Hyrcanus II. Antipater II convinced Hyrcanus II that he was unjustly deprived of his right to rule by Aristobulus II. Furthermore, Antipater II promised to help him regain that position. With the help of the Arabian king, Aretas, Aristobulus II was defeated in 65 B.C.

With the advent of Roman power in the East (*see* Roman East), each brother (Hyrcanus II and Aristobulus II) asked Pompey, the Roman general, to side with him against the other. After having some trouble with Aristobulus II, Pompey joined forces with Hyrcanus II (Josephus *Ant.* 14.3. §§46-47) and after three months, in the autumn of 63 B.C., they defeated Aristobulus II. This marked the end of the Jewish independence that had first been gained in 142 B.C. (*see* Jewish History: Greek Period). Pompey entered the holy of holies of the temple but did not plunder it. In fact, he ordered its cleansing, the resumption of the *sacrifices, and he reinstated Hyrcanus II as high priest (Josephus *Ant.* 14.4.4 §§69-73; *J.W.* 1.6.5—7.6 §133-53; Tacitus *Hist.* 5.9; Appian *Mith. W.* 106, 114; Florus 1.40.30; Livy *Hist.* 102; Plutarch *Pomp.* 39; cf. Dio Cassius *Hist.* 37.15-17).

In 48 B.C., with the defeat of Pompey by Julius Caesar, Hyrcanus II and Antipater II attached themselves to the new ruler, who in turn reconfirmed Hyrcanus II as high priest, giving him the title of Ethnarch of the Jews, and recognized Antipater II as administrator of Judea (Josephus *Ant.* 14.8.1-5 §§127-55; 10.2 §191; *J.W.* 1.9.3.—10.4 §§187-203). Although publicly Antipater II enjoined the people to honor Hyrcanus II, he began to show his dynastic ambitions in 47 B.C. by appointing his son, Phasael, as governor of *Jerusalem and his second son, Herod, as governor of *Galilee (Josephus *Ant.* 14.9.1-2 §§156-58; *J.W.* 1.10.4 §§201-3).

1.2. Herod's Rule.

1.2.1. Herod's Governorship of Galilee (47-37 B.C.). Although only twenty-five years of age, Herod was admired by the Galilean Jews and the Romans for the leadership he demonstrated in removing the brigand leader Ezekias and his followers (47-46 B.C.). Some in Hyrcanus's court felt that Herod was becoming too powerful, and he was brought to trial before the *Sanhedrin. However, Sextus Caesar, governor of Syria, forced Hyrcanus II to acquit him. After that Herod joined Sextus Caesar in Damascus, where he was appointed governor of Coele-Syria and thus became involved with Roman affairs in Syria (Josephus *Ant.* 14.9.2-5 §§158-84; *J.W.* 1.10.5-9 §§204-15; *b. Qidd.* 43a). He again proved himself to Rome as an able leader in collecting taxes and suppressing revolts.

After Cassius and Brutus murdered Julius Caesar in 44 B.C., Cassius went to Syria and assumed the leadership there. In need of money, he reappointed Herod as governor of Coele-Syria to collect more revenue. He promised to make Herod king after he and Brutus defeated Octavian and Antony. New disturbances in Judea were quelled by Herod (43-42 B.C.), and he received praise from the people and from Hyrcanus II (Josephus *Ant.* 14.11.3—12.1 §§277-99; *J.W.* 1.11—1.12.3 §§220-40).

In 42 B.C. Antony defeated Cassius. About this time Herod and Phasael were accused by the Jewish leaders of usurping governmental powers and leaving Hyrcanus II with only titular honors. But Herod was acquitted (Josephus *Ant.* 14.12.2-6 §§301-23; *J.W.* 1.12.4-6 §§242-45; Plutarch *Anton.* 24; Dio Cassius *Hist.* 48.24; Appian *Civ. W.* 5.30-38). In 41 B.C. new accusations were made against Herod, and he was tried in *Antioch with Antony present. Antony asked Hyrcanus II who would be the best qualified ruler, and Hyrcanus II suggested Herod and Phasael. As a result, Antony appointed them as tetrarchs of Judea (Josephus *J.W.* 1.12.5 §§243-44; *Ant.* 14.13.1 §§324-26).

New troubles arose in 40 B.C. when the Parthians arrived in Syria. The Parthians were joined by Antigonus (the son of Hyrcanus II's deposed brother Aristobulus II), who wanted to remove Hyrcanus. Jerusalem was besieged and the Parthians asked for peace. However, Herod was suspicious of the offer while, on the other hand, Phasael and Hyrcanus II met the Parthians but were betrayed by them and put in chains. On hearing this, Herod and his family fled to Masada and then Petra. Antigonus was made king, and he mutilated his uncle Hyrcanus's ears in order to prevent him from being restored as the high priest and then carried him off to Parthia. Phasael died either of suicide or poisoning (Josephus *Ant.* 14.13.3-10 §§335-69; 15.2.1 §12; *J.W.* 1.13.2-11 §§250-73; Dio Cassius *Hist.* 48.26, 41).

Herod went to Rome, where Antony, Octavian and the senate designated him king of Judea (Josephus *Ant.* 14.14.6 §§381-85; *J.W.* 1.14.4 §§282-85; cf. Strabo *Geog.* 26.2.46; Appian *Civ. W.* 5.74; Tacitus *Hist.* 5.9). Herod returned to Palestine, recaptured Galilee and finally captured Jerusalem in the summer of 37 B.C. Just before capturing Jerusalem, he married Mariamne I, niece of Antigonus, to whom he had been betrothed for five years. Not only was this a contemptuous move against Antigonus, but also since she was a Hasmonean, it strengthened his claim to the throne. Herod beheaded Antigonus, thus ending the Hasmonean rule and ensuring his position as king of the Jews (Josephus *Ant.* 14.15.8—16.2 §§439-80; *J.W.* 1.16.7—18.3 §§320-57; Dio Cassius *Hist.* 49.22; Plutarch *Anton.* 36).

1.2.2. Herod's Kingship (37-4 B.C.). The reign of Herod is divided into three periods: (1) consolidation from 37 to 25 B.C.; (2) prosperity from 25 to 12 B.C.; and (3) the period of domestic troubles from 14 to 4 B.C.

The period of consolidation lasted from his accession as king in 37 B.C. to the death of the sons of Babas, the last male representatives of the Hasmonean family, in 25 B.C. The first adversaries, the people and the *Pharisees, objected both to his being an Idumean, a half-Jew, as well as his friendship with the Romans. Those who opposed him were punished, and those who took his side were rewarded with favors and honors (Josephus *Ant.* 15.1.1 §§2-3; *J.W.* 1.18.4 §358).

The second adversaries were those of the aristocracy who sided with Antigonus. Herod executed forty-five of the wealthiest and confiscated their properties, thereby replenishing his own coffers (Josephus *Ant.* 15.1.2 §§5-6; cf. 14.9.4 §175; *J.W.* 1.18.4 §358).

The third group of adversaries was the Hasmonean family. His mother-in-law Alexandra was the main problem. She forced him, through Cleopatra's influence, to appoint her son Aristobulus as high priest even though he was only sixteen years old. After officiating a successful Feast of Tabernacles (*see* Festivals and Holy Days), Aristobulus supposedly accidentally drowned at Herod's palace in Jericho—a story never believed by Alexandra (Josephus *Ant.* 15.3.2-4 §§42-61; *J.W.* 1.22.2 §437). Alexandra told her friend Cleopatra of Herod's misdeeds, and thus Herod had to appear before Antony at Laodicea (on the coast of Syria). Not knowing what his fate might be, he ordered his uncle Joseph to kill Mariamne if he were sentenced to death. Mariamne heard of Herod's order for her execution and resented it. But through gifts and eloquence Herod was able to convince Antony that he was not guilty (Josephus *Ant.* 15.3.5-9 §§62-87; *J.W.* 1.22.4-5 §§441-44).

Herod's final adversary was Cleopatra. She had cooperated with Alexandra in the matter of Aristobulus. Next she asked Antony to increase her territory by eliminating Herod and Malchus of Arabia in order to possess their land. Antony did not permit this but did give her the rich district of Jericho and a part of Arabia (Josephus *Ant.* 15.4.1-2 §§88-103). When in 32 B.C. civil war erupted between Antony and Octavian, Herod wanted to help Antony, but he was prevented by Cleopatra for she wanted Herod to make war against Malchus, who had failed to pay his tribute to her. When she saw Herod winning, she ordered her troops to help Malchus, hoping to weaken both parties so that she could absorb both. In the spring of 31 B.C. there was a devastating earthquake in Herod's land, killing 30,000 people. Malchus took advantage of the situation and attacked. But in the end Herod won (Josephus *Ant.* 15.5.2-5 §§121-60; *J.W.* 1.19.3-6 §§369-85).

Soon after, on September 2, 31 B.C., Antony was defeated by Octavian in the battle of Actium. Herod now had to ingratiate himself to Octavian and persuade him that he was the rightful ruler of Judea. In the spring of 30 B.C. he set out for Rhodes and persuaded Octavian that he had not actually fought Octavian because of his skirmish with Malchus and that he had been loyal to Rome for many years. Octavian was convinced and confirmed Herod's royal rank. When Octavian came through Palestine on his way to Egypt, Herod met him at Ptolemais and gave him 800 talents, a gesture much appreciated by Octavian (Josephus *Ant.* 15.6.6-7 §§188-201; *J.W.* 1.20.1-3 §§387-95). Following Octavian's defeat of Antony in Egypt, Herod went to Egypt to congratulate him, and Octavian returned Jericho (which Cleopatra had taken) to Herod, adding to it Gadara, Hippos, Samaria, Gaza, Anthedon, Joppa and Strato's Tower (which later became Caesarea Maritima) (Josephus *Ant.* 15.7.3 §§215-17; *JW* 1.20.3 §396).

During this time Herod continued to have domestic problems. While he was at Rhodes, his wife Mariamne discovered that Herod had again ordered that she be killed if he did not return. Her bitterness toward Herod was increased, and when it became evident to Herod, he placed her on trial for adultery and had her executed toward the end of 29 B.C. (Josephus *Ant.* 15.7.1-5 §§202-36). In 28 B.C. he had his mother-in-law, Alexandra, executed. And Herod's sister Salome, wanting to get rid of her husband Costobarus, convinced Herod that Costobarus was concealing and protecting the influential sons of Babas, who were loyal to Antigonus and who spoke ill of Herod. Herod executed Costobarus and the sons of Babas in 25 B.C., making it impossible for any of Hyrcanus's descendants to become king (Josephus *Ant.* 15.7.6-10 §§237-66).

The second period of Herod's reign was one of prosperity, lasting from 25 to 12 B.C. The first thing Josephus mentions of this period is Herod's violations of the Jewish law in introducing the quinquennial games in Caesar's honor as well as the fact that he built *theaters, amphitheaters and hippodromes (Josephus *Ant.* 15.8.1 §§267-76; 17.10.3 §255; *J.W.* 2.3.1 §44). Herod rebuilt many fortresses in the land and temples in Gentile territories, including the rebuilding of Strato's Tower, which was renamed Caesarea Maritima. In 24 B.C. he built for himself a royal palace in Jerusalem (Josephus *Ant.* 15.8.5—9.6 §§292-341). According to Josephus the most notable achievement of Herod was the building of the *temple in Jerusalem, which was begun in 20/19 B.C. and finished in A.D. 63, long after his death (Josephus *Ant.* 15.11.1-6 §§380-425). The rabbis are recorded saying, "He who has not seen the temple of Herod has never seen a beautiful building" (*b. B. Bat.* 4a), and they saw its construction as an "atonement for having slain so many sages of Israel" (*Midr. Num. Rab.* 14:8).

Herod acquainted himself with Greek culture by surrounding himself with men accomplished in Greek literature and *art (*see* Hellenism). In 22 B.C. Herod sent his sons by Mariamne I, Alexander and Aristobulus, to Rome for their education. They were personally received by Caesar. About this time Augustus (Octavian's newly acquired title) gave Herod the territories of Trachonitis, Batanea and Auranitis (Josephus *Ant.* 15.10.1-2 §§343-49; *J.W.* 1.20.4 §398). Two years later (20 B.C.) Augustus came to Syria and bestowed on Herod the former territory belonging to Zenodorus that lay between Trachonitis and Galilee (containing Ulatha and Paneas) and the adjacent area north and northeast of the Lake of Gennesaret. Augustus also made the procurators of Syria responsible to Herod for all their actions (Josephus *Ant.* 15.10.3 §§354-60; *J.W.* 1.20.4 §§399-400; Dio Cassius *Hist.* 54.7.4-6; 9.3). In addition Herod obtained the tetrarchy of Perea for his brother Pheroras (Josephus *Ant.* 15.10.3 §§362; *J.W.* 1.24.5 §483). In a show of gratitude for Augustus's generosity, Herod built a beautiful temple (*see* Temples, Greco-Roman) for Augustus in the territory of Zenodorus, near the place called Paneion (Josephus *Ant.* 15.10.3 §363; *J.W.* 1.21.3 §§404-6). It was around this time that Herod reduced the taxes by a third under the pretext of a crop failure, but in reality it is more likely he did this to promote goodwill among those who were displeased with his emphasis on Greco-Roman culture and religion (Josephus *Ant.* 15.10.4 §§365-72). In 14 B.C. Herod again reduced taxes by one-fourth (Josephus *Ant.* 16.2.5 §§64-65). In conclusion, this period was marked by prosperity in building and success in ruling the country.

The third period of Herod's reign was characterized by domestic problems (14-4 B.C.). Many of the problems arose because he had ten wives, each wanting her son(s) to succeed him (Josephus *Ant.* 17.1.3 §§19-22; *J.W.* 1.28.4 §§562-63). His first wife, Doris, had only one son, Antipater (Josephus *Ant.* 14.12.1 §300). In 37 B.C. Herod repudiated Doris and Antipater and married Mariamne I, permitting Doris and Antipater to visit Jerusalem only during the festivals (Josephus *J.W.* 1.22.1 §433). Mariamne was the granddaughter of Hyrcanus II, and she had five children: two daughters and three sons. In late 24 B.C. Herod married his third wife, Mariamne II, by whom he had Herod (Philip). His fourth wife, Malthace, was a Samaritan who bore Archelaus and Herod Antipas. His fifth wife, Cleopatra of Jerusalem, bore Philip the tetrarch. Of the remaining five wives, only Pallas, Phaedra and Elpsis are known by name, but they play an insignificant role (Josephus *Ant.* 17.1.3 §§19-22; *J.W.* 1.28.4 §§562-63).

Of all the sons of Herod, Alexander and Aristobulus, the sons of Mariamne I, were his favorites. However, they were hated by Salome, Herod's sister, even though her daughter Bernice was married to Aristobulus. The reason for her hatred is that she wanted her son to succeed her brother, Herod the Great. Salome spread rumors that Alexander and Aristobulus had never forgiven Herod for his murder of their mother and they were seeking to avenge it by bringing charges against him before Caesar, which would lead to his losing the throne (Josephus *Ant.* 16.3.1-2 §§66-77). Because of this, Herod recalled his exiled son Antipater to show Alexander and Aristobulus that there could be another heir to the throne (14 B.C.). Antipater took full advantage of the situation and used every means to acquire the coveted throne.

In 13 B.C. Herod made his second will, whereby he designated Antipater as the sole heir. Herod sent Antipater with Agrippa (a friend of Augustus) to Rome to have this will ratified. While in Rome Antipater wrote slanderous letters against Alexander and Aristobulus. Herod became more aggravated with these two sons, and finally in 12 B.C. he brought them before Augustus in Aquileia (near Venice) to be tried. Rather than being executed, the two brothers were reconciled to their father.

Herod made his third will, naming all three sons as successors (Josephus *Ant.* 16.3.3—4.6 §§86-135; *J.W.* 1.23.2-5 §§451-66). Shortly thereafter (c. 11/10 B.C.) Herod again became suspicious of Alexander and Aristobulus when the slanderous accusation that they were going to kill and succeed Herod was brought against them by Antipater and Herod's sister Salome. Herod imprisoned Alexander, but Alexander's father-in-law, the king of Cappadocia, being concerned about his daughter's welfare, interceded and was able to reconcile Herod and Alexander (Josephus *Ant.* 16.7.2—8.6 §§188-270; *J.W.* 1.24.2—25.6 §§467-512). This brought peace to the Herodian household only temporarily. A certain Eurycles from Lacedemon and other troublemakers aroused in Herod's mind new suspicions against Alexander and Aristobulus. Consequently, Herod imprisoned them and sent a report to the emperor of their involvement in treasonable plots (Josephus *Ant.* 16.10.1-5 §§300-24; *J.W.* 1.26.1—27.1 §§513-35; cf. also Pausanias *Descr.* 2.3.5; Strabo *Geog.* 8.5.1; Plutarch *Anton.* 67).

Herod had lost favor with the emperor because of the accusations of Herod's Arab neighbor, Syllaeus, that Herod had invaded his territory for no reason. However, Herod's teacher, friend and counsellor, Nicolaus of Damascus, went to Rome and convinced Augustus that Syllaeus's case was false, and Herod regained the emperor's favor. Nicolaus also presented Herod's accusations against his two sons, and Herod was given permission to have them tried outside of Herod's territory. Herod had them tried at Berytus (Beirut) before a Roman court. They were found guilty and were executed by strangulation in Sebaste (Samaria) c. 7 B.C. It was there that Herod had married their mother Mariamne I thirty years earlier (Josephus *Ant.* 16.10.6—11.8 §§324-404; *J.W.* 1.27.1-6 §§536-51).

Herod made his fourth will by naming Antipater as the sole heir. But becoming impatient to gain the throne, Antipater attempted to poison Herod. However, this plot failed when Herod's brother, Pheroras, drank the poison by mistake. Herod imprisoned Antipater and reported this attempt on his life to the emperor (c. 5 B.C.). Becoming very ill, Herod drew up the fifth will in which he bypassed his oldest sons, Archelaus and Philip, because Antipater had turned Herod's mind against them, and chose his youngest son, Antipas, to succeed him as king (Josephus *Ant.* 17.1.1—6.1 §§1-146; *J.W.* 1.28.1—29.32 §§552-646).

It is against this background of palace intrigue that Matthew recounts the circumstances surrounding the birth of Jesus. Matthew relates that shortly before Herod's death, magi arrived in Judea, looking for the newborn king of the Jews. Herod instructed them to inform him of the location of this child. But being warned in a dream, they did not report back to Herod but returned to their homes via another route (Mt 2:1-8, 12). God warned Joseph (husband of Jesus' mother) to flee to Egypt because of Herod's intention to kill Jesus (Mt 2:13-15). Soon after Joseph left Bethlehem, Herod killed all the male children in Bethlehem who were two years old and under (Mt 2:16).

Herod steadily grew more ill. He received permission from Rome to execute Antipater, which he promptly did. Herod then wrote his sixth will, making Archelaus king, Antipas tetrarch of Galilee and Perea, and Philip tetrarch of Gaulanitis, Trachonitis, Batanea and Paneas. In the spring of 4 B.C., five days after Antipater's execution, Herod died at Jericho The people made Archelaus their king. Herod's reign of thirty-three or thirty-four years had been marked with violence, not unlike those of most of his contemporary rulers.

1.2.3. Herod's Wills. Herod had written six wills, and the sixth will was only a codicil of the fifth. Since the sixth will was made only five days before Herod's death, it did not have the ratification of the emperor. When Herod died, Archelaus assumed leadership but refused to be crowned king (Josephus *Ant.* 17.8.4 §§202-3; *J.W.* 2.1.1 §3). Immediately after the Passover, Archelaus and Antipas went to Rome to contest the will while Philip took care of the home front. Archelaus felt that Augustus should ratify Herod's sixth will because it expressed Herod's wish immediately preceding his death. On the other hand, Antipas argued that Herod had not been of sound mind when he wrote the sixth will. To further complicate the situation, a revolt broke out in Palestine and a Jewish delegate went to Rome asking for national autonomy and a union with the province of Syria. After much discussion, Augustus formulated a compromise whereby Archelaus was designated ethnarch of Idumea, Judea and Samaria, with the promise to be made king if he proved worthy; Antipas was made tetrarch of Galilee and Perea; and Philip was appointed tetrarch over Gaulanitis, Trachonitis, Batanea and Paneas (Josephus *Ant.* 17.11.4 §§317-20; *J.W.* 2.6.3 §§93-100). Thus Antipas, while losing his claim to be king, did prevent Archelaus from becoming king over the entire realm.

2. Archelaus (4 B.C.-A.D. 6).

2.1. Archelaus's Rule. Archelaus (born c. 22 B.C.), the son of Herod the Great and Malthace (a Samaritan), was made ethnarch over Idumea, Judea and Samaria with the promise to be made king if he ruled with prudence. But Archelaus got off to a bad start. Even before he left for Rome to contest Herod's final will, he overreacted to an uprising in the temple at Passover by sending in his troops and cavalry and killing about three thousand pilgrims. While he was in Rome, a revolt broke out again in Jerusalem at the feast of Pentecost, this time against Caesar's procurator Sabinus, and spread to Judea, Galilee and Perea.

Archelaus's brutal treatment of the Jews and the Samaritans (Josephus *J.W.* 2.7.3 §111) is in keeping with what Matthew tells of Joseph, who heard that Archelaus was ruling Judea and was afraid to go there. Being warned in a dream on his return from Egypt, Joseph, Mary and Jesus went to live in Nazareth in Galilee (Mt 2:20-23).

Soon after his return from Rome, Archelaus removed the high priest, Joazar, blaming him for siding with the rebels. He replaced him with Joazar's brother, Eleazar, and later replaced Eleazar with Jesus, son of See. Around this same time Archelaus divorced Mariamne and married Glaphyra, daughter of King Archelaus of Cappadocia. She was the former wife of Alexander, Herod's son and Archelaus's half-brother. This was a transgression of ancestral law (Josephus *Ant.* 17.13.1, 4-5 §§339-41, 350-53; *J.W.* 2.7.4 §§114-16). Either or both of these last two incidents may have caused the unrest that erupted. Archelaus used oppressive measures to quell the opposition.

Archelaus followed his father's example in building projects. He rebuilt the royal palace at Jericho in splendid fashion and diverted half of the water of the village of Neara into the newly planted palm trees in the plain of Jericho. He also created a village and honored himself by naming it Archelais (Josephus *Ant.* 17.13.1 §340).

*2.2. **Archelaus's Demise.*** Because of his continued oppressive rule, he was finally deposed in A.D. 6. A delegation of Jews and Samaritans complained to Augustus about Archelaus's brutality and tyranny. For these two enemies to cooperate in this matter indicates the seriousness of the complaint. Also, Archelaus's brothers, Antipas and Philip, went to Rome to complain about him, presumably resenting his oversight of them in his role as ethnarch or Roman representative for Palestine. As a result, Archelaus was banished to Vienna in Gaul (modern Vienne on the Rhône, south of Lyons). Antipas and Philip retained their domains while Archelaus's territories were reduced to an imperial province under the rule of prefects (Josephus *Ant.* 17.13.1-5 §§342-55; *J.W.* 2.7.3—8.1 §§111-18; Strabo *Geog.* 16.2.46; Dio Cassius *Hist.* 55.27.6).

3. Philip the Tetrarch (4 B.C.-A.D. 34).
Philip the tetrarch was the son of Herod the Great and Cleopatra of Jerusalem and was born around 22/21 B.C. As a result of the debate over Herod's will, Augustus made him tetrarch over the northeastern part of Herod the Great's domain, Gaulanitis, Auranitis, Batanea, Trachonitis, Paneas and Iturea (Josephus *Ant.* 17.9.4 §319; *J.W.* 2.6.3 §95; cf. Lk 3:1). His subjects were mainly Syrian and Greek (i.e., non-Jewish), and hence he was the first and only Herodian to have the emperor's as well as his own image on his coins.

Philip built two cities (Josephus *Ant.* 18.2.1 §28; *J.W.* 2.9.1 §168). The first city was a rebuilding and enlarging of Paneas (near the source of the Jordan), which he renamed Caesarea Philippi in honor of the Roman emperor and to distinguish it from the coastal Caesarea. It was there that Peter made his confession of faith to Jesus (Mt 16:13-20; Mk 8:27-30). The second city was the rebuilding and enlarging of the fishing village of Bethsaida (where the Jordan flows into the Sea of Galilee). Philip gave it the status of a Greek *polis* and renamed it Julias in honor of Augustus's daughter Julia. There Jesus would heal the blind man (Mk 8:22-26), and in a nearby desert place Jesus would feed the five thousand (Lk 9:10). Also, it may have been in the southern portion of Philip's territory that Jesus fed the four thousand.

Philip did not possess the ambitious and scheming character of his brothers. He ruled his domain with moderation and tranquility and was well liked by his subjects (Josephus *Ant.* 18.4.6 §§106-8). He married Herodias's daughter Salome, whose dance led to the beheading of John the Baptist (Mt 14:3-12; Mk 6:17-29; Lk 3:19-20; Josephus *Ant.* 18.5.2 §§116-19). They had no children (Josephus *Ant.* 18.5.4 §§137). When Philip died in A.D. 34 the emperor Tiberius annexed his territory to Syria, and when Caligula became emperor in A.D. 37, Philip's territory was given to Herod Agrippa I, brother of Herodias.

4. Herod Antipas (4 B.C.-A.D. 39).

*4.1. **Antipas's Realm.*** Herod Antipas, the younger brother of Archelaus, was born c. 20 B.C. He was made tetrarch of Galilee and Perea and ruled from 4 B.C. to A.D. 39. These were the territories where both Jesus and John the Baptist concentrated their ministries. On his return from Rome, Antipas had to restore order and rebuild what had been destroyed at the Feast of Pentecost in 4 B.C. Like his father, he founded cities. He rebuilt Sepphoris (c. A.D. 8-10; *see* Galilee), which was the largest city in Galilee and was the capital of his territories until he built *Tiberias. Joseph, Mary's husband, living in Nazareth only four miles SSW of Sepphoris may well have used his skill as a carpenter (Mt 13:55; Mk 6:3) during its rebuilding. The second city Antipas rebuilt was Livias (or Julias) of Perea in honor of Augustus's wife Livia. This was completed c. A.D. 13 (Josephus *Ant.* 18.2.1 §27). Although the Herodian family had built twelve cities, Tiberias was the first city in Jewish history to be founded within the municipal pattern of the Greek *polis.* In the process of building the city an ancient cemetery was struck, and subsequently Antipas had difficulty in populating it because the Jews regarded it as an unclean area. Antipas offered free houses and lands as well as exemption from taxes for the first few years for anyone who would move into the new city. Named in honor of the emperor Tiberius, it was completed around A.D. 25 and served as Antipas's capital (Josephus *Ant.* 18.2.3 §§36-38).

*4.2. **Antipas's Reign.*** As far as Rome was concerned, Herod Antipas was a good ruler who reigned over the territories of Galilee and Perea from 4 B.C. to A.D. 39.

4.2.1. Antipas and Archelaus. The only important recorded event early in Antipas's reign was the deposition of his brother Archelaus in A.D. 6. Together with his half-brother, Philip the tetrarch, and a Jewish and Samaritan delegation, he went to Rome to complain about Archelaus to Tiberius (Josephus *Ant.* 18.13.2 §§342-44; *J.W.* 2.7.3 §111). Although Antipas hoped to receive the title of *king*, Tiberius allowed Antipas to have the dynastic title of *Herod* (cf. Josephus *J.W.* 2.9.1 §167; *Ant.* 18.2.1 §27), which was significant for both his subjects and the political and social circles of the Roman world.

4.2.2. Antipas and John the Baptist. In the Gospels Herod Antipas is best known for his imprisonment and beheading of John the Baptist (Mt 14:3-12; Mk 6:17-29; Lk 3:19-20; Josephus *Ant.* 18.5.2 §§116-19). Antipas had been married to the daughter of the Nabatean king Aretas IV, a marriage probably arranged by Augustus in order to gain peace between Jews and Arabs and provide a buffer zone between Rome and the Parthians. This marriage would have taken place before Augustus's death in A.D. 14. When Antipas traveled to Rome in c. A.D. 29, he visited his brother Herod (Philip), who apparently lived in one of the coastal cities of Palestine. While there he fell in love with his niece, who was also his brother's wife, Herodias. She agreed to marry Antipas when he returned from Rome provided that he divorce his first wife (Josephus *Ant.* 18.5.1 §§109-10). Antipas's first wife learned of the plan and fled to her father, Aretas IV, who considered the matter a personal insult and later retaliated against Antipas.

When Antipas married Herodias, John the Baptist boldly criticized him for marrying his brother's wife, and as a result John was imprisoned by Antipas. The Mosaic law prohibited a man from marrying a brother's wife (Lev 18:16; 20:21) except in the case of levirate marriages (Deut 25:5; Mk 12:19; *see* Adultery, Divorce). Since Antipas's brother had a daughter Salome and, more pointedly, his brother was still living, the levirate marriage did not apply.

There is a problem in identifying Herodias's first husband. The Gospels designate him as Philip (Mt 14:3; Mk 6:17), but Josephus lists him as Herod, son of Herod the Great and Mariamne II, daughter of Simon the high priest (Josephus *Ant.* 18.5 §109). Since the Herodian family line is complicated, many think that the Gospel writers confused this Herod with Philip the tetrarch, who later married Herodias's daughter Salome. However, although this may seem plausible at first, it is untenable for several reasons.

First, the Gospels would be guilty of three historical blunders, namely, (1) confusing this Herod with his half-brother Philip the tetrarch, (2) making Philip the tetrarch the husband of Herodias instead of the husband of her daughter Salome and (3) assuming that Salome was the daughter of Philip the tetrarch, who, according to Josephus, had no children. These errors would be incredible in the light of the Gospel writers' familiarity with other historical details of the era. Furthermore, the early Christian community included people like Joanna, wife of Chuza, Antipas's financial minister (Lk 8:3), and Manaen, a close friend of Antipas (Acts 13:1), who would have known the details and would have prevented such historical error.

Third, some argue that Herod the Great would not have two of his sons with the same name. But this is untenable because, although the two sons had the same father, they had different mothers. This is substantiated by the facts that Herod the Great did have two sons named Antipas/Antipater and two sons named Herod, all of whom had different mothers.

Fourth, it is highly probable that Herodias's first husband was called both Herod and Philip or, in other words, Herod Philip. Although some would argue that double names were not used, no one argues that Herod of Acts 12:1, 6, 11, 19-21 is the Agrippa of Josephus nor that Archelaus is Herod Archelaus. Double names were used of emperors like Caesar Augustus.

Fifth, if the Evangelists intended that Herodias's former husband was actually Philip the tetrarch, why did they not call him "Philip the tetrarch" as they had called Herod Antipas first "tetrarch" and then "king" within the same pericope (cf. Mt 14:1, 9; Mk 6:14, 26)?

Therefore, it seems most reasonable to conclude that the Philip in the Gospels and the Herod in Josephus are one and the same person, otherwise it would be hopelessly confusing.

Antipas's imprisonment of John the Baptist was not enough for Herodias. At the appropriate time, probably Antipas's birthday, at Machaerus in Perea, Herodias arranged for a banquet for Antipas in order to eliminate John the Baptist. When Herodias's daughter danced before the guests, Antipas was overwhelmed and promised under oath to give her anything she wanted, up to half of his kingdom. With the advice of her mother, Salome asked for the head of John the Baptist on a platter. Although Antipas was sorry for his rash promise, he granted the request to save face before his guests. John was beheaded in A.D. 31 or 32.

4.2.3. Antipas and Jesus. Antipas's relationship to Jesus is seen in three events. First, Antipas heard of Jesus' ministry and concluded, with some irony, that Jesus was John the Baptist resurrected (Mt 14:1-2; Mk 6:14-16; Lk 9:7-9). Antipas had silenced John the Baptist's movement, and now there appeared to be a more successful people's preacher on the horizon. Hence, Antipas concluded that it was John the Baptist all over again. Antipas wanted to see Jesus, but Jesus withdrew from Antipas's territories. Antipas did not want to use force, fearing that his citizens would again resent his treatment as they had with his treatment of John the Baptist.

The second incident was Jesus' final journey to Jerusalem. While Jesus was in Antipas's territories, some of the Pharisees came to warn Jesus that he should leave because Antipas wanted to kill him (Lk 13:31-33). Jesus told them to "Go tell that fox" that he would continue his ministry of casting out demons and healing for a short time longer, and when he had finished, he would then go to Jerusalem to die.

The third event was Jesus' trial by Antipas in A.D. 33 (Lk 23:6-12). Although some scholars think this pericope is legendary because it is not mentioned in the other Gospels, its occurrence in Luke's Gospel makes historical sense. Luke was writing to Theophilus, probably a Roman official, who would have been interested in the relationships between the Herods and the prefects of Judea, especially since this pericope reports the reconciliation between Antipas and Pilate (Lk 23:12). Since the account reports no progress in the trial, it is understandable why the other Gospel writers left it out. Some scholars think the source for this incident is from the *Gospel of Peter*. But that Gospel presents no real parallel with Luke's account of Antipas's trial of Jesus. In fact the *Gospel of Peter* holds Antipas responsible for Jesus' death, whereas there is nothing of this in Luke.

In Luke's account, Pilate, knowing Antipas was in Jerusalem for the Passover and hearing that Jesus was from Antipas's territory, Galilee, sent Jesus to him. Pilate was not legally obligated to do so, but he wanted to extricate himself from an awkward situation in which the Jews wanted to crucify Jesus while Pilate felt that he was innocent. Furthermore, Pilate needed to improve his relationship with Antipas. The relationship had been strained by Pilate's massacre of some of Antipas's subjects (Lk 13:1), and it was further aggravated when Antipas reported to Tiberius the trouble Pilate had caused the Jews when he brought votive shields to Jerusalem. Subsequently Tiberius had ordered their immediate removal in c. A.D. 32 (Philo *Leg. Gai.* 299-304). Hence Pilate had overstepped his bounds and needed to appease Antipas. On the other hand, Antipas did not want to give Pilate any reason to report him to the emperor, and so after mocking Jesus, he sent him back to Pilate without comment, thereby paving the road for reconciliation between the two leaders from that day forward (Lk 23:12).

4.2.4. Antipas and Exile. In A.D. 36 Aretas IV attacked and defeated Antipas's army. The Jews considered this divine punishment for Antipas's execution of John the Baptist (Josephus *Ant.* 18.5.1-2 §§116-19). Tiberius commanded Vitellius, governor of Syria, to help Antipas against Aretas. However, before this could be accomplished Tiberius had died and Vitellius withheld his aid until he received orders from the new emperor Caligula.

When Caligula became emperor (A.D. 37), he gave his friend Agrippa I, brother of Herodias and nephew of Antipas, the land of Philip the tetrarch as well as the tetrarch of Lysanius with the title *king* (Josephus *Ant.* 18.6.10 §§225-39). Later Agrippa went to Palestine (c. August of 38) to see his newly acquired domain. His presence in the land provoked Herodias's jealousy because he had obtained the much-coveted title *king*, which Antipas had never received, although he had ruled well and faithfully since 4 B.C. Finally, under Herodias's persuasion, Antipas and Herodias went to Rome in A.D. 39 to seek the same honor. Agrippa heard of this and sent an envoy to Rome to bring accusations against Antipas. This action resulted in the banishment of Antipas and Herodias to Lugdunum Convenarum, now Saint-Bertrand de Comminges in southern France, in the foothills of the Pyrenees. Caligula learned that Herodias was the sister of Agrippa I and excused her from the exile, but she chose to follow her husband. As a result, Agrippa I obtained Antipas's territories of Galilee and Perea (Josephus *Ant.* 18.7.1-2 §§240-55; *J.W.* 2.9.6 §§181-83).

5. The Herodians.

The Herodians were influential men who were partisans of the Herodian dynasty. They are mentioned three times in the NT, dealing with two incidents where they joined with the Pharisees in their opposition to Jesus. The first incident took place in Galilee immediately after Jesus healed the man with the withered hand, and the Herodians and the Pharisees sought to destroy Jesus (Mk 3:6). The second episode was in Jerusalem when the Pharisees and the Herodians tried to incriminate Jesus regarding the lawfulness of paying taxes to Caesar (Mt 22:16 par. Mk 12:13). The Herodians are not mentioned in Luke or John.

The origin of the name has been debated. Some think that the ending of their name reflects the Latin suffix *-ianus*, which is appended to adjectives, thus making it a substantive meaning that they were of the household of Herod, that is, domestic servants. Others think that it is a Greek suffix meaning that they were officers or agents of Herod. However, in the Gospel narratives they are not portrayed as either domestic servants or officers of Herod but as influential people whose outlook was friendly to the Herodian rule and consequently to the Roman rule upon which it rested.

The issue comes to the forefront in Mark 8:15 and Matthew 16:6, where in Mark we read of the "leaven of Herod" and the Matthean parallel refers to the "leaven of the Sadducees." This problem becomes more critical if the secondary Markan reading, "leaven of the Herodians" (P^{45}, W, Θ $f^{1,\,13}$), is the correct one. The problem with this passage is not the interpretation but the question of whether the *Sadducees and the Herod(ians) are the same? At first this seems impossible because Herod the Great tried to discredit the Hasmonean house. Furthermore, he and his grandson Agrippa I never selected a high priest from among the Sadducees, who were pro-Hasmonean, but rather from the house of Boethus. However, a reversal of this policy occurred between Herod's son Archelaus's deposition in A.D. 6 and Agrippa I's acquisition of Judea in A.D. 41.

At that time most of the high priests came from the Sadducean house of Annas because the province of Judea was not under Herodian rule but under direct Roman rule of the prefects. It seems probable, then, that the Boethusians, being pro-Herodian, were really the Herodians and the Sadducees were pro-Hasmonean. Actually, later rabbinic sources used the Boethusian name interchangeably with that of the Sadducees (*m. Menaḥ.* 10:3). It may well be that the Sadducees and the Herodians would have been close if not identical religiously and economically. Thus the Herodians were politically affiliated with the Herodian house, but they were religiously and economically affiliated with the Sadducees. However, the political distinctions between the Sadducees and Herodians were blurred with the marriage of Herod Antipas and Herodias (a Hasmonean on her mother's side). It could be that Herod Antipas married Herodias to gain Sadducean support. Hence the Herodians and the Sadducees would have been on the same side politically, against the *Pharisees, the Herodians being pro-Herodian government while the Pharisees were both anti-Hasmonean and anti-Herodian. This is borne out in Mark 8:15 and Matthew 16:6, 12, where the Pharisees and the Sadducees/Herodians are contrary parties opposing Jesus.

In summary, the Herodians were theologically in agreement with the Sadducees, and politically both of these parties would have been the opposite of the Pharisees, who were anti-Hasmonean, anti-Herodian and anti-Roman. The Pharisees looked for a cataclysmic messianic kingdom to remove the rule of the Herods and Rome, whereas the Herodians wanted to preserve the Herodian rule. However, the Herodians and the Pharisees worked together to oppose Jesus because he was introducing a new kingdom that neither wanted.

See also HASMONEANS; JEWISH HISTORY: ROMAN PERIOD; REVOLUTIONARY MOVEMENTS.

BIBLIOGRAPHY. W. J. Bennett, "Herodians of Mark's Gospel," *NovT* 17 (1975) 9-14; P. M. Bernegger, "Affirmation of Herod's Death in 4 B.C.," *JTS* 34 (1983) 526-31; D. C. Braund, "Four Notes on the Herods," *CQ* 33 (1983) 239-42; idem, "Herodian Dynasty," in *ABD* 3:173-74; idem, *Rome and the Friendly King* (New York: St. Martin's, 1984); F. F. Bruce, "Herod Antipas, Tetrarch of Galilee and Perea," *ALUOS* 5 (1963-65) 6-23; C. Daniel, "Les 'Hérodiens' du Nouveau

Testament sont-ils des Esséniens?" *RQ* 6 (1967) 31-53; J. D. M. Derrett, "Herod's Oath and the Baptist's Head," *BZ* NF 9 (1965) 49-59, 233-46; R. T. France, "Herod and the Children of Bethlehem," *NovT* 21 (1979) 98-120; M. Grant, *Herod the Great* (New York: American Heritage, 1971); H. W. Hoehner, "The Date of the Death of Herod the Great," in *Chronos, Kairos, Christos: Nativity and Chronological Studies Presented to Jack Finegan*, ed. J. Vardaman and E. M. Yamauchi (Winona Lake, IN: Eisenbrauns, 1989) 101-11; idem, *Herod Antipas* (SNTSMS 17; Cambridge: Cambridge University Press, 1972); A. H. M. Jones, *The Herods of Judea* (Oxford: Oxford University Press, 1938); A. Negoită and C. Daniel, "L'énigme du levain," *NovT* 9 (1967) 306-14; P. Parker, "Herod Antipas and the Death of Jesus," in *Jesus, the Gospels, and the Church: Essays in Honor of William R. Farmer* (Macon, GA: Mercer University Press, 1987) 197-208; S. Perowne, *The Later Herods* (London: Hodder & Stoughton, 1958); idem, *The Life and Times of Herod the Great* (London: Hodder & Stoughton, 1957); P. Richardson, *Herod: King of the Jews and Friend of the Romans* (Columbia: University of South Carolina Press, 1996); H. H. Rowley, "The Herodians in the Gospels," *JTS* 41 (1940) 14-27; S. Sandmel, *Herod: Profile of a Tyrant* (Philadelphia: J. B. Lippincott, 1987); A. Schalit, *König Herodes: Der Mann und sein Werk* (SJ 4; Berlin, 1969); E. Schürer, *The History of the Jewish People in the Age of Jesus Christ (175 B.C.-A.D. 135)*, rev. and ed. G. Vermes, F. Millar and M. Goodman (3 vols.; Edinburgh: T & T Clark, 1973-87) 1:287-357; M. Stern, "The Reign of Herod and the Herodian Dynasty," in *The Jewish People in the First Century*, ed. S. Safrai and M. Stern (2 vols.; CRINT 1; Philadelphia: Fortress, 1974-76) 1:216-307.

H. W. Hoehner

HERODIANS. *See* HERODIAN DYNASTY.

HERODOTUS OF HALICARNASSUS. *See* HISTORIANS, GRECO-ROMAN.

HEROES

Every civilization and culture has its heroes of the past. These renowned dead are the prominent characters of a given culture's traditional narratives (written and/or oral, fictional and historical) that provide stories of origins, explain national identity and religion and may express many of its moral and civil virtues. The heroes of these narratives stand out from others for many reasons: moral, religious or intellectual superiority, great deeds of courage and faith, and celebrated accomplishments on behalf of their nation and descendants. As societies use and reuse such traditional narratives, the stories themselves are evaluated, repeated, edited and supplemented. In manifold ways the hero traditions are thus reflected and refracted in light of contemporary knowledge, intellectual currents, and social and religious needs of later generations.

1. Greek Heroes
2. Jewish Heroes
3. Heroes in the New Testament

1. Greek Heroes.

The centuries preceding the turn of the era, and the first century itself, saw among Jewish authors a great outpouring of literature concerning their own culture's traditional heroes. It was also a time of great intellectual ferment in the Greco-Roman world and of expanding interaction among Hellenistic, Roman and Jewish cultures. Such cultural intercourse encouraged the practice of relating and comparing the narratives and heroes of one culture to those of another. For some Greek historians, this intellectual enterprise of the *Hellenistic era saw Greek historians writing universal histories and taking a keen interest in foreign peoples and cultures (Momigliano 1975, 1-6). Within this dynamic climate early Christians lived and the books of the NT were composed.

Some Greek authors used the sobriquet *heroes* with reference to a particular class of characters from Greek tradition. For Hesiod (seventh century B.C.) the heroes were the Fourth Age of men who fell prior to the destruction of Thebes and Troy and who were superior in all ways to the current race. For Pindar (fifth century B.C.), heroes were identical to demigods. Much later, the word *hero* came to be used popularly to refer to minor local deities or city founders. But Jewish heroes are not best thought of with these specific associations.

In more general historiographic terms, at least since the fifth century B.C., Greek historians divided history into two eras, the prehistoric age of heroes and myth prior to the mid-twelfth century B.C. and the historical time to the present. The age of heroes, of whom Heracles (Lat. Hercules) was the most prominent, was not formally abandoned by historians; it was left to individual writers to make of the confusing and improbable legends what they would (Fornara, 7-10). In the popular and not strictly historical mind, the hero stories, such as those of Homer, still functioned either as general history or as source material for sundry forms of allegorical or didactic interpretation.

2. Jewish Heroes.

*Judaism looked to its sacred and traditional writings for its heroes. Though distinctions were not made between a heroic age and a historical period, Jewish writers did not just repeat their hero stories. In a variety of manners they too were reading and rewriting their narratives in light of later times and interests. In Israel's sacred literature, many figures exhibited heroic qualities, but certain ones tend to stand out: Noah, Abraham, *Moses, Elijah, David and Solomon. In the Hellenistic period there was an increased interest in such ideal figures (Nickelsburg, 4).

Though the eponymous ancestors of the Jews were Eber (Gen 10:24; 11:14-17), Israel and Judah, Abraham was considered the father of the nation and by many its greatest hero. The Abraham stories of Genesis 12—25 were repeated orally in synagogue readings and many other settings. They were also embellished in works such as the **Genesis Apocryphon* (1QapGen), found among the *Dead Sea Scrolls. In that work, Abram's sojourn in Egypt, elliptically narrated in Genesis (Gen 12:10-20), is expansively rewritten to include chronological detail, justification of Abram's lie, explicit description of Sarai's beauty and unequivocal protection of her chastity. Such stories reveal careful interaction with the biblical text, as well as contemporary concerns for chronography and exegetical solutions for various problems raised in Genesis. The terseness and elliptical nature of many a biblical story invited speculation and attempts to read between the lines so as to fill out the tantalizing narratives.

Some Jewish Hellenistic authors wrote with distinctly Hellenistic concerns about Jewish heroes. For example, in the context of the Hellenistic historiographic efforts to trace the origin and spread of philosophy and science, Abraham is presented as a member of a class of international intelligentsia, a wise sage who taught the Egyptians the art of astronomy (Pseudo-Eupolemus; Artapanus; Josephus *Ant.* 1.8.2 §165). In the context of another contemporary issue, the recording of universal genealogy, Abraham is related to the Greek hero Heracles by the marriage of his granddaughter to this most famous of all Greek heroes. It is clear that in much Jewish Hellenistic literature, including Josephus (Feldman, 143) Abraham, like other biblical figures, was transformed into a hero particularly suited for the Hellenistic environment of the authors.

Other contemporary texts, not written for a Greek audience, are more traditional in their depiction of biblical heroes, in that they focus on the religious aspects of the biblical characters. In the literature often grouped under the rubrics deuterocanonical or *Apocrypha and Pseudepigrapha, the hero Abraham is primarily represented as the covenant-making ancestor, the incessantly faithful-to-God father of the nation and the revelation-receiving sage. In Genesis and the rest of biblical literature, Abraham's faith in and covenant with God are the dominant themes with which he is associated. These emphases and the picture of Abraham as an ideal religious figure continue in the **Testaments of the Twelve Patriarchs, *Jubilees,* the **Apocalypse of Abraham,* the **Damascus Document* (CD, 4Q266-272) and other *Qumran texts (Sandmel, 37-38, 49).

The process of idealization, intrinsic to heroic literature, began in canonical texts, as one can easily see by comparing the figure of David in Kings with the highly idealized and pious David of the Chronicler. For the community using the Qumran Psalter (11Q5 27), David is said to have been "wise, and bright as the sun, a scribe, and discerning man, blameless in all his ways before God and men." He is then credited with composing 4,050 songs and psalms. In the most extensive catalog and description of heroic figures of Israel, Ben Sira (=*Ecclesiasticus, *Sirach) 44—50, the ancestors of Israel are praised usually for their piety, faithfulness and wisdom in a great hymn that begins: "Let us now laud famous men, and our ancestors in their generations. The Lord appointed to them much glory, his greatness from eternity. There were those who ruled and were famous men because of their valor; those who counseled because of their understanding; those who proclaimed prophecies" (Sir 44:1-3). Finally, even obscure figures in the biblical text, such as *Enoch and

*Melchizedek, were to become heroes in their own right, inspiring an extensive literature (*1-3 Enoch,* 11QMelchizedek).

Another interesting feature of the Jewish appreciation of its heroes was the popularity of *pseudepigraphic works composed in the name of Jewish heroes during the Greco-Roman era. This literary device was extremely common as witnessed in the mass of literature claiming the authorship of some ancient worthy, such as Adam, Enoch, Abraham, Jacob, Joseph, David, Solomon, Ezra, and many others.

*Philo, the prolific Jewish exegete and philosopher of *Alexandria (first century A.D.), displays a different side of the Greco-Jewish appreciation of heroes. Utilizing common Hellenistic interpretive conventions used first for the works of Homer, Philo allegorized the biblical text and thus made Abraham in his departure from Ur a philosopher's hero, a symbol of the soul that rejects the lower physical world as the ultimate reality and seeks the higher world of the mind (Philo *Abr.* 66, 84).

3. Heroes in the New Testament.

NT authors frequently look back to their national narratives and in so doing they generally fall in line with the deuterocanonical or apocryphal and pseudepigraphic literature as appreciators of Israel's heroes primarily for their religious qualities, albeit sometimes with distinctly Christian concerns. The famous catalog of heroes in Hebrews 11 hearkens back to Sirach 44—50. Abraham retains his prominence among NT authors, particularly for his faith and thus as the spiritual father even of Christians (Rom 4:13-25). James 2:23 uses an epithet for Abraham ("God's friend"), which apparently arose in the traditions developing around the person of Abraham (see Is 41:8; 2 Chron 20:7). But the heroics of the obscure were also considered, as is shown in the case of Melchizedek in Hebrews 7. The pseudepigraphic tradition that grew up around heroes is represented in the NT by the author of Jude (14-15), who quotes as authoritative the work of Enoch (*1 Enoch* 1:9).

The heroic David influenced profoundly *messianic notions of Christians, as can be seen in the Gospel narratives of Jesus' entry into Jerusalem (Mt 21:1-11; Mk 11:1-10). But stories about David could also be put to other uses. For example, David's procurement of the sacred bread of the presence (1 Sam 21:1-6) becomes Jesus' example of the legitimate breaking of the sabbath code of Exodus 20:8-11 (Mt 12:3-4 par.). All of the NT writings reflect the appreciative and creative use of Jewish heroic traditions within the contours of emerging Christianity.

See also MOSES; RELIGION, GRECO-ROMAN; REWRITTEN BIBLE IN PSEUDEPIGRAPHA AND QUMRAN.

BIBLIOGRAPHY. E. Bickerman, "The Jewish Historian Demetrios," in *Christianity, Judaism and Other Greco-Roman Cults,* ed. J. Neusner (Leiden: E. J. Brill, 1975); J. E. Bowley, "The Compositions of Abraham," in *Tracing the Threads: Studies in the Vitality of Jewish Pseudepigrapha,* ed. J. Reeves (Atlanta: Scholars Press, 1994); J. Charlesworth, ed., *The Old Testament Pseudepigrapha* (2 vols.; Garden City, NY: Doubleday, 1983-85); L. Feldman, "Abraham the Greek Philosopher in Josephus," *TAPA* 99 (1968) 143-56; C. Fornara, *The Nature of History in Ancient Greece and Rome* (Berkeley and Los Angeles: University of California, 1983); A. C. Haddon et al., "Heroes and Hero-Gods," *Encyclopedia of Religion and Ethics,* ed. J. Hastings (13 vols.; Edinburgh: T & T Clark, 1908-27) 6:633-68; B. M. Metzger, "Literary Forgeries and Canonical Pseudepigrapha," *JBL* 91 (1972) 3-24; A. Momigliano, *Alien Wisdom* (London: Cambridge University Press, 1975); idem, "The Origins of Universal History," in *On Pagans, Jews and Christians* (Middletown, CT: Wesleyan University Press, 1987) 31-57; G. Nickelsburg and J. Collins, eds., *Ideal Figures in Ancient Judaism* (Chico, CA: Scholars Press, 1980); S. Sandmel, *Philo's Place in Judaism: A Study of Conceptions of Abraham in Jewish Literature* (rev. ed.; New York: Ktav, 1971).

J. E. Bowley

HILLEL, HOUSE OF

Hillel the Elder flourished in the time of *Herod the Great. He is the founder of one of the principal houses or schools that laid the foundation on which later rabbinic Judaism would build and is famous for his seven rules of exegesis. He was regarded as the ideal sage.

1. Hillel the Person
2. The House of Hillel

1. Hillel the Person.

Hillel was born in Babylonia and as a young man went to Israel to study Scripture and the oral law. Very little is known of his life and personality. The earliest materials, mostly found in the Mishnah and Tosefta, record his legal opinions on various topics (*see* Rabbinic Literature: Mishnah and Tosefta). Stories about his life, usually with a moral lesson, are found in later sources and should be viewed with skepticism (Neusner, 286). The claim that Hillel was a descendant of David is in all probability an invention intended to enhance the great scholar's reputation.

That Hillel emerged as a major figure in Jewish law cannot be denied. He is regarded as *nasi*ʾ, "prince" (cf. *b. Pesaḥ.* 66a), which is probably a title retroactively applied to him. But this tradition accurately reflects Hillel's leadership and prominence. Later generations compared him with *Moses and Ezra. Another important indication of his leadership is seen in the enduring House of Hillel that continued to defend and develop his teaching.

2. The House of Hillel.

Hillel was well known for his teachings on the rules of *sacrifice and the *prozbul.* In the case of the former, he taught that the paschal lamb may be slaughtered on the *sabbath (*t. Pesaḥ.* 4:13; *y. Pesaḥ.* 6:1; *b. Pesaḥ.* 66a) and that one must lay hands on the sacrificial animal before presenting it to the priest (*b. Beṣa* 20a-b). In the case of the latter, he taught that one could circumvent the Jubilee remission of debt, for the Jubilee law induced people not to lend as the Jubilee drew near (*m. Šeb.* 10:2-4; contrast the teaching of Jesus in Luke 6:35: "Love your enemies, and do good, and lend, expecting nothing in return"). It is conceivable that Hillel's teaching that one must lay hands upon the animal of sacrifice before presenting it to the priest may shed light on Jesus' action in the *temple precincts, an action that appears to have been centered on the sellers of sacrificial animals (Mk 11:15-18; Jn 2:13-22).

Hillel is remembered to have enjoined his students, "Be among the disciples of Aaron, who loved peace and pursued it" (*m*ʾ*Abot* 1:12) and to have told a pest who demanded that Hillel teach him the whole of Torah in a single statement: "Do not do to another what you would not wish done to yourself; that is the whole Torah. The rest is commentary; go and study" (*b. Šabb.* 31a). Hillel's negative formulation of this principle finds a parallel in the somewhat older Tobit 4:15a: "And what you hate, do not do to any one" (*see* Tobit). In Jesus' teaching, the principle is expressed positively: "Whatever you wish that people would do to you, do so to them; for this is the law and the prophets" (Mt 7:12). The admonition to "go and study" is also found in Matthew 9:13 ("Go and learn"). Another saying credited to Hillel may parallel dominical tradition: "If I am not for myself, who is for me?" (*m* ʾ*Abot* 1:14). One is immediately reminded of Jesus' saying: "He who is not with me is against me, and he who does not gather with me scatters" (Mt 12:30 par. Lk 11:23).

Following the *destruction of Jerusalem and the temple in A.D. 70, the House of Hillel gained ascendancy over the House of *Shammai. We are told that the academy at Usha decided that the legal rulings of the House of Hillel were to be followed (*y. Ber.* 1:7). Often the rulings of the House of Hillel stand alongside (almost always following) the rulings of the House of Shammai. The editing of rabbinic literature suggests that the Shammaite rulings are older and at one time held sway and that the Hillelite rulings are later and came to hold sway.

Tradition has held that the House of Hillel, following the lead of its founder, taught more lenient views than did the House of Shammai. However, that is not always true. It has been estimated that in about 20 percent of their rulings, the House of Hillel ruled more stringently. Seven rules of exegesis, or *middot* ("measurements"), are attributed to Hillel (cf. *t. Sanh.* 7:11). These rules probably took their formal shape after Hillel's time, though it is possible some of them derive from the famous sage (*see* Biblical Interpretation, Jewish).

See also SHAMMAI, HOUSE OF; RABBINIC LITERATURE: MIDRASHIM; RABBINIC LITERATURE: MISHNAH AND TOSEFTA; RABBIS.

BIBLIOGRAPHY. D. Flusser, "Hillel and Jesus: Two Ways of Self-Awareness," in *Hillel and Jesus: Comparisons of Two Major Religious Leaders,* ed. J. H. Charlesworth and L. L. Johns (Minneapolis: Fortress, 1997) 71-107; R. Goldenberg, "Hillel the Elder," *ABD* 3:201-2; A. Goshen-Gottstein, "Hillel and Jesus: Are Comparisons Possible?" in *Hillel and Jesus: Comparisons of Two Major Religious Leaders,* ed. J. H. Charlesworth and L. L. Johns (Minneapolis: Fortress, 1997) 31-55; "Hillel and Shammai, Houses of" and "Hillel the Elder," *DJBP* 293-94; J. Neusner, *The Rabbinic Traditions About the Pharisees Before 70,* vol. 1 (Leiden: E. J. Brill, 1971); C. Safrai, "Sayings and Legends in the Hillel Tradition," in *Hillel and*

Jesus: Comparisons of Two Major Religious Leaders, ed. J. H. Charlesworth and L. L. Johns (Minneapolis: Fortress, 1997) 306-20; S. Safrai, "The Sayings of Hillel: Their Transmission and Reinterpretation," in *Hillel and Jesus: Comparisons of Two Major Religious Leaders*, ed. J. H. Charlesworth and L. L. Johns (Minneapolis: Fortress, 1997) 321-34; A. J. Saldarini, *Pharisees, Scribes and Sadducees in Palestinian Society: A Sociological Approach* (Wilmington, DE: Glazier, 1988) 204-7; D. R. Schwartz, "Hillel and Scripture: From Authority to Exegesis," in *Hillel and Jesus: Comparisons of Two Major Religious Leaders*, ed. J. H. Charlesworth and L. L. Johns (Minneapolis: Fortress, 1997) 335-62; E. E. Urbach, *The Sages: Their Concepts and Beliefs* (Cambridge, MA: Harvard University Press, 1973; 2d ed., Jerusalem: Magnes, 1979) 576-648; B. T. Viviano, "Hillel and Jesus on Prayer," in *Hillel and Jesus: Comparison of Two Major Religious Leaders*, ed. J. H. Charlesworth and L. L. Johns (Minneapolis: Fortress, 1997) 427-57. C. A. Evans

HIPPOCRATIC LETTERS

In his life of Hippocrates, the second-century A.D. Greek physician and historian Soranus refers to Hippocrates as the father of medicine and dates his birth to the equivalent of 460 B.C. He notes that Hippocrates was a member of a guild or a society known as the Asclepiades (= sons of Asclepius). Asclepius may have been a historical figure, since he is mentioned as a physician in the *Iliad* of Homer, but he came to be regarded as a deity, as attested by the renowned Temple of Asclepius on the island of Cos. Those with diseases offered sacrifices to him, and many slept in his temple, expecting the deity to visit and heal them. Hippocrates was said to have been descended from Asclepius on his father's side and from Heracles on his mother's side. Hippocrates' many writings on medical subjects resulted in his being venerated as a descendant of Asclepius. He was clearly regarded with respect by some ancient intellectuals, as is evident from his being mentioned twice by *Plato (in the *Protagoras* and the *Phaedrus*) and once by *Aristotle (in *Politics*).

The various editions of the Hippocratic collection of writings attributed to this man run from seventy to one hundred treatises, and the scholarly opinions about their authenticity has been a matter of debate since ancient times. In addition to treatises on explicitly medical subjects—such as *Epidemics, Fractures, Ulcers, Sacred Disease* [epilepsy]—there were letters from and to Hippocrates, including communications from rulers and officials. The latter convey assumptions about supernatural and miraculous actions in human experience, such as overcoming plagues and healing monarchs.

Galen (A.D. 129-195) traced to Asclepius his call to medicine and built on the main body of the Hippocratic tradition but regarded the letters as spurious. Born in Pergamum, he spent time at the medical school in *Alexandria and settled in *Rome. While he affirmed the perceptions of Hippocrates and traced their history in his own writings, he acknowledged that there were many works falsely attributed to him. Paracelsus (1493-1541), who taught medicine in Basel, reacted in the opposite way. He affirmed that God had revealed the truth about nature through such men as Hippocrates, while rationalists, such as Aristotle and Galen, had turned away from nature. He was drawn particularly to the Aphorisms, attributed to Hippocrates, which he saw as offering timeless truth, rather than to the Hippocratic analyses of human ailments. What one can see taking place in these shifting attitudes and strategies for handling the Hippocratic tradition might well be called the quest for the historical Hippocrates.

W. D. Smith has traced the historical evolution of the literature attributed to Hippocrates. By the seventeenth century, for example, there developed skepticism concerning the reports of supernatural achievements of Hippocrates, as is evident in the opinion of Jean Baptist van Belmont (1571-1644), who dismissed as spurious the letter of Hippocrates in which he reports how he had accomplished the cure of a plague. In the post-Enlightenment era, however, the conceptual and methodological issues concerning the Hippocratic tradition came into sharper focus. This is evident in the mid-nineteenth-century edition of the complete works of Hippocrates prepared by M. P. E. Littre, with the Greek text, translation in French and interpretive notes, published in 1861; it includes *Letters, Decrees* and the *Harangue*. Littre characterizes these writings, attributed to Hippocrates, as apocryphal and pseudonymous. He says that they are ancient, but the date and author(s) of them are unknown (308), and they probably range from the late fifth century B.C. down into the third century B.C.

Similarly, in the introduction by E. C. Kelly to F. Adam's translation of *The Genuine Works of Hippocrates* there is offered a reconstruction of the evolving role of medicine in Greek culture (v-viii). He states that in the fifth century B.C., "in the Golden Age of Greece," medicine began to sever its direct connection with religion and its control by the priesthood. Health resorts were developing on the shores of the Aegean and on islands, resembling modern spas. Hydrotherapy was taught, and relaxation from worry was encouraged. These resorts were controlled by priest-physicians: Asclepiads, who had dedicated their lives to *Aesculapius,* the god of medicine. Knowledge was passed on to sons and to a few disciples.

One such figure was Hippocrates, at the health resort/medical hospital on the island of Cos. Little was known about his life, but stories emerged that he was the son of a physician and the pupil of Gorgias the Sophist and Democritus the philosopher. He traveled widely but achieved his greatest fame by bringing to an end a plague in *Athens. The king of Persia, Artaxerxes, tried to lure him there as court physician, but Hippocrates was loyal to the Greek tradition and declined the invitation. He was said to have died in Thessaly at the age of 104.

When the writings of the ancients were being assembled for the library in Alexandria (*see* Alexandrian Library) two hundred years after Hippocrates' death, many writings attributed to him were found. Characteristic of works by him or attributed to him was the direct, personal study of disease, including the appearance of the stricken and an account of the course of the disease. This mode of analysis was in sharp contrast to the description of disease in religious terms and as a consequence of divine rebuke. In his translation of the works of Hippocrates, Kelly grouped those attributed to Hippocrates according to the probability of their being genuine or at least representing accurately the point of view of Hippocrates and his immediate successors. The epistles, however, and other public documents included in the Hippocratic collection he perceived to be almost certainly spurious, although they were probably composed within a century or so after his death.

The powerful factor that united these diverse documents was the high esteem in which Hippocrates was held, and—although Kelly does not make the point—the link of Hippocrates with the sacred figure of *Aesculapius,* the god of healing. His fame was enhanced by these letters purporting to have been sent to him by royal and political leaders, such as the *Letter from the Senate and People of Abdera to Hippocrates.* The expansion of the works attributed to him and the extension of reports of contacts with him by leaders who were his contemporaries are analogous to what happened in the evolution of the Jesus tradition. In the apocryphal Gospels the miraculous actions of Jesus are expanded and his alleged contacts with religious and political leaders of his time, as well as their recognition of his extraordinary powers, are set forth in this ongoing evolution of the Gospel tradition. Analogously, the emergence in the post-Enlightenment era of critical views concerning the authenticity and reliability of works attributed to Hippocrates parallel in time and intent the development of critical methods for evaluating and interpreting the traditions concerning Jesus.

BIBLIOGRAPHY. F. Adam, trans., with introduction by E. C. Kelly, *The Genuine Works of Hippocrates* (Baltimore: Williams & Wilkins, 1938); M. P. E. Littre, *Oeuvres Complete d'Hippocrate* (10 vols.; Paris: J. B. Bailliere et Fils, 1861); W. D. Smith, *The Hippocratic Tradition* (Ithaca, NY: Cornell University Press, 1979); J. B. van Belmont, *Aufgang der Artzney-Kunst* [The Exit of Medical Art] (Sulzbach, 1683). H. C. Kee

HISTORIANS, GRECO-ROMAN

Greco-Roman historians are important for the understanding of Christian origins in several ways. They provide *geographical, topographical and historical information that enables us to reconstruct the larger world in which Second Temple Judaism and early Christianity flourished. They also provide the basis for understanding the conventions of Jewish and early Christian historians upon whose works our understanding of early Christian origins is founded.

1. Origins
2. Classes of History
3. Conclusion

1. Origins.

The origins of historical writing must be reconstructed from limited fragmentary evidence and the testimonia of later authors. Its origins are bound up with the beginning of prose, as are many other genres of writing.

1.1. Precursors. The first prose author was Anaximander of Miletus (c. 610-540 B.C.), who applied the insights of Ionian philosophy to the world as he knew it. According to ancient testimonia, Anaximander made a map of the world and wrote a summary of its geography (e.g., Diogenes Laertius *Vit.* 2.1-2). His project was advanced in the second half of the sixth century B.C. by Hecataeus of Miletus, who also made a map of the world (FGrH 1 T 1) and wrote a commentary on it. Fragments of *The Geographical Description of the World* (*Periēgēsis gēs*) have come down to us from two volumes: one devoted to Europe and the other to Asia. These probably represent Hecataeus's perception of the world in two continents. The work is an ethnographic survey of the Mediterranean basin. It moves along the seacoast, describing the coast, the interior, major cities and points of interest, the history of the people and their customs.

1.2. The Development of "Historical" Genres. Since the work of F. Jacoby (*Fragmente der griechischen Historiker* [FGrH], 1923-), most scholars have recognized four related genres of writing that evolved out of these early Ionian works. In addition to *The Geographical Description of the World,* Hecataeus wrote a *Genealogies* in which he attempted to determine the mythical and historical periods (FGrH 1 FF 1-35). Genealogy dealt with the mythical period by attempting to work out the relationships among the heroes. Others followed suit, for example, Acusilaeus of Argos (FGrH 2) and Pherecydes of Athens (FGrH 3). Other prose authors drew their inspiration from *The Geographical Description of the World* and developed the ethnographic treatments of individual peoples by writing ethnography. The works were typically entitled by the adjectival form of the name of the people, such as Charon of Lampsacus, who wrote an *Ethiopica* and a two-volume *Persica* (FGrH 262 T 1), and Xanthus of Lydia, who wrote a four-volume *Lydiaca* (FGrH 765 FF 1-30). Still others began writing horography, or local histories, chronicling the stories of a city year by year, such as the local historians of Athens (Atthidographers): Hellanicus, Cleidemus, Androtion, Phanodemus, Melanthius, Demon and Philochorus (FGrH 323a-28). The attempt to write a sequential narrative led to the development of chronology. The most famous figure is Eratosthenes (275-194 B.C.), the head of the *Alexandrian library, who was the first to attempt to provide specific dates for literary and political figures (FGrH 241).

1.3. The Development of History. There is a fifth genre that Jacoby was reluctant to acknowledge but which most contemporary scholars recognize: history. The most famous successor to Hecataeus was Herodotus of Halicarnassus (c. 484-c. 430 B.C.). Herodotus knew Hecataeus's work (e.g., FGrH 1 F 305/Herodotus *Hist.* 2.155.2-156.2). He used some of the same methodology as his predecessor and incorporated at least eighteen ethnographic treatments of different peoples. At the same time, his work is far more than an extension of the Ionian's. Herodotus focused on people rather than geography. He not only related the events of the Persian wars but attempted to explain the conflict between the East and the West. The first sentence of his work is justly famous: "This is the publication of the research [*historia*] of Herodotus of Halicarnassus so that human affairs will not fade in time and the great and marvelous deeds that were displayed by both Greeks and barbarians will not lack renown, especially the reason why they fought with one another" (Herodotus *Hist.* 1.1). It is for this reason that *Cicero properly called Herodotus the *pater historiae* (Cicero *De Leg.* 1.5).

1.4. History and Related Genres. The relationships between history and other genres was not firm. There are several reasons for this. History was not a firmly defined discipline in antiquity. Cicero thought of history as a subset of *rhetoric (Cicero *De Orat.* 2.62). The distinction between history and the four genres of prose above are often vague: horography can be considered a subgenre of history and is conflated with history in some instances; ethnography was often a constituent element of history, e.g., Thucydides (*Hist.* 6.2-5) provided a sketch of Sicily, Hieronymous of Cardia regularly inserted ethnographies in his history of Alexander's successors (FGrH 154), and Polybius devoted one book to an ethnography (*Hist.* 34). The issue is what is placed in the foreground and what is set in the background. Even the distinction between history and other more distant genres can be problematic. For example, it is not always easy to distinguish history and *biography (although see Polybius *Hist.* 10.21.5-8; Plutarch, *Alex.* 1.2). At the same time, the ancients were aware of the task of the historian. Some wrote treatises on the principles that should govern historical writing (e.g., Dionysius of Halicarnassus, *Letter to Gnaeus Pompeius* 3-6; Lucian, *How to Write History*). Historians often made observations about their task, particularly in critiques of fellow practitioners.

2. Classes of History.

Among these observations are a number of comments that indicate the types of historical writing that ancient historians recognized. Dionysius of Halicarnassus distinguished three types: histories of individual cities or peoples, universal histories and histories of wars (Dionysius of Halicarnassus *Thuc.* 5-6). Content is the basic criterion in his assessment. Others distinguished between writing about antiquity and contemporary events (e.g., Polybius *Hist.* 9.2.1-7; Diodorus Siculus *Bib. Hist.* 4.1.1-4), making scope the decisive criterion. Still others distinguished between histories written by Greek authors and histories written by Easterners (e.g., Josephus, *Ag. Ap.* 1 §27), championing perspective as the normative criterion. While these distinctions do not constitute a full-scale analysis of the historical works from the Greco-Roman world, they do provide us with a scheme of classification that permits us to group many of the histories that have come down to us or about which ancients inform us.

2.1. Histories of Individual Cities or Peoples. The first group which Dionysius mentioned is the histories of individual cities or peoples. In other words, he lumped horography and ethnography together. While this lacks the precision of modern analyses, it has the advantage of providing a large category for works that deal with specific groups.

2.1.1. Local Histories. Local histories developed the possibility latent in the annals of cities by attempting to write the history of a specific city year by year. Most are characterized by parochialism: they were written by individuals who admired the city and wanted to set out its records. Like the annals they used, their works are simply written: they lack the rhetorical flourish that would characterize so much of Greek historiography. One of the best examples is Hellanicus of Lesbos (fl. fifth century B.C.). Hellanicus was a prolific author who is credited with more than twenty different works. He was the first to write an *Atthis*, or history of Attica (FGrH 323a). Hellanicus's effort was more than an expression of admiration for Athens: he attempted to use a scientific spirit to extend state records back into the remote past and bring them down to his own time, a reconstruction that earned Thucydides' stricture (*Hist.* 1.97.2).

The use of annals appealed to the Romans, who began writing horographies at least as early as Cassius Hemina (fl. second century B.C.). Hemina traced the history of Rome from the earliest period down through the Second Punic War (218-201 B.C.) and perhaps beyond. Pliny called him the oldest annalist (*Nat. Hist.* 13.84). There was, however, a difference between the Greek and Roman practices. The Greeks kept horography and history proper separate; the Romans did not. While the Romans used annals as a basis for their works, they did not feel bound by the conventions of Greek horography that simply chronicled the events of a year; rather, they chose to write about human affairs more freely but to do so in an annalistic form.

2.1.2. Histories of Peoples. The other group consists of ethnographies and histories of specific people. These were distinct, even though Dionysius did not address the differences. Ethnographies were written by Greeks who were interested in other peoples. They continued to use the Ionian method of reporting hearsay. They were obligated to cover the standard topics of the genre: geography, history, wonder and customs of the people. Histories were different. Historians were required to analyze causes, not simply report. They did not follow the fourfold pattern of ethnography. Finally, their perspective is quite different from that of ethnographies; they are Greeks writing about Greeks, not Greeks writing about non-Greeks.

The works in this subcategory are known as *Hellenica.* They are continuations of Thucydides' *History of the Peloponnesian War,* which ended abruptly in 411 B.C. The anonymous Oxyrhynchus historian, Theopompus, and Xenophon changed the scope of Thucydides' work by enlarging it to the affairs of the Greeks generally rather than focusing on a single war. The identity of the historian who wrote the 900 lines that were discovered on a papyrus at Oxyrhynchus in 1906 has never been solved (FGrH 66). The lengthy fragment is characterized by a sobriety of judgment and critical acumen that is rare in antiquity. It is not unfair to say that the Oxyrhynchus historian, Thucydides and Polybius are the ancient world's closest analogues to modern historians and constitute an exception rather than a rule in ancient historiography.

Theopompus was a student of Isocrates who thought that history should be subordinated to politics (FGrH 115). Xenophon's work is a roughly united work that consists of three major sections that set out the affairs of the Greeks from 411 to 362 B.C. The significance of these works is that they broadened history from the war monograph (see below) to the larger story of a people.

2.1.3. Archaic Histories of Peoples. The next subgroup is problematic. F. Jacoby considered the histories of Sicily to be ethnographies (FGrH 554-77). However, C. Fornara has made a reasonable case for considering them as a separate subgroup. Unlike *Hellenica* that addressed recent events, the *Sicilica* contained *archaeologiae*, or accounts of the earliest period. Since a number of historians considered *archaeologiae* to be distinct from works that concentrate on recent history, we may place these in a separate subgroup.

The most important of these historians was Timaeus of Tauromenium (c. 356-c. 260 B.C.). Timaeus's thirty-eight volume history extended the perspective of the *Hellenica* both chronologically and geographically (FGrH 566). He argued that the Greeks in the West had made notable contributions to Hellenism. The work thus had an apologetic edge: the Greek west was important and should not be ignored (see FF 40 and 94). It was natural that a work that dealt with Sicily, Italy and northern Africa would have an impact on Roman historians and those Greeks who were interested in Rome. It was significant enough that Polybius felt compelled to engage in a major polemic against Timaeus (Polybius *Hist.* 12.3.1—16.14; 23.1—28.10).

2.1.4. Apologetic Histories. The apologetic dimension of Timaeus reflects an inside debate among Greeks. What happened when the debate was extended to non-Greeks? In the course of a major polemic against Greek historians, Josephus claimed that groups from the East had a superior historiography (Josephus *Ag. Ap.* 1 §§6-56). While the Greeks were superior rhetors, they did not record ancient history accurately. Josephus claimed that Eastern historians did. The three most important representatives were Berossus (c. 350-c. 280 B.C.), who wrote a *Babylonica* (FGrH 680); Manetho (fl. c. 280 B.C.), who wrote an *Aigyptiaca* (FGrH 609); and Josephus (A.D. 37/38-c. 96), who wrote a twenty-volume *Jewish Antiquities*. All were priests who used the records of their own people to write their histories. In each case they recast their indigenous stories in Hellenic form in an effort to offer a self-definition that would win higher respect and acceptance for the group in the Greco-Roman world.

2.2. Universal Histories. The second category that Dionysius used was universal histories. These were works that had a geographical/ethnographical scope that extended beyond specific cities or peoples to incorporate the world as it was known. There are at least two forces that helped to create a worldwide perspective.

2.2.1. Persia. The first was Persia's encroachment on Greek soil. The expansion of Persia made the Greeks aware of other peoples in ways that they had not been prior to the end of the sixth century B.C. The work of Hecataeus of Miletus is at least indirectly indebted to Persia. The decisive step was taken by Herodotus, whose *Histories* are Dionysius's parade example of a universal history. While we might consider them a war monograph, they do describe the world as Herodotus knew it.

The real honor for writing the first universal history should go to Ephorus (c. 405-330 B.C.). At least Polybius claimed that he was his only predecessor (Polybius *Hist.* 5.32.2), and Diodorus of Siculus considered him an important model (Diodorus Siculus *Bib. Hist.* 5.1.4). Ephorus wrote a thirty-volume history of the world from the return of the Heracleidae in the eleventh century B.C. to 341 B.C. (FGrH 70). One of the most pressing difficulties Ephorus had to address in such an undertaking was the organization of diverse and independent material. He solved the problem by aligning topics with specific books (Diodorus Siculus *Bib. Hist.* 5.1.4). This topical arrangement was a break with the chronological arrangement of his predecessors, but its practical utility was apparent enough to his successors that they adopted it.

2.2.2. Rome. The second power that forced the Greeks to think in universal terms was Rome. The impact of Rome was not lost on a Greek military officer who had been captured during the Third Macedonian War. Polybius wrote: "For what human being is so small or indifferent that he or she would not want to know how and by what type of government almost the entire world came under the single rule of the Romans in less than fifty-three years—something that had never happened before" (Polybius *Hist.* 1.1.5; cf. also 6.2.3 and 39.8.7). In particular, he felt compelled to explain Rome's rise to his fellow Greeks, a compulsion he answered in a complex work of forty books. He thought that the uniqueness of the events necessitated a new synthesis: "For what is unique in my work and what is amazing about our time is this: just as Fortune has bent almost every historical event in the known world into one direction and has compelled everything to incline to one and the same goal, so," he continued, "it is necessary to bring the administration of Fortune which she has used for the completion of her universal tasks, under one synoptic perspective for the readers through a history" (Polybius *Hist.* 1.4.1-2).

Polybius's most important successor was the Middle Stoic philosopher, Poseidonius (c. 135-51/50 B.C.). Poseidonius began where Polybius left off at 146 B.C. and continued to c. 80 B.C. Like Polybius, he believed in the unity of history. However, he worked out his understanding of history in a more philosophically sophisticated form than his military predecessor had. For Poseidonius, the Roman Empire represented the unity of humanity and reflected the cosmopolis of God.

Polybius's and Poseidonius's perspectives were universal spatially but not temporally. Polybius began his narrative proper in 220 B.C., providing a preface of the Punic Wars in the first two books (see Polybius *Hist.* 1.3.8), while Poseidonius began in 146 B.C. Another Greek thought that this gap should be filled. Like Polybius, Dionysius of Halicarnassus spent an appreciable part of his adult life in Rome. Dionysius agreed with Polybius that the accomplishment of Rome merited special attention (Dionysius of Halicarnassus *Ant. Rom.* 1.2.1-3.6). Unlike Polybius, he had not come to Rome as a captive; rather, he had been well received. He saw a cultural unity in the Greco-Roman world that he attempted to demonstrate in both his rhetorical treatises and his history. Dionysius believed that the Greeks did not know the early period of Rome adequately. For this reason he wrote his *Roman Antiquities* in twenty books (Dionysius of Halicarnassus *Ant. Rom.* 1.4.1-6.5, esp. 4.1-3; 6.1-2). One of his basic arguments was that the Romans were originally Greeks (Dionysius of Halicarnassus *Ant. Rom.* 1.5.1-4; 7.70.1-73.5). While we might be tempted to smile at such an argument, we should remember that Greek culture had so pervaded Rome that his argument was not without power.

Not all Greeks were so enthralled by Rome. Diodorus Siculus (fl. first century B.C.) wrote a forty-volume *Bibliothēkē* that covered the known world. For years, Diodorus's excessive dependence on sources led modern scholars to devalue his work. More recently a number of studies have argued that the *Bibliothēkē* is not a pastische of sources but a work that has been shaped by definite ideas. This has led to a reassessment of Diodorus's attitude toward Rome. Diodorus lacks the notion of the inevitable rise of Rome. While he includes praise of Rome, these statements are probably those of his sources; his own view appears to be much more guarded if not negative.

These Greek efforts were not without a corresponding tradition among the Romans. The most famous Latin historian of Rome is Livy (64/59 B.C.-A.D. 12/17). His 142-book *Ab urbe condita libri* covered Rome from the origins of the city to his own period. Unlike Polybius and Dionysius, who were concerned about the impact of Rome on Greeks, Livy was unnerved by the end of the republic. While he has often been called an "Augustan historian," his sympathies were with the republic. His work depends heavily on sources that are often incorporated without adequate critical analysis.

The later story of Rome has an interesting twist. The story of early imperial Rome is told by *Tacitus (A.D. c. 56-c. 115). While his approximately thirty-volume *Histories* and *Annals* that relate the history of Rome from A.D. 14 to 96 are not universal histories, they serve as the predecessor for the important universal history of Ammianus Marcellinus (A.D. c. 330-395). Ammianus's thirty-volume history began where Tactius left off at A.D. 96 and continued to A.D. 378. While a great deal of his work has been lost, what we have suggests that he worked carefully with a great deal of attention to detail. It is fitting that a Greek who wrote a history of Rome in Latin should write the last great universal history of the Greco-Roman world.

2.3. Histories of Wars. The third and final category that Dionysius mentioned was the war monograph. The paradigm is Thucydides (c. 460/455-c. 400 B.C.), the Athenian general who wrote an incomplete eight-volume history of the Peloponnesian War (431-404 B.C.). Thucydides took the theme of war introduced by Herodotus, but reduced Herodotus's global perspective to a limited time and place. He matched the intensification of his scope with the rigor of his analysis. He is open about his preferences, thorough in his research and critical in his analyses. Perhaps the most famous example is his comments about the speeches of his characters (Thucydides *Hist.* 1.22.1; cf. also Polybius *Hist.* 12.25a.5-25b.1). This does not mean that he is without fault, but it does indicate that he set a new standard in historical writing.

He was followed by many successors. Two of the most important from the standpoint of the NT are the Roman senator Sallust, who wrote two monographs, *Cataline's Conspiracy* and *Jugurtha's War*, and the Jewish priest-general-historian *Josephus, who wrote an account of the First Jewish Revolt (A.D. 66-70) in seven volumes, *The Jewish War*. In all of these cases, the author was a either a participant or eyewitness of the events that he describes.

3. Conclusion.

There are several caveats that we should keep in mind when reading ancient historians. We still lack all of the texts. It has only been in recent years that the task of completing Jacoby's monumental collection of Greek fragments has been undertaken. While scholarship has studied the major historians in detail, it has not explored many of the less significant historians adequately. The result is that we often work with generalizations that were created by the prejudices of an earlier generation of scholars without the benefit of full-scale analyses. There is still a good deal of work to do in the field of Hellenistic historiography.

See also BIOGRAPHY, ANCIENT; GEOGRAPHICAL PERSPECTIVES IN LATE ANTIQUITY; JEWISH LITERATURE: HISTORIANS AND POETS; JOSEPHUS: INTERPRETIVE METHODS AND TENDENCIES; JOSEPHUS: VALUE FOR NEW TESTAMENT STUDY; REWRITTEN BIBLE IN PSEUDEPIGRAPHA AND QUMRAN; SCHOLARSHIP, GREEK AND ROMAN; SUETONIUS; TACITUS; WRITING AND LITERATURE: GRECO-ROMAN; WRITING AND LITERATURE: JEWISH.

BIBLIOGRAPHY. **Editions.** Most Greek and Latin texts are in one of the three major series: the Collection des Univerités de France (Budé), the Oxford Classical Library, and the Teubner Series. The major authors are all in the Loeb Classical Library. F. Jacoby, *Die Fragmente der griechischen Historiker* (3 vols. in 16 parts; Leiden: E. J. Brill, 1923-69) is incomplete, but the work has been resumed. **General Bibliography.** R. Drews, *The Greek Accounts of Eastern History* (Washington, D.C.: Center for Hellenic Studies, 1973); C. Fornara, *The Nature of History in Ancient Greece and Rome* (Berkeley and Los Angeles: University of California Press, 1983); F. Jacoby, "Über die Entwicklung der griechischen Historiographie. . . ," *Klio* 9 (1909) 80-123; A. Momigliano, *The Classical Foundations of Modern Historiography* (SCL 54; Berkeley and Los Angeles: University of California Press, 1990); idem, *Studies in Historiography* (London: Weidenfeld and Nicolson, 1966); G. E. Sterling, *Historiography and Self-definition: Josephos, Luke-Acts and Apologetic Historiography* (NovTSup 64; Leiden: E. J. Brill, 1992). **Studies of Individual Historians.** P. Bilde, *Flavius Josephus between Jerusalem and Rome* (JSPSup 2; Sheffield: Sheffield Academic Press, 1988); E. Gabba, *Dionysius and* The History of Archaic Rome (SCL 56; Berkeley and Los Angeles: University of California Press, 1991); A. W. Gomme, A. Andrewes and K. J. Dover, *A Historical Commentary on Thucydides* (5 vols.; Oxford: Clarendon Press, 1945-81); J. Malitz, *Die Historien des Poseidonios* (Zetemata 79; München: C. H. Beck, 1983); R. Martin, *Tacitus* (Berkeley and Los Angeles: University of California Press, 1981); S. Mason, ed., *Flavius Josephus: Translation and Commentary* (10 vols.; Leiden: E. J. Brill, 2000-); K. Sacks, *Diodorus Siculus and the First Century* (Princeton, NJ: Princeton University Press, 1990); idem, *Polybius on the Writing of History* (UCPCS 24; Berkeley and Los Angeles: University of California Press, 1981); W. F. Walbank, *A Historical Commentary on Polybius* (3 vols.; Oxford: Clarendon Press, 1957-79); idem, *Polybius* (SCL 42; Berkeley and Los Angeles: University of California Press, 1972); P. G. Walsh, *Livy: His Historical Aims and Methods* (Cambridge: Cambridge University Press, 1961); K. H. Waters, *Herodotos: His Problems, Methods and Originality* (Norman, OK: University of Oklahoma Press, 1985).

G. E. Sterling

HISTORIANS, JEWISH. *See* JEWISH LITERATURE: HISTORIANS AND POETS; JOSEPHUS: INTERPRETIVE METHODS AND TENDENCIES; JOSEPHUS: VALUE FOR NEW TESTAMENT STUDY.

HISTORIOGRAPHY, ANCIENT. *See* HISTORIANS, GRECO-ROMAN; JOSEPHUS: INTERPRETIVE METHODS AND TENDENCIES.

HISTORY, JEWISH. *See* JEWISH HISTORY: GREEK PERIOD; JEWISH HISTORY: PERSIAN PERIOD; JEWISH HISTORY: ROMAN PERIOD.

HOLY DAYS. *See* FESTIVALS AND HOLY DAYS: GRECO-ROMAN; FESTIVALS AND HOLY DAYS: JEWISH.

HOLY LAND. *See* ISRAEL, LAND OF.

HOLY MEN, JEWISH

Several Jewish holy men in the time of Jesus were well known for mighty acts and remarkable answers to *prayer. The lives and activities of five of them compare in various ways with the life and ministry of Jesus. These five are Ḥoni ha-Meʿaggel (first century B.C.); Abba Ḥilqiah, grandson of Ḥoni (late first century B.C., early first century A.D.); Ḥanan ha-Neḥba, grandson of Ḥoni (late first century B.C., early first century A.D.); Ḥanina ben Dosa (first century A.D.) and Eleazar the Exorcist (first century A.D.).

1. Ḥoni ha-Meʿaggel
2. Abba Ḥilqiah, Grandson of Ḥoni
3. Ḥanan ha-Neḥba
4. Ḥanina ben Dosa
5. Eleazar the Exorcist

1. Ḥoni ha-Meʿaggel.

In the rabbinic literature Ḥoni is called ha-Meʿaggel ("the circle drawer"). *Josephus refers to him as "Onias, a righteous man beloved by God." He was remembered for praying for rain during a time of severe drought. When his prayer initially went unheeded, he drew a circle on the ground and told God that he would not leave it until rain came (perhaps following the example of Habakkuk; Hab 2:1). Soon it did rain. The story is found in the *Mishnah (*m. Taʿan.* 3:8; cf. *b. Taʿan.* 23a) and is mentioned by Josephus.

The earliest account is provided by Josephus, who is primarily interested in the Jewish civil war, not Ḥoni's answered prayer. His allusion to the holy man and to the belief that through his prayer God sent rain attests to the antiquity of the tradition and offers an important measure of support for its authenticity. According to Josephus (*Ant.* 14.2.1 §§22-24):

> Now there was a certain man named Onias, who was righteous and beloved of God, who at one time during a rainless period prayed to end the drought; and hearing, God sent rain. This man hid himself because he saw that the civil war continued unabated, but taken up to the camp of the Judeans he was asked, just as he ended the drought through prayer, similarly to place a curse on Aristobulus and his partisans. But though refusing and trying to beg off, he was compelled by the mob. Standing in their midst, he said: "O God, King of the universe, since those who are now standing with me are Your people and those who are besieged are Your priests, I beseech You neither to hearken to those men against these nor (to hearken to) what these men are asking (You) to perform against those." And the wicked among the Judeans who stood by stoned him for praying these things.

The Mishnaic account shows no interest in the political issues; its interest is much more theological. According to *m. Taʿanit* 3:8:

> Once they said to Ḥoni the Circle-Drawer, "Pray that rain may fall." He said to them, "Go out and bring in the Passover ovens that they may not be softened." He prayed, but rain did not come down. What did he do? He drew a circle and stood within it and said, "Lord of the universe, Your sons have turned their faces to me, for I am as a son of the house before You. I swear by Your great name that I will not move from here until You have mercy on Your sons." Rain began dripping. He said, "Not for this have I prayed, but for rain [that fills] cisterns, pits, and caverns." It began to come down violently. He said, "Not for this have I prayed, but for rain of goodwill, blessing, and plenty." It came down in moderation until Israel went up from Jerusalem to the Mount of the House because of the rain.

What is of concern to the Mishnaic tradition is Ḥoni's apparent familiarity with heaven. We are told that a certain Simeon ben Shetah expressed disapprobation: "Had you not been Ḥoni, I would have pronounced a ban against you! For were these years like those concerning which Elijah said no rain should fall—for the keys to rainfall were in his hands—would not the result of your action have been the desecration of God's name? But what can I do with you, since you importune God and he performs your will, like a son that importunes his father and he performs his will."

Ḥoni's life and activities present a few points

of comparison with the life and ministry of Jesus. Ḥoni's persistence in praying for rain parallels Jesus' similar teaching, as seen in the parables of the persistent friend (Lk 11:5-8) and the importunate widow (Lk 18:1-8). Ḥoni's filial relationship with God is also interesting. Jesus taught his disciples to pray to God as "Father" (Mt 6:9; Mk 14:36) and was regarded as God's Son (Mk 1:11).

2. Abba Ḥilqiah, Grandson of Ḥoni.
Abba Ḥilqiah, grandson of Ḥoni (son of Ḥoni's son), was a very pious and poor man who worked for hire, wore a borrowed coat and had insufficient food for guests. He was requested by the rabbis to pray for rain. He and his wife went upstairs and, from opposite corners, prayed. Soon clouds began to form (*b. Ta ʿan.* 23a-23b). Part of the story reads:

> He said to his wife, "I know that the rabbis have come on account of rain. Let us go up to the roof and pray. Perhaps the Holy One, blessed be He, will have mercy and rain will come down, without credit given to us." They went up to the roof. He stood in one corner; she [stood] in another corner. At first the clouds appeared over the corner where his wife [stood] . . . . They said to him, "We know that the rain [has come] on your account."

Poverty is a feature common to most of the traditions of the holy men. Jesus' lifestyle was also one of poverty: "Foxes have holes, and birds of the air have nests; but the Son of Man has nowhere to lay his head" (Mt 8:20 NRSV; Lk 9:58).

3. Ḥanan ha-Neḥba.
Ḥanan ha-Neḥba (i.e., Ḥanan "the hidden"), grandson of Ḥoni (son of Ḥoni's daugher), was a modest man who used to hide from public view. Like his famous grandfather, Ḥanan gained a reputation for bringing down rain through his prayers (*b. Ta ʿan.* 23b):

> Ḥanan ha-Neḥba was the son of the daughter of Ḥoni the Circle-Drawer. When the world needed rain the rabbis would send school children to him and they would seize the hem of his cloak and say to him, "Father, Father, give us rain!" Then he would petition the Holy One, blessed be He, "Master of the universe, give rain for the sake of these children who do not even know enough to distinguish between a Father who gives rain and a father who does not."

The action of the little children who come to Ḥanan ha-Neḥba, seize the hem of his cloak and make a request parallels Synoptic tradition: "They . . . begged him that they might touch even the fringe of his cloak; and all who touched it were healed" (Mk 6:56 NRSV).

4. Ḥanina ben Dosa.
Ḥanina, probably the most famous of the holy men, lived in the town of Arab, a small Galilean village about 10 miles north of Nazareth. In *m. Soṭa* 9:15 he is remembered as one of the "men of deeds": "When Rabbi Ḥanina ben Dosa died, the men of [great] deeds ceased." The description "men of deeds" (*ʾanšê ma ʿaseh*) refers to the miracles that were effected through his prayers. Ḥanina was especially famous for his prayers that resulted in healing (*m. Ber.* 5:5):

> They say about Rabbi Ḥanina ben Dosa that he used to pray over the sick and say, "This one will live," or "That one will die." They said to him, "How do you know?" He said to them, "If my prayer is fluent in my mouth, I know that he is accepted; and if it is not, I know that he is rejected."

On one occasion he prayed for the son of Gamaliel II (or possibly Gamaliel the Elder). Because the words of his prayer in this instance came fluently, he knew he had been answered. Gamaliel's disciples noted the time and returned to their master to discover that the boy had recovered at the very hour Ḥanina had spoken (*b. Ber.* 34b; cf. *y. Ber.* 5:5):

> The Rabbis taught: Once the son of Rabban Gamaliel became ill. He sent two scholars to Rabbi Ḥanina ben Dosa to ask him to pray for him. As soon as he saw them, he went up to an upper room and prayed for him. When he came down, he said to them, "Go, the fever has left him." They said to him, "Are you a prophet?" He said to them, "I am neither a prophet nor the son of a prophet. But this I have accepted: If my prayer is fluent in my mouth, I know that he is accepted; and if not, I know that he is rejected." They sat down and wrote down the exact time. And when they came to Rabban Gamaliel, he said to them, "[By] the [temple] service! You are neither short nor long, but so it was. At that exact time the fever left him and he asked us for water to drink."

The healing of Gamaliel's son at the very "hour" that Ḥanina announced to the disciples that he would recover parallels the Jesus tradition: "The father realized that was the hour when Jesus had said to him, 'Your son will live'" (Jn 4:46-53 NRSV; cf. Mt 8:5-13; Lk 7:1-10). The statement itself, "Your son will live," parallels Ḥanina's alternating pronouncements, "This one will live" or "That one will die."

Another early story tells of Ḥanina's encounter with a poisonous lizard (*t. Ber.* 3:20; cf. *m. Ber.* 5:1):

> They say about Rabbi Ḥanina ben Dosa that once while he was standing and praying, a poisonous lizard bit him, but he did not interrupt [his prayer]. His disciples went and found it dead at the mouth of its hole. They said, "Woe to the man who is bitten by a lizard. Woe to the lizard that bit ben Dosa!"

The Talmudic gemara richly embellishes the Ḥanina ben Dosa tradition. He stretches boards, bans the "queen of the demons" from the land, daily hears the heavenly voice cry out, "My son" (cf. *b. Ber.* 34b; *y. Ber.* 5:5; *b. Pesaḥ.* 112b; *b. Ta* ʿ*an.* 24b-25a).

5. Eleazar the Exorcist.

Josephus tells us of a certain Eleazar who followed the incantations of Solomon and could draw out demons through a person's nostrils, through the use of the Baaras root (further described in *J.W.* 7.6.3 §§180-85). Josephus explains that God gave Solomon "knowledge of the art used against demons for the benefit and healing of humans. He also composed incantations by which illnesses are relieved, and left behind forms of exorcisms with which those possessed by demons drive them out, never to return" (Josephus *Ant.* 8.2.5 §45). Josephus says that Eleazar "adjured the demon, speaking Solomon's name and repeating the incantations which he had composed, never to re-enter him" and proved the success of his exorcism by commanding the departing spirit to upset a cup of water or a foot basin (Josephus *Ant.* 8.2.5 §§46-49).

A few of the details recounted by Josephus parallel certain features that appear in the stories of Jesus' exorcisms. Like Eleazar, Jesus was well known for his ability to cast out "demons" (Mk 1:34), though in the specific Gospel episodes themselves "evil spirit" and "unclean spirit" are the preferred terms (e.g., Mk 5:8; Lk 7:21). The possessed falls down (Mk 3:11; 9:20). The exorcist adjures the demon (Mk 5:7) and warns it not to return or reenter (Mk 9:25; Mt 12:44-45 par. Lk 11:24-26). The demon is cast out in Jesus' name (Mk 9:38-39). Eleazar commanded the demon to tip over the washbasin; Jesus ordered the demon to be silent (e.g., Mk 3:12).

See also APOLLONIUS OF TYANA; MAGICAL PAPYRI; RABBIS.

BIBLIOGRAPHY. C. Brown, "Synoptic Miracles Stories: A Jewish Religious and Social Setting," *Forum* 2 (1986) 55-76; P. Fiebig, *Jüdische Wundergeschichten des neutestamentlichen Zeitalters* (Tübingen: Mohr Siebeck, 1911); M. J. Geller, "Jesus' Theurgic Powers: Parallels in the Talmud and Incantation Bowls," *JJS* 28 (1977) 141-55; G. H. Twelftree, *Jesus the Exorcist: A Contribution to the Study of the Historical Jesus* (WUNT 2.54; Tübingen: Mohr Siebeck, 1993; repr. Peabody, MA: Hendrickson, 1993) esp. 209-12; G. Vermes, "Ḥanina ben Dosa," in *Post-Biblical Jewish Studies* (SJLA 8; Leiden: E. J. Brill, 1975) 178-214; idem, *Jesus the Jew: A Historian's Reading of the Gospels* (Philadelphia: Fortress, 1973) 58-82.

C. A. Evans

HOLY SPIRIT

This analysis is intended to expose the most significant issues related to NT conceptions of the Holy Spirit with respect to their Jewish and Greco-Roman milieus. In the first century the expression *holy spirit* was not a *terminus technicus* but an expression that could be construed in a variety of ways, from *nepeš* to an *eschatological agent of purification. Jews during the first century did not uniformly believe that they lived during an era bereft of the Holy Spirit. Jewish concepts of *pneuma* were extraordinarily flexible during the first century, due in no small measure to the Greco-Roman milieu that inevitably influenced large segments of early *Judaism. The spirit, however its nature was construed, was associated with a wide variety of effects, including but not limited to prophecy; inspired exegesis; creation; purity, conversion, and initiation; and an eschatological figure.

1. Diverse Conceptions of the Holy Spirit
2. The Alleged Absence of the Holy Spirit
3. A Variegated Milieu
4. Varieties of Effects

1. Diverse Conceptions of the Holy Spirit.

In the NT the word *spirit* (*pneuma*) is to be understood as the spirit of God approximately 275 times; in as many as 92 of these occurrences, the expression is "holy spirit" (*pneuma hagion*). This impressive frequency of references should not lead, however, to the incorrect inference that the words *pneuma* or *pneuma hagion* were *termini technici* to which were attached a relatively established cluster of meanings. The scenario is to the contrary.

Even references to "holy spirit" in the *Hebrew Bible (MT Ps 51:13; Is 63:10, 11) suggest widely varying applications of this designation. In Psalm 51, the holy spirit is that which vivifies individual human beings. The psalmist therefore implores, "Do not cast me away from your presence/Do not take your holy spirit away from me" (Ps 51:13). In Isaiah 63:7-14, in contrast, the holy spirit is similar to the angel of Exodus 23 that guided Israel through the wilderness. The prophet's recollection that Israel "rebelled and grieved his holy spirit," in a context permeated by exodus and wilderness imagery, is reminiscent of the command that Israel "not rebel against" the angel sent to guard Israel on its wilderness sojourn (Ex 23:20-23). The further recollection that "the spirit of the LORD gave them rest" (Is 63:14) is reminiscent of Exodus 33:14, according to which God's presence gave Israel rest.

During the centuries preceding the first century A.D., this flexibility with respect to conceptions of the holy spirit persisted, as the Dead Sea Scrolls illustrate. In the **Damascus Document* (CD 7:4; 5:11-13) the term "holy spirit" replaces the biblical term *nepeš* to describe that which can be defiled. While Leviticus 11:43 and 20:25 contain the command not to defile the *nepeš,* CD 7:4 describes sinners who defile "their holy spirit, for with blasphemous tongue they have opened their mouth against the statutes of God's covenant" (see CD 5:11-13; 12:11). Compare this with the hymn writer's thanks to God that he is "strengthened by the spirit of holiness" (1QH 16:15; *see* Thanksgiving Hymns) or the words of praise that God has chosen "to purify me with your holy spirit" (1QH 16:20).

Still further afield from the anthropological interpretation of the term "holy spirit" in CD 7:4 is the belief expressed in the **Rule of the Community* (1QS 4:21), according to which the holy spirit is the eschatological agent of purification. The scrolls provide, therefore, a window into the diversity that characterized the era that gave birth to Christianity. The holy spirit could be conceived as a constituent dimension of human life (*nepeš*) from birth to death, as that power that strengthens and purifies those who join themselves to the community of *Qumran coven-anters and as that which will bring eschatological purification.

2. The Alleged Absence of the Holy Spirit.

Much of NT scholarship has adhered to the hypothesis that Jews during the NT era believed that the holy spirit had departed from Israel in the distant past and would return only in the eschatological future. J. Jeremias, for instance, subtitled a portion of his *New Testament Theology* (New York: Scribner's, 1971) "The Return of the Quenched Spirit," and aptly summarized this view: "With the death of the last writing prophets, Haggai, Zechariah and Malachi, *the spirit was quenched* because of the sin of Israel. After that time, it was believed, God still spoke only through the 'echo of his voice' . . . a poor substitute" (Jeremias, 81).

The earliest literature that allegedly espouses this position belongs to a *rabbinic compilation known as the Tosefta, which was compiled possibly in the fourth century A.D. but no doubt contains earlier traditions (*see* Rabbinic Literature: Mishnah and Tosefta). The text reads:

> When Haggai, Zechariah, and Malachi, the last of the prophets, died, the Holy Spirit ceased in [from] Israel. Nevertheless, a Bath Qol was heard by them: It once happened that the sages entered a house in Jericho and they heard a Bath Qol, saying, "There is a man here who is worthy of the Holy Spirit, but there is no one in his generation righteous." Thereupon, they set their eyes upon Hillel (*t. Soṭa* 13:2-4).

Interpreted alongside other texts of disparate provenance and date of composition (Ps 74:9; Pr Azar 15; 1 Macc 4:46; 9:27; 14:41; Josephus *Ag. Ap.* 1.8 §§37-41; *2 Bar.* 85:3), this text is alleged to state that with the end of the succession of the canonical prophets, the holy spirit was replaced by an inferior voice, the *bath qol* (*bat qōl*). The *bath qol* informs the sages who are gathered together that *Hillel is worthy of the spirit but cannot receive it because of the evil generation to which he belongs.

The problem with this interpretation is that it ignores the literary context of *t. Soṭa* 13:2-4 and therefore violates the straightforward principle this text is intended to illustrate: "When a righteous person comes into the world, good comes into the world . . . and retribution departs from the world" (*t. Soṭa* 10:1). The compiler illustrates this principle by means of a historical survey that extends from Noah to the *Sanhedrin (*t. Soṭa* 10:1—15:7).

If *t. Soṭa* 13:2-4 be interpreted in light of this principle, according to which the presence of the righteous in the world brings the presence of good, then the word that Hillel is worthy of the holy spirit should be interpreted to mean that the holy spirit which withdrew with the death of Haggai, Zechariah and Malachi has now returned because someone—Hillel—is again present who is worthy to warrant the return of the spirit. Interpreted within its literary context, *t. Soṭa* 13:2-4 is an affirmation that with the presence once again of the righteous in the first century A.D., the holy spirit could reappear following its temporary withdrawal after the death of the latter prophets.

The advent of the Spirit at the baptism of Jesus ought not then to be construed as the beginning of Christian spiritual vitality in the midst of an arid Judaism (*see DJG,* Holy Spirit). Rather, this Tosefta text corresponds to the situation portrayed in the Synoptic Gospels (Mt 3; Lk 3): in both there appears one who is worthy of the Holy Spirit in the midst of an evil generation. In the Tosefta, this one is Hillel; in the Gospels, Jesus.

3. A Variegated Milieu.

Essential to any study of conceptions of the Spirit in the NT is the realization that many of the forms of Judaism that birthed Christianity were indelibly impressed by Greco-Roman conceptions of inspiration.

A dominant philosophy during the first centuries B.C. and A.D. was *Stoicism, which inherited specific conceptions of the spirit. The Roman statesman *Seneca devoted one of his letters to this *sacer spiritus:* "a holy spirit indwells within us, one who marks our good and bad deeds, and is our guardian. As we treat this spirit, so are we treated" (Seneca *Ep. Mor.* 41.2). Seneca's subsequent discussion (*Ep. Mor.* 41.8) indicates that this spirit "is soul, and reason brought to perfection in the soul." Seneca could espouse this view because he, like many of his Stoic forebears, believed that the soul was a portion of the rational and divine *pneuma,* "which wholly pervades it [the cosmos] and by which the universe is made coherent and kept together" (Alexander of Aphrodisias *On Mixture* 216.14-17, summarizing the view of Chrysippus). This point of view had an impact upon the Alexandrian author of *Wisdom of Solomon, according to whom "the spirit of the Lord has filled the world, and that which holds all things together knows what is said" (Wis 1:7). This impact is evident as well in *Philo of Alexandria's interpretation of Exodus 31:3. While the biblical text describes Bezalel as filled with the spirit of wisdom, Philo employs Exodus 31:3 as a point of departure for defining that spirit in Stoic terms as "susceptible of neither severance nor division, diffused in its fullness everywhere and through all things" (Philo *Gig.* 27).

Another example of the early Jewish assimilation of Greco-Roman conceptions of inspiration concerns the ancient and auspicious shrine at Delphi. Several explanations were proffered to account for the power of this shrine, as well as the first-century realization that prophetic activity at Delphi had decreased. Cleombrotus, in Plutarch's *On the Defection of Oracles,* attributes the lessening of oracular activity in Delphi, compared with earlier centuries, to the withdrawal of the angelic beings (*daemones*) who, he believed, utilized the Delphic prophetesses as passive instruments of inspiration. He argues: "coincidently with the total defection [withdrawal] of the guardian spirits assigned to the oracles and prophetic shrines, occurs the defection of the oracles themselves; and when the spirits flee or go to another place, the oracles themselves lose their power" (Plutarch *Def. Orac.* 418C-D). He later explains, "For what was said then [i.e., earlier], that when the demigods withdraw and forsake the oracles, these lie idle and inarticulate like the instruments of musicians" (Plutarch *Def. Orac.* 431A-B).

Josephus and Philo appear to have adopted a conception of inspiration similar to this in their interpretations of Numbers 22—24, in which the angel promises to place words in Balaam's mouth (Num 22:35), and the spirit of God subsequently comes upon Balaam (Num 24:2). Philo draws an integral relationship between the prediction of the angel and its fulfillment by the spirit. In an expanded version of Numbers 22:35, the angel predicts: "I shall prompt the needful words without your mind's consent, and direct your organs of speech as justice and convenience require. I shall guide the reins of speech, and, though you understand it not, employ your tongue for each prophetic utterance"

(Philo *Vit. Mos.* 1.274). This prediction is fulfilled when Balaam "advanced outside, and straightway became possessed, and there fell upon him the truly prophetic spirit which banished utterly from his soul his art of wizardry" (Philo *Vit. Mos.* 1.277). In Philo's version the angel who had promised to prompt Balaam's words accomplished this when it reappeared, designated appropriately in this new context as the prophetic spirit.

Josephus arrives at a similar identification of the angel and spirit of Numbers 22—24. In *Antiquities* 4.6.3 §108, he carefully draws a parallel between the initial approach of the divine angel and the ass's perception of the divine spirit: "But on the road an angel of God confronted him in a narrow place, enclosed by stone walls on either side, and the ass whereon Balaam rode, conscious of the divine spirit approaching her, turning aside thrust Balaam against one of these fences, insensible to the blows with which the seer belabored her." In this summary, Josephus shows no reluctance to use the expressions "angel of God" and "divine spirit" interchangeably.

In addition to this identification of the angel with the inspiring spirit, the interpretations of Philo and Josephus underscore the passivity of Balaam. Philo's angel predicts Balaam's experience with such words as "without your mind's consent . . . though you understand it not . . . employ your tongue." Balaam in Josephus's version explains to Balak: "that spirit gives utterance to such language and words as it will, whereof we are all unconscious" (Josephus *Ant.* 4.6.5 §119).

This coalescence of ingredients—an angelic spirit and the loss of mental control—may well be the product of interpreting the biblical text in light of Greco-Roman discussions of Delphic inspiration. This scenario seems best to explain the transformation that the spirit of Numbers 24:2 undergoes in the interpretations of Philo and Josephus.

Still further evidence of the combustion of biblical and Greco-Roman elements is apparent in Philo's autobiographical reflections on the inspiration he alleges to receive in order to interpret the Scriptures. In *De Somniis* 2.252, Philo refers to the invisible voice that he hears: "I hear once more the voice of the invisible spirit, the familiar secret tenant, saying, 'Friend, it would seem that there is a matter great and precious of which thou knowest nothing, and this I will ungrudgingly shew thee, for many other well-timed lessons have I given thee.'" This form of inspiration is different from Balaam's, for Philo's experience involves instructing, rather than bypassing, his mind.

Moreover, Philo regards the spirit as a "familiar" or "customary" figure. This designation is evocative of Socrates' inspiration, for Socrates referred to "the customary prophetic inspiration of the daemon" (Plato *Apol.* 40A), "the daemonic and customary sign" (Plato *Phaed.* 242B) and "my customary daemonic sign" (Plato *Euthyd.* 272E). Further, in a discussion of the nature of Socrates' inspiration, in Plutarch's *On the Genius of Socrates,* Simmias explains that "the messages of daemons pass through all other people but find an echo in those only whose character is untroubled and soul unruffled, the very people in fact we call holy and daemonic" (Plutarch *Gen. Socr.* 589D). The affinities between the renowned Socrates and Philo, in his own estimation, include an untroubled mind that is taught by the presence of a customary friend. Once again, then, the inspiring spirit has undergone a transformation through its coalescence with Greco-Roman conceptions of inspiration.

The inspiration of Joshua in the first-century Palestinian version of Genesis—1 Samuel, known as *Liber Antiquitatum Biblicarum* (*see* Pseudo-Philo) provides still another example of the melding of biblical and Greco-Roman ingredients by early Jewish writers. To the straightforward text of Deuteronomy 34:9a, "Joshua son of Nun was full of the spirit of wisdom," Pseudo-Philo adds, "And when he clothed himself with it [the garments of wisdom], his mind was afire and his spirit was moved, and he said" (Pseudo-Philo *Bib. Ant.* 20.3). These elements have no place in Deuteronomy 34. They echo rather the juxtaposition of images that characterize the ecstatic soul in *Cicero's *On Divination* 1.114: the winged soul is "inflamed and aroused." This juxtaposition of frenzy and fire reappears in Plutarch's discussion of enthusiasm, according to which the "soul becomes hot and fiery and throws aside the caution that human intelligence lays upon it" (Plutarch *Def. Orac.* 432E-F). Cicero's *On Divination* and Plutarch's *On the Defection of Oracles,* then, contain the conceptions of prophetic inspiration that explain Pseudo-Philo's expansion of Deuteronomy 34:9.

The century that spawned early Christianity was characterized by enormous diversity with respect to conceptions of inspiration. The inspiring spirit (*pneuma*) could be interpreted as an angelic spirit that ousts thought, as a customary friend that instructs the untroubled mind and as a catalyst to prophetic oracles that inflames and arouses. Studies of the NT therefore must acknowledge that references to the holy spirit are not homogeneous but reflect rather the complex situation of the milieu of the NT, in which various adherents of early Judaism conceived of the spirit differently from one another, due often to the nature of their indebtedness to a diverse and influential Greco-Roman milieu.

4. Varieties of Effects.

The explosive diversity associated with the divine spirit in first-century Judaism can best be grasped by an exploration of the various effects that were attributed to the spirit, even when the particular nature of that spirit is left unexplained. The spirit could be so construed as to bring about effects as diverse as the ascent of a philosopher's mind (Philo *Plant.* 18-26); the ascent of a prophet's mind (Pseudo-Philo *Bib. Ant.* 28.6-10); a coalescence of internal and external beauty characteristic of kingship and rhetorical prowess (Philo *Virt.* 217-19); extraordinary military capabilities (Pseudo-Philo *Bib. Ant.* 27.9-10); and praise (Pseudo-Philo *Bib. Ant.* 32.14). The others, which are here outlined in more detail, include the association of the spirit with prophecy; creation; purity, conversion, and communal initiation; and a messianic figure.

4.1. Prophecy. Although the spirit produces an assortment of effects, prophecy is the most pervasive of them. The postexilic author of the book of Nehemiah had already incorporated a *prayer in which God is said to have been patient with Israel for many years and to have "warned them by your spirit through the prophets" (Neh 9:30). This conviction is echoed by the Qumran sectarians: "This is the study of the law which he commanded through the hand of Moses, in order to act in compliance with all that has been revealed from age to age, and according to what the prophets have revealed through his holy spirit" (1QS 8:15-16).

In the book of **Jubilees,* "a spirit of truth descended upon the mouth" of Rebecca so that she could bless her children (*Jub.* 25:14), and Jacob blessed Levi and Judah when "a spirit of prophecy came down upon his mouth" (*Jub.* 31:11). A section of *1 Enoch* begins when Enoch commands, "Now, my son Methuselah, [please] summon all your brothers on my behalf, and gather together to me all the sons of your mother; for a voice calls me, and the spirit is poured over me so that I may show you everything that shall happen to you forever" (*1 Enoch* 91:1; *see* Enoch, Books of). In a humorous portion of the **Testament of Abraham,* in which the archangel Michael cannot find the resources to convince Abraham that he will die, God says to Michael: "And I shall send my holy spirit upon his son Isaac, and I shall thrust the mention of his death into Isaac's heart, so that he will see his father's death in a dream" (*T. Abr.* A 4:8).

According to Philo, Balaam became possessed when "there fell upon him the truly prophetic spirit which banished utterly from his soul his art of wizardry" (Philo *Vit. Mos.* 1.277). *Moses cannot be excluded from this prophetic race, for he too spoke "when possessed by God and carried away out of himself" because he experienced "that divine possession in virtue of which he is chiefly and in the strict sense considered a prophet" (Philo *Vit. Mos.* 2.191). The experience that the false diviner Balaam and the truest of prophets Moses have in common is characteristic of the prophetic race: "This is what regularly befalls the fellowship of the prophets. The mind is evicted at the arrival of the divine Spirit, but when that departs the mind returns to its tenancy" (Philo *Her.* 265; see *Spec. Leg.* 1.65; 4.49; *Quaest. in Gen.* 3.9).

Josephus also closely associates the work of the spirit with prophecy. On some occasions, Josephus adds references to prophecy in contexts that focus upon the effects of the spirit. For example, while 1 Samuel 16:13 recounts that "the spirit of the Lord came mightily upon David from that day forward," Josephus relates that David, "when the divine spirit had removed to him, began to prophesy" (Josephus *Ant.* 6.8.2 §166). While Zedekiah, the false prophet, asks Micaiah in 1 Kings 22:24 (LXX), "What sort of spirit of the Lord speaks in you?" Josephus explicitly relates the spirit with prophecy: "But you shall know whether he is really a true prophet and has the power of the divine spirit" (Josephus *Ant.* 8.15.4 §408). Although he reduces the number of references to the spirit in his version of the book of Daniel, he does nonetheless preserve a reference to the spirit and emphasizes Daniel's place as "one of the greatest prophets" (Josephus *Ant.* 10.11.7 §266). On other occasions, Josephus preserves the element of prophecy that is already included in a biblical narrative, such as in the story of Saul's pursuit of David (Josephus *Ant.* 6.11.5 §§222-23).

This association between the spirit and prophecy is evident as well in the *Liber Antiquitatum Biblicarum* (Pseudo-Philo). In extrabiblical additions, the spirit comes upon Miriam to be the recipient of a dream in which the birth of Moses is predicted (Pseudo-Philo *Bib. Ant.* 9.10), and Deborah is said explicitly to have predicted Sisera's demise by the inspiration of the spirit (Pseudo-Philo *Bib. Ant.* 31.9). Pseudo-Philo also creates *de novo* the association of prophecy and the spirit in a biblical text, Judges 3:9-10, in which the spirit is associated only with judging Israel. According to Pseudo-Philo's version, "when they had sat down, a holy spirit came upon Kenaz . . . and he began to prophesy" (Pseudo-Philo *Bib. Ant.* 28.6). The attentiveness of Pseudo-Philo is evident, furthermore, in his interpretation of Deuteronomy 34:9, where an explicit reference to the spirit of wisdom is thoughtfully supplanted by allusions to 1 Samuel 10:6 and Judges 6:34, other biblical texts that refer to the spirit, and followed by a prophetic utterance of Joshua (Pseudo-Philo *Bib. Ant.* 20.2-3). Even in a highly abbreviated account of Saul's pursuit of David, Pseudo-Philo preserves the explicit association of prophecy and the spirit: "And [a] spirit abided in Saul, and he prophesied" (Pseudo-Philo *Bib. Ant.* 62.2).

Rabbinic literature, though it was composed later than the first century A.D., maintains as well this association between the spirit and prophecy. In a discussion of Miriam in *Mekilta de-Rabbi Ishmael,* tractate *Shirata* 10:58-73, for example, the question is raised concerning where in Torah Miriam is said to have been a prophetess. The biblical text quoted, Exodus 2:1-3, has nothing to do with prophecy. Nevertheless, the rabbis are able to detect a reference to prophecy in an alleged reference to the holy spirit in the vocabulary of Exodus 2:4, such as the words "afar off," which are said to express the holy spirit's presence because, in Jeremiah 31:2, it is said, "From afar the Lord appeared to me." Miriam's prophetic abilities in Exodus 2:1-4 are evident in a veiled reference to the holy spirit in Jeremiah 31:2 by means of the exegetical principle *gezerah shawah,* an argument from analogy drawn from two passages that contain similar expression. This association of the spirit with prophecy is characteristic as well of the *targumim; the designation "spirit of prophecy" occurs consistently in *Targum Onqelos,* while in *Targum Pseudo-Jonathan* the expression "holy spirit" occurs fifteen times and "spirit of prophecy" eleven times.

4.2. Inspired Exegesis. Although the association of the spirit with the ability to interpret Scripture is implicit in several texts (Ezra 9:20; Josephus *J.W.* 3.8.3 §§351-53; 1QS 5:9; 1QH 12:11-13), three discussions in particular adhere to the conviction that interpretation requires the inspiration of the spirit.

First, prior to the Maccabean rebellion, Ben Sira espouses a conception of inspired interpretation when he, in self-conscious reflection upon his scribal calling, writes: "he [the scribe] will be filled by a spirit of understanding/he will pour out his own words of wisdom. . . . He will make known the instruction of what he has learned" (Sir 39:6-8). The importance of the Scriptures in the encomium on the scribe, of which this text is a part, is evident in references to elements of the three portions of scripture: the Torah (Sir 38:34); prophecies (Sir 39:1); and elements of the Writings, namely, wisdom, such as parables and proverbs (Sir 39:2-3). Against this sort of inspiration, which requires a mind alert and scriptural texts, Ben Sira sets the false knowledge of omens and *dreams (Sir 34:1-2, 5).

Second, we observed already that in *De Somniis* 2.252, Philo claims to be taught by his customary friend, the spirit. In this autobiographical reflection, Philo lets the reader know that the immediate task is to solve an exegetical dilemma, such as why the biblical text refers to two cherubim rather than to one cherub that the spirit teaches him; and that this teaching is directed toward his mind (see also Philo *Spec. Leg.* 3.1-6; *Cher.* 27-29; *Som.* 1.164-65; *Fug.* 53-58).

Third, the conviction of 4 Ezra 14 is that Ezra's mind is inspired in a wakeful state to write ninety-four books in response to his prayer for the holy spirit (4 Ezra 14:22; *see* Esdras, Books of). Prior to this inspiration, Ezra is given the promise that the lamp of understanding will remain lit throughout his experience. The process itself begins as he drinks the cup given to him, his heart pours forth understanding and wisdom increases within him. Following his experience, it is said that these ninety-four books contain "the spring of understanding, the fountain of wisdom and the river of knowledge" (4 Ezra 14:47). The conviction that Ezra is inspired in a conscious state is confirmed by the significant detail that Ezra's understanding and wisdom overflowed because his own spirit retained its memory. From start to finish, then, Ezra composed ninety-four books by means of a form of inspiration that heightened his intellectual capacity.

4.3. Creation. The spirit is associated with creation. The influence of Genesis 1:2 is apparent in *2 Baruch* 21:4 and 23:5, Baruch's address to God, "you who created the earth, the one who fixed the firmament by the word and fastened the height of heaven by the spirit," and God's response to this prayer, "For my spirit creates the living." Ezra in 4 Ezra 6:39 similarly recalls the earliest creative activity of God: "And then the Spirit was hovering, and darkness and silence embraced everything; the sound of a human voice was not yet there. Then you commanded that a ray of light be brought forth." In Judith 16:14, it is not Genesis 1:2 but Genesis 2:7, mediated through Psalm 104:29-30, that influences the depiction of the spirit's relation to creation. Judith praises God: "You sent forth your spirit, and it formed them/there is none that can resist your voice."

The spirit's function vis-à-vis creation is, according to Wisdom of Solomon 1:7-8, not only to grant life but also to convict wrongdoers: "the spirit of the Lord has filled the world/and that which holds all things together knows what is said." In the words of the Sibyl composed by another Egyptian author, "Nor is anything left unaccomplished that God so much as puts in mind/for the spirit of God which knows no falsehood is throughout the world" (*Sib. Or.* 3:696-701).

4.4. Purity, Conversion and Initiation. In many other early Jewish texts, the spirit is related to *purity, individual conversion and communal initiation. In the *Rule of the Community* from Qumran the spirit is integrally tied to purification, which transpires upon entry into the community: "by the spirit of holiness which links him with the truth he is cleansed of all his sins. And by the spirit of uprightness and of humility his sin is atoned" (3:7-8; see 9:3-4). The association of the spirit with initiation into the Qumran community is evident, moreover, in the Qumran hymns, the vocabulary of which can be understood to indicate drawing near to God through initiation into the community, such as in 1QH 14:13-14: "in your kindness toward humankind/you have enlarged his share with the spirit of your holiness./Thus, you make me approach your intelligence,/and to the degree that I approach/my fervor against all those who act wickedly." The sixteenth hymn is particularly rich with such language: "to be strengthened by the spirit of holiness/to adhere to the truth of your covenant/to serve you in truth, with a perfect heart . . . to purify me with your holy spirit/to approach your will according to the extent of your kindnesses" (1QH 16:15, 19-20).

Far from the shores of the Dead Sea, the spirit was associated with conversion to Judaism. In the romantic tale **Joseph and Aseneth*, Aseneth, the daughter of Pentephres (the biblical Potiphar), is converted to Judaism. In this story, Joseph places his hand upon her head and prays, "and renew her by your spirit/and form her anew by your hidden hand/and make her alive again by your life" (*Jos. and As.* 8:9). Later Aseneth is led by a heavenly man to a room with a marvelous honeycomb. He says to her, "Happy are you, Aseneth, because the ineffable mysteries of the Most High have been revealed to you, and happy [are] all who attach themselves to the Lord God in repentance, because they will eat from this comb. For this comb is [full of the] spirit of life" (*Jos. and As.* 16:14). Finally, at a climactic moment, "Joseph kissed Aseneth and gave her spirit of life, and he kissed her the second time and gave her spirit of wisdom, and he kissed her the third time and gave her spirit of truth" (*Jos. and As.* 19:10-11). In this lovely romance, then, the spirit purifies and draws people into the sphere of the faithful.

This purifying power does not conclude with admittance to the community of faith. In the Mishnah (tractate *Soṭa* 9:15), "Heedfulness leads to cleanliness, and cleanliness leads to purity, and purity to abstinence, and abstinence leads to holiness, and holiness leads to humility, and humility leads to the shunning of sin, and the shunning of sin leads to saintliness, and saintliness leads to [the gift of] the Holy Spirit, and the Holy Spirit leads to the resurrection of the dead." Rabbi Nehemiah, in *Mekilta de-Rabbi Ishmael,* tractate *Bešallaḥ* 7:134-36, associates obedience with reception of the spirit: "For as a reward for the faith with which Israel believed in God, the Holy Spirit rested upon them. R. Nehemiah says: Whence can you prove that whosoever accepts even one single commandment with true faith is deserving of having the Holy Spirit rest upon them." In the **Testaments of the*

Twelve Patriarchs, Benjamin attributes sexual purity to the spirit: "He has no pollution in his heart, because upon him is resting the spirit of God" (*T. Benj.* 8:3).

This association of the spirit with purity is invested with a communal dimension in *Jubilees* 1:20-21, where Moses, echoing Psalm 51, intercedes for Israel, "O Lord, let your mercy be lifted up upon your people, and create for them an upright spirit. . . . Create a pure heart and a holy spirit for them. And do not let them be ensnared by their sin henceforth and forever." God responds (*Jub.* 1:22-25) by echoing Psalm 51 and Ezekiel 11:19-20: "And I shall create for them a holy spirit, and I shall purify them so that they will not turn away from following me from that day and forever. And their souls will cleave to me and to all my commandments."

4.5. Wisdom and Messiah. A particularly focused association of the spirit with wisdom emerges from the prediction of a just Davidic ruler who will bring in the wake of his reign both human and cosmic peace (Is 11:1-9): "The spirit of the LORD shall rest on him/the spirit of wisdom and understanding/the spirit of counsel and might/the spirit of knowledge and the fear of the LORD" (Is 11:2). Although later developments of this figure in Isaiah preserve the relationship between justice, mercy and the knowledge of God, the defining feature that predominates is justice. Wisdom is supplanted by justice in the exilic description of the so-called messianic servant in whom God delights: "I have put my spirit upon him; he will bring forth justice to the nations" (Is 42:1b-c). This servant will not grow weary "until he has established justice in the earth" (Is 42:1d). The elusive yet related prophetic figure of Isaiah 61:1-7 also holds justice rather than wisdom to be the fundamental project of his calling: "The spirit of the Lord GOD is upon me/because the LORD has anointed me/he has sent me to bring good news to the oppressed" (Is 61:1).

Despite the ascendancy of justice at the expense of wisdom in Isaiah, early Jewish appropriations of these texts preserve the original association of the spirit with wisdom. The spirit that dwells upon the Elect One, the central eschatological character of the Similitudes of *Enoch,* is depicted principally, in language reminiscent of Isaiah 11, as a spirit of wisdom: "The Elect One stands before the Lord of the Spirits; his glory is forever and ever and his power is unto all generations. In him dwells the spirit of wisdom, the spirit which gives thoughtfulness, the spirit of knowledge and strength, and the spirit of those who have fallen asleep in righteousness" (*1 Enoch* 49:2-3).

Poetic depictions of the anticipated *messianic deliverer, redolent of the images of Isaiah 11, emerge as well in the literature of Judaism. The author of the **Psalms of Solomon* preserves the association of the spirit and wisdom: "And he will not weaken in his days, [relying] upon his God/for God made him powerful in the holy spirit/and wise in the counsel of understanding/with strength and righteousness" (*Pss. Sol.* 17:37). So too does the author of the *Testament of Levi:* "And the glory of the Most High shall burst forth upon him./And the spirit of understanding and sanctification/shall rest upon him . . . / And he shall open the gates of paradise/he shall remove the sword that has threatened since Adam/and he will grant to the saints to eat of the tree of life./The spirit of holiness shall be upon them./And Beliar shall be bound by him./ And he shall grant to his children the authority to trample on wicked spirits" (*T. Levi* 18:7, 10-12). In the *Traditions of *Melchizedek* (11QMelch), the figure of Isaiah 61 is transformed into a warrior figure who will destroy *Belial and his entourage of evil spirits. These texts project an emphasis upon strength or power, which, though consistent with their own eschatological expectations of deliverance, cannot be said to arise genetically from Isaiah 11, 42 or 61.

See also ESCHATOLOGIES OF LATE ANTIQUITY; MESSIANISM; PROPHETS AND PROPHECY.

BIBLIOGRAPHY. D. E. Aune, *Prophecy in Early Christianity and the Ancient Mediterranean World* (Grand Rapids, MI: Eerdmans, 1983); F. Baumgärten et al. "πνεύμα, πνευματικός κτλ," *TDNT* 6:332-451; C. Forbes, *Prophecy and Inspired Speech: In Early Christianity and Its Hellenistic Environment* (Peabody, MA: Hendrickson, 1997); H. Gunkel, *The Influence of the Holy Spirit: The Popular View of the Apostolic Age and the Teaching of the Apostle Paul* (Philadelphia: Fortress, 1979); F. W. Horn, "Holy Spirit," *ABD* 3:260-80; M. Isaacs, *The Concept of Spirit: A Study of Pneuma in Hellenistic Judaism and Its Bearing on the New Testament* (London: Heythrop College, 1976); C. S. Keener, *The Spirit in the Gospels and Acts: Divine Purity and Power* (Peabody, MA: Hendrickson, 1997); H. Leisegang, *Der Heilige Geist: Das Wesen und Werden der mystisch-intuitiven Erkenntnis in der Philosophie und*

Religion der Griechen (Leipzig: Teubner, 1919); idem, *Pneuma Hagion: der Ursprung des Geistbegriffs der synoptischen Evangelien aus der griechischen Mystik* (Hildesheim: G. Olms, 1970); J. R. Levison, "Did the Spirit Withdraw from Israel? An Evaluation of the Earliest Jewish Data," *NTS* 43 (1997) 35-57; idem, *The Spirit in First Century Judaism* (AGAJU 29; Leiden: E. J. Brill, 1997); R. P. Menzies, *The Development of Early Christian Pneumatology: With Special Reference to Luke-Acts* (JSNTSup 54; Sheffield: Sheffield Academic Press, 1991); G. T. Montague, *Holy Spirit: Growth of a Biblical Tradition* (Peabody, MA: Hendrickson, 1976); P. Schäfer, *Die Vorstellung vom heiligen Geist in der rabbinischen Literatur* (SANT 28; Munich: Kösel, 1972); A. E. Sekki, *The Meaning of* Ruaḥ *at Qumran* (SBLDS 110; Atlanta: Scholars Press, 1989); M. M. B. Turner, *Power from on High: The Spirit in Israel's Restoration and Witness in Luke-Acts* (JPTSup 9; Sheffield: Sheffield Academic Press, 1996); G. Verbeke, *L'évolution de la Doctrine du Pneuma du Stoïcisme à S. Augustin* (Paris: Desclée de Brouwer, 1945); P. Volz, *Der Geist Gottes und die verwandten Erscheinungen im Alten Testament und im anschliessenden Judentum* (Tübingen: Mohr Siebeck, 1910).

J. R. Levison

HOMILY, ANCIENT

While there is evidence for the existence of the homily in both the *synagogue and the church prior to the second century A.D., its nature during this period is disputed. However, there is firm evidence for the homily in both Jewish and Christian circles from the second century A.D. onward. These homilies show a Greek *rhetorical basis with Jewish motifs.

1. The Jewish Homily Before A.D. 70
2. The Christian Homily in the First Century
3. The Jewish Homily After A.D. 70
4. The Christian Homily After the First Century
5. Conclusions

1. The Jewish Homily Before A.D. 70.

Before A.D. 70 there is little purely Jewish evidence for the homily that is not based on extrapolation from later *rabbinic literature. The major exception is the homiletic form identified by P. Borgen (51) in *Philo, especially in *Legum Allegoriae* 3.162-68 and *De Mutatione Nominum* 253-63, although wrongly called the proem form (Stegner, 67). During this period the *synagogue (i.e., Jewish community gathering) existed as a less formal institution, sometimes meeting in homes and sometimes in structures (at times an adapted house) devoted to study and *prayer (Oster; cf. Levine, 426-43, who argues that it developed from communal gatherings in the city gate as the architecture of city gates changed). The degree to which such meetings were religious or liturgical versus the transaction of communal business is debated. Some scholars argue for a developed service complete with something like the triennial lectionary cycle (Heinemann), but such a portrait depends upon accepting the historical reliability of a number of later talmudic and midrashic references to the first century, which may in fact have read later patterns back into earlier material.

There is firmer evidence that one of the synagogue activities, wherever the gathering met, was *Torah reading and exposition (Levine, 431-32, 439-41). Thus one can argue with reasonable certainty that Jews in both Palestine and the *Diaspora did meet and that in those meetings Scripture was read and discussed. This discussion or exposition is the earliest form of the Jewish homily; unfortunately, no undisputed examples survive from the pre-A.D. 70 period. While some scholars have pointed to *4 Maccabees as an example, its lack of a scriptural text makes this unlikely; Philo's *Quaestiones in Genesin* has a better claim in that each short exposition is built around a Torah text, although the brevity makes it difficult to judge whether they demonstrate a specific homiletic form (Schürer, 3:539, 818, 830; Borgen, 28-58).

At a later date, in the more formal liturgical setting of Jewish worship, questions could be put to the speaker and congregational reaction is recorded. Thus it is likely that the early Jewish homily was at least somewhat interactive. However, the practice of commenting on a text of Scripture and developing this exposition through the citation of other Scriptures according to accepted rules of exegesis (e.g., the seven rules of Hillel, which probably reflect practices of the first century and earlier) characterized the homiletic form from an early date (Philo *Spec. Leg.* 2.15 §62; *Omn. Prob. Lib.* 12 §§81-82; Schürer, 2:424-27, although the citation of Ps 74:8 is questionable, 448).

There are also a number of early Christian references to the exposition of Scripture in Jewish synagogues during the pre-70 period (Mk

1:21; 6:2; Lk 4:16-22, 31; 6:6; 13:10; Acts 13:14-16, 27, 42, 44; 15:21; 16:13; 17:2; 18:4). While this Christian evidence has been disputed as a reading of post-70 developments into the earlier period (Kee), none of these passages claim more than that in both Palestine and Diaspora settings Jews gathered on the *sabbath to read and expound the Scriptures. In this these passages are consonant with both *archaeological data and the meager literary data that we possess (Oster). However, all of these references, with the exception of Luke 4:16-22, either give no evidence as to the form of the Jewish homily or else present Christian missionary preaching in a synagogue context.

2. The Christian Homily in the First Century.
Early Christian evidence for the homily is of two types. First, there are reference to Christian preaching. Most of this is missionary preaching taking place within the synagogue setting (e.g., Acts 13:15-41) and thus is Luke's example of preaching within the synagogue service. The most important of these references is in Acts 13:15, in which the invitation requests a "word of exhortation" *(logos paraklēseōs)* and connects it to the reading of "the law and the prophets," which is the relationship to Scripture that many homilies had in later synagogue worship. This suggests that later Jewish homiletic forms may have found their roots in the pre-70 synagogue.

Second, there are Christian sermons, both those embedded in Acts (although the degree to which these reflect pre-70 Christian preaching is debated) and those observed in other works, for example, John 6 (Borgen), James 2 (Wessel, 78-91; Davids, 23, 105-34) and Hebrews as a whole (see Attridge; Lane; Wills). Hebrews designates itself as a "word of exhortation" *(tou logou tēs paraklēseōs)* which, as comparison with Acts 13:15 (cf. Acts 13:16-41) indicates, was one way to refer to a homily.

Examination of this Christian material gives us our best evidence for Jewish and Christian homiletic forms. J. W. Bowker, for example, sees the *yelammedenu* form in Acts 13, while P. H. Davids points out that James 2:1-13 and James 2:14-27 each contain a similar structure of opening statement, short narrative, theological argument, two OT citations (one of which at least is from the Pentateuch) and final summary, which is similar to later Jewish homiletic material. In particular this structure is similar to the *yelammedenu* form minus the formal introduction, which starts with a question and moves through a series of texts to the Torah reading of the day (*seder;* see 3 below).

However, while there are similarities to the later Jewish homily, it is clear that these passages are also dependent upon Greco-Roman rhetorical forms. The homily in Acts 13 can be analyzed in this way (Black); the passages in James have often been described as diatribes, although the *diatribe was not a formally recognized rhetorical form; and while the exact type of rhetoric (deliberative or epideictic) in Hebrews has been debated, modern commentators are quick to point out how closely the work conforms to rhetorical structures (e.g., deSilva). This observation raises the probability that the Jewish homily itself developed under the influence of Greek rhetoric, especially in the Diaspora synagogue, but also in Palestine, where *Hellenistic influence was far more pervasive than was once thought. The content (for example, the use of Scripture and the principles of exegesis) would be distinctively Jewish, but the rhetorical form likely came from the surrounding culture. This is H. W. Attridge's explanation for our inability to decisively identify the form of rhetoric in Hebrews.

The picture that emerges, then, is that of the synagogue as originally a gathering and then a gathering place of the local Jewish community for numerous purposes, but chief among them was instruction in Scripture (Levine). As leaders began to give discourses on Scripture, they utilized both their Jewish tradition and the forms of discourse that were in the air, namely, Greek rhetoric. The resultant homiletic form was adopted by the church, which at first was a synagogue that believed Jesus was the Messiah. It is not that the leaders of either the first-century synagogues or the early church were highly trained in rhetoric, although some of them were, but that this rhetoric shaped the speeches that they heard and whatever schooling they had, resulting in their absorbing some of the principles and methods, formally or informally.

3. The Jewish Homily After A.D. 70.
There is abundant later Jewish evidence for the use of the homily, especially after A.D. 200 (Wessel, 79-89, although there is far more data now than when he wrote). The proem *(petiḥta)* begins with a text from the hagiographa that is

then linked by haggadic interpretation with the first verse of the *seder* and thus gives a specific example for the general idea of that verse (cf. Bowker, 100, for more detail). The *yelammedenu* (which begins with halakic questions rather than a specific text, although it often moves toward a specific text through intermediate citations, Stegner, 54-55) forms are clearly in evidence, as well as a form beginning with a benediction and a simple expositional form (a verse of the Torah reading *[seder]* followed by a verse from elsewhere in the Scripture, which is used to interpret the first verse). Generally the materials we have are not complete sermons, especially since the proem form appears to have functioned as either the peroration to the sermon (its function in some of the homiletical midrashim) or more likely originally an introduction to the Torah reading. Instead we have outlines or parts of sermons later edited into larger units by the editors of the homiletic midrashim. Complete sermons, such as the one found in *b. Šabbat* 30 a-b, are rare (Heinemann).

All of these forms assume congregational interaction. The *yelammedenu* form begins with the term (*yelammedenu* = "Let [our rabbi] teach us") plus a halakic question, which appears at times to have been a question from the congregation. As the sermon progressed it was responded to, positively or negatively. This fits with a major original function of the synagogue as a gathering for communal study.

The proem was used extensively between 200 and 500 and thus is reflected in the NT only to the extent that it illustrates some of the same traditional exegetical principles found in both bodies of literature (*see* Biblical Interpretation, Jewish). The *yelammedenu* form is found mostly in *Tanḥuma* and thus is very late (post-sixth century) in its present form. However, its basic structure has been argued to exist in the NT (Bowker) and other first-century Jewish literature (Wills), perhaps because the developed form is built on earlier, simpler expositional forms known at least by the time the NT books were composed.

4. The Christian Homily After the First Century.
The systematic study of the Christian homily begins with some of the *apostolic fathers and develops from that point. While much of the focus of this study has been on the fourth century and later (e.g., Chrysostom), Melito of Sardis (*see DLNTD*, Melito of Sardis) and other second-century writers are significant in the development. What is clear in examining these writers is that Greek rhetoric came to play an increasingly explicit role in the formation of the Christian homily. While this would lead to conflict within the church by the end of the second century, it was also a mark that the church fit into its cultural setting (Overman).

In this case also the homily meant not simply communication of information but also interaction with the congregation, who expressed their approval or disapproval of the preacher verbally or via facial expressions. Homiletic development took place more in urban than in rural settings, and a variety of rhetorical types suited to various church occasions were used. Given that the homily was an adaptation of Greek forms, it is not surprising to discover that the forms of judicial, deliberative and epideictic rhetoric were often mixed (Allen and Mayer).

5. Conclusions.
It is likely that the origins of the homily can be traced to the synagogues of the Second Temple period, when culturally available Greek rhetorical forms were adapted to the purpose of scriptural exposition for the Jewish community. This cultural form was taken over by the church, which continued in contact with the synagogue for more than two centuries and thus may have had some continuing influence. The oldest homiletic literature we possess is that embedded in Philo and the NT, but its similarity to later Jewish homiletic material indicates that some form of the Jewish homily existed before A.D. 70. Yet the Christian homily soon diverged under the direct influence of the Greek rhetorical tradition (e.g., dropping some of the characteristics of Jewish exegetical practice), reaching its high point in the fourth and fifth centuries. However, it would be anachronistic to retroject this developed homily into the formative period of the first century.

See also BIBLICAL INTERPRETATION, JEWISH; LITURGY: QUMRAN; LITURGY: RABBINIC; RABBINIC LITERATURE: TARGUMIM; SYNAGOGUES.

BIBLIOGRAPHY. P. Allen and W. Mayer, "Computer and Homily: Accessing the Everyday Life of Early Christians," 47 (1993) 260-80; K. Atkinson, "On Further Defining the First-Century C.E. Synagogue: Fact or Fiction?" *NTS* 43 (1997) 491-502; H. W. Attridge, "Paraenesis in a Homily (*logos parakleseos*): The Possible Location of, and Socialization in, the 'Epistle to the Hebrews,'" *Semeia* 50 (1990) 211-26; C. C. Black II, "The Rhetorical Form of the Hellenistic Jewish and Early Christian Sermon: A Response to Lawrence Wills," *HTR* 81 (1988) 1-18; P. Borgen, *Bread from Heaven: An Exegetical Study of the Concept of Manna in the Gospel of John and the Writings of Philo* (NovTSup 10; Leiden: E. J. Brill, 1965); J. W. Bowker, *The Targums and Rabbinic Literature: An Introduction to Jewish Interpretations of Scripture* (Cambridge: Cambridge University Press, 1969); P. H. Davids, *The Epistle of James* (NIGTC; Grand Rapids, MI: Eerdmans, 1982); D. A. deSilva, *Despising Shame: Honor Discourse and Community Maintenance in the Epistle to the Hebrews* (SBLDS 152; Atlanta: Scholars Press, 1995); idem, *Perseverance in Gratitude: A Socio-Rhetorical Commentary on the Epistle to the Hebrews* (Grand Rapids, MI: Eerdmans, 2000); A. Goldberg, "Form-Analysis of Midrashic Literature as a Method of Description," *JJS* 36 (1985) 159-74; J. Heinemann, "Preaching. In the Talmudic Period," *EncJud* 13:994-98; H. C. Kee, "The Transformation of the Synagogue After 70 C.E.: Its Import for Early Christianity," *NTS* 36 (1990) 1-24; W. L. Lane, "Hebrews: A Sermon in Search of a Setting," *SWJT* 28 (1985) 13-18; L. I. Levine, "The Nature and Origin of the Palestinian Synagogue Reconsidered," *JBL* 115 (1996) 425-48; R. E. Oster, "Supposed Anachronism in Luke-Acts' Use of *synagoge:* A Rejoinder to H. C. Kee," *NTS* 39 (1993) 178-208; J. A. Overman, "Homily Form (Hellenistic and Early Christian)," *ABD* 3:280-82; E. Schürer, *The History of the Jewish People in the Age of Jesus Christ, (175 B.C.-A.D. 135)* rev. and ed. G. Vermes, F. Miller, M. Goodman (3 vols.; Edinburgh: T & T Clark, 1973-87); W. R. Stegner, "The Ancient Jewish Synagogue Homily," in *Greco-Roman Literature and the New Testament: Selected Forms and Genres,* ed. D. E. Aune (SBLSBS 21; Atlanta: Scholars Press, 1988) 51-69; H. Thyan, *Der Stil der Jüdisch-Hellenistischen Homilie* (Göttingen: Vandenhoeck & Ruprecht, 1955); W. W. Wessel, "An Inquiry into the Origin, Literary Character, Historical and Religious Significance of the Epistle of James" (Ph.D. diss., University of Edinburgh, 1953); L. Wills, "The Form of the Sermon in Hellenistic Judaism and Early Christianity," *HTR* 77 (1984) 277-99; W. Wuellner, "Haggadic Homily Genre in 1 Corinthians 1—3," *JBL* 89 (1970) 199-204.

P. H. Davids

HOMOEROTICISM. *See* ADULTERY, DIVORCE.

HOMOSEXUAL INTERCOURSE. *See* ADULTERY, DIVORCE

ḤONI THE CIRCLE DRAWER. *See* HOLY MEN, JEWISH.

HONOR AND SHAME

Honor refers to the public acknowledgment of a person's worth, granted on the basis of how fully that individual embodies qualities and behaviors valued by the group. First-century Mediterranean people were oriented from early childhood to seek honor and avoid disgrace, meaning that they would be sensitive to public recognition or reproach. Where different cultures with different values existed side by side, it became extremely important to insulate one's own group members against the desire for honor or avoidance of dishonor in the eyes of outsiders, since only by so doing could one remain wholly committed to the distinctive culture and values of the group. This struggle is particularly evident in the NT, as church leaders seek to affirm the honor of Christians on the basis of their adherence to Jesus while insulating them from the disapproval they face from non-Christian Jews and Gentiles alike.

1. Honor and Group Values
2. Honor Discourse Among Competing Cultures
3. Honor Discourse in the Early Church

1. Honor and Group Values.

A person born into the first-century Mediterranean world, whether Gentile or Jewish, was trained from childhood to seek honor and to avoid disgrace. Honor is essentially the affirmation of one's worth by one's peers and society, awarded on the basis of the individual's ability to embody the virtues and attributes that his or her society values. Certain of these attributes are ascribed and are frequently beyond the individual's control (e.g., birth into a powerful or wealthy family); other attributes or virtues, such as piety, courage and reliability, are accessible to all, and individuals will strive to achieve honor by pursuing them (Malina and Neyrey 1991b). The definitions of which behaviors are honorable and which disgraceful vary among cultures and over time, but honor remains an abiding concern. In most cultures, male honor and female honor are defined differently, with shame (in the sense of modesty and chastity) being presented as a primary female virtue (cf. Sir 26:10-16; 42:9-12; 4 Macc 18:6-8; Thucydides *Hist.* 2.45.2; Moxnes 1993).

Honor and dishonor represent the primary means of social control in the ancient Mediterranean world (Aristotle *Rhet.* 2.6.26: "there are many things which [people] either do or do not do owing to the feeling of shame which [their neighbors] inspire"). A society upholds its values by rewarding with greater degrees of honor those who embody those values in greater degrees. Dishonor represents a group's disapproval of a member based on his or her lack of conformity with those values deemed essential for the group's continued existence. Since people are reared in a world where honor is of great importance to a person's sense of worth, the social group is in a strong position to motivate conformity among its individual members. An individual has self-respect on the basis of his or her perception of how fully he or she has embodied the culture's ideals (Williams); that individual has honor on the basis of the society's recognition of that person's conformity with essential values (Pitt-Rivers).

The threat of dishonor supports a society's prohibitions of socially disruptive behavior. For example, *adultery—the violation of the sanctity and peace of a bond that is foundational to society—often carries the threat of disgrace (cf. Prov 6:32-33). Agreement and unity, essential values for the orderly life of a city, are lauded as honorable, while dissensions and strife bring the threat of disgrace for the city (cf. Dio Chrysostom *Or.* 48.5-6; Phil 1:27—2:4). Similarly, courage in battle, necessary for a city's survival, wins honor and lasting remembrance (cf. Thucydides *Hist.* 2.35-42). In a society that has as its basic building block the patron-client relationship (Seneca *Ben.* 1.4.2; *see* Patronage), the demonstration of gratitude to one's patron is supported by the threat of irrevocable dishonor and therefore exclusion from future patronage (Dio Chrysostom *Or.* 31; Heb 6:4-8; 10:26-31).

Honor becomes the umbrella that extends over the set of behaviors, commitments and attitudes that preserve a given culture and society; individuals reared with a desire for honor will seek the good of the larger group, willingly embodying the group's values, as the path to self-fulfillment. It is the first principle in discussions of ethics, for "the honorable is cherished for no other reason than because it is honorable" (Seneca *Ben.* 4.16.2). Ancient collections of advice, from Pseudo-Isocrates' *Ad Demonicam* to the more familiar Proverbs, label actions either with the positive sanction "noble" or with the negative sanction "disgraceful." By such means, the author sets before the reader a model of existence that acts always in the best interest of the public trust, honors the established authorities on which the state rests (gods, parents, laws) and restrains the expenditure of resources on that which brings pleasure only to the self and not benefit to others as well. Those who follow such a model are promised society's approval and affirmation, that is, honor.

Greco-Roman manuals on *rhetoric attest to the importance of honor and to the way an orator would play on the audience's desire for honor in order to achieve persuasion (deSilva 1995a; 1995b; 1999). An audience could be won to the orator's recommended course of action (deliberative rhetoric) if the orator demonstrated that it would lead to honor or to greater honor than an alternative course being promoted by a rival (Aristotle *Rhet.* 1.9.35-36; *Eth. Nic.* 2.3.7; Quintilian *Inst. Orat.* 3.7.28; 3.8.1; Pseudo-Cicero *Rhet. Ad Herren* 3.2.3). Conversely, showing how a certain course of action would result in dishonor created a strong deterrent. Another rhetorical genre, epideictic rhetoric, was associated with the praise and censure of particular individuals or groups. Orators reinforced society's values by holding up as praiseworthy those people who had exemplified a particular value. Hearing others praised—that is, honored—led the hearers to recommit themselves to the virtue or behavior that led to praise. Similarly, hearing some person censured or reproached would lead hearers to beware of falling into those behaviors that led to reproach and loss of honor. The two genres often work together, as orators, including the NT authors, use examples to illustrate the benefits of following or dangers of departing from the course they promote.

2. Honor Discourse Among Competing Cultures.

The first-century Mediterranean was far from monolithic: within a dominant Romanized Hellenistic culture, one found the ethnic subculture of Judaism, *philosophical schools and the

Christian minority culture, among others. All of these groups defined what was honorable or dishonorable in different ways. Even if groups agreed that piety was an essential virtue and component of honor, different groups defined piety quite differently (respect for the traditional gods and the *emperor; worship of the God of Israel through observance of *Torah; worship of the God of Jews and Gentiles through obedience to Jesus). Even within groups, there would be differences (e.g., Paul's conflicts with Christian Judaizers).

In such a world, it became essential to define carefully who constituted one's group of significant others—those people whose approval or disapproval mattered—and to insulate group members from concern about the honor or dishonor in which they were held by outsiders (Seneca *Const.* 13.2, 5; Epictetus *Ench.* 24.1; Moxnes 1993). If one seeks status in the eyes of the larger society, one will seek to maintain the values and fulfill the expectations of the dominant (pagan) culture. If one has been brought into a minority culture (e.g., a philosophical school or a voluntary association like the early Christian community) or has been born into an ethnic subculture (such as Judaism), then one's adherence to the group's values and ideals will remain strong only if one redefines the constituency of one's circle of significant others. The court of reputation must be limited to group members, who will support the group values in their grants of honor and censure (Plato *Cri.* 46C-47D). Including some suprasocial entity in this group (e.g., God, reason or nature) offsets the minority (and therefore deviant) status of the group's opinion. The opinion of one's fellow group members is thus fortified by and anchored in a higher court of reputation, whose judgments are of greater importance and more lasting consequence than the opinion of the disapproving majority or the dominant culture (Plato *Gorg.* 526D-527A; Epictetus *Diss.* 1.30.1; Sir 2:15-17; 23:18-19; Wis 2:12—3:5; 4:16—5:8; 4 Macc 13:3, 17; 17:5). Both Greco-Roman philosophers and Jewish authors routinely point to the opinion of God as a support for the minority culture's values. Both admonish group members to remain committed to the group's values, for that is what God looks for and honors in a person.

Where the values and commitments of a minority culture differ from those of a dominant or other alternative culture, members of that minority culture must be moved to disregard the opinion of nonmembers about their behavior (Seneca *Const.* 11.2—12.1; Epictetus *Diss.* 1.29.50-54). All groups will seek to use honor and disgrace to enforce the values of their particular culture, so each group must insulate its members from the pull of the opinion of nonmembers. Those who do not hold to the values and the construals of reality embodied in the group are excluded from the court of reputation as shameless or errant—approval or disapproval in their eyes must count for nothing, as it rests on error, and the representative of the minority culture can look forward to the vindication of his or her honor when the extent of that error is revealed (e.g., at a last judgment; 4 Macc 11:4-6; 12:11-13). When, for example, the dominant Greco-Roman culture holds a group like the Jews in contempt, the effect is a constant pressure upon individual Jews to give up their Jewishness and join in those behaviors that will then be greeted as honorable by the members of the dominant culture. Jewish authors will urge their fellow Jews to set their hearts on the opinion of the congregation and the opinion of God and so be able to resist the pull of the Gentile world.

Members of this clearly defined court of reputation must have frequent and meaningful interaction within the group. They must encourage one another to pursue group values and ideals and honor one another on that basis. Those who begin to show signs of slackening in their commitment to the values of the group out of a growing regard for the opinion of outsiders must be made to feel ashamed by the members of the group and thus pulled back from assimilation. Such people will need reminders that the realm outside the group is also outside the sphere of God's approval (Moxnes 1988). Encouragement within the group must outweigh the discouragement that comes to the individual from outside the group. Relationships within the group—the sense of connectedness and belonging so essential to the social being—must offset the sense of disconnectedness and alienation from the society that, in the case of converts, formerly provided one's primary reference group. The negative opinion of outsiders may even be transformed into a badge of honor within the group, often through the use of *athletic metaphors: insult and abuse become a competition in which the minority culture's members must endure unto victory (4 Macc 16:16; 17:11-16;

Heb 10:32). Group members are still encouraged to fulfill their desire for honor, but in terms of how the group defines honorable behavior. Thus Jews, for example, are encouraged to seek honor through obedience to Torah and enabled to resist the pressure exerted upon them by the dominant culture's contempt (Sir 10:19-24; 25:10-11; 41:6-8; deSilva 1996a).

3. Honor Discourse in the Early Church.
Honor is depicted in the NT as the result of a life of loyalty to Jesus and obedience to his teachings and example (Mt 10:32-33; Jn 12:26; 2 Tim 4:7-8). Commitment and service to fellow believers (Mt 20:25-28), witnessing to the favor of God in Christ (Rev 20:4-6) and embodying the mind of Christ, which seeks the interest of others (Phil 2:5-11), are promoted as the path to honor. The approval of God and God's Messiah, typically announced at a last judgment but also affirmed in the present by early Christian authors, alone matters for the establishment of one's honor (Mt 25:14-46; 2 Cor 5:9-10). Believers are urged to encourage and honor one another as each embodies the attributes of Christian discipleship (Phil 2:29-30; 1 Thess 5:12-13; Heb 10:24-25) and are reminded frequently of the honor they have inherited as "children of God" (Jn 1:12-13; Rom 8:14-17; Gal 3:26; Heb 2:10; 1 Jn 3:1-2) and "partners of Christ" (Heb 3:6, 14). They were called as well to honor their divine Patron and their Mediator in their lives (1 Cor 6:20) and to take care not to show contempt for the Giver by undervaluing the gift as this would result in their own dishonor before God's court (Heb 10:26-31).

The Greco-Roman society frequently reacts against these communities, often informally by insulting, reproaching, abusing and harassing the Christians (Heb 10:32-34; 1 Pet 2:11-12; 4:1-4). These represent society's attempts to draw the believers back to a life in line with traditional Greco-Roman virtues (e.g., piety, expressions of civic loyalty through cult). Similar pressures could be brought to bear on Christian Jews by the *synagogue (Jn 12:42-43; Acts 5:40-41; Rev 2:9). Christian authors, however, sought to insulate the believers from these attempts at shaming by presenting persecution as expected (Mt 10:24-25; 24:9-10; Jn 16:2-4; 1 Thess 3:3-4), as a contest in which an honorable victory may be won (Heb 12:1-4; Rev 2:26-28; 12:10-11) or as an imitation of the passion of Jesus that held the assurance of the same vindication Jesus enjoyed (Mt 5:11-12; Rom 8:17; Phil 1:29; 2:5-11; 3:10-11; 2 Tim 2:11-12; Heb 12:1-2; 1 Pet 3:18-22; 4:13-14). Close bonds between believers (e.g., as "brothers and sisters") were essential, for relationships within the group had to be of greater importance for the individual than relationships outside the group. Exhortations directed at augmenting love, encouragement and support within the group (1 Thess 4:9-10; 5:11, 14; Heb 3:13; 10:24-25; 13:1-3) aim at making the Christian court of reputation stronger than the opinion of the outside world, so that individual believers might remain committed to the way of the cross.

See also PATRONAGE; SOCIAL VALUES AND STRUCTURES; VICE AND VIRTUE LISTS.

BIBLIOGRAPHY. A. W. Adkins, *Merit and Responsibility: A Study in Greek Values* (Oxford: Clarendon Press, 1960); D. A. deSilva, *Despising Shame: Honor Discourse and Community Maintenance in the Epistle to the Hebrews* (SBLDS 152; Atlanta: Scholars Press, 1995a); idem, *Honor, Patronage, Kinship and Purity: Unlocking New Testament Culture* (Downers Grove, IL: InterVarsity Press, 2000); idem, *The Hope of Glory: Honor Discourse and New Testament Interpretation* (Collegeville, MN: Liturgical Press, 1999); idem, "Investigating Honor Discourse: Guidelines from Classical Rhetoricians," *SBLSP* 36 (1997) 491-525; idem, "The Noble Contest: Honor, Shame and the Rhetorical Strategy of 4 Maccabees," *JSP* 13 (1995b) 31-57; idem, "The Wisdom of Ben Sira: Honor, Shame and the Maintenance of the Values of a Minority Culture," *CBQ* 58 (1996a) 433-55; idem, "Worthy of His Kingdom: Honor Discourse and Social Engineering in 1 Thessalonians," *JSNT* 64 (1996b) 49-79; E. R. Dodds, *The Greeks and the Irrational* (Berkeley and Los Angeles: University of California Press, 1966); B. J. Malina and J. H. Neyrey, "Conflict in Luke-Acts: Labeling and Deviance Theory," in *The Social World of Luke-Acts: Models for Interpretation,* ed. J. H. Neyrey (Peabody, MA: Hendrickson, 1991a) 97-124; idem, "Honor and Shame in Luke-Acts: Pivotal Values of the Mediterranean World," in *The Social World of Luke-Acts: Models for Interpretation,* ed. J. H. Neyrey (Peabody, MA: Hendrickson, 1991b) 25-66; H. Moxnes, "Honor and Righteousness in Romans," *JSNT* 32 (1988b) 61-77; idem, "Honor and Shame," *BTB* 23 (1993) 167-76; idem, "Honor, Shame and the Outside World in Paul's Letter to the Romans," in *The Social World of Formative Christianity and*

Judaism, ed. J. Neusner et al. (Philadelphia: Fortress, 1988a) 207-18; J. H. Neyrey, "Despising the Shame of the Cross: Honor and Shame in the Johannine Passion Narrative," *Semeia* 68 (1996) 113-37; idem, *Honor and Shame in the Gospel of Matthew* (Louisville: Westminster John Knox, 1998); idem, *2 Peter, Jude* (AB 37C; Garden City, NY: Doubleday, 1993); J. Pitt-Rivers, "Honor and Social Status," in *Honor and Shame: The Values of Mediterranean Society,* ed. J. G. Peristiany (London: Weidenfeld & Nicolson, 1965) 21-77; B. Williams, *Shame and Necessity* (Berkeley and Los Angeles: University of California, 1993).

D. A. deSilva

HOROGRAPHY, ANCIENT. *See* HISTORIANS, GRECO-ROMAN.

HOROSCOPE TEXT (4Q186). *See* DEAD SEA SCROLLS: GENERAL INTRODUCTION.

HOSPITALITY

Hospitality is a universal phenomenon, practiced to varying degrees by all the world's cultures (Pitt-Rivers). Of the various types of hospitality that existed in the ancient Mediterranean world, five receive emphasis in the following survey. The first is public hospitality, which was practiced by states as part of their foreign policy. The second is temple hospitality, which was designed to facilitate pilgrimages to holy places. The third is commercial hospitality, which enabled travelers to obtain food and lodging for a fee. The fourth is private hospitality, which was widely esteemed and encouraged throughout the ancient world as a moral virtue. The fifth is theoxenic hospitality, in which humans were said to provide hospitality to gods, heroes and various semi-divine guests. All five types are attested in Greek, Roman and Jewish sources.

1. Greek and Roman Hospitality
2. Jewish Hospitality

1. Greek and Roman Hospitality.

The basic Greek word for hospitality is *xenia,* which is cognate with *xenos (xeinos),* the Greek word for "stranger" (Baslez; Stählin). This suggests that *xenia* originally designated hospitality to strangers, that is, guests not previously known by the host. One of the chief conventions of the Homeric hospitality scene is the revelation of the anonymous guest's identity, a disclosure that properly occurs only after the consumption of the meal and in response to the host's inquiries about the guest's name, homeland and parentage (Homer *Odys.* 1.123-24; 3.69-74; 4.60-62; 7.226-39; 14.45-47; 16.54-59). Some instances of hospitality are thus theoxenies, with the unknown guest later revealed as a god in disguise. In such cases the visit constitutes a divine test of human character, with the virtuous receiving a reward for their hospitality and the unworthy meriting punishment because of their inhospitality (Homer *Odys.* 17.484-87; Plato *Soph.* 216A-B; Ovid *Met.* 8.611-724; Silius Italicus *Pun.* 7.162-211; Acts 13:2).

Another Greek term for hospitality is *philoxenia,* which indicates that the host is friendly to the guest, treating the stranger as though he were a friend *(philos).* In Homeric times the host's friendly treatment of the guest created a formal bond of friendship between them (Fitzgerald). The establishment of this pact of guest friendship was cemented and symbolized by a gift that the host bestowed on the departing guest (Homer *Odys.* 1.311-13). The acceptance of the gift obligated the guest to remember the host (Homer *Odys.* 4.589-92; 8.430-32; 15.51-55) and to reciprocate his hospitality and generosity at a later time (Homer *Odys.* 1.316-18; 24.284-86). The resulting alliance between host and guest was transgenerational, so that even descendants of the original guest and host were bound by the obligations of guest friendship (Homer *Il.* 6.119-236). Hereditary ties of hospitality *(hospitium)* likewise existed between prominent Romans and non-Romans (Caesar *B. Civ.* 2.25; Cicero *Rosc. Am.* 6.15; Livy *Hist.* 1.1.1; 42.1.10), and both Greek and Roman travelers frequently carried tokens of hospitality *(symbola, tessarae hospitales)* that served to identify them to former hosts and their descendants as guest friends entitled to hospitality (Scholiast on Euripides *Med.* 613; Plautus *Poen.* 958, 1045-55; Gauthier). Only a formal renunciation of the relationship, sometimes accompanied by the breaking of the token (Plautus *Cist.* 503), terminated the obligations of guest friendship (Cicero *Verr.* 2.2.36 §§88-89; Livy *Hist.* 25.18.4-5).

From the beginning, therefore, the practice of hospitality was linked to *friendship, serving originally to establish a reciprocal relationship between individuals previously unknown to one another and later extended to nurture both affective and nonaffective associations between known parties. Such friendly treatment of strangers stood in vivid contrast to *xenophobia*, a fear of strangers that often resulted in them being neglected or abused (Bolchazy 1978). The wayfarer in a foreign land was in a highly vulnerable situation. Consequently, to extend hospitality and friendship to a stranger was a magnanimous act by the host; conversely, for a stranger to abuse or take advantage of the host was an egregious act that utterly violated the pact of guest friendship. The most notorious instance of such a violation of a host's hospitality was Paris's seduction of Helen, which was so outrageous that it resulted in the Trojan War.

Hospitality played a major role in aristocratic circles in ancient Greece, so that it is not surprising that it appears as an important theme in the Homeric corpus; the latter contains eighteen major scenes in which the rituals of hospitality are prominent. S. Reece has identified thirty-eight conventional elements that occur in the Homeric hospitality scenes. Among the more important conventions are the guest's arrival and waiting at the threshold, the reception by the host, seating, feasting, toasting, revelation of the guest's identity, exchange of information, entertainment, the guest's blessing of the host and participation in a libation or sacrifice, bed and bath, the giving of gifts to the guest, departure meal and libation, farewell blessing and escort to the guest's next destination. Many of these ritualized actions, such as the meal and farewell blessing, remained characteristic features of hospitality in the following centuries.

As an aristocratic institution, guest friendship (also known as ritualized friendship) created strong alliances between families living in different lands (Herman). In addition, it contributed to the rise of proxeny *(proxenia),* an official pact of friendship and hospitality with certain individuals as part of the foreign policy of a number of Greek states (Walbank; Wallace). Whereas modern states typically appoint their own citizens to reside in foreign lands and represent their national and commercial interests, many ancient Greek states formed alliances with citizens from other states for this same purpose. The local individual with whom this pact was formed was known as a *proxenos* ("friend of a foreign state"), and he promoted the interests of the foreign power within his own country and provided hospitality to envoys and distinguished visitors from the state that he represented (Herodotus *Hist.* 8.136, 143; Plato *Leg.* 1.642B-C; 12.953B-C; Xenophon *Hell.* 5.4.22; *Symp.* 8.40; Athenaeus *Deipn.* 13.603F). In some cases, Greek states also appointed a *proxenos* in their own lands to provide public hospitality to foreign residents and guests (Herodotus *Hist.* 6.57). A similar kind of public hospitality *(hospitium publicum)* existed in the Roman world (Cicero *Balb.* 18.41; *Div. in Caecil.* 20.66-67; Livy *Hist.* 5.28.4-5; Diodorus Siculus *Bib. Hist.* 14.93.4-5), which in various ways emphasized state hospitality (Livy *Hist.* 1.45.2; 5.50.3; 32.27.4; 37.54.5; 42.1.7-12).

There were also *proxenoi* at important religious sites in Greece, especially Delphi (Euripides *Ion* 551, 1039; *Androm.* 1103; Gauthier, 46-52), and religious pilgrimages to various holy places prompted the establishment of inns in or near temples where pilgrims could find lodging (Thucydides *Hist.* 3.68.3; Plato *Leg.* 12.953A).

Most travel, however, was not religiously motivated, and the number of travelers increased greatly as a result of *Rome's rise to power. Rome's establishment of an elaborate network of roads and sea routes made travel relatively easy, and an extensive system of hostels and inns offering commercial hospitality developed in response to this enhanced physical mobility. Although the accommodations offered by some of these commercial establishments were pleasant (Epictetus *Diss.* 2.23.36), most were far from ideal (Livy *Hist.* 45.22.2; *Acts Jn.* 60) and some were no more than brothels (Strabo *Geog.* 12.17; 17.1.17; *see also* Theophrastus *Char.* 6.5; Plutarch *Demetr.* 26.3; Pollux *Onom.* 9.34). In addition, they posed a number of dangers, including robbery and murder (Cicero *De Inv.* 2.4.14-15; *De Div.* 1.27.57).

Many, especially the wealthy, thus preferred to lodge with friends, who often entertained them in grand style (Xenophon *Oec.* 2.5; Vitruvius *De Arch.* 6.7.4); as a result, private hospitality was widely practiced despite the proliferation of inns in the Greco-Roman period. It was common for people to write letters of recommendation on behalf of friends who were traveling to places where other friends lived; these letters commended the travelers and requested hospitality and other favors for them (Kim, 76-77; see also Plato *Cri.* 45C). Yet the practice of extending hospitality to complete strangers also continued (Aelian *V.H.* 4.9), strongly encouraged by the conviction that hospitality was not only a sign of a generous (Cicero *De Offic.* 2.18.64) and philanthropic nature (Acts 28:7) but also a religious act by which one paid homage to the divine (esp. Zeus Xenios = Jupiter Hospitalis) as the protector and avenger of the stranger (Homer *Odys.* 9.270-71; 14.57-58, 283-84, 389; Plato *Leg.* 5.729E-730A; 12.953E; Apollonius of Rhodes *Arg.* 2.1131-33; Cicero *Deiot.* 6.18; *Q. Fr.* 2.12; Aelian *V.H.* 4.1; 2 Macc 6:2; see also Pausanias *Descr.* 7.27.4; Cicero *Verr.* 2.4.22 § 48; Ovid *Met.* 5.45; Livy *Hist.* 39.51.12; Tacitus *Ann.* 15.52). Only in exceptional cases was a violation of the code of hospitality defended and celebrated (Livy *Hist.* 1.9.1-16).

2. Jewish Hospitality.

The ancient Israelite practice of state hospitality (1 Kings 10:1-13; 2 Kings 20:12-13) was noted by *Josephus (Josephus *Ant.* 7.1.4 §30; 8.15.3 §398; 9.3.1 §§30-31; 9.4.3 §59; 10.9.4 §§168-69; see also 4.6.2 §105; Philo *Vit. Mos.* 1.275), who likewise emphasized the importance of this practice in subsequent Jewish history (Josephus *Ant.* 12.4.2-3 §§165-74), especially during the Roman period when Antipater (Josephus *J.W.* 1.8.9 §181; 1.9.3 §187; *Ant.* 14.5.1 §81; 14.7.3 §122) and his descendants used public hospitality and guest friendship to form strong political alliances with prominent Romans, including Marc Antony (Josephus *J.W.* 1.12.5 §244; 1.14.4 §282; *Ant.* 14.13.1 §326; 14.14.4 §381), Augustus (Josephus *J.W.* 1.14.4 §283; *Ant.* 14.14.4 §383; 15.6.7 §§199-200; 16.4.5 §128), Marcus Agrippa (Josephus *Ant.* 16.2.1 §12) and Vespasian (Josephus *J.W.* 3.9.7 §§443-45). Although this practice created a number of problems for the *Herodians (Josephus *J.W.* 1.13.3 §254; 1.26.1-2 §§513-25; *Ant.* 14.13.4 §341), Herod's commitment to it is evident from the fact that his palace was built with bedchambers for one hundred guests (Josephus *J.W.* 5.4.4 §177; see also *Ant.* 15.6.7 §199). Like the Romans, the Jews used letters to request hospitality for various people (Josephus *J.W.* 2.21.6 §615), including Roman generals and their armies (Josephus *Ant.* 14.8.1 §131).

Following the exile, most Jews lived outside of the Holy Land, and many of these made pilgrimages to *Jerusalem. At least one of the *synagogues in Jerusalem was built in such a way as to address this situation; in an inscription (*CIJ* 1404), Theodotus claims that he built "the guest-house and the rooms and the water supplies as an inn for those who have need when they come from abroad" (Barrett, 54).

Roman roads were built in Palestine, and inns offering hospitality for a fee appeared soon thereafter (Luke 10:34-35; see also 2:7). Yet the emphasis in Judaism remained on the exercise of private hospitality, especially to aliens and strangers, as an obligation that was enjoined by the *Torah (Lev 19:33-34) and underscored by the depiction of Yahweh as the protector of strangers (Deut 10:17-19; Philo *Abr.* 96; *Vit. Mos.* 1.36). Hospitality was viewed as a byproduct of personal piety toward God (Philo *Abr.* 114), and Josephus's depiction of the pious *Essenes accordingly gave emphasis to their hospitality (Josephus *J.W.* 2.8.4-5 §§125, 132).

To practice hospitality, therefore, was worthy of praise, even self-praise (Job 31:32), whereas the failure to do so evoked condemnation (Job 22:7), especially in circles where hospitality was regarded as superior to fasting (Is 58:6-7). For models of hospitality and inhospitality, Jews of the Greco-Roman period drew heavily on the OT. Particularly important was the theoxeny of Genesis 18:1-8, where Abraham is praised as an extraordinarily attentive and gracious host (Philo *Abr.* 107-67; Josephus *Ant.* 1.11.2 §196). Lot's theoxenic hospitality (Gen 19:1-11) was also noted (Josephus *Ant.* 1.11.3 §200), including his placement of the security of his guests above that of his own daughters (cf. Aulus Gellius *Noc. Att.* 5.13.2, 5). Others singled out for their hospitality included Melchizedek (Gen 14:17-24; Josephus *Ant.* 1.10.2 §181), Rebekah (Gen 24:16-25; Josephus *Ant.* 1.16.2 §§246, 250-51), the prostitute Rahab (Josh 2), whose house, in view of her profession, was called an inn (Josephus *Ant.* 5.1.2 §§7-8, 10, 13; see also 3.12.2 §276), Manoah (Judg 13; Josephus *Ant.* 5.8.3 §§282-84), Boaz (Josephus *Ant.* 5.9.2 §323) and the Shunammite woman (2 Kings 4:8-17).

Models of OT inhospitality included the Sodomites (Gen 19:1-11; Wis 19:14-15; Philo *Conf. Ling.* 27), the Egyptians (Gen 12:10-20; Ex 1—2; Wis 19:13-16; Philo *Abr.* 94, 107; *Vit. Mos.* 1.34-36; *Spec. Leg.* 2.146; Josephus *Ant.* 1.8.1 §164), Abimelech (Gen 20; Josephus *Ant.* 1.12.1 §208), Jethro's daughters (Ex 2:20; Philo *Vit. Mos.* 1.58) and the Gibeahites (Judg 19:22-30; Josephus *Ant.* 5.2.8 §§136-49). Celebrations of a breach of hospitality were extremely rare (Judg 4:17-22; 5:24-31).

In practice the guest-host relationship was not without its problems. *Sirach (Sir 29:21-28), for example, complains of rude treatment of guests by hosts, and Joseph's brothers were recalled as those who had been falsely accused of mistreating their host (Gen 44:4; Philo *Jos.* 163-257; Josephus *Ant.* 2.6.7-8 §§128, 136). Despite problems and abuses, hospitality remained a highly esteemed practice and was enthusiastically commended in later *rabbinic literature (e.g., *m. ʾAbot* 1:5).

See also BANQUETS; FAMILY AND HOUSEHOLD; FRIENDSHIP; TRAVEL AND TRADE.

BIBLIOGRAPHY. C. K. Barrett, ed., *The New Testament Background: Writings from Ancient Greece and the Roman Empire That Illuminate Christian Origins* (rev. ed.; San Francisco: HarperSanFrancisco, 1989); M.-F. Baslez, *L'étranger dans la Grèce antique* (Realia; Paris: Société d'Édition "Les Belles Lettres," 1984); L. J. Bolchazy, "From Xenophobia to Altruism: Homeric and Roman Hospitality," *The Ancient World* 1 (1978) 45-64; idem, *Hospitality in Early Rome: Livy's Concept of Its Humanizing Force* (Chicago: Ares, 1977); J. T. Fitzgerald, "Friendship in the Greek World Prior to Aristotle," in *Greco-Roman Perspectives on Friendship,* ed. J. T. Fitzgerald (SBLRBS 34; Atlanta: Scholars Press, 1997) 13-34; P. Gauthier, *Symbola: Les étrangers et la justice dans les cités grecques* (Annales de l'Est, Mémoire 42; Nancy: Université de Nancy, 1972); G. Herman, *Ritualised Friendship and the Greek City* (Cambridge: Cambridge University Press, 1987); O. Hiltbrunner, D. Gorce and H. Wehr, "Gastfreundschaft," *RAC* 8:1061-1123; C.-H. Kim, *Form and Structure of the Familiar Greek Letter of Recommendation* (SBLDS 4; Missoula, MT: SBL, 1972); J. B. Mathews, "Hospitality and the New Testament Church: An Historical and Exegetical Study" (Th.D. diss., Princeton Theological Seminary, 1964); O. E. Nybakken, "The Moral Basis of *Hospitium Privatum,*" *CJ* 41 (1945-46) 248-53; J. Pitt-Rivers, "The Law of Hospitality," in *The Fate of Shechem or The Politics of Sex: Essays in the Anthropology of the Mediterranean* (Cambridge: Cambridge University Press, 1977) 94-112; S. Reece, *The Stranger's Welcome: Oral Theory and the Aesthetics of the Homeric Hospitality Scene* (Michigan Monographs in Classical Antiquity; Ann Arbor: University of Michigan Press, 1993); L. Schmitz, H. Hager and W. Wayte, "Hospitium," *A Dictionary of Greek and Roman Antiquities,* ed. W. Smith, W. Wayte and G. E. Marindin (3d ed.; 2 vols.; London: John Murray, 1890) 1:977-82; G. Stählin, "ξένος κτλ," *TDNT* 5:1-36; M. B. Walbank, *Athenian Proxenies of the Fifth Century B.C.* (Toronto: Samuel Stevens, 1978); M. B. Wallace, "Early Greek *Proxenoi,*" *Phoenix* 24 (1970) 189-208.

J. T. Fitzgerald

HOUSEHOLD. *See* FAMILY AND HOUSEHOLD.

HOUSEHOLD CODES. *See* FAMILY AND HOUSEHOLD.

HOUSEHOLD CULT. *See* DOMESTIC RELIGION AND PRACTICES.

HUSBANDS. *See* MARRIAGE.

HYMNS. *See* CREEDS AND HYMNS; PSALMS AND HYMNS OF QUMRAN; THANKSGIVING HYMNS (1QH).

I

IDOLATRY, JEWISH CONCEPTION OF

The religious use of icons, or idols, as they are often called in biblical literature, was offensive to Jews, for any image of God or a divine being violated the second of the Ten Commandments (cf. Ex 20:4-5), and by implication violated the first as well (cf. Ex 20:3). In the course of Israel's history, controversy and polemic developed in response to the idolatry that was part of the ancient Near East.

1. Key Passages in Jewish Literature
2. Jewish Anti-Idolatry in the Setting of the Greco-Roman World

1. Key Passages in Jewish Literature.

The Hebrew Bible frequently dwells on an anti-idolatry theme, though the most developed and later influential form of this polemic is to be found in prophetic texts such as Isaiah 44—46 and Jeremiah 10. Numerous other passages are worthy of mention, including, but not limited to, the following: Epistle of Jeremiah; Wisdom 11:15-16; 12:24, 27; 13:10-14; 14:8; 15:18—16:1; *Epistle of Aristeas* 138; *1 Enoch* 99:6-10; *Sibylline Oracles* 3:6-35; *2 Baruch* 54:17-22; and Philo *De Decalogo* 76-80 and *Bel and the Dragon*. These texts are not all of a kind. Some of them seem to be directly related to OT prophetic anti-idolatry texts such as those mentioned from Isaiah and Jeremiah (e.g., Ep Jer; *1 Enoch* 99:6-10 [Wis 13:10-14; 14:8-29 also have strong parallels with Is 44—46, but there is reason to judge that there are additional elements accrued to this tradition which merit further investigation, as argued below]). The clearest reflection of the biblical castigation of idolatry is that found in the general attitude of later rabbinic literature (e.g., *b. Šabb.* 72b-73a; 82a-b; *b. Ketub.* 45b). Yet many of the other texts we have mentioned above seem to be more fully situated within the setting of the Greco-Roman world and its concerns than they are within the purview of concerns expressed in the Hebrew Bible/Old Testament.

2. Jewish Anti-Idolatry in the Setting of the Greco-Roman World.

Despite the assumption on the part of most students and scholars of biblical texts that Judaism is simply by nature anti-idolatry, much of this is an impressionistic rendering of the OT's rhetorical program and owes little to a developed understanding of *Judaism in the Greek and Roman periods. A more developed understanding might help to illuminate more clearly some of the reasons for the continuation and development of Jewish anti-idolatry in the Second Temple period. Typically, NT scholars discussing the phenomenon of idol worship in the Greco-Roman world make little distinction between kinds of idol-worship. However, this unfortunate conflation is not indicative of the state-of-play in the Greco-Roman period. The import and export of religious ideas throughout the Mediterranean basin in the wake of *Alexander the Great's conquest of the Persian world brought to the fore not just similarities between the cultures of this area but also differences. One source of conflict in the Roman period revolved around such a difference, namely, the differences between ancient Roman religious sensibility and the equally ancient Egyptian zooalatry (worship of animal gods). For the purposes of this brief article, and because of its important place within the history of religion in the Roman period, we will focus on the Jewish interaction with both Egyptian idolatry and the Roman attitudes toward it as a test case to help develop an understanding of the Jewish attitude toward idolatry in this period.

2.1. Roman Attitudes Toward Egyptian Idolatry. The Roman author Diodorus Siculus's discussion of Egyptian zoomorphic (i.e., animal-shaped) idolatry provides a striking backdrop for discussion (Diodorus Siculus *Bib. Hist.* 1.86-87). One of the most interesting passages in this discussion is a section discussing the *reasons* for the worship of the individual animals. In this context, Diodorus apparently reflects a typical Roman confusion regarding the *reasons* for worshiping each of the various animals, and records three explanations. The first two are mythical, but the third is quite practical: "The third cause which they adduce in connection with the dispute in question is the service which each of these animals renders for the benefit of community life and of mankind" (Diodorus Siculus *Bib. Hist.* 1.87.1, LCL). He proceeds to explain how the following animals are useful to humankind and hence worthy of honor (Diodorus Siculus *Bib. Hist.* 1.87-88; cf. Witt, 27-35 for the identification of various gods/goddesses and their animal forms).

Clearly this rationalistic, euhemeristic approach is the most acceptable form of explaining Egyptian animal worship for Diodorus. However, "useful" animals are not the only animals worshiped by the Egyptians. In addition, the crocodile and lion, among other less savory characters, were also accorded worship. Diodorus deals with only one of these—the crocodile. He suggests that, as "these beasts eat the flesh of men," the worship of the crocodile is "a subject regarding which most men are entirely at a loss to explain how . . . it ever became the law to honor like the gods creatures of the most revolting habits" (Diodorus Siculus *Bib. Hist.* 1.89.1). He presents two explanations, one mythical (with the primeval king, Menas, being carried on the back of a crocodile to escape an angry pack of dogs, Diodorus Siculus *Bib. Hist.* 1.89.3), and one practical—the Nile, infested with crocodiles, formed a naturally impenetrable frontier for most of Egypt's eastern border (Diodorus Siculus *Bib. Hist.* 1.89.2). The mythical explanation is given by Diodorus to explain certain monuments that have obviously been attached to the legend of the crocodile ferry-ride by Menas; yet it is clear by his "strange though it may seem [this is what they say]" (Diodorus Siculus *Bib. Hist.* 1.89.3) style of language that he is clearly in favor of the first explanation. Regardless of the rationality of Diodorus's first explanation, however, the fact that he tries to unravel this problem "which most men are entirely at a loss to explain" shows that there must exist in both his sources and his contemporaries' minds some question concerning the worship of these animals.

In contrast to Diodorus's detached, scholarly approach to the explanation of Egyptian idolatry, another author of importance is Plutarch, who, in his *Isis and Osiris* (377D–378A; 379B-D), has an extended discussion of idols, atheism and superstition, and then, in 379D–382D, of animals and idols (esp. 382B-C, regarding the equality of animate and inanimate representation of the gods). Although Plutarch does not try to explain the reasons for the worship of each of the animals as do Diodorus and Philo (see below), opting instead for mythical explanations, his reasoned discussion regarding the nature of idolatry stands in contrast to the kind of vitriol we find in Jewish literature of the period. It also highlights the need that many Jewish authors must have felt to make their point regarding idolatry, and perhaps one of the reasons for overstating their case (cf. the passages listed above in section 1).

2.2 Jewish Attitudes Toward Egyptian Idolatry. Like the Roman literature briefly surveyed here, various Jewish authors treat the idea of idolatry differently. Wisdom 11:15-16 reflects a reasoning similar to Diodorus's concerning the reasons for the worship of various animals: "In return for their foolish and wicked thoughts, which led them astray to worship irrational serpents and worthless animals, you sent upon them a multitude of irrational creatures to punish them, that they might learn that one is punished by the very things by which he sins" (see also Wis 12:24, 27). Philo's discussion in *De Decalogo* 76-80, specifically anti-Egyptian, is also relevant in this regard. Like Diodorus, he is (grudgingly) able to understand the deification of domestic animals, but not of the vicious beasts like the crocodile or lion: "the Egyptians are rightly charged not only on the count to which every country is liable [i.e., idolatry], but also on another peculiar to themselves. For in addition to wooden and other images, they have advanced to divine honors irrational animals, bulls and rams and goats, and invented for each some famous legend of wonder. And with these perhaps there might be some reason, for they are thoroughly domesticated and useful for our livelihood" (Philo *Decal.* 76-77, LCL). Philo goes on to describe the various uses of these animals, then resumes his discussion of the various Egyptian animal divinities: "But actually the Egyptians have gone to a further excess and chosen the fiercest and most savage of wild animals, lions and crocodiles and among reptiles the venomous asp, all of which they dignify with temples, sacred precincts, sacrifices, assemblies, processions and the like" (Philo *Decal.* 78, LCL). He continues his polemic against zooalatry with those animals he can neither understand nor ridicule as vicious, and records the reaction of foreigners to the Egyptian predilection for animal worship:

> Many other animals too they have deified, dogs, cats, wolves and among the birds, ibises and hawks; fishes too, either their whole bodies or particular parts. What could be more ridiculous than this? Indeed strangers on their first arrival in Egypt before the vanity of the land has gained a lodgement in their minds are like to die with laughing at it, while anyone who knows the flavor of right instruction, horrified at this veneration of things so much the reverse of venerable, pities those who render it and regards them with good reason as more miserable than the creatures they honor, as men with souls transformed into the nature of those creatures, so that as they pass before him, they seem beasts in human shape. (Philo *Decal.* 79-80, LCL)

The extensive success of Egyptian cults both in Hellenized Egypt itself and throughout the rest of the Greco-Roman world makes this kind of argument on Philo's part unsurprising. That many of the visitors to Alexandria in Philo's time would be Romans goes without saying, and the existence in a Roman author such as Diodorus of similar argumentation (although dispassionate in comparison to Philo) suggests that this kind of argumentation was more widespread than simply these two authors. It seems that neither of them is actually furnishing new arguments, but, rather, each makes use of a generally accepted way of speaking about Egyptian religion.

Why, though, focus on Egyptians and Romans like this? On the surface, a simpler answer to the question, What were Jewish attitudes to idolatry in the Greco-Roman period? would be to simply point out the OT passages relevant to this concern and be done with it. This, however, is not an exclusively sufficient basis for study of Jewish attitudes in the Greco-Roman period. Although it is obvious that the anti-Egyptian levels of discourse in, for instance, Wisdom, are partly structured on the story of the plagues visited on the Egyptians in Exodus, it should be noticed that this new application of this discourse emerged in a very different historical and cultural situation.

2.3. Roman Religious Xenophobia and Jewish Attitudes Toward Idolatry. While space precludes a full examination of the characteristics of this period, the phenomenon of Roman religious xenophobia calls for attention. While Rome enjoyed its status as the center of the known world, it seems relatively clear that the implications of this hublike position were not always well received by the Romans themselves. Rome was full of different people groups and all of their accompanying elements: ethnic dress, cultural practices, religions, food, work habits, languages, etc. We read of Roman suspicion of especially religious practice on multiple occasions, the most obvious for the NT being the expulsion of all Jews from Rome under Claudius (Priscilla and Aquila, who left Italy and came to Corinth [Acts 18:2] were probably part of this expulsion; cf. Cicero *Flac.* 28.66-67; Horace *Sat.* 1.4.142-43; 1.5.100; 1.9.67-72 for Roman anti-Semitism or -Judaism). Roman xenophobia was not limited to the Jews, however. We have many examples of alien cults receiving stringent criticism (e.g., Livy 39.15.3, regarding alien cults in general; and Dionysius of Halicarnassus *Ant. Rom.* 2.19, regarding worship of the Phrygian mother, who was, in an expression of the Roman equivocation on these matters, later highly honored by the Claudian emperors; cf. La Piana, 397-402). But the Egyptian cults seem to have received special attention (cf. Roullet, 1-12). This was probably due to a variety of factors: some religious and cultural, others economic (especially with regard to the dependence of Rome upon the grain supply from Egypt).

From a religious and cultural perspective, however, Egyptian zooalatry seems to have been particularly repugnant to the Roman mind. When visiting Egypt, Augustus is recorded to have refused to visit the temple of Anubis, since the worship of a dog was completely beneath him (Dio Cassius *Hist.* 51.16). Juvenal, in his *Satires* 15.1-8, 11-13, presents a particularly scathing attack and mockery of the Egyptian predilection for animal worship. In addition, in *Satires* 6.489, 526-41, he specifically connects the worship of Egyptian gods with illicit sexual license (cf. Grant, 35). We also have evidence that there was *official* resistance to the importation to Rome of the Egyptian gods as well as popular support for them (cf. Tertullian, *Ad Nat.* 1.10; *Apol. I* 6; Valerius Maximus 1.3.4). Still, it seems that the Romans could also display respect for the dedication with which the Egyptians (and non-Egyptian initiates of the Egyptian religions) viewed their zoomorphic gods. In the mid-first century, the remaining members of the first Triumvirate, in need of public support after the death of Caesar, built the people of Rome a temple of Isis and Sarapis (Dio Cassius *Hist.* 47.15).

The dominant political and military power in the Mediterranean world had a tradition of anti-Egyptian sentiment. In this cultural-semantic context we may very well have precedents in the OT that lend themselves to reinterpretation in light of the current cultural situation, but as components in other thematics of fresh origin. It is unlikely that it was the OT/Jewish critique of Egyptian religion that spurred the Romans into their anti-Egyptian polemic. We must not forget that the Jews themselves came under the same Roman prejudicial judgment as did the Egyptians. They were even ridiculed by Juvenal in the same context as the Egyptians (Juvenal *Sat.* 6.542-47, directly after the passage mentioned above with regard to the Egyptians). Moreover, this conflation of Jews and followers of the Egyptian cults is reflected in a series of expulsions which took place in the late republic and early imperial periods. As Tacitus records in *Annals* 2.85, relating the "expulsion of Egyptian and Jewish rites [under Tiberius in A.D. 19; on the dating here, cf. Slingerland, 50-51 n. 42] the senate declared that four thousand adult ex-slaves tainted with those superstitions should be transported to Sardinia. . . . The rest, unless they repudiated their unholy practices by a given date, must leave Italy."

The trend towards intercultural quarrels between the conquered people groups of the *Roman East is likely the motivating factor in this regard. First under the Greeks, then under the Romans, the various groups were forced to vie for respect in the eyes of their overlords (both of which were notoriously "young" culturally, at least in comparison to their Eastern subjects) (cf. [pseudo]Eupolemus frag. 1 [Eusebius *Praep. Ev.* 9.17.8-9]; and Bickerman, 218-36). It follows from this presuppositional perspective that one people group would make use of the overlord's own denigration of another threatening people group both to obtain favor in the eyes of the overlord and to position themselves above the other group. This is an effective—if sycophantic—strategy. While we would not suggest that this is the only motivation for Jewish attitudes toward idolatry, its consideration is lacking in modern scholarship.

See also JUDAISM AND THE NEW TESTAMENT; POLYTHEISM, GRECO-ROMAN; RELIGION, GRECO-ROMAN; RELIGION, PERSONAL.

BIBLIOGRAPHY. E. J. Bickerman, *The Jews in the Greek Age* (Cambridge, MA: Harvard University Press, 1988); R. M. Grant, *Gods and the One God* (Philadelphia: Westminster, 1986); G. La Piana, "Foreign Groups in Ancient Rome During the First Centuries of the Empire," *HTR* 20.4 (1927) 183-403; A. Roullet, *The Egyptian and Egyptianizing Monuments of Imperial Rome* (EPRO 20; Leiden: E. J. Brill, 1972); H. D. Slingerland, *Claudian Policymaking and the Early Imperial Repression of Judaism at Rome* (SFSHJ 160; Atlanta: Scholars Press, 1997); R. E. Witt, *Isis in the Graeco-Roman World* (Ithaca, NY: Cornell University Press, 1971) [= *Isis in the Ancient World* (Baltimore and London: Johns Hopkins University Press, 1997)]. B. W. R. Pearson

INCEST. *See* ADULTERY, DIVORCE.

INFANTICIDE. *See* FAMILY AND HOUSEHOLD.

INSCRIPTIONS AND PAPYRI: GRECO-ROMAN

Inscriptions and papyri are two of the most important sources for study of the background of the NT, yet they remain widely neglected and misunderstood by many NT scholars. An understanding of their place within the ancient world, as well as some of the basic principles of their interpretation, is a desideratum for NT scholarship.

1. Inscriptions
2. Papyri
3. Implications for Study of the New Testament

1. Inscriptions.

Inscriptions in many ways served the same purpose as the mass media do for modern culture and society. There are major flaws with this analogy in terms of the process required for dissemination, but inscriptions were widely used as a means of propagating news. They included edicts by rulers, correspondence between distant potentates and a local population, laws and proscriptions regarding behavior, and general information regarding individuals and groups, including information about their lives and deaths.

1.1. Discovery and Classification. The nineteenth century has been described as the century for inscriptions. This pronouncement by the historian and epigrapher T. Mommsen accurately captures the climate of academic discovery during that century (van Minnen, 5). In conjunction with the building of modern empires and the resulting power and economic influence that such empire building entailed, a number of countries were able to sponsor various archaeological ventures and to support scholars in exploration of the territory around the Mediterranean. During this time major archaeological excavations occurred in *Greece, *Asia Minor and elsewhere in the greater Mediterranean area, with the result that numerous sites were dug, their contents cataloged and the findings published for wider dissemination.

Among the major findings were numerous inscriptions (many inscriptions were already known and housed in museums around the world, but this marked the advent of serious and widespread scholarly interest in them). Inscriptions consisted of various texts that were inscribed on stone or other similar hard surfaces, often with the intention of the stone providing a permanent and nonportable record of what was written. Inscriptions, however, are also written on a number of other surfaces, such as pottery, metal and wood. Although there are inscriptions from a range of people groups, dating back to earliest times, those of greatest interest to NT scholars are those in Greek and Latin and possibly in several local languages of the regions related to NT study such as Asia Minor and Palestine. Because of their prominence, travelers have long been interested in inscriptions, with the first collections of Greek and Latin inscriptions made in the ninth or tenth centuries A.D. During the nineteenth century, as well as into the twentieth century, numerous inscriptions were found and/or recorded and then disseminated in a wide range of publications, many of them established during the nineteenth century. One of the most important categories of inscriptions is grave inscriptions, of which thousands have been discovered in the greater Mediterranean area. These could range from a simple stone marking a place of burial to an elaborate and highly decorated family mausoleum (see van der Horst for Jewish epitaphs; *see* Burial Practices, Jewish; Art and Architecture: Jewish).

Inscriptions have been, and continue to be, published in a wide variety of places (see Woodhead, 94-107). The three major venues are the collections of inscriptions from a given site or collection, anthologies of inscriptions (often thematically arranged) and individual inscriptions published in various archaeological or classical studies journals. Several of the major publishing projects of inscriptions related to sites or collections include the inscriptions from *Athens in the *Inscriptiones Graecae* (*IG*), now being revised in multiple volumes. There is also the *Collection of Ancient Greek Inscriptions in the British Museum* (4 vols.). For a collection from Asia Minor, one should consult *Monumenta Asiae Minoris Antiqua.* Many of the major sites have their own publications, including collections from such places as *Corinth, Cos, *Ephesus, Magnesia, Olympia, Pergamum and Priene, among many others. Useful and standard collections of inscriptions include the *Corpus Inscriptionum Graecarum* (*CIG*) and the *Corpus Inscriptionum Latinarum* (*CIL*), as well as several volumes made by the German scholar W. Dittenberger, including *Orientis Graeci Inscriptiones Selectae* (*OGIS*), and the second and third editions of *Sylloge Inscriptionum Graecarum* (*SIG*), and one by H. Dessau, *Inscriptiones Latinae Selectae* (*ILS*). There is also a valuable collection of inscriptions related to the Jews and Judaism in *Corpus Inscriptionum Judaicarum* (*CIJ*). C. B. Welles's *Royal Correspondence in the Hellenistic Period* is also an important collection for the period.

Useful for students of the NT in particular are the recently published texts in L. Boffo, *Iscrizioni Greche e Latine,* the occasional inscriptions with commentary treated in *New Documents Illustrating Early Christianity* (*NewDocs* 1-8), and A. Deissmann's classic *Light from the Ancient East.* A number of volumes have inscriptional material relevant to the time (Ehrenberg and Jones; Charlesworth; McCrum and Woodhead). The range of journals to consult is vast. Some of the more important are the *Journal of Hellenic Studies,* the *Journal of Roman Studies* and *Gnomon,* among many others. One should also consult *Supplementum Epigraphicum Graecum* (*SEG*), which attempts to chronicle recent publications in this area, and the relevant sections in the *L'Année Épigraphique* and *L'Année Philologique.* The proliferation of finds and the undertaking of numerous publication projects, as well as personal finds and publications, has resulted in a wealth of information, much of it difficult to access, since there is no systematic referencing system for inscriptions yet devised. Even several of the sources noted above have conflicting referencing systems, and some inscriptions are found in several different, overlapping sources.

1.2. Process of Inscribing a Stone. Once an edict or pronouncement had been passed by a city council or proclaimed by a ruler, or a person had died and an epitaph had been written, and it was determined that these needed fixed proclamation, the process of creating an inscription took place. This would involve selecting a stone suitable in terms of size and material. Many of the ancient inscriptions from Greece and Italy are on marble, no doubt due to its availability as well as its beauty and permanence. But other kinds of stone were used as well, including granite, obsidian, chalk and limestone. The stonecutter employed could range in skill from the very good to the very poor, as indicated by the quality and consistency of the letters cut in the stone. A declaration regarding the accomplishments of a city in battle might involve an expert stonecutter employed by the city, but a grave inscription might involve someone who did not take as much care or even have the necessary skill.

The cutting of the stone can be evaluated along several different lines. These include the size and shape of the letters (there was a difference in technique required to inscribe larger as opposed to smaller letters); the regularity with which they are cut into the stone, both in terms of the shape of the letters and their depth; the alphabet and style of letters used; and the ability to accurately judge the spacing of the letters, lines and text on the stone. Regional and temporal distinctions can also be made on the basis of the kind of lettering used by the stonecutter. S. V. Tracy's recent study shows that different stonecutters can be recognized by the way in which they inscribed their letters.

Once the text to be inscribed was established, the stonecutter proceeded to cut the stone (see Woodhead, 24-34). Many early Greek inscriptions used a technique called boustrophedon, in which the inscription is to be read line by line left to right and then right to left. This practice seems to have ended during the sixth to fifth centuries B.C., with subsequent inscriptions written to be read left to right. Many of these inscriptions, certainly in Attica, are written in what is called *stoichedon* or semi-*stoichedon* style, with the same number of letters in each line and each letter lined up vertically with the one above. Early Latin inscriptions used the Greek forms of letters and had peculiarities such as writing right to left or up and down. The Augustan age marked a high point in the formal presentation of Latin inscriptions, when a standard monumental alphabet was often used (see Sandys, 34-57). Less formal Greek and Latin inscriptions, and especially some from outlying areas, are often not written in such regular and well-spaced lettering, with some tending toward a cursive style.

If in the process of cutting the stone there was a change made in the text or the stonecutter made an error, he would need to chisel away the old letter or inscribe the new letter more deeply into the stone. Even with careful attention to detail by the stonecutter, it is not uncommon to discover errors in inscriptions. These can include incorrect but also incomplete letters (e.g., the crossbar of a letter has been overlooked). When the lettering was complete, sometimes the letters were highlighted in paint or by filling them in with a contrasting material to make them stand out. Many of the features of the process of creating an inscription must be taken into account in interpreting them.

1.3. Process of Reading and Interpreting Inscriptions. As for any ancient document, interpretation of an inscription is not an easy task. It assumes knowledge of the language that is being used. Earlier inscriptions in the Greek dialects have a number of peculiarities particular to the dialect involved, including letters not familiar to students of later Greek. However, even with a knowledge of this language, reading an inscription is often more difficult than reading the text of a standard author, as found in a modern printed edition. The reasons for this are several and can be divided into three major categories. The first is with regard to the conventions of writing an inscription, the second is with regard to the state of preservation, and the third is with regard to the language and context.

The conventions of writing an inscription in Greek follow those of many ancient texts. In other words, they are usually written in a continuous lettering, without word division, punctuation or accentuation, in capital letters. Usually inscriptions are to be read left to right line by line, but some earlier inscriptions are written left to right and right to left and even in circular fashion. All of these standard features of inscriptions require that the reader master these details before reading and interpreting the text. In printed editions of Greek inscriptions the editors have often regularized and standardized these texts by writing *boustrophedon* lines all left to right and even standardizing to the Ionic alphabet. This practice obviously helps the reader, but it also involves the editor in making a number of interpretive judgments, including those related to word division, accentuation and punctuation, and even interpretation of the meaning of the text.

The second set of difficulties concerns the state of preservation of the inscription. Many inscriptions are fragmentary, with only part of the inscription to be found. It is fortunate if a number of fragments of an inscription can be found and joined—although even here one must be careful that the reconstruction has been done accurately. Often, however, what is found of an inscription is incomplete. For example, since inscriptions are often inscribed on stone, these stones have often been reused, sometimes for other inscriptions but more often simply as stone for building material. Inscriptions have been found embedded in walls as rubble or forming the part of another structure (e.g., the Rosetta Stone). It is not unknown for parts of the same inscription to be found widely separated from each other. In their fragmentary state, often the beginning and ending of the inscription is missing, as well as the beginnings and endings of lines. All of these difficulties must be addressed in deciphering the inscription.

The third factor to consider in deciphering inscriptions is the language and context. *Literacy was very limited in the ancient world at the best of times, with probably not much more than 20 percent of the male population of a city being literate. There has been much scholarly debate regarding whether most of these literate people would have been able to read the inscriptions erected around the city. One of the major reasons for raising this question is that many inscriptions, especially those from classical Greek times, are written in a highly artificial dialect. The suspicion by many scholars is that many inscriptions used a form of literary or inscriptional language, perhaps seen to be appropriate to the solemnity of the subject matter, rather than the kind of language that the average person was accustomed to speaking and possibly reading and writing. It is true that inscriptions often use formulaic language. Therefore, there have been a number of analyses of the language of the Greek inscriptions, noting its particular linguistic features (see Meisterhans; Threatte). These include variations at all levels, including phonological/morphological features and syntactical features. Some of these are related to the Greek dialect in use, and others are related to the peculiarities of the language of the one erecting the inscription.

A further difficulty is that inscriptions often lack a context. Scholars have been fortunate to find a number of inscriptions that make reference to historical figures of interest (such as Pilate [*see* Roman Governors of Palestine], Gallio and possibly Erastus [Rom 16:23]), but many inscriptions do not have such clear indications. They may refer to unclear events or to people (such as in grave inscriptions) who are now lost in time. This makes it more difficult to establish the significance of the inscription. Nevertheless, just because historically unknown or now unimportant people and events are apparently referred to in inscriptions does not mean that they are not of importance for interpreting the NT.

1.4. Important Inscriptions for Interpreting the NT. There are numerous inscriptions of importance for interpreting the NT. Some of these have interest because they help to establish the identity or certainty of particular people or events. Others are important because they offer other insights into the world or culture of the time, including the language and conventions of public discourse. Here only a small number of important inscriptions can be cited to give some idea of their larger importance. For each inscription a reference to an accessible standard edition is given, but they are found elsewhere as well.

1.4.1. Rosetta Stone (OGIS 90). The Rosetta Stone, an irregular slab of black basalt now housed in the British Museum, is one of the most well-known and also one of the most important inscriptions from the ancient world (see Wallis Budge for history, text and translation). Discovered in 1799 by the French in Rosetta,

Egypt, the stone was taken to Britain in 1802 after the defeat of the French in Egypt. The importance of the Rosetta Stone was recognized from the time of its discovery. This fragmentary stele, which at the turn of the twenty-first century was reconstructed in its entirety for an exhibit at the British Museum, contains an inscription written in three languages: Egyptian hieroglyphics, Egyptian Demotic and Greek. When this stone was discovered, Egyptian hieroglyphics were indecipherable by scholars, although ancient Greek was widely known. The assumption used was that these three inscriptions were the same in content. This proved to be a well-founded assumption, since it was commonly known that rulers often propagated their decrees to their people in several languages to ensure that everyone was aware of it. The Romans typically had their decrees translated from Latin into Greek, and the assumption was that the *Ptolemies as Greek rulers did the same for the local population. The French scholar Jean Francois Champollion, basing his work on that of the Englishman Thomas Young, went through a process of discovery in which he rejected the alphabetic character of the language and instead focused on the royal names and titles (these pictograms were encircled in what is called a cartouche). This led to the cracking of the code of the hieroglyphs.

The inscription itself is interesting for several other reasons, including the clear attestation of deification of oriental rulers (in this case Ptolemy V Epiphanes, 203-181 B.C., who made the decree), as well as some features of the language and the customs of the time, but the major importance is the fact that this inscription led to the decipherment of Egyptian hieroglyphics.

1.4.2. Priene Inscription (*OGIS* 458). The so-called Priene Inscription, now housed in the Berlin Museum, is one of several versions of a bilingual (Greek and Latin) calendar inscription promulgated in Asia Minor in celebration of the birthday of Augustus in 9 B.C. (*see* Roman Emperors). The several versions of the inscription (from Priene, Apamea, Eumeneia and Dorylaeum) have various interesting differences among them, including differences of crucial wording (see Ehrenberg and Jones, 81-83). Often the several versions are used synoptically for reconstructing the entire inscription, since the individual inscriptions are fragmentary. What is noteworthy about this inscription, however, is what it says regarding Augustus. The inscription says, so far as the Greek reconstructions can be relied upon (see Ehrenberg and Jones, 82), that it seemed good to the Greeks of Asia to give thanks for providence sending Augustus as a savior (*sōtēr*) and that his appearance (*epiphanein*) surpassed expectations, since the birthday of the god (*tou theou*) was the beginning of the good news (*euangelia*) for the world. This inscription is consistent with a number of other inscriptions, as well as papyri, that use language of divination with regard to the emperors (*see* Ruler Cult). The words of significance have been noted above, and their resonance with the wording at the beginning of Mark's Gospel and the opening section of Romans cannot be missed.

1.4.3. Jerusalem Temple Inscription (OGIS 598; CIJ 1400; Boffo, 284). The Jerusalem Temple Inscription exists in two versions in Greek, one being housed in Istanbul and the other in Jerusalem. *Josephus also reports that the inscription was written in Latin (Josephus *J.W.* 5.5.2 §§193-94), but this version has not been found. That it was written in Latin is consistent with the way that official decrees were promulgated during Roman times. This inscription was written in the early Roman imperial period as a warning to non-Jews of the death penalty for entry into the inner court of the *temple. There is some question of whether the Jews or the Romans erected the inscription and whether it was written only for non-Jews. Although it is apparently complete, the inscription contains the edict, not information regarding who erected it, such as is often contained on other inscriptions. It is likely that the Jews had it erected, in the language that those who were not Jewish would be expected to read or have read to them, as well as it being available in a language that numerous Jews, especially those from outside of Palestine, would have been able to read as well. This inscription offers insights into some of the linguistic and cultural issues at play in first-century Palestine. Besides the historical interest that this inscription holds, it also reflects a number of linguistic features of interest, including phonetically based spelling and the imperatival use of the infinitive.

1.4.4. Gallio Inscription (SIG^3 801; Boffo, 248-49). The Gallio Inscription is highly fragmentary, with at least seven different pieces that need to be reassembled. This Greek inscription was found at the Greek city of Delphi and is housed in the museum there. The significance of this inscription is less in what the inscription says than in the fact that it mentions in lines 5-6 a person named Lucius Junius Gallio, proconsul of Achaia. The inscription records an edict by the Roman emperor Claudius (A.D. 41-54) referring to Gallio as proconsul. The significance of this inscription for establishing certain facts and dates in early Christian chronology, especially in the book of Acts, cannot be overlooked. Unfortunately, placing this inscription within its chronology is dependent upon other temporal calculations. However, most scholars are confident that, on the basis of this inscription, as well as the fact that proconsuls usually served one-year terms, it is possible to date Gallio's term of office as proconsul of Corinth to A.D. 51/52.

1.4.5. Theodotus Inscription (CIJ 1404; Boffo, 275). No inscription related to NT study has generated so much interest lately as the Theodotus Inscription. This inscription, found at the end of the nineteenth century, had suffered the misfortune of someone attempting to cut it into three pieces in ancient times and being placed at the bottom of a well. It contains an inscription commemorating a Greek-speaking Jew named Theodotus. Theodotus was a son of Vettenos, a *priest and head of the *synagogue, the son and grandson of the head of the synagogue, who himself built a synagogue for the reading of the law and study of the commandments. Even though this inscription is well preserved, as with many inscriptions the context of where and when it was originally erected is unknown. The vast majority of scholars, from those who first discovered it to the present, have accepted that it was probably erected before A.D. 70, since this is the best explanation of what the inscription says, why it would have been written and why it was found in the condition it was. (Some experts have argued that the inscription was placed in the well as a sort of storage place for such sacred items, thus accounting for its being carefully cut into three pieces.) Recently this dating has been called into question by several scholars, but this response is probably predicated on their wishing to see the usage of the term *synagogue* for a building as a late development, rather than on their firsthand study of the inscription (see McKay for references to recent discussion on this and related issues).

1.4.6. Pilate Inscription (Boffo, 219). This Latin inscription of only four lines was found in 1961 in the Roman *theater in *Caesarea Maritima and attests to the fact that Pontius Pilate was prefect of Judea. This inscription is important because it is the only direct evidence from the time that Pilate was the Roman governor of Judea, apart from references in the NT and other writers such as Josephus and *Tacitus. It also confirms the title of the governor of this region as a prefect (*praefectus*), as well as providing evidence possibly for the word *Tiberium,* or at least that a building project occurred in *Tiberias (Boffo, 220).

1.4.7. Jerusalem Inscription of the Tenth Legion (Boffo, 315). This Latin inscription on a pillar attests to Vespasian and Titus as emperors. The fifth line of the inscription was erased in antiquity. The original editors thought that it attested to L. Flavius Silva, the governor who captured Masada, but more recent scholarship has shown that this reconstruction is not possible and that it probably read L. Antonius Saturninus, referring to the governor of Judea from A.D. 78-81 who led a failed rebellion in A.D. 89, thus leading to his name being erased (*NewDocs* 3 [1978] no. 95).

This survey of inscriptions has obviously excluded a large number of important ones that merit discussion and could easily have been introduced and surveyed here. The above are offered as opening gambits for those needing to be introduced to the important world of inscriptions for understanding the NT.

2. Papyri.

Whereas the nineteenth century was the century for inscriptions, to a large extent the twentieth century was the one for papyri (see van Minnen). Interest in the papyri ran high for NT scholars in the early part of the century, especially in light of the work of such scholars as J. H. Moulton and A. Deissmann, among others, but this interest was not as pronounced in the second part of the century. Yet there is much to learn from these documents, and they are in many ways vital for the study of the NT.

2.1. Discovery and Classification. Although the majority of papyri were discovered in the mid-nineteenth century to early twentieth century and many of the major collections were begun at that time, most of the major publication series did not get underway until around the turn of the twentieth century. Since then, there has been a steady stream of publication. It depends upon how one counts the fragments available, but there are probably somewhere around two hundred thousand papyri in total that have been discovered, with roughly about 40 percent of those discovered having been published. The vast majority of the papyri have been discovered in Egypt, where the geological and climatological conditions are ideal for preservation of the papyri. We know from other evidence, including comments by ancient writers, that papyrus was used throughout the larger Mediterranean world at the time of the NT, and some of the Egyptian papyrus documents originated outside that area.

One of the first major discoveries of papyri took place in the eighteenth century, when carbonized papyri were discovered in Herculaneum, in Italy, the result of the eruption of Vesuvius in A.D. 79. There have also been a number of other finds of papyri outside of Egypt, including a number of significant finds in Palestine (e.g., the Bar Kokhba letters [P. Yadin*], the Minor Prophets Scroll [DJD 8] and the Babatha archive [P. Yadin], among others [*see* Papyri, Palestinian]). The *Dead Sea Scrolls constitute a papyrus archive in which there are mostly *Hebrew and *Aramaic manuscripts, as well as *Greek. Whereas the vast majority of papyri are in Greek, with a significant number also in *Latin, the term is not limited to manuscripts in those languages and includes manuscripts relevant for the study of the NT in such languages as Nabatean, Arabic, Coptic, Syriac and others.

Whereas referencing inscriptions is often quite difficult, there is much more order to the classification system for papyri. Most papyri are referred to by the abbreviation of their place of publication or archive and an accession or catalog number. Thus, P.Oxy. 1 refers to the Papyrus Oxyrhynchus collection, papyrus one (found in volume 1, which is sometimes also indicated; this is the famous Oxyrhynchus Sayings of Jesus papyrus, published in 1898). Many papyri, however, may also be known by popular names or by other identifying numbers. For example, all of the NT papyri have their own identification in terms of the collection of which they are a part (e.g., P.Ryl. Greek 457), but also by a Gregory-Aland number, given to each NT papyrus (e.g., 52, which is the same as the Rylands papyrus noted above). As with the inscriptions, there are a number of important series of papyri, some named according to their archive (e.g., P.Oxy.) but most named after the library that houses the archive (e.g., MPER from the Austrian National Library; *PSI* from Florence, Italy; BGU from Berlin).

A number of other collections of papyri have been made for various specific purposes, such as the *Corpus Papyrorum Judaicarum.* Many of the collections mentioned above under inscriptions, such as A. Deissmann's *Light from the Ancient East* and *New Documents,* also contain papyri important for NT study, as does J. L. White's *Light from Ancient Letters,* the most recent collection of this type. Most of the Latin papyri are contained in the *Corpus Papyrorum Latinarum* (the numbers are much smaller than those in Greek).

Whereas the term *inscription* is used to refer to any inscribed material (though usually stone) designed to have lasting value, the term *papyrus* is used to describe portable documents that were not designed for longevity and that are written on a number of different surfaces. The kinds of writing materials included under the term *papyri* are papyrus, an ancient form of paperlike writing material made from pressed strips of the papyrus plant, found in abundance in Egypt; parchment, the cured skins of animals; ostraca, shards of broken pottery, of which there was an abundance; wood, often used for identity tags; leather; bone; small stones of various types, upon which ink was used (rather than the stone being inscribed); and similar kinds of materials (see Bagnall; Kenyon).

2.2. Literary Papyri. Two major types of papyri are to be mentioned, although the categories are not watertight. The first are literary papyri. Literary papyri consist of works of some kind of literary merit. Some of the most important literary papyri to have been discovered include biblical manuscripts of both the OT and NT; *apocryphal biblical works such as Gospels (*see* Apocryphal Gospels) and other writings; other sacred and religious writings, such as those by the church fathers and devotional works of various sorts; and ancient secular authors, such as Homer, the Greek tragedians and other poets, the Latin writers *Cicero and Virgil, as well as a number of other Greek and Latin authors. Most of the literary papyri have provided further and for the most part earlier texts for known authors, although a number of previously unknown authors and works have been discovered as well. Some of these documents include those of unknown authors of apocryphal Gospels (e.g., the Fayyum fragment housed in the Vienna collection [P.Vindob. G 2325], the Egerton Papyrus in the British Library [P.Egerton 2], and the Oxyrhynchus Sayings of Jesus, now identified as part of the *Gospel of Thomas* [P.Oxy. 1, as well as 654, 655]), some previously unknown works by known authors (e.g., the *Athenian Politics* by *Aristotle [London Papyrus CXXXI]) and works by previously unknown authors (e.g., the Oxyrhynchus Historian, who continues the account of the Peloponnesian war [*P. Oxy.* 842]).

Literary papyri are categorized according to content, but there are other characteristics as well. Although the texts as discovered are often fragmentary, they come from larger documents. Many papyrus documents were originally written on scrolls, which consisted of various pieces of papyrus (*kollemata*) connected together to form a long strip. There were obvious limitations in terms of reference (if one was at one end of a papyrus and wanted to check something at the other end of the text, one had to wind through the entire scroll) and ease of handling associated with the scroll. In large part motivated by the Christian writings, the codex, or bound book, was developed. Rather than connecting pieces of papyrus end to end, the codex consisted of a number of sheets of papyrus folded over to form a quire, or gathering. The size of the codex would be determined by the number of sheets in a gathering and the number of gatherings put together. These were then bound on the end, much like a modern book. If more sheets were needed, other gatherings could be added. Some codices were quite small in size, while others were large. As opposed to scrolls, on which one wrote on only one side, writing could be done on both sides of a sheet in a codex, although there are differences in the quality of the writing surface of the front and back of a sheet of papyrus, as well as the front and back of a parchment sheet. Some of the most noteworthy codices are those of Codex Sinaiticus, Codex Alexandrinus, and Codex Vaticanus, fourth- and fifth-century biblical manuscripts.

The hand used in writing these literary documents is often distinguishable as following a particular literary style of handwriting, as well as being more carefully done than nonliterary documents. A number of styles of writing are found even on literary papyri, reflective of developments in the Greek bookhand, including the influences of other languages, such as the use of Coptic from the fifth century on. What distinguishes at least the early literary papyri, however, is the continuous form of writing without word division, with very little punctuation and accentuation. The punctuation and accentuation tend to increase the later the papyri are dated. Some Christian manuscripts were also used as liturgical texts, and these manuscripts sometimes carry what is called ekphonetic notation (this began in the sixth century and reached its full form in the tenth century; see Wellesz). This notation consists of various diacritical marks made on the manuscript to guide those who read or chanted the manuscript so that they would know how to phrase or intone the text. Christian manuscripts also made use of what has been called *nomina sacra.* These are shortened forms for such words as Jesus, Lord, Christ and God, and over time they were extended to include such words as heaven, man, cross and the like (see Paap). Although these shortened forms look like abbreviations, there is some question whether they should be treated as such, since considerations of length do not seem to have been important. Perhaps a better way to classify them is as a particular form of Christian script.

It should be clear from what has been said above that the literary papyri are essential for NT study, since the NT manuscripts themselves are a subcategory of these manuscripts. Thus NT textual critics are quite familiar with these literary documents (*see* Textual Criticism).

2.3. Documentary Papyri. The documentary papyri are less well known to NT scholars but in many ways are just as important. The documentary papyri cover those documents that were not written with literary intentions in mind, in terms of a wider reading public or for posterity. These documents cover a wide range of types of texts, including such things as personal letters, business accounts, receipts, wills, personal identification documents, census reports, student exercise books, and other such documents.

Perhaps the most important collection of documentary texts, and the largest to have been found, is the *Zenon papyrus collection. This collection of texts is not to be found in any one library but has been published in a number of different papyrus collections, united by the fact that they all involve Zenon and his correspondence. Zenon was the estate manager for Apollonios, the state treasurer for Ptolemy II Philadelphus (282-246 B.C.), and managed holdings that extended as far as Palestine. The archive contains letters sent between Zenon and others, recording various transactions and other business necessary to the management of a huge estate. However, many other collections of smaller size, as well as a huge number of random documents, have been found as well.

The documentary papyri give insight into not only the personal characteristics of those involved but also the economic situation of the time, the terminology used to transact such business (some of it with application to categories in the NT) and the language used by various people who had no notion of creating documents that would be read two thousand years later. Many of these documents are brief. It has been estimated, for example, that the average personal *letter in Greco-Roman times was only about 250 words in length. That is, the average letter was significantly shorter than any letter in the NT, including Philemon, which has about 325 words. Receipts are often not only quite brief but highly elliptical, since they may only refer in abbreviated sentences to the items being recorded. Other documents were considerably longer, however, extending to many sheets of papyrus.

The writing to be found on the documentary papyri varies considerably (see Thompson). The papyri were written in a continuous hand, often with letters that formed almost a kind of cursive script. An extensive set of abbreviations also was used. These abbreviations included not only such things as units of measure but also various common words and terminology. The quality of the writing often varies depending on the educational level and amount of training of the one writing. Writing on papyrus was a skill that had to be learned, so there was an industry in being a professional scribe, who was trained in the mechanics of preparing a papyrus and stylus for writing and mixing various types of ink as well as in the proper forms and formulas to be used in writing such documents as letters. Often scribes were hired to write for those who were illiterate. One of the conventions of letter writing was to note at the end of a letter that one had written the letter for another, because of the illiteracy of the one who signed the letter.

Nevertheless, even if one is aware of all of the conventions of writing documentary texts in the Greco-Roman world, the difficulties in deciphering a papyrus can still be immense. The manuscripts themselves are often fragmentary and have suffered severe damage through abrasion or weathering. Often pieces are broken away, or there are holes where insects have eaten them. There is the further difficulty of deciphering the hand and then attempting to read a text that may well have characteristics of other texts but also have features unique to itself that provide further difficulties. Several grammars have been prepared to help in studying the Greek of the papyri (see Mayser; Gignac).

2.4. Important Papyri for Interpreting the NT. A number of papyri could be discussed in this section because of their importance for NT study. The following selection of one literary and one documentary papyrus is for the sake of illustration.

2.4.1. Fayyum Fragment (P. Vindob. G 2325). This apocryphal Gospel fragment was the first discovered and the first to be published (1885). It is a small fragmentary text (4.5 cm x 3.6 cm) of only seven incomplete lines, written on only one side of the papyrus (and thus possibly from a scroll rather than a codex). The text is a conflation of Mark 14:26-30 and Matthew 26:30-34, and it has been dated to the third century A.D. Several of the peculiarities of this document, besides its conflation of the biblical texts, is its use of the *nomen sacrum* for Peter in line 5 in red ink, rather than the black ink used for the rest of the text. This small document offers much insight into the processes of textual transmission in the early church, including the tendency to harmonize traditions and the early veneration offered at least in some places to such figures as Peter. The use of the red ink for Peter's name is consistent with the tendency in Egyptian religious texts to use red for divine names.

2.4.2. Letter from Theon to His Father Theon (P. Oxy. 119). This rightly well-known papyrus letter is from young Theon to his father, also named Theon. It was written in the second or third century A.D. and offers rare insight into interpersonal relations. If nothing else, it shows that human personality has been consistent from ancient times to the present. In the letter, young Theon, using sarcasm, exaggeration and threats, attempts to make his father feel guilty for not taking him with him to *Alexandria. The letter is written in conformity with the Hellenistic letter form. It begins with the formulaic "A to B, greetings" (Theon to Theon his father, *chairein*). The health wish is abbreviated to a reprimand regarding not taking him to Alexandria. The body of the letter is taken up with Theon's threats not to speak to his father again. The letter then closes with a form of the standard health wish ("I pray that you be well"). This letter is only about 110 words in length, but it captures so much, in terms of both personal relations and the conventions of the Greco-Roman world. One can recognize in this letter the basic model from which Paul took his letter form and expanded it into the Christian letter form that it became.

3. Implications for Study of the New Testament. The implications for study of the NT of knowledge of inscriptions and papyri are great (see Bagnall; Cary, regarding method in using these types of documents). Three merit brief mention. The first is that these documents are roughly contemporary with the NT. Whereas the original NT documents are no longer extant, many of the documents mentioned above are the actual document that was created in the world of that time. These documents offer a window into the ancient world by providing direct and immediate access to those who lived, worked and wrote during that time.

The second is that these documents help to remind us of the interpretive difficulties in dealing with an ancient civilization that wrote in another language or languages. It is easy, with the wealth of secondary literature available today, and reasonably widespread biblical knowledge, to take for granted that interpreting the NT as an ancient text is a relatively straightforward exercise. When confronted by a previously unread or untranscribed papyrus from the same time period, however, one is brought back to the reality that our fortunate state of current interpretive ease has been built on much hard work involving the study of primary sources. These papyri and inscriptions are essential documents in that storehouse of primary texts.

The third implication is that these documents, since they are primary texts often unsanitized by subsequent scholarship, provide a fund of useful information regarding a range of important issues. These include indications of the kinds of personal, social and religious relations that existed in the ancient world; the kinds of values that were important to its inhabitants; and even the kinds and types of language that they used to communicate these ideas. There is much still to be learned from ancient inscriptions and papyri regarding the world of the NT.

See also INSCRIPTIONS AND PAPYRI: JEWISH; LETTERS, GRECO-ROMAN; PAPYRI, PALESTINIAN; ZENON PAPYRI.

BIBLIOGRAPHY. R. S. Bagnall, *Reading Papyri, Writing Ancient History* (London: Routledge, 1995); B. Bischoff, *Latin Palaeography: Antiquity and the Middle Ages* (Cambridge: Cambridge University Press, 1990); L. Boffo, *Iscrizioni Greche e Latine per lo Studio della Bibbia* (Biblioteca de Storia e Storiografia dei Tempi Biblici 9; Brescia: Paideia, 1994); M. Cary, *The Documentary Sources of Greek History* (New York: Greenwood, 1969 [1927]); M. P. Charlesworth, *Documents Illustrating the Reigns of Claudius and Nero* (Cambridge: Cambridge University Press, 1951); B. F. Cook, *Greek Inscriptions* (London: British Museum Publications, 1987); A. Deissmann, *Light from the Ancient East* (4th ed.; London: Hodder & Stoughton, 1927); V. Ehrenberg and A. H. M. Jones, *Documents Illustrating the Reigns of Augustus and Tiberius* (2d ed.; Oxford: Clarendon Press, 1955); I. Gallo, *Greek and Latin Papyrology* (Classical Handbook 1; London: Institute of Classical Studies, 1986); F. T. Gignac, *A Grammar of the Greek Papyri of the Roman and Byzantine Periods* (2 vols. to date; Milan: Cisalpino, 1976-); G. H. R. Horsley et al., eds., *New Documents Illustrating Early Christianity* (8 vols. to date; New South Wales, Australia: Macquarie University, 1981-); P. van der Horst, *Ancient Jewish Epitaphs: An Introductory Survey of a Millennium of Jewish Funerary Epigraphy (300 B.C.E.-700 C.E.)* (Kampen: Kok Pharos, 1991); F. G. Kenyon, *The Paleography of Greek Papyri* (Oxford: Clarendon Press, 1899); M. McCrum and A. G. Woodhead, *Select Documents of the Principates of the Flavian Emperors A.D. 68-96* (Cambridge: Cambridge University Press, 1966); H. A. McKay, "Ancient Synagogues: The Continuing Dialectic Between Two Major Views," *Currents in Research: Biblical Studies* 6 (1998) 103-42; E. Mayser, *Grammatik der griechischen Papyri aus der Ptolemäerzeit* (3 vols., with vol. 1 rev. H. Schmoll; Berlin: Walter de Gruyter, 1906-70); K. Meisterhans, *Grammatik der attischen Inschriften* (3d ed.; Berlin: Walter de Gruyter, 1900); P. van Minnen, "The Century of Papyrology (1892-1922)," *BASP* 30 (1993) 5-18; A. H. R. E. Paap,

Nomina Sacra in the Greek Papyri of the First Five Centuries A.D.*: The Sources and Some Deductions* (Papyrologica Lugduno-Batava 8; Leiden: E. J. Brill, 1959); J. E. Sandys, *Latin Epigraphy: An Introduction to the Study of Latin Inscriptions* (Cambridge: Cambridge University Press, 1919); E. M. Thompson, *An Introduction to Greek and Latin Palaeography* (Oxford: Clarendon Press, 1912); L. Threatte, *The Grammar of Attic Inscriptions* (2 vols. to date; Berlin: Walter de Gruyter, 1980-); S. V. Tracy, *Attic Letter-Cutters of 229 to 86* B.C. (Berkeley and Los Angeles: University of California Press, 1990); E. G. Turner, *Greek Papyri: An Introduction* (Oxford: Clarendon Press, 1968); E. A. Wallis Budge, *The Rosetta Stone* (New York: Dover, 1989 [1929]); C. B. Welles, *Royal Correspondence in the Hellenistic Period: A Study in Greek Epigraphy* (New Haven, CT: Yale University Press, 1934); E. Wellesz, *A History of Byzantine Music and Hymnography* (2d ed.; Oxford: Clarendon Press, 1961); J. L. White, *Light from Ancient Letters* (Philadelphia: Fortress, 1986); A. G. Woodhead, *The Study of Greek Inscriptions* (2d ed.; Cambridge: Cambridge University Press, 1981).

S. E. Porter

INSCRIPTIONS AND PAPYRI: JEWISH

Jews, like all the inhabitants of the *Roman Empire and its surroundings, used inscriptions to create a written record of events that they wished to be remembered indefinitely and papyri and ostraca to record matters of more temporary importance. Inscriptions are mainly epitaphs, written on the walls of tombs or (in Judea) on ossuaries (*see* Burial Practices, Jewish), but they can also record the erection or refurbishment of communal buildings, honors for individuals and the emancipation of *slaves. A number of inscriptions that were presumably displayed in synagogues honor the reigning *emperor; all datable ones are from the Severan period. Papyri may include deeds of sale and gift, leases and contracts, petitions to officials and records of tax payments. Most inscriptions and papyri are in *Greek, the lingua franca of the eastern Mediterranean. Some are in *Aramaic or *Hebrew, but Latin was rarely written by Jews before the third century A.D.

The identification of such documents as Jewish or not can be problematic, since distinctively Jewish symbols such as the menorah were not normally used before the second century A.D. The following criteria are usually accepted as indicating the presence of a Jew: the use of descriptions such as *Ioudaios* or *Hebraios;* reference to specifically Jewish institutions such as the *synagogue, usually called *proseuchē,* or Mosaic law; the use of Hebrew; the presence of distinctively Jewish names such as Joseph or Salome. Inscriptions and papyri that were never intended for a Jewish audience can still illuminate Jewish history: the epitaph from Rome of a procurator for the Jewish tax (*JIWE* ii 603) or a letter from a woman to her son who was serving in the Egyptian militia fighting the Jewish revolt of A.D. 115-117 (*CPJ* 437).

1. Inscriptions
2. Papyri

1. Inscriptions.

1.1. Publications. The main corpus of Jewish inscriptions from the Roman Empire *(CIJ)* has now been partially superseded by regional or local corpora and studies (*BSh, CJZC, JIGRE, JIWE,* Trebilco, Levinskaya) but remains the most accessible collection for Judea and Syria.

1.2. Judea. The practice of *burial in ossuaries flourished in the Jerusalem area in the first centuries B.C. and A.D. Although they are often elaborately decorated, ossuaries rarely have more than a name and patronymic inscribed on them. Members of priestly or high-priestly families might also have their rank given, allowing occasional identification with people known from the NT or *Josephus (van der Horst, 140-43). An ossuary found on the Mount of Olives (*JIGRE* 153) commemorates "Nicanor the Alexandrian who made the gates," presumably a reference to the bronze Gate of Nicanor in the *temple.

At Jerusalem, a man named Theodotos son of Vettenus put up an inscription recording his refurbishment of a synagogue founded by his "fathers," in order to provide room for the reading of the law, teaching of the commandments and accommodation for visitors from abroad (*CIJ* 1404). Theodotos was "priest and *archisynagōgos,*" and his father and grandfather both held the title of *archisynagōgos.* This inscription is presumably from before A.D. 70, but the title, attested in Mark, Luke and Acts, was a common one for the leaders of Jewish communities for centuries afterward.

1.3. Europe. Most identifiably Jewish epitaphs from Europe are from the third century A.D. or later. There are, however, earlier manumission inscriptions from Greece and the Crimea. At Stobi in Macedonia, probably in the second century A.D., Ti. Claudius Polycharmus built a synagogue, reserving for his family the right to live in the upper story (*CIJ* 694). The donation to the synagogue at Ostia of an "ark for the holy law" was also recorded in a second-century inscription (*JIWE* i 13).

1.4. Asia Minor and North Africa. There are also synagogue inscriptions from Egypt, Cyrenaica and western and southern *Asia Minor. A full publication of the numerous inscriptions from the Sardis synagogue is still awaited. At Acmonia, the first-century A.D. synagogue was built by a woman named Julia Severa (Trebilco, 58-60), who was also high priestess of the imperial cult. An inscription from Berenice in Cyrenaica records honors given by the Jewish community to the Roman governor M. Tittius (*CJZC* 71).

A number of epitaphs come from the area of Leontopolis in the southern Nile Delta, where Josephus records the existence of an alternative Jewish temple founded in the second century B.C. and closed in A.D. 73/74. The genuineness of Josephus's account (Josephus *Ant.* 13.3.1 §67) may be supported by the fact that he makes the founder Onias IV promise to build the temple *hyper* ("on behalf of") the king and queen, exactly the formula used in the dedicatory inscriptions of a number of Egyptian synagogues of the third and second centuries B.C., although the formula was long obsolete in Josephus's day. While the epitaphs say little of how the community was organized and nothing of the running of the temple beyond the epitaph of a *hierisa* (either "priestess" or "woman of priestly family"), they show a Jewish society well integrated into its surroundings, producing epitaphs similar to those of its pagan contemporaries, even to the extent of using references to Hades and Charon.

1.5. Godfearers. The existence of a group of people on the fringes of Judaism is shown by the recurrence of the term *theosebēs* ("Godfearer") in a long inscription from Aphrodisias, probably third or fourth century A.D., listing the contributors to some sort of Jewish communal institution, possibly a soup kitchen (*see* Proselytism and Godfearers). There are epitaphs for people described as *theosebēs* from various dates and places, and the term is now generally accepted to be synonymous with the descriptions in Acts of people who "feared God." Other inscriptions record the worship of *Theos Hypsistos* ("Most High God"), a term used for the Jewish God in the *Septuagint but perhaps of epigraphic use to Godfearers and even pagans as well. There are also epitaphs for proselytes (sixteen are listed by Levinskaya, 25).

2. Papyri.

2.1. Publications. Jewish papyri and ostraca from Egypt were collected in *CPJ*. There have been few Egyptian additions since then but many from Judea (one group is published by Lewis).

2.2. Jewish Tax and the Revolt of A.D. 115-117. After the destruction of the temple in A.D. 70, Vespasian imposed an annual Jewish *tax of two denarii (two drachmae) on all Jews in the Roman Empire. Ostraca from Egypt, particularly from Apollinopolis Magna (Edfu), are the main source of information about how the tax worked: it was paid by both males and females over the age of three, slaves as well as free. Its scope was thus much greater than that of the temple tax, which it nominally replaced. Payment is first recorded in A.D. 71/72, and it ceased in May A.D. 116 during the revolt against Trajan (*CPJ* 160-229). Papyri give some idea of how Egypt was affected by that revolt, and the defeat of the Jews was still being celebrated annually at Oxyrhynchus in A.D. 199/200 (*CPJ* 450). The devastating effects on the Jews of Egypt are illustrated by the dearth of papyrological evidence after A.D. 117.

2.3. Edict of Claudius. One exception to the rule that papyri record information of less lasting importance than inscriptions is *CPJ* 153, a papyrus record (which was presumably converted into or taken from a now lost marble inscription) of the edict of Claudius of A.D. 41 dealing with relations between Greeks and Jews at *Alexandria. This document is paraphrased by Josephus (Josephus *Ant.* 19.5.2-3 §§278-85), and the selective nature of Josephus's reporting is clear: he records Claudius's confirmation of the Jews' existing rights but not his drastic warnings about their future conduct.

2.4. Babatha. At Naḥal Ḥever near the west shore of the Dead Sea, a collection of thirty-five papyri carefully hidden in a cave proved to belong to a wealthy woman named Babatha who took refuge there at the start of the Bar Kokhba revolt in A.D. 132. Most are in Greek, with a few in Aramaic or Nabatean; Babatha came from

Maoza at the southern end of the Dead Sea, part of the Nabatean kingdom, which became the Roman province of Arabia in A.D. 106. These papyri record property transactions, petitions to Roman officials and dealings concerning the guardianship of Babatha's son. Babatha's second husband, Judah, appears (although this interpretation is not universally accepted) already to have had another wife at the time of their marriage, and at his death in c. A.D. 130 complications ensued about the rights of the two women. Babatha and her relatives had numerous dealings with non-Jews, and their lives and transactions were heavily influenced by Greek custom and Roman law, but there are occasional signs of distinctively Jewish practice: her Aramaic marriage contract says that her marriage was "according to the law of Moses and the Jews."

2.5. Bar Kokhba Letters. Slightly further north, at Wadi Murabaʿat, a number of letters from Bar Kokhba himself were discovered (listed with bibliography by Millar, 545-52). These illustrate, among other things, that his "official" name was Simeon bar Kosiba, that he took an interest in the observation of religious *festivals (one letter makes arrangements for the supply of palm branches and citrons for Tabernacles) and that his followers included people who could write Hebrew, Aramaic and Greek (*see* Simon ben Kosiba).

See also ARCHAEOLOGY OF THE LAND OF ISRAEL; DEAD SEA SCROLLS: GENERAL INTRODUCTION; INSCRIPTIONS AND PAPYRI: GRECO-ROMAN.

BIBLIOGRAPHY. J. B. Frey, *Corpus Inscriptionum Judaicarum* (2 vols.; Sussidi allo Studio di Antichità Cristiane 1 & 3; Vatican City: Pontificio Istituto di Archeologia Cristiana, 1936, 1952; vol. 1 reprinted with prolegomenon by B. Lifshitz, New York: Ktav, 1975); E. L. Gibson, *The Jewish Manumission Inscriptions of the Bosporus Kingdom* (TSAJ 75; Tübingen: Mohr Siebeck, 1999); W. Horbury and D. Noy, *Jewish Inscriptions of Graeco-Roman Egypt* (Cambridge: Cambridge University Press, 1992); P. W. van der Horst, *Ancient Jewish Epitaphs* (Kampen: Kok Pharos, 1991); I. Levinskaya, *The Book of Acts in Its Diaspora Setting* (BAFCS 5; Grand Rapids, MI: Eerdmans, 1996); N. Lewis, ed., *The Documents from the Bar Kokhba Period in the Cave of Letters* (Judean Desert Studies; Jerusalem: Israel Exploration Society, 1989); G. Lüderitz and J. M. Reynolds, *Corpus jüdischer Zeugnisse aus der Cyrenaika* (Beihefte zum Tübinger Atlas des vorderen Orients, Reihe B Nr 53; Wiesbaden: Dr Lüdwig Reichert Verlag, 1983); F. Millar, *The Roman Near East 31 B.C.—A.D. 337* (Cambridge, MA: Harvard University Press, 1993); D. Noy, *Jewish Inscriptions of Western Europe* (2 vols.; Cambridge: Cambridge University Press, 1993, 1995); L. Y. Rahmani, *A Catalogue of Jewish Ossuaries in the Collections of the State of Israel* (Jerusalem: Israel Antiquities Authority/Israel Academy of Sciences and Humanities, 1994); T. Rajak and D. Noy, "*Archisynagogoi:* Office, Title and Social Status in the Greco-Jewish Synagogue," *JRS* 83 (1993) 75-93; J. Reynolds and R. Tannenbaum, *Jews and Godfearers at Aphrodisias* (Cambridge: Cambridge Philological Society, 1987); A. J. Saldarini, "Babatha's Story," *BAR* 24.2 (1998) 29-37, 72-74; M. Schwabe and B. Lifshitz, *Beth She'arim, 2: The Greek Inscriptions* (New Brunswick, NJ: Rutgers University Press, 1974); V. Tcherikover, A. Fuks and M. Stern, *Corpus Papyrorum Judaicarum* (3 vols.; Cambridge, MA: Harvard University Press, 1957-64); P. M. Trebilco, *Jewish Communities in Asia Minor* (SNTSMS 69; Cambridge: Cambridge University Press, 1991); Y. Yadin, J. C. Greenfield and A. Yardeni, "Babatha's Ketubba," *IEJ* 46 (1994) 75-101.

D. Noy

INSTRUCTION AND DISCIPLINE. *See* EDUCATION: JEWISH AND GRECO-ROMAN; FAMILY AND HOUSEHOLD.

INTERTEXTUALITY, BIBLICAL

The literature of the NT was shaped within a Jewish interpretive culture whose teachers sought to clarify and make relevant God's intended meaning of the Scriptures for current audiences. The present result is a Christian Bible that resonates with echoes of earlier texts, forming reflexive intertexts that enable today's interpreter to understand more fully the theological meaning of a biblical text.

1. Definition: Intertextuality
2. The Formation of Biblical Literature: The Intertextuality of Midrash
3. The Final Form of the Christian Bible: The Intertextuality of Scripture
4. Case Study: The Function of Habakkuk 1:5 (LXX) in the Book of Acts

1. Definition: Intertextuality.

A technical definition of intertextuality is difficult to state with precision. In part this is because the term was only recently coined by poststructuralist literary critics (Kristeva; Barthes) to describe every literary text whose existence and meaning is predicated in relationship to other texts, whether spoken or written, earlier or later. At its essence, literature's constant recourse to other literature merely confirms that no text is an island, composed in isolation from a preexisting body of other texts. Further, it is supposed that every writer employs *rhetorical phenomena known since antiquity (e.g., citations of or allusions to antecedent texts) not merely to repeat them as important markers and makers of meaning but also to amplify and even to revise their original meaning in order to reconstitute different texts as parts of one continuous written text of shared images, stories and meanings.

Poststructuralist reading strategies, however idiosyncratic, suppose the intertextuality of a particular text (or intertext) subverts the essentially historical boundaries that modern interpreters tend to place around it to facilitate conversation about the normative meaning of a text, or the identity of the author and the intended readers or the precise date when it was written and the real reasons why. According to postmodern convention, however, to speak of a text as an intertext posits meaning in the text qua text, not at its point of origin, and so within a much wider literary field constituted by other texts that are related together by literary pattern, linguistic correspondence or thematic similarity. Rather than constricting the plausible meaning of a single text to a single or thin conception as determined by reconstructing what it might have first meant, this field of related texts establishes a more complex matrix of interconnected textuality, the *via media* by which its current reader thickens a text's (multivalent) meaning.

The term *intertextuality* has since entered the vocabulary of biblical scholarship as a broad reference to the various ways by which biblical writers presume the continuing authority of their Scripture that is cited or "echoed" (Hays) when it is exegeted to amplify the meaning of this sacred tradition *(traditium)* as the word of God *(traditio)* for new readers or auditors (Fishbane). J. A. Sanders's cautionary distinction between the "stability" and "adaptability" of biblical tradition, envisaged by Scripture's own "unrecorded hermeneutics," is helpful in qualifying what M. Fishbane means by the transforming and generative powers of "inner-biblical exegesis." On the one hand, it is no longer disputed that biblical writers found new and different meanings in the texts and stories of their Scripture from those originally scored by their authors for their first audiences. The existential necessity and eschatological urgency of God's word, mediated by this textual *traditium,* is formative of theological understanding yet constantly requires talented interpreters (= biblical writers) to seek out from the old, old gospel story those new meanings *(traditio)* that are "adaptable to the life" of today's believers who continue to submit to their inspired Scriptures as the word of the Lord God Almighty.

On the other hand, this same biblical tradition is canonical, a persistent and stable rule of faith and life for all God's people in each age and every place. The essential theological subject matter of the biblical word does not change: Scripture in all its parts bears witness to one God, one Lord Christ, one Holy Spirit. The inherent subjectivity of the interpretive enterprise, by which the individual interpreter seeks out the meaning of Scripture for a particular situation, is constrained not by consistent application of certain hermeneutical rules but by certain core convictions about God disclosed through Scripture's narrative of God's salvation of all things through Christ. Biblical texts do not bear witness to the interpreter but to the interpreter's God, "who was and who is and who is to come."

In this sense, the canon consciousness of NT writers obligates them to pick up again and again their biblical texts and stories to repeat them as integral to their compositions, not only to demonstrate the *traditium*'s continuing authority as *via medium* of God's word to their audiences but also to give it new meaning and different relevance for still other congregations of believers. This interpretive act hardly subverts the Bible's witness to God but rather intends to confirm the church's rule of faith that the God of Israel to whom his biblical tradition bears witness is the same God who is incarnate in the Lord Jesus Christ. The purpose of this article is to draw out and illustrate the most important implications of this textual phenomenon for NT interpretation.

2. The Formation of Biblical Literature: The Intertextuality of Midrash.

Even a cursory reading of the NT discloses the

routine use the writers made of their own biblical witness. Earliest Christianity retained Jewish Scriptures as the word of God, the symbolic universe within which its faith and life took shape and found direction. Its own literature naturally reused, reinterpreted and reapplied their sacred writings to bring clarity and direction to the new period that dawned with Jesus. Earliest Christian interpreters inherited the OT from Jesus and with Jesus; they were compelled in submission to their risen Lord to use his Bible to interpret his messiahship and themselves in relationship to it. Thus, every NT writing quotes or echoes texts or stories from antecedent biblical (together with Jesus) traditions in order to help believers understand what it means to believe as Jesus did and to behave as he did.

2.1. Jewish Community of Interpretation. What remains perplexing for the modern interpreter is why NT writers appropriated Scripture so creatively, without due consideration of its original meaning. In response to this problem and in keeping with critical scholarship's historical interest, standard discussions (Longenecker; Ellis; Vermes; Patte; Bruce) are careful to locate the hermeneutics of NT writers and writings within an ancient Jewish interpretive culture (*see* Biblical Interpretation, Jewish). The study of sacred Scripture, especially *Torah, was central to the different parties of religious Jews, who sought out God's requirements for every aspect of life and faith although with different methods to support different theological beliefs. This guiding perspective toward Scripture, especially envisaged by the *Pharisaic interpretation of Scripture, coupled with appropriate exegetical strategies used to search out God's will from the biblical text, were more or less followed by NT writers.

Most recent discussions of the NT interpretation of the OT follow this more historical and descriptive interest and typically seek to relate NT writings to extant Jewish literature under two rubrics: writings from Second Temple (pre-A.D. 70) *Judaism, including the *Septuagint, the OT *Apocrypha and Pseudepigrapha, the *Dead Sea Scrolls, early rabbinical midrashim; and writings from rabbinical (post-A.D. 70) Judaism (*Talmud, Aramaic *targumim and *midrashim), all of which reflect first-century oral interpretation of the Jewish Bible and are therefore contemporary with the writing of the NT (Evans). Well-known interpretive strategies (or hermeneutical *middoth*; *see* Biblical Interpretation, Jewish) of Jewish scribes as well as the various genres of this literature are also summarized, which are then compared favorably to NT writers who use these same exegetical methods and literary conventions when appropriating their Scriptures for a new (i.e., Christian) situation. According to these genres and techniques, then, the two essential purposes of Jewish interpretation are clarified as halakah (how to live) and haggadah (what to believe). Further, by comparing the subject matter of midrashim from different teachers, certain schools of interpretation are defined, whether *Alexandrian (Philo) or *Pharisaic (Hillel) or *Qumran (DSS) or Christian (NT) as well as different theological tendencies within each (e.g., Samaritans or Pauline Christianity).

Two qualifications should be added to make this connection between Jewish Scriptures and the NT even more precise. While evincing the literary conventions and hermeneutical interests of Jewish exegesis, NT literature, like earliest Christianity, emerges from a *Hellenistic world as well. "The Christianity of the New Testament is a creative combination of Jewish and Hellenistic traditions transformed into a *tertium quid* ('a third something'): that is, a reality related to two known things but transcending them both" (Aune, 12). NT writings, then, envisage neither Jewish nor Hellenistic contexts exclusively but are in every case creative combinations of both literary and interpretive cultures. It is doubtful that any rhetorical device of the Second Temple period is any longer considered a uniquely Jewish literary convention.

The same can be said of the Hellenized Judaism from which earliest Christianity emerged. The Judaism of the NT is hardly a monolithic movement, but is in Sanders's phrase, a "pluralizing monotheism." The fluidity of Jewish culture and of its canonical Scriptures, not yet stabilized in the first century, is generally reflected in its biblical tradition, still fluid, and exegetical practice, still experimental. Text-centered exegesis became the norm within the early church only after the canonical process resulted in a fixed text (*see* Canonical Formation of the New Testament). Thus, what the reader of the NT will sometimes find is more like the *rewritten Bible of apocryphal literature, where the focus of the writer's use of a cited text is not the received text but a modified or supplemented one and where perceived gaps in the biblical narrative are filled in by the writer in an attempt to complete the historical record. T. L. Brodie has even argued, for example, that the author of Luke-Acts narrates the story of Jesus and his apostolic successors by imitating or rewriting the story of his Bible (LXX).

2.2. Canon Consciousness of New Testament Writers. Even if the boundaries around the biblical canon of its writers were not yet fixed when the NT literature was written, clearly they use their Bible as a normative guide to faith and witness; it is for them a sufficient and trusted medium of God's word that communicated what it means to be God's people and to do as God's people ought. At no time is it possible for the interpreter to divorce the writer's citation of or allusion to Scripture from these core convictions about Scripture: the authority of the biblical text and the act of interpreting it are joined together. While demonstrating considerable creativity in adapting the meaning of their biblical texts to every new situation, biblical writers also reveal considerable selectivity in which texts are used and show meticulous care in doing so—characteristics of what G. Sheppard has referred to as the writer's "canon-consciousness" (Sheppard, 109-19).

Further, the canon consciousness of the NT writers must be a factor in determining the deeper logic of their exegetical activity. The interpreter should not presume that NT writers thought of their stories or letters as literary creations, which arise ex nihilo as if every new historical event obligates a brand new text to narrate or interpret it; rather, this literature is written in conceptual continuity with or mimesis of extant biblical tradition because its writers and audiences believed that the "things that have happened among us" continue Israel's history and God's revelation, witnessed to by that tradition, into a new dispensation of God's promised salvation.

NT writers are heirs of a sacred tradition, whose mind-set and methods are also nurtured within a living, dynamic interpretative culture. We make a mistake supposing that they picked up biblical texts to find a new meaning for another audience in isolation from the prior interpretations of earlier tradents. The Tanahk supplies the literary texts of a sacred tradition that is always received from others who have already found it to be the Word of God for their own communities of believers. Usually implicit in a writer's use of Scripture is his profound regard for these earlier tradents. That is, NT writers typically interpret an interpreted Scripture, especially interpretations received from their rewritten (e.g., OT Pseudepigrapha and Apocrypha) or translated (e.g., Aramaic targums and Greek Septuagint) Bibles. Even the midrashim of early rabbinical Judaism, which postdates the NT, recalls interpretations from an earlier period that is shared by NT writers.

The precious memories of Jesus and perhaps certain writings from his apostolic successors (2 Pet 3:15-16) form yet another deposit of sacred tradition that NT writers reinterpret for new situations. The phenomenon of interbiblical exegesis that Fishbane recognizes in the OT may well be true of the NT, especially if certain writings are read as pseudepigraphical (*see* Pseudonimity and Pseudepigraphy). For example, does the author of 1 Timothy rewrite Pauline tradition, already accepted as normative for Gentile Christianity, for the catholicizing church of a post-Pauline situation? Does its author compose Acts as a narrative setting for a community's reading of Paul's Romans and in particular his interpretation of God's faithfulness to a spiritual Israel? Even though lacking in explicit references to Jesus, are portions of James written in conversation with authoritative Jesus tradition? Perhaps. In any case, the interpreter should listen for echoes of an emerging *traditium* of Christian texts as a sacred complement to those inherited from Judaism.

2.3. The Intertextuality of Midrash. The NT writings are midrashic literature in this sense: they are written in response to the urgent needs and questions of the present moment under the light shed by antecedent texts, which writers deemed normative for faith and divine in origin (Bloch). In particular, biblical writers find meaning in these canonical texts that not only coheres around the core convictions of a Christian theological tradition but also enters into a sometimes playful conversation with other interpretations of these same texts (Sanders). This broader definition of midrash follows current literary theory, which terms midrashic any interpretive act that interprets earlier texts by means of narrative or discursive augmentation in a way that renders meaning in culturally and ideologically determined ways. Midrash is no longer limited by this definition to a particular exegetical method or literary genre (e.g., haggadoth or halakoth) that transmits determinate and timeless interpretations of specific, biblical texts to no particular audience. NT interpreters are increasingly more apt to draw comparisons between the texts and topics of OT literature with those of NT literature, ever more sensitive to the subtle and clever ways biblical writers appropriated these sacred traditions to make clearer and more authoritative their own words.

According to D. Boyarin the essential characteristic of midrash, understood in its broader sense, is its intertextuality (Boyarin, 12). He posits three senses to his definition of the "intertextuality of midrash." (1) A literary text is always a "mosaic" of conscious and unconscious citation of earlier discourse; no single text carriers a self-contained meaning. (2) Therefore, a text is always in conversation with other texts; no single text is the objective mimesis of truth. Meaning is funded by all relevant texts, one glossing the other texts, which in turn add sublayers of meaning to the one. (3) A new text is produced within and for a new culture of readers; the writer "slips" into the gaps of antecedent texts to interpret and "re-code" them for his own day and audience. The more important these antecedent texts, the more important is the interpretive task of slipping into and filling their evident gaps. NT writers believed that their Scriptures mediated the word of God to their audiences; their conscious or unconscious citation of biblical texts or types is in demonstration of this belief but also to invite an intertextual reading of what they have written as the context for readers to reflect upon the fuller, more textured meaning of what is written.

3. The Final Form of the Christian Bible: The Intertextuality of Scripture.

To this point the NT has been described as a collection of hermeneutical writings, each shaped by the interpretive strategies and theological conceptions of their authors as much as by the historical circumstances and literary conventions to which each responds and by which each is composed. That is, the intertextuality of NT writings is the literary precipitate of a Jewish interpretive culture in which these NT texts were written in conversation with a writer's antecedent sacred tradition in order to support and add an inherent depth of understanding to his reinterpretation of God's word for the theological crisis of his day.

This next section shifts focus from the NT's Jewish *Sitz im Leben* to its current address in the Christian biblical canon. Even as intertextuality is an important feature in the production of different NT writings, it is currently an important feature of the NT canon. Scripture's special role within the life of the church qualifies to some extent the value we posit for Scripture's inherent intertextuality. In saying this, I contend that Scripture's authority for the faithful is not only as a revelatory word by which one acquires theological understanding; it also supplies its readers with interpretive models that continue to facilitate their reading of Scripture as God's Word. In this light, I want to press for the importance of the NT's intertextuality as a salient feature of Scripture's own unrecorded hermeneutics and therefore its importance for the alert exegete who aims at the theological formation of those who in faith seek understanding.

To read a biblical text on its own terms requires its current exegete to construct meaning in light of the writer's conception and use of Scripture. An interest in Scripture's intertextuality tilts the interpreter to a particular approach to NT interpretation that presumes that every NT book is a midrashic writing, the textual precipitate of its writer's own interpretation of his biblical canon, rendered in ways to address a new situation with a word from God. In recognizing this the clarity of our perception of the audience's spiritual crisis is sharpened and our understanding the author's theological response to this crisis is deepened. In most cases we can hardly understand the theological subject matter of a particular NT composition apart from a critical analysis of the persistent interplay of ancient texts with the text as well as its rhetorical design and theological aim.

3.1. Old Testament and New Testament as a Canonical Intertext. The ultimate referentiality of the biblical canon, however, is not historical, with meanings posited at the point of origin, but theological, with meanings that result from Scripture's performance as the word of God for its canonical audience. The stakes of this discussion of the NT's intertextuality acquire greater importance if they are framed as a feature of Scripture's ongoing mediation of God's word. That is, the intertextuality of Scripture's final literary (or canonical) form is an inherent feature of its revelatory powers and must be understood by its current interpreters in terms other than a particular writer's exegetical strategy or the intended meaning of his writing for his first readers or auditors (however, see Childs, 76).

The intertextuality of the NT does not simply add a new and interesting angle to the historical-critical enterprise; it points us toward a hermeneutical model in which OT and NT are an interdependent (or intertextual) medium of the word of the Lord. The current reductionism of interpreting the OT or NT in isolation from the other, thereby regarding the NT's relationship to the *Hebrew Bible as insignificant, is subverted by the NT's appeal to and exegesis of the OT. Sharply put, the Scriptures of the NT writers are "neither superseded nor nullified but transformed into a witness of the gospel" (Hays, 157). On a canonical level of authority, this point funds our hermeneutical model, rather than our exegetical methods per se, for our ongoing consideration of the relationship between OT and NT within the church's Christian Bible.

Several features of this interpretive emphasis should be noted. The OT is the *via medium* of God's Word, which is now "brought near" to God's people through its christological interpretation, and its current authority for God's people is constantly demonstrated by the confession "Jesus is Lord" that it evokes from them (Rom 10:8-9). The theological authority of the OT presumes its trustworthy witness to the God who is now incarnate in Jesus; as such, and only as such, can the OT function as Christian Scripture. The theological subject matter and perspicuity of OT and NT cohere around this single christological confession that brings to maturity the interpreter's perception of Scripture's own intertextuality.

This same Jesus refuses to decanonize the OT (Mt 5:17-18); rather, we have received the OT from and with him as the normative context in which his people deepen their faith in him as Lord (see Watson, 181-85).

Paul's difficult claim that Christ is the *telos* of the biblical law (Rom 10:4; Gal 3:24) may provide another biblical analog for relating NT (Christ) and OT (law). In this statement, both Christ and law function as Pauline metaphors for particular patterns of salvation, the one worked out in the history of Israel and the other on the cross. For Paul, the Christ event is the climax of God's redemptive purpose for Israel, and this Christ event insinuates itself upon the sacred writings that bear authoritative witness to that divine intent. The function of law is no longer the object of the community's devotion to God; Christ is. The role of law in this new age is rather to reveal the hard beginnings of God's redemption of creation, which now has its climax in Christ. In a similar way, the NT is the *telos* of the OT within the Christian Bible.

That is, in a narrative sense, the OT and NT are incomplete without the other, and together they form an irreducible and self-sufficient whole: we expect no third testament beyond these two. Thus, what is new about the NT's testimony to the Messiah's *kairos* and kerygma can be adequately discerned by the biblical interpreter only in relationship to what has become old about the OT as a result. From this perspective, the Christ event is the climax of a variegated history whose beginning is narrated by the OT.

The Christian Bible, which narrates the beginnings of God's reconciliation of all things (OT) that climaxes with Jesus' messianic mission (NT), heralds the consummation of this history with the coming triumph of God on earth as now in heaven, to which all Scripture bears proleptic witness.

In a kerygmatic sense, the theological subtext and deeper logic of NT proclamation is the OT narrative of God's response to a fallen creation and to an elect people, Israel, whom God has called out of this broken and sinful world as a light to all the nations. Every redemptive *typos* claimed by the OT prophets is embodied by Jesus, and every promise made by God through them is fulfilled through him.

While it is nowhere about Jesus, the OT must be understood entirely in relationship to this gospel typology about him. That is, the "truth and grace" now disclosed in the messianic event, to which the NT bears normative witness, establishes a theological and historical continuity with the truth and grace disclosed in the Israel event, to which the OT bears normative witness.

The intertextuality of OT and NT, then, is this: the OT supplies the NT with its normative theological and historical markers, while the NT witness to the risen Messiah supplies the subject matter for a Christian hermeneutic by which the OT is rendered as Christian Scripture. The old meaning of the OT is now relativized and made new by this christological midrash.

3.2. The Simultaneity of Scripture. Recalling that the aim of Scripture is theological understanding and not historical reconstruction and that hermeneutical practice is constrained by one's theological commitments rather than by adherence to accepted exegetical rules, two other related features of this hermeneutical model are advanced for NT exegesis. Even as NT writers approach Scripture as the revelation of God's Word, their formulaic references to particular prophets to introduce citations of Scripture do not envisage a modern historical-critical concern for authorial identity and intent; rather, they presume these OT figures were those who gave voice to the word of the Lord. God is the actual author of their sacred tradition; their midrashim of Scripture presume only to clarify and contemporize what is God's intended meaning for a new, post-Easter address and for their particular audiences who struggle to remain faithful to their Lord.

In this restricted sense, I would argue that the anonymity of the OT and the insinuation of divine authorship by the NT writers are useful tools in shifting the locus of normative meaning from the text's human author to the inspired text itself as the *via medium* of God's Word (Levenson). By divine authorship I do not mean that God mechanically produced biblical texts, whether by dictation or some other literary process whereby the production of Scripture is by God's direct and miraculous intervention; rather, the purpose of approaching biblical texts in terms of their divine authorship postulates a theological norm that subverts the modern tendency to posit a text's normative meaning in the mind of a text's "real" author.

In this sense, the authorship concerns of the modern critic are theologically laden projects, having to do with the location of a text's normative meaning for today's readers. The stated historical problematic of the modern critic is to identify the one who should take responsibility for the production of a particular text; the unstated theological problematic is to posit the place and time for the normative meaning of that text. The authorial fallacy is to suppose that the meaning of a text and the basis of its continuing authority resides with its human author. The preoccupation with these questions extends to the postcritical interpretive culture, which has shifted focus from authorship to interpreter, who now is the principal broker, even locus, of a text's meaning.

The normative meaning of Scripture for the church is not fixed in the author's mind for all time; nor in the constantly shifting locations of various interpreters. Scripture is special precisely because we recognize its revelatory power to convey God's intended meaning to the current readers via the canonical text. If the meaning of Scripture is divinely intended and mediated by the inspired text itself, then it is the task of every faithful interpreter to seek after it. The act of reinterpreting Scripture as God's Word, however provisional and seemingly tentative, is the courageous act of finding God's intended meaning for a community who in faith seeks theological understanding.

If God's intended meaning is posited in the whole of the text itself, OT and NT, then the intertextuality of Scripture suggests their simultaneity. Rather than signifying common meanings, the simultaneity of OT and NT conveys rather a sense that there is no perceived chasm between what Scripture meant and what it now means. The text received and a text that reinterprets it for theological understanding are equally valued texts in the dynamic process that seeks to hear and then submit to the Word of the Lord God Almighty—a Word that Christians believe is incarnate in God's Son, Jesus of Nazareth, and is made ever new by God's Spirit.

4. Case Study: The Function of Habakkuk 1:5 (LXX) in the Book of Acts.

4.1. Theology of Scripture According to Acts. The function of Scripture within a particular NT writing is first of all discerned by the writer's own theology of Scripture: the exegesis of antecedent tradition is constrained as much by prior theological commitments as by current exegetical technique or methodological interests. Although it is also shaped by the concerns and conventions of the Greco-Roman world, Acts is substantially Jewish in theological conception (Jervell), in historical methodology and literary design (Evans and Sanders). Not only does its author follow Jewish exegetical practices when using Scripture; his understanding of Scripture's importance for theological understanding is also Jewish. His canon consciousness results in a narrative written in the style of his Bible (Brodie) and in reflexive conversation with its texts, all of which promise a salvation that he now recognizes is being fulfilled in those events following from Jesus' resurrection. Luke's commitment to composing a narrative in the idiom and ideology of his own sacred text leads J. Jervell to call him "the fundamentalist within the NT."

The use of antecedent tradition in Acts is distinctive within the NT, not only in form (Jervell, 62-63) but also in substance (Bock). According to its narrator, Scripture is authored by a living God who continues to address God's people by its prophetic interpreters, who render its true meaning in public proclamation under the light of Jesus' suffering and resurrection (Acts 17:3). Not only does the Spirit of God produce what Scripture says, but also the Spirit continues to inspire its right interpretation—a continuity of divine activity that ensures the perspicuity of Christian theological understanding: the promises God intended Scripture to make, these Spirit-filled interpreters rightly discern, are now being fulfilled in the "events that are fulfilled among us" (Lk 1:1).

Luke's belief in the simultaneity of these sacred texts is made clear by the several formulae that claim all Scripture is rightly interpreted by a Christian theological typology (Acts 24:14; 26:22) or, similarly, that all Scripture speaks about the Christ event or those events that follow after him (Acts 3:18, 24; 10:43; 17:3; 18:28; 24:14; 26:23). Luke's composition, then, is itself a Christian midrash of selected biblical texts, a synecdoche for all Scripture, which demonstrates this is the case: not only are all the prophecies of Scripture being fulfilled, but also their intended meaning is now being interpreted by the history of Jesus and his apostolic successors according as "reported" (see *diēgēsis,* Lk 1:1) by the Evangelist. The tragic irony for Luke is that even though Scripture belongs to Israel, Israel fails to understand its true, christological meaning. The salvation of Israel is at stake when Scripture is not understood by the messiahship of Jesus and the experiences of his converted people who now live under the aegis of the Spirit. Likewise, the identity of a true Israel, constituted by those Christian converts, is disclosed by a believing response to Scripture's prophetic message.

4.2. The Function of Habakkuk 1:5 in Acts. The important use of Habakkuk 1:5 (LXX) in Acts 13:41 to conclude Paul's inaugural speech in Acts typifies how Luke uses biblical tradition. Paul's appeal to Scripture settles two theological problems that continued to provoke controversy in the church's Jewish mission. The first problem participated in a wider intramural debate within Judaism between messianic and nonmessianic Jews and is envisaged in Acts by the fact that Paul's interpretation of Scripture is typically located within the Jewish synagogue of the Diaspora and with Jewish conversation partners. Within this Jewish setting, Paul's strategy is to posit as a proof from prophecy that it is necessary (*dei*) that the Christ should suffer and that God would raise him from the dead and that this prophesied Christ is realized in the suffering and resurrection of Jesus of Nazareth. Besides this christological meaning, Scripture is used to explain the conflict and conversion that result from the christological midrashim of Jesus' apostolic successors. This speech not only is programmatic of Paul's message in Acts but also introduces the motif of Israel's misunderstanding as a justification project for the Gentile mission, which results in Paul's declaration in Acts 13:46 that unbelieving Jews "judge yourselves unworthy of eternal life; therefore, we now turn to the Gentiles" (cf. Acts 18:6; 28:28).

The original prophetic setting issues God's warning of imminent destruction of disobedient Israel. This text begins an oracle of judgment addressed to the prophet's Judean community by observing with fearful "astonishment" that the Chaldeans have become a national enemy of considerable power and resolve. The prophet notes in particular the execution of a violent "work" about to be experienced in Judah—a "report" of coming calamity that they in their pride and unrighteousness will not "believe" (Hab 2:4). The prophet's intent is to bring about the repentance and faith that will avert the imminent disaster.

The new meaning given to this oracle by the Lukan Paul does not entirely subvert its original meaning and function. The intertextuality of Scripture presumes the interdependence of its theological subject matter: following Habakkuk, then, the text functions in Acts as a warning to a Jewish community, whose pride results in the rejection of God's work in their midst (Acts 13:45), even though faith would have resulted in eternal life (Acts 13:38-39). Moreover, Paul and the prophet share this similar vocation: they are reporters of God's work, which stands as the rule of faith for this community prone by pride to disbelieve. In this essential way the theological meaning of the antecedent text has insinuated itself upon Acts to make more clear to its reader that the stakes for hearing the prophetic word of God remain as high as ever.

In Acts, however, the earlier prophetic text has an expanded role. Critically, Luke has rewritten Scripture by adding another "work" to indicate more clearly its current role as a theological catchword in his narrative, linking this citation to an earlier use of "work" in Acts 13:2 while anticipating a subsequent echo in Acts 14:26. The same Spirit who spoke the prophetic text speaks again in calling Paul to begin the work that would fulfill his commission (Acts 9:15-16). In this new setting, the work of Habakkuk is reinterpreted in reference to its most controversial element: the innovations of Paul's Gentile mission, where clean goes out among unclean. This new work of God goes to the heart of a Jewish identity, which Paul's mission among the Gentiles seems to imperil and for which he is ultimately arrested and tried.

The prophetic warning of God, mediated through the biblical word, has a new object—namely, Paul's mission—that will "astonish" Israel and will provoke their unbelief. The subsequent repetition of "work" in Acts 14:26 supplies with Acts 13:2 the other bracket that frames the prophetic citation. In this case, both the Spirit's earlier word, which commissions Paul's work, and the biblical citation, which warns another Jewish community of the peril of its unbelief, are said to have been fulfilled.

The texture of the citation's meaning is thickened when the alert reader hears the resonance of its language in earlier texts of Acts. The repetition of prophetic catchwords within Acts is also reflexive in intent; earlier texts gloss subsequent texts in the dynamic unfolding of a story's meaning and theological importance. That is, earlier allusions to the prophet's cited vocabulary add layers to the full meaning of his oracle in Acts as it unfolds piecemeal throughout the narrative. The deeper logic and coherence of Scripture cited and echoed for a new setting (intertext) are discerned by the interpreter who is ever attentive to the sequence and sum of language within a text (intratext). No text is an island.

Consider, for example, the antecedent uses of "wonder" in Acts (Acts 2:7; 3:12; 4:13; 7:31), which may supply an important subtext that glosses the prophecy from Habakkuk in Acts 13:41. In every case, the word is used in Acts to characterize an affective and ambivalent response of outsiders to the Spirit's activity when empowering the apostolic witness to the risen Christ. Here is Paul, whom this same Spirit has charged to proclaim the risen Christ in Jewish synagogues. By reading the citation within Acts, the interpreter slips into a gap to anticipate before the text narrates it that Scripture's prophetic warning will not be heeded by all: some who listen have already responded to Paul in "wonder" rather than in faith, and the reader knows perhaps before they do that their response has marked them out as outsiders to the salvation of God.

Similarly the phrase "in your days" recalls the opening formula "in these last days" that Luke adds to the critical citation from Joel (Acts 2:17) to frame its prophecy of the Spirit's outpouring as heralding the day of the Lord as a day of universal salvation. This implicit interplay between Joel and Habakkuk presumes that Israel's misunderstanding of Paul's mission and message is a feature of the last days, which are days not only of conversion but of conflict as well.

Finally, the biblical reader should note that the citation's "believe" recalls its prior and positive use in Acts 13:38-39, which echoes Habakkuk 2:4 and anticipates its programmatic interpretation by Paul in Romans 1:17 (Wall 1998). Important here is the implicit conflict between Moses and belief in Christ in matters of salvation; Habakkuk supplies a fuller biblical setting in which Paul's interpretation of God's salvation, promised to David, is rendered by Acts. That is, through their belief that Jesus is God's Messiah and not through their observance of Torah alone, Israelites experience God's forgiveness. As will soon be evinced in Acts 15, this conflict between faith and law stands at the center of Paul's continuing conflict with the Jews.

4.3. Hearing an Echo of Habakkuk 1:5 in Acts 15:3. The importance of Acts 15 in this narrative of earliest Christianity can hardly be exaggerated, and it remains a storm center of Acts criticism. On the face of it, the success of Paul's first mission, which concludes with a grand declaration of all that God had done among the Gentiles (Acts 14:27), provokes a protest in *Antioch between teachers of the Jewish church and Paul's supporters there (Acts 15:2). The apparent conflict is over the continuing status of the Torah and circumcision within these new Gentile congregations founded by the Antiochean mission (Acts 15:1).

This disagreement is repeated in Jerusalem (Acts 15:4), where Paul and Barnabas have come to meet with the church's apostles and elders to bear witness to their mission and in particular to their direct experiences of Gentile conversion (Acts 15:12). However, after they relate all that God has done with them (Acts 15:4 par. Acts 14:27), a faction of Jewish believers, in this case from the Pharisees, assert that Gentile proselytes, like those Gentiles who convert to Judaism, must be circumcised and observe the Torah. Most interpreters suppose that this Jewish protest against Paul's mission among the Gentiles stems from their perception that Paul circumvents the protocol of Judaism, which constitutes a political threat to the future of a Christian mission among Gentiles (since Judaism did not sponsor one) as well as undermines Judaism's pattern of salvation. For these reasons most think that the eventual resolution of this conflict is critical to the eventual expansion of the Christian mission to Rome and beyond. This criticism of Paul's Gentile mission is already subverted when it is glossed by Peter's earlier Pentecostal citation of Joel's prophecy of the day of the Lord (cf. Acts 2:17-21). According to this prophecy, interpreted by Luke's subsequent narrative of conversion, any person, whether Jew or Gentile, who calls upon the name of the Lord Jesus in faith will be saved from his or her sins (cf. Acts 2:21).

Yet modern interpreters of Acts fail to note the importance of Luke's brief travel summary sandwiched between his repetition of the conflict thematic, which notes that on their way Paul and Barnabas "reported the conversion of the Gentiles" (Acts 15:3). Critically, this phrase echoes the final phrase of the earlier citation of Habakkuk 1:5, "even if someone reports [a work] to you," an intertext the reader recognizes by their common verb, *ekdiēgeomai* ("report"). The repetition of this unusual verb, used only in these two NT texts, suggests that Luke's description of the Jewish church's protest over Paul's mission among the Gentiles continues his exegesis of Habakkuk 1:5; the meaning and function of this prophetic citation in its earlier setting in Acts 13 informs Luke's handling of this watershed moment in the history of earliest Christianity.

In its earlier setting in Acts the "work" cited by Habakkuk now refers to Paul's mission and message (Acts 13:2), the success of which among the Gentiles is reported by Paul and Barnabas on their way to Jerusalem (Acts 15:3). The echo of Habakkuk 1:5 underscores what the reader already knows: Paul's work among the Gentiles, which has provoked protests from certain groups within the Jewish church, is commissioned by the Spirit to broker the saving grace of God for the Gentiles (Acts 14:26-27). Paul's mission demonstrates the radical extent to which God's promise of universal salvation is now being fulfilled.

The primary function of Habakkuk 1:5 in Acts is to issue a stern warning to Paul's Jewish audience to heed his report of God's work or face God's imminent judgment. The echo in Acts 15:3 recalls this same prophetic function but in another setting for another Jewish audience—this one Christian. The urgency of the present situation is framed by Luke's rhetorical shaping of its rejection thematic in Acts. Recalling a conventional formulation of rejection, God's messenger is sent twice to visit the people; a people are graciously given two chances to accept God's saving word. The first time the people reject the prophet, only then to return again in greater power to determine once for all the redemptive status of his people (Acts 7:35-39; cf. Acts 3:15-20). Consistent with this narrative thematic in Acts, Paul's poor reception by the Jews in Pisidia on "the next sabbath" (Acts 13:44-45) leads Paul to condemn them as "unworthy of eternal life" (Acts 13:46).

The currency of the prophecy from Habakkuk in this new narrative setting adds another layer of meaning to our perception of the real crisis settled at the Jerusalem council. The rhetorical effect of placing the echo (Acts 15:3) between a repetition of the conflict thematic (Acts 14:27—15:2; 15:4-5) is to stress the urgency of Paul's report for those very Jewish believers who protest the terms of his mission. Recall also that Peter's conversion of the Gentile Cornelius, rehearsed again at the Jerusalem council (Acts 15:6-11), has already been criticized by a similar group in the Jerusalem church (Acts 11:2). The apparent resolution of this earlier intramural conflict in Jerusalem is obviously short lived; the volume of their protest seems to have escalated from "criticism" (Acts 11:2, *diakrinomai*) to outright "conflict" (Acts 15:2, *stasis*). In effect, the importance of the Jerusalem council is to give this particular group of Jewish believers another chance to respond favorably to Peter's second report of what God is doing among the Gentiles (Acts 15:6-11), which is strengthened by Paul's direct testimony (Acts 15:12). The subtext of the Jerusalem council according to Acts comes to light by this echo of the prophetic text: the failure of certain Jewish believers to accept the divinely appointed work of Paul among the Gentiles, which he along with other witnesses reports to them, will surely result in divine judgment and perhaps even the forfeiture of eternal life (cf. Acts 13:46).

See also BIBLICAL INTERPRETATION, JEWISH; REWRITTEN BIBLE IN PSEUDEPIGRAPHA AND QUMRAN; WRITING AND LITERATURE: JEWISH.

BIBLIOGRAPHY. D. E. Aune, *The New Testament in Its Literary Environment* (LEC 8; Philadelphia: Westminster, 1987); R. Barthes, "The Death of the Author," in *Image, Music, Text* (New York: Hill & Wang, 1977) 142-48; J. Barton, "Judaism and Christianity: Prophecy and Fulfillment," *Theology* 79 (1976) 260-66; R. Bloch, "Midrash" and "Methodological Note for the Study of Rabbinic Literature," in *Approaches in Ancient Judaism,* ed. W. Green (Missoula, MT: Scholars Press, 1978) 29-50, 51-75; D. L. Bock, *Proclamation from Prophecy and Pattern: Lukan Old Testament Christology* (JSNTSup 12; Sheffield: Sheffield Academic Press, 1987); J. W. Bowker, *The Targums and Rabbinic Literature: An Introduction to Jewish Interpretation of Scripture* (Cambridge: Cambridge Uni-versity Press, 1969); D. Boyarin, *Intertextuality and the Reading of Midrash* (Bloomington: Indiana University Press, 1990); T. L. Brodie, *Luke the Literary Interpreter: Luke-Acts as a Systematic Rewriting and Updating of the Elisha-Elijah Narrative* (Rome: Pontifical University, 1987); F. F. Bruce, *Biblical Exegesis in the Qumran Texts* (Grand Rapids, MI: Eerdmans, 1959); B. Childs, *Biblical Theology of the Old and New Testaments: Theological Reflection on the Christian Bible* (Minneapolis: Fortress, 1992); E. E. Ellis, *Paul's Use of the Old Testament* (Grand Rapids, MI: Eerdmans, 1957); C. A. Evans, *Noncanonical Writings and New Testament Interpretation* (Peabody, MA: Hendrickson, 1992); C. A. Evans and J. A. Sanders, *Luke and Scripture* (Minneapolis: Fortress, 1993); M. Fishbane, *The Garments of Torah: Essays in Biblical Hermeneutics* (Bloomington: Indiana University Press, 1989); R. B. Hays, *Echoes of Scripture in the Letters of Paul* (New Haven, CT: Yale University Press, 1989); J. Jervell, *The Theology of the Acts of the Apostles* (NTT; Cambridge: Cambridge University Press, 1996); J. Kristeva, *Desire in Language: A Semiotic Approach to Literature and Art* (New York: Columbia University Press, 1980); J. L. Kugel and R. A. Greer, *Early Biblical Interpretation* (LEC 3; Philadelphia: Westminster, 1986); J. Levenson, *The Hebrew Bible, the Old Testament and Historical Criticism* (Louisville, KY: Westminster John Knox, 1993); R. N. Longenecker, *Biblical Exegesis in the Apostolic Period* (Grand Rapids, MI: Eerdmans, 1975); D. Patte, *Early Jewish Hermeneutic in Palestine* (SBLDS 22; Missoula, MT: Scholars Press, 1975); J. P. Rosenblatt and J. C. Sitterson Jr., eds., *"Not In Heaven": Coherence and Complexity in Biblical Narrative* (Bloomington: Indiana University Press, 1991); J. A. Sanders, *From Sacred Story to Sacred Text* (Philadelphia: Fortress, 1987); G. Sheppard, *Wisdom as a Hermeneutical Construct* (BZAW 151; Berlin: Walter de Gruyter, 1980); G. Vermes, *Scripture and Tradition in Judaism* (Leiden: E. J. Brill, 1983); R. W. Wall, "Israel and the Gentile Mission According to Acts and Paul," in *Witness to the Gospel: The Theology of Acts,* ed. I. H. Marshall and D. Peterson (Grand Rapids, MI: Eerdmans, 1998) 437-57; idem, "New Testament Use of the Old Testament," in *Mercer Dictionary of the Bible,* ed. W. Mills (Macon, GA: Mercer University Press, 1990) 614-16; F. Watson, *Text and Truth: Redefining Biblical Theology* (Grand Rapids, MI: Eerdmans, 1997).

R. W. Wall

ISAIAH SCROLLS (1QISAIAH[a,b])

The manuscripts 1QIsaiah[a] and 1QIsaiah[b] are two Hebrew scrolls of the book of Isaiah found in Cave 1 at *Qumran, near the northwestern shore of the Dead Sea in 1947, and they are two of the most important and dramatic scrolls discovered. 1QIsaiah[a] is the only biblical scroll completely preserved. These two scrolls were among the first ones published, thus exerting great influence in biblical studies, and they provided with abundant and unmistakable evidence two of our principal insights into the biblical text in antiquity. Moreover, the discovery of these scrolls was important because Isaiah served the NT authors as one of the richest resources for understanding and portraying Jesus. Finally, the numerous Isaiah scrolls recovered at Qumran showed that the NT's heavy and pervasive use of Isaiah fit into a larger context shared by other Jewish groups at the time.

The discussion that follows will examine the character of these two manuscripts, their place within the context of other Isaiah scrolls, what they have taught us about the development of the biblical text and their significance for NT studies.

1. The Character of 1QIsaiah[a] and 1QIsaiah[b]
2. The Other Isaiah Scrolls
3. History of the Biblical Text
4. Significance for New Testament Studies

1. The Character of 1QIsaiah[a] and 1QIsaiah[b].

1.1. 1QIsaiah[a]. Except for a few minor lacunae here and there 1QIsaiah[a] preserves the full sixty-six chapters of the biblical book in their entirety; no other biblical manuscript is even half so well preserved. This scroll also can claim to be the oldest manuscript of the book of Isaiah, dating from about 125 B.C. Its text differs in more than a thousand instances from the received Masoretic Text (MT) of Isaiah, though mostly in minor ways. Although many of these differences are of minimal significance, some are dramatic, showing that the MT has incorporated whole sentences or more as the text developed through history.

1.1.1. Types of Variants. The most frequent type of difference is in orthography (i.e., alternate legitimate spellings of the same word, parallel to "honor"/"honour" or "catalog"/"catalogue"). But every category of text-critical variant is displayed: differences in person, gender or number; misspellings, accidental omissions or additions; different word, phrase or verse division; synonyms, minor clarifications, euphemistic or derogatory substitutes, attempts at smoothing or harmonizing. In all these categories, sometimes the traditional MT has the correct form, but sometimes 1QIsaiah[a] has the correct form and offers valuable evidence for Bible translators.

1.1.2. Examples of Significant Variants. Two of the many large variants illuminated by 1QIsaiah[a] are these:

Isaiah 2:9b-10: Do not forgive them! Enter into the rock and hide in the dust before the terror and glorious majesty of the Lord.

This verse and a half are not yet in 1QIsaiah[a] and show that the MT and the *Septuagint (LXX) have incorporated a secondary addition.

Isaiah 2:22: Cease dealing with humans, who have only breath in their nostrils, for of what account are they?

This verse is in 1QIsaiah[a] and the MT but not in the LXX, showing that the Hebrew text behind the Greek version had not yet incorporated this secondary reflection.

1.2. 1QIsaiah[b]. Dating from the turn of the era and surviving only in fragments, 1QIsaiah[b] is much closer to what scholars at mid-century expected (see 4.1 below). It agrees with the consonantal text transmitted in the MT much more closely than 1QIsaiah[a] does; it is often described as virtually identical with the MT. But there are more than a hundred differences in orthography and more than another hundred textual variants, mostly minor. There are also more variants than usually thought because its (twentieth-century) editor apparently supplied from the MT letters that were minimally preserved; often they are correct, sometimes not.

2. The Other Isaiah Scrolls.

2.1. Scrolls from Other Caves. The main cave at Qumran, Cave 4, provided eighteen more fragmentary copies of Isaiah (4QIsa[a-r]). A couple of small fragments of one more copy were found in the adjacent Cave 5, and a cave at Murabbaʿat to the south yielded fragments of yet another. These twenty-two manuscripts of the book of Isaiah comprise about 10 percent of the approximately 227 biblical scrolls, and they show a spectrum of variants that range between the many of 1QIsaiah[a] and the comparably few of 1QIsaiah[b].

2.2. Scrolls with Commentaries on Isaiah. Already at Qumran the concept of commentaries on books of Scripture is documented. The **Rule of the Community* mandates study of the biblical texts one-third of the nights (1QS 6:6-8), and the community attests its obedience to this rule in the form of *pesharim ("commentaries"). Short portions of a prophetic text are quoted sequentially, each followed by an interpretation of that passage unique to the particular circumstances of the community and its history or destiny; the interpretation is generally not interested in the original meaning intended by the *prophet but in the application of the prophetic word to the events taking place in the end time in which they were living (*see* Pesharim). One such commentary was found in Cave 3 (3Q4) and five in Cave 4 (4Q161-165), for a total of six commentaries on Isaiah—more than on any other book.

3. History of the Biblical Text.

3.1. The Text of Isaiah and Other Individual

Books. The textual form displayed by 1QIsaiah^{b} and especially by 1QIsaiah^{a} demonstrated immediately upon their discovery that the biblical text in antiquity had been pluriform (*see* Hebrew Bible). Some scholars reacted by labeling 1QIsaiah^{a} "a vulgar text," relegating it to the margins in understanding the history of the biblical text. The assumption was that the MT was the real text and variation from it meant aberrance. But as scroll after scroll of other books was analyzed, it eventually became clear that there had been two phases in the development of the text. The overwhelming amount of variants, especially variant literary editions of many books, illustrated the earlier phase of textual pluriformity, when creativity was still at work. Qumran shows us the compositional process of the biblical texts still in their developmental phase. Clues for this first phase had been available all along in the Samaritan Pentateuch (*see* Samaritan Literature), the LXX and other sources, such as *Josephus's recasting of the biblical narrative in his *Antiquities*. The biblical text was pluriform when the NT authors were using it and quoting from it. 1QIsaiah^{a} and many other scrolls amply document and illustrate this first phase.

Then a second phase set in around the second Jewish revolt (A.D. 132-135; *see* Jewish Wars with Rome), a time that saw very little development in the Hebrew textual forms adopted by the rabbis. These latter became the texts eventually standardized and transmitted to modernity as the basis of most Bible translations. From the second century until the emergence of extant Masoretic manuscripts at the end of the ninth century, no evidence remains of growth in the Hebrew text, and it appears that the text preserved in that tradition transmitted the rabbinic text with amazing accuracy. But it must be kept in mind that only one form of the text as it existed in NT times has been transmitted. 1QIsaiah^{b} illustrates the form that has been transmitted by the rabbis.

3.2. The Collection of Books of the Law and the Prophets. During the life of Jesus and the composition of the NT, just as the text of the Scriptures (i.e., the OT) was still pluriform, so too the collection of Scriptures (what would become the canon) was largely but not fully established. The NT term for the collection is "the Law and the Prophets," the latter probably including more than is now placed in that category. Only in Luke 24:44 does there begin to be a mention of more: "all must be fulfilled that is written in the law of Moses and the prophets and psalms about me."

4. Significance for New Testament Studies.

4.1. Apocalyptic Thought. The book of Isaiah was a major source for the Jewish *apocalyptic thinking that pervades the NT. Deutero-Isaiah had attempted to raise the morale of the Babylonian *exiles for salvation and return by promising salvation from their oppressors through God's "messiah" Cyrus (Is 45:1), heralding that God was planning a "new creation" (Is 65:17) and was about to do "new things" (Is 42:9; 43:19; 48:6). When read in subsequent centuries in similar situations of oppression, these appealing promises (Is 46:11) in the face of intolerable oppression provided fuel for the apocalyptic mindset. Moreover, it is not difficult to appreciate that the early Christians saw the promises as being actualized in their day (cf. Mt 1:22-23; 3:3).

4.2. Quotations of Isaiah in the New Testament. Just as the books of Psalms, Deuteronomy and Isaiah are the books with most manuscripts attested at Qumran, so too those three books rank the highest for NT quotations. Also, like the *Rule of the Community* at Qumran, all four Gospels (though with application to John the Baptist) quote Isaiah 40:3 for self-identity. NT authors and other Christians would probably find no difficulty with the statement in *4QFlorilegium 1:15: "as it is written in the book of Isaiah the prophet for the End of Days"; Luke lacks only the last element: "as it is written in the book of the words of Isaiah the prophet" (Lk 3:4).

4.3. Reliability of the Septuagint. The LXX was the form of the OT predominantly used by NT authors. Frequently 1QIsaiah^{a} and other scrolls provide readings in Hebrew that confirm the LXX as a faithful translation of its ancient Hebrew parent text, though it may differ from the form transmitted in the MT. The reputation of the LXX had suffered when compared with the MT due to the assumption that the MT was the single, original Hebrew text. But 1QIsaiah^{a} provides a much more realistic image of the Hebrew text and its challenges which the Greek translator worked with than does *Biblia Hebraica Stuttgartensia* with its clear print, accents, verse divisions and stichometric arrangement.

4.4. Pervasiveness of Isaiah in the Portrait of Jesus. In composing the kerygma, from before his birth (cf. Mt 1:22-23) to after his resurrection (cf. Lk 24:44-45), the NT authors found in the book of Isaiah one of the most potent resources and illustrations that "God does nothing without revealing his plan through his servants the prophets" (Amos 3:7). From antiquity God had foreshadowed through the prophet's words: his birth from the virgin who would name him Emmanuel (Is 7:14 = Mt 1:22-23); John the Baptist as "the voice of one announcing in the wilderness" to prepare his way (Is 40:3 = Mt 3:3; Mk 1:3; Lk 3:4-6; Jn 1:23; cf. 1QS 8:13-14); the Spirit of God upon him and the voice at his baptism (Is 11:2; 42:1 = Mt 3:16-17); the reading from the scroll of Isaiah (which would have looked much like 1QIsaiah[a]) in the Nazareth *synagogue, inaugurating his ministry (Is 61:1-2; 58:6 = Lk 4:16-21); and numerous similar features up to his death as the Suffering Servant (Is 52:13—53:12); and after his death and resurrection, for the two disciples on the road to Emmaus, undoubtedly playing a prominent role in their "opening of minds to understand the Scriptures" (Lk 24:44-46).

See also HEBREW BIBLE; SEPTUAGINT/GREEK OLD TESTAMENT.

BIBLIOGRAPHY. M. Abegg Jr., P. Flint and E. Ulrich, *The Dead Sea Scrolls Bible: The Oldest Known Bible Translated for the First Time into English* (San Francisco: HarperSanFrancisco, 1999); D. Barthélemy and J. T. Milik, *Qumrân Cave 1* (DJD 1; Oxford: Clarendon Press, 1955) includes an edition of further fragments of 1QIsa[b] recovered in the excavation of Cave 1 and thus supplements Sukenik's edition; G. J. Brooke, "Isaiah 40:3 and the Wilderness Community," in *New Qumran Texts and Studies: Proceedings of the First Meeting of the International Organization for Qumran Studies. Paris 1992,* ed. G. J. Brooke with F. García Martínez (STDJ 15; Leiden: E. J. Brill, 1994) 117-32; C. C. Broyles and C. A. Evans, eds., *Writing and Reading the Scroll of Isaiah: Studies of an Interpretive Tradition* (FIOTL 1 and 2 = VTSup 70.1-2; Leiden: E. J. Brill, 1997); F. M. Cross, D. N. Freedman and J. A. Sanders, eds., *Scrolls from Qumran Cave 1: The Great Isaiah Scroll, the Order of the Community, the Pesher to Habakkuk, from Photographs by J. C. Trever* (Jerusalem: Albright Institute of Archaeological Research and Shrine of the Book, 1972); C. A. Evans and J. A. Sanders, *Luke and Scripture: The Function of Sacred Tradition in Luke-Acts* (Minneapolis: Fortress, 1993); J. A. Fitzmyer, "The Use of Explicit Old Testament Quotations in Qumran Literature and in the New Testament," *NTS* 7 (1961) 297-333; M. P. Horgan, *Pesharim: Qumran Interpretations of Biblical Books* (CBQMS 8; Washington, DC: Catholic Biblical Association, 1979); E. Y. Kutscher, *The Language and Linguistic Background of the Isaiah Scroll (1QIsa[a])* (STDJ 6; Leiden: E. J. Brill, 1974); D. W. Parry and E. Qimron, eds., *The Great Isaiah Scroll (1QIsa[a]): A New Edition* (STDJ 32; Leiden: E. J. Brill, 1999); E. Qimron, *The Language and Linguistic Background of the Isaiah Scroll by E. Y. Kutscher: Indices and Corrections* (STDJ 6A; Leiden: E. J. Brill, 1979); E. L. Sukenik, *The Dead Sea Scrolls of the Hebrew University,* ed. N. Avigad and Y. Yadin (Jerusalem: Hebrew University and Magnes, 1955); E. Tov, "The Text of Isaiah at Qumran," in *Writing and Reading the Scroll of Isaiah: Studies of an Interpretive Tradition,* ed. C. C. Broyles and C. A. Evans (FIOTL 2 = VTSup 70.2; Leiden: E. J. Brill, 1997) 491-511; idem, *Textual Criticism of the Hebrew Bible* (Minneapolis: Fortress, 1992); E. Ulrich, *The Dead Sea Scrolls and the Origins of the Bible* (SDSSRL 2; Grand Rapids, MI: Eerdmans; Leiden: E. J. Brill, 1999); idem, "Isaiah, Book of," in *Encyclopedia of the Dead Sea Scrolls,* ed. L. H. Schiffman and J. C. VanderKam (New York: Oxford University Press, 2000); E. Ulrich et al., *Qumran Cave 4.10: The Prophets* (DJD 15; Oxford: Clarendon Press, 1997).

E. Ulrich

ISRAEL, LAND OF

The land of Israel evokes thematic and theological concepts, quite apart from mere geographical issues. The "land" alludes to God's promise to Abraham and becomes a symbol of Israel's covenant. This tradition is rooted in Scripture itself, but is extended in important ways in later traditions.

1. Hebrew Biblical Evidence
2. Apocrypha and Pseudepigrapha
3. Qumran Scrolls
4. New Testament
5. Rabbinic Literature

1. Hebrew Biblical Evidence.

The term *Israel,* Hebrew *Yisra'el,* was used in the Hebrew Bible as the collective name for the twelve tribes who traced their ancestry to Jacob. His name was changed to Israel after he wrestled with an angel (Gen 32:28; 35:10). The Israelites were also known as "children of Israel," often translated "people of Israel." While this term often designated the nation as a whole, during the period of the divided monarchy (924-721 B.C.), it referred only to the northern kingdom, as distinct from Judah, the southern kingdom. After the destruction of the North, the term *Israel* was again used for the entire people. In accord with this usage, the land occupied by the people of Israel was termed the land of Israel in the Prophets and the Writings. In Second Temple Jewish sources, Israel was synonymous with the Jewish people (or with the nonpriestly and nonlevitical members of the Jewish people), and the term *land of Israel* (Hebrew *Eretz Yisrael*) was used to denote its ancestral homeland.

In the biblical account, God promises Abraham a land that will be given to his descendants. Genesis 15:18-21 states that Abram's descendants, who had previously been likened to the stars of the heavens in number, will inherit the land between the Nile and the Euphrates (Gen 15:18), which was then in the hands of various Canaanite peoples. In fact, in Genesis 12:5 and 23:2 it is known as the land of Canaan. Numbers 34, however, excludes the territory of Transjordan, following the borders of the Egyptian province of Canaan. Abraham is assured that the land will be his and his descendants' "for an everlasting possession" (Gen 17:8). Deuteronomy further confirms this promise (Deut 4:40). The commandments given at Sinai are to be scrupulously observed in the land that the Israelites will enter. In fact, the commandments are the means by which the land will be governed, and they include laws directly relating to the land such as sabbatical (Ex 23:10-11) and Jubilee years (Lev 25:8-55).

Abandonment of the commandments will cause the land to expel its inhabitants (Lev 22—26), a judgment that was meted out to the undeserving nations that preceded the Israelites (Deut 9:45). Joshua 23:13-14 states that one such severe transgression would be the intermarriage of Israelites with the people who inhabit the land. Leviticus cites contact with unclean beasts (Lev 20:22-26) and harlotry (Lev 19:29), and Deuteronomy adds the shedding of innocent blood (Deut 21:69) and the prohibition of leaving a corpse hanging overnight (Deut 1:22-23). All of these things, and other transgressions, defile the Holy Land.

The concept of the holiness of the land is intrinsic and is not linked merely to the biblical commandments. The *Torah understands the Israelite victory as succeeding in part because the land itself was so holy that it vomited out the inhabitants who defiled it by their abominable practices (Lev 18:28; Deut 9:45). Yet Moses assures the people that even the neglect of the commandments will not utterly negate God's promise. The children of Israel cannot be destroyed, and the land is a heritage for all time (Deut 9:24-29).

The land belongs to God himself, who states in Leviticus 25:23: "The land shall not be sold in perpetuity; for the land is mine; for you are strangers and sojourners with me." God demands the tithes and the firstfruits as owner of the land. In fact, God himself conquered the land for the Israelites. He helped Joshua win each and every military victory, but in Exodus 23:29-30 he also allowed the Canaanites to be driven out gradually so that the land would not suffer for lack of inhabitants. Indeed, in Joshua 24:13 we are reminded that the land given to the Israelites already had cities, vineyards and olive groves on it which the people were able to take advantage of although they did not construct them. As described in Numbers 26:52-56; Joshua 11:23; 13:78 and Ezekiel 48:29, when the tribes of Israel had taken possession of the land, they were to divide it up and distribute it by tribe. Only the tribe of Levi did not receive this property, but instead they were given certain levitical cities, ministered in the temple and received tithes.

The Hebrew Bible often refers to the promised land as the "land of milk and [date] honey" (Ex 3:17). The presumption here is that God bequeathed to his people a land blessed with abundant produce. In Deuteronomy 11:10-12 we are told that it is a well-irrigated land with ample crops, blessed also with natural resources in the form of metals.

The period of the judges was a struggle, mainly with the Philistines, over the land, and Israel's victories were understood to depend on their obedience to God. Judges 1:1—2:5 accuses the Israelites of failure to dispossess the Canaanites and subsequent intermarriage with them (Judg 3:5-6). In Samuel and Kings the empire of David and Solomon is established, and later kings are measured by David's faithfulness. When they fall short, it is inevitable that the land will suffer devastation and its inhabitants will be exiled. The prime example of injustice in distributing the land and its produce is Ahab's confiscation of Naboth's inheritance (1 Kings 21).

The prophets Amos, Isaiah and Micah castigate the people for abuse by the powerful against the small landowners and announce that God will punish his people with exile. Hosea and Jeremiah add the sin of idolatry. Jeremiah 38:2 depicts the exile as God's will, for most Israelites are forced to live in Babylon, and the minority who remain in Jerusalem perish.

Nevertheless Jerusalem will not be forgotten, and the promise to return to her will not be abnegated. The children of Israel will yet return to their land. Several prophets foretold restoration—Hosea, Isaiah, Ezekiel and Amos. Amos 9:14-15 expresses a vision of the restoration of Israel, of rebuilt cities and fruitful gardens, in which Israel is God's plant: " 'I will plant them upon their land, and they shall never again be plucked up out of the land which I have given them,' says the Lord your God." The dispersed and exiled of Israel will be reunited in their own land, and the land shall be cleansed of its abominations which caused the dispersion. Furthermore, Israel and God shall be reconciled, and the land will become fertile, peaceful and secure. Isaiah 9:7 would restore the house of David to rule over the newly established kingdom.

The restoration of Israel to its land redounds to the honor of God whose promises must be fulfilled before the nations. One of the themes of Ezekiel is the ingathering of the dispersed from the lands to which they were taken by their captors. In Ezekiel 17:22-23 God takes a sprig from the top of a cedar and plants it on the mountain to become a noble tree representing the reestablishment of the people of Israel on their land. Ezekiel 48:18, 23-27 sets out an idealized view of the reallocation of the land to the tribes of Israel which differs from that in the book of Joshua. Ezekiel assumes that each tribe occupies an east-west strip of land so that the entire country is covered.

In every prophetic message the prophecy of judgment and doom is tempered by the prophecy of consolation and restoration. Like the dry bones in Ezekiel's vision (Ezek 37:1-14), the old community of Israel will be restored, and from it the future generations will grow and flourish. The land will be cleansed of its pollution and sin, and it will welcome home its scattered people and become repopulated. Isaiah announces a second exodus through the wilderness to the promised land. God, who had "exiled" himself along with his people, returns to dwell in Jerusalem (Is 52:8), the center of the earth. The primary emphasis turned to the restoration of the temple and its cult and the rebuilding of the city of Jerusalem.

2. Apocrypha and Pseudepigrapha.
The connection of the people of Israel and the land of Israel in the *Apocrypha and pseudepigrapha is strong. The term *Holy Land* appears in Wisdom of Solomon 13:3, 4, 7 and *2 Baruch* 65:9-10, and the land is praised for its goodness (Tob 14:45; *Jub.* 13:2, 6), pleasantness (*1 Enoch* 89:40) and beauty (*Ep. Arist.* 107). *Jubilees* makes the connection between the failure to obey God's commandments and the punishment of forfeiture of the land (*Jub.* 6:12-13). Wisdom 2:7 and *1 Enoch* 90:20 associate the punishment of the Canaanite inhabitants for their sins with the conquest of their land by the Israelites. The Apocrypha and pseudepigrapha strengthen the idea that God will be vindicated in the sight of the nations of the world by the restoration of his people to the land. *Psalms of Solomon* 17:26-28 prophesies that God will fulfill all his promises by gathering his people together, planting them in the land according to tribe, and since they are all righteous, he will banish the aliens and wicked from among them. The land itself will protect its inhabitants, and that land will be surrounded by God's presence (*2 Bar.* 9:2; 71:1). 4 Ezra 9:79 and 13:48 states that at the end of days, the saved shall be those who dwell within the borders of the land of Israel. There will be erected the throne of God (*1 Enoch* 90:20) to stand for all time.

3. Qumran Scrolls.
The biblical usage of the expression *land of Israel* (*Eretz Yisrael*) became increasingly prominent in the Second Temple period and is used in the scrolls. This expression occurs only rarely in the preserved Qumran scrolls (cf. 4Q382, para-Kings frag. 1 4 [restored]). Often the area of Judea is termed "land of Judah" in the scrolls, apparently a reference to the political realities of the Greco-Roman period. In 4QMMT B, *land of Israel* serves as a legal term for the area which is subject according to Jewish law to the laws of tithing of produce and the offering of fourth-year produce. While this legal usage certainly in-

dicates a geographical entity, it need not assume a governmental or administrative significance. In the *Temple Scroll* (11QTemple 58:6) it is used as a geographical and governmental term for the area under the sovereignty of the ideal king of Israel, whose constitution is set forth in the law of the king (11QTemple 56—59).

The *Temple Scroll* presents an ideal vision of how the people of Israel should live in the land of Israel. Throughout, the author is informed by a notion of concentric spheres of holiness, as well as by distinct concern for the sanctity of the entire land of Israel as sacred space. The preserved portion of the *Temple Scroll* begins with the assertion of God's covenant with Israel regarding the land of Israel (11QTemple 2), a motif that was common in the Hebrew Bible, as noted above. This section, adapted from Exodus 34:10-16 and Deuteronomy 7:5, 25, relates that God will expel the Canaanite nations from the land of Israel. The Israelites, in turn, are commanded to destroy pagan cult objects and to avoid any covenants with the Canaanite nations since such alliances would lead to *idolatry and intermarriage. The laws of war in the scroll (11QTemple 60:9-16) concern the destruction of the pagan inhabitants of the land as well.

The notion that Israel is given the land conditionally also appears in the scroll. Bribery and corruption in judgment must be avoided, "in order that you might live, and come and take (or retain) possession of the land which I am giving you as a possession for ever" (11QTemple 51:15-16). In other words, judicial corruption will result in the destruction of the land and exile. Only after repentance will Israel return to its land (11QTemple 59:2-11).

For the *Temple Scroll,* the central point of the land of Israel was the temple and the surrounding complex. The scroll provides for a temple plan of very different proportions from that which existed in First or Second Temple times. This new temple plan would be characterized by the enclosure of the temple building itself by three concentric courtyards. This entire plan has behind it the assumption that the temple is the center of sanctity for the entire land. The scroll makes clear repeatedly that it is the indwelling of the divine presence in the temple which imparts to the land this level of sanctity.

Beyond the temple city which, for the scroll, symbolized the desert camp, was located the hinterland of Israel. Ezekiel had adopted an ideal view of the land but for its author it is most likely that the tribes were to dwell outside the respective gates through which they were to enter the temple precincts. Indeed, it was through these gates that the tribal territory was to be tied to the sanctity of the central shrine and the divine presence which dwelled there.

The *Temple Scroll* envisaged the people, including priests and Levites, as living in the cities of Israel, which were to be scattered about the central sanctuary, each tribe opposite its respective gate. Burial in the cities was forbidden (11QTemple 48:11). Burial places were to be set aside one for each four cities (11QTemple 48:11-13). The limitation of burial to specified places was designed to avoid rendering the land impure (11QTemple 48:10).

All in all the authors of the various sectarian texts found at Qumran saw both the people and land of Israel in ideal terms. They expected that as the true Israel, separated from both errant Jews and from the non-Jewish world, they could live a life of perfect holiness and sanctity in their ancestral land. Yet in the eyes of the author/redactor of the *Temple Scroll,* this land, even before the end of days, had to be reconfigured and idealized in order to represent the level of holiness to which the sectarians aspired.

4. New Testament.

The land of Israel is not a major theme in the NT (*see DLNTD,* Land in Early Christianity). In fact, the exact phrase, "land of Israel," occurs only in Matthew 2:20-21, where the angel directs Joseph to return to Israel. However, there are important allusions in Hebrews 3—4, where the author warns Jewish Christians not to fall away from faith in Christ and so fail to enter God's "rest." This exegesis is based on Psalm 95:7-11, which itself is a reflection on Israel's wilderness wanderings. The implication is that if God's people obey the voice of the Lord, they will enter God's "rest," which is a theologized development of the promised land (see Davies).

5. Rabbinic Literature.

Rabbinic literature presumes a close connection between the land of Israel and the people who called it their ancestral land. *Mishnah Ḥalla* 4:78 debates the borders of the land subject to the tithe. The halakic relevance of the Torah's commandments pertaining to agricultural produce in the land of Israel continued to occupy the sages throughout late antiquity.

Although Philo had said that Jewish "colonies" were established because the land of Israel was overpopulated, some rabbis strongly condemned those who left the land, even to perform a commandment (*y. Mo'ed Qaṭ.* 3:81c). Demonstrations of love of the land, such as kissing the ground on arriving there, are found in rabbinic literature, and praises of the land point to its superior attributes. The ritual and historical centrality of the land for many early rabbinic sages was a major part of their religious outlook.

Nevertheless, statements by tannaim who lived before the Bar Kokhba revolt (*see* Simon ben Kosiba), Yohanan ben Zakkai, R. Joshua, R. Eliezer, R. Eleazar ben Azariah, and R. Akiba, actually express minimal praise of the land in supernatural terms and do not allude often to the centrality of the land and Jewish commitment to live there. Babylonia is even mentioned as another possible Jewish homeland. But Eleazar ha-Moda'i states that the land of Israel is a reward for keeping the sabbath (*Mek. Beshalah*).

The disciples of Rabbi Akiba, who lived after the Bar Kokhba revolt, however, begin to stress the requirement to live in the land of Israel and not to leave it, it being preferable to live in the land in a town inhabited mostly by Gentiles than in a Jewish town outside the land (*t. ʿAbod. Zar.* 4:3). A statement attributed to Shimon Bar Yohai (*t. ʿAbod. Zar.* 4:4) derives the necessity of staying in the land of Israel from Ruth 1:1. There we read that Elimelech left during the famine, but he and his sons died in exile while the inhabitants of the land were ultimately sustained. *Tosefta Ketubbot* 12:5 rules that in a *marriage the law is on the side of either party who wishes to force the other to stay in the land or to immigrate there. Laws concerning the possession of confiscated land (*sicaricon*) listed in Mishnah tractate *Giṭin* 5:6 also are constructed to try to maintain the Jewish presence in the land after the devastation of the Bar Kokhba revolt. These laws made it easier for a Jew to purchase property when the original Jewish owner was illegally dispossessed of his land and was no longer present. It was known that even some significant *rabbis went abroad after the revolt. *Tosefta ʿAboda Zara* 4:3 declares that "dwelling in the land of Israel is equivalent to (observing) all the commandments." Their opinions were an expression of commitment to the land for fear that the majority of its inhabitants would no longer be Jewish, and the Jewish claim to the land would be whittled away. According to *Sifre Deuteronomy* 333, "he who lives in the land of Israel, recites the Shema morning and evening, and speaks in the holy tongue is assured of his place in the next world."

While these statements applied to times of economic distress, *Tosefta ʿAboda Zara* 4:5 emphasizes that it is even more important to live in the land in times of relative well-being. *Tosefta Berakot* 3:15 teaches that those who live abroad must direct their prayers toward the land of Israel, and within its boundaries toward Jerusalem, the site of the temple.

All of these texts refer to an actual land, not a spiritualized land. This is the case even in passages that refer to idealized schemes or messianic times. This land would have at its center the Jerusalem temple, which was for classical Judaism a symbol of God's eternal spiritual presence among them.

See also JERUSALEM; TEMPLE, JEWISH; TEMPLE SCROLL (11QTEMPLE).

BIBLIOGRAPHY. W. D. Davies, *The Gospel and the Land* (BSem 25; Sheffield: JSOT, 1994 [1974]); I. M. Gafni, *Land, Center and Diaspora* (JSPSup 21; Sheffield: Sheffield Academic Press, 1997); E. Qimron and J. Strugnell, *Qumran Cave 4.5: Miqṣat Maʿaśe ha-Torah* (DJD 10; Oxford: Clarendon Press, 1994) 88; L. H. Schiffman, "Sacred Space: The Land of Israel in the Temple Scroll," in *Biblical Archaeology Today, 1990: Proceedings of the Second International Congress on Biblical Archaeology, Jerusalem, June-July 1990*, ed. A. Biran (Jerusalem: Israel Exploration Society, 1993) 398-410; M. Weinfeld, *The Promise of the Land* (Berkeley and Los Angeles: University of California Press, 1993).

L. H. Schiffman

J

JEREMIAH, ADDITIONS TO. *See* DANIEL, ESTHER AND JEREMIAH, ADDITIONS TO.

JERUSALEM

Jerusalem, the Holy City, is sacred to Judaism, Christianity and Islam, three of the world's monotheistic religions. Located in Israel 25 miles east of the Mediterranean Sea, Jerusalem is perched atop the central north/south mountain range at an elevation of approximately 800 meters and is not on a major trade route. Near the Judean desert, the climate is arid; the land is poor for agriculture and without valuable minerals. However, the limestone has for thousands of years provided excellent building material. The limited fresh water for the ancient city came from the Gihon Spring in the Kidron Valley to the east. Numerous cisterns supplemented this supply.

1. Early History
2. Hellenistic Period
3. Roman Period
4. Jerusalem in the New Testament

1. Early History.

The oldest literary mention of Jerusalem is in the Egyptian Execration Texts (nineteenth to eighteenth centuries B.C.) and in the Armana Tablets (fourteenth century). Assyrian texts record Sennacherib's siege of Jerusalem (*Ursalimmu*) in 701. The first specific biblical reference to Jerusalem is in Joshua 10:3, where King Adonizedek organized a coalition of five Amorite kings to attack Gibeon. Joshua defeated them. Also, Genesis 14:18 identifies Melchizedek as the king of Salem, probably an abbreviated reference to Jerusalem (see Ps 76:2).

The etymology of the name *Jerusalem* (Heb. *yᵉrûšālayim*) is disputed but appears to be Western Semitic or Canaanite and means "founded or established by the god Salem," a god mentioned in the Ugaritic texts (fourteenth century B.C.).

Pottery dated to the Early Bronze Age indicates that the earliest settlement of Jerusalem was on the Ophel ("bulge") west of the Gihon Spring between 3000 and 2000 B.C. It is difficult to reconstruct the history of the city from archaeological evidence due to several destructions and continuous rebuilding and expansions. David captured the Jebusite city in 1000 B.C. and made Jerusalem the capital of his kingdom, combining political and religious authorities. The City of David initially included about 12 acres with a population of one thousand but was soon enlarged to 15 acres to accommodate the growing number of residences. Solomon extended the city limits to incorporate 32 acres in order to provide adequate space for the *temple and his own palace as well as other major constructions.

The civil war following Solomon's death (922 B.C.) divided the united kingdom into northern and southern kingdoms with Jerusalem continuing as the capital of the south and the seat of the Davidic dynasty. In 598 B.C. the Babylonians, led by Nebuchadnezzar, captured and plundered Jerusalem and subsequently destroyed the city in 587 B.C., taking the most influential and skilled people into Babylonian captivity. A half century later (539 B.C.) Babylon fell before the onslaught of Persia. The new ruler, Cyrus II, issued an edict (538 B.C.) granting permission for the Jews to return and rebuild Jerusalem. The importance of the city derived primarily from its religious heritage rather than its political influence. Zerubbabel, the governor and a descendant of the royal house of David, rebuilt the temple (Second Temple) and dedicated it in 515 B.C. Jerusalem under enlightened Persian rule enjoyed political stability and prosperity, although tensions sharpened between the Jews who returned from Babylonian exile and those who had stayed behind in Jerusalem (*see* Jewish History: Persian Period).

2. Hellenistic Period.

The capture of Jerusalem by *Alexander the Great (332 B.C.) ushered in the Hellenistic period (332-63 B.C.). Following Alexander's death (323 B.C.), Jerusalem came under the successive control of two dynasties established by his generals, the *Ptolemies in Egypt (c. 320-198 B.C.) and the *Seleucids in Syria (198-135 B.C.). The pervasive and attractive influence of Hellenization precipitated a conflict between the Jews who embraced Greek culture—building a stadium (*see* Athletics) and *gymnasium in Jerusalem and renaming the city Antioch—and those Jews violently opposed to Hellenization (*see* Jewish History: Greek Period).

The Seleucid rulers initially tolerated Jewish customs and religious practices, even providing financial support to restore the temple and rebuild Jerusalem. Taxes were suspended for three years. Jason, the high priest, promoted Hellenization and reorganized Jerusalem as a Greek city-state (*polis*). The Seleucids did not force Hellenization on the Jews, but those who welcomed Hellenistic culture, adopting Greek styles and values, provoked the open antagonism of the anti-Hellenists.

Smoldering resentment flared into open rebellion when Mattathias, an old Jewish priest, aided by his five sons, initiated a revolt in 167 B.C. to prevent the spread of Hellenization. Antiochus IV Epiphanes, the Seleucid king, attempted to crush the insurrection and end Jewish religious practices. He captured Jerusalem, confiscated the temple gold and dedicated the temple to Olympian Zeus. Leadership of the resistance movement fell to Judas, one of the five sons who received the name Maccabeus (the "hammer") because of his successful guerrilla tactics. In 164 B.C. he recaptured Jerusalem, purified the sanctuary and reinstituted *sacrificial rites—an event commemorated at Hanukkah. For a century Jerusalem remained the capital of Judea enjoying political and religious freedom under *Hasmonean rule. The Hasmoneans were a dynasty of priest-kings named for Hasmon, the tribal surname of Mattathias. In 63 B.C. the Roman general Pompey settled a dispute between rival Hasmonean factions by annexing Judea to Rome, thus bringing Hasmonean rule under Roman protection (*see* Jewish History: Roman Period).

3. Roman Period.

The Roman senate appointed *Herod the Great king of Judea in 40 B.C. Herod returned to Judea, gathered an army and captured Jerusalem in 37 B.C., sending the last Hasmonean king, Antigonus, to Antony to be executed. Once in control of Jerusalem Herod launched several massive and extensive building projects (*see* Archaeology of the Land of Israel). He extended and fortified the city walls. The Baris, the Hasmonean fortress north of the Temple Mount, was renovated and named The Antonia in honor of his friend and benefactor Marc Antony. Herod constructed his own secure and luxurious palace, the Citadel, in the Upper City near the present-day Jaffa Gate, where the wealthiest and most prominent people resided. A new aqueduct brought water from pools near Bethlehem, greatly improving Jerusalem's water supply.

Following Octavian's (Augustus's; *see* Roman Emperors) defeat of Antony and Cleopatra on September 2, 31 B.C., in the naval battle fought off the western coast of Greece near Actium, Herod skillfully switched his loyalty and support from Antony to Octavian. To commemorate this decisive victory, Herod celebrated the Actium Games in Jerusalem. He constructed the necessary buildings—a *theater, amphitheater, hippodrome and even a zoo—and awarded lucrative prizes to the winners of competitions. The elaborate spectacles greatly pleased the Romans and Hellenists but further alienated the more conservative Jews.

Courting Jewish favor, Herod began in 20 B.C. to rebuild the temple, the centerpiece of his vast urban renewal project (see below). He doubled the size of the temple platform to 34 acres by constructing massive retaining walls of huge embossed ashlars laid without mortar. The western wall (*kotel*) stands today as a silent witness to the skill of Herod's architects and engineers.

Following Herod's death in 4 B.C., his son Archelaus became ethnarch (ruler of a people) of Judea and Samaria and ruled ineptly for a decade until he was removed from power and replaced by Roman prefects who transferred the capital to *Caesarea Maritima, Herod's seaport on the

Mediterranean. Pontius Pilate, who condemned Jesus to crucifixion, was one of a series of prefects (*see* Roman Governors of Palestine). The last prefect, Gessius Florus, stole from the temple treasury and provoked a revolt (A.D. 66) that resulted in the destruction in A.D. 70 of Jerusalem and the temple by Roman troops led by Titus (*see* Jewish Wars with Rome). The Tenth Legion was stationed in Jerusalem to enforce the peace.

Hadrian visited Jerusalem in A.D. 129-130 and rebuilt the city on the plan of a Roman military camp. On the Temple Mount he erected a temple dedicated to Jupiter Capitolinus and nearby a second temple honoring the goddess Aphrodite. Hadrian renamed Jerusalem Aelia Capitolina, a designation that combined one of his names with Rome's Capitoline triad: Jupiter, Juno and Minerva. Hadrian's actions and policies provoked a second revolt by the Jews in A.D. 132. Led by Bar Kokhba, the Jewish troops succeeded in taking control of Jerusalem briefly but were soon (A.D. 135) crushed by the superior Roman army. After this decisive defeat it became a capital offense for a Jew to set foot in Jerusalem.

4. Jerusalem in the New Testament.
In Jerusalem Jesus meets his fate, a possibility that he evidently anticipated: "Behold, we are going up to Jerusalem; and the Son of Man will be delivered to the chief priests and the scribes, and they will condemn him to death and deliver him to the Gentiles" (Mk 10:34; cf. Mt 23:37: "O Jerusalem, Jerusalem, killing the prophets and stoning those who are sent to you!"). The Christian church begins in Jerusalem, having awaited the empowerment of the Holy Spirit (Acts 1:4-5, 8; 2:4, 17-18) and having begun the proclamation of the resurrection of Jesus on the day of Pentecost (Acts 2:14-38). (*See DJG,* Archeology and Geography.)

Paul refers to Jerusalem ten times in his epistles. In Romans 15:19 he claims that "from Jerusalem and as far round as Illyricum I have fully preached the gospel of Christ." The apostle is especially concerned with the Gentiles' gift of aid for the church of Jerusalem (cf. Rom 15:25-26, 31; 1 Cor 16:3). But in Galatians he refers to Jerusalem in an allegorical sense (Gal 4:25-26).

Jerusalem is the venue for one, possibly two important church councils, concerned with the question of the admission of Gentiles into the Church (Acts 11) and of how Gentiles should behave (Acts 15). James, the brother of Jesus, emerges as the leader of the church centered in Jerusalem. With the destruction of Jerusalem in A.D. 70 the Jewish branch of the church begins to decline and is eventually eclipsed by Gentile Christianity.

See also DESTRUCTION OF JERUSALEM; JUDEA; NEW JERUSALEM TEXTS; TEMPLE, JEWISH.

BIBLIOGRAPHY. D. Bahat, "Jerusalem," *Oxford Encyclopedia of Archaeology in the Near East,* ed. E. M. Meyers (5 vols.; New York: Oxford University Press, 1997) 3:224-38; D. Baldi, *Enchiridion Locorum Sanctorum* (3d ed.; Jerusalem: Franciscan Printing Press, 1982); G. Dalman, *Sacred Sites and Ways: Studies in the Topography of the Gospels* (New York: Macmillan, 1935); W. D. Davies, *The Gospel and the Land* (Berkeley and Los Angeles: University of California Press, 1974); H. Eshel, "Aelia Capitolina, Jerusalem No More," *BAR* 22 (1997) 46-48, 73; H. Geva, "Roman Jerusalem," *BAR* 22 (1997) 34-45, 72, 73; M. Hengel, "Luke the Historian and the Geography of Palestine in the Acts of the Apostles," in *Between Jesus and Paul* (Philadelphia: Fortress, 1983) 97-128; J. Jeremias, *Jerusalem in the Time of Jesus* (Philadelphia: Fortress, 1969); P. J. King, "Jerusalem," *ABD* 3:747-66; C. Kopp, *The Holy Places of the Gospels* (Edinburgh: Nelson, n.d.); G. Kroll, *Auf den Spuren Jesu* (llth ed.; Leipzig: St. Benno, 1990); R. H. Lightfoot, *Locality and Doctrine in the Gospels* (London: Hodder & Stoughton, 1938); B. Pixner, *Wege des Messias und Stätten der Urkirche* (Giessen: Brunnen, 1991); R. Riesner, "Bethany Beyond the Jordan," *TynB* 38 (1987) 29-63; idem, "Galiläa," *GBL* 1:406-7; idem, "Jerusalem," *GBL* 2:661-77; idem, "Judäa," *GBL* 2:735-36; J. A. T. Robinson, *The Priority of John* (Yorktown Heights, NY: Meyer-Stone, 1987); E. Ruckstuhl, *Chronology of the Last Days of Jesus* (New York: Desclée, 1965); W. Sanday, *Sacred Sites of the Gospels* (Oxford: Clarendon Press, 1903); B. E. Schein, *Following the Way* (Minneapolis: Augsburg, 1980); G. Theissen, *The Gospels in Context: Social and Political History in the Synoptic Tradition* (Minneapolis: Fortress, 1991).

R. A. Batey

JESUS BEN ANANIAS

According to *Josephus (*J.W.* 6.5.3 §§300), during the Feast of Tabernacles in the year A.D. 62 "one Jesus son of Ananias, an untrained peasant" stood in the *temple precints and "suddenly began to cry out, 'A voice from the east, a voice from the west, a voice from the four winds, a voice against Jerusalem and the sanctuary, a voice against the bridegroom and the bride, a voice against all the people.'" Jesus' words are based on Jeremiah 7:34: "I will bring to an end the sound of mirth and gladness, the voice of the bride and bridegroom in the cities of Judah and in the streets of Jerusalem; for the land shall become a waste." The citizens of *Jerusalem were incensed, especially those of the upper class. Jesus was seized and beaten but still continued his plaintive cry. Finally, the "rulers" (by which Josephus probably means ruling *priests) brought Jesus before the Roman governor Albinus, who questioned and flogged the prophet of doom. Convinced that the man was a harmless lunatic, the governor released him (*see* Roman Governors of Palestine). Jesus ben Ananias continued his gloomy ministry for seven years, especially crying out during the *feasts, until he was struck and killed by a Roman siege stone in A.D. 69, less than a year before the city was captured and destroyed (*see* Destruction of Jerusalem).

There are several important parallels between the temple-related experiences of Jesus of Nazareth and Jesus son of Ananias. Both entered the precincts of the temple (*to hieron:* Mk 11:11, 15, 27; 12:35; 13:1; 14:49; Josephus *J.W.* 6.5.3 §301) at the time of a religious festival (*heortē:* Mk 14:2; 15:6; Jn 2:23; Josephus *J.W.* 6.5.3 §300). Both spoke of the doom of Jerusalem (Lk 19:41-44; 21:20-24; Josephus *J.W.* 6.5.3 §301), the sanctuary (*naos:* Mk 13:2; 14:58; Josephus *J.W.* 6.5.3 §301) and the people (*laos:* Mk 13:17; Lk 19:44; 23:28-31; Josephus *J.W.* 6.5.3 §301). Both apparently alluded to Jeremiah 7, where the prophet condemned the temple establishment of his day ("cave of robbers": Jer 7:11 in Mk 11:17; "the voice against the bridegroom and the bride": Jer 7:34 in Josephus *J.W.* 6.5.3 §301). Both were "arrested" by the authority of Jewish (Horsley, 451)—not Roman—leaders (*syllambanei:* Mk 14:48; Jn 18:12; Josephus *J.W.* 6.5.3 §302). Both were beaten by the Jewish authorities (*paiein:* Mt 26:68; Mk 14:65; Josephus *J.W.* 6.5.3 §302). Both were handed over to the Roman governor (*ēgagon auton epi ton Pilato*: Lk 23:1; *anagousin . . . epi ton . . . eparcho:* Josephus *J.W.* 6.5.3 §303). Both were interrogated by the Roman governor (*eperōta:* Mk 15:4; Josephus *J.W.* 6.5.3 §305). Both refused to answer the governor (*ouden apokrinesthai:* Mk 15:5; Josephus *J.W.* 6.5.3 §305). Both were scourged by the governor (*mastigoun/masti:* Jn 19:1; Josephus *J.W.* 6.5.3 §304). Pilate apparently offered to release Jesus of Nazareth but did not; Albinus did release Jesus son of Ananias (*apolyein:* Mk 15:9; Josephus *J.W.* 6.5.3 §305).

The experience of Jesus ben Ananias provides independent corroboration for the juridical process described in the NT Gospels. It also reveals how little tolerated were appeals to Jeremiah 7 and talk of judgment upon the temple. The initial reaction of Jewish and Roman authorities to Jesus of Nazareth is scarcely different from their reaction to Jesus son of Ananias. Had Albinus found the son of Ananias sane and dangerous, in all probability he would have had him executed as well. But in the case of Jesus of Nazareth, who entertained *messianic ideas and spoke of a new kingdom, who had a following, who challenged the polity of the chief priests and who evidently was found sane and dangerous, execution was deemed expedient.

See also DESTRUCTION OF JERUSALEM; TEMPLE, JEWISH.

BIBLIOGRAPHY. C. A. Evans, "Jesus and the 'Cave of Robbers': Toward a Jewish Context for the Temple Action," *BBR* 3 (1993) 93-110; R. A. Horsley, "'Like One of the Prophets of Old': Two Types of Popular Prophets at the Time of Jesus," *CBQ* 47 (1985) 435-63; R. A. Horsley and J. S. Hanson, *Bandits, Prophets and Messiahs: Popular Movements at the Time of Jesus* (NVBS; Minneapolis: Winston, 1985; repr. San Francisco: Harper & Row, 1988) 172-87.

C. A. Evans

JEWISH COMMUNITIES IN ASIA MINOR

By the NT period, there were numerous Jewish communities in *Asia Minor that testify to the diversity and strength of this part of the Jewish *Diaspora. We have evidence for Jewish communities in more than fifty places in Asia Minor, and doubtless there were many more. Some of these communities seem to have thrived, while others were small. Yet many were at home in Asia Minor while still exhibiting a strong Jewish identity. These communities provide significant evidence concerning Jewish identity, the importance of the synagogue, the place of Godfearers, the position of women in the community, the interaction between the community and the wider city and relations with Christians. Given the early and significant growth of Christian communities in Asia Minor, the literature of the NT that is probably associated with Asia Minor in some way (John, Galatians, Ephesians, Colossians, the Pastoral Epistles, 1 Peter, the Johannine epistles and Revelation) and that Jewish communities were a significant feature of the context of early Christianity, our understanding of the NT will be enriched by a greater understanding of these Jewish communities in Asia Minor.

1. Sources
2. The Beginnings and Extent of Jewish Settlement in Asia Minor
3. Synagogue Buildings in Sardis and Priene
4. Facets of Jewish Identity
5. Other Facets of the Life of the Jewish Communities
6. Conclusions

1. Sources.

Our main sources of evidence for Jewish communities in Asia Minor are literary, archaeological and epigraphic. *Sibylline Oracles* 1—2, written around the turn of the era, is the only literary document to be preserved whose provenance can be assigned to a Jew from Asia Minor. Other literary texts also provide evidence, particularly *Josephus, *Philo, Greco-Roman authors such as *Cicero and Strabo, the NT and early Christian writers such as Ignatius, Justin Martyr, Melito and the *Martyrdom of Polycarp*. Synagogue buildings have also been discovered in Sardis and Priene, and we have more than 135 Jewish *inscriptions from Asia Minor. Seven of these are in Hebrew, but the vast majority are in Greek and are grave epitaphs or concern donations to synagogues, although in some cases we cannot be certain of their Jewish provenance. This evidence is limited and often problematic, and much of it comes from after the first century A.D. The matters that are dealt with here are those for which we have the most significant evidence.

2. The Beginnings and Extent of Jewish Settlement in Asia Minor.

The earliest probably reliable evidence of Jewish settlement in Asia Minor comes from Josephus, who informs us that Antiochus III transferred two thousand Jewish families from Mesopotamia and Babylonia to Lydia and Phrygia as military settlers sometime between 210 and 205 B.C. (Josephus *Ant.* 12.3.4 §§147-53). These Jews were settled on favorable terms, such as being allowed to use their own laws, which probably gave these new communities an opportunity to become well established.

First Maccabees 15:16-23 may indicate that by 139-138 B.C. Jews lived in the kingdom, cities and areas listed in Asia Minor, but this is disputed. We have evidence for a Jewish community in Pergamum between 139 and 95 B.C. from a decree of the city cited by Josephus (Josephus *Ant.* 14.10.22 §§247-55). Shortly after 88 B.C. Mithridates seized a huge amount of money on Cos; Josephus claimed the money had been deposited there for safe keeping by Asian Jews. If Josephus is correct about the origin of the money, then the Jewish communities in Asia had by this time accumulated significant financial resources (Josephus *Ant.* 14.7.2 §§110-14). In *Pro Flacco* 28.66-69, Cicero writes that in 62 B.C. the Roman governor Flaccus seized the Jewish *temple tax from Apamea, Adramyttium, Laodicea and Pergamum; in some cases the amounts were considerable. Josephus and Philo also preserve some generally authentic documents that provide evidence for a number of Jewish communities in Asia Minor. These were written by emperors, Roman administrators (*see* Roman Administration) or the cities themselves and are generally to be dated from 49 B.C. to A.D. 2/3 (Josephus *Ant.* 14.10.1-26 §§185-267; 16.6.1-8 §§160-78; Philo *Leg. Gai.* 315; cf. Josephus *Ant.* 16.2.3-5 §§27-61). They show that there were Jewish communities in *Ephesus, Halicarnassus, Laodicea, Miletus, Sardis and Tralles (cf. Philo *Leg. Gai.* 245, 281-82). A speech by Nicholas of Damascus shows some Jews in Ionia had a reputation for prosperity (Josephus *Ant.* 16.2.4 §§31-57; see Barclay, 268-69).

From the NT we have information about Jewish communities in Pisidian *Antioch, Iconium, Ephesus, Smyrna, Philadelphia and perhaps Lystra (Acts 13—14; 16:1-5; 18:19—19:41; Rev 2:9; 3:9), and Acts 2:9-10 and 6:9-15 indicate that Jews lived in Cappadocia, Pontus, Asia, Phrygia, Pamphylia and Cilicia. From some passages written by Ignatius early in the second century, we can probably infer the existence of Jewish communities in the vicinity of Philadelphia and Magnesia ad Maeander and their influence on local Christians (Ign. *Phld.* 6.1-2; 8.2; Ign. *Magn.* 8.1; 9.1-2; 10.1-3). Passages in the *Martyrdom of Polycarp* and the *Martyrdom of Pionius* give evidence for the Jewish community in Smyrna in the second and third centuries A.D.

Synagogues have been discovered in Sardis

and Priene, and inscriptions often provide us with evidence for communities about which the literary sources are silent. We have particularly significant inscriptional evidence from Acmonia, Apamea, Aphrodisias, Corycus, Hierapolis and Sardis.

P. W. van der Horst (166-67) estimates that about one million Jews lived in Asia Minor in the first century A.D., and although this is only an estimate, it may be compared with the general estimate of the total Jewish population of the Diaspora at this time of five to six million.

3. Synagogue Buildings in Sardis and Priene. Josephus preserved three decrees concerning the Jewish community in Sardis that suggest that in the first century B.C. the community was well established and had some autonomy and its own building (Josephus *Ant.* 14.10.17 §235; 14.10.24 §§259-61; 16.6.6 §171). In 1962 the largest synagogue building extant from antiquity was discovered in Sardis. It was an integral part of the bath-gymnasium complex, which occupied a central position on a major thoroughfare. The building was begun in the late second century A.D. and originally served as a Roman civil basilica. Around A.D. 270 it was remodeled and probably became a synagogue. We do not know exactly when or how the Jewish community acquired this notable building. Further remodeling was done by the Jewish community between A.D. 320 and 380. An atrium-like forecourt, colonnaded on all four sides and with a central fountain, led into the main hall, which was 59 x 18 meters and could accommodate more than one thousand people. The hall contained two shrines, which were probably used for the *Torah and for a menorah, a large apse lined with semicircular benches and a large marble table flanked by Lydian stone lions in reuse. Elaborate mosaics covered the floor, and the walls were decorated with marble revetments. The overall effect of the building must have been impressive. Despite the growing strength of Christianity in Sardis, the community continued to use the synagogue until the destruction of the city in A.D. 616. This shows the enduring vitality of the Jewish community.

The building differs considerably from other synagogues. Its style has been determined by the building's previous history, by local architectural idioms and by the local community. The building contained more than eighty inscriptions, some in Hebrew, but the vast majority in Greek, which mainly concern donations and date from the fourth century A.D. and later. These inscriptions and the building itself reveal a large, prosperous and influential Jewish community that had considerable social status and was active in civic and political affairs. The community seems to have been integrated into the economic, social and political life of Sardis to an unusual degree. Yet the strength of the Jewish identity of this community is also clear from the building itself. We can also note that Melito, the bishop of Sardis in the latter part of the second century, was strongly polemical toward Israel in his *Peri Pascha* (*see DLNTD,* Melito of Sardis). This work can be seen in part as a reaction to the Jewish community in the city.

The only other synagogue that has been discovered in Asia Minor is a remodeled house at Priene, probably to be dated to the third century A.D. A small forecourt led into the main room, which was 10 x 14 meters. The main features in the otherwise plain room were a bench and a Torah niche in the Jerusalem-facing wall. The contrast between this building and the Sardis synagogue is striking. The two buildings show the diversity of Judaism in Asia Minor and also indicate that the local history of the community and local factors had a formative influence on Jewish communities. Early in the twentieth century von Gerkan identified a small building in Miletus as a synagogue, but positive evidence that it was ever a synagogue is lacking.

4. Facets of Jewish Identity. Factors that enabled Diaspora Jewish communities to retain their identity include ethnicity, the life of the local Jewish community, links with Jerusalem and other Diaspora communities, the Torah and key Jewish practices and beliefs such as worship of the one God of Israel, dietary laws, circumcision and *sabbath observance (see Barclay, 399-444). Although our evidence is limited, we can suggest that many of these key facets of Jewish identity were important for the communities in Asia Minor.

Jews in Asia Minor regarded themselves as belonging to a "people" or a "race," and this was also recognized by their cities and by the Romans in their documents about Jewish communities (see, e.g., Josephus *Ant.* 14.10.24 §§259-61; cf. Acts 16:1-3 for one example of exogamy). The importance of the local Jewish community for the preservation of identity is clear, for example, from the fact that communities petitioned the Roman authorities for the right to assemble and to govern their own communal life (Josephus *Ant.* 14.10.8 §§213-16). Synagogue buildings, *festivals (e.g., Josephus *Ant.* 14.10.23 §§256-58; *CIJ* 777) and sabbath gatherings also played a part in fostering community life.

Links were maintained by Jews in Asia Minor with Jerusalem. Communities in Asia Minor seem to have faithfully paid the annual temple tax to Jerusalem; on one occasion some Jewish communities were willing to defy Roman law in order to obey their own law on this matter (Cicero *Flac.* 28.66-69), thus showing the significance of the temple and its worship and of Jerusalem to these communities (see also Josephus *Ant.* 16.6.4 §§167-68). Other evidence also points to the significant links between Jewish communities in Judea and Asia Minor (e.g., Josephus *Ant.* 14.10.20 §§241-42; cf. Acts 2:9-11).

The Torah was vital for Jewish identity in Asia Minor. The importance of the law and the temple is shown by the opposition of Jews from Asia and Cilicia, as well as elsewhere, to Stephen (*see DLNTD,* Stephen) when they thought he was attacking the temple and the unalterable nature of the law (Acts 6:9-15). Jews in Asia Minor almost certainly opposed Paul (Acts 13:45, 50; 14:2-5, 19) because he did not require Gentiles to come under the law (cf. Gal 5:11; 6:12), showing the significance of the law for the Jews who opposed him (cf. Acts 21:27-29). A number of Jewish epitaphs contain grave curses (*see* Burial Practices: Jewish; Art and Architecture: Jewish) that often draw on or allude to passages in the *Septuagint. Thus, a group of third-century A.D. inscriptions from Acmonia speak of the curses that "are written in Deuteronomy," which refers to Deuteronomy 27—29, and others speak of "the sickle of the curse," referring to Zechariah 5:1-5 (LXX, although this inscription could perhaps be Christian; see Trebilco, 60-76). These inscriptions suggest that the Scriptures functioned as an authority and guide for these communities. Further, at Aphrodisias in the early third century A.D. there was a Jewish group of "students [or disciples or sages] of the law," which shows the importance of study of the law for a group of Jews there. In both the Sardis and Priene synagogues, provision for the Law were significant features.

We have evidence that key Jewish practices and beliefs were important for the identity of the Jewish communities in Asia Minor. Worship of the one God of Israel was a feature of these communities (Josephus *Ant.* 12.3.2 §126). Further, there is no clear evidence that these Jewish communities were syncretistic, as has sometimes been suggested, and the link that earlier scholars saw between the Sabazios cult and Jewish communities is unfounded (see Trebilco, 127-44). The importance of the sabbath (Josephus *Ant.* 14.10.24 §§259-61), food laws (Josephus *Ant.* 14.10.12 §§225-27) and of following their "ancestral tradition" (Josephus *Ant.* 14.10.25 §§262-64) for Jews in Asia Minor is shown by the fact that Jews sought permission from the Roman authorities with regard to these matters. Jews at times sought to gain exemptions from military service and from other activities that would make observance of the Jewish law impossible (Josephus *Ant.* 14.10.11-12 §§223-27), showing their commitment to Jewish practices.

Clear evidence for the retention of Jewish identity by these communities begins in the first century B.C. and continues through the fourth century A.D. and later. Thus these communities clearly understood themselves as being Jewish. We can note that we lack clear evidence that Jewish communities in Asia Minor knew or followed *rabbinic teaching, which in any case was not the normative form of Judaism in this period.

5. Other Facets of the Life of the Jewish Communities.

5.1. Women Leaders in Jewish Communities. Some inscriptions tell us about women leaders of Jewish communities. In the second or third century A.D. Rufina was *archisynagōgos,* or ruler of the synagogue, in Smyrna, and in the fourth century or later Theopempte held the same office in Myndos. The *archisynagōgos* was a leading official who had a role in making arrangements for the services of the synagogue (Acts 13:15) and was often a wealthy person of influence and standing in the community, was a *benefactor or *patron (see Rajak in Lieu, North and Rajak, 22-24). Although some scholars have argued that a woman held this title in an honorary sense, there is no evidence for this, and it seems most likely that they actively fulfilled the office.

In Aphrodisias in the early third century A.D. a person named Jael, who was probably a woman (although some argue the name is here used of a man), held the title of *prostatēs,* which means Jael was either president or patron of a group. At Phocaea in Ionia in the third century, Tation built a synagogue for the community and was given a golden crown and the privilege of sitting in the seat of honor. We also know of nineteen women who made other donations to synagogues, either by themselves or jointly with their husbands. Thus women had a significant degree of involvement and leadership in some of the Jewish communities in Asia Minor (see Trebilco, 104-13). One reason for this was probably the prominence of women as benefactors and leaders in social and political life in Asia Minor in general. Thus the Jewish communities were probably influenced by their environment in their openness to the leadership of women.

5.2. Godfearers. A recently discovered inscription to be dated early in third century A.D. from Aphrodisias lists, along with a number of Jews (as is evident from many of their names), fifty-four Gentiles who are called *theosebis,* or "pious" (see Reynolds and Tannenbaum). Although some scholars argue that the title here means the Gentiles concerned have simply expressed their support for the Jews as fellow townspeople, it seems much more likely that the term indicates that these Gentiles were associated in some formal way with the Jewish community, without being proselytes. They seem to come into the category of Godfearers, that is, Gentiles who could be formally associated with the Jewish community, were involved in at least some facets of synagogue life and adopted some Jewish practices without becoming proselytes who joined the community (see Trebilco, 145-66).

Other inscriptions from Asia Minor in which there is a strong probability that *theosebēs* designates a Godfearer come from Tralles, Sardis and Miletus, and Godfearers are most likely mentioned in Asia Minor in Acts 13:16, 26, 50; 14:1, although Luke uses different terms (see also Josephus *Ant.* 14.7.2 §110). Although Diaspora Jews in general do not seem to have been involved in an organized, active mission to convert Gentiles (see Goodman in Lieu, North and Rajak, 53-78), they do seem to have welcomed Gentiles who were attracted to the Jewish com-munity, either as Godfearers or proselytes, and this seems to have occurred most notably in Asia Minor. The existence of Godfearers points to the attractiveness to Gentiles of some Jewish communities in Asia Minor and the openness of Jews to the involvement of Gentiles in their communities.

5.3. Jewish Communities in the Greek City in Asia Minor. We have no clear evidence that Jews in Asia Minor possessed *citizenship as a body in any Greek city. Josephus's statements that suggest they did have citizenship (e.g., Josephus *Ant.* 12.3.1 §119; 12.3.2 §§125-26; 16.6.1 §160; *Ag. Ap.* 2.4 §§37-39) are historically dubious or ambiguous (see Safrai and Stern, 440-81). However, some individuals did obtain citizenship in their cities (e.g., Paul [Acts 21:39]; Trebilco, 172). Some Jews in Asia Minor were also Roman citizens, "sufficiently many to make it worthwhile to issue special directives about them" (Barclay, 271; see Josephus *Ant.* 14.10.13-19 §§228-40). Jews in Asia Minor, as elsewhere, generally organized themselves into communities, although the constitutional position of these communities varied from place to place and over time. The position of the Jewish community within any city probably depended on local factors such as when, how, and for what purpose the Jewish community became established in that locality. Generally, the position of the Jews in a city is best compared with that of other associations of immigrants who lived as foreign people in a city. The form of communal life probably varied from place to place, as is shown by the variety of terms used to express the notion of community, including the terms "the Jews," "the people," *synodos, katoikia,* "the *ethnos*" and "the *synagōgē*."

The documents preserved by Josephus and Philo concerning Jews in Asia Minor, to be dated from 49 B.C. to A.D. 2/3 (Josephus *Ant.* 12.3.2 §§125-28; 14.10.1-26 §§185-267; 16.2.3-5 §§27-61; 16.6.1-8 §§160-78; Philo *Leg. Gai.* 315) reveal that the Jewish communities in view experienced a significant degree of ongoing hostility from the cities in which they lived during this period, concerning matters such as synagogue assembly, the temple tax and observing the sabbath. At least three factors seem to have caused such hostility (see Barclay, 270-77). First, that prosperous Jewish communities (see Josephus *Ant.* 16.2.3-4 §§28-41) wished to export the temple tax to Jerusalem at times when cities in the province of Asia were experiencing severe economic problems led to hostility. Second, hostility grew from a lack of tolerance on the part of the city toward communities that were distinctive and did not worship pagan gods and so were seen as unpatriotic. Third, that, for example, sabbath observance by Jews became an issue suggests that some Jewish communities were a significant group within the city, with some members being of social and economic importance. A city can ignore or coerce small and insignificant communities, but "one senses the presence of Jews sufficiently prominent in city life for it to be exceptionally awkward when they refuse to attend court or do business on the Sabbath" (Barclay, 271), and this led to hostility. Yet the Jewish communities concerned were also well organized and sufficiently well connected to have been able to lobby the Roman authorities, who granted them various rights and privileges that enabled them to live according to their own laws.

However, we have no evidence for hostility after A.D. 2, and the marked improvement of social and economic conditions in Asia during the Augustan era may have eased the pressure against Jewish communities from their cities. Further, positive evidence for good relations begins in the mid-first century A.D. (Julia Severa's benefaction and the evidence from Acts; see below) and continues through the end of the third century and shows a marked degree of coherence and consistency. We should also note that Jewish communities in Asia Minor did not support the Jews of Palestine in the war of A.D. 66-70 or in the Bar Kokhba war of A.D. 132-135 (*see* Jewish Wars with Rome). Further, the Diaspora revolt of A.D. 115-117 against the local authorities and Rome did not occur, as far as we know, in Asia Minor. We can suggest that the hostility experienced by the Jewish communities in the first century B.C. was confined to that period and that after that time Jewish communities in Asia Minor lived peaceably and interacted positively with their wider communities, which was one factor that enabled them to flourish. In contrast to the situation in Palestine and Jewish communities in Egypt, Cyrenaica and Cyprus, the situation in Asia Minor seems to have been marked by peace and respect rather than ongoing tension and hostility. The reduction in hostility in Asia Minor probably advanced the integration and social assimilation of Asian Jews into the life of their cities. We will now review the evidence for good relations.

Some Jews and some Jewish communities took an active part in city life, into which they were integrated and socially assimilated to quite some degree. As we have noted, J. M. G. Barclay (271-78) argues that in the first century B.C. one of the reasons that Jews experienced hostility from their cities was because they were a significant group within the city, with some members being socially and economically prominent. The opposition Jews encountered thus testifies to the significance and influence of the Jewish communities in their cities, even in the first century B.C. Barclay (276-77) suggests: "The controversies which arose in these Asian cities reflect the significant integration of such Jews into civic life: it is as business-partners, litigants, market-users, even potential 'liturgists' that the Jews are noticed and their peculiarities resented."

We also know of Jews from the third century A.D. onward who held significant offices, such as being presiding officer of the city council, a member of the governing committee of the city council, the controller of the market, city councilor, official public doctor and controller of the weight of money in Acmonia, Corycos, Ephesus, Hypaepa, Sardis and Side (e.g., *CII* 745, 748, 770; Trebilco, 37-103). We note also that the prominent position of the Sardis synagogue and its inscriptions suggest relations between the city and the Jews were harmonious and that the community was a respected element in the city. Since the epigraphic record always gives us only a partial picture, we can suggest that there were many more Jews similarly involved in the civic and political affairs of their cities.

There is also evidence of Jews being what may be called good residents who participated in the civic and cultural life of their cities. In 12 B.C. Jews of Asia passed a resolution in honor of the emperor Augustus (Josephus *Ant.* 16.6.2 §165; *see* Roman Emperors), thus showing themselves to be his loyal supporters. At Acmonia some Jews made a donation to the city and in doing so called Acmonia their *patris,* or home city, which shows both their involvement in the life of the city and a strong sense of "at homeness." In Miletus, probably in the second century A.D., some Jews had the privilege of good reserved seats in the city's *theater, which suggests that they were prominent members of the theater audiences and regularly attended this center of the social and cultural life of the city. At Iasos and Hypaepa some Jews were involved in the *gymnasium (Trebilco, 173-77).

A unique series of *coins minted in Apamea from the end of the second century A.D. suggest the local Jewish community was influential in the city. These coins portray Noah, his wife and the ark and are the only known coins that portray a biblical scene. They suggest that the city of Apamea accepted the Jewish flood story as its own; the Jewish community seems to have been influential and respected in the city and able to convince the city of the validity of its own traditions (Trebilco, 86-95). *Sibylline Oracles* 1.261-67 also locates the place where the ark landed after the flood as Apamea.

Further evidence of relations with the wider society is provided by the fact that important non-Jews acted as patrons of or were involved in or influenced by Jewish communities. In Acmonia in the mid-first century A.D. the Gentile Julia Severa, who belonged to a nexus of leading families, built a synagogue for the Jewish community. She can be seen as a Gentile patron of the Jewish community, and this fact shows that they had friends in the highest social circles. According to Acts, some Jewish communities were able to stir up opposition to Christian preaching among Gentiles, including some in high places, which suggests the Jewish communities concerned had influential contacts in their city (Acts 13:50; 14:2, 5, 19). The Godfearers mentioned in Acts might suggest that at this time the Jews were a respected group in their cities (Acts 13:16, 48-50; 14:1). At Aphrodisias nine Godfearers were city council members and thus had significant social standing, which suggests that the Jewish community was a respected and influential group. These nine Gentile Godfearers were involved in the synagogue while also holding important positions in the city. That there were Godfearers in some synagogues also suggests that these communities had not withdrawn into themselves but were open to Gentiles attending the synagogue.

Another area that points to strong relationships between Jewish communities and the wider society is provided by the number of ways in which Jewish communities were influenced by the customs of their local city. In a number of areas we can see that Jews in Asia Minor did certain things or adopted a particular practice because of the influence of their environment. These include the way *benefactors were honored, the way graves were decorated, the form of some grave curses, the formation and practices of a burial society, some of the symbolism used in the Sardis synagogue and openness to the leadership of women. Taken with the evidence of involvement in city life, these points suggest the Jewish communities had strong links with the wider society in which they lived.

We conclude that in Asia Minor Jewish communities were not isolated, insular groups but rather interacted regularly with Gentiles and were involved to a significant degree in city life. Some Jewish communities in Asia Minor were influential and respected in their cities, where they were very much at home and made a significant social contribution. They were part of the social networks of the city and shared in many of the characteristics of everyday life. This seems to have occurred more in Asia Minor than in most other Mediterranean centers where Jews lived. It seems also that local factors were a strong formative influence on these Jewish communities. Yet the evidence suggests the Jewish communities generally did not abandon an active attention to Jewish tradition or compromise their Jewish identity. Proximity with pagan neighbors both sprang from and led to clarity in the definition of Judaism and to an inner self-assurance and not to syncretism or assimilation to paganism. It was as Jews that they were part of the life of the city.

We can note that one consequence of the degree of Jewish communities' integration in and interaction with their cities is that it is sometimes difficult to determine if an inscription is Jewish or not, since Jews and non-Jews could share a great deal in common, including grave formulas that have been used to identify inscriptions as Jewish.

5.4. Relations with Christians. Some members of Jewish communities in Asia Minor responded to Paul's preaching (Acts 13:43; 14:1; 18:27; 19:8-10; cf. 1 Cor 9:20), while others rejected his message and on some occasions stirred up opposition to Paul among Gentiles (e.g., Acts 13:45, 50; 14:2-5, 19; 19:9; 20:19; cf. 2 Cor 6:4-5; 11:24). Revelation 2:9 and 3:9 suggest that around A.D. 95 the Jewish communities in Smyrna and Philadelphia actively opposed Christians. In some difficult passages written early in the second century, Ignatius seems to refer to Gentile Judaizers in Philadelphia and Magnesia ad Maeander (Ign. *Phld.* 6.1-2; 8.2; Ign. *Magn.* 8.1; 9.1-2; 10.1-3). It seems likely that these Gentile Christians were tempted to go to the synagogue and adopt Jewish customs because of the influence of Jewish communities in the area. In these cases, the

Jewish communities were probably attractive to Christians and had an impact on the churches.

According to the *Martyrdom of Polycarp,* the Jews of Smyrna had a part in Polycarp's death, sometime between A.D. 156 and 167 (see *Mart. Pol.* 12.2; 13.2; 17.2—18.1) The Jews in the city may have had contacts in high places in the city and have been prepared to work with Gentiles against the Christians. The *Martyrdom of Pionius,* set in Smyrna around A.D. 250, suggests that the Jewish community in the city had a continuing interest in attracting Christians to Judaism and was involved in polemic against the Christians about Jesus and his resurrection.

6. Conclusions.

The strength and vitality of many of the Jewish communities in Asia Minor is clear from the evidence. The Sardis community, with its impressive synagogue, is perhaps the most revealing. And yet some communities, such as the community at Priene, were undoubtedly small. This underlines the diversity of the communities. Some flourished; others did not. Local factors, such as the date and conditions under which the communities were founded, the attitudes of the local cities and the size of the community were significant in determining the nature of these communities.

We have also shown that rather than forming introverted groups, these communities were at home in their local cities and interacted with the wider society. Some communities were influential and respected in their cities, and some attracted Godfearers; many were influenced by their environment. Yet in many cases there is strong evidence for the retention of Jewish identity. It was as *Jewish* communities that they were a part of the life of their cities. These communities can be seen as worthy and legitimate but distinctive heirs of OT faith.

Finally, the evidence suggests the presence of local Jewish communities was often a real factor in the life of the early Christian churches in Asia Minor, and Jewish communities often had a significant influence on the churches. Christians often formed and preserved their identity in the context of visible and attractive Jewish communities that were rival interpreters of the Jewish tradition and competitors for supporters. We can suggest that, given their significance, Jewish communities in Asia Minor were often much part of the foreground of the life of the early churches.

See also ALEXANDRIA; ASIA MINOR; DIASPORA JUDAISM; HELLENISTIC JUDAISM; JERUSALEM; PHILO; SYNAGOGUES; TAXATION, JEWISH.

BIBLIOGRAPHY. J. M. G. Barclay, *Jews in the Mediterranean Diaspora from Alexander to Trajan (323 B.C.E.—117 A.D.)* (Edinburgh: T & T Clark, 1996); B. J. Brooten, *Women Leaders in the Ancient Synagogues: Inscriptional Evidence and Background Issues* (BJS 36; Chico, CA: Scholars Press, 1982); L. H. Feldman, *Jew and Gentile in the Ancient World: Attitudes and Interactions from Alexander to Justinian* (Princeton, NJ: Princeton University Press, 1993); J. B. Frey, *Corpus Inscriptionum Judaicarum* (2 vols.; vol. 1, originally published 1936, rev. B. Lifshitz; New York: Ktav, 1975; vol. 2, Rome: Pontificio Instituto di archaeologia christiana, 1952); I. Levinskaya, *Diaspora Setting* (BAFCS 5; Grand Rapids, MI: Eerdmans, 1996); J. Lieu, J. North and T. Rajak, eds., *The Jews Among Pagans and Christians in the Roman Empire* (London: Routledge, 1992); J. A. Overman and R. S. MacLennan, *Diaspora Jews and Judaism: Essays in Honor of, and in Dialogue with, A. Thomas Kraabel* (SFSHJ 41; Atlanta: Scholars Press, 1992); J. Reynolds and R. Tannenbaum, *Jews and Godfearers at Aphrodisias* (Cambridge Philological Society Supplementary Volume 12; Cambridge: Cambridge Philological Society, 1987); L. V. Rutgers, *The Hidden Heritage of Diaspora Judaism* (CBET 20; Leuven: Peeters, 1998); S. Safrai and M. Stern, eds., *The Jewish People in the First Century* (2 vols.; CRINT 1; Assen: Van Gorcum; Philadelphia: Fortress, 1974-76); E. Schürer, *The History of the Jewish People in the Age of Jesus Christ (175 B.C.— A.D. 135),* rev. and ed. G. Vermes, F. Millar, M. Black, M. Goodman (3 vols.; Edinburgh: T & T Clark, 1973-87); A. R. Seager, et al., *The Synagogue and Its Setting* (Archaeological Exploration of Sardis, Report 4; Cambridge, MA: Harvard University Press, forthcoming); M. Stern, *Greek and Latin Authors on Jews and Judaism* (3 vols.; Jerusalem: Israel Academy of Sciences and Humanities, 1974, 1981, 1984); P. R. Trebilco, *Jewish Communities in Asia Minor* (SNTSMS 69; Cambridge: Cambridge University Press, 1991); P. W. van der Horst, *Essays on the Jewish World of Early Christianity* (NTOA 14; Freiburg: Universitätsverlag; Göttingen: Vandenhoeck & Ruprecht, 1990); J. W. van Henten and P. W. van der Horst, eds., *Studies in Early Jewish Epigraphy* (AGJU 21; Leiden: E. J. Brill, 1994).

P. R. Trebilco

JEWISH HISTORY: GREEK PERIOD

The Greek period of Jewish history extends from the conquest of *Alexander the Great until the taking of *Jerusalem by Pompey (333-63 B.C.), a period of more than two and a half centuries. This encompasses the initial conquest by Alexander and the period of his successors, the time of *Ptolemaic rule, the transfer to *Seleucid rule and the *Maccabean revolt and the *Hasmonean kingdom. Each of these periods will be treated separately, since the sources and characteristics are often different. Each section will begin with a discussion of historical sources and the problems involved in trying to reconstruct a history of the period.

1. Alexander and the Diadochi
2. The Ptolemaic Period
3. Seleucid Rule and the Hasmonean Kingdom

1. Alexander and the Diadochi.

1.1. Sources. The first half century of Greek rule is well documented by the historians, mainly Arrian of Alexander, and by the writers about the wars of the successors (Gk *diadochoi,* usually given in its Latin form as *Diadochi), mainly Diodorus Siculus. Our knowledge of the Jews, however, has to be inferred from a few miscellaneous pieces of data whose interpretation is often uncertain. *Josephus gives us some bits of information. The most extensive is the legend that Alexander visited Jerusalem and bowed to the high priest (Josephus *Ant.* 11.8.1-6 §§304-45). Modern scholars have been practically unanimous in rejecting this as fictional. There was not time between the siege of Tyre and the siege of Gaza for such an expedition to Jerusalem; in any case, other historians would have mentioned it since they had no hesitation in recording Alexander's visits to shrines or his other religious undertakings.

Apart from this story Josephus gives us only a few quotes (Josephus *Ag. Ap.* 1.22 §§183-204). One of these is from Agartharchides of Cnidus and states that at some point during the fighting, Ptolemy I was allowed to enter Jerusalem because the Jews would not fight on the sabbath. No date is given, but if this is historically accurate, this was probably the period 315 to 301 B.C. He also claims to quote Hecateus of Abdera to the effect that the high priest Hezekiah (Ezekias in Greek) was allowed by Ptolemy to migrate to Egypt with a great many Jews who settled there. This was after the battle of Gaza in 312 B.C. The authenticity of Josephus's quotations of Hecateus are suspect and probably come from a Jewish writer around 100 (Bar-Kochva).

1.2. Historical Reconstruction. On the whole, all we can do is make some intelligent guesses about the Jews through this period. Alexander crossed into Asia Minor in 334. The next year he defeated Darius III at Issus and then laid siege to Tyre. After taking Tyre he moved rapidly south along the coast, taking Gaza and reaching Egypt, where he wintered. It is reasonable that representatives of the Jewish state met Alexander or his lieutenants and gave their formal submission while he was on his way to Egypt, as would have been normal for a new conqueror, though the story of Alexander's visit to Jerusalem after the siege of Tyre can be considered only legendary in the light of present evidence. The next year Samaria revolted and was destroyed, bringing Greek troops into central Palestine, but they would not necessarily have gone into Judah. Alexander himself continued his conquests for another several years, possibly with Jewish recruits among his soldiers (Josephus *Ag. Ap.* 1.22 §§192, 201-4). Darius III was finally defeated and killed in 331, but Alexander continued to march east, reaching northern India; however, his soldiers had had enough, and he reluctantly returned to Babylonia to consolidate his empire. There he died in 323 B.C.

For the next forty years the *Diadochi fought among themselves for control of Alexander's empire, eventually splitting it three ways: Ptolemy got Egypt, Palestine and southern Syria; Seleucus controlled most of Asia Minor, northern Syria, Mesopotamia and the rest of the eastern empire; the Antigonids held mainland Greece, Thrace and some other territory. Judah may well have been affected by the march of armies through Palestine during this time, though we hear of little specific. The story that Ptolemy I took Jerusalem may be true, but Josephus gives no context or explanation why this should have happened. What we do know is that in 301 B.C. Ptolemy took Palestine and, despite legal claims by the Seleucids, held the territory for the next century. The settlement of Jews in Egypt (apart from those at Elephantine) may have begun at this time, though we have no precise information.

2. The Ptolemaic Period.

2.1. Sources. In some ways the Ptolemaic period is almost as unknown as the Persian period. We know little about the day-to-day events and life of the Jewish people. What we do have are three invaluable sources, though the evaluation of the last one is not an easy task. First is the account of Hecateus of Abdera, a Greek writer about 300 B.C., who produced a work on the Egyptians (his work is now lost but a portion is quoted in Diodorus Siculus *Bib. Hist.* 40.3). In it he mentions the Jews in Palestine in a positive way and briefly describes their society, giving a short glimpse of it at a crucial time. A second source is the archive of *Zenon, an agent of Apollonius the Egyptian finance minister. He took a tour of Palestine and southern Syria about 259 B.C. and continued to correspond with some of those he met for a good many years afterward. Finally, we have the Tobiad family history or romance as used by Josephus (Josephus *Ant.* 12.4.1-11 §§157-236). It contains novelistic elements that may be entertaining to readers, but it does not resolve the question of how much of it is historical. Although scholars recognize that the account has been embellished, the general view is that the story is credible in its main outline.

2.2. Historical Reconstruction. Hecateus of Abdera describes the Jewish community as it apparently was in his time. Whether he knew it directly is uncertain, but his account shows some evidence of inside knowledge and is positive in its description. It has been suggested that he used a Jewish source, possibly an oral description by priests. He says that the country was founded by *Moses, who led a group of disaffected Egyptians out of the country to Judea, where he founded the city of Jerusalem and a *temple. He asserts that the Jews have never had a king (showing that he knows nothing of the contents of Samuel and Kings) but elect the wisest of the priests to lead them. They have a law that they follow faithfully. They have no images of their God but worship the heavens. This description fits well the other sources we have for the community in Palestine in the Persian and Greek periods, showing the structure of a theocracy in which the high priest was the main leader of the people and its representative to the Greek overlords.

Apart from Hecateus, who describes the community but no historical events, we have almost no information until about 260 B.C., when Zenon comes on the scene. The Zenon papyri are invaluable because they represent genuine, original sources; their worth is mainly not for historical events but for social and economic data. Thanks to them we know much more about the social and economic situation in Egypt during this period than in many other areas. On his journey through Palestine Zenon's entourage was given *hospitality by a Tobias in the Transjordanian area. This Tobias headed a cleruchy, or military colony, and was a power on the local scene. He later sent a gift of *slaves to Apollonius (Zenon's superior) and even a gift of exotic animals to the king himself. His letters are in good Greek. Since he would have used a Greek scribe, we cannot be sure that he knew Greek himself, but he may well have.

Judging by his name and the location of his estate, Tobias was a part of an old aristocratic family, one of whose ancesters was the Tobiah opposed by Nehemiah. This inference is confirmed by the Tobiad romance. According to it the high priest Onias II refused to pay a tribute to the Ptolemaic government. Since punishment for this could have affected the province as a whole, an individual of the Tobiad family named Joseph borrowed money and paid the tribute himself. (Joseph was the nephew of the high priest, showing that the Tobiad family had intermarried with the high-priestly family.) Ptolemy II was impressed by Joseph and, according to one interpretation, even took away the financial office for Judea from the high priest and gave it to Joseph. More importantly Joseph was able to bid for and win the tax-farming rights to the whole region of Palestine and southern Syria. The Ptolemies had found that it was most efficient to put the collection of certain taxes out to tender to the highest bidder. The tax farmer agreed to pay a certain amount to the king. If he collected more tax than this, he kept it as profit; if he collected less, he had to make it up from his own resources. When Joseph secured the tax-farming rights for the region, he became an important and eventually a wealthy man.

Joseph had eight sons, the last of whom was Hyrcanus. This son turned out to be a clever and entrepreneurial individual who managed to wrestle the regional tax-farming rights from his father. This instigated a quarrel with Hyrcanus on one side and Joseph and his other sons on the other. However, the matter went deeper than business practices. Based on the general history of the period, it has been concluded that Joseph and his other sons had become pro-Seleucid, taking the view that the Seleucids would soon take over the region; Hyrcanus remained pro-Ptolemaic. Despite his astuteness, Hyrcanus was the one who miscalculated. In 200 Antiochus III defeated the armies of Ptolemy V and took over Palestine and southern Syria, territories for which the Seleucids had originally been given title a century earlier.

3. Seleucid Rule and the Hasmonean Kingdom.

3.1. Sources. Our major sources for the period from about 200 to 135 B.C. are the books of *Maccabees. First Maccabees covers mainly the period 175 to 135 B.C. and is usually taken to be the most trustworthy. Second Maccabees covers a shorter period (about 175 to 162 B.C.) and has novelistic and theological elements. For this reason, scholars have generally preferred 1 Maccabees. They are probably right in this, but 2 Maccabees gives the most detail on the period leading up to the Maccabean revolt; also the straightforwardness of 1 Maccabees is sometimes deceptive, masking the prejudices and agenda of the writer. Both books must be used critically. The book of Daniel gives brief but important information, especially in Daniel 11. Josephus quotes a decree of Antiochus III on behalf of the Jews, which looks genuine. In the *War* he gives a brief account of the Maccabean revolt to which scholars have not given much credence. In the *Antiquities,* however, he gives a close paraphrase of most of 1 Maccabees. Both the *War* and the *Antiquities* give the only detailed account of Hasmonean history and are extremely important sources for this period. The source seems to be mainly Nicolaus of Damascus, who was secretary to *Herod the Great, though the lost histories of Strabo were also used in the *Antiquities.*

3.2. Historical Reconstruction. Many Jews welcomed the new Seleucid rulers. A decree of Antiochus III (221-187 B.C.), quoted by Josephus (Josephus *Ant.* 12.3.3-4 §§138-46) and generally accepted as genuine, grants certain concessions to the Jews because they opened the gates of Jerusalem to him. There had apparently been fighting, perhaps even with pro-Ptolemaic Jews, leaving damage in Jerusalem. Antiochus gave a temporary remission of taxes to assist in paying for repairs. The one who carried out these repairs was the high priest Simon II, who was probably the son of the Onias who was uncle to Joseph Tobiad and had refused to pay the tribute to Ptolemy (Sir 50:1-21).

From all the information we have the Jews were content with the first part of Seleucid rule. Second Maccabees 3 records an incident in which Seleucus IV (187-175 B.C.) sends his financial minister to confiscate the temple treasury. The reasons for this are not clear, though one seems to be that Hyrcanus Tobiad had a large sum deposited in the temple. The exact sequence of events is also unclear, though it seems that the treasury was spared (2 Macc ascribes it to a miracle). Apart from this we hear of no incidents until the reign of Antiochus IV (175-164 B.C.). Much nonsense has been written about Antiochus IV and the Jews. The first thing to remember is that Antiochus was not a rabid Hellenizer, and he seems to have had no interest in the Jews initially. He got involved in Jewish affairs because they approached him.

When Antiochus came to the throne, the high priest was Onias III. Shortly afterward the high priest's brother Jason (Heb Jeshua) approached the king and offered to pay a certain sum to be given the office in place of his brother. Jason also paid a further sum to make Jerusalem into a Greek city *(polis).* Antiochus agreed to both these requests, and thus began what has been called the *Hellenistic reform. A good deal written on this subject is not based on a critical reading of the sources or the most recent studies.

First, it should be noted that Hellenization had been going on for more than 150 years when Antiochus IV took the throne. The Jews had been as much influenced as were any other Near Eastern peoples. That is, the upper classes would have been most affected, but the average Jew who was a peasant or laborer or craftsman saw little change in lifestyle, only in the overlord to whom taxes were paid. A few Jews obtained a Greek education (e.g., Joseph Tobiad and his sons evidently spoke Greek and seem at home in the Greek world), many more learned some Greek in order to trade or deal with the administration, but Greek did not displace the native languages of *Aramaic and *Hebrew. Much of the administration at the lower level was carried out in the native languages. The process of Hellenization was not the displacement of native culture by Greek but rather the addition of Greek to the cultural mixture that already existed. The Greek and the native coexisted for centuries in a happy partnership (*see* Hellenistic Judaism).

Second, Jason's reform was a cultural one and did not affect the religion. The books of Maccabees, especially 2 Maccabees 4, allege that *Judaism was abandoned and great sins committed. But when their bias is taken into account and the reader cuts through the rhetoric, no specific breaches of the law are named. No pagan practices were introduced, the daily *tamid* offering continued, individual sacrifices were still brought, and the cult functioned as normal. It was not in Jason's interest to interfere with the cult that was both his power base and financial support. His Hellenistic reform caused changes to the city government, introduced an institute of Greek *education (the *gymnasium) and changed the lifestyle of many citizens of Jerusalem (apparently for the better, in their view), but the practice of religion continued as before.

Third, Jason's reform was widely welcomed. Many of the inhabitants of Jerusalem became citizens, and no opposition is mentioned. Readers may have read that "the orthodox Jews were appalled" at this. Not only does this beg the question of what is orthodox, but it is also speculation. There may have been a variety of reactions to Jason's actions, but if there were negative reactions, we do not know of them. The negative view comes from the books of Maccabees, which were written decades later, after the bitter events of the Maccabean revolt.

Having taken the high priesthood, Jason was displaced by Menelaus, who offered Antiochus even more money. Unlike Jason, Menelaus does seem to have broken the law, apparently even selling off vessels from the temple. When this happened, the people of Jerusalem (i.e., the citizens of Jason's Hellenistic city) rioted and killed Menelaus's brother, who tried to quell the riot, showing that the citizens were not indifferent to religion. However, the situation was overtaken by events: Antiochus invaded Egypt in 170 B.C. and was highly successful, but the regime he established quickly collapsed, and he invaded again in 168 B.C. This time the Romans forced him to withdraw. In the meantime, Jason attacked Menelaus in Jerusalem to take back the office of high priest, and Antiochus sent an army to put down what he thought was a rebellion.

We now enter one of the most puzzling episodes of Jewish history. Not only did Antiochus suppress what he thought was a revolt, but he then went on to order the suppression of Judaism as a religion. Why this happened has not been satisfactorily explained, even though there have been many suggestions. It has even been suggested that Menelaus instigated the religious measures. Whatever the reason, the temple was desecrated with a pagan cult (called the "abomination of desolation"), and any who practiced Judaism were persecuted. The Jews rebelled. Whether the family of the Maccabees began the revolt, as alleged by the pro-Hasmonean books of Maccabees, is not certain, but they eventually took it over. In the short space of three years they managed to retake the temple and restore the cult (probably in December 165 B.C.), and Antiochus's decree against Judaism was withdrawn. At this point many Jews were content to stop fighting, but the Maccabees had now shifted their goal to national independence.

What followed was a long battle in which the Maccabees had initially only small support. Judas Maccabeus was killed in 162 B.C. His brother Jonathan took up the leadership but began to gain success only when a rival Seleucid dynasty arose, a situation that he exploited by playing one side against the other. He was given the office of high priest and other concessions but was eventually killed by trickery in 143 B.C. The third brother, Simon, now took the leadership; in the third year of his office (c. 140 B.C.) a decree was issued on behalf of the Jewish people that declared their freedom from foreign rule. This was highly symbolic, and the reality was that Seleucid claims had not been given up. Simon was assassinated, and his son John Hyrcanus I took over.

John Hyrcanus (135-104 B.C.) was quite successful, establishing the theory of Jewish independence as a fact, and he began to take over neighboring territories. Although he had only the title of high priest, he acted like a king over what was now called the Hasmonean state (after Hasmon, an ancestor of the Maccabees). His son Aristobulus I ruled only briefly (104-103 B.C.) but according to some sources took the title of king. Alexander Janneus (103-76 B.C.) expanded the Hasmonean kingdom to its largest extent but was troubled by a good deal of internal opposition, including from the *Pharisees. On his deathbed, he turned the kingdom over to his wife, Alexandra Salome (76-67 B.C.), who was dominated by the Pharisees. She made her eldest son Hyrcanus II high priest, but her younger son, Aristobulus II, rebelled. Her death left them to fight each other for the throne, which led to disastrous consequences (*see* Jewish History: Roman Period).

See also ALEXANDER THE GREAT; DIADOCHI; HASMONEANS; HELLENISM; HELLENISTIC JUDAISM; 1 & 2 MACCABEES; PTOLEMIES; SELEUCIDS AND ANTIOCHIDS.

BIBLIOGRAPHY. B. Bar-Kochva, *Judas Maccabeus: The Jewish Struggle Against the Seleucids* (Cambridge: Cambridge University Press, 1989); E. Bickerman, *The Jews in the Greek Age* (Cambridge, MA: Harvard University Press, 1988); W. D. Davies and L. Finkelstein, eds., *Cambridge History of Judaism,* 2: *The Hellenistic Age* (Cambridge: Cambridge University Press, 1989); L. L. Grabbe, "The Hellenistic City of Jerusalem," in *Jews in the Hellenistic and Roman Cities,* ed. S. Freyne (Royal Irish Academy; London: Routledge, 2000); idem, *Judaism from Cyrus to Hadrian,* 1: *Persian and Greek Periods;* 2: *Roman Period* (Minneapolis: Fortress, 1992); idem, M. Hengel, *Judaism and Hellenism* (2 vols.; Philadelphia: Fortress, 1974); E. Schürer, *The History of the Jewish People in the Age of Jesus Christ, (175 B.C.-A.D. 135)* rev. and ed. by G. Vermes F. Millar and M. Good-man (3 vols.; Edinburgh: T & T Clark, 1973-87); J. Sievers, *The Hasmoneans and Their Supporters* (SFSHJ 6; Atlanta: Scholars Press, 1990); V. A. Tcherikover, *Hellenistic Civilization and the Jews* (Philadelphia: Jewish Publication Society of America, 1959). L. L. Grabbe

JEWISH HISTORY: PERSIAN PERIOD

The Persian period is probably the most unknown period in the history of the Jews for the past three thousand years. This is for two reasons: our sources are skimpy for this period, and what sources we do have are of doubtful historical value in some cases. There are few Persian sources; thus, for much of our knowledge of chronology and political events of the Persian Empire in general we are dependent on the Greek historians. For the history of the Jews we have a few brief references in external sources. Otherwise we have to depend on the biblical material, which sometimes has little that relates to actual events and in other cases poses historical problems.

1. Extrabiblical Sources
2. Biblical Sources

1. Extrabiblical Sources.

The extrabiblical sources include the papyri left by a Jewish colony in Egypt at Elephantine. This provides valuable original material, especially in the way of legal documents and references to the colony itself, but little of it throws direct light on events in Palestine. The Wadi Daliyeh papyri are also mainly legal documents (with only two so far published), though there are references to important persons in the documents and the seal impressions. A number of *coins were issued in Judah itself and mention the name of the province (Yehud); a few mention Hezekiah the governor, and there is one with the name of Johanan the priest.

A Jewish military colony lived on the island of Elephantine in southern Egypt. It may have been founded before the fall of Jerusalem in 587 B.C., though its origins are obscure. They worshiped Yahweh but did so in their own local temple. When this was destroyed as a conspiracy of the priesthood of the local Egyptian cult, they wrote to the governor asking permission to rebuild it. They also wrote to "the high priest and his companions the priests who are in Jerusalem and to Ostan the brother of Anan and the nobles of the Jews" and "to Delaiah and Shemaiah sons of Sanballat governor of Samaria" (Porten and Yardeni, 68-71). Their letter indicates that the high priest, the other priests and the Jerusalem nobility were in charge of the community even though a Persian governor had also been appointed over the province. It also shows, in contrast to the book of Nehemiah, that Sanballat was an important official in the Persian local government. Interestingly, the Jerusalem establishment did not reply, perhaps because they were opposed to the Elephantine temple. The only record of an answer is a memorandum jointly from Bagohi and Delaiah, permitting the temple to be rebuilt and resume some offerings but not those of blood *sacrifice (Porten and Yardeni, 76-77).

For the last century of Persian rule, we have almost nothing relating to Jerusalem. The Wadi Daliyeh papyri seem to have been left by refugees from Samaria fleeing from *Alexander the Great's soldiers. These relate to the last days of Persian rule but are mainly legal material, concern only Samaria and have been only partially published. They do show that a second Sanballat was governor of Samaria around the middle of the fourth century. It has been suggested that in about 350 B.C. Judah was involved in a widespread rebellion against Persian rule known as the Tennes rebellion; however, the arguments for this are not well founded (Grainger, 24-31; Grabbe 1992, 99-100).

2. Biblical Sources.

Of the biblical sources, the most important are the prophets Haggai and Zechariah 1—8 and the books of Ezra and Nehemiah. Chronicles are often dated to the Persian period (though the Greek period seems more likely), as are a number of other books or sections of books such as Isaiah 56—66, Job, Jonah, Malachi, and possibly Esther, Ruth and the Song of Songs. Many scholars think the framework parts of Haggai and Zechariah may have been written much later, but in any case each is set to a narrow period of time around 520 B.C. It is widely accepted that at the core of Nehemiah is a writing of Nehemiah himself (the Nehemiah Memoir/Memorial, found mainly in Neh 1—2, 4—6 and portions of 12; whether 13 belongs is debated). The extent of historicity in Ezra is fiercely debated at the moment, and many find little or nothing reliable in the book.

Although the decree of Cyrus (Ezra 1:1-4) is widely regarded as an invention of the editor, most scholars think there was a return of some Jews to Palestine fairly soon after Cyrus took Babylon in 539 B.C. This seems to have been led by Sheshbazzar, who may have been appointed governor of the province and who supposedly laid the foundations for rebuilding the temple (Ezra 5:14-16). Yet we are told that almost twenty years later nothing had happened (Hag 1:1-13). Ezra 3 credits Joshua and Zerubbabel with the rebuilding and says nothing about any building work having been done by Sheshbazzar. Ezra 4—6 is also a narrative about the opposition of unspecified enemies. A peculiar feature is the use of letters from the time of Artaxerxes, at least three quarters of a century later, to stop the building work in the time of Darius. Supposedly the temple was finished within four years and completed in the fifth year of king Darius's reign. However, it is doubtful that sufficient resources were available to rebuild it in so short a time.

The books of Haggai and Zechariah give a somewhat different picture. They say nothing of opposition from foreigners but suggest that the people themselves are to blame. They also show local materials being used rather than imported wood from Lebanon and the like (Hag 1:8 vs. Ezra 3:7). The one fact that seems reasonably secure is that the temple was rebuilt in the early Persian period.

One particular feature of Ezra is puzzling and looks like an attempt to blacken the descendants of the Jews who had remained in the land. In a number of places, but especially Ezra 4—6, the book speaks of enemies who are the "people[s] of the land[s]." The "peoples of the land" is a term well known and widely in use in later Judaism, but it always has Jews as its object (Oppenheimer). But Ezra does not seem to recognize anyone as legitimate who is not a part of the returnee community. Yet we know a large number of Jews—probably the majority—were left in the land by the Babylonians. Their descendants continued to live in the land and to bear the name Jews (Barstad). For some reason, the writer of Ezra does not want them to be a part of the Jewish community in Palestine.

The figure of Ezra becomes harder to pin down the closer one looks (Grabbe 1998a, esp. chap. 6). Nehemiah knows nothing of him even though he was supposed to be there at the same time. He appears to be a high priest, but he does not preside over the temple. He comes across as a governor—even a satrap—but when a crisis arises, he can only mourn and pray while others take action. He comes to Jerusalem with a law that was already being observed; with priests and Levites, when there were already plenty there; and temple vessels and great treasure for the temple, when it had been functioning there for six decades. Some scholars have tried to resolve the problem by dating Ezra to 398 B.C. (the seventh year of Artaxerxes II), but the basic enigma remains.

Nehemiah is different, however, since it looks as if a genuine writing of Nehemiah lies at the core of the book. Like Sheshbazzar and Zerubbabel before him, he was governor of the province. He seems to have been a difficult figure to work with. Many of the local people saw no reason why they should cut their ties with such figures as Tobiah, who was a Jew from an old, aristocratic family. Two books that are frequently dated to the Persian period take a rather different point of view from Nehemiah's: Jonah argues for tolerance toward Gentiles, and Ruth traces David's own ancestry to a Moabite. These and other sources from the next couple of centuries indicate that Nehemiah's vision of an isolated community refusing to have anything to do with the surrounding peoples did not prevail (Grabbe 1998b, though after the fall of Jerusalem in A.D. 70, this attitude helped to preserve the Jewish community from assimilation).

Nehemiah's mission may be partially explained in the light of the Egyptian revolts of 460 to 456 B.C. (Hoglund). From the archaeological evidence for Persian fortifications constructed all over the eastern Mediterranean seaboard at this time and from other data, it is inferred that the Persians were concerned about threats from a Greek-led coalition. According to this interpretation, Nehemiah's mission was to fortify Jerusalem to maintain Persian interests and policy, though the biblical writers interpreted events from their own theological perspective.

See also JEWISH HISTORY: GREEK PERIOD; JEWISH HISTORY: ROMAN PERIOD.

BIBLIOGRAPHY. P. R. Ackroyd, *Exile and Restoration* (Philadelphia: Westminster, 1968); H. M. Barstad, *The Myth of the Empty Land: A Study in the History and Archaeology of Judah During the "Exilic" Period* (SO 28; Oslo and Cambridge, MA: Scandinavian University Press, 1996); W. D. Davies and L. Finkelstein, eds., *Cambridge History of Judaism,* 1: *The Persian Period* (Cambridge: Cambridge University Press, 1984); I. Gershevitch, ed., *Cambridge History of Iran,* 2: *The Median and Achaemenian Periods* (Cambridge: Cambridge University Press, 1985); L. L. Grabbe, *Ezra-Nehemiah* (Readings; New York: Routledge, 1998a); idem, *Judaism from Cyrus to Hadrian,* 1: *Persian and Greek Periods;* 2: *Roman Period* (Minneapolis: Fortress, 1992); idem, "Triumph of the Pious or Failure of the Xenophobes? The Ezra/Nehemiah Reforms and Their *Nachgeschichte,*" in *Studies in Jewish Local Patriotism and Self-Identification in the Greco-Roman Period,* ed. S. Jones and S. Pearce (JSPSup 31; Sheffield: Sheffield Academic Press, 1998b) 50-65; J. D. Grainger, *Hellenistic Phoenicia* (Oxford: Clarendon Press, 1991); K. G. Hoglund, *Achaemenid Imperial Administration in Syria-Palestine and the Missions of Ezra and Nehemiah* (SBLDS 125; Atlanta: Scholars Press, 1992); A. Oppenheimer, *The 'Am ha-Aretz: A Study in the Social History of the Jewish People in the Hellenistic-Roman Period* (ALGHJ 8; Leiden: E. J. Brill, 1977); B. Porten and A. Yardeni, *Textbook of Aramaic Documents from Ancient Egypt* (vols. 1- ; Hebrew University, Department of the History of the Jewish People, Texts and Studies for Students; Jerusalem: Hebrew University, 1986-); E. Stern, *Material Culture of the Land of the Bible in the Persian Period 538-332 B.C.* (Jerusalem: Israel Exploration Society, 1982); E. M. Yamauchi, *Persia and the Bible* (Grand Rapids, MI: Baker, 1990).

L. L. Grabbe

JEWISH HISTORY: ROMAN PERIOD

The Jews in Judea came under Roman rule in 63 B.C. and remained so until the Arab conquest in the seventh century. The most dramatic events in Jewish history took place in the first two centuries or so, however, including the loss of nationhood, the destruction of the *temple and the final revolt that sealed any hope of national revival for many centuries. This article will tell the story to about A.D. 200, which is the period of most interest to students of the NT.

1. The Hasmoneans and Rome
2. Palestine and the Roman Republic
3. Herod the Great
4. A Province, Then a Kingdom
5. Revolts and Religious Regrouping

1. Tha Hasmoneans and Rome.

The intervention of Rome into Jewish affairs was inevitable, given the steady expansion of the Roman sphere of influence and control (*see* Roman Empire). The early *Hasmoneans had already made contact with Rome, perhaps even as early as the time of Judas Maccabeus (1 Macc 8, though not everyone accepts this statement). The treaty with the Romans was renewed several times (cf. 1 Macc 12:1-4; 14:16-19). Yet the immediate cause for Rome to take a hand in Judea was a request by the Jews themselves. After the death of Alexandra Salome (67 B.C.), her two sons fought over the succession, the younger son Aristobulus II seeming to get the upper hand at first but the elder Hyrcanus II fighting back with the aid and advice of Antipater, governor of Idumea and father of *Herod the Great. Eventually, they both appealed to *Pompey, the Roman legate in Syria. When Pompey decided in favor of Hyrcanus, Aristobulus at first refused to yield. When he finally gave in, some of his followers still held out in *Jerusalem, which was then besieged and taken by the Romans in 63 B.C. This marked the official end of the Hasmonean state.

2. Palestine and the Roman Republic.

In the next thirty years the Jews of Palestine were caught up in the final throes of the Roman republic, in which the civil war raged over the whole of the Mediterranean. Pompey died fighting Julius Caesar in 48 B.C., a fact the **Psalms of Solomon* 17:7-18 record with some satisfaction. After the death of Caesar, one of the Roman triumvirate of leaders, Cassius, was in control and extracted a great deal of money in a special taxation to support his fight against Marc Antony and Octavian. The Jewish leader was nominally Hyrcanus II, though Antipater and his two sons Phasael and Herod impressed the Roman leadership of the region with their vigorous administration. The Hasmonean family had not given up its claim to rule, however, and first Aristobulus and then his sons Alexander and Antigonus led rebellions periodically. In 41 B.C. Antigonus allied with the Parthians, who invaded the eastern Mediterranean and took Judea. By this time Antipater was dead, and the Parthians captured Phasael by trickery; he then committed suicide. But Herod escaped and made his way to Rome, where he was made king by Octavian and Marc Antony in 40 B.C. He returned to Judea, which had been quitted by the Parthians, leaving Antigonus in control. Herod took the city in 37 B.C. and had Antigonus executed.

Marc Antony was in charge of the east. Herod served him faithfully, but Cleopatra made life difficult for him. She persuaded Antony to remove various areas from Herod's possession and put them under her control. She also attempted to maintain a Hasmonean presence near the throne by making Antigonus's son high *priest (Hyrcanus II had been mutilated by the Parthians and was thus now ineligible to be high priest). However, he was soon drowned under suspicious circumstances while swimming. It was probably only Herod's usefulness to Antony that let him keep his throne under such determined opposition. Herod happened to be fighting the Nabateans in the final confrontation between Octavian and Antony at Actium in 31 B.C. Although he was officially Antony's man and on the losing side, he took the bold step of going to Rhodes to meet Octavian and declaring that he would serve him as faithfully as he had served Antony. Octavian (Augustus; *see* Roman Emperors) was an astute leader and recognized the value of a person of Herod's caliber. He confirmed Herod in his position.

3. Herod the Great.

Herod's reign has often been seen and judged through the polemic of the NT and the negative statements of *Josephus. However, a proper historical evaluation must see him in all his complexity, recognizing his positive as well as negative achievements, and also apply the standards of other rulers of his time. Herod ruled as friendly king of Rome; that is, he was ultimately responsible to the Romans and restricted in actions on the international scene, but within his own realm he was absolute ruler. He countenanced no opposition and was ruthless with those who seemed to present a danger to his rule, but in this he hardly differed from other rulers. He was no doubt hated by many Jews—but then so were the Hasmoneans.

What is clear from our perspective is that Herod did much good for the Jews, and his rule was much preferable to direct Roman rule. He spoke up for the Jews of the *Diaspora on more than one occasion. His many building activities brought a certain prestige to his kingdom and employment for many local people (*see* Art and Architecture: Jewish; Archaeology of the Land of Israel; Caesarea Maritima; Caesarea Philippi). This especially applies to his refurbishment of the temple, which seems to be almost a rebuilding of it. Many of these activities were paid for by *taxes, but his taxes do not seem to have been more burdensome than those of previous or later rulers, and he reduced them in times of economic problems for the people. Herod's precise ancestry is debated (the statement that he was a "half Jew" was made by enemies), but he lived as a Jew and strictly observed Jewish law, at least in his own kingdom. His bad characteristics are obvious, but his positive accomplishments are often overlooked.

Herod's last years were troubled by ill health and by difficulties within his own family. He accused some of his sons of treason and even had several executed; it looks as if there was a basis for the charges brought against them in some cases. He died in 4 B.C., and his remaining sons immediately rushed to Rome, each with a claim to the throne. Augustus decided not to bestow kingship on anyone immediately. Instead he appointed Archelaus ethnarch of Judea; Herod Antipas tetrarch of the Galilean area; and Philip tetrarch over the territory in southern Syria, which had few Jews among its inhabitants. Philip ruled his area until his death in A.D. 34, and Herod Antipas held office until A.D. 37. Archelaus might have hoped eventually to gain the title of king, but after a reign of ten years Augustus removed him from office and exiled him for reasons that are not entirely clear, though his own subjects apparently complained to Rome about his rule.

4. A Province, Then a Kingdom.

In A.D. 6 Judea was turned into a Roman province with a Roman governor (*see* Roman Administration; Roman Governors of Palestine). It was now brought under the Roman tax administration, which required a census. This census was carried out by Quirinius, the Syrian legate, and seems to lie behind the event mentioned in Luke 2:1-3. Some Jews opposed this as contrary to their religious beliefs, but the high priest of the time helped to calm the people. We know almost nothing about the twenty years between this event and the governorship of Pontius Pilate, a significant gap from the point of view of NT study. Pilate was governor for ten years, and even the Roman writers seem to think he was not very successful. He caused several confrontations with the Jewish leadership over religious matters. When he was finally recalled by Tiberius, he reached Rome only after Tiberius's death.

Tiberius was succeeded in office by Gaius Caligula (A.D. 37-41). Caligula has become notorious in history, some of his reputation being deserved and some of it probably due only to senatorial slander. However, he had been a childhood friend of Agrippa, the grandson of Herod the Great. Agrippa had been imprisoned by Tiberius. Caligula released him and made him king over the realm of Philip. Shortly afterward, Herod Antipas was removed from his rule (Agrippa is alleged to have had a hand in bringing this about), and his territory also given to Agrippa (now Agrippa I). In A.D. 41 Agrippa helped to avert one of the gravest crises since the time of Antiochus Epiphanes: the attempt by Caligula to set up his statue in the Jerusalem temple.

Misunderstanding surrounds the episode of Caligula, partly because modern historians have not always known what to make of the emperor. It was easy to dismiss his actions as those of a madman and as simply a capricious anti-Semitic action. Neither of these suggestions is likely to be correct. Recent studies of Caligula have indicated that he was far from being insane and that his reign of terror among the Roman ruling class is a gross exaggeration. His background had not prepared him to be emperor, and his personality was not suited to the task (he seems to have had a strange sense of humor), but the Roman historians who wrote of his reign have indulged a strong class bias. The same applies to writers such as *Philo and Josephus with regard to the episode of the statue in the temple.

It was most likely not mere whim that made Caligula act as he did. Rather, it was a response to the actions of some young Jewish activists who destroyed a pagan altar in a non-Jewish part of Palestine. Rome tolerated most religions, including *Judaism, but they required them to be law-abiding. Pagan altars were not allowed in Judea proper in deference to Jewish sensibilities; in return it was expected that Jews would not interfere with lawful cults outside their own territory. This reciprocal understanding was broken, and Caligula intended to inflict punishment. Why he chose to do so by putting his statue in the temple is not clear, but he probably saw this as an appropriate reaction.

The description of events is somewhat parallel in our two main sources, Josephus (who has two rather different accounts) and Philo. Apparently the local people nonviolently resisted Petronius, the Roman commander who came to do the deed. Philo led a delegation to the emperor (originally for another purpose, but this crisis came up in the meantime) and claimed to be in fear of his life, but his description of the meeting belies this interpretation. Evidently Agrippa, as a close friend of the emperor, had a large hand in persuading him to give up the plan. Although the sources report that Caligula abandoned the plan only reluctantly and even secretly planned to go ahead anyway, there is no real evidence for this claim. In any case, Caligula's assassination in early A.D. 41 put paid to any further repercussions.

The new emperor, Claudius (A.D. 41-54), made Agrippa I king over Judea, as well as the territories he already ruled, and his kingdom now became as large as that of his grandfather Herod the Great. All the reports from antiquity are positive, which seems a bit odd since Agrippa was not particularly a good manager—before becoming king he kept spending large amounts of money and was constantly needing to borrow—and his tax burden was no less than Herod the Great's. Perhaps the reason for his reputation is that he lived to rule only another three years. But this short reign was welcomed by the Jews, and it made the return of direct Roman rule even more difficult. According to Acts 12 (unaccountably called "Herod" here—his other names were Julius Marcus, and the frequent designation of him as "Herod Agrippa" is incorrect), Agrippa persecuted Christians, but there is no confirmation of this in other sources. The description of his death in Acts 12:19-23 is similar to that in Josephus, though it is given a Christian interpretation.

Claudius decided not to give the kingdom to Agrippa's young son Agrippa II, and Judea became a Roman province once again. The description of the next twenty years in our sources is one of deteriorating relations between Jews and the Roman administration and considerable violence against Romans and, especially, those Jews in leadership positions who tried to cooperate with Roman administration, with the sect called the Sicarii ("assassins") targeting even members of the high priest's family for assassination or kidnapping. The Roman governors are all described as of poor quality and generally corrupt. However much this picture may be something of a caricature, it could not have been a very happy time and was no doubt a contributing cause to the war.

5. Revolts and Religious Regrouping.
In many ways the revolt that began in A.D. 66 was inevitable since it was only a matter of time and the right circumstances before the inhabitants of Judea would try for independence once again. In other ways, it is surprising that intelligent people could think that they could defeat Rome (*see* Jewish Wars with Rome).

The A.D. 66-70 war with Rome was one of the most significant events in Jewish history. The fall of the temple in A.D. 70 marks a watershed that affects all aspects of Jewish history, whether political or religious. Although Judea was no longer a kingdom ruled by a native king, it was not impossible that it could have become such again under Roman rule. The A.D. 66-70 revolt confirmed to the Romans that the Jews had to be ruled with a firm hand. The year A.D. 70 also serves as a significant benchmark in the religious history of Judaism. In retrospect we see great changes after A.D. 70, despite an undoubted continuity in many areas. A large number of the strands in the multifaceted religious scene were cut off, the centrality of the *temple cult in worship came to an end, and the whole set of power relationships in religious leadership changed. The power of the priesthood and dependent groups (the *Sadducees?) whose power base was the temple quickly waned. Some of the important pre-70 religious sects seem to have been destroyed by the war itself (the *Essenes, the Fourth Philosophy, many of the revolutionary groups). Sects with a religious system that did not depend on an active temple cult were in a good position to thrive in the new environment. This applied particularly to the *Pharisees and the Christians.

The period between A.D. 70 and the Bar Kokhba revolt was a time of great religious regrouping. The indication is that the traditional Judean leadership, the priests and the Herodian family, attempted to reassert itself but was unsuccessful (Schwartz). Instead a new religious entity was born in the small coastal town of Yavneh: *rabbinic Judaism. Rabbinic Judaism had its roots in the pre-70 religious situation, apparently drawing heavily on Pharisaic tradition but also incorporating ideas or mentalities of scribalism, the priesthood and perhaps even groups such as the Essenes. Thus, many of the elements of rabbinic Judaism were not new, but it represented a new synthesis that did not correspond to any pre-70 group. The frequent assumption that rabbinic Judaism is interchangeable with Pharisaism is mistaken. Many of the traditions that are likely to have gone back to the Pharisees are found in early rabbinic Judaism, but they occur in a new context. Especially important is the centrality of *Torah study as a religious act in rabbinic Judaism, which does not seem to have been the case with Pharisaism, though it might have been more so with the *Qumran community, the Essenes and that strange group called the scribes.

The reconstruction of Judaism going on in Yavneh did not have an immediate effect on the Jews as a whole. Looking back from modern times, one can see the importance of the Yavnean period as the place of seminal development for what became the dominant form of Judaism, but this took centuries. The Jews as a whole seem to have recovered from the A.D. 66-70 war fairly quickly. The destruction of Jerusalem and its surroundings was great, but much of the rest of the country had got off relatively lightly. The Jews in many of the regional cities had suffered, and some had been wiped out;

however, the Jewish communities outside the Palestinian area had generally been affected only indirectly. The extent of the recovery both in the economic situation and the general morale is attested by the revolts in the first part of the second century A.D.

A widespread set of revolts took place beginning in A.D. 115 in Egypt and Mesopotamia, including Cyrenaica and Cyprus. We do not have a lot of details since no Jewish author describes these, but they seem to have been bloody and, whatever the initial successes, ultimately a disaster for the Jewish communities that participated. The great synagogue and much of the large Jewish community in *Alexandria were destroyed. According to the Roman source, many thousands of non-Jews were killed in Cyprus before the revolt was crushed. Archaeology in Cyrenaica has partially confirmed the literary sources.

Palestine does not seem to have participated in the A.D. 115-117 revolts, but a decade and a half later the Jews tried again to throw off the Roman yoke (*see* Jewish Wars with Rome for the details of this revolt and the possible reasons for it). It seems to have devastated the country and people to a much greater degree than the 66-70 war. Jerusalem was turned into a Roman city, and Jews were forbidden to enter it. It was now clear that no national entity or temple would be possible for centuries. The energies of the people, such as there were, went into the development of their religion.

The site of the new reconstruction was a village in Galilee called Usha. Most of the leaders of the Yavnean period were dead, many of them killed in the Bar Kokhba revolt. The developments of the Yavnean period continued, but Usha also had a different perspective, as was inevitable after the Bar Kokhba revolt. One of the traditional strands of Judaism—belief in an *apocalyptic intervention by God to exalt his people and destroy their enemies—seems to have been dropped or suppressed (the messianism of later rabbinic literature has a different nature [Neusner]). After two crushing defeats that were at least in part inspired by *eschatological speculations, this is hardly surprising. The new rabbinic worldview was quite different from that of many of the pre-70 strands of Judaism (Judaisms).

See also HASMONEANS; HERODIAN DYNASTY; JERUSALEM; JEWISH WARS WITH ROME; PAX ROMANA; REVOLUTIONARY MOVEMENTS, JEWISH; ROMAN ADMINISTRATION; ROMAN EAST; ROMAN EMPERORS; ROMAN EMPIRE; ROMAN GOVERNORS OF PALESTINE; TAXATION, GRECO-ROMAN; TEMPLE, JEWISH.

BIBLIOGRAPHY. M. Goodman, *The Ruling Class of Judaea* (New York: Cambridge University Press, 1987); L. L. Grabbe, *Judaism from Cyrus to Hadrian,* 1: *Persian and Greek Periods;* 2: *Roman Period* (Minneapolis: Fortress, 1992) esp. chaps. 7-9; J. Neusner, *Messiah in Context: Israel's History and Destiny in Formative Judaism* (Philadelphia: Fortress, 1984); S. Schwartz, *Josephus and Judean Politics* (CSCT 18; Leiden: E. J. Brill, 1990); E. M. Smallwood, *The Jews Under Roman Rule: From Pompey to Diocletian* (SJLA 20; Leiden: E. J. Brill, 1981).

L. L. Grabbe

JEWISH HOLY MEN. *See* HOLY MEN, JEWISH.

JEWISH LITERATURE: HISTORIANS AND POETS

The Jewish historians and poets dealt with here are all authors writing in Greek who lived in the period from the third century B.C. to the first century A.D. Most of them were Diaspora-based Jews; some of them, however, were of Palestinian provenance. *Josephus and the books of the *Maccabees are left aside here, as is the *Letter of *Aristeas.* The works of most of these authors have been preserved only fragmentarily, in the form of excerpts by the first-century B.C. pagan scholar Alexander Polyhistor. Polyhistor's work *(On the Jews)* is lost as well, but Christian authors, primarily Clement of Alexandria and Eusebius of Caesarea, preserve extensive quotes from it. They are the main sources for our knowledge of these authors. The complex tradition history of the text of their works creates many uncertainties, especially in prose works—poetry is less subject to alteration—but what has been handed down to us suffices to give a clear idea of a fascinating variety of ways in which these writers appropriated the biblical tradition and tried to reshape it in Greek literary modes.

1. Historians
2. Poets

1. Historians.

1.1. Demetrius. *Demetrius the chronographer is almost certainly the earliest Jewish author (in the last decades of the third century B.C.) we know to have written in Greek. While dealing with biblical material, he tries to combine two Hellenistic genres: *erotapokriseis* and description of the history of a non-Greek people in Greek by one of its own members. The first is a genre in which a topic is dealt with in a question-and-answer format, popular in exegesis of Homer (cf., e.g., Philo's *Quaest. in Gen.*); the second is a genre known from the works of the Egyptian Manetho, the Babylonian Berossus and the Roman Fabius Pictor (cf. Josephus's *Ant.*). In the latter genre the emphasis is often on matters of chronology (the older a tradition of a nation, the better; see Aristotle *Metaphysics* A 3, 983b32), and this explains why in the six fragments of Demetrius there is so much computation of years and attention to genealogy (e.g., in fragment 2 we find a calculation of the number of years from the creation until Jacob's arrival in Egypt, a genealogy from Jacob to Moses, a calculation of the length of Israel's sojourn in Egypt and of the time lapse between Abraham's departure from Ur and the exodus). The main emphasis in Demetrius is on the credibility of the Bible as a historical record. His style is sober and dry, and there is no evidence of syncretism.

*1.2. **Eupolemus.*** Eupolemus is probably identical with the priest called Eupolemus mentioned in 1 Maccabees 8:17-18 as the man sent by Judas Maccabeus to Rome in order to conclude a Roman-Jewish friendship treaty in 161 B.C. (*see* Jewish History: Roman Period). He is important in that he shows that being an adherent of the Maccabees did not necessarily imply a rejection of anything Greek and that a member of an important priestly family in *Jerusalem could be critical of the biblical traditions and did not hesitate to rewrite them in order to glorify the great figures of Israel's past, Solomon in particular. He represents Moses not only as the first lawgiver but also as the inventor of the alphabet (the Jews passed it on to the Phoenicians). But the largest fragment (2) focuses on Solomon's building of the *temple as the religious and political center of the Jewish people. It contains among other things a detailed description of its construction that is at variance with the biblical account, but his outlook is clearly a priestly one. The biblical story is interspersed with the letters exchanged between Solomon and Pharaoh Ouaphres and King Suron (= Hiram) of Tyre. Solomon writes severely, as to client kings; the others submissively, to "the great king." The builder of the Jerusalem temple is presented by this Jerusalem priest as if he were an emperor with subordinate vassal kings. The center of the Jewish religion deserved nothing less.

*1.3. **Pseudo-Eupolemus.*** Pseudo-Eupolemus is the name given by modern scholars to the author of two fragments, one of which is attributed by Alexander Polyhistor (or Eusebius) to Eupolemus and the other to an anonymous writer. They need therefore not derive from the same author. The first fragment deals primarily with Abraham, and it intersperses the biblical stories with Greek and Babylonian mythological elements. For example, Kronos is incorporated into the genealogy of Genesis 10, Enoch is identified with Atlas and is the inventor of astrology (*see* Enoch, Books of), and Abraham is received (by Melchizedek?) in the temple at Mt. Gerizim, here explicitly identified as "mount of the Most High." This syncretistic concoction most probably derives from a second-century B.C. Samaritan author in view of the emphasis on Mt. Gerizim. The second fragment has Babylon built by the giants (see Gen 6:4; 10:8-10; 11:1-9), to whom Abraham traced his pedigree. Since it says that these giants were destroyed by the "gods," a reference to the pagan myth of the *gigantomachia* ("battle of the giants" [against the gods]) may be implied here. In both fragments the openness to non-Jewish traditions is remarkable.

*1.4. **Artapanus.*** Artapanus is the most curious of these Jewish historians. He goes further than any of his co-religionists in deviating from the Bible in his portrayals of the patriarchs and especially of Moses as inventors and founders of human civilization and culture in general. Abraham invented and taught astrology, and Moses was the inventor of ships, quarrying instruments, hydraulic machinery, weapons of war, hieroglyphs, *philosophy, even of the Egyptian animal cult, and for that reason the Egyptian priests called him Hermes (= Thoth). Moses is here not so much a lawgiver as a great teacher to whom the Egyptians owe their culture, their religion, their arts and their economy. One senses here a counterattack on the account of Moses given by the Egyptian priest Manetho (or similar anti-Jewish Greco-Egyptian writers), who depicted the Jewish leader as the embodiment of hostility to Egypt. In order to make his point this author goes so far as to make it difficult for us to draw a sharp line between what is Jewish or Jewish syncretistic or pagan.

*1.5. **Cleodemus-Malchus.*** The only surviving

fragment of Cleodemus-Malchus presents not only a reshuffling of the data of the genealogy in Genesis 25:1-6 but also an expansion of it with pagan personalities. The most striking feature is the attempt to forge a genealogical link between Abraham and Heracles, who marries Abraham's granddaughter. There is a clear tendency to make several peoples descend from Abraham and so to create kinship between the Jews and these other peoples.

1.6. Aristeas. Aristeas presents us in the only fragment preserved with a small piece of postbiblical Job haggadah. He identifies Job with the Edomite king Jobab, who is Esau's son (cf. Job 42:17b-e LXX), thus placing Job in the patriarchal period, a tradition also found elsewhere (Pseudo-Philo *Bib. Ant.* 8.8; *T. Job* 1:6).

2. Poets.

2.1. Ezekiel the Tragedian. Ezekiel the Tragedian is the name of a second-century B.C. playwright who wrote a classical Greek drama on the exodus from Egypt, called *Exagōgē*. Only 269 iambic trimeters have been preserved. It is the only Jewish play known to us from antiquity, and it was probably intended to be staged, not just read. The drama follows the *Septuagint version of Exodus 1—15 fairly closely but adds several interesting haggadic motifs, such as the appearance of the mythical phoenix, which heralds the inauguration of a new era in salvation history. The most striking and controversial scene is a dream of Moses in which he sees God upon his throne on the top of Mt. Sinai; God beckons Moses to come to his throne, hands him his regalia and, leaving the throne himself, seats Moses upon it, whereupon all heavenly powers prostrate before Moses. It would seem that this indicates that according to Ezekiel all power in heaven and on earth has been handed over to Moses, who acts here as the viceregent or plenipotentiary of God (cf. Mt 28:18). The synthesis of biblical story, Greek literary form, postbiblical haggadah and theological speculation makes this play into one of the most typical products of Jewish *Hellenism.

2.2. Philo the Epic Poet. Philo is a second-century B.C. epic poet who wrote a lengthy epos on Jerusalem in what is sometimes almost unintelligible Greek. He has a tortuous style and obscure diction, but the 24 hexameters extant show that the author identified the land Moriah (Gen 22:2) with the Temple Mount (cf. 2 Chron 3:1) and that he felt a great admiration for the complex water supply systems in the holy city. Philo is the first to apply the Hellenistic genre of an epic poem on the history of a city to a biblical city.

2.3. Theodotus. Theodotus is a representative of the same genre, but he employs it for a Samaritan city, Shechem. It is highly likely that the author was a *Samaritan. The 47 lines extant (in six fragments) describe the surroundings and walls of Shechem in the framework of a summary of Jacob's history, but the most extensive part is a free rendering of the story of the murdering of the Shechemites by Levi and Simeon (Gen 34). Even though the Bible is very critical of these brothers' behavior (Gen 34:30; 49:5-6), Theodotus justifies their act by stating that God himself commanded them to kill the Shechemites, because they were godless. This kind of whitewashing of the Jewish patriarchs or Moses is found more often in postbiblical haggadah. The poem can be read as a piece of Samaritan propaganda in which the author presents the ancestors of his co-religionists as zealous Israelites.

2.4. Pseudo-Orpheus. Pseudo-Orpheus is the name given to a piece of Jewish hexametric poetry, in which Orpheus gives esoteric information to his son Musaeus. There are three or four different recensions, varying in length from 36 to 46 lines, all of them known only from quotations by patristic authors. Eusebius of Caesarea asserts that he found the poem in a work by the Jewish philosopher Aristobulus, who lived in *Alexandria. The oldest version of the poem therefore may go back to the second century B.C., but the dating of the recensions is a controversial matter. The poet emphasizes the oneness and greatness of God, who is the invisible creator and ruler of everything, and says that of all humankind only Abraham (or Moses, in the later recensions), owing to his great astrological knowledge, has been able to see God. The importance of the text lies in the Jewish appropriation of Orpheus and language from the mystery cults in order to serve as vehicles of Jewish monotheism. There are several points of similarity with the Areopagus speech in Acts 17.

2.5. Pseudo-Phocylides. Under the mask of the sixth-century B.C. Greek gnomic poet Phocylides, renowned for the wisdom of his ethical maxims, around the turn of the era a Jewish author wrote a gnomic wisdom poem of 230 hexametric sentences in the old Ionic dialect (*see* Pseudo-Phocylides). It shares the characteristics of both Greek gnomologies and Jewish wisdom literature and is as such a typical example of cross-cultural didactic poetry. A striking characteristic of this poem is that on the one hand it draws heavily upon the Pentateuch (esp. Lev 18—20 and the Decalogue), but on the other hand it consistently avoids references to specifically Jewish precepts such as *sabbath observance, circumcision and kashrut. All cultic precepts are passed over in silence; only moral precepts for daily life are presented, with a strong emphasis on sexual ethics. Mixed with biblical rules are precepts of originally pagan Greek provenance, which are also presented as God's law, exactly as in the "summaries of the Law" in Philo's *Hypothetica* and Josephus's *Against Apion* 2.190-219 (with which Pseudo-Phocylides has significant overlap). The author's purpose is unclear and debated. Maybe he wanted to prove to strongly Hellenized Jews that biblical and Greek ethics could go hand in hand; that for that reason even the famous pagan poet Phocylides could promulgate biblical ethics; and that it therefore made sense to remain attached to Judaism. Maybe he intended his sentences for schoolroom instruction, as was often the purpose of gnomologies.

Other pseudonyms used by Jewish Hellenistic poets include Homer, Hesiod, Pythagoras, Aeschylus, Sophocles, Euripides and Menander. Church fathers quote various fragments that proclaim the unity and transcendence of God and the reality of divine justice while emphasizing the futility of pagan worship and mythology.

By way of conclusion it can be noticed that these early examples of Judeo-Greek literature, in spite of all their variety of form and outlook, have several things in common. Their literary level is not very high, but they were pioneers in the difficult task of putting a Greek dress upon biblical materials. Their concern was to bolster Jewish self-consciousness and self-confidence in an often inimical environment by repeated assertions that several inventions of major cultural importance (such as astrology and the art of writing) were made by Abraham or Moses and were therefore Jewish discoveries. Many cultures, including Greek civilization, were thus ultimately dependent upon Moses. For that reason their co-religionists *Aristobulus (frag. 3) and Pseudo-Aristeas (30.313-16) state explicitly that the great Greek philosophers derived all their insights from the books of Moses.

Yet there is little emphasis on the significance of the *Torah as a book of commandments. Moses is not so much presented as the one to whom God revealed his Torah but rather as the first sage, a cultural benefactor, an inventor, a great king, even a cosmic ruler. This absence of emphasis on the centrality of the Torah makes these early Jewish writings so different from later *rabbinic literature. As far as we can judge from the few fragments, these writers focused on the nonhalakic parts of the Torah (Genesis and the first half of Exodus), whereas the rabbis focused on the other parts of the Pentateuch. Even so we can see that several haggadic motifs in rabbinic literature find their first attestations in these Judeo-Greek authors and may even derive from them.

See also APOCRYPHA AND PSEUDEPIGRAPHA; ARISTEAS, EPISTLE OF; DEMETRIUS; JEWISH HISTORY; JOSEPHUS; 1 & 2 MACCABEES; PHILO; POETRY, HELLENISTIC; PSEUDO-PHILO; PSEUDO-PHOCYLIDES; WRITING AND LITERATURE: JEWISH.

BIBLIOGRAPHY. J. M. G. Barclay, *Jews in the Mediterranean Diaspora from Alexander to Trajan (323 B.C.-A.D. 117)* (Edinburgh: T & T Clark, 1996); J. R. Bartlett, *Jews in the Hellenistic World* (Cambridge: Cambridge University Press, 1985); E. J. Bickerman, "The Jewish Historian Demetrios," in *Studies in Jewish and Christian History* (AGJU 9; Leiden: E. J. Brill, 1980) 2:347-58; J. H. Charlesworth, ed., *The Old Testament Pseudepigrapha* (2 vols.; Garden City, NY: Doubleday, 1985) vol. 2; J. J. Collins, *Between Athens and Jerusalem: Jewish Identity in the Hellenistic Diaspora* (New York: Crossroad, 1986); A.-M. Denis, *Introduction aux Pseudépigraphes Grecs d'Ancien Testament* (Leiden: E. J. Brill, 1970); L. H. Feldman and M. Reinhold, *Jewish Life and Thought Among Greeks and Romans* (Minneapolis: Fortress, 1996); M. Goodman, "Jewish Literature Composed in Greek," in E. Schürer, *The History of the Jewish People in the Age of Jesus Christ (175 B.C.-A.D. 135)*, rev. and ed. G. Vermes, F. Millar and M. Goodman (3 vols.; Edinburgh: T & T Clark, 1973-87) 3.1:470-704; E. S. Gruen, *Heritage and Hellenism: The Reinvention of Jewish Tradition* (Berkeley and Los Angeles: University of California Press, 1998); M. Hengel, *Judaism and Hellenism* (Philadelphia: Fortress, 1974); C. R. Holladay, *Fragments from Hellenistic Jewish Authors* (4 vols.; Atlanta: Scholars Press, 1983-96); P. W. van der

Horst, "The Interpretation of the Bible by the Minor Hellenistic Jewish Authors," in *Mikra,* ed. M. J. Mulder (CRINT 2.1; Assen: Van Gorcum; Philadelphia: Fortress, 1988) 519-46 (= idem, *Essays on the Jewish World of Early Christianity* [NTOA 14; Freiburg: Universitätsverlag; Göttingen: Vandenhoeck & Ruprecht, 1990] 187-219); idem, *The Sentences of Pseudo-Phocylides* (SVTP 4; Leiden: E. J. Brill, 1978); H. Jacobson, *The Exagoge of Ezekiel* (Cambridge: Cambridge University Press, 1983); G. E. Sterling, *Historiography and Self-Definition: Josephus, Luke-Acts and Apologetic Historiography* (NovTSup 64; Leiden: E. J. Brill, 1992); B. Z. Wacholder, *Eupolemos: A Study of Judeo-Greek Literature* (Cincinnati: Hebrew Union College Press, 1974); N. Walter, nine contributions in *Jüdische Schriften aus hellenistisch-römischer Zeit* 1.2, 3.2, 4.3 (Gütersloh: Gütersloher Verlagshaus, 1975-83). P. W. van der Horst

JEWISH WARS WITH ROME

For many centuries after the fall of the first *temple and the end of the kingdom of Judah, the Jews seem to have been essentially peaceful under the rule of various Near Eastern empires. Perhaps the reason is that they had no other choice: rebellion would have gained nothing. There are reports that some Jews served in *Hellenistic armies, either as mercenaries or because they were required to do so (Josephus *Ant.* 13.10.4 §§284-87; *Ag. Ap.* 1.22 §§192, 201-4; *CPJ* 1.11-15, 118-21, 147-78), but the Jews as a people do not appear as a war-making community in the sources. This changed with the Maccabean revolt. Threatened with the suppression and destruction of their religion, the Jews of Palestine revolted against their *Seleucid rulers and eventually gained sufficient autonomy to form an independent Jewish state with a standing army and a policy of expansion.

The *Hasmonean state was brought to an end by the Roman general *Pompey in 63 B.C., and the Jews were under Roman rule (*see* Jewish History: Roman Period). Over the next two centuries, they tried in three major encounters and several minor ones to throw off Roman rule—without success. These wars with Rome shaped Jewish history in a significant way, and the defeats that resulted had a great effect on the Jewish communities.

1. From Pompey's Intervention to Herod's Rule (63-31 B.C.)
2. From the Death of Herod to the First Revolt (4 B.C.-A.D. 66)
3. The First Revolt (A.D. 66-70)
4. Revolts Under Trajan (A.D. 115-117)
5. The Bar Kokhba Revolt (A.D. 132-135)

1. From Pompey's Intervention to Herod's Rule (63-31 B.C.).

The initial military encounter between the Jews and Romans happened almost by accident, though with the continued expansion of Rome into the Near East it was perhaps bound to happen (*see* Roman East). At the end of the Hasmonean kingdom, Alexandra Salome took the throne as queen (76-67 B.C.). Since she could not be high *priest as previous Hasmoneans had been, she appointed her eldest son, Hyrcanus II, as high priest. His younger brother, Aristobulus II, did not accept this but bided his time; when his mother became ill, he seized a number of the country's fortresses and began a rebellion. After her death, the two brothers struggled with one another for the throne. Aristobulus prevailed at first, but Hyrcanus fought back successfully. Pompey was in Syria as legate of the Roman senate, fighting the Armenians, and each of the Hasmonean brothers appealed to him to adjudicate, seeking to influence his judgment with substantial bribes. Pompey eventually sided with Hyrcanus, at which point Aristobulus left in such a manner as to suggest that he was prepared to resist implementing the Roman decision. Pompey pursued him. Aristobulus himself then surrendered to Pompey's troops, but some of his followers took charge of Jerusalem and shut the gates in the face of the Roman army.

Pompey besieged the city for three months. In the final onslaught the priests continued to carry out their cultic duties, and many were slain around the altar. Pompey went into the temple itself. However, this was probably a matter of curiosity, because the treasury was not touched, and the next day he told the priests to ritually purify the sanctuary and continue with the regular cult. Many of the Jews regarded Pompey's actions as an insult to God and rejoiced a few years later when he was killed and his body cast out into the open (*Pss. Sol.* 17:7-18).

For the next quarter of a century the last of the Hasmoneans attempted to regain some ground against the Romans but with little success. During this period Aristobulus and his sons Alexander and (somewhat later) Antigonus staged revolts and attempted revolts. It was not difficult to gather a large following in a short period of time, indicating the Hasmoneans were still popular among the Jewish people. Aristobulus was initially taken captive to Rome, but Alexander escaped and in 57 B.C. gathered an army sufficiently large to take Jerusalem. Defeated by the Romans, he was taken to Rome. But then the next year both Aristobulus and Alexander escaped and fostered another revolt. They were defeated and Aristobulus returned to Rome, but his sons were left free to promote further revolts. Caesar attempted to use Aristobulus when the Roman civil war began in 49 B.C., but the latter was poisoned by Pompey's followers, who also executed Alexander.

In 40 B.C. the Parthians invaded, taking over Palestine and setting Antigonus on the throne. Herod escaped and fled to Rome, where he was made king of Judea by the Romans. His first task was to establish his rule over Antigonus, who was still in control of Jerusalem, though the Parthians had withdrawn. Although taking not only his own troops but also a Roman force, Herod found retaking Palestine a far from easy task, and one of his brothers was killed in the fighting. He besieged Jerusalem for a number of months in the summer of 37 B.C. The city finally fell about the beginning of September, though Herod managed to prevent the looting of the city by the Roman soldiers (which would have been considered their right of conquest) by paying them from his own resources. Herod had Antigonus executed. This was the last investment of Jerusalem by Roman troops for a century, though Roman troops were often involved in police actions in the city.

2. From the Death of Herod to the First Revolt (4 B.C.-A.D. 66).
Herod kept a tight rein on those under his rule, and there were no significant internal rebellions while he was alive. However, as soon as he died in 4 B.C. a series of revolts broke out in Judah over demands about the reduction of taxes and the release of prisoners. After a quick show of force, Archelaus and the other sons of Herod rushed to Rome to try to obtain the throne, leaving the Roman Sabinus in charge. The unrest did not quiet down but increased, with a full-scale revolt developing. Even some of Herod's Idumean veterans participated. This was not a coordinated rebellion but rather a series of individual movements with separate, independent leaders. Some of the leaders seem even to have had certain messianic pretensions. The revolt grew so extensive that the governor of Syria, Varus, was sent to suppress it, which he did with the expected efficiency and ruthlessness. Nevertheless, some groups continued to cause trouble for years, and the "war of Varus" was still remembered in later Jewish literature (e.g., the *Seder Olam Rabbah*).

Archelaus reigned for about a decade before being removed, and Judea turned into a Roman province in A.D. 6. Rather than a native ruler, the country now had a Roman governor and came under the Roman system of taxation, which required a tax census to be made of the region (*see* Roman Administration; Roman Governors of Palestine). The memory of that census probably gave rise to Luke's "census in the time of Augustus" (Lk 2:1-2). Some Jews resisted this with the slogan that only God could rule them. Two leaders in particular were Judas the Galilean and Simon the Pharisee, who founded what Josephus calls the "fourth philosophy," a sect that he places alongside the *Sadducees, *Pharisees and *Essenes (Josephus *Ant.* 18.1.1 §§4-10; 18.1.6 §23; cf. Acts 5:37).

Throughout the next decades there seem to have been various *revolutionary groups who resisted Roman rule at different times. These do not always seem to have been organized groups, and they did not often last long. For example, we hear of Theudas, who gained a following but apparently was short-lived (Josephus *Ant.* 20.5.1 §§97-99; cf. Acts 5:36). The members of these groups are often called "bandits" (Gk *lēstēs)*, and it is not always clear whether those referred to as bandits or robbers should be literally so designated or whether we should think rather of revolutionaries (the distinction was not always clear-cut, however). The Gospels mention that a certain Barabbas, who seems to have been a political rebel, was released (Mk 15:7) while two "thieves" (members of revolutionary groups?) were crucified with Jesus (Mk 15:27).

Especially in the period after the death of Agrippa I (A.D. 44), various resistance groups seem to become even more prominent. One of the tasks faced by each new Roman governor was to try to clear the country of the bandits who were threatening the social order. These include the Sicarii ("assassins"), who, according to Josephus, arose from the fourth philosophy, though this is not certain. The Sicarii targeted Roman officials in a few cases but mainly Jewish officials who cooperated with the Roman regime. In a manner reminiscent of some modern terrorist groups, they financed their activities by kidnaping members of leading families and holding them for ransom. They are also said to have been hired both by the Roman governors and by the high priests—the very authorities supposedly trying to get rid of them—to carry out certain nefarious actions.

3. The First Revolt (A.D. 66-70).

The A.D. 66-70 revolt against Rome did not begin suddenly but was preceded by a long series of incidents, including the revolutionary activities mentioned in the preceding section and a line of bad governors. Then in A.D. 66 occurred in succession a major incident regarding the synagogue in Caesarea, the seizure of the temple treasury to help make up for the arrears of tribute and the halting of the traditional *sacrifices for the emperor and his family (*see* Ruler Cult). This eventually led to Agrippa II's being driven from Jerusalem and finally a massacre of Roman soldiers in August. The Romans responded by sending Cestius with two legions to Jerusalem. He came within sight of the city and, according to Josephus, could easily have taken the city; however, he suddenly decided to withdraw, laying himself open to harassment by Jewish guerrilla tactics and losing a considerable number of his troops. It also gave the Jews time to set up a revolutionary government and make plans for defense.

Josephus wants us to believe that the war was caused on the Jewish side by a handful of unrestrained, hotheaded bandits who forced a reluctant leading class of priests and nobles, as well as the people at large, into the conflict. This picture has been questioned by a number of scholars in recent times, but a full study has now demonstrated the extent to which Josephus has painted a false picture (Price). Although a few members of the leading classes did oppose the war, Josephus's own data show that the leadership of the country as a whole was overwhelmingly in favor of the fight against the occupying forces, even those who had earlier cooperated with the Romans. Josephus alleges that he was against the revolt, yet all his actions on the contrary argue much louder than words for an enthusiastic supporter of the rebellion. The leaders of the new revolutionary government were overwhelmingly from the upper-class priests and lay nobility.

This does not mean that the leadership was united. On the contrary, old feuds persisted, and the previously existing revolutionary groups, whom the leaders tried to control and use for their particular purposes, often pursued their own objectives. Josephus's detailed account of his activities in Galilee illustrates how enmity with other Jewish leaders was more important than the Roman threat. Thus, much energy was expended in fighting each other. This continued to be true until the final siege of Jerusalem, when they fought bravely and even unitedly—but by then it was too late.

To put down the revolt Nero appointed Vespasian, who took a systematic approach to the task. He assembled three legions and many other troops and began his attack in Galilee. His main opponent here was Josephus, who was besieged in the city of Jotapata and taken prisoner in July 67. After subduing the rest of Galilee, Vespasian advanced south, quickly taking the defended areas outside of Jerusalem. Many refugees fled to Jerusalem, which Vespasian surrounded in the summer of 68. But then news of Nero's death came, and Vespasian felt unable to carry on the war until the political situation in Rome was clarified. He had been appointed by Nero, who was now dead, and Nero's successor might issue new orders. Over the next year there were several different claimants to the office of emperor; the year 69 has sometimes been referred to as the year of the three emperors (*see* Roman Emperors). In the summer of 69 Vespasian decided to get on with the siege of Jerusalem. But when word came that Vitellius had overcome Galba, Vespasian was declared emperor by his troops, though this was clearly stage managed. He set out for Rome to confront Vitellius, leaving Titus with four legions to finish conquering Jerusalem.

Josephus describes the final siege of Jerusalem in great detail (Josephus *J.W.* 5-6). We know that by this time the city was divided among three factions with three different leaders: Eleazer son of Simon, John of Gischala (Josephus's old enemy), and Simon son of Gioras. Each was in control of a different part of the city, and each was willing to kill other Jews to retain and extend his power. A group called the Zealots had emerged at some point. (Some writers have used the term *Zealot* incorrectly to describe any revolutionary group, but Josephus is clear that it was a specific group, though we are not given its history.) By this time, the Zealots seem to have become divided among the various factional leaders. Interestingly, the Sicarii seem to have left the city toward the beginning of the revolt and to have made Masada their base (*see* Revolutionary Movements).

Titus besieged Jerusalem through the spring and summer of 70. The city was well defended, and the fighters—now working in concert—fought well, but the Romans had the resources and the technical skill needed. When the city fell in August, Josephus claims that it was Titus's intent to spare the temple but that the actions of soldiers and rebels set it on fire. However, another source gives the more realistic story that Titus met with his commanders to discuss the destruction of the temple, since it was seen as the root of much of the revolutionary feeling. Three fortresses continued in rebel hands. Herodium surrendered without much resistance, but Machaerus decided to hold out and had to be taken after a siege. Masada did not fall until 73 in a remarkable feat of siege warfare by the Romans. Most of the defenders committed suicide before the final assault, however.

4. Revolts Under Trajan (A.D. 115-117).
One of the purposes of Josephus's *War* was to deliver the message that Rome could not be defeated and revolt was useless. This might seem a strange thing to write about only a few years after a devastating war, yet his perspicacity became evident when less than fifty years later another series of revolts caused great suffering to Jewish communities in a number of places. The areas mainly affected were Cyrenaica, Egypt, Cyprus and Mesopotamia. We have only a few fragments of information that are subject to more than one explanation.

The prevailing hypothesis has been that the revolt began in Egypt in A.D. 115; that this may not have had any connection with Mesopotamia, which revolted after Trajan's conquest of certain areas; that Palestine was not involved; and that peace was finally established in 117. The study by T. D. Barnes has now challenged that. He argues that the revolt did not begin until 116 and originated in Mesopotamia. The revolt here was not of the Jews alone; they were only part of a broader group, including the Parthians and other natives of the region.

We know most about the situation in Egypt and North Africa, where we have some *papyri and also archaeology. The revolt in this region apparently began in Cyrenaica and only then affected Egypt. We know of civil disorder in *Alexandria in 115, but it may not have been directly connected with the revolt, if Barnes is right. There was a great deal of destruction in both areas, and it took the arrival of a second legion to quell the disturbances in Egypt.

As in Cyrenaica, the revolt in Cyprus was apparently led by an individual who declared himself king. The huge numbers of those said to have been killed by the Jews (a quarter of a million) are probably exaggerated but indicate the massive slaughter. After the defeat of the Jews, a decree was passed forbidding them to settle on Cyprus.

5. The Bar Kokhba Revolt (A.D. 132-135).
The Bar Kokhba revolt was apparently a devastating war from both the Jewish and Roman point of view; no Josephus recorded it, and our knowledge is made up of incomplete information. We now know from a Greek letter written by the leader himself that his name was *Simeon ben Kosiba. *Rabbinic and Christian sources indicate that Simon was proclaimed the messiah and took the title "Bar Kokhba" (Aramaic "son of the star"), in a play on Numbers 24:17. If so, a religious motivation and expectation may have blinded the participants to the military realities. Yet the finds of correspondence from and with Simeon give no such indication of messianic claims. Only the symbols on some of the *coins may suggest messianic pretensions.

The cause(s) of the revolt are uncertain. The popular explanation, that Hadrian forbade circumcision, has been rejected in several recent studies. Hadrian may have intended turning Jerusalem into a Romanized city called Aelia Capitolina; we know this happened after the revolt, but this may have been only the realization of what was planned earlier and sparked a violent reaction. The skimpiness of our sources makes it difficult to be sure.

The territory held by Simon seems to have been primarily south and southeast of Jerusalem, centering on the Judean desert west of the Dead Sea. Some scholars have argued that he took and held Jerusalem for a time, but this now seems unlikely. A favorite fighting tactic was to build secret underground hiding places from which quick attacks could be made on the enemy (Kloner; Gichon). A final stand seems to have been made at Bethar, 6 or 7 miles southwest of Jerusalem. An enormous number of Jews were killed by the fighting, famine and disease, but the Roman losses were also so severe that Hadrian dropped the customary greeting in his report to the senate, "I and the legions are well." Jerusalem was turned into a Roman city, and Jews were excluded for many centuries.

See also JERUSALEM; JEWISH HISTORY: ROMAN PERIOD; JOSEPHUS; REVOLUTIONARY MOVEMENTS, JEWISH; TEMPLE, JEWISH.

BIBLIOGRAPHY. B. Bar-Kochva, *Judas Maccabeus: The Jewish Struggle Against the Seleucids* (Cambridge: Cambridge University Press, 1989); idem, *The Seleucid Army: Organization and Tactics in the Great Campaigns* (Cambridge Classical Studies; Cambridge: Cambridge University Press, 1976); T. D. Barnes, "Trajan and the Jews," *JJS* 40 (1989) 145-62; M. Gichon, "New Insight into the Bar Kokhba War and a Reappraisal of Dio Cassius 69.12-13," *JQR* 77 (1986-87) 15-43; L. L. Grabbe, *Judaism from Cyrus to Hadrian,* 1: *Persian and Greek Periods;* 2: *Roman Period* (Minneapolis: Fortress, 1992); A. Kloner, "The Subterranean Hideaways of the Judean Foothills and the Bar-Kokhba Revolt," *The Jerusalem Cathedra* 3 (1983) 83-96; idem, "Underground Hiding Complexes from the Bar Kokhba War in the Judean Shephelah," *BA* 46 (1983) 210-21; J. T. Price, *Jerusalem Under Siege: The Collapse of the Jewish State A.D. 66-70* (BSJS 3; Leiden: E. J. Brill, 1992); I. Shatzman, *The Armies of the Hasmoneans and Herod: From Hellenistic to Roman Frameworks* (TSAJ 25; Tübingen: Mohr Siebeck, 1991).

L. L. Grabbe

JOB. *See* ARAMAIC TARGUMIM; TESTAMENT OF JOB.

JONATHAN THE REFUGEE. *See* REVOLUTIONARY MOVEMENTS, JEWISH.

JOSEPH AND ASENETH

Interest in this book has grown considerably over the last fifty years, and critical studies of its genre, new translations and attempts to date it and place it in its environment have all brought about a consensus, although not unanimity. Critical to the discussion is finding a date for the book. Conclusions range from 100 B.C. to A.D. 200. Persuasive arguments have been made by R. D. Chesnutt that it was written in Egypt prior to A.D. 115 and likely before A.D. 38. Since it betrays a heavy dependence on the *Septuagint it must have been written after 100 B.C. It locale is likely Egypt. Once a date has been established it is easier to determine to what extent Christian writers may have been influenced by this fundamentally Jewish book. A few scholars, like T. Holtz, find Christian interpolations in the book. The manuscript tradition, especially their dating, is also critical to our understanding of the book's relation to Jewish and Christian history.

1. Structure of the Book
2. Significance for New Testament Studies

1. Structure of the Book.

The book is divided into two distinct parts. Chapters 1—21 are a touching love story describing what brought Joseph and Aseneth together and how they overcame the obstacles to their union. Joseph could not marry a pagan, and that obstacle is removed by Aseneth's conversion. Aseneth displays a streak of independence and occasionally apologizes for her *parrēsia* ("boldness"), a trait for which, according to *Josephus, one of *Herod's wives paid with her life (Klassen 1996), and Aseneth is not about to allow her father to select a mate for her sight unseen. Her resistance is removed once she sees how handsome Joseph is. Beyond the romantic motif is clearly the issue of, How can this famous Jewish patriarch have married a non-Jewish woman, and how does this apply to the men in our community who are also tempted to marry outside the Jewish community? Aseneth not only emerges as a strong person in her own right but also becomes a genuine convert to *Judaism and an eloquent defender of its values.

The second part of the book deals with the jealousy that Joseph and Aseneth have to deal with from Pharaoh's son, who recruits Joseph's brothers to murder both Joseph and Aseneth. The plot draws on the popular motif that God is a warrior who defends them at critical times. Pharaoh's son is mortally wounded, and when Pharaoh himself dies of grief, Joseph becomes king of Egypt.

Throughout the book the motif "it is not proper for the one who worships God" is used frequently to convey Jewish law and customs. That applies to whether a good male can kiss a pagan female (*Jos. and As.* 8:5), retaliate against an attacker or eat certain foods. The book is one of the strongest affirmations of the role of a pagan female convert in Judaism and was designed to rebut those who felt that Jews should not marry outside the faith. There remain insoluble mysteries in the book, such as the scene of Aseneth eating the honeycomb (*Jos. and As.* 16:17-23) and the unusual behavior of the bees. Most likely these are symbolic ways of describing or summarizing Jewish life.

2. Significance for New Testament Studies.

The current prominence of the book as a resource for studying the NT derives from the fact that it is almost certainly coterminous with the time during which the NT was written or slightly before. It sheds light on such important issues as the teaching on vengeance by this circle of Jews from which it emerged, and it puts some balance into the widespread portrayal of Joseph's gentleness, kindness and moderation. It portrays a powerful and sensitive woman who is worthy of being considered a Jew. By choosing the model of a love story or a romance it joins the book of Ruth in assuring itself an immortal place not only in Jewish literature but also in world literature. Moreover, it balances stories like that of *Judith, in which her strength comes from her doing manly things such as cutting the head off the enemy. Aseneth has to instruct the patriarchs that it is not right to harm an enemy; rather it is incumbent upon them to heal and to forgive the enemy. Simon asks in disbelief: "Why does our mistress speak good on behalf of her enemies?" (*Jos. and As.* 28:12).

Nowhere in Jewish or Christian literature of that early period is the issue of love of enemies, retaliation and revenge more clearly faced than here (Zerbe, 72-97). There are also strong indications that the application of this mandate goes far beyond relations between two people and also applies to group attitudes and religious competitors. The impetus for this came not only from direct conflicts between both Jews and outsiders but also from conflicts within the Jewish community. But the answers were drawn from their careful reading of the Septuagint and their use of both the wisdom tradition as well as the haggadah. Later definitions of the enemy included "the enemy is one who hasn't spoken to the neighbor for three days" (*m. Sanh.* 3:5). This story is more specific and has the traditional enemy of Jews, the Egyptians, trying to give Jews a lesson on how important it is that goodness can overcome evil when the enemy's healing is considered important. Most important, however, is the religious and spiritual undergirding that this ethical action receives, since it derives its ultimate sanction from God, who also provides strength to carry it out.

See also JUDITH; ROMANCES/NOVELS, ANCIENT; WRITING AND LITERATURE: JEWISH.

BIBLIOGRAPHY. V. Aptowitzer, "Asenath the Wife of Joseph: A Haggadic Literary-Historical Study," *HUCA* 1 (1924) 239-306; G. Bohak, *Joseph and Aseneth and the Jewish Temple in Heliopolis* (SBLEJL 10; Atlanta: Scholars Press, 1996); C. Burchard, *Gesammelte Studien zu Joseph und Aseneth,* ed. C. Burfeind (Leiden: E. J. Brill, 1996); idem, "The Importance of Joseph and Aseneth for the Study of the New Testament," *NTS* 33 (1987) 102-34; idem, ed. and trans., "Joseph and Aseneth," in *OTP* 2:177-247; R. D. Chesnutt, "Joseph and Aseneth," *ABD* 3:969-71 (extensive bibliography); idem, "The Social Setting and Purpose of Joseph and Aseneth," *JSP* 2 (1988) 21-48; T. Holtz, "Christliche Interpolationen in JA," *NTS* 14 (1968) 482-97; E. M. Humphrey, *The Ladies and the Cities: Transformation and Apocalyptic Identity in Joseph and Aseneth* (JSPSup 17; Sheffield: Sheffield Academic Press, 1995); T. Ilan, *Jewish Women in Greco-Roman Palestine* (Peabody, MA: Hendrickson, 1995) 81-83 passim; H. C. Kee, "The Social-Cultural Setting of Joseph and Aseneth," *NTS* 29 (1983) 394-413; W. Klassen, *Love of Enemies: The Way to Peace* (Philadelphia: Fortress, 1986) 53-57; idem, "*parrēsia* in the Johannine Corpus," in *Friendship, Flattery and Frankness of Speech: Studies in Friendship in the New Testament World,* ed. J. T. Fitzgerald (Leiden: E. J. Brill, 1996) 227-54; R. I. Pervo, "Aseneth and Her Sisters: Women in Jewish Narratives and in the Greek Novels," in *"Women Like This." New Perspectives on Jewish Women in the Greco-Roman World,* ed. A.-J. Levine (SBLEJL 1; Atlanta: Scholars Press, 1991) 145-60; M. Philonenko, *Joseph et Aséneth* (SPB 13; Leiden: E. J. Brill, 1968); D. Sänger, *Antikes Judentum und die Mysterien, Religionsgeschichtliche Untersuchungen zu JundA,* (WUNT 2.5; Berlin: Walter de Gruyter, 1980); G. Zerbe, *Nonretaliation in Early Jewish and New Testament Texts: Ethical Themes in Social Contexts* (JSPSup 13; Sheffield: JSOT , 1993).

W. Klassen

JOSEPHUS: INTERPRETIVE METHODS AND TENDENCIES

There are three major reasons why Josephus (A.D. 37-c. 100) is important for students of the background of the NT. First, he presents by far the most comprehensive and systematic history of the Jewish people from their beginnings to his own day and is especially full for the period just before, during and immediately after the lifetime of Jesus, especially concerning such personalities as *Herod and such events as the census of Quirinius. Second, he is the earliest non-Christian writer who mentions John the Baptist, Jesus, James the brother of Jesus, Judas the Galilean, Theudas and the Egyptian prophet. Third, he presents the earliest systematic and comprehensive paraphrase and interpretation of the Bible.

Whereas the overwhelming majority of classical works have been lost, everything that Josephus wrote has come down to us. This is because the Christian church found him extremely useful in filling in the gap of history between the chronological close of the Jewish Scriptures in the fifth century B.C. and the birth of Christianity. In particular his work was useful in confirming the historicity of Jesus and John the Baptist and in establishing the view that the terrible sufferings of the Jews during the war against the Romans and of the destruction of the *temple were in fulfillment of the prophecies of Jesus and were inflicted by God upon the Jews for their rejection of Jesus.

1. Josephus as Historian
2. Josephus and the New Testament
3. Josephus as Interpreter of the Bible

1. Josephus as Historian.

Josephus is the author of four works: the *Jewish War,* in seven books, covering the period from the reign of Antiochus IV Epiphanes (175 B.C.) to the aftermath of the fall of Masada (A.D. 74) and concentrating on the war against the Romans culminating in the destruction of the temple in Jerusalem (A.D. 70); the *Antiquities of the Jews,* in twenty books, covering the period from creation to the outbreak of the war against the Romans in A.D. 66; the *Life,* in one book, the earliest extant autobiography from antiquity (*see* Biography, Ancient), concentrating on Josephus's role as general in Galilee in the war against the Romans; *Against Apion,* in two books, attempting to refute the anti-Jewish charges of Manetho, Lysimachus, Chaeremon, Apion and others.

Josephus was, to judge from his autobiography, excellently equipped to write his histories. He was descended on his mother's side from the *Hasmonean kings (Josephus *Life* 1 §2) and was a personal friend of Agrippa II, the last Jewish king, who is said to have written no fewer than sixty-two *letters testifying to the accuracy of Josephus's history of the Jewish war (Josephus *Life* 65 §364). On his father's side he belonged to the first of the twenty-four courses of *priests (Josephus *Life* 1 §2) in an era when priestly status was a source of great prestige.

Josephus received an excellent *education in traditional Jewish learning and at the tender age of fourteen was already consulted by the chief priests and other leaders for interpretations of Jewish law (Josephus *Life* 2 §9). He spent three years gaining first hand experience of the three leading sects of Jews—*Pharisees, *Sadducees and *Essenes (Josephus *Life* 2 §§10-11). At the age of twenty-seven he was chosen to go to *Rome to secure the freedom of some priests and proved successful (Josephus *Life* 3 §§13-16). Though he had no first hand experience as a soldier he was chosen at twenty-nine to be general of the Jewish forces in *Galilee (Josephus *J.W.* 2.20.3 §563; *Life* 7 §§28-29). He gained the favor of the Roman generals—later *emperors—Vespasian and Titus, whose family name, Flavius, he adopted and who presumably gave him a good deal of first hand historical information; and he spent the last thirty years of his life living in Rome on a pension granted to him by them (Josephus *Life* 76 §423).

In Rome he had a *patron, Epaphroditus, who is said to have had a library of some thirty thousand books. He also gained a good knowledge of Greek literature, particularly Homer, Thucydides, *Plato and the Greek tragedians. Scholars are generally suspicious of his accounts of events in which he directly participated, such as the siege of Jotapata; but for other events, notably his account of the siege of Masada, where we can compare his account with the excavations of Y. Yadin in 1963 to 1965, he has generally proven to be accurate. The fact that in the introduction to his *Jewish War* he is so critical of his predecessors who wrote the history of that war (Josephus *J.W.* 1.pref.1 §§1-2) and that in his essay *Against Apion* (1.2-5 §§6-27) he is so critical of Greek historians would indicate that he himself had to make a special effort to be fair and accurate lest he be laughed out of court.

2. Josephus and the New Testament.
Few scholars have doubted the authenticity of the reference to John the Baptist (Josephus *Ant.* 18.5.2 §§116-19), since the language is particularly typical of this part of the *Antiquities.* If a Christian had interpolated it, it is hard to explain why he would have made it almost twice as long as the passage about Jesus, why he should have contradicted the Gospels' account as to why John was put to death (Josephus says that he was condemned by Herod Antipas because the latter saw that John was attracting such large crowds, and he feared that this would lead to sedition) and why he should have said nothing about the connection of John with Jesus. As to the passage about the condemnation by a *Sanhedrin of James (Josephus *Ant.* 20.9.1 §200), who is referred to as the brother of Jesus, who was called the Christ, virtually all scholars have accepted its authenticity.

As to the passage (the so-called *Testimonium Flavianum*) about Jesus (Josephus *Ant.* 18.3.3 §§63-64), which is found in all 42 of the extant Greek manuscripts containing this portion of the *Antiquities* (the earliest of which dates from the eleventh century), as well as in all 171 extant manuscripts of the Latin translation, which was done in the sixth century under the sponsorship of Cassiodorus, scholars have increasingly concluded that it is authentic in part. It says that during the procuratorship of Pontius Pilate "there lived Jesus, a wise man, if indeed one ought to call him a man." It notes that he wrought miracles and won over many Jews and many of the Greeks and then bluntly states that "he was the Messiah." It reports that Pilate had him crucified upon hearing him accused by men of the highest standing among the Jews. It then adds that on the third day Jesus appeared to his followers restored to life, in accordance with the prophecies of the prophets.

Such a passage, as it stands, should have been vital for Christian apologists, such as Justin Martyr, seeking to answer the charge that Jesus was a figment of imagination. And yet, of eleven Christian church fathers who lived prior to or contemporary with the fourth-century Eusebius of Caesarea and who cite passages from Josephus, including the *Antiquities,* none refers to this passage. Moreover, Origen, who knew book 18 of the *Antiquities* and who cites five passages from it, expresses wonder that Josephus did not admit "Jesus to be the Christ" (Origen *Comm. Mt.* 10:17) and states that Josephus "disbelieved in Jesus as Christ" (Origen *Cont. Cels.* 1.47).

A clue to the original wording may be found in Jerome (Jerome *Vir.* 13), who cites Josephus as saying not that Jesus was the Messiah but that "he was believed to be the Messiah." A further clue may be found in a tenth-century history of the world in Arabic by a Christian named Agapius. He omits "if indeed we ought to call him a man," as well as the reference to Jesus' miracles and to the role of the Jewish leaders in accusing Jesus; and he says not that Jesus appeared to his disciples on the third day but that his disciples reported this event. Most important, his version declares not that Jesus was the Messiah but that "he was perhaps the Messiah." Two centuries later a twelfth-century chronicle in Syriac by a Christian named Michael the Syrian, in its version of the *Testimonium,* has language similar to that of Jerome: "He was thought to be the Messiah."

3. Josephus as Interpreter of the Bible.
Josephus solemnly assures his readers that he has set forth the precise details of the Scriptures, neither adding nor omitting anything (Josephus *Ant.* 1.proem.3 §17), whereas in fact he adds, subtracts and modifies, usually in minor respects but sometimes in major shifts as well. One such case is that of Jehoash, who in the Bible (2 Kings 13:11) is said to have done evil in the sight of the Lord. Yet in Josephus he is described as a good man (*Ant.* 9.8.6 §178). Again, Josephus goes so far as to transform Jehoiachin, who in the Bible is said to have done evil in the sight of the Lord (2 Kings 24:9; 2 Chron 36:9), into a king who is described as kind and just (*Ant.* 10.7.1 §100).

It seems hardly convincing, in view of the highly competitive nature of the craft of historian, to say that Josephus is not telling the truth or that he is careless or that he depends upon the ignorance of his readers, knowing how difficult it would be for them to check up on him, with manuscripts being relatively scarce and with there being no indices. Apparently this kind of programmatic statement, as we see in other historians of the era (e.g., Dionysius of Halicarnassus *Thuc.* 5 and 8), is intended to assure the reader that the historian has done his research honestly.

Moreover, in taking such liberties, Josephus

had the precedent of the Bible itself, namely, the book of Chronicles, which often differs in attitude and in specific details with the corresponding treatments in the books of Samuel and Kings. Other precedents were to be found in the *Septuagint, in such historians (usually regarded as Jewish) as Demetrius, Artapanus, Eupolemus, Pseudo-Eupolemus, Cleodemus Malchus and Pseudo-Hecataeus (*see* Jewish Literature: Historians and Poets); in such *Dead Sea Scrolls as the **Genesis Apocryphon;* in the book of **Jubilees;* in *Pseudo-Philo's *Biblical Antiquities;* and in traditions embodied in the *targumim and *midrashim. The practice of rewriting the Bible was apparently well established among the Dead Sea sect, so that it is frequently impossible to tell whether a given fragment represents an alternate reading of a text or an interpretation of it (*see* Rewritten Bible in Pseudepigrapha and Qumran).

In addition, as we see in *Cicero's famous letter to his friend Lucceius (Cicero *Fam.* 5.12), there is precedent even in the much admired historian Polybius for exaggerating and for disregarding the canons of history when writing a monograph. Apparently Josephus has extended this to writing the history of a whole people, the Jews.

Finally, in his rewriting of the sacred text, Josephus has the precedent of the Greek tragedians, with whom he was well acquainted. Even at the religious festivals of the god Dionysus, they did not hesitate unabashedly to remold the familiar myths as they saw fit. Even Plato (Plato *Rep.* 2.377) and the *Stoics, who object to the degrading portrayal of the gods, do not object to the fact that the myths are interpreted with such latitude and seek to have them interpreted even more liberally.

Among the factors that influenced Josephus most in his rewriting of the Bible in the first half of the *Antiquities* we may note his audience. That his audience consisted primarily of non-Jews is clear from the statement that his work was undertaken in the belief that the whole Greek-speaking world would find it worthy of attention (Josephus *Ant.* 1.proem.2 §5). Josephus states as the precedent for his work the translation of the Pentateuch known as the Septuagint, which was undertaken at the behest of a non-Jewish king, Ptolemy II Philadelphus (*Ant.* 1.proem.3 §10).

To be sure, his secondary audience consisted of Jews, as we see from his apology for rearranging the order of the biblical narrative; he states that perhaps "any of my countrymen who read this work should reproach me" (Josephus *Ant.* 4.8.4 §197). Moreover, he is apparently addressing Jews in his audience in his accounts of the Israelites' sin with the Midianite women, which he has increased in length from nine verses (Num 25:1-9) to twenty-five paragraphs (*Ant.* 4.6.7-12 §§131-55), Samson's affairs with non-Jewish women (*Ant.* 5.8.5-11 §§286-313) and Solomon's excesses of passion (*Ant.* 8.7.5 §§191-98), all of which stress the dangers of assimilation and intermarriage. Finally, only Jews would appreciate the cryptic references to the fall of the Roman Empire in Balaam's prophecy (*Ant.* 4.6.5 §125) and in Nebuchadnezzar's dream (*Ant.* 10.10.4 §210), and in the latter passage's invitation to read the book of Daniel.

Because eminent intellectuals, such as Apollonius Molon and Apion, had accused the Jews of not having produced any outstanding inventors in the arts or eminent sages and of not having added anything useful to human civilization (Josephus *Ag. Ap.* 2.12 §135; 2.14 §148), Josephus felt a need to prove, through his delineation of biblical personalities, that the Jews had indeed produced such virtuous and outstanding leaders. Thus he elevates the genealogy of Abraham (*Ant.* 1.6.5 §148), Rebekah (*Ant.* 1.16.2 §247), Jacob (*Ant.* 1.19.4 §§288-90), Joseph (*Ant.* 2.2.1 §9), Amram (*Ant.* 2.9.3 §210), Moses (*Ant.* 2.9.6 §229), Aaron (*Ant.* 4.2.4 §26), Gideon (*Ant.* 5.6.2 §213), Jephthah (*Ant.* 5.7.8 §257), Samson (*Ant.* 5.8.2 §276), Saul (*Ant.* 6.4.1 §45), Shallum (*Ant.* 10.4.2 §59), Gedaliah (*Ant.* 10.9.1 §155) and Esther (*Ant.* 11.6.1 §185). Among biblical figures whose precocity he emphasizes are Moses (*Ant.* 2.9.7 §233), who, though only an infant, throws down the crown placed upon his head by Pharaoh, and Josiah (*Ant.* 10.4.1 §50), who, though only twelve years old, showed his piety by endeavoring to have the people give up their belief in idols.

Moreover, the importance for the Greeks of beautiful appearance may be discerned from Plato's remark that the philosopher-kings in his ideal state should, if at all possible, be the most handsome persons (Plato *Rep.* 7.535). To Josephus it is Joseph's handsomeness that made him especially beloved to his father (Josephus *Ant.* 2.2.1 §9) as well as to Potiphar's wife (*Ant.* 2.4.2 §41). Pharaoh's daughter is enchanted with the beauty of the infant Moses (*Ant.* 2.9.5 §224).

Likewise Josephus calls attention to Saul's and David's handsomeness (*Ant.* 6.4.1 §45; 6.8.1 §164). Absalom's beauty, we are told, surpassed even those who lived in great luxury (*Ant.* 7.8.5 §189).

In particular Josephus aggrandizes the cardinal virtues possessed by his biblical heroes. Abraham is a veritable philosopher (Josephus *Ant.* 1.7.1 §154) who presents an original proof of the existence of God (*Ant.* 1.7.1 §156). Jacob shows wisdom in understanding the significance of Joseph's dreams (*Ant.* 2.2.3 §15). Joseph's wisdom is likewise manifest in his interpretation of the dreams of the butler, the baker and Pharaoh (*Ant.* 2.5.1-2 §§63-65; 2.5.6-7 §§84-87). Moses is said to have surpassed all others in understanding (*Ant.* 4.8.49 §328). Among others whose wisdom is stressed are Saul (*Ant.* 6.4.1 §45), Abner (*Ant.* 7.1.5 §31), David (*Ant.* 7.7.4 §158) and especially Solomon (*Ant.* 8.2.2 §34).

Josephus felt a particular need to emphasize the courage of his biblical heroes because Jews had been reproached with cowardice by such influential intellectuals as Apollonius Molon (Josephus *Ag. Ap.* 2.14 §148). Furthermore, Josephus himself had been similarly accused (*J.W.* 3.8.4 §358). Hence he expatiates the description of the courage of Abraham in his fight against the Assyrians (*Ant.* 1.9.1 §172), of Abraham's sons (*Ant.* 1.15.1 §§239-41) in their joint effort with the renowned Heracles and in the long account of Moses' expedition against the Ethiopians (*Ant.* 2.10.1-2 §§238-51) and in Moses' conduct of war after the exodus from Egypt (*Ant.* 2.15.3—16.3 §§320-44).

The stress that the Greeks placed upon temperance may be seen in the motto inscribed in Delphi: *mēden agan.* Moses is praised for his command of his passions (Josephus *Ant.* 4.8.47-49 §§318-29). The Bible has an embarrassing scene in which Elisha loses his self-control and curses some little boys who jeered him for his baldness (*Ant.* 8.15.5 §414); Josephus, who clearly admires Elisha, omits the incident. In the case of Jehu, whom Josephus seeks to rehabilitate, both the Hebrew and Septuagint texts (2 Kings 9:20) indicate that he drove his chariot madly; Josephus says that he drove slowly and in good order (*Ant.* 9.6.3 §117). The virtue of modesty, which is allied with that of temperance, is particularly to be seen in Moses (*Ant.* 4.8.49 §§328-29), Gideon (*Ant.* 5.6.6 §230), Saul (*Ant.* 6.4.5 §63), David (*Ant.* 7.15.2 §391) and Solomon (*Ant.* 8.5.3 §§146-49), the last most remarkably in recognizing that he had proven inferior to a Tyrian lad, Abdemon, in proposing and in solving riddles.

The fact that justice is the subject of the most famous and most influential of Plato's dialogues, *The Republic,* is an indication of the importance of this virtue, which is central in Josephus's depiction of most of the major personalities of the Bible, such as Abraham (Josephus *Ant.* 1.7.2 §158), Moses (*Ant.* 3.4.1 §§66-67), Samuel (*Ant.* 6.3.3 §36; 6.13.5 §294), Saul (*Ant.* 6.11.2 §212), David (*Ant.* 6.13.4 §290; 7.5.4 §110), Solomon (*Ant.* 8.2.1 §21), Josiah (*Ant.* 10.4.1 §50), Gedaliah (*Ant.* 10.9.1 §155), Daniel (*Ant.* 10.11.4 §246), Ezra (*Ant.* 11.5.1 §121) and Nehemiah (*Ant.* 11.5.8 §183).

The presence of *philanthrōpia* ("humanity"), which is so closely connected with justice, is particularly important to Josephus in his answer to the charge that Jews hate other peoples (Josephus *Ag. Ap.* 2.10 §121; 2.14 §148). Hence this virtue is ascribed to Rebekah (*Ant.* 1.16.2 §250), Joseph (*Ant.* 2.6.3 §101; 2.6.8 §§136, 145), David (*Ant.* 6.13.6 §299; 6.13.7 §304; 7.6.1 §118; 7.8.4 §184; 7.15.2 §391), Solomon (*Ant.* 8.4.3 §§116-17), Gedaliah (*Ant.* 10.9.3 §§163-64) and Zerubbabel (*Ant.* 11.4.3 §87). In the case of Gedaliah, for example, the returnees to Judea are so impressed with his kindness *(chrēstotēs)* and friendliness *(philanthrōpia)* that they develop a very great affection for him. Indeed, generosity is a prime quality of Samuel (*Ant.* 6.10.1 §194), Jehonadab (*Ant.* 9.6.7 §133), Jehoiada (*Ant.* 9.8.3 §166) and Hezekiah (*Ant.* 9.13.1 §260).

One aspect of *philanthrōpia* that was of special significance for the ancients was *hospitality, as we see, for example, in the concept of guest-friendship as enunciated in the meeting of Glaucus and Diomedes in book 6 of Homer's *Iliad* and in the reception accorded Odysseus by the Phaeacians in books 6-8 of the *Odyssey.* Josephus is particularly eager to answer the charge of inhospitality, as found in such writers as Juvenal (Juvenal *Sat.* 14.103-4), that the Jews show the way or a fountain to none except fellow Jews. Hence he stresses the presence of this quality in such key figures as Moses (Josephus *Ant.* 3.3.1 §63), Boaz (*Ant.* 5.9.3 §330) and David (*Ant.* 7.2.2 §54). It is particularly prominent in Gedaliah, who, when warned of the plot against his life by Ishmael, responds that he prefers to die by Ishmael's hands rather than to put to death a man, namely, Ishmael, who had taken refuge with him and had entrusted his very life to him. Likewise, we see the importance of regard for a suppliant in Josephus's expansion (*Ant.* 8.14.4 §386) of the reception Ahab gave to Ben-hadad.

Another important aspect of justice is gratefulness. This is displayed, in extrabiblical additions, by Joseph (Josephus *Ant.* 2.6.8 §152), Jethro's daughters (*Ant.* 2.11.2 §262), Moses (*Ant.* 2.11.2 §262), Joshua (*Ant.* 5.1.7 §30; 5.1.25 §95), Saul (*Ant.* 6.7.4 §145), David (*Ant.* 7.3.3 §69; 7.5.5 §111; 7.7.5 §160; 7.11.4 §§272-74), Jehoshaphat (*Ant.* 9.1.1 §2) and Mordecai (*Ant.* 11.6.13 §294).

That piety is to be regarded as the fifth of the cardinal virtues is clear from Plato (*Protag.* 330B, 349B). Moreover, that *pietas* is the great Roman virtue is clear from the fact that it is the key quality of Aeneas in the great national epic of the Romans, Virgil's *Aeneid.* It was particularly important for Josephus to stress this virtue in his biblical heroes inasmuch as the Jews had been accused of teaching impiety (Josephus *Ag. Ap.* 2.41 §291). Thus Josephus makes a point of stressing that it is especially in piety that Moses trained the Israelites (*Ant.* 1.proem.2 §6). Again, Jehoshaphat shows his piety in that he tells his people that they must show their faith in the prophet Jahaziel by not even drawing themselves up for battle (*Ant.* 9.1.3 §12). Conversely, because it clearly implies impiety, Josephus is careful to omit the account of Gideon's making of an ephod out of the earrings formed from spoils of war (*Ant.* 5.6.7 §232).

Above all, in his rewriting of the Bible, Josephus preaches a realistic attitude and even a high regard for the superpower of the day. Thus, in his reworking of the narrative of Gedaliah, the client governor of Judea appointed by Nebuchadnezzar, and with clear implications for the contemporary position of Jews vis-à-vis the Romans, Josephus stresses that it is a matter of military necessity for the Jews to remain subservient to the superpower. Again, despite the Bible's strongly positive view of Hezekiah, Josephus is clearly critical of Hezekiah for not realistically accommodating himself to the superior power of that day, Assyria; and, drawing a parallel to the situation of the Jews vis-à-vis the Romans, Josephus is less than enthusiastic about him, even going to the point of asserting that it was cowardice that influenced Hezekiah not to come out himself to meet the Assyrians (Josephus *Ant.* 10.1.2 §5). The fact that Hezekiah was encouraged by the prophet Isaiah to resist the Assyrians may help to explain Josephus's relative downgrading of Isaiah's importance.

Josephus, in contrast to the Bible (2 Kings 14:9; 2 Chron 36:9), presents a very positive view of Jehoiachin (Josephus *Ant.* 10.7.1 §100), presumably because he saw a striking parallel between the events surrounding the destruction of the two temples and because Jehoiachin, as Josephus himself did later, realized the power of the enemy and surrendered to him in order to save the temple from destruction; significantly, in his address to his fellow Jews urging the Jews to surrender, the one precedent he cites is that of Jehoiachin (*J.W.* 6.2.1 §§103-4). Josephus justifies the subservience of Gedaliah to the Babylonians, where Gedaliah is a thinly veiled version of Josephus, and Ishmael, his assassin, is a thinly veiled version of John of Gischala (*Ant.* 10.9.3 §§164-66). Significantly, the same damning epithets are applied to Ishmael, the assassin of Gedaliah, as are used of John (*Ant.* 10.9.2 §160 = *Life;* 16 §85; 21 §102; *J.W.* 2.21.1 §585; 4.3.13 §208; 4.7.1 §389; 5.10.4 §441).

One of the recurring charges against Jews was that they had an implacable hatred of non-Jews. To answer this charge, as made by Apollonius Molon and Lysimachus (Josephus *Ag. Ap.* 2.14 §145) and repeated by Tacitus (Tacitus *Hist.* 5.5.1), Josephus goes out of his way to stress that Jews show compassion for non-Jews. Joseph sells grain to all people and not merely to native Egyptians (*Ant.* 2.6.1 §94; 2.6.3 §101). Jethro is seen in a most favorable light; when he wishes to criticize the way in which Moses is administering justice, he shows remarkable sensitivity in taking him aside so as not to embarrass him. Again, Solomon, in dedicating the temple, asks that God grant the prayers not only of Jews but also of non-Jews (*Ant.* 8.4.3 §§116-17). Furthermore, when Mesha, the king of the Moabites, sacrifices his own son to his god, the Bible says nothing about the reaction of Jehoshaphat and Jehoram (2 Kings 3:27); Josephus calls attention to their humanity and compassion (*Ant.* 9.3.2 §43).

Philanthrōpia is a quality that Josephus ascribes to Cyrus (Josephus *Ag. Ap.* 1.20 §153) and Xerxes (*Ant.* 11.5.1 §123). The other non-Jewish leaders whom Josephus presents in a more favorable light include Balaam, Eglon the king of Moab, Nebuchadnezzar, Belshazzar, Darius, Ahasuerus, and even the various pharaohs (especially the one connected with Joseph) that are mentioned in the Bible. For example, Josephus stresses Ahasuerus's undeviating respect for law (*Ant.* 11.6.2 §195), portrays his relationship with Esther as a lawful marriage (*Ant.* 11.6.2 §202), stresses his tender concern for her (*Ant.* 11.6.9 §236) and depicts him as the ideal ruler who is totally concerned with peace, good government and the welfare of his subjects (*Ant.* 11.6.6 §216; 11.6.5 §213). Where he does criticize non-Jewish leaders he usually puts the blame on their advisers.

Moreover, in an interpretation of Exodus 22:27 [28], wherein he follows the Septuagint, Josephus declares that Jews are forbidden to speak ill of the religion of Gentiles out of respect for the very word *god* (Josephus *Ant.* 4.8.10 §207; *Ag. Ap.* 2.33 §237). Thus Josephus omits the passage in which Gideon, upon instructions from God, pulls down the altar of Baal and the Asherah tree that was worshiped beside it (Judg 6:25-32). Inasmuch as *mystery cults were held in such high regard by many non-Jews, it is not surprising that Josephus omits the statement, as found in the Septuagint translation, that Asa ended the mystery cults (1 Kings 15:12). Furthermore, he omits the statement that Jehoshaphat removed the pagan high places and Asherahs (2 Chron 17:6 vs. *Ant.* 9.1.1 §1). He likewise omits Jehu's conversion of the temple of Baal into an outhouse (2 Kings 10:27).

Furthermore, in his effort to establish better relations between Jews and non-Jews Josephus emphasizes that Gentile nations are not motivated by hatred of the Jews. Thus Balak and Balaam are motivated not by hatred but rather by a desire to defeat the Jews militarily (Josephus *Ant.* 4.6.4 §112). In Josephus's view, Balaam's readiness to curse the Israelites is due not to hatred for them but rather to his friendship with Balak (*Ant.* 4.6.5 §§120-21). Again, Haman's hatred for the Jews is presented not as part of an eternal Jewish-Gentile conflict but rather as a personal grudge, since he is an Amalekite (*Ant.* 11.6.5 §212).

It is particularly effective to have the Jews complimented by non-Jews. Jethro is so impressed with Moses that he even adopts him as his son (Josephus *Ant.* 2.11.2 §263). Again, Balaam, who has been sent to curse the Jews, declares that they have been invested by God with superior bravery (*Ant.* 4.6.4 §117). Finally, the supreme example of compliments directed toward Jews by non-Jews is to be found in connection with Solomon. Thus we read that the Queen of Sheba's strong desire to see Solomon arose from the daily reports that she received about his country (*Ant.* 8.6.5 §165). Furthermore, we read of the compliment paid to Solomon by a certain Dios, who wrote a history of Phoenicia and who reported how honest and modest Solomon was in acknowledging that he had been bested in the solving of riddles by a Tyrian lad named Abdemon (*Ant.* 8.5.3 §149; *Ag. Ap.* 1.17 §§114-15).

Thus Josephus's second edition of the Bible, so to speak, is particularly designed at once to answer critics of the Jews and to instill in Jews a sense of pride in their history and to teach them how to avoid the mistakes of the past and to learn from them.

See also HISTORIANS: GRECO-ROMAN; JEWISH LITERATURE: HISTORIANS AND POETS; JOSEPHUS: VALUE FOR NEW TESTAMENT STUDY; REWRITTEN BIBLE IN PSEUDEPIGRAPHA AND QUMRAN.

BIBLIOGRAPHY. **Bibliographies:** L. H. Feldman, *Josephus and Modern Scholarship (1937-1980)* (Berlin: Walter de Gruyter, 1984); idem, *Josephus: A Supplementary Bibliography* (New York: Garland, 1986); idem, "A Selective Critical Bibliography of Josephus," in *Josephus, the Bible and History,* ed. L. H. Feldman and G. Hata (Detroit: Wayne State University Press, 1989) 330-448; H. Schreckenberg, *Bibliographie zu Flavius Josephus* (Leiden: E. J. Brill, 1968); idem, *Bibliographie zu Flavius Josephus: Supplementband mit Gesamtregister* (Leiden: E. J. Brill, 1979). **Studies:** P. Bilde, *Flavius Josephus Between Jerusalem and Rome: His Life, His Works and Their Importance* (Sheffield: Sheffield Academic Press, 1988); S. J. D. Cohen, *Josephus in Galilee and Rome: His Vita and Development as a Historian* (Leiden: E. J. Brill, 1979); L. H. Feldman, "Flavius Josephus Revisited: The Man, His Writings and His Significance," *ANRW* 2.21.2, (1984) 763-862; idem, *Josephus's Interpretation of the Bible* (HCS 27; Berkeley and Los Angeles: University of California Press, 1998); idem, *Studies in Josephus' Rewritten Bible* (Leiden: E. J. Brill, 1998); L. H. Feldman and G. Hata, eds., *Josephus, Judaism and Christianity* (Detroit: Wayne State University Press, 1987); idem, *Josephus, the Bible and History* (Detroit: Wayne State University Press, 1989); M. Hadas-Lebel, *Flavius Josephus: Eyewitness to Rome's First-Century Conquest of Judea*

(New York: Macmillan, 1993); S. Mason, *Flavius Josephus on the Pharisees: A Composition-Critical Study* (Leiden: E. J. Brill, 1991); idem, *Josephus and the New Testament* (Peabody, MA: Hendrickson, 1992); T. Rajak, *Josephus: The Historian and His Society* (London: Duckworth, 1983); S. Schwartz, *Josephus and Judaean Politics* (Leiden: E. J. Brill, 1990); P. Spilsbury, *The Image of the Jew in Flavius Josephus' Paraphrase of the Bible* (Tübingen: Mohr Siebeck, 1998); G. E. Sterling, *Historiography and Self-Definition: Josephos, Luke-Acts and Apologetic Historiography* (Leiden: E. J. Brill, 1992); H. St. J. Thackeray, *Josephus, the Man and the Historian* (New York: Jewish Institute of Religion, 1929).

L. H. Feldman

JOSEPHUS: VALUE FOR NEW TESTAMENT STUDY

The writings of Flavius *Josephus (A.D. 37-c. 100) constitute by far the most important body of literature for the background of Christianity. It is Josephus who tells us almost everything we know about the non-Christian figures, groups, institutions, customs, geographical areas and events mentioned in the NT. He is the only surviving contemporary writer, for example, who describes John the Baptist, the Jewish high *priests of the first century, the *Pharisees and *Sadducees, the various regions of Judea, *Samaria and *Galilee, *Herod the Great, Agrippa II and Berenice, the Jerusalem *temple renovated by Herod and its destruction in the revolt of 66-74, the census under Quirinius, Judas the Galilean, Theudas and the Egyptian prophet (*see* Revolutionary Movements). Although his older contemporary *Philo mentions Pontius Pilate and Agrippa I, even there Josephus's evidence is critical for reconstruction.

These pieces of information may not, however, turn out to be the most important contributions of Josephus to the study of NT backgrounds. For scholars are coming to realize that Josephus writes about these matters because he has stories to tell. And those stories represent the most fully articulated statements of first-century Judaism in Judea that we possess. They are told by a contemporary of the first and second Christian generations who came from circles very different from Jesus' followers: from a member of the governing aristocratic priesthood. Josephus's narratives are important, then, both because they represent a different view of the same conditions that the NT mentions and because they provide the indispensable context for understanding what Josephus says about Herod, Pilate, the temple, and so on. We cannot use this information without first understanding what it means as Josephus tells it.

This article will first introduce each of Josephus's surviving works in their social and literary contexts in Rome. Then we shall consider the suggestive parallels between Josephus and Luke-Acts.

1. Josephus's Writings
2. The Life and Character of Josephus
3. Josephus and the New Testament

1. Josephus's Writings.

1.1. **Jewish War.** We first encounter Josephus in his seven-volume account of the *Jewish War*, the core of which he wrote between A.D. 75 and 79 but which he completed during the reigns of Titus (A.D. 79-81) and Domitian (A.D. 81-96; *see* Roman Emperors). We are fairly confident of the following sketch. He led one group of Galileans in the revolt against Rome. He surrendered to the Romans in July 67. After serving as a Roman prisoner and intelligence assistant, he was liberated (late 69) and taken back to Rome in 71. There he first wrote an account of the war in Aramaic, for Parthians and the Jews living among them. Then he wrote a Greek account of the war, which was an essentially new work in relation to the Aramaic. He was treated decently, but not conspicuously well, by successive Flavian rulers in Rome. Although he was given space to live in Vespasian's former private house, along with Roman *citizenship, a stipend, some tax relief and land in the conquered Judea, neither he nor his sons received any of the standard Roman benefits for exceptional service or *friendship (e.g., land in Italy, equestrian or senatorial status).

Post-70 Rome was evidently a difficult place for members of the expatriate Judean community there. They witnessed the spectacular *triumphal marches commemorating the submission of Jerusalem, the minting of celebratory *coins ("Judea Capta!"), the erection of a massive arch memorializing Titus's victory and the aggressive collection of the Jewish tax, now diverted for the support of the temple to Jupiter Capitolinus in Rome. Roman writers reveled in the Judean defeat on two grounds: first, the revolt seemed to embody what they saw as the Jews' national character, bellicose and oddly withdrawn from the rest of the world's culture; second, the Roman triumph represented the obvious victory of Roman virtue over Judean misanthropy and of the Roman gods over the Judean God, who had made his people so hostile to other deities.

This was the situation in which Josephus wrote the *War*. Although many scholars have read this work as pro-Roman propaganda, there is considerable evidence in the book's context and content for a different reading. Josephus claims that he writes in order to counter anti-Judean and pro-Roman accounts already in existence (Josephus *J.W.* pref.1.3 §§1-3, 7-9). And his two main theses directly challenge the two accusations that the Judeans are hated by the gods (or serve a defeated God) and that the revolt confirmed their hostility toward the rest of the *Roman Empire. Josephus counters, first, that the revolt was engineered by a small handful of power-seeking tyrants who by various means were able to lead the people away from their historic and legitimate priestly-aristocratic leadership, with catastrophic results (*see* Jewish Wars with Rome). The argument is not simplistic but allows that loyalty of the Judeans was sorely tested by corrupt and incompetent governors. Nevertheless, the ancient Judean tradition favored peaceful good citizenship and faithfulness.

In support of this claim Josephus provides detailed examples of the national character: the early *Hasmoneans, who fought off a vicious oppressor (and the Romans' old enemy) and quickly made an ally of the Romans (Josephus *J.W.* 1.1.4 §38); Herod, whose friendship with several Roman rulers was famous and full of consequence, for he won guarantees and exemptions for all Jews in the empire; the *Essenes, who led exemplary lives as models of peace and order (Josephus *J.W.* 2.8.2-13 §§119-61); and several members of the upper priesthood and royalty, who courageously spoke out for peace against the fickleness of the masses (e.g., Josephus *J.W.* 2.15.4—17.4 §§321-421).

The reason why Jews can tolerate the rule of various powers, as Josephus says in speeches attributed to several characters, is that they have a profound belief in God's control of human history *(pronoia heimarmenē)*. Convinced that no nation achieves power without divine aid (Josephus *J.W.* 2.8.7 §140), they are willing to observe the rise and fall of world powers under the sovereignty of God (Josephus *J.W.* 2.16.4 §§365-87), and they know that they themselves would only ever achieve freedom if God brought it to pass—that their own militancy would be doomed to fail (Josephus *J.W.* 5.9.3—9.4 §§362-419). This view of history has many affiliations with biblical Jeremiah and Daniel, and Josephus sees himself as a latter-day Jeremiah (Josephus *J.W.* 5.9.4 §§392-93). So, against the position that the Judean God now stands defeated, Josephus declares that the Romans too serve him, in this case as instruments for cleansing his temple from the pollutions created by the rebel leaders.

Although Josephus unquestionably includes in his narrative the flattery of Vespasian and Titus that was unavoidable in Flavian Rome, his *War* appears to be mainly a bid for recognizing the Judeans as good citizens of the empire and so for the cessation of any hostilities toward them. He evinces much concern about reprisals in various places around the Mediterranean (Josephus *J.W.* 2.18.1-7 §§457-93). Rather than serving as Roman propaganda, therefore, the *War* may well have been intended as a courageous presentation in behalf of his people. It is not clear exactly who first read or heard him recite his account, although King Agrippa II, who seems to have been involved in the development of the book, may have been his primary patron. The imperial family received copies after its completion and endorsed it; presumably its message of peace, good citizenship and avoidance of reprisal was also in their interests. As with all ancient texts, we should probably assume that Josephus expected a friendly or at least malleable first audience, so that his aim would be not so much to convince the powerfully disaffected but to give well-wishers a way of conceiving the conflict that would help them answer critics.

1.2. Antiquities** and **Life. We next encounter Josephus in his twenty-one-volume magnum opus, the *Antiquities of the Jews* and *Life*, which he completed during the last years of Domitian's reign (A.D. 93), the years that were most difficult for many in the senatorial aristocracy. In the prologue, Josephus claims that those interested in Judean culture have pressed him to provide an account of the Judean constitution *(politeia;* Josephus *Ant.* 1.pref.2-3 §§5-17). These "lovers of learning" are led by one Epaphroditus, whose identity is uncertain. His name and what Josephus says about him, including the form of address "most excellent" *(kratiste),* suggest a freedman of some wealth and social prominence who has experienced marked turns of fortune. This description would best suit Nero's former correspondence secretary of that name, who would die at Domitian's hand in 95, but we cannot be sure. Another candidate is a grammarian who died in about 97. The latter half of the prologue (Josephus *Ant.* 1.pref.4 §§18-26) begins to develop the philosophical underpinnings of the Judean constitution. Josephus sets out to show that this constitution is unique in the world: more ancient than others, philosophically purer and universally effective in its punishment of vice and reward of virtue, in contrast to the codes of other nations.

The *Antiquities* engages directly, therefore, a long-standing Greek and Roman debate about the best kind of constitution: monarchy, aristocracy or democracy. The problem was not abstract but of immediate import in Josephus's Rome. The old aristocratic republic of the Roman city-state had begun to falter as the empire grew so rapidly in the second century B.C. Various individuals came to unusual positions of great prominence over their fellows, thus straining to the limit the collegial model of leadership. From Augustus onward, a sort of compromise was reached between republican forms and the real executive power of the *princeps,* but the problem persevered. In Josephus's Rome, where Domitian had taken on many trappings of monarchy, where many senators longed silently for the older system, constitutional questions were on the minds of all educated people.

In presenting the Judean constitution, Josephus displays little caution, again assuming a friendly audience. The Judeans have a senatorial priestly aristocracy that is older and purer than any other, one that does not tolerate monarchy (Josephus *Ant.* 4.7.17 §223; 6.3.3 §36). He begins with the antecedents in creation and the patriarchs: Abraham set the stage by deducing that God was one and by bringing the sciences to the Egyptians, whence they reached the Greeks. The constitution itself is elaborately presented in volumes 3 and 4, as a uniquely just but humane code. *Moses entrusted this to the college of priests, led by the high priest, in whose care it has remained ever since. The priests formed a senate, consulted by the best leaders. Although the constitution called for aristocracy, the Judeans experimented with monarchy from time to time, but this was always disastrous. Even Herod the Great now appears as an illegitimate king who departed from the laws (Josephus *Ant.* 14.15.2 §403). And Josephus pointedly uses the case of Gaius Caligula to include a Roman discussion of constitutions and the pitfalls of monarchy (Josephus *Ant.* 19.2.5—4.6 §§201-62).

Although it is not ideal, monarchy could be tolerable for a time when the ruler was also a philosopher. Thus Solomon was a remarkable ruler, a man wiser than any other in his understanding of nature and people, though he too went astray by placing his own wishes above the laws. All of the Judeans' famous figures, whether military leaders, kings, prophets or priests, lived philosophical lives: Abraham, Joseph, Moses, Joshua, David, Solomon, Jeremiah and Daniel.

This Greek primer in the Judean constitution falls neatly into two halves. The former ten volumes describe the first commonwealth, the regimes that led to the building of the first temple and then its destruction; the latter ten volumes describe the second commonwealth—to the eve of the Second Temple's recent destruction. The halfway point, significantly, is taken by Josephus's ruminations on the exilic prophet Daniel. Completely unaware of the later date that would be ascribed to Daniel by the *Platonist philosopher Porphyry (and by modern scholarship), Josephus appears deeply impressed by the fact that Daniel accurately predicted events under Antiochus IV Epiphanes so long before the fact. He takes this as decisive proof of his basic thesis: that the God of the Judean constitution not only controls all of history but also has encoded that history in the sacred Judean books (Josephus *Ant.* 10.11.7 §§277-81). From beginning to end, the *Antiquities* demonstrates the efficacy of these laws: the peril of those who violate them and the reward of those who follow them. He even includes near the end a compelling story concerning a prominent Gentile family who converted to adopt these laws as their own; they were especially protected and honored by God (Josephus *Ant.* 20.2.1—4.3 §§17-96).

At the end of the *Antiquities,* Josephus introduces an appendix on his own life and character. The main significance of this appears to be that he wishes to illustrate the Judean constitution by his own ancestry, public career (*Life* 2 §12: *polis, politeuesthai)* and character (Josephus *Ant.* 20.12.1 §266; *Life* 76 §430). A full member of the ancient Judean priestly aristocracy himself, and fully trained in the constitution's philosophical principles, he naturally led a stellar, albeit brief, public life in the period preceding his surrender. He experienced divine favor and protection, along with the friendship of important people; although assailed by unworthy, envious challengers who resorted to bribery and all sorts of other vices (John of Gischala, the delegation from Jerusalem, Justus of Tiberias), he succeeded where they failed miserably. His audience in Rome can take comfort from his credentials as a representative of this attractive Judean constitution.

1.3. **Against Apion.** Josephus's final two-volume work is traditionally known as *Against Apion,* although only about a quarter of it deals with Apion; Josephus apparently called it something like *On the Antiquity of the Judeans.* This is an effort to restate in much more systematic form the theses of *Antiquities:* extreme Judean antiquity, the nobility of Judean origins, the purity of the priestly line that preserves the constitution, the peerless moral excellence of the constitution and Judeans as the primary source of the world's best values. In the course of this systematic presentation, however, Josephus devotes the middle half of the book to refuting the Judeans' more prominent Egyptian slanderers, in order and by name.

Although scholars often take this argumentative focus as evidence that the work has a defensive aim, we note that as a sequel to the *Antiquities,* it appears to expect the same, already favorable audience; it is hard to imagine a real social context in which this work would reach the Jews' literary detractors; many of Josephus's particular arguments assume uncritical, well-disposed hearers; and ancient *rhetoric called for rebuttal and challenge even where there was no serious threat. On balance, then, it seems preferable to take *Against Apion* as a further composition for Gentiles interested in Judaism, so that they would have ready answers to common slanders. The book further encourages the interest of such Gentiles and even celebrates the reception given to converts (Josephus *Ag. Ap.* 2.28, 36, 38 §§209-10, 261, 282).

2. The Life and Character of Josephus.

The foregoing presentation differs from many in that it deals primarily with Josephus's writings, whereas most begin with his life. The common judgment that he was a traitor and informer strongly colors assessment of his writings—as propagandistic, opportunistic and perhaps even shamed attempts at rehabilitation. It makes better sense methodologically, however, to begin with what we have—his writings—and move only cautiously from there to the events of his life. He tells the story of his life quite differently in the *War* and in the *Life,* just as he tells most other stories differently in the parallel sections of *War* and *Antiquities.* This retelling of the same story with entirely new moral points and emphases, even contradicting what one had said before, was commonplace in Roman rhetoric, and there is no evidence that Josephus was embarrassed by it. In particular, we probably ought not to take his happy stories of duplicity, ruses, lies and dissembling as if it were incriminating. He tells these stories only to win points within the rules of the ancient rhetorical game. In the process, he has rendered much of his life unrecoverable to us.

3. Josephus and the New Testament.

In the NT, the most suggestive parallels with Josephus's writings are to be found in Luke-Acts. That work, too, is self-consciously historical (Lk 1:1-4) and addresses itself to an interested and somewhat informed *patron, who appears also to be an equestrian freedman: Theophilus. The author has the similar broad aim of conveying what is trustworthy or reliable about his group's way of life. Most interestingly, the author of Luke-Acts, when making reference to outside figures, happens to choose many of the people and events featured by Josephus: the watershed census under Quirinius, which sparked Judas the Galilean's revolt; Pilate; Herod Antipas; Theudas; and the Egyptian. It is an old debate whether the author knew Josephus's writings, and most scholars think that he did not. If he did, the writings in question would include *Antiquities* 18-20, which would put the composition of Luke-Acts after A.D. 93.

In any event, Josephus's works are extremely useful for reading along with Luke-Acts. Josephus writes from the inner circle of the ancient priestly aristocracy, the only legitimate leadership, for whom the Pharisees occupy an outer circle of tolerable but often disliked demagogues; they are still preferable to the various popular leaders, messiahs, false prophets and bandits with their ad hoc constituencies (*see* Revolutionary Movements). The Gospel of Luke looks at things from the other end: popular leader Jesus, though critical of the influential Pharisees, is able to converse with them as a fellow teacher, whereas the powerful Jerusalem priesthood appears as the very heart of darkness.

See also JOSEPHUS: INTERPRETIVE METHODS AND TENDENCIES.

BIBLIOGRAPHY. H. W. Attridge, *The Interpretation of Biblical History in the Antiquitates Judaicae of Flavius Josephus* (HDR 7; Missoula, MT: Scholars Press, 1976); P. Bilde, *Flavius Josephus Between Jerusalem and Rome: His Life, His Works and their Importance* (JSPSup 2; Sheffield: JSOT, 1988); S. J. D. Cohen, *Josephus in Galilee and Rome: His Vita and His Development as a Historian* (CSCT 8; Leiden: E. J. Brill, 1979); L. H. Feldman and G. Hata, eds., *Josephus, Judaism and Christianity* (Detroit: Wayne State University Press, 1987); idem, *Josephus, the Bible and History* (Detroit: Wayne State University Press, 1989); L. H. Feldman and J. R. Levison, eds., *Josephus's Contra Apionem: Studies in Its Character and Context with a Latin Concordance to the Portion Missing in Greek* (AGJU 34; Leiden: E. J. Brill, 1996); R. Laqueur, *Der jüdische Historiker Flavius Josephus: Ein biographischer Versuch auf neuer Quellenkritischer Grundlage* (Darmstadt: Wissenschaftlicher Buchgesellschaft, 1979 repr.); H. Lindner, *Die Geschichtsauffassung des Flavius Josephus im Bellum Judaicum* (AGJU 12; Leiden: E. J. Brill, 1972); S. Mason, *Flavius Josephus on the Pharisees: A Composition-Critical Study* (SPB 39; Leiden: E. J. Brill, 1991); idem, *Josephus and the New Testament* (Peabody, MA: Hendrickson, 1992); idem, "'Should Anyone Wish to Enquire Further. . .' (*Ant.* 1.25): The Aim and Audience of Josephus's *Judean Antiquities*," in *Understanding Josephus: Seven Perspectives*, ed. S. Mason (Sheffield: Sheffield Academic Press, 1998); F. Parente and J. Sievers, *Josephus and the History of the Greco-Roman Period: Essays in Memory of Morton Smith* (SPB 41; Leiden: E. J. Brill, 1994); T. Rajak, *Josephus: The Man and His Society* (London: Duckworth, 1983); S. Schwartz, *Josephus and Judaean Politics* (CSCT 18; Leiden: E. J. Brill, 1990); G. E. Sterling, *Historiography and Self-Definition: Josephos, Luke-Acts and Apologetic Historiography* (NovTSup 44; Leiden: E. J. Brill, 1992); H. St. J. Thackeray, *Josephus: The Man and the Historian* (New York; Ktav, 1967 repr.).

S. Mason

JUBILEES

The book of *Jubilees* is a rewriting of Genesis 1—Exodus 19 (*see* Rewritten Bible in Pseudepigrapha and Qumran). A prefatory chapter indicates that the *pseudepigraphic setting for the work is the scene in Exodus 24, with *Moses on Mt. Sinai. There the Lord predicts Israel's apostasy, and Moses intercedes for the people. After he describes what will happen at the end, the Lord tells an angel of the presence to dictate the contents of the heavenly tablets to Moses. The angelic dictation begins with the creation story and continues with the biblical account until the Israelites arrive at Mt. Sinai. By having Moses record the biblical narrative, the writer indicates that Mosaic authorship of Genesis and the first part of Exodus was an idea known already when *Jubilees* was composed.

1. Date
2. Versions
3. Characteristics
4. Jubilees and the New Testament

1. Date.

There is reason to believe that *Jubilees* was written in Hebrew in approximately 150 B.C. Before the *Dead Sea Scrolls were found, it was thought that the original Hebrew form of the book had not survived, but among the scroll fragments fourteen or fifteen copies of the book have been identified. Two of these were found in Cave 1 (1Q17-18), two in Cave 2 (2Q19-20), one in Cave 3 (3Q5), eight or nine in Cave 4 (4Q176 frags. 19-21; 4Q216, 4Q218, 4Q219, 4Q220, 4Q221, 4Q222 and 4Q223-224; 4Q217 may be another copy, but this is uncertain) and one in Cave 11 (11Q12). The most ancient of these copies is 4Q216, which can be dated on the basis of its script to approximately 125-100 B.C.

Another indicator of the book's date is the fact that the **Damascus Document* (CD 16.2-4) cites *Jubilees* as an authority, and the earliest copy of this dates from the early to middle first century B.C. The author of *Jubilees* does seem to know the Enochic Animal Apocalypse (*1 Enoch* 85—90), which was written in the late 160s B.C. (*see* Enoch, Books of). *Jubilees* was thus composed between the late 160s B.C. and the time of the earliest surviving copy of it (125-100 B.C.). It appears to have been written before the *Qumran community went to the wilderness; the number of copies found there and the influence *Jubilees* exercised on Qumran thought suggest that it was considered an important work by the members of that group and probably a highly authoritative one.

2. Versions.

At some point Hebrew *Jubilees* was translated into Greek. No manuscript of the Greek version is available, but a number of ancient writers cited from it and thus verify that it once existed. From Greek the book was rendered into Latin (one manuscript with part of the translation has survived) and Geʿez, the classical language of Ethiopia, the only version in which the book is fully extant. In the Christian church of Ethiopia *Jubilees* (called *kufāle* [Divisions]) was regarded as one of the books of the OT. It is possible that a Syriac translation was made from the Hebrew; it has, however, survived only in a series of quotations in other Syriac texts. Comparison of the Hebrew fragments of the book with the versions, especially the Ethiopic, shows that the ancient translators did their work very accurately. Because of this and because *Jubilees* cites Genesis and Exodus so frequently, the book has become an important witness to the wording of the biblical text in the second century B.C.

3. Characteristics.

Jubilees presents itself as a divine revelation: God speaks directly with Moses in *Jubilees* 1, and in the remaining chapters an angel of the presence dictates the contents of the book to him. The source for the angel's revelation is the tablets of heaven.

*3.1. **Chronology.*** The book provides a complete system of chronology for the first books of the Bible. For the author a Jubilee was a forty-nine-year period; each of these he divided into seven "weeks" of years. He uses this system to date a long series of events in biblical history. His entire chronology covers the initial forty-nine Jubilees and the first few years of the fiftieth; the fiftieth Jubilee, which begins just before the exodus, is the time when the Israelite *slaves are freed from Egypt and when they will enter the promised land that had been assigned to their ancestors in the division of the earth after the flood (*Jub.* 8:12-21). By including these two events in the fiftieth Jubilee the author transfers onto a national level the two events that, according to biblical legislation, occurred for the individual in the Jubilee year: release of Hebrew slaves and repossession of alienated family property.

*3.2. **Calendar.*** A related feature is the annual solar calendar that underlies the Jubilee calculations. The writer claims that God had revealed to Enoch before the flood that the year consisted of 364 days (*Jub.* 4:17-18, 21) and that only the sun, not the moon, was to be used for calendrical purposes (*Jub.* 6:28-38). The 364-day solar year includes four quarters of 91 days each, and within a quarter the first and second months contain 30 days each and the third lasts 31 days. In this system, there are exactly 52 weeks in a year, so that in every year a particular date will fall on the same day of the week; as it turns out, no *festival ever falls on the *sabbath.

*3.3. **Earlier Laws.*** *Jubilees* also regularly antedates biblical legislation by claiming that laws and festivals that in the Bible were not revealed until Moses' time had already been disclosed to the patriarchs of Genesis. For example, the laws about a woman's purification after childbirth (Lev 12) are traced to the time of Adam and Eve (*Jub.* 3:8-14). Also, the pilgrimage festivals of Unleavened Bread, Weeks and Tabernacles are said to have been practiced long before the time of Moses (by Noah for the Festival of Weeks [*Jub.* 6:17-22] and by Abraham for all three [*Jub.* 18:17-19; 15:1-10; 16:15-31]). Although there is usually a textual trigger in Genesis that gives some justification for the writer to place the origins of the laws where he does, his larger purpose seems to have been to stress that the law was not a later accretion to biblical religion but an integral part of it from earliest times.

*3.4. **Covenant.*** *Jubilees* reserves a central place for the one eternal covenant that governs the relations between God and his people. The covenant was first made with Noah after the flood and renewed with Abraham, Isaac, Jacob and Israel. It embraced a set of laws that grew with time, and the author insists on strictest obedience to them. All of the covenantal ceremonies in *Jubilees* take place in the third month of the year. Several are specifically dated to the middle of this month, that is, the fifteenth day. This was the date on which the Festival of Weeks was celebrated in *Jubilees,* with the result that it became associated with remembering and renewing the covenant. Covenant ceremonies in *Jubilees* are accompanied by oaths; the Hebrew words for "oaths" *(š^{e}būʿôt)* and "weeks" *(šābūʿôt)* are very similar and may have encouraged the association. *Jubilees* is the earliest text to document this dating of the Festival of Weeks; the same date is also found in calendar texts among the Dead Sea Scrolls. *Jubilees'* strong condemnation of a calendar based on lunar observation, however, does not agree with the Qumran calendars, which correlate both lunar and solar arrangements.

3.5. Exegesis. *Jubilees* is one of the oldest witnesses to the expository methods used by Jewish experts in interpreting Genesis and Exodus, and in a number of places the writer shows his knowledge of how they solved some problems in the text (*see* Biblical Interpretation, Jewish). For example, one of the most important topics is sabbath law, which, as in the Bible, is introduced in connection with the seventh day of creation (*Jub.* 2:17-33; the book also ends with a section on sabbath legislation [*Jub.* 50:6-13]). One biblical passage that could prove disconcerting in this regard is Genesis 2:2: "on the seventh day God finished the work that he had done" (NRSV). From it one could conclude that God had violated the first sabbath by completing his creative work on it. The solution to this difficulty in *Jubilees* and in other sources is to change the ordinal so that God finishes his work on the sixth day (*Jub.* 2:1).

It is important to note that the author, as he rewrote and interpreted Genesis and Exodus, felt free to add and subtract passages. He adds lengthy sections on topics such as the calendar and festivals and omits details that might diminish the reputations of biblical heroes (e.g., he omits Abram's lie about his wife's identity [*Jub.* 13:11-15]). One of the longest additions in *Jubilees* is the section that deals with Jacob's son Levi (much of *Jub.* 30:1—32:9). According to biblical legislation, the male descendants of Levi served as *priests in Israel, but Genesis had little to say about their eponymous ancestor other than to criticize him for his part in the slaughter at Shechem (Gen 49:5-7). *Jubilees* rehabilitates Levi, making him into a model patriarch who is appointed priest and carries out priestly functions for his father and other family members. Levi is also presented as a member of a long priestly line through whom the writings of the ancestors were transmitted and preserved (see *Jub.* 45:16). It seems likely that the author of Jubilees was himself a priest.

3.6. Purity of the Chosen Line. *Jubilees* adds the names of many women to the biblical text (e.g., for the wives of the antediluvian patriarchs in Gen 5) and gives details about their genealogies. The concern was to document and guarantee the purity of the elect family and to show that when marriages outside acceptable limits took place, serious problems resulted (Halpern-Amaru).

4. Jubilees and the New Testament.

There is no clear evidence that NT writers were aware of the book of *Jubilees,* but some passages could be illumined from the information contained in it. One possibility is the notion mentioned in three places in the NT (Acts 7:38; Gal 3:19; Heb 2:2) that angels revealed the law on Mt. Sinai, as the angel of the presence reveals almost all of *Jubilees* to Moses. It was once thought that *Jubilees'* 364-day calendar might provide a solution to the problem that, while the Synoptic Gospels make Jesus' last supper a Passover meal, John places it on the day before Passover. A. Jaubert proposed that the Evangelists assumed different calendars, with John using the standard lunar-solar calendar of the time and the Synoptic Evangelists employing *Jubilees'* system. However, it is more likely that John's desire to present Jesus as the Passover lamb who was slain (they were being *sacrificed at the time he was crucified) led to the differing chronologies for the passion week. *Jubilees,* with its insistence on precise and full obedience to the law, may serve as an example of the kind of legal *piety that the apostle Paul opposed (see, for example, Col 2:16).

See also APOCRYPHA AND PSEUDEPIGRAPHA; BIBLICAL INTERPRETATION, JEWISH; REWRITTEN BIBLE IN PSEUDEPIGRAPHA AND QUMRAN.

BIBLIOGRAPHY. R. H. Charles, *The Book of Jubilees or the Little Genesis* (London: Adam & Charles Black, 1902); G. L. Davenport, *The Eschatology of the Book of Jubilees* (SPB 20; Leiden: E. J. Brill, 1971); J. C. Endres, *Biblical Interpretation in the Book of Jubilees* (CBQMS 18; Washington, DC: Catholic Biblical Association, 1987); B. Halpern-Amaru, *The Empowerment of Women in the Book of Jubilees* (SJSJ 60; Leiden: E. J. Brill, 1999); idem, "The First Woman, Wives and Mothers in *Jubilees,*" *JBL* 113 (1994) 609-26; A. Jaubert, *La Date de la Cène* (Paris: Librairie LeCoffre, 1957 [ET: *The Date of the Last Supper* (Staten Island, NY: Alba House, 1965)]); J. Kugel, "Levi's Elevation to the Priesthood in Second Temple Writings," *HTR* 86 (1993) 1-64; B. Noack, "The Day of Pentecost in Jubilees, Qumran and Acts," *ASTI* (1962) 73-95; C. Rabin, "Jubilees," in *The Apocryphal Old Testament,* ed. H. F. D. Sparks (Oxford: Clarendon Press, 1984) 1-139; S. Talmon, "The Calendar Reckoning of the Sect from the

Judean Desert," in *Aspects of the Dead Sea Scrolls,* ed. C. Rabin and Y. Yadin (ScrHier 4; Jerusalem: Magnes, 1958) 162-99; J. C. VanderKam, *The Book of Jubilees* (2 vols.; CSCO 510–11, Scriptores Aethiopici 87-88; Louvain: Peeters, 1989); idem, "Jubilees, Book of," *ABD* 3:1030-32; idem, *Textual and Historical Studies in the Book of Jubilees* (HSM 14; Missoula, MT: Scholars Press, 1977); J. C. VanderKam and J. T. Milik, "Jubilees," in *Qumran Cave 4VIII: Parabiblical Texts Part I* (DJD 13; Oxford: Clarendon Press, 1994) 1-140; O. Wintermute, "Jubilees," in *The Old Testament Pseudepigrapha,* ed. J. H. Charlesworth (2 vols.; Garden City, NY: Doubleday, 1983, 1985) 2:35-142. J. C. VanderKam

JUDAISM AND THE NEW TESTAMENT

Judaism in antiquity is a complex phenomenon, involving religious, social, economic, historical and ethnic aspects of the life of a people whose influence has greatly exceeded their power.

That influence is most obvious today in the literary remains of ancient Judaism, canonical and noncanonical, which continue to have a formative impact upon the very definition of human culture. But Judaism itself must not be equated directly with the religions of those Judaic sources that happen to remain; in order to assess those sources, to appreciate the significance of Judaism within the task of understanding Jesus and the NT and to gauge its influence more generally, a different approach is necessary. We need to uncover those religious systems of beliefs, reactions, social conventions, ways of thinking and habits of feeling that the literary sources and the history of the people manifest; moreover, those systems must be appraised with reference to their dramatic transitions over time, or not at all. The present article is to deal with Judaism through the time of the NT, that is, prior to the emergence of *rabbinic Judaism (*see DJG,* Rabbinic Traditions and Writings §1). Judaism in the time of the NT can be appreciated only on the basis of its procession from earlier forms. Accordingly, we must first turn our attention to the root of Judaism, the religion of *Israel, taking account of the delay between the emergence of that religion and the probable dates of its sources.

Judaism in every period is rooted in the notion that Israel is chosen. The perennial paradox in the study of Judaism is that the notion of election is more persistent than any definition of what Israel might be. We might be thinking of an extended family of Arameans that departed from Mesopotamia in order to settle westward, of their initial settlement in Canaan, of the migrant group in Egypt, of those who departed from Egypt, of those who struggled for control of the land of Canaan, of the nation and its eventual monarchy and consequent civil war, of the dispossessed peoples in Babylonia, of the ideal Israel that the Scriptures of the exile project and/or of those people both in the land and in the Diaspora who read those Scriptures as their own, for whom Israel was and is an identification of self.

Each of the moments of the development of Israel named above and each of several other stages has been the object of particular, scholarly attention. But we may, as a convenience, cope with the topic of Judaism under four stages: the period of prehistory, between the scriptural Abrahamic family and the scriptural people led by judges; the period of nationalization and monarchy; the period of dispossession and the canonization of Scripture; and the period of radical pluralization, which is widely referred to today as early Judaism.

1. The Prehistory of Israel: From Family to People
2. Nationalization and Monarchy
3. Dispossession and Canonization
4. Radical Pluralization
5. Early Judaism and the New Testament

1. The Prehistory of Israel: From Family to People.

If the conviction of being divinely elect is a condition *sine qua non* of Judaism, then the traditional notion that Abraham is the father of all Jews is a useful point of departure. After all, he is remembered as being partner to the covenant involving both God's gift of the land that would be called Israel and the sign of circumcision (Gen 15:1-21; 17:1-14). But the assumption of Genesis is that Abraham and the patriarchs are seminomadic, in the sense that they migrate and cultivate land. Just that style of living is what brings Israel, the children of Jacob, who was renamed in a struggle with God (Gen 32:22-32), down to Egypt. The emphasis throughout the patriarchal cycle is upon the literal kinship of the entire group that may be called Israel.

*Moses is particularly associated with the liberation of Israel from Egypt, but, just as the quality of the sojourn in that land changed (cf. Exod 1:8-10), so did the constitution of the people. The estimate of more than a half million warriors in Numbers 1:45-46 may well be hyperbolic, but an increase of population during a period described biblically as of more than four centuries (Ex 12:40) meant that any system of strictly familial lineage was out of the question. Moses was therefore responsible not simply for the liberation from Egypt but also for the reconstitution of Israel as a people, rather than simply a family, on the basis of his revelation.

The Mosaic constitution or covenant would become paradigmatic for every age of Judaism that followed. Tribal lineage, on the assumption that the tribes were descended from the sons of Jacob/Israel, replaced familial lineage as the operative definition of the group, and that was an evolution that the weight of numbers alone probably effected. But the tribal arrangement by itself was unsystematic and needed to be balanced by a centripetal impulse in order for Israel to emerge as a functional entity. Moses is the emblem of centralized *sacrifice and judgment. His claims upon Pharaoh are predicated upon sacrifice (Ex 3:18), and his relation to Jethro (or "Reuel," in the passage in question), the Midianite priest, makes his cultic interests manifest (Ex 2:15b-22). The notion of "the people" sacrificing creates the notion of the people; apart from some common action, there would be families, extended families, villages and "stems" (or "staffs," as the tribes are called in the *Hebrew Bible), but no organic whole.

The Mosaic constitution established the stem of Levi as the guardians of the sanctuary (cf. Num 4:1-49) and also assured that the conception of one God would be coextensive with the conviction of one people. If sacrifice was the charter of liberation, then a declension into multiple gods would return Israel to the division of Egypt (cf. Ex 20:2, 3, 22-26). A corollary of the unity of God and his people is that there should be a single sanctuary, but in the premonarchial phase we can speak only of the preeminence of the pan-tribal shrine, since worship at other sites is also attested. At the same time, the tribal stems of Israel were coordinated at the cultic center in a system of judgment (Ex 18:13-26), so that disputes could be regulated and the appropriate integrity of Israel could be maintained. That Israel should be whole, an integer of divine revelation, becomes the central imperative of the Mosaic covenant.

Sacrifice, within the Mosaic system, is the place of meeting between God and Israel (Ex 24:1-11), such that only what is clean may be involved (cf. Lev 11—15), and much of it passes to divine ownership (cf. Lev 3:1-17). Not only parts of things offered but the cultic instruments themselves (Ex 25—31) and the entire tribe of Levi (cf. Num 3:45) are God's. Moreover, the declared aim of entry into the land of promise is to cleanse it of what is not acceptable to God. Everything else, people, beasts and property, is to be "devoted," that is, extirpated (cf. Josh 6, 7). The pentateuchal emphasis upon that "devotion" (*ḥerem*) has confused some modern discussion. There has been a tendency to refer to the conquest of Canaan, but much of the language of destruction—which is undoubtedly present—needs to be understood in its sacrificial context, as a cleansing of the land.

Joshua and Judges reflect the situation in Canaan much more directly, in their stories of intertribal rivalries and wars, accommodations with the indigenous populations, the desire for booty and the problems inherent in the tendency to erect local shrines. Those glimpses into the turmoil in the midst of which the nation emerged have led to the evolution of distinct, scholarly theories concerning how Canaan was settled by Hebrew-speakers. M. Noth is associated with the theory of an amphictyony (such as existed in ancient Greece), an association of twelve tribes for cultic purposes. The number twelve is problematic, however. Greek amphictyonies of other numbers are known, and the number within Israel was largely theoretical, perhaps derived from sacrificial practice (cf. Josh 4:9, 20).

Levi was left out from the point of view of a geographical inheritance, and Joseph in standard lists could be counted three times, as Ephraim and the two half-tribes of Manasseh (cf. Josh 17:17, 18; 22:1-6). Unusual lists, such as Judges 1:16-36, have the tribes deviate from the number, names and kinship presupposed ordinarily in the Mosaic covenant. In addition, the point of Levi within Israel is to provide a fixed arrangement of cultic personnel for a moving sanctuary, while in Noth's Greek analogy tribes took turns in providing for a settled sanctuary. But with those crucial allowances, Noth's theory has been the most influential of the twentieth century. Crucial changes, however, have been suggested by G. Mendenhall and by N. Gottwald. The former envisages the occupation of the land as an instance of peasants' revolt, while the latter thinks in terms of a union between disenfranchised local elements and migrants from Egypt in opposition to Canaanite hegemony.

The Israel that (dis)possessed the land of Canaan, then, was an amalgam of groups that claimed such affinity with Abraham, pursued the worship of God laid down by Moses and on that basis sought to rid the land of Canaan of all but its own. Its destruction of other material cultures, particularly urban cultures (as in the case of Jericho; Josh 6), was its hallmark. Leadership consisted in the intervention of judges who defended the possession of a given stem or stems, rooted out elements of Canaanite worship or attacked non-Israelite powers. The authority of the judges seems to have resided in their success in pursuing one or more of those aims, which success might be attributed to possession by the Spirit of God (cf. Judg 11).

2. Nationalization and Monarchy.

Judges takes a particularly dim view of the institution that obviously would have provided greater stability: the monarchy. The removable ark of the covenant, which provided the center of Israel's loyalty and devotion, was vulnerable to attack, and the unsystematic convention of judges, while it might answer to the occasional onslaught of disorganized foes, was no answer to the centralized attack of even a petty kingdom. But the book of Judges casts monarchy as an essentially apostate institution, in that it implicitly involves denying the sovereignty of the Lord (cf. Judg 8:22—9:57).

The prophet Samuel is portrayed as intimately connected with the rise of the monarchy in Israel. He is closely associated with the ark of the covenant and the priesthood of Eli. Evidently worship effects the proximity of the Lord, whose will Samuel is then held to interpret (1 Sam 3:1—4:1). Samuel is a fully priestly figure (and a judge, 1 Sam 7:15—8:2), in that he offers sacrifice himself, and it is notable that he does so in sites other than the central shrine (1 Sam 7; 9:3—10:24; 16). Assertions about the future are involved in his interpretation of God's presence in sacrifice, but interpretation is by no means limited to prediction. Samuel's period of prophecy corresponds to the capture of the ark in war and its removal to Ashdod, a city with a fixed temple for its god, Dagon (1 Sam 4, 5). The ultimate release of the ark, after it was held to cause harm to the inhabitants of any city in which is was held, ends the regular practice of bringing it into battle (1 Sam 7:1-2; cf. 14:18-22), and a desire for monarchy grows thereafter (1 Sam 8:4-22). Samuel resists but ultimately gives in, on God's behalf, to popular desire and anoints Saul (1 Sam 10). Saul is a physically big man (1 Sam 9:1-2), in the tradition of the judges, but also a failure. He usurps the function of sacrifice (1 Sam 13:8-15; 14:31-35); fails to devote what he should (that is, destroy captives and spoil that was incompatible with God's sanctity; 1 Sam 15); he also becomes ambitious for his own family (1 Sam 18—20). God, by means of Samuel, rejects Saul and anoints David (1 Sam 16:1-13).

2.1. The Davidic Monarchy. The Davidic monarchy itself becomes the object of a solemn oath in 2 Samuel 7, where the prophet Nathan promises God's protection of David's progeny. It is notable that the promise is occasioned by David's undertaking to build a *temple. The offer itself is accepted but deferred: Solomon is to accomplish the task (2 Sam 7:13). But the function of the king in protecting, not leading, worship is established, and the role of prophecy as the guide of the king is confirmed. Precisely in those aspects, David differs from Saul, and the promise to David is integrated within the covenant generally.

The centralization of the sacrificial cult in David's city, *Jerusalem (2 Sam 6), had both positive and negative effects, from the point of view of faithfulness to the covenant. Positive, because the new center became the focus of codification. In addition to the court history, an account of David's reign produced shortly after his death (2 Sam 9—1 Kings 2), the source known to scholarship as J was produced. J (named after its putative author or authors, the "Yahwist" [earlier spelled with a "j" in the Latin manner]) first linked in literary form the people of the Davidic kingdom with creation, the patriarchs, the exodus and the possession of the land. Earlier, shorter books had been compiled to be recited at cultic centers, so that a treaty, or regulations of purity or ethics, or alleged genealogical connections or victories or other formative events might be remembered in association with sacrifice. But a single center involved a collection of such materials during the tenth century, and an early attempt to present them more coherently, for presentation at Jerusalem for the *feasts that were primarily celebrated there. But there is also a negative side to the settlement in Jerusalem. With monarchy there came the pressure to trade and compete with other cities: the multiplication of cults—and the de facto acceptance of their deities—was a feature of Solomon's otherwise auspicious reign (1 Kings 11).

First Kings lays the blame for the division of united Israel into Israel in the north and Judah in the south upon Solomon's apostasy (1 Kings 11:29-40), and there is a thematic link in Scripture between marriage to non-Israelite women and idolatry. But the kings, north and south, undermined their own authority by their recourse to *slavery and their conspicuous consumption, not only their idolatry. The last aspect is nonetheless an especially emphasized feature in the careers of the worst kings. Ahab in the north, with his wife Jezebel, fomented the worship of Baal and was opposed by the prophet Elijah (1 Kings 16:29—22:40); in the south, Ahaz renovated the temple to look like the one in Damascus and may even have practiced human sacrifice (2 Kings 16:1-20). It is evident that the alliance of Ahab with Sidon and of Ahaz with Damascus was a formative influence in their respective religious policies.

2.2. The Prophetic Movement. Prophecy found its voice as a movement in its opposition to the monarchs it regarded as apostate. Prior to the crystallizing impact of that opposition, prophets appear to have been identified as those who spoke for God, often in association with worship in particular sanctuaries. Their prophetic ministry might to a greater or lesser extent involve unusual states of consciousness or atypical behavior, sometimes with the use of music and dance. But first the association with David, and then the antagonism of kings in the north and south, made of prophecy a startlingly coherent movement.

The emergence of prophecy as a literary genre is to be dated to the eighth century and the message of Amos. Fundamentally a prophet of doom against the northern kingdom, Amos foretold judgment against Israel's apostate kings, and the prophet Hosea vividly generalized that theme to include the nation as a whole. They were quickly followed in the south by Micah and Isaiah, and an urgent appeal for social justice became a hallmark of prophecy in the south.

The doom announced against the north by an Amos or a Hosea must have appeared idle during periods of prosperity, but when, in 722 B.C., the capital of the north was taken and the northern kingdom was subjected to a policy of exile, the prophetic message appeared to have been vindicated. The works of the northern prophets were preserved in the south, together with extensive pentateuchal traditions of Israel's beginnings that had been treasured in the north. There were those in the north, priests and prophets and scribes, who were not taken in by the royal attempt at syncretism. Nonetheless, the prophetic attack upon deceitful prophets and cultic hypocrisy is eloquent testimony to the power of that attempt.

Spurred on by the demise of Israel in the north, whose people were lost to history, the prophets in Judah attempted to purify the life of their people. Isaiah urgently argued against foreign alliances and insisted that fidelity to God alone would save Jerusalem; Jeremiah ceaselessly denounced faithlessness and was prosecuted for his trouble; Ezekiel's enactments of coming disaster won him a reputation as a crank. But in the reign of Josiah, a royal reformation backed much of the critique of the prophets (2 Kings 22:1—23:30; 2 Chron 34:1—35:27). Josiah restored worship in the temple according to covenantal norms; he centralized sacrifice, even of the Passover, in Jerusalem; he tolerated no foreign incursions. In his program he was guided by a scroll of the law, which was found in the temple during the restoration, a scroll that has since antiquity been associated with the present book of Deuteronomy, which presses an agenda of radical centralization and separation from foreign nations such as impelled Josiah. But in 609 B.C., Josiah was killed in battle in an attempt to block the alliance between Pharaoh Neco and the Assyrians at a place called Megiddo. The impact of his death may be gauged by the impact of that name upon the *apocalyptic tradition (see 4.1.1 below), in the form Armageddon (Rev 16:16; cf. Zech 12:11).

3. Dispossession and Canonization.

3.1. Exile and the Vision of Classic Israel: The Pentateuch. The end of the kingdom of Judah came quickly after the death of Josiah. Culminating in 587/586 B.C., the Babylonian Empire, which had succeeded the Assyrians (see the prophetic book of Nahum), implemented a policy of exile, subsequent to their siege of Jerusalem and their destruction of the temple. Had the course of events then followed what happened to Israel, there would today be no Judaism to study. Paradoxically, however, the forces that must have seemed sure to destroy the religion of the covenant with the Lord instead assured its survival and nurtured its international dimension. During the Babylonian exile, priestly and prophetic movements joined forces to form a united program of restoration that put a form of Israel back on the map within a generation. Out of this restoration a vision of an ideal Israel, memorialized in the Pentateuch as we know it, emerged as a truly canonical standard for Judaism.

3.2. Restoration and New Visions for the Future: The Prophets. The dispossession of Judah to Babylon set up the priestly and prophetic hegemony that made restoration possible. But just as the Pentateuch sets out particularly priestly concerns, the prophetic movement also brought a distinctive message to the canon. The prophets generally agreed with their priestly confederates that the land was to be possessed again, and postexilic additions to the books of Isaiah (Is 40—55), Jeremiah (Jer 23:1-8; 31) and Ezekiel (Ezek 40—48) constitute eloquent motivations for return to the land.

But the previous abuses of the kings and their sanctuaries made the prophetic movement insist that righteousness was the prior requirement of sacrifice and that the events of the recent past were a warning. A Zechariah might be happy to set out the hope of a priestly messiah beside the Davidic king who was to rule (Zech 3; 4), but the predominant emphasis fell on the crucial necessity of loyalty to the worship of God (Zech 8). Moreover, *eschatology became characteristic of the prophetic movement, both in additions to biblical prophets, such as Isaiah and Ezekiel, and in fresh works, such as Joel and Malachi. The contemporary governance, whether *Persian, *Ptolemaic or *Seleucid, and the present temple were provisional, until an anointed king and an anointed priest would rule properly. Just the image of a priestly orientation redefined by the prophets is seen in the career of Ezra in the books of Ezra and Nehemiah: prophet, priest and scribe become one in their insistence on the vision of classic Israel, centered on the restored *temple.

The temple as restored (beginning in 520 B.C.) was, however, far from anyone's ideal. Some who remembered the splendor of Solomon's edifice are reported to have wept when they saw the results of the efforts under Ezra (Ezra 3:10-13). That imperfect focus nonetheless served to attract a permanent priesthood, and the notion of a canon provided focus to the prophetic movement. Now a body of literature, which could be interpreted, was held to provide the guidance that individual prophets formerly gave. It is notable that Ezra's own ministry involved guiding Israel on the basis of scriptural interpretation. The scribe emerges as something of a judge: the dominant, religious personality, as the warrant of true prophecy and the arbiter of priestly conduct (Neh 8—13).

3.3. Voices from Outside the Priestly-Prophetic Hegemony: The Writings. But the appearance that scribal leadership was settled is more superficial than representative. Battles concerning the proper conduct of the cult and the proper personnel of the priesthood raged during the period of restored Israel, and powerful movements produced literatures outside of scribal control. While the final form of the Pentateuch and what are called the Former Prophets (Joshua—2 Kings) and the Latter Prophets within Judaism may be attributed to the hegemony of priestly and prophetic interests that has been described, the category of Writings (the last in the three biblical divisions of traditional Judaism), together with the *Apocrypha and the pseudepigrapha, best characterizes other facets of the religion.

The book of Psalms represents a cultic *piety centered on just those aspects that levitical instructions exclude: the *music, dance, poetry, *prayer and praise (the term *psalms, t*^{e}*hillîm,* means "songs of praise") that the temple attracted. They speak more eloquently of the emotional affect of and popular participation in sacrificial worship than does any other document in the Bible. Proverbs also represents a nonpriestly, nonprophetic focus of piety in restored Israel, defined by prudential wisdom. Job and Ecclesiastes are other examples within the canon.

Initially wisdom is understood to be an aspect of God, which by knowing one can become familiar with God. "Wisdom" in Hebrew is a feminine noun and came to be personified as a woman; by the time of Ecclesiasticus (or Ben

Sira, from the early second century B.C.; *see* Sirach) and the *Wisdom of Solomon (from the late first century B.C. or somewhat later), she is considered a fundamental means of access to God. The Wisdom of Solomon was composed in Greek, but the focus upon Wisdom is by no means unique to what is commonly called *Hellenistic Judaism. Contacts with Egyptian and Babylonian inquiries into divine wisdom do probably date from the time of the Israelite and Judean kings, as part of their characteristic syncretism. But unlike idolatry and polygyny, Wisdom survived and prospered as a suitable and fertile means of communion with God after the notion of the unique covenant with Israel had triumphed.

In the case of *Philo of Alexandria, whose lifetime straddled the end of the last era and the beginning of our own, the pursuit of wisdom became a philosophical articulation of Judaism; he contributed an awareness of how Judaism and Hellenistic culture (*see* Hellenistic Judaism)—whose contact is already obvious in the Apocrypha and pseudepigrapha—might be related. Philo is unusually learned in his representation of a basic development of the Judaism of his period. His simultaneously Greco-Roman and Judaic notion of the logos is a case in point (see Philo *Op. Mund.*).

3.4. Threats to Cultic Purity and Priestly Unity. The question of the priesthood in the restored temple, meanwhile, became increasingly fraught. The Persian regime gave way to *Alexander the Great. Among the dynasties of the generals who succeeded him (*see* Diadochoi), first the Egyptian Ptolemies and then the Syrian Seleucids largely maintained the enlightened settlement of the Persians. The Seleucid monarch Antiochus IV (surnamed Epiphanes) is commonly portrayed as a great exception to the policy, and he did unquestionably occupy Jerusalem and arrange for a foreign cult in the sanctuary in 167 B.C., which included the sacrifice of swine (a Hellenistic delicacy; 1 Macc 1:20-64; Josephus *Ant.* 12.5.4 §§248-56). But Antiochus intervened in the city at first as the protector of a high-priestly family, the Tobiads, who were then in dispute with the Oniad family (Josephus *J.W.* 1.1-2 §§31-35). Dispossessed, the latter group moved to Egypt, where a temple was built at Heliopolis, in a form different from the restored temple in Jerusalem (Josephus *J.W.* 1.1 §33; 7.10.2-3 §§420-32). The cult of Onias appears to have been of limited influence, but the mere existence in the period of restored Israel of an alternative cult, manned by legitimate pretenders to the high priesthood in Jerusalem, is eloquent testimony of deep divisions within the sacerdotal ranks and within Judaism generally.

4. Radical Pluralization.

Early Judaism may conveniently be dated from 167 B.C., with the entry of Antiochus's officer, named Apollonius (2 Macc 5:24-25), into Jerusalem and his desecration of the temple, but it is evident that the radical pluralization of Judaism prior to Jesus, and of which Jesus was both a symptom and a result, is rooted in the flawed unity of restored Israel during the previous period. But Antiochus's campaign triggered both a fissure of interests and a reconfiguration of those interests in a way that made pluralism the order of the day. The temple of Onias at Heliopolis is only one example, but one that shows that how sacrifice was offered, and by whom, was held by one, familial group to be a better measure of the acceptability of worship than where sacrifice was offered.

4.1. The Rise of the Hasmoneans and the Response of the Faithful. In Israel, however, there was another group, defined by a desire to remain loyal to *sacrifice in Jerusalem by an appropriate priesthood and a resistance to the demands of Antiochus, known as "the faithful" (the famous Hasidim). Attempts have been made in the history of scholarship to identify the Hasidim with a particular sect of Judaism during the period of the Second Temple, such as the *Essenes or the *Pharisees, but the adjective *faithful* cannot usefully or legitimately be limited to any one specific group. In the context of reaction to Antiochus, however, the sense of the term clearly related to one's adherence to covenantal norms of sacrifice, as part of a vehement resistance.

Among the resisters was Mattathias, a country priest from Modin, whose son, Judas Maccabeus ("the hammer") introduced the most powerful priestly rule Judaism has ever known, which was known under the name of Hasmoneus, Mattathias's ancestor (1 Macc 2:1—9:18; Josephus *Ant.* 12.6.1 §265; 16.7.1 §187; 20.8.11 §190; 20.10.1 §§238, 247). Judas, as is well known, turned piety into disciplined revolt, including an alliance with Rome (1 Macc 8) and a willingness to break the *sabbath for military reasons (1 Macc 2:41), which saw the restoration of worship within the covenant in the temple in 164 B.C. (1 Macc 4:36-61). After his death, his brother Jonathan was named high priest (1 Macc 10:20-21), and from that time until the period of Roman rule (*see* Jewish History: Roman Period), the high priesthood was a *Hasmonean prerogative.

Those events were too rapid for some and unacceptable in the view of others. In strictly familial terms, the Hasmoneans could not claim the high priesthood as a right, and therefore competition with other families of priests was a factor. Moreover, the suspension of the sabbath for military purposes (see Josephus *J.W.* 1.7.3 §146) and the arrogation of the high priesthood and the monarchy by the non-Davidic Hasmoneans seemed particularly vicious to many Jews (Josephus *J.W.* 1.3.1 §70). Antiochus had sanctioned apostasy, and the Hasmonean regime appeared to be compounding apostasy both in its initial resistance and its consolidation of power.

4.1.1. Apocalyptic Resistance. The book of Daniel does not express overt opposition to the Hasmoneans, but it does represent the less activist, apocalyptic stance that many pious Jews adopted as an alternative to the nationalistic and militaristic policy of the Hasmoneans. The eschatology of the prophets during the period of restored Israel is here transformed into a scenario of the end time, in which the temple would be restored by miraculous means, with the archangel Michael's triumph capped by the resurrection of the just and the unjust (Dan 12:1-4). Folk Judaism of the period also anticipated providential interventions (*see* Tobit), but Daniel elevates and specifies that anticipation until it becomes a program of patient attention and fidelity, warranted by both heavenly vision and the sage named Daniel of the Babylonian period (cf. Ezek 14:14).

4.1.2. Essenes. In the case of the Essenes, opposition to the Hasmoneans became overt. They pursued their own system of purity, ethics and initiation, followed their own calendar and withdrew into their own communities, either within cities or in isolated sites such as *Qumran. There they awaited a coming apocalyptic war, when they, as "the sons of light," would triumph over "the sons of darkness": not only the Gentiles but anyone not of their vision (*War Scroll* [1QM]; *Rule of the Community* [1QS]). The culmination of those efforts was to be complete control of Jerusalem and the temple, where worship would be offered according to their revelation, the correct understanding of the law of Moses (cf. CD 5:17—6:11). Their insistence upon a doctrine of two *messiahs, one of Israel and one of Aaron, would suggest that it was particularly the Hasmoneans' arrogation of priestly and royal powers that alienated the Essenes.

4.1.3. Pharisees. Most of those who resisted the Seleucids or who sympathized with the resistance were neither of priestly families nor of Essene temperament. Nonetheless, the unchecked rule of the Hasmonean priests in the temple was not entirely acceptable to them. For that large group, the pharisaic movement held a great attraction. The Pharisees, in their attempt to influence what the Hasmoneans did rather than to replace them definitively, appear as much more conservative than the Essenes or competing priestly families. Their focus was upon the issue of *purity, as defined principally in their oral tradition and their interpretation of Scripture. Since issues of purity were bound to be complicated in the Hasmonean combination of secular government and sacrificial worship, disputes were inevitable.

*Josephus, for example, reports that the Pharisees made known their displeasure at Alexander Janneus by inciting a crowd to pelt him with lemons (at hand for a festal procession) at the time he should have been offering sacrifice (Josephus *Ant.* 13.13.5 §§372-73). Josephus also relates, from a later period, the teaching of the rabbis (probably Pharisees) who were implicated in dismantling the eagle Herod had erected over a gate of the temple (Josephus *J.W.* 1.33.2-4 §§648-55; *Ant.* 17.6.2-4 §§149-67). This gesture was both less subversive of the established authority in the cult than what earlier Pharisees had done and more pointedly a challenge to Herod. Paradoxically, the willingness of the Pharisees to consider the Hasmoneans in their priestly function, in distinction from the Essenes, involved them not only in symbolic disputes but also in vocal and bloody confrontations. Alexander Janneus is reported to have executed by crucifixion eight hundred opponents, either Pharisees or those with whom the Pharisees sympathized, and to have slaughtered their families; but his wife came to an accommodation with the Pharisees that guaranteed them considerable influence (Josephus *J.W.* 1.4.6—1.5.3 §§96-114).

It seems clear that within the Hasmonean period, purity was a political issue and to some extent a symbol. The acquiescence of one of the dynasty to any pharisaic stricture implicitly acknowledged that the Hasmonean priesthood was provisional, and the pharisaic movement probably found its original political expression in opposition to that priesthood (Josephus *Ant.* 13.10.5-6 §§288-98). The Pharisees accepted and developed the notion that with the end of the canon, the age of prophecy in the classical sense had ceased (cf. 1 Macc 4:46). For that reason they plausibly saw Ezra as their source and their own interpretative movement as an extension of his program of restoration (cf. *m. ʾAbot* 1:1-18; 2 Esdr 14). But in two vital respects, the Pharisees need to be distinguished from the reforms of Ezra. First, they identified themselves with no specific priestly or political figure. Their program was its own guide and was not to be subservient to any particular family or dynasty. Second, pharisaic interpretation was not limited to the Scriptures, nor was its characteristic focus scriptural: the principal point of departure was the recollection of earlier teaching of those called sages.

Ultimately, after the period of the NT, the ideology of the rabbis, as the Pharisees came to be called, had it that Moses conveyed two Torahs on Sinai, one written and one oral. Even before that understanding, however, the sages treated as normative the teachings of their predecessors in chains of tradition. It was not so much that oral tradition was set alongside Scripture as that oral tradition *was* Scripture until the canon itself could no longer be ignored as the functional standard of Judaism (*see* Hebrew Bible).

4.2. Judaism Under Roman Rule. Factionalism among the Hasmoneans, which resulted in rival claims to the high priesthood between Aristobulus and Hyrcanus, the sons of Alexandra, culminated in an appeal by both sides to *Pompey, who obliged by taking Jerusalem for Rome and entering the sanctuary in 63 B.C. (Josephus *J.W.* 1.7.6 §§152-54).

4.2.1. Opposition and Accommodation. The **Psalms of Solomon* represents a common, pious expression of horror at the events of 63 B.C., which was probably shared by most Pharisees (whether or not the *Psalms* should be taken as specifically pharisaic). From that period and all through the reign of Herod and his relatives, the Pharisees' attitude to the government was ambivalent. Some appear to have engaged in a principled opposition to Roman rule and its representatives as such. Today that group is known as the Zealots, but the term is a misnomer.

The Zealots were a priestly group of *revolutionaries, not rebellious Pharisees, who were associated with Eleazar, son of Simon, during the revolt of A.D. 66-73 (Josephus *J.W.* 2.20.3 §§564-65; 4.4.1 §§224-25). The rebellious Pharisees are also to be distinguished from the movements of prophetic pretenders who claimed divine inspiration for their efforts to free the land of the Romans (Josephus *J.W.* 2.13.4-6 §§258-65; 7.11.1-2 §§437-46). Other Pharisees normally accommodated to the new regime, but resisted—sometimes violently—Herodian excesses, such as the erection of a golden eagle on a gate of the temple (Josephus *J.W.* 1.33.2-4 §§648-55). Nonetheless, an apparently pharisaic group is called "the Herodians" (Mt 22:16; Mk 3:6; 12:13), which presumably signals its partisanship of the interests of the royal family as a considerable support of their teaching of purity. They may be associated with rabbis who enjoyed the protection of Herod and his house; the authorities referred to in rabbinic literature as the "sons of Bathyra" (cf. *b. B. Meṣ.* 85a) may have been such a group.

Others still largely cooperated with the Romans and with the priestly administration of the temple, although they might fall out regarding such questions as whether the priestly vestments should be kept under Roman or local control (Josephus *Ant.* 18.4.3 §§90-95; 20.1.1-2 §§6-14) or the price of doves for sacrifice (*m. Ker.* 1:7).

4.2.2. The Fracturing of the Priesthood: Sadducees, High Priests and Priestly Nationalists. The priesthood itself, meanwhile, was fractured further in its response to the fact of Roman governance. Some priests, especially among the privileged families in Jerusalem, were notoriously pro-Roman. The story of sons of the high priest having the surgery called *epispasm* in order to restore the appearance of a foreskin (for gymnastic purposes) is well known (cf. 1 Macc 1:14-15; Josephus *Ant.* 12.5.1 §§240-41). There is little doubt but that such families, the most prominent of which were the *Sadducees and Boethusians, were not highly regarded by most Jews (*b. Pesaḥ.* 57a). They are typically portrayed in a negative light, as not teaching the resurrection of the dead (Josephus *J.W.* 2.8.14 §165; Mt 22:23; Mk 12:18; Lk 20:27; Acts 23:8), but the issue may have been one of emphasis. The Torah had stressed that correct worship in the temple would bring with it material prosperity, and the elite priests attempted to realize that promise. Appeal to apocalyptic schemes or revelations would never have been accepted by the Sadducees as equivalent to or comparable with the Torah. Arrangements in the temple gave them such consistent control that they became known as high priests, although there was only one high priest. But Josephus indulges in the plural usage, as well as the Gospels, so that it should not be taken as an inaccuracy: the plural is a cultic mistake but a sociological fact.

Caiaphas held a historically long tenure as high priest during the period (Josephus *Ant.* 18.2.2 §35; 18.4.3 §95), and the frequent change of personnel reflects the collective nature of the priestly leadership as well as Roman caution in respect of a post that might at any time have produced a national leader. Herod himself understood the possibilities of the high priesthood in that regard, which is why he had Jonathan and Hyrcanus, potential rivals (albeit relatives by marriage), murdered, and why he married Mariamne (Josephus *J.W.* 1.22.1-5 §§431-37; *Ant.* 20.10.1 §§247-49). His ambition was for a new Hasmonean dynasty, and it appears that only the notorious greed of his sons, combined with his willingness to have them executed, thwarted its realization. As it was, Herod's grandson and namesake, king of Chalcis, did maintain the residual power of selecting the high priest, although as king of Chalcis he had no ordinary authority over Jerusalem (Josephus *Ant.* 20.1.3 §§15-16).

Several priests were also prominent in the revolt against Rome, however, and it should not be thought that such priestly nationalists, among whom were Joseph bar Matthias, better known as Flavius Josephus, emerged only at the end of the sixties (Josephus *J.W.* 2.20.3-4 §§562-68). The precedent of the Hasmoneans was there for any priestly family to see as a possible alternative to Roman rule, direct or indirect. Some priests were not only nationalists but also revolutionaries who joined with the Essenes or with rebellious Pharisees, although any alliance of priests with a prophetic pretender is perhaps not a likely supposition.

4.2.3. The Growing Influence of the Pharisees. The Pharisees' mastery of the oral medium made them the most successful—in terms of popularity—of the tendencies within pluralized Judaism. In the period before written communication was standard among the generality of Jews, the use of memorization and recitation was far more prominent. The Pharisees were in a position to communicate guidance in respect of purity, an emerging understanding of Scripture (in the targumim, whose development they influenced) and their own sense of the authority of the sages, without requiring general literacy. There is no reason to suppose, for example, that rabbis of the first century such as Hillel and Ḥanina ben Dosa were able to read fluently, although each was a formative member of the pharisaic, and therefore later of the rabbinic, movements. The Pharisees' willingness to live by craft rather than by status (cf. *m. ʾAbot* 2:2)—the most prominent example being Hillel's menial labor (*b. Yoma* 35b)—also meant that they could move from town to town, promulgating their views. In some respects, their occasional itineracy was comparable in Israel to that of the Greco-Roman philosophers of the Mediterranean world (*Stoic, Pythagorean and/or *Cynic).

The success of the Pharisees in small towns became all the more pronounced as their power was largely ceded to priestly interests in Jerusalem. Many local scribes, but not all, were likely Pharisees, and the majority would have to account for pharisaic views. Scribes are men who can read and write, a skill that in antiquity represented some social and educational attainment (*see* Literacy and Book Culture). In Israel, given the Roman encouragement of local government, scribes emerged in towns and villages as a focus of judicial and religious power; their role might be characterized as that of a judge or a magistrate. From the time of the writing of the Torah itself, it was accepted that both aspects of God's rule, the legal and the cultic, were articulated by Moses. The ability of the scribes to read and write made them ideal judges, adjuncts to priests, teachers and leaders of worship.

All those functions were probably discharged by an interactive group of scribes, people of priestly lineage and Pharisees and other elders in any given village. It was likely in the same place in a town that cases were settled, purity or impurity declared, lessons given and the Torah recited from the written form and from memory in Aramaic. There, too, disputes would take place among scribes, judges, priests, Pharisees and elders, concerning how the Torah was to be understood and applied. Later rabbinic literature tends to reduce the disputes of the period to the "houses" of *Hillel and *Shammai, but that is evidently a schematic presentation; because they lacked any central leadership in the period before A.D. 70, Pharisees differed from movement to movement, town to town, rabbi to rabbi, and to some extent even day to day.

4.2.4. The Sanhedrin. The structure of a local council also prevailed under Roman rule in Jerusalem, and the Greek term *synedrion* was applied to it and it has become known as the *Sanhedrin, largely as a result of the *Mishnah. Mishnah, a document of the second century, cannot be taken as a sure guide of events and institutions during the first century (*see DJG,* Rabbinic Traditions and Writings §1), but it does seem clear, from the Gospels and Josephus with the Mishnah, that the council in Jerusalem was largely controlled by the high priests. Elders or aristocrats of the city also participated, among whom were Pharisees and some scribes, who may or may not have been priests, elders or Pharisees. Whether there were seventy-one members of the Sanhedrin (as in rabbinic literature) cannot be known with certainty, and the extent of its capital jurisdiction is not known. But the Romans appear to have given the council the authority to order the execution of perpetrators of blatant sacrilege (Josephus *J.W.* 2.12.2 §§228-31; 5.5.2 §194; *Ant.* 15.11.5 §417).

The authority of the council of Jerusalem outside of the city followed the prestige of the city itself and the acknowledged centrality of the temple. But a ruling of the council there was not automatically binding upon those in the countryside and in other major cities; acceptance of a given teaching, precept by precept, was the path of influence. Pharisees also taught in and around the temple, the focus of their discussion of purity, and the Pharisees in Jerusalem were the most prestigious in the movement.

5. Early Judaism and the New Testament.

5.1. Jesus in the Temple Within the Context of Early Judaism. Hillel, an older contemporary of Jesus, is reported to have taught that offerings (as in the case of his own *ʿōlâ,* sacrifice by fire) should be brought to the temple, where the owners would lay hands on them and then give them over to priests for slaughter (cf. *t. Ḥag.* 2:11; *y. Ḥag.* 2:3; *y. Beṣa* 2:4; *b. Beṣa* 20a, b). His perennial and stereotypical disputants, the school of Shammai, resist, insisting that the animals might be handed over directly. One of the school of Shammai (named Baba ben Buta in the Babylonian Talmud and Tosefta), however, was so struck by the rectitude of Hillel's position that he had three thousand animals (a number specified only in the Jerusalem Talmud) brought to the temple, and he gave them to those who were willing to lay hands on them in advance of sacrifice.

Generally the Haggadah (narrative, or instructional tale) concerning Hillel, Baba ben Buta and the sheep is characteristic of the pharisaic/rabbinic program. Moreover, the broad attestation of the story within the two Talmuds and its appearance in the Tosefta constitute an indication that it may reflect an actual dispute. Finally, although Hillel's disputants are stereotypical, it is striking that in *b. Beṣa* 20a, Hillel pretends the animal is a female, for a shared sacrifice rather than a sacrifice by fire, in order to get it by the disciples of Shammai. That is, the Babli's version of the story assumes that the followers of Shammai are in better control of what worshipers do in the temple than are followers of Hillel. The Haggadah is a far cry from the sort of tale, also instanced in rabbinic literature, in which Hillel is portrayed as the prototypical patriarchate of rabbinic Judaism.

In one sense, the tradition concerning Hillel envisages a movement opposite from that of Jesus in the temple (Mt 21:12, 13; Mk 11:15-17; Lk 19:45, 46; Jn 2:13-17): animals are introduced, rather than their traders expelled. But the purpose of the action by Hillel's partisan is to enforce a certain understanding of correct worship, and that is also the motivation attributed to Jesus in the Gospels. Hillel's Halakah, in effect, insists upon the participation of the offerer by virtue of his ownership of what is offered, an ownership of which the laying on of hands is a definitive gesture (cf. *b. Pesaḥ* 66b and the abundant anthropological evidence for this sacrificial gesture, some of which is cited in Chilton 1992, 27-42). "The house of Shammai" is portrayed as sanctioning sacrifice without mandating that sort of emphatic participation on the part of the offerer. Although nothing like the violence of Jesus is attributed to Baba ben Buta, he does offer an analogy for a forcible attempt to insist upon correct worship in the temple on the part of a Pharisee.

Mishnah itself reflects a concern to control

commercial arrangements connected with the temple, and such concern is also somewhat analogous to Jesus' action in the exterior court. The following story is told concerning one of the successors of Hillel (*m. Ker.* 1:7):

> Once in Jerusalem a pair of doves cost a golden denar. Rabban Simeon ben Gamaliel said: By this Place! I will not rest this night before they cost but a [silver] denar. He went into the court and taught: If a woman suffered five miscarriages that were not in doubt or five issues that were not in doubt, she need bring but one offering, and she may then eat of the sacrifices; and the rest is not required of her. And the same day the price of a pair of doves stood at a quarter denar each.

Although the story requires more effort to understand than does the one concerning Hillel, it rewards the attention required. The assumption of the tale is that a pair of doves might be offered by a woman as both a burnt offering and a sacrifice for sin, in order to be purified after childbirth; the second of the two would be offered normally, while the first, in the case of poverty, might take the place of a yearling lamb (Lev 12:6-8). The story also assumes that miscarriages and unusual issues of blood akin to miscarriages should be treated under the category of childbirth, from the point of view of purity. That interest is characteristically pharisaic, as is the question of when the woman might be considered entitled to eat of offerings. The Pharisees defined purity as fitness to take part in sacrifice and in meals that in their teaching were extensions of the holiness of the temple.

Simeon's anger, which causes him to swear by the temple (cf. Mt 23:16-22), is therefore motivated to some extent by economic considerations, and his response is, like Jesus', to teach in the court of the temple, to which point such offerings would be brought. But his action there is far less direct than Hillel's or Jesus'. Instead of importing more birds or releasing those bought at an extortionate price, he promulgates a Halakah designed to reduce the trade in doves, no matter what their price.

If a woman may await several (up to five) miscarriages or flows of blood, offer a single pair of doves and be considered pure enough to eat of the animal offering, the potential revenue from sales of doves would obviously decline. In effect Simeon counters inflationary prices with sacrificial monetarism. The political lesson was quickly appreciated (on the very day, if we believe the story), and prices went lower even than Simeon had intended. Presumably there was no reason for him to continue promulgating his view in the court of the temple, and both he and the traders were content with the settlement.

The dating of the Mishah, as compared with the Tosefta, the *Yerushalmi* and the *Babli* (the Jerusalem and Babylonian Talmuds respectively) makes its material, when in any way comparable to the Gospels, of immediate interest to the student of Jesus' life and teaching. For all its complexity, the Haggadah in *Keritot* is vital for appreciating the sort of pharisaic intervention in the operation of the temple that was considered possible during the first century according to the testimony of the Mishnah. (Perhaps the story concerning Simeon is more complicated precisely because it is closer to particulars of pharisaic concern than is the Haggadah concerning Hillel and Baba ben Buta, which is available only in later sources.) Hillel, Simeon and Jesus are all portrayed as interested in the animals offered in the temple to the extent that they intervene (or, in the case of Hillel, a surrogate intervenes) in the exterior court in order to influence the ordinary course of worship. To that extent, it may be said that rabbinic traditions and writings provide a context within which it is possible to interpret a well-attested action of Jesus.

5.2. Paul and the Temple Within Early Judaism. When Paul conceives of Jesus' death sacrificially, he does so as a sacrifice for sin (Rom 8:3). By the time he came to compose Romans, he had been referring to Jesus' death in that way for five years (cf. Gal 1:4, written about A.D. 53, following Papyrus 46 and Sinaiticus). Paul uses precisely the phrase used in the *Septuagint to refer to a sacrifice for sin (*peri hamartias;* cf. Lev 16:3, 5, 6, 9, 11, 15). Paul cites the Hebrew Scriptures in a paradigmatically Septuagintal version, so that the identity of phrasing might alone be taken to suggest that he presented Jesus' death as a sacrifice for sin. In addition, both Galatians and Romans conceive of Jesus' death in a manner congruent with the image of a sacrifice for sin. In Galatians 1:4, the purpose of his death is redemption from the present evil age, while Romans 8:3 contrasts God's sending his Son with the flesh of sacrifice.

But Paul did not conceive of that death as a

replacement of the cult, for the simple reason that Paul believed he had a role to play within the service of the temple. His preaching of the gospel is depicted in Romans 15:16 as a kind of priestly service, in that it is to result in "the offering of the nations, pleasing, sanctified in Holy Spirit." Contextually Paul's characterization of his own ministry as sacrificial is associated with his "serving the saints in Jerusalem" (Rom 15:25), by means of a collection in Macedonia and Asia for the poorer community in return for its spiritual treasure (Rom 15:26, 27). That done, Paul expects to come to Rome "in the fullness of Christ's blessing" and to proceed to Spain (Rom 15:28, 29), there to engage in the same priestly service (cf. Rom 15:19). Paul's program is known conventionally as the collection, after Galatians 2:10; 1 Corinthians 16:1, 2; 2 Corinthians 8, 9; and Romans 15:26, and the assumption has been that the purpose of the program was purely practical: Paul agreed to provide material support in exchange for recognition by Peter, James and John (cf. Gal 2:9) and used priestly language as a rhetorical device.

Paul was unquestionably capable of using cultic language as metaphor. Romans 12:1 provides the example of the addressees being called to present their bodies as "a living sacrifice, holy and acceptable to God." Romans 15:16 itself can only refer to Paul's priestly service metaphorically, as the agency by which the offering of the nations might be completed, since Paul did not claim priestly lineage. But is "the offering of the nations" itself to be taken only as a metaphor? Paul may be capable of priestly service only in the figurative sense that he brings support to the community of Jesus' followers in Jerusalem, who in turn offer sacrifice within the temple. But the fact would remain that the offering of that community was a sacrifice according to the Torah in the direct and usual sense.

The hope of a climactic disclosure of divine power, signaled in the willingness of nations to worship on Mt. Zion, is attested within Judaic sources extant by the first century. Chief among them, from the point of view of its influence upon the NT, is the book of Zechariah. It can be argued that Zechariah provided a point of departure for Jesus' inclusive program of purity and forgiveness as the occasions of the kingdom (see Chilton 1992, 113-36). Jesus is said to have mentioned the prophet by name (cf. Mt 23:34-36; Lk 11:49-51). The book programmatically concerns the establishment of restored worship in the temple, especially at the feast of Sukkoth (Zech 14:16-19).

"All the nations" are to go up to Jerusalem annually for worship (Zech 14:16), and the transformation of which that worship is part involves the provision of "living waters" from the city (Zech 14:8; cf. Jn 4:10, 14). That image is related to an earlier "fountain opened for the house of David and the inhabitants of Jerusalem in view of sin and uncleanness" (Zech 13:1). Here is the association of forgiveness and purity that is a feature of Jesus' program, as well as the notion of an immediate release, without any mention of sacrifice, from what keeps Israel from God. (There is also an indication of how the issue of Davidic ancestry might have featured in Jesus' ministry, aside from a formally messianic claim.) God himself is held to arrange the purity he requires, so that the sacrifice he desires might take place.

Zechariah features the commissioning of a priest (Zech 3; cf. Mt 16:18, 19), an oracle against swearing (Zech 5:3, 4; cf. Mt 5:33-37), a vision of a king humbly riding an ass (Zech 9:9; cf. Mt 21:1-9; Mk 11:1-10; Lk 19:28-40; Jn 12:12-19), the prophetic receipt of thirty shekels of silver in witness against the owners of sheep (Zech 11:4-17; cf. Mt 26:14-16; 27:3-10; Mk 14:10, 11; Lk 22:3-6). It is obvious that the connections between Jesus' ministry and Zechariah do not amount to a completely common agenda in every detail, and Matthew reflects a tendency to tailor the fit between the two. But the similarities may be suggestive of Jesus' appropriation of Zechariah's prophecy of eschatological purity, as a final, more fundamental connection would indicate. The climactic vision of Zechariah insists that every vessel in Jerusalem will belong to the Lord and become a fit vessel for sacrifice. As part of that insistence, the text asserts that no trader will be allowed in the temple (Zech 14:20, 21). In the light of Zechariah, Jesus' occupation of the temple appears an enactment of prophetic purity in the face of a commercial innovation, a vigorous insistence that God would prepare his own people and vessels for eschatological worship.

Notably, the *Targum of Zechariah* specifically includes reference to God's kingdom at Zechariah 14:9, and that provides another programmatic link with Jesus. It is clear that Jesus understood the essential affect of sacrifice to derive from a purity and a forgiveness that God extended to Israel in anticipation of the climax of worship. In those understandings, Jesus was no doubt unusual in his immediate application of a prophetic program to the temple, but far from unique. His precise demands concerning the provision of animals as offerings, however, show how the issue of purity was for him pragmatic as well as affective. And it was in that pharisaic vein that he confronted the authorities in the temple with the claim that their management was a scandal and that the direct provision of animals by a forgiven, purified Israel was what was required for the experience of holiness and the reality of the covenant to be achieved.

Whether or not Jesus' program was a direct precedent for Paul's, the mere existence of Zechariah, which Paul alludes to (cf. Rom 8:36; 1 Cor 2:11; 11:25; 13:5; 14:25), opens the possibility that Paul might have included an offering from the Gentiles in Jerusalem as a part of his program and therefore as part of his meaning in Romans 15:16. The reading of the *Targum of Zechariah* is particularly pertinent at this point, aside from the question of its relationship to Jesus' preaching. This section of the *Targum of Zechariah* is agreed to reflect the earliest development of the targumim, from the first century onward, and this theme is also represented independently of the book of Zechariah, within the book of *Tobit (Tob 13:8-11). It is evident that within *Hellenistic Judaism the consolation of Jerusalem and the sacrificial recognition of God as king by the nations were motifs that could be and were associated. The significance of the prominence of a similar theme in the *Targum of Zechariah* shows that the association was not merely Hellenistic and that it survived through the first century. More generally, *Jubilees* 4:26 establishes that the global range of the sanctuary was an expectation within early Judaism.

Targum Jonathan, together with Tobit and **Jubilees,* establishes clearly that an expectation of global worship in the temple was a feature of early Judaism, so that it is within the range of plausibility that Paul aimed to promote a literal offering of the nations by means of his collection for the needs of the church in Jerusalem. The book of Acts is at pains to exculpate Paul from the charge that he introduced Gentiles into the precincts of the temple (Acts 21:27-30), but precisely that accusation, mounted by Jews from Asia who were in a position to know what Paul intended (Acts 21:27), is what in Acts produces the attempt to kill Paul and his subsequent (as it turned out, definitive) arrest (Acts 21:31-32). The conflicted picture Acts conveys at this point may be said to be consistent with the finding from Paul's own letters that he intended that Gentiles should be joined within the sacrificial worship of Israel.

Paul's assertion in Romans 3:25, that God appointed Jesus a cultic appeasement through faith in his blood, is therefore not to be understood as positing a formal replacement of the cult by Jesus' death. The standard references to similar usages in *2 Maccabees (2 Macc 3:33) and *4 Maccabees (4 Macc 6:28, 29; 17:20-22) ought long ago to have warned commentators against any reading that involves such notions. Second Maccabees 3:33 speaks of a high priest "making appeasement" by cultic means. Even 4 Maccabees, which is probably too late a composition to be used as representing the milieu that was the matrix of Paul's thought, maintains a distinction between God's pleasure in sacrifice and the means of that sacrifice. In 4 Maccabees 6:28, God is asked to be pleased with his people by Eleazar and on that basis to make his blood their purification and his life their ransom (4 Macc 6:29). Then, in 4 Maccabees 17, it is said of the seven brothers that, in the manner of Eleazar, they purified the homeland in that they became a ransom for the sin of the nation (4 Macc 17:21). The language of purification and ransom is consistently used, in 4 Maccabees 6 and 17, to refer to the deaths of martyrs in cultic and salvific terms. That salvation did not involve the replacement of cultic sacrifice but its reestablishment in the temple.

Jesus for Paul in Romans 3:25 is a *hilastērion* because he provides the occasion on which God may be appeased, an opportunity for the correct offering of sacrifice in Jerusalem. Precisely that rectitude lies behind the emphasis upon God's righteousness. "The righteous" are held within the *Targum of Isaiah* to be the recipients of that joy whose epicenter is the sanctuary (cf. Is 24:16; 5:17; 66:24). More particularly, the establishment of correct worship in the temple is signaled in Daniel 8:14 as involving a divine justification. Danielic usage presents God as both righteous (cf. Dan 9:7, 14, 16) and making righteous (Dan 9:24; cf. 12:3) an unrighteous nation (Dan 9:7, 16, 18).

5.3. Summary. The utility of the documents of early Judaism and rabbinic Judaism in assessing Jesus and Paul is qualified by three critical considerations, each of which has been instanced in the examples developed here. First, the relatively late date of rabbinic literature must be taken into account, although the continuities between rabbinic Judaism and Pharisaism during the first century rule out any global refusal to countenance analogies between the Gospels and rabbinica. Second, a recognition of the social and religious transformations involved in the emergence of rabbinic Judaism must alert the reader to the possibility of anachronistic attributions or to the presentation of early teachers as spokesmen of later theologies. And finally, the initial target of inquiry must be understood to be the recovery not so much of particular events and sayings paralleled in the Gospels but of the milieu of early Judaism, reflected indirectly both in the Gospels and in rabbinica, which was the matrix of the Christian faith.

See also APOCRYPHA AND PSEUDEPIGRAPHA; FESTIVALS AND HOLY DAYS: JEWISH; HASMONEANS; HEBREW BIBLE; JEWISH HISTORY; MESSIANISM; PHARISEES; RABBINIC LITERATURE; RABBIS; SACRIFICE AND TEMPLE SERVICE; TEMPLE, JEWISH; TORAH; THEOLOGIES AND SECTS, JEWISH; WRITING AND LITERATURE: JEWISH.

BIBLIOGRAPHY. E. Auerbach, *Moses* (Detroit: Wayne State University Press, 1975); J. Bright, *A History of Israel* (Philadelphia: Westminster, 1981); B. D. Chilton, "Aramaic and Targumic Antecedents of Pauline 'Justification,'" in *The Aramaic Bible: The Targums in Their Historical Context* (JSOTSup 166; Sheffield: Sheffield Academic Press, 1994) 379-97; idem, *The Isaiah Targum: Introduction, Translation, Apparatus and Notes* (ArBib 11; Wilmington, DE: Michael Glazier, 1987); idem, *The Temple of Jesus: His Sacrificial Program Within a Cultural History of Sacrifice* (University Park: Pennsylvania State University Press, 1992); S. J. D. Cohen, *From the Maccabees to the Mishnah* (LEC 7; Philadelphia: Westminster, 1987); W. D. Davies and L. Finkelstein, eds., *The Cambridge History of Judaism,* 1: *Introduction; the Persian Period* (London and New York: Cambridge University Press, 1984); A. Finkel, *The Pharisees and the Teacher of Nazareth* (AGSU 4; Leiden: E. J. Brill, 1964); V. P. Furnish, *2 Corinthians* (AB; Garden City, NY: Doubleday, 1984); E. R. Goodenough, *An Introduction to Philo Judaeus* (BCJ; Lanham, MD: University Press of America, 1986); N. K. Gottwald, *The Tribes of Yahweh: A Sociology of the Religion of Liberated Israel 1250-1050 B.C.* (Maryknoll, NY: Orbis, 1979); R. A. Kraft and G. W. E. Nickelsburg, *Early Judaism and Its Modern Interpreters* (The Bible and Its Modern Interpreters 2; Atlanta: Scholars Press, 1986); A. R. C. Leany, *The Jewish and Christian World 200 B.C. to A.D. 200* (CCWJCW 7; Cambridge and New York: Cambridge University Press, 1984); N. P. Lemche, *Early Israel: Anthropological and Historical Studies on the Israelite Society Before the Monarchy* (VTSup; Leiden: E. J. Brill, 1985); L. I. Levine, *The Rabbinic Class of Roman Palestine in Late Antiquity* (New York: Jewish Theological Seminary of America, 1989); M. McNamara, *Palestinian Judaism and the New Testament* (GNS 4; Wilmington, DE: Michael Glazier, 1983); G. E. Mendenhall, "The Hebrew Conquest of Palestine," *The Biblical Archaeologist Reader* 3 (1962) 100-120; J. Neusner, "Josephus' Pharisees: A Complete Repertoire," in *Josephus, Judaism and Christianity,* ed. L. H. Feldman and G. Hata (Detroit: Wayne State University Press, 1987) 274-92; idem, *The Pharisees: Rabbinic Perspectives* (SAJ; Hoboken, NJ: Ktav, 1984); M. Noth, *The History of Israel* (London: Adam & Charles Black, 1959); E. Schürer, *The History of the Jewish People in the Age of Jesus Christ* (175 B.C.-A.D. 135), ed. G. Vermes, F. Millar and M. Goodman (3 vols.; Edinburgh: T & T Clark, 1973-87); R. M. Seltzer, ed., *Judaism: A People and Its History* (New York: Macmillan, 1989); R. R. Wilson, *Sociological Approaches to the Old Testament* (Philadelphia: Fortress, 1984).

B. D. Chilton

JUDAS THE GALILEAN. *See* REVOLUTIONARY MOVEMENTS, JEWISH.

JUDEA

Judea is the Latinized spelling of Judah (Lat *Iudaea,* Gk *Ioudaia,* Aramaic *Y^ehud,* Heb *Y^ehudah),* the Israelite territory that became the seat of the Davidic kingdom, terminated by the Babylonian conquest of 587 B.C. Comprising the regions immediately surrounding the city of *Jerusalem, Judea encompassed the hill country and desert fringe dividing the Shephelah from the Dead Sea. Intermittently, during periods of *Hasmonean, *Herodian and Roman rule, "Judea" could also be used to designate the totality of regions controlled by Jerusalem's monarch or the Roman governor at *Caesarea

Maritima (*see* Roman Administration; Roman Governors of Palestine). At various times, these possessions included Idumea, Samaria, Galilee and portions of the Mediterranean coast and Transjordan.

It is important to keep in mind that this region never ceased to be referred to as Judea under Babylonian rule; nor did it cease to be inhabited by Judeans, in spite of the deportation of its ruling house and a substantial number of hangers-on to Mesopotamia. Nevertheless, the restoration of Jerusalem and its *temple under Persian auspices marks an important break with the intervening years and is the proper starting point for an overview of what is now commonly referred to as the Second Temple period (516 B.C.-A.D. 70).

1. Judea Under Persian Rule
2. Conquests of Alexander the Great
3. Ptolemaic Rule of Judea
4. Judea Under Seleucid Rule
5. The Hasmonean Revolt
6. Conquest by Pompey
7. Herodian Rule
8. Judea Under Roman Rule
9. Jewish Rebellions

1. Judea Under Persian Rule.
Despite the fact that the Persian kings held Judea as part of their vast Near Eastern empire for a full two centuries (539-332 B.C.), no continuous historical narrative of this period has survived. The biblical books of Ezra and Nehemiah remain the primary literary sources, but their depiction of events is episodic, often confusing and almost always rendered according to the ideological or apologetic agendas of their authors. Archaeology is beginning to provide a counterbalance to these limitations, but its application to the Persian period is still in its infancy (*see* Jewish History: Persian Period).

In 539 B.C., Babylon was conquered by King Cyrus of Persia, the founder of the Achaemenid dynasty. Cyrus's decision to restore Jerusalem was part of a wider propaganda campaign to legitimize his seizure of power. By setting himself up as the *patron and protector of various native cults, Cyrus secured the loyalty of his new subjects. In addition to authorizing the rebuilding of Jerusalem's temple, Cyrus permitted deported Judeans in Mesopotamia to resettle their ancestral homeland. The biblical sources place the number of returnees in the neighborhood of forty-two thousand (Ezra 2:1-67; Neh 7:5-69). Recent demographic analysis based on known site distribution from this period, however, has made it clear that the biblical statistics are greatly exaggerated not only as estimates for the number of the returning exiles but also for the entire population of Judea at any time during the Persian era. C. E. Carter proposes a total population of about eleven thousand under the early Achaemenids and about seventeen thousand during the mid-fifth century.

More important than the absolute size of Judea's population is the question of the proportion of returnees in relation to the Judeans and neighboring northern Israelites who had never been deported, and how the settlement of these groups was distributed. The biblical sources grudgingly concede the existence of the latter, only to derogate them as "people of the land" (Ezra 6:21; Neh 10:28) or even to deny their Israelite identity outright (Ezra 4:1-3; cf. Josephus *Ant.* 10.9.7 §§183-85). The degree to which imperial goals may have played a role in encouraging such an exclusionary policy is an important issue that still requires an adequate exposition.

As the Persian Empire grew, Judea came to occupy a frontier zone between the Achaemenids and the frequently rebellious satrapy of Egypt. The disruptive potential of this frontier came to a head when the Athenian fleet allied itself with an Egyptian revolt in 460 B.C. The Peace of Callias that followed the conflict (449 B.C.) left the Achaemenids eager to prevent this corner of their empire from slipping out of their control again. Archaeological remains attest to an extensive fortification of Judea at this time, and Nehemiah's mission to rebuild the walls of Jerusalem in 445 B.C. is best understood within this larger context.

2. Conquests of Alexander the Great.
Achaemenid rule over Judea came to an abrupt end with the conquests of *Alexander the Great, king of Macedon, who in 332 B.C. triumphantly marched through Syria, besieging and capturing any cities that still held out for Persia. Two years later, Alexander decisively shattered Achaemenid power and assumed the Persian diadem; seven years later (323 B.C.), Alexander died suddenly and without an heir. For a time his generals took up the challenge of holding together the vast world empire they had inherited, but their unity of purpose was ultimately under-

mined and they fell to fighting one another for supremacy or survival. Virtually nothing is known about Judea's involvement in this era of titanic conflicts. *Josephus preserves a tradition about a meeting between Alexander and the Judeans, but most scholars regard the incident as fictitious.

The partition of Alexander's empire among his surviving generals at the battle of Ipsus (301 B.C.) did not end their conflicts, but the division of spoils resulting from it set the stage for Judea's geopolitical role for the remaining two centuries of the Hellenistic age (*see* Diadochi): as an object of repeated contestation between the superpowers of north and south—the *Seleucids of Syria and the *Ptolemies of Egypt. In accordance with the agreement at Ipsus, Seleucus was to enjoy suzerainty over the whole of Syria and the Phoenician coast; but Ptolemy refused to give up southern Syria, which his own forces were then holding. Consequently Judea became part of the Ptolemaic Empire for the next hundred years (*see* Jewish History: Greek Period).

3. Ptolemaic Rule of Judea.

The period of Ptolemaic rule over Judea suffers from gaping silences in the historical record comparable to those framing the Persian era that preceded it. Two windows on this period are the *Zenon papyri (penned in the 250s by an agent of Ptolemy II's financial minister) and a lengthy section in Josephus purporting to document the fortunes of the Tobiads, a wealthy family of Transjordanian tax farmers with ties to both Jerusalem and the Ptolemies (Josephus *Ant.* 12.4.1—4.11 §§157-236). The latter, however, is patently fictional in many respects, and its dubious temporal setting makes it problematic as a source for chronology.

The Ptolemies were interested in Judea for the same reasons as the Achaemenids before them: as a military frontier to be secured and a source of revenue to be controlled. A Ptolemaic garrison is known to have existed in Jerusalem in 200 B.C. (Josephus *Ant.* 12.3.3 §138); whether this had been a permanent feature or was the result of the immediate military conflict in which it is mentioned is not determinable. The Ptolemies exercised economic control by allowing only Ptolemaic *coinage to be recognized in Syria and Phoenicia and sought to maximize their revenues by the institution of a tax-farming system. If Josephus's account is to be believed, the high *priest in Jerusalem was initially responsible for paying Judea's tribute, a role described as the *prostasia* (Josephus *Ant.* 12.4.1-2 §§158, 161). Subsequently, we are told, this position was taken over by the Tobiad family. If this is true, it illustrates how imperial economic goals could erode prerogatives traditionally held by the high priest and thus enable other sectors of Judean society to achieve prominence in political life.

4. Judea Under Seleucid Rule.

The Ptolemies lost their Near Eastern holdings to the Seleucids in the so-called Fifth Syrian War (202-200 B.C.). The inhabitants of Jerusalem sided with the victors at a crucial moment in that conflict and were amply rewarded by Antiochus III, the Seleucid king, who renewed the Achaemenid precedent of patronizing the temple and its personnel and endorsing local jurisdiction in accordance with Judean ancestral laws (Josephus *Ant.* 12.3.3 §§138-44). Recent excavations suggest that at some point during Antiochus III's reign, the Israelites of *Samaria (Samaritans) built a temple on the summit of Mt. Gerizim in rivalry to Judean pretensions of Jerusalem being the sole authentic shrine for the worship of Yahweh. This development points to an escalation during this period (first intimated by Ezra and Nehemiah) of competing claims to the biblical heritage as a basis for cult and jurisdiction in Palestine.

Continued involvement with the Seleucid court gave new scope for political rivalry in Jerusalem. The most marked indications of this are the successes of Jason (brother of the high priest) and subsequently of Menelaus (brother of a temple officer) in persuading King Antiochus IV through bribery to summarily depose the incumbent high priest and to install them instead. By the same token, this practice served to undermine the high priest's authority in Judean eyes, because possession of the office was seen to be dependent upon the favor of the Seleucid monarch. This was made manifest by Menelaus's complicity with Antiochus's sack of the temple treasury in 169 B.C. and by Jason's attempt to regain his position a year later when he heard a rumor that Antiochus had died.

The civil strife ensuing from Jason's and Menelaus's feud triggered an unprecedented reaction from the Seleucid king. The civil strife was violently repressed and a Syrian garrison was installed in Jerusalem; Antiochus is said to have issued an edict outlawing the observance of Torah, installing a cult of Zeus Olympias in the Jerusalem temple and compelling the performance of acts designed to violate Judean laws. It is difficult to interpret Antiochus's motivation for enacting this decree. Second Maccabees offers no explanation other than hubris, and the reason alleged by 1 Maccabees 1:41-42—that Antiochus sought to dissolve ethnic differences throughout his realm—is disproved by evidence for the continuity of native cults elsewhere in the Seleucid Empire at this time. The extreme nature of the decree does not appear to follow logically either from the events that immediately preceded it or from prior Seleucid policy. Whatever Antiochus's intent, the implementation of the decree drove a significant number of Judeans to militant rebellion under the leadership of the Hasmoneans.

5. The Hasmonean Revolt.

The *Hasmonean revolt, led first by Judas Maccabeus and subsequently by his brothers, was simultaneously a power play by the Hasmonean family to gain control of the high priesthood. Their heroic military victories and pious rededication of the Jerusalem temple gave them a powerful advantage over their rivals in terms of popularity, yet they remained beholden to the Seleucid dynasty for their legitimacy, just as Jason and Menelaus before them. Hasmonean aspirations became patent when Judas continued to organize armed resistance in spite of the fact that Antiochus's decree was eventually rescinded (163 B.C.) and a new high priest, Alcimus, was appointed by Antiochus's successor (162 B.C.). Judas counterbalanced Alcimus's authority by appealing to *Rome for a token alliance that recognized the Hasmoneans to be the legitimate representatives of the Judeans—a gesture that had no practical effect but great propaganda value for Judas and his family. His brothers would continue to emulate Judas in this practice even after they had become established as Seleucid vassals.

Following Alcimus's death in 160 B.C., the Hasmoneans began to capitalize on repeated dynastic quarrels among the Seleucids, currying the favor of rival contenders in order to bolster their own status and political prestige. This led to their acquisition of the high priesthood, territorial additions and finally ostensible independence from the Seleucids in 143/2 B.C. Yet all of these advances were obtained as Seleucid benefactions, and arbitrary retraction of privileges was a frequent occurrence. Even after the Hasmoneans appeared to have entrenched their power, other Judeans continued to regard the Seleucids as a viable means of usurping or deposing them. This can be seen in the actions of Ptolemy, who murdered his Hasmonean uncle and then appealed to the Seleucids for support in 135/4 B.C. (1 Macc 16:18), and in 88 B.C., when the Judean populace appealed to the Seleucid monarch to assist them in deposing Alexander Janneus (Josephus *J.W.* 1.4.4-5 §§92-95; *Ant.* 13.5—14.1 §§376-78).

Eventually the Hasmoneans felt sufficiently secure to assert royal honors and to engage in large-scale expansion of their Judea-centered domain. The impact this expansion had upon Idumea, Samaria, Galilee and parts of Transjordan, and the consequent attitudes of their inhabitants towards Jerusalem, varied. The rival temple on Mt. Gerizim was destroyed by John Hyrcanus in about 111 B.C. (Josephus *Ant.* 13.9.1 §256), though the Samaritans themselves continued to exist as an ethnic group with distinct cultic traditions. Josephus also reports that the Hasmonean conquest of Idumea and later of Iturea was accompanied by a mass compulsory circumcision of the indigenous male populace and the enforcement of Judean laws (Josephus *Ant.* 13.9.1 §257; 13.5.3 §138). It is noteworthy, however, that both of these groups continue to be referred to as Idumeans and Itureans, not as Judeans. Their ostensible incorporation into the Abrahamic covenant did not erase existing ethnic distinctions. No surviving literary source documents the Hasmonean acquisition of Galilee, unless Josephus's passing reference to Judas Aristobulus's Iturean campaign is to be understood as having taken place within Galilee. Both the Maccabean literature and Josephus assume that region to be inhabited, at least in part, by fellow Israelites.

The consolidation of Hasmonean rule in Judea did not go unchallenged, nor was their control of the high priesthood endorsed by all Judeans. In addition to widespread popular opposition under Alexander Janneus (103-76 B.C.), this era also saw the emergence of sectarian groups, such as *Pharisees, *Essenes and the *Qumran community. During the reign of Shelamzion Alexandra (76-67 B.C.), it appears that the Pharisees managed to gain a significant amount of political power (Josephus *J.W.* 1.5.2 §§110-12; *Ant.* 13.15.5 §§401-4; 13.16.2 §§410-11). Yet in spite of the diversity of their relationships with the ruling family, these groups shared some degree of dissatisfaction with Hasmonean management of the Jerusalem temple, which led them to develop alternative strategies for maintaining the cultic purity and social integrity of Israel. Another effect of the resurgence of a native Judean monarchy was the development or amplification in sectarian literature of royal, as distinct from priestly, models of divinely authorized rule. Dissatisfaction with the existing regime gave new relevance to the biblical monarchic heritage as an ideological foil to Hasmonean and later to Herodian rule (e.g., *Pss. Sol.* 17; 4QpGen[a]; 4QFlor; 4QpIsa[a]; 4QSerek HaMilḥamah).

6. Conquest by Pompey.

The political gains of the later Hasmoneans owed much to the power vacuum resulting from the final throes of the Seleucid Empire. This window of opportunity proved to be short-lived, however, and was soon closed by the arrival of Roman military might in the Near East, occasioned by the Third Mithridatic War (74/3-66 B.C.). Having defeated Mithridates of Pontus and Tigranes of Armenia, the Roman general *Pompey advanced southward in 64 B.C. for the purpose of rearranging the political map of Syria in Rome's favor in order to prevent the Parthians, the new rising imperial power of the East, from doing the same.

Pompey found the Hasmonean house divided. Aristobulus II and Hyrcanus II, the sons of Shelamzion Alexandra, were contending against each other for the kingship, and both appealed to Pompey for support. It was Hyrcanus who succeeded in winning Pompey's favor. Aristobulus's refusal to abide by this verdict elicited a strong Roman reaction. With the assistance of Hyrcanus and his Judean supporters, Jerusalem fell quickly to Pompey in 63 B.C., and Aristobulus was sent to Rome in chains. Pompey then confirmed Hyrcanus as high priest but denied him royal honors, assigning to him instead the less elevated title of *ethnarch* ("ruler of the people"). Pompey further reduced the resources of the Hasmonean state by restoring many of its territorial acquisitions to their native Greco-Syrian citizenries and by imposing tribute on Judea, which was now placed under the supervision of the Roman proconsul in Syria.

Josephus places great weight on Pompey's actions as marking an end to Judean independence (Josephus *Ant.* 14.4.5 §§77-78; 14.16.4 §§490-91; *J.W.* 2.16.4 §§355-57). This construal of events, however, is an exaggeration reflecting Josephus's pro-Hasmonean bias. Rome continued to rely on native rulers for governing Judea and its neighboring regions for more than a century after Pompey's reinstallation of Hyrcanus in 63 B.C. The scope for political involvement of these native regimes under Roman rule was no less genuine in principle than the autonomy exercised by Judean leaders under the Persian or Hellenistic empires. The significant shift in Judean history that Pompey's arrival did inaugurate was the reorientation of Judea's geopolitical importance from a north-south (Seleucid-Ptolemaic) to an east-west (Roman-Parthian) axis and the gradual supplanting of Hasmonean rule by the Idumean strongman Antipater and his son, Herod the Great (*see* Jewish History: Roman Period).

7. Herodian Rule.

The rise of Antipater and *Herod was made possible by a combination of internal and external circumstances. Tenacious military opposition to Hyrcanus led by surviving members of Aristobulus's family polarized Judean loyalties and left the political climate susceptible to manipulation by the larger Parthian-Roman conflict. More crucial to Herod's success were the protracted civil wars of Rome, in which the resources of Syria and Judea would play no small part.

Antipater's involvement with Hyrcanus began during the initial power struggle with Aristobulus, just prior to Pompey's arrival. Antipater first gained Roman notice by his timely military support for Julius Caesar during the Alexandrian War (48-47 B.C.). In gratitude for this, Caesar conferred substantial vice-regal powers upon Antipater and confirmed Hyrcanus as high priest. Caesar's murder in 44 B.C. left Syria in the hands of the assassins. Antipater bent with the changing political wind and dutifully collected tribute to fund Cassius's imminent war with Octavian and Mark Antony but was himself murdered by a rival potentate in Judea. Herod wasted no time in drawing upon Cassius's support to aid him in avenging his father's death.

Following the battle of Philippi (42 B.C.), Herod was quick to reverse his allegiance yet again in favor of the victorious Antony, winning him over through a combination of bribery and the support of Hyrcanus. Two years later, all of Herod's gains in Judea were undermined by a Parthian invasionary force that agreed to set up Antigonus, the last surviving son of Aristobulus, as king. Hyrcanus was captured and mutilated so that he could no longer serve as high priest, and Herod was compelled to flee to Rome. Eager to counter the Parthians' move, the Roman senate, under advisement from both Antony and Octavian, nominated Herod king of the Judeans *(basileus Ioudaiōn),* promising him military assistance for Antigonus's deposition. So while Antony endeavored to repulse the Parthians in Syria, Herod made war on Antigonus. Three years later (37 B.C.) Jerusalem was taken and Antigonus executed. The Roman political situation had not yet settled, however, and Herod found himself forced once more into a dramatic change of allegiance when Octavian defeated Antony at the battle of Actium in 31 B.C. Octavian (soon to be the emperor Augustus; *see* Roman Emperors) reconfirmed Herod in his kingship, and Herodian rule over Judea continued unchallenged.

Herod ruled Judea and its satellite territories (increased on three separate occasions by Augustus) for twenty-six years following his reconfirmation. His reign was marked by an extravagant program of building and *benefactions throughout the eastern Mediterranean, the greatest work of which was the restoration and expansion of the Jerusalem temple (which was not finished until long after Herod's death). The majority of this activity, however, was concentrated outside of Judea and was calculated to advertise Herod's personal prestige within the Greek world. Another, less glorious side to Herod's reign was his gradual elimination of all surviving Hasmoneans, including Hyrcanus, his own wife Mariamme and his two sons by her. Beginning with the defeat of Antigonus in 37 B.C., Herod introduced a significant innovation to the institution of the high priesthood. Brooking no potential rival to his absolute rule, Herod began appointing and deposing high priests at his discretion, selecting candidates from families who had no political influence in Judea, so that they would be dependent upon him. This practice severely undercut the legitimacy of the high priesthood in the eyes of many Judeans. How widespread native opposition may have been to Herod during his reign is difficult to determine, but the aftermath of his death in 4 B.C. revealed strongly anti-Herodian sentiments from within both popular and elite sectors of Judean society.

Herod wrote more than one will during his reign, and this fact became a source of contention among his children after his death. Archelaus, the chosen successor in Herod's last will, was challenged by Antipas, named heir in an earlier dispensation. The issue was submitted to the emperor Augustus for judgment, but the situation was complicated by Archelaus's failure to maintain order in Jerusalem just prior to his voyage to Rome, an incident that resulted in a mass slaughter of Judeans and the involvement of Roman troops. Violence escalated in places into open revolt against Herodian rule. Order was restored with the aid of the Syrian governor, who permitted a Judean delegation to be sent to Rome to appeal to the emperor to attach Judea to the province of Syria and allow it to be administered by non-Herodian native governors *(hēgemones).* Augustus opted to retain Archelaus but reduced his territory by dividing it among his siblings, confining Archelaus to Judea, Samaria and Idumea and probationally demoting him to the rank of *ethnarch* until he could prove his worth. Archelaus, however, failed at the test; after a rule of only ten years, Augustus deposed and exiled him in response to complaints of misrule from his subjects. Not sufficiently confident in the abilities of Herod's remaining children, Augustus placed Judea under provincial rule in A.D. 6.

8. Judea Under Roman Rule.

Apart from a brief interval during which Herodian rule was restored, Judea was administered throughout the first century by Roman prefects stationed at Caesarea Maritima who were subordinate to the governor of Syria. In A.D. 66, Jerusalem and much of Palestine rose in armed rebellion against Roman rule (*see* Revolutionary Movements, Jewish). This revolt culminated in the destruction of Jerusalem and its temple four years later.

A balanced reconstruction of this period is hampered by the skewed perspective placed on it by the Gospels and by the writings of Josephus, all of which (albeit for different reasons) regard Jerusalem's destruction in A.D. 70 as the inevitable climax to much earlier developments. Josephus in particular retrojects this outcome onto his interpretation of events as far back as the inception of Roman rule in A.D. 6. Consequently Josephus's narrative is selectively biased toward documenting incidents that support a scenario of inexorably escalating tensions within Judean society and between that society and its Roman rulers. In all probability there is much truth to Josephus's picture; however, to adopt his interpretive framework as the sole perspective from which to examine and characterize first-century Judea is to risk oversimplification of a far more complex situation and to ignore or downplay strategies of accommodation to imperial rule that Judeans of this period shared in common with those of previous periods.

A key element of both continuity and discontinuity from A.D. 6 to 66 was the importance of the Judean aristocracy in mediating Roman rule. The Herodians shared in this role throughout the period, though not as directly as Herod the Great had done. The exception to this pattern was Agrippa I, who ruled Judea as its king from A.D. 41 until his death three years later. However, even after Judea's reversion to provincial status, members of the Herodian family (whose realms lay outside Judea's boundaries) were given a degree of control over the Jerusalem temple. Chief among their prerogatives was the power to appoint or depose high priests, just as Herod had done. Yet the impact of this practice was markedly different from its exercise under Herod.

While it is true that such overt control of priestly office, a power also enjoyed by the Roman procurators during the years prior to Agrippa I's reign, advertised the dependency of the candidate upon the one appointing him, the nonmonarchic character of Roman Judea removed the imperative, so clearly manifested in Herod the Great's behavior, of appointing individuals without public influence. On the contrary, the indispensability of the high priest for maintaining public order meant that prospective candidates would be selected only from among the wealthy and the powerful. The result was that the political clout of the high priesthood rose substantially during the first century A.D., and with this development came to prominence a group, hitherto unattested in Judean history, referred to by Josephus and the NT as the *archiereis* ("the chief/ruling priests").

Also elevated in prestige at this time were ex-high priests, a novel phenomenon whose existence was ironically dependent on the instability of their tenure. The cumulative effect of these developments was the expansion of political involvement by priests in Judean society and the corresponding enhancement of the priesthood as a source of mediation for Rome's administration. The politically important stratum of Judean society, however, was by no means confined to those of priestly descent. Individuals of nonpriestly background were just as prominent in the resolution of crises. What is perhaps most striking about the first century is the minimal extent of Roman military-administrative presence in Judea outside of Caesarea and the degree to which Rome relied upon influential priests and laity to maintain the peace.

While it is clear that many native elites benefited politically from the removal of Herodian rule from Judea, it is less easy to ascertain the impact of Roman administration on the Judean populace. Josephus's numerous references to rural brigandage, especially during the post-Agrippa era, suggest increasing economic hardship for the peasantry. The precise causes and dynamics of the situation, however, are not directly accessible and must be reconstructed on the basis of inference and circumstantial evidence. One likely factor contributing to such conditions was the increased importance of wealth in aristocratic competition for Roman or Herodian favor, and the pressure this would have placed on elites to consolidate large, revenue-producing estates. Another factor possibly conducive to worsening conditions may have been the failure of the Roman prefects to respond adequately to economic crises, such as the great famine of the 40s.

Other indications of dissatisfaction with direct Roman rule and its aristocratic Judean collaborators do not point exclusively to material grievances. Ideological factors could be equally relevant, as can be seen in the reaction of certain individuals to the imposition of a Roman census in A.D. 6, who regarded acquiescence to the assessment as being incompatible with the acknowledgment of Yahweh's supremacy (Josephus *J.W.* 2.8.1 §118; cf. *Ant.* 18.1.1 §4). Ironically, the prime exponent of this view, a certain Judas, was not himself affected by the census, as he did not live in Judea. Josephus seeks to make Judas the wellspring of the revolt of A.D. 66 but provides little evidence of this in his narration of events, suggesting that whatever popular reaction Judas may have inspired in A.D. 6 was ephemeral.

Nevertheless, the ideal of freedom (*eleutheria*) appears to have played a role in other expressions of discontent that the Roman government regarded with greater seriousness. Josephus makes reference to popular prophetic figures who appeared in the Judean desert in the 40s and 50s, apparently reenacting with their followers significant episodes of the biblical past that portended Israel's liberation (Josephus *J.W.* 2.13.4-5 §§259-63; *Ant.* 20.5.1 §§97-98; 20.8.6 §§168-71; *see* Revolutionary Movements). Finally, there was a Jerusalem-based terrorist group popularly known as Sicarii ("dagger-men") who assassinated several notables, including at least one high priest (Josephus *J.W.* 2.13.3 §§254-57) and who later played a role in the revolt of A.D. 66-70. A recurrent element in the activities of these groups (with the exception of Judas, about whom very little is known) is that their anti-Roman stance went hand in hand with opposition, explicit or implicit, to the existing Judean leadership, in particular to the priesthood. This point is crucial to an analysis of the outbreak of the revolt in A.D. 66, because however symptomatic these or other expressions of discontent may have been, the instigation of the revolt came from none of these groups but from the Jerusalem priesthood itself.

9. Jewish Rebellions.

The rebellion of A.D. 66-70, dubbed by Josephus the Judean War against the Romans and by modern scholarship also as the First Revolt or the Great Revolt, took place in several stages. This was in part due to its coincidence with severe political upheaval in Rome, triggered by the emperor Nero's suicide in A.D. 68, which ushered in a succession of short-lived regimes culminating in the seizure of power by Vespasian, the general whom Nero had commissioned to suppress the revolt in Judea. Vespasian's rule initiated a new dynasty of Roman emperors, the Flavians, and for that reason the punishment of Judea became a showpiece for Flavian claims to have reestablished law and order.

Josephus's participation in the rebellion, his capture by the Romans and his subsequent role as a Flavian protégé have proved as much of a hindrance as a help to modern attempts at understanding the instigation and progress of the revolt from the Judean side. Bent on rehabilitating the image of his people as law-abiding Roman subjects, Josephus frequently took pains to obfuscate the identities and aims of the rebels so as to make them appear unrepresentative of the Judean majority. However, Josephus is unable to conceal the fact that the revolt was begun and led by prominent Jerusalem elites, including most significantly the son of the high priest. Why those who considered as a class stood to benefit most—socially, politically, economically—from the status quo should have ended up at the forefront of a concerted anti-Roman undertaking is perhaps the most puzzling aspect of the revolt.

At the same time, it must be recognized that no single group or individual dominated the scene, and much of the rebel energies were squandered on internecine power struggles. The motivational emphasis of the various groups also appears to have varied. For some leaders, like Menachem, possession of the city of Jerusalem (with possible monarchic aspirations) was the main objective; for others, like the priestly-led Zealots, control of the temple and a probably biblically inspired restructuring of the high-priestly office was paramount. An element of class conflict or at least an appeal to economic grievances may also have been present in the actions of some of the rebel groups, such as the burning of the public debt archives and Herodian residences in Jerusalem by the Sicarii. Yet in spite of their internal divisions, many of the rebel leaders managed to collaborate against the Roman reprisal.

The Jerusalem leaders had a good deal of time to prepare because the Romans would first have to secure the regions surrounding Judea. The initial assault on Jerusalem was led by Cestius Gallus, the governor of Syria, who reached the city late in A.D. 66. He was, however, repulsed by the defenders and forced to withdraw. In the spring of the following year, Nero dispatched Vespasian to handle the situation. The campaign was interrupted by Nero's death and the ensuing political chaos in Rome, which ultimately led Vespasian to entrust the war in Judea to his son Titus. It was not until A.D. 70 that Titus was able to begin the siege of Jerusalem. The temple fell to Titus's troops sometime in August of that year and was put to the torch. By the end of the following month, the remainder of the city was subdued. Surviving rebels continued to hold out in the fortresses of Herodium, Masada and Machaerus but were eventually crushed.

Although the temple's destruction marked the end of Herodian involvement in Judea and terminated the role of its priesthood, it did not signal the end of Judea itself, nor even of Jerusalem. Judeans continued to inhabit both for more than half a century. A Roman legion now occupied Jerusalem, and some Judean territory was confiscated for Roman usage (Josephus *J.W.* 6.3.5 §216), yet those Judean aristocrats who had surrendered to the Roman forces prior to the conclusion of the war were promised eventual restoration of their property (Josephus *J.W.* 6.2.2 §115). It was not until the reign of the emperor Hadrian, who proposed to transform Jerusalem into a pagan city, that the inhabitants of Judea entered into conflict with Rome once again. No extensive literary source survives for the second revolt (A.D. 132-135), but epigraphic and numismatic testimony from the Judean desert evinces strong continuity with the ideology of the first revolt—the liberation/redemption of Zion—and reveals the name of its leader, Simeon bar Kosibah (known from other contemporary sources as Bar Kokbba; *see* Simon ben Kosiba). The Roman suppression of the second revolt resulted in the effective end of Judea. Judeans were excluded from inhabiting the territory, which was now renamed Syria Palaestina; Jerusalem became Aelia Capitolina. The center of Judean settlement in southern Syria shifted to Galilee, which would come to foster rabbinic Judaism.

See also HASMONEANS; HERODIAN DYNASTY; JEWISH HISTORY; JEWISH WARS WITH ROME; JOSEPHUS; REVOLUTIONARY MOVEMENTS, JEWISH; SIMON BEN KOSIBA.

BIBLIOGRAPHY. R. S. Bagnall, *The Administration of the Ptolemaic Possessions Outside Egypt* (Leiden: E. J. Brill, 1976); A. I. Baumgarten, *The Flourishing of Jewish Sects in the Maccabean Era: An Interpretation* (Leiden: E. J. Brill, 1997); E. J. Bickerman, "La Charte Séleucide de Jérusalem," in *Studies in Jewish and Christian History* (3 vols. Leiden: E. J. Brill, 1976-86) 2; C. E. Carter, *The Emergence of Yehud in the Persian Period: A Social and Demographic Study* (Sheffield: Sheffield Academic Press, 1999); J. Elayi and J. Sapin, *Beyond the River: New Perspectives on Transeuphratene* (Sheffield: Sheffield University Press, 1998); M. Goodman, *The Ruling Class of Judea: The Origins of the Jewish Revolt Against Rome A.D. 66-70* (Cambridge: Cambridge University Press, 1987); L. L. Grabbe, *Judaism from Cyrus to Hadrian* (2 vols.; Minneapolis: Fortress, 1992); E. S. Gruen, "Hellenism and Persecution: Antiochus IV and the Jews," in *Hellenistic History and Culture,* ed. P. Green (Berkeley and Los Angeles: University of California Press, 1993); K. G. Hoglund, *Achaemenid Imperial Administration in Syria-Palestine and the Missions of Ezra and Nehemiah* (Atlanta: Scholars Press, 1992); R. H. Horsley with J. S. Hanson, *Bandits, Prophets and Messiahs: Popular Movements in the Time of Jesus* (San Francisco: Harper & Row, 1985); J. S. McLaren, *Power and Politics in Palestine: The Jews and the Governing of Their Land 100 B.C.-A.D. 70* (Sheffield: Sheffield Academic Press, 1991); idem, *Turbulent Times? Josephus and Scholarship on Judea in the First Century A.D.* (Sheffield: Sheffield Academic Press, 1998); F. Millar, *The Roman Near East: 31 B.C.-A.D. 337* (Cambridge, MA: Harvard University Press, 1993); J. Pastor, *Land and Economy in Ancient Palestine* (London: Routledge, 1997); K. E. Pomykala, *The Davidic Dynasty Tradition in Early Judaism: Its History and Significance for Messianism* (Atlanta: Scholars Press, 1995); J. J. Price, *Jerusalem Under Siege: The Collapse of the Jewish State 66-70 A.D.* (Leiden: E. J. Brill, 1992); A. N. Sherwin-White, *Roman Foreign Policy in the East: 168 B.C. to A.D. 1* (London: Duckworth, 1984); E. M. Smallwood, *The Jews Under Roman Rule from Pompey to Diocletian: A Study in Political Relations* (Leiden: E. J. Brill, 1981). C. Seeman

JUDITH

The art of early Jewish storytelling rises to a new level in this literary gem. The tale narrates Judith's single-handed deliverance of the Jewish people from an invasion by the Assyrians. Though ostensibly historical, it is clearly a fictional work. The plot moves rather slowly until Judith makes her appearance, but from that moment on the storyteller spins the tale with escalating suspense, right up to the spine-tingling climax.

Judith is reckoned as deuterocanonical by Roman and Eastern Orthodox Christians but is assigned to the *Apocrypha by Protestants. Though it is extant only in Greek and later versions, it clearly had a Semitic, probably Hebrew, original. א, B and A represent the three best

Greek versions, each of which is slightly different. In the *Septuagint, Judith is placed among the historical books, after Ezra-Nehemiah, in this order: Esther, Judith and *Tobit. In the Vulgate, the order is Ezra-Nehemiah, Tobit, Judith and Esther.

1. Summary of Contents
2. Author, Date and Place
3. Purpose
4. Use of Irony
5. Relevance for the New Testament

1. Summary of Contents.
The book falls into two parts: the first seven chapters narrate the invasion of the Assyrians; chapters 8—16 recount Judith's deliverance. Because the western nations, including Judea, refused assistance in a war against Arphaxad, Nebuchadnezzar (in reality a Neo-Babylonian, not an Assyrian) dispatches his general Holofernes to punish them (Jdt 1—2). The rebels sue for peace and become vassals, except for Judea (Jdt 3).

Left to face retribution alone, the Israelites cry out to God for deliverance and prepare for invasion (Jdt 4). Holofernes consults Achior the Ammonite for an assessment of Israelite strength and resolve. Infuriated by Achior's high regard for and warning about the God of Israel, Holofernes banishes Achior to Bethulia, a Jewish city guarding the pass to the hill country of Judea (Jdt 5—6). Holofernes lays siege to Bethulia, cutting off its water supply. The leaders hearken to the pleas of the people to surrender if rescue does not come within five days (Jdt 7).

At this point the beautiful and pious widow Judith enters the story. One is reminded of 2 Maccabees 5:27 and the *Assumption of Moses* 9:1, in which the introduction of Judas and Taxo, respectively, signals a turning point in the narrative. Hearing of the planned capitulation, she determines to save the city by her own device (Jdt 8). After securing permission from the elders and offering up a *prayer for success, she arrays herself in stunning attire and, with her maidservant and a supply of kosher food, enters Holofernes's camp. Displaying her charms to good effect and under the pretext of having secret information that will prove the undoing of the Israelites, she obtains an audience with Holofernes (Jdt 9—10).

Holofernes, captivated by Judith's beauty, invites her to a banquet and intends to seduce her (Jdt 11—12). Once alone with the general, who falls into a drunken stupor, Judith decapitates him with his own sword. Owing to a cleverly established pattern of ritual observance, she is able to slip out of the camp unchallenged, carrying Holofernes's head in her kosher food bag (Jdt 13). Back in Bethulia, Achior beholds Holofernes's face and becomes a proselyte. The Assyrians, meanwhile, discover the decapitated Holofernes and flee in panic, hotly pursued by the Israelites. Judith is honored by the high *priest and grateful nation (Jdt 14—15). The book concludes with Judith's celebratory song, her dedication of the spoils to the temple and a tribute to her fame and *piety (Jdt 16).

2. Author, Date and Place.
Judith is an anonymous work. Internal evidence suggests that the author was a Palestinian Jew. Though some scholars have placed Judith in the Persian period (*see* Jewish History: Persian Period), the conversion of Achior suggests a date well after the time of Ezra, when conversion of Ammonites to *Judaism was unthinkable (cf. Ezra 9—10 with Deut 23:3). Furthermore, the concerns and atmosphere of the book seem to reflect the trauma of the Maccabean revolt. A widely accepted date is about 150 B.C. The fact, however, that the story is placed in Samaria, with no indication of sectarian strife within Judaism, may point to the reign of John Hyrcanus (135-104 B.C.; *see* Hasmoneans). Hyrcanus captured Shechem, sometimes identified with the otherwise unknown city of Bethulia, and destroyed the Samaritan temple on Mt. Gerizim in 128 B.C. Later he conquered and incorporated Samaria into his kingdom (109 B.C.; cf. Josephus *Ant.* 13.8.4—9.1 §§249-58). This would account for Jews living in a city lying within the former province of Samaria. Achior's conversion may also be a reflex of the forced conversion of the Idumeans living in southern Judea in about 128 B.C. (see 4 below).

3. Purpose.
This rousing story combines a clarion call for militant defense of political and religious freedom with a scrupulous observance of Torah. A tale of impending annihilation thinly veils a real-time danger for observant Jews. Through the lens of Nebuchadnezzar, we glimpse the menacing figure of Antiochus IV Epiphanes.

Holofernes conjures up reminiscences of Nicanor, Antiochus's general, whom Judas beheaded (cf. 2 Macc 15:30-35). The narrative breathes the atmosphere of the stirring deeds of the Maccabean brothers. Standing in a line of ancient worthies like Deborah, Jael and Esther, Judith confronts the dark forces of *Hellenistic imperialism. The keynote of Judith is the conviction that God will intervene and defend his people if they but faithfully observe his law. This divine intervention, however, includes militant activism on the part of individuals.

4. Use of Irony.

That the army of Nebuchadnezzar, which had reduced powerful kingdoms to rubble, could be routed by a small Jewish town in Samaria leads off a series of ironies. The supreme irony lies in the thematic verse: "But the Lord Almighty has foiled them by the hand of a woman" (Jdt 16:5 NRSV). This woman, a pious widow of whom no one spoke any ill (Jdt 8:8), lived a celibate life until the day she died (at 105). And yet she possessed such seductive charm that every male who laid eyes upon her was smitten.

The story is framed by the figure of Achior, an Ammonite, who, remarkably, testifies to the power of Israel's God and their invincibility when they obey him (Jdt 5:5-21). The haughty Holofernes expels him to Bethulia with this death sentence: "you shall not see my face again from this day until I take revenge on this race that came out of Egypt. Then at my return the sword of my army and the spear of my servants shall pierce your sides, and you shall fall among their wounded" (Jdt 6:5b-6 NRSV). The next time Achior does see Holofernes's face, Holofernes is bodiless—Achior falls on his face and promptly converts to Judaism (Jdt 14:10). This ironic touch may reflect the conquest of Medaba, near the ancestral home of the Ammonites, and the forced conversion of the Idumeans living in the southern regions of Judea.

Several lines in the story are good examples of double entendre (Jdt 11:6, 16, 19; 12:4, 14, 18). These become apparent after the tale is fully told and add a humorous touch to an otherwise grim plot. Jewish readers would certainly relish the irony of Judith escaping the Assyrian camp with Holofernes's head in her kosher food bag (Jdt 13:10). Perhaps the most delightful irony in Judith surfaces in the realization that Holofernes "lost his head" before he lost his head (Jdt 12:16).

5. Relevance for the New Testament.

Judith is not a historical figure but rather a personification (her name means "Jewess"). As such, she embodies the ideals of a religious community. We are overhearing the concerns and theology of a group similar to the *Pharisees. One of the difficult issues in historical research of early Judaism and Christianity has been an accurate reconstruction of Second Temple Pharisaism. Judith is valuable in this connection because it seems to portray an earlier phase of Pharisaism than that depicted in the NT and in later *rabbinic sources.

For example, Judith's practice of rigorous fasting (Jdt 8:6) exceeds that enjoined in the OT and conforms to the injunctions of the Pharisees as portrayed in the NT (cf. Mk 2:18 par. Mt 9:14-17; Lk 5:33-39; and see Mt 6:16-18). In this regard, Jesus' relaxation of fasting requirements for his disciples was highly controversial (cf. Mk 2:19-20). Judith's fidelity to the ritual purity laws is especially noteworthy. Besides adherence to food laws (Jdt 12:2-4), we read of ritual bathing in running water before *prayer (Jdt 12:6-9), as required by Pharisaic halakah. The NT refers to rules governing table fellowship and ritual purity in Jewish society (cf. Gal 2:11-14; Mk 7:1-5; Lk 11:38; Jn 2:6). These rules generally conform to the Pharisaic position, which, as *Josephus informs us, was acknowledged by the majority of Jews as "the most accurate" (Josephus *Ant.* 13.10.5 §288).

Judith also observed special times of prayer, coinciding with the burning of incense at the *Jerusalem temple (Jdt 9:1), a practice continued by the earliest Jerusalem church (Acts 3:1). Judith's revelation to Holofernes, that the elders of Bethulia were about to commit a grave sin by eating food tithed to God, refers to the Pharisaic practice of meticulously tithing all produce grown in the Holy Land (cf. Mt 23:23; Lk 11:42). We should also mention that Achior's conversion assumes a Judaism that is open to proselytizing—a stance reflected in NT literature (cf. Mt 23:15; Acts 2:10; 6:5; 13:43).

Although no NT document compares with Judith in terms of genre, two writings share a similar intensity and urgency: Hebrews and the Apocalypse. In both, feminine figures and imagery play a role in the rhetorical strategy of exhorting the faithful (cf. Heb 11; Rev 19—21).

The main question that Judith raises is ethical: Are Judith's actions compatible with NT ethical teaching? The general tenor of NT paraenesis with respect to Christian involvement in violence and the role of Christian *women in Greco-Roman society might suggest pacifism (cf. Mt 5:38-48 par. Lk 6:29-30; Mt 26:52; Rom 12:17-21; 1 Pet 2:13-25; 3:1-6, 9; Heb 11:35; 1 Tim 2:9-15; Rev 13:10). However, Christian insistence that the state has the right to punish evildoers has some relevant implications for our question (Rom 13:1-5; 1 Pet 2:13-17). Christian ethicists must search for underlying theological principles in the teachings of Jesus and the apostles and employ philosophical argumentation in working out a response to this difficult issue. What is clear is that in Second Temple Judaism a significant number of Jews viewed Judith's actions as embodying the noblest form of piety. In this they have been joined by some prominent figures in Christian church history (cf. *1 Clem.* 55.3-5).

See also APOCRYPHA AND PSEUDEPIGRAPHA; WOMEN IN GRECO-ROMAN WORLD AND JUDAISM.

BIBLIOGRAPHY. **Text and Translations:** R. Hanhart, *Iudith* (Septuaginta 8.4; Göttingen: Vandenhoeck & Ruprecht, 1979); B. M. Metzger and R. E. Murphy, eds., *The New Oxford Annotated Bible with the Apocryphal/Deuterocanonical Books: New Revised Standard Version* (New York: Oxford University Press, 1991) Apocrypha: 20-40; A. Rahlfs, *Iudith* (Septuaginta; Stuttgart: Deutsche Bibelgesellschaft, 1935, 1979); M. J. Suggs, K. D. Sakenfeld and J. R. Meuller, eds., *The Oxford Study Bible: Revised English Bible with the Apocrypha* (New York: Oxford University Press, 1992) 1071-86. **Commentaries and Studies:** L. Alonso-Schöckel, "Narrative Structures in the Book of Judith," in *The Center for Hermeneutical Studies in Hellenistic and Modern Culture* (Colloquy 11; Berkeley: Graduate Theological Union, 1975) 1-20; J. Craghan, *Esther, Judith, Tobit, Jonah, Ruth* (OTM 16; Wilmington, DE: Michael Glazier, 1982) 64-126; T. Craven, "Artistry and Faith in the Book of Judith," *Semeia* 8 (1977) 75-101; R. Doran, "Narrative Literature," in *Early Judaism and Its Modern Interpreters,* ed. R. A. Kraft and G. W. E. Nickelsburg (Atlanta: Scholars Press, 1985) 302-4; A.-M. Dubarle, *Judith* (2 vols.; AnBib 24; Rome: Biblical Institute, 1966); M. S. Enslin and S. Zeitlin, *The Book of Judith* (JAL 8; Leiden: E. J. Brill, 1972); J. M. Grintz, "Judith, Book of," *EncJud* 10:451-59; B. M. Metzger, *An Introduction to the Apocrypha* (New York; Oxford University Press, 1957) 43-53; C. A. Moore, *Judith: A New Translation with Introduction and Commentary* (AB 40; Garden City, NY: Doubleday, 1985); idem, "Judith, Book of," *ABD* 3:1117-25; G. W. E. Nickelsburg, *Jewish Literature Between the Bible and the Mishnah: A Historical and Literary Introduction* (Philadelphia: Fortress, 1981) 105-9; idem, "Stories of Biblical and Early Postbiblical Times," in *Jewish Writings of the Second Temple Period,* ed. M. E. Stone (CRINT 2.2; Assen: Van Gorcum; Philadelphia: Fortress, 1984) 46-52; J. C. VanderKam, ed., *"No One Spoke Ill of Her": Essays on Judith* (EJL 2; Atlanta: Scholars Press, 1992); L. M. Wills, "The Jewish Novellas," in *Greek Fiction: The Greek Novel in Context* (New York: Routledge, 1994) 223-38.

L. R. Helyer

K

KINGDOM OF GOD. *See* APOCALYPTICISM.

KINSHIP. *See* FAMILY AND HOUSEHOLD.

KISSING

Although readers of the NT will be familiar with the practice of the "holy kiss" (Rom 16:16; 1 Cor 16:20; 2 Cor 13:12; 1 Thess 5:26) or "kiss of love" (1 Pet 5:14) and many will recognize it as a cultural practice, fewer readers understand the cultural framework in which such a custom made sense.

In a somewhat later period, the "kiss of peace" assumed a liturgical function in church services (Justin Martyr *Apol. I.* 65). Because the practice in its earliest form was probably not restricted to one's own gender (Tertullian *Ad Ux.* 2.4), it was sometimes abused, drawing condemnations of those who kissed a second time (Athenagoras *Suppl.* 32); eventually it was restricted to members of one's own gender (*Apost. Const.* 2.7.57). Such restrictions were important especially given false accusations the church combated, such as incest (Athenagoras *Suppl.* 3; Theophilus of Antioch *Autol.* 3.4; Minucius Felix *Oct.* 31.1; Tertullian *Apol.* 2.5, 20). But before Paul's instructions ever were adapted for liturgical use, they reflected a broader cultural use in greetings for family and friends.

1. Family and Friends
2. A Respectful Greeting
3. The Nature of Kissing

1. Family and Friends.

Kissing was normally intended to express love; the term *phileō* can mean either "kiss" or "love" and occasionally appears as a play on words that means both (Diodorus Siculus *Bib. Hist.* 9.37.1). Kissing was a standard familial greeting (Longus *Daphn. Chl.* 4.22-23); thus, for example, Roman women kissed kinsmen (Plutarch *Quaest. Rom.* 6, *Mor.* 265B). A child was expected to kiss his mother (Ovid *Met.* 10.525) and father (Euripides *Androm.* 416). Likewise, fathers kissed their children (Virgil *Geor.* 2.523). One might rise and kiss a cousin who had greeted him (Achilles Tatius *Leuc.* 1.7.3).

Jewish people also counted it natural for a father to kiss and embrace a son he loved (*Jub.* 31:21; *Song Rab.* 5:16 §3) or for a son to kiss his father (Gen 27:26-27; *Jub.* 22:10-11; 26:21). Such kissing provided a natural greeting for close relatives such as children (*T. Sim.* 1:2), between sisters (*Num. Rab.* 9:9) or between sister and brother (Song 8:1; *Jos. and As.* 8:4/3). One expected such displays of affection all the more in dramatic circumstances. One might kiss a relative who had just arrived from a distant land, weeping for joy (Gen 33:4; Tob 7:6-7) or any other relative one had not seen for a long time (Ex 4:27; 18:7). Likewise one might kiss a child (Gen 31:28, 55; Tob 10:13) or other relative (Ruth 1:9, 14; 1 Kings 19:20) who was about to depart. A sister might embrace a brother whom she learned was safe, falling on his neck and kissing him (*Song Rab.* 8:1 §1).

That the father kisses his son in Luke 15:20 is therefore hardly surprising, except for the exceptional circumstances this kiss implies, including the father's forgiveness of the son's radically antisocial behavior. A kiss might also function as an affirmation (e.g., 1 Sam 10:1) or welcoming back into fellowship (2 Sam 14:33), as when John kisses the repentant Callimachus in *Acts of John* 78.

Kissing and embracing friends in greeting was also natural; hence pagans thought it signified a good omen in a dream (Artemidorus *Oneir.* 2.2). Kissing thus functioned as an intimate greeting for someone with whom one was close (Homer *Odys.* 21.224-27); Jewish friends also kissed at separation (1 Sam 20:4; Acts 20:37) and in greeting (2 Sam 15:5; 19:39; 20:9).

2. A Respectful Greeting.

Kisses further served as respectful greetings to one of higher status (Arrian *Alex.* 4.11.3; cf. Lk 7:38, 45); congratulatory kisses might be offered on the neck, hands, eyes or other body parts (mocked in Epictetus *Disc.* 1.19.24). In one Jewish story Abraham, in respectfully kissing Death's hand, died (*T. Abr.* 20, A). One might kiss one who pleased him; thus God is said to have kissed some Israelites who were circumcised (*Ex. Rab.* 19:5). One source similarly reports that Miriam's father kissed her hand when he thought her prophecy fulfilled, though he struck her head when he later wrongly concluded it a false prophecy (*b. Soṭa* 13a). A kiss was generally seen as pleasant (Prov 24:26) and hence might function as a suitable reward.

A king might rise to kiss a teacher whose wise discourse had pleased him (1 Esdr 4:47). A rabbi might rise and kiss the head of a student who expounded well; this is reported of Johanan ben Zakkai (*t. Ḥag.* 2:1; ARN 6 A; ARN 13 §32 B; *b. Ḥag.* 14b; *y. Ḥag.* 2:1 §4), R. Gamaliel II (*y. Roš Haš.* 2:9 §2), R. Simeon ben Yohai (*Pesiq. Rab Kah.* 1:3) and R. Abba bar Kahana (*y. Hor.* 3:5 §3; *Koh. Rab.* 6:2 §1). A student might also kiss a teacher on the head (*Qoh. Rab.* 9:5 §1). Such a practice seems relevant to Judas's betrayal kiss in Matthew 26:48-49 (par. Mk 14:44-45; Lk 22:47-48): that the outward act should have signified friendship, respect or devotion made the treachery all the more heinous (cf. Prov 27:6).

3. The Nature of Kissing.

The nature of kissing may also differ in many cases from modern readers' expectations. It is possible that the first Christian kisses of greeting, like many kisses in biblical tradition, were light kisses on the cheek (see Ellington). But whether in an early period or a later one, it is likely that some kisses, especially in the Roman West, involved more. Roman women kissed kinsmen on the lips (Plutarch *Quaest. Rom.* 6, *Mor.* 265B); mothers kissed daughters on the lips (Ovid *Met.* 2.356-57). Sources tell us the same of Roman fathers: one might kiss his son on the lips, albeit lightly (Virgil *Aen.* 12.434), or his daughter on the lips in pure innocence (Ovid *Met.* 10.362). A mourning Greek sister might wish to kiss her dead brother on the mouth (Euripides *Phoen.* 1671); children might do the same with a deceased mother (Euripides *Alc.* 403-4) or father (cf. facial kissing in Gen 50:1). Despite the common use of lips, the kiss of a sister (Ovid *Met.* 4.334) or mother (Ovid *Met.* 4.222) is naturally said to be less passionate than that of a lover. Maidens kiss one another on the lips, but only modestly; thus a lustful deity in disguise might give himself away (Ovid *Met.* 2.430-31). A *Hellenistic Jewish document can thus take for granted that one would kiss relatives on the lips (*Jos. and As.* 8:6).

Conversely, an aged priestess might kiss a departing hero merely on the hand (Apollonius of Rhodes *Arg.* 1.313). Some Jewish teachers seem uncomfortable with some forms of kissing; R. Akiba reportedly respected the Medes because they kissed only on the hand (*b. Ber.* 8b). Kisses of greeting could become the occasion for lustful abuses (Chariton *Chaer.* 2.7.7; cf. *Jos. and As.* 8:3-7).

Romans generally considered sexual kissing (also practiced in traditional Jewish culture; cf. Prov 7:13; Song 1:2) to be a private matter. Traditionalists opined that a man should not kiss his wife in public, though Cato's expulsion from the senate of a man for kissing his own wife in front of their daughter was generally deemed excessive (Plutarch *Bride* 13, *Mor.* 139E). Some erotic kissing did occur at *banquets. "The erotic banquet kiss, the *basium,* was completely different from the *osculum,* the innocent kiss that members of the same family would give each other on the mouth." The *basium* "may have been just a slight brushing of the lips," a hint pointing to something more (Dupont, 285).

See also FAMILY AND HOUSEHOLD; FRIENDSHIP.

BIBLIOGRAPHY. F. Dupont, *Daily Life in Ancient Rome* (Oxford: Blackwell, 1992); J. Ellington, "Kissing in the Bible: Form and Meaning," *BT* 41 (1990): 409-16.

C. S. Keener

L

LAND OF ISRAEL. *See* Israel, Land of.

LANGUAGES. *See* Aramaic Language; Grammarians, Hellenistic Greek; Greek of the New Testament; Hebrew Language; Latin Language.

LATIN LANGUAGE

The standard opinion of scholars is that Latin had relatively no influence on the language milieu of first-century Palestine and has little to inform our understanding of the language Jesus used. This position has recently been questioned, and the evidence deserves examination. It is now widely recognized that *Aramaic and *Greek, with some *Hebrew, were the major languages in use in Palestine in the first century. Aramaic was used by many if not most Jews of the time, with many Jews as well as the non-Jewish population using Greek. Hebrew was probably used in various religious contexts, but there is not clear evidence that it was used much more widely than that. The use of Latin remains disputed.

1. Use for Official Purposes
2. Use in Papyri, the Gospels and Other Documents

1. Use for Official Purposes.

The view of J. A. Fitzmyer is usually cited as representative of the position on Latin. He contends that the evidence indicates that Latin was used "mainly by the Romans who occupied the land and for more or less official purposes" (Fitzmyer, 129). The evidence that he cites in support of this contention is the inscriptional material in Latin found on buildings and aqueducts, funerary inscriptions on the tombstones of Roman legionnaires in Palestine, milestones and Roman tiles with the abbreviation of the Tenth Legion. Several inscriptions he cites are from *Caesarea Maritima, one of them noting that Pilate had erected a building in honor of Tiberius. This is in keeping with *Josephus's noting that the inscription forbidding non-Jews to enter the *Jerusalem *temple was written in Greek and in Latin characters (Josephus *J.W.* 5.5.2 §§193-94). It also, according to Fitzmyer, makes sense of Pilate's writing the title on Jesus' cross in Latin (Jn 19:20). Fitzmyer thus concludes that this evidence, which he claims is not abundant, says "little about the amount of Latin that might have been spoken in Palestine by the indigenous population, despite the long time since the Roman occupation began in 63 B.C." (Fitzmyer, 133), a situation he attributes to the widespread use of Greek as the *lingua franca* in the Roman East.

2. Use in Papyri, the Gospels and Other Documents.

Recent research has accepted the evidence that Fitzmyer has marshaled but extends it to conclude that not only did the Roman officials use Latin, but that there was some knowledge of Latin among those of the lower social orders as well. In an important and provocative article, A. Millard cites three types of evidence in support of this position: *papyri and *inscriptions pointing to lower societal levels knowing Latin; Latin terms in the Gospels; and Latin in other documents. These three lines of evidence can be summarized briefly.

As evidence that those other than Roman officials knew Latin, Millard cites the jars in the cellar in *Herod's palace at Masada, which were labeled in Latin. It stands to reason, he thinks, that the servants responsible for serving Herod would have needed to know what the labels said in order to carry out their duties properly. Millard also notes that a number of Latin fragments from Masada indicate that others than the officials read or wrote Latin. Included here is a papyrus fragment of one or two lines of Virgil. In the papyri from the Cave of Letters, dated to the time of the Bar Kokhba revolt (A.D. 132-35; *see* Jewish Wars with Rome), there are Latinisms noted in the Greek texts, including use of *basilika* (Lat. *basilica;* no. 16 lines 2, 4), *apo aktōn* (Lat. *ablex actis;* no. 12 lines 1, 4), *praisidion* (Lat. *praesidium;* no. 11, lines 6,19), *tribounalion* (Lat. *tribunal;* no. 14 lines 12-13, 31), as well as Latin terms for money, such as *dēnarion* (Lat. *denarius).*

Regarding the evidence in the Gospels (see Blass and Debrunner, 4-6; Robertson, 108-11 for a detailed listing), Millard draws attention to several types of evidence. First he notes that the presence of words and terms for money, measure and the military are easily explained but are nevertheless to be noted, since the same penetration is not found in the Hebrew and Aramaic of the *Dead Sea Scrolls or the writings of *Philo and Josephus. Second, Mark's Gospel has ten of the eighteen Latin words to appear in the Gospels. Some scholars have taken this as evidence for Mark's Roman provenance. Millard, however, reexamines the evidence, noting that Matthew has as many Latin words but not all of them in parallel passages to Mark. He contends further that investigation shows that a number of these Latin words appear in Greek texts for the first time in the first century and often first or only in the Gospels (e.g., *kēnsos*/Lat. *census; koustōdia*/Lat. *custodia; ksestēs*/Lat. *sextarius; praitōrion*/Lat. *praetorium; soudarion*/Lat. *sudarium; spekoulatōr*/Lat. *speculator; titlos*/Lat. *tit(u)lus; phragellion*/Lat. *flagellium; phragelloun*/ Lat. *flagellare).* These words are distributed throughout all four Gospels and sometimes occur in places where Synoptic passages have a different word.

Millard also notes several places in the Mishnah and other *rabbinic writings where Latin loanwords are found. Thus he concludes that, unlike the Greek of Egypt, the Greek and local languages of Palestine seem to have been more open to Latinisms and that "the presence of these Latin words in the Gospels reflects the linguistic picture of Palestine in the first century C.E. . . . We may deduce, therefore, that such Latin words as the ones used in the Gospels were current in the Greek spoken in Palestine early in the first century, C.E., even during the lifetime of Jesus of Nazareth" (Millard, 458).

Although even on Millard's accounting one cannot further argue that Jesus had anything other than a superficial knowledge of Latin or anything other than knowledge of just a few words of Latin, it is plausible to examine again the question of how much Latin was in use in first-century Palestine. Knowledge of Latin may not have been widespread at all societal levels, but there may well have been a greater influence of Latin on other languages of the time than has previously been thought.

See also ARAMAIC LANGUAGE; GRAMMARIANS, HELLENISTIC GREEK; GREEK OF THE NEW TESTAMENT; HEBREW LANGUAGE.

BIBLIOGRAPHY. F. Blass and A. Debrunner, *A Greek Grammar of the New Testament and Other Early Christian Literature* (Chicago: University of Chicago Press, 1961); J. A. Fitzmyer, "The Languages of Palestine in the First Century A.D.," *CBQ* 32 (1970) 501-31 [repr. in J. A. Fitzmyer, *A Wandering Aramean: Collected Aramaic Essays* (Missoula, MT: Scholars Press, 1979) 29-56; and *The Language of the New Testament: Classic Essays,* ed. S. E. Porter (JSNTSup 60; Sheffield; JSOT, 1991) 126-62 (cited here)]; A. Millard, "Latin in First-Century Palestine," in *Solving Riddles and Untying Knots: Biblical, Epigraphic and Semitic Studies in Honor of Jonas C. Greenfield,* ed. Z. Zevit, S. Gitin and M. Sokoloff (Winona Lake, IN: Eisenbrauns, 1995) 451-58; A. T. Robertson, *A Grammar of the Greek New Testament in the Light of Historical Research* (4th ed.; Nashville: Broadman, 1934). S. E. Porter

LATIN NEW TESTAMENT. *See* NEW TESTAMENT VERSIONS, ANCIENT.

LAW/NOMOS IN GRECO-ROMAN WORLD

Law in the Greco-Roman world was predominantly the law of *Rome. While Roman law originated as a function of the pontiffs or priests during the period of the kings (753-509 B.C.), it developed into a legal system concerned almost entirely with secular matters. The Roman jurist Gaius (second century A.D.), for instance, rarely refers to religious matters in his *Institutes* and never mentions a god. Religious communities in the Greco-Roman world had their own laws, the Jews being a prime example, but we are not concerned with such manifestations of law (*see* Torah).

1. The Role of Law
2. Law, Custom and Social Context

3. The Roman Empire and Roman Law
4. Greek Reflection on Law

1. The Role of Law.
Understanding the role that law played in the lives of ancient Mediterranean peoples is vital to an appreciation of several NT writings. The Gospels and Acts refer to various aspects of Roman law when describing Jesus' life and death and the lives of the first Christians. Paul's metaphors for explaining the Christian life often rely on legal terminology, for instance, heredity, guardianship, adoption, and a will. Specific texts such as 1 Corinthians 6:1-8 and 2 Corinthians 13:1 are better appreciated when certain features of Roman law are understood. Particular themes, such as partnership (*koinōnia*), when they are credited with their legal connotations, become even more theologically fertile. Even those terms that we think of in primarily theological categories, such as redemption and judgment, take on richer semantic texture when it is recognized that they originated as legal categories.

The ancients recognized both implicitly and explicitly that social behavior was not regulated by laws alone. In the Greco-Roman world one's *honor was often as valuable as one's life. Consequently concern for staying within social norms, even if they were not legal norms, played a strong regulatory role.

Much of what we know about law in the Greco-Roman world we know because the writings of the law-making and social elite are those that remain. It is difficult to ascertain whether the ordinary *citizen and noncitizen considered the laws to be just or capable of representing their needs and interests. We do know, however, that the distinction between law and justice was one that the *philosophers and jurists understood. Epicurus (341-270 B.C.), for one, understood that law and justice do not coincide. He distinguishes between laws and justice, noting that some laws are too general to apply to individual situations and some too particular (Porphyry *On Abstinence* 1.10ff. The Cynics with their anti-establishment lifestyle thought it just to act outside of the law. *Cicero (106-43 B.C.) recognized that some laws were contrary to natural law (Cicero *De Leg.* 2.5.13-14). Furthermore, the Roman jurists themselves understood that a legal decision could be reached that accorded with legal principle but was not fair.

2. Law, Custom and Social Context.
The Greek word usually rendered "law" by the translators of the NT is *nomos*. This word meant both "law" and "custom" and so could refer to the laws of a society and to that society's habits and customs. Custom was one of the cornerstones of law in the Greco-Roman world: "The commonwealth of Rome is founded firm, On ancient customs and on men of might" (Ennius; quoted in Cicero *De Rep.* 5.1). If custom was not identified with law, it was treated with respect and seen as integral to the rule of law. Gaius's *Institutes* begin this way: "Every people that is governed by statutes and custom observes partly its own peculiar law, and partly common law of all mankind" (*The Institutes of Gaius,* trans. F. de Zulueta [Oxford: Clarendon Press, 1946]). Along with equity, decided cases and legislation Cicero lists custom among the sources of law, that is, the places to which a jurist could go to find out what the law is.

Law always has an organic relationship to its social context. The fact that custom had (and has) such persuasive force in legal matters demonstrates this. One of the features that most separates the Greco-Roman social context from that of the modern Western world was its hierarchical nature. The rule of law did not mean equality for all under the law. Cicero wrote that "equality of legal rights . . . cannot be maintained" since there are "great distinctions among men. . . . For when equal honor is given to the highest and the lowest . . . then this very 'fairness' is most unfair" (Cicero *De Rep.* 1.34.54, LCL, trans. C. W. Keyes). He goes on to advise that every citizen should learn to be content "in his own station" (Cicero *De Rep.* 1.45.69). The Roman legal system has often been characterized as evidencing class jurisprudence. The Romans understood people as essentially unequal—fathers had more status than sons, *patrons than clients, masters than *slaves, men than *women. The development and maintenance of class privilege protected by law is one of the features of the history of Roman law.

Another distinguishing feature of law in the Greco-Roman world is that much of what the modern Western world considers to be public law was private in the ancient Mediterranean world. For example, there were no divorce courts. Neither *marriage nor divorce required public authorization.

3. The Roman Empire and Roman Law.

The Greco-Roman world is the world of the *Roman Empire, a world that began as Rome became dominant through its conquests and acquisitions of territories and as it changed from republic to principate, to governance by oligarchy to governance by emperor (*see* Roman Emperors). Caesar Octavius, who came to be called Augustus, through his remarkable military victories and the changes he brought about in the Roman system of government, marks the beginning of the Greco-Roman world. In 27 B.C. Octavian, ostensibly to restore the republic, gave back the extraordinary powers he had assumed during the civil wars. Effectively, however, this action was the beginning of the empire, for in 23 B.C. he was voted tribunician power for life, and his command was recognized as superior to any other. The age of the Greco-Roman world, in which Rome's authority and influence was felt throughout the known world, began with Augustus. In this age the NT writings were composed.

3.1. Impact of Empire on Roman Law. One of the chief impacts of the spread of Rome's power was the concomitant growth in significance of Roman law. Rome's dominance meant that by and large law in the Greco-Roman world was Roman law. While not all provinces of Rome took on the Roman legal system, Judea being a case in point, all were ultimately under the rule of Rome's law. The *Roman governors of Judea, for instance, had the authority of imperial legates or proconsuls. Furthermore, provincial governors almost invariably had held office in Rome prior to their appointment. A Roman provincial governor might take into account the customs of his province when making legal decisions, but in the end he sought to enforce Roman legal ideas.

Another significant result of the principate was the change in the legal procedure of Roman law, with ultimate power resting in the hands of the emperor. The history of Roman law goes back to the monarchy (753-509 B.C.). The kings produced some legislation, and the pontiffs administered the law, both sacred and secular. After the last king, Tarquin the Proud, was expelled from Rome in 509 B.C. the city was organized as a republic, which it remained until 27 B.C. During this period Rome came into increasing contact with other city-states. Its law broadened to include provisions for relations with foreigners—the *ius genitum,* the law of all people—a law that acknowledged that some legal principles were valid for all people. At this time the population was divided between the patricians, who knew and administered the law, and the plebians. As a result of conflict between the patricians and the plebians at least some private law was put in writing. This part of the Roman legal tradition was published in the forum in 450 B.C. and came to be called the Twelve Tables.

The effect of this codification was at least twofold: the law was taken out of the hands of the priests, and a need was created for interpretation. The office of praetor arose in order to provide for official legal interpretation. The praetor did not act as a judge but rather oversaw the legal procedure. He was elected by popular vote for one year and upon assuming office published an edict that would remain in force for the tenure of his office. The core of the edict, however, was traditional, and consequently there was relative consistency in the law. In addition to the praetor there developed a body of jurists, wealthy citizens who, without financial rewards, gave legal advice, taught and wrote on the law and assisted in the legal process. The praetor and the jurists built up the Roman civil law.

When the republic was replaced by the principate the law continued to be influenced by the praetor and the jurists, but increasingly the emperor became the source of law. Augustus, for instance, introduced the *ius respondendi,* the right to give legal opinions as emperor. He also gave to several jurists the right to use his authority in their legal dealings. While the senate was given law-making powers in the early empire, many of its actions were dictated by the emperor. Although the emperor was not immediately involved with either legal administration or codification of the law, he was the final court of appeal for those of the senatorial class and for provincial legal matters. Eventually the emperor became the only source of law, as the following ancient adages made plain: "the emperor's will is as good as a statute" and "the emperor is not bound by statutes." Despite the authority of law resting with the emperor the jurists were active during the principate, at least until Diocletian. Their writings are one of the reasons that the period of the principate is called the classical period of Roman law. The most significant work from this period is that of the jurist Gaius, whose

Institutes (c. A.D. 161) came to serve as the model for Justinian's *Digest* (A.D. 533), the chief source of our knowledge of Roman law.

3.2. Impact of Imperial Roman Law on Society. One of the developments in the legal process of the principate was the continuation of what had begun in 149 B.C. with the establishment of standing courts specializing in different types of offenses. Whereas previously the people had been directly involved in deciding legal cases, increasingly legal decision making was in the hands of the privileged, the juries in the standing courts being largely made up of members of the senate and other privileged orders. Furthermore, the principle of inequality became more firmly entrenched, with differentiation in ranks and status making for different juridical privileges.

3.3. Social Significance of Legal Knowledge. In retrospect we recognize that Rome's great legacy is its legal system, preserved for us by Justinian. Rome's legacy rests on its deep and abiding interest in the law. Legal interpretation was one of the few acceptable pastimes for the rich, and excellence in legal knowledge increased one's social stature. As Edward Gibbon put so well in his chapter on Roman law: "arms, eloquence, and the study of civil law, promoted a citizen to the honours of the Roman state" (*Survey of the Roman, or Civil Law; An Extract from Gibbon's History of the Decline and Fall of the Roman Empire* [Littleton, CO: Rothman, 1996] 44).

Moreover, the social significance attached to knowledge of the law rested on the tradition that the original interpreters of the law had been the pontiffs and also on the high cultural value placed on law throughout the ancient Mediterranean world. The Roman playwright Plautus (second century B.C.) writes about how parents ambitious for their children spare no pains or expense in giving "lots of schooling: arts and letters, legal lore to build his brain" (Plautus *Mostell.* 125; trans. E. Segal). In another play he speaks of the duty of appearing in court on behalf of another (Plautus *Cas.* 563). By the time of Cicero we have evidence that the study of law is widely regarded as the most important study for the state's leaders.

Furthermore, the patron-client system meant that a patron needed knowledge of the law in order to manage matters regarding his clients. Dionysius of Halicarnassus (born c. 20 B.C.) put it this way: "it was the duty of the patricians to explain to their clients the laws, of which they were ignorant; . . . doing everything for them that fathers do for their sons with regard both to money and the contracts that related to money; to bring suit on behalf of their clients when they were wronged" (Dionysius of Halicarnassus *Ant. Rom.* 11.10; LCL, trans. E. Carey).

3.4. Cultural Regard for Law. The Romans did not place law in a preeminent position in their society only because of social and practical considerations. They thought of the rule of law as synonymous with a state of harmony. Some, like the poet Ovid (43 B.C.-A.D. 17/18), wrote of a primitive golden age when people obeyed the law naturally: "Golden was that first age which unconstrained, With heart and soul, obedient to no law, Gave honour to good faith and righteousness" (Ovid *Met.* 1.90; trans. A. D. Melville). Others, like the Stoic *Seneca (55 B.C.-c. A.D. 37), identified law with reason or nature and wrote that "nature produced us related to one another, since she created us from the same source and to the same end. . . . She established fairness and justice" (Seneca *Ep. Mor.* 95.52). The purpose of human life is to learn and conform to these "laws of life" (Seneca *Ep. Mor.* 57).

4. Greek Reflection on Law.

4.1. The Poets. High regard for law was found not only among the Roman people. The ancient Greek poet Hesiod, in his *Works and Days,* writes: "for this usage [*nomos*] did the son of Cronus grant to people: fishes and land animals and winged birds eat each other because *dikē* [law] is not in them. But to people he gave *dikē,* which is by much the best thing" (276-80; trans. D. W. Tandy and W. C. Neale). Demosthenes (384-322 B.C.) is reputed to have addressed a jury of Athenians with these words:

> The whole life of men, Athenians, whether they dwell in a large state or a small one, is governed by nature and by the laws. Of these, nature is something irregular and incalculable, and peculiar to each individual; but the laws are something universal, definite, and the same for all. . . . Laws desire what is just and honourable and salutary; they seek for it, and when they find it, they set it forth as a general commandment, equal and identical for all. . . . Every law is an invention and gift of the gods, a tenet of wise men, a corrective of errors voluntary and involuntary, and a general covenant of the

whole State, in accordance with which all men in that State ought to regulate their lives. (Demosthenes *Arist.* 1.15-16; LCL, trans. J. H. Vince)

The rule of law was often identified with the civilized life. One of the greatest fears of an ancient Greek was of being exiled from his city and its laws, for then one's life was little better than that of an animal. In Euripides' play *Electra* Orestes asks who can be more wretched than a fugitive who cannot call upon his city's laws (lines 234 and 1194).

4.2. Plato. Both *Plato and *Aristotle devoted themselves to the study of law and its significance. Neither thought of the philosophical task as including involvement in the details of law, but both considered thinking about law essential to reflecting on the good human life. In the *Crito,* which discusses the question of whether the innocent Socrates should submit to his city's laws and be executed or escape, Plato examines the significance of a city's laws. Socrates expresses the view that since he owes his existence to laws such as those that protect marriage and the procreation of children, and his development to laws that have provided for his *education, he owes the city his obedience to the laws. The laws are not to be disobeyed, even if one believes oneself wrongly accused by them.

In the *Republic* Plato attempts to formulate a definition of justice. Plato understands there to be an inseparable relationship between the state and the individual who is a member of the state. Justice stems from and shapes the individual's soul in relation to how it is embodied and enacted in the community in which the individual lives. And so Plato seeks to determine the best relation between different members or classes in the state so as to find the more harmonious balance.

In the *Laws* Plato applies his idea that a state reflects the composition of its individuals' souls just as its individuals' souls are shaped by the state. He prescribes that laws should include an explanatory preamble explaining the reasons for their enactment (Plato *Leg.* 722D-723B), for since there is an organic relationship between the health of the individual and the health of the state it is equally important that the community member understand and willingly obey the law as it is that the law exist. Plato sought to help individuals be just, that is, to find a way for reason to control the passions so that the common good was the desire of each individual. Related to this, Plato's goal was to construct a system of law that would be so well suited and effective for its society that eventually the laws themselves would become obsolete. Plato hoped for a time when the laws would have become self-evident to those trained in them (Plato *Leg.* 798A, B).

4.3. Aristotle. Aristotle's interest in law extended from the scientific collection and categorizing of different legal constitutions (he is said to have collected 158 different constitutions as preparation for his *Politics,* of which only the Constitution of Athens survives), to philosophical thinking about the nature and function of law. In the *Rhetoric* Aristotle, in distinction from Plato, invests forensic *rhetoric with a certain dignity. Aristotle's *Ethics* are an attempt to understand the way that citizens can be prepared for goodness, through self-understanding, education and the laws. For Aristotle well-devised laws encourage and direct a virtuous and well-ordered life in community. In Aristotle's view ethics and politics are intimately related. His *Politics* is necessarily preceded by his *Ethics* because moral education is essential for the proper working of the state, and laws are a critical factor in training in virtue (Aristotle *Eth. Nic.* 1102a).

4.4. Stoicism. *Stoicism, which may have affected Roman law more than any other trend in Greek philosophy, considered that there was a universal law of nature that human reason could appropriate and that formed the basis of all good laws. The Roman *ius genitum* reflected this conception. Chrysippus is said to have written in *De Iure et Lege,* "Law is king of all things human and divine. Law must preside over what is honourable and base . . . and thus be the standard of what is just and unjust' (Chrysippus *Stoicorum Veterum Fragmenta,* 1. *Arnim,* 3.314). As Cicero, whose work evidences many Stoic leanings, wrote: "True law is right reason in agreement with nature; it is of universal application, unchanging and everlasting" (Cicero *De Rep.* 3.22; LCL, trans. C. W. Keyes).

Greek reflections on law may not have had a direct impact on Roman jurisprudence, but they nourished the high regard for law that was one of the features of the Greco-Roman culture. The writers of the NT were undoubtedly influenced by both the Roman legal system and the Greco-Roman attitude toward law.

See also ROMAN LAW AND LEGAL SYSTEM; TORAH.

BIBLIOGRAPHY. W. W. Buckland, *A Textbook of Roman Law from Augustus to Justinian* (Cambridge: Cambridge University Press, 1963); P. Garnsey, *Social Status and Legal Privilege in the Roman Empire* (Oxford: Clarendon Press, 1970); A. Giardina, ed., *The Romans* (Chicago: University of Chicago Press, 1989); H. F. Jolowicz, *Historical Introduction to the Study of Roman Law* (Cambridge: Cambridge University Press, 1932); J. W. Jones, *The Law and Legal Theory of the Greeks* (Oxford: Clarendon Press, 1956); A. Laks and M. Scholfield, eds., *Justice and Generosity: Studies in Hellenistic Social and Political Philosophy* (Cambridge: Cambridge University Press, 1995); C. Nicolet, *The World of the Citizen in Republican Rome* (Berkeley and Los Angeles: University of California Press, 1980); O. F. Robinson, *The Sources of Roman Law: Problems and Methods For Ancient Historians* (New York: Routledge, 1997); P. Sampley, *Pauline Partnership in Christ: Christian Community and Commitment in Light of Roman Law* (Philadelphia: Fortress, 1980); A. N. Sherwin-White, *Roman Society and Roman Law in the New Testament* (Oxford: Clarendon Press, 1963); P. J. Thomas, *Introduction to Roman Law* (Deventer: Kluwer Law and Taxation Publishers, 1986); A. Watson, *The Law of the Ancient Romans* (Dallas: Southern Methodist University Press, 1970); idem, *The Spirit of Roman Law* (Athens, GA: University of Georgia Press, 1995). L. A. Jervis

LEGAL TEXTS AT QUMRAN

The centrality of Jewish law (termed by the rabbis *halakah*) at *Qumran, among those sectarians usually identified by scholars with the *Essenes, is evident from the legal materials in both major, well-preserved scrolls and in texts which survive in only fragmentary condition. Even the phylacteries and mezuzot and the biblical scrolls reveal much information, mainly on the scribal Halakah of the times.

1. Corpus of Legal Texts
2. Contents of the Legal Texts

1. Corpus of Legal Texts.

A wide variety of legal texts or texts containing Jewish legal rulings are found in the Qumran corpus. Best known are the so-called Serek, or "Rule," scrolls: 1QS, 1QSa and 1QSb. These scrolls more or less systematically provide a constitution whereby the community conducted itself. The *Damascus Document*, the *War Scroll*, the *Halakic Letter* (or 4QMMT), and the *Temple Scroll* are among the most important documents. However, there are many more.

2. Contents of the Legal Texts.

2.1. **Rule of the Community *(1QS).*** Also known as the *Manual of Discipline* or *Serekh ha-Yaḥad,* the **Rule of the Community* was one of the first Qumran scrolls to be discovered and dates from the beginning of the first century B.C. In addition, it exists in fragmentary copies, ten in Cave 4 (4Q255–264) and two in Cave 5 (5Q11), which testify to its centrality to the life of the Qumran sectarians. The text sets out the rules for entry into the community, regulations for sectarian organization and a penal code. The penal code prescribes punishment by a banishment from pure liquid or solid food of the community, tantamount to exclusion from the communal meals, a reduction of the food ration for specified periods and even an expulsion from the sect. The initiation rites of the *Rule of the Community* reveal information on the purity system of the sectarians as well as about their understanding of the theology of Jewish law. The community in the wilderness was devoted to the study and observance of the law as a means of expiation for the land and the attainment of purity and perfection in the pre-messianic age.

2.2. **Rule of the Congregation *(1QSa or 1Q28a).*** Also known as the *Messianic Rule* or *Serek ha-ʿEdah,* the **Rule of the Congregation* was appended to the *Rule of the Community.* A *messianic document, it sets out a kind of eschatological Halakah describing the ritual purity that must be maintained due to the presence of *angels among the sectarians. At the end of days, the Zadokite priests and their families will gather to read the law at a covenant-renewal ceremony. The text also specifies the ages at which the sectarian attains the right to marry, participate in the military, become an official or leader, and retire. Special roles are assigned to the Levites. The council of the community is appointed to legislate and declare war, but some members of the sect are disqualified from certain duties because they are old, infirm or impure, again emphasizing the strict *purity of the camp. There follows the description of the communal *banquet which, while held in the present, premessianic age, is also the enactment of the messianic meal. The priest blesses the bread and wine and receives the first portion, and the

Messiah of Israel takes his portion and distributes the rest among the sectarians according to their rank.

2.3. **The War of the Sons of Light Against the Sons of Darkness *or* War Scroll *(1QM).*** This is one of the longest preserved sectarian scrolls at approximately twenty columns long. In addition to its version in Cave 1, there are also fragments from Cave 4 (4Q491–496) and other related texts describing a final war, such as 4Q285 and 4Q497. However, all of these are certainly different manuscripts copied at different times and slightly different in content; some of them may even be sources of the **War Scroll.* 1QM contains an entire version of the Deuteronomic laws of war as understood and adapted by the sectarians. Predicated upon a forty-year battle between the Sons of Light/Israel and the Sons of Darkness/nations of the world, the victory of Israel frees them from the domination of their traditional enemies, Edom, Ammon, Moab, Philistia and the "Kittim," used to refer to Egypt, Syria or Rome. While the battles are more idealistic than realistic, they contain much information about military tactics and weaponry of the era. In addition, the *War Scroll* alludes to sacrificial law and rules of ritual impurity. It shares some of the organizational aspects of the military units and the ages of service for officials and leaders with the *Rule of the Congregation.*

2.4. **Damascus Document.** Cave 4 at Qumran yielded eight manuscripts of the **Damascus Document* (also known as the *Zadokite Fragments* or CD) which had been found in two partial manuscripts in the Cairo genizah long before the discovery of their counterparts in the caves of Qumran. Cave 5 held one fragmentary text (5Q12), and Cave 6 added five fragments of CD (6Q15). The legal sections of CD describe an entire system of Jewish law, including *priests and their functions such as their diagnosis of skin diseases, laws of the harvest such as gleaning and tithes, impurity of *idolatry and corpses, rules for the proper observance of the *sabbath, oaths and vows, *marriage, judicial procedures, and the purity of the *temple and the temple city. Some of the laws are similar to those of the rabbinic oral law, such as beginning the sabbath some time before sunset, and others disagree with the rabbinic viewpoint such as the statement that the ashes of the red cow cannot be prepared by a minor, a practice which according to tannaitic sources (*m. Parah* 3:2) was customary in the Second Temple. The laws are mostly stated without scriptural references, and often they are found under rubrics announcing their subject matter, making this one of the first postbiblical Jewish legal codes organized by topic. The communal life described here appears to be of families observing the Torah. This text includes a penal code very similar to that in the *Rule of the Community.*

2.5. Miqṣat Maʿaśê ha-Torah *(4QMMT).* Literally rendered "Some Precepts of the Torah," and also known as the *Halakic Letter,* 4QMMT purports to be a letter sent from the leaders of the sectarian community to the leaders of the Jerusalem establishment (*see* Miqsat Maʿasey ha-Torah [4QMMT]). It reports some twenty disputes regarding sacrificial and purification laws in a sectarian context, exhorting the leaders in Jerusalem to follow sectarian law. In a number of significant cases, tannaitic sources allow us to identify the sectarian view with that of the *Sadducees and the view of the opponents of the sect with that of the *Pharisees. Dating from the late *Hasmonean to the early *Herodian period (second half of the first century B.C.), the six manuscripts of this document may represent the foundation document of the Qumran sect or may have been written later to justify the sect's removal from Jerusalem. The arguments presented here show how the sect differed from the Jerusalem establishment so that they refused to participate in the Jerusalem temple. For example, the sect disallowed a priest from officiating in the temple if he had just completed a purification ritual, and the sun had not yet set on his last day of purification. The pharisaic-rabbinic tradition would have allowed a priest still awaiting sunset on his last day of purification to perform the ritual. The Sadducees and those who followed their halakic tradition disagreed. 4QMMT shows the importance of matters of Jewish law as sources of schism within Judaism in Second Temple times.

2.6. **Temple Scroll *(11Q19-21; 4Q524, 4Q365a).*** Caves 11 and 4 yielded manuscripts of the *Temple Scroll.* 11Q19 is the longest scroll, running about 26 feet (8 meters). A rewriting of the Torah designed to put forward the author's views on Jewish law, the scroll is written as if it were God's word, changing the third person of the biblical text into the first person. The *Temple Scroll* has four main themes: the construction of the temple, its courtyards, altar, etc.; the cycle of *festivals; the *purity laws for the temple and the temple city; and a rewriting of the diverse laws contained in Deuteronomy 12—23, emphasizing the law of the king (Deut 17:14-20). Besides the Torah, the author/redactor used several other sources such as a festival calendar including *festivals not mentioned in the Bible (new wheat, wine, oil and the wood offering). Other sources contain laws that were in use in the group to which the author/redactor belonged. The author hoped that the temple would be rebuilt according to his specifications. The interest in *sacrificial law, the architecture of the temple and temple rituals, and the desire to see the monarch subordinated to the priesthood would seem to point to a priestly origin. The text also has a decidedly anti-Hasmonean polemic, a distinct Halakah of its own, and a unique vocabulary, although some of its legal prescriptions agree with Qumran sectarian texts and Sadducean traditions. The best explanation for this phenomenon is to posit that the *Temple Scroll*, like 4QMMT, was compiled by priestly circles early in the history of the Qumran sect, before its removal from Jerusalem.

*2.7. **4QMiscellaneous Rules.*** The initial editors of 4QMiscellaneous Rules (4Q265, or *Serek-Damascus*) assumed that it was a combination of the *Serek ha-Yaḥad* (*Rule of the Community*) and *Damascus Document*. While the text might be a composite based on these documents, it might also be an independent redaction made up of the building blocks (*serakîm*) of these larger texts. The manuscript is in Late Herodian script and should be dated to the first half of the first century A.D. The text prohibits men below twenty or women of any age from eating of the paschal sacrifice, contrary to the actual practice of Second Temple Judaism but perhaps in accord with the wider Sadducean trend in Halakah (*see* Sacrifice and Temple Service). The text also describes the entry process for joining the sect, parallel to the version in the *Rule of the Community*. Several sabbath prohibitions parallel the sabbath code preserved in both the medieval Cairo genizah version of the *Damascus Document* and the Qumran manuscripts. Appended to this section is a prohibition on eating nonsacral meat in the vicinity of the temple, a regulation also found in the *Temple Scroll*. Like the *Rule of the Community*, 4Q265 requires that there be a learned priest wherever there are ten sectarians and that a minimum of fifteen comprise the council of the community. The final section is a statement of the laws of the parturient, the woman who has just given birth, following Leviticus 12:1-6 and *Jubilees* 3:9-14.

2.8. **Ordinances** *(4Q159, 4Q513, 4Q514).* Three manuscripts of *Ordinances* deal with assorted Halakoth. A sample of laws can be assembled from one manuscript: atonement rituals, the produce given to the poor, the donation of the half-shekel upon reaching the majority of twenty years of age, the prohibition of selling Israelite slaves to non-Jews, the court of appeals in capital cases, the prohibition of a man's wearing women's clothes and the case of the husband who claims that his bride was not a virgin. Some of the materials are more biblical in style while others are closer to the formulations common in sectarian texts.

2.9. 4Q Halakha A (4Q251). This text contains many prescriptions which overlap with laws known from the *Damascus Document*, *Miscellaneous Rules*, *Temple Scroll*, 4QMMT and Sadducean-type laws in the sectarian materials. The literary form of this text is close to that of *rewritten Bible, in many ways similar to some portions of the *Temple Scroll*. After some sabbath laws, there is a reference to what seems to be public scriptural reading on the sabbath. Most of the preserved text is a rewriting of various laws in Exodus 21—22. Also discussed here are laws of firstfruits and new grain, following a scheme similar to that in the Festival Calendar of the *Temple Scroll*. Other laws discuss the selling of ancestral lands, the giving of fourth-year produce to priests (as opposed to eating it in Jerusalem as the Pharisees required), a practice also mandated in the *Temple Scroll* and 4QMMT. The text also prohibits eating an animal that did not live for seven days and the slaughter of pregnant animals, prohibitions shared with the *Temple Scroll* and 4QMMT but permitted by pharisaic-rabbinic Halakah. The text also includes a list of forbidden consanguineous marriages similar to that in the *Temple Scroll*. Among the laws here are a prohibition of intermarriage with non-Jews and of a priest giving his daughter in marriage to a nonpriest.

2.10. Purification Rules (Tohorot) A (4Q274). This is a fragmentary text dealing with the laws of impurity resulting from the skin disease *ṣāraʿat*, usually mistranslated as "leprosy." As in the *Temple Scroll*, this text provides for special places for the quarantine of those with this disease who must stay away from the pure food. Such people are forbidden to come in contact even with those already impure, as they would still require ritual cleansing from such contact. This indicates that impurity can be contracted in successively stronger layers, so that those with lesser impurity may not come in contact with those with this skin disease. The requirement of separation, even for the impure, indicates a consciousness also of the contagious nature of such diseases. Similarly a woman with a nonmenstrual discharge of blood may not touch a gonorrheic or anything which he touched. If she does, she must undergo purification, even if she remains in her own original state of impurity. The text goes into several examples to make this general point. Other issues discussed in this text, also found in the *Temple Scroll,* are the method of purification and the impurity of semen and reptiles.

*2.11. **Purification Rules.*** Tohorot B[a] (4Q276) and B[b] (4Q277) describe the ritual of the red cow as the means of purification from impurity of the dead according to Numbers 19. 4Q276 seems to refer at the beginning to the high priest who ministers at this ritual. The text describes the slaughter of the animal and the sprinkling of its blood, as well as other aspects of the ritual as prescribed in the Torah. 4Q277 mentions the fact that those who perform the ritual of the red cow are rendered impure as a result, a paradox mentioned already in the Bible. Also hinted at here is the requirement, specified also in 4QMMT, that the priest who officiates must be totally pure himself. Further, the text lists a number of ways in which the impurity of the dead can be passed from one person to another.

4Q275 (Tohorot B), as presently preserved, has no specific legal content, but does refer to the inspector (*mebaqqer*) and to the cursing of someone, perhaps one who is being expelled from the community. Expulsion as a punishment is mentioned in the *Rule of the Community* and *Damascus Document.* 4QTohorot C (4Q278) is extremely fragmentary and relates to impurity that can be transferred by contact.

2.12. Harvesting, Leqet (4Q284a). This text, although extremely fragmentary, apparently deals with the requirements for gleaning. According to Leviticus 19:9-10 and 23:22, grain left in the field may not be collected after the harvest is completed but must be left for the poor. The Bible supplies no specific requirements for the gleaners, but this text requires that they be ritually pure. Little more can be derived from this text, but it no doubt included specifics of this requirement and may have included other agricultural laws.

2.13. Rebukes by the Overseer (4Q477). This text clearly stems from the Qumran sectarian community and records actual dockets reflecting sectarian legal proceedings against those who violated the sect's prescriptions. According to sectarian law as detailed in the *Damascus Document,* it was required to perform reproof of those who violated the law, in front of the overseer (*mebaqqer*) and in front of witnesses. Only if this procedure had taken place could a sectarian be punished for a later infraction of the same law. This fragmentary text lists by name specific individuals who had been rebuked as well as their transgressions.

The nature of the law in Qumran documents was revealed in greater and greater detail as more and more pieces of the Dead Sea Scrolls puzzle were put into place. These scroll materials all help to clarify legal issues which arise in tannaitic texts and rabbinic Judaism (*see* Rabbis), such as the historical development of Halakah, the theological underpinnings of the law according to the different religious sects of the time, the later formulation of midrash and Mishnah (*see* Rabbinic Literature: Midrashim; Rabbinic Literature: Mishnah), the effect of the cataclysm of A.D. 70 on the history of Judaism, and the role of purity in Second Temple Judaism.

See also DAMASCUS DOCUMENT (CD AND QD); DEAD SEA SCROLLS; LAW/NOMOS IN THE GRECO-ROMAN WORLD; PURITY; RULE OF THE COMMUNITY/MANUAL OF DISCIPLINE (1QS); RULE OF THE CONGREGATION/MESSIANIC RULE (1QSA); THEOLOGIES AND SECTS, JEWISH; TORAH.

BIBLIOGRAPHY. P. S. Alexander and G. Vermes, *Qumran Cave 4.19: 4QSerekh ha-Yaḥad and Two Related Texts* (DJD 26; Oxford: Clarendon Press, 1998); J. M. Baumgarten et al., *Qumran Cave 4.25: Halakhic Texts* (DJD 25; Oxford: Clarendon Press, 1999); E. Eshel, "4Q477: The Rebukes of the Overseer," *JJS* 45 (1994) 111-22; J. Licht, *The Rule Scroll* [Hebrew] (Jerusalem: The Bialik Institute, 1965); E. Qimron and J. Strugnell, *Qumran Cave 4.5: Miqṣat Maʿaśe ha-Torah* (DJD 10; Oxford: Clarendon Press, 1994); C. Rabin, *The Zadokite Documents* (Oxford: Clarendon Press, 1954); L. H. Schiffman, *Reclaiming the*

Dead Sea Scrolls (Philadelphia: Jewish Publication Society of America, 1994) 243-312; Y. Yadin, *The Temple Scroll* (3 vols.; Jerusalem: Israel Exploration Society, 1983).

L. H. Schiffman

LEGION. *See* ROMAN MILITARY.

LEGIONARY. *See* ROMAN MILITARY.

LEQET/HARVESTING TEXT (4Q284a). *See* LEGAL TEXTS AT QUMRAN

LETTERS, GRECO-ROMAN

The popularity of the letter form increased significantly during the *Hellenistic period due to a variety of factors: the increase in scribal learning and influence, the growing availability and relatively inexpensive cost of papyrus as a writing material, the need to monitor accurately expansions in the area of trade and commerce and the desire of political leaders to spread imperial propaganda. The Roman period witnessed an even greater rise in this literary form as the letter increasingly became a common means of communication among people of all stations of life, thereby causing one modern scholar to note that "letter writing was almost a disease" (Brooke, 17). The popularity of the letter form during the Greco-Roman period is also evident in the fact that twenty of the twenty-seven documents found in the NT purport to be letters and two of the remaining documents (Acts, Apocalypse of John) contain letters within them.

1. Epistolary Types
2. Epistolary Conventions
3. Summary

1. Epistolary Types.

The classification of Greco-Roman letters is a difficult matter, since letters can be categorized according to several criteria that often overlap: writing materials (papyri or parchment), character (private, official or public), style of writing (plain, middle or grand), purpose (e.g., commendatory, reproachful, consoling, apologetic) or agreement with one of the three types of *rhetoric (judicial, deliberative or epideictic). The few ancient writers who address this issue of classification fail to provide any real help, as their discussions contain no agreement of categories (*see* Epistolary Theory). A similar lack of consensus exists among modern scholars of ancient epistolography. Although no typology is completely free from criticism, it seems best to classify Greco-Roman letters according to three broad categories: private letters, official letters and literary letters.

1.1. Private Letters. Private or documentary letters (i.e., nonliterary writings, or correspondence not intended for publication) constitute the papyrus letters, at least a few thousand in number, that have been preserved in the dry Egyptian climate and that provide the primary source of our knowledge of the common letter tradition in the ancient world. The designation *private* needs to be understood in an extensive fashion so that it includes all correspondence in the personal domain, whether it concerns business or family matters. Private letters are commonly divided into the following subcategories on the basis of subject matter: family letters, letters of petition, letters of introduction and business letters. Since these private or documentary letters are widely recognized as the most important of the three types for a comparative analysis with NT letters, one example of each of the four kinds of private letters is provided below. These letters also illustrate well many of the epistolary conventions discussed in the second half of this article.

1.1.1. Family Letters. Many private letters consist of correspondence between family members, here illustrated by P.Mich 490 (second century A.D.), a letter from a young Greco-Egyptian recruit to his mother:

> Apollinarious to his mother, Taesion, many greetings. Before anything else I wish that you are well, making obeisance on your behalf to all the gods. And when I found someone who was journeying to you from Cyrene, I thought it a necessity to inform you about my welfare; you must inform me at once, in turn, about your safety and that of my brothers. And now I am writing to you from Portus, for I have not yet gone up to Rome and been assigned. When I am assigned and know where I will be, I will tell you immediately; and, for your part, do not hesitate to write about your welfare and that of my brothers. If you do not find someone coming to me, write to Socrates and he will transmit it to me. I greet my brothers much, and Apollinarious and his children, and Kalalas and his children, and all your

friends. Asklepiades greets you. I pray that you are well. I arrived in Portus on Pachon 25.

[2d hand] Know that I have been assigned to Misenus, for I found out later [i.e., after the letter had been written].

1.1.2. Letters of Petition. A second type of private letter that frequently occurs is the letter of petition. In this example from P.Enteux 32 (200 B.C.), a woman appeals to the king for justice in a personal matter in which she feels wronged:

> To King Ptolemy, greetings from Philista, daughter of Lysis, resident in Trikomia. I am wronged by Petechon. For as I was bathing in the baths of the aforesaid village, on Tybi 7 of the year 1, and had stepped out to soap myself, he, being bathman in the women's rotunda and having brought in the jugs of hot water, emptied one over me and scalded my belly and my left thigh down to the knee, so that my life was in danger. On finding him, I gave him into the custody of Nechthosiris, the chief policeman of the village, in the presence of Simon the epistates. I appeal to you therefore, O king, if it pleases you, as a suppliant who has sought your protection, not to suffer me, who am a working woman, to be treated so lawlessly, but to order Diophanes the strategos to instruct Simon the epistates and Nechthosiris the policeman to bring Petechon before him that Diophanes may inquire into the case, hoping that, having sought your protection, O king, the common benefactor, I may obtain justice. Farewell.

1.1.3. Letters of Introduction. The prevalence of the *patronage system and the reciprocity ethic (favors bestowed incurred obligation) ensured that *commendationes,* or letters of recommendation, played an important role in society, as illustrated here by P.Oxy. 292 (c. A.D. 25):

> Theon to the most honored Tyrannos, many greetings. Herakledies, who carries this letter to you, is my brother. Therefore, I appeal to you with all my power to regard him as recommended. I have also asked your brother Hermias through correspondence to talk with you about him. You will grant the greatest favor to me if he receives your attention. Above all I pray that you may have good health and prosperity. Farewell.

1.1.4. Business Letters. Rapid growth in trade and commerce contributed to the popularity of the business letter, an epistolary type illustrated by P.Oxy. 264 (A.D. 54), which deals with the sale of a loom:

> Ammonius, son of Ammonius, to Tryphon, son of Dionysius: Greetings. I agree that I have sold to you the weaver's loom belonging to me, measuring three weavers' cubits less two palms, and containing two rollers and two beams, and I acknowledge the receipt from you through the bank of Sarapion, son of Lochus, near the Serapeum at Oxyrhynchus, of the price of it agreed upon between us, namely, twenty silver drachmae of the Imperial and Ptolemaic coinage; and that I will guarantee to you the sale with every guarantee, under penalty of payment to you of the price which I have received from you increased by half its amount, and of the damages. This note of hand is valid. The fourteenth year of Tiberius Claudius Caesar Augustus Germanicus Imperator, the fifteenth of the month Caesareus.
>
> [2d hand] I, Ammonius, son of Ammonius, have sold the loom, and have received the price of twenty drachmae of silver and will guarantee the sale as aforesaid. I, Heraclides, son of Dionysius, wrote for him as he was illiterate.

1.2. Official Letters. Official letters, the second of the three broad classes of letters, include correspondence written for the conduct of state business and sent between kings, government officials, military officers or ambassadors in the exercise of their duties. The traditional view is that official letters developed out of private letters. There is some evidence, however, in support of the opposite opinion, namely, that official letters were the generating source for the other classes of letters, as diplomatic correspondence was soon adapted to meet personal and other more broadly literary needs.

During the Hellenistic period, official letters were typically written by royal secretaries who not only drafted such letters but also kept copies of all royal correspondence. Although some of these official letters were initiated by the king, more often they were written in response to an oral or a written request from a city or foreign state. The king would prepare a rough draft of his reply, the royal secretaries would put the letter in its finished form, and finally the king would then add the closing farewell wish in his own hand. Many of these official letters were inscribed on stone after delivery and placed in prominent places for public viewing. Cities regularly published royal letters in this way, both out of respect for the kings who had written them and to guarantee for themselves whatever privileges such letters contained.

In the later Roman period official letters continued to be used widely. Imperial letters *(epistulae principum)*, along with epistolary responses to the queries of officials *(rescripta)*, were the primary means by which the *emperor conveyed his will and influenced public policy and opinion. Senatorial decrees and other official decisions were typically translated into Greek, a measure taken for no other language group under Roman authority, and published in epistolary form.

1.3. Literary Letters. Literary letters encompass a wide variety of epistolary works that were preserved and transmitted through literary channels. This is a bit of a catch-all category that includes a variety of letters that do not belong to the more clearly defined categories of private and official letters. Yet literary letters share in common with each other their obvious literary character and the intention that such correspondence be copied and distributed to a wider audience. One example of this epistolary type are letter essays, treatises that make use of epistolary conventions, especially in their openings and closings (e.g., writings by *Seneca, Dionysius of Halicarnassus, *Plutarch). There are also philosophical letters written by moral *philosophers who increasingly made use of the letter form as a means for instruction (e.g., *Plato, *Aristotle, *Epicurus). Literary letters also include novelistic letters—fictional, often *pseudepigraphical documents cast in an epistolary format that present interesting stories and anecdotes about important historical figures. Some of these novelistic letters were written as part of school exercises in the training of philosophy and rhetoric.

2. Epistolary Conventions.

Despite the diversity of epistolary types, one of the striking features of Greco-Roman letters is how similar and formulaic they are, both in their overall structure (letter opening, letter body, letter closing) and in their constituent epistolary conventions. Many of these stereotyped formulas reappear in either an identical or an adapted form in NT letters.

2.1. Letter Opening. Whereas the letter body contains the specific, situational occasion of the letter (which could be quite diverse), the letter opening, along with the letter closing, is primarily concerned with establishing or enhancing personal contact with the letter recipient (what Koskenniemi called "philophronesis," the expression of friendly relationship). Given this rather uniform purpose of the letter opening, it is not surprising that this section of the letter became stereotyped in nature. Three epistolary conventions found in the letter opening include the prescript, the health wish and sometimes the thanksgiving formula.

2.1.1. Prescript. All letters open with the prescript, which consists of three elements: the sender, the recipient and the salutation. The resulting formula is almost always: "X [nominative] to Y [dative], greetings [*chairein*]." An exception to this pattern is found in letters of petition where, because the document is written to a superior, the name of the recipient is given before that of the sender. All three elements of the prescript are frequently expanded: the sender and recipient through the addition of titles or terms of relationship, endearment and honor; the salutation by adding adverbs emphasizing degree ("warmest greetings") or by combining it with the health wish ("greetings and good health").

2.1.2. Health Wish. The health wish *(formula valetudinis)* expresses concern about the welfare of the letter recipient, with an assurance of the letter writer's own well-being often included as well. Although the health wish exhibits variety, its basic form in the letter opening is "If you are well, it would be good. I too am well."

2.1.3. Thanksgiving Formula. A third epistolary convention sometimes found in the letter opening is the thanksgiving formula. This formula is not nearly as fixed as are the other epistolary conventions found in the letter opening, but it involves some mention of thanksgiving, worship (*proskynēma*) or prayer to the gods, usually for good health or safe travel.

2.2. Letter Body. The letter body deals with the specific historical context and purpose(s) of the letter. Since these settings and purposes can be diverse, the letter body is understandably much less stereotyped than are the opening and closing sections. Nevertheless a number of epistolary formulas can be identified in the body of ancient letters. Space restraints permit the mention of only a few of these body formulas here, with an emphasis on those stereotypical expressions that also appear in NT letters.

2.2.1. Disclosure Formula. The disclosure formula makes use of a verb of knowing and derives its names from the fact that the writer wishes to make known to the recipient some information. Although this formula exhibits some variety, its most common form is: "I want you to know that . . ." This specific form of the disclosure formula frequently introduces the letter body (see Rom 1:13; 2 Cor 1:8; Gal 1:11; Phil 1:12; 1 Thess 2:1).

2.2.2. Appeal Formula. The appeal formula, common in both private and official letters, typically consists of four elements: the verb *parakaleō* ("I appeal") or its synonyms, the person(s) addressed, a prepositional phrase indicating the authority by which the appeal is made (this element is found in official letters only) and the content of the appeal. This formula was used to express a more friendly, less heavy-handed tone than would be conveyed through an explicit command (see Rom 12:1; 15:30; 1 Cor 1:10; 1 Thess 4:1; Philem 9-10).

2.2.3. Confidence Formula. The confidence formula typically consists of four elements: the emphatic use of the first person pronoun ("I"), a verb of confidence ("I am confident"), the reason(s) for the writer's confidence and the course of action that the writer is confident the recipient will take. This formula functions to strengthen the letter's request or admonition by creating a sense of obligation through praise: the recipient feels some indirect pressure to live up to the confidence that the sender has in him or her (see Rom 15:14; Gal 5:10; 2 Thess 3:4; Philem 21).

2.2.4. Peri de *Formula.* A simple formula frequently used as a topic marker—a shorthand way of introducing the next subject of discussion—is *peri de* ("now about/concerning"), normally pulled to the front of the sentence for emphasis. Although this formula often signals a reply to an issue raised in a preceding letter, it is not restricted to this use (see 1 Cor 7:1, 25; 8:1; 12:1; 16:1, 12; 1 Thess 4:9, 13; 5:1).

2.2.5. Ta de loipa *Formula.* Another topic-changing formula is *ta de loipa* ("finally/for the rest") and its variations. This concluding transitional formula often introduces the last item or subject matter to be treated in the letter body (see 2 Cor 13:11; Gal 6:17; Phil 4:8; 1 Thess 4:1; 2 Thess 3:1).

2.3. Letter Closing. The letter closing, like the opening section of a letter, is primarily concerned with reestablishing the sender's relationship with the recipient, and this function has similarly resulted in closings that are stereotyped. A number of epistolary conventions belong to the closings of ancient letters: a farewell wish, a health wish, secondary greetings, an autograph and an illiteracy formula. Yet the instances in which all or even most of these occur simultaneously are rare.

2.3.1. Farewell Wish. The farewell wish served to signal the definitive end of a letter, somewhat akin to our modern expressions "sincerely" or "yours truly." This formula occurs in two basic forms, *errōsso* or *eutychei,* which, despite literally meaning "Be strong!" and "Prosper!" can be translated as "farewell" because of their function in bringing a letter to a close. These two basic forms of the farewell wish were often subject to the expansion and elaboration that also takes place in the prescript.

2.3.2. Health Wish. Despite its presence in the letter opening, the health wish is frequently repeated in the letter closing. The basic form of this formula ("Take care of yourself in order that you may be healthy") in the letter closing differs slightly from its use in the letter opening in that it makes no reference to the writer's own health and also exhibits much less variety than does its counterpart in the letter opening.

2.3.3. Secondary Greetings. In addition to the salutation or primary greeting in the letter opening (*chairein*), the letter closing often contains secondary greetings, normally expressed by the *aspazesthai* ("greeting") formula. The sender either greets someone directly (first-person greetings), exhorts the recipient to greet someone else on his or her behalf (second-person greetings) or becomes an agent through whom a third party greets the recipient or even some fourth party (third-person greetings).

2.3.4. Autograph. In letters that were written with the help of a secretary or amanuensis (a widespread practice in that day), it was common for the letter closing to contain an autograph—some final remarks written by the sender in his or her own hand. Since this change of script would have been obvious to the reader of the letter, there was no reason to state explicitly that the author was now writing rather than the secretary. We do not find among the ancient letters, therefore, an autograph formula or fixed phrase typically given to indicate that the author has begun writing. The extent of an autograph section varies greatly, normally consisting just of the farewell wish but at times including other items such as greetings, a date or postscriptive remarks.

2.3.5. Illiteracy Formula. Many people did not possess the ability to write and so, despite the assistance of a secretary, were unable to close the letter in their own hand. In such situations, a secretary would often include an illiteracy formula—a brief note explaining that a secretary had written the correspondence because of the illiteracy of the person who commissioned the letter ("X wrote for Y because he did not know how to write"). This formula does not occur in family letters but appears to have been a requirement of business and official letters.

3. Summary.

The epistolary handbooks, the rhetorical writings and the educational curriculum reveal a genuine interest in epistolary theory—the ideal characteristics and style of a letter. Nevertheless, the epistolary theorists and rhetoricians did not appear to have much impact on the practice of writing letters and very little about this subject can be learned from the training received in the schools. A more accurate understanding of letter writing, therefore, requires an analysis of the several thousand actual letters from antiquity that have survived.

See also EPISTOLARY THEORY; LITERACY AND BOOK CULTURE.

BIBLIOGRAPHY. D. E. Aune, "Letters in the Ancient World," in *The New Testament in Its Literary Environment* (LEC 8; Philadelphia: Westminster, 1987) 158-82; D. Brooke, *Private Letters Pagan and Christian* (London: Benn, 1929); A. Deis-smann, *Light from the Ancient East* (London: Hodder & Stoughton, 1910); W. G. Doty, *Letters in Primitive Christianity* (Philadelphia: Fortress, 1973); F. X. J. Exler, *The Form of the Ancient Greek Letter* (Washington, DC: Catholic University of America, 1923); H. Koskenniemi, *Studien zur Idee und Phraseologie des griechischen Briefes bis 400 n. Chrs.* (Helsinki: Akateeminen Kirjakauppa, 1956); M. L. Stirewalt, *Studies in Ancient Greek Epistolography* (Atlanta: Scholars Press, 1993); S. K. Stowers, *Letter Writing in Greco-Roman Antiquity* (LEC 5; Philadelphia: Westminster, 1986); K. Thraede, *Grundzüge griechish-römischer Brieftopik* (Munich: C. H. Beck, 1970); C. B. Wells, *Royal Correspondence in the Hellenistic Period* (New Haven, CT: Yale University Press, 1934); J. L. White, "Ancient Greek Letters," *Greco-Roman Literature and the New Testament,* ed. D. E. Aune (Atlanta: Scholars Press, 1988) 85-105; idem, *The Body of the Greek Letter* (Missoula, MT: Scholars Press, 1972); idem, *The Form and Structure of the Official Petition* (Missoula, MT: Scholars Press, 1972); idem, *Light from Ancient Letters* (Philadelphia: Fortress, 1986).

J. A. D. Weima

LITERACY AND BOOK CULTURE

In Greco-Roman antiquity generally literacy was narrowly limited and heavily concentrated in the aristocratic classes. Although the levels and extent of literacy may have varied somewhat with period and region, in no ancient society was there mass literacy. Book culture was similarly limited, being contingent not only on literacy but also on the cost and availability of hand-produced books.

1. Literacy
2. The Uses of Literacy
3. Literacy and Orality
4. Book Culture

1. Literacy.

Literacy in the ancient world is difficult to estimate, owing both to different definitions of literacy and to the incidental nature of available evidence. Literacy can be understood to mean anything from signature literacy (the ability to write one's name), to the capacity to puzzle out a brief and pointed message, to the functional literacy of craftspersons, to the developed skills of reading and comprehending lengthy literary texts. Granting varied types and gradations of literacy, if literacy is understood as the capacity to read with comprehension a text of average complexity, then it seems to have been possessed by relatively few. A further complication in estimating literacy in antiquity is the multilingual character of much of the Mediterranean world, especially in the *Hellenistic and *Roman periods. In many areas several languages were current (in Egypt, for example: Coptic, Greek and Latin), and literacy and its levels varied according to the language in question.

W. V. Harris, using a broad definition of literacy and drawing on evidence partly explicit, partly circumstantial and partly comparative, has concluded that over the whole period of classical antiquity the extent of literacy rarely exceeded 10 percent of the population. In the special circumstances of a few Hellenistic cities it may have approximated 20 to 30 percent, while in the western provinces of the *Roman Empire it may not have been as high as 5 to 10 percent. Such quantifications are necessarily tentative, but this estimate now commands broad assent. Even if the rate were twice as high, literacy would have characterized only a small minority, and it is beyond dispute that the ancient world knew nothing remotely like mass literacy. Apart from explicit evidence, literacy has historically been a function of social class and of *education, and any appreciable extent of literacy within a society requires institutions and incentives to foster it. These were largely lacking in ancient societies, which made no provisions for general public education and offered no strong or broad-based social and economic stimuli to the acquisition of literacy. Moreover, the means for acquiring literacy and the leisure to exercise it belonged only to some, and texts were not readily available or affordable to all.

Although literacy occurred principally within the aristocratic elite and among males of that class, it was not confined to them. There were literate *women of the aristocracy, but the extent of literacy among women was considerably less than among men at all social levels. Beyond the social elite, literacy must have been fairly common also among members of the retainer class who were in the service of the elite. Among the lower social echelons literacy was rare. Yet some *slaves were literate and often also could write, having been specifically trained for duties requiring those skills. Some technical professions had special uses for literacy: engineers, doctors, surveyors and magicians were frequently literate, as were some well-to-do tradespersons. But there is evidence also that some artisans and craftspersons were literate, and even some farmers possessed low levels of literacy.

2. The Uses of Literacy.

The need of literacy, when it was not routinely gained through the education available to the small upper class, depended on its practical uses. Chief among these was the importance of writing and reading in the operations of government, especially in imperial and provincial administration (*see* Roman Administration). Official correspondence, administrative record keeping and the public dissemination of decrees, *laws and regulations were essential tasks. Relatedly, there was apparently an above-average rate of literacy in the Roman army (*see* Roman Military), where it had obvious uses in the communication of orders and in maintaining rosters and records, as well as probably counting in recruitment and promotion. The sheer expanse of the empire placed a premium on writing and reading for long-distance communi-cation, not only in trade but also between family members and friends at far removes (*see* Letters, Greco-Roman).

But locally the general population had little or no need of literacy to negotiate the ordinary business of life. When such skills were required (e.g., in writing contracts or business letters, recording *marriages or *divorces, drawing wills) the assistance of a professional scribe was accessible almost anywhere, and the great number of documentary papyri attest to the regularity of such recourse. In addition, but almost entirely among the elite, literacy was essential to the pursuit of the arts and higher learning. The cultivation and appreciation of history, *poetry, *philosophy, philology and other forms of literature were by definition dependent upon literate skills and also presupposed a leisure that could be devoted to them. Literacy also had a role to play in *religion, though in Greek and Roman religions generally writing played only a small role and literate skills were important principally for priests or hierarchs who had use of calendars, ritual manuals, temple archives or oracular records.

In addition to its diverse pragmatic uses, literacy possessed structural and symbolic values. Because of its restricted accessibility, what was written easily acquired significance in excess of content alone: it had features of the esoteric, of uncommon stability and permanence and of authority. Hence literacy and texts also furnished a medium for the construction, configuration and exercise of power. On one side this can be understood as a power over texts, exercised by controlling access to texts and regulating their use but also by maintaining an exegetical hegemony over their meaning and application. On the other side power was exercised through texts in various ways, for example, through the impressive prominence of monumental inscriptions, the development of intricate bureaucracies and their records, the emergence of scribal classes, the formation of canons of texts or the creation of vernacular literatures.

3. Literacy and Orality.

The culture of the ancient Mediterranean was a traditionally oral culture into which literacy had made a strong advance, and although literacy was mostly concentrated in the social and political elite, society at large was characterized by a lively synergism of the oral and the written. Modern theoretical models of a fundamental disjunction or opposition between the oral and literate modes (whether social, linguistic, cognitive or hermeneutical) fail to illuminate either their manifest coexistence or their fluid interaction in the Greco-Roman period and offer no adequate account of the ways in which the literate participated in oral culture or the illiterate participated in literate culture. In the ancient world writing and reading were closely related to the spoken word: texts were commonly inscribed from dictation and, once inscribed, were normally read aloud, so that at the level of composition and use the oral and the written were interpenetrating. Similarly, the illiterate and semiliterate found access to the world of literacy not only through public readings of poetry and prose, official inscriptions, public oratory and dramatic performances but also through quotidian familiarity with the documentation entailed by commercial and legal transactions.

Form criticism strongly promoted the idea that early Christianity was a nonliterate folk culture that cultivated oral tradition and had little or no investment in literacy or texts. Without denying the currency of oral tradition, it is increasingly recognized that Christianity, which emerged from a textually oriented *Judaism and whose constituency comprised a rough cross-section of Greco-Roman society, was also early engaged in the use, interpretation and production of texts. Appeals to Jewish Scripture and the exegesis of Jewish texts appear to have been an aspect of Christian activity from the beginning. There was frequent epistolary communication with Christian communities by their founders or overseers and among the far-flung communities spawned by the Christian mission; and various pre-Gospel textual redactions of tradition (small collections of sayings, miracle stories, testimonia) furnished materials later employed in the composition of full-blown Gospels.

In respect of its interest in texts, as well as in other ways, early Christianity more closely resembled a scholastic movement or philosophical school than did other religious groups of the period. Christianity's concern with texts was practical and functional rather than literary in the high sense: texts served the needs of communication, teaching, evangelism, apologetics and worship. Not least in connection with worship a small fund of texts would have been indispensable in virtually every Christian community. Although the vast majority of Christians were, like the larger society, illiterate, through the public reading, interpretation and exposition of texts in worship and catechesis they were strongly exposed to texts and participated in book culture to an unusual degree.

4. Book Culture.

In a context where literacy was restricted and all texts were individually produced by hand, book culture was naturally limited. Beyond literacy, the cost of books and the leisure to use them meant that book culture was mainly confined to the upper classes.

The standard form of the book in antiquity was the roll, a strip of papyrus 8 to 10 inches high and up to about 30 feet long, inscribed on the inside (recto) in tall, narrow columns 2 to 4 inches wide with 25 to 45 lines per column. Near the end of the first century an alternative form, the codex, or leaf book, made an appearance. Constructed by stacking sheets of papyrus, folding them and stitching them along the fold, the codex enabled the leaves to be inscribed on both sides, usually in one broad column to the page, and thus made for a more economical, capacious and convenient book. The codex, which served originally as a notebook, only slowly replaced the roll in general usage but caught on very early in Christian circles. Judging from extant early Christian manuscripts, it appears to have been the preferred and nearly exclusive format for Christian writings.

There was no mass production of books in antiquity. An author who wished to publish a text engaged the services of a professional scribe and furnished the text to be copied. Publication (*ekdosis*) consisted in giving such a copy to a *patron or a friend, who then made it available to be copied at the initiative of other interested parties. In this way copies of the book were multiplied seriatim, one at a time. Once a text was in circulation and available for copying, anyone who had an interest in and access to it could have a copy made. Thus books were produced and acquired through an informal and unregulated process. Commercial interests played a very small role. Although there were some booksellers, because the market was limited and copying was unregulated they commonly produced books to order rather than stocking large numbers of copies of any work, and throughout the period books were routinely obtained privately, through channels of friendship among persons of literary interests.

The acquisition and use of books depended upon literacy, leisure, financial means and otherwise on need. The educated aristocracy valued and collected belletristic books—of poetry, prose, history, philosophy—for aesthetic and intellectual purposes. Scholars and certain professionals (e.g., physicians, architects, magicians) also required books, including technical manuals. Novelistic literature had a readership, though in a largely illiterate society it hardly qualified as popular in the broad sense. Because literature was a symbol of social status, books were sometimes avidly collected and ostentatiously displayed by the upwardly mobile and *nouveaux riches*. Yet a true book culture flourished only among the literati and among scholars.

Reading in antiquity was customarily done aloud, even if privately. The reason is that texts were written in continuous script (*scriptio continua*), without divisions between words, phrases, clauses or paragraphs, and without punctuation, so that the syllables needed to be sounded and heard in order to be organized into recognizable semantic patterns. Correspondingly, almost all ancient texts were composed in consideration of how they would sound when read aloud. In general it was more common to hear a text read than to read it oneself. There were various occasions of public reading when the illiterate or semiliterate might hear a text and have contact with literary culture.

Books were variously accumulated into libraries, both personal and institutional. Personal libraries of any size were exceptional and rarely exceeded some hundreds of rolls, though a few larger ones are reported. The great institutional libraries of the ancient world not only harbored very large collections of books but also carefully established texts from the best manuscripts and catalogued their holdings. The renowned *Alexandrian library reputedly held some half a million items, housed a scriptorium and sponsored technical philological scholarship. The rival library at Pergamum was not so large but pursued similar textual, philological and bibliographical work. Roman institutional libraries were smaller and on the whole less notable for technical scholarship. There is no reason to think that ancient institutional libraries were public in the modern sense: their use was limited de facto to a small number of literate and leisured persons, and one of their principal functions was to serve as cultural and political symbols.

See also ALEXANDRIAN LIBRARY; ALEXANDRIAN SCHOLARSHIP; BIBLIOMANCY; LETTERS, GRECO-ROMAN; RABBINIC LITERATURE; SCHOLARSHIP, GREEK AND ROMAN; WRITING AND LITERATURE: GREEK AND ROMAN; WRITING AND LITERATURE: JEWISH.

BIBLIOGRAPHY. P. J. Achtemeier, "*Omne Verbum Sonat:* The New Testament and the Oral Environment of Late Western Antiquity," *JBL* 109 (1990) 3-27; H. Blanck, *Das Buch in der Antike* (Munich: C. H. Beck, 1992); A. K. Bowman and G. Woolf, eds., *Literacy and Power in the Ancient World* (Cambridge: Cambridge University Press, 1994); J. Dewey, ed., *Orality and Textuality in Early Christian Literature* (Semeia 65; Atlanta: Scholars Press, 1995); H. Gamble, *Books and Readers in the Early Church: A History of Early Christian Texts* (New Haven, CT: Yale University Press, 1995); W. V. Harris, *Ancient Literacy* (Cambridge, MA: Harvard University Press, 1989); J. Humphrey, ed., *Literacy in the Roman World* (JRA Supplementary Series 3; Ann Arbor: University of Michigan Press, 1991); T. M. Lentz, *Orality and Literacy in Hellenic Greece* (Carbondale: Southern Illinois University Press, 1989); C. H. Roberts, *Manuscript, Society and Belief in Early Christian Egypt* (London: Oxford University Press, 1979); C. H. Roberts and T. C. Skeat, *The Birth of the Codex* (Oxford: Oxford University Press, 1983); R. J. Starr, "The Circulation of Literary Texts in the Roman World," *CQ* 27 (1987) 213-23; R. Thomas, *Oral Tradition and Written Record in Classical Athens* (Cambridge: Cambridge University Press, 1989); E. G. Turner, *Greek Manuscripts of the Ancient World*, ed. P. Parsons (2d ed.; London: University of London Institute of Classical Studies, 1987); idem, *The*

Typology of the Early Codex (Philadelphia: University of Pennsylvania Press, 1977).

H. Gamble

LITERATURE. *See* WRITING AND LITERATURE: GRECO-ROMAN; WRITING AND LITERATURE: JEWISH.

LITURGY: QUMRAN

Liturgy, religious speech which is by its nature fixed rather than spontaneous, is rare in the Hebrew Bible. The rabbis identified only eight instances (*m. Soṭa* 7:2) that they accepted as liturgical: the paragraph of the firstfruits (Deut 26:3, 5-10), the rite of *halitzah* (Deut 25:7, 9), the blessings and the cursings (Deut 27:14-26), the priestly blessing (Num 6:24-26), the blessing of the high priest on the Day of Atonement (Lev 16), the paragraph of the king (Deut 17:14-20), the paragraph of the heifer whose neck was to be broken (Deut 21:7-8), and the address of the priest who was anointed for battle when he spoke before the troops (Deut 20:2-7). The determining factor for these passages was the presence (either actual or assumed by argument) of the introductory formula,"they/you/she shall answer and say."

1. Postbiblical Liturgical Ceremonies
2. Development of Institutionalized Prayers
3. Daily and Occasional Prayers

1. Postbiblical Liturgical Ceremonies.

The first concrete evidence for extrabiblical Jewish liturgy is found among the Dead Sea Scrolls. The sectarians evidently noted the same biblical formula later recognized by the rabbis and couched their liturgical compositions in the language of the Bible. In addition to the introductory formula, they also emphasized the antiphonal nature of some liturgy by appending "amen, amen" to the statements (Num 5:22; Neh 8:6). The function of Qumran liturgy can in large part be determined by the distribution and modification of these formulas.

1.1. Initiation Ceremony. The Qumran initiation ceremony incorporated both the plural initial formula, "they shall answer and say," as well as the twofold "amen" closing. 1QS 1:22—3:12 is by and large a confessional prayer developed from the liturgical rites of the Day of Atonement described in Leviticus 16 (*see* Sacrifice and Temple Service). The blessing texts from Cave 4 (4Q286; 4Q287; 4Q289), which include the same formulas, may be evidence of an earlier stage in the development of the sectarian initiation. These latter texts are themselves founded on the blessings and the cursings of Deuteronomy 27:14-26. It may be that the fragmentary 4Q275, *Communal Ceremony*, should be included here as well, despite the fact that the bifold "amen" was not preserved among its fragments.

1.2. Thanksgiving Ceremony. Both 4Q502, *Ritual of Marriage*, and 4Q503, *Daily Prayers*, incorporate a plural introduction, "they shall answer and say," with no "amen, amen" response. Some have posed an alternative purpose for the extremely fragmentary 4Q502, suggesting that it is a Golden Age ritual in thanksgiving for longevity (Baumgarten 1983). 4Q503, although entitled *Daily Prayers*, is more accurately a series of community thanksgiving responses for each day of the month, praising God for the sunrise and sunset and plotted according to the changing phases of the moon. In addition to the similar form and corporate setting of these two compositions, the thanksgivings addressed to the "God of Israel" is a common element.

1.3. Purification Ceremony. A singular introductory formula, "he shall answer and say," with no bifold "amen" response defines a group of texts which are all purification liturgies: 4Q284, *Purification Liturgy*; 4Q414, *Ritual Purity A*; and 4Q512, *Ritual Purity B*. These liturgies are for individual use and were recited during ritual bathing. They are also directed to God, incorporating the common phrase, "You are the God of Israel." Numbers 5:2 identified the three areas of ritual uncleanness: leprosy, bodily discharges of any kind, and contact with the dead. The extant purity rituals from Qumran are concerned with these very issues.

2. Development of Institutionalized Prayers.

Although personal prayer is attested on numerous occasions in the Hebrew Bible (e.g., Gen 20:7; 32:11; 1 Sam 1:11; Jer 14:11, etc.), the beginnings of institutionalized prayer have been more difficult to pinpoint. Prayers on special occasions—new moons, sabbaths, assemblies and festivals—are cited (Is 1:13-15), but the fact remains that there are no institutionalized communal prayers in the biblical record and certainly no mention of individual daily prayers until the postexilic period. That there are no prayers or commands to pray as part of the instructions for *sacrifice suggests that the temple was a place where silence reigned. The theory that institutionalized prayer began in Babylonian exile and was brought about by the destruction of the temple and a need for a substitution for sacrifice has become widely accepted, but, although reasonable, it is without any evidence. However, the later data from the scroll manuscripts do attest to this sort of substitution, but for a different reason than that of forced exile and destruction. The Qumran sectarians had separated themselves from normative Judaism likely due to calendar issues (*see* Calendars, Jewish), a non-Zadokite ruling *priesthood, and a constellation of *legal debates linked to the temple cult (4QMMT). Although a preoccupation with the temple is evident in the community's literature (11QTemple), there would not likely have been any thought of replacing the Jerusalem sanctuary (1 Kings 11:36). Perhaps Proverbs 15:8 (quoted at CD 11:20-21) provided the catalyst for a solution to the lack of temple access:

> The sacrifice of the wicked [i.e., normative Judaism] is an abomination to the LORD;
> But the prayer of the upright [i.e., the Qumran sect] is his delight.

Although there is some scattered evidence that the priests continued their officiating role as prayer began to substitute for sacrifice (1QSa 2:17-21, 1QS 6:2-8; CD 13:2-3; 1QM 10:2, 4Q289 frag. 1 4), generally it would appear that they were not singled out as having special prerogative either in prayer or other liturgical functions. The absence of a presiding priest in the text of virtually every Qumran liturgical composition is certainly noteworthy.

An additional surprise is the lack of any indication that a reading of the law was a part of the liturgy of the public meeting, such as it became in the synagogue service (see Neh 9). Rather than a *bêt kenneset*, or synagogue, where the reading of the law was at the center, the scrolls call the place of meeting the *bêt hištaḥ^{a}wût*, or "house of worship" (CD 11:22, 4Q271 frag. 5 i 15), where prayer was central.

3. Daily and Occasional Prayers.

3.1. Communal Prayers. Liturgy that exhibits an absence of the initial formula ("they answered and said") but with a direct address to the Lord (always *Adonai*) clearly functions as prayer. A set of occasional prayers ending in the bifold "amen" evidences elements that suggest a setting of public worship. 4Q504, *Words of the Heavenly Lights*, is a collection of daily prayers that incorporates both prayers of confession and celebration. 4Q507-509 are festival prayers; only prayers for the Day of Atonement and Weeks (Pentecost) are explicitly mentioned among the fragments.

3.2 Prayers of the Instructor. The *Songs of the Sage*, 4Q510-511, are prayers specifically composed for the instructor *(maśkîl)* to intercede for the community to protect it against the power of evil spirits.

3.3 Personal Daily Prayers. Although a manuscript containing personal daily prayers has not been recognized among the Qumran documents, S. Talmon has suggested that 1QS 9:26—10:3 records the six daily occasions for personal prayer. The three daytime prayers are suggested by the biblical text (Dan 5:10; Ps 55:16-17) and also became a part of rabbinic Judaism as attested by the *ʿAmidah.*

(1) Morning Prayer: when day begins its dominion

(2) Midday Prayer: within the sun's circuit

(3) Evening Prayer: when the sun is regathered into its dwelling place

The Qumran sect also recited prayers during the night hours, dividing it like the day into three watches:

(4) First Night Prayer: when the night watches begin

(5) Second Night Prayer: within its circuit when the stars shine brightest

(6) End of Night Prayer: when the stars are gathered to their dwelling place

See also LITURGY: RABBINIC; SACRIFICE AND TEMPLE SERVICE; SYNAGOGUES.

BIBLIOGRAPHY. J. Baumgarten, "4Q502, Marriage or Golden Age Ritual?" *JJS* 34 (1983) 125-35; idem, "The Purification Liturgies," in *The Dead Sea Scrolls After Fifty Years: A Comprehensive Assessment*, ed. P. Flint and J. VanderKam (2 vols.; Leiden: E. J. Brill, 1999) 2:200-12; E. Chazon, "Prayers from Qumran and Their Historical Implications," *DSD* 1 (1994) 265-84; E. Schuller, "Prayer, Hymnic and Liturgical Texts from Qumran," in *The Community of the Renewed Covenant: The Notre Dame Symposium on the Dead Sea Scrolls*, ed. E. Ulrich and J. VanderKam (Notre Dame, IN: University of Notre Dame Press, 1994) 153-71; S. Talmon, "The Emergence of Institutionalized Prayer in Israel in the Light of the Qumran Literature," in *Qumran: Sa piété, sa théologie et son milieu*, ed. M. Delcor (Paris: Leuven

University Press, 1978) 265-84; M. Weinfeld, "Prayer and Liturgical Practice in the Qumran Sect," in *The Dead Sea Scrolls: Forty Years of Research,* ed. D. Dimant and U. Rappaport (Leiden: E. J. Brill; Jerusalem: Magnes, 1992) 241-58.

M. G. Abegg Jr.

LITURGY: RABBINIC

Traditional Jewish liturgy took shape in various stages over a number of centuries. Arguably the most important achievement of rabbinical *Judaism was the establishment and institutionalization of the basic liturgical form of communal worship. This process took place after the destruction of the Second *Temple in A.D. 70 and involved the formulation of the major liturgical pattern and its moral and spiritual principles.

Prior to 70 a certain order of communal prayer existed. In the *Jerusalem temple, sacrifices were accompanied by set *prayers and ceremonies administered by temple *priests (*m. Tamid* 5:1; Sir 50:19; Josephus *Ag. Ap.* 2.24 §196; Lk 1:10). Rituals of early *synagogues, as well, incorporated diverse forms of communal prayer (Mt 6:5; Josephus *Life* 54 §277; *Ag. Ap.* 2.2 §10).

1. Emergence of the Liturgy
2. Form of the Liturgy

1. Emergence of the Liturgy.

The *destruction of the Jerusalem temple placed the rabbis in a position of religious leadership. They strove to form a liturgical system that would function without reliance on the temple as a uniting religious focal point and that would still be acceptable to the people as an effective and authentic method of Jewish worship. Supported by the biblical verse "And serve him with all your heart" (Deut 11:13), the rabbis redefined the act of prayer as the *avodah,* or "service" of the heart, implying that the act of prayer can function independently of geographical location and can thus substitute for the temple service (*b. Ber.* 32b). With the multiple inspiration of Scripture, forms of individual petitions and prayers, existing patterns of *synagogue worship, mystical notions and the ancient temple ceremonies, the rabbis created the basic Jewish liturgical system.

Liturgy and communal worship became central to Jewish religious life. Prayers replaced temple worship, and gradually acquired a fixed and obligatory pattern (*b. Ber.* 21a). Set times for the recital of prayers were defined: twice a day, at sunrise and sunset, according to one tradition (*m. Ber.* 1:4; cf. 4Q503; Josephus *Ant.* 4.13 §212), and three times a day according to another (*m. Ber.* 4:1; compare *2 Enoch* 51:4; Acts 10:9; *Did.* 8:3). Basic liturgical themes were standardized and the synagogue (lit., "house of meeting") became the major center of communal prayer and worship.

The development of specific prayers in the liturgy was gradual. The liturgy grew in a process of constant additions and rewritings and initially underwent a period of relative fluidity in which various alternative forms of liturgical expression were used interchangeably in Palestine and Babylon. Although it is impossible to trace the roots and authorship of specific prayers, sources such as the early *rabbinical literature, *Josephus, *Philo and the NT all attest to the existence of an established structure of rabbinic public worship and its crystallization in several central prayers. Of these, the following prayers can be considered core elements of the liturgy.

The *Shema,* a prayer so called after its opening words "Hear *[sᵉmaʿ]* O Israel, the Lord is our God, the Lord is one" (Deut 6:4) had existed before the destruction of the Second Temple but became central in the new liturgy (*m. Meg.* 4:3; Josephus *Ant.* 4.13 §213; Lk 10:27). It declares a confession of faith and an ultimate acceptance of God's kingship. The *Shema* consists of three Torah passages, Deuteronomy 6:4-9, Deuteronomy 11:13-21 and Numbers 15:37-41, sections which express the oneness of God, the supreme obligation to serve him, as well as notions of reward, punishment and redemption (*m. Ber.* 2:2; *m. Tamid* 5:1). These biblical passages are framed by various blessings composed by the sages of the rabbinical period. The *Shema* is to be recited twice a day, in the morning and evening time, by every adult male (*m. Ber.* 1:1-4).

The *Shemoneh Esreh,* or Eighteen Benedictions, probably reached its final iteration between A.D. 70 and 100, but it consists of much older traditions. It included originally eighteen separate paragraphs, usually called blessings (*berakhot; m. Ber.* 4:3; *m. Taʿan.* 2:2). Toward the end of the first century a nineteenth paragraph was appended—a curse against heretics, or *minîm* (*b. Ber.* 28b). As a pivotal prayer of the liturgy, the *Shemoneh Esreh* was known by the rabbis simply as the Prayer or the Amidah (standing) since it is recited while standing. The *Shemoneh Esreh* is divided into three sections: praises, requests and thanksgiving. It is recited by every member of the congregation three times a day with additional times on the *sabbath and holy days. These times were associated with the original times of the ritual sacrifices of the temple (*b. Ber.* 26b; *t. Ber.* 3:1-2).

2. Form of the Liturgy.

To the *Shema* and the *Shemoneh Esreh,* probably the original components of the public worship in rabbinic times, other liturgical material was added. Public reading of Scripture became part of the service in rabbinic Judaism and was required on the morning of sabbaths, festivals, Mondays, Thursdays, new moons and all special feast and fast days. It consisted of readings from the Torah (*b. Meg.* 29b) and from the Prophets (*m. Meg.* 4:1-5; Lk 4:17; Acts 13:15) as well as public readings of their Aramaic *translations* (**targum*), since the Hebrew language of the Scripture was no longer familiar to all audiences (*m. Meg.* 4:4, 6, 10). These readings were followed by an exposition on the Scripture, *drashah,* in which the passage was interpreted (*m. Soṭa* 9:15; Lk 4:20).

The blessing of the priests (Num 6:22-26; *m. Soṭa* 7:6 = *m. Tamid* 7:2) usually concluded the service. If no priest was present in the congregation, the blessing was replaced by words of benediction recited by the leader of the prayer.

The *Kaddish,* a prayer for the future establishment of God's ultimate kingship on earth, began as a popular prayer recited in the houses of study. It was offered at the conclusion of the daily study of the Torah, fundamentally as an expression of hope for a time when God will be recognized and accepted by all. The *Kaddish* appears in many variations. Its ancient Aramaic verses express clearly the rabbinical concept of sanctifying the name of God *(Kiddush ha-Shem).* This prayer is often associated with the Lord's Prayer formulated by Jesus (Mt 6:9-13 par. Lk 11:2-4).

Between the third and the sixth centuries A.D. poets began to use basic themes of the prayer in poetic patterns known as *piyyutim.* Several of these poetic compositions and others that followed were incorporated later into the formal liturgy.

Early rabbinical Judaism attempted to define the place of liturgy in the framework of its religious philosophy and basic ideology. Rabbinic discussion of liturgy presupposes that God hears all forms of prayers, yet humans are instructed to submit their prayer according to specific ethical and spiritual standards. Prayers directed to harm others are not permitted, even those that request the fall of one's enemies (*m. ʾAbot* 4:19). Prayers that aim to affect that which is determined or has already occurred are regarded as vain (*m. Ber.* 9:3). Prayers for the benefit of others are encouraged (*b. Ber.* 29b-30a). Private personal prayer is acceptable within the framework of the liturgical service, but communal prayers are considered to be of greater significance (*b. Ber.* 6a, 8a; *y. Ber.* 5:1; *Deut. Rab.* 2:12). Prayers that are concerned with the holiness of God can be recited only in the presence of a *minyan,* the minimum quorum of ten adults that, according to the tradition, symbolically represents the whole community.

Prayers must be said with sincerity and offered with proper concentration and intention, *kavana* (*b. Ber.* 31a; *b. ʿErub.* 65a). A routine and mechanical recitation of the prayers is not acceptable: "He that makes his prayer a fixed task, his prayer is not supplication" (*m. Ber.* 4:4; *m. ʾAbot* 2:13). The language of Jewish prayer is Hebrew, but it is permissible to pray in any language (*m. Soṭa.* 7:1; *t. Soṭa.* 7:7; *y. Soṭa.* 21b).

Clear evidence regarding the degree of female participation in liturgical acts does not exist. References to segregation of women are found (Philo *Vit. Cont.* 9 [69]), yet specific acts of prayer are recorded on the part of women in several sources (*t. Ber.* 16b-17a; *t. Soṭa.* 22a). Recent evidence indicates that in the *Diaspora synagogues, women were not segregated and participated in the functional roles of prayer side by side with the men (Brooten).

Normative formulation of the liturgy seems to include elements from early Jewish *mystical traditions associated with the *Hekhalot* and *Merkabah* literature (*see* Mysticism). Ancient mystical traditions, as well as Second Temple period *apocalyptic traditions and texts from *Qumran, present an understanding of prayer as an angelic liturgy in which human beings join the *angels in the celestial act of praising God (*see* Heavenly Ascent). These mystical sources also describe acts of ascending to heaven and beholding the presence of God, accompanied and achieved through the recitation of prayers and blessings. Verses and themes from the *Hekhalot* and *Merkabah* mystical traditions correspond directly to several prayers of rabbinical Judaism. Thus they probably reflect a process in which mystical and nonmystical traditions influenced one another (Bar-Ilan; Swartz).

Even though a fairly fixed order for prayer was established in rabbinical Judaism, official liturgical texts did not exist. Only in the ninth century, the Geonim created a prayer book known as the *Siddur* (order) and thus canonized the entire system of Jewish liturgy.

See also LITURGY: QUMRAN; MUSIC; SYNAGOGUES; TEMPLE, JEWISH; SACRIFICE AND TEMPLE SERVICE.

BIBLIOGRAPHY. M. Bar-Ilan, *The Mysteries of Jewish Prayer and Hekhalot* (Ramat Gan, Israel: Bar Ilan University Press, 1987 [Hebrew]); P. F. Bradshaw and L. A. Hoffman, eds., *The Making of Jewish and Christian Worship* (Notre Dame, IN: University of Notre Dame Press, 1991); B. Brooten, *Women Leaders in the Ancient Synagogues: Inscriptional Evidence and Background Issues* (Chico, CA: Scholars Press, 1982); J. H. Charlesworth, "Jewish Prayers in the Time of Jesus," *PSB* supp. 2 (1992) 36-55; I. Elbogen, *Jewish Liturgy: A Comprehensive History,* ed. J. Heinemann et al. (based on the 1913 German edition and the 1972 Hebrew edition; Philadelphia: Jewish Publication Society of America; New York: Jewish Theological Seminary of America, 1993); R. Hammer, *Entering Jewish Prayer: A Guide to Personal Devotion and the Worship Service* (New York: Schocken, 1994); J. Heinemann, *Prayer in the Talmud: Forms and Patterns* (New York: Walter de Gruyter, 1977); R. Langer, *To Worship God Properly: Tensions Between Liturgical Custom and Halakhah in Judaism* (Cincinnati: Hebrew Union College Press, 1998); J. Neusner, *Judaic Law from Jesus to the Mishnah* (SFSHJ 84; Atlanta: Scholars Press, 1993); J. J. Petuchowski, "The Liturgy of the Synagogue: History, Structure and Contents," in *Approaches to Ancient Judaism,* vol. 4: *Studies in Liturgy, Exegesis and Talmudic Narrative,* ed. W. S. Green (Chico, CA: Scholars Press, 1983) 1-64; S. Reif, *Judaism and Hebrew Prayer: New Perspectives on Jewish Liturgical History* (New York: Cambridge University Press, 1993); M. D. Swartz, *Mystical Prayer in Early Judaism: An Analysis of Ma'ashe Merkavah* (Tübingen: Mohr Siebeck, 1992); T. Zahavy, *Studies in Jewish Prayer* (Lanham, MD: University Press of America, 1990).

D. V. Arbel

LIVES OF THE PROPHETS

Lives of the Prophets, often referred to by its Latin name *Vitae Prophetarum,* is a brief Jewish writing from the first century A.D. Its intention is indicated by the opening line: "The names of the prophets, and where they are from, and where they died and how, and where they lie" (all quotations of this document are taken from D. R. A. Hare). These biographical "facts" are sometimes supplemented by reports of miracles performed by the prophet or for him, portents associated with him or prophecies he made concerning the end time. Included are all the literary prophets and seven nonliterary prophets (Nathan, Abijah, Joad, Azariah, Elijah, Elisha and Zechariah son of Jehoiada). In some instances the entry is very brief: "Hosea. This man was from Belemoth of the tribe of Issachar, and he was buried in his own district in peace. And he gave a portent, that the Lord would arrive upon the earth if ever the oak which is in Shiloh were divided from itself, and twelve oaks came to be" (*Liv. Proph.* 5:1-2). The longest entries are devoted to Isaiah, Jeremiah, Ezekiel, Daniel, Jonah, Habakkuk, Elijah and Elisha.

The writing has received relatively little attention in the English-speaking world. R. H. Charles did not include it in his *Apocrypha and Pseudepigrapha.* The translation by C. C. Torrey was not easily accessible. Not until 1985 was an English version of the *Lives,* prepared by D. R. A. Hare, readily available in *The Old Testament Pseudepigrapha* (ed. J. H. Charlesworth). More attention has been paid to the document in Europe. Recently a full-length commentary has been undertaken by A. M. Schwemer. The first volume, dealing with the major prophets, appeared in 1995.

This article will present a brief discussion of the original language, earliest sources, probable date, place of origin and the document's significance for students of the NT.

1. Original Language
2. Earliest Sources
3. Probable Date
4. Place of Origin
5. The Document's Significance

1. Original Language.

Although some scholars have argued that *Lives of the Prophets* was written in a Semitic language (Hebrew or Aramaic), this thesis has not stood up under careful examination of the earliest sources, all of which are Greek. The scholarly consensus is that, whether or not the author had access to earlier materials in a Semitic language, the present work was created in Greek. Early versions of the work are extant in Syriac, Ethiopic, Latin and Armenian, but these are all based on Greek originals.

2. Earliest Sources.

The many Greek manuscripts are sorted into four recensions. Two are associated with Epiphanius of Salamis. The longer of these is best represented by Codex Paris. Gk. 1115 in the Bibliothèque Nationale, Paris. The primary witness of the shorter recension is Codex Coisl. 120, also deposited in the Bibliothèque Nationale. A third recension, attributed to Dorotheus, is found in purest form in Codex Vindob. Theol. Gk. 40, located in Vienna. The fourth is referred to as the anonymous recension, since its witnesses are not associated with the name of a church father. The best example of this recension is Codex Marchalianus, Codex Vaticanus Gk. 2125, in the Vatican library.

Although the text is generally well preserved in these manuscripts, they differ remarkably in the order in which the prophets are treated and regarding which nonliterary prophets are included. The longer Epiphanian recension includes John the Baptist, his father, Zechariah, and Simeon (Lk 2:25). A critical text is available in T. Schermann.

Since all of the surviving witnesses are from Christian scribes (none of the work has been preserved in Jewish sources), it is not surprising that many contain Christian interpolations, some of which are more obvious than others. In the Life of Jeremiah, for example, the Dorotheus recension supplements the prophet's prediction of the collapse of Egyptian idolatry with the promise that this will happen "through a savior, a child born of a virgin, in a manger."

3. Probable Date.

It is generally agreed by scholars that this writing can hardly be older than the Maccabean period, nor more recent than A.D. 70, since there in no allusion to the *destruction of Jerusalem that must be taken as prophecy after the fact. Within this period scholars tend to prefer the first half of the first century.

A further narrowing of the range of dates is based on two allusions that can be related to historical data. The Life of Isaiah (*Liv. Proph.* 1:1-8) implies that the spring of Siloam is outside the Jerusalem wall. If this reflects the time of writing rather than simply preserving an uncorrected earlier tradition, a date prior to the new south wall, erected during the rule of Herod Agrippa (A.D. 41-44) is required. The same passage reports that "the nation also buried him [Isaiah] nearby with care and great honor." The wording suggests the erection of a memorial of some kind. A saying of Jesus rebukes his contemporaries for building monuments for prophets whom their ancestors had murdered (Mt 23:29-31; Lk 11:47-48). An associated saying mentions a specific martyr, "Zechariah, who perished between the altar and the sanctuary" (Lk 11:51; cf. Mt 23:35).

J. Jeremias has argued that these sayings refer to the martyrdoms and Jerusalem burials of Isaiah and Zechariah son of Jehoiada (2 Chron 24:20-22); the practice of building memorials to these martyrs was perhaps stimulated by the monuments dedicated to the Maccabean martyrs and by the costly structure built by Herod the Great at the entrance to David's tomb (Josephus *Ant.* 16.7.1 §182; Jeremias, 66, 68). Since the Life of Zechariah son of Jehoiada does not mention a monument, Jeremias infers that the *Lives of the Prophets* must have been written earlier, that is, before Jesus' public ministry. If this argument is accepted, the document was probably written in the first quarter of the first century.

4. Place of Origin.

Although the author's scriptural allusions sometimes reflect the Hebrew text, at other points his work clearly relies upon the *Septuagint. This by no means proves that the work originated in the *Diaspora. Palestine was multilingual. The author's familiarity with the geography of Palestine and his detailed knowledge of Jerusalem suggest that despite the fact that Greek was probably his first language, he was resident in Palestine, and probably in Jerusalem. He may, however, have employed sources deriving from the Diaspora. Recently this has been strongly argued by Schwemer (1:165-236) for the Egyptian portions of the Life of Jeremiah.

5. The Document's Significance.

The chief value of this writing derives from the glimpses it provides of first-century Jewish popular religion. Although it manifests little interest in theology, it seems to belong in the mainstream of Judaism with respect to its views on God, *angels, *Satan, idolatry, the resurrection of the dead and judgment. Again, it has little to say about the *Torah, but nothing suggests that the author supported lax observance. His interest lies in the fate of the prophets, not in their scriptural teaching. He is particularly interested in miracles, prodigies, portents and end-time prophecies, and it is proper to assume that he wrote for a public that shared his interests.

Students of the NT will be interested to learn that brief birth narratives are supplied for both Elijah and Elisha. The one concerning Elijah is particularly noteworthy, since it includes a prophecy regarding Elijah's *eschatological role: "When he was to be born, his father Sobacha saw that men of shining white appearance were greeting him and wrapping him in fire, and they gave him flames of fire to eat. And he went and reported (this) in Jerusalem, and the oracle told him, 'Do not be afraid, for his dwelling will be light and his word judgment, and he will judge Israel'" (*Liv. Proph.* 21:2-3; most manuscripts add "with sword and fire"). This passage provides further evidence that first-century Jews did not find reprehensible the idea that God would employ one or more human deputies at the eschatological judgment (cf. Acts 17:31).

Historians of religion are interested in possible pagan antecedents for elements of the stories in Matthew 1—2 and Luke 1—2 concerning Jesus' birth. Some have proposed that the statement in the Life of Jeremiah that the Egyptians "revere a virgin giving birth and, placing an infant in a manger, they worship" (*Liv. Proph.* 2:9) is irrelevant to the question because it is a Christian interpolation. Schwemer argues that this Jewish document was probably referring to a well-known practice of Egyptian religion honoring the "virgin" Isis and her son Horus. Even the reference to a manger need not be secondary, since the myth located the birth of the divine child in the Delta and declared that the baby was born between two animals and was raised by shepherds. Schwemer (1:197-98) proposes that this passage in the *Lives* constitutes the "missing link" between the Egyptian myth and the birth stories in Matthew and Luke. The document's treatment of the prophets as heroes of the faith, whose graves may be profitably visited by pilgrims, suggests a Jewish background for the later Christian practice of the veneration of the saints.

See also APOCRYPHA AND PSEUDEPIGRAPHA; WRITING AND LITERATURE: JEWISH.

BIBLIOGRAPHY. D. R. A. Hare, "The Lives of the Prophets: A New Translation and Introduction," *OTP* 2:379-99; J. Jeremias, *Heiligengräber in Jesu Umwelt* (Göttingen: Vandenhoeck & Ruprecht, 1958); T. Schermann, *Prophetarum Vitae Fabulosae Indices Apostolorum Discipulorumque Domini Dorotheo, Epiphanio, Hyppolyto Aliisque Vindicate* (Leipzig: Teubner, 1907); A. M. Schwemer, *Studien zu den frühjüdischen Prophetenlegenden* Vitae Prophetarum (TSAJ 49; Tübingen: Mohr Siebeck, 1995); C. C. Torrey, *The Lives of the Prophets: Greek Text and Translation* (JBLMS 1; Philadelphia: Society of Biblical Literature and Exegesis, 1946).

D. R. A. Hare

LUCIAN OF SAMOSATA

A prolific satirist of the second century A.D., Lucian's writings are of value to students of the NT for their preservation of numerous insights into religion, philosophy, rhetoric and daily life in the Roman Empire.

1. Life
2. Writings
3. Satire
4. Interpretation
5. Usefulness

1. Life.

Freeborn (c. A.D. 120/125-c. 185) in Syria, in a city located on the Euphrates yet touched by Greek culture, Lucian left home and his uncle's workshop to pursue oratory. He may have begun practicing in *Antioch before moving on to Ionia, *Greece, Italy and Gaul, becoming so accomplished that he received Greek citizenship and eliminated his Syrian accent. Perhaps during his tenure in Gaul Lucian attained his greatest wealth and reputation. Though Lucian eventually settled in *Athens, he continued to travel, including a return to Syria and a governmental position in Egypt.

Further comment on Lucian's life flounders on two dangers. First, dating Lucian's works typically depends on a theory of Lucian's development, a dubious enterprise (see Hall). Second, Lucian's literary artifices afford few straightforward autobiographical insights. Even the nature and results of Lucian's alleged conversion to *philosophy around the age of forty are ambiguous.

2. Writings.

A large corpus of Lucian's writings survives.

M. D. Macleod's edition lists eighty-six treatises, of which at least ten are spurious. The genuine writings include *prolaliai* (i.e., prefaces used to introduce longer speeches), encomia (i.e., speeches of praise) and defense speeches, which together display brilliantly Lucian's *rhetoric. His enduring reputation, however, rests on his criticism and formal innovations. In diatribes, pamphlets and novels, Lucian unleashes parody and satire to lampoon and censure. Lucian shines brightest, however, in his satiric dialogues, which imaginatively blend Menippean elements with philosophic form to abuse and amuse. Lucian grins as he bites (*Bis Acc.* 33).

3. Satire.
As a satirist, Lucian generally highlights human foibles. He often laughs at human desires for wealth (*Gall.*, *Tim.*, *Cont.*), expressing standard objections such as worry, cares, envy and distrust (*Nav.*). He skewers flatterers (*Tim.*, *Nigr.*; cf. *Par.*, *Pr. Im.*) and charlatans (*Alex.*), mocks pretentiousness (*Ind.*) and attitudes to death (*Dial. Mort.*) and is amused by the convoluted ways of love (*Dial. Meretr.*).

Common fare from the critique of paganism arises in Lucian's handling of religion. He criticizes oracles as ignorant and deceitful, feeding on weakness and credulity. Lucian also enters into the philosophical-religious debate about Fate (*J. Conf.*; *J. Tr.*), as well as the censure of sacrificial and funerary practices (*Sacr.*; *Luct.*). Lucian also disparages Hesiod and viciously maligns the prophet Alexander and the economics of temple practices.

Lucian often scoffs at philosophy. Sometimes he criticizes contradictory cosmologies (*Icar.*), more often contradictory behavior (*Symp.*). In *Vitarum Auctio* he ridicules every philosophical position he knows; *Piscator* and especially *Hermotimus* continue this attack. The latter presses the problem that philosophical schools hold mutually exclusive positions, the analysis and comparison of which are beyond human capability, yet unnecessary because philosophy fails to make people more virtuous anyway.

In the wake of his satires, Lucian has little positive to offer. He does, however, advocate a common-sense view of life: one should accept one's lot in life, shunning the pursuits of wealth, power or speculative philosophy. Pride is evil, dogma foolish, simplicity good. Accordingly, Lucian holds a Delphic anthropology ("Know thyself"), an ethic of moderation expressed by the mythical flights of Icarus and Daedalus; moreover, he commends the social criticism of the Platonist Nigrinus and the model life and wisdom of the unaffiliated Socratic Demonax. In short, Lucian grew to regard the life of the common person as best while nevertheless admiring the virtues educated culture inculcated.

4. Interpretation.
Lucian reflects the second sophistic (i.e., the educated culture) of which he was part. Infatuated with ancient Greece (i.e., Atticism), Lucian looked back particularly to Homer, Aristophanes, *Plato, Demosthenes and Menander, drawing as well on Menippus, for both the substance and style of his work, quoting often and imitating habitually (*mimēsis*). Much of the charm of his writings lies in the creative, erudite and witty way he treated old stories, themes and styles. This sophisticated use of tradition characterized his era.

Lucian's obvious participation in Atticizing educated culture (*paideia*) raises the key problem in Lucianic criticism: How real are his observations on life? Did Lucian offer only esoteric comments based on and in dialogue with books, or did he have living targets in view? J. Bompaire's monograph argued that Lucian's dependence on previous literature placed Lucian in conversation with literary culture and left little room for reality in his writings. Recent literature disagrees. B. Baldwin, L. Robert, C. P. Jones and others have documented many comments in Lucian's writings particular to the historical context in which Lucian lived. G. Anderson adds perspective to this debate: on the one hand realists draw their evidence from only a portion of Lucian's writings, while on the other hand nonrealists must concede that engaging the past was the fashion among educated people of Lucian's day and thus a part of Lucian's contemporary reality.

5. Usefulness.
Myriad insights into the background of early Christianity appear in Lucian's writings. For example, he speaks about ancient athletics (*Anach.*), pantomime (*Salt.*), images (*Im.*) and historiography (*Hist. Conscr.*). More obviously, Lucian's writings reveal the social conditions of public speaking (*Ind.*, *Peregr.*, *Scyth.*, *Herod.*, *Sat.*): he records the competitive nature of sophists

and their insults, the possibilities of a peripatetic lifestyle or attachment to great houses, voluntary poverty or potential riches, as well as the popularity and range of audiences. He also demonstrates the attraction of apophthegms (*Demon.*). Lucian's own rhetoric displays a polished Atticism and the ability to make the worse argument the better (e.g., *Phal.*), while his *prolaliai* (e.g., *Zeux.*) and encomia (e.g., *Musc. Enc.*) exemplify the art of embellishment. His invective further trades in standard rhetoric, for example, caricature and charges of inconsistency, murder or sexual malfeasance.

Religious subjects appear throughout Lucian's writings. Greek ideas about the gods and the afterlife fill his works, extending Greek mythology in creative fashion (e.g., *Ver. Hist.*, *Cat.*, *Dial. Deor.*). Lucian's frequent references to gods, oracles, healings, relics, mysteries, rites, sanctuaries and festivals reveal the common features of religion (e.g., *Sat.*, *Alex.*); he also provides narratives that illuminate ancient magic (*Philops.*, *Nec.*). Lucian's observations on how the human and divine realms are bridged contribute to the history-of-religions construction of the divine man (*Alex.*, *Peregr.*, *Philops.*, *Deor. Conc.*; *Demon.* 44, 63, 67; *Nigr.* 3, 38; *Dial. Mort.* 3, 13-16, 28; *Tox.* 3-4; *Herm.* 7).

Specific notice of Christianity (called a *kainē teletē*) appears in *Peregrinus* (11-16) and *Alexander* (25, 38). In typical slander, the latter associates Christians with atheists and Epicureans as scapegoats and the enemies of traditional religion, while the former treatise tells about the time Peregrinus spent as a Christian. Lucian knows about Christian beliefs and practices and evaluates Christians as simpletons (*idiōtai*) and easy prey for a charlatan (*goēs*). These essays earned Lucian the label blasphemer.

See also RHETORIC.

BIBLIOGRAPHY. G. Anderson, "Lucian: Tradition Versus Reality," *ANRW* 2.34.2 (1994) 1422-47; B. Baldwin, *Studies in Lucian* (Toronto: Hakkert, 1973); H.-D. Betz, "Lukian von Samosata und das Christentum," *NovT* 3 (1959) 226-37; idem, *Lukian von Samosata und das Neue Testament: Religionsgeschichtliche und paränetische Parallelen, ein Beitrag zum Corpus Hellenisticum Novi Testamenti* (TU 76; Berlin: Akademie Verlag, 1961); A. Billault, ed., *Lucien de Samosate* (CERGR, n.s. 13; Lyon: Université Jean-Moulin; Paris: Boccard, 1994); J. Bompaire, *Lucien écrivain: imitation et création* (BEFAR 190; Paris: Boccard, 1958); idem, *Lucien: Oeuvres* (Budé; Paris: Les Belles Lettres, 1993-); R. B. Branham, *Unruly Eloquence: Lucian and the Comedy of Traditions* (Cambridge, MA: Harvard University Press, 1989); J. A. Hall, *Lucian's Satire* (New York: Arno, 1981); C. P. Jones, *Culture and Society in Lucian* (Cambridge, MA: Harvard University Press, 1986); M. D. Macleod, *Luciani Opera* (SCBO; 4 vols.; Oxford: Oxford University Press, 1972-87); idem, "Lucianic Studies Since 1930," *ANRW* 2.34.2 (1994) 1362-421; J. C. Relihan, *Ancient Menippean Satire* (Baltimore: Johns Hopkins University Press, 1993); L. Robert, *À travers l'Asie Mineure: poètes et prosateurs, monnaies grecques, voyageurs et géographie* (BEFAR 239; Paris: Boccard, 1980).

D. D. Walker

M

1 AND 2 MACCABEES

The books of 1 and 2 Maccabees are two of the most important works relating to Jewish history during the Greek period (*see* Jewish History: Greek Period). Virtually all that we know about *Seleucid rule, the Maccabean revolt and the rise of the *Hasmonean kingdom come from them. Their value is further enhanced in that they seem to have been written relatively soon after the events they purport to describe. As examples of *Jewish literature, they take their place alongside the many other writings of the Second Temple period that did not become a part of the Hebrew canon, though they feature among the deuterocanonical writings in the Roman Catholic and Greek Orthodox canons.

The two books are independent writings but cover a good deal of the same ground. First Maccabees begins with the accession of Antiochus IV (175-164 B.C.), under whose reign great changes rocked the Jewish community in Judah, and ends with the accession of John Hyrcanus (135-104 B.C.) to the high priesthood and leadership of the nation, thus covering almost fifty years. Second Maccabees begins with the reign of Seleucus IV (187-175 B.C.) and ends before the death of Judas Maccabeus in 162 B.C., thus embracing the much shorter period of about a quarter of a century. Apart from the fact that both are fiercely pro-Maccabean and overlapping for one of the most significant periods of the revolt, the aims and content of the two books are quite different in many ways.

1. First Maccabees
2. Second Maccabees

1. First Maccabees.

In the text itself there is no indication of who wrote the book; however, it is evident that the author was a devotee of the Hasmonean dynasty who justifies and extols the exploits of the Maccabean brothers. Since the book ends at the beginning of John Hyrcanus's reign, it is likely to have been completed sometime during that ruler's reign, perhaps about 125 B.C. (some scholars would date it to the beginning of Alexander Janneus's reign, or about 100 B.C.). It has been argued that a number of the battle scenes show the knowledge of an eyewitness (Bar-Kochva, 158-62, though this has been disputed by Schwartz, 37 n. 64). However, even if this argument is correct, this may only indicate sources used by the author, not that the author himself had been the witness to the battle.

The style of the Greek text indicates that it was composed originally in Hebrew. No certain portions of that text are extant; the story is referred to in *rabbinic literature, but these allusions do not indicate that the text of the book was known at this time. Some textual difficulties in the Greek have been resolved by attempting to determine the Hebrew text behind the translation. The nature of the narrative indicates that the author used narrative texts of the OT (e.g., Joshua, 1 and 2 Samuel) as a model for his account. Although *piety and theology are not as intrusive in 1 Maccabees as in 2 Maccabees, they are there in a low-key but pervasive manner. God is not referred to directly but as "heaven" (e.g., 1 Macc 3:18; 4:10). Judas and the people pray before battle and even read the law (1 Macc 3:44-54). Heaven gives victory to the righteous even over great odds (1 Macc 3:18-22).

The book contains a summary of the origin and process of the Maccabean struggle, climaxing in the statement of independence in 1 Maccabees 14:27-47 and the affirmation of Maccabean leadership. In 1 Maccabees 1 there is a brief account of the preliminary events, beginning with *Alexander the Great's invasion, but it quickly skips to the time of the wicked Antiochus Epiphanes when Jewish apostates built a *gymnasium and followed Greek ways. Then Antiochus attacked Jerusalem, issued a decree imposing the Greek way and set up an "abomination of desolation" in the temple.

In 1 Maccabees 2 the resistance began under Mattathias, but he soon died. First Maccabees 3—4 describe Judas's fight against the Syrian armies in which he finally retakes the temple and reconsecrates it, ending the abomination of desolation. The continuing story of Judas and his fight to prevent the envious Gentiles from wiping out the Jews is related in 1 Maccabees 5—8. Judas's death is recounted in 1 Maccabees 9:1-22, and Jonathan's story is told in 1 Maccabees 9:13—12:53. Simon's story follows in 1 Maccabees 13—14, and one might have thought that the book would end here; Josephus's copy may have done just that, for in the *Antiquities* he follows 1 Maccabees closely almost to the end of chapter 13 but then picks up another source for the continuing story of the Hasmoneans. First Maccabees 15—16 form a sort of epilogue about the rest of Simon's reign, describing recognition of the new Jewish state by the Seleucid ruler Antiochus VII Sidetes and by envoys from *Rome. However, Antiochus VII then reneged on his acknowledgment of Jewish independence and was defeated by an army led by John Hyrcanus, Simon's son. The book ends with the death of Simon and the accession of John to the office of high *priest.

The story thus focuses on the Maccabean family, especially the three brothers who each led the people in turn. It is mainly a chronological narrative of events without reflection on what they mean. No clear reason is given for Antiochus's attack on the Jewish religion, and the rightness of the Maccabean actions is taken for granted. The persuasive strength of the book lies in its apparent ingenuousness: it seems straightforward and honest. But this is a part of its *rhetoric of persuasion. A simple narrative also allows the writer's own perspective to prevail without intrusion on the reader's consciousness. The book is very pro-Maccabean, though it does not particularly favor Judas in the way that 2 Maccabees does. Although Judas is given a central position, the phrase "Judas and his brothers" or other phrases in which Judas acts in concert with others occur frequently (1 Macc 3:25, 42; 4:16, 36, 59; 5:16, 25, 28, 63, 65). When those not a part of the Maccabean family attempt to take the lead, disaster invariably befalls them (1 Macc 5:55-62). Each Maccabean brother is chosen in turn by "the people" (1 Macc 3:2; 9:28-31; 13:1-9; 14:27-47).

Much has been made of the David-and-Goliath-like nature of the conflict and the victories of a small group of Jews against a great empire. This is a part of the myth created by the book. As has been well demonstrated (Bar-Kochva), the victories of Judas were not miraculous but usually fit the normal military criteria for success. In a few cases, defeats have been treated as victories (e.g., 1 Macc 4:28-35 par. 2 Macc 11). The success of the Maccabees was due neither to supernatural intervention nor to superhuman powers on the part of the Jewish fighters. Judas's greatest achievement was in building up and training a regular army skilled in the conventional military techniques of the *Hellenistic period. His brother Jonathan's achievements were in exploiting the divisions in the Seleucid dynasty to his own ends.

The book also makes a close association between ancient Israel and the Jewish nation of the second century. The term **Israel* is used frequently as a designation of the Jewish people, especially in a religious or ideological context. The ideological nature of the usage is indicated by the fact that none of the alleged treaties or letters relating to outsiders use anything but "Jews" (e.g., 1 Macc 8:23-32; 10:18-20, 25-45; 11:30-37; 12:6-23; 13:36-40; 14:20-23; 15:2-9, 15-21).

The figure of Antiochus IV looms large in both books, in which his actions are described in satanic terms. First Maccabees presents him as one who is determined to Hellenize his kingdom and replace all local customs with Greek ones (cf. 1 Macc 1:41-42), and many modern scholars have referred to his Hellenizing policy. However, this statement in 1 Maccabees is not supported by other sources. There is no evidence that Antiochus was a particular champion of Hellenization or that he had a policy of suppressing native customs (Bickerman, 30-31). Nor is there any indication that he had a special interest in the Jews; the initial approach to Hellenize Jerusalem came from the Jews themselves (*see* Hellenistic Judaism). Yet Antiochus did issue a decree forbidding Judaism, at least in Judah itself, and persecuted those who disobeyed. Why he issued this decree is still debated, but it occasioned one of the greatest religious crises for the Jews of antiquity (*see* Jewish History: Greek Period).

First Maccabees is also an important source for establishing the chronology of Jewish history for the period. It has become widespread in the past fifty years to date the Maccabean revolt to 167-164 B.C. This is a complex calculation, based on the *Seleucid dating used in both books, though we now know that Antiochus died in November-December 164 B.C.. However, it has been recently argued that the correct dating is 168-165 B.C., in line with an earlier generation of scholars (Grabbe 1991).

Of particular interest are a number of documents and letters allegedly quoted in 1 Maccabees 8 and 1 Maccabees 10—15, including a treaty with Rome and *letters between Hasmonean and Seleucid rulers and even with the king of Sparta. Most of the letters have been accepted as genuine, though whether the original wording is preserved is a question since they would have been translated into Hebrew and retranslated into Greek. The two main documents questioned are the supposed treaty with Rome made by Judas (1 Macc 8:23-32) and the letter from the Spartan king (1 Macc 12:20-23). Although a treaty between Rome and the Maccabean state was eventually concluded, the question is whether it was as early as the time of Judas. Many scholars feel it was not until at least the time of Simon. It also seems likely that Jonathan wrote to the king of Sparta, but whether he had a reply and whether this is it are two questions still very much disputed.

One of the most puzzling groups in the book are the *Asidaioi* or Hasidim (1 Macc 2:42; 7:13; 2 Macc 14:6). Hardly has another group about which so little is known been so used in theories and historical reconstructions. Apart from the fact that they were "mighty warriors" *(ischyroi dynamei),* we know hardly anything about them (Davies). The Greek word probably represents Hebrew *ḥesed,* which can mean "pious." It may be that *Hasidim* was a term not referring to members of a specific narrow sect but a more generic term applied to anyone exhibiting certain characteristics of piety or a particular attitude toward the law. In 2 Maccabees 14:6 the term is applied to Judas Maccabeus, though we cannot be sure that the term is being used in exactly the same way it is in 1 Maccabees. In the end, we must be careful not to build significant theories on a group about which we really know so little.

2. Second Maccabees.

Superficially, 2 Maccabees seems to be a shorter version of 1 Maccabees, since it covers a shorter period of time, yet there are significant differences not only of content but also of outlook and approach. The book is divided into two clear parts: 2 Maccabees 1:1—2:18 is made up of parts of several letters written by the Palestinian community to the Jews in Egypt, calling on them to celebrate the "Feast of Tabernacles in the month of Kislev" (i.e., Hanukkah; *see* Festivals and Holy Days); 2 Maccabees 3:1—15:39 describes the events of Jewish history, beginning with an episode in the reign of Seleucus IV and ending with Judas Maccabeus's defeat of the Seleucid general Nicanor in the spring of 162 B.C. Second Maccabees 3 is a sort of pre-Maccabean episode that tells how Seleucus IV sent an officer to confiscate the treasury of the Jerusalem temple but was prevented by divine intervention. The rest of the book is on the events leading up to the Maccabean revolt and on the revolt itself. Second Maccabees 4 describes the Hellenistic reform in which Jason took the high priesthood from his brother Onias (III), built a gymnasium and turned Jerusalem into a Greek *polis.* Second Maccabees 5:1—6:11 describes how Jewish worship was suppressed by Antiochus IV. We then come to a description of several martyrdoms in 2 Maccabees 6:12—7:42. Second Maccabees 8—15 is devoted to the exploits of Judas, ending with the great victory over Nicanor.

According to 2:19-31, 2 Maccabees is an epitome or abridged version of a five-volume history of Jason of Cyrene; unfortunately, nothing else is known of this Jason beyond what can be gleaned from 2 Maccabees itself. It is clear, however, that the book was composed originally in Greek and is not a translation like 1 Maccabees. It is debated as to whether the letters that begin the book (2 Macc 1:1—2:18) were a part of Jason's work or were added only to the epitome. Nevertheless, in the present book they form an integral part of the story and message, and they may be a key to its genre.

The exact genre of the book has been debated. It fits the genre of apologetic historiography in many ways, especially in that it defends and exalts a native tradition while using Greek rhetoric to do so (cf. Sterling, 16-19, though he does not explicitly discuss 2 Maccabees in this context; van Henten 1997, 20). It has been argued that it is "temple propaganda" (Doran), possibly against the temple of Leontopolis in Egypt founded by Onias IV after his father Onias III was murdered (Josephus *Ant.* 12.9.7 §387, though Doran rejects the idea that it is directed against the Leontopolis temple). One of its aims is to commend the celebration of Hanukkah to the Jews of Egypt. This has led to the argument that the book originated as a Jewish parallel to a well-known Hellenistic literary convention, the recommendation to celebrate a *sōtēria* festival ("salvation festival"). The *sōtēria* festival was a local celebration well-known in the Greek world in which the deliverance of a city from grave danger was accomplished by the god(s) and the people, fighting against a foreign power, and was celebrated both by inviting a wide group of neighbors to participate and also by composing a history to chronicle the deliverance (van Henten, 47-50, 248-54, 263-65). If this is correct, 2 Maccabees 1:1—2:18 forms the letter of invitation and 2 Maccabees 3—15 is the document chronicling the event being celebrated.

Since the letter prefacing the book is dated to "year 188 [of the Seleucid era]" or about 125 B.C., the book is no earlier than this time. The book also presupposes Jewish independence, which did not become a reality until the reign of John Hyrcanus (135-104 B.C.). However, the Romans are referred to favorably throughout the book, suggesting it was before they were seen as an enemy, which was the view after the Roman conquest of Jerusalem in 63 B.C. There seems no reason not to assign the date to a time near 125 B.C., that is, the late second century, or approximately the same time as 1 Maccabees.

Several characteristics of 2 Maccabees distinguish it from 1 Maccabees. As already noted, the main focus is on Judas Maccabeus, who is singled out as a great Jewish hero in a way that he is not in 1 Maccabees. Mattathias is ignored, and very little is said about the other brothers. It is Judas who leads the successful restoration of the temple cult and the destruction of the Syrian army. The author has deliberately told the story to end on a high note with his victory over Nicanor, which was not all that long before Judas's death, rather than because he did not know of Judas's death. By the time that 2 Maccabees was written, the story of Judas's death would have been well known, yet it is ignored even though it came not long after the defeat of Nicanor. Another important theme is that of martyrdom. The last part of 1 Maccabees 6 and especially 1 Maccabees 7 go into painful and even gruesome detail about the deaths of several individuals, especially the mother and her seven sons. This section is extremely important to the book, however, because the deaths of the martyrs are essential for the recovery of Judah. The sins of the Jews have created a breach between them and God, and before future obedience can be given its due the old breach must be repaired. The blood of the martyrs is a vital ingredient for this reconciliation (cf. van Henten, 27).

One section that is widely misunderstood is that of the Hellenistic reform (primarily 1 Macc 4). This episode is often misinterpreted because of the bias of the book itself as well as that of many modern scholars. The initial event was illegal: Jason took the high priesthood from his brother by offering a large sum of money to Antiochus. He also obtained permission to found a gymnasium and turn Jerusalem into a Greek city, or *polis*. Yet from all we can tell, Jason remained firmly committed to the traditional Jewish religion, however much the Greek lifestyle may have been adopted in other respects by some Jews (see Grabbe 1992, 277-81; Grabbe 2000).

The book quotes letters in 1 Maccabees 1:1—2:18, 9 and 11. The first letter (1 Macc 1:1-10a) is probably authentic, but 1 Maccabees 1:10b-2:18 seems to be made of parts of several letters (van Henten, 37). The letters of 1 Maccabees 11 have been widely accepted, but questions remain. Some find a problem with the letter of Antiochus IV (1 Macc 9:19-29), not that he withdrew the decree prohibiting the practice of Judaism but that some aspects of the letter do not fit known Seleucid correspondence. Probably the most questionable is the alleged letter of Antiochus V to Lysias (1 Macc 11:22-26). The dates on the other letters are also a problem, which makes the sequence of letters difficult to sort out; a variety of schemes have been proposed (Grabbe 1992, 262).

See also JEWISH HISTORY: GREEK PERIOD; JUDEA; 3 AND 4 MACCABEES.

BIBLIOGRAPHY. B. Bar-Kochva, *Judas Maccabeus: The Jewish Struggle Against the Seleucids* (Cambridge: Cambridge University Press, 1989); J. R. Bartlett, *1 Maccabees* (GAP; Sheffield Academic Press, 1998); E. J. Bickerman, *The God of the Maccabees* (SJLA 32; Leiden: E. J. Brill, 1979); P. R. Davies, "*Hasidim* in the Maccabean Period,"

JJS 28 (1977) 127-40; R. Doran, *Temple Propaganda: The Purpose and Character of 2 Maccabees* (CBQMS 12; Washington, DC: Catholic Biblical Association, 1981); J. A. Goldstein, *1 Maccabees* (AB 41; Garden City, NY: Doubleday, 1976); idem, *2 Maccabees* (AB 41A; Garden City, NY: Doubleday, 1983, 1985); L. L. Grabbe, "The Hellenistic City of Jerusalem," in *Jews in the Hellenistic and Roman Cities*, ed. S. Freyne (Royal Irish Academy; London: Routledge, 2000); idem, *Judaism from Cyrus to Hadrian*, 1: *Persian and Greek Periods;* 2: *Roman Period* (Minneapolis: Fortress, 1992); idem, "Maccabean Chronology: 167-164 or 168-165 BCE?" *JBL* 110 (1991) 59-74; J. W. van Henten, *The Maccabean Martyrs as Saviors of the Jewish People: A Study of 2 and 4 Maccabees* (SJSJ 57; Leiden: E. J. Brill, 1997); S. Schwartz, "Israel and the Nations Roundabout: 1 Maccabees and the Hasmonean Expansion," *JJS* 42 (1991) 16-38; G. E. Sterling, *Historiography and Self-Definition: Josephus, Luke-Acts and Apologetic Historiography* (NovTSup 64; Leiden: E. J. Brill, 1992).

L. L. Grabbe

3 AND 4 MACCABEES

Third Maccabees and 4 Maccabees are windows into the challenges and concerns of *Diaspora Jews seeking to maintain their identity as God's chosen people. The titles of both are misnomers, as the former deals with Jews under *Ptolemaic rule in Egypt well before the rise of Judas Maccabeus, and the latter celebrates not the military heroes of the Hellenization crisis but rather its steadfast victims. Due to similarities in story and theme, however, these works came to be grouped together with *1 and 2 Maccabees in several *Septuagint codices. Both strongly support strict observance of *Torah and look disfavorably upon compromise of any kind for the sake of the temporary benefits of complete assimilation. Though quite different in content and strategy, both witness to the need of Diaspora Jews to remember who they are and why they must remain separate from the nations around them.

1. Third Maccabees
2. Fourth Maccabees

1. Third Maccabees.

1.1. Synopsis. Third Maccabees opens abruptly with Ptolemy IV Philopator's advance against the forces of Antiochus III at Raphia, near Gaza. After a plot against his life is thwarted through the timely warning of a lapsed Jew, Ptolemy defeats Antiochus III and goes through the cities in that region to confirm their loyalty to his throne and to encourage them in the aftermath of the war (3 Macc 1:1-8). As was customary for Hellenistic monarchs, he visits sacred sites in order to confer gifts to increase morale. This becomes a problem for the author when Ptolemy enters *Jerusalem and desires to enter the holy place of the *temple there, contrary to local law (Torah). The people flock to the streets in protest and prayer, and Simon, the high *priest, successfully arouses divine intervention. Ptolemy is chastised by invisible forces and, upon recovery, returns to Egypt vowing to inflict vengeance upon the Jewish population there for the repulse he suffered in Jerusalem (3 Macc 1:8—2:24).

Ptolemy's vengeance takes the form of clarifying the civic status of Jews in *Alexandria and the Fayum: those who will assimilate to Hellenistic customs, symbolized by participation in the Dionysus cult, will be enrolled as full citizens; those who do not will be reduced to the status of *slaves, branded as such, and executed if they object. About three hundred Jews accept the benefit of full citizenship at the cost of exclusive commitment to one God; most prefer to suffer loss for their ancestral covenant and even show open contempt for those few who accept the king's offer (3 Macc 2:25-33). This assures Ptolemy of the nation's ill will, so that he now proposes to assemble all the Jews living in his kingdom (save for the apostates) and execute them in the hippodrome (3 Macc 3:1—4:13).

At this point, God's intervention on behalf of his people in Egypt begins. During the registration of the Jews, the king's agents run out of papyrus and pens, allowing some, perhaps, to escape detection (3 Macc 4:14-21). The Jews are herded into the racetrack, and the elephants, which are gathered to trample the Jews to death, are prepared with wine and drugs. In response to prayer, God frustrates Ptolemy's plans first by causing him to sleep through the time appointed for the execution, then by causing the king to forget his plan and become temporarily deranged (3 Macc 5:1-35). On the third day, the king manages to give the order to release the elephants upon the Jews, a sight that fills the victims with a terror portrayed by the author with great pathos (3 Macc 5:36-51). An aged priest named Eleazar silences the screams of the people to lead them in *prayer, after which *angels, visible to all but the Jews, frighten the elephants and turn them back on Ptolemy's soldiers (3 Macc 6:1-21). The king repents of his plan, blames his courtiers for leading him into this self-destructive plan and releases the Jews, providing for a seven-day feast for all the Jews and issuing a decree protecting Jewish rights thenceforth (3 Macc 6:22—7:9). The king allows the Jews to execute their co-religionists who had voluntarily apostatized (3 Macc 7:10-16; cf. Deut 13:6-18). Those who were leaving Alexandria celebrated a second seven-day festival as they began their journey (3 Macc 7:17-23).

1.2. Date and Setting. The extreme limits of dating 3 Maccabees are 217 B.C., the battle of Raphia to which the book refers, and A.D. 70, the destruction of the temple, of which the book gives not the slightest hint. Third Maccabees shows striking similarities with 2 Maccabees and the *Letter of *Aristeas,* both frequently associated with Alexandria: it shares vocabulary and phrases found nowhere else in the Septuagint with each of these books, together with common sets of interests (Emmet collects some remarkable data in this regard), and peculiarities of Greek composition (for example, crasis of the definite article). Moreover, it preserves a peculiar epistolary greeting in the king's edicts, which is documented in papyri from 160 to 60 B.C. (Williams). Given these data, a date in the first half of the first century B.C. and a provenance in Alexandria seem most likely. A number of scholars favor a date in the Roman period (Hadas; Tcherikover) mainly on account of the threat of *laographia,* the registration and poll tax that the Romans introduced in 24 B.C. Others, however, point to the regular execution of censuses under the Ptolemies and to the absence of any connection of the *laographia* with taxes in 3 Maccabees (Anderson; Williams). Finally, some scholars have been tempted to link this book with the threat facing Jews under Caligula, but this crisis theory has been ably called into question by H. Anderson and D. S. Williams. Third Maccabees, then, is best read as a work of Egyptian Judaism from the first century B.C. with broader applicability for Jews living in the Diaspora than can be limited to any particular crisis facing the community.

1.3. Genre and Historicity. The genre of 3 Maccabees has been identified as "historical romance" (Hadas): the author was not seeking to write history but an edifying tale loosely anchored in history. The lack of a single hero or love interest can be ascribed to the author's peculiar moral interests, speaking to the place of the people of *Israel in God's providence and in Diaspora life. While some stress the plausibility of the basic historical outline of the story (e.g., Hadas), others see within the narrative a free expansion of a number of episodes originally unconnected—Ptolemy's victory at Raphia, his census of his kingdom fifteen years later, an isolated episode of persecution under Ptolemy VI Physcon (see Josephus *Ag. Ap.* 2. §§51-55)—now brought together for a specific purpose (Emmet; Williams). Similarities with Esther and 2 Maccabees also suggest conscious literary creativity and patterning rather than historiographical interest.

1.4. Purposes. D. S. Williams's proposal that 3 Maccabees presents a defense of Diaspora Judaism must, in some form, be accepted. He suggests that this book responds to Palestinian Jewish criticism of Jews in the Diaspora who follow not Torah but an imperfect translation of it (cf. the prologue to Ben Sira; *see* Sirach) and whose very location in exile bears witness to God's lingering displeasure (cf. 2 Macc 1:1-9). The artificial connection of the three events related above strongly supports this thesis. The author opens the scene in the Jerusalem temple, linking the trials of Jews in Egypt with the holy place; similarly, Ptolemy's vow to destroy the Jerusalem temple after he eradicates Egyptian Jewry further links the destiny of the holy place with Diaspora Jews. Furthermore, the main theme of the author is God's protection of these faithful Diaspora Jews: God is quick to hear and answer their prayers for deliverance, a sure sign of God's acceptance of their performance of Torah and fully restored favor. The fact that 3 Maccabees is parallel at almost every point to 2 Maccabees 3:1—10:9 (cf. Ptolemy's attempt on the temple to Heliodorus's repulse in 2 Macc 3:1-40; the choice of apostasy or punishment for fidelity to Torah; the persecution of faithful Jews; the efficacious prayer of an aged priest named Eleazar; God's victory over the Gentile forces; the establishment of a festival commemorating deliverance) suggests that it was composed as a sort of parallel saga for Egyptian Judaism.

Third Maccabees served a second function, reinforcing boundaries between the Jewish population and their Gentile neighbors. The book holds out the themes of divine election, especially in the prayers of Simon and Eleazar (3 Macc 2:2-20; 6:2-15), providence, the dangers of apostasy (3 Macc 2:31-33; 7:10-16) and the error of Gentile religious thinking in order to strengthen commitment to Jewish custom and Torah among the readers and to challenge the view that assimilation to Hellenism brought advantage (*see* Hellenistic Judaism). In light of this, it is almost certain that it was not intended for a Gentile readership, which would only be repulsed by the dim light in which non-Jews are presented throughout the narrative (vs. Anderson).

1.5. Value as Witness to Ethnic Tensions Between Jew and Gentile. While 3 Maccabees appears to have little or no influence on later Jewish or Christian authors, it is a valuable window into the world of Egyptian Judaism and its social tensions, providing essential information on the environment of early Christianity.

Gentiles are "alienated from the truth" concerning the one God and true religion (3 Macc 4:16)—a theme that will appear again in *Wisdom of Solomon and Paul's letter to the Romans (cf. Rom 1:21, 25, 28). Provoking the one God through their neglect of true worship, disregard for Jerusalem and hostility toward God's elect people, the Gentiles are "arrogant" as well (3 Macc 1:25-26; 2:2-9; 5:13; 6:9). This is not merely a character flaw but a base vice. In 3 Maccabees we also are given an astonishingly balanced view from the Gentile side. Because of their dietary regulations and exclusive worship of one God, Jews tended to stand apart from the larger society, neither mingling in everyday intercourse nor appearing at public festivals (3 Macc 3:3-7). This *amixia* was interpreted negatively as misanthropy, as rejection of the virtue of civic unity and even as a sign of potential seditiousness. The larger community felt as though the Jews in their midst were not fellow citizens concerned about the common good of the city or reliable friends.

Ptolemy also stands as a frustrated *benefactor of the Jewish nation, and the transformation of his favor into wrath may reveal another source of tension between Jews and Gentile rulers. Ptolemy approaches the temple as a beneficent *patron: the peculiar customs of the place baffle him, and the refusal of the Jews to allow him access to the holy place strikes him as a singular offense. This incompatibility of norms and values appears also in the different perspectives on citizenship and the cost of acquiring citizenship (3 Macc 2:27; 3:23). What Ptolemy sees as the benefaction of the "priceless citizenship," the Jewish author regards as "inflicting public disgrace" because it involves joining fully in the civic life of an idolatrous culture. He comes to regard the Jews as ungrateful (3 Macc 3:17-19), which is the cardinal sin in a society where patronage and clientage makes the world go round (*see* Patronage). They "disdain what is good" in rejecting the benefits of full participation in Greek society and thus show themselves baseminded (3 Macc 3:15-24). These tensions within the narrative world reveal sources of mutual misunderstanding in the real world.

The hostility of faithful Jews toward apostate Jews in 3 Maccabees—to the point of enforcing the injunctions of Deuteronomy 13:6-18 against the lapsed—provides important background for the hostility of both Christian and non-Christian Jews to such phenomena as the Pauline mission, which sought to eliminate boundaries and prejudices that had been in place for centuries. Paul's relaxation of Torah observance for Jews within the church no doubt appeared as another Hellenizing movement, another threat to the integrity of the covenant people of God.

2. Fourth Maccabees.

2.1. Synopsis. Fourth Maccabees is not an attempt at historiography but at philosophical demonstration (4 Macc 1:1, 7-8) of the thesis that "pious reason is sovereign over the *pathē*," a term that includes emotions, desires and physical sensations. The author argues that the reasoning faculty that is trained in the Jewish Torah is able to achieve domination over these passions, enabling the person to live a life full of virtue. He discusses at some length how specific Mosaic laws train the adherent in different virtues and sets forth the examples of Joseph, *Moses and David to demonstrate how the mind subject to Torah can overcome lust, anger and irrational desire (4 Macc 1:13—2:18). The author cites as the examples that best prove his thesis those who were martyred under Antiochus IV during the Hellenization crisis of 175 to 164 B.C. (4 Macc 1:7-12; 5:1—18:5; cf. 2 Macc 6:18—7:42).

After setting the scene by recounting the apostasy of the nation's leadership (4 Macc 3:19—4:26), the author tells of the martyrdoms of the aged priest Eleazar, the seven brothers and finally the mother of the seven (4 Macc 5:1—6:30; 8:1—12:19; 14:11—17:1). The author expands the narrative by creating lengthy dialogues between Antiochus, the representative of Hellenistic culture and criticism, and the martyrs, who respond courageously and cogently to the king's arguments and choose loyalty to God and Torah in the face of extreme tortures. The author returns to his demonstration after the deaths of Eleazar, the seven and the mother (4 Macc 6:31—7:23; 13:1—14:10; 16:1-4) in order to celebrate the achievements of the reason dedicated to Torah in the face of the storm of passions, emotions and sensations. He concludes with an exhortation to the readers to devote themselves to Torah, so as to achieve fullness of virtue and the honors that attend it (4 Macc 18:1-2).

*2.2. **Date and Setting.*** The authorship of 4 Maccabees is unknown: while some early church fathers attribute it to *Josephus, this has been almost universally rejected on account of certain historical inaccuracies, different styles and radically different stances toward accommodation to Gentile culture (Townshend; Anderson). The author was a devout Jew who was skilled in Greek composition and *rhetoric (Klauck) and who was conversant in the "philosophical *koinē*" of his time (Renehan). While some scholars favor a date in the Hadrianic period (Dupont-Sommer; Breitenstein), the strongest evidence for establishing a date has been provided by E. J. Bickerman. He places the work between A.D. 19 and 54 on account of the use of certain terms *(nomikos, thrēskeia)* and the joining of Cilicia, Syria and Phoenicia into one administrative unit (4 Macc 4:2; cf. 2 Macc 3:5). Attempts to narrow this further to the reign of Caligula are based on the false premise that it must respond to a period of crisis or persecution (so rightly O'Hagan). The author does not suggest that his hearers become martyrs themselves but rather emulate their devotion to the Torah so as to become similarly impervious to the passions that weaken devotion to virtue in any circumstance. The choice of these primary examples suggests tension, even despair of rapprochement between the races, but does not necessitate a period of violent persecution. Many are tempted to place the work at Alexandria (Townshend) or *Antioch (Dupont-Sommer): the former because of the work's interest in *philosophy, the latter because the relics of the martyrs were said to be preserved there. But given the flow of popular philosophy through all major cities of the Mediterranean and the presence of Jewish populations in many, we cannot be certain concerning its provenance.

*2.3. **Genre and Purpose.*** Fourth Maccabees describes itself using the language of "demonstration" and "praise" (4 Macc 1:1, 2, 10; 3:19; 16:2) and so falls within the category of epideictic *rhetoric. It may best be described as a protreptic discourse, an oration that recommends a certain way of life and seeks to arouse commitment to pursue that way of life. Like *Seneca's *De Constantia Sapientis,* 4 Maccabees sets out to demonstrate a proposition of philosophical ethics, uses examples of adherents to the philosophy to prove the proposition and seeks to convert the addressee to the way of life espoused by those examples. Some have suggested that it was composed as a sermon for a festival commemorating the martyrs (Hadas; Dupont-Sommer); it would also have been appropriate for the celebration of Hanukah, particularly in the Diaspora and particularly after the Maccabean line fell into disrepute; its message would also have been timely for a festival celebrating the giving of the Torah (like Shavuot or Simchat-hattorah). Ultimately, however, it cannot be bound with certainty to any particular occasion. An oration that emphasized the nobility of Torah and the Jewish philosophy would always have been in season as a support for Jews resisting the pressures of assimilation, seeking to maintain self-respect among Gentiles who frequently found their customs and religion dishonorable and incomprehensible (Klauck; deSilva). The author addresses his work to his fellow Jews (4 Macc 7:19; 18:1-2) in order to encourage them to remain loyal to their particular customs, knowing that it produces in them the virtues admired by the Greek world and leads to benefits far surpassing anything the Gentiles can offer.

*2.4. **Torah and Greco-Roman Ethical Philosophy.*** The author's thesis is familiar to Greco-Roman ethics (Renehan; Hadas; Dupont-Sommer; deSilva). Stoics and Peripatetics (disciples of Aristotelian ethics) alike stress the danger that the *pathē* pose to virtue: fear or pain can disenable courage and endurance; anger can frustrate prudence; pleasure can subvert temperance. For the person to live a life of virtue, it is necessary for reason to gain the upper hand

and control (*Aristotle, *Plutarch and some *Stoics like Poseidonius) or destroy (*Cicero and other Stoics) the passions. Fourth Maccabees clearly lines up with the former school: since the emotions and inclinations are part of God's design, they are not to be eradicated but controlled (4 Macc 2:21). The author is not merely arguing a Greek thesis, however: he sets out to demonstrate that "pious" reason masters the passions and directs one's steps in virtue (4 Macc 1:1; 6:31; 13:1; 16:1; 18:2). This adjective signals the author's main contribution: it is specifically the mind that has been trained by the Jewish Torah that is able to achieve the anthropological and ethical goal almost universally admired by Greek and Roman ethicists (4 Macc 1:15-17; 2:21-23; 5:22-24; 7:18-19; 9:18).

The very laws that Gentiles ridicule, especially Jewish dietary laws (4 Macc 5:5-13), are shown to equip the mind for victory over the passions and for the exercise of every virtue (4 Macc 1:30b—2:14; 5:22-26). The Torah is shown to be a superior guide to virtue than the Stoic law of nature, whose spokesperson in this story is Antiochus himself (4 Macc 5:8-11). Nature, however, teaches love for siblings and love for offspring (described here in terms very similar to those found in Aristotle's *Nicomachean Ethics* and Plutarch's "On Affection for Offspring" and "On Fraternal Affection"; Klauck; deSilva) and thus can even inhibit the domination of reason over these *pathē* (4 Macc 13:19-27; 14:13—15:10, 23-28). Torah is not merely a local, ethnic law inferior to the law of nature (cf. Dio Chrysostom *Or.* 80.5-6) but a law superior to nature as it comes from the Creator of nature (4 Macc 5:25-26). The devout Jew will thus attain every virtue and become the enfleshment of the Stoic sage, unconquered (4 Macc 11:24-27) and uninjured (4 Macc 9:7-9). Those who despise or abuse these paragons of virtue will be the ones to be ashamed (4 Macc 11:4-6; 12:11-14; cf. Plato *Gorg.* 508c-e; Seneca *Const.* 16.3).

Fourth Maccabees' engagement with philosophy helps Jews reject the Gentile society's lack of regard and hold fast to Judaism as the true means of attaining *honor, based on virtues that even Greeks should recognize. The criticism from without is turned back against the detractors, as Jews are now equipped to see in their religion the fulfillment of the virtues that Greek culture lauds as honorable. They may ask themselves why the Gentiles fail to recognize their worth, but they will not be as sorely tempted to seek Gentile validation of their worth.

2.5. Fourth Maccabees and Early Christianity. The early church appears to have known and appreciated 4 Maccabees. Paul's opponents in Galatia may have used arguments very similar to those found in 4 Maccabees to persuade the Gentile converts that taking on the yoke of Torah would lead them on to perfection (Gal 3:3) by providing them with what was lacking in Paul's gospel—a reliable means of making progress toward virtue and overcoming the "passions of the flesh" (Gal 5:16-17). Fourth Maccabees 2:4-6 provides an instructive parallel to Romans 7:7-24: one Jewish author claims that the very commandment proves that reason can conquer the passions and attain the virtue for which God calls, the other claims that the same commandment awakes the passions and leads to sin.

The letter to the Hebrews bears some striking similarities to 4 Maccabees, both in certain phrases (cf. Heb 12:2 with 4 Macc 9:9; Heb 3:6, 14 with 4 Macc 17:4; Heb 11:35b with 4 Macc 6:12-23 and 9:16) and in the definition of faith as loyalty to the divine Patron (cf. 4 Macc 16:18-22 with Heb 11:6, 35). Most striking, however, is the use of the language of vicarious atonement for the deaths of the martyrs (4 Macc 6:27-29; 17:21-22), which represents a bridge and an important development between the Servant Song of Isaiah 52:13—53:12 and early Christian reflection on the death of Jesus (e.g., Rom 3:25; Heb 1:3; 9:11-15; 1 Pet 1:19; 1 Jn 1:7). NT reflection on Jesus' death shares with 4 Maccabees an emphasis not on blood itself as atoning but on the blood of a specifically righteous person who remains loyal to God, which moves the Deity to accept and deliver God's people (4 Macc 17:21-22; Heb 10:4-10).

Fourth Maccabees shares with NT authors several important rhetorical features, although here the latter provides evidence for a common cultural milieu rather than any suggestion of dependence. In both, *athletic imagery becomes a useful image for transforming the endurance of pain, opposition and hostility from one's peers and society into a contest for a noble victory (4 Macc 16:20; 17:11-16; cf. Heb 12:1-4; Phil 3:12-14; 1 Cor 9:24-27). Both use military imagery to turn physical defeat into spiritual victory (4 Macc 1:1; 7:4; 9:23-24, 30; 11:24-27; 16:14; 18:4; cf. Rev 5:5-10; 12:10-11; 15:2). Both also explicitly contrast temporal advantage or disadvantage with eternal advantage or disadvantage in order to strengthen commitment to the one God in the face of opposition (4 Macc 13:14-15; 15:2-3, 8, 26-27; cf. 2 Cor 4:7-18; Heb 10:34; 11:16, 25-26, 35).

Unlike 3 Maccabees, 4 Maccabees enjoys great popularity into the Nicene period, being alluded to or echoed in varying degrees in the *Martyrdom of Polycarp,* Origen's *Exhortation to Martyrdom* and Eusebius's *Ecclesiastical History* (5.1.53-55). The book forms the basis for sermons by John Chrysostom and Gregory of Nazianzus (Townshend), and the martyrs themselves continued to be venerated in numerous circles of the church.

See also DIASPORA JUDAISM; HELLENISTIC JUDAISM; 1 AND 2 MACCABEES; WRITING AND LITERATURE: JEWISH.

BIBLIOGRAPHY. H. Anderson, "4 Maccabees (First Century A.D.): A New Translation and Introduction," in *OTP* 2:531-64; idem, "3 Maccabees: A New Translation and Introduction," in *The Old Testament Pseudepigrapha,* ed. J. H. Charlesworth (2 vols.; Garden City, NY: Doubleday, 1985) 2:509-29; E. J. Bickerman, "The Date of Fourth Maccabees," in *Studies in Jewish and Christian History* (3 vols.; AGJU 9; Leiden: E. J. Brill, 1976-86) 1:275-81; U. Breitenstein, *Beobachtungen zu Sprache, Stil und Gedankengut des Vierten Makkabäerbuchs* (Basel and Stuttgart: Schwabe, 1978); A. Deissman, "Das vierte Makkabäerbuch," in *Die Apokryphen und Pseudepigraphen des Alten Testaments,* ed. E. Kautzsch (Hildesheim: Georg Olms, 1962 repr.) 2:149-76; D. A. deSilva, *4 Maccabees* (Sheffield: Sheffield Academic Press, 1998); idem, "The Noble Contest: Honor, Shame and the Rhetorical Strategy of 4 Maccabees," *JSP* 13 (1995) 31-57; A. Dupont-Sommer, *Le Quatrième Livre des Machabées* (Paris: Librairie Ancienne Honoré Champion, 1939); C. W. Emmet, "The Third Book of Maccabees," in *The Apocrypha and Pseudepigrapha of the Old Testament in English,* ed. R. H. Charles (2 vols.; Oxford: Clarendon Press, 1913), 1:155-73; M. Gilbert, "4 Maccabees," in *Jewish Writings of the Second Temple Period,* ed. M. E. Stone (CLINT 2.2; Assen: Van Gorcum; Philadelphia: Fortress, 1984) 316-19; M. Hadas, *The Third and Fourth Books of Maccabees* (New York: Harper, 1953); J. W. van Henton, *The Maccabean Martyrs as Saviors of the Jewish People: A Study of 2 and 4 Maccabees* (Leiden: E. J. Brill, 1997); H.-J. Klauck, "Brotherly Love in Plutarch and in 4 Maccabees," in *Greeks, Romans, Christians,* ed. D. L. Balch, E. Ferguson and W. A. Meeks (Minneapolis: Fortress, 1990) 144-56; idem, *4 Makkabäerbuch* (Jüdische Schriften aus hellenistisch-römischer Zeit 3.6; Gütersloh: Gerd Mohn, 1989); A. O'Hagan, "The Martyr in the Fourth Book of Maccabees," *SBFLA* 24 (194) 94-120; P. D. Redditt, "The Concept of *Nomos* in Fourth Maccabees," *CBQ* 45 (1983) 249-70; R. Renehan, "The Greek Philosophic Background of Fourth Maccabees," *Rheinisches Museum für Philologie* 115 (1972) 223-38; D. Seely, *The Noble Death: Greco-Roman Martyrology and Paul's Concept of Salvation* (JSNTSup 28; Sheffield: Sheffield Acadmic Press, 1990); V. Tcherikover, *Hellenistic Civilization and the Jews* (New York: Atheneum, 1977 [1961]); R. B. Townshend, "The Fourth Book of Maccabees," in *The Apocrypha and Pseudepigrapha of the Old Testament in English,* ed. R. H. Charles (2 vols.; Oxford: Clarendon Press, 1913) 2:653-85; D. S. Williams, "3 Maccabees: A Defense of Diaspora Judaism?" *JSP* 13 (1995) 17-29.

D. A. deSilva

MACEDON. *See* GREECE AND MACEDON.

MAGICAL PAPYRI

The magical papyri are a collection of documents from Greco-Roman antiquity that have come to be recognized as important witnesses to the common folk beliefs and practices of the NT era. Their contents include incantations, rituals, formulas, spells, hymns and a variety of magical symbols, characters and names. The majority of these texts were written in Greek, but some were composed in Demotic, Coptic and even *Aramaic. Written on paper made from the papyrus reeds grown in the Nile region of Egypt, these texts are part of a broader set of witnesses attesting to magic. In addition to parchment manuscripts and the many literary references to magic, there are numerous curse tablets, amulets and a variety of magical items that provide further perspective on the practice of magic.

1. Description of the Papyri
2. The Date
3. The Nature and Significance of Magic
4. Jewish Influence
5. The Magical Papyri and the New Testament

1. Description of the Papyri.

The discovery of magical texts written on papyrus took place simultaneous to the discovery of many other papyrus documents, including NT fragments, in the early 1800s in Egypt. The largest and most significant find occurred in the 1820s in Thebes, where some villagers discovered a large number of papyrus rolls in a tomb. Bought by Giovanni Anastasi, the Anastasi collection was subsequently sold in 1828 to a number of libraries throughout Europe, including the Rijksmuseum in Leiden, the Bibliothèque Nationale in Paris and the British Museum. Since then, many additional discoveries have been made. There are now about 230 extant magical papyri.

The Great Paris Magical Papyrus (*P. Bibl. Nat. Suppl. Gr.* 574; *PGM* IV) has garnered the most attention. The longest of all the texts yet discovered, *PGM* IV is a papyrus codex containing 36 leaves written on both sides with a total of 3,274 lines. Each leaf measures roughly 30 x 13 centimeters (11.7 x 5 inches). The book appears to have been a collection of magical incantations and formulas belonging to one magician in ancient Egypt. Dating to the early fourth century A.D., the document contains a wide variety of magical traditions from much earlier sources.

The definitive critical edition of the magical papyri was compiled by K. Preisendanz in two volumes titled *Papyri Graecae Magicae: Die Griech-ischen Zauberpapyri,* published in 1928 and 1931 and now appearing in a second edition by A. Heinrichs (1973-74). References to the magical papyri are customarily cited by the abbreviation of Preisendanz's work (*PGM*). A projected third volume with indexes was scheduled to be printed, but the Teubner publishing house in Leipzig was destroyed in an Allied bombing raid in World War II. The few surviving galley proofs were never reset and printed. R. W. Daniel and F. Maltomini have begun a reedition of some *PGM* texts under the title *Supplementum Magicum.*

H.-D. Betz of the University of Chicago gathered a team of scholars to translate into English the Preisendanz texts, some Demotic papyri and a few other magical papyri appearing since Preisendanz's edition. *The Greek Magical Papyri in Translation* (*GMPT*) has become the indispensable source for NT students wanting easy access to the contents of these distinctive texts.

2. The Date.

Some NT scholars dismiss the relevance of the magical papyri for NT interpretation because the majority of the documents postdate the NT. But this response fails to recognize how crucial these documents are for understanding the worldview of the masses in the Greco-Roman empire. There are a number of good reasons for affirming the importance of these texts for NT interpretation.

First, a number of these documents can be dated to the first century A.D. and before. The earliest papyrus is known as the curse of Artemisia (*PGM* XL) and should be dated to the late fourth century B.C. (see Brashear 1995, 3413). It was incorrectly labeled as fourth century A.D. in the *GMPT.* A few magical papyri can be dated to the first century B.C. (*PGM* XX, CXVII and CXXII) and the first century A.D. (*PGM* XVI and CXI). A comparison of these texts with the others demonstrates a strong affinity of vocabulary, forms and rituals. The only observable difference is that there is a development of *voces magicae* (magical use of vowels) and *characteres* (magical symbols) in the later texts (Brashear 1995, 3414).

Second, unlike *Gnosticism, which did not emerge as a religious system until the second century, magic not only existed but also was widely practiced for centuries leading up to the time of Jesus and the apostles. There are numerous references to magical practices in a variety of literary sources. The existence of magical scrolls in the first century is corroborated in part by *Suetonius, who says that Augustus ordered two thousand magical scrolls to be burned in 13 B.C. (Suetonius *Augustus* 31.1; see Betz 1992, xli). In the mid-first century, *Pliny complained that "the fraudulent art has held sway throughout the world for many ages" (Pliny *Nat. Hist.* 30.1.1). He also speaks of "the greatness of its influence" in his day (Pliny *Nat. Hist.* 30.1.1), noting that "magic rose to such a height that even today it has sway over a great part of mankind" (Pliny *Nat. Hist.* 30.1.2; see also 30.4.13).

Third, many of the magical papyri are recipes for the creation of amulets and lead curse tablets. Archaeologists have unearthed more than fifteen hundred of these curse tablets, many dating as early as the fifth century B.C. Hundreds of amulets have also been discovered. These material witnesses have demonstrated that the kind of magic illustrated in the magical papyri was practiced all over the Mediterranean world throughout the *Hellenistic and Roman periods.

Finally, magicians prided themselves on the

antiquity of the traditions they used. Classicists agree that the collections of traditions found in the scrolls have been handed down for generations. G. Luck concludes, "they reflect much older ideas, and the doctrines and techniques they embody were probably developed in the late Hellenistic period. Many are considered to be copies of copies" (Luck, 16).

3. The Nature and Significance of Magic.
In the Roman era, magic was a set of rituals and practices that enabled people to coerce the gods and spirit powers to accomplish whatever they might ask. Fundamental to magic is an animistic worldview. Spirits are everywhere and involved in everything. Spirit beings are associated with the sun, moon, stars and planets; they populate the underworld; they are involved with animal life, plants and the elements. The magical papyri ostensibly provide the directions for managing the spirit realm as it touches on every facet of daily life.

F. Graf notes that "the practice of magic was omnipresent in classical antiquity" (Graf, 1). The magical papyri are particularly valuable in providing us with a window on popular beliefs and practices in the Greco-Roman period. They are the primary source documents of folk belief in the lives of people living at the time of Jesus and the apostles. A. D. Nock went so far as to emphasize the necessity of using the magical texts to interpret the religion of the common people. He writes, "We may and must make use of magical papyri in our attempt to reconstruct the religious attitude of the mass of mankind in the Roman world" (Nock, 34).

Many of the spells in the papyri prescribe rituals and formulas for protection from curses, malevolent spirits and disembodied souls (*biaiothanatoi*) that could cause harm. Such apotropaic, or protective, spells typically involved the performance of a ritual, the uttering of magical words and names of spirits or deities and often the creation of an amulet to be worn. *PGM* IV.1932-54 illustrates some of these elements:

> I call upon you, lord Helios, and your holy angels on this day, in this very hour: Preserve me, NN [insert name], for I am *thenor,* and you are holy angels, guardians of the *ardimalecha* and [nine lines of *voces magicae* follow], I beg you, lord Helios, hear me NN and grant me power over the spirit of this man who died a violent death [*biaiothanatos*], from whose tent I hold [this], so that I may keep him with me, [NN] as helper and avenger for whatever business I crave from him.

Related to these protective charms are spells designed to expel harmful spirits and for obtaining healing from various ailments, especially fevers and headaches. Spirits and sickness were seldom separated in the magical texts. Indeed, the spirits were believed to be behind the afflictions.

There are also numerous love spells of attraction in the magical papyri. In these the suppliant summons infernal powers to compel the person who is the object of desire to submit herself to the conjurer. A variety of other forms of maleficent magic fill the pages of the papyri. These consist primarily of curses against enemies (slanderers, thieves, economic competitors, adversaries at a trial and competitors in the games). A recipe for a lead curse tablet (*PGM* XXXVI.231-55) prescribes a ritual involving bat's blood and the body of a frog. Along with the performance of the ritual, the conjurer is instructed to inscribe this curse on the lead tablet: "Supreme angels, just as this frog drips with blood and dries up, so also will the body of him, NN whom NN bore, because I conjure you, who are in command of fire *maskelli maskello.*"

The magical papyri are also filled with recipes for the conjuring of a dream vision and the appearance of a spirit guide *(paredros).* The spirit assistant is said to come and reside with the one who accomplishes the bidding.

4. Jewish Influence.
Many Jews, in Palestine and throughout the Diaspora, participated in the magical arts. W. M. Brashear states that "the repute of Jewish magicians exceeded even that of Egyptian sorcerers" (Brashear 1995, 3426). In his study of Jewish magic, P. S. Alexander notes, "Magic flourished among the Jews despite strong and persistent condemnation by the religious authority" (Alexander, 342).

Two magical papyri written in Aramaic have recently been discovered in Egypt, one at Oxyrhynchus and another of unknown provenance (see Brashear 1995, 3428). It is likely that some of the recipes in the Greek magical papyri may have been created by Jews. Alexander lists more than a dozen texts from the *PGM* that were probably composed by a Jew based on the overwhelmingly Jewish content of the texts (Alexander, 357-59). The most noteworthy example is

PGM IV.3007-86, a charm to be used by someone possessed by demons (*see* Demonology). The demons are conjured by "the God of the Hebrews," and the text makes allusions to the exodus and other key figures and events in the history of Israel.

Of even greater significance is the pervasive influence of Jewish ideas on magic as it was practiced all over the Mediterranean world and is evidenced in the magical papyri. Egyptian sorcerers had great respect for the names of the supernatural powers in Judaism. References to Iao (for YHWH), Sabaoth, Adonai, *Moses, Solomon, Michael, Gabriel, angels, archangels, cherubim and seraphim abound in the texts.

Jewish magic continued into the following centuries and is evidenced in such documents as *Sefer ha-Razim, Harba de Mosheh, Testament of Solomon* and the magical texts found in the Cairo Genizah (see Schäfer and Shaked).

5. The Magical Papyri and the New Testament. The importance of the magical papyri for NT interpretation lies in their ability to illuminate folk belief. Alexander aptly states, "they open up areas of popular religion which are often inadequately represented in the official literary texts, and which are in consequence frequently ignored by historians. As an indicator of the spiritual atmosphere in which large sections of the populace lived—rich and poor, educated and ignorant—their importance can hardly be overestimated" (Alexander, 342).

M. Smith made extensive use of the magical papyri to develop the thesis that Jesus' contemporaries understood him to be a magician. This view has been rightly rejected because it fails to take into account the whole of what Jesus said and did, the essential Jewishness of Jesus' teaching and the many dissimilarities of method and worldview between Jesus and contemporary magicians.

A more productive approach has been to use the magical texts to illuminate passages in the Gospels that speak about demons and exorcism, even if for distinguishing Jesus from contemporary beliefs and practices. The magical texts give us insight into the worldview assumptions of people bringing demon-possessed persons to Jesus and the nature of cursing. The texts also help to explain specific lexical items such as *selēniazomai* (e.g., Mt 4:24; "to be moonstruck," but often understood to be an epileptic seizure). The moon goddess Selene figures prominently in the magical papyri and was believed to cause people to go mad.

In the book of Acts, the magical papyri illustrate the kind of texts burned by the *Ephesian believers (Acts 19:19). But the texts also illustrate many features of certain narratives explicitly involving exorcism and magic, such as Simon the Magus (Acts 9:9-25), Paul's encounter with Elymas the magician (Acts 13:6-12), the failed exorcism of Sceva and his sons (Acts 19:13-16), Paul's exorcism of the *slave girl with the spirit of divination (Acts 16:16-21), and many other passages. S. R. Garrett in particular has made good use of the magical papyri to illustrate some of these features.

Many aspects of the Pauline epistles (*see DPL*, Magic) and the rest of the NT (*see DLNTD*, Magic and Astrology) can be illuminated through the use of the magical papyri.

See also BELIAL, BELIAR, DEVIL, SATAN; DEMONOLOGY; RELIGION, GRECO-ROMAN; RELIGION, PERSONAL.

BIBLIOGRAPHY. P. S. Alexander, "Incantations and Books of Magic," in *The History of the Jewish People in the Age of Jesus Christ,* rev. and ed. G. Vermes, F. Millar and M. Goodman (3 vols.; Edinburgh: T & T Clark, 1986) 3.1:342-79; C. E. Arnold, *Ephesians: Power and Magic* (SNTSMS 63; Cambridge: Cambridge University Press, 1989; repr., Grand Rapids, MI: Baker, 1992); D. E. Aune, "Magic in Early Christianity," *ANRW* 2.23.2 (1980) 1507-57; H.-D. Betz, ed., *The Greek Magical Papyri in Translation,* 1: *Text* (2d ed.; Chicago: University of Chicago Press, 1992); idem, "Magic and Mystery in the Greek Magical Papyri," in *Hellenismus und Urchristentum: Gesammelte Aufsätze I* (Tübingen: Mohr Siebeck, 1990) 209-29; W. M. Brashear, "The Greek Magical Papyri: An Introduction and Survey; Annotated Bibliography (1928-1994)," *ANRW* 2.18.5(1995) 3380-3603; idem, *Magica Varia* (PB 25; Brussels: Fondation Égyptologique Reine Élisabeth, 1991); R. Daniel and F. Maltomini, *Supplementum Magicum* (2 vols; ARWAW; Sonderreihe, Papyrological Coloniensia 16.1, 16.2; Opladen: Westdeutscher Verlag, 1990, 1992); C. A. Faraone and D. Obbink, eds., *Magika Hiera: Ancient Greek Magic and Religion* (New York: Oxford University Press, 1991); J. G. Gager, *Curse Tablets and Binding Spells from the Ancient World* (New York: Oxford University Press, 1992); S. R. Garrett, *The Demise of the Devil: Magic and the Demonic in Luke's*

Writings (Minneapolis: Fortress, 1989); E. R. Goodenough, *Jewish Symbols in the Greco-Roman Period, 2: The Archaeological Evidence from the Diaspora* (BS 37; New York: Bollingen Foundation, 1953); F. Graf, *Magic in the Ancient World* (RA 10; Cambridge, MA: Harvard University Press, 1997); F. L. Griffith and H. Thompson, *The Leyden Papyrus: An Egyptian Magical Book* (New York: Dover, 1974); idem, *The Demotic Magical Papyrus of London and Leiden* (London: H. Grevel, 1904); H. G. Gundel, *Weltbild und Astrologie in den griechischen Zauberpapyri* (MBPAR 53; Munich: C. H. Beck, 1968); T. Hopfner, *Griechisch-Ägyptischer Offenbarungszauber* (SPP 21; Amsterdam: Hakkert, 1974 [1921]); G. Luck, *Arcana Mundi* (Baltimore: Johns Hopkins University Press, 1985); R. Merkelbach and M. Totti, *Abrasax: Ausgewählte Papyri Religiösen und Magischen Inhalts* (3 vols.; ARWAW; Sonderreihe, Papyrological Colonìensia 17.1, 17.2, 17.3; Opladen: Westdeutscher Verlag, 1990, 1991, 1992); M. W. Meyer and P. Mirecki, *Ancient Magic and Ritual Power* (RGRW 129; Leiden: E. J. Brill, 1995); M. W. Meyer and R. Smith, *Ancient Christian Magic: Coptic Texts of Ritual Power* (San Francisco: Harper, 1994); A. D. Nock, "Studies in the Greco-Roman Beliefs of the Empire," *Arthur Darby Nock: Essays on Religion and the Ancient World,* ed. Z. Stewart (Oxford: Clarendon Press, 1972) 32-48 (= *JHS* 48 [1928] 84-101); K. Preisendanz, *Papyri Graecae Magicae: Die Griechischen Zauberpapyri* (Leipzig: Teubner, 1: 1928; 2: 1931; 3: 1942 [2d rev. ed., A. Heinrichs, Stuttgart: Teubner 1973-74]); P. Schäfer and S. Shaked, *Magische Texte aus der Kairoer Geniza* (TSAJ 42; Tübingen: Mohr Siebeck, 1994) vol. 1; G. Twelftree, *Jesus the Exorcist: A Contribution to the Study of the Historical Jesus* (Peabody, MA: Hendrickson, 1993 [originally WUNT 2.54; Tübingen: Mohr Siebeck, 1993]).

C. E. Arnold

MANASSEH. *See* PRAYER OF MANASSEH.

MANUAL OF DISCIPLINE. *See* RULE OF THE COMMUNITY (1QS)

MANUMISSION. *See* FAMILY AND HOUSEHOLD; SLAVERY.

MANUSCRIPTS, GREEK NEW TESTAMENT

There are approximately fifty-five hundred manuscripts of the Greek NT, depending upon how they are counted. The number is larger than for any other ancient Greek or Latin author or book. This wealth of material for reconstructing the text of the NT, as well as tracing its development, also presents a number of problems due to the varied nature of these artifacts. Here is offered a discussion of the physical character of the manuscripts, a summary of the means by which these manuscripts are classified and then a list and description of several of the most important manuscripts.

1. The Physical Character and Description of the Manuscripts
2. Manuscript Types
3. List of the Most Important Manuscripts
4. Conclusion

1. The Physical Character and Description of the Manuscripts.

There are two major problems in describing the manuscripts of the NT (see Epp 1997, 64-67). These stem from the material on which they are written and the character of the writing on them. There is also the third problem of how pages of material were assembled.

NT manuscripts are written on three major kinds of materials: papyrus, parchment and paper (see Kenyon 1899 for description and plates; see Metzger 1981; Skeat 1995). Papyrus was a readily available writing material, made from cutting the papyrus plant into strips that were then laid together in two layers running vertically and horizontally, pressed and dried. The side with the strips of papyrus running horizontally (often referred to as the recto) was considered the preferable side for writing as opposed to that with the strips running vertically (verso). Parchment was made from animal skins, which were skinned, treated, dried and prepared for writing. The side without hair was preferred for writing, since even though the hair had been removed, pores and other imperfections disrupted the smooth surface of the hair side. However, history has shown that the ink adhered better to the hair side, so that often reading parchments on the side without hair requires deciphering surfaces where only a trace or shadow of ink is present. Once paper had been invented, it too became a surface on which to write manuscripts.

Several factors complicate this differentiation of materials. The first is that the term *papyrus* or *papyri* has come to be used for any material upon which nonpermanent writing was made.

Thus, for example, even though the series is referred to as the Oxyrhynchus Papyri (abbreviated P. Oxy.), many of the texts are written on parchment, as well as papyrus. There also was not a clear-cut time when papyrus gave way to the use of parchment and then to paper. Although papyrus appears to have been the earliest writing surface for NT manuscripts, there was significant overlap between papyrus and parchment, at least from the fourth to the eighth centuries. The same is true, although much later, for parchment and paper.

At the outset NT manuscripts were written in a continuous hand of capital letters, or majuscules (distinctions are sometimes made between capitals and majuscules, and majuscules and uncials, but these will not be discussed here). Occasionally accents or punctuation was indicated on manuscripts, and occasionally there was some word separation and even paragraph separation. Around the sixth century manuscripts began also to be used for liturgical purposes. The result was that further diacritical marks began to be added to the manuscript to indicate intonation patterns, besides the addition of various lectionary markings (the Gospel manuscripts also began to incorporate the Eusebian numbers as well). This liturgical marking was fully developed by the tenth century. From the ninth century, manuscripts also were produced in noncapital or minuscule letters in a connected or cursive fashion. Although the latest in date, the vast majority of NT manuscripts are written in minuscule letters.

In discussing NT manuscripts some confusion occurs regarding materials and handwriting due to the fact that all of the papyri are written in majuscule letters, although they are not categorized with the manuscripts written in majuscule hand on parchment. Similarly, majuscule or minuscule hands may be found on parchment or paper. At first NT manuscripts were probably written on scrolls, although it is disputed whether we have any manuscripts that were actually scrolls. We have some papyri that have writing of the NT text on only one side (see below), but these are thought to be opistographs, that is, manuscripts written on reused papyrus (Aland and Aland, 102). The rise of Christianity as a book religion was probably at least in part responsible for development of the book form, called the codex (see Roberts and Skeat; Skeat 1994). Rather than having a set of horizontally connected sheets of papyrus rolled into a scroll with writing on one side only, the codex bound gatherings of pages on the end and allowed for writing on both sides of the sheet (*see* Literacy and Book Culture).

In referring to particular manuscripts of the NT, however, there are also potential difficulties. One first must note that each of the manuscripts is given a form of identification according to the library in which it is held or the collection in which it is published. However, in the nineteenth century, when textual criticism began to develop, scholars who were editing critical texts of the NT realized that they needed more broadly encompassing schemes for classifying manuscripts. Although several different systems have been used, the one begun by the American/German scholar C. R. Gregory at around the turn of the nineteenth and twentieth centuries and continued by K. Aland is the one most widely used today (Aland and Aland, 72-75). Each manuscript is given a Gregory-Aland designation.

Manuscripts are classified in the Gregory-Aland scheme as belonging to one of four categories. The first is the papyri (designated with a P) (on the papyri, see Porter, forthcoming). The majority of papyri came to light as part of the vast discoveries of thousands and thousands of papyri in Egypt during the nineteenth and early twentieth centuries. There are now about 116 Greek NT papyri (although some of these are bilingual with Coptic). The first was published in 1868 by C. Tischendorf (Russian National Library Greek 258A; now known in NT textual criticism as P^{11}) and the latest, to our knowledge, in 2000 by Papathomas (P. Vindob. G 42417).

The majuscules, often referred to as uncials, are the next category. These are often associated with the codex form, although as noted above, virtually all NT manuscripts were part of codices. The majuscules, designated by a letter for the most well known, as well as a number beginning with 0, include the major codices, such as Codex Sinaiticus (א 01), discovered by Tischendorf in St. Catharine's monastery in Sinai; Codex Alexandrinus (A 02), housed in the British Library; Codex Vaticanus (B 03), long held in the Vatican library; and Codex Bezae (D 05), a bilingual Greek and Latin manuscript, as well as several hundred more (see below).

The third category is minuscules. This category, designated simply with a number (1, 2, 3, etc.), comprises a huge number of manuscripts written in a lower case and interconnected (cursive) hand. These manuscripts also are in codex or book form, and some of them are beautifully prepared. Their beauty includes not only their handwriting but also the decorations and illuminations that often are part of the presentation.

The fourth category of manuscripts is lectionaries. Lectionaries, designated with *l*, themselves can be written in majuscule or minuscule hands and are also in codex, or book, form. What distinguishes a lectionary is its division into lections for liturgical use.

Besides the several difficulties already noted in terms of inconsistencies regarding handwriting and materials, a number of other specific difficulties emerge. To qualify as a Greek NT manuscript in the first three categories (papyrus, majuscule and minuscule), the manuscript is to have continuous text of the NT on it. What distinguishes the lectionaries is their lack of continuous NT text; they have lections, that is, selections of text used for liturgical purposes, often indicated with division lines and other types of identification. This kind of distinction is not as simple as it first seems. One difficulty is that a number of the papyri have been categorized under the Gregory-Aland system as Greek NT papyri when there is serious question of whether they should be seen as having continuous text. For example, a number of these papyri are small fragments, making it very difficult to know if they had continuous text, even if there is text on the other side. They may not have had continuous text or may have been one small excerpt.

There have also been various questions raised about a number of the papyri: P^2, P^3 and P^{44} have been suspected as lectionaries; P^{12}, P^{13}, P^{18} and P^{22} are opistographs (P^{12} is also thought to be notes); P^{55}, P^{59}, P^{60}, P^{63}, P^{76} and P^{80} have been suspected of being commentaries, especially since a number of these manuscripts of John's Gospel have the word *hermeneia* on them (Metzger 1992, 266, disputes this interpretation); P^7 has been suspected of being a patristic rendition, P^{10} of being a writing exercise, P^{25} of being from the *Diatessaron*, P^{42} of being a song, P^{43} and P^{62} of being merely selections and P^{50} and P^{78} of being talismans (see Aland and Aland, 102, 85).

A similar kind of situation applies to some majuscules, where there is commentary with the biblical text, in some cases interspersed and breaking up its continuousness (e.g., K 018; X 033; 075). This means that roughly one-fifth of the designated Greek NT papyri are possibly misclassified, as well as some majuscules. It also means that the categorization system may have been unduly harsh on those labeled lectionaries, possibly because they provided larger sections than mere fragments.

Some other manuscripts have been excluded from classification as NT manuscripts but might have some bearing on the textual question. These include, for example, the apocryphal Gospel manuscripts (*see* Apocryphal Gospels). Some recent scholars have wanted to elevate the status of some of these manuscripts (e.g., the *Gospel of Thomas* found in Greek fragments P. Oxy. 1, 654, 655; P. Egerton 2; portions of the *Gospel of Peter* P. Cair. 10759) to priority over, if not equality with, the Greek NT manuscripts in terms of being the earliest Christian documents. Their priority is seriously questioned by other scholars, most of them seeing the apocryphal Gospels, even the earliest ones, as probably derived from the canonical Gospels.

Nevertheless, such apocryphal Gospel manuscripts may have a potentially important role to play in NT textual criticism. According to the classification schemes used presently, there is no place for them to fit within such a scheme, but one also runs the risk of losing sight of important papyri if the ones mentioned above are demoted and have their Gregory-Aland number revoked. As a result, it has been suggested that it might be wise to introduce a layered classificatory system, in which those manuscripts that clearly are continuous Greek NT manuscripts are included in one category but that other related manuscripts of importance—such as some of the problematic papyri noted above or the apocryphal Gospels—are classified in a second category, so that their importance is not overlooked (Porter, forthcoming; cf. also the scheme found in van Haelst).

2. Manuscript Types.

There have been a number of systems for classification of NT manuscript types. One of the most enduring has been that connected with the Majority Text. Those who subscribe to the Majority Text essentially believe that the text of the Greek NT should follow that of the majority of the manuscripts. Of the approximately fifty-five hundred extant Greek NT manuscripts, approximately 80 percent (or more) of them have common features. The Textus Receptus, a label given to an edition of Erasmus's Greek NT, follows a limited number of manuscripts that fall within this category of the majority of manuscripts (see Wallace, 297-320, in Ehrman and Holmes).

Most textual critics today do not follow the Majority Text but instead recognize a number of different manuscript types (see Metzger 1992 for a history of discussion). In the eighteenth century J. J. Griesbach was instrumental in formulating principles that led to the development of modern textual criticism. In the course of his investigation of the text and transmission of the Greek NT, he grouped manuscripts into a number of different categories. He at one time thought there were five or six different groups but eventually confined himself to three: the Alexandrian, Western and Byzantine types. Griesbach's work was instrumental in both breaking the hold of the Textus Receptus on NT textual criticism (the Textus Receptus fit within his Byzantine group, which he believed was a later combination of the Alexandrian and the Western) and led to further differentiations of manuscript types.

These developments included a number of important events. One was the compiling of comprehensive lists of Greek NT manuscripts. The first to do so was J. M. A. Scholz, and this work is continued in the Gregory-Aland system (see above). There was also much attention paid to tracing the origins and lines of developments of the manuscripts. Sometimes these origins were associated with particular people and sometimes with places. For example, the Alexandrian manuscript tradition has been associated with Origen, who was said to have taken manuscripts of this type with him from Alexandria. B. H. Streeter (27-50) went the furthest, perhaps, in terms of locating manuscripts with places, in his developing a theory of local texts. Related to this was also much work, in the spirit of classical textual criticism, given to tracing the genealogical relationships (hence reference to families of manuscripts) that existed among texts, a method that persists in classical textual criticism (West) and was used in an earlier period of NT textual criticism (e.g., Kenyon, Westcott and Hort, among others; see Colwell, 63-84) but is not as widely relied upon today.

The most important and lasting classification scheme is that developed by B. F. Westcott and F. J. A. Hort in 1881 (see Metzger 1992, 132-35). Westcott and Hort differentiated four textual types: the Neutral, the Alexandrian, the Western and the Syrian. The Syrian, the latest of the four, is a conflation of the other textual types, made to harmonize the textual tradition. The Textus Receptus followed this tradition and is found in the Gospel portion of Codex Alexandrinus (A 02). The Western text, dated very early, probably in the second century, was an ancient and widespread textual type. This textual type is best known through the bilingual (Greek and Latin) Codex Bezae (D 05). The Alexandrian text, apparently under the influence of Alexandrian literary scholarship, reveals the greatest philological precision (*see* Alexandrian Scholarship). The Neutral text is the textual type that, at least ostensibly, has raised the most questions regarding Westcott and Hort's method.

According to Westcott and Hort, the Neutral text came closest to the original manuscripts and hence was the one freest from corruption in transmission. This textual type is represented by Codex Sinaiticus (א 01) and Codex Vaticanus (B 03). Hence, in their edition, they usually follow these two manuscripts, except in a few places where they note otherwise. These exceptional places they have labeled "Western noninterpolations," recognizing that the Western text preserves an earlier reading. It is worth noting, however, that although most textual critics reject the notion of the Neutral text, the standard editions used today, the Nestle-Aland and the United Bible Societies' Greek New Testament, show surprisingly few deviances from the Westcott and Hort edition, especially considering the fact that only one of the papyri had been discovered and published before the publication of the Westcott and Hort edition in 1881. Hence these editions retain the Neutral text in fact if not in principle (Epp, 13-14, in Ehrman and Holmes).

Most textual critics today would recognize three, and possibly four, textual types (see Metzger 1992, 213-16; Epp 1989, 97-100). These are the Alexandrian, the Western, the Byzantine and possibly the Caesarean text types. The Alexandrian text type is still considered by most textual critics to be the most reliable. Discovery of several papyri that have been dated to the late second or early third centuries have confirmed the earliness of this manuscript tradition, which is thought to go back to the early second century. B. M. Metzger (1992, 216) notes that what is called the proto-Alexandrian form of this text has generally shorter readings and does not have the characteristics of later philological improvement that characterize some later Alexandrian texts. The highly regarded place of the Alexandrian text and the dependence of the standard modern editions of the Greek NT upon it have led some textual critics to the belief that the text currently in use is virtually the same as the original. Many would find this to be an overly optimistic position, however.

The second text type is the Western. The Western text has been the subject of much discussion, especially in terms of its widely divergent text for the book of Acts. The tendency of this text toward longer readings has led to much speculation about its origin. Some have thought that it was the result of deliberate editing of an earlier text. However, most scholars today do not see the necessary cohesiveness in the text to commend such a conclusion and believe that it was the result of growth in the manuscript tradition. The Western text did not fare well in the hands of Westcott and Hort, but many textual critics today would give it much higher recognition as preserving original readings in a number of instances. The text appears to have been known fairly early over a wide area of the Mediterranean world, including the East, from the second century on (especially in the church fathers). Some have even posited that the Western version of Acts is at least as original as the one found in the Alexandrian tradition.

The third text type, the Caesarean, earlier in the twentieth century was considered to be a distinct text type. It was often identified with Origen, who had brought it from Egypt where it originated, to Caesarea and then to Jerusalem. The Caesarean text was recognized as having a mixture of Western and Alexandrian readings. Because of this diverse mixture, the text as a type was seen as the least homogeneous. As a result, recent textual criticism has wanted to distance itself even further from seeing this as a distinctive textual type, although without losing sight of the important readings to be found in manuscripts previously put in this category, and referring to them as pre-Caesarean (see Metzger 1992, 290).

The final text type is the Byzantine. This text, called the Syrian by Westcott and Hort and also referred to as the Koine, encompasses the vast majority of manuscripts, including a number of majuscules, and most minuscules. As mentioned above, it is thought that more than 80 percent of Greek NT manuscripts are of this type, and it is especially found in late manuscripts. Some textual critics have attempted to revive the fortunes of the Byzantine text through reconsidering the quality of its witness (Sturz) or editing and disseminating the Majority Text according to more refined text-critical principles than have sometimes been used in advocacy of this kind of text (Hodges and Farstad).

It is probably fair to say that most textual critics today would recognize far more interpenetration between these text types than would some earlier textual critics. The tendency is far less to try to categorize these manuscripts according to location or genealogy and much more to have them represent a tradition of transmission, regardless of how that transmission took place. Nevertheless, the Alexandrian text type, especially as it is found in the two major codices, Sinaiticus and Vaticanus, and confirmed by discovery of several major papyri, including P^{66} and P^{75}, continues to be relied upon in NT textual criticism.

3. List of the Most Important Manuscripts. This list cannot discuss all or even a substantial portion of the extant NT Greek manuscripts. However, a number of these manuscripts merit brief mention because of their importance in the history of discussion (see esp. Metzger 1992; Kenyon 1975; Aland and Aland, where much of the following information is found).

3.1. Papyri. The papyri have been widely discussed in NT textual criticism, even if they have not been fully appreciated in the task of establishing the Greek text commonly used (see Epp 1989, 103-6). The following are a number that merit discussion (see Epp, 3-21, in Ehrman and Holmes).

P^4, P^{64}, P^{67}. Some but not all papyrologists would put these three separately numbered and separately housed fragments together, and virtually all put P^{64} and P^{67} together (see Comfort, 43-54). P^4 is housed in the National Library in Paris, P^{64} is housed in Magdalen College in Oxford and P^{67} is in Barcelona. P^4 contains parts of Luke, and P^{64} and P^{67} consist of parts of Matthew. P^{64} and P^{67} were once used in the ancient world to bind together a manuscript of *Philo. Recently C. P. Thiede has argued that the Magdalen papyrus should be dated possibly to

the mid to late first century (see Thiede, 29-42; cf. Thiede, 55-57). His view has not been followed by most scholars (see Head; Skeat 1997).

P^{11}. This papyrus from the seventh century has parts of 1 Corinthians. Its significance lies in the fact that it was the first NT Greek papyrus to be published, by Tischendorf in 1868. It is housed in St. Petersburg in the Russian National Library.

P^{45}. Chester Beatty I consists of parts of thirty leaves of a papyrus codex. The manuscript, apart from one portion of several fragments in the Vienna collection, is housed in Dublin. Metzger (1992, 37) describes it as being of the Caesarean type for Mark and between the Alexandrian and Western for Matthew, Luke and John, whereas Acts is Alexandrian. The manuscript has been dated to the early third century and is one of the largest Gospels papyri extant.

P^{46}. Chester Beatty II consists of eighty-six leaves of the Pauline letters, beginning at Romans 5 and continuing to 1 Thessalonians, with Hebrews after Romans and Ephesians before Galatians. This manuscript has been variously dated, but the general scholarly opinion is that it is to be dated to around A.D. 200, with some scholars wanting to date it earlier. The most controversial aspect of this papyrus codex is whether it ever contained the Pastoral Epistles. Many scholars have noted the fact that this codex does not have the Pastoral Epistles and appears never to have done so, since the composition of the codex gives a fairly clear idea of how many pages it originally included. However, J. Duff has argued that there is a chance the manuscript did have space for the Pastoral Epistles, since the scribe's writing gets more compact as the manuscript proceeds. There is also the possibility that extra pages were added, a feature that the codex form allowed for. About two-thirds of the leaves of this papyrus are in Dublin, with the rest in the University of Michigan collection.

P^{52}. This papyrus in the John Rylands Library in Manchester is generally thought to be the earliest papyrus fragment of the Greek NT, being dated by most papyrologists to somewhere in the first half of the second century (see on P^4). This is a fragment from John's Gospel, the finding of which has implications for the dating and provenance of that Gospel. It makes it difficult to accept a date much later than the end of the first century, since the Gospel had to be transmitted from its place of authorship, thought by many scholars to be Ephesus in Asia Minor, to Egypt.

P^{66}. This number is given to a number of manuscripts. The largest part is the Bodmer Papyrus II located in Cologny-Geneva, with other portions housed as part of the Chester Beatty collection. In all there are parts of about 150 pages. This is an important manuscript because it contains a large portion of John's Gospel and has been dated to around A.D. 200. One of the noteworthy features of this manuscript is the abundance of correction, apparently by the scribe who wrote it out. This manuscript has a mixture of Alexandrian and Western readings.

P^{75}. This papyrus manuscript is also housed in the Bodmer collection in Cologny-Geneva and is known as Bodmer Papyrus XIV, XV. This manuscript has been dated from the late second to the early third centuries, and its 102 pages contain large portions of Luke and John. The dating may make it the earliest manuscript of Luke's Gospel (cf. P^{45}). This manuscript follows the Alexandrian textual tradition.

There are many other papyri worth mentioning. Already mentioned above are some that have peculiarities that make them questionable for inclusion in this category. There are also new papyri being published, and these deserve attention as well.

3.2. Majuscule Codices. The majuscule codices are impressive documents, many of them having been in the possession of important libraries, nations or even individuals for a number of years—sometimes for so many years that their origins before then are unknown. They were obviously valued both for their intrinsic worth as documents but also often for their beauty (see Parker, 22-42, in Ehrman and Holmes).

Codex Sinaiticus (א 01). This manuscript is a beautifully written and prepared codex from the fourth century, with a combination of Alexandrian and Western readings. It contains a portion of the OT and all of the NT, plus the *Epistle of Barnabas* and parts of the *Shepherd of Hermas.* Much could be said about Codex Sinaiticus, since its history has been filled with intrigue and adventure. It was discovered in the mid-nineteenth century by Tischendorf at St. Catharine's Monastery on Mt. Sinai. His story was that he saved it from being burned by the monks for heating. When he had a chance to examine the manuscript, he realized its significance. The manuscript apparently at one time included the complete Bible in Greek, but some of the pages are now missing (according to Tischendorf's story, the monks told him they had already burned some pages—pages from the first half of the OT are the ones that are most noticeably missing). Nevertheless, the manuscript still preserves a complete Greek NT, the only complete majuscule NT.

It took Tischendorf several trips back to the monastery and enlisting the patronage of the czar of Russia before he was able to locate the entire manuscript. According to Tischendorf, he was able to persuade the monks to make a gift of the manuscript to the czar, who then paid for it to be published and rewarded the monks. Others contend, however, that Tischendorf in some way tricked the monks into handing over the manuscript, possibly with the promise of returning it. The reception of the payment by the monastery, a supposed receipt from Tischendorf only appearing in 1964, and the general behavior and character of Tischendorf make it difficult to accept the revisionist view of what transpired. In any event, the Soviet Union sold the manuscript to the British Museum in 1933 for one hundred thousand pounds (see Tischendorf; Bell). The entire manuscript of 199 leaves, apart from 43 leaves that Tischendorf had secured on his first visit and that are in the Leipzig University library and 3 leaves still in Leningrad, is now on display in the British Museum. It has been thought by some that Sinaiticus was one of the fifty copies of the Bible commissioned by Constantine for Eusebius to produce in Caesarea.

Codex Alexandrinus (A 02). This beautiful manuscript from the fifth century has been in British possession since the seventeenth century and the reign of King Charles I. Its history before that time is unknown. The manuscript contains most of the OT and much of the NT. In the NT, the manuscript in the Gospels follows the Byzantine text but for Acts, the Pauline letters, and the rest of the NT it follows the Alexandrian text.

Codex Vaticanus (B 03). This fourth-century manuscript is an important Alexandrian text, although its beauty as a majuscule codex was ruined when a later scribe retraced all the letters. It also lacks any of the ornamentation that is often found on codex manuscripts. This has led some to suspect that this manuscript was also one of the fifty commissioned by Constantine, but that it was rejected. In any event, this manuscript has been in the possession of the Vatican Library since at least the fifteenth century. The manuscript contained the entire Bible at one time but now is missing some of Genesis, the Psalms and several books in the NT (some of Hebrews, the Pastoral Epistles, Philemon and Revelation).

Codex Ephraemi (C 04). This fifth-century manuscript has an interesting history that makes it important to note. In the twelfth century this manuscript was erased, and some of Ephraem's (Ephraem the Syrian) sermons were copied onto it, therefore making it a palimpsest. A number of scholars tried to decipher the writing underneath, but it was not until Tischendorf attempted the task that reasonable success was attained (see Tischendorf). Since that time, further work has been done on deciphering the text and correcting Tischendorf's work.

Codex Bezae, or Cantabrigiensis (D 05). This fifth- or sixth-century manuscript contains most of the four Gospels and Acts and a small fragment of 3 John, with the Gospels in the order Matthew, John, Luke and Mark. It is a bilingual manuscript, written in both Greek and Latin (Greek text on the verso), with the writing in cola, or sense units, rather than continuous uninterrupted lettering. This manuscript was given to the library of the University of Cambridge in 1581 by Theodore Beza, Calvin's successor in Geneva. It is interesting to note that although Beza possessed this text, he does not appear to have used it in his own text-critical work. The text of this manuscript is the best representative of the Western tradition (see above).

Purple Codex (N 022). This sixth-century manuscript, called *Purpureus Petropolitanus,* has silver lettering on purple parchment, with gold ink used for the *nomina sacra* (or sacred names, reduced forms of special words used by scribes in copying manuscripts). The result is a striking and beautiful manuscript. Portions of it are now located in a number of different libraries, including the Russian National Library in St. Petersburg, Patmos, the Vatican Library, the British Museum, the Austrian National Library and individual sheets in a number of other places. Roughly half of the original leaves are now extant, of what was a codex with the four Gospels. The text type is Byzantine.

Many other majuscule codices of importance

could be noted here. Most standard textual-criticism volumes have a description of most of these, including Metzger (1992), Kenyon (1975) and Aland and Aland.

*3.3. **Minuscules.*** As noted above, there are many minuscule manuscripts. There is differing opinion among textual critics on their value for textual criticism of the Greek NT. One factor seems to be clear: regardless of how much value one places on them for NT textual criticism, as a whole they have been neglected as manuscripts in their own right (see Aland and Wachtel, 43-60, in Ehrman and Holmes). For the purposes of NT textual criticism, some scholars have noticed that a number of minuscules have a close relationship and so they have put them together into families.

Family 1. This family consists of four minuscules from the twelfth to the fourteenth centuries. They seem to reflect a common text that some have thought could go back to Caesarea in the third and fourth centuries.

Family 13. Originally Family 13 consisted of four medieval minuscule manuscripts, but since then this group, known as the Ferrar group after its first identifier, has been expanded to about a dozen minuscules, copied between the eleventh and fifteenth centuries.

*3.4. **Lectionaries.*** Many lectionaries could be discussed. Apart from the early lectionaries, dated to the fourth to sixth centuries (*l*1604, *l*1403, *l*1276, *l*1347, *l*1354), most of them are thought to be significantly later, around the eighth to eleventh centuries, and hence not as valuable in the text-critical endeavor (see Osburn, 61-74, in Ehrman and Holmes). One lectionary (*l*1403), dated to the fifth century, is the second oldest. Now housed in the Austrian National Library, it consists of excerpts from the four Gospels. It is a bilingual lectionary, with Greek lections followed by Coptic lections.

4. Conclusion.

NT textual criticism is fortunate to have an abundance of materials. The abundance of materials also raises a number of questions regarding the data and handling of them. There is not only the difficulty caused by the sheer abundance of evidence, but also a variety of classificatory and methodological problems must be confronted. One of these is the tendency to rely upon the standard critical editions in circulation today, without realizing the manuscript traditions that go into their makeup. As noted above, the two major codices, Sinaiticus and Vaticanus, are the basis of these modern editions. Even though more than one hundred papyri have been published since Westcott and Hort first published their edition of the Greek NT, these papyri have not apparently influenced the modern textual tradition as much as some scholars may have thought they should. A second area is to be aware of the peculiarities of a given manuscript, rather than simply classifying it according to its type as designated above. There is a tendency in textual criticism to put into fixed categories the various manuscripts and then to use these categorizations in a determinative way for making text-critical judgments. As a result, the peculiarities of the given manuscript can be overlooked.

See also INSCRIPTIONS AND PAPYRI: GRECO-ROMAN; LITERACY AND BOOK CULTURE; NEW TESTAMENT VERSIONS, ANCIENT; OLD TESTAMENT VERSIONS, ANCIENT; TEXTUAL CRITICISM.

BIBLIOGRAPHY. K. Aland and B. Aland, *The Text of the New Testament* (2d ed.; Grand Rapids, MI: Eerdmans, 1989); H. I. Bell, *The Codex Sinaiticus and the Codex Alexandrinus,* ed. T. C. Skeat (London: British Museum Publications, 1955); E. C. Colwell, *Studies in Methodology in Textual Criticism of the New Testament* (NTTS 9; Leiden: E. J. Brill, 1969); P. W. Comfort, "Exploring the Common Identification of Three New Testament Manuscripts: P^4, P^{64} and P^{67}," *TynB* 46.1 (1995) 43-54; J. Duff, "P^{46} and the Pastorals: A Misleading Consensus?" *NTS* 44 (1998) 578-90; B. D. Ehrman and M. W. Holmes, eds., *The Text of the New Testament in Contemporary Research: Essays on the Status Quaestionis* (Grand Rapids, MI: Eerdmans, 1995); E. J. Epp, "Textual Criticism," in *The New Testament and its Modern Interpreters,* ed. E. J. Epp and G. W. MacRae (Atlanta: Scholars Press, 1989) 75-126; idem, "Textual Criticism in the Exegesis of the New Testament, with an Excursus on Canon," in *Handbook to Exegesis of the New Testament,* ed. S. E. Porter (NTTS 25; Leiden: E. J. Brill, 1997) 45-98; J. van Haelst, *Catalogue des Papyrus Littéraires Juifs et Chrétiens* (Université de Paris IV Paris-Sorbonne Série "Papyrologie" 1; Paris: Sorbonne, 1976); P. M. Head, "The Date of the Magdalen Papyrus of Matthew (*P. Magd. Gr.* 17 = P^{64}): A Response to C. P. Thiede," *TynB* 46.2 (1995) 251-85; Z. C. Hodges and A. L. Farstad, eds., *The Greek New Testament According to the Majority Text* (2d ed.;

Nashville: Nelson, 1985); F. G. Kenyon, *The Paleography of Greek Papyri* (Oxford: Clarendon Press, 1899); idem, *The Text of the Greek Bible* (3d ed.; London: Duckworth, 1975); B. M. Metzger, *Manuscripts of the Greek Bible: An Introduction to Greek Paleography* (New York: Oxford University Press, 1981); idem, *The Text of the New Testament: Its Transmission, Corruption and Restoration* (3d ed.; New York: Oxford University Press, 1992); A. Papathomas, "A New Testimony to the Letter to the Hebrews," *JGRCJ* 1 (2000) 18-24; S. E. Porter, "The Greek Apocryphal Gospels Papyri: The Need for a Critical Edition," *Akten des 21. Internationalen Papyrologenkongresses Berlin, 13.-19.8.1995,* ed. B. Kramer et al. (2 vols.; APB 3; Stuttgart and Leipzig: Teubner, 1997) 2:795-803; idem, "Why So Many Holes in the Papyrological Evidence for the Greek New Testament?" in *The Bible as Book: The Transmission of the Greek Text,* ed. K. van Kampen and S. McKendrick (London: British Library Publications; Grand Haven, MI: Scriptorium, forthcoming); C. H. Roberts and T. C. Skeat, *The Birth of the Codex* (London: Oxford University Press, 1983); T. C. Skeat, "The Oldest Manuscript of the Four Gospels?" *NTS* 43 (1997) 1-34; idem, "The Origin of the Christian Codex," *ZPE* 102 (1994) 263-68; idem, "Was Papyrus Regarded as 'Cheap' or 'Expensive' in the Ancient World?" *Aegyptus* 75 (1995) 75-93; B. H. Streeter, *The Four Gospels: A Study of Origins* (London: Macmillan, 1930); H. A. Sturz, *The Byzantine Text-Type and New Testament Textual Criticism* (Nashville: Nelson, 1984); C. P. Thiede, "Notes on P^{4} = Bibliothèque Nationale Paris, Supplementum Graece 1120/5," *TynB* 46.1 (1995) 55-58; idem, "Papyrus Magdalen Greek 17 (Gregory-Aland P^{64}): A Reappraisal," *TynB* 46.1 (1995) 29-42; C. Tischendorf, *Codex Sinaiticus: The Ancient Biblical Manuscript Now in the British Museum* (London: Lutterworth, n.d.); M. L. West, *Textual Criticism and Editorial Technique* (Stuttgart: Teubner, 1973); B. F. Westcott and F. J. A. Hort, *The New Testament in the Original Greek* (2 vols.; Cambridge: Macmillan, 1881).

S. E. Porter

MANUSCRIPTS, GREEK OLD TESTAMENT

Manuscripts for establishing the text of the Greek OT (Septuagint) continue to increase in number, especially due to papyrological finds in Egypt and in the Judean Desert. The major categories of Greek manuscripts for the Greek OT include papyri (whether actually written on papyrus or leather, etc.), majuscule codices and minuscules (see Jellicoe, 175-242; Tov 1992, 137-39; Kenyon, 13-53, for the following information). There are also a limited number of manuscripts that contain later versions of the Greek OT.

Discoveries and publication of papyri from Egypt and more recently from the Judean Desert have increased the number of Greek manuscripts to be used in establishing the text of the Greek OT. For years the earliest manuscript was considered P. Rylands Greek 458, a fragment of Deuteronomy dated to the second century B.C., followed by P. Fouad 266, possibly also a second-century B.C. fragment of Deuteronomy. With the publication of several fragments of the Greek OT from the Judean Desert, there are a number of other early fragments to consider, some of which are possibly to be dated to the second century B.C., the latest date being the first century A.D. These include 4QLXXLev^{a}, 4QLXXLev^{b}, 4QLXXNum, 4QLXXDeut, 7QLXXExod, 7QLXXEpJer, and possibly others of the Greek fragments found in Cave 7, as well as pap4QparExod, a Greek paraphrase of Exodus (Fitzmyer). These manuscripts are important for textual criticism because some seem to attest various versions of the Greek Bible, and they are also significant for establishing the history and development of the text of the Greek OT, including the use of the Greek OT at *Qumran. A very important manuscript for textual criticism is 8ḤevXIIgr, the so-called Minor Prophets Scroll found in Naḥal Ḥever (Tov 1990), dated to around the turn of the era, and probably associated with the later Bar Kokhba revolt (A.D. 132-135) and having significance regarding the multilingual context of the first and second centuries A.D. (Porter; Pearson). This document, which has fragments of Jonah, Micah, Nahum, Habakkuk, Zephaniah and Zechariah, seems to attest to a proto-Masoretic form of the Minor Prophets in use at this time, often called the *kaige*-Theodotion recension. Papyrus manuscripts of the Greek OT continue to be published, and many of these are of importance, although some are of later date. Important among these are: P. Oxy. 3522, a second-century fragment of Job; Berlin Staatsbibliothek Gr. fol. 66 I, II, with fragments of Genesis from the third century; the Freer Greek MS V, with the Minor Prophets, also from the third century; and the Chester Beatty Papyri IV, V, VI, VII, VIII, IX, X, XI, with portions of Genesis, Numbers, Deuteronomy, Isaiah, Jeremiah, Daniel, Esther and Ecclesiasticus, and dating to the second to fourth centuries.

Before the discovery and publication of the papyri noted above, textual criticism of the Greek OT was dependent for the most part on the major majuscule codex manuscripts. The most important of these is Codex Vaticanus (fourth century A.D.), which is nearly complete for the Septuagint (it lacks much of Genesis and some of Psalms), and seems to reflect a fairly early Alexandrian text type, although it has some intrusions reflective of Origen's *Hexapla*. Also of importance for its text type is Codex Sinaiticus (fourth century A.D.), although this manuscript now only contains about one-third of the OT and is thought to reflect some later textual developments. There is controversy over the origins and relations of these manuscripts, both in terms of where they were written (Alexandria or Caesarea as two of the fifty manuscripts produced by Eusebius for Constantine) and why Vaticanus is in the condition it is (perhaps unfinished, and written over by a later scribe; see Skeat). Next in importance is Codex Alexandrinus (fifth century A.D.), a nearly complete manuscript (it only lacks about ten leaves), but one that is thought to reflect later translational influences, such as from the *Hexapla*. There are a number of other majuscule codices that also are important for textual criticism, but they are later than these, and hence of relatively less importance. These three major codices, especially Codex Vaticanus, are the ones that have formed the basis for the major critical editions of the Greek OT, such as those of Swete, Rahlfs and Brooke-McLean Thackeray.

The number of minuscule manuscripts (or portions) of the Greek OT is large, perhaps totaling 2,000. However, although there may be occasional important readings found in these minuscules, for the most part they are of tertiary importance in textual criticism, due to their late date and the high proportion that reflect later versions, such as the Hexaplaric and Lucianic. The Alexandrian minuscules are relatively few.

The textual evidence for later versions of the Greek OT is relatively sparce. For example, Aquila's version must be reconstructed from marginalia in a few tenth-century Hexaplaric manuscripts and from citations in the church fathers. Theodotion's version is found complete in a tenth-century Vatican minuscule, partially in a third-century manuscript (Chester Beatty IX, X), as well as in Syriac translation and some readings in other manuscripts. Symmachus's translation is the least well attested, being found only in fragmentary form in the church fathers.

See also HEBREW BIBLE; MANUSCRIPTS, GREEK NEW TESTAMENT; OLD TESTAMENT VERSIONS, ANCIENT; SEPTUAGINT/GREEK OLD TESTAMENT.

BIBLIOGRAPHY. J. A. Fitzmyer, *The Dead Sea Scrolls: Major Publications and Tools for Study* (SBLRBS 20; Atlanta: Scholars Press, 1990); S. Jellicoe, *The Septuagint and Modern Study* (Oxford: Clarendon Press, 1968); F. G. Kenyon, *The Text of the Greek Bible*, rev. A. W. Adams (3d ed.; London: Duckworth, 1975); B. Pearson, "The Book of the Twelve, Aqiba's Messianic Interpretations, and the Refuge Caves of the Second Jewish War," in *The Scrolls and the Scriptures: Qumran Fifty Years After*, ed. S. E. Porter and C. A. Evans (JSPSup 26; RILP 3; Sheffield: Sheffield Academic Press, 1997) 221-39; S. E. Porter, "The Greek Papyri of the Judaean Desert and the World of the Roman East," in *The Scrolls and the Scriptures: Qumran Fifty Years After*, ed. S. E. Porter and C. A. Evans (JSPSup 26; RILP 3; Sheffield: Sheffield Academic Press, 1997) 293-316; T. Skeat, "The Codex Sinaiticus, the Codex Vaticanus, and Constantine," *JTS* 50 (1999) 583-625; E. Tov, *The Greek Minor Prophets Scroll from Nahal Hever (8HevXIIgr)* (DJD 8; Oxford: Clarendon Press, 1990); idem, *Textual Criticism of the Hebrew Bible* (Minneapolis: Fortress; Assen/Maastricht: Van Gorcum, 1992).

S. E. Porter

MARIA THE JEWISH ALCHEMIST

This long-neglected author is important in more than one respect. First, Maria is the first nonfictitious alchemist of the Western world; and second, she is the first Jewish woman in history we know to have written and published under her own name. Although her works are lost, extensive quotations and excerpts from them have been preserved in the works of later Greco-Roman alchemists, most notably Zosimus of Panopolis (Egypt, c. A.D. 300), who held her in the highest esteem. It is impossible to say exactly when and where she lived, but Egypt and the period from the first century B.C. until the second century A.D. are reasonable guesses.

We know of the existence of other Jewish alchemists in Greco-Roman Egypt, but only Maria rose to great fame among alchemists of late antiquity and the Middle Ages, which is primarily due to her invention of several types of ovens and boiling and distilling devices made of metal, clay and glass, and to her extraordinary skill. Her most famous invention (or at least description) is that of the *balneum Mariae,* a water bath consisting of a double vessel, of which the outer one is filled with water while the inner vessel contains the substance that must be heated to a moderate degree (the French expression *au bain Marie* derives from it).

Zosimus usually refers to her as Maria but sometimes as Maria Hebraia or even the divine Maria (others call her the Hebrew prophetess). Her Jewishness is also apparent from the fact that she says that the Jews are the chosen people and that only they, not the Gentiles, should know the deepest alchemical secrets. She is reported to have told others not to touch the philosophers' stone with their hands, "since you are not of our race, you are not of the race of Abraham." Maria claims that alchemical procedures were revealed directly to her by God, thus laying the foundation for a long tradition of alchemical esotericism in which Jews played such a significant role. From the quotations by later authors Maria appears as an erudite person, well versed in the traditions and lore of her science (she is the first to mention hydrochloric acid), for whom alchemy was more than an attempt at transmuting base metals into gold. It was a comprehensive religious worldview that assumed an essential unity underlying all of nature and in which the God of Israel acted as guarantor of this unity. In subsequent centuries, Maria became identified with Miriam (= Maria), the sister of Moses.

See also WOMEN IN GRECO-ROMAN WORLD AND JUDAISM.

BIBLIOGRAPHY. M. Berthelot and C. E. Ruelle, *Collection des Anciens Alchimistes Grecs* (Osnabrück: Otto Zeller, 1967 [= the Paris 1888 ed.]) vols. 2-3, index *s.v.*; M. Mertens, *Les Alchimistes Grecs,* 4: *Zosime de Panopolis, Mémoires Authentiques* (Paris: Les Belles Lettres, 1995) index *s.v.*; R. Patai, *The Jewish Alchemists* (Princeton, NJ: Princeton University Press, 1994) 60-91; B. Suler, "Alchemy," *EncJud* 2: 542-49, esp. 546.

P. W. van der Horst

MARRIAGE

Although ancient Mediterranean marriages and gender roles were quite different from those in modern Western nations, they also varied among themselves. This article examines ancient Mediterranean views concerning marriage, childbearing, singleness, celibacy and monogamy; the beginning of marriage; and gender roles in marriages.

1. Marriage, Childbearing and Celibacy
2. Beginning Marriage
3. Gender Roles in Marriage
4. Summary

1. Marriage, Childbearing and Celibacy.

1.1. Marriage as a Norm in Greek and Roman Sources. Most people in the ancient Mediterranean world felt that marriage was the norm. Early *Rome required Romans to marry and rear their children (Dionysius of Halicarnassus 9.22.2); the later republic continued to advocate marriage (Aulus Gellius *Noc. Att.* 1.6). In the early empire (*see* Roman Empire; Roman Emperors), propagandists for the policies of the Roman state advocated marriage, as did Augustus's laws, at least for the aristocracy (e.g., Dixon, 22, 24, 71-103). Most young women reportedly longed for marriage (Apuleius *Met.* 4.32), and tomb *inscriptions underline the tragedy of dying unmarried (e.g., Lefkowitz and Fant, 11). It was also tragic for young men to die unmarried (Pseudo-Demosthenes *Against Leochares* 18).

1.2. Preference for Celibacy or Singleness in Greek and Roman Sources. Marriage remained the norm, but some people did refuse to marry because they feared broken trust (Plutarch *Dinner of Seven Wise Men* 21, *Mor.* 164B); others preferred exclusively homosexual practices (e.g., Clinias in Achilles Tatius *Leuc.* 1.8.1-2). Celibacy for religious reasons was considered praiseworthy, as evidenced specifically by Rome's vestal virgins (e.g., Livy *Hist.* 4.44.11-12; Appian *Rom. Hist.* 1.1.2; *Civ. W.* 1.6.54); the divine displeasure incurred by their voluntary defilement could be propitiated only by death (Dionysius of Halicarnassus 2.67; 9.40.3-4; Livy *Hist.* 8.15.7-8; 14; Plutarch *Quaest. Rom.* 83, 96, *Mor.* 284A-C, 286EF; Dio Cassius *Hist.* 67.3.3-4; Herodian *Hist.* 4.6.4). Some other cult priestesses were also virgins, whether until puberty (Pausanias *Descr.* 2.33.2) or until death (Pausanias *Descr.* 9.27.6). Normally a man could not embrace a sacred figure executing her duties (Euripides *Iph. Taur.* 798-99), and worshipers of many deities had to abstain from sex during the rites (Propertius *Elegies* 2.33.1-6; Ovid *Met.* 10.431-35). The priests of Cybele, the Galli, were pledged to celibacy: their initiation rite included their castration (e.g., Lucian *Syrian Goddess* 51; Lucretius *Nat.* 2.614-15); but in contrast to the vestal virgins, the Galli usually elicited merely crude satire (e.g., Horace *Sat.* 1.2.120-21; Martial *Epigr.* 1.35.15; 3.24.13).

Some classical Greek *philosophers had reservations about marriage (Diogenes Laertius *Vit.* 4.48; 6.1.3; 10.119; Aulus Gellius *Noc. Att.* 5.11.2); this was especially true of the Cynics, who complained that it involved distraction (Diogenes Laertius *Vit.* 6.2.54; Epictetus *Disc.* 3.22.69-76; Diogenes *Ep.* 47). Cynics had other ways of relieving their sexual appetites, sometimes even publicly, so their singleness does not represent a pledge to celibacy (Diogenes Laertius *Vit.* 6.2.46, 69). But it does indicate that not everyone shared the prevailing Greco-Roman emphasis on marriage. Even Cynics made at least one exception: despite the skepticism of her male colleagues, the woman Hipparchia proved able to embrace the Cynic lifestyle, and the head of the Cynic school married her (Diogenes Laertius *Vit.* 6.7.96-97). Some philosophers also discouraged intercourse, at least during much of the year (Diogenes Laertius *Vit.* 8.1.9). Others, especially *Stoics, sometimes defend marriage or intercourse (Epictetus *Disc.* 3.7.19; Diogenes Laertius *Vit.* 7.1.121); like Paul, they felt that marriage was better for some, celibacy for others (1 Cor 7:7; see Balch 1983; on celibacy and marriage in antiquity, see Keener 1991, 68-78).

1.3. Marriage and Procreation in Mediterranean Antiquity. Although few people viewed marriage as purely for procreation, procreation provided one vital incentive for pursuing it. Hesiod had warned that avoiding marriage left one childless (Hesiod *Theog.* 602-6), although having a wife and children had its own disadvantages (Hesiod *Theog.* 607-12). Many philosophers, among them the Pythagoreans, emphasized the importance of begetting children to propagate society (*Pythagorean Sentences* 29; Thom, 109). Some of more conservative moral bent did limit the purpose of intercourse to procreation (Lucan *Civ. W.* 2.387-88). In the period of the early empire, Augustus enacted laws to encourage the aristocracy to marry and produce children (e.g., Dio Cassius *Hist.* 54.16.1, 7; Gaius *Inst.* 2.286a; Rawson, 9). Some scholars attribute the low birth rate in Rome in this period to the regular practice of hot baths, which can reportedly reduce male fertility (see Devine).

Not everyone wanted more children; some resisted the new emphasis on childbearing (see Dixon, 22-23). Some resorted to magical contraceptives (*PGM* LXIII.24-28) or other contraceptive means they thought were medically sounder (e.g., *b. Nid.* 45a; contraception and abortion were not as widespread as some have argued [see Frier]). Child abandonment was frequent (e.g., Quintilian *Inst. Orat.* 8.1.14; Juvenal *Sat.* 6.602-9). Nevertheless, the debate over such practices appears to have been heated. Stoics (Malherbe, 99), Egyptians (Diodorus Siculus *Bib. Hist.* 1.80.3) and Jews (e.g., *Sib. Or.* 3.765-66) condemned child abandonment; *Judaism also condemned abortions (e.g., Josephus *Ag. Ap.* 2.25 §202; *Pseud,-Phoc.* 184-85; in early Christianity, see Lindemann). Many philosophers (e.g., Heraclitus *Ep.* 7; Den Boer, 272), physicians (see Gorman 19-32), and others (e.g., Chariton *Chaer.* 2.8.6—9.11) disliked abortion; ancients debated whether the embryo was a person and therefore whether or not abortion should be legal (Theon *Progymn.* 2.96-99).

1.4. Marriage and Childbearing as a Norm in Early Judaism. Early Judaism emphasized childbearing even more than imperial propaganda did (see Ilan, 105-7). *Josephus claimed that biblical law allowed intercourse only for procreation (Josephus *Ag. Ap.* 2.25 §199). *Philo claims that a man who knowingly marries a woman who cannot bear children is an enemy of God and nature and acts like an impassioned animal (Philo *Spec. Leg.* 3.6 §36).

The later *rabbis also remained emphatic about the importance of procreation. Rabbis attributed the necessity of procreation to God's command to be fruitful and multiply, because humans are made in God's image (e.g., *m. Yebam.* 6:6; *Pesiq. Rab Kah.* 22:2; cf. *m. Giṭ* 4:5); reportedly as early as the late first century, it was taught that one who refrained from seeking children was "as though he had diminished the image of God" (*Gen. Rab.* 34:14). Thus starting with Adam, begetting children was a divinely ordained duty (*Gen. Rab.* 23:4), and neglecting to beget children came to be viewed as nearly equivalent to killing them (*Ex. Rab.* 1:13; cf. Josephus *Ant.* 4.8.40 §290; *'Abot R. Nat.* 31A). One late rabbi said that God nearly let Hezekiah die young to punish him for not trying to have children sooner (*b. Ber.* 10a). Others claimed that one should remarry and continue siring children in old age (*b. Yebam.* 62b, possibly tannaitic tradition). P. E. Harrell cites one Jewish source as saying that procreation was more meritorious than building the *temple had been (Harrell, 62). One should not marry on holy days when one could not procreate (*y. Giṭ.* 4:5 §2).

Whereas Roman *law permitted but did not require *divorce for childlessness (Rawson, 32; Gardner, 81; Appian *Civ. W.* 2.14.99; Aulus Gellius *Noc. Att.* 4.3.2), rabbis required husbands to divorce their wives who proved unable to bear children, although they were to allow a trial period of ten years (*m. Yebam.* 6:6). Such divorce was sometimes viewed as a tragic necessity (*Pesiq. Rab Kah.* 22:2), but any form of wasting semen was a terrible sin (*b. Nid.* 13a; some argue that the practice was probably less stringent than this—Baskin). The basic custom of divorce for childlessness undoubtedly predates the rabbis: Pseudo-Philo claims that a wife in Judges 13:2 who could bear no children was on the verge of being divorced (Pseudo-Philo *Bib. Ant.* 42:1). Likewise, the only specific offense Josephus mentions when he notes that he divorced his wife for her behavior is that two of the three children she had borne him had died (Josephus *Life* 76 §426).

1.5. Celibacy in Early Judaism. Marriage was the norm for most Judean and Galilean Jews in the Roman period (*see* Jewish History: Roman Period), but exceptions existed. Under particular circumstances, even some rabbis sometimes allowed prolonged abstinence (cf. Ostmeyer, though they normally recommended divorce if the husband withheld intercourse more than two weeks—*m. Ketub.* 5:6). If they had the permission of their wives, married men sometimes left home to study with a rabbi (e.g., stories about second-century rabbis in *ARN* 6A; *Gen. Rab.* 95 MSV), as did Jesus' disciples in the first century (Mk 1:18-20; 10:28-29). One early second-century teacher reportedly agreed with the *rabbinic consensus that procreation was a sacred duty yet personally abstained to allow himself more time to study Torah, much to his colleagues' disdain (*t. Yebam.* 8:7).

Rabbis also sometimes permitted temporary celibacy under extreme circumstances. Because women were often considered unreliable, one second-century rabbi hiding from the Romans allegedly kept his whereabouts a secret from his wife (*b. Šabb.* 33b); while in the ark, Noah had to abstain from intercourse (*y. Ta'an.* 1:6 §8; cf. *Num. Rab.* 14:12). Although they did not approve of the practice in their own time, some rabbis apparently thought biblical prophets might temporarily abstain to secure divine revelation (Vermes, 100-1; *ARN* 2A; 2 §10B).

Some first-century, prerabbinic traditions seem more open to celibacy than the rabbis were (McArthur). Some scholars have argued that circles as diverse as those represented in *1 Enoch* and Philo promoted temporary abstinence to secure revelations (Marx), yet this was hardly widespread. Others find in Philo an apparent sexual asceticism, modeled especially by the Therapeutae and dependent on a spiritual marriage with Wisdom (R. A. Horsley). Some other Jewish traditions refer specifically to emergencies: because Pharaoh was killing their sons, the Israelites in Egypt began abstaining (Pseudo-Philo *Bib Ant.* 9:2, but cf. 9:5). In one pre-Christian source, Jacob abstained from marriage until he was more than sixty years old so as to avoid marrying a Canaanite (*Jub.* 25:4; cf. *T. Iss.* 2:1-2). Probably mirroring some Greek conceptions, *2 Baruch* misinterprets Genesis so that parental passion and conceiving children resulted from the fall (*2 Bar.* 56:6), but the writer nowhere advocates celibacy.

Many of these exceptions are temporary and emergency concessions, and none of them seems to have been widespread or well-known. More well-known, though still exceptional, would have been the undoubted celibacy of wilderness prophets like Banus (Josephus *Life* 2 §11) and John the Baptist (Mk 1:4-6). In antiquity, however, the most widely cited example of Jewish celibacy was the *Essenes (Josephus *Ant.* 18.1.5 §21; Philo *Hypoth.* 11.14-18; Pliny *Nat. Hist.* 5.15.73). Some scholars dispute whether the Essenes were celibate or at least were celibate in all periods (Marx; Hübner), yet various ancient sources converge to indicate that some Essenes were celibate. The evidence suggests both celibate and married Essenes, as Josephus also indicates (Josephus *J.W.* 2.8.2 §§120-21, 13); it is possible that many Essenes who lived in the cities were married (in the **Damascus Document* and **Temple Scroll*), whereas most of those in the wilderness were celibate (the **Rule of the Community*). Even at *Qumran in the wilderness, some women's skeletons indicate that in some period of the community's history, a few women lived there (perhaps a third of the tombs—Elder); some of the texts appear to agree (Baumgarten). But the skeletal evidence also suggests that women were the minority and probably exceptional (perhaps in one period some already married men were permitted to bring their wives). Some Greek thought may have influenced the ideal of celibacy among Qumran's Essenes, but elements of the Israelite prophetic tradition (Thiering) are also possible antecedents.

Mirroring the rise of sexual asceticism in some circles in late antiquity, some early Christians regarded abstention from intercourse as pious (1 Cor 7:5-6; *Acts Jn.* 63; *Acts of Paul* 3.5-8, 12), although others clearly indicated that Christians could marry and bear children (1 Cor 7:27-28; 1 Tim 5:14; *Diogn.* 5), as well as be celibate (Mt 19:10-12; 1 Cor 7:25-40).

1.6. Monogamy. Some peoples on the periphery of the empire reportedly practiced polygamy, including Thracians, Numidians and Moors (Sallust *Iug.* 80.6; Sextus Empiricus *Pyr.* 3.213; cf. Diodorus Siculus *Bib. Hist.* 1.80.3 on Egypt); writers also alleged that some distant peoples merely held children in common (Diodorus Siculus *Bib. Hist.* 2.58.1). Although a few Greek philosophers supported group marriage (Diogenes Laertius *Vit.* 6.2.72; 7.1.131; 8.1.33), Greek culture as a whole forbade it (e.g., Euripides *Androm.* 465-93, 909). Likewise, Roman law prohibited polygamy, which bore as its minimum penalty *infamia* (Gardner, 92-93; Gaius *Inst.* 1.63; Dionysius of Halicarnassus 11.28.4); Roman wives found the notion of polygamy abhorrent (Aulus Gellius *Noc. Att.* 1.23.8).

Although the practice was not common, early Palestinian Judaism allowed polygamy (*m. Sanh.* 2:4), and it was practiced at least by some wealthy kings (Josephus *J.W.* 1.28.4 §562). The early sage Hillel reportedly complained against polygamy, but mainly because he felt wives could be dangerous, especially in large numbers (*m. ʾAbot* 2:7). Nevertheless, the vast majority of Jewish men and all Jewish women were monogamous, and some conservative sectarians forbade polygamy, including for rulers (CD 4:20—5:2; 11QTemple 56:18-19). More significantly, Jewish people outside Palestine followed the regular Greek practice of avoiding polygamous unions (cf. Frey, cxii).

Other kinds of multiple sexual arrangements were more common than polygamy, although they were not always legal. Greeks did not always approve of holding concubines, but they recognized the practice among other peoples (Athenaeus *Deipn.* 13.556b-57e). Roman law also forbade holding a concubine in addition to a wife (Gardner, 56-57), and early Romans regarded concubines as infamous (Aulus Gellius *Noc. Att.* 4.3.3). Jewish legal experts refer to concubinage in biblical times, but in their literature treat as a contemporary parallel only intercourse with female *slaves, which they condemn (Safrai, 748-49).

Nevertheless, many men in this period, especially those of lower social status, acquired concubines (Gardner, 57-58). Their unions lacked legal standing, but custom elevated them above merely temporary affairs (O'Rourke, 182). Concubinage was especially common in the military (see, e.g., *OGIS* 674; Lewis, 141), since soldiers could not legally marry until they had completed their term of military service, a period that lasted more than twenty years. Two decades was a long time to wait, and romances were consequently more readily forgiven (Fabius Maximus 4, in Plutarch *Sayings of Romans, Mor.* 195E-F), though it was better to avoid them (cf. Scipio the Elder 2, in Plutarch *Sayings of Romans, Mor.* 196B). In some military discharge documents from the first century Roman officials grant soldiers the legalization of their prior unions as marriages, adding the stipulation that they have only one woman each (Sherk, 99-100, 154; Gaius *Inst.* 1.57). Similarly, *Pseudo-Phocylides* 181 warns against having intercourse with one's father's concubines (plural).

2. Beginning Marriage.

2.1. Age at Marriage. Greeks and Romans were familiar with other cultures that married women around age fifteen (*Ninus Romance* frag. A-3) and reportedly much earlier (Arrian *Ind.* 9.1). In classical Greek culture, Athenian girls usually married younger than did Spartan girls, often before fifteen (Den Boer, 39, 269); the average age, however, was probably late teens (Hesiod *Op.* 698). In the Roman period, a high percentage of Roman girls were married in or by their late teens (Shaw); thus, for example, Quintilian mourns that his wife died after bearing him two sons and before the age of nineteen (pref. 4). Augustus's laws permitted girls to be betrothed as young as the age of ten and married as young as twelve (Gardner, 38; Rawson, 21), and many girls were married by the age of fifteen (Pomeroy 1975, 14; cf. Ovid *Met.* 9.714). In samples with the higher figures (not all run this high), nearly 40 percent of women were married before age fifteen and nearly 75 percent before age nineteen; in one sample 8 percent were married in some sense before age twelve (Gardner, 39). Seventeen or eighteen was a common age of marriage for most upper-class women, though Augustus's legislation did not penalize them for singleness until the age of twenty (Rawson, 22).

Roman boys could not legally marry before fourteen or physical signs of puberty (Gardner, 38), but Roman males were usually older, often twenty-five or older (Saller). Although Greek men could marry by eighteen (*Mantitheus Against Boeotus* 2.12 in Demosthenes, LCL 4:488-89), thirty seems to have been most common (Hesiod *Op.* 695-97). Some scholars have proposed that Greek men tended to be at least a decade older than women because of a shortage of women due to the more frequent abandonment of female infants (see Lewis, 54-55).

Jewish writers and teachers advocated marrying early, partly to propagate one's family name (e.g., *Pseud.-Phoc.* 175-76; *b. Pesaḥ.* 113b) and partly to protect young men from sexual passion (Sir 7:23; *b. Qidd.* 29b; *b. Yebam.* 63ab). Eighteen to twenty was considered an appropriate age for a man's marriage (*m. ʾAbot* 5:21; cf. 1QSa 1:10; *see* Rule of the Congregation). Though men sometimes married later than twenty (e.g., *CIJ* 1:409 §553), many later rabbis complained that men who were twenty or older and still not married were sinning against God (*b. Qidd.* 29b-30a, from the second-century school of Rabbi Ishmael). Women usually married in their teens, such as at thirteen or sixteen, but some were older than twenty (Ilan, 67-69).

2.2. Potential Marriage Partners. Many ancient male writers expressed a preference for virgins (Hesiod *Op.* 699). Jewish men usually seem to have preferred virgins (Josephus *Ant.* 4.8.23 §244); *priests could marry only virgins or the widows of priests, and the high priest could marry only a virgin (Josephus *Ant.* 3.14.2 §277).

Contrary to what one might expect, not all men preferred marrying a wealthy woman. That Plutarch warns against wives relying on their dowry, or wealth brought into the marriage, suggests that some must have done so (*Bride* 22, *Mor.* 141AB). Josephus claims that the law forbids marrying a wife on account of money (Josephus *Ag. Ap.* 2.25 §200), though one wonders the degree to which he followed this advice (Josephus *Life* 76 §427). Some men considered a wealthy wife to be worse; if the marriage did not turn out well, her dowry could become a deterrent from being able to divorce her (*Pseud.-Phoc.* 199-200).

Greeks and Romans recognized some days as more auspicious for marriage than others (Apuleius *Met.* 2.12; cf. Plutarch *Quaest. Rom.* 86, *Mor.* 284F), and Roman widows married on a different day of the week than did virgins (Plutarch *Quaest. Rom.* 105, *Mor.* 289A). If later rabbinic passages may reflect more widespread Palestinian Jewish customs in the first century A.D. in this case, Palestinian Jewish virgins were married on the fourth day and widows on the fifth (*m. Ketub.* 1:1; *b. Ketub.* 2a; *y. Ketub.* 1:1 §1; *Pesiq. Rab Kah.* 26:2).

The ancient Mediterranean world knew nothing of the modern prejudice against interracial marriage, which presupposes a concept of race equally foreign to them (see Snowden, 94-97). But ancients often contemplated the complications of marriage across class lines. Thus a maxim warned against marrying a wife of higher status than oneself (Plutarch *Lib. Educ.* 19, *Mor.* 13F-14A). Likewise, legislators regularly addressed the status of the children of socially mixed marriages. In earlier days, patricians and plebeians could not intermarry (Dionysius of Halicarnassus 11.28.4), though this prohibition was no longer in effect. When both parents were Romans, the child adopted the father's legal status; when neither was Roman, the child adopted the mother's status (Ulpian *Rules* 5.8-9 in Lefkowitz and Fant, 192). Only Roman citizens normally contracted official Roman marriages, but Romans sometimes granted such marriages to Latins and foreigners marrying Romans, out of concern for the status of the children (Gardner, 32). Marriages between free Romans and slaves who had not yet been freed were not legal (Weaver, 149-51).

Jewish legal experts also discussed the suitability of intermarriage among classes, especially among lay Israelites, Levites and priests (*t. Sanh.* 4:7); a few questioned whether children of earlier competing *Pharisaic schools should have intermarried (*y. Qidd.* 1:1 §8). Rabbis warned against marrying a daughter of an *am haaretz* (one who ignored the rabbinic understanding of the law) lest one die and one's children be reared badly (*b. Pesaḥ.* 49a, *Bar.*)

But the issue for Jewish interpreters became most serious when it involved intermarriage between Jews and Gentiles. For some teachers, the offspring of pagans would neither live nor be judged in the world to come (*t. Sanh.* 13:2), but marriage between Jews and Gentiles complicated the question. Some rabbis claimed that a child that an Israelite woman bore to a Gentile or a slave was illegitimate (*y. Giṭ.* 1:4 §2). A child conceived in the womb of a proselyte was himself a full Israelite, but if his mother converted between his conception and his birth or if his father fulfilled only part of the conversion ritual, his Jewish status was incomplete (*b. Sanh.* 58a; *y. Qidd.* 3:12 §8); the son of Esther and Ahasuerus was thus only half pure (*Esther Rab.* 8:3). This is probably what Paul means in 1 Corinthians 7:14, where he probably implies that children with one believing parent remain within the sphere of the gospel's influence.

That some of the Corinthian Christians may have wished to divorce on the grounds of spiritual incompatibility (1 Cor 7:12-14) may reflect a tradition of Jewish interpretation: one text claims that it is God's will for Israelite men to divorce pagan wives they wrongly married (1 Esdr 9:9); a husband might also divorce his wife for behavior that he regarded as ungodly (Sir 26:1-3; *t. Dem.* 3:9). Under Roman law, children normally went to the father in the case of divorce (Pomeroy 1975, 158, 169).

2.3. Betrothals, Dowries and Other Arrangements. Tannaitic interpreters, probably reflecting broader social custom on family matters, recognized women as persons but in legal matters disposed of their sexuality as chattel (see Wegner, 40-70), as required by traditional Middle Eastern and Greco-Roman customs regarding bride price and dowry.

From the time of Augustus, who desired to replenish especially the aristocracy, Roman law required marriage within two years after betrothal (Dio Cassius *Hist.* 54.16.7). Jewish couples probably normally married a year after their betrothal (*m. Ketub.* 5:2; *m. Ned.* 10:5; Safrai, 757).

Greek custom required a family provide a daughter with a dowry at marriage (Diodorus Siculus *Bib. Hist.* 32.10.2); affluent families often showered her with wealth, but some poor families abandoned infant daughters on trash heaps because they would not be able to provide a dowry (Lewis, 55). The girl's dowry usually corresponded to the degree to which she was considered attractive (Pseudo-Demosthenes *Or.* 59, *Against Neaera* 113). Because of potential conflicts of interest, Roman spouses could not receive gifts from one another or from most in-laws (Plutarch *Quaest. Rom.* 7-8, *Mor.* 265E-266A).

Husbands controlled all the property (Plutarch *Bride* 20, *Mor.* 140-41), and a dowry was a gift from the in-laws—socially expected but not legally required—to help the new husband cover the expenses he was incurring by getting a wife (Gardner, 97). But if a husband divorced his wife, he would have to release her, paying her back her dowry (e.g., *CPJ* 1:236-38 §128), and some contracts required him to add half to it if he had mistreated her in violation of the contract (Lewis, 55). Because the dowry was usually spent by this point, it provided a monetary deterrent against frivolous divorce. Rabbinic law on dowries to a great extent reflects the larger Mediterranean and Middle Eastern legal milieu of which it was a part (Cohen, 348-76; Geller). By preparing to divorce Mary privately rather than taking her before judges, Joseph may have forfeited his legal right to impound an allegedly unfaithful fiancée's dowry (rabbis said she could lose it for as little as speaking with another man [*m. Ketub.* 7:6]) in order to avoid her humiliation (Mt 1:19).

In Hellenistic Egypt, men and women often contracted the marriage directly with each other (Verner, 36-37). Parents usually arranged Palestinian Jewish marriages through intermediaries (agents; *t. Yebam.* 4:4). Both Roman and Jewish law recognized the use of agents, or intermediary marriage brokers, in betrothals (Cohen, 295-96). Betrothal was legally binding and left the survivor of the man's death a widow (*m. Ketub.* 1:2; *m. Yebam.* 4:10; 6:4). Although a betrothed couple like Joseph and Mary did not live together or have intercourse, their union was as binding as marriage and could thus be dissolved only through death or divorce (*m. Giṭ.* 6:2; *Ketub.* 1:2; *Yebam.* 2:6).

2.4. Weddings. Jewish weddings normally lasted seven days (cf. Tob 11:19; *Jos. and As.* 21:8 in *OTP,* 21:6 in Greek text; *Sipra Behuq. pq.* 5.266.1.7); the fourteen days of Tobit 8:19-20 was apparently exceptional, a celebration due to Sara's deliverance. Many of the closest associates of the bride and groom remained the full seven days (*t. Ber.* 2:10), but extant tradition suggests that blessings would be repeated for those who arrived later in the feast (Safrai, 760). The first night was presumably the most essential, however; if traditional Middle Eastern weddings provide a clue, feasting during the wedding night itself may have been the most important (Eickelman, 174; cf. Mt 25:10-12). Palestinian Jewish wedding parties included the *shoshbin,* apparently an esteemed friend (*m. Sanh.* 3:5; cf. Jn 3:29), though all one's friends would join in the joy of the wedding (1 Macc 9:39). A *shoshbin* of higher status than the groom seems to have been preferred (*b. Yebam.* 63a).

Well-to-do fathers and *patrons were known to invite large numbers of people, sometimes whole villages, to celebrations, including a child's wedding (Chariton *Chaer.* 3.2.10; Diodorus Siculus *Bib. Hist.* 16.91.4; 16.92.1; Pliny *Ep.* 10.116); refusal to come, especially after responding positively to an invitation (cf. Mt 22:2-7), constituted an insult. If others thought as highly of the sages' profession as the sages themselves did, their writings testify that some considered it meritorious to show hospitality to sages and their disciples (*Sipre Deut.* 1.10.1); hence it would prove natural to invite a scholar to a wedding (*b. Ketub.* 17b; *Koh. Rab.* 1:3 §1; Jn 2:2). The rabbis assumed the importance of wine for festal celebrations, including in the blessing for *sabbath meals (*t. Ber.* 3:8) and at weddings (Safrai, 747). It was customary to have food left over at weddings (*t. Šabb.* 17:4), and one who urged a neighbor to attend his wedding without showing proper *hospitality is listed among thieves (*t. B. Qam.* 7:8); running out of wine at a wedding was thus a serious problem (Jn 2:3).

The rites of passage that inaugurated most Roman marriages were often less formal than we would expect (O'Rourke, 181). By contrast, Jewish people emphasized joyous celebration at wedding feasts; texts often use weddings to symbolize the greatest joy, in contrast to the epitome of sorrow, grief at a funeral (1 Macc 9:39-41; Josephus *J.W.* 6.5.3 §301). As one must mourn with the bereaved, one was also obligated to celebrate with the couple at a wedding (*y. Ketub.* 1:1 §6). Like funeral processions, bridal processions were so important that later rabbis even interrupted their schools on this account (*ARN* 4 A; 8 §22 B); God's patronage of Adam and Eve's wedding showed the importance of weddings (*ARN* 8 §23 B; *b. B. Bat.* 75a). Rabbis even exempted the wedding party from *festal obligations (*b. Sukk.* 25b; *p. Sukk.* 2:5 §1) and many ritual obligations, though only the groom was exempt from the Shema (*m. Ber.* 2:5; *t. Ber.* 2:10).

2.5. Intercourse and Passion. It was customary to consummate one's marriage quickly. As in later Middle Eastern practice (Eickelman, 174), blood on the sheet probably proved the validity of the consummation (Deut 22:15; cf. *y. Ketub.* 1:1 §§7-8), though later rabbis always ruled in favor of women when they claimed exceptional reasons for a hymen not bleeding on the first night (Ilan, 98-99). Mary and Joseph chose to forgo this evidence for the honor of God's Messiah (Mt 1:25).

Musonius Rufus thought that sexual desire was inappropriate in marriage except for purposes of procreation (Ward, 284); some Jewish writers (*Pseud.-Phoc.* 193-94) and second-century Christians echoed the attitude (*Sentius Sextus* 231). Such views were not, however, the prevailing ones in the early empire. Love charms were widespread (Theocritus *The Spell),* especially in the *magical papyri (*PGM* XIII.304; XXXVI.69-133, 187-210, 295-311). Such magical love spells were used to secure the attention of persons single (e.g., *PGM* XXXVI.69-160, 187-210, 295-311) or sometimes married (*PDM* LXI.197-216 = *PGM* LXI.39-71; Euripides *Hipp.* 513-16).

Still, even nonphilosophers recognized that the passion of love drowned reason (Publilius Syrus *Publii* 15, 22, 131, 314). Although many people based their desire for marriage on beauty (Babrius *Fables* 32.5-6; Judg 14:3), moralists warned that attraction on merely physical grounds was bound to fade after the beginning of a marriage (Plutarch *Bride* 4, *Mor.* 138F). Women could be said to rule or enslave men through men's passion for them (1 Esdr 4:14-33; Josephus *Ant.* 4.6.7 §133; Sir 47:19; Sophocles *Ant.* 756; cf. Sophocles *Trach.* 488-89; Appian *Civ. W.* 5.1.8-9), though many philosophers warned against such behavior (1 Cor 6:12; Diodorus Siculus *Bib. Hist.* 10.9.4; Philo *Op. Mund.* 59-60 §§165-67). Even a married man who failed to deny his wife anything was but a "slave" (insultingly, in Cicero *Parad.* 36; Diodorus Siculus *Bib. Hist.* 32.10.9; Philo *Hypoth.* 11.16-17).

Ancient literature regularly described the passion of love as burning (Apollonius of Rhodes *Arg.* 3.774; Virgil *Aen.* 4.2, 23, 54, 66, 68; *Ecl.* 8.83; Lucan *Civ. W.* 10.71; Plutarch *Dialogue on Love* 16, *Mor.* 759B), including in romance novels (Longus *Daphn. Chl.* 2.7; 3.10; Achilles Tatius *Leuc.* 1.5.5-6; 1.11.3; Chariton *Chaer.* 1.1.8; 2.3.8; Apuleius *Met.* 2.5, 7; 5.23; *Alexandrian Erotic Fragment* col. 1) and Jewish texts (Sir 9:8; *T. Jos.* 2:2); Paul adopts the same image for passion

(1 Cor 7:9). Such texts sometimes describe romantic passion as wounds (Chariton *Chaer.* 1.1.7) or sickness (Longus *Daphn. Chl.* 1.32; Propertius *Eleg.* 2.1.57-58; Song 2:5; *b. Sanh.* 75a; *y. 'Abod. Zar.* 2:2 §3), sometimes from the arrows, often flaming arrows, of Cupid or Eros (Apollonius of Rhodes *Arg.* 3.287; Virgil *Aen.* 4.69; Ovid *Met.* 1.453-65; Propertius *Eleg.* 2.12.9; 2.13.1-2; Longus *Daphn. Chl.* 1.7; 2.6; Achilles Tatius *Leuc.* 1.17.1; 4.6.1). But such descriptions frequently apply to unmarried passions; some texts also apply them to homoerotic desire (Sextus Empiricus *Pyr.* 3.199). Some Gentiles also excused their passion as uncontrollable (e.g., Sophocles *Trach.* 441-48; Herodian *Hist.* 5.6.2) and believed people could die if their passions remained unfulfilled (Parthenius *L.R.* 16.1; 17.2; see other details in Keener 1999, 186-87, on Mt 5:28).

Greek legend claimed that the seer Teiresias had been both male and female and that he testified that women enjoy intercourse ten times as much as men do (e.g., Hesiod *The Melampodia* 3). Nevertheless, one might recognize that a virgin might not find intercourse pleasurable at first, until she continued the practice with her husband for some time (Apuleius *Met.* 5.4); also, a wife should not make advances to her husband (Plutarch *Bride* 18, *Mor.* 140CD). Greek men preferred for their wives to submit to intercourse without signs of reluctance (Artemidorus *Oneir.* 1.78); arguments were known to occur in the bedchamber, though Plutarch advises both husbands and wives against this (Plutarch *Bride* 39, *Mor.* 143E).

Among the husband's duties demanded by Jewish legal scholars, the husband must provide his wife with intercourse (*Sipre Deut.* 231.2.1-2). Classical Athenian law urged husbands to provide intercourse with their wives three times a month, for procreation (Pomeroy 1975, 87). Jewish scholars were more emphatic, however: if a husband abstained from intercourse with his wife for more than one or two weeks, the Pharisees felt that he was obligated to grant her a divorce (*m. Ketub.* 5:6). Many believed that women were more susceptible to passion than were men (Euripides *Androm.* 218-21).

Ancient Mediterranean writers celebrated married love (Dixon, 2-3; Rawson, 26). Wives should love their husbands (e.g., *IG* 14 cited in G. H. R. Horsley 4:35 §10; Dio Chrysostom frag. in LCL, 5:348-49); in the late republic and early empire willingness to die with one's husband grew as an ideal (Dixon, 3; Petronius *Sat.* 111). Husbands should also love their wives (Homer *Il.* 9.341-42; Cato collection of distichs 20; *Pseud.-Phoc.* 195; *Grk. Anth.* 7.340), which involves more than merely sexual union (as in Athenaeus *Deipn.* 13.557E); the first and most critical family union is between husband and wife (Cicero *De Offic.* 1.17.54). Jewish epitaphs also emphasize married love (Frey, cxvi; *CIJ* 1:118 §166; 1:137 §195). One Diaspora Jewish source attributes domestic disturbances to demonic instigation (*T. Sol.* 18:15).

3. Gender Roles in Marriage.

3.1. Greco-Roman Household Codes. *Aristotle established household codes to advise aristocratic men how to rule their wives, children and slaves (see Balch 1981, 1988). Although there were differences (e.g., Aristotle *Pol.* 1.1.2, 1252a), these codes concerning household management could be linked with the broader category of advice on city management, as in the context in Aristotle (Aristotle *Pol.* 1.2.1, 1253b) and some other works (Lührmann; Lycurgus 21 in Plutarch *Sayings of Spartans, Mor.* 228CD). Aristotle and others thought that order in the household would produce order in society.

Household codes probably also affected the formulation of some official laws in terms of relationships among children, wives and slaves (Gaius *Inst.* 1.48-51, 108-19). Josephus's apologetic included an emphasis on biblical law's great virtues (Josephus *Ag. Ap.* 2.291-96), and it is not surprising that Jewish writers with Greek or Hellenized audiences stressed such codes as a way of identifying Judaism with the prevailing values of the dominant culture (see Balch 1988, 28-31). Paul adapts the content of the codes but retains their structure (Eph 5:21—6:9; Col 3:18—4:1), possibly to help Christians witness within their culture (1 Cor 9:19-23; Tit 2:5, 8).

Even outside the context of such household codes, it was understood that wives should subject themselves to their husbands and husbands should tenderly rule their wives the way the soul rules the body (Plutarch *Bride* 33, *Mor.* 142E).

3.2. Relative Rank of Gentile Husbands and Wives. In classical *Athens (Verner, 30-33) and traditional Roman families (Verner, 33-34), the husband had authority over the household. Under the traditional Roman *manus* marriage, marriage freed a bride from her father's authority (*patria potestas*) to bring her under her husband's authority (Verner, 33). One's dependents thus included both those "in marital submission" (*in manu*) and servants (*in mancipio,* Gaius *Inst.* 1.49). But by the period of the early empire most marriages abandoned this arrangement, officially leaving the bride under her father's household. Because she was living with her husband rather than her father, this arrangement increased the wife's freedom in practice; aristocratic wives could accumulate wealth and establish some independence from their husbands (Verner, 39). Some ideals, however, endured over time.

Many ancient writers attributed women's appropriate inferiority of rank in marriage and society to an inferiority inherent in nature (e.g., Aristotle *Eth. Nic.* 8.12.7, 1162a; *Pol.* 1.2.12, 1254b; Aelian *De Nat. Anim.* 11.26). Many viewed women as weaker emotionally (Euripides *Med.* 928; Virgil *Aen.* 4.569-70) or as unfit for battle (Virgil *Aen.* 9.617; 11.734; Livy *Hist.* 25.36.9; Aulus Gellius *Noc. Att.* 17.21.33; Phaedrus *Fables* 4.17.6) or the law court (*P. Oxy.* 261). Writers did report the exploits of women, but generally as unusual. A few men viewed women as a curse to men (Hesiod *Theog.* 570-612; Euripides *Or.* 605-6); a woman might count her own life less valuable than those of male warriors (Euripides *Iph. Aul.* 1393-94). Women's moral weaknesses were also proverbial (e.g., Sir 42:12-14; Hesiod *Theog.* 601-2; *Op.* 375; Publilius Syrus *Publii* 20, 365, 376; Juvenal *Sat.* 6.242-43; Babrius *Fables* 22.13-15; Avianus *Fables* 15-16; in contemporary Middle Eastern culture, Delaney, 41; Eickelman, 205-6, 243), and one woman's behavior could be held to reflect badly on her gender (Homer *Odys.* 11.432-34). Thus Plutarch, a more progressive voice by the standards of his male aristocratic contemporaries, urges a young husband to attend to his bride's learning (*Bride* 48, *Mor.* 145C), for if left to themselves without a husband's input, women produce only base passions and folly (*Bride* 48, *Mor.* 145D-E).

The classical Greek ideal was that women should be shy and retiring, easily injured by hearing foul language (Demosthenes *Meid.* 79) or being insulted (*hubridzōn,* Demosthenes *Aristoc.* 141). In common classical Athenian opinion, a woman's virtue includes being an obedient and dutiful housewife (Meno in Plato *Meno* 71). Well-to-do men slept with high-class prostitutes for pleasure, concubines for bodily health and wives to bear children and rule domestic matters (Pseudo-Demosthenes *Orat.* 59, *Neaer.* 122). A virtuous wife sought to perform whatever her husband wished (Pseudo-Melissa, *Letter to Kleareta* in Malherbe, 83). Traditional Roman ideals also presented women as being submissive and subservient (Hallett, 241-42). Wives should obey their husbands (e.g., Marcus Aurelius *Med.* 1.17.7; Artemidorus *Oneir.* 1.24; Apuleius *Met.* 5.5), including submission in all social and religious matters (Plutarch *Bride* 19, *Mor.* 140D). Good wives prefer such submission to the freedom created by widowhood (Livy *Hist.* 34.7.12).

Thus when women acted boldly, they could be said to be acting like men (Apuleius *Met.* 5.22); some male writers condemned this behavior as a lack of modesty (e.g., Homer *Odys.* 19.91; Valerius Maximus *Fact. ac Dict.* 8.3; Aulus Gellius *Noc. Att.* 10.6). Various first-century writers satirized women who exercised too much power, especially over their husbands (Petronius *Sat.* 37; frag. 6; Juvenal *Sat.* 4.30-37; 6.219-24, 246-305, 474-85). Such writers, committed to the traditional task of preserving the social order (in earlier times, e.g., Isocrates *Ad Nic.* 55, *Or.* 3.38) and perhaps their own role in it, were resisting changes taking place in women's roles in their society (see Reekmans). In so doing, they apparently perpetuated earlier complaints that Roman women were not submissive enough (Cato the Elder 3 in Plutarch *Sayings of Romans, Mor.* 198D). Socialization undoubtedly reaffirmed such gender roles even as it does in the same region today, rewarding quiet and submissive behavior on the part of women (Giovannini, 67).

Daily practice was never quite what the ideals may have prescribed. Thus the emperor Augustus, promoting traditional Roman values, told men to command their wives as they wished, especially with regard to modest dress and behavior. But it was widely known that Augustus did not admonish the empress Livia in this manner (Dio Cassius *Hist.* 54.16.4-5). Livia was an exception in some respects; after Augustus's death she shared with the new emperor Tiberius in honoring her deceased husband as if she shared in power (*autarchousa,* Dio Cassius *Hist.* 56.47.1); she also controlled a massive estate (Treggiari). Even Philo exempted Livia from his usual standards for gender, albeit by noting that she had become virtually masculine in her wisdom (Philo *Leg. Gai.* 320). Yet there were limits to her power; even Livia's intercession did not always persuade Augustus to act against tradition (Sherk, 7). Augustus used Livia for propaganda while maintaining a conservative social policy (Flory).

Britons might have women authority figures like Boudicca (Tacitus *Ann.* 14.31-37); pre-Roman *Alexandria hosted *Macedonian women authority figures of the *Ptolemaic dynasty, including the most famous Cleopatra. To a lesser extent, Roman women also held higher positions than did classical Greek women (e.g., Lefkowitz and Fant, 244-47), and the Roman aristocracy produced powerful women like Livia, Messalina and both first-century Agrippinas (Balsdon). But the degree to which the authority of such public figures affected average marriages remains unclear.

Nevertheless, other indications further render doubtful the assumption that classical ideals always represented social reality. Even the Homeric portrait of Penelope's relationship with Odysseus suggests some degree of mutual respect (Arthur, 15); likewise, some suggest that men in classical Athens felt less secure in their dominance than some texts would suggest (Gould, 52-57). In the first-century Roman world, women had advanced considerably both economically and socially, although a conservative backlash apparently reversed this in early second century A.D. (see Boatwright). The old *manus* marriage largely faded from use, and husbands' authority over their wives was roughly the same as their authority over male children; further, not all husbands would have abused their authority in the ways the laws could have permitted (Gardner, 5). In the period of the early empire some writers also introduced ideals of greater feminine freedom (Hallett, 244); some writers, such as Pliny, proved more favorable toward women than did others (Dobson).

Nevertheless, funerary *inscriptions of the imperial period largely commemorate women in their roles as wives, mothers and daughters, the primary roles through which the predominantly male elite of society related to them (Kleiner; cf., e.g., *CIL* 6.10230). Even when Plutarch, a relatively progressive writer, advocated harmonious consent and mutual agreement in marriage, he expected the husband to lead (Plutarch *Bride* 11, *Mor.* 139CD); even writers like Plutarch and Roman *Stoics who advocated theoretical equality of the sexes usually encouraged wifely subordination in practice (Balch 1981, 143-49). Women were not always dramatically subordinate; this does not, however, imply that Greco-Roman antiquity shared modern Western egalitarian ideals.

Ancient writers were also aware of geographical variations in marital gender roles. Women exercised more freedom in the western than the eastern Mediterranean (see, e.g., Salles), and Greeks recognized that historically Roman women were more influential than were Greek women (Appian *Rom. Hist.* 3.11.1). Even in Sparta women ran the city while the men were away, much to Aristotle's disdain (Aristotle *Pol.* 2.6.7, 1269b; though cf. Gorgo 5 and anonymous 22 in Plutarch *Sayings of Spartan Women, Mor.* 240E, 242B). Sparta's long-term cultural influence was limited; the Greek cultural ideals most recited in the Hellenistic eastern Mediterranean stemmed especially from Athens. Yet Greeks were aware of other customs elsewhere; some they considered savagely repressive toward women, such as bride burning in India (Diodorus Siculus *Bib. Hist.* 17.91.3). But other cases struck the Greeks as odd or inappropriate because they permitted wives undue freedom.

In contrast to the Greeks, Ligurian women worked the fields alongside their husbands because their soil was poor (Diodorus Siculus *Bib. Hist.* 4.20). Making a living at distaff and loom was difficult (Terence *And.* 73-74), but women often worked in rural areas (Longus *Daphn. Chl.* 3.25; *P. Fay.* 91; Scheidel). A writer could criticize the king of old Persia for ruling all his subjects except the one he ought to have ruled most of all, his wife (Plutarch *Uneducated Ruler* 2, *Mor.* 780C). Greeks were so amazed by the greater relative freedom among Egyptian women that they portrayed Egyptian women as ruling *(kyrieuein)* their husbands and Egyptian marriage contracts as stipulating that men obey their wives in all things (*peitharchēsein . . . hapanta,* Diodorus Siculus *Bib. Hist.* 1.27.2). This was an exaggeration but underlines the greater freedom of Egyptian women in contrast to that of Greek women.

But long before the Roman period, Greek culture had pervaded the eastern Mediterranean, including urban Egypt (i.e., Alexandria and the Hellenistic elite in Egypt's nomes). Thus although women in general in Roman Egypt wielded considerably greater economic power than they did in classical Athens (Pomeroy 1981), first- and second-century B.C. marriage contracts from Egypt list among requirements for wives submission to their husbands, not leaving the home without their permission, and so forth (Verner, 38, 64-65; Lewis, 55). Although more such documents were preserved in Egypt, however, the wives' promise to obey their husbands was hardly limited to Egypt.

3.3. Gender Roles in Palestinian and Geographically Related Jewish Traditions. Views on gender roles varied significantly in early Jewish sources (see van der Horst 1993). Philo and Josephus provide examples of Jewish people writing for Hellenistic-Roman or Hellenized audiences. Philo believes that Moses' law enjoins wives to serve and obey their husbands (Philo *Hypoth.* 7.3); child rearing necessarily also subordinates wives to their husbands (Philo *Op. Mund.* 167). That such subservience would, he believed, be good for women undoubtedly stems from his conviction that women are less rational than men (Philo *Omn. Prob. Lib.* 18 §117); his use of feminine imagery connotes women's inferiority by nature (see most extensively Baer), which reflects a broader pattern of Greco-Roman thought. The difficulties of bearing and rearing children also necessarily subject the wife in obedience to her husband (Philo *Op. Mund.* 60 §167). Essenes do not marry, he noted, because women are selfish and devote all their energy to leading their husbands into error (Philo *Hypoth.* 11.14-17).

Josephus also views women as inferior in moral character to men (Josephus *Ant.* 4.8.15 §219). Because women are inferior in all things, the law prescribes the husband's authority and wife's submission for the wife's own good (Josephus *Ag. Ap.* 2.25 §§200-201); thus Josephus believed that God punished both Adam and Herod Antipas for being so weak as to have heeded their wives (Josephus *Ant.* 1.1.4 §49; 18.7.2 §255; cf. *Adam and Eve* 26:2). Josephus may have felt personal existential reasons for his opinions; although he later found a wealthy Jewish woman he believed to be of nobler character than most other women (Josephus *Life* 76 §427), he divorced another wife, displeased with her behavior (Josephus *Life* 76 §426). Yet he was hardly alone in his opinions; negative views of women predominate in Sirach (e.g., Sir 42:13) and probably the *Testament of Job* (Garrett; but cf. van der Horst 1986), though positive pictures appear in Tobit (Sara; Edna; Anna) and Pseudo-Philo (van der Horst 1989). Samaritan marriage contracts require full obedience from the wife (Bowman, 311).

The rabbis also assume that husbands rule their wives (*Sipra Qed.* par. 1.195.2.2; cf. Graetz; 4Q416 frag. 2 iv 2) and complain that a man ruled by his wife has no life (*b. Beṣa* 32b, *Bar.)* But these sources easily appear more nuanced than Josephus or Philo. The husband had to respect his wife (Safrai, 763-64, citing *b. Yebam.* 62b, *Bar.;* cf. Montefiore and Loewe, 507-15). Second-century rabbis were concerned for women's legal, especially property, rights (see Langer). Likewise, nonliterary evidence suggests the participation of Diaspora Jewish women in community life (Kraemer).

Some sources may reflect broader ancient Mediterranean mistrust of women's moral character. A rash or impudent *(thrasus)* woman shamed her father and husband and invited their loathing (Sir 22:5), and various sources warn about the talkative wife (*Syr. Men. Sent.* 118-21; *Gen. Rab.* 45:5; 80:5). Such women will falsely accuse their husbands (*Sent. Syr. Men.* 336-39). But a husband should appreciate a good wife (Sir 7:19; 26:1-4).

3.4. Respective Duties of Husband and Wife. Classical Athenian culture idealized women's seclusion to the domestic sphere, though it was never fully realized in practice; probably partly to retain the wife's exclusive allegiance to her husband, much of the Greek-speaking eastern Mediterranean of the early empire, however, was less restrictive (Keener 1992, 22-24). Nevertheless, most married women outside the urban elite covered their heads to prevent the lust of males other than their husbands (Keener 1992, 28-30).

The Stoic Hierocles also expects the husband to rule external affairs while the matron rules domestic affairs, but in contrast to many others, he refuses to observe this distinction rigidly (Hierocles *On Duties* Household Management, in Malherbe, 97-98).

Early Palestinian Judaism did not restrict women's movement the way classical Greek culture did (see *m. Ketub.* 1:10; 9:4); it also provided women some rights not common in broader Mediterranean culture (see Verner, 45). Nevertheless, the wife's standard duties are largely domestic: grinding wheat, cooking, washing, nursing and sewing (*m. Ketub.* 5:5; late first-century adaptations of these duties suggest that the original list was accepted among first-century Pharisees).

But Jewish law also required husbands to

provide their wives with expected comforts (Goodman, 36; cf. *Adam and Eve* 2:1). This custom contrasts starkly with Roman law, which provided the wife no claim to maintenance (Gardner, 68). Some divisions of labor may also have been less strict in Galilean village life, especially around harvest time. In southern Lebanon, even today peasant men and women often share interchangeable roles (see Eickelman, 194).

4. Summary.

Betrothal and marriage were commercial and legal as well as romantic matters. Some Gentiles advocated singleness, and a few advocated celibacy; some Jews also advocated celibate singleness. But the Roman world emphasized marriage and the bearing of children, and many Jewish teachers took this emphasis further. Roman laws expected sensitivity to class and citizenship issues in marriage. Greeks, Romans and the vast majority of Jews were officially monogamous. Husbands were expected to rule their homes, though wives could exercise considerable control over domestic matters. Although Palestinian Jewish customs differed in many respects from those of Greece and Rome, they also share much in common with their broader Mediterranean milieu, and Diaspora Jewish customs reflected that milieu even more closely.

See also ADULTERY, DIVORCE; FAMILY AND HOUSEHOLD; WOMEN IN GRECO-ROMAN WORLD AND JUDAISM.

BIIBLIOGRAPHY. M. B. Arthur, "Early Greece: The Origins of the Western Attitude Toward Women," in *Women in the Ancient World: The Arethusa Papers,* ed. J. Peradotto and J. P. Sullivan (SUNYSCS; Albany, NY: State University of New York Press, 1984) 7-58; R. A. Baer, *Philo's Use of the Categories Male and Female* (ALGHJ 3; Leiden: E. J. Brill, 1970); D. L. Balch, "1 Corinthians 7:32-35 and Stoic Debates About Marriage, Anxiety and Distraction," *JBL* 102 (1983) 429-39; idem, "Household Codes," in *Greco-Roman Literature and the New Testament: Selected Forms and Genres,* ed. D. E. Aune (SBLSBS 21; Atlanta: Scholars Press, 1988) 25-50; idem, *Let Wives Be Submissive: The Domestic Code in 1 Peter* (SBLMS 26; Chico, CA: Scholars Press, 1981); J. P. V. D. Balsdon, "Women in Imperial Rome," *History Today* 10 (1960) 24-31; J. R. Baskin, "Rabbinic Reflections on the Barren Wife," *HTR* 82 (1989) 101-14; J. M. Baumgarten, "4Q 502, Marriage or Golden Age Ritual?" *JJS* 34 (1983) 125-35; M. T. Boatwright, "The Imperial Women of the Early Second Century A.D.," *AJP* 112 (1991) 513-40; J. Bowman, trans. and ed., *Samaritan Documents Relating to Their History, Religion and Life* (Pittsburgh Original Texts and Translations Series 2; Pittsburgh: Pickwick, 1977); J. Carcopino, *Daily Life in Ancient Rome,* ed. H. T. Rowell (New Haven, CT: Yale University Press, 1940); B. Cohen, *Jewish and Roman Law: A Comparative Study* (2 vols.; New York: Jewish Theological Seminary of America, 1966); C. Delaney, "Seeds of Honor, Fields of Shame," in *Honor and Shame and the Unity of the Mediterranean,* ed. D. D. Gilmore (AAA 22; Washington, DC: American Anthropological Association, 1987) 35-48; W. Den Boer, *Private Morality in Greece and Rome: Some Historical Aspects* (MBCB Supplementum Quinquagesimum Septimum; Leiden: E. J. Brill, 1979); A. M. Devine, "The Low Birth Rate in Ancient Rome: A Possible Contributing Factor," *RMP* 128 (1985) 313-17; S. Dixon, *The Roman Mother* (Norman: Oklahoma University Press, 1988); E. S. Dobson, "Pliny the Younger's Depiction of Women," *CB* 58 (1982) 81-85; D. F. Eickelman, *The Middle East: An Anthropological Approach* (2d ed.; Englewood Cliffs, NJ: Prentice-Hall, 1989); L. B. Elder, "The Woman Question and Female Ascetics Among Essenes," *BA* 57 (1995) 220-34; M. B. Flory, "Livia and the History of Public Honorific Statues for Women in Rome," *TAPA* 123 (1993) 287-308; P. J.-B. Frey, ed., *Corpus Inscriptionum Iudaicarum: Recueil des Inscriptions Juives qui vont du IIIe Siècle de Notre ère* (3 vols.; Rome: Pontificio Istituto di Archeologa Cristiana, 1936-52); B. W. Frier, "Natural Fertility and Family Limitation in Roman Marriage," *CP* 89 (1994) 318-33; J. F. Gardner, *Women in Roman Law and Society* (Bloomington: Indiana University Press, 1986); S. R. Garrett, "The 'Weaker Sex' in the *Testament of Job," JBL* 112 (1993) 55-70; M. J. Geller, "New Sources for the Origins of the Rabbinic Ketubah," *HUCA* 49 (1978) 227-45; M. J. Giovannini, "Female Chastity Codes in the Circum-Mediterranean: Comparative Perspectives," in *Honor and Shame and the Unity of the Mediterranean,* ed. D. D. Gilmore (AAA 22; Washington, DC: American Anthropological Association, 1987), 61-74; M. Goodman, *State and Society in Roman Galilee, A.D. 132-212* (Oxford Center for Postgraduate Hebrew Studies; Totowa, NJ: Rowman & Allanfield, 1983); M. J. Gorman, *Abortion and the Early Church: Pagan, Jewish and*

Christian Attitudes in the Greco-Roman World (Downers Grove, IL: InterVarsity Press, 1982); J. Gould, "Law, Custom and Myth: Aspects of the Social Position of Women in Classical Athens," *JHS* 100 (1980) 38-59; N. Graetz, "Miriam: Guilty or Not Guilty?" *Judaism* 40 (1991) 184-92; J. P. Hallett, "The Role of Women in Roman Elegy: Counter-Cultural Feminism," in *Women in the Ancient World: The Arethusa Papers,* ed. J. Peradotto and J. P. Sullivan (SUNYSCS; Albany, NY: State University of New York Press, 1984) 241-62; P. E. Harrell, *Divorce and Remarriage in the Early Church: A History of Divorce and Remarriage in the Ante-Nicene Church* (Austin: R. B. Sweet Company, 1967); G. H. R. Horsley, ed., *New Documents Illustrating Early Christianity: A Review of the Greek Inscriptions and Papyri published in 1979* (North Ryde, N.S.W.: The Ancient History Documentary Research Centre, Macquarie University, 1987) vol. 4; R. A. Horsley, "Spiritual Marriage with Sophia," *VC* 33 (1979) 30-54; P. W. van der Horst, "Einige Beobachtungen zum Thema Frauen im antiken Judentum," *BTZ* 10 (1993) 77-93; idem, "Portraits of Biblical Women in Pseudo-Philo's *Liber Antiquitatum Biblicarum,*" *JSP* 5 (1989) 29-46; idem, "The Role of Women in the Testament of Job," *NedTTs* 40 (1986) 273-89; H. Hübner, "Zölibat in Qumran?" *NTS* 17 (1971) 153-67; T. Ilan, *Jewish Women in Greco-Roman Palestine* (Peabody, MA: Hendrickson, 1996); C. S. Keener, . . . *And Marries Another: Divorce and Remarriage in the Teaching of the New Testament* (Peabody, MA: Hendrickson, 1991); idem, *A Commentary on the Gospel of Matthew* (Grand Rapids, MI: Eerdmans, 1999); idem, *Paul, Women and Wives: Marriage and Women's Ministry in the Letters of Paul* (Peabody, MA: Hendrickson, 1992); D. E. E. Kleiner, "Women and Family Life on Roman Imperial Funerary Altars," *Latomus* 46 (1987) 545-54; R. S. Kraemer, "Nonliterary Evidence for Jewish Women in Rome and Egypt," *Helios* 13 (1986) 85-101; G. Langer, "Zum Vermögensrecht von Frauen in der Ehe am Beispiel des Mischna-und-Tosefta-Traktates Ketubbot," *Kairos* 34-35 (1992-93) 27-63; M. R. Lefkowitz and M. B. Fant, *Women's Life in Greece and Rome* (Baltimore: Johns Hopkins University Press, 1982); N. Lewis, *Life in Egypt Under Roman Rule* (Oxford: Clarendon Press, 1983); A. Lindemann, " 'Do Not Let a Woman Destroy the Unborn Babe in Her Belly': Abortion in Ancient Judaism and Christianity," *ST* 49 (1995) 253-71; D. Lührmann, "Neutestamentliche Haustafeln und antike Ökonomie," *NTS* 27 (1980) 83-97; A. J. Malherbe, *Moral Exhortation, A Greco-Roman Sourcebook* (LEC 4; Philadelphia: Westminster, 1986); A. Marx, "Les Racines du Célibat Essénien," *RevQ* 7 (1970) 323-42; H. McArthur, "Celibacy in Judaism at the Time of Christian Beginnings," *AUSS* 25 (1987) 163-81; M. McDonnell, "Divorce Initiated by Women in Rome," *AJAH* 8 (1983) 54-80; C. G. Montefiore and H. Loewe, *A Rabbinic Anthology* (London: Macmillan, 1938); J. J. O'Rourke, "Roman Law and the Early Church," in *The Catacombs and the Colosseum: The Roman Empire as the Setting of Primitive Christianity,* ed. S. Benko and J. J. O'Rourke (Valley Forge, PA: Judson, 1971) 165-86; K.-H. Ostmeyer, "Die Sexualethik des antiken Judentims im Licht des Babylonischen Talmuds," *BTZ* 12 (1995) 167-85; S. B. Pomeroy, *Goddesses, Whores, Wives and Slaves: Women in Classical Antiquity* (New York: Schocken, 1975); idem, "Women in Roman Egypt: A Preliminary Study Based on Papyri," in *Reflections of Women in Antiquity,* ed. H. P. Foley (New York: Gordon and Breach Science Publishers, 1981) 303-22; B. Rawson, "The Roman Family," in *The Family in Ancient Rome: New Perspectives,* ed. B. Rawson (Ithaca, NY: Cornell University Press, 1986) 1-57; T. Reekmans, "Juvenal's Views on Social Change," *AS* 2 (1971) 117-61; A. Richlin, "Approaches to the Sources on Adultery at Rome," *WS* 8 (1981) 225-50; S. Safrai, "Home and Family," in *The Jewish People in the First Century: Historical Geography, Political History, Social, Cultural and Religious Life and Institutions,* ed. S. Safrai and M. Stern (2 vols.; CRINT 1.1: Assen: Van Gorcum; Philadelphia: Fortress, 1974, 1976) 728-92; R. P. Saller, "Men's Age at Marriage and Its Consequences in the Roman Family," *CP* 82 (1987) 21-34; C. Salles, "La Diversité de la Situation des Femmes dans l'empire Romain aux 1er et 2e Siècles," *Foi et Vie* 88 (1989) 43-48; W. Scheidel, "The Most Silent Women of Greece and Rome: Rural Labor and Women's Life in the Ancient World (I)," *GR* 42 (1995) 202-17; B. D. Shaw, "The Age of Roman Girls at Marriage: Some Reconsiderations," *JRS* 77 (1987) 30-46; R. K. Sherk, ed. and trans., *The Roman Empire: Augustus to Hadrian* (TDGR 6; New York: Cambridge University Press, 1988); F. M. Snowden Jr., *Before Color Prejudice: The Ancient View of Blacks* (Cambridge, MA: Harvard University Press, 1983); B. Thiering, "The Biblical Source of Qumran Asceticism," *JBL* 93 (1974) 429-44; J. C. Thom, " 'Don't Walk on the Highways': The Pythagorean *Akousmata* and Early Christian Literature," *JBL* 113 (1994) 93-112; S. Treggiari, "Jobs in the Household of Livia," *PBSR* 43 (1975) 48-77; G. Vermes, *Jesus the Jew: A Historian's Reading of the Gospels* (Philadelphia: Fortress, 1973); D. C. Verner, *The Household of God: The Social World of the Pastoral Epistles* (SBLDS 71; Chico, CA: Scholars Press, 1983); R. B. Ward, "Musonius and Paul on Marriage," *NTS* 36 (1990) 281-89; P. R. C. Weaver, "The Status of Children in Mixed Marriages," in *The Family in Ancient Rome: New Perspectives,* ed. B. Rawson (Ithaca, NY: Cornell University Press, 1986) 145-69; J. R. Wegner, *Chattel or Person? The Status of Women in the Mishnah* (New York: Oxford University Press, 1988). C. S. Keener

MARTYRDOM TRADITION, JEWISH. *See* REVOLUTIONARY MOVEMENTS, JEWISH.

MASADA. *See* JEWISH WARS WITH ROME.

MASADA TEXTS. *See* PAPYRI, PALESTINIAN.

MASORETIC TEXT. *See* HEBREW BIBLE.

MATTHEW'S GOSPEL IN HEBREW. *See* HEBREW MATTHEW.

MELCHIZEDEK, TRADITIONS OF

The figure of Melchizedek was king and priest of God Most High in the city of Salem. He appears briefly in the OT, and his story was then elaborated upon by early Jewish *apocalyptic literature. He became particularly pivotal in the development of early Christian *messianism and the formulation of christology.

1. Old Testament Traditions
2. *Second Enoch*
3. Melchizedek in Qumran Literature
4. Other Jewish Literature
5. Melchizedek in the New Testament

1. Old Testament Traditions.

The Melchizedek traditions begin with the enigmatic appearance of Melchizedek in Genesis 14:18-20. After Abraham's conquest of the five kings (Gen 14:1-17), Abraham gives Melchizedek a tithe of the booty. The name *Melchizedek,* which means "king of righteousness," may be understood as either a personal name or a title; it is intended to underscore the symbolic or perhaps allegorical nature of the figure. The city of Salem is understood by all later Jewish tradition to have been *Jerusalem. Consequently some commentators understand the Melchizedek tradition in Genesis 14:18-20 as justifying a high priesthood in Jerusalem predating the Solomonic temple and even Abraham; however, it is difficult to understand why the Zadokite priests would have promulgated tradition that ultimately undermined their own authority.

In Psalm 110, God apparently designates a Davidic ruler—although this is not explicit—"you are a priest forever in the order of Melchizedek." Some commentators would like to see Psalm 110 as a *Hasmonean composition that justifies the secular and priestly leadership of Simon Maccabeus (c. 142-134 B.C.) because Psalm 110:1-4 can be read as an acrostic, *šmʿn* ("Simeon"); however, such a late date has not been widely accepted. Still, it is possible that the peculiar versification that gives rise to the possible acrostic identification with Simeon was Hasmonean. The Melchizedek tradition was a natural mine to excavate in the attempt to legitimate the Hasmonean pedigree. Indeed, the mystery surrounding Melchizedek in both Genesis 14 and Psalm 110 left ample interpretative room for divergent early Jewish communities to fill out his pedigree.

2. Second Enoch.

The earliest and most extensive extrabiblical tradition about Melchizedek is found in *2 Enoch* 71—72 (A and J manuscripts; *see* Enoch, Books of). Melchizedek is described as born "fully developed" as a three-year old. He has the mark of the high priesthood on him from birth and must be hidden lest the wicked kill him. God, through the agency of an archangel, hides the child Melchizedek in the garden of Eden for seven years. This child is finally placed at the head of the high priests of the future in the "center of the earth where Adam was created" (*2 Enoch* 71:35 [J]). In these texts Melchizedek is a title. There are multiple Melchizedeks "according to the order of Melchizedek," though the greatest of these is the aforementioned.

3. Melchizedek in Qumran Literature.

Although fragments of Enoch dating to the early third century B.C. are found among the *Dead Sea Scrolls, *2 Enoch* is not found and is usually considered a later composition (c. A.D. 100-200). Still, it seems likely that the traditions in *2 Enoch* have their origins in the Second Temple period, given other evidence for highly developed Melchizedek traditions in *Qumran literature.

The most prominent development of the Melchizedek traditions in Qumran literature are found in a thematic *midrash *(pesher)* known as 11QMelchizedek (11Q13; van der Woude 1965). The midrash is quite fragmentary, with only one column of text well represented. It was apparently organized around Isaiah 61, which is cited repeatedly (see lines 4, 9, 14, 19-20). The passage from Isaiah raises the issue of the release (citing Lev 25:13; Deut 15:2), which points to the ten Jubilee periods that will end in "the day of the vengeance of *ʾ ᵉlōhênû*." Although the plain sense would suggest that *ʾ ᵉlōhênû* means "our God," the Qumran interpreter takes it as a reference to Melchizedek (note lines 24-25), citing passages where he understands *ʾ ᵉlōhîm* to refer to the holy *angels who will judge the fallen angels (Pss 82:1; 7:8-9; 82:2; Is 52:7). Melchizedek is presented as the judge of both the saints of God and the fallen angels. The faithful of God will be included in Melchizedek's lot, while the fallen angels are part of the lot of *Belial. There is a similarity between the roles of Melchizedek and the archangel Michael in the **War Scroll* (1QM 9:14-16), though the two are never explicitly equated in Qumranic literature. F. García Martínez has suggested that Melchizedek may be identified with the "Son of God" in another Qumran composition, the *Aramaic Apocalypse* (4Q "Son of God" [4Q246]).

An underlying dualism in the Melchizedek traditions is evident by the appearance of the anti-figure Melchireshaʿ ("king of wickedness") in 4QAmram (4Q543-548) and 4QBenedictions[f] (4Q280). 4QAmram is quite fragmentary, yet a few observations can be recovered. In 4QAmram, the father of *Moses, Amram, describes his vision of the Watchers, including the chief Angel of Darkness. One of the three names of this angel is Melchireshaʿ (the other two names are lost). Melchireshaʿ addresses the leader of the army of light, who also has three names. One of the names of Melchireshaʿ's counterpart, the leader of the army of light, was probably Melchizedek (and also perhaps Michael), but his three names are also lost. 4QBenedictions is also fragmentary, but it suggests that Melchireshaʿ is set apart "from the sons of light for evil because he turned away from following God." In other words, it suggests that the Qumran sectarians read the Melchizedek traditions as part of the myth of the fallen angels (see Gen 6:1-4).

4. Other Jewish Literature.

The Palestinian Jew turned historian, Flavius *Josephus, took a purely human interpretation of Melchizedek. He writes that Abraham "was received by the king of Solyma, Melchizedek, whose name means righteous king, and such he was by common consent, inasmuch as for this reason he was moreover made priest of God; Solyma was in fact the place afterward called Hierosolyma [that is, Jerusalem]" (Josephus *Ant.* 1.10.2 §180).

*Philo Judaeus lived in *Alexandria and was roughly a contemporary with Jesus as well as the later stages of the Qumran community. He also took a strictly this-worldly view of Melchizedek: "God has also made Melchizedek both king of peace, for that is the meaning of Salem, and his own priest. . . . For he is named 'the righteous king' [= Melchizedek], and a king is one who is opposed to the tyrant; the one is the author of laws, the other of lawlessness" (Philo *Leg. All.* 3.25-26 §§79-82).

Both the second-century Aramaic *Targum Neofiti* and the *Fragment Targum* identify Melchizedek with Noah's son Shem in its translation of Genesis 14:18: "The king of Righteousness (Melka-sedek), the king of Jerusalem—he is Shem, the great one—brought out bread and wine, for he was the priest who served in the High Priesthood before the Most High God" (also the later *Targum Pseudo-Jonathan).*

Later *rabbinic traditions understand the high priesthood to have first been given to Shem-Melchizedek (Gen 14:18-20) but then transferred to Aaron through Abraham. Psalm 110:4 was read, "You [Abraham] are a priest forever" (see *b. Zebaḥ.* 62a). From manuscripts of *b. Sukkah* 52b, we learn that Melchizedek is a righteous priest who was apparently translated into heaven and who would reappear in the messianic age. But he is a purely human figure. The connection of the Melchizedek tradition with the traditions about the fallen angels was thus marginalized by rabbinic *Judaism, perhaps even in response to the prominence they were given in early Christianity.

5. Melchizedek in the New Testament.

The importance of the Melchizedek traditions

in early Christianity begins already in the Gospels, when Jesus baffles the *Pharisees with his question from Psalm 110: "What do you think of the Messiah? Whose son is he?" The Pharisees responded, "The son of David." He said to them, "How is it then that David by the Spirit calls him Lord, saying, 'The Lord said to my Lord, "Sit at my right hand, until I put your enemies under your feet"?' If David thus calls him Lord, how can he be his son?" (Mt 22:41-45). Jesus uses the enigmatic and debated interpretation of the Melchizedek traditions in early Judaism in order to raise questions about the character of the expected Davidic Messiah.

The figure of Melchizedek becomes central in the book of Hebrews' development of christology (esp. Heb 5, 7). The ambiguity in the OT traditions about Melchizedek, as well as the debate among early Jewish interpreters, left an ideal opening for the author of Hebrews to chart a new way. Melchizedek provides a way for combining the royal and priestly offices ostensibly held by separate individuals. To be sure, the Hasmonean priest-kings had already combined these offices, though they were opposed in part for that reason. The fact that Melchizedek appears suddenly in Genesis 14 gave rise to his identification with an angel in early Jewish apocalyptic literature; for the author of Hebrews, however, it points to Jesus' timelessness; that is, Melchizedek is "without father, without mother, without genealogy, having neither beginning of days nor end of life, but resembling the Son of God, he remains a priest forever" (Heb 7:3).

Hence Hebrews argues that there are two changes in priesthood, one from Melchizedek to Abraham, as in Jewish tradition, but a further transference to Jesus. Since Jesus is the one and only eternal high priest there need be no further transference of the priesthood (Heb 7:12). The emphasis on Jesus as priest in Hebrews undoubtedly responds to the weakness in his messianic claims; that is, by genealogy he was a Davidic messiah, but what about the Messiah of Aaron? Melchizedek provides the way through (see Yadin; Delcor; Gieschen).

See also BELIAL, BELIAR, DEVIL, SATAN; ANGELS OF THE NATIONS; VISIONS OF AMRAM (4Q543-548); WAR SCROLL (1QM).

BIBLIOGRAPHY. M. Delcor, "Melchizedek from Genesis to the Qumran Texts and the Epistle to the Hebrews," *JSJ* 2 (1971) 115-35; D. Flusser, "Melchizedek and the Son of Man," in *Judaism and the Origins of Christianity* (Jerusalem: Magnes, 1988) 186-92; C. A. Gieschen, "The Different Functions of a Similar Melchizedek Tradition in 2 Enoch and the Epistle to the Hebrews," in *Early Christian Interpretation of the Scriptures of Israel: Investigations and Proposals,* ed. C. A. Evans and J. A. Sanders (JSNTSup 148; Sheffield: JSOT, 1997) 364-79; R. Hayward, "Shem, Melchizedek and Concern with Christianity in the Pentateuchal Targumim," in *Targumic and Cognate Studies: Essays in Honor of Martin McNamara,* ed. K. J. Cathcart and M. Maher (JSOTSup 230; Sheffield: Sheffield Academic Press, 1996) 67-80; F. L. Horton Jr., *The Melchizedek Tradition* (SNTSMS 30; Cambridge: Cambridge University Press, 1976); P. J. Kobelski, *Melchizedek and Melchireša*ʿ (CBQMS 10; Washington, DC: The Catholic Biblical Association of America, 1981); J. L. Marshall, "Melchizedek in Hebrews, Philo and Justin Martyr," *SE* 7 (1982) 339-42; P. J. Nel, "Psalm 110 and the Melchizedek Tradition," *JNSL* 22 (1996) 1-14; M. J. Paul, "The Order of Melchizedek (Ps 110:4 and Heb 7:3)," *WTJ* 49 (1987) 195-211; B. A. Pearson, "The Figure of Melchizedek in Gnostic Literature," in *Gnosticism, Judaism and Egyptian Christianity* (Minneapolis: Fortress, 1990) 108-23; E. Puech, "Notes sur le Manuscrit de 11Q Melkisédeq," *RevQ* 12 (1987) 483-513; S. E. Robinson, "The Apocryphal Story of Melchizedek," *JSJ* 18 (1987) 26-39; A. S. van der Woude, "Melchisedek als himmlische Erlösergestalt in den neugefunden eschatologischen Midraschim aus Qumran Höhle XI," כה *1940-1965* (OS 14; Leiden: E. J. Brill, 1965) 354-73; A. S. van der Woude and M. de Jonge, "11Q Melchizedek and the New Testament," *NTS* (1966) 301-26; Y. Yadin, "The Dead Sea Scrolls and the Epistle to the Hebrews," *ScrHier* 4 (1958) 36-55. W. M. Schniedewind

MESSIANIC APOCALYPSE (4Q521)

The so-called *Messianic Apocalypse* (4Q521) has generated interest among NT interpreters because of its reference to a messiah to whom "heaven and earth will listen." The text is sometimes referred to as the *Works of the Messiah* or *On Resurrection.* The text, which dates to 75 to 50 B.C. and may have been produced at *Qumran, was published in 1992 and is frequently discussed in connection to Jesus' reply to the imprisoned John the Baptist.

1. Contents of the *Messianic Apocalypse* (4Q521)
2. Interpretations of the *Messianic Apocalypse*
3. The *Messianic Apocalypse* and the New Testament

1. Contents of the *Messianic Apocalypse* (4Q521). The *Messianic Apocalypse* (4Q521) consists of seventeen or eighteen fragments. Of these fragments the best known is fragment 2, which contains the greater part of fourteen lines that make up column 2 (with a few words and letters in column 1 and seven partially preserved lines in column 3; see PAM 41.676 and 43.604). This column, alluding to Psalm 146:6-8, speaks of "his [probably God's] Messiah," to whom "heaven and earth will listen, [and all th]at is in them will not turn away from the commandment of the holy ones" (lines 1-2). The text goes on to speak of an era of blessing and restoration, a time when God "will glorify the pious on the throne of an eternal kingdom, releasing captives, giving sight to the blind and raising up those who are bo[wed down]" (lines 7-8). The "Lord will do as he s[aid], for he will heal the wounded, give life to the dead, and preach good news to the poor" (lines 11-12). Lines 7-8 and 11-12 allude to several passages from Isaiah, such as Isaiah 35:5-6 ("the eyes of the blind shall be opened"), Isaiah 61:1 ("anointed . . . to preach good news to the poor"), Isaiah 26:19 ("your dead shall live, their bodies shall rise") and possibly Isaiah 53:5 ("he was wounded . . . and with his stripes we are healed").

Fragment 2 column 3 alludes to Malachi 4:5-6, with the promise that "the fathers will return to the sons" (line 2). The day of judgment appears to be in view in fragments 7 + 5, which speak of "those who do the good before the Lord" (line 4), those who are "the accursed" and have been set aside "for death" (line 5) and the Lord "who gives life to the dead of his people" (line 6). We probably have contact here with Daniel 12:2, which promises resurrection and "everlasting life" for some and "everlasting contempt" for others. Lines 1-3 ("the earth and all that is in it, the seals and all they contain") parallel the opening lines of fragment 2. Fragment 8 refers to "all his anointed ones" (line 9), which is probably a reference to the prophets (see line 10, which says they "will speak the word of the Lord"), though the reference to "holy vessels" in the previous line may suggest that the "anointed ones" are priests (so Puech, 1992, 509).

2. Interpretations of the *Messianic Apocalypse*. E. Puech (1992, 497) and others have understood the Messiah of 4Q521 2 ii as the traditional, royal figure ("Messiah-king") whom the awaited Elijah-like prophet will announce. In his most recent discussion, Puech (2000, 543) thinks "his (or its) messiah" *(m^e^sîḥô)* may be plural ("its messiahs," *m^e^sîḥaw*), in which case reference is to the two anointed figures, the king and the priest (as in 1 QS 9:11: "until the coming of the prophet and the anointed ones of Aaron and of Israel"). If the word is read as a singular, then it is probably to be read in reference to the "priest-prophet of messianic times." The latter option is close to what J. J. Collins (1995a, 117-22; 1998, 112-16) has contended. He thinks the "anointed" figure of this scroll is himself an anointed prophet, probably on the model of the *eschatological Elijah, through whom God will heal and raise the dead.

Collins observes that the principal task of this anointed figure is to "preach good news to the poor" (line 12), which alludes to Isaiah 61:1, a text understood to be referring to the eschatological prophet. In the Aramaic paraphrase, this passage is understood explicitly as referring to the prophet: "*The prophet said,* 'A spirit *of prophecy before the Lord God* is upon me, because the Lord has *exalted* me to announce good news to the poor . . .'" (*Tg. Isa.* 61:1, with italics denoting departures from the Hebrew). Not only are the words "the prophet" and "a spirit of prophecy" added to the text, but also "anointed" has been replaced with "exalted," perhaps to avoid confusing the eschatological prophet with the Messiah. In any case it is clear that the task outlined in Isaiah 61:1 is understood to be the duty of the eschatological prophet, not that of the awaited royal Messiah.

Collins's interpretation gains further support from the allusion to Malachi in 4Q521 2 iii 2: "it is su[re]: The fathers will return to the sons." According to Malachi 4:5-6 (Heb 3:23-24), when Elijah comes, "he will turn the hearts of fathers to their children and the hearts of children to their fathers." This feature of Elijah's eschatological ministry is mentioned in Sirach 48:10, "you are ready at the appointed time . . . to turn the heart of the father to the son and to restore the tribes of Jacob" and is echoed in Luke 1:16-17, in reference to the promised birth of John the Baptist: "And he will turn many of the sons of Israel to the Lord their God, and he will go before him in the spirit and power of Elijah, to turn the hearts of the fathers to the children . . . tc make ready for the Lord a people prepared."

Collins (1995a, 118-19) suspects that the author of 4Q521 understands lines 11-12 ("the Lord will do as he s[aid], for he will heal the wounded, give life to the dead, and preach good news to the poor") as God acting through his agent the anointed prophet. This understanding is consistent with Jewish messianism seen in other texts, such as in *y. Ketubbot* 12:3, which says "the dead will come to life in the time of the Messiah," in *m. Soṭa* 9:15, which says "the resurrection of the dead comes through Elijah," and in 1QS 9:11, which speaks of the coming of "the Prophet and the anointed ones of Aaron and of Israel" (*see* Rule of the Community). A prophet is expected to come in the power of Elijah, through whom Israel's healing and restoration will take place, and the Messiah is to come, who will rule Israel faithfully.

3. The *Messianic Apocalypse* and the New Testament.

Jesus' reply to the imprisoned John the Baptist contains three Isaianic phrases also found in 4Q521: the blind receiving sight, the raising of the dead and the preaching of good news to the poor. The Matthean Evangelist explains that John queried Jesus because he had heard of the "deeds of the Messiah." Reference to the Messiah (or anointed) gives us yet a fourth parallel. From these parallels many interpreters have concluded that Jesus and the author of 4Q521 share a similar eschatological and messianic expectation. The story is found in the Synoptic double tradition: John "sent word by his disciples and said to him, 'Are you he who is to come, or shall we look for another?' And Jesus answered them, 'Go and tell John what you hear and see: the blind receive their sight and the lame walk, lepers are cleansed and the deaf hear, and the dead are raised up, and the poor have good news preached to them. And blessed is he who takes no offense at me'" (Mt 11:2-6; cf. Lk 7:19-23).

The authenticity of the double tradition is assured by the improbability that the early church would create tradition in which such a significant figure as John the Baptist, Jesus' mentor and (in more theological terms) "forerunner," would express doubt in Jesus. Moreover, one would expect to find a more direct and enhanced testimony to Jesus in a piece of fictional and confessional material.

Because 4Q521 introduces the blessings of the eschatological period as the time when "heaven and earth will listen to his Messiah" and because these blessings match closely those mentioned by Jesus, scholars now conclude that Jesus' reply to the Baptist was indeed messianic in nature. Thus 4Q521 makes a significant contribution to research into Jesus' self-understanding. This new evidence suggests that Jesus did understand himself in messianic terms. However, the precise nature of this messianism remains unclear. It is probable that it is a prophetic messianism, perhaps even modeled after Malachi's promise of the return of Elijah. In the NT Gospels John denies that he is Elijah (Jn 1:21) and speaks of the coming of one "mightier" than himself (Mk 1:7; Mt 3:11-12; Lk 3:16-17). Moreover, Jesus refers to himself as a prophet (Mk 6:4) and was even regarded by some as Elijah or some other prophet (Mk 6:15; 8:28). Although it is possible that at a later stage in his ministry Jesus began to view John as Elijah (Mk 9:11-13) and himself in more exalted, even royal terms (cf. Mk 11:1-10, where Jesus enters *Jerusalem on an ass, in fulfillment of Zech 9:9), at the outset of his ministry in which he proclaims the kingdom he may have seen himself as the eschatological Elijah.

See also MESSIANISM.

BIBLIOGRAPHY. M. Becker, "4Q521 und die Gesalbten," *RevQ* 18 (1997) 73-96; R. Bergmeier, "Beobachtungen zu 4Q521 f 2, II, 1–13," *ZDMG* 145 (1995) 38-48; J. J. Collins, "Jesus, Messianism and the Dead Sea Scrolls," in *Qumran-Messianism: Studies on the Messianic Expectations in the Dead Sea Scrolls*, ed. J. H. Charlesworth, H. Lichtenberger and G. S. Oegema (Tübingen: Mohr Siebeck, 1998) 100-120, esp. 112-16; idem, *The Scepter and the Star: The Messiahs of the Dead Sea Scrolls and Other Ancient Literature* (ABRL 10; New York: Doubleday, 1995a) 117-22; idem, "The Works of the Messiah," *DSD* 1 (1995b) 98-112; J. Duhaime, "Le messie et les saints dans un fragment apocalyptique de Qumrân (4Q 521 2)," in *Ce Dieu qui vient: mélanges offerts à Bernard Renaud,* ed. R. Kuntzmann (LD 159; Paris: Editions du Cerf, 1995) 265-73; C. A. Evans, " 'Go and Tell John What You See and Hear': Jesus, the Kingdom and 4Q521," in *Jars of Clay: The New Testament's Use of the Old in Its Historical-Hermeneutical Milieu,* ed. P. E. Enns (Grand Rapids, MI: Zondervan, forthcoming); K.-W. Niebuhr, "4Q521,2 II—Ein Eschatologischer Psalm," in *Mogilany 1995,* ed. Z. J. Kapera (Krakow: Enigma, 1998) 151-68; E. Puech, "Une apocalypse messianique (4Q521)," *RevQ* 15 (1992) 475-519; idem, *La croyance des Esséniens en la vie future,* vol. 2 (EB 22; Paris: Gabalda, 1993) 627-92; idem, "Messianic Apocalypse," in *Encyclopedia of the Dead Sea Scrolls,* ed. L. H. Schiffman and J. C. VanderKam (2 vols., Oxford: Oxford University Press, 2000) 1:543-44; idem, "Messianism, Resurrection and Eschatology at Qumran and in the New Testament," in *The Community of the Renewed Covenant: The Notre Dame Symposium on the Dead Sea Scrolls,* ed. E. Ulrich and J. C. VanderKam (CJAS 10; Notre Dame, IN: University of Notre Dame Press, 1994) 235-56; E. Puech, ed., *Textes Hébreux (4Q521-4Q528, 4Q576-4Q579)* (DJD 25; Oxford: Oxford University Press, forthcoming); J. D. Tabor and M. O. Wise, "4Q521 'On Resurrection' and the Synoptic Gospel Tradition: A Preliminary Study," *JSP* 10 (1992) 149-62; G. Vermes, "Qumran Forum Miscellanea I," *JJS* 43 (1992) 299-305.

C. A. Evans

MESSIANIC RULE. *See* RULE OF THE CONGREGATION/MESSIANIC RULE (1QSa).

MESSIANISM

Messianism is the expectation of a coming anointed person or persons who will redeem Israel and/or the church. The appearance of this anointed figure is usually understood to be part of a larger eschatological drama whereby human activity on earth is appreciably altered. At that time God's will on earth will be more tangibly and perhaps permanently experienced, often under the rubric "kingdom of God." It is usually believed that this anointed figure is part of the climax of human history and will not be succeeded by other anointed figures.

1. Derivation of the Term *Messiah*
2. Origins of Messianism
3. Anachronisms in Jewish and Christian Interpretation
4. Varieties of Messianism
5. Messianism and New Testament Christology

1. Derivation of the Term *Messiah*.

The word "messiah" comes from the Greek *messias* (cf. Jn 1:41; 4:25), which is itself a transliteration of the Hebrew *māšîaḥ* (2 Sam 22:51; 23:1), meaning one who is "smeared" or "anointed" (with oil). *Māšîaḥ* occurs some 38 times in the OT. The Greek equivalent is *christos* (cf. LXX 2 Sam 22:51; 23:1), which occurs some 529 times in the NT (about half in Paul; more than half, if one includes the Pastorals). The nominal form is derived from the verbs *māšaḥ* (Hebrew) and *chriein* (Greek), which mean "to anoint" or "to smear (with oil)." When the nominal form is definite (Heb. *hammāšîaḥ*; Aram. *m*^{a}*šîḥāʾ*), it is usually translated "the Messiah." The Greek definite form, *ho christos,* is usually translated "the Christ."

Israel's tradition of anointing the *priest is ancient (cf. Ex 28:41; 30:30; 40:13-15; Lev 16:32; Num 3:3). Of special interest is the anointing of the high priest (Ex 40:13; Lev 7:35), who in Numbers 35:25 is said to be "anointed with holy oil." Yeshua ben Sira eulogizes Aaron, stating that "Moses ordained him, and anointed him with holy oil" (Sir 45:15). Early rabbinic literature is keenly interested in the "anointed (high) priest" (cf. *m. Hor.* 2:1, 2, 3, 6, 7; 3:1, 2, 4, 6; *m. Zebaḥ.* 4:3; *m. Menaḥ.* 5:3, 5; 6:2, 4; *m. Meʿil.* 2:9) much more than it is in the royal Messiah (cf. *m. Soṭa* 9:15; on this point, see Neusner 1984).

The kings of Judah and Israel were "anointed," usually by prophets, as well as by priests. Especially important is Samuel's anointing of Saul (1 Sam 9:9, 16; 10:1; 15:1, 17) and David (1 Sam 16:1-3, 12-13; 2 Sam 12:7; cf. Sir 46:13). Nathan the prophet and Zadok the priest anointed Solomon (1 Kings 1:34; cf. 1:39, 45). Elijah was commanded to anoint Hazael to be king over Syria and Jehu to be king over Israel (1 Kings 19:15-16), though it would be Elisha who carried out the task (2 Kings 9:1-3, 6, 12; cf. Sir 48:8). Even in the period of the judges we find tradition of someone being anointed king (Judg 9:8, 15). Frequently the anointed king is called "the Lord's anointed" (1 Sam 16:6; 24:6, 10; 26:9, 11, 16, 23; 2 Sam 1:14, 16; 19:21; cf. Ps 2:2; 18:50; 20:6; 28:8). The psalmist, on behalf of the "anointed," sometimes appeals to God for help (Ps 84:9; 89:38, 51; 132:10, 17).

Elijah was told to anoint Elisha, his prophetic successor, though the deed itself is not actually narrated (1 Kings 19:15-16; cf. 2 Kings 9:1-3, 6, 12). The anointing of Elisha is the only instance of an anointed prophet. However, one should recall that the prophetic speaker in Isaiah 61 claims to have the Spirit of the Lord and to have been "anointed" to preach (cf. *Tg. Isa.* 61:1: "The prophet said: 'A spirit of prophecy before the Lord God is upon me'"). The association in a sermon, which is attributed to Jesus (Luke 4:18-27), of this passage from Isaiah with the ministries of Elijah and Elisha is probably not accidental but reflects the tradition of the anointed prophet.

2. Origins of Messianism.

Messianism originates in the OT, which speaks of anointed priests, kings and prophets. But none of these anointed persons are to be understood as eschatological figures of deliverance. Sometime in the third or second century B.C. "messiah" takes on this eschatological nuance (though hopes for a new Davidic king, expressed in some of the prophets, made important contributions to the messianism that would eventually emerge). In reaction to the oppression of Greek and Roman rule, and in response to what was perceived as usurpation of the high priesthood on the part of the Hasmoneans and their successors, hopes for the appearance of a righteous king and/or priest began to be expressed. The later usurpation of Israel's throne by Herod and his successors only fueled these hopes. The literature of this time speaks of the appearance of worthy anointed persons through whom the restoration of Israel might take place. These hopes and predictions drew upon passages of Scripture that spoke of anointed persons and upon passages that spoke in more indirect ways of individuals or symbols that lent themselves to eschatological or salvific interpretations.

Three passages in particular played an important, generative role in the rise of messianism: Genesis 49:10; Numbers 24:17 and Isaiah 11:1-6. All of these passages are interpreted in a messianic sense in the Dead Sea Scrolls and other early Jewish and Christian writings.

2.1. Genesis 49:10. In 4Q252 5:1-7, Gen 49:10-11 is cited and is understood to refer to the "Branch of David." The passage may also be alluded to in 4QpIsa[a] (4Q161) frags. 7–10 iii 25, again in a messianic sense. The messianic potential appears to have been enhanced in the LXX. All four targums to the Pentateuch render the passage in an explicitly messianic sense ("king messiah" is mentioned in Gen 49:10, 11, and 12). Jacob's blessing (Gen 49:8-12) is referred to in *Testament of Judah* 1:6 ("my father declared to me, 'You shall be king'") and in *Testament of Judah* 22:3 seems to be understood in a messianic sense. The description of the warrior Messiah in Revelation 19:11-16 may have this passage, as well as Isaiah 11, in mind (compare Rev 19:13 with Gen 49:11); and it may be alluded to in Hebrews 7:14. Christian messianic interpretation of the passage becomes commonplace in the second century (cf. Justin Martyr *Apol. I* 32, 54; *Dial. Tryph.* 52, 120; Clement of Alexandria *Paed.* 1.5, 6; Irenaeus *Haer.* 4.10.2).

2.2. Numbers 24:17. The interpretation of Numbers 24:17 is similar to that of Genesis 49:10. All four Pentateuch targums paraphrase the passage in explicitly messianic terms. The Hebrew text's "a star shall come forth out of Jacob, and a scepter shall rise out of Israel" becomes in the Aramaic "a king shall arise out of Jacob and be anointed the Messiah out of Israel" (*Tg. Onq.*; cf. *Tgs. Neof., Ps. J., Frg.*). Messianic interpretation of Numbers 24:17 is widely attested in traditions dating to the first century and earlier (*T. Jud.* 24:1-6; CD 7:20; 1QSb 5:27-28; 1QM 11:4-9; 4Q175 1:9-13; possibly Philo *Vit. Mos.* 1.52 §290; *Praem. Poen.* 16 §95; *Orphica* 31 = Aristobulus frag. 4:5). It is probably to this passage that Josephus refers when he says that his countrymen were misled by an "ambiguous oracle," which promised that "one from their country would become ruler of the world" (Josephus *J.W.* 6.5.4 §§312-13; cf. 3.8.9 §§400-402). The "star" that "stood over the city" of Jerusalem would have only fueled such speculation (Josephus *J.W.* 6.5.3 §289). At issue was not the messianic orientation of the oracle; rather, the question was to whom the oracle applied. Of course, Josephus here is being disingenuous. It is very probable that he too understood the passage in the way his contemporaries did (at least at the beginning of the Jewish War). Instead, Josephus deliberately distanced himself from popular Jewish interpretation and applied the oracle to General Vespasian, his patron, "who was proclaimed emperor on Jewish soil." Early Christians were also aware of the passage's messianic potential, as seen in the "star" of Matthew 2:2 and the magis' assumption that it pointed to the birthplace of the "king of the Jews." *Simon ben Kosiba's nickname *bar kokhba* ("son of the star") apparently was inspired by this passage. According to rabbinic tradition, this man claimed to be the Messiah, or at least was proclaimed as such by some of his following (cf. *y.*

Ta'an. 4:5 §8; *b. Sanh.* 93b; Justin Martyr *Apol. I* 31; *Dial. Tryph.* 106; Irenaeus *Haer.* 3.9.2), though in the wake of his defeat his sobriquet was changed to *bar kozibah* ("son of the lie").

2.3. Isaiah 11:1-6. In the Hebrew text, the oracle of Isaiah 11 anticipates the coming forth of "a shoot from the stump of Jesse, even a branch (that) shall grow out of his roots" (*Isa.* 11:1). The Isaiah targum renders the verse, "And a king shall come forth from the sons of Jesse, and the Messiah shall be exalted from the sons of his sons" (cf. *Tg.* Is 11:6: "In the days of the Messiah of Israel"). Much earlier the LXX had enhanced the messianic potential of Isaiah 11:10: "And there shall be in that day the root of Jesse, even he who arises to rule over nations"). Paul quotes this passage and applies it to "Christ" (Rom 15:12; cf. Rev 5:5; 22:16; Clement of Alexandria *Strom.* 5.6). Isaiah 11 is taken in a messianic sense in 4QpIsa[a] frags. 7–10 iii 22-29 and is echoed in 1QSb 5:21-26, a passage which describes the blessing that is to be pronounced upon the Prince of the congregation. In 4 Ezra 13:2-10, Isaiah 11:4 is alluded to and applied to the man who "flew with the clouds of heaven" (cf. Dan 7:13). Messianic interpretation of Isaiah 11 probably underlies 4Q285 5:1-6 and *Testament of Levi* 18:7 as well. Early Christian writers were especially fond of Isaiah 11 (for Is 11:1, cf. Mt 2:23; Acts 13:23; Heb 7:14; Rev 5:5; 22:16; Justin Martyr *Apol. I* 32; *Dial. Tryph.* 87; Clement of Alexandria *Paed.* 1.7; Irenaeus *Haer.* 3.9.3; *Sib. Or.* 6:8, 16; 7:38; 8:254; for Is 11:2, cf. Eph 1:17; 1 Pet 4:14; Irenaeus *Haer.* 3.17.1; for Is 11:3, cf. Jn 7:24; Clement of Alexandria *Paed.* 1.7; for Is 11:4, cf. Jn 7:24; Eph 6:17; 2 Thess 2:8; Rev 19:11; Clement of Alexandria *Paed.* 1.7; Irenaeus *Haer.* 4.33.1; for Is 11:5, cf. Eph 6:14).

The data therefore suggest that the messianism attested in early sources, such as the Dead Sea Scrolls, coheres with what can be ascertained from other Jewish sources from this period of time (such as some of the pseudepigrapha and NT writings) and even later (such as the targums and rabbinic literature). The Scrolls contain some distinctive ideas in certain details (such as the nature of the final war at the end of days and the Messiah's role in it, or the Messiah's submission to the priests), but it would appear that in most of the major points, Qumran messianism is not much different from that held by other pious, hopeful Jews (on this point, see Collins 1995b).

3. Anachronisms in Jewish and Christian Interpretation.

Until relatively recent times, Jewish and Christian interpreters often read messianic ideas of later periods back into the first century. Jewish interpreters assumed that the messianism of the rabbinic literature (the diversity of which was itself often unappreciated) was "normative" and reached back to the times of *Shammai and *Hillel, and perhaps back even further. Christian interpreters sometimes assumed that aspects of Chalcedonian christology were operative in the messianism of Jesus' contemporaries.

Many of the beliefs regarding the supernatural identity and/or abilities of the Messiah in both Jewish and Christian traditions do not reflect pre-A.D. 70 ideas. The Messiah was not expected to perform miracles, though miracles might occur when he appeared (as assumed in 4Q521; cf. Jesus' reply to the imprisoned John the Baptist in Mt 11:5 par. Lk 7:22). Belief that the Messiah is divine is a Christian idea; it is not Jewish, even if in traditions like those of *1 Enoch*, the Messiah appears to enjoy a heavenly co-regency. Belief that the Messiah would suffer death in behalf of his people is largely a Christian idea, though the possibilities for such thinking may be traced to Jewish ideas of the suffering and martyrdom of the righteous (as in 2 Macc 6—7; 4 Macc 5—8). Ideas of the Messiah's existence before his birth, or even before the creation of the world, are post-A.D. 70 and appear in various ways in both Jewish and Christian contexts. For the latter, it becomes an integral part of christology, with its earliest explicit expression found in the Gospel of John (esp. Jn 1:1-18) and an even earlier implicit expression found in Paul (Col 1:15-17). Even in these instances, however, Christian ideas are rooted in Jewish traditions of the eternal Word or Wisdom of God (cf. Sir 24).

The important point is to take into account the diversity of Jewish messianism prior to Christianity and to recognize the development of Christian messianism in the aftermath of Jesus' ministry, death and resurrection. What became christology in the NT writings and in the later creeds must be carefully distinguished from pre-A.D. 70 Jewish messianism.

4. Varieties of Messianism.

Messianism developed in the postexilic period and seems to have taken on fresh vigor and variety in the Greek and Roman periods. The Dead

Sea Scrolls and various "intertestamental" writings, many of which are related in some ways to the Scrolls, offer a variety of messianic expectations.

4.1. Texts That Speak of an "Anointed" Figure.

4.1.1. Pseudepigrapha. There are seven early and important texts in the OT pseudepigrapha that speak of the Messiah. The reference in *1 Enoch* 48:10 ("For they have denied the Lord of the Spirits and his Messiah") appears to reflect the language of Psalm 2:2: "The kings of the earth set themselves, and the rulers take counsel together, against the LORD and his anointed." The reference in *1 Enoch* 52:4 ("All these things you have seen happen by the authority of his Messiah so that he may give orders and be praised upon the earth") may reflect the idea that the "son of man" will receive authority (cf. Dan 7:13-14).

The textually uncertain 4 Ezra 7:28-29 reads: "For my son the Messiah shall be revealed with those who are with him, and those who remain shall rejoice four hundred years. And after these years my son the Messiah shall die, and all who draw human breath." Although it is possible that the epithet "my son the Messiah," instead of something more simple like "my servant," is due to Christian alteration of the text, we may have a genuine Jewish reading, which alludes to Psalm 2:2 ("the Lord and his anointed") and 2:7 ("You are my son, today I have begotten you"). In 4 Ezra 12:32 the "lion" (of the vision in 4 Ezra 11:1—12:3) is identified as "the Messiah whom the Most High has kept until the end of days, who will arise from the posterity of David." Here we probably have an allusion to Isaiah 11:1 ("a shoot from the stump of Jesse") and Genesis 49:9 ("as a lion").

The Messiah of the **Psalms of Solomon* is explicitly Davidic (*Pss. Sol.* 17:4, 21). The awaited Davidic king of Israel "shall be the Lord Messiah" (*Pss. Sol.* 17:32), who will appear in "the appointed day" (*Pss. Sol.* 18:5). He will drive out the wicked (*Pss. Sol.* 17:27), will purge Jerusalem of sinners (*Pss. Sol.* 17:30, 32, 36; 18:5), and will lead Israel (*Pss. Sol.* 17:26), judging the tribes of the people (*Pss. Sol.* 17:26), who will be distributed upon the land according to their tribes (*Pss. Sol.* 17:28). Happy are those who will be born in those days, to live "under the rod of discipline of the Lord Messiah" (*Pss. Sol.* 18:7; cf. 17:42). Some scholars believe it is necessary to emend *Psalms of Solomon* 17:32 and 18:7 to read "the Lord's Messiah." However, Greek and Syriac MSS uniformly read "the Lord Messiah." "Lord" here should not be understood in the later Christian sense, or in reference to Yahweh. It is rather part of the Messiah's honorific title and may in fact be modeled after 1 Kings 1:31, 37, 43, 47, where we find the address "lord king David."

4.1.2. Qumran. Some thirty texts in the Dead Sea Scrolls speak of anointed personages. About half of these are in reference to what is probably the traditional, royal Messiah. Most of the other texts are in reference to the prophets. A few refer to the priest and one is in reference to Moses. The texts that speak of an awaited anointed person, probably the royal Messiah, are as follows:

(1) CD 12:23—13:1: "until the appearance of the anointed of Aaron and of Israel."

(2) CD 14:19 (= 4Q266 frag.18 iii 12): "[until the anoin]ted of Aaron and of Israel appears and expiates their iniquity."

(3) CD 19:10-11: "others will be delivered up to the sword at the coming of the anointed of Aaron and of Israel."

(4) CD 20:1: "the anointed of Aaron and of Israel appears."

(5) 1QS 9:11: "until the coming of the prophet and the anointed ones of Aaron and of Israel."

(6) 1QSa 2:11-12: "when [God] will have be[got]ten the anointed one among them." This text has been vigorously debated, with several emendations proposed for *yôlîd* ("begotten"). However, these emendations are hardly necessary, for not only is *yôlîd* the most probable original reading, the language of the passage seems to be an unmistakable allusion to Psalm 2:2, 7: "the Lord and his Messiah . . . 'You are my son; today I have begotten you.' "

(7) 1QSa 2:14-15: "afterward the [anoin]ted one of Israel will [enter]; and the chiefs of the cl[ans (*or* thousands) of Israel] will sit before him."

(8) 1QSa 2:20-21: "afterwar[d] the anointed one of Israel [will str]etch out his hands over the bread."

(9) 4Q252 frag.1 v. 3-4: "until the coming of the anointed one of righteousness, the branch of David."

(10) 4Q381 frag.15 7: "and I your anointed one have gained understanding."

(11) 4Q382 frag.16 2: "[an]ointed one of Isra[e]l."

(12) 4Q458 frag.2 ii 6: "one anointed with the oil of the kingdom."

(13) 4Q521 frags. 2 + 4 ii 1: "[hea]ven and earth will obey his anointed one."

(14) 4Q521 frag.7 3: "you shall fall[?] by the hand of [his anoin]ted."

4.2. Texts That Speak of Messianic Figures Who Are Not Said to Be "Anointed." There are several other texts that speak of the Messiah, but without using the word "anointed." Many of these texts employ the epithet "Prince" *(nāśî)*; most of them are found in the Dead Sea Scrolls:

(1) CD 7:19-20 (= 4Q266 frag. 3 iv 9): "'a rod is risen from Israel' [Num 24:17]. The rod is the prince of the whole congregation."

(2) 1QSb 5:20: "for the Instructor to bless the prince of the congregation."

(3) 1QM 3:16: "the name of the prince of the myriad."

(4) 1QM 5:1: "and on the st[af]f of the prince of the whole congregation they shall write [his] name."

(5) 4Q496 frag. 10 3-4 (cf. 1QM 3:11-15): "the [great standard of the pri]nce who heads [. . .] 'People [of God' and the name of Isra]e[l and] Aaro[n] and [the name of] the prince."

(6) 4Q161 frags. 2-6 ii 17: "the 'rod' [is] the prince of the congregation. And afterwards he will dep[a]rt from them."

(7) 4Q285 frag. 4 2: "the [pr]ince of the congregation as far as the [Great] Sea."

(8) 4Q285 frag. 4 6: "then they will bring him before the prince of the [congregation]."

(9) 4Q285 frag. 5 4: "and the prince of the congregation, the Bran[ch of David,] will put him to death."

(10) 4Q285 frag. 6 2: "the [prin]ce of the congregation and all Israel."

(11) 4Q376 frag. 1 iii 1: "and if the prince of the whole congregation is in the camp."

(12) 4Q376 frag. 1 iii 3: "to the prince"

(13) *Jubilees* 31:18: Jacob blesses his Judah and says, "be a prince, you and one of your sons."

(14) *Sibylline Oracles* 3:469: "a holy prince will come to gain sway over the scepters of the earth."

4.3. Texts That Speak of a Branch of David. The "Branch of David" *(ṣemaḥ dāwîd)* is another favorite epithet for the expected Messiah:

(1) 4Q161 frags. 7-10 iii 22: "[its interpretation concerns the Branch] of David who will arise at the en[d of days]."

(2) 4Q174 frags. 1-3 i 11: "'I [will be] a father to him and he shall be a son to me' [2 Sam 7:14a]. This is the 'Branch of David' who will arise with the interpreter of the law."

(3) 4Q252 frag. 1 v 3-4: "'until' [Gen 49:10] the coming of the anointed one of righteousness, the Branch of David."

(4) 4Q285 frag. 5 3: "the Branch of David. Then [all forces of Belial] shall be judged."

(5) 4Q285 frag. 5 4: "and the prince of the congregation, the Bran[ch of David,] will put him to death."

4.4. The Scepter. The awaited Messiah is sometimes referred to as the "scepter," *šebeṭ* (cf. CD 7:19-20 = 4Q266 frag. 3 iv 9):

(1) 1QSb 5:27-28: "for God has established you as a scepter over the rulers."

(2) 4Q161 frags. 2-6 ii 17: "[the scepter is] the prince of the congregation."

4.5. Son of God. Much disputed are the "Son" texts in 4Q246, as well as the "firstborn" text in 4Q369. All of them may refer to a messianic figure, and the texts in 4Q246 probably do (*see* Son of God Text). The "firstborn son" of 4Q369 may refer either to the historical figure David or to Israel.

(1) 4Q246 1:9: "and he shall be called '[son of] the [gr]eat [God].'"

(2) 4Q246 2:1: "he shall be hailed 'the Son of God.'"

(3) 4Q246 2:1: "and they shall call him 'Son of (the) Most High.'"

(4) 4Q369 frag. 1 ii 6: "and you made him a firstbo[rn] son to you."

4.6. Son of Man and Chosen One. Mention must also be made of the one like a "son of man" in Daniel 7:13, who is alluded to in a messianic sense in *1 Enoch* 46—71 (esp. *1 Enoch* 46:1-5; 52:4; 62:1-15; 63:11; 71:17) and in 4 Ezra 13:3 ("I looked, and behold, that man flew with the clouds of heaven") and 4 Ezra 13:6 ("he carved out for himself a great mountain, and flew upon it"), which also alludes to the mountain of Daniel 2, a mountain that smashes the pagan empires. This man who flies to the mountain will slay God's enemies with his mouth (4 Ezra 13:9-11), an allusion this time to Isaiah 11:4. Finally, the "son of man" figure in *1 Enoch* is frequently designated by the sobriquet "Elect One" or "Chosen One" (e.g., *1 Enoch* 48:6; 49:2, 4; 52:6; 53:6; 55:4; 61:8, 10; 62:1; cf. *Apoc. Abr.* 31:1, whose "chosen one" is probably a messianic figure). This sobriquet probably derives from Isaiah 42:1.

4.7. Diarchic Messianism at Qumran. When the Dead Sea Scrolls first came to light, there was much interest in references to two Messiahs, one priestly and the other royal (e.g., 1QS 9:11 "until there come the Prophet and the Messiahs of Aaron and Israel"; cf. CD 12:23—13:1; 14:19; 19:10-11; 20:1). This diarchic messianism, however, is not innovative, but was envisioned by the prophets Jeremiah, Zechariah and Haggai. The former anticipates a righteous Branch of David and a faithful priest (Jer 33:15-18). The second speaks of "two olive trees," "two branches" and "two sons of oil" (Zech 4:11-14); and the coming of a man whose name is "Branch," who will build the temple, and a "priest by his throne," between whom there will be understanding (Zech 6:12-13). The reference here is to Zerubbabel, through whom the restoration of the Davidic dynasty was expected, and to Joshua, through whom the restoration of the Zadokite high priesthood was expected. The prophet Haggai reassures Zerubbabel and Joshua that the Lord is with them and his Spirit abides among them (Hag 2:1-7). In all probability, Qumran's messianism reflects the diarchism of these prophets and is thus unexceptional. The probability increases with the discovery of a reference to the "two sons of oil" of Zechariah 4:14 in part of a commentary on Jacob's blessing of Judah (cf. 4Q254 frag. 4). The messianic interpretation of this blessing (Gen 49:8-12) has already been noted.

4.8. A Slain Messiah at Qumran? From A. Dupont-Sommer (1950) to M. O. Wise (1999), comparison between the Teacher of Righteousness and Jesus of Nazareth has been made. That the life and thought of the Teacher of Righteousness, to the extent that these can be established, shed light on the context of Jesus can hardly be disputed. But claims that the Scrolls actually speak elliptically of Jesus and his contemporaries are farfetched and rest on no clear evidence. Moreover, the more recent and sensational claim that 4Q285 speaks of a slain Messiah rests on a misreading of the Hebrew and a failure to appreciate the context of the fragment in question. The text reads, beginning with a quotation from Isaiah:

> "A shoot shall come out from the stump of Jesse [and a branch shall grow out of his roots" (Is 11:1). This is the] Branch of David. Then [all forces of Belial] shall be judged, [and the king of the Kittim shall stand for judgment] and the Prince of the community—the Bra[nch of David]—will have him put to death. [Then all Israel shall come out with timbrel]s and dancers, and the [high] priest shall order [them to cleanse their bodies from the guilty blood of the c]orpse[s of] the Kittim. (4Q285 frag. 5 2-6)

Far from anticipating the coming of a suffering Messiah, Qumran messianism was traditional in all major respects. A triumphant, conquering Messiah, who of course would submit himself to Qumran's understanding of the renewed covenant, was awaited.

5. Messianism and New Testament Christology. Most of the components that we have surveyed contribute to early Christian messianism and lay the groundwork upon which later christology will be constructed. The portrait of the militant Messiah, who is expected to vanquish Israel's enemies, especially the hated Romans (as in 4Q285 and *Pss. Sol.* 17—18), is subordinated to highly symbolic scenarios, such as what we have in the book of Revelation.

5.1. Davidic Descent. The Davidic descent of Jesus is affirmed in the NT and is rooted in the gospel story itself. Blind Bartimaeus hails Jesus as "son of David" (Mk 10:47, 48). The request for healing presupposes Jesus' healing ministry and may play on ideas regarding David's famous son Solomon, whose healing and exorcistic powers had over the course of time taken on epic proportions in Jewish tradition. Jesus enters Jerusalem amidst shouts about the "kingdom of our father David that is coming!" (Mk 11:10). Jesus' questioning of the scribal tendency to refer to the Messiah as "son of David" (Mk 12:35-37) should not be understood as either a rejection of the Davidic descent of the Messiah or Jesus' rejection of Davidic lineage. His point has to do with the adequacy of the epithet itself, for the Messiah is greater than David and not lesser (as, according to the conventions of the time, *son* of David implies).

The Davidic descent of Jesus is so firmly entrenched in the tradition, Paul can refer to it almost in passing (Rom 1:3, in reference to God's "Son, who was descended from David according to the flesh"). Alluding to this very verse, the Pauline school augments the Christian catechism: "Remember Jesus Christ, risen from the dead, descended from David, as preached in my gospel" (2 Tim 2:8). The Matthean and Lukan

Evangelists incorporate Davidic descent in their respective genealogies (esp. Mt 1:1, 20; Lk 1:32, 69; 2:11), with each supplementing the tradition in his own fashion (Mt 15:22; 21:9, 15; Acts 13:34; 15:16). The author of the Apocalypse testifies to Jesus' Davidic descent (Rev 3:7; 5:5). Indeed, the exalted Christ at the conclusion of the vision declares: "I, Jesus . . . am the root and the offspring of David" (Rev 22:16).

*5.2. **Messiah.*** The idea that Jesus is "anointed" of God and that therefore he is the Messiah is everywhere attested in the NT, so much so in the epistles, especially the Pauline epistles, that "Christ" becomes a quasi name, not just a title. Notwithstanding some critical opinion, the messianic understanding of Jesus is rooted in the teaching and activity of Jesus himself and not simply in the post-Easter reflection of the early church.

In the Synoptic tradition we have Peter's famous confession: "You are the Messiah" (Mk 8:29). When asked by high priest Caiaphas, "Are you the Messiah, the Son of the Blessed?" Jesus answers "I am" (Mk 14:61-61). Some critics claim that these traditions are post-Easter confessions, but the crucifixion of Jesus as the "king of the Jews" (Mk 15:26) suggests otherwise. The epithet "king of the Jews" played no role in early Christian confession or christology; nor does it reflect Jewish messianism (cf. Mk 15:32). The epithet is Roman, and its appearance in the crucifixion scene is historical, arguing strongly that by the time Jesus had entered Jerusalem his disciples were speaking of him as Israel's Messiah.

Jesus' allusive use of Isaiah 61:1-2 in his reply to the imprisoned John the Baptist (Mt 11:5 = Lk 7:22; cf. Lk 4:18-19) is another compelling indication of messianic self-understanding. Not only does the speaker of Isaiah 61:1 think of himself as anointed ("the spirit of the Lord is upon me, for he has anointed me to preach"), but phrases of this passage appear in 4Q521, a passage that describes what will take place when God's Messiah, whom "heaven and earth will obey," appears.

*5.3. **Son of Man.*** Jesus' favorite self-designation was "the Son of Man." Although the epithet lacks the definite article in Daniel 7:13, whence it is derived, it appears consistently with the article in the Gospels. This articularity is not technical, as though "son of man" is a messianic title (though later it becomes that, as attested in the Similitudes of *Enoch*); rather, it is specific. When Jesus speaks of *the* Son of Man, he refers specifically to the one in the vision of Daniel 7. This explains why Jesus declares that as Son of Man he has "authority on earth" to forgive sins (Mk 2:10) and to make sabbath rulings (Mk 2:27-28). Furthermore, as Son of Man, Jesus has received God's kingdom and authority, permitting him to act on behalf of God's people in the cosmic struggle against Satan's kingdom, as envisioned in Daniel 7 and attested in various sayings in the dominical tradition (e.g., Mk 3:27; Lk 11:20).

*5.4. **Chosen/Elect One.*** The NT also speaks of Jesus as God's "elect" or "chosen." Once again, the tradition may derive from Jesus himself, or the experience of his disciples. The most probable context was during or shortly after the baptism, when the heavenly voice said: "You are my beloved Son; with you I am well pleased" (Mk 1:11). These words probably echo Isaiah 42:1: "Behold my servant, whom I uphold, my chosen, in whom my soul delights; I have put my Spirit upon him, he will bring forth justice to the nations." Mark's "my beloved" is the equivalent of Isaiah's "my chosen" (which the Lukan Evangelist makes explicit in his version of the heavenly voice in Lk 9:35: "This is my Son, my Chosen"). Mark's "with you I am well pleased" is the equivalent of Isaiah's "in whom my soul delights." However, the idea that Jesus was God's chosen one was not influential in the development of NT christology. Luke adds the epithet to the priestly taunting of the crucified Jesus: "He saved others; let him save himself, if he is the Christ of God, his Chosen One!" (Lk 23:35). The author of 1 Peter indirectly refers to Jesus as "chosen" in applying to him Isaiah 28:16: "Behold, I am laying in Zion a stone, a cornerstone chosen and precious, and he who believes in him will not be put to shame" (1 Pet 2:6).

*5.5. **Priestly Messianism.*** Finally, the christology and apologetics of the book of Hebrews approximates features of Qumran's priestly messianism (see Heb 5:6, 10; 6:20; 7:1-17). One should take note especially of the exaltation of the mysterious figure Melchizedek, who may have a messianic function (see esp. 11QMelch 2:5-9, 13, 25). Note too that in this scroll Melchizedek's appearance is linked to Isaiah 61:1-2.

See also APOCALYPTIC LITERATURE; DEAD SEA SCROLLS: GENERAL INTRODUCTION; ESCHATOLOGIES OF LATE ANTIQUITY; NARRATIVE A (4Q458); PSALMS OF SOLOMON; SIMON BEN KOSIBA; REVO-

LUTIONARY MOVEMENTS; SON OF GOD TEXT (4Q246).

BIBLIOGRAPHY. M. G. Abegg Jr., "The Messiah at Qumran: Are We Still Seeing Double?" *DSD* 2 (1995) 125-44; idem, "Messianic Hope and 4Q285: A Reassessment," *JBL* 113 (1994) 81-91; R. Bauckham, "The Messianic Interpretation of Isa. 10:34 in the Dead Sea Scrolls, 2 Baruch and the Preaching of John the Baptist," *DSD* 2 (1995) 202-16; K. Berger, "Die königlichen Messiastraditionen des Neuen Testaments," *NTS* 29 (1973-74) 1-44; M. Black, "The Messianism of the Parables of Enoch: Their Date and Contributions to Christological Origins," in *The Messiah: Developments in Earliest Judaism and Christianity*, ed. J. H. Charlesworth (Minneapolis: Fortress, 1992) 145-68; M. Bockmuehl, "A 'Slain Messiah' in 4Q Serekh Milhamah (4Q285)?" *TynB* 43 (1992) 155-69; G. J. Brooke, "The Messiah of Aaron in the Damascus Document," *RevQ* 15 (1991) 215-30; R. E. Brown, "J. Starcky's Theory of Qumran Messianic Development," *CBQ* 28 (1966) 51-57; W. H. Brownlee, "Messianic Motifs of Qumran and the New Testament," *NTS* 3 (1956-57) 12-30; A. Caquot, "Le messianisme Qumrânien," in *Qumrân: Sa piété, sa théologie et son milieu*, ed. M. Delcor (BETL 46; Paris and Gembloux: Duculot and Leuven University Press, 1978) 231-47; J. H. Charlesworth, "From Jewish Messianology to Christian Christology: Some Caveats and Perspectives," in *Judaisms and Their Messiahs*, ed. J. Neusner et al. (Cambridge: Cambridge University Press, 1987) 225-64; idem, "The Messiah in the Pseudepigrapha," *ANRW* 2.19.2 (1979) 188-218; idem, ed., *The Messiah: Developments in Earliest Judaism and Christianity* (Minneapolis: Fortress, 1992); idem, ed., *Qumran-Messianism: Studies on the Messianic Expectations in the Dead Sea Scrolls* (Tübingen: Mohr Siebeck, 1998); A. Chester, "Jewish Messianic Expectations and Mediatorian Figures," in *Paulus und das antike Judentum*, ed. M. Hengel and U. Heckel (Tübingen: Mohr Siebeck, 1991) 17-89; J. J. Collins, "'He Shall Not Judge by What His Eyes See': Messianic Authority in the Dead Sea Scrolls," *DSD* 2 (1995a) 145-64; idem, "Jesus and the Messiahs of Israel," in *Geschichte—Tradition—Reflection, 3: Frühes Christentum*, ed. H. Cancik et. al. (Tübingen: Mohr Siebeck, 1996) 287-302; idem, "Messianism in the Maccabean Period," in *Judaisms and Their Messiahs*, ed. J. Neusner et al. (Cambridge: Cambridge University Press, 1987) 97-109; idem, *The Scepter and the Star: The Messiahs of the Dead Sea Scrolls and Other Ancient Literature* (ABRL; New York: Doubleday, 1995b); idem, "The Works of the Messiah," *DSD* 1 (1995c) 98-112; N. A. Dahl, "Messianic Ideas and the Crucifixion of Jesus," in *The Messiah: Developments in Earliest Judaism and Christianity*, ed. J. H. Charlesworth (Minneapolis: Fortress, 1992) 382-403; G. L. Davenport, "The 'Anointed of the Lord' in Psalms of 17," in *Ideal Figures in Ancient Judaism*, ed. J. J. Collins and G. W. Nickelsburg (Chico, CA: Scholars Press, 1980) 67-92; J. D. G. Dunn, "Messianic Ideas and Their Influence on the Jesus of History," in *Messiah: Developments in Earliest Judaism and Christianity*, ed. J. H. Charlesworth (Minneapolis: Fortress, 1992) 365-81; A. Dupont-Sommer, *The Dead Sea Scrolls: A Preliminary Sketch* (Oxford: Blackwell, 1952 [French orig. 1950]) 97-100; C. A. Evans, *Jesus and His Contemporaries: Comparative Studies* (AGJU 25; Leiden: E. J. Brill, 1995) 53-181; idem, "Mishna and Messiah 'in Context': Some Comments on Jacob Neusner's Proposals," *JBL* 112 (1993) 267-89; idem, "A Note on the 'First-Born Son' of 4Q369," *DSD* 2 (1995) 185-201; C. A. Evans and M. G. Abegg Jr., "Messianic Passages in the Dead Sea Scrolls," in *Qumran-Messianism: Studies on the Messianic Expectations in the Dead Sea Scrolls*, ed. J. H. Charlesworth (Tübingen: Mohr Siebeck, 1998) 191-203; J. A. Fitzmyer, "4Q246: The 'Son of God' Document from Qumran," *Bib* 74 (1993) 153-74 [= idem, *The Dead Sea Scrolls and Christian Origins* (SDSSRL; Grand Rapids, MI: Eerdmans, 2000) 41-61]; idem, "Qumran Messianism," in *The Dead Sea Scrolls and Christian Origins* (SDSSRL; Grand Rapids, MI: Eerdmans, 2000) 73-110; F. García Martínez, "Messianic Hopes in the Qumran Writings," in F. García Martínez and J. Trebolle Barrera, *The People of the Dead Sea Scrolls* (Leiden: E. J. Brill, 1995) 159-89; J. A. Goldstein, "How the Authors of 1 and 2 Maccabees Treated the 'Messianic' Promises," in *Judaisms and Their Messiahs*, ed. J. Neusner et al. (Cambridge: Cambridge University Press, 1987) 69-96; W. S. Green, "Introduction: Messiah in Judaism: Rethinking the Question," in *Judaisms and Their Messiahs*, ed. J. Neusner et al. (Cambridge: Cambridge University Press, 1987) 1-13; I. Gruenwald, "From Priesthood to Messianism: The Anti-Priestly Polemic and the Messianic Factor," in *Messiah and Christos: Studies in the Jewish Origins of Christianity*, ed. I. Gruenwald et al. (TSAJ 32; Tübingen: Mohr Siebeck, 1992) 75-93;

I. Gruenwald et al., eds., *Messiah and Christos: Studies in the Jewish Origins of Christianity* (TSAJ 32; Tübingen: Mohr Siebeck, 1992); P. D. Hanson, "Messiahs and Messianic Figures in Proto-Apocalypticism," in *The Messiah: Developments in Earliest Judaism and Christianity*, ed. J. H. Charlesworth (Minneapolis: Fortress, 1992) 67-78; M. Hengel, *The Son of God* (Philadelphia: Fortress, 1976); W. Horbury, *Jewish Messianism and the Cult of Christ* (London: SCM, 1998); R. A. Horsley, "'Messianic' Figures and Movements in First-Century Palestine," in *The Messiah: Developments in Earliest Judaism and Christianity*, ed. J. H. Charlesworth (Minneapolis: Fortress, 1992) 276-95; M. de Jonge, "The Earliest Christian Use of *Christos*: Some Suggestions," *NTS* 32 (1986) 321-43; idem, "Messiah," in *ABD* 4:777-88; idem, "The Role of Intermediaries in God's Final Intervention in the Future According to the Qumran Scrolls," in *Studies on the Jewish Background of the New Testament*, ed., O. Michel et al. (Assen: Van Gorcum, 1969) 44-63; idem, "Two Messiahs in the Testaments of the Twelve Patriarchs?" in *Tradition and Reinterpretation in Jewish and Early Christian Literature*, ed. J. W. van Henten et al. (SPB 36; Leiden: E. J. Brill, 1986) 150-62 [= idem, *Jewish Eschatology, Early Christian Christology and the Testaments of the Twelve Patriarchs: Collected Essays* (NovTSup 63; Leiden: E. J. Brill, 1991) 191-203]; idem, "The Use of the Word 'Anointed' in the Time of Jesus," *NovT* 8 (1966) 132-48; M. A. Knibb, "Messianism in the Pseudepigrapha in the Light of the Scrolls," *DSD* 2 (1995) 165-84; idem, "The Teacher of Righteousness—a Messianic Title?" in *A Tribute to Geza Vermes: Essays on Jewish and Christian Literature and History*, ed. P. R. Davies and R. T. White (JSOTSup 100; Sheffield: JSOT, 1990) 51-65; K. G. Kuhn, "The Two Messiahs of Aaron and Israel," *NTS* 1 (1954-55) 168-80 [= *The Scrolls and the New Testament*, ed. K. Stendahl (New York: Crossroad, 1992 {1957]) 54-64, 256-59]; L. Landman, ed., *Messianism in the Talmudic Era* (New York: Ktav, 1979); S. H. Levey, *The Messiah: An Aramaic Interpretation. The Messianic Exegesis of the Targum* (MHUC 2; Cincinnati: Hebrew Union College/Jewish Institute of Religion, 1974); J. Liver, "The Doctrine of the Two Messiahs in Sectarian Literature in the Time of the Second Commonwealth," *HTR* 52 (1959) 149-85 [= L. Landman, ed., *Messianism in the Talmudic Era* (New York: Ktav, 1979) 354-90]; J. Lust, "Messianism and Septuagint," in *Congress Volume Salamanca (1983)*, ed. J. A. Emerton (VTSup 36; Leiden: E. J. Brill, 1985) 174-91; E. Massaux et al., eds., *La venue du Messie: Messianisme et eschatologie* (RechBib 6; Paris: Gabalda, 1962); D. Mendels, "Pseudo-Philo's *Biblical Antiquities*, the 'Fourth Philosophy,' and the Political Messianism of the First Century C.E.," in *The Messiah: Developments in Earliest Judaism and Christianity*, ed. J. H. Charlesworth (Minneapolis: Fortress, 1992) 261-75; J. Neusner, *Messiah in Context* (Philadelphia: Fortress, 1984); J. Neusner et al., eds., *Judaisms and Their Messiahs at the Turn of the Christian Era* (Cambridge: Cambridge University Press, 1987); G. W. E. Nickelsburg, "Salvation with and Without a Messiah: Developing Beliefs in Writings Ascribed to Enoch," in *Judaisms and Their Messiahs*, ed. J. Neusner et al. (Cambridge: Cambridge University Press, 1987) 49-68; G. S. Oegema, *The Anointed and His People: Messianic Expectations from the Maccabees to Bar Kochba* (JSPSup 27; Sheffield: Sheffield Academic Press, 1998); E. Puech, "Messianism, Resurrection, and Eschatology at Qumran and in the New Testament," in *The Community of the Renewed Covenant: The Notre Dame Symposium on the Dead Sea Scrolls*, ed. E. Ulrich and J. C. VanderKam (Notre Dame, IN: University of Notre Dame Press, 1994) 235-56; J. J. M. Roberts, "The Old Testament's Contribution to Messianic Expectations," in *The Messiah: Developments in Earliest Judaism and Christianity*, ed. J. H. Charlesworth (Minneapolis: Fortress, 1992) 39-51; L. H. Schiffman, "Messianic Figures and Ideas in the Qumran Scrolls," in *The Messiah: Developments in Earliest Judaism and Christianity*, ed. J. H. Charlesworth (Minneapolis: Fortress, 1992) 116-29; G. Scholem, *The Messianic Idea in Judaism and Other Essays on Jewish Spirituality* (New York: Schocken, 1971); M. Smith, "What Is Implied by the Variety of Messianic Figures?" *JBL* 78 (1959) 66-72; J. Starcky, "Les quatres étapes du messianisme à Qumrân," *RB* 70 (1963) 481-505; M. E. Stone, "The Concept of the Messiah in IV Ezra," in *Religions in Antiquity: Essays in Memory of Erwin Ramsdell Goodenough*, ed. J. Neusner (NumSup 14; Leiden: E. J. Brill, 1968) 295-312; idem, "The Question of the Messiah in 4 Ezra," in *Judaisms and Their Messiahs*, ed. J. Neusner et al. (Cambridge: Cambridge University Press, 1987) 209-24; S. Talmon, "The Concept of *Māšîaḥ* and Messianism in Early Judaism," in *The Messiah: Developments in Earliest Judaism and Christianity*, ed. J. H. Charlesworth (Minneapolis: Fortress, 1992) 79-115; idem,

"Types of Messianic Expectation at the Turn of the Era," in *King, Cult and Calendar in Ancient Israel*, ed. S. Talmon (Jerusalem: Magnes, 1986) 202-24; idem, "Waiting for the Messiah at Qumran," in *The World of Qumran from Within* (Jerusalem: Magnes; Leiden: E. J. Brill, 1989) 273-300; J. C. VanderKam, "Jubilees and the Priestly Messiah of Qumran," *RevQ* 13 (1988) 353-65; idem, "Messianism in the Scrolls," in *The Community of the Renewed Covenant: The Notre Dame Symposium on the Dead Sea Scrolls*, ed. E. Ulrich and J. C. VanderKam (Notre Dame, IN: University of Notre Dame Press, 1994) 211-34; idem, "Righteous One, Messiah, Chosen One, and Son of Man in 1 Enoch 37–71," in *The Messiah: Developments in Earliest Judaism and Christianity*, ed. J. H. Charlesworth (Minneapolis: Fortress, 1992) 169-91; M. O. Wise, *The First Messiah: Investigating the Savior Before Christ* (San Francisco: HarperCollins, 1999); M. O. Wise and J. D. Tabor, "The Messiah at Qumran," *BAR* 18.6 (1992) 60-65; A. S. van der Woude, *Die messianischen Vorstellungen der Gemeinde von Qumrân* (SSN 3; Assen: Van Gorcum, 1957). C. A. Evans

MIDRASHIM. *See* RABBINIC LITERATURE: MIDRASHIM.

MILITARY, ROMAN. *See* ROMAN MILITARY.

MILK

The Hebrew Bible described the promised land as a land of milk and honey (twenty times in the OT, e.g., Ex 3:8, 17; 13:5; 33:5; Lev 20:24). This meant that it would be a prosperous land (cf. Sinuhe 80-83; Homer *Odys.* 15.403-14; Euripides *Bacch.* 142-45), not requiring irrigation to the same degree as did Egypt or Mesopotamia (Aharoni, 4). Israelites used milk from sheep, cows (Deut 32:14) and probably especially goats (Prov 27:27). Milk was offered for *hospitality (Gen 18:8), and it was more valuable than mere water (Judg 4:19). Drunk fresh but souring quickly in the warm climate, milk was often curdled for cheese (1 Sam 17:18; 2 Sam 17:29; Job 10:10) or for curds (Gen 18:8; Deut 32:14; Job 20:17; Is 7:15, 22), which are similar to yogurt.

1. Ancient Practices
2. Nursing
3. New Testament References

1. Ancient Practices.

The prohibition against boiling a kid in its mother's milk (Ex 23:19; 34:26; Deut 14:21) may stem from humanitarian considerations (cf. Deut 22:6-7), but as early as Maimonides some commentators have seen in it a warning against a pagan practice. Canaanite evidence previously cited for this practice (*UT* 52:14) was based on a reconstructed and mistranslated text (Gordon, 173; Craigie, 74-76), yet it is possible that a Thraco-Phrygian Dionysiac ceremony involved ritual boiling of milk in the worship of a mother goddess (Guthrie, 209). Boiling milk in general may have been common (Sinuhe 25-28).

Extrabiblical sources provide much information on ancient Mediterranean practices. Although some goat's milk would be taken to town (*Priapea* 2.10-11), milk was more easily preserved and used in the countryside, especially in the form of goat's and sheep's milk (Cary and Haarhoff, 93). Cow's milk was known (e.g., *b. Šabb.* 143b) but not usually preferred in the eastern Mediterranean. Greeks consumed most cow's milk raw, preferring goat's and sheep's milk for cheeses; Romans, by contrast, preferred cheeses from cow's milk (Lewis, 131). Most sheep and goat milk was curdled and pressed into cheeses (Longus *Daphn. Chl.* 1.23; Epictetus *Disc.* 1.16.8). Thus Mediterranean cultures generally found unusual the behavior of such peoples as the Scythians, who depended on wild mares' milk (Strabo *Geog.* 7.300-302).

2. Nursing.

Young children, however, normally required fresh, human milk. Nursing was a common practice in Greco-Roman antiquity (Marcus Aurelius *Med.* 5.4; Lefkowitz and Fant, 164-68; Bradley; *see* Slavery). Though moralists often promoted maternal breastfeeding, most well-to-do homes and many poorer homes preferred nurses (Dixon, 3, 120; Treggiari, 87). Nursing contracts sometimes specified that the woman would nurse the child in her own home for a particular period and prohibited her from becoming pregnant or nursing another child (*CPJ* 2:15-19 §146). The most common duration of nursing was about two years (e.g., Pseudo-Philo *Bib. Ant.* 51:1), but contracts ranged from six months to three years (Lewis, 146). Jewish mothers normally nursed their own children (4 Macc 13:20; 4 Ezra 8:10; *T. Benj.* 1:3; *m. Ketub.* 5:5; for nursing in *rabbinic sources, see Ilan, 119-21). Some Jewish teachers disapproved of Jewish women nursing Gentiles, because this would nurture future idolaters, but they allowed the reverse practice (*m. 'Abod. Zar.* 2:1); other Jewish traditions suggest a Jewish preference for avoiding idolaters' milk (Josephus *Ant.* 2.9.5 §226).

Only in ancient legends did sources other than human breasts supply milk for human infants. Pagans included stories of animals that provided milk for lost human babies; these included goats (Longus *Daphn. Chl.* 1.2) and sheep (Longus *Daphn. Chl.* 1.5). In such accounts a goat suckled Zeus (Longus *Daphn. Chl.* 1.16); most often recounted, a wolf suckled Romulus and Remus (Livy *Hist.* 1.4.6; Propertius *Elegies* 4.1.55-56). A man without a wife nursed his child with a wild mare's milk, squeezing the udder himself (Virgil *Aen.* 11.570-72). Later Jewish sages occasionally told of men who miraculously breastfed infants when no mothers were available (*b Šabb.* 53b, *Bar.; Gen. Rab.* 30:8), or of Sarah, who miraculously breastfed the whole world and so converted many Gentiles to the worship of the true God (*Gen. Rab.* 53:9; *Pesiq. Rab Kah.* 22:1). Unlimited milk functioned as a figure for prosperity (Job 29:6; Song 5:12; *T. Job* 13) and was part of the Jewish vision of *eschatological abundance (Joel 3:18; *Sib. Or.* 3.749).

3. New Testament References.

Milk is mentioned several times in the NT. In 1 Corinthians 3:2 Paul probably compares himself with a mother or a nurse breastfeeding a baby. Such feminine images for males were not unusual or necessarily demeaning (e.g., Homer *Il.* 8.271-72; *Odys.* 20.14-16; cf. Malherbe on 1 Thess 2:7). The image does, however, call the Corinthian Christians to account: comparing an adult with a baby (e.g., Homer *Il.* 16.7-8) or a child (Aristophanes *Nub.* 821; Epictetus *Disc.* 2.16.39) was generally insulting. Perhaps the Corinthian Christians felt that Paul's meat was little better than his milk, wanting something deeper than his teaching (cf. Hooker), but for Paul no message could prove deeper than the message of the cross (1 Cor 1:17—2:16). The writer of Hebrews similarly notes that his audience remains dependent on milk (Heb 5:12-13) but in his exposition about the heavenly priest like *Melchizedek warns them that he must supply them deeper teachings lest their failure to press deeper result in their destruction (Heb 6:1-12).

Less relevantly, some scholars have related such NT images to pagan religious images (e.g., Reitzenstein 417-18). For example, some ancients employed divine lactation as a symbol for intimacy with a deity (Apuleius *Met.* 11.10; see Goodenough, 6:117-22; 8:75-77; Corrington). In what is probably a twist on this image, in some early Christian texts Christ metaphorically offers holy milk from his breasts (*Odes Sol.* 8:14), or the Spirit milked the Father to incarnate Christ in Mary's womb (*Odes Sol.* 19.1-7). J. D. M. Derrett thinks the pagan association of milk with Dionysus restricted the Jewish emphasis on milk and honey in the early Roman period.

What is more likely in view in the NT texts is the ancient use of milk as a metaphor for the elementary studies, appropriate only for novices (Philo *Agric.* 9; *Congr.* 19; *Migr. Abr.* 29; Quintilian *Inst. Orat.* 2.4.5-6). In a more positive vein, as in 1 Peter 2:2, some Jewish teachers compared the *Torah with milk (*Sipre Deut.* 321.8.5). Papyri and inscriptions attest that the adjective applied to milk in 1 Peter 2:2, when used of foodstuffs, refers to their pure and unadulterated character.

BIBLIOGRAPHY. Y. Aharoni, *The Archaeology of the Land of Israel* (Philadelphia: Westminster, 1982); K. R. Bradley, "Wet-Nursing at Rome: A Study in Social Relations," in *The Family in Ancient Rome: New Perspectives,* ed. B. Rawson (Ithaca, NY: Cornell University Press, 1986) 201-29; M. Cary and T. J. Haarhoff, *Life and Thought in the Greek and Roman World* (4th ed.; London: Methuen, 1946); G. P. Corrington, "The Milk of Salvation: Redemption by the Mother in Late Antiquity and Early Christianity," *HTR* 82 (1989) 393-420; P. C. Craigie, *Ugarit and the Old Testament* (Grand Rapids. MI: Eerdmans, 1983); J. D. M. Derrett, "Whatever Happened to the Land Flowing with Milk and Honey?" *VC* 38 (1984) 178-84; S. Dixon, *The Roman Mother* (Norman: Oklahoma University Press, 1988); E. R. Goodenough, *Jewish Symbols in the Greco-Roman Period* (13 vols.; BS 37, vols. 1-12 New York: Pantheon, for Bollingen Foundation, 1953-65; vol. 13: Princeton, NJ: Princeton University Press, for Bollingen Foundation, 1968); C. H. Gordon, *The Common Background of Greek and Hebrew Civilizations* (New York: Norton, 1965); W. K. C. Guthrie, *Orpheus and Greek Religion: A Study of the Orphic Movement* (2d ed.; New York: Norton, 1966); M. D. Hooker, "Hard Sayings: 1 Corinthians 3:2," *Theology* (London) 69 (1966) 19-22; T. Ilan, *Jewish Women in Greco-Roman Palestine* (Peabody, MA: Hendrickson, 1996); M. R. Lefkowitz and M. B. Fant, *Women's Life in Greece and Rome* (Baltimore: Johns Hopkins University Press, 1982); N.

Lewis, *Life in Egypt Under Roman Rule* (Oxford: Clarendon Press, 1983); A. J. Malherbe, "'Gentle as a Nurse': The Cynic Background to 1 Thessalonians 2," *NovT* 12 (1970) 203-17; R. Reitzenstein, *Hellenistic Mystery-Religions: Their Basic Ideas and Significance* (PTMS 15; Pittsburgh: Pickwick, 1978); S. Treggiari, "Jobs for Women," *AJAH* 1 (1976) 76-104. C. S. Keener

MIQṢAT MA'AŚEY HA-TORAH (4QMMT)

Known commonly by its abbreviation 4QMMT, this work is undoubtedly the most important document to come to light since the "rediscovery" of the Dead Sea Scrolls in 1991.

1. Description of the Manuscript Evidence
2. Genre
3. Contents
4. Conclusions

1. Description of the Manuscript Evidence.

Six copies of the text were discovered in Cave 4 in 1952 (4Q394-399), but it seems that even the official editors were not fully aware of its significance until the mid-1980s. Its circulation began in bootleg copies of a handwritten manuscript (c. 1986) followed by two unauthorized publications (1990, 1991) before the official edition finally appeared in 1994 (Qimron and Strugnell). None of the six manuscripts is complete, but together they preserve perhaps as much as 50 percent of the original. Two of the manuscripts (4Q394-395) have been dated paleographically to the mid-first century B.C. (Qimron and Strugnell). However, many researchers believe that the document dates to the earliest days of the Qumran sect (c. 160 B.C.).

2. Genre.

4QMMT is a letter of exhortation that gives evidence of having been composed by the leadership of the Qumran sect for the purpose of warning the addressee ("you") concerning differences of opinion respecting legal issues that the addressee was violating, having come under the influence of a third party.

3. Contents.

Calendar (A1-21)

I. Legal Body: Do not mix the holy with the profane. (B1-C4)
(At least twenty-four paragraphs detailing issues of Halakhah)

II. Warning I: Transgression brings destruction, therefore we have separated. (C5-9)

III. Exhortation I: Separate yourself. (C10-21a)

IV. Warning II: The last days are upon us. (C21b-26a)

V. Exhortation II: Keep away from the counsel of Belial. (C26b-32)

*3.1. **The Calendar.*** One of the six manuscripts contains a calendar preceding the opening passages of the letter itself. As the letter does not mention calendrical matters and instead deals with issues related to purity, it remains doubtful whether it is an integral part of 4QMMT. It is of note that the calendar is the 364-day sectarian form (*see* Calendars, Jewish) found in numerous other documents among the Dead Sea Scrolls (*see* Dead Sea Scrolls §1.2.6). This fact alone makes it relatively certain that 4QMMT is a work composed by the Qumran sect.

*3.2. **The Legal Body.*** Although the law and various discussions pertaining to it are plentiful in the Dead Sea corpus, only 4QMMT directly challenges the position of another religious group. Because of the potentially defining nature of such a challenge, scholars have hoped to find in 4QMMT a basis for a definitive identification of the group behind the sectarian scrolls.

3.2.1. Sadducean Theory. L. Schiffman has shaken the long-standing "Essene consensus" by suggesting, "The author of the MMT is usually more stringent than the later Rabbis and where we can check is parallel to the Sadducees in his views." The problems posed by this conclusion are significant. The Sadducees known from ancient sources (Josephus, NT) stand opposed to several foundational doctrines of the Qumran sect. Josephus wrote that the Sadducees "say there is no such thing as fate" (Josephus *Ant.* 13.5.9 §173), whereas the Qumran sect gloried in the fact that God ordered all things, "a destiny impossible to change" (1QS 3:15-23, see also CD 2:7-10). Matthew 22:23 makes it clear that the Sadducees did not believe in the resurrection, whereas the Qumran sect hoped in the resurrection of the dead (4Q521 2+4 ii 12) followed by eternal blessings (1QS 4:7-8).

3.2.2. Weak Point of the Sadducean Theory. A possible problem with the Sadducean theory of Qumran origins is that the similarities in doctrine between the Sadducees and the Qumran sectarians may not be significant enough for identification. As an example, 4QMMT (B13-17) stipulates that the priest who was to prepare the ashes of the red cow must bathe and wait until sunset before setting to the task of burning the cow. *Mishnah Parah* 3:7 discloses that the priest was to burn the cow before the setting of the sun and the completion of his cleansing, simply because the Sadducees waited until after. There is certainly a notable similarity between the Sadducees and the Qumran sectarians. However, Numbers 19:10-11 stipulates that the gathering of the resultant ashes was to be done by someone clean. This cannot be those who prepared ashes, as the text clearly states that this duty has made them unclean and that they must bathe and wait until evening to be clean once again. If the gathering must be done by a clean individual, it would stand to reason that the preparation was to be done by those who were clean as well. Not so, says the Mishnah, "because of the Sadducees." It would appear that the rabbis (Pharisees) were the odd party in this scenario and that the Sadducees and Qumran sectarians were true to the spirit of the biblical text. Thus the similarity may not be specific enough for identification.

3.2.3. Essene Theory. The matter is not settled, but the standard Qumran sect = Essene hypothesis still appears to be the best explanation of the data. Accordingly, 4QMMT was written by Essenes opposing the legal teaching of the Pharisees.

3.3. Warning and Exhortation. The clear message of the final portion of the text is that uncleanness and the impending last days have compelled the author and his group to separate from the rest of the people (C7). The author encourages the addressee—whom he says has "insight and knowledge of the law" (C28)—to do likewise, else he would stand in danger of discovering the writer's words to be true in the end of time (C30). The last two lines then propose: "And it will be reckoned to you as righteousness, in that you have done what is right and good before him, to your own benefit and to that of Israel" (C31-32).

3.3.1. Works of the Law. Contextually, "doing what is right and good" refers to the two dozen or more legal discussions in the body of the document. In line C27 these are called "some of the works of the law," the very phrase which gives the composition its name. The similarity of this statement to passages in Paul's letters to the Romans and Galatians must not be overlooked: "Knowing that a man is not justified by *works of the law*, but rather by faith in Jesus Christ, even we have believed in Jesus Christ, in order that we might be justified by faith in Christ and not by *works of the law*, because by *works of the law* no flesh shall be justified" (Gal 2:16).

There is virtually no doubt that the Hebrew phrase *maʿaśey ha-tôrah* ("works of the law") is equivalent to the Greek phrase *erga nomou* (also, "works of the law"). The importance of this fact can hardly be overstated. Prior to the discovery of 4QMMT, the only ancient documents which contained this phrase were Romans and Galatians and subsequent Christian literature. On the basis of this, some have suggested that Paul had built a straw man, or perhaps that he was not well informed concerning Palestinian Judaism.

3.3.2. Reckoned Righteous. In addition to this clear link between the language of Paul and 4QMMT, the significance of the works of the law to the Qumran writer was that the doing of them brought the "reckoning of righteousness" (C31). The echo of this discussion cannot be denied in Galatians 2:16. This statement places the Qumran writer and Paul in a virtual face-off: 4QMMT claims that it is by works of the law that one is reckoned righteous, while Paul counters directly: not works, but faith in Christ. Paul's ancient opponents—or rather their theology—has been found.

3.3.3. Salvation by Works? The next step of investigation into this matter may be the most significant. Given the existence of an ancient Jewish group that was a theological parallel to Paul's "false brethren" (Gal 2:4), what do their own writings claim one gained by keeping the law. Was salvation by works? "Surely a man's way is not his own; neither can any person firm his own step. Surely justification is of God; by his power is the way made perfect. All that shall be, he foreknows, all that is, his plans establish; apart from him is nothing done. As for me, if I stumble, God's lovingkindness forever shall save me. If through sin of the flesh I fall, my justification will be by the righteousness of God which endures for all time" (1QS 11:11-12, see also 1QS 2:25—3:4; 10:20-21; 1QH 12:30-31; CD 2:4-5).

The emphasis on the need for repentance and focus on God's grace in this and other Qumran writings should convince that a knee-jerk reaction which suggests that 4QMMT reflects a "works-earn-righteousness" religion is hardly justified. Before the publication of 4QMMT, E. P. Sanders challenged this firmly entrenched notion. The place of obedience to the law in Qumran literature—as well as for other expressions of Palestinian Judaism—"is always the same: it is the consequence of being in the covenant and the requirement for remaining in the covenant" (Sanders).

The following excerpt from the *Damascus Document* makes it clear that Sanders' assessment of Qumran Judaism is correct: "Such is the fate for all who join the company of the men of holy perfection and then become sick of obeying virtuous rules. This is the type of person who 'melts in the crucible' [Ezek 22:21]. When his actions become evident he shall be sent away from the company as if his lot had never fallen among the disciples of God" (CD 20:1b-4a, see also CD 19:33—20:1a, 4b-10).

Thus "works of the law," according to the only ancient Jewish group of record that used the term, was not the initiator of a relationship with God; it was the requirement of such a relationship. Paul counters the first century A.D. proponents of this position, writing that both the initial step (Gal 3:2) and the continuing relationship (Gal 3:3) were "by faith in Christ Jesus." The keynote to Paul's position is encapsulated in the quote from Habakkuk 3:11, "The righteous shall live [conduct oneself] by faith."

4. Conclusions.

4.1 Pauline Studies. For Pauline studies, 4QMMT is important in that it shows that Luther's reaction to Catholicism which has been traditionally projected onto first century Judaism is not supported by an examination of the only Jewish community of record which used the vocabulary reflected in Paul's discussions of law and righteousness.

4.2 Qumran Studies. Most scroll researchers have concluded that 4QMMT was directed to the Jerusalem establishment and possibly to the office of the high priest himself. Noting, however, that repentance plays no part in the argument of the writer of 4QMMT, the document appears rather to be directed to one who had been influenced by the counsel of a third party and had begun to turn away from the position of the author. Thus the letter is more likely a warning to a fellow covenanter (and the group he represents) who had fallen under the influence of pharisaic thought.

See also DEAD SEA SCROLLS; LEGAL TEXTS AT QUMRAN; TORAH.

BIBLIOGRAPHY. M. G. Abegg Jr., "4QMMT C27, 31 and 'Works Righteousness,'" *DSD* 6 (1999) 139-47; idem, "Paul, Works of the Law, and the MMT," *BAR* 20.6 (1994) 52-55, 82; J. Kampen and M. J. Bernstein, eds., *Reading 4QMMT: New Perspectives on Qumran Law and History* (SBLSymS 2; Atlanta: Scholars Press, 1996); E. Qimron and J. Strugnell. *Qumran Cave 4.5: Miqṣat Maʿase ha-Torah* (DJD 10, Oxford: Clarendon Press, 1994); E. P. Sanders, *Paul and Palestinian Judaism* (Philadelphia: Fortress, 1977); L. H. Schiffman, "The New Halakhic Letter (4QMMT) and the Origins of the Dead Sea Sect," *BA* 53 (1990) 64-73; idem, "The Place of 4QMMT in the Corpus of Qumran Manuscripts," in *Reading 4QMMT: New Perspectives on Qumran Law and History,* ed. J Kampen and M. J. Bernstein (SBLSymS 2; Atlanta: Scholars Press, 1996) 81-98; J. Sussmann, "The History of the Halakha and the Dead Sea Scrolls: Preliminary Talmudic Observations on Miqṣat Maʿase ha-Torah (4QMMT)," in *Qumran Cave 4.5: Miqṣat Maʿase ha-Torah,* ed. E. Qimron and J. Strugnell (DJD 10; Oxford: Clarendon Press, 1994) 179–200; J. C. VanderKam, "The People of the Dead Sea Scrolls: Essenes or Sadducees?" in *Understanding the Dead Sea Scrolls,* ed. H. Shanks (New York: Random House, 1992) 50-62.

M. G. Abegg Jr.

MIRACLES AND HEALING. *See* RELIGION, PERSONAL.

MISHNAH AND TOSEFTA. *See* RABBINIC LITERATURE: MISHNAH AND TOSEFTA.

MMT. *See* MIQSAT MAʿASEY HA-TORAH (4QMMT).

MONOGAMY. *See* MARRIAGE.

MOSES. *See* APOCRYPHA OF MOSES (1Q29; 4Q374-377, 4Q408); REWRITTEN BIBLE IN PSEUDEPIGRAPHA AND QUMRAN; TESTAMENT OF MOSES; TORAH; WORDS OF MOSES (1Q22).

MUSIC

Investigation of the music of the early church has drawn on the efforts of liturgical scholars, musicologists and historians, as well as biblical scholars, in attempting to find out what the music of the earliest Christian church consisted of and where it came from. There are still many questions to be answered, and perhaps many questions yet to be asked.

The distance of time and culture makes the task of identifying or reconstructing the musical fiber of the early Christian church particularly elusive. While interest in the subject is rising and investigation of it is increasingly sophisticated, essential features of this music still remain largely unknown to us. For instance, what did the music sound like? What melodies did it use? Was the music Jewish? These most basic of questions and others like them form the basis of scholarly discussion about music in the early Christian church, for even elementary characteristics of the music remain somewhat of a mystery. Essays on this topic frequently begin by saying that the early Christian church was a singing church, but what that means is hard to define.

The sources of information on the subject of music in the early Christian church are limited. Some require much lateral thinking in order to interpret the possible relevance they may have for the subject, and this is one area in which comparative musicology has played a role. Musical texts are likely preserved in the Bible and in other related literature, but how they were used is unclear.

Finally, scholarly discussion about the music of the early Christian church inevitably turns to the question of backgrounds and influences; that is, based on the religious and cultural backgrounds against which the early Christian church was set and within which it thrived, determining which of these influenced its music.

1. Voices and Instruments
2. Sources and Traditions
3. Origins and Influences

1. Voices and Instruments.

The most essential element of music—that is, to experience it, either by hearing it or by participating in it—is what we know the least about when it comes to the music of the early Christian church. The kind of singing, the descriptive terms that were used, and the use of musical instruments all merit attention.

1.1. Singing with One Voice. J. Quasten's classic work on the music and worship found in pagan and Christian antiquity devotes some discussion to the kind of singing that was likely in the early Christian church (Quasten, 66-72). He writes, "the ideal of early Christian singing was unity or monophony" (Quasten, 68), and this thought is based in part on some of the church fathers' use of the term "one voice," which is seen to be an indication of singing in unison. For instance, Clement of Rome (fl. c. A.D. 96) states: "Let us, therefore, gathered together in concord by conscience, cry out earnestly to him as if with one voice, so that we might come to share in his great and glorious promises" (McKinnon 1987, no. 20). Later, Eusebius of Caesarea (c. A.D. 260-c. 340) uses similar language to describe Christian singing (McKinnon 1987, no. 206; see also Quasten for further examples and discussion). E. Werner also writes that "the ideal of the early Church was, according to the Apostolic literature, the *koinōnia* i.e. the congregation singing in unison" (Werner 1947, 431). Even Paul is thought by some to support this view, where he writes, "so that with one heart and mouth you may glorify the God and Father of our Lord Jesus Christ" (Rom 15:5-6).

Most scholars also think that singing was unaccompanied, although the surest evidence for this view comes generally from third- and fourth-century documents, not from the first century. Quasten, for instance, points out that in Revelation 5:8 John speaks of a "new song" and that he "expressly mentions that it is accompanied by the music of the cithara" (Quasten, 72).

1.2. Psalms, Hymns and Spiritual Songs. Perspectives on these three terms, "psalms, hymns and spiritual songs" (Eph 5:19; Col 3:16), ranged widely over the twentieth century. From a musicological perspective, E. Wellesz proposed that the terms were specific in meaning. He defined psalmody as "the cantillation of the Jewish psalms and of the canticles and doxologies modelled on them"; hymns as "songs of praise of a syllabic type, i.e. each syllable is sung to one or two notes of melody"; and spiritual songs as "Alleluias and other chants of a jubilant or ecstatic character, richly ornamented" (Wellesz 1955, 2). It is thought that Wellesz's distinctions are typical of later Christian chant but not necessarily early Christian chant (see J. A. Smith 1994), and it has also been argued linguistically that the three words seem to be synonyms (see Meeks, 144). Wellesz was aware of the view that the three words are synonyms but suggests that "the individuality of psalm, hymn, and spiritual song is obvious to the student of comparative liturgiology" (Wellesz 1961, 33-34). At this point, therefore, it remains unknown exactly what musical form may have been meant by any of these three terms, if any, although it is possible that Wellesz's proposal was too easily dismissed.

*1.3. **Psalmody.*** P. F. Bradshaw comments that "liturgical and musical historians have tended to assert confidently that psalmody was a standard part of the early *synagogue. . . . There is, however, an almost total lack of documentary evidence for the inclusion of psalms in synagogue worship. . . . While the *Hallel* seems to have been taken over into the domestic Passover meal at an early date, and apparently also into the festal synagogue liturgy, the first mention of the adoption of the daily psalms in the synagogue is not until the eighth century" (1987, 22-23; see also McKinnon 1986; J. A. Smith 1984). Most scholars think that the Jewish psalmody of the synagogue is what the first Christians sang, and as the earliest Christians were Jews, it is reasonable to think that Jewish psalmody was the basis of their music. Evidence of psalmody in the Christian church is cited from writers in the first centuries outside of the Jewish tradition who describe psalmody as an unusual form of music, while writers from within the Jewish tradition find nothing exceptional about it, which suggests that it is familiar to them.

However, if Bradshaw's assessment is correct, it is difficult to know what role psalmody had in early Christian services. Justin Martyr (c. A.D. 100-c. 165), for instance, gives a detailed description of a eucharistic service at Rome but makes no mention of music or psalm singing (*Apol. I* I 65-66). His description may not be representative of the first century or of other locations and gatherings. Nonetheless, psalmody seems to have played some role in the early church, for it is mentioned in later writers, Jewish and Christian, although it may not have had a large established role until one or two centuries after Christ. *Philo's detailed description of an evening gathering of the *Therapeutae is often considered an indication of musical practices in religious gatherings of the time of the NT and is thought to shed light on early Christian gatherings (Philo *Vit. Cont.* 10.80-81). J. W. McKinnon suggests that in "Judaism the psalmody that accompanied sacrifice in the late Temple was music in the fullest sense, but the psalms recited in the synagogues, and in the early Christian gatherings as well, were more scripture than song. They were no doubt recited with some sort of cantillation, but so was all scripture; it would take several centuries in each of the religions before psalmody became music in a selfconscious sense" (McKinnon 1990, 10).

Another area of the church gatherings where music may have been fostered was at the common meals. For instance, the Synoptic accounts of the Last Supper (Mt 26:30 par. Mk 14:26) mention that Jesus and his disciples sang a hymn before they went out, which is thought by many scholars to be an allusion to the psalms of the Jewish *Hallel.* Similarly, several second- and third-century accounts describe psalmody as a part of common Christian meals (McKinnon 1987, 9).

*1.4. **Musical Instruments.*** It is commonly thought that musical instruments were banned from the early church on account of their worldly nature. Some scholars believe that instruments were banned throughout the first century; others, that they were banned after the *destruction of the temple as a way of expressing disapproval. Of the Jews, Werner says that "rabbinic sources explain the strict prohibition of any instrumental music in the Synagogue as an expression of mourning for the loss of the Temple and land, but the present writer has been able to show that a certain animosity against all instrumental music existed well before the fall of the Temple. . . . It seems that this enmity towards instrumental music was a defence against the musical and orgiastic mystery cults in which Syrian and Mesopotamian Jews not infrequently participated." Werner adds, "The primitive Christian community held the same view, as we know from apostolic and postapostolic literature: instrumental music was thought unfit for religious services" (Werner 1966, 315; see also Werner 1947, 468).

However, McKinnon's search of early rabbinical writings and other contemporaneous literature has found no support for the idea that instruments were banned in the synagogue, but also no evidence that musical instruments were ever employed in the ancient synagogue. As a result, he observes that the central element of the service, the simple declamation of Scripture, had no call for the use of instruments in any case (McKinnon 1979-80; 1986). He further clarifies the position of some of the church fathers against musical instruments: "Music historians have tended to assume . . . that ecclesiastical authorities consciously strove to maintain their music free from incursion of musical instruments. There is little evidence of this in the sources however. What one observes there are two separate phenomena: a consistent condemnation of instruments . . . and an ecclesiastical psalmody obviously free of instrumental involvement. . . . The truth remains that the polemic against musical instruments and the vocal performance of early Christian psalmody were—for whatever reasons—unrelated in the minds of the church fathers" (McKinnon 1987, 3).

2. Sources and Traditions.

2.1. Written Sources. Sources that may be relevant to studying music in the early Christian church are spread far and wide. How to determine which are truly relevant and what they can tell us is the difficulty. Ordered somewhat chronologically, some sources that are used are the OT (Sendrey; J. A. Smith 1998); ancient writings and musical artifacts of ancient cultures (e.g., Sachs 1943; Farmer; Galpin); ancient Greek literature on musical subjects or literature that incorporates either written music or texts that are written to be sung (Henderson); the *Apocrypha (intertestamental literature); the NT (W. S. Smith); the *apocryphal NT books; musical fragments from around the time of Christ (e.g., West 1992a,); the *Dead Sea Scrolls (Werner 1957); *letters (van Beeck); later collections of hymns (Wellesz 1961); writings of the church fathers (McKinnon 1965; 1987); written records of later liturgical practices; frescoes and funerary sculptures that depict musical scenes (Quasten); Jewish writings such as the Talmud and Mishnah (Werner 1959, 1984); and later chant books and other liturgical books that preserve the ancient rites of branches of the Christian church (Wellesz 1967).

Each of these sources poses numerous difficulties. One would think that the NT would be the most authoritative source on music in the early Christian church, but where music is referred to at all, there are more questions than certainties as to what is meant. NT passages include the parallel passages mentioned above about Jesus and his disciples having sung a hymn before going to the Mount of Olives (Mt 26:30 par. Mk 14:26); Paul and Silas praying and singing hymns in prison at midnight (Acts 16:25); Paul's discourse on praying and singing both with the spirit and with the mind (1 Cor 14:15); his reference to having a hymn as part of one's contribution to the strengthening of the church (1 Cor 14:26); his reference to psalms, hymns and spiritual songs (Eph 5:19; Col 3:16); a comment in the book of James on the appropriateness of singing songs of praise when one is happy (Jas 5:13); and instances of singing a new song, singing in a loud voice and singing the song of Moses (Rev 5:9, 12; 14:3; 15:3).

Similarly, there are limited references to musical instruments in the NT, but some that are mentioned are the Greek *aulos* (thought by some to be equivalent to the Roman *tibia,* although the modern equivalent is the oboe; see McKinnon 1990, 7; Scott), harp, kithara, lyre, pipe and timbrel (see Sachs 1940; Sadie 1984; Werner, *IDB,* 469-76). These each have a long history preceding the time of the NT and can be found in various forms in ancient cultures (see, e.g., Schlesinger on the Greek *aulos;* and McKinnon and Anderson; Wulstan on the Babylonian harp; and recently West 1994). NT references to playing musical instruments or to the instruments themselves are found in the pericope where Jesus finds *aulos* players in attendance over a dead girl (Mt 9:23-24); parallel Synoptic passages that quote a children's ditty sung in the marketplace that mentions playing the *aulos* (Mt 11:16-17 par. Lk 7:32); music and dancing in the home of the prodigal son (Lk 15:25); the clanging gong and noisy cymbals mentioned in Paul's discourse on love (see Werner 1960, who argues that Paul detested musical instruments); Paul's discussion about using intelligible words, comparing instruments such as the *aulos,* harp and trumpet that require delineation of notes in order to know the melody (*aulos,* harp) or to recognize a call to battle (trumpet; 1 Cor 14:7-9; see also Porter); and a declaration that harpists and musicians, flute players and trumpeters will not be heard again (Rev 18:22).

Other musical references are found in the Apocrypha in such books as *Judith and *Maccabees. The *Apocryphal Acts of John the Evangelist* (first century) mentions the playing of the *aulos* and dancing in relation to hymn singing (Apel, 39). The OT is replete with musical references, as well as several quotations of canticles (J. A. Smith 1998). The book of Psalms in the OT is thought by many to be the musical texts that were used by early Christians (J. A. Smith 1990). Depictions of musical scenes that are thought to take place near to the time of Christ give some insight into musical practices of the time, sometimes related to certain cult activities and religious rites (Quasten). Musical fragments that show notation of some of the music in the centuries surrounding the time of Christ may contain insights into the kind of music used by early Christians (West 1992a; for some examples of ancient but undated Jewish melodies, see Davison and Apel, 8; for a transcription of the Greek "First Delphic Hymn," c. 138 B.C. and of Mesomedes's "Hymn to the Sun," c. A.D. 130, as well as "Seikilos Song," first century A.D., see Davison and Apel, 9-10).

Although some of these sources are particularly relevant for early Christian music, it is rare that they can provide conclusive evidence on an issue. For example, the fragmentary notated Christian hymn found on the *papyrus at Oxyrhynchus, first published in 1922 (P.Oxy. 1786; Grenfell and Hunt) is still one of the most significant finds pertaining to the music of early Christianity, yet there is no consensus as to what it tells us or whether it is representative of music of the third-century Christian church or earlier. On its discovery and publication it was thought to show close ties with Greek culture and religion, in particular because of its Greek musical notation (see early discussions in Grenfell and Hunt; Abert; Reinach; more recently, Pöhlmann; but see also Werner IDB; Wellesz 1961, 156). It also has been argued that the hymn is a failed attempt to apply Greek notation to a Christian hymn (Holleman 1972). Recent study, however, has again shown aspects of the Greek hypothesis to have merit (West 1992a).

*2.2. **Oral Tradition.*** Some scholars think that certain Jewish oral traditions that have been handed down through the centuries may have changed very little. If this is true, it makes it possible that the singing of some isolated Jewish communities may preserve ancient forms of Jewish psalmody (Idelsohn, followed by Werner 1959, 1984) and therefore reflect psalmody of the earliest churches in Christianity. A. Z. Idelsohn's transcriptions and recordings of Jewish music in the first two decades of the twentieth century were based in part on this premise. The real sound of the music of antiquity is hidden in the past, yet hints of it may exist and be reconstructed from formulaic patterns of notes that have been woven into the various oral traditions of the Jews (see Werner 1981). The inherent difficulty in this approach is that historical threads must be connected over very long periods of time, and move backwards in time, in order to show that melodies and musical patterns of the Jews were taken over by the early Christian church.

Similar connections must be made (e.g., Wellesz 1967) in order to show that the early church's musical roots exist in the traditional music of branches of the Christian church that have retained the most ancient forms of liturgy, such as may be found in Syrian church music (see, e.g., Husmann). In this regard, comparative musicology has attempted to analyze ancient musical traditions that are thought to be preserved in various languages and cultural settings, which include not only Syrian but also Georgian (Jeffery), Armenian (Hannick) and Byzantine (Strunk, 151-64), as well as branches of Judaism (e.g., Werner 1981), to identify common roots and to determine the chronology of their development (see Sendrey; Werner 1959, 1984; Jeffery; for discussion in general on oral tradition, see Treitler). There are many difficulties to be worked out in tracing oral tradition back to its most primitive sources—specifically, the lack of written records—but it is becoming recognized that new approaches must be developed in this regard.

3. Origins and Influences.

This discussion leads directly back to the question that has dominated discussions about music of the early Christian church—the question of origins and influences. Is the music Jewish? Is it Greek? Or is it a combination of these and other influences?

The twentieth century saw a tremendous increase in scholarly writings on Jewish origins of the music of the early Christian church. These include the groundbreaking work in comparative musicology by Idelsohn, which showed links between the music of isolated Jewish communities that are thought to preserve Jewish chant from before the rise of the Christian church (but cf. Hucke's analysis and critique, 438-39). Similarly, the work of Wellesz (1967) and Werner (1959, 1984; plus numerous other publications by both Wellesz and Werner, and others) represents a vast field of study in musical and liturgical origins, particularly Jewish. It is no surprise to find Jewish origins in the musical traditions of the Christian church. As R. T. Beckwith states, "At its origin, Christianity was a Jewish religion.

Jesus Christ was a Jew, and his first followers were Jews" (Beckwith, 39). It is equally unsurprising, however, to find influences of the Greco-Roman multicultural environment within which the Christian church was situated. Some of these are discussed below.

4.1. The Influence of the Jewish Temple. The Jewish temple is frequently cited as being highly influential in the music of the early Christian church, but the temple music was formal music, performed by professional musicians. There seems to be little reason to think that this had much influence on the early church, partly because Christianity only began in the early thirties and the temple was destroyed in A.D. 70, and partly because the early church was not a formal or formalized institution. The earliest church consisted of small, informal gatherings, while the temple was a highly regularized formal institution, therefore allowing for little direct influence. Nonetheless, the early church may have incorporated the cantillation of Scripture (e.g., Maxwell, 2; Werner 1966), which is something that would have been learned originally through the formal training and traditions of the temple. Werner writes that both cantillation and psalmody directly influenced the early Christian church: "Not only are these two elements, the core of the ancient musical liturgy, common to both Synagogue and Church, they also are by far the best preserved and most authentic features" (Werner 1947, 438; but cf. McKinnon on cantillation, 1990, 10).

4.2. The Influence of the Synagogue. Two common assumptions regarding the continuity of practices in the Jewish *synagogue and the early Christian church have come under recent scrutiny. The first is that the liturgy of the Jewish synagogue was carried over directly to the Christian church (e.g., Dugmore; Dix; *see* Liturgy: Rabbinic). R. P. Martin, for instance, writes that "Christianity entered into the inheritance of an already existing pattern of worship, provided by the Temple ritual and synagogue Liturgy" (Martin 1974, 19). The NT makes clear that Jesus frequently attended and taught in the synagogue on the sabbath (Lk 4:15-16), as did Paul (Acts 17:2), so it is reasonable to think that its liturgical practices were carried on in the early church. But there are difficulties with this seemingly straightforward view.

The synagogue in the first century seems to have been known as a place of study, a place of prayer (but cf. McKinnon 1986) and also as a place where discussions and certain kinds of general business took place. However, current research on the first-century synagogue recognizes several unsolved problems. There is some question as to the exact nature of the synagogue, even as to its formal existence before the destruction of the temple in A.D. 70 (van der Horst; Bradshaw 1992; see the recent review of discussion in McKay), and recent liturgical scholarship has found little evidence of an established synagogue liturgy. Bradshaw questions the confidence Christian liturgical scholars place on the sure foundations of Jewish liturgical research by pointing out that Jewish scholars are not nearly so certain of a single *Urtext* of this liturgy as has been thought (Bradshaw 1987). The idea of a single pattern from which all later liturgical practices and documents evolved has been found to be unlikely; more likely is that there has always been more than one pattern, even from the earliest days.

The outcome of the discussion on the liturgy of the synagogue will have repercussions on the second assumption: that there was a continuing tradition of music from the Jewish synagogue to the early church (Dix; Martin 1974, 45). Here again difficulties have been encountered. There is doubt, for instance, regarding the role that formal psalmody had in the synagogue of the first century, particularly if there was no formal liturgy (J. A. Smith 1984; McKinnon 1986; Bradshaw 1992; some acknowledgment from Martin 1974, 41, who says, "we admit that there is some doubt as to the extent to which the singing of divine praises had developed in the Palestinian synagogues of the first century"; cf. Dix). McKinnon's observation is that there seems to have been no singing in the synagogue.

However, none of this denies the influence of Judaism on the early church but suggests that it may not have occurred in the manner that is commonly thought, for it is not only the formal liturgy and formal psalmody of the synagogue that may have influenced the Christian church. For instance, musical practices such as psalmody were also a part of the family observance of religious life (*see* Piety, Jewish). The most significant Jewish influence may have been through the music that was a part of Christian family meals (e.g., J. A. Smith 1994).

4.3. The Influence of the Greco-Roman World. It has been mentioned above that in the earlier part of the twentieth century, the discovery of a third-century Greek papyrus with a fragment of a Christian hymn using Greek musical notation (Grenfell and Hunt) contributed to the idea that early Christian music was highly influenced by Greek music. Later, scholars questioned whether the single papyrus fragment represented a tradition or whether it was a single deviation from that tradition (Hollmann 1972). However, recent investigation suggests that a complete move away from the former possibility may have been premature (West 1998).

However, a less compartmentalized view acknowledges that Jewish religion and culture were highly significant components of the early music of Christianity but also recognizes the influence of the surrounding Greco-Roman culture, a confluence of religious and cultural ingredients that may have combined both contemporary and ancient practices. The position that acknowledges a combination of influences has untidy edges and nondiscrete boundaries, but it is the most consistent with the multicultural environment in which Christianity first began, as well as the fact that Christianity had some things in common with Judaism while it held other things directly in conflict with Judaism. This is the direction in studies of early Christian music that may bring us closest to its origins.

See also CREEDS AND HYMNS; LITURGY: QUMRAN; LITURGY: RABBINIC; PSALMS AND HYMNS OF QUMRAN.

BIBLIOGRAPHY. H. Abert, "Ein neu entdeckter frühchristlicher Hymnus mit Antiken Musiknoten," *ZMW* 4 (1921-22) 524-29; W. Apel, *Gregorian Chant* (Bloomington: Indiana University Press, 1958); D. E. Aune, "Worship, Early Christian," *ABD* 6:973-89; R. T. Beckwith, "The Jewish Background to Christian Worship," in *The Study of Liturgy*, ed. C. Jones, G. Wainwright and E. Yarnold (London: SPCK, 1983 [1978]) 39-51; F. J. van Beeck, "The Worship of Christians in Pliny's Letter," *SL* 18 (1988) 121-31; P. F. Bradshaw, "The Search for the Origins of Christian Liturgy: Some Methodological Reflections," *SL* 17 (1987) 26-34; idem, *The Search for the Origins of Christian Worship: Sources and Methods for the Study of Early Liturgy* (Oxford: Oxford University Press, 1992); A. T. Davison and W. Apel, eds., *Historical Anthology of Music*, vol. 1: *Oriental, Medieval and Renaissance Music* (rev. ed.; Cambridge, MA: Harvard University Press, 1977); G. Dix, *The Shape of the Liturgy* (Westminster: Dacre, 1954); C. W. Dugmore, *The Influence of the Synagogue upon the Divine Office* (London: Faith Press, 1964 [1944]); F. G. Farmer, "The Music of Ancient Egypt" and "The Music of Ancient Mesopotamia," in *Ancient and Oriental Music*, ed. E. Wellesz (1; London and Oxford: Oxford University Press, 1966 [1957]) 255-82, 228-54; F. W. Galpin, *The Music of the Sumerians and Their Immediate Successors the Babylonians and Assyrians* (Cambridge: Cambridge University Press, 1937); J. Gelineau, "Music and Singing in the Liturgy," in *The Study of Liturgy*, ed. C. Jones, G. Wainwright and E. Yarnold (London: SPCK, 1983 [1978]) 440-54; B. P. Grenfell and A. S. Hunt, "Christian Hymn with Musical Notation," in *The Oxyrhynchus Papyri*, XV (Egyptian Exploration Society Greco-Roman Memoirs; London: Egypt Exploration Society, 1922), no. 1786, 21-25; C. Hannick, "Armenian Rite, Music of the," in *The New Grove Dictionary of Music and Musicians* 1:596-99; idem, "Christian Church, Music of the Early," in *The New Grove Dictionary of Music and Musicians* 4:363-71; I. Henderson, "Ancient Greek Music," in *Ancient and Oriental Music*, ed. E. Wellesz (NOHM 1; London and Oxford: Oxford University Press, 1966 [1957]) 336-403; A. W. J. Holleman, "Early Christian Liturgical Music," *SL* 8 (1971) 185-92; idem, "The Oxyrhynchus Papyrus 1786 and the Relationship Between Ancient Greek and Early Christian Music," *VC* 26 (1972) 1-17; P. W. van der Horst, "Was the Synagogue a Place of Worship Before 70 C.E.?" in *Jews, Christians, and Polytheists in the Ancient Synagogue: Cultural Interaction During the Greco-Roman Period*, ed. S. Fine (London: Routledge, 1999) 18-43; H. Hucke, "Toward a New Historical View of Gregorian Chant," *Journal of the American Musicological Society* 33 (1980) 437-67; H. Husmann, "Syrian Church Music," in *The New Grove Dictionary of Music and Musicians* 18:472-81; A. Z. Idelsohn, *Jewish Music in Its Historical Development* (New York: Schocken, 1967 [1929]); P. Jeffery, "The Earliest Christian Chant Repertory Recovered: The Georgian Witnesses to Jerusalem Chant," *Journal of the American Musicological Society* 47 (1994) 1-38; C. Jones, G. Wainwright and E. Yarnold, eds., *The Study of Liturgy* (London: SPCK, 1983 [1978]); I. H. Jones, "Music and Musical Instruments," *ABD* 4:934-39; A. D. Kilmer, "Music," *IDBSup* 610-12; A. D. Kilmer and D. A. Foxveg, "Music," HBD 665-71; C. H. Kraeling and L. Mowry, "Music in the Bible," in *Ancient and Oriental Music,* ed. E. Wellesz (NOHM 1; London and Oxford: Oxford University Press, 1966 [1957]) 283-312; R. P. Martin, "Aspects of Worship in the New Testament Church," *VoxEv* 2 (1963) 6-32; idem, "Patterns of Worship in New Testament Churches," *JSNT* 37 (1989) 59-85; idem, *Worship in the Early Church* (Grand Rapids, MI: Eerdmans, 1974 [1964]); V. M. Matthews, "Music in the Bible," *ABD* 4:930; W. D. Maxwell, *An Outline of Christian Worship: Its Developments and Forms* (London: Oxford University Press, 1965 [1936]); H. A. McKay, "Ancient Synagogues: The Continuing Dialectic Between Two Major Views," *Currents in Research: Biblical Studies* 6 (1998) 103-42; J. W. McKinnon, "Early Western Civilization," in *Antiquity and the Middle Ages: From Ancient Greece to the Fifteenth Century,* ed. J. W. McKinnon (Man and Music; Basingstoke, Hampshire: Macmillan, 1990); idem, "The Exclusion of Musical Instruments from the Ancient Synagogue," *Proceedings of the Royal Musical Association* 106 (1979-80) 77-87; idem, "The Meaning of the Patristic Polemic Against Musical Instruments," *Current Musicology* 1 (1965) 69-82; idem, "On the Question of Psalmody in the Ancient Synagogue," *Early Music History* 6 (1986) 159-91; J. W. McKinnon, ed., *Music in Early Christian Literature* (Cambridge Studies in the Literature of Music; Cambridge: Cambridge University Press, 1987); J. W. McKinnon and R. Anderson, "Aulos," in *New Grove Dictionary of Musical Instruments* 1:85-87; W. A. Meeks, *The First Urban Christians: The Social World of the Apostle Paul* (New Haven, CT: Yale University Press, 1983); E. Pöhlmann, *Denkmäler altgriechischer Musik: Sammlung, Übertragung und Erläuterung aller Fragmente und Fälshchungen* (Nürnberg: Verlag Hans Carl, 1970) 106-9; W. J. Porter, "λαλέω: A Word About Women, Music and Sensuality in the Early Church," in *Religion and Sexuality,* ed. M. A. Hayes, W. J. Porter and D. Tombs (RILP 4; STS 2; Sheffield: Sheffield Academic Press, 1998) 101-24; J. Quasten, *Music and Worship in Pagan and Christian Antiquity* (2d ed.; Washington DC: National Association of Pastoral Musicians, 1980); T. Reinach, *La Musique Greque* (Editions d'aujourd'hui; Paris: Payot, 1926); A. Robertson, "Psalmody," in *A Dictionary of Liturgy and Worship,* ed. J. G. Davies (London: SCM, 1972); C. Sachs, *The History of Musical Instruments* (New York: Norton, 1940); idem, *The Rise of Music in the Ancient World East and West* (New York: Norton, 1943); S. Sadie, ed., *The New Grove Dictionary of Music and Musicians* (20 vols.; London: Macmillan, 1980); idem, *The New Grove Dictionary of Musical Instruments* (New York: Macmillan, 1984); K. Schlesinger, *The Greek Aulos: A Study of Mechanism and of Its Relation to the Modal System of Ancient Greek Music* (London: Methuen, 1939); J. E. Scott, "Roman Music," in *Ancient and Oriental Music,* ed. E. Wellesz (NOHM 1; London and Oxford: Oxford University Press, 1966 [1957]) 404-20; A. Sendrey, *Music in Ancient Israel* (New York: Philosophical Library, 1969); J. A. Smith, "The Ancient Synagogue, the Early Church and Singing," *Music & Letters* 65 (1984) 1-16; idem, "First-Century Christian Singing and Its Relationship to Contemporary Jewish Religious Song," *Music & Letters* 75 (1994) 1-15; idem, "Musical Aspects of Old Testament Canticles in Their Biblical Setting," *Early Music History* 17 (1998) 221-64; idem, "Which Psalms Were Sung in the Temple?" *Music & Letters* 71 (1990) 167-86; W. S. Smith, *Musical Aspects of the New Testament* (Amsterdam: W. Ten Have, 1962); O. Strunk, *Essays on Music in the Byzantine World* (New York: Norton, 1977); L. Treitler, "Homer and Gregory: The Transmission of Epic Poetry and Plainchant," *Musical Quarterly* 40 (1974) 333-72; E. Wellesz, "Early Christian Music," in *Early Medieval Music up to 1300,* ed. A. Hughes (NOHM 2; rev. ed.; London: Oxford University Press, 1955) 1-13; idem, *Eastern Elements in Western Chant: Studies in the Early History of Ecclesiastical Music* (Copenhagen: Ejnar Munksgaard, 1967 [1947]); idem, *A History of Byzantine Music and Hymnography* (2d ed.; Oxford: Clarendon Press, 1961); E. Wellesz, ed., *Ancient and Oriental Music* (NOHM 1; London and Oxford: Oxford University Press, 1966 [1957]); E. Werner, "The Common Ground in the Chant of Church and Synagogue," repr. in E. Werner, *Three Ages of Musical Thought: Essays on Ethics and Aesthetics* (New York: Da Capo Press, 1981) 3-15; idem, "The Conflict Between Hellenism and Judaism in the Music of the Early Christian Church," *HUCA* 20 (1947) 407-70; idem, " 'If I Speak in the Tongues of Men . . . ': St. Paul's Attitude to Music," *Journal of the American Musicological Society* 13 (1960) 18-23; idem, "Jewish Music. I. Liturgical," in *The New Grove Dictionary of Music and Musicians* 9:614-34; idem, "Music," *IDB* 3:457; idem, "The Music of Post-Biblical Judaism," in *Ancient and Oriental Music,* ed. E. Wellesz (NOHM 1; London and Oxford: Oxford University Press, 1966 [1957]) 313-35; idem, "Musical

Aspects of the Dead Sea Scrolls," *Musical Quarterly* 43 (1957) 21-37; idem, "Musical Instruments," *IDB* 3:469-76; idem, *The Sacred Bridge: The Interdependence of Liturgy and Music in Synagogue and Church During the First Millenium* (vol. 1, New York: Columbia University Press, 1959; vol. 2, New York: Ktav, 1984); M. L. West, "Analecta Musica," *ZPE* 92 (1992a) 1-54; idem, *Ancient Greek Music* (Oxford: Clarendon Press, 1992b) 14-21; idem, "The Babylonian Musical Notation and the Hurrian Melodic Texts," *Music & Letters* 75 (1994) 161-79; idem, "Texts with Musical Notation," in *Oxyrhynchus Papyri*, LXV, ed. M. W. Haslam et al. (Egypt Exploration Society Greco-Roman Memoirs 85; London: Egypt Exploration Society, 1998) 81-102; D. Wulstan, "The Tuning of the Babylonian Harp," *Iraq* 30 (1968) 215-28.

W. J. Porter

MUSONIUS RUFUS

C. Musonius Rufus, a knight of equestrian rank who lived in the first century A.D., for a time in *Rome, and was roughly a contemporary of Paul, zealously embraced *Stoic dogma and avidly pursued Stoic philosophy. Judging by both the number and the quality of the students whom he attracted and tutored—Rubellius Plautus, *Pliny the Younger, Minicius Fundanus, the teacher of Fronto, Athenodotus, Euphrates (an opponent of Appollonius), Timocrates, Artimedorus (his future son-in-law) and above all *Epictetus—but most of all by the imprint he left on his contemporaries, he was an unusual man. His dialogues have been preserved by his students; he himself wrote nothing. If Stoics would have introduced saints, he would have been one of them. He was co-opted into the Christian church by men like Clement of Alexandria and called a "model of the highest form of life" by Origen; one might expect him to have enjoyed at least as good a reputation in the subsequent history of the church as did *Seneca. But such was not the case.

1. Assessments of Musonius
2. Ethical Teachings

1. Assessments of Musonius.

The reception Musonius has received from modern scholars and even historians who have tried to depict the variegated picture of Stoicism has been, with some exceptions, modest. M. P. Charlesworth, however, in his five character studies from the Roman Empire, selects him as the philosopher and finds "something noble and attractive in the figure of Musonius, a simplicity and strength of character . . . single-minded throughout. . . . living hard and nobly. . . . It was a good life he lived, and he held before his pupils no low or light ideal" (Charlesworth, 60). A major book on Stoicism describes him as "a spirit whom certainly none excelled." M. Pohlenz described him as "a man cast in a unique mold who in the midst of a servile world went his own way . . . and without following any doctrinaire approach . . . actualised stoic philosophy in life. No wonder that he made a powerful impact on his contemporaries" (Pohlenz, 1:303).

More than one author has drawn a parallel between Musonius and Socrates, but apparently R. Hirzel first called him explicitly the "Roman Socrates." This designation has achieved a certain popularity since it was used as a title for the first extensive monograph (Lutz 1947) ever published on him in English.

2. Ethical Teachings.

As a popular teacher of ethics Musonius believed in teaching and living the simple life, keeping clothes, furniture and a dwelling place to the bare necessities so that he had more to give to the poor and the needy. He taught that men and *women were equal, should have equal opportunities in *education and work and, rejecting pederasty, that married love between male and female was the highest form of love humans could attain. For in *marriage not only do two bodies unite but their spirits, minds and wills as well. He rejected the double standard of behavior in sexual matters and argued that if a female slave owner is not allowed to treat her male *slave as sexual property, then neither can the male slave owner do so.

Musonius was a popular ethicist advocating a high folk morality and had little time for the complex ethical debates of the Sophists. Nevertheless the imitation of Socrates was important to him, and he firmly believed that the virtues of God could be emulated. He rejected violence not only in principle but also by intervening bodily in one conflict by interposing himself between two warring armies. He argued that good people must help offenders, for the bad person's sole hope rests in the way the good person treats him or her.

In his sexual ethics Musonius comes closest to Paul, differing only in that Musonius urged that sexual intercourse be restricted to childbearing, while Paul urged that it be engaged in whenever either party desired (1 Cor 7:1-5), as long as there was mutual desire and consent. But Musonius has a higher view of the model of partnership in marriage (cf. Genesis), which seems not to have figured very largely in Paul's view. Paul seems to have viewed marriage as an anodyne to sexual drives. Both viewed marriage as an arrangement under divine appointment and therefore a violation of marriage vows was a breach of the divine will leading to human misery. In short, Musonius had a theological bent, which in itself set him apart from both the Stoics (although clearly Epictetus followed his teacher), but also made it easier for later Christians to be attracted to him. His influence is not directly seen in the NT; there is no doubt that the same people may have been attracted to both Musonius and preachers from the early church, like Paul. At the same time Musonius seems to have addressed ethical dilemmas of the wealthy, whereas most of the early Christian ethical directives were formed to meet the needs of simpler and poorer people.

See also PHILOSOPHY; STOICISM.

BIBLIOGRAPHY. D. L. Balch, *let Wives Be Submissive* (Chico, CA: Scholars Press, 1981) 143-45; M. P. Charlesworth, *Five Men: Character Studies from the Roman Empire* (Cambridge, MA: Harvard University Press, 1936); A. C. van Geytenbeek, *Musonius Rufus and Greek Diatribe* (Wijgerige Teksten en Studies 8; Assen: Van Gorcum, 1963); P. W. van der Horst, "Musonius Rufus and the New Testament," *NovT* 16 (1974) 306-15; W. Klassen, "A 'Child of Peace' (Luke 10:6) in First-Century Context," *NTS* 27 (1981) 488-506; idem, "Foundations for Pauline Sexual Ethics as Seen in 1 Thessalonians 4:18," *SBLSP* (1978) 159-81; idem, "Humanitas as Seen by Epictetus and Musonius Rufus," in *Studi Storico Religiosi* 1, 1 (Rome, 1977) 63-82; idem, "Musonius Rufus and the Living Law," *SR* 14 (1985) 63-71; idem, "Musonius Rufus, Jesus and Paul: Three First-Century Feminists," in *From Jesus to Paul: Studies in Honor of Francis Wright Beare,* ed. P. Richardson and J. C. Hurd (Waterloo, ON: Wilfrid Laurier Press, 1984) 185-206; idem, "Παρρησια in the Johannine Corpus," in *Friendship, Flattery and Frankness of Speech: Studies in Friendship in the New Testament World,* ed. J. T. Fitzgerald (Leiden: E. J. Brill, 1996) 227-54; C. Lutz, "Musonius Rufus, 'The Roman Socrates,'" *Yale Classical Studies* 10 (1947) 3-147; A. J. Malherbe, *Moral Exhortation: A Greco-Roman Sourcebook* (Philadelphia: Westminster, 1986) provides six lengthy sections from Musonius; M. Pohlenz, *Die Stoa: Geschichte einer geistigen Bewegung* (2 vols.; Göttingen: Vandenhoeck & Ruprecht, 1970); L. Vaage, "Musonius Rufus, On Training (Discourse VI)," in *Ascetic Behavior in Greco-Roman Antiquity: A Sourcebook,* ed. V. Wimbush (Minneapolis, Fortress, 1990) 129-33; R. B. Ward, "Musonius and Paul on Marriage," *NTS* 36 (1990) 281-89; D. Wiens, "Musonius and Genuine Education" (Ph.D. diss., University of Chicago, 1970).

W. Klassen

MYSTERIES

The mysteries, or mystery religions, were secretive religions that flourished alongside official, public religions during the Greco-Roman period. The mysteries varied in matters of geographical origin, historical development and theological orientation, and they championed deities from all around the Mediterranean world and the ancient Middle East. Nonetheless, authors ancient and modern have classified and discussed the mysteries together because they represent a particular form of religion. The mysteries advocated salvation for individual followers who chose to seek initiation into the mysteries and thus to draw close to the divine and to each other. Apparently rooted in ancient tribal and fertility rituals, the mysteries celebrated the death and new life that may be experienced not only in nature but also in the world of humankind. On account of their profound experiences within the mysteries, initiates were enjoined to keep the mysteries secret and not to divulge them to the profane. Some interpreters have suggested that Christianity may be considered to be a mystery religion.

1. Descriptions of the Mysteries
2. Greek Mysteries
3. Mysteries of Middle Eastern Origin
4. The Mysteries and Early Christianity

1. Descriptions of the Mysteries.

In contrast to official Greco-Roman religions, in which people expressed public devotion to the deities of the state, the mysteries were in large part private affairs. In the main the mysteries looked inward, within the persons initiated and within the groups of initiates, to find religious fulfillment. The groups within the mysteries frequently were close-knit and egalitarian, and the members of these groups typically shared in rituals that included public and especially private ceremonies. Ancient sources freely depict parades and processions, with music and dance, and various preliminary rituals of purification and sacrifice. For example, in his *Metamorphoses,* commonly referred to as *The Golden Ass,* Apuleius of Madaura describes a parade in honor of the Egyptian goddess Isis, with a devoted band of singers, instrumentalists and folks in costume, and with parade officials calling for people to make way for the goddess. As described by Apuleius, the procession was a colorful event, and accompanying the goddess were some participants who were dressed to resemble Egyptian deities and others who carried religious symbols and a chest containing the sacred and secret things of the Egyptian goddess.

Ancient sources say comparatively little, however, about the private ceremonies of the mysteries, and the details of these ceremonies remain largely unknown. A few early Christian authors who had once been initiated or who claimed to know the things that went on in the mysteries sometimes divulged what they believed to be ungodly secrets of the mysteries, but even these sources say relatively little. In descriptions of the Eleusinian mysteries it is said in general that among the experiences within the private ceremonies of the mysteries were "things recited," "things shown" and "things performed," and presumably these sorts of things were a part of other mysteries as well.

Occasionally ancient sources give formulas or symbols *(symbola)* that purportedly were spoken during the private ceremonies, but these formulas are difficult to interpret out of context. Often a sacred meal was shared by the followers of the mysteries, and in at least some of the mysteries there were ceremonies in which participants were said to go through death and rebirth. In a literary fragment attributed to *Plutarch, initiation into the mysteries is compared to the experience of death. Plutarch notes the similarity of the Greek verbs "to be initiated" *(teleisthai)* and "to die" *(teleutan),* and he compares the transformations of those who are initiated and those who die:

> At first there is wandering, and wearisome roaming, and fearful traveling through darkness with no end to be found. Then, just before the consummation, there is every sort of terror, shuddering and trembling and sweating and being alarmed. But after this a marvelous light appears, and open places and meadows await, with voices and dances and the solemnities of sacred utterances and holy visions. In that place one walks about at will, now perfect and initiated and free, and wearing a crown, one celebrates religious rituals, and joins with pure and pious people.

*Aristotle confirms that initiation into the mysteries could be a deeply moving emotional experience. In a fragment preserved in Synesius, Aristotle claims that initiates into the mysteries did not really learn anything, but rather they underwent some kind of experience and they were put into a particular state of mind.

The word *mystery* (*mystērion*) derives from the Greek verb *myein,* "to close," and it can be interpreted to refer to the closing of the lips, for secrecy or the closing and subsequent opening of the eyes, for enlightenment. The word *mystery* is also used in the OT, the NT and the *Dead Sea Scrolls (see Brown). In 1 Corinthians 15:51, in his discussion of the resurrection of Christ and Christians, Paul states that the resurrection is a mystery: "Look, I tell you a mystery. We shall not all sleep, but we shall all be changed." Elsewhere in this discussion Paul uses other language that is reminiscent of the ancient mysteries.

2. Greek Mysteries.

Ancient Greek mysteries were celebrated from very early times through Roman antiquity. The most well known of the Greek mysteries are the Eleusinian mysteries, the Andanian mysteries and the mysteries of Dionysus. Also of considerable significance are the mysteries from Samothrace, which featured the Great Gods, the Kabeiroi, or Cabiri. Further, in his satire *Alexander the False Prophet,* *Lucian of Samosata describes mysteries that employed themes that recall the Eleusinian mysteries but that were founded by Alexander of Abonoteichos, in honor of the serpent Glykon, an incarnation of the Greek god of healing, Asclepius.

2.1. Eleusinian Mysteries. The Eleusinian mysteries, the most prominent of the Greek mysteries, were observed at Eleusis, near *Athens. The Eleusinian mysteries incorporated rituals like those of the old agricultural religion of Eleusis, which commemorated the life cycle and the transformation of grain, but the Eleusinian mysteries applied these agricultural interests to the life cycle and transformation of people. The sacred mythic account *(hieros logos)* used in the Eleusinian mysteries most likely rehearsed the dramatic story of Demeter, the Grain Mother, and her dying and rising daughter Kore, the Maiden. In this story, as told in the *Homeric Hymn to Demeter,* Kore is seized by Hades (or Plouton, the Wealthy One), but the grieving Demeter finds Kore, who eventually is made to spend part of the year with the dead and part of the year with the living. These agricultural themes remained in the Eleusinian mysteries, it would seem, for the Christian author Hippolytus of Rome observes that among the things shown in the mysteries was a single head of grain beheld in silence by the initiates. The emphasis upon life and death also remained, *Cicero observes, when he indicates that from the Eleusinian mysteries people learned the fundamentals of life, and they grasped "the basis not only for living with joy but also for dying with a better hope." In time Athens took control of the Eleusinian mysteries, and later mysteries of Demeter and Kore were celebrated at a site, also named Eleusis, in *Alexandria, Egypt.

*2.2. **Andanian Mysteries.*** The author Pausanias and the inscription called the Rule of the Andanian Mysteries depict Greek mysteries celebrated at Andania in the southwestern Peloponnesus. The Andanian mysteries were dedicated to Demeter, Hermes, Apollo Karneios, Hagna (Holy One or Pure One) and the Great Gods. The Rule of the Andanian Mysteries is a public documentation of the regulations that governed the mysteries. The rule thus outlines the formal features of the mysteries (oaths, clothing, processions, tents, funds, sacrifices, musicians, the sacred meal, and so on) and the means by which regulations were to be enforced, but no secrets are disclosed in the rule. As a public document, the rule openly discusses only external aspects of the Andanian mysteries, and when it refers to the private ceremonies, it does so with such cryptic expressions as "the things pertaining to the initiation" and "the things pertaining to the sacrifices."

*2.3. **Mysteries of Dionysus.*** The mysteries of Dionysus, or Bacchus, must have been remarkably diverse in character. Euripides' *Bacchae* dramatizes aspects of what might be mysteries of Dionysus in which female followers of Dionysus (Bacchae, or maenads, that is, women in an ecstatic state of mind) are portrayed as embodying the raw power of Dionysus. Livy's *History of Rome* states that the Roman senate adopted a decree, *Senatus Consultum de Bacchanalibus,* because of suspicions regarding sexual irregularities within the mysteries of Dionysus. Conversely, frescoes in the Villa of the Mysteries at Pompeii make use of Dionysian themes to suggest more domesticated mysteries of sexuality, and the Rule of the Iobacchoi presents the regulations of an Athenian Bacchic club that met together to enjoy the Dionysian pleasures of wine, food and drama. The Orphics considered the Dionysian stories of tearing apart flesh and consuming it raw to reflect the original sin committed by the Titans against Dionysus. Hence, an Orphic lamella from Thessaly has a dead person's soul comment on the dual nature of a human being, who consists of earth, or Titanic flesh, and heaven, or Dionysian divinity: "I am a child of earth and of starry heaven, but my race is of heaven." This Orphic view of the dual nature of a human being may be compared with the view of *Plato.

3. Mysteries of Middle Eastern Origin.
Mysteries of Middle Eastern origin were popular during the *Hellenistic and Roman periods as some religious people of the Mediterranean world became increasingly fascinated with foreign and sometimes exotic religious traditions. These mysteries came, directly or indirectly, from such places as Asia Minor, Syria, Egypt and Persia, and the most important of the mysteries of Middle Eastern origin include the mysteries of the Great Mother and Attis, the mysteries of Isis and Osiris and the mysteries of Mithras. In addition, the mysteries of the Syrian goddess and the slain youth Adonis were also important, and they appear to have been similar in some respects to the mysteries of the Great Mother and Attis.

*3.1. **Mysteries of the Great Mother and Attis.*** The mysteries of the Great Mother and Attis come from Phrygia in Asia Minor and feature the Great Mother *(Magna Mater),* often named Kybele (Cybele or Kybebe), and her young lover Attis. During Roman times these mysteries spread to various parts of the Roman world, and they became infamous for their unusual festivals and flamboyant followers, or Galli, who imitated the mythological act of Attis by castrating themselves and becoming eunuchs of the Great Mother. The Christian poet Prudentius describes the ritual slaughter of a bull (the *taurobo-*

lium) in which an initiate descended into a pit to be drenched with the blood of the sacrificed bull. An inscription dated to A.D. 376 maintains that a person thus bathed in the bull's blood was "reborn for eternity." The private ceremonies of the mysteries of the Great Mother and Attis are unknown, but Clement of Alexandria cites a formula with tantalizing hints: "I have eaten from the drum (or tambourine), I have drunk from the cymbal, I have carried the sacred dish, I have stolen into the inner chamber" (variant readings of this formula are to be read in Firmicus Maternus).

3.2. Mysteries of Isis and Osiris. The mysteries of Isis and Osiris from the Greco-Roman world built upon the Egyptian worship of these Egyptian deities, but the Greco-Roman mysteries differ from the ancient Egyptian mysteries of succession and mummification in substantial ways. The goddess Isis was revered during Greco-Roman times, and she retained aspects of her Egyptian nature but also assumed characteristics of a Greco-Roman goddess. The god Osiris, brother and lover of Isis and lord of the realm of death, also attracted many followers in the Greco-Roman period, and sometimes he was worshiped as Sarapis or Osiris-Apis (Osiris joined to the Apis bull). Apuleius of Madaura has the initiate Lucius recount, in guarded terms, what happened during the private ceremonies in the mysteries of Isis and Osiris: "I approached the border of death; I stepped across the threshold of Proserpine and, carried through all the elements, I returned. In the middle of the night I saw the sun shining with dazzling light. I approached the gods below and the gods above and, while near them, I worshiped them." This statement, though deliberately obscure, explains initiation as an experience of moving from darkness to light and from death to life. Elsewhere Apuleius states that Lucius is "reborn" or "born again."

3.3. Mysteries of Mithras. The mysteries of Mithras as found in the Roman world are Roman mysteries that recall some features of Persian sources but appear to represent Roman values. Men, especially soldiers, sailors and imperial officers, were attracted to the worship of Mithras, probably because Mithras was a warrior on behalf of light, truth and justice, and these followers of Mithras entered sanctuaries of Mithras (Mithraea) in order to participate in initiatory rituals and other ceremonies. According to Tertullian, these Mithraic rituals included lustrations, ordeals and tests of courage; Justin Martyr describes a sacred meal in which initiates partake of bread and a cup of water or a cup of water and wine and recite certain formulas.

Initiation into the mysteries of Mithras specified several stages or grades of initiation. Often seven are enumerated: raven, bridegroom (or occult), soldier, lion, Persian, courier of the sun and father. These seven stages or grades may have corresponded to the seven stations that decorate Mithraea at Ostia Antica, the seven gates of heaven and seven planets and metals associated with the soul's ascent in Origen's citation of Celsus, and the seven stages of ascent in the Mithras Liturgy. The Mithraea often were richly decorated, most notably with astronomical and astrological imagery, and the apse of a Mithraeum usually contained a scene of Mithras slaying a bull (Mithras *tauroktonos).* Recent studies of Mithraism (R. Beck; D. Ulansey) propose astronomical and astrological interpre-tations of the mysteries of Mithras instead of the traditional dualistic, Zoroastrian interpretations (F. Cumont). An inscription from the Mithraeum of Santa Prisca in *Rome may suggest a soteriological interpretation of the slaying of the bull: "and having shed eternal blood, you [Mithras] have saved us." Another fragmentary inscription may understand salvation as rebirth and creation, perhaps through partaking of the sacred meal: "one piously reborn and created by sweet things."

4. The Mysteries and Early Christianity.

Early Christianity developed as a Greco-Roman religion, with Jewish roots, in the same world as the mystery religions, and it shows clear affinities with the mysteries. Like the mysteries, early Christianity developed as a religion of salvation and personal choice. Early Christian initiates participated in ceremonies of purification, fasting and baptism, and some of these ceremonies were private and secretive. Like groups within the mysteries, early Christian communities could also proclaim that they were egalitarian and lived in unity, and Paul preached that in Christ "there is neither Jew nor Greek, there is neither slave nor free person, there is not male and female" (Gal 3:28). For Paul and other early Christians, baptism could be understood as a death experience that anticipated the experience of resurrection and new life. In 1 Corinthians 15 Paul interprets this *apocalyptically and terms it a mystery.

Early Christian believers also shared in a sacred meal, the Eucharist, with the elements bread and wine linked to the death of Christ. Thus early Christians could articulate their salvation to be an experience of dying and rising with Christ, so that Paul writes about being "in Christ" and John discusses being "born again" or "born from above" (*gennēthē anōthen*). Paul's discussion of the Christian mystery of dying and rising involves a comparison, calling to mind the Eleusinian mysteries, with the planting and sprouting of seed (1 Cor 15:36-38), and John likewise has Jesus announce, "In truth, in truth I tell you, unless a kernel of wheat falls into the ground and dies, it remains a single seed, but if it dies, it yields much produce" (Jn 12:24). Further, John's portrayal of Jesus performing the sign of changing water into wine (Jn 2:1-11) duplicates accounts of the famous miracle the Greek god Dionysus, and early Christian depictions of the Virgin Mary and young Jesus recall representations of the Egyptian deities Isis and Horus, and Mary, like Isis, could be acclaimed the queen of heaven.

Ancient and modern interpreters sometimes have tried to explain these similarities by proposing theories of dependence. Early Christian authors such as Tertullian and Justin Martyr explained the similarities between early Christianity and Mithraism as being due to demonic imitation of Christianity, and some modern scholars have also proposed that followers of early Christianity and the mysteries may have borrowed from each other. The Christian author Clement of Alexandria affirms that Christianity is a mystery religion with "truly sacred mysteries," but he grants a privileged status to Christianity by asserting that Christianity is the only true mystery, in contrast to the shameless and corrupt Greco-Roman mysteries.

A balanced interpretation of the relationship between the mysteries and early Christianity acknowledges the similarities but avoids simplistic conclusions about dependence. Borrowing of certain religious ideas and practices may well have occurred in the syncretistic world of Greco-Roman antiquity, and it seems clear that from the fourth century on Christianity appropriated a goodly amount from other religions. Yet many of the similarities between the mysteries and early Christianity may be attributed to the fact that they were equally religions of the Greco-Roman world. As such, the mysteries and early Christianity often faced similar religious and social challenges, proposed similar ways of salvation and transformation and shared points of similarity in their visions of the way to light and life.

See also MYSTICISM; RELIGION, GRECO-ROMAN; RELIGION, PERSONAL.

BIBLIOGRAPHY. R. Beck, *Planetary Gods and Planetary Orders in the Mysteries of Mithras* (Leiden: E. J. Brill, 1988); U. Bianchi, *The Greek Mysteries* (IR:GR 3; Leiden: E. J. Brill, 1976); W. Bousset, *Kyrios Christos* (Nashville: Abingdon, 1970 [1913]); R. E. Brown, *The Semitic Background of the Term "Mystery" in the New Testament* (FB, Biblical Series 21; Philadelphia: Fortress, 1968); W. Burkert, *Ancient Mystery Cults* (Cambridge, MA: Harvard University Press, 1987); F. Cumont, *The Oriental Religions in Roman Paganism* (New York: Dover, 1956 [1911]); E. J. Epp, "Mystery Religions of the Greco-Roman World," in *Sourcebook of Texts for the Comparative Study of the Gospels,* ed. D. L. Dungan and D. R. Cartlidge (SBLSBS 1; Missoula, MT: Scholars Press, 1974) 355-74; W. K. C. Guthrie, *Orpheus and Greek Religion: A Study of the Orphic Movement* (2d ed.; London: Methuen, 1952); C. Kerényi, *Eleusis: Archetypal Image of Mother and Daughter* (New York: Schocken, 1977); K. Lehmann, ed., *Samothrace* (BS 60; New York: Pantheon, 1958); R. Merkelbach, *Mithras* (Königstein: Hain, 1984); B. M. Metzger, "A Classified Bibliography of the Greco-Roman Mystery Religions 1924-1973 with a Supplement 1974-77," *ANRW* 2.17.3 (1984) 1259-1423; idem, "Methodology in the Study of the Mystery Religions and Early Christianity," in *Historical and Literary Studies: Pagan, Jewish, and Christian* (NTTS 8; Leiden: E. J. Brill, 1968) 1-24; M. Meyer, ed., *The Ancient Mysteries: A Sourcebook of Sacred Texts* (Philadelphia: University of Pennsylvania Press, 1999); G. E. Mylonas, *Eleusis and the Eleusinian Mysteries* (Princeton, NJ: Princeton University Press, 1961); M. P. Nilsson, *The Dionysiac Mysteries of the Hellenistic and Roman Age* (New York: Arno, 1975); A. D. Nock, *Early Gentile Christianity and Its Hellenistic Background* (New York: Harper & Row, 1964 [1927]); idem, *Essays on Religion and the Ancient World,* ed. Z. Stewart (2 vols.; Cambridge, MA: Harvard University Press, 1972); W. F. Otto, *Dionysos: Myth and Cult* (Bloomington: Indiana University Press, 1965); R. Reitzenstein, *Hellenistic Mystery Religions: Their Basic Ideas and Significance* (PTMS 18; Pittsburgh:

Pickwick, 1978 [1927]); J. Z. Smith, *Drudgery Divine: On the Comparison of Early Christianities and the Religions of Late Antiquity* (CSHJ; Chicago: University of Chicago Press, 1990); F. Solmsen, *Isis Among the Greeks and Romans* (MCL 25; Cambridge, MA: Harvard University Press, 1979); D. Ulansey, *The Origins of the Mithraic Mysteries: Cosmology and Salvation in the Ancient World* (New York: Oxford University Press, 1989); M. J. Vermaseren, *Cybele and Attis: The Myth and the Cult* (New York: Thames & Hudson, 1977); R. E. Witt, *Isis in the Greco-Roman World* (Ithaca, NY: Cornell University Press, 1971). M. Meyer

MYSTICISM

There are two broad problems in confronting the subject of mysticism as background to the NT. The first concerns the definition of mysticism as such, a notoriously elusive idea but one that in turn defines the materials to be handled. The second concerns the treatment of the historical mysticisms thus defined. The following article will therefore begin with a discussion of definition followed by a treatment of Jewish mysticism, particularly Merkabah mysticism.

On *Hellenistic forms of mysticism, including the *mystery religions, see B. McGinn (23-61). Specifically regarding *Philo's own brand of mysticism, see D. Winston. These latter strands are of greater importance to the study of postapostolic mystical developments within Christianity, although at a variety of points Philo's writings bear on if they do not reflect some of the same ideas that will be touched on in this article.

1. Definition
2. Merkabah Mysticism
3. Mysticism and the New Testament

1. Definition.

No movement existed anywhere in biblical times under the name of mysticism. The noun *mysticism (la mystique)* is of recent derivation (according to McGinn, xvi, 266-67, it dates to early seventeenth-century France), though the qualifier *mystical* was used by Christians from the late second century on. Of greater interest than the history of words, including the Greek and Hebrew words related to the idea of mystery, is the way we choose to define the idea we will call mysticism (for the terms used by the Jewish mystics themselves, see Scholem 1974, 6-7; on terminology, *see DPL,* Mystery; Mysticism; *DLNTD,* Mystery; a lengthy survey of modern theories of mysticism is given by McGinn under the headings of theological approaches [266-91], philosophical approaches [291-326] and comparativist and psychological approaches [326-43]).

Like *Gnosticism and *apocalypticism, their suspected cousin mysticism has not allowed a consensus on definition. In the first of his proposed four volumes on the history of Western Christian mysticism, McGinn offers a working definition: "The mystical element in Christianity is that part of its belief and practices that concerns the preparation for, the consciousness of, and the reaction to what can be described as the immediate or direct presence of God" (xvii). By this definition mysticism does not exist as a distinct religion but is an element that can exist within the various religions.

Significantly, McGinn stops short of including in his definition the idea of union with God, "particularly a union of absorption or identity in which the individual personality is lost." Given the history of what is commonly called by this name, "at the very least, it is necessary to expand the notion of union, recognizing that there are several, perhaps even many, understandings of union with God held by Christians over the centuries" (McGinn, xvi). A constant feature in mystical texts is the claim that the mystic's "mode of access to God is radically different from that found in ordinary consciousness, even from the awareness of God gained through the usual activities of prayer, sacraments, and other rituals. As believers they affirm that God does become present in these activities, but not in any direct or immediate fashion" (McGinn, xix). It deserves notice for the purposes of this article that according to McGinn's reading of the materials, "Christian mysticism in the proper sense was the result of a historical process that was not complete for several centuries," though "from the start Christianity contained a mystical element" or at least was amenable to mystical interpretations (McGinn, 7).

Though other attempts at definition could be noted (see McGinn; Dunn 1998, 394), McGinn's attempt merits special mention as it is based on probably the widest historical survey of Western Christian mysticism yet undertaken. It cannot be assumed that a definition based on a study of Christian mysticism will be a reliable guide to the presence of non-Christian mysticisms during the first century and earlier, but it provides a place to start, and it is an appropriate starting point so long as we ask our questions from within an overtly Christian frame of reference.

The leading name among scholars of Jewish mysticism, G. Scholem (1897-1982), takes up the question of definition in the first chapter of *Major Trends in Jewish Mysticism* (1954, from which the following summary derives; *see also* Scholem 1974, which is an expanded reprint of his contributions to the *Encyclopaedia Judaica;* Scholem 1965). In preliminary fashion Scholem rejects as too broad an equation of mysticism with any experiential form of religion that is concerned with humanity's immediate experience of a divine presence, and he rejects as too narrow any definition that is restricted to an ultimate loss of the mystic's individuality through union with God. Moreover, and significantly, there can be no thought of an abstract mystical religion: "there is only the mysticism of a particular religious system, Christian, Islamic, Jewish mysticism and so on" (Scholem 1954, 6). This is not to deny that there are common characteristics among the mysticisms, but it is to deny that there is any such thing as an ideal mysticism of which the various manifestations are imperfect forms.

Scholem's own definition proceeds from the basic conviction that "mysticism is a definite stage in the historical development of religion and makes its appearance under certain well-defined conditions. It is connected with, and inseparable from, a certain stage of the religious consciousness" (Scholem 1954, 7). According to this evolutionary model, the initial, mythical stage of religion posits no abyss between humanity and deity. Humanity and the gods relate directly so that mysticism is excluded.

The second stage, classical religion, involves the creation of the abyss that cannot be bridged. The religious community "becomes aware of a fundamental duality, of a vast gulf which can be crossed by nothing but the *voice*" of God in revelation and the voice of humanity in *prayer (Scholem 1954, 7). The creation of this abyss, which is the "supreme function" of religion, is antithetical to mysticism.

It is the third, the romantic epoch, that, recognizing the abyss, "proceeds to a quest for the secret that will close it in, the hidden path that will span it" (Scholem 1954, 8). This is the mystical stage, involving the discovery of new religious impulses that reinterpret the old religious values of the classical stage and suggest new meanings in line with the directness of mystical experience. "Mystical religion seeks to transform the God whom it encounters in the peculiar religious consciousness of its own social environment from an object of dogmatic knowledge into a novel and living experience and intuition. In addition, it also seeks to interpret this experience in a new way" (Scholem 1954, 10; Gruenwald 1995, 8, comments similarly that "mysticism may be described as a live realization of theological notions or entities").

Thus Jewish mysticism "in its various forms represents an attempt to interpret the religious values of Judaism in terms of mystical values" (Scholem 1954, 10). Concentrating on the idea of God who manifests himself in the acts of creation, revelation and redemption, Jewish mystical meditation ultimately "gives birth to the conception of a sphere, a whole realm of divinity, which underlies the world of our sense-data and which is present and active in all that exists" (Scholem 1954, 10-11; this last comment relates especially to the *Sefirot,* which will be mentioned in 2.1 below). Associated with this enterprise is a distinctive technique that employs unique symbols and rituals and brings about the state of ecstasy necessary for the experience.

This is not the place to explain further or critique this definition of Jewish mysticism, but it will be clear from the foregoing that in Scholem's view Jewish mysticism is a necessary stage in the evolution of the Jewish religion (and religions can pass through this sequence more than once), and that as such it is sui generis. It is enough to have noted the attempts of two outstanding students of the subject and so to have been reminded of the difficulty of defining this area and of the linkage between definition and historical investigation.

2. Merkabah Mysticism.

The history of Jewish mysticism will depend on our definition of mysticism as such, and in Scholem's model the first phase of Jewish mysticism, Merkabah mysticism, runs from the first century B.C. to the tenth century A.D., having its roots in the end of the Second Temple era when the conditions of Scholem's third stage of religion prevailed; he notes "the struggle taking place in this period between different religious forces, and . . . the tendency then current to delve more deeply into original religious speculation" (Scholem 1974, 10); differing definitions will trace Jewish mysticism into the OT period (see 2.2.1 below), and one must also allow for other strands within early *Judaism.

2.1. Synopsis. It will be helpful to provide a synopsis of what we mean by Merkabah mysticism before surveying the evidence adduced for its existence and development. The following summary uses Scholem's seminal characterization as a starting point with certain qualifications added from the more recent models, some of which depart in significant ways from Scholem's work. The main lines of this profile are drawn from the fifth century and later *Hekhalot* texts, which are themselves inharmonious, but at various points there is assumed an essential continuity with earlier apocalyptic and *rabbinic sources.

Merkabah mysticism "is used to refer to an esoteric, visionary-mystical tradition centred upon the vision of God seated on the celestial throne or Merkabah" (Morray-Jones 1992, 2). "Its essence is not absorbed contemplation of God's true nature, but perception of his appearance on the throne, as described by Ezekiel, and cognition of the mysteries of the celestial throne-world. . . . God's pre-existing throne, which embodies and exemplifies all forms of creation, is at once the goal and the theme of his mystical vision" (Scholem 1954, 44). The term *Merkabah* ("throne-chariot") is not used in the text of Ezekiel but is first used in reference to Ezekiel's vision in Sirach 49:8 (cf. 1 Chron 28:18; *see* Sirach) and also frequently in the scrolls from *Qumran. The term *hammerkabah* is often used in Talmudic literature as a shorthand title for Ezekiel 1.

The expression *Maaseh Merkabah* ("the Account of the Chariot") refers to the esoteric tradition of exegesis of Ezekiel 1 and related texts (esp. Dan 7; Is 6), exegesis that could be related to mystical experiences and practices of *ascent to the throne. The ascent through seven heavens is characteristic of these texts, and correspondingly there is mention of seven Merkabah along with the *Hekhalot* ("chambers," "palaces," "temples") of the Merkabah. The latter idea of the *Hekhalot* is possibly a later development, but it became dominant. Though scholarship has traced these mystical practices or traditions into the first century A.D. and earlier, its classical period ran from the fourth to sixth centuries, and its outstanding documents were edited in the fifth and sixth centuries. These documents are among the *Hekhalot* tracts (seee 2.2.6 below), so named because of the importance of "descriptions of the *hekhaloth,* the heavenly halls or palaces through which the visionary passes and in the seventh and last of which there rises the throne of divine glory" (Scholem 1954, 45).

Recent scholarship has preferred to stress that the *Hekhalot* texts represent just one development of the Merkabah tradition along with the apocalypses and other Jewish, Christian and gnostic texts (Morray-Jones 1992, 2; note for example that the term *Merkabah* features prominently in the relevant Qumran materials), though the relationship of the ideas expressed in these sources and the continuity of the movement are matters of dispute.

A strand of speculation related to *Maaseh Merkabah* and also developing during the first six centuries was *Maaseh Bereshit* ("the Account of Creation"). Focusing chiefly on the Genesis account of creation, this was an esoteric and theoretical approach to the problems of cosmology and cosmogony. Little of this teaching was leaked to outsiders, but an important exception is *Sefer Yetsirah* (The Book of Creation), which has been variously dated from the late second/early third century A.D. (in an earlier form) to the ninth century. The work is thought to have been written by and for educated rabbis as an explanation of the creation story of Genesis and as instruction in creative *magic (on permissible magic, see *b. Sanh.* 67a). "Its chief subject matters are the elements of the world, which are sought in the ten elementary and primordial numbers—*Sefiroth,* as the book calls them—and the 22 letters of the Hebrew alphabet. These together represent the mysterious forces whose convergence has produced the various combinations observable throughout the whole of creation; they are the 'thirty-two secret paths of wisdom,' through which God has created all that exists" (Scholem 1954, 76; see further Blumenthal, 6-46; through comparison with Assyrian materials, Parpola [1993], has traced the roots of the Sefirotic Tree, a symbolic configuration of the Sefirot, into the early thirteenth century B.C.).

This inauguration of the Sefirot terminology is noted by I. Gruenwald (1995, 10) as the turning point in the history of Jewish mysticism, leading to a distinct phase of Jewish mysticism, subsequent to the Merkabah phase, namely,

Kabbalah ("reception," "tradition"; on the need to distinguish these phases see Gruenwald 1995, 10), although it must be noted that the term *Kabbalah* is sometimes used to cover the whole mystical movement of Judaism from Talmudic times to the present.

It is argued that behind the tradition of Merkabah mysticism existed a movement, originating in Palestine and organized into esoteric groups making up a school of mystics who were not prepared to reveal their secret knowledge due to its controversial nature. These mystics came to refer to themselves as *Yorde Merkabah,* "Descenders to the Merkabah," though the choice of the descent motif rather than ascent has resisted explanation (the motif of descent might have originated c. A.D. 500). These groups were organized around a master who initiated his group into the tradition's teachings and also demonstrated in their presence the ascent to the Merkabah. Entrance into these groups was conditioned on certain criteria, especially intellectual conditions and age limits ("life's half-way stage"), as well as moral and physical criteria (the latter including physiognomy and chiromancy).

Those who passed the test were worthy to make the ascent, and the primary interests of the *Hekhalot* texts are their preparation and technique for the ascent as well as what was perceived on the voyage. Preparation for the ascent involved fasting, eating special foods or bathing. The ascent was then effected by techniques that would seem designed to effect a trancelike state, especially the recitation of hymns, *prayers or magical incantations that featured the rhythmical repetition of words, sounds or ideas, possibly whispered while placing the head between the knees (cf. 1 Kings 18:42; Gilgamesh, in the Epic of Gilgamesh, uses a similar technique for attaining dreams; see Parpola 1993, 192 n. 120). In the resulting state of ecstasy the journey took place.

The *Hekhalot* texts do not give much information about the ascent through the heavens, but they do describe the movement of the soul through the seven concentrically arranged *Hekhalot* (palaces) in the seventh heaven (aside from *3 Enoch* [an apocalypse; *see* Enoch, Books of] and *Massekhet Hekhalot* [a *midrashic compilation] the instructional *Hekhalot* texts appear to equate the *Hekhalot* with the heavenly levels rather than locating them in the seventh heaven; cf. Morray-Jones 1993, 179-80). The progress of the soul is blocked by a series of angelic gatekeepers. Success in the journey depends, then, on the knowledge of secret names, magic seals derived from the Merkabah itself that function as passes and put the hostile *angels to flight.

As the journey progresses the struggle increases with the result that longer and more complicated magical formulas are needed in order to break through. Theurgy is prominent throughout this literature (theurgy is a form of magic, roughly described "as the 'science' of coercing the gods, and particularly of bringing about changes in divine realms"; see further Gruenwald 1995, 40-41). The journey is perilous, not only because of the hostile angels but also because the mystic must undergo a fiery transformation that threatens to devour the unworthy (on transformation, see 2.2.2; 2.2.5; 2.2.6; 3 below). The entire experience takes place in an atmosphere of majesty, fear and trembling, with an almost exclusive focus on God's otherness. Even the climax of the ascent involves a seeing and hearing in the presence of the throne with no suggestion of absorption or mystical union. Correspondingly there is in this literature no focus on the presence of God or on love of God but primarily an occupation with God as the holy King.

The purpose of the ascent could vary between the mere desire to view God's glory and join in the heavenly angelic worship, the more practical desire to gain knowledge of benefit to oneself (e.g., knowledge of what was about to happen) and the desire to gain revelatory knowledge of more ultimate consequence. The vision of the celestial realm, the songs of the angels and the structure of the Merkabah were among the subjects of esoteric knowledge, and of equal importance to these was the appearance of God in his aspect of Creator enthroned on the Merkabah. The description of this gigantic human form (cf. Ezek 1:26-28) became the subject of the *Shiur Komah* ("Dimensions of the Body") texts and passages, which drew on the imagery and language of OT passages such as Isaiah 6:1-4; 66:1 and especially Song of Solomon 5 (in this connection, the defense of Song of Solomon's canonicity by Rabbi Akiba [*t. Sanh.* 12:10], one of the early rabbis associated with Merkabah mysticism, is significant; Scholem 1965, 38-40, notes other evidence for the dating of these traditions as early as the third century A.D.).

In the *Hekhalot* texts a distinction is maintained between God as he is in himself and his visible, corporeal manifestation upon his descent to the seventh heaven so as to be worshiped by his creation. This manifestation of God on the throne was referred to as "the Glory," "the Great Glory" or "the Power" (cf. Ezek 1:28; *T. Levi* 2:4; *1 Enoch* 14:20-21; some associate the Simon of Acts 8:10 with this idea), which in some sources could be identified with the "Name" or "Word/Logos" of God (Morray-Jones 1992, 2-5).

A variety of other aspects of this speculation are brought forth for comparison with NT texts, but space forbids even a summary of them here. Just one more will be mentioned: the figure of Metatron-Enoch. The etymology and meaning of the name *Metatron* is not yet clear, but there appear to be two main sides to his character (see Morray-Jones 1992, 7-14). He is the "Angel of the Lord" or "Prince of the Presence," a Name-bearing angel (Ex 23:21) who mediates and to some extent embodies the divine Glory. The Judaism represented by the Babylonian Talmud is suspicious of this figure, associating him in two of its three allusions to him with the heretical notion that another Power existed in heaven equal to God (the so-called Two Powers heresy; the three references are *b. 'Abod. Zar.* 3b; *b. Ḥag.* 15a [cf. *3 Enoch* 16]; *b. Sanh.* 38b), but this negative attitude is understood to confirm the existence of more positive interest in Metatron by other early strands of Judaism. Presumably the latter would be the esoteric strand of Merkabah mystics who would later give birth to the *Hekhalot* texts.

However, some texts relate how the famous *Enoch was transformed in the course of his ascent into an angelic figure and go on to identify Metatron with the transformed Enoch (e.g., *3 Enoch* 7—15). Once again, it is possible to find indications in earlier rabbinic and apocalyptic traditions that this idea of the transformation of an exceptionally righteous person into an angelic figure, possibly even identified with the enthroned Glory *(kābôd)*, has early roots (see Morray-Jones 1992, 10-11, where he also draws the parallel with the Jesus traditions in 2 Cor 4:3-6; Col 1:15; 2:9; Jn 17:6-12; Phil 2:9-11; Heb 1:2-4).

It was mentioned that rabbinic texts appear to indicate an unease with aspects of Merkabah mysticism. It would seem that possible causes of this unease would be the threat of new revelation and the perceived tendency to compromise monotheism. Yet the authors of the *Hekhalot* literature were concerned to stress their continuity with rabbinic Judaism by associating their teachings with names such as Rabbi Akiba, Rabbi Ishmael and Rabbi Johanan ben Zakkai (all late first to early second century A.D.; these connections are attested by *Talmud and *midrash as well), by striving to remain within the bounds of monotheism and by paying due respect to *Torah. It is probable that some within this movement did operate from within orthodox Judaism, and the official tendency seems to have been to control rather than ban these teachings. (On the relationship of Merkabah mysticism and Gnosticism, see Scholem 1965; P. Alexander, 236-38; Gruenwald 1982. On the forces giving shape to Merkabah mysticism, see Alexander, 238-39.)

2.2. Literary Evidence. Since we have no continuous literary evidence of Jewish mysticism from its earliest to its later forms there is great difficulty in speaking of historical continuity and a real question as to how much of the later material can be read back into the first century. An additional complication for the NT scholar stems from the growing tendency to use the NT itself as evidence for the first-century currency of Jewish ideas. The latter tendency is methodologically sound from the standpoint of writing a general history of thought, but it is difficult to avoid allowing this circular argument to become viciously circular. Until further evidence comes to light we are without sufficient external controls on the largely speculative reconstructions surrounding, for example, 2 Corinthians 12. At the same time it should be recalled that the Jewish esoteric traditions that found expression in the rabbinic literature were purposely not written down until well after the first century, and in this article we are dealing with Jewish esoteric traditions. The later date of the *Hekhalot* texts should not be overpressed against the case for the early origins of the ideas expressed therein.

For his part Scholem (1954, 43) speaks of three stages in the development of early Jewish Merkabah mysticism: "the anonymous conventicles of the old apocalyptics; the Merkabah speculation of the Mishnaic teachers who are known to us by name; and the Merkabah mysticism of late and post-Talmudic times, as reflected in the literature which has come down to us." Taken together, the three stages manifest an "essential continuity of thought." D. Halperin, however, argues that there is no evidence within the tannaitic literature itself for the practice of ascent or for its association with *Maaseh Merkabah.* In this period *Maaseh Merkabah* involved simply the public exegesis of Ezekiel 1. This does not mean that Scholem's model is wrong, but it would remove positive evidence for the middle stage. And I. Gruenwald issues the caveat that "literary similarity [between earlier and later texts] may point to historical affiliation, but need not of necessity do so" (1995, 32 n. 55). He adds, "generally speaking, scholarly work has still a long way to go before a clear cut case can be made concerning the evidential historical-continuity between trends spread out over hundreds of years, and more."

When speaking of Merkabah mysticism we might treat the strands of evidence as follows: OT, apocalyptic, Qumran, NT, rabbinic and *Hekhalot* texts.

2.2.1. Old Testament. OT texts that became a focus or springboard for the later mysticism are Ezekiel 1; 3:12-13; 10; Isaiah 6:1-4; Exodus 24:10-11; and Daniel 7:9-14. Others deserving mention are 1 Kings 22 and Job 1. Though some scholars have argued that these and other OT texts evidence the existence of mystical trends in OT times, Scholem himself stated that "it is almost certain that the phenomena which they connected with mysticism . . . belong to other strands in the history of religion" (Scholem 1974, 10). Yet Gruenwald, on the basis of a "relaxed definition" (Gruenwald 1995, 27) of mysticism, argues in favor of the idea "that there are mystical elements in [OT] Scripture itself." Of related interest is the recent work of S. Parpola on Assyrian prophecies, in which he seeks "to correlate the Assyrian data with related phenomena, especially OT prophecy, Gnosticism and Jewish mysticism" (Parpola 1997, XVI; cf. Parpola 1993).

2.2.2. Apocalyptic Literature. The earliest Jewish account of an ascent to heaven and vision of the divine throne outside of the *Hebrew Bible is *1 Enoch* 14:8-25 (*1 Enoch* 71:5-11 is thought to depend on this passage; see also *1 Enoch* 18:8), which draws on Ezekiel 1 and 10, Isaiah 6 and Daniel 7:9-10. Parpola (1993, 195) believes that the secret of the ascent to heaven "was the precious secret that Gilgamesh brought back from his journey to Utnapishtim." The only other pre-Christian description of an ascent in a Semitic language is Levi's in the Aramaic Levi apocryphon from Qumran (cf. *T. Levi* 2—3). At the least these passages evidence interest in the idea of an ascent to the throne of God, and possibly the currency of the mystical practice.

If we broaden our view to include early but not necessarily pre-Christian apocalyptic passages, a variety of features can be found that parallel the picture derived from the later sources (for the following, see esp. Alexander, 247-49). In *1 Enoch* 61:10-12 (Book of the Similitudes; end of the first century A.D.) we encounter a similar angelology. Likewise the transformation of Enoch in *1 Enoch* 70—71 into the Son of Man can be placed alongside the later mystical idea that "exceptionally worthy human beings or 'men of righteousness' were able to achieve a transformation into the likeness of the divine Glory" (Morray-Jones 1992, 20; on this idea of transformation and apotheosis, see also J. J. Collins; cf. *3 Enoch* 3—15). The Slavonic Apocalypse of Enoch (*2 Enoch;* no consensus on date, but probably stemming back to the late first century A.D. in part) contains a number of similarities to *3 Enoch,* which belongs among the *Hekhalot* texts. Enoch travels through seven heavens—a motif that is fundamental to the later Merkabah texts—to the throne of God, where he is transformed and instructed in matters of nature and creation *(Maaseh Bereshit).*

Likewise the *Testament of Levi* 2:6—5:3 in its portrayal of Levi's ascent to the "throne of glory" and in several details of that narrative runs parallel to the later Merkabah texts. *Ascension of Isaiah* 6—11 (probably a Christian composition dating to the second century), *Apocalypse of Abraham* 15—29 (the basic edition probably stemming back to the late first century A.D.), *Life of Adam and Eve* ([Latin] 25—29, [Greek] 31—40, original composition dated to end of first century A.D.), *3 Baruch* (original Jewish work dated to the first and second centuries A.D.), *Testament of Abraham* 10 (c. A.D. 100), and *Testament of Job* 48—50 (original dating to the first century B.C., but 46—53 may be a Montanist addition) all contain a significant amount of material similar to that in the later texts of Merkabah mysticism. There is enough here to justify the claim that ideas of ascent to heaven involving themes important to the later Merkabah speculation were current already in the late first century A.D.

within apocalypticism.

Some of the general differences between these apocalyptic texts and the later Merkabah speculation in the *Hekhalot* texts are enumerated by Alexander (235). He mentions a different ethos, namely, a concentration on the mysteries of heaven and a description of God's throne in the Merkabah texts contrasted with the *eschatological themes (last judgment, resurrection, messianic kingdom, world to come) that are so important in the earlier apocalyptic texts. The difference is one of emphasis, but the contrast is marked. Likewise cosmology is given more attention in apocalyptic than in classic Merkabah texts. Alexander notes also that the theurgic element with its focus on preparation and techniques for ascent is much more pronounced in the later Merkabah texts, though again it is not missing in apocalyptic. Additionally, "the familiar pattern of ascent through a numbered series of heavens, usually seven, is not attested in Judaism before the Christian era" (J. J. Collins, 46). The tradition of seven heavens itself is basic in the *Hekhalot* texts, but it cannot be confirmed earlier than the first century A.D. (Aune, 279, 317-19; cf. A. Y. Collins).

Notwithstanding such differences, C. R. A. Morray-Jones affirms the essential unity of the apocalyptic traditions and the *Hekhalot* writings. It is merely a matter of one mystical tradition giving rise to two *genres of literature: the apocalypse, which functions as a descriptive narrative, subordinating the description of the heavenly vision to the writer's didactic purpose, and the *Hekhalot* writings, which serve as technical guides for mystics (Morray-Jones 1992, 24; see 2.2.6 below).

2.2.3. Qumran. That most of our present book of *1 Enoch* (excluding 37—71, the Similitudes) predated the Qumran settlement and that the sect had an interest in this work in general is evidenced by the Aramaic fragments found at Qumran. Among these are fragments of the ascent passage of *1 Enoch* 14 as well as the allusion to the throne of God in *1 Enoch* 18:8 (Schiffman, 353-54). Likewise, among the Aramaic fragments of the *Testament of Levi* there is preserved at least one text giving an account of Levi's ascent (4Q213 [TLevi[a] ar] 1 ii 11-18; cf. A. Y. Collins, 62-66).

An interest in elements that would later feature in the *Hekhalot* texts is more specifically evidenced by several types of texts. The work called *Pseudo-Ezekiel* contains a treatment of Ezekiel's vision of the divine throne-chariot (4Q385 4), which is noteworthy as the oldest extant example of exegesis of Ezekiel 1, set apart from *1 Enoch* 14 and similar texts by its explicit and intentional reworking of the biblical text (Dimant and Strugnell). D. Dimant and J. Strugnell observe that there does not appear to be anything sectarian about this text, which permits the supposition that this kind of interest in Ezekiel 1 was not necessarily unique to the Qumran sect. Also sharing an interest in the "chariots of your glory" is 4Q286 (cf. also 4Q287).

Among the *Festival Prayers* fragments is a text that connects the renewal of the covenant with "the vision of your glory," though the meaning and significance of this brief allusion is not clear (4Q509 97-98 i 7-8; cf. Schiffman, 355, for one view, though his translation differs from some others). Additionally, several passages in the scrolls express an important belief that the community experienced communion with the angelic hosts (for this see Dunn 1996, 171-87; Newsom, 1-83, esp. 59-72; cf. esp. 1QSa 2:8-9; 4QFl or 1:2-5; CD 15:15-17; 4QCD[b]; 1QM 7:4-6; 1QH 3:21-23; 11:10-13, 25; 1QS 11:7-8; 1QSb 3:25-26; 4:24-26; *see* Book of Blessings; Damascus Document; Rule of the Congregation; Thanksgiving Hymns). Some of the last mentioned texts look to the last days, and some focus on the experience of the priests in particular, but there is a sense in which the holiness of the entire community, all of which is priestly in an extended sense, is defined by the presence of the angels in the present. "Life in the community becomes in some sense priestly service before God shared with the angels" (Newsom, 63).

None of these strands of evidence gives a clear indication of the practice of mystical ascent by individuals. In contrast, 4Q491 [4QM[a]] 11 i 8-24 evidently records the claims of a teacher within the community (probably not the Teacher of Righteousness) to have undergone deification through enthronement in heaven. The text gives no description of heaven or of an ascent, but it might be an adaptation of traditions found in Ezekiel the Tragedian's *Exagoge* 68—89 concerning the enthronement and deification of Moses (on which see J. J. Collins). The latter text is identified by Collins as the only "scene of heavenly enthronement in pre-Christian Judaism that is not, or is not necessarily, eschatological" (50).

The most important group of texts relating to the themes of the Merkabah are the *Songs of the Sabbath Sacrifice (see esp. Newsom). The *Songs of the Sabbath Sacrifice,* also called the *Angelic Liturgy,* is a partial reconstruction of a liturgical text using 4Q400-407, 11Q17 (11QShirShabb) and a fragment of the same work that was found at Masada (Masada ShirShabb). The major critical edition and study of this text is by C. A. Newsom, upon whose work (esp. Newsom, 1-83) the following comments are based. The text appears to have been written by and for the Qumran sect as a sequence of thirteen *sabbath day readings, specifically for the first quarter of the year. Of present interest are the numerous parallels between these songs and the later *Hekhalot* texts, not least in the strong reliance on Ezekiel's vision of the Merkabah in Ezekiel 1 and 10, as well as other parts of Ezekiel (esp. Ezek 40—48). Much of the text focuses on descriptions of the angelic praise of God toward the end of fostering a type of "communal mysticism." This is accomplished by means of a lengthy period of "preparation" (songs 1-8, though it must be remembered that the recitation of the respective songs is separated by intervals of a week) followed by what can be called a "temple tour" (Newsom, 19). The description of the Merkabah itself runs in part as follows (the following is taken from the penultimate song):

> The cherubim lie prostrate before him, and bless when they rise. The voice of a divine silence is heard, and there is the uproar of excitement when they raise their wings, the voice of a divine silence. They bless the image of the throne-chariot (which is) above the vault of the cherubim, and they sing [the splen]dour of the shining vault (which is) beneath the seat of his glory. And when the *ofanim* move forward, the holy angels go back; they emerge among the glorious wheels with the likeness of fire, the spirits of the holy of holies. Around them, the likeness of a stream of fire like electrum, and a luminous substance with glorious colours, wonderfully intermingled, brightly combined. The spirits of the living gods move constantly with the glory of the wonderful chariots. (4Q405 20-21-22:7-11; García Martínez, 429)

It is intriguing that in this same community apocalyptic works containing accounts of ascents to heaven (e.g., *1 Enoch* 14) are apparently being read, even if the songs differ from the latter in that the songs function as acts of worship (Newsom, esp. 59, 65). There are interests in these songs that will later be shared by the Merkabah mystics, and with the discovery of a fragment of this collection of texts at Masada we may justifiably imagine that precisely these texts or tendencies fed into the later speculation.

Yet there are distinctive features of the songs that are important to note. While these songs may indicate a kind of mysticism relating to the vision of the divine throne, it is not the individual mysticism characteristic of the *Hekalot* texts. It is impossible to say what individuals participating in the liturgical readings might have "experienced" as individuals, but the texts appear to be directed toward a communal experience of being in God's presence "with the perpetual host and the [everlasting] spirits . . . and with those who know in a community of jubilation" (1QH 11:13-14; García Martínez, 353). It is questionable whether the idea of ascent is relevant in such a setting, if that word is being used in the sense of the later mystical practices. In addition, it might be of significance that the vision of the chariot-throne does not form the goal of the composition. Rather, the sequence of songs culminates in song 13 with a brief description of the heavenly sacrificial service followed by a lengthy description of the vestments of the high-priestly angels who offer the *sacrifice. There does not appear to be an idea of coparticipation in the heavenly cult itself nor a common recitation of a liturgical formula with the angels. The purpose of these liturgical readings was rather the attempt to mount a "literary or rhetorical argument for the legitimation, idealization, or glorification" of the sect's priesthood, a literary function that is paralleled in Zechariah 3, *Jubilees* (esp. *Jub.* 31:13-14; 2:17-19, 21; 6:18; 15:26-27) and the *Apocryphon of Levi,* all of which were known to the Qumran community (Newsom, 67-72).

There are parallels between the *Songs of the Sabbath Sacrifice* and the later Merkabah texts (see Newsom, 237, 314, 329, and elsewhere). But there are also differences, and the extent to which the songs indicate interests (in this particular form) cherished outside of Qumran earlier than A.D. 70 is not yet clear.

2.2.4. New Testament. Several NT texts or ideas are currently being explained with reference to Merkabah mysticism (see 3 below). Two texts, however, stand out as the only firsthand autobiographical accounts of ascent to heaven in all the earliest Jewish and Christian literature, namely, 2 Corinthians 12:2-4 and Revelation 4. Another might be Akiba's account of his ascent, if the reconstruction of that tradition noted below (see 2.2.5) is correct.

2.2.4.1. 2 Corinthians 12. It is not clear why Paul would bring up "visions and revelations" and discuss the topic as he does unless he felt compelled to do so. The probable occasion for his doing so would be an appeal to such experiences by his opponents (2 Cor 11:5 et passim) as a part of their attempt to authenticate their ministerial claims, although what they claimed to derive from their visions is not evident from 2 Corinthians. Paul had appealed to his vision of Christ as a credential of apostleship (e.g., 1 Cor 9:1), and Luke records a vision in connection with Paul's original Corinthian ministry (Acts 18:9-10).

Paul mentions neither of these in 2 Corinthians 12 but instead cites an experience dating well before his work in Corinth and seemingly takes pains to downplay its significance for the issue of apostolic credentials. Positioned at the climax of his "fool's speech" (2 Cor 11:1—12:13) the whole account of his ascent rapidly bypasses any hint of positive benefit in order to focus on the lesson learned through the "thorn" in his flesh: "My grace is sufficient for you, for my power is made perfect in weakness" (2 Cor 12:9 NIV). On the latter lesson the argument of the epistle (assumed in this article to be unified) pivots, and by that argument the appeal to "visions and revelations" is neutralized. Without denying the reality of such experiences in general or diminishing their God-givenness, Paul rejects any suggestion that they authenticate new covenant ministry.

That being the thrust of Paul's argument in 2 Corinthians 12 it is difficult to accept that he is pointing the attention of the Corinthians to an experience, Merkabah or otherwise, that was foundational and formative for his apostleship (as argued esp. by Morray-Jones 1993, who associates 2 Cor 12 with Acts 22:17-18). Nothing here suggests that as of the writing of 2 Corinthians Paul would routinely pursue or promote such experiences, and much suggests that he would now transfer what was thought to be of value in them to another type of experience: turning to the Spirit (2 Cor 3:7-18).

Not only does he not report anything seen or heard during his journey, but Paul also stresses that nothing reportable resulted. Without denigrating the speech heard in paradise (2 Cor 12:4) he probably means to suggest that the experience was of little or no pastoral benefit (cf. 1 Cor 14:18-19). It has been suggested that the thorn (2 Cor 12:7) may correspond to the perils tradition assigned to Merkabah ascents through the seven (versus Paul's three) heavens and *Hekhalot,* but it is not clear that the thorn resulted from the particular ascent narrated (note the plural used in 2 Cor 12:7: "revelations") or that it was inflicted in the course of any ascent. What we know is that the thorn was associated by Paul with his visions and revelations and it functioned as a watershed in his Christian missiology: the prayers of 2 Corinthians 12:8 and the declarations of 2 Corinthians 12:10 represent the two sides of that watershed. As for the connection with Acts 22:17-18, this depends on treating 2 Corinthians 10—13 as a separate letter dating to just before the Jerusalem council of Acts 15 and a generally negative evaluation of Acts' historical reliability touching the chronology of Paul's ministry.

It is apparent that Paul had had mystical experiences (2 Cor 12:1-10 among them; cf. Acts 9:3-9, 12; 16:9-10; 18:9-10; 22:17-21; 23:11; 26:19; 27:23-24; Gal 1:12; 2:1; as did other Christians, e.g., Ananias [Acts 9:10-16], Peter [Acts 10:9-16] and the Seer of Revelation) and he valued them as "surpassingly great," but of greater benefit to the churches and of greater relevance to the subject of authentic new covenant apostleship was the revelation of the thorn. The attempt to correlate details of Paul's account in 2 Corinthians 12 with the Merkabah traditions are strained but possible. It could be that Paul had earlier practiced a kind of mysticism such as we encounter in these traditions—this might explain the various parallels between his writings in general and the Merkabah texts—but that the experience of the thorn had effected the shift in evaluation that he now encourages the Corinthians to accept.

2.2.4.2. Revelation. According to the analysis of D. E. Aune, most of the book of Revelation consists of a "single extended vision narrative" (Rev 1:9—22:9), within which Revelation 4:1-2a introduces a new phase, "The Disclosure of God's Eschatological Plan" (Rev 4:1—22:9). The heavenly journey of Revelation 4:1-2a serves as an introduction to both the seal narrative of Revelation 4:2b—6:17 and Revelation 4:2b—22:9. Formally, Revelation 4:1—6:17 is labeled a "literary throne scene, i.e., the primarily literary use of the throne vision is as a vehicle for commenting on earthly events in the narrative" (Aune, 278). The accounts of the divine throne room (Rev 4:1—5:14; 8:2-5; 15:1-8) establish the sovereignty of God over the events unfolding on earth. Within Revelation 4—6 we are given a depiction of the heavenly worship of God (Rev 4:2b-11) and the investiture of the Lamb (Rev 5:1-14).

In Revelation 4:1-2a God opens the door of heaven (cf. *1 Enoch* 14:14b-15, 18-25) and a voice identified as the angelic voice of Revelation 1:10-11 summons the Seer to heaven so that he might be shown "what must happen after these things" (cf. Dan 2:29). Immediately the Seer falls into a "prophetic trance" (Aune, 82-83, 283-84; cf. Rev 1:10; 17:3; 21:10; and also Acts 10:10; 11:5; 22:17), designating an experience that took place "in the spirit" rather than "in the body." Ritual preparations that might have attended this experience go unmentioned, if there were any. The journey itself, which involves one rather than seven heavens, passes undescribed; the Seer is immediately in the throne room. The vision that follows verbally recalls the OT passages of Ezekiel 1; 10; Isaiah 6; Daniel 7 and 1 Kings 22:19 and parallels features found in some of the other literature surveyed in this article (e.g., cf. Rev 4:3b with Ezek 1:27-28 and 4Q405 20-21-22:10-11; on the same verse see *1 Enoch* 71:6-8; *3 Enoch* 33:1—34:2; see further Aune, 279-374). In contrast to Ezekiel this account does not attempt to describe God.

Thus this passage contains both similarities and dissimilarities to the various sources of information about Merkabah mysticism, and it contains unique elements as well (Aune, 278-79). More study is needed before we can say that this account is either borrowing from or contrasting itself with a movement or set of traditions continuous with what we encounter in the later *Hekhalot* texts, nor can we say whether this text records a unique experience within the Christian circles associated with this book. Some scholars deny that this text is the voice of experience; it is rather a literary construct borrowing from a variety of traditions, including the Merkabah traditions.

2.2.5. Rabbinic Literature. A variety of rabbinic texts are brought into consideration by those investigating the roots of Jewish mysticism (see, e.g., Scholem 1965 and 1974, 373-74, and the articles by Morray-Jones). A significant passage is *b. Ḥag.* 11b-16a (cf. *y. Ḥag.* 2; *b. Šabb.* 80b), which supplies a lengthy discussion of the seven heavens (*Maaseh Bereshit*), discusses *Maaseh Merkabah* and passes on stories of famous individuals associated with these teachings. Yet in these and other texts there are hints at the existence of esoteric traditions in the background. Of central interest is a story of four who ascended to paradise in heaven, which the Tosefta and both Talmuds attach to a restriction articulated in the Mishnah at *m. Ḥag.* 2:1 (for related restrictions, see *b. Šabb.* 80b; *y. Ḥag.* 77a.46; *b. Ḥag.* 13a).

M. Ḥag. 2:1 reads: "They do not expound upon the laws of prohibited relationships [Lev 18] before three persons, the works of creation [Gen 1] before two, or the chariot [Ezek 1] before one, unless he was a sage and understands of his own knowledge. Whoever reflects upon four things would have been better off had he not been born: what is above, what is below, what is before, and what is beyond. And whoever has no concern for the glory of his Maker— would have been better off had he not been born" (Neusner, 330).

It is argued that this Mishnah assumes the currency of *Maaseh Bereshit* (works of creation) and *Maaseh Merkabah* (the chariot), and while it issues stern warnings in connection with the public exposition of these portions of Scripture it includes such exposition within the fold of rabbinic orthodoxy. In the judgment of Morray-Jones the first sentence of the above translation "originally meant that no individual (or ascetic) was competent to expound (that is, teach about, or express an opinion concerning) Ezekiel's vision unless he was a mantic sage [such as Daniel] who could do so on the basis of his own visionary-mystical experience and esoteric knowledge" (Morray-Jones 1993, 188). This part of the paragraph derived from the pre-first century A.D. apocalyptic tradition and was modified when taken up into rabbinism. The last two sentences are additions that represent a later strand of opinion "that was hostile toward the esoteric and mystical traditions, especially as it was developed in circles outside rabbinic control" (Morray-Jones 1993, 190), including Christians and Gnostics.

The Tosefta and both Talmuds attach to *m. Ḥag.* 2:1 the above-mentioned story of four who went into paradise during life, only one of whom made the round-trip journey "in peace" (*t. Ḥag.* 2:1-4; *y. Ḥag.* 77b; *b. Ḥag.* 14b-15b). This story is also contained in *Song of Songs Rabbah (Cant. Rab.* 1:28 [= 1:4:1]) and in two *Hekhalot* texts (*Hekhalot Zutarti* and *Merkabah Rabbah*). A translation of these texts is supplied by Morray-Jones (1993, 196-98, 210-15). It is possible to interpret this story as originally nonmystical, understanding it, for example, as an allegory of four types of rabbinic scholarship (for some of these alternatives with their principal representatives, see Morray-Jones 1993, 192-93; Halperin's view would fit here). Several scholars, however, take the view that this story is an ancient (early third century A.D. or earlier) witness to the practice of mystical ascents to paradise and that the story's association of this type of practice with Akiba (late first and early second century A.D.) is not unlikely.

The sources mentioned in the preceding paragraph represent different versions of the story, and a reconstruction of an earliest version appears to be less than straightforward. One possibility (argued by Morray-Jones 1993) is that the *Hekhalot* texts, though later, contain an earlier version of the story. This was a first-person account of Akiba's ascent in the face of angelic opposition to the heavenly holy of holies to behold the glory of God on the Merkabah. This version left the other three men unnamed and attributed Akiba's success (versus their failure) to the merit of his deeds. This story was later adapted as an illustration of the Mishnah's restriction (*m Ḥag.* 2:1), which by that time had come to be interpreted as saying that only an ordained rabbi could become involved in *Maaseh Merkabah.* Therefore the previously unnamed three were assigned identities of famous but unordained teachers. According to Morray-Jones, this tradition, going back to its earliest form, is continuous with apocalyptic and mystical traditions predating the first century (assuming continuity with texts such as *1 Enoch* 14).

Key issues here are the related problems of the interpretation of individual texts and the reconstruction of the history of the hypothetical traditions. The same must be said for the further attempt to trace through the rabbinic literature the experience of transformation into angels that certain practitioners of ascents were said to undergo (see esp. Morray-Jones 1992). The transformation of Enoch has already been noted (*1 Enoch* 70—71), and another early text important to the case for the pre-Christian origins of the transformation motif is Ezekiel the Tragedian's *Exagoge* (second century B.C.; cf. Segal, 102; J. J. Collins, 50-53). Possibly 4Q491 (4QM^{a}) 11, noted above, confirms its early origins as well. According to A. Segal, "there is adequate evidence . . . that many Jewish mystics and apocalypticists sensed a relationship between the heavenly figure on the throne and important figures in the life of their community. The roots of this tradition are pre-Christian" (Segal, 107-8, for whom the NT itself evidences the antiquity of this tradition).

Likewise, Morray-Jones (1992, 26) summarizes a review of several relevant texts by noting that the story of Enoch's transformation "may represent the ultimate aspiration of the Merkabah mystic." The evidence suggests "that a variety of mythical and historical figures were credited with having achieved such a transformation on what might be called a 'cosmic' scale and with having become veritable incarnations of the Name or Power of God. An analogous, though lesser, transformation was promised to the righteous in the world to come. But it seems that such a transformation was also considered possible, if only temporarily, for exceptionally holy individuals in this life. Such men were gifted with supernatural power and knowledge, and became intercessors between the divine and human worlds, because they had been conformed to the divine Image or *kābôd* and, like the High Priest in the Temple sanctuary, had been vested with the Name of God." Note that the experience of mystical transformation is a foretaste of the final transformation of the righteous and the benefits to the mystic.

Assuming an essential continuity between apocalyptic texts such as *1 Enoch* 14 and the later *Hekhalot* writings, Morray-Jones (1992, 1) argues that the mystical aspirations mentioned "were inherited from apocalyptic circles and enthusiastically developed by some Tannaim, but were opposed by others, mainly because the same traditions were being developed by groups whom they regarded as heretical, including the various forms of Christianity and Gnosticism. The Hekhalot writings represent the development of these traditions within rabbinism." Thus the negative tone of certain rabbinic texts with respect to mystical beliefs and practices, some of which are related to the Two-Power heresy (e.g., *b. Sukk.* 45b; *b. Sanh.* 63a; *Ex. Rab.* 43:3; *b. Ḥag.*

15a; *m. Meg.* 4:10; *b. H[ag.* 13a; cf. *3 Enoch* 16) represents only one viewpoint from within rabbinism while those very texts attest the currency of these traditions.

In sum, it is possible to make a case from the rabbinic literature for the existence of mystical-visionary beliefs and practices within first-century Judaism, beliefs that are essentially continuous with those later expressed in the *Hekhalot* texts. Confirmation of this hypothesis would open the way for a fresh reading of several NT texts, as some scholars have already proposed. To return to 2 Corinthians, Paul's description of the process of glorification associated with seeing God in 2 Corinthians 3:7-18 coupled with the evident claim to authority made by his opponents based on their "visions and revelations" (2 Cor 12:1-6)—to mention just two important features—might seem to some to be most at home in this matrix of reconstructed mysticism. The way is then opened to read a number of other details scattered about the NT along the same lines.

2.2.6. The Hekhalot *Literature.* On the whole, these writings have been described as technical guides or manuals for mystics that give little space to narrative descriptions of ascent or the transformation of the mystic (see 2.2.2 above). The exception to this rule is *3 Enoch,* which is a fairly late product of the same mystical-visionary movement but which is itself an apocalypse.

Viewing the texts of Jewish mysticism collectively (not restricted to the *Hekhalot* texts), one is confronted with "a religious phenomenon that is contained in hundreds of books and in thousands of manuscripts, many of which are still unpublished" (Gruenwald 1995, 6), and fewer of which have been translated (for a list of published texts and translations relating to Merkabah mysticism, see Morray-Jones 1993). Scholem characterizes the *Hekhalot* sources as follows: "All our material is in the form of brief tracts, or scattered fragments of varying lengths from what may have been voluminous works; in addition there is a good deal of almost shapeless literary raw material" (Scholem 1954, 44-45). He enumerates eight of the most important *Hekhalot* texts (Scholem 1965, 5-7), giving special mention to the *Lesser Hekhalot,* the *Greater Hekhalot* and *3 Enoch.* The dating of the material is difficult, but the "outstanding documents of the movement appear to have been edited in the fifth and sixth centuries" (Scholem 1954, 44). The relative inaccessibility of this literature, the lack of a consensus among specialists regarding the origins and dates of the traditions and literary strata and dispute over whether there is one text behind the various extant manuscripts has hindered work with this material by NT scholars. Further, "as a matter of general rule and practice, mysticism is a highly and densely encoded domain. No justice can be done to it by simply translating mystical texts . . . from one language into another, particularly when those translations are made by people who know more about the language than about the 'inner grammar' that is used in mystical formations" (Gruenwald 1995, 29).

A fuller account of the profile of the mysticism encountered in this literature has already been given. And as has already been stated, the key question for those interested in NT background concerns the measure of continuity one can assume between the mysticism encountered in these *Hekhalot* materials and any mysticism that some scholars detect in the other and largely earlier strands of literature surveyed here. Components of the *Hekhalot* traditions had very early origins, but the question of the continuity of a movement, not unlike questions relating to the history of Gnosticism, has not yet received a firm answer.

3. Mysticism and the New Testament.

Second Corinthians 12 (along with 2 Cor 3:7-18; 4:4-6) and Revelation 4 have already been noted as NT texts that have received attention in connection with Merkabah mysticism. In addition to these a number of other NT texts and ideas have been brought into this discussion in the literature, on which see the works mentioned in the bibliography and standard commentaries. In particular, the exaltation of Jesus in a variety of NT texts is paralleled with the transformation of Enoch and his identification with the divine Glory. In addition to 2 Corinthians 12, Paul's experience on the Damascus road has been viewed in this light, as well as his language of baptismal transformation (e.g., Col 3:9-10; cf. Rom 8:29; 2 Cor 3:18), his descriptions of the body of Christ (e.g., Eph 4:12-13, which is paralleled with the *Shiur Komah* doctrine and related ideas), his christology (e.g., Phil 2:9-11, noting especially the bestowal of the divine name, the tetragrammaton, YHWH) and the implied idea of a celestial family of angels in Ephesians 3:14-15 (cf. *3 Enoch* 12:5; 18:21).

Some scholars have sought to explain the mixture of ideas being confronted in Colossians (esp. Col 2:16-19) against the background of Merkabah mysticism. If connections like these can be established, others will almost certainly follow, for example, the "snatching up" of the saints in 1 Thessalonians 4:17 (cf. the use of the same verb in 2 Cor 12:2 and the idea that mystical ascents were a foretaste of the transformation of the righteous). A recent treatment of Paul's so-called Christ mysticism, by contrast, appears to owe little to the background of Merkabah mysticism (Dunn 1998, 390-412; *see DPL*, Mysticism). The book of Hebrews has been placed in this context, with emphasis on among other things the importance of its interest in angels, the importance of the throne and the allusions to the heavenly curtain, which is also important in the *Hekhalot* texts. Elements of John's Gospel have also been related to Merkabah mysticism, for example, features of John 6 and 14:1 (cf. with the latter *3 Enoch* 1:1 with its idea of God's heavenly dwellings with their chambers; on the question of John's Gospel, see Kanagaraj). Among other issues in all of this would be the issues of magic and theurgy, which imbued Merka-bah mysticism, within apostolic Christianity.

While considerable work remains to be done in the area of Jewish mysticism as background for the NT, enough has been done to show that it could have been current in the apostolic period in some form and that it holds potential for an improved understanding of some NT texts.

See also HEAVENLY ASCENT IN JEWISH AND PAGAN TRADITIONS; MYSTERIES; SONGS OF THE SABBATH SACRIFICE (4Q400-407).

BIBLIOGRAPHY. P. Alexander, "3 (Hebrew Apocalypse of) Enoch," *OTP* 1:223-315; D. E. Aune, *Revelation 1—5* (WBC 52; Dallas: Word, 1997); D. Blumenthal, *Understanding Jewish Mysticism, a Source Reader: The Merkabah Tradition and the Zoharic Tradition* (New York: Ktav, 1978); A. Y. Collins, "The Seven Heavens in Jewish and Christian Apocalypses," in *Death, Ecstasy and Other-Worldly Journeys,* ed. J. J. Collins and M. Fishbane (Albany: State University of New York Press, 1995) 59-93; J. J. Collins, "A Throne in the Heavens: Apotheosis in Pre-Christian Judaism," in *Death, Ecstasy and Other-Worldly Journeys,* ed. J. J. Collins and M. Fishbane (Albany: State University of New York Press, 1995) 43-58; D. Dim-ant and J. Strugnell, "The Merkabah Vision in *Second Ezekiel* (4Q385 4)," *RevQ* 14 (1990) 331-48; J. D. G. Dunn, *The Epistles to the Colossians and to Philemon* (NIGTC; Grand Rapids, MI: Eerdmans, 1996); idem, *The Theology of Paul the Apostle* (Grand Rapids, MI: Eerdmans, 1998); F. García Martínez, *The Dead Sea Scrolls Translated* (2d ed.; Grand Rapids, MI: Eerdmans, 1996); I. Gruenwald, *Apocalyptic and Merkavah Mysticism* (Leiden: E. J. Brill, 1980); idem, "Jewish Merkavah Mysticism and Gnosticism," in *Studies in Jewish Mysticism,* ed. J. Dan and F. Talmage (Association for Jewish Studies; Cambridge, MA; Harvard University Press, 1982) 41-55; idem, "Major Issues in the Study and Understanding of Jewish Mysticism," in *Historical Syntheses,* part 2 of *Judaism in Late Antiquity,* ed. J. Neusner (HOS; The Near and Middle East 17; Leiden: E. J. Brill, 1995) 1-49; D. Halperin, *The Merkabah in Rabbinic Literature* (AOS 62; New Haven, CT: American Oriental Society, 1980); J. J. Kanagaraj, *"Mysticism" in the Gospel of John: An Inquiry into its Background* (JSNTSup 158; Sheffield: Sheffield Academic Press, 1998); B. McGinn, *The Foundations of Mysticism: Origins to the Fifth Century* (TPG 1; New York: Crossroad, 1991); C. R. A. Morray-Jones, "Paradise Revisited (2 Cor 12:1-12): The Jewish Mystical Background of Paul's Apostolate," *HTR* 86 (1993) 177-217, 265-92; idem, "Transformational Mysticism in the Apocalyptic-Merkabah Tradition," *JJS* 43 (1992) 1-31; J. Neusner, *The Mishnah: A New Translation* (New Haven, CT: Yale University Press, 1988); C. Newsom, *Songs of the Sabbath Sacrifice: A Critical Edition* (HSS 27; Atlanta: Scholars Press, 1985); S. Parpola, *Assyrian Prophecies* (State Archives of Assyria 9; Helsinki: Helsinki University Press, 1997); idem, "The Assyrian Tree of Life: Tracing the Origins of Jewish Monotheism and Greek Philosophy," *JNES* 52 (1993) 161-208; L. H. Schiffman, *Reclaiming the Dead Sea Scrolls* (ABRL; New York: Doubleday, 1994, 1995); G. Scholem, *Jewish Gnosticism, Merkabah Mysticism and Talmudic Tradition* (2d ed.; New York: Jewish Theological Seminary of America, 1965); idem, *Kabbalah* (Jerusalem: Keter, 1974); idem, *Major Trends in Jewish Mysticism* (3d ed.; New York: Schocken, 1954); A. Segal, "Paul and the Beginning of Jewish Mysticism," in *Death, Ecstasy and Other-Worldly Journeys,* ed. J. J. Collins and M. Fishbane (Albany, NY: State University of New York Press, 1995) 95-122; D. Winston, "Was Philo a Mystic?" in *Studies in Jewish Mysticism,* ed. J. Dan and F. Talmage (Association for Jewish Studies; Cambridge, MA: Harvard University Press, 1982) 15-39.

J. Laansma

N

NABONIDUS. See Prayer of Nabonidus (4Q242) and Pseudo-Daniel (4Q243-245).

NARRATIVE A (4Q458)

4Q458 consists of some seventeen fragments. Only fragments 1 and 2 preserve significant amounts of text, with fragment 2 preserving portions of two columns. The official designation of 4Q458 is "Narrative A." However, R. H. Eisenman and M. O. Wise (46) refer to it as the "Tree of Evil" (from frag. 1, line 9) and classify it not as narrative but as apocalypse. Fragments 1 and 2, which is all that Eisenman and Wise cite and translate, have an *apocalyptic orientation, but the other fragments seem to be part of a narrative, with reference to the patriarchs. It may be that the document originally contained both narrative and apocalyptic elements.

Lines 8 and 9 of fragment 1 do create an apocalyptic impression: "And the fir[st] angel will throw down [or: will send] . . . laid waste, and he will cut down the tree of evil. . . ." Some of the words and phrases in fragment 2, column 1, seem to contribute to this (possibly) apocalyptic scenario: "terrify them" (line 1), "[the moo]n and the stars" (line 2) and "the immorality" (line 6). Column 2 of the second fragment seems to envision a final, possibly messianic battle: "and he will destroy him, and his army . . . and it will swallow up all the uncircumcised ones, and it will . . . and they will be justified. And he walked upon the mountains . . . anointed with the oil of the kingdom of the . . ." (lines 3-6). It is difficult to determine the context, even the appropriate tense of the verbs (should they be treated as future or as past?). The person referred to as "anointed with the oil of the kingdom" may be a historical personage, perhaps even David himself. We may have an allusion to Psalm 89:21(ET 89:20): "I have found David my servant, with my holy oil I have anointed him." 11QPs[a] 28:11 should also be noted: "he will anoint me with holy oil." Moreover, Psalm 89:28 (ET 89:27) goes on to refer to David as God's "firstborn," an epithet that occurs also in 4Q458 frag. 15. If these fragments have an apocalyptic orientation, then a *messianic figure may be in view.

It is possible that the first two fragments depict a scene related in some way to the garden of Eden, in which Adam and Eve ate from the tree of the knowledge of good and evil and were then driven out by an angel. In the end time this "tree of evil" will be cut down and Israel's enemies overthrown. A review of Israel's history then follows this futuristic scenario. (Because the order of the fragments is uncertain, the sequence may actually be the reverse.)

There is little else that can be gleaned from these fragments. Fragment 15 (line 1) probably reads "my first-born" (cf. 4Q369 frag. 1 ii 6), which could refer either to Israel (as in Ex 4:22; Jer 31:9) or to Israel's Davidic king (as in Ps 89:27). "Prophetess" or "prophecy" appears in the next line. "Judah" and "Reuben abhorred[?]" appear in fragment 14, lines 3 and 4, and possibly "Joseph" in line 5. We may have here an allusion to Genesis 49. A few other words scattered among the fragments can be picked out (e.g., "heaven" in frag. 3, line 1; "breathe on them" in frag. 4, line 2; "twelfth day" in frag. 4, line 3; "from the east and from the north" in frag. 9, line 2 [cf. Dan 11:44]; "Israel" in frag. 10, line 2; "from his evil" in frag. 11, line 3; "Meshech[?]" in frag. 17, line 2), but with no sense of context or flow of thought.

See also MESSIANISM.

BIBLIOGRAPHY. R. H. Eisenman and M. O. Wise, *The Dead Sea Scrolls Uncovered: The First Complete Translation and Interpretation of 50 Key Documents Withheld for Over 35 Years* (Shaftesbury and Rockport: Element, 1992) 46-49; F. García Martínez and E. J. C. Tigchelaar, *The Dead Sea*

Scrolls Study Edition, 2: *4Q274-11Q31* (Leiden: E. J. Brill, 1998) 934-37; B. Z. Wacholder and M. G. Abegg Jr., *A Preliminary Edition of the Unpublished Dead Sea Scrolls: The Hebrew and Aramaic Texts from Cave Four* (4 fascicles; Washington, DC: Biblical Archaeology Society, 1991-96) 2:287-91. C. A. Evans

NARRATIVE AND PSALMIC WORK (4Q371-372, 539). *See* APOCRYPHON OF JOSEPH (4Q371-372, 539)

NAVY, ROMAN. *See* ROMAN MILITARY.

NAḤAL ḤEVER TEXTS. *See* INSCRIPTIONS AND PAPYRI: JEWISH; PAPYRI, PALESTINIAN.

NEO-PYTHAGOREANISM

Neo-Pythagoreanism refers to the revival of the philosophy of Pythagoras, which began in the first century B.C. and continued until it merged with Neo-Platonism in the third century A.D. This revival did not, however, constitute an organized movement; the representatives of Neo-Pythagoreanism appear as individuals who show no awareness of one another. Neither was there a systematic or distinctive body of doctrines; Neo-Pythagoreanism derived much from *Platonic and *Stoic thought as well as from Pythagoras.

1. Pythagorean Antecedents
2. Leading Figures and Ideas
3. Comparisons and Contrasts
4. Apollonius of Tyana
5. Literary Analogies

1. Pythagorean Antecedents.

Pythagoras, a devotee of Apollo, founded a religious society in Croton (southern Italy) in the latter half of the sixth century B.C. If he produced any writings, none has survived, but admiring *poets, *philosophers and *historians testify to his belief in metempsychosis, or the transmigration of the soul. He believed the soul to be a fallen divinity imprisoned in the body as a tomb and condemned to a cycle of reincarnation. Only by devotion to Apollo could one hope to escape. A second major emphasis of Pythagoras was the interpretation of the world as a whole through numbers, a mathematicization of reality. This resulted from his discovery of the numerical ratios of the intervals in the musical scale. The society he established practiced a distinctive ascetic and reflective way of life, but political opposition led to its dissolution in the latter half of the fifth century B.C.

2. Leading Figures and Ideas.

Neo-Pythagoreans were often more concerned with religious rather than philosophical speculation. They glorified Pythagoras as the bringer of a revelation and the founder of their way of life. Several figures have been identified as Neo-Pythagoreans, beginning with Nigidius Figulus in the mid-first century B.C. He seems to be the only significant Neo-Pythagorean to predate the Christian era. He was an abstruse scholar, a *mystic and a dabbler in astrology. His writings in *grammar, theology and natural science survive only in fragments. Nicomachus, an arithmetician of the late first/early second century A.D., wrote several works on the Pythagorean theory of numbers, portions of which have survived. Numenius of Apamea (in Syria) was active in the mid-second century. Significant fragments of his work survive. His treatise *On the Good* is a dialogue on the "First Principle" or "the Good." Numenius taught a doctrine of three gods. In addition to the Supreme God there is a Demiurge who is divided between the second and third divinities, creator and creation respectively. The Supreme God is the Father of the creator god. Numenius viewed matter not as neutral but as a positive evil; the descent of the immaterial soul into a material body was a great misfortune.

3. Comparisons and Contrasts.

Neo-Pythagorean life and thought have some similarities to and important differences from early Christianity. Obviously the close-knit community of followers with common commitments and practices has a parallel in Jesus' disciples and the nascent church. The asceticism of the Pythagoreans calls to mind John the Baptist (Mk 1:6), but the latter did not share the Pythagorean rejection of clothing from animal products. Jesus lived the relatively austere life of an itinerant preacher (Mt 8:18-20) but was by no means an ascetic (Mt 11:18-19). The concepts of metempsychosis and reincarnation are foreign to the NT. Neither does the Pythagorean preoccupation with numbers have a parallel in the NT. A clear instance of Pythagorean influence in this respect is found not in the NT but in *Philo (Philo *Op. Mund.* 99-100).

Neo-Pythagoreanism's negative view of the body may have been an influence on *Gnosticism, which was developing simultaneously. The view of the NT stands in contrast to this (Jn 1:14; 1 Cor 6:12-20; Col 2:9); the body is fallen but not intrinsically evil.

The Neo-Pythagorean triad of divinities, apparently an original contribution of Numenius, catches the eye of the Christian interpreter. This reflects the tendency to posit intermediary daimons between the transcendent, supreme God and the world of human beings. The personification of Wisdom and the Johannine Logos function similarly. But beyond this there is no significant correspondence between Numenius's trinity and the concept emerging in Christian thought. Although Numenius does employ relational language similar to the Father/Son terminology of the NT (forefather, offspring, descendant), other comments show that only the second and third members form a unity. The First God is self-existent, indivisible and uninvolved in creation, which is the work of the second deity. Numenius's trinity is necessitated by his negative view of matter: the First God, being truly "the Good," can have no involvement with an evil material world.

The affinities between Neo-Pythagoreanism and the NT are of interest but hardly remarkable. The primary importance of Neo-Pythagoreanism for the study of the NT pertains to the most famous Neo-Pythagorean figure and to certain literary considerations.

4. Apollonius of Tyana.

Apollonius of Tyana, a wandering sage and wonder worker of the first century A.D., combined Pythagorean ideas with the lifestyle of a charismatic prophet. The chief source of information about Apollonius is the idealized and somewhat legendary biography by Philostratus, the *Life of Apollonius*. Philostratus wrote during the reign of Septimius Severus (A.D. 193-211) at the instigation of the emperor's wife, Julia Domna. He was especially concerned to refute the charge that Apollonius was a practitioner of *magic and instead to attribute his miracles to supernatural power (cf. Mk 3:22). The work is apologetic but also laudatory and didactic.

4.1. Comparisons to Christ. The importance of the figure of Apollonius of Tyana for NT studies is twofold: individual passages that are reminiscent of Gospel stories and the *theios anēr* ("divine man") concept, of which Apollonius is the principal first-century representative.

A number of stories in the *Life of Apollonius* may be paralleled with Gospel accounts. Miraculous portents, including divine apparitions and dreams, surrounded the birth of Apollonius (Philostratus *Vit. Ap.* 1.4-5). Similarities with the birth narratives of Matthew and Luke are apparent (Mt 1:20; 2:13, 19; Lk 1:26-38). A number of miracles and healings are attributed to Apollonius (Philostratus *Vit. Ap.* 3.39). The most detailed and, for our purposes, most significant account is the passage that relates the raising of a dead girl in Rome (Philostratus *Vit. Ap.* 4.45). A girl who had apparently died in the hour of her marriage was being carried away for *burial. Apollonius halted the procession, touched the girl, spoke something over her secretly, then awakened her from her seeming death. A close parallel in the NT is found in Luke 7:11-17. A widow's only son has died; he is being carried forth; a large crowd of mourners accompanies them. Jesus calls for the weeping to cease, touches the bier and addresses the young man out loud. In both cases the resuscitated person immediately speaks and is returned to his or her household.

A significant difference between the two narratives is the view of the narrator toward the narrated event. Luke tells his story with an ingenuousness or naiveté that presumes the miraculous nature of the event. Philostratus, while clearly wanting to relate a spectacular occurrence, deliberately leaves the nature of the event ambiguous. This is achieved in the narration itself and even more so in the concluding reflection that neither he nor those present could determine precisely what had occurred.

Finally, the end of Apollonius's life offers a fascinating parallel to the resurrection of Jesus. At the close of his work, Philostratus reaches a point at which his alleged source, the memoirs of Damis the Assyrian, comes to an end. But since that source related nothing about the death of the sage, Philostratus felt compelled to append some stories about Apollonius's denouement that were popular in the author's day. These, he admits, are contradictory; neither the age of Apollonius nor the site of his death is reliably known. After relating competing versions of the philosopher's death or translation, Philostratus concludes with a postmortem appearance story.

After the death of Apollonius, a young man engaged the sage's followers in heated discussions about the immortality of the soul, openly and emphatically rejecting the idea. After one such debate he fell asleep. Some time later he awoke suddenly and with much disorientation and distress claimed to see the departed Apollonius present among them, orating on the immortality of the soul. The others present, though desirous, did not share in the vision. The once-skeptical youth transmits a few lines of the sage's utterance, affirming the immortality of the soul and, in true Pythagorean tradition, describing death as liberation from the body.

This passage bears clear similarities to the NT story of doubting Thomas (Jn 20:24-29): an openly skeptical follower becomes convinced of his teacher's immortality by means of a postmortem revelation. But in certain respects the stories differ. Whereas the young doubter's vision and audition of Apollonius are described as a private experience in which no one else present shares, the appearance of Jesus to Thomas is presumably perceived by others as well. Secondly, the skeptical follower of Apollonius is said to have awakened suddenly from sleep, perspiring and raving. Jesus appears to Thomas when the latter is presumably in a normal, wakeful state. Finally, the appearance to Thomas refers to tactile verification of Jesus' reality (cf. Lk 24:39-43). This starkly somatic conception of resurrection contrasts with the Neo-Pythagorean understanding of the immortal soul enduring a "spell of harsh and painful servitude" in the body (Philostratus *Vit. Ap.* 8.31).

4.2. Divine Men. A second way in which Apollonius of Tyana impinges upon NT study relates to the concept of the *theios anēr.* This title refers to a worker of miracles and/or a person with divine wisdom. It occurs twice with reference to Apollonius. In the *Epistles* of Apollonius (of doubtful authenticity) the sage supposedly writes of himself, "Even the gods have spoken of me as of a divine man, not only on many occasions to private individuals, but also in public" (*Ep.* 48). Similarly, Philostratus speaks of how Apollonius came to be considered "a supernatural and divine being" (Philostratus *Vit. Ap.* 1.20). When followers of Apollonius raise the issue of his divinity, he repudiates the idea (Philostratus *Vit. Ap.* 8.7).

The term "divine man" does not occur in the NT, but some scholars have seen its substance in Jesus' remarkable spiritual insight and ministry of healing. These scholars hypothesize that in the *Hellenistic world the divine man was a widespread and popular concept with a recognizable set of traits such as close affiliation with the divine, ability to work miracles and superior wisdom. Through the impact of Hellenization, Jews, who normally would have regarded the concept as contradictory if not blasphemous, supposedly began to reinterpret their ancient biblical heroes, especially *Moses, such that these heroes were presented to non-Jews as divine men.

According to the hypothesis, this change in Jewish thinking enabled Christianity to conceive of Jesus in similar terms. But recent study has called this hypothesis into question on two counts. First, Hellenization among Jews seems to have strengthened, not weakened, the dualism between the divine and the human (Holladay). It would be unlikely that Hellenistic *Judaism paved the way for Christianity to appropriate the divine man category and apply it to Jesus. Second, the existence of the divine man model has been questioned (Tiede). Characteristics have sometimes been indiscriminately combined to produce a profile that exists only in the minds of modern scholars. Comparisons between Jesus and other charismatic sages of antiquity will continue to intrigue and illuminate, but the sources of NT christology are probably to be sought elsewhere than in the divine man hypothesis.

5. Literary Analogies.

Neo-Pythagorean writings play a role in discussions about certain NT literary forms. Philostratus's *Life of Apollonius* is sometimes regarded as the closest literary analogue to the NT Gospels. One possible category for both is that of aretalogy, a collection of miracle stories whose function is to praise a performer of miraculous deeds. But the existence of the literary form aretalogy has been questioned (Kee), since the common description has no fully representative example. The three most essential features, a wise teacher who also has the ability to work miracles and who dies a martyr's death, are not found together. Ultimately the Gospels resist easy categorization. The Evangelists used recognizable subforms (chreiai, miracle stories), but their end product lacks clear literary precedents, and it must be remembered that the *Life of Apol-*

lonius postdates the canonical Gospels by approximately a century.

Finally, a recent study (Balch) has shown that the household codes of Neo-Pythagorean moralists have much in common with those of the NT (*see* Family and Household). Among other things, the subordination of *women to their husbands and the elevation of a woman's inner character over her external adornment are common to both.

See also PHILOSOPHY; STOICISM.

BIBLIOGRAPHY. D. L. Balch, "Neo-Pythagorean Moralists and the New Testament Household Codes," *ANRW* 2.26.1 (1992) 380-411; B. Blackburn, *Theios Aner and the Markan Miracle Traditions* (Tübingen: Mohr Siebeck, 1991); E. L. Bowie, "Apollonius of Tyana: Tradition and Reality," *ANRW* 2.16.2 (1978) 1652-99; G. P. Corrington, *The "Divine Man": His Origin and Function in Hellenistic Popular Religion* (New York: Peter Lang, 1986); J. M. Dillon, *The Middle Platonists* (rev. ed.; Ithaca, NY: Cornell University Press, 1996); M. Dzielska, *Apollonius of Tyana in Legend and History* (Rome: "L'Erma" di Bretschneider, 1986); C. R. Holladay, *Theios Aner in Hellenistic Judaism: A Critique of the Use of This Category in New Testament Christology* (Missoula, MT: Scholars Press, 1977); H. C. Kee, "Aretalogy and Gospel," *JBL* 92 (1973) 402-22; R. J. Penella, *The Letters of Apollonius of Tyana* (Leiden: E. J. Brill, 1979); G. Petzke, *Die Traditionen über Apollonius von Tyana und Das Neue Testament* (Leiden: E. J. Brill, 1970); Philostratus, *The Life of Apollonius of Tyana* (2 vols.; LCL; Cambridge, MA: Harvard University Press, 1912); M. Smith, "Prolegomena to a Discussion of Aretalogies, Divine Men, the Gospels and Jesus," *JBL* 90 (1971) 174-99; H. Thesleff, *An Introduction to the Pythagorean Writings of the Hellenistic Period* (Abo: Abo Akademi, 1961); idem, *The Pythagorean Texts of the Hellenistic Period* (Åbo: Åbo Akademi, 1961); D. L. Tiede, *The Charismatic Figure as Miracle Worker* (Missoula, MT: SBL, 1972).

N. C. Croy

NEW JERUSALEM TEXTS

Fragments of one or more works describing an ideal future city, presumably *Jerusalem (the name never appears), have been discovered in Qumran Caves 1, 2, 4, 5 and 11. Written in *Aramaic, the texts provide a verbal blueprint for an enormous temple city, mandating the design of its walls, gates, towers and other structures, including the *temple, though almost nothing of that structure's details survive. Some of the fragments describe *priestly ceremonies, ritual actions and Jewish *festivals known from neither the Bible nor any other source.

A total of seven *Qumran manuscripts are subsumed under the rubric "New Jerusalem" (1Q32, 2Q24, 4Q554-555a, 5Q15 and 11Q18). Apart from general archaeological considerations, the only way to date these manuscripts is by paleography, or analysis of the letter forms in the writing. This is an imprecise art, but it suggests that the earliest of the copies date to about 25 B.C. This is the date of the copies; the time of original composition can only be inferred by literary analysis and the observation that the New Jerusalem descriptions evidently served as a source for another *Dead Sea Scroll, the **Temple Scroll*. A date in the early to mid-second century B.C. is probable for the original writing(s), though there may have been subsequent redaction. The work possesses none of the diagnostic features of language or ideology that would brand it a sectarian composition such as are the **Rule of the Community* and **Damascus Document*.

1. Background and Description
2. Significance

1. Background and Description.

"In the twenty-fifth year of our exile," wrote Ezekiel the prophet, "the hand of the Lord was upon me, and he brought me by means of angelic visions to the land of Israel, and set me down upon an exceedingly high mountain" (Ezek 40:1-2). The mountain was Zion, whence Ezekiel looked out upon what none other could see. His visions of a new temple set within a new temple city comprise Ezekiel 40—48. Isaiah, too, looked for a new Jerusalem, encrusted with all manner of precious stone (Is 54:11-12); and the *apocryphal book of *Tobit longed for the day when "Jerusalem and the Temple of God will be rebuilt in splendor, just as the prophets have said" (Tob 14:6-7). In part these ideas were a reaction to the comparatively modest temple the Jews were able to build upon their return from exile in Babylon. It was no match, said contemporaries, for the splendid structure of old, erected by Solomon and destroyed by Nebuchadnezzar. For centuries notions of a future, wondrous temple were nurtured and grew, particularly in *priestly circles. Such circles produced the New Jerusalem work(s).

The largest surviving fragments of the New Jerusalem works derive from Qumran Cave 4. These portions have yet to be published in an *editio princeps,* though preliminary publications are available (Eisenman and Wise; Beyer). Fragments from Cave 11 are also of great significance, but they nowhere overlap those from Cave 4, nor is their own order certain. Recently a reconstruction by M. Chyutin has attempted to fit all surviving fragments into a hypothetical twenty-two-line, twenty-two-column scroll. The suggested reconstruction is very problematic, and his ordering of the fragments, largely based on corresponding points of damage, is at best uncertain; nor does Chyutin convincingly reconstruct the Aramaic morphology and syntax at every juncture. Nevertheless, his work has a certain value and includes some intriguing suggestions for the understanding of the New Jerusalem text as a whole, particularly its temple ceremonies. One way of understanding the setting and contents of the New Jerusalem text is as follows.

An angelic figure guides a visionary—unnamed, but possibly to be understood as Ezekiel—around the city, measuring its structures with a seven-cubit cane and revealing to him the ceremonies conducted within it. According to Chyutin, the earliest surviving fragments describe ceremonies held inside the temple; descriptions of the inner court of the temple and of aspects of the temple itself follow. Columns 9-14 of Chyutin's hypothetical twenty-two-column scroll concern ceremonies held within the innermost of three temple courts; column 15 then provides a snapshot of the other two courts. Columns 15-17 detail the fortification wall that surrounds the entire city, measuring about 19 x 13 miles and pierced by twelve gates named after the sons of Jacob; the next several columns consider the city plan with its residential structures, buildings and gates. After a digression to depict certain structures of the outer enclosure (including its 1,432 towers), the last column contains a scenario for the final battle against Jerusalem, led by the Kittim and including among enemy forces Babylon, Edom, Moab and the sons of Ammon.

In Chyutin's reconstruction the New Jerusalem fragments from Cave 11 constitute the initial columns. Notable among these fragmentarily preserved descriptions are several ceremonies that, unlike any described in the Bible, take place within the temple itself. They have only priestly onlookers, lay attendance being forbidden. In a series of rituals that celebrate the investiture of a new high priest and perhaps also the consecration of the new temple described by lost portions of the New Jerusalem, the high priest is dressed in his father's holy garments and crowned with seven successive diadems. He then takes his seat upon a high-priestly throne in the outer room of the temple (Aramaic *hêklâ*). He may read from a scroll (of the law?) that the New Jerusalem situates in that same outer room. The priests receive gifts, and a ceremonial changing of the priestly courses follows. The New Jerusalem text implies twenty-six priestly courses, as in the **War Scroll,* contrasting with the twenty-four courses of the later biblical sources (Chronicles), the Qumran priestly calendars, or *mishmarot,* and *rabbinic literature. Chyutin makes the intriguing but questionable suggestion that the high priest ends the ceremony by entering the holy of holies as final confirmation of receiving his office, whereupon all the priests prostrate themselves.

The New Jerusalem text's description of the Passover is notable for its attention to the ceremony of cooking the *sacrifices (*see* Festivals). The work requires the use of seven glasses, seven cups and seven cisterns, details mentioned in no other Jewish sources. The congregation is pictured eating their portions of the sacrifices within the temple confines, as in the *Temple Scroll* (17:6-9) and **Jubilees* (*Jub.* 49:20), and not throughout the entire city of Jerusalem as rabbinic law permitted. Notable here is the numbering of the congregation as 32,900. This number implies representative, not full lay participation, since the total population of the ideal city according to Chyutin's reconstruction (reasonable at this point) is about six hundred thousand.

The New Jerusalem text's description of the inner court of the temple, as with its architecture more generally, enjoys numerous points of contact with other descriptions of the ideal city, including that of Revelation. The inner court is surrounded by a wall built of white stone and penetrated by twelve gates, compared with the four of the *Temple Scroll.* A roofed and gold-plated stoa connects the gates to each other. One of the gates is called the Sapphire Gate, recalling the sapphire in Tobit's future Jerusalem (Tob 14:17) and the foundations of the walls in

Isaiah (Is 54:11-12) and Revelation (second of the twelve foundations of the wall, Rev 21:19). The dimensions of the white wall are identical to those of the *Temple Scroll's* inner court wall. Located within the inner court are a House of the Laver, where the priests would purify themselves—a structure otherwise mentioned only in the *Temple Scroll*—and a slaughterhouse installation integrating twelve pillars and rings to hold the animals, again paralleling the *Temple Scroll* description.

The fortification wall surrounding the city of the New Jerusalem text is the same height as that of the outer court in the *Temple Scroll,* but twice as wide. The wall is built of amber, sapphire and jacinth and overlaid with gold. The gates are named after the twelve sons of Jacob, with Levi in the place of honor: the central gate on the east side. The precise order of the gates accords with no other biblical or extrabiblical gated structure or listing of the tribes; the *Temple Scroll* with its named gates is closest (one small change).

Broadly conceived, the plan of the New Jerusalem text considers in varying detail three architectural complexes—if Chyutin is correct, moving from the innermost outward (as does the *Temple Scroll,* but the opposite of Ezekiel). The outermost complex is the enclosure wall, forming a rectangle. A relatively small square at the center of this rectangle represents the other two complexes combined. One complex is a residential area of 240 blocks shaped as squares. The other is a substantial temple environs having the temple and its courts at its center. The residential area stands to the north of the temple environs, such that this holy zone comprises roughly the southern third of the city. The temple with its three courts presumably formed a square. Thus the New Jerusalem text is the earliest known example of a square planning tradition for the ideal city that is attested by various Jewish and Jewish Christian sources, including Revelation.

2. Significance.

The New Jerusalem text evidences a strain of apocalyptic thinking in Second Temple Judaism that originated in priestly circles and looked forward to an ultimate restoration of Jerusalem and its temple in ideal form. This hope was a straightforward development from the words of Israel's prophets taken at face value. From this restored Jerusalem the Jews were to rule the surrounding Gentile nations, who in turn would offer their worship and the finest of their goods to the God of Israel. This was a mundane as opposed to ultramundane-utopian or millennial concept. The book of Revelation developed this thinking in new directions but used older imagery, at least some deriving, it seems, from extrabiblical Jewish sources. The New Jerusalem text provides us a glimpse of architectural aspects of that older pool of imagery. The New Jerusalem text's tradition of an *angel guiding and measuring the ideal city, ultimately deriving from Ezekiel, also appears in Revelation.

For an understanding of the Judaism of NT times the New Jerusalem text offers more than meets the eye. For its city plan was intended as an expression of number *mysticism reminiscent of *Pythagorean ideas. If Chyutin is correct, the ideal dimensions of the human body lay behind its design, derived ultimately from a much older Egyptian tradition. The numbers seven and eleven are the most important in this mysticism. Moreover, the relation 11:7, which the New Jerusalem text adopts as the relation between the sides of the residential area, solves one of the two main geometrical problems of the ancient world: how to square a circle. The dimensions of the fortification wall of the New Jerusalem are 7:5, creating an oblong that is initially surprising in a square building tradition. But this oblong is deliberate, for it presents a solution to the second major geometric problem of the ancient world: the relation between the lengths of the diagonal and the side of any given square. The ratio 7:5 was the value accepted by *Plato in his *Republic* (546) and by rabbinic sages in the *Talmud. For the author of the New Jerusalem text, a man was, if not the measure of all things, at least that of the city of God.

See also JERUSALEM; TEMPLE, JEWISH; TEMPLE SCROLL (11QTEMPLE).

BIBLIOGRAPHY. M. Baillet, "Description de la Jérusalem Nouvelle," in *"Les Petites Grotte" de Qumrân,* ed. M. Baillet, J. T. Milik and R. de Vaux (DJD 3; Oxford: Clarendon Press, 1962) 84-89; K. Beyer, *Die aramäischen Texte vom Toten Meer: Ergänzungsband* (Göttingen: Vandenhoeck & Ruprecht, 1994); M. Chyutin, "The New Jerusalem: Ideal City," *Dead Sea Discoveries* 1 (1994) 71-97; idem, *The New Jerusalem Scroll from Qumran: A Comprehensive Reconstruction* (JSPS 25; Sheffield: Sheffield Academic Press, 1997); R. Eisenman and M. Wise, *The Dead Sea Scrolls Uncovered* (Shaftesbury, Dorset, England: Element, 1992); J. A. Fitzmyer and D. J. Harrington, *A Manual of Palestinian Aramaic Texts* (BibO 34; Rome: Biblical Institute Press, 1978); F. García Martínez, "The Last Surviving Columns of 11 QNJ," in *The Scriptures and the Scrolls*, ed. F. García Martínez (Leiden: E. J. Brill, 1992) 178-92; J. C. Greenfield, "The Small Caves of Qumran," *JAOS* 89 (1969) 132-35; B. Jongeling, "Publication Provisoire d'un Fragment Provenant de la Grotte 11 de Qumran," *JSJ* 1 (1970) 58-64; J. Licht, "The Ideal Town Plan from Qumran: The Description of the New Jerusalem," *IEJ* 29 (1979) 47-59; J. T. Milik, "Description de la Jérusalem Nouvelle," in *Les "Petites Grottes" de Qumrân*, ed. M. Baillet, J. T. Milik and R. de Vaux (DJD 3; Oxford: Clarendon Press, 1962) 184-93; J. Starcky, "Jerusalem et les Manuscrits de la Mer Morte," *Le Monde de la Bible* 1 (1977) 38-40; E. Tigchelaar, review of Chyutin, *The New Jerusalem Scroll from Qumran, RevQ* 18 (1998) 453-57; M. O. Wise, *A Critical Study of the Temple Scroll from Qumran Cave 11* (Chicago: Oriental Institute, 1990). M. O. Wise

NEW TESTAMENT VERSIONS, ANCIENT

There are numerous ancient versions or translations of the NT that were produced in a variety of languages. Some of these are quite early, dating possibly to the second century A.D. As a result many textual critics believe that these versions have a significant role to play in textual criticism of the NT by providing another form of external evidence to complement that provided by the Greek manuscripts.

1. The Use of the Versions
2. The Extant Versions
3. Conclusion

1. The Use of the Versions.

The versions or translations of the Greek NT into other languages offer significant evidence for textual critics. The earliest translations were made by Christian missionaries who prepared these versions to aid them in their attempts to propagate Christianity among those for whom Greek was not a first language. As Metzger notes (1992, 67), the Bible being translated into Syriac, Latin and Coptic from the second century on is very important for tracing the history of interpretation of the Bible. However, it is also important for the textual critic, because many of these translations were made very early in the development of the textual tradition of Christianity. We can see the importance of these versions when we consider that the earliest complete or nearly complete codices of the Greek NT date to the fourth century A.D., by which time some of the versions were already well established. Thus, access to manuscripts that were sympathetically prepared in order to represent Christianity accurately, and made at such an early date, seem to offer much to the textual critic. Nevertheless, despite these possibilities, the versions tend to have been neglected in most textual criticism, from Westcott and Hort to the present. A survey of the major NT textual critics indicates that right up to the present the versions have often been only haphazardly or incompletely drawn upon in the critical apparatuses of published Greek NT texts (see Birdsall, 118).

The reasons for the apparent neglect of the versions can perhaps be accounted for in light of a number of difficulties connected with these documents. The first concerns the difficulties in translation itself. Although many people, especially in the ancient world, were able to communicate in several languages, this does not necessarily mean that they could prepare accurate and faithful translations. In fact, translation is a far more difficult task than is often realized, and for some versions it is questionable whether those who performed the translation had a grasp of Greek adequate enough to provide a faithful rendering into their receptor language.

The second difficulty relates to the demands of textual criticism. Even if one were confident that the rendering into the receptor language were able to capture the essence of the original text, in order for the versions to be useful for NT textual criticism, they must capture the original text in a fairly literalistic way. However, the lack of iconistic correlation between Greek and a number of the other languages into which it was rendered means that such a literalism is by definition virtually excluded. For example (see Metzger 1992, 67-68; Epp, 67), Greek has an article, but Latin does not. Greek distinguishes the aorist and perfect tense-forms, but Syriac and Latin do not. Greek also has a future form, but Gothic does not. Greek has three grammaticalized voices, including a passive voice, but Coptic does not have the passive voice form and uses a syntactical construction to render this concept. Greek has comparative and superlative forms for adjectives, but Syriac has neither. Greek is an inflected language, with a full case system, but Syriac and Coptic do not have case endings. Greek has a relatively flexible word order depending on a variety of pragmatic features, but Coptic relies on a strict word order (since it does not have case endings). These kinds of variances between Greek and other languages mean that while it might be evident that a version contains a given pericope, and even a given sentence or phrase, it may not be possible to determine the exact Greek wording behind such a text.

A third mitigating factor for the use of the versions is that some of these translations were probably not made directly from the Greek NT but were derived from another translation. It is possible that the Armenian version is derived from the Syriac version and the Georgian from either Armenian or Syriac or both (Epp, 67). A fourth difficulty is the number of manuscripts available in the versions. The numbers exceed those of the Greek NT itself and present a whole host of text-critical questions to be answered in their own right before they can be used. These include questions of whether later versions were checked against Greek manuscripts, and which ones, and how much contamination occurred between manuscripts of the version concerned. For these reasons, due caution must be exercised when drawing upon the versions in textual criticism of the NT.

2. The Extant Versions.

There are a number of versions of the Greek NT that merit discussion. These will be categorized according to their relative importance. For each of these versions there is a wealth of historical discussion that has preceded our arrival at the *status quaestionis*. The current state of scholarship, as gleaned from recent research, will be cited below, with sources listed for further consultation.

2.1. **Diatessaron**. (Metzger 1977, 10-36; Petersen, 77-96 in Ehrman and Holmes; Birdsall, 127-30.) Although no longer extant and reconstructed through secondary witnesses (possibly apart from a Greek fragment found at Dura-Europos in 1933, considered by some as close as one can get to the earliest text), Tatian's *Diatessaron* has been the subject of much continued discussion. The consensus today is that Tatian composed this harmony of the Gospels in Syriac in about A.D. 172. Whereas it was once thought, more by default than anything else, that he had composed it in Rome, there is now reason for thinking that he composed it in the East or on his way to the East after being expelled from the Roman church. Tatian's *Diatessaron*, according to the reconstructed evidence, has a number of readings that deviate from those in the canonical Gospels, which has prompted speculation on his sources. Some have suspected that he used a noncanonical Gospel, while others think that he may have had a canonical Gospel containing readings that deviated from those found in the major codices. In any event, the *Diatessaron* was highly influential in the East and possibly in the West. In the East it influenced, directly or indirectly, all of the later Syriac texts, as well as the Georgian and Arabic texts, and possibly the Armenian. In the West, the influence of the *Diatessaron* had to compete with other influences, such as Justin's harmony of the Gospels, which may account for Diatessaronic readings found in various traditions, such as the Latin, Middle Dutch, Old French, Old and Middle German, Middle English and Middle Italian.

2.2. ***Syriac***. (Metzger 1977, 36-98; Metzger 1992, 68-71, 269-70; Birdsall, 123-32; Baarda, 97-112 in Ehrman and Holmes.) The Peshitta Syriac (fifth century A.D.) version is still considered the standard version of the Syriac-speaking church, but two earlier manuscripts reveal that there was an earlier Old Syriac text. The first manuscript is the Cureton manuscript of the British Library (Syr^c, fifth century A.D.), published in 1858, and the second is a palimpsest (overwritten) manuscript in St. Catherine's Monastery in Sinai, discovered by Mrs. Agnes Smith Lewis (Syr^s, fourth century) and published in 1910. These both contain portions of the Gospels, but there is nothing else of the Old Syriac for other portions of the NT, except through citations found in church fathers and reconstructions from other versions, such as Armenian.

The Peshitta version dates to about the fifth century and probably was (so Metzger) prepared to replace the divergent Old Syriac version. The Peshitta does not include 2 Peter, 2 and 3 John, Jude and Revelation. The Peshitta exists in more than 350 manuscripts, some dating to the fifth and sixth centuries. According to Metzger, it follows the Byzantine tradition in the Gospels and the Western tradition in Acts. In the sixth and seventh centuries, there were two revisions of the Peshitta made, the Philoxenian version and the Harclean. The relation between these two versions is complex. Some think that the

Philoxenia was prepared for Bishop Philoxenus of Mabbug and then was reissued by Thomas of Harkel, a later bishop of Mabbug, who added marginal notes gained from several Greek manuscripts. However, a competing theory is that Thomas thoroughly revised the earlier version. As Metzger says, the first theory contends that there was one version with variant readings, but the second theory contends that there are two versions. The difficulty is compounded by the fact that the Philoxenian version has very little manuscript evidence, apart from some marginalia in Harclean manuscripts.

Finally, there is the Palestinian Syriac version. This Aramaic version is known from a Gospel lectionary found primarily in three manuscripts from the eleventh and twelfth centuries, although there are also other fragmentary manuscripts of the rest of the NT. Some speculate that this version dates from the fifth century. According to Metzger, it appears to follow the Caesarean text type and is independent of the other Syriac versions.

2.3. Latin. (Metzger 1977, 285-374; Metzger 1992, 72-79, 270-72; Petzer, in Ehrman and Holmes, 113-30; Birdsall, 118-22). With over ten thousand extant manuscripts, the Latin tradition is the best attested of any of the versions. Although there has been some terminological confusion occasioned by the terms used to refer to the Latin versions, the two major distinctions are the Old Latin (OL), with its European and African traditions, and the Vulgate (Vg). There are over fifty manuscripts of the Old Latin version, dating from the fourth to the thirteen centuries (Epp, 68), although there is no extant complete Old Latin Bible. Some parts of the Greek NT appear to have been translated into Latin as early as the late second century, and Tertullian cites the NT in Latin in the third century. However, it is not until the mid-third century that there appears to be an identifiable text of the Latin Bible. The Old Latin tradition is divided into the African and European texts. Although called the African text because of association with Cyprian, who was bishop of Carthage, recent scholarship thinks that the text may have been produced in Italy and probably not Africa. According to Petzer, the African version is distinguished by distinct vocabulary and diction that indicate the age of the version. This African version was subjected to revision, which produced the European version. As with the African, the origins of the European Old Latin version are unknown. It evidences great diversity in the tradition, with numerous divergent readings from manuscript to manuscript. This diversity led to other minor revisions of this tradition, often having only local influence. Despite this great diversity in this very widely disseminated tradition, as Petzer notes, it is thought that the Old Latin tradition in all its diversity sprang from a single translation from Greek into Latin. Nevertheless, even Jerome complained to Pope Damasus that there were as many versions as manuscripts, prompting the pope in A.D. 382 to commission Jerome to revise the Latin Bible (Vulgate). Whereas Jerome's Latin OT is a translation from Hebrew, the NT is a revision of the European version. Metzger notes that in his explanation of his principles of revision for the Gospels, Jerome indicates he used a relatively good Latin text, compared it with some Greek manuscripts, and revised in a conservative way, retaining the Latin text except where the meaning was distorted. Many scholars now doubt that Jerome was responsible for the entire NT, with someone else doing the Pauline and other letters. The goal of Jerome's work originally was to bring unity to the diverse textual tradition. This was not accomplished, however. The Old Latin version continued to be used and transmitted, and the Vulgate itself underwent a number of revisions, promoting further textual diversity. One instance noted by Petzer is the apparent use in Peregrinus's Spanish revision of an Old Latin manuscript to revise the Vulgate.

2.4. Coptic. (Metzger 1977, 99-152, with an essay by Plumley, 141-52 on problems in translation of Greek into Coptic; Metzger 1992, 79-81, 272-74; Wisse, 131-41 in Ehrman and Holmes; Birdsall, 132-35.) Coptic, though the latest form of the ancient Egyptian language, adopted the Greek alphabet in the first and second centuries, supplementing it with seven characters from the Demotic script. It was used in Egypt but in a context that had been heavily influenced by Greek language and culture, so that Coptic had many Greek loanwords (estimated at 15 percent of its total vocabulary). One might have thought that, as a result, the Coptic version would be the most unproblematic in terms of tracing its relationship with the Greek NT textual tradition. However, the opposite appears to be the case. Because of the deep penetration of Greek language and culture into Egypt, there were many native Copts who used Greek instead, with the result that the earliest Coptic manuscripts did not appear until the fourth century. Because of the interpenetration of languages, there is also a difficulty in using the Coptic text to reconstruct the Greek text, because after the Coptic translation was completed, the Greek could continue to be in use, thus possibly distorting the Coptic version. There are also many linguistic differences (noted above, such as Coptic not being a case but a word-order language, etc.) that make iconic translation difficult.

Wisse notes four stages in the development of the Coptic tradition. The first is the pre-classical stage (A.D. 250-350), during which there were several uncoordinated efforts at producing a Coptic version, resulting in odd selections from the NT. Wisse thinks it is not appropriate to speak of a Coptic version at this point. The next stage is the classical Sahidic and Fayumic stage (A.D. 350-450). During this period the Coptic shifted from bilingual to monolingual Coptic members, along with the growth of the monastic movement. Thus, a Coptic translation was needed, and the most widely used dialect, Sahidic, was used. The Sahidic seems to follow the Alexandrian text, but with Western readings in the Gospels and Acts. Of the other versions in Coptic that took place during this period, the Fayumic was the most important, probably for the same reasons as the Sahidic, but for the relatively isolated Fayum area. The third period is the final Sahidic and Fayumic stage (A.D. 450-1000). With the Arab conquest of Egypt in the seventh century, the Coptic language began its decline, with Bohairic becoming the liturgical language of the Coptic church. The fourth period is the Bohairic version (after A.D. 800). The earliest evidence of a true Bohairic version is from the ninth century. Wisse attributes the shift from Greek to Bohairic as the language of the Coptic church as the reason for the origin and spread of the Bohairic version as an ecclesiastical version.

*2.5. **Other Versions.*** (Metzger 1977, 153-282, 375-460; Metzger 1992, 81-86, 274-76; Zuurmund, 142-56, Alexanian, 157-72, and Birdsall, 173-87, all in Ehrman and Holmes; Birdsall, 135-37.) Other versions worth noting are the Gothic version, which is well represented by the fifth- or sixth-century Codex Argenteus; the Armenian version, in which there are over 1200 manuscripts, second of the versions only to Latin, possibly dating from the fifth century, though possibly a rendering of the Syriac version; the Georgian version, of which little is known, with its earliest manuscript from the ninth century; the Ethiopic version, which though it may have been directly translated from Greek relatively early (fourth century?) is only represented in late manuscripts; Church Slavonic, the result of the work of Saints Cyril and Methodius, to whom are accredited the Glagolitic and Cyrillic alphabets, and the translation in the ninth century into Old Bulgarian or Old Slavonic.

3. Conclusion.

There are two major issues one must confront in the study of the versions. First is how and in what ways they are useful for determining the text of the Greek NT and tracing its development. Second is the state of scholarship regarding the individual versions. Some of the versions have been studied more thoroughly than others, some of which have been virtually neglected. The wealth of evidence in Greek manuscripts mitigates the efforts that will or can be spent on some of these other versions as well.

See also MANUSCRIPTS, GREEK NEW TESTAMENT; OLD TESTAMENT VERSIONS, ANCIENT; TEXTUAL CRITICISM.

BIBLIOGRAPHY. K. Aland and B. Aland, *The Text of the New Testament* (2d ed.; Grand Rapids, MI: Eerdmans, 1989); J. N. Birdsall, "The Recent History of New Testament Textual Criticism (from Westcott and Hort, 1881, to the Present)," *ANRW* 2.26.1 (1992) 99-197; B. D. Ehrman and M. W. Holmes, eds., *The Text of the New Testament in Contemporary Research: Essays on the Status Quaestionis* (SD 46; Grand Rapids, MI: Eerdmans, 1995); E. J. Epp, "Textual Criticism in Exegesis of the New Testament, with an Excursus on Canon," *Handbook to Exegesis of the New Testament*, ed. S. E. Porter (NTTS 25; Leiden: E. J. Brill, 1997) 45-97; B. M. Metzger, *The Early Versions of the New Testament: Their Origin, Transmission and Limitations* (New York: Oxford University Press, 1977); idem, *The Text of the New Testament: Its Transmission, Corruption, and Restoration* (3d ed.; New York: Oxford University Press, 1992).

S. E. Porter

NOMOS. *See* LAW/NOMOS IN GRECO-ROMAN WORLD.

NOVELS. *See* ROMANCES/NOVELS, ANCIENT.

NURSES, WET. *See* FAMILY AND HOUSEHOLD.

O

ODES OF SOLOMON

The *Odes of Solomon* (*Odes*) are preserved in four manuscripts: two are in Syriac, but neither preserves the whole collection of *Odes*; one is in Greek, but it preserves only one ode; and one is in Coptic, but it consists of excerpts in the *Pistis Sophia.* There is in addition only one quotation; it is in Latin. Thus, only forty of the original forty-two *Odes* are extant. *Ode* 1 may be preserved in a Coptic citation in the *Pistis Sophia,* but all of *Ode* 2 and the beginning of *Ode* 3 are lost. The collection was perhaps attributed by the author, the Odist, to Solomon. It is characterized by the joy and love experienced at the appearance of the Beloved who is the Messiah (*Ode* 7:1-2). Since the *Odes* were discovered in a Syriac manuscript in 1909, scholars have published widely different assessments of them, ranging from a Jewish composition of the first century A.D. or earlier to a *gnostic text of the third century A.D. Thus, the *Odes* are hailed as a most important hymnbook, but scholars have not been able to decide if they are Jewish, Christian or gnostic. The debate is not easy to follow, since during the twentieth century each of these terms were defined, redefined and sometimes claimed as misleading for documents composed in the first two centuries.

1. Original Language
2. Date
3. Provenance
4. Relation to the Dead Sea Scrolls
5. Jewish, Christian, Gnostic?
6. Importance

1. Original Language.

The original language of the *Odes of Solomon* is perhaps Greek but most likely an early form of Aramaic-Syriac. The extant Greek seems to represent Semitisms that suggest an earlier manuscript in Syriac or better Aramaic-Syriac; perhaps it was in the original language. The Syriac text abounds in paronomasia, assonance, rhythm and other linguistic features that indicate either the scribe was an unusually gifted translator or was composing these *Odes* in an early form of Aramaic-Syriac (*see* Aramaic Language).

2. Date.

After some confusion and speculations, those focusing their research on the *Odes* now agree that the collection was completed in the second century and most likely before A.D. 125. The Greek manuscript (Bodmer Papyrus XI), which dates from the third century, was copied from an earlier Greek manuscript that would most likely take us back into the second century A.D. That is evident since the scribe inadvertently omits, and later adds in the margins, a portion of the ode. If the original language is not Greek, then we must allow for some time for the *Odes* to be composed and then later translated into Greek. If the *Odes* antedate A.D. 125, then the question to be researched is the date of the odes in the collection. That is, how early does the collection go into the first century? It is clear that the hymns in a hymnbook were not written when they were collected into a hymnbook.

3. Provenance.

If the *Odes* were composed in Greek, they could have been written virtually anywhere, including Egypt, Syria or Palestine. If they were composed in Aramaic-Syriac, then they may have been composed in Palestine, perhaps in Galilee, or in western Syria. Scholars cannot discover their provenance. As with most works in the OT *pseudepigrapha, scholars find it practically impossible to discern the place in which a work was written. Long before the *Odes* were composed, the first world culture appeared: the Hellenistic world. Commerce and the movement of ideas traveled from Parthia in the East to *Rome in the West. After the end of the first century B.C. piracy on the high seas was abolished and substantial roads still evident connected the East with the West. Hence, it is not clear where a document was composed. The situation applies not only to the documents in the OT pseudepigrapha but also to those in the NT.

4. Relation to the Dead Sea Scrolls.

The abundant links with the *Dead Sea Scrolls, especially those composed at *Qumran—the **Rule of the Community* (1QS) and the *Hodayot,* or **Thanksgiving Hymns* (1QH)—suggest some influence from the Qumranites or, better, *Essenes. The dualism seems to reflect that developed in 1QS 3-4, and the poetry is similar to that found in 1QH. J. Carmignac concluded that the Odist was once a member of the Qumran community. J. H. Charlesworth contends that the Odist may not have been a Qumranite but seems to have been an Essene—that is, he was once a member of the larger Essene community that lived on the fringes of towns or cities (as *Philo and *Josephus reported).

5. Jewish, Christian, Gnostic?

Some scholars claimed that the *Odes* were originally Jewish but later edited by a Christian (esp. Harnack) or Jewish-Christian as now extant. Some specialists were convinced the *Odes* should be declared to be gnostic (Gunkel and Rudolph). Most scholars contend that they are Christian (Charlesworth and Emerton). Strictly speaking, the labels "Jewish," "gnostic" and "Christian" seem to be ill suited to this collection of forty-two odes attributed to Solomon. Some passages are deeply Jewish, others apparently gnostic, and yet others patently influenced by Christian ideas and teachings. Thus the *Odes* seem to have been composed when Judaism, gnostic ideas [not Gnosticism of the second century] and Christian affirmation were mixing easily.

Note how "the Messiah" is mentioned in the *Odes.* The reference to the Messiah seems only symbolically Christian. In *Ode* 9:3 the Odist mentions "the Messiah" for the first time:

The word of the Lord and his desires,
The holy thought which he has thought concerning his Messiah.

The thought is fundamentally Jewish. The mention of "his Messiah"—which appears also in *Ode* 41:3-4—is reminiscent of "his Messiah" of the **Psalms of Solomon,* which always subordinates the Messiah to the Lord (cf. *Pss. Sol.* 18:5) Yahweh. Who is "the Lord" in the ode? In antiquity some readers may have taken the noun to refer to Yahweh, others to Jesus. Thus it is not wise to label the Odist as a Christian without discussion and clarification.

In *Ode* 17:17 the noun *Messiah* appears in a doxology:

Glory to you, our Head, O Lord Messiah.

Not only a Jew, expecting the coming of the Messiah, but also a Christian could have recited this doxology. We should remember that the Jew who composed the *Psalms of Solomon* called the Messiah "the Lord Messiah" (*Pss. Sol.* 17:32; 18:7). If the *Odes* are to be labeled Christian, then we need to also stress that the Christianity of the *Odes* is articulated so that a Jew could join in chanting them. In contrast to the apocryphal NT compositions, which are frequently anti-Jewish, the *Odes* are not anti-Christian; they are sometimes anti-Gentile (*Ode* 10:4-6).

In *Ode* 24:1 the Odist mentions how

The dove fluttered over the head of our Lord Messiah,
Because he was her head.

Again, "Lord Messiah" is mentioned, but there is no clear reference to Jesus. This passage, however, is surely a poetic reflection on the baptism of Jesus, highlighted by the descent of the Spirit as a dove, which is described in the Gospels (Mt 3:16; Mk 1:10; Lk 3:22; Jn 1:32). Yet the passage is only obliquely Christian, and there seem to be gnostic overtones in the exegesis of the verse in the following verses. Note especially verses 9-12:

And all of them who were lacking perished,
Because they were not able to express the word so that they might remain.
And the Lord destroyed the thoughts,
Of all those who had not the truth with them.
For they were lacking in wisdom,
They who exalted themselves in their mind.
So they were rejected,
Because the truth was not with them.

We do not know much about the full extent of Christianity at the turn of the first to the second centuries. Some scholars may argue that we should expect a Christian to stress the salvation the Messiah brought to those on earth. Instead, the Odist stresses the punishment the Messiah brings to those who do not have the truth or wisdom. This idea seems strange in light of the Christian confession that the Messiah brings the truth or is the truth. Thus these verses in *Ode* 24 do seem quasi-gnostic or maybe naively gnostic—that is, if the *Ode* seems distant from Christian claims, it is also far from Gnosticism.

In *Ode* 39:11-12 we find another allusion, again veiled, to another aspect of the charismatic dimension or pneumatic quality of Jesus' life, according to the Gospels:

> On this side and on that the waves were lifted up,
> But the footsteps of our Lord Messiah were standing firm.
> And they are neither blotted out,
> Nor destroyed. (*Ode* 39:11-12)

Obviously, readers who are familiar with the NT will see an allusion to the account of Jesus walking on the water, found in Matthew 14:22-33, Mark 6:45-52 and John 6:16-21 (but not in Luke). Again, the allusion is only oblique and the mention of the Messiah is as "Lord Messiah" (as in the *Pss. Sol.* 17:32; 18:7).

The Odist mentions the Messiah twice in his next to last ode, *Ode* 41:

> We live in the Lord by his grace,
> And life we receive by his Messiah.
> For a great day has shined upon us,
> And wonderful is he who has given to us of his glory. (*Ode* 41:3-4)
> The Man who humbled himself,
> But was raised because of his own righteousness.
> The Son of the Most High appeared
> In the perfection of his Father.
> And light dawned from the Word
> That was before time in him.
> The Messiah in truth is one.
> And he was known before the foundations of the world,
> That he might give life to persons forever by the truth of his name. (*Ode* 41:12-15)

As in *Ode* 9:3, so here we hear about "his Messiah" (cf. *Pss. Sol.* 18:5). *Ode* 41 is clearly the most Christian interpretation of the Messiah in the *Odes*—note the joyous tone at the appearance of the Messiah, the poetic vision of Jesus' crucifixion, the sonship christology, and the Word christology (similar to the protology of the prologue of the Gospel of John). Yet the name *Jesus* does not appear here or anywhere in the *Odes*. The thin veneer of Christian theology seems deliberate, and this seems so pro-Jewish in light of the growing hostility to Jews in Matthew and John (that is, Gospels written just before or contemporaneous with the composition of the *Odes*). If one needs a label for the Odist, I would suggest a Jew, perhaps once an Essene, who was ecstatic about the appearance of God's Messiah, whose sacrifice and righteousness brought love and life to all who have knowledge (e.g., *Odes* 8:8-12; 9:7; 11:4; 12:3, etc.) and love the Lord (e.g., *Odes* 3:3-5; 5:1; 6:2; 8:20-22, etc).

6. Importance.

The importance of the *Odes* seems evident. They mark a fork in the road in the development of Western culture. The Odist seems to stand at a three-way junction: some will proceed ahead to Judaism, others will move on to full-blown Gnosticism, and others will progress to orthodox Christianity. The beauty of the *Odes* seems to lie in their naive, spontaneous and joyous affirmation that the long-awaited Messiah has come to God's people, the Jews:

> My joy is the Lord and my course is toward him,
> This way of mine is beautiful.
> For there is a Helper for me, the Lord.
> He has generously shown himself to me in his simplicity,
> Because his kindness has diminished his grandeur.
> He became like me, that I might receive him.
> In form he was considered like me, that I might put him on.
> And I trembled not when I saw him.
> Because he was gracious to me.
> Like my nature he became, that I might understand him.
> And like my form, that I might not turn away from him. (*Ode* 7:2-6)

See also APOCRYPHA AND PSEUDEPIGRAPHA; PSALMS OF SOLOMON.

BIBLIOGRAPHY. J. Carmignac, "Un qumrânien converti au christianisme: L'Auteur des Odes de Salomon," in *Qumran-Probleme,* ed. H. Bardtke (DAWB 42; Berlin: Akademie Verlag, 1963) 75-108; J. H. Charlesworth, *Critical Reflections on the Odes of Solomon,* vol. 1: *Literary Setting, Textual Studies, Gnosticism, the Dead Sea Scrolls and the Gospel of John* (JSPSup 22 [The Distinguished Scholars Collection]; Sheffield: Sheffield Academic Press, 1998); idem, *The Odes of Solomon* (Oxford: Clarendon Press, 1977 [1973]), contains the critical text and translation as well as a bibliography; idem, "The Odes of Solomon," in *The Old Testament Pseudepigrapha,* ed. J. H. Charlesworth (2 vols.; Garden City, NY: Doubleday, 1983, 1985) 2:725-71; J. H. Charlesworth, ed., *Papyri and Leather Manuscripts of the Odes of Solomon* (Dickerson Series of Photographs 1; Durham, NC: Hunter Publishing Co., 1981); J. A. Emerton, "The Odes of Solomon," in *The Apocryphal Old Testament,* ed. H. F. D. Sparks (Oxford: Clarendon Press, 1984) 683-731; H. Gunkel, "Salomo Oden," in *RGG*[2] 5:87-90; A. Harnack and J. Fleming, *Ein jüdisch-christliches Psalmbuch aus dem ersten Jahrhundert* (TU 34.4; Leipzig: Hinrichs 1910); M. Lattke, *Die Oden Salomos in ihrer Bedeutung für Neues Testament und Gnosis* (OBO 25.1, 25.1a, 25.2, 25.3; Frieburg: Universitatsverlag Freiburg Schweiz; Göttingen: Vandenhoeck & Ruprecht, 1979-86); idem, *Oden Salomos: Text, Übersetzung, Kommentar: Teil 1 Oden 1 und 3-14* (NTOA 41/1; Freiburg: Universitätsverlag Freiburg Schweiz; Göttingen: Vandenhoeck & Ruprecht, 1999); K. Rudolf, "War der Verfasser der Oden Salomos ein 'Qumran-Christ'? Ein Beitrag zur Diskussion um die Anfänge der Gnosis," *RevQ* 4 (1964) 523-55.

J. H. Charlesworth

OLD TESTAMENT VERSIONS, ANCIENT

The writers of the NT were convinced that God had revealed himself in earlier Scripture (sacred writing) and that important portions of this Scripture applied directly to themselves and their community. It is not surprising that the NT is filled with references, direct and otherwise, to what today's Christians call the OT and Jews, the *Hebrew Bible. In this article we explore the textual resources for Scripture available to NT writers. By the first century A.D., much if not all of the Hebrew Bible had been translated into Greek and/or Aramaic. The seeds of other foreign-language versions may also have been sown by this time. Additionally, although not technically versions, there were differing Hebrew texts as well. Such diversity, which was exegetical as well as textual, offered a rich array of possibilities for NT authors.

1. Greek Versions
2. Aramaic Versions
3. Syriac Versions
4. Latin Versions
5. Hebrew-Language Versions
6. Transmission of the New Testament

1. Greek Versions.

The earliest translation of the Hebrew Bible, the *Septuagint, dates to the first quarter of the third century B.C., when, in *Alexandria, Egypt, the Torah or Pentateuch was rendered into Greek, primarily, we may suppose, for the benefit of members of that city's large Jewish population who were no longer fluent in the Hebrew language. In subsequent decades the remainder of the Hebrew Bible was translated, although the circumstances and chronology of this process are still obscure. Eventually the term *Septuagint* (relating to the tradition that seventy or seventy-two Jewish elders prepared the Greek version of the Torah) was applied to the Greek translation of the entire OT as well as to materials originally composed in Greek.

The first translators of the Pentateuch adopted a fairly literal approach toward that text, although not without introducing some interpretive elements that would bridge the gap between ancient *Israel and *Hellenistic Egypt. A number of other translators also tended toward the literal representation of their Hebrew *Vorlage,* that is, the Hebrew text that lay before them. Fairly early, however, perhaps before the Hebrew Bible was completely translated for a first time, efforts were made to retranslate it or to revise earlier forms of the Greek version. Such efforts arose from the fact that the Septuagint, or more precisely the Old Greek, did not always conform to the Hebrew text coming into popular use especially in *Jerusalem. This occurred primarily when the Old Greek translators had access to a Hebrew different from the developing standard, later to be called the Masoretic Text, but also as a result of conscious efforts to update or modify the Hebrew for cultural, theological or other ideological reasons. In this way several alternative Greek versions of various OT books came into being.

It is not clear that even a careful ancient reader would have been able, even if he or she had wanted to, to distinguish between original Old Greek and later revisional or translational activity. Almost everything in Greek, so it appears, could be called Septuagint. In some cases, a later text all but replaced an earlier one (as is true for the book of Daniel) or usurped the place originally occupied by the Old Greek (as with Ecclesiastes). It cannot be proven to be so, but it is reasonable to maintain that the Greek text, whatever its precise origins, would be viewed by many first-century Jews as equal in authority to the Hebrew. Such a view goes back at least as far as the second century B.C. **Epistle of Aristeas*, which describes the reception of the Greek Pentateuch at Alexandria in language unmistakably reminiscent of Moses' giving of the Ten Commandments at Sinai. The first-century A.D. Jewish philosopher *Philo was surely not alone in maintaining that those responsible for the Septuagint were more than mere translators—they had functioned as authentic and true *prophets.

It is not surprising, given this information, to learn that the Septuagint broadly defined is a constant source of OT citations in the NT. It would be natural for those writing in Greek to have recourse to Scripture in that language. A number of caveats or provisos must, however, be kept in mind when dealing with this important issue. (1) Most, if not all, NT authors were familiar with Hebrew. On their own initiative they could have prepared and incorporated Greek translations of Hebrew texts, both those like our standard Masoretic text and those in agreement with the differing *Vorlage* of the Greek translators. (2) On occasion, NT authors cited from memory or modified an OT passage to fit into its context (literary, theological, and other) within the NT. (3) To speak of NT usage of the Septuagint can lead to the trap of envisioning the Septuagint as a monolithic composition, an artificial construction we have sought to abolish.

In short, no careful reader can fully comprehend the NT without knowledge and appreciation for the Greek version known as the Septuagint. In a world for which and in which the divinely inspired word conveyed life-defining meaning and instruction, it was frequently the word as conveyed in Greek that formed the essence of the NT and the later versions that derived from it.

2. Aramaic Versions.

Because *Aramaic was the dominant language in the Near East considerably before the advent of the Hellenistic period, it is logical to assume that some sort of translation of the Hebrew Bible into that language took place even earlier than the Septuagint. Nehemiah 8 portrays Ezra as reading from the Book of the Law (a form of our Pentateuch?) in front of Jerusalem's Water Gate, with others providing an explanation of the text for the benefit of the huge crowd gathered on this occasion. Many scholars understand this event, which took place in the mid-fifth century B.C., to refer to the origins of the practice of supplementing with Aramaic translation or interpretation the reading of the Hebrew biblical text. Although Hebrew and Aramaic are closely related Semitic languages (far closer to each other than either is to Indo-European languages like Greek), knowledge of one does not guarantee understanding of the other.

Our textual evidence for Aramaic translations or interpretations of the Hebrew Bible, which are generally called targums (*targumim) from the Aramaic term for "translation," in pre-Christian centuries is scant. Tradition records that the Pentateuch or Torah was the first portion to be rendered in either oral or written form into Aramaic. The process apparently followed by those who produced the Septuagint, as well as the near universal prominence accorded to the Torah in almost all branches of Judaism, gives considerable support to this tradition. Some confirmation is provided by two small fragments of the Dead Sea Scrolls; found in Cave 4, they preserve a targum to the book of Leviticus. But the most extensive remains of early targumic texts, also found at *Qumran, are from the book of Job (*see* Targum of Job). Be that as it may, there are extant several important targumim to the Torah from both Palestine and Babylonia. The Former Prophets (roughly equivalent to the historical books in the Christian tradition) and the Latter Prophets are also well represented, as are the Writings (Ketubim, the third part into which the Hebrew Bible is divided in Jewish tradition).

In their present form all of these texts, to the extent they are datable, stem from periods well after the formation of the NT. But it is demonstrable that several of them contain material that derives from pre-Christian times and that would therefore have been available to writers of the NT. In addition to specific instances in which dependence on an Aramaic source seems likely on the part of such writers, there is the more general observation that Aramaic was bound to exert at least some influence in the world of the NT, where many, perhaps most, people were functionally bilingual or even trilingual, with Aramaic being the common tongue.

It is often asserted that the targumim exhibit a uniformly periphrastic style in rendering the Hebrew. This is not the case. Although it is difficult to go beyond speculation, it seems that those responsible for the targumim rather carefully represented what appeared in their *Vorlage,* to which they added in widely varying degrees all manner of exegetical and other interpretive material. This accords well with an understanding of targumic origins as complementary to/accompanying the Hebrew text rather than as its replacement. It is also true that many targumim display circumlocutions for references to the divine, presumably reflecting (as do added materials) beliefs and practices contemporary with the targumim's creation or compilation.

3. Syriac Versions.
There is no sure evidence to support the view that other foreign-language versions of the Hebrew Bible were in circulation within the Jewish community during the time when the NT was being composed. Nonetheless, it is possible that some books had already received Jewish renderings from Hebrew to Syriac (Eastern Aramaic) by the end of the first century A.D. The process that produced the Peshitta, as the standard version of the Syriac became known in Eastern churches, was a long and varied one, similar in that respect to what appears to have occurred with the Septuagint (*see* Syriac Bible). But this takes us beyond the background period of the NT.

4. Latin Versions.
The same holds true for Latin translations, although their genesis seems to have been about a century later, that is, second century A.D., than the early Syriac renderings. Moreover, there are no Latin biblical texts that can be surely connected with Jewish communities. It is not, however, impossible that some Jews in Roman North Africa, where Latin texts first appear among Christians, attempted to produce biblical materials for their non-Semitic speaking/understanding communities.

5. Hebrew-Language Versions.
Writers of the NT had at their disposal not only texts and traditions circulating in Greek and one form or another of Aramaic, but also a number (possibly a considerable number) of texts in Hebrew. Although not technically versions, this material must be taken into account in any evaluation of OT citations or quotations in the NT. Recent discoveries have made it clear that textual diversity characterized the Bible for almost all Jews until the end of the first century A.D. (with the destruction of the *temple and its leadership), when one textual tradition was selected by leading rabbis for each book or block of material and nearly all others were suppressed.

As Jews, NT writers might well have come into contact, for example, with the expansive Hebrew text of the *Torah that later became identified with the *Samaritans. And there is no reason to believe that the array of textual evidence uncovered at Qumran was restricted to that community and its adherents. Full recognition of this phenomenon makes it increasingly difficult to state unequivocally that a given NT quotation of the OT is Septuagintal, since it is possible that the NT writer had access to the same Hebrew *Vorlage* as the did Old Greek translators.

6. Transmission of the New Testament.
Ancient versions, including the two post-NT ones enumerated, play another role with respect to the NT. As the NT was copied over and over again in its Greek original, to say nothing of its numerous translations, some scribes would feel empowered or impelled to correct OT citations on the basis of the biblical text in circulation within the Christian community contemporary with them. To the extent that this text had been influenced at some point by the Septuagint, the targumim, the Peshitta or the Latin, the ancient versions would continue their influence on the NT far after its composition.

See also ARAMAIC LANGUAGE; ARAMAIC TARGUMIM: QUMRAN; HEBREW BIBLE; NEW TESTAMENT VERSIONS, ANCIENT; RABBINIC LITERATURE: TARGUMIM; SEPTUAGINT/GREEK OLD TESTAMENT; SYRIAC BIBLE.

BIBLIOGRAPHY. P. S. Alexander, "Jewish Aramaic Translations of Hebrew Scriptures," in *Mikra,* ed. M. J. Mulder (CRINT 2.1; Assen: Van Gorcum; Philadelphia: Fortress, 1988) 217-54; idem, "Targum, Targumim," *ABD* 6:320-31; D. Barthelemy, *Les devanciers d'Aquila* (VTSup 10; Leiden: E. J. Brill, 1963); D. R. G. Beattie and M. J. McNamara, eds., *The Aramaic Bible: Targums in Their Historical Context* (JSOTSup 166; Sheffield: JSOT, 1994); J. N. Birdsall, "Versions, Ancient (Survey)," *ABD* 6:787-93; J. Bowker, *The Targums and Rabbinic Literature* (Cambridge: Cambridge University Press, 1969); S. P. Brock, *The Bible in the Syriac Tradition* (SEERI Correspondence Course on the Syrian Christian Heritage 1; Kottayam, 1989); idem, "Versions, Ancient (Syriac)," *ABD* 6:794-99; P. B. Dirksen, *An Annotated Bibliography of the Peshitta of the Old Testament* (MPI 5; Leiden: E. J. Brill, 1989); P. B. Dirksen and M. J. Mulder, eds., *The Peshitta* (MPI 4; Leiden: E. J. Brill, 1988); C. Dogniez, *Bibliography of the Septuagint/Bibliographie de la Septante (1970-1993)* (VTSup 60; Leiden: E. J. Brill, 1995); F. Fernandez Marcos, *Introduccion a las Versiones Griegas de la Biblia* (TECC 23; Madrid: CSIC, 1979); L. J. Greenspoon, "Versions, Ancient (Greek)," *ABD* 6:793-94; M. Harl, G. Dorival and O. Munnich, *La Bible Grecque des Septante: Du Judaisme Hellenistique au Christianisme ancien* (ICA; 2d ed.; Paris: Editions du Cerf, 1994); S. Jellicoe, *The Septuagint and Modern Study* (Oxford: Oxford University Press, 1968); B. M. Metzger, "Versions, Ancient," *IDB* 4:749-60; M. K. H. Peters, "Septuagint," *ABD* 5:1093-1104; E. Tov, "The Septuagint," in *Mikra,* ed. M. J. Mulder (CRINT 2.1; Assen: Van Gorcum; Philadelphia: Fortress, 1988) 161-88; idem, *The Text-Critical Use of the Septuagint in Biblical Research* (BSt 8; 2d ed.; Jerusalem: Simor, 1997); M. P. Weitzman, *The Syriac Version of the Old Testament: An Introduction* (UCOP 56; Cambridge: Cambridge University Press, 1999).

L. J. Greenspoon

ORACLES. *See* PROPHETS AND PROPHECY; RELIGION, GRECO-ROMAN; RELIGION, PERSONAL.

ORDINANCES (4Q159, 4Q513, 4Q514). *See* LEGAL TEXTS AT QUMRAN.

OSSUARIES. *See* BURIAL PRACTICES, JEWISH; CAIAPHAS OSSUARY.

P

PAGAN SOURCES IN THE NEW TESTAMENT

Students of the Bible are understandably inclined, given the Jewish matrix of early Christianity, to read the NT wholly in terms of language and idiom found in the *Hebrew Bible and postbiblical *Judaism. These two domains thus constitute the primary, if not lone, ancient source with which the student is typically familiar. If, however, the NT is framed against the background of pan-Hellenic culture, it is reasonable to assume that its ideas, conventions, metaphors, language, literary genre, style and technique mirror that cultural milieu. An early Christian writer expressed the relationship of Christianity to the surrounding world in the following way: "Christians are distinguished from other men neither by country, nor by language, nor by customs. For nowhere do they inhabit cities of their own, nor do they make use of any exceptional dialect, nor do they practice a conspicuous mode of life" (*Diogn.* 5). The NT can be understood as "a book of peasants, fishermen, artisans, travellers by land and sea, fighters and martyrs, . . . [a book] in cosmopolitan Greek with marks of Semitic origin, . . . [a book] of the Imperial age, written at Antioch, Ephesus, Corinth, Rome" (Deissmann, 392).

Language cannot exist independently of culture; nor can culture exist apart from its expression through language. Appreciating the extent to which the NT mirrors the language and idiom of the Greco-Roman world is the thrust of the examination that follows. Probing this relationship will serve to illuminate the world of the NT and thus confirm the maxim that "five words in an original source are worth a thousand words in a secondary source" (Ferguson, xv). The early Christian community, which emerged and proliferated in Greco-Roman culture, expressed itself in the language and thought mode of that cultural context.

1. Assessing Convergence Between Pagan and Early Christian Texts
2. Classifying Convergence Between Pagan and Early Christian Texts
3. Examples of Convergence Between Pagan and Early Christian Texts

1. Assessing Convergence Between Pagan and Early Christian Texts.

The inherent value of studying the NT against the background of extrabiblical tradition material is multifaceted. It can elucidate the meaning of concepts, themes, words and literary strategy. In addition it can shed light on the social, political and religious history of late antiquity, thereby aiding the exegetical and hermeneutical task.

Even though the reader is less likely to explore the NT writers' appropriation of pagan sources than their reliance on the OT or Judaistic texts, a word of caution is in order. Whether one is analyzing classical texts that circulated in the Hellenistic world, texts from the Hebrew Bible or *rabbinic parallels that surface in the NT, a common temptation accompanies the examination of ancient sources. Superficial but erroneous parallels that appear to illuminate the NT might be discovered by unconsciously importing contemporary cultural assumptions into the world of antiquity. Texts that are alien to the NT are to be understood in their own terms and not apart from their literary environment. The tendency of the modern reader may be to describe source and derivation "as if implying literary connection flowing in an inevitable or predetermined direction" (Sandmel, 1). The cautionary reminders of D. E. Aune and F. W. Danker need restatement: there exists the perennial danger that those whose primary interest is early Christian literature will "seize only the more easily portable valuables found in random raids on ancient texts" (Aune 1988, ii); those who have explored the labyrinth of Greco-Roman studies will be familiar with the hazards that await the enthusiastic but unwary seeker (Danker, 7).

While few people have the luxury of being steeped in classical literature, investigating points of contact between Hellenistic and NT writers nevertheless promises rich returns for the study of the NT. Demonstrating the relevance and fruitfulness of comparing NT writings with diverse ancient sources serves as a reminder that all ancient texts, including sacred Scripture, are a reflection of the literary, social, religious and political culture to which they belong. It is this pluriform cultural backdrop that the writers of the NT share with their contemporaries. The greater our capacity to enter the world of the NT equipped with both knowledge and imagination, the more rewarding will be our study and appreciation of the NT as literature.

In seeking to persuade their contemporaries, the NT writers employ not only the language of that era but also the generic forms, stylistic features and literary conventions of their day. Inasmuch as apologetic and evangelistic motives underlay their writings, they adapt, accommodate and modify these tools as part of a literary arsenal in the service of a greater, overriding theological purpose.

Touchpoints between ancient literary genre and that of the NT include story, biography, epistolography, poetry, hymns, *apocalyptic and historiography. Among the literary-rhetorical conventions that are common to both fields are the household code, the diatribe, paraenesis, the chreia, the rhetorical question, the imaginary dialogue, the parable, riddle or proverb, inclusio, the concealment motif and tragedy. On a broader level, the student of the NT encounters an enormously wide range of vocabulary and imagery common to both pagan and early Christian texts. Metaphors of the slave market and institutional *slavery, the wealthy *benefactor, the military, agriculture, the Isthmian games, the *athlete, the *marriage relationship, commerce, circumcision, the *mystery cults, the priesthood, the *ruler cult, medicine and the Asclepius cult are but a few points of literary contact worthy of note.

Similarly, NT writers exploit for their own purposes the rich semantic fields of words and word pictures—for example, *skandalon* ("scandal"), *logos* ("word," "mind," "reason"), *gnōsis* ("knowledge"), *diathēkē* ("covenant"), *autarkeia* ("self-sufficiency"), *stoicheia* ("elemental substances," "heavenly bodies"), *chorēgos* ("wealthy local benefactor"), *prōtotokos* ("firstborn"), *ekklēsia* ("assembly"), *arrabōn* ("deposit," "engagement ring"), *leitourgia* ("public service"), *biastēs* ("violent person") *thriambos* ("military triumph")—that have the effect of translating for the reader the kaleidoscopic implications of the Christian gospel.

2. Classifying Convergence Between Pagan and Early Christian Texts.

Neat and clean distinctions between varieties of literary convergence elude the reader and resist being pressed too far. Such might be illustrated by the distinction between borrowing, adaptation and citation. Any finer distinctions that may be made serve to highlight the redactive interests of the NT writer and the new literary context in which the appropriation is found. General distinctions can be observed and classified according to the following categories, none of which are intended to be all-inclusive or exhaustive.

2.1. Common Idea or Concept. Pagan and NT texts may reflect common themes, concepts or traditions that have divergent theological assumptions. Examples include the broader ancient Near Eastern wisdom tradition (Gospels and James), the idea of dying and rising deities (Gospels and Pauline epistles), the notion of covenant or testament (Gospels, Pauline epistles and Hebrews), Greco-Roman attitudes toward *women (1 Cor 11; 1 Tim 2), and slave-master relationships (Pauline and Pastoral Epistles).

2.2. Common Convention. Elements, customs or conventions from common culture are frequently utilized by the writers of the NT because of their form and function. Among common literary-rhetorical conventions are the household code (Col 3:18—4:1; 1 Pet 2:11—3:12), catalogs of vice and virtue (e.g., Rom 1:29-31; Gal 5:19-21, 22-23; 2 Cor 6:6-8; Phil 4:8; 1 Tim 1:9-10; 4:12; 6:11; 2 Tim 2:22; 3:2-5; 2 Pet 1:5-7), the rhetoric of boasting (2 Cor 10—13), diatribe (e.g., Rom 2:1-16, 17-29; 1 Cor 15:19-33) and imaginary dialogue (e.g., Rom 11:19-21; Tit 1:13-17; Jas 2:1-9, 14-26).

Exemplary cultural customs deriving from

Greco-Roman society that provide the context for particular NT teaching include the eating of meat sold in the marketplace (1 Cor 8:1-13; Acts 15:20, 29) and the veiling of the head (1 Cor 11:2-16). Typically viewed by the modern reader as some form of obscure cultural oddity, the veiling of the head would have been known to Paul from his upbringing in the city of Tarsus, the capital seat of the province of Cilicia. A "university" city, Tarsus was markedly cosmopolitan. Due to its location, the city was a center of trade and commerce and served as a gateway to the East and West. Writing approximately A.D. 110, the *historian Dio Chrysostom, upon visiting the city, makes note of one particular aspect of Tarsian social etiquette. He lavishly praises the conspicuously modest dress of Tarsian women, who are always deeply veiled when they appear in public (Dio Chrysostom *Or.* 7.89). Doubtless this practice would have left a notable impression on Paul when he was confronted with matters of impropriety in the Christian community at Corinth (*see* Head Coverings).

*2.3. **Expansion.*** Concepts or terms may take on high visibility or central importance in the NT that possess marginal significance in broader culture. Notable examples are the Christian virtues of *agapē* and *pistis* (e.g., 1 Cor 13; Col 3:19; Eph 5:25), as well as humility and poverty of spirit (cf., e.g., the introductory chapters of *Aristotle's *Eth. Nic.* over against Mt 5:3-10).

*2.4. **Reminiscence.*** The reminiscence bears slight resemblance to another tradition, story, concept or occurrence from common culture. In the Lukan account of Paul's work in *Athens, the apostle to the Gentiles is portrayed as adapting himself in a fluid manner to the dialectical habits of Athenian life, where he "disputed . . . in the agora daily with any whom he encountered" (Acts 17:17). It was in the agora, Athens's marketplace, that Socrates argued and carried on discourse. Perhaps Luke (Acts 17:18: "Others said [of Paul], 'He seems to be a preacher of foreign deities'") has in mind the tradition regarding Socrates, recounted by Xenophon: "Socrates does wrongly, for he does not acknowledge the gods which the state acknowledges; rather, he introduces other new-fashioned gods" (Xenophon *Mem.* 1.1.1). Not only Socrates but also Anaxagoras (500-428 B.C.) and Protagoras (480-410 B.C.) were accused in Athens of introducing "foreign gods." A century prior to Paul, *Cicero had criticized the *Stoic philosopher Chrysippus for embracing "unknown gods" (Cicero *Nat. Deor.* 1.15.39). Luke may well be attempting to present Paul in the great philosophic tradition.

Paul's dialectical habits are displayed in his epistle to the Romans as well. A faint resemblance to *Aristotle's discussion of the unwritten law of nature (Aristotle *Rhet.* 1.15.8) can be detected in Romans 2:12-15. Aristotle writes that "it is part of a better man to make use of and abide by the unwritten rather than the written law."

*2.5. **Parallel.*** A parallel shows direct correspondence to certain elements of a tradition, concept, form or function. Representative NT parallels to pagan tradition material include miracles stories (Gospels), walking on water (Gospels; cf. in Hesiod [*Astron.* 4.182] the grandson of Poseidon possessing the power to walk on the waves of the sea) and the Last Supper (Gospels) as contrasted with pagan cultic meals.

In form and function, the household codes of Colossians 3:18—4:1 and 1 Peter 2:11—3:12 mirror discussions on household management that appear in Aristotle (Aristotle *Pol.* I 1253b 1-14; *Eth. Nic.* V 1134b 9-18; VIII 1160a-1161a), *Seneca (*Ep.* 94.1-3) and other Stoic writers. The NT writers' appropriation of the household management code would appear to have an apologetic function; it serves as part of a response to Greco-Roman critics who may be slandering the Christian community. This response entails attitudes toward authority and how to rightly order social relationships (*see* Family and Household).

*2.6. **Borrowing.*** NT writers may borrow a pagan tradition, concept or convention without any clarification or explanation for the reader and without transposing or adapting it to a different literary context. Background knowledge on the part of the audience would appear to be assumed. Numerous examples of borrowing in the NT can be cited. Religious superstition (*deisidaimonia*) is viewed positively in antiquity by some and negatively by others. Writing in the second century B.C., Polybius (*Hist.* 6.56) understands *deisidaimonia* as a contributing factor in the success and cohesion of the *Roman Empire: "The quality in which the Roman commonwealth is the most distinctly superior is in my opinion the nature of their religious convictions. I believe that it is the very thing which among other peoples is an object of reproach. I mean superstition [*deisidaimonia*], which maintains the cohesion of the Roman state" (LCL).

Cicero observes that Roman citizens "in piety, in devotion to religion, . . . have excelled every race and every nation" (Cicero *De Div.* 9.19 [LCL]). Exploiting this positive sense of *deisidaimonia* in his opening remarks to the Council of the Areopagus, of which Cicero had been a member one hundred years earlier, the apostle Paul commends his audience: "Men of Athens, I perceive that in every respect you are very religious [*deisidaimonesterous*], for as I passed along and observed your objects of devotion" (Acts 17:22b-23a). Properly understood, this reference is a commendation, intended to build a bridge with the audience.

NT themes are dependent on borrowing as well. The message of the NT Apocalypse is framed against the backdrop of the imperial cult, which supplies the principal motif and ancillary imagery that are critical to John's presentation of the Lamb. Asian readers are painfully aware of the all-encompassing nature, majesty and irresistible character of the Roman imperium. In Titus 1:12, meant to illustrate the need for integrity in the life of an elder, the reader encounters a popular byword about Cretans ("Cretans are always liars, evil beasts, lazy gluttons"), attributed to the sixth-century B.C. *poet Epimenides of Crete and borrowed for the sake of comparison. Some NT scholars attribute the proverb to the third-century B.C. poet Callimachus, whose *Hymn to Zeus* contains only the expression "Cretans are always liars."

Perhaps most frequently borrowed by the writers of the NT are sundry images that derive from metropolitan life in the first century. Imagery abounds from Corinthian life as mirrored in Paul's letters to the church in Corinth. Polished bronze mirrors, the theater, the proconsul's judgment seat, agriculture, *architecture and building, the Isthmian Games and local *temples all add color to Pauline correspondence. Given the apostle's emphasis on unity and diversity among different members of Christ's body, it would be natural for him to conceive of unity and diversity in terms of the local Asclepius temple in Corinth. In 1 Corinthians 12:12-31 Paul mentions ears, eyes, hands and more honorable and less honorable parts of the body. It is plausible that he is alluding to the huge number of clay figurines of dismembered body parts scattered throughout the Asclepion that represented afflicted members cured by the deity. In Paul's day, these terra cotta offerings consisted of heads, hands and feet, arms and legs, breasts and genitals, eyes and ears. Against the background of the Asclepion the Corinthian believers would have been reminded in the most vivid of terms of what they should not be—divided, dead, unconnected members of the body (Murphy-O'Connor, 161-67). The Asclepius cult provides the apostle with forceful imagery to underscore the need for Christian unity.

In his exhortations to the Philippian believers, Paul "forgets what lies behind" and "stretches forward, pressing on for the prize" (Phil 3:13-14). The apostle may well have in mind not the *athletic contests of the Greek games, as many commentators have assumed, rather the chariot racing of either *Rome or the Isthmian Games, which depict a much more perilous sport and supply graphic imagery to the audience in *Philippi, an intensely loyal Roman colony. Standing braced on a small platform over the chariot's wheels and axle, the charioteer bent forward with arms outstretched toward the horses' rumps, reins wrapped tightly—lethally—around the arms. The driver, in accordance with his skills, was fully at the mercy of his charging steeds. Should he fall or be pulled from the chariot, his fate was often an excruciating death. Any ill-timed glance behind at the competition, any distraction by the roaring crowd, could be fatal (cf. the graphic description of the chariot race in Ovid *Met.* 15). One thing and one thing alone remained in the eye of the driver: to reach the end of the race.

Not least, the *letters to the seven churches in the NT Apocalypse are replete with contemporary images meaningful to the audience. The initial letter, addressed to the Ephesian Christians, appropriates the image imprinted on *coins of Ephesus showing a date palm, sacred to Artemis and symbol of her life: "To the one overcoming I will give to eat from the tree of life" (Rev 2:7). Similarly, the concluding letter, addressed to Christians in Laodicea (Rev 3:14-22), borrows multiple images from the city's banking industry (3:17, 18), inadequate water source and hot springs (3:15, 16), garment industry (3:17, 18) and medical school (3:17, 18).

2.7. Transposition. Material or traditions might be transplanted by the NT writers into a new literary context with a different thematic emphasis. Examples of transposition abound in Paul's ministry. In his speech before the Areopagus Council (Acts 17:22-31), the apostle borrows from literary sources meaningful to his audience. His qualification of the divine nature entails a strategy utilizing common ground sustained by partial citations from well-known poets. The statement "In him we live, move and have our being" (Acts 17:28a) expresses the Stoic belief in kinship with God. No pagan *philosopher would reject this assertion, since any Stoic worth his salt readily conceded that the divine fills the universe, allowing a union to exist. This saying is generally attributed to the poet Epimenides of Crete (*Clem. Misc.* 1.14.59), with traces of resemblance in Callimachus.

The second literary allusion at the Areopagus, "We are his offspring," stems from the third-century B.C. Stoic philosopher Aratus, who hailed from Paul's native Cilicia. Written in honor of Zeus and titled *Phaenomena,* Aratus's poetry is an interpretation of constellations and weather signs. The poetic verse from which Paul borrows reads "In all things each of us needs Zeus, for we are also his offspring" (Aratus *Phaen.* 5), and it closely resembles the verse of Cleanthes, a contemporary of Aratus, whose *Hymn to Zeus* reads, "Unto you may all flesh speak, for we are your offspring." M. E. Boring and others note the generally widespread use of the works of Aratus in the pedagogy of late antiquity. Transposed by the apostle, the words "his offspring" are sure to resonate with any Stoic present in his audience.

*2.8. **Adaptation.*** Material that is adapted mirrors a less direct correspondence than does material that is borrowed. Adapted material is adjusted or modified to the theological and redactive purposes of the NT writer. Writing the Christians at Colossae, Paul uses the metaphor of a commercial loan to interpret the redemptive work of Christ, wherein the debt that stood against us has been cancelled (Col 2:14); the apostle's wording implies that the *cheirographon,* the bond, has been publicly displayed as cancelled. A second image follows on the heels of the *cheirographon* (Col 2:15): that of the Roman victory procession, in which conquered military leaders and prisoners were paraded through the city behind the chariot of their victor, free for all to behold (*see* Roman Triumph). Tacitus (*Ann.* 8.36) describes one such triumphal procession occurring during the reign of Claudius, in the year 51, roughly a decade before the epistle to the Colossians is thought to have been penned (see also 2 Cor 2:14-16).

The worthy-hymn of Revelation 5 adapts language and imagery derived from the imperial cult (Aune 1983; Charles 1993). With the scroll of Revelation 5, which has been sealed in accordance with Roman stipulations and represents history from the divine standpoint, the absolute sovereignty of the one sitting on the throne and the Lamb is in focus. The vision of the Lamb mediated by John is heavily imbued with imperial overtones. The Lion-Lamb who is simultaneously savior and conqueror is revealed in terms that are poignantly familiar to a first-century audience. Extolling the Lamb in categories normally reserved for the Caesar—"might," "power," "strength," "glory," "honor," "riches," "wisdom" and "blessing"—John portrays Jesus in a manner that causes even the glories of the imperial throne to pale by contrast.

*2.9. **Imitation.*** The category of imitation implies a strong correspondence in literary-linguistic form or structure without any correspondence to substance or content. The dominant genre employed by NT writers, the epistle (twenty-one of twenty-seven NT documents), reflects the widespread use of epistolography in Greco-Roman culture, whether diplomatic *letters, petitions, family letters or letters of introduction and recommendation. Epistolary treatises and letter essays are known to have steadily increased in later antiquity. The NT epistle, while comparable to the Greek letter in terms of fixed formal patterns, phraseology and function, tends to be somewhat longer than its pagan counterpart, a phenomenon attributable in large measure to its purpose (i.e., theological instruction).

In addition to imitating generic form, NT writers also employ standard literary-rhetorical conventions such as the *rhetorical question, the diatribe or the imaginary dialogue. The latter two features figure prominently in Romans and James, where discussions of God's justice (Rom 2), an individual's justification (Rom 3), the function of the law (Rom 7) and the relationship of faith and works (Jas 2) proceed.

*2.10. **Allusion or Citation.*** This category consists of traditional material utilized by the NT writer in which the reference is clearly to a known text or source, verbatim or near-verbatim and the literary context is not significantly altered. The citation by Paul of Menander ("Bad company corrupts good character," 1 Cor 15:33b), who had introduced the New Comedy in Athens, rings true regardless of culture, era or audience and certainly in Corinth (see *Fragments of Menander* [LCL]). Similarly, 1 Timothy 6:10 is an echo of Bion, the first-century B.C. Greek poet, quoted in Stobaeus (*Anth.* 3.417): "Bion the Sophist said, 'The love of money is the matrix of all evils.'" This timeless maxim holds true cross-culturally, much the same way as that of Menander.

3. Examples of Convergence Between Pagan and Early Christian Texts.

3.1. Gospels. Mt 5:25-26 = Lk 12:57-59 (Synoptic reflections of duties and liability as spelled out by Roman law, on which see Wolff)

Mt 8:18-20 (*chreia*); 8:21-22 (*chreia*)

Mt 13:1-52 = Mk 4:1-34 = Lk 8:1-18 (cf. Hellenistic analogies to Jesus' parables but without the *eschatological element; see Aesop's fables, which remind the hearer of moral choices, the frequent necessity of personal sacrifice and the priority of wisdom in social dealings; see Ernst)

Mt 14:22-33 = Mk 6:45-52 = Jn 6:15-21 (cf. Hesiod *Astron.* 4.182, in which Orion, grandson of Poseidon, has power to walk on the waves of the sea as on dry ground)

Mt 15:19 = Mk 7:21-22 (catalog of vices)

Jn 1:1-4, 14 (cf. Stoic cosmology; Zeno in Diogenes Laertius *Vit.* 7.87; Cicero *De Fin. Bon. et Mal.* 3.6; Epictetus *Diss.* 1.20; Diogenes Laertius *Vit.* 7.88; Eusebius *Praep. Ev.* 15.15—by which the *logos,* Reason and Purpose, were understood to pervade the universe; a seed of this universal principle, *logos spermatikos,* was thought to dwell within humans)

Jn 4:43-44 (*chreia*)

Jn 19:12 (according to Philo *Leg. Gai.* 161, and Josephus *Ant.* 18.3.1-2, 5 §§55-62, 85-89, in A.D. 31 the emperor Tiberius deposed his turncoat, anti-Jewish confidant Sejanus, head of the Praetorian Guard, and ordered provincial *governors to treat the Jews with more respect; the Jews' success in crucifying Jesus required the assistance of Pilate, who, as political realities would have it, was a close confidant of Sejanus; hence the politically loaded reference to "a friend of Caesar")

3.2. Luke-Acts. Lk 3:10-11 (*chreia*)

Lk 9:49-50 (*chreia*)

Acts 14:11-13 (cf. Ovid *Met.* 8.610-700, a late first-century B.C. depiction of a similar appearance of the incognito god, with Jupiter and Mercury corresponding to Zeus and Hermes)

Acts 17:17-18 (cf. Xenophon *Mem.* 1.1.1, and Cicero *Nat. Deor.* 1.15.39, regarding the charge of preaching "foreign" or "unknown" deities)

Acts 17:22 (cf. Polybius *Hist.* 6.56, and Cicero *De Div.* 9.19, regarding *deisidaimonia,* religous superstition/devotion, conceived as a positive Roman virtue)

Acts 17:28-29 (cf. Aratus *Phaen.* 5; Cleanthes *Hymn to Zeus;* Callimachus *Hymn to Zeus;* and *Clement. Misc.* 1.14.59, regarding Paul's appropriation of Stoic philosopher-poets)

Acts 18:2 (cf. Suetonius *Claudius* 25, which reports on the Claudian edict resulting in the expulsion of Jews from Rome arising from disturbances instigated by one "Chrestus" [*impulsore Christo*])

3.3. Pauline Epistles. Rom 1:26-27 (cf. Plato *Leg.* 1.636; 8.841; *Phaed.* 251, on the analogous argument from the animal world and belief that same-sex relationships are contrary to nature)

Rom 1:29-31 (catalog of vices)

Rom 2:1-5, 17-24 (imaginary dialog)

Rom 2:12-15 (cf. Aristotle *Rhet.* 1.15.3-8, on a parallel understanding of the "unwritten law" of nature)

Rom 7:7-25 (imaginary dialog)

Rom 11:19-21 (imaginary dialog)

Rom 13:4 (cf. Tacitus *Hist.* 3.68, regarding the use of the technical term *ius gladii,* the "law of the sword," by which was conveyed magisterial sentence of punishment by death)

1 Cor 1:18—2:16 (discourse against the background of Greek notions of wisdom)

1 Cor 3:5-15 (building and agriculture metaphors)

1 Cor 3:16-17 (the temple metaphor)

1 Cor 4:15 (cf. descriptions of the *paidagōgos,* the guardian, guide or tutor, in Xenophon *Laced.* 3.1: "When a boy ceases to be child, and begins to be a lad, others release him from his moral tutor and his schoolmaster: he is then no longer under a ruler and is allowed to go his own way"; also Plato *Lys.* 208; Diogenes Laertius *Vit.* 3.92; and Philo *Leg. Gai.* 53)

1 Cor 5:10-11 (catalog of vices)

1 Cor 6:9-10 (catalog of vices)

1 Cor 6:19-20 (the temple metaphor)

1 Cor 7:22-23 (the slave metaphor)

1 Cor 8:1-13 (wordplay on *gnōsis*)

1 Cor 9:24-27 (the Isthmian Games metaphor)

1 Cor 11:2-16 (common convention: the veiling of the head)

1 Cor 12:12-27 (the body metaphor most

likely borrowed from the Asclepion)

1 Cor 15:32a (a possible rhetorical metaphor for ideological conflict; cf. Ign. *Rom.* 5.1)

1 Cor 15:32b (possible citation from Plutarch *Mor.* 1098)

1 Cor 15:33 (citation from the New Comedian Menander *Thais* [*Fragments of Menander*, LCL])

1 Cor 15:35 (imaginary dialog)

2 Cor 1:22 (adaptation of the *arrabōn* ["deposit," "down payment," "wedding ring"] metaphor)

2 Cor 2:14-16 (the triumphal procession metaphor; cf. Tacitus *Ann.* 8.36)

2 Cor 6:6-8, 9-10 (catalogs of virtue and vice)

2 Cor 10—13 (the rhetoric of boasting; cf. Cicero *De Inv.* 1.16.22, and the textbook *Ad Herennium* 1.5.8, on specific ways to influence an audience with self-reference and self-praise respectively)

2 Cor 12:20-21 (catalogs of vice)

Gal 3:24 (the *paidagōgos* metaphor; see 1 Cor 4:15)

Gal 5:19-21, 22-23 (catalogs of vice and virtue)

Eph 1:14 (adaptation of the *arrabōn* metaphor; see 2 Cor 1:22)

Eph 2:19-22 (the citizenship and building metaphors)

Eph 4:31 (catalog of vices)

Eph 4:32 (catalog of virtues)

Eph 5:9 (catalog of virtues)

Eph 5:22-33 (the marriage metaphor)

Eph 6:11-17 (the soldier metaphor)

Phil 1:21 (cf. Aeschylus *Prom.* 747, and Sophocles *Antig.* 463-64, in which death is gain because of life filled with suffering)

Phil 2:17 (the libation metaphor; cf. Ign. *Rom.* 2.2, where cultic associations appear to be confirmed)

Phil 3:13-14 (cf. the description in Ovid *Met.* 15, of the driver in a chariot race; see 2.6 above)

Phil 4:8 (catalog of virtues)

Col 2:14 (the bond metaphor; see 2.8 above)

Col 2:15 (the triumph metaphor; see 2.8 above)

Col 3:12 (catalog of virtues)

Col 3:18—4:1 (household code)

1 Thess 2:6-7 (cf. Dio Chrysostom *Or.* 32, on Stoic and Cynic recourse to gentleness over harshness)

1 Thess 5:3 (the words "For when they are saying 'Peace and safety'" may be an allusion to the OT *prophets' denunciation of those who say "peace when there is no peace" [e.g., Jer 6:14; Ezek 13:10]; however, it may be a reference to the peace and safety, i.e., an absence of war based on **Pax Romana*, popularly associated with Roman imperium)

1 Thess 5:8 (the soldier metaphor; see Eph 6:11-17)

2 Thess 2:5-12 (plausibly an allusion to the restraining influence of Roman imperium, which maintains social order; cf. Rom 13:1-7)

3.4. Pastoral Epistles. 1 Tim 6:10 (cf. Bion in Stobaeus *Anth.* 3.417 on *philargyrian,* the love of money as the "matrix of all evils")

1 Tim 6:11 (catalog of virtues)

1 Tim 6:12 (the soldier metaphor)

2 Tim 2:22 (catalog of virtues)

2 Tim 3:10-11 (catalog of virtues)

2 Tim 4:6 (the libation metaphor; see Phil 2:17)

Tit 1:12 (citation of Epimenides of Crete, echoes of which appear also in Callimachus's *Hymn to Zeus)*

Tit 1:13 (imaginary dialog)

Tit 3:3 (catalog of vices)

3.5. ***General Epistles.*** Jas 1:19-20, 22-25, 26; 3:1-12 (cf. Plutarch *The Education of Children,* which utilizes the "mirror of remembrance" as a teaching device in the context of moral *education, wherein, significantly, control of the tongue and control of one's anger are incorporated)

Jas 2:1-9 (imaginary dialog with rhetorical questions)

Jas 2:14-26 (imaginary dialog with rhetorical questions)

Jas 3:15, 17 (catalogs of vice and virtue)

1 Pet 2:1 (catalog of vices)

1 Pet 2:11—3:12 (household code)

1 Pet 3:8 (catalog of virtues)

1 Pet 4:3, 14 (catalogs of vice)

2 Pet 1:5-7 (catalog of virtues)

2 Pet 2:22 (cf. *Ahiq.* 8.18 [Syr.]; also Horace *Ep.* 1.2.26)

2 Pet 3:3-4 (cf. Diogenes Laertius *Vit.* 10.73 on the Epicurean cosmological argument against divine providence)

2 Pet 3:5-7 (Seneca *Nat. Quaest.* 3.29; Plutarch *Mor.* 1077; and Diogenes Laertius *Vit.* 7.134 on Stoic notions of cosmic conflagration)

Jude 13 (cf. the grotesque account in Hesiod *Theog.* 147-206, of Aphrodite's birth and parallels to Jude's "wild waves of the sea, casting up the foam of their shame")

3.6. ***Revelation.*** Rev 2:7—3:11 (cf. Ramsay 1904; Blaiklock 1951; and Hemer for background to the abundance of imagery drawn from cosmopolitan life in the cities of *Asia Minor)

Rev 4—5 (the imperial cult motif)

See also ART AND ARCHITECTURE: GRECO-ROMAN; ATHLETICS; BENEFACTOR; CIRCUSES AND GAMES; CIVIC CULTS; DIATRIBE; EDUCATION: JEWISH AND GRECO-ROMAN; EPISTOLARY THEORY; FAMILY AND HOUSEHOLD; GYMNASIA AND BATHS; HEAD COVERINGS; HOSPITALITY; INSCRIPTIONS AND PAPYRI: GRECO-ROMAN; MARRIAGE; PATRONAGE; PHILOSOPHY; POETRY, HELLENISTIC; PROPHECY, GRECO-ROMAN; RELIGION, GRECO-ROMAN; RELIGION, PERSONAL; ROMANCES/NOVELS, ANCIENT; RULER CULT; SCHOLARSHIP, GREEK AND ROMAN; SOCIAL VALUES AND STRUCTURES; TEMPLES, GRECO-ROMAN; THEATERS; TRAVEL AND TRADE; VICE AND VIRTUE LISTS; WRITING AND LITERATURE: GRECO-ROMAN.

BIBLIOGRAPHY. D. E. Aune, ed., *Greco-Roman Literature and the New Testament* (SBLSBS 21; Atlanta: Scholars Press, 1988); idem, "The Influence of Roman Imperial Court Ceremonial on the Apocalypse of John," *BR* 28 (1983) 5-26; idem, *The New Testament in Its Literary Environment* (LEC 8; Philadelphia: Westminster, 1987); C. K. Barrett, ed., *The New Testament Background: Selected Documents* (rev. ed.; San Francisco: Harper & Row, 1987); C. K. Barrett and C.-J. Thornton, eds., *Texte zur Umwelt des Neuen Testaments* (UTB; 2d ed.; Tübingen: Mohr Siebeck, 1991); E. M. Blaiklock, *Cities of the New Testament* (Westwood, NJ: Revell, 1965); idem, *The Seven Churches* (London: Marshall, Morgan & Scott, 1951); M. E. Boring et al., eds., *Hellenistic Commentary to the New Testament* (Nashville: Abingdon, 1995); J. D. Charles, "Engaging the (Neo)Pagan Mind: Paul's Encounter with Athenian Culture as a Model of Cultural Apologetics," *TJ* n.s. 16 (1995) 47-62; idem, "Imperial Pretensions and the Throne-Vision of the Lamb: Observations on the Function of Revelation 5," *CTR* 7 (1993) 85-97; F. W. Danker, *Benefactor: Epigraphic Study of a Greco-Roman and New Testament Semantic Field* (St. Louis: Clayton, 1982); G. A. Deissmann, *Bible Studies: Contributions Chiefly from Papyri and Inscriptions to the History of the Language, the Literature and the Religion of Hellenistic Judaism and Primitive Christianity* (Edinburgh: T & T Clark, 1901); M. Ernst, "Hellenistische Analogien zu neutestamentlichen Gleichnissen," in *Ein Gott, Eine Offenbarung: Beiträge zur biblischen Exegese, Theologie und Spiritualität,* ed. F. V. Reiterer (Würzburg: Echter, 1991) 461-80; E. Ferguson, *Backgrounds of Early Christianity* (Grand Rapids, MI: Eerdmans, 1987); D. E. Garland, "Background Studies and New Testament Interpretation," in *New Testament Criticism and Interpretation,* ed. D. A. Black and D. S. Dockery (Grand Rapids, MI: Zondervan, 1991) 349-76; D. W. J. Gill and C. Gempf, eds., *The Book of Acts in Its Graeco-Roman Setting* (BAFCS 2; Grand Rapids, MI: Eerdmans, 1994); W. R. Halliday, *The Pagan Background of Early Christianity* (Liverpool: University of Liverpool, 1925); C. Hemer, *The Letters to the Seven Churches of Asia in Their Local Setting* (JSNTSup 11; Sheffield: JSOT, 1986); M. Hengel, *Jews, Greeks and Barbarians: Aspects of the Hellenization of Judaism in the Pre-Christian Period* (Philadelphia: Fortress, 1980); G. H. R. Horsley, ed., *New Documents Illustrating Early Christianity* (Marrickville, Australia: Macquarie University, 1989) vol. 5; H. G. Kippenberg and G. A. Wewers, *Textbuch zur neutestamentlichen Zeitgeschichte* (NTD 8; Göttingen: Vandenhoeck & Ruprecht, 1979); S. R. Llewelyn, ed., *New Documents Illustrating Early Christianity* (Marrickville: Macquarie University, 1992) vol. 6; S. R. Llewelyn and R. A. Kearsley, eds., *New Documents Illustrating Early Christianity* (Marrickville: Macquarie University, 1993) vol. 7; P. Marshall, *Enmity at Corinth: Social Conventions in Paul's Relations with the Corinthians* (WUNT 2.23; Tübingen: Mohr Siebeck, 1987); J. Murphy-O'Connor, *St. Paul's Corinth: Texts and Archaeology* (GNS 6; Wilmington, DE: Michael Glazier, 1983); J. H. Neyrey, "The Form and Background of the Polemic in 2 Peter," *JBL* 99 (1980) 407-31; W. M. Ramsay, *The Cities of St. Paul: Their Influence on His Life and Thought* (London: Hodder & Stoughton, 1907); idem, *The Letters to the Seven Churches of Asia* (London: Hodder & Stoughton, 1904); S. Sandmel, "Parallelomania," *JBL* 81 (1962) 1-13; G. Strecker and U. Schnelle, eds., *Neuer Wettstein: Texte zum Neuen Testament aus Griechentum und Hellenismus* (2 vols.; Berlin: Walter de Gruyter, 1995, 1997); P. Wendland, *Die hellenistisch-römische Kultur in ihren Beziehungen zu Judentum und Christentum* (HNT 1.2; Tübingen: Mohr Siebeck, 1907); J. Wiseman, "Corinth and Rome I: 228 BC—AD 267," *ANRW* 2.7.1 (1979) 438-548; H. J. Wolff, "Consensual Contracts in the Papyri?" *TAPA* 72 (1941) 56-71.

J. D. Charles

PANTHEON, GREEK AND ROMAN. *See* POLYTHEISM.

PAPYRI, PALESTINIAN

When one thinks of the papyri documents, one typically thinks of those found in Egypt. Whereas the vast majority of papyrus documents have come from Egypt, there have been a number of significant discoveries in Palestine as well. Their importance for understanding the background to the NT cannot be underestimated.

1. Greek Papyri Found in Palestine
2. Significant Manuscript Archives
3. Conclusion

1. Greek Papyri Found in Palestine.
A survey of the papyrological finds of the Roman Near East (Cotton, Cockle and Millar) shows that more than six hundred documentary texts have been discovered in that area. The documents cover a wide range, from a few letters or a simple list of names to lengthier contracts, and the like. The substances on which these documents are written covers the usual range of ephemeral materials, including papyrus, wood, leather and ostraka. The languages also cover Greek, Latin, Hebrew, a number of Aramaic dialects and a few scraps of others.

What is most significant to note, however, is that *Greek is the dominant language of these papyri. Of the roughly 600 documents, 400 of them are in Greek. Of the roughly 155 documents found in Judea/Syria Palestina from the first to the third centuries A.D., around 54 of these are in Greek. What becomes clear through this evidence is the widespread use of Greek throughout the Roman world of the time, including in the eastern part of the empire (*see* Roman East), of which Palestine was a part. To be sure, some of these documents were written by non-Jews who came from outside of the area (e.g., DJD 2 [= P.Mur.], no. 114, a document acknowledging a debt written by a Roman soldier), and some are written later than is germane for the period being investigated here.

Nevertheless, a number of others are of more direct relevance. For example, there are letters in Greek that have been found at Masada and are thought mostly to originate with Jews. One document from Masada in Greek may be from as early as A.D. 25-35 (Doc. Masada 740), but the vast majority are from the period of the First Jewish Revolt (A.D. 66-73; *see* Jewish Wars with Rome). These include a letter from Judah to Abascantus regarding a delivery of lettuce (Doc. Masada 741), instructions regarding a delivery (Doc. Masada 248; cf. Doc. Masada 249) and several ledgers or lists of names (Doc. Masada 244, 247 [bilingual with Latin], 250, 251, 254), as well as a number of fragmentary texts. What is especially interesting to note is that at least one of these documents is an abecedaria (Doc. Masada 782-83).

There are also a number of legal and other financial texts written in Greek that involve Jews. Some of these are records of accounts and the like (e.g., DJD 2 [= P.Mur.], nos. 89-107, 118-21, 123-25). There is also possibly a school exercise in this group (DJD 2 [= P.Mur.], no. 122). One is a double deed contract dated to A.D. 124 for remarriage (a double deed contract involved the contract being written twice, with one copy sealed as a permanent record and the other exposed for reference) between two Jews, Elaios and Salome, who had been divorced and then reconciled, along with payment of a dowry (DJD 2 [= P.Mur.], no. 115). The original editors note that this rare practice of remarriage (*see* Marriage) is paralleled by a few other papyri from Egypt (e.g., BGU IV 1101 [13 B.C.]), and seems to reflect typically Greco-Roman practices even by Jews. (The editors refer here to syncretism, but this appears to be an instance of Jews living by the legal conventions of the Greco-Roman world, as might have been expected.) Similar is a fragmentary cancelled marriage double deed contract between two Jews, Aqabas and Selampious (?), dated to A.D. 130 (DJD 27 [= XḤev/Se Gr.], no. 69, probably from the Naḥal Ḥever Cave of Letters). This text also probably originated near Hebron. Another marriage contract also involves a woman named Salome, here marrying a man named Aurelius (DJD 2 [= P. Mur.], no. 116). The fragmentary text cannot be dated precisely but probably dates to the first half of the second century.

A last example is an example of legal proceedings between two Jewish women, Mariam and Salome, and a Roman soldier (DJD 2 [= P.Mur.], no. 113). The fragmentary nature of the text makes it uncertain regarding the nature of the litigation. Paleographically the text has been dated to the second half of the second century A.D.

2. Significant Manuscript Archives.
Among these significant findings in Palestine of

Greek papyrus letters and documents, there are two particular archives worth noting.

2.1. The Bar Kokhba Letters in Greek. One of the most significant papyrus finds in Palestine has been the *Hebrew, *Aramaic and especially Greek letters from the so-called Cave of Letters in Wadi Habra/Naḥal Ḥever from the Bar Kokhba archive (designated P.Yadin). Among the fifteen letters found in the Bar Kokhba archive, two of the letters are in Greek. Arguably the most interesting of all of these documents is P. Yadin *52 (= 5/6Ḥev 52 and SB VIII 9843). The second Greek letter is P. Yadin *59 (= 5/6Ḥev 59 = SB VIII 9844). The first letter is from a certain Soumaios to Jonathe and Masabala. Although this letter has been edited numerous times, there are still difficulties with it. The issues can only be summarized here. One concerns whether the author of the letter, Soumaios, is Simon Ben Kosiba, the leader of the Second Jewish revolt (A.D. 132-35). A second factor is the reconstruction of line 13, which seems to indicate the reason for the letter's having been written in Greek: "I have written the letter in Greek because the [blank] was not found to write in Hebrew." Proposals to fill this gap have included the word *desire* (*horman*); a name, such as Herman (*herman*), although any name of suitable length could do; and the word *opportunity* (*ophormas*). A third and final issue to mention is the use of the opening *chairein* ("greeting") and the closing *errōso* ("farewell"), which are the standard Greek epistolary formulas.

Although the letter remains problematic, several conclusions can be drawn from it. The first is that the letter is clearly written in the form of the standard Hellenistic *letter, with the usual epistolary formulas (including greetings and closing). Second, the letter confirms the multilingual milieu of first- and second-century Palestine. We may still not know the reason the letter was written in Greek, but written in Greek it was. Third, this letter helps to dispute attempts to link language, ethnicity and region in a simplistic or unitary way (see Porter for recent discussion, including an edition and translation of the letter).

2.2. The Babatha Archive. The Babatha archive (see Lewis; Porter), arguably the most important archive for a discussion of this nature, comes from the so-called Cave of Letters in Wadi Habra/Naḥal Ḥever (designated alternatively as P.Yadin or P.Babatha), to which further similar texts have been added in recent publications (designated P. Se'elim, although they probably also originated in the Cave of Letters; DJD 27). The Babatha archive has texts in Nabatean, Palestinian Aramaic and Greek. A second, somewhat similar archive has recently been identified and published from the Cave of Letters, but it contains only six Greek documents (DJD 27 nos. 60-65, plus one in Aramaic, DJD 27 no. 12). The Babatha archive consists of thirty-six or thirty-seven items, twenty-six of which are Greek documents (nine of these with subscriptions and signatures in Aramaic and/or Nabatean), the rest being in Nabatean and Aramaic.

Babatha was a woman of some financial status, although not from the upper or noble class of Jewish residents of the province of Arabia. She was apparently married twice. Her first husband, Joshua, died, leaving her with an orphaned son placed in the care of guardians. She married a second time, to a man named Judah, who was already married to a woman named Miriam (polygamy was apparently more widespread among Jews during this time than many have recognized). When he died two years later, Babatha became embroiled in a number of legal battles, since her husband's second wife and family failed to provide her with the dowry to which she was legally entitled, including providing an adequate means of support for her son. As a result, she was sued and countersued, through a guardian or lord, as per Roman law.

Babatha's archive spans the years of A.D. 94 to 132, many articles being precisely dated, and some of the documents apparently overlap with the start of the Second Jewish revolt. Her residence was in Arabia, in the village of Maoza on the southeastern side of the Dead Sea. It appears that, when the revolution broke out, she, along with other villagers, may have gone to Engedi, which was a stronghold of the revolutionaries, probably fleeing to the caves when events turned against them. She apparently took her most important legal documents, spanning almost forty years of litigation and establishing her legal claim to a variety of properties, along with a number of valuable artifacts, for a time when she might need them to establish her claims. Whether she died in the Cave of Letters is not known.

Included in the archive are the following Greek documents, many of them double documents: a series of texts regarding her orphaned son and his guardians (P.Yadin 27-30), including extracts of council minutes on the appointments of the guardians (P.Yadin 12), a petition to the Roman governor regarding the care of the son (P.Yadin 13), a summons of the guardians (P.Yadin 14) and a deposition (P.Yadin 15); several financial documents, including a census report that establishes her wealth (P.Yadin 16); two documents regarding her first husband's daughter (P.Yadin 18, 19), perhaps implying that the daughter was also in the cave; and a series of litigation-related documents concerning Babatha's inheritance when her second husband died (P.Yadin 20-26). A number of fragmentary texts also appear to be financial or administrative documents (P.Yadin 31-35). There was also a marriage contract for Salome Komaise (P.Yadin 37), a woman from the same village (her archive has now been published as well).

This archive indicates that Babatha was fully conversant with and involved in the Roman legal system of the time, even if she herself did not speak or write Greek (this cannot be determined). This social-political system apparently allowed for, or even encouraged, the suitable documents to be recorded, filed and preserved in Greek, no matter what other languages may also have been used. Since Arabia had only been a province since A.D. 106, by the time of direct Roman rule over the area there was already a distinct and clear understanding and use of the Roman legal system. Whereas indigenous Semitic languages continued to be used, these documents illustrate that the language of commerce, trade and governmental administration, including the courts, was Greek.

3. Conclusion.

Most NT interpreters associate Greek documentary papyri with the abundant finds in Egypt from the nineteenth and twentieth centuries. The result of this categorization has led some to think that the Egyptian situation is distinctly different from that of the eastern Mediterranean. The find of significant numbers and types of documentary papyri from the Roman East has confirmed that in many respects the Egyptian papyrological situation can probably stand as representative for the rest of the Mediterranean world of the time. The finds from the Roman East well illustrate that Greco-Roman influence was widespread, and deep in many areas. This factor must be taken into account when studying and analyzing life in Palestine in the first century.

See also GREEK OF THE NEW TESTAMENT; INSCRIPTIONS AND PAPYRI: GRECO-ROMAN; INSCRIPTIONS AND PAPYRI: JEWISH.

BIBLIOGRAPHY. P. Benoit, J. T. Milik and R. de Vaux, eds., *Les Grottes de Murabba'ât* (DJD 2; 2 vols.; Oxford: Clarendon Press, 1961); H. M. Cotton, W. E. H. Cockle and F. G. B. Millar, "The Papyrology of the Roman Near East: A Survey," *JRS* 85 (1995) 214-35; H. M. Cotton and A. Yardeni, eds., *Aramaic, Hebrew and Greek Documentary Texts from Nahal Hever and Other Sites* (Seiyal Collection 2; DJD 27; Oxford: Clarendon Press, 1997); N. Lewis, *The Documents from the Bar Kokhba Period in the Cave of Letters: Greek Papyri* (Jerusalem: Israel Exploration Society, Hebrew University of Jerusalem, Shrine of the Book, 1989); S. E. Porter, "The Greek Papyri of the Judean Desert and the World of the Roman East," in *The Scrolls and the Scriptures: Qumran Fifty Years After*, ed. S. E. Porter and C. A. Evans (RILP 3; JSPSup 26; Sheffield: Sheffield Academic Press, 1997) 293-316.

S. E. Porter

PAPYRI. *See* INSCRIPTIONS AND PAPYRI: GRECO-ROMAN; INSCRIPTIONS AND PAPYRI, JEWISH; PAPYRI, PALESTINIAN; ZENON PAPYRI.

PARABLES. *See* RABBINIC PARABLES.

PARENTS. *See* FAMILY AND HOUSEHOLD; MARRIAGE.

PATERFAMILIAS. *See* FAMILY AND HOUSEHOLD.

PATRONAGE

The patron-client relationship is the basic building block of Greco-Roman society. In an economy in which most of the resources are held by a fraction of the population, attaching oneself to a patron would be essential to ensure the well-being of oneself and one's family. In a culture in which prestige and *honor were highly valued, patrons would be willing to exchange material goods or other assistance for the honor, loyalty and service that a client would provide. This form of beneficence, which involved mutual loyalty and personal connection, stood alongside the practice of public *benefaction, in which giving brought recognition but did not involve the formation of patron-client bonds. The social institution of patronage becomes relevant for reading the NT since, for example, the language of "grace" and "faith" are central terms in both.

1. Patron-Client Scripts
2. Patronage and Salvation in the New Testament
3. Patronage Within the New Community

1. Patron-Client Scripts.

1.1. Patrons, Brokers and Clients. *Seneca speaks of the giving and receiving of benefactions as "the practice that constitutes the chief bond of human society" (Seneca *Ben.* 1.4.2; cf. 5.11.5; 6.41.2). The Greco-Roman world was a patronal society, supported by an infrastructure of networks of favor and loyalty. These relationships were regarded as an essential element of security (Seneca *Ben.* 4.18.1). Such bonds existed between social equals who call each other friends (*see* Friendship) and for whom the dictum "friends possess all things in common" holds true. Partners in such relationships exchanged favors as needed, with neither party being in an inferior, dependent role (Saller).

Such bonds were also forged between social unequals, in which one party was clearly the patron of the other. These relationships might still employ the language of friendship out of sensitivity to the person in the inferior role (e.g., when Pilate is called "Caesar's friend," Jn 19:12). The system did not lend itself to precise evaluations of favors (Seneca *Ben.* 3.9.3), such that mutual commitment tended to be long-term. The point of the institution was not even exchange but ongoing exchange (Seneca *Ben.* 2.18.5). Mutual bonds of favor and the accompanying bonds of indebtedness provided the glue that maintained social cohesion (Saller). In such a society, gratitude becomes an essential virtue, and ingratitude the cardinal social and political sin (Seneca *Ben.* 7.31.1; 4.18.1).

In a world in which wealth and property were concentrated into the hands of a very small percentage of the population, the majority of people often found themselves in need of assistance in one form or another and therefore had to seek the patronage of someone who was better placed in the world than himself or herself. Patrons might be asked to provide money, grain, employment or land; the better connected persons could be sought out as patrons for the opportunities they would give for professional or social advancement (Stambaugh and Balch). One who received such a benefit became a client to the patron, accepting the obligation to publicize the favor and his or her gratitude for it, thus contributing to the patron's reputation. The client also accepted the obligation of loyalty to a patron and could be called upon to perform services for the patron, thus contributing to the patron's power. The reception of a gift and the acceptance of the obligation of gratitude are inseparable (cf. Seneca *Ben.* 2.25.3).

A third figure in this network of patronage has been called the "broker" (Boissevain) or mediator. This mediator acts as a patron, but his or her primary gift to the client is access to a more suitable or powerful patron. This second patron will be a friend (in the technical sense) of the broker, a member of the broker's family or the broker's own patron. Brokerage was common and personal in the ancient world. The letters of *Pliny the Younger, *Cicero and Fronto are filled with these authors' attempts to connect a client with one of their friends or patrons (de Ste. Croix). Pliny's letters to Trajan, for example, document Pliny's attempts to gain imperial *beneficia* (benefits) for Pliny's own friends and clients. In *Epistles* 10.4, Pliny asks Trajan to grant a senatorial office to Voconius Romanus. He addresses Trajan clearly as a client addressing his patron and proceeds to ask a favor for Romanus. Pliny offers his own character as a guarantee of his client's character, and Trajan's assessment of the secondhand client is inseparable from his assessment of Pliny—Trajan's "favorable judgment" of Pliny (not Romanus) is the basis for Trajan's granting of this favor.

Such considerations in the patron-client exchange have an obvious corollary in the church's christology and soteriology, wherein God, the Patron, accepts Christ's clients (i.e., the Christians) on the basis of the mediator's merit. Within these webs of patronage, indebtedness remains within each patron-client (or friend-to-friend) relationship. Voconius Romanus will be indebted to Pliny as well as Trajan, and Pliny will be indebted further to Trajan. The broker, or mediator, at the same time incurs a debt and increases his own honor through the indebtedness of his or her client. Brokerage occurs also between friends and associates in private life. A familiar example appears in Paul's letter to Philemon, in which Paul approaches his friend Philemon on behalf of Paul's new client, Onesimus: "if you consider me your partner, welcome him as you would welcome me" (Philem 17).

1.2. Grace and Patronage. A term of central importance for discourse about patronage is *charis,* frequently translated "grace." Classical and Hellenistic Greek authors use this word primarily as an expression of the dynamics within the patron-client or friendship relationship. Within this social context, *charis* has three distinct meanings. First, it is the benefactor's favorable disposition toward the petitioner (Aristotle *Rhet.* 2.7.1-2). Second, the term can be used to refer to the gift or benefit conferred (as frequently in honorary inscriptions; see Danker; *TDNT* 9:375; cf. 2 Cor 8:19). The third meaning is the reciprocal of the first, namely, the response of the client, the necessary and appropriate return for favor shown. In this sense the term is best translated as "gratitude" (Demosthenes *De Cor.* 131; Rom 6:17; 7:25; Heb 12:28).

According to ancient ethicists on giving, patrons were to give without calculation of reward. That is, giving was to be in the interest of the recipient, not motivated by self-interest (Aristotle *Eth. Nic.* 1385a35-1385b3; Seneca *Ben.* 3.15.4). Patrons were, however, cautioned to select their beneficiaries well—people who had a reputation for honoring the giver with gratitude (Isocrates *Dem.* 29). Even *Seneca, however, could exhort the patron to consider giving to a proven ingrate, thus imitating the generosity of the gods (Seneca *Ben.* 1.1.9; 4.26.1—4.28.1) and possibly arousing a grateful response with a second gift (Seneca *Ben.* 7.32).

A person who received "grace" (a patron's favor) knew also that "grace" (gratitude) must be returned (Aristotle *Eth. Nic.* 1163b12-15; Cicero *De Offic.* 1.47-48; Seneca *Ben.* 2.25.3). According to Seneca, the three Graces dance with their arms linked in an unbroken circle because a benefit "passing from hand to hand nevertheless returns to the giver; the beauty of the whole is destroyed if the course is anywhere broken" (Seneca *Ben.* 1.3.3-4). Gratitude was a sacred obligation, and the client who failed to show gratitude appropriately was considered base and impious (Dio Chrysostom *Or.* 31.37; Seneca *Ben.* 1.4.4). The greater the benefit bestowed, the greater should be the response of gratitude.

Gratitude in the ancient world involves the demonstration of respect for the benefactor (Aristotle *Eth. Nic.* 1163b1-5; Danker), acting in such a way as to enhance his or her *honor and avoiding any course of action that would bring him or her into dishonor. A client who showed disregard for a patron would exchange favor for wrath (Aristotle *Rhet.* 2.2.8). The client would return this gift of honor not only in his or her own demeanor and actions but also in public testimony to the benefactor (Seneca *Ben.* 2.22.1; 2.24.2). Gratitude also involves intense personal loyalty to the patron, even if that loyalty should lead one to lose one's place in one's homeland, one's physical well-being, one's wealth and one's reputation (Seneca *Ep. Mor.* 81.27; *Ben.* 4.20.2; 4.24.2). This is the level of gratitude and loyalty that the NT authors claim should be given to Jesus and, through him, to God. Finally, making a fair return for a gift meant giving something in exchange, whether another gift, or, as was more usual for clients, some appropriate acts of service (Seneca *Ben.* 2.35.1). "Grace," therefore, has specific meanings for the authors and readers of the NT, who are themselves part of a world in which patronage is a primary social bond.

1.3. Faith and Patronage. While not as dominant as *charis* in discussions of patronage, *pistis* (usually translated as "faith") and its related words also receive specific meanings within the context of the patron-client relationship (Danker). To place *pistis* in a patron is to trust him or her to be able and willing to provide what he or she has promised. It means to entrust one's cause or future to a patron (cf. 4 Macc 8:5-7), to give oneself over into his or her care. *Pistis* also represents the response of loyalty on the part of the client. Having received benefits from a patron, the client must demonstrate *pistis* ("loyalty") toward the patron (Latin *fides,* Seneca *Ben.* 3.14.2; cf. 4 Macc 16:18-22; 7:19; 15:24; 17:2-3). In this context, then, *pistis* speaks to the firmness, reliability and faithfulness of both parties in the patron-client relationship or the relationship of friends.

The opposite of *pistis* is *apistia.* This refers in one sense to "distrust" toward a patron or client. It would entail a negative evaluation of the character and reliability of the other person and could be insulting in the extreme. However, it was also recognized that one had to be prudent concerning the placement of trust (cf. Dio Chrysostom *Or.* 74, "Concerning Distrust"), just as a patron would need to weigh carefully whether or not to accept the responsibility of a client's or a friend's "trust" (Seneca *Ben.* 1.1.2; 4.8.2; Dio Chrysostom *Or.* 73). The term may also refer, in its second sense, to disloyalty or unfaithfulness, as when clients fail to remain steadfast in their commitment to their patron or prove untrustworthy in their service.

2. Patronage and Salvation in the New Testament.

In order to give expression to supernatural or unseen realities, people in the ancient world used the language of everyday realities. The world beyond was understood by analogy to known quantities in the world at hand. The relationship between human and divine beings, cosmic inferiors and superiors as it were, was expressed in terms of the closest analogy in the world of social interaction, namely, patronage, so that we find talk of "patron deities" by individuals and groups (e.g., associations or cities; Saller). This holds true also for the way NT authors give expression to the relationship between the one God and the people of God. Even its use of *family imagery connects with the image of the patron who brings a host of clients into the household, although now with the special status of daughters and sons.

2.1. God as Patron. The Hebrew Scriptures speak of God as the Patron of *Israel who protects and provides for the people with whom God has formed this special relationship of favor. When Israel does not make the proper response (i.e., by failing to return honor, exclusive loyalty and service in the form of obedience to Torah), God responds by punishing them. What is remarkable is God's loyalty to the relationship: though that relationship is breached on one side, God never abandons the nation despite its ingratitude.

Both the Jewish and Greco-Roman backgrounds lead the early church to view God in a similar fashion. God is the Patron of all, since God has given to all the matchless gift of existence and sustenance (Rev 4:11). God will be the benefactor of all who seek and trust God's favor (Heb 11:6). God is celebrated as the Patron whose favor and benefits are sought in *prayer and whose favorable response to prayer is assured (Lk 1:13, 25, 28, 30; 11:9-13; Heb 4:14-16). The songs in the Lukan infancy narratives (Lk 1:46-55, 68-75) are primarily songs about God's patronage. They represent the response of gratitude to God for God's favor but also describe God as the patron of the weak and the poor, a portrait that ties closely with Luke's overall emphasis on caring for the poor. God is also celebrated as the Patron of Israel in both Mary's and Zechariah's songs, for God has brought the help that the people have needed so desperately.

God's favor is astonishing not in that God gives "freely" or "uncoerced": every benefactor, in theory at least, did this. Rather, it is in God's determination to bring benefit to those who have affronted God in the extreme. God goes far beyond the high-water mark of generosity set by Seneca, which was for virtuous people to consider even giving to the ungrateful (*if* they had resources to spare after benefiting the virtuous). To provide some modest assistance to those who had failed to be grateful in the past would be accounted a proof of great generosity, but God shows the supreme, fullest generosity (giving his most costly gift, the life of his Son) toward those who are not merely ungrateful but who have been actively hostile to God and God's desires. This is an outgrowth of God's determination to be "kind" even "toward the ungrateful [*acharistous*] and the wicked" (Lk 6:35).

A second distinctive aspect of God's favor is God's initiative in effecting reconciliation with those who have affronted God's honor. God does not wait for the offenders to make an overture or to offer some token acknowledging their own disgrace and shame in acting against God in the first place. Rather, God sets aside his anger in setting forth Jesus, providing an opportunity for people to come into favor and escape the consequences of having previously acted as enemies (hence the choice of "deliverance," *sōtēria*, as a dominant image for God's gift).

Not all, however, honor God as the Patron merits (cf. Rom 1:18-25; Rev 9:20-11; 14:9-11); even the special covenant people have brought God's name into dishonor on account of disloyalty and disobedience (Rom 2:17-24). Nevertheless, God remains faithful to those whom he has benefitted in the past, continuing to offer favor, even the gift of adoption into God's household, for those who return to God in trust and gratitude. Those who persist in responding ungracefully to the divine Patron, however, will ultimately face wrath.

2.2. Jesus as Mediator. Jesus is presented likewise as a patron of the Christian community. The author of Hebrews, for example, presents Jesus as one who "lays hold of the descendants of Abraham" (Heb 2:16) and comes "to the aid of those who are tempted" (Heb 2:18). He supplies for the Christians what is wanting in their own resources. Jesus' patronage may be more precisely defined, however, as brokerage. He is the mediator (Heb 8:6; 9:15; 12:24) who secures favor from God on behalf of those who have committed themselves to Jesus as client dependents. As God's Son, who is placed closest to the head of the household, Jesus' successful mediation is assured. Jesus' gift of access to God (Heb 4:14-16; cf. Heb 10:19-22) affords the community access to resources for endurance in faith in the present world so that they may receive the benefactions promised for the future, to be awarded before God's court at the end of the age. The believers may draw near to God and expect to "receive mercy and find favor"—that is, the disposition of God to give assistance—"for timely help" (Heb 4:16). Christians have been brought into God's household (Heb 3:6) through their clientage to the Son and are thus under God's protection and provision (deSilva 1999).

Other NT authors share the conviction that Jesus is the one who mediates the favor of God. One gains access to God only through the Son, and apart from Jesus there is none who can secure for us God's favor (Lk 9:48; 10:22; Jn 13:20; 14:6). Paul, in his formulation of "salvation by grace," uses this background to articulate the gospel. Being "saved by grace" points to God's uncoerced initiative in reaching out to form a people from all nations through God's anointed agent, Jesus. The role of "faith" in this process is Jesus' reliability as broker of God's favor and our trust in and loyalty toward Jesus. Paul reacts so strongly against requiring circumcision and observance of dietary laws for Gentile converts because this "displaces the favor of God" (Gal 2:21), evidenced in the benefaction of the Holy Spirit (Gal 3:1-5), which Jesus has gained for his faithful clients (Gal 2:21; 5:2-4). It casts doubt on Jesus' ability to secure God's favor by his own mediation and thus shows distrust toward Jesus.

2.3. The Obligation of Gratitude. The proper response toward a patron is gratitude: offering honor, loyalty, testimony and service to the patron. Reciprocity is such a part of this relationship that failure to return "grace" ("gratitude") for "grace" ("favor") results in a breach of the patron-client relationship. God's favor seeks a response of faithfulness *(pistis)* and service from God's clients. Paul speaks, for example, of the "obedience of faith" (Rom 1:5; 16:26) as the goal of his mission, calling forth the proper response of those who have benefitted from God's gift. The recipients of God's favor are called to offer up their whole selves to God's service, to do what is righteous in God's sight (Rom 6:1-14; 12:1). This response centers not only on honoring God but also on love, generosity and loyal service toward one's fellow believers (Gal 5:13-14; 6:2; Rom 13:9-10).

The author of Hebrews also calls Christians to remain firm in their trust and loyalty (Heb 10:35-39; 11), to take great care not to dishonor the Giver nor show contempt for the gift won at such cost to the Broker (Heb 10:26-31) through apostasy, to avoid "distrust" (Heb 3:19—4:2) and to "show gratitude" (Heb 12:28) to God by continuing to bear witness to their Benefactor in a hostile world (Heb 13:15) and by assisting one another by love and service, encouraging and supporting one another in the face of an unsupportive society (Heb 6:10; 13:1-3, 16). While God's favor remains free and uncoerced, the first-century hearer knows that to accept a gift meant accepting also the obligation to respond properly.

3. Patronage Within the New Community.
The Christian mission depended on the financial support of its richer converts. Individuals might provide some important service or financial aid for the community and so be remembered honorably (cf. Acts 4:34-36; 1 Cor 16:17-18; Phil 2:29-30; Philem 7). Householders within the movement would host the meetings of the group (Rom 16:23; 1 Cor 16:19; Philem 1) and provide *hospitality for missionaries and teachers (Philem 22; 3 Jn 5-8, 10b). Paul sought to develop relationships of reciprocity between churches, so that beneficence between Christians might span the Mediterranean. The collection of relief funds for the churches in Judea is presented as an act of reciprocity for the spiritual benefits that went out from those Judean churches to the Gentiles (Rom 15:25-29); similarly, Paul assures the Achaian churches that their contributions to other churches will establish ties of reciprocity for the future (2 Cor 8:13-14). Churches are to act as collectives of friends who share all things in common. Paul presents himself frequently as a partner or a friend who brings spiritual benefits and receives material support (Phil 1:5-7; 4:15; Philem 17), but he is also conscious of his role as patron or "father" (1 Cor 4:15) to the converts since he has provided the gift of access to Jesus that has saved

them from God's wrath (Philem 19).

Patronage within the church is not, however, meant to be pursued as a means of advancing one's own honor or power within the group. Acts of love and service toward one's fellow believers was the service enjoined upon the clients by the divine Patron. Giving to fellow believers is presented as a reflection of Christ's own act on our behalf (2 Cor 8:9-14), and Paul presents giving as itself a spiritual gift (Rom 12:8). Patrons within the church are acting as stewards of God's gifts (2 Cor 9:8-10). Christians are also urged to extend their own beneficence to the outside world (1 Thess 5:15; 1 Pet 2:14-16; Rom 13:3-4), not only as a reflection of the generosity of God but also as a sign that Christians, too, were honorable people who contributed to the welfare of all (Winter).

See also BENEFACTOR; FAMILY AND HOUSEHOLD; FRIENDSHIP; HONOR AND SHAME; SOCIAL VALUES AND STRUCTURES.

BIBLIOGRAPHY. J. Boissevain, *Friends of Friends: Networks, Manipulators and Coalitions* (New York: St. Martin's, 1974); J. K. Chow, *Patronage and Power: A Study of Social Networks in Corinth* (JSNTSup 75; Sheffield: Sheffield Academic Press, 1992); F. W. Danker, *Benefactor: Epigraphic Study of a Greco-Roman and New Testament Semantic Field* (St. Louis: Clayton, 1982); J. Davis, *The People of the Mediterranean: An Essay in Comparative Social Anthropology* (London: Routledge & Kegan Paul, 1977); G. E. M. de Ste. Croix, "Suffragium: From Vote to Patronage," *British Journal of Sociology* 5 (1954) 33-48; D. A. deSilva, "Exchanging Favor for Wrath: Apostasy in Hebrews and Patron-Client Relations," *JBL* 115 (1996) 91-116; ibid, "Hebrews 6:4-8: A Socio-rhetorical Investigation," *TynB* 50 (1999) 33-57, 225-35; idem, *Honor, Patronage, Kinship and Purity: Unlocking New Testament Culture* (Downers Grove, IL: InterVarsity Press, 2000); M. Hals, *Grace and Faith in the Old Testament* (Minneapolis: Fortress, 1980); B. Levick, *The Government of the Roman Empire: A Sourcebook* (London: Croom Helm, 1985) 137-51; H. Moxnes, "Patron-Client Relations and the New Community in Luke-Acts," in *The Social World of Luke-Acts,* ed. J. H. Neyrey (Peabody, MA: Hendrickson, 1991) 241-68; R. P. Saller, *Personal Patronage Under the Early Empire* (Cambridge: Cambridge University Press, 1982); J. E. Stambaugh and D. L. Balch, *The New Testament in Its Social Environment* (LEC 2; Philadelphia: Westminster, 1986); B. W. Winter, *Seek the Welfare of the City: Christians as Benefactors and Citizens* (Grand Rapids, MI: Eerdmans, 1994).

D. A. deSilva

PAX ROMANA

The *Pax Romana* ("Roman peace") is a term used to designate Roman political rule in the Mediterranean world beginning with the reign of Caesar Augustus and lasting for the next two and a half centuries. The term, original to the Romans, reflects both imperial ideal and propaganda toward its own *citizens and its imperial holdings (*see* Roman Emperors; Roman Empire). "Pax" is also used of a Roman cult that was the religious support for the governing ideal. The pax is most closely associated with Caesar Augustus, and its benefits are enshrined in the traditional sobriquet for the period of Augustus's rule (27 B.C.-A.D. 14), "the Augustan Golden Age."

1. The Ideal of Pax Romana
2. The Pax Cult
3. The Pax Romana and New Testament Writings

1. The Ideal of Pax Romana.

1.1. Pax Romana and the Empire of Augustus. A standard assessment of the achievements of Augustus is to be found in M. Grant's *History of Rome.* Grant writes that "by his reorganization . . . of the entire machinery of civilian government, he had proved himself one of the most gifted administrators the world has ever seen and the most influential single figure in the entire history of Rome. The gigantic work of reform that he carried out in every branch of Italian and provincial life not only transformed the decaying republic into a new regime with many centuries of existence ahead of it, but also created a durable efficient Roman peace. It was this *Pax Romana* or *Pax Augusta* that insured the survival and eventual transmission of the classical heritage, Greek and Roman alike, and made possible the diffusion of Christianity, of which the founder, Jesus, was born during this reign" (Grant, 256-58).

An appreciation of Augustus's achievement from a Roman perspective is gained by comparing the internal stability of Roman politics in the Augustan Age with the chaotic two decades of civil war and unrest in the years preceding his rule. In those years the Roman world was torn by "disruption and uncertainty, pillage and slaughter, near-anarchy and the ever-present threat of disintegration, years in which the rule of law was set aside and justice was merely 'the interest of the stronger'" (Stockton, 532). After Augustus's triumph, "the mass of the inhabitants of Italy and the Empire welcomed the peace and stability, material prosperity, and increased administrative efficiency which came with the Principate. . . . It was his achievement that . . . gave to the Roman world a freedom from war and the fear of war unmatched in its duration, and that freedom under the law, one of the ideals of classical Greece and republican Rome, was still an ideal of the Principate" (Stockton, 539).

In the centuries following Augustus, this ideal of imperial peace, best defined as security within the empire, remained intact even as the empire, which already dominated the lands surrounding the Mediterranean, grew. The influential English historian of the late eighteenth century, Edward Gibbon, made the famous and fantastic claim that in the second century A.D. (from Domitian's death in 96 to Commodus's accession in 176), when Rome spread its imperial wings over the largest territory, the world saw its greatest happiness and prosperity (*History of the Decline and Fall of the Roman Empire,* chap. 3).

Most important for understanding how the imperial peace was understood by Augustus are his own words published in the *Res Gestae* ("Works Accomplished"). This composition, written to be read in the senate after his death and intended for display at the entrance to his mausoleum in *Rome, now survives in partial inscriptional evidence from the provinces. It testifies to the emperor's desire to be known and remembered as the architect of a government that created and sustained peace.

> (paragraph 3) I undertook many wars, civil and foreign, by land and sea, in every part of the world; and as victor I pardoned all citizens who sought mercy. Foreign peoples who could safely be pardoned, I preferred to spare rather than put to the sword.
>
> (paragraph 12) On my return to Rome from Spain and Gaul [13 B.C.] . . . , after the successful conclusion of affairs in those provinces, the Senate in honour of my return decreed that an altar to the Peace of Augustus should be consecrated on the Campus Martius, where it commanded magistrates and priests and the Vestal virgins to perform an annual sacrifice.
>
> (paragraph 13) The temple of Janus Geminus, which our ancestors resolved should be closed whenever peace with victory was secured throughout the empire of the Roman people by land and sea, and which before my birth according to tradition has been closed only twice in all since the founding of Rome, was ordered by the Senate to be closed three times during my Principate.
>
> (paragraph 25) I brought peace to the seas by freeing them from pirates.
>
> (paragraph 26) I pacified the provinces of Gaul and Spain, and likewise Germany. . . . I pacified the Alps from the region next to the Adriatic sea to the Tuscan sea, without waging war unjustly on any people.
>
> (paragraph 32) Numerous other peoples, with whom hitherto there had been no exchange of embassies or friendship with the Roman people, also enjoyed the good faith of the Roman people during my Principate. (translation by A. Lentin from Chisholm and Ferguson, 4-10)

1.2. The Pax Romana and Roman Writers: Ideal and Reality. The theme of peace, so apparent in Augustus's words, became conventional in Roman thought and writings concerning the empire. The popular ideal can be defined as "Rome's mission of peace in the world, with concord, prosperity, and ordered life" and led many Romans to see their empire as the great benefactor of the world (Syme, 2:529). The poet Virgil (70-19 B.C.) immortalized Augustus in his national epic, the *Aeneid.* He lauds Augustus as he who "is destined to bound his domain with the ocean"; in his reign "wars shall cease" (1.280-90) for he "shall rebuild the golden age" (6.793). Virgil calls his fellow Romans to the imperial ideal with these words: "Remember, Romans, your arts shall be: to rule the nations as their masters, to establish the law of peace, to show clemency to the conquered, and to conquer the proud" (6.851-853). Similarly, the patriotic *historian Livy (59-17 B.C.) held that the Romans were "children of destiny, lords of creation, fated to prevail over all other peoples," and it was the will of heaven that Rome would be "the capital of the world" (Livy *Hist.* 1.4.1; Hadas, 230). With such a view of Rome's divine destiny, it is perhaps not surprising that Livy could overlook or excuse Roman atrocities abroad (Syme, 2:529). Panegyrics to the Roman state and its rule of peace continue in the next centuries and are perhaps at their most fulsome in the encomium of Publius Aelius Aristides (A.D. 117-181), titled "To Rome."

Other Roman authors were more critical (see Wengst). Tacitus (c. A.D. 56-120), for example, gave Roman injustices no disguise. He is sympathetic with those for whom the Roman peace was experienced as brute force and calls the *Pax Romana* a thing to be feared (Tacitus *Ann.* 12.33) and speaks instead of *vis Romana* ("Roman power," Tacitus *Ann.* 3.60). In his first monograph, Tacitus speaks forthrightly in references to the Roman conquest of Caldonia thus: "the Romans call it empire, it is in fact murder and rapine and profit; they make a desolation and they call it peace" (*Agric.* 30.7; Syme 2:529). So also the *Dissertationes* (3.22.55) of *Epictetus (mid-first to second century) note the incongruities between the Roman ideal and reality.

In the Republican Era, prior to any official state doctrine of pax, the orator and historian Cato (234-149 B.C.) had criticized the oppression of Roman governors sent to rule Rhodes from then republican Rome. A century later, the orator *Cicero (106-43 B.C.) "declares how bitterly and how justly the empire of the Romans is detested in all the lands: the provinces make lamentation, free peoples complain, and kings are indignant" (Cicero *Verr.* 2.3.207, *De Imp. Cn. Pomp.* 65; Syme, 2:527-29). It is clear from events in Judea and from writers such as Tacitus that oppression by governors continued apace after Augustus. Thus, what could be hailed by Romans at home as an empire of strength and peace was characterized otherwise by many of its subjects, experiencing oppression and foreign taxation, both before and after Augustus (Shelton, 236, 241, 249, 287-88).

1.3. Pax Romana in the Provinces. In the provinces of the Roman Empire the *Pax Romana* was not uniformly experienced as tranquility in the best interest of indigenous peoples. In addition to the inevitable difficulties associated with rule by a foreign nation, the Roman system of provincial rule was prone to abuse (*see* Roman Administration). *Roman governors, usually called proconsuls, were placed over foreign territories, and their freedom to rule was almost unfettered. "Few bounds were set to the free exercise of their *imperium* ["command"]. Unless the proconsul offended the wealthy magnates of his province, he was unlikely to be called to account at Rome for abuse of power when his proconsulship was over. He was under no compulsion to consult the Senate, which was his nominal director, and still less the *Princeps*. . . . The proconsul had the total power of administration, jurisdiction, defense—in so far as that arose—and the maintenance of public order" (Sherwin-White, 2).

This created a system of governing that was only as good as the character of the governor. During this period, *Judea, which had come under Roman dominion in 63 B.C., when not under Rome's client king (e.g., *Herod, 27-4 B.C.) was governed by a prefect (after Claudius, A.D. 41-54, called procurator). The prefects were of lesser Roman rank than the proconsuls and were commissioned to smaller territories or areas that required special treatment (Sherwin-White, 6). Formally under the emperor, "they had been given powers similar to those of the proconsuls" (Sherwin-White, 7; Josephus *J.W.* 2.8.1 §117; *see* Roman Governors of Palestine).

Thus in Judea, the experience of the eulogized Roman peace was mediated by the ruling client king or current prefect. *Flavius Josephus (A.D. 37-c. 100), the Jewish historian who wrote his history of the Jewish revolt (A.D. 66-70) under Roman *patronage, while blaming the war on a few Jewish renegades and tyrants (Josephus *J.W.* 1.1.4, 11 §§10-11, 27), does not fail to record the provocations to violence by Roman governors, client kings and even emperors (Josephus *J.W.* 2.3.1 §41; 2.6.2 §§84-92; 2.9.2 §§169-77; 2.10.1 §184; 2.12.7 §§245-46; 2.14.1-2 §§272-77). Of the Roman governors in Judea, E. Schürer writes that the good intentions of emperors [i.e., their ideals of peace and goodwill] "were always foiled by the ineptitude of the governors, and not infrequently also by gross miscarriages of justice on their part. These officials of lower rank were, like all petty rulers, above all conscious of their own arbitrary power, and through their infringements they in the end so aggravated the people that in wild despair they plunged into a war of self-annihilation" (Schürer, 1:356-57; cf. 455). In the next century, in the midst of what Gibbon declared to be the time when the human race was most happy, the second Jewish revolt, provoked by Roman interference in Jewish custom, was put down ruthlessly (A.D. 132-135), and *Jerusalem was divested of its Jewish inhabitants.

2. The Pax Cult.

Not to be overlooked is the association of the institutions of religion with the imperial pax. *Pax Augusta,* often generalized as *Pax Romana,* was a cult centered around the goddess Pax, the personification of political security and peace. The *Res Gestae* of Augustus (paragraph 13; see 1.1. above) mentions the founding of her temple, the *Ara Pacis Augustae* ("Augustan Peace Altar"), which was voted by the senate in 13 B.C., finished in 9 B.C. and is today beautifully restored. Though Pax was not unknown prior to the principate (note the Greek goddess Eirene, "Peace"), the cult was given solid imperial standing by Augustus. From its name and the situation surrounding its establishment, it is clear that the cult was profoundly political and supportive of the Roman imperial view of its governance at home and abroad. Augustus and his successors for obvious political purposes fostered the worship of divine abstractions with which they associated themselves (Ferguson, 72). As to the monument itself, it is considered "one of the major products of Augustan public art" in Rome, and its reliefs are called the "highest achievement of Roman decorative art that is known to us" (Platner, 32; for a photograph, see Cornell and Matthews, 77).

But the cult, as evidence of its value in Roman culture, was not limited to the Julio-Claudian patronage. Another temple, also in Rome, the *Templum Pacis* ("Peace Temple"), was founded in A.D. 71 by Vespasian, the first of the Flavian emperors, after the battle for Jerusalem at the conclusion of the great revolt of the Jews against Roman rule (A.D. 68-70). Completed in 75, this temple housed a library, antique art and spoils of war brought by Vespasian from Jerusalem. According to *Pliny the Elder (A.D. 23-79) it was one of the most beautiful monuments in Rome (Pliny *Nat. Hist.* 36.102). Josephus, equally impressed with the shrine's magnificence, describes the erection of this temple of Peace (*temnos Eirēnēs*) as following upon the firm "establishment of the Roman empire" after the war with the Jews (Josephus *J.W.* 7.5.7 §158). Such a description is apt from the Roman perspective, for peace meant imperial security.

3. The Pax Romana and New Testament Writings.

The complex realities of the Roman empire—with ideals of strength, peace, clemency, the freedom of movement, times of prosperity but also repression and both good and bad governors—form the political backdrop of the drama of the NT. The spread of Christianity was served by the security and stability of the empire. Yet NT writers do not discuss the Roman peace, either as a political policy or as a religious cult. Certain texts, however, are given added perspective when they are read against the background of the Roman ideal of peace. For example, those who suffered the brutal enforcement of the pax Romana must have heard with hope the words of Jesus contrasting his peace with that of the current world order: "Peace I impart to you, my peace I give to you; not like the world gives, I give to you" (Jn 14:27).

For those early Christians whose experience with Roman governance was mainly positive, the concept of *Pax Romana* would also have been positive. The apostle Paul was a native of the important city of Tarsus (Acts 21:39; 22:3), capital of the Roman province of Cilicia and a prominent city with a vibrant intellectual life and prosperous position in the empire (cf. Strabo *Geog.* 14.673-74). Furthermore, according to Acts, Paul's status as a citizen of the Roman Empire benefitted him greatly (Acts 22:27-29), and so we are not surprised by his generous opinion of the Roman authorities (cf. Rom 13:1-7, "for the rulers are not a threat to doing good but to doing bad. . . . It [the government] is God's servant for your own good."). In contrast, the author of Revelation is much more critical of the imperial rule (Rev 13).

But it cannot be assumed that Paul would have been always uncritical of Roman authority. Having experienced no small amount of suffering (cf. 2 Cor 11:23-33), Paul saw himself not ultimately as a citizen of Rome but of a different empire not of this world (Gal 4:26; Eph 2:19; Phil 2:20). Finally, Paul's familiar benediction, "The God of peace be with you" (Rom 15:33; 16:20; 1 Cor 14:33; 2 Cor 13:11; Phil 4:9; 1 Thess 5:23; 2 Thess 3:16), while not referring to the Roman goddess Pax, would have registered with those familiar with the Roman cult as a subtle claim that divine peace for the world is not found in the rule or cult of Rome but in the rule of the God proclaimed by Paul.

See also ROMAN EMPIRE; ROMAN TRIUMPH.

BIBLIOGRAPHY. K. Chisholm and J. Ferguson, eds., *Rome, The Augustan Age* (New York: Oxford

University Press, 1981); T. Cornell and J. Matthews, *Atlas of the Roman World* (New York: Facts on File, 1982); J. Ferguson, *The Religions of the Roman Empire* (Ithaca, NY: Cornell University Press, 1970); W. Foerster, "εἰρηνή κτλ," *TDNT* 2:400-420; M. Grant, *History of Rome* (New York: Charles Scribner's Sons, 1978); M. Hadas, *A History of Latin Literature* (New York: Columbia University Press, 1952); C. Koch, "Pax," in *Paulys Realencyclopädie der classischen Altertumswissenschaft* (Stuttgart: Druckenmüller, 1949); S. Platner, *Topographical Dictionary of Ancient Rome* (London: Oxford University Press, 1929); B. Reicke, *The New Testament Era* (Philadelphia: Fortress, 1968); E. Schürer, *The History of the Jewish People in the Age of Jesus Christ*, rev. and ed. G. Vermes et al. (3 vols.; Edinburgh: T & T Clark, 1973-87); J. Shelton, *As the Romans Did* (New York: Oxford University Press, 1988); D. Stockton, "The Founding of the Empire," in *The Oxford History of the Classical World*, ed. J. Boardman et al. (New York: Oxford University Press, 1986) 531-59; A. N. Sherwin-White, *Roman Law and Roman Society in the New Testament* (Oxford: Clarendon Press, 1963); R. Syme, *Tacitus* (2 vols.; Oxford: Clarendon Press, 1958); K. Wengst, *Pax Romana and the Peace of Jesus Christ* (London: SCM, 1987).

J. E. Bowley

PEREGRINI. *See* ROMAN SOCIAL CLASSES.

PERSECUTION

The experience of persecution, suffering for one's religious beliefs or behavior, is widely attested in the pages of the NT. Jews suffered because of their fidelity to their ancestral religion (Heb 11:35-38), Christians were persecuted by Jews (Acts 5:17-42; 6:8—8:1; 17:1-14; 18:12-17; 21:27-36; 2 Cor 11:24; Gal 5:11; 6:12; 1 Thess 2:14-16), and Christians suffered under Roman officials (Heb 10:32-35; 12:3-7; 1 Pet 1:6; 4:12-19; Rev 2:10; 6:9-11; 17:1-6; 20:4). Extrabiblical writings provide important background information about these persecutions.

1. Jewish Experience of Persecution
2. Jewish Persecution of Christians
3. Roman Persecution of Christians
4. Relevance for the Interpretation of the New Testament

1. Jewish Experience of Persecution.

1.1. Under Ptolemaic and Seleucid Rulers. Jewish people suffered persecution for their beliefs under both *Ptolemaic and *Seleucid rulers in the second century B.C. Ptolemy Philopater, for example, having been prevented from entering the inner sanctuary of the Jerusalem *temple, returned to Egypt and set in motion plans to exterminate Jews in *Alexandria (3 Macc 3:1—4:15). The Seleucid ruler Antiochus IV Epiphanes is remembered as the most infamous persecutor of the Jews. He proscribed Jewish practices (1 Macc 1:44-49; 2 Macc 6:1, 10-11), plundered and desecrated the temple in Jerusalem (1 Macc 1:20-24, 50, 54-55; 2 Macc 6:2-6), banned the possession of the book of the covenant (1 Macc 1:56-57) and demanded that Jewish people offer sacrifice to pagan gods (2 Macc 6:7-8). All these things were enforced on threat of death (1 Macc 1:57, 60-61). His actions precipitated the Maccabean revolt (1 Macc 2:15-28; *see* Revolutionary Movements, Jewish).

Many Jews saw Antiochus as one bent upon destroying their ancestral religion. Antiochus was more concerned, initially at least, about uniting his kingdom with a common culture (1 Macc 1:41-43) and supplementing his finances by plundering the temple treasury (1 Macc 1:20-24). He probably did not understand the long struggle against Hellenization that had been going on among the Jews when he sought to impose Greek practices upon them (Frend). Antiochus shared the Greek view that Jews were by nature the enemies of all nations (3 Macc 7:4) and therefore deserved to be punished.

While some Jews capitulated to the process of Hellenization (1 Macc 2:23; 2 Macc 4:15), pious Jews chose to suffer and die rather than transgress the laws of their ancestors (1 Macc 2:29-38, 49-50; 2 Macc 6:18-31; 7:1-42). They believed that those who suffered would be rewarded in the age to come (2 Macc 7:9, 14, 20-29) and that the blood of their martyrs would become, by divine providence, an expiation for the sins of the nation (4 Macc 6:24-30; 17:17-22; 18:3-4).

1.2. Under the Romans. The Romans allowed the Jewish people a great deal of autonomy in local affairs as long as they did not rebel (Josephus *J.W.* 6.6.2 §§323-50). They supported Jewish rights when threatened by others, as in the case of the dispute between the Greek and Jewish communities in Alexandria in A.D. 113 and 115. On that occasion the emperor Trajan and his local prefect adopted severe attitudes toward the Greeks who initiated the conflict (Ze'ev). The Romans made concessions to accommodate

Jewish beliefs. Nevertheless, many educated Romans despised Jews because of their strange customs, proselytizing and exclusiveness ("haters of the human race") and because they showed no respect to Roman gods (Tacitus *Hist.* 5.8; Quintilian *Inst. Orat.* 3.7.21; Suetonius *Claudius* 25.4; Juvenal *Sat.* 14.96-104). Romans had cause to be wary of the Jews in the light of repeated Jewish attempts to throw off the Roman yoke (as they attempted to do in A.D. 66-73, 115-117 and 132-135).

Jewish attitudes toward the Romans varied considerably. There were those of the ruling elite who cooperated with the Romans and had sacrifices made to Israel's God for the well being of the emperor (Philo *Leg. Gai.* 357). But there were others who were prepared to resist the Romans to the last drop of blood. Jews like these brought about the cessation of the offerings for the *emperor in the Jerusalem temple at the outbreak of the Jewish war of A.D. 66 to 73 (Josephus *J.W.* 2.17.2 §§409-410) and made a last stand against the Romans at Masada in A.D. 73, choosing to die rather than call Caesar Lord (Josephus *J.W.* 7.8.6 §§320-336; *see* Jewish Wars with Rome).

1.3. Jewish Persecution of Fellow Jews. Zealous Jews in the time of Antiochus IV put to death renegade Jews who broke God's laws in obedience to Antiochus's edicts (1 Macc 2:23-26). They believed they were following the godly example of Phinehas (Num 25:1-13). Zeal for the law also lead them to forcibly circumcise Jews who had not yet been circumcised to prevent the desecration of the holy land (1 Macc 2:45-46). Zealous Jews, know as *sicarii,* were responsible for the murder of other Jews who collaborated with the Romans (Josephus *J.W.* 2.13.3 §§254-57), sometimes after mock trials (Josephus *J.W.* 4.5.4 §§335-44).

2. Jewish Persecution of Christians.

Extrabiblical sources, like parts of the NT (Acts 24:5, 14; 28:22), indicate that in the early years other Jews regarded Jewish Christians as sectarians *(minim).* They continued to do this even after many Christians saw themselves as separate from the Jewish community (Setzer). Toward the end of the first century the Eighteen Benedictions used in *synagogue prayers were reworded to include a curse upon Nazarenes and heretics.

In the early years of the Christian church, Jewish Christians saw themselves as part of Judaism (Acts 2:46—3:1; 20:16; 21:17-26), though the relationship between Christians and Jews became increasingly tense as time went on. Christian attitudes toward the temple probably prevented them opposing Caligula's attempt to desecrate the temple in A.D. 39/40 and contributed to the ultimate separation of Judaism and Christianity (N. H. Taylor). If Eusebius's tradition concerning the flight of Jewish Christians from Jerusalem to Pella at the outbreak of the Jewish war of A.D. 66 to 73 (*Hist. Eccl.* 3.5.3) is true, this incident would have further contributed to the separation (*see DLNTD,* Pella, Flight to). The writings of the apostolic fathers contain polemic passages directed against Jews (*Diogn.* 3.1-5; 4.1-6; Ign. *Magn.* 8.1; 10.2-3; Ign. *Phld.* 6.1-2), but these may not accurately reflect living Judaism of the time but rather a symbolic Judaism constructed by the fathers to make points for their Christian readers (M. S. Taylor). The Jews are portrayed as partly responsible for the martyrdom of Polycarp (*Mart. Pol.* 12.2; 13.1).

3. Roman Persecution of Christians.

The Romans had a stronger dislike for Christians than they did for Jews. They regarded the Jews as an ancient people who had remained faithful to their ancestral traditions. The Christians by contrast had abandoned their ancestral religions to become followers of the Crucified. Christians refused to worship Roman gods, representing them as either nonexistent or *demonic, and would not even acknowledge that others ought to do so (de Ste. Croix). To the Romans this was atheism (*Mart. Pol.* 3.2; Justin Martyr *Apol. I* 6; *Apol. II* 3). It alienated the gods upon whom the well-being of the empire depended. However, Roman hostility was not a reaction to Christians' atheism only, but to a mélange of other Christian characteristics that also affronted them: their aggressive proselytizing, antipagan polemics and the disruption their beliefs produced in families (Walsh). Nevertheless, it was rarely Roman policy to seek out Christians for punishment. The process depended on accusations from the populace, not official inquisitions. No action was taken against Christians unless formal denunciations were made by people who were not only prepared to inform but also to conduct the prosecution and to risk the charge of malicious prosecution if their cases failed (de Ste. Croix). It is a sad fact that sometimes Jews were more zealous than

Roman officials in seeing Christians put to death (*Mart. Pol.* 13.2).

The correspondence between *Pliny (proconsul of Bithynia and Pontus, A.D. 111-112) and Trajan (emperor, A.D. 98-117) reflects a policy of not seeking out Christians for punishment (Pliny *Ep.* 10.97.2). If Christians, once accused, refused to recant by offering sacrifices to Roman gods and the statue of the emperor, they were to be punished. Pliny's practice, endorsed by Trajan, was to execute those who refused to recant or, if they were Roman *citizens, to send them to *Rome for trial. This Pliny did, not because of the beliefs or practices of the Christians but because of their obstinate refusal to make offerings of wine and incense to Roman gods (Pliny *Ep.* 10.96.3-4).

The major sources outside the NT for information concerning Christian attitudes toward persecution by the Romans are Ignatius's *Letter to the Romans,* Polycarp's *Letter to the Philippians* and the *Martyrdom of Polycarp.* Ignatius speaks of his desire for martyrdom (Ign. *Rom.* 8.1) and urges his readers not to intervene to prevent it because he wants to become a "true disciple of Christ" (Ign. *Rom.* 4:1-3) and "attain to Jesus Christ" (Ign. *Rom.* 5.3; *see DLNTD,* Ignatius of Antioch). Polycarp wrote to the Philippians shortly after Ignatius's death. He speaks of suffering persecution as an imitation of the endurance of Christ (Pol. *Phil.* 8.2) and urges his readers to obey "the word of righteousness" by following the example of the martyrs (Pol. *Phil.* 9:1). The *Martyrdom of Polycarp* speaks of the blessedness and noble example of the martyrs (*Mart. Pol.* 2.1-2) and the privilege of being numbered among them (*Mart. Pol.* 14.1-2). By a single hour of worldly tortures they purchase everlasting life (*Mart. Pol.* 2.3). By their endurance they "overcome" unrighteous rulers, gain immortality and glorify God (*Mart. Pol.* 19.2). Christians choose martyrdom rather than deny their Lord (*Mart. Pol.* 9.3; *see DLNTD,* Polycarp of Smyrna). It is a choice between the Lord and Caesar. Martyrdom was a special gift from God (Osiek), but this did not mean that Christians should court martyrdom by voluntarily "giving themselves up," a practice that Marcus Aurelius (emperor, A.D. 161-180) later described as "stage heroics" (*Med.* 11.3). This practice was not commanded in the gospel (*Mart. Pol.* 14.1-2). While martyrdom in the first centuries was probably something that most Christians heard about, it was something that most never witnessed (Osiek).

4. Relevance for the Interpretation of the New Testament.

Hebrews draws upon the example of the faithful Jews of the Maccabean period (Heb 11:35-38) to encourage Christians to stand firm in face of persecution (Heb 10:32-35). They must be prepared to give their lives (Heb 12:4) rather than deny their faith in Christ. The Maccabean belief that those who suffered because of their faithfulness to God would be rewarded in the age to come has counterparts in the NT (Mt 5:10-12; Mk 10:30; Acts 14:22; Rom 8:17b; 2 Thess 1:5; 2 Tim 3:12), as does the view that there is an absolute choice to be made between faithfulness to the Lord and compromise with idolatry (1 Cor 6:9; 2 Cor 6:16). This belief carries over into the postapostolic period, when Christians had to choose between the demands of Caesar and allegiance to Christ (*Mart. Pol.* 9.3).

Jewish persecution of Jesus (Jn 5:16), Stephen (Acts 6:13-14), Paul (Gal 5:11; 2 Cor 11:24, 26) and other Jewish Christians (Gal 6:12) because they were thought to speak against or neglect the law may be understood against the background of Jewish zeal for the law. Paul's failure to preach circumcision (Gal 5:11) made him the object of verbal attack by Jewish Christians, who themselves wanted to avoid persecution by unbelieving Jews (Gal 6:12). Jesus' and Paul's criticisms of some of their Jewish kinspeople (Mt 15:12-14; 23:1-36; Gal 4:22-26; 2 Thess 2:14-16), as well as Paul's negative comments about the value of Jewish pedigree and piety (Phil 3:2-11), probably provided some impetus for anti-Jewish writings by Gentile Christians in the postapostolic period (*Diogn.* 3.1-5; 4.1-6; Ign. *Magn.* 8.1; 10.2-3; Ign. *Phld.* 6.1-2).

The term "the word of righteousness" found in Hebrews 5:13 is best understood in the light of Polycarp's exhortation to obey "the word of righteousness" by following the example of the martyrs' endurance (Pol. *Phil.* 9.1). If this is the case, the readers of Hebrews were described as "unskilled in the word of righteousness" because they had forgotten how to endure persecution for the sake of Christ.

The persecutions reflected in 1 Peter are best understood to have been initiated by people who, for various reasons, had grudges against Christians and brought accusations against them to Roman governors, who then acted as

Pliny did. The nature of the persecutions reflected in Revelation might best be understood in the same way, as supporting evidence for the tradition that Domitian actively persecuted Christians is rather scant (Bruce).

See also ARENAS; JEWISH WARS WITH ROME; 1 & 2 MACCABEES; ROMAN LAW AND LEGAL SYSTEM; SLAVERY.

BIBLIOGRAPHY. F. F. Bruce, *New Testament History* (Garden City, NY: Doubleday, 1971); F. G. Downing, "Pliny's Prosecutions of Christians: Revelation and 1 Peter," *JSNT* 34 (1988) 105-23; W. H. C. Frend, *Martyrdom and Persecution in the Early Church: A Study of a Conflict from the Maccabees to Donatus* (Oxford: Blackwell, 1965); M. Hengel, *The Zealots: Investigations into the Jewish Freedom Movement in the Period from Herod I Until A.D. 70* (Edinburgh: T & T Clark, 1989); R. Jewett, "The Agitators and the Galatian Congregation," *NTS* 17 (1970-71) 198-212; E. A. Judge, "Judaism and the Rise of Christianity: A Roman Perspective," *TynB* 45 (1994) 355-68; P. Keresztes, *Imperial Rome and the Christians from Herod the Great to About A.D. 200* (Lanham, MD: University Press of America, 1989) vol. 1; C. Osiek, "Early Christian Theology of Martyrdom," *TBT* 28 (1990) 153-57; C. J. Setzer, *Jewish Responses to Early Christians: History and Polemics, 30-150 C.E.* (Minneapolis: Fortress, 1994); A. N. Sherwin-White, *Roman Society and Roman Law in the New Testament* (Oxford: Oxford University Press, 1963); G. E. M. de Ste. Croix, "Why Were the Early Christians Persecuted?" *Past and Present* 26 (1963) 6-38; M. S. Taylor, *Anti-Judaism and Early Christian Identity: A Critique of the Scholarly Consensus* (SPB 46; Leiden: E. J. Brill, 1995); J. J. Walsh, "On Christian Atheism," *VC* 45 (1991) 255-77; N. H. Taylor, "Palestinian Christianity and the Caligula Crisis, Part 1: Social and Historical Reconstruction," *JSNT* 61 (1996) 101-24; M. P. ben Ze'ev, "Greek Attacks Against Alexandrian Jews During Emperor Trajan's Reign," *JSJ* 20 (1989) 31-48.

C. G. Kruse

PESHARIM

The term *pesher* (pl. *pesharim*) is a noun from the root *pšr*, a root that is attested in several Semitic languages and has the basic meaning of "loosen." The extended meaning of "interpret, interpretation" is found in Akkadian of the mid-second millennium B.C. The term only occurs in biblical Hebrew as a noun (Eccles 8:1; cf. Sir 38:14) but in biblical Aramaic both as a noun (e.g., Dan 4:3; 5:15, 26) and as a verb (Dan 5:12, 16). In the book of Daniel it is consistently used of the "interpretation" of dreams, a contextual meaning that has also been clearly recognized in Akkadian texts more than a thousand years earlier. The term is also used of dream interpretation in 4QEnGiants[b] frags. 7-8 ii 14, 23 and iii 10. In the Bible the Hebrew cognate root *ptr* occurs only in relation to the "interpretation" of dreams in Genesis 40—41. Pesher is "interpretation," and more specifically "dream interpretation." In the sectarian compositions from *Qumran the term *pesher* is used almost exclusively in technical formulas that introduce the interpretation of biblical texts; the exception is 4Q180 frag. 1 1, 7 where the term introduces whole units of summarized interpretation. By extension the term has come to be used in modern scholarship of a literary genre of biblical commentary and the exegetical techniques used in it. The closer definition and significance of such a genre is the subject of the rest of this article.

1. Definition of the Genre
2. Kinds of Pesher
3. The New Testament

1. Definition of the Genre.

Among the first seven scrolls to come to light from Cave 1 in 1947, one was found to contain a commentary on the first two chapters of the prophet Habakkuk (1QpHab; *see* Habakkuk Commentary). The commentary had a distinctive form: each small section (lemma) of text was followed by a few sentences of commentary introduced formulaically, in each case by a phrase including the word *pesher*. The significant occurrence of the term used in a technical way gave its name to this type of commentary. Other examples were found, also using similar formulas. As scholars sought to define this new genre more closely, several different facets of this kind of commentary were described. The discussion about *pšr* has been controlled by observations made about 1QpHab, but as M. P. Horgan neatly points out (part 2) the diversity and range of all the evidence needs to be carefully described and assessed.

Several factors contribute to the definition of the genre.

1.1. Form and Structure. The most obvious feature of 1QpHab is its structural form (see Brooke 1979-81). The manuscript of 1QpHab is comparatively well preserved, so it is easy to see that the whole of Habakkuk 1—2 is broken into small units and presented in its biblical sequence with each unit of prophetic text interleaved with interpretation. After the explicit quotation of the prophetic text each segment of interpretation is introduced by a formula such as "its interpretation concerns" (*pšrw ʿl*) or "the interpretation of the word is" (*pšr hdbr*). In some sections of interpretation part of the scriptural quotation is repeated and then precise interpretation given, again usually introduced by a formula that includes the word *pesher,* such as "its interpretation is that" (*pšrw ʾšr*). Though this formal arrangement seems strict, there are many minor variations, even in 1QpHab, which appears to be one of the most consistently structured of the pesharim. For example, sometimes a pronoun rather than a pesher formula will introduce a subsection of interpretation.

The variations to this formal arrangement are most obvious in compositions, such as 4Q174 and 11QMelchizedek (*see* Florilegium; Melchizedek, Traditions of), where the biblical quotations are selected thematically and the pesher formulae are used more intermittently.

1.2. Content. Apart from form, content has been the most widely discussed criterion for defining pesher. Such discussions have considered both the biblical text being interpreted and the content of the interpretations themselves. Working with 1QpHab and some fragmentary pesharim from Cave 1 (1QpMic, 1QpZeph, 1QpPs) as well as the more extensive range of examples found in Cave 4 (4QpIsa^{a-e}, 4QpHos^{a-b}, 4QpNah, 4QpZeph and 4QpPs^{a-b}), it has often been noted that all the biblical texts that receive interpretation in the form of pesher are from the prophets (including the Psalms considered as prophecy; cf. 11QPs^{a} 27:11; Acts 2:30). Furthermore, in the pesharim these prophetic texts are treated as being fully understood only by the Qumran commentator. As with those who dream (Finkel), so the prophets are portrayed as not knowing the significance of the *mysteries that they spoke or saw; only the Qumran interpreter can make this known.

More closely defined, it is possible to see that pesher is usually given only to what were considered to be partially or completely unfulfilled prophecies, blessings and curses; an oft-cited exception is 4Q159 frag. 5 1, which seems to offer an interpretation of Leviticus 16:1, but the context is not large enough for detailed comment. Part of the exhortation in the so-called halakic letter (4QMMT; *see Miqṣat Maʿaśey haTorah*) is significant in this overall respect: "And we recognize that some of the blessings and curses which are written in the book of Moses have been fulfilled" (4Q398 frags. 11-13 3-4). The sectarian authors of this letter claim that they can discern between those items that have already been fulfilled and those that are yet to happen.

As for the interpretation itself, this is uniformly concerned with the circumstances of the interpreter's present or immediate future, both of which are conceived as belonging to the *eschatological age. Thus the prophets, including *Moses, and the psalmists are understood as predictively uttering mysteries concerning the end times, rather than as speaking to the Israelites of their own generations.

1.3. Character. Other interpreters (Betz) have stressed the distinctive way in which interpretation in the form of pesher assumes a particular view of revelation. Not only is the original prophecy inspired by God, but also the interpretation could be considered to be equally inspired. Such an understanding was encouraged by taking at face value the claims made by the author of the *Habakkuk Commentary* on behalf of the Teacher of Righteousness. He is the one "to whom God made known all the mysteries of the words of his servants the prophets" (1QpHab 7:4-5). This aspect of defining the genre minimizes the role of the careful exegete and emphasizes the experiential side of the interpretative process. Like those who originally received the oracles or visions, the sectarian interpreter is given the interpretation directly by God. In this way the interpretation can claim to have as great an authority as the text that is interpreted. This fact may lie behind the use of small sections of pesher-like interpretation in some of the other sectarian compositions. Most notably in the **Damascus Document* various exegetical units, such as the so-called Amos—Numbers *midrash (CD 7:14—8:3), are woven into the composition's comments on the movement's history, its particular interpretations of the law and its eschatological hopes.

1.4. Interpreter. Through noting that the interpretation might be as inspired as the prophetic text, attention in defining the genre of pesher has sometimes been given to the identification of the interpreter. Some scholars have supposed that all the pesharim were authored by the Teacher of Righteousness, since the *Habbakuk Commentary* (1QpHab 7:3-5) claims that it was to him, albeit in the third person, that God made known all the mysteries of his servants the prophets. Since it was sometimes wrongly believed that only one copy of any of the pesharim has survived, this view was often accompanied by the explicit assumption that the manuscripts of the pesharim are all autographs, as if dictated by the Teacher. This is highly unlikely. Not only are there several different copies of pesharim for Isaiah, but also manuscripts such as 1QpHab preserve marginal markings that seem to reflect some aspect of the copying process. Nevertheless, the place of the interpreter should not be underestimated as a significant part of the definition of the genre. Only a group of teachers learned in the Scriptures and in the techniques of how their secrets could be unlocked could have produced such intricate interpretations.

1.5. Interpretative Techniques. Those who do not want to identify the pesharim too closely with just one inspired interpreter often tend to stress the exegetical techniques that are apparent in many places in these works (Brownlee). Thus rather than thinking that an inspired teacher discloses meaning after flashes of divine insight, the sectarian commentator may be more appropriately described as an expert in unlocking ancient texts by applying appropriate methods. Several of these methods anticipate those found in the later *rabbinic midrashim and strongly suggest that the increasing acceptance in rabbinic circles of various hermeneutical methods was the result of the rabbis recognizing what many Jews were already practicing, rather than being their own innovations (Brooke 1985, 8-17).

A few examples of these exegetical techniques can be cited. In 4Q174, where the Psalms receive interpretation introduced by a pesher formula, the interpretation contains the subsidiary quotation of other scriptural passages such as Isaiah 8:11 and Ezekiel 37:23. These quotations are not cited arbitrarily but on the basis of key catchwords or phrases that can be directly compared with the Psalms text that is being interpreted; this is akin to the rabbinic technique of *gĕzēra= šāwa=* (analogy). The use of a quotation of Zechariah in the commentary on Isaiah 14:26-27 in 4QpIsa[c] frags. 8-10 lines 4-9 is another example of the same phenomenon. In 1QpHab there are several examples of paronomasia, playing on the polyvalence of some Hebrew roots: for example, the Hebrew *mšl* of Habakkuk 2:6, where it means "proverb," is taken in the commentary to mean "rule" (1QpHab 8:9), which the same three letters can signify. Or there seem to be instances of the rearrangement of the letters of a word (anagram): so, for example, the consonants *hykl* ("temple," Hab 2:20) are rearranged in the interpretation as *yklh* ("he will destroy," 1QpHab 13:4), suggesting that when God is rightly acknowledged as present in the *temple, then idolaters are put to destruction. This method is akin to the later rabbinic technique of *ḥilluf*. The rabbinic approach of *ʿal tiqrēʾ* (don't read this, but read that) is anticipated in the pesharim. For example, in 1QpHab 4:9 the commentator reads *wyšm*, "he will make waste," instead of *wʾšm*, "and guilt," of Habakkuk 1:11, but in the interpretation both words are understood, as there is description of the "house of guilt" (*ʾšm*) and "laying waste" (*lšḥyt*).

The widespread use of such exegetical techniques, together with the formal similarities between Qumran pesher and rabbinic descriptions of dream interpretation (Finkel), has caused several scholars to highlight the similarities between the Qumran compositions and later rabbinic texts. The nontechnical use of the label *midrash* in 4Q174 frags. 1-3 i 14 has also encouraged the view that pesher should be viewed as an early part of a trajectory of Jewish biblical interpretation that runs through to the medieval period and beyond. Caution should be exercised, however, before anachronistic terminology is used to describe this distinctive Qumran phenomenon.

2. Kinds of Pesher.

Having considered these various grounds for appreciating pesher as a literary genre, many scholars have agreed with J. Carmignac (Dimant) that the phenomenon at Qumran is visible in two kinds. The first is the continuous interpretation of a single prophetic text. Here the influence of 1QpHab is obvious: it is a continuous interpretation of the whole of Habakkuk 1—2. Other more fragmentary manuscripts probably fall straightforwardly into this category, such as 4QpIsa[a] (on Is 10:20—11:5), 4QpHos[a] (on Hos 2:7-14), and 4QpNah (on Nah 1:3—3:14). The second kind of pesher commentary Carmignac designated as thematic. Several compositions could be grouped in this category. Among those most often referred to as thematic pesharim is 4QFlorilegium (4Q174, sometimes known as 4QEschatological Midrash), of which the principal fragment contains some quotations from and interpretation of parts of 2 Samuel 7 and some pesher commentary on the Psalms, which are cited by their opening verses. Another composition that is commonly described as a thematic pesher is 11QMelchizedek (*see* Melchizedek, Traditions of). The principal extant fragment of 11QMelchizedek contains an elaborate interpretation of Leviticus 25; parts of the interpretation contain the quotation of secondary biblical passages that are then themselves interpreted. In two cases (Ps 82:2 in 11QMelch 2:11-12; Is 52:7 in 11QMelch 2:15-17) the interpretations of these secondary quotations are introduced by a technical formula using the term *pesher*.

Although the two categories of continuous and thematic pesher are convenient, a better appreciation of the character of pesher is obtained by considering it formally as a kind of interpretation of a wide variety of kinds (Bernstein). There is no such thing as pesher in a narrowly defined sense against which all forms of commentary can be assessed. It is true that some compositions are readily recognized as pesher, others less obviously so, but it is important to recognize the diversity of the phenomenon. At one end of the range are the most obviously continuous and formulaically regular kinds of commentary such as 1QpHab. However, even in 1QpHab it is clear that the commentary is often heavily reliant on allusions to other parts of Scripture: for example, in 1QpHab 6:10-12 the interpretation of Habakkuk 1:17 is in large part an implicit quotation of Isaiah 13:18. Several commentaries at Qumran follow the form and structure of 1QpHab, but it should be noted, for example, that although 4QpIsa^b 1 ii seems to be a continuous commentary, it only covers excerpts from Isaiah 5, not the complete text. Perhaps it should be classified as more thematic than continuous. Rather than a strict classification into two kinds, scholars should reckon that the term *pesher* covers a spectrum of prophetic commentaries or sections of commentaries in which at one end there is something easily defined formally (1QpHab) and at the other the form is much more varied (4Q174 frags. 1-3 i 14—ii 5) with only excerpts of the base text being given exegesis and that exegesis commonly using subsidiary scriptural quotations.

Discussion of pesher should include the wider character of compositions such as the *Damascus Document* and the *Commentary on Genesis A*. In the *Damascus Document* there are frequent uses of sections of biblical interpretation, including one, the quotation and interpretation of Isaiah 24:17 (CD 4:14-19), in which there is technical use of the term *pesher*. In the *Commentary on Genesis A* the formal section of pesher interpretation, which is an exegesis of the unfulfilled blessings of Jacob from Genesis 49, is combined with other kinds of interpretation that have other purposes: there is a rewritten version of the flood narrative that fits all the events of the flood into a 364-day year, there are chronisitic reworkings of some sections from the Abram narratives, there is a poetic adaptation of the curse of Canaan that magisterially combines Genesis 9:24-25, 9:1, 9:27 and 2 Chronicles 20:7, and there is a legal adaptation of the story of the destruction of Sodom and Gomorrah through the use of relevant phraseology from Deuteronomy 13:16-17 and 20:11-14 (Brooke 1994). It is clear that neither the *Damascus Document* nor the *Commentary on Genesis A* can be simply labeled as pesher. Rather both compositions show the wide variety of forms of biblical interpretation to be found in the sectarian scrolls, of which pesher forms a part, and a very distinctive part at that, concerned with the interpretation of partially or completely unfulfilled blessings, curses and prophecies of all kinds.

On the basis of this variety it is important that modern commentators do not use the term *pesher* loosely, as if it could ever cover all that there is to understand and catalog in Qumran biblical interpretation. Pesher describes one distinctive kind of interpretation among others (Gabrion; Fishbane). Commonly, studies have focused almost exclusively on pesher as Qumran exegesis and thereby missed the wealth of ways in which Scripture is used in the sectarian and nonsectarian scrolls found in the Qumran library. The interpretation of legal texts, the reuse of biblical poetic images in new hymns and psalms, the homiletic use of scriptural examples and the retelling of biblical stories with a certain amount of embellishment, all these are among the variety of scriptural interpretation in the Qumran literary corpus. None of them is pesher.

3. The New Testament.
The warning about the careful use of the term *pesher* applies especially in relation to the various kinds of biblical interpretation found in the NT (sound usage is adopted by Fitzmyer; Lim). The argument of this article implies that the term can be applied only in cases where the NT author engages in the interpretation of unfulfilled or partially fulfilled blessings, curses and other prophecies. Perhaps it is important to note that most of the scriptural interpretation in the NT that is usually associated with the Qumran pesharim depicts the Scriptures as having been fulfilled. It is no surprise, therefore, that the order of presentation in Matthew's infancy narrative, for example, is not a quotation of Scripture and then its interpretation as in the pesharim. It is rather a description of an event that has already taken place for which a prophetic text is provided as a prooftext. Scripture is not searched for information about what will happen but plundered to explain what has already taken place. In many ways what is found in NT passages such as Matthew's infancy narrative is more akin to the use of scriptural material in parts of compositions like the *Damascus Document,* where at least some of the experiences described are in the past, than it is close to the more explicitly continuous pesharim like 1QpHab, in which the scriptural text acts as much more of a control over the whole content of the commentary.

Furthermore, some modern NT commentators suggest that the existence of certain exegetical techniques in some passages of the NT, such as the use of catchwords in the catena in Romans 3:10-18, aligns such passages with the pesharim. But it has been noted above that the use of such techniques is not a sufficient criterion for defining a piece of exegesis as pesher.

See also BIBLICAL INTERPRETATION, JEWISH; HABAKKUK COMMENTARY (1QPHAB); RABBINIC LITERATURE: MIDRASHIM.

BIBLIOGRAPHY. M. Bernstein, "Introductory Formulas for Citation and Re-citation of Biblical Verses in the Qumran Pesharim," *DSD* 1 (1994) 30-70; O. Betz, *Offenbarung und Schriftforschung in der Qumransekte* (WUNT 6; Tübingen: Mohr Siebeck, 1960); G. J. Brooke, *Exegesis at Qumran: 4QFlorilegium in Its Jewish Context* (JSOTSup 29; Sheffield: JSOT, 1985); idem, "The Genre of 4Q252: From Poetry to Pesher," *DSD* 1 (1994) 160-79; idem, "Qumran Pesher: Toward the Redefinition of a Genre," *RevQ* 10 (1979-81) 483-503; W. H. Brownlee, *The Midrash Pesher of Habakkuk* (SBLMS 24; Missoula, MT: Scholars Press, 1979); F. F. Bruce, *Biblical Exegesis in the Qumran Texts* (Exegetica 3.1; Grand Rapids, MI: Eerdmans, 1959); J. Carmignac, "Le Document de Qumrân sur Melkisédeq," *RevQ* 7 (1969-71) 343-78; D. Dimant, "Pesharim, Qumran," *ABD* 5:244-51; A. Finkel, "The Pesher of Dreams and Scriptures," *RevQ* 4 (1963-64) 357-70; M. Fishbane, "Use, Authority and Interpretation of Mikra at Qumran," in *Mikra: Text, Translation, Reading and Interpretation of the Hebrew Bible in Ancient Judaism and Early Christianity,* ed. M. J. Mulder (CRINT 2.1; Assen: Van Gorcum; Philadelphia: Fortress, 1988) 339-77; J. A. Fitzmyer, "The Use of Explicit Old Testament Quotations in Qumran Literature and in the New Testament," *NTS* 7 (1960-61) 297-333; most recently reprinted in J. A. Fitzmyer, *The Semitic Background of the New Testament* (Biblical Resource Series; Grand Rapids, MI: Eerdmans; Livonia: Dove, 1997); H. Gabrion, "L'interprétation de l'Écriture dans la littérature de Qumrân," *ANRW* 2.19.1 (1979) 779-848; M. P. Horgan, *Pesharim: Qumran Interpretations of Biblical Books* (CBQMS 8; Washington DC: Catholic Biblical Association of America, 1979); T. H. Lim, *Holy Scripture in the Qumran Commentaries and Pauline Letters* (Oxford: Clarendon Press, 1997); G. Vermes, "Bible Interpretation at Qumran," *ErIs* 20 (1989) 184-91; idem, "Biblical Proof-Texts in Qumran Literature," *JSS* 34 (1989) 493-508.

G. J. Brooke

PESHER HABAKKUK. *See* HABAKKUK COMMENTARY (1QpHab).

PESHITTA. *See* NEW TESTAMENT VERSIONS, ANCIENT.

PHARISEES

Although the name of the Pharisees and the main sources about them have been known for about two thousand years, scholars are only now beginning to reconstruct the group's aims and history. From the rise of critical scholarship on this matter in the nineteenth century until the 1960s, there was a growing consensus on some issues and growing disagreement on others. It was broadly agreed, for example, that the Pharisees formed the core of the rabbinic movement, so that first-century Pharisaic perspectives could be read out of *rabbinic literature—even though that was admittedly published only in the third to sixth centuries and later. Most scholars also held that the Pharisees dominated Jewish society, having supplanted the *priests, who had long since ceased to be effective leaders. The Pharisee-sages were the authorized teachers of Jesus' time, exercising their influence through the *Sanhedrin, the *synagogues (held to be Pharisaic institutions, over against the *temple) and the schools.

1. Origins and Sources
2. Josephus
3. New Testament Evidence
4. Rabbinic Literature
5. Conclusion

1. Origins and Sources.
If these points were agreed upon, disagreement proliferated on most other matters. The origin of the Pharisees was variously traced to conflicts between high priests in Solomon's time (1000 B.C.), to the early postexilic period (500 B.C.) or to the *Hasmonean era (c. 150 B.C.). Even though the majority of scholars preferred the last option, they disagreed widely about the circumstances of and reasons for the Pharisees' emergence and about the group's relation to the Asideans described in 1 and 2 Maccabees (1 Macc 2:42; 7:13; 2 Macc 14:6). The name of the Pharisees similarly was much debated: even though most critics (not all) traced it to the Hebrew *p*ᵉ*rûšîm* of the rabbinic literature, they did not agree about the meaning of this word's root ("separation," "consecration," "secession," "interpretation," "specification"); perhaps it means something else altogether: Persian! Even more vigorous debates occurred over the questions: whether the Pharisees had an interest in *apocalypticism and wrote such literature; how much they were involved in the political life of the nation or endorsed a political program (pacifism? militancy?); their connection with the rebels; and above all, whether they were a progressive reforming movement or a virtual establishment trying to protect its narrow, legalistic traditions.

An important change occurred in scholarship on the Pharisees in the 1970s, with the work of J. Neusner and E. Rivkin. In various articles and books, both critics made the observation that any sound historical results would need to proceed from a prior, disciplined analysis of the best sources. The only sources that name the Pharisees and have some claim to independent knowledge of the group are the works of the first-century priest Flavius *Josephus; the NT texts, especially the Gospels; and the early rabbinic literature. One needs to understand each source collection's portrait of the Pharisees in context before proceeding to historical reconstruction. Much of the debate of the preceding decades stemmed from seemingly arbitrary choices of sources: many scholars assumed that certain apocalyptic texts were Pharisaic, whereas others thought them anti-Pharisaic; some used the *Dead Sea Scrolls, on certain assumptions about those texts' authors and opponents, whereas others did not. And even among those who used Josephus, the NT and the rabbinic literature, some arbitrarily gave more weight to one of these than to the others.

Neusner and Rivkin were both experts in rabbinic literature, but they also undertook to analyze the Pharisees in other sources in order to be true to their avowed methods. Even though they came to radically opposite conclusions, they sealed the methodological agenda for coming decades. Neusner in particular showed that even what had been agreed upon by previous scholarship, the easy Pharisee/rabbi tandem, could not be sustained. He and his students, among others, have now undermined the old consensus with the following arguments: that synagogues before A.D. 70, of which not many have been found, were not Pharisaic institutions; that the rabbinic movement was a coalition of groups, not the Pharisees alone, between 70 and 200; that rabbinic literature reflected the particular concerns of its authors in particular social circumstances; and that many other Jews did not recognize the earlier rabbis without further ado—they took different views. The degree of the Pharisees' influence in pre-70 society remains a matter of debate, but the general trend today is to minimize that influence over against the old consensus.

Because we have no surviving text written by a committed Pharisee and no archaeological finds that mention Pharisees, the reconstruction of their aims and views must depend on the writings of the third parties mentioned. Because none of these outsiders was primarily interested in explaining who the Pharisees were, we must be careful to interpret their evidence against their motives and larger contexts.

2. Josephus.
Josephus, a representative of the priestly aristoc-

racy, wrote the *Jewish War* in the late A.D. 70s to persuade Greek readers that the recent Jewish loss to Rome (A.D. 66-74) was not a defeat of the Jewish God and that most Jews had no desire to revolt (*see* Jewish Wars with Rome). In recounting earlier history as evidence of the Jews' good citizenship, Josephus mentions the Pharisees incidentally as a destructive force, because of the inordinate power they wielded under the Hasmonean queen Alexandra (Josephus *J.W.* 1.5.2 §§110-14) and later under *Herod (Josephus *J.W.* 1.29.2 §571). When the revolt against *Rome finally broke out, however, the most eminent Pharisees joined with the temple authorities in trying to dissuade the revolutionaries, but they were all equally unsuccessful (Josephus *J.W.* 2.17.3 §411).

Describing the Jews' philosophical traditions in this same work, Josephus devotes the greatest attention to the *Pythagorean-like *Essenes but includes brief mention of the Pharisees. He says that they, in contrast to the *Sadducees, believe in life after death, judgment and fate or providence (Josephus *J.W.* 2.8.14 §§162-66).

In the *Antiquities of the Jews/Life,* completed fifteen to twenty years after the *War,* Josephus offers a primer in Judean history and culture, with an appendix portraying his own life and character. He describes the Judean constitution as priestly and aristocratic: the proper form of government is through the priestly senate; monarchy is to be avoided, and democracy is ill advised (apparently) in view of Josephus's general disdain for the fickleness of the masses.

Antiquities expands *War*'s narrative for the period from the Hasmoneans to the revolt by six times (Josephus *Ant.* 13—20; *Life),* so it includes a good deal more information than did *War* about the Pharisees. In both the narrative accounts and Josephus's editorial comments, the Pharisees appear as the most influential of the Jewish parties, even though they do not officially control the organs of power, which are centered in the temple. Every time Josephus mentions the Pharisees' activities, under the Hasmonean prince John Hyrcanus, Queen Alexandra, Herod the Great or himself as commander of Galilean forces in the revolt, he caustically repudiates them: they allegedly use their vast popular support to cause problems for the proper leaders—that is, for Josephus and other aristocrats (Josephus *Ant.* 13.10.5, 15.5—16.6 §§288, 400-432; 17.2.2 §§41-45; *Life* 38-39 §§189-98).

In his descriptions of the Pharisees' views, Josephus continues to mention their doctrine of the afterlife, which he claims endears them to the masses, and he also introduces their special extrabiblical tradition "from the fathers" (Josephus *Ant.* 13.10.6 §§297-98; 18.1.3-4 §§12-17). Throughout his works, Josephus repeats that the Pharisees have the reputation for being the most precise of the schools in their interpretation of the laws (Josephus *J.W.* 1.5.2 §110; 2.8.14 §162; *Ant.* 17.2.4 §41; *Life* 38 §191), though this priest-expert is not willing to concede that they are legitimate teachers of the constitution.

Scholars who wish to challenge the old consensus view of the Pharisees' virtual hegemony in Judean society with the argument that they actually had little influence before A.D. 70 must explain Josephus's portrayal in some way. The most common solution is to propose that Josephus exaggerated their power in his *Antiquities* (completed in A.D. 93) because he was trying then to throw in his lot with the new rabbinic movement at Yavneh in Judea, which was allegedly grounded in the surviving Pharisees. Thus Josephus drew attention to the Pharisees' power in order to alert the Romans to the importance of this group, to make a bid for Roman support of them as the new power brokers in postwar Judea.

The problems with this theory are legion, however. As we have seen, Josephus does not speak positively of the Pharisees' power but complains about it from his aristocratic perspective. It is far from clear why Roman authorities (which ones?) should have persevered through the long biblical paraphrase (Josephus *Ant.* 1—11) to reach the sections concerning Pharisees at the time of the Hasmoneans and Herods, understood these sections as praise or understood that these Pharisees were to be identified with the rabbinic movement in Judea. And we have seen that scholarship on early rabbinism has denied that it was exclusively Pharisaic. It is not so easy to dismiss Josephus's complaints about the Pharisees' great influence with the people. And the Gospels, from quite different perspectives, tend to agree about that influence.

3. New Testament Evidence.
The NT authors use the Pharisees mainly as a negative foil for Jesus, but there are considerable differences among them. Paul is the only writer known to us who lived as a Pharisee (Phil

3:5), so we might hope to find traces of his Pharisaic past in what he writes as a Christian—for example, in his apocalyptic orientation toward the imminent end of this evil age. But because his writings are conditioned by his encounter with the risen Christ and he dismisses his Pharisaic past as "dung" (Phil 3:8), it is hazardous to make inferences about Pharisaism from them. Paul's expert biblical knowledge doubtless comes from his former life as a Pharisee; he cites allegiance to the Pharisees as if it were a token of superior legal training (Phil 3:5). Since other sources include belief in resurrection or some sort of afterlife and spiritual powers among Pharisaic beliefs, these features of Paul's worldview probably also continue from his past as a Pharisee.

Of the Gospels, Mark and John portray the Pharisees as key elements of the cosmic battle between Jesus and the evil spirits. Lumped together in a scarcely differentiated Jewish leadership, they are presented as hostile to Jesus from the outset and in league with the devil (Mk 3:6, 19-30; Jn 8:13, 22, 44). For historical purposes it is noteworthy that the Pharisees appear in both texts as the most prominent Jewish group in Jesus' environment. And Mark, among the minor distinctions that it retains, shows them as preoccupied with issues of purity, tithing and legal interpretation (Mk 2:1—3:6). This Gospel also attributes to them a special extrabiblical tradition that Jesus denounces as a merely human accretion to the divine law (Mk 7:5-8).

Matthew often couples the Pharisees with the Sadducees, even with the chief priests, to portray them all as the leadership of old *Israel (Mt 3:7; 16:1, 6), the ones from whom the kingdom will be taken away (Mt 8:12; 21:43-45). His linking of the Pharisees and Sadducees as partners is historically problematic in view of what other sources say about the typical hostility and class differences between these two groups (Josephus *Ant.* 13.10.6 §298; Acts 23:7-9). Within Matthew's portrayal tensions remain, however, perhaps partly as a result of Matthew's conflicting sources. The Pharisees are both "blind guides" whose teachings are harmful (Mt 15:14; 16:11-12) and those who "sit on Moses' seat," whose teachings should be observed even while their practices are eschewed (Mt 23:2-3). Matthew introduces specific remarks about the Pharisees' wearing of phylacteries (small boxes containing Scripture portions, ancient examples of which have been found) and fringes (corner tassels on men's shirts), and also about their concern for tithing (Mt 23:5, 23). Like Mark and John, this Gospel assumes their prominence in Galilean-Judean life.

So does Luke-Acts. Luke's portrayal of the Pharisees recalls portraits of the Sophists in Hellenistic texts. They are the respected teachers of the common people who come out to scrutinize Jesus' activities (Lk 5:17). Though sometimes critical of him, they nevertheless address him respectfully as a fellow teacher, regularly invite him to dinner and even try to help him when he is in trouble (Lk 7:36; 11:37; 13:31; 14:1; 19:39). Jesus is much more strident in his critique of them for typical sophists' faults—allegedly for being money-hungry, complacent and ineffective in bringing about real change (Lk 11:39-44; 12:1; 16:14-15; 18:9-14). The Pharisees of Luke remain outside Jerusalem and so are sharply distinguished from the Sadducee-related temple authorities, who immediately plan to kill Jesus upon his arrival (Lk 20:47).

In Acts this openness continues at first, especially in the person of Gamaliel, an influential member of the Sanhedrin (Acts 5:33-39). But with the execution of Stephen, Acts presents a galvanizing Jewish opposition to the Christian "Path" (Acts 8:1-3). Some Pharisees convert, and they remain zealous for the precise observance of Torah (Acts 15:5). Acts claims that the Pharisees are the most scrupulously precise of the schools (Acts 22:3; 26:5). When he is brought before the Sanhedrin, Acts' Paul is able to make clever use of the Pharisees' famous opposition to the Sadducees on the issue of resurrection (and angels, the author notes) to deflect the charges against him.

4. Rabbinic Literature.

Rabbinic literature is complex and multilayered. It was written in *Hebrew and *Aramaic from the third to the sixth centuries A.D., in Galilee and Babylonia. Because this literature mentions among its founding figures some men who are elsewhere connected with the Pharisees, especially Hillel and Shammai, as well as the family of Gamaliel, scholars have traditionally more or less identified the Pharisees with the rabbis. Those who liked what they found in rabbinic literature saw the Pharisees as a progressive party committed to making the Torah practicable for everyone. Those who were baffled and alienated by rabbinic style found support for their view of the Pharisees as petty legalists. Curiously, when these texts refer to a group called the *pᵉrûšîm* (Heb), more often than not the tone is unfavorable (e.g., *m. Soṭa.* 3:4); the rabbis do not call their own forebears *pᵉrûšîm*. Scholars disagree, also for linguistic reasons, on the extent to which these *pᵉrûšîm* should even be identified with the Pharisees (Gk *Pharisaioi)* of Josephus and the NT.

Neusner's work on the various rabbinic compositions pointed out that because each of these rabbinic texts had its particular historical context and reasons for being written and because it used highly stylized presentations of rabbinic opinion to support these aims, one could only distill information about the Pharisees before A.D. 70 by applying thoroughgoing suspicion and rigorous logic. In a monumental study, he distinguished layers of oral tradition going back to the first consolidation of a rabbinic group at Yavneh (Jamnia) after the Judean revolt. He argued that the few surviving traditions about likely Pharisees before A.D. 70 portray them as a small association concerned with applying priestly codes of purity to their own table fellowship. Neusner's more recent work on rabbinic literature has made it even more difficult to abstract reliable information about the first-century Pharisees from rabbinic literature; he focuses increasingly on the ways in which the aims of the final authors have decisively shaped those texts.

The general trend today is to see early rabbinic literature as the product of a small elite that gradually came to exert influence over larger circles of Jews toward the end of the second century A.D. That elite claimed notable Pharisees among its founders, but it also took over the role of temple-related teaching. It probably originated not simply among the Pharisees but in a coalition of priests, scribes, Pharisees, Sadducees, and others who survived the destruction of the temple. Rabbinic literature should no longer be used, therefore, as transparent evidence for the Pharisees.

5. Conclusion.

Reconstruction of the historical Pharisees turns mainly on the use of these three bodies of literature. The most vigorously contested issue concerns the degree and manner of the Pharisees' influence over the Judean-Galilean populace in the time of Jesus and Paul. But all three source collections, although they understand the Pharisees differently, support the conclusions that: they were a lay, not priestly, association who were thought to be expert in the laws; they were in a sociological sense brokers of power between the aristocracy and the masses; they promoted their special living tradition in addition to the biblical laws; they were interested in issues of ritual purity and tithing; and they believed in afterlife, judgment and a densely populated, organized spirit world.

Few critics today, however, would make the confident statements that characterized scholarship of a generation ago concerning the meaning of the Pharisees' name (separatists, the consecrated, Persians, specifiers), the date and circumstances of their origin (in Ezra's time, after the Maccabean revolt, from the Hasidim), the degree of their involvement with apocalypticism and their political platform. It is plausible that the Pharisees emerged from the turmoil following the Maccabean revolt, but no more can be said at this point.

See also JEWISH HISTORY; JOSEPHUS; JUDAISM AND THE NEW TESTAMENT; RABBINIC LITERATURE; RABBIS; SADDUCEES; THEOLOGIES AND SECTS, JEWISH.

BIBLIOGRAPHY. A. I. Baumgarten, *The Flourishing of Jewish Sects in the Maccabean Era: An Interpretation* (SJSJ 55; Leiden: E. J. Brill, 1997); J. Bowker, *Jesus and the Pharisees* (Cambridge: Cambridge University Press, 1973); L. L. Grabbe, *Judaism from Cyrus to Hadrian* (2 vols.; Philadelphia: Fortress, 1992); J. Lightstone, "Sadducees Versus Pharisees: The Tannaitic Sources," in *Christianity, Judaism and Other Greco-Roman Cults: Studies for Morton Smith at Sixty,* ed. J. Neusner (Leiden: E. J. Brill, 1975) 3:206-17; S. Mason, "Chief Priests, Pharisees, Sadducees and Sanhedrin in Acts," in *The Book of Acts in Its Palestinian Setting,* ed. R. Bauckham (BAFCS 4; Grand Rapids, MI: Eerdmans, 1995) 115-78; idem, *Josephus on the Pharisees: A Composition-Critical Study* (SPB 39; Leiden: E. J. Brill, 1991); idem, "The Problem of the Pharisees in Modern Scholarship," in *Approaches to Ancient Judaism,* 3: *Historical and Literary Studies,* ed. J. Neusner (SFSHJ 56; Atlanta: Scholars Press, 1993) 103-40; J. Neusner, *Rabbinic Traditions About the Pharisees* (3 vols.; Leiden: E. J. Brill, 1971); E. Rivkin, "Defining the Pharisees: The Tannaitic Sources," *HUCA* 40 (1969) 205-49; idem, *A Hidden Revolu-*

tion (Nashville: Abingdon, 1978); A. J. Saldarini, *Pharisees, Scribes and Sadducees in Palestinian Society: A Sociological Approach* (Wilmington, DE: Michael Glazier, 1988); E. P. Sanders, *Judaism: Practice and Belief, 63 B.C.—A.D. 66* (Philadelphia: Trinity Press International, 1992); G. Stemberger, *Jewish Contemporaries of Jesus: Pharisees, Sadducees, Essenes* (Minneapolis: Fortress, 1995).

S. Mason

PHILIP THE TETRARCH. *See* HERODIAN DYNASTY.

PHILIPPI

Philippi is situated in eastern Macedonia on the Via Egnatia that overlooks an inland plain to the east of Mt. Pangaeus/Pangaion. It was founded by immigrants from Thrace and known for its rich gold mines as well as for its many springs of water that rise in its hills (Strabo *Geog.* 7.34). This ancient community was surrounded by mountains on three sides and an open plain to the west.

1. Macedonian Influence
2. Roman Influence
3. The Church in Philippi
4. Archaeological Features

1. Macedonian Influence.

The current site was settled about 360 B.C., when residents from Thasos annexed the territory and called it Crenides because of its springs (Gk *krenai).* It was also known for a brief period as Datum or Daton (Strabo *Geog.* 7.34). Later, when its citizens called upon Philip II of Macedon, the father of *Alexander the Great, for help against the Thracians, he came to their aid but also enlarged their city and renamed it after himself. He built a wall around the city, some of which still remains, though it was later reinforced by the Romans. Except for the wealth derived from the gold mines, Philippi was relatively unimportant until the Roman conquest of the region in 168-167 B.C. According to Diodorus Siculus (*Bib. Hist.* 16.3.7, 8.6), Philip II received one thousand talents a year from the rich mines in the vicinity and treated Philippi as a free city within his kingdom. The wealth received here enabled him to enlarge his army and unify his kingdom. Pausanias, who traveled *Greece during the reign of Hadrian (A.D. 117-138), called the city the "youngest city in Macedonia." The city is mentioned in a number of ancient authors (Dio Cassius *Hist.* 47.35-49; Appian *Civ.W.* 4.102-138; Plutarch *Brutus* 38-53).

2. Roman Influence.

When work was completed on the famous Via Egnatia (begun c. 145 B.C. and completed c. 130), which connected Byzantium (later Constantinople) with the Adriatic ports that led to Italy and became *Rome's primary route to the east, Philippi became a major stopping place on the way. Besides making it possible to move troops more rapidly throughout the empire, this route was the one Paul traveled on his missionary journey from Neapolis to Philippi, Amphipolis, Apollonia and Thessalonica (Acts 16:12; 17:1) but abandoned when he departed for Berea (Acts 17:10).

With the emergence of the second triumvirate made up of Octavian (later Augustus; *see* Roman Emperors), Marc Antony (Marcus Antonius) and Marcus Aemilius Lepidus in 43 B.C., and following their proscriptions that led to the executions of three hundred senators and two thousand knights in Rome, they had secured their control of Rome. The only remaining threat to their control was the republican army led by Cassius Longinus and Iunius Brutus, the murderers of Julius Caesar. Leaving Lepidus to guard Rome, Octavian and Antony engaged the republican forces just west of Philippi in two battles. After their defeat, both Cassius and Brutus committed suicide (Horace *Odes* 2.7.9-12).

Following the battles, Antony settled many veterans from his army in Philippi and enlarged and fortified the city, made it a Roman colony that included Neapolis, Oisyme and Apollonia, and offered land to many of the triumviral soldiers from Rome who had earlier lost their land in Italy (Strabo *Geog.* 7.41; Pliny *Nat. Hist.* 4.42; Diodorus Siculus *Bib. Hist.* 51.4.6). Following his victory over Antony at Actium in 31 B.C., Octavian moved more settlers from Italy to Philippi. Its colonial status brought with it the significant benefit of equal status with the Italian communities and freedom of its citizens and lands from direct taxation. This was known as the *ius italicum,* which conferred the same rights as those granted to Italian cities (Acts 16:12)—the highest privilege possible for a Roman province. The new settlers, along with the previous residents, constituted the newly reformed colony that became known as *Colonia Augusta Julia Philippensis.* It was common in those days for the Romans to build or reconstitute communities as Roman colonies and then offer property to veteran soldiers and other *citizens of Rome.

The official language of Philippi in the first century was Latin, the language of more than half of the inscriptions found there, but the marketplace language and that of the surrounding community continued to be Greek. The city was serviced both by the nearby port of Neapolis, modern Kavalla (Acts 16:11), some 10 miles southeast of the city and by the Via Egnatia. Remains from the Macedonian, Roman and Byzantine periods, including remains of a sanctuary of the Egyptian gods Serapis and Isis, have been found on the acropolis at Philippi.

3. The Church in Philippi.
Following his vision at Troas (Acts 16:8-10), the apostle Paul started the first church in ancient Greece at Philippi (c. A.D. 49-50, Acts 16:11-40). Although he was shamefully treated at Philippi (1 Thess 2:2; cf. Acts 16:19-24), he nevertheless had a significant ministry in the city. His best known converts at Philippi included Lydia, in whose house he began the church; the jailer and his family (Acts 16:14-15, 27-34); Epaphroditus (Phil 2:25-30); Euodia and Syntyche, who were at odds with one another after Paul's departure; Clement; and others who served with Paul and Silas at Philippi (Phil 4:2-3). The Philippian church contributed substantially to Paul's subsequent missionary activity (Phil 4:15-18) and became very dear to him. He visited here at least one more time (1 Cor 16:5-6; 2 Cor 2:13; 7:5; Acts 20:1-6) and, on the same trip, may have gone west to Illyricum (Rom 15:19). He may have written his letter(s) to the leaders of the church at Philippi (c. 54-55) from Ephesus or later while he was at Rome (c. 60). The letter itself originally may have been two or more separate letters that were brought together into one document after the death of Paul (*see DPL*, Philippians, Letter to the).

In the second century, Ignatius, bishop of *Antioch of Syria, passed through Philippi on his way to Rome to face martyrdom. The Philippian church later sent a letter to Polycarp, bishop of Smyrna, requesting his assistance in collecting Ignatius's letters. Polycarp responded favorably to their request in his only letter that has survived (see Pol. *Phil.* 13.2), though Irenaeus claims that he wrote several others (Irenaeus *Haer.* 5.33.4). Polycarp's letter (c. the mid-second century A.D.) is helpful in understanding the continuing witness of the church in Philippi in the second century, its concern for those in prison because of their faith and its *hospitality. Like Paul, Polycarp also addressed the presbyters (bishops) and deacons (Pol. *Phil.* 5.2-3; 6.1; cf. Paul's Phil 1:1; *see DLNTD*, Polycarp of Smyrna). In the post-Nicene era, the city became an important Christian center and had a metropolitan bishop.

4. Archaeological Features.
In the reigns of Trajan (A.D. 97-117) and Hadrian (A.D. 117-138) extensive repairs to the Via Egnatia in the vicinity of Philippi were made, and later Marcus Aurelius made many building additions and improvements at Philippi. Several of the remains at Philippi date from the second century, but most come from the fourth to the sixth centuries. These remains include a large forum (230 x 485 feet) and a rostrum for public speaking, with other buildings that can be dated to the time of Marcus Aurelius (A.D. 161-180). Philippi also has a large theater that dates from the time of Philip II (382-336 B.C.). It later was enlarged by the Romans in the second century. The location where Paul and Silas were imprisoned may possibly be identified with a Roman crypt found just west of Basilica A on the north side of the forum. Portions of the Neapolis gate, through which they entered the city from the east, have also been discovered. Philippi also has four large basilicas and a section of the ancient Via Egnatia, but nothing that remains at the ancient site sheds light on the church's organization, life, worship and ministries in the first century.

Among the most significant discoveries at this site are seven churches dating from the fourth to the sixth centuries, the most prominent of which are commonly identified as Basilicas A and B. A number of other buildings were found, as well as tombs of both Christians and pagans dating from the fifth and sixth centuries. In the fourth century, the city was an important economic and cultural center and was praised for the purity of Greek spoken there. The fate of Philippi after the seventh century is obscure, though the Slavs settled in much of the area in the seventh century, and the Bulgarian invasions of 812 forced the residents to flee the city and its fortress. The city was finally captured by the Ottomans in 1387.

See also CITIES, GRECO-ROMAN; GREECE AND MACEDON.

BIBLIOGRAPHY. R. E. Brown, *An Introduction to the New Testament* (ABRL; Garden City, NY: Doubleday, 1997); P. Collart, *Philippes: Ville de Macédoine depuis ses origines jusqu' à la fin de la l'époque romaine* (Paris: Boccard, 1937); H. L. Hendrix, "Philippi," *ABD* 5:313-17; A. H. M. Jones, *The Cities of the Eastern Roman Provinces* (2d ed.; Oxford: Clarendon Press, 1971); P. Lemerle, *Philippes et la Macédoine orientale à l'époque Chretienne et Byzantine* (BEFAR 158; Paris: Boccard, 1945); J. McRay, *Archaeology and the New Testament* (Grand Rapids, MI: Baker, 1991) 283-88; idem, "Philippi, Philippians," *Encyclopedia of Early Christianity* (2d ed.; New York: Garland, 1997) 2:910-12; J. E. Stambaugh and D. L. Balch, *The New Testament in Its Social Environment* (LEC 2; Philadelphia: Westminster, 1986); R. A. Wild, "Philippi," *HarperCollins Bible Dictionary*, ed. P. Achtemeier (New York: HarperCollins, 1996) 844-45.

L. M. McDonald

PHILO

Philo (c. 20 B.C.-c. A.D. 50) is an important witness of Greek-speaking Judaism in the Second Temple period. The expansiveness of his corpus and its preservation by Christians make it a significant source both for the world of early Christianity and for determining the extent to which Christianity developed from Greek-speaking Judaism.

1. The Life of Philo
2. The Philonic Corpus
3. Philo and Early Christianity

1. The Life of Philo.

There is no ancient *bios* of Philo. We can reconstruct a sketch of his life from occasional autobiographical asides, ancient *testimonia* and the indirect evidence provided by our knowledge of his family.

1.1. Philo's Family. Philo was a member of the most prominent family of the Jewish community of *Alexandria. Eusebius accurately says that he "was inferior to none of the illustrious people in office in Alexandria" (Eusebius *Hist. Eccl.* 2.4.2). His brother, Julius Gaius Alexander, held a responsible governmental position in Alexandria (Josephus *Ant.* 20.5.2 §100; *CPJ* 420). His name suggests that Julius Gaius Caesar bestowed citizenship on the family, possibly on Alexander's and Philo's grandfather for assistance during the Alexandrian war (48-47 B.C.). Since the family could not have received Roman *citizenship without first holding Alexandrian citizenship (Pliny *Ep.* 10.5-7, 10), members of the family must have held triple citizenships in the Jewish community of Alexandria, the Greek city of Alexandria and *Rome. The privileged position of the family is confirmed by the careers of Alexander's sons: Tiberius Julius Alexander worked his way up the *cursus honorum* through governorships of Judea, Syria and Egypt, until he became Titus's chief of staff during the first Jewish revolt (A.D. 66-70; *see* Jewish Wars with Rome; Roman Administration) and the prefect of the praetorian guard in Rome; Marcus Julius Alexander died at an early age but not before he married Berenice, the daughter of *Herod Agrippa I. It was undoubtedly the social standing of the family that led the Jewish community to select Philo, Alexander and the young Tiberius Julius Alexander as members of the embassy to Gaius in A.D. 39-41 (Philo *Leg. Gai.* 182, 370; *Anim.* 54).

1.2. Philo's Life. As a member of this family, Philo received both a Greek (Philo *Congr.* 74-76; *Spec. Leg.* 2.229-30) and a Jewish *education. His Greek education would have taken place in three stages: training in a *gymnasium, a one-year *ephebeia* that in Alexandria normally occurred when a boy was thirteen or fourteen and advanced training in *rhetoric and *philosophy. The latter was particularly important for Philo, who embraced the basic positions of Middle Platonism (c. 80 B.C.-A.D. 220), which became a vibrant intellectual force in Alexandria with Eudorus (fl. c. 25 B.C.). He also received training in his ancestral traditions, although not in Aramaic or Hebrew. His thorough knowledge of the *Septuagint (LXX) suggests that he learned it from the cradle. Philo did not believe that Platonism and Judaism were antagonistic systems; rather, he held that *Moses and *Plato understood the same realities. This does not mean that they stood on equal footing—Philo was first and foremost a Jew—but that Philo's commitment to Moses was not to a Hebraic Moses but to a Platonic Moses. Ancient authors recognized this in the famous aphorism, "Either Plato philonizes or Philo platonizes" (e.g., Jerome *Vir.* 11.7).

Philo's Greek education and social position invited him to embrace many aspects of Greek culture. He mentions his participation in banquets (e.g., Philo *Leg. All.* 3.156; *Fug.* 31-32), theater productions (e.g., Philo *Ebr.* 177; *Omn. Prob.*

Lib. 141), and athletic contests (e.g., Philo *Omn. Prob. Lib.* 26; *Prov.* 2.58). Like most Jews in this period, he did not believe such activities constituted a threat to his Jewish identity. The latter remained secure through observance of Jewish practices (e.g., Philo *Vit. Mos.* 1.31) including a pilgrimage to the *temple in *Jerusalem (Philo *Prov.* 2.64).

While Philo served the Jewish community in the famous embassy and possibly in other civic positions, his heart lay in the contemplative life (Philo *Spec. Leg.* 3.1-6). We know that there was a tradition of Jewish works in Alexandria that extended from the third century B.C., when the translation of the LXX began, to the dismantling of the Alexandrian Jewish community in A.D. 115 to 117. Although Philo does not mention his predecessors by name, his works betray knowledge of several, including *Aristobulus, Pseudo-Aristeas and Ezekiel the Tragedian (*see* Jewish Literature: Historians and Poets). Even more important are the anonymous exegetes to whom he alludes and whose exegetical traditions he incorporates (e.g., Philo *Op. Mund.* 26 for literalists; *Migr. Abr.* 89-93 for radical allegorizers). We should therefore not view his work as an isolated effort but as the apex of a long and rich tradition. The specific social locale for Philo's study and writing is debated. While the meagerness of the evidence permits only speculation, the best suggestion is that he operated an advanced school of exegesis in his home or in a privately owned building as philosophers and physicians often did (e.g., the *Epicurean Philodemus, the *Stoic *Epictetus, the Neo-Platonist Plotinus or the physician Galen). His students were probably potential leaders of the Jewish community.

2. The Philonic Corpus.

Some such setting must be posited given the extensive nature of Philo's corpus. We know that he wrote more than seventy treatises: thirty-seven of these survive in Greek manuscripts and twelve in a rather literal sixth-century Armenian translation. We have excerpts of another work in Greek and fragments of two more in Armenian. The remainder are known only from references in either the extant treatises or *testimonia.* It is likely that lacunae in the commentary series point to others about which we have no evidence. The corpus can be subdivided into five major groups: three commentary series, philosophical works and apologetic treatises. The three commentary series are Philo's own literary designs; the philosophical and apologetic groupings are modern constructs used to group treatises that are conceptually similar but literarily independent. The interrelationship among these groups, especially the commentary series, is complex. We should probably think of them as independent projects that were written simultaneously throughout his career rather than single projects that were completed before he moved on to the next series.

The bulk of the treatises belong to the commentary series. Philo provided a general introduction to all three sets in his two-volume *Life of Moses* (*De Vita Mosis*). The biography provided an orientation to the works of Moses in much the same way that Porphyry's *Life of Plotinus* prepares the reader for the *Enneads.* The implied audience of this *biography is large and probably included members of the wider Jewish community and possibly interested non-Jews.

***2.1.* The Questions and Answers on Genesis and Exodus.** The simplest of the commentary series is the twelve-book *The Questions and Answers on Genesis and Exodus* (*Quaestiones et Solutiones in Exodum, Quaestiones et Solutiones in Genesin*), a running commentary on Genesis 2:4—28:9 and Exodus 6:2—30:10. Ten of the twelve books are extant in the Armenian translation and in some Greek fragments. The commentary uses the question-and-answer format in the literary tradition that began with Aristotle's *Homeric Problems* and is best represented in Plutarch's zetematic works. Jewish predecessors such as Demetrius (frags. 2 and 5) and Aristobulus (frag. 2) had used the question-and-answer format within a larger work, but Philo's commentary is the first known zetematic work in Judaism. The questions take two forms: a citation of the biblical text prefaced with an interrogative or a fully formed question that includes the rationale for the query. The answers are relatively brief and frequently contain both literal and allegorical interpretations. The work was probably intended as a beginning commentary for students in Philo's school or for members of the larger Jewish community.

***2.2. The* Allegorical Commentary.** The most famous commentary series is the *Allegorical Commentary,* a running commentary on Genesis 2:1—41:24. Of the thirty-one books whose titles have come down to us, twenty are preserved in

Greek and a fragment of another in Armenian. Like the *Questions and Answers*, the *Allegorical Commentary* uses the question-and-answer device; however, it does so differently. The questions are now subsumed in the exegesis. The answers are greatly expanded through the incorporation of observations on secondary biblical texts (*lemmata*) in which allegorical readings dominate the exposition. While earlier Jews such as Aristobulus and Pseudo-Aristeas used allegorical interpretation, the particular form of Philo's commentary is closest to that of commentaries in the philosophical tradition (e.g., the Platonic *Anonymous Theaetetus Commentary*, Plutarch's *On the Generation of the Soul in the Timaeus* and Porphyry's *On the Cave of Nymphs*). However, the similarities are not complete; for example, Philo attempted to connect his exegetical treatments into an unbroken chain. The series was probably intended for advanced students of Philo's school or for other Jewish exegetes.

2.3. The **Exposition of the Law.** The third commentary series is the *Exposition of the Law*. We have twelve of the fifteen books preserved in Greek. This series is significantly different from the other two: it is systematic in its organization and literal in its interpretation. Philo divides the series into three parts (*Praem.* 1—3). The first is an account of creation since the cosmos is in harmony with the law (*Creation/De Opificio Mundi*). The second is historical or biographical: the patriarchs (Abraham, Isaac and Jacob) are embodiments of the unwritten law (*Abraham/De Abrahamo*), and Joseph is a politician (*Joseph/De Iosepho*). The third is legislative. It opens with *On the Decalogue* (*De Decalogo*). Each of the Ten Commandments subsequently serves as a heading for other laws in the four-volume *On the Special Laws* (*De Specialibus Legibus*). The remaining legal material appears in several appendices under the headings of various virtues (*Virtues/De Virtutibus*). *On Rewards and Punishments* (*De Praemiis et Poenis*) functions as the finale in imitation of Deuteronomy. It is possible that these works were written for a wider Jewish audience.

2.4. Philosophical Works. The fourth group comprises Philo's philosophical works. Of the eight books we know that he wrote we have two in Greek, two in Armenian and an Armenian fragment of another. These have several features that set them apart from the commentary series: the subject matter consists of philosophical themes, the sources are primarily Greek, and the literary forms are those of the philosophical tradition (e.g., arithmology, *Numbers/De Arithmis*; dialogue, *Providence/De Providentia* and *Animals/De Animalibus*; thesis, a work which sets out a thesis along with the arguments pro and con, *Eternity/De Aeternitate Mundi*; and a discourse, *That Every Good Person Is Free/Quod Omnis Probus Liber Sit*). They were probably intended for students in Philo's school.

2.5. Apologetic Works. The final category consists of works that are explicitly apologetic. We have three of the eight books extant in Greek (*On the Contemplative Life/De Vita Contemplativa*, *Flaccus/In Flaccum* and *Embassy/Legatio ad Gaium*) and excerpts from a fourth (*Hypothetica*). The majority of these were probably written in connection with the pogrom at Alexandria and the subsequent embassy in A.D. 38-41.

3. Philo and Early Christianity.

At an early date, probably prior to the destruction of the Alexandrian Jewish community in 115 to 117, Philo's works passed into Christian hands. A legend soon developed that he was a Christian (e.g., Eusebius *Hist. Eccl.* 2.16.2—17.2). In a number of Byzantine catenae he is called Philo the bishop. His works directly influenced a number of significant early Christian thinkers, including Clement of Alexandria, Origen, Eusebius, Didymus, Gregory of Nyssa and Ambrose. Indirectly they influenced far more. While the legend of Philo Christianus is an anachronistic effort to christen a remarkable Jew, it points out the importance that Philo had for early Christians. What about his relationship to the NT authors and communities?

3.1. The Debate. Scholars have long recognized the relevance of Philo's treatises for the interpretation of the NT. One of the most important initial works was C. F. Loesnerus, *Observationes ad Novum Testamentum e Philone Alexandrino* (1777). The place of Philo in NT studies reached a zenith in the first half of the twentieth century in the works of C. Spicq on Hebrews, C. H. Dodd on John and E. R. Goodenough on the history of religions. The discovery of the *Dead Sea Scrolls and the archaeological discoveries of the century have challenged earlier assessments. The scrolls provided a different set of texts against which the NT could be read. In particular scholars pointed out that the *apocalyptic eschatology of the scrolls was much closer to the perspective of NT authors than was the Platonic ontology of Philo. Further, the scrolls and archaeological discoveries established the diversity of Judaism. When M. Hengel erased the distinction between Hellenistic and Palestinian Judaism (*see* Hellenistic Judaism), Philo's place in Judaism became problematic.

The issue is not whether Philo's works are important for understanding the world of early Christians; they constitute a mine of information on interpretative traditions, Jewish ethics and *Hellenistic moral philosophy, and historical matters. The issue is whether Philo attests a form of *Judaism that directly influenced the development of Christianity. Philonic specialists have argued that Philo's works are representative in a number of areas (Borgen, Sterling). While he is not socially representative of the larger Jewish world, he incorporated perspectives that were widely held.

3.2. The History of Religions. The following examples suggest some of the perspectives that were common to Philo, Greek-speaking Judaism and early Christians.

3.2.1. The Corinthians. The earliest example is the anthropology of the Corinthian community (Pearson; Horsley; Sellin; Sterling). The clearest example is in 1 Corinthians 15:44-49, where Paul's eschatological orientation led him to argue against the Corinthians' understanding of Genesis 1:26-27 and Genesis 2:7. The latter became the focal point of a controversy between the apostle and the community. Paul quoted the text but reversed clauses c and b (1 Cor 15:45). He explained, "The spiritual is not first, but the natural." For Paul the natural is Adam and the spiritual is Christ. The apostle's polemic on order suggests that the Corinthians had a different order. They identified the spiritual with the human of Genesis 1:26-27 and the natural with the human of Genesis 2:7. The closest analogy to their view is Philo, who distinguished between the intelligible human of Genesis 1:26-27 and the sense-perceptible human of Genesis 2:7 (e.g., Philo *Op. Mund.* 134-35). It was probably this type of Platonizing exegesis that led the Corinthians to devalue the corruptible body and deny the resurrection.

3.2.2. Hebrews. The major issue comes into sharp relief in Hebrews: Does this early homily use an apocalyptic eschatology (Hurst) or a Platonizing ontology (Thompson)? It may not be a case of either-or but of both-and. Two texts use the famous Platonic metaphor of "shadow" (Plato *Rep.* 7.515a-b) but in different ways. The first occurs in the discussion of the tabernacle, when the author refers to the priests on earth "who serve in a shadowy copy of the heavenly (tabernacle)" (Heb 8:5). It is difficult to miss the Platonism of this statement: it uses a Platonic image ("shadow") and an earthly/heavenly contrast and cites Exodus 25:40 as a textual basis for the distinction. Philo made the same Platonic distinction from the same text (Plato *Leg.* 3.102-3; Philo *Quaest. in Ex.* 2.82). It may have been a well-known interpretation in some circles. The second text uses identical imagery but juxtaposes it with an eschatological perspective that operates temporally: "For the law was a shadow of the good things to come, not the very image of the things" (Heb 10:1). The imagery of the contrast is again Platonic: "shadow" (Plato *Rep.* 7.515a-b) versus "image" (Plato *Crat.* 439a), but the application is eschatological: the Mosaic cult and law are a shadowy reflection of a future reality ("image"). The relationship between the ontological distinction of Hebrews 8:5 and the eschatological distinction of Hebrews 10:1 is problematic. It may be that both the audience and author accepted the Platonic distinction but that the author added an eschatological twist in keeping with a christological understanding of history.

3.2.3. Luke-Acts. H. Conzelmann pointed out the importance of repentance (*metanoeō, metanoia*) for Luke-Acts. The third Evangelist used the word group to denote a turning to God involving a moral transformation (e.g., Acts 26:20). While some philosophers used the language to describe moral improvement (e.g., Pseudo-Cebes *Tabula* 10.4—11.1-2; Plutarch *Mor.* 26d, 27a, 204a, 551d, 712c), the closest parallels are Second Temple Jewish authors who found this to be a natural way to speak of conversion from paganism to Judaism (*Jos. and As.* 9:2; 15:6-8; 16.7; Pr Man; Philo *Virt.* 175-86). The most striking parallels are in Philo. Luke-Acts appears to reflect a view common in Greek-speaking Judaism.

3.2.4. John. A final example occurs in the *hymnic prologue of John. There are three significant parallels to Philo. First, the use of Logos for the intermediary between God and the cosmos and humanity is striking. It is not only the common term but the similar functions of the Logos that make the parallel powerful (Tobin). Second, the prologue distinguishes between the eternal Logos and the temporal creation through a Platonic distinction between "was" (*ēn*) in verses 1-2 and "became" (*egeneto*) in verse 3. The shift in tenses is not accidental: it is maintained throughout the prologue (the Logos *was* [Jn 1:1, 2, 3, 9, 10, 15, 18] versus the world *became* [Jn 1:3, 6, 10, 14, 17]) and possibly in the main text (Jn 8:24, 28, 58; 13:19). This shift is reminiscent of Plato's famous question "whether the cosmos always was [*ēn*], having no beginning, or became [*gegenon*], having begun from a certain beginning" (Plato *Tim.* 28b). Philo of Alexandria used the same word play to make the distinction between the two worlds (Philo *Op. Mund.* 12; *Poster. C.* 30; *Gig.* 42). Third, the prologue uses prepositional metaphysics (the use of different prepositions to denote different metaphysical causes) to present the Logos as the agent of creation (Jn 1:3, 10). Philo uses the same prepositional phrase to denote the agency of the Logos in creation (Philo *Sacr.* 8; *Spec. Leg.* 1.81).

Examples such as these suggest that our changed understanding of Judaism should redirect but not eliminate the use that we make of Philo's works in reconstructing Christian origins.

See also ALEXANDRIA; ALEXANDRIAN SCHOLARSHIP; HELLENISTIC JUDAISM; PLATO, PLATONISM.

BIBLIOGRAPHY. **Bibliographies.** H. L. Goodhart and E. R. Goodenough, "A General Bibliography of Philo Judaeus," in E. R. Goodenough, *The Politics of Philo Judaeus: Practice and Theory* (New Haven, CT: Yale University Press, 1938) 125-321; R. Radice and D. T. Runia, *Philo of Alexandria: An Annotated Bibliography 1937-1986* (VCSup 8; Leiden: E. J. Brill, 1988); D. T. Runia et al., "A Bibliography of Philonic Studies," *Studia Philonica Annual* 1 (1989) 95-123; 2 (1990) 141-75; 3 (1991) 347-74; 4 (1992) 97-124; 5 (1993) 180-218; 6 (1994) 122-59; 7 (1995) 186-222; 8 (1996) 122-54; 9 (1997) 332-66; 10 (1998) 135-75; 11 (1999) 121-60. **Editions.** R. Arnaldez, C. Mondéseret and J. Pouilloux, eds., *Les Œuvres de Philon d'Alexandrie* (34 vols.; Paris: Editions du Cerf, 1961-92); L. Cohn et al., eds., *Philonis Alexandrini Opera Quae Supersunt* (7 vols.; Berlin: George Reimer, 1896-1930; 2d ed., 1962); F. H. Colson, G. H. Whitaker and R. Markus, eds. *Philo* (10 vols. and 2 supplementary vols.; LCL; Cambridge, MA: Harvard University Press, 1929-62). **Concordance.** P. Borgen, K. Fuglseth and R. Skarsten, *The Philo Index: A Complete Greek Word Index to the Writings of Philo of Alexandria* (Grand Rapids, MI: Eerdmans; Leiden: E. J. Brill, 2000). **Major Journals and Series on Philo.** D. Hay, ed., The *Studia Philonica* Monograph Series (BJS; Atlanta: Scholars Press, 1995-). E. Hilgert, ed., *The Studia Philonica* 1-6 (1972-80); R. Berchman and F. Calabi, eds., *Studies in Philo of Alexandria and Mediterranean Antiquity* (SFSHJ; Lanham, MD: University Press of America, 1998-); D. T. Runia and G. E. Sterling, eds., *The Studia Philonica Annual* 1- (1989-). **Studies on Philo and the New Testament.** P. Borgen, *Bread from Heaven: An Exegetical Study of the Concept of Manna in the Gospel of John and the Writings of Philo* (NovTSup 10; Leiden: E. J. Brill, 1965); idem, *Early Christianity and Hellenistic Judaism* (Edinburgh: T & T Clark, 1996); L. D. Hurst, *The Epistle to the Hebrews: Its Background of Thought* (SNTSMS 65; Cambridge: Cambridge University Press, 1990); B. A. Pearson, *The Pneumatikos-Psychikos Terminology in 1 Corinthians* (SBLDS 12; Missoula, MT: Scholars Press, 1973); D. T. Runia, *Philo in Early Christian Literature: A Survey* (CRINT 3.3; Minneapolis: Fortress, 1993); T. Seland, *Establishment Violence in Philo and Luke: A Study of Non-Conformity to the Torah and Jewish Vigilante Reactions* (BIS 15; Leiden: E. J. Brill, 1995); G. Sellin, *Der Streit um die Auferstehung der Toten: Eine religionsgeschichtliche und exegetische Untersuchung von 1 Kor 15* (FRLANT 138; Göttingen: Vandenhoeck & Ruprecht, 1986); G. E. Sterling, "'Wisdom Among the Perfect': Creation Traditions in Alexandrian Judaism and Corinthian Christianity," *NovT* 37 (1995) 355-84; J. W. Thompson, *The Beginnings of Christian Philosophy: The Epistle to the Hebrews* (CBQMS 13; Washington, DC: Catholic Biblical Association, 1982); T. J. Tobin, "The Prologue of John and Hellenistic Jewish Speculation," *CBQ* 52 (1990) 252-69.

G. E. Sterling

PHILOSOPHY

The subject matter of philosophy, as it emerges in *Greece from the beginning of the sixth century, with Thales of Miletus (fl. c. 585 B.C.), is grouped around three basic questions: What is there?—that is to say, what is the world made of, what is its origin and what is its end, if any? What ought we to do?—that is, what are the bases, natural or conventional, of personal and social morality? How can we know?—that is, what is the criterion of knowledge, as opposed to opinion, and what are the laws of reasoning and of proof? From these basic philosophical questions arise in this historical order the topics respectively of physics, including metaphysics, ethics and logic. The earliest philosophizing was really physics in this broad sense, and much of what constitutes pre-Socratic philosophy has more to do with the origins of science than with philosophy in the sense relevant to this article.

1. The Pre-Socratic Period
2. Plato and Aristotle
3. Hellenistic Philosophy: Stoics and Epicureans
4. The Philosophies of the Roman Empire

1. The Pre-Socratic Period.

The term *philosophia,* or "love of wisdom," as well as much of the substance behind that term is an invention not of the earliest recorded philosophers, the Milesian school of Thales and his successors, but rather of Pythagoras (fl. c. 520) and his followers in southern Italy, around the end of the sixth century B.C. The significance of this neologism, in Pythagoras's mind, was that he felt, in contrast to the early physicists and other contemporary experts (who would have called themselves *sophoi*) that wisdom (*sophia*) properly belonged to God alone, and that humans could only aspire to being seekers after wisdom (*philosophos*).

For Pythagoras and the tradition stemming from him, including that of *Plato, this search for wisdom involved not only the postulation of certain principles but also the adoption of a distinct moral code, or way of life (*bios*). In the case of the original Pythagoreans this *bios* meant a strictly regulated communal life, anticipating in many ways that of later Christian monastic communities; abstention from animal food because of a belief in reincarnation and the kinship of all souls, human and animal; and a series of taboos, such as that against the eating of beans, probably devised by Pythagoras to give his followers a sense of distinctness.

Such a degree of discipline, however, remained peculiar to the Pythagoreans. Their philosophical doctrines became widely influential through commending themselves to Plato. Pythagoras's chief philosophical insight was that the world was held together and given coherence by the operation of harmony and proportion, which could be expressed in terms of mathematical ratios. The dominant creative principle was One, or unity (the Monad), which acted on an archetypal, formless substratum, symbolized by the number Two (the Dyad). The union of these two generated primarily the whole system of numbers and secondarily the world of physical objects, which, for the early Pythagoreans, were to be regarded as numbers.

Pythagoras was also the first to give philosophical underpinning to the originally shamanistic notion of the soul as something separable from the body, which is not just an insubstantial shade but the true repository of the personality. For him, and for Plato after him, immortality for the soul was inextricably involved with reincarnation, into both human and (in the case of unsatisfactory humans) animal bodies. The problems about personal identity that this involves do not seem to have bothered ancient thinkers.

2. Plato and Aristotle.

Plato (427-347 B.C.) is the spiritual heir to Pythagoras, but in constructing his philosophy he was also much influenced by the intellectual challenges laid down by Parmenides of Elea (c. 515-445 B.C.) and Heraclitus of Ephesus (fl. c. 500 B.C.). Heraclitus seems to have been the first to view the world (*kosmos*) as a system: in constant flux but held together in a tension of opposites, by a force that he termed *logos* ("ratio," "reason," "word"). Parmenides focused on the problem of being, what must be the characteristics of what is, and declared that it must be one, eternal, uniform and motionless, and that only what is can be known: there can be no knowledge of what is not. The true subject of these mysterious pronouncements remained a puzzle for subsequent thinkers, but they make best sense if they are taken to concern the totality of what is. To confuse matters, Parmenides also composed an account of the physical world, which for him was a realm of illusion, and Plato took up the challenge thus posed by postulating first an intelligible realm of true Being, which fulfilled Parmenides' prescription, and served as home of the Forms, ideal archetypes of all physical reality, and then a sense-perceptible realm of Becoming, in which we dwell, which is in constant (Heraclitean) flux but held together nonetheless by the system of Forms, which project themselves upon a material substratum in the form of geometrical structures (the basic triangles and their combinations described in his dialogue *Timaeus*).

However, Pythagoras is the dominant influence on Plato and his immediate successors, Speusippus and Xenocrates, under whom Platonism becomes properly a system. All their works have perished, but we can see from the titles that are preserved their formalizing tendency, of Xenocrates in particular, and that propensity for reinterpreting Pythagoras to accord with their doctrines that is the origin of *Neo-Pythagoreanism. Speusippus advanced a doctrine of the first principle, that it is a unity beyond being, which finds no support in mainline Platonism before Plotinus but which seems to have found echoes in less orthodox Neo-Pythagorean and platonizing gnostic circles. Xenocrates, perhaps influenced to some extent by *Aristotle, postulated as a first principle a monad that is also an intellect and whose contents were probably, though not certainly, envisaged as being the Forms (this is the case in the Platonism of such figures as Antiochus and Eudorus in the first century B.C.).

Plato's most distinguished successor, however, was his most dissident one, *Aristotle (384-322 B.C.). Aristotle, son of a distinguished doctor from Stagira in the north of Greece, had joined Plato's Academy in 367 B.C., at the age of seventeen, and remained with him until his death, though showing an increasing tendency to argue with him on basic issues. After a period abroad, Aristotle set up his own rival school across town, the Lyceum or Peripatos, in 335 B.C. Aristotle greatly advanced all departments of philosophy, metaphysics, physics, ethics and logic, but, despite his polemical stance toward Plato, his disagreements with him chiefly concern the theory of Forms, the general tendency to mathematicize the universe (evident particularly in Plato's other successors) and the doctrine of the separable nature of the soul. Later Platonists managed to appropriate most of Aristotelian philosophy into a common Academic synthesis, even contriving to downplay his objections to the Forms and his denial of the separate existence of the soul. In the former case, he was held to be referring to the immanent form (*eidos*), a projection into matter of the transcendent form (*idea*); in the latter, likewise, his analysis (in the *De Anima)* is thought to concern only the soul in its embodied mode—a triumphant exercise of the late antique philosophical conviction that great minds must at all costs think alike, as well as being entirely consistent with themselves!

Aristotle's doctrine of the supreme principle, or God, as a mind thinking itself becomes standard Platonic doctrine up to the time of Plotinus, when a doctrine stemming from Speusippus is reasserted, of a unitary first principle, above being and intellection, the self-thinking mind being relegated to second place in the universe. Such doctrines as those of the four causes, of matter, of potentiality and actuality, and the whole of Aristotelian logic, are also taken on board. In the sphere of ethics, the doctrines advanced in the *Nicomachean Ethics,* such as those of virtue as a mean, the moderation of the passions and contemplation (*theoria*) as the supreme purpose of human life, are accepted likewise. It was felt by later Platonists that in all these areas Aristotle was formalizing the common doctrine of the Academy.

3. Hellenistic Philosophy: Stoics and Epicureans.

During the *Hellenistic era, dating broadly from the death of *Alexander the Great in 323 B.C. to the defeat of Antony and Cleopatra by Augustus in 31 B.C., the cutting edge of philosophy was represented not by either the Academy (which after Polemon deviated into skepticism) or by the Lyceum (which after Aristotle's successor, Theophrastus, declined into antiquarianism and triviality) but rather by the rival schools of *Stoics and *Epicureans, the one founded by Zeno of Kition, in Cyprus (335-263 B.C.), a creative admirer of the Cynic movement, the other by the Athenian Epicurus (341-270 B.C.), a dissident follower of the Atomists, but both based in Athens.

Of these, the Epicureans have little to offer from the perspective of Christianity—being materialists, constructive atheists (Epicurus held that the gods existed but were not concerned with humans) and devotees of pleasure as the highest aim of human life—except for their advancement of certain arguments that they developed against the existence of the traditional Greek gods, which are borrowed gratefully by the church fathers. The Stoics, by contrast, despite their materialism, are of great importance. In metaphysics, their conception of the Logos, or creative reason-principle of God, which is borrowed back by later Platonists as a demythologized version of the Demiurge of Plato's *Timaeus,* becomes crucial for the development of christological doctrine from the Fourth Gospel on and causes difficulties later about the relation of the Son to the Father.

In epistemology, the Stoics' most important contribution was to postulate the concept of the "cognitive impression" (*katalēptikē phantasia*), the essential feature of which was that it could not have come from anything other than that of which it did in fact come. On this basis they were able to construct a system involving propositions of which one could be certain, such as "gods exist" and "they exercise providential care over the world"—this in the face of the pervasive skepticism being advanced by the Platonic Academy of the time.

In ethics, too, the Stoics set up an ideal of the extirpation of the passions (*apatheia*), as against the less extreme Aristotelian ideal of their moderation (*metriopatheia*), which proved attractive both to many Platonists and to many of the church fathers. The Stoics propounded an ideal of the Sage as self-sufficient and impervious to the blows of fortune, an ideal that was in one way attractive to Christian ascetics but in another way antithetical to the Christian ideal of brotherly love and concern for one's fellow humans.

5. The Philosophies of the Roman Empire. In the first century B.C., various important developments took place. The Platonist Antiochus of Ascalon (c. 130-69 B.C.), much influenced by Stoic thought, turned Platonism back to dogmatism in a way that was to prove fruitful for later ages, though a transcendental element derived from Neo-Pythagoreanism, which reestablished a supreme deity as immaterial and external to the physical world, needed to be added before the synthetic philosophical system known as Middle Platonism could emerge in the first centuries A.D. and exercise a significant influence on emergent Christianity. At the same time, a revitalized Stoicism, the most notable representatives of which were the Roman nobleman *Seneca (c. 4 B.C.-A.D. 65), the freed slave *Epictetus (mid-first to mid-second century A.D.), and the emperor Marcus Aurelius Antoninus (A.D. 121-180), popularized and developed the basic principles of Stoic ethics in such a way as to influence both Platonism and Christianity.

In many ways, the new synthesis developed by the third-century Platonist Plotinus (A.D. 204-269), taking in many concepts from both Aristotelianism and Stoicism but adding also a strongly transcendentalist element derived from the Neo-Pythagoreanism of Numenius (fl. c. A.D. 150) provided a stimulus for later Christian thinkers such as the Cappadocian fathers. In Plotinus we find for the first time, in a coherent form, the concept of a first principle superior to intellect, the One, adumbrated by Plato's successor Speusippus but overlaid then by the Aristotelian concept of God as a self-thinking intellect. This development, however, which becomes a distinguishing mark of later Platonism, was one that Christian thinkers were disinclined to follow, as it conflicted with the concept of a personal God. Only in the writings of the mysterious sixth-century Christian Platonist going under the name of Dionysius the Areopagite is this concept taken on board, with fantastic results.

For Plotinus, as for most other philosophers of the period, philosophy is a matter of seeking the best way of purifying the soul from the influences of the body and the external world and leading it back to its source in the intelligible world. Both his ethical theory and his epistemology are directed to that end. He expends much effort in trying to bring us to a realization of our true nature, being that of a strictly impassive soul immured in a body animated by a sort of emanation from this soul, which is the seat of "vulgar" consciousness, involving passions and sense perceptions but which does not properly constitute the core of our being. Such a scenario, while considerably more austere than the normal Christian view, presents a challenge that a number of the more Platonically minded fathers, such as the Cappadocians, found stimulating.

See also ARISTOTLE, ARISTOTELIANISM; CYNIC EPISTLES; CYNICISM AND SKEPTICISM; EPICTETUS; EPICUREANISM; NEO-PYTHAGOREANISM; PLATO, PLATONISM; SENECA; STOICISM.

BIBLIOGRAPHY. A. H. Armstrong, *An Introduction to Greek Philosophy* (London: Methuen, 1947); idem, ed., *The Cambridge History of Late Ancient and Early Medieval Philosophy* (Cambridge: Cambridge University Press, 1967); J. M. Dillon, *The Middle Platonists* (Ithaca, NY: Cornell University Press, 1977); W. K. C. Guthrie, *A History of Greek Philosophy* (Cambridge: Cambridge University Press, 1962). J. M. Dillon

PHYLACTERIES/TEPILLIN, QUMRAN. *See* DEAD SEA SCROLLS: GENERAL INTRODUCTION.

PIETY, JEWISH

For ancient *Judaism piety, or devotion to God, was understood to embrace every aspect of life:

"Piety governs all our actions and occupations and speech; none of these things did our lawgiver leave unexamined or indeterminate" (Josephus *Ag. Ap.* 2.16 §171). In a more narrow sense, piety (*eusebeia;* cf. "holiness," *hosiotēs*) could refer to duty to God, although true piety was inseparable from its corollary, duty to fellow human beings ("justice," *dikaiosynē,* and "love of humanity," *philanthrōpia*; *Ep. Arist.* 131; cf. 24, 215; Josephus *Ant.* 18.5.2 §117; Philo *Spec. Leg.* 2.15 §63; Mk 12:28-34 par.). Although our focus will be on piety more narrowly conceived, a full picture of ancient Judaism must also include its strong emphasis on love of neighbor (Lev 19:18) and stranger (Lev 19:34) as essential to the right worship of God (*m. ʾAbot* 1:2). The following discussion is divided among the three major spheres of life in which piety was practiced: temple, synagogue and daily life.

1. The Context of Piety
2. The Practice of Piety in the Temple
3. The Practice of Piety in the Synagogue
4. The Practice of Piety in Daily Life
5. Jewish Piety After A.D. 70

1. The Context of Piety.

1.1. Diversity and Unity. Critical use of our major sources—Jewish writings of the Second Temple period (*Josephus, *Philo, the *Apocrypha and Pseudepigrapha, *Dead Sea Scrolls), the NT, *rabbinic literature and pagan writers who discuss Jews and Judaism—reveals vibrant, developing and often diverse practices and beliefs, such that broad generalizations about Judaism are difficult and potentially misleading. Interpretations of the Torah varied, and surviving documents reveal often vigorous debates concerning correct practices (**Miqsat Maʿasey ha-Torah* [4QMMT]; Mk 7:1-23 par.; Mt 23; cf. the debates between the school of Hillel and the school of Shammai in rabbinic literature [see Neusner 1971]). Furthermore, the vast majority of Jews who lived in this period left no written records; the extent to which their various understandings of piety are reflected in our sources is a matter for conjecture.

In highlighting the diversity within Judaism, it must be emphasized that important core beliefs (particularly monotheism and election) and practices (e.g., circumcision, dietary observances, *sabbath) clearly set the Jewish people as a whole apart from surrounding cultures. Below we will focus on the core of generally shared practices; more information on diversity of practice within Second Temple Judaism can be found herein under articles treating various groups and sects and in the works cited in the bibliography.

1.2. Obedience as a Response to Grace. The overarching context for Jewish piety was the belief that the one true God had graciously chosen *Israel to be his people. Monotheism—exclusive devotion to Yahweh—resulted in a strong abhorrence of Gentile idolatry, although the degree of participation in surrounding cultures varied widely (see Barclay; Kasher). *Rome generally exempted Jews from direct participation in the emperor cult (*see* Ruler Cult). The attempt of Gaius Caligula to install his statue in the Jerusalem *temple (c. A.D. 41) nearly touched off a worldwide uprising of Jews (Philo *Leg. Gai.* 31 §§213-17; cf. Mt 24:15 par.). After Gaius's death brought this crisis to an end, the right of the Jews to worship Yahweh alone was reaffirmed (Josephus *Ant.* 19.5.2 §§284-85).

Along with belief in Yahweh as the one true God came the conviction that this God had chosen Israel out of all the nations of the world and made a covenant with them. This conviction is crucial for a correct understanding of the place of the law in early Judaism (*see* Torah). Jewish piety has often been unfairly characterized as legalism—the attempt to acquire merit before God through the performance of various rituals and practices. This reconstruction of Judaism is founded primarily on a particular reading of polemical passages in the Gospels and in Paul's writings. When all of our available sources are considered, however, a much different picture results. In a series of major studies investigating a wide range of Jewish texts from approximately 200 B.C. to A.D. 200, E. P. Sanders has persuasively argued that obedience to the law was widely understood in Second Temple Judaism not as a way to earn God's favor but rather as a response to God's prior election of Israel (Sanders 1977, 1990, 1992; cf. Moore; *see DPL,* Law).

Obedience to the commandments was viewed as a sign of membership in God's covenant, but the covenant itself had its origin in God's grace, not in Israel's worthiness: "Thou hast shown us mercy, for we had no meritorious deeds to show. . . . For the whole world is Thine, and yet Thou hast no other people than Israel, as it is said, 'The people which I formed for Myself' (Is 43:21)" (*Mekilta Shirata* 9 [Lauterbach

2:69]). Likewise, while human obedience was a necessary response to God, the maintenance of the covenant ultimately depended on God's mercy and faithfulness: "As for me, if I stumble, the mercies of God shall be my eternal salvation. If I stagger because of the sin of flesh, my justification shall be by the righteousness of God which endures forever. . . . He will draw me near by His grace, and by His mercy will He bring my justification. He will judge me in the righteousness of His truth and in the greatness of His goodness He will pardon all my sins" (1QS 11:11-14, Vermes). Similar views are expressed in a multitude of texts, many of which are cited and discussed in detail by Sanders. That individual Jews, much like the adherents of any other faith, did not always live up to the ideals expressed in their theology is not to be doubted. However, criticisms of Jewish practices and beliefs, whether found in the NT or in other early Jewish literature, must be interpreted in light of the widespread and foundational Jewish conviction that obedience to the commandments was above all a response of love and devotion to the God who out of his abundant mercy and grace had chosen Israel to be his covenant people.

2. The Practice of Piety in the Temple.

2.1. One God, One Temple. The Second Temple was built after the exile on the site of Solomon's temple (516 B.C.; Ezra 6:14-18). *Herod began a massive expansion of the temple complex (20/19 B.C.; Josephus *Ant.* 15.11.1-7 §§380-425) that was not completed until about A.D. 64 (Josephus *Ant.* 20.9.7 §219; cf. Jn 2:20). What was most notable about the Jerusalem temple, however, was not its size and magnificence but the fact that it stood as the sole official temple of Yahweh, in stark contrast to the multitude of temples and shrines to other gods found throughout the Greco-Roman world (Acts 17:16, 22-23). "Since God is one, there should likewise be only one temple," remarks Philo (*Spec. Leg.* 1.12 §67; cf. Josephus *Ag. Ap.* 2.23 §193). Even groups who bitterly opposed the current temple leadership did not normally establish alternate temples, although the hope for a new or renewed temple was a common *eschatological expectation (Tob 13:16-18; *1 Enoch* 90:28-29; *Jub.* 1:17, 29; 11QTemple 29:7-10; *Sib. Or.* 5:420-33; contrast Rev 21:22). Other Jewish temples, such as those at Araq el-Emir (second century B.C.) and Leontopolis (c. 160 B.C.-A.D. 73), never seriously rivaled the Jerusalem temple. Diaspora Jews looked to Jerusalem and its temple as the spiritual center of Judaism (Philo *Spec. Leg.* 1.12 §§68-70).

2.2. Sacrifice, Prayer and Festivals. Temple activities centered around *sacrifice. The daily sacrifice of two male yearling lambs along with offerings of flour, oil and wine (one lamb in the morning and one in the late afternoon) was accompanied by *prayers and by the recitation of the *Shemaʿ* and the Ten Commandments (Ex 29:38-46; Num 28:1-8; Josephus *Ant.* 14.4.3 §65; *Ag. Ap.* 2.23 §§196-97; *m. Tamid* 4:1—5:1). In connection with these daily sacrifices, the *priests burned incense before the Most Holy Place inside the temple (Ex 30:7-8; Jdt 9:1; Lk 1:8-11). Special sacrifices were offered on the sabbath, at the new moon, at the New Year, on the Day of Atonement and during the three major pilgrimage *festivals (Lev 23; Num 28:9—29:40; Josephus *Ant.* 3.10.1-7 §§237-57). Individual worshipers brought various offerings for purification (Mk 1:44; Lk 2:22-24; Acts 21:23-26), for transgressions or for thanksgiving (Lev 1—7; Josephus *Ant.* 3.9.1-4 §§224-36). Proper sacrifice was understood to require the right intentions, such as repentance for sin and reconciliation with others, on the part of the worshiper (Philo *Spec. Leg.* 1.53 §§290-95; Mt 5:23-24).

Laypeople came to pray in the temple precincts at the times of the daily sacrifices (Sir 50:5-21; Lk 1:10; Acts 3:1; cf. Acts 2:42) and throughout the day (Lk 2:37). Psalms continued to be sung in the temple as well (Sir 50:18). The temple courts and porticoes served as a location for Jesus' teaching (Mk 11:27; 14:49; Jn 10:23), for the apostles' preaching (Acts 5:42) and for gatherings of the Jerusalem church (Acts 2:46).

The three great pilgrimage feasts (Passover/Unleavened Bread, Weeks or Pentecost and Tabernacles), which recalled the exodus, wilderness journeys and the gift of the land (Ex 12:1—13:10; Num 28:16-31; 29:12-38; Deut 16:1-17), brought great crowds to Jerusalem. The increased numbers and heightened sense of national identity made these festivals prime occasions for protest and even revolt (Josephus *Ant.* 13.13.5 §§372-73; 17.9.3 §§213-18; 17.10.2 §§254-64; 20.5.3 §§105-12; cf. Mk 14:1-2 par.). As a result, the Roman governor (*see* Roman Governors of Palestine), who normally resided in *Caesarea Maritima, brought extra troops to Jerusalem for the feasts.

Although the Torah requires attendance at all three major festivals, those who lived far from Jerusalem probably found it difficult to come to more than one festival per year, while most *Diaspora Jews might have made the pilgrimage only once, if at all. The pilgrimage was both a worshipful and a festive experience. Families would spend their "second tithe" money in Jerusalem (Deut 14:22-26; *Jub.* 32:10-14; Josephus *Ant.* 4.8.8 §205) and also use the visit to bring their sacrifices, which in the case of shared sacrifices and the Passover sacrifice resulted in a relatively rare opportunity to enjoy red meat. The difficulty involved in bringing sacrificial animals long distances created a demand for suitable animals that could be bought in Jerusalem (Mk 11:15 par.; *see* Festivals).

Gentiles could and did bring gifts and sacrifices to the temple (Josephus *Ag. Ap.* 2.5 §48; *J.W.* 2.17.3 §§412-14; 5.13.6 §§562-63; cf. Is 56:7; Mk 11:17 par.), though they were prevented from moving beyond the outer court by a barrier carrying a strict warning that to proceed further would result in a death sentence (Josephus *Ant.* 15.11.5 §417; Philo *Leg. Gai.* 31 §212; cf. Acts 21:27-29; Eph 2:14). Rome subsidized a daily sacrifice at the temple for the emperor and the Roman people (Philo *Leg. Gai.* 23 §157; 40 §317; cf. 32 §232; 36 §291; 45 §§356-57; Josephus *Ag. Ap.* 2.6 §77; *J.W.* 2.10.4 §197); the priests' decision in A.D. 66 to cease this sacrifice signaled their fixed intent to go to war with Rome (Josephus *J.W.* 2.17.2-3 §§408-16; *see* Jewish History: Roman Period; Jewish Wars with Rome).

2.3. Financial Support of the Temple. The Torah, as interpreted in the Second Temple period, stipulated that a tenth of each nonsabbatical year's produce be given for the support of the Levites, who in turn tithed to the priests (Num 18:21-32; Neh 10:37-39; Josephus *Ant.* 4.4.4 §69). The priests also received the firstfruits of produce (Num 18:13), the firstborn of clean animals (unclean animals and firstborn children were redeemed with money, Ex 13:11-16; Num 18:15-18), heave offering (Num 18:11-12; Neh 10:37; *m. Ter.*) and portions of many of the sacrifices and offerings brought to the temple (Josephus *Ant.* 4.4.4 §§69-75). People could also dedicate property to the temple (Mk 7:11 par.).

A yearly temple tax of a half shekel (2 denarii), required of every male Israelite over twenty, directly supported the temple operations (Ex 30:11-16; Neh 10:32). This tax appears to have been paid faithfully, even by Diaspora Jews, and it served as a marker of Jewish identity. Rome helped to ensure the Jews' right to send money to Jerusalem despite the local tensions caused by this large outflow of cash (Philo *Spec. Leg.* 1.14 §§76-78; *Leg. Gai.* 23 §§156-57; 31 §216; 36 §291; 40 §§311-16; Josephus *Ant.* 14.10.8 §§213-16; 16.6.2-3 §§163, 166; Cicero *Flac.* 28; on payment of the tax by Babylonian Jews, see Josephus *Ant.* 18.9.1 §§312-13; Philo *Leg. Gai.* 31 §216). The rich temple treasury found itself the object of plunder by foreigners more than once (1 Macc 1:20-24; Josephus *J.W.* 2.9.4 §175; 2.14.6 §293; *Ant.* 17.10.2 §264). After the destruction of the temple, the Romans collected an equivalent tax on all Jews to be paid to the temple of Jupiter Capitolinus (Josephus *J.W.* 7.6.6 §218; Dio Cassius *Hist.* 66.7.2). Jesus' payment of the temple tax is the subject of a curious exchange in Matthew 17:24-27 (*see* Taxation, Jewish; see also Sanders 1992. For attitudes toward the temple, *see* Temple, Jewish).

3. The Practice of Piety in the Synagogue.
While its origins remain obscure, the synagogue was an established, if continually developing, institution by the Second Temple period in both the Diaspora and Palestine. The functions associated with the synagogue varied from place to place and from time to time, with the synagogue's importance to the Jewish community likely increasing the greater the distance from Jerusalem. The right of Jews to assemble was protected by Roman law, even in Rome itself, where other religious societies were forbidden to meet (Josephus *Ant.* 14.10.8 §§213-16; Philo *Leg. Gai.* 40 §§311-16). Sabbath assembly was regarded by some as a Mosaic decree (*Bib. Ant.* 11:8; Philo *Hypoth.* 7.12-13; *Op. Mund.* 43 §128; Josephus *Ag. Ap.* 2.17 §175).

Remains of synagogues from the first century A.D. have been discovered, but in many cases Jews may have met on the sabbath in private homes or in buildings used on other days for different purposes (*see* Synagogues; see also Fine; Levine 1987 and 1999; Urman and Flesher). In the Diaspora, synagogues were often located by water, perhaps for purification rituals (Josephus *Ant.* 14.10.23 §258; *Ep. Arist.* 305-6; Acts 16:13). Leadership may have been primarily by laypeople, although the Theodotus inscription from Jerusalem (in Greek, usually dated first century A.D.) indicates several generations of priestly leadership at that particular synagogue (cf. Philo *Hypoth.* 7.12-13; *see* Inscriptions and Papyri: Jewish). Leadership of synagogues by *Pharisees is suggested by some passages in the Gospels (Mt 23:2, 6), but not all (Mk 5:21-24, 35-43 par.; Lk 13:14). *Women appear to have participated in leadership roles in the synagogue to varying degrees (cf. Acts 16:13-14; 17:4, 12; 18:26; see Brooten; Kraemer; Feldman 1996, 56-58).

3.1. Study of Torah. During the pre-70 period, the reading and exposition of *Torah was the primary sabbath activity of the synagogue (Philo *Op. Mund.* 43 §128; *Spec. Leg.* 2.15 §§61-64; Josephus *Ag. Ap.* 2.17 §175; Acts 15:21). Portions of the Torah and Prophets were read, although there was not yet a standard lectionary. The origin of the *Septuagint and of the *targumim is probably to be traced back to the necessity of providing translations of Scriptures in the vernacular (*m. Meg.* 4:4; *see* Septuagint/Greek Old Testament; Aramaic Language). Exposition and exhortation would follow, perhaps with several people speaking in turn. The NT provides important early evidence for the structure of a synagogue service (Lk 4:16-27; Acts 13:14-43; cf. 1 Cor 14:26-33a). The Dead Sea sect was notable for its devotion to the study of Torah, legislating continual study and exposition by some members of the group (1QS 6:6-8; 8:12-16).

3.2. Prayer. The most common Greek term for what we know as a synagogue is *proseuchē*, "[place of] prayer" (see Acts 16:13, 16), yet the role of communal prayer in the synagogue service of the pre-70 period is unclear. The Dead Sea sect appears to have had a fixed liturgy for corporate prayer, but similar evidence for other groups is lacking before A.D. 70 (see Liturgy: Qumran). Even if they did not attain a fixed form this early, however, the main themes of later rabbinic prayers such as the Eighteen Benedictions—creation, revelation, election, redemption—were likely widespread. These later prayers share common features with the Lord's Prayer as well as with prayers known from the Dead Sea Scrolls (*see* Prayer; Liturgy: Rabbinic).

3.3. Other Communal Activities. Particularly in the Diaspora, the synagogue functioned as a center for community life in a manner similar to that of Greco-Roman associations, providing a site for communal meals and for the celebration of holy days (Josephus *Ant.* 14.10.8 §§213-16; cf. Mt 23:6; 1 Cor 11:17-34; *see* Associations) and serving as a collection point for alms (Mt 6:2) and for the temple tax (Philo *Leg. Gai.* 23 §156; Josephus *Ant.* 14.10.8 §215; 16.6.2 §§163-64). The synagogue also served as a law court for community matters, with authority to mete out punishments such as the thirty-nine lashes suffered repeatedly by Paul (2 Cor 11:24; cf. Mt 10:17; Acts 22:19; *m. Mak.* 3:10-11). The Theodotus inscription indicates that the synagogue provided accommodations for visitors to Jerusalem, most likely from the Greek-speaking Diaspora.

3.4. Gentiles and the Synagogue. Jewish piety evoked both scorn and admiration from Gentiles (see Feldman 1993; Whittaker). Instances of violence against Jews and their synagogues are known from this period (e.g., in *Alexandria, A.D. 38, Philo *Leg. Gai.* §§132-39; *Flacc.* §§41-53; Caesarea, A.D. 66, Josephus *J.W.* 2.14.4-5 §§284-92), yet a sizable number of Gentiles appear to have attended synagogues and to have observed some Jewish practices (Josephus *Ag. Ap.* 2.39 §282; *J.W.* 7.3.3 §45; *see* Proselytism and Godfearers; see also Feldman 1993).

4. The Practice of Piety in Daily Life.

4.1. Circumcision. Though it was practiced by other peoples in the ancient world (e.g., by Arabs and by Egyptian priests, Josephus *Ant.* 1.12.2 §214; *Ag. Ap.* 2.13 §141), circumcision was particularly associated with the Jews. According to Genesis 17:9-14, circumcision on the eighth day was given to Abraham by God as a sign of the covenant. Thus, to forego circumcision would be to renounce the covenant (Gen 17:14; cf. Acts 21:20-24; *m. Ker.* 1:1). That it served as a clear marker of Jewish identity can be seen in Antiochus IV Epiphanes' prohibition of the practice (1 Macc 1:48) and in the attempt of some Hellenizing Jews surgically to remove the evidence of circumcision (1 Macc 1:15). Circumcision was the mark that distinguished Gentile proselytes from sympathizers (Josephus *Ant.* 20.2.4 §§38-48; 20.7.1 §139; see Nolland).

4.2. Dietary Observances. Another distinguishing mark of Jewish identity was observance of biblical restrictions on allowable foods (Lev 11:1-47; Deut 14:3-21; *see DJG*, Clean and Unclean). Particularly notable in the ancient world (and often the subject of mockery—cf. Philo *Leg. Gai.* 45 §§361-62) was Jewish avoidance of pork. During the *Hasmonean revolt, pious Jews chose death rather than violate this stricture (2 Macc 7; 4 Macc 5:1—6:30).

While observance of dietary laws was fairly uncomplicated in Palestine, Diaspora Jews had more difficulty obtaining acceptable food, as is evidenced by a number of decrees designed to ensure that Jews had access to their ancestral food (Josephus *Ant.* 14.10.12, 21, 24 §§226, 245, 261). Eating with Gentiles would have been acceptable as long as Jewish food was available (Jdt 10:5; 12:2, 9, 19; *Ep. Arist.* 180-81), although in practice the food laws probably limited social interaction between Jews and Gentiles (3 Macc 3:3-7). Eating Gentile meat would have posed difficulties both because most of the meat in the Greco-Roman world had been sacrificed in connection with a religious ceremony (1 Cor 8, 10) and because Jews suspected Gentile slaughtering methods of leaving blood in the meat (Lev 7:26-27; 17:10-14; Acts 15:20). The common practice of offering a libation to the gods would have made Gentile wine objectionable as well. Gentile oil was also avoided by many Jews, perhaps for purity reasons (Josephus *Life* 13 §74; *J.W.* 2.21.2 §591; *Ant.* 12.3.1 §120). Where proper food was unavailable, pious Jews probably ate vegetables and drank water (Josephus *Life* 3 §14; cf. Dan 1:8-16; Rom 14:2). Josephus mentions observance of at least some of the Jewish dietary laws by Gentile sympathizers as a fairly common phenomenon (Josephus *Ag. Ap.* 2.39 §282).

4.3. ***Purity.*** Biblical purity laws also continued to be observed in our period (e.g., Lev 11—15; Num 19; *see DJG,* Clean and Unclean; see also Sanders 1992). Purity primarily had to do with one's ability to participate in the temple cult, since no impure Israelite could enter the temple precincts (Lev 15:31; *m. Parah* 11:4). Because impurity was contracted in the course of everyday activities, however, most people were impure most of the time. It is crucial to realize that to be in a state of impurity was not sinful in and of itself. Many activities that in themselves were pious and good (e.g., caring for the dead; sexual intercourse; childbirth) resulted in impurity. Depending on the type of impurity, purification could require some or all of the following: immersion, washing clothes, the passage of set time periods, inspection by a priest and sacrifice (cf. Mk 1:44). Corpse impurity required a seven-day purification period and sprinkling with a special mixture of water and the ashes of the red heifer sacrifice (Num 19). Only the high priest was prohibited from contracting corpse impurity altogether (Lev 21:10-12), but priests were expected to avoid it except in the case of a close relative's death (Lev 21:1-4). This stricture may help to explain the behavior of the priest and Levite in Jesus' parable of the Good Samaritan (Lk 10:25-37).

Although impurity was in many cases unavoidable and not in itself sinful, purity was generally seen as a desirable state, and many people may have immersed regularly (Jdt 12:7-9). Archaeological investigation has turned up numerous immersion pools both in Jerusalem and in areas of Palestine far from the temple. Groups such as the Pharisees and the Dead Sea sectarians elaborated purity laws to a greater extent than most Jews observed (*see* Pharisees; Essenes). The Pharisees as well as other groups of pious Jews (Is 66:20; Jdt 11:13; *m. Parah* 11:4-5; CD 11:18-21) tried to handle the priests' food in a state of ritual purity, though to what extent they attempted to eat their own food in purity is debated (see Neusner 1973; Sanders 1990). Nothing suggests that the Pharisees forced everyone to follow their purity rules or considered those who did not to be "sinners" (*m. Parah* 11:5); even the schools of Hillel and Shammai disagreed on correct practices, yet they continued to associate and intermarry with each other (*m. Yebam.* 1:4). Jesus debated with Pharisees over issues involving purity (*see DJG,* Clean and Unclean; see also Sanders 1990; Fredriksen).

In the Diaspora, Jews developed extrabiblical purifications such as handwashing and sprinkling (*Ep. Arist.* 305-6; *Sib. Or.* 3.591-93; Philo *Spec. Leg.* 3.10 §63; 36 §§205-6; cf. Mk 7:1-4), evincing a desire for purity even apart from direct participation in the temple cult. Writers such as *Philo emphasized that outward purity is valueless without purity of one's heart (Philo *Spec. Leg.* 1.49 §§262-66; *Quaest. in Ex.* 1.2; cf. 1QS 2:25—3:12; Ps 24:4; Jas 4:8). Gentiles were apparently not thought to be subject to purity laws. The major Jewish concern in social relationships with Gentile neighbors would have been to avoid idolatry and impure food (see Sanders 1992, 72-76).

4.4. ***Prayer.*** In addition to spontaneous, private prayer, the practice of fixed times of prayer was widespread by this period. Prayers were joined with recitation of the *Shema*ʿ (Deut 6:4-9), a passage that affirms the core beliefs of monotheism and election. Saying the *Shema*ʿ in the morning and evening follows from a literal interpretation of Deuteronomy 6:7b-9, as does the wearing of *tefillin* (phylacteries) on arm and forehead and the use of *mezuzot* on doorposts, both of which contained portions of Scripture (*m. Ber.* 1:1-4; 1QS 9:26—10:3; 4Q128-155; *Ep. Arist.* 158-60; Josephus *Ant.* 4.8.13 §§212-13; Mt 23:5). Some evidence connects regular times of prayer with the daily sacrifices in the morning and late afternoon (Jdt 9:1; *t. Ber.* 3:1; cf. *m. Ber.* 4:1). Other sources suggest that three times of prayer were observed (*m. Ber.* 4:1; cf. Dan 6:10, 13; Ps 55:17; Acts 10:9). Mealtimes provided yet another opportunity for prayer and thanksgiving (1QS 6:4-6; Josephus *J.W.* 2.8.5 §131; Mk 6:41 par.; Mk 8:6-7 par.; Mk 14:22-23 par.; Rom 14:6). The proliferation of hymns and prayers in Second Temple period texts attests the vibrancy of prayer and praise in this era (cf. 1QH; Lk 1:46-55, 67-79; 2:28-32; *see* Prayer).

4.5. Sabbath. The Torah establishes observance of a day of rest as a mark of the covenant, linking it both with creation (Ex 20:8-11) and with the redemption of Israel at the exodus (Deut 5:12-15). The prohibition of work on the sabbath, elaborated in later periods (Jer 17:19-27; Neh 10:31; 13:15-22), continued to be further specified in the Second Temple period, though not everyone observed the same restrictions. For example, the practice of the Essenes was notable for its strictness (Josephus *J.W.* 2.8.9 §147; cf. CD 10:14—11:18). Rabbinic evidence indicates that certain religious duties and any actions necessary to protect life, even when the danger to life was doubtful, took precedence over sabbath observance (*m. Yoma* 8:6; *m. Šabb.* 18:3—19:5; *m. Pesaḥ.* 5—6).

Observance of the sabbath was a conspicuous marker of Jewish identity. During the Hasmonean revolt, some pious Jews refused even to defend themselves on the sabbath and were slaughtered (1 Macc 2:29-38). The subsequent decision to allow self-defense (1 Macc 2:39-41) covered only direct assault; thus, in 63 B.C., *Pompey's army was able to capture the temple by building siege works on the sabbath, when they were unhindered by the Jews' missiles (Josephus *J.W.* 1.7.3 §§145-47; Dio Cassius *Hist.* 37.16.1-4). The Romans exempted Jews from military service because of their refusal to carry arms or march on the sabbath (Josephus *Ant.* 14.10.12 §226; *see* Roman Military), and Josephus mentions decrees allowing Jews to assemble on the sabbath (Josephus *Ant.* 14.10.23-24 §§258, 261) and exempting them from being called into court on the sabbath (Josephus *Ant.* 16.6.2 §163). In addition to the weekly sabbath, every seventh year the land was to have a rest from cultivation (Ex 23:10-11; Lev 25:1-7). That this was generally observed is suggested by Caesar's remission of taxes on Herod's domain in the seventh year (Josephus *Ant.* 14.10.6 §202).

Although some pagans mistook the sabbath for a fast day, in reality it was a day for rest and festive dining with family and friends (cf. Lk 14:1; Jdt 8:6). *ʿErubin*, a Pharisaic device allowing houses with a common courtyard to be considered as one dwelling (thus permitting the carrying of vessels between the houses), facilitated communal dining, even though it relaxed the sabbath restriction that prohibited carrying vessels out of a house (Jer 17:22; *m. ʿErub.*). Other groups, such as the *Sadducees, who did not recognize this custom (cf. *m. ʿErub.* 6:1-2), probably considered the Pharisees to be breaking one of the commandments regulating the sabbath. Yet this, like most minor differences of practice, appears to have been met with toleration. Sabbath observance was one of the practices often adopted by Gentile sympathizers (Josephus *Ag. Ap.* 2.39 §282; Philo *Vit. Mos.* 2.4 §§20-22; cf. Rom 14:5-6; Gal 4:10; Col 2:16).

5. Jewish Piety After A.D. 70.

The sacrificial cult ceased with the destruction of the temple in 70, yet hopes for the imminent rebuilding of the temple and the renewal of *sacrifice persisted at least until after the Bar Kokhba revolt. A saying attributed to Rabbi Johanan ben Zakkai indicates one way in which Jewish piety came to terms with the loss of temple and sacrifice: "We have another atonement in place of [the temple cult]. . . . 'For I desire lovingkindness and not sacrifice (Hos 6:6)' " (*ʾAbot R. Nat.* A, 4 [B, 8]; cf. Pr Azar 15-18; Sir 35:1-5; Tob 4:11). In Justin's *Dialogue with Trypho* (c. 160), Trypho notes that even without the temple the Jews continue to observe practices such as circumcision, sabbath, new moon festivals and some purificatory washings (Justin Martyr *Dial. Tryph.* 46.2); in addition, continued observance of dietary laws is presupposed by rabbinic literature. As synagogue worship gradually became more central to Jewish piety, its liturgy was expanded and standardized to a greater degree than in the pre-70 period. In the decades following the first war with Rome, rabbinic Judaism increasingly became the dominant, though not the exclusive, form of Judaism; even so, the debates preserved in the Mishnah and related literature show that rabbinic Judaism continued to be characterized to a significant degree by diversity of practice.

See also JEWISH COMMUNITIES IN ASIA MINOR; LITURGY: QUMRAN; LITURGY: RABBINIC; SABBATH; SYNAGOGUES; TORAH.

BIBLIOGRAPHY. J. M. G. Barclay, *Jews in the Mediterranean Diaspora: From Alexander to Trajan (323 B.C.E.-C.E. 117)* (Edinburgh: T & T Clark, 1996); B. J. Brooten, *Women Leaders in the Ancient Synagogue* (BJS 36; Chico, CA: Scholars Press, 1982); L. H. Feldman, "Diaspora Synagogues: New Light from Inscriptions and Papyri," in *Sacred Realm: The Emergence of the Synagogue in the Ancient World,* ed. S. Fine (Oxford: Oxford University Press, 1996) 48-66, reprinted in L. H. Feldman, *Studies in Hellenistic Judaism* (AGJU 30; Leiden: E. J. Brill, 1996) 577-602; idem, *Jew and Gentile in the Ancient World: Attitudes and Interactions from Alexander to Justinian* (Princeton, NJ: Princeton University Press, 1993); S. Fine, ed., *Sacred Realm: The Emergence of the Synagogue in the Ancient World* (Oxford: Oxford University Press, 1996); P. Fredriksen, "Did Jesus Oppose the Purity Laws?" *BRev* 11 (1995) 19-25, 42-47; J. Heinemann, *Prayer in the Talmud* (SJ 9; Berlin: Walter de Gruyter, 1977); J. Heinemann and J. J. Petuchowski, *Literature of the Synagogue* (New York: Behrman House, 1975); M. Hengel and R. Deines, "E. P. Sanders's 'Common Judaism', Jesus, and the Pharisees," *JTS* 46 (1995) 1-70; A. Kasher, *Jews and Hellenistic Cities in Eretz-Israel* (Tübingen: Mohr Siebeck, 1990); R. S. Kraemer, *Her Share of the Blessings: Women's Religions Among Pagans, Jews, and Christians in the Greco-Roman World* (Oxford: Oxford University Press, 1992); R. A. Kraft and G. W. E. Nickelsburg, eds., *Early Judaism and Its Modern Interpreters* (Atlanta: Scholars Press, 1986); J. Z. Lauterbach, ed. and trans., *Mekilta de-Rabbi Ishmael* (3 vols.; Philadelphia: Jewish Publication Society of America, 1933); L. I. Levine, *The Ancient Synagogue: The First Thousand Years* (New Haven, CT: Yale University Press, 1999); idem, *The Synagogue in Late Antiquity* (Philadelphia: American Schools of Oriental Research, 1987); G. F. Moore, *Judaism in the First Centuries of the Christian Era: The Age of the Tannaim* (3 vols.; Peabody, MA: Hendrickson, 1997 [1932-40]); J. Neusner, *From Politics to Piety: The Emergence of Pharisaic Judaism* (Englewood Cliffs, NJ: Prentice-Hall, 1973); idem, *Rabbinic Traditions About the Pharisees Before 70* (3 vols.; Leiden: E. J. Brill, 1971); G. W. E. Nickelsburg and M. E. Stone, *Faith and Piety in Early Judaism: Texts and Documents* (Philadelphia: Fortress, 1983); J. Nolland, "Uncircumcised Proselytes?" *JSJ* 12 (1981) 173-94; S. Safrai and M. Stern, eds., *The Jewish People in the First Century* (2 vols., CRINT 1.1-2; Assen: Van Gorcum; Philadelphia: Fortress, 1974-76); E. P. Sanders, *Jewish Law from Jesus to the Mishnah* (Philadelphia: Trinity Press International, 1990); idem, *Judaism: Practice and Belief 63 B.C.-A.D. 66* (Philadelphia: Trinity Press International, 1992); idem, *Paul and Palestinian Judaism* (Philadelphia: Fortress, 1977); E. Schürer, *The History of the Jewish People in the Age of Jesus Christ: A New English Edition* (3 vols. in 4 parts; rev. and ed. G. Vermes et al.; Edinburgh: T & T Clark, 1973-87); E. M. Smallwood, *The Jews Under Roman Rule* (SJLA 20; Leiden: E. J. Brill, 1976); E. Urbach, *The Sages: Their Concepts and Beliefs* (Jerusalem: Magnes, 1975); D. Urman and P. V. M. Flesher, eds., *Ancient Synagogues: Historical Analysis and Archaeological Discovery* (2 vols.; SPB 47; Leiden: E. J. Brill, 1995); G. Vermes, *The Dead Sea Scrolls in English* (4th ed.; Sheffield: Sheffield Academic Press, 1995); M. Whittaker, *Jews and Christians: Graeco-Roman Views* (CCWJCW 6; Cambridge: Cambridge University Press, 1984); M. H. Williams, *The Jews among the Greeks and Romans: A Diaspora Sourcebook* (London: Duckworth, 1998).

J. R. Wagner

PILATE INSCRIPTION

Pontius Pilate, governor of Judea, notorious for his role in condemning Jesus to the cross (Mt 27:1-2, 11-26 par. Mk 15:1-15; Lk 23:1-7, 13-25; Jn 18:28—19:16; cf. Acts 3:13; 4:27; 13:28; 1 Tim 6:13), succeeded Valerius Gratus in A.D. 26 (*see* Roman Governors of Palestine). Pilate was dismissed by Vitellius, legate of Syria, in late A.D. 36 or early 37. The immediate cause for Pilate's removal was his violent action taken against the *Samaritans who had gathered at the foot of Mt. Gerizim in hopes of finding the lost vessels of the Samaritan temple, which had been destroyed by the *Hasmoneans some 150 years earlier. Pilate was involved in at least two serious encounters with the Jewish people (Josephus *J.W.* 2.9.2-3 §§171-74; *Ant.* 18.3.1—2 §§55-62; Philo *Leg. Gai.* 38 §§299-305; Lk 13:1).

In the Gospels, Pilate is called a *hēgemōn* (cf. Mt 27:2; Lk 3:1), a general term that means "leader" or "governor" and can serve as the

Greek equivalent for either prefect or procurator. *Josephus calls Gratus, Pilate's predecessor, an *eparchos* (Josephus *Ant.* 18.2.2 §33) but elsewhere refers to Pilate as an *eiptropos* (Josephus *J.W.* 2.9.2 §169), the word *Philo uses (*Leg. Gai.* 38 §299). The Roman historian Cornelius *Tacitus (c. 56-c. 118) states that "Christus . . . had suffered the death penalty during the reign of Tiberius, by sentence of the procurator Pontius Pilate" (*per procuratorem Pontium Pilatum, Ann.* 15.44). Some scholars suspected that Tacitus was in error and that Pilate was a governor of the rank of prefect, not procurator.

An inscription found at *Caesarea Maritima in 1961 confirmed this suspicion. Inscribed on a partially effaced stone that had been used as a step in the theater are the following words:

STIBERIÉVM
TIVSPILATVS
ECTVSIVDA[EA]E
É

A. Frova has restored most of the text accordingly:

[Caesarien]STIBERIÉVM
[PON]TIVSPILATVS
[PRAEF]ECTVSIVDA[EA]E
[D]É[DIT]

This restoration reads:

[Caesarean]s' Tiberieum
[Pon]tius Pilate,
[Pref]ect of Juda[ea]
[d]e[dicates]

Several other restorations of the first word have been proposed. S. Bartina: [opu]s Tiberieum—"The Tiberieum building"; A. Degrassi, [Dis Augusti]s Tiberieum—"The Tiberieum of the Divine Augusti" (i.e., Caesar Augustus and Livia his wife, the mother of Tiberius); E. Weber, [Kal(endis) Iulii]s Tiberiéum—"The Tiberieum of July First"; V. Burr, [nemu]s Tiberieum—"The Tiberieum of the (sacred) grove"; C. Gatti, [Iudaei]s Tiberieum—"The Tiberieum of the Jews"; G. Labbé, [munu]s Tiberieum—"The Tiberieum (erected for the people)"; G. Alföldy, [nauti]s Tiberieum—"The seamen's Tiberieum." The last proposed reconstruction has much to commend it. Alföldy believes that the Seamen's Tiberieum in all probability was the lighthouse that guided ships into the harbor at Caesarea Maritima. Alföldy restores the word in the last line *refecit* ("restores"), concluding that the restoration of the lighthouse was only part of a major renovation of the harbor, over which Pilate gave oversight.

The Pilate inscription thus confirms the governor's rank as prefect, and it may also provide an important indication of what major projects occupied the attention of the governor of Judea.

See also INSCRIPTIONS AND PAPYRI: GRECO ROMAN; ROMAN GOVERNORS OF PALESTINE.

BIBLIOGRAPHY. G. Alföldy, "Pontius Pilatus und das Tiberieum von Caesarea Maritima," *Studia Classica Israelica* 18 (1999) 85-108; S. Bartina, "Poncio Pilato en Una Inscripción Monumentaria Palestinense," *Cultura Bíblica* 19 (1962) 170-75; V. Burr, "Epigraphischer Beitrag zur neueren Pontius-Pilatus-Forschung," in *Vergangenheit, Gegenwart, Zukunft,* ed. W. Burr (Würzburg: Echter, 1972) 37-41; A. Degrassi, "Sull'iscrizione di Ponzio Pilato," *Rendiconti dell' Accademia Nazionale dei Lincei. Classe di Scienze morali, storiche e filologiche series* 8 (1964) 59-65; I. Di Stefano Manzella, "Pontius Pilatus nell'iscrizione di Cesarea di Palestina," in *Le iscrizioni dei cristiani in Vaticano: Materiali e contributi scientifici per un mostra epigrafica,* ed. I. Di Stefano Manzella (Vatican City: Edizioni Quasar, 1997) 209-15 + fig. 3.1.2; A. Frova, "L'iscrizione di Ponzio Pilato a Cesarea," *Rendiconti dell'Istituto Lombardo* 95 (1961) 419-34; C. Gatti, "A proposito di una rilettura dell'epigrafe di Ponzio Pilato," *Aevum* 55 (1981) 13-21; G. Labbé, "Ponce Pilate et la munificence de Tibère: l'inscription de Césarée," *Revue des Études Anciennes* 93 (1991) 277-97; J.-P. Lémonon, "Ponce Pilate: Documents profanes, Nouveau Testament et traditions ecclésiales," *ANRW* 2.26.1 (1992) 748-52. B. Lifshitz, "Inscriptions latines de Césarée (Caesarea Palaestinae)," *Latomus* 22 (1963) 783-84 + plates LXIII–LXIV; J. Vardaman, "A New Inscription Which Mentions Pilate as 'Prefect,'" *JBL* 81 (1962) 70-71; H. Volkmann, "Die Pilatusinschrift von Caesarea Maritima," *Gymnasium* 75 (1968) 124-35 + plates XIII–XV; E. Weber, "Zur Inschrift des Pontius Pilatus," *Bonner Jahrbücher* 171 (1971) 194-200.

C. A. Evans

PISIDIAN ANTIOCH. *See* ANTIOCH (PISIDIA).

PLATO, PLATONISM

The system of philosophy founded by Plato is perhaps the greatest philosophical edifice ever erected in the Western intellectual tradition. Its influence even on thinkers who rejected its principles, beginning with Aristotle, has been profound. Contemporary Platonism helped to shape Christian theology in the first centuries A.D. and heavily influenced European thought thereafter, down to Descartes, Kant and Hegel.

1. Plato
2. Platonism

1. Plato.

Plato (427-347 B.C.), an Athenian philosopher, was of aristocratic and antidemocratic background. In his youth he fell under the spell of *Socrates, and this led him first to abandon literature and then, after Socrates' death in 399 B.C., to give up any thought of political activity. From Socrates he learned to subordinate the concerns of the body to those of the soul, as the true seat of the personality, and to seek for truth though the formulation of definitions of key concepts, such as justice, courage and beauty, through the practice of dialectic, or the radical questioning of uncritically held assumptions by means of dialogue, which was Socrates' own method of philosophizing. After Socrates' execution, Plato left *Athens for some years and traveled widely, chiefly to southern Italy and Sicily, where he came into contact with Pythagorean philosophers, such as Archytas of Tarentum, who gave a new direction to his thought.

Socrates had not much concerned himself with the ontological status of the definitions that he was seeking. Now Plato was stimulated to postulate that they must relate to real objects in an intelligible world (Forms or Ideas) and that this was the level of reality at which the soul is truly itself. He was also attracted by the Pythagorean mathematization of the universe, whereby things were in some sense numbers, or mathematical formulas, and all was held together by a cosmic harmony. While he considerably refined these Pythagorean concepts, they remain basic for his later thought.

On returning to Athens in 387 B.C., Plato established a philosophical school, the Academy, and gathered around him a distinguished group of pupils, including his immediate successors Speusippus and Xenocrates, the distinguished mathematician Eudoxus, and *Aristotle, who, though Plato's pupil for twenty years, was later to set up a rival school. Plato presided over this establishment for forty years, with only two interruptions, so far as we know, in the form of two further visits to Sicily, in 367 and 361, in a futile attempt to convert the tyrant of Syracuse, Dionysius II, into an ideal ruler.

Plato produced a steady stream of works—not straightforward treatises, however, but dialogues, in which his own views are generally not unequivocally presented. This device enables him to honor Socrates' aversion to writing and the memory of Socrates himself, while still preserving for posterity something of his philosophical positions. This problematic body of work seems to be preserved in full and amounts to fully twenty-seven works, of varying length and importance. Their dates of composition are unknown, but they are conventionally divided into three broad groups, early, middle and late. The most important works for later Greek philosophy, and for early Christianity, are in the latter two groups: *Phaedo, Symposium, Republic, Phaedrus, Parmenides, Theaetetus* (middle); and *Sophist, Statesman, Timaeus, Philebus, Laws* (late). Of special interest also is the seventh in a collection of Plato's letters, which contains some autobiographical material and a statement of his philosophical position.

The most important aspects of his philosophy from the point of view of Christianity are his emphasis on the immortality of the soul and the paramount importance of "tending" it by the practice of virtue (see esp. *Phaedo, Republic*); the existence of an intelligible realm, in which are situated the Forms, paramount among which is the Form of the Good; and that this material world is a realm of flux and imperfection about which nothing certain can be known—knowledge is of perfect and permanent objects of knowledge, namely, the Forms. His political philosophy—his advocacy of rational absolutism—is also of some importance as a basis for theories of absolute monarchy.

2. Platonism.

As a coherent and structured philosophical system, Platonism should be regarded as beginning not with Plato himself but rather among his immediate successors in the Academy, in particular with its third head, Xenocrates, who presided over the Academy from 339 to 314 B.C. We may divide Platonism in the ancient world, up to about A.D. 250, into three main periods—a fourth, Neo-Platonism (c. A.D. 250-600), falls outside the scope of the present survey.

2.1. The Old Academy (347-267 B.C.). Plato's followers continued to develop his ideas freely after his death. After the formal secession of Ar-

istotle in 335 B.C. to found his own school, however, a process of codification of doctrine seems to have begun under Xenocrates, who was probably responsible for the definitive edition of Plato's works and who published many works himself (all now lost) that sound like dogmatic treatises on various basic issues. The other heads of the Old Academy were Speusippus, who led from 347 to 339 B.C., and Polemon, who presided longest, from 314 to 267 B.C.
The complex of doctrines that emerges is as follows:

1. In metaphysics, a first principle is termed a Monad or One, but it is also a self-thinking intellect like Aristotle's god, the contents of whose mind are probably the Platonic Forms, and from whose interaction with a secondary principle (an indefinite Dyad), the whole cosmos, at its various levels, is derived. We also find the doctrine of soul as a self-motive number—a formulation probably intended to bring together the definitions of soul in Plato's *Phaedrus* and *Timaeus*.

2. In ethics we find a recognition of "the primary natural instincts" as a basis for conduct, in a way that seems to anticipate the *Stoics, though without involving the rejection of physical or external goods. In fact, Old Academic ethics remained closer to Aristotelian principles, and this continued to be the case in later times.

3. In logic, the Old Academicians remained faithful to the Platonic processes of collection and division. The Aristotelian system of categories and the syllogism do not seem to have been adopted until the Middle Platonic period.

2.2. The New Academy (267-80 B.C.). With Polemon's successor Arcesilaus (scholarch 267-241 B.C.), the Platonist tradition takes a remarkable turn, though one that could and did reasonably appeal for authority to the Socratic, aporetic aspect of Plato's teaching. What precisely set this off is not clear, but it is probably a reaction to the dogmatic tendencies of contemporary Stoicism. The main thrust of Arcesilaus's philosophical activity was polemical, his chief targets being the Stoic theory of knowledge, specifically the doctrines of *enargeia* ("certainty") and *synkatathesis* ("assent to impressions"). He asserted that the sort of certainty claimed by the Stoics was not attainable and that the only rational attitude to physical phenomena was to withhold assent (*epochē*). Like Socrates, he published nothing but was enormously influential nonetheless. Of his followers, only Carneades (scholarch c. 160-129 B.C.) made any original contribution. He seems to have devised a system of three levels of "probability" (*pithanotēs*), by observance of which one would be enabled to make practical decisions without assenting to the perspicuity of impressions.

2.3. Middle Platonism (c. 80 B.C.-A.D. 250). The New Academy's position was effectively undermined by its last scholarch, Philo of Larissa, who went so far as to deny that Platonists claimed that things were nonapprehensible but only that the Stoic criterion of certainty was unworkable. His precise position is not easy to recover, but it left the way open for his dissident successor, Antiochus of Ascalon (c. 130-69 B.C.), to reassert the dogmatic tradition of Platonism, augmented by Stoic influences, thus inaugurating the amalgam known as Middle Platonism. This is the period of Platonism most influential on the earliest generations of Christian thinkers. Antiochus claimed to be returning the Academy to its Platonic roots, but in reality he was much influenced by Stoicism, to the extent that it is not clear that he believed in immaterial reality. Certainly he accepted a Stoic-style system of an active and passive principle within the universe, taking the creator-god of Plato's *Timaeus* as representing the Stoic *Logos,* a concept influential in Christianity from St. John onwards. He also adopted the Stoic formulation of the purpose of human life as "living in accordance with nature."

However, over the next generation or so, beginning with such a figure as Eudorus of Alexandria (fl. c. 25 B.C.), a much more transcendental tendency manifests itself, which leads also to a revival of respect for Pythagoras within Platonism. This comes to a head in the second century A.D. In metaphysics, the view of God is as a self-thinking intellect on the Aristotelian model, whose thoughts are the Platonic Forms, this divine intellect being also a perfect unity (the Pythagorean Monad), for which a source was found in the Good of Plato's *Republic.* A secondary divinity, either a demiurgic figure derived from the *Timaeus* or a version of the Stoic *Logos* (which had some influence on the role of Christ in the thinking of the church fathers) and a World-Soul, is also derived from the *Timaeus* but owes something as well to the Pythagorean Indefinite Dyad.

In ethics, we find Aristotelian doctrine widely accepted as Platonism, notably by such a figure as *Plutarch, though others, such as the second-century Atticus, championed the Stoic ideals of impassivity and the self-sufficiency of virtue. In logic, Aristotelian syllogistic, as amplified by Theophrastus, reigns supreme, though there is some tendency also to adopt the basic argument-forms of Stoic logic.

Within the Middle Platonic spectrum, a special place must be accorded to the *Neo-Pythagorean tradition, the most notable representative of which is Numenius of Apamea (fl. c. A.D. 150), and which, while accepting the broad lines of Platonic doctrine, advocated a much more ascetic and structured lifestyle, modeled on the old Pythagorean communities of south Italy. Numenius was a major influence on the founder of Neo-Platonism, Plotinus.

A series of Christian thinkers in the first two and a half centuries A.D., from Justin and Tatian to Clement and Origen, were influenced to varying degrees by contemporary Platonism and are often themselves valuable witnesses to developments in Platonic doctrine.

See also ARISTOTLE, ARISTOTELIANISM; CYNIC EPISTLES; CYNICISM AND SKEPTICISM; EPICTETUS; EPICUREANISM; NEO-PYTHAGOREANISM; PHILOSOPHY; SENECA; STOICISM.

BIBLIOGRAPHY. A. H. Armstrong, ed., *The Cambridge History of Later Greek and Early Medieval Philosophy* (Cambridge: Cambridge University Press, 1967); H. Chadwick, *Early Christianity and the Classical Tradition* (Oxford: Oxford University Press, 1966); J. Dillon, *The Middle Platonists* (2d ed.; Ithaca, NY: Cornell University Press, 1996); S. Gersh, *Middle Platonism and Neoplatonism: The Latin Tradition* (Notre Dame, IN: Notre Dame University Press, 1986); G. M. A. Grube, *Plato's Thought* (Indianapolis: Hackett, 1980); A. A. Long, *Hellenistic Philosophy* (2d ed.; Berkeley and Los Angeles: University of California Press, 1986); P. Merlan, *From Platonism to Neoplatonism* (The Hague: M. Nijhoff, 1953).

J. M. Dillon

PLATONISM. *See* PLATO, PLATONISM.

PLEBS. *See* ROMAN SOCIAL CLASSES.

PLINY THE ELDER

Gaius Plinius Secundus (A.D. 23/24-79) was born in Nouum Comum in Cisalpine Gaul. Of equestrian rank, he followed a public career in the army, law, provincial administration and the navy. His literary works included a history of the Roman wars against the Germans in twenty books and a general history in thirty-one books, beginning perhaps with the 30s. But his only surviving work is an encyclopedia of practical knowledge, the *Natural History (Naturalis Historia)* in thirty-seven books, dedicated to the future emperor Titus in 77 (pref. 1-3) but published posthumously according to a manuscript note to book 34. Book 1 is a table of contents for the remaining thirty-six books. For each book there is a list of topics followed more briefly by a list of authors consulted as sources. The procedure shows that in general the writing is a compendium rather than the result of independent research, despite Pliny's occasional claims to originality (e.g., *Nat. Hist.* 2.71). The contents are the universe as a whole (book 2); the geography of the earth (books 3-6); humankind (book 7); other animals (books 8-11); botany in general (books 12-19); drugs obtained from plants (books 20-27); drugs obtained from animals (books 28-32); metals, stones and their uses (books 33-37).

Pliny makes no mention of Christians in his surviving work. However, there are references relevant to the Jewish and Judean background of Christianity. There are primarily geographical references to the external boundaries of Judea (*Nat. Hist.* 5.66-70; 6.13; 12.100), to towns and toparchies (*Nat. Hist.* 5.68-70; 6.13; 9.11; 12.64) and to physical features (*Nat. Hist.* 5.71-72; 31.24), especially the Dead Sea (*Nat. Hist.* 2.226; 5.72). Major natural products receive particular attention, apparently because of their economic significance: bitumen from the Dead Sea (*Nat. Hist.* 2.226; 5.72; 7.65; 28.80; 35.178), the balsam shrub (*Nat. Hist.* 12.111-24) and palm trees (*Nat. Hist.* 13.26-49). The information reflects sources of different periods and is not always accurate (for details see Stern, chap. 78).

The most notable passage concerns the *Essenes (*Nat. Hist.* 5.73). This occurs within the geographical section of the work. Pliny follows the course of the River Jordan from north to south to its termination in the Dead Sea (*Nat. Hist.* 5.71-73). On the west side of the sea, away from the shore, is the "isolated group" *(gens sola)* of the Essenes. Pliny is the only extant pagan writer who independently connects the Essenes with the Dead Sea. According to Synesius *Life of Dio,* Dio Chrysostom praised the Essenes, "a *polis* situated by the Dead Sea" (Stern, 1:539). However, it is not clear that this alleged account was independent of Pliny: *polis* may mean "community" rather than a city and may correspond to Pliny's *gens*. Nor is it clear that Pliny regarded the Essenes as a separate nation, since *gens* may also mean a type or class of people. And, if *sola* meant "unique" here, it would be redundant with the coordinate phrase, "and remarkable in all the world beyond others"; it therefore more probably means "isolated."

In describing the Essenes as "without any woman" *(sine ulla femina)* and "having rejected all sexual love" *(omni uenere abdicata)*, Pliny's account corresponds to *Philo in Eusebius (*Praep. Ev.* 8.11.4) and to *Josephus (*J.W.* 2.8.2 §120). Pliny's description of the Essenes as being "without money" *(sine pecunia)* is usually understood as a reference not to poverty but to communal sharing of resources. This corresponds to Philo *That Every Good Man Is Free* 76-77; Philo in Eusebius (*Praep. Ev.* 8.11.4-5); Josephus (*J.W.* 2.8.3 §122). Pliny is struck by the paradox that the membership of the community remains stable, even though no one is born into it. Daily recruitment compensates for any deaths. But Pliny exaggerates when he says that this has been going on "for thousands of generations/ages/centuries" *(per saeculorum milia)*. As he acknowledges, this is "unbelievable to say" *(incredibile dictu)*. In conclusion, repeating the point, "others' weariness of life is fruitful for them." The phrase "weariness of life" *(uitae paenitentia)* corresponds to the preceding phrase "weary of life" *(uita fessos)*; it can hardly mean "repentance . . . for their past lives" (contrary to Vermes and Goodman, 33).

Pliny rounds off his treatment of Judea by mentioning the town of Engedi and the fortress of Masada; "and that is as far as Judaea goes." The location of Engedi "below" *(infra)* the Essenes has caused debate. But Pliny's discussion has been proceeding southward, and that is a standard application of the term *infra*.

Pliny's account thus gives a single location for the Essenes, which corresponds to the site of *Qumran: on the west of the Dead Sea, away from the shore, and north of Engedi and in turn Masada. The isolated nature of the community described by Pliny also fits in with the site of Qumran. The portrayal of the Essenes as male celibates who shared their property corresponds to Philo's description and to one of the two subgroups described by Josephus (*J.W.* 2.8.2-4 §§120-127; 2.8.13 §§160-61). In the light of the *Dead Sea Scrolls and of the archaeology of Qumran, it is likely that there was a stricter group of Essenes at Qumran from an early date and a more open order of marrying Essenes with private property living in towns (see Schürer, 2:577-79; Vermes, 45). Pliny's description suits only the stricter group at a single site. But if Qumran was devastated by the Romans in the summer of A.D. 68, then Pliny's account, though accurate, was out of date by the time it was published in or after 79.

Apart from the preface to *Natural History*, the most useful ancient information about Pliny the Elder comes from two letters of *Pliny the Younger. *Epistles* 3.5 lists Pliny the Elder's writings in chronological sequence and describes his method of study. *Epistles* 6.16 is written in reply to a request by *Tacitus for information about the death of Pliny the Elder at the time of the eruption of Mt. Vesuvius in A.D. 79.

See also ESSENES; GEOGRAPHICAL PERSPECTIVES IN LATE ANTIQUITY; PLINY THE YOUNGER.

BIBLIOGRAPHY. **Texts and Translations.** Plinius der Ältere, *Naturkunde/Naturalis Historia*, ed. R. König, K. Bayer and J. Hopp (31 vols.; Düsseldorf: Artemis, 1976-97) (text); Pliny, *Natural History* (10 vols.; Cambridge, MA: Harvard University Press, 1949-63) (translation). **Studies.** M. Beagon, *Roman Nature: The Thought of Pliny the Elder* (Oxford: Clarendon Press, 1992); E. Schürer, *The History of the Jewish People in the Age of Jesus Christ 175 B.C.-A.D. 135*, ed. G. Vermes, F. Millar and M. Goodman (3 vols.; Edinburgh: T & T Clark, 1973-87); G. Serbat, "Pline l'Ancien: État Présent des Études sur sa Vie, son Œuvre et Son Influence," *ANRW* 2.32.4 (1986) 2069-2200; M. Stern, *Greek and Latin Authors on Jews and Judaism* (3 vols.; Jerusalem: The Israel Academy of Sciences and Humanities, 1976-84); R. Syme, "Pliny the Procurator," *Harvard Studies in Classical Philology* 73 (1969) 201-36, reprinted in R. Syme, *Roman Papers* II, ed. E. Badian (Oxford: Clarendon Press, 1979) 742-73; G. Vermes, *The Complete Dead Sea Scrolls in English* (London: Penguin, 1997); G. Vermes and M. D. Goodman, *The Essenes According to the Classical Sources* (Sheffield: JSOT, 1989).

D. W. Palmer

PLINY THE YOUNGER

Pliny the Younger was a Roman administrator of the early second century A.D. His published letters convey the ethos of the man and his times.

An exchange of correspondence with the emperor Trajan is of particular interest for the social setting of early Christianity in an eastern Roman province.

1. Life
2. Writings
3. Pliny on Christians

1. Life.

Pliny the Younger lived from A.D. 61/62 to about A.D. 113. His father, Lucius Caecilius, died during Pliny's boyhood. An official guardian, Verginius Rufus, was appointed for Pliny by his father's will (*Ep.* 2.1.8). Although the guardian lived until A.D. 97, Pliny and his mother were living with the mother's brother, *Pliny the Elder, at the time of the latter's death in A.D. 79. And it is assumed that the uncle had some responsibility for his nephew's education. Pliny the Younger was in his eighteenth year when his uncle died (*Ep.* 6.20.5). His career in law, in public administration and even in the army was especially concerned with financial issues. He was the first of his family to attain senatorial rank, which he achieved as a result of his quaestorship (probably A.D. 90). He was one of several supplementary consuls (*consul suffectus*) in A.D. 100. But he held no provincial governorship until about ten years later. He presumably died in office no later than A.D. 113. Pliny mentions only once the fact of his adoption by his uncle (*Ep.* 5.8.5). This may have occurred in accordance with the uncle's will. Hence Pliny the Younger is both a Plinius (by adoption) and a Caecilius (by birth). But he continues to refer to Pliny the Elder as uncle.

Bithynia and Pontus on the southern rim of the Black Sea had formed a single Roman province since A.D. 63. The culture remained Greek and barbarian. Individual cities were prosperous but competitive. Roman governors had been appointed by the senate. However, in the early empire, procurators (independent of the governor) played a large role in the management of the emperor's properties in the province (*see* Roman Administration; Roman Emperors). With the appointment of Pliny by the emperor Trajan the status of the province in effect changed from senatorial to imperial. It was Pliny's financial and administrative skills rather than his limited military experience that justified the appointment. His brief was to improve the organization and efficiency of the province. His period of office fell within three calendar years, most probably A.D. 109 to 111, but conceivably A.D. 110 to 112 or 111 to 113.

2. Writings.

Pliny mentions having written a Greek tragedy at the age of fourteen (*Ep.* 7.4.2). He also wrote light verse and two short biographies besides revising some of his speeches for publication (references in Sherwin-White, 51). The only surviving speech is the *Panegyricus.* This is an expanded form of the speech given in the Roman senate in gratitude for Pliny's appointment as consul in A.D. 100, but it largely consists of praise of Trajan, especially by contrast with the former emperor Domitian (A.D. 81-96). However, Pliny is best known for his *letters published in ten books. Books 1-9 appeared spasmodically between A.D. 104/5 and Pliny's departure for Bithynia. All the letters in books 1-9 are written by Pliny himself to a variety of addressees. There is a wide range of topics (for a classification see Sherwin-White, 43-45). While books 1-9 are chronological, the letters within each book are arranged to achieve an aesthetic balance. Book 10 is different. It is probably a complete set of correspondence between Pliny and the emperor Trajan. *Epistles* 10.1-14 comprise eleven letters from Pliny to Trajan and three of Trajan's replies between A.D. 98 (Trajan's accession) and the beginning of Pliny's governorship. The remaining 109 letters of book 10 (including 17B and 86B) all belong to the period of the governorship and include 61 from Pliny to Trajan and 48 replies. The letters of book 10 have perhaps not been revised and were probably published posthumously.

3. Pliny on Christians.

*Judaism is not a topic of Pliny's correspondence. But an exchange of letters at *Epistles* 10.96-97 is directly concerned with Christianity. Indeed, it is noticeable that Christianity is not considered in relation to Judaism but as a voluntary association of the same social status as a fire brigade (*Ep.* 10.96.7; cf. 10.34). The term *Christian* occurs for the first time in extant Latin literature at *Epistles* 10.96.1, 2, 3, 5, 6; also 10.97.1, 2. On the assumption that the letters in book 10 are arranged chronologically and that Pliny is proceeding on an administrative circuit, *Epistles* 10.96 will have been written between September 18 of the second calendar year of Pliny's office and the following January 3, and either from Amisus (*Ep.* 10.92) or from Amastris (*Ep.* 10.98). Both places are Greek towns of the former kingdom of Pontus in the eastern part of the province (*see* Asia Minor).

Pliny begins by noting that it is his regular practice to refer all doubtful matters to the emperor. This is not a sign of incompetence on Pliny's part but is in keeping with the current imperial policy of centralized administration. Pliny then states that he has never participated in trials concerning Christians. The type of trial indicated (*cognitio*) involved the emperor or his deputy sitting in council (*consilium*), hearing charges and making a decision. Pliny had served on the emperor's council for such trials at Vienne in Gaul (*Ep.* 4.22), at *Rome (*Ep.* 6.22, presumably) and at Centum Cellae in Etruria (*Ep.* 6.31); and in his own jurisdiction as prefect of Saturn (*Ep.* 1.10.10). A moderate interpretation of Pliny's statement would be that he had participated in trials of the *cognitio* type, but never concerning Christians. More extreme views have been taken. "This implies that Pliny knew that such trials had taken place within the period of his public career, and hence at Rome" (Sherwin-White, 694). W. Williams (139) follows this view. But according to K. Wellesley (489) the "exact contrary could be implied with equal logic."

Pliny therefore does not know the usual nature and extent of investigation and punishment of Christians. He is unsure whether quite young persons should be treated in the same way as the more mature. This implies that persons within such an age range, perhaps families, have been brought to the attention of Pliny. He also expresses uncertainty whether allowance (or pardon, *venia*) should be made for those who have withdrawn from their commitment to Christianity. This indicates that both present and former Christians have been reported to him. Finally, Pliny wants to know whether the mere status (*nomen,* lit. "name") of being a Christian without any shameful actions (*flagitia*; the term does not mean "crimes" as such) requires punishment or whether only *flagitia* connected with the *nomen* should be punished. Confusion is already evident in Pliny's opening four questions. "Punishment" is mentioned in the first and fourth. In the first, Pliny assumes that punishment is appropriate. In the fourth, he allows that Christianity may exist without any shameful action. On the other hand, he thinks that there are shameful actions "connected with" (*cohaerentia*) Christianity. And he still seeks advice on whether punishment is appropriate either for the alleged shameful actions or even for being a Christian without any such actions (*Ep.* 10.96.1-2).

Pliny next outlines the procedure that he has been following so far (*Ep.* 10.96.2-4). When any persons are accused before him as being Christians, he asks them whether they are so; if they admit it, he threatens punishment and repeats the question twice more. If they persist, he orders them to be led (away for punishment?). His rationale is that whatever they confess to, they ought at any rate to be punished for their "persistence and unbending stubbornness." Many modern scholars see Pliny's action as a normal exercise of *coercitio,* summary punishment for refusal to obey a lawful command. But Pliny has not issued any command; he has merely asked the accused whether they are Christians. His rationale seems unjustified. Williams (140-41) regards this as "a retrospective account of his attitude, written . . . after he had become convinced of the desirability of making Christians apostatise rather than confess." All this applies to Christians who were not Roman *citizens. But "there were others of similar madness, whom, since they were Roman citizens, I designated to be referred to the city" (of Rome) (*Ep.* 10.96.4). This is a case of referral by the governor, not appeal to the emperor by the accused, for which, in general, evidence is limited.

However, once Pliny began to deal with the matter, allegations increased. First, an anonymous notice containing many names was posted (*Ep.* 10.96.5). Pliny does not comment on any persistent Christians from this group. But he dismissed those who denied that they were or had been Christians, after they had called on the gods, made offerings of incense and wine to Trajan's statue and insulted Christ; for real Christians could not be compelled to do any of these things. These tests are applied only to those who deny that they are Christians. If all or some of this group were really not Christians, it remains a question who falsely accused them and why. And the implication stands, that Christianity was socially unacceptable.

A second group of alleged Christians was reported to Pliny by an informer (*Ep.* 10.96.6). These all admitted to being Christians but subsequently denied. The denial is essentially a clarification: they had been Christians but ceased to be so three or more or even twenty years earlier. The maximum period shows that people in this region not only had been converted to Christianity in the later first century but had already begun dropping out by about A.D. 90. No reason is given for their falling away. Members of this group seem not to have been reluctant to admit that they had been Christians. And the following description of their former activity seems harmless from a Roman point of view. However, they all demonstrated their lapsed status by venerating the statues of the emperor and the gods and by insulting Christ. "Moreover, they asserted that this had been the extent of their fault or error" (*Ep.* 10.96.7). Pliny's phrasing suggests that he did not regard their Christian activity as a very serious matter. They reported regular meetings before dawn; the singing of a *hymn to Christ as to a god; and an oath concerning theft, adultery, breach of trust and refusal to repay a deposit. There was a separate meeting later in the day to take food, which was "nevertheless ordinary and harmless." They had abandoned even this practice after Pliny's decree (*edictum*) in accordance with Trajan's instructions (*mandata*) forbidding voluntary associations (*hetaeriae*) (*Ep.* 10.96.7).

Such an edict could only have been issued within the preceding year or so (cf. *Ep.* 10.33-34; 10.92-93) and thus would affect only those who were still practicing Christians at that period. Three aspects of the practice of these lapsed Christians (no adultery, no strange food and perhaps veneration of Christ as a god) anticipate the allegations that will soon be defended in the apologists (sexual immorality, cannibalism and atheism).

Because of the apparently harmless nature of Christianity, Pliny pressed his inquiry by the normal method of interrogating slaves under torture: "servants [*ancillae*] who were called assistants [*ministrae*]" (*Ep.* 10.96.8). Both terms are feminine. Pliny may be translating Greek terms into Latin. The phrasing suggests that he first uses a general term, then a synonymous but technical term denoting deaconesses. Pliny does not specify whether these women belonged to the lapsed group. His conclusion was that the Christians constituted "nothing other than a misguided and extreme cult" (*nihil aliud . . . quam superstitionem pravam et immodicam, Ep.* 10.96.8).

In his concluding paragraph Pliny states that he has postponed the trial pending consultation with the emperor. But he also gives a further indication of the extent of the spread of Christianity, its effect on pagan religion and the prospects for reform (*Ep.* 10.96.8-10). There is a large number of persons "on trial" (*periclitantium*): "many of every age, every rank, both sexes are still being summoned and will be summoned to trial [*periculum*]." "And the infection of that cult has spread not only through the cities but also through the villages and the countryside." Thus Pliny is confident that further denunciations will be made as he continues his administrative circuit. But he believes that the tide is turning: abandoned temples are becoming crowded, sacred rites are being performed again and the "flesh" (*carnem,* an editorial insertion) of victims is on sale everywhere. Although the language of this description is inflated, that seems to be due to Pliny rather than to his informants (against Williams, 143). Pliny is supporting his view that "if there were opportunity for a change of attitude, . . . a crowd of people could be reformed."

In his brief reply, Trajan gives general approval to the procedure that Pliny has followed; no fixed rule of universal application is possible (*Ep.* 10.97.1). He does not answer Pliny's question concerning differentiation according to age. More precisely, Christians are not to be hunted out (*conquirendi*) but are to be punished if they are reported and convicted (*Ep.* 10.97.2). So government officials are not to take the initiative in prosecuting Christians. Moreover, anyone who denies that he or she is a Christian and demonstrates this by making offerings to the gods is to be pardoned. Trajan's brevity becomes confusing here, since non-Christians should not need pardon along with lapsed Christians. Finally, anonymous notices are not a valid form of accusation.

These letters of Pliny and Trajan give a picture of Christianity in an eastern province of the Roman Empire in the early second century. There is evidence of liturgical and ethical practice. Christianity is not portrayed as a crime. Nor is any evidence presented for crimes connected with the movement. Although modern scholars often assume that Pliny has already executed some Christians at the time of writing, the term "to be led" (*duci, Ep.* 10.96.3) does not necessarily imply punishment (it may allude to detention); Pliny does not specify any particular form of punishment for Christians; and Roman citizens are to be sent to Rome (*Ep.* 10.96.4). Christianity in the province is simultaneously flourishing and declining: some have lapsed as long as twenty years previously, but accusations are continuing to be made; the large number of Christians is distributed through city and country, but pagan worship is beginning to recover. The main basis for proceeding against Christians is an ill-defined social unacceptability and their stubborn refusal to recant. A governor may punish them by virtue of the imperial authority vested in him, despite the lack of any crime on the part of the Christians. However, Pliny would welcome recantations as the easiest way of dealing with the problem. Apart from confessed Christians, others have been falsely accused. This reflects the litigious character of the province of Bithynia Pontus (Johnson).

See also PERSECUTION; PLINY THE ELDER; ROMAN ADMINISTRATION.

BIBLIOGRAPHY. **Texts and Translations.** *C. Plini Caecili Secundi Epistularum Libri Decem,* ed. R. A. B. Mynors (Oxford: Clarendon Press, 1963; corrected 1966) (text); Pliny, *Correspondence with Trajan from Bithynia* (Epistles X), translated, with introduction and commentary, by W. Williams (Warminster: Aris & Phillips, 1990); Pliny, *Letters and Panegyricus* (2 vols.; Cambridge, MA: Harvard University Press, 1972) (translation). **Studies.** E. Aubrion, "La 'Correspondance' de Pline le Jeune: Problèmes et Orientations Actuelles de la Recherche," *ANRW* 2.33.1 (1989) 304-74; F. G. Downing, "Pliny's Persecutions of Christians: Revelation and 1 Peter," *JSNT* 34 (1988) 105-33; G. J. Johnson, "*De Conspiratione Delatorum:* Pliny and the Christians Revisited," *Latomus* 47 (1988) 417-22; A. N. Sherwin-White, *The Letters of Pliny: A Historical and Social Commentary* (Oxford: Clarendon Press, 1966); K. Wellesley, review of Pliny, *Correspondence,* trans. W. Williams, *Classical Review* 41 (1991) 488-90.

D. W. Palmer

PLUTARCH

Plutarch of Chaironeia, famous essayist, biographer and philosopher, was born about A.D. 45. Much of his life, especially the later years until his death (ca. 120), were spent in this town of central *Greece where his well-to-do family had long resided. He studied at *Athens with the *Platonist Ammonius and taught at Rome. Through the consular L. Mestrius Florus, one of his influential friends, Plutarch acquired Roman *citizenship and the name Mestrius.

Plutarch advocated partnership between Greece and Rome, and his two patriotisms are reflected in his *Lives* or biographies, most of which belong to a series of parallels of Greek and Roman heroes and statesmen, often with comparisons (*synkriseis*). Plutarch viewed history as a kind of mirror and tried to fashion his own life in conformity with the virtues depicted in his *Lives* (see *Aem.* 1–2).

For about the last thirty years of his life, Plutarch was a priest at Delphi and helped to revive this shrine of Apollo in Trajanic times. His special interest in religious and theological matters is found, for example, in the Pythian dialogues (e.g., *E Delph.,* which together with works of quite varied content, form the so-called *Moralia* (*Ethica* in Greek).

Although Christianity began its expansion shortly before Plutarch's lifetime, he never mentions it in his extant writings, and like many of his contemporaries, he probably took little or no notice of it. Yet scholars of Christianity have often been struck by similarities between it and Plutarch's thought and have sought for parallels between his writings and early Christian literature focusing on forms of composition, language and style, and topics such as ethics and theology.

Plutarch was a Platonist who despite opposing *Aristotelianism and *Stoicism was indirectly indebted to them. Among the main themes of Plutarch's thought is that the purpose or goal of life (*telos*) is "likeness to God." For Plutarch, God was the One (or monadic intellect) and the Good, opposed by an evil principle, the Indefinite Dyad representing disorder and multiplicity, similar to but not simply Matter. Intermediate between God and mortals are good and evil *daemons* (guardian spirits) involved in human affairs so that God remains serene and untroubled. On divine providence, fate and free will, Plutarch's beliefs cannot be fully determined, but his ethical teaching is clear: "likeness to God" is the goal of human existence, and in order to attain this state of well-being, external and bodily goods as well as virtues that involve moderation of the passions are in some measure required.

In sum, Plutarch's works are important for understanding some *philosophical and religious beliefs of the Greco-Roman world, in which the NT and other early Christian literature took their origin. Moreover, Plutarch has always had a strong appeal to Christian thinkers such as Clement of Alexandria and other Greek church fathers and Byzantine and Renaissance scholars such as Michael Planudes and Erasmus.

See also PLATO, PLATONISM; SCHOLARSHIP, GREEK AND ROMAN.

BIBLIOGRAPHY. **Texts and Editions.** *Moralia* in LCL (15 vols.; Cambridge, MA: Harvard University Press, 1927-76); *Moralia* (7 vols.; Stuttgart and Leipzig: Teubner, 1971); *The Parallel Lives* in LCL (11 vols.; Cambridge, MA: Harvard University Press, 1914-26); *Vitae Parallelae,* ed. K. Ziegler and H. Gärtner (4 vols.; Stuttgart and Leipzig: Teubner, 1957). **Studies.** H. Almquist, *Plutarch und das Neue Testament: Ein Beitrag zum Corpus Hellenisticum Novi Testamenti* (ASNU 15; Uppsala: Appelbergs, 1946); D. Babut, *Plutarque et le Stoicisme* (Paris: Presses Universitaires de France, 1969); H.-D. Betz, ed., *Plutarch's Ethical Writings and Early Christian Literature* (Leiden: E. J. Brill, 1978); idem, ed., *Plutarch's Theological Writings and Early Christian Literature* (Leiden: E. J. Brill, 1975); F. Brenk, *In Mist Apparelled: Religious Themes in Plutarch's* Moralia *and* Lives (Leiden: E. J. Brill, 1977); J. Dillon, *The Middle Platonists, 80 B.C.-A.D. 220* (rev. ed.; Ithaca, NY: Cornell University Press, 1996); O. Gréad, *De la* Morale *de Plutarque* (Paris: Hachette, 1866); C. P. Jones, *Plutarch and Rome* (Oxford: Clarendon Press, 1971); R. M. Jones, *The Platonism of Plutarch* (Menasha, WI: George Banta Publishing, 1916); D. A. Russell, *Plutarch* (London: Duckworth, 1973); B. Scardigli, ed., *Essays on Plutarch's* Lives (Oxford: Clarendon Press, 1995); G. Soury, *La Démonologie de Plutarque* (Paris, 1942); F. Ziegler, "Plutarchos," in *Realenzyklopädie,* ed. P. Wissowa (1952; rev. 1964). J. P. Hershbell

POETRY, HELLENISTIC

*Plato's attack on poets as technicians who offered no real knowledge to their readers reflected the Hellenistic age's forsaking of poetry for the more disciplined studies of science and philosophy. Poets of the Hellenistic age were not only greeted with skepticism but also were faced with the daunting certainty of having their work compared unfavorably with the great epic, lyrical and dramatic works of the classical age. No longer was the poet a reputable source of insight, wisdom or moral authority, and no longer was poetry intimately connected with Greek *religion. Hence Hellenistic poetry is marked by a preoccupation with style and technical virtuosity and a discarding of traditional religion and mythology.

Despite the poet's diminished cultural role, the Hellenistic period produced works of daring innovation and technical brilliance. The most celebrated source was the school of poetry centered in the new city of *Alexandria, where the foundation of the library offered the age's best poets a professional security impossible elsewhere (*see* Alexandrian Library). But while Alexandria as an intellectual center offered poets a secure office to practice their art, it also comprised their entire audience. These poets wrote for a scholarly elite, and their works reflect the erudition of their audience. Unlike their classic predecessors, the Hellenistic poets' work was doomed to be time-bound. To modern tastes, the poetry of this era can seem sterile and irrelevant. Among the Alexandrian scholar-poets were the three greatest of the age: Callimachus, Apollonius and Theocritus.

1. Callimachus
2. Apollonius
3. Theocritus
4. Paul and the Poets

1. Callimachus.

Callimachus (third century B.C.) was born in Cyrene and educated in *Athens. Although he is reputed to have written more than 800 books of prose, including his 120-volume catalog of the library at Alexandria, only portions of his poetry continue to exist. Callimachus composed in several genres of poetry but is best known for his epigrams, which have come to be recognized as the characteristic Hellenistic form. Sensing, perhaps, that no new works could compete with the epic poetry of the past, Callimachus championed the value of brevity in poetry. "A great book," he insisted, "is a great evil." In one of his epigrams he points out that the waters of the great Assyrian river are muddied but that a trickling stream is pure and undefiled. For Callimachus, if poetry was to remain relevant in this new age, it would be through technical perfection, rigorous scholarship and distilled meaning, none of which he found in the epics of his contemporaries.

Of Callimachus's poetic works, six hymns and nearly sixty epigrams remain extant. Based on the elegiac couplet, Callimachus's epigrams gained renown for their striking wit and terseness. Forgoing the mythological and heroic, these epigrams celebrated the lives and concerns of ordinary people. Of his six existing hymns, which have no true religious content but are rather political poems addressed to specific gods, five are composed of hexameters and one of elegiac couplets. Also extant are several sections of *Aetia,* a collection of legends in elegiac verse, and his brief epic, *Hecale.* Judging by the frequency with which Callimachus's poetry is quoted by later scholars and the large number of papyri that bear recognizable fragments of his work, Callimachus's reputation likely eclipsed that of any other Hellenistic poet. Callimachus's epigrams greatly influenced many Roman poets, most notably Catullus (c. 84-c. 54 B.C.), Ovid (43 B.C.-A.D. 17) and Propertius (c. 50-c. 15 B.C.).

2. Apollonius.

Apollonius of Rhodes (?295-215 B.C.) likely began his career as a student of Callimachus but soon became his teacher's superior when he was appointed director of the library around 260 B.C. A violent quarrel ensued between the two poets, culminating in Callimachus's accusations of plagiary. Callimachus seems to have gained the upper hand early in the quarrel, and Apollonius retired to Rhodes.

While Callimachus championed short poems, Apollonius, in what seems clearly an act of rebellion against his teacher, imitated the epic poetry of Homer, the length of which enabled him to revel in the Hellenistic tendency toward erudition. In his only extant work, *Argonautica,* Apollonius retells the myth of Jason, leader of the Argonauts, who, with the assistance of the princess Medea, obtains the golden fleece. Unlike the traditional treatments of the myth, however, Apollonius's version is distinctly Hellenistic in tone. While previous treatments focused on war and heroism, Apollonius's version is psychological and romantic in nature, focusing on the love story between Jason and Medea. Apollonius exerted a great influence on the Roman poet Virgil (70-19 B.C.).

3. Theocritus.

Theocritus (c. 310-c. 250 B.C.) is generally recognized today as the finest of the Alexandrian poets and is noted for his elegance and grace. While Callimachus likely enjoyed a greater reputation in his day, Theocritus answers best to modern tastes, due largely to his avoidance of the Hellenistic tendency toward the esoteric and scholarly. Of his work, two dozen epigrams and thirty idyllic poems remain extant.

Theocritus is credited with the invention of the pastoral poem, which celebrates rural life and focuses on the loves of shepherds and shepherdesses, although precursors of the genre can be found in earlier works attributed to the Sicilian poets Epiharmus and Sophron. Theocritus's pastoral *Idylls* are most likely drawn from his memories of childhood in Sicily. Penned for the city dweller nostalgic for the rustic, the *Idylls* are not entirely escapist but rather find a balance between idealized and realistic pictures of rural life. The shepherds in the *Idylls* express themselves as shepherds; their speech is full of village proverbs and superstition, and so the *Idylls* manage to avoid the scholarly tone that marks most poetry of the age. Love and nature are the focus of these poems, and so they strike the modern reader as more relevant. Theocritus's pastoral poetry influenced subsequent Greek pastoral poets, including Moschus of Syracuse (c. 150 B.C.) and Bion of Phlossa (c. ?100 B.C.). He also exerted a great influence on Latin poetry, most notably in the pastoral works of Virgil. *Idyll* 1 especially has demonstrated remarkable influence even on English poetry, being the model for Milton's *Lycidas* and Shelley's *Adonais.*

4. Paul and the Poets.

Paul makes four references to Greek poets in the NT. While preaching to the Athenians (Acts 17:28), Paul quotes Aratus (c. 315-c. 240 B.C.), an Athenian whose *Phaenomena* describes the major constellations in Greek astronomy. Paul's use of the plural ("poets") is thought to indicate an acquaintance with the work of Cleanthes (c. 331-c. 232 B.C.), the founder of *Stoicism, who is best known for a surviving fragment of a hymn to Zeus that advocates a disinterested, stoic outlook in a world governed by a sovereign god. Menander (342-c. 292 B.C.), alluded to in 1 Corinthians 15:33, is a comic playwright who composed in iambic verse, and Paul's quote "Cretans are always liars" (Tit 1:12) is thought to refer to the work of Epimenides (fifth century B.C.), the legendary Cretan mystic poet and wonder worker.

See also HELLENISM; SCHOLARSHIP, GREEK AND ROMAN; WRITING AND LITERATURE, GRECO-ROMAN.

BIBLIOGRAPHY. A. Bonnard, *Greek Civilization: From Euripides to Alexandria* (London: Allen & Unwin, 1962); G. D. Hutchinson, *Hellenistic Poetry* (Oxford: Clarendon Press, 1988); A. Körte, *Hellenistic Poetry* (New York: Columbia University Press, 1929); T. B. L. Webster, *Hellenistic Poetry and Art* (New York: Barnes & Noble, 1965); H. White, *Essays in Hellenistic Poetry* (Amsterdam: Gieben, 1980); idem, *New Essays in Hellenistic Poetry* (Amsterdam: Gieben, 1985).

P. Buchanan

POETS, JEWISH. *See* JEWISH LITERATURE: HISTORIANS AND POETS.

POLITICAL SYSTEM, ROMAN. *See* ROMAN POLITICAL SYSTEM.

POLYTHEISM, GRECO-ROMAN

Greco-Roman polytheism was a complex interplay of not only the pantheons of Greece and Rome, but also the many foreign gods and goddesses of other cultures, such as Egypt, Israel and the many indigenous groups of Asia Minor.

1. The Greek Pantheon
2. The Roman Pantheon
3. Greco-Roman Polytheism and the New Testament

1. The Greek Pantheon.

In the earliest phases of extant Greek literature, there are clear traces of connections with cult and religious belief from a much earlier phase of development. In recent years, since the decipherment of Mycenean Linear B, there has been a growing awareness that the Greeks of the archaic period (up to the sixth century B.C.) had inherited something of the religion of the Mycenean/Minoan period. Although impossible to uncover fully, the *Iliad* and the *Odyssey* contain much that reflects the religion of this now lost civilization. However, Hesiod, another writer almost contemporary with Homer, wrote what are probably the earliest records of Greek polytheistic belief.

Hesiod's *Theogony* is especially valuable for understanding the generation of the gods, their various groupings, and their relationships with one another. Hesiod records the following as the "family tree" of the gods: In the beginning was Chaos, and from Chaos came Earth (Gaia) and Heaven (Uranos). The mating of these two primordial figures produced, in turn, the twelve Titans: Oceanus and Tethys, Hyperion and Thia, Crios and Eurybia (or Mnemosyne), Coeos and Phoebe, Iapetos and Themis, and Cronos and Rhea. Uranos, unhappy with the potential for competition from his offspring, imprisons each of his children in Tartarus, the underworld. Gaia, understandably unhappy with Uranos's imprisonment of her children, convinced Cronos to castrate Uranos, in an effort to take revenge on him for his shameful treatment of his children. This he does, and, according to Hesiod, when the severed testicles of Uranos land on the ocean, Aphrodite is "born" from them (though other versions of Aphrodite's genesis suggest that she is the daughter of Zeus and Dione). There are, in Hesiod, also two other orders of "earth-born" (i.e., born of Gaia): the Cyclopes (one-eyed) and the Hacatonchires (hundred-handed). These were also imprisoned by Uranos, but were not released by Cronos when he attained mastery over his father.

In time, all of the Titans mate with each other, and from the union of Cronos and Rhea descend the twelve gods who will eventually be known as "Olympian": Zeus, Poseidon, Hera, Hephaestus, Ares, Apollo, Aphrodite, Demeter, Hermes, Hestia, Artemis, Pallas Athena, and some lists also include Hades as an Olympian. Cronos, like his father Uranos before him, was afraid of the possibility of being usurped from his kingly position by his children and so swallowed each of them as they were born. Rhea, no more happy with this than was Gaia with Uranos, consults with her parents on an appropriate way to stop Cronos. The plan which is hatched and carried through is as follows: instead of her last child to be born, Cronos will be handed a stone, wrapped in swaddling clothes, to swallow, while the child is whisked away to Crete to be raised. This child, of course, is Zeus, and upon reaching maturity he came back and caused his father to vomit up all of his siblings, as well as the rock that Cronos had thought was Zeus (this rock, known as the Omphalus, was thought to be the very same stone which, in the NT period, was still in the temple of Apollo at Delphi [Plutarch *E Delph.*).

Zeus and his siblings, supported by the Cyclopes and the Hecatonchires whom he freed from prison, made war on the Titans in a battle known as the Titanomachy or the Gigantomachy. At the end of this battle, the Titans were reimprisoned in Tartarus, and Zeus and his siblings reign from this point onwards on Mount Olympus. It is these Olympian gods that are active in the Homeric literature and who form the basis of most popular conceptions of Greek polytheism from the archaic period right into NT times. However, this was not the only way in which Greeks formulated their theogonies. There were several different theogonies that played different roles for different groups.

One of the most well-known alternatives is the Rhapsodic Theogony of the Orphic cult. The Rhapsodic Theogony seems to have existed as early as the first century B.C., and though it bears some relationship to more "conventional" theogonies like that recorded in Hesiod, it is far more complex. In this version, the world was made by the Manifest (Phanes), or the Firstborn (Protogonos), who was swallowed by Zeus, who went on to create the world in which humans live. This form of theogony had special currency with Neo-Platonic philosophy, which saw in this a reflection of the Platonic doctrine of ideals (i.e., the world of Phanes corresponds to this world, while the world that Zeus created is the world in which we live). These stories of genesis have an obvious correlation to the biblical stories of creation and primordial times, and this sort of connection was an important feature of much Jewish literature of the Second Temple period (cf. Pearson 1999).

In Greek literature, there is a plethora of divine beings. Not only the twelve Titans and the Olympian gods are considered deities. For instance, Hesiod has long lists of the gods and goddesses sprung from various unions among the Titans and the Olympian gods, but these, such as Night, Dawn, the Nymphs, etc., are not on the same level as the Olympian gods. As a result, we read in Homer of the "goddess" Calypso, who is clearly not an Olympian (Homer *Odys.* 5), and Odysseus proclaims his devotion to the Nymphs. These are the "goddesses" who are believed to be resident in the sacred cave on Ithaca, next to which he is put ashore by the Phaicean sailors on his return to Ithaca, despite the fact that he is, at that time, in the company of Athena, one of the second-generation Olympian goddesses.

Homeric religion is somewhat of a mystery in many aspects, even if Homer devotes great detail to describing things like libations and sacrifices and makes it fairly clear what the family relationships are among the Olympian gods. Zeus, clearly king of the gods, is closely related to Poseidon, and acts at times in collusion with him, and at times keeps clear of Poseidon's wishes. Athena, clearly a friend of the Achaeans (Greeks), and in particular of Odysseus, is afraid to act against her uncle, and she only truly reveals herself to Odysseus when Poseidon's vengeance is apparently assuaged, after he has turned the Phaecian ship to stone, and (apparently) ringed Phaecia itself with impenetrable mountains. There is a clear tension in Homer over the way in which humans devote themselves to the gods and the way in which the gods act toward humans.

The developments of Greek polytheism during the Hellenistic period are simply too complex to address here. As with so many things, the way the Greeks sublimated everything into their own cultural framework—the *interpretatio graeca*—led to widespread identifications between Greek gods and those of their subjects and neighbors. Perhaps the most famous of these, however, is the relationship between the Greek and Roman pantheons.

2. The Roman Pantheon.

Because of this, Roman religion is often misunderstood as a rough cognate of Greek religion, but with Latin names. The assimilation of Roman gods to their Greek counterparts—e.g., Zeus = Jupiter, Hera = Minerva, Ares = Mars—has been so deeply ingrained in modern Western culture that a recovery of the *Roman* pantheon becomes not only an exercise in the history of ancient religions, but a countercultural move as well. This assimilation can be found as early as the work of the poet Ennius (239-169 B.C.), but became characteristic of the Hellenistic period and the later Augustan age. Nevertheless, this recovery is possible and instructive for those interested in the world that gave birth to the NT and eventually elevated its religion to primacy.

Kerényi's comments (219-20) outline one of the clichés of comparison between Greek and Roman religion: "With the Greeks it is their poetry which provides a basis for characterizing the form of the relation between god and man. . . . In the acts of the Greek cult . . . primordial things are always to some extent still present. . . . The cult was still essentially representation, but it was always mythology. . . . In the Roman cult the picture is quite different. Here mythology and art seem to be lacking." This lack of extant mythology has led, in many cases, to uncertainty about the roles of and relations between the Roman gods and goddesses. This has led many to consider Roman religion to be without mythology, and even, by nature, confused and uncertain when it came to understanding its own gods. Nevertheless, as the great scholar of Roman religion G. Dumézil (48) characterizes it, "our uncertainty is the result of a weakening, an aging produced by the forgetting of definitions and functions which had earlier been clear, complex, and harmonious."

The earliest structure of archaic Roman religion is the triad of Jupiter, Mars and Quirinus, but this structure is, by the NT period, no longer much in evidence. The chief gods of the Romans in the NT period are known as the Capitoline Triad, which is made up of Jupiter, Juno and Minerva. Juno played the role of queen of the gods, and would, under later Greek influence, play conjugal mate to Jupiter (as Hera did to Zeus), while Minerva was a goddess of the arts and trades and of their practitioners. Minerva was identified with Pallas Athena of the Greek pantheon.

The origins of the Capitoline Triad are obscure. Dumézil's detailed discussion (Dumézil, 306-10) of all archaic aspects of Roman religion only surely connects this with the Etruscans, but can establish little else that is firm. Although it is clear that three was a sacred number to both the early Etruscans and their Roman successors, beyond this "We can only imagine" the original significance of the triad (Dumézil, 309). Regardless, it is clear that the temple of Jupiter Optimus Maximus on the Capitol hill of Rome was the chief temple of the triad and formed the political and religious center of Roman cult. Each of the three gods had a section (or *cella*) of the *temple dedicated to themselves.

Jupiter was the sky-father king god, whose epithets included various features of the heavens: *Tonans* ("Thunderer"), *Fulgur* ("Lightning"), *Feretrius* ("Striker"?) (cf. Ferguson 33). Jupiter, whatever his precise origins and archaic function in the original triad with Mars and Quirinus, is nevertheless the chief national divinity of Rome. Yet, as Dumézil states (1:198): "Even before he took two goddesses as his associates on the Capitol, Jupiter was not alone in his majestic sovereignty. Surrounding him on his own level, and forming theological structures with him, were several Entities, autonomous divinities more or less absorbed by him, or aspects more or less detached from him." Still, despite Dumézil's use of Roman theology to try and reconstruct this original structure, the lack of extant ancient mythology makes this a difficult task. Dumézil himself recognizes this, and his conception of the state-of-play in the NT period is central (Dumézil, 1:48, cf. 1:197): "In the era when it was fixed in literature, a great part of the Roman pantheon was on its way to dissolution. The Greek flood had submerged everything and had destroyed the taste for and awareness of traditional explanations. The most original forms, those which had not been able to receive an *interpretatio graeca*, were destined to disappear or to survive only in rites which became less and less intelligible."

3. Greco-Roman Polytheism and the New Testament.

This "Greek flood," or, as Momigliano put it, "alien wisdom," is in the NT period really the more important movement to understand, for it was in the widely accessible and appropriated medium of Greek or Graecized culture that the theologies of the first century were being argued and established. "Greco-Roman," while not an ancient term, nevertheless describes well the complex interplay between especially these two cultures, but also the many cultures of the eastern Mediterranean. In this kind of setting, many more pantheons play a role than merely the Greek or Roman—the Egyptian gods and goddesses, the Jewish God, the new God of the Christians, various mother-goddesses, ruler and emperor worship, etc., all play a role in the intricate dance of deities competing for adherents, status and recognition.

It would be impossible here to outline this drama in any detail, but two contrasting examples from the writings of Paul are illustrative of the role that interaction with these various factors plays in the writings of the apostle to the Gentiles. Both of these represent interpretive positions unusual in contemporary NT scholarship, which only underlines the complexity of this aspect of the ancient world and the degree to which facility with ancient religious culture may ultimately be one of the most important aspects of the work of any NT scholar.

The first of these is found in Romans 1:23, in Paul's apparently summative condemnation of idolatry: "Claiming to be wise, they became fools, and exchanged the glory of the immortal God for images resembling mortal man or birds or animals or reptiles" (RSV). There are two usual approaches to contextualizing Paul's meaning here, but these two are really only alternative versions of the same solution: Paul is reflecting traditional Jewish invective against pagan idolatry. It is typically suggested either that the argumentative framework here is simply antipagan (*see* Idolatry) or that the condemnation of Israel is in view. These approaches have masked the true identity of Paul's dialogue with the Roman church and ignored vital evidence for the reconstruction of the religious milieu in which the earliest church existed. Anyone versed in the cultic imagery of the Roman world will note that the idolatrous images listed in this passage exist together *only* in one group of cults in the Roman world: those originating in Egypt, and typically centered around the worship of the chief god and goddess, Sarapis and Isis (see Witt, 255). Nevertheless, this is not a typical position in the scholarship of this passage. As Pearson shows (forthcoming, ch. 6), there is much potential fruit in understanding this contextualization, both for the interpretation of Romans and for our understanding of the character of Paul's religious milieux.

Likewise, the second chapter of Philippians, with its famous christological hymn (or so-called hymn), is another example where Paul's interaction with Romans on a religious level is directly predicated upon polemic against Roman religious practice. Paul's characterization of Christ's humility and humiliation in this passage—whatever the interest that this has had for modern theologians—was originally written to members of a church in a Roman *colonia*, whose understanding of and devotion to the emperor cult (*see* Ruler Cult) must have played a dramatic role in their lives both prior to and, to a different degree, after their conversion to Christianity. Paul is also writing this letter at a time when, of course, he is in prison, likely in Rome, having appealed to the emperor Nero. Nero's well-known self-aggrandizement and desired divination (cf. Suetonius *Nero*) did not sit well with his subjects. Long before his suicide/assassination in A.D. 68, there were stirrings of discontent. In this setting, Paul characterizes Christ as once a god, but taking the form of a human, even a slave!; emptying himself, not counting equality with God something to be grasped at (*harpagmos*); humbling himself to death, even death on a cross (on the social status of crucifixion, see Hengel, 62). In direct and polemical contrast to the attitudes of Nero, whose ideas about himself could be easily construed as the contradiction of this characterization of Christ, Paul asserts that this *via negativa* is the reason that God has "highly exalted him and bestowed on him the name which is above every name, that at the name of Jesus every knee should bow, in heaven and on earth and under the earth, and every tongue confess that Jesus Christ is Lord, to the glory of God the Father" (Phil 2:9-11 RSV).

Paul is not only aware of Greco-Roman religious sensibilities, he is able in at least two circumstances to manipulate and polemicize against one aspect of Greco-Roman religion for the purpose of speaking to another group. The investigation of other NT writings that engage in similar polemics with Greco-Roman polytheism is a burgeoning area for research.

See also CIVIC CULTS; DOMESTIC RELIGION AND PRACTICES; IDOLATRY, JEWISH CONCEPTION OF; RELIGION, GRECO-ROMAN; RELIGION, PERSONAL; RULER CULT.

BIBLIOGRAPHY. G. Dumézil, *Archaic Roman Religion* (2 vols.; Chicago: University of Chicago Press, 1970 [1966]); J. Ferguson, *The Religions of the Roman Empire* (London: Thames & Hudson, 1970); M. Grant, *Myths of the Greeks and Romans* (London: Weidenfeld & Nicolson, 1962); M. Hengel, *Crucifixion* (London: SCM, 1977); C. Kerényi, *The Religion of the Greeks and Romans* (London: Thames & Hudson, 1962); A. Momigliano, *Alien Wisdom: The Limits of Hellenization* (Cambridge: Cambridge University Press, 1975); B. W. R. Pearson, *Paul, Dialectic, and Gadamer: Conversation and Play in the Study of Paul in the Ancient World* (forthcoming); idem, "Resurrection and the Judgment of the Titans: ἡ γῆ τῶν ἀσεβῶν in LXX Isaiah 26.19," in *Resurrection*, ed. S. E. Porter, M. A. Hayes and D. Tombs (RILP 5; JSNTSup 186; Sheffield: Sheffield Academic Press, 1999) 33-51; R.. E. Witt, *Isis in the Ancient World* (Baltimore and London: Johns Hopkins University Press, 1997 [1971]).

B. W. R. Pearson

POMPEY

In the history of the Jews, Pompey is most significant as the Roman general who brought to an end the waning power of the *Hasmonean dynasty and the first Gentile to penetrate into the holy of holies of the Jewish *temple since its purification after the Maccabean revolt.

1. Career
2. Interaction with the Jews

1. Career.
Born in 106 B.C., Gnaeus Pompeius was the son of the Roman general Strabo. He appears to have been a gifted youth and obtained much early distinction in a variety of military exploits. The 80s were a period of unrest in the *Roman Empire, with one tyrant after another seizing power. During this period, at the age of twenty-three, Pompey attached himself to one of these figures, the tyrant Sulla. He did so only after winning a victory in Sulla's interest as a self-appointed general against Sulla's enemy, Carbo, and further defeating an offensive force led by three generals (Plutarch *Pomp.* 6.3—7.3). His career after this risky but well-calculated beginning continued with striking success as a general in Sulla's service (83–79 B.C., during which he was given the cognomen "the Great," in obvious suggestion of his similarity with *Alexander the Great).

Against precedent, as he held only knightly, equestrian rank (see Roman Social Classes), and only those of consular or praetorian rank were allowed to triumph, he was allowed to triumph in Rome after successful campaigning in northern Africa, while still in his mid-twenties (*see* Roman Triumph).

After the death of Sulla in 78 B.C., Pompey was appointed by the senate to campaign against a pretender to Sulla's former power, Lepidus (whom Pompey had earlier backed, against Sulla's wishes, in a consular election). Later (76 B.C.) he was enlisted again to face the rebellious general Sertorius, who, in the power vacuum after the passing of Sulla, was threatening Rome from Spain. This campaign dragged on for several years until 71 B.C., when Sertorius was killed by intimates, who then tried to continue in his place. Pompey dealt with the ringleader, Perpenna, in a single battle. Returning from Spain, he became involved in the mop-up operations against the Spartican revolt.

His reception in Rome was a wary one, as the possibility of Pompey claiming the power of Sulla was a very real one now that he had dealt with Sertorius. In response Pompey promised to disband his army if he was granted a consulship and a second triumph, to which the senate agreed. In the process, the statesman Crassus, formerly above Pompey in both rank and personal pride, was forced to turn to Pompey to gain support in his bid to become a consul.

After the cessation of this office, Pompey's hitherto unchecked success began to flag—it seems his role as a peacetime statesman was ill-fitted to his soldierly temperament, and he withdrew from an active political life. However, in 67 B.C. he was called upon again to deal with the extensive piratical activity in the Mediterranean centered in Cilicia, which was flourishing as a result of extended Roman inattention in the wake of the Mithridatic wars (88–85, 83–81, 74 B.C.; Plutarch *Pomp.* 24). Pompey was given virtual hegemony over the Mediterranean and its coastal areas, as well as a large fleet and fighting force. He effected the destruction of the pirate fleets, showing forbearance and humanness in dealing with the different groups of pirates and the towns that had lent them support, even resettling many of them in areas depopulated as a result of various conflicts (Plutarch *Pomp.* 27.4—28.4).

Upon these successes, Pompey was given the command of the forces aligned against Mithridates and Tigranes, together with all of the territories of *Asia Minor, while still retaining the command of his naval forces. Over the next four years, he defeated not only the territory of Mithridates and Tigranes but, in pursuit of the fleeing Mithridates, took Syria and Judea as well. Upon Mithridates' suicide in 62 B.C., Pompey returned to Rome, where he celebrated his third triumph in 61 B.C. These victories of Pompey's, in which he subdued fourteen nations, brought back twenty thousand talents to Rome and almost doubled its annual income.

In Rome, however, he faced opposition on account of senatorial disapproval of some of his actions while in command of the eastern portion of the empire. In response, the First Triumvirate, consisting of Pompey, Crassus and Julius Caesar, came into being. This uneasy alliance allowed each of these powerful figures the support he needed to circumvent the senate and was active until the death of Crassus in 53 B.C. During the intervening years, while Caesar had been campaigning against the Gauls and the Germans, Pompey had steadily been losing political ground in Rome. Ever the soldier, his political acumen seems again to have lacked the force necessary to survive the senatorial infighting, as well as the increasing popularity of Caesar. After the death of Crassus, the senate aligned itself behind Pompey as sole consul in 52 B.C. Caesar invaded three years later, and Pompey withdrew to *Greece, where the final battle of the civil war was concluded in 48 B.C. Pompey fled with his wife and a few loyal retainers, only to die as the result of treachery in Egypt later that year.

2. Interaction with the Jews.

During his pursuit of Mithridates in 64/63 B.C., Pompey became involved in the struggles between the Hasmoneans Aristobulus and Hyrcanus. Josephus (*J.W.* 1.6.3—7.7 §§128-58; *Ant.* 15.2.3—4.4 §§29-76), Plutarch (*Pomp.* 30.2), Strabo (*Geog.* 16.763), and Dio Cassius (*Epit.* 37.15.2—19.3), with varying degrees of concern and detail, all record his subjugation of *Judea, with the result that it was placed under the governorship of the governor of Syria and made to pay tribute to Rome, although it was allowed to exist with some independence as a temple state under Hyrcanus's leadership.

Although all of the available historical sources (save Plutarch, who merely states that Judea was subjugated) record that the defenders of the temple were captured as a result of their unwillingness on the *sabbath to prevent the Romans from building up earthworks, some have thought that Dio Cassius disagrees with Josephus and Strabo in suggesting that Pompey plundered the temple. However, the language of Dio Cassius does not necessitate such an interpretation—he makes no explicit reference to Pompey's tour of the holy of holies with all of its treasures, nor does he contradict other sources that suggest that he left these treasures intact.

Pompey took Aristobulus as a captive and displayed him, along with other notable captives, in his third triumph (Plutarch *Pomp.* 65.4). In addition, he reorganized many of the territories that had been captured by the Hasmoneans, including the coastal towns of Gaza, Joppa, Dora and Strato's Tower (later *Caesarea Philippi); rebuilt Gadara in response to a request from a favorite freedman, Demetrius, who was a native of that city; and restored many of the cities to their former inhabitants of what was later known as the *Decapolis, as well as other non-Jewish cities.

The **Psalms of Solomon* were probably written just after Pompey's Palestinian conquests, and Pompey himself is probably the "foreign" conqueror mentioned in them (see esp. *Ps. Sol.* 2). In addition, it is probable that the pesher on Habakkuk from *Qumran (1QpHab; *see* Habakkuk Commentary) dates from the period immediately following the taking of Jerusalem by Pompey (see esp. 1QpHab 9:2-7).

See also JEWISH HISTORY: ROMAN PERIOD; ROMAN EAST.

BIBLIOGRAPHY. W. S. Anderson, *Pompey, His Friends, and the Literature of the First Century B.C.* (University of California Publications in Classical Philology 19.1; Berkeley and Los Angeles: University of California Press, 1963); P. A. L. Greenhalgh, *Pompey: The Republican Prince* (London: Weidenfeld & Nicolson, 1981); idem, *Pompey: The Roman Alexander* (London: Weidenfeld & Nicolson, 1980); R. Seager, *Pompey: A Political Biography* (Oxford: Blackwell, 1979).

B. W. R. Pearson

PONTIUS PILATE. *See* ROMAN GOVERNORS OF PALESTINE.

PORCIUS FESTUS. *See* ROMAN GOVERNORS OF PALESTINE.

PRAETORIAN GUARD. *See* ROMAN MILITARY.

PRAYER OF ENOSH (4Q369 + 4Q458)

Prayer of Enosh (4Q369 + 4Q458) consists of ten leather fragments. Fragment 1 is the largest and contains portions of two columns. In the second column there is reference to a "firstborn son." H. Attridge and J. Strugnell (353) have named the document the *Prayer of Enosh.* According to *Jubilees* 4:12, Enosh was the "first to call upon the name of the Lord" (*see* Jubilees). This tradition, which represents an elaboration on Genesis 5, is probably what underlies 4Q369. It is probable that this document represents what is imagined to have been uttered by Enosh when he called upon the name of the Lord. However, the contents of column ii may in fact be a prayer uttered by Enoch.

What is disputed in this book is its perspective. Does Enosh foresee the historical Israel, or does he foresee the Davidic Messiah (*see* Messianism)? Attridge, Strugnell and C. A. Evans opt for the latter alternative; J. L. Kugel opts for the former. Kugel believes that the "firstborn son" of fragment 1 ii 6 refers to Israel (perhaps alluding to Ex 4:22), not to David or to a Davidic Messiah, and that the whole of column ii concerns the history of Israel as a nation. The reference to "goodly statutes" and "righteous laws" in fragment 1 ii 5 and 10 is to the Sinai covenant, not to some special preparation of the Messiah. God has taught his people his laws (cf. Deut 8:5). Kugel further notes that the perspective of 4Q369 is similar to 4Q504 (the *Words of the Luminaries*), which also speaks of Israel as God's "firstborn son" among the nations. Kugel also cites Sirach 17:17-18, which in some manuscripts speaks of Israel as God's "firstborn," brought up with discipline. Thus it may be argued that Israel is firstborn "by dint of discipline" in the Torah (Kugel, 129-30). 4Q369's "eternal light" may be in reference to the guiding light of Torah, as in Proverbs 6:23 and later interpretive traditions, such as in Wisdom 18:4, *Testament of Levi* 14:4 or *Pseudo-Philo's *Biblical Antiquities* 11:11 (*see* Sirach; Wisdom of Solomon; Testaments of the Twelve Patriarchs).

Although Kugel's interpretation may be correct, some factors support the eschatological interpretation. The words "until the decreed time of judgment" in fragment 1 i 6 and the appearance of Enoch, of the seventh generation, at the conclusion of the genealogy in fragment 1 i 10 suggest an eschatological orientation, which in turn supports a messianic understanding of the "firstborn son" in column ii. References to the land of Israel do not compete with this interpretation. The exact words, "in/with eternal light," appear in 1QM 17:6 and 1QS 4:8, again in eschatological contexts (*see* War Scroll; Rule of the Community). In the Hebrew Bible David is called God's "firstborn," as in Psalm 89:21, 27-28 (Eng. vv. 20, 26-27): "I have found David, my servant; with holy oil I have anointed him . . . he shall cry to me, 'You are my Father . . .' and I will make him the firstborn, the highest of the kings of the earth." Psalm 89 offers three important parallels with 4Q369 frag. 1 ii 6-10: David calls God his father, which parallels line 10, "as a father to his son"; the psalmist says that God "will make him the firstborn," which parallels line 6, "You made him a firstborn son to you"; and the psalmist says that God's firstborn will be "the highest of the kings of the earth," which finds a partial parallel in line 7, "a prince and ruler in all your earthly land." Finally, the words in fragment 3, line 3, "from your hand is all the dominion," may hint at eschatological deliverance.

See also MESSIANISM; SON OF GOD TEXT (4Q246).

BIBLIOGRAPHY. H. Attridge and J. Strugnell, "The Prayer of Enosh," in *Qumran Cave 4.8: Parabiblical Texts, Part 1,* ed. H. Attridge et al. (DJD 13; Oxford: Clarendon Press, 1994) 353-62; C. A. Evans, "A Note on the 'First-Born Son' of 4Q369," *DSD* 2 (1995) 185-201; J. L. Kugel, "4Q369 'Prayer of Enosh' and Ancient Biblical Interpretation," *DSD* 5 (1998) 119-48.

C. A. Evans

PRAYER OF MANASSEH

The Prayer of Manasseh is an individual penitential prayer ascribed to Manasseh, king of Judah (687-642 B.C.). According to 2 Chronicles, Manasseh, a king notorious for his sin and idolatry (2 Kings 21), was taken prisoner to Babylon, where he repented and prayed for forgiveness (2 Chron 33:11-13). The account also refers to two annals that contain "his prayer to God" (2 Chron 33:18-19). Though the Prayer of Manasseh purports to be this prayer uttered by the king in prison, there is little doubt that it is a pseudonymous work composed many centuries later.

1. Structure of the Prayer
2. Composition of the Prayer

1. Structure of the Prayer.

The structure of the prayer is similar to what we find in other postexilic and early Jewish prayers (cf. Dan 9:4-19; Neh 9:6-37; Tob 3:2-6; Pr Azar):

1. Invocation (v. 1)
2. Ascription of praise, mentioning God's work in creation, his wrath and his mercy (vv. 2-7)
3. Confession of sin (vv. 8-10)
4. Petition for forgiveness (v. 11-15a)
5. Doxology (v. 15b)

While most other penitential prayers contain a collective confession of sin, the Prayer of Manasseh is strictly individual: Manasseh stresses his own sinfulness in opposition to the righteous patriarchs (Pr Man 8; cf. Lk 5:32; 15:7). And while he paints himself as the worst of sinners, "unworthy" of God's grace (Pr Man 9, 14; cf. *Jos. and As.* 12:5; Lk 15:19), he knows that God is "compassionate, long-suffering, and very merciful" (Pr Man 7; cf. Ex 34:6), the "God of those who repent" (Pr Man 13). The intention of the prayer is apparently to proclaim God's willingness to forgive repenting sinners.

2. Composition of the Prayer.

There is no consensus with regard to original language; it may be Hebrew, but most likely the prayer was composed in Greek. This is supported by the author's apparent acquaintance with the *Septuagint (cf. Pr Man 7 and Joel 2:13/Jon 4:2; Pr Man 10, 11, 14 and Ps 50 (51):1, 5, 6) and by the occurrence of Greek words that are unusual in translation from the Hebrew.

Though the prayer is not found in any Jewish writings, it was probably composed by a Jew. This is indicated by the lack of any specific Christian elements, the parallels in Jewish prayers, for example, *Joseph and Aseneth* 12, the *Hellenistic *synagogal prayers (preserved in the *Apos. Con.* 7.33-38; cf. 7.33.2; 35.1), the *Shemoneh Esreh* (sixth benediction) and the existence of a similar, fragmentary Prayer of Manasseh in *Qumran (4Q381 33:8-11). It should also be noted that the most peculiar statement found in the prayer—the sinlessness of the patriarchs (Pr Man 8)—has its closest parallels in other early Jewish texts (cf. *T. Abr.* 10:13; *T. Iss.* 7:1; *T. Zeb.* 1:4; cf. also *Jub.* 23:10; 35:12). All these parallels point to a date of composition sometime between 200 B.C. and A.D. 100.

The earliest attestation of the prayer is in the Syriac *Didascalia Apostolorum* (early third century A.D.; originally written in Greek) and later incorporated in the *Apostolic Constitutions* (c. 350-380). There the prayer is found as part of the story of Manasseh, retold on the basis of 2 Kings and 2 Chronicles, though it is supplemented by other material that has some parallels in *rabbinic works (e.g., *Tg. Chron.* 33; *b. Sanh.* 103a). In all probability the prayer was originally composed and transmitted in such a context and not as a separate prayer later ascribed to Manasseh. This is supported by the links between the prayer and the story in 2 Chronicles (cf. Pr Man 1, 10, and 2 Chron 33:6, 11, 12; 35:19c LXX).

Despite the links to the story of Manasseh, the influence from other texts in the LXX (esp. the Psalms) has given the prayer a rather general tone. Consequently it could easily be used as a general penitential prayer. A Christian liturgical use is attested by its place among the Odes added to the Psalms in some manuscripts of the LXX (e.g., Codex Alexandrinum and Codex Turicensis) and in many separate editions of these Odes or Canticles in various languages (see Mearns). According to John of Damascus (*Sacra Parallela; PG* 95.1436.35), already Julius Africanus (c. A.D. 160-240) knew the prayer as an "ode."

In the Eastern Orthodox churches the Prayer of Manasseh is regarded as canonical, and in many Protestant Bibles (e.g. the Bible of Luther, KJV, RSV) it is part of the OT *Apocrypha. In the early printed editions of the Vulgate it is found at the end of 2 Chronicles; after the Council of Trent, which did not list it as canonical, it is placed as an appendix following the NT in the Vulgate.

See also APOCRYPHA AND PSEUDEPIGRAPHA; PRAYER OF NABONIDUS AND PSEUDO-DANIEL (4Q242-245).

BIBLIOGRAPHY. P. Bogaert, "La Légende de Manassé," *Apocalypse de Baruch* (SC 144; Paris: Éditions du Cerf, 1969) 296-319; H. N. Bream, "Manasseh and His Prayer," *Lutheran Theological Seminary Bulletin* 66 (1986) 5-47; J. H. Charlesworth, "Prayer of Manasseh," *OTP* 2:625-37; R. H. Connolly, *Didascalia Apostolorum* (Oxford: Clarendon Press, 1929); J. C. Dancy, *The Shorter Books of the Apocrypha* (CBC; Cambridge: Cambridge University Press, 1972) 242-48; D. A. Fiensy, *Prayers Alleged to be Jewish: An Examination of the Constitutiones Apostolorum* (BJS 65; Chico, CA: Scholars Press, 1985); D. J. Harrington, "Prayer of Manasseh," *HBC* 872-74; J. Mearns, *The Canticles of the Christian Church* (Cambridge: Cambridge University Press, 1914); M. Metzger, *Les Constitutions Apostoliques I* (SC 320; Paris: Éditions du Cerf, 1985); E. Oswald, "Gebet Manasses," *JSHRZ* 4 (1973) 15-27; A. Rahlfs, ed., *Septuaginta vol. 10: Psalmi cum Odis* (Göttingen: Vandenhoeck & Ruprecht, 1967) 361-63; H. E. Ryle, "Prayer of Manasses," *APOT* 1:612-24; E. M. Schuller, *Noncanonical Psalms from Qumran: A Pseudepigraphic Collection* (HSS 28; Atlanta: Scholars Press, 1986) 146-62; E. Schürer, *A History of the Jewish People in the Time of Jesus Christ (175 B.C.-A.D. 135)*, rev. and ed. G. Vermes et al. (3 vols.; Edinburgh: T & T Clark, 1973-87) 3.2:730-33; A. Vööbus, *The Didascalia Apostolorum in Syriac* (CSCO 401-2; 407-8; Louvain: Secrétariat du CorpusSCO, 1979).

R. Hvalvik

PRAYER OF NABONIDUS (4Q242) AND PSEUDO-DANIEL (4Q243-245)

As many as nine Dead Sea Scrolls, all written in Aramaic, are associated with the book of Daniel or with traditions about Daniel. The first four of these manuscripts, comprising three distinct works, are the focus of this article (see table).

1. 4Q242 (4QPrNab ar, "The Prayer of Nabonidus")
2. The *Pseudo-Daniel* Scrolls

Table of Danielic Writings at Qumran

Manuscript	*Number*	*Date Copied*
PrNab ar	4Q242	72–50 B.C.
psDan[a] ar	4Q243	early 1st cent. A.D.
psDan[b] ar	4Q244	early 1st cent. A.D.
psDan[c] ar	4Q245	early 1st cent. A.D.
apocrDan ar	4Q246	last 3d of 1st cent. B.C.
papApocalypse ar	4Q489	c. 50 A.D.
DanSuz? ar	4Q551	late 1st cent. B.C.
Four Kingdoms[a] ar	4Q552	c. early 1st cent. A.D.
Four Kingdoms[b] ar	4Q553	c. early 1st cent. A.D.

1. 4Q242 (4QPrNab ar, "The Prayer of Nabonidus").
Although this text does not mention Daniel by name, it shares several features with the book of Daniel: a Babylonian king who is afflicted for seven years, his recovery due to the intervention of a Jewish exile, a king who speaks in the first person, a written proclamation in praise of the true God, and possibly the king becoming like a "beast" (line 3, restored). The text opens with "The words of the pray[er] which Nabonidus, king [of Baby]lon, the [great k]ing, prayed [when he was smitten] with a bad disease by the decree of [Go]d in Teima." In the book of Daniel, however, it is King Nebuchadnezzar, not Nabonidus, who was afflicted. The overall relevance of 4QPrNab ar is to the literary pre-history of Daniel 4.

2. The *Pseudo-Daniel* Scrolls.
Unlike 4QPrNab ar, the three *Pseudo-Daniel* scrolls contain clear references to Daniel. The first composition is represented by 4Q243 and 4Q244, with at least one overlapping passage. When these two manuscripts are viewed together, the main components of the composition may be divided into five sections: (1) The Court Setting, where Daniel addresses King Bel-shazzar and his court and explains a writing or book which probably contained the overview of biblical history that follows. (2) The Primeval History, dealing with the events or material found in Genesis 5—11 (including *Enoch, the flood and the Tower of Babel). (3) From the Patriarchs to the *Exile, including the time in Egypt, crossing the Jordan, the wilderness wanderings, Nebuchadnezzar's conquest and the exile. (4) The Hellenistic Era, which is distinguished from the preceding ones by the presentation of events as yet to come and by the presence of Greek proper names (e.g., *Balakros*). (5) The Eschatological Period, which specifies a time of oppression, but then how God will save his people "with his great hand."

The second pseudo-Daniel composition is in 4QpsDan[c] (4Q245). Only two fragments are preserved, the first of which mentions Daniel and presents a list of *priests ([Lev]i, Qahath, Bukki, Uzzi, [Zado]k, Abiathar, Hi[l]kiah, Onias, [Jona]than, Simon) in lines 5-10. The missing text contained other names, most of which occur in the priestly list in 1 Chronicles 6:1-15 (Heb 5:27-41), and probably extended to Jehozadak, Judah's last high priest before the exile (cf. 1 Chron 6:15 [MT 5:41]). The extant text suggests that Onias followed in the line of Zadokite high priests. A list of kings (David, Solomon, Ahazia[h], [Joa]sh) follows in lines 11-12. In view of the royal list found in 1 Chronicles 10—16, it is reasonable to conclude that the list continued beyond line 12 down to Zedekiah, the last king of Judah.

The second fragment presents an eschatological conclusion to the work:

1. [ ]. .[
2. [ ]to exterminate wickedness
3. [ ]these in blindness, and they have gone astray
4. [th]ese then will arise
5. [ ]the [h]oly [ ], and they will return
6. [ ] iniquity.

This language is clearly eschatological and describes two groups of people. The extermination of wickedness (line 2) is clearly an eschatological theme (cf. 1QS 4:18: "But in the mysteries of his understanding, and in his glorious wisdom, God has ordained an end for evil, and at the time of the visitation he will destroy it for ever"). The notion of a blind man losing his way (cf. line 3) is common in the Hebrew Bible (e.g.,

Deut 27:18; 28:29; Is 59:10; Zeph 1:17; Lam 4:14) and occurs elsewhere in the scrolls (CD 1:10-11: "And they were like the blind and like those who grope their way," referring to the remnant of Israel).

Two groups ("these . . . [th]ese") seem to be contrasted in lines 3-4. *These* must either be understood in the context of final judgment or may reflect the parting of the ways when an elect group arises in the end time. Line 4 preserves the words "[th]ese then will arise," which some commentators see as an allusion to Daniel 12 and the resurrection of the dead. However, Daniel 12:2 uses a different verb ("they will awake"); furthermore, in Daniel the other group will awake "to shame and everlasting contempt," while in 4Q245 (line 3) they are in blindness and have gone astray. It seems here that contrast is not between two groups who are resurrected, but between some who persist in error and others who rise and walk in the way of truth (cf. CD 1:11-15). Although lines 5-6 are fragmentary, the references to the "holy kingdom" and a return have strong eschatological connotations. "Iniquity" may well be the last word in the manuscript, which suggests that the composition ended with the extermination of wickedness (cf. line 2).

The lists in fragment 1 must be understood in light of the eschatological conclusion in fragment 2. The return of one group at the end suggests a reversal of the course of history, as in apocalyptic and pseudo-prophetic texts (e.g., the Apocalypse of Weeks in *1 Enoch* and Daniel 10—12). The list of legitimate priests in 4Q245 must have ended with Simon, suggesting that subsequent priests were unacceptable since the boundary between priesthood and kingship had been transgressed. Thus fragment 2 anticipates the eschatological restoration in accordance with the divine order, which would include a priesthood that was legitimate in the eyes of God.

See also DANIEL, ESTHER AND JEREMIAH, ADDITIONS TO.

BIBLIOGRAPHY. J. J. Collins, "Nabonidus, Prayer of (4QPrNab)," *ABD* 4:976-77; idem, "Pseudo-Daniel Revisited," *RevQ* 17 (1996) 111-36; E. Cook, "The Vision of Daniel," in *The Dead Sea Scrolls: A New Translation*, M. O. Wise, M. G. Abegg Jr. and E. Cook (San Francisco: HarperCollins, 1996) 266-68; F. M. Cross, "Fragments of the Prayer of Nabonidas," *IEJ* 34 (1984) 260-64; P. W. Flint, "4QPseudo-Daniel ar[c] (4Q245) and the Restoration of the Priesthood," *RevQ* 17 (1996) 137-50; idem, "The Prophet Daniel at Qumran," in *Eschatology, Messianism, and the Dead Sea Scrolls*, ed. C. A. Evans and P. W. Flint (SDSSRL 1; Grand Rapids, MI: Eerdmans, 1997) 41-60; F. García Martínez, "Daniel et Susanne à Qumrân," in *De la Tôrah au Messie: Mélanges Henri Cazelles*, ed. M. Carrez, J. Doré and P. Grelot (Paris: Desclée, 1981) 337-59; idem, "The Prayer of Nabonidus: A New Synthesis," in *Qumran and Apocalyptic: Studies on the Aramaic Texts from Qumran* (STDJ 9; Leiden: E. J. Brill, 1992) 116-36; R. Meyer, *Das Gebet des Nabonid* (Berlin: Akademie Verlag, 1962); J. T. Milik, "'Prière de Nabonide' et autres écrits d'un cycle de Daniel," *RB* 63 (1956) 411-15; E. Puech, "La prière de Nabonide (4Q242)," in *Targumic and Cognate Studies: Essays in Honour of Martin McNamara*, ed. K. J. Cathcart and M. Maher (JSOTSup 230; Sheffield: Sheffield Academic Press, 1996) 208-27; E. Ulrich, "Daniel Manuscripts from Qumran. Part 1: Preliminary Edition of 4QDan[a]," *BASOR* 268 (1987) 17–37; idem, "Daniel Manuscripts from Qumran. Part 2: Preliminary Edition of 4QDan[b] and 4QDan[c]," *BASOR* 274 (1989) 3–26; M. O. Wise, "The Healing of King Nabonidus," in *The Dead Sea Scrolls: A New Translation*, M. O. Wise, M. G. Abegg Jr. and E. Cook (San Francisco: HarperCollins, 1996) 265-66.

P. W. Flint

PREFECT. *See* ROMAN ADMINISTRATION; ROMAN GOVERNORS OF PALESTINE.

PREMARITAL SEXUAL INTERCOURSE. *See* ADULTERY, DIVORCE.

PRIENE INSCRIPTION. *See* INSCRIPTIONS AND PAPYRI: GRECO-ROMAN.

PRIESTS AND PRIESTHOOD, JEWISH

This entry deals with the traditional view of the priesthood as it emerges from ancient biblical commentaries and age-old tradition. These sources illuminate our understanding of the NT.

1. Descent and Duties of the Priests
2. The High Priest
3. New Testament and Talmudic References to Priests

1. Descent and Duties of the Priests.

The priesthood is a male, hereditary clique,

each member descended from *Moses' brother Aaron and his male children, themselves descendants of Levi the son of Jacob the patriarch (that is, they belong to the tribe of Levites). Their major duty, in times when *sacrifices were offered, was to attend to the sacrificial rites in whatever places were designated as public sanctuaries (Deut 10:8). They did not officiate at high places of private individuals where altars were constructed. They came to participate according to a rotation on weeks or courses set up for the various families. The families were named after the progenitor of the course. Priests sprinkled blood of purification on the ark covers, altars, ark of the covenant, and on those with designated plagues. They prepared and burned incense on the inner altar, lit the candelabra and offered advice on religious matters. They performed the elaborate rituals of sacrifice, instructed the people, judged certain cases—particularly cases involving *temple matters—blessed the nation, examined and purified lepers and helped the high priest in teaching the oracles of the Lord that were entrusted to him.

In later times, priests were not the only ones to instruct and judge the people, even matters involving just priests. The class of scribes eventually assumed authority for this and even supervised the priests in the temple at certain times. The priests received priestly gifts of food from produce and animals that people ate, as well as a portion in certain sacrifices. Some had special duties during wars. They set out and consumed shewbread on the temple table and were given parts of certain sacrifices to eat. Priests also administered the rites of the suspected adulteress who wanted to clear herself of suspicion (Num 5:11). When they received firstfruits they were to listen to a specific liturgy detailing the heroic exploits of God in saving his people and bringing them to the land. They were the administrators of the Lord's manor, watching to see that everyone understood their security depended on the Lord. Nevertheless, they were not to own property themselves but to tend the vineyard of the Lord. Yet they were given dwelling places, and Joshua 21 mentions thirteen towns. An elevated priest, specifically anointed for the purpose, addressed the people at the beginnings of wars.

Priests were anointed with the sprinkling of oil on their vestments, but the high priest was anointed with oil also being poured on his head (Ex 29:29). According to tradition this pouring ritual ceased during the reign of King Josiah during biblical times. Many priests were entrusted with looking after ritual items and overseeing certain duties of other priests. There was an assistant high priest as well who had very few cultic duties but many administrative ones. In essence the priest's job was to effect atonement for sins, private and public, and to maintain the institution of covenant. In this regard they joined with kings and prophets in early biblical periods of the first temple. Their job was to ensure the sanctity of the temple and the obedience of the people so that God would dwell among the nation.

Priests had designated duties in the temple and rotated their presence according to a well worked out scheme. They were not to enter the sanctuary except for the purposes of fulfilling their duties, nor were they to leave until their ministrations were completed. Priests were enjoined from strong drink, from growing long hair, from wearing ragged clothing and from having contact with most corpses. Priests with certain physical defects were not permitted to offer sacrifices.

Today, long after the destruction of the temple, descendants of priestly families themselves holding the status of priest with potential to serve in a rebuilt temple hold special privileges in the *synagogue, where their hereditary honor is respected and acknowledged. The integrity of the priestly line and their family traditions have been bolstered by modern genetic studies that have shown that the male group has a marked tendency to have a chromosome marker statistically unique to Jews claiming priestly descent.

2. The High Priest.

The high priest was the foremost priest and had special rites on the Day of Atonement. The high priest wore specific garments for certain ministrations; ordinary priests wore a different arrangement of clothes. Every day he offered a cake offering of flour and oil both in the morning and in the evening. While both ordinary priests and high priests were not to marry divorcees, loose women or the daughters of priests who broke these marriage rules, high priests were not supposed to marry widows although ordinary priests might. The high priesthood, during the time of Solomon's temple, was the right of the family of Zadok (2 Sam 15:24).

During the period of the restoration, when

Palestine was ruled by monarchs of Persian and then Hellenist cultures, the high priest served as head of state, incorporating the duties of king and prophet since his office was the only remaining office of first temple times (*see* Jewish History: Greek Period; Jewish History: Persian Period). He enjoyed unprecedented power, and now families vied over the office and problems developed. As the high priesthood developed into a highly political office serving the needs of the ruling Syrians, strife and war broke out.

Eventually the *Hasmonean family established themselves officially as high priests and kings of Israel, although they were entitled to do so neither by the rules or long-established practice. They were neither of the high-priestly clan of Zadok nor of the kingly tribe of Judah. The last of the Hasmoneans was deposed by *Herod, who made himself king and appointed high priests. High priests were no longer groomed for the position nor sanctioned by official judicial powers, and the office lent itself to corruption, although not all appointed high priests were corrupt. An early Talmudic source (*t. Menaḥ.* 13:21) mentions the oppression of the people by some *Sadducean high priests. Since high priests came and went year by year after Herod, the families of the once high priests, including these priests themselves, formed an aristocracy of chief priests. Eventually the Sanhedrin, the official *Pharisaic judicial power, gained control over the appointments long after Herod's death, but with the destruction of the temple this privilege came to an abrupt end.

3. New Testament and Talmudic References to Priests.

The NT refers to priests within many contexts, but the while Gospels do not refer to the sense of a minister of the Christian sacraments, Paul does regard himself as carrying out a priestly role (Rom 15:16). The development of the priesthood in Catholicism, East and West, requires special treatment beyond the focus of this article. The modern-day Catholic priesthood is heir to a Christian institution whose roots are based on a kind of imitation of the Jewish priesthood, including the papal office as a kind of high priesthood.

The Talmud mentions not only priestly courses but also the method of drawing lots for the various services in the temple. References to these institutions are noted in Luke 1. The Talmud also mentions the institution of lay prayer at the time of various offerings, and this also is noted in Luke 1. Indeed, the Talmud noted that a priest who got to offer incense was deemed very fortunate, as that honor would surely bring him miraculous joy, so that once a priest had received that honor he was not to participate in that lottery again until every other priest had at least had a turn. In the Gospel trial scenes mention is made of chief priests, elders, scribes and the high priest. We must assume that the trial envisioned here is one in which the high priest convened his own council and not the official Pharisaic court or *Sanhedrin mentioned in the Talmud to have existed in the latter days of the Second Temple.

In the Synoptic Gospels, Jesus does not assume priestly roles. For instance, Matthew 8:4 (Mk 1:44; Lk 5:14) and Luke 17:14 tell that Jesus sent lepers to the priest for examination to be declared pure. He did not declare them such himself. However in 1 Peter 2:5-9 Christians are seen as a priesthood with Jesus as the chief priest by which sacrifices might be offered. The passage makes it clear that a spiritual, nonphysical sacrificial rite is at the core here, and so it is in Revelation 1:6.

The book of Hebrews (Heb 5, 7) is unique in that it claims Jesus has superseded the levitical priesthood of the Jewish temple and the universal, Gentile priesthood of *Melchizedek. The previous orders of serving God, whether by Jew or Gentile, was said to be encompassed in the priestly figure of Jesus Christ. There were many traditions concerning Genesis 14:18-19. According to some *Melchizedek, king of Salem, was none other than Shem the son of Noah. He was fluent in all the laws of the priesthood and acted as one. The rabbis interpreted Psalm 110:4 to mean that he eventually handed the authority of the eternal priesthood to Abraham. One senses here an attempt to defuse the personage of Melchizedek from the Christian model. The author of Hebrews used Psalm 110 to claim that Melchizedek prefigured Jesus as the eternal and universal high priest.

See also HASMONEANS; LITURGY: QUMRAN; LITURGY: RABBINIC; MELCHIZEDEK, TRADITIONS OF; PURITY; SACRIFICE AND TEMPLE SERVICE; SANHEDRIN; TEMPLE, JEWISH.

BIBLIOGRAPHY. J. D. Eisenstein, *Ozar Dinim u-Minhagim: A Digest of Jewish Laws and Customs* (New York: J. D. Eisenstein, 1938) 175-77; idem,

"Priests and Priesthood," *EncJud* 13:1069-91; E. P. Sanders, *Judaism: Practice and Belief 63 BCE-66 CE* (Philadelphia: Trinity Press International. 1992) 7-102, 170-89; H. L. Strack and P. Billerbeck, *Commentar zum Neuen Testament* (6 vols.; Munich: C. H. Beck, 1924-56) 4:452-65. H. W. Basser

PRISON, PRISONER

Jesus prophesied that his disciples would experience imprisonment (Lk 21:12). This prophecy was recurrently fulfilled in the experience of the Twelve (Acts 4:3; 5:18-25; 12:1-19; cf. Rev 1:9-10), Paul and his associates (Acts 16:16-40; 20:23; 21:11-13; 21:27—28:31; 2 Cor 6:5; 11:23; cf. Col 4:10; Philem 23) and many other believers (Acts 8:3; 9:2, 14; 22:4-5; 26:10; Heb 10:34). Moreover, of the thirteen letters attributed to Paul in the NT, five are written in the context of custody. Historical knowledge of the nature and variety of imprisonment practices in antiquity is critical to an understanding of the life impact and theological significance of the earliest Christian experiences.

1. The Process of Going to Prison
2. The Purposes and Places of Imprisonment
3. The Privations of Custody and Prisoner Pastimes
4. The Shame of Bonds and Christian Responses

1. The Process of Going to Prison.

As with the administration of justice (e.g., Pliny *Ep.* 9.5; 10.96), custodial arrangements in the Greco-Roman world were made based on legal and social factors. The Roman jurist Ulpian writes that the proconsul normally determined the custody of accused persons "by reference to the nature of the charge brought, the honorable status, or the great wealth, or the harmlessness, or the rank of the accused" (Justinian *Dig.* 48.3.1).

1.1. Charges. Serious crimes usually merited heavier custody and less serious crimes lighter custody. A charge could be deemed "serious" in itself (e.g., murder) or in virtue of the one against whom it had been committed (e.g., striking a senator). Some crimes were eminently worthy of imprisonment: war, rebellion and civil disturbance; treason (*maiestas minuta*), which diminished or endangered the dignity, grandeur or power of *Rome and/or the *emperor; conjuring harm to the emperor through *philosophy or occult practices; murder and poisoning; theft, brigandage, piracy and sacrilege; fiscal offenses and debt; and sundry other charges, including Christianity (Rapske 1994, 41-46).

1.2. Identity. An individual's identity was determined not only by the civil law (whether one was free or *slave, *citizen or alien) but also by background and status, as noted by Ulpian. Where "upper-class" (*honestiores*) and "lower-class" (*humiliores*) distinctions using Ulpian's measures cut across the divide between citizens and aliens, conflicts inevitably arose (Garnsey). For example, citizens had trusted in legal provisions that protected them from bonds, scourging and summary execution (Livy *Hist.* 10.9.3-5; Cicero *Verr.* 2.5.170; Justinian *Dig.* 48.6.7-8; Paulus *Sent.* 5.26.1-2). However, a citizenship unadorned by upper-class attachments might make it difficult to come to one's rights. The more extensive grant of Roman citizenship over time (Tacitus *Ann.* 3.40.2) also tended to erode its currency in litigation and custodial assignments.

The class indicators noted by Ulpian may be defined thus: "Honorable status" (*honor*) related to offices held and the public esteem they commanded. "Great wealth" (*amplissimae facultates*) reflected material superabundance. "Harmlessness" (*innocentia*) probably denoted what a magistrate might positively presume of an individual. "Rank" (*dignitas*) indicated one's place relative to others in Roman society. All of these were in various ways inheritable.

Citizens generally fared better than noncitizens and the wealthy better than the poor in the setting of custodial arrangements. It must also be kept in mind that magistrates were interested in the relative status of both accused and accuser.

1.3. Negative Influences. Custodial determinations might be corrupted by the sinister forces of influence (*potentia*), favoritism (*gratia*) and bribery (*pecunia*). Despite laws against it (e.g., Justinian *Dig.* 48.11.7 *prol.*), judicial corruption was rife (Josephus *Ant.* 20.21.5 §215; *J.W.* 2.14.1 §273; 2.14.4-9 §§284-308; Pliny *Ep.* 2.11). Additionally, for magistrates who possessed capital jurisdiction and immunity from prosecution during office and who governed at a distance from Rome, there was great temptation to wrongdoing.

2. The Purposes and Places of Imprisonment.

2.1. Purposes. In antiquity custody had several purposes: protection against threat from others or oneself; remand against the risk of flight; the place to await ratification or execution of sentence; the place of execution; and an instrument of extrajudicial coercion (*coercitio*). While Roman criminal law did not formally recognize imprisonment as a punishment for free persons, delays in trial, sentence and execution effectively turned imprisonment into a punishment (Rapske 1994, 10-20).

*2.2. **Places.*** Ulpian indicates a range of options in setting custody, "whether someone is to be lodged in prison, handed over to the military, entrusted to sureties, or even on his own recognizances" (Justinian *Dig.* 48.3.1). Ulpian's sequence runs from most to least severe.

Prison (*carcer*) was the most severe form of custody. Rome's oldest state prison (the *Carcer*), consisting of an upper structure and a subterranean death cell (the *Tullianum*), had the worst appointments and housed the worst criminals. Rome's quarry prison (*lautumia*) and prison of the Hundred (*carcer centumviralis*), the ancient prison on the site of the Theater of Marcellus, and the prison cells of the regional fire stations were less severe. Like Rome, other cities, towns and municipalities had their prisons. The wearing of chains (*vincula, catenae;* Gk *desma/oi, halyseis*) seems more consistently to have been associated with confinement in the *Carcer* rather than in the prisons of lighter custody (*libera custodia*), but this is far from invariable. Generally, however, imprisonment without chains was a concession to high status.

The next most severe form of incarceration, military custody (*custodia militaris*), was a development of the imperial period. It could be more or less severe depending upon whether it was within a barracks or camp, in transit to a provincial capital or Rome, in a place of exile or relegation or in one's own home. The rank, experience and number of soldiers assigned to guard a prisoner corresponded with his or her importance or status. Prisoners and guards were frequently manacled together (Josephus *Ant.* 18.6.6-10 §§189-237; Ign. *Rom.* 5.1; Seneca *Ep.* 5.7; Seneca *Tranq.* 10.3). Guards who allowed their prisoners to escape or kill themselves were subject to a graduated penalty system based upon level of culpability (Justinian *Dig.* 48.3.12, 14; Petronius *Sat.* 112).

Less severe yet was entrustment to sureties (*fideiusoribus committenda*), where an accused person of rank was transferred into the custody of a higher-ranking person. The security and safety of the prisoner were paramount, and the surety had absolute control over the manner of detention and its modalities, which could be comfortable or quite miserable (Dio Cassius *Hist.* 58.3.5-6; Tacitus *Ann.* 6.3.3, 22; Suetonius *Vitellius* 7.2.3; Justinian *Dig.* 1.18.14).

The least severe custodial option Ulpian mentions is release of an accused on his own recognizances (*etiam sibi*). Where an accused was restricted from appearance in public or travel it showed itself to be a true form of custody.

3. The Privations of Custody and Prisoner Pastimes.

*3.1. **Privations of Custody.*** Prisoners suffered various privations in custody. War and civil disturbance, the enforcement of condemnatory edicts and delay in processing cases owing to volume, incompetence or sheer malice could pack prisons far beyond reasonable capacity. Poor ventilation created conditions of dangerously stale air, suffocating heat and dehydration. Prisons were sleepless places. Where pallets were not available one slept on the floor, perhaps using one's outer cloak as a cover against the cold (Josephus *Ant.* 18.6.7 §204; cf. Acts 12:8; 2 Tim 4:13). Chains and stocks (*xyla*) also hindered sleep (Lucian of Samosata *Tox.* 29; Acts 16:24-25).

Most prisons were devoid of much natural light. In their inner cells and underground chambers, light was nonexistent. Small wonder that *tenebrae* ("darkness") can be rendered "dungeon" in some passages (e.g., Cicero *Cat.* 4.10). Nightfall robbed prisoners of natural light, and the requirements of security forbade them artificial light (Tertullian *Ad Mart.* 2; *Mart. Let. Lyons et Vienne* 27-28; *Mart. Perp. et Felic.* 3.5; cf. Acts 16:29).

The chaining of prisoners caused varied consequent sufferings. Iron chafed and corroded the skin over time (Lucan *Civ. W.* 72—73; Seneca *Contr.* 1.6.2; cf. Phil. 1:17). Tightly fixed, chains were a means of torture (*Cod. Theod.* 9.3.1). Prisoners could also be weighed down with such heavy chains as to exhaust or cripple them (*ARS* 8—XII Tables 3.3; Ovid *Con. Liv.* 273-74; Suetonius *Nero* 36.2; Seneca *Contr.* 1.6.2; Philostratus *Vit. Ap.* 7.36).

Without recourse to personal resources or the help of friends on the outside for food or drink (Josephus *Ant.* 18.6.7 §204; *Life* 3 §§13-14; Lucian of Samosata *Peregr.* 12; Tertullian *De Je-*

jun. 12; *b. Mo'ed Qaṭ.* 3:1-2; *b. Mo'ed* III: *'Erub.* 21b; cf. Acts 16:34; 24:23; 27:3), the prisoner's prospects could be grim. The officially provided daily prison ration (*solo fiscalis*) was poor and intended not for health but bare survival. Its denial could be a punishment, a form of torture or even a means of execution (Dio Cassius *Hist.* 58.3.5-6; Tertullian *De Jejun.* 12; Christian Martyr Literature passim; Heliodorus *Aeth.* 8.6.2; Cyprian *Ep.* 21.2; 33.2; cf. Acts 16:25, 33-34).

Prisons were places of squalor and appalling filth (Cicero *Verr.* 2.5.21; Tertullian *Ad Mart.* 2; Cyprian *Ep.* 47.3). The permissions of a lighter custody might allow for new clothing and visits to the public baths (Josephus *Ant.* 18.6.7 §203; 18.6.10 §228; Tertullian *De Jejun.* 12; Justinian *Dig.* 48.20.2, 6), but barber's knives were a risk and so haircuts were denied (Martial *Epigr.* 3.74; Josephus *Ant.* 16.11.16 §§387-88; 18.6.10 §237; Lucian of Samosata *Tox.* 30; *m. Mo'ed Qaṭ.* 3:1). Clothing quickly turned to rags in severe custody so prisoners came to look more dead than alive (Lucian of Samosata *Tox.* 30). Even before entering custody, the action of mobs and the normal process of punitive or coercive flogging left clothing and bodies torn (Seneca *Contr.* 9.2.21; Acts 16:22; 21:30-32; 22:24-25).

It is not a surprise that these awful conditions caused such profound distress of body and soul that prisoners, if they did not become sick and die (Seneca *Contr.* 9.1; Plutarch *Vit. Cim.* 4.3; Philostratus *Vit. Ap.* 4.35; 7.26; 8.22; cf. Mt 25:36, 43), wished themselves dead or actively sought suicide (Philostratus *Vit. Ap.* 7.26; Lucian of Samosata *Tox.* 30; Tacitus *Ann.* 6.5.8; Suetonius *Vitellius* 7.2.3; *Tiberius* 61.5; Dio Cassius *Hist.* 58.3.5-6; Justinian *Dig.* 48.3.8; 48.3.14.3-5).

3.2. Prisoner Pastimes. Extended imprisonment created yawning periods of unoccupied time. Prisoners would not have been permitted to pursue a trade and especially not one like tent making, which called for the use of dangerous tools (Acts 18:3; cf. Justinian *Dig.* 2.11.4.1; 4.6.1.1, 10; 22.1.23; 49.14.45.1). Prisoners in antiquity are known to have written petitions for release (PLund. 2:354; PPetr. 3:36a verso; P. Cair. Zen. 2:59275; 3:59482; 4:59492, 59601, 59626; *Sammelb.* 3:6787; PLBat. 20:29; Keenan). It is unlikely that Paul so engaged himself. While other prisoners might prepare their cases in prison (Philostratus *Vit. Ap.* 7; 8.6-7; Achilles Tatius *Leuc.* 7.2.1-4), Jesus had forbidden such activity to Christian prisoners (Lk 21:14-15). It is also a fact that prisoners occupied their time by playing games (Seneca *Tranq.* 14.6-7; Plutarch *Mor. Sera* 554.D), reading and conversing (Plato *Phaed.* 61.B; Suetonius *Tiberius* 61.4; Arrian *Epict. Diss.* 2.6.27; Lucian of Samosata *Peregr.* 12; cf. 2 Tim 4:13).

Prisoners also engaged in the philosophical and religious disciplines of prayer, song and fasting (Plato *Phaed.* 60.D-E; 61.A-B; 117.B-C; Philostratus *Vit. Ap.* 7.31, 38; Tibullus 2.6.25-26; cf. Christian Martyr Literature passim). The Pauline pattern in prayer and song is evident in both Acts and the captivity epistles. Related to the above were philosophical and religious ministrations to others in writing (Plato *Phaed.* 60.D-E; Cicero *Verr.* 2.5.112; Tacitus *Ann.* 6.39; Philostratus *Vit. Ap.* 4.46; Pol. *Phil.* 13.2; Ign. passim; Christian Martyr Literature passim) and conversation (Plato *Crito*; *Phaed.*; Philostratus *Vit. Ap.* 7.26-42; *b. Naš.* I: *Yebam.* II:104a, 108b; *m. Giṭ.* 6:7; cf. Christian Martyr Literature passim). The book of Acts and the captivity epistles are particularly rich in their indications that time in custody was not dead time for the apostle.

4. The Shame of Bonds and Christian Responses.

4.1. The Shame of Bonds. Mediterranean culture was significantly driven by *honor and shame concerns, and in such a context the experience of custody and bonds carried devastating dishonor and shame connotations. Prisons and shame are closely identified in the literature (Plutarch *Vit. Sol.* 15.2-3; Pausanius *Test.* 6.13.1; Cicero *Verr.* 2.5.148; Arrian *Epict.* 1.4.23-24; 2.1.35; 2.6.25; Suetonius *Vitellius* 7.17; Seneca *Ep. Lucil.* 85.41). Damaging connotations and insult attached to prisoners irrespective of their deserts because prison was by definition for social deviants (Dio Cassius *Hist.* 58.11.1; Seneca *Contr.* 9.4.20-21; Suetonius *Vitellius* 7.17.1; Philostratus *Vit. Ap.* 7.34). The process of being publicly conducted in chains was intended to degrade prisoners (Dio Cassius *Hist.* 58.11.1.F; Suetonius *Vitellius* 7.17.1; cf. Josephus *J.W.* 2.12.7 §246), and it inspired a general and sometimes lifelong revulsion of the prisoner (Philostratus *Vit. Ap.* 7.34-37; Dio Chrysostom *De Ser.* 1.22 [§14]). Terms for prison and its accoutrements were applied derisively, including "jail guard" (*custos carceris*), "fetter farmer" (*catenarum colonus*), "ex-convict and jail bird" (*ex compedibus atque ergastulo*) and "jail bird" (*desmotes*). Even friends and close associates experienced great pressure to abandon the prisoner (Seneca *Ep. Lucil.* 9.9; Philostratus *Vit. Ap.* 4.37; Lucian of Samosata *Tox.* 18, 28-29; Antiphon *De Caed. Her.* 18; *Mart. Perp. et Felic.* 5.2). It might be added that the same connotations attended those who had been publicly stripped and flogged (Justinian *Dig.* 48.19.28; 50.2.12).

4.2. Christian Responses. The shame associations from imprisonment and bonds also threatened Christian prisoners in the NT (Acts 16:37; 26:29; 1 Thess 2:2; Phil 1:29-30; Heb 10:33-34; 2 Tim 1:8-12; 2:9). Brothers and sisters were taught that service to the Christian prisoner was service to Christ (Mt 25:31-46). While numbers were celebrated for courageously doing just that (Acts; Phil 1:14; 2:19-30; Col 4:7-15; 2 Tim 2:9; 4:11; Philem 23-24; Heb 10:33-34; 13:3; cf. Rapske 1991), others abandoned their incarcerated fellows (Phil 1:15, 17; 2:21; 2 Tim 4:9-10, 16).

The damage of going into custody, the rigors and restrictions of being in custody and the shame and dishonor of being a prisoner resulted in significant theological reflection, particularly for Luke and Paul. Acts shows that not only is Paul unflaggingly for the Lord, but also the Lord is decidedly for his imprisoned apostle. Paul is moved to account for his imprisonments and bonds to individuals and to churches, demonstrating that his status, credibility and effectiveness as missionary accommodates to and shows the divine purpose of these trials. This is demonstrable in Paul's terminology of self-designation (Eph 3:1; 4:1; 6:20; Philem 1, 9), his reflections on suffering and mission (Phil 1:12-13, 16, 29; Col 1:24; Philem 13; cf. Eph 4:7-13) and the terminology with which he affirms those who courageously continue to support and help him in his bonds (Col 4:10; Philem 23; cf. Rom 16:7).

See also ROMAN LAW AND LEGAL SYSTEM.

BIBLIOGRAPHY. S. Arbandt, W. Macheiner and C. Colpe, "Gefangenschaft," *RAC* 9 (1976) 318-45; G. Bertram, "φυλάσσω, φυλακή," *TDNT* 9:236-44; W. von Eisenhut, "Die römische Gefängnisstrafe," *ANRW* 1.2 (1972) 268-82; P. Garnsey, *Social Status and Legal Privilege in the Roman Empire* (Oxford: Clarendon Press, 1970); B. H. D. Hermesdorf, "Paulus Vinctus," *StudCath* 29 (1954) 120-33; F. H. Hitzig, "Carcer 1)," *PW* 3:1576-81; idem, "Custodia," *PW* 4:1896-99; Chr. Hülsen, "Carcer 2)," *PW* 3:1581-82; J. G. Keenan, "12. Petition from a Prisoner: New Evidence on Ptolemy Philometor's Accession," in *Collectanea Papyrologica: Texts Published in Honor of H. C. Youtie, Part One, Numbers 1-65,* ed. A. E. Hanson (Bonn: Rudolph Habelt, 1976) 91-102; J. M. Kelly, *Roman Litigation* (Oxford: Clarendon Press, 1966); G. Kittel, "αἰχμάλωτος κτλ," *TDNT* 1:195-97; idem, "δεσμός, δέσμιος," *TDNT* 2:43; F. A. K. Krauss, *Die Gefangenen und die Verbrecher unter dem Einfluss des Christenthums. Geschichtlicher Ueberblick, umfassend die ersten siebzehn Jahrhunderte* (Heidelberg: G. Weiss, 1889); idem, *Im Kerker vor und nach Christus. Schatten und Licht aus den profanen und kirchlichen Culture und Rechtsleben vergang. Zeiten.* (Tübingen: Mohr Siebeck, 1895); G.-H. Link et al., "Slave, Servant, Captive, Prisoner, Freedman," *NIDNTT* 3:589-599; G. Lopuszanski, "La Police Romaine et les Chrétiens," *L'Antiquité Classique* 20 (1951) 5- 46; R. MacMullen, *Enemies of the Roman Order: Treason, Unrest and Alienation in the Empire* (Cambridge, MA: Harvard University Press, 1967); Th. Mayer-Maly, "Carcer," in *Der Kleine Pauly,* ed. K. Ziegler and W. Sontheimer (Stuttgart: Druckenmüller, 1964) 1:1053; B. Rapske, *The Book of Acts and Paul in Roman Custody,* (BAFCS 3; Grand Rapids, MI: Eerdmans, 1994); idem, "The Importance of Helpers to the Imprisoned Paul in the Book of Acts," *TynB* 42 (1991) 3-30; A. N. Sherwin-White, *Roman Society and Roman Law in the New Testament* (Oxford: Clarendon Press, 1963); R. Taubenschlag, "63. L'Emprisonnement dans le Droit Gréco-Égyptien," in *Opera Minora: II Band Spezieller Teil* (Warsaw: Pánstwowe Wydawnictwo Naukowe, 1959) 713-19; idem, "64. Le procès de l'Apôtre Paul en lumière des papyri," in *Opera Minora: II Band Spezieller Teil* (Warsaw: Pánstwowe Wydawnictwo Naukowe, 1959) 721-26; R. Whiston and W. Wayte, "Carcer," *DGRA* 1:362-63; E. A. Whittuck, "Custodia," *DGRA* 1:589.

B. M. Rapske

PROCONSUL. *See* ROMAN ADMINISTRATION; ROMAN GOVERNORS OF PALESTINE.

PROCURATOR. *See* ROMAN ADMINISTRATION; ROMAN GOVERNORS OF PALESTINE.

PROMISED LAND. *See* ISRAEL, LAND OF.

PROPHETS AND PROPHECY

Prophecy is the proclamation of divine revelation. At the time of nascent Christianity, it was an established and a ubiquitous phenomenon; in the *Hellenic world, oracular sites had been operative for centuries and continued to provide guidance to enquirers, while in Rome the Sibylline Oracles had long furnished the senate with direction (*see* Mysteries). Within the milieu of Second Temple Judaism, the writings of *Josephus, *Philo and the *Dead Sea community reveal that prophecy had not died out but continued as a viable, if diverse, phenomenon. This very diversity both in the pagan and Jewish records helps in part to account for the variegated conceptions of prophecy present within the NT.

1. Terminology
2. The Nature of Pagan Oracles
3. False Prophecy in the Greco-Roman World
4. Sibylline Prophecy
5. Intertestamental Prophecy
6. Prophecy in the Dead Sea Scrolls
7. Prophecy in the Writings of Josephus
8. Prophecy in the Writings of Philo
9. Prophecy and the New Testament

1. Terminology.

In the Hellenistic pagan world, prophecy was but one of a large number of divinatory practices (*mantikē*) employed to elicit messages and guidance from the gods. The word *prophecy* (*prophēteia*) is derived from Greek *pro* and *phēmi*, with *pro* signifying "on behalf of" and the root *phēm-* meaning "speak." A prophet is, therefore, "one who speaks on behalf of" someone. It is not until the NT itself that the prophet becomes largely associated with foretelling (Acts 11:27-28; 21:10-12; though cf. Plato *Charm.* 173C). Rather, *prophētēs* ("prophet") signifies a spokesperson or interpreter, and hence the spokesperson of a god. Typically, such a spokesperson was associated with oracular shrines, either as a mouthpiece or a functionary. Somewhat confusingly, in the classical milieu the word *prophet* only occasionally refers to the inspired speaker. The inspired priestess of Apollo at Delphi, the Pythia, for instance, is sometimes designated as a prophet (*prophētis,* Plato *Phaed.* 244A; Euripides *Ion* 42.321), but the term is more frequently used of temple functionaries who may have had little or nothing to do with the Pythia's inspired utterance. Itinerant seers are commonly characterized not as prophets but as *mantikoi,* and oracle mongers as *chrēsmologoi.* The following discussion, therefore, will not restrict itself to the word *prophētēs* and its cognates but will assume a broader purview.

2. The Nature of Pagan Oracles.

*2.1. **Oracles.*** An "oracle" can refer either to the shrine where the gods were consulted for advice or prophecy or to the response furnished by a deity. Prophecy at oracular shrines was widespread in the ancient world both temporally and geographically. Oracular sites are attested as early as Homer (c. 750 B.C.; Homer *Il.* 16.233-5; *Odys.* 14.327-28 = 19.296-97) and continued until they were proscribed in the fourth century A.D. While there was a certain falling off in popularity with some of the shrines, especially Delphi about the turn of the common era, due, among other factors, to the increasing influence of astrology (cf. Juvenal *Sat.* 6.553-56), this decline has been unduly emphasized (e.g., by Boring, 50). The second century marked a notable resurgence of interest in the established oracles, particularly in *Asia Minor (Lane Fox, 168-261).

Geographically, oracular sites were widely distributed throughout the Mediterranean world. While oracles to Apollo (Delphi, Claros, Didyma, Corope, Argos) were most common, there were also famous sanctuaries dedicated to Zeus (Dodona, Olympia; and Siwa to Zeus-Ammon) and to heroes such as Amphiaraos and Trophonius. Intriguingly, as Y. Hajjar has demonstrated, oracular sites in Syria and Phoenicia were also abundant, even if our archaeological record is limited.

*2.2. **Oracular Procedure.*** The methods of oracular consultation were remarkably varied. At the oracle of Trophonius, for instance, the consultant would himself descend into a chasm to encounter the hero (cf. Pausanias *Descr.* 9.39.4, for a firsthand account). At Boura, by contrast, there was a dice oracle that used knucklebones and an interpretive tablet (Pausanias *Descr.* 7.25.10). While the consultation process at the most famous of ancient oracles, Delphi, is the best known, even its specifics are still far from certain (for reconstructions based on syntheses of the available evidence, see Parke and Wormell).

2.2.1. Oracular Questions. The questions brought to oracles were both public and private in nature. Some oracles, such as Dodona, were largely consulted about private matters, with most of the extant oracular queries formulated in the form of yes-or-no questions: "is it better, and more appropriate to?" Delphi was distinctive because of its large proportion of public enquiries about how cities were to cope when confronted with natural catastrophes, divine prodigies or war; and how they were to sanction legislation, found colonies or please the gods. Naturally, Delphi also had its share of private queries typically, according to *Plutarch, whether "one ought to marry, or to start on a voyage, or to make a loan" (Plutarch *Mor.* 408C).

2.2.2. Oracular Replies. Heraclitus (frag. 93) claims that at Delphi, Apollo "neither conceals nor reveals, but signifies." His elliptical remark suggests that the oracle straddled the line between clarity and obscurity. While it has been argued (e.g., by Fontenrose, who discounts the historian Herodotus's testimony) that the replies given at Delphi were not ambiguous, it is more likely that some were (Plutarch *Mor.* 406E; 407A-B). The longer replies in particular, delivered in dactylic hexameter, were decidedly cryptic and allusive (cf. Herodotus *Hist.* 1.61), though it must be borne in mind that our evidence is heavily reliant upon literary sources. The shorter replies, perhaps because they were obtained by lot-oracle, tended to be more straightforward.

2.3. Manic or Mantic? The nature and character of the Pythia's inspiration continue to be debated. Some scholars still adhere to nineteenth-century conceptions that have the Pythia, rapt in an ecstatic trance, blurt out frenzied and inarticulate utterances, which are then rendered into hexameter verse by attendant prophets. This reconstruction is not without ancient attestation (Lucan *Civ. W.* 5.165-224; Strabo *Geog.* 9.3.5). Plutarch tells us, for instance, that an uneducated girl was chosen to be the Pythia (Plutarch *Mor.* 405C) and alludes to various poets in the vicinity of the oracle who would versify (Plutarch *Mor.* 407B), while *Plato further claims that the Pythia did not know what she was saying (Plato *Phaed.* 244B-C).

All of this could indicate that the Pythia was merely the unwitting mouthpiece for the vatic and unintelligible utterances of Apollo. Such a reconstruction, however, is undeniably problematic. L. Maurizio has rightly argued that not one ancient source describes anyone but the Pythia issuing oracular responses at Delphi. That these responses originated with her is also substantiated by accounts of the Pythia being suborned (Herodotus *Hist.* 6.66, 75), since there would be little point in bribing her if her pronouncements were unintelligible. Whether she would be capable of producing verse in dactylic hexameter is debated, but is not without precedents (cf. Dodds, 92-93 #70; and Tacitus *Ann.* 2.54 of the "illiterate" priest of Apollo at Claros ignorant of meter), especially given Plutarch's remarks on the poor quality of the verse (Plutarch *Mor.* 396D).

Further, Plato's account of inspiration (Plato *Phaed.* 244; *Tim.* 71-72) has been unduly influential among modern interpreters, but it is idiosyncratic and obviously calculated to promote his own distinction between *philosophers who possess understanding and those who are inspired (poets, prophets) but who do not fully comprehend what they utter. Recent examinations of the phenomenon of inspiration suggest that, Plato apart, poets were regarded as having conscious control over their productions, while at the same time acknowledging their dependence on the divine. The Pythia, then, is best regarded as figuring among their number (cf. Forbes, though his attempt to dissociate prophecy from ecstasy is misguided).

3. False Prophecy in the Greco-Roman World. While the political motivations and accuracy of the Delphic oracle have sometimes appeared suspect to moderns, in the oracle's heyday these factors appear to have been little questioned. As in the mythological record, Delphi's authority was considered unimpeachable, and much the same could be said for almost all of the ancient oracles. Celsus enthusiastically vouches for them all when he asks, "How many cities have been built by oracles, and have gotten rid of disease and famines, and how many that have neglected or forgotten them have suffered terrible destruction? How many have been sent to form a colony and have prospered by attending to their commands? How many that have been distressed at being childless have come to possess that for which they prayed and escaped the wrath of demons?" (Celsus apud Origen *Cont. Cels.* 8.45, trans. Chadwick).

Despite Celsus's glowing testimonial, false prophets and dubious oracles were widely recognized in the ancient world. *Chrēsmologoi* were thought to add oracles of their own (Herodotus *Hist.* 7.6) or to interpret written oracles in self-serving fashion (Aristophanes *Av.* 959-91; *Pax* 1095; *Eq.* 997-1099). If *Lucian of Samosata is to be believed, there were even bogus oracular sites. His *Alexander* recounts in detail how Alexander of Abonoteichos established his own oracle to the snake(-oil) deity Glykon, the "new Asklepios," and gulled the public with sham oracles. The entire work provides us with an admirable manifesto of sharp practice.

4. Sibylline Prophecy.

In addition to the prophets at oracular shrines, the postclassical period saw the widespread emergence and circulation of written oracles and Sibylline prophecies. "Sibyl" may have originally been a proper name, but by the early fourth century B.C. it had become a generic term for an inspired prophetess. Varro, for instance, is able to list ten sibyls (frag. 56 apud Lactantius *Div. Inst.* 1.6.8-12). If largely mythical, the sibyls were nonetheless extraordinarily influential through the prophetic writings that circulated in their names.

The written oracles of the Cumaean Sibyl became duly famous because of their influence in *Rome. Reputedly sold by the Cumaean Sibyl to Tarquinus Superbus (Pliny *Nat. Hist.* 13.88), they were entrusted to the priestly college of the *Quindecimviri sacris faciundis.* When divine prodigies were brought to the attention of the senate, the college would, on the latter's instruction, consult the Sibylline oracles to establish what the state needed to do. Though the collection perished in 83 B.C., it was reassembled and continued to be consulted until at least A.D. 363 (Ammianus Marcellinus 23.1.7). Augustus's destruction of more than two thousand prophetic books and his editing of the explicitly Sibylline writings in 13 B.C. (Suetonius *Augustus* 31) indicate the pervasiveness of such collections, Sibylline and otherwise, and implicitly their considerable influence. That Tiberius apparently had to embark on a similar proceeding a mere thirty years later (Dio Cassius *Hist.* 57.18.5) is no small indication of their popularity.

Where the Sibylline writings differed from oracular prophecy was in their spontaneous and unsolicited vaticinations. If oracular prophecy was the product of specific queries, the Sibylline and related oracles often independently predicted future natural catastrophes, wars and the rise and fall of kingdoms. Given some of the obvious affinities with traditional Hebrew prophecy and *apocalyptic writings, particularly the prognostic and *eschatological elements, the form was readily appropriated and recast by Jewish authors (c. second century B.C.) and later by Christians.

5. Intertestamental Prophecy.

It is now generally recognized (Sommer's protests notwithstanding) that the so-called cessation of prophecy between the Testaments has been greatly exaggerated. Although *b. Yoma* (9b) states that "after the later prophets, Haggai, Zechariah, and Malachi had died, the Holy Spirit departed from Israel," sources nearer the time of the Second Temple period suggest otherwise (*see* Holy Spirit). In addition to the examples adduced below, there is evidence in *Josephus for prophetic types of activity among the *Pharisees of Herod's day (Josephus *Ant.* 17.2.4 §43), the Zealots (Josephus *J.W.* 6.5.2 §286) and the Samaritans (Josephus *Ant.* 18.4.1 §§85-87). Prophecy continued, therefore, albeit in a variety of guises. As attempts to categorize the various types of prophet and prophecy have generally proved inadequate (see Webb, 312-16, his own attempt being overly arbitrary), the following examination is drawn from our primary sources for the period: the Dead Sea Scrolls, Josephus and Philo.

6. Prophecy in the Dead Sea Scrolls.

6.1. Charismatic Exegesis. For the Essenes, the Teacher of Righteousness was the inspired interpreter of prophetic secrets. The **Habakkuk Commentary* depicts him as the one to whom "God revealed all the mysteries of his servants the prophets" (1QpHab 7:1-5). He, by means of "charismatic exegesis," was able to make known to later generations what God "would do to the last generation, the congregation of traitors" (CD 1:12-13; *see* Damascus Document). So even if he is not explicitly styled a prophet, the Teacher's inspired insight into the writings of the OT prophets and into eschatological mysteries show him to be the possessor and expounder of God-given insights.

6.2. False Prophecy. Several fragments of the DSS are cognizant of false prophets. One fragment apparently contains a ceremonial procedure employed to help distinguish between true and false prophets (4Q375). Another fragment (4Q339) lists eight false prophets, including Balaam. The final name on the list is damaged but has plausibly been reconstructed as "John, son of Simon." If so, the reference is likely to John Hyrcanus, who was famed for his prophetic abilities (Josephus *Ant.* 13.10.7 §§299-300; *J.W.* 1.2.8 §§68-69, though ironically Josephus lauds Hyrcanus as a true prophet: "for the Deity was with him and enabled him to foresee and foretell the future").

6.3. Prognostication. In addition to the evidence provided by the DSS, Josephus maintains that some of the Essenes were gifted with prognostication. He attributes this gift to their "being versed from their early years in holy books, various forms of purification and apothegms of prophets" (Josephus *J.W.* 2.8.12 §159). He specifically cites two individuals, Judas (Josephus *J.W.* 1.3.5 §§78-80; *Ant.* 13.11.2 §§311-13) and Menahem (Josephus *Ant.* 15.10.5 §§373-79), and provides detailed accounts of their predictions.

7. Prophecy in the Writings of Josephus.

Generally speaking, Josephus, mindful of the LXX equation of the Hebrew *nābîʾ* ("prophet") with *prophētēs,* confines his use of the latter term to the prophets of the Hebrew Scriptures (though cf. the anomalous *prophētai* at Josephus *J.W.* 6.5.2 §286). In doing so, he appears to accord a special status to the OT prophets and to their writings. This should not, however, be taken to mean that Josephus regards prophecy as having ceased. Rather, in part because he is uncertain about prophetic continuity (Josephus *Ag. Ap.* 1.8 §41), he employs different terms (chiefly *mantis* and cognate forms) to account for the phenomenon. As R. Gray (167) aptly observes, for Josephus "the differences between ancient and modern prophetic figures were differences of degree, not of kind."

7.1. Josephus as Prophet. Remarkably, Josephus claimed to be able to foretell the future himself. Not only does he profess to have predicted the fall of Jotapata after a forty-seven-day siege, but also he alleges that he reneged on a suicide pact because of his conviction that he had been called by God to prophesy to Vespasian. His predictions that the Roman general and his son Titus would both accede to the imperial throne (Josephus *J.W.* 3.8.9 §§399-408) did transpire.

7.2. Sign Prophets. Josephus is our chief source for the so-called Sign Prophets (the designation is coined by Barnett), who were leaders of popular movements in the decades preceding the outbreak of the first revolt against Rome (*see* Revolutionary Movements, Jewish). Two of these figures, Theudas and the Egyptian, are also mentioned in Acts (Acts 5:36; 21:38; cf. Josephus *Ant.* 20.5.1 §§97-99; *J.W.* 2.13.4 §§258-60; *Ant.* 20.8.5 §§169-72). The Sign Prophets include Jonathan, active just after the war (Josephus *J.W.* 7.11.1-2 §§437-50; *Life* 76 §§424-25), as well as a variety of unnamed individuals who came to prominence under the procuratorships of Felix (Josephus *Ant.* 20.8.6 §§167-68; *J.W.* 2.13.4 §§258-60) and Festus (Josephus *Ant.* 20.8.10 §188).

As P. W. Barnett's designation implies, these figures were united both in their claims to be prophets and in their promises of signs or miracles to their followers. Typically they would lead the faithful to a set locale (the Jordan, the Mount of Olives, the wilderness) promising redemption and an imminent divine deliverance. Josephus dismisses them as "deceivers" *(planoi)* or "false prophets" *(pseudoprophētai),* using as his chief *discrimen* the failure of their prophecies to come true. As most of the Sign Prophets were put to death and their followers killed or dispersed, his judgment is hardly unexpected. By contrast, he takes the case of *Jesus ben Ananias more seriously. The latter, dismissed as mad by the procurator Albinus, ceaselessly proclaimed "woe to the city of Jerusalem." He was killed by a Roman missile during the siege of Jerusalem, his last words being "and woe to me also" (Josephus *J.W.* 6.5.3 §309). All of the foregoing indicates, therefore, that for Josephus prognostication is one of the distinguishing hallmarks of prophecy in the Second Temple period. The true prophet is divinely gifted with knowledge of the future.

8. Prophecy in the Writings of Philo.

Like the DSS and Josephus, Philo recognizes the unquestioned prophetic authority of Moses and the prophets. Philo's own approach to prophecy is distinctive in that he presupposes that prophetic experience is mediated through ecstasy and that it is open to every good (*asteios*) man (cf. Philo *Rer. Div. Her.* 259). In the course of the prophet's ecstatic experience, ecstasy, divine possession and madness overshadow him or her, and "the mind is evicted at the arrival of the divine spirit" (Philo *Rer. Div. Her.* 265). Philo's Greek terminology here echoes Plato and testifies to his indebtedness to a Platonic understanding of mantic inspiration. Further passages, however, may indicate that Philo also recognizes instances in which the mind is not entirely eclipsed. In his *Life of Moses* he outlines three different modes in which God communicates with Moses, including questions with oracular responses and the possession of Moses by God, where Moses apparently retains at least some of his faculties (Philo

Vit. Mos. 2.188-90; cf. Winston).

Philo also expatiates on the character of false prophets. Basing his remarks on Deuteronomy 13:1, he remarks that a false prophet appears to "be inspired and possessed by the Holy Spirit" but incites the people to worship false (Greek?) gods (Philo *Spec. Leg.* 1.315). All told, therefore, Philo's prophetic paradigm is an intriguing composite of Greek and Jewish perspectives.

9. Prophecy and the New Testament.

Taken as a whole, the above conceptions of prophecy are remarkably diverse. Even among the Jewish authors, who uniformly acknowledge the authority of the OT prophets, there is little agreement. That they also uniformly express divergent, even contradictory, perspectives on the nature, hallmarks and manifestations of true and false prophecy is revealing and helps to demonstrate something of the fluid conceptions of prophecy characteristic of the late Second Temple period. When the influence of pagan prophecy is further factored into the equation, it becomes evident just how wide-ranging a conceptual framework the NT authors had to draw upon. The diversity of our record, therefore, helps in some measure to account for the variegated conceptions of prophecy present within the NT and within emergent Christianity itself.

See also APOCALYPTIC LITERATURE; APOCALYPTICISM; HOLY MEN, JEWISH; HOLY SPIRIT; JESUS BEN ANANIAS; REVOLUTIONARY MOVEMENTS, JEWISH; SIBYLLINE ORACLES.

BIBLIOGRAPHY. D. E. Aune, *Prophecy in Early Christianity and the Ancient Mediterranean World* (Grand Rapids, MI: Eerdmans, 1983); P. W. Barnett, "The Jewish Sign Prophets—A.D. 40-70: Their Intentions and Origin," *NTS* 27 (1980-81) 679-97; H. Barstad, "Prophecy at Qumran?" in *In the Last Days,* ed. K. Jeppesen et al. (Aarhus: Aarhus University Press, 1994) 104-20; R. M. Berchman, "Arcana Mundi: Prophecy and Divination in the *Vita Mosis* of Philo of Alexandria," *AW* 26 (1995) 150-79. M. Eugene Boring, *The Continuing Voice of Jesus* (Louisville, KY: Westminster John Knox, 1991); J. J. Collins, *Seers, Sibyls and Sages in Hellenistic-Roman Judaism* (JSJS 54; Leiden: E. J. Brill, 1997); E. R. Dodds, *The Greeks and the Irrational* (Berkeley and Los Angeles: University of California Press, 1951); J. Fontenrose, *The Delphic Oracle* (Berkeley and Los Angeles: University of California Press, 1978); C. Forbes, *Prophecy and Inspired Speech in Early Christianity and Its Hellenistic Environment* (Peabody, MA: Hendrickson, 1997); G. Friedrich et al., "Προφήτης κτλ," *TDNT* 6:781-861; R. Gray, *Prophetic Figures in Late Second Temple Palestine: The Evidence from Josephus* (New York: Oxford University Press, 1993); Y. Hajjar, "Divinités oraculaires et rites divinatoires en Syrie et en Phénicie à l'époque Gréco-Romaine," *ANRW* 2.18.4 (1990) 2236-2320; R. Lane Fox, *Pagans and Christians* (London: Penguin, 1986); S. Levin, "The Old Greek Oracles in Decline," *ANRW* 2.18.2 (1989) 1599-1649; L. Maurizio, "Anthropology and Spirit Possession: A Reconsideration of the Pythia's Role at Delphi," *JHS* 115 (1995) 69-86; H. W. Parke, *Sibyls and Sibylline Prophecy in Classical Antiquity* (London: Routledge, 1988); H. W. Parke and D. E. W. Wormell, *The Delphic Oracle* (2 vols.; Oxford: Blackwell, 1956); D. Potter, *Prophets and Emperors: Human and Divine Authority from Augustus to Theodosius* (Cambridge, MA: Harvard University Press, 1994); B. Sommer, "Did Prophecy Cease? Evaluating a Reevaluation," *JBL* 115 (1996) 31-47; R. L. Webb, *John the Baptist and Prophet: A Socio-Historical Study* (JSNTS 62; Sheffield: JSOT, 1991); D. Winston, "Two Types of Mosaic Prophecy According to Philo," *JSP* 4 (1989) 49-67. J. R. C. Cousland

PROSELYTISM AND GODFEARERS

"Proselytizing" refers to active attempts on the part of Jews to recruit or evangelize Gentiles as new religious members of *Judaism. Recent discussion of the nature and extent of Jewish proselytzing has focused on whether or not Judaism is a missionary religion and, for historians of the development of the Christian faith, to what degree Christian practice is indebted to Jewish ideology and practice. "Godfearer" describes a Gentile with a certain level of adherence to Judaism, in particular to incomplete commitment to Judaism but with a corresponding commitment to the Jewish community. In effect Godfearers are Gentiles who stand between pagan Gentiles and faithful Jews.

1. History of Scholarship
2. Judaism and the Gentile
3. Judaism and Proselytes
4. Methods of Proselytizing
5. Requirements for Proselytes
6. Levels of Adherence

1. History of Scholarship.

While scholarship has addressed more than the

issue of whether or not Judaism was a missionary religion, the specific points of the discussion (e.g., requirements, numbers of proselytes, the meaning of the Lukan expression *Godfearers*) neatly arrange themselves around this issue.

1.1. The Older Scholarly Consensus. Older scholarship, especially that of Protestant Germany in the nineteenth and early twentieth centuries, univocally affirmed, assumed and sought to explain the rise of Christianity on the basis of the perception that Judaism was a missionary religion. Accompanying the assertion that Judaism evolved into a monotheistic religion with universalistic dimensions was the consistent contention that Judaism and individual Jews actively recruited Gentiles to Judaism. *Diaspora Judaism was given prominence of place in this evolution of Judaism to a universalistic faith that naturally evolved into the Christian mission to the world (see Bertholet; Jeremias; Hahn; Georgi).

While this strand of scholarship affirmed that Judaism was a missionary religion in impulse, it was also argued by some of these scholars that Judaism was inferior to Christianity because it either did not live out its natural impulse to evangelize the world or because, when Christianity emerged as more powerful than Judaism or when *Bar Kokhba's revolt failed, it then abandoned its universalistic impulse to become a nationalistic and introverted religion. Jewish scholars countered this Protestant propaganda by demonstrating both the openness to proselytes in Jewish formative texts, especially the *Talmudim and *Midrashim, as well as the fundamental kindness of individual Jews to Gentiles, both ancient and modern. The most important studies of Jewish scholars are those of B. J. Bamberger, W. G. Braude, J. S. Raisin, J. R. Rosenbloom and L. H. Feldman. A conclusion from a well-known Christian scholar of Judaism, G. F. Moore, perhaps crystallizes this view the best when he says that "the belief in the future universality of the true religion . . . led to efforts to convert the Gentiles to the worship of the one true God and to faith and obedience according to the revelation he had given, and made Judaism the first great missionary religion of the Mediterranean world" (Moore, 1:323-24).

An even more influential articulation of this view was penned by J. Jeremias, whose standing in Christian perceptions of Judaism was without peer for nearly a generation (though that standing has now been shifted as a result of the work of E. P. Sanders): "Jesus grew up in the midst of a people actively engaged, both by the spoken and written word, in a Gentile mission, whose impelling force was a profound sense of their obligation to glorify their God in the Gentile world." He can also maintain that "Jesus thus came upon the scene in the midst of what was *par excellence* the missionary age of Jewish history" (Jeremias, 17, 11).

Although Feldman's recent study does not make such exaggerated claims, his book establishes the conclusion that Judaism was a missionary religion and was actively involved in proselytizing Gentiles in a manner that helped shape the identity of Judaism (Feldman, 288-341). Feldman's case is based on two major items: demographics and the evidence found in literature. Recognizing the strength of the arguments against the view that Judaism was a missionary religion, Feldman offers a massive concession: "However, although there is, in truth, no single item of conclusive evidence, as we shall see, the cumulative evidence—both demographic and literary—for such activity is considerable" (Feldman, 293).

The literary evidence will be explained in a contrasting manner below, but a word ought to be said here about the demographic evidence. Feldman's argument is simple: since the population statistics of numerical growth cannot be explained on the basis of normal birth and survival patterns, there must have been some other factor that contributed to the blossoming of Jews around the Mediterranean. That other factor, he contends, must have been conversion as the result of Jewish missionary activity. The weaknesses of this argument are that it assumes (1) accurate estimations of Jewish populations from two different periods of history (so a comparison could be made) throughout the Mediterranean basin (all Jews need to be numbered) so that the second larger number would require special explanation; (2) an accurate knowledge of survival rates; and (3) accurate perceptions of immigrations and emigrations, not to mention knowledge of survival after famines, earthquakes, plagues and other disasters. None of these items can be known with the kind of precision needed in order to have sufficient disparity that could be explained by Jewish missionary successes. For example, our knowledge of Jewish population lacks precision at every point; all that we have is rough estimations that cannot be taken seriously enough for the kind of comparison required (Rosenbloom). Thus an argument for Jewish missionary activity on the basis of demographics lacks credibility (McKnight forthcoming).

1.2. The Recent Scholarly Consensus. Though the assertion that Judaism was a missionary religion has garnered significant support in the last two centuries of scholarship, that conclusion has recently been challenged to such a degree that it may be said to have been overturned and the consensus today is that Judaism was not a missionary religion. Even if some German Protestant scholars polemically contended that Judaism failed to live up to its inherent universalistic impulse, recent studies that contend that Judaism was not a missionary religion argue so on the basis of a variety of ancient evidence and not in order to support an ideology.

One of the earliest voices to be heard in this regard was that of A. T. Kraabel, who after exploring the archaeological data at the site of Sardis, concluded that much of what scholars, particularly Christian, were saying about Jewish missionary activity could not be justified on the basis of evidence, either literary or archaeological (Kraabel 1982, 1983). His insights were then confirmed by three monograph studies of Jewish missionary activity, each of which contended that Judaism was not a missionary religion (McKnight 1991; Goodman; Porton). S. McKnight (1991) offers a comprehensive survey of the evidence that has been used to describe Jewish missionary activity, arranging his separate studies around the following topics: Judaism and the Gentile, Judaism and proselytes, methods, requirements, levels of adherence and the evidence for Jewish missionary activity in the NT. One result of this study is a more careful approach to terms, including "missionary religion" (a self-conscious religion that defines itself in part in terms of missionary practice) and "conversion" (involves cognitive agreement, socialization into a new group and personal-biographical reconstruction). The result of McKnight's study is the contention that Judaism, though it evinced acceptance of Gentiles and proselytes who came to Judaism, (1) was never a missionary religion, (2) occasionally had persons who were involved in what we might call missionary activity and (3) did not set the stage in any substantial manner for early Christian missionary practice (McKnight 1991).

M. Goodman's study, though it approaches the data from a different angle, comes to the same conclusion: Judaism was not a missionary religion; in addition, he argues that Christianity itself was not always everywhere a missionary religion. The fresh perspective of Goodman is that he approaches the issue from the angle of the ancient Greco-Roman world and seeks to understand not just Jewish practice but also how ancient religious and philosophical groups sought to recruit adherents (if they did). In addition, Goodman introduces nuance into each discussion, especially seeing the historical and social factors at work in Judaism, whether in his approach to the development of missionary work along the lines of Christianity in connection with Nerva or in his insight into the various concerns of missions (information, education, apologetics) or in his conclusion that the imposition of social order should not be confused with religious conversion.

A final study is that of G. Porton, who presents a nuanced socio-rhetorical analysis of the convert within *rabbinic texts, a convert whose legal ambiguity prompts the title of his book as *The Stranger Within Your Gates*. Diversity is a leitmotif for Porton. Thus, "indeed, even within each of these documents, various strands of Jewish thought and life, representing disparate locations, periods of time, populations, cultural views, and intellectual environments, have been joined together. . . . Therefore, it is most correct to speak of the rabbinic *views* on conversion" (193). This diversity is enhanced by his contention that Judaism, as a national religion with national and ethnic identity, could not by nature be a missionary religion. Porton's book replaces the older studies of Bamberger, Raisin and Braude because the texts are analyzed with a more critical approach that considers not just ostensive reference but also rhetorical and sociological strategy. These three studies converge in one important way: Judaism was not a missionary religion.

2. Judaism and the Gentile.

Before the historian can describe the relationship of Jews to proselytes, the relationship of Jews and Gentiles in general needs to be analyzed. This relationship can be characterized as both an integrating tendency as well as a resisting tendency, and this observation needs to take into account the important perception that Judaism was diverse (cf. McKnight 1991, 11-29). What for one group was something to be resisted was for another group something to be welcomed; on top of this we need to note that individual groups changed over time so that a constant vacillation characterizes Judaism. Consequently it is historically inaccurate to contend that any one view characterizes Judaism in its relationship to the Gentiles. Instead we are more accurate if we describe Judaism (some would say Judaisms) as a diversity with various approaches to how Jews related to the Gentile world. In light of these observations, these two features of how they related take on special nuance, but in so describing various dimensions of the integrating and resisting tendencies, specific groups are not in view (i.e., *Philo integrates whereas the *Pharisees resist).

2.1. Integrating Tendencies. For nearly two centuries scholars have compared the Hellenistic movement with Jewish culture and religion. Most notable in this regard is the work of M. Hengel, who proved that Judaism, even in Palestine, was heavily influenced by the pervasive influence of *Hellenism. At least six features of this interaction can be observed.

2.1.1. A Growing Universalism. Within Judaism scholars have observed a growing universalism on the part of its various branches. That is, while the *Hebrew Bible has always included the notion that Yahweh is God of the world and that he rules over all the nations (Gen 12:1-3; Is 42; 56), Judaism developed a more precise perception of God and his relation to the world in which not only is God's truth revealed to the nation of *Israel but also that God's truth in all its dimensions was perceived, even if to a lesser degree, by some Gentiles as well. Ben Sira may speak of God's compassion being showered upon everyone (Sir 13:15), but Philo can say that all "created things . . . are brothers, since they have all one Father, the Maker of the universe" (Philo *Decal.* 64; cf. *Spec. Leg.* 1.169; *Praem. Poen.* 9; *Prov.* 2.6); even further: "they can claim to be children of the one common mother of mankind, nature" (Philo *Decal.* 41).

2.1.2. Friendliness. These statements are to be differentiated from friendliness, or even love, being shown to other nations, since in the latter category Israel is sharply distinguished from the nations (e.g., Josephus *Ag. Ap.* 2 §146). Philo reveals the same kind of distinction when he speaks of general benevolence (Philo *Flacc.* 94; *Virt.* 109-15, 147). From the archaeological evidence discovered at Sardis one can see a similar kind of friendliness, a socioreligious distinction of groups that nonetheless broke down as Jews and Gentiles interacted freely, even to the point of pushing against religious boundaries. At Sardis the Jewish *synagogue was connected to a Gentile *gymnasium, revealing a breathtaking integration of two cultures and a friendly cooperation. The evidence from Sardis also suggests that Jews had the same jobs that Gentiles had and that Jews were members of the city council, holding positions of considerable influence (Kraabel 1983; Trebilco).

2.1.3. Participation. This illustration of integration from the Sardis evidence leads to an observation that Jews regularly permitted Gentiles to participate in the Jewish religion. Even if the balustrade surrounding the inner court of the *temple warned Gentiles not to penetrate any further into the temple, such a prohibition did not prevent Jews from permitting Gentiles, especially the powerful, from offering sacrifices (Josephus *J.W.* 2.17.3 §§412-16; 5.13.6 §563; *Ant.* 13.5.4 §§145-47; 13.5.8 §168; 13.8.2 §242). *Josephus can claim that the Jerusalem temple "flung wide its gates to every foreigner for worship" (Josephus *J.W.* 4.4.4 §275). If the evidence from Sardis suggests an intermingling of Jews with Gentiles in the context of their synagogue, other evidence suggests that Gentiles found famous Jewish religious institutions as something in which they could join (e.g., *sabbath; *CPJ* 3.43-87).

2.1.4. Integration. Integration into foreign culture finds a primary crystallization when Jews became *citizens and found official recognition. If Philo can describe legal protection in *Alexandria as "the sole mooring on which our life was secured" (Philo *Flacc.* 74), Josephus can confirm the same desire for legal protection in the familiar pursuit at the hands of other governments (Josephus *Ant.* 8.2.6-7 §§50-54; 12.4.2-10 §§160-224; 12.10.6 §§414-19). We should probably infer from this desire for citizenship or recognition the need for Jews to find protection, but we would not be far off in also inferring that the Gentile governments at whose hands the Jews wanted protection also benefitted from having Jews as citizens, as opposed to malcontents. The benefits worked both ways.

2.1.5. Education. If our knowledge of Judaism

came exclusively from the rabbinic documents, especially the Mishnah and Tosefta, we might think that Jews abhorred Gentile *education, but the surviving evidence from Philo and Josephus especially reveals that many Jews, particularly those from landed families, were educated in the Greco-Roman manner (Bonner). Thus, in addition to the Torah, Jewish children in Alexandria were educated in the encyclical (Philo *Vit. Mos.* 1.23-24; *Spec. Leg.* 2.228-30; *Leg. All.* 3.244; *Migr. Abr.* 72; *Rer. Div. Her.* 274; *Omn. Prob. Lib.* 143). *Herod, Archelaus and Philip each had a Roman education (Josephus *Ant.* 15.10.5 §373; *J.W.* 1.31.1 §602). Though this approach is not always approved (Josephus *Ant.* 18.5.4 §141), the foundation is laid here for the kind of education that every aspiring politician would need. Such an education is legitimated by Josephus when he says that Joseph, the patriarch, was given a "liberal education" in Alexandria (Josephus *Ant.* 2.4.1 §39); *Moses received the same (Josephus *Ant.* 2.9.3 §216).

2.1.6. Intermarriage. *Marriages took place for different reasons in the ancient world: in addition to marrying for love, one married also for political, religious and social alliances. Thus intermarriage becomes one further illustration of Jewish integration into the Gentile world. Even if the tradition connected to Ezra and Nehemiah shapes one perception of how Jews should relate to the ancient Gentile world, not all followed that path of curbing social contact. Jews regularly and consistently intermarried with women of other nations and religions. Josephus mentions at least the following: Joseph (*Ant.* 2.6.1 §§91-92), Antipater (*J.W.* 1.8.9 §181) and Herod (*Ant.* 17.1.3 §20). Esther's marriage, according to Josephus, however, was not a source for pride (*Ant.* 11.6.2 §§198-204).

Integration, however, can become a problem for Judaism. At times integration slides rather easily into assimilation and adaptation of the Jewish faith in ways unacceptable to many or even outright apostasy. To be sure, this process might be defined differently by various Jewish persons, but lines were nonetheless drawn, even if not by some authorized orthodoxy. Philo finds a "backsliding" (*paranomia*), or apostasy, when some were "spurning their ancestral customs and seeking admission to the rites of a fabulous religion" (Philo *Spec. Leg.* 1.56-57). Antiochus of *Antioch converted to Hellenism, detested Jewish customs and sacrificed in the manner of the Greeks, according to Josephus (*J.W.* 7.3.3 §§50-53). In times of *persecution, apostasy becomes a socially acute issue, and on at least one occasion the bare decision to eat pork was a surrender of the Jewish nation and faith (Philo *Flacc.* 96).

2.2. Resisting Tendencies. Resistance to the various forms of Hellenism no doubt provoked the charge that Jews were misanthropists, but the charges, however observant of special features of Jewish identity, are not founded in fact. Rather, Jewish resistance is not so much a reflection of Jewish attitudes toward Gentiles as it is one of their own identity as the people of God, of their role in the world and of their commitment to the Torah for divine protection (e.g., Deut). At least five features are notable.

2.2.1. Separation. For different reasons, usually pertaining to purity, Jews separated themselves from Gentiles in various ways. In fact, the *Epistle of Aristeas* claims that the Torah was given to Israel "that we might not mingle at all with any of the other nations" (139, *APOT;* cf. 151). At times this separation emerges into nationalism (cf. *2 Bar.* 62:7), which can be seen full force in the documents discovered at *Qumran and its environs (esp. 1QM; cf. also CD 6:14, 15; 7:13; 1QS 1:4; 5:1-2; 1QH 14:21-22; 11QTemple 48:7-13; 60:16-21; *see* Rule of the Community; Temple Scroll; Thanksgiving Hymns). In the **War Scroll* the Gentiles seem to be assigned by God to his wrath (cf. 1QM 2:7; 4:12; 6:6; 9:9). The list of derogatory comments about other nations is nearly endless in Jewish literature; one example is Philo's attitude toward Egyptians, the people with whom he had to live (Philo *Flacc.* 17, 29, 96; *Spec. Leg.* 162, 166; *Sacr.* 51; *Poster. C.* 96, 113; *Spec. Leg.* 3.110; *Virt.* 131-133).

2.2.2. Restricted Access to the Temple. However much the Jews permitted the Gentiles to participate in their religious customs and no matter how much they integrated themselves into the various cultures surrounding them, they remained adamant that Gentiles could not enter into the holiest parts of the *temple. This evinces a clear consciousness of separation and of being the elect of God (cf. Josephus *J.W.* 1.7.6 §152; 1.18.3 §354; *Ant.* 3.15.3 §§318-22). Memorialized on a wall at regular intervals around the holy place, there was a sign in the temple prohibiting Gentile entrance, and "death without appeal" was the consequence for transgression (Bickerman).

2.2.3. Idolatry. Especially repudiated among

Jewish authors is the worship of other gods and the practice of other *religions. The polemic against idolatry appears in every dimension of Jewish literature (e.g., Wis Sol 14:12-31; *Jos. and As.* 8:5-7) and is surely the most common form of Jewish resistance.

2.2.4. Prohibitions of Intermarriage. Because of consistent Jewish integration into the Gentile world and the consequent occurrence of intermarriage, we regularly find warnings and prohibitions of intermarriage; the decision not to marry a Gentile woman was a significant public act on the part of a male Jew. Though not a clear teaching of the Pentateuch (cf. Ex 34:11-17; Deut 7:3-4; 23:2-9), the absolute prohibition of intermarriage in the reform of Ezra and Nehemiah became a rallying cry for national purity (Ezra 9—10). For instance, in *Tobit we find a consistent prohibition of intermarriage (Tob 1:9; 3:10; 4:12; 5:11, 13; 6:12; 7:13). Philo, writing where intermarriage was both practiced as well as a source for constant alarm, legitimates such a prohibition by appealing to its eventual deleterious affect on the sons and daughters (Philo *Spec. Leg.* 3.29).

2.2.5. Uprisings and Wars. The bluntest form of resistance is military uprisings and national wars. At no place is this given greater prominence than in the *Maccabean literature and war stories (1-2 Macc). The marvelous legend of the Jewish boys who die, one by one, in the presence of their mother for honoring their faith undoubtedly stirred the hearts of many Jews (cf. 4 Macc 8:8; 14:11—17:6). And Pilate learned from his own Jewish contemporaries the willingness of Jews to fight if faithfulness to their traditions was under threat (Josephus *J.W.* 2.9.2 §§169-74). Undoubtedly this is how many Jews saw the fight with Rome in A.D. 66-73: Jewish resistance against Roman imposition of order (*see* Jewish Wars with Rome).

In summary, we are on sure ground when we stand on the following convictions: Jews were convinced that they were the people of God; and because they were the people of God they were different from the rest of the world, especially but not only in their religious customs. However, those two convictions did not lead Jews as a rule to cut off all relations to Gentiles, nor did it lead them to hate Gentiles. Rather, though Jews as a rule accepted Gentiles and lived with and dealt with them in business, they knew that deep in their own identity was a conviction that God had chosen them as a light among the Gentiles.

3. Judaism and Proselytes.

In a context of integration, yet not without a corresponding resistance, Jews found "proselytes" in their midst (McKnight 1991, 30-48; Feldman, 177-382). Did they favor this development, or did they discourage it?

3.1. Names of Proselytes. Names of proselytes appear in nearly every major facet of Jewish evidence (e.g., Jdt 14:10, Achior the Ammonite; Philo *Abr.* 251, Hagar; Josephus *Ant.* 20.2.1-5 §§17-53, the royal family of Adiabene; *CIJ* 523, Veturia Paulla; *b. Giṭ* 56a, Nero). But what can be made of names? Some have argued that the presence of names everywhere reveals consistent missionary activity, but surely this outstrips the evidence. It may be the case that names are given because of their exceptional status. The evidence of names is like the evidence of demographics: too much can be made of too little. A more secure foundation must be found to construct a view that Judaism was a missionary religion or that Jews on the whole were regularly proselytzing their Gentile neighbors.

3.2. Favorable Attitudes. Much evidence can be brought to the table on this topic, but a selection will provide the essential contours. Tobit, when visiting *Jerusalem, gave his second tithe in money to needy people (Tob 1:7), among whom were "proselytes who attached themselves to the sons of Israel" (Tob 1:8). And Tobit 13:11 reads: "A bright light will shine over all the regions of the earth; many nations will come from far away, from all the ends of the earth, to dwell close to the holy name of the Lord God, with gifts in their hands for the King of heaven." While this surely reveals a positive attitude toward proselytism, it divulges nothing about how people became proselytes and even less about the nature of a Judaism that identified itself as a missionary religion.

In the *Testament of Levi* we find a text that asks what will happen to the world if Jews become pervasively disobedient. The author responds by relating the Jewish mission to the world. *Testament of Levi* 14:4 reads: "For what will all the nations do if you become darkened with impiety? You will bring down a curse on our nation, because you want to destroy the light of the Law which was granted to you for the enlightenment of every man." Here conversion is something that will take place in the future (as in *T. Jud.* 24:6; 25:5; *T. Dan* 5:11; 6:7; *T. Asher* 7:3; *T. Zeb.* 9:8), but there is no evidence of Jewish missionaries, of Jewish missionary practice and of only one convert (*T. Naph.* 1:10). Rather, what this text expresses is the typical Jewish view that Gentile conversions will take place on the Day of the Lord; when God comes to Zion, Gentiles will swarm to the temple to praise Yahweh and bring gifts to his people.

Philo, who had abundant opportunity to engage in Jewish proselytizing activities, speaks only occasionally of proselytes. He has a fairly relaxed attitude toward Gentile participation in Judaism and sees the Jewish nation as having a purpose of revealing what is good (Philo *Vit. Mos.* 1.149; 2.36). Philo perceives a philosophical-religious element to conversion to Judaism when one becomes enlightened (Philo *Spec. Leg.* 1.51-53; *Praem. Poen.* 61). In particular Philo sees a special revelation to the world in the translation of the Torah from Hebrew to Greek (Philo *Vit. Mos.* 2.44). However, he knows of restrictions even for proselytes: it takes three generations for a convert's family to become fully Jewish (Philo *Virt.* 108), though it is possible that Philo sees this restriction only for Egyptian converts.

With pride Josephus relates that "they [i.e., the Antiochenes] were constantly attracting to their religious ceremonies multitudes of Greeks, and they had in some measure incorporated with themselves" (Josephus *J.W.* 7.3.3 §45). What this text affirms is hard to discern: that Gentiles converted—probably; that Gentiles were attracted to Jewish customs and were not repelled—certainly; but that Judaism was therefore a missionary religion or that Jewish missionaries are at work here—clearly not. The evidence does not permit the latter surmises.

We may take the legendary story about Hillel and Shammai as a reflection of rabbinic attitudes toward proselytism and proselytes (cf. *b. Šabb.* 31a; *ʾAbot R. Nat.* 24ab, p. 91). A Gentile wants to be taught the whole Torah while he stands on one foot. Shammai repulses him; Hillel expresses the whole law in a negative form of the Golden Rule and accepts him. When another Gentile asks to wear priestly garments Shammai rejects him; Hillel teaches him the law and the heathen converts, learns the special prerogative of *priests and abandons his desire for power. While the texts surely represent the Hillelitic viewpoint, the two positions are common sense enough for us to say that within Judaism there were those who did not want proselytes and those who did. It is likely that Hillel was more open on this issue.

3.3. Unfavorable Attitudes. While the favorable attitude prevails in Judaism, there is evidence that at times Jews either despised proselytes or disapproved of them. We are justified in our suspicion that more often than not unfavorable attitudes toward proselytes probably are the result of bad experiences with either Gentiles or proselytes in particular. Accordingly, in the diverse setting of ancient Judaisms it is nearly unassailable that Jews favored proselytes and only rarely did they disapprove of them. However, acceptance of proselytes does not entail an easy transition or an unthinking incorporation of them into the Jewish community (e.g., Porton).

When Philo discusses the exodus from Egypt he describes the travelers as comprised of a diverse lot, and he looked down on "the children of Egyptian women by Hebrew fathers into whose families they had been adopted" and another group who had converted as a result of miracles from God or his supernatural judgments (Philo *Vit. Mos.* 1.147). This latter observation leads one to think of the much later rabbinical category of "lion proselytes" and reveals a much earlier reflection by Jews on the various motives, some of which are not approved, for conversion. What we find in Philo is not a rejection of proselytes but an unfavorable attitude toward certain motives for conversion.

Historically, the negative evidence found in the rabbis has played a major role in Christian reconstructions of post-Bar Kokhba Judaism with respect to its missionary practices. Thus, Shammai's repulsing of the would-be proselyte (*b. Šabb.* 31a), R. Eliezer b. Hyrcanus's exclusion of Amalekites (*Mek. Amalek,* par. 2, lines 177-86), R. Akiba's rejection of proselytes (*Mek. Shirata,* par. 3, lines 49-63) and R. Helbo's infamous comment that "Proselytes are as hard for Israel as a sore" (*b. Yebam.* 47a; *b. Qidd.* 70b) are used to suggest that the fundamental approach of rabbinic Judaism was unfavorable toward proselytes. It is much more likely, however, that these few statements need to be overwhelmed by the positive attitude found throughout rabbinic literature. That is, these statements are occasional exceptions, probably stemming from negative experiences with proselytes.

Just as the positive attitude toward Gentiles

was tempered by religious and ethical strictures, so also with proselytes: proselytes could come into the fold of Judaism, but certain moral and theological prescriptions were necessary for an acceptable conversion. There is no evidence that Jews repulsed would-be proselytes who wanted to convert for good reasons; those who wanted to convert for marriage, for political advantages or because they were scared of God's power were discouraged by some. But this gives no solid basis for considering Jews unfavorable toward proselytes. There is almost no evidence that Jews actively recruited new members or that they aggressively proselytized Gentiles in order that they might become members of Judaism. Rather, for Judaism conversion was resocialization, and that was nationalization. If Gentiles wanted to join the Jewish nation, to follow its laws, to worship in its temple, to marry its children ethnically and to fight for its causes, then let them in. But it ought to be noted that a leitmotif of proselyte evidence in Judaism is that Gentile conversion is a massive act that will take place on the Day of the Lord rather than an ongoing challenge to the nation (e.g., Tob 13:11; Sir 36:11-17; 4 Ezra 6:26). For the Jews of this time, they were a light among the nations, not a light to the nations.

4. Methods of Proselytizing.

That Judaism was not a missionary religion does not mean that no missionary activity took place. In fact, there are occasional acts of proselytization that not only reveal dimensions of Judaism but also may well have been the stock of information drawn on by early Christian missionaries. A survey of the evidence reveals at least eight methods of converting Gentiles to Judaism and the Jewish nation.

4.1. God's Intervention. Above all, Jews believed that when Gentiles did convert, especially on the Day of the Lord, it would be the result of God's intervention in the world. On the last day, Gentiles will stream to Zion (Tob 13:11; *1 Enoch* 48:4-5; 50:1-5; 62:9-13; 90:30-33; 91:14), even if at times the theme is more triumphalistic than evangelistic (cf. *Jub.* 26:23; 39:4; *T. Sim.* 7:2; *T. Levi* 2:11; 4:3-4; 18:1-9).

4.2. Evangelization. Did Jews evangelize Gentiles? Is there evidence for Jewish missionaries? If we believe the older literature (see 1 above), we would argue that there were missionaries who evangelized Gentiles. But the consensus today is twofold: not only is "evangelism" an anachronistic term for ancient Judaism, but also active proselytization was only a rare exception in Judaism. Though Feldman contends that Judaism was a missionary religion in some sense, he is perplexed by the absence of missionaries: "one of the great puzzles of the proselytizing movement is how to explain the existence of a mass movement [of conversions to Judaism] when we do not know the name of a single Jewish missionary" (see McKnight 1991, 52).

Though some scholars have pointed to a variety of evidence (e.g., Sir 39:4; *Ep. Arist.* 266; *T. Levi* 14:4; Wis Sol 18:4; *Sib.Or.* 3:5-10; 1QS 10:17-18; Philo *Spec. Leg.* 1.320-23; *Omn. Prob. Lib.* 74), by far the most probable piece of evidence can be found in Ananias, a Jewish merchant, who won over Izates (Josephus *Ant.* 20.2.3-4 §§35-48). Ananias can profitably be compared with the Christian missionary/apostle Paul, who used his profession as a tentmaker as a platform for evangelism. After winning over some women of the royal court, Ananias also converted King Izates. Later, a certain Eleazar, knowing that Izates had not yet been circumcised, urged the king to convert completely and be circumcised; and he was. In my judgment, Ananias and perhaps Eleazar may be used as evidence for Jewish missionaries, but only in a guarded sense. It is far more likely that they were merchants who used their professions as opportunities to teach others the customs of the Jews than that they were self-defined missionaries. In this sense, they differ from Paul, who was only tangentially a tentmaker.

However, it is perhaps nitpicking to refuse assignment of these two teachers of the Torah to the category of missionary. But we need to observe that these are the only two missionaries that we have a record of, if they were even that. That ordinary Jews occasionally spoke up in defense of their religion, that they occasionally explained their religion and practices to others and that they occasionally wanted Gentiles to convert to their religion and took active steps to convert them seems historically plausible. There is no evidence, however, that Jews enlisted missionaries in the Christian sense of the term.

4.3. Distributing Literature. Distributing literature for the purpose of converting Gentiles has been regularly considered a method of Jewish proselytism. Documents considered to have been written for this purpose include at least the following: the nonextant Philo, *Apologia hyper Ioudaion,* Josephus, *Contra Apionem,* the **Epistle of Aristeas,* and **Sibylline Oracles,* as well as the various texts of *Demetrius, Eupolemus and *Aristobulus. However, the scholarly classification, definition and explanation, not to mention the historical context from which such literature supposedly emerges, have not yet been delineated with sufficient scholarly rigor to be used in a critical reconstruction of Jewish missionary activity. What has taken place is that scholars have assumed that this literature was designed for Jewish apologetics and for Jewish proselytization when that assumption is hardly capable of proof. If a given document defends Judaism against Gentile charges, that alone does not prove that the piece of literature was written to convince Gentiles to convert to Judaism.

There is an insurmountable fact, a phenomenon of the contemporary world, that virtually eliminates such a view from consideration: namely, literature was too expensive to be produced and given to an enemy who may destroy the document (Tcherikover; *see* Literacy and Book Culture). We do not need to argue that Jews did not respond to charges against them, but we do need to exercise caution when considering whether they produced literature to convince the opponents to convert. Simple logic reveals that the bulk of apologetic literature fosters internal legitimation rather than external conversion. From a later Christian world, Tertullian comments on the use of apologetical literature: "to which [literature] no one comes for guidance unless he is already a Christian" (Tertullian *Test.* 1). The same scenario best explains the supposed apologetical literature of Judaism. (On Philo and Josephus, see McKnight 1991, 68-73.)

4.4. Synagogue Influence. Moore once said, "Their [the Jews] religious influence was exerted chiefly through the synagogues, which they set up for themselves, but which were open to all whom curiosity drew to their services" (Moore, 1:324). Nearly a half century later, however, Kraabel argued the opposite: "There is no evidence from the excavations of attempts to recruit gentiles by means of these buildings. In the inscriptions the word 'proselyte' is very rare: it appears in but one per cent of the Jewish inscriptions from Italy, the largest sample available; and it does not occur in the synagogue inscriptions at all" (1982, 458). We need not ask whether Gentiles were converted, led to conversion or catechized after their conversion in the synagogue: if they attended the synagogue those kinds of things happened. What we need to know is whether the synagogue was intentionally a place for proselytization.

Several pieces of evidence have been offered in defense of the synagogue as a place of intentional proselytizing through the exposition of Torah (see Georgi, 83-90): Philo *Spec. Leg.* 2.62-63; Horace *Sat.* 1.4.138-43; Juvenal *Sat.* 14.96-106; Josephus *J.W.* 7.3.3 §45. However, the evidence is not as clear as some would have it: (1) Philo's text says nothing about Gentiles, though it does say much about Jewish intensity; (2) Horace's text does not deal with synagogues or with interpreting the Torah in synagogues; in fact, J. Nolland's recent study suggests that it is concerned with political agitation; (3) Juvenal's comments are also not about synagogues; finally, (4) Josephus's comments may lend credence to synagogue proselytizing, but the text falls short of affirming this as the intention of the activity in the synagogues. It needs to be reiterated that it is probably the case that Gentiles were converted in synagogues, but that the Jews saw their synagogue meetings as designed to reach out to their Gentile community with the hope of conversion goes well beyond the evidence. The synagogue was for Jews; if Gentiles wanted to attend and to behave themselves accordingly so that the service could go on without distraction, they were welcomed; that in so attending some found their interest perked or that some of them converted seems reasonable. But that is a long way from arguing that Jews used the synagogue as a missionary platform (McKnight 1998).

4.5. Education. It cannot be demonstrated with probity that the synagogue was used to proselytize; it remains nonetheless the case that *education was used in proselytizing. If becoming a Jew involved learning the *Torah, comprehending the nature of God's dealing with Israel and appreciating the nature of the temple's sacrificial system, then it is undoubtedly the case that concomitant to becoming a proselyte was being educated in Judaism. The story of Shammai and Hillel illustrates the point adequately: when the would-be proselyte wants to learn Torah or wear priestly vestments, according to Hillel, he needs to be educated—either as to the essence of Torah or to the significance of a specialized priesthood. Philo prides himself on the educational value of the Torah for humankind: it was translated so "that the greater part, or even the whole, of the human race might be profited and led to a better life" (Philo *Vit. Mos.* 2.36). A distinctive feature of Judaism was the discovering of *asufi* ("foundlings") and educating them into Judaism (Josephus *J.W.* 2.8.2 §120; *m. Qidd.* 4:1-3).

4.6. Good Works. Probably the most effective, even if fundamentally unconscious, method of attracting Gentiles was through the power of good works and a morally attractive life. The author of the *Epistle of Aristeas* has expressed this clearly: "My belief is that we must (also) show liberal charity to our opponents so that in this manner we may convert them to what is proper and fitting to them. You must pray God that these things be brought to pass, for he rules the minds of all" (226, *APOT;* but cf. *OTP* for a different rendering; see also *T. Ben.* 5:1-5). Philo, with his unconquerable praise of the Torah's virtues, contends that good behavior led to the translation of the Torah, but "in course of time, the daily, unbroken regularity of practice exercised by those who observed them [the laws] brought them to the knowledge of others, and their fame began to spread on every side" (Philo *Vit. Mos.* 2.27). The son of a Gentile Godfearer described by Juvenal eventually becomes a proselyte as a result of observing the behavior of others (Juvenal *Sat.* 14.96-106).

4.7. Intermarriage. Besides the above-mentioned methods of converting Gentiles, we cannot fail to mention that intermarriage was a common means by which a Gentile chose to convert (*m. Qidd.* 3:5; *b. Yebam.* 92b; *B. Meṣ.* 16b), and the romantic legend **Joseph and Aseneth,* in which Aseneth converts as a result of her encounter with the wise Joseph, may have legitimated such practice. However, it would be historically unjustified to contend that intermarriage was an intentional method of converting Gentiles.

4.8. Force. At certain periods in history certain Jewish movements, led by charismatic or politically powerful heroes, many conversions took place as the result of force. However triumphalistic the writers' concepts might be, the conversions recorded in Judith (Jdt 14:10) and Esther (Esther 8:17) resulted from force. Hyrcanus, Aristobulus I and Alexander Jannaeus each forced Gentiles to convert and be circumcised, even if they saw such as part of an *eschatological program or political purgation (Josephus *Ant.* 13.9.1 §§257-58; 13.9.3 §§318-19; 13.15.4 §397; 15.7.9 §§253-54).

In summary, it is likely that the predominant method for conversion in ancient Judaism was God's stupendous acts in history, especially the future Day of the Lord. It is reasonable to infer from this observation that expectation for conversion in the future emerges from the lack of conversions in the present: that is, since Judaism was true, since Yahweh was the one God of the universe and since Gentiles are not now converting to Judaism, they will someday. But there is sufficient evidence of converts, not to mention rules and regulations about them (which imply converts), to contend that some methods were effective in the present. The evidence suggests that the power of good deeds led some Gentiles to inquire about Judaism, and the natural place for their education to occur would be through social discussion or synagogue activities. It is very doubtful, however, that Jews wrote literature for the express purpose of converting Gentiles, and it is even more doubtful that there were Jewish missionaries.

5. Requirements for Proselytes.

Conversion theory requires that most religious conversions be accompanied by demonstration events, symbolic actions that communicate the reality of conversion and a commitment to the new religious group. That is, ritual marks the transition from one social body to another and the resocialization process that is thereby implied. Christian scholars need, however, to beware of the common practice of imputing to Judaism the very ritual that marks the transition into the Christian faith. The evidence from antiquity reveals rather a diverse set of requirements that differ from time and place so that it is no longer accurate to speak of Judaism requiring circumcision, baptism and a sacrifice in the temple (replaced by almsgiving after the temple's destruction). Not only is this evidence sparse; it is also skewed in an androcentric direction since the concerns of *women in conversion are silenced.

5.1. Circumcision. We can be sure that converts were circumcised (Jdt 14:10), but the ambiguity of certain authors about the rite reveals that it was not perceived as a necessary requirement by all Jews for all converts (cf. Philo *Som.* 2.25; *Spec. Leg.* 1.304-6; *Quaest. in Ex.* 2.2; but cf.

Migr. Abr. 92; see also Josephus *Ant.* 20.2.3-4 §§35-49). Circumcision as a conversion ritual becomes confused with how Jews perceived the nation: the act and national identity are not easy to separate (Josephus *J.W.* 2.17.10 §454), but when King Izates becomes serious about his commitment to Judaism he undergoes circumcision (Josephus *Ant.* 20.2.3-4 §§35-49). I suspect that Paul's contention that converts to Messiah Jesus did not have to be circumcised would not have been either a startling innovation or unacceptable to all, even if it caused no small disturbance for the Jerusalem converts (Gal 5:2, 6, 12; 6:15; Phil 3:2; cf. Acts 15:1-2). The evidence from the rabbis, though hardly plentiful, suggests that even though there was dispute about how quickly the convert needed to submit to the rite, circumcision was required because it was in Torah (cf. *m. ʿEd.* 5:2; *m. Pesaḥ.* 8:8; *b. Pesaḥ.* 92a; *t. Pesaḥ.* 7:14; *b. Šabb.* 135a; later see *b. Yebam.* 46a; 71a). A safe historical inference is that circumcision was required but there were dissenting voices at different times for special reasons.

5.2. Baptism. The evidence for proselyte baptism is even less clear. Water lustrations were clearly a part of Judaism, and ceremonial cleansings were knit deeply into the fabric of Judaism. Therefore a transition rite, such as baptism, seems reasonable, but the evidence is not as clear as this. Baptism is understood in Christianity as a one-time, unrepeatable initiation rite, but the evidence for Judaism practicing baptism in this manner is either unavailable or (which is more likely) nonexistent because it was not a feature of Judaism until after the Bar Kokhba revolt.

It seems possible that *Sibylline Oracles* 4:162-65 refers to a pre-Christian proselyte baptismal rite. It reads: "Ah, wretched mortals, change these things, and do not lead the great God to all sorts of anger, but abandon daggers and groanings, murders and outrages, and *wash your whole bodies in perennial rivers*" (italics added). Not only is the date of this passage unclear (probably around A.D. 80), but also the heavy use of metaphor makes one wonder if a physical act is involved. Apart from this text, the evidence from Philo, Josephus (where Izates is not baptized) and *Joseph and Aseneth* (where Aseneth is not baptized) show a uniform absence of the rite as a conversion act. The rabbinic evidence gains clarity over time: the earliest texts are ambiguous (e.g., *t. Pesaḥ.* 7:13; *m. ʿEd.* 5:2; *m. Pesaḥ.* 8:8; *b. Pesaḥ.* 92a), while the latter ones show a rite prescribed for converts (*b. Yebam.* 46a; 71a). It is reasonable then to argue that baptism, as an initiation rite, was a symbolic rite in progress in Judaism when John, probably Jesus and certainly early Christians like Paul began to use the rite as the prevailing entry rite into the newfound movement.

5.3. Sacrifices. Judaism was dominated by temple, and that meant *sacrifice; it seems reasonable that Judaism may have required converts to offer a first sacrifice as part of their conversion process. But the evidence is shaky, and the reality of the situation mitigates against sacrifice being a conversion requirement. However important temple was to Judaism, sacrifice was not an integral part of religious life for most Jews, especially those who had no opportunity to visit the temple. Consequently, the voice of Philo may well represent if not a studied view at least a common-sense response: "What is precious in the sight of God is not the number of victims immolated but the true purity of a rational spirit in him who makes the sacrifice" (Philo *Spec. Leg.* 1.277). Thus, "if he is pure of heart and just, this sacrifice stands firm . . . even if no victim at all is brought to the altar" (Philo *Vit. Mos.* 2.107-8). Though Helene of Adiabene offered a sacrifice when she visited Jerusalem there is no evidence that she did so to fulfill some duty (Josephus *Ant.* 20.2.5 §49).

The evidence of the rabbis is explicably silent regarding first-century practice: why prescribe what can't be done when the temple is no longer standing? Thus we are justified to agree with Moore: "The offering of a sacrifice is, thus, not one of the conditions of becoming a proselyte, but only a condition precedent to the exercise of one of the rights which belong to him as a proselyte, namely, the participation in a sacrificial meal" (Moore 1:332). Later rabbis, however, assume the practice and grant a substitute in almsgiving (cf. *m. Ker.* 2:1; *b. Ker.* 8a-9a; *b. Roš Haš.* 31b).

In conclusion, the requirements for proselytes varied from time to time and according to the dominating customs of local culture. It can be said, however, that all Jews would have expected repentance, obedience and social integration into the Jewish community if one wanted to become a proselyte (cf. Philo *Det. Pot. Ins.* 97; *Spec. Leg.* 1.277; *Cher.* 95-96; *Jos. and As.*). It can also be maintained that the absence of data about requirements perhaps reflects the scarcity of conversions and proselytes.

6. Levels of Adherence.

The rabbis made several distinctions among proselytes, including the following: the true proselyte (*ger sedeq;* see *b. Pesaḥ.* 21b; *b. Giṭ.* 57b), the resident alien (*ger toshab;* see *b. ʿAbod. Zar.* 64b; *b. Giṭ.* 57b), the lion/fear proselyte (*ger 'arayot;* see *b. Qidd.* 75ab) and the dream proselyte (*ger halomot;* see *b. Yebam.* 24b; *b. Menaḥ.* 44a). The first is the proselyte who converts for the right reasons and lives righteously according to the Torah; the second is the Gentile who lives appropriately in the land of Israel; the third, stemming from 2 Kings 17:25, converts out of fear or as a result of seeing a miracle, and the conversion is not perceived as complete; the fourth refers to those who convert to their own advantage. While this categorization may prove helpful to later rabbis, there is no evidence that any of these terms were used in the first century. Two kinds of evidence are extant, however, that permit us to see that first-century Jews saw levels of adherence among proselytes and these categories allowed them to define the true Jew more accurately as well as the kinds of conversions that were being made.

6.1. Motives for Conversion. From Philo's exegesis of Exodus 12:38 ("a mixed crowd [*ʿēreb rab*] also went up with them," *Vit. Mos.* 1.147) we can see that Philo himself saw at least two different motives for conversion (see McKnight 1989). The text reads: "They were accompanied by a promiscuous, nondescript and menial crowd, a bastard host, so to speak, associated with the true-born. These were (1) the children of Egyptian women by Hebrew fathers into whose families they had been adopted, (2) also those who, reverencing the divine favor shown to the people, had come over to them, (3) and such as were converted and brought to a wiser mind by the magnitude and the number of the successive punishments." As a result of an apparent contact with what we now find in the targumic tradition (cf. *Tg. Neof.* on Ex 12:38) Philo has revolutionized a group: from a "mixed crowd" to three separable groups, two of which are kinds of proselytes! Thus we have children educated into Judaism, proselytes who converted as a result of miracles and proselytes who converted after seeing God's punishments. Another distinction, that between the true proselyte and the resident alien, seems to be made by Philo (*Virt.* 102-8). Thus we can safely conclude that some Jews knew of levels of adherence to Judaism and categorized proselytes accordingly.

6.2. Godfearers. The issue of the meaning of Godfearers has recently been revisited and deserves consideration (Trebilco, 145-66; McKnight 1991, 110-14). A standard perception of the Godfearer is that it is a technical term, describing a Gentile who has only partly committed himself or herself to Judaism, but this definition has been overturned. In general, scholars are convinced that the Jewish communities, especially in the Diaspora (Barclay), attracted in various ways a diversity of Gentiles who may accurately be termed "sympathizers" (Feldman, 342-82). The term *Godfearer* describes either Jews or Gentiles and apparently most of the time on the basis of observable piety (*Jos. and As.* 4:7; 23:3-13; 27:1; 28:7; 29:3; Josephus *Ant.* 20.2.4 §41). The question now is what it means when used of a Gentile and whether that term is technical for a specific class of partial converts.

In the Acts of the Apostles the term *Godfearer* is used of Gentiles who honor God in various ways (including almsgiving and synagogue participation) who are distinguished from run-of-the-mill Gentiles, and the term seems to be nearly synonymous with "proselyte" or a category of proselytes; that is, for Luke the Godfearer is a quasi-official sympathizer with Judaism (Acts 10:2, 22; 13:16, 26, 43, 50; 17:4, 17; 18:7).

This quasi-official participation in Judaism has been recently confirmed by the discovery in Aphrodisias of a stele that dates to about A.D. 210 (Reynolds and Tannenbaum). In a list of subscribers to a Jewish institution, perhaps a soup kitchen or a *burial society, there are three proselytes (*a.* lines 13, 17, 22) and two "Godfearers" (*theosebēs,* lines 19-20). On face *b.* of the stele there is a list of fifty-four Jews and, after a break, a list of fifty Godfearers whose names are either Greek or Greco-Roman, suggesting a Gentile origin for the group. This text reveals there is a distinction, for this community, between Gentiles and Jews, between Jews and proselytes and between proselytes and Godfearers. We do not have hard data about much else regarding this group, such as the nature and degree of their participation or how they became associated with Judaism, but we do now have independent data that suggests, with Luke, that the distinction between proselytes and Godfearers was being made.

See also ARISTEAS, EPISTLE OF; DIASPORA; EDUCATION: JEWISH AND GRECO-ROMAN; JEWISH COMMUNITIES IN ASIA MINOR; LITERACY AND BOOK CULTURE; PERSECUTION; RELIGION, GRECO-ROMAN; RELIGION, PERSONAL; THEOLOGIES AND SECTS, JEWISH.

BIBLIOGRAPHY. B. J. Bamberger, *Proselytism in the Talmudic Era* (2d ed.; New York: Ktav, 1968); J. G. M. Barclay, *Jews in the Mediterranean Diaspora* (Edinburgh: T & T Clark, 1996); A. Bertholet, *Die Stellung der Israeliten und der Juden zu den Fremden* (Freiburg and Leipzig: Mohr Siebeck, 1896); E. Bickerman, "The Warning Inscriptions of Herod's Temple," *JQR* 37 (1946-47) 387-405; S. F. Bonner, *Education in Ancient Rome: From the Elder Cato to the Younger Pliny* (Berkeley and Los Angeles: University of California Press, 1977); W. G. Braude, *Jewish Proselytizing in the First Five Centuries of the Common Era, the Age of the Tannaim and the Amoraim* (BUS 6; Providence, RI: Brown University Press, 1940); L. H. Feldman, *Jew and Gentile in the Ancient World: Attitudes and Interactions from Alexander to Jutinian* (Princeton, NJ: Princeton University Press, 1993); D. Georgi, *The Opponents of Paul in Second Corinthians* (Philadelphia: Fortress, 1986); M. Goodman, *Mission and Conversion: Proselytizing in the Religious History of the Roman Empire* (Oxford: Clarendon Press, 1994); F. Hahn, *Mission in the New Testament* (SBT 47; London: SCM, 1981); M. Hengel, *Judaism and Hellenism: Studies in Their Encounter in Palestine During the Early Hellenistic Period* (2 vols.; Philadelphia: Fortress, 1980); J. Jeremias, *Jesus' Promise to the Nations* (SBT 24; London: SCM, 1958); A. T. Kraabel, "The Impact of the Discovery at Sardis," in *Sardis from Prehistoric to Roman Times: Results of the Archaeological Exploration of Sardis, 1958-1975*, ed. G. M. Hanfmann and W. E. Mierse (Cambridge, MA: Harvard University Press, 1983) 178-90; idem, "The Roman Diaspora: Six Questionable Assumptions," *JJS* 33 (1982) 445-64; S. McKnight, "*De Vita Mosis* 1.147: Lion Proselytes in Philo?" in *The Studia Philonica Annual: Studies in Hellenistic Judaism* 1 (1989) 58-62; idem, "Jewish Missionary Activity: The Evidence of Demographics and Synagogues," in *Jewish Proselytism*, ed. A.-J. Levine and R. Pervo (Atlanta: Scholars Press, forthcoming); idem, *A Light Among the Gentiles: Jewish Missionary Activity in the Second Temple Period* (Minneapolis: Fortress, 1991); G. F. Moore, *Judaism in the First Centuries of the Christian Era: The Age of the Tannaim* (3 vols.; Cambridge, MA: Harvard University Press, 1927-1930); J. Nolland, "Proselytism or Politics in Horace *Satires* 1.4.138-43?" *VC* 33 (1979) 347-55; G. Porton, *The Stranger Within Your Gates: Converts and Conversion in Rabbinic Literature* (CSHJ; Chicago: University of Chicago Press, 1994); J. S. Raisin, *Gentile Reactions to Jewish Ideals, with Special Reference to Proselytes*, ed. H. Hailperin (New York: Philosophical Library, 1953); J. Reynolds and R. F. Tannenbaum, *Jews and Godfearers at Aphrodisias: Greek Inscriptions with Commentary* (CPSSV 12; Cambridge: Cambridge Philological Society, 1987); J. R. Rosenbloom, *Conversion to Judaism: From the Biblical Period to the Present* (HUCAS: Cincinnati: Hebrew Union College Press, 1978); E. P. Sanders, *Judaism: Practice and Belief: 63 B.C.E.—66 C.E.* (Philadelphia: Trinity Press International, 1992); V. Tcherikover, "Jewish Apologetic Literature Reconsidered," *Eos* 48 (1956) 169-93; P. Trebilco, *Jewish Communities in Asia Minor* (SNTSMS 69; Cambridge: Cambridge University Press, 1991).

S. McKnight

PROSTITUTION. *See* ADULTERY, DIVORCE.

PROVERBS. *See* RABBINIC PROVERBS.

PSALMS AND HYMNS OF QUMRAN

Among the hundreds of scrolls found in the region of the Dead Sea, dozens contain psalms and hymns. Many of these are the psalms that Jews and Christians would later regard as canonical, but a great many were unknown until the discovery of the scrolls. These various psalms and hymns have implications for our understanding of the Psalter and its recognition as canonical literature, as well as for our understanding of the NT and the world of the early church.

1. The Psalms Scrolls
2. Implications for our Understanding of the Psalter
3. Use and Interpretation of the Psalter at Qumran
4. Relationship to the New Testament
5. "Apocryphal" Psalms
6. Other Hymns and Songs

1. The Psalms Scrolls.

A total of thirty-nine psalm scrolls or manuscripts incorporating psalms were found among the Dead Sea Scrolls. Thirty-six were discovered in eight caves at Qumran: three in Cave 1, one each in the minor Caves 2, 3, 5, 6 and 8, twenty-three in Cave 4 and five in Cave 11. Three additional psalms scrolls were discovered further south: two at Masada and one at Naḥal Ḥever. Analysis of these manuscripts reveals interesting features:

*1.1. **Comparative Datings.*** At least thirteen psalms manuscripts were copied before the first century B.C. The oldest two are 4QPs^{a} and 4QPs^{w}, which date from the second century B.C., while the remaining eleven were copied in first century B.C. (1QPs^{a}, 4QPs^{b}, 4QPs^{d}, 4QPs^{f}, 4QPs^{k}, 4QPs^{l}, 4QPs^{n}, 4QPs^{o}, 4QPs^{u}, 4Q522, MasPs^{b}). Six scrolls are generally classified as Herodian (1QPs^{c}, 2QPs, 4QPs^{h}, 4QPs^{m}, 4QPs^{p}, 4QPs^{r}), and four were copied in the first century A.D. (1QPs^{b}, 3QPs, 5QPs, 8QPs). More specifically, ten scrolls are dated from the early to mid-first century A.D. (4QPs^{e}, 4QPs^{g}, 4QPs^{j}, 4QPs^{q}, 4QPs^{t}, 11QPs^{a}, 11QPs^{b}, 11QPs^{c}, 11QPs^{d}, MasPs^{a}) and four from the mid-first century A.D. onward (4QPs^{c}, 4QPs^{s}, 11QapocPs, 5/6ḤevPs).

*1.2. **Original Contents.*** Some psalms scrolls originally contained only a few compositions or part of a psalter (e.g., 4QPs^{g}, 4QPs^{h}, 5QPs probably contained only Ps 119).

*1.3. **Quantity Preserved.*** In decreasing order, scrolls with the greatest number of verses preserved (whether wholly or in part) are the *Great Psalms Scroll* from Cave 11 (11QPs^{a}), followed by 4QPs^{a}, 5/6ḤevPs, 4QPs^{b}, 4QPs^{c} and 4QPs^{e}.

*1.4. **Compositions in these Manuscripts.*** Of the 150 psalms found in the Masoretic Text (MT-150 Psalter hereafter; i.e., the traditional book of Psalms that appears in modern Bibles), 126 are represented in the thirty-nine psalms scrolls or other relevant manuscripts such as the *Pesharim.* The remaining twenty-four psalms were most likely included, but are now lost due to deterioration and damage: Psalms 3—4, 20—21, 32, 41, 46, 55, 58, 61, 64—65, 70, 72—75, 80, 87, 90, 108?, 110, 111 and 117. At least fifteen "apocryphal" psalms or compositions are also distributed among five manuscripts (11QPs^{a}, 4QPs^{f}, 4Q522, 11QPs^{b}, 11QapocPs). Six of these pieces were previously familiar to scholars: Psalms 151A, 151B, 154, 155, David's Last Words (= 2 Sam 23:1-7) and Sirach 51:13-30. The remaining nine were completely unknown prior to the discovery of the Dead Sea Scrolls: the *Apostrophe to Judah, Apostrophe to Zion, David's Compositions, Eschatological Hymn, Hymn to the Creator, Plea for Deliverance* and *Three Songs Against Demons.* (For more details on these pieces, see section 6 below.)

*1.5. **Major Disagreements with the Masoretic Psalter.*** In comparison with the MT-150 Psalter, twelve scrolls contain major disagreements. Variations in *content* (the inclusion of compositions not found in the MT) occur in two scrolls from Cave 4 and another from Cave 11 (4QPs^{f}, 4Q522, 11QapocPs), for example, the *Apostrophe to Judah* in 4QPs^{f}. Differences in the *order* of psalms appear in seven scrolls from Cave 4 (4QPs^{a}, 4QPs^{b}, 4QPs^{d}, 4QPs^{e}, 4QPs^{k}, 4QPs^{n}, 4QPs^{q}), for instance, Psalm 31 followed directly by Psalm 33 in 4QPs^{a} and 4QPs^{q}. Differences in both *order* and *content* are present in two manuscripts from Cave 11 (11QPs^{a} and 11QPs^{b}).

*1.6. **Variant Readings.*** The psalms scrolls preserve hundreds of variant readings (not counting orthography) that often involve single words but sometimes extend to entire verses. Many are relatively minor, but several are significant for our understanding of the text of the Psalter: for example, the missing *nun*-verse of the acrostic Psalm 145:13 is preserved in 17:2-3 of 11QPs^{a}.

2. Implications for Our Understanding of the Psalter.

The publication of 11QPs^{a} in 1965 by J. A. Sanders (see bibliography) showed how this manuscript greatly diverges from the Masoretic Psalter in both the ordering of contents and the presence of additional compositions. In a series of articles commencing in 1966, Sanders developed a hypothesis that challenged traditional views of the text and canonization of the book of Psalms. According to this hypothesis, the Qumran Psalter was regarded by those who used it as "canonical" (since it incorporated Psalms 1—89, which had been finalized), yet also as "open" (able to admit additional contents or arrangements, since Psalms 90 and following were still fluid). Furthermore, the gathering of Psalms 90 and beyond developed independently in two directions, resulting in two collections or editions that had Psalms 1—89 in common but differed from Psalm 90 onward. These two collections are what Sanders termed the "Qumran Psalter," of which almost all the second half is represented by 11QPs^{a}, and the Psalter found in the Received Text whose second half comprises Psalms 90—150. Subsequent discussion on the psalms scrolls has been centered on four main areas:

2.1. Gradual Stabilization. According to Sanders, 11QPs[a] and certain other scrolls witness to a Psalter that was being gradually stabilized, from beginning to end. Agreements between the Masoretic Text and the psalms scrolls may be regarded as indicative of stability (e.g., Ps 5 followed by Ps 6 in 4QPs[a]), while disagreements in order or content provide evidence of fluidity (e.g., Ps 147 followed by 104 in 4QPs[d] and Ps 150 followed by the *Hymn to the Creator* in 11QPs[a]). With respect to arrangement, the small number of disagreements with the MT-150 Psalter for Books I–III contrasts markedly with the high incidence of variation for Books IV–V: thirty-six consecutive psalms are in the same arrangement as in the Masoretic Text as opposed to only three in a conflicting order. For Books IV–V, however, only thirty-one consecutive psalms support the Masoretic arrangement, while forty-nine are in a conflicting order. This fluidity following Book III of the Psalter is underscored by the presence of compositions not found in the Masoretic Psalter in eleven consecutive arrangements with compositions (e.g., the *Apostrophe to Zion*) that appear in Psalms 90—150 of the Masoretic Text, but never with any of Psalms 1—89. The psalms scrolls thus show that the order and content of Psalms 1—89 vary little from that of the MT-150 Psalter, but for Psalm 90 and beyond many divergences are evident. This evidence indicates that during the Qumran period Books I–III were stabilized, but Books IV–V remained fluid, although the precise cutoff point is not certain. Comparison of the older and later psalms scrolls shows that this stabilization did not take place gradually but in two distinct stages: Psalms 1—89 (or so) prior to the first century B.C., and Psalm 90 onward toward the end of the first century A.D.

2.2. Two or More Editions of the Psalter. The psalms scrolls attest not to a single, finalized Psalter, but to more than one literary edition of the book of Psalms: the "11QPs[a] Psalter," the "MT-150 collection" and possibly others besides. With a literary edition defined as an intentional reworking of an older form of a book according to a specific editorial agenda or for specific purposes, the identification of different literary editions depends mainly upon an assessment of individual variant readings. In the psalms scrolls and the Masoretic Psalter, two types of variation are prominent: differences in the order of adjoining psalms, and the presence or absence of entire compositions. A comparative analysis suggests the existence of three major collections:

(a) An early Psalter comprising Psalms 1 to 89 (or thereabouts) that was stabilized well before the second century B.C.

(b) The MT-150 Psalter. Note that none of the psalms scrolls *unambiguously* confirms the longer order of the received Masoretic Text (Psalms 1—150) against 11QPs[a]; such evidence is only found at Masada, where MasPs[b] represents a Psalter ending with Psalm 150.

(c) The 11QPs[a]-Psalter. Containing both Psalms 1—89 and the arrangement found in 11QPs[a], this Psalter is found in at least three manuscripts: 11QPs[a], 11QPs[b] (includes the *Catena, Plea for Deliverance,* the *Apostrophe to Zion,* and the sequence of Psalms 141–133–144), and 4QPs[e] (note the sequence of Psalms 118–104–[147]–105–146). Both the MT-150 Psalter and the 11QPs[a] Psalter seem to have been completed prior to the Qumran period; it seems impossible to decide which was earlier.

2.3. Provenance of the 11QPs[a]-Psalter. There is no clear evidence that 11QPs[a] was actually compiled at Qumran and thus may be termed the "Qumran Psalter." The possibility that the 11QPs[a]-Psalter was assembled by the Qumran covenanters is allowed by its occurrence in at least three manuscripts (4QPs[e], 11QPs[a], and 11QPs[b]), and the 364-day solar *calendar evident in *David's Compositions* (col. 27); however, neither of these is a necessary indicator of Qumran provenance. Other factors make it more likely that the collection was compiled and used by wider Jewish circles—including those at Qumran—who advocated the solar calendar; for example, the individual compositions in 11QPs[a] all predate the Qumran period, the absence of "sectually explicit" references (e.g., to the Teacher of Righteousness) suggests that none of the pieces was actually composed there, and the 364-day solar calendar is also attested in other Jewish writings that arose before the founding of the community (*1 *Enoch, *Jubilees,* the **Temple Scroll*). The notion of a 11QPs[a]-Psalter that was used not only at Qumran, but also among other Jewish circles advocating the solar calendar, attests to a widespread type of Judaism which possibly included the *Sadducees. This is in marked contrast to the *Pharisees and *rabbis with their 354-day lunar calendar and cannot be viewed as sectarian (cf. Flint 1997, 198-201). However, as regards the production of individual *scrolls*, it is very possible that 11QPs[a] and the other two representatives of the 11QPs[a]-Psalter (4QPs[e], 11QPs[b]) were copied at Qumran in view of the popularity of the 11QPs[a]-Psalter among the covenanters and because scrolls were produced at the site.

2.4. 11QPs[a] as Part of a Scriptural Psalter. 11QPs[a] contains the latter part of a true scriptural Psalter, and it is not a secondary collection dependent upon Psalms 1—150 as found in the Received Text. This proposal has produced numerous challengers, including S. Talmon (1966), M. H. Goshen-Gottstein (1966), P. Skehan (several articles, see bibliography) and B. Z. Wacholder (1988). For example, Talmon proposed that 11QPs[a] contains material that is supplementary to Scripture, while Skehan sought to demonstrate that the MT-150 Psalter is chronologically prior to 11QPs[a], which he classified as a "library edition," an "instruction book" containing the supposed works of David or "an instruction book for budding Levite choristers" at the temple in about 200 B.C. In contrast, G. H. Wilson (1985), taking into account 11QPs[a-d] and most of the Cave 4 scrolls, concluded that the psalms scrolls attest to overall stability for Psalms 1—89 and to general fluidity for Psalm 90 onward, and that 11QPs[a] was organized in accordance with principles similar to those in Books IV and V in the MT-150 Psalter.

The analysis of P. Flint (1997) affirms Sanders's view that 11QPs[a] represents a scriptural Psalter and that the 11QPs[a]-Psalter is an edition of the book of Psalms on three main grounds: the attribution to David, structural principles and usage (i.e., quotations and allusions). For example, *David's Compositions* implies that all the pieces in 11QPs[a] originated with David by asserting that 4,050 pieces—which surely included those in 11QPs[a]—were spoken by David "through prophecy" (27:11). He finds the attempts by earlier scholars to show that 11QPs[a] is not a true scriptural Psalter but a secondary liturgical compilation to be ultimately unconvincing because all presume that the arrangement of the MT-150 Psalter, or even its textual form, had been finalized and was accepted by virtually all Jews as the "book of Psalms" well before the second century B.C., which is simply not the case.

3. Use and Interpretation of the Psalter at Qumran.

There are several indications that the book of Psalms was widely used and most influential within the Qumran community. First, there are more manuscripts of the Psalms among the Dead Sea Scrolls (thirty-six from Qumran, plus three more from other sites) than of any other book, which is a sure indication of the popularity of the Psalter. Second, the Psalter was the model for other books composed at Qumran, the prime example being the *Hodayot.* Third, the Qumran caves yielded three *pesharim, or commentaries, written on the Psalms: 1QpPs, 4QpPs[a] and 4QpPs[b]. This may emphasize the prophetic nature of the Psalter among the Qumran community, since all the other pesharim were written on prophetic books, and we are told in *David's Compositions* that he spoke the compositions in 11QPs[a]—and many others besides—"through prophecy" (27:11).

The largest fragments of 4QpPs[a] preserve a running commentary on Psalm 37, which encourages the righteous to keep faith in God despite the apparent prosperity of the wicked. The pesher associates "wickedness" and "the wicked" with the Man of the Lie (frags. 1-10 i 26 and iv 14), the ruthless ones of the covenant (frags. 1-10 ii 14 and iii 12) and the ruthless ones of the Gentiles (frags. 1-10 ii 20). In contrast, "the righteous" are associated with the Teacher of Righteousness (frags. 1-10 iii [15], [19]), the Interpreter of Knowledge (frags. 1-10 i 27), the congregation of the elect (frags. 1-10 ii 5 and iii 5), the congregation of the poor ones (frags. 1-10 ii 10 and iii 10) and the Priest and his partisans (frags. 1-10 ii 19). God will ensure that the wicked will receive punishment, and the righteous will receive their inheritance (frags. 1-10 iii 1, 10). The pesher thus interprets a psalm of instruction and personal tribulation in an eschatological manner.

4. Relationship to the New Testament.

There are similarities between the book of Psalms at Qumran and in the NT with respect to textual forms and interpretation. Although no Greek Psalms are preserved in the scrolls, some features in the Hebrew correspond with the *Septuagint Psalter that was used and quoted by the NT writers. Most prominent is Psalm 151, which ends both the Septuagint Psalter and the 11QPs[a]-Psalter (but for the Qumran scroll in the form of two psalms: 151A and 151B). Another example is Psalm 145:13, where the required *nun* verse in this acrostic psalm, which is missing from the Masoretic Text, is found in 11QPs^a ("God is faithful in his words, and gracious in all his deeds") and in the Septuagint ("The LORD is faithful in all his words, and gracious in all his deeds") that was used by the NT writers.

Like the Psalms pesharim (e.g. 4QpPs^a), the NT writers tend to interpret the Psalms eschatologically; however, whereas 4QpPs^a relates Psalm 37 to the Teacher of Righteousness, the NT writers often connect passages from the Psalms as pointing to Jesus the Messiah. This is especially evident with respect to Psalm 22, which is alluded to by Jesus or the Evangelists in relation to the crucifixion (see Mk 15:24 [Ps 22:18], 29 [Ps 22:7], 34 [Ps 22:1] and parallels).

5. "Apocryphal" Psalms.

11QPs^a includes six pieces that were previously familiar to scholars, all of which are grouped with psalms now found in the MT-150 Psalter:

Psalms 151A and 151B (known from the Greek, Syriac and Latin). Accepted as canonical by the Orthodox churches, this is the final composition in the Septuagint Psalter and the 11QPs^a-Psalter (col. 28).

Psalms 154 and 155 (previously known from the Syriac). Psalm 154 is a wisdom composition that calls the faithful to glorify God by gathering to proclaim his greatness (vv. 1-3) and to instruct the ignorant (vv. 4-8). It goes on to describe the nature and characteristics of wisdom (vv. 12-15) and to affirm God's protection over the godly, humble and pure (vv. 16-20). Psalm 155 is a psalm of thanksgiving that incorporates a plea for deliverance and is reminiscent of Psalms 22 and 51.

David's Last Words (= 2 Sam 23:1-7). Together with *David's Compositions* that follows it (see 6 below), this piece serves to affirm the Davidic authority and authorship of the 11QPs^a-Psalter. Like those of patriarchs such as Jacob, David's final words carried special authority.

Sirach 51:13-30 (previously known from the Greek, Syriac and Latin). This is the second canticle of the Wisdom of Ben Sira (also known as Ecclesiasticus or *Sirach), part of the OT in Roman Catholic and Orthodox Bibles and one of the Apocrypha for Protestants. This text describes how a celibate young man is able, through discipline, to devote his bodily passions and appetites to the pursuit of wisdom instead of sexual pleasure (a theme found earlier in Genesis, Proverbs and the Song of Songs). The description in 11QPs^a is more erotic than the other versions, which suggests that provocative portions of the original Hebrew version were modified by a later editor. It appears that this piece was originally an independent poem that was both incorporated into the 11QPs^a–Psalter and appended to Ben Sira.

6. Other Hymns and Songs.

The Dead Sea Scrolls also include many hymns or songs that are not grouped with psalms now found in the canonical book of Psalms. Several of these are grouped with psalms now found in the MT-150 Psalter.

The *Apostrophe to Judah*. Preserved only in 4QPs^f, the *Apostrophe* calls on all creation and on Judah to give praise at the coming destruction of Belial and evildoers, and affirms the eternal nature of Yahweh and his glory.

The *Apostrophe to Zion*. The *Apostrophe* appears in one scroll from Cave 4 (4QPs^f) and one from Cave 11 (11QPs^a). It is a love poem addressed to Zion in a style reminiscent of the three apostrophes to Zion found in Isaiah (Is 54:1-8; 60:1-22; 62:1-8).

David's Compositions. This piece functions as a prose epilogue to 11QPs^a, although it appears in the second to last inscribed column (27) of the manuscript. The epilogue affirms the Davidic authority and authorship of the 11QPs^a-Psalter and states that he composed a total of 4,050 compositions in accordance with the 364-day solar calendar.

The *Eschatological Hymn*. Found only in 4QPs^f, this hymn apparently belongs to the category of *hallel* or *halleluyah* psalms, but has marked eschatological features.

The *Hymn to the Creator*. Preserved in 11QPs^a, this hymn is a Jewish sapiential poem that has many affinities with the *Thanksgiving Hymns* (1QH and 4QH).

The *Plea for Deliverance*. Found in 11QPs^a and 11QPs^b, the *Plea* is a prayer for deliverance from Satan and sin, and includes praise and thanksgiving for experiences of salvation in the past.

Three *Songs Against Demons*. These three pieces are grouped together with Psalm 91 in 11QapocPs, with the function of exorcism. They are in all probability the four songs "for making music over the stricken" that are referred to in

David's Compositions (11QPs^{a}, 27:9-10).

Two more important manuscripts are 4Q380 and 4Q381, which are probably from different parts of a single collection, although two different collections cannot be ruled out. Seven fragments of 4Q380 remain, containing portions of at least three distinct psalms, while the approximately 100 fragments of 4Q381 preserve parts of at least twelve psalms. The original collection or collections were certainly larger. The psalms in these two scrolls are very similar to biblical psalms in vocabulary, style, theme and content. One such theme is Zion, as in 4Q380 fragment 1: "[For the na]me of Yahweh is invoked upon it (= Zion), ^{6}[and his glory] is seen upon Jerusalem" (lines 5-6). Penitential psalms or lamentations are also evident, as in 381 fragments 33+35: "For (my) transgressions are too many for me, and [. . .]. But you, my God, will send your spir[it] and [you will give your compassions] ^{5}to the son of your handmaiden, and your mercies to the servant near to you" (lines 4-5. See also frags. 15, 24, 31, 45).

Precisely when the psalms of 4Q380 and 4Q381, all written in Hebrew, were composed is difficult to determine, since they contain virtually no historical references or special themes (4Q380 and 4Q381 were both copied in mid- to late-Hasmonean times, c. 100–30 B.C.). Like several biblical psalms, the general linguistic features are characteristic of Late Biblical and Qumranic Hebrew (*see* Hebrew Language), suggesting a date in the Persian or early Hellenistic periods. The complete absence of references to the afterlife suggests a relatively early date of composition.

See also CREEDS AND HYMNS; DEAD SEA SCROLLS: GENERAL INTRODUCTION; HEBREW BIBLE; LITURGY: QUMRAN; MUSIC; THANKSGIVING HYMNS (1QH).

BIBLIOGRAPHY. **Editions.** M. Baillet, J. T. Milik and R. de Vaux, *Les "Petites Grottes" de Qumrân: Exploration de la falaise Les grottes 2Q, 3Q, 5Q, 6Q, 7Q, à 10Q, Le rouleau de cuivre* (DJD 3; Oxford: Clarendon Press, 1962); D. Barthélemy and J. T. Milik, *Qumran Cave 1* (DJD 1; Oxford: Clarendon Press, 1955); P. W. Flint, "The Biblical Scrolls from Naḥal Ḥever (including 'Wadi Seiyal')," in *Qumran Cave 4.26: Miscellaneous Texts, Part 2* (DJD 36; Oxford: Clarendon Press, 2000); idem, "The Book of Psalms in the Light of the Dead Sea Scrolls," *VT* 48 (1998) 453–72; F. García Martínez, E. J. C. Tigchelaar and A. S. van der Woude, "11QPsalms^{a} Fragments E, F; 11QPsalms^{b}; 11QPsalms^{c}; 11QPsalms^{d}; 11QPsalms^{e}?," in *Qumran Cave 11.2: 11Q2-18, 11Q20-31* (DJD 23; Oxford: Clarendon Press, 1998; J. A. Sanders, *The Dead Sea Psalms Scroll* (Ithaca, NY: Cornell University Press, 1967); idem, "Non-Masoretic Psalms," in *The Dead Sea Scrolls: Pseudepigraphic and Non-Masoretic Psalms and Prayers*, ed. J. H. Charlesworth et al. (PTSDSS 4A; Tübingen: Mohr Siebeck; Louisville: Westminster John Knox, 1997) 155-215; idem, *The Psalms Scroll of Qumrân Cave 11 (11QPs^{a})* (DJD 4; Oxford: Clarendon Press, 1965); E. M. Schuller, *Non-Canonical Psalms from Qumran: A Pseudepigraphic Collection* (HSS 28; Atlanta: Scholars Press, 1986); P. W. Skehan, E. Ulrich and P. W. Flint, "The Cave 4 Psalms Scrolls," in *Qumran Cave 4.11: Psalms to Chronicles*, ed. E. Ulrich (DJD 16; Oxford: Clarendon Press, 2000); S. Talmon, "The Psalms Scrolls from Masada," in *Masada VI: The Yigael Yadin Excavations 1963-1965, Final Reports. Hebrew Fragments from Masada*, ed. S. Talmon and Y. Yadin (Jerusalem: Israel Exploration Society, 1999); Y. Yadin, "Another Fragment (E) of the Psalms Scroll from Qumran Cave 11 (11QPs^{a})," *Text* 5 (1966) 1–10 + plates I–V. **Studies.** W. H. Brownlee, "The Significance of 'David's Compositions,'" *RevQ* 20 (1966) 569–74; M. Chyutin, "The Redaction of the Qumranic and the Traditional Book of Psalms as a Calendar," *RevQ* 63 (1994) 367–95; P. W. Flint, *The Dead Sea Psalms Scrolls and the Book of Psalms* (STDJ 17; Leiden: E. J. Brill, 1997) 135–241; D. Flusser, "Psalms, Hymns and Prayers," in *Jewish Writings of the Second Temple Period*, ed. M. E. Stone (CRINT 2.2; Assen: Van Gorcum; Philadelphia: Fortress, 1984) 551–77; M. H. Goshen-Gottstein, "The Psalms Scroll (11QPs^{a}). A Problem of Canon and Text," *Text* 5 (1966) 22–33; M. Haran, "11QPs^{a} and the Canonical Book of Psalms," in *Minḥah le-Naḥum: Biblical and Other Studies Presented to Nahum M. Sarna in Honour of His 70th Birthday*, ed. M. Brettler and M. Fishbane (JSOTSup 154; Sheffield: Sheffield Academic Press, 1993) 93–201; M. P. Horgan, *Pesharim: Qumran Interpretations of Biblical Books* (CBQMS 8; Washington, DC: Catholic Biblical Associaiton); S. C. Pigué, "Psalms, Syriac (Apocryphal)," *ABD* 5:536–37; R. Polzin, "Notes on the Dating of the Non-Masoretic Psalms of 11QPs^{a}," *HTR* 60 (1967) 468–76; J. A. Sanders, "Psalm 154 Revisited," in *Biblische Theologie und gesellschaftlicher Wandel. Für Norbert Lohfink S.J.*, ed. G. Braulik, W.

Gross, and S. McEvenue (Freiburg: Herder, 1993) 296–306; idem, "The Qumran Psalms Scroll (11QPs[a]) Reviewed," in *On Language, Culture, and Religion: In Honor of Eugene A. Nida*, ed. M. Black and W. A. Smalley (The Hague and Paris: Mouton, 1974) 79–99; P. W. Skehan, "The Divine Name at Qumran, in the Masada Scroll, and in the Septuagint," *BIOSCS* 13 (1980) 14–44, esp. 42; idem, "A Liturgical Complex in 11QPs[a]," *CBQ* 34 (1973)195–205; idem, "Qumran and Old Testament Criticism," in *Qumrân. Sa piété, sa théologie et son milieu*, ed. M. Delcor (BETL 46; Paris and Leuven: Duculot, 1978) 163–82; M. Smith, "Psalm 151, David, Jesus, and Orpheus," *ZAW* 93 (1981) 247–53; S. Talmon, "Pisqah Be'emsa' Pasuq and 11QPs[a]," *Text* 5 (1966) 11–21; idem, "The Textual Study of the Bible—A New Outlook," in *Qumran and the History of the Biblical Text*, ed. F. M. Cross and S. Talmon (Cambridge, MA: Harvard University Press, 1975) 321–400; E. Ulrich, "The Bible in the Making: The Scriptures at Qumran," in *The Community of the Renewed Covenant: The Notre Dame Symposium on the Dead Sea Scrolls*, ed. E. Ulrich and J. VanderKam (CJA 10; Notre Dame, IN: University of Notre Dame Press, 1994) 77–93; idem, "Multiple Literary Editions: Reflections Toward a Theory of the History of the Biblical Text," in *Current Research and Technological Developments on the Dead Sea Scrolls: Conference on the Texts from the Judean Desert, Jerusalem, 30 April 1995*, ed., D. Parry and S. Ricks (STDJ 20; Leiden: E. J. Brill, 1996) 78–105 + plates i–ii; B. Z. Wacholder, "David's Eschatological Psalter: 11QPsalms[a]," *HUCA* 59 (1988) 23–72; G. H. Wilson, *The Editing of the Hebrew Psalter* (SBLDS 76; Chico, CA: Scholars Press, 1985). P. W. Flint

PSALMS OF SOLOMON

Composed in Hebrew in the first century B.C., these Jewish poems have been assembled into a collection of eighteen so-called psalms. Today they are available only in Greek and Syriac translations. If *1 Baruch* 5:5-8 is dependent on *Psalms of Solomon* 11:2-5 the Greek version must have existed before the end of the first century A.D. Otherwise the earliest evidence, often overlooked, is given with the Coptic-Gnostic *Pistis Sophia*, which originated in Greek in the third century A.D. As a Jewish but not necessarily *Pharisaic source the *Psalms of Solomon* are of greatest importance, both by similarity and contrast, for NT christology, theology and anthropology.

1. Evidence of the Text
2. *Psalms of Solomon* as Poetry
3. Hebrew Forms and Jewish Content
4. Historical Allusions and Dating
5. Impact on the New Testament

1. Evidence of the Text.

Although easily accessible in volume 2 of A. Rahlfs's *Septuaginta* (2:471-89) and in part 4, fascicle 6 of *The Old Testament in Syriac* (Baars, 26 pp., between Apocryphal Psalms and *Tobit), the small collection of eighteen pseudo-Solomonic poems has never been part of any *Septuagint version or *Syriac translation of the Bible (Peshitta, etc.). Before the *editio princeps* in 1626 by the Spanish Jesuit J. L. de la Cerda (on the basis of only one Vienna MS) these so-called psalms were lost without any textual trace. There was, however, some evidence of their existence.

1.1. Canon Lists. The table of contents of the Greek Bible Codex A (Alexandrinus, fifth century A.D.; not Vaticanus [Schürer, 196]) mentions at the end—after twenty-nine NT writings, including *1 Clement* and *2 Clement*—as a kind of appendix *Psalmoi Solomōntos iē* ("Eighteen Psalms of Solomon") that must have been regarded as texts very close to the NT.

In the so-called Synopsis of Pseudo-Athanasius (sixth-seventh century A.D.) "Psalms and Odes of Solomon" appear between 1-4 Maccabees and Susanna, among the *antilegomena* ("disputed writings") of the OT.

The appendix to the Greek list of sixty canonical books (seventh century A.D.) contains *Psalmoi Solomōntos* ("Psalms of Solomon") as one of twenty-five *apokrypha* ("apocryphal writings"). This group of twenty-five NT and OT *apocrypha and pseudepigrapha is separated from nine books "outside the sixty," namely, *Wisdom of Solomon, *Sirach, 1-4 *Maccabees, Esther, *Judith and *Tobit. There might be some significance in the number of sixty ("sixty books" as a name of the Bible) even with regard to the early collections of eighteen psalms and forty-two odes (or, forty-two odes and eighteen psalms) of Solomon.

In the *Stichometria* of Patriarch Nicephorus (ninth century A.D.) "Psalms and Odes of Solomon" are again listed as one group of eight OT writings, *hosai antilegontai kai ouk ekklēsiazontai* ("which are disputed and not canonized"), in this case preceded by 1-3 Maccabees, Wisdom of

Solomon and Wisdom of Jesus Sirach and followed by Esther, Judith, Susanna and Tobit.

1.2. **Pistis Sophia.** However, since 1909, the year which saw the *editio princeps* of the Syriac *Odes and Psalms of Solomon,* another witness to the existence of the eighteen poems can be identified that is considerably earlier than Codex A. In the Coptic-Gnostic *Pistis Sophia,* which came gradually to light in the nineteenth century, there is a short quotation from the "Nineteenth Ode of Solomon," which is, however, not identical with any text of Ode 19. The only possible conclusion from this erroneous citation is that a collection of Greek psalms and odes of Solomon must have existed as early as the third century A.D. And it is far from certain whether this collection distinguished between *psalmoi* ("psalms") and *ōdai* ("odes"). That is, it is unknown at which time the specific title *Psalms* was given to the eighteen poems ascribed to the poet-king Solomon (cf. 1 Kings 5:12) and originally composed in Hebrew in the first century B.C., probably by several Jewish authors from Palestine or even Jerusalem.

*1.3. **Manuscripts.*** If the Hebrew original carried already a general heading given to it by a Jewish collector or redactor, the title might have contained the plural of *mizmōr* ("psalm"; cf. the Syriac title *mazmōrē,* "Psalms," in two of three fragments [Baars, v-vi]). It has to be noted, however, that the only two Syriac manuscripts containing larger parts of the *Psalms of Solomon* as a continuation of the *Odes of Solomon* subsume both the forty-two odes and the eighteen psalms under the title *z*ᵉ*mīrtā* ("ode"; plural *z*ᵉ*mīrātā,* "odes"). The question of whether the Syriac version is "primarily" based on a Hebrew text (so again, after Kuhn; Trafton 1985, 207; 1986, 234) or is a translation of a Greek version (cf. Begrich 1939; Holm-Nielsen, 55, "more probable") must be regarded as an open problem.

A Greek translation also produced by Jews was probably "available by the mid first century A.D." (Wright, 640). In its general title the LXX term *psalmoi* ("psalms") would have been used, although in three of the eleven Greek manuscripts known today the superscription is *sophia Solomōntos* ("Wisdom of Solomon"; cf. Trafton 1985, 6-9; Hann 1982, 3-6). Part of this confusion goes back to the secondary titles of *Psalms of Solomon* 2—18 (a title of 1 is not preserved). Only 2, 3, 5, 13, 15, 17 and 18 show *psalmos* ("psalm") in their respective superscriptions, whereas all extant single titles contain the name of Solomon. In the headings of 15 and 17 an additional *meta ōdēs* ("with song") is found, and *hymnos* ("hymn") serves as superscription of 10, 14 and 16 (cf. Lattke 1991, 116). All these musicological or hymnological terms are as insignificant as the rhetorical term *dialogē* ("conver-sation") appearing in the title of 4 (one MS reads the traditional *psalmos,* "psalm"). It is difficult to explain why neither of them has been used for 6—9 and 11—13.

2. Psalms of Solomon as Poetry.

With the exception of 5, 10 and 14, there is some further indication of the contents in the psalms' headings. However, these key words are more or less arbitrary and have apparently been taken from the total of some six hundred lines, most of which are without any meter. The only poetical device clearly recognizable in all eighteen poems of different length (and without strophical subdivisions) is *parallelismus membrorum* in various forms, namely, antithetical, synonymous and synthetical parallelism (cf. Eissfeldt, 57). As to future research, a "comprehensive critical edition of the *Pss. Sol.,* using both the Greek and the Syriac, is clearly needed," and a "sensitive reading of the *Pss. Sol.* as poetry, rather than history or theology, would be in order" (Trafton 1994, 12-13). With R. B. Wright's new edition of the Greek text still awaiting publication, the following outline of historical and theological issues is still dependent on O. von Gebhardt's textual-critical edition of 1895 (from then only eight MSS) forming also the basis of Rahlfs's text.

3. Hebrew Forms and Jewish Content.

In all of their redaction-critical stages (Schüpphaus, 138-53; Trafton 1994, 6) these poems are dependent on well-established Hebrew forms such as "lament," "praise" and "thanksgiving" (Trafton 1994, 5-6) and to an even larger extent on the contents of earlier Jewish texts, including wisdom literature (cf. index of OT passages and extracanonical writings in Holm-Nielsen, 110-12; Jansen, 9-55). Bearing this in mind one has to be very cautious in drawing conclusions with regard to historical and geographical details. Apart from the name of the holy city Jerusalem (*Pss. Sol.* 2:3, 11, 13, 19, 22; 8:4, 15, 17-22; 9:1 [v.l.]; 11:1-2, 7-8; 17:14, 22, 30) and "the mountains of Egypt" (*Pss. Sol.* 2:26) there is hardly anything of a concrete and direct nature in the so-called psalms that deals mainly with God's righteousness, justice and help and the contrast between the *dikaios* ("righteous") and the *hamartōlos* ("sinner") (*Pss. Sol.* 2:34 and passim, also in different terms, cf. Trafton *ABD*, 116). Biblical names such as Abraham (*Pss. Sol.* 9:9; 18:3), Jacob (*Pss. Sol.* 7:10; 15:1) and David (*Pss. Sol.* 17:4, 6, 21) appear along with *Israel (*Pss. Sol.* 7:8; 8:26, 28, 34; 9:1-2, 8, 11; 10:5-8; 11:1, 6-9; 12:6; 14:5; 16:3; 17:4, 21, 42, 44-45; 18:1, 3, 5), demonstrating nothing else than the self-understanding of Jews over against the *ethnē* ("Gentiles," *Pss. Sol.* 1:8; 2:2, 6, 19; 7:3, 6; 8:23, 30; 9:2, 9; 17:14-15, 22, 29).

4. Historical Allusions and Dating.

4.1. Pompey. However, there are a few passages within the monotonous flow of lamenting ethics, thanksgiving hope and praising although "unstable theodicy" (Wright, 643) that can be interpreted as encoded allusions to certain historical circumstances, events and sufferings, thus allowing a more specific dating of at least some parts of the whole collection whose first piece seems to be incomplete (Holm-Nielsen, 62). The violent *hamartōlos* ("sinner") of *Psalms of Solomon* 2:1 is probably the Roman conqueror *Pompey (cf. *Pss. Sol.* 2:24), who invaded Jerusalem in 63 B.C. and was killed in Egypt in 48 B.C. Therefore it is also highly probable that *Psalms of Solomon* 2:25-29 is an allusion to the shameful death of Pompey, who wanted to "be Lord of land and sea" (*Pss. Sol.* 2:29), not understanding that *theos* ("God") is *basileus epi tōn ouranōn*, "king over the heavens" (*Pss. Sol.* 2:29-30; cf. Lattke, 85-86; addition in the Syriac translation: "and over the earth"). References to "the sound of war" (see also *Pss. Sol.* 1:2), the "one who attacks in strength" and the murderous defilement of Jerusalem in *Psalms of Solomon* 8:1-22 (esp. 1, 15, 22) also remind the reader of "the capture of Jerusalem and the Temple by Pompey" (Wright 658).

4.2. Herodian Era. More difficult and controversial is the case of *Psalms of Solomon* 17, "commonly considered to describe (1) the succession of the sinful *Hasmoneans, (2) their punishment by the hand of Pompey, who was himself a sinner, and (3) from vs. 21 onward, the (future) Davidic Messiah, who will remove Pompey and restore Israel to its glorious state" (Tromp, 346). This view has recently been challenged by J. Tromp and K. Atkinson, who date this most important messianological/christological psalm to the early Herodian era (37-4 B.C.). While the former thinks of "the Parthians" who "invaded Palestine in 40 B.C.E." (Tromp, 360-61), the latter argues "that Ps. Sol. 17 actually describes the siege of Jerusalem by Herod the Great and the Roman general Sosius in 37 B.C.E., and Herod's subsequent extermination of the remaining Hasmonean descendants" (Atkinson 1996, 314). This alternative hypothesis "places the writing of Ps. Sol. 17 within the narrow confines between 37-30 B.C.E." (Atkinson 1996, 322; but cf. already Begrich 1931, 90; Braun 1961, 1342; Eissfeldt, 612).

4.3. Psalms of the Pharisees? It has often been assumed "that the *Pss. Sol.* are the classical source of Pharisaism" (Trafton 1994, 7; cf. Ryle and James; Kittel, 128; Beer, 236; Gray, 630; esp. Schüpphaus, 127-37; *see* Pharisees). However, "voices have been raised in protest against interpreting all the poems as Pharisaic attacks on the Sadducees," and more than once warnings have been issued against too great a confidence in tracing them to Pharisaic circles, "the more so since the Psalms of Solomon show many points of contact with the Qumran texts" (Eissfeldt, 613; cf. Begrich 1931, 91; Braun 1961, 1343; O'Dell; Wright, 641-42, 648-49). In the 1980s a new debate flared up about the community and the *Sitz im Leben* of the Jewish poems (cf. Trafton 1994, 7-8). According to R. R. Hann (1988), the movement that composed them might have had its deepest roots in "a second-century proto-Essene protest of disenfranchised priests against the Hasmonean high priesthood" (Trafton 1994, 7; *see* Essenes). The other extreme to the drawing of sharp trajectories is a position that goes beyond the "conventional Pharisee—Sadducee—Essene categorization" and ascribes the composition to a Jewish "school" of "otherwise 'unknown' groups" (Brock, 651).

5. Impact on the New Testament.

5.1. The Messiah of Psalms 17 and 18. As indicated above, psalm 17 (with one hundred lines, the longest one) is "an especially important witness to pre-Christian Jewish messianism" (Trafton *ABD*, 116; see also Trafton 1994, 8-10; *see* Messianism). It must be seen together with 18:1-9, which is followed by the traditional musical and cultic term *diapsalma* ("pause," as after *Pss. Sol.* 17:29; cf. Eissfeldt, 611) and a short hymnological appendix (*Pss. Sol.* 18:10-12; cf. Wright, 641).

Although the poem emphasizes by *inclusio* that the Lord (God) himself is *basileus hēmōn* ("our king") for ever and ever (*Pss. Sol.* 17:1, 46; cf. 17:3, 34), it also speaks about David's kingship over Israel (*Pss. Sol.* 17:4) and prays for a new *basileus* ("king") as a son of David, *basileusai* ("to rule") over Israel (*Pss. Sol.* 17:21) and *katharisai* ("to purge") Jerusalem from Gentiles (*Pss. Sol.* 17:22; cf. 17:30; 18:5). This king will gather *laon hagion* ("a holy people") and judge *phylas* ("the tribes") of his own sanctified *laos* ("people," 17:26). Like a new Joshua (Holm-Nielsen, 103) he will distribute the tribes of Israel upon the land purged of foreigners (*Pss. Sol.* 17:28). This contradicts the vision that *ethnē* ("nations") will come from the ends of the earth to see his *doxa* ("glory," *Pss. Sol.* 17:31). The appointed king will be *dikaios* ("righteous, just") and *didaktos hypo theou* ("taught by God"). Then all will be *hagioi* ("holy," cf. 1 Pet 2:9), and *basileus autōn* ("their king") will be *christos kyrios* ("Messiah, Lord," *Pss. Sol.* 17:32; cf. relevant NT passages in Fitzmyer, 330).

There is no need to regard the apocalyptic title "Lord Messiah" (Wright, 667, 669; Prigent, 989 ["le Messie Seigneur"]; cf. Lk 2:11) as a Christian emendation and to change it against the evidence of the Syriac and nine Greek manuscripts to *christos kyriou* ("Messiah of the Lord," Rahlfs, 488; Holm-Nielsen, 104). Although the expected Messiah shall be *christos kyriou* ("Messiah of the Lord [God = Yahweh]," *Pss. Sol.* 18:7; cf. 18:5-6, 8, and secondary superscription of 18), he himself can be called *kyrios* ("Lord" = *ʾādôn* in Heb, *mārjā* in Aramaic/Syriac; cf. Fitzmyer, 330; Hann 1985, 623, 625). The ambivalence is similar to the use of the title *basileus* ("king") for both God (Yahweh) and his appointed-anointed one.

5.2. Righteousness and Mercy. Apart from the complex issue of eschatological messianism (cf. Braun 1950-51, 42-50 = 1967, 56-64) and a few passages that might have influenced NT authors and redactors, the most important NT background problem is a fair understanding and interpretation of "righteousness" (cf. Trafton 1994, 10-12), which is partly dependent on the question of authorship. The frequent noun *dikaiosynē* ("righteousness," cf. *Pss. Sol.* 1:2-3; 2:15; 4:24; 5:17; 8:6, 24-26; 9:2, 5; 17:19, 26, 40; 18:7-8), the equally frequent adjective *dikaios* ("righteous," cf. *Pss. Sol.* 2:18, 32, 35; 3:3-7; 4:8; 5:1; 8:9; 9:2; 10:3, 5; 13:7-11; 14:9; 15:6-7; 16:15), as well as the much less frequent verb *dikaioō* ("to justify," cf., with direct object in brackets, *Pss. Sol.* 2:15 [God]; 3:5 [Lord]; 4:8 [God's judgment]; 8:7 [God in his judgments]; 8:26 [God's name]; cf. also the passive, with God as subject, in *Pss. Sol.* 8:23 and 9:2), are primarily forensic terms and must be seen in context with other synonyms and the concept of God's mercy (cf. Braun 1950-51 = 1967, passim).

5.3. Further Impact. In addition to NT parallels listed elsewhere (cf. Braun 1950-51, 54 = 1967, 69; Holm-Nielsen, 112; Wright, 651-70), attention may be drawn to two passages that might also have some bearing on NT texts. The statement of *Psalms of Solomon* 15:7 that *limos kai rhomphaia kai thanatos apo dikaiōn makran* ("famine and sword and death shall be far from the righteous") may have influenced Paul's wording of Romans 8:35-39. And the incestuous phenomenon of *Psalms of Solomon* 8:9 that *hyios meta mētros kai patēr meta thygatros synephyronto* ("son with mother and father with daughter mingled sexually") may in part explain the harsh and far-reaching reaction of Paul in 1 Corinthians 5:1-5 (cf. also Lane, passim, on Paul).

See also APOCRYPHA AND PSEUDEPIGRAPHA; MESSIANISM; PHARISEES; POMPEY.

BIBLIOGRAPHY. K. Atkinson, "Herod the Great, Sosius and the Siege of Jerusalem (37 B.C.E.) in Psalm of Solomon 17," *NovT* 38 (1996) 313-22; idem, "On the Herodian Origin of Militant Davidic Messianism at Qumran: New Light from *Psalm of Solomon* 17," *JBL* 118 (1999) 435-460; idem, "Toward a Redating of the Psalms of Solomon: Implications for Understanding the 'Sitz im Leben' of an Unknown Jewish sect," *JSP* 17 (1998) 95-112; W. Baars, "Psalms of Solomon," in *The Old Testament in Syriac* (Leiden: E. J. Brill, 1972) 4.6; G. Beer, "Pseudepigraphen des Alten Testaments," *RE* (3d ed., 1905) 16:229-65; J. Begrich, "Salomo-Psalmen," *RGG* (2d ed., 1931) 5:90-91; idem, "Der Text der Psalmen Salomos," *ZNW* 38 (1939) 131-64; H. Braun, "Vom Erbarmen Gottes über den Gerechten: Zur Theologie der Psalmen Salomos," *ZNW* 43 (1950-51) 1-54 = *Gesammelte Studien zum Neuen Testament und seiner Umwelt* (2d ed.; Tübingen: Mohr Siebeck, 1967) 8-65; idem, "Salomo-Psalmen," *RGG* (3d ed.; 1961) 5:1342-43; S. P. Brock, "The Psalms of Solomon," in *The Apocryphal Old Testament,* ed. H. F. D. Sparks (Oxford: Clarendon Press, 1984)

649-82; O. Eissfeldt, *The Old Testament: An Introduction* (Oxford: Blackwell, 1974); J. A. Fitzmyer, "κυριος," *EDNT* 2:328-31; O. von Gebhardt, ed., *Psalmoi Solomōntos: Die Psalmen Salomos, zum ersten Male mit Benutzung der Athoshandschriften und des Codex Casanatensis* (TU 13.2; Leipzig: Hinrichs, 1895); G. B. Gray, "The Psalms of Solomon," *APOT* 2:625-52; R. R. Hann, "Christos Kyrios in PsSol 17.32: 'The Lord's Anointed' Reconsidered," *NTS* 31 (1985) 620-27; idem, "The Community of the Pious: The Social Setting of the Psalms of Solomon," *SR* 17 (1988) 169-89; idem, *The Manuscript History of the Psalms of Solomon* (SBLSCS 13; Chico, CA: Scholars Press, 1982); R. Harris and A. Mingana, eds., *The Odes and Psalms of Solomon* (Manchester: Manchester University Press, 1916, 1920) vols. 1-2; S. Holm-Nielsen, *Die Psalmen Salomos* (JSHRZ 4.2; Gütersloh: Gerd Mohn, 1977); H. L. Jansen, *Die spätjüdische Psalmendichtung: Ihr Entstehungskreis und ihr "Sitz im Leben": Eine literaturgeschichtlich-soziologische Untersuchung* (SNVAO.HF 1937; no. 3; Oslo: Jacob Dybwad, 1937); R. Kittel, "Die Psalmen Salomos," *APAT* 2 (1900 = 2d repr. 1962) 127-48; K. G. Kuhn, *Die älteste Textgestalt der Psalmen Salomos: Insbesondere auf Grund der syrischen Übersetzung neu untersucht* (BWANT 73; Stuttgart: Kohlhammer, 1937); W. L. Lane, "Paul's Legacy from Pharisaism: Light from the Psalms of Solomon," *ConJ* 8 (1982) 130-38; M. Lattke, *Hymnus: Materialien zu einer Geschichte der antiken Hymnologie* (NTOA 19; Freiburg: Universitätsverlag; Göttingen: Vandenhoeck & Ruprecht, 1991); idem, "On the Jewish Background of the Synoptic Concept 'The Kingdom of God,'" in *The Kingdom of God in the Teaching of Jesus,* ed. B. Chilton (IRT 5; Philadelphia: Fortress, 1984) 72-91; idem, "Salomo III. Apokryphe Schriften," *LTK*[3] 8:1492; G. T. Milazzo, "Psalms of Solomon," in *Dictionary of Biblical Interpretation,* ed. J. H. Hays (2 vols.; Nashville: Abingdon, 1999) 2:329-331; J. O'Dell, "The Religious Background of the Psalms of Solomon (Re-evaluated in the Light of the Qumran Texts)," *RevQ* 3 (1961-62) 241-57; P. Prigent, "Psaumes de Salomon," in *La Bible, Ecrits Intertestamentaires,* ed. A. Dupont-Sommer et al. (BP; Paris: Gallimard, 1987) 945-92; A. Rahlfs, ed., *Septuaginta: Id est Vetus Testamentum graece iuxta LXX interpretes* (ed. octava; Stuttgart: Württembergische Bibelanstalt, 1965) vols. 1-2; H. E. Ryle and M. R. James, *Psalmoi Solomōntos: Psalms of the Pharisees, Commonly Called the Psalms of Solomon* (Cambridge: Cambridge University Press, 1891); J. Schröter, "Gerechtigkeit und Barmherzigkeit: Das Gottesbild der Psalmen Salomos in seinem Verhältnis zu Qumran und Paulus," *NTS* 44 (1998) 566-67; J. Schüpphaus, *Die Psalmen Salomos: Ein Zeugnis Jerusalemer Theologie und Frömmigkeit in der Mitte des vorchristlichen Jahrhunderts* (ALGHJ 7; Leiden: E. J. Brill, 1977); E. Schürer, *The History of the Jewish People in the Age of Jesus Christ (175 B.C.—A.D. 135),* rev. and ed. G. Vermes, F. Millar and M. Goodman (3 vols.; Edinburgh: T & T Clark, 1973-87) vol. 3.1; J. L. Trafton, "The *Psalms of Solomon* in Recent Research," *JSP* 12 (1994) 3-19; idem, "The Psalms of Solomon: New Light from the Syriac Version?" *JBL* 105 (1986) 227-37; idem, "Solomon, Psalms of," *ABD* 6:115-17; idem, *The Syriac Version of the Psalms of Solomon: A Critical Evaluation* (SBLSCS 11; Atlanta: Scholars Press, 1985); J. Tromp, "The Sinners and the Lawless in Psalm of Solomon 17," *NovT* 35 (1993) 344-61; M. Winninge, *Sinners and the Righteous: A Comparative Study of the Psalms of Solomon and Paul's Letters* (ConBNT 26; Stockholm: Almquist & Wiksell, 1995); R. B. Wright, "Psalms of Solomon (First Century B.C.): A New Translation and Introduction," *OTP* 2:639-70.

M. Lattke

PSEUDO-DANIEL (4Q243-245). *See* PRAYER OF NABONIDUS (4Q242) AND PSEUDO-DANIEL (4Q243-245).

PSEUDO-EUPOLEMUS. *See* JEWISH LITERATURE: HISTORIANS AND POETS

PSEUDO-EZEKIEL. *See* PSEUDO-PROPHETS (4Q385-388, 390-391)

PSEUDONYMITY AND PSEUDEPIGRAPHY

Pseudonymity and pseudepigraphy denote the practice of ascribing written works to someone other than the author—that is, the works in question are falsely (*pseud-*) named (*onoma,* "name") or attributed (*epigraphos,* "superscription"). This must not be confused with anonymity, in which no formal claim is made (e.g., Matthew, John and Hebrews are all formally anonymous). Similarly one must distinguish between pseudepigraphical and *apocryphal works. The word *apocrypha* is tied rather more to notions of canon than to notions of authenticity. The matter of false attribution played little or no part in the identification of the fourteen or fifteen books or parts of books that constitute the Apocrypha, most of which Roman Catholics view as deuterocanonical. A book is either canonical or apocryphal (or, for Roman Catholics, deuterocanonical), regardless of whether or not it is pseudepigraphical.

Although pseudonymity and pseudepigraphy are today used almost synonymously, only the latter term has been traced back to antiquity (as early as an inscription from the second century B.C., found at Priene). Apart from the intrinsic interest of the subject—by what criteria do scholars decide that a document makes false claims regarding its authorship?—its bearing on NT interpretation arises from the fact that a majority of contemporary scholars hold that some of the NT books are pseudonymous. The list of books varies considerably, but a broad consensus would label Ephesians and the Pastoral Epistles (attributed to Paul) pseudepigraphical, as well as 2 Peter (attributed to Peter). Some would add other books: Colossians, 2 Thessalonians, 1 Peter.

1. Extrabiblical Evidence
2. The Stance of the Church Fathers
3. Evidence Internal to the New Testament Documents
4. Some Contemporary Theories

1. Extrabiblical Evidence.

1.1. Preliminary Observations. Given the broadest definition, pseudonymity is a more extensive phenomenon than some have thought. It embraces every false claim of authorship, whether for good motive or ill, and whether advanced by the real author or by some later historical accident. It includes every instance of an author adopting, for whatever reason, a nom de plum—Mary Ann Evans writing under the name of George Eliot or the three Brontë sisters (Charlotte, Emily and Anne) publishing their poems under the title *Poems by Currier, Ellis and Acton Bell,* or the English scholar Gervase Fen writing detective fiction under the name of Edmund Crispin. According to Galen, a learned physician from the second century A.D., literary forgeries first circulated in large numbers when *Alexandria and Pergamum began a race to outdo each other by increasing the number of volumes in their respective libraries (*see* Alexandrian Library): the *Ptolemies of Egypt and King Eumenes of Pergamum offered large sums to acquire copies of the works of ancient authors. Among other things, Galen feels outraged and betrayed by the interpolations and corruptions introduced into the medical works he and Hippocrates had written (in Hippocrates *Nat. Hom.* 1.42).

At this juncture it is vital to distinguish between pseudepigraphical works and literary forgeries (Metzger, 4). A literary forgery is a work written or modified with the intent to deceive. All literary forgeries are pseudepigraphical, but not all pseudepigrapha are literary forgeries. There is a substantial class of pseudepigraphical writings that, in the course of their transmission, somehow became associated with some figure or other. These connections between a text and an ancient figure, however fallacious, were judgments made with the best will in the world. We do not know how the commentaries of Pelagius on Paul came to be associated with the name of Jerome (who violently opposed Pelagius), but that is what happened. Most hold that Lobon of Argos wrote the *Hymn to Poseidon* in the third century B.C., even though the hymn is widely attributed to Arion; but it is doubtful that Lobon himself had anything to do with the attribution. The reason this distinction is important is that debates over the authenticity of NT books are tied up with the motives of actual authors, since the texts are so early and so stable that the putative author's name is there from the beginning. For the purposes of this article, then, it will be well to focus only on cases where demonstrable intent is involved and thus to exclude all pseudepigrapha that have become such owing to nothing more than the irretrievable accidents of history.

The motives of pseudepigraphers, ancient and modern, have been highly diverse and include the following. (1) Sometimes literary forgeries have been crafted out of pure malice. According to Pausanias (*Descr.* 6.18.2-6) and Josephus (*Ag. Ap.* 1.24 §221), in the fourth century B.C. Anaximenes of Lampsacus destroyed the reputation of a contemporary historian, Theopompus of Chios, by writing, under the name of his rival, horrible invectives against three Greek cities (Athens, Sparta and Thebes) and circulating them. Eusebius (*Hist. Eccl.* 9.5.1) reports that in the fourth century the *Acts of Pilate* began to circulate (possibly written by the apostate Theotecnus), full of bitter slanders against the moral character of Jesus. In modern times, czarist Russia produced the "Protocols of the Learned Elders of Zion."

(2) More commonly, as we have already seen, literary forgeries were prompted by promise of financial payment.

(3) Sometimes the pseudepigrapher used an ancient name to gain credence for his writing in order to support a position he knew to be false. According to Strabo (*Geog.* 9.1.10), in the sixth century B.C. either Solon or Pisistratus inserted a verse in Homer's *Iliad* (book B, line 258) in order to support the Athenian claim to the island of Salamis. Herodotus (*Hist.* 7.6) says that Onomacritus was banished from Athens when it was shown he had interpolated a passage into the Oracles of Musaeus predicting that the islands off Lemnos would sink into the sea. This third motive has some overtones of the first.

(4) Similarly the pseudepigrapher sometimes used an ancient name to gain credence for his writing in order to support a position he judged to be true. This was especially the case in ancient schools in which the founder was highly venerated. Very few of the *Neo-Pythagoreans published their works under their own names. They attributed them to Pythagorus himself, even though he had been dead for centuries (so Iamblichus, c. A.D. 250-325: *De Vita Pythagorica* 198, following Deubner's edition). In the sixth century A.D. several works appeared claiming to be written by Dionysius the Areopagite (cf. Acts 17:34), though drawing on much later Neo-Platonic argumentation.

(5) A more idiosyncratic case of the same thing has occasionally occurred when an individual has ostensibly hidden his or her own name out of modesty, using the name of another. Perhaps the most famous instance is that of an encyclical that began to circulate about A.D. 440, ostensibly written by someone who identified himself as "Timothy, least of the servants of God." Bishop Salonius guessed the author was Salvian, a priest in Marseilles. Without admitting anything, Salvian responded to the bishop's sharp queries by saying that he thought authors, out of humility and modesty, might be justified in using the name of another, so as not to seek glory for themselves (cf. Haefner). One may perhaps be excused for thinking this is a trifle disingenuous. It is a strange modesty that thinks one's own writings are so good that they could and should be attributed to an ancient biblical hero.

One easily imagines that this motive runs into another: (6) A deep desire to get published and be widely read, for both personal and ideological reasons, doubtless characterizes more authors than the Brontë sisters and may be the motive behind the motive of Salvian.

(7) More difficult to assign are the substantial numbers of pseudepigraphical writings that belong to specific genres. Doubtless more than one of the preceding motives were involved. But it is difficult to overlook what might almost be called a genre incentive. In the post-Aristotle period, the rise of the great Attic orators generated high interest in *rhetoric and oratory. Students were taught to compose speeches based on models left by the ancient orators. The most skillful of these were doubtless difficult to distinguish from the originals. This drifted over into the reconstruction, by historians, of speeches that their subjects probably would have made (in the view of the historians). Some historians, of course, were more reflective about such practices than others (cf. Thucydides *Hist.* 1.22). L. Alexander has shown that from Isocrates on, one can distinguish between a more scientific historiography and a looser, more creative form—and Luke, at least (she insists), fits into the former category.

Further, if complex motives were involved in the creation of pseudonymous speeches, the same can be said of *letters. At least in the classical period, great leaders and thinkers were credited with important and voluminous correspondence. One hundred forty-eight letters are attributed to the sixth-century B.C. tyrant Phalaris of Acragas (= Agrigentum), portraying him as a gentle and kind man and as a patron of the arts—though since the end of the seventeenth century scholars have known that these letters were almost certainly composed in the second century A.D., probably by a Sophist (see the work of Bentley). The phenomenon is less common in *Hellenistic times, but see below.

(8) Finally, several bodies of writings are ascribed to some philosophical-religious-mythical figure, especially Orpheus, the Sibyl and Hermes Trismegistus (see esp. Sint, Speyer and some essays in Brox).

1.2. Jewish Examples. Jewish literature evinces a fairly high occurrence of pseudepigraphical literature from about the middle of the third century B.C. to the third century A.D., much of it belonging to the genre of *apocalyptic (broadly defined). One thinks of the **Psalms of Solomon, 1 Enoch, 2 Enoch, 3 Enoch* (*see* Enoch, Books of), the works of the Ezra cycle (e.g., 4 Ezra; *see* Esdras, Books of), the **Treatise of Shem,* the **Apocalypse of Zephaniah,* the **Apocalypse of Abraham,* the *Apocalypse of Adam* (*see* Adam and Eve, Literature Concerning) and many more. We may include here the various testaments, most of which have apocalyptic sections (e.g., **Testaments of the Twelve Patriarchs,* **Testament of Job,* **Testament of Moses, Testament of Solomon).* Yet other genres are not unrepresented (e.g., *Wisdom of Solomon). Some works are of such mixed genre they are variously classified. The **Sibylline Oracles,* for example, appears to be made up of a strange mix of pagan oracles from various countries, Jewish writings from a wide spread of dates and Christian moralizing interpolations—yet all the while the document maintains the claim that this conglomeration is the utterance of the Sibyl, an ancient prophetess, sometimes represented as the daughter-in-law of Noah. This arrangement is transparently designed to gain credence for the oracles as genuine *prophecies.

The wide variety of expansions of OT narratives are not normally pseudepigraphical, but some of the expansions that are also *prayers must be placed in that category: *Prayer of Manasseh, *Prayer of Joseph, Odes of Solomon* (*see* Psalms of Solomon). Occasionally a later, nonbiblical, literary figure finds his name forged: today's scholars read not only *Philo but *Pseudo-Philo (first century A.D., like the real Philo).

Examples of pseudepigraphical letters from this milieu are harder to come by. The two cited by everyone are *Epistle of *Aristeas* and *Epistle of Jeremy,* neither of which is really a letter.

1.3. Early Christian Examples. About the middle of the second century A.D., pseudonymous Christian works began to multiply, often associated with a great Christian leader. We are not here concerned with works that purport to tell us about esteemed Christian figures without making claims as to authorship but only with those that are clearly pseudepigraphical. Some of these are apocalypses (e.g., the *Apocalypse of Peter,* the *Apocalypse of Paul);* some are gospels (e.g., *Gospel of Peter; Gospel of Thomas,* which is really no gospel but mostly a collection of sayings attributed to Jesus; *see* Apocryphal Gospels). Several are letters claiming to be written by Paul: *3 Corinthians, Epistle to the Alexandrians, Epistle to the Laodiceans* (*see* Apocryphal Acts and Epistles). The latter was almost certainly written to provide the document mentioned in Colossians 4:16. It is a brief and rough compilation of Pauline phrases and passages, primarily from Philippians. The largest collection of pseudonymous epistles from the early period of the church's history is the set of fourteen letters of correspondence between the apostle Paul and *Seneca. They are referred to by both Jerome (*Vir.* 12) and Augustine (*Ep.* 153). The *Muratorian Canon* (c. A.D. 170-200) refers to the *Epistle to the Alexandrians* and the *Epistle to the Laodiceans* as "both forged in Paul's name" (*Mur. Can.* 64-65), and so the *canon will not allow them to be included. This last observation leads to the next heading.

2. The Stance of the Church Fathers.

All sides agree that pseudepigraphy was common in the ancient world. Nevertheless, in Jewish and Christian circles it was *not* so common in epistles—and it is in the epistolary genre where the subject impinges on the NT documents. But does pseudonymity occur in the NT?

From a mere listing of pseudepigraphical sources, one might unwittingly infer that no one cared. But that is not the case. "Both Greeks and Romans show great concern to maintain the authenticity of their collections of writings from the past, but the sheer number of the pseudepigrapha made the task difficult" (Donelson, 11). Similarly J. Duff: "It simply cannot be maintained that in the pagan culture surrounding the early Christians there was no sense of literary propriety, or no concern over authenticity" (Duff, 278). Referring both to Christian and non-Christian sources, L. R. Donelson goes so far as to say, "No one ever seems to have accepted a document as religiously and philosophically prescriptive which was known to be forged. I do not know a single example" (Donelson, 11).

This is virulently the case in early Christian circles. We have already observed the stance of the *Muratorian Canon* and of Bishop Salonius. When Asian elders examined the author of an *Acts of Paul,* which included the pseudonymous *3 Corinthians,* they condemned him for presuming to write in Paul's name. When about A.D. 200 Serapion, bishop of Antioch, first read *Gospel of Peter,* he thought it might be genuine. When further investigation led him to conclude it was not, he rejected it and provided a rationale for the church of Rhossus in Cilicia: "For we, brothers, receive both Peter and the other apostles as Christ. But pseudepigrapha in their name we reject, as men of experience, knowing that we did not receive such [from the tradition]" (Eusebius *Hist. Eccl.* 6.12.3; cf. 2.25.4-7—widely cited in the literature). Tertullian is blistering against the Asian elder who confesses that he wrote *Acts of Paul and Thecla.* All the elder's protestations that he had done so out of great love for the apostle did not prevent him from being deposed from the ministry (Tertullian *De Bapt.* 17). Similarly, when Cyril of Jerusalem provides a list of canonical books, he allows only four Gospels, for the rest are "falsely written and hurtful" (*pseudepigrapha kai blabera;* Cyril of Jerusalem *Cat.* 4.36).

I know of no exception to the evidence, which is far more extensive than this brief summary suggests. Ostensible exceptions turn out, under close inspection, to be unconvincing. For instance, M. Kiley (17-18) rightly observes that the *Muratorian Canon* attaches to its list of NT books the Wisdom of Solomon, observing that it was written by the "friends of Solomon in his honor"—which surely, he suggests, demonstrates that "at least portions of the early church were able to detect the pseudepigraphical process." But where it is clear that a "pseudepigraphical process" is observed by the fathers, the fathers universally condemn it. In this case, as Kiley himself observes in an extended footnote, the reference in the *Muratorian Canon* may not be to our Wisdom of Solomon but to the book of Proverbs, which was at that time sometimes referred to as the Wisdom of Solomon. But in that case pseudonymity is not an issue, since the book itself frankly distinguishes various collections of proverbs by different authors.

Similarly, some have argued that Tertullian's words admit the legitimacy of at least some kinds of pseudonymity: "It is allowable that that which pupils publish should be regarded as their master's work" (Tertullian *Marc.* 4.5). But D. Guthrie has rightly shown that this is to misunderstand Tertullian. Tertullian is discussing how Peter stands behind Mark's Gospel and how Paul informs Luke's writing. He does not suggest that the church received the second Gospel as if it had been written by Peter when in fact it was written by Mark.

The view that the NT includes some pseudepigrapha was not mooted until two centuries ago (by Evanson in 1792) and became popular with the work of F. C. Baur. But so far as the evidence of the fathers goes, when they explicitly evaluated a work for its authenticity, canonicity and pseudonymity proved mutually exclusive.

3. Evidence Internal to the New Testament Documents.

All sides acknowledge that, however they are taken, the extrabiblical examples of pseudonymity cannot establish the ostensible pseudonymity of any NT document. Such material provides no more than a social world of plausibility (or implausibility!) for the acceptance of pseudepigrapha into the NT. The pseudepigraphical character of any particular document is established on other grounds: anachronisms; a high percentage of words or phrases not found in the known writings of the author; a high number of words and phrases found in the ostensible author's agreed writings but used in quite different ways; forms of thought and emphasis that seem at odds with the dominant strains of the agreed writings; and more of the same.

Although some scholars view such evidence as having no more weight than that which affects the balance of probabilities, many judge it to be so strong that there is no doubt in their minds that some NT books are pseudepigraphical (e.g. Charlesworth, Donelson, Meade, Metzger, Speyer). In some cases, those who disagree with them are dismissed as beyond the pale, unworthy and perhaps incompetent opponents. But the issues are complex and interlocking. One might usefully gain insight into the nature of the debate at its best by reading the respective commentaries on Ephesians by A. T. Lincoln and P. T. O'Brien—not only their introductions, but their exegeses wherever understanding of the text is affected by, or affects, the questions of authorship; or by reading the exchange between S. E. Porter and R. W. Wall; or standard introductions, such as those by W. G. Kümmel and Guthrie (esp. the latter's appendix C: "Epistolary Pseudepigraphy," 1011-28).

The entire complex apparatus of technical scholarship and historical criticism, not to say theology and worldview, impinge on a complex string of judgments that bear on the question of whether or not there are pseudepigrapha among the NT documents. Scholars who answer yes are inclined to argue that, say, Ephesians has far too much realized *eschatology for it to be Pauline; scholars who answer no highlight all the passages that retain futurist eschatology and argue that whatever differences that remain are nothing more than different locations on the Pauline spectrum, variously applied by the apostle himself in different ways to meet certain pastoral needs. Scholars who answer yes carefully list all the *hapax legomena* in Ephesians; scholars who answer no point out that Ephesians has no more *hapax legomena* than do some undisputed Pauline letters. Such matters cannot be addressed here, yet it is important to see that they impinge on our topic and that the evidence is spun by scholars in different ways and given very different weight.

Two other bits of internal evidence bear on the discussion. (1) The author of 2 Thessalonians is aware of forgeries made in his own name. He therefore warns his readers "not to become easily unsettled or alarmed by some prophecy, report or letter supposed to have come from us" (2 Thess 2:1-2) and provides them with some signature or token to enable them to distinguish which letters purporting to come from him were authentic and which were not (2 Tim 3:17). If the author was not Paul, as many scholars think, then our pseudonymous author is in the odd position of condemning pseudonymous authors; a literary forgery damns literary forgeries. If the author was Paul, then the apostle himself makes it clear that he is aware of pseudonymity and condemns the practice, at least when people are using his name. (2) It is clear that Paul and perhaps other NT writers used amanuenses (e.g., Rom 16:22). There is a long and complex literature about how much freedom amanuenses enjoyed in the ancient world—much as I might give my secretary detailed dictation or simply ask her to write a letter along such and such a line, which becomes mine once I have read it and signed it. These questions have a bearing on many critical debates and cannot be overlooked in discussion of, say, the authenticity of the Pastorals.

4. Some Contemporary Theories.

Some scholars are convinced that the NT contains many examples of literary forgeries and are unembarrassed by this conclusion. On this view, the pseudonymous author of 2 Peter, for instance, was trying to deceive his readers into thinking that the apostle wrote the missive (so Charlesworth): he was a hypocrite. Similarly Donelson on the Pastorals: the pseudonymous author, in "the interest of deception . . . fabricated all the personal notes, all the fine moments of deep piety, and all the careless but effective commonplaces in the letter. . . . [He] is quite self-consciously employing pseudonymity in order to deceive" (24). W. A. Meeks on Colossians is similar.

On the other side are those who similarly point out how often deception plays a role in pseudepigraphy but recall how the church universally rejected any hint of such deception (e.g., Ellis). This is not to deny the complexity of motives that stand behind the various forms of pseudepigraphy lightly sketched above. It is to say that the letters of the NT, where pseudonymity is alleged to have taken place, are not educational exercises designed to ape the rhetorical styles of Attic orators. Nor are they writings that belong to a certain school of thought with a great but deceased head (whether Paul or Peter): the NT documents make concrete claims that the apostle is the author. Rather, the nature of the ostensibly pseudonymous claim is such that we must conclude that if the documents are pseudonymous, the writers intended to deceive in a way that is morally reprehensible—and given the nature of the documents, this is not credible. Thus in Ephesians, the author refers to his earlier ministry, written and oral (Eph 3:3-4), his chains, his arrangement of the ministry of other of Paul's men (e.g., Tychicus, Eph 6:21-22). He exhorts his readers to pray for his (Paul's!) needs (Eph 6:19-20), when, on the assumptions of pseudonymity, the apostle was already dead. Yet he also exhorts his readers to put off falsehood and to speak truthfully (Eph 4:25; cf. also 4:15, 24; 5:9; 6:14). Similar things can be said about all the ostensibly pseudepigraphical works in the NT. It seems better to take the documents at face value, respect the opinion and care of the church fathers in this regard and read the historical-critical evidence for pseudonymity with historical-critical discernment.

In recent years several mediating positions have been advanced. K. Aland and others have argued that the Holy Spirit breached the gap from ostensible author to real author. Provided the Spirit inspired the text, what difference does it make who the human author was? But this solution is awkward. It ignores the widespread recognition within earliest Christianity that there was such a thing as false prophecy. Worse, it overlooks that these "inspired" prophets were making historical claims that were either true or not true.

D. G. Meade argues that the most believable background to NT pseudepigraphy is neither the body of Greco-Roman parallels nor the corpus of Second Temple Jewish pseudepigraphy but the process within Jewish writing whereby an original deposit (oral or written) has been enlarged upon, with all the later material being attributed to the earliest author. This pattern, he argues, began within the OT itself: Isaiah, the Solomonic corpus, Daniel. But in every case the ostensible parallels break down. On Meade's assumptions, the prophecy of Isaiah of Jerusalem was enlarged by contributions made more than a century later by others who followed in his train. But Ephesians or 2 Thessalonians or the Pastorals are not additions to a book, additions that seek to make contemporary the prophetic word of someone long dead. They are independent documents, written, even under Meade's assumptions, within a decade or so of the apostle's death. Nor is there anything like the personal claims and historical reminiscences of Ephesians or the Pastorals in Isaiah 40 and following chapters. Meade's theory sounds like an attempt to make the results work out after one has already bought into the dominant historical-critical assumptions.

The mediating position that is perhaps most widely followed today is some form of school theory (e.g. Dunn, Farmer, Bauckham; *see DLNTD,* Pauline Legacy and School; 2 Peter). Those who espouse it concur with the majority opinion that certain NT documents are pseudonymous, but they argue that no deception was involved because within the school of those churches or writers everyone who needed to know understood that the writing was not really from the ostensible author. There was a kind of living tradition that allowed for its expansion in this way, and its adherents understood the process.

If this position were genuinely sustainable, it would have its attractions. In reality it presents more problems than it resolves. The school terminology suitable to the Neo-Pythagoreans does not transfer very well to the church: the former constituted a closed, disciplined society. Moreover, even if the Neo-Pythagoreans understood that some new publication was not penned by Pythagorus, doubtless some outsiders were duped. If the school mode of transmission was so ubiquitous and easily understood, why did none of the church fathers who addressed questions of authencity view it as an appropriate model for their grasp of the NT documents? Moreover, the new treatises published by the Neo-Pythagoreans did not attempt the personal claims and allusions happily thrown in by the NT writers. Their new truths were tied up with new insights into numbers, not comments on Pythagorus's prison conditions or solicitations that the readers pray for him. One must not fly in the face of the evidence. J. D. G. Dunn (*see DLNTD,* Pseudepigraphy, 978), for instance, writes, "It is hard to believe that such a convention was not recognized, at least by most thoughtful readers, in the case of the Enoch corpus, the *Testaments of the Twelve Patriarchs* or the *Apocalypse of Adam,* all written probably between second century B.C. and second century A.D." But the fact is that when "the most thoughtful readers" discuss the authenticity of various documents, where they become convinced that a document is pseudonymous it is invariably judged ineligible for inclusion in the canon.

In short, the search for parallels to justify the view that the intended readers of some NT documents would have understood them to be pseudonymous, so that no deception took place, has proved a failure. The hard evidence demands that we conclude either that some NT documents are pseudonymous and that the real authors intended to deceive their readers, or that the real authors intended to speak the truth and that pseudonymity is not attested in the NT.

See also APOCRYPHA AND PSEUDEPIGRAPHA; APOCRYPHAL ACTS AND EPISTLES; APOCRYPHAL GOSPELS; CANONICAL FORMATION OF THE NEW TESTAMENT; LITERACY AND BOOK CULTURE; SCHOLARSHIP, GREEK AND ROMAN; WRITING AND LITERATURE: JEWISH.

BIBLIOGRAPHY. K. Aland, "The Problem of Anonymity and Pseudonymity in Christian Literature of the First Two Centuries," in *The Authorship and Integrity of the New Testament,* by K. Aland et al. (TC 4; London: SPCK, 1965) 1-13; L. Alexander, *The Preface to Luke's Gospel: Literary Convention and Social Context in Luke 1:1-4 and Acts 1:1* (SNTSMS 78; Cambridge: Cambridge University Press, 1993); H. R. Balz, "Anonymität und Pseudepigraphie im Urchristentum," *ZTK* 66 (1969) 403-36; M. Barker, "Pseudonymity," in *A Dictionary of Biblical Interpretation,* ed. R. J. C. Coggins and J. L. Houlden (Philadelphia: Trinity Press International, 1990) 568-71; R. Bauckham, *Jude, 2 Peter* (WBC 50; Waco: Word, 1986); R. Bentley, *Dissertations upon the Epistles of Phalaris . . .*, ed. with introduction and notes by W. Wagner (Berlin: S. Calvary, 1874 [1697-99]); L. H. Brockington, "The Problem of Pseudonymity," *JTS* 4 (1953) 15-22; N. Brox, ed., *Pseudepigraphie in der heidnischen und jüdisch-christlichen Antike* (WF 484; Darmstadt: Wissenschaftliche Buchgesellschaft, 1977); J. H. Charlesworth, "Pseudonymity and Pseudepigraphy," *ABD* 5:540-41; M. L. Clarke, *Higher Education in the Ancient World* (London: Routledge & Kegan Paul, 1971); L. R. Donelson, *Pseudepigraphy and Ethical Argument in the Pastoral Epistles* (HUT 22; Tübingen: Mohr Siebeck, 1986); J. Duff, "A Critical Examination of Pseudepigrapy in First- and Second-Century Christianity and the Approaches to it of Twentieth-Century Scholars" (D.Phil. diss.; Oxford University, 1998); E. E. Ellis, "Pseudonymity and Canonicity of New Testament Documents," in *Worship, Theology and Ministry in the Early Church,* ed. M. J. Wilkins and T. Paige (Sheffield: JSOT, 1992) 212-14; E. Evanson, *The Dissonance of the Four Generally Received Evangelists* (Ipswich: G. Jermyn, 1792); D. Farkasfalvy, "The Ecclesial Setting of Pseudepigraphy in Second Peter and Its Role in the Formation of the Canon," *SecCent* 5 (1986) 3-29, response by W. R. Farmer, 30-46; C. Gempf, "Pseudonymity and the New Testament," *Them* 17.2 (1992) 8-10; D. Guthrie, "The Development of the Idea of Canonical Pseudepigrapha in New Testament Criticism," in *The Authorship and Integrity of the New Testament,* ed. K. Aland et al. (TC 4; London: SPCK, 1965) 14-39; idem, *New Testament Introduction* (Leicester: Apollos, 1990); idem, "Tertullian and Pseudonymity," *ExpT* 67 (1955-56) 341-42; A. E. Haefner, "A Unique Source for the Study of Ancient Pseudonymity," *ATR* 16 (1934) 8-15; M. Kiley, *Colossians as Pseudepigraphy* (Sheffield: JSOT, 1986); W. G. Kümmel, *Introduction to the New Testament* (London: SCM, 1975); A. T. Lincoln, *Ephesians* (WBC 42; Dallas: Word, 1990); D. G. Meade, *Pseudonymity and Canon: An Investigation into the Relationship of Authorship and Authority in Jewish and Early Christian Tradition* (WUNT 39; Tübingen: Mohr Siebeck, 1986); W. A. Meeks, " 'To Walk Worthily of the Lord': Moral Formation in the Pauline School Exemplified by the Letter to the Colossians," in *Hermes and Athena: Biblical Exegesis and Philosophical Theology,* ed. E. Stump and T. P. Flint (UNDSPR 7; Notre Dame, IN: University of Notre Dame Press, 1993) 37-58; B. M. Metzger, "Literary Forgeries and Canonical Pseudepigrapha," *JBL* 91 (1972) 3-24; P. T. O'Brien, *Ephesians* (PNTC; Grand Rapids, MI: Eerdmans, forthcoming); S. E. Porter, "Pauline Authorship and the Pastoral Epistles: Implications for Canon," *BBR* 5 (1995) 105-23; idem, "Pauline Authorship and the Pastoral Epistles: A Response to R. W. Wall's Response," *BBR* 6 (1996) 133-38; M. Rist, "Pseudepigraphy and the Early Christians," in *Studies in New Testament and Early Christian Literature,* ed. D. E. Aune (Leiden: E. J. Brill, 1972) 75-91; J. A. Sint, *Pseudonymität im Altertum, ihre Formen und ihre Gründe* (Innsbruck: Universitätsverlag, 1960); W. Speyer, *Die literarische Fälschung im heidnischen und christlichen Altertum: Ein Versuch ihrer Deutung* (Munich: C. H. Beck, 1971); E. Stump, "Moral Authority and Pseudonymity: Comments on the Paper of Wayne A. Meeks," in *Hermes and Athena: Biblical Exegesis and Philosophical Theology,* ed. E. Stump and T. P. Flint (UNDSPR 7; Notre Dame, IN: University of Notre Dame Press, 1993) 59-74; R. W. Wall, "Pauline Authorship and the Pastoral Epistles: A Response to S. E. Porter," *BBR* 5 (1995) 125-28; M. Wolter, "Die anonymen Schriften des Neuen Testaments: Annäherungsversuch an ein literarisches Phänomen," *ZNW* 79 (1988) 1-16.

D. A. Carson

PSEUDO-ORPHEUS. *See* JEWISH LITERATURE: HISTORIANS AND POETS

PSEUDO-PHILO

Pseudo-Philo is the name given the unknown author of *Biblical Antiquities* (also known as *Liber Antiquitatum Biblicarum),* a selective narrative of Israel's history from Adam to David, composed in Hebrew around A.D. 70 in Palestine. Attempts at connecting the work with a specific Jewish group (*Essenes, *Pharisees, *Samaritans) have not been successful. Rather it is best seen as a reflection of how Palestinian Jews in the first century A.D. interpreted the Jewish Scriptures, as a source for the popular biblical theology of the period and as a repository for motifs and legends that are paralleled or even unique in ancient Jewish literature. For NT study it is important chiefly for its birth narratives; treatment of the Abraham-Isaac episode in Genesis 22; attitude toward *women, *angelology and *eschatology, as well as for its verbal, literary and theological affinities with

Luke-Acts and other NT texts.

1. *Biblical Antiquities*
2. Pseudo-Philo and the New Testament

1. *Biblical Antiquities.*

1.1. Title. Neither the ascription to *Philo nor the Latin title *Liber Antiquitatum Biblicarum (LAB)* appears to be original (Jacobson, 257-73). At no place does the author identify himself as Philo of *Alexandria, and the approach to the biblical text and the theology are different from those of Philo (Cohn, 277-332). Rather, both the ascription and the title probably rest only on a very general analogy perceived between this work and Josephus's *Jewish Antiquities* at a time when among Christians Philo and *Josephus were the best-known Jewish authors from NT times. In the Latin manuscript tradition the work circulated along with Philo's genuine writings.

1.2. Text. *Biblical Antiquities* exists in eighteen complete and three fragmentary Latin manuscripts (Harrington and Cazeaux). All date from the eleventh to the fifteenth centuries, and all are of German or Austrian origin. The Latin manuscripts fall into two major groups, and good readings can be found on both sides of the stemma. There is substantial evidence that the Latin version was translated from Greek and that the Greek version was based on a Hebrew original (Harrington 1970, 503-14). The Hebrew excerpts contained in the *Chronicles of Jerhameel* (Harrington 1974) are more likely retroversions from the Latin translation than remnants of the Hebrew original. The complete manuscripts all break off in an abrupt manner at *Biblical Antiquities* 65:5, just before Saul's death, leaving in doubt whether the original ending has been lost.

1.3. Content. *Biblical Antiquities* is a selective retelling of the biblical story from Genesis through 1 Samuel (Murphy; Reinmuth). It covers the narratives from *Adam to Joseph (*Bib. Ant.* 1—8), through *Moses (*Bib. Ant.* 9—19), Joshua (*Bib. Ant.* 20—24), Kenaz (*Bib. Ant.* 25—29) and Deborah (*Bib. Ant.* 30—33), and then from Aod to the ascension of Phinehas (*Bib. Ant.* 34—48) and from Samuel to David (*Bib. Ant.* 49—65). Rather than telling the whole biblical story, the author chooses certain episodes and expands some greatly while summarizing others quite concisely.

1.4. Genre. As a rewriting of the biblical narrative from Adam to David, *Biblical Antiquities* is closest in literary form to Josephus's *Jewish Antiquities,* the *Qumran **Genesis Apocryphon* and **Jubilees.* These works are often described as examples of the "rewritten Bible" (Murphy; *see* Rewritten Bible). They are sometimes also called *"midrash" (Bauckham, 33-76) or *targum, with both terms used loosely. Whether any or all of these three terms define a literary genre and whether *Biblical Antiquities* fits into it are matters of dispute. At any rate, Pseudo-Philo uses biblical episodes creatively to illustrate issues that he regarded as especially instructive for his audience.

1.5. Aim. The central theological theme is God's fidelity to the covenant with *Israel. The disasters that befell Israel in its early history from Adam to David were appropriate punishments for its sins, especially idolatry, and so serve to uphold the justice of God. The positive ideal for Israel is absolute faith in God and faithful observance of God's law. And so the author appears especially interested in biblical narratives that deal with sin and punishment on a collective or national level (Jacobson, 241-53). Whether these lessons demand a date after the destruction of the Jerusalem *temple in A.D. 70 or could fit just as well at other times in Israel's history is a matter of debate.

1.6. Date and Place. The Latin version of *Biblical Antiquities* was very likely produced by a Christian translator in the fourth century A.D. (Jacobson, 277-80). The Greek version seems to have been made by a Jew on the basis of the Hebrew original (Jacobson, 215-24). There is general agreement that the work was composed in Palestine in the first or early second century A.D. Favoring a pre-A.D. 70 composition (Perrot and Bogaert, 66-74) are the free attitude toward the biblical text, interest in *sacrifices and other cultic matters and the apparent silence about the events of 70. Favoring a post-70 date (Jacobson, 199-210) are the parallels with *4 Ezra and **2 Baruch* (both post-70 works) and what some regard as allusions to the temple's destruction (*Bib. Ant.* 19:7; 26:13).

1.7. Background. The author's primary source and focus of interest was the Hebrew Bible (Jacobson, 224-41). He was thoroughly familiar with the biblical text and with the popular traditions that were attached to it. His language is biblical, and he assumes his audience's familiarity with the Hebrew Bible. For his own literary and theological purposes he rearranges, simplifies and expands various biblical passages. He sometimes refers to events that are past from his narrative perspective (flashbacks), and at other points he looks forward to the future (anticipations). Some nonbiblical elements in the narrative may indicate the author's knowledge of the religious beliefs and practices of the pagan population of Palestine (see *Bib. Ant.* 25—26, 44). And he may also have been familiar with some Greco-Roman mythology and *magical practices (Jacobson, 213-15; *see* Religion, Greco-Roman).

2. Pseudo-Philo and the New Testament.

2.1. General Relationship. It cannot be established that any NT author used *Biblical Antiquities* as a source or that Pseudo-Philo knew any NT book. Rather, Pseudo-Philo's *Biblical Antiquities* provides parallels to NT writings from roughly the same time (first century A.D.) and from roughly the same milieu, especially for the Jesus traditions in the Gospels and for the early chapters of Acts.

2.2. Birth Narratives.

2.2.1. Moses and Jesus. Biblical Antiquities is an important source for expanded versions of biblical narratives about the births of biblical heroes (Perrot, 481-518). In retelling the biblical narrative about Moses' birth (Ex 2:1-10), Pseudo-Philo in 9:9-16 solves some puzzles in the biblical text by supplying the names of Moses' parents (Amram and Jochebed; see Ex 6:20), by explaining why Pharaoh's daughter recognized Moses as one of the Hebrew children (because he was born circumcised; see *Bib. Ant.* 9:13, 15) and by giving Moses the Hebrew name Melchiel (*Bib. Ant.* 9:16). He also adds some motifs to the biblical account of Moses' birth: The Spirit of God initiates the course of events (*Bib. Ant.* 9:10); God communicates to Miriam (*Bib. Ant.* 9:10) and to Pharaoh's daughter (*Bib. Ant.* 9:15) by dreams; a connection is made between Moses' name and his mission (*Bib. Ant.* 19:10); and the slaughter of the Hebrew children is presented not merely as a threat but as an actual event (*Bib. Ant.* 9:15). These features also appear in Matthew's infancy narrative (Mt 1:18, 20 and 2:13, 19; 1:21 and 2:16-18), thus contributing to the Moses-Jesus typology.

2.2.2. Samson and John the Baptist. A Samson-John the Baptist typology is prominent in Luke 1. And again there are illuminating parallels with *Biblical Antiquities* 42 as seen in its rewriting of Judges 13. In the cases of both Samson and John the Baptist the mother is regarded as sterile (*Bib. Ant.* 42:1; Lk 1:7); the birth announcement is an answer to prayer (*Bib. Ant.* 42:2, 5; Lk 1:10); an angel announces the hero's birth and describes his future mission (*Bib. Ant.* 42:3; Lk 1:13, 15-18); the child will abstain from wine and strong drink (*Bib. Ant.* 42:3; Lk 1:15); and a parent is silenced (*Bib. Ant.* 42:4; Lk 1:20, 22). The genealogies of Jesus in Matthew 1:1-17 and Luke 3:23-38, especially where there are no biblical sources (Mt 1:13-16; Lk 3:23-27), are amply paralleled not only by Samson's genealogy (*Bib. Ant.* 42:1) but also by the many genealogies in the early chapters of the work (*Bib. Ant.* 1—2, 4—5, 8).

2.3. The Sacrifice of Isaac. The story of God's command to Abraham to sacrifice his son Isaac in Genesis 22 has fascinated Jewish and Christian interpreters throughout the centuries (Daly, 45-75). Perhaps under the influence of the Fourth Servant Song (Is 52:13—53:12) or in the light of the Jewish Passover and New Year's festivals, Pseudo-Philo portrayed Isaac as a martyr who willingly offers himself as a sacrifice to God (see *Bib. Ant.* 18:5; 32:3; 40:2). In general, this motif parallels the NT concept of Jesus' death as a voluntary sacrifice. The specific Abraham-Isaac typology, however, is not as prominent in the NT as one might expect, though it may be present in Romans 8:32 ("He who did not spare his own Son but gave him up for us all"; see also Jas 2:21-23; Heb 11:17-20).

2.4. Women. In comparison with the biblical sources, as in the birth stories of Moses and Samson, Pseudo-Philo often expands the roles of *women (Brown). For example, he gives particular attention to Deborah (*Bib. Ant.* 30—33), Jephthah's daughter Seila (*Bib. Ant.* 39—40) and Hannah (*Bib. Ant.* 50). He offers "feminist" versions of biblical cliches to produce such expressions as "woman of God" (*Bib. Ant.* 33:1) and the "bosom of her mothers" (*Bib. Ant.* 40:4). While relatively open to the place of women in Israel's early history, Pseudo-Philo shared the androcentric and patriarchal assumptions of his society, as did most of the NT writers, despite Galatians 3:28. He was adamantly opposed to *marriage with Gentiles. He claims that Tamar had sexual relations with her father-in-law rather than with Gentiles (*Bib. Ant.* 9:5). Balaam plots to have the Midianite women lead Israel astray (*Bib. Ant.* 18:13-14), and the list of evils in *Biblical Antiquities* 44:7 culminates in lust after foreign wives. The Levite's concubine is said to have been abused because she had intercourse with Amalekites (*Bib. Ant.* 45:3); for other criticisms of sexual relations with Gentiles, see *Biblical Antiquities* 6:11; 27:7, 15; 45:3; and 49:5.

2.5. Angelology. Angels not only figure in the announcements of the births of Moses and Samson (*Bib. Ant.* 9:10; 42:3, 6-7) but also appear in other contexts throughout the work (as in the Gospels and Acts). Angels lament the death of Moses (*Bib. Ant.* 19:16) and are jealous of Abraham (*Bib. Ant.* 32:1-2). They serve as guardians (*Bib. Ant.* 11:12; 59:4) but will not intercede for sinners (*Bib. Ant.* 15:5). Four angels are named: Ingethel and Zeruel (*Bib. Ant.* 27:10), Nathaniel (*Bib. Ant.* 38:3) and Fadahel (*Bib. Ant.* 42:10). Holy spirits assist in the prophecies of Balaam (*Bib. Ant.* 18:3, 11), Kenaz (*Bib. Ant.* 28:6) and Deborah (*Bib. Ant.* 32:14). Evil spirits (*Bib. Ant.* 53:3-4; 60:1) were created on the second day of creation (*Bib. Ant.* 60:3). Condemned angels help humans in their sorcery (*Bib. Ant.* 34:3), and two angels assist the witch of Endor in raising Samuel from the dead (*Bib. Ant.* 64:6). There is little interest in a chief evil angel such as *Satan who exercises leadership over the forces of evil.

2.6. Eschatology. Pseudo-Philo's teachings on the end time are scattered throughout the work; see, for example, the Apocalypse of Noah in *Biblical Antiquities* 3:9-10 and the Testament of Deborah in *Biblical Antiquities* 33:1-6. He shows no obvious interest in an eschatological messiah or in the political implications of eschatology. The framework is set by the two ages: the present and the world to come (*Bib. Ant.* 3:10; 16:3; 19:7, 13; 32:17; 62:9). His special interest is in what happens to the person after death and then during the eschatological visitation. After death the soul is separated from the body, and all are judged according to their deeds (*Bib. Ant.* 44:10). There is no chance to repent after death, and not even Israel's ancestors can mediate on behalf of sinful Israel (*Bib. Ant.* 33:2-5). The souls of the just are at peace until God's visitation, while the wicked undergo punishment for their sins. After the final judgment the just dwell with God (*Bib. Ant.* 19:12-13) and with the ancestors (*Bib. Ant.* 23:13), whereas the wicked are annihilated (*Bib. Ant.* 16:3).

2.7. Luke-Acts. Pseudo-Philo wrote a history of early Israel from Adam to David with reference to major figures—much as Luke did in writing his two-volume presentation of the Jesus movement and the early church (Perrot and Bogaert, 30). Likewise, there are common interests between Pseudo-Philo and Luke not only in the births of biblical heroes but also in the themes such as *prayer, the *Holy Spirit, *prophecy, divine providence, and so forth. E. Reinmuth finds many affinities between these works in their literary patterns, motifs and the use of Scripture as well as close parallels between specific episodes (e.g., the calls of OT figures and the call of Peter in Lk 5:1-11, and various motifs in Stephen's speech in Acts 7). So impressive are these parallels to Reinmuth that he concludes that the roots of Luke-Acts should be sought in early Judaism rather than describing it as the work of a Hellenist or a Gentile Christian.

2.8. Other Parallels. The following list is but a sample of verbal coincidences between Pseudo-Philo and other NT texts (James, LVI-LVIII): "May your blood be upon your own head" (*Bib. Ant.* 6:11; Mt 27:25); "and brought forth a well of water to follow them" (*Bib. Ant.* 10:7/11:5; 1 Cor 10:4); "on the third day" as the equivalent of "after three days" (*Bib. Ant.* 11:2; Mt 27:63 par.); the list of gems (*Bib. Ant.* 26:9-11; Rev 21:19-20); the wife taking the initiative in a divorce proceeding (*Bib. Ant.* 42:1; Mk 10:12); and "he who restrains" (*Bib. Ant.* 51:5; 2 Thess 2:6-7). Most of the examples reflect a common background in the OT and in Judaism rather than representing a direct borrowing or a unique coincidence.

See also APOCRYPHA AND PSEUDEPIGRAPHA; JEWISH LITERATURE: HISTORIANS AND POETS; JOSEPHUS; REWRITTEN BIBLE IN PSEUDEPIGRAPHA AND QUMRAN.

BIBLIOGRAPHY. R. J. Bauckham, "The *Liber Antiquitatum Biblicarum* of Pseudo-Philo and the Gospels as 'Midrash,'" in *Gospel Perspectives 3: Studies in Midrash and Historiography,* ed. R. T. France and D. Wenham (Sheffield: JSOT, 1983) 33-76; C. A. Brown, *No Longer Be Silent: First-Century Jewish Portraits of Biblical Women* (Louisville, KY: Westminster John Knox, 1992); L. Cohn, "An Apocryphal Work Ascribed to Philo of Alexandria," *JQR* 10 (1898) 277-332; R. J. Daly, "The Soteriological Significance of the Sacrifice of Isaac," *CBQ* 39 (1977) 45-75; D. J. Harrington, *The Hebrew Fragments of Pseudo-Philo's Liber Antiquitatum Biblicarum Preserved in the Chronicles of Jerahmeel* (SBLTT 3; Cambridge, MA: SBL, 1974); idem, "The Original Language of Pseudo-Philo's *Liber Antiquitatum Biblicarum,*" *HTR* 63

(1970) 503-14; idem, "Pseudo-Philo," in *OTP* 2:297-377; D. J. Harrington and J. Cazeaux, *Pseudo-Philon: Les Antiquités Bibliques,* 1*: Introduction et Texte Critiques; Traduction* (SC 229; Paris: Editions du Cerf, 1976); H. Jacobson, *A Commentary on Pseudo-Philo's Liber Antiquitatum Biblicarum with Latin Text and English Translation* (AGJU 31; Leiden: E. J. Brill, 1996); M. R. James, *The Biblical Antiquities of Philo* (New York: Ktav, 1971), with a prolegomenon by L. H. Feldman on pp. VII-CLXIX; G. Kisch, *Pseudo-Philo's Liber Antiquitatum Biblicarum* (Notre Dame, IN: University of Notre Dame Press, 1949); F. J. Murphy, *Pseudo-Philo: Rewriting the Bible* (New York: Oxford University Press, 1993); C. Perrot, "Les Récits d'enfance dans la Haggada antérieure au IIe siècle de Notre ère," *RSR* 55 (1967) 481-518; C. Perrot and P.-M. Bogaert, *Pseudo-Philon: Les Antiquités Bibliques,* 2*: Introduction Littéraire, Commentaire et Index* (SC 230; Paris: Editions du Cerf, 1976); E. Reinmuth, *Pseudo-Philo und Lukas: Studien zum Liber Antiquitatum Biblicarum und seiner Bedeutung für die Interpretation des lukanischen Doppelwerkes* (WUNT 74; Tübingen: Mohr Siebeck, 1994). D. J. Harrington

PSEUDO-PHOCYLIDES

The Greek gnomic poet and bard Phocylides lived in Miletus in Ionia in the middle of the sixth century B.C. and was regarded as a great authority concerning ethical matters and correct behavior in daily living (see, e.g., Plato *Rep.* 407a7; and Aristotle *Pol.* 4.11.1295b34). Only a very few lines of his poetry remain extant.

The poem itself, consisting of 230 verses, serves as the principal formation of practical wisdom stemming from the Hellenistic *Diaspora (Collins, 158). The first known quotation of the poem is by Stobaeus (fifth century A.D.). The work contains similarities found in both Greek gnomologies and Jewish wisdom literature and can therefore be regarded as a "typical example of cross-cultural didactic poetry" (van der Horst 1978, 77). Under the assumption that the work was genuinely written by the hand of Phocylides himself, it achieved wide popularity in the later Middle Ages and was commonly used as a schoolbook (van der Horst 1978, 6).

The work's authenticity was first seriously questioned by J. Scaliger, who in 1606 concluded that in light of the poem's biblical undertones (see sections of the Pentateuch such as Lev 18—20 and the Decalogue) and its dependence upon the *Septuagint, it was a Christian forgery (Scaliger). After waning interest, study of the poem was revived in 1856 by J. Bernays. Although accepting the poem's reliance upon the LXX, the importance of Bernays's work was to challenge the notion of its Christian authorship (Bernays). Although the Jewish authorship of Pseudo-Phocylides was still disputed into the early twentieth century, this view is presently unchallenged and holds universal acceptance (Collins, 158).

A number of examples exist where Jewish writings from the Hellenistic Diaspora are pseudonymously attributed to prestigious pagan figures, including Sibyl, Orpheus and the great tragedians (Collins, 159). In similar fashion, a Jewish wisdom poet has here invoked the name of Phocylides. Although the author makes a skillful and excellent attempt at antiquating the poem by writing in the old Ionic dialect of Phocylides, he occasionally betrays himself and the work's later compilation date by using Hellenistic or early imperial period vocabulary, meter and syntax; and by employing OT, LXX and *Stoic influences (van der Horst 1978, 55-58). In view of these considerations it seems reasonable to suggest a date of compilation falling sometime between 200 B.C. and A.D. 150, and more specifically between 30 B.C. and A.D. 40 (van der Horst 1978, 81-83). Although *Alexandria has been tentatively suggested as the poem's place of origin, this is uncertain.

Perhaps the most problematic issue concerning the poem, and a matter of much debate, is the question of its purpose. P. W. van der Horst poignantly stresses the dilemma when he asks why a Jewish author wrote a summary of the *Torah, mixed with nonbiblical ethical rules, under a heathen pseudonym. A variety of suggestions have been made, including the author wrote primarily for the pleasure of writing; he wrote to reassure his fellow Jews that Greek and Jewish ethics closely corresponded and therefore there was no need to look beyond their own traditions; he wrote to the pagan public in order to explain Judaism's ethical consensus with Greek thought and to encourage sympathy toward the Jewish faith; the author was a Godfearer (*see* Proselytism and Godfearers) who accepted elements of Judaism but not the full ritual law and desired to win converts to his particular view; consistent with the purpose of gnomologies, the author wrote a schoolbook for children; and lastly, the author wrote in order to prevent defection from Judaism toward Hellenistic culture with all its attractions (Collins, 175). Regardless of the poem's actual purpose, it serves as an important source for our understanding of ethics and morality in daily living within the context of Diaspora Judaism and also provides a background for several paraenetic texts found in the NT.

See also JEWISH LITERATURE: HISTORIANS AND POETS; HELLENISTIC JUDAISM.

BIBLIOGRAPHY. J. Bernays, *Über das phokylideische Gedicht: Ein Beitrag zur hellenistischen Literatur* (Berlin, 1856); D. G. Castanien, "Quevedo's Translation of the Pseudo-Phocylides," *PQ* 40 (1961) 44-52; J. J. Collins, *Jewish Wisdom in the Hellenistic Age* (Louisville, KY: Westminster John Knox, 1997); P. Derron, "Inventaire des manuscripts du Pseudo-Phocylides," *Revue d'histoire des textes* 10 (1980) 237-47; idem, *Pseudo-Phocylides: Sentences* (Paris: Les Belles Lettres, 1986) xxii; B. S. Easton, "Pseudo-Phocylides," *ATR* 14 (1932) 222-28; P. W. van der Horst, "Pseudo-Phocylides Revisited," *JSP* 3 (1988) 3-30; idem, *The Sentences of Pseudo-Phocylides* (SVTP 4; Leiden: E. J. Brill, 1978); J. Scaliger, "Animadversiones in Chronologica Eusebii," in *Thesaurus Temporum* (Leiden, 1606).

K. D. Clarke

PSEUDO-PROPHETS (4Q385-388, 390-391)

This group of manuscripts was originally identified by John Strugnell as copies of the same composition and given the title *Pseudo-Ezekiel*. Subsequent editing by D. Dimant (Strugnell and Dimant 1988) has shown that the group is actually two distinct literary works, *Pseudo-Ezekiel* and the *Apocryphon of Jeremiah*, with perhaps as many as five manuscripts of the first and six of the second. The oldest manuscripts date to the middle of the first century B.C., while the contents are nearly a century older.

1. *Pseudo-Ezekiel*
2. *Apocryphon of Jeremiah*

1. *Pseudo-Ezekiel.*

Manuscripts 4Q385, 4Q385b, 4Q385c, 4Q386 and 4Q388 echo aspects of Ezekiel 37—38 in the same first-person format as the biblical book. The vision of the dry bones, their resurrection, and the judgment of the nations are all rehearsed. The addition of a *merkabah* (chariot) vision, which apparently follows these elements, is of special note. It is likely that the return of the glory of the Lord to the eschatological temple foretold at Ezekiel 43:1-5 is expanded to reflect the prophet's two previous *merkabah* visions (Ezek 1 and 10; *see* Mysticism).

1.1. Resurrection of the Dead. The interpretive aspects of the text are of great importance. When (pseudo-) Ezekiel poses the question, "When will [th]ese things come to pass? How shall their faithfulness be rewarded?" (4Q385 frag. 2 3), the ambiguous nature of the biblical dry bones vision of Ezekiel 37:1-14—is the revival figurative only of Israel's national revival or does it exemplify a belief in the resurrection of the dead?—is clarified. The vision was understood by the ancient author to mean that the resurrection was the reward of righteous individuals. This text thus stands with 4Q521 as the only manuscripts from Qumran that speak explicitly of the resurrection. It is of note that neither of these compositions are characterized by sectarian language, suggesting that the doctrine was widely held in the Jewish community rather than by the Qumran community alone.

1.2. Shortening of the End. *Pseudo-Ezekiel* records that God had promised a shortening of the time of the end due to the difficulties associated with the last days (4Q385 frag. 3 2-5). This concept presages the same theme of difficulties (birth pangs) associated with the end of the age and return of Jesus in the Gospel accounts (Mt 24:22, Mk 13:20).

1.3. Son of Belial. In context of the judgment of the nations, 4Q386 frag. 1 ii 3 mentions a "son of Belial" who comes to Israel as an oppressor (*see* Belial, Beliar, Devil, Satan). Normally found in the plural in Qumran literature in reference to recalcitrant Jews, this singular instance might refer to some historical oppressor—perhaps Antiochus IV Epiphanes (175–164 B.C.).

2. *Apocryphon of Jeremiah.*

Manuscripts 4Q385a, 4Q387, 4Q387a, 4Q388a, 4Q389 and 4Q390 have been assessed by D. Dimant as witnesses to the *Apocryphon of Jeremiah*.

2.1. Historical Review. One portion of the work reviews the sinful history of Israel, mentioning such historical figures as Abraham, Isaac, Jacob, Samuel and Solomon. These end with Nebuzaradan, the fall of Jerusalem and the *exile to Babylon. Jeremiah's biblical role of preparing the Jewish deportees for exile in Egypt is expanded to include Babylon in the *Apocryphon of Jeremiah.* This addition to the biblical account is also found in later *apocryphal and pseudepigraphal works such as 2 *Maccabees, the Epistle of Jeremiah and *2 *Baruch.*

2.2. **Vaticinium ex Eventu.** The second half of the work turns to the future but is in large part *vaticinium ex eventu.* An example of this genre, a two-column section from 4Q387 (frag. 3 ii-iii) preserves a prophecy of the *Gadfan* (Blasphemer) who was to come ten full Jubilees after the destruction of the *temple (587/6 B.C.). Given the forty-nine-year period delimited by the Qumran Jubilee (*see* Calendars, Jewish), a literal reckoning would suggest a date of 97/6 B.C. and place the fulfillment during the reign of Alexander Janneus (103-76 B.C.). The title *Gadfan* is, however, more appropriate for the Syrian king Antiochus IV Epiphanes who initiated a persecution of the Jews in 168 B.C. (*see* Jewish History: Greek Period) and portrayed himself as divine (thus a blasphemer). On the other hand, the schematic basis of the prophecy suggests that the character may be intentionally ambiguous, pointing mainly to the hopeless nature of the last days apart from God's intervention. It is of special note that the period of ten Jubilees—490 years—echoes Daniel 9:24. Only the starting point is different: for the *Apocryphon* the *terminus a quo* is the destruction of the temple, for Daniel it is the "decree to rebuild and restore Jerusalem."

2.3. Sectarian Origins. In concert with much of Qumran literature, it is the view of the writer of the *Apocryphon* that Israel once again fell into sin during the Second Temple period. This state of steady decline led finally to the loss of statehood, the oppression of the *Gadfan* and subjection to the Angels of Mastemot in the second century B.C. (4Q387 frag. 2 iii 4). The reference to a "remnant" that was rescued rather than destroyed in God's wrath during this time is contextually the same as that mentioned at CD 1:4, the Qumran sectarians. Thus *Apocryphon of Jeremiah* is likely a sectarian document.

See also DEAD SEA SCROLLS; MYSTICISM.

BIBLIOGRAPHY. D. Dimant, "An Apocryphon of Jeremiah from Cave 4 (4Q385B = 4Q385 16)," in *New Qumran Texts and Studies,* ed. G. J. Brooke (STDJ 15; Leiden: E. J. Brill, 1994) 11-30; idem, "New Light from Qumran on the Jewish Pseudepigrapha—4Q390," in *The Madrid Qumran Congress: Proceedings of the International Congress on the Dead Sea Scrolls, Madrid 18-21, 1991,* vol. 2, ed. by J. Trebolle Barrera and L. Vegas Montaner (STDJ 11.2; Leiden: E. J. Brill, 1992) 405-47; idem, *Qumran Cave 4.21: Parabiblical Texts, Part 4* (DJD; Oxford: Clarendon Press, forthcoming); idem, "A Quotation from Nahum 3:8-10 in the Fragment 4Q386 6 from Qumran," in *The Bible in the Light of Its Interpreters: Sara Kamin Memorial Volume,* ed. S. Japhet (Jerusalem: Magnes, 1995) 31-7 (Hebrew); D. Dimant and J. Strugnell, "The Merkhabah Vision in Second Ezekiel (4Q385 4)," *RevQ* 14 (1990) 331-48; M. Kister and E. Qimron, "Observations on 4QSecond Ezekiel," *RevQ* 15 (1992) 595-602; J. Strugnell and D. Dimant, "4Q Second Ezekiel," *RevQ* 13 (1988) 45-58. M. G. Abegg Jr.

PTOLEMIES

From the Greek takeover of the Persian Empire in the late fourth century B.C. to the Roman annexation of Egypt in the mid-first century B.C., Egypt was ruled by a succession of kings and queens from a family of outsiders. The dynasty was fathered by Ptolemy, a high-ranking Macedonian general and long-time confidant of *Alexander the Great (*see* Greece and Macedon). Ptolemaic Egypt endured for three centuries, approximately one-half of the era designated as *Hellenistic Egypt.

1. Accession to Power
2. Land and Administration
3. Special Concerns

1. Accession to Power.

Upon the unexpected death of Alexander in 323 B.C., Ptolemy became embroiled in the struggles for who would succeed the essentially heirless Alexander. Unlike the other would-be successors (*see* Diadochi), Ptolemy was content to secure control of the region that he foresaw as having the most potential. It was a gamble, but in the end it was a wise and strategic move. Under the Ptolemies, Egypt rivaled the *Seleucids as the dominant kingdom in the Mediterranean world and was the last to succumb to *Rome. Had Octavian not been successful against Antony and Cleopatra, Ptolemaic Egypt may have prevailed in the eastern Mediterranean.

When Ptolemy hijacked Alexander's corpse and began construction of a fitting tomb in *Alexandria for the great king, he was the satrap over Egypt (using the former Persian terminology). But he was prepared to defend his position of supreme ruler if necessary—and it became necessary when Perdiccas, one of his former comrades, unsuccessfully attacked in 321 B.C. Ptolemy eventually assumed the title of king in 305 B.C. and subsequently dated events during his reign from that year. Each of the kings in the Ptolemaic dynasty used the name Ptolemy, and seven of the queens used the name Cleopatra. For ease of reference, the Ptolemies have been assigned Roman numerals, such as Ptolemy II and Cleopatra VII. But their own way of distinguishing each other was by epithet. The epithets for the first five Ptolemies were Soter (savior), Philadelphus (sister-loving), Euergetes (benefactor), Philopator (father-loving) and Epiphanes ([god] manifest). Though the adjective *philadelphus* in this context denoted an incestuous relationship, the noun *philadelphia* appears in the NT for Christian love.

2. Land and Administration.

The assumption of authority over Egypt by the Greek and Macedonian rulers was a strange and awkward time. To the Greeks, Egypt was an enigma with its far-reaching floods, towering pyramids, stick-figured hieroglyphs and mummified crocodiles. To the Egyptians, the new conquerors were equally suspect, partly because of differences in culture but more because of their inexperience in administering Egypt. The issue was whether the newly arrived rulers could figure out how to manage this strange but fertile land and whether the two distinct ethnic groups, cultures and languages could become a functioning society to make Egypt prosperous. The somewhat surprising answer was a profound yes, even with the unique requirements for making Egypt productive agriculturally.

As part of the vast desert stretching across North Africa, Egypt would not be inhabited were it not for the great river flowing north through it. Even so, the only hospitable areas of Egypt were near water, including the river—which transformed the strip of land a few miles on either side into valuable ground for agriculture; the delta in Lower Egypt—where the river fans out to provide large areas of arable land; the lake in the depression known as the Fayum, to the southwest of the delta—which gets its water from the Nile; occasional oases in the desert; and the Mediterranean Sea. With so little functional land, it was up to the Ptolemies to manage what could be farmed to produce as high yields as possible. Success depended on the annual flooding of the Nile and the silt that was deposited. The summer rainy season deep within the African continent would cause the Nile to begin rising in June, with the peak of the flood not arriving until August or September. The river was generally back within its banks by the end of October. As the river receded, canals and dikes were utilized to retain the water for the agricultural work about to begin. In the areas inundated by the flood, the growing season was November through May. With careful management, areas not touched by the flood could be irrigated with canals and lifting devices, in some cases allowing for two and three crops annually.

The Ptolemaic success in developing Egypt into a world power—especially during the reigns of Ptolemies II and III, with dominion over Cyrenaica, Cyprus, most of the Aegean islands, parts of Asia Minor and Palestine—depended to a great extent on the success of managing the internal concerns of the country. One feature of the domestic policy was to leave in place as much of the native control as possible, from temples and priests to officials overseeing agriculture. In one sense the Ptolemies had to be true Greeks and run the country as such, but in another sense they had to take on the bearing of Egyptian pharaohs and maintain as much tradition as possible. Most of the natives remained in their respective occupations and positions, and except for taxes many were affected only indirectly by the presence of the new rulers. Essential to the Ptolemies' management of Egypt was agriculture and the water supply it depended on. To the government's credit, engineers were able to enlarge and improve on the pharaonic irrigation system so that more of Egypt than ever before could be used for agriculture. All arable parcels of land were carefully registered and classed as royal land (often leased to peasants for farming), sacred land (for the use of temples), allotments to soldiers (cleruchs), civil gift-estates (*doreai*) and (the smallest amount of all) private land.

The notion that the Ptolemies succeeded by running a tightly organized, rigidly centralized bureaucracy—as suggested, for example, by the longest surviving papyrus, known as the Revenue Laws—is an exaggeration. One part of the economy that the Ptolemies attempted to monopolize was oil, used especially in lamps—primarily castor oil, sesame oil and olive oil. The papyri permit detailed analysis of oil crops and oil production for some areas and time periods. Whereas the Revenue Laws was an attempt to micromanage everything about oils—specifying amounts of seed to be planted, fixing prices of seed and oil, regulating oil factories—the evidence in other papyri suggests that this was an unrealized ideal. For example, some sources of oil prescribed in the Revenue Laws (gourd seed oil and linseed oil) are unattested elsewhere in the papyri. Nevertheless, the Ptolemies were able to impose controls on many aspects of the economy, such as banking and imports and exports.

3. Special Concerns.

Taxes on everything possible were a burden on the populace but a source of significant wealth for the government. The system of tax collection instituted by the Ptolemies was adopted from the Greek homeland. On a yearly basis the government auctioned off to the highest bidders various areas of the country and the right to the taxes from those areas. The entrepreneur who purchased the contract for the taxes (referred to as a tax farmer) thereby guaranteed to the government the amount of the bid, to be paid in installments or in one lump sum. Throughout the year local officials and special agents collected taxes, depositing them in a local bank. If all went well, the purchaser of the contract recouped his outlay plus enough for a healthy profit. If it was a bad year, the entrepreneur had to bear the brunt of the shortfall. The result was that the government's tax revenue did not fluctuate with the variation in Nile flooding and in the harvests.

As a member of the Macedonian aristocracy, Ptolemy I received the best *education the Greek world could offer. But that kind of education was lacking in Egypt. So on behalf of their heirs and their Greek and Macedonian subjects, the Ptolemies offered royal patronage to the intelligentsia of the Greek world in order to entice them to move to Alexandria. The Ptolemies wanted to make Alexandria a showcase to the world of learning and culture, and they were successful. The library with its unrivaled collection of scrolls and the museum with unrivaled advancements in learning were a significant achievement (*see* Alexandrian Library; Alexandrian Scholarship). Demetrius of Phalerum is one example of many who relocated to Alexandria. He was a prominent philosopher and statesman in Athens, but at the urging of Ptolemy he moved to Alexandria and was instrumental in shaping the developing scholarship (*see* Scholarship, Greek and Roman).

Regarding religion, the Ptolemies encouraged traditional Egyptian cults to continue without change. The creation of their own patron deity, the cult of Sarapis, showed the intentional syncretism of Egyptian and Greek *religion. Similar to the cult of the deified Alexander, the Ptolemies were gradually recognized as descendants of gods. It was a cult with religious and political overtones, part of the strategy to maintain control over both Greek and Egyptian subjects. The Ptolemies' use of epithets like "savior" and "god manifest" supported this cult of living rulers (*see* Ruler Cult).

Of the fifteen Ptolemies and seven Cleopatras, Ptolemy II Philadelphus is the best documented, partly due to the *Zenon papyri. Zenon was the top administrator of the affairs of Apollonius, who as minister of finance was one of the highest government officials. Apollonius had extensive business interests in Palestine and the Fayum, and the Zenon archive documents much of the details of managing those interests. During the reign of Ptolemy V Epiphanes—crowned king at the age of five—serious internal and external problems took their toll on the fading glory of Egypt. In Upper Egypt a revolt lasted for several years, and Egypt's possessions in the Aegean, Asia Minor and Palestine were lost. Even more telling, Rome was easing its way into Ptolemaic politics. It was a trend that would continue with each of the successive Ptolemies, with Egypt in essence becoming a client state of Rome. The most promising ruler of the end of the Ptolemaic dynasty was Cleopatra VII. The Egyptian economy was once again surging, and the peasants were suddenly supportive of the queen. But Cleopatra's ambitions were her downfall. Pursuing a dream to be queen of the Roman world, she courted Julius Caesar and then Marc Antony. But when both of them died and when Octavian could not be enticed, she reportedly took her own life. By doing so, she in effect turned Egypt over to the Romans.

See also ALEXANDRIA; DIADOCHI; HELLENISTIC EGYPT; JEWISH HISTORY: GREEK PERIOD; SELEUCIDS AND ANTIOCHIDS; ZENON PAPYRI.

BIBLIOGRAPHY. R. S. Bianchi, *Cleopatra's Egypt: Age of the Ptolemies* (New York: Brooklyn Museum, 1988); A. K. Bowman, *Egypt After the*

Ptolemies: 332 B.C.—A.D. 642 from Alexander to the Arab Conquest (Berkeley and Loss Angeles: University of California Press, 1986); W. M. Ellis, *Ptolemy of Egypt* (London: Routledge, 1994); P. M. Fraser, *Ptolemaic Alexandria* (Oxford: Clarendon Press, 1972); P. Green, *Alexander to Actium: The Historical Evolution of the Hellenistic Age* (Berkeley and Los Angeles: University of California Press, 1990); N. Lewis, *Greeks in Ptolemaic Egypt: Case Studies in the Social History of the Hellenistic World* (Oxford: Clarendon Press, 1986); J. F. Oates, *The Ptolemaic Basilikos Grammateus* (BASPSup 8; Atlanta: Scholars Press, 1995); E. E. Rice, *The Grand Procession of Ptolemy Philadelphus* (New York: Oxford University Press, 1983); M. Rostovtzeff, *The Social and Economic History of the Hellenistic World* (3 vols.; Oxford: Clarendon Press, 1941); A. E. Samuel, *From Athens to Alexandria: Hellenism and Social Goals in Ptolemaic Egypt* (SH 26; Louvain, 1983); D. B. Sandy, *The Production and Use of Vegetable Oils in Ptolemaic Egypt* (BASP Sup 6; Atlanta: Scholars Press, 1989); D. J. Thompson, *Memphis Under the Ptolemies* (Princeton, NJ: Princeton University Press, 1988). D. B. Sandy

PUBLICANI. *See* TAXATION, GRECO-ROMAN.

PURIFICATION LITURGY (4Q284). *See* LITURGY: QUMRAN; PURIFICATION TEXTS (4Q274-279, 281-284, 512-514).

PURIFICATION TEXTS (4Q274-279, 281-284, 512-514)

In continuity with Pentateuchal legislation and with later *rabbinic halakah, numerous *Qumran documents from a variety of genres reveal a community for whom obedience to God and recognition of God's holiness and presence entailed maintenance of ritual *purity. Some texts are of a legal genre and articulate specific regulations concerning males rendered impure by bodily emissions (4Q274, 4Q514), menstruating women (4Q274, 4Q278, 4Q284), removal of impurity by water containing ashes of a red heifer (4Q276-277), purification after sexual intercourse (4Q284), corpse uncleanness (4Q284), crop gleaning by those ritually impure (4Q284a), liturgy for purification rituals (4Q512) and purity status of priests' daughters married to foreigners (4Q513).

The Qumran community was well attuned to the religious value of ritual purity in the Torah as well as to the specificity of the ritual code. The sect noted, for example, that a menstruating women and a man with a discharge were considered unclean for a set period and so had a ritually defiling effect on what they contacted during that time (Lev 15:2-33). But determining their status vis-à-vis one another during their unclean period and how their status affected their interaction and other daily activities is not spelled out in the Pentateuchal legislation. In response, one ruling (4Q274 frag 1 i 7-9) enjoins avoidance of contact between two ritually unclean persons and prescribes ritual baths and garment washing should such contact occur. In this manner, the Qumran community promulgated laws that clarified and supplemented the Mosaic code, making it practical for their time and circumstances. The dozens of laws in these texts are examples of careful reading of the law of *Moses and demonstrate that their interpretations are organic outgrowths of their authoritative texts (Harrington, 261-62).

For the study of the NT, these laws of ritual purity illustrate at least three important facts of first-century *Judaism that were recognized even before the discovery of the *Dead Sea Scrolls and are now beginning to make their rightful impact on the study of the NT. First, in late Second Temple Judaism "sectarian law was a living, developing phenomenon constantly giving rise to new compilations of lists of laws" (Schiffman, 280-81). The dynamic nature of Jewish law was characteristic not only of the community responsible for the Dead Sea Scrolls but also of their Jewish contemporaries.

Second, concerning ritual purity and other matters of Jewish practice, there was a variety of viewpoints (cf. 4QMMT; *see* Miqsat Maʿasey ha-Torah) and the differences between the Qumran sectarians, *Pharisees, *Sadducees, Jesus of Nazareth and early Jewish Christians should be seen as various degrees on the spectrum of religious observance. On this spectrum, the Qumran purity regulations are comparatively strict (Harrington, 264). Third, the scrolls help to "dispel a common misconception about the Jewish laws of ritual purity and impurity—that they lack ethical and religious dimensions" (Schiffman, 299). Indeed, 4Q512 is a liturgical composition for use in prescribed purification rituals and expressive of inner spiritual *piety.

It is in this context of a constantly developing, expanding and reforming law; of lively debate; and of genuine spiritual interest that one must read Gospel narratives, the interlocutions of Jesus with his contemporaries and early Christian discussions on such subjects. The immersion of John the baptizer, for example, while focused on ethical repentance (Mk 1:4-5), was like the Qumran washings in that it was a symbolic ritual act and also made use of the familiar forms of ablutions of ritual purity. In the NT one observes the movement away from the ideas of ritual purity toward the characteristically Christian (especially Gentile) emphasis, namely, purity as exclusively a moral category.

See also ESSENES; PHARISEES; PURITY; TEMPLE, JEWISH; THEOLOGIES AND SECTS, JEWISH; VICE AND VIRTUE LISTS.

BIBLIOGRAPHY. J. Baumgarten, "The Laws About Fluxes in 4QTohora[a] (4Q274)," in *Time to Prepare the Way in the Wilderness,* ed. D. Dimant and L. H. Schiffman (Leiden: E. J. Brill, 1985) 1-8; idem, "Liquids and Susceptibility to Defilement in New 4Q Texts," *JQR* 85 (1994) 96-99; idem, "The Red Cow Purification Rites in Qumran Texts," *JJS* 46 (1995) 112-19; H. Harrington, *The Impurity Systems of Qumran and the Rabbis* (Atlanta: Scholars Press, 1993); J. Milgrom, "4QTohora[a]: An Unpublished Qumran Text on Purities," in *Time to Prepare the Way in the Wilderness,* ed. D. Dimant and L. H. Schiffman (Leiden: E. J. Brill, 1985) 59-68; L. Schiffman, *Reclaiming the Dead Sea Scrolls* (Philadelphia: Jewish Publication Society of America, 1994). J. E. Bowley

PURITY

Purity is best understood as the condition that God demands of his people for contact with him. In the case of *Israel, specific foods, objects and physical characteristics are demanded for any approach of the divine. Even then, *priests mediate in the final acts of *sacrifice, because greater purity is required the closer one comes to God's holiness.

Two sorts of impurity threaten Israel: impurity by contagion and impurity by holiness. Impurity by contagion results from contact with anything that should not exist. A corpse or a monstrous beast, for example, are not a part of the created order intended by God and must not be brought near God. But it is equally dangerous to approach what belongs to God alone: blood, for example, threatens Israel's existence because it is too holy to be eaten, not because it is essentially impure.

Both forms of impurity can be mortal, unless they are prevented or dealt with once they emerge. Nadab and Abihu offer an unwarranted sacrifice, and they are consumed by fire (Lev 10:1-3). But God also "broke out" against Uzzah, because he had touched the ark in order to steady it during transport (2 Sam 6:6-10). Such stories show that Israel's purity was a balance on a knife's edge. On the one side were the basic impurities whose existence God would not tolerate. On the other side was the holiness that destroyed even what was pure by simple contact. Defining what is pure was held to be Israel's charter of existence. Earlier inhabitants of the land had been expelled because they did not attend to the purity required by God (see Lev 18:24-30). That belief clearly marks the systemic importance of the observation of the clean and the unclean within Israel.

Issues related to the overall definition of purity were prominent within Jesus' discussions and disputes with his contemporaries. His stance in regard to those questions was so coherent as to amount to a program. As the cultural milieu of Jesus' movement changed after the resurrection, the principal circles of the primitive church (represented by Peter, James and Paul) developed distinctive understandings of purity. Tensions among those positions were resolved in the equation of purity with virtue. That resolution is one of the most important theological achievements of the NT.

1. Strategies of Purity Within Early Judaism
2. Jesus' Program of Purity
3. The Conflicting Strategies of Peter, James and Paul
4. The Resolution of Purity and Virtue in Hellenistic Christianity

1. Strategies of Purity Within Early Judaism. That purity is required of Israel is axiomatic within the *Hebrew Bible, but distinct strategies of defining, achieving and maintaining purity were developed. The best-known and most comprehensive strategy is the priestly scheme represented in the book of Leviticus, and most discussions understandably begin at that point (*see DJG,* Clean and Unclean). But that picture is to be supplemented by the alternative strategies of other circles within Israel. Ezekiel, Leviticus and Deuteronomy provide patterns of understanding that were classic within the understanding of Israel and formative for several groups within *Judaism during the time the NT emerged.

In Ezekiel 40—48, a vision establishes the purity by which Israel gains access to the holy, the powerful source of its inheritance. Only Zadokite priests are to serve God in his sanctuary (Ezek 44:15-16). Foreigners are to be excluded, as "foreskinned in heart and foreskinned in flesh" (Ezek 44:9). Levites are relegated to an ancillary function, owing to their previous involvement in idolatry (Ezek 44:10-14): service in the funeral cult of dead kings (Ezek 43:6-9). The Zadokite priests in turn are carefully regulated in respect of their clothing (Ezek 44:17-18), coiffeur (Ezek 44:20), temperance (Ezek 44:21) and marriages (Ezek 44:22).

The priests are to leave their clothing in sacred chambers and put on other clothing before they meet the people in the outer court, "lest they make the people holy with their garments" (Ezek 44:19). Purity and sanctity are complementary and yet distinct. What is pure is accessible to the holy and for that very reason must be protected from the holy. The priests are also charged with teaching the people the difference between the holy and the profane and with making known the difference between the defiled and the clean (Ezek 44:23). Both basic impurity and any outbreak of holiness are dangers that must be guarded against.

Priestly concerns with the logic of cleanness are developed further in Leviticus. Certain things, such as blood and the parts of beasts that are to be offered, are unclean because they belong to the divine alone (see, e.g., Lev 7:22-27; 17:10-14). But other things, impure beasts and carcasses, are not fit for consumption, whether human (Israelite) or divine (Lev 7:19-21; 17:15-16). But whether viewed from the perspective of impurity or of holiness, the thread of the argument is the same: the laws of cleanness are Israel's means of maintaining a solidarity of sacrifice with God, apart from which the land may not be retained. Indeed, the claim is here explicitly made that the former inhabitants of the land failed to keep the rules of purity and for that reason were expelled, so that Israel might suffer the same fate (Lev 18:24-30). The land, in Leviticus, is not for Israel; Israel is for the service of God in his land. The conditionality of Israel's presence is cognate with the fierce emphasis on cutting off what is unclean (cf., e.g., Lev 7:19-21, 22-27) and separating from the Gentiles (cf., again as mere instances, Lev 18:3; 20:23).

Holiness is a curiously ambivalent force. It is what gives Israel the land but also what destroys anything that is not compatible with it. The priests are to be the instruments of Israel's compatibility with the holy, and for that reason they are both oddly privileged and fiercely punished. They partake of holy sacrifices and are held to a higher order of sanctity than the generality of Israel (Lev 21:6, 8, 14, 15, 22, 23). When Nadab and Abihu, sons of Aaron, offer incense in a foreign manner, they are consumed in fire, and God announces without remorse, "I will be sanctified among those who are near me, and I will be glorified before all the people" (Lev 10:1-3). Death then becomes the sanction for breaking the specific requirements of priesthood (cf. Lev 10:6-11; 16:1-2). God's desire is to consume a part of what is pure, but he will extirpate the impure, and his destruction of what he does not want is more comprehensive than his consumption of what he sets aside for himself. The priests are to keep those laws of purity that they teach, and more, because they are the guardians of Israel's cleanness, the peoples' tenuous compatibility with the holy (Lev 10:10, 11).

The notion that there are three *feasts that all male Israelites are to keep is paradigmatic within the Torah (cf. Ex 23:14-17; Lev 23; Num 28, 29), but Deuteronomy 16 is especially plain in its requirement. In Deuteronomy, the emphasis is not on what is offered to God, as in Leviticus and Numbers, nor on appearing before him, as in Exodus, but on the fact that a pilgrimage is necessary (for further discussion, *see* Temple). From the perspective of Moses, of course, Jerusalem itself is not at issue, but readers or hearers can only identify that city with the single "place" *(hamāqôm)* where God is to be worshiped (Deut 12:5-14). Because the ambit of activity in Deuteronomy extends far from Jerusalem, the slaughter and consumption of animals outside of Jerusalem, explicitly as nonsacrificial, is permitted, provided the blood is poured out and the beast concerned is not owed as a sacrifice (Deut 12:15-28).

The assumption of Leviticus is quite different; the priestly focus of its scheme imagines all meat being offered in sacrifice prior to consumption (see Lev 17:1-9). Just as Deuteronomy replaces that impracticable requirement with a concept of a secular meal, so it widens the definition of the meat that may be eaten. The gazelle and the hart are specifically authorized for eating in Deuteronomy 12:22, although they are not mentioned in Leviticus 11. Deuteronomy establishes a conception of purity that functions as related but not identical to the category of what may be sacrificed. Ezekiel, Leviticus and Deuteronomy all represent the covenantal regulation of sacrifice and make the *temple in Jerusalem the sole focus of that regulation.

Sacrifice includes certain pragmatics, things offered in the appropriate place by certain people. The pragmatic offering is associated with specific emotions and is justified by articulated ideologies. Ezekiel defines a particular space and its priests by visionary means; the pragmatics of Leviticus are the animals offered by specified procedures; Deuteronomy motivates Israel to join in sacrifice on festive occasions. Ezekiel looks forward to an affect of security, Leviticus to separation from Gentiles, Deuteronomy to the joy of households. What justifies the particular sacrifices of each book? The memory of idolatry in Ezekiel; the recollection of those expelled from the land in Leviticus; the anticipation of prosperity in Deuteronomy.

The Hebrew Bible attests, then, that the single covenant with Israel was consistent with varying emphases and practices within the conception of purity. Variation in that regard was also characteristic of well-known Judaic groups in the first century (*see DJG*, Judaism §4). *Priests, *Essenes and *Pharisees evolved characteristic concerns of purity. The parable of the Good Samaritan presents a priest and Levite avoiding a man left for dead on the side of the road; their fear of contamination from an unclean corpse overcame their compassion (Lk 10:31-32). Similar attitudes may be the source of *Josephus's complaint that the *Sadducees generally are boorish and suspicious (see Josephus *J.W.* 2.8.14 §166). Josephus also describes the Essenes' peculiar habits in regard to purity: among other things, he specifies the avoidance of oil, the practice of ablution and changing clothes prior to ritual meals and the treatment of the eating hall "as if it were a holy temple" (Josephus *J.W.* 2.8.3-5 §§123-31). The Pharisees also used changing clothes as a marker of purity: an associate was not to accept the *hospitality of a person of the land and could only receive a person of the land as a guest if a fresh clothing was provided for the guest (see *m. Dem.* 2:3).

2. Jesus' Program of Purity.

Jesus' circle was centered in *Galilee and was characterized by fellowship at meals involving various people with different practices of purity (see Mt 11:18-19 par. Lk 7:33-35). That description applies to the period of Jesus' own activity and also to the period after his death when Peter appears to lead the movement. In either phase, the circle of Jesus needed to cope with the social issue of possible defilement as one member of Israel with one set of practices met another member of Israel with a different set of practices.

One of the best attested of Jesus' sayings is his assertion that defilement is a matter of what comes from within, not from without (Mk 7:14-15). The point of this saying (and those to which it may be compared, Mt 15:10-11; Lk 11:40-41) is that there is a link between integrity and cleanness: that Israelites are properly understood as pure and that what extends from a person, what he or she is and does and has, manifests that purity.

Paul was to write some twenty-five years later and for his own purposes, "Do you not know that your body is a temple of the Holy Spirit within you, which you have from God?" (1 Cor 6:19). Paul may be alluding to a particular saying of Jesus (cf. Jn 2:21) or to what he takes to be a theme of Jesus; in either case he refers his readers to what he assumes to be elementary knowledge of the gospel. That Jesus and especially Paul, who associated himself with the Pharisees (cf. Phil 3:5) speak from such a perspective is not unusual. It is said that Hillel took a similar point of view and expressed it in a more heterodox manner. He defended an Israelite's right to bathe in Roman installations (*see* Gymnasia and Baths) on the grounds that if Gentiles deem it an honor to wash the idols of their gods, Israelites should similarly deem it an honor (indeed, a duty) to wash their bodies, the image of God (*Lev. Rab.* 34.3 [on Lev 25:25]). In other words, bathing does not make one pure but celebrates the fact of purity; in their different ways, Hillel and Paul demonstrate that representatives of the Pharisaic movement could conceive of purity as a condition that Israelites could be assumed to enjoy and out of which they should act. Fundamentally Jesus' concern appears similarly to have been with cleanness as a matter of production rather than of consumption.

Jesus' interest in the definition of purity is

also evident in the Synoptic story of what is known as Jesus' cleansing of a leper (Mt 8:2-4; Mk 1:40-44; Lk 5:12-14). In the story, a leper approaches Jesus and for no stated reason asserts that Jesus is able to cleanse him. Jesus assents, touching the man and pronouncing him clean, ordering him to show himself to a priest and to offer the sacrifice prescribed by Moses for cleansing. The terms of reference of the actions described are explicitly given with the book of Leviticus (Lev 13, 14).

The assumption of Leviticus 13—14, and therefore of the story in the Synoptics, is that leprosy, which might more literally be rendered "outbreak" (*ṣāraʿat*) comes and goes and that its presence and absence can be detected. In Leviticus 13, when the issue is "outbreak" in humans as distinct from cloth and houses, it is clear that the great concern and the cause of uncleanness is broken flesh (Lev 13:15). The suspicion of "outbreak" arises when there is a change in the pigmentation of the skin and accompanying hair, but a total change signals a return to cleanness (Lev 13:12-13), since the fundamental concern is broken flesh, to which no human correctly has access. Accordingly, sufferers are banned (Lev 13:45-46).

In the event one is declared clean by a priest, two distinct offerings are enjoined in Leviticus 14. The first is a local sacrifice and may take place wherever there is running water. The priest kills a bird in a earthen vessel over the water and dips a living bird in its blood, having beforehand attached cedar, scarlet and hyssop to it. He then sprinkles the sufferer from "outbreak" with the living bird and releases it (Lev 14:1-8). Purification follows (cf. Lev 14:9), after which the sufferer needs to offer two male lambs, a ewe, cereal and oil; together they constitute a sacrifice for guilt, a sacrifice for sin, a burnt sacrifice and a cereal sacrifice, all with the sufferer particularly in view (Lev 14:10-20). Exceptional provisions are made for instances of poverty (Lev 14:21-32), but the requirement of ownership remains onerous.

Within the setting envisaged in Leviticus, the story concerning Jesus therefore refers to a specific moment. The sufferer from "outbreak" attributes to Jesus the ability to adjudicate the status of his skin, and Jesus accepts the responsibility of telling him he may proceed directly to the sacrificial moment that is to occur after cleanness has been declared. Although Jesus is not portrayed as taking over any sacrificial function, he is explicitly assigned—within the terms of reference the story itself establishes—the authority to pronounce on matters of purity. Pharisees were similarly involved, as an entire tractate of the Mishnah *(Negaʿim)* attests.

Jesus and his circle appear to have been keenly concerned with purity as such, in a manner similar to the Pharisees (although purity was generally a focus of discussion and controversy within early Judaism). Jesus' stance is perhaps more similar to the Pharisees' than to the sectarians' of Qumran, who separated from ordinary worship in the temple, or the priests', who perpetuated that worship, but the formal categorization of Jesus as a Pharisee is not warranted.

The essential assumption in Jesus' cleansing of the man with "outbreak" is that purity is not merely a function of diagnosis by observation. The integrity of the skin proceeds from the integrity that animates the skin. Others concerned with purity might tell priests how to declare on the basis of their observations, advise concerning the removal of suspicious growths or counsel when the priest could best be visited (so the tractate *Negaʿim);* Jesus appears in the story to hold that the determinative factor is the man's approach in the expectation of purity and his own agreement to purification by contact with the man. The link between purity and righteousness is implicit within the sacrificial systems of the Hebrew Bible, and Psalms brings to open expression the systemic association of righteousness and purity (cf. Pss 18:21 [v. 20 in English versions]; 24:3-6; 26:4-7; 51:4, 8, 9, 12 [English vv. 2, 6, 7, 10]; 119:9).

Jesus' perspective in regard to purity is reflected within a passage that is also common to the Synoptics but that is particularly articulated in the source of Jesus' teaching commonly called Q. (Q is principally attested in Matthew and Luke, but parts of the source are also reflected in Mark.) In the commission to his twelve followers (and in Luke, seventy followers) to preach and heal, Jesus specifically commands them to remain in whatever house they are received within a given village, until they depart (Mt 10:11-14; Mk 6:10; Lk 9:4; 10:5-7). That commandment by itself is a notable development compared with a Pharisaic construction of purity, because it presupposes that what the disciples eat, within any house that might perceive them, is clean. Jesus' itineracy and that of his disciples, treated in much recent literature as if it were an obviously Greco-Roman practice, was a profound statement of the general purity of food in Israel.

The sayings source underscores that statement by having the disciples pronounce their peace upon the house in question (Mt 10:12, 13; Lk 10:5, 6), and Luke's Jesus particularly insists that the disciples should eat what is set before them in whatever town they might enter (Lk 10:7-8; see also *Gos. Thom.* §14). The pronouncement of peace and the injunction not to go from house to house within a given community (cf. Lk 10:7) but to stay put until the visit is over had obvious utility within the missionary concerns of the movement after the resurrection. (The message of the resurrection proved to be more divisive than Jesus' own preaching. The temptation to try to find especially sympathetic households prior to settling into a mission must have been great.) But the particular focus upon purity, all but obscured in Q with missionary directives, appears to have been Jesus'.

A last peculiarity of the commission in Q, which has long seemed incomprehensible, finds its sense under our analysis. Although Mark's Jesus has the disciples without bread, bag, money or a change of clothes, he does permit them a staff and sandals (Mk 6:8-9). In the mishnaic source of Jesus' sayings, however, just those obviously necessary items are singled out for exclusion (cf. Mt 10:9-10; Lk 9:3; 10:4). The traditional attempt to explain differences within the lists as the result of missionary practices within the early church is reasonable superficially, but that attempt only diverts attention from the obvious fact that the commission makes extremely poor sense as a missionary instrument. Why tell people not to take what on any journey they, practically speaking, might need? But if we understand the commission to treat every village they might enter as clean, as purely Israel as the temple itself, the perplexing structure of the commission makes eminent sense. The disciples are to enter villages exactly as pilgrims were to enter the temple within Pharisaic teaching: without the sandals, the staffs, the garments, the bags and the money (cf. *m. Ber.* 9:5; *b. Yebam.* 6b) that would normally accompany a journey. Q makes Jesus' commission into a missionary discourse; within his ministry, it was designed to be an enacted parable of Israel's purity.

Whether in the triply attested material of the Synoptics (a probable reflection of Petrine tradition) or in the doubly attested mishnaic source known as Q, a circle of concern associated with Jesus is held to see purity as proceeding from Israel. Once one is identified with Israel, it is not that which is without that defiles but those things that come from oneself. Separation from that which is outside one does not therefore assure purity, and non-Jews in the mixed environment of Galilee pose no particular danger to Israel. The circle of Jesus frames its rhetoric for its specific, social circumstance of Israel in the midst of the nations. Defilement here is a matter of failing to recognize the others of Israel, refusing to produce from within and to contact on that basis the pure Israel that those others represent.

3. The Conflicting Strategies of Peter, James and Paul.

Peter shared with Jesus the hope of a climactic disclosure of divine power, signaled in the willingness of nations to worship on Mt. Zion. That hope is attested within sources extant by the first century. Chief among them, from the point of view of its influence upon the NT, is the book of Zechariah.

Zechariah provided the point of departure for Jesus' inclusive program of purity and forgiveness as the occasions of the kingdom. Jesus is said to have mentioned the prophet by name (see Mt 23:34-36; Lk 11:49-51). The book of Zechariah programmatically concerns the establishment of restored worship in the temple, especially at the feast of Sukkoth (Zech 14:16-19). "All the nations" are to go up to Jerusalem annually for worship (Zech 14:16), and the transformation of which that worship is part involves the provision of "living waters" from the city (Zech 14:8; cf. Jn 4:10, 14). That image is related to an earlier "fountain opened for the house of David and the inhabitants of Jerusalem in view of sin and uncleanness" (Zech 13:1). Here we see the association of forgiveness and purity that is a feature of Jesus' program, as well as the notion of an immediate release, without any mention of sacrifice, from what keeps Israel from God. God himself is held to arrange the purity he requires, so that the sacrifice he desires might take place.

Zechariah features the commissioning of a priest (Zech 3; see Mt 16:18-19), an oracle against swearing (Zech 5:3-4; see Mt 5:33-37), a vision of a king humbly riding an ass (Zech 9:9; see Mt 21:1-9; Mk 11:1-10; Lk 19:28-40; Jn 12:12-19), the prophetic receipt of thirty shekels of silver in witness against the owners of sheep (Zech 11:4-17; see Mt 26:14-16; 27:3-10; cf. Mk 14:10-11; Lk 22:3-6). It is obvious that the connections between Jesus' ministry and Zechariah do not amount to a common agenda, and Matthew clearly reflects a tendency to increase the fit between the two. But the similarities are suggestive of Jesus' appropriation of Zechariah's prophecy of eschatological purity, as a final, more fundamental connection would indicate. The climactic vision of Zechariah insists that every vessel in Jerusalem will belong to the Lord and become a fit vessel for sacrifice. As part of that insistence, the text asserts that no trader will be allowed in the temple (Zech 14:20-21). In the light of Zechariah, Jesus' occupation of the temple appears an enactment of prophetic purity in the face of a commercial innovation, a vigorous insistence that God would prepare his own people and vessels for eschatological worship (see *see DLNTD*, Temple §2).

Peter perpetuated that vision by means of his fidelity both to breaking bread at home with the disciples and in worship within the temple. At the same time, Acts portrays Peter's activity much further afield (*see DLNTD*, Temple §3). The key to connection between Peter's residence in Jerusalem and his activity in Syria and beyond is provided by the vision that he relates as the warrant for his visit to the house of Cornelius, the Roman centurion (Acts 10:1-48). Peter is praying on a rooftop in Joppa around noon. His vision occurs while he is hungry and concerns a linen lowering from heaven, filled with four-footed animals, reptiles and birds. A voice says, "Arise, Peter, slaughter and eat," and he refuses (in words reminiscent of Ezek 4:14). But a voice again says, "What God has cleansed, you will not defile" (see Acts 10:9-16).

Peter defends his baptisms in the house of Cornelius on the basis of his vision in the course of a dispute with those who argued that circumcision was a requirement of adherence to the movement (Acts 11:1-18). He cites his activity among non-Jews at a later point, in the context of what has come to be called the apostolic council (Acts 15:7-11). Throughout, the position of Peter appears to have been consistent: God may make, and has made, eschatological exceptions to the usual practice of purity. Those exceptions include the acceptance of uncircumcised men in baptism and fellowship with them.

The policy of accepting non-Jews, who were baptized but not circumcised, was perhaps the most important decision that the primitive church made. It is presented as formalized in the book of Acts in a single session (Acts 15:1-35), but the reference to the dispute earlier (in Acts 11:1-3) shows that the policy was framed over a number of years. Moreover, what appears as a single meeting in Acts 15 addresses two distinct issues. The first issue was whether non-Jews might be baptized without being circumcised (see Acts 15:1-12). The second issue was whether such baptized Gentiles could be embraced in a single fellowship with Jews who had been baptized (see Acts 15:13-29).

In his letter to the Galatians, Paul reflects the discussion and dispute over the two issues as a vitally concerned participant (Gal 2:1-10). Paul records the agreement of the "pillars" of the church in Jerusalem that there should be an apostolate to the uncircumcised, represented by Paul, as well as to the circumcised, represented by Peter. Of course, other apostolates—such as James's—also concentrated on the circumcised; Paul's point is that Peter was especially concerned with the circumcised outside of Jerusalem and even beyond territorial Israel. Those pillars include James, Jesus' brother; Peter; and John. Paul goes on to describe the contention that emerged in *Antioch, a dispute that split the church for decades, but the remarkable agreement on a central point should not be overlooked: James, Peter and Paul agreed that there was a place for non-Jews within the movement. Those who disagreed with them, the adherents to the Abrahamic requirement of circumcision (see Gen 17:10-14), were not silenced and maintained their position (see Acts 11:2-3; 15:1; Gal 5:2-12). Ebionite Christianity, however, appears to have been the only wing of the church in the second century in which their stance prevailed (see Irenaeus *Haer.* 1.26.2; *see DLNTD*, Ebionites). However much the position of the circumcisers could claim the warrant of Scripture, the vision of Peter represents the dominant tendency toward an acceptance of non-Jews.

The inevitable question emerged: did the acceptance of non-Jews imply their full fellowship of Jewish believers? In their response to that question, Peter, James and Paul went their separate ways. Paul reports favorably on the practice in Antioch before emissaries from James came, when meals could be conducted with common fellowship among Jewish and non-Jewish followers of Jesus (see Gal 2:12). According to Paul, the arrival of those emissaries caused Peter to separate from non-Jews, and even Barnabas acceded to the separation (Gal 2:12-13). The tendency of Hellenistic communities of Christians to mix their Jewish and non-Jewish constituencies, and therefore to relax or ignore issues of purity in foods, is here documented by Paul (c. A.D. 53).

When Acts gives an account of the Jacobean policy toward Gentiles, James appears much more sympathetic but nonetheless rigorous. The occasion of his statement of policy is said to be the suggestion that one must be circumcised in order to be saved (Acts 15:1), a suggestion that is associated with a form of Christian Pharisaism (Acts 15:5). Peter is said to side with Paul, with the argument that Gentiles who receive the Holy Spirit should not have the burdens laid on them "which neither our fathers nor we were able to bear" (Acts 15:10, within Acts 15:7-11). Peter sounds remarkably Pauline at this juncture: Paul uses a similar line of argument against Peter in Galatians 2:14-21, and Peter according to Acts 15:11 sums up by averring that both Jews and Gentiles are to be saved "through the grace of the Lord Jesus" (cf. Eph 2:5). Whatever the precise relationship between Acts 15 and Galatians 2, it is apparent that the Lukan portrayal of Peter has been framed in the interests of an accommodation with a Pauline perspective. James in Acts agrees that Gentiles who turn to God are not to be encumbered (Acts 15:19), and yet he insists they be instructed by letter to abstain "from the pollutions of idols, and from fornication, and from what is strangled, and from blood" (Acts 15:20).

The grounds given for the Jacobean policy are that the law of Moses is commonly acknowledged (Acts 15:21); the implication is that to disregard such elemental considerations of purity as James specifies would be to dishonor Moses. Judas Barsabbas and Silas are then dispatched with Paul and Barnabas to deliver the letter in Antioch along with their personal testimony (Acts 15:22-29), and they are said particularly to continue their instruction as prophets (Acts 15:32-33). They refer to the regulations of purity as necessities (Acts 15:28), and no amount of Lukan gloss can conceal that what they insist upon is a serious reversal of Paul's position (see 1 Cor 8). The dispatch of Judas and Silas implicitly undermines the standing of Paul and Barnabas, and James's policy amounts to a constraint upon the behavior of Gentiles who joined the movement. The constraints are sometimes compared to the so-called Noachic commandments of *b. Sanhedrin* 56a-b, which are held to be binding on non-Jews.

While Paul held that there was a new "Israel of God" (Gal 6:16), defined by having faith in Jesus just as Abraham had faith in God (Gal 3:6-9), Peter conceived of the acceptance of non-Jews in baptism more as a gracious inclusion than the "new creation" of which Paul spoke (Gal 6:15). Once non-Jews had been accepted in baptism, Peter might sometimes have fellowship with them, and sometimes not. As an apostle, such contact might be necessary; as a faithful Jew, it was not natural. Within Paul's perspective, that was hypocrisy; within Peter's perspective, it was a consistent consequence of proceeding by the revelation of whom and what God accepts and when, rather than a predetermined policy. James, while accepting the baptism of non-Jews, nonetheless maintained that a policy of their separation from Jews should be followed, unless they observed enough of the commonly acknowledged rules of purity to honor in practice the status of the Torah as the revelation to Moses, warranted in Scripture.

4. The Resolution of Purity and Virtue in Hellenistic Christianity.

The logical extension of Paul's conception was that all things are pure to the pure, precisely the formulation attributed to him in Titus 1:15. But Paul's practice turned out to be otherwise. In 1 Corinthians 8 he departs from the policy of James by accepting that food offered to idols might be eaten on the grounds that idols represent entirely fictional gods (1 Cor 8:4-6). But he also warns against eating such food if some who believe in such gods are confirmed in their idolatry, "and their conscience, being weak, is defiled" (1 Cor 8:7-13, especially v. 7). The defilement here is internal and moral rather than pragmatic, but it is nonetheless dangerous; Paul declares that he would prefer not to eat meat at all rather than cause a brother to sin (1 Cor 8:13; see the restatement of the principle in Rom 14:13-23). By means of his own, characteristic argument, Paul approximates to what the rabbis would come to teach concerning the danger of idolatrous feasts (see *b. ʿAbod. Zar.* 8a, instruction in the name of R. Ishmael).

Paul in this aspect reflects a more general tendency in Hellenistic Christianity. In his letters and in letters attributed to him there is an express connection between named vices, which are cataloged, and "impurity" (Rom 1:24; Gal 5:19; Eph 4:19; 5:3; Col 3:5). Early Christianity saw a shift in the understanding of the medium of impurity: no longer foods but moral intentions conveyed the danger of defilement. And those intentions are as specifically identified in the NT as impure foods are discussed in rabbinic literature, because the danger in both cases was understood to be an impurity that made a real and dangerous separation from God.

The cataloguing of sins, and their classification with impurity, is scarcely a Christian invention (*see* Vice and Virtue Lists). It is represented, for example, in Wisdom 14:22-31. But the genre is mastered to brilliant effect in Romans 1:24-32; Galatians 5:19-21; Ephesians 5:3-5; Colossians 3:5-6, and is taken up in the period after the NT (see *Did.* 5; *Herm. Man.* 8; *see DLNTD*, Virtues and Vices). What is striking in each case is not only the equation of impurity and sin but also a clear indication that impurity as such remains a fundamental category: sexual contact, a concern from at least the time of Leviticus 18, survives the declining significance of alimentary purity, even within Paul's thought. There is no question, therefore, of purity being abstracted into the realm of intention. Rather, intentionality of practice, as well as observation of the integrity of one's body, are together held to define an ambit of purity. On such an understanding, one's body was indeed a temple of the Holy Spirit (see 1 Cor 6:18-20; cf 1 Cor 3:16-17), and a rigorous attitude toward *marriage is coherent with the emphasis that a new purity is required by God for the inheritance of his kingdom (see Mt 5:27-28, 31-32; 19:3-12; Mk 10:2-12; Lk 16:18; 1 Cor 7:10-16).

The success of the gospel of Jesus within the Hellenistic environment of primitive Christianity was in no small measure a function of its ability to frame a rational, practical but stringent system of purity. The marketplace is declared pure in itself, provided it does not encourage the defilement of idolatry, and the requirements of James are largely forgotten. But moral, and especially sexual, requirements make it clear that purity has not been abandoned as a regulatory system, despite the efforts of Paul in regard to alimentary purity.

The success of the resolution of virtue and purity within primitive Christianity was sealed by the attribution to Jesus of the identification between the two. The attribution appears in Mark and the Matthean parallel just after Jesus' own teaching about what truly defiles (Mk 7:15). First by means of comment in response to a question (Mk 7:17-19) and then by means of comment and catalog (Mk 7:20-23), the rhetoric attributes the shift in the medium of impurity to Jesus himself. The rhetoric is the product of an interpretative community, a circle sufficiently influential to cast what it had been taught concerning Jesus' principle into the terms of reference of the Hellenistic mission.

The circle is concerned with issues of fellowship at meals but is unwilling to dismiss purity as a divine category, as Pauline rhetoric could do (see Rom 14:14). The circle responsible for Mark 7:20-23 insists upon the danger of impurity but sees the contagion in moral terms. Such an attitude is closer to that of the lists of vices that Paul repeats than it is to the innovative aspects of his argument and rhetoric. The identification of the authority behind the circle is obviously a matter of inference, but—among the possibilities given by Paul in Galatians 2—the most plausible suggestion is that it represents the apostolate of Barnabas. Barnabas is described by Paul as being less engaged with the dispute than either James or Peter but also as having been taken up in their "hypocrisy" (Gal 2:11-13). In effect, once Jesus enters the house in Mark 7:17, a new social setting is addressed, and the point of his teaching, as commented upon and expanded by means of a catalog, is that vices rather than foods are sources of impurity. The categories of the pure and the impure are maintained, but they are worked out on the basis of moral rather than alimentary materials.

The dramatic shift in rhetoric and meaning within the Barnaban circle could not have succeeded by means of the comment (Mk 7:17-19) and the catalog (Mk 7:20-23) alone. After all, they were by way of appendix to the principal matter of the emerging text, which still concerned qorban (Mk 7:6-13) and the direction of impurity (Mk 7:14-15). In order to recast the whole of the tradition as an assertion of a new medium of impurity, defined on Jesus' authority, a rhetorical method needed to be found that would point all of the arguments in the same direction that the latest developments indicated.

The solution was a synthetic device of enormous power: narrative context. The arguments generally, with their varying rhetorics and different topics, are presented in the context of a single dispute. Pharisees and scribes observe that Jesus' disciples do not wash their hands before meals; they object, and Jesus goes on to reply by means of the narrative material (Mk 7:1-2, 5). The new context has nothing precisely to do with the arguments that are then attributed to Jesus. Qorban, the direction of defilement, the comparative danger of foods and vices are all interesting matters, more or less related by a common interest in what true purity is, but none of those arguments answers the Pharisaic/scribal objection to not washing prior to a meal. The narrative context proceeds on the assurance that the readership already understands that all Pharisaic/scribal practices are to be grouped together and accorded the same sort of weight one would attribute to washing one's hands.

The power of the rhetoric is demonstrated by the fact that Jesus never answers the question that is posed to him. The response needs to be filled in by the hearer or reader, who has been catechized to the point that it seems evident that there is a new, inner purity of moral intention that supersedes the practices of Judaism. The Gospels, as well as the more obviously Hellenistic documents of the NT, attest the resolution of virtue and purity that was a vital part of the genius of Christianity.

See also JUDAISM AND THE NEW TESTAMENT; PHARISEES; PRIESTS AND PRIESTHOOD, JEWISH; PURIFICATION TEXTS; SACRIFICE AND TEMPLE SERVICE; TEMPLE, JEWISH; VICE AND VIRTUE LISTS.

BIBLIOGRAPHY. R. P. Booth, *Jesus and the Laws of Purity: Tradition and Legal History in Mark 7* (JSNTSup 13; Sheffield: JSOT, 1986); A. Büchler, *Studies in Sin and Atonement* (New York: Ktav, 1967); R. Caillois, *L'homme et le sacré: Edition augmenté de trois appendices sur le sexe, le jeu, la guerre dans leurs rapport avec le sacré* (Paris: Gallimard, 1989); D. Catchpole, "Paul, James and the Apostolic Decree," *NTS* 23 (1977) 428-44; B. Chilton, *A Feast of Meanings: Eucharistic Theologies from Jesus Through Johannine Circles* (NovTSup 72; Leiden: E. J. Brill, 1994); M. Detienne and J.-P. Vernant (with J.-L. Durand, S. Georgoudi, F. Hartog, J. Svenbro), *La cuisine du sacrifice en pays grec: Bibliothèque des histoires* (Paris: Gallimard, 1979); M. Hengel, "Jakobus der Herrenbruder—der erste "Papst"? in *Glaube und Eschatologie: Festschrift für Werner Georg Kümmel zum 80. Geburtstag,* ed. E. Grässer and O. Merk (Tübingen: Mohr Siebeck, 1985) 71-104; J. D. Levenson, *Theology of the Program of Restoration of Ezekiel 40—48* (HSM 10; Atlanta: Scholars Press, 1986); J. Milgrom, *Studies in Cultic Theology and Terminology* (Leiden: E. J. Brill, 1983); E. P. Sanders, *Jewish Law from Jesus to the Mishnah: Five Studies* (Philadelphia: Trinity Press International, 1990); J. Z. Smith, *To Take Place: Toward Theory in Ritual* (Chicago: University of Chicago Press, 1987); D. P. Wright, *The Disposal of Impurity: Elimination Rites in the Bible and in Hittite and Mesopotamian Literature* (SBLDS 101; Atlanta: Scholars Press, 1987).

B. D. Chilton

PYTHAGOREANISM. *See* NEW-PYTHAGOREANISM.

PYTHIAN ORACLES. *See* PROPHETS AND PROPHECY.

QAHAT. *See* TESTAMENT OF QAHAT.

QUMRAN CAVE 7. *See* CAVE 7 FRAGMENTS (QUMRAN).

QUMRAN: PLACE AND HISTORY

Nestled above the northwest shore of the Dead Sea, this archaeological site first attracted attention after the discovery of the *Dead Sea Scrolls in 1947. Since then it has been the object of enormous interest and controversy. Its interest for NT studies lies chiefly in what it permits us to know about the people of the Dead Sea Scrolls who were an integral part of the historical context into which the early Christian movement emerged.

1. Physical Location
2. Relationship to the Caves
3. The Excavation of the Site
4. History of the Site: The Consensus View
5. History of the Site: Alternative Hypotheses
6. Related Site: Ain Feshka

1. Physical Location.

The ruins at Qumran (Khirbet Qumran) are located nearly 30 kilometers east of *Jerusalem. The ruins sit atop the north edge of Wadi Qumran, the drainage for the Plain of Buqeiʿa. The wadi runs into the Dead Sea several kilometers north of Ain Feshka, a site thought to be related to Khirbet Qumran.

2. Relationship to the Caves.

Of the nearly three hundred caves explored in the surrounding region, eleven have yielded scrolls. Caves 1 and 2 are located about 2 kilometers north of Khirbet Qumran, and Caves 11 and 3 are over 1 kilometer further to the north. Caves 4 and 5 and 7 through 10 are situated in the cliffs that lead down from the site to the bottom of the wadi. Cave 6 is located in an eastward-facing cliff due west of Caves 4 and 5 and 7 through 10. When the location of Cave 1 was first established in early 1949 the connection between it and the Qumran site was at first rejected. But in time more observers considered it likely that there was some connection between the two, and so in 1951 R. de Vaux of the École Biblique in Jerusalem led the first season's excavation. That undertaking established the link between the caves, the site and the *Essenes mentioned in the classical sources (Philo *Omn. Prob. Lib.* 75-91; *Hypoth.* 11.1-18; Josephus *J.W.* 2.8.2-13 §§119-61; *Ant* 18.1.5 §§18-22; Hippolytus *Haer.* 9.18.2—28.2; Pliny *Nat. Hist.* 5.15.73).

3. The Excavation of the Site.

After the 1951 campaign de Vaux did not return to the site to excavate until the 1953 season. He was forced to devote the 1952 season to Cave 4, thanks to its discovery by the bedouin earlier in the same year. Then beginning in 1953 de Vaux and his team excavated at Khirbet Qumran for four consecutive seasons. The complete results of those efforts were never published in de Vaux's lifetime, although his 1959 Scweich Lectures summarize his findings (de Vaux). Only now are the full excavation reports being published (Humbert and Chambon). In any case, de Vaux's fieldwork laid the foundation for the standard view regarding the history of the site and its relationship to the life of the Essene community at Qumran.

4. History of the Site: The Consensus View.

According to de Vaux there were three periods of habitation at Qumran associated with the people of the scrolls (Periods Ia, Ib and II). In addition there was another period that preceded the first Essene occupation of the site (the Israelite period) and three more that followed their residence between A.D. 69 and 134 (Periods II and III and the second revolt).

4.1. Israelite Period. The details of this period of habitation remain sketchy. That it came to a close at the time of the Babylonian conquest of Judah in 586 B.C. seems assured since de Vaux's excavations turned up scattered pottery fragments datable to the sixth century B.C. in an ash layer indicative of violent destruction. During the Israelite period the site consisted of an enclosure that encompassed at its northwest end a large round cistern, a single large room to the east of the cistern, up to eight smaller enclosed spaces at its eastern end and some additional rooms on its north and south sides. De Vaux also dated a wall running from the southeast corner of the enclosure down to Wadi Qumran to this period.

The remains from this period are associated with one of the cities mentioned in Joshua 15:61-62. The passage mentions six cities located "in the desert," one of which is Ain Gedi, a site further up the Dead Sea from Qumran. Thus it is assumed that the phrase "in the wilderness" situates the cities in the Dead Sea region. Additional evidence supporting this conclusion comes from a survey of other Israelite-period strongholds located on the "Plain of the Buqeiʿa, on the plateau which dominates Qumran" (de Vaux, 2; Cross and Milik). De Vaux and most others have assumed this site to be the City of Salt mentioned in Joshua 15:62, but whether that is true can hardly be determined with certainty. In any case, the site was occupied in the preexilic period and probably functioned as an outpost like the other sites surveyed by F. M. Cross and J. T. Milik.

4.2. Period Ia. According to de Vaux the site remained unoccupied for centuries, only to be resettled some time in the second half of the second century B.C. The modest installation during this period was built around the remains of the earlier settlement. North and east of the round cistern two new rectangular water basins were added, and the original round cistern was restored to use. Rudimentary aqueducts were installed to collect the runoff from the plain to the west and to channel the water among the cisterns. A decantation basin to collect the silt from all three cisterns was added. Several small rooms were constructed around the cisterns, and in the southeast corner, in the space formerly occupied by the small rooms at the east end of the Israelite period settlement, two pottery kilns were constructed. De Vaux notes that the few pottery sherds from this period are of the same type as those produced in Period Ib, making it impossible to use them to date the beginning of this era. However, because he dates the beginning of the next phase of occupation to around 100 B.C. and the evidence for this phase is so sparse, he concludes that it cannot have lasted long and that it began no earlier than the middle of the second century B.C.

4.3. Period Ib. De Vaux remarks that it was during this period "when the buildings at Khirbet Qumran acquired what was virtually their definitive form" (5; see fig. Qumran Site, Period Ib). From the evidence of the site it is presumed that an influx of new community members necessitated an expansion of the existing facilities. The new construction developed around the basic structural outlines of Period Ia.

One new feature of this period is the addition of a well-defined entryway to the community site. Just to the east of the existing cistern complex is an entrance from the north. This opens to a corridor that runs between the cistern complex and the now walled-off enclosure of Period Ia. The corridor extends to the southern edge of the Period Ia settlement and continues, after a jog to the east, into Period Ib buildings south of the earlier enclosure.

A second new feature is the considerable expansion and articulation of the large Period Ia enclosure that formed the easternmost part of the settlement. There are several new features within the enclosure. A fortified tower was built in the northwest corner, adjacent to the new entryway. Access to its lower two stories could be had only from within the tower, indicating the structure's defensive purpose. South of the tower several new rooms on two levels were added. Further to the south, but still within the Period Ia enclosure, a new, large cistern was added. Another cistern was installed over the old pottery kiln in the southeast corner of the enclosure. Finally, another complex of rooms was developed in the eastern half of the old enclosure, among which were a kitchen and workshops. Outside of the Period Ia courtyard there were small expansions to the north and east of the tower. To the east of the old enclosure and west of the Period Ia wall that ran to the wadi a pottery workshop was added, and south of that a large cistern was installed. On the south side of the Period Ia en-

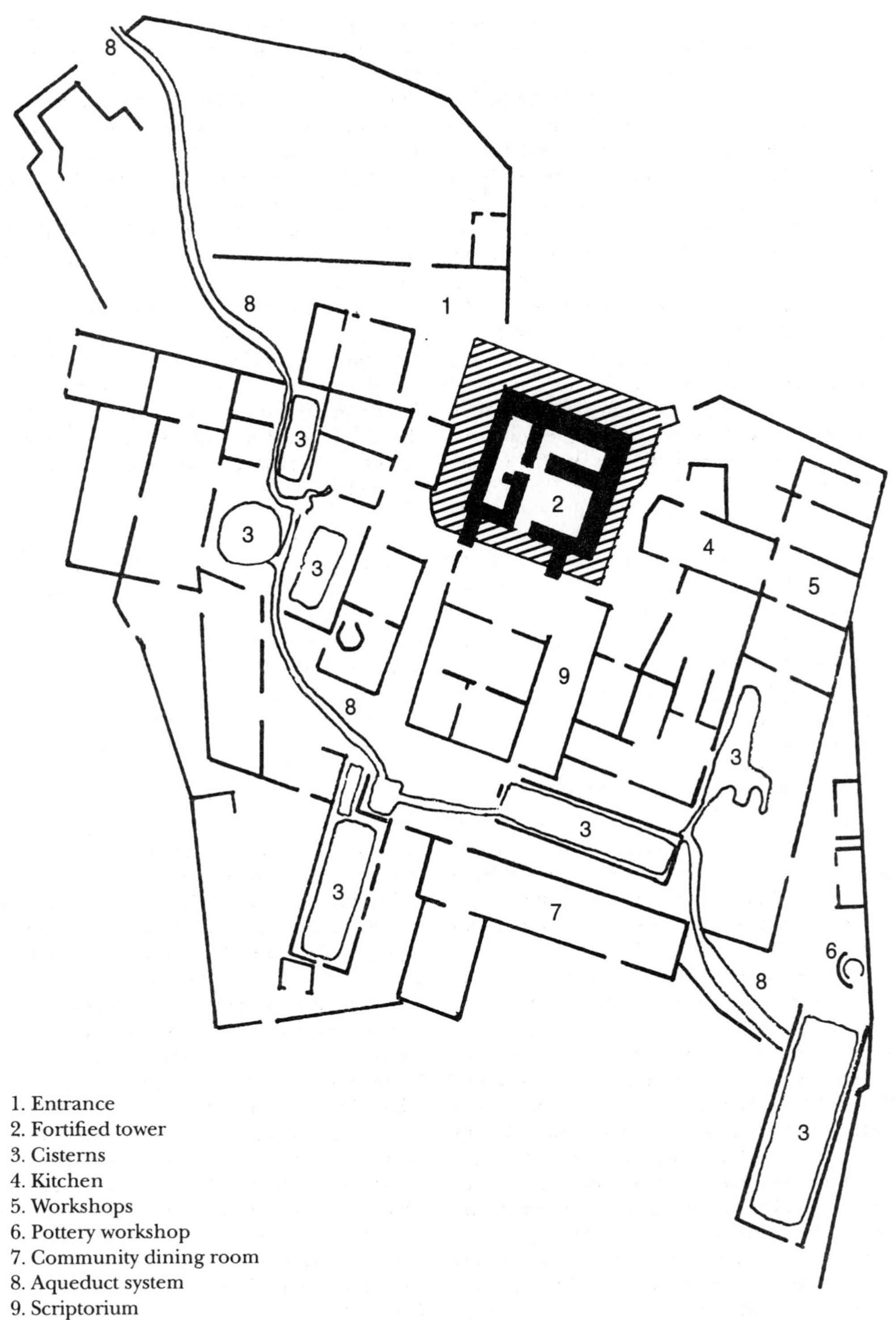

QUMRAN SITE, PERIOD IB

closure the community dining room was added. Supporting the latter identification was the additional room off the southwest corner of the dining hall that contained hundreds of pieces of crockery. An additional cistern was added to the west of the dining hall and due south of the original cistern complex, and still further to the west was a corral area for livestock.

Additional expansion in this period took place to the west and north of the existing cistern complex. A courtyard was added west of the original circular cistern, and to the west of the courtyard storerooms were constructed. To the north of the cistern complex an enclosed courtyard was added, as were decantation basins and a bath, all of which served to catch the water flowing into the community from the newly constructed aqueduct that brought runoff from the hillside. The increased numbers of site users necessitated construction of the aqueduct, as well as the new cisterns.

De Vaux made a complex argument involving the pottery and coin evidence to date the beginning of this period to the reign of John Hyrcanus (*see* Hasmoneans), although he was inclined by the evidence to go as late as the beginning of the first century B.C. To date the end of Period Ib de Vaux correlates the testimony of *Josephus with signs of an earthquake and a fire at the site. Josephus records that an earthquake struck the region in 31 B.C. (*Ant.* 15.5. §§121-47; *War* 1.19. §§370-80), and there is abundant evidence of a seismic event in the site that was followed almost immediately by a fire. While de Vaux acknowledges that the two events could have been separated by some time, he insists that the simplest explanation of the evidence is that the earthquake caused a devastating fire to break out. This single episode marked the end of the Period Ib.

4.4. Period II. Relying once more on a complicated argument involving the *coins found at the site, de Vaux suggests that the site was reoccupied during the early part of the reign of Archelaus, perhaps around 4 B.C. Roman arrowheads within a layer of ash, coins from the third year of the war between *Rome and the Jews and Josephus's account of Vespasian's military activities in the region (*J.W.* 3.4. §447) convince de Vaux that Period II drew to a violent close in A.D. 68 (*see* Jewish Wars with Rome).

During this period little new was added to the site. The main adjustments seem to have been aimed at compensating for the losses incurred as a result of the earthquake and fire that ended the previous period of habitation. Rooms that were no longer useful were closed off, and other spaces that had been open were covered over to create new indoor areas. Walls weakened by the earthquake were fortified, especially those around the tower. Decantation basins overrun with silt during the period of abandonment were repaired or replaced. De Vaux also thinks that the room in the central part of the settlement he defined as a scriptorium was constructed in this period. He identified the room as a scriptorium on the basis of several structures that he thought were suitable as writing tables. Further confirmation came in two inkwells unearthed in the rubble of the room (see fig. Qumran Site, Period Ib).

4.5. Period III. The presence of coins from *Caesarea and Roman arrowheads above the destruction layer that indicates the end of Period IIb suggested to de Vaux that the site was remodeled by the Romans as a garrison after their attack on the community in A.D. 68. The latest coin found within the settlement dates to A.D. 72/73, indicating to de Vaux that use of the site ceased not much later, certainly by the end of the war. During this period most of the site was leveled or left to decay, and only the fortified tower and rooms to the south and east of it were refurbished for use by the soldiers stationed there. That the aqueduct was simplified to channel all of the runoff from the hillside into the cistern at the southeastern corner of the site further indicates the more limited use of the site during this period.

4.6. The Second Revolt. Once again a small cache of coins helps prove that the site was inhabited during the period in question. A bowl containing ten coins was found in a ground-floor room in the fortified tower. Among them was one silver denarius of the second revolt, one denarius of Vespasian and three denarii of Trajan. The coins suggest that this was one of the sites that provided refuge for Jews fleeing the Roman legions as they advanced across the land to extirpate the remaining pockets of resistance. A letter from Wadi Murabbat is interpreted to refer to this site when it mentions a "Fortress of the Pious" (Milik 1960, 163-64). Whatever its name at the time, it was only briefly occupied during the revolt, and there is no sign that its inhabitants did anything to adjust the structures to their needs.

4.7. The Cemetery. A large cemetery was located by the community just to the east of the settlement. It contains around eleven hundred graves and is generally associated with Periods I and II (Steckoll). The few graves that have been excavated within the cemetery proper all contained male remains that were more or less interred in the same manner. A north-south orientation shaft of 1 to 2 meters was dug into the marl terrace, at the bottom of which was carved out a cavity under the east wall. The body was laid in the cavity, and the cavity was covered over with stone slabs or bricks. The bodies were placed with their heads to the south. (On burial practices at Qumran, see Hachlili.) An extension to the east of this large cemetery contains bodies in much shallower east-west orientation graves. The remains in those graves were of women and children, raising questions regarding the community's admission of nonmale members. However, recently those remains have proven to be no more than two centuries old, and probably those of bedouin who traveled the area in the recent past (Zias). Two additional cemeteries north and south of the settlement hold another forty-five graves altogether.

5. History of the Site: Alternative Hypotheses.

Not everyone has accepted de Vaux's judgments. There are two kinds of alternative hypotheses. Some reject his identification of the site with the Essenes, and one other merely disagrees with his site chronology.

5.1. Alternative Identifications. Several alternative theories have been proposed, but because they all stumble over some of the most obvious aspects of the site, none of them presents real challenges to the Essene hypothesis. P. Donceel-Voûte and J.-B. Humbert interpret the site as a country villa, N. Golb determines it to be a fortress, A. Crown and L. Cansdale speculate that it was a commercial trading post, and E. Cook has suggested that it served as a ritual purification center. The fortified tower and lack of ornamentation speak against the villa hypothesis; the lack of fortification apart from the tower undermines Golb's suggestion; insufficient evidence of trading activity eliminates the Crown and Cansdale theory; and the evidence for wider use of the site than for ritual cleansing casts doubt on Cook's notion.

5.2. Alternative Chronology. A much stiffer challenge to de Vaux's theory comes from J. Magness, who offers a revised chronology for the site (1998, 57-59). She notes, as have others, that the absence of habitation from 31 B.C. (the earthquake and fire) to 4 B.C. is difficult to explain. Moreover, she notes that the hoard of silver coins found beneath Period II and above Period Ib include Tyrian tetradrachmas dating from 126 B.C. to 9/8 B.C., when *Herod's reign ended. De Vaux said that these must have been placed there at the beginning of Period II. Magness makes the observation that hoards are most likely placed in situ during periods of stress and that 9/8 B.C., the end of Herod's reign and the time of the latest coins in the hoard, was just such a passage of time. So she suggests that the earthquake of 31 B.C. did damage the site but that there was no fire at the time and the site was not abandoned then. Rather the repairs de Vaux associates with Period II were made shortly after the seismic event, and it was only in 9/8 B.C. that fire and violence descended upon the site as a result of the disturbances connected with Herod's demise. Thus the site would have been abandoned no more than a few years at most, since we are confident of habitation beginning again in 4 B.C. On the basis of ceramic evidence Magness also rejects de Vaux's Period Ia, suggesting instead that the settlement was first inhabited by the people of the Dead Sea Scrolls in the first half of the first century B.C. (1998, 64-65).

6. Related Site: Ain Feshka.

Down the hill from Qumran and slightly to the south is a related site, Ain Feshka. It was in use during Periods Ib and II of the Qumran site. There is no sign of the fire that de Vaux thinks brought Period Ib to a close. There is, however, evidence of destruction in A.D. 68. Magness suggests that this site was developed only after the earthquake of 31 B.C. (Magness 1997).

The installation is made up of a central building or courtyard with rooms around it. De Vaux found some evidence that the site served as a date-ripening facility. Another building to the north contains a water-control box with waterways and a pool. Just what this part of the installation was used for is not clear, although some speculate that it was a tannery (de Vaux), while another suggests it served as a fish farm (Zeuner). In any case, it seems to have been utilized for some unspecified industrial use supportive to the residents at the Qumran site.

See also DEAD SEA SCROLLS: GENERAL INTRODUCTION; ESSENES.

BIBLIOGRAPHY. E. Cook, "What Was Qumran? A Ritual Purification Center," *BAR* 22 (1996) 39, 48-51, 73-75; F. M. Cross and J. T. Milik, "Explorations in the Judean Buqêʿah," *BASOR* 142 (1956) 5-17; A. Crown and L. Cansdale, "Qumran—Was It an Essene Settlement?" *BAR* 20 (1994) 24-36, 73-78; P. Donceel-Voûte, "Les ruines de Qumran réinterprétées," *Archeologia* 298 (1994) 24-35; N. Golb, *Who Wrote the Dead Sea Scrolls?* (New York: Simon & Schuster, 1995); R. Hachlili, "Burial Practices at Qumran," *RevQ* 62 (1993) 247-64; J.-B. Humbert, "L'espace sacré à Qumràn," *RB* 101-2 (1994) 161-214; J.-B. Humbert and A. Chambon, *Fouilles de Khirbet Qumrân et de Aïn Feshkha* (NTOA Series Archaeologica 1; Freiburg: Editions Universitaires; Göttingen: Vandenhoeck & Ruprecht, 1994-); J. Magness, "The Chronology of Qumran, Ein Feshka and Ein el-Ghuweir," *The Qumran Chronicle* 8 (1997) 7-21; idem, "Qumran Archaeology: Past Perspectives and Future Prospects," in *The Dead Sea Scrolls: A Comprehensive Assessment After Fifty Years,* ed. P. W. Flint and J. C. VanderKam (2 vols; Leiden: E. J. Brill, 1998, 1999) 1:47-77; J. T. Milik, *Ten Years of Discovery in the Wilderness of Judaea* (SBT 26; London: SCM, 1959); idem, "Textes hébreux et araméens," in *Les Grottes de Murabbaʿât,* ed. P. Benoit, J. T. Milik and R. de Vaux (DJD 2; Oxford: Clarendon Press, 1960) 67-205; S. H. Steckoll, "Preliminary Excavation Report in the Qumran Cemetery," *RevQ* 23 (1968) 323-36; R. de Vaux, *Archaeology and the Dead Sea Scrolls* (London: Oxford University Press, 1973); F. E. Zeuner, "Notes on Qumran," *PEQ* 92 (1960) 27-36; J. Zias, "The Cemeteries of Qumran and Celibacy: Confusion Laid to Rest?" *DSD* 7 (2000) forthcoming.

R. A. Kugler

R

RABBINIC LITERATURE: MIDRASHIM

The noun *midrash* derives from the Hebrew root *drš*, which means "to seek" or "to inquire." The root *drš* occurs more than 150 times in the *Hebrew Bible; however, the noun *mdrš* appears only twice (2 Chron 13:22; 24:27). Both passages refer to items "written in the midrash of," but it is impossible for us to know the contents or nature of these two midrashic texts. *Mdrš* appears a few times in the literature from *Qumran, where it denotes the study of *law, judicial investigation or interpretation of Scripture. In Mishnah, *mdrš* refers to an interpretation or explanation. In the earliest midrashic collections—*Mekilta, Sipra* and *Sipre*—it denotes interpretation of statutes, *ḥûqîm,* or a collection of these interpretations, and it often carries the same two meanings in the Babylonian Talmud. While *midrash* may mean study or inquiry in general, by the time of the compilation of the Babylonian Talmud it most frequently refers to scriptural interpretation or to collections of such interpretations; that is, it names an intellectual activity, the product of that activity and a collection of those products.

1. Midrash as a Type of Literature
2. Types of Rabbinic Literature
3. Midrash as a Literary and Religious Activity
4. Midrashic Collections

1. Midrash as a Type of Literature.

At present we have only literary examples of midrash and the midrashic processes. As a literary phenomenon, midrash is best defined as "a type of literature, oral or written, that stands in direct relationship to a fixed, canonical text, considered to be the authoritative and revealed word of God by the midrashist and his (or today, her) audience, and in which this canonical text is explicitly cited or clearly alluded to" (Porton 1979, 112). Midrash stands in opposition to those texts of rabbinic Judaism, such as Mishnah and Tosefta, that do not frequently cite biblical texts in support of their rulings or as elements in their pericopes (*see* Rabbinic Literature: Mishnah and Tosefta). Some passages within large literary collections may be midrashic, while other sections are not.

The midrashic enterprise begins within the Hebrew Bible itself. Deuteronomy reworks passages from Exodus and Numbers, Chronicles retells many of the stories found in the books of Kings, the later prophets often build upon the earlier prophets, and the titles of some of the psalms are commentaries on the psalms' contents. Although the exact relationship between intrabiblical and extrabiblical midrash has not been fully examined, it is likely that the Bible does not comment upon itself in exactly the same manner as do the later texts that view it as a sacred and canonical whole.

The Samaritan Pentateuch, 1 Maccabees 1:56 ("The books of the law which they found they tore to pieces and burned with fire"), the appearance of every biblical book with the exception of Esther at Qumran, the importance of the OT for the nascent Christian communities and the centrality of the Bible for *Philo, *Josephus and rabbinic Judaism testify to the importance of the Hebrew Bible during the *Hellenistic period and in late antiquity. However, this does not justify the claim that the Bible was the charter, constitution or sole source of inspiration and law for the postexilic Jewish communities. The *Apocrypha and Pseudepigrapha, the texts from Qumran, the Christian Bible and the rabbinic collections all include many nonbiblical traditions. Midrash often brings these two sources, biblical and nonbiblical traditions, into juxtaposition.

There are several types of Palestinian Jewish

midrashic activity in the postbiblical period. As Ben Sira's grandson noted (*see* Sirach), all translations involve interpretation, "for things once expressed in Hebrew do not have the same force in them when put into another language." The *Septuagint and the targumin (*see* Rabbinic Literature: Targumim) are examples of this type of midrash. Another class of midrash involves rewriting the biblical narratives (*see* Rewritten Bible). The book of **Jubilees*, *Pseudo-Philo's *Liber Antiquitatum Biblicarum* and the **Genesis Apocryphon* are perfect illustrations of this type of midrashic activity. Because Josephus's *Antiquities of the Jews* and Philo's *Life of Moses* seem to be directed to non-Jews, they do not fall into our definition of midrash. The pesharim found at Qumran and similar eschatological interpretations of the Hebrew Bible represent another kind of midrashic activity. Finally, rabbinic midrash fits into its own category, and this is the type of midrash we normally think of.

2. Types of Rabbinic Literature.

In general terms there are two major types of rabbinic literature: midrashic and nonmidrashic, frequently referred to as mishnaic. Previous scholars have distinguished between *midrash halakhah,* the legal midrashic collections of *Sipre, Sipra* and *Mekilta,* and *midrash aggadah,* nonlegal midrashic collections, such as *Genesis Rabbah, Leviticus Rabbah,* the *Pesiqta de Rab Kahana* and the *Pesiqta Rabbati.* However, this distinction is meaningless because the so-called halakic midrashim contain a good deal of nonlegal material and comment upon nonlegal passages in the Bible, and the so-called haggadic midrashim include a fair amount of explicit halakah and even more implicit halakah. Similarly, the label "tannaitic midrashim," which is often used to refer to the halakic midrashim, should be abandoned. The date of the compilation of some of these texts is far from certain. They do contain only interpretations attributed to Tannaim, Palestinian sages of the first two centuries A.D., but the later texts also contain Tannaim along with Amoraim, Babylonian and Palestinian rabbis of the third through the eighth centuries. Some include major sections that cite only tannaitic authorities and may be tannaitic creations.

The most useful distinction among the midrashic collections is between the homiletical and the expositional midrashim. An expositional midrash follows the text of a given biblical book. It is a running commentary on the book or a major section of the book. While individual sections may have been created in settings different from their present contexts and may have no real relationship to the comments that surround them, a relationship has been imposed on them by the order of the biblical text. The homiletical midrashim are collections of independent units that do not form a running commentary on the biblical books. Each unit's coherence stems from its relationship to a given topic, theme or holy day. *Sipra, Sipre, Mekilta, Genesis Rabbah* and the midrash on Lamentations are the major expositional midrashim. The *Pesiqta de Rab Kahana,* the *Pesiqta Rabbati, Leviticus Rabbah* and *Deuteronomy Rabbah* are the best examples of the homiletical midrashim.

3. Midrash as a Literary and Religious Activity.

The homiletic midrashim we have are literary creations; we have no evidence that they were originally oral rabbinic sermons. No rabbinic sources from late antiquity support the contention that the rabbis preached in *synagogues. There are few texts that place rabbis within the context of a synagogue, and none of them describe a rabbi preaching a sermon. More likely the rabbis created midrash for other sages within the context of their schoolhouses. Midrash reflects the rabbis' fascination with the Hebrew Bible as God's revelation. One of the rabbis' tasks was to make the Bible applicable and comprehensible in the age in which they lived. The rabbis also sought to demonstrate their intimate knowledge of the text and their mastery of God's revelation. Their knowledge of the whole of revelation, both the written Torahand the oral torah, distinguished the rabbis from other Jews, who at most knew only the written Torah. Their knowledge of Torah was the source of the rabbis' authority within the Jewish community, as well as the blueprint for the community they wished to create.

Midrash is a religious activity, and it reflects the rabbis' intimate interaction with the written record of God's revelation. The styles and methods of rabbinic interpretation did not differ greatly from the Greek *rhetoricians' investigations of Homer. The Hebrew exegetical terms are often Hebrew translations of the rhetoricians' technical vocabulary. The major difference between the two enterprises was the rabbis' belief that the Bible was God's revelation to humanity and that it contained, along with the oral torah, God's plan and expectations for the whole of humankind. The Bible was God's everlasting, perfect truth, and it formed the foundation of the world the rabbis sought to create. Midrash was based on and reinforced these truths. It was a means of bringing the Bible into the rabbis' world in a more direct way than did Mishnah or other nonmidrashic intellectual activities.

Jewish groups in the ancient world distinguished themselves from one another through their readings of the Hebrew Bible and their interpretative schemes. Josephus tells us that a major difference between the *Sadducees and the *Pharisees was the former's rejection of laws "which were not recorded in the Law of Moses." The Mishnah states that those who deny that resurrection is a biblical doctrine will not enter the world to come. A defining difference between Judaism and Christianity was their mutually exclusive interpretations of the Hebrew Bible. The covenanters at Qumran and the Jews in Jerusalem had radically different ideas about the Bible's calendar and its theory of election. Even Philo distinguishes himself from others in *Alexandria based on their methods of biblical exegesis. Interpretation of Scripture was a literary and theological activity of great consequence for Jews in antiquity.

Those who engaged in midrash accepted the divinity of the Torah and the belief that the only way to discover God's plan was through exegeting Scripture. The biblical text had to be examined and reexamined until every nuance had been elucidated and their implications fully spelled out. Those who composed nonmidrashic texts, such as Mishnah, assumed that human rationality and reason could uncover God's will and plan. While the authors of Mishnah drew heavily on Scripture, we could not perceive the topics they chose to elucidate merely by studying the Bible. They moved in directions and on trajectories unlimited by the biblical text and its priorities. Those who created midrash sought to demonstrate that everything they imagined or created was firmly based in and even originated in the biblical text. The human mind could not create the Jewish community or follow God's plan unaided by revelation.

4. Midrashic Collections.

It is impossible for us to review in detail the major midrashic collections from the rabbinic period. At this point, we only wish to mention something about the most frequently cited collections for purposes of studying Judaism and its relationship to early Christianity. We must remember, however, that these collections date at the earliest from the third century, so that it is often difficult to know what parts of their content originated earlier. They were all created in Palestine.

Sipra is an early collection of exegetical statements on Leviticus. *Sipra* means "the book," an early designation for the book of Leviticus. The *Sipra* we now have comments on the entire book of Leviticus, verse by verse, often word by word. *Sipra* is either contemporaneous with Mishnah or slightly postdates it.

Mekilta is an exegesis of parts of the book of Exodus, specifically Exodus 12:1—23:19, 31:12-17 and 35:1-3. *Mekilta* is the Aramaic word for "rule" or "norm." In the postrabbinic age, the word carries the meaning of a rule derived from Scripture or of halakic exegesis. Although *mekilta* occurs in the Talmudim, it does not refer to our exegetical collection. The earliest clear reference to our present *Mekilta* comes from the eleventh century. The work is called the *Mekilta of Rabbi Ishmael* because the body of the collection was considered to have begun with the second section, which opens with a reference to Ishmael. *Mekilta* does not cover all of the legal portions of Exodus, especially omitting the building of the tabernacle, and it contains an exegesis of some of the narrative portions of the biblical book, especially the Song of the Sea (Ex 15). The *Mekilta* we have has undergone numerous redactions, beginning in the Amoraic period; therefore, it is difficult to determine the date of its origin as an exegetical collection. However, most would place its origins somewhere in the second to the third centuries.

Sipre means "books," and in the Babylonian Talmud it refers to a commentary on Exodus, Numbers and Deuteronomy. By the Middle Ages, however, the term was limited to commentaries on only the latter two books of the Torah. *Sipre Numbers* begins with Numbers 5:1, the first legal material in the book, and covers Numbers 5—12, 15, 18—19, 25:1-13, 26:52—31:24 and 35:9-34. The consensus of scholarly opinion dates the midrash after the middle of the third century. *Sipre Deuteronomy* is a midrash on Deuteronomy 1:1-30, 3:23-29, 6:4-9, 11:10—26:15

and 31:14—32:34; therefore, it covers both legal and narrative portions of the biblical book. Most scholars believe that the exegetical portions at the beginning and the end of the collection are of a different origin from the midrash's central legal core. The collection is usually dated to the late third century.

Genesis Rabbah is a midrash on the book of Genesis. The meaning of the word *rabbah* in its title is a matter of dispute. Some have argued that this is the "great" midrash on Genesis, while others have suggested that the name comes from Rabbi Oshayah Rabbah, a sage cited early in the collection. The midrash includes everything from close readings of verses, sometimes word by word, to elaborate expositions that have little connection to the text of Genesis. The redactor of this collection seems to have drawn material from a wide range of rabbinic texts. Although direct quotations are difficult to demonstrate, especially given the state of the manuscripts we now have, it seems that those behind *Genesis Rabbah* knew the contents of Mishnah, Tosefta, *Sipra, Sipre, Mekilta* and the targumim. Because *Genesis Rabbah* does not quote our present version of the Palestinian Talmud but does know the content of even its most recent layers, the two texts were most likely redacted at about the same time, probably in the first half of the fifth century.

Leviticus Rabbah is constructed around themes. It does not necessarily follow the order of the biblical text, and it often deals with only the first few verses of a section of the Bible. *Leviticus Rabbah* consists of thirty-seven homilies. Most scholars agree that *Leviticus Rabbah* was redacted sometime in the fifth century. The *Pesiqta de Rab Kahana* is a homiletical midrash constructed around the biblical readings for the *festivals and the special *sabbaths. In addition to sections for the festivals, there are homilies for the four sabbaths after Hanukkah, the three sabbaths before the ninth of Av, the fast day on which Jews recall the destructions of the first and second temples, the seven sabbaths of comfort after the ninth of Av and the two sabbaths after the New Year. The *Pisiqta* has five chapters in common with *Leviticus Rabbah.* Most contemporary scholars would date the core of the midrash to the fifth century, about the same time as the redaction of *Leviticus Rabbah.*

See also BIBLICAL INTERPRETATION, JEWISH; RABBINIC LITERATURE: MISHNAH AND TOSEFTA; RABBINIC LITERATURE: TALMUD; RABBINIC LITERATURE: TARGUMIM; SCHOLARSHIP, GREEK AND ROMAN; TORAH; WRITING AND LITERATURE: JEWISH.

BIBLIOGRAPHY. H. Basser, *Sifre Haazinu: Midrashic Interpretations of the Song of Moses* (New York: Peter Lang, 1984); D. Boyarin, *Intertextuality and the Reading of Midrash* (Bloomington: Indiana University Press, 1990); W. G. Braude and I. J. Kapstein, *Pesikta de-Rab Kahana: R. Kahana's Compilation of Discourses for Sabbaths and Festal Days* (Philadelphia: Jewish Publication Society of America, 1975); W. H. Brownlee, "Biblical Interpretation Among the Sectaries of the Dead Sea Scrolls," *BA* 14 (1951) 54-76; G. L. Bruns, "The Hermeneutics of Midrash," in *The Book and the Text: The Bible and Literary Theory,* ed. R. Schwartz (Oxford: Blackwell, 1990) 189-213; D. Daube, "Rabbinic Methods of Interpretation and Hellenistic Rhetoric," *HUCA* 22 (1949) 234-64; M. Fishbane, *Biblical Interpretation in Ancient Israel* (Oxford: Clarendon Press, 1985); idem, *The Midrashic Imagination: Jewish Exegesis, Thought and History* (Albany, NY: State University of New York Press, 1993); S. D. Fraade, *From Tradition to Commentary: Torah and Its Interpretation in the Midrash Sifre to Deuteronomy* (Albany, NY: State University of New York Press, 1991); H. Freedman, *Midrash Rabbah* (10 vols.; London: Soncino, 1931-39); J. Goldin, *The Song at the Sea* (New Haven, CT: Yale University Press, 1971); W. S. Green, "Romancing the Tome: Rabbinic Hermeneutics and the Theory of Literature," *Semeia* 40 (1987) 147-68; R. Hammer, *Sifre: A Tannaitic Commentary on the Book of Deuteronomy* (New Haven, CT: Yale University Press, 1986); S. A. Handelman, *The Slayers of Moses: The Emergence of Rabbinic Interpretation in Modern Literary Theory* (Albany, NY: State University of New York Press, 1982); G. H. Hartman and S. Budick, *Midrash and Literature* (New Haven, CT: Yale University Press, 1986); J. Z. Lauterbach, *Mekhilta de-Rabbi Ishmael* (Philadelphia: Jewish Publication Society of America, 1933); P. P. Levertoff, *Midrash Sifre on Numbers* (London: A. Golub, 1926); J. Neusner, *Genesis Rabbah: The Judaic Commentary to the Book of Genesis, A New American Translation* (Atlanta: Scholars Press, 1985); idem, *Introduction to Rabbinic Literature* (ABRL; New York: Doubleday, 1994); idem, *Invitation to Midrash: The Working of Rabbinic Bible Interpretation, A Teaching Book* (San Francisco: Harper & Row, 1988); idem, *Judaism and Scripture: The Evidence of Leviticus Rabbah* (Chicago: University of Chicago Press, 1986); idem, *Mekhilta Attributed to R. Ishmael: An Analytical Translation* (Atlanta: Scholars Press, 1988); idem, *Midrash in Context: Exegesis in Formative Judaism* (Philadelphia: Fortress, 1983); idem, *A Midrash Reader* (Minneapolis: Fortress, 1990); idem, *Pesiqta deRab Kahana: An Analytical Translation and Explanation* (Atlanta: Scholars Press, 1987); idem, *Sifra: An Analytical Translation* (Atlanta: Scholars Press, 1988); idem, *Sifre to Deuteronomy: An Analytical Translation* (Atlanta: Scholars Press, 1987); idem, *Sifre to Numbers: An American Translation and Explanation* (Atlanta: Scholars Press, 1986); G. G. Porton, "Midrash: Palestinian Jews and the Hebrew Bible in the Greco-Roman Period," in *ANRW* 2.19.2 (1979) 103-38; idem, "Rabbinic Midrash," in *History of Biblical Interpretation,* ed. A. J. Hauser and D. F. Watson (Grand Rapids, MI: Eerdmans, 2000) vol. 1; idem, *Understanding Rabbinic Midrash: Text and Commentary* (Hoboken, NJ: Ktav, 1985); R. Sarason, "The Petihot in Leviticus Rabba: Oral Homilies or Redactional Constructions?" *JJS* 33 (1982) 557-67; idem, "Road to a New Agendum for the Study of Rabbinic Midrashic Literature," in *Studies in Aggadah, Targum and Jewish Liturgy in Memory of Joseph Heinemann,* ed. J. J. Petuchowski and E. Fleischer (Jerusalem: Magnes, 1981) 55-73; H. Strack and G. Stemberger, *Introduction to the Talmud and Midrash* (Edinburgh: T & T Clark, 1991); G. Vermes, "Bible and Midrash: Early Old Testament Exegesis," in *Cambridge History of the Bible,* 1: *From the Beginnings to Jerome,* ed. P. R. Ackroyd and C. F. Evans (Cambridge: Cambridge University Press, 1970) 199-231; idem, *Scripture and Tradition in Judaism* (Leiden: E. J. Brill, 1961).

G. G. Porton

RABBINIC LITERATURE: MISHNAH AND TOSEFTA

The Mishnah is the principal source of the law of Judaism in ancient times. The Tosefta is a compilation of clarifications of mishnaic law and supplements to them.

1. The Mishnah
2. The Tosefta

1. The Mishnah.

The primary law code of Judaism from its closure in about A.D. 200 to the present, the Mishnah is a collection of sixty-two treatises on norms of action and attitude that all together set forth a philosophy of hierarchical classification. That philosophy sets forth through inductive analysis a philosophy of monotheism. That religious philosophy shows through practical rules how all things flow upward to one thing or how from one thing all things emanate downward, the result of hierarchical classification. When the framers of the Mishnah take up any topic, they collect the relevant facts and then form these facts into groups through a process of classification by indicative traits, working from the species to the genus. At the next stage, the groups are formed into lists of things in hierarchical order. The whole therefore holds together through syllogistic logic applied to the analysis of the traits of things: applied reason and practical logic.

The Mishnah's laws cover both theoretical matters, bearing no practical consequence at the time of the formation of the code, as well as highly practical topics. Organized by topic, the laws fall into six principal categories: the conduct of the agricultural economy in accord with the commandments of God to *Moses set forth in the Torah of Sinai; the observance of holy time, specifically, the *sabbath and *festivals; the sanctification of *marriage and *family life; the institutions of civil government and the resolution of conflict in a just and righteous society; the sacred offerings of the *temple and maintenance of the building and the cults; and the levitical rules of *purity and uncleanness pertinent both to the temple and sexual life.

1.1.* Zeraim: *Agriculture. The critical issue in the economic life, which means in farming, is in two parts, revealed in the first division. First, Israel, as tenant on God's Holy Land, maintains that property in the ways God requires, keeping the rules that mark the land and its crops as holy. Next, the hour at which the sanctification of the land comes to form a critical mass, namely, in the ripened crops, is the moment most ponderous with danger and heightened holiness. Israel's will so affects the crops as to mark a part of them as holy, the rest of them as available for common use. The human will is determinative in the process of sanctification.

1.2.* Moed: *Appointed Times or Holy Seasons. What happens in the land at appointed times marks off spaces of the land as holy in yet another way. The center of the land and the focus of its sanctification is the temple. There the produce of the land is received and given back to

God, the One who created and sanctified the land. At these unusual moments of sanctification, the inhabitants of the land in their social being in villages enter a state of spatial sanctification. That is to say, the village boundaries mark off holy space, within which one must remain during the holy time. This is expressed in two ways. First, the temple itself observes and expresses the special, recurring holy time. Second, the villages of the land are brought into alignment with the temple, forming a complement and completion to the temple's sacred being. The advent of the appointed times precipitates a spatial reordering of the land, so that the boundaries of the sacred are matched and mirrored in village and in temple. At the heightened holiness marked by these moments of appointed times, therefore, the occasion for an affective sanctification is worked out. Like the harvest, the advent of an appointed time such as a pilgrim festival, also a sacred season, is made to express that regular, orderly and predictable sort of sanctification for Israel that the system as a whole seeks.

1.3. **Nashim:** ***Women and Neziqin: Damages.*** These take their place in the structure of the whole by showing the congruence, within the larger framework of regularity and order, of human concerns of family and farm, politics and workaday transactions among ordinary people. For without attending to these matters, the Mishnah's system does not encompass what is meant to comprehend and order. So what is at issue is fully cogent with the rest. In the case of *women, the third division, attention focuses upon the point of disorder marked by the transfer of that disordering anomaly, woman, from the regular status provided by one man to the equally trustworthy status provided by another. That is the point at which the Mishnah's interests are aroused: once more, predictably, the moment of disorder. In the case of damages, the fourth division, there are two important concerns. First, there is the paramount interest in preventing, so far as possible, the disorderly rise of one person and fall of another and in sustaining the status quo of the economy, the house and household, of Israel, the holy society in eternal stasis. Second, there is the necessary concomitant in the provision of a system of political institutions to carry out the laws that preserve the balance and steady state of persons.

The third and fourth divisions, which take up topics of concrete and material concern, the formation and dissolution of families and the transfer of property in that connection, the transactions, both through torts and through commerce, that lead to exchanges of property and the potential dislocation of the state of families in society, are both locative and utopian. They deal with the concrete locations in which people make their lives, household and street and field, the sexual and commercial exchanges of a given village. But they pertain to the life of all Israel, both in the land and otherwise. These two divisions, together with the household ones of appointed times, constitute the sole opening outward toward the life of utopian Israel, that *Diaspora in the far reaches of the ancient world, in the endless span of time. This community from the Mishnah's perspective is not only in exile but also unaccounted for, outside the system, for the Mishnah declines to recognize and take it into account. Israelites who dwell in the land of (unclean) death instead of in the Holy Land fall outside of the range of (holy) life. *Priests, who must remain cultically clean, may not leave the land, and neither may most of the Mishnah.

1.4. **Qodoshim:** ***Holy Things and Tohorot: Purities.*** These form the counterpart of the divisions of agriculture and appointed times, for they deal with the everyday and the ordinary, as against the special moments of harvest and special time or season. The fifth division is specifically about the temple on ordinary days. The work of the temple, the locus of sanctification, is conducted in a wholly routine and trustworthy, punctilious manner. The one thing that may unsettle matters is the intention and will of the human actor. This is subjected to carefully prescribed limitations and remedies. The division of holy things generates its companion, the sixth division, the one on cultic cleanness, purities. The relationship between the two is like that between agriculture and appointed times, the former locative, the latter utopian, the former dealing with the fields, the latter with the interplay between fields and altar.

Here too, in the sixth division, once we speak of the one place of the temple, we address the cleanness that pertains to every place. A system of cleanness, taking into account what imparts uncleanness and how this is done, what is subject to uncleanness and how that state is overcome, that system is fully expressed in response to the participation of the human will. Without the wish and act of a human being, the system does not function. It is inert. Sources of uncleanness, which come naturally and not by volition, and modes of purification, which work naturally and not by human intervention, remain inert until human will has imparted susceptibility to uncleanness. The movement from sanctification to uncleanness takes place when human will and work precipitate it.

2. The Tosefta.

Reaching closure some time, perhaps fifty years (hence c. A.D. 250), after the Mishnah, the Tosefta ("supplements") provides a compilation of statements pertinent to rulings of the Mishnah or their problems or their themes. Some of these statements are freestanding, but most of them presuppose counterpart statements in the Mishnah and form commentaries to them. It follows that the Tosefta is a collection of statements on the general problems addressed in the Mishnah, ordered in large topical formations, or tractates, that correspond to those of the Mishnah and treating only the topics addressed in the Mishnah and no others.

The document contains three kinds of materials, in descending order of frequency. The first is citation of a sentence of the Mishnah and a paraphrase and gloss of that sentence, thus, commentary in the simplest form; such writing is incomprehensible on its own but makes good sense in relationship to the Mishnah's sentence, which defines its context and meaning. The second is freestanding sentence(s), which can be understood in their own terms but that, on closer reading, can be fully understood and shown to be coherent only when brought into juxtaposition with a counterpart statement in the Mishnah. The third is autonomous sets of sentences that make full and complete sense standing on their own, with no point of intersection with the Mishnah except in general topic. We do not need to open the Mishnah to understand the statements of such aggregates of cogent sentences, forming entirely coherent paragraphs.

2.1. How the Tosefta Is Organized. The Tosefta holds together in one of two ways. First, sentences cohere not to one another but only to the Mishnah, forming glosses, pure and simple; we know that they cohere only to the Mishnah because if we rearranged the sentences, putting first last and last first, they would make as much or as little sense as they do now. But, in relationship to the Mishnah, they make perfect sense. Then the Mishnah's order dictates the Tosefta's sentences' sequence. Second, sentences cohere to one another but make sense only when we read the corresponding Mishnah paragraph. The coherence is general, but if we set forth the same sentences in some other order than the one they now have, they would make sense just as well or just as little. So we know that the full sense of a set of sentences emerges only in response to the uncited but omnipresent Mishnah paragraph, because their present order is explained or is best explained when we bring the discrete sentences into relationship to the Mishnah. Then the order, which at first seems random, turns out to be necessary; we can explain that order and show that that, and no other sequence, is necessary.

2.2. The Oral Torah. The laws of the Mishnah and the Tosefta are represented by tractate *ʾAbot,* the Fathers (c. A.D. 250), as deriving by oral tradition from God through Moses and the prophets and sages. Presented as part of the Mishnah but standing on its own and autonomous of the Mishnah's forms and entire topical program, tractate *ʾAbot* contains wise sayings attributed to sages in a chain of tradition beginning, "Moses received Torah from Sinai and handed it on to Joshua" and ending with the names of authorities of the first and second centuries. Some of these, in particular Gamaliel and his son Simeon, are known to us as *Pharisees.

While the Mishnah contains laws deriving from a variety of sources, beginning with Scripture itself, and while much of the document is worked out in the names of authorities who flourished in the second century, three areas of the law focus upon topics important to the Pharisees as represented by the Gospels: tithing, cultic cleanness and sabbath observance. These bodies of law are portrayed as subject to dispute between Jesus and the Pharisees, and much that the Mishnah records as normative law intersects in topic, problematic and even proposition with sayings attributed to Jesus. That explains why, once the Gospels indicate points of intersection with the rules of the Mishnah or the Tosefta, we may ask those rules to help us understand that to which the Gospels' stories make reference. The Mishnah's and Tosefta's information may then define the context in which statements in the Gospels take on concrete meaning.

2.3. The Mishnah and the Gospels: A Case Study. Numerous stories and sayings in the Gospels presuppose information that comes to us only in the Mishnah and its supplement. To give a single example, Matthew 23:25-26 has "Woe to you, scribes and Pharisees, hypocrites! For you cleanse the outside of the cup and of the plate but inside they are full of extortion and rapacity . . . first cleanse the inside of the cup and of the plate, that the outside also may be clean."

The saying thus presupposes that Pharisees concern themselves with the cleanness of cups and plates, and since the setting is not cultic (temple cleanness) but quotidian, the premise of the saying directs attention to the application to domestic affairs of levitical rules of cultic cleanness that in Scripture apply only to the temple. The saying further takes for granted Pharisees distinguish between the inside and the outside of a cup or plate; they cleanse first of all the outside. To uncover the relevance of the saying we turn to Mishnah tractate *Kelim* 25:1, which states, "All utensils have outsides and an inside." The matter is further clarified at *m. Kelim* 25:6: "A utensil, the outer parts of which have been made unclean with liquids—the outer parts are unclean. Its inside, its rims, hangers, and handles are clean. [If] its inside is made unclean, the whole is unclean." To this Tosefta *Kelim Baba Batra* 3:12 adds, "Utensils used for Holy Things have no [distinctions among] an outer part or an inner part." A further statement in the same context is assigned to first-century figures: "This testimony did Hezekiah Abi Iqqesh present before Rabban Gamaliel in Yavneh, which he stated in the name of Rabban Gamaliel the Elder, 'Whatever has no inside among clay utensils also has no outer parts [that are subject to becoming unclean. Such a flat clay object is insusceptible entirely]'" (*Sifra* CXIV:1.6). So the premise of the statement attributed to Jesus, that we deal with everyday objects, is reenforced by this explicit statement of the law.

In the present instance, therefore, the notion that we make distinctions among the parts of a utensil is attested to the first century by Matthew, and the details of what it means to make such a distinction are contributed by the later rabbinic law code and its commentary. But a point of conflict emerges. The saying attributed to Jesus takes for granted that Pharisees first or only cleanse the outside of the cup. If it were taken for granted that Pharisees first cleanse the inside of the cup before they cleanse the outside or do not cleanse the outside, then the saying makes no sense. If people do clean the inside first, then the saying "first cleanse the inside" bears no weight. But all parties to the discussion of the rabbinic law concur that if the outside is unclean, the inside of the utensil is unaffected. If the inside is unclean, the entire utensil is unclean. Now that conception is precisely the one advocated—metaphorically for the moral condition of humanity—by Jesus. So the actual law taken as normative by the authorities of the Mishnah contradicts the law that the saying attributed to Jesus imputes to the Pharisees.

But there are Pharisees who maintain that the outer part of the utensil may be clean even while the inner part is unclean. These are the disciples of Shammai, the first-century debating partner of Hillel, organized as the house of Shammai, opponents of the house of Hillel. They take the view that even if the inner part of the utensil is unclean, the outer part is clean. That position emerges at Mishnah tractate *Berakot* 8:2. In preparing the meal, the house of Shammai maintains that people are to wash hands and then mix the cup of wine, and the house of Hillel hold that one mixes the cup and afterward washes the hands. The reason of the house of Shammai is given by the Tosefta to the same passage: "So that the liquids that are on the outer side of the cup may not be made unclean by his hands and then go and make the cup unclean." The house of Shammai does not want unclean hands to touch the liquid on the outer part of the cup, which will go and make the cup unclean; so the state of the inner part is not decisive (just the opposite of what Jesus says). The house of Hillel, by contrast, holds that the outer side of the cup is always unclean (so the Tosefta), so all that what matters is the condition of the inside of the cup (exactly what Jesus says in his metaphor).

The saying of Matthew has called our attention to the corresponding passages in the Mishnah and the Tosefta, and these have imparted concreteness to the saying attributed to Jesus and shown the practical foundations for his moral metaphor.

We cannot uncritically cite the Mishnah and the Tosefta for a factual account of the state of the law in the time of Jesus. The Mishnah's attributions cannot be taken at face value, and the sources of the Mishnah's law and the state of its conception of the law prior to closure remain questions subject to considerable study. No final answers dictate that a given rule tells us about the law in remote antiquity, or in the first century or only in the early third century, when the document reached closure. And the Tosefta is temporally and logically subordinate to the Mishnah. The Gospels stand closer in time to the first century than do the Mishnah and the Tosefta as we now have them. Nor can we automatically deem as a factual account of first-century times a saying attributed to a first-century authority by a third-century compilation. But at numerous specific points exegesis of the Gospels does find valuable information and even sharp perspective in those documents, just as the Gospels richly contribute to the exegesis of the Mishnah.

See also PURITY; RABBINIC LITERATURE: TALMUD; RABBIS; TORAH.

BIBLIOGRAPHY. **Translations.** H. Danby, *The Mishnah* (Oxford: Oxford University Press, 1933); J. Neusner, *The Mishnah: A New Translation* (New Haven, CT: Yale University Press, 1987); J. Neusner and R. S. Sarason, eds., *The Tosefta: Translated from the Hebrew,* 1: *The First Division (Zeraim)* (New York: Ktav, 1985); J. Neusner, *The Tosefta: Translated from the Hebrew,* 2: *Second Division (Moed)*; idem, *The Tosefta: Translated from the Hebrew,* 3: *Third Division (Nashim)*; idem, *The Tosefta: Translated from the Hebrew,* 4: *Fourth Division (Neziqin)*; idem, *The Tosefta: Translated from the Hebrew,* 5: *Fifth Division (Qodoshim)* (2nd printing; Atlanta: Scholars Press for USF Academic Commentary Series, 1995); idem, *The Tosefta: Translated from the Hebrew,* 6: *Sixth Division (Tohorot)* (2nd printing: Atlanta: Scholars Press for South Florida Studies in the History of Judaism, 1990, with a new preface). **Studies.** W. S. Green, "The Talmudic Historians," in *The Modern Study of the Mishnah,* ed. J. Neusner (Leiden: E. J. Brill, 1973); M. D. Heer, "Tosefta," *EncJud* 15:1283-85; G. F. Moore, *Judaism in the First Centuries of the Christian Era: The Age of the Tannaim* (Cambridge, MA: Harvard University Press, 1927); J. Neusner, *Form Analysis and Exegesis: A Fresh Approach to the Interpretation of Mishnah* (Minneapolis: University of Minnesota Press, 1980); idem, *A History of the Mishnaic Law of Appointed Times,* 5: *The Mishnaic System of Appointed Times* (Leiden: E. J. Brill, 1981); idem, *A History of the Mishnaic Law of Damages,* 5: *The Mishnaic System of Damages* (Leiden: E. J. Brill, 1985); idem, *A History of the Mishnaic Law of Holy Things,* 6: *The Mishnaic System of Sacrifice and Sanctuary* (Leiden: E. J. Brill, 1969); idem, *A History of the Mishnaic Law of Purities,* 21: *The Redaction and Formulation of the Order of Purities in the Mishnah and Tosefta* (Leiden: E. J. Brill, 1977); idem, *A History of the Mishnaic Law of Purities,* 22: *The Mishnaic System of Uncleanness: Its Context and History* (Leiden: E. J. Brill, 1977); idem, *A History of the Mishnaic Law of Women,* 5: *The Mishnaic System of Women* (Leiden: E. J. Brill, 1980); idem, *Judaism: The Evidence of the Mishnah* (Chicago: University of Chicago Press, 1981); J. Neusner, ed., *The Modern Study of the Mishnah* (Leiden: E. J. Brill, 1973); F. C. Porter, Review of Moore, *Judaism, JR* 8 (1928) 30-62; G. G. Porton, "The Mishnah as a Law Code," in *The Modern Study of the Mishnah,* ed. J. Neusner (Leiden: E. J. Brill, 1973); E. P. Sanders, *Paul and Palestinian Judaism* (London: SCM, 1977); S. Schulman, Review of Moore, *Judaism, JQR* 18 (1927-28) 339-55; H. L. Strack and G. Stemberger, *Introduction to the Talmud and Midrash* (Minneapolis: Fortress, 1992); E. E. Urbach, "Mishnah," *EncJud* 12:93-109; idem, *The Sages: Their Concepts and Beliefs* (Jerusalem: Magnes, 1969); E. Schürer, *The History of the Jewish People in the Age of Jesus Christ (175 B.C.-A.D. 135),* rev. and ed. G. Vermes and F. Millar (3 vols., Edinburgh: T & T Clark, 1973-87).

J. Neusner

RABBINIC LITERATURE: TALMUD

The Talmud (lit. "learning," or what is to be "learned," from *lāmad,* "to learn") is a compendium of rabbinic law and lore that combines Mishnah and *gemara* ("completion"), as well as portions of the Tosefta (*see* Rabbinic Literature: Mishnah and Tosefta). The mishnaic material derives from the tannaitic rabbis and sages (c. 50 B.C. to A.D. 200), while the *gemara* derives mostly from the amoraic rabbis of a later period (c. A.D. 200-500). Included in the *gemara* are tannaitic sayings not included in the Mishnah. These traditions are called *baraitoth* ("external [sayings]"), in that they reach back to the tannaitic period but are *external* to the Mishnah. Although the Talmud postdates the NT by several centuries, it offers potentially useful background material.

1. The Two Talmuds
2. The Relevance of the Talmuds for New Testament Study
3. Jesus' Teaching and Rabbinic Thought
4. Paul and Rabbinic Teaching

5. Historical Relevance of the Talmuds

1. The Two Talmuds.

Although it is conventional to refer to "the Talmud," as though it is a single recension, there are in fact two recensions, one from the land of Israel, called Talmud Yerushalmi, the other from Babylon, called Talmud Babli. Although very similar in format, as seen in how each follows a program of citing a paragraph of Mishnah and then adding several explanatory paragraphs of *gemara*, the two recensions of the Talmud are quite different. These differences are seen in the ground that is covered (i.e., how many and which tractates of the Mishnah are actually treated), how extensive the *gemara* is, the text of the underlying Mishnah, the sages who are cited, the respective lengths (Babli is much longer) and the degree to which the recension has been edited and finalized (Babli is much more edited and polished).

1.1. Talmud Yerushalmi. The oldest recension is the one prepared in the land of Israel. The name "Talmud of the Land of Israel" is actually found on one of the oldest surviving manuscripts. However, this recension has been linked with Jerusalem and so traditionally has been called Yerushalmi. Much of this recension probably dates to A.D. 400, or just a generation or two after the time of the compilation of the Tosefta. The later parts of Yerushalmi probably date closer to A.D. 450. As the name of this recension suggests, most of the cited rabbinic authorities lived in Palestine.

Yerushalmi comments on the first, second, third and fourth divisions of the Mishnah. The compilers and editors of Yerushalmi are interested in the reading of the Mishnah (textual criticism), in the meaning of the Mishnah, in augmenting the Mishnah's arguments with scriptural proof texts and in harmonizing mishnaic traditions.

1.2. Talmud Babli. The Babylonian Talmud was edited sometime after A.D. 500 and up to A.D. 600. As the name suggests, it was produced in Babylon, where a large Jewish population developed in the aftermath of the Babylonian capture of Jerusalem and *destruction of the Jewish temple in 586 B.C. Most of the cited rabbinic authorities were from Babylon, though Palestinian authorities are also cited.

Babli comments and expands upon the second, third, fourth and fifth divisions of the Mishnah, as well as part of the first division. Babli interprets and embellishes the Mishnah, exegetes Scripture, identifies anonymous authorities and discusses a variety of topics that fall outside the subject of the Mishnah. Whereas there is almost no *messianic tradition in the Mishnah (see the later insertion at *m. Soṭa* 9:15), there is comparatively a great deal of messianic lore in Babli.

2. The Relevance of the Talmuds for New Testament Study.

Because of the late date of rabbinic literature, especially the recensions of the Talmud, the question of the relevance of the Talmuds for NT study must be addressed.

2.1. The Problem of Date. The Mishnah was edited and published between A.D. 200 and 220, while other major rabbinic works, including the Tosefta, the halakic midrashim, the two Talmuds, and the homiletic midrashim were composed in the period A.D. 300-1000. These dates of composition might seem to rule out the rabbinic literature as providing background material for the NT, leaving us with only *Apocrypha, *pseudepigrapha, *Dead Sea Scrolls, *Philo and *Josephus as roughly contemporaneous literature. Such a conclusion, however, would be mistaken, because the rabbinic literature consists of compilations of material, much of which stems from or is strongly related to periods far earlier than the date of redaction. Moreover, the *targumim (Aramaic translations of the Bible, some parts of which date from the first century) should be reckoned as part of rabbinic literature, and much evidence can be gleaned from them about early rabbinic and pharisaic attitudes. Problems of dating exist, since even material purporting to be early may be late, but scholarly methods exist to cope with such problems in all ancient texts. Thus, after due allowance has been made for legendary or pseudepigraphic elements, a wealth of material remains in the rabbinic literature throwing light on the background of Jesus' sayings and on the circumstances of his lifetime.

2.2. Pharisees and Rabbis. A related question is, What degree of continuity existed between the Pharisees of Jesus' day, who included such figures as *Hillel, *Shammai and Gamaliel I, and the rabbinic movement of the post-temple period, which included Gamaliel II, Akiba and Meir? Scholarly opinions have varied much.

H. Strack and P. Billerbeck had no doubt that sufficient continuity existed for rabbinic material to throw light on the *Pharisees. Some of their work, it is now recognized, was biased by their desire to find evidence supporting NT criticism of the Pharisees. Later scholars, notably E. P. Sanders (1977), showed that the rabbinic literature does not support such criticism. Some scholars (e.g., Fitzmyer; Neusner) have resorted to a theory of complete discontinuity between Pharisees and *rabbis. This has proved unsustainable (see Vermes; Sanders 1992), and it seems clear that the lack of compatibility between rabbinic literature and the NT Pharisees should be explained in terms of NT bias or selective treatment rather than Jewish discontinuity. Further, many of the features of Jesus' preaching, even when ostensibly anti-Pharisee, can best be understood as arising from a background of pharisaic thought.

3. Jesus' Teaching and Rabbinic Thought. At many points there is overlap between Jesus' teaching and rabbinic thought. Evidence of overlap may be traced through the two Talmuds to the oldest rabbinic literature.

3.1. The Lord's Prayer. A prominent example of affinity between Jesus and the rabbinic movement is the prayer Jesus composed, known as the Lord's Prayer. Scarcely a single phrase in this prayer does not have its parallel in rabbinic sources (see Petuchowski and Brocke). The Lord's Prayer was composed by Jesus in response to a request from his disciples to provide them with a prayer "as John also taught his disciples" (Lk 11:2-4 AV). Rabbis often composed a prayer for their disciples, not to supersede the regular daily prayers but as an addition to them. Neither John nor Jesus wanted to abolish the regular prayers, consisting mainly of the Shema, which was prized by Jesus (Mt 22:37), and the Amidah, or supplications (*see* Liturgy: Rabbinic). It was only in the later church that the Lord's Prayer was given liturgical centrality.

Some scholars, noting parallels between rabbinic prayer and the Lord's Prayer, conclude that Jesus had an influence on the rabbis, rather than the reverse (see 3.3 below). This, however, ignores the communal nature of rabbinic thinking, by which patterns of creativity derive from mutual exchange and tradition rather than from an individual. Each rabbi had his own measure of creativity and originality, set within a framework of societal patterning. It is highly unlikely that Jesus invented new patterns that were then adopted by the rabbis; much more likely he exercised his own individuality within existing patterns, just as they did.

3.2. Modes of Expression. If we can find in Jesus' reported utterances strong affinities to rabbinic style, as found in the Talmud and other rabbinic literature, we shall be justified in postulating that Jesus moved in a milieu that was saturated with rabbinic culture.

Examples may be found in Jesus' use of metaphor and hyperbole. When he says that it is easier for a camel to go through the eye of a needle than for a rich man to enter heaven (Mt 19:24), this extravagant turn of phrase is typically rabbinic. Indeed, the parallel rabbinic phrase expressing impossibility is even more extravagant, involving an elephant and a needle (*b. Ber.* 55b; *b. B. Meṣ.* 38b). In another passage, the animal is a camel, but instead of going through the eye of a needle, it dances in a tiny area (*b. Yebam.* 45a). Exegetes who have tried to reduce the extravagance of Jesus' simile (by saying that the camel means "rope" or that the needle was the name of a gate in Jerusalem) fail to appreciate the authentically exuberant rabbinic idiom of Jesus' saying.

Similarly, Jesus' sayings on hypocrites have a genuinely rabbinic air. He says (Mt 7:4 AV), "Thou hypocrite, first cast the beam out of thine own eye; and then shalt thou see clearly to cast out the mote out of thy brother's eye." The rabbinic parallel runs,

Rabbi Tarfon said, "I wonder if anyone in this generation knows how to accept reproof. If anyone says to him, 'Take the splinter from between your eyes,' he replies, 'Take the beam from between *your* eyes'" (*b. ʿArak.* 16b).

Here the charge of hypocrisy is made in order to avoid a just reproof. Yet, despite the somewhat broader context, the metaphor for hypocrisy is almost identical.

Similarly, Jesus refers to hypocrites as "whited sepulchres, which indeed appear beautiful outward, but are within full of dead men's bones, and of all uncleanness" (Mt 23:27 AV). The rabbis used very similar imagery, as is shown by the dream of Rabban Gamaliel in which he saw "white pitchers full of ashes." This was in a context where he had issued a proclamation, "No disciple may enter the House of Learning unless his inside is like his outside" (*b. Ber.* 28a).

3.3. Parables. We do not find parables in the pseudepigrapha or in the Dead Sea Scrolls, but we do find them in profusion in the rabbinic writings, especially the Midrashim (*see* Rabbinic Parables).

Here again the question of dating has given rise to controversy. Some scholars, notably J. Jeremias, have argued that there is no evidence of the use of parables among the Pharisees of Jesus' day and that the frequent parables of the second-century rabbis show that they were influenced in this aspect by Jesus himself. However, there is evidence that the second-century rabbis were carrying on an established tradition of preaching in their use of parables. Moreover, a rabbinic version of a parable can sometimes throw light on parables that appear in the Gospels in a version modified by the ideological aims of the Gospel redactor. The full range of the parable genre is much better displayed in the rabbinic literature, which contains thousands of examples, than in the NT, which contains only thirty-one.

An example is the following:

> Rabban Johanan ben Zakkai said: This may be compared to a king who summoned his servants to a banquet without appointing a time. The wise ones adorned themselves and sat at the door of the palace. Said they, Is anything lacking in a royal palace? The fools went about their work, saying, Can there be a banquet without preparations? Suddenly the king desired [the presence of] his servants: the wise entered adorned, while the fools entered soiled. The king rejoiced at the wise but was angry with the fools. Those who adorned themselves for the banquet, ordered he, let them sit, eat and drink. But those who did not adorn themselves for the banquet, let them stand and watch. (*b. Šabb.* 153a, Soncino translation)

This parable shows affinities to two Gospel parables: that of the virgins (Mt 25:1-12) and that of the wedding (Mt 22:2-14). It is interesting that this Talmudic parable is attributed to Rabban Johanan ben Zakkai, who was a contemporary of Jesus and was well known for his knowledge of parables and fables, though most of them were lost. Certain puzzling or redundant features in the Gospel versions suggest that the simpler Talmudic version is the earliest.

3.4. Halakah. The arguments attributed to Jesus in the Gospels often have strong affinities to the kind of legal argument associated with the pharisaic and rabbinic Halakah (lit. "way" or "going").

An example is Jesus' argument for healing on the *sabbath, based on the analogy of circumcision. In this saying (Jn 7:22-23) Jesus refers to the ruling that circumcision overrules the sabbath law: that though incisions are usually forbidden on the sabbath, an exception is made when a child's circumcision day (the eighth from birth) coincides with the sabbath. Now this particular ruling, or Halakah, features elsewhere only in the rabbinic literature. Nothing is said in the Hebrew Bible or the intertestamental literature about what to do if the circumcision day coincides with the sabbath. This is thus a typical piece of rabbinic decision making, to which Jesus refers as a matter already known to his hearers.

Even more interesting is that the inference that Jesus then proceeds to make (that healing should be allowed on the sabbath) is also to be found in the rabbinic literature:

> Whence do we know that the duty of saving life annuls the sabbath? Rabbi Eleazar ben Azariah answered: If circumcision, which affects only one member of the body annuls the sabbath, how much more so for the rest of the body! Rabbi Simeon ben Menasia says: Behold it is said, "And you shall keep the sabbath for it is holy to you" (Ex 31:14). To you the sabbath is handed over, but you are not handed over to the sabbath. (*Mek. Abbeta* on Ex 31:13)

Though the rabbis quoted here belong to the second century, the arguments they use were part of the rabbinic stock, on which Jesus also was drawing. It is noteworthy that the second argument quoted, that of Rabbi Simeon ben Menasia, is almost identical with another saying of Jesus in the incident of the corn plucking. When Jesus said, "The Sabbath was made for man, not man for the Sabbath" (Mk 2:27 AV), he was quoting from the pharisaic heritage, for a pharisaic purpose, namely, the mitigation of the law of the sabbath in situations dangerous to human life (see Maccoby, 40-42, for a detailed analysis of the corn-plucking incident).

3.5. Theology: Kingdom of God. The rabbinic writings can also throw light on Jesus' religious aims and teaching. When Jesus first came on the public scene, he was proclaiming, "Repent, for the kingdom of heaven is at hand" (Mt 4:17 AV). The expression "kingdom of heaven" *(malkût šāmayim)* is found in many places in rabbinic literature, where it means "the rule of God as King." Jesus, like John the Baptist before him (Mt 3:2), was prophesying the messianic era on earth, when the commands of God (i.e., the Torah) would be obeyed, rather than the commands of the Roman emperor (*see* Roman Emperors). The whole this-worldly, revolutionary emphasis of the expression "kingdom of heaven" is lost in later "spiritualizing" interpretations, but can be recovered through study of the Talmud. The emphasis on repentance in Jesus' preaching is indissolubly tied to his proclamation of the coming rule of God. All Jewish messianic campaigns began with an emphasis on repentance, or "return" (*tᵉšûbâ*).

3.6. Jesus and Christian Study of the Talmud. On the other hand, the intensive effort of Christian scholars, especially by the Dominicans in the Middle Ages, to find Talmudic support for specifically Christian doctrines was a failure. The chief literary product of this school was the monumental *Pugio Fidei* of R. Martini, and the chief public use of the method for conversionary purposes was the Barcelona Disputation of 1263. An example is the citing of the Talmudic legend (*b. Yoma* 39b) that forty years before the destruction of the *temple, certain miracles associated with the service of the temple ceased. The date was equated with that of the death of Jesus and the NT account of the rending of the temple "veil" (Mk 25:38); and Talmudic authority was thus claimed for the supersession of the temple by the salvific death of Jesus. Tendentious though such associations were, they led to an interesting phase of Talmudic study by Christians, foreshadowing the modern scientific interest in the Talmud as background to the NT.

3.7. The Talmud and Re-Judaizing the New Testament. For some scholars the use of Talmudic material tends to throw light on the essential Jewishness of Jesus' teaching and activity but to cast doubt on the historicity of his conflicts with the Pharisees. The question has been raised, however, especially by the school of form criticism, whether the rabbinic aspects of Jesus are authentic or later accretions in the Gospel narratives. It is argued that we have here a phenomenon of re-Judaization, by which the radical aspects of Jesus' thinking have been tempered and reconciled with mainstream Judaism. Certain early Christian communities, it is argued, did not wish to sever their links with Judaism, and it was for the benefit of such communities that the Jewish Jesus was created. For example, in the corn-plucking incident, Matthew adds to Mark's account by saying that the disciples were hungry, an addition that would bring Jesus' action within the scope of rabbinic laws allowing sabbath breaking in extreme conditions. Yet, it should be observed, Mark's account of the incident is closer in other respects to rabbinic thought than Matthew's, so such argument is not decisive. At any rate, the value of the Talmudic background to NT exegesis is not affected, since even if it were only relevant to re-Judaized material, it would still throw light on important elements in the NT. The form-critical approach, however, while valuable in principle, has been seen recently as biased in its attempts to eliminate the Jewish aspects of Jesus.

4. Paul and Rabbinic Teaching.

While the rabbinic quality of Jesus' teaching has been questioned or, where it is acknowledged as unquestionable, relegated to the re-Judaizing activity of the Gospel writers, Paul's writings have always been a hunting ground for rabbinic allusions, and most NT scholars (both Christian and Jewish) have assumed that Paul was someone whose texture of thought was essentially rabbinic. This is because Paul himself claimed to have had an upbringing as a Pharisee and even to have reached the peak of Pharisee education. According to Acts, he was a pupil of Gamaliel, though Paul himself does not make this claim in his letters, and most scholars have discounted it, especially in view of the problem of why Paul (Saul) was so intolerant to the followers of Jesus when Gamaliel was so tolerant (Acts 5).

A celebrated attempt to establish the rabbinic credentials of Paul is that of W. D. Davies, which concentrates on alleged links between Paul's christology and rabbinic (and prerabbinic) messianism. More recent attempts to substantiate Paul as a Pharisee (e.g., Segal) have acknowledged a conceptual gap between Paul and rabbinism and have thus been led to postulate a prerabbinic Pharisaism, for which the chief evidence is Paul's own writings. This approach, which has been criticized as circular, abandons the rabbinic writings as too late to provide background to Paul's kind of Pharisaism. However, Jesus' own style of preaching (even if it is re-Judaized by the redactors) testifies to the existence of rabbinism in the first century (see the introductory paragraphs and 3.7 above), so it is hard to see why Paul had a Pharisaism so devoid of rabbinism. Some scholars (e.g., Montefiore, Maccoby) have seen Paul as primarily employing *Hellenistic styles of thought and argument but as occasionally attempting to argue in rabbinic style (e.g., Rom 7:1-6). On this view, Paul's claim to special Pharisee expertness must be regarded as a stance that he thought helpful to his missionary campaigns. The debate on Paul's Pharisaism continues.

5. Historical Relevance of the Talmuds.

The rabbinic writings are not of a historical or biographical nature and thus do not provide the kind of direct historical data relevant to NT studies that we find in *Josephus or even *Philo. Nevertheless, much incidental material found in the rabbinic writings is relevant. An example is the character of Gamaliel, referred to in the NT as a Pharisee "held in high regard by all the people" (Acts 5:34 NEB). Acts describes how Gamaliel intervened to save Peter and his companions from the high priest. Even here one may discern that he was an influential figure, that he was sympathetic to Jesus and other messianic figures aiming at Jewish liberation and that he led the opposition to the high priest. This picture, which is at odds with other NT portrayals of Pharisees, is much enhanced by recourse to the rabbinic writings, in which Gamaliel is a prominent and respected figure: grandson of Hillel, progenitor of Gamaliel II and Judah the Prince, and author of many seminal pronouncements. Among other Talmudic topics useful for NT studies are the conflict between Pharisees and *Sadducees; the *Samaritan issue; the nature of *messianic hopes; the position of the high priest as a temple administrator who carried no religious authority among the Jewish masses (*see* Sacrifice and Temple Service).

In conclusion, the rabbinic literature, especially the two recensions of the Talmud, is the depository of many centuries of Jewish thought and life. Though late in time of composition and final redaction, it is of great value, if read critically, as evidence of social, religious and political conditions in first-century Palestine. It is therefore an indispensable source for NT research.

See also JUDAISM AND THE NEW TESTAMENT; LAW/NOMOS IN GRECO-ROMAN WORLD; LEGAL TEXTS AT QUMRAN; RABBINIC LITERATURE: MIDRASHIM; RABBINIC LITERATURE: MISHNAH AND TOSEFTA; RABBINIC LITERATURE: TARGUMIM; RABBINIC PARABLES; RABBINIC PROVERBS; RABBIS; SEMITIC INFLUENCE ON THE NEW TESTAMENT; TORAH; WRITING AND LITERATURE: JEWISH.

BIBLIOGRAPHY. I. Abrahams, *Studies in Pharisaism and the Gospels* (2d ed.; Cambridge: Cambridge University Press, 1967); D. Daube, *The New Testament and Rabbinic Judaism* (London: Athlone, 1956); W. D. Davies, *Paul and Rabbinic Judaism: Some Rabbinic Elements in Pauline Theology* (4th ed.; Philadelphia: Fortress, 1980); J. A. Fitzmyer, *Essays on the Semitic Background of the New Testament* (Missoula, MT: Scholars Press, 1974); J. Jeremias, *The Parables of Jesus* (rev. ed.; London, SCM, 1972); H. Maccoby, *Early Rabbinic Writings* (Cambridge: Cambridge University Press, 1988); idem, *Paul and Hellenism* (London: SCM, 1991); C. G. Montefiore, *Rabbinic Literature and Gospel Teachings* (London: Macmillan, 1930); idem, *The Synoptic Gospels* (2d ed.; 2 vols.; London, Macmillan, 1968); J. Neusner, *Judaism: The Evidence of the Mishnah* (Chicago: University of Chicago Press, 1981); J. J. Petuchowski and M. Brocke, *The Lord's Prayer and Jewish Liturgy* (London: Burns & Oates, 1978); A. J. Saldarini, *Pharisees, Scribes and Sadducees in Palestinian Society* (Wilmington, DE: Michael Glazier, 1988); E. P. Sanders, *Judaism: Practice and Belief 63 B.C.-A.D. 66* (Philadelphia: Trinity Press International, 1992); idem, *Paul and Palestinian Judaism* (Philadelphia: Fortress, 1977); S. Sandmel, *Judaism and Christian Beginnings* (New York: Oxford University Press, 1978); A. E. Segal, *Paul the Convert* (New Haven, CT: Yale University Press, 1990); H. Strack and P. Billerbeck, *Kommentar zum Neuen Testament aus Talmud und Midrasch* (6 vols.; Munich: Oscar Beck, 1922-61); H. L. Strack and G. Stemberger, *Introduction to the Talmud and Midrash* (Edinburgh: T & T Clark, 1991); G. Vermes, *The Religion of Jesus the Jew* (London: SCM, 1993).

H. Maccoby

RABBINIC LITERATURE: TARGUMIM

The term *targum* simply means "translation" in Aramaic, but the type and purpose of the rendering involved in Judaism was distinctive. The general phenomenon of targum needs to be appreciated, and the specific documents involved (targumim) need to be described before the question of targumic influence upon Jesus and the Gospels may be taken up.

1. The Purpose of Targumic Production
2. Categories of Targumim
3. Significance of the Targumim
4. The Targumim and Aspects of Judaism
5. The Targumim and Paul

1. The Purpose of Targumic Production.
*Aramaic survived the demise of the Persian Empire as a *lingua franca* in the Near East. It had been embraced enthusiastically by Jews as by other peoples, such as Nabateans and Palmyrenes, and the Aramaic portions of the Hebrew Bible (in Ezra and Daniel) testify to a significant change in the linguistic constitution of *Judaism. Abraham himself had been an Aramean, although the variants of the Aramaic language during its history are stunning. Conceivably, one reason for Jewish enthusiasm in embracing Aramaic was a distant memory of its affiliation with *Hebrew, but it should always be borne in mind that Hebrew is quite a different language. By the time of Jesus, Aramaic appears to have been the common language of *Judea, *Samaria and *Galilee, although distinctive dialects were spoken; Hebrew was understood by an educated and/or perhaps a nationalistic stratum of the population, and some familiarity with Greek was a cultural—especially a commercial and bureaucratic—necessity.

The linguistic situation in Judea and Galilee demanded that translation be effected for the purpose of popular study and worship. Although fragments of Leviticus and Job in Aramaic, which have been discovered at *Qumran, are technically targumim, the fact is that they are unrepresentative of the genre targum in literary terms (*see* Aramaic Targums: Qumran). They are reasonably literal renderings; that is, there is some attempt at formal correspondence between the Hebrew rendered and the Aramaic that is presented. The targumim that are extant, as documents deliberately guarded within rabbinic Judaism, are of a different character.

In that the aim of targumic production was to give the sense of the Hebrew Scriptures, paraphrase is characteristic of the targumim. Theoretically, a passage of Scripture was to be rendered orally by an interpreter (meturgeman) after the reading in Hebrew; the meturgeman was not to be confused with the reader, lest the congregation mistake the interpretation with the original text (cf. *m. Meg.* 4:4-10 and *b. Meg.* 23b-25b). Regulations that specify the number of verses that may be read prior to the delivery of a targum probably date from well after the period of the NT. Although the renderings so delivered were oral in principle, over the course of time traditions in important centers of learning became fixed and coalescence became possible.

Moreover, the emergence of the rabbis as the dominant leaders within Judaism after A.D. 70 provided a centralizing tendency without which literary targumim could never have been produced. The targumim preserved by the rabbis are notoriously difficult to characterize. They are paraphrases, but the theological programs conveyed are not always consistent, even within a given targum. Although the rabbis attempted to control targumic activity, the extant targumim themselves sometimes contradict rabbinic proscriptions. For example, *Mishnah Megilla* 4:9 insists that Leviticus 18:21 ("You must not give of your seed, to deliver it to Moloch") should not be interpreted in respect of sexual intercourse with Gentiles; the *Targum Pseudo-Jonathan*—a late work, produced long after rabbinic authority had been established—takes just that line. The targumim evince such oddities because they are the products of a dialectical interaction between folk practice and rabbinic supervision—sometimes mediated through a love of dramatic and inventive speculation, a dynamic tension that continued over centuries. Each of the extant targumim crystallizes that complex relationship at a given moment.

2. Categories of Targumim.
The targumim may conveniently be divided among those of the Torah (the Pentateuch), those of the Prophets (both Former Prophets, or the so-called historical works, and the Latter Prophets, or the Prophets as commonly designated in English) and those of the Writings (or Hagiographa), following the conventional designations of the Hebrew Bible in Judaism. The fact needs to be stressed at the outset, however, that although the Hebrew Bible is almost entirely rendered by the targumim in aggregate, there was no single moment and no particular movement that produced a comprehensive Bible in Aramaic. The targumim are irreducibly complex in proveniences, purposes and dialects of Aramaic.

Among the targumim to the Pentateuch, *Targum Onqelos* is a suitable point of departure. *Onqelos* appears to correspond best of all the targumim to rabbinic ideals of translation. Although paraphrase is evident, especially in order to describe God and his revelation in suitably reverent terms, the high degree of correspondence with the Hebrew of the Masoretic Text (and, presumably, with the Hebrew text current in antiquity) is striking. The dialect of *Onqelos* is commonly called Middle Aramaic, which would place the targum between the first century B.C. and A.D. 200. A better designation, however, would be Transitional Aramaic (200 B.C.-A.D. 200), embracing the various dialects (*Hasmonean, Nabatean, Palmyrene, Arsacid, *Essene, as well as targumic) that came to be used during the period, since what followed was a strong regionalization in dialects of Aramaic, which we can logically refer to as Regional Aramaic (A.D. 200-700).

Because it was transitional, various targumim were produced in Transitional Aramaic *after* its demise as a common language. For that reason, the year 200 is not a firm date, after which a targum in Transitional Aramaic cannot have been composed. *Onqelos* should probably be dated toward the end of the third century, in the wake of similar efforts to produce a literal Greek rendering during the second century, and well after any strict construal of the principle that targumim were to be oral. By contrast with the rabbinic ethos that permitted the creation and preservation of *Onqelos,* one might recall the story of Rabbi Gamaliel, who is said during the first century to have immured a targum of Job in a wall of the temple *(t. Šabb. 115a).*

The *Targum Neofiti I* was discovered in 1949 by A. Díez Macho in the Library of the Neophytes in Rome. The paraphrases of *Neofiti* are substantially different from those of *Onqelos.* Entire paragraphs are added, as when Cain and Abel argue in the field prior to the first case of murder (Gen 4:8); such renderings are substantial additions, and it is impossible to predict when remarkable freedom of this kind is to be indulged. The dialect of *Neofiti* is known as Palestinian Aramaic (and was produced during the period of Regional Aramaic, A.D. 200-700), to distinguish it from the Babylonian Aramaic of *Onqelos.* That distinction between Palestinian and Babylonian manifests the nascent regionalization in the Aramaic language to which we have referred. But *Neofiti* is produced in a frankly Regional Aramaic, while *Onqelos* appears in a Transitional Aramaic that is on the way to becoming Regional. Yet the chronology of the two targumim is about the same, although *Neofiti* appears somewhat later; the differences between them are a function more of program than dating. The rabbis of Babylonia, who called *Onqelos* "our targum," exerted greater influence there than did their colleagues in the west.

The latest representative of the type of expansive rendering found in *Neofiti* is *Targum Pseudo-Jonathan.* Its reference to the names of Muhammad's wife and daughter in Genesis 21:21 puts its final composition sometime after the seventh century A.D. (This oddly designated targum is so called in that the name *Jonathan* was attributed to it during the Middle Ages, because its name was abbreviated with a *yod.* But the letter probably stood for Jerusalem, although that designation is also not established critically. The title *Pseudo-Jonathan* is therefore an admission of uncertainty.) *Neofiti* and *Pseudo-Jonathan* are together known as Palestinian targumim, to distinguish their dialects and their style of interpretation from those of *Onqelos.* In fact, however, *Pseudo-Jonathan* was produced at the dawn of the period of Academic Aramaic (A.D. 700-1500), during which rabbinic usage continued to develop the language in a literary idiom after it had been supplanted by Arabic as a *lingua franca* in the Near East.

Neofiti and *Pseudo-Jonathan* are to be associated with two other targumim, or to be more precise, groups of targumim. The first group, in chronological order, consists of the fragments of the Cairo Genizah. They were originally part of more complete works, dating between the seventh and the eleventh centuries, that were deposited in the Genizah of the Old Synagogue in Cairo. In the type and substance of its interpretation, these fragments are comparable to the other targumim of the Palestinian type. The same may be said of the *Fragmentary Targum,* which was collected as a miscellany of targumic readings during the Middle Ages. An interesting feature of the targumim of the Palestinian type is that their relationship might be described as a synoptic one, in some ways comparable to the relationship among the Gospels. All four of the Palestinian targumim, for example, convey a debate between Cain and Abel, and they do so with those variations of order and wording that are well known to students of the Synoptic Gospels.

Both the Former and the Latter Prophets are extant in Aramaic in a single collection, although the date and character of each targum within the collection needs to be studied individually. The entire corpus, however, is ascribed by rabbinic tradition (*b. Meg.* 3a) to Jonathan ben Uzziel, a disciple of Hillel, the famous contemporary of Jesus. There are passages of the *Targum of the Prophets* that accord precisely with renderings given in the name of Joseph bar Ḥiyya, a rabbi of the fourth century (cf. *Tg. Isa.* 5:17b and *b. Pesaḥ.* 68a).

As it happens, *Targum Isaiah,* which has been subjected to more study than any of the Prophets' targumim, shows signs of a nationalistic *eschatology that was current just after the destruction of the temple in A.D. 70 and of the more settled perspective of the rabbis in Babylon some three hundred years later. It appears that *Targum Jonathan* as a whole is the result of two major periods of collecting and editing interpretations by the rabbis, the first period being tannaitic, and the second amoraic.

After *Targum Jonathan* was composed, probably around the same time the *Fragmentary Targum* (to the Pentateuch) was assembled, targumic addenda were appended in certain of its manuscripts; they are represented in the Codex Reuchlinianus and in a manuscript in the Bibliothèque Nationale (mis)labed *Hébreu 75.*

Of the three categories of targumim, that of the Writings is without question the most diverse. Although the targum to Psalms is formally a translation, substantially it is better described as a midrash, while the targum to Proverbs appears to be a fairly straightforward rendition of the Peshitta (*see* Syriac Bible), and the targum(im) to Esther seems designed for use within a celebration of the liturgy of Purim. The targumim to the Writings are the most problematic within modern study, but they are also of the least interest of the three general categories of targumim from the point of view of understanding the NT, in view of their late (in most cases, medieval) date.

3. Significance of the Targumim.

The significance of the targumim for appreciating Jesus and the Gospels follows naturally from assessing their purpose and provenience. Fundamentally, the targumim constitute evidence of the first importance for the way in which the Hebrew Scriptures were understood, not simply among rabbis but more commonly by the congregations for whom the targumim were intended. Insofar as what is reflected in a targum is representative of the reception of Scripture in the first century, that targumic material is of crucial importance for any student of the NT. But care must also be taken, lest the perspective of later materials be accepted uncritically as representative of an earlier period: that would result in anachronistic exegeses. There are clearly readings in the targumim that presuppose events long after the death of Jesus. One example of such a reading is *Targum Isaiah* 53:4, 5, 10-11a, which clearly anticipates that the reader takes the destruction of the temple as given.

A particular problem is posed for modern study by the persistent notion that there is somewhere extant today a Palestinian targum that substantially represents the understanding of the Hebrew Bible in the time of Jesus. There was a time when that was a comprehensible position, because it was taken that Palestinian Aramaic was more ancient than Babylonian Aramaic. Today, however, the discoveries at Qumran have cast a new light on *Onqelos* and *Jonathan,* which makes them appear more ancient than was supposed some sixty years ago and more similar to Aramaic as spoken in Palestine. *Onqelos* and *Jonathan,* insofar as they represent Transitional Aramaic, convey an earlier form of the language than what we find in the Cairo Genizah, *Pseudo-Jonathan* and the *Fragmentary Targum.* To the same extent that the last three targumim are Palestinian, they also represent the later, Regional dialect of Aramaic. Moreover, the present understanding of early Judaism is that it was too variegated to allow the formation of a single, authoritative tradition of rendering, such as the designation "Palestinian Targum" would suggest. *Pseudo-Jonathan* appears to represent a more recent tendency, not only in language but also in its historical allusions and its form.

The difficulty of assessing the precise form of targumic tradition(s) within the first century should also make us wary of any claim that we know the precise dialect(s) of Aramaic current in that period. The literary remains of the language are sporadic, dialectical variation was great, and there sometimes appears to have been a significant difference between the language as spoken and the language as written.

For all those reasons, attempts to retranslate the Greek Gospels into Jesus' own language are extremely speculative; when the targumim are appealed to by way of antecedent, speculation is piled upon speculation. In purely linguistic terms, it is evident that the Aramaic of Qumran, rather than that of any of the targumim, offers a useful guide in the exercise of retroversion.

The composite nature of the targumim is nonetheless such that upon occasion one may discern in them the survival of materials that did circulate in the time of Jesus and therefore influenced his teaching and/or the memory of that teaching among those disciples who were familiar with such traditions. Whatever Qumran may tell us of the language of Jesus, his thought and its environment are often better represented by the targumim. An example of such a survival might be Leviticus 22:28 in *Pseudo-Jonathan,* "My people, children of Israel, since our father is merciful in heaven, so should you be merciful upon the earth." The expansion in the targum is unquestionably innovative, as compared with what may be read in the Masoretic Text, so that the possible echo in Luke 6:36, within the address known conventionally as the Sermon on the Plain, is with the targum or with nothing at all. It is theoretically possible that the saying originated with Jesus and was then anonymously taken up within the targum.

Without doubt, the statement is rhetorically more at home within Luke than in *Pseudo-Jonathan,* where it appears unmotivated. But it seems inherently unlikely that *Pseudo-Jonathan,* which of all the Pentateuchal targumim is perhaps the most influenced by a concern to guard and articulate Judaic integrity, would inadvertently convey a saying of Jesus. More probably, both *Pseudo-Jonathan* and Luke's Jesus are here independently passing on the wisdom of a proverbial statement. The targumic echo is therefore not the source of Jesus' statement, but it may help us to describe the nature of Jesus' statement.

Examples such as Leviticus 22:28 demonstrate that the targumim might have a heuristic value in illustrating the sort of Judaism that Jesus and his followers took for granted. Recent study has greatly increased the catalog of such instances. But there are also cases in which Jesus appears to have cited a form of the book of Isaiah that is closer to the targum than to any other extant source; in such cases, an awareness of the fact helps us better to understand his preaching. *Targum Isaiah* 6:9, 10 is an especially famous example, and it helps to explain Mark 4:11, 12. The statement in Mark could be taken to mean that Jesus told parables with the purpose that (*hina*) people might see and not perceive, hear and not understand, lest they turn and be forgiven:

> And he was saying to them, "To you the mystery has been given of the kingdom of God, but to those outside, everything comes in parables, so that (*hina*) while seeing they see and not perceive, and while hearing they hear and do not understand, lest they repent and it be forgiven them."

The targum also, unlike the Masoretic Text and the *Septuagint, refers to people not being "forgiven" (rather than not being "healed"), and that suggests that the targum may give the key to the meaning supposed in Mark. The relevant clause in the targum refers to people who behave in such a way "so that" (*d* in Aramaic) they see and do not perceive, hear and do not understand, lest they repent and they be forgiven. It appears that Jesus was characterizing people in the targumic manner, as he characterizes his own fate similarly in Mark with a clause employing *hina* (cf. Mk 9:12), not acting in order to be misunderstood.

In this famous case from Mark, then, the underlying Aramaism of using the clause with *d* caused the saying of Jesus to use the term *hina* in Greek, which may mean "in order that" or "so that." If the former meaning obtains, Mark's Jesus speaks so as not to be understood and deliberately to preclude the forgiveness of those who do not understand. If the latter meaning obtains, then Jesus uses the reference from Isaiah in its targumic form in order to characterize the kind of people who do not respond to his message and what happens to them. The fact of the similarity in word with the targum shows us that the second meaning is preferable, as does the fact that Jesus elsewhere in Mark refers to his own followers as being hard-hearted, with unseeing eyes and unseeing ears (Mk 8:17-18). His point in alluding once again to Isaiah 6 is given at the end of the rebuke, "Do you not yet understand?" (Mk 8:21). Jesus' citation of Isaiah 6 in its targumic form was intended to rouse hearers to understanding, not to make their misunderstanding into his own program.

Another example of overlap with the teaching of Jesus is provided by the final verse of the book of Isaiah targum, which clearly identifies who will suffer where at the end of time, when it says "the wicked shall be judged in Gehenna until the righteous will say concerning them, 'We have seen enough'" (*Tg. Isa.* 66:24). "Gehenna" is just what Jesus associates with the phrase "their worm will not die, and their fire will not be quenched" (Mk 9:48, and see vv. 44, 46 in many manuscripts), which is taken from the same verse of Isaiah. The term *Gehenna* refers in a literal sense to the Valley of Hinnom in the Kidron Valley, just across from the temple in Jerusalem. But because that had been a place where idolatrous human sacrifice by fire had taken place (see 2 Kings 16:3; 21:6), the site was deliberately destroyed and desecrated by King Josiah as part of his cultic reform during the seventh century B.C. (see 2 Kings 23:10). As a result, Gehenna came to be known as the place of the definitive punishment of the wicked.

Apart from James 3:6, the term appears only in sayings of Jesus in the NT; otherwise, only the *Pseudepigrapha and rabbinic literature (especially the book of **1 Enoch*) provide us with examples of the usage from the same period or near the same period that enable us to see what the usage means. Gehenna is the place of fiery torment for the wicked. But it is not known as such in the Septuagint, *Josephus or even *Philo: evidently the usage is at home in an Aramaic environment. Rabbi Aqiba also is said to have associated Gehenna with the end of the book of Isaiah (in the Mishnah, see *ʿEd.* 2:10). Aqiba, however, refers to punishment in Gehenna having a limit, of twelve months; for Jesus, as in *Targum Isaiah,* part of the threat of Gehenna was that its limit could not be determined in advance.

Time and again the targumim present a synoptic relationship among their materials, be it in the instance of the dispute between Cain and Abel (as already mentioned), the Aqedah (Gen 22 in the Palestinian targumim and Isaiah 33:7 in the margin of Reuchlinianus) or the Poem of the Four Nights (Ex 12:32 in the Palestinian targumim). In that the synopticity of the targumim is evinced among four documents, not three (as in the case of the relationship among the Gospels), it is even more complicated to trace a purely documentary, rigidly literary relationship among the texts. The study of the synoptic aspect of the targumim remains in its infancy, but it appears possible that, once it is better understood, we will find that we also conceive of the literary relationship among the Gospels in a different way.

4. The Targumim and Aspects of Judaism.

The targumim are a rich source of that form of early Judaism and rabbinic Judaism where the folk and the expert aspects of the religion met. For that reason, serious students of the NT might well read them as helping them to comprehend the context within which Jesus taught and his movement first developed, before the transition to a Hellenistic compass and to the Greek language. In particular cases, the targumim uniquely present material that helps to illuminate Jesus' teaching. (In other instances, they may support what we know from other sources.) It might be that a targum happens to preserve proverbial material that Jesus cites or alludes to (*see* Rabbinic Proverbs). But there are also cases in which Jesus seems to have been influenced by a specifically targumic understanding of the Bible. Finally, apart from what they may tell us of particular passages in the Gospels, the targumim give us an example of how composite documents evolved within Judaism, and to that extent they may provide an analogy for understanding the Gospels themselves.

5. The Targumim and Paul.

Paul also is sometimes better understood in the light of the targumim than he can be otherwise. In his letter to the Galatians, Paul uses the phrase "hanging upon a tree" in order to describe Jesus' execution. The wording itself comes from Deuteronomy 21:23, and Paul applies it to argue that, in being crucified, Jesus was subject to the curse of "everyone who hangs upon a tree" (Gal 3:13, which follows the LXX in its wording). The argument assumes that crucifixion carries with it some sanction of Judaic law, and that is just what we find in the Ruth targum, when Naomi says, "We have four kinds of death for the guilty, stoning with stones, burning with fire, execution by the sword and hanging upon a tree." In his commentary, D. R. G. Beattie observes the contradiction of the Mishnah (*Sanh.* 7:1) in equating crucifixion with the punishment envisaged in Deuteronomy. That is a principal support of his suggestion of "an ancient origin, at least for that part of the Targum."

The argument is vitiated by the severe criticism that has recently been leveled at any form of the assertion that a statement that appears to be antimishnaic in content must be premishnaic in origin. The logic of midrash may explore almost any logical and historical possibility, precisely because it is not identified with halakic authority. And the Ruth targum is late, midrashic in nature; it represents the later interpretative tendency in Academic Aramaic, probably during the eighth century, of incorporating selected midrashic passages within a rendering that was generally more restrained.

But Beattie's basic insight can be supported by reference to what Paul himself says. Here is an indisputably first-century usage in which the midrashic connection between crucifixion and Deuteronomy 21:23 is explicitly made. Taken together, Galatians and the Ruth targum show us that this connection is as ancient as Beattie suggests and that Paul was making an argument that was within the idiom of midrashic possibility.

But perhaps the most evocative overlap between Paul and the targumim corresponds to the equally telling comparison between Jesus and the targumim: reference to the kingdom of God. The phrase conveys the central category of Jesus' theology and also appears in the form "kingdom of the Lord" in the targumim (see *Tg. Onq.*, Ex 15:18; *Tg. Ps.-J.*, Is 24:23; 31:4; 40:9; 52:7; Ezek 7:7; Obad 21; Zech 14:9). The first usage in *Targum Isaiah (Tg. Isa.* 24:23) associates the theologoumenon of the kingdom of God with God's self-revelation on Mt. Zion, where his appearing is to occasion a feast for all nations (see Is 25:6-8). The association of the kingdom with a festal image is comparable to Jesus' promise in Matthew 8:11 and Luke 13:28-29 that many will come from the ends of the earth to feast with Abraham, Isaac and Jacob in the kingdom of God.

The Masoretic Text develops a picture of the Lord descending upon Mt. Zion as a lion that is not afraid of the shepherds who attempt to protect the prey. That arresting image is referred explicitly to the kingdom in *Targum Isaiah (Tg. Isa.* 31:4):

> As a lion, a young lion roars over its prey, and, when a band of shepherds are appointed against it, it is not broken up at their shouting or checked at their tumult, so the kingdom of the Lord of hosts will be revealed to settle upon the Mount of Zion and upon its hill.

This passage refutes the outworn generalization that the kingdom within Judaic usage was static in nature and that the dynamic aspect was Jesus' innovation. The kingdom's dynamism was not original with Jesus; his particular contribution was in his portrayal of how the kingdom comes.

The dynamic nature of the kingdom in the targumim explicitly involves eschatological judgment. In the case of Paul, the emphasis falls more unequivocally on the aspect of judgment involved in the kingdom than it does in the case of Jesus (see Gal 5:21; 1 Cor 6:9-11; 15:24, 50). At the same time, Paul understands that the kingdom is also active as a force in the present, involving both divine power (see 1 Cor 4:20) and human response to that power through the Holy Spirit (Rom 14:17). In their mutual reference to the kingdom of God as the dynamic strength of God's rule, Jesus and Paul show themselves to have inherited and evolved the idiom of the targumim.

See also ARAMAIC LANGUAGE; ARAMAIC TARGUMS: QUMRAN; OLD TESTAMENT VERSIONS, ANCIENT; RABBINIC LITERATURE.

BIBLIOGRAPHY. J. Ådna, "Der Gottesknecht als triumphierender and interzessorischer Messias. Die Rezeption von Jes 53 im Targum Jonathan untersucht mit besonderer Berücksichtigung des Messiasbildes," in *Die leidende Gottesknecht: Jesaja 53 und seine Wirkungsgeschichte,* ed. B. Janowski and P. Stuhlmacher (FAT 14; Tübingen: Mohr Siebeck, 1996) 129-58; D. R. G. Beattie, *The Targum of Ruth: Translated, with Introduction, Apparatus and Notes* (ArBib 19; Collegeville, MN: Liturgical Press, 1994); K. Beyer, *Die Aramäische Texte vom Toten Meer samt den Inschriften aus Palästina, dem Testament Levis und der Kairoer Geniza, der Fastenrolle und den alten talmudischen Zitaten* (Göttingen: Vandenhoeck & Ruprecht, 1984); J. Bowker, *The Targums and Rabbinic Literature: An Introduction to Jewish Interpretation of Scripture* (Cambridge: Cambridge University Press, 1969); B. D. Chilton, *A Galilean Rabbi and His Bible: Jesus' Use of the Interpreted Scripture of His Time* (GNS 8; Wilmington, DE: Michael Glazier, 1986); idem, *The Glory of Israel: The Theology and Provenience of the Isaiah Targum* (JSOTSup 23; Sheffield: JSOT, 1982); idem, *God in Strength: Jesus' Announcement of the Kingdom* (SNTU 1; Freistadt: Plochl, 1979); idem, *Targumic Approaches to the Gospels: Essays in the Mutual Definition of Judaism and Christianity* (Studies in

Judaism; Lanham, MD: University Press of America, 1986); C. A. Evans, *To See and Not Perceive: Isaiah 6:9-10 in Early Jewish and Christian Interpretation* (JSOTSup 64; Sheffield: Sheffield Academic Press, 1989); J. A. Fitzmyer, *Essays on the Semitic Background of the New Testament* (Sources for Biblical Study 5; Missoula, MT: Scholars Press, 1974); idem, *A Wandering Aramean: Collected Aramaic Essays* (SBLMS 25; (Missoula, MT: Scholars Press, 1979); M. McNamara, *The New Testament and the Palestinian Targum to the Pentateuch* (AnBib 27; Rome: Pontifical Biblical Institute, 1966); idem, *Targum and Testament: Aramaic Paraphrases of the Hebrew Bible: A Light on the New Testament* (Grand Rapids, MI: Eerdmans, 1972); A. D. York, "The Dating of Targumic Literature," *JSJ* 5 (1974) 49-62; idem, "The Targum in the Synagogue and the School," *JSJ* 10 (1979) 74-86.

B. D. Chilton

RABBINIC PARABLES

Parables are "short fictitious stories that illustrate a moral attitude or religious principle" (*Webster's Third New International Dictionary*). Normally they have two levels of meaning, popularly the "earthly story" and the "heavenly meaning."

1. Frequency
2. Variety
3. Parables as Analogies
4. Parables as Mini-Dramas
5. Caricature
6. Stock Metaphors
7. Function and Audience
8. Comparison with Jesus' Parables

1. Frequency.

In the ancient Greco-Roman world parables occur frequently in the teaching of Jesus and the rabbinic literature but only rarely elsewhere. More than 1,500 rabbinic parables survive, though only 324 of these date before A.D. 200. These earlier parables are given in R. M. Johnston (1977). Only three date before the time of Jesus, from R. Hillel in the generation immediately preceding. Thus the 60 parables of Jesus in the Synoptic Gospels are among the earliest known. Yet Jesus' audience realized he was speaking in parables (Mt 13:10), so the form was apparently well known at that time. Perhaps parables were common in the *synagogue sermons of Jesus' day, as they were later. We have too little information from this early period to be sure.

2. Variety.

In Jewish usage, the Greek word *parabolē*, like its Hebrew counterpart *māšāl*, is broader in meaning than the English word *parable*. Both also include proverb and paradox, and *māšāl* can mean byword or prophetic poem as well. Here we confine ourselves to parables in the narrower sense, illustrative stories ranging in length from a sentence or two (a similitude) to a short story of a few hundred words (story parable). These may make a single point or several; they may be rather allegorical or not. To conserve space here, the parables quoted are the shorter ones.

3. Parables as Analogies.

Most parables have two levels of meaning. As J. W. Sider notes, parables typically make their points by means of analogy or proportion, using some situation in everyday life to picture something in the moral or spiritual realm. "R. Jacob said: 'This world is like a lobby before the world to come. Prepare yourself in the lobby that you may enter the banquet hall'" (J116 [indicates the number of the parable cataloged in Johnston's work]; *m. ʾAbot* 4:16) Here the analogy is:

> this world: the world to come = lobby: banquet hall.

The left side of the equation is the reality part (tenor, *nimšal);* the right side is the picture part (vehicle, *māšāl).* The speaker is making one or more points of comparison through this proportion. His main point here is (1) we need to get ready in the first before we enter the second. Some other points are probably implied: (2) we have to pass out of the first to get into the second; (3) the second is far more important than the first, or even the (3a) second is what the first is all about.

4. Parables as Mini-Dramas.

B. H. Young notes that many parables have a structure like that of a miniature drama. They often begin with an introductory formula, followed by the presentation of the main characters and setting. A crisis is developed and then resolved. Finally, the parable is applied.

> Judah ha-Nasi said: "Unto what is the matter like? It is like a king who was judging his son, and the accuser was standing and indicting him. When the tutor of the prince saw that his pupil was being condemned, he thrust the accuser outside the court and put himself in

his place in order to plead on his behalf. Even so, when Israel made the Golden Calf, Satan stood before God accusing him, while Moses remained without. What then did Moses do? He arose and thrust Satan away and put himself in his place." (J267; *Ex. Rab.* 43:1)

5. Caricature.

Parables are typically stories drawn from everyday life, but often they have some unusual character or exaggerated action designed to draw attention to a particular point. The best ones are short and memorable creations of experienced storytellers.

It is said, "Will you be angry with the entire assembly when only one man sins?" (Num 16:22). R. Simeon b. Yohai taught: "A parable. It is like men sitting in a ship. One took a drill and began boring beneath his seat. His fellow-travelers said, 'What are you doing?' He responded, 'What does it matter to you? It's my seat I'm boring under!' They said, 'The water will come in and drown us all!' " (J271; *Lev. Rab.* 4:6)

6. Stock Metaphors.

Parable stories often have characters and actions that are based on common metaphors. Many of these are drawn from the OT, and they help the listener understand what the point is. Among Johnston's 324 early rabbinic parables, by far the commonest metaphor is that of a king (161 times), nearly always standing for God. Other common pictures for God are husband and father. For Israel, the stock metaphors are son, wife, daughter and servant. *Moses is often pictured as a friend, steward or tutor. A banquet is used with some variety, but a common meaning is the age to come. Inheritance sometimes pictures the promised land, sometimes Israelites and once the future reward. The skillful parable maker would often weave together a consistent set of these motifs into a story to teach a lesson.

> A philosopher asked R. Gamaliel, "Why is your God jealous of idol-worshipers rather than of the idol itself?" He answered, "I will tell you a parable. To what is the matter like? It is like a king who had a son, and his son raised a dog whom he named for his father. Whenever the son took an oath, he said, 'By the life of this dog, my father!' When the king heard of it, with whom was he angry, his son or the dog? Surely his son!" (J174; *Mek. Bahodesh* 6:113ff.).

7. Function and Audience.

Among the rabbis, parables are commonly used in two ways—as illustrations and as arguments. The rabbi's audience might be his disciples in a teaching situation, a congregation listening to a synagogue sermon or some outsider in an encounter or debate. We see the last of these in the parable cited in §6 above. The teaching situation is probably the occasion for §§4-5, which are explaining Scripture passages, and the setting of §3 is likely to have been sermonic (*see* Homily, Ancient).

8. Comparison with Jesus' Parables.

The sorts of parables used by the rabbis are often similar to those used by Jesus, and each can cast some light on the interpretation of the other. In fact, most of what has been said above applies to the parables of Jesus.

8.1. Fables. One type of rabbinic parable not found in the Gospels is the fable, a story featuring animals or plants acting in human ways. When one rabbi warned R. Akiba for violating the Roman decree against studying the Torah, the latter responded,

> Unto what is the matter like? It is like a fox who was walking alongside a river, and he saw fish going in swarms from one place to another [fleeing the fishermen]. He said to them, "Would you like to come on to the dry land . . . ?" They said to him, " . . . If we are afraid in the element in which we live, how much more in the element in which we would die!" So it is with us. . . . If we go and neglect the Torah [which is our life], how much worse off we shall be. (J148; *b. Ber.* 61b)

This type of parable is occasionally found in the OT (e.g., Judg 9:8-15), but is best known in the collection ascribed to Aesop (sixth century B.C.).

8.2. Sample Parables. A type of parable used by Jesus but not apparently by the rabbis is the sample, or paradigm, parable. In these, the story operates only on a single level, being already a moral or religious story without the use of analogy. Instead, a sample of the sort of behavior to be approved or condemned is given (e.g., the parables of the Good Samaritan, Lk 10:30-36, and the Rich Fool, Lk 12:16-21), and the recipient is expected to generalize the lesson from this concrete example. These have a background in the case law of the OT and in the sample stories of Proverbs (e.g., Prov 7:6-23).

8.3. Similar Parables. Stock metaphors (§6

above) are used by Jesus as well as the rabbis, and in a few cases, a similar cluster of such metaphors results in a very similar parable. Compare R. Tarfon's saying, "The day is short, the task is great, the laborers are idle, the wage is abundant, and the master of the house is urgent" (*m. ʾAbot* 2:15) with Jesus' "The harvest is plentiful, but the workers are few. Ask the Lord of the harvest, therefore, to send out workers into his harvest field" (Lk 10:2). Or consider the following parable:

> A king had a vineyard for which he engaged many laborers, one of whom was especially apt and skillful. What did the king do? He took this laborer from his work and walked through the vineyard with him. When the laborers came for their hire in the evening, the skillful laborer also appeared among them and received a full day's wages from the king. The other laborers were angry at this and said, "We have toiled the whole day, while this man has worked but two hours; why does the king give him the full hire, even as to us?" The king said to them, "Why are you angry? Through his skill he has done more in two hours than you have all day." (*y. Ber.* 2:5)

The story is very similar to that of Jesus in Matthew 20:1-16, but the lesson is very different.

See also Rabbinic Proverbs.

Bibliography. R. M. Johnston, "Parabolic Interpretations Attributed to Tannaim" (Ph.D. thesis, Hartford Seminary Foundation, 1977; available from University Microfilms International); J. Z. Lauterbach, "Parable," *JE* 9:512-14; H. K. MacArthur and R. M. Johnston, *They Also Taught in Parables: Rabbinic Parables from the First Centuries of the Christian Era* (Grand Rapids, MI: Zondervan, 1990); R. B. Y. Scott and L. I. Rabinowitz, "Parable," *EncJud* 13:72-77; J. W. Sider, *Interpreting the Parables: A Hermeneutical Guide to Their Meaning* (Grand Rapids, MI: Zondervan, 1995); D. Stern, *Parables in Midrash* (Cambridge, MA: Harvard University Press, 1991); B. H. Young, *Jesus and His Jewish Parables: Rediscovering the Roots of Jesus' Teaching* (TI; New York: Paulist, 1989).

R. C. Newman

RABBINIC PROVERBS

The word *proverb* suggests a gem of popular wisdom, a short, pithy statement that encapsulates a keen observation about nature and/or human nature, and is memorable and often repeated.

Rabbinic proverbs are part of a long tradition linking Jewish wisdom teaching with Torah. The biblical proverbs are paradigmatic as exhortations to correct moral choices; this emphasis continues from the Old Testament period into the first centuries A.D. As they appear in selected texts from late antiquity, rabbinic proverbs illustrate the richness of practical instruction and illuminate our study of Jesus as the consummate teacher of wisdom.

1. Definition
2. A Literary/Historical Survey
3. Characteristics of Rabbinic Proverbs
4. Selected Parallels: Rabbinic Proverbs and the Teaching of Jesus

1. Definition.

The Hebrew word translated "proverb" is *māšāl,* a term that covers a wide spectrum of literary products. While the fundamental meaning of this word implies "likeness" (Johnson, 162-63), the various means of articulating that likeness are manifold. *Māšāl* frequently indicates a *parable, a literary form that significantly develops the comparison. This study of rabbinic proverbs, however, will focus on decidedly brief but pungent and memorable statements, only some of which are labeled *mᵉšālîm.* Certain of these are introduced in the rabbinic collections by *(hayyenu) de ʾamre ʿinše,* "according to the popular saying," indicating they were often repeated.

2. A Literary/Historical Survey.

The same features that characterize biblical proverbs are reflected in their rabbinic counterparts.

2.1. Attributed Collections. A majority of biblical proverbs are found in collections and are attributed to named individuals whose reputation for wisdom gives credence to the statements. Portions of the book of Proverbs are attributed to Solomon (Prov 10:1; 25:1) and to "the wise" (Prov 22:17). Likewise, the wisdom sayings collected in *Pirqe ʾAbot* (*Sayings of the Fathers*) are attributed to significant sages of the first centuries B.C. and A.D.

2.2. Isolated Statements. At the same time, the biblical text contains singular instances of popular sayings. One example is Ezekiel 18:2b: "the fathers eat sour grapes, and the teeth of the children are set on edge." So also, popular sayings appear individually in the rabbinic literature, often introduced by *(hayyenu) de ʾamre ʿinše.*

2.3. Topics. Biblical wisdom texts deal with

knowledge and wisdom, righteousness, truth, justice and humility; the rabbinic collections of proverbs address the same profound concerns, starting with the necessity of knowing and practicing Torah. Many of the biblical and rabbinic proverbs are founded upon observations about the natural world. Often the proverbs focus on the implicit order and predictable character of that world and then note the reversals introduced by humanity.

*2.4. **Extrabiblical Sources.*** The long tradition of Jewish texts that contain proverbs includes *Sirach (Ben Sira) and the *Wisdom of Solomon from the intertestamental period. Indicative of the perceived importance of these pursuits, Sirach 39:1-3 describes the sage who devoted himself to the study of the law of the Most High: "He seeks out the wisdom of all the ancients . . . he seeks out the hidden meanings of proverbs [*apocrypha paroimiōn*] and is at home with the obscurities of parables" (NRSV).

The rabbinic texts cited below include the Mishnah, compiled about A.D. 220; *Mekilta de Rabbi Ishmael,* an exegetical commentary on the book of Exodus that most likely dates to the second half of the third century; and the Babylonian Talmud, compiled around A.D. 500. While the names of the sages suggest that some of these traditions may be representative of the first century, they have undergone centuries of oral development.

3. Characteristics of Rabbinic Proverbs.

3.1. Collections with a Biblical Foundation.

3.1.1. ʾAbot. The best known collection of rabbinic proverbs is *ʾAbot,* a tractate in the Mishnah, one purpose of which seems to have been to establish the authority of oral tradition by linking it with written Torah (Lerner, 273). The named individuals whose wise sayings are cited span the period from Ezra to the production of the Mishnah by Rabbi Judah the Prince, thus demonstrating this continuity. The major subjects addressed have to do with the study and practice of Torah, the importance of a teacher, care with words, choosing to do good, wisdom and the fear of heaven, honoring other people, justice and humility. Chapter 5 presents these gems of wisdom in numbered lists, a pattern found in Proverbs and an aid to memory.

Hillel's words are prominent in the early chapters: "A name made great is a name destroyed, and he that increases not decreases, and he that learns not is worthy of death, and he that makes worldly use of the crown shall perish" (*m. ʾAbot* 1:13) and "do not judge your fellow until you have come into his place" (*m. ʾAbot* 2:5b). Further expositions of *ʾAbot*'s wisdom sayings appear in *ʾAbot de Rabbi Nathan,* one of the minor tractates of the Babylonian Talmud.

3.1.2. The Babylonian Talmud. Later collections of rabbinic proverbs appear in *Derek Ereṣ Rabba* and *Baba Qamma* 92a-b, tractates of the Babylonian Talmud. Chapter 2 of *Derek Ereṣ Rabba* is a series of character descriptions, each of which is grounded in a biblical text. These are similar to traits described in Proverbs, and parts of the chapter also resonate with Jesus' Sermon on the Mount. "Concerning them who are merciful, who feed the hungry, give drink to the thirsty, clothe the naked and distribute alms Scripture declares, *Say of the righteous, that it shall be well with him*" [Is 3:10] (*b. Der. Er. Rab.* 2:21).

In the *Baba Qamma* collection, several features are significant. First, some of them are cited as popular sayings, while others are attributed to the sages. Second, in both cases there is an intentional effort to link them with biblical texts as their bases. Note the following examples:

> Raba said to Rabbah bar Mari: "Whence can be derived the popular saying that together with the thorn the cabbage is smitten?" He replied: "As it is written, *Why will you strive with Me? You all have transgressed against Me, says the Lord*" [Jer 2:29]. (*b. B. Qam.* 92a)

This prooftext and those that follow in the ensuing discussion draw on a plural pronoun in the biblical text to conclude that all are worthy of punishment.

> Raba said to Rabbah bar Mari: "Whence can be derived the saying of the rabbis: 'If your fellow calls you an ass, put a saddle on your back'?"

The response quotes Genesis 16:8-9, in which Hagar, addressed by the angel as the handmaid of Sarai, calls Sarai her mistress, accepting the role (*b. B. Qam.* 92b).

3.2. Isolated Statements. Apart from the collections of proverbs, we occasionally find single maxims that are cited in the context of biblical text analyses. For example, as the sages discussed the name Di-Zahab (Deut 1:1),

> the school of Yannai said: "Moses said before The Holy One Blessed Be He: 'Master of the Universe, it was because of the silver and

gold that you poured out on Israel until they said: Enough! that they were led to make a god of gold.'" A *mashal*: The lion does not tear and roar out of a basket of straw, but out of a basket of meat. (*b. Sanh.* 102a)

The Hebrew word for "enough" is related to Di; Zahab is "gold." The moral is that they were overwhelmed by the abundant presence of that which tempted them to sin. The proverb drawn from the natural world graphically illustrates the point.

*3.3. **Incongruities and Paradoxes.*** Folk proverbs often point out incongruities and paradoxes. "Though the wine belongs to the master, the thanks are given to the butler" (*b. B. Qam.* 92b). Hillel's words in *m. ʾAbot* 1:13 (cited above) are illustrative of a recognizable set of paradoxes.

*3.4. **Hebrew and Aramaic.*** Although the Mishnah is an essentially Hebrew text, some of the maxims quoted by Hillel in *ʾAbot* are in Aramaic. In other words, those sayings that were reflective of the earlier discussions in academic circles were preserved in Hebrew, while the popular culture and language only occasionally emerged in the text. In the Babylonian Talmud, compiled later and in a different geographical context, both the proverbs and the sages' discussion are primarily in Aramaic.

4. Selected Parallels: Rabbinic Proverbs and the Teaching of Jesus.

*4.1. **Paradoxes.*** Some of Jesus' proverbs highlighted the reversals of life in the kingdom of God: "The first shall be last, and the last first" (Mt 19:30; 20:16); and "whoever wants to save his life will lose it, but whoever loses his life for me will find it" (Mt 16:25).

*4.2. **Measure for Measure.*** A maxim that appears with great frequency in the rabbinic texts is the assurance that "according to the measure that a person has used, so it will be measured to him." This is followed by citations of multiple biblical examples to demonstrate that God's justice is balanced and the measures of punishment and reward fit the human activity (*m. Soṭa* 1:7-9; *Mek. Bešallah* 1; *Mek. Širta* 2). Overall, there is a qualitative balance in all of God's dispensations of justice. In those contexts, however, the rabbis also emphasized that the measure of reward for good was always greater than the measure of punishment for a crime. This was in keeping with Exodus 20:5-6.

When Jesus used this expression in Matthew 7:1-2, simple balanced justice is evident. "Do not judge, so that you may not be judged. For with the judgment you make you will be judged, and the measure you give will be the measure you get" (NRSV). In Mark 4, Jesus' reference to measure for measure engaged both the aspects of balance and greater measure. Following his disclosure of the meaning of the parable of the sower, Jesus says: "For there is nothing hidden, except to be disclosed; nor is anything secret, except to come to light. . . . the measure you give will be the measure you get. For to those who have, more will be given; and from those who have nothing, even what they have will be taken away" (Mk 4:22-25 NRSV).

*4.3. **The Sabbath.*** Jesus' use of proverbs was occasionally prompted by disputes. One example was the ongoing sabbath controversy. After the *Pharisees challenged the actions of his disciples on the sabbath, Jesus responded with several biblical examples and then made a summary statement in Mark 2:27 (NRSV): "The sabbath was made for humankind, and not humankind for the sabbath." This is echoed in *Mekilta* in conjunction with its commentary on Exodus 31:13. The question for the sages was what activities ought to supersede the sabbath and why. Following that discussion, R. Shimon ben Menasiah said: "The verse says: *Keep the Sabbath because it is holy for you.* The Sabbath has been given for you; you haven't been given for the Sabbath" (*Mek. Šabta* 1).

See also RABBINIC PARABLES.

BIBLIOGRAPHY. C. Albeck, ed., *Shishah Sidrei Mishnah* (Heb; 6 vols.; Jerusalem: The Bialik Institute, 1954-59); R. Bultmann, *The History of the Synoptic Tradition* (5th ed.; Oxford: Blackwell, 1963); A. Cohen, ed., *The Babylonian Talmud* (Heb/Eng ed.; London: Soncino, 1984); H. Danby, trans., *The Mishnah* (London: Oxford University Press, 1933); J. Goldin, trans., *The Fathers According to Rabbi Nathan* (New Haven, CT: Yale University Press, 1955); H. S. Horovitz and I. A. Rabin, eds., *Mechilta d'Rabbi Ismael* (Heb; Jerusalem: Bamberger & Wahrman, 1960); A. R. Johnson, "Mashal," in *Wisdom in Israel and in the Ancient Near East,* ed. M. Noth and D. W. Thomas (Leiden: E. J. Brill, 1955); M. B. Lerner, "The Tractate Avot," in *The Literature of the Sages,* ed. S. Safrai (CRINT 2.3; Assen: Van Gorcum; Philadelphia: Fortress, 1987); R. H. Stein, *The Method and Message of Jesus' Teachings* (rev. ed.; Louisville, KY: Westminster John Knox, 1994); A. Strikovsky, "Talmudic Proverbs," *EncJud* 13:1273-76.

E. A. Phillips

RABBIS

The term "rabbi" has ignited controversy in the study of the NT. Although it appears frequently within the Gospels in reference to Jesus, some scholars deny that earliest Christianity can be described in rabbinic terms at all. Others have been prepared to assume, as part of the background of the NT, the existence of rabbinic institutions that only developed after the destruction of the temple in A.D. 70. Considering the history of the term's actual usage during this period enables us to negotiate this impasse.

1. The Pharisees Within Early Judaism
2. The Transition to Rabbinic Judaism

1. The Pharisees Within Early Judaism.

The rabbinic movement in its earliest phase is to be identified with Pharisaism. The *Pharisees are portrayed by *Josephus as being critical of the *Hasmonean *priesthood. Their expression was at first political (Josephus *Ant.* 13.10.5-6 §§288-98) and could extend to violent action, as in the demand that the counselors who advised Alexander Janneus to kill some of their sympathizers should themselves be executed (Josephus *J.W.* 1.5.2-3 §§110-14). At base, however, the orientation of the Pharisees was toward the achievement and maintenance of *purity.

The purity they strived for had fundamentally to do with making offerings, people and priests fit for the cult of *sacrifice in the *temple. For that reason, the issues of the personnel of the priesthood, the sorts of animals and goods that might be brought and their permitted proximity to all sources of uncleanness were vitally important.

By the dawn of the present era, the Pharisees found a distinguished teacher in *Jerusalem in the person of Hillel. Hillel is justly famous for the dictum, uttered some twenty years before Jesus, "That which you hate, do not do to your fellow; that is the whole Torah, while all the rest is commentary thereon" (*b. Šabb.* 31a). The story is striking, but it can also be misleading. First, Hillel in the tale is talking to an impatient proselyte who wished to learn the Torah while he stands on one foot; his impatience has just won him a cuff with a measuring rod from Shammai, the rabbi with whom Hillel is programmatically contrasted in Mishnah. Obviously Hillel has no overt desire to reduce the Torah on the grounds of principle, and he tells the proselyte, "Go and learn it." In other words, the Gentile is told that the revelation to *Moses is the expression of the best ethics, and for that reason the whole should be mastered.

In any case, Hillel was understood among the Pharisees as having come to prominence for adjudicating a distinct issue: whether the Passover (*see* Festivals and Holy Days: Jewish) could be offered on the *sabbath. Hillel first offers a scriptural argument for accepting the practice: since other forms of priestly service are permitted, so is the slaying of the lamb. His hearers are unimpressed, until he states that he learned the position in Babylon, from Shemaiah and Abtalion, distinguished predecessors in the movement. Their authority is sufficient to displace the current leaders of Pharisaic opinion, the sons of Bathyra (cf. *t. Pesaḥ.* 4:13, 14; *y. Pesaḥ.* 6:1; *y. Šabb.* 19:1; *b. Pesaḥ.* 66a, b).

The latter story may appear the more arcane to most readers, but it is also more redolent of Pharisaic culture. Hillel consistently involved himself in cultic questions and disputes in Jerusalem. His position also is said to have convinced another teacher, Baba ben Buta, to provide cultically correct beasts in great numbers for slaughter, with the stipulation (against the school of Shammai) that the offerer lay hands on the victim immediately prior to the killing (cf. *t. Ḥag.* 2:11; *y. Ḥag.* 2:3; *y. Beṣa* 2:4; *b. Beṣa* 20a, b). Moreover, the basis of Hillel's authority was not so much any scriptural expertise as his mastery of what he had been taught by previous masters. Hillel embodies the Pharisaic principle that the "chains" of their tradition were normative for purity. Such chains were understood to have been developed from Moses to Ezra, after that by "the men of the great congregation" and then by teachers who were generally invoked as "pairs" (*m. ʾAbot* 1:1-18). The last pair was Hillel and Shammai, from which point the Pharisees acknowledged that division increased in Israel (*b. Soṭa* 47b; *b. Sanh.* 88b; *t. Soṭa* 14:9; *t. Ḥag.* 2:9; *t. Sanh.* 7:1; *y. Ḥag.* 2:2; *y. Sanh.* 1:4). The notion of primeval unity disturbed by recent faction is probably mythical, but it is plain that the Pharisees developed their oral tradition by means of a structured understanding of the past, as well as by mnemonic techniques.

The term *Pharisee* is probably an outsiders'

name for the movement and may mean "separatist" or "purist"; participants in the movement appear to have referred to their ancient predecessors (after Ezra) as "the sages" or "the wise" and to their more recent predecessors and contemporaries as "teachers" (cf. *rab* in *m. ʾAbot* 1:6, 16; *sophistēs* in Josephus). The normal, respectful address of a teacher was "my great one," or "my master," *rabbi*. Jesus is so addressed in the Gospels more than by any other designation; moreover, he had a characteristic interest in purity, and a dispute concerning appropriate sacrifice in the temple cost him his life.

That Jesus' followers called him rabbi (Mt 26:25, 49; Mk 9:5; 10:51; 11:21; 14:45; Jn 1:38, 49; 3:2; 4:31; 6:25; 9:2; 11:8) is a straightforward deduction from the Gospels as they stand; that he is most naturally to be associated with the Pharisees of his period is an equally straightforward inference. When, during the course of the twentieth century, scholars have expressed reservations in respect of that finding, they have had in mind the danger of identifying Jesus with the rabbinic movement after A.D. 70, which was more systematized than before that time and which amounted to the established power within Judaism. Unfortunately, anxiety in respect of that anachronism can result in the far greater error of bracketing Jesus within "sectarian" Judaism (as if "orthodoxy" existed in early, pluralized Judaism) or—worse still—of placing him within no Judaism at all (*see* Theologies and Sects, Jewish).

2. The Transition to Rabbinic Judaism.

During the time of Hillel and Shammai and until A.D. 70, Pharisaic teaching was targeted at the conduct of the cult in the temple, but its influence was limited. Nonetheless, Pharisees appeared to have succeeded reasonably well in towns and villages, even in Galilee, where they urged local populations to maintain the sort of purity that would permit them to participate rightly in the cult. Josephus's fellow in the armed resistance against Rome and archrival, John of Gischala, may well have been representing Pharisaic interests when he arranged for Jews in Syria to purchase oil exclusively from Galilean sources (Josephus *J.W.* 2.21.2 §§591-94). In any case, it does appear plain that some Pharisees supported the revolt of A.D. 66-70, while others did not (*see* Jewish Wars with Rome). But while many priests and *Essenes perished in the internecine strife of the revolt and in the war with the Romans, and while the aristocracy of scribes and elders in Jerusalem was discredited and decimated, the Pharisees survived the war better than did any other single group. They were well accepted locally, had long ago accommodated to some marginality and survived with their personnel and their traditions comparatively intact.

Rabbinic literature itself personifies the survival of the movement in a story concerning Rabbi Yoḥanan ben Zakkai. According to the story, Yoḥanan had himself borne out of Jerusalem on the pretense he was dead, only to hail Vespasian as king; on his ascent to power, Vespasian granted Yoḥanan his wish of settlement in the town of Yavneh. In that Josephus claims similarly to have flattered Vespasian (Josephus *J.W.* 3.8.9 §§399-408) and to have seen in his coming the fulfillment of messianic prophecy (Jospehus *J.W.* 6.5.4 §§310-15), the tale is to be used with caution, but it remains expressive of the rabbinic ethos.

With the foundation of academies such as the one at Yavneh after A.D. 70, one may speak of the transition of Pharisaism to rabbinic Judaism. The rabbis, those who directly contributed to rabbinic literature and to the Judaism that is framed by that literature, belonged to a movement much changed from the popular Puritanism of the Pharisees, initially for reasons not of their own making. The sort of leadership that a Yoḥanan ben Zakkai might offer became suddenly attractive, in the absence of priestly, Essene or scribal alternatives. The target of the tradition's application became correspondingly wider as the Pharisaic/rabbinic program was applied not simply to issues of purity and sacrifice but also to worship generally, ethics and daily living. To Yoḥanan is explicitly attributed the view that the world, which had been sustained by the temple, the law and deeds of faithful love, now was to be supported only by the last two of the three (*ʾAbot R. Nat.* 4). Moreover, he specifically adjudicated, on the basis of his tradition, how feasts might be kept in the gathering for reading, prayer and discussion that was called a congregation or *synagogue (*kenesset,* also applied to buildings erected for the purpose of such gatherings; cf. *m. Sukk.* 3:12; *m. Roš Haš.* 4:1, 3, 4).

The development of that sort of worship, as a replacement for activity within the temple, was not without analogy during the period prior to

A.D. 70. Mishnah (*m. Taʿan.* 4:2) envisages a system in which priests, Levites and laypeople alike gathered in local synagogues while their representatives were in Jerusalem. The priestly system of courses of service was perhaps the germ of such *piety: it allowed for a substantial population of priests, which it divided into twenty-four courses. While a few priests from each group were chosen to officiate in Jerusalem during the course of the week that the group was appointed to cover, the remainder may have gathered and read the appropriate lections in the villages of Judea and Galilee where they normally lived (1 Chron 24:1-19; Josephus *Ant.* 7.14.17 §§365-67). The inclusion of the faithful in *Israel generally in such meetings was a natural development under the rabbis, and general meetings for prayer and instruction had long been a customary feature of Judaism in the *Diaspora. The development of worship in synagogues as something of a replacement for worship in the temple was therefore natural.

The transition from Pharisaism to rabbinic Judaism, however, was not accomplished immediately after A.D. 70, nor was it a matter of the same movement with the same personnel carrying on in a totally new environment. The environment was new and favored the emerging authority of rabbis uniquely. But the Pharisees of the period before A.D. 70 also were sufficiently flexible to accommodate an influx of priests and scribes into their ranks. The priestly interest of the Pharisaic movement was historically organic, and the references to priests in stories and teachings from the time of Yoḥanan (cf. Rabbi Yosi the Priest, *m. ʾAbot* 2:8) and well into the second century is striking.

Moreover, the consolidation of the rabbis' power after A.D. 70, predicated as it was on local influence, could be assured only by means of the control of local adjudication, as well as worship and study. The tendency of scribes to align themselves with the Pharisees, together with priestly adherents and sympathizers with the movement, assured the emergence and the success of the rabbis. At the same time, the triumph of rabbinic authority assured the continuing influence of the priests in decisions regarding purity, in blessings and in receipts of payment of redemption and of tithe, while scribal influence, in the production of written materials and the convocation of formal courts, is also striking. Nonetheless, the functional consolidation of the power of the old groups and factions was achieved only during the time of Rabbi Judah, with the emergence of a patriarchate recognized and supported by the Romans.

In the wake of A.D. 70 and the Roman confiscation of the tax formerly paid for the temple, neither Jerusalem nor its environs was amenable to the maintenance of a hub of the movement, and even Yavneh was eclipsed during the second century by centers in prosperous Galilee, such as Usha and Beth She'arim. Later, metropolitan cities such as Sepphoris and Tiberias were the foci of leadership. There was at first nothing like a central leadership or even a common policy, but rabbinic Judaism was constituted in the Pharisaic, priestly and scribal quest for the purity of the nation. The health of the movement required a shift from the highly personal authority of the Pharisees to some notion of learned consensus.

Just that shift is reflected in a Talmudic story concerning a great teacher, Rabbi Eliezer ben Hyrcanus. The story has it that, against a majority of his colleagues, Eliezer held that a ceramic stove, once polluted, might be reassembled, provided the tiles were separated by sand. The majority taught that the result would be unclean; such materials should never be used again. Eliezer's correctness was demonstrated by a tree that was uprooted at his behest, by a stream that ran backwards at his command, by a building he similarly demolished and by a voice from heaven. Despite all that, the majority held that its decision was binding (*b. B. Meṣ.* 59a, b). As the rudiments of an institution emerged, Eliezer's personal authority clearly diminished; the rabbis of the second century were to stress a rational, consensual achievement of purity, and by the time of the Talmud that was held to be a greater purity than charismatic authority could achieve.

The historic concern for the temple as the focus of purity nonetheless resulted in a final and nearly disastrous attempt—encouraged by some rabbis—to free and restore the holy site. The most prominent rabbinic supporter of that attempt was a student of Eliezer's renowned for his expertise in the tradition, Aqiba. Aqiba supported the claims of one *Simeon bar Kosiba to be the new prince of Israel, acting in conjunction with a priest named Eleazar. Simeon's supporters referred to him as Bar Kokhba, "son of a star," projecting onto him the messianic expectations of Numbers 24:17, while his detractors came to know him as Bar Koziba, "son of a lie." His initial success and military acumen is attested in letters he sent his commanders during his revolt and regime, which lasted from A.D. 132 until 135. In the shape of Hadrian, the response of the empire was even more definitive than it had been in A.D. 70. The remnants of the temple were taken apart, and new shrines were built in the city; Jerusalem itself was now called Aelia Capitolina, Jews were denied entry, and Judea became Syria Palaestina.

The rabbis survived by disowning the aspirations embodied by Aqiba but keeping much of his teaching. "Aqiba, grass will grow out of your jaw, before the son of David comes" (*y. Ta ʿan.* 4:7; *Lam. Rab.* 2.2.4); that is to say, the messiah is to be of David, not of popular choosing, and his time cannot be pressed. But the greatness of the rabbinic response to national defeat and their consequent redefinition of Judaism consisted less in their formulation of a particular teaching regarding *messianism, which emerges in any case from time to time in many forms of Judaism, than in their textual constitution of a form of thought, discipline and life, the Mishnah (*see* Rabbinic Literature: Mishnah and Tosefta).

See also PHARISEES; RABBINIC LITERATURE: MISHNAH AND TOSEFTA.

BIBLIOGRAPHY. A. Finkel, *The Pharisees and the Teacher of Nazareth* (AGSU 4; Leiden: E. J. Brill, 1964); J. A. Fitzmyer, "The Bar Cochba Period," *Essays on the Semitic Background of the New Testament* (SBLSBS 5; Missoula, MT: Scholars Press, 1974) 305-54; J. Goldin, *The Fathers According to Rabbi Nathan* (New York: Schocken, 1974); L. I. Levine, *The Rabbinic Class of Roman Palestine in Late Antiquity* (New York: Jewish Theological Seminary of America, 1989); J. N. Neusner, *The Pharisees: Rabbinic Perspectives* (Hoboken, NJ: Ktav, 1973); idem, *Torah: From Scroll to Symbol in Formative Judaism: The Foundations of Judaism* (Philadelphia: Fortress, 1985); E. Schürer, *A History of the Jewish People in the Age of Jesus Christ,* ed. G. Vermes, F. Millar, et al. (3 vols.; Edinburgh: T & T Clark, 1973-87).

B. D. Chilton

READING. *See* LITERACY AND BOOK CULTURE.

REBUKES BY THE OVERSEER (4Q477). *See* LEGAL TEXTS AT QUMRAN.

RELIGION, GRECO-ROMAN

The adjective *Greco-Roman* indicates that the cults discussed in this article are those which were practiced in the ancient Mediterranean world during the Hellenistic and Roman periods (i.e., from the late fourth century B.C. through the fifth century A.D.). These were periods of complex political and cultural change and syncretism in which first the Greeks and then the Romans provided the dominant political and cultural frameworks for life in the ancient Mediterranean world. Thus Greco-Roman religions include not only those public and private cults which had developed out of archaic and classical Greek and Roman religious practices, but also the many native cults and *mystery religions which had arisen on ancient Near Eastern soil and which had subsequently spread to the major urban areas of the Mediterranean world, including early Judaism and early Christianity.

1. Political and Cultural Setting
2. Greek Religion
3. Roman Religion
4. Hellenistic Religions

1. Political and Cultural Setting.

The political and cultural situation of the Mediterranean world changed radically following the victorious campaign which *Alexander the Great, king of Macedonia, waged against the massive Persian Empire beginning in 334 B.C. when Alexander invaded Anatolia with a force of 37,000. His father, Philip II, had earlier defeated the Greeks at the battle of Chaeronea in 338 B.C., and upon his death in 336 B.C. he was succeeded by his son Alexander III. Alexander was successful at the battle of Granicus in Anatolia in 334 B.C., where he first clashed with the Persian army under Darius and won decisively; the final blow was delivered at the battle of Gaugamela near the Ganges river in 331 B.C. Following the premature death of Alexander in 323 B.C., his empire crumbled.

The **diadochoi*, or Greek "successors," of Alexander fought among themselves in the attempt to gain control of ever larger parts of the vast region which Alexander had conquered. The more important among these successors were able to found dynastic kingdoms in which a Greco-Macedonian elite ruled over extensive native populations until the Roman conquest of the eastern Mediterranean. Ptolemy founded the Ptolemaic dynasty, which ruled Egypt (and Palestine until 201 B.C.; *see* Hellenistic Egypt); Seleucus founded the Seleucid dynasty, which ruled the territories from Syria to India; Antigonus founded the Antigonid dynasty, which ruled Macedonia, shorn of its empire; and Lysimachus and his successors ruled Armenia and Thrace.

After Rome had taken control of most of Italy shortly after the beginning of the third century B.C., she embarked on a series of wars with Punic Carthage in North Africa for control of the western Mediterranean. Following Roman victories in the First Punic War (264-241 B.C.) and the Second Punic War (220-201 B.C.), Rome turned to the eastern Mediterranean initially to punish Philip of Macedonia for the military assistance he had provided to Hannibal, the Carthaginian general. Rome fought a series of three Macedonian wars (214-205, 200-196 and 148-146 B.C.). After the conclusion of the Third Macedonian War in 146 B.C. (which included the complete destruction of Hellenistic Corinth in 146 B.C.), Rome turned Macedonia and Greece into Roman provinces. At the same time Rome permanently eliminated the economic competition afforded her by Carthage by completely destroying this Punic North African city in 146 B.C.

After the decisive Roman victories over Macedonia, Greece and Carthage in 146 B.C., Rome slowly began annexing the Hellenistic kingdoms which had achieved independence following the crumbling of Alexander's Greco-Macedonian empire. The last Hellenistic kingdom to be defeated was Ptolemaic Egypt; Octavian, the Roman general who was later to become the first Roman emperor and assume the titular name Augustus (meaning "venerable"), defeated Mark Antony and Cleopatra VII (the last Ptolemaic dynast) at the battle of Actium in 31 B.C. At this point the Romans began to refer to the Mediterranean as *mare nostrum* ("our sea").

Rome had undergone profound changes since the city was founded c. 753 B.C. (the date preferred by the Roman antiquarian Varro, 116-27 B.C.). The period of the monarchy lasted from 753 to 509 B.C., when Tarquinius Superbus, the last of seven kings, was overthrown. The monarchy was succeeded by the republic, which lasted from 509 B.C. until it collapsed during the political and military chaos of 133-31 B.C. Following the battle of Actium in 31 B.C., Octavian took firm control of political and military affairs in Rome. In 27 B.C. he became the first of a series of Roman emperors to rule until the collapse of the western empire in A.D. 476, when the last Roman emperor Romulus Augustulus was deposed.

2. Greek Religion.

The Greek world consisted of hundreds of *poleis*, or "city-states," on the Greek peninsula and islands, on the west coast of Asia Minor, Sicily and in Magna Graecia in Italy (*see* Cities, Greco-Roman). Each *polis* was fiercely independent. Each had its own distinctive internal political and religious structure. Originating c. 750 B.C., perhaps linked to the transition from monarchy to aristocracy throughout much of the Greek world, the *polis* reached a fully developed form by the late sixth century B.C., and typically included such features as an acropolis, walls, a market, temples, a theater and a gymnasium (Pausanias *Descr.* 10.4.1). There were, in addition, a number of interstate religious institutions and sanctuaries which did not function primarily for the benefit of a particular *polis*. These institutions provided the hundreds of Greek communities, separated both by distance and topography, with a variety of cult centers which, along with the use of a common language (in many dialects), contributed to the development of Hellenic national consciousness (Herodotus *Hist.* 8.144). The religious and cultural institutions accessible to all Greeks included the pan-Hellenic games held at intervals of from two to four years (the Olympian games, the most famous, were held every four years beginning in 776 B.C.), the oracle of Apollo at Delphi, the healing cult of Asclepius at Epidauros and the Eleusinian mysteries at Eleusis in Attica. Another pan-Hellenic religious development was the institution of the *civic cult of the Twelve Gods instituted in a number of Greek cities beginning in the late sixth century B.C. In general, Greek religion was not organized around a set of coherent doctrines, but rather centered in the observance of traditional rituals such as processions, prayers, libations, sacrifice and feasting.

2.1. The Gods. The Greek notion of deity contrasts sharply with traditional Jewish and Christian conceptions. For the Greeks the gods were not transcendent and passive, but rather immanent and active. They did not create the cosmos (which was thought to be eternal), but came into being after the cosmos. Consequently gods such as the sun, moon and stars were considered "eternals," while gods such as Zeus, Hera and Poseidon were considered "immortals." Though the Greek gods were thought to be more powerful than humans, both were subject to *moira* ("fate"). Further, gods were sustained by ambrosia and nectar, usually inaccessible to mortals, and "ichor" rather than blood flowed in their veins. Though considered very powerful and very wise, they were neither omnipotent nor omniscient. Human beings were considered mortal, while the Greek gods were considered immortal; in archaic and classical Greek religion, immortality was not a possibility for mortals. The scores of deities worshiped by various Greek cities were placed into a comprehensive genealogical relationship by Hesiod in his *Theogony*. In the *Iliad* and *Odyssey*, epic poems created by a series of bards collectively designated "Homer," a synthetic presentation of the many originally local divinities was depicted as a pantheon of Olympian gods (though chthonic deities such as Demeter and Dionysus are not mentioned). The cult of Twelve Gods, however, first appears in the late sixth century; literary and archaeological evidence indicates than an altar to the Twelve Gods was dedicated c. 520 B.C. (Herodotus *Hist.* 6.108; Thucydides *Hist.* 6.54.6; Plutarch *Nic.* 13.2). However, this group of Twelve, while they were probably major Attic deities, was not identical with the later pantheon of twelve Olympians (which typically included Zeus, Hera, Poseidon, Hades, Apollo, Artemis, Hephaestus, Athena, Ares, Aphrodite, Hermes, Hestia). The earth deities Demeter and Dionysus (absent from Homer) are sometimes substituted for Hades and Hestia. The earliest complete list of the Twelve Olympians comes from 217 B.C. in connection with the list of gods honored at the *lectisternium* (a sacred banquet where the gods were made guests at a meal; Livy *Hist.* 22.10.9-10; Quintus Ennius *Ann.* 7.240-41).

The Greeks recognized three kinds of deities: Olympian gods, chthonic ("earth") gods and heroes. Some of the Olympian gods were of Indo-European origin and were brought with the Greeks when they migrated into the Greek peninsula c. 2000 B.C. The most important Greek deity, for example, was Zeus (the genitive form is Dios, a cognate of the old Sanskrit term *dyaus*, "bright sky"), who corresponds to the central Roman god Jupiter (derived from *Dieu* + *pater*, i.e., "Zeus Father"). Other Olympians, such as Athena, Apollo, Artemis and Poseidon, were indigenous to the Greek peninsula or western Anatolia. Most of the chthonic gods, including Demeter and Dionysus, appear to have been deities indigenous to the Greek world and associated with the earth, crops and the underworld. The heroes were thought originally to have been mortals (usually with one divine parent) who were deified upon death and received cultic honors at the supposed site of their tomb. The major exception to this generalization is Heracles, a mythological figure who was worshiped as a god in some places but as a hero in others, even though he had no known tomb (Herodotus *Hist.* 2.43-45; Apollodorus *Bib.* 2.7.7). Some heroes appear to have originally been considered gods who subsequently "faded" to heroic status (e.g., Asclepius, Helen), some are mythical (e.g., Perseus, Achilles, Orestes, Oedipus, Theseus; on the last two see Sophocles *Oed. Col.* 1590-1666; Plutarch *Thes.* 35-36), while yet others are historical (the Spartan heroes Brasidas and Lysander).

In general the Greeks were extremely open to new deities and cults and often identified their own deities with some of the major foreign deities which they encountered. During the long contact that the Greeks had with Egypt, they developed an *interpretatio Graeca*, "Greek interpretation," of Egyptian religion in which they regarded various native Egyptian deities as identical with traditional Greek deities. For example, Demeter was thought to be the Greek equivalent of Isis, Athena of Thoeris, Zeus of Ammon and Hermes of Thoth. The pantheon of Olympian gods was the creation of the Homeric poets, who produced a synthetic assembly of divinities unknown before the seventh century B.C.

2.2. Prayer. From Homer on, Greek prayer involved formulas that were intended to ensure that the god addressed would not be offended by an incorrect invocation. The hymn to Zeus in the *Agamemnon* of Aeschylus is introduced in this manner: "Zeus, whoever he is, if this name pleases him in invocation." Here the liturgical formula *hostis pot' estin*, "whoever he is," occurs (lines 160-61). An earlier example of this formula occurs in *Odyssey* 5.445: "Hear, Lord, whoever you are." In Plato *Cratylus* 400d-e, a distinction is made between the names the gods use of themselves, which are unknown to humans, and the customary names that humans use in prayers since the true names of the gods are unknown. Prayers were uttered aloud in connection with great public sacrifices, at the beginning of public assemblies (Aristophanes *Thes.* 295-305) and before battle (Aeschylus *Sept. c. Theb.* 252-60; Thucydides *Hist.* 6.32).

*2.3. **Sacrifice.*** The primary type of sacrifice practiced in Greek religious rituals was the slaughter of approved types of domestic animals, part of which was burned on an altar and part of which was consumed by those who offered the sacrifice. Such sacrifices could be part of domestic or public religious ritual. Certain animals were thought to be required of particular divinities. Cows were sacrificed to Athena, while pigs were sacrificed to Demeter. In the Greek protocol of sacrifice a distinction was made between sacrifices made to Olympian or to chthonic (earth) deities. Sacrifices to Olympians were made on a raised altar (*bomos*) during the day; the sacrificial animals were light colored; their throats were slit upward so that the blood would spurt toward the sky before running down on the altar. Sacrifices to chthonic deities, on the other hand, were made on a low altar (*eschara*) during the evening; the sacrificial animals were dark colored; their throats were slit downward so that the blood would spurt down upon the low altar or pit. The central event of many of the great civic religious festivals, such as the Hyacinthia at Sparta or the Panathenaia at Athens, was a great procession in which the priests and civic officials led the sacrificial victims to the altar, followed by the citizens. After the ritual slaughter, parts of the victims were burned on the altar, while the edible portions were divided up equally among the populace. These portions of meat were sometimes cooked and eaten on the spot or were taken to private homes for cooking and eating.

*2.4. **Festivals.*** In the *polis* of Athens, about which most is known, approximately 120 days of the calendar were devoted to religious festivals, and the number may have been even greater. Most of these festivals originated as rural, agricultural celebrations. The single festival found more frequently than any other throughout the Greek world was the Thesmophoria, celebrated in honor of Demeter, an indigenous Aegean earth goddess (*see* Festivals and Holy Days: Greco-Roman).

*2.5. **Temples.*** The Greek temple, a free-standing architectural form, originated in the early eighth century B.C., perhaps in conjunction with the rise of the *polis*. Most temples were rectangular (the Telesterion of Demeter at Eleusis was square), and in a central room, called the *cella*, was located a cult-statue of the divinity to whom the temple was dedicated, usually larger than life-size. The temple functioned primarily as a house for the god. Inside the temple various types of offerings and dedications to the deity were stored, and incense was burned in honor of the god. Altars where animals were sacrificed were always located in the open air, usually in front of the temple. Worshipers gathered outside the temple for festivals and sacrifices, never inside (*see* Temples, Greco-Roman).

*2.6. **Divination.*** Oracles and divination played an important role in the lives of the Greeks from the archaic period until the triumph of Christianity in the fourth century A.D. Divination is the art or science of interpreting symbolic messages from the gods; often these messages are of an unpredictable or even trivial nature. Some of the more typical forms of divination included cleromancy (casting lots), ornithomancy (observing the flight of birds), hieromancy (observing the behavior of sacrificial animals and the condition of their internal organs before and after sacrifice), cledonomancy (interpreting random omens or sounds) and oneiromancy (dream interpretation). The general Greek term for the diviner was *mantis*, a word which is translated "diviner," "soothsayer," "seer" and "prophet." Greeks and Romans often distinguished between "technical divination" (the interpretation of signs, sacrifices, dreams, omens and prodigies) and "natural divination" (the direct inspiration of the *mantis* through trance, ecstasy or vision), though in practice there was no rigid distinction between these two types of divine revelation.

The term *oracle* could refer both to the verbal response of a god to a query as well as to the sacred place where the god was consulted. Local oracles were of several types: lot oracles, incubation oracles and inspired oracles. One of the most famous incubation oracles of antiquity was the sanctuary of Asclepius at Epidauros. There healing was believed to be accomplished through the nocturnal appearance of the god to the patient, who was often given instructions about what he or she must do to be cured. The most famous inspired oracle of ancient Greece, which was combined with a lot oracle, was the pan-Hellenic oracle of Apollo at Delphi. There on the seventh day of each month, inquirers could pose questions to the Pythia, a priestess believed to be the spokesperson for Apollo when seated on Apollo's throne-tripod. The male priests who assisted the Pythia would convey her responses, often in verse, in oral or written form to the inquirer. Apollo gave advice on such matters of state concern as the founding of colonies, the waging of war and on issues of sacrificial ritual and protocol, and on such private matters as business trips, occupations, marriages and the whereabouts of stolen property. Thousands of such oracles have survived, most of them in literary sources, though most of them are not authentic. Since oracles were often phrased enigmatically, oracle interpreters (*chresmologoi*) would explain their meaning for a fee (*see* Prophecy, Greco-Roman).

2.7. Domestic Cults. The ancient Greek extended *family (the *oikos*, or household) was the context for a form of cult which focused on the hearth and the tomb. The hearth was the place where meals were cooked over a fire that was kept burning for an entire year. It was ritually extinguished each year only to be rekindled again the same day for the next year. Prayers were said before the hearth at the beginning and end of each day, and libations (drink offerings usually consisting of a mixture of wine and water) were poured out on the ground or on the hearth, which functioned as a domestic altar (Hesiod *Op.* 722-24). The male head of the household functioned as a priest, and such offerings were often made to deceased ancestors, who had been made divine upon death. Offerings to these ancestors were also made at the site of their tombs, located on land owned by the family.

3. Roman Religion.

Though Rome was a single city-state that became the political seat and administrative center of an enormous empire which surrounded the Mediterranean Sea and extended north and northeast into Europe, native Roman religious cults and cultic practices were never adopted in any significant way by those who were not Roman citizens. Even when citizenship was extended to all adult male inhabitants of the Roman Empire by the emperor Caracalla in A.D. 212, the practice of the traditional Roman forms of public worship (religious rituals performed on behalf of the state by members of the college of priests and the magistrates, and rituals celebrated by all citizens) and private worship (the *sacra domestica*, "domestic worship," practiced by families and clans) remained almost exclusively the concern of those who were ethnically Roman. The following description of the public and private aspects of Roman religion focuses on the stage of development which had been reached by the reign of Augustus (27 B.C.-A.D. 14).

3.1. Central Features. One of the central features of Roman religion throughout its long history was an emphasis on the *pax deorum* ("peace with the gods"), that is, the conviction that the maintenance of a harmonious relationship with the gods was the basis for temporal prosperity and success. All public disasters were assumed to have been caused by a breach in the relationship between the Roman people and the gods, and the reasons for these breaches must be diagnosed through divination and rectified by specific cultic measures. The *pax deorum* was maintained by following a number of measures: (1) deities must be placated by sacrifice and prayer; (2) all vows and oaths must be fulfilled exactly; (3) the city must be preserved from hostile influences by the ritual of *lustratio* and (4) strict attention must be paid to all outward signs of the will of the gods. By the imperial period, the most important aspect of the *pax deorum* was the support and protection of the emperor by the gods.

3.2. Roman Deities. The ancient Romans recognized three categories of divine beings. The first type was composed of the autonomous divinities, often arranged in triads (following the Etruscan model), such as Jupiter, Mars and Quirinus, or Jupiter, Juno and Minerva. These deities had a relatively fixed character and were individually honored but (unlike Greek divinities), though they could be called "Father" and "Mother," they did not have marital relationships or offspring. Consequently, the Romans had no native mythology recounting the adventures of the gods (Dionysius of Halicarnassus *Ant. Rom.* 2.19-20). Though they later absorbed Greek myths about the gods, their deities could never be arranged genealogically. Roman mythology took the form of historical accounts with a pervasive legendary component (e.g., Virgil's account of the origins of Rome in the *Aeneid*). The most important Roman god, Jupiter Optimus Maximus ("Jupiter Best and Greatest") had two partners (not wives), Juno and Minerva. Archaic Roman religion grouped Jupiter with Mars and Quirinus. There is evidence attributed to Quintus Ennius (early second century B.C.) for the introduction of the Greek grouping of Twelve Gods in Rome, called *di consentes* ("united gods"), under the names Juno (= Hera), Vesta (= Hestia), Minerva (= Athena), Ceres (= Demeter), Diana (= Artemis), Venus (= Aphrodite), Mars (= Ares), Mercury (= Hermes), Jupiter (= Zeus), Neptune (= Poseidon), Vulcan (= Hephaestus) and Apollo (Ennius *Ann.* 7.240-41 [ed. O. Skutsch]). During the terrifying days of Hannibal's invasion of Italy in 217 B.C. during the Second Punic War, the Greek municipal cult of the Twelve Gods was incorporated into the *lectisternium* of the Twelve Gods in Rome (previous *lectisternia* honored only six gods). A *lectisternium* was a "sacred banquet," held only at times of political or social crisis, at which the images of the Twelve Gods were placed in pairs on each of six couches (Livy *Hist.* 22.10.9-10); *lectisternia* were celebrated until at least A.D. 166 (see *Scriptores Historiae Augustae, Marcus Antoninus,* 13.1-2).

The second type of Roman divinity was to be found in the countless numbers of secret beings that were jealous of their anonymity and were constantly helping or hindering the Roman people in their various undertakings. The Romans, though, were at a disadvantage because they were unable to name them and so control them through the appropriate ritual.

The third category of divinities consisted of the so-called *indigitimenta,* teams of minor deities (found in extensive lists), each with a minor function in assisting or hindering in each activity or fraction of various human activities, particularly those characteristic of rural areas and those involving private life (Tertullian *Ad Nat.* 11; *De An.* 37-39; Augustine *Civ. D.* 4.11).

3.3. Priests. There were two different terms for "priest" in Roman religion: *pontifex* (a member of a college of priests holding supreme authority in public religious matters in Rome, and later a term for an inferior grade of priest) and *flamen* (a priest charged with carrying out the sacrificial ritual of a particular deity and in the imperial period a priest of a deceased or living Roman emperor). The offices of priest and magistrate were not mutually exclusive, so that all priesthoods, with two exceptions (the *rex sacrorum,* "king of sacrifices," and the *flamen Dialis,* "priest of Jupiter"), were part-time positions which could be held for life (with the exception of the six Vestal virgins who held office for thirty years). These customs ensured that no priestly class ever developed in Rome, just as none had developed in Greece.

During the late period of the republic and during the empire there were four main colleges of priests that developed: (1) The *collegium pontificum,* or "college of priests," consisted eventually of sixteen *flamines,* including three *flamines maiores,* "major priests," the *flamen Dialis,* "priest of Jupiter" (Aulus Gellius *Noc. Att.* 10.15), the *flamen Martialis,* "priest of Mars," and the *flamen Quirinalis,* "priest of Quirinus" (reflecting the archaic triad of Jupiter, Mars and Quirinus), together with twelve *flamines minores,* minor priests. Other members of this college included the *rex sacrorum,* "king of sacrifices" (a survival of one function of the Roman kings) and six *virgines vestales.* This college was under the jurisdiction of the *pontifex maximus,* "high priest" (Cicero *Phil.* 11.18), an office regularly held by the emperor during the imperial period. There were also (2) the college of sixteen *augures,* (3) *quindecemviri sacris faciendis,* a college of fifteen men "for conducting sacrifices," and (4) the *septemviri epulones,* a college of seven, and later ten, "supervisors of public feasts." Only the emperor could belong to all of the priestly colleges simultaneously (Augustus *Res Gest.* 7.3).

Public divination, the *ius divinum,* was an important part of Roman civic religion, for divination was the primary means for diagnosing the causes that were thought to have interrupted "peace with the gods," and for interpreting prodigies, signs sent by the gods. There were three types of public diviners whose chief task was to proclaim divine approval or displeasure by interpreting various types of symbolic messages sent by the gods: the *augures,* who interpreted the flight of birds and the meaning of thunder and lightning (Cicero *De Leg.* 2.30); *haruspices,* who interpreted the entrails of sacrificial animals; and the *quindecimviri,* who kept and interpreted the Sibylline books.

3.4. Prayer. The invocation of a god or gods by name is a universal feature of prayer. When Romans prayed or sacrificed, they always did so with their heads covered. In the polytheistic system of Roman religion, it was necessary to discover which deity one wanted to influence through invoking his or her name (Varro in Augustine *Civ. D.* 4.22; Horace *Odes* 1.2.25-26). The Romans used a kind of "to whom it may concern" prayer formula so that their prayers would be properly addressed. This formula is usually phrased *sive deus sive dea*, or *si deus si dea*, "whether a god or goddess" (Livy *Hist.* 7.26.4; Cicero *Rab. Perd.* 5; Aulus Gellius *Noc. Att.* 2.28.3) or *sive quo alio nomine te appellari volueris*, "or whatever name you want to be called" (Virgil *Aen.* 2.351; 4.576; Catullus 34.21-22). A regular part of the structure of ancient prayer was the reasons given why a deity should respond favorably to the request. Two common reasons are: (1) because the god had done so in the past and (2) because it was within his competence to do so now. In Roman religious ritual, Janus was the first deity invoked in prayers and invocations (followed by Jupiter, Mars and Quirinus), while Vesta was the last.

3.5. Sacrifice and Temples. Sacrifice was one of the most important aspects of Roman religion, both public and private. One invariable rule was that male animals were offered to male deities and female animals to female deities. It was considered a good sign if animals went willingly to their slaughter. According to the Roman antiquarian Varro, the early Romans worshiped the gods without statues or temples for 170 years (Augustine *Civ. D.* 4.31), when the Etruscan king Tarquinius Priscus vowed to erect a temple to Jupiter on the capitol (Livy *Hist.* 1.38.7). Roman temples were usually rectangular buildings constructed on a raised platform and had four main features: (1) the inner room, or *cella*, contained the statue of the god to whom the temple was dedicated together with an altar for the burning of incense; (2) a room or rooms behind the *cella* for the preservation of treasures; (3) an anteroom located in front of the *cella*, surrounded by (4) a roofed colonnade, oblong in Italian temples, but square in Romano-Celtic temples. A stone altar was usually located in front of the temple, where animal sacrifices were made. With the sacrifice of smaller animals, such as goats or lambs, the priest and the sacrificers could eat the edible portions of the sacrifice. The sacrifice of larger animals, such as oxen, provided a feast for a larger number of people, and often the excess meat was sold to the public in the market.

3.6. The Imperial Cult. The antecedents of the Roman imperial cult are to be found in the civic cults of the Hellenistic kings (see 4.2 below). The Hellenistic period is characterized in part by a tendency to blur the traditional Greek distinction between mortal and immortal. From the end of the third century B.C. on, there were many cults of Roman magistrates instituted by the Greek cities they controlled. The deified Julius Caesar and the deified Augustus, who were consecrated by official acts of the Roman senate, became part of the official pantheon of the Roman people. The imperial cult was of far greater importance in the provinces than in Rome itself. In Roman Asia in particular, the imperial cult provided a presence for an absent emperor. In the traditional form of the imperial cult, the emperor was worshiped as a god only after his death and apotheosis. In the imperial cults in Anatolia, the divinized emperor was usually associated with other, more traditional, gods such as Dea Roma or various groups of Olympian deities (*see* Ruler Cult).

4. Hellenistic Religions.

4.1. Introduction. The Hellenistic period began with the conquests of Alexander the Great during the late fourth century B.C. Technically it concluded with the Roman conquest of the last independent Hellenistic kingdom, Ptolemaic Egypt, at the battle of Actium in 31 B.C. Nevertheless, it actually continued on into the Roman period because of the enormous cultural influence which the Greeks had on their Roman conquerors. The immense political, social and cultural changes accompanying the conquests of Alexander meant that the tension between continuity and change was one of the central features of the Hellenistic age.

4.2. Hellenistic Ruler Cults. The development of the ruler cult of Alexander the Great, followed by the cults of subsequent Hellenistic kings, was in many respects an adjustment to the political reality that the cities were no longer independent. As such they required a type of cult appropriate to their subordinate status. One of the major forms of this adjustment is reflected in the development of the ruler cult. Such cults (with priests, processions, sacrifices and often games) were founded in honor of various Greek rulers such as Lysander of Sparta and Dion of Syracuse. Alexander the Great both requested and was granted a cult with divine honors. Greek cities often benefitted from various privileges and *benefactions from those Hellenistic rulers in whose honor they established cults. Cities normally took the initiative in founding ruler cults, and these cults were integral to the affairs of each city-state. After the death of Ptolemy I (c. 280 B.C.), his son and successor Ptolemy II Philadelphus arranged for the formal deification of his father Ptolemy I and his mother Berenike, as *theoi sōteres*, "savior gods." In the 270s B.C., Ptolemy II and his wife Arsinoe II were officially deified while yet living as *theoi adelphoi*, "sibling gods," and were offered divine worship in the shrine of Alexander the Great. After Ptolemy II, each successive Ptolemaic king and queen was deified upon accession and worshiped as part of the royal household.

*4.3. **Private Associations.*** During the Hellenistic and Roman period there were three types of voluntary associations (*collegia*), each of which had a religious character: (1) professional corporations or guilds (fishermen, fruit growers, ship owners, etc.), (2) funerary societies (*collegia tenuiorum*), and (3) religious or cult societies (*collegia sodalicia*), which centered in the worship of a deity.

*4.4. **Mystery Religions.*** *Mystery religion* is a general term for a variety of ancient public and private cults which shared a number of common features (*see* Mysteries). The term *mystery* is based on the Greek term *mystēs*, meaning "initiant," from which is derived the term *mystērion*, meaning "ritual of initiation," that is, the secret rites which formed the center of such cults. In contrast to the public character of most traditional cults of the Greek city-states, the mystery religions were private associations into which interested individuals could be initiated by undergoing a secret ritual. The mystery religions did not appear suddenly in the Mediterranean world during the Hellenistic period, though the period of their greatest popularity appears to have been the first through the third centuries A.D. Many of the mystery cults in the Greek world were profoundly influenced by the oldest of all mystery cults (referred to as "*the* mysteries"), the Eleusinian mysteries with their cult center in Eleusis in Attica. While very little is known about these rituals of initiation (called *telete*), they appear to have consisted of three interrelated features of a mystery cult initiation ritual: (1) *drōmena*, "things acted out," or the enactment of the myth on which the cult was based; (2) *legomena*, "things spoken," or the oral presentation of the myth on which the cult was based; and (3) *deiknymena*, "things shown," or the ritual presentation of symbolic objects to the initiant. Initiants who experienced the central mystery ritual became convinced that they would enjoy *sōtēria*, "salvation," both in the sense of health and prosperity in this life as well as a blissful afterlife (Firmicus Maternus *De Errore Prof. Rel.* 22.1). Mystery religions were once thought to share a common focus in a divinity who represented the annual decay and renewal of vegetation through his or her death and restoration to life. In recent years the great diversity among those cults formerly lumped together as "mystery cults" has become increasingly apparent. Though there were many mystery cults in antiquity, only the Eleusinian Mysteries and the Mysteries of Mithra will be summarized.

4.4.1. The Eleusinian Mysteries. This cult was native to Attica until it was taken over by Athenians upon the unification of Attica under Athens. Originating as early as the fifteenth century B.C., the cult continued to flourish until the Telesterion, the rectangular temple in Eleusis which served as the center for the cult, was destroyed by the Goths in A.D. 395. The earliest literary evidence for this cult is found in the Homeric *Hymn to Demeter*, which originated c. 550 B.C. A story about the goddess Demeter and her daughter Persephone served as the central myth of the cult. Hades, the god of the underworld, seized Persephone and took her down into the underworld as his wife. Grieving for her daughter, Demeter sought her whereabouts for nine days, when Helios (the sun god) revealed to Demeter what had happened to her daughter. In anger Demeter left Olympus and caused a drought which deprived humans of food and gods of sacrifices. Zeus therefore sent Hermes to strike a compromise with Hades. Persephone was returned to her mother on the condition that she spend one-third of every year in the underworld with Hades. In this myth Demeter is literally the "earth mother," while Persephone represents grain. Persephone's presence with her mother for two-thirds of the year represents the rainy season (primarily during the winter) when crops flourish, while her descent to Hades each year represents the dry, dormant season of the year (Hesiod *Op.* 582-88).

These vegetation deities were understood as metaphors for life and death, and those initiants who voluntarily participated in this cult believed that their ritual identification with Persephone would guarantee them a blissful afterlife (Isocrates *Paneg.* 28-29). One fragment of Sophocles (found in Plutarch *How to Study Poetry* 22F) emphasizes the salvific benefits of initiation: "Thrice blest are those who go to Hades after beholding these rites. For them alone is there life there; for all others there is only evil" (see also Pindar in Clement of Alexandria *Strom.* 3.3.17).

Initiation into the Eleusinian mysteries was a voluntary, two-staged process. The first stage involved initiation into the Lesser Mysteries, celebrated annually during the month Anthesterion. After the interval of at least one year, a candidate could be initiated into the Greater Mysteries, which took place during the month Boedromion (September/October). The ritual began in Athens with a gathering of the initiants and the offering of a sacrificial pig in honor of Demeter. Thereafter there was a torchlight parade to Eleusis, culminating at the Telesterion, or "hall of initiation." The initiation concluded when the initiants were led into the Telesterion, and to the innermost room of that temple called the Anaktoron. There the initiation was completed. Though ancient sources divulge very little information about the specific character of the initiation ritual, the *drōmena* ("things enacted") probably consisted of a nocturnal drama depicting Demeter's sufferings, the *legomena* ("things spoken") possibly consisted of a recitation of a myth similar to that preserved in the Homeric *Hymn to Demeter*, and the *deiknymena* ("things shown") may have consisted of the display of symbolic ritual objects such as an ear of grain.

4.4.2. The Mysteries of Mithra. Mithras was worshiped as the sun god, and the name is of Iranian origin. The actual Iranian connections of this cult are dubious, however. Though the earliest datable evidence for the existence of the Mithraic mysteries is the first century A.D., it is likely that this cult originated in the first century B.C. This mystery cult flourished in the second through the fourth centuries A.D., after which the triumph of Christianity resulted in its ultimate disappearance. Information about this cult is primarily available through archaeological evidence, which suggests that it was particularly popular in Italy and in the region of the Danube. Epigraphical evidence indicates that members of the cult included soldiers, bureaucrats, merchants and slaves (women were excluded). The central focus of the cult was the preparation for astral salvation, which would be realized upon death when the soul would ascend through the seven planetary spheres to the place of its origin. Members of the cult were initiated into seven ascending levels or grades of initiation, each of which had the protection of a planetary god: (1) *corax*, "raven" (Mercury); (2) *nymphus*, "bride" (Venus); (3) *miles*, "soldier" (Mars); (4) *leo*, "lion" (Jupiter); (5) *Perses*, "Persian" (Moon); (6) *heliodromus*, "courier of the sun" (Sun); and (7) *pater*, "father" (Saturn). This cult worshiped in artificial caverns, structures called mithraea (fifty-eight of which have been identified by archaeologists), located below grade. Every Mithraeum had an artistic representation of the *tauroctony*, or "bull-slaying" scene, in which Mithras is portrayed as slaying a bull, and it was probably the experience of this event, presented through the medium of a ritual, that constituted the central salvific events for adherents to the cult.

See also CIVIC CULTS; FESTIVALS AND HOLY DAYS: GRECO-ROMAN; IDOLATRY, JEWISH CONCEPTION OF; MYSTERIES; POLYTHEISM, GRECO-ROMAN; PROPHETS AND PROPHECY; RELIGION, PERSONAL; RULER CULT; TEMPLES, GRECO-ROMAN.

BIBLIOGRAPHY. S. Angus, *The Mystery-Religions and Christianity: A Study in the Religious Background of Early Christianity* (London: John Murray, 1925); idem, *The Religious Quests of the Graeco-Roman World: A Study in the Historical Background of Early Christianity* (London: John Murray, 1929); H. Böhlig, *Die Geisteskultur von Tarsos im augusteischen Zeitalter mit Berücksichtigung der paulinischen Schriften* (FRLANT 19; Göttingen: Vandenhoeck & Ruprecht, 1913); W. Burkert, *Ancient Mystery Cults* (Cambridge, MA: Harvard University Press, 1987); idem, *Greek Religion* (Cambridge, MA: Harvard University Press, 1985); F. Cumont, *The Mysteries of Mithra* (New York: Dover, 1956); idem, *Oriental Religions in Roman Paganism* (New York: Dover, 1956); E. J. Edelstein and L. Edelstein, *Asclepius: A Collection and Interpretation of the Testimonies* (Salem, NH: Ayer, 1988); J. Ferguson, *The Religions of the Roman Empire* (Ithaca, NY: Cornell University Press, 1970); J. Finegan, *Myth & Mystery: An Introduction to the Pagan Religions of the Biblical World* (Grand Rapids, MI: Baker, 1989); J. Fontenrose, *The Delphic Oracle: Its Responses and Operations* (Berkeley and Los Angeles: University of California Press, 1978); J. G. Frazer, *Adonis, Attis, Osiris: Studies in the History of Oriental Religion* (London: Macmillan, 1906); T. R. Glover, *The*

Conflict of Religions in the Early Roman Empire (10th ed.; London: Methuen, 1923); idem, *Progress in Religion to the Christian Era* (London: SCM, 1922); R. M. Grant, *Gods and the One God* (Philadelphia: Westminster, 1986); W. K. C. Guthrie, *The Greeks and Their Gods* (Boston: Beacon, 1950); J. E. Harrison, *Prolegomena to the Study of Greek Religion* (Cambridge: Cambridge University Press, 1922); P. W. van der Horst, "The Altar of the 'Unknown God' in Athens (Acts 17:23) and the Cult of 'Unknown Gods' in the Hellenistic and Roman Periods," *ANRW* 2.18.2 (1989) 1426-56; idem, *Hellenism—Judaism—Christianity: Essays on Their Interaction* (2d ed.; Leuven: Peeters, 1998); H.-J. Klauck, *The Religious Context of Early Christianity: A Guide to Graeco-Roman Religions* (Edinburgh: T & T Clark, 2000); J. H. W. G. Liebeschuetz, *Continuity and Change in Roman Religion* (Oxford: Clarendon Press, 1979); G. Luck, *Arcana Mundi: Magic and the Occult in the Greek and Roman World* (Baltimore: Johns Hopkins University Press, 1985); J. G. Machen, *The Origin of Paul's Religion* (New York: Macmillan, 1921); R. MacMullen, *Paganism in the Roman Empire* (New Haven, CT: Yale University Press, 1981); G. Murray, *Five Stages of Greek Religion* (London: Watts, 1935); M. P. Nilsson, *The Dionysiac Mysteries of the Hellenistic and Roman Age* (Salem, NH: Ayer, 1985 [1957]); idem, *Greek Folk Religion* (Philadelphia: University of Pennsylvania Press, 1940); idem, *A History of Greek Religion* (2d ed.; Oxford: Clarendon Press, 1949); A. D. Nock, *Conversion: The Old and the New in Religion from Alexander the Great to Augustine of Hippo* (London: Oxford University Press, 1933); W. O. E. Oesterley and T. H. Robinson, *Hebrew Religion: Its Origin and Development* (2d ed.; London: SPCK, 1937); R. M. Ogilvie, *The Romans and Their Gods* (London: Book Club, 1979 [1969]); R. Reitzenstein, *Hellenistic Mystery-Religions: Their Basic Ideas and Significance* (Pittsburgh: Pickwick, 1978); H. J. Rose, *Ancient Greek Religion* (London: Hutchinson, 1946); idem, *Ancient Roman Religion* (London: Hutchinson, 1948); D. Ulansey, *The Origins of the Mithraic Mysteries: Cosmology and Salvation in the Ancient World* (New York: Oxford University Press, 1989); A. Wardman, *Religion and Statecraft Among the Romans* (Baltimore: Johns Hopkins University Press, 1982); A. J. M. Wedderburn, *Baptism and Resurrection: Studies in Pauline Theology Against Its Graeco-Roman Background* (WUNT I.44; Tübingen: Mohr Siebeck, 1987); R. W. Witt, *Isis in the Ancient World* (Baltimore: Johns Hopkins University Press, 1971); L. B. Zaidman and P. S. Pantel, *Religion in the Ancient Greek City* (Cambridge: Cambridge University Press, 1992).

D. E. Aune

RELIGION, PERSONAL

Personal religion refers to those beliefs and practices of ordinary persons that were not primarily related to formal religious systems or institutions. Here piety was more a matter of voluntary and individual involvement as opposed to those religious practices in which tradition and civic responsibility played a large role. Personal religion and formal religion admittedly overlap; *prayer, for example, is common to both. However, other articles in this dictionary will treat the more formal and institutional expressions of religion (*see* Religion, Greco-Roman). The many phenomena gathered under the rubric of Personal Religion are loosely related to one another, and the arrangement in this article is only one way in which they can be organized.

1. Discerning the Deity's Will
2. Securing the Deity's Help
3. Beliefs and Hopes
4. Conclusion

1. Discerning the Deity's Will.

Pagans in the *Hellenistic era were by no means irreligious persons; many of them sought divine guidance in their everyday lives. The various means that individuals used to discern the deity's will included oracles, prayer, dreams and divination.

1.1. Oracles. An oracle is either an utterance given through a human mediator but presumed to be from the deity, given in response to an inquiry, or the site at which the response is given. In the classical period oracles often were consulted by official delegations concerning political and religious matters of the state; in the Hellenistic era oracles more often served the needs of individuals and communities. The most famous oracular site in antiquity was Delphi, the cultic center of Apollo, the god of prophecy (*see* Prophecy, Greco-Roman). It was located on the north coast of the Gulf of Corinth. Although Delphi provides the richest source of information about oracles, there were many others in *Greece and *Asia Minor. Oracles of Apollo included Didyma, Claros and Daphne; oracles of Zeus included Olympia, Dodona and Siwa, an oasis in the Sahara Desert where the Egyptian god Ammon came to be identified with the chief god of the Greeks' pantheon.

Oracles such as the one at Delphi were sought out to obtain advice on matters of business, *marriage or *travel, or even to solve questions of paternity (Plutarch *Mor.* 386C, 407D, 408C). While the procedure for receiving a response varied and could be as simple as casting lots, some oracles had elaborate rituals. At Delphi a prophetess known as the Pythia (see Acts 16:16) would take a seat on a tripod in an underground chamber of the oracle and would enter a trance by some means not fully understood. Inquirers, after purification and sacrifices, would enter the sanctuary, separated from the Pythia, and pose their questions to priestly attendants. These mediators would relay the requests to the prophetess and return with a response interpreting her utterances. Although some Delphic responses were famous for their ambiguous or cryptic language, more often they were practical and straightforward, advising the best course between two options or prescribing the cultic observances necessary to achieve one's aim.

The popularity of oracles declined in the Roman period and became defunct in the third century A.D. Already in the early second century, *Plutarch could write an essay on the *Obsolescence of Oracles.* Fraudulent practices and disbelief may have contributed to the decline. *Lucian of Samosata wrote a treatise in the latter half of the second century, describing a certain Alexander Abonuteichos who engineered an elaborate ploy to present himself as a prophet of Asclepius. Alexander set up a cult, including an oracle, with the help of a large, mechanical snake constructed to appear partially human, which would deliver the responses. Lucian portrays Alexander as a charlatan who exploited the popular interest in oracles.

1.2. Dreams. Although not all dreams were thought to be significant, some were regarded as revelatory communications whose meanings could be given by oracles or other professional interpreters. Plutarch stated plainly, "The majority believe that the divine spirit inspires people when they are asleep" (Plutarch *Mor.* 589D). The widespread nature of this belief is evident in the various dream manuals that were written from the classical period into the Byzantine era. The only extant example of the latter is the *Oneirocriticon* (dream interpretation) of Artemidorus of the late second century A.D. Artemidorus traveled extensively and collected anecdotes about dreams and the meanings commonly ascribed to them.

When dreams were regarded as revelatory, they had a variety of functions. Often they warned of an impending crisis such as death (Appian *Civ. W.* 1.105; 2.115; Pausanius *Descr.* 9.23.3; 10.2.6; Xenophon *Cyr.* 7.1-2). Dreams might also encourage a military leader to advance (Quintus Curtius 3.3.7; 4.2.17), reveal the perpetrator of a crime (Appian *Pun.* 1), inspire someone to found a city (Pausanias *Descr.* 7.5.1-2) or even effect healing for diseases (Pausanias *Descr.* 10.33.11).

In NT narratives dreams are often regarded as revelatory. The Greek word *onar* ("dream") is found only in Matthew. In that Gospel Joseph is reassured and instructed in a dream to take Mary as his wife (Mt 1:20-4); later both the magi and Joseph are warned in dreams about the threat of *Herod (Mt 2:12-15). Near the end of the same Gospel, Pilate's wife speaks of a troubling dream she has had that compels her to urge a hands-off policy toward Jesus (Mt 27:19). In the book of Acts several visions are mentioned, some of which occur at night and can probably be classed as dreams. (Note that in antiquity dreams are often distinguished from waking visions; see Pausanias *Descr.* 10.38.13 and LSJ, "*hypar,*" 1853.) These dreams supply direction and impetus to the Pauline mission (Acts 16:9-10; 23:11; 27:23-4). Finally, in the quotation from Joel in Acts 2:17, dreams (Gk *enypnion)* are associated with the outpouring of the Spirit in the last days. In general the NT writers shared the popular ancient perspective that dreams could be revelatory communications from God.

1.3. Divination. In the broadest sense divination could include any means of discerning the deity's will: prayer, dreams, prophecy. The term is used here in the sense of augury: the belief that divine communication could be observed in everyday events and phenomena. Some people regarded divination as the way in which common folk could receive by observation the kind of revealed knowledge that prophets received directly (Plutarch *Mor.* 593D). Divination was considered important enough that Rome had an official board of *augures,* whose job was the interpretation of such events. *Augures* would observe signs and determine which of two possible courses of action should be taken. Common forms of augury included the casting of dice; the interpretation of heavenly, tectonic or meteorological signs; observing the flight or other behavior of birds (*auspicium*); and observing the entrails of sacrificial animals (extispicy or haruspicy). Even something as innocent as a sneeze, because it was involuntary and thought to be divinely caused, could constitute an omen (Xenophon *Anab.* 3.2.8-9).

Omens were taken seriously by most of the ancients. Xenophon regarded them as among the greatest benefits given by the gods (Xenophon *Mem.* 4.3.12; *Eq. Mag.* 9.9; *Symp.* 4.47-8). They were considered so essential to military decisions that sacred birds, usually chickens, accompanied armies for use in divination (Livy *Hist.* 10.40.1-5; Suetonius *Tiberius* 2.2). Not all were convinced, however, of the validity of divination. In addition to those who denied divination outright (Xenophanes, the Epicureans), there were occasional critics. *Cicero, whose *On Divination* is the most significant ancient source on the subject, regarded it as part error, part superstition and a large measure of fraud (Cicero *De Div.* 2.39.83). The elder *Pliny noted the highly subjective nature of the interpretations: the meaning of the omens largely resided in the eye of the diviners (Pliny *Nat. Hist.* 28.4.17). In the NT there is little that resembles divination. In Acts 1:23-26, however, the apostles resort to sortilege to choose a replacement for Judas Iscariot.

2. Securing the Deity's Help.

2.1. Prayer. Prayer was one of the most common expressions of personal religion. It was often closely associated with sacrifice and other rituals. The earliest literary example of prayer is found in the *Iliad* (1.37-42), the prayer of Chryses to Apollo when the former is grieved at the insolent treatment he has received at the hands of Agamemnon. In this prayer and numerous others, scholars have observed the following formal elements: an address or invocation usually employing divine titles, epithets and descriptions of the deity's parentage and/or attributes; the argument or rationale, usually an appeal to the worshiper's pious deeds or to the deity's past beneficence; and the petition proper, which may ask for some salutary benefit for the worshiper or something baneful for the enemies of the worshiper. In the example from the *Iliad,* Chryses seeks and obtains a judgment against the Greeks; Apollo strikes their camp with a plague that lasts for several days. Thus petitions in prayer could involve either blessings, curses or both.

But prayers in Greco-Roman antiquity were by no means limited to selfish requests for personal advantage or punishment for enemies. There were also expressions of earnest, lofty piety and true reverence for deity. Socrates' prayer to Pan asks for inner beauty, harmony and wisdom above wealth (Plato *Phaed.* 279B-C). Cleanthes, one of the early *Stoics, is famous for his *Hymn to Zeus,* a majestic prayer that extols the deity's creative power, reason and love. Ancient prayers were usually spoken aloud; silent prayer was employed for indecent petitions or imprecations. The posture of prayer was generally standing with one's arms outstretched.

2.2. Magic, Miracles and Healing. Magic in antiquity is notoriously difficult to define. The boundary between magic and religion in particular is not completely distinct. But H. S. Versnel (*OCD,* 3d ed., 909) provides a serviceable definition: "[Magic is] a manipulative strategy to influence the course of nature by supernatural ('occult') means." The manipulative or coercive aspect of magic generally distinguishes it from religion. The premise of magic is that occult formulas and rites effectively compel spiritual forces to act.

The Greek terms *magos* and *mageia* originally referred to Persian wise men and their mysterious arts without necessarily carrying a negative connotation (e.g., Mt 2:7). Nevertheless, magic gathered negative associations and came to be viewed by many as deviant; the pejorative force of the term *goēs* ("sorcerer, wizard, charlatan") reflects this sentiment. Ultimately the perspective of the speaker or writer evaluates a miraculous or mysterious act. Christian miracles were sometimes vilified as the work of magic or the devil (Mk 3:22; Justin Martyr *Apol. I* 30); Christians in turn denounced pagan miracles (2 Thess 2:9-10; Rev 13:11-14; 19:20).

In Greek myth the Olympian deities generally did not engage in magic, but Hermes, who occasionally was portrayed bearing a magic wand, was a partial exception. Hecate, however, was a goddess who was frequently associated with magic and sorcery (Euripides *Med.* 394). Female characters figure prominently in the magical arts, most famously Medea of Euripedes' play and Circe of Homer's *Odyssey* (10.274-574). In literature of a later period, two works of Apuleius provide insight on the subject of magic. His *Apology* is a speech defending himself (successfully) against the charge of sorcery. The *Metamorphoses*, or *The Golden Ass*, is a delightful and humorous novel containing many scenes involving magical spells and cures.

For details and actual examples of how magic was practiced in the Hellenistic age, as opposed to its literary portrayal, one may consult the *Greek Magical Papyri* (*see* Magical Papyri). Here one learns that the means of magic were verbal, material and performative. Verbal means involved elaborate invocations of deities using multiple divine names. Some of the invocations in the Greek magical papyri even used forms of the name Jesus or Yahweh (cf. Acts 19:13-20). In addition to divine names, verbal means included mysterious and most likely meaningless strings of syllables that were presumed to be powerful, foreign incantations (see Cato the Elder *Agr.* 160). Material means of magic included amulets, tablets, dolls and a wide variety of folk medicines. "Performative" refers to the ritual actions that employed both verbal and material means to effect the magical cures, spells or curses.

The aims of magic were many. They could be more or less benign: obtaining healing, power or wealth, securing the affections of another person, averting evil. Amulets and phylacteries were especially common as apotropaics, means of warding off evil. Alternately, the aims of magic could be harmful. Curse tablets, usually made of thin sheets of lead on which the name of the intended victim was inscribed, often invoked the gods of the underworld to do harm in revenge for injustices or injuries received. Curses might also target contingent behavior, such as funerary *inscriptions that forbid violation of a grave under penalty of divine retribution. Baneful magic was of two types: imitative, or sympathetic, and contagious. Imitative magic employed objects such as tablets and dolls, whose destruction was to have a sympathetic effect of causing similar suffering in the victim (see Plato *Leg.* 933B; Theocritus *Id.* 2). Contagious magic operated on the principle of the part affecting the whole; material from the victim (hair, fingernails, clothing) was destroyed to effect the same in the person (see Virgil *Aen.* 4.494-521; Theocritus *Id.* 2.53-56).

Healing of diseases was one of many aims of the magical arts, but healing deserves additional brief discussion because of its special association with certain deities and cultic centers. In Greece, the god Apollo was associated with healing and sometimes bore the epithet *iētros* ("physician"). Other gods and heroes, both Greek (Demeter, Heracles, Amphiarus) and Egyptian (Isis, Sarapis), were occasionally invoked for specific cures, but pride of place goes to Asclepius, a hero/deity whose specialty was the healing arts.

Asclepius was a benevolent deity who took a strong interest in human well-being and consequently aroused deep devotion in his followers. His cult flourished in the period of the empire. A staff entwined by a snake was a common attribute of Asclepius in art. This son of Apollo, according to myth, had sanctuaries in Epidaurus, Cos and Pergamum. These sanctuaries featured temples, springs, baths and gymnasia; they were the ancient equivalents of health resorts or sanitariums. Healing was effected by a process that involved purifications, offerings and incubation (see Aristophanes *Plut.* 653-747). In incubation the patient slept in a private room and received a dream vision of the god and instructions for healing. Some of the cures obtained at Asclepius's sanctuaries may have involved autosuggestion, but there were also some genuinely therapeutic treatments not unlike those practiced by physicians of that time. Suitably, then, physicians were sometimes referred to by the patronymic Asclepiadae, or sons of Asclepius.

3. Beliefs and Hopes.

All of these practices imply certain beliefs held by people in the Hellenistic world. They were generally *polytheistic and believed that the gods were knowledgeable and powerful far beyond human capabilities and that they were able to intervene in human affairs. But beyond these fundamental and nearly universal tenets, certain other beliefs must be mentioned.

3.1. Superstition, Astrology and Fate. Superstition in antiquity referred to a servile attitude toward supernatural powers, an excessive and irrational fear of the divine, sometimes accompanied by a gullibility to being exploited by those who would prey on the religious. Plutarch's essay *On Superstition* is one of the most valuable sources on the topic. He condemns superstition as more harmful than atheism. The

Greek word for superstition (*deisidaimonia*) etymologically denotes "fear of demons." This reflects the popular notion that demons were present throughout the world causing ill of all sorts. Disease, especially little-understood ailments such as epilepsy, were commonly attributed to the work of *demons. The superstitious believed that the noxious effects of demons had to be countered by some means: amulets or phylacteries, verbal formulas and other precautions (see Pliny *Nat. Hist.* 28.5.23-29).

Astrology is the observation of celestial phenomena for the purpose of predicting human events. It was based on the belief that heavenly and terrestrial events are linked by a kind of universal sympathy. It was imported to the Mediterranean world from Babylon in the East (cf. Mt 2:1-10) but eventually developed a distinctive Greek form. Astrology became a sophisticated art and gained widespread popularity with all social classes. The modern distinction between astronomy as science and astrology as something dubious was unknown in antiquity. A common form of astrology was to predict the events of persons' lives based on the position of the stars and planets at the time of their births. Astrology depended on a kind of determinism: the course of human affairs had been fixed by the movements of heavenly bodies.

Fate was closely related to the determinism of astrology. The Greeks had several words throughout their history for this idea. *Moira* referred to one's share or portion in life. An untimely death or a reversal of fortune was thus explained as the action of fate. *Moira* was eventually personified as a group of women, the Fates, usually three, Atropos, Clotho and Lachesis, although the number and names vary. *Tychē,* another word used by the Greeks, was equivalent to the Latin *fortuna* and meant "chance" or "luck," an outcome usually unrelated to human effort. *Tychē* was also personified as a goddess. Finally, from the fourth century B.C. on, the dominant word was *heimarmenē*. This word approached the modern sense of fate, a force ruling the world in a deterministic fashion. Between the influences of demons and the sympathetic action of the stars, many of the ancients probably thought of human events as largely determined. This kind of fatalism may strike us as undercutting meaning and motivation, but it may be that some in the Hellenistic age found it a comforting and reassuring thought.

3.2. Death and the Afterlife. Death was understood in Greco-Roman times as the separation of the body from the soul, however the latter was understood. Proper funeral rites for the dead were essential, and the lack thereof was deemed a great indignity (see Sophocles' *Antigone).* Greeks practiced both *burial and cremation. In the Roman world, cremation was more popular in the era of the republic and early empire, with inhumation becoming dominant in the late first century A.D.

Views about the destiny of the dead varied (*see* Afterlife). The earliest view was that the dead live on in the tomb. A related idea, which became the popular *eschatology of antiquity, was that the good and the evil dead live on in the bleak, shadowy realm of Hades (see Homer *Odys.* 11). But Homer, along with Hesiod, also speaks of "the Isles of the Blessed," located at the ends of the earth, to which divinely favored heroes are translated. The Eleusinian *mysteries promised their initiates a happy afterlife, apparently one of continual celebration of the mysteries in the underworld. Orphism and *Pythagoreanism developed a dualistic eschatology in which the immortal soul would receive its due in the afterlife. *Plato supplied this notion with a philosophical foundation. *Aristotle limited immortality to the intellectual part of the human tripartite soul, and even it would lack sensibility in the afterlife. In the Roman era there were those who dismissed the notion of the soul surviving death (*Epicureans) and those who held that the souls of at least some persons enjoyed a postmortem existence of some duration (*Stoics). Thus, while there was nothing like a consensus, at least some inhabitants of the Greco-Roman world would have found the Christian proclamation of a resurrected Lord intriguing.

4. Conclusion.

Personal religion in Hellenistic times took many forms. It was sometimes primitive and superstitious but sometimes earnest and contemplative. The occasional biblical portrayal of Gentiles as irreligious (e.g., 1 Thess 4:5) reflects the polemical perspective of Jews and Christians. Although this caricature may have been true of some, more often it was the piety or religiosity of the Hellenistic world that made it fertile soil for the early Christian mission.

See also DOMESTIC RELIGION AND PRACTICES; ESCHATOLOGIES OF LATE ANTIQUITY; HEAVENLY ASCENT IN JEWISH AND PAGAN TRADITIONS; MAGICAL PAPYRI; MYSTERIES; PHILOSOPHY; POLYTHEISM, GRECO-ROMAN; PRAYER; PROPHECY, GRECO-ROMAN; RELIGION, GRECO-ROMAN; RULER CULT; TEMPLES, GRECO-ROMAN.

BIBLIOGRAPHY. Artemidorus, *The Interpretation of Dreams: Oneirocritica*, trans. and commentary by R. J. White (Park Ridge, NJ: Noyes, 1975); D. E. Aune, "Magic in Early Christianity," *ANRW* 2.23.2 (1980) 1507-57; T. S. Barton, *Ancient Astrology* (London: Routledge, 1994); H.-D. Betz, ed., *The Greek Magical Papyri in Translation* (Chicago: University of Chicago Press, 1986); E. R. Dodds, *The Greeks and the Irrational* (Berkeley and Los Angeles: University of California Press, 1951); C. A. Faraone and D. Obbink, eds., *Magika Hiera: Ancient Greek Magic and Religion* (Oxford: Oxford University Press, 1991); E. Ferguson, *Demonology of the Early Christian World* (Lewiston, NY: Edwin Mellen Press, 1984); A. J. Festugière, *Personal Religion among the Greeks* (Berkeley and Los Angeles: University of California Press, 1954); R. Flacelière, *Greek Oracles* (London: Elek, 1965); F. Graf, *Magic in the Ancient World* (Cambridge, MA: Harvard University Press, 1997); H. C. Kee, *Medicine, Miracle and Magic in New Testament Times* (Cambridge: Cambridge University Press, 1986); M. Kelsey, *God, Dreams and Revelation* (rev. ed.; Minneapolis: Augsburg, 1991); G. Luck, *Arcana Mundi: Magic and the Occult in the Greek and Roman Worlds* (Baltimore: Johns Hopkins University Press, 1985); E. Vermeule, *Greek Attitudes Toward Death* (Berkeley: University of Berkeley Press, 1979); H. S. Versnel, "Religious Mentality in Ancient Prayer," in *Faith, Hope and Worship: Aspects of Religious Mentality in the Ancient World*, ed. H. S. Versnel (Leiden: E. J. Brill, 1981) 1-64.

N. C. Croy

RESTORATION OF ISRAEL. *See* EXILE; ISRAEL, LAND OF.

RESURRECTION

Resurrection became the cardinal belief for the early church by virtue of the Easter event. But Jewish ideas of resurrection prior to Christianity were diverse, and the idea itself was not universally held. The resurrection of Jesus and the Christian belief that his resurrection was but the firstfruits of a general resurrection have given rise to intense interest in the origins of the idea and its meaning in the time of Jesus and the early church.

1. Resurrection in the Old Testament
2. Resurrection in Second Temple Judaism
3. Resurrection and Afterlife in the Sayings of Jesus

1. Resurrection in the Old Testament.

Evidence from the Hebrew Scriptures indicates that Israel did not dwell on the question of the afterlife until late in the OT period. Rather they stressed the involvement of Yahweh in this life. The blessing of the righteous and punishment of the wicked were seen as taking place in the present age. Life and death were also related primarily to this life.

This does not mean that Israelites believed in annihilation after death. The OT maintains that in one sense death is the cessation of life—at death a person returns to the "dust" (Gen 3:19; Ps 90:3). In another sense it is not the absolute end of life, for existence continues—at death the person descends to Sheol (*šᵉʾôl*), a term at times synonymous with "death" (Gen 42:38; Ps 89:48), the "grave" (Gen 37:35; Is 14:11) or the "netherworld" (Ezek 32:21; perhaps Ps 86:13). In some cases the dead are said to dwell in Sheol as *rᵉpāʾîm* or "shades" (Job 26:5; Ps 88:10; Prov 9:18; Is 26:14)—possibly either a shadowy, wraithlike existence or a synonym for "the dead" (Ugaritic parallels favor the former). These references to *rᵉpʾāîm* and Sheol suggest a burgeoning view of afterlife.

But while the OT does not give explicit witness to an early belief in existence after death, neither does it deny it. Moreover, two figures were "taken up" to be with God and do not experience death—Enoch (Gen 5:24) and Elijah (2 Kings 2:9-11). While these narratives do not theologically reflect on the implications of these events (we read that Enoch "was no more, for God took him"), later Judaism (cf. Heb 11:5) interpreted this as an "assumption" to eternal life. The incident in 1 Samuel 28:1-25, where Saul attempts to consult Samuel through the medium of Endor, provides further evidence for popular belief that death was not the end of existence.

Several OT statements affirm resurrection in the sense of a corporate preservation rather than individual afterlife. For instance, Hosea 6:1-3 states, "After two days he will revive us; on the third day he will restore us, that we may live in his presence." Similarly, Hosea 13:14 promises, "I will ransom them from the power of the grave; I will redeem them from death" (cf. RSV). In both cases the redemption of Israel from exile is envisaged in terms of deliverance from death (exile) to life (national restoration). In the same way Ezekiel's famous vision of the dry bones coming to life (Ezek 37:1-14) depicts the national reconstitution of Israel. Other passages are often used as evidence of a resurrection hope but seem to refer to rescue from life-threatening situations (Deut 32:39; 1 Sam 2:6).

The basic question is stated in Job 14:14, "If a man dies, will he live again?" A tentative answer is given in Job's response to Bildad in Job 19:25-27, "I know that my Redeemer *(gōʾēl)* lives, and that in the end he will stand upon the earth. And after my skin has been destroyed, yet in my flesh I will see God." It is likely that the "redeemer" is God and that the time of deliverance is after death, thereby constituting a confession of belief in life after death.

The Psalms contain many similar statements. In Psalm 49:15 clearly and in Psalms 16:10 and 73:24 implicitly, a belief in resurrection is apparent, though without any speculation regarding the form the afterlife will take. As G. E. Ladd put it,

> The hope is based on confidence in God's power over death, not on a view of something immortal in man. The Psalmists do not reflect on what *part* of man survives death—his soul or spirit; nor is there any reflection on the nature of life after death. There is merely the confidence that even death cannot destroy the reality of fellowship with the living God. (Ladd, 47)

The prophets provide additional testimony to a resurrection faith. In the so-called Isaiah Apocalypse (Is 24:1—27:13) there are two statements, Isaiah 25:8 and 26:19. The former says that Yahweh will "swallow up death forever" and is used by Paul of the resurrection (1 Cor 15:54). This leads to the affirmation of Isaiah 26:19, "But your dead will live, their bodies will rise. You who dwell in the dust, wake up and shout for joy." However, this resurrection is restricted to God's people. The next two verses (Is 26:20-21) speak of God's wrath upon "the people of the earth" but mention no resurrection to judgment. Less certain is Isaiah 53:10, which asserts that the Servant of Yahweh, after being "assigned a grave with the wicked" (Is 53:9), will "see his offspring and prolong his days." Most agree that "prolong his days" refers to eternal life, but there is disagreement as to whether the song refers to an individual or corporate figure, the nation or the remnant.

The resurrection faith attested in the prophets climaxes in Daniel 12:1-3, 13. Here the first complete statement of a resurrection of the just and the unjust appears: "Multitudes who sleep in the dust of the earth will awake; some to everlasting life, others to shame and everlasting contempt" (Dan 12:2). There is some question whether "many" is restricted to Israel or the righteous remnant ("many *among* those who sleep") or refers to a general resurrection ("many, *namely* those who sleep"). Verse 13 adds the promise that "at the end of your days you will rise to receive your allotted inheritance."

In conclusion, the OT stresses the presence of God in the daily affairs of this life and tends thereby to ignore the larger issue of life after death. Nevertheless, it is not entirely silent, and several passages demonstrate that at a later period in Israel's history a belief in resurrection became more explicit. Two emphases emerge: (1) a close connection between the corporate and individual aspect of resurrection (i.e., national restoration and individual resurrection) and (2) a link between ethics and eschatology (i.e., resurrection is associated with reward and punishment).

2. Resurrection in Second Temple Judaism. While Second Temple Jewish literature witnesses to a great deal more speculation regarding the afterlife, there is clearly no uniformity in the views expressed. This may be due in part to the emphasis in Judaism upon Torah and orthopraxy (correct practice) rather than orthodoxy (correct doctrine) (Ladd, 52).

Indeed, like the Sadducees of Jesus' day (see Josephus *Ant.* 18.1.4 §16 as well as Acts 4:1-2; 23:8), some Jews did not believe in a resurrection. Jesus ben *Sirach wrote in his first book that at death the person abides in Sheol, a place of unending sleep (Sir 30:17; 46:19) and silence (Sir 17:27-28); and immortality is restricted to the nation and the person's good name (Sir 37:26; 39:9; 44:8-15).

Other texts show the influence of *Hellenism, speaking of the afterlife in terms of immortality without linking it to a physical resurrection. 4 *Maccabees, in describing the same seven martyrs mentioned in 2 Maccabees, seemingly substitutes an immortality of the soul where 2 Maccabees spoke of a physical resurrection (cf. 4 Macc 10:15 with 2 Macc 7:14; cf. also 4 Macc 9:22; 16:13; 18:23). Likewise, *Wisdom of Solomon speaks of the righteous finding peace (Wis 3:1-4) and an incorruptible existence (Wis 2:23-24; cf. 5:5; 6:19; and Philo *Op. Mund.* 135; *Gig.* 14). In the last book of *Enoch (*1 Enoch* 91—104; notice that the five books contain quite variant views on this topic), there is language that at first glance seems to suggest a physical resurrection (e.g., *1 Enoch* 92:3-5; 104:2, 4), but in *1 Enoch* 103:4 we learn that it is their "spirits" that will "live and rejoice" and will "not perish."

Of those texts which do speak of a resurrection, some restrict it to Israel or "the saints" (*1 Enoch* 22:13; 46:6; 51:1-2; *Pss. Sol.* 3:11-16; 13:9-11; 14:4-10; 15:12-15), while several from the first century and later attest belief in the resurrection of the righteous and the wicked (4 Ezra 4:41-43; 7:32-38 cf. *T. Benj.* 10:6-9; *2 Bar.* 49:2—51:12; 85:13). While the possibility of some Christian influence and interpolation cannot be discounted, the resurrection of the righteous and the wicked is itself essentially Jewish, reflecting the *eschatology of Daniel 12:2-3. Finally, an extremely literalistic concept of bodily resurrection can be found in 2 Maccabees, which speaks not only of the raising of the body but even the restoration of missing limbs or other body parts (2 Macc 7:10-11; 14:46). Similarly, the *Sibylline Oracles* states that the resurrection body will be fashioned exactly after the earthly body (*Sib. Or.* 4:176-82).

Clearly Second Temple Judaism showed a much greater interest than does the Hebrew Bible in the question of the afterlife, with interest centering on the theme of God vindicating his people. In addition, a variety of viewpoints emerged. This variety is reflected in the beliefs of the various parties or sects within the Judaism of Jesus' time. The *Sadducees rejected any idea of an afterlife (Acts 23:8; 26:8; Josephus *Ant.* 18.1.4 §16; *b. Sanh.* 90b). The *Pharisees taught a resurrection and eternal reward for Israel in the age to come, excluding only apostates (Acts 23:6-8; Josephus *Ant.* 18.1.3 §14; *b. Sanh.* 90b; *b. Ketub.* 111b). The *Essene view on the matter was not clear, as exemplified in the *Dead Sea Scrolls. Josephus asserts that they held to the immortality of the soul (Josephus *J.W.* 18.1.5 §18), but many scholars maintain that statements referring to the habitation of the faithful with the angels (1QS 2:25; 1QH 3:19-23; 11:10-14) should be understood as the sectarians' experience in this life rather than an eschatological hope.

3. Resurrection and Afterlife in the Sayings of Jesus.

Jesus followed in the tradition extending from Daniel to the Pharisees, teaching that there would be a twofold resurrection: the righteous to reward and the wicked to judgment.

3.1. Sayings of the Triple Tradition. The clearest discussion of resurrection in Jesus' teaching can be found in the triple-tradition story of his controversy with the Sadducees (Mk 12:18-27 par. Mt 22:23-33 and Lk 20:27-38). Even those who maintain that the final form is a later catechetical elaboration accept the first pronouncement ("become like angels") as authentic. Luke in particular stresses the contrast between the "people of this age" and those "worthy of taking part in that age and in the resurrection from the dead" (Lk 20:34-35), a distinct reference to eschatological views of an afterlife. Yet the major question is the significance of the phrase "like the angels in heaven." Some conclude from this that Jesus believed in a spiritual rather than physical resurrection or that he had a view, like some within Judaism, that in heaven there would be no consciousness of prior existence. However, this reads more into the passage than is intended, since the phrase is contrasting marriage on earth with marriage in heaven rather than teaching the state of the resurrection body.

Sayings on reward and judgment also appear in the triple tradition. The query of the wealthy young man in Mark 10:17 (par. Mt 19:16 and Lk 18:18), "What must I do to inherit eternal life?" is often understood as a desire to "enter the kingdom" in its realized presence. While this is certainly part of the meaning, it does not exhaust its thrust. Jesus' final statement in Mark 10:30 (par. Mt 19:29 and Lk 18:30), "and in the age to come eternal life," forms an inclusio with the young man's question and clearly refers to the afterlife. There is both a present and future connotation in "eternal life" in Mark 10:17, 30 and parallels. The other side, resurrection to judgment, is found in the Gehenna warning of Mark 9:43, 45, 47 (par. Mt 18:8, 9; omitted in Luke). Using successive metaphors of the hand, foot and eye, Jesus exhorts the disciples to disciplined resistance against temptation, lest one (Mark and Matthew both stress the singular "you") be cast into "hell, where the fire never goes out" (Mk 9:43; cf. Matthew's "eternal fire," Mt 18:8).

3.2. The Passion Predictions. The best-known tradition is the threefold passion prediction of Mark 8:31; 9:31; 10:33, 34 and parallels. Many interpreters have understood these as *vaticinium ex eventu* (prophecy after the event), but the absence of the type of theological elaboration found in the creeds (e.g., "for our sins," "according to the Scriptures" and the exaltation theme) makes it more likely that these are indeed historical reminiscences. The one constant in all three accounts is Jesus' prediction that "three days after" his death he would be vindicated by resurrection. The third-day theme (cf. 1 Cor 15:4) may reflect Hosea 6:2 ("on the third day he will raise us"), a more general allusion to the OT theme of the third day as a day of deliverance (cf. Gen 22:4; 42:17-18; Is 2:16; Jon 2:1), or more simply a reference on Jesus' part to a brief period of time.

Added to these direct predictions are the numerous parallel passages where Jesus presumes his future resurrection, such as Mark 9:9 (tell no one of his transfiguration "until the Son of Man has risen from the dead"); Mark 12:10-11 ("the stone the builders rejected has become the capstone"); Mark 13:26 ("the Son of man coming in clouds with great power and glory"); Mark 14:25 ("when I drink it [the eschatological cup] anew in the kingdom of God"); Mark 14:28 ("after I have arisen I will go before you into Galilee") and Mark 14:62 ("you will see the Son of man sitting at the right hand of the Mighty One and coming on the clouds of heaven").

One of the most remarkable prophecies of Jesus is not found in Luke but is recorded indirectly in Mark (Mk 14:58; 15:29) and a Matthean parallel (Mt 26:61; 27:40) and directly in John 2:19: "Destroy this temple, and I will raise it again in three days." John 2:21, 22 explains that this direct prophecy of physical resurrection was not understood by the disciples until after the resurrection itself (ironically, the chief priests and Pharisees according to Mt 27:63 correctly interpreted this saying before the disciples did). In summation, according to the Gospels, Jesus clearly expected to be vindicated by resurrection.

3.3. The Q Tradition. The Q tradition contains similar teaching. The "sign of Jonah" (Mt 12:39-42 par. Lk 11:29-32) is problematic because only Matthew spells out the sign as a cryptic reference to the resurrection ("the Son of Man will be three days and three nights in the heart of the earth," Mt 12:40). But it is just as likely that Luke has omitted the Q statement on resurrection (due to the difficulty of "three days and three nights" for his readers) as Matthew has added it.

There are also several Q passages on final reward and punishment, such as those found at the end of Matthew's Olivet Discourse. At the end of the exhortation to watchfulness (Mt 24:40-44 par. Lk 17:34-37), we have three successive short parables (men in the field, women grinding, two in a bed) demonstrating that "one will be taken, the other left." These form a severe warning regarding the sudden, unexpected separation at the Parousia (cf. Mt 24:44; cf. Lk 12:40) between those receiving salvation and those doomed for judgment. This contrast is further emphasized in the parable of the good and wicked servants (Mt 24:45-51 par. Lk 12:41-46), in which the faithful servant is given a share in Jesus' future authority while the wicked servant will be "dismembered" (Lk 12:46) and placed with the unfaithful. Finally, Matthew 10:28 and Luke 12:5 add a further saying on Gehenna, that the disciple should fear not those who can kill the body but the one who "can destroy both soul and body in hell." These passages show that Jesus followed Daniel 12:2 regarding the resurrection of good and evil alike, one to vindication and the other to judgment.

3.4. The M and L Traditions. The source material peculiar to Matthew (M) and Luke (L) adds further data. In the M tradition judgment will be universal; both good and evil people will be accountable "on the day of judgment for every careless word they have spoken" (Mt 12:35-37). While evil or "careless" speech is stressed, the "acquittal" or "condemnation" (Mt 12:37) of all speech is in mind. Two further parables address the radical separation of believer from unbeliever at the last judgment. The parable of the weeds in Matthew 13:24-30, 36-43 teaches that only at "the end of the age" (Mt 13:43) will the wicked finally be separated from the good, the former headed for "the fiery furnace" and the latter for glory (Mt 13:42-43). The parable of the sheep and the goats (also called "the judgment of the nations") has a similar theme but adds that the judgment will be determined also by the way the nations have treated God's people (the "least of these" of Mt 13:40, 45). The reward for the merciful will be "your inheritance, the kingdom prepared for you since the creation of the world" (Mt 13:34); the punishment for the merciless will be "the eternal fire prepared for the devil and his angels" (Mt 13:41).

Several L passages demonstrate the Lukan theme of the reversal of roles at the final resurrection. At the conclusion of the sayings on proper conduct at banquets (Lk 14:7-14), Jesus says that those who invite the poor and the crippled "will be repaid at the resurrection of the righteous" (Lk 14:14). While there may be no thanks in this life, God will vindicate good deeds at the eschaton. The key is a life of servanthood which seeks the lesser rather than the greater place (Lk 14:8-11) and is oriented to the dispossessed rather than the wealthy (Lk 14:12-14).

This theme is taken further in the parable of the rich man and Lazarus in Luke 16:19-31. The rich man, who undoubtedly had a lavish earthly funeral, is described in terse clauses: "died and was buried and in Hades." The poor man, who seemingly is not buried at all, has exactly the opposite afterlife: "angels carried him to Abraham's side." There are two concurrent emphases in this parable: the reversal of roles at the final resurrection and the radical faith demands of the kingdom message. Similar warnings of final judgment are addressed to the rich and to all disciples in Luke 3:7-14; 6:24-26 (cf. 1:51-53); 12:16-21, 32-34, 42-48; 16:8-9. The implications of this parable for a doctrine of the afterlife cannot be pressed too far. The picture of a compartmentalized "Hades" does not describe "the way it is" but is a feature of the parable probably derived from a popular Jewish conception of Sheol.

3.5. The Johannine Tradition. The Johannine tradition contains a few sayings that relate to the resurrection theology of Jesus and the early church. While the Fourth Gospel primarily sets forth a realized eschatology, a growing consensus of scholarship has detected a future eschatology within this characteristic Johannine matrix. In John 5:28-29, Jesus speaks of the "coming time" when the dead will hear his voice and "come out—those who have done good will rise to live, and those who have done evil will rise to be condemned." The context centers on Jesus as the eschatological Judge in the present (Jn 5:19-24) and the future (Jn 5:25-30). Then in John 6:40, 44, 54—within a context emphasizing the united sovereignty of the Father and Son in the salvation process (cf. "will never die" in 11:25, 26)—Jesus thrice repeats that he will "raise" the faithful "at the last day."

The other side is found in John 12:48, in which the unbeliever is warned that Jesus' words will "condemn him at the last day." Finally, Jesus promises in John 14:2, 3 that he is "preparing a place" for his disciples and "will come back" to bring them to his side. Some have interpreted this of the Paraclete/Holy Spirit (*see* Holy Spirit) "coming back" as Jesus' representative, but the consensus is that this is a reference to the Parousia. Bultmann and others have long argued that these futuristic passages were added by a later redactor and that realized passages like John 12:31 and 16:11 (the judgment "*now*" of the "prince of this world") are original. Yet there is no reason why the two cannot stand side by side, with present salvation and future promise interrelated.

Jesus' sayings related to resurrection teaching into the ongoing tradition from Daniel through the Pharisees, attesting to the general pattern of physical resurrection of God's people to reward and of the resurrection of the ungodly to final judgment.

See also BURIAL PRACTICES, JEWISH; ESCHATOLOGIES OF LATE ANTIQUITY; HEAVENLY ASCENT IN JEWISH AND PAGAN TRADITIONS.

BIBLIOGRAPHY. J. E. Alsup, *The Post-Resurrection Appearance Stories of the Gospel Tradition: A History-of-Tradition Analysis* (Stuttgart: Calwer, 1975); A. Avery Peck and J. Neusner, eds., *Judaism in Late Antiquity: Death, Life-After-Death, Resurrection and the World-to-Come in the Judaisms of Late Antiquity* (Leiden: E. J. Brill, 1999); R. Bauckham, *The Fate of the Dead: Studies on the Jewish and Christian Apocalypses* (NovTSup 93; Leiden: E. J. Brill, 1998); idem, "Life, Death and the Afterlife in Second Temple Judaism" in *Life in the Face of Death*, ed. R. N. Longenecker (Grand Rapids, MI: Eerdmans, 1998) 80-95; S. Davis, D. Kendall and G. O'Collins, eds., *The Resurrection: An Interdisciplinary Symposium on the Resurrection of Jesus* (2d ed.; New York: Oxford University Press, 1999); M. J. Harris, *From Grave to Glory: Resurrection in the New Testament* (Grand Rapids, MI: Zondervan, 1990); idem, *Raised Immortal: Resurrection and Immortality in the New Testament* (Grand Rapids, MI: Eerdmans, 1985); G. E. Ladd, *I Believe in the Resurrection of Jesus* (Grand Rapids, MI: Eerdmans, 1975); R. N. Longenecker, ed., *Life in the Face of Death: The Resurrection Message of the New*

Testament (Grand Rapids, MI: Eerdmans, 1998); R. Martin-Achard, *From Death to Life* (Edinburgh: Oliver & Boyd, 1960); E. Nickelsburg, *Resurrection, Immortality, and Eternal Life in Intertestamental Judaism* (HTS 26; Cambridge, MA: Harvard University Press, 1972); G. R. Osborne, *The Resurrection Narratives: A Redactional Study* (Grand Rapids, MI: Baker, 1984); P. Perkins, *Resurrection: New Testament Witness and Contemporary Reflection* (New York: Doubleday, 1984); S. E. Porter, M. A. Hayes and D. Tombs, eds., *Resurrection* (JSNTSup 186; Sheffield: Sheffield Academic Press, 1999); A. F. Segal, "Life After Death: The Social Sources," in *The Resurrection: An Interdisciplinary Symposium on the Resurrection of Jesus*, ed. S. Davis, D. Kendall and G. O'Collins (2d ed.; New York: Oxford University Press, 1999) 90-125; idem, "Paul's Thinking About Resurrection in Its Jewish Context" *NTS* 44 (1998) 400-19; K. Stendahl, ed., *Immortality and Resurrection* (New York: Macmillan, 1965); E. Sutcliffe, *The Old Testament and the Future Life* (London: Barnes, Oates & Washborn, 1964); N. J. Tromp, *Primitive Conceptions of Death and the Nether World in the Old Testament* (Rome: Pontifical Biblical Institute, 1969); A. J. M. Wedderburn, *Beyond Resurrection* (Peabody, MA: Hendrickson, 1999); N. T. Wright, *The New Testament and the People of God* (COQG 1; Minneapolis: Fortress, 1992) esp. 320-34; idem, "The Resurrection of the Messiah," *STR* 41.2 (1998) 107-56. G. R. Osborne

REVOLUTIONARY MOVEMENTS, JEWISH

Revolutionary movements were a Jewish response to the injustice of Israel's oppressors, particularly the Roman Empire. The first century was one of the most violent epochs of Jewish history, with the cauldron of unrest reaching its apex in the *destruction of Jerusalem by the Romans in A.D. 70. This in turn was punctuated by the mass suicide of Jewish rebel forces at Masada in A.D. 74. Sixty years later the smoldering embers from this war were fanned into flame by the Jewish leader *Simon ben Kosiba, who led the second revolt against the Romans in A.D. 132-135.

The causes of this unrest were many and varied, but the following factors contributed to a milieu ripe for revolution: foreign military occupation, class conflicts, misconduct of Jewish and Roman officials, Hellenization (*see* Hellenism), burdensome taxation (*see* Taxes) and the *Samaritan situation. When the Roman army occupied a land, it was accompanied by thousands of civilians (wives, children, doctors, merchants, etc.). The army lived off the occupied country, pilfering its natural resources, enslaving members of its population, raping women and generally terrorizing the populace. The gentry of Palestine collaborated with the occupying forces and, in exchange for personal safety and affluence, aided Israel's oppressors. This collusion led to class conflict between the rich and the poor, the faithful and the unfaithful, the rulers and the people (see Horsley and Hanson).

With conditions so difficult for the average Palestinian Jew, it is not surprising that a good deal of revolutionary activity arose. This took a variety of forms.

1. Social Bandits
2. Messianic Pretenders
3. Revolutionary Prophets
4. Apocalypticists
5. The Fourth Philosophy and the Martyr Tradition
6. Sicarii
7. Zealots

1. Social Bandits.

Generally speaking, social banditry arises in agrarian societies where peasants are exploited by the government or ruling class. Social bandits are the "Robin Hoods" of the land and usually increase during times of economic crisis, famine, high taxation and social disruption. The people of the land usually side with the bandits since they are champions of justice for the common people. These brigands usually symbolize the country's fundamental sense of justice and its basic religious loyalties.

In 57 B.C. Gabinius, proconsul in Syria, gave increased power to the nobility, thereby putting extreme pressure on the peasantry. In response the peasantry rebelled and not until a decade later was Palestine able to effectively govern itself again. It is therefore not surprising to find social banditry on the rise during and after this period of civil war and economic hardship. In fact, *Josephus reports that a certain Hezekiah led a band of social bandits who raided the Syrian border (Josephus *J.W.* 1.10.5-7 §§204-11; *Ant.* 14.9.2-4 §§159-74). Herod (*see* Herodian Dynasty), when he was governing *Galilee, caught and killed Hezekiah and many of his cohorts. These deaths, however, did not mark the end of social banditry. Years later Herod was still trying to exterminate the brigands (Josephus *J.W.* 1.16.2 §304). In 39-38 B.C. Herod assembled an army to track down these social bandits in order to consolidate his power as Rome's client king. Josephus notes that there was a "large force of brigands" (Josephus *J.W.* 1.16.1-2 §§303-4). Undoubtedly these social bandits were attacking the gentry, who were in league with Herod.

The brigands retreated to the caves near Arbela but were strong enough to continue to harass the gentry and challenge Herod's complete control of the land. Herod, not to be defied, formulated a strategy which Josephus narrates:

> With ropes he lowered [over the cliffs] the toughest of his men in large baskets until they reached the mouths of the caves; they then slaughtered the brigands and their families, and threw firebrands at those who resisted. . . . Not a one of them voluntarily surrendered and of those brought out forcibly, many preferred death to captivity. (Josephus *J.W.* 1.16.4 §311)
>
> An old man who had been caught inside one of the caves with his wife and seven children . . . stood at the entrance and cut down each of his sons as they came to the mouth of the cave, and then his wife. After throwing their dead bodies down the steep slope, he threw himself down too, thus submitting to death rather than slavery. (Josephus *Ant.* 14.15.5 §§429-30)

Since sources from Herod's reign contain no references to social bandits, this attack may have extinguished them, but it is an argument from silence. Indeed, until the end of the reign of Agrippa I (A.D. 44), there is very little evidence for active resistance through social banditry. In Mark 15:27, however, two "bandits" are mentioned. Josephus also mentions a certain Tholomaus as a bandit leader (Josephus *Ant.* 20.1.1 §5). Tholomaus was likely not the only one because we read that Fadus (A.D. 44-46) set out to purge the "whole of Judea" of brigands (Josephus *Ant.* 20.1.1 §5). It seems that around the middle of the first century, probably as a result of a severe famine, social banditry sharply increased. Eleazar was one of these brigands, and he enjoyed a twenty-year career (Josephus *J.W.* 2.13.2 §253). Actions taken by the authorities seem to have only proliferated Palestinian banditry. Cumanus (A.D. 48-52) took aggressive military action against the brigands, but they merely retreated into their strongholds and "from then on the whole of Judea was infested with brigands" (Josephus *Ant.* 20.6.1 §124).

Just before the Jewish revolt the rich and the poor were sharply polarized, taxation was very high, Roman oppression was grievous, justice was perverted and poverty was widespread. Consequently, Jewish banditry swelled to epidemic proportions so that a sizable number of the population were outlaws. This situation obviously took its toll on the gentry and contributed to the spiraling social unrest. Without doubt, social banditry is a major factor to be considered in any study of the First Jewish Revolt.

As the revolt broke out the bandits played an important role in resisting the Roman army's forays into Judea and Galilee, with brigand groups dominating the region of Galilee. The effectiveness of the brigands against Rome was due not only to their impressive military strength, but also to their favorable relationship with the peasants and their ability to build alliances with other rebel forces. The most important contribution made by these social bandits was their highly effective use of guerrilla warfare, which they demonstrated in routing the army of Cestius Gallus in A.D. 66. Ultimately, however, the brigands failed in their attempt to free Palestine from Roman rule.

2. Messianic Pretenders.

In Judaism prior to the first century there was no single messianic expectation held by Jews (*see* Messianism). Furthermore, messiah, as a title, does not appear frequently in pre-Christian literature. Only after the destruction of Jerusalem in A.D. 70, when *rabbinic theological reflection standardized and popularized the term, does *messiah* appear frequently with essentially the same meaning in each usage. The scarcity of the term, however, *does not* suggest that there were no expectations of an anointed royal Jewish leader. The OT had begun to shape an expectation with its promises of a "branch" that God would raise for David. This notion can be seen in Jeremiah 23:5-6 and Isaiah 11:2-9, where the "shoot from the stump of Jesse" shall "judge the poor with righteousness." Micah also contributed to the expectation by identifying Bethlehem as the home town of Messiah (Mic 5:2). But it is inappropriate to speak of a widespread OT expectation of a messiah.

During the period of Persian and Hellenistic domination, there is also little evidence of a messianic hope. The promises to David and the prophecies of a future Davidic king were known during these periods (cf. Sir 47:11, 22; 1 Macc 2:57), but the fulfillment was postponed to the distant future. This is also probably the case during the persecution by Antiochus Epiphanes, although a few references may be interpreted otherwise (cf. *1 Enoch* 90:9, 37-38; 1 Macc. 3:4; see Jewish History: Greek Period). During the *Hasmonean period, however, the hope of an anointed royal figure who would deliver Israel became more prominent. At Qumran (*see* Dead Sea Scrolls) there were apparently two anointed figures: a high-priestly messiah and the Prince of the Congregation, a lay head of the eschatological community. And in other Jewish literature of the period an anointed royal figure begins to emerge (*Pss. Sol.* 17). But among extant writings, only those coming from the period following the death of Herod (4 B.C.) refer unambiguously to a promised anointed figure.

After the death of Herod in 4 B.C. the Jews pressed Herod's son and heir apparent, Archelaus, for a number of reforms. During the Passover, when the demands reached a feverish pitch, Archelaus sent his armies into Jerusalem and massacred thousands of worshiping pilgrims. This action catalyzed revolt in every major area of Herod's kingdom, and some of these revolts took the form of messianic movements. Josephus identifies several leaders of these movements: Judas, the son of Ezekias (Josephus *Ant.* 17.10.5 §§271-72; *J.W.* 2.4.1 §56); Simon, servant of King Herod (Josephus *Ant.* 17.10.6 §§273-76); and Athronges (Josephus *Ant.* 17.7 §§278-85). Josephus clearly indicates that they aspired to be Israel's king (Josephus *J.W.* 2.4.1 §55; *Ant.* 17.10.8 §285). All of these messianic figures were of humble origins, and their followers were primarily peasants (see Barnett).

The principal goal of these revolutionaries was to overthrow Herodian and Roman domination of Palestine. In addition to fighting the Romans, these revolutionaries attacked the mansions of the aristocracy and the royal residences. This undoubtedly reveals the frustration of years of social inequality. In response, Varus, legate of Syria, dispatched two legions (6,000 troops each) and four regiments of cavalry (500 each). This was in addition to the troops already in Judea and the auxiliary troops provided by the city-states and client kings in the area. In spite of this military might these messianic movements were difficult to subdue.

Because of the lack of sources it is difficult to identify any messianic movements between the above-mentioned revolts and those surrounding the First Jewish Revolt (except, of course, the followers of Jesus). With regard to the First Jewish Revolt, Josephus notes two messianic movements that bear mentioning. The first is Menahem, son of Judas, the Galilean, who

> took his followers and marched off to Masada. There he broke open king Herod's arsenal and armed other brigands, in addition to his own group. With these men as his bodyguards, he returned to Jerusalem as a king, and becoming a leader of the insurrection, he organized the siege of the palace. (Josephus *J.W.* 2.17.8 §§433-34; cf. 2.17.5 §§422-42)

The second messianic movement mentioned by Josephus was built around Simon bar Giora (i.e., "Simon son of a proselyte"). In A.D. 66, at the outbreak of the war, Simon helped aid the Jews against Cestius by attacking the Roman rear guard. Simon's messianic movement was also motivated by the social oppression exerted by Israel's aristocracy. When Simon had gained control of the Judean and Idumean countryside, the citizens of Jerusalem invited him to lead the defense against Rome. After a power struggle in which he forced the Zealots and John of Gischala aside, Simon took control of Jerusalem. Simon was a strict disciplinarian and did well in his struggle against the Romans, but the Roman army was overwhelmingly powerful. Adorned in a white tunic and a purple cape as the king of the Jews, Simon surrendered and was taken to Rome. There he was ritually executed. The messianic movement led by Simon was the largest of all the movements described by Josephus, lasting nearly two years. It may have been fueled by eschatological hopes. [W. J. Heard]

During the reign of Trajan, the Jewish inhabitants of Judea, Egypt, and Cyrene revolted (A.D. 114 or 115). According to Eusebius, they rallied to one Lukuas, "their king" (Eusebius *Hist. Eccl.* 4.2.1-4). Dio Cassius mentions this revolt, but calls the Jewish leader Andreas (Dio Cassius *Hist.* 68.32; 69.12-13). Eusebius says that General Marcius Turbo "waged war vigorously against [the Jews] in many battles for a considerable time and killed many thousands" (Eusebius *Hist. Eccl.* 4.2.4). Although Dio's claim that hundreds of thousands perished is probably an exaggeration, the papyri and archaeological evidence confirm that the revolt was widespread and very destructive (see Schürer, 1:530-33). [C. A. Evans]

The final messianic movement in recorded Jewish antiquity (A.D. 132–35) was led by Simon ben Kosiba. Rabbi Aqiba proclaimed that Simon was indeed the Messiah, and a large portion of the Judean peasantry responded to the claim. Simon had three years of independence and even minted coins (inscribed "Year 1 of the liberation of Israel"). When Rome sent in a massive army, Simon resorted to guerrilla warfare and forced the Romans into a prolonged war of attrition. Nevertheless, the Romans finally did "annihilate, exterminate and eradicate" them from the land (Dio Cassius *Hist.* 59.13.3).

3. Revolutionary Prophets.

Despite the amount of prophetic activity prior to the first century, there is virtually no evidence for a Jewish expectation of the imminent return of the promised eschatological prophet. Nor were there vivid expectations for the appearance of the prophet like *Moses mentioned in Deuteronomy 18:18. There may have been some expectations for the return of Elijah, but a claimant to this identity never materialized. Thus the appearance of any popular prophet of reputed eschatological significance was more than just the fulfillment of a popular expectation.

R. A. Horsley has helpfully distinguished between "popular prophetic movements" and "oracular prophets." The latter group were similar in character to the classical oracular prophets such as Hosea or Jeremiah; they prophesied either judgment or deliverance. Oracular prophets proclaiming deliverance appeared just prior to and during the First Jewish Revolt. Typically those oracular prophets who pronounced judgment were not well received, being perceived by the establishment as a threat and consequently silenced.

3.1. Popular Prophets. Popular prophetic movements, on the other hand, had leaders who led sizeable movements of peasants. The political authorities generally viewed this activity as an insurrection and therefore forced a military confrontation. These prophets and their followers generally arose in anticipation of the appearance of God's eschatological liberation. This liberation was perceived as imminent, and when it arrived the Jews would be freed from their political bondage and would again govern Palestine, the land God had given to them as their own possession. The leaders of these popular prophetic movements are described by Josephus in general terms:

> Impostors and demagogues, under the guise of divine inspiration, provoked revolutionary actions and impelled the masses to act like madmen. They led them out into the wilderness so that there God would show them signs of imminent liberation. (Josephus *J.W.* 2.13.4 §259; cf. *Ant.* 20.8.6 §168)

These popular prophets, preying upon social conditions, apparently taught that God was about to transform their society—characterized by oppression and social injustice—into a society marked by peace, prosperity and righteousness. Responding to the call, large numbers of

c. 4 B.C.	Archelaus massacres Passover pilgrims in Jerusalem.
c. 36 A.D.	The Samaritan leads followers to Mt. Gerizim.
40	Caligula attempts to set up his statue in the temple
44	Herod Agrippa, the last Jewish king, dies.
45	Theudas persuades followers to accompany him to Jordan.
50s	The Egyptian leads followers to Mt. of Olives to experience fall of Jerusalem's walls.
c. 60-62	Unnamed prophet leads people into wilderness to receive salvation.
66	Florus, procurator, antagonizes Jews by taking from temple treasury.
66-68	Simon bar Giora is popularly acclaimed king and later will play a leadership role in Jerusalem.
66 August	Jewish insurgents capture Antonia; Cestius, Syrian legate, attacks Jerusalem and retreats.
67 spring-fall	Roman army under Vespasian subdues Galilee.
67-68 winter	Zealot party formed under Eleazar controls Jerusalem.
69 spring	Turmoil divides Jerusalem with three parties vying for power.
70 spring-fall	Titus conquers and destroys temple and Jerusalem.
74	Jewish rebels at Masada commit mass suicide.
132-135	Bar Kokhba leads second revolt against Rome.

Jewish revolutionary movements and conflict with Rome

peasants left their homes, their work and their communities to follow these charismatic leaders into the desert. There in the wilderness they awaited God to manifest his presence through signs and wonders, purify his people and unveil the eschatological plan of redemption which he had previously revealed to his prophet. At this juncture God himself would act and defeat Israel's enemies.

3.1.1. The Samaritan. The first of these prophets appeared when Pontius Pilate was procurator. Interestingly, this first movement appeared among the Samaritans. The Samaritans, like the Jews, revered Moses as the prophet and cultivated hopes for a future Mosaic prophet who was discussed in terms of "the restorer" *(taheb).* The *Taheb* would appear and restore Solomon's temple on Mt. Gerizim. Josephus has described one such Samaritan prophetic movement:

> Nor was the Samaritan nation free from disturbance. For a man who had no qualms about deceit, and freely used it to sway the crowd, commanded them to go up with him as a group to Mount Gerizim, which is for them the most sacred mountain. He promised to show them, when they got there, the holy vessels buried at the spot where Moses had put them. Those who thought his speech convincing came with arms and stationed themselves at a village called Tirathana. There they welcomed late-comers so that they might make the climb up the mountain in a great throng. But Pilate was quick to prevent their ascent with a contingent of cavalry and armed infantry. They attacked those who had assembled beforehand in the village, killed some, routed others, and took many into captivity. From this group Pilate executed the ringleaders as well as the most able among the fugitives. (Josephus *Ant.* 18.4.1 §§85-87)

3.1.2. Theudas. Perhaps ten years later, about A.D. 45, a second major prophetic movement began. A certain Theudas (probably not the Theudas mentioned in Acts 5:36) organized one of these prophetic movements during the reign of Fadus (A.D. 44-46). Josephus also describes this prophet's ministry:

> When Fadus was governor of Judea, a charlatan named Theudas persuaded most of the common people to take their possessions and follow him to the Jordan River. He said he was a prophet, and that at his command the river would be divided and allow them an easy crossing. Through such words he deceived many. But Fadus hardly let them consummate such foolishness. He sent out a cavalry unit against them, which killed many in a surprise attack, though they also took many alive. Having captured Theudas himself, they cut off his head and carried it off to Jerusalem. (Josephus *Ant.* 20.5.1 §§97-98)

Obviously Theudas's movement attracted large numbers of Jews, so much so that Josephus hyperbolically states that Theudas deceived "most of the common people." Perhaps Theudas, in some sort of reverse exodus, saw himself as the new Moses leading the people out of bondage (like Egypt) and across the Jordan (like the Red Sea) into the wilderness to be divinely prepared for the new conquest. Fadus, not taking any chances, acted decisively, thus showing his fear of such movements. The movement's swift annihilation almost certainly indicates that, unlike the messianic movements, this prophetic band was unarmed. Theudas's posthumous public humiliation by the ceremonial parading of his severed head was intended to send a stern warning to any would-be leaders of similar prophetic movements.

3.1.3. The Egyptian. Another movement, about ten years later, involved a Jewish prophet who originated from Egypt (Josephus *Ant.* 20.8.6 §§169-71; *J.W.* 2.13.5 §§261-63; cf. Acts 21:38). Josephus records that this prophet had a following of thirty thousand who were to march from the wilderness to the Mount of Olives and then into Jerusalem. Felix sent Roman troops to slaughter all those involved in the movement. The Roman army easily defeated this prophetic band even though the Egyptian himself escaped.

It seems fairly clear that these prophetic movements viewed themselves as acting in some sort of continuity with Israel's past great historical deliverances. They also had an eschatological dimension in their claim that God was about to deliver Israel and grant their autonomy in the promised land. [W. J. Heard]

3.1.4. Jonathan the Refugee. Following the Roman victory over Israel, a certain Jonathan fled to Cyrene. According to Josephus, this man, by trade a weaver, was one of the *sicarii* (see 6 below). He persuaded many of the poorer Jews to follow him out into the desert, "promising to show them signs and apparitions" (Josephus *J.W.* 7.11.1 §§437-38; *Life* 76 §§424-25). Catallus, the Roman governor, dispatched troops who routed Jonathan's following and eventually captured the leader himself (Josephus *J.W.* 7.11.1 §§439-42). Although Josephus does not describe Jonathan as a (false) prophet, it is likely that Jonathan viewed himself as a prophet, as the desert summons seems to imply. [C. A. Evans]

*3.2. **Oracular Prophets.*** The second category of prophets, the oracular prophets, pronounced imminent divine deliverance; these prophets were concentrated around the First Jewish Revolt. Josephus (*J.W.* 6.5.3 §§300-9) recalls with considerable detail a prophet named Jesus, son of Hananiah (*see* Jesus ben Ananias). This Jesus appeared four years before the First Revolt, during a time when Jerusalem "was enjoying great peace and prosperity," and prophesied against Jerusalem for seven years and five months. In the end he was struck by a stone from one of the Roman "missile engines" and was killed. As the war began and the number of prophets increased, the Jews were urged to await help from God (Josephus *J.W.* 6.5.2 §§286-87). Even at the end of the war, when the temple had already been sacked and set on fire, a prophet pronounced to six thousand refugees that they would receive "tokens of their deliverance" and "help from God." Every one of those six thousand perished (Josephus *J.W.* 6.5.2 §§283-84).

4. Apocalypticists.

The apocalypticists do not seem to have been a party per se, but many of the Jews in the period 200 B.C.-A.D. 100, including some of the oracular prophets, apparently became persuaded of apocalyptic eschatology (*see* Apocalypticism). For the apocalypticists, Israel's situation looked funereal. It was a depressing period of unfulfilled hopes, shattered eschatological dreams, conflict with the ruling class, with no authorized prophetic spokesperson and, above all, buffeted by persecution of the righteous who remained faithful to the *Torah. At the same time the Hellenized and severely compromised Jewish aristocracy was prospering. This situation, perceived as a crisis by some within Israel, forced a search for creative solutions. This gave rise to an apocalyptic eschatology that represented a new interpretation of human history and destiny with new emphases and insights. While maintaining continuity with the prophetic eschatology of the past, it developed in a direction that was at once dualistic, cosmic, universalistic, transcendental and individualistic.

Apocalyptic eschatology led to an emphasis on other-worldliness and a disinterest in temporal affairs. With its stress on cosmic dualism, the apocalypticists understood the real battle to be in the heavenlies between the spiritual powers. They were called upon therefore to participate with Michael and the heavenly host in the battle against evil (*see* Belial, Beliar, Devil, Satan). The primary weapon of this warfare was prayer, but it also included personal holiness and faithfulness to the Torah even if that meant severe trial. In this way the apocalypticists could defeat Israel's oppressor and rightly be classified a "revolutionary movement."

5. The Fourth Philosophy and the Martyr Tradition.

Josephus mentions, in addition to the *Pharisees, *Sadducees and *Essenes, a "Fourth Philosophy." Although many have linked this Fourth Philosophy with the Zealots and the *sicarii,* recently Horsley has persuasively argued that this identification is not correct. Horsley notes that, on the one hand, Judas the Galilean was a teacher with his own party (Josephus *J.W.* 2.3.3 §118), but on the other, Judas, as part of the Fourth Philosophy, "agreed with the views of the Pharisees in everything except their unconquerable passion for freedom since they take God as their only leader and master" (Josephus *Ant.* 18.1.6 §23). At least prima facie this Fourth Philosophy was a branch of Pharisaism in which certain teachers (e.g., Judas, Saddok, etc.) advocated a strongly proactive stance against Roman rule. Horsley suggests that the advocacy of resistance against Rome was rooted in four interrelated concepts.

The first concept was related to *taxation: to pay tax was equivalent to slavery. Moreover, it was argued that Scripture prohibited it (2 Sam 24). Taxes therefore should not be paid to Rome. Second, Israel was a theocracy and to be ruled solely by God. To submit to foreign rule was no less than idolatry and a violation of the first commandment: "Thou shalt have no other gods before me." Third, God would work synergistically through his faithful people if they would stand firm and actively resist their oppressors. Fourth, if Israel would demonstrate their resistance, God would work through them to establish his kingdom on earth. If the worst case occurred, and they ended in ruin, they would "at least have honor and glory for their high ideals" (Josephus *Ant.* 18.1.1 §§5-7).

This resistance, Horsley notes, is never stated by Josephus as armed rebellion. In fact they seem instead to be willing sufferers: "They shrug off submitting to unusual forms of death and stand firm in the face of torture of relatives and friends, all for refusing to call any man master" (Josephus *Ant.* 18.1.6 §23). The assumption that the Fourth Philosophy called people to armed rebellion has led to the mistaken identification of this Fourth Philosophy with the Zealots, with Judas as the founder of the movement. Instead of armed resistance, proponents of the Fourth Philosophy felt that if they remained firm and resisted Rome through obedience to the Torah, "God would eagerly join in promoting the success of their plans, especially if they did not shrink from the slaughter that might come upon them" (Josephus *Ant.* 18.1.1 §5). If this understanding of the Fourth Philosophy is correct, this group traced its lineage to the martyrs under Antiochus IV Epiphanes .

The martyrological tradition, though it had antecedents, largely developed in the second century B.C. when Israel was experiencing severe persecution. The aristocracy had compromised its faith and was cooperating with the oppressing nation while those faithful to Torah were experiencing severe persecution. The suffering of the righteous, however, was interpreted as "warfare." Part of the worldview of these pious Jews was the belief that their innocent suffering would be so heinous that it would almost—in a reflex action—force God to act. This notion is most obvious in the **Testament of Moses*:

> If we . . . die, our blood will be avenged before the Lord and then his kingdom shall appear throughout all his creation . . . he shall . . . avenge them of their enemies . . . he will go forth from his holy habitation with indignation and wrath on account of his sons. (*T. Mos.* 9:7—10:3)

Underlying Taxo's speech to his sons is the belief that God is the kinsman redeemer of the righteous. This doctrine of divine vengeance taught that God protects and avenges the innocent and the vulnerable when they are victimized by social injustice (Ps 9:21; Is 5:4-5; 16:1-6; Jer 11:20; 15:15) or the spilling of blood (Gen 4:9; Deut 32:43; 2 Kings 9:7-10; Ps 9:11-12; Ezek 24:7-11; Joel 3:19-20). God is portrayed as not responding to the crime itself but to the prayers of the oppressed and the cry emanating from the slain victim's blood: "You shall not afflict any widow or orphan. If you afflict him at all, and if he does cry out to me, I will surely hear his cry . . . and I will kill you with the sword" (Ex 22:22-23). It is clear, therefore, that the martyrdom of the innocent Taxo and his sons was portrayed by the author of the *Testament of Moses* to provoke God to action because of the cry of innocent blood. God's response would be no less than the complete annihilation of Israel's enemies and the appearance of the eschatological kingdom. This perspective also appears in literature from this period, especially 4 Maccabees (*see* 3 & 4 Maccabees).

4 Maccabees was written sometime just before the First Jewish Revolt as an encomium to the martyrs under Antiochus IV. The purpose of the book was not only to apotheosize the martyrs, but also to encourage those who were facing similar trials to stand firm and fight against the opposition with the weapons of obedience and suffering. In 4 Maccabees 9 the eldest brother, after enduring a series of appalling acts of cruelty, encourages his compatriots: "Fight the sacred and noble battle for religion. Thereby the just Providence of our ancestors may become merciful to our nation and take vengeance on the accursed tyrant" (4 Macc 9:24 NRSV).

In this verse the brother is exhorting the others not to compromise nor fight with illicit means. Rather, they are to hold fast and endure righteous suffering. In so doing they will defeat the king, because God will take vengeance upon the despot. This is equally as clear in the fourth brother's response to his torture and torments:

> Even if you remove my organ of speech, God hears also those who are mute. See, here is my tongue; cut it off, for in spite of this you will not make our reason speechless. Gladly, for the sake of God, we let our bodily members be mutilated. God will visit you swiftly, for you are cutting out a tongue that has been melodious with divine hymns. (4 Macc 10:18-21 NRSV; cf. 9:9)

Again, it is the innocent suffering which elicits God's response, and therefore his judgment is precipitated upon Israel's persecutors.

Atrocities against the innocent accumulate, and the cries for vengeance rise to heaven. Thus, as each martyr dies, he knows that the testimony against the tyrant is strengthened, and judgment upon the king has been brought nearer. We also see this clearly in 4 Maccabees 11:3, the fifth brother's speech: "I have come of my own accord, so that by murdering me you will incur punishment from the heavenly justice for even more crimes" (NRSV). This martyr believed that by his righteous suffering the perpetrator of the grave evil, Antiochus, would increase his guilt, which would soon reach the level whereupon the divine Judge would necessarily act on behalf of justice. We can see this same theological construct operating in the sixth brother's poignant speech: "I also, equipped with nobility, will die with my brothers, and I myself will bring a great avenger upon you, you inventor of tortures and enemy of those who are truly devout" (4 Macc 11:22-23 NRSV; cf. 9:32).

The strength of this avenger is found in his armor, namely, his virtue. The *innocent* death of the martyrs promptly precipitates the avenging wrath of God; the righteous victims need not wait indefinitely—judgment is at hand. This fact obviously had motivated the fourth brother as he endured the agony: "Gladly, for the sake of God, we let our bodily members be mutilated. God will visit you swiftly" (4 Macc 10:20-21 NRSV; cf. 12:20). Vengeance has even been personified as one in pursuit of the arch-villain. The author intimates that it does not take long for vengeance to stalk its prey and administer justice, "The tyrant Antiochus was both punished on earth and is being chastised after his death" (4 Macc 18:5 NRSV). And again in the same chapter we read, "For these crimes divine justice pursued and will pursue the accursed tyrant" (4 Macc 18:22 NRSV).

The author clearly perceives the martyrs' struggle as nothing less than *war*. It is a conflict of good against evil, God against Satan. This is again made clear from his comment after recounting the martyrs' eulogy:

> Indeed it would be proper to inscribe on their tomb these words as a reminder to the people of our nation: "Here lie buried an aged priest and an aged woman and seven sons, because of the violence of the tyrant who wished to destroy the way of life of the Hebrews. They vindicated their nation, looking to God and enduring torture even to death. Truly the contest in which they were engaged was divine." (4 Macc 17:8-11 NRSV)

The mother of the seven sons has earned the complete respect of the author as an assailant in the battle against Antiochus. He gives her the title "warrior" and remarks in amazement at her spirited combat. The writer goes so far as to credit her with the victory in the national struggle against the despot:

> O mother, soldier of God in the cause of religion, elder and woman! By steadfastness you have conquered even a tyrant . . . you stood and watched Eleazar being tortured, and said to your sons in the Hebrew language, "My sons, noble is the contest to which you are called to bear witness for the nation. Fight zealously for our ancestral law." (4 Macc 16:14-16 NRSV)

In the battle against Antiochus the martyrs' role is to endure suffering and die; they are not to compromise nor take up arms. The martyrs are merely to acquiesce to the tyrant's torture and sword. In performing this function they provide the key element in the battle which will defeat the enemies' forces and deliver the nation from their oppressors. This is a consistent theme throughout the book. Note these representative texts:

> [the martyrs are] the cause of the downfall of tyranny over their nation, they conquered the tyrant. (4 Macc 1:11 NRSV)

> O mother, who with your seven sons nullified the violence of the tyrant, frustrated his evil designs. (4 Macc 17:2 NRSV; cf. 9:30)

In most of the passages commenting on the effect of the martyrs' deaths, the martyrs themselves are the agents of victory. Thus the contribution of the martyrs is the cardinal contribution in the war effort. It justifies the amount of time devoted in 4 Maccabees to the martyrs' heroics. Without them victory would have been impossible. In the author's opinion the martyrs single-handedly defeat Antiochus and his evil forces. They accomplish his downfall by clinging to their law, not compromising and giving clear testimony to their faith. Righteousness is the lethal weapon in their struggle. They fight by persevering in their righteousness and patiently enduring torture and martyrdom; these are the martyrs' only weapons. Their foe is Antiochus, to be sure, but only insofar as he is in league with evil. The martyrs' real enemy is Satan, and their souls are at stake in the war. The heavenly host aids their effort, and by dying the martyrs are assured of victory. The picture is nearly identical to that contained in the martyrological literature written earlier.

This evidence suggests that the martyrs, by their innocent suffering, participated in the war against Antiochus and were the principle agents of victory. Their suffering was the decisive factor in the war effort. If Horsley is indeed correct in his identification of the Fourth Philosophy, these martyrs with their theology of martyrdom are likely to have been its antecedents and the Fourth Philosophy held many, if not all, of the above-mentioned theological constructs. Although this was principally a theology of suffering, the outcome was victory over Israel's enemies and therefore no less a revolutionary movement than any other.

6. ***Sicarii.***

The name *sicarii* was derived from the weapon that they employed, a curved dagger like the Roman *sicae* (Josephus *Ant.* 20.8.10 §186). Josephus describes them thus:

> A different type of bandit sprang up in Jerusalem known as *sicarii.* This group murdered people in broad daylight right in the middle of the city. Mixing with the crowds, especially during the festivals, they would conceal small daggers beneath their garments and stealthily stab their opponents. Then, when their victims fell, the murderers simply melted into the outraged crowds, undetected because of the naturalness of their presence. The first to have his throat cut was Jonathan the high priest, and after him many were murdered daily. (Josephus *J.W.* 2.13.3 §§254-56)

Some have identified these *sicarii* with the Zealots, others with social bandits, but as Horsley points out, these *sicarii* are a "different type" of bandit. As noted earlier, ordinary banditry is a rural activity in which the bandits pillage the wealthy. Because of their notoriety they normally congregate in hideouts and are always on the move. The *sicarii,* however, were urban assassins, or terrorists (not rural bandits), who, because of their secrecy, could live apparently normal lives (without fleeing to a hideout).

Obviously these violent tactics are not those of the Fourth Philosophy. Josephus, however, seems to suggest a connection in the leadership: "Menahem, leader of the sicarii at the outbreak of the revolt, was Judas' of Galilee grandson or perhaps son" (Josephus *J.W.* 7.8.1 §§253-54). If this conclusion is correct, it means that there must be some degree of correspondence between the religio-political orientation of these two groups. The assassination strategy is, however, a new development.

The tactics of assassinations first appeared during the reign of Felix in the 50s (cf. Josephus *J.W.* 2.13.3 §§254-57; 2.13.6 §§264-65; *Ant.* 20.8.5 §§163-65; 20.8.10 §§187-88). Unlike the social bandits who preyed on Roman petty officials and supply trains, the *sicarii* apparently attacked the Jewish aristocracy. These attacks took one of three forms. First, there were the selective assassinations of the ruling elite. The assassination of the high priest Jonathan is an example. Second, the *sicarii* slaughtered selected pro-Roman members of the Jewish aristocracy who lived in the countryside. These attacks also included plundering and burning selected aristocratic estates (Josephus *J.W.* 2.13.6 §§264-66; *Ant.* 20.8.6 §172). Third, the *sicarii* practiced terrorist hostage taking.

These attacks of the *sicarii* helped precipitate a revolutionary situation. They led to distrust among the ruling elite, fear among the aristocracy and catalyzed the fragmentation of the social order. That which normally provided the upper class with security began to erode, and vague feelings of anxiety and insecurity came in their place. Anyone could be next. The fragmentation of the ruling class was inevitable; individual personal safety became society's most important value. Thus, instead of cooperative efforts to protect their interests, the ecclesiastical aristocracy and ruling class began hiring personal armies to protect their interests (Josephus *Ant.* 20.9.2 §§206-7). By responding with force and violence, the ruling class further contributed to the breakdown of the social fiber and helped set the stage for the First Jewish Revolt.

The *sicarii*'s role in the revolt itself seems quite limited. Apparently, at first they were not in the midst of the fray, but before long they entered the action. They helped in the siege of the upper city and its aristocratic inhabitants (Josephus *J.W.* 2.17.6 §425); they also helped raze the royal palaces and the residence of the high priest Ananias. Shortly thereafter conflict broke out between the *sicarii* and the rest of the revolutionary forces. Within weeks the main body of the *sicarii* either had been executed, had retreated to Masada or had fled into hiding. The *sicarii* who occupied Masada sat out the rest of the war and preyed upon the surrounding countryside for their food supplies. In A.D. 73 the Romans attacked Masada, one of the last holdouts, only to discover that all of its occupants had committed suicide (Josephus *J.W.* 7.8.6—9.1 §§320-401).

7. Zealots.

Although Luke mentions a certain Simon "the zealot" (Lk 6:15; Acts 1:13) this is probably a characterizing name (namely, Simon was zealous), rather than a technical term identifying his affiliation with a revolutionary party. The Zealot party per se was not formed until the winter of A.D. 67-68. The party's origins can be traced back to the clash between the Roman procurator Florus (A.D. 64-66) and the Jerusalem citizenry. During his term Florus had pilfered the temple treasury, allowed his army to loot the city and attempted to capture and control the temple. With such abuses left without redress and the city in a rebellious mood, the lower priests began to agitate for war. The temple captain, Eleazar, son of Ananias, provided leadership and, together with the lower priests and the revolutionary leaders of the populace, decided to terminate the *sacrifices offered twice each day on behalf of Rome and the Roman emperor (Josephus *J.W.* 2.17.2 §§409-10). Previously, the offering of this sacrifice had been negotiated as a satisfactory substitute for emperor worship and therefore was a tangible sign of Jewish loyalty to Rome (*see* Ruler Cult). Thus the refusal to offer sacrifices was tantamount to a declaration of war; it broke the peace treaty and Israel was now regarded outside the *Roman Empire (Josephus *J.W.* 2.17.3 §415). The temple was subsequently cleansed, and Israel was again showing her absolute fidelity to the Torah. God was about to shower the nation with blessing.

The chief priests and leading Pharisees, however, resisted the changes, and civil war soon broke out. Eleazar was joined by the *sicarii* (Josephus *J.W.* 2.17.5 §423), and together they defeated their rivals. But a power struggle ensued, with the *sicarii* battling Eleazar and his faithful; the *sicarii* were defeated and took refuge in Masada. Eleazar was now in control in Jerusalem. In August of A.D. 66, however, Cestius, the governor of Syria, bolstered with Roman forces, attacked Jerusalem. Through an unexpected turn of events Cestius abandoned the siege of Jerusalem and, in the process of retreat, lost a good number of troops. Buoyed by their success, most of Jerusalem and Judea rallied around the revolutionary cause. Now basically unified, the nation named Ananus, the high priest, as its head. The traditional high priests resumed their positions and Eleazar joined them as general to Idumea (Josephus *J.W.* 2.20.4 §566).

The Romans then began their reconquest. During the summer and fall of A.D. 67 they had subdued Galilee and were marching through Judea. The brigands and revolutionary forces in these areas were retreating. As these fugitives, as well as those from Idumea and Perea, took refuge in the city, their own views seemed to resonate with those lower priests who had started the revolt with the cessation of the sacrifices on behalf of Rome. This new coalition is the group Josephus calls "Zealots." The Zealots agitated against the ecclesiastical aristocracy and soon decided to assert themselves. First, they attacked some Herodian nobles against whom they still had some "ancient quarrel" and who also were accused of treason (Josephus *J.W.* 4.3.4-5 §§140-46). These "ancient quarrels" almost certainly were focused on those members of the nobility who were wealthy landowners with a large number of peasants indebted to them. The Zealots, regardless of the Roman threat, were also fighting a class war against the Jewish aristocracy.

Obviously, this activity against the Herodian nobility would give rise to anxiety throughout the rest of Israel's upper class. If this discriminate violence were not enough, the Zealots elected by lot their own people to priestly offices—even installing an uneducated layperson in the office of high priest. Without doubt the Zealots were conspiring for political control. Given the inflammatory nature of this Zealot activity, it is no surprise that the Jewish aristocracy immediately turned on the Zealots and viciously attacked them (Josephus *J.W.* 4.3.6-8 §§147-57). Incited by Ananus and Jesus son of Gamala, both high priests, the people of Jerusalem forced the zealots into the inner court (Josephus *J.W.* 4.3.12 §§197-204). Trapped in the temple, the Zealots contacted sympathizers outside of Jerusalem to free them (Josephus *J.W.* 4.4.1 §§224-32). The Idumeans responded, freed the Zealots and slaughtered Ananus and Jesus son of Gamala. While they were at it, they also assassinated a number of other nobles (Josephus *J.W.* 4.4.2-3 §§233-53). There was yet another purge of Jerusalem's nobility, and this one also included many who were formerly in power, as well as the wealthy.

Within the Zealot ranks, however, all was not well. Many of the Zealots were not responsive to the dictatorial ways of John of Gischala. Since John could not gain absolute authority among the Zealots, he broke away to form his own revolutionary faction (Josephus *J.W.* 4.7.1 §§389-96). John's independence, however, was short lived. The messianic movement by Simon bar Giora was a threat to the Zealot regime in Jerusalem, and a good part of John's army deserted so that John and the Zealots again formed an alliance. This alliance, however, did not prevent Simon bar Giora from attempting to liberate the city from the Zealots and John of Gischala (Josephus *J.W.* 4.9.11 §§571-76). Simon was able to force the Zealots back into the temple (Josephus *J.W.* 4.9.12 §§577-84). The faction-prone Zealots split over the leadership of John. Josephus records that for a time there was even a three-way battle raging. Simon bar Giora, in control of Jerusalem, pressing in upon John of Gischala, who was fighting to control the temple courtyard and was caught between Simon and the rest of the Zealot party who were in the inner court above the temple (Josephus *J.W.* 5.1.1-3 §§1-12). Shortly thereafter, John was able to reconcile himself to the rest of the Zealot party, although he was only able to accomplish it by way of trickery. John of Gischala was now the Zealot leader again (Josephus *J.W.* 5.2.3—3.2 §§67-106).

By this time the Romans were at Jerusalem's gates. This threat galvanized the rival factions to form a united front. The Jews, however, were no match for the Romans. During the siege the Zealots were the smallest of the rival groups and therefore had the least significant role to play (2,400 Zealots, 6,000 under John of Gischala, 15,000 under Simon bar Giora). Nevertheless, the Zealots, in spite of their less significant role, did fight courageously to the end in cooperation with their Jewish rivals against the overwhelming military strength of the Romans (Josephus *J.W.* 5.6.1—9.3 §§248-374).

The Zealots should be remembered primarily for their thwarting of the nobility's plan to negotiate a settlement with the Romans. Moreover, the Zealots were not the Fourth Philosophy mentioned by Josephus; indeed, they were not a sect or philosophy at all. Furthermore, the Zealots were not in the vanguard among those who were agitating for rebellion, but once the revolt was underway and the only choice was to fight or to flee, they stayed and fought to the death.

The centuries leading up to the First and Second Jewish Revolts were very painful for the Jewish nation. The political subjugation by foreign nations was extremely difficult as well as the erosion of religious, cultural and socioeconomic structures. Israel's general response to the unrest was revolt, but not always via armed rebellion. The social bandits, Zealots, *sicarii* and messianic pretenders generally advocated armed rebellion and agitated for a military solution. These groups, however, often fought among themselves, significantly weakening their impact. The other response, generally advocated by the apocalypticists, prophets and martyrs, believed in waiting upon God, who, they believed, was about to intervene and personally defeat the enemy. The Fourth Philosophy, generally identifiable as having a genealogical link with the Maccabean martyrs, advocated suffering and martyrdom in order to move God to deliver Israel. None of these responses, however, was adequate to deal with the Roman threat. After the Second Jewish Revolt (A.D. 132-135) Israel lost its political identity for almost two millennia. [W. J. Heard]

See also APOCALYPTICISM; DESTRUCTION OF JERUSALEM; ECONOMICS OF PALESTINE; JEWISH WARS WITH ROME; JUDAISM AND THE NEW TESTAMENT; ROMAN ADMINISTRATION; ROMAN EAST; ROMAN GOVERNORS OF PALESTINE; ROMAN LAW AND LEGAL SYSTEM; SIMON BEN KOSIBA.

BIBLIOGRAPHY. S. A. Applebaum, "The Zealots: The Case for Reevaluation," *JRS* 61 (1971) 165; E. Bammel and C. F. D. Moule, eds., *Jesus and the Politics of His Day* (Cambridge: Cambridge University Press, 1984); P. W. Barnett, "The Jewish Sign Prophets—A.D. 40-70—Their Intentions and Origin," *NTS* 27 (1981) 679-97; S. G. F. Brandon, *Jesus and the Zealots* (Manchester: Manchester University Press, 1967); O. Cullmann, *Jesus and the Revolutionaries* (New York: Harper & Row, 1970); C. A. Evans, "Messianic Claimants of the First and Second Centuries," in *Jesus and His Contemporaries: Comparative Studies* (AGJU 25; Leiden: E. J. Brill, 1995) 53-81; W. R. Farmer, *Maccabees, Zealots and Josephus* (New York: Columbia University Press, 1956); W. J. Heard, "The Maccabean Martyrs' Contribution to Holy War," *EvQ* 58 (1986) 291-318; D. Hellholm, ed., *Apocalypticism in the Mediterranean World and the Near East* (Tübingen: Mohr Siebeck, 1983); M. Hengel, *Was Jesus a Revolutionist?*

(Philadelphia: Fortress, 1971); idem, *The Zealots* (Edinburgh: T & T Clark, 1988); R. A. Horsely, "'Messianic' Figures and Movements in First-Century Palestine," in *The Messiah: Developments in Earliest Judaism and Christianity*, ed. J. H. Charlesworth (Minneapolis: Fortress, 1992) 276-95; idem, "Popular Messianic Movements Around the Time of Jesus," *CBQ* 46 (1984) 471-95; R. A. Horsley and J. S. Hanson, *Bandits, Prophets and Messiahs* (New York: Winston, 1985); M. de Jonge, "Messianic Ideas in Later Judaism," *TDNT* 9:509-17; P. Kingdon, "Who Were the Zealots and Their Leaders in A.D. 66?," *NTS* 17 (1970) 60-75; J. Neusner, *Messiah in Context* (Philadelphia: Fortress, 1984); J. Neusner, ed., *Judaisms and Their Messiahs at the Turn of the Christian Era* (Cambridge: Cambridge University Press, 1987); G. S. Oegema, *The Anointed and His People: Messianic Expectations from the Maccabees to Bar Kochba* (JSPSup 27; Sheffield: Sheffield Academic Press, 1998); D. M. Rhoads, *Israel in Revolution: 6-74 C.E.* (Philadelphia: Fortress, 1976); D. S. Russell, *The Message and Method of Jewish Apocalyptic* (Philadelphia: Fortress, 1974); S. Safrai and M. Stern, *The Jewish People in the First Century* (2 vols.; CRINT 1; Assen: Van Gorcum; Philadelphia: Fortress, 1974-76); E. Schürer, *The History of the Jewish People in the Age of Jesus Christ (175 B.C.-A.D. 135)*, rev. and ed. G. Vermes, F. Millar and M. Goodman (3 vols.; Edinburgh: T & T Clark, 1973-87); M. Smith, "Zealots and Sicarii, Their Origins and Relations," *HTR* 64 (1971) 1-19.

W. J. Heard and C. A. Evans

REVOLUTIONARY PROPHETS. *See* REVOLUTIONARY MOVEMENTS, JEWISH.

REWORKED PENTATEUCH (4Q158, 4Q364-367). *See* DEAD SEA SCROLLS: GENERAL INTRODUCTION; REWRITTEN BIBLE IN PSEUDEPIGRAPHA AND QUMRAN.

REWRITTEN BIBLE IN PSEUDEPIGRAPHA AND QUMRAN

Scattered among the Jewish writings of the period 250 B.C. to A.D. 135 is a loose collection of narrative texts that retell and reinterpret the biblical story. These works, known most commonly as "rewritten Bible," open a window on early Jewish exegesis around the turn of the era and demonstrate the deeply held conviction that the ancient stories bore a message for the present day. Pride of place within this corpus goes to three compositions: **Jubilees*, *Pseudo-Philo's *Biblical Antiquities* and, among the *Qumran scrolls, the **Genesis Apocryphon* (1QapGen).

1. Basic Characteristics of Rewritten Bible
2. Exemplars Among the Pseudepigrapha and Dead Sea Scrolls
3. Rewritten Bible as Biblical Exegesis

1. Basic Characteristics of Rewritten Bible. Works of rewritten Bible are remarkably diverse; they share a narrative framework but differ widely in manner of biblical citation, extent of narrative embellishment, apparent purpose and in what they demand of their readers. Accordingly, efforts to define and delimit rewritten Bible as a literary genre have produced little consensus. What follows are four fundamental characteristics.

1.1. Literary Framework: An Extended Biblical Narrative. Works of rewritten Bible offer a coherent and sustained retelling of substantial portions of OT narrative, generally in chronological sequence and in accord with the narrative framework of Scripture itself. By this criterion, compositions modeled on biblical law (e.g., 11QTemple [*see* Temple Scroll]), poetry (e.g., **Psalms of Solomon*, 1QH [*see* Thanksgiving Hymns], 11QPs151, *Prayer of Manasseh) or wisdom (e.g., 11QTargum of Job, 4Q184-185) would be excluded.

Using biblical narrative as literary framework does not mean, however, that the biblical account is treated evenly; lengthy sections of narrative can be summarized in a few lines or passed over. For example, Pseudo-Philo allots only three chapters (Pseudo-Philo *Bib. Ant.* 6—8) to the patriarchs but thirty (Pseudo-Philo *Bib. Ant.* 20—49) to the period of Joshua and the judges. By contrast, more than half of *Jubilees* (19—45) concerns Jacob and his twelve sons. Each composition reiterates episodes and details that advance its own interests.

Expansions and summaries of biblical narrative could also be embedded within compositions of different genres. For example, the story of Reuben's intercourse with Bilhah (Gen 35:22) is expanded in *Jubilees* 33:1-9 but also in the *Testament of Reuben* 3:11-15. *Jubilees* (33:16) explains why Reuben and Bilhah are not executed, in accord with the law; the *Testament* (*T. Reub.* 4:2-4) emphasizes Reuben's contrition and warns readers of the pitfalls of promiscuity. Many important examples of early Jewish narrative exegesis are thus preserved outside of rewritten Bible, in other sorts of compositions. Contrast, for example, interpretations of the rape of Dinah (Gen 34) in *Jubilees* 30, Judith 9:2-4 and *Testament of Levi* 2:1-2; 5:7. Likewise, different rewritings of the Judah/Tamar episode (Gen 38) occur in *Jubilees* 41, Pseudo-Philo's *Biblical Antiquities* 9:5 and *Testament of Judah* 10—15. And Abraham's rejection of idolatry (cf. Josh 24:2-3, 14-15) is expounded in *Jubilees* 11—12, *Biblical Antiquities* 6 and **Apocalypse of Abraham* 1—8.

*1.2. **Composition: An Integration of Biblical Episodes and Extrabiblical Traditions.*** Works of rewritten Bible construct a coherent narrative by weaving into the laconic biblical storyline extrabiblical traditions. The result is a seamless, unified composition that disguises the boundaries between biblical text (whether quoted or paraphrased) and secondary elements. C. Perrot (24-26) calls such works "texte continua" to distinguish them from "texte explique," works that alternate between explicit biblical citations and commentary (e.g., Qumran pesharim, Philo's commentaries, many NT citations of the OT and later *rabbinic midrashim). D. Dimant (382-83) likewise contrasts this "compositional" use of Scripture that predominates in the *Apocrypha and pseudepigrapha with the "expositional" use of Scripture in various early commentaries.

*1.3. **Relation to Scripture: Implicit, Rather Than Explicit, Exegesis.*** The rich yield of early Jewish haggadic traditions preserved in rewritten Bible is not merely a loose collection of detached legends inserted at convenient points along the biblical storyline. Rather, narrative additions function as implicit biblical exegesis, by filling gaps, solving problems and explaining connections in the biblical text. Whether extrabiblical elements are novel or traditional, they arose almost certainly from a meticulous reading of the biblical story, informed by a profound familiarity with the rest of Scripture. In contrast to later rabbinic exegesis, the narrative shape of rewritten Bible generally precludes the offering of more than one interpretation and prevents the author from setting forth the exegetical reasoning behind his exegesis.

*1.4. **Function: Companion to, Rather Than Replacement of, Scripture.*** Although the storyline is largely intelligible without prior biblical knowledge, works of rewritten Bible do not seek to displace Scripture but rather offer a fuller, smoother version of the sacred story. Except for the predominantly non-Jewish audience of *Josephus's *Antiquities*, readers of rewritten Bible would be expected to recognize and recall the underlying biblical narrative, even if they were not always sure where the embellishments began and ended. Explicitly marked scriptural citations are rare in rewritten Bible (e.g., *Jub.* 30:12, citing Gen 34:14). Pseudo-Philo typically has one of his characters recite divine sayings in Scripture (e.g., Pseudo-Philo *Bib. Ant.* 9:3 cites Gen 15:13; *Bib. Ant.* 9:8 cites Gen 6:3; *Bib. Ant.* 15:6 cites Gen 1:9), and *Jubilees* has the angel refer to what is written on the heavenly tablets (e.g., *Jub.* 4:30 cites Gen 2:17; *Jub.* 16:29 cites Lev 23:42). Occasionally biblical books are mentioned directly. *Jubilees* speaks of the "first law" (*Jub.* 6:22) and of words already written down (*Jub.* 30:12, 21; 50:6), presumably referring to the Pentateuch. Pseudo-Philo mentions by name both Judges (Pseudo-Philo *Bib. Ant.* 35:7; 43:4) and Kings (Pseudo-Philo *Bib. Ant.* 56:7; 63:5; cf. *T. Mos.* 1:5).

Some episodes assume prior knowledge of the biblical account. *Jubilees* 29:4 omits Rachel's theft of Laban's idols (Gen 31:19, 30-35) but later mentions it in passing (*Jub.* 31:2; cf. Gen 35:1-4). The language of *Jubilees* 30:3-4, 12, 23 seems to presuppose knowledge of Genesis 34:13-27. Likewise, Pseudo-Philo's passing reference to Cain "[after he had killed Abel his brother"] (Pseudo-Philo *Bib. Ant.* 2:1) assumes familiarity with Genesis 4; the offering of Isaac (Gen 22) is omitted from *Biblical Antiquities* 8:3 but invoked three times later (Pseudo-Philo *Bib. Ant.* 18:5; 32:2-4; 40:2; cf. *Bib. Ant.* 9:3; 12:5).

2. Exemplars Among the Pseudepigrapha and Dead Sea Scrolls.

The practice of biblical rewriting is as old as Scripture itself. Deuteronomy takes up and reshapes portions of Exodus, Leviticus and Numbers; Chronicles rewrites Samuel-Kings; and the apocryphal 1 Esdras (*see* Esdras, Books of) appears to be a modest revision of parts of 2 Chronicles, Ezra and Nehemiah. See also the narrative summaries in Joshua 24, Nehemiah 9, Psalms 78, 105, 106 and 3 Maccabees 2. (On this "innerbiblical" rewriting, see esp. Fishbane.) Accordingly, the rewritten Bible of early *Judaism followed the precedent set within Scripture itself, in order to reinterpret and apply the sacred text for subsequent generations. The shape of this reinterpretation, however, varied with each new composition, as the following survey illustrates.

2.1. **Jubilees.** This reworking of Genesis 1—Exodus 16:1, dating from the second century B.C., claims to be the transcript of revelations made by the angel of the presence to *Moses during his time on Mt. Sinai (cf. Ex 24:18). This claim to inspired status (*Jub.* 1:5, 7, 26-27; 2:1; 50:13), apparently affirmed in CD 16:2-3 (and perhaps also 4Q228; *see* Damascus Document), is not a challenge to the authority of Torah, however. The aim was to supplement, not to supplant, Scripture (see *Jub.* 6:22). Biblical warrant for the idea of a "second written" Torah might have been found in the Torah itself: Exodus 24:12; 31:18; 32:16; 34:1 and Deuteronomy 9:10; 10:2, 4 portray God writing on the Sinai tablets, but Exodus 34:27 depicts God telling Moses to do the writing.

Jubilees has much in common with the *Genesis Apocryphon* but differs in its pervasive interest in halakic and calendrical matters and in its tendency to use narrative episodes as warrant for legal rulings. For example, Israel's laws prohibiting nakedness (e.g., Ex 20:26; 28:42-43) are grounded in God's clothing of Adam and Eve (*Jub.* 3:31; cf. Gen 3:21). Also linked to narrative episodes are laws regarding purification (*Jub.* 3:8, 10, 13), murder (*Jub.* 4:5), retaliation (*Jub.* 4:32), eating blood (*Jub.* 6:11), circumcision (*Jub.* 15:25-34), *marriage (*Jub.* 28:6), incest (*Jub.* 33:10-17) and *feasts (*Jub.* 6:17; 16:29). Narrative expansions thus serve to demonstrate the preexistence, even eternality, of Torah. They also serve to idealize biblical figures (*Jub.* 11:15—12:21; 17:17-18), explain difficulties in the text (*Jub.* 4:29-30; 17:15-18) and promote various doctrines, for example, about *eschatology (*Jub.* 1:7-18, 22-25), idolatry (*Jub.* 11:16-17; 12:2-14), *demons (*Jub.* 5:6-11; 10:1-13) and *sabbath (*Jub.* 50:1-13).

2.2. Pseudo-Philo's **Biblical Antiquities.** Often referred to by its Latin title *Liber Antiquitatum Biblicarum* (hence *LAB*), this work was originally written in Hebrew, probably in Palestine shortly before or soon after the Jewish war of A.D. 70 (*see* Jewish Wars with Rome). It selectively rewrites Genesis through 2 Samuel, bypassing some portions (e.g., Gen 1—3; almost all of Lev and Deut) and heavily compressing others (cf. Ex 3—13 and Pseudo-Philo *Bib. Ant.* 10:1; Josh 1—21 and *Bib. Ant.* 20:1-10). In sharp contrast to *Jubilees,* Pseudo-Philo omits almost all pentateuchal legal material (see Pseudo-Philo *Bib. Ant.* 11; 13). Most notably, Pseudo-Philo devotes about one-third of the work (Pseudo-Philo *Bib. Ant.* 25—49) to rewriting Judges. The work ends, intriguingly, with the death of Saul (Pseudo-Philo *Bib. Ant.* 65; 2 Sam 1:10), though some scholars (e.g., James, Harrington; contra C. Perrot, Jacobson, Murphy) contend the original ending has been lost.

Pseudo-Philo's rewriting emphasizes Israel's covenant status (Pseudo-Philo *Bib. Ant.* 4:5; 7:4; 8:3; 9:3; 11:5; contrast Josephus), the dangers of idolatry (Pseudo-Philo *Bib. Ant.* 6:1-5; 12:1-10; 25:7-13; 44; cf. *Jub.*) and the importance of moral leadership (Pseudo-Philo *Bib. Ant.* 6; 9). It has not been successfully tied to any one school or party (e.g., *Pharisees, *Sadducees, *Essenes, Samaritans), nor does it attack the Jewish *priesthood, *temple cult or monarchy. The view of Perrot, that Pseudo-Philo *Biblical Antiquities* emerged from a pre-70 Palestinian synagogal context, although speculative, underlines the nonsectarian, homiletical tone of the work.

A distinctive feature of Pseudo-Philo's composition is his use of Scriptures from far-removed contexts to illuminate and interpret his rewritten narrative. For example, Amram draws wisdom from the story of Tamar (Gen 38) during the crisis under Pharaoh (Pseudo-Philo *Bib. Ant.* 9:5-6; cf. Ex 1). And the episode of the molten calf (Ex 32) is portrayed as a "fulfillment" of God's words to the Babel generation (Pseudo-Philo *Bib. Ant.* 12:3; Gen 11:6). These secondary texts in Pseudo-Philo may appear as explicit citations (perhaps with fulfillment formulas), unmarked allusions, biblical echoes and narrative flashbacks. Many are unique to *Biblical Antiquities.*

2.3. **Genesis Apocryphon.** This fragmentary Aramaic scroll from Cave 1 of the Dead Sea caves (*see* Dead Sea Scrolls) is an embellished paraphrase of Genesis, composed around the turn of the era. The six best-preserved columns (2, 12, 19-22) rewrite the biblical accounts of Noah and Abraham (Gen 5:28—15:4), solving what are perceived to be problems in the narrative and idealizing biblical characters. Earlier portions (through col. 20, line 22) are substantially expanded, first-person accounts, paralleling both *Jubilees* and *1 Enoch* 106—107. Thereafter the work abruptly shifts to the third person and resembles the more restrained style of the targumim (*see* Rabbinic Literature: Targumim). Evidence of halakic (legal) interest or sectarian bias is lacking.

*2.4. **Other Dead Sea Scrolls.*** 1Q22 (1QDM) is a fragmentary scroll rewriting Moses' final farewell based on Deuteronomy. The extant fragments correspond to Deuteronony 1:3 (1Q22 1:1-4); 1:9-18 (2:5-11); 4:25-28 (1:5-9); 6:10-11 (2:1-5); 11:17 (2:5-11); 27:9-19 (2:1-5); 28:15 (1:9-11); 31:7 (1:11-12).

4Q158 (4QRP[a]) is a fragmentary scroll rewriting narrative and legal portions of Genesis and Exodus, interwoven with excerpts from Deuteronomy. Fragment 1 rewrites Genesis 32:25-33 and Exodus 4:27-28; fragment 6, Exodus 20:19-21 and Deuteronomy 18:18-22; fragments 7—8, Exodus 20:12-17, Deuteronomy 5:30-31, Exodus 20:22-26; 21:1-10; fragments 10—12, Exodus 21:32—22:13.

4Q225 (4QpsJub[a]) is a fragmentary scroll of three columns named *Pseudo-Jubilees* by its editors that recounts the binding of Isaac (Gen 22) with details not in *Jubilees* 17—18, including (following Vermes's reconstruction) Isaac's request that his hands be tied and the attendance of holy angels. 4Q225 has obvious relevance for assessing the development of Aqedah traditions at the turn of the era.

4Q252 (4QpGen[a]) has six surviving columns corresponding to Genesis 6:3—8:18; 9:24-27; 11:31—12:4; 18:16-33; 22:10-12; 49:2-4, 10, 20-21. Chronological details of the flood narrative are painstakingly retold to support the solar *calendar (1:1—2:5; cf. *Jub.* 5:31). 4Q254 parallels 4Q252 columns 1-2.

4Q364-365 (4QRP[b, c]) are fragmentary scrolls that originally may have spanned the entire Pentateuch. Some are rearrangements of the biblical order. Rewritten narrative portions include Genesis 25:18-19; 28:6; 30:14; Exodus 9:9-10; 14:10, 12-20; 25:1-2; Numbers 4:47-49; 7:1; 36:1-2.

*2.5. **Related Compositions.*** Across the spectrum of early Jewish literature, many works embed rewritten biblical narratives within larger compositions. The following list is representative but by no means comprehensive. Omitted are works of a primarily legendary nature, such as **Joseph and Aseneth*, the *Ladder of Jacob*, *Jannes and Jambres*, the **Martyrdom of Isaiah* and the **Lives of the Prophets*.

2.5.1. 1 Enoch. Several sections of this important collection rewrite and expand portions of scripture: *1 Enoch* 6—11 offer an apocalyptic expansion of Genesis 6—9; Enoch's wildly symbolic animal vision of chapters 85—90 summarizes all of biblical history; and chapters 106—107 recount legends about Noah's birth, built up from Genesis 5:28-29 (cf. 1QapGen 2—5). Noah traditions are also found in *1 Enoch* 65—67 (*see* Enoch, Books of).

2.5.2. Testament of Moses. Heavily dependent upon Deuteronomy 31—34 but influenced by other scriptures (e.g., Dan 9:4-19), **Testament of Moses* uses the transfer of leadership from Moses to Joshua as the occasion for a rapid overview of Israel's history, from the conquest under Joshua (*T. Mos.* 2:1) to the exile (*T. Mos.* 3:3), the return (*T. Mos.* 4:7) and the *Hasmonean and *Herodian dynasties (*T. Mos.* 5—6).

2.5.3. Books of Adam and Eve. Preserved in two distinct recensions, the Greek (so-called) *Apocalypse of Moses* and the Latin *Life of Adam and Eve,* this composition retells and midrashically embellishes portions of Genesis 1—5, reflecting nonsectarian Jewish theology (perhaps Palestinian and Pharisaic) from approximately the first century A.D. (*see* Adam and Eve) Most striking, perhaps, is the work's moving portrayal of Eve; she not only takes the blame (*Apoc. Mos.* 11:1-2; 14:2; 21:6; *Adam and Eve* 38:1-3; 44:2) but also accepts major responsibility for the Fall (*Apoc. Mos.* 9:2; 21:2; 23:4; 32:1-3; 3:1; 5:2; 35:3; 37:2). The devil even speaks through Eve to Adam (*Apoc. Mos.* 21:3).

2.5.4. The Exagoge *of Ezekiel the Tragedian.* Originating sometime between the third and first centuries B.C. but preserved now only in Eusebius's *Praeparatio Evangelica,* this work combines features of Jewish rewritten Bible with Greek drama to produce a poetic-narrative work the surviving fragments of which rewrite and reinterpret portions of Genesis 46 to Exodus 15. The *Exagoge* represents a creative attempt to interpret Jewish traditions for a Greek audience.

2.5.5. Demetrius the Chronographer. Five excerpts attributed to *Demetrius the chronographer are preserved by Eusebius (*Praep. Ev.* 9), and a sixth survives in Clement of Alexandria's *Stromata* (1.141.1-2). These fragments of a longer work, probably dating from the late third century B.C., retell several patriarchal tales (esp. Gen 22, 27—35, 41, 43, 46; Ex 12, 14, 15). The rewritten narratives are marked by brevity, minimal theological reflection and especially by a relentless concern to clarify details of chronology and genealogy.

2.5.6. Jewish Antiquities *of Josephus.* An introduction to rewritten Bible must include at least brief mention of Josephus. Of the twenty books of the *Antiquities*, the first thirteen (Josephus *Ant.* 1.1.1 §27—11.7.2 §303; 12.5.1 §241—13.6.7 §214) are devoted to paraphrasing the biblical story from Genesis through 1 Maccabees for the Greek-speaking world. Thus his account is not only embellished by midrashic traditions (whether oral or written) but also shaped by Josephus's own apologetic concerns and editorial license, and perhaps it is influenced by other *Hellenistic Jewish sources, including *Philo. Although Josephus promises his readers at the outset to provide a precise rendering of the Scriptures without additions or omissions (*Ant.* 1 Proem 3 §17; cf. 1 Proem 2 §5; 20.12.1 §261), *Antiquities* includes innumerable departures from the biblical precursor. If his promise of fidelity to his sources was not an essentially meaningless stock formula, Josephus likely conceived of himself as interpreter of Israel's story, in rewritten Bible tradition, and not merely as translator.

2.5.7. Philo's Life of Moses (De Vita Mosis). This work also merits inclusion because of the way it integrates biblical episodes with early Jewish tradition about Moses. Philo's introductory remarks bear repeating since they so clearly articulate an essential feature of rewritten Bible: "I will . . . tell the story of Moses as I have learned it, both from the sacred books [*ek biblōn tōn hierōn*] . . . and from some of the elders of the nation: (*para tinōn apo tou ethnous presbyterōn*); for "I always interwove what I was told with what I read [*ta . . . legomena tois anaginoskomenois aei synyphainon*], and thus believed myself to have a closer knowledge than others of his life's history" (Philo *Vit. Mos.* 1.4). *Life of Moses* also integrates numerous features of the Greek *bios* (biographical novel; *see* Biography, Ancient).

3. Rewritten Bible as Biblical Exegesis.

It is helpful to identify various reading techniques or interpretive strategies at work in rewritten Bible, not only because they illuminate the nature of early Jewish exegesis, but also because they compare at numerous points with strategies employed in early Christian readings of both the OT and the Jesus traditions.

3.1. Problem Solving. Much of early Jewish exegesis could be described as the tradents' responses to perceived ambiguities and gaps in the biblical text. This sort of biblical problem solving is ubiquitous in rewritten Bible. For example, the scandal of having God demand Isaac as a holocaust (Gen 22:1-2) is explained in *Jubilees* as God's decision to prove Abraham's faithfulness before Satan (*Jub.* 17:15—18:16; cf. 4Q225). And Pseudo-Philo solves the problem of having Moses break the divinely inscribed stone tablets (Ex 32:19) by having the script first disappear (Pseudo-Philo *Bib. Ant.* 12:5; 19:7). Why did God allow Jephthah's daughter to be first out of the tent (Judg 11:34)? According to Pseudo-Philo's *Biblical Antiquities* 39:10-11, it was divine punishment for Jephthah's irreverent vow. And, according to 4Q252 2:5-7, God's curse fell on Canaan instead of Ham (Gen 9:26) because God's irrevocable blessing had already fallen on Noah's three sons (Gen 9:1). In many such cases, the rewritten version does not contradict Scripture but fills in its gaps with traditional material. (For additional examples, *see* Genesis Apocryphon 4.2.2.)

When a biblical episode reflected poorly upon the patriarchs, the problem could be solved by omission. Thus Abraham's dubious scheme to pass Sarai off as his sister (Gen 12:10-20) disappears from *Jubilees* 13:11-15, just as the conflict between the shepherds of Abraham and Lot (Gen 13:5-11a) drops out of *Jubilees* 13:17-18. Similarly, Pseudo-Philo neglects to mention how Simeon and Levi duped Shechem by requiring circumcision before they put them to the sword (Pseudo-Philo *Bib. Ant.* 8:7; cf. Gen 34). Josephus's omission of the molten calf (Josephus *Ant.* 3.5.7-8 §§95-101; cf. Ex 32) is only the most blatant example of this phenomenon in his work.

3.2. Exploiting Biblical Juxtapositions. Underlying many ancient rewritings was the assumption that adjacent scriptural episodes were meaningfully related and thus mutually illuminating. Accordingly, biblical juxtapositions could be exploited in the interest of exegesis. Thus, *Jubilees* 24:2-3 explains Esau's hunger and willingness to sell his birthright to Jacob (Gen 25:29-34) by reading that episode in light of the subsequent mention of the famine (Gen 26:1). Similarly, when Pseudo-Philo inserts Abraham into the Babel episode (Pseudo-Philo *Bib. Ant.* 6:3-18; 7:4), he clearly assumes a link between Genesis 11 and 12. And *Biblical Antiquities* 16:1 explains Korah's rebellion (Num 16:1-3) as a reaction to the garment fringe legislation of the previous pericope (Num 15:37-41). Judges 17—18 and

Judges 19—21 are linked in Pseudo-Philo *Biblical Antiquities* 44—48. This reading strategy would become formalized in rabbinic exegesis (see Fishbane, 399-403).

3.3. Interpreting Scripture by Scripture. For the authors of rewritten Bible, Scripture was a single, unified story, so that interpreting one passage could readily entail citing or alluding to several others. Some of these intertexts are predictable: 1QapGen 20:22-33 imports elements from Genesis 20 in its rewriting of the parallel story in Genesis 12; 4Q158 (frags. 7-8) inserts Deuteronomy 5:30-31 between citations of Exodus 20; and 4Q252 forges links between Genesis 49:3-4 and Genesis 35:22. Other connections are imaginative, as when *Jubilees* 4:30 invokes Psalm 90:4 to explain how God kept the promise of Genesis 2:17 ("on the day you eat of it you shall surely die") even though Adam did not die the same day he sinned.

Pseudo-Philo makes extensive use of intertextual reference (see 2.2 above). He explains Moses' transfigured countenance (Ex 34:29-35) by comparing it with Joseph's appearance before his brothers (Pseudo-Philo *Bib. Ant.* 12:1; cf. Gen 42:8) and likens the parting of the Red Sea (Ex 14:21) to God's separating the waters at creation (Pseudo-Philo *Bib. Ant.* 15:6; cf. Gen 1:9). When *Biblical Antiquities* 12:7 describes Moses' destruction of the molten calf and Israel's drinking of its dust (Exod 32:19-20), we can hear echoes of Numbers 5:11-31, the bitter water rite for the suspected adulteress. Thus a ritual act of idol destruction and humiliation becomes a tribunal that rendered verdicts upon idolatrous Israel (see also Pseudo-Philo *Bib. Ant.* 11:8; 14:2; 19:11).

3.4. Idealizing Biblical Characters. Many narrative expansions idealize Scripture's central characters. Patriarchs, matriarchs and kings become model law keepers (e.g., Abraham and Jacob in *Jubilees*), exemplary leaders (e.g., Moses in Pseudo-Philo *Bib. Ant.*), healers (Abraham in 1QapGen) and champions of virtue (Sarai in 1QapGen; Moses, David and Solomon in Josephus). They deliver eloquent speeches and moving testaments, rehearsing God's deeds or calling the people to obedience (*Jub.* 20—22; 25; 36; Pseudo-Philo *Bib. Ant.* 23; 32). Their birth narratives are expanded (1QapGen 2—5; Pseudo-Philo *Bib. Ant.* 9:13; 42; 50) or created (*Jub.* 11:14-17; Pseudo-Philo *Bib. Ant.* 4:11). Their sins and character flaws are passed over or explained away (*Jub.* 13:10-13; 41:23-24; 1QapGen 19:13-19). Angels mourn their deaths (Pseudo-Philo *Bib. Ant.* 19:16). Praiseworthy qualities of one biblical figure are transferred to another. Even lesser figures may benefit from idealization (e.g., Enoch in 1QapGen; Tamar in Pseudo-Philo *Bib. Ant.* 9; Jephthah's daughter in *Bib. Ant.* 40).

See also ADAM AND EVE, LITERATURE CONCERNING; DEMETRIUS; ENOCH, BOOKS OF; GENESIS APOCRYPHON (1QAPGEN); JEWISH LITERATURE: HISTORIANS AND POETS; JOSEPHUS; JUBILEES; PHILO; PSEUDO-PHILO; RABBINIC LITERATURE: TARGUMIM; TESTAMENT OF MOSES .

BIBLIOGRAPHY. P. S. Alexander, "Retelling the Old Testament," in *It Is Written: Scripture Citing Scripture,* ed. D. A. Carson and H. G. Williamson (Cambridge: Cambridge University Press, 1988) 99-121; G. A. Anderson, "The Status of the Torah Before Sinai: The Retelling of the Bible in the Damascus Covenant and the Book of Jubilees," *DSD* 1 (1994) 1-29; R. Bauckham, "The *Liber Antiquitatum Biblicarum* of Pseudo-Philo and the Gospels as 'Midrash,'" in *Gospel Perspectives III: Studies in Midrash and Historiography,* ed. R. T. France and D. Wenham (Sheffield: JSOT, 1983) 33-76; M. J. Bernstein, "4Q252: From Rewritten Bible to Biblical Commentary," *JJS* 45 (1994) 1-27; J. H. Charlesworth, "The Pseudepigrapha as Biblical Exegesis," in *Early Jewish and Christian Exegesis,* ed. C. A. Evans and W. F. Stinespring (Atlanta: Scholars Press, 1987) 139-52; J. H. Charlesworth, ed., *The Old Testament Pseudepigrapha* (2 vols.; Garden City, NY: Doubleday, 1983, 1985) vol. 2; D. Dimant, "Use and Interpretation of 'Mikra' in the Apocrypha and Pseudepigrapha," in *Mikra: Text, Translation, Reading and Interpretation of the Hebrew Bible in Ancient Judaism and Early Christianity,* ed. M. J. Moulder (CRINT 2.1; Assen: Van Gorcum; Minneapolis: Fortress, 1990) 379-419; R. Eisenman and M. Wise, *The Dead Sea Scrolls Uncovered* (New York: Penguin, 1992) 77-89, 104-5 (on 4Q252); J. C. Endres, *Biblical Interpretation in the Book of Jubilees* (CBQMS 18; Washington, DC: Catholic Biblical Association, 1987); C. A. Evans, "Luke and the Rewritten Bible: Aspects of Lukan Hagiography," in *The Pseudepigrapha and Early Biblical Interpretation,* ed. J. H. Charlesworth and C. A. Evans (Sheffield: JSOT, 1993) 170-201; M. Fishbane, *Biblical Interpretation in Ancient Israel* (Oxford: Clarendon Press, 1985) 281-440; B. N. Fisk, "Scripture Shaping Scripture: The

Interpretive Role of Biblical Citations in Pseudo-Philo's Episode of the Golden Calf," *JSP* 17 (1988) 3-23; B. Halpern-Amaru, *Rewriting the Bible: Land and Covenant in Postbiblical Jewish Literature* (Valley Forge, PA: Trinity Press International, 1994); D. J. Harrington and M. P. Horgan, "Palestinian Adaptations of Biblical Narratives and Prophecies," in *Early Judaism and Its Modern Interpreters,* ed. R. A. Kraft and G. W. E. Nickelsburg (Philadelphia: Fortress, 1986) 239-58; H. C. Kee, "Appropriating the History of God's People: A Survey of Interpretations of the History of Israel in the Pseudepigrapha, Apocrypha and the New Testament," in *The Pseudepigrapha and Early Biblical Interpretation,* ed. J. H. Charlesworth and C. A. Evans (Sheffield: JSOT, 1993) 44-64; J. L. Kugel, *The Bible as It Was* (Cambridge, MA: Harvard University Press, 1997); idem, *In Potiphar's House: The Interpretive Life of Biblical Texts* (San Francisco: HarperCollins, 1990); idem, "Two Introductions to Midrash," in *Midrash and Literature,* ed. G. H. Hartman and S. Budick (New Haven, CT: Yale University Press, 1986) 77-103; F. J. Murphy, *Pseudo-Philo: Rewriting the Bible* (New York: Oxford University Press, 1993); G. W. E. Nickelsburg, "The Bible Rewritten and Expanded," in *Jewish Writings of the Second Temple Period,* ed. M. E. Stone (CRINT 2.2; Assen: Van Gorcum; Philadelphia: Fortress, 1984) 89-156; C. Perrot and P.-M. Bogaert, *Pseudo-Philon, Les Antiquiteas Bibliques, Tome II* (SC 230; Paris: Editions du Cerf, 1976); E. Reinmuth, *Pseudo-Philo und Lukas: Studien zum Liber Antiquitatum Biblicarum und seiner Bedeutung für die Interpretation des lukanischen Doppelwerks* (WUNT; Tübingen: Mohr Siebeck, 1994); E. Schürer, *The History of the Jewish People in the Age of Jesus Christ,* rev. and ed. G. Vermes, et al. (Edinburgh: T & T Clark, 1986) 3.1:308-41; G. Vermes, "New Light on the Sacrifice of Isaac from 4Q225," *JJS* 47 (1996) 140-46; idem, *Postbiblical Jewish Studies* (SJLA 8; Leiden: E. J. Brill, 1975); idem, *Scripture and Tradition in Judaism: Haggadic Studies* (SPB 1961; rev. ed., Leiden: E. J. Brill, 1973); M. Wadsworth, "Making and Interpreting Scripture," in *Ways of Reading the Bible,* ed. M. Wadsworth (Totowa, NJ: Barnes & Noble, 1981) 7-22. B. N. Fisk

RHETORIC

Throughout the history of biblical studies, especially in the early church fathers, in German biblical criticism of the eighteenth through the early twentieth centuries, and most recently in the latter part of the twentieth century, the study of rhetoric has been seen as an important background for interpreting the NT. By rhetoric it is usually meant ancient rhetorical theory, which emerged as a specific field of study during the Greek and Roman empires, what is often called classical rhetoric. The Greeks in particular developed *technē logōn* ("art of words/speech"), which was the exploration of human communication through language. This interest in communication is evident in early Greek literature like Homer's *Iliad* and in Greek drama. Various social constructs that emerged in the Greek city state also contributed to the importance of oral communication with the lawcourt, political assembly and public ceremonies as key contexts for oral discourse. It was in the fourth century B.C. that this oral discourse came to be labeled as *rhētorikē* ("rhetoric"), defined in particular as *peithō* ("persuasion") (Plato, *Gorg.* 453a2).

This article will examine classical rhetoric in order to evaluate its importance as a historical communicative context for the NT.

1. History and Development of Classical Rhetoric
2. The Practice of Rhetoric in the First Century A.D.
3. Jewish Rhetoric
4. The Distinctives of Christian Rhetoric
5. Relevance for New Testament Interpretation Today

1. History and Development of Classical Rhetoric.

1.1. The Sophists and Early Greek Rhetoric (Fifth Century B.C.). In fifth-century Athens, a group of teachers who came to be known as Sophists set themselves up as instructors in wisdom and eloquence in order to help male Athenians succeed in civic life. Their focus was on bringing thought or ideas to expression through techniques of proof or devices of argument revealing the two sides to every question. Their teaching style mostly included imitation of good literature or speeches and memorizing certain rhetorical formulaic devices. Aristotle criticizes their style for lacking art and being unsystematic (Aristotle *Soph. Elench.* 183a-184b).

Some of the key figures are Protagoras, Antiphon, Gorgias and Isocrates, the latter two being the more influential. Gorgias (485-380 B.C.) linked eloquence and virtue as companion qualities. The Gorgias style used parallelism and antitheses expressed in ornate schemes or figures of speech marked by their clever and poetic sound patterns: making the ideas sound good was persuasive. His model speeches that are extant include *The Encomium of Helen* and *The Defense of Palamedes*. Isocrates' (436-338 B.C.) main contribution was to establish rhetoric as a key educational method (see his *Antidosis*). He also laid the foundation for three of the major elements of rhetoric: invention (the thought), arrangement (ways to join them together) and style (ways to adorn the speech) (Isocrates *Soph.* 13.16-17). He downplayed the ornate style of Gorgias and developed the periodic style in which the main subject and/or verb are withheld until the end of the sentence, creating suspense in the listener.

The sophistic approach to rhetoric—wisdom as eloquence is persuasive—continued as a prominent school of rhetoric throughout the history of rhetoric. In fact, there was a period known as the second sophistic, which began around the early second century A.D. In an environment of repressed freedom of speech due to empire politics, rhetoric moved toward oratorical excess in which the emphasis was on style and delivery rather than on content.

1.2. Plato (427-347 B.C.). The move away from the sophistic style to a more philosophical (and moral) rhetoric was inaugurated by Socrates. His pupil, Plato, perfected the Socratic method: using questions and answers in dialogue or dialectic to move toward the truth of an idea. He wrote two works that had an emphasis on rhetoric, *Gorgias* and *Phaedrus*. The earlier work, *Gorgias*, focuses on the orator and by implication contains a fairly negative perspective on rhetoric suggesting it is mostly art without knowledge, a form of flattery that produces pleasure in an audience and plays upon the ignorance of the audience (see especially, *Gorg.* 462-66). In the *Phaedrus* there is a more sustained and focused discussion of rhetoric as a subject (see esp. *Phaedr.* 260-64). Plato recognizes the potential for rhetoric to "lead the soul" if practiced with the correct principles: knowledge, logic, structure (unity of the parts).

1.3. Aristotle (394-322 B.C.). It is in the writings of Aristotle, particularly *Rhetoric*, that rhetoric as a topic is given systematic treatment. Most significantly, rather than positing rhetoric against dialectic (as in Plato's *Gorgias*), he suggests that rhetoric is a counterpoint to dialectic. By so saying, he elevates rhetoric as part of philosophy. *Rhetoric* is not an easy work to understand as it appears unpolished, with an elliptical style, possibly indicating it was a set of lecture notes. Internal contradictions also suggest this and possibly imply the influence of editorial hands in the extant text. Nonetheless, it remains a most significant and foundational treatise. Book 1 is essentially an introduction. He first establishes rhetoric as art (again contra the *Gorgias*) with concomitant uses. Next he sets forth a practical definition of rhetoric: "the ability in each case to see the available means of persuasion" (Aristotle *Rhet.* 1.2.1355b25-26). He sets out proofs as artistic (ethos, pathos and logos) and inartistic (direct evidence). He divides logical proofs into two types: examples (used in inductive arguments) and enthymemes (deductive syllogisms). Next, he proposes a theory of three categories of topics. Finally, he identifies the three genres, or species, of rhetoric: deliberative (a judgment about the future, usually with respect to an action), judicial (a judgment about the past) and epideictic (demonstration in the present of what is honorable). It is his concept of genres that influences almost all future theory on rhetoric. Book 2 examines material premises in depth, first as they relate to the three kinds of discourses, then as they establish ethos, then pathos, followed by a more general discussion. Book 3 looks in detail at forms of argument, in particular, enthymemes. Book 4 studies the language (or style) for presenting proofs. Book 5 discusses arrangement of proofs. Though there is a great deal that is significant, much of the terminology, definitions and categories are not found in later rhetorical theory, possibly due to the book's lack of circulation until his personal library was rediscovered in the first century B.C.

1.4. Development of Technical Rhetoric in the Roman Period (First Century B.C. to Second Century A.D.).

1.4.1. Rhetorica ad Alexandrum. While handbooks on rhetoric are alluded to as early as the fifth century B.C. through to the late classical and Hellenistic periods, the only extant one of this time is *Rhetorica ad Alexandrum* (late fourth or early third century B.C.). It also is important to mention Hermagoras of Temnos, who apparently wrote on rhetorical theory in the late second century B.C. but whose work is lost. From

Cicero and Quintilian we know he developed a theory of *stasis*, which sought to determine the question at issue in a speech; this is at the heart of rhetorical invention. Hermagoras provides a key transition from Greek to Roman rhetoric. It is during the Roman period that follows (first to fourth centuries A.D.) that the theory of rhetoric becomes standardized through the influence of handbooks and influential rhetoricians.

1.4.2. Rhetorica ad Herennium. One of the most important works on rhetorical theory in the Roman period is *Rhetorica ad Herennium* (late first century B.C.), written in Latin. It is the earliest extant text that sets out the standard five elements of the practice of rhetoric: invention (identifying the subject, thesis or position to be adopted, and the arguments to be used), arrangement (ordering the components into an effective whole), style (configuring and enhancing the components through the choice of words, figures of speech and various devices), memory (memorizing the speech for effect and naturalness) and delivery (use of the voice and gestures).

One of the important aspects of arrangement was the theory regarding the standard form for the rhetorical speech. Based primarily on the judicial genre, the standard pattern consisted of six parts (Quintilian *Inst. Orat.* 3.9.1-6): *exordium, narratio, partitio, probatio, refutatio, peroratio.* The *partitio* is sometimes seen as part of the *narratio,* and the *refutatio* as part of the *probatio.* The *exordium* is like an introduction, which seeks to set the scene, favorably dispose the audience and establish the ethos of the speaker. The *narratio* is a statement of the case at hand, clarifying the specific question or *stasis* to be addressed. The *partitio,* or *propositio,* establishes the proposition. The *probatio,* or *confirmatio,* marshals arguments in order to confirm through conventional strategies and topics the case being argued. The *refutatio* attacks the proof of the opponent's argument by anticipation or through a response. The conclusion, or *peroratio,* recapitulates the main arguments and appeals for their acceptance. Rhetorical criticism then includes the attempt to analyse a speech or text by identifying its various parts (Mack, 41-48).

1.4.3. Cicero (106-44 B.C.). *Cicero, who stands in this same tradition, combines sophistic and philosophical rhetoric with technical elaboration. He wrote seven influential works on rhetoric, chief of which are *De Inventione* and *De Oratore.* Cicero not only influenced the theory of rhetoric but also espoused and embodied the duties of a civil orator.

1.4.4. Demetrius. Another important work of this time is Demetrius's *De Elocutione* ("On Style"), which is pseudonymous and of uncertain dating but most likely from the first century B.C. It is primarily a study of the four kinds of style: elevated, plain, elegant and forceful. Unusually, and of interest for NT studies, the section on plain style includes a discussion of letter-writing. He defines a letter as one half of a dialogue, but distinctive from conversation in its more studied character (Demetrius *Eloc.* 224).

1.4.5. Marcus Fabius Quintilianus (c. A.D. 40-96). Quintilian is credited with the longest Latin writing on rhetoric, *Institutio Oratoria,* or *Education of the Orator.* He was a teacher of rhetoric and held an official government-sponsored chair of rhetoric in Rome. After retirement he published his lectures as a treatise extending over twelve books. His work is important because it represents the culmination of technical rhetoric in its standard, even canonical tradition, showing little distinctive innovation but solid and helpful insight on rhetorical theory in general. His work also gives a helpful historical perspective by often providing a historical survey of the subject he discusses. Interestingly, he reveals his direct dependence on both Cicero and Greek classical rhetoric. In Books 1 and 2, he sets the study of rhetoric in a complete educational context from birth to the grammar school, and he outlines the required training and education for a good rhetorician. In Books 3 through 11, he traverses the standard fivefold elements of rhetorical theory and practice. In Book 12 he describes the perfect orator. He gives a very sophistic definition of rhetoric himself, "the knowledge of speaking well" (Quintilian *Inst. Orat.* 2.15.34). For Quintilian, Cicero is the ideal rhetor: "Cicero is not the name of a man, but of eloquence" (Quintilian *Inst. Orat.* 10.1.112).

2. The Practice of Rhetoric in the First Century A.D.

2.1. Rhetoric and Hellenistic Society. It is difficult to discern how widespread the knowledge and practice of rhetoric was in the Greco-Roman world. In the upper spheres of Hellenistic society, among the free citizens and the wealthy, rhetoric played a key role. But this sector of society would comprise, at most, 10 percent of the population, probably less. And the extant literature of this period on this subject tends to be from the important political and cultural urban centers like *Athens, *Rome, *Alexandria or *Antioch. As the three genres of rhetoric imply, the main areas of life where important rhetorical oratory operated were the courtroom, the civil assembly and the important public civil and religious celebrations. To those who inhabited this realm of social life, rhetoric was perceived as being everywhere (Dio Chrysostom *Disc.* 27.6; Juvenal *Sat.* 15.110-12). Life in the provinces and rural parts of the empire probably did not experience the place of rhetoric in the same way as the major centers, but there is good archaeological evidence of Hellenistic *cities with amphitheaters, *gymnasia and markets where speech making was important. Whatever the experience of formal rhetorical theory and practice in Hellenistic society, it did influence many forms of communication.

It must be asked, however, how much the 90 percent knew and understood about rhetorical theory and practice. Even though literacy was more widespread than once thought, the literacy was limited and often very function specific, like *letter writing or business accounts (*see* Literacy and Book Culture). No doubt effective communication was important to all people, and imitation of communication skills and forms of discourse, such as those possibly overheard in the marketplace, would have occurred even without specific technical knowledge and training.

2.2. Rhetoric as Part of the Education Program. An important factor that contributed to the high profile of rhetoric in the upper social spheres was its place as a primary subject in the education program (*see* Education: Jewish and Greco-Roman). It is difficult to determine how early in the education of children aspects of formal rhetorical theory were introduced. Between the ages of twelve and fourteen, Hellenistic education appears to have included various composition exercises known as "first exercises," or "preliminary exercises," later known as *progymnasmata.* Essentially a student would begin copying and later imitating various kinds of literature in order to learn a variety of writing techniques and literary or rhetorical concepts, such as fable, tale, chreia (or anecdote), proverb, refutation/confirmation, etc. As each stage was mastered, the exercises increased in length and complexity (see Theon [first century A.D.], Hermogenes of Tarsus [second century A.D.] and Aphthonius of Antioch [fifth century A.D.]). These exercises were the building blocks for the more advanced exercises of declamation, the creation and performance of complete practice orations on assigned topics, either political (*suasoriae*) or judicial (*controversiae*). These advanced exercises were mostly in the next stage of education between the years of sixteen and eighteen. Declamation also became a form of public entertainment during the Roman Empire.

It is clear that mastery of oral communication was very important to the education program, but this program, especially after the age of twelve, was primarily for the wealthy or elite (*see* Roman Social Classes). When certain Latin writers of the first century A.D. discuss the popularity of rhetoric (as in Pliny *Ep.* 3.18.7), they are referring to the interests of the wealthy—it was the people with both the leisure and money who could linger in the marketplace or attend the courtroom or assembly to listen to speeches. So while rhetoric was pervasive in Greco-Roman society, it is unlikely that formal rhetorical theory and skills were widespread among the general population.

3. Jewish Rhetoric.

3.1. Jewish Argumentation. There is no real evidence that Greco-Roman classical rhetorical theory or practice pervaded Jewish literary or oral discourse, though this remains an important area of future research. Jewish discourse had its own literary genres and forms of argumentation. The area where there may be some cultural interchange and influence through rhetoric is the midrashic practice of Halakah (*see* Rabbinic Literature: Midrashim). This consisted of applying a statement of law given in the Bible or from oral tradition (midrash) to some aspect of daily life. The process involved oral discourse in which the *rabbis and students engaged in lecture, disputation and discussion.

3.2. Rhetorical Analysis of Jewish Oral Discourse. Looking at practice through the rhetorical terms, such as argument, proof, style, delivery and memory, several insights emerge. Generally, argumentation included citing respected authorities, authoritative writings and presentation of facts from life. Proof, as such, was practiced, centered on quoting an accepted scale of authorities. The best style was the clear, logical presentation of correctly cited sources, with the ability to reason out conclusions from them. There is limited use of figures and tropes, but generally the use of such rhetorical devices is condemned. Delivery was based on a loud and clear voice with precision in pronunciation. Though the speaker often planned around the subject area, it appears such discourse was generally extempore with the interruption of questions and arguments providing unplanned diversions. Because of the unpredictable interruptions, memory did not play an important part except through the recall of memorized biblical and Mishnaic material. Reconstructing the practice of such oral discourse is difficult because the sources, generally related to Talmudic writings, postdate the NT period (*see* Rabbinic Literature: Talmud). It is also questionable whether it is appropriate to speak of this form of Jewish discourse in classical rhetorical categories, but it does elucidate the distinctives of Jewish oral argumentation from Greco-Roman rhetoric.

4. The Distinctives of Christian Rhetoric.

4.1. The Appeal to Authority. The general modes of discourse in the NT—Gospels, various forms of epistles and the Apocalypse—are not recognized forms of rhetorical discourse according to the ancient Greco-Roman rhetorical handbooks. Nevertheless, it is clear that the NT texts are written to be persuasive. The question is the means of that persuasion and its distinctive character, if any. In general, the one distinction which many commentators note with regard to Christian rhetoric is its appeal to authority. This authority has been variously defined: God, Jesus, Holy Spirit, Hebrew Scripture, Christian tradition. In terms of rhetoric, an additional key question is whether there is a different rhetorical strategy or appeal in the different genres of the NT writings (Kennedy 1984; Mack).

4.2. Radical Christian Rhetoric. G. A. Kennedy, a classical scholar, has posited a definition of Christian rhetoric over against classical rhetoric: "Christian preaching is thus not persuasion, but proclamation, and is based on authority and grace, not on proof" (Kennedy 1980, 127). In a later book, Kennedy refined this wholesale distinction of Christian rhetoric from classical rhetoric to a notion that within the scriptural writings there is Christian rhetoric that uses classical rhetorical persuasion and there is radical Christian rhetoric (Kennedy 1984, 6-8). Still using the idea of Christian rhetoric as proclamation, Kennedy notes that some parts of the Bible "give a reason why the proclamation should be received and thus appeals, at least in part, to human rationality" (Kennedy 1984, 7). Radical Christian rhetoric is different in that it does not appeal to rational argument: "When a doctrine is purely proclaimed and not couched in enthymemes I call the technique radical Christian rhetoric (Kennedy 1984, 7).

4.3. Distinctive Argumentation. Taking a different approach, B. Mack and A. Eriksson have noted that Christian rhetoric uses authoritative appeals to the Christian kerygma or Christian traditions as a core conviction (Mack, 96-98; Eriksson, 273-76). Where Mack and Eriksson depart is that Mack sees this appeal as outside the cultural conventions of Greco-Roman rhetoric, that is, outside the norms of rationality (Mack, 96-97), and Eriksson sees this appeal as according to such cultural convention, at least in terms of the use of logos, ethos and pathos, and more particularly as appeal to special topics (Eriksson, 273-76). T. Olbricht refers to the distinctive nature of Christian rhetoric as "church" rhetoric (Olbricht, 226-27). By this term Olbricht is hardly dismissing Aristotelian rhetoric; rather he is asserting that Greco-Roman rhetorical theory is insufficient for fully understanding the nature of Christian rhetoric. But Olbricht, like Mack, Eriksson and even Kennedy, notes that Christian rhetoric is distinctive in that it operates within a particular worldview: "God (through God's son and the Spirit) carries out divine purposes among humans" (Olbricht, 226). Olbricht is happy to use Aristotelian rhetorical theory to analyze Christian rhetoric, but he recognizes that it may not be completely sufficient to ascertain the full gamut of persuasive strategies within the NT writings. What all these scholars agree on is that there is a distinctive form of argumentation, but the question is the degree of correspondence with Greco-Roman rhetorical convention. The question regarding the distinctive nature of Christian rhetoric in the NT writings remains an open question.

5. Relevance for New Testament Interpretation Today.

5.1. Different Rhetorical-Critical Approaches to

the New Testament. The study of the NT that attempts to analyze the rhetoric of the different NT texts is called rhetorical criticism (*see DLNTD*, Rhetoric, Rhetorical Criticism). Assessing the rhetoric of the NT depends on the perspective one adopts about the influence of Greco-Roman rhetorical practice on the NT writings and about the nature of rhetoric. The primary debate is whether the writers themselves intended to use Greco-Roman rhetorical practice or whether they implicitly mirrored the communication context of the Hellenistic period that is to some degree rhetorical in the classical sense, or whether it is entirely inappropriate to use the categories of Greco-Roman rhetoric to analyze the NT writings. Another way to approach the question regarding the rhetorical nature of the NT is to use classical rhetorical categories to analyze the persuasive and argumentative form of the texts, either because that is the intention of the writers or because that was the universal communication practice of the time or because such categories provide a universal or heuristic means for analyzing any argumentation in any age (Stamps, 135-51). An interesting and growing rhetorical-critical perspective is socio-rhetorical criticism, which attempts to interpret and evaluate the rhetoric of the NT as a means to create a new sociocultural construct and as a text within a culture of social and literary convention and ideology (Robbins). There are others who adopt a modern rhetorical perspective to analyze the argumentation, forsaking classical rhetorical categories (Amador).

5.2. Rhetoric and the Genre of the New Testament Writings. Part of the debate concerning the rhetoric of the NT is focused on the *genre of the NT writings (Porter, 507-632). As noted above, epistles, or letter writing, seemed to be excluded from Greco-Roman rhetorical theory and practice (*see* Epistolary Theory). The Gospels, whether a unique genre or an adapted Greco-Roman genre like *bios* (*see* Biography, Ancient) also stand outside classical rhetorical theory because of the primary use of narrative discourse. Similarly, Revelation as an apocalypse or revelatory prophetic letter (*see* Apocalyptic Literature) is not a common form of Greco-Roman rhetorical discourse. If these issues regarding genre are so, it is questionable whether such classical rhetorical conventions should be used to analyze the NT texts (however, *see DJG*, Rhetorical Criticism, and *DPL*, Rhetorical Criticism).

There is no way to solve the debate as to the extent Greco-Roman rhetorical theory and practice has influenced the NT writings. At present, NT rhetorical criticism is practiced from several different perspectives. Rhetoric is part of the literary and communication context of the Hellenistic world that played some role, whether to a large degree or small degree, in the writing of the NT.

See also ARISTOTLE, ARISTOTELIANISM; BIOGRAPHY, ANCIENT; CICERO; DIATRIBE; EDUCATION: JEWISH AND GRECO-ROMAN; EPISTOLARY THEORY; GENRES OF THE NEW TESTAMENT; LETTERS, GRECO-ROMAN; LITERACY AND BOOK CULTURE; SCHOLARSHIP, GREEK AND ROMAN.

BIBLIOGRAPHY. J. D. H. Amador, *Academic Constraints in Rhetorical Criticism of the New Testament: An Introduction to a Rhetoric of Power* (JSNTSup 174; Sheffield: Sheffield Academic Press, 1999); R. D. Anderson Jr., *Ancient Rhetorical Theory and Paul* (rev. ed.; CBET 18; Leuven: Peeters, 1998); A. Eriksson, "Special Topics in 1 Corinthians 8-10," in *The Rhetorical Interpretation of Scripture: Essays from the 1996 Malibu Conference*, ed. S. E. Porter and D. L. Stamps (JSNTSup 180; Sheffield: Sheffield Academic Press, 1999) 272-301; G. A. Kennedy, *Classical Rhetoric and Its Christian and Secular Tradition from Ancient to Modern Times* (Chapel Hill: University of North Carolina Press, 1980); idem, *A New History of Classical Rhetoric* (Princeton, NJ: Princeton University Press, 1994); idem, *New Testament Interpretation Through Rhetorical Criticism* (SR; Chapel Hill: University of North Carolina Press, 1984); D. Litfin, *St. Paul's Theology of Proclamation: 1 Corinthians 1—4 and Greco-Roman Rhetoric* (SNTSMS 79: Cambridge: Cambridge University Press, 1994); B. L. Mack, *Rhetoric and the New Testament* (GBS; Minneapolis: Augsburg Fortress, 1990); J. J. Murphy, ed., *A Synoptic History of Classical Rhetoric* (Davis, CA: Hermagoras, 1983); T. S. Olbricht, " An Aristotelian Rhetorical Analysis of 1 Thessalonians," in *Greeks, Romans and Christians: Essays in Honor of A. J. Malherbe*, ed. D. Balch, E. Ferguson and W. Meeks (Minneapolis: Fortress, 1990) 216-37; C. Perelman and L. Olbrechts-Tyteca, *The New Rhetoric: A Treatise on Argumentation* (Notre Dame, IN: University of Notre Dame Press, 1969); S. E. Porter, ed., *Handbook of Classical Rhetoric in the Hellenistic Period 330 B.C.-A.D. 400* (Leiden: E. J. Brill, 1997); V. K. Robbins, *The Tapestry of Early Christian Discourse: Rhetoric, Society and Ideology* (London and New York: Routledge, 1996); D. L. Stamps, "Rhetorical Criticism of the New Testament: Ancient and Modern Evaluations of Argumentation," in *Approaches to New Testament Study,* ed. S. E. Porter and D. Tombs (JSNTSup 120; Sheffield: Sheffield Academic Press, 1995) 129-69; B. Vickers, *In Defence of Rhetoric* (Oxford: Clarendon Press, 1988); D. F. Watson and A. J. Hauser, *Rhetorical Criticism of the Bible: A Comprehensive Bibliography with Notes on History and Method* (BIS 4; Leiden: E. J. Brill, 1994). D. L. Stamps

RITUAL OF MARRIAGE (4Q502). *See* LITURGY: QUMRAN.

RITUAL PURITY A & B (4Q414, 512). *See* LITURGY: QUMRAN.

ROMAN ADMINISTRATION

While passages such as Polybius (*Hist.* 6.11-18) and *Cicero's *De Legibus* are useful in understanding Roman administration, much of our knowledge comes from scattered literary, epigraphic and *papyrological evidence.

1. Administration at Rome
2. Provincial Administration

1. Administration at Rome.

During the Roman republic the quaestors, aediles, tribunes, praetors and consuls were the most prominent executors of the will of the senate and people of *Rome, and these offices were not formally curtailed by Augustus (*see* Roman Emperors). In reality, however, the emperor became the chief legislator and the chief executive officer of the empire. New departments and officers were added in a way that made the executive branch loyal to him. Magisterial elections continued, and even though the emperor ensured the election of some candidates, many offices were still filled by genuine elections. While senators still held many of the top positions, the *equites* (traditionally translated as "knights") played increasing roles in the administration of the empire. Of equal importance was the use of the imperial freedmen and imperial *slaves, the *familia Caesaris,* in running much of the bureaucracy at Rome, especially the imperial *fiscus* and records. These were inherited by Tiberius and his successors and provided a continuity that was missing in the traditional Roman system of annual magistracies. This may have been the "Caesar's household" referred to by Paul in Philippians 4:22.

1.1. Finance. By Claudius's day there were two distinct treasuries. The *aerarium,* the traditional treasury, declined in importance while the *fiscus Caesaris,* the emperor's personal exchequer, became more prominent, though it is difficult to distinguish which revenues and which expenses were associated with each.

The chief financial officers of the *aerarium* were still the quaestors, normally twenty in number. Two served as the urban quaestors in Rome; others served in the senatorial provinces. Eventually the *aerarium* was handed over to a *praefectus aerarii.* The chief of accounts (*a rationibus*) for the *fiscus Caesaris* became the real minister of finance. Three prefects controlled a military treasury (*aerarium militare*) that paid the soldiers' discharge benefits.

1.2. Military and Police. The urban prefect (*praefectus urbi*), a senator of consular rank, commanded the three urban cohorts charged with keeping peace and order in the city. Beneath him a *praefectus vigilum* supervised seven cohorts of *vigiles* who served as a fire brigade and perhaps as a night watch. Augustus also created the praetorian guard, an imperial bodyguard of nine cohorts. It was usually led by two *praefecti praetorio* and was supplemented by a small number of cavalry and by the emperor's mounted German guard.

1.3. Public Works and Records. Although in the early empire they lost their police function, the aediles continued their function of overseeing the city streets, markets and public games, as well as supervising eating establishments, bars and inns. They divided these responsibilities with the praetors and tribunes, each taking a particular part of the city. They were assisted by street commissioners who did the work of cleaning and repairing streets and saving burned buildings.

New administrators, *curatores,* were gradually added during the early empire to oversee other important aspects of the city infrastructure, usually serving in pairs or groups of three. The *curatores viarum* oversaw the maintenance of the streets and roads outside the city walls. The *curatores aedium sacrarum et operum publicorum* supervised and maintained public buildings and shrines. The aqueduct system was maintained by the *curatores aquarum,* while a board of five senators (*curatores riparum*) was appointed to oversee the riverbed, banks and towpaths of the

Tiber. The imperial postal system (*cursus publicus*) was organized and run by the *praefectus vehiculorum* and his staff. To ensure a steady supply of grain at a stable price, a *praefectus annonae* was appointed by A.D. 14. He organized the transport and delivery of the grain dole to the populace, selling any excess on the open market. There were also three curators of public records, and the imperial archives were directed by the *a memoria*. The extensive imperial correspondence was handled by the *ab epistulis* and *a libellis*. Additional but less important posts included the *a studiis, a cognitionibus, a codicillis* and *a diplomatibus*. Each of these employed imperial slaves and freedmen in lesser roles.

2. Provincial Administration.

In the late republic, the word *provincia*, previously used of the geographical area in which a consul could exercise his military command (*imperium*), denoted a district under formal Roman administration (Gk *eparcheia* or *eparcheios*, Acts 23:34; 25:1). As the number of such areas increased, the consuls had to be supplemented by praetors. The Sullan reforms of 81 B.C. provided for a second year to be added to the duties of consuls and praetors. This was to be spent administering the provinces in place of a consul (*pro consule*) or praetor (*pro praetore*).

When Augustus laid aside the consulship in 23 B.C., the senate augmented his *imperium proconsulare*, allowing him to keep his *imperium* even while in Rome itself and making his *imperium* superior (*maius*) in relation to the other proconsuls. In 19 B.C. the senate seems to have made his *imperium* equal to that of the consuls, extending his sway over Rome and Italy as well. Thus he became commander-in-chief of the army and could interfere at will in the governing of all the provinces. Some provinces he ruled directly through his personal appointees; others had governors appointed by the senate. Still other areas were left in the hands of local dynasts, such as the *Herods. Rome would officially confirm them in their kingdoms as "kings, allies, and friends of the Roman people," yet they were expected to support the policies and actions of the neighboring Roman governors (*see* Roman Governors of Palestine).

*2.1. **Senatorial Provinces.*** Augustus and his successors left in the hands of the senate the administration of those provinces in which legions were not permanently stationed. These were governed by senators, usually ex-consuls or ex-praetors, elected by their peers and given the rank of proconsul and a normal term of one year. The senate voted funds from the *aerarium* for the governor to carry out his duties, and he was to submit an accounting upon his return. This provincial *fiscus* was augmented by the taxes collected in the province, the balance of which were forwarded to Rome.

When an area was incorporated as a province, a *lex provinciae* was issued by the conquering general, first governor or an ad hoc senatorial commission, and then approved by the Senate. It spelled out the initial terms of organization and taxation. Subsequent governors, as well as direct legislation in Rome, would add to or amend this *lex provinciae*, spelling out the current administration's policies in administering the province.

The province's chief financial officer was a *quaestor* or *procurator* who was responsible for revenues with which the emperor was directly concerned, and, by Claudius's time, over wider fiscal matters. He could communicate directly with the emperor and so at times was viewed as a spy on the governor. He could also be granted small bodies of troops to carry out his duties. A freedman procurator would often serve as an assistant to the equestrian procurator.

The governor would take along a personal staff, essentially a smaller version of his family, friends and clients (*see* Patronage), but the daily routine was handled by the governor's legates, who also formed his advisory council (*concilium* or *symboulion*, as in Acts 25:12). A legal advisor and an orderly ran his office, and he would stay in touch with the emperor by sending letters over the *cursus publicus* to the *ab epistulis* in Rome. His priorities were always to preserve Roman supremacy and military security and to protect and administer justice for Roman *citizens and Italian allies. His jurisdiction extended over local disputes, and he could appoint judges and juries, take securities and pledges, make arrests and physically punish criminals. Normally, however, he would limit his intervention to cases in which Rome or Roman citizens had a substantial interest or in which appeal was made to him, though even then he might decline to hear a case (as Gallio did in Acts 18).

*2.2. **Imperial Provinces.*** The imperial provinces were also governed by senators of consular or praetorian rank. Their terms, however, were indefinite, and they were appointed by the emperor as *legatus Augusti pro praetore.* An exception was Egypt, where an equestrian served as *praefectus Aegypti;* the latter was also exceptional in being granted command of Egypt's three legions. Senators who headed provinces in which a single legion was stationed usually served as legionary commander (*legatus legionis*) and governor simultaneously.

In some smaller provinces (Mauretania, Thrace, Raetia, Noricum and Judea), *equites* governed with the title *praefectus* or *pro legato* and commanded the local troops. They were subject to some extent to the adjacent senatorial governors. Sometimes one man would serve as both prefect and procurator (chief financial officer) simultaneously. Pilate did both, according to *Josephus (Josephus *Ant.* 18.3.2 §60; *J.W.* 2.9.4 §175). Under Claudius, the title of this office changed to *procurator Augusti.* Thus we find Felix called the procurator in Acts 23—24 though he was obviously not just a financial officer. He was a freedman, the brother of Claudius's *a rationibus* (Pliny *Ep.* 4.12), though he may have been granted equestrian status before his appointment.

Each *legatus Augusti pro praetore* would have a staff (*officium*) made up principally of soldiers seconded from their other duties. His office was mostly involved in judicial and police duties (Acts 21:31-36). The emperor directly appointed all the important officers in the imperial provinces. His legates could draw funds from local *fisci* as necessary, and, until Nero, an accounting (*rationes imperii*) was published (Suetonius *Caligula* 16; Dio Cassius *Hist.* 59.9).

The other important department was that of the financial procurator, who represented the imperial *fiscus* and was responsible for financial accounts and seeing that revenues (taxes, mine revenues, rents) were properly collected.

Both imperial and senatorial provinces were divided into administrative districts (*conventus* or *dioceses*) in which governors convoked appeals courts with assemblies of local Roman *equites* and other respected Romans of the district. The Romans served as assessors or jurors and were presided over by a curator. They took up cases in which Rome or Romans had a vested interest or in which appeal was made to the governor. Other local matters of administration and justice were seen to by local agencies that Rome allowed to continue or helped establish. Provincial *concilia* were also formed from the local aristocracy, and at times appointed *inquisitores* investigated cases of corruption or illegal activities (such as the Christians in Bithynia under Pliny). The *koinon* of Asia was a provincial body functioning already in the mid-first century B.C. both to coordinate embassies to Rome and to distribute information from Rome to the Asiatic cities. Its members were given the title Asiarchs (Acts 19:31). In Judea the traditional Sanhedrin and religious courts were allowed to take care of many local tasks. When the provincials were dissatisfied by a governor's decisions, action or lack of action, appeals could be made directly to Rome, in theory, but this seldom happened during the republic. Under the empire more formal systems of appeal were developed, though the exact legal status of Paul's appeal to Caesar is still debated.

2.3. Cities. While provincial government was important, city government and citizenship played a larger role for most provincials, and these structures differed according to the official status of each city. In the western empire, cities were often favored by the grant of "Latin rights" (the families of magistrates were given Roman citizenship) or by being given the status of *municipia* (citizens received citizenship and the city kept a form of its constitution). The two types of special status in the east were those of colonies and free cities.

Roman colonies were new foundations or cities in which Roman settlers were added. Their name often reflected this status. Originally colonies were armed garrisons, but by the early empire they were frequently settlements of veterans and freedmen, such as at *Philippi and *Corinth. The colonies were thus important bases for the Romanization of the provinces. Further along in the principate, new colonies were no longer necessarily associated with the army and often were mere upgradings of an existing town's rank.

The concept of the free city, a city that was part of an alliance or kingdom but was internally autonomous and not subject to exactions or tribute, had developed in the Hellenistic world (*see* Cities, Greco-Roman). Rome continued to grant this title to select cities, such as when in 196 B.C. Flamininus declared the Greek cities free, that is, free to live under their own laws and free from Roman garrisons and tribute (Polybius *Hist.* 18.46.5). However, there was still a master-subject relationship, and the status could be revoked, as happened to Corinth and the other Greek cities that rebelled in 147-146 B.C. From Sulla on, however, the specific favors granted to a free city of *Greece, Asia or other provinces were less comprehensive and had to be spelled out for each city individually. By the late republic the advantage of being a free city had been reduced to the exemption from the billeting of troops and the enjoyment of some judicial autonomy.

Cities with no special rights were termed *stipendariae* (payers of tribute). They usually retained their constitutions, as in Asia, and continued their local citizenship rolls with citizens organized into tribes. In some areas popular assemblies still voted on local measures, but more often the important business was conducted by a town council made up of the elite. Annual magistrates were elected to serve as executive officers, judges, city treasurers, priests of public cults and overseers of public buildings and festivals. Local finances relied on election fees paid by council members and magistrates, rental of city-owned land, fines and other minor fees, but especially *benefactions by the leading citizens and its Roman patrons. By the second century these benefactory services to the city (*munera* or *leitourgiai)* had become less than voluntary in many instances and instead were required privileges that could be avoided only with ingenuity and loss of face.

2.4. Towns and Countryside. Smaller towns and villages could have single or collegial administrators. Village assemblies, whether formal or informal, gathered and deliberated as needed. Terms such as "the village" (*komē*), "the people" (*dēmos* or *koinon*) and the assembly (*boulē*) are the most common in inscriptions. At least some villages had a common treasury fattened by one or more of the following: honoraria given by magistrates entering office, fines, benefactory gifts, the rent of public buildings, lands or pastures, water fees or compulsory subscriptions to public works. As with the larger cities, public works were often assisted by local benefactors. The head tax had to be paid to Rome, either directly or through the city in whose *territorium* the village was located. The other additional taxes Rome levied on the province were applicable also to most villages, not to mention other taxes that the local city might impose for itself.

See also ROMAN EMPERORS; ROMAN EMPIRE; ROMAN GOVERNORS OF PALESTINE; ROMAN LAW AND LEGAL SYSTEM; ROMAN POLITICAL SYSTEM; ROMAN SOCIAL CLASSES.

BIBLIOGRAPHY. F. F. Abbott and A. C. Johnson, *Municipal Administration in the Roman Empire* (Princeton, NJ: Princeton University Press, 1926); A. Bowman, "Provincial Administration and Taxation," *Cambridge Ancient History* (2d ed.; Cambridge: Cambridge University Press, 1996) 10:344-70; P. A. Brunt, "The Fiscus and Its Development," *JRS* 56 (1966) 75-91; J. Gaudemet, *Institutions de L'antiquite* (Paris: Sirey, 1967); A. H. M. Jones, *Studies in Roman Government and Law* (Oxford: Blackwell, 1960); A. Lintott, *Imperium Romanum: Politics and Administration* (London: Routledge, 1993); F. Millar, *The Emperor in the Roman World* (Ithaca, NY: Cornell University Press, 1977); D. Rathbone, "The Imperial Finances," *Cambridge Ancient History* (2d ed.; Cambridge: Cambridge University Press, 1996) 10:309-23; J. Richardson, "The Administration of the Empire," *Cambridge Ancient History* (2d. ed.; Cambridge: Cambridge University Press, 1994) 9:564-98; M. Rostovtzeff, *Social and Economic History of the Roman Empire,* ed. P. Fraser (2d ed.; Oxford: Clarendon Press, 1957); G. H. Stevenson, *Roman Provincial Administration Till the Age of the Antonines* (Oxford: Blackwell, 1939); P. R. C. Weaver, *Familia Caesaris* (Cambridge: Cambridge University Press, 1972). G. L. Thompson

ROMAN EAST

By 200 B.C., Rome had emerged as the dominant power in the western Mediterranean and began to play a larger role in Eastern affairs as well. At that time, the *Hellenistic world consisted of a network of states and city-states in a tenuous balance of power. Aggression by one ruler or state would cause a wave of realignments rippling outward from the East and often reaching Roman interests or Rome itself. By the birth of Jesus, Rome not only dominated Eastern politics but also had annexed much of the East in the form of new provinces. We will treat Rome's entire expansion eastward (with the exception of Illyricum, which was culturally part of the West), as well as its formal organization through the first century A.D.

1. The Progress of Roman Expansion
2. Motivation for Roman Expansion
3. Policies in the East
4. Influence on Life
5. Attitudes Toward Rome

1. The Progress of Roman Expansion.

1.1. Macedonia and Greece. Rome first made military contact with the Greek world when Pyrrhus of Epirus was called into Italy to help the city of Tarentum fight Rome (270s B.C.). In the following decades Rome spread its influence southward, overrunning all of southern Italy and Sicily. The fleets that Rome had built to challenge Carthage also sailed into Eastern political waters when Macedon allied itself with Carthage, and Rome then joined the Aetolian league and Pergamum in keeping Macedon in check (First Macedonian War, 215-205 B.C.; *see* Greece and Macedon). Three more Macedonian wars would follow before Rome would organize Macedon as a province in 148 B.C. Four administrative districts were formed and boards of *politarchs* (Acts 17:6) oversaw the administration of the cities. The Egnatian Way, which passed through the important cities of *Philippi and *Thessalonica, was built to span the province and connect it to the Adriatic. Further campaigns down to 102 B.C. expanded the province at the expense of the Thracians.

Contact with the Greeks of Aetolia and Pergamum was renewed soon after the First Macedonian War. In 200 B.C. a delegation reached Rome seeking aid in rebuffing new incursions into Greece by Macedon and the *Seleucids. Although the Roman army eventually routed Macedon (Second Macedonian War, 200-197 B.C.) and Rome declared the Greeks free (i.e., free from direct administrative control), Greece remained weak and disunited. After their short-lived revolt in 146 B.C. (the Achean War), Rome imposed harsh conditions on much of Greece (*Corinth was razed, to be refounded as a Roman colony a century later by Julius Caesar); however, a long-term peace was established. For a time the councils of the regional leagues were disbanded, oligarchic governments were imposed in many places, and indemnities and tribute were imposed upon the ringleaders, as well as a general taxation. The governor of Macedon would intervene as necessary until a separate province of Achaia was formalized in Augustus's settlement of 27 B.C. Augustus added Macedonia and Achaia to the province of Moesia about 15 B.C., but they were made separate provinces again in A.D. 44. Achaia was freed in A.D. 67 by Nero, but this had no political significance.

1.2. Asia Minor. By the early second century B.C., *Asia Minor was also a site of Roman interests. About 190 B.C. Rome joined Pergamum in a major battle against the expansion of the Seleucid Antiochus III. This left Pergamum the major power in western Asia Minor, and at his death in 133 B.C. Attalus III of Pergamum bequeathed his vast royal lands to the Roman people. This became the province of Asia in 129 B.C. Many cities (including the NT cities of *Ephesus, Laodicea and Pergamum) were made autonomous and left free from tribute. The kingdoms of Cappadocia, Bithynia and Pontus remained independent, the latter even being granted much of Phrygia until about 120 B.C. Lycaonia and perhaps Pamphylia were added to the province of Asia by the end of the second century B.C.

However, the conflicting interests of Rome, Bithynia and Pontus led eventually to yet another major conflict (First Mithridatic War, 89-85 B.C.). Mithridates VI of Pontus took the field in 88 B.C., overrunning Asia, instigating the massacre of tens of thousands of Roman citizens and allies, and even gaining control of much of southern and central Greece. Sulla eventually expelled Mithridates and imposed far heavier taxes on Asia, except for the few cities that had remained loyal to Rome. In 75 B.C. Nicomedes III willed Bithynia to Rome, but the efforts of Mithridates VI to occupy it led to a Third Mithridatic War (73-66 B.C.). The Roman general Lucullus defeated the Pontic king and, when Mithridates fled to Armenia, took a Roman army beyond the Taurus Mountains for the first time. Few Asian cities had supported Mithridates this time, and in reward Lucullus helped improve their economic lot.

While numerous principalities in the eastern two-thirds of Asia Minor (Pontus, Cappadocia, Cilicia Tracheia, Paphlagonia, Armenia Minor) would continue to be passed back and forth between hereditary royal families for another century, Rome gradually took more and more under direct rule. *Pompey was responsible for the first major reorganization of the area from 64 to 62 B.C. Pontus was divided, the western half being added to the new province of Bithynia. The eastern half was added to the kingdom of the *Galatians (a group of Celts who had seized central Asia Minor in the third century), but it reverted to a client fiefdom in 40 B.C. Pompey also enlarged Cilicia, which had permanently become a province about 85 B.C. In about 56 B.C. Cyprus was added to Cilicia. Galatia was finally made into a province after the death of King

Amyntas in 25 B.C.; Pisidian *Antioch (Acts 13) and Lystra (Acts 14) were among the Roman colonies established there soon after. Cappadocia was annexed in A.D. 17 and on strategic grounds was joined to Galatia as a single province in A.D. 54. Lycia, a federation of cities, remained autonomous until it was annexed and joined to Pamphilia in A.D. 43. Commagene, whose king had been recognized by Rome since Pompey's day, was annexed in A.D. 18; in succeeding decades its hereditary rulers were repeatedly deposed and restored by Rome. Eventually Vespasian added Commagene and Armenia Minor to the province of Syria, giving Rome a unified border along the upper Euphrates.

1.3. Syria and Palestine. Rome had had dealings with the faltering Seleucid dynasty for more than a century before Pompey ended its history by his annexing of Syria in 64 B.C. The new province included parts of Palestine taken from the *Hasmoneans, the Jewish dynasts whose continual bickering had weakened their realm since their first contacts with Rome in the mid-second century. The Roman civil wars and the incursions of the Parthians deprived the area of much of its prosperity and peace until Augustus's accession. From 27 B.C. on, the governorship of Syria was entrusted to a senator of consular rank who was appointed by the emperor (*see* Roman Administration; Roman Governors of Palestine). He was the most important Roman official in the East and was based in Syrian *Antioch, the political and cultural capital of the Roman Middle East (as well as an early Christian center; see Acts 11:19-30). The province of Syria was slowly extended at the expense of small kingdoms and tetrarchies so that by Vespasian's day the middle Euphrates became an effective and stable border with Parthia.

When possible, Rome used client states in the area of Palestine as elsewhere. By 43 B.C., Antipater had become the effective ruler of the former Hasmonean realm. Marc Antony made Antipater's son, Herod, king of *Judea, and Octavian later confirmed and augmented his realm. Upon Herod's death in 4 B.C., his son Archelaus became ethnarch of Judea, Samaria and Iturea (Mt 2:22). Two other local dynasts, Philip (d. A.D. 33) and Antipas (deposed A.D. 39), were given tetrarchies in Iturea and Galilee respectively (Lk 3:1; *see* Herods). Arabia Petraia (Nabatea) and Emesa remained independent kingdoms for another century. Archelaus was deposed in A.D. 6, and Judea was made into an equestrian province governed by a prefect. From A.D. 41 to 44 Judea and the tetrarchies were reunited under Agrippa I, but at his death they reverted to a province. The Jewish revolt of A.D. 66 ended in the destruction of the *temple in A.D. 70 but effected no weakening of Roman control (*see* Jewish Wars with Rome). Meanwhile, Agrippa II had been given Chalchis to rule, and later small areas of Galilee were added by Claudius and Nero. At his death in the 90s these areas were reattached to Judea.

1.4. Armenia and Parthia. Tigranes of Armenia had submitted to Pompey in 66 B.C. and been allowed to keep his kingdom as a friend and ally of Rome. His successor Artavasdes abandoned Antony during the latter's invasion of Parthia in 36 B.C., and two years later Antony overran Armenia and deposed the king. A coup d'état took place soon after, and most Roman citizens were massacred. Rather than intervene directly, Augustus decided to support a rival claimant and eventually sent Tiberius to crown him (20 B.C.). Rome crowned new kings again in 1 B.C. and A.D. 18. Both by its Armenian policy and by the strengthening of the province of Syria, Rome sought to secure this wealthy province against its most powerful eastern neighbor, Parthia, which had a long-standing interest in the region. Crassus had led a Roman invasion during a dispute over the throne in 53 B.C. but was himself killed along with much of his army. Parthia in turn interfered repeatedly in Armenia from A.D. 35 on. More stable relations were finally brokered in A.D. 65 when the Parthian claimant to the throne of Armenia agreed to be crowned in Rome, thus beginning a period of more peaceful coexistence in the region that would last through the end of the first century A.D.

1.5. Egypt and Cyrene. On the northeast coast of Africa the *Ptolemaic kingdom crumbled from within during the second and first centuries B.C., creating a vacuum that Rome would eventually fill. Cyrenaica was willed to Rome in 96 B.C., but it was not organized and administered as a province until between 75 and 67 B.C. It was made a joint province with Crete in 27 B.C. Egypt became a "friend and ally" in 59 B.C. but was formally annexed by Octavian in 30 B.C. It had a unique status as a personal holding of the emperor, who governed through an equestrian prefect. Soon the province was extended southward to near the second cataract of the Nile, and, after some skirmishing, Rome accepted the kingdom of Meroe (the Ethiopia of Acts 8:27) under Roman protection.

2. Motivation for Roman Expansion.

The reason behind Roman expansion in the East has been heatedly debated in recent decades. W. V. Harris has argued that aggression had become a way of life during the republic and that warfare and its resultant glory and booty had become a psychological, social and economic necessity in Roman culture. Roman expansion in the East was due to the need for new triumphs to win, new economies to exploit and new captives to bolster its *slave economy. E. S. Gruen, building on the arguments of T. Frank, has argued that Rome expanded eastward almost against its will and eventually was forced to fill the vacuum of power. As he sees it, Rome almost never took the initiative in the East, constructed no Eastern policy and avoided making commitments wherever and whenever possible, often declining opportunities to form new provinces.

Both of these viewpoints have contributed important truths to the discussion. Rome in the later republican period truly was a nation built on war. It needed constant military opportunity for its citizen army with its aristocratic leadership. Throughout the last two centuries of the republic, there was an increasing demand for both slaves and booty. Both of these spoils of war fed the generals and soldiery as much as the state treasury. The chaotic first century B.C. shows us an Italy in which extremely wealthy generals, by means of military prowess but even more by the spoils of war, kept their troops loyal to themselves rather than to the state (*see* Roman Military). The East was an important area of operations in this evolving system. And a senatorial comment recorded by Livy indicates that when a province's tax receipts were eaten up by local military expenditures, the situation was viewed as unacceptable (Livy *Hist.* 23.48.7). A profit was expected.

At the same time, for most of this period Rome had more than enough military opportunities in the West. Even after the protracted engagements with Carthage, the ongoing operations in Spain, Gaul and North Africa left it few extended periods for systematic exploitation of the East. When it did commit itself there, it was usually for a limited time. In doing so it gained booty and exacted monetary payments from the defeated. Its citizens also established economic outposts from which to exploit the opportunities the East provided. But Rome usually viewed long-term commitments as counterproductive to its economic and political interests; better to stabilize the balance of power with occasional incursions to check aggressors and enjoy the fruits of those opportunities than to take over the administration and protection of large areas far from home. Stationing legions far from home would involve serious financial and manpower commitments, and especially the latter were hard to justify while Rome was involved in numerous Western conflicts.

Thus Rome was both militaristic and pragmatic. The Roman system required that generals and legions be kept busy amassing glory and wealth. Yet it had a finite number of experienced troops and good generals. The late republic also showed the dangers of committing too many troops to a talented but ambitious general. In addition, foreign policy had until that time been firmly controlled by the senate, a group of aristocrats who spent most of their lives in Italy and often had their own agendas. Many of its members had military experience, but they met far from the fields of battle and were supplied with limited information on the realities at the front. In such a situation one would not expect that Rome could have developed and maintained a coherent long-term policy about the East. Except when serious loss of Roman life, income or political stability was at stake, decisive action far from home would not be seriously considered. Rome neither jeopardized its own excellent economic status quo by rash annexations of new area nor played Good Samaritan to distant states.

3. Policies in the East.

The complex interstate relationships of the *Hellenistic world were not based on treaties as much as on declarations of *friendship *(philia)* and military mutual-support alliances *(symmachia)*. Gruen has shown how Rome used these same categories in its relationships in the East. Until 168 B.C. it tried to keep the major powers in balance but then began to show favors more to the minor powers. Wherever possible, this took the form of backing local dynasts who could be trusted to keep the peace and not support other powers at the expense of Rome. When disagreements did arise between states, third-party arbitration was the increasingly popular Hellenistic solution. As the second century progressed, Rome often became that third party, and its role was remembered in the many cities that hailed Rome as a *benefactor. Cities or areas could also be freed, left autonomous and without direct administrative control by Rome yet subject in other ways.

Where Roman interests were especially strong or when local dynasts failed to keep the peace, Rome turned to annexation. From Sulla on, a proconsul (a consul whose *imperium* was extended for a further year of service) would be sent to administer the province for Rome. He might have a limited entourage with him, or he might have several legions, depending on the prospects for peace in the region. Under the Augustan settlement, the emperor, through the office of legate, directly ruled areas where troops were garrisoned. In the East Augustus stationed two legions in Galatia, three or four in Syria and three in Egypt. The solid lines representing the external borders of the Roman Empire that we see on our maps were in places rather fluid and "porous," to use F. Millar's expression. Tribal raiders and adjacent dynasties could make incursions into border areas and not always meet with immediate opposition or Roman reaction. Cities and fertile farmland were what provinces were made of, and in the East the frontiers (*limes*) were drawn wherever possible with buffers to assure the peace of urban areas and farms. However, as B. Isaac has shown, areas of constant unrest such as Judea would be garrisoned with an army of occupation, and Roman roads would be constructed to allow the quick movement of supplies and troops to trouble spots. Troops were deployed in such areas to keep the peace rather than to repel invaders.

4. Influence on Life.

In many areas of the East there was little outward change when Rome took over. There was little in the way of a Roman bureaucracy that descended on the new provinces and imposed new systems. Rome in general left the people to live, work and worship as they had previously. In most provinces a few Roman colonies would be founded upon which the legionary and auxiliary veterans would be settled. Such a colony could serve as an army reserve unit if needed and also brought some additional Roman culture into the region. Outside the colonies and the handful of cities in which legions and auxiliary units were stationed, the Roman military was not visible. Dynasts would have their own troops and might be granted some auxiliary troops to keep order.

*Taxation was where the Roman presence would be most noticeably felt, including a tax on expected harvests, a poll tax, a tax on cattle grazing on public land, as well as harbor and border excises. In addition there were the irregular burdens of billeting Roman officials and troops, and at times providing board, entertainment and transport for them (Mt 5:41). In Asia, the right to collect taxes was auctioned off to groups of Roman businessmen, the hated *publicani.* In other areas, previous methods of collection were continued, but later the proconsul or legate usually took over the responsibility for the collection. These officials, however, would expect the taxes to be gathered by the cities and other administrative districts themselves, and the locals who served as collectors were often termed *publicani* (the *telōnai* of the Gospels) and considered cheats. Although unscrupulous governors and *publicani* were common, especially under the republic, the general prosperity of most provinces would indicate that Rome's tax burden, while not insignificant, was probably not much worse than that exacted by the previous Hellenistic and local dynasts.

In general the East became increasingly Hellenized rather than Romanized during the late republic and early empire. Roman citizenship was granted to select natives in the East (e.g., Paul of Tarsus), but during our period few Eastern provincials received advancement to the Roman aristocracy as knights or senators, and most of those were from the province of Asia. While Latin became an official political language, local languages continued to flourish and Greek remained the cultural and economic *lingua franca* of the eastern empire. Only in the colonies do we find many inscriptions in Latin. Local and Hellenistic cults, festivals and entertainments were to be found side by side. A few Roman elements were added, such as gladitorial contests and chariot races (*see* Arenas), the cult of Roma and the imperial cults (which began in the East, modeled on Hellenistic *ruler cults, and spread back to Italy). At *Jerusalem, Herod had inaugurated a daily *sacrifice in the temple for the emperor's well-being. Despite such indications, however, Rome never matched the influence that the language and culture of Greece had on the East.

5. Attitudes Toward Rome.

Most of the sentiments of Easterners toward Rome that have come down to us have done so through Roman or at least pro-Roman filters. After considering the natural traits of the Romans, the Greek *historian Polybius concluded that Rome was destined to become a superpower and wrote his history to show how it happened. *Josephus led a Galilean army against Rome in the Jewish revolt but wrote his historical works after his surrender, when he had become pro-Roman and even gained Roman *citizenship. These men and their likes prove that not all the intelligentsia could see only horror in Roman domination. There were other Greek writers who were hostile to Rome, however, even though their works have, as a result, come down to us in much more fragmentary form.

The NT writings are themselves an important source for provincial attitudes toward Roman rule, especially since they convey attitudes of the non-elite. The Gospels and Acts reveal an uneasy peace: Jews despise the tax collectors and only grudgingly give to Caesar; some can respect the piety of a centurion (Lk 7:1-5; Acts 10:1-2), yet many eagerly await a new, independent Jewish state (Acts 1:6); life continues rather peaceably, but provocation by Rome (Lk 13:1) or by Jewish nationalists (the *sicarii* of Acts 21:38) is never far away, and it is thought plausible that the next confrontation might cause Rome to "take away our temple and our nationhood" (Jn 11:48).

Paul's life and letters sketch a picture of life in the bustling provinces of Galatia, Asia, Macedonia and Achaia, where the Christian message causes strong reactions among the Jewish *Diaspora and among Gentiles whose livelihood seems threatened by it (Acts 19:25-41). The Roman authorities are portrayed as mostly impartial and fairly competent, although Roman citizens regularly receive preferential treatment not afforded the average provincial (Acts 16:37-40; 22:25-29). Paul is writing to Christians in Rome when he argues that if one lives an upright life and prays for and obeys the government, one need fear nothing from it (Rom 13:1-4).

James discusses economic inequalities and social unrest yet never places the blame at the door of Rome. First Peter specifically commands obedience to the authority of human government and the emperor (1 Pet 2:13) yet invokes a mass of extremely negative connotations by referring to Rome as Babylon (1 Pet 5:13). All in all, the testimony is what we might expect—undercurrents of nationalistic tensions and economic hardships within the Jewish community are mixed with accounts of prosperous civic life in other Eastern provinces. First-century provincials saw Rome to various degrees as a master with whom one could live or as a satanic oppressor. The NT writers, however, saw spiritual oppression manifested by sin as the universal human predicament, and the Christian message was one of spiritual liberation leading to an emancipation of life in the present and in the age to come. Both the positive and negative sides of Rome's lordship were seen as only secondary elements.

The Jewish revolt was perhaps the only Eastern revolt against direct Roman rule that could match the scale and intensity of the revolt of Rome's own Italian allies (the Social War of 91-89 B.C.) and the several slave revolts in Sicily and Campania. A Pontic or Parthian king invading Roman land would not always find the local non-Roman populace awaiting his arrival with open gates. Roman rule was in many cases apparently viewed as no worse than that of other outsiders. After the late Hellenistic period, which had been one extended political melee in Greece, Asia Minor and the Near East, the stability that the Roman Empire brought was probably appreciated by many. The basic truth behind the **Pax Romana* made it into effective propaganda. Whenever Rome's local representatives were not too overbearing or insensitive to local culture and when the harvests and economy were good (and these seem to have been true over wide areas during the first century A.D.), many locals probably brought sacrifices to the cult of Roma without pressure and with little duplicity.

See also GEOGRAPHICAL PERSPECTIVES IN LATE ANTIQUITY; PAX ROMANA; ROMAN ADMINISTRATION; ROMAN EMPIRE; ROMAN GOVERNORS OF PALESTINE; ROMAN LAW AND LEGAL SYSTEM; ROMAN MILITARY; ROMAN POLITICAL SYSTEM; RULER CULT.

BIBLIOGRAPHY. B. Forte, *Rome and the Romans as the Greeks Saw Them* (Papers and Monographs of the American Academy in Rome 24; Rome:

American Academy, 1972); E. S. Gruen, "The Expansion of the Empire under Augustus," *Cambridge Ancient History* (2d ed.; Cambridge: Cambridge University Press, 1996) 10:147-97; idem, *The Hellenistic World and the Coming of Rome* (2 vols.; Berkeley and Los Angeles: University of California Press, 1984); W. V. Harris, *War and Imperialism in Republican Rome, 327-70 B.C.* (Oxford: Oxford University Press, 1979); J. Hind, "Mithridates," *Cambridge Ancient History* (2d ed.; Cambridge: Cambridge University Press, 1994) 9:129-64; B. Isaac, *The Limits of Empire: The Roman Army in the East* (2d ed.; Oxford: Oxford University Press, 1992); R. Kallet-Marx, *Hegemony to Empire: The Development of the Roman Imperium in the East from 148 to 62 B.C.* (Berkeley and Los Angeles: University of California Press, 1995); A. Kuhrt and S. Sherwin White, eds., *Hellenism in the East* (Berkeley and Los Angeles: University of California Press, 1987); D. Kennedy, "Syria," *Cambridge Ancient History* (2d ed.; Cambridge: Cambridge University Press, 1996) 10:703-36; B. Levick, "Greece," *Cambridge Ancient History* (2d ed.; Cambridge: Cambridge University Press, 1996) 10:641-75; D. Magie, *Roman Rule in Asia Minor* (2 vols.; Princeton, NJ: Princeton University Press, 1985 [1950]); F. Millar, *The Roman Near East: 31 B.C.-A.D. 337* (Cambridge, MA: Harvard University Press, 1993); C. Nicolet, *Rome et la conquête du monde méditerranéen: 264-27 avant J.-C.* (2 vols.; Paris: Presses Universitaires de France, 1977-78); R. K. Sherk, *Roman Documents from the Greek East* (Baltimore: Johns Hopkins University Press, 1969); idem, *Translated Documents of Greece and Rome,* 4: *Rome and the Greek East to the Death of Augustus* (Cambridge: Cambridge University Press, 1984); A. N. Sherwin-White, "Lucullus, Pompey and the East," *Cambridge Ancient History* (2d ed.; Cambridge: Cambridge University Press, 1994) 9:229-73; idem, *Roman Foreign Policy in the East* (London: Duckworth, 1984); F. W. Walbank, "Polybius and Rome's Eastern Policy," *JRS* 53 (1963) 1-13. G. L. Thompson

ROMAN EMPERORS

During the advent of Christianity, *Rome was experiencing a tumultuous revolution in its constitution from republican order to the rule of autocracy. The political environment of Jesus and the NT writers was far from consistent and reflects many transitions in power and the general fluidity of Roman policy and society.

1. The Beginning of Empire
2. Transitions in Power
3. Religion and Power

1. The Beginning of Empire.

1.1. Gaius Julius Caesar (100-44 B.C.). The social and civil wars of the early first century gave rise to Julius Caesar, the son of an unnoted patrician family (Suetonius *Caesar;* Dio Cassius *Hist.* 36—44). When Caesar's attempts to build his reputation through the courts were overshadowed by *Cicero, he adopted a populist approach. As aedile (65 B.C.) he funded extrava-gant games (*see* Circuses and Games), but this expense along with that of the intense campaigning for the offices of the pontifex maximus (63 B.C.) and the praetor (62 B.C.) left him in debt to Crassus. When the senate attempted to block Caesar's bid for the consulship (60 B.C.), he formed a coalition with *Pompey and Crassus (the first triumvirate), which not only secured the consulship (59 B.C.) but also dominated politics for the next decade. Caesar spent these years in his proconsular provinces of Cisalpine and Transalpine Gaul and Illyricum. He quieted all uprisings and subjugated the entirety, which won him great wealth and a reputation as a general beyond equal (Caesar *B. Gall.*).

The triumvirate disintegrated. Crassus was killed in his campaign against the Parthians (53 B.C.), and Pompey began favoring the conservative optimates. On January 1, 49 B.C., the senate ordered Caesar to relinquish his province before standing again for the consulship. Caesar marched on Rome. The following year he defeated Pompey at Pharsalus and became dictator (Caesar *B. Civ.*).

Caesar's dictatorship (48-44 B.C.) restored stability to Rome, which was ravaged by years of civil war. Caesar disbanded his bodyguard and implemented a policy of clemency: he pardoned many opponents and appointed some to office. He eased the problem of personal debt that had impoverished many citizens. Still, although the dictator was part of a revolution against the oligarchic control of the nobles, he was not disposed to restore the powers of the assembly but commenced an autocracy. For this he was assassinated.

1.2. (Gaius Octavius) Augustus (Caesar, 63 B.C.-A.D. 14). Caesar's murder did not restore the republic, but civil war continued for more than ten years between the Republicans and Caesareans.

Gaius Octavius, the dictator's greatnephew and adopted heir, acted quickly (Suetonius *Augustus;* Dio Cassius *Hist.* 45—56). Bolstered by Caesar's money, armies and political supporters (Caesar was deified in 42 B.C.), Octavius avenged Caesar's murder (Augustus *Res Gest.* 1-3), and when the senate limited his power, he formed a triumvirate with Marcus Antonius and Marcus Lepidus (43 B.C.). Octavius was ambitious to complete the Caesarean revolution, and thus the triumvirate was in constant turmoil. After intrigues with the younger Pompeius, Lepidus was forced into a mostly private life, and Octavius set his coalition against Antonius, whom he defeated at Actium along with Cleopatra (31 B.C.). Octavius was the sole *imperator,* a title ratified by the senate (29 B.C.).

Republican freedom was lost, but there was peace and the opportunity to revitalize the empire's infrastructure. Octavius rebuilt temples and public buildings, revived religion, reorganized the senate and expanded and settled the borders. He claimed to have restored the republic to the people, for which he was honored with the name *Augustus* (27 B.C.). Although he did resign the consulate (23 B.C.), he never relinquished tribunician power (Augustus *Res Gest.* 34-35). The poets Virgil, Horace and Varius extolled the peace, but Ovid was exiled. Liberty had a new definition.

2. Transitions in Power.

2.1. The Julio-Claudian Dynasty.

2.1.1. (Tiberius) Claudius Nero (42 B.C.-A.D. 37). Tiberius, the Caesar during the time of Jesus, was the son of Tiberius Claudius Nero and Livia. He enjoyed a distinguished military career particularly in the German campaigns but never was the favorite of Augustus, who seemed intent on leaving the *imperium* to one of his grandsons. Livia, determined to see her son at the head of the empire, arranged that Tiberius divorce Vipsania, the mother of his only son Drusus, and marry Julia, Augustus's daughter. The marriage was not happy (Augustus exiled Julia for *adultery), but Tiberius had become part of the Augustan family (A.D. 4), and when both of his grandsons died, Augustus officially adopted him (Tacitus *Ann.* 1.1-5). When Augustus died (A.D. 14), although Tiberius immediately began conducting imperial affairs, there was a month-long debate in the senate before he was proclaimed emperor. Tiberius never recovered from this insult and was haunted by his fear of revolutionary plots. He eventually abandoned Rome and ruled his last ten years from the isolation of Capri (Suetonius *Tiberius* 39-72). Even there Tiberius maintained his hold on Rome and managed without returning to put down Sejanus's revolt (Tacitus *Ann.* 4.1—6.50). He commanded enough loyalty or fear to stay at the head of the unwieldy large empire.

2.1.2. (Gaius) Caligula (Julius Caesar Germanicus, A.D. 12-41). Rome, weary of the reclusive Tiberius, welcomed the accession of Gaius Caligula (A.D. 37), son of the popular Nero Claudius Germanicus (15 B.C.- A.D. 19) and Agrippina. Caligula promised an open policy. In his first year he recalled exiles, allowed censored writings to be published, made public the imperial budget and allowed more popular control of the magistracies (Suetonius *Caligula* 13-21; Dio Cassius *Hist.* 59.6-7). His promises of constitutional reform appeared genuine but collapsed later that same year, when a serious illness was followed by the deaths of several relatives and close advisers. Caligula quickly transformed the principate into kingship. With capricious cruelty, he eliminated all competitors. His extravagance depleted the vast imperial wealth, which he replenished by plundering his own leading citizens (Suetonius *Caligula* 34-42; Dio Cassius *Hist.* 59.9-10). He reveled in deification and revived in the provinces the language and practices of the Hellenistic *ruler cults to such an extent that the Jews of the empire were victimized politically and physically (Josephus *Ant.* 18.8.1-9 §§257-309; Philo *Leg. Gai.* 261-337). After only three years, Caligula was so hated that he was assassinated by members of his own guard (January A.D. 41).

2.1.3. Tiberius Claudius (Nero Germanicus, 10 B.C.-A.D. 54). Claudius succeeded his nephew Gaius Caligula by accident rather than achievement. Claudius, cowering in the palace and expecting the same fate as Gaius, was discovered by members of the praetorian guard, who spirited him to their camp and saluted him as emperor (Suetonius *Claudius* 10). Claudius had little political experience (Suetonius *Claudius* 4-7; Dio Cassius *Hist.* 59.6-7; Tacitus *Ann.* 1.54), since the imperial family considered his sickliness and reputation as a dullard a liability (exaggerated by the sources: Suetonius *Claudius* 2; Dio Cassius *Hist.* 60.2; Seneca *Apocol.* 6).

As emperor he extended the Augustan program: maintain an appearance of traditional constitutionalism but continue to centralize power under the leading citizen. Claudius stabilized imperial control by creating an executive staff, which effectively ended any senatorial power. This dichotomy of traditionalism combined with aggressive imperialism is clearly evident in his policy toward the Jews. Immediately after his accession (A.D. 41), which was supported by Agrippa (Josephus *Ant.* 19.4.2 §§236-45), Claudius reaffirmed that the *Alexandrian Jews were exempt from the imperial cult as under Augustus, but in the same edict he warned the Jews not to expand their privileges (P. Lond. 1912 [Smallwood, 370]; Josephus *Ant.* 19.5.2-3 §§279-91). Claudius consistently opposed *proselytizing, and when disturbances continued in the Roman Jewish community, he exiled those responsible (Suetonius *Claudius* 25.4: *Iudaeos impulsore Chresto assidue tumultantis Roma expulit,* "he expelled the Jews from Rome because they were in constant uproar at the instigation of Chrestus"; Acts 18:2) and banned meetings (Dio Cassius *Hist.* 60.6.6).

2.1.4. Nero (Claudius Caesar, A.D. 37-68). Nero's atrocities are among the most remembered acts of the Caesars and are largely responsible for Rome's image as an intolerable despot (Tacitus *Ann.* 15.37; Suetonius *Nero* 20-49; Dio Cassius *Hist.* 62.15). There was, however, no opposition to his proclamation as emperor (A.D. 54), as the transition to power was well prepared by his mother, the younger Agrippina, and Burrus, the commander of the praetorian guard (Suetonius *Nero* 6-7). At first, his management of the empire was exemplary: treasury administration was reformed, grain importation and distribution improved, there was tax relief, and able governors were appointed (Tacitus *Ann.* 13.50-52; Suetonius *Nero* 10-19).

Then, Nero, who had always nursed his vices, murdered his interfering mother (A.D. 59), and when Burrus died and his influential adviser *Seneca retired (A.D. 62), the worst of the autocrat emerged. Nero ignored the provinces and armies, while he spent imperial wealth on his love for games and the *theater (Tacitus *Ann.* 14.16; 15.2-5; Suetonius *Nero* 52; Josephus *J.W.* 2.13.1 §§250-51). Rome burned (A.D. 64), and although Nero blamed the Christians (Tacitus *Ann.* 15.38-44; Suetonius *Nero* 16), the people suspected Nero (Pliny *Nat. Hist.* 17.1.5; Suetonius *Nero* 38; Dio Cassius *Hist.* 62.6). Britain (A.D. 60), Judea (A.D. 66; *see* Jewish Wars with Rome) and finally his own armies revolted. The disgraced emperor committed suicide (A.D. 68), and since he had massacred all the members of the Julio-Claudian family and much of the nobility, the competition to replace him plunged the empire back into civil war.

2.2. The Flavian Dynasty.

2.2.1. (Titus Flavius) Vespasianus (A.D. 9-79). The year A.D. 69 witnessed four emperors: Otho ousted and murdered Galba, but then facing certain defeat by Vitellius, commander of the German legions, he committed suicide. Vitellius entered Rome that June, but by July 1 the Alexandrian legions hailed Vespasian, and the Judean legions quickly followed. Before Vespasian reached Italy his allied forces had overthrown and assassinated the emperor (Tacitus *Hist.* 2—4). Vespasian had survived well the reigns of Caligula and Claudius but was threatened by Nero after he fell asleep at one of the emperor's recitals. Soon afterward, however, Nero commissioned him to end the Judean revolt (A.D. 67), which was no favor given the rebellious history of the region and the increasing messianic fervor (Suetonius *Vespasian* 4). Vespasian restored Roman rule, but *Jerusalem and the other hill fortresses fell later to his son Titus (A.D. 70; Suetonius *Vespasian* 4-5; Dio Cassius *Hist.* 65.4-7; Josephus *J.W.* 5.6-13 §§248-572). Vespasian's attention turned to the restoration of the empire: he regained public confidence by his simple and tolerant manner (Suetonius *Vespasian* 11-12, 14, 22-23; Dio Cassius *Hist.* 8—9, 11; Josephus *Ant.* 12.3.1 §§119-24), secured the borders and brought economic stability by new taxes and frugal spending policy (Suetonius *Vespasian* 16-17; Dio Cassisus *Hist.* 65.2, 8). To his credit, he rebuilt the physical and political infrastructure of Rome (Suetonius *Vespasian* 9-10, 17-19; Dio Cassius *Hist.* 65.10).

2.2.2. Titus (Flavius Vespasianus, A.D. 39-81). Vespasian secured dynastic succession for his sons, first Titus and then Domitian, by making them partners in government (Suetonius *Titus* 6). Titus distinguished himself as a general, serving in Germany, Britain and most notably in the Judean campaign. After Vespasian returned to Rome, Titus captured Jerusalem, after he twice attempted to negotiate a settlement, and ended the Jewish revolt (A.D. 70). The tax previously paid by the Jews to their *temple in Jerusalem, now in ruins, was redirected to that of Jupiter

Capitolinus in Rome (the *fiscus Iudaicus*). Upon his return from the east, Titus shared a triumph (*see* Roman Triumph) with his father, commemorated by the Arch of Titus built under Domitian (A.D. 81), and assumed many imperial duties, including seven co-consulates (Suetonius *Titus* 4-5; Dio Cassius *Hist.* 65.4-7). His passionate affair with Berenice, the sister of Herod Agrippa, was notorious (Suetonius *Titus* 7; Dio Cassius *Hist.* 66.19). As the praetorian commander, he was feared for the swift execution of his father's critics. As emperor (A.D. 79-81), however, he was generous, murdered none and banished all informers (Suetonius *Titus* 8-9; Dio Cassius *Hist.* 66.18-19). His relief efforts for the destruction caused by the eruption of Vesuvius (A.D. 79) and another fire in Rome (A.D. 80) contrasted sharply to Nero's self-indulgence (Dio Cassius *Hist.* 66.21-24). When he died of fever, all of Rome mourned.

2.2.3. (Titus Flavius) Domitianus (A.D. 51-96). After Flavian forces secured Rome (December A.D. 69), Domitian governed until the return of his father the following year (September). Then, divested of all responsibilities, he waited for his brother to relinquish the empire (Suetonius *Domitian* 1-3; Tacitus *Hist.* 4.59-86; Dio Cassius *Hist.* 66.2-9; Josephus *J.W.* 4.11.4 §§645-49). Domitian coveted imperial power, and when Titus died (A.D. 81), he quickly reversed the open policy and returned to the autocracy of the earlier emperors. He ignored the senate and often held court outside Rome at his villa, known as the Alban fortress (Tacitus *Agric.* 45; Juvenal *Sat.* 4.145) and now the papal retreat of Castel Gandolfo. Domitian pursued a conservative policy (Suetonius *Domitian* 9).

In religion, Domitian punished Vestals for immorality and especially honored Minerva, while he relished the imperial cult and filled Rome with his statues (Suetonius *Domitian* 13; Dio Cassius *Hist.* 67.4; 8.1). His censorship heightened the hypocrisy of his own immorality (Suetonius *Domitian* 7-8). As for finances, he revalued currency to its Augustan level, which was too restrictive given imperial expenses (Suetonius *Domitian* 7, 12; Dio Cassius *Hist.* 67.4.5): an extensive building program, public banquets and games and military pay increases. Financial stress resulted in an aggressive tax policy, which included expanding the *fiscus Iudaicus* (Suetonius *Domitian* 12.2; Dio Cassius *Hist.* 65.7.2; Josephus *J.W.* 7.6.6 §218). His cruelty only increased sedition, which worsened his fear of supposed rivals (Pliny *Panegyr.* 49), such as Flavius Clemens, charged with atheism, a convenient allegation for many murders (Suetonius *Domitian* 15.1; Dio Cassius *Hist.* 67.14.1-3). Domitian was killed by his own court (A.D. 96).

2.3. Three Good Emperors.

2.3.1. (Marcus Cocceius) Nerva (A.D. 30-98). The senate, acting quickly, named as emperor one of its own (A.D. 96, Tacitus *Ann.* 15.72; Pliny *Ep.* 4.22.4-7). Nerva ended the terror of Domitian and restored a more constitutional government. He forbade all charges of treason, including those against the Jewish way of life, and restricted the *fiscus Iudaicus* to practicing Jews. Statues of Domitian were torn down, exiles recalled and property returned (Dio Cassius *Hist.* 68.1). Further, Nerva envisioned an imperial *alimenta,* which would allow small farmers to secure loans at low interest, used in turn to fund grants for poor children. The senate had its champion (Dio Cassius *Hist.* 68.2). The army, however, threatened mutiny (Pliny *Ep.* 9.13.11; Dio Cassius *Hist.* 68.3), and Nerva, lacking the military experience that could give him credibility with troops loyal to the Flavians, granted their demands to punish Domitian's assassins. To prevent a coup, he ignored the tradition of dynastic succession and adopted a Spanish provincial, Trajan, a distinguished soldier and the governor of Upper Germany. In his reign of only sixteen months, Nerva set a tone of reconciliation that dominated the next century.

2.3.2. (Marcus Ulpius) Traianus (A.D. 53-117). The sources universally acclaim the moderate reign (A.D. 98-117) and the unrivaled success of Trajan, whom the senate proclaimed *optimus princeps* for his victories in Armenia (A.D. 114). Although the formulaic and hyperbolic manner of the panegyrists obscures Trajan's private life, his public policy demonstrates a renewed imperialism. Trajan was chosen emperor because of political expediency and his ability, not dynastic succession, and his Spanish origin signaled an equilibrium between Italy and the provinces. Such balance opened trade, increased urbanization and created an economic boon for the empire. The renewed economy, strengthened further by the plunder of war, funded an extensive building program, a lasting memorial to Trajan: a forum, library, basilica, baths, harbor at Ostia and countless roads and bridges.

Trajan was master of the army, which he expanded and led on two major campaigns, the first against Dacia (A.D. 101-106) and later Parthia (A.D. 114), an expedition that spread to Mesopotamia and advanced to the Persian Gulf (A.D. 116-117). Before Trajan even returned from the East, violent revolts in Parthia and the Diaspora Jewish communities throughout Cyrenaica, Egypt, Cyprus and Mesopotamia (A.D. 115-117; Dio Cassius *Hist.* 68.32; Orosius *Hist.* 7.12.6-7; Eus. *Chron.* 2.164) once again destabilized the entire region. Trajan withdrew, but he died before he could return to Rome.

Trajan's response to Pliny on the prosecution of Christians (Pliny *Ep.* 96, 97), the oldest existing official document on the subject, exemplifies his moderate approach. Trajan avoided establishing any universal rule against Christianity but presumed a personal confession was punishable by death. His concern was with the manner of investigation. Charges had to be brought by individuals; there could be no governmental searches. Further, he directed Pliny to ignore the problem of past transgressions by confining questions to the defendant's present status. Those charged need not curse Christ but only sacrifice to the gods to prove their innocence.

2.3.3. (Publius Aelius) Hadrianus (A.D. 76-138). Hadrian quieted the empire and governed it well for more than thirty years (A.D. 117-138): his fiscal policy was sound; he was renowned for his building program (the temple of Venus and Roma, the temple of Neptune, the reconstruction of the Pantheon, Castel Sant' Angelo); he secured the borders, toured the provinces more extensively than any other emperor and extended the rights of Roman *citizenship (Dio Cassius *Hist.* 69.1-9). Hadrian immediately abandoned Trajan's expansionist policy (Dio Cassius *Hist.* 69.5; Pausanius *Descr.* 1.5.5; Spartianus *SHA Hadr.* 10) and settled the East by giving up the provinces of Armenia, Mesopotamia and Assyria. He conceded the lower part of Moesia beyond the Danube and continued to pull back to the Flavian boundaries, which he strengthened with long palisades, fortified walls and garrisons. The empire had reached its zenith.

When Hadrian gave up the trans-Euphrates provinces and replaced the harsh *governor of Palestine, Lusius Quietus, with his favorite Q. Marcius Turbo, he fired the Jewish messianic fervor and its hope for liberation, which just recently had caused vast destruction (A.D. 115-117; Eusebius *Hist. Eccl.* 4.2-3). Hadrian's policy more than disappointed, it antagonized (Dio Cassius *Hist.* 69.12; *Gen. Rab.* 64). He finished the temple of Antiochus Epiphanes in Athens and on his tour through Palestinian regions erected a monument over the burial mound of Pompey the Great, who himself had desecrated the temple (63 B.C.). The Jews began to militarize under the leadership of another messiah, Bar Kokhba (Dio Cassius *Hist.* 69.12-13; Eusebius *Hist. Eccl.* 4.6.1-4; *Lam. Rab.* 2; *see* Simon ben Kosiba). Hadrian issued a series of decrees aimed at limiting the practice and growth of Judaism, which included a proscription against circumcision. Guerrilla attacks against Roman forces turned to open revolt, which lasted almost four years (A.D. 131-135). Not only was the loss of life on both sides catastrophic, but also large numbers of the surviving Jews were sold into *slavery. Most settlements in Judea were destroyed, and Hadrian built a new Roman town, Aelia Capitolina, with its temple to Jupiter on the site that had been *Jerusalem (Dio Cassius *Hist.* 69.14-15).

3. Religion and Power.

3.1. The Roman Empire and the Kingdom of Israel. The Romans, particularly in the republic and early years of the empire, had treated Judaism with tolerance and even respect, if only for its antiquity. Jews were exempted from obeisance to the gods, given allowances for *sabbath observances and later excused from worshiping the emperor. Conflict, however, was inevitable, since neither the Romans nor Jews separated their religion from the existence and welfare of the state. The power of one's god(s) was evidenced in the strength of the nation. For the Jews this included control over the land promised to them in the Abrahamic covenant (Gen 12:1-7).

The NT environment is one of increasing tension between Rome and Judaism, which is reflected in the Jewish leaders' hostility to Jesus (Jn 11:47-50; Mt 24:1-2; 25:59-61). Pontius Pilate, appointed by Sejanus under Tiberius, circulated *coins and displayed standards with the image of the emperor. Caligula determined that the Jews would worship his image and was only barely dissuaded by Agrippa (Josephus *Ant.* 18.8.7-8 §§289-304). When the Jews revolted in the time of Nero (66; Josephus *J.W.* 2.16.4 §§345-401), the ultimate price was paid in the sack of Jerusalem and the destruction of the temple (A.D. 70). Still, a messianic hope survived and led the Diaspora Jews to revolt (A.D. 115-117) and later pushed

Hadrian to a final solution, when in the aftermath of the Bar Kokhba revolt he attempted the Romanization of Jerusalem (A.D. 135).

*3.2. **The Roman Empire and the Kingdom of Heaven.*** In contrast to Judaism, the ascent of Christianity was aided by a certain compatibility to the Roman concept of empire. Roman *ingenium* (spirit), never monolithic but a mixture of diverse influences, Etruscan, native Italic and Greek, harshly criticized Judaism for its exclusivity and sense of superiority (Cicero *Flac.* 66-69; Horace *Sat.* 1.4.141-43; Juvenal *Sat.* 14; Tacitus *Hist.* 5.5). It was dangerous to defy Rome's authority, but Rome did not strip the provinces of their own identity. Christianity, nurtured by its Caesarean-styled clemency (Mk 9:40; Suetonius *Caesar* 75.3-6) and mission to the Gentiles (Mt 8:11-13; Acts 15:1-29; Eph 3:1-10), was likewise inclusive and quickly began to bridge territorial and cultural boundaries.

This is not to dismiss any conflict. It was not until the Neronian *persecution that Rome made any distinction between the Christians and Jews, and it is likely that both suffered together under Domitian's religious conservatism (Suetonius *Domitian* 15.1; Dio Cassius *Hist.* 67.14.1-3). Christians, especially in the eastern provinces (*see* Roman East), were subjected to intense local persecutions often provoked by their proselytizing, and even though emperors restricted state-sponsored investigations, they still considered Christianity a divisive superstition deserving capital punishment (Trajan [Pliny *Ep.* 96, 97]; Hadrian [Justin Martyr *Apol. I* 68.6-10; Eusebius *Hist. Eccl.* 4.9.1-3]). Within the confrontational context of the earthbound kingdoms of Rome and Judea, the Christian writers advanced the superiority of a spiritual kingdom not ruled by Caesars (Lk 20:19-26; Jn 18:35-36; 19:10-11; Eph 6:12) or the priestly hierarchy (1 Pet 2:5; Rev 5:9-10). Christians could respect these rulers as representatives of a lesser power, while they regarded them as subservient to the will of their God (Rom 13:1-7; 1 Tim 2:1-2; 1 Pet 2:13-14). Caesar Augustus took a census and consecrated it with a *lustrum,* practices that had been neglected during the republic; Mary and Joseph traveled to Bethlehem, where, in accordance with Scripture, the promised Messiah was born.

See also PAX ROMANA; ROMAN ADMINISTRATION; ROMAN EMPIRE; ROMAN GOVERNORS OF PALESTINE; ROMAN LAW AND LEGAL SYSTEM; ROMAN MILITARY; ROMAN POLITICAL SYSTEM; ROME; RULER CULT.

BIBLIOGRAPHY. T. D. Barnes, *Early Christianity and the Roman Empire* (London: Variorum Reprints, 1984); S. Benko, "Pagan Criticism of Christianity During the First Two Centuries A.D.," *ANRW* 2.23.2 (1980) 1054-1118; idem, *Pagan Rome and the Early Christians* (Bloomington: Indiana University Press, 1984); E. J. Bickerman, "Trajan, Hadrian and the Christians," in *Studies in Jewish and Christian History* (AGJU 9.3; Leiden: E. J. Brill, 1986) 152-71; G. W. Bowersock, *Martyrdom and Rome* (Cambridge: Cambridge University Press, 1995); P. Brown, *Power and Persuasion in Late Antiquity: Toward a Christian Empire* (Madison: University of Wisconsin Press, 1992); D. R. Edwards, *Religion and Power: Pagans, Jews and Christians in the Greek East* (Oxford: Oxford University Press, 1996); D. C. Feeney, *The Gods in Epic: Poets and Critics of the Classical Tradition* (Oxford: Oxford University Press, 1991); A. Fuks, "Aspects of the Jewish Revolt in A.D. 115-117," in *History of the Jews in the Second Century of the Common Era,* ed. J. Neusner and W. S. Green (Origins of Judaism 7; New York: Garland, 1990) 58-64; A. Garzetti, *From Tiberius to the Antonines: A History of the Roman Empire A.D. 14-192* (London: Methuen, 1974); M. Goodman, "The First Jewish Revolt: Social Conflict and the Problem of Debt," *JJS* 33 (1982) 417-27; P. Keresztes, *Imperial Rome and the Christians from Herod the Great to About 200 A.D.* (Lanham, MD: University Press of America, 1989); H. J. Leon, *The Jews of Ancient Rome* (Philadelphia: Jewish Publication Society of America, 1960); H. Mantel, "The Causes of the Bar Kokba Revolt," in *History of the Jews in the Second Century of the Common Era,* ed. J. Neusner and W. S. Green (Origins of Judaism 7; New York: Garland, 1990) 338-80; K. Raaflaub and M. Toher, eds., *Between Republic and Empire: Interpretations of Augustus and His Principate* (Berkeley and Los Angeles: University of California Press, 1990); V. Rudich, *Political Dissidence Under Nero: The Price of Dissimulation* (New York: Routledge, 1993); P. Schäfer, *Judeophobia: Attitudes Toward the Jews in the Ancient World* (Cambridge, MA: Harvard University Press, 1997); E. M. Smallwood, *Documents Illustrating the Principates of Gaius, Claudius and Nero* (London: Cambridge University Press, 1967); M. Sordi, *The Christians and the Roman Empire* (Norman: University of Oklahoma Press, 1986); R. Syme, *The Augustine Aristocracy* (Oxford: Oxford University Press, 1986); B. Wardy, "Jewish Religion in Pagan Literature During the Late Republic and Early Empire," *ANRW* 2.19.1 (1979) 613-35.

T. S. Johnson

ROMAN EMPIRE

*Rome was a city in the west-central coastal area of Italy that rose from a small agricultural settlement in the eighth century B.C. to become a world power dominating the Mediterranean and beyond by the birth of Christ. The Roman Empire dominated the background of the ministry of Jesus and the development of the early church, as attested by everything from the crucifixion of Jesus for treason to the persecutions of early Christians.

1. Archaic or Pre-Republican Rome (753-509 B.C.)
2. The Roman Republic (509-31 B.C.)
3. The Late Roman Republic
4. The Empire (31 B.C.-mid-fifth century A.D.)
5. The Late Empire

1. Archaic or Pre-Republican Rome (753-509 B.C.).

The earliest period of Roman history is only known through the works of historians who lived in the first century B.C. and later—more than five hundred years beyond the founding of Rome. History and legend are not easily separated in these accounts. M. Terentius Varro (first century B.C.) claimed that Romulus founded Rome in 753 B.C. as a fortified settlement on the Palatine Hill. Historians do not have archaeological evidence sufficient to establish the date independently of such literary accounts, but archaeology dates a settlement on the site to the end of the Bronze Age (1000 B.C.).

In any case, Rome was founded on the Tiber River by Latin peoples as a small agricultural village. There was initial conflict with the Sabines, another Latin people, which led to the combining of the towns and villages of these Latin peoples into a capital called Rome. Rome was ruled as a monarchy with elected kings who received advice from a council, the senate (*senatus*), composed of the male heads or elders (*patres*) of prominent clans (*gentes*), and from a civic council, the *comitia curiata,* composed of all the official *citizens of Rome.

The Etruscans, a commercial and industrial people, came to prominence in Rome about 600 B.C. and developed it into a prominent city-state dominating central Italy. The swamps between the hills of Rome were drained to provide suitable foundations for a city of brick and stone. The Etruscans placed a wall around the city, paved its streets and erected public buildings. They also built the institutions of Rome by adapting their legal and religious systems to the needs of the city. Their direct influence ended in 510 B.C. with the expulsion of the Etruscan king, due in part to the unwelcome adoption by the Etruscans of the tyrannical model of kingship from *Greece.

2. The Roman Republic (509-31 B.C.).

The monarchy was ended by an aristocratic coup, and republican Rome was established in 509 B.C. as an oligarchy of patricians. It lasted almost five centuries. The king was replaced by two magistrates called *praetors* (later *consuls*) elected annually. The senate was now more than a consulting body—it was the real power of the government.

The oligarchy was modified in the mid-fourth century B.C., when conflict escalated between the two social classes, the patricians, from whose ranks the consuls were elected and religion controlled, and plebeians (*plebs*). The wealthy plebeians wanted more voice in the government, and the poorer plebeians wanted debt reduction, equitable land distribution and relief from food shortages. The plebeians made moves to secede to form an alternative state. This conflict resulted in new lands being used to form colonies peopled by the plebeians and elimination of debt bondage. Also, the constitution was modified and the plebeian assembly, the *concilium plebis,* was recognized as a legislative body. Eventually influential plebeians were included in the government, even as consuls. This reform process was completed in 287 B.C., when legislation of the *concilium plebis* became binding on the people. The patrician and plebeian elite consolidated their power, dominating the senate and higher offices.

After the fall of the monarchy Rome found itself in conflict with its Latin neighbors. During this time the city-state of Rome began to unify the Italian peninsula and its Latin peoples under its control, using alliances or military might. As territory came under its control, Rome established colonies connected by military roads in order to secure its influence. Each subject community was treated as benefited Rome, some receiving full citizenship and others having their relationship to Rome outlined by treaty. Local aristocrats who proved useful were left in power. All new territories were required to supply soldiers for the Roman army. All of the Italian peninsula south of the Rubicon was united by 270 B.C.

Once the Roman peninsula was united, Rome set its sight on expansion beyond Italy. This included wars with Greece, the three Macedonian wars (214-205, 200-197 and 171-167 B.C.) resulting in Macedonia and Greece becoming Roman provinces. The chief rival of Rome was the Phoenician city of Carthage in North Africa. Within the span of just over a century Rome waged three wars with Carthage, initially for control of Sicily. Together these wars were known as the Punic Wars (264-241, 218-201 and 149-146 B.C.) and ended with the defeat of Carthage and the annexing of its territory as a province of Rome. The defeat of Carthage gave Rome dominion over the eastern Mediterranean (*see* Roman East), including northwest Africa, Spain and southern Gaul (France). Rome governed these subject lands directly through a succession of senatorial proconsuls and propraetors. These administrators were responsible for maintaining order and collecting taxes. Some areas were governed by client kings and aristocrats subject to the senate.

By the middle of the second century Rome had become a cosmopolitan city and the center of culture, trade and industry. Hellenistic influence was evident everywhere in this growth in architecture, the arts and literature, especially in historiography, epic poetry and drama. Along with urbanization Rome had an increasing problem with landless urbanites who began life in agriculture, came to the city and were unemployable in urban trades. They relied upon the public dole and became a powerful source of votes for local politicians. The problem was aggravated by the new emphasis upon absentee landlords holding vast landed estates that created a land distribution problem and mass displacement of small farmers.

3. The Late Roman Republic.

In its last century the republic was destabilized by many factors. There was competition between social classes and their interests, especially at Rome. The wealthy senatorial class and the equestrian class (a privileged class once providing cavalry for the legions of Rome) were trying to retain their privileged status and large estates while the urban poor were seeking land and more public dole. There was provincial unrest due to a lack of a bureaucracy capable of administering an empire (*see* Roman Administration) and autocratic and corrupt provincial *governors. Allies demanded *citizenship and threatened to withdraw from the empire. German tribes in the north and Pontus in the east posed military threats from without the empire. The senate had too little power to effectively deal with these economic and military difficulties.

Three civil wars were waged to resolve these social and political tensions. The Social or Marsian War (91-89 B.C.) was fought to stop Italian peoples from taking arms and leaving the republic because they had not received citizenship. After the war they were awarded citizenship. The other two wars were waged over the control of the government, including Marius against Sulla (80s B.C.) and Caesar against *Pompey (40s B.C.). The *military was reformed from mandatory service that was due from landowning citizens to a volunteer army in which allegiance was to the commander. This reform made the military a vital force for solving political problems in which the commander was involved.

These civil wars marked the transition from the republic to the empire. Julius Caesar's struggles with Pompey had the consequence of adding much territory in the western Mediterranean to the empire and creating political stability. In the end Caesar was named king (*dictator perpetuus*), but his assassination for his monarchial tendencies resulted in a new round of civil wars, this time between Octavian, his adopted son, in league with Marc Antony and others seeking to reestablish the republic. After a parting of the ways, Octavian defeated Antony, his chief rival, and Cleopatra VII, queen of Egypt, at the battle of Actium (31 B.C.). Egypt itself was incorporated as a Roman province. Octavian took the title *princeps* ("first citizen") and became known as Imperator Augustus Caesar. His consolidation of power marks the true beginning of the empire.

When the civil wars were over, all of Italy was united politically, culturally and economically. It was a time of great literary achievement in *rhetoric and *poetry, witnessing the works of *Cicero, Caesar, Virgil and Varro, to name a few. It also witnessed a great shift in the economy from small farm agriculture to large agricultural tracts run by tenant farmers. A business and commercial class arose. Industry was limited largely to supplying agriculture and the military. Finance and investment were well-developed in the republic and centered at Rome.

4. The Empire (31 B.C.-mid-fifth century A.D.). Augustus established the Julio-Claudian emperors. At the death of Nero and the civil war caused in part by his excesses and tyranny, the Julio-Claudian emperors were replaced by the Flavian emperors in A.D. 69. At the end of the first century the Flavians were replaced by emperors who were elected by the senate and were themselves senators. These emperors ruled according to constitutional forms and the help of the senatorial and equestrian orders. However, with few exceptions the power was passed in dynastic succession from emperor to son or adopted son.

Although Augustus was the sole ruler, his government was outwardly similar to that of the republic. He shared power with the senate. He controlled the military, foreign policy and supervision of the government. The senate was given legislative and judicial roles, controlled government administration and was consulted on policy. Augustus and his successors controlled the provinces that had military power through appointment of governors from men of consular or praetorian rank, with the length of term determined by the emperor. The senate controlled the provinces that did not have military power, usually in Asia and Africa, through its appointment of proconsuls or propraetors appointed as governors for one-year terms. Governorships of important imperial or senatorial provinces were staffed by ex-consuls. A governor kept the peace of his province, commanded troops in its borders, applied the law and collected the taxes. Any decision of a governor could be overruled at any time by the emperor, who had *imperium maius* ("superior command"). Much of the administration of the empire was performed by freedmen of the imperial household, in charge of finance, roads, public works and aqueducts. No large-scale bureaucracy was established. This form of government was called the principate and lasted into the third century A.D. (*see* Roman Administration).

The senate created the laws for the emperor and also provided judicial functions, becoming the highest court. Its laws did not have to be ratified by the popular assemblies (*comitia*). Legislation by the popular assemblies became infrequent. Augustus reconfigured a man's career path to the senate. He entered the senate by being elected a *quaester* (finance) around the age of twenty-five, then an *aedile* or tribune (municipal administration) and at about age thirty a *praetor* (judicial). A former praetor could become a governor of a province or a commander of a legion. The most sought-after positions in the government of the empire were the two consulships, or heads of state, that opened up each year to men age forty-two or older. Praetors and consuls had *imperium,* which gave them power to administer laws and command in war in the provinces that they served.

Augustus reformed the system of *taxation. He used the census to create a system of assessment and direct taxation (cf. the tax census decreed by Augustus in Lk 2:1). Tax money and his own resources were used to buy tracts of land for colonization by retiring soldiers and to provide the grain dole to the inhabitants of Rome. This helped solve the problem of land distribution and the plight of the urban poor—two key problems of the late republic. Augustus also instituted a professional army with set terms of service. He maintained loyalty by appointing all the senior commanding officers and limiting legion commanders and governors of military provinces to three-year terms of service.

Augustus used his new military to complete the conquest of Spain. However, for the most part Rome maintained its traditional boundaries. During the first century A.D. the Roman Empire encompassed the entire Mediterranean basin and surrounding territory. It extended as far north as Britain, with the Rhine and Danube Rivers forming the boundary with the Germanic tribes, east with the Euphrates River forming the boundary with the Parthian Empire, south to Egypt and northern Africa and west to Spain. Legions were stationed at the frontier borders of the empire and worked in conjunction with local garrisons to protect the boundaries.

Whereas Rome was the administrative center for the entire empire, *Antioch in Syria served as the administrative center for the eastern portion of the empire. The empire was divided into provinces ruled by governors of senatorial ranking who relied heavily upon local officials for administration and tax collection. Each province had a provincial council composed of aristocrats from key cities. It could appeal directly to the emperor about its needs or abuses of the governor, independent of the governor.

After a century of civil war the populace welcomed the empire. It brought a long-lasting peace and economic prosperity, including urbanization and massive building projects throughout the empire, even to the extent of building entire cities. The capital of Rome was transformed in gleaming marble. Rome is estimated to have had a population of one million people and Antioch in Syria, Carthage and *Alexandria, Egypt, to have had populations of perhaps half that. The population of the empire is estimated to have been between fifty and sixty million. *Travel was slow, but all regions of the empire were accessible. Regional languages continued, with Latin in the west and Greek in the east providing a common language, especially among the upper classes. This confluence of accessibility and common language greatly facilitated the early missionary work of Christianity, as the travel and ministry of Paul attest.

Divisions in society were along economic lines rather than ethnic or nationalistic lines. There was an enormous gap between the upper classes of senators and equestrians and the lower classes of free men, freedmen and *slaves. The one notable exception was the Jews of Judea, with which Rome fought two wars (A.D. 66-73 and 132-135; *see* Jewish Wars with Rome), where social division was along ethnic and nationalistic lines. The Roman economy was mainly based on agriculture with an admixture of light industry. Poverty was rampant in the big cities.

Within the population there was an increasing dissatisfaction with traditional religion, its pantheon and its worldview. Religions offering a personal relationship with deity were increasingly popular, including Christianity and Mithraism (*see* Mysteries; Religion, Personal). The Christian gospel offered a personal relationship with deity, as well as the promise of participation in the kingdom of God that gave the poor masses a hopeful worldview. Emperor worship became popular in the first century A.D., and its claims for the divinity of the emperor were antithetical to Christianity's claim that Jesus was Lord (*see* Ruler Cult). This tension led in part to sporadic *persecutions of Christians throughout the empire. It was during the persecution of Nero, who blamed Christians for the burning of Rome in A.D. 64, that Paul and Peter lost their lives, and the book of Revelation helps the churches of *Asia Minor cope with the persecution under Domitian, who demanded worship as "Lord and God" (c. A.D. 95-96).

One of the most lasting contributions of the empire was its rule of *law (*see* Roman Law and Legal System). The body of law amassed by legislation and decree was administered by the praetors. The method of adjudication of cases was to appeal to legal precedent and the interpretation of legal experts. Both the civil and criminal law were different for Roman citizens and noncitizens. Citizens enjoyed the full measure of the law, but noncitizens did not. We may compare Paul's appeal to his citizenship and ultimately to the emperor, a privilege he invoked as a Roman citizen when he realized that local jurisdiction was not going to be impartial (Acts 25:11). And we may also note the dismay of the Philippian magistrates when they discovered that Paul and Silas were Roman citizens after they had treated them as a noncitizens—stripping, flogging and imprisoning them (Acts 16:35-39). The distinction between citizen and noncitizens broke down in the third century, when most free inhabitants of the empire were given citizenship by the *Constitutio Antoniniana* of A.D. 212. Social status became the major distinction in administering the law. The propertied classes (*honestiores*) were treated less harshly by the law than were the poorer classes (*humiliores*). Slaves had no rights under the law.

5. The Late Empire.

The third century A.D. saw great instability in the empire. There was a rapid succession of emperors ruling in Rome between the death of Severus Alexander (A.D. 235) and the accession of Diocletian (A.D. 284), as well as would-be emperors and local rulers governing areas of the empire that Rome could no longer control. Civil wars were common. The Parthians to the east and Germanic hordes to the north took much territory from Rome. Its frontier garrisons fought among themselves for rival claimants to power, destroying both the economy and the frontier defenses. Aurelian (A.D. 270-275) and his successors regained this territory. Diocletian (A.D. 284-305) reestablished stability. He reformed the military by creating mobile armies that could be moved to the frontier to help local garrisons defend the boundaries. He formed a tetrarchy of emperors who administered smaller portions of the empire called dioceses, which were in turn composed of provinces. This system of government led to a decade of rivalries between emperors, civil war and persecution of the Christians. Constantine (A.D. 306-337) emerged to reunify the empire under one emperor and established Byzantium (Constantinople) rather than Rome as the capital of the empire. Christianity was now a recognized religion of the empire.

The late empire witnessed many economic and social changes that were the precursors of the feudalism of the Middle Ages. Urban life declined as agriculture thrived. People became less socially and physically mobile. They were tied to their land and the jobs of their ancestors. Local aristocrats provided the military protection for their geographical locations until the mobile Roman forces could arrive. Cities near the frontier of the empire thrived as the resources of the empire were directed there to bolster the frontier defenses. Professional bureaucracy increased with greater delineation of roles and functions. There was stability in education, trade, administration and the judiciary. Christianity provided a common culture and ideology of power to ruler and ruled alike.

The western portion of the empire was finally overrun by Germanic tribes in the fifth century. The eastern portion continued until 1453, when Byzantium was conquered by the Turks. However, Roman culture and the Christian faith that it eventually adopted have been major influences on Western civilization ever since.

See also PAX ROMANA; ROMAN ADMINISTRATION; ROMAN EMPERORS; ROMAN GOVERNORS OF PALESTINE; ROMAN LAW AND LEGAL SYSTEM; ROMAN MILITARY; ROMAN POLITICAL SYSTEM; ROME.

BIBLIOGRAPHY. G. Alföldy, *The Social History of Rome* (rev. ed.; Baltimore: Johns Hopkins University Press, 1988); A. E. Astin et al., eds., *Rome and the Mediterranean to 133 B.C.* (2d ed.; *CAH* 8; Cambridge: Cambridge University Press, 1989); M. Beard and M. Crawford, *Rome in the Late Republic* (Ithaca, NY: Cornell University Press, 1985); J. Boardman, J. Griffin and O. Murray, eds., *The Oxford History of the Roman World* (Oxford: Oxford University Press, 1991); A. K. Bowman, E. Champlin and A. Lintott, eds., *The Augustan Empire, 43 B.C.-A.D. 69* (2d ed.; *CAH* 10; Cambridge: Cambridge University Press, 1996); A. Cameron, *The Later Roman Empire, A.D. 284-430* (Cambridge, MA: Harvard University Press, 1993); A. Cameron and P. Garnsey, eds., *The Late Empire: A.D. 337-425* (*CAH* 13; Cambridge: Cambridge University Press, 1997); T. Cornell, *The Beginnings of Rome* (London: Routledge, 1995); M. Crawford, *The Roman Republic* (2d ed.; Cambridge, MA: Harvard University Press, 1993); J. A. Crook, A. Lintott and E. Rawson, eds., *The Last Age of the Roman Republic: 146-43 B.C.* (2d ed.; *CAH* 9; Cambridge: Cambridge University Press, 1994); P. Garnsey and R. Saller, *The Roman Empire: Economy, Society and Culture* (Berkeley and Los Angeles: University of California Press, 1987); A. Garzetti, *From Tiberius to the Antonines: A History of the Roman Empire* (London: Methuen, 1974); W. V. Harris, *War and Imperialism in Republican Rome* (Oxford: Clarendon Press, 1979); A. H. M. Jones, *The Later Roman Empire: A Social, Economic and Administrative Survey* (Norman: University of Oklahoma Press, 1964); R. M. Ogilvie, *Early Rome and the Etruscans* (London: Fontana, 1976); R. MacMullen, *Roman Government's Response to Crisis, A.D. 235-337* (New Haven, CT: Yale University Press, 1976); F. Millar, *The Emperor in the Roman World (31 B.C.-A.D. 337)* (2d ed.; London: Duckworth, 1992); idem, *The Roman Empire and Its Neighbors* (2d ed.; London: Duckworth, 1981); K. Raabflaub, *Social Struggles in Archaic Rome* (Berkeley and Los Angeles: University of California Press, 1986); E. T. Salmon, *The Making of Roman Italy* (Ithaca, NY: Cornell University Press, 1982); F. W. Walbank et al., eds., *The Rise of Rome to 220 B.C.* (2d ed.; *CAH* 7.2; Cambridge: Cambridge University Press, 1990); C. Wells, *The Roman Empire* (2d ed.; Cambridge, MA: Harvard University Press, 1995).

D. F. Watson

ROMAN GOVERNORS OF PALESTINE

The office of the Roman governor in the first century A.D. was the most prominent and distinctive expression of the dominion of Rome over the land and people of the Jews. Through this office and with the varied nuances of consideration or brutality that each appointee brought to it, the will of the *emperor and the Roman people was enforced. In this article the office of Roman governor and the governance of three particular appointees will be considered.

1. Rome and the Jewish State
2. Roman Governors in Palestine
3. Pontius Pilatus

4. Antonius or Claudius Felix
5. Porcius Festus

1. Rome and the Jewish State.

1.1. Early Roman-Jewish Relations. *Rome's presence in the Near East was at first seen to be a comfort to the Maccabean rulers of Palestine who early sought a friendship treaty and several times renewed it for the protections it might afford (1 Macc 8; 13:36; Josephus *Ant.* 12.10.6 §§414-19; 13.5.8 §§163-65; 13.9.2 §§259-66). All changed, however, in 63 B.C., when against the resistance of Aristobulus II, *Pompey took *Jerusalem by force (Josephus *Ant.* 14.4.1-5 §§54-79). Thereafter the Jewish people were ruled by Rome, whether they were constituted a province or a client kingdom under nominated royals (Tacitus *Hist.* 5.9).

1.2. Orientation Within the Roman Orbit. The NT period begins with the Idumean ruler *Herod the Great. The young Herod's successes in governing Galilee from 47 B.C. resulted in the Roman senate's voting him king of the Jews in 40 B.C. Herod's de facto reign as king from 37 B.C. until his death in 4 B.C. was characterized by zeal for Rome and an absolutely ruthless elimination of threats, whether these were Arab designs on territory, real or supposed intrigues of political leaders, friends and family, or news of the birth of a Davidic claimant to the throne (Mt 2). Herod died master of an extensive and generally stable kingdom whose subject population for the most part hated him.

At his death, Herod's three sons went to Rome to vie for the sole kingship (Josephus *Ant.* 17.9.3-4 §§219-27; 17.11.1 §303). Augustus (*see* Roman Emperors) divided the kingdom between Herod's sons but withheld the royal title. Archelaus was made ethnarch of about half of Herod's kingdom, comprising Idumea, *Judea and *Samaria. Antipas became tetrarch of *Galilee and Perea. Philip was made tetrarch of Batanea, Trachonitis and Auranitis (Josephus *Ant.* 17.11.4 §§317-20; cf. Lk 3:1).

Archelaus's government was brutal and tyrannical. It lasted ten years. He was deposed in A.D. 6 by Augustus on the successful complaint of a Samaritan and Jewish delegation (Josephus *Ant.* 17.13.1-5 §§339-55; *J.W.* 2.7.3 §111). Excepting the brief reign of Herod Agrippa I from A.D. 41 to 44 over a much enlarged Jewish realm (Josephus *Ant.* 18.6.10 §237; 19.5.1 §§274-77; *J.W.* 2.9.6 §§181-83; 2.11.5-6 §§214-20), the area of Idumea, Judea and Samaria, including much of the rest of Herod's domain (Josephus *J.W.* 2.11.6 §§218-20; 2.12.8 §247), was after A.D. 44 ruled by Roman governors.

1.3. Provincial Status. Augustus's options for the governance of the former ethnarchy of Archelaus were several. At the death of Herod the Great, some Jews pled that Augustus annex the kingdom to Syria (Josephus *J.W.* 2.6.1 §§80-92; cf. Zeitlin, 2:128). This was not done. But documents describing the territory after Archelaus's deposition call it both a province (Josephus *J.W.* 2.8.1 §117; 2.9.1 §167; cf. Tacitus *Ann.* 2.42; *Hist.* 5.9; Suetonius *Claudius* 28) and an annex to Syria (Josephus *Ant.* 17.13.5 §355; 18.1.1 §1). Records attest to the significant interventions of Syrian governors in its politics throughout the NT period. Syrian legates made military incursions to keep the peace, entertained the appeals and complaints of Jewish delegations and exercised power over both governors and high *priests. The Syrian legate Vibius Marsus even dissolved a gathering of client kings, which included Herod Agrippa I (Josephus *Ant.* 19.8.1 §§338-42; cf. Stern, 314, on the motives). After the Bar Kokhba revolt (*see* Simon ben Kosiba), it received a governor holding the formal title of *legatus Augusti pro praetore provinciae Iudaea* who possessed, in addition to full civilian powers, military charge over legionary forces (*ILS* 1035-36, 1056).

1.4. Provincial Seat. While Palestine's governors occupied the palace built by Herod the Great on the west side of Jerusalem during *festivals and for the conduct of official business, their normal residence was Herod's praetorium (Burrell; Acts 23:35) at *Caesarea Maritima, the administrative seat of the province (Josephus *Ant.* 18.3.1 §57; 20.5.4 §116; *J.W.* 2.9.2 §171; 2.12.2 §230; Tacitus *Hist.* 2.78).

2. Roman Governors in Palestine.

2.1. Title. The Roman governors in Palestine are variously designated. The title *hēgemōn* is a general term and indicates a governor, whether a Roman proconsul (Lk 2:2; cf. Acts 18:12), a legate (Josephus *Ant.* 15.11.4 §405; 18.4.2 §88) or some more subordinate Roman official (e.g., Mt 27:2; Mk 13:9; Lk 3:1; 20:20; Acts 23:24, 26; 26:30; 1 Pet 2:14; Josephus *Ant.* 18.3.1 §55). Two more specific designations for governors of Palestine were *praefectus* (*eparchos*), appropriate to a military commander of five hundred to one thousand auxiliary troops, and *procurator* (*epitropos*), which referred to a financial officer of a province or a governor (*see DJG*, "Pontius Pilate"). The 1961 discovery of a Latin inscription at Caesarea referring to Pontius Pilatus as *praefectus* has led to an inference that pre-Claudian governors in Palestine were officially known as prefects (= *eparchos:* Josephus *Ant.* 18.2.2 §33) but thereafter as procurators (= *epitropos:* Josephus *J.W.* 2.11.6 §220; 2.12.1 §223; 2.12.8 §247; 2.14.1 §272; *Ant.* 15.11.4 §406; 20.1.2 §14; 20.5.1 §97). On this assumption, the descriptions of Coponius and Pilatus as procurators (Josephus *J.W.* 2.8.1 §117; 2.9.2 §169; Tacitus *Ann.* 15.44) and Cuspius Fadus and Lucceius Albinus as prefects (Josephus *Ant.* 19.9.2 §363; 20.9.1 §197) are anachronistic.

*2.2. **Qualifications and Appointment.*** Except for the imperial freedman Felix, the governors of Palestine belonged to the Roman equestrian order. They were persons of military and administrative experience whose abilities and/or connections recommended them. While the governors of Palestine up to the reign of Claudius were Italians or Latins, at least three of the seven thereafter were of Greek or Oriental origin. The Jewish apostate Tiberius Julius Alexander (A.D. 46-48) governed the Jews with some sensitivity (Josephus *J.W.* 2.11.6 §220). But Greco-Roman prejudice generally prevailed, and grinding tension is the context to first-century A.D. events.

The governors were appointed and dismissed directly by the emperor (e.g., Josephus *J.W.* 2.9.2 §169; 2.12.6-8 §§244-47; *Ant.* 20.1.2 §14; 20.8.5, 9 §§162, 182) or his surrogate (Reicke, 175). In exceptional circumstances, the Syrian legate might send an errant governor to Rome and install a caretaker (Josephus *Ant.* 18.4.2 §89). Their term of office varied according to imperial policy. Augustus's Palestinian appointees served an average of three years. In the twenty-four years of Tiberius's reign, however, there were only two governors (on his motives, see Tacitus *Ann.* 1.80; Josephus *Ant.* 18.6.5 §§170-77). In the post-Tiberian period, outside of Marullus (A.D. 37-41), Ventidius Cumanus (A.D. 48-52) and Felix (A.D. 52-60), the terms were for two years.

*2.3. **Powers.*** The governor of Palestine had no recourse to legions, only auxiliary forces levied largely from the Greek populations of Caesarea and Sebaste and probably led by a Roman citizen officer class. The bulk of these forces were normally garrisoned at Caesarea but wintered in Jerusalem (Josephus *Ant.* 18.3.1 §55). One cohort, however, was permanently quartered in Jerusalem in the Fortress Antonia attached to the temple precincts. Their peacekeeping had special focus to monitoring temple officiants and worshipers (Josephus *Ant.* 20.8.11 §192; *J.W.* 5.5.8 §§244-45; Acts 21:31-37).

Except where a non-Jew desecrated the temple by entering beyond the barrier (Josephus *Ant.* 12.3.4 §145; 15.11.5 §417; *J.W.* 5.5.2 §§193-94; 6.2.4 §§124-26; Philo *Leg. Gai.* 31 §212; Eph 2:14), capital punishment was the exclusive preserve of the governor (Josephus *J.W.* 2.8.1 §117-16; *Ant.* 18.1.1 §2). The emblems of this power were the right to wear a military uniform and to carry a sword (Dio Cassius *Hist.* 53.13.6-7; 53.14.5; Rom 13:4). The power was absolute over non-Roman provincials (Mt 27; Mk 15; Lk 23; Jn 18—19). It probably also included the right to execute both citizen soldiers and civilians after due process. In the case of citizen civilians, governors could try, condemn and execute provided there was no appeal (Garnsey 1966, 54; cf. Acts 22—26).

The power to nominate and depose high priests and administer the high-priestly vestments were rights delegated by Rome. From Josephus's record (*Ant.* 18.4.3 §93; 18.2.2 §§34-35) we learn that these significant powers resided directly in the hands of Roman governors from A.D. 6 (Coponius) to A.D. 36 (Pilatus). Before Coponius, they were the responsibility of Herod the Great and Archelaus (Josephus *Ant.* 18.4.3 §92; 20.10.5 §247). After Pilatus, the Syrian legate Vitellius possessed the power but relinquished control of the vestments to the Jewish priests (Josephus *Ant.* 18.4.3 §§90-95). At the death of Herod Agrippa I, who as monarch possessed all the powers, the governor Cuspius Fadus and Syrian legate Cassius Longinus petitioned Claudius to regain control. Claudius refused the request in favor of Herod Agrippa II (Josephus *Ant.* 15.11.4 §407; 20.8.8, 11 §179, §196; 20.9.1, 4, §§197-203, §213, §§222-23).

The governors of Palestine were responsible for the province's financial affairs, including the levying of various taxes (see Zeitlin, 2:137, on the types). After Archelaus, a census was taken to that end (Josephus *Ant.* 17.13.5 §335; Tacitus *Ann.* 6.41). Collections were farmed out to state contractors called publicans (*publicani*) and their agents (*conductores*). While Romans were at the top of the ladder, Jews were hired for direct collections (e.g. Mk 3:13-19; Lk 19:1-10).

The governors of Palestine also possessed the right to mint *coinage. Jewish religious scruples called for the avoidance of pagan symbols on coins. This was generally followed by even the harshest of the governors.

*2.4. **Salaries and Accountability.*** As agents of the emperor, procurators were paid an annual stipend from the treasury. The title of their procuratorial grade or rank actually reflected the amount of their annual stipend. They were known as *sexagenarii, centenarii, ducenarii* or *trice-narii,* indicating that they received 60,000, 100,000, 200,000 or 300,000 *sesterces* respectively (Dio Cassius *Hist.* 53.15.1 [cf. LCL 6:231 n.2]; Suetonius *Claudius* 24 [cf. LCL 2:46-47, n.c]). The equestrian governors of Palestine probably got an annual salary of 100,000 *sestertii,* in keeping with their military grade and the forces in their charge (Stern, 320). Legitimate salaries, however, were invariably supplemented incredibly by means of illicit exactions. In a factionalized province a governor could multiply the take by playing sides. The administrations of Felix, Albinus and Florus illustrate the problem well.

Herod Agrippa II declared that it was not by Rome's order that a governor was harsh but that Rome could not easily see or hear of oppressions committed at a great distance (Josephus *J.W.* 2.16.4 §§352-53). Governors were generally immune from prosecution while in office. Only in the year following their return to Rome could they be prosecuted (Josephus *Ant.* 20.8.9 §182). Term renewals and promotions only extended this immunity. Appeals against a governor by cities and even whole provinces needed approval from the offending governor himself (Josephus *Ant.* 20.8.11 §§193-94) or his nearest superior (Josephus *Ant.* 18.4.2 §§88-89; *J.W.* 2.12.5-7 §§239-46). Unsanctioned embassies were both less successful and more risky. A fair trial and conviction was remote given the governor's being an imperial appointee and the judges his peers. Moreover, money and/or influence could purchase acquittal (Josephus *Ant.* 20.8.9 §§182-83).

3. Pontius Pilatus.

*3.1. **Dates.*** Pontius Pilatus, the fifth prefect of Judea, came to his appointment in the year A.D. 26 and served until A.D. 36. What we know of his career comes from Josephus (*Ant.* 18.2.2 §35; 18.3.1-3 §§55-64; 18.4.1-2 §§85-89; *J.W.* 2.9.2-4 §§169-77), *Philo of *Alexandria (*Leg. Gai.* 38 §§299-305), Tacitus (*Ann.* 15.44), the 1961 *praefectus* inscription from Caesarea and the NT (Gospels passim; Acts 3:13; 4:27; 13:28; 1 Tim 6:13). Information on Pilate from later church tradition and *apocryphal literature is of doubtful veracity (Sandmel, 3:813-14).

*3.2. **Origin and Appointment.*** The *nomen* Pontius suggests that Pilatus was from the region of Samnium in central Italy. While governorship was an imperial appointment (Josephus *J.W.* 2.9.2 §169), Pilatus's preferment was probably sponsored by Tiberius's anti-Semitic praetorian commander Sejanus (Philo *Leg. Gai.* 24 §§159-61). The notice that Pilatus's wife accompanied him (Mt 27:19) is confirmed by a policy change in A.D. 21 that permitted such an arrangement (Tacitus *Ann.* 3.33-34).

*3.3. **Governance.*** Pilatus was contemptuous of Jewish religious sensibilities and deliberately provocative. Under cover of darkness and against the practice of earlier Roman governors, Pilatus on one occasion brought military standards bearing images of the emperor into Jerusalem. He ignored the demonstrations and rebuffed the pleas of those who pursued him to Caesarea. Secretly surrounding the Jews who gathered before his tribunal in the stadium with troops, he threatened them with death. Jewish resolve to get satisfaction even if it meant a wholesale slaughter, however, caused Pilate to remove the standards (Josephus *Ant.* 18.3.1 §§55-62; *J.W.* 2.9.2-3 §§169-74).

Pilatus provoked further hatred by financing the construction of an aqueduct through the seizure of Jewish sacred funds. Protests were met with brutal force, resulting in a panic that took many Jewish lives (Josephus *Ant.* 18.3.2 §§60-62; *J.W.* 2.9.4 §§175-77). Some identify this event with the NT notice of Pilatus's slaughter of certain Galileans (Lk 13:1-2; 23:12).

Even in the minting of coins, Pilatus was careless of Jewish sensibilities. Coins during the period A.D. 29 to 31 feature Roman religious emblems. Serious Jews were scandalized (Wheaton, 1230).

Soon after Sejanus's execution in A.D. 31, Pilatus erected a set of golden votive shields at his Jerusalem residence bearing the names of Tiberius and himself. Protests were again registered by the Jewish elites, including Herod's four sons, and letters of supplication were sent to Tiberius. The emperor was sorely displeased with Pilatus's action and ordered that the shields be immediately removed to Caesarea (Philo *Leg.*

Gai. 38 §§299-305).

Pilatus's dismissal came about over a military action against the Samaritans. In A.D. 36 a certain Samaritan commanded an armed following by declaring he knew the whereabouts of sacred vessels hidden by *Moses near Mt. Gerizim. Pilatus blocked their way, and in the ensuing battle many Samaritans were slaughtered or taken prisoner and their leaders executed. A subsequent Samaritan deputation brought complaint to the Syrian legate, representing Pilatus's action as a vicious slaughter of innocents. Vitellius (Tacitus *Ann.* 6.31-32) ordered Pilatus to Rome and sent Marcellus as caretaker (Josephus *Ant.* 18.4.1-2 §§85-89). Tiberius died (March 16, A.D. 37) before Pilatus reached Rome. We know nothing more of him after this.

3.4. Characteristics of Governance. Philo describes Pilatus as a proud and vindictive man who possessed a fiery temper, and in describing his administration speaks of "the briberies, the insults, the robberies, the outrages and wanton injuries, the executions without trial constantly repeated, the ceaseless and supremely grievous cruelty" (Philo *Leg. Gai.* 38 §§302-3). Actions were engaged provocatively and resistance was met with brinkmanship that led either to embarrassing climbdowns or appalling bloodshed. The duration of Pilatus's oversight was more a reflection of Tiberius's inattention and policy of not changing governors quickly than of Pilatus's success in governance.

3.5. New Testament Record. The NT accounts of Pilatus's conduct in the trial and condemnation of Jesus fit well the other notices of his governorship. The relationship between Pilatus and Herod Antipas in the referral of Jesus (Lk 23:12), Pilatus's malleability under Jewish threats (Mt 27:15-26; Mk 15:6-15; Lk 23:13-25; Jn 18:39—19:12) and the cynical and provocative phrase he placed on Jesus' *titulus*, the inscription on the cross (Mt 27:38; Mk 15:26; Lk 23:38; Jn 19:19-22), exemplify the consistency.

4. Antonius or Claudius Felix.

4.1. Dates. There is disagreement on the dates of the eleventh governor Felix. Tacitus describes a shared governance, with Felix in charge of Samaria from A.D. 48 and Ventidius Cumanus in charge of Galilee. In A.D. 52, the Syrian legate Quadratus removed Cumanus on charges of provincial maladministration and elevated Felix to oversight of the entire area (Tacitus *Ann.* 12.54). Josephus has Felix newly arrived from Rome as successor to the disgraced Cumanus with a remit over Judea, Samaria, Galilee and Patrea (Josephus *J.W.* 2.12.8 §247; *Ant.* 20.7.1 §137; 20.8.5 §§162-63).

Some scholars have argued for Felix's earlier dismissal from office in A.D. 55 because his brother Pallas was removed from administering the imperial *fiscus* that year. Pallas could not have protected Felix against Jewish accusations after that. Several things can be said, however, in defense of Felix's remaining in office until A.D. 59 or 60. Pallas's dismissal was not a fall or disgrace; it was a political and policy move (Josephus *Ant.* 20.7.1 §137; 20.8.9 §§182-84; Tacitus *Ann.* 13.2, 14). Pallas left office honored, "exonerated" and fabulously wealthy (Tacitus *Ann.* 13.14, 23; Dio Cassius *Hist.* 62.14.3; Pliny *Ep.* 7.29; 8.6). His murder in A.D. 62 was more out of Nero's greed than hostility (Dio Cassius *Hist.* 62.14.3; Tacitus *Ann.* 14.64-65). If one assumes the earlier dismissal date, Josephus's *War* (2.13 §§250-70) reports too many activities for the one year when Nero was emperor and Felix governor. Changes in Judean coinage also seem to favor the date of A.D. 59 or 60. Finally, Paul's *captatio benevolentiae* at Acts 24:10—better taken to be accurate and influential historical summary rather than a risky piece of insincere fawning (see Winter)—in speaking of the "many years" that Felix had been judge over "this nation," probably refers to a period of eight or nine years rather than a half time less.

4.2. Origin and Appointment. Tacitus gives the name Antonius Felix (*Hist.* 5.9), suggesting that, like his brother Pallas (Josephus *Ant.* 18.6.6 §182), Felix had received his freedom from Antonia, the mother of Claudius. Notice of Felix's marriage to the granddaughter of Antony and Cleopatra appears to reinforce the Antonian connection (Tacitus *Hist.* 5.9). However, some manuscripts of Josephus (*Ant.* 20.7.1 §137) and Suidas refer to him as Claudius Felix, and a Greek inscription notes an *epitropos* named Tiberius Claudius (Schürer, 1:460 n. 19).

In any event, favorable connections to the imperial household not only garnered Felix the governorship that the Jewish high priest Jonathan had requested for him (Josephus *Ant.* 20.8.5 §162) but also ensured its continuation beyond Claudius's death and that its excesses would be ultimately survivable. Among his three marriages to royal women (Suetonius *Claudius*

28) was a liaison in Judea that may have purposely connected him with the Herodian dynasty (Josephus *Ant.* 20.7.2 §§141-44).

4.3. Governance. Felix pacified the countryside by capturing bandit leaders and sending them on to Rome, crucifying their followers and punishing their supporters. Eleazar the son of Deinaeus, who had ranged the province for twenty years, was captured by a ruse (Josephus *Ant.* 20.8.5 §§160-61; *J.W.* 2.13.2 §253). Felix also put down less militant movements by slaughter (Josephus *J.W.* 2.13.4 §§258-60). About the year 54, he dealt with a popular movement led by a self-proclaimed prophet from Egypt. Many were killed and a good number taken prisoner, excepting the Egyptian who escaped. This action renewed banditry in the countryside (Josephus *Ant.* 20.8.6 §§167-72; *J.W.* 2.13.5-6 §§261-65). Several years later, the apostle Paul was mistaken for the Egyptian (Acts 21:38; *see* Revolutionary Movements, Jewish).

Felix both fought against and at times collaborated with urban terrorists known as *sicarii* (*sica* = a curved dagger). The high priest Jonathan was assassinated by *sicarii*, at Felix's instigation, when Jonathan grew openly restive about Felix's actions (Josephus *Ant.* 20.8.5 §162; *J.W.* 2.13.3 §§254-57).

Near the end of Felix's tenure, the substantial Jewish population of Caesarea claimed proprietary rights over the city against Greco-Syrian counterclaims. Local magistrates having failed to keep the peace, Felix intervened. He put down the disturbances by military means. Many Jews were killed, and the soldiers were permitted to plunder their property. Felix was eventually moved by certain Jewish notables to recall his forces (Josephus *Ant.* 20.8.7 §§173-78; *J.W.* 2.13.7 §§266-70).

4.4. Characteristics of Governance. Tacitus's comment that Felix "practiced every kind of cruelty and lust, wielding the power of a king with all the instincts of a slave" (Tacitus *Hist.* 5.10) is heavy with upper-class disdain. But Felix's crimes were more than the expression of character flaws. His imperial connections gave him a sense of invincibility and encouraged a disposition to harshness (Tacitus *Ann.* 12.54). His confidence was well founded. The Caesarean Jewish delegation that accused Felix of provincial maladministration before Nero was unsuccessful (Josephus *Ant.* 20.8.9 §182).

4.5. New Testament Record. While the rhetor Tertullus and the apostle Paul could refer in general to Felix's peacekeeping and legal reforms (Acts 24:2; cf. Acts 21:38) and his judicial equity and competence (Acts 24:10) respectively without blushing, Felix's reaction to the Pauline preaching on justice, self-control and future judgment (Acts 24:25) hints at the truthfulness of the excesses of secular description. Moreover, notice of Felix's play for a bribe (Acts 24:26) and his grant of the "favor" of Paul's continued imprisonment (Acts 24:27) compare with the general practice of "sweating" individuals or factions for personal advantage (cf. Josephus *J.W.* 2.14.1 §273; *Ant.* 20.9.5 §215).

5. Porcius Festus.

5.1. Dates. Porcius Festus succeeded Felix, probably around A.D. 59 or 60, as the twelfth governor. At his death in A.D. 62, he was succeeded by Lucceius Albinus.

5.2. Governance. Festus came to a province again convulsed by banditry and assassinations. He bent considerable efforts to capture and execute large numbers of malefactors. Josephus notes how he also pursued and slaughtered a self-proclaimed messiah and all his followers (Josephus *Ant.* 20.8.10 §§185-88; *J.W.* 2.14.1 §271).

Festus sided with Herod Agrippa II against the priests on one occasion. Agrippa had built an addition to his palace that allowed him to observe priestly activity and particularly the temple sacrifices. The offended priests blocked Agrippa's view by erecting a wall on the inner temple arcade. This also blocked the view of Roman patrols on the porticoes, so Festus ordered the wall's destruction. The priests refused, arguing that this was tantamount to ordering the temple's destruction. Nero sided with the priestly deputation out of deference to his wife Poppaea, who was "religious" (*theosebēs:* Josephus *Ant.* 20.8.11 §§189-96).

5.3. Characteristics of Governance. Festus comes off better in the scanty sources than both his immediate predecessor and any of the governors who followed him. But it was too little and too late as the province continued to plunge toward war with Rome.

5.4. New Testament Record. The NT gives the reader a view of Festus's first days of governance. While he was courteous to the Jewish ruling elites (Acts 25:1), swift in trying cases (Acts 25:6) and cognizant of due process (Acts 25:16), it is clear that the newly arrived Festus was vulnerable to influence and power (Acts 25:1-6; cf. Kelly). This was the value in the "favor" of Felix's leaving Paul in prison, and it raised sufficient alarm to trigger Paul's unusual appeal (Acts 25:9-12). The formal reception of Agrippa II and his queen Berenice and the showcasing of Paul for Agrippa's assessment probably served a dual function—to furnish information for a document specifying charges (Acts 25:26; on *litterae dimissoriae* see Justinian *Dig.* 49.6.1) and to encourage warm official relations.

See also CAESAREA MARITIMA; HERODIAN DYNASTY; REVOLUTIONARY MOVEMENTS, JEWISH; ROMAN ADMINISTRATION; ROMAN EAST; ROMAN LAW AND LEGAL SYSTEM; ROMAN POLITICAL SYSTEM.

BIBLIOGRAPHY. S. Applebaum, "Judea as a Roman Province; the Countryside as a Political and Economic Factor," *ANRW* 2.8 (1977) 355-96; E. Bammel, "The Trial Before Pilate," in *Jesus and the Politics of His Day,* ed. E. Bammel and C. F. D. Moule (Cambridge: Cambridge University Press, 1984) 415-51; H. K. Bond, *Pontius Pilate in History and Interpretation* (SNTSMS 100; Cambridge: Cambridge University Press, 1998); P. A. Brunt, "Charges of Provincial Maladministration," *Historia* 10 (1961) 189-227; B. Burrell et al., "Uncovering Herod's Seaside Palace," *BAR* 193 (1993); P. D. A. Garnsey, "The Criminal Jurisdiction of Governors," *JRS* 58 (1966) 51-59; idem, *Social Status and Legal Privilege in the Roman Empire* (Oxford: Clarendon Press, 1970); D. W. J. Gill, "Acts and Roman Policy in Judea," in *The Book of Acts in Its Palestinian Setting,* ed. R. Bauckham (BAFCS 4; Grand Rapids, MI: Eerdmans, 1995) 15-26; E. M. B. Green and C. J. Hemer, "Felix," *IBD* 1:505; C. J. Hemer, "Festus," *IBD* 1:505-506; J. M. Kelly, *Roman Litigation* (Oxford: Clarendon Press, 1966); F. Millar, *The Roman Empire and Its Neighbors* (London: Duckworth, 1981); S. I. Oost, "The Career of M. Antonius Pallas," *AJP* 79 (1958) 113-39; B. Reicke, *The New Testament Era* (Philadelphia: Fortress, 1968); S. Sandmel, "Felix, Antonius," *IDB* 2:264; idem, "Pilate, Acts of," *IDB* 3:813-14; idem, "Festus, Porcius," *IDB* 2:264-66; idem, "Pilate, Pontius," *IDB* 3:811-13; E. Schürer, *The History of the Jewish People in the Age of Jesus Christ (175 B.C.-A.D. 135),* rev. and ed. G. Vermes et al. (3 vols.; Edinburgh: T & T Clark, 1973-87) vol. 1; E. M. Smallwood, *The Jews Under Roman Rule* (Leiden: E. J. Brill, 1976); M. Stern, "The Province of Judea," in *The Jewish People in the First Century,* ed. S Safrai and M. Stern (CRINT 1.1; Assen: Van Gorcum; Philadelphia: Fortress, 1974) 308-76; R. D. Sullivan, "The Dynasty of Judea in the First Century," *ANRW* 2.8 (1977) 296-354; E. G. Turner, "Tiberius Iulius Alexander," *JRS* 44 (1954) 54-64; D. H. Wheaton, "Pilate," *IBD* 3:1229-31; B. W. Winter, "The Importance of the *Captatio Beneuolentiae* in the Speeches of Tertullus and Paul in Acts 24:1-21," *JTS* 42 (1991) 505-31; C. U. Wolf, "Governor," *IDB* 2:462-63; S. Zeitlin, *The Rise and Fall of the Judean State* (2 vols.; Philadelphia: Jewish Publication Society of America, 1969) vol. 2.

B. M. Rapske

ROMAN LAW AND LEGAL SYSTEM

"Roman law" refers neither to all legal systems within the *Roman Empire nor to the legal procedures of Italy but rather to the law of imperial *citizens, Roman colonies and governors' courts throughout the Roman Empire.

The brightest in *Greece turned to *philosophy; the brightest in Rome, to law (*see* Law/Nomos in Greco-Roman World). The practical nature of the Romans and their concern for tolerance led to the development of a set of generally consistent rules—involving both statute and juristic law—within a flexible and distinctive legal system.

At the same time, Roman law was not consistent throughout the empire; provincial law differed from place to place. As a result, it frequently is difficult to know what laws were valid in a particular province. When the Gospel of John presents the Jewish leaders in *Jerusalem as saying "We are not permitted to put anyone to death" (Jn 18:31), that may well have been the case (Stephen and James may have been lynched). Examples from other provinces—of locals having the right to engage in capital punishment—do not serve as ultimately compelling evidence. Laws differed from province to province.

In examining Roman law and the NT, it is initially helpful to recognize extant sources of Roman law and to see how the Roman legal system developed in the principate. An overview of trial procedure in the provinces will then serve to illuminate a number of examples of various trials and courtroom activity within the NT. A discussion of legal metaphors and allusions in the NT, particularly in Paul's epistles, will follow, with some concluding remarks on one later trajectory: Constantine and Roman law in the service of the church.

1. Sources of Roman Law

2. General Characteristics of Roman Trials in the Provinces
3. Trials and Courtrooms in the New Testament
4. Allusions to Roman Law and Legal Processes in the New Testament
5. Constantine and Roman Law in the Service of the Church

1. Sources of Roman Law.
Christians who lived during the so-called classical period of the empire, during the first and second centuries A.D., were most familiar with Roman law and legal procedures from mundane sources: from Roman officials, from urban life and from fellow Christians.

In the announcement of edicts and the development of policy, Roman officials throughout the empire would have communicated the law: *emperors (Augustus, Claudius, Tiberius, Nero), provincial *governors (Felix, Festus, Pilate and Quirinius) and proconsuls (Gallio and Sergius Paulus)—all mentioned in the NT—would have had occasion to make public declarations of Roman law.

With Rome as capital of the empire, with *Corinth, *Philippi and the cities of *Galatia as Roman colonies, with *Thessalonica as a province capital and with *Ephesus and other cities as major trade centers, urban life would have left many Christians familiar with fundamental concepts in Roman law. Interest in the law was not reserved for the elite: the comic playwright Plautus filled his plays with legal jokes and parodies.

Finally, Christians would have heard about Roman legal procedure from others in the faith: some of whom were Roman citizens; some of whom could read; some of whom were trained in the law; some of whom had been persecuted or had been taken to trial.

Modern readers' knowledge of Roman law and legal institutions comes primarily from written sources: numismatics, ancient art and archaeological remains are only of limited use. Allusions to Roman law and legal practices are frequently indirect. Historians like Livy, *Josephus, *Tacitus and *Suetonius and *rhetoricians like *Cicero and Quintilian all refer to law and legal traditions familiar to them. In addition, the epistle exchanges between the emperor Trajan and *Pliny the Younger (preserved as book 10 of Pliny's letters), along with private and public *papyri, contain numerous references to Roman law, practices and customs.

Our primary sources for understanding written law are statutes and *plebiscita* (state-enacted law), *edicta* (pronouncements from magistrates), *senatusconsulta* (decrees of the senate), the decisions of the emperors and *interpretatio* (the replies of the jurists).

Roman law was shaped by legal developments during the republic and by basic legal principles dating from the Law of the Twelve Tables (451-450 B.C.). In addition, during the first two centuries of the empire, decrees of the senate (*senatusconsulta*) and emperors' pronouncements also came to have the force of law (cf. Gaius *Inst.* 1.5). The emperor's judicial decisions (*decreta*) on individual lawsuits, his written responses (*rescripta, epistulae, subscriptiones*) to requests or an embassy and his instructions (*mandata*) to officials throughout the empire came to have binding effect.

During the principate, however, the most significant development in Roman law came from jurists, who were under the authority and guidance of the emperor. Augustus gave special status to the *responsa* of specific jurists who received legal questions from judges and, by the time of Hadrian, these responses were collected, standardized and binding. Because of the imperial backing, there was much juristic literary activity in the first 250 years of the empire: numerous textbooks, legal monographs and commentaries on praetorian edicts came from this classical period; from jurists such as Salvius Julianus (second century), Gaius (second century) and Ulpian (early third century).

The standard textbook on Roman law, the only complete lawbook from the classical period, was a manual known as Gaius's *Institutes* (*Institutionum Commentarii Quattuor;* c. A.D. 161). Although nothing is known about Gaius himself, this work consists of four books, each reflecting the law of the previous century.

The collection and organization of many jurists' materials is most evident in the codes of Theodosius (fourth century) and of Justinian (sixth century). Justinian's work (A.D. 527-565) is the most impressive legal codification of the ancient world. Now known as the *Corpus Iuris Civilis,* this work consists of three parts: the *Digest,* the *Code* and the *Institutes.* The *Digest* (A.D. 533) records excerpts from jurists of the first three centuries. These excerpts, arranged by topic, are said to have come from the researching of some two thousand books. The *Digest* preserves earlier traditions, but it also does so with an eye towards the function of the law for the present. Some revision and editing occurred; laws were altered and adapted. Justinian's *Code* (final form, A.D. 534) is a collection of imperial legislation from the second through the sixth centuries, and the *Institutes* (A.D. 533) essentially reflect Gaius's second-century textbook, supplemented with other examples and sources.

2. General Characteristics of Roman Trials in the Provinces.

During the early principate, the *praetores* oversaw the courts in Rome; the *governors, in the provinces. Because of the provinces' significance for the NT, trial procedures in province courts are particularly illuminating. In the provinces, Romans tended to let local indigenous laws and legal customs prevail, challenging them only when they posed a threat to the empire. Thus, local magistrates followed their own systems of law. Governors, whether proconsuls, imperial legates or equestrian procurators, were involved primarily in serious cases, frequently capital trials, that involved the defense and preservation of public order.

There were no public prosecutors in the Roman legal system, so the procedure of both civil and criminal trials had to be initiated by a private party who drew up charges and then brought a formal accusation (*delatio*) against the defendant. As a safeguard against abuse of this system, those who made false accusations would themselves bear the brunt of the penalty of their accusations. Before approaching the governor, the accusing party would need to state the charges in a manner such that the governor would be sympathetic and willing to hear the case. When a governor took office, he would issue an edict, stating what *formula* he would find acceptable and what sorts of court cases he would be willing to hear. It would be wise for the accusing party to refer to that edict before presenting charges.

In determining whether to accept the charge, the governor had to decide whether the alleged act was a crime. Thus, in Corinth, when the proconsul Annius Gallio had Paul brought before him (Acts 18:12-17), he subsequently chose to dismiss the case, seeing the affair as an internal dispute between Jews.

If the governor felt there was justification and grounds for the charge, both parties would appear in court. After the governor announced the terms and parameters of the trial's proceedings, a civil case could be tried either by a judge or a jury. Judges and jury members generally were of a higher social status: jury members needed to be male, over twenty-five years of age and owners of property worth not less than seventy-five hundred denarii. As might be assumed, judges and jury members tended to favor plaintiffs who were also of a higher social status. The magistrate would then decide the punishment or penalties to be imposed.

If the governor felt there was justification for a criminal case, he would hear the case while seated on his tribunal (Jn 19:13; Acts 18:12), frequently surrounded by a *consilium*, a council of friends and officials who served as legal consultants. With criminal cases, the governor had two options in terms of procedure: he could look to precedents established by the Roman *ordo judiciorum publicorum* (a list of crimes, procedures and punishments, established and binding in Rome), or he could go outside the *ordo* (*cognitio extra ordinem*), particularly in cases where he felt there was no adequate precedent. The governor was not bound to follow the *ordo*, in part because such legislation might interfere with local laws or customs or with gubernatorial legal precedent within that particular province. In trials heard *extra ordinem*, the magistrate had no limitations placed on how he came to his knowledge (*cognitio*) of the crime.

With the authority of the *imperium*, the governor found himself accountable only to the emperor and the senate. Just as magistrates in the city of Rome had imperium related to their sphere of charges, just as they formulated policies and law, so, within the provinces of the Roman Empire, governors had been given the absolute authority of imperium. This allowed them to make decisions and determine the law as they saw fit. Because each governor exercised the authority of imperium, because there was no set manual that he would follow, there was a great deal of latitude involved in the penalties and punishment for crimes, just as there was in determining charges and procedures.

Furthermore, the penalties themselves frequently depended less on the crime committed than on the person who was alleged to have committed it. The rank of both the accuser and the accused had bearing on the case. The concept "equal before the law" was not assumed in Roman society. Differences in treatment under the law are particularly evident in areas related to social rank and status, citizenship and legal status.

Before a person could testify, he was asked what his place in society was. The higher one's rank, the greater one's opportunities in the courtroom. A plaintiff of lower social status generally was not allowed to initiate an action against a superior, nor could he have afforded to do so. In general, those of higher rank (*honestiores*) were treated better and not punished as severely as those of lower rank (*humiliores*). Honestiores were not to be tortured, they were frequently sent into exile rather than face execution, and if they did face the death penalty, they were killed in as painless a manner as possible. Although legislation at the end of the second century A.D. made these differences in punishment into law, previous to such formal distinctions there was still a de facto recognition that status played a large role in determining how one was to be treated.

Citizens (*cives Romani*) and aliens (*peregrini*) also were treated differently. Initially, the only Roman citizens were those patricians who lived in Rome. Others became citizens by holding certain offices, by being army veterans, by being manumitted from slavery, by having been born of citizens or by having bought their citizenship (Lysias in Acts 22:28). The emperor, the senate or a general in the field also had the right to confer citizenship on individuals or entire cities. Finally, in A.D. 212, the *Constitutio Antoniniana* made citizens of almost all persons who were subject to Rome.

During the time of the writing of the NT, Roman citizenship had some distinct advantages. Citizens could vote in popular assemblies, they were exempt from payment of certain taxes, they could be tried by either local or Roman courts, they could appeal capital sentences, and they were protected from scourging, whipping, torture and injury. In capital cases, a Roman citizen had the right of appeal (*provocatio*). There is not a scholarly consensus on whether the terms *provocatio* and *appellatio* could have been used interchangeably for the same appeals process, or whether *provocatio* involved an appeal before the trial (as in Paul's case, Acts 25:11) and *appellatio* involved one after the trial and sentence. Most scholars seem to see the existence of two different types of appeals, with the latter type (*appellatio*) developing in the later empire.

Finally, *slave and free were treated differently. Slaves could be crucified, they could be tortured during trial, they could be treated like property.

At other times, status per se did not have as much to do with how one was treated. *Pecunia* (judicial bribery) was expected, and such bribes served to speed up the judicial process, to pay for lawyers, witnesses, judges, juries or the opponents' counsel. In Acts 24:26 Felix is presented as being receptive to financial favors; he hopes to get some money from Paul.

A magistrate's ability to act according to his own discretion, coupled with an accepted concept of inequality before the law, allowed for a wide degree of differences in terms of what charges were heard in court, how trials were conducted and how individuals were treated, both prior to and after sentencing.

3. Trials and Courtrooms in the New Testament.

3.1. The Trial of Jesus. Trials in the NT can be understood best by acknowledging the governor's imperium in both setting the parameters of a trial and arriving at a verdict. The accounts of Jesus' trial before Pontius Pilate reflect the typical process of *cognitio*.

The accusers—the Jewish officials—had an initial deliberation, referred to as a trial, among themselves, where they determined what charges the governor would be most likely to find acceptable. After they had made their case, Pilate could have stopped the trial, seeing the charges as unjustifiable. He chose not to: the accompanying charges of treason or sedition (described only in Lk 23:2 and Jn 19:2) linked religious with political concerns and in the process may have given Pilate the excuse to listen to the more influential of the parties before him. Jesus' noncitizenship and his apparent lack of defense, coupled with the sort of threat made in John 19:12, only helped make Pilate's eventual decision easier.

How Pilate conducted the trial and how he determined the punishment both fell within the jurisdiction of his imperium. Outside of Rome, Pilate could follow less formal and technical procedures, having the right to conduct the trial as he saw fit. The punishment, similarly, could have fallen across a wide range of punishments, since there are wide degrees of interpretation on laws of treason, but crucifixion clearly could be seen as an option available.

One of the freedoms the governor had was to ask for advice. In Luke 23:6-12, Jesus is said to have been tried by Herod Antipas, the tetrarch of Galilee and Perea. Because Jesus came from Galilee, under *Herod's authority, scholars have debated whether Jesus legally needed to be tried by Herod. Some claim that the accused needed to be tried in the *forum domicilii,* the province in which he lived. Others believe that the accused was to be tried in the *forum delicti,* the province in which the crime was said to have been committed. It does appear that accused criminals were transferred only rarely. In Acts 23—24, Felix finds out that Paul is a Cilician, but he does not feel in any way obliged to send the case to Syria-Cilicia. Apparently Pilate was under no legal obligation to turn Jesus over to Antipas. Rather, in dealing with an awkward case, he followed the *extra ordinem* parameters and turned to Antipas for advice.

3.2. The Trials of Paul. Paul's Roman citizenship allowed him rights and opportunities not available to the majority of provincials. Roman citizens could not be examined under torture. If they were, their tormentors could be severely punished. After being beaten with rods in *Philippi (Acts 16:37-39) and when faced with the possibility of a scourging in Jerusalem (Acts 22:25-29), Paul appealed to his citizenship. In both cases the magistrates, aware of the consequences of their actions, were afraid.

Paul's other encounters with magistrates represent fairly typical processes of Roman law in the first century. This can be seen in his encounters with Gallio, Lysias, Felix and Festus.

In Acts 18:12-17, when Gallio was proconsul of Achaia, a group of Jews accused Paul of "persuading people to worship God contrary to the law." This formulation of the charge seems to be an attempt to anticipate what charges Gallio would have been willing to consider. Gallio, however, saw the disagreement as an inter-Jewish squabble. Because he did not have to listen to the case, he chose not to, driving the accusers away from the tribunal. Under the procedure *extra ordinem,* Gallio had considerable flexibility in his decisions, with such decisions clearly being shaped by political considerations.

Conversely, when the tribune Claudius Lysias knew that Paul was a Roman citizen, he commanded a special meeting of the chief priests and the *Sanhedrin in Jerusalem, so he could understand better why these people had brought accusations against Paul (Acts 22:30—23:10). Although this encounter is not a trial, it too represents the sort of evidence-gathering possible under a system of *extra ordinem.*

The trial before Felix followed the *cognitio* procedure: the plaintiffs were required to prosecute and the accused defended himself. The trial would not take place unless the accusers were present (Acts 23:30-35; cf. 25:5, 16). Ananias, some elders and Tertullus—an orator—accused Paul before Felix. The charges (Acts 24:5-7) were framed in political terms, intending to show Paul as an agitator and a threat to the government, and designed to appeal to Roman concerns about security. Paul refuted the charges, and Felix postponed a decision on the case until Lysias arrived (Acts 24:22). Lysias, as an independent witness to the disruption that had occurred, could have been seen as a necessary part of the trial.

Felix kept Paul imprisoned, apparently expecting a bribe. When none came and when he was succeeded by Porcius Festus, he left Paul in prison, as a favor to the Jews (Acts 24:25-26). When Festus took office, some Jews from Jerusalem initiated proceedings against Paul and raised serious charges. Paul pleaded his innocence and then, when Festus considered sending Paul to Jerusalem to be tried on a capital charge, Paul said "I appeal to Caesar" (Acts 25:11).

Paul's statement here is seen as the best example of a Roman citizen's right of appeal (*provocatio*). This allowed Festus to pass a delicate issue on to a higher authority in Rome, and it allowed Paul to have his case removed to a place that, for him, would have been a safer jurisdiction, free from political pressures. Before Festus, the charge against Paul was a political one; the evidence, theological. Thus it is not surprising that, before sending Paul to Rome, he felt the need to consult with King Herod Agrippa II (Acts 25:13—26:32).

3.3. First Corinthians 6:1-11. Some Christians willingly went to provincial courts, where they brought civil litigation against other Christians. That is the situation Paul faced in Corinth (1 Cor 6:1-11). Higher-status Christians were bringing litigation against those of lower status.

Here Paul asks the Corinthians to turn to private arbitration instead of provincial courts (he implies that some Christians in Corinth could serve as arbitrators; 1 Cor 6:2; cf. 6:5). Such an extrajudicial procedure, available under Roman law, eliminated the expenses and biases faced by those who appeared in secular courts. In addition, it helped members of the lower class, and it ensured that the mores of the world would not define what constituted Christian behavior and relationships.

3.4. Romans and 1 Peter. Although Paul discourages the Corinthians from having outsiders resolve their differences, in Romans 13:1-7 he implores Christians to recognize the government's right to engage in criminal litigation. The imperium is seen both as divine imperium and as necessity.

Romans 13:1-7, emphasizing respect for government authorities, is closely related to the admonitions in Romans 12:14-21, which emphasize moral behavior. This connection is particularly understandable in light of charges made against Christians in Roman trials. As governor of Bithynia, Pliny the Younger had Christians brought before him as criminals, but he was unsure what, in their case, constituted a crime under Roman law. In his letter to Trajan (Pliny *Ep.* 10.96), he asks if it is a crime simply to be a Christian, if the crime is the immoral behavior associated with the name *Christian* (regardless if the behavior actually occurred) or if the Christians' obstinacy was enough to justify charges against them.

Just as Romans 13:1-7 sees the state as correcting immoral behavior, just as these verses exhort their readers to respect the state's criminal proceedings, so the author of 1 Peter encourages his readers to be subject, for the Lord's sake, both to the emperor and to governors (1 Pet 2:13-14). The author of 1 Peter also encourages his readers to be ready to defend themselves (1 Pet 3:15-17) and in doing so to be clear to the magistrates that they suffer only for the Christian name, not because of immoral behavior (1 Pet 4:15-16). Pliny may have faced "inflexible obstinacy" from some Christians, but 1 Peter encourages readers to state their defense "with gentleness and reverence" (1 Pet 3:16).

Romans 12:14—13:7 and 1 Peter 2:13-14 encourage Christians to respect the criminal proceedings of the state and to clearly articulate their faith in such a manner so that they will not be persecuted for inappropriate reasons.

4. Allusions to Roman Law and Legal Processes in the New Testament.

In the NT, legal concepts are also used rhetorically and metaphorically. Paul, a Roman citizen with a background in Jewish law, had a particular interest in Roman law. In writing to Gentiles and others in Roman colonies, Paul's allusions can be seen in terms of both forensic rhetoric and specific legal themes.

4.1. Forensic Rhetoric. Paul's epistle to the Galatians has a form that would have been familiar to its first readers but becomes clear to us only with a basic knowledge of court speeches and legal procedures in the Roman Empire. Paul's defense of himself in Galatians follows the same rhetorical strategies seen in ancient handbooks for courtroom success. This letter functions as a defense speech, an example of forensic rhetoric, which sees its readers, Paul and his opponents as, respectively, jury, defendant and accusers. Paul's defense of himself in Galatians 1 is underscored with an oath, an oath being one of three ways in which a trial could be shortened.

4.2. Citizenship. According to the book of Acts, Paul's Roman *citizenship shaped how he was treated: it protected him from a variety of punishments and gave him a number of legal rights. Writing to a Roman colony like Philippi, Paul refers to Christians' citizenship in heaven (Phil 3:20), knowing that the Philippians would have valued such a metaphor. The author of Ephesians, similarly, acknowledges that his readers are "fellow citizens with the saints and members of the household of God" (Eph 2:19; cf. 2:12; 4:18).

That citizenship is not to be found in this world is particularly clear from non-Pauline writings. Hebrews repeatedly makes that point by referring to the city that is to come (Heb 11:9-10; 12:2; 13:14). The addressees of 1 Peter are seen as a "chosen race . . . God's own people" (1 Pet 2:9), but they are also seen as "aliens and exiles" (1 Pet 2:11), who should be subject to the emperor and governors in this world (1 Pet 2:13-18).

Citizenship was highly valued in the Roman Empire. The NT writers use this desideratum to acknowledge that citizenship is important, but only the citizenship that is conferred on those who are people of God. All Christians in this world, even those who are Roman citizens, are aliens. Their true citizenship is in heaven.

4.3. **Societas** *and Commercial Language.* Familiarity with *societas* (*koinōnia,* in Greek) illuminates Paul's description of three of his relationships. In Roman law, *societas* refers to a unique, voluntary partnership contract that did not require witnesses, written documents or a public announcement and that could be made even with slaves (Justinian *Dig.* 17.2.58.3). Most characteristic of such contracts was that each partner contributed, frequently financially, with a view toward a shared goal.

When Paul refers to the "giving of the right hand" to James, Cephas and John (Gal 2:9-10), such an expression does not make sense within Jewish tradition but does appear in the papyri as a means of establishing contract. Paul's arrangement with "the pillars" is seen as an example of *societas,* with clearly articulated goals and expectations.

Similarly, the imprisoned apostle also sees his relationship with the Philippians in terms of *societas:* he writes a receipt for their gift to him (Phil 4:10-20); he uses *koinōnia* in the sense of a *societas* contract (Phil 1:5; cf. 1:7; 4:15); and he employs terminology (e.g., "to have the same mind," Phil 2:5) characteristic of *societas.* Later, again in a prison epistle, Paul discusses a partnership with Philemon (Philem 17), using legal language of commerce and accounting (Philem 18-19).

Through the terminology of *societas,* Paul emphasizes his concern about sharing the gospel, a goal he shared with the pillars in Jerusalem, with the Philippians and with Philemon.

4.4. Slavery. Paul's epistles contain many references to slaves: to those born of slaves; to those who willingly choose *slavery; to those who should see themselves as slaves of Christ; and to those who should see themselves as freedmen.

In the allegory of Hagar and Sarah (Gal 4:21-31), Paul draws on the notion that a person who was born to a slave mother would take on that status at birth. The legal institution of slavery thus clarifies a theological point: Christians are born of faith, not of law; they should not enslave themselves to something that had nothing to do with their birth in the faith.

In Romans 6:15-23 Paul emphasizes that his readers are not to be slaves of sin. In discussing human choosing to sin, Paul alludes to another provision of Roman law: if one pretended to be a slave, that status could be confirmed; if one sold oneself into slavery, in order to receive money for one's family, for instance, one would be considered a slave. In a world in which slavery was not an attractive option, the metaphor was particularly strong.

At the same time Paul acknowledges that not all slavery is bad, since his readers, who had been "slaves of sin," were "set free from sin and have become slaves of God" (Rom 6:22; cf. Tit 1:1; note also the references to "slaves of Christ" in Rom 1:1; Phil 1:1; Eph 6:5-8). Gaius, *Institutiones* 1.52-57 notes that slaves are in the power of their masters. Paul is concerned in Romans (cf. 1 Cor 7:23) that those Christians who had been "bought with a price" may return to their previous lives of slavery, enslaved either to sin or to humans.

Paul's admonitions in 1 Corinthians 7:22 make sense only under Roman law: "For he who was called in the Lord while a slave is a freedman of the Lord. Likewise he who was free when called is a slave of Christ." Under Roman law, a freed slave still maintained a relationship with his former owner; those ties served as security for the former slave. Thus Paul does not simply say that slaves have become free. By referring to slaves as freedmen of the Lord, he recognizes that a new relationship has developed, a relationship based on security with a new master.

4.5. Adoption. Under Roman law, if a man were adopted at any age, his relationship to his natural parents would end, his previous debts would be cancelled, he would start a new life, take a new family name and be entitled to an inheritance. The new father (*paterfamilias*) would then expect the same of him and provide the same for him as he would any natural children: he would claim his property, control his personal relationships and assume responsibility and liability for his actions (*see* Family and Household). After the *paterfamilias* died, the son would continue to represent his adopted family before the family god.

The apostle Paul found the legal principle of adoption to serve well in expressing theological principles. In Romans 9:4, the Israelites are seen as having been adopted; believers in Christ are seen as adopted (Rom 8:15; Gal 4:5-6; Eph 1:5); and believers are also seen as "groaning inwardly, waiting eagerly for adoption as sons, the redemption of our bodies" (Rom 8:23). Just as Jesus was known as the Son of God, so believers come to be seen as sons by adoption: God has paternal rights over believers; all that believers have and are belong to God.

4.6. Inheritance. In many legal systems an heir does not exist until after a person dies; until then, there exists only an heir apparent. Under Roman law, however, the heir was seen as a continuation of the *paterfamilias*'s legal personality, not as a separate legal entity, and, as a result, he had legal standing as heir during the life of the *paterfamilias*. One was heir not through the father's death but through one's own birth or adoption.

In Romans 8:16-17 Paul writes, "we are children of God, and if children, then heirs." In Galatians 4:7 he says, "you are no longer a slave but a son, then also an heir, through God" (cf. Eph 3:6; Tit 3:7). Paul's references to heirship make best sense within Roman law: there is no implication that heirship necessitates the death of God. Christians' status as heirs comes from their relationship with God: birth and unity of personality create this relationship.

5. Constantine and Roman Law in the Service of the Church.

Before Decius, in A.D. 250, there was no formal legal foundation for a systematic, empire-wide persecution of Christians. Under the *cognitio* system in Roman law, provincial governors chose whether or not they would hear cases against Christians. Some did; some did not.

After the Decian and Diocletian persecutions ended and after the rise of Constantine, specific legal structures developed to support Christian social ideals. Roman law came to forbid crucifixion, gladiatorial shows, the branding of slaves' faces and abandonment of infants. Constantine also repealed Augustus's *marriage laws, which penalized celibates, childless couples and widows who did not remarry. Sunday labor was discouraged except where it was necessary on farms, and in A.D. 321 a law was passed that closed all courts on Sundays, unless they were engaged in freeing slaves.

The church itself came to play a greater role in public life. It was given public grants, property that had been taken away was restored, new buildings and copies of the Bible were financed by the government. In addition, bishops and deacons were given new privileges and came to resemble their secular counterparts. Canon law mirrored Roman law, the clergy's role and vestments were similar to that of their counterparts in civil life, and, from A.D. 318, bishops were permitted to rule in civil suits. Eventually, through Theodosius's edict of A.D. 380, Roman law ensured the dominance of Christianity and the silencing of its rivals.

See also CITIZENSHIP, ROMAN; LAW/NOMOS IN GRECO-ROMAN WORLD; ROMAN ADMINISTRATION; ROMAN EMPIRE; ROMAN GOVERNORS OF PALESTINE.

BIBLIOGRAPHY. H. D. Betz, *Galatians* (Herm; Philadelphia: Fortress, 1979); A. H. M. Jones, *The Criminal Courts of the Roman Republic and Principate* (Totowa, NJ: Rowman & Littlefield, 1972); idem, *Studies in Roman Government and Law* (New York: Praeger, 1960); A. W. Lintott, "Provocatio: From the Struggle of the Orders to the Principate," *ANRW* 1.2 (1972) 226-67; F. Lyall, *Slaves, Citizens, Sons: Legal Metaphors in the Epistles* (Grand Rapids, MI: Zondervan, 1984); A. C. Mitchell, "Rich and Poor in the Courts of Corinth: Litigiousness and Status in 1 Corinthians 6:1-11," *NTS* 39 (1993) 562-86; T. Mommsen, *Römisches Strafrecht* (Leipzig: Duncker & Humblot, 1899); T. Mommsen, P. Kreuger and A. Watson, eds., *The Digest of Justinian* (4 vols.; Philadelphia; University of Pennsylvania Press, 1985); B. Rapske, *The Books of Acts and Paul in Roman Custody* (BAFCS 3; Grand Rapids, MI: Eerdmans, 1994); J. P. Sampley, *Pauline Partnership in Christ: Christian Community and Commitment in Light of Roman Law* (Philadelphia: Fortress, 1980); S. L. Sass, "Research in Roman Law: A Guide to the Sources and Their English Translations," *Law Library Journal* 56 (1963) 210-33; A. N. Sherwin-White, *Roman Society and Roman Law in the New Testament* (Oxford: Oxford University Press, 1963); idem, "Why Were the Early Christians Persecuted?—An Amendment," *Past and Present* 27 (1964) 23-27; G. E. M. de Ste. Croix, "Why Were the Early Christians Persecuted?" *Past and Present* 26 (1963) 6-38; idem, "Why Were the Early Christians Persecuted?—A Rejoinder," *Past and Present* 27 (1964) 28-33; A. Watson, *The Law of the Ancient Romans* (Dallas: Southern Methodist University Press, 1970); B. W. Winter, "Civil Litigation in Secular Corinth and the Church," *NTS* 37 (1991) 559-72.

C. S. Wansink

ROMAN MILITARY

The specter of the Roman military machine was seen and felt across the NT world. According to Matthew, Jesus himself compared his heavenly Father's angelic army to the vast number of the

Roman legions (Mt 26:53). The Roman army reached new heights of might, organization and efficiency for which it remains proverbial to our own day.

1. Sources
2. The Legion
3. The Legionary
4. Other Military Units
5. The Army in Peacetime

1. Sources.

The most important extant ancient literary sources on the Roman military are the *Summary of Military Matters* of Vegetius, Arrian's *Tactics,* the treatise on legionary camps by Pseudo-Hyginus, Josephus's *Jewish War* (especially *J.W.* 3.4-5 §§59-109 and 5.1.6—2.3 §§39-70) and book 6 of Polybius. Other written sources of major importance are the *Code* of Justinian, the many tombstones of soldiers, bronze military diplomas, military *papyri and the wooden tablets from Vindolanda. Among archaeological contributions must be mentioned the numerous excavated forts and camps, especially in Britain and Germany; the increasing amount of armor and weaponry that has been discovered; and the pictures on Trajan's Column in Rome.

2. The Legion.

2.1. Organization and Deployment. The basic army unit of the Romans, the famous legion, was organized as follows. A unit of 8 men was called a *contubernium,* sharing a mule and a tent or two rooms in a permanent barracks. Ten *contubernia* made up one *century* (80 men), six *centuries* made up one *cohort* (480 men), and ten *cohorts* made up one *legion* (4,800 men). Included in this number were 120 horsemen distributed among the centuries to serve as scouts, escorts and messengers. Many of the legionaries were also trained to serve in special capacities as doctors, surveyors, masons, smiths and engineers, though these would be counted among the normal legionaries and would serve in the ranks during battle. At some time during the first century the first *cohort* was changed to six double *centuries* (960 men), raising the total to 5,280 fighting men at full strength. Still higher numbers quoted in some ancient sources probably include the *slaves assigned to the legion, as J. Roth has argued. They helped with the transport of tents and supplies, performed menial functions for the soldiers and guarded the camp during battle.

Augustus (*see* Roman Emperors) had parts of sixty legions under his command at the time of his accession, and he reduced these eventually to twenty-five. Tacitus lists their deployment in A.D. 23: eight were on the Rhine, three in Spain, two in Africa, two in Egypt, four in Syria, two in Pannonia, two in Moesia and two in Dalmatia (Tacitus *Ann.* 4.5). Each legion was numbered (I-XXII), though often several had the same number and were distinguished by nicknames or *cognomina.* Seven or eight new legions were established and an equal number were disbanded during the first century, keeping the overall strength at about twenty-five legions.

When troops were deployed for battle, a triple or double battle line was normally used, the first line being made up of cohorts 1 to 5 arranged from right to left, and behind them the sixth to the tenth, again ranged from right to left. The least-seasoned troops were usually put in cohorts 2, 4, 7 and 9, all of which had seasoned troops on either side. A frontal charge by the seasoned troops was augmented by the cavalry attacking on the wings and attempting to outflank and encircle the enemy. A reserve unit was maintained wherever possible to be deployed as needed. The legion always camped within a wall surrounded by a trench. Within were two main intersecting streets leading to four gates, and with headquarters (*praetorium*) at the intersection. The legions were usually divided into smaller units for winter quartering and reassembled in the spring.

The legionary standards (*signa*) were poles bearing emblems that served as a rallying point and helped identify one's friends during the dusty confusion of an ancient battlefield. They were also thought to embody the soul (*genius*) of the legion and hence were given honor and kept in a special shrine in the camp. Among the standards belonging to each legion was an eagle; a hand symbolizing the vow of loyalty, which was renewed each year; and designs distinctive to each cohort of the legion. The image of the emperor was borne on a similar shaft and included among the standards.

2.2. Command Structure. The commander of a legion (*legatus legionis*) was usually a senator in his late twenties or early thirties and with prior experience as a Roman magistrate, usually as *praetor.* He was appointed by the emperor and given total command in the emperor's place (*imperium,* *epitagē*; cf. Rom 16:26; 1 Tim 1:1; Tit 1:3; 2:15), with a normal term of office of three to four years. His top assistants were the senior tribune, a senator designate who served in this position before entering the senate as a quaestor, and the prefect of the camp. The latter, an elder soldier who had risen through the ranks to become the top centurion and would retire after serving in this position, saw to the food supply, munitions, weapons training and equipment maintenance, general camp or fortress maintenance and medical services. An additional five tribunes, usually *equites*, rounded out the senior staff, taking care of administrative and judicial functions. Additional legates would command other troops as assigned by the legionary commander.

The most important officers from a military standpoint were the sixty centurions (Gk *kentyrion* [Mk 15:39-47] and *hekatontarchos/-ēs* [Mt 8:5, etc.]). Each had full responsibility over his *century*—command in battle, administration, training and discipline. All centurions were graded, the highest being the *primus pilus*, the centurion of the first century of the first cohort. This one-year appointment held wide responsibilities and great honor and led to a discharge with a bonus sufficient to qualify for equestrian rank. Beneath him, in order of rank and honor, were the other centurions of the first cohort, followed by the centurions of the other cohorts. The centurion of the first century of each cohort had command of the entire cohort. Centurions received double the pay of the ordinary soldier and were regularly posted from legion to legion over great distances, often remaining in the army until death. On the basis of past service or outstanding merit, the legionary commander or provincial governor appointed the centurions from the ranks of the lesser officers or from the praetorian guard, or from among civilians (especially the *equites*) as an act of *patronage. It often took fifteen to twenty years for a soldier to work his way up to centurion rank. A centurion who was not a harsh, haughty man was an exception (Lk 7:2-9; Acts 10:1-2).

Below the centurion were the lesser officers (*principales*), the two chief ones being the head standardbearer (*signifer*), who also did the paperwork necessary for the century, and the assistant commander (*optio*), who took charge in the centurion's absence. Also of importance were the sentry and picket supervisor and the weapons and armory chief.

3. The Legionary.

While Roman *citizenship was a prerequisite for service as a legionary, by the early first century one-third came from outside Italy, and by the end of the century Roman citizens from the provinces made up 80 percent of all legionaries. Recruits had to be in good health, have an adequate physique with a minimum height of 6 Roman feet (5'10"), and were usually eighteen to twenty-three years old. A candidate with all the qualifications except *citizenship could be awarded the latter during the interview process (*probatio*); he was enrolled in the Pollian tribe with his birthplace given as the military camp (*castra*). All recruits would take an oath of loyalty (*sacramentum*) to the legionary standards and to the emperor as commander-in-chief, swearing to obey his orders and to protect the state. Breaking this oath was a religious as well as a military crime. The recruit would then receive traveling money to reach his unit. His training would include marching in step, parading, traveling twenty miles in five hours, swimming, basic tactics, battle maneuvers and hand-to-hand combat.

The legionary wore a linen undergarment covered by a knee-length woolen tunic, and he wore boots. His battle armor (*panoplia*, Eph 6:11, 13) included a breastplate (*thōrax*, Eph 6:14) of mail or, from Claudius on, of articulated iron strips, and an iron or bronze helmet (*perikephalaia*, Eph 6:17) with long cheek protectors and a wide flaring neck protector in the back. He carried a large rectangular shield (*scutum, thyreos*, Eph 6:16) and two six-foot javelins (*logchē*, Jn 19:34), and he had a short two-edged sword (*gladius, machaira*, Eph 6:17), as well as a dagger at his belt.

Rank and special honors were indicated by armbands, gold or silver bosses or similar military decorations. A legionary who was first into a besieged town, saved the life of a citizen or did some other heroic act might be awarded a crown. The spoils of war distributed to the troops during the republic were for the most part replaced by imperial donatives given on an emperor's accession and on other special occasions. The triumph (*see* Roman Triumph) granted republican commanders and their armies for extraordinary victories turned into imperial propaganda parades (cf. 2 Cor 2:14; Col 2:15); a scaled-down version was the ovation.

During the course of the first century, the

minimum term of service for legionaries rose from sixteen years plus four years as reservists to twenty years plus five as reservists. Pay during that same period rose from 900 to 1,200 sesterces annually. At retirement a soldier received a plot of land (individually or in a colony) or more commonly a cash gratuity (12,000 sesterces under Augustus). In addition they continued to be exempt from some taxes and personal services and immune from some punishments. Most retirees remained in the provinces, settling near their last camp. To encourage a single-minded loyalty and mobility, soldiers could not legally marry (*see* Marriage). Nonlegal unions, however, were common; a complicated series of laws was enacted to deal with matters of civil rights and inheritance for soldiers, veterans and their offspring. In other ways also, especially with the formal requirements for making wills and the buying and selling of property, soldiers were given legal privileges not enjoyed by ordinary citizens. They were often shown favor in provincial courts and hence could take advantage of the local population.

An army calendar from Dura-Europos shows that festivals in honor of the traditional Roman deities were part of legionary life (*see* Religion, Greco-Roman). Of especial importance were the Capitoline triad (Jupiter, Juno and Minerva), Urbs Roma and imperial cults (*see* Ruler Cult). Foreign cults, especially those of Jupiter Dolichenos and Mithras (*see* Mysteries), while not officially encouraged, were widespread in the army. The lower ranks formed one of the last strongholds of paganism after the Christianization of the empire.

4. Other Military Units.

4.1. Auxiliaries. The *auxilia* made up for the traditional Roman lack of sufficient cavalry and light-armed troops. They were recruited from the provinces, initially remaining as ethnic units and stationed in their areas of origin, though a few units were made up of Roman citizens. While units were of varying type and function, gradually these became more standardized. The basic types were (1) the more elite cavalry, grouped in wings (*alae*) of five hundred (later in the first century often one thousand) and subdivided into squadrons (*turmae*); (2) the similarly sized *cohortes* of light-armed infantry; (3) equestrian cohorts combining cavalry and infantry; and (4) groups of archers and slingers. By the mid-first century, units of double size were also in existence. Local nobles and, later, Roman *equites* commanded the auxiliary units, while its smaller divisions were led by decurions and centurions.

*Herod the Great and his successors had troops that were used as auxiliaries when needed, and they included Thracians, Germans and Gauls, as well as local troops, with some Roman officers (Josephus *J.W.* 1.33.9 §672; 2.3.4 §52). Before the Jewish uprising, such auxiliary units were probably the only Roman troops stationed in Palestine. A centurion named Cornelius was part of the Italian Cohort (Gk *speira*) stationed in *Caesarea Maritima (Acts 10:1). In Acts 27:1 Paul is sent to Italy under guard of a centurion named Julius from the *Sebastēs* Cohort (either the descendants of the crack troops from Samaria mentioned by *Josephus [*J.W.* 2.3.4 §52, etc.] or a cohort named after Augustus, as Jerome translates it). The unit manning the Fortress Antonia when Paul was arrested was commanded by a Roman tribune (Gk *chiliarch*, Acts 21:31), Claudius Lysias, probably an equestrian, who was in charge of at least a double equestrian cohort and several centurions (Acts 21:32; 23:23-26). The troops that arrested Jesus, even though John calls the commander a *chiliarch* and the soldiers a *speira*, was made up "both of men from the high priest's service and from the Pharisees" (Jn 18:3), and thus were not regular Roman auxiliaries.

From Claudius on, all auxiliaries were given citizenship upon their discharge. Their new status was spelled out on two bronze tablets (*diplomata militaria*) verifying their military service, honorable discharge, grant of citizenship for themselves and their existing children and their right to be legally married. On the march, cavalry would make up a forward party and rear guard, while the legionary cavalry preceded the infantry and the *alae* followed the latter. In battle they often charged, first using their lance-like spears and then engaging in hand-to-hand combat with their long broadswords. They were also often used for rear-guard actions or in outflanking or surrounding the enemy.

4.2. Navy. Augustus organized two main standing fleets with a combined strength of seventy-five to one hundred ships. One was based on the Gulf of Naples at Misenum and was responsible for the western Mediterranean; the other was based at Ravenna and controlled the

Adriatic and eastern Mediterranean. For a while another base at Fréjus on the south coast of Gaul had some importance. The fleet commanders were equestrians, often ex-tribunes with experience in the auxiliary forces, and held the rank of prefect. Under Vespasian the commander of the Misenum fleet became one of the highest equestrian posts. Squadron commander and ship captain were also coveted ranks, and retirees were highly honored in their municipalities. The crew itself was recruited from the lower strata of freemen, and often from non-Italian stock, with the term of service rising through the century to twenty-six years, followed by retirement with citizenship. Smaller fleets patrolled the Black Sea, the Rhine and the Danube.

*4.3. **Praetorian Guard.*** The praetorian guard served as the emperor's personal troops and bodyguard. They were recruited mainly from Italy, served for a period of sixteen years and enjoyed significantly higher pay and status than did normal legionaries, as well as the immense donatives given them by new emperors. They were normally commanded by two praetorian prefects of equestrian status. Augustus kept three cohorts, probably of 480 men each, in Rome, with one of them always on guard at the palace. Six other cohorts were stationed in nearby towns. Tiberius built a praetorian camp on the edge of Rome for the entire corps. If Philippians was indeed written from Rome, the statement in Philippians 1:13 would indicate that Paul's preaching infiltrated the praetorian guard. The *speculatores Augusti* were an elite group of praetorian horsemen who cleared the emperor's way through the streets, and, until A.D. 69, the *Germani corporis custodes* formed an additional mounted guard, hand-picked from the auxiliary *alae.*

5. The Army in Peacetime.

In peacetime, the routine duties for legionaries and auxiliaries included guard duty, patrols, foraging expeditions, serving as messengers and guards for the provincial governor (Acts 27:1) and manning outposts. In addition there might be road and bridge building and maintenance, as well as routine maintenance of the camp structures and facilities, including brick and tile making and smithing. A centurion could be seconded by a provincial governor to serve in a police or security function, to help with tax and tribute collections or to be used as a diplomatic envoy. A provincial who met a soldier or an army unit on a road might well became nervous of having his property confiscated for "official use" (Lk 3:14; Apuleius *Met.* 9:39-40; Juvenal *Sat.* 16), or of being himself forced to do labor (*aggareuō,* cf. Mt. 5:41, or Simon of Cyrene in Mt 27:32).

See also JEWISH WARS WITH ROME; ROMAN EMPIRE; ROMAN TRIUMPH.

BIBLIOGRAPHY. M. Bishop and J. Coulston, *Roman Military Equipment from the Punic Wars to the Fall of Rome* (London: Batsford, 1993); B. Campbell, *The Roman Army, 31 B.C.-A.D. 337: A Sourcebook* (London: Routledge, 1994); R. W. Davies, *Service in the Roman Army* (New York: Columbia University Press, 1989); R. O. Fink, *Roman Military Records on Papyrus* (Cleveland: American Philological Association, 1971); A. Goldsworthy, *The Roman Army at War, 100 B.C.-A.D. 200* (Oxford: Oxford University Press, 1996); P. Holder, *Studies in the Auxilia of the Roman Army from Augustus to Trajan* (BAR International Series 70; Oxford: BAR, 1980); L. Keppie, *The Making of the Roman Army: From Republic to Empire* (Totowa, NJ: Barnes & Noble, 1984); Y. Le Bohec, *The Imperial Roman Army* (London: Batsford, 1994); J. Roth, *The Logistics of the Roman Army at War (264 B.C.-A.D. 235)* (Leiden: E. J. Brill, 1998); D. B. Saddington, "The Development of the Roman Auxiliary Forces from Augustus to Trajan," *ANRW* 2.3 (1975) 176-201; C. F. Starr, *The Roman Imperial Navy, 31 B.C.-A.D. 324* (2d ed.; New York: Barnes & Noble, 1960); G. R. Watson, *The Roman Soldier* (Ithaca, NY: Cornell University Press, 1969); G. Webster, *The Roman Imperial Army* (3d ed.; Totowa, NJ: Barnes & Noble, 1985).

G. L. Thompson

ROMAN POLITICAL SYSTEM

The immediate background to the NT is the *Roman Empire under the control of an emperor (*see* Roman Emperors). This control had emerged from the republic, which had been removed during the civil war between Julius Caesar and Gnaeus *Pompey and which had seen the emergence of the emperor Augustus. Many of the Roman political institutions and offices can be traced back to the republican period, though in scope and power there had been many changes.

1. The Senate and Consuls
2. The Emperor
3. Provincial Administration

4. Client Kingdoms
5. Colonies and Cities

1. The Senate and Consuls.
Under the republic the senate had been the main political body of the state. The people had been able to express their view in the political process; however, this effectively ceased under the empire. Although the nature of the senate changed, it nevertheless continued to have a role in the life of *Rome, often as a champion of traditional values; it is noteworthy that all emperors down to the early third century had first been a member of the senate. Most emperors sought to have good relations with the senate, and technically the senate confirmed the emperor in his office. This can be detected with the accession of Tiberius on the death of Augustus in A.D. 14, as up to this point there had been no precedent. However, the acclamation of the emperor by his troops, for example in the case of Vespasian in A.D. 69, might predate the senate's decision.

The conferring of power to the emperor by the senate is well illustrated by the record of a decree (termed in this case a *lex*) of the senate that indicates the range of power for Vespasian (*CIL* 6. 930). This included the right to conclude treaties, to convene the senate, to put and refer proposals to the senate and to expand the empire. Often the titles used by an emperor were awarded by the senate. After the emperor's death, the senate voted on whether or not to grant him deification or, in some cases, damnation (as was the case for Domitian in A.D. 96). Alongside this was the confirmation or annulment of the actions of the deceased emperor.

Although the senate was largely without power of its own, during the first century A.D. there are two key moments when it sought to make changes to the existing Roman political system. The first was in A.D. 41, when Gaius (Caligula) had been murdered and the senate discussed the possibility of returning to a republic; Claudius received his acclamation by the praetorian guard. The second came when Nero fled Rome and the senate gave its support to Galba.

The senate met twice a month, and attendance was technically obligatory. Surviving attendance records show that this was not adhered to; for example, in A.D. 45 only 383 senators attended. In the imperial period, the emperor presented legislation through a formal speech to the senate, and the legislation was usually accepted without emendation. Apart from legislation the senate made decisions on matters pertaining to the provinces, such as religious festivals; it also received formal embassies from cities and provinces. It became responsible for investigating corruption of provincial governors as well as for looking into acts of treason.

Membership of the senate was based on a property valuation of 1,000,000 or 1,200,000 sesterces. Members had usually held a magistracy. Often this was linked to holding the post of quaestor, a financial post associated with provincial proconsuls, which could first be held at the age of twenty-five (*see* Roman Administration). Senators were excluded from certain activities, including commerce. They were eligible to be appointed as provincial governors—with the exception of Egypt, which for historical reasons could be governed only by a member of the equestrian order—as well as to take command of legions (*see* Roman Military). As Roman *citizenship expanded, so the senate became open to provincials.

The two consuls remained the chief magistrates of the city of Rome, and they were responsible for presiding over the senate. In effect the emperor acquired some of the functions of the consul or even held one of the posts himself.

2. The Emperor.
The role of emperor had been established by Augustus. It assumed the powers of proconsuls as well as of the tribunes. The emperor could also hold the office of consul. The emperor held a number of titles of a religious, political and military nature: he was *pontifex maximus* in charge of Roman religious ritual, as well as being *pater patriae,* father of his country. He also assumed the title *imperator,* or commander.

It was to the emperor that Paul appealed (Acts 25:12). Interestingly the book of Acts (Acts 25:21, 25) also uses the Greek form *Sebastos,* or *Augustus* (and see Lk 2:1), an honorific title of the emperor. Elsewhere in the NT the term *Caesar* (Gk *Kaisar*) is used (e.g., on Roman *coinage, Mt 22:21).

3. Provincial Administration.
Provinces (*provinciae*) had first formed part of the Roman political structure in the late third century with the acquisition of the islands of Sic-

ily, Sardinia and Corsica. These areas were placed under the authority of a Roman magistrate. As Rome expanded in the East new provinces such as *Macedonia or *Asia were added.

3.1. Governors. Augustus's reforms in 27 B.C. included the return to certain republican practices, including the appointment of governorships by lot; those appointed were known as proconsuls, and their provinces are usually designated as senatorial. However, the emperor retained the right to appoint to some provinces—known as imperial—especially those where there were concentrations of legions. Strabo (*Geog.* 17.3.24-25) made the point that imperial provinces needed a military garrison either because the territory bordered on territory yet to be subdued or because it might be the center of rebellion; in reality the distinction between the two types of provinces was more complex. In the east Syria was one of the more important imperial provinces. The governors of these imperial provinces, though they were also of senatorial rank and had usually held the rank of either praetor or consul, had a different title and were known as *legati Augusti.* They held office until they were recalled by the emperor.

In spite of this apparent distinction between the types of province, in the imperial period both types of governor received *mandata,* or instructions, from the emperor. For example, the proconsul Gnaeus Domitius Corbulo, proconsul of Asia under Claudius, had to draw attention to his *mandata* when the people of the island of Cos appealed to the emperor (Oliver 1979); he pointed out that matters for the emperor had "first to be submitted to the provincial governors." The governor himself was expected to conduct his authority in the light of the *lex provinciae,* which was established when the province was incorporated.

There were two types of provincial governors in the Roman Empire. The first, more usual type, was drawn from the senatorial class and had usually held other positions prior to their appointment. The governor was conceived of as having proconsular power in the fashion of the governors of the Roman republic. There were set protocols to be adopted by the senatorial governors. For example, they had to announce the day on which they were expected to arrive in their province. The arrival itself was carefully controlled; for example, the governor of Asia had to arrive at Ephesus. There were set protocols to avoid people being seen before the governor arrived in their city; this was to avoid the problems of favoritism and corruption. Finally, the proconsul was expected to administer justice until his successor arrived in the province. The usual Greek word for governor was *anthypatos* (i.e., proconsul), which is how it is applied to Sergius Paulus for Cyprus (Acts 13:7, 8, 12) and L. Junius Gallio for Achaia (Acts 18:12); proconsuls, presumably of the province of Asia, are alluded to by the clerk of the city of Ephesus during the riot (Acts 19:38). Quirinius, governor of the imperial province of Syria, is referred to as *hēgemōn* (Lk 2:2).

The second type of provincial governor, notably in the eastern Mediterranean for Egypt and Judea, was drawn from the equestrian class. He normally was given the title of prefect (Gk *eparchos* or *epitropos*), although in the case of Judea, the title was changed in the middle of the first century A.D. to procurator. Pontius Pilatus is described as prefect in a Latin inscription found in the theater at *Caesarea Maritima. The NT often uses the Greek term *hēgemōn* to refer to the prefect of Judea, whether Pontius Pilatus (e.g., Mt 27; Lk 20:20; cf. Lk 3:1), M. Antonius Felix (Acts 23:24, 26, 33; 24:1, 10) or Porcius Festus (Acts 26:30). Felix was an imperial freedman, and his brother Pallas had been freed by the emperor Claudius.

Governors had a judicial function, and there were set circuits where they had to hear cases. It was deemed to be a privilege to have such hearings in a city (in the Greek east they were known as *metropoleis*) especially as people gathered from over a wide area for the event. It was to be in this capacity that Jesus' disciples were to be brought before governors (Mt 10:18; Mk 13:9; Lk 21:12). In effect the authority of the governor was an extension of that of the emperor (see 1 Pet 2:14). Governors might be expected to intervene in the affairs of individual cities during times of crisis. One such example is the case of Pisidian *Antioch when the governor, Lucius Antistius Rusticus, had to intervene in A.D. 93 during a time of food shortage due to a harsh winter (Sherk no. 107). Individuals were to declare how much grain they had in store, and the price of grain was restricted. Sextus Sotidius Strabo Libuscidianus, governor of Galatia in A.D. 14-15, had to pass an edict about the abuse of requisitioned transport in the province. Details about the duties of the governor were written by

Ulpian (from Tyre) in the early third century A.D. This is preserved within the Roman *Digest* that was issued in 533 by Justinian.

*3.2. **Provincial Officials.*** In senatorial provinces the governor was assisted by a magistrate, the quaestor, also of senatorial rank (usually an ex-praetor; see Strabo *Geog.* 3.4.20) and also chosen by lot and serving for one year. He was usually in charge of the finances of the province. The quaestor might later become the governor of a province in his own right, as in the case of Lucius Novius Crispinus Martialis Saturninus, who served as quaestor of the province of Macedonia in the early second century A.D. (*ILS* 1070). He had previously held a number of offices at Rome, including being part of the board responsible for road maintenance, and a military tribuneship in the Ninth Legion. Subsequently he held the praetorship at Rome, judicial posts in Spain, command of a legion in Lower Germany and then in Africa, and proconsul for Narbonensian Gaul; he finally held the consulship in A.D. 150. Altogether he was active in six different provinces over a period of about twelve years.

Also part of the administrative team was a procurator who was in charge of properties belonging to the emperor. As the procurator could have his own staff, he could challenge the role of the proconsul. An example of a procurator for the province of Asia is presented by the honorific statue awarded to Gaius Minicius Italus by his hometown of Aquileia in Italy in A.D. 105 (*CIL* V 875). He had been prefect of Egypt and was procurator of two separate provinces; when in Asia he had to act as governor when Gaius Vettulenus Civica Cerealis was put to death by Domitian in A.D. 89.

In an imperial province the financial side of the administration was looked after by a procurator. As imperial provinces often contained large numbers of troops he would be responsible for their payment (see Strabo *Geog.* 3.4.20). These procurators were of a lower rank than the quaestors, being drawn from the equestrian order, who had a property qualification of 400,000 sesterces; in some cases they were imperial freedmen, that is, former *slaves of the emperor's household. Imperial property, such as mines, would also be their responsibility. The *mandata* for Claudius Athenodoros, procurator of the imperial province of Syria and dating to the reign of Domitian, was found at Epiphaneia. It records instructions about how to deal with the issue of transport through the province, and in particular the concern that the province should not be overburdened.

Attached to the governor of both types of province was a small number of military officials under a centurion. The governor himself might be accompanied by friends from Rome or even recruit members of the local elite to act as his advisers. An inscription, dated to May 1, A.D. 165, from the sanctuary of the Great Gods on the island of Samothrace, records the proconsul of Macedonia, Publius Antius Orestes, attending the *mysteries attended by four friends who are clearly all Roman citizens, several lictors carrying his badge of authority, several messengers, fifteen slaves, five auxiliary soldiers (one a deputy centurion) and an imperial slave. Further individuals are clearly attached to the governor's friends.

*3.3. **Provincial Councils.*** Within a province there could be loose provincial councils that might come together to present a single voice on behalf of several cities. For example, in Asia there was a council of the Hellenes, that is, the Greek cities of the province. Influential figures in the province of Asia were the Asiarchs who appear at Ephesus (Acts 19:31).

4. Client Kingdoms.

Alongside provinces, Rome sought to maintain friendly relations with free kingdoms that adjoined its territory. Special alliances could be formed, giving the rulers the official title "king, friend and ally of the Roman people." Augustus particularly encouraged client kings as part of his control of the empire (Suetonius *Augustus* 48). For example, Cappadocia continued to be a client kingdom until A.D. 17. *Herod the Great (e.g., Mt 2:1) was appointed king of the Jews by Marcus Antonius and Octavian (who was later to become the emperor Augustus); on Herod's death in 4 B.C., the emperor Augustus ratified Herod's will to allow his sons Archelaus, Herod Antipas and Philip to rule their specified territories. Agrippa I of Judea was brought up with members of the imperial household. Some territories were controlled by a federation of cities, such as Lycia in southwest Turkey (Strabo *Geog.* 14.3.2), which remained independent until A.D. 43. The Nabatean kingdom to the east of the province of Judea for a short time included Damascus (cf. 2 Cor 11:32).

5. Colonies and Cities.

Traditional forms of civic administration continued in the Greek cities (Gk *poleis,* Lat *civitates*) of the Roman East (*see* Roman East). There are recognizable bodies such as the *demos* ("people"), which might meet as the *ekklēsia* ("assembly"). There would normally be a representative body, commonly known as the *boulē*, in which decisions would be made. A personification of these groups appears on the first-century A.D. funeral monument of C. Julius Zoilos at Aphrodisias, a freedman of Augustus. There the *boulē* and *demos* of the Aphrodisians come to honor Zoilos, who is dressed in Greek style.

A number of magistrates, sometimes known as *archōn,* would be appointed to the city (see Acts 16:19, at the Roman colony of *Philippi). In Macedonia one of the regular terms for civic magistrates who were elected on an annual basis was the *politarch.* Many of the examples of individuals holding this post come from *Thessalonica (Acts 17:6-9), but not exclusively so. There would also be a number of officers to carry out the operations of the city. For example, at Ephesus the *grammateus* (city clerk) tried to calm the rioting crowd in the theater (Acts 19:35).

The urban landscape of the provinces included a number of new colonies established by Rome to settle its veteran soldiers. These had a Roman form of government that in many ways reflected the political structures of Rome itself. The *populus* of a colony had two main elements, the *cives*, or colonists, and the other inhabitants, or *incolae.* The *populus* was divided into tribes—for example, at *Corinth twelve tribes are attested—which voted as a body in the *comitia tributa,* the equivalent of the Greek *ekklēsia.* This body was responsible for electing magistrates, most significantly the *duoviri.* The colony itself was administered by a committee or *decurio* (Gk *boulē*); it was responsible for the finance of the colony as well as building projects. Like the senate at Rome, membership of the *decurio* was based on a property qualification. Below the *duoviri* were the *aediles,* who were in charge of the financial arrangements for the city. The land of the colony was considered to be under *ius Italicum,* which meant that it was exempt from Roman tribute as those to whom it belonged were Roman citizens.

A possible civic official at Corinth appears in the form of Erastus, who is referred to as *oikonomos tēs poleōs* (Rom 16:23). The *oikonomos* may have been in charge of estates belonging to the colony; this may solve earlier attempts at arguing that the *oikonomos* was the Greek translation of the Latin *aedile.* Roman colonies such as Corinth, Philippi and Pisidian Antioch feature in the NT.

See also ROMAN ADMINISTRATION; ROMAN EAST; ROMAN EMPERORS; ROMAN GOVERNORS OF PALESTINE; ROMAN LAW AND LEGAL SYSTEM.

BIBLIOGRAPHY. D. Braund, ed., *The Administration of the Roman Empire (241 B.C.-A.D. 193)* (ESH 18; Exeter: University of Exeter, 1988); P. A. Brunt, "Lex de Imperio Vespasiani," *JRS* 67 (1977) 95-116; G. P. Burton, "The Issuing of Mandata to Proconsuls and a New Inscription from Cos," *ZPE* 21 (1976) 63-68; K. Galinsky, *Augustan Culture: An Interpretative Introduction* (Princeton, NJ: Princeton University Press, 1996); D. W. J. Gill, "The Roman Empire as a Context for the New Testament," in *Handbook to Exegesis of the New Testament,* ed. S. E. Porter (NTTS 25; Leiden: E. J. Brill, 1997) 389-406; M. Goodman, *The Roman World 44 B.C.-A.D. 180* (London: Routledge, 1997); A. H. M. Jones, *The Greek City from Alexander to Justinian* (Oxford: Clarendon Press, 1940); A. Lintott, *Imperium Romanum: Politics and Administration* (London: Routledge, 1993); F. Millar, *The Emperor in the Roman World* (2d ed.; London: Duckworth, 1992); idem, *The Roman Empire and Its Neighbors* (2d ed.; London: Duckworth, 1981); J. H. Oliver, "Greek applications for Roman trials," *AJP* 100 (1979) 542-58; idem, "A Roman governor visits Samothrace," *AJP* 87 (1966) 75-80; R. K. Sherk, *The Roman Empire: Augustus to Hadrian* (Cambridge: Cambridge University Press, 1988).

D. W. J. Gill

ROMAN SOCIAL CLASSES

Roman social stratification was assessed according to economic class (access to wealth and means of production), status and power. Roman social classes in the late republic and early imperial periods were determined primarily by birth and legal status rather than by *education, wealth or ethnic background as social class is determined today. Being born into a social class with its legally determined privileges, duties and parameters was generally more socially determinative than personal achievement in education or amassing of wealth. Some social mobility was built into the system and usually granted from the top down.

The Roman world had two main classifications of people: the upper and lower classes or orders (*ordines*). The very small upper classes controlled the vast majority of the property, wealth, power and status and constituted less than 1 percent of the population. As a way of establishing and reinforcing status the wealthy were expected to contribute financially to local schools, baths, *temples, feasts and games (*see* Athletics). They sat in the best seats at public events and received more of the public doles. The lower classes had little or no property, wealth, power and status and constituted 99 percent of the population. Early Christians fell almost exclusively within the lower classes.

1. The Three Upper Classes
2. The Lower Classes
3. Social Mobility
4. The Social Level of the Early Christians

1. The Three Upper Classes.
The three aristocratic classes or orders established by law and qualifications of property ownership, especially under Augustus, were called the *honestiores* ("possessors of honor"). These were the *ordo senatorius* ("senators") and the *ordo equester* ("equestrians" or *equites*) of *Rome, and the *decurions,* the provincial aristocracy. By the first century A.D., most wealth was concentrated in the Italian homeland in the hands of the senators and equestrians. Wealth in all three orders was kept primarily in the form of land—country estates worked by *slaves and furnishing the means for the owner to live in luxury in the city.

The rich despised manual labor. They upheld the life of leisure as the truly satisfying one because it is self-sufficient and allows attendance to virtue. Their occupations revolved around social, *political and *military activities, as well as gentleman farming, trading (in small quantity) and advanced teaching and architecture.

Members of the upper orders were entitled to more at any imperial dole of cash, food or wine. Compare Jesus' words: "For to those who have, more will be given" (Mk 4:25 par. Mt 13:12; Lk 8:18 NRSV). They had the preferential seats at theater productions and *banquets, where they were also served better food. They were tried in different courts and given more lenient sentences for convictions of the same crimes as members of the lower classes (*see* Roman Law and Legal System).

1.1. The Senatorial Order. During the republic the senators were magistrates who represented the aristocratic families of the Roman city-state (patricians). In the emperor's fight to consolidate power during the early days of the empire, many of these senators were purged and replaced by senators from outside the city of Rome and even by those of non-Roman origin. During the empire senators were appointed by the emperor as representatives from all over the *Roman Empire. They were six hundred to nine hundred in number, with qualification for the order being 250,000 denarii worth of property (a denarii is roughly a day's wage for a laborer), the equivalent of 1,000,000 sesterces. Because the empire was an agricultural economy, the senators' money was usually built and maintained from landed estates. They held the highest government offices in Rome, running the legions (praetorians), administering the provinces (consulars) and functioning as ceremonial priests. R. MacMullen estimates that senators made up less than two-thousandths of 1 percent of the population.

1.2. The Equestrian Order. The equestrians were originally wealthy landowners who could afford to ride to war on a horse. During the republic they were rich Romans who had not entered political or military life. Unlike the senatorial order, there was no set number of equestrians. The emperor could appoint anyone to this order who met the qualifications of being a *citizen of free birth with property worth at least 100,000 denarii (= 400,000 sesterces). During the reign of Tiberius, to keep too many freedmen from aspiring to be equestrians, the qualification was modified to two generations free. MacMullen estimates that the equestrians comprised less than one-tenth of 1 percent of the population.

Like that of the senatorial order, the wealth of equestrians was usually built from agriculture on landed estates. They usually held a series of salaried positions, including in the army, procuratorial appointments involving financial administration (especially in small provinces that did not need large numbers of troops), appointments involving food doles in Rome and to the imperial fleets, and, at the highest levels, prefectures of Egypt and the praetorian guard. Senators were frequently replenished from this order.

1.3. Decurions. Decurions were provincial,

monied aristocrats. They obtained their fortunes through inheritance, landowning (the main source of wealth), trading and manufacturing. Rome utilized decurions to administrate the provinces. They served as magistrates on the local council that formed the highest local authority, working alongside the popular assembly. There were about one hundred decurions to a council, but the number could range from thirty to five hundred and was generally larger in the East. The property requirement was usually 25,000 denarii, or one-tenth that needed to be a senator. Decurions collected taxes, supervised markets and harbors and served as ambassadors. For a job well done and with other necessary qualifications met, the emperor could appoint decurions to the equestrian order. The decurions probably constituted less than 5 percent of the population of the provincial cities.

1.4. Caesar and His Household. Of course the emperor was at the top of the social order. His honorable status was shared by members of his imperial household and officials of the central administration, the *Servi Caesaris* or *Familia Caesaris,* who lived very comfortably on his property. At one time his household numbered about 20,000 and was mainly composed of slaves. Their roles ranged from being domestics to heads of state bureaus, supervising the emperor's property and collecting his revenue. As a boy, a slave received training in Latin, Greek and mathematics and worked in domestic service. From ages twenty to thirty he occupied minor posts in civil service. He was manumitted at thirty but could move to more important posts such as record officer, accountant, paymaster or correspondent. Upon manumission these former members of the imperial household usually became prominent among the monied freedmen.

2. The Lower Classes.

The lower classes, the *humiliores* ("of lowly birth and status") constituted the vast majority of the population. These classes were distinguishable yet overlapping. There was no middle class within the urban commercial and industrial portions of society as we would think of middle class. There was intermediate wealth represented by the aristocracy of smaller cities and towns. Also, within the lower classes there were small landowners, craftsmen, shopkeepers and soldiers with some economic means. However, none of these formed a middle class. There was an enormous chasm between their wealth and power and even the decurions at the lower end of the three upper orders.

2.1. Owners of Small Farms and Businesses. At the top of the lower classes were owners of small farms and businesses. These owners usually employed slaves, whether the owners were the masters of the slaves or the owners were free men or freedmen hiring slave labor. Sometimes these farms and businesses were run by free men or freedmen for their rich *patrons. The small businesses included such ventures as auctioneer, baker, barber, butcher, dyer, fuller, grocer, innkeeper, moneylender, potter, shipper, smith, tanner, trader, weaver and wine and oil exporter. These artisans and craftsmen took pride in their work and handed down the trade to their children. They could rise to be magistrates and decurions in the aristocracy of their local communities. These often formed *collegia,* or guilds, that were social organizations formed around a shared trade (*see* Associations).

2.2. Free Poor. The plebs were freeborn Roman citizens, both urban and rural. As much as one-third of the population of Rome may have fallen into this category. Socially the plebs had an advantage over freedmen, slaves and freeborn non-Roman citizens (*peregrini*), but economically they were disadvantaged. Slave labor was cheaper, and plebs could not get funding to engage in business activities as freely as could freedmen. Freedmen could more readily obtain financing from their savings during slavery or from their former masters.

The free poor often had no means of production and relied upon work on farms and docks and in construction. They were often fishermen, fowlers, hunters, shoemakers, barbers and other occupations in which the equipment was not expensive. Their lot was uncertain, depending as it did upon the availability of work and the beneficence of others. They could attach themselves as clients to patrons, which would make their lot more reliable, or they could beg or steal. If they were Roman citizens within the cities they could be fed by the Roman monthly grain dole, which supplied about two-fifths of their food needs. Those faring better owned means of production and employed slaves, such as bakers or those in construction where they could be superintendents of buildings, dressers of stone or plasterers.

*2.3. **Freedmen.*** The freedmen (*libertini*) were a class of former slaves who had been manumitted. Their lot was mixed. While they were slaves, some were taught a trade, given a wage and were able to leave slavery to practice their professions or start their own businesses. They could also remain in the business ventures of their former masters as agents in business transactions thought too unseemly for the master to be conducting in person. Others found themselves as day laborers without the certainty of food, clothing and shelter that they enjoyed as slaves; that is, they found their lot even less than a slave's lot. In the upheaval of the last century of the republic large numbers of slaves were manumitted, and the class grew enormously, causing considerable social dislocation.

*2.4. **Slaves.*** Slaves were legally classified as commodities (*res*). They were of two main types: those born in *slavery to a family already in slavery and rooted in society, and those reduced to slavery by conquest or pirates. Possibly a quarter of the population of the Roman Empire consisted of slaves, and within Rome it may have been 25 to 40 percent. They were workers on farms, road construction, harbors, shipping and mining. Slaves in rich households could count on shelter, food, clothing, some wages and advancement for their children. Many were well-educated and often themselves served as tutors to the children of their masters (especially those of Caesar's household) and were managers of their masters' households. Usually overlooked is the fact that even poor free men and freedmen had their own slaves working within their small farms and businesses. Thus slave ownership was found among people of widely divergent economic means.

Slaves were primarily occupied with agricultural crops and domestic service on large estates. Other jobs filled by slaves (rarely by freedmen) revolved around food and clothing, in both the household and in business. Slaves provided food as fishermen, fowlers and hunters; prepared food as millers and bakers; and served food, whether in a household or a bakery business. They provided clothing as spinners, weavers, fullers, menders and cobblers, whether in the household or a small shop. They also provided domestic service on large estates and worked in inns and baths. In transportation, slaves took care of horses in stables and drove mules and wagons.

3. Social Mobility.

The upper and lower classes were separated by a number of legal and cultural barriers (e.g., those of the senatorial class could not marry former slaves). However, as P. Garnsey, P. R. C. Weaver and J. E. Stambaugh have pointed out, some social mobility did exist. *Peregrini* could become citizens, slaves could become freedmen, plebs and freedmen could become equestrians, and equestrians could become senators.

One could move up the social scale by *marriage to someone further up the social scale. *Women could gain wealth and power through inheritance or investment but were expected to remain in private life and not assume public office. However, many became involved in manufacture and commerce and became *benefactors to cities by providing public buildings and temples. Even before manumission, slaves of the household of Caesar could marry a freeborn woman, own slaves and acquire wealth; and after manumission they continued in government positions. This put them ahead socially, beyond others in the lower classes.

Usually mobility was initiated by a person in a higher social position who sponsored a person of a lower class on the basis of the latter's great personal achievement. For example, the emperor could appoint a notable person to the senatorial or equestrian order. Locally some people could rise to the local aristocracy by appointment of the governor or emperor on the advice of worthy citizens and on the basis of meritorious achievement or service.

Obtaining Roman citizenship was also a factor in social mobility. Citizenship could be granted from the emperor, senate or generals to individuals or whole communities. Citizenship was also acquired upon discharge from military service or upon manumission from slavery. During the empire, however, citizenship did not confer significant or enforced privileges.

Manumission from slavery made slaves freedmen. Freedmen from Caesar's household had great opportunities for upward social mobility that other segments of the population did not. However, generally the social mobility of freedmen was restricted. They became patrons of their former masters, and these obligations could be litigated if not performed. Freedmen could not hold public office or serve in the Roman legions. They could not join the equestrian order no matter how much wealth they garnered. They could not marry within the senatorial order. The children of freedmen were free from birth, so unlike their parents, they could rise to the equestrian and senatorial orders. Many of these restrictions were created to keep the freedmen from overwhelming the aristocracy.

It must also be noted that social mobility moved in both directions. People could also move down the social scale by losing their fortunes or through conviction as criminals. The emperor could remove a person from the senatorial or equestrian orders.

4. The Social Level of the Early Christians.
The second-century pagan author Celsus wrote against Christianity, seeing it as a religion of "the foolish, dishonourable and stupid, and only slaves, women, and little children" led by "wool-workers, cobblers, laundry-workers, and the most illiterate and bucolic yokels" (Origen *Cont. Cels.* 3.44, 55, trans. Chadwick 1965), that is, a lower-class movement of slaves, women and children; of uneducated day workers. In the last century, A. Deissmann, noting that the language of the NT is akin to the language of the common people of the nonliterary *papyri (*koinē*), concluded that the early Christians were poor, uneducated and dispossessed within Roman society. Until recently this has been the assessment in NT studies.

However, *Pliny (Pliny *Ep.* 10.96.9; c. A.D. 112) said that Christians were of every social rank. When addressing the Corinthians, Paul said "not many of you were wise by human standards, not many were powerful, not many were of noble birth" (1 Cor 1:26 NRSV), a statement implying that some Christians did fit this description. *Koine* Greek was also the language of very educated people within the upper classes. These indications and recent study, especially of Paul's letters by W. A. Meeks, A. J. Malherbe and G. Theissen, among others, indicate that Christianity was drawn from a cross-section of the population. The upper classes of Greco-Roman society do not seem to be represented in Paul's letters: senators, equestrians and decurions. The extreme bottom is also not well-represented: the subsistence day laborers. The groups that are present are the slaves, freeborn poor, freedmen, small business owners and some of moderate wealth. This assessment is confirmed in the second century by Justin Martyr (*Apol. II* 10.8), Tatian (*Or. Graec.* 32), and Minucius Felix (*Oct.* 8.3-4; 31.6). It was not until the third century that Christians appear within the upper orders of Roman society.

Some early Christians were wealthy (although not aristocracy) as indicated by their possessing houses able to accommodate church meetings, ownership of slaves and ability to travel. Some Christians were rich patrons who accommodated Paul and the fledgling church in their homes, including the mother of John Mark (Acts 12:12), Lydia (Acts 16:15, 40), Jason (Acts 17:5-9), Titius Justus (Acts 18:7), Nympha (Col 4:15), Philemon (Philem 2) and Aquila and Priscilla (Acts 18:2-3, 18; Rom 16:5; 1 Cor 16:19). Several could travel: Aquila and Priscilla (Acts 18:18-19; Rom 16:3-5; 1 Cor 16:19), Phoebe (Rom 16:1-2) and Chloe's people (1 Cor 1:11). As Theissen has pointed out, social stratification explains several of the conflicts in the Corinthian church. For example, at the agape feast and Lord's Supper the wealthy may have excluded the poor. The problem may have been that a wealthy patron of the agape feast acted like a patron at a banquet and only allowed food distribution according to social status—the best for the rich, the worst for the poor (1 Cor 11:17-34).

Small business and crafts people were well-represented in the early church. There are references to Jesus as a "carpenter's son" (Mt 13:55), Simon a tanner (Acts 9:43), Paul and Aquila and Priscilla as leather workers (Acts 18:2-3; *see DPL,* Tentmaking) and Lydia as a dealer of luxury textiles (Acts 16:14). There were slaves and freedmen of the household of Caesar in the church (Phil 4:22), as well as slaves and slaveowners (Onesimus and Philemon). Paul even legislates for slaves and masters in the church (1 Cor 7:20-24; Eph 6:5-9; Col 3:22-25). Erastus in *Corinth (Rom 16:23) may be the aedile (superintendent of public works) who paved the courtyard outside the theater of Corinth. He may have been a freedman with Roman citizenship. Paul addresses several passages to those who work with their hands, perhaps as artisans and day laborers (Eph 4:28; 1 Thess 4:11; 2 Thess 3:6-13).

See also BENEFACTOR; CITIZENSHIP, ROMAN; PATRONAGE; ROMAN POLITICAL SYSTEM; SLAVERY; SOCIAL VALUES AND STRUCTURES.

BIBLIOGRAPHY. J. H. D'Arms, *Commerce and Social Standing in Ancient Rome* (Cambridge, MA: Harvard University Press, 1981); M. I. Finley, *The Ancient Economy* (Sather Classical Lectures 43;

Berkeley and Los Angeles: University of California Press, 1973); J. Gagé, *Les Classes sociales dans L'empire Romain* (Bibliothèque Historique; Paris: Payot, 1964); J. G. Gager, *Kingdom and Community: The Social World of Early Christianity* (Prentice-Hall Studies in Religion Series; Englewood Cliffs, NJ: Prentice-Hall, 1975) 93-113; P. Garnsey, *Social Status and Legal Privilege in the Roman Empire* (Oxford: Clarendon Press, 1970); P. Garnsey and R. Saller, *The Roman Empire: Economy, Society and Culture* (Berkeley and Los Angeles: University of California Press, 1987); J. S. Jeffers, *Conflict at Rome: Social Order and Hierarchy in Early Christianity* (Minneapolis: Fortress, 1991); E. A. Judge, "The Social Identity of the First Christians: A Question of Method in Religious History," *JRH* 11 (1980) 201-17; R. MacMullen, *Roman Social Relations 50 B.C. to A.D. 284* (New Haven, CT: Yale University Press, 1974) 88-120; A. J. Malherbe, *Social Aspects of Early Christianity* (2d ed.; Philadelphia: Fortress, 1983) 29-59; M. Maxey, *Occupations of the Lower Classes in Roman Society* (Chicago: University of Chicago Press, 1938) [M. E. Park and M. Maxey, *Two Studies on the Roman Lower Classes* (New York: Arno, 1975) chap. 1]; W. A. Meeks, *The First Urban Christians: The Social World of the Apostle Paul* (New Haven, CT: Yale University Press, 1983) 51-73; C. Nicolet, ed., *Recherches sur les structures sociales dans l'antiquite classique* (Paris: Éditions du centre national de la recherche scientifique, 1970); M. Rostovtzeff, *The Social and Economic History of the Roman Empire* (2 vols.; 2d ed.; rev. P. M. Fraser; Oxford: Clarendon Press, 1957); J. E. Stambaugh and D. L. Balch, *The New Testament in Its Social Environment* (LEC 2; Philadelphia: Westminster, 1986) 107-37; G. Theissen, *The Social Setting of Pauline Christianity: Essays on Corinth* (Philadelphia: Fortress, 1982) 69-119; P. R. C. Weaver, *Familia Caesaris: A Social Study of the Emperor's Freedmen and Slaves* (Cambridge: Cambridge University Press, 1972); idem, "Social Mobility in the Early Roman Empire: The Evidence of the Imperial Freedman and Slaves," *Past and Present* 37 (1967) 3-20 [=*Studies in Ancient Society*, ed. M. I. Finley (London: Routledge & Kegan Paul, 1974) 121-40]. D. F. Watson

ROMAN TRIUMPH

By the time of the NT, the spectacular parades that entered through the *Porta Triumphalis* ("triumphal gate") of *Rome had become perhaps the most important and well-known political-religious institution of the period. Images of the *emperor in a triumphal chariot were even frequently used on imperial *coins. These lavish pageants or triumphal processions, known as the Roman triumph (Gk *thriambos;* Lat *triumphus),* were carried out by special decree of the city of Rome in order to celebrate great victories, to honor the general, consul or emperor who had achieved them and to render thanksgiving to the deity who had granted them. According to the ancient historian Orosius (A.D. 385-418[?]), 320 such triumphs were celebrated between the founding of Rome and the reign of Vespasian in A.D. 69-79 (Orosius *Hist.* 7.9). It is widely recognized that there are two explicit references to the institution of the Roman triumph in the NT: 2 Corinthians 2:14 and Colossians 2:15. In addition, J. R. White has argued that it informs the corresponding metaphor of death in 1 Corinthians 15:29-31. Finally, T. E. Schmidt has suggested that the imagery of the Roman triumph is implicit in Mark 15:16-32. An understanding of these important passages is therefore dependent on an awareness of the nature of the Roman triumph itself and of what it meant to lead and to be led through the streets of Rome in such a procession.

1. The Nature of the Roman Triumph
2. The Use of the Triumph Imagery in the New Testament

1. The Nature of the Roman Triumph.

H. S. Versnel has argued that the Roman triumph in the *Hellenistic period was the result of a long development that extends back into the pre-Roman period of the Etruscan dynasties (late sixth century B.C.). Originally, the triumph was most likely a sacral New Year's festival in which the king, dressed to represent the deity in his yearly arrival or renewal, was carried into the city in anticipation of a sacrifice, at which time there was a cry for the epiphany of the god in his triumph (Gk *thriambe;* Lat *triumpe).* This rite was later transferred to Zeus in *Greece, to Dionysus in Egypt and then to Jupiter in Rome (*see* Religion, Greco-Roman).

But during the days of the republic, the idea of a human being representing a deity, not to mention embodying his or her presence, was offensive to Roman sensibilities (cf. Diodorus Siculus *Bib. Hist.* 14.117.6; Livy *Hist.* 5.23.5; Plutarch *Cam.* 7.1; Dio Cassius *Hist.* 52.13.3). As a result, the victorious generals now took the place of the god, so that the triumph celebrated their military triumphs and the political supremacy of Rome rather than being directly linked to the enthronement of a deity. The triumphator's former role as an epiphany of the deity was now replaced by his identity as the bearer of good fortune who returns to bring welfare to Rome and who in turn leads in the worship of Jupiter for his blessing (cf. Tacitus *Hist.* 4.58.6; Livy *Hist.* 45.39.10). However, by 20 B.C. the triumphs had again become the exclusive privilege of the emperor, forming an essential part of the imperial quest for power. By the mid-first century A.D. the significance of the triumph had therefore come full circle, since once again the triumph portrayed the ruler as a god. But now the triumph not only publicized the caesar's conquest and domination but also pictured his own deification.

Central to the Roman triumph, in contrast to the minor triumph or ovation awarded for lesser feats, was the portrayal of the general, consul or caesar as victor and savior (*sōtēr,* in the sense of one who brings good fortune). As the focal point of the procession, the triumphator rode the triumph in a chariot. He was dressed in a purple toga, wore a tunic stitched with gold palm motifs and had a crown upon his head. His face was painted red and he carried an eagle-crowned scepter in his hand, all of which were elements taken from the depiction of Jupiter in the temple of Jupiter Capitolinus. The victor was surrounded by his soldiers and by leading exhibits of the spoils of war, graphic representations of the significant battle(s) on billboards and placards announcing the peoples conquered.

Most significantly, the victor led in his triumph representative samples of the vanquished foes and leaders, the former being paraded through the streets as *slaves, the latter in mockery of their former royalty. The parade route ended at the temple of Jupiter Capitolinus, where the people offered sacrifices of thanksgiving and petitions for the future health of Rome. At the climax of the pageant, those prisoners and royalty who had been led in triumph and were not destined to be sold into slavery were executed in honor to the victor as the ultimate sign of his conquest and in homage to Rome's deity (Versnel, 58-63, 83-87). Indeed, the accounts of the NT period often highlighted the fact that the Roman triumph culminated in the death of those captives being led in it (cf., e.g., Plutarch *Aem.* 33.3—34.2; 36.6; *Anton.* 84.2-4; and esp. Josephus *J.W.* 6.9.4 §§433-34; 7.5.4 §§123-57, which details Titus's triumph after his victory over the Jews and is the most extensive of the extant ancient accounts). The glories of the spoils, the story of the battles, the strength of the prisoners of war, the humiliation of the conquered rulers and the final sacrifices and death of the captives were all meant to display vividly the glory, wisdom, power and sovereignty of Rome and its leaders.

Moreover, the entire event took place in recognition of the favor of the supreme god, to whom the triumph as a whole was intended to be an act of worship. Thus, as Versnel has observed, "In no other Roman ceremony do god and man approach each other as closely as they do in the triumph" (Versnel, 1). Hence to be granted such a triumph was the greatest honor Rome could bestow (Livy *Hist.* 30.15.12). Conversely, to be led to death in such a triumphal procession was the ultimate act of defeat and humiliation.

2. The Use of the Triumph Imagery in the New Testament.

Though the noun *thriambos* (the triumph) is not found in the NT, its corresponding verb *thriambeuō* ("to lead in a triumphal procession," cf. Plutarch *Rom.* 25.4; *Thes.* 4.2; *Pomp.* 45.1-5) occurs in both 2 Corinthians 2:14 and Colossians 2:15, where Paul employs the image of the Roman triumph metaphorically to describe God's role as the sole, divine ruler and sovereign victor over his enemies. It is striking, however, that in both these texts the focus is on the direct object of the verb, thereby calling attention to the role of those led in triumph in revealing, ultimately through their death, the glory of the one who had conquered them. Read against this cultural backdrop, Colossians 2:15 affirms that God, having previously conquered and disarmed the rulers and authorities of this age, is now leading them in a triumphal procession (*thriambeuō*). Just as being led in a triumphal procession meant being led to death, so too the result of God's triumph over the rulers of this age is the manifestation of his sovereign glory through the public display of their destruction.

In 2 Corinthians 2:14 Paul himself in his role as an apostle (hence the use of the literary or apostolic plural in this verse) is now the object of the verb: "But thanks be to God who always leads us in his triumphal procession (*thriam-*

beuō) in Christ and [in this way] makes known through us the fragrance of the knowledge of him in every place." In addition, some scholars have taken the image of the fragrance in this passage (cf. 2 Cor 2:14-16a) to refer to the incense that was sometimes carried along in the triumph, while others (more correctly in my opinion) view it as a reference to the incense of the OT sacrifice.

But ever since John Calvin found it impossible to imagine that Paul could be praising God for leading him like a prisoner of war in such a triumphal procession, the more significant issue has been the application of the metaphor of the Roman triumph itself. Calvin himself, for theological reasons, gave the verb a causative sense, which he recognized was different from the common meaning of the verb, and translated the verse, "Thanks be to God who causes us to triumph." Rather than being led in the triumph to his death, Paul was now portrayed as sharing in God's triumph like a general walking alongside of the chariot.

Although such a rendering is impossible both linguistically (in 1879 Findlay demonstrated that *thriambeuō,* being a transitive verb, was never used in such a factitive sense) and historically (those led in triumph were not the victors), this reading of the text has influenced the translation and interpretation of the passage ever since (cf. Egan's attempt to redefine it to mean "display," "noise abroad" or "publicize," even though there is no textual or linguistic support for such a reading).

More recently, J. M. Scott has argued that although Paul does picture himself as being led in triumph, the image refers not to being led to death but to Paul's vision of the triumphator's chariot in front of him, which in the Roman triumph helped to symbolize the deity. Taken in this way, the metaphor points to Paul's experiences of a Jewish *merkabah* (= chariot) mysticism, as in 2 Corinthians 12:1-6, since Paul associated the Roman chariot with the chariot vision of God's glory in Ezekiel 1:15-21 as picked up in the imagery of Psalm 68(67):18-19 (cf. Eph 4:8). In 2 Corinthians 2:14, Paul is thus speaking of being led into mystical experiences of God's glory, by which he makes God known to others. On the other hand, C. Breytenbach has argued that the metaphor should not be pressed so far but refers simply to Paul's role as the one who reveals God's glory as victor, without including the other images of the Roman triumph. In his view, Paul is referring only to his ministry as an apostolic mediator of the knowledge of God in a general sense.

However, such attempts to emphasize a different aspect of the triumph other than Paul's being led to death as the key to the metaphorical image in 2 Corinthians 2:14 cannot do justice to the immediate context of 2 Corinthians 2:12-13, where Paul has just described his anxiety over the welfare of the Corinthians as he awaited news from Titus, which he reminds the Corinthians in 2 Corinthians 11:28 was one of his greatest experiences of suffering. For Paul, to be led into such situations of suffering as an apostle is to be led to his "death" in Christ and for the sake of the gospel. Nor can it make sense out of the exact parallels between 2 Corinthians 2:14 and 1 Corinthians 4:9 and 2 Corinthians 4:10-11, where Paul's suffering as an apostle is also pictured in terms of being sentenced to death or delivered over to death as the means by which God reveals his resurrection power (= life) in the world.

In light of these parallels and within the context of 2 Corinthians 2:14 itself, it becomes clear that for Paul, being delivered over to death is a metonymy for suffering (see too 2 Cor 1:8-11). In 2 Corinthians 2:14 Paul praises God for his suffering because, rather than calling his apostolic ministry into question, Paul's suffering is the very means through which God reveals himself in the world (cf. Duff's helpful analysis of the force of the metaphor as an epiphany procession). Only if the image is taken here in all of its grim reality does the text make sense within its own context and within Paul's larger apologetic for his legitimacy as an apostle. As the former enemy of God's people who had been conquered by God in his conversion call on the road to Damascus, Paul, now a "slave of Christ" (his favorite term for himself in his role as an apostle), was always being led by God in a triumphal procession "to death" (i.e., into situations of weakness and suffering; cf. 1 Cor 15:31).

In this way Paul makes known the majesty, power and glory of his conqueror, either through his experiences of divine deliverance (cf. 2 Cor 2:8-11) or through his divinely enabled endurance in the midst of adversity (cf. 1 Cor 2:2-5; 4:8-13; 2 Cor 4:7-15; 6:3-10; 11:23-33; 12:7-10; Phil 1:12; 2:25-30; *see DPL,* Suffering). Hence, 2 Corinthians 2:14 is not an abrupt break in

Paul's argument but the necessary and logical response to the suffering introduced in 2 Corinthians 2:12-13 (Hafemann, 35-72, 80-83). In 2 Corinthians 2:14 Paul praises God for the very thing his opponents maintained called his apostleship into question.

This interpretation of 2 Corinthians 2:14 has found confirmation in White's argument that this same Pauline use of "death" as a metonymy for suffering is the key to understanding not only 1 Corinthians 15:31 ("I die every day") but also the image of "being baptized on account of the dead" in 1 Corinthians 15:29. Instead of being an obscure reference to an unknown ritual lost in history, Paul is referring to the Corinthians' baptism under the ministry of Paul, here pictured in terms of his suffering (i.e., his being dead) as an essential, legitimizing aspect of his apostolic calling and of the gospel of the resurrection that he preached. To be baptized in Christ also meant being identified with those who preached Christ and suffered for his people (cf. 2 Cor 4:5). Thus 1 Corinthians 15:29 refers to the convert's identification with Paul's ministry as an apostle, once again pictured in terms of "death" as a metonymy for the daily suffering that Paul endures in hope of the resurrection and final reign of God in Christ (cf. 1 Cor 15:28, 30-32). In Paul's words, "For what will those do who are being baptized on account of the 'dead' [i.e., in response to the ministry of the apostles who suffer for the sake of the gospel]? If the truly dead are not being raised, why then are people being baptized on account of them [i.e., on account of the apostles, since their gospel offers no hope]?" (1 Cor 15:29). Paul would not willingly suffer, and the Corinthian believers would not have accepted his suffering as legitimate, being baptized as a result, were it not for the truth of Paul's gospel.

Finally, Schmidt has speculated that Mark selected and arranged key elements of the passion narrative in Mark 15:16-32 to recall the image of the Roman triumph: the gathering of the whole guard in Mark 15:16; the ceremonial royal robe and crown in Mark 15:17; the real mockery by the soldiers in Mark 15:18-19, who in the triumph would deride the victor to keep him humble; the offer and refusal of the myrrhed wine in Mark 15:23, which in the triumph was given to and refused by the victor and then poured out on the altar of sacrifice; and the placement on the right and left of those crucified with Jesus in Mark 15:27, in mock parallel to those who sometimes surrounded the enthroned ruler in these positions of power during the triumph. For Mark's Roman audience, these elements would highlight that the death of Jesus took place in ways that ironically recalled the adoration of the emperor who led the triumphal procession in his attempts at self-glorification and even deification. Now, however, the real triumph had been celebrated by a defeated king who, though executed himself, was in reality the true Son of God. Against the backdrop of the triumph, "Mark is presenting an *anti*-triumph in reaction to the contemporary offensive self-divinization efforts of Gaius and especially Nero" (Schmidt, 16). The purpose of such a portrayal is clear: one of the same Roman soldiers who first mocked Jesus as a triumphant king is the one who joins God himself in confessing Jesus' lordship.

See also ROMAN EMPERORS; ROMAN EMPIRE; ROMAN MILITARY.

BIBLIOGRAPHY. C. Breytenbach, "Paul's Proclamation and God's *Thriambos* (Notes on 2 Corinthians 2:14-16b)," *Neot* 24 (1990) 257-71; J. Calvin, *The Second Epistle of Paul the Apostle to the Corinthians and the Epistles to Timothy, Titus and Philemon* (CNTC 10; Grand Rapids, MI: Eerdmans, 1964); K. Dahn and H.-G. Link, "*thriambeuō*," *NIDNTT* 1:649-50; R. B. Egan, "Lexical Evidence on Two Pauline Passages," *NovT* 19 (1977) 34-62; P. B. Duff, "Metaphor, Motif and Meaning: The Rhetorical Strategy behind the Image 'Led in Triumph' in 2 Corinthians 2:14," *CBQ* 53 (1991) 79-92; G. G. Findlay, "St. Paul's use of *Thriambeuō*," *Exp* 10 (1879) 403-21; S. J. Hafemann, *Suffering and Ministry in the Spirit: Paul's Defense of His Ministry in 2 Corinthians 2:14—3:3* (Grand Rapids, MI: Eerdmans, 1990); P. Marshall, "A Metaphor of Social Shame: *Thriambeuein* in 2 Cor 2:14," *NovT* 25 (1983) 302-17; T. E. Schmidt, "Mark 15:16-32: The Crucifixion Narrative and the Roman Triumphal Procession," *NTS* 41 (1995) 1-18; J. M. Scott, "The Triumph of God in 2 Cor 2:14: Additional Evidence of Merkabah Mysticism in Paul," *NTS* 42 (1996) 260-81; "Triumphus," in *Paulys Realencyclopädie der classischen Altertumswissenschaft,* 2. Reihe, Bd. 7.1:493-511; H. S. Versnel, *Triumphus: An Inquiry into the Origin, Development and Meaning of the Roman Triumph* (Leiden: E. J. Brill, 1970); E. Wallisch, "Name und Herkunft des römischen Triumphes," *Philologus* 99 (1954-55) 245-58; J. R. White, " 'Baptized on Account of the Dead': The Meaning of Co-rinthians 15:29 in Its Context," *JBL* 116 (1997) 487-99; L. Williamson Jr., "Led in Triumph, Paul's Use of *Thriambeuō*," *Int* 22 (1968) 317-32.

S. J. Hafemann

ROMANCES/NOVELS, ANCIENT

Ancient romances, or novels, are modern terms that scholars use for a number of ancient narratives that typically involve an extraordinarily beautiful young couple who fall in love but who must endure various temptations, hardships and humiliations before they, with the help of the gods, can live happily ever after.

1. Romances and Related Narratives
2. Recent Scholarship on the Romances
3. The Romances and the New Testament

1. Romances and Related Narratives.

1.1. Extant Romances. Five classic Greek romances have survived intact and are readily available in English translation (see Reardon 1989, 17-588). They are, in chronological sequence, Chariton's *Chaereas and Callirhoe*, Xenophon's *Ephesian Tale*, Achilles Tatius's *Leucippe and Cleitophon*, Longus's *Daphnis and Chloe* and Heliodorus's *Ethiopian Story*. Chariton may have written his romance as early as the mid-first century A.D. and certainly by the early second. The next three—Xenophon, Achilles Tatius and Longus—all belong to the second century A.D., the first two to the early part, the last to the latter part of the century. Heliodorus's dates have been less secure, vacillating between the third and fourth century, but recently resolved in favor of the fourth (Bowersock, 149-55).

1.2. Evidence of Further Romances. These five complete romances are the most important examples of the genre, but hardly the only ones. References in literature point to other romances—for example, Philostratus mentions a romance called *Araspes and Panthea* and attributes it to the early second-century sophist Dionysius of Miletus (*Vit. Soph.* 524). Summaries of still other romances are preserved in the *Bibliotheca* of Photius, ninth-century patriarch of Constantinople (Reardon 1989, 773-97). But it is the sands of Egypt that continue to provide new, if very fragmentary, papyrus evidence of previously unknown novels, about a dozen to date, all of which are now readily available (see Stephens and Winkler; Reardon 1989, 799-827).

1.3. Related Narratives. Finally, a number of related narratives are often included with the romances, such as Dio Chrysostom's "Hunters of Euboea" (= *Or.* 7.1-80), the *Alexander Romance*, the epistolary novel of Chion of Heraklea, the Jewish novella **Joseph and Aseneth* and the Christian apocryphal Acts (see Morgan and Stoneman, 117-271; *see* Apocryphal Acts and Epistles).

2. Recent Scholarship on the Romances.

Scholarship on this considerable body of literature was long dormant, despite occasional contributions, most notably E. Rohde's massive and erudite *Der griechische Roman und seine Vorläufer* and B. Perry's *Ancient Romances*. Since the 1970s, however, interest in the romances has burgeoned, so much so that they have become, as one recent assessment puts it, "one of the hottest properties in town" (Bowie and Harrison, 159). The reasons for this renewed interest are many: the current interest in the Second Sophistic, which is the broader literary and intellectual context for the romances; the fascination with contemporary literary theory that has grown out of studies of the romances' contemporary counterpart, the modern novel; and the increased communication and collaboration among scholars that has been fostered by international conferences and bibliographical newsletters like G. Schmeling's *Petronian Society Newsletter*.

In any case, scholarship on the romances is growing rapidly, and the growth has not outrun sophisticated and insightful analysis. For example, new editions of the texts continue to appear, including the recent addition of Chariton's *Callirhoe* in the Loeb Classical Library (Goold). In addition, excellent introductory studies of the romances are now available (Hägg; Holzberg; Schmeling), and scholarship on individual romances progresses on a number of fronts. Not surprisingly, much of this scholarship is concentrated on literary analysis, both of the genre of romance and of specific narratological techniques in the romances (Reardon 1991; Bartsch; Schmeling), but scholars are also using the romances as sources for reconstructing ancient social life, in particular their portrayal of *women, their understanding of love and their conventions of *marriage (Egger; Konstan; Schmeling).

3. The Romances and the New Testament.

Consequently, given the ready availability of texts and translations, along with an extensive and impressive secondary literature, it is a good time for NT scholars to become more familiar with the romances and to appreciate their value for understanding the NT at a variety of levels.

*3.1. **Romances as Sources for Social Life.*** Taken as a whole, the romances provide a detailed, comprehensive and coherent account of the lives of people in the regions that witnessed the spread of Christianity in the first and early second centuries. The romances place us in *Antioch, Tyre, Tarsus, *Ephesus, Miletus, *Alexandria, Paphos, Syracuse and Tarentum, to name just a few of the cities that the romances and NT share. We observe people in these regions at all social levels—from leisurely aristocrats and their households in the cities to the most marginalized shepherds and brigands in the countryside and beyond. Moreover, the stories involving these people are so detailed that we can discover the specific conventions that govern their attitudes and behavior; we observe them, for example, attending symposia (*see* Banquets), *travel-ing, being attacked by brigands, abusing *slaves, being put on trial, celebrating festivals, *burying loved ones and being engaged in harvests. Perhaps no other source is as rich in data of social life as the romances are.

*3.2. **Specific Parallels.*** But the romances provide more than a general if comprehensive picture of life during NT times. They also corroborate and clarify many specific NT texts, from minor matters of Greek grammar to the central concern of christology. A sampling of specific parallels will illustrate the value of reading ancient romances, as is beginning to be realized (see Hock et al.).

3.2.1. Linguistic Parallels. For example, the romances share many features of Koine Greek with the NT: the partitive use of *apo* or *ek* ("of") with a suppressed *tines* ("some") (Mt 23:34; Mk 12:2; Jn 7:40; cf. Longus *Daphn. Chl.* 4.15.4); the ascensive use of *alla* ("but") in the phrase *alla kai* ("and what is more") (Lk 16:21; cf. Xenophon *Ephesian Tale* 1.5.8); the perfective sense of the present *pareisin* ("have come") (Acts 17:6; cf. Chariton *Chaer.* 1.1.14); and the identical litotes that Paul uses when describing Tarsus as "no mean city" (*ouk asēmou poleōs*) (Acts 21:39; cf. Achilles Tatius *Leuc.* 8.3.1).

3.2.2. Social Parallels. The parallels, however, go beyond language to various social conventions, thereby corroborating many social details in the NT: counting seeds to judge the quality of a harvest (Mk 4:8; cf. Longus *Daphn. Chl.* 3.30); being interested in different burial practices (Jn 19:40; cf. Xenophon *Ephesian Tale* 5.1.10); and using various epistolary conventions—writing a letter with tears (2 Cor 2:4; cf. Chariton *Chaer.* 4.6.6), sending greetings to individuals (Rom 16:3-16; cf. Chariton *Chaer.* 8.4.6), closing with an authenticating sentence or two in one's own hand (1 Cor 16:21-24; Philem 19; cf. Chariton *Chaer.* 8.4.6), sending letters by means of slaves (Eph 6:21; cf. Xenophon *Ephesian Tale* 2.12.1; Achilles Tatius *Leuc.* 1.3.5; 4.11.1) and giving them oral messages to deliver as well (Eph 6:21; cf. Chariton *Chaer.* 8.4.9; Achilles Tatius *Leuc.* 5.21.1).

At times parallels from the romances do more than corroborate; they also clarify. For example, the brief mention of a pit into which a sheep might fall (Mt 12:11) finds clarification in Longus's romance, where the practice of digging pits is more fully described: they are the work of a whole village, are six feet across and four times as deep, are camouflaged with branches and are designed to trap marauding wolves (Longus *Daphn. Chl.* 1.11.1-2).

3.2.3. A Christological Parallel. Clarification extends to the central concern of christology. For example, the christological claims of the so-called Philippians hymn (Phil 2:6-11) find considerable clarification from both the narrative structure of the romances and their detailed accounts of master-slave conventions. Structurally, the protagonists of the romances belong to the highest social classes at the beginning of the story but soon suffer the humiliations of capture and enslavement before some deity raises them back to their original status at the end of the story. The Philippians hymn is similarly structured: at the beginning Jesus' status is virtually equal to that of God (Phil 2:6), but then he accepts the humiliation of being an obedient slave (Phil 2:7-8) before God raises him to a status so high that all beings—in heaven, on earth and under the earth—bow at the sound of his name and confess him as "Lord" (*kyrios,* Phil 2:9-11), the same title used by slaves for their "master" (*kyrios;* cf. Chariton *Chaer.* 2.3.5-6).

An incident in Xenophon's romance provides further clarification: Habrocomes, after being enslaved and then punished severely for supposedly raping his master's daughter, finds himself locked up and near death (Xenophon *Ephesian Tale* 1.13.6; 2.3-7); the master, however, soon learns of his innocence and then quickly summons him, apologizes to him and makes him manager of his household, where he rules everyone (Xenophon *Ephesian Tale* 2.10.1-3). In other words, here are the precise social conventions that provide plausibility to the religious claims of the Philippians hymn: just as Habrocomes, enslaved and near death, can have his status reversed so quickly and completely so that he rules all in the household, so could Jesus, enslaved and obedient to death by crucifixion, be raised up by God to the status of master of all in creation. Consequently, the romances are valuable indeed if they can help clarify, as here, the meaning and truth of the christological claims of the NT.

See also JOSEPH AND ASENETH; LITERACY AND BOOK CULTURE; WRITING AND LITERATURE: GRECO-ROMAN.

BIBLIOGRAPHY. S. Bartsch, *Decoding the Ancient Novel: The Reader and the Role of Description in Heliodorus and Achilles Tatius* (Princeton, NJ: Princeton University Press, 1989); G. Bowersock, *Fiction as History: Nero to Julian* (Berkeley and Los Angeles: University of California Press, 1994); E. L. Bowie and S. J. Harrison, "The Romance of the Novel," *JRS* 83 (1993) 159-78; B. Egger, "Women and Marriage in the Greek Novels," in *The Search for the Ancient Novel*, ed. J. Tatum (Baltimore: Johns Hopkins University Press, 1994) 260-80; G. P. Goold, ed. and trans., *Chariton, Callirhoe* (LCL; Cambridge, MA: Harvard University Press, 1995); T. Hägg, *The Novel in Antiquity* (Berkeley and Los Angeles: University of California Press, 1983); R. F. Hock et al., eds., *Ancient Fiction and Early Christian Narrative* (SS 6; Atlanta: Scholars Press, 1998); N. Holzberg, *The Ancient Novel: An Introduction* (London: Routledge, 1995); D. Konstan, *Sexual Symmetry: Love in the Ancient Novel and Related Genres* (Princeton, NJ: Princeton University Press, 1994); D. MacDonald, *The Homeric Epics and the Gospel of Mark* (New Haven, CT: Yale University Press, 2000); J. R. Morgan and R. Stoneman, eds., *Greek Fiction: The Greek Novel in Context* (London: Routledge, 1994); B. Perry, *The Ancient Romances: A Literary-Historical Account of Their Origins* (Berkeley and Los Angeles: University of California Press, 1967); B. P. Reardon, ed., *Collected Ancient Greek Novels* (Berkeley and Los Angeles: University of California Press, 1989); idem, *The Form of Greek Romance* (Princeton, NJ: Princeton University Press, 1991); E. Rohde, *Der griechische Roman und seine Vorläufer* (3d ed.; Leipzig: Breitkopf & Hartel, 1914); G. Schmeling, ed., *The Novel in the Ancient World* (Leiden: E. J. Brill, 1997); S. Stephens and J. Winkler, eds., *Ancient Greek Novels: The Fragments* (Princeton, NJ: Princeton University Press, 1995); L. M. Wills, *The Quest of the Historical Gospel: Mark, John and the Origins of the Gospel Genre* (New York: Routledge, 1997).

R. F. Hock

ROME: OVERVIEW

Rome was the chief city in Italy and the capital of the *Roman Empire. Because of its prestige and importance its name is used both for the city and for Roman civilization.

1. Historical and Cultural Background of the City and the Empire
2. The City of Rome in the First Century A.D.
3. The Romans in Palestine

1. Historical and Cultural Background of the City and the Empire.

1.1. The Roman Republic. Rome began as a small settlement on the east bank of the Tiber River. Traditionally founded by Romulus by about 753 B.C. and ruled by kings, Rome became a republic in 509 B.C., governed by a senate under two consuls. It rapidly expanded, conquering its neighbors and establishing the dominance of its language, Latin. In the third to second centuries, Rome became a naval power, defeating its rival Carthage in two Punic wars. The Romans also gained ascendancy in the East with the defeat of Antiochus III of Syria and the conquest of *Macedon and *Greece (in 146 B.C. *Corinth was sacked). By this time Rome had a highly efficient and well-disciplined professional army.

After class struggles, political rivalries and civil wars, the republic came to an end in a contest for power, initially among *Pompey, Crassus and Julius Caesar (assassinated 44 B.C.), and then between Marc Antony and Octavian, who emerged victor at Actium (31 B.C.). In 27 B.C. Octavian, taking the surname Augustus, or "venerable" (cf. Lk 2:1), "restored the republic." This was the beginning of an empire that was to last for many centuries.

1.2. The Early Empire. For the purposes of studying the background to the NT, only the first phase of the Roman Empire, notably the Julio-Claudian and Flavian dynasties, is of direct importance. Knowledge of this period is indebted especially to *Tacitus's *Annals* and *Histories*, Suetonius's *Lives of the Caesars,* Cassius Dio's *Histories* and *Josephus's *Jewish War* and *Antiquities,* and to *inscriptions, papyri and data derived from *coins and other material remains (see Balsdon; Jones and Milns; Avi-Yonah).

Augustus (27 B.C.-A.D. 14) is rightly famous for establishing and maintaining peace (the **pax Romana,* although this was not kept without a price; see Wengst); for his efficient administration, including legal and financial reforms; his upholding of traditional Roman values and morality; and his patronage of the arts. Modest in his lifestyle, he preferred to be known as *princeps,* "first citizen," rather than *imperator,* "emperor." The principate of his stepson Tiberius (A.D. 14-37) proved more tyrannical and ended in a reign of terror. The evils of autocratic power became still more evident under Gaius (Caligula, A.D. 37-41), who may have been insane. He offended the Jews by ordering his statue to be placed in the *temple at *Jerusalem (the Syrian legate Petronius averted a confrontation by delaying tactics). After Gaius's assassination, Claudius's reign (A.D. 41-54) provided stability with the development of the civil service, the strengthening of empire and the generous extension of Roman *citizenship. He continued Augustus's policy of allowing the Jews freedom of worship and was a friend of Herod Agrippa I, whom he set up as king (see below). In the later part of his reign, he expelled the Jews from Rome, an event that Suetonius (*Claudius* 25.4) claims was precipitated by disturbances caused by Chrestus ("at the instigation of Chrestus" *[impulsore Chresto],* perhaps a distortion of "Christ," although this is not certain; see Stern, 113-17). Nero's eccentric and extravagant reign (A.D. 54-68) was marked by a great fire at Rome, probably accidental but attributed to Christians. It led to the first concentrated Roman persecutions of Christians.

On Nero's death different military factions fought over the succession (A.D. 68-69, the Year of the Four Emperors), until Vespasian, a plebeian and commander of the army in the East, emerged victorious (reigned A.D. 69-79). This period saw the Jewish revolt of A.D. 66 to 70 with the brutal sack of Jerusalem by Vespasian's son Titus, who commemorated the event by his arch in Rome (*see* Jewish Wars with Rome). After this, Judea became an imperial Roman province. Titus reigned only two years (A.D. 79-81) and was followed by his brother Domitian (A.D. 81-96), an efficient administrator who carried out a public building program. But his rule, like that of Tiberius, ended in a reign of terror. He claimed the title "lord and god" (Suetonius *Domitian* 13) and was responsible for a major persecution of Christians. In contrast, the reigns of Nerva (A.D. 96-98) and Trajan (A.D. 98-117) brought peace and stability.

One can understand why the Romans are famous for their military and administrative abilities, their law and their skills in architecture, engineering and road building (*see* Roman Administration; Roman Emperors; Roman Law and Legal System; Roman Military; Roman Political System; Art and Architecture: Greco-Roman). Deeply indebted to Greece in the areas of literature, *philosophy and the creative arts, they nevertheless had their own gift for the lucid expression of ideas in precise and elegant language (see Howatson; Bandinelli). Traditionally the Romans valued family life and the virtues of *gravitas* ("dignity") and *pietas* ("devotion" or "dutifulness"). But like all peoples they had their darker side, and many instances are recorded of corruption, sexual immorality, brutality and murder. One should be wary of either idealizing or denigrating them as a people or in terms of their accomplishments.

1.3. Roman Religion and Politics.

1.3.1. Religion and Politics. Roman religion was originally animistic, involving the spirits of the woods, springs and mountains. The Romans also worshiped anthropomorphic gods such as Jupiter, Juno, Mars and Minerva, whom they identified with their Greek counterparts. They came successively under the influence of the Etruscans, the Greeks and various Eastern peoples and imported foreign cults, including those of Cybele, Isis and Mithras, so long as these were compatible with state policies. Roman religion and the state's policies toward religion affected the reception that the Roman people gave to foreign religions, including *Judaism and Christianity, since Roman religion was closely bound up with the government of Rome. A good example of this linkage is emperor worship (*see DLNTD,* Emperor, Emperor Cult), which seems to have originated in the East, where *Hellenistic monarchs had long been recognized as divine saviors. In the empire it became a focus and test of political loyalty (Pliny *Ep.* 10.96-97), even though at Rome it was at first restricted either to the deceased emperor (cf. the earlier worship of ancestors) or his "genius" (guardian spirit). In the provinces and later at Rome also, the emperor often shared his cult with the goddess Roma, personification of the power and spirit of Rome. [R. B. Edwards]

The tie between religion and politics was felt in other ways, however. The priests of the state religion served as advisors to the senate. They were consulted for discerning the divine will through signs and purifying significant areas (*augures*), setting the calendar and establishing religious law (*pontifices*), making war in religiously correct ways (*fetiales*) and keeping and interpreting the Sibylline Books (*duoviri* [later *decemviri*] *sacris faciundis*). Priests, by their function of interpreting foreign books, especially in the third century B.C., called for the acceptance of certain foreign religions into Rome. At the end of the republican age the *haruspices* (lit., "soothsayers") were organized as a priestly college. Its members were trained to discern the divine will from the entrails of sacrificial animals.

Everywhere in first-century Rome there were reminders of the gods. On the hill known as Capitolium a large temple was dedicated to Jupiter, Juno and Minerva in the first year of the republic. Though it burned in 83 B.C., a new temple was built in 69 B.C. This was repaired and embellished by Augustus in 26 and 9 B.C.. The temple therefore dominated the city when Christianity first made inroads there. On the southern border of the political center, the forum, were temples of Saturn, the Castores, Vesta and the office spaces of the *pontifices* and another member of their priestly college, the *rex sacrorum* ("king of sacred things," a religious post representing the ancient kings of Rome). Privately, the *lares* (shrines for dead family members) and *di penates* (gods of the family cupboard) were constant reminders in the home of the connection in the Roman religious mind between this world and the other.

Participation in religious ritual was a way of life for Romans. The possibility of choosing a religion and joining a group defined only for its religious identity was unknown. Groups that were organized solely for religious purposes, with the exception of vocational priesthoods in the state religion, Jewish *synagogues, and later the churches, were unknown. Though there were *collegia* named after certain deities, the members of such associations were joined by a common occupation or ethnic background. The churches in Rome arguably showed their faith as the organizing principle more than synagogues, since the churches likely consisted of a greater variety in ethnic and class backgrounds.

1.3.2. Legal Orientation. In public and in private, Roman religion was in essence the performance of ritual; hence there was great emphasis on the proper observance of ritual (Pliny *Nat. Hist.* 13.10). The priesthoods were closely linked with the legislative government; this fact and the elaborate rules within Roman religion point to the essential legal character of religion. Far from espousing a personal relationship with the gods, Roman religion taught that if one followed the rituals correctly, a contract would be made that obtained the "peace of the gods" (*pax deorum*; cf. Rom 5:1-2, where Paul states that believers have "peace with God" on the basis of faith).

Since the Romans considered religion as essentially a legal matter, it is possible to interpret Paul's presentation of his gospel in the book of Romans in legal terms: God's general moral law (Rom 2:14-16), Torah (Rom 3:21; 10:4) and political law (Rom 13:1-7). Paul's focus on questions of law (Rom 2:12-27; 4:13-16; 7 passim) and his acknowledgment that his readers "know law" (Rom 7:1) may not simply reflect the Jewish preoccupation with Torah or the high percentage of secular lawyers in Roman society but Paul's recognition that Romans viewed religion as a matter of law. The Roman emphasis on legal etiquette in religion presupposed that the gods were rational, a point not shared with most foreign cults introduced to Rome. The religious vow of 217 B.C. (Livy *Hist.* 22.10) illustrates how a Roman priest could treat the gods as rational bargaining partners, much as one person would reason with another. Paul's *letter to the Romans emphasizes being rational in religion. The rational God hands over those who ignore him "to an unfit mind" (Rom 1:28); acting against one's mind is perceived as acting against God (Rom 7:20-24); and presenting one's body to God is reasonable religion, accompanied by a renewed mind (Rom 12:1-2).

1.3.3. Roman Policies and Attitudes to Foreign Religions. As one of the later foreign religions to seek entrance into Rome, Christianity inherited stereotypes and government policies developed from past encounters between the Roman government and foreign religions, such as Judaism.

Any study of church-state relations not only must begin with the state religion of Rome but also must include the reception Rome gave to the foreign religions that antedated Christianity, since foreign religions could not be introduced in Rome without official approval from the senate and Romans viewed religion as a concern of the state. Since the late republic, Rome looked at all foreign religions with much suspicion. At the same time, it was ready to attempt the introduction of a foreign religion when it perceived that cults offered a solution to an unmet need in Rome. For example, the Asclepius cult (known in Rome as *Aesculapius*) was brought from Epidaurus to Rome when in 293 B.C. the Roman priests who kept the Sibylline Books called for its importation to quell a plague. Its temple on the island of Tiber was dedicated on January 1, 291 B.C.. The minor deity Hygieia was also worshiped there, to whom the Romans later attached the name of their Italian goddess, Salus.

The official importation of a new cult did not mean that the state religion was abandoned. There was no mechanism in Roman religion for abolishing any traditional practice. Rather, new cults were brought to Rome and new interpretations of state religion were made as history progressed. Religious exclusivism, such as was found in Judaism and Christianity, was therefore unheard of to the Roman religious mind. While earlier more tolerant, Rome was more cautious regarding new religions after events in 186 B.C. that raised the government's suspicions about foreign religions. In this year, the Roman senate forbade the practice of the Dionysian *orgia,* or *bacchanalia.* The Dionysus cult had entered Rome from Campanian Italy. In response to the senate's measures (*CIL* 1.196; *ILS* 18), the people of Rome reacted violently, and an outbreak of crime spread through the city (Livy *Hist.* 39.8-18). This incident, known now as the Bacchanalia, helped shape the Roman stereotype that foreign religions inevitably brought disorder. Hence, when Christianity entered Rome, it too was viewed with suspicion. [M. Reasoner]

1.4. Roman Provincial Administration. The first Roman provinces, in the West, were acquired in the third century B.C. After Rome's expansion into the East, Asia (i.e., western Turkey), Cilicia and Bithynia were added, followed by Syria and Egypt. Augustus annexed several more provinces, and Claudius added Britain (A.D. 43).

Under the empire provinces were of two kinds: public or consular, governed by proconsuls under the authority of the senate (these were generally the richer and more settled provinces); or imperial, governed by legates, appointed by the emperor (mostly frontier provinces, such as Syria, where legions were stationed). Both these types of governor were of senatorial rank. There was a third class of governors, known as prefects or procurators, of lower equestrian rank, who were in charge of smaller provinces (e.g., Judea). These were often experts in financial administration. All governors had judicial and military powers. The number of troops available might be quite small (e.g., one cohort, consisting of three hundred to six hundred men) but in frontier provinces could rise to three or four legions (a legion consisting of some three thousand to six thousand infantry and one hundred to two hundred cavalry). Governors could not be prosecuted for mismanagement until after their term of office.

Roman provincial government has been described as "supervisory rather than executive" (Sherwin-White, *ISBE* 3:1027), which meant that few Roman officials were involved, detailed administration being in the hands of municipal authorities or, in the case of Judea, councils of elders grouped into toparchies. Revenue was raised by a system of tax farming. Local laws and religious customs were usually respected as long as they did not interfere with smooth government. Roman citizens came under Roman law. Citizenship could be granted both to whole communities and to individuals (e.g., to men with long service in auxiliary units of the army) and was passed down from father to son. In the Eastern provinces members of the wealthy upper classes often acquired their citizenship through influence. [R. B. Edwards]

2. The City of Rome in the First Century A.D.

2.1. Size and Character. With a population of about one million people, the city of Rome in the first century drew people from every corner of the empire and beyond. During Augustus's reign an urban police force *(cohortes urbanae)* and fire prevention units *(vigiles)* were added to keep order in the growing city. Like the great cities of today, Rome was the place to visit in the imperial period. Paul's declaration that he had intended many times to visit the Roman Christians before writing his letter to them (Rom 1:13) was therefore similar to what any provincial would say before making final arrangements for a trip to Rome.

From at least the third century B.C., Rome had been a drawing point for people of a variety of ethnic backgrounds. The immigration of provincial Italians and Greeks that was occurring under the republic was eclipsed in the early principate by immigration from Syria, *Asia Minor (modern Turkey), Egypt, Africa, Spain and later Gaul and Germany. Juvenal's statement that "long ago the Orontes has overflowed into the Tiber" (Juvenal *Sat.* 3.62) shows his perception of the high number of Semitic people living in first-century Rome. Record of a Jewish presence in Rome dates from 139 B.C., and it is known that the number of Jewish residents in Rome increased when, in 62 B.C., Pompey brought back a large number of Jewish captives for use as *slaves. By the time *Cicero defended Flaccus in 59 B.C., it appears that the Jews were a significant political interest group in Rome (Cicero *Flac.* 66). In the civil war that began in 49 B.C., the Jews in Rome and throughout the Mediterranean world supported Julius Caesar against Pompey, thus explaining why Jews mourned the death of Caesar in 44 B.C. (Suetonius *Julius* 84.5). It is estimated that there were at least forty thousand Jews in Rome during the first century A.D. Literary sources from the late republic and early empire show, however, that these foreign residents in Rome *(peregrini)* were not fully accepted and experienced racial discrimination. Africans were reportedly despised (Livy *Hist.* 30.12.18; Sallust *Iug.* 91.7), the Jews were the victims of such discrimination (Cicero *Flac.* 66-69; Horace *Sat.* 1.9.71-72), and even Greeks received slurs (Cicero *Ep.* 16.4.2; *Tusc.* 2.65; *De Orat.* 1.105; 2.13).

2.2. Judaism in Rome. Scholars disagree whether Judaism had been accorded the status of a legal religion *(religio licita),* but it appears that Jews were given tacit permission to meet for religious purposes in their synagogues, and the Jews' observance of the *sabbath was not used to their disadvantage. It is true that Jews were expelled from Rome in 139 B.C. (Valerius Maximus *Fact. ac Dict.* 1.3.2), in A.D. 19 (Josephus *Ant.* 18.3.5 §§81-84; Tacitus *Ann.* 2.85.5; Suetonius *Tiberius* 36; Dio Cassius *Hist.* 57.18.5) and in A.D. 49 (Suetonius *Claudius* 25.4; Acts 18:1-2; some scholars think this expulsion took place in A.D. 41). The first two cases were probably a Roman response to active proselytizing by the Jews, but the third was perhaps due to unrest within the Jewish community about Christianity (see above). But these expulsions were not permanent measures, and at least in the latter two cases probably did not apply to Jews who were Roman citizens.

Judaism in Rome was also closely tied to Judaism in Jerusalem. Around 140 B.C., the high priests in Jerusalem sent emissaries to Rome in order to offset the power of the *Seleucids. Later, ruling priests in the first century politically endorsed Julius Caesar (and not Pompey, who had entered the temple in 63 B..C.), and *Herod the Great was in political alliance with Augustus. In the first century A.D., princes in the family of Herod such as Agrippa II, who would later hold the rights of appointing high priests in Jerusalem, were reared in Rome under imperial patronage. Far from being an unruly cousin of Judaism in Jerusalem, then, Judaism in Rome was rather a devoted son. Within the synagogues of Rome, Christianity first gained its inroads there.

2.3. Christians in Rome. Although Christianity first appeared as a sect of Judaism, the Roman church by the time of Paul's initial visit (A.D. 60) was already making its break with Judaism, a break that must have been complete by A.D. 64, when Nero focused persecution on Christians, blaming them for the fire in the city. The churches in Rome represented a body of Christianity that Paul could not ignore. Their strategic potential came from their close connection with Jerusalem, their location in the world capital and their connections with the rest of the empire through people groups represented in Rome's congregations.

2.3.1. Origins. The connection between the Jews in Rome and Jerusalem and the Jewish element within early Roman Christianity lead to the probable conclusion that Christianity was brought to Rome by Jewish Christians from Palestine. This is confirmed by the note that Jews from Rome were in Peter's audience in Jerusalem at Pentecost (Acts 2:10). Jewish Christians most probably entered into dialogue with fellow Jews, and this resulted in tumultuous encounters and some conversions. One such encounter possibly occurred in A.D. 49, when Claudius expelled the Jews from Rome. Suetonius's brief description of this event (see above) is generally taken to mean that the Jews were arguing among themselves about Christ. As a result,

Priscilla and Aquila, two Jewish Christians, left Italy when Claudius expelled the Jews from Rome (Acts 18:2).

The Jewish component in early Roman Christianity suggests that house churches may have developed in association with various synagogues, indicating that Christianity in Rome arose not in a single church but in a plurality of house churches. Paul's greeting in the letter to the Romans is given not to a church (cf. 1 Cor 1:2; 2 Cor 1:1) but to "all those who are in Rome, beloved of God, chosen saints" (Rom 1:7). Paul still used the singular "church" to describe the Christians who met in Rome, while acknowledging that they did so probably in a variety of places.

2.3.2. Jewish Presence. Because of its likely origin in the synagogues of Rome, Jewish Christianity retained a close connection with its Jewish roots in Jerusalem. Paul's letter to the church is evidence for this (Rom 1:16; 3:1-30; 9—11). Half a century later, when Tacitus describes Christianity, he links it to Judea (Tacitus *Ann.* 15.44.2). Roman Christianity must have included a distinctly Jewish element. Theologically such a presence within the church most representative of the world's peoples forced Paul to outline his gospel in a manner that accounted for God's dealings with all people (Rom 2:1-16; 15:7-13). A letter and visit to this church provided apologetic opportunities for Paul to defend himself to people with close ties to the groups that most criticized and resisted Paul's ministry, the Judaism and Christianity of Jerusalem. Thus, for the Romans, Paul defends his theology (Rom 6:1-2) and mission strategy (Rom 15:14-24). His upcoming visit to Jerusalem is explained and addressed to them as a worthwhile and spiritual endeavor (Rom 15:25-32). While Roman Christianity was primarily composed of Gentiles, as Paul's letter shows, it is probable that there was an ethnically Jewish presence in the Roman churches.

2.3.3. Servile Presence. Since many Jews first came to Rome as slaves, it is likely that some of the Jews within the Roman churches were of the servile classes (either slaves or freedmen and freedwomen). The slaves in Rome were primarily of foreign origin in the first century of the principate. While there were some freeborn foreigners in Rome, the possibility that many were servile foreigners fits with Suetonius's conviction that Nero administered Roman law properly when crucifying Christians (Suetonius *Nero* 16.2; 19.3), since Roman law prohibited crucifixion of its citizens. Further evidence for the servile nature of the Roman church are the references to those of certain "households" (Rom 16:10-11), a standard euphemism for the servile classes.

2.3.4. Asceticism. G. La Piana has suggested an ascetic element within the first-century Roman church. This seems fully in accordance with extrabiblical evidence and indications in Paul's letter to the Romans. Vegetarianism was taught in the school of Quintus Sextius in the early first century. The philosopher Sotion led *Seneca to practice vegetarianism for a time (Seneca *Ep.* 108.22). Another philosopher who was influential during the reign of Nero, *Musonius Rufus, also taught vegetarianism (*Peri Trophes,* ed. Hense, 95). Vegetarianism is reflected in *1 Clement* 20.4, while asceticism in dress is mentioned in *1 Clement* 17.1. Biblical evidence for asceticism in Roman Christianity comes from Hebrews 13:9 and Romans 14:1-3, 21. In the latter reference the strong and weak are differentiated within the Roman church by different postures toward ascetic practice. The mind/body dualism common to ascetics is found in Romans 1:24; 6:19; 7:23-24; 12:1-2. The ascetic tendencies of Roman Christianity were later worked out in one of its leaders, Tatian (fl. in Rome A.D. 160-172). The ascetic movement within the Roman church at the time Paul wrote his letter may well have prompted him to delineate an ethic of responsibility in which the strong in conscience was to respect the weak, more ascetic, Christians (Rom 14:14-17; 15:1-3).

2.3.5. Influence. By the time Paul wrote Romans, it is clear that the Roman church was ascendant in influence among churches of the Mediterranean world. Paul's uncharacteristic desire to visit the church in Rome that he had not founded (Rom 1:9-13; cf. 15:20) and his need for the Roman church's endorsement and support (Rom 15:22-24) show the influence that this church carried in the Mediterranean world. The influence of the Roman church is also seen in *1 Clement,* a letter written as early as A.D. 96, in which the Roman church expects its directives to its sister church in *Corinth to be followed (*1 Clem.* 7.1-3; 62.1-3; 65.1).

Though the church in Rome was not founded by an apostle, Paul is associated with its early history. As apostle to the Gentiles, he considered this within his sphere of ministry (Rom 1:11-15). One's understanding of the relationship that Paul had with Roman Christianity before his visit in A.D. 60 affects one's conception of early church history and hence one's interpretation of the letter to the Romans. While it is true that Romans is the most systematic of Paul's letters, its occasional nature cannot be denied. The influence that Roman Christianity enjoyed likely meant that Christians throughout the empire knew something about the Roman church. Paul's statement "your faith is announced throughout the whole world" (Rom 1:8) is probably more than epistolary flattery. Paul met Christians from Rome at least by A.D. 50, after Aquila and Priscilla had come to Corinth from Rome (Acts 18:1-2; cf. Rom 16:3-5). Christians in Pauline circles no doubt had associations with other Christians in Rome. While Romans 16 has been assigned an *Ephesian destination by T. W. Manson, later works by H. Gamble, P. Lampe and W.-H. Ollrog have demonstrated the integrity of this chapter with the rest of the letter. On the basis of Romans 16, then, it is probable that Paul knew a number of people in Rome. The letter is written in order to strengthen an existing relationship.

By the time Paul arrived in Rome in about A.D. 60 (Acts 28:14-16) in order to stand trial before Nero's representative, the praetorian prefect, Nero had murdered his mother, his advisor Burrus had died, and Seneca had retired. Rumors were probably spreading that the imperial government did not seem as stable as in the earlier part of Nero's reign. According to tradition, Paul was freed after his first trial. From the testimony that Paul "reached the limits of the West" (*1 Clem.* 5:7), it is possible that Paul then reached Spain as intended (Rom 15:24). It is then most likely that Paul was arrested and imprisoned again at Rome, where he was executed sometime between A.D. 64 and 67. *First Clement* 5:2-5, in citing "pillars of the church," mentions Peter first and then Paul as examples of endurance under suffering. Today one can see a carving of both apostles baptizing their jailers in the Mamertine Prison (Rome's state prison), testimony to the tradition that both men suffered for their faith in Rome. The details of Paul's second trial (if he had one) and martyrdom are unknown. Tradition tells us that he was beheaded on the Ostian Way at about the same time and place as Peter (Eusebius *Hist. Eccl.* 2.25.7-8). [M. Reasoner]

3. The Romans in Palestine.

3.1. To Herod the Great. The history of the Roman government of Palestine is complex. In 66 to 63 B.C., Pompey conducted his celebrated Eastern campaign, during which he was called into Palestine by the two sons of Salome Alexandra in their dispute over the succession (*see* Hasmoneans). He captured Jerusalem and entered the temple but ordered its cleansing and reinstated Hyrcanus as high priest. After this, Syria became a Roman imperial province, with the Decapolis and *Samaria, now freed from Jewish rule, under its wing. Judea, Galilee, Idumea and Perea were retained by the Jews as client kingdoms, dependent on Rome. Julius Caesar appointed Antipater procurator of Judea. His son *Herod, who had been governor of Galilee, won from Rome the title king of the Jews, a title which he had to make a reality by force of arms. Herod reigned from 37 to 4 B.C.; he extended his territories and restored the Jerusalem temple on a lavish scale, including Greco-Roman architectural features (*see* Archaeology of the Land of Israel; Art and Architecture: Greco-Roman; Art and Architecture: Jewish). Herod was both a lover of *Hellenism and an admirer of Roman culture. He encouraged Hellenistic education and social mores; he built *theaters, amphitheaters and other civic amenities such as aqueducts. Under his rule, Judea was materially prosperous. But he was also violent and cruel. The massacre of the innocents at Bethlehem (Mt 2), though not confirmed by external sources, is consistent with his character.

3.2. After Herod the Great. On Herod's death his kingdom was split into three with Herod Antipas as tetrarch of Galilee and Perea (4 B.C.-A.D. 39); Philip tetrarch of Trachonitis and Iturea (4 B.C.-A.D. 34); and Archelaus ethnarch in Judea, Idumea and Samaria (4 B.C.-A.D. 6; cf. Mt 2:22; Lk 3:1). Archelaus's rule ended in riots, and he was banished. Judea now came under the control of Roman governors (*see* Roman Governors of Palestine).

Pontius Pilate was governor of Judea from A.D. 26/27 to 36. Tacitus (*Ann.* 15.44) refers to him as procurator and mentions that "Christus" was put to death by him when Tiberius was emperor. However, an inscription from *Caesarea, the Roman capital of Judea, shows that his title was more correctly prefect. He was of equestrian rank, presumably a former military tribune, and had five cohorts of infantry and a cavalry regiment under his command. He had absolute authority in his own province but was responsible to the legate in Syria. *Josephus and *Philo say that his governorship was marred by bloodshed, including a massacre of some Galileans (possibly alluded to in Lk 13:1) and the slaughter of many Samaritans in an ugly incident that resulted in protests to the legate Vitellius in Syria and Pilate's recall to Rome. According to Eusebius he later committed suicide.

In A.D. 41, Herod Agrippa I, who had previously governed northern Palestine and Galilee, was made king of the Jews (cf. Acts 12), but in A.D. 44 Palestine reverted to Roman governors. In A.D. 66 to 70 the tragic Jewish war erupted, with the siege and fall of Jerusalem in A.D. 70 (*see* Jewish Revolts). The Jewish patriots held out at Masada until A.D. 73 and committed suicide rather than submit to Rome. In A.D. 132 to 135 the Bar Kokhba revolt finally sealed the fate of Judea, and Jerusalem became a Roman colony (Aelia Capitolina) inhabited by non-Jews.

In Palestine the Jewish leaders and people varied immensely in their attitudes to the Romans. The Herodian rulers and their party were naturally pro-Roman. The high priests also generally favored cooperation, as did the *Sadducees. At least some of the *Essenes withdrew to the desert, while the Zealots worked for armed rebellion. The *Pharisees saw as their first loyalty absolute adherence to the Mosaic law and traditions, so they refused to take an oath of loyalty to Herod (Josephus *Ant.* 17.42); some actively resisted Roman rule, but others were more acquiescent. The common people must have simply scraped a living in a society where there was great inequality between rich and poor and much scope for oppression (*see* Econmics of Palestine). [R. B. Edwards]

See also ROMAN ADMINISTRATION; ROMAN EAST; ROMAN EMPERORS; ROMAN EMPIRE; ROMAN GOVERNORS OF PALESTINE; ROMAN LAW AND LEGAL SYSTEM;; ROMAN MILITARY; ROMAN POLITICAL SYSTEM; ROMAN SOCIAL CLASSES.

BIBLIOGRAPHY. L. Adkins and R. A. Adkins, *Dictionary of Roman Religion* (New York: Facts on File, 1996); W. T. Arnold, *The Roman System of Provincial Administration* (Oxford: Blackwell, 1906); M. Avi-Yonah, *Gazetteer of Roman Palestine* (*Qedem* 5; Jerusalem: Hebrew University, 1976); J. P. V. D. Balsdon, *Rome: The Story of an Empire* (London: Weidenfeld & Nicolson, 1970); E. Bammel and C. F. D. Moule, eds., *Jesus and the Politics of His Day* (Cambridge: Cambridge University Press, 1984); R. B. Bandinelli, *Rome, The Center of Power* (London: Thames & Hudson, 1970); M. Beard and M. Crawford, *Rome in the Late Republic* (London: Duckworth, 1985); K. R. Bradley, *Slaves and Masters in the Roman Empire: A Study in Social Control* (New York: Oxford University Press, 1987); R. E. Brown and J. P. Meier, *Antioch and Rome: New Testament Cradles of Catholic Christianity* (New York: Paulist, 1983); M. Cary, *A History of Rome Down to the Reign of Constantine* (2d ed.; London: Macmillan, 1967); M. P. Charlesworth, *Documents Illustrating the Reigns of Claudius and Nero* (Cambridge: Cambridge University Press, 1951); G. Edmundson, *The Church in Rome in the First Century* (London: Longmans, Green, 1913); V. Ehrenberg and A. H. M. Jones, *Documents Illustrating the Reigns of Augustus and Tiberius* (2d ed.; Oxford: Clarendon Press, 1955); S. Freyne, *Galilee from Alexander the Great to Hadrian* (Wilmington, DE: Michael Glazier; Notre Dame, IN: University of Notre Dame Press, 1980); J. Ferguson, *The Religions of the Roman Empire* (Ithaca, NY: Cornell University Press, 1970); H. Gamble Jr., *The Textual History of the Letter to the Romans* (Grand Rapids, MI: Eerdmans, 1977); P. Garnsey and R. Saller, *The Roman Empire: Economy, Society and Culture* (Berkeley and Los Angeles: University of California Press, 1987); T. R. Glover, *The Conflict of Religions in the Early Roman Empire* (London: Methuen, 1909); F. C. Grant, *Roman Hellenism and the New Testament* (Edinburgh: Oliver & Boyd, 1962); M. Grant, *The Twelve Caesars* (London: Weidenfeld & Nicolson, 1975); R. M. Grant, *Early Christianity and Society* (London: Collins, 1978); M. C. Howatson, ed., *The Oxford Companion to Classical Literature* (2d ed.; Oxford: Oxford University Press, 1989); A. H. M. Jones, *Augustus* (London: Chatto & Windus, 1970); idem, *Cities of the Eastern Roman Provinces* (Oxford: Clarendon Press, 1937); B. W. Jones and R. D. Milns, *The Use of Documentary Evidence in the Study of Roman Imperial History* (Sydney: Sydney University Press, 1984); N. Kokkinos, *The Herodian Dynasty: Origins, Role in Society and Eclipse* (JSPSup 30; Sheffield: Sheffield Academic Press, 1998); L. J. Kreitzer, *Striking New Images: Roman Imperial Coinage and the New Testament World* (JSNTSup 134; Sheffield: Sheffield Academic Press, 1996); P. Lampe, *Die stadtrömischen Christen in den ersten beiden Jahrhunderten: Untersuchungen zur Sozialgeschichte* (WUNT 2.18; 2d ed.; Tübingen: Mohr Siebeck,

1989); G. La Piana, "Foreign Groups in Rome During the First Centuries of the Empire," *HTR* 20 (1927) 183-403; idem, "La Primitiva Communità Cristiana di Roma e L'epistola ai Romani," *Ricerche Religiose* 1 (1925) 209-26; 305-26; H. J. Leon, *The Jews of Ancient Rome* (Philadelphia: Jewish Publication Society of America, 1960); J. H. W. G. Liebeschuetz, *Continuity and Change in Roman Religion* (Oxford: Clarendon Press, 1979); A. Linder, *The Jews in Roman Imperial Legislation* (Detroit: Wayne State University Press, 1987); E. Lohse, *The New Testament Environment* (Nashville: Abingdon, 1976); R. MacMullen, *Christianizing the Roman Empire (A.D. 100-400)* (New Haven, CT: Yale University Press, 1984); idem, *Paganism in the Roman Empire* (New Haven, CT: Yale University Press, 1981); idem, *Roman Social Relations 50 B.C. to A.D. 284* (New Haven, CT: Yale University Press, 1974); T. W. Manson, "St. Paul's Letter to the Romans—and Others," in *The Romans Debate*, ed. K. P. Donfried (Minneapolis: Augsburg, 1978) 1-16; M. McCrum and A. G. Woodhead, *Select Documents of the Principates of the Flavian Emperors Including the Year of Revolution A.D. 68-96* (Cambridge: Cambridge University Press, 1966); F. Millar, *The Roman Empire and Its Neighbors* (2d ed.; London: Gerald Duckworth, 1981); idem, *The Roman Near East 31 B.C.-A.D. 337* (Cambridge, MA: Harvard University Press, 1993); T. Mommsen, *The Provinces of the Roman Empire from Casesar to Diocletian* (2 vols.; London: Macmillan, 1909); M. P. Nilsson, *The Dionysiac Mysteries of the Hellenistic and Roman Age* (Salem, NH: Ayer, 1985); idem, *Imperial Rome* (London: Bell, 1926); J. A. North, "Conservatism and Change in Roman Religion," *PBSR* 44 (1976) 1-12; idem, "Religion in Republican Rome," in *CAH* 7.2:573-624; W.-H. Ollrog, "Die Abfassungsverhältnisse von Röm 16," in *Kirche*, Festschrift for G. Bornkamm, ed. D. Lührmann and G. Strecker (Tübingen Mohr Siebeck, 1980) 221-44; A. M. Rostovtzeff, *Social and Economic History of the Roman Empire* (2d ed.; 2 vols.; Oxford: Clarendon Press, 1957); R. K. Sherk, ed., *Rome and the Greek East to the Death of Augustus* (Cambridge: Cambridge University Press, 1984); idem, *The Roman Empire: Augustus to Hadrian* (Cambridge: Cambridge University Press, 1988); A. N. Sherwin-White, "Provinces, Roman," *ISBE* 3:1026-28; idem, *Roman Society and Roman Law in the New Testament* (Oxford: Clarendon Press, 1963); M. Stern, ed., *Greek and Latin Authors on Jews and Judaism*, vol. 2 (Jerusalem: Israel Academy of Sciences and Humanities, 1980); A. Watson, *The Law of the Ancient Romans* (Dallas: Southern Methodist University Press, 1970); K. Wengst, *Pax Romana and the Peace of Jesus Christ* (London: SCM, 1987); R. L. Wilken, *The Christians as the Romans Saw Them* (New Haven, CT: Yale University Press, 1984); M. H. Williams, *The Jews Among the Greeks and Romans: A Diasporan Sourcebook* (London: Duckworth, 1998).

R. B. Edwards and M. Reasoner, rev. S. E. Porter

ROSETTA STONE. *See* INSCRIPTIONS AND PAPYRI: GRECO-ROMAN.

RULE OF THE COMMUNITY/MANUAL OF DISCIPLINE (1QS)

The *Serek ha-yaḥad* (*Rule of the Community*) is a document that records the beliefs and rules of the *Essene community living at Khirbet *Qumran near the Dead Sea at the period before, during and after the life of Jesus of Nazareth (c. 150 B.C.-A.D. 68). It is important not only for understanding the Essenes but also for shedding light on the NT at many significant points.

1. The Preserved Manuscripts and Their Publication History
2. The Contents of the Best-Preserved Manuscript (1QS)
3. The Textual History of the Document
4. The Relationship to Other Texts of the Qumran Community
5. The Relevance of the Document for New Testament Studies

1. The Preserved Manuscripts and Their Publication History.

The *Rule of the Community* (1QS) was among the first manuscripts found at Qumran in 1947, and it was published in 1951. It is almost completely preserved and comprises eleven columns written on five leather sheets stitched together. It was first entitled the *Manual of Discipline*, which aptly describes its contents, for the majority of its sections contain regulations governing the life and order of the community. The currently used title, the *Rule of the Community*, translates the Hebrew title in the opening line of the document.

A total of twelve copies were found: in addition to the complete copy from Cave 1, ten fragmentary copies were found in Cave 4 (4QS$^{a\text{-}j}$) and another in Cave 5 (5QS). The manuscript from Cave 5 was published in 1962, but due to its fragmentary nature it has been of fairly limited use for the analysis of the *Rule*, or *Serek*. The DJD volume containing the Cave 4 manuscripts was published in 1998, and their analysis is still at an early stage, but it is clear that some of them show remarkable differences compared with the copy from Cave 1.

2. The Contents of the Best-Preserved Manuscript (1QS).

1QS 1:1-15. The main manuscript starts with an introduction that mentions several topics essential for life in the community. The centrality of the law of *Moses is emphasized; the community is dualistic in its thinking, and this involves strict separation between "the sons of light" and "the sons of darkness," that is, the community members and those outside. The community understands itself as the true keeper of the covenant, and its members strive for perfection in their ritual conduct. A command is given for proper observance of cultic *festivals according to the (solar) *calendar used in the community. The members of the community hand over their property to the community.

1QS 1:16—3:12. The liturgical section is divided into three parts. The first part contains a ceremony for entry into the covenant. The second part describes the annual renewal of the covenant, which presumably took place in the same ceremony. The third part includes condemnation of those who (after the novitiate period?) refuse to enter into the covenant.

1QS 3:13—4:26. A theological section expounds the doctrine of the Two Spirits. The basis for the doctrine is the assumption that while God is predestinator of all, there are two opposing superhuman powers working in the world, the spirit of truth and the spirit of wickedness, also called the spirit of light and the spirit of darkness, that influence the life and destiny of every human being. The perspectives are both cosmological and anthropological. On the one hand, every person is allotted to the dominion of either one or the other of the two spirits. On the other hand, every person is simultaneously influenced by both of the spirits: the spirits fight in the heart of a person who does either good or evil according to which of the spirits dominates more. A wrongdoing committed by a righteous person is to be understood as caused by the angel of darkness.

The dualism of the *Rule of the Community* is not absolute in the sense that evil would be considered as an independent force, for it is explicitly stated that God created both the spirit of light and the spirit of darkness. They have been appointed to influence the lives of human beings until the predetermined end of the existence of the spirit of darkness, after which the spirit of truth will reign. The dualistic beliefs of the community seem to have been closely related to the community's conviction that they were living in the end time and that God would soon intervene in the course of human history, destroy evil and create an era where his dominion would not be challenged.

1QS 5:1—6:23. The order of the community is expounded in columns 5 and 6, commencing with an introductory account of the principles of the community's life. This is followed by a passage describing the oath to be taken by each member: "to return to the law of Moses with all his heart and soul, following all that he has commanded, and in accordance with all that has been revealed from it to the sons of Zadok, the priests who keep the covenant and seek his will, and to the multitude of the men of their covenant who together willingly offer themselves for his truth and to walk according to his will" (1QS 5:8-10). Further regulations of community life continue, such as rules for separation from outsiders, for the meeting of the full members of the community, "the many" (*ha-rabbîm*) and for accepting new members into the community. The manuscripts $4QS^b$ and $4QS^d$ provide a shorter and perhaps more original form of the text for these columns.

In order to become accepted as a full member of the community, the novice was tested through a lengthy probationary period. After the "the officer in charge" (*ha-paqîd*) at the head of the many had preliminarily accepted the candidate, he was investigated by the many. If the many also approved of the candidate, he was able to begin his first probationary year. During this period the candidate was not allowed to "touch the purity of the many," which mainly involved the common cultic meal. After the probationary year the candidate was reexamined, now by the *priests and the many. If he was accepted, his property was handed over to "the overseer" (*ha-m̆ᵉbaqqēr*) to be listed in the community records. The final decision as to whether the candidate was accepted into the full membership of the community took place after the second year. The only decision maker mentioned in this connection is the many.

1QS 6:24-7:25. The section containing the penal code of the community is connected to the preceding section of columns 5—6 in that together they form the set of regulations governing the inner life of the community (5—7). The penal code is very heterogeneous, the rules apparently having been collected somewhat haphazardly, but all of them reflect tensions in the community's life. The penal code may have been compiled as the result of the court proceedings in the meetings of the many. The penalties vary from the punishment of ten days—the exact meaning of which is unclear, possibly it involved cutting the food ration—to permanent expulsion. The literary genre of this secti on is that of casuistic law, as paralleled, for example, in the Book of the Covenant (Ex 20:22—23:33).

1QS 8:1—9:26a. A major part of the material in columns 8 and 9 may have been inserted into the composition fairly late, for 1QS 8:15—9:11 is not included in the manuscript 4QS[e]. The scribe who inserted the section into the *Rule of the Community* apparently borrowed an older source. A number of scholars maintain that the text originates in the period when the founding of the community still lay ahead, and they label the section a manifesto or the program of the new community. The section begins with an introduction that, like the one at the beginning of column 5, lists the basic principles of the community's life and is followed by a penal code, the regulations of which are set out in far more general terms than those of the penal code of column 6. The section is characterized by strong idealism that could indicate that the movement was still at an early stage. The latter part of column 9 comprises two sections addressed to the "wise leader" (*ha-maskîl*). They describe the qualities and responsibilities of the community's spiritual leader.

1QS 9:26b—11:22. The document concludes with a *hymn, which includes a calendric section listing the community's times of *prayer. In the manuscript 4QS[e], the hymn is replaced by the calendric text *Otot.*

3. The Textual History of the Document.
E. F. Sutcliffe proposed in 1959 that columns 8—9 of 1QS represent the earliest material of the *Rule.* J. Murphy-O'Connor in 1969 argued that there was a three-stage development from the nucleus or manifesto formed by 8:1-16 and 9:3—10:8 (1QS 8:16—9:2; 1QS 5:1-13 + 5:15—7:25; 1QS 1:1—4:26 + 10:9—11:22). The redactional stages corresponded to the archaeological phases of Khirbet Qumran. His theory was developed and modified in the 1970s and 1980s in publications by various scholars, but no one presented a serious alternative.

The evidence of the Cave 4 copies both illuminates and complicates the textual history. J. T. Milik in 1977 suggested that 4QS[b,d] with a shorter text represent an earlier form of the document than 1QS. G. Vermes agreed in 1991, paying special attention to a variant referring to the authority of the community: the words "according to the many" in 4QS[b,d] were replaced by a longer formulation in 1QS 5:2-3: "according to the sons of Zadok, the priests who keep the covenant, and to the multitude of the men of the community who hold fast to the covenant; on their word the decision shall be taken on any matter having to do with the law, with wealth, or with justice." Whereas Vermes speaks of two different traditions, C. Hempel has developed the thought further, speaking of a Zadokite recension, the marks of which she also detects in the text of the *Rule of the Congregation* (1QSa), a different manuscript copied on the same scroll with 1QS.

P. S. Alexander begins from the principle that the order in which the manuscripts were copied holds the key to the order in which the different recensions were created. 1QS, which is generally dated to about 100 to 75 B.C., contains a longer version. The manuscripts 4QS[b] and 4QS[d], which are dated a half century later, to the last third of the last century B.C., have preserved a shorter version of the document than 1QS. Alexander, in contrast to Milik and Vermes, considers 4QS[b,d] a result of intentional omissions from the longer document. His explanation of the variant in 1QS 5:2-3 versus 4QS[b,d] (above) is that 1QS reflects an early stage in the history of the community when the Zadokites held a leading position, whereas 4QS[b,d] belong to a later stage when their position had weakened. The manuscript 4QS[e] lacks the large section 8:15—9:11 in 1QS. Alexander thinks that this was an intentional omission, after the redactor observed contradictions and repetitions in that section. As to the relationship between 4QS[b,d] and 4QS[e], Alexander sees 4QS[e] as the latest redactional stage. Thus, his suggestion of the order of the MSS is 1QS (oldest), $4QS^{(b),d}$, $4QS^{e}$ (youngest).

S. Metso, in a literary- and redaction-critical analysis of the Cave 4 manuscripts ($4QS^{a\text{-}j}$), presents a comprehensive treatment of all the *Serek* variants. She sees 1QS as a relatively late stage in the development of the document and considers the forms transmitted by $4QS^{e}$ and $4QS^{b,d}$ as forerunners of that in 1QS. The main characteristic of the redaction that can be detected by comparing $4QS^{b,d}$ and 1QS was the need to provide scriptural legitimization for the rules of the community and to strengthen the group's self-understanding as the true keeper of the covenant and the law. The redaction observed by comparing $4QS^{e}$ and 1QS, however, aimed at bringing the text up to date. Thus $4QS^{e}$ and $4QS^{b,d}$ represent two lines of tradition that derive from an earlier version, a version that (1) as witnessed by $4QS^{d}$ did not include the material parallel to 1QS 1—4; (2) as witnessed by $4QS^{d}$ commenced with the text parallel to 1QS 5 and was addressed to the *maśkîl*; (3) as witnessed by $4QS^{b,d}$ did not yet have the scriptural quotations or the additions aimed at strengthening the community's self-understanding; (4) as witnessed by $4QS^{e}$ did not yet include the section parallel to 1QS 8:15—9:11; and (5) as witnessed by $4QS^{e}$ lacked the final psalm found in 1QS 10—11 but possibly included (as does $4QS^{e}$) the calendric text *Otot.* The redaction as found in 1QS is a combination of both lines of tradition as in $4QS^{e}$ and $4QS^{b,d}$ and thus includes both the final psalm and the scriptural quotations and community-oriented additions. The latest stage of redaction is to be seen in the revisions and additions made even later by the scribal corrector in 1QS 7—8. Thus the plurality of textual forms indicates that the community had continued copying older versions even when newer, expanded versions were available. In this she points to the parallel of the biblical manuscripts, where the same phenomenon is documented.

4. The Relationship to Other Texts of the Qumran Community.

Two other works, the *Rule of the Congregation* (1QSa) and the *Book of Blessings* (1QSb), were copied on the same scroll as 1QS, and scholars question the rationale for compiling these works together. Are 1QSa and 1QSb to be seen as independent works in a collection with 1QS or as two appendices to 1QS? The question has even been raised whether the community that created 1QS was the same as the community behind 1QSa. The three works share some common vocabulary, yet there are significant differences between them. The literary genre of 1QSb is different from that of 1QS and 1QSa, and, while 1QSa describes an *eschatological community, 1QS describes the historical community that lived at Qumran.

The **Damascus Document* (CD) shares many features with the *Rule of the Community* in vocabulary, themes and theology, but there are clear dissimilarities as well. The *Damascus Document* has long sections describing the history of the community, whereas the *Rule of the Community* shows no particular interest in the events of the community's past. The CD has references to *women and *children, whereas 1QS never mentions them. There is nothing comparable to the doctrine of the Two Spirits (1QS 3:13—4:26) in the *Damascus Document.* Puzzling differences occur in the thematically parallel sections found in both 1QS and CD. For example, the novitiate for membership in the community is longer according to the *Rule of the Community* than according to the Damascus Document; and in 1QS it is the many (*ha-rabbîm*) but in CD it is the "the overseer" (*ha-mᵉbaqqēr*) who approves candidates for membership. The differences in the organizational terminology (e.g., the different functions attributed to *ha-mᵉbaqqēr, ha-paqîd, ha-maśkîl* and *ha-rabbîm*) are particularly difficult to explain.

The differences between the two documents have often been explained using sociological and historical factors. That is, 1QS was viewed as written for the community centered at Qumran, whereas CD was aimed at the larger Essene membership in the towns. Some of the recently published Cave 4 documents that were previously unknown, however, do not seem to represent clearly either one group or the other. A manuscript called *Miscellaneous Rules* (4Q265; *olim Serek Dameseq*), for example, contains features from both the *Rule of the Community* and the *Damascus Document. Miscellaneous Rules* includes rules that are typical for the *Damascus Document* (e.g., *sabbath regulations), and like the *Damascus Document* mentions women and children. However, it lists transgressions that occur in the *Rule of the Community*, such as complaining against those ranked higher in the community, lying about a neighbor, insulting or betraying a neighbor, falling asleep in the community meeting and guffawing stupidly. Similarly, two Cave 4 manuscripts of the *Damascus Document* (4Q266 = 4QD[a] and 4Q270 = 4QD[e]) include a penal code, which does not have a parallel in CD but is clearly based on the same text as the one in 1QS 7. Although the parallel sections in 4QD contain some regulations that are absent in 1QS, the order of the regulations is the same. The analysis of the parallel sections clearly indicates that the writers behind 1QS and 4QD[a,e] used the same source.

These complexities have implications for methodology in studying rule texts. Since different groups used common sources and borrowed material from each other, it is problematic to distinguish and identify the specific groups behind the manuscripts. If whole blocks of material in manuscripts are borrowed and adapted, what are the criteria that make it possible to assign a manuscript to a particular group (e.g., a celibate community versus a community where *marriage was a common practice)? The composite nature of the documents needs to be taken into account, and analyses should concentrate on separate passages, acknowledging the developmental history of texts rather than only on the complete final redaction.

5. The Relevance of the Document for New Testament Studies.

At least four areas can be mentioned where it is fruitful to compare the NT material with the *Rule of the Community.*

5.1. Citations of the Old Testament. First, the *Rule of the Community* as well as other rule texts found at Qumran (e.g., CD and 1QM), which combine citations into a prose narrative, come close to the way citations are used in the NT. Often an OT citation serves to bolster up or illustrate an argument, or it may act as a kind of prooftext. For example, both 1QS and all four Gospels cite Isaiah 40:3. In 1QS 8:12-16 it is used for the Qumran community's self-understanding in its withdrawal into the desert. In the NT the same verse is used by all four Evangelists to explain John the Baptist's presence in the desert (Mt 3:3; Mk 1:3; Lk 3:4-6; Jn 1:23). Deutero-Isaiah's original proclamation was that Yahweh was about to put himself at the head of his people and lead them to freedom from exile across the desert, as he did at the exodus from Egypt into the promised land. Both the *Rule of the Community* and the four Evangelists have in analogous ways disregarded the historical context, detached the verse from its original message and accommodated it into their new environments—the Qumran community to explain its withdrawal into the desert, and the Evangelists to explain John the Baptist's annunciation of the coming Lord.

5.2. Concepts and Theological Ideas. There are many concepts and theological ideas held in common. The strongly dualistic language of the doctrine of the Two Spirits (1QS 3:13—4:26) has similarities with the ethical and eschatological dualism in the Gospel of John:

> God created man to rule the world, and he assigned two spirits to him that he might walk by them until the appointed time of his visitation; they are the spirits of truth and of injustice. From a spring of light come the generations of truth, and from a well of darkness the generations of injustice. Control over all the sons of righteousness lies in the hand of the prince of lights, and they walk in the ways of light; complete control over the sons of injustice lies in the hand of the angel of darkness, and they walk in the ways of darkness. (1QS 3:17-21, trans. M. A. Knibb)

For the opposition of light and darkness in John, see John 1:4-5; 3:19; 12:35-36 (see also 1 Jn 1:5-6) and of truth and falsehood, see John 3:21; 8:44 (see also 1 Jn 2:21, 27; 4:6). But though some parallels are striking (e.g., "spirit of truth" in Jn 14:17; 15:26; 16:13 and 1QS 3:18-19; 4:21, 23; "sons of light" in Jn 12:36 and 1QS 3:13, 24, 25), Johannine dualism—in which Jesus is truth incarnate—is not identical with that of the Essenes, for whom the truth is revealed in the Torah. Dualistic thinking is broadly attested in Judaism and later Christianity, as can be seen in **Jubilees* 7—12, *Sirach 33, *1 Enoch* 2—5 and 41—48 (*see* Enoch, Books of) and **Testaments of the Twelve Patriarchs* (*T. Jud.* 20:1-4; *T. Asher* 1:3—6:5; 3—6; *T. Benj.* 4:1—8:3). Moreover, this dualistic thinking can be compared with the idea of the Two Ways expressed in Matthew 7:13-14 and in later Christian literature, such as *Didache* 1—6 and *Epistle of Barnabas* 18—21.

A transition toward Paul's central belief of justification by divine grace (e.g., Rom 3:21-31) can be seen, for example, in 1QS 11:9-15. Though based on OT ideas, the Qumran theology shows a Palestinian Jewish development that has risen to a new plane, having synthesized the ideas of universal sinfulness, dependence on the mercy of a gracious God and a new state of righteousness derivative from that of God:

> And I belong to the Adam of wickedness and to the assembly of evil flesh. My iniquities, my transgressions, my sins along with the perversities of my heart belong to the assembly of worms and of those who walk in darkness. . . . To God belongs judgement and from his hands comes perfection of way. . . . But for me, if I falter—the mercies of God are my salvation for ever; and if I stumble in the iniquity of flesh, my judgement is with the righteousness of God, which shall endure for ever. . . . In his compassion he has drawn me near and in his mercies he will bring in my judgement. In the righteousness of his truth he will judge me and in his great goodness he will cover for ever all my iniquities; and in his righteousness he will purify me from the uncleanness of mankind and the sin of the sons of men, that I may praise God for his righteousness and the most high for his majesty. (trans. A. R. C. Leaney)

The idea of *mysteries that are revealed only to the chosen of God but hidden from others, which has its prototype in the book of Daniel (e.g., Dan 2:19, 28-30, 47) and is a theme used in Matthew and Luke (e.g., Mt 10:26 par. Lk 12:2; Mt 11:25 par. Lk 10:21; Mt 11:27 par. Lk 10:22; Mt 13:35; Lk 18:34), may be compared with that in the *Rule of the Community* and other Qumran writings (1QS 4:6; 5:11-12; 1QH 9:21; 20:13; 4QpHab 7:4-5).

5.3. Hebrew/Aramaic Expressions. Some expressions attested in the *Rule of the Community* and other Qumran writings provide the Hebrew or Aramaic equivalents of NT phrases, documenting that these Hebrew or Aramaic expressions were in use in the period when the NT writings were being formulated. Fitzmyer lists, for example, the Pauline expressions "deeds of the law" (*erga nomou;* Rom 3:20, 28; Gal 2:16; 3:2, 5, 10; cf. 4QFlor 1:7, 4QMMT C 27; 1QS 5:21; 6:18), "the righteousness of God" (*dikaiosynē theou;* Rom 1:17; 3:5, 21, 22; 10:3; 2 Cor 5:21) and "a spirit of holiness" (*pneuma hagiōsynēs* in parallelism with *kata sarka;* Rom 1:3-4; 1QS 4:21; 8:16; 9:3).

5.4. Community Structures and Practices. Certain community structures and practices are similar in the *Rule of the Community* and the NT. At Qumran the term "the many" (*ha-rabbîm*) designates the group of full community members that had judicial functions (e.g., 1QS 6:11-12; see 2 above). This Hebrew word probably lies behind Paul's reference in 2 Corinthians 2:5-6 to a discipline by "the majority" (see also Acts 6:2, 5; 15:12, 30). Again, the eucharistic words "my blood of the covenant that is poured out for many" in Matthew 26:27-28 and Mark 14:23-24 may echo the way this term was used at Qumran. Though the designation of "the many" is somewhat unclear in Matthew and Mark, the parallel in Luke 22:20, "poured out for you," suggests that Luke understood "the many" as referring to the group of disciples. Likewise, the Hebrew word for "the overseer" (*ha-m*ᵉ*baqqēr*) is the translational equivalent of *episkopos* ("overseer/ bishop") in the NT (Phil 1:1; 1 Tim 3:1-7; Tit 1:7-9).

Another feature in common with the Essenes and the followers of Jesus and the early church is the division into twelve (Jas 1:1; Mt 19:28; Lk 22:30). According to 1QS 8:1 there should be twelve men and three priests in the council of the community, apparently signifying the twelve tribes of *Israel and the three clans of the tribe of Levi (cf. Num 3:17-20).

Finally, the practice of sharing property in common is attested at Qumran (1QS 1:11-13; 6:16-23, 24-25). The correlation between spirituality and one's attitude toward wealth is parallel to that seen in Acts 2:44-47; 4:34-37; 5:1-11 (see also Lk 3:10-14; 8:1-3; 12:33).

See also DAMASCUS DOCUMENT (CD AND QD); RULE OF THE CONGREGATION/MESSIANIC RULE (1QSA).

BIBLIOGRAPHY. P. S. Alexander, "The Redaction History of Serekh Ha-Yaḥad. A Proposal," *RevQ* 17 (1996) 437-56; P. S. Alexander and G. Vermes, *Qumran Cave 4.19: 4QSerekh Ha-Yaḥad and Two Related Texts* (DJD 26; Oxford: Clarendon Press, 1998); D. Barthélemy and J. T. Milik, "Annexes à la Règle de la Communauté," in *Qumran Cave I* (DJD 1; Oxford: Clarendon Press, 1955) 107-30, plates XXII-XXIX; J. M. Baumgarten, "The Cave 4 Versions of the Qumran Penal Code," *JJS* 43 (1992) 268-76; idem, "Miscellaneous Rules," in *Cave 4.25: Halakhic Texts* (DJD 35; Oxford: Clarendon Press, 1999) 57-78, plates V-VIII; J. M. Baumgarten, with J. T. Milik, S. Pfann and A. Yardeni, *Qumran Cave 4. 13: The Damascus Document (4Q266-273)* (DJD 18; Oxford: Clarendon Press, 1996); M. Burrows with J. C. Trever and W. H. Brownlee, *The Dead Sea Scrolls of St. Mark's Monastery,* vol. 2: *Fasc. 2. Plates and Transcription of the Manual of Discipline* (New Haven, CT: American Schools of Oriental Research, 1951); P. R. Davies, "Communities in the Qumran Scrolls," *Proceedings of the Irish Biblical Association* 17 (1994) 55-68; C. A. Evans, "The Synoptic Gospels and the Dead Sea Scrolls," in *The Bible and the Dead Sea Scrolls,* vol. 5: *Jesus and the Origins of Christianity,* ed. J. H. Charlesworth (North Richland Hills, TX: BIBAL, forthcoming); J. A. Fitzmyer, "Paul and the Dead Sea Scrolls," in *The Dead Sea Scrolls After Fifty Years: A Comprehensive Assessment,* ed. P. W. Flint and J. C. VanderKam (2 vols.; Leiden: E. J. Brill, 1998) 2:599-621; F. García Martínez and J. Trebolle Barrera, *The People of the Dead Sea Scrolls: Their Writings, Beliefs and Practices* (Leiden, E. J. Brill, 1995); C. Hempel, "The Earthly Essene Nucleus of 1QSa," *DSD* 3 (1996) 253-69; M. A. Knibb, *The Qumran Community* (CCJC 2; Cambridge: Cambridge University Press, 1987); idem, "Rule of the Community," *Encyclopedia of the Dead Sea Scrolls* (New York: Oxford University Press, 2000) 793-97; A. R. C. Leaney, *The Rule of Qumran and Its Meaning. Introduction, Translation and Commentary* (London: SCM, 1966); S. Metso, *The Textual Development of the Qumran Community Rule* (STDJ 21; Leiden: E. J. Brill, 1997); J. T. Milik, "Numérotation des feuilles des rouleaux dans le scriptorium de Qumrân," *Semitica* 27 (1977) 75-81; idem, "Règle de la Communauté," in *Les "Petites Grottes" de Qumran: Textes,* ed. M. Baillet, J. T. Milik and R. de Vaux (DJD 3; Oxford: Clarendon Press, 1962) 180-181, plate xxxviii; idem, "Texte des Variantes des Dix Manuscrits de la Règle de la Communauté trouvés dans la Grotte 4. Recension de P.Wernberg-Møller, The Manual of Discipline," *RB* 67 (1960) 410-16; J. Murphy-O'Connor, "La Genèse Littéraire de la Règle de la Communauté," *RB* 76 (1969) 528- 49; J. Pouilly, *La Règle de la Communauté: Son Evolution Littéraire* (CRB 17; Paris: Gabalda, 1976); E. Qimron and J. H. Charlesworth, with an appendix by F. M. Cross, "Cave IV Fragments (4Q255-264 = 4QS MSS A-J)," in *The Dead Sea Scrolls: Hebrew, Aramaic and Greek Texts with English Translations,* vol. 1: *Rule of the Community and Related Documents,* ed. J. H. Charlesworth et al. (Louisville, KY: John Knox, 1994) 53-103; H. Stegemann, *Die Essener, Qumran, Johannes der Täufer und Jesus: Ein Sachbuch* (Freiburg: Herder, 1993); E. F. Sutcliffe, "The First Fifteen Members of the Qumran Community: A Note on 1QS 8:1ff.," *JSS* 4 (1959) 134-38; G. Vermes, "Preliminary Remarks on Unpublished Fragments of the Community Rule from Qumran Cave 4," *JJS* 42 (1991) 250-55.

S. Metso

RULE OF THE CONGREGATION/ MESSIANIC RULE (1QSA)

The *Rule of the Congregation* (1QSa) is part of one of the original seven scrolls found in Cave 1 near Khirbet *Qumran. It is also known as the *Messianic Rule* as well as the *Messianic Banquet.* Its relationship to NT literature may be attributed to a common Jewish background that begins with the OT. The scroll is important for the insights it gives us into early Jewish messianic expectations.

1. Text, Title and Content
2. Contribution to New Testament Studies
3. The Congregational Meal

1. Text, Title and Content.

The text was originally published by D. Barthélemy (1955). A critical edition has been done by J. H. Charlesworth and L. Stuckenbruck (1994), but the most extensive and important study of the text was done by L. H. Schiffman (1989).

The composition is two columns long (51 lines) and was originally included on the same scroll as the larger, more well-known **Rule of the Community* (1QS) along with the **Book of Blessings* (1QSb). This short text was composed in Hebrew sometime before 75 B.C. The scroll has proved one of the more enigmatic of the Qumran scrolls for a variety of reasons, including the poor state of preservation and the carelessness of the scribe. The language is archaizing, recalling OT literature, albeit in an indirect way (e.g., cf. 1QSa 1:11 and Ex 30:11-16; 1QSa 2:11-12 and Ps 2:7).

The *Rule of the Congregation* gets its title from the opening words of the text: "This is the rule of the whole congregation of Israel in the last days" (1QSa 1:1). This also indicates one of the main interests of the scrolls, namely, proper conduct in the eschaton. What follows suggests that the writer assumed that his readers, by following the community rules, were preparing the way for and living proleptically in the final messianic age (*see* Eschatologies).

The content of 1QSa may be outlined as follows: (1) introduction (1:1-5), (2) stages of life before full initiation into the community (1:6-18), (3) disqualifications from the community (1:19-22), (4) the work of the Levites (1:22-25), (5) purity of the convocation (1:25-27), (6) those invited (1:27—2:3), (7) those not invited (2:3-10) and (8) proper conduct at the messianic banquet (2:11-22). The stages of life here are paralleled by a similar list in Mishnah *ʾAbot* 5:21, where a person is supposed to begin Scripture study at age five, Mishnah study at age ten, to take up business at age twenty, and so on until the age of one hundred. Another example of this genre is found in the rabbinic midrash on Ecclesiates illustrating the widespread use of the genre (see *Eccles. Rab.* 1:2 §1). We may assume that each list was shaped by the views of its authors; in the case of the Qumranites this meant outlining the gradual induction into "the holy congregation" (e.g., 1QSa 1:12-13).

2. Contribution to New Testament Studies.

The *Rule of the Congregation* is clearly a Qumran sectarian composition. Two other documents on the scroll, the *Rule of the Community* (1QS) and *Blessings* (1QSb), are the most important for contextualizing the text. Other important texts include the **War Scroll* (1QM) and the **Temple Scroll* (11QTemple) (e.g., 1QSa 1:14-18 with 1QM 6:12-13 and 1QSa 2:3-4 with 1QM 7:3-6 and 11QTemple 45:7-18). These and other parallels are discussed at length by Schiffman. The parallels, however, do not suggest direct dependence between the various scrolls but rather point to a common background within the Qumran community.

Perhaps one of the most interesting aspects of the *Rule of the Congregation* is the role of *women. When the Men of God's Counsel assemble, they are supposed to bring "children along with women" and all will hear the "statutes of the covenant" (1QSa 1:4-5). Likewise, the restriction that a fledgling of the community should not lie with a woman until age twenty implies *marriage among the community (1QSa 1:9-10). This all flies in the face of the conventional wisdom, no doubt heavily influenced by *Pliny's and *Josephus's descriptions of the *Essenes, that the Qumran sectarians lived without women. It is clear that the rule speaks of the messianic age so that one must admit that women and children had a place at the messianic banquet of the final eschaton.

In spite of its fragmentary condition, the *Rule of the Congregation* contributes to our understanding of Qumran sectarian *messianism. First, the text strengthens the conventional interpretation of Qumran messianism as configured with two messiahs, royal and priestly. Second, it describes the otherwise unknown messianic banquet in the last days. There has been much debate about an apparent lack of unanimity across the whole Qumran corpus about messianic expectations, particularly whether there was one or two messiahs (e.g., Abegg). Much of this problem stems from the diversity of the corpus, which stretches over at least three centuries and which includes clearly nonsectarian compositions (most obviously biblical books, **Enoch, *Jubilees*). There seems more unanimity among scrolls of unquestioned sectarian origin (e.g., 1QS 9:11; 4QFlorilegium; CD 7:14-21; *see* Damascus Document). 1QSa focuses particularly on the role of the Messiah of Israel; the role of a priestly messiah in the messianic banquet is secondary and unfortunately appears in some of the most heavily damaged parts of the text (1QSa 2:11-13, 19).

One point of particular contention in 1QSa concerns Barthélemy's original reading of the last word column 2, line 11 as "begets" (Heb *yôlîd*); hence, God begets the Messiah. The text here is broken and difficult, and ironically computer enhancement of the scroll has supposedly helped both confirm (Vermes) and correct the reading (Charlesworth, who reads "leads forth" [Heb *yôlîk*]). In truth, the text is so badly damaged that even computer enhancement does not completely vindicate any reading. The original reading is certainly in accord with the idea of the Messiah as "son of God" (*see* Son of God Text [4Q246]), and it is even anticipated by Psalm 2:7 (also Ps 110:3), in which God declares to his anointed: "You are my son, today I have begotten you [Heb *yᵉlidtîkā*]." Such ideas certainly run against the grain of rabbinic conceptions of the Messiah. The idea of Jesus as "begotten" stems from the OT and gave rise to early developments in christology and to later christological debates (see, for example, *1 Clem.* 36; *Letter of Arius to Eusebius*, c. A.D. 321).

3. The Congregational Meal.

The idea of a congregational meal was critical not only to the messianic age but also to the present age of both the Qumran community and the early Christian church. For the Qumran sectarians, the ideal of a community meal undoubtedly meant that their present age was intended to mirror the expected messianic age (*see* Banquets). The same was true for the early Christian community. Indeed, Jesus' parables that refer to the royal wedding banquet in the kingdom of heaven (Mt 22:1-14; 25:1-12) and the common meal of the early Christians (Acts 2:46) should now be read in light of the Qumran community meal and their vision of a messianic banquet.

See also DEAD SEA SCROLLS: GENERAL INTRODUCTION; MESSIANISM; QUMRAN: PLACE AND HISTORY.

BIBLIOGRAPHY. M. G. Abegg Jr., "The Messiah at Qumran: Are We Still Seeing Double?" *DSD* 2 (1995) 125-44; D. Barthélemy, "Règle de la Congrégation (1QSa)," in *Qumran Cave 1,* ed., D. Barthélemy and J. T. Milik (*DJD* 1; Oxford: Clarendon Press, 1955) 107-18, plates XXII-XXIV; J. H. Charlesworth and L. Stuckenbruck, "The Rule of the Congregation," in *The Dead Sea Scrolls,* 1: *Rule of the Community and Related Documents,* ed. J. H. Charlesworth (Tübingen: Mohr Siebeck; Louisville, KY: Westminister, 1994) 108-17; P. R. Davies and J. E. Taylor, "On the Testimony of Women in 1QSa," *DSD* 3 (1996) 223-35; É. Puech, "Préséance Sacerdotale et Messie—Roi dans la Règle de la Congrégation (1QSa ii 11-22)," *RevQ* 16 (1994) 351-65; L. H. Schiffman, *The Eschatological Community of the Dead Sea Scrolls: A Study of the Rule of the Congregation* (SBLMS 38; Atlanta: Scholars Press, 1989); H. Stegemann, "Some Remarks to 1QSa, to 1QSb and to Qumran Messianism," *RevQ* 17 (1996) 479-505; G. Vermes, *The Complete Dead Sea Scrolls in English* (New York: Penguin, 1997).

W. M. Schniedewind

RULER CULT

The imperial cult was an important expression of loyalty and gratitude toward the *emperor: since his gifts matched those of the gods, so also should the thankful response. The cult both articulated the position of the emperor in the world and provided provincial elites with a language for diplomacy and strategy for developing relations with this powerful figure. For those who were committed to the worship of one God, however, imperial cult became a point of high tension with the larger society.

1. Ruler Cult in the Greco-Roman World
2. The Imperial Cult and the Jews
3. The Imperial Cult and the Early Church

1. Ruler Cult in the Greco-Roman World.

The cult of the Roman emperor, the form of ruler cult most important for the NT and its environment, was primarily a sacral articulation of the role and significance of the emperor within the *Roman Empire. It gave visual and ritual expression to the stature of this imposing figure and provided a language for understanding one's relatedness to this figure, whether as beneficent *patron or as *paterfamilias,* the head of a vastly extended family. The specific form of the cult differed in the various parts of the empire, especially between the eastern provinces, which had a long history of offering divine honors to rulers, and the western provinces, especially Italy (Earl). Nevertheless, imperial cult in all parts of the empire focused attention on the emperor as the patron of the world. Since his gifts matched those of the deities, it was deemed only fitting that the expressions of gratitude and loyalty should take on the forms used to communicate with the patron deities themselves.

1.1. Eastern Provinces. The East had a long history of ascribing divine honors to powerful figures. Most pronounced in Egypt, where pharaohs had been hailed as sons of the Sun God for many centuries, this became more common in the other territories of the eastern Mediterranean after the career of *Alexander the Great. Such honors were rooted first in the awareness of the power of a ruler. A papyrus fragment, apparently from a child's book, reads: "What is a god? That which is powerful. What is a king? He who is equal to the divine." The person who can do exponentially more than others, whether a governor, a general, a pharaoh or a Hellenistic monarch, was placed by such thinking close to the deities, having more in common with that order of being than with the common person. The power that the Roman emperor had over the known world—legions moving at his command, movement of enormous amounts of resources at his direction, and so forth—would make the distinction between himself and the gods all the more blurred.

Cultic honors were also rooted in the more basic institution of *patronage. If a rich person provides grain for a poor family in times of famine, that family owes a deep debt of loyalty, gratitude and obedience to the patron. The family is obliged to spread the good report of the patron's virtue and beneficence, to serve the patron when called upon and to remain loyal to the patron against his or her rivals. When a general liberates a city from tyranny, or a governor provides ongoing stability, or a benefactor provides relief for an entire province in times of famine, how can the beneficiaries show ample gratitude? The honors due the gods seemed the only appropriate form of thanks for a patron who gave gifts such as were normally sought from the gods. When *Athens greeted its successful general, Demetrius Poliorketes, it used cultic language:

> The other gods must be far distant, or have no ears, or even do not exist, or, if they do, care nothing for us—but you we see as living and present among us, not of wood or of stone, but truly present. Thus we pray: above all, make peace, Most Beloved, for you are Lord [*kyrios*]. (*FHG* 76 F13)

The city's safety and continued peace rested on the efforts of this military figure, and since he provided what people normally looked to the gods to provide, it was deemed fitting to render thanks worthy of the divine.

A similar picture emerges from Nicolaus of Damascus's firsthand observations concerning the origin of the cult of Augustus:

> People gave him the name [Augustus] in view of his claim to honor; and, scattered over islands and continents, through city and trive, they revere him by building temples and by sacrificing to him, thus requiting him for his great virtue and acts of kindness toward them. (Nicolaus of Damascus *Life of Augustus* 1)

The *pax Augusti* (*see* Pax Romana) was viewed as relief of divine proportions, and the return of thanks must be equal to the gift. Augustus thus succeeded in the East to the tradition of according divine honors to benefactors, generals and, during the Roman republic, governors (Bowersock). As long as the emperor was strong and his clients faithful, peace and prosperity would remain and the horrors of civil war and foreign invasion be prevented.

The imperial cult brings together these two aspects of power and patronage. The cult gave expression to the power of the emperor over the life of the province and the dependence of provincials on his favor and aid. The cult, however, also provided a means of access to the emperor. The language of the imperial cult became the language of diplomacy (Price). Provinces sought imperial aid (benefactions) through the mediation of the priests of the imperial cult, who both officiated at a distance and became the official ambassadors to Rome on behalf of the province (Price; Thompson). The cult not only provided the province with a representation of its emperor, but it also provided the emperor with a representation of the province (Thompson). It was essential that this image be one of uncompromising loyalty and gratitude, so that the province could be assured of ongoing favor. The Jewish author of *Wisdom of Solomon, a nonparticipant observer of the ruler cult, provides an intriguing testimony (Wis 14:17-21) supporting the interpretation of the cult as the forging of links of patronage between province and *princeps* (emperor).

The imperial cult was embedded in the cults of the traditional deities. Frequently, the statues of the emperor and traditional deities shared the same sacred space, emphasizing their connectedness. The emperor was not simply a god but the vessel by which the traditional gods established order and showered their gifts upon humanity. He was himself an object of veneration but also the chief priest of the Roman world, *pontifex maximus*, and therefore he stood as mediator between the gods and the human race (*see* Patronage). *Coins often feature the portrait of the emperor with his titles (including *divi filius*, "son of the deified," and *pontifex maximus*) on the obverse and portraits of one or another deity on the reverse, showing that his rule was grounded in the rule of all gods. He ruled by divine right, and his achievements were signs of divine favor.

Roman imperial ideology expressed itself not only in the cult of the emperor but also in the cult of Roma. Smyrna appears to have been the first to design a cult for Rome, raising a temple to her in 195 B.C. (Earl). Augustus refused to have any temple consecrated to himself, except in tandem with the goddess Roma. *Rome was chosen by the gods to rule the world, to subdue all nations and lead them into a golden age, united under its banner. Temples everywhere were dedicated to *Roma Aeterna*, "Eternal Rome," which would reign forever. Her dominion over the earth was thus promoted and welcomed as the will of the gods and the cause of lasting peace and well-being.

Imperial cult was not imposed on the eastern provinces by the emperor or his staff. Divine honors and cult were motivated from below and from the periphery of the empire as a means of establishing meaningful and favorable connection with the center of power and beneficence. Local provincial elites fostered active cults, enjoying the opportunities that holding priesthoods in these cults brought for advancing their prestige and ambitions for higher offices in the emperor's administration. At the same time, the fear of the return of civil disorder and the ever-present threat of invasion from foreign kingdoms like Parthia made the strength of Rome a welcome bulwark for those under its protection. Rome's power meant order and security, and the cult of the *Augusti et Roma* became an important expression of loyalty to that sheltering power. The emperors needed only to regulate this cult, and most of them push in the direction of moderation rather than intensification of cultic honors.

1.2. Rome and the West. In Italy, the custom of according divine honors to a living person had no precedent. Here, imperial cult took shape around the well-established family religion of the *genius*. Each family performed rites honoring its *genius,* the guardian spirit of the head of the household, and its *lar,* the spirit of the family's founding ancestor. When Augustus became the head of the state, rites began to be offered in public sites and in private homes to his *genius*. This articulated Augustus's role as head of the vastly extended family of the Roman state. He was the *pater patriae,* "father" or "patron of the country," the *paterfamilias* of the empire. Such cultic honors practiced throughout Rome and Italy "took natural root as an expression of that Roman gratitude for peace and stability established and guaranteed by the person and power of Augustus" (Earl, 174). Imperial cult failed to take substantial root in Gaul or the German frontier regions, there being nothing in the local, tribal, indigenous religions to which to attach the figure of the emperor. Cultic centers were established in the more Romanized areas but never reached the fervor that the cult enjoyed in the East (*see* Roman East).

2. The Imperial Cult and the Jews.

The Jewish people, because of their exclusive commitment to one God, offered sacrifices to this God on behalf of the emperor rather than to the emperor, and these were accepted by most emperors as a suitable display of loyalty and goodwill. Jews throughout the empire were officially given the same consideration, although this did not guarantee that local populations of Greek cities would accept the Jews, who refused to take part in the cults of the traditional gods and the emperor, as fellow citizens and equal sharers in the life of the city.

Two incidents involving imperial cult deserve attention, since the impression these made on Jews was widespread and long-lasting. *Josephus (*J.W.* 2.10.1-5 §§184-203; *Ant.* 18.8.2-9 §§261-309) tells of Gaius Caligula's attempt to erect a statue of himself in the Jerusalem *temple, thus giving the God of the Jews a face that would also link the site with imperial cult. The Jews refused to allow the installation of the statue, which would have been another "desolating sacrilege." When Petronius, the governor of Syria, realized that carrying out the emperor's order would result in massive loss of life, he appealed to Gaius to reconsider. Only the timely assassination of Gaius averted a disaster in Judea.

*Philo (*Leg. Gai.* 133-54; *Flacc.* 41-52) and Josephus (*Ant.* 18.8.1 §§257-60) both record how imperial cult was used as a weapon against Jews in Egypt during the escalating ethnic violence there between A.D. 38 and 41. Some anti-Jewish elements seized upon Gaius's zeal for divine honors as an excuse to break into the *synagogues of *Alexandria and install statues of Gaius and other tokens of imperial cult. The Jews could not remove them, which would be punishable as sacrilege, nor could they use the sites for their own worship while the idolatrous trappings were in place. Philo served on an embassy to Gaius seeking the restoration of their privileges under his predecessors, but only Gaius's death and the accession of Claudius brought a return to normalcy in Alexandria for the Jewish population. The riots in Alexandria, occasioned in part by Jewish attempts to clarify their position as full citizens of the Greek city, also highlight the connection of cult and citizenship: Jewish abstinence from the cults of the traditional gods and the emperor was a sign of their lack of any claim to "equal citizenship" in the eyes of many non-Jewish neighbors (Josephus *Ant.* 12.3.1-2 §§121-26).

3. The Imperial Cult and the Early Church.

3.1. Gospels. The command of Jesus to "give back to Caesar what belongs to Caesar and to God what belongs to God" (Mt 22:21 par.), while responding in the first instance to the narrower question of paying taxes to a foreign Gentile power, articulated a basic distinction between the emperor and God and between the honors due to each. Jesus also set the fear of God above the fear of any mortal with the *ius gladium,* the authority to execute the body (Mt 10:28 par.). Such sayings would reinforce the Christian commitment to offer divine honor exclusively to the one God and to protect that exclusivity with one's life should the need arise.

Luke's infancy narrative resonates with, and tends to supplant, claims for a Golden Age inaugurated by Augustus. An inscription from Priene in *Asia Minor bears witness to the attribution of Augustus's rule to the generous provision of providence, speaking of Augustus as the virtuous benefactor of the human race and bringer of peace. Augustus has surpassed the hopes of preceding generations and leaves no expectation that his benefactions will be surpassed in the future. The "birthday of the god" signifies for the world the "beginning of his good news." Luke declares in narrative form that God's provision for the benefit of humanity arrives not in Augustus but in Jesus, the announcement of whose birth is truly *euangelion* ("good news") and the sign of God's favor. The divine gift of *salus* ("well-being") becomes available not in the emperor but in Jesus, the Savior and Benefactor of the human race. It is in Jesus that all former hopes for a time of blessedness (articulated in the Jewish prophets) find fulfillment and whose provision for deliverance and wholeness make it impossible ever to hope for better. Such a text again serves to direct highest honors toward Jesus and the one God, calling for a more moderate assessment of the emperor's importance.

3.2. Epistles. Romans and 1 Peter contribute to an alternative ideology of the emperor, one that will allow the Christian to honor the emperor within the framework of an exclusive worship of God and God's Anointed. The authorities are "servants of God" (Rom 13:4, 6) who restrain bad deeds and promote doing good (Rom 13:3-4; 1 Pet 2:14). The Christian response is to be subject to them precisely as God's agents (Rom 13:1, 5) and to give them the taxes, respect and honor that is their due. This is, however, precisely to give the emperor less than the Christians' neighbors believe to be his due, namely, cultic honors. Such obedience, which should show the unbelieving critics of the church that Christians are not a dissident and base element (1 Pet 2:15), is at the same time a critique of the extravagant and idolatrous displays of loyalty and obedience. While the emperor may be supreme among human authorities, the Christian's response to the emperor is qualitatively different from his or her response to God: "Revere God; honor the emperor" (1 Pet 2:17).

3.3. Revelation. Imperial cult was extremely active in the province of Asia Minor: most of the cities addressed by Revelation contain archaeological evidence of a highly active imperial cult (Price; Friesen), and several were already in competition for the title of *neokoros,* "temple warden," of the provincial imperial cult. Ephesus and Pergamum were each honored as "twice *neokoros*" by the end of Trajan's reign (A.D. 117; Ferguson). Christians were routinely exposed to the cult and faced strong pressures to participate lest they arouse the ill will of their neighbors and local elites.

John's visions provide a cosmic perspective on this prominent phenomenon, undermining the imperial ideology at every point (deSilva 1991; Krodel; Cuss). The true center of power is not the emperor in Rome but God and the Lamb (deSilva 1993), who have an unrivaled claim to cultic honors as the creator and redeemer of humankind (Rev 4:1—5:14). They alone are "worthy" of acclamation as "savior" and "creator" (the first being used of civic benefactors, the second of "founders" of cities or colonies). Revelation 13 presents the imperial household and its cult (organized locally by the provincial government) as the manifestations not of divine governance but of Satan's rebellion against divine order (Rev 12:7—13:2). The emperor is not a model and object of piety but rather a blasphemer whose titles are an affront to the one God (Rev 13:2, 4-6). The imperial cult that sought to unify the empire in loyalty to its center (Rev 13:7, 12) competes with the church as God's means of unifying the world in true worship (Rev 5:9-10). Imperial cult is not a manifestation of divine power at work but a manufactured cult imposed by the local elites (notably not by the emperor, even here) upon the population (Rev 13:11-17).

The emperor's partner in worship, the goddess Roma, is unveiled as a prostitute whose reign means corruption. Rome and its emperors have brought not peace, law and security, but rather stand under God's judgment for their violence, economic injustice and corruption of the known world. Revelation calls for ongoing critique of the imperial regime and the ideology that supports it. Incensed that God's honor has been so severely assaulted, John calls for protest and nonparticipation, sending the churches on a course of escalating tension with the larger society over the issue of who is worthy of worship (deSilva 1991; 1993).

3.4. Second-Century Developments. Imperial cult became increasingly a focus of confrontation and resistance in the second century. Pliny, governor of Bithynia and Pontus in A.D. 110, writes a revealing letter to the emperor Trajan concerning charges brought against Christians (Pliny *Ep.* 10.96). Pliny allows those who are so denounced the opportunity to repudiate Christ and to demonstrate their loyalty by offering wine and incense before the images of Trajan and the traditional gods. According to Pliny's report, many accept his invitation. Trajan confirms Pliny's procedure—releasing those who offer cultic displays of loyalty, punishing those who refuse—and thus sets a troublesome precedent for the legal prosecution of Christians (Downing).

The *Martyrdom of Polycarp* shows this policy at work several decades later (*see DLNTD*, Polycarp). After Polycarp is denounced and arrested, the chief of police counsels him to say "Caesar is Lord" and to offer incense so as to save his life (*Mart. Pol.* 8). The governor urges him likewise to take an oath "by the fortune of Caesar" (*Mart. Pol.* 9-10). Polycarp dies witnessing both to the civil obedience of Christians, "taught to pay due respect to God's appointed rulers and authorities" (*Mart. Pol.* 10), but also to the qualitative difference between the honor due to emperor and the honor due God and God's Christ. Such confrontations again serve to highlight the political and civic importance of cultic expressions of loyalty to the emperor.

See also CIVIC CULTS; RELIGION, GRECO-ROMAN; ROMAN EMPERORS.

BIBLIOGRAPHY. G. W. Bowersock, "The Imperial Cult: Perceptions and Persistence," in *Jewish and Christian Self-Definition*, ed. B. F. Meyer and E. P. Sanders (3 vols.; Philadelphia: Fortress, 1982) 3:171-83; A. Y. Collins, *Crisis and Catharsis* (Philadelphia: Westminster, 1984); D. Cuss, *Imperial Cult and Honorary Terms in the New Testament* (Fribourg: Fribourg University Press, 1974); W. Den Boer, ed., *Le Culte des Souverains dans l'Empire Romain* (Geneva: Fondation Hardt, 1973); D. A. deSilva, "The Construction and Social Function of a Counter-Cosmos in the Revelation of John," *Forum* 9 (1993) 47-61; idem, "The Image of the Beast and the Christians in Asia Minor," *TJ* n.s. 12 (1991) 185-206; F. G. Downing, "Pliny's Prosecutions of Christians," *JSNT* 34 (1988) 105-23; D. Earl, *The Age of Augustus* (New York: Exeter, 1968) 166-76; J. Ferguson, *The Religions of the Roman Empire* (Ithaca, NY: Cornell University Press, 1970) 89-98; S. J. Friesen, *Twice Neokoros: Ephesus, Asia and the Cult of the Flavian Imperial Family* (Leiden: E. J. Brill, 1993); C. J. Hemer, *The Letters to the Seven Churches of Asia in Their Local Setting* (Sheffield: JSOT, 1986); D. L. Jones, "Christianity and the Roman Imperial Cult," in *ANRW* 2.23.2 (1980) 1023-54; P. Keresztes, *Imperial Rome and the Christians* (Lanham, MD: University Press of America, 1989); L. Kreitzer, "Apotheosis of the Roman Emperor," *BA* 58 (1990) 211-17; G. Krodel, *Revelation* (ACNT; Minneapolis: Augsburg, 1989); S. R. F. Price, *Rituals and Power: The Roman Imperial Cult in Asia Minor* (Cambridge: Cambridge University Press, 1984); S. J. Scherrer, "Signs and Wonders in the Imperial Cult: A New Look at a Roman Religious Institution in the Light of Rev 13:13-15," *JBL* 103 (1984) 599-610; K. Scott, *The Imperial Cult Under the Flavians* (Stuttgart: Kohlhammer, 1936); E. Stauffer, *Christus und die Caesaren* (Hamburg: Friedrich Wittig, 1952); L. R. Taylor, *The Divinity of the Roman Emperor* (Middletown, CT: American Philological Association, 1931); L. L. Thompson, *The Book of Revelation: Apocalypse and Empire* (Oxford: Oxford University Press, 1990).

D. A. deSilva

S

SABBATH

The English "sabbath," like the Greek *sabbaton*, is a transliteration of the Hebrew *šabbāt*. The term designates the seventh day of the Jewish week, a day marked by the cessation of work and by religious and ceremonial observances. All four Gospels depict Jesus in conflict with his contemporaries on matters of sabbath observance. The traditions, rooted in Jesus' ministry, are used to accentuate themes central to each Evangelist.

1. Sabbath Law
2. Sabbath in the Gospels
3. Sabbath in Acts and the Epistles

1. Sabbath Law.

A prohibition of work on the sabbath is found in the Decalogue (Ex 20:8-11; Deut 5:12-15) and several other OT texts (e.g., Ex 31:12-17; 35:2), and its transgression is treated in the law codes as a capital offense (Ex 31:14-15; 35:2; cf. Num 15:32-36). Different motivations for the interruption of normal activities on the seventh day are given. The Israelite community was to be allowed to rest (the emphasis of Deut 5:12-15; cf. Ex 23:12); but the day was also to be considered holy (Ex 20:8; Deut 5:12), a portion of the Israelites' time which was consecrated to Yahweh (Ex 20:10; 35:2) just as the tithe of their produce was to be reserved for him. Israel's observance of the sabbath was to be a sign of its special covenantal relationship with Yahweh (Ex 31:12-17; Ezek 20:12, 20), an imitation of God's own rest after the completion of his creative work (Gen 2:2-3; Ex 20:11) and a reminder of the relief God granted his people in delivering them from slavery in Egypt (Deut 5:15). Those whose vision failed to extend beyond their pursuit of business naturally found the interruption an irritation to be evaded (Amos 8:5; cf. Jer 17:19-27; Neh 13:15-22). For Yahweh's faithful, however, the day's observance was a delight (Is 58:13-14).

In the Second Temple period (515 B.C.-A.D. 70) the words of Scripture became the object of interpretation by legal experts (*see* Scribes). Their goal was to spell out the duties of God's people by defining the terms and limits of God's revealed commands. The sabbath provided a significant challenge since, from this point of view, the faithful needed to know precisely what constituted the "work" which was to be avoided if the command was not to be transgressed. Lists were drawn up (*Jub.* 2:29-30; 50:6-13; CD 10:14—11:18). Scripture itself provided some guidelines. Fires were not to be lit (Ex 35:3). Burdens were not to be carried (Jer 17:21-22), though from this point of view the term "burden" now needed legal definition. Similarly, a general prohibition of travel could be derived from Isaiah 58:13 (and see Ex 16:29). When such a prohibition took on the force of a legal statute, it became necessary to define the limits of a legitimate journey (cf. a "sabbath day's journey," Acts 1:12). That sowing and reaping are forbidden could be based on Exodus 34:21 (cf. Ex 16:25-30).

Further problems arose when the prohibition of work on the sabbath was perceived to conflict with other commands or with considerations of practicality or prudence. The principle that the prohibition may be disregarded when human life is in danger became well established (see 1 Macc 2:29-41). The service of the *temple was conceded to take precedence over the sabbath (cf. Num 28:9-10; 1 Chron 23:31), as was circumcision. The extent to which considerations of practicality were allowed to influence sabbath regulations varied considerably with different interpreters. [S. Westerholm]

Sabbath law was interpreted very strictly at Qumran. According to the **Damascus Document* (esp. CD 10:14–11:18), prohibitions included walking further than 1,000 cubits (CD 10:21), wearing perfume (CD 11:9-10), lifting a stone or dust at home (CD 11:10-11), aiding an animal in giving birth (CD 11:13) or lifting an animal that has fallen into a pit (CD 11:13-14). On this latter point, compare Jesus' remark in Luke 14:5. The **Songs of the Sabbath Sacrifice* from Masada and from Qumran's Cave 4 present heaven itself and its angelic liturgies in a sabbath framework. The **Temple Scroll* (11Q19) adds several interesting features pertaining to sabbath law and *calendar. [C. A. Evans]

Jewish observance of the sabbath was well known and distinctive in the ancient world. It called forth both admiration (Josephus *Ag. Ap.* 2.39 §282; Philo, *Vit. Mos.* 2.21) and scorn (Josephus *Ag. Ap.* 2.2 §20-21) from outsiders and led, for example, to the excusal of Jews from service in foreign military forces (Jews would neither march forbidden lengths nor carry arms on the sabbath; see Josephus *Ant.* 14.10.12 §226-27). With laws whose scriptural background seemed clear, and with customs long and widely established, many Jews could be expected to comply. It can also be seen, however, that questions of proper observance were often a matter of interpretation. The various religious parties of Jesus' day not infrequently differed in their practice. And though each group doubtless pressed on others the claims of its interpretation to represent the will of heaven, such claims in our period were terrestrially unenforceable.

Positively, Jews met in *synagogues on the sabbath day for prayer, Scripture readings and edifying discourses. The welter of prohibitions may strike the outsider, and surely struck the half-hearted, as a burden grievous to be borne; still, it should not be doubted that faithful Jews continued to find in their observance an occasion for joy.

2. Sabbath in the Gospels.

2.1. Mark. Jesus is said to have participated in synagogue services on the sabbath in Mark 1:21; 3:1 and 6:2. Instances of sabbath observance may be noted in Mark 1:32 (the people wait until sabbath is over to carry the sick to Jesus) and Mark 16:1 (the women wait until sabbath has passed before attending to the body of Jesus). Interestingly, Mark connects no queries with the sabbath healings reported in Mark 1:21-28 and 29-31. In the latter case, Jesus is depicted among friends; in the former, he is in the synagogue. That not every record of a sabbath healing is linked with a dispute suggests that Jesus' activities were not in flagrant transgression of existing formulations of sabbath law and that, perhaps in the initial stages of his career, public enthusiasm may have silenced whatever private compunctions may have been felt. That objections are recorded on other occasions suggests that healing was liable to be construed as work and that in the absence of a life-threatening situation the scrupulous might well find cause for offense.

The issue in Mark 2:23-28 appears more clear-cut. Though gleaning in the fields of another was expressly permitted by pentateuchal law (Lev 19:9-10; 23:22), such activity on the sabbath breached the prohibition of sabbath reaping. Since the prohibition has a scriptural base (Ex 34:21; cf. 16:25-29), it is hazardous to apply the claim here that Jesus merely challenges scribal additions while conforming to scriptural commands. Nor does the defense of the disciples' activity in Mark 2:25-28 follow that tack (David's transgression, cited as a precedent, was clearly of pentateuchal law). Rather a precedent is cited from Scripture (1 Sam 21:1-6) for activity which, on the strict application of scriptural commands, was "not lawful."

The force of the illustration has been differently construed. (1) Some see the point of the comparison in the hunger felt by both Jesus' followers and those of David. The point would then be that, though the sabbath prohibitions insisted on by Jesus' opponents are valid in principle, they must yield to the higher claims of human need. But Mark makes no mention of the disciples' hunger, as he would surely have done if hunger had been the crux of the defense. Nothing suggests that their need was so extreme as to legitimate the transgression of the law. And indeed the unlawfulness of what David did is explicitly mentioned (Mk 2:26) in the defense of the disciples' activity. The point can hardly be that when the extenuating circumstances are taken into account, nothing unlawful has been done.

(2) Others note that the illustration records the behavior of David and suggest that Jesus is tacitly claiming a similar right as David's son, the Messiah, to somehow transcend the law. But the necessary implication of this view is that David was entitled by his calling or office to transgress divine commands applicable to other people, a point which neither scriptural law nor its later interpreters would concede.

(3) Most likely is the view that the example illustrates how Scripture itself countenances the breaking of the law strictly construed and thus calls in question the facile identification of God's will with a rigid interpretation of the terms of the law. Verse 27 (perhaps an independent logion introduced here because it was felt appropriate; so at least the new introduction and the absence of the logion from the parallels in Matthew and Luke may suggest) can be construed as advancing the previous argument on either the first or third reading given above. The divine origin of the sabbath is granted on either reading. Following interpretation (1) above, the logion represents a fresh insistence that humanitarian concerns must take priority over sabbath commands. In the case of the third interpretation proposed above, the point would now be that God's design in giving the sabbath for his people's good is overthrown when human behavior is subjected to rules developed in the casuistic interpretation of the law.

Finally, Mark 2:28 clearly and remarkably insists on Jesus' superiority as Son of Man over the sabbath law. It is not evident whether the verse is intended to represent a claim on Jesus' own lips or one added by the Christian community as a commentary on the preceding episode.

According to Mark 3:1-6 a healing performed by Jesus on the sabbath was found objectionable and occasioned the plotting of *Pharisees and Herodians (*see* Herodian Dynasty) against his life. For his part Jesus is said to be grieved by the attitude of those more concerned with the niceties of the law than with the well-being of a person (Mk 3:5). The defense of Jesus' activity given in Mark 3:4 is striking. No attempt is made to show that the healing does not overstep the command prohibiting "work." The interpretation of the terms of the command, by which the legal experts of contemporary *Judaism defined the divine will, is not here an issue. Rather, the Markan Jesus insists that God can hardly be offended or his will transgressed by the doing of good and the restoring of health on the sabbath (regardless, apparently, of whether or not the deed may be construed as "work"). God's will is rather disobeyed when evil is done or life "killed." It is debated whether the "evil" intended is that of leaving unperformed the miracle of healing or the active plotting against Jesus' life in which, according to the pericope, his opponents were involved on the sabbath.

It seems unlikely that sabbath observance was a significant issue for the Second Evangelist or the community for which he wrote. The two relevant episodes do not appear to focus on the community's need of either guidance or a defense for its sabbath behavior. Rather, the first incident celebrates the authority of the community's Lord over the institutions of Israel's law; the second is clearly meant to account for the hostility which Jesus' ministry aroused.

2.2. Matthew. For Matthew and his community, on the other hand, proper sabbath observance may well have remained an issue. Admittedly, the prayer in Matthew 24:20 (that the community's flight might not occur on the sabbath) does not point unambiguously in that direction. Even a Christian congregation not observing the sabbath would be exposed to hardship and danger if its people attempted to flee on that day in a Jewish environment. Nor does Matthew's Gospel preserve instances of sabbath conflict or discussions of proper sabbath behavior not found in Mark. But the parallels to Mark 2:23-28 and 3:1-6 in Matthew 12:1-14 show differences designed apparently to show that the sabbath command, when properly interpreted, had not been transgressed. Its continuing relevance may therefore be implied.

Perhaps the explicit reference to the hunger of Jesus' disciples (Mt 12:1) is intended to provide a humanitarian legitimation for their behavior. Matthew 12:5 adds an illustration from the Torah (cf. Num 28:9-10) by which priests violate the sabbath law without incurring guilt. Verse 6 then at least claims that the coming of the kingdom ("something greater than the temple") in the person of Jesus causes the sabbath laws to pale in significance. But perhaps the legal argument is implied that the activity of those in the service of the kingdom, like that of *priests in the temple, takes precedence over sabbath laws. In verse 7 a favorite Matthean OT citation (Hos 6:6) is repeated, indicating that sabbath laws are to be interpreted in such a way that divine mercy is emphasized rather than strict conformity with ritual prescriptions.

In the second pericope (Mt 12:9-14) verse 12 preserves but a fragment of the argument of Mark 3:4. The main emphasis in the Matthean account falls rather on a logion shared with Luke (Lk 14:5) which Matthew introduces here. Though the stricter construction of the law forbade the drawing up on the sabbath of an animal from a pit (CD 11:13-14; *t. Šabb.* 14:3), the logion assumes that in ordinary practice compassion prevailed and assistance was given. This being the case, no objection should be raised when a human being (who is, after all, worth far more than a sheep) is healed on the holy day. Proper sabbath observance does seem here to be a concern, but priority is given to claims of compassion over strict adherence to sabbath rules.

2.3. Luke. In the two conflict pericopes common to the three Synoptic Gospels, Luke (Lk 6:1-5, 6-11) follows Mark quite closely without the Matthean additions. But two new instances of controversy arising from sabbath healings are recorded. In Luke 13:10-17 the ruler of the synagogue objects to the healing of a woman with a chronic deformity. Work is allowed, he says, on six days of the week, and healings are then in order. There is therefore no need to desecrate the sabbath with such activity. The Lukan Jesus finds the objection hypocritical, noting that domestic animals are commonly "unbound" and led to water on the sabbath. Far more justified, surely, is the "unbinding" of a daughter of Abraham from a satanic affliction. Jesus' opponents are said to have been shamed by the response and the crowd delighted by the whole episode. In Luke 14:1-6 a variant of the argument presented in Matthew 12:11-12 is presented and leaves potential objectors speechless. The sabbath discussions in Luke seem designed to show compassion on the part of Jesus, the ready acceptance it meets from the crowds and the speechless shame to which opponents are reduced.

2.4. John. Johannine irony is undoubtedly to be seen in John 19:31 (cf. Jn 18:28), where punctilious sabbath observance is grimly juxtaposed with the crucifixion of God's Son. Sabbath healings lead to disputes in John 5 and 9; the former is recalled in John 7:22-23. In no case does the Evangelist evince a concern for guiding the sabbath behavior of his readers. In John 5 offense is first raised when, at Jesus' command, a pallet is carried on the sabbath (Jn 5:10) and exacerbated when it is learned that Jesus has healed on that day (Jn 5:15-16). Remarkably, the Johannine Jesus concedes that he "works" on the sabbath (Jn 5:17)—precisely what the law prohibits—but claims that he is merely acting as God his Father does. The charge that Jesus breaks the sabbath is thus conceded (Jn 5:18), but the interest of the Evangelist is rather on the christological claim to which it leads.

In John 7:22-23 the unreasonableness of Jesus' opponents seems the point: they permit sabbath circumcision but object to the restoration of a man's health. Similarly, in John 9 the sabbath healing gives the Evangelist the opportunity to show Jesus' opponents as blind to the manifest workings of God in their midst (Jn 9:30-33), a blindness induced by their insistence that a divine representative must conform to the niceties of the old code (Jn 9:16). The memory of sabbath disputes aroused by Jesus is preserved in John, but it becomes the starting point for the pursuit of favorite Johannine themes: the divine sonship of Jesus and the necessity of faith in him.

2.5 Conclusion. As we have seen, sabbath controversies are found in Mark (Mk 2:23-28; 3:1-6), in material common to Matthew and Luke (Mt 12:11-12 par. Lk 14:5), in material unique to Matthew (Mt 12:5-7) and Luke (Lk 13:10-17; the incident of Lk 14:1-6), and in John (Jn 5; 7:22-23; 9). Furthermore, the authenticity of crucial logia (Mk 2:27; 3:4, etc.) is widely conceded. At the roots of the Gospel tradition, then, are memories of opposition to Jesus' sabbath behavior aroused among his contemporaries.

Opponents saw the divine will as requiring conformity with the terms of Torah's statutes as interpreted by legal authorities. Hence activities which could be construed as the "work" which Torah forbade were to be avoided unless extenuating circumstances (as defined by the legal experts) could be found to legitimate the activity. Jesus' behavior (and, according to one story, that of his disciples) was found to violate this stricture. The basic line of Jesus' defense as portrayed in the Gospels shows a different approach to the understanding of the divine will. No more than Jesus allows the terminology of Deuteronomy 24:1-4 to define the propriety of divorce (Mk 10:1-12) or the terminology of scriptural law to define norms for oaths (Mt 5:33-36), does he allow that the divine will for the sabbath rests in the proper interpretation of the word "work." When opposed he does not reply by arguing that, counter to his opponents' claims, "work" has not been done nor the command transgressed. He insists that doing "good" can never be wrong on the sabbath (Mk 3:4—a criterion quite different from the question whether or not "work" has been done), that compassion is a better guide to proper behavior than rules defined by legal experts (Mt 12:10-11), that God's intentions with the sabbath are distorted when humans are subjected to a rigid code (Mk 2:27). Implicit in each case, and explicit at various points in the Gospel narrative, is the claim that Jesus has authority to interpret the divine will.

Only for Matthew is it likely that proper sabbath observance remained an issue. Only in this Gospel is it likely that the relevant pericopes were intended to provide guidance in the matter. In the other Gospels the traditional material serves other ends. Sabbath discussions provide the opportunity to highlight Jesus' authority, his compassion and the nature of his opposition. [S. Westerholm]

3. Sabbath in Acts and the Epistles.

3.1. Sabbath in Acts. Christian observance of the sabbath is presupposed in the book of Acts. Paul is portrayed as routinely entering synagogues on the sabbath, in order to preach the Christian gospel (e.g., Acts 13:14, 42, 44; 17:2 ["as was his custom"]; 18:4). There is no direct evidence that the sabbath had been abrogated by early Christians (Turner, 135-37), though the gathering "on the first day of the week" (Acts 20:7-12) may suggest that Christians had begun gathering on Sunday, in addition to attendance of the synagogue on Saturdays.

3.2. Sabbath in the Epistles. There are very few references to the sabbath in the NT epistles.

3.2.1. Paul. In Colossians 2:16 Paul urges his readers not to allow themselves to be judged "in questions of food and drink or with regard to a festival or a new moon or a sabbath" (RSV). The meaning of this verse is disputed; it does not necessarily teach that Christians should not assemble on the sabbath.

In 1 Corinthians 16:2, Paul commands the Christians of Corinth, "On the first day of every week *[mian sabbatou]*, each of you is to put something aside and store it up, as he may prosper, so that contributions need not be made when I come" (RSV). This passage may presuppose Christian assembly on Sunday (as possibly in Acts 20:7-12), but it is not clear that assembly is in fact in view. In any case, nothing is said directly concerning observance of the sabbath.

3.2.2 Hebrews. The author of Hebrews admonishes Jewish Christians to enter God's "rest" (Heb 3—4). The author infers from Scripture and Israel's history that "there remains a sabbath rest [*sabbatismos*] for the people of God" (Heb 4:9). The reference here is not to weekly sabbaths or to any particular holy day, but to the eschatological fulfillment of God's will. At this time all believers will enter God's rest, or sabbath. [C. A. Evans]

See also CALENDARS, JEWISH; FESTIVALS AND HOLY DAYS: JEWISH; SACRIFICE AND TEMPLE SERVICE; TORAH.

BIBLIOGRAPHY. S. Bacchiocchi, *From Sabbath to Sunday: A Historical Investigation of the Rise of Sunday Observance in Early Christianity* (Rome: Pontifical Gregorian University Press, 1977); R. Banks, *Jesus and the Law in the Synoptic Tradition* (SNTSMS 28; Cambridge: Cambridge University Press, 1975) 113-31; D. A. Carson, "Jesus and the Sabbath in the Four Grospels," in *From Sabbath to Lord's Day: A Biblical, Historical, and Theological Investigation,* ed. D. A. Carson (Grand Rapids, MI: Zondervan, 1982) 57-97; D. M. Cohn-Sherbok, "An Analysis of Jesus' Arguments Concerning the Plucking of Grain on the Sabbath," *JSNT* 2 (1979) 31-41; S. B. Hoenig, "The Designated Number of Kinds of Labor Prohibited on the Sabbath," *JQR* 68 (1978) 193-208; S. T. Kimbrough, "The Concept of the Sabbath at Qumran," *RevQ* 6 (1966) 483-502; F. Neirynck, "Jesus and the Sabbath: Some Observations on Mark II, 27," in *Jésus aux origines de la christologie,* ed. J. Dupont (Louvain: Louvain University Press, 1975) 227-270; H. Riesenfeld, "The Sabbath and the Lord's Day in Judaism, the Preaching of Jesus and Early Christianity," in *The Gospel Tradition* (Philadelphia: Fortress, 1970) 111-37; C. Rowland, "A Summary of Sabbath Observance in Judaism at the Beginning of the Christian Era," in *From Sabbath to Lord's Day: A Biblical, Historical, and Theological Investigation,* ed. D. A. Carson (Grand Rapids, MI: Zondervan, 1982) 44-55; L. H. Schiffman, *The Halakhah at Qumran* (SJLA 16; Leiden: E. J. Brill, 1975) 77-133; P. Sigal, *The Halakah of Jesus of Nazareth according to the Gospel of Matthew* (Lanham, MD: University Press of America, 1986); M. M. B. Turner, "The Sabbath, Sunday, and the Law in Luke/Acts," in *From Sabbath to Lord's Day: A Biblical, Historical, and Theological Investigation,* ed. D. A. Carson (Grand Rapids, MI: Zondervan, 1982) 99-157; S. Westerholm, *Jesus and Scribal Authority* (ConBNT 10; Lund: Gleerup, 1978) 92-103.

S. Westerholm and C. A. Evans

SABBATH SACRIFICE, SONGS OF THE *See* SONGS OF THE SABBATH SACRIFICE (4Q400-407, 11Q17, MAS1K).

SACRED SPACE. *See* ISRAEL, LAND OF; TEMPLE, JEWISH; TEMPLES, GRECO-ROMAN.

SACRIFICE AND TEMPLE SERVICE

Prior to the destruction of the temple in A.D. 70, the temple, its services and its priesthood lay at the heart of any identifiable "common" Jewish vision of Israel's life rightly ordered before God. Even Jews who lived at some distance from Jerusalem and its temple would have regarded the temple as the center of sacred space and of their mental map of the world (e.g., Dan 6:10; 9:21; Ezra 9:5; Jdt 9:1; *m. Kelim* 1:6-9; *see* Israel, Land of). Synagogue worship functioned as a sort of mirror site of the temple, reflecting aspects of temple worship and drawing its authority from the temple while also adding its own innovations. Central to temple worship was the liturgical act of sacrifice or offering.

Our knowledge of the duties of priests and Levites, the actual practice of sacrifice and worship, as well as the daily functioning of the temple is incomplete. The Torah, particularly in Leviticus and Numbers, provides a starting point for understanding the sacrifices and priestly service. Yet the Torah implicitly allowed for some variation in interpretation and implementation, and while Chronicles and Nehemiah offer occasional insights, we must reckon with centuries of historical development as well as the innovations of the Herodian temple. Various sources, such as Josephus (who was of a priestly family) and Philo in the first century A.D., the *Letter of Aristeas* from about the second century B.C. and *Jubilees* from about the middle of the second century B.C., provide insights into actual practices (see Hayward for selection of relevant texts). The Dead Sea Scrolls, such as the *Temple Scroll,* sometimes offer reflexive views of sacrifice and temple service. Later rabbinic sources, particularly Mishnah (c. A.D. 200), afford intriguing and sometimes detailed considerations of what went on in the temple. Although Mishnah views the temple service through nearly a century and a half of rabbinic tradition and debate, ideals and imagination, its recountings of temple services such as the daily sacrifices and the Day of Atonement are priceless for giving structure to our own critically informed historical imagination. In this article we will follow Mishnah in several instances, posting the caution here that in many cases we cannot discern which details are historical and which are not.

1. Function and Meaning of Sacrifice
2. Types of Sacrifice
3. Appointed Sacrifices
4. Provisions for Sacrifice and Temple Service
5. Access to Worship
6. Officiants: Levites, Priests and High Priests

1. Function and Meaning of Sacrifice.

A distinction can be drawn between sacrifices and other gifts, or oblations, to God. Sacrifices (Heb *z*[e]*baḥ*) are gifts that are presented in whole or in part on the altar *(mizbēaḥ).* These would include the burnt offerings, peace offerings, purification offerings, reparation offerings and grain offerings. Distinguished from these sacrifices proper are the gifts of firstfruits, wave offerings, heave offerings and tithes. We should observe that although the shedding of blood was an important element in the Israelite conception of sacrifice, this criterion does not prove adequate in distinguishing sacrifices from other gifts, for grain was also burned on the altar and was acceptable as a purification/sin offering for those who were very poor and could not afford two doves or pigeons (Lev 5:11-13; see below).

Numerous theories of Israelite sacrifice have been constructed, frequently answering the impulse to find a unified or underlying meaning for the variety of forms of sacrifice and how they evolved. As our purpose here is primarily to set out the phenomena of sacrifice and temple worship, we will not explore this question in any detail. Some fundamental features of Israelite and Jewish sacrifice should, however, be noted:

(1) Sacrifices and other oblations are gifts offered by humans to God, and their type, occasion and manner of presentation are prescribed by God.

(2) The offering of sacrifice is mediated by a male priesthood, and the layers of mediation were greater for Israelite women than for men.

(3) The giving, or "offering," of a sacrifice implies a personal cost and intentionality on the part of the one who offers, and in the most ideal circumstances the thing offered represents the labor or investment of the person's own time and labor (a relationship that is preserved in theory but indirect in experience when an animal, grain or wine is purchased at the temple).

(4) In sacrifices involving the slaying of an animal, perhaps particularly from the flock or herd, there is evoked a strong sense of substitution or representation of the animal's life for the

person or community, particularly symbolized in the action of placing hands on the head of the animal.

(5) The shedding of blood had particular atoning significance. Israelites were reminded that "life is in the blood," and blood was not to be consumed (Lev 17:11; Deut 12:23; *Jub.* 21:17-19; 1QapGen 11:17) but was reserved for God alone, the giver and Lord of life. Blood evoked the presence of a numinous power in animate life, and in cultic sacrifice it could symbolize expiation of sin or a purification from an unclean condition. Its use and disposal was strictly regulated.

(6) Where the sacrifice is offered for particular or for generalized sins, it is implicit that the animal is paying a price for an offense committed by the person or community offering it (though this is mitigated in the case of grain offered by the poor). The prevailing and strong impression is that, apart from the gift of divine forgiveness, sin would ultimately result in estrangement from God and death. (This perspective find its counterpart in the numerous scenes of judgment in Hebrew Scripture [e.g., Num 25:6-13], including the "ban," or "devotion" to Yahweh, of the Canaanite peoples in the wars of Yahweh [cf. Is 34:1-7; Ezek 39:17-20].)

(7) Israelite sacrifice (like that of other ancient Mediterranean cultures) evokes the notion of food offered to God (with the altar as table), and in all but the burnt offering or a sin/purity offering for the priest or community, this food is shared by humans, whether by priests exclusively or by the person and family of the one who offers it (peace offerings and Passover). While a literal understanding of this image is subverted in Israel's Scriptures by a passage such as Psalm 50:12-14, the archetype of table fellowship with a deity was significant for Judaism as it was also for Jesus and the early church (*see* Banquets).

Despite the centrality of sacrifice for Jewish worship, when the temple was destroyed by the Romans in A.D. 70, sacrifice ceased as an actual element in Jewish worship. Torah had prescribed that sacrifice was to be conducted at the "place" of God's choosing, where God would cause the divine name to "dwell" (Deut 12:15-17), and this place was the Jerusalem temple. When the temple no longer existed, and Jews no longer had access to its sacred site, sacrifice ceased. Some evidence suggests, however, that by the first century the centrality of the temple and its sacrifices had suffered a degree of ambiguity (see Scott, 152-58). We learn of a rival temple at Leontopolis, Egypt, founded by a Zadokite priest (Josephus *J.W.* 1.1.1 §33; 7.10.2-3 §§423-36) and perhaps even viewed as the fulfillment of a prophetic text (Is 19:18-23). But this would not have been regarded as acceptable by the mainstream of Jews, whether in the Diaspora or in the land of Israel. From the Dead Sea Scrolls we learn that the priestly oriented Essenes of Qumran, galvanized in their opinion that the current temple and its leadership were corrupt, had withdrawn themselves from participation in the temple services, adopted an interim mode of worship and life that excluded animal sacrifice (1QS 9:4-5; Josephus *Ant.* 18.15 §§18-19) and awaited the establishment of a new temple (11QTemple). Nevertheless, their perspective was focused on the centrality of the temple in Jerusalem and the hope of a new Jerusalem and restored temple. We should also bear in mind that some Jews living in Diaspora communities might seldom or never visit the temple. Despite all that may be affirmed of the central role of sacrifice in temple worship and the importance of the temple for Judaism of the first century, prior to the fall of Jerusalem there already existed modes and strategies for living faithfully as a Jew while not participating directly in temple sacrifice. Some of these perspectives and practices had been initially shaped during the experience of Babylonian exile.

Chief among these strategies was the association of prayer with sacrifice. Within the context of the temple cult, the morning and evening sacrifice was an occasion for prayer by the priests and the gathered laypeople (see Falk, 285-92). There is good reason to conclude that synagogue prayers in the first century were also conducted along the same lines, in correspondence with temple worship (see Safrai, 904-5). The Essene community of Qumran could speak of itself as constituting a spiritual temple engaged in a spiritual worship apart from the temple (1QS 8:1-10), and the *Songs of the Sabbath Sacrifice* envision an angelic worship in a heavenly sanctuary where atonement is made (apart from animal sacrifices) "for those who repent of sin" (4Q400 frag. 1 ii 16). These lines of evidence suggest that the early church and post-A.D. 70 Judaism found ready vectors within the Jewish tradition for an understanding of spiritual sacrifice apart from the temple.

2. Types of Sacrifice.

The Torah does not neatly categorize the sacrifices and present them all in one place. While Leviticus may have functioned as a sort of handbook for priests, sacrificial instructions are also found in Numbers, and relevant material occurs elsewhere in the Pentateuch. Some fundamental patterns and distinctions appear and are helpful to keep in mind regarding sacrifices. First is the basic distinction between sacrifices offered on behalf of the individual and the community. Second, some sacrifices were occasional, called forth by particular sins or blessings or deliverances, and others were regularly prescribed, such as the daily morning and evening sacrifices, the weekly sabbath sacrifices, the monthly new-moon sacrifices, or the yearly Passover and Day of Atonement sacrifices. Third, not all sacrifices were specifically an atonement for sin or guilt; some were for worship and communion with God, for thanksgiving and celebration. Finally, the things sacrificed varied also, from the four-legged animals of the herd (cattle) and flock (sheep and goats) to the birds of the air (doves or pigeons) to the inanimate (and thus bloodless) produce of the field (grain) and vineyard (wine). In some cases the object of sacrifice was determined by a scale of economic means, with those who were financially able offering a sheep and the poor offering a bird or even grain (for pagan sacrifice, *see* Religions, Greco-Roman).

2.1. Burnt, or Holocaust, Offering (ʿōlâ). The Hebrew term for this type of sacrifice suggests an "ascending" sacrifice, evoking the conveyance of the burning sacrifice "up" to God as the smoke ascends skyward. This sacrifice was to be a male without defect of the herd or flock, or it could be two birds. After the animal was slain, its blood was thrown against the altar; it was skinned (hides were never offered but were the priest's portion), cut in pieces, washed and salted (as were all sacrifices salted with the "salt of the covenant": Lev 2:13; *Jub.* 21:11; Josephus *Ant.* 3.9.1 §227) and placed on the altar. In the case of birds, the head was wrung off and placed on the altar, the crop (and probably the feathers) discarded, the body torn open and the whole placed on the altar to be burned; no part of a burnt offering was to be consumed by priests (Lev 1:3-17; Josephus *Ant.* 3.9.1 §§226-27).

As Leviticus states, the burnt offering "makes atonement" (NIV) for the one who brings it (Lev 1:4), and it is "an aroma pleasing to the LORD" (Lev 1:9, 13, 17 NIV). This "atonement" might suggest that the offering is for sin, perhaps sins in general. But the Hebrew term *kippēr* may more accurately be translated "to purge," and the broader contexts for which this sacrifice is prescribed or voluntarily given suggest it functions as a means of approaching Yahweh with an entreaty. Josephus does not indicate it is an atonement for sins, and Philo regards the burnt offering as rendering honor *(timē)* to God apart from any other motive or self-interest (Philo *Spec. Leg.* 1.195-97). This may well have been its significance, at least in the first century.

2.2. Peace Offering (šᵉlāmîm). Sometimes called a "fellowship" offering, this type of sacrifice was offered with cakes and wafers, the blood of the animal (a male or female from the flock or herd) was sprinkled against the sides of the altar, the fat burned on the altar and the breast "waved" before the altar (as an act of presentation to the Lord). The right thigh was then presented to the officiating priest as his portion to be consumed and the breast given to be shared among the priests in general for their family ("sons and daughters," Num 18:18-19; see 4Q513 for restriction against priests' daughters who married Gentiles) consumption (Lev 7:28-36; cf. Deut 18:3, includes jowls and maw; *m. Ḥul.* 10:1). The remainder of the meat was then returned to the offerer to be consumed as a meal with his family and friends for up to two days, after which any remainder was to be burned (Lev 7:11-21, 28-36; Josephus *Ant.* 3.9.2 §§228-29). This offering epitomizes the notion that sacrifice is a shared meal of communion between God and humans. The occasion for such a sacrifice could be thanksgiving *(tôdâ)* for a blessing received, the completion of a vow to the Lord or simply the freewill offering of a glad heart.

2.3. Purification/Sin Offering (ḥaṭṭāʾt). For unwitting sins committed or for specified states of impurity, a purification offering was to be made. The common designation of *sin offering* is less satisfactory because it does not adequately account for conditions of uncleanness for which this offering was made, such as childbirth (a dove or pigeon, along with a burnt offering, Lev 12:6-8), infectious skin disease (with a guilt and burnt offering, Lev 14:19-20), bodily discharge (with a burnt offering, Lev 15:14-15) or unusual menstrual flow (with a burnt offering, Lev 15:29-30).

The purification/sin offering might be occasioned by and offered for various parties, with an appropriate sacrifice assigned to each instance: for the unwitting sin of a priest/high priest, a young bull (Lev 4:3-12); for the entire community, a young bull (Lev 4:13-21); for a leader of Israel, a male goat (Lev 4:22-26); for an individual, a female goat or lamb (Lev 4:27-35). In each instance the procedure was basically the same: the individual (or the elders of the community) laid a hand on the head of the animal and slaughtered it (with a deft cut of the jugular vein, and a bowl ready to capture the blood). In the case of the sin of a priest or the community, the priest sprinkled some of the blood seven times in front of the sanctuary curtain, but in all cases the priest took some of the blood and put it on the "horns" of the altar and then poured the rest at the base of the altar. The fat with the kidneys was then taken from the animal and burned on the altar. In the case of the sin offering for the priest or the community, the entire remainder of the carcass, including the hide, was taken outside the sanctuary to a designated, ceremonially clean place (where ashes were dumped), and it was burned on a wood fire (Lev 4:11-12, 21; see 4QMMT, where taking the ashes "outside the camp" is interpreted as "outside Jerusalem"). But in the case of sacrifices for a leader or an individual, the meat was to be eaten by the priest who offered it or by any male of his family, but it was only to be eaten within the sanctuary, for it was "holy" (Lev 6:24-30).

*2.4. **Reparation/Guilt Offering (ʾāšām).*** This offering is prescribed for unintentional violations and sins of sacrilege regarding "any of the LORD's holy things" (NIV, Lev 5:14) or against "any of the LORD's commands" (NIV, Lev 5:17) or for sins against one's "neighbor" involving a breach of faith, such as cheating, stealing, swearing falsely, deceiving regarding property held in trust, dealing dishonestly with lost property that one finds or any like sin in which one seeks gain at the expense of another member of the covenant community. Restitution is to be made to the offended party with a fifth of the value added (cf. Num 5:5-9; see Ex 22:1, 7, 9 for examples of restitution in cases where guilt is not voluntarily confessed), and a reparation/guilt offering is to be made (Lev 5:16, 18; 6:1-5). In the case of "holy things," restitution is to be made to the temple. The fault is to be confessed to the priest, and the prescribed sacrifice is a ram (i.e., a male sheep) without defect (Lev 5:15, 18; 6:6). The procedure for slaughtering the ram was the same as for the purification/sin offering, with the individual placing his hand on the head of the ram. The blood was collected and sprinkled against all four sides of the altar, and the fat along with the kidneys was to be offered on the fire of the altar (Lev 7:1-5). The meat was to be eaten by the officiating priest and any male of his family in a "holy" place, and the hide became the property of the priest (Lev 7:7-8). There were other instances in which the reparation/guilt offering was prescribed, such as a cleansing from an infectious skin disease (Lev 14:10, 12-14) and a Nazirite cleansing him or herself from corpse impurity (Num 6:12).

*2.5. **Grain Offering.*** Grain offerings were offered in various contexts, either alone or accompanying animal sacrifice. The grain (semolina, or grits) could be presented as uncooked, as baked cakes or wafers, or as cooked on a griddle or fried in a pan. In most cases (but not for a sin offering, Lev 5:11) it was prepared with olive oil, and depending on the preparation, the grain was mixed, spread or fried in the oil. In most cases (but again, not for a sin offering, Lev 5:11) incense was offered with the grain. Never was the offering to contain yeast or honey (Lev 2:11), and (as with other sacrifices) it was always to be salted (Lev 2:13). The priest placed a "memorial portion" of the offering on the altar, along with all of the incense, and kept the rest of the offering for consumption "in a holy place" in the courtyard of the sanctuary (Lev 6:14-18), unless, of course, it was offered on behalf of the priest, in which case it was all burned on the altar (Lev 6:19-23). A grain offering could be made by a poor person in lieu of a burnt animal offering, and a very poor person, who could not afford two doves or pigeons, could make a purification/sin offering of grain without oil or incense (Lev 5:11-13). The status of this "bloodless" offering is illuminated by latter rabbinic tradition (*Lev. Rab.* 3:5 [on Lev 1:17]): "Once a woman brought a handful of fine flour, and the priest despised her, saying: 'See what she offers! What is there in this to eat? What is there in this to offer up?' It was shown to him in a dream: 'Do not despise her! It is regarded as if she had sacrificed her own life'" (see also *Sipra* §62 [on Lev 5:11-13]).

*2.6. **Firstfruits and Firstborn Offering.** (Ex 22:29-30; 23:16, 19; 34:22; Num 18:12-19).* The firstfruits of the harvest and every firstborn son of Israel and male of domestic animals was to be devoted to Yahweh. The firstfruits of the harvest (grain, oil and wine, Num 18:12) were to be brought to the sanctuary and given to the priests as their portion. The firstborn son was to be redeemed by a monetary payment (Num 18:15-16). The firstborn of unclean animals were to be redeemed by a set price (Num 18:15-16; Ex 13:13, for a firstborn donkey, allows a lamb offering or killing the animal). But the firstborn of clean animals—the ox, sheep or goat—were to be presented at the sanctuary as a sacrifice. The blood was to be sprinkled on the altar, the fat burned upon the altar and the meat presented to the priest for household consumption (Num 18:18-19). The firstfruit and firstborn offerings thus provided food for the priests, who had no land inheritance in Israel (Num 18:20).

According to Deuteronomy 26, one is to present the firstfruits of one's harvest to the priest at "the place" (i.e., the temple, which of course in Deuteronomy's storyline is not yet built) and make the "confession" in which one recites how God made a covenant with Abraham and rescued his descendants from Egypt and how one has remained loyal to the covenant. This confession (or declaration/avowal) of Deuteronomy 26 is discussed in Mishnah at *Bikkurim* 1:1—3:12 and *Ma ʿaśer Šeni* 5:10-15 and offers a plausible setting for the Pharisee and publican in Jesus' parable (Lk 18:9-14).

3. Appointed Sacrifices.

3.1. Morning and Evening Burnt Sacrifice. Exodus 29:38-43 commands the Israelite community to offer a daily morning and evening sacrifice of a year-old lamb without defect, a tenth of an ephah of flour mixed with a quarter hin of olive oil and a quarter hin of wine. These daily burnt offerings (*ʿōlat hattāmîd*, Num 28:10) were to be made at dawn and at about three in the afternoon (about the ninth hour: Josephus *Ant.* 14.4.3 §65; *m. Pesaḥ.* 5:1; earlier it had been at dusk), and thus opened and closed the day of temple service throughout the year. Numbers 28:3-8 repeats and expands the instruction of Exodus, pointing out that these sacrifices are an aroma pleasing to the Lord (Num 28:6, 8). The procedures for carrying out these daily sacrifices were developed over time and in continuity with the principles laid out in Torah. Mishnah tractate *Tamid* describes the procedure in great detail, and though it is perhaps idealized and elaborated in this memorialized tradition of the sages, the description is probably reliable in its basic outline. Because of its central role in the functioning of the temple cult (it was being carried out daily even as the temple was falling to the Romans in A.D. 70; Josephus *J.W.* 6.2.1 §§94-95), it is worth outlining the morning sacrifice in some detail. Included with this offering was the morning and evening offering of the high priest, which consisted of flat cakes of grain mixed with oil (Lev 6:12-16; Sir 45:14).

Before dawn the priests who had spent the night in the temple immersed themselves in a purification pool and cast lots in the Chamber of Hewn Stone to determine which priests would perform the tasks, the first of which was to clean and arrange the altar that had remained smoldering through the night. The appointed priest entered the courtyard in darkness, and two groups of priests filed along the east and west colonnades of the court, inspecting the premises for any infractions of purity. After he had purified his hands and feet with water from the bronze basin, the appointed priest took up the utensil and began work on the altar. At a prescribed moment he was joined by others, and the remaining sacrificial portions on the altar were placed aside, the ashes removed, new wood carefully arranged and then ignited from the hot embers, and the unconsumed portions of sacrifice were placed back on the altar fire. Choice pieces of fig wood from the altar of sacrifice were set aside to ignite the altar of incense. Meanwhile the grain cakes of the high priest's offering were being prepared in a chamber designated for that task near the Nicanor Gate.

Their work completed, the priests returned to their chamber to again draw lots, this time to choose thirteen priests who would perform the next phase of work: the slaughter of the lamb, the sprinkling of the blood, the tending of the altar of incense, the cleaning of the lampstand and the carrying of the various sacrificial portions (parts of the lamb as well as flour, cakes and wine) to the altar (cf. *m. Yoma* 2:1-3).

After the selection, a lookout was sent to see if the sun had lit the horizon "as far as Hebron" (*m. Tamid* 3:2; *m. Yoma* 3:1), which was the signal to begin the sacrifice. The preselected, unblemished lamb, which had been inspected the night before, was fetched from its chamber, the ninety-three (so *m. Tamid* 3:4) silver and gold utensils were brought forth, and the lamb was given a drink of water from a golden bowl and then reinspected. A procession of priests went forward, led by the two who would prepare the altar of incense and lampstand (bearing utensils, ash bin, oil and keys for the gate) and followed by the appointed priest with the lamb and the entourage of those who would offer the parts. The lamb was taken to the area north of the altar where there were slaughterhouse fixtures: rings for tying the beasts, hooks on pillars for suspending their carcasses and marble tables for preparing and cleaning the slain animal parts for sacrifice (*m. Tamid* 3:5). Ascending the steps to the porch of the sanctuary, the appointed priest opened the great gate and entered with his companions to tend the altar of incense and lampstand. Meanwhile, in the court of priests the lamb was slaughtered, with the blood carefully caught in a bowl. Blood was sprinkled on the sides of the altar and the remainder poured at the base of the altar. The slain lamb was skinned and carved into its prescribed parts, which were then given to the six appointed priests, who carried them in procession up the altar ramp, along with three priests carrying the flour, the grain cakes and the wine, and laid them on the ramp. There all the offerings but the wine were salted.

All of the participating priests then returned to the Chamber of Hewn Stone to recite the Shema and various prayers and blessings. Lots were again cast to choose one from among the priests who had not yet had the privilege of offering the incense. Once chosen, the appointed priest carried the incense while one of his two companions went to the altar of sacrifice and placed burning cinders into a golden fire pan. They then proceeded with the appointed priest to enter the sanctuary and perform the ritual of burning the incense. (This is the privilege, Luke tell us, that had fallen to Zechariah, the father of John the Baptist, to perform [Lk 1:8], during which the angel Gabriel appeared to him at the right of the altar of incense [Lk 1:11-20].) In the morning the incense was to be offered first, before the offerings on the altar of sacrifice; in the evening it was to be offered last, thus bracketing the day of temple service. Only a few of the flames on the candelabra were left burning during the day, and in the evening all seven were lit. As the priests proceeded to the altar of incense, a signal was sounded for the Levites to gather for singing, the priests from about the temple to assemble and the people who were to be purified that day (e.g., women and those healed of skin disease) to gather at the eastern gate called Nicanor (cf. Lk 1:10). Within the holy place the altar of incense was lit (two others also returned to finish their work on the lamps) and the appointed priest was then left alone to offer the incense (see *m. Tamid* 6:1-3 for details). Meanwhile the designated priests returned to the altar to prepare to make the offering on the altar. The priests who had entered the holy place now had returned to stand on the steps facing the Court of Priests, and raising their hands, they said a blessing (Num 6:24-26) on the people, so uttering the divine name Yahweh (cf. Lk 1:21-22 and Zechariah's silence). The priests at the altar could now offer the pieces of lamb as well as the flour, cakes and wine. At a signal, two trumpets sounded and the people and priests who had assembled before the court prostrated themselves. As the wine was poured out, the Levites broke out in song (one of the set psalms determined by the day of the week), accompanied by stringed instruments. At pauses in the singing the trumpets blasted, and the people fell prostrate (*m. Tamid* 7:3). Thus began the day of temple service, and the work of offering the people's individual sacrifices was underway. The pattern of the morning sacrifice was repeated with only small variation in the afternoon for the evening sacrifice, which closed the day of temple service ("the time of prayer" at the "ninth hour," when Peter and John go up to the temple in Acts 3:1). The same priests served in the afternoon as in the morning, with the exception of a new appointment for the offering of incense.

3.2. Sabbath Sacrifice. On the sabbath, in addition to the daily morning and evening sacrifices (see 3.1 above), an additional sacrifice of two lambs a year old, along with a wine offering and grain offering, were offered on behalf of Israel. This ritual followed the daily morning sacrifice, and these were the only sacrifices offered on the sabbath (sacrifices for individuals were not offered). The sabbath was also the time designated for the changing of the priestly divisions, which took place after the sabbath offering. As the new division began service, they replaced the previous week's twelve loaves of shewbread with fresh loaves (Lev 24:5-9; *m. Menaḥ.* 11), accompanied by the burning of frankincense. The previous week's loaves were given to the priests to eat within the sanctuary.

3.3. Day of Atonement Sacrifices. On the tenth day of the seventh month, five days prior to the Feast of Booths, the annual Day of Atonement was observed. From the evening of the ninth day until the evening of the tenth was a fast day on which Israelites were not to work (Lev 16:29; 23:26-32; Num 29:7) and, according to Mishnah, were forbidden to eat, drink, bathe, put on oil or sandals, or engage in sexual relations (*m. Yoma* 8:1-7). It was not a pilgrimage festival, but it was to be observed throughout Israel, with attention focused on confession of sin. The central enactment of the observance was carried out in the temple, and there the focus of attention was on the high priest, who performed the vital rite for himself, his household, the priesthood and all Israel. It was an annual day of purification for the temple, its altars, furnishings, instruments, its officiants and an atoning for the sins of Israel (Lev 16:30; *m. Śabb.* 1:6-7). It was the only day of the year on which the high priest entered the holy of holies (and he was the only one ever permitted to enter). The evidence from Mishnah tractate *Yoma* reflects the extreme care with which the rite would have been carried out in the first century A.D., for it was fundamental to the maintenance of the status of Israel before God and, in the eyes of many, the fulfillment of Israel's promised redemption.

Seven days prior to the Day of Atonement (*m. Yoma* 1:1) the high priest took up residence in his chamber within the temple (along the southern edge of the sanctuary, adjoining the Chamber of Hewn Stone) in order to carefully maintain his ritual purity. During that time he carried out the daily morning and evening offerings and, under the tutelage of the elders of the priesthood, reviewed and memorized the rite of the coming Day. (This practice, related by Mishnah, gains historical plausibility when we remember that the office of high priest was filled by Herodian or Roman appointments during the NT era, and many of these were short lived; see 6.2 below). The high priest was not allowed to sleep the night before the Day of Atonement lest he jeopardize his cultic purity by a nocturnal emission (see Josephus *Ant.* 17.6.4 §§165-66). At dawn the high priest carried out the daily morning offering (see 3.1 above), and when that was completed, he bathed, dressed in linen and turned to the centerpiece of the day's activity: the sacrifice of a young bull for a sin offering for himself and his household, a ram for a burnt offering (Lev 16:3) and the sacrifice for Israel of two male goats for a sin offering (one a sacrifice and one a scapegoat) and a ram for a burnt offering (Lev 16:5; each of these sacrifices accompanied by specified grain offerings).

Briefly outlined, the high priest first confessed his sins over the bull, then cast lots to determine which of the goats would be sacrificed and which would be the scapegoat (*m. Yoma* 3:9; 4:1). He returned to the bull, confessed his sins again, and slaughtered it (its blood was captured in a bowl). Then he entered the holy of holies to place a censer of burning incense on the stone where the ark of the covenant had once rested (*m. Yoma* 5:2). He returned to get the blood of the bull, reentered the holy of holies, and sprinkled some of the blood in the direction of the stone (*m. Yoma* 5:3). Now he returned to the sacrificial goat, slaughtered it, captured its blood and took the blood into the holy of holies, where he sprinkled it on the stone and on the curtain. The blood of both bull and goat was then mixed and used to sanctify the altar, with blood being applied to the four horns of the altar as well as sprinkled against its sides and the remainder being poured out at the base. The high priest then put his hands on the head of the scapegoat and confessed the sins of Israel. A designated person then led the goat out into the "wilderness." Mishnah speaks of ten "booths," or stations, along the goat's processional way to the ravine into which it was pushed head over heels to its death (*m. Yoma* 6:3-6). Meanwhile the high priest shed his linen garments, bathed, and put on his regular high-priestly garments (Lev 16:23-24). He then placed the fat from the bull and goat on the burning altar as a sin offering along with their respective grain offerings, and the remainder of the animals, including the hide, was taken out of the temple and burned completely. Mishnah tractate *Yoma* tells us that the high priest then proceeded to the Court of Women, where the people were assembled, and he read the instructions for the Day of Atonement from the Torah—Leviticus 16; 23:26-52 and Numbers 29:7-11—and uttered eight blessings (for a somewhat different picture, see Sir 50:14-21). What followed was a matter of disagreement among the sages. Rabbi Eliezer maintained that it was now that the high priest offered his ram and the ram of the people as a burnt offering (Lev 16:24) along with the seven lambs (Num 29:8). But Rabbi Aqiba held that the lambs had already been offered with the daily offerings at dawn, and the bull, goat and burnt offerings of rams were made with the daily evening sacrifice in the afternoon (*m. Yoma* 7:3).

It remained for the high priest to take off his clothes, don white garments, purify his hands and feet, and return to the holy of holies, where he retrieved the incense censer. Then, after another immersion and change of clothes (now in his full high-priestly regalia), he proceeded to offer incense on the golden incense altar and light the candelabra for the evening (see 3.1 above). After a final immersion and change into his own clothes, the high priest went home for a feast with his friends, celebrating the safe accomplishment of his duties (*m. Yoma* 7:4). Thus ended the high point of the cultic year. It is this event the author of Hebrews has in mind when he speaks of the high priest entering the inner room of the earthly tabernacle once a year, but Christ entering once into the most holy place of the heavenly tabernacle with his own blood rather than the blood of bulls and goats (Heb 9:6-14). When Paul in Romans 3:25 speaks of Christ being set forth as a *hilastērion,* he has in mind the "mercy seat," or covering of the ark of the covenant, on which the blood was originally to be sprinkled in the holy of holies on the Day of Atonement. Jesus is the mercy seat of the new temple, and by the blood of his death he fulfills this yearly rite of atonement, far surpassing it in finality and scope.

3.4. Passover Sacrifice. Passover, with Tabernacles and Pentecost, was one of the great festivals of Israel's calendar. The prominence of the Passover sacrifice in the life of Israel and the Gospel accounts calls for some comment here (for festivals in general, *see* Festivals and Holy Days: Jewish). Deuteronomy instructs the Israelites to sacrifice the Passover animal "at the place the LORD will choose as a dwelling for his Name" (Deut 16:2 NIV; cf. Ex 12:14-20; Lev 23:4-8; Num 28:16-25). This "place," as it turns out, is the temple in Jerusalem, and in the first century Jews who were able made a pilgrimage to Jerusalem to celebrate the Passover on the fourteenth day of Nisan (see Mk 14:12-15 par.; Jn 2:13; 11:55-56). The seven days following Passover were the Feast of Unleavened Bread.

The sacrifice of the prescribed "lamb" (a year-old male goat or sheep, Ex 12:5) took place in the temple, and the crowds that kept this festival necessitated their being divided into three groups who would successively enter the court and carry out the sacrifice en masse (as described and discussed in *m. Pesaḥ.*; but see discussion in Sanders, 136-37). Each Passover lamb was to be shared by a household or group, generally including at least ten men (*m. Pesaḥ.* 8:7; cf. Jesus and the Twelve celebrating Passover), though 4Q265 frag. 4 expresses a sectarian view in prohibiting "a young boy or a woman" from eating the Passover. The sacrifice took place between the ninth and eleventh hours (roughly 4:00 to 6:00 p.m.; Josephus *J.W.* 6.9.3 §423). Mishnah tells us that when the first group entered the court (it is not clear which court, the Court of Israel seems far too small, and a larger area of the temple may have been sanctified for this purpose), the gate was closed behind them. The choir of Levites was assembled and sang the Hallel, Psalms 113—118 (or Songs of Ascent). At the sounding of the shofar, the priests lined up in rows, with gold or silver basins in their hands. Each Israelite male representative would slit the throat of his group's lamb, and a priest would catch the blood in a bowl. The bowl was then handed down the line of priests, and the one closest to the altar would throw the blood against the altar. The priest would then hang the lamb on a hook, slit it open, remove the sacrificial portions of fat and place them on the altar fire. The lamb was then returned to its owner, and when the entire group had finished, the gates would be opened and the second group would enter. The lamb was taken to the household's selected spot within the walls of Jerusalem, roasted over a fire, and eaten with unleavened bread, bitter herbs, a fruit puree, salt water and wine—the prescribed foods of Passover. By one estimate, there were approximately 300,000 pilgrims and Jerusalemites who would gather for Passover, which would represent approximately 30,000 lambs needing to be slaughtered within a two-hour period (Sanders, 136). The activity of the priests, the bleating of lambs, the flow of blood and the traffic within the temple courts is staggering to imagine. It is easy to see why at Passover (and the other major festivals) all of the priests and Levites were on duty. Moreover, we should not forget that pilgrims would take the opportunity while in Jerusalem to offer other sacrifices. In addition, the required daily sacrifices during Passover and Unleavened Bread were augmented by two young bulls, one ram and seven male lambs for a burnt offering, and a male goat as a sin offering (Num 28:19-24). There is evidence that Jews in the Diaspora, for whom a regular pilgrimage to the temple was impractical or prohibitive, celebrated the Passover within their homes. In this case, every house became a temple and every Israelite male a priest (Philo *Spec. Leg.* 2.145-49; cf. Josephus *Ant.* 14.10.24 §260). For this they could appeal to precedent in the origin of the festival as a household event at the time of the exodus from Egypt.

4. Provisions for Sacrifice and Temple Service.

4.1. Animals. The needs of the temple and individuals for specific and unblemished animals—both four-legged and birds—was one of the most obvious features of the functioning of the temple. Numerous doves, sheep, goats and, to a lesser extent, cattle were daily being led through the courts of the temple toward the altar. Jews who lived in the environs of Jerusalem would perhaps be most likely to bring their own animals to the temple for sacrifice. But pilgrims from more distant places such as Galilee, and certainly the Diaspora, would welcome the opportunity to buy their animals in Jerusalem. Not the least of a worshiper's concerns would be whether the animal was unblemished by priestly standards, and if the owner (or local priest) did not overlook a blemish before starting out on the journey to Jerusalem, the hazards of travel could well result in an injury that would disqualify the beast from the altar. In Jerusalem, say our rabbinic sources, they could buy rams from Moab, calves from Sharon, sheep from Hebron and doves from the Mount of Anointing (see Safrai, 882).

The Gospels, in the scene of Jesus' temple "cleansing" (Mt 21:10-17; Mk 11:11, 15-17; Lk 19:45-46; Jn 2:13-17), give us a snapshot of animals being sold within the temple precincts. Matthew and Mark speak only of doves being sold (and moneychangers, see 4.6 below), but John adds "cattle and sheep" (Jn 2:14-15). As we have seen, it is easy to see how the sale of animals within the temple precincts, perhaps in the porticos around the perimeter of the exterior Court of the Gentiles, would have been a valuable service to worshipers. The authenticity of the Gospel scene, particularly John's introduction of "cattle and sheep," has been questioned (for objections see, e.g., Sanders, 86-89). Not the least of the apparent problems is that maintaining animals in their stalls (even if only during the daylight hours) would have polluted the sacred space of the temple with dung, fodder and noise. Formerly the sale of the animals had taken place in an area called the Hanuth, on the Mount of Olives, but there is some rabbinic evidence that the innovation of selling within the temple precincts was undertaken during the tenure of Caiaphas the high priest, some forty years prior to the destruction of Jerusalem (see Eppstein; Jeremias, 48-49; Chilton; *see DLNTD,* Temple §2). Such a practice would no doubt have disturbed some pious Jews, not least the Pharisees with their concern for purity, and probably Jesus also. For the administration of the temple, this commerce—whether operated or simply licensed by the high priest—represented another stream of revenue.

4.2. Salt, Oil, Grain, Wine and Incense. In addition to animals for sacrifice, the temple service required a steady supply of salt, oil, grain, wine and incense. All of these items were required for the offerings that were part of the regular functioning of the temple on behalf of Israel, and except for the incense and salt, which were supplied by the temple, these items were called for in various offerings of individuals. Worshipers might bring their own oil, grain or wine, but if they were traveling a distance they would find it more convenient to purchase it when they arrived, and in so doing they would be better assured that it met the strict temple standards for quality. This need was also accommodated at the temple.

Salt was a constant necessity since all offerings on the altar were accompanied by salt, and it was also used to preserve the hides that became the priests' property. Rabbinic sources mention that the salt was supplied from Sodom, near the Dead Sea, the incense (including frankincense) came from Arabia, the olive oil from Tekoa and Gush Halav in Galilee, and the grain and wine from Judea. The procurement and quality of these supplies was regulated by the temple administration, as was its sale. For example, we read in Mishnah that those who wished to offer a drink offering would pay for it at an office in the temple, receive a token and then exchange the token for the drink offering at another place (*m. Šeqal.* 5:4). All of these daily material needs of the altar, not to speak of vestments, gold, silver, curtains, furnishings, building supplies for the protracted construction and finishing of Herod's temple, and the "tourist" trade of pilgrims in Jerusalem, contributed to making the temple a vital centerpiece of the local and regional economy (see Hanson and Oakman, 146-54; *see* Economics of Palestine).

4.3. Wood. The altar of sacrifice burned daily and consumed vast quantities of wood throughout the course of a year. The wood was routinely supplied by particular families in Israel (listed in *m. Ta'an.* 4:5; cf. Neh 10:3), for whom it was regarded a privilege (see Safrai, 882-83). The wood was delivered to the temple with ceremony, and the fifteenth of the month of Ab was a day designated for Israel in general to bring their offerings of wood to the temple (Josephus *J.W.* 2.17.6 §425). The *Temple Scroll* of Qumran calls for a festival of wood offering in its vision of an ideal temple (11QTemple 23; also 4Q325). The types of wood accepted are listed in *Jubilees* 21:12-15 and *Testament of Levi* 9:12, but Mishnah allows any wood but olive or vine for the altar of sacrifice (*m. Tamid* 2:3) and specifies only fig wood for the altar of incense (*m. Tamid* 2:5). Within the temple the wood was stored in bulk in the Chamber of Wood located in the northeast corner of the Court of Women. There it was inspected, and worm-eaten pieces were culled by priests who were disqualified from service within the sanctuary due to their own physical blemishes (*m. Midid* 2:5). Individual worshipers could also offer a sacrifice of wood for the altar, which they could purchase in the temple.

4.4. Water. Large volumes of water were necessary for the operation of the temple (*Ep. Arist.* 88-90). Most prominently, water was needed for filling the great bronze laver in the Court of Priests, for the immersion pools used by the priests, and for the pools used for the ritual cleansing of every person who entered the temple courts. Water for the laver was drawn up from below the floor level of the temple by a wheeled mechanism located in a chamber immediately south of the laver (*m. Mid.* 5:4). In addition, water was needed for cleaning the floor of the temple, particularly the area north of the altar where the animals were slaughtered. By the first century, the water was supplied from two sources: cisterns that captured rain water (*m. Mid.* 5:4 and *m. 'Erub.* 10:14 mention two large cisterns, and over thirty have been discovered by archaeologists) and a sophisticated aqueduct system that transported water from Solomon's Pools, south of Bethlehem and twelve miles south of Jerusalem. The *Letter of Aristeas* speaks of a complex of channels running beneath the temple and being able to hear the rush of the waters from a certain spot about eight hundred yards outside the city (*Ep. Arist.* 90).

4.5. Blood and Animal Waste Disposal. The blood that was poured at the base of the altar descended through two drains. Aristeas (writing in the second century B.C.) comments that the drains (*m. Mid.* 3:2) operated with the effect that "large amounts of blood which collected from the sacrifices were all cleansed by the downward pressure and momentum" (*Ep. Arist.* 90; cf. *m. Yoma* 5:6). The blood, mixed with water, then flowed into the Brook Kidron where, Mishnah states, the accumulated blood product was collected and sold to farmers as fertilizer (*m. Yoma* 5:6). Ash from the altar (as well as from the fires in the Chamber of the Hearth and Chamber of Baked Cakes) needed to be collected and disposed of, and this was taken outside the temple. The tremendous amount of animal waste, particularly at a festival season, no doubt posed a challenge. That which was not to be offered on the altar or consumed by the priests was to be burned at a designated and "holy" spot outside the temple. In picturing the scene we should not miss an obvious fact: the smell of a slaughterhouse would have permeated the Court of Priests and its surroundings, particularly on a warm day, and most twenty-first-century westerners placed on the scene would find it revolting.

4.6. Temple Treasury. Some of the expense of the temple services was borne by direct gifts (such as wood), the portions of sacrifices that were the priests' allotment and perhaps income from the sale of items and animals for offerings. In addition, freewill offerings of money could be made by depositing them in one of the thirteen trumpet-shaped coffers located in the temple (see Mk 12:41-44 par. Lk 21:1-4). But the most significant source of temple revenue was the annual half-shekel tax levied on every Israelite male, whether in the land of Israel or in the Diaspora. Though this was the prevailing practice, it was not beyond dispute. 4Q159 maintains that it should be paid only once in a lifetime, probably appealing to its origin as a onetime payment in Exodus 30:13-14, and this opinion may have been shared by Jesus (Mt 17:24-27; see also *m. Šeqal.* 1:4; *Mek.* on Ex 19:1; *b. Menaḥ.* 65a). In Diaspora communities the tax was collected and transported to Jerusalem with ceremony (*Ep. Arist.* 40; Josephus *Ant.* 14.7.2 §§110-14; 16.2.3-4 §§28-41; *see* Jewish Communities in Asia Minor §2). Other Jews, such as Galileans on their yearly pilgrimage to the temple, could pay the tax on the temple grounds. The standard currency for this tax, and for any other donations to the temple, was a Tyrian coinage of silver (*m. Bek.* 8:7), which could be acquired at the temple, though an exchange fee was involved (thus the money changers whose tables Jesus overturned in the temple courts). This money was deposited in the temple treasury and was chiefly used to support the daily morning and evening sacrifices of the temple. In this manner all of Israel joined in offering ceaseless corporate worship to Yahweh.

The amount of money that was received and paid out in various transactions, including purchasing temple provisions, selling sacrificial elements, disbursing charity to the poor, as well as the business affairs related to temple land holdings, would have required a substantial office, chief treasurer(s), accountants, purchasers and other personnel (*m. Šeq.* 5:2; Josephus *Ant.* 15.11.4 §408; 20.8.11 §194). The treasury was also responsible for the safekeeping of valuables related to worship, such as the high priest's vestments. In fact this arm of the temple operated much like a bank, with private funds also being held on deposit (2 Macc. 3:6, 10-12, 15, 22; 4 Macc. 4:3; cf. Josephus *J.W.* 6.5.2. §282).

5. Access to Worship.

5.1. Males and Females. Sacrifice, the central act of worship, was carried out by an exclusively male priesthood, and Israelite males were the only ones allowed in the Court of Israel, which immediately bordered on the Court of Priests. Only a male Israelite was allowed to place his hands on the head of the sacrificial victim (probably by leaning over a low barrier separating the Court of Israel from the Court of Priests), confess his sins and slay the animal. Women and children could look on from the Court of Women or perhaps from elevated galleries (*m. Mid.* 2:5), if they in fact existed. In any case, the inner courts were progressively elevated and the altar was situated near the center so that it was at least partially visible through the gateway. Gentiles, on the other hand, were kept at some distance, being forbidden (on pain of death) from crossing beyond the balustrade that separated the Court of the Gentiles from the Court of Women.

5.2. Restricted Persons. Mishnah tractate *Menaḥot* 9:8 specifies that the deaf mute, idiot, minor, blind person, Gentile, slave, agent and woman may not lay their hands on the head of the sacrificial animal, and consequently may not slay the animal (cf. *m. Ḥul.* 1:1). This restriction reflects the categories of people who were restricted from the Court of Israel (and for some, the Court of Women). The Qumran sectarian document 4QMMT is of a stricter opinion, applying the levitical restrictions on priestly service (Lev 21:17-23) to Israel as a whole. Banned from entrance to the temple are not only the Ammonite and Moabite (Deut 23:3) but those with impure male conditions (e.g., a bastard or one with crushed testicles or a severed penis). Neither should the blind and the deaf be permitted to enter the temple, for the deaf have not heard the laws of purity and the blind cannot visibly discern impurities and so are helpless to guard against defilement. Both are judged a hazard to maintaining the sanctity of the temple and its functions. David's restriction of the "blind and lame" from entering the house of God (2 Sam 5:8; rendered "sinners and guilty" in *Tg.*), where the temple would eventually be built, finds a reversal in the "Son of David" who heals the "blind and lame" at the temple, probably in the Court of the Gentiles (Mt 21:14-15).

5.3. Gentile Offerings. Gentiles, particularly those of influence and power, were known to have their sacrifices accepted by the temple. In fact, Josephus tells us, the votive offerings of prominent Gentiles had long adorned the temple. Tellingly, the refusal of these sacrifices and offerings marked the outbreak of the Jewish revolt of A.D. 66 (Josephus *J.W.* 2.17.3 §§48-21; 5.13.6 §563; *Ant.* 13.5.4 §§145-47; 13.5.8 §168; 13.8.2 §242; see Schürer, 2:309-13). Mishnah indicates that Gentiles could bring freewill or votive offerings (*m. Šeqal.* 1:5). These would have included drink offerings, grain offerings and burnt offerings (*m. Šeqal.* 7:6; *m. Menaḥ.* 5:3, 5, 6; 6:1; 9:8) but not purification, reparation and peace offerings. The Qumran sectarian document 4QMMT expresses a dissenting opinion against any offerings of Gentiles in the temple. The evidence is somewhat ambiguous regarding the rights of full proselyte males (Gentile converts who had been circumcised) to offer sacrifices in the Court of Israel. We do know that proselytes offered sacrifices, but we cannot be certain that they did so on the same footing as Israelites by descent.

The emperor Augustus instituted a daily burnt offering of two lambs and a bull "for the Emperor and the Roman people" (Philo *Leg. Gai.* 23.157; 40:317; Josephus *J.W.* 2.10.4 §197). By this means the Jews were able to honor the emperor and yet avoid sacrificing *to* the emperor (*see* Ruler Cult), though the practice had more ancient precedent (Ezra 6:9-10; Josephus *Ant.* 3.3 §140; *Ep. Arist.* 45; 1 Macc 7:33). Philo tells us this sacrifice was undertaken at the emperor's expense (Philo *Leg. Gai.* 23.157), but Josephus holds that it was borne by the Jewish people (Josephus *Ag. Ap.* 2.6 §77). Perhaps the truth lies in the middle, with the sacrifices being paid out of the Roman taxation of the Jews.

6. Officiants: Levites, Priests and High Priests.

6.1. Priests and Levites. Priests and Levites served in the temple according to a set schedule. Each priest and Levite was a member of one of twenty-four "courses," or divisions (1 Chron 24:7-19; Josephus *Life* 1 §2; *Ant.* 7.14.7 §366), and each course served a one-week period twice a year (see 4Q328, 329 for sectarian opinion on the rotation of priestly families). However, during the major festivals of Passover, Weeks and Booths, all priests and Levites were on duty at the temple. This meant that, apart from four or five weeks of the year, much of the time priests and Levites were at home and otherwise occupied. Their place of residence might be anywhere in the land of Israel (or even outside the land, e.g., Joseph, called Barnabas, of Cyprus, Acts 4:36). For example, we learn that Zechariah, the father of John the Baptist, lived in "a Judean town in the hill country" (Lk 1:39 NRSV) and that he was serving in the temple as his division (Gk. *ephēmeria*, Lk 1:8) was on duty. We may picture, then, a number of priests and Levites scattered throughout the cities, towns and villages of Judea and Galilee (excluding a place such as *Tiberias, which was ritually defiled by reason of being built over a graveyard). However, it appears a great number of them lived in Jerusalem or its immediate environs (e.g., even at the time of Nehemiah, there were approximately 1,500 priests and Levites in Jerusalem; Neh 11:10-18). Since the priests and Levites were not given a family inheritance within the land of Israel, they were not farmers. Some of them were probably engaged in common and honorable trades, and we know that Herod had priests trained as stonecutters and carpenters for the construction of the inner courts of the temple (Josephus *Ant.* 15.11.2 §390). But it is reasonable to assume that a good number of the priests and Levites, and particularly the priests, served in capacities adjunct to their holy calling (see Sanders, 170-82): as teachers of Torah (Deut 31:19, 25; Sir. 45:17; Josephus *Ant.* 4.8.44 §304), village magistrates (Josephus *Ag. Ap.* 2.22 §187; 2.24 §194), scribes (which included a number of functions) and synagogue leaders (Philo *Hypoth.* 7.13; Theodotus inscription). Their support from tithes and offerings (see Schürer, 2:257-74) allowed them to undertake these functions that were strategic for Israel's corporate life before God. Dispersed among the various communities of Israel, priests would have been ready resources for teaching, advising and ruling in matters of purity (e.g., skin diseases), sacrifice and the numerous facets of Torah, as well as providing a vital link to the inner life of the temple, the heart of Judaism.

A priest who was a teacher of Torah and lived in Jerusalem might spend a good deal of time within the temple's outer courts, where instruction and reading of the Torah was carried out. For example, we read that Rabbi Johanan ben Zakkai (though not identified as a priest) would "sit and teach in the shadow of the sanctuary" (*b. Pesaḥ.* 26a), and in the NT we find Jesus and the apostles teaching on the temple grounds (Mt 26:55; Lk 21:37; Acts 2—4). The Theodotus inscription, discovered in Jerusalem, informs us that Theodotus was a priest and third-generation ruler of a Greek-speaking synagogue established for "reading of the law and for teaching of the commandments." Although there were other synagogues in Jerusalem where instruction also took place, the temple, with its porticos and open areas, its worshipers and its gradations of sacred space, was a natural venue for instruction in Torah (Lk 2:46-47). The Jerusalem temple was not exceptional in this regard, for Greek and Roman education also took place in public venues such as temple environs.

Scriptures were kept in the temple (Josephus *Ant.* 3.1.7 §38; 5.1.17 §61; *J.W.* 7.5.5 §150), and we can safely surmise that scribal activity of all sorts was carried out in the temple, probably by priests and Levites who were professional scribes apart from their routine temple duties.

The psalm scrolls from which the Levites sang needed to be copied, stored and cared for. The priestly genealogies (Josephus *Ag. Ap.* 1.6-7 §§28-37), temple records and documents, and all sorts of work related to copying and preserving sacred Scriptures (including a master copy of the Scriptures) would have kept scribes well occupied. It is not impossible that some of the biblical scrolls found at Qumran were produced by the hands of temple scribes.

In general, the Levites' work was to assist the priests. Like the priests, they were not allotted land within Israel. They were supported by the tithe but did not receive a share of the sacrifices as did the priests. The Levites may have assisted in ushering animals to the Court of Priests and in taking the sacrifices of women to the priests. They carried firewood, swept the grounds and cleaned up refuse. They were responsible for the festal branches at the Feast of Tabernacles. We know that some of them sang in choirs and played instruments, and they would also have cared for the psalm scrolls and instruments. They manned the gates of the temple, keeping the keys, opening the gates in the morning, closing them in the evening, guarding them throughout the day (Philo *Spec. Leg.* 1.156), checking to see that worshipers carried nothing into the temple grounds that was unrelated to sacrifice and making certain that unauthorized persons did not trespass upon courts where they were forbidden. Levites were likely a part of the armed temple guard, and we may surmise that during festivals the Levites would have been responsible for crowd control. Rabbinic sources indicate that some Levites occupied permanent positions in the temple, and this seems historically probable. For instance, there was a "director of music," a "director of singers," a "chief doorkeeper," a "keeper of the keys" and a jailer, who was also in charge of administering the scourge (see Jeremias, 167-72; see Hanson and Oakman, 141, for an organizational chart of the temple).

We have already observed many of the duties of the priests as they engaged in offering sacrifices and other functions within the Court of Priests and sanctuary. Clearly the task of struggling with reluctant animals, lifting carcasses, skinning and cutting, carrying portions up to the altar, transporting wood and working around the heat of the altar while always being observant of purity regulations was not for the physically frail. In fact it called for strength, fitness, efficiency and perspiration. Working in linen garments, with sleeves laced tightly around their arms, they engaged in "a combination of liturgical worship and expert butchery, mostly the latter" (Sanders, 79). The *Letter of Aristeas* 92-93 gives us a glimpse of their work in the second or third century B.C. For the priests, a day of work in the temple was demanding and tiring, though *Aristeas* tells us that a "break room" was set aside for their rest, and they rotated in and out of duty. *Aristeas* speaks of "more than seven hundred ministers" being on duty at one time (*Ep. Arist.* 95), an improbable number if we are to think of them all in the Court of Priests at one time or even half of them resting (Sanders, 79). But the figure likely includes Levites, and it may be derived from the combined number of priests and Levites in each of their twenty-four courses. If we consider the probability that each course was divided into daily courses for the week of service, and half of these were on duty while the other half rested, a more manageable figure of approximately fifty priests and Levites working at one time comes into view (Jeremias, 200). But this too is conjecture; we simply do not know. During important feasts, when all of the priests and Levites were on duty (serving on shifts), their numbers must have been impressive. Josephus tells us that there were about twenty thousand priests during the time of Jesus (Josephus *Ag. Ap.* 2.108), but we do not know whether these were all fit for service or if some were retired. The accuracy of this figure simply cannot be tested reliably (see Jeremias, 200-205; Sanders, 78-79).

6.2. High Priest and Chief Priests. Beginning with Jonathan in 153/152 B.C. and extending for 120 years, the high priesthood was filled by *Hasmoneans, who joined priestly privilege with kingship. Traditionally the office had been filled by priests of the lineage of Zadok (*see* Priests and Priesthood). There were dissenters to this change, and it is probably around this time that the *Essenes of Qumran formed their priestly community in response to this perceived crisis. Over time the supporters of the Hasmoneans, including some priestly families in Jerusalem, came to enjoy the benefits of elite status, power and wealth (splendid homes of priests have been excavated on the Western Hill of Jerusalem). When Herod the Great became king, he overcame this power bloc by various means, including replacing the Hasmoneans with priests of his own appointment and eventually eliminating the male heirs of the Hasmonean house. A total of eight high priests were appointed during the reign of Herod, and Josephus counts twenty-eight high priests from Herod the Great to the fall of Jerusalem, with several lasting only one year (Josephus *Ant.* 20.10 §§247-51). After Herod the Great, the high priests were appointed by Archelaus (4 B.C.-A.D. 6), then by Roman legates or prefects (A.D. 6-41), and then (by permission and under authority of the Romans) by Agrippa I (A.D. 41-44), Herod of Chalcis (A.D. 44-48) and Agrippa II (A.D. 48-66). The effect of this circulation of high priests was that there could be a number of individuals living at one time who had served as high priest and might be referred to as such (e.g., Annas, the father-in-law of Caiaphas, the high priest that year, Jn 18:12-24; *see* Caiaphas Ossuary).

The Gospels refer to "chief priests," which in Greek is the plural form *(archiereis)* of the word used for high priest *(archiereus).* In the Gospels the chief priests appear in conjunction with "elders" (nobility or lay aristocracy), scribes and Pharisees. Josephus mentions them in conjunction with "the powerful" and "best known men" (i.e., the Gospels' "elders"), the Pharisees and "the council" (or Sanhedrin). The most likely identification of the chief priests is that they were male members of the three or four priestly families (Phiabi, Boethus, Ananus/Annas, Camith) from which the high priests were chosen (see Sanders, 328; Goodman, 120; Schürer, 2:232-36; contra Jeremias, 179). The chief priests would thus have included former and future high priests as well as others of this priestly aristocracy, with the current high priest having a status of "first among equals." Their concentration of power was in Jerusalem, but their influence extended throughout Judea. Many of them were probably Sadducees. Their rise to power seems to have been concurrent with the direct rule of Judea under Roman procurators (A.D. 6-41). Under this direct Roman rule, the appointed high priest was responsible for mediating Roman rule by governing the temple and Jerusalem and keeping the peace (cf. Lk 23:2; Jn 11:48), while the prefect or procurator resided for much of the year in Caesarea. Placed between Rome and Israel, the high priest used whatever means of diplomacy were available, attempting to please Rome, on the one hand, and his fellow Jews on the other. He carried out his charge with the assistance of the chief priests (see Sanders, 327-32, 481-90) and a council. One of these chief priests was the "captain of the temple" (*stratēgos tou hierou,* Acts 5:24, 26; cf. Lk 22:4, 52), a deputy of the high priest who was placed over the temple guard and was responsible for policing the temple and enforcing the jurisdiction of the high priest (cf. leaders in 1QM 2:1-2).

The primary liturgical role of the high priest was conducting the ceremony of the Day of Atonement (see 3.3 above). There was a daily grain offering of the high priest (see 3.1 above), but that was usually offered on his behalf by the priests performing the daily sacrifices. During the Second Temple period the office of high priest extended well beyond a liturgical role in the temple (and the office was never only that) and took on the authority of political leadership, first in the wedding of priesthood and kingship by the Hasmoneans and later in the role of political go-between during the era of direct Roman rule. A prominent duty of the high priest was to preside over the *Sanhedrin. Nevertheless, in the eyes of the faithful in Israel, the high priest's role in the temple, as a representative of corporate Israel, was fundamental for Israel's atonement and hope of restoration. *Jubilees* (3:12, 26-27; 4:25-26; 8:19) even evokes cosmic overtones by applying Edenic imagery to the temple (see Hayward, 88-107). And as if to fill out this picture, Sirach 49:15—50:26 portrays the Hasmonean high priest Onias as an Adamic figure, clad in his "robe of glory" (Sir 50:11) and ministering at the altar in Edenic splendor (see Hayward, 73-84 for text and commentary). For later rabbinic Judaism, heaven and earth intersected at the altar. "The Temple sacrifices celebrate creation, leading to Eden" and "priests serve as bearers of the sin and embodiment of the atonement of Israel" (Neusner, 1291-92). At the apex of this representation of Israel is the high priest.

See also FESTIVALS AND HOLY DAYS: JEWISH; JUDAISM AND THE NEW TESTAMENT; LITURGY: QUMRAN; LITURGY: RABBINIC; RELIGION, GRECO-ROMAN; SYNAGOGUES; TEMPLE, JEWISH; TEMPLE SCROLL (11QTEMPLE).

BIBLIOGRAPHY. G. A. Anderson, "Sacrifice and Sacrificial Offerings (OT)," *ABD* 5:870-86; B. Chilton, *The Temple of Jesus: His Sacrificial Program Within a Cultural History of Sacrifice* (University Park: Pennsylvania State University Press, 1992); A. Edersheim, *The Temple: Its Ministry and Services as They Were at the Time of Jesus Christ*, introduction J. J. Bimson (Grand Rapids, MI: Kregel, 1997 [1874]); V. Eppstein, "The Historicity of the Gospel Account of the Cleansing of the Temple," *ZNW* 55 (1964) 42-58; D. K. Falk, "Jewish Prayer Literature and the Jerusalem Church in Acts," in *The Book of Acts in Its Palestinian Setting*, ed. R. J. Bauckham (BAFCS 4; Grand Rapids, MI: Eerdmans, 1995); M. Goodman, *The Ruling Class of Judea: The Origins of the Jewish Revolt Against Rome A.D. 66-70* (Cambridge: Cambridge University Press, 1987); K. C. Hanson and D. E. Oakman, *Palestine in the Time of Jesus: Social Structures and Social Conflicts* (Minneapolis: Fortress, 1998); C. T. R. Hayward, *The Jewish Temple: A Non-Biblical Sourcebook* (London and New York: Routledge, 1996); W. Horbury, ed., *Templum Amicitiae: Essays on the Second Temple Presented to Ernst Bammel* (JSNTSup 48; Sheffield: Sheffield Academic Press, 1991); J. Jeremias, *Jerusalem in the Time of Jesus* (Philadelphia: Fortress, 1969); B. Mazar, *The Mountain of the Lord* (Garden City, NY: Doubleday, 1975); J. Neusner, "Sacrifice and Temple in Rabbinic Judaism," in *The Encyclopedia of Judaism*, ed. J. Neusner, A. J. Avery-Peck and W. S. Green (3 vols.; New York: Continuum, 1999) 1290-1302; S. Safrai, "The Temple," in *The Jewish People in the First Century: Historical Geography; Political History; Social, Cultural and Religious Life and Institutions*, ed. S. Satvai and M. Stern (2 vols.; CRINT 1; Assen: Van Gorcum; Philadelphia: Fortress, 1974-76) 2:865-907; E. P. Sanders, *Judaism: Practice and Belief 63 BCE-66 CE* (Philadelphia: Trinity Press International, 1992); E. Schürer, *The History of the Jewish People in the Age of Jesus Christ (175 B.C.-A.D. 135)*, rev. and ed. G. Vermes, F. Millar, M. Goodman (3 vol.; Edinburgh: T & T Clark, 1973-87) 2:292-313; J. J. Scott Jr., *Customs and Controversies: Intertestamental Jewish Backgrounds of the New Testament* (Grand Rapids, MI: Baker, 1995).

D. G. Reid

SACRIFICES, PAGAN. *See* RELIGIONS, GRECO-ROMAN.

SADDUCEES

The Sadducees were a group of Jews that arose sometime during the Maccabean period and disappeared sometime in the first two centuries of the common era. The Hebrew is *ṣadûqî*, so that they have often been related to *Ṣadoq*, David's high priest; however, there is little justification for this connection. *Josephus and the *rabbinic texts often place them in opposition to the *Pharisees. We know relatively little about the Sadducees, and all of the documents we now have suggest that they were much less important than the Pharisees. However, because we do not have any Sadducean documents, all of our information comes from texts written by people who were not Sadducees and some of whom actively opposed them. Josephus, the Gospels and Acts and the rabbinic texts provide our information about the Sadducees.

1. Beliefs
2. Place in Jewish Society
3. Exegetical Traditions

1. Beliefs.

Josephus identifies the Sadducees as one of the three varieties of *Judaism that existed during the Maccabean period and enumerates their beliefs in four places (Josephus *J.W.* 2.8.14 §164; *Ant.* 13.5.9 §173; 13.10.6 §293; 18.1.4 §§16-17); however, not one element of the Sadducean system of beliefs so impressed Josephus or his source(s) that it immediately came to mind when he wrote about the Sadducees. Josephus tells us that the Sadducees (1) rejected the concept of fate and accepted the idea of free will, so that God could not be held responsible for evil, (2) did not believe that the soul exists after death and (3) did not believe that there were rewards and punishments after one died. Josephus also mentions that the Sadducees observed nothing apart from the law and that they considered it a virtue to dispute with their teachers. He further states that the Sadducees did not have the support of the masses, that they only enjoyed the "confidence of the wealthy" (Josephus *Ant.* 13.10.6 §297), and that only a few men of the "highest standing" know the Sadducean doctrines (Josephus *Ant.* 18.1.4 §17). He claims that the Sadducees were "boorish" (Josephus *J.W.* 2.8.14 §166) and "more heartless" than other Jews (*Ant.* 20.9.1 §199). He claims that the Sadducees frequently accepted Pharisaic doctrine. He names only one high priest, Ananas, as a Sadducee.

The NT considers the Sadducees' rejection of resurrection as their primary characteristic, for the issue of resurrection was central to the early church. The Gospel of Mark does not place the

Sadducees in opposition to the Pharisees, and Matthew often places them together as if they were two similar groups. Luke mentions the Sadducees only in his discussion of resurrection. John does not mention the Sadducees. Only in Acts do we find the two groups disagreeing; however, the disagreement centers only on the issue of resurrection. While some Sadducees seem to be attached to the *temple, the NT does not equate them with the priests, or the priests with them.

The *Mishnah contains several passages in which the Sadducees disagreed with the Pharisees, frequently over matters of purity: *Yadayim* 4:6, whether or not Scripture renders the hands unclean; whether or not the bones of an ass or the high priest are clean; *Yadayim* 4:7, whether or not certain types of water are unclean; *Parah* 3:7, the importance of the setting of the sun in rendering one clean; *Niddah* 4:2, the state of cleanness of Sadducean *women. They also disputed some matters of civil law: *Yadayim* 3:7, whether or not a *slave's master is responsible for the damage caused by the slave and *Makkot* 1:6, whether or not a false witness is executed only when the one against whom he testified is executed. The Mishnah contains only one reference to a disagreement concerning a matter of holiday law: *ʿErubin* 6:1 suggests that the Sadducees hold their own views concerning the *ʿerub,* the establishment of the *sabbath limit. Tosefta records disputes only on matters of purity.

The early midrashim add some new information. *Sipre Numbers* 112 takes Numbers 15:31, "for he despised the word of Yahweh," as a reference to the Sadducees; this is our earliest reference in the rabbinic texts to the position that some accepted that the Sadducees did not follow the Word of God. *Sipre Deuteronomy* 190 contains a story about a Sadducean high priest who did not burn the incense on the Day of Atonement in accordance with the sages' rules.

The Babylonian Talmud contains a number of references to the Sadducees; however, the medieval censors often replaced the words "Gentiles" and "heretics" with "Sadducees." The following are those passages in which the reference to the Sadducees is not suspect. *ʿErubin* 68b concludes that the Sadducees should be equated with Gentiles in matters of the sabbath limit, for neither know rabbinic law. *B. Yoma* 19b informs us that the Sadducean high priests who offered incense on the Day of Atonement were afraid of the Pharisees and generally followed the rulings of the latter. The high priest who ignored Pharisaic tradition when he offered the incense soon died.

B. Niddah 33b informs us that if the attitude of a Sadducean woman is unknown, she is considered to have followed the rules concerning her menstrual period to which all other Israelite women adhere, that is, the Pharisaic/rabbinic injunctions. The Sadducean view concerning the importance of the sun's setting in matters of cleanness is discussed on *b. Yoma* 2b, *b. Ḥagiga* 23a and *b. Zebaḥim* 21a.

On *b. Yoma* 4a the Sadducees are excluded from the "students of the sages" and "the students of Moses." *b. Ḥagiga* 16b and *b. Makkot* 8b refer to the matter of the execution of the false witness. On *b. Baba Batra* 1 15b we learn that the Sadducees and the Pharisees disagreed concerning a daughter's right of inheritance in certain circumstances. On *b. Sanhedrin* 52b, R. Joseph, a third-generation Babylonian Amora, refers to a Sadducean court; however, he had no firsthand knowledge of the court system in the first century. *B. Menaḥot* 65a tells us that the Sadducees believed that individuals, and not the community, should pay for the daily offering. *B. Horayot* 4a and *b. Sanhedrin* 33b discuss a court that incorrectly ruled according to Sadducean law.

B. Sanhedrin 90b refers to the Sadducees' rejection of resurrection. The Palestinian Talmud does not add any new information, except that a Boethusian high priest lights the incense incorrectly.

The *ʾAbot de Rabbi Nathan* version A, 5 states that Antigonus of Soko had two disciples who "arose and withdrew from the Torah" forming two groups: the Sadducees and the Boethusians. The Sadducees derive their name from Zadok, one of the disciples, and the Boethusians take their name from Boethus, the other disciple. The split was over the issue of resurrection. We are further told that "they," the Boethusians and/or Sadducees, used silver and gold vessels not because they were ostentatious, but because it was Pharisaic tradition to inflict themselves in this world, hoping to receive a reward in the world to come. *ʾAbot de Rabbi Nathan* version B contains a shorter version and omits the reference to the gold and silver vessels.

2. Place in Jewish Society.

Based on Josephus's remarks with a slight nod

to the *ʾAbot de Rabbi Nathan*, scholars have often claimed that the Sadducees were the priestly aristocracy of Jewish society; however, Josephus named only one Sadducean priest, and the rabbinic texts know many priests who were Pharisees. Also, the NT sometimes connects Sadducees with the temple, at times implies that the Pharisees acted in concord with the priests and also indicates that the priests acted on their own. Josephus alone argues that the Sadducees influenced the aristocracy, although he pictures the Pharisees as politically influential at times. But this is as much to underscore the support that the Pharisees have with the populace as to provide us information about the Sadducees.

Scholars have made a good deal about the opposition between the Pharisees and the Sadducees; however, the disputes are few and limited to minute details of law. We have no information about the matters they agreed upon, which given what we have must have been extensive. The Gospel writers do not draw clear and consistent distinctions between the two groups, which suggests that from the outside they must have looked similar. The earliest rabbinic texts suggest that the groups differed over small details of purity law, civil law and sabbath law. The further removed in time we get from the first century, the more extensively these disputes are detailed. Newly published materials from *Qumran have brought to light a few parallels between the legal positions at Qumran and those assigned to the Sadducees in the rabbinic documents. But one cannot claim a clear relationship between Qumran and the Sadducees or even that both reflect priestly law.

3. Exegetical Traditions.

Following Josephus, many have argued that the Sadducees were biblical literalists, but we have no evidence for that other than Josephus's claim that they held that resurrection was not a biblical concept. The few exegetical comments assigned to them do not make them biblical literalists; but again, we have little evidence about them. While one may claim that they rejected the Pharisaic or some of the Pharisaic scriptural interpretations and legal exegeses, one must also assume that like those at Qumran, the Pharisees and the early Christians, the Sadducees had their own exegetical traditions, some of which probably deviated quite a bit from the literal meaning of the biblical text, as did many of the exegetical remarks of all of the other Jews from whom we have information (*see* Biblical Interpretation, Jewish).

See also PHARISEES; PRIESTS AND PRIESTHOOD, JEWISH; THEOLOGIES AND SECTS, JEWISH; TEMPLE, JEWISH.

BIBLIOGRAPHY. B. J. Bamberger, "The Sadducees and the Belief in Angels," *JBL* 82 (1964) 433-35; G. Baumbach, "Der Sadduczaische Konservatismus," *Literature und Religion des Fruhjudentums,* ed. J. Maier and J. Schreiner (Würzburg: Echter, 1973); V. Eppstein, "When and How the Sadducees Were Excommunicated," *JBL* 85 (1966) 213-24; S. Isenberg, "An Anti-Sadducean Polemic in the Palestinian Targum Tradition," *HTR* 63 (1970) 433-44; J. Jeremias, *Jerusalem in the Time of Jesus* (Philadelphia: Fortress, 1977); J. Le Moyne, *Les Sadduceens* (Paris: Librarie Lecoffre, 1972); J. Lightstone, "Sadducees versus Pharisees: The Tannaitic Sources," *Christianity, Judaism and Other Greco-Roman Cults: Studies for Morton Smith at Sixty,* ed. J. Neusner (4 vols.; Leiden: E. J. Brill, 1975), 3:206-17; M. Mansoor, "Sadducees," *EncJud* 14:620-22; J. Patrich, "A Sadducean Halakha and the Jerusalem Aqueduct," *The Jerusalem Cathedra: Studies in the History, Archaeology, Geography and Ethnography of the Land of Israel 2,* ed. L. I. Levine (Detroit: Wayne State University Press, 1982) 25-39; G. G. Porton, "Sadducees," *ABD* 5:892-95; idem, "Sects and Sectarianism During the Period of the Second Temple: The Case of the Sadducees," in *The Solomon Goldman Lectures: Perspectives in Jewish Learning Volume IV,* ed. N. Stampfer (Chicago: Spertus College of Judaica Press, 1985) 119-34; E. Rivkin, "Defining the Pharisees: The Tannaitic Sources," *HUCA* 40-41 (1969-70) 204-49; A. J. Saldarini, *Pharisees, Scribes and Sadducees in Palestinian Society: A Sociological Approach* (Wilmington, DE: Michael Glazier, 1988); G. Stemberger, *Jewish Contemporaries of Jesus: Pharisees, Sadducees, Essenes* (Minneapolis: Fortress, 1995); A. C. Sundberg, "Sadducees," *IDB* 4:160-63.

G. G. Porton

SAMARITAN LITERATURE

The relationship between the first-century Samaritans and the community that produced the NT becomes clearer with the help of comments on the Samaritans by *Josephus; early *rabbinical literature; the literature of the Samaritan community, including the Samaritan Pentateuch, which would predate the NT; and later

Samaritan theological works and chronicles. In the latter part of the twentieth century, the literature regarding that relationship is far too rich to ignore. More than one scholar has compared the value of Samaritan studies to that of the *Dead Sea Scrolls from *Qumran and the *gnostic materials from Nag Hammadi as a source of illumination of the NT (e.g., Scobie, 414).

1. Josephus's Comments on the Samaritans
2. Early Rabbinical Literature on the Samaritans
3. The Samaritan Pentateuch
4. Later Samaritan Literature
5. The New Testament and the Samaritans
6. Conclusions

1. Josephus's Comments on the Samaritans.

The first-century Jewish historian Josephus provides one of the few contemporary glimpses of the Samaritans in the NT period and reflects the animosity or at best condescension of the Jews toward the Samaritans. To explain the background of the Samaritans, Josephus essentially relates the biblical account of 2 Kings 17, which claimed that the inhabitants of Samaria were foreigners forcibly transported there by the Assyrians in the eighth century B.C. In *Antiquities* 11.4.3 §84, which tends to be pro-Jewish and anti-Samaritan, Josephus identifies the enemies of Judah who request to be partners in the rebuilding of the Jerusalem *temple in Ezra 4:1 (where they are unnamed) as the Samaritans. When the Jews rejected the request, the Samaritans reported the building project to the king and continued their own harassment of the Jews. According to Josephus, they also hindered Nehemiah when he was rebuilding the walls of the city of Jerusalem (Josephus *Ant.* 11.5.8 §174).

Josephus characterizes the Samaritans as pro-Greek, a fact that would not endear them to the Jews of the first century, who would well remember their own oppression under the Greeks and their partial deliverance under the leadership of the Maccabees, a Jewish rebel family of the second century B.C. (*see* Jewish History: Greek Period). Josephus helps make the connection by giving an account (Josephus *Ant.* 12.7.1 §§287-92) of a Samaritan general, Apollonius, attacking the Maccabees during the time of their first leader, Judas. Apollonius was defeated. In *Antiquities* 12.5.5 §261 Josephus reports that the Samaritans asked to have their temple named Jupiter Hellenius in honor of a Greek deity.

Josephus reports disparagingly on *Herod's close relationship to Samaritans. Herod had a Samaritan wife (Josephus *Ant.* 17.1.3 §20; *J.W.* 1.28.4 §562), even though Jews were prohibited from marrying Samaritans. Further, he had a Samaritan tutor for his son (Josephus *J.W.* 1.30.5 §592). He reports that the Samaritans defiled the temple by strewing bones in it (Josephus *Ant.* 18.2.2 §29) and that Agrippa I borrowed money from a Samaritan (Josephus *Ant.* 18.6.4 §167).

In the *Jewish War,* which tends to be pro-Roman and more sympathetic to the Samaritans (perhaps he is using a *Hellenistic source), Josephus describes two incidents in which Samaritans were massacred by Roman troops, the latter episode leading to the dismissal of Pontius Pilate (Josephus *J.W.* 3.7.32 §§307-15; *Ant.* 18.4.1-2 §§85-89).

2. Early Rabbinical Literature on the Samaritans.

Jewish self-consciousness of its difference from Samaritanism is expressed in the Talmudic sources that emerged from the second to the sixth century A.D. Samaritans were welcome to seek the advice of rabbinical authorities in settling disputes (*b. B. Meṣ.* 69a), but *marriage between the two groups was forbidden by the same rabbinical authorities (*b. Qidd.* 4.3). Some of the concern felt by Jews regarding the Samaritans involved rituals. Jews felt that Samaritans were not ritually clean (*b. Nid.* 4.1), that they made unacceptable offerings (*b. Bek.* 7.1), did not observe *holy days correctly (*b. Roš Haš.* 22b) and could not be relied on to give legal testimony (*b. Giṭ.* 1.5). A booklet in the Babylonian Talmud summarized the basic differences with the Samaritans by asking when the Samaritans would be acceptable to the Jews. The response: "When they renounce Mount Gerizim, and confess Jerusalem and the resurrection of the dead" (the conclusion of the *Masseket Kutim).*

3. The Samaritan Pentateuch.

The final revision of the Samaritan Pentateuch probably dates to the latter part of the second century B.C. The text type reflected there has been found among the Dead Sea Scrolls, and although it may not have been unique to the Samaritans (for example, it shares many readings with the *Septuagint), its presence both at Qumran and in certain NT passages strongly suggests the possibility of Samaritan influence. There are several thousand variants between the Samaritan Pentateuch and the Masoretic Text, though most of them are minor differences in spelling. Those differences do make it possible to identify which text type is used in many quotations. Its use by NT writers is suspected in Acts 7:4, 5, 32, 37 and Hebrews 9:3-4. The first reference (Acts 7:4) is found in Stephen's speech, which has other indications of sensitivity to Samaritans. He emphasized Samaritan heroes and modified the Hebrew text in favor of Samaritan concerns. Many scholars deduce that he is either of Samaritan background or targeting an audience of Samaritan background. If Stephen was a member of a Samaritan Christian group, he was uniquely equipped to bring a *Hellenized Christianity to Jerusalem, but also equipped to arouse the resentment from Jerusalem-based Jews that led to his martyrdom. Stephen's identity has been a central focus in Samaritan studies.

4. Later Samaritan Literature.

Samaritan works other than the Pentateuch date later than the NT period, clustering primarily during periods of Samaritan renaissance in the fourth century under the leadership of Baba Raba and the fourteenth century led by the high priest Phineas. These later works contain likely vestiges of interaction between the Samaritans and the NT documents, particularly as they highlight vocabulary and ideas that are prominent in the NT.

4.1. The **Memar Marqah.** The *Memar Marqah* contains the thought and biblical interpretation of the third- or fourth-century Samaritan theologian Marqah. It reflects the Samaritan acceptance of many NT terms, especially from the Gospel of John and the book of Hebrews. This leads some scholars to conclude that both of these NT books were written with Samaritan Christians very much in mind. They share with the *Memar Marqah* references to the waters of life, the glorification of the dead or elect upon the arrival of the Messiah, the curious supernatural powers, the importance of the Word, the equation of belief in Jesus (or for the Samaritans, *Moses) as belief in God and naming of each as the Word and the Light of the world and Son of God (Marqah calls Moses son of the house of God). This close tie of Samaritan and Christian theological terminology may be a significant key to understanding early Christianity.

4.2. The Samaritan Chronicles. The Samaritan Chronicles, particularly that of Abu'l Fath, contain a few comments about Jesus and the NT period, and the general temper is sympathetic. Abu'l Fath, commissioned to organize various Samaritan traditions and chronicles in the middle of the fourteenth century, preserved some Samaritan memories of first-century Christianity. He refers to Jesus as the Messiah, son of Mary and Joseph, born in Bethlehem and claiming messiahship in Nazareth. His numbering of the disciples is curious, referring to seven in one place, fifteen in another and commenting that Jesus was crucified with twelve of his companions. He notes that another source says that only two were crucified with him. The chronicles also have brief comments on John the Baptist. The sources are unknown, but they do reflect a tradition of amity between Christians and Samaritans. That amity is reflected on the Christian side as well, both in the NT and in early Christian interpretations of the story of the Good Samaritan. Very early Irenaeus (c. 180), Clement of Alexandria, Origen (c. 200) and Ambrose of Milan (c. 400) were depicting the Good Samaritan as Jesus rescuing the earthly traveler beset by temptations after the priest and Levite, representing the OT, failed. Likewise in the earliest visual depiction of this scene, in the Codex Rossanensis, the role of the Good Samaritan is portrayed by Jesus.

5. The New Testament and the Samaritans.

The vocabulary and concepts drawn from these Samaritan sources illuminate the NT, and many scholars have written on these issues. The Gospel of John has been the focus of major works by J. Bowman, G. Buchanan, E. Freed, J. MacDonald, W. Meeks, H. Odeburg and J. Purvis. Attention has been given to Stephen's speech by R. Coggins, S. Lowy, W. Mare, Purvis, E. Richard, A. Spiro and D. Sylva. The book of Hebrews has been the subject of studies by R. Eccles, M. Haran, E. Knox, C. H. H. Scobie and R. Trotter.

The NT has several explicit references to Samaritans, and they could be the sometime referent to the terms "Israelite," "Hebrew" and even "Galilean." Several terms characteristically used by the Samaritans in their later writings (e.g., *topos* ["place"]); the use of the demonstrative pronoun "this" before a proper name, as in "this Jesus" (which occurs six times in Stephen's speech) and "this" *Melchizedek (Heb 7:1); and "our Father" (several places in John) could be used intentionally to appeal to the Samaritans. The several passages condemning the temple in Jerusalem would have been attractive to the Samaritans, whether they influenced them or not. Abraham, Moses and Joshua have particular significance for the Samaritans, and each has been seen as a sign of influence on the NT. Luke may have emphasized the priestly parenthood of John the Baptist and the priesthood in general to appeal to the priestly-centered Samaritans (Bowman, 70-71).

Detailed NT information on the Samaritan sect is sparse and ambiguous. They are not mentioned in Mark. Matthew alludes to their cities, along with pagan cities, as places the disciples should not visit (Mt 10:5). Only Luke-Acts and John describe Christian experience of the Samaritans and imply Christian attitudes toward them. The cryptic account in Luke 9:51-56 almost certainly involves representatives from the Samaritan sect rather than simply inhabitants of Samaria, for it is only upon hearing mention of Jerusalem that they refuse hospitality to Jesus and his disciples. One of the significant aspects of the story is the refusal of Jesus to allow the disciples any form of retaliation, implying a conciliatory stance taken by Jesus (and probably the early church) toward the Samaritan sect. Luke's stories of the Good Samaritan (Lk 10) and the thankful Samaritan leper (Lk 17) also imply an openness to the Samaritans.

Samaritans, both in the sense of inhabitants of Samaria and as members of the sect focused at Mt. Gerizim, were viable and actual converts to Christianity. John 4:9 implies that many Samaritans were drawn to Christianity by Jesus himself. In that story it is clear that Jesus is dealing with members of the Samaritan sect. The woman in the conversation with Jesus at the well is aware of the distinction between Jew and Samaritan (Jn 4:9), and that self-conscious distinction involves the preference of Gerizim over Jerusalem as the proper place of worship (Jn 4:20). Finally, John 4:39 implies that "Samaritan" is not coequal with inhabitants of the region, for the Samaritans were not the only inhabitants of the city in which the woman made her home.

It is very likely that some Samaritans were an audience and soon participants in Christianity. *Galilee was the early point of origin and focus for Christianity, and the Samaritans were geographical neighbors. Acts 8:5-6 indicates that the first converts to Christianity from among the Samaritans were a result of the preaching of Philip.

There are good arguments that Mark, John and Q, the hypothetical unique source that many believe was used by Matthew and Luke, are products of Galilee. In the Gospel of John, Galileans and Samaritans are equated (Purvis, 171-72). C. H. H. Scobie argues for another hypothetical source, akin to Q and sharing the same provenance, that was the Samaritan source used by Luke (Scobie, 397). This would confirm that Samaritans were involved in the Christian movement very early. Certainly their low economic-social status would predispose them to the appeal of the Christian message.

Several scholars believe John was intentionally creating a bridge between Samaritans and Jews in the person of Jesus. Salvation may be from the Jews but is for all Israel, the former northern kingdom, home of the Samaritans, as well as the Jews of the southern kingdom. Therefore John emphasized many Samaritan concepts such as "light" and "word" and a preexistent Christ (echoing a preexistent Moses for the Samaritans); he diminished the role of Peter and exalted the role of the "beloved disciple"; he implied that Jesus was rejected only in Jerusalem and not in Galilee and Samaria; he made a conscious attempt to relate Galileans and Samaritans and possibly used the Samaritan ascent/descent motif to facilitate Samaritan receptivity to the gospel. Jesus specifies that his ultimate audience is the Israelites, the total of the twelve tribes, which could be understood as part of an early Christian polemic against orthodox *Judaism but is more likely an expression of Jesus' vision of inclusiveness. Inspired by Ezekiel and his vision of a unification of all Israel, John used Ezekiel's term "Son of Man" for the Messiah.

Simon Magus (Acts 8:9-24) and *Melchizedek (an important focus of Hebrews) may tie together Gnosticism, Christianity and the Samaritans. That Simon was a Samaritan is implied by the fourteenth-century Samaritan Chronicler Abu'l Fath and by the early church fathers who also identified him as a Gnostic, though both labels are still debated. Simon and Stephen represent diametrically opposed expressions of Samaritan Christianity—gnostic versus historical Christianity.

Gnosticism, which denied Jesus a real body, Jewish or otherwise, would have allowed members of a gnostic Samaritan Christian sect to dejudaize Jesus and elevate him above the Samaritan-Jewish conflict. Separated from a hostile Jewish context, Jesus would be more acceptable to the such Samaritans. It is possible that the Gnosticism that Paul seems so often to attack is one form of Samaritanism.

6. Conclusions.
Later Samaritan literature, brought into dialogue with Josephus, early rabbinical literature and the NT itself, illuminates the first-century Samaritan community and its relationship to early Christianity, suggesting strong ties and mutual appreciation. Later Samaritan literature gives us a Samaritan vocabulary of words and concepts that clue us to recognize a wider Samaritan presence in some NT works addressed to or by the Samaritans or Samaritan Christians. Further, the text type of the Samaritan Pentateuch is detectable in some parts of the NT, further implying significant Samaritan presence or influence.

See also SAMARITANS.

BIBLIOGRAPHY. R. Anderson, "Samaritan Studies and Early Christianity," in *New Samaritan Studies,* ed. A. Crown and L. Davey (Sydney: Mandelbaum Publishing, University of Sydney, 1995) 121-31; J. Bowman, *The Samaritan Problem* (Pittsburg: Pickwick, 1975); A. Crown, *The Samaritans* (Tübingen: Mohr Siebeck, 1989); E. Freed, "Did John Write His Gospel Partly to Win Samaritan Converts?" *NovT* 12 (1970) 241-56; idem, "Samaritan Influence in the Gospel of John," *CBQ* 30 (1968) 580-87; B. Hall, "Some Thoughts About Samaritanism and the Johannine Community," in *New Samaritan Studies,* ed. A. Crown and L. Davey (Sydney: Mandelbaum Publishing, University of Sydney, 1995) 207-15; E. Knox, "The Samaritans and the Epistle to the Hebrews," *Churchman* (1927) 184-93; J. MacDonald, *Memar Marqah: The Teaching of Marqah* (Berlin: Töpelmann, 1963); idem, *The Samaritan Chronicle No II (or Sepher Ha-Yamim from Joshua to Nebuchadnezzar* (BZAW 107; Berlin: Walter de Gruyter, 1969); idem, *The Theology of the Samaritans* (London: SCM, 1964); W. Mare, "Acts 7: Jewish or Samaritan in Character?" *WTJ* 34 (1971) 21; J. Purvis, "The Fourth Gospel and the Samaritans," *NovT* 17 (1975) 161-98; E. Richard, "Acts 7: An Investigation of the Samaritan Evidence," *CBQ* 39 (1977) 190-208; C. H. H. Scobie, "The Origins and Development of Samaritan Christianity," *NTS* 19 (1973) 390-414; P. Stenhouse, trans., *The Kitab Al-Tarikh of Abu'l Fath* (Sydney: Mandelbaum Trust, 1985). R. T. Anderson

SAMARITAN, THE. *See* REVOLUTIONARY MOVEMENTS, JEWISH.

SAMARITANS

In NT times the Samaritans were a substantial religious group inhabiting parts of the central hill country of Samaria between *Galilee to the north and Judea to the south, but with *Diaspora communities in addition. Physically, they focused on Mt. Gerizim, close to the ancient town of Shechem, while religiously the focus of their faith was on a form of the law of Moses, the Pentateuch, which differed only slightly, but in one or two respects crucially, from the form of the Pentateuch familiar to us from its Masoretic recension.

1. Sources and Their Difficulties
2. Origins and Early History
3. Varieties of Samaritanism and Principal Beliefs
4. Jewish-Samaritan Conflicts and Polemics
5. Samaritans in the Gospels
6. Samaritans in the Book of Acts

1. Sources and Their Difficulties.
Despite the explosion in recent years in the publication of Samaritan texts and secondary discussions based upon them, considerable problems still confront us regarding most questions relating to the Samaritans in the first half of the first century A.D.

1.1. Samaritan Sources. Apart from the Samaritan Pentateuch itself, all Samaritan sources date from periods considerably later than the NT. Moreover, many of these sources, whether historical, doctrinal or liturgical, are known only from manuscripts of far more recent date still. In addition, it must be remembered that the Samaritan community has survived in unbroken continuity to this very day and that during its history it has both developed internally and, being usually a minority group, has inevitably been influenced by external pressures in its quest for survival. Scholars thus disagree, often quite widely, over the extent to which these sources can help in reconstructing early Samaritan history and belief.

Among the more important texts which incorporate valuable earlier traditions are (1) the *Memar Marqah,* a fourth-century composition but also including later material; it is an expansive retelling of the biblical account of Moses, incorporating many midrashic supplements (*see* Rabbinic Literature: Midrashim); (2) the *Kitab al-Ta'rikh* ("annals") of Abu'l-Fath, composed in A.D. 1355, and now generally recognized as the most valuable of the various Samaritan "Chronicles"; and (3) the *Samaritan Targum* (*see* Rabbinic Literature: Targumim). Of course, even though the greatest caution has to be exercised before historical conclusions can be drawn from these and other such Samaritan sources, they have considerable significance on their own account in terms of heightening our appreciation of the Samaritans' sense of self-awareness.

1.2. Jewish Sources. Pride of place here belongs to *Josephus, who both recounts a version of the origin of the Samaritans and includes frequent references to them in his *Antiquities* and *Jewish War.* This material has to be evaluated in the light of Josephus's evident anti-Samaritan stance and his historical confusion (which can be independently verified) surrounding especially the last part of the Persian period and the start of the Hellenistic period, precisely the time in which he locates the most important step in the development of the Samaritan community.

There are also references of varied significance in the Second Temple literature and in the later Mishnah and Talmud (*see* Rabbinic Literature). Though generally negative, scholars have frequently remarked on the fact that several of these are a good deal more ambivalent than might at first have been supposed, reflecting, no doubt, the fact that the status of the Samaritans was extremely problematic from a Jewish point of view.

1.3. Other Sources. The NT itself contains important material from a historical point of view. In the context of our present discussion, we need therefore to be particularly aware of the dangers of circular argumentation. Some of the early church fathers also include potentially relevant material. Finally, archaeology is a particularly important source of information in an area where the textual data are so uncertain. Shechem has been extensively excavated, and work is currently in progress unearthing the remains of a substantial Hellenistic town on Mt. Gerizim itself, so that we may hope for further advances in our understanding in the coming years.

A full survey of all these sources is now available in *The Samaritans,* a magisterial compendium by a number of leading experts and edited by A. D. Crown (1989).

2. Origins and Early History.

Several views of Samaritan origins are attested in antiquity. Though each contains problems from a modern perspective, they retain their importance as evidence for how the situation was perceived in the first century. The following survey represents a heavy simplification for the sake of clarity.

2.1. Samaritan Views. The Samaritans have always believed that they are the direct descendants of a faithful nucleus of ancient Israel. From their perspective, Israel's apostasy began as early as the time of Eli (eleventh century B.C.), when the nation's cultic center was removed from Gerizim to Shiloh (and thence eventually to Jerusalem); they would thus not have regarded themselves as the remnant of the old northern kingdom of Israel but as a separate group alongside them. This helps explain their acceptance of the Pentateuch alone as authoritative. For them, therefore, the question of origins should be directed more toward *Judaism than to themselves.

2.2. Jewish Traditions. The origins of the Samaritans are linked with the account in 2 Kings 17:24-41 about how, following their conquest of the northern kingdom, the Assyrians colonized the area by settling it with people from a number of Mesopotamian towns, including Cuthah. These colonists adopted the Israelite faith alongside their own religion (1 Kings 17:41), and their descendants, often called "Cuthaeans" in Jewish polemical sources, are the Samaritans of later times. The hostilities between Judah and her northern neighbor recorded in the books of Ezra and Nehemiah demonstrate the antiquity of the division between the two groups.

2.3. Josephus. While sharing the previous opinion, Josephus adds a further significant ingredient, namely, that at the end of the Persian period the priest Manasseh was expelled from Jerusalem and that a sanctuary was built for him shortly thereafter at the start of the Hellenistic period by Sanballat, his father-in-law, on Mt. Gerizim. Over the course of time other priests from Jerusalem joined him there. Josephus thus recognizes a certain degree of Samaritan priestly legitimacy (at least in terms of descent), and his account helps him explain the Jewish character of much Samaritan practice.

2.4. Critical Reconstruction. After decades of discussion (which cannot be surveyed here) as new pieces of evidence have come to light, scholars are now agreed that none of these positions can be maintained as an accurate reflection of the situation. While disagreement inevitably remains, there is a widespread measure of agreement on some of the salient issues, the upshot of which for our present purposes is that the situation as reflected in the NT developed far more recently than had previously been thought and that the division was by no means as clear-cut as the earlier views might be thought to imply. The following points deserve notice.

2.4.1. The Question of 2 Kings 17. The account in 2 Kings 17 should be discounted in discussions of Samaritan origins. (1) The word *haššômrônîm* in 2 Kings 17:29, often translated "the Samaritans," seems merely to mean "inhabitants of [the city or province of] Samaria," and this fits the context best. (2) There is no evidence to link the later Samaritans with Samaria. The earliest certain references to them all point clearly to their residence at Shechem, as we should expect on the basis of their theology (Sir 50:26; 2 Macc 5:22-23; 6:2), and one of Josephus's sources refers to them as "Shechemites" (Josephus *Ant.* 11.8.6 §§340-47; 12.1.1 §10). Shechem was rebuilt only in the early Hellenistic period, following an interruption in settlement of some 150 years. (3) Despite earlier mistaken suggestions, it is now clear that nothing of later Samaritan religion and practice owes anything to the proposed pagan influence of 2 Kings 17 or Ezra 4.

2.4.2. The Resettlement of Shechem. It is not known for certain precisely who resettled Shechem (and Mt. Gerizim itself?) at the start of the Hellenistic period. Most probably an important element comprised a group of religious purists who were descendants of the original Israelite population in the north who had not been exiled by the Assyrians (that there were some is recognized by the OT itself; cf., for instance, 2 Chron 30; 34:6; Jer 40:5). Following the severe suppression of a revolt in Samaria in the time of Alexander the Great and the complete Hellenization of this city, the ancient site of Shechem would have been an obvious place to settle. "It often happened that when a Greek colony was established, native villages under its control formed a union around an ancestral sanctuary" (Bickerman, 43-44). The discovery of over two hundred skeletons in a cave in the *Wâdī ed-Dâliyeh* is generally thought to reflect part of this same upheaval.

Less certain, but in the present writer's view very attractive, is the suggestion that they were joined, or even preceded, by a group of *priests from Jerusalem who had been forced to leave the *temple service there because of the rigorous policies of those who succeeded Ezra and Nehemiah. Josephus's account may include some memory of this; there is strong circumstantial evidence in the OT for a major reorganization of the Jerusalem priesthood at about this time; it would help account for Samaritan claims to a legitimate priesthood, their close association with a number of inner-Jewish developments (e.g., in Halakah), and the apparently continuing inner-Samaritan tensions between the priesthood and the laity (see below). The later establishment of the Qumran community (*see* Dead Sea Scrolls), this time by a more strict group of priests and their followers, forms an interesting parallel development.

2.4.3. Conflict and Identity. The formation of this community and the building of a temple soon after would not of themselves have caused a decisive breach or schism. Purvis (1986), however, notes four possible reasons for a steadily deteriorating situation during the third and second centuries B.C.: (1) political tensions because of different alliances with the Ptolemies and the Seleucids; (2) Jewish resentment because of Samaritan acceptance of a greater degree of Hellenization and their consequent failure to join in the resistance to Antiochus IV Epiphanes; (3) tensions between their respective Diaspora communities; and (4) Hasmonean expansion.

This last element was probably decisive, for in 128 B.C. John Hyrcanus captured Shechem and destroyed the sanctuary on Mt. Gerizim. Apart from natural resentment, this drove the Samaritans to a closer religious rationale of their situation (compare the effect of the destruction of the Jerusalem temple in A.D. 70; *see* Destruction of Jerusalem). As Purvis (1968) has shown, it was at this period that the Samaritan Pentateuch began its own separate history in terms of script, orthography and, crucially, textual tradition and recension. From this point on, therefore, though one should certainly continue to regard Samaritanism as a form of Judaism ("sect" would be an anachronistic term to use), it became crystallized as by far the most distinct by virtue of its wholesale rejection of the Jerusalem-centered *Heilsgeschichte,* something which cannot be said of any other variety of Judaism in antiquity.

Not surprisingly, relations continued thereafter at a low ebb, and isolated events that are recorded from the first century A.D. may be regarded as symptomatic, though told from a Jewish standpoint. For instance, between A.D. 6 and 7, some Samaritans scattered bones in the Jerusalem temple during Passover (Josephus *Ant.* 18.2.2 §§29-30), while in A.D. 52 Samaritans massacred a group of Galilean pilgrims at *Engannîm* (Josephus *Ant.* 20.6.1 §118).

3. Varieties of Samaritanism and Principal Beliefs.

Just as it is clearly mistaken to speak of normative Judaism in the first century in view of the number of groups which often differed quite sharply from one another, so recent research has suggested that the same was probably true of the Samaritans (cf. Kippenberg; Isser).

3.1. The Dositheans. Because of the fragmentary nature and late date of all our relevant sources, it is not possible to go beyond informed conjecture, but Isser has made out a strong case for the view that "Dositheus was an early first century A.D. eschatological figure among the Samaritans, who applied the 'Prophet like Moses' passage of Dt. 18 to himself" (Isser, 163). He further argues that he became prominent within a Samaritan sect which had already been formed during the previous century and which, as a *synagogue-based lay movement, was somewhat akin to the pharisaic movement within Judaism, in contradistinction to the more Sadducee-like orthodox Samaritans, who were no doubt predominantly priestly and centered on Gerizim.

Such distinctions need to be borne in mind when evaluating references to contacts between the Samaritans and Jesus or the first Christians as well as between Jews and Samaritans, for the degrees of affinity between different groups across the divide may have varied far more than our severely fragmented knowledge allows us to recognize.

3.2. Principal Beliefs. The previous remarks also mean that it is difficult to speak in general terms about Samaritan beliefs. However, from the Samaritan Pentateuch, whose primary recension should be dated, as we have seen, earlier than the first century, a few comments may be made. From the text-type of the Pentateuch which they elected to adopt for themselves, it is probable that already the passage in Deuteronomy 18:18-22 about a future "prophet like Moses" had been joined to the Exodus version of the Sinai account (following Ex 20:21). They will themselves, however, have added to the Decalogue the commandment, based on Deuteronomy 27, to build an altar on Gerizim.

Thus we can be reasonably certain that the following elements of their later creed were already established in early times: belief in one God, in Moses the prophet, in the law and in Mt. Gerizim as the place appointed by God for *sacrifice. The other two elements of the creed are less certain: the day of judgment and recompense, and the return of Moses as *Taheb* (the "restorer" or "returning one"). The latter is of particular interest in view of what we have seen about Dositheus, while in addition we may note the unrelated report of Josephus (*Ant.* 18.4.1 §§85-87) that in A.D. 36 a Samaritan fanatic assembled a crowd on Gerizim, promising to reveal the sacred vessels thought to have been hidden there by Moses. These indications, coupled with the Samaritan Pentateuch, suggest that from early times an important element of Samaritan belief, especially amongst the laity, was the coming of the "prophet like Moses," but that only later did this develop into the more crystallized concept of the *Taheb* (cf. Dexinger in Crown); beyond that it would be hazardous to speculate. [H. G. M. Williamson]

4. Jewish-Samaritan Conflicts and Polemics.

Jewish-Samaritan polemics emerged in the postexilic period, from time to time exploding into violence. Because of these hostilities, Jewish pilgrims from Galilee often crossed over to the East Bank of the Jordan River in order to detour around Samaria. Those who chose to pass through Samaritan territory did so at great risk. According to Josephus, "Hatred also arose between the Samaritans and the Jews for the following reason. It was the custom of the Galileans at the time of the festival to pass through the Samaritan territory on their way to the Holy City. On one occasion, while they were passing through, certain of the [Samaritan] inhabitants of a village . . . joined battle with the Galileans and slew a great number of them" (*Ant.* 20.6.1 §118; see also *J.W.* 2.12.3 §232).

Some Jews regarded the Samaritans with contempt, considering them fools (Sir 50:25-26; *T. Levi* 7:2) and idolaters (*Gen. Rab.* 81:3 [on Gen 35:4]), who were killed with divine approval (*Jub.* 30:5-6, 23). Later traditions in rabbinic literature regard Samaritans as apostate, wholly unclean and destined for Gehenna. [C. A. Evans]

5. Samaritans in the Gospels.

Although we have sought not to go beyond the available evidence in our treatment of Samaritan history and belief, we probably now have enough data to do justice to the references to the Samaritans in the Gospels.

5.1. The Synoptic Gospels. In the first three Gospels there are references to the Samaritans at Matthew 10:5; Luke 9:52; 10:33 and 17:16. These can all be understood against the background described above, once it is additionally borne in mind that they are told from a predominantly Jewish standpoint. Thus, in order to make a point similar to that in Luke 7:1-10, the foreignness of the grateful Samaritan is emphasized in Luke 17:11-19, even though he is instructed according to Jewish law along with the other nine lepers in v. 14. Similarly, Jesus' instruction to his disciples to go only to "the lost sheep of the house of Israel" (Mt 10:6) is contrasted not only with the negative command concerning the Gentiles but also, as in a separate and distinctive category, "any city of the Samaritans" (Mt 10:5). The incident in Luke 9:51-56 reflects typical Jewish-Samaritan personal antipathies of the time, though it is of interest to note both here and elsewhere that Jesus did not always bypass Samaritan territory (by taking a circuitous route through Transjordan) as many Galilean pilgrims to Jerusalem did. At the same popular level, the selection of a Samaritan for the positive role in the parable told in answer to the question "who is my neighbor?" (Lk 10:25-37) is telling and in a veiled manner anticipates the Jewish acknowledgment (recorded much later) that the Samaritans were often more punctilious in their observance of the law than the Jews (*b. Qidd.* 76a).

5.2. John. It is John 4 that gives the most extended account of an encounter of Jesus with the Samaritans (the only other reference in this Gospel being Jn 8:48). Despite its popularity, the title "woman of Samaria" is misleading. The incident takes place at Sychar (Jn 4:5), clearly identified as being close to Shechem and Mt. Gerizim (cf. Jn 4:5-6, 20; Gen 48:22 [LXX]). The parenthetical comment in John 4:9 about Jewish-Samaritan relations following the woman's expression of surprise that Jesus should ask her for a drink is probably not a general statement, but reflects a halakic ruling (mid-first century?) that "the daughters of the Samaritans are menstruants from their cradle" (*b. Nid.* 31b) and hence that the vessels which they handle are unclean. If so, the comment may reflect more the time of the Evangelist than of Jesus himself, and the woman's surprise may not have been so specifically motivated. The woman's question about the right place to worship (Jn 4:20) is, as we have seen, entirely appropriate as reflecting the issue that stood at the heart of Samaritan identity and is just the kind of easily grasped popular polemic which someone of her status might have been expected to raise. Her response to Jesus' reply (Jn 4:25), however, is more problematic; talk of a "messiah" would probably have been foreign to a Samaritan (though our earlier caveat about diversity in this particular area of eschatology must be borne in mind). If historical tradition lies behind the saying, its present expression must be regarded as a Johannine paraphrase for his more Jewish-orientated readership. A reference to the prophet like Moses in the context of a discussion of the right place and mode of worship would have fitted well here, as is clear from our earlier discussion. [H. G. M. Williamson]

6. Samaritans in the Book of Acts.

In the book of Acts, Samaria plays a significant role in the report of the progress of the gospel. We see this in Acts 1:8, where the risen Christ tells his disciples that they shall be his "witnesses in Jerusalem and in all Judea and Samaria and to the end of the earth" (RSV). Here Samaria appears to function as a bridge between the Jewish people and the Gentiles. Persecution in Judea scatters the young church into Samaria (Acts 8:1, 5, 14, 25), where Simon the magician makes his appearance in the narrative (Acts 8:9). We are later told that the "church throughout all Judea and Galilee and Samaria had peace and was built up; and walking in the fear of the Lord and in the comfort of the Holy Spirit it was multiplied" (Acts 9:31; cf. 15:3). [C. A. Evans]

See also JUDAISM AND THE NEW TESTAMENT; SAMARITAN LITERATURE.

BIBLIOGRAPHY. R. T. Anderson, "Samaritans," *ABD* 5:940-47; E. Bickerman, *From Ezra to the Last of the Maccabees* (New York: Schocken, 1962); R. J. Coggins, *Samaritans and Jews: The Origins of Samaritanism Reconsidered* (Atlanta: John Knox, 1975); A. D. Crown, *A Bibliography of the Samaritans* (ATLABibS 10; Metuchen, NJ: American Theological Library Association and Scarecrow, 1984); idem, ed., *The Samaritans* (Tübingen: Mohr Siebeck, 1989); F. Dexinger, "Limits of Tolerance in Judaism: The Samaritan Example" in *Jewish and Christian Self-Definition*, 2: *Aspects of Judaism in the Graeco-Roman Period*, ed. E. P. Sanders (Philadelphia: Fortress, 1981) 88-114; K. Haacker, "Samaritan, Samaria," in *NIDNTT* 3:449-67; S. J. Isser, *The Dositheans: A Samaritan Sect in Late Antiquity* (SJLA 17; Leiden: E. J. Brill, 1976); H. G. Kippenberg, *Garizim und Synagoge: Traditionsgeschichtliche Untersuchungen zur samaritanischen Religion der aramäischen Periode* (RVV 30; Berlin: Walter de Gruyter, 1971); J. MacDonald, *Theology of the Samaritans* (NTL; London: SCM, 1964); A. Montgomery, *The Samaritans: The Earliest Jewish Sect* (Philadelphia: J. C. Winston, 1907); R. Pummer, "The Present State of Samaritan Studies," *JSS* 21 (1976) 39-61; 22 (1977) 27-47; J. D. Purvis, *The Samaritan Pentateuch and the Origin of the Samaritan Sect* (HSM 2; Cambridge, MA: Harvard University Press, 1968); idem, "The Samaritans and Judaism," in *Early Judaism and Its Modern Interpreters*, ed. R. A. Kraft and G. W. E. Nickelsburg (Philadelphia: Fortress; Atlanta: Scholars Press, 1986) 81-98.

H. G. M. Williamson and C. A. Evans

SANHEDRIN

The sanhedrin was the supreme Jewish religious, political and legal council in Jerusalem in NT times. The term was also used of the smaller courts governing the affairs of the Jewish communities throughout Palestine and the *Diaspora.

1. Terminology
2. Theories
3. Origin and History
4. Membership
5. Powers and Functions
6. Times and Procedures

1. Terminology.

There are a number of Greek terms that may refer to various religious and political groups. In the NT a variety of these Greek terms is used but not all with reference to the body we know as the Sanhedrin.

1.1. Synedrion. In the LXX *synedrion* (*syn*, "together," and *hedra*, "a seat") had no fixed meaning and translated a variety of Hebrew words (*mat*, Ps 25(26):4; *sôd*, Prov 11:13; *dîn*, Prov 22:10; *qāhāl*, 26:26). By the end of the Maccabean period *synedrion* is widespread in the Greek literature for the supreme Jerusalem council. The Hebrew word *sanhēdrîn*, a transliteration of *synedrion*, is also used in the Mishnah for the Jerusalem court (*m. Soṭa* 9:11).

In the Gospels *synedrion* refers to the Jerusalem council (Mt 26:59; Mk 15:1; Jn 11:47; cf. Acts 5:27). In Matthew 5:22 and 10:17 (par. Mk 13:9) any judicial body may be in mind, such as the Sanhedrin, a local Jewish council or a group in the Christian community. In Luke 22:66 *synedrion* probably refers to the assembly room.

Synedrion occurs some fourteen times in the book of Acts, with the same meaning as found in the Gospels. The Twelve are brought before the Sanhedrin and commanded to stop proclaiming the gospel (Acts 4:1-22). The apostles continue to preach and are again brought before the Sanhedrin (Acts 5:27-41). Stephen is also brought before the Sanhedrin (Acts 6:12), as well as Paul on various occasions (Acts 22:30; 23:1, 6, 15, 20, 28; 24:20). In Acts we are told that Pharisees and Sadducees number among the members of the Sanhedrin (Acts 5:34; 23:6).

Josephus also uses the term for the Jerusalem council (Josephus *Ant.* 14.9.2-4 §§167-80; *Vit.* §62) and for the five districts and councils created in Palestine by Gabinius (Josephus *Ant.* 14.5.4 §§89-91). In other Greek literature of the period a sanhedrin was often a council of representatives from various constituencies (e.g., Diodorus Siculus *Bib. Hist.* 16:41).

1.2. Gerousia. Generally translated as "senate" or "council," *gerousia* was a word used mainly for the Greek and Roman nondemocratic senates (Aristotle *Pol.* 2.6.15) and was an older term than *synedrion* for the Jerusalem council from the end of the Persian period and the beginning of the Hellenistic period (Josephus *Ant.* 12.3.3 §138 and especially the Apocrypha, Jdt 4:8; 2 Macc 11:27). Only in a puzzling verse in Acts 5:21 is the term used in the NT where the high *priest "called together the council *[synedrion]* and all the senate *[gerousia]* of the sons of Israel." Luke may have thought there were two supreme bodies in Jerusalem, though it is more likely that, for the sake of his Greek readers, he means to say "the Sanhedrin, that is, all the senate."

1.3. Presbyterion. In Luke 22:66 *presbyterion* ("council of elders"; also Acts 22:5 and 1 Tim 4:14) may refer to the group of elders, one of the constituents of the Sanhedrin, but probably refers to the supreme Jerusalem council.

1.4. Boulē. Josephus often uses *boulē* ("council") for the senate in Rome (Josephus *J.W.* 1.14.4 §284; *Ant.* 13.5.8 §164), local Roman city councils (Josephus *Ant.* 14.10.13 §230), local Jewish city councils (Jospehus *Vit.* §64), the Jerusalem Sanhedrin (Josephus *J.W.* 5.13.1 §532) and its meeting place (*bouleutērion,* Josephus *J.W.* 5.4.2 §144). However, the NT does not use the word in this way (cf. Lk 7:30; 23:51).

2. Theories.

According to the Greek literature (Apocrypha, NT and Josephus) there was a single body in Jerusalem. However, the Mishnah says that there were two major courts in Jerusalem: "The greater Sanhedrin was made up of one and seventy [judges] and the lesser [Sanhedrin] of three and twenty" (*m. Sanh.* 1:6). The conflicting sources and multitude of terms has resulted in a number of theories about the Sanhedrin. A. Büchler proposed that before A.D. 70 there was a political body *(boulē),* a college of mostly priests *(synedrion),* and the Great Sanhedrin, which oversaw Jewish religious life. M. Wolff argued that the high priest presided over a little Sanhedrin and there was also a Great Sanhedrin *(gerousia)* of *scribes that condemned Jesus. S. B. Hoenig's theory was that there were three Sanhedrins: a political as well as a priestly and also a scribal one, which was the Great Sanhedrin. However, it is difficult to determine how far the Mishnah has preserved reliable traditions on the Sanhedrin, for it is now generally agreed that it is reflecting the entirely different situation at Jamnia, not that in Jerusalem before A.D. 70. On the other hand the Greek sources are more contemporaneous to the time of Jesus and are therefore to be favored in reconstructing the history of the Sanhedrin before A.D. 70.

3. Origin and History.

The rabbis at Jamnia legitimized their governing body by tracing it back to Moses and his seventy elders (Deut 27:1; *m. Sanh.* 1:6). However, apart from a supreme law court in Jerusalem (Deut 17:8-13; 19:15-21) and the occasional mention of "elders" (Ex 3:16; Deut 5:23), there is no hint of the existence of such an institution as the Sanhedrin in this period.

The actual seeds of the Jerusalem Sanhedrin in the time of Jesus were planted in the time of Ezra and Nehemiah. Joshua the high priest and the Davidic governor of Jerusalem, Zerubbabel, ruled the community together (Hag 1:1; Zech 4:14). The community was headed by a priestly nobility that formed an aristocratic council (Neh 2:16; 5:7) representing the people in negotiations with the Persian provincial governor, Tattenai, in the reconstruction of the *temple (Ezra 5:5, 9; 6:7-8, 14). With the death of Zerubbabel the house of David came to an end and the high priest emerged as the head of the *gerousia* and Jewish state (1 Macc 12:6).

From Hecataeus of Abdera, a contemporary of *Alexander the Great, we learn that the council was dominated by the priests: "He [Moses] picked out the men of most refinement and with the greatest ability to head the entire nation, and appointed them priests. . . . These same men he appointed to be judges in all major disputes, and entrusted to them the guardianship of the laws and customs. For this reason the Jews have never had a king, and authority over the people is regularly vested in whichever priest is regarded as superior to his colleagues in wisdom and virtue. They call this man the high priest" (Diodorus Siculus *Bib. Hist.* 40.3.4-5).

Under the relative freedom provided by the Hellenistic Kings, the influence of the Jerusalem court increased. The Seleucid king, Antiochus III (223-187 B.C.), said that it was his will that the Jewish nation "shall have a form of government in accordance with the laws of their country, and the senate [*gerousia*], the priests, the scribes of the temple and the temple-singers shall be relieved from poll-tax" (Josephus *Ant.* 12.3.3 §142).

From the beginning of the Maccabean revolt (167 B.C.) the power of the high priest increased (1 Macc 12:6) and with Simon being established as high priest, military chief and ethnarch (140 B.C.), the power of the Sanhedrin was reduced (1 Macc 14:24-49). With the reign of Queen Alexandra (76-67 B.C.) the Sanhedrin's power increased and the domination of the priests and nobility was exchanged for that of the *Pharisees. Alexandra permitted "the Pharisees to do as they liked in all matters, and also commanded the people to obey them; and whatever regulations, introduced by the Pharisees in accordance with the traditions of their fathers, had been abolished by her father-in-law Hyrcanus, these she again restored" (Josephus *Ant.* 13.16.2 §408).

Gabinius (57-55 B.C.), the Roman governor in Syria, divided the nation into five districts with councils (*synedria*) in Jerusalem, Gadara, Amathus, Jericho and Sepphoris (Josephus *Ant.* 14.5.4 §91). In 47 B.C. Caesar overturned this arrangement so that the high priest and the Jerusalem council were responsible for the affairs of the whole nation even though these local councils survived (Josephus *Ant.* 14.10.2 §§192-95). The Sanhedrin became sufficiently confident in its authority that the high priest and ethnarch Hyrcanus II (63-40 B.C.) summoned Herod to stand trial on capital sentences he had passed without the Sanhedrin's authority (Josephus *J.W.* 1.10.5-9 §§204-15). When *Herod took Jerusalem in 37 B.C. he retaliated by killing the entire membership of the Sanhedrin (Josephus *Ant.* 14.9.4 §174, though *Ant.* 15.1.2 §6 says only forty-five leading men were killed). Herod abolished the privilege of serving as high priest for life and appointed high priests with ceremonial duties and no political power.

Under the Roman procurators (A.D. 6-41), the Sanhedrin's power increased again (Josephus *Ant.* 20.9.1 §200; 20.10.1 §251). So, in the NT the Sanhedrin is represented as the supreme court of justice (Mk 14:55).

After the destruction of Jerusalem and the temple in A.D. 70 (*see* Destruction of Jerusalem), the Sanhedrin was recreated at Jamnia (Yavneh in the OT; 2 Chron 26:6) in the northwest of Judea (*m. Soṭa* 9:11; *m. Sanh.* 11:4) before moving to Galilee in A.D. 118.

4. Membership.
The Mishnah is probably correct in saying that prior to A.D. 70 the Sanhedrin in Jerusalem had seventy-one members (cf. Num 11:16; Josephus *J.W.* 2.18.6 §482; *Ep. Arist.* 46-50; *m. Sanh.* 1:6).

After the exile the Jerusalem council was composed of Levites, priests and heads of families (2 Chron 19:5-11). In the Maccabean period the Sanhedrin consisted of lay aristocracy and priests of Sadducean sympathy (1 Macc 7:33; 11:23; 14:28). In the time of Queen Alexandra, pharisaic scribes belonged to the assembly.

Both the NT and Josephus agree that in the first century the chief priests (*archiereis*) were the key figures in the Sanhedrin (Mt 27:41; Mk 14:53; Josephus *J.W.* 2.14.8 §301; 2.15.2—16.3 §§316-42). These were probably the former high priests and members of the priestly aristocracy from which the high priests were chosen and belonged to the party of the Sadducees (Acts 4:1; 5:17; Josephus *Ant.* 20.9.1 §199). The scribes (*grammateis*) were the second major component of the Sanhedrin and dominated the body (Acts 5:34; 23:6; Josephus *Ant.* 18.1.4 §17; *J.W.* 2.17.3 §411). In the Persian period all the members of the Sanhedrin (*gerousia*) were called "elders" (*presbyteroi*, 1 Macc 14:20; 2 Macc 4:44). By NT times the term "elders" was used for a third group consisting of priests and lay members of the nobility (Mt 26:3; 27:1; 28:11-12) within the Sanhedrin. From observing the synonyms for these elders we learn that they are leading men of the people (Lk 19:47; Josephus *Life* §194), the leading men of Jerusalem, the powerful and the dignitaries (Josephus *J.W.* 2.15.2 §316; 2.17.2 §410; *Life* §9).

Josephus says that, along with Ishmael the high priest and Helcias the treasurer, ten leading men were sent on a delegation to Nero (Josephus *Ant.* 20.8.11 §194). Also, as Greek cities had a committee of ten leading men, there may have been a group of the ten foremost members within the Sanhedrin.

The high priest was always the president of the Sanhedrin (1 Macc 14:44; Mt 26:57; Acts 5:17; 24:1; Josephus *Ag. Ap.* 2.24 §194; *Ant.* 20.9.1 §200; 20.10.1 §251). From the time of Herod the Great the high priest was often appointed arbitrarily and out of political considerations. Otherwise, the office was hereditary (Num 3:32; 25:11-13; 35:25, 28; Neh 12:10-11) and the Palestinian Talmud says that the high priest would not be elected high priest if he had not first been captain of the temple (*y. Yoma* 3:8, 41a. 5; cf. Josephus *J.W.* 2.17.2 §409).

Second in rank to the high priest was the captain of the temple (Hebrew, *sāgān* or *segen*, Aramaic *sĕgan*, Greek, *stratēgos*, Josephus *Ant.* 20.6.2 §131; Lk 22:4, 52; Acts 4:1, 24, 26; *m. Yoma* 3:1). Josephus also mentions a secretary of the Sanhedrin (Josephus *J.W.* 5.13.1 §532).

We know little of how people were appointed to the Sanhedrin, though they may have been co-opted (*m. Sanh.* 4:4) from among those of legitimate Israelite descent (*m. Qidd.* 4:5). Actual admission was through the laying on of hands (*m. Sanh.* 4:4; cf. Num 27:18-23; Deut 34:9).

5. Powers and Functions.

At least theoretically, the Jerusalem Sanhedrin's sphere of authority extended over the spiritual, political and legal affairs of all Jews (*m. Ta ʿan.* 3:6). Thus, the Mishnah says that where members of a local court disagreed on a point of law, the matter was referred to the Jerusalem court which sat at the gate of the Temple Mount. If the dispute could not be resolved, it went to the court which sat at the gate of the temple court. If a resolution was still not found, the Sanhedrin heard the dispute. Thereafter, on the pain of death, local judges were to follow the decision (*m. Sanh.* 11:2; cf. Josephus *Ant.* 4.10.8 §§214-18; *J.W.* 2.20.5 §§570-1). However, the sphere of authority and geographical area over which the Jerusalem Sanhedrin exercised jurisdiction varied greatly over time according to the relative freedom of the Jews in relation to the succession of foreign oppressors.

In the time of the Hasmonean rulers the whole of Palestine was a single political unit over which the Sanhedrin exercised oversight. When Gabinius (57-55 B.C.) divided Jewish territory into five areas, the authority of the Jerusalem Sanhedrin may have covered only one third of Judea (Josephus *Ant.* 14.15.4 §91; *J.W.* 1.8.5 §170). From the death of Herod the Great, Galilee and Perea were separate administrative regions so that the civil jurisdiction of the Jerusalem Sanhedrin did not extend beyond Judea. Thus while Jesus remained in Galilee, the Sanhedrin had no judicial authority over him. Even so, Luke says that the Sanhedrin authorized Paul to arrest Christians in Damascus (Acts 9:1-2; 22:5). Then Josephus says that in a peaceful period after the first stages of the Jewish War in A.D. 60, magistrates and members of the Sanhedrin dispersed from Jerusalem and collected the Roman taxes from the whole of Judea (Josephus *J.W.* 2.17.1 §405).

In A.D. 6 Augustus appointed a procurator for Judea "with full powers, including the affliction of capital punishment" (Josephus *J.W.* 2.8.1 §117). That the Sanhedrin could no longer order and execute a capital sentence is reflected in John 18:31 and in the rabbinic literature (*y. Sanh.* 18a; 24b; *b. Sanh.* 41a; *b. ʿAbod. Zar.* 8b). On the other hand, Josephus says (Josephus *J.W.* 5.5.2 §§193-94) that the second court of the temple was surrounded by a stone balustrade on which at regular intervals stood slabs giving warning in Greek and Latin: "No foreigner is to enter within the forecourt and the balustrade around the sanctuary. Whoever is caught will have himself to blame for his subsequent death" (*CIJ,* 1400 n. 85). This could be a special case granted to the Jews. In any case it is more likely to be a warning against being lynched (cf. Acts 6:8—8:2; Jn 10:31).

Also, Josephus says that the Sanhedrin condemned James, the brother of Jesus, to be stoned. In this case the procurator Porcius Festus had died and Ananus took the opportunity of convening the Sanhedrin before Albinus the new procurator had arrived (Josephus *Ant.* 20.9.1 §§197-203). Further, the Mishnah relates the burning of a priest's daughter convicted of adultery (*m. Sanh.* 7:2). Those who argue that the Sanhedrin did not have the power of death under the Roman procurators suggest that this took place during the brief reign of Agrippa I (A.D. 41-44) when the Jews had their own independent state. Whether or not the Sanhedrin was able to execute capital punishment, the Romans maintained the right to intervene when a political crime was suspected (Acts 22:30; 23:15; 20:28).

6. Times and Procedures.

The Sanhedrin probably met on the western boundary of the Temple Mount (Josephus *J.W.* 5.4.2 §144; 6.6.3 §354) in the "Hall of Hewn Stone" (*lishkat ha-gazit*), indicating that it was next to the gymnasium or Xystus (*gazit* = *xystos,* 1 Chron 22:2; Amos 5:11).

The night meeting in Mark 14:53 (par. Mt 26:57; Lk 22:54) was probably to be considered a preliminary hearing in the high priest's palace because trials could only be held in the hours of daylight (cf. Mk 15:1; *m. Sanh.* 4:1).

No record remains of the proceedings of the Jerusalem Sanhedrin. However, the Mishnah gives details of the judicial procedure of the lesser Sanhedrin of Twenty-Three, which may reflect procedure of the Jerusalem Sanhedrin before A.D. 70. Members sat in a half-circle so they could see each other. Before them stood two scribes, one writing down what was said in favor and the other what was said against the accused. Before them sat three rows of students, who could participate in noncapital trials (*m. Sanh.* 4:1-4).

Noncapital trials began with either case, but capital trials were to begin with the case for acquittal. A majority of one was sufficient in noncapital trials to acquit the accused of a capital charge. A majority of two was required for a guilty verdict on a capital charge. Verdicts could be reversed but not from an acquittal to a conviction in a capital trial. Those participating in the case could speak for and against the accused in noncapital trials. In capital trials a speaker in favor of conviction could only change and argue in favor of the accused, not the reverse. In non-capital cases the daytime trial could be followed by reaching a verdict that same night. In capital cases the verdict for an acquittal could be reached that night, but a verdict of conviction had to wait until the following day (*m. Sanh.* 4:1). In that way members of the Sanhedrin could go off in pairs to eat a little (no wine was permitted) and discuss the matter all night before meeting in court early next morning (*m. Sanh.* 5:5). Therefore, trials were not to be held on the days before a *sabbath or *festival (*m. Sanh.* 4:1). In capital cases voting began with the most junior members standing, each giving their verdict (*m. Sanh.* 5:5).

See also PRIESTS AND PRIESTHOOD, JEWISH; SCRIBES.

BIBLIOGRAPHY. E. Bammel, ed., *The Trial of Jesus* (London: SCM, 1970); J. Blinzler, *The Trial of Jesus* (Cork, U.K.: Mercer Press, 1959); T. A. Burkill, "The Competence of the Sanhedrin," *VC* 10 (1956) 80-96; D. R. Catchpole, *The Trial of Jesus* (Leiden: E. J. Brill, 1971); H. Danby, "The Bearing of the Rabbinical Criminal Code on the Jewish Trial Narratives in the Gospels," *JTS* 21 (1919-20) 51-76; S. B. Hoenig, *The Great Sanhedrin* (Philadelphia: Dropsie College, 1953); J. S. Kennard, "The Jewish Provincial Assembly," *ZNW* 53 (1962) 25-51; E. Lohse, "συνέδριον," *TDNT* 7:860-71; H. Mantel, *Studies in the History of the Sanhedrin* (Cambridge MA: Harvard University Press, 1961); E. Schürer, *The History of the Jewish People in the Age of Jesus Christ (175 B.C.-A.D. 135)*, rev. and ed. G. Vermes, F. Millar and M. Goodman (3 vols.; Edinburgh: T & T Clark, 1973-87) 2:199-226; P. Winter, *On the Trial of Jesus* (Berlin: Walter de Gruyter, 1974).

G. H. Twelftree

SAPIENTIAL WORK A. *See* APOCRYPHON OF MOSES; SECRET OF EXISTENCE (4Q412-413, 415-421).

SATAN. *See* BELIAL, BELIAR, DEVIL, SATAN.

SCHOLARSHIP, GREEK AND ROMAN

In a broad definition, encompassing the whole range of the intellectual activities of the human mind, the scholarship of late antiquity would undoubtedly include the analysis, systematization, codification and conservation of hitherto attained knowledge as well as new expressions of literary and other scientific accomplishments. This broad perspective would necessitate a discussion of all the different fields of literature and natural sciences—inasmuch as these too have come down to us in writing—in which important advances were made during the period under our purview, such as the various types of poetry and prose, literary criticism, grammar, lexicography, historiography, music, mathematics, geometry, geodesy, geography, astronomy, physics, mechanics, pneumatics, medicine, pharmacology, jurisprudence, *philosophy and *rhetoric. In this way the grandiose achievement of the *Hellenistic age and its significance as the matrix of the NT literature and its thought would come to its rightful place. However, the limits imposed upon the present article make it imperative to abandon the broader perspective and to concentrate instead on what is normally perceived to be the peculiarly original contribution of the times, that is, the scientification of the various literary disciplines. Nevertheless, a brief treatment of certain scientific discoveries, important for the worldview current in NT times, can hardly be omitted.

1. Greek Scholarship
1.1. Beginnings: Athens
1.2. Alexandrian Scholarship
1.3. Scholarship in Other Greek Centers
1.4. Greek Scholarship in the First and Second Centuries A.D.
1.5. A Few Other Types of Literary Writing

2. Latin Scholarship
2.1. The Beginnings of Latin Literatsure
2.2. Grammatical and Lexicographical Scholarship
2.3. Libraries in Rome
2.4. Latin Literature and Scholarship at Its Height
2.5. The Decline of Latin Literature in the First and Second Centuries A.D.

1. Greek Scholarship.

1.1. Beginnings: Athens. The rudimentary beginnings of textual, literary, grammatical, lexical and stylistic criticism were made in *Athens. The incentive was undoubtedly given by the collection of the Homeric epics and later also Hesiodic epics, which were made the basis of the *educational system. This, according to one view, probably went back to Solon (fl. 594/3 B.C.), who had decreed how the epics were to be recited (Diogenes Laertius Vit. 1.57) at the Panathenaea (Plato *Hipparch.* 228 b); according to another view (Cicero *De Orat.* 3.137; Pausanias *Descr.* 7.26) to Peisistratos (ruled 560-527 B.C.), who had committed the task to Onomacritus (Tzetzes *Prolegomena on Aristophanes*). The first concern was to produce an edition of the "scattered" Homeric texts (Pausanias Descr. 7.26); however, tampering with old texts was not unknown (cf. Herodotus *Hist.* 7.6) and may even have been considered necessary.

1.1.1. Textual Criticism. The influence of Homer on later poets—Alcman (fl. 657 B.C.), Archilochus (fl. 650 B.C.), Stesichorus (fl. 620 B.C.), Pindar (518-443 B.C.), to mention only a few—was enormous. The great tragedians Aeschylus (c. 535-456 B.C.), Sophocles (496-406 B.C.) and Euripides (c. 485-?406 B.C.), especially the former two, often exploited his themes in their verse, though the last frequently showed independence. Aristophanes freely admitted his debt (*Frogs* 1034ff.), while historians such as Herodotus (c. 484-post 430 B.C.) and Thucydides (c. 460-400 B.C.) were indebted to him. Homer's influence on Athenian and generally on Greek *paideia* was without rival: the motto of excellence in competition having being inspired from *Iliad* 6.208: "May you always excel and surpass (all) others." In his expeditions *Alexander the Great slept with a copy of *Aristotle's edition of the *Iliad* under his pillow (Plutarch *Alex.* 8). Of this edition we hear from Strabo (64 B.C.-A.D. 21; *Geog.* 13.1.27) and Plutarch (A.D. 46-120). The first philological critic, who is also credited with the first known edition (recension?) of Homer (Ἱστορία τοῦ ἑλληνικοῦ ἔθνους 5.306) was the epic-elegiac poet and scholar Antimachus of Colophon (born c. 444 B.C.). *Plato's interest in this poet was great enough to send Heraclides to Colophon to collect his works (Proclus *In Tim.* 1.90). All this implies not only that Homer and other poets were widely read and studied but also copied, edited and disseminated.

1.1.2. Criticism-Commentary. Although we can hardly speak of a strictly literary-critical treatment of ancient works at this period, Homer, Hesiod and other poets had had their critics, some friendly, others more hostile. One of the earliest admirers of Homer, who appreciated the poet's genius and lofty diction, was the atomic philosopher Democritus (460-357 B.C.) (cf. Dio Chrysostom *Or.* 53.1). The orator Isocrates (436-338 B.C.) extolled Homer for eulogizing those who had fought against foreign enemies, attributing to this the high esteem in which he was held at Athens (Isocrates *Paneg.* 159; *Panath.* 33-34). One of the foremost rhapsodists of classical times, Ion, claimed to be divinely inspired in transmitting the poet's inspired interpretation of the gods to the listeners (Plato *Ion* 533-535). He had apparently written the earliest commentary on Homer.

1.1.3. Sachkritik. Among the earliest critics of Homer's pantheon was Xenophanes of Colophon (c. 570-470 B.C.). In rationalistic fashion he accused Homer and Hesiod of having created their gods in human form, attributing to them "whatever is shameful among men" (Xenophanes frag. 11.2). Heraclitus of Ephesus (540-480 B.C.) declared that Homer should be "expelled from the contests and be beaten" (Heraclitus frag. 42), while the most merciless critics of Homer's theology were Euripides (e.g., Euripides frag. 63, *Heracl.* 211) and Aristophanes (e.g., Aristophanes *Pax* 57-63; *Av.* 554-60; *Eq.* 32-34, *Nub.* 366). Plato detested the Homeric pantheon (e.g., Plato *Leg.* 10.903, see also 885 c.) and had no place for Homer or Hesiod in his ideal state (e.g., Plato *Rep.* 377d-378e; 607a). Here we have the beginnings of the higher-critical occupation with Homer's ideas, theology and morals, that is, the beginnings of *Sachkritik* ("content criticism").

1.1.4. Literary Criticism. Literary criticism too makes its first appearance in Athens. The award of prizes at the various rhapsodical, lyric and dramatic contests presupposes competence in literary criticism. A decisive step is taken by Plato and Aristotle, but even here the subject is treated more or less as an interesting aside rather than as a serious scientific pursuit. Plato's view of poetry has its point of departure in his idealistic philosophy and his conception of the ideal state. It is true that in several of his dialogues (Plato *Phaed.* 245a; *Apol.* 22a-c; *Leg.* 719c, and especially in *Ion* 533-34d), Plato looks upon the poet as inspired, possessed, out of his mind, completely under the control of the Muses. But when he comes to speak of the poets' and the dramatists' place in his state, he speaks of their work not as inspiration and possession but as imitation. However, imitation has no place in his state because it is an imitation of the imitations of the real (Plato *Rep.* 394-95; 597e). Plato is also the first to treat of grammar in a broader sense. In his *Cratylus* he takes up a number of terms for etymological analysis. Although many of his etymologies are quite fanciful, the importance of the work is that words and in a sense language begin to attract attention as worthy objects of scientific inquiry.

Aristotle had inherited Plato's idea of poetry and other arts as imitation, but in his hands such artistic creations become the vehicle of universal truth (Aristotle *Poet.* 9). Hence, in his *Poetica* Aristotle takes up poetry for detailed analysis: "Severely scientific and masterly in method . . . it . . . stands out conspicuously in Greek literature as the earliest example of a systematic criticism of poetry . . . we shall find nothing in Greek literature until, in the Roman age, we ultimately reach the celebrated treatise *On the Sublime*" (Sandys, 1:75).

1.1.5. Rhetoric. The contribution of *rhetoric in this connection is not negligible. Brought from Sicily by Gorgias (483-376 B.C.), the celebrated pupil of Teisias, rhetoric took firm root in Athens. At least one of the great orators of the canon, Isocrates, was Gorgias's disciple. The Sicilian school had the tendency to intermingle poetical elements in their prose aiming at achieving beauty of language (*euepeia*), whereas the other branch of rhetorician-Sophists whose leader was Protagoras (c. 485-415 B.C.) and his disciples Prodikos (fifth century), Hippias (481-411 B.C.), the most encyclopedic teacher of his day, and possibly the Sophist Antiphon (fifth century; not to be confused with the orator Antiphon of Rhamnus) aimed at correctness of language (*orthoepeia*). If some of these authors had the tendency to succumb to an involved and ponderous style, such as the one we find in Thucydides, others, among them Lysias (459-380 B.C.), captivate by their simplicity and straightforwardness. Thrasymachus of Chalcedon (457-400 B.C.) chose a middle course, and in this he was followed by Isocrates and Plato. Lacking the natural gifts required for addressing great crowds, Isocrates established the first rhetorical school in Athens, which became duly famous, and through his many speeches he influenced as few others the political climate during his long life.

Prodicus is important for his etymological studies and his analysis of synonyms, while Hippias appears to have written one of the earliest handbooks on rhetoric (not extant). Other handbooks on rhetoric include those of Isocrates (lost); Anaximenes of Lampsacus's *Rhetoric to Alexander* (before 340 B.C.), wrongly attributed to Aristotle; and Aristotle's *Rhetorica* (both extant), which develops ideas put forth by Plato in his *Phaedrus.* The rhetoricians and Sophists contributed in particular by their analysis of speech into several parts and their emphasis on a cultivated and effective use of language aimed at gaining control over the minds of the listeners. With them words, etymology, synonyms, syntax and the effective use of oratory become subjects of analysis and inquiry.

1.1.6. Grammar. With respect to grammar, the Sophists were the first to distinguish gender in nouns: male, female and things. Plato distinguished between noun (or more correctly subject) and verb (predicate) (Plato *Soph.* 261e-262c) and between substantive and adjective (Plato *Parm.* 131a; *Soph.* 225d; *Phaed.* 238a). He recognized number (Plato *Soph.* 237d), tenses (Plato *Soph.* 262d; *Parm.* 151e; 156a) and active-passive (Plato *Soph.* 219b; *Phileb.* 26e).

In his *Cratylus* Plato touches on the problem of the meaning of words, on derivation and on etymology, and discerns onomatopoetic words. He seems to hold that language is based on nature (*physis*) but that it is modified by convention (*nomos*). Words normally have their meaning from their nature, but many of them are conventionally so named.

Aristotle categorizes the letters and speaks of declensions and conjugations, but these passages are thought to be interpolations. Elsewhere he speaks of the parts of speech as noun, verb and conjunctions. He is the first to have drawn a clear distinction between the subject (*hypokeimenon*) and the predicate (*kategoroumenon*) (Aristotle *Int.* 17-21).

1.2. Alexandrian Scholarship. With the Alexandrian age Greek scholarship passes from its faltering, rudimentary beginnings to a mature and sure handling of the various disciplines, from amateurish attempts at literary and grammatical criticism to a methodical, scientific treatment.

Alexandrian scholarship is connected with two famous institutions: the museum and the library (*see* Alexandrian Library; Alexandrian Scholarship).

1.2.1. Precursors of the Alexandrian Library: Early Book Collections and Libraries. The dissemination of the Homeric epics in archaic times presupposes the art of book production. During classical times we hear of bookstores in Athens selling works of contemporaries cheaply (Eupolis [430 B.C.], frag. 304; Plato *Apol.* 26d; *Phaed.* 97b; Aristomenes frag. 9; Nicophon frag. 14.9; Theopompos frag. 77), and around 400 B.C. cargos of books shipped to Pontos (Xenophon *Anab.* 7.5.14). This need not mean that books were published in large editions or that the majority of people owned books. However, men of letters and persons in high positions must have had their private libraries. We hear of the book collections of Polycrates of Samos (fl. 540 B.C.), Peisistratos of Athens (fl. 560-527 B.C.), Euripides (485-406 B.C.), Euclides, the Athenian Archon, who in 403 B.C. ratified the twenty-four-letter alphabet still in use, and Nicocrates of Cyprus (Athenaeus *Deipn.* 1.3a). Seleucus Nicanor had the books taken by Xerxes from Athens (480 B.C.) returned to their place (Aulus Gellius *Noc. Att.* 7.171-72). This implies the existence at the time of a public library or at least of book collections. It is assumed that Plato had his own library at the Academy. Aristotle (384-322 B.C.) had his private library, which he bequeathed to his pupil Theophrastus (372-288 B.C.), who in turn left it to Neleas (Strabo *Geog.* 13.1.54; Athenaeus *Deipn.* 1.3a; Diogenes Laertius *Vit.* 5.52). Epaphroditus of Chaeronea (first century A.D.) is said to have amassed a private library of some thirty thousand volumes (*Suda* E 2004; see also *OCD*^{3}, Libraries).

One of the first public libraries was apparently founded by Clearchus of Heraclea in Pontus (390-353 B.C.) (Memnon 1.1, 2; Photius *Bibl.* 222b). At a later date libraries were found in Pella, *Antioch, Rhodes, Cyprus and especially in Pergamum. Cities such as *Ephesus, Smyrna and Tarsus were renowned for their rhetorical schools, which imply the existence of libraries, some of them founded after the Alexandrian one. The Alexandrian museum and library thus constitute the apogee of a long tradition of centers of learning and research.

1.2.2. The Museum and the Library. In Greece the museum was a sanctuary for the worship of the Muses. It had an altar and open colonnades and was adorned with various statues. The Muses, nine in number (see Hesiod *Theog.* 75ff.), were deities, daughters of Zeus and Mnemosyne (= Memory), and were connected with music, dance, poetry and other fine arts. Being patrons of intellectual activities, they were the center around which both Plato's Academy and Aristotle's Lyceum (or Peripatos) were structured.

The link between Athens and *Alexandria was Demetrius Phalereus (c. 350-?283 B.C.), a pupil of Aristotle. Having been Cassander's regent in Athens (318-308 B.C.), this able politician and scholar took up service under Ptolemy I Soter, around 297 B.C., and was probably the instigator of the museum and the library (cf. Strabo *Geog.* 17.1.8; Plutarch *Mor.* 1095d-e, which do not, however, mention Demetrius). Having advised against the succession of Ptolemy II Philadelphus on the accession of the latter prince, Demetrius was banished and died soon thereafter. The museum, whose director was a priest, had a large number of researchers, who were furnished with free meals, received a high annual salary and were exempted from taxes.

The library, which was probably a separate institution but housed in the museum complex, was under the directorship of a librarian (see Fraser, 1:305-35; 2:462-94). The **Epistle of Aristeas* (9—10) states that Demetrius was the first librarian, but this is considered at least unlikely. The library's holdings are given for the time of Philadelphus as two hundred thousand books *(Ep. Arist.* 10), for the time of Callimachus as four hundred thousand (Tzetzes *Prolegomena to Scholia on Aristophanes* 11a.2.10-11), and in the first century B.C. as seven hundred thousand (Aulus Gellius *Noc. Att.* 6.17). This was a research library situated in the Broucheion district, where the palace was, there being another, smaller library with about forty thousand books, in the Serapeion district, open to the public.

To stock the library, the *Ptolemies spent large sums of money (though Aristeas's information of the mythical sums paid for the *Septuagint [LXX] is unworthy of credit), but sometimes they also resorted to deceitful means (e.g., they borrowed the Athenian edition of the tragedians to copy it, giving fifteen talents as guarantee for its return, but then kept the original, sending back a copy and relinquishing the fifteen talents). They were also in the habit of confiscating all books found in ships visiting Alexandria (Galen *Hypomn. Hippoc., Epid. III,* Kühn, 17a:606-7). It was their ambition to include not only all Greek literature but also all literature written in any language. It is against this greater context that the translation of the LXX ought to be viewed.

Henceforth the history of scholarship is more or less bound up with the work of the Alexandrian librarians and other museum scholars. The main sources for Alexandrian scholarship are the few remains of their many and varied works, the scholia of Byzantine scholiasts, which take up their text editions or recensions, treatises, commentaries, grammars and lexica; the erudite Byzantine scholar Ioannes Tzetzes; and the *Suda* lexicon. The dates of the librarians and certain other scholars are only approximate.

Who the librarians were and in which order they succeeded one another had long been a standing problem until the discovery of *Oxyrhyncus Papyrus* 1241 (second century A.D.). According to the second column of this document the librarians were

> [Apollo]n[i]os the Alexandrian, son of Silleus, called Rhodios—he was succeeded by Eratosthenes, who was followed by Aristophanes Byzantios, son of Appelos, and Aristarchos; thereafter Apollonios the Alexandrian, called [E]idographos; after him Aristarchos the Alexandrian, son of Aristarchos (originally Samothrax)—after him Kydas one of the Lancers; under the ninth [k]ing there flourished the Grammarians: Ammo[ni]os, Zeno[dotus], Dio[kl]es, and Apollo[d]oros.

This document is problematic: the list begins with Apollonius of Rhodes, but we know that Zenodotus had preceded him (*Suda* Z 74). It is therefore generally surmised that the name of Zenodotus was written at the end of the first column, now lost. Moreover, between Aristophanes of Byzantium and Apollonius of Eidographus the papyrus interjects another Aristarchus, who has never existed.

Alexandrian scholarship is usually divided into three periods: the formative period, the period of maturity and the period of decline.

1.2.2.1. The Formative Period. Zenodotus of Ephesus (325-260 B.C.), pupil of Philitas, is the first librarian (284-?260 B.C.) and the first great scholar. His *Glossai,* a kind of alphabetically arranged glossary on rare Homeric words, was probably the first attempt at a lexicon, giving impetus to the critical study of language. His lasting work was his recension of Homer (he also edited Hesiod, Anacreon and Pindar), the first critical edition ever by means of collation of different manuscripts. Zenodotus is probably the scholar who gave the definitive form to the *Iliad* and the *Odyssey,* dividing them into twenty-four books each. Of even greater importance was his introduction of critical marks (developed further by Aristophanes of Byzantium and Aristarchus), like *obeloi* (-), asterisks (*) and *diple* (>), to mark doubtful lines. (Similar critical marks were later used by Origen, who was nurtured in the Alexandrian tradition, in his edition of his *Hexapla).* Zenodotus's scientific insight and objectivity is attested by the fact that he did not remove any text that appeared to him suspect, but he marked it and left it in place, thus enabling future scholars to continue their critical work. He occasionally emended the text, for which he has been maligned by ancients and disparaged by moderns, but many of his rejected corrections have now turned up in old papyri. He is the link between the older tradition of the Homeric text—not available to later scholars—and the Alexandrian recensions. With no prototype to follow, he was the great pioneer.

Apollonius of Rhodes (born c. 295 B.C.), disciple of Callimachus, succeeded Zenodotus around 270 or 260 B.C. and, following his quarrel with Callimachus, retired to Rhodes around 247 B.C. He is the greatest epic poet of this period through his celebrated *Argonautica,* an epic of 5,834 dactylic hexameters. As a scholar his main work seems to have been an attack on Zenodotus's edition of Homer. He preferred the pre-Zenodotian form of Homer, and he worked on Hesiod and Archilochus. In Rhodes he exerted considerable influence on scholarship.

Callimachus of Cyrene (c. 305-240 B.C.), one of the most illustrious Alexandrian poet-scholars, worked in the library, though according to *Oxyrhyncus Papyrus* 1241 he never served as librarian. He wrote on antiquities, language and literary criticism. Drawing inspiration and models from works of the past, he produced a novel, independent and exquisite poetry (e.g., *Aeitia,* fragments survive). His main work, and his significance from the standpoint of scholarship is, however, the *Pinakes (Tables of Persons Illustrious in Every Department of Learning, as Well as of Their Writings)* in 120 books. Of this important and influential work (see Pfeiffer, 127-34)—a first scientific attempt at literary history—which must have been of inestimable value in cataloging the library and classifying its treasures, almost nothing remains. These *Pinakes* may have been the source for many biographical details found in later authors (e.g., Hesychios, *Suda*, Tzetzes). He also wrote another, similar *Pinakes* on *Didaskaloi* (dramatic poets). In the area of prose Callimachus wrote several books on strange and paradoxical phenomena in various places. According to *Suda* (K 227) he wrote more than eight hundred books.

The successor of Apollonius of Rhodes was Eratosthenes, also of Cyrene (285-194 B.C.). Eratosthenes, a pupil of the philosopher Ariston, the grammarian Lysanias and Callimachus

Years	**Kings of Egypt**	**Years**	**Grammarians & Other Scholars (according to P Oxy 1241)**
305			
	Ptolemy I Soter I		
285		285	
	Ptolemy II Philadelphus		Zenodotus (325-260 B.C.
		270	Apollonius of Rhodes (c. 295-240 B.C.)
246		245	
	Ptolemy III Euergetes		Eratosthenes (285-194 B.C.
221			
	Ptolemy IV Philopator		
204			
	Ptolemy V Epiphanes		
		194	
			Aristophanes of Byzantium (257-180 B.C.)
180		180	
	Ptolemy VI Philopator		Apollonius Eidographus
		153	
			Aristarchus of Samothrace (217-145 B.C.)
145		145	
	Ptolemy VII New Philopator		Cydas the Lancer (Librarian?)
145			
	Ptolemy VIII Euergetes II		
116		116	
	Ptolemy IX Stoer II		Ammonius (2nd cent. B.C.)
			Zenodotus (2nd-1st cent. B.C.)
			Diocles (2nd cent. B.C.)
			Apollodorus Athenaius (180?-109 B.C.)
107		107	
	Ptolemy X Alexander I		
88			
	Ptolemy IX. Soter II		
80			
	Ptolemy XI. Alexander II?		Dionysius Thrax (170-90 B.C.)
80			(Pupil of Aristarchus)
	Ptolemy XII. New Dionysus		
51			
	Ptolemy XIII/Cleopatra VII?		Didymus Chalkenteros (80-10 B.C.)
47			(Aristarchian
	Ptolemy XIV/Cleopatra VII		
44			
	Cleopatra VII		
31			

SCHOLARS OF ALEXANDRIA

(*Suda* E 2898), was the first real scholar whose research interests were truly universalistic: as chronographer he was the first author to disregard the mythical element in his *History* from the fall of Troy to Alexander the Great; he was the first writer to treat geography in a scientific way. He was a not inconsiderable mathematician, astronomer (e.g., he compiled a list 675 stars) and geodesist, and he succeeded in measuring the circumference of the earth with stupendous precision; as poet he was praised by that excellent literary critic [pseudo-] Longinus [hence "Longinos"] *(Peri Hypsous)*. As philosopher he belonged to the Platonic school; finally, as a literary critic he wrote his masterpiece on Old Comedy in twelve books, in which he corrected previous views (Lycophron, Callimachus), on such questions as authorship, dating, textual criticism and subject matter. He was the first to assume the title of *philologos,* that is, a man of erudition. He also had a modern outlook on Homer: asked about the wanderings of Odysseus, he replied: "The scenes of Odysseus' wanderings will be found when you find the cobbler who sewed up the bag of winds, and not before" (Strabo *Geog.* 1.2.14).

With Eratosthenes ends the first period of Alexandrian scholarship. The museum and the library had now been established as renowned institutions of research, unique in the world; books had been amassed as never before; the fundamental authors in Greek education had been edited and recensions seeking to establish the original text had followed one upon another. Principles of criticism had been laid down, commentary work had been commenced; lexicography and grammar had seen the light of day; and literary analysis had become an established science. Applied mathematics and natural sciences—geography, geodesy, astronomy and others—had advanced, and the answers presented had become more satisfactory. In short, the worldview of the times was beginning to wear a modern garb.

It now remained to consolidate the gains and to push the frontiers of research further, nearer the ultimate goal. This was to be achieved in the next period, the period of maturity.

1.2.2.2. The Period of Maturity. With Aristophanes of Byzantium (257-180 B.C.), successor of Eratosthenes and pupil of Zenodotus and Callimachus, we pass into the era of maturity. Aristophanes was a mature scholar of sixty-two when he became head of the library. He carried the work of his predecessors so far that he overshadowed their contributions. His work was many-sided. He improved on Eratosthenes in the edition of Homer, in which, like him, instead of removing lines or taking to conjectures, he indicated his critical work and preferences by means of critical symbols in the margins, augmenting Eratosthenes' text-critical sign-system considerably. He is also the scholar who established the use of punctuation marks (some of which are witnessed in very early inscriptions, are mentioned by classical scholars and are used occasionally in early papyri) and was the first to use accents. His editions of the lyric poets surpassed even his work on Homer, and he was the first scholar to divide the songs into colometric lines. Not much of his work on the tragic poets remains, but some of his plots to the various plays survive. Through his work *Lexeis* ("Words") he opened up a new area of research, which addressed the evolution of the Greek language: it treated old, dialectal and colloquial forms of his time, morphology and etymology. He also propounded the linguistic theory of analogy, that is, the regularity of declension of substantives. Aristophanes was one of the greatest scholars of the Hellenistic age.

Aristophanes was succeeded (c. 180 B.C.) by his pupil Apollonius Eidographos (i.e., Classifier). We know practically nothing of his work, except that he had special abilities in classifying the holdings of the library according to their literary genre—a service that must at this stage have been most welcome.

One of the greatest scholars of late antiquity is Aristarchus of Samothrace (217-145 B.C.), the successor of Apollonius Eidographos (in 153 B.C.) and a disciple of Aristophanes. With Aristarchus's philological work we reach the zenith of literary scholarship. His work covers many areas: grammar, orthography, etymology, and literary and philological criticism. He was called *Grammatikotatos* (the Grammarian par excellence), as well as *Mantis* ("wizard") on account of his critical and hermeneutical excellence. He surpassed the previous librarians in pure scientific knowledge. Among his writings may be mentioned recensions, commentaries and treatises on Homer and other authors. It is said that he wrote more than eight hundred commentaries on authors down to his own time (*Suda* A 3892). He used polemics against earlier scholars, especially those who denied the unity of Homer. He was the first to comment on a prose author such as Herodotus (possibly also Thucydides). In his grammarian's work he developed further Aristophanes' declension rules and recognized eight parts of speech. He developed further Aristophanes' principle of analogy in the declension of substantives and verbs, and he drew the attacks of the Pergamene scholars, who propounded the opposite principle of anomaly or irregularity in declension.

1.2.2.3. The Period of Decline. With Aristarchus ends the period of maturity, and scholarship is set on trial. Ptolemy VIII Euergetes II (Physcon) (145-116 B.C.) broke the benevolent tradition of the Ptolemies toward the intelligentsia, and the persecuted Alexandrian scholars found themselves scattered in various parts of the Greek world. This led to the establishment of many institutions of learning in other Greek cities such as Rhodes. The *Oxyrhyncus Papyrus* 1241 speaks of Cydas, the next person in charge of the library, as one of the lancers. Nothing is known of this person, and it is surmised that he served in some capacity other than as an ordinary librarian. There was apparently a hiatus in the function of the library, since the successor to Aristarchus, his disciple Ammonius, is said to have flourished together with his own successors—Zenodotus, Diocles and Apollodorus—during the reign of Ptolemy IX Soter (116-107 B.C.). Nine years is a brief period for four librarians, and there is the added difficulty that Apollodorus had left Alexandria in 145 B.C. for Pergamum and Athens, apparently never to return to Alexandria. Perhaps this document, which has been taken as basic for the order of the librarians, is not so well informed after all.

Dionysius Thrax (170-90 B.C.) is one of the better known pupils of Aristarchus and the only Alexandrian whose *Grammatikē Technē* (sometimes attributed to another) has survived. Being the oldest grammarian, he defines grammar as an *empeiria* ("experience," "acquaintance," "knowledge," "practice") "of the usual subject matter found in poets and prose authors" *(Grammatikē estin empeiria tōn para poietais te kai syngrafeusin hōs epi to poly legomenōn).* He treats letters and syllables, the parts of speech, cases (four, to which he adds the vocative), moods, tenses, accents, spirits and stops. The article includes the relative pronoun. His book takes up declensions and conjugations but contains nothing about syntax. This grammar reigned supreme and through Latin came to influence the grammatical terminology and approach to grammar in most European languages. Dionysius migrated to Rhodes probably during Euergetes II's persecution of the Alexandrian scholars.

The last great Alexandrian is Didymus Alexandreus (80-10 B.C.). He lacked somewhat in originality, but he had an enormous capacity for work, earning the sobriquet *Chalkenteros* ("having intestines of bronze"), and his works are computed to more than thirty-five hundred books (*Suda* D 872). Among his works may be mentioned his lexica on rare and obscure terms, as well as on the tragic and comic poets. His commentaries were steeped in literary, philological, mythological and historical notes. As the last in the long line of eminent Alexandrian scholars, he summarizes their great and lasting achievement.

With the fall of Egypt, the center of interest moves to various Greek cities as well as to Rome.

1.3. Scholarship in Other Greek Centers.

1.3.1. Pergamum. No sooner had the foundation of Pergamum as the capital of the new kingdom by that name been laid than its kings conceived the design of establishing their city as a center of learning, able to compete with Alexandria. Already its first ruler, Eumenes I (263-241 B.C.), showed himself a patron of letters, while his successor, Attalos I (241-197 B.C.), the first king properly speaking, made strenuous efforts to attract men of letters to his city and began collecting books. The library was apparently erected under his successor, Eumenes II (197-159 B.C.) (Strabo *Geog.* 13.1.54; 4.2). In its greatest extent the library had some two hundred thousand volumes. The scholar who set his stamp upon Pergamene scholarship was Crates of Mallus, a follower of *Stoic teaching. He introduced the allegorical interpretation of Homer. He was an opponent of the great Alexandrians Aristophanes and Aristarchus in this as well as in propounding anomaly against their principle of analogy in grammar. This dispute was bequeathed to their successors. His visit to *Rome (c. 168 B.C.) had unexpected results: owing to an accident, he took to lecturing during his recuperation (Suetonius *Gram.* 2). These lectures awakened the Romans' interest in scholarship and libraries.

Pergamum is usually credited with the momentous invention of parchment (Gk *perga-*

mēnē), when Ptolemy V Epiphanes refused to export papyrus to Eumenes II (Varro, according to Pliny *Nat. Hist.* 13.70). However, since parchment had been used as writing material earlier in the Greek world, Pergamum's contribution may have been a more refined method of producing such material.

Other famous scholars in Pergamum were Crates' disciple Panaetius (185-110 B.C.), as well as Apollodorus of Pergamum (102-20 B.C.) and Alexander Polyhistor (105-c. 35 B.C.), both of whom settled in Rome. The interests of the school of Pergamum differed from those of Alexandria. Besides literary matters, they attended to such pursuits as the history of art (Antigonus of Carystus), the study of inscriptions and travel (Polemon of Ilion), chronology (Apollodorus of Athens) and topography (Demetrius of Scepsis).

1.3.2. Athens. As the mother of arts, Athens held throughout antiquity its place of honor. In importance of scholarship, however, it could not compete with Alexandria or Pergamum. Nevertheless, it was the home of the four schools of philosophy, the Academy (Platonists), the Peripatos (Aristotelians), the Stoa (Stoics) and the Garden (Kēpos) (*Epicureans). The first and oldest of these was also the last to close down (in 529 A.D. under Justinian).

1.3.3. Pella. The *Macedonian capital was a literary center only during the reign of Antigonus Gonatas (275-239 B.C.). The king, himself a pupil of Megarian philosopher Euphantus, and a friend of Zenon, attracted to his capital philosophers and poets such as Timon of Phlius, Alexander Aetolus and Aratus (315-?240 B.C.), whose *Phaenomena* (1.5) is quoted in Acts 17:28.

1.3.4. Rhodes. Already in the mid-third century B.C. Rhodes had welcomed the greatest epic author of Hellenistic times, Apollonius of Rhodes, while a century later it received a new impulse from another Alexandrian, Dionysius Thrax (Strabo *Geog.* 14.2.13), who helped establish Rhodian scholarship and was teacher of Panaetius. Rhodes was also famous as a school of rhetoric, and among its celebrities it numbered the Stoic Panaetius, his disciple, the great Poseidonius (138-45 B.C.), and Molon, the last two of whom had taught such Romans as *Cicero, *Pompey and Castor and (esp. Poseidonius) deeply influenced Caesar, Sallust, Lucretius and Livy.

1.3.5. Antioch. Little is known of Antiochean scholarship, but it is well-established that the *Seleucids were patrons not only of medicine but also of the literary arts. We know of a public library that reckoned as one of its librarians Euphorion of Chalcis (born 276 B.C.) under Antiochus the Great (224-181 B.C.) (cf. *Suda* E 3801).

1.3.6. Tarsus. Tarsus was well known for its philosophical and rhetorical schools, but it catered only to native pupils—foreigners were not attracted to it—and even these completed their education in other cities, with most of them never returning to their native city (Strabo *Geog.* 14.5.10-15).

1.4. Greek Scholarship in the First and Second Centuries A.D. The first two centuries of the Christian era see a change in the interests of scholarship. It is above all the age of grammar and lexicography, as well as of literary criticism.

1.4.1. Grammar and Lexicography. One of the main grammarians of this period was Theon (first century A.D.) son of the Tarsian grammarian Artemidorus. He wrote commentaries on epic as well as Hellenistic writers; lexica on tragedy and comedy and one of the earliest works on syntax. Another writer on syntax was Lesbonax (first century A.D.). He treated difficult points of syntax, important for researching the spoken language as well as various dialects.

Apollonius Dyscolus and his son Herodianus are the greatest grammarians of the second century. Apollonius, who died in extreme poverty in what once was a thriving center of learning, the quarter of the Alexandrian library, had one of the finest scientific minds and a deep dedication to his work. Of some twenty important contributions only portions of four have survived: on pronouns, conjunctions, adverbs and syntax. But these give us a sufficiently clear view of his greatness. He put the study of grammar and syntax in particular on a scientific basis. Herodianus's main work was his *Katholikē Prosōdia,* in twenty-one books, fragments of which survive through later citations. In this work he dealt with the accentuation of sixty thousand words. The rest of his works treat the parts of speech, figures, conjunctions and declensions, as well as include an Atticist lexicon *(Philetairos).* He was a moderate adherent of analogy, disagreeing with his father's extreme position. He was the last great, original grammarian.

With regard to lexicography, from this period dates the great lexicon produced by Pamphilus (fl. 50 A.D., lost) in ninety-five books. This lexicon was condensed by Diogenianus (second century A.D.) into five books, whose edition was used by Hesychius (fifth century A.D.) for his own lexicon (extant: fifty-three thousand lemmata), and later by *Suda* and Photius. Other authors of this period include Herennius of Byblos (first to second centuries A.D.), who wrote a lexicon on synonyms, on which a certain Ammonius based his own work; Polydeuces of Naucratis (second century A.D.) wrote an *Onomastikon,* extant in summary form, and Harpocration (first to second centuries A.D.), an epitome of whose lexicon on the ten orators has come down to us.

Of strict Atticist lexicographers mention may be made of Phrynichus and Moiris. Phrynichus (fl. 180 A.D.) wrote his *Sophistic Preparation,* a lexicon in thirty-seven books, parts of which are preserved by Photius, as well as his *Attikistēs* (extant), in which he condemns un-Attic forms (many of which occur in the NT). Of the work of Moiris (slightly younger than Phrynichus), his *Attic Words* (extant) investigates points of diction and style, the choice of correct vocabulary, which must be Attic, and other topics.

1.4.2. Rhetoric, Asianism and Second Sophistic. *Rhetoric had been attacked by Plato as unphilosophical and unethical in its pursuits (e.g., *Gorg.* 461b-481b; *Phaedr.* 259e-262c), though his relations to Isocrates, the leading rhetorician of his day with a school, are not quite clear. By his strictly scientific *Technē Rhētorikē* Aristotle had raised rhetoric to the level of a serious discipline based on philosophical foundations. However, by the middle of the third century B.C. rhetoric had lost its original, fresh charm and was reduced to a scholastic enterprise. This transformation was effected by a new current that flowed from certain cities in Asia Minor, which gave it the name "Asianist zeal" (Plutarch *Anton.* 2.5). Asianism was characterized by profuse, bombastic and flowery styles, which had no interest in the subject matter, their chief purpose being to flatter and persuade ("to tickle the ears," Aelius Aristides *Or.* 50, 405). This new genre, initiated chiefly by Hegesias of Magnesia (fl. 250 B.C.; cf. Strabo *Geog.* 14.1.41; for criticism of Hegesias see Dionysius of Halicarnassus *Comp.* 18; *Ant. Or.* 1). Later Asianists include M. Antonius (Plutarch *Anton.* 2.5), Polemon of Laodicea (A.D. 90-145; cf. *Suda* P 1889) and (partly) Aelius Aristides (cf. his *Or.* 14: *Encomium of Rome* and *Or.* 15: *On Smyrna),* who became a model for later times, and came to dominate Greek education. This led to a renewed attack by the philosophical schools, but this attack was soon offset by Hermagoras's (fl. 150 B.C.) reforming measures, which paid greater attention to the subject matter of speeches. From the following century on the Romans became interested in it, not least the *emperors, who needed the rhetoricians to sing their praise, and this gave rhetoric not merely a new lease of life but a period of popularity and luster. Rhetoric had triumphed over philosophy.

Many of these rhetoricians, having lost their political independence, now also surrendered their personal freedom and abjectly served the base interests of their *patrons, overlooking Roman corruption and injustice (their wretched life is depicted in Lucian *Salaried Posts,* passim. For similar treatment of Romans, see Juvenal *Sat.* 1.1-5). In the words of "Longinus's" philosopher friend (Longinus *Subl.* 44.1-3), who echoed the current view, "democracy is the good nurturer of greatness, and great authors flourished with democracy and died with it . . . we who live now . . . seem to have learned in our infancy to live under justified slavery . . . we end up as masters of flattery." His maxim was "No slave should be a rhetor!" Even more serious rhetoricians like Dio Chrysostom (A.D. 40-112) and Aelius Aristides (c. A.D. 129-181), who occasionally pointed out injustice (e.g. Dio Chrysostom *Or.* 34.51: "fellow slaves"; 38.37: "use you like small children") not infrequently sang encomia on Romans and counseled Greek cities to submission (e.g., Dio Chrysostom *Or.* 1.15-36; 34.45-51; Aelius Aristides *Or.* 14). The times and the political situation made impossible the exercise of true rhetoric. The days of Demosthenes were long past.

This bitter experience led already in the middle of the first century B.C. to the Atticist revival. This movement rejected Asianism in all its forms, advocating a return to the classical standards. But even this new direction was exploited in the interests of rhetoric. Early in the second century A.D. begins the last phase of old rhetoric. It is now known as the Second Sophistic; its chief representatives are Herodes Atticus (A.D. 101-177) and Aelius Aristides (on the sophists see Philostratus's *Lives of the Sophists).* Having established itself in the educational system and having drawn inspiration from the Atticist revival, it came under the influence of such Asiatic centers as Ephesus, Smyrna and Tarsus. It gave up its earlier doctrines and was reduced to a scholastic movement, whose chief contributions to theory and practice were the *Progymnasmata,* that is, preliminary exercises (cf. Theon, Hermogenes, et al.).

1.4.3. Atticism and Literary Criticism. The Atticist movement was not solely a reaction to Asianist rhetoric. It was also a reaction to a new double-faceted situation. The unification of the Greek states under Alexander had led to the amalgamation of the Greek dialects producing a new linguistic medium, the *Koinē,* in which Attic formed the basic understructure. In Alexander's vast empire the majority of Greeks spoke a language that was relatively different in vocabulary, form and syntax from Attic Greek. This was now felt to be a downgrade development. To crown it all, Alexander's conquests had brought under the Greek umbrella countless types of peoples of diverse linguistic backgrounds and varying proficiency in Greek, who consciously or unconsciously had introduced barbarous elements into the Greek language (cf. the Egyptian papyri). This situation continued to obtain even after the Roman conquest.

The other reason was political. The Roman conquest proved a traumatic experience to most Greeks. Having been nurtured in the spirit of democracy, many Greeks found themselves caught up first in Macedonian despotism and then in Roman imperialism. All that went to make a free citizen with dignity and honor, they felt, was denied to them. Unqualified freedom in debate, which had been the Greeks' sphere of life, was stifled. The hopelessness of ever being able to free themselves from the Roman yoke induced many of them to play along to survive.

Thus, the same historical reality that had reduced rhetoric, Asianist or otherwise, to encomiastic compositions singing the praises of their Roman "benefactors" was also at work behind the Atticist revival, though here it took the opposite course. The Atticist revival was a reawakening of the Greeks' national consciousness. It was an outlet for their frustrations. The climate not being conducive to creative and original intellectual work, they turned to dreaming of their glorious past, extolling their ancestors, reassuming their Greek names, which they had abandoned for Roman ones (cf. the criticisms of Apollonius of Tyana *Ep.* 71, and of the Stoics generally) and voicing their opinion that a higher civilization had been defeated by an inferior one (cf. the young Stoic's taunt "The Latin race in general were uncivilized rustics," Aulus Gellius *Noc. Att.* 1.2.4; *IEE* 6:560-81). The astute Romans not only allowed this but even encouraged it, because it had the potential for peace: the turning of the Greeks' attention to their glorious past correspondingly took it away from their present predicament and made their plight more bearable. Further, the Romans' adopting of the Greek culture—which was inevitable, given its superiority and ubiquity—and the opening of the highest offices of the empire (consul and senator; *see* Roman Empire) to Greeks were also promulgated consciously in order to render impossible any permanent rift between them and the Greek world.

But notwithstanding what the causes that had brought about the Atticist revival were, Atticism became a powerful movement, reaching its peak in the second century A.D., though its force was all expended on linguistic battles and never took any other form, political or military. Nevertheless, Atticism, Asianism, literary criticism and rhetoric and Second Sophistic were all entangled in a literary tug of war, and it is this intellectual climate that formed the context, the stage in which Christianity and the NT appeared. Atticism had many advocates who distinguished themselves in various literary fields: Dionysius of Halicarnassus: literary theory and criticism, rhetoric; Plutarch (A.D. 46-post 120): moral philosophy; Herodes Atticus: the most famous representative of the Second Sophistic; Dio Chrysostom and Aelius Aristides: rhetoric; Harpocration (? second century A.D.) and Polydeuces (late second century A.D.): lexicography; Phrynichus (fl. 180 A.D.) and Moiris (fl. 185 A.D.): Attic diction; Lucian (c. A.D. 120-post 180): criticism and satire; Athenaeus (fl. 200 A.D.): banqueting sophists; Philostratus (A.D. 160-244): biography.

The achievement of the Atticist movement was that it arrested the downgrade course that the Greek language had taken through its multifarious users. It set a stop to the importation of foreign elements for which there were Greek equivalents; it condemned forms and syntax not witnessed in the best classical authors; it preserved the high ideals of linguistic perfection set in classical times; in short, it preserved the language intact throughout Byzantine and into modern Greek times (the *Katharevousa,* pure or Atticistic Modern Greek). This puristic movement received a mortal blow in the legislation of 1975, whereby the popular, Demotic form of Greek (descended from Koine Greek) was declared the official language of Greece in place of *Katharevousa,* but it is still not quite dead.

The Atticist revival has often been criticized for looking back, especially by advocates of the Demotic form of Modern Greek. However, its beneficial influence upon the Greek language cannot be overestimated. It is thanks to the Atticist movement that Modern Greek is, after more than two thousand years, still Greek, in fact, closer to ancient Greek than any other European language is to its own past of only a few centuries.

Of the many important Atticists, only a few specimens will be taken up briefly, to illustrate their contribution to scholarship in general and to literary criticism in particular.

In the four centuries that elapsed between Aristotle's *Technē Rhētorikē* and "Longinus" *Peri Hypsous* (or *On the Sublime*) no other writer addressed literary criticism as successfully as did Dionysius of Halicarnassus (fl. 30-8 B.C.). His work covers many areas: history, rhetoric, literary criticism, grammar. His literary theories are expounded in his *On Literary Composition* and *Comments on the Ancient Orators.* As one of the founders of the Atticist movement, Dionysius's main aim was to portray the Attic authors, and in particular Demosthenes, as the highest example of prose to follow. His writings reveal a genuine feeling for style best achieved in charm (*hēdonē*) (Dionysius of Halicarnassus *Comp.* 10), that is, freshness, gracefulness, euphony, sweetness, persuasiveness (*Comp.* 11) and beauty (*to kalon*): grandeur, forcefulness, solemnity, dignity (*Comp.* 10). This was partly directed against the bombastic traits of the Asianist movement in rhetoric, though Dionysius's concerns were constructive rather than polemical, and his work has been greatly appreciated in ancient, medieval and even modern times.

Another Atticist was Dionysius's friend probably of Jewish background, Caecilius of Caleacte, Sicily, who wrote on the Ten Orators of the Canon, a *Technē Rhētorikē, Against the Phrygians,* attacking Asianism, a lexicon on Attic Greek with the Hellenistic Greek equivalents, as well as a treatise, *Peri Hypsous* (or *On the Sublime*) criticized with some appreciation by "Longinus" in his own work by that title.

Plutarch of Chaeronea, one of the most popular authors of antiquity, was a Platonist with a deep concern for ethics. His preserved works fall into two parts: his *Lives* (or *Vitae*) and his ethical writings (*Moralia*). His *Lives* contain twenty-two pairs of one Greek and one Roman, usually with a comparison, with a view to drawing ethical conclusions. To these must be added four more single biographies. The second part of his work, his ethical writings, take up a wide variety of ethical questions (where Plutarch's pedagogical concerns are obvious) and even literary aspects. He has thus preserved many quotations of works otherwise lost; he treats of Homer and other poets (disapproving of Aristophanes as a model on account of his coarse language), making literary remarks on them, but these are always subordinate to his chief aim, to moralize. Plutarch's relevance for NT studies lies in the genre of his biographies, preceded by Aristoxenos, fourth century B.C. and followed by Suetonius, Diogenes Laertius, Philostratus, Eunapius, et al., in which he states his purpose to be to present portraits of character rather than merely historical facts (Plutarch *Alex.* 1.2-3; see also *Nic.* 1.5), the relevance of which is obvious for the Gospel genre (*see* Biography, Ancient), and in his ethical writings, which were found by many church fathers to be precursors of Christian teaching.

*Lucian of Samosata is a most versatile author, but above all the great satirist of Sophists and rhetors. He parodied the superficiality of the Sophists, the affectations of rhetors and the blunders of fanatic Atticists, although he was an Atticist himself. His writings exhibit considerable wit, but he has not given us much of special value as far as literary criticism is concerned.

The greatest piece of literary criticism in antiquity is a brief writing of which only two-thirds survive: *Peri Hypsous* (*On the Sublime*). The manuscripts often bear the doubtful ascription "Dionysius [i.e., Dionysius of Halicarnassus] or Longinus" (i.e., Cassius Longinus, d. 273 A.D.), while a Florentine manuscript ascribes it to an anonymous author. It is usually assigned to the first century A.D. The aim of the author is to treat of literary criticism in general, but with special emphasis on the qualities that make style elevated. These qualities are grandeur in conception, intensity of emotion, elegance, nobility in diction and dignified and elevated composition (Longinus *Subl.* 8.1-2). Negatively, it implies the avoidance of bombastry, puerility, inelegance, bad taste and the like (*Subl.* 3-5; cf. 41-43). He subjects a great number of classical passages to a penetrating criticism to illustrate sublimity and the absence of it. According to the author sublimity is the absolute criterion of real poetry. It is the echo of a great soul (*Subl.* 9.1). Sublimity is thus akin to divine high-mindedness. Sublimity is possible only for a poet with a great, heroic nature. Real genius is aware of the laws governing literary composition but is never enslaved to them. In his worldview the author seems to admire not so much the order and harmony of each part as the magnitude and grandeur of the whole. In all this the influence of the Stoa is perhaps to be suspected. This writing is unique in pagan literature in quoting a biblical text. At 9.9 it cites Genesis 1:3: "God said: 'Let there be light,' and there was light," as an example of true sublimity. With "Longinus's" *Peri Hypsous* we reach the zenith of literary theory and criticism in poetry as well as prose. His precepts are equally valid for rhetoric.

1.5. A Few Other Types of Literary Writing.

1.5.1. Historiography. The long tradition of Greek historiography (Hecataeus, Hellanicus, Herodotus, Thucydides, Xenophon), was continued during our period by such authors as Polybius (203-120 B.C.), Poseidonius (first to second centuries B.C.), Diodorus Siculus (first century B.C.), Dionysius of Halicarnassus, Appian (first to second century A.D.), Arrian (first to second centuries A.D.), and others. Polybius was the first historian to perceive the new situation that faced the world with Rome's victory over Hannibal and its meddling in Greek affairs, and he braced himself to present this new reality. It was now seen that Rome had come to stay for some considerable time. The centralized rule of Rome and its intercommunication system give an awareness of the unity of the world, and from now on history assumes a world perspective absent in previous history writing. Ancient historiography as a particular genre of ancient writing has once again become relevant for interpreting the Acts of the Apostles. Luke not only shares the universalistic perspectives of the historians of Rome, he even transcends it, when he paints the onward march of the gospel in conquering not merely the Roman Empire but also the whole world. Another important area of comparison are the speeches of Acts as compared with those of ancient history writing.

1.5.2. Astronomy. Scientific astronomy begins with Thales of Miletus (fl. c. 600 B.C.), who predicted the sun eclipse of May 28, 585 (Herodotus *Hist.* 1.74). Anaximander (b. 610 B.C.) taught that the sun was purest fire. First the Pythagorians (around 525 B.C.) declared the sphericity of the earth (as well as of all heavenly bodies), which was demonstrated by Aristotle (*Cael.* 297a). Hicetas (? fifth to fourth centuries B.C.) and Ecphantus (fourth century B.C.), both of Syracuse, were first in propounding the theory that the earth revolved around its axis (also Plato *Tim.* 40c), while Heraclides of Pontus (390-310 B.C.) specified that this happened in twenty-four hours, while the sun was stationary. Plato and Aristotle, as Anaximander before them, believed the universe to be spherical (e.g. Plato *Phaedr.* 247d; *Phaed.* 109a; *Rep.* 616a-e; Aristotle *Cael.* 2.4).

With the preceding positions taken for granted, the astronomers of our period went on to achieve greater exactness. Aristarchus of Samos (310-230 B.C.) argued that the earth makes one revolution around the sun each year (the same applied to other planets). Hipparchus (second century B.C.), the greatest astronomer of antiquity (worked in Rhodes and Alexandria), who, however, went back to the geocentric theory, founded applied trigonometry, perfected the instruments of measurement, mapped 850 stars and discovered the precession of the equinoxes. He also determined the solar year to be 365 days, 5 hours and 55 minutes, not 365 days and 6 hours, as was believed until then. Finally, studying a lunar eclipse Hipparchus calculated the distance to the moon to be 59 times that of the earth's radius. This gives 6,378 x 59 = 376,302 kilometers (confirmed by Ptolemy, who applied the method of triangulation). The distance of the moon as known today is 384,400 kilometers. The last great astronomer was Ptolemy (Claudius Ptolemaeus, second century A.D.). Working in Alexandria, he systematized the findings of earlier astronomers, particularly those of Hipparchus, added his own observations, enlarged Hipparchus's list of stars to more than one thousand and produced a book on astronomy that was standard until the time of Copernicus.

It is obvious that the Greek view of the universe has importance for the interpretation of certain passages of the NT. For example, Greek astronomy knew that the moon had no light of its own but reflected that of the sun (e.g., Plato *Crat.* 409b). It is interesting to find that Matthew 24:29 (= Mk 13:24) has changed the wording of

(LXX) Isaiah 13:10, in particular *phōs* to *pheggos,* making the inability of the moon to shine the result of the sun's being darkened (*pheggos* = properly the weak reflection of light from the moon; cf. Plato *Rep.* 508c; Xenophon *Symp.* 1.9; *Cyn.* 5.4; Hesychius s.v.; A. E. Sophocles *Greek Lexicon of the Roman and Byzantine Periods* s.v.; in medieval and modern Greek *pheggari* [*on*] = the moon).

1.5.3. Geography and Geodesy. Greek geography begins early in the first millennium B.C. with the colonization of the Mediterranean and the Euxine (or Black) Sea and continues with voyages in the Atlantic, north to the British Isles and Thule, "near the Frozen Sea" (= Norway, Iceland or Hebrides?) (Pytheas, fourth century B.C.), and in Hellenistic times with the exploration of the Red Sea, the Persian Gulf, the East of Africa down to Mozambique, and of India, Malaysia and China. The maps that were created (the first by Anaximander, c. 550 B.C.) were very imperfect, though Hecataeus of Miletus (fourth to fifth centuries B.C.) had concluded that the dry land was surrounded by water.

Aristotle divided the earth into zones; Dicaearchus (fl. 310 B.C.) drew a basic latitude from Gibraltar to Rhodes, Issus and the Himalayas; Eratosthenes added several latitudes as well as meridians and divided the earth into two hemispheres, while Hipparchus (150 B.C.) divided Eratosthenes's main latitudes into 360 degrees. To Eratosthenes we owe the measurement of the earth. Learning that in the summer solstice the sun cast no shadow from a perpendicular gnomom in Syene, Upper Egypt, which he calculated to be five thousand stadia from Alexandria, he found that in Alexandria the sun's rays had an angle of 7°12 v. This figure, being 1/50th of the 360° of the circle, gave him 50 x 50.000 = 250.000 stadia as the earth's circumference (Cleomedes 96-100; Strabo *Geog.* 2.5.7). We are uncertain as to the length of his stadion, but if Pliny's figure is correct (Pliny *Nat. Hist.* 12.53), it was 157 1/7 meters, giving about 39,690 kilometers. If, as there is also reason to believe, 10 stadia equaled 1 mile, then 250,000 stadia = 25,000 miles = 40,233 kilometers (see Fraser, 1:414-15 and 2:597-600). The circumference of the earth, as known today, is 40,072 kilometers. The work of Eratosthenes has been preserved in the summaries of Strabo (66 B.C.-A.D. 24). Strabo discussed critically his predecessors, adding his own observations from his extensive travels. He describes Europe, Asia and Africa. His work is not confined to geographical features but is what might be called an ethnological and cultural geography. Strabo's work was continued by Ptolemy's more exact descriptions and measurements. He gives a list of no fewer than eight thousand place names and directed the drawing of ten maps for Europe, four for Africa and twelve for Asia. Ptolemy's geography became a standard book for fifteen hundred years.

1.5.4. Medicine. As in other disciplines, so in medicine, the concern of the Hellenistic age was to conserve the research of the past by editing, copying and commenting on the works of previous doctors and to carry research further. Medicine was practiced in Greece before Hippocrates (c. 460-370 B.C., or later). Even granting that many or most of the writings in the Hippocratic corpus are not his own (*see* Hippocratic Letters), Hippocrates must have dealt with many of the main areas of medicine: natural causation, diagnosis, diet, climate, the importance of the organism in the process of healing, which needs the assistance of medicines. He was apparently the first to assert that epilepsy had its natural causes rather than (as was thought) possession. The scientific seriousness that characterized Hippocrates may be seen in the ethos he inspired in his pupils, a concrete example of which is found in the famous Hippocratic Oath.

It is in the Alexandrian period that medicine becomes properly speaking a science. The great anatomist, Herophilus (fourth to third centuries B.C.), was the first to dissect human bodies (only animals had been dissected previously) and to write a manual of anatomy. He discovered the nervous system with its sensor and motor functions as well as that the brain was the seat of thinking; he described accurately the eye, the brain and the genitals, and he discovered the pulse. Erasistratus (fl. early third century B.C.) maintained that the body was composed of minute atoms that were surrounded by vacuum. He described the heart (the circulation of the blood was obviously already known; cf. Plato *Tim.* 70b) and contributed further to physiology, pathology and pathological anatomy. Soranus (first to second centuries A.D.) of Ephesus specialized in gynecology and obstetrics.

It is at this time that the science of pharmacology develops. Among its representatives may be mentioned Heraclides of Tarentum (fl. 75 B.C.), an empiricist physician; Crateuas (second to first centuries B.C.), whose work contained color drawings of pharmacological plants; and Pedanius Dioscurides (first century A.D.), who wrote the most important book on medicines in antiquity.

Surgery also followed on the advances of anatomy. Hegetor (second century B.C.) operated on the hip, while Archigenes (first to second centuries A.D.) describes amputations. Heliodorus (first to second centuries A.D.) performed skull operations; Antyllus (second century A.D.) operated on eye cataracts. The book by Aulus Cornelius Celsus, written in Latin, summarizing Hellenistic medicine, describes operations for goiter, stones in the bladder, probably tonsils and facial operations as well as dentistry.

The last great physician of antiquity was Galen of Pergamum (A.D. 129-199). In the huge corpus that is attributed to him, he dealt with almost every conceivable area of medicine. He summarized the work of his predecessors, and as the undisputed master of physicians of his day, added his own observations and experience. His medicine was standard for Europe until the end of the Middle Ages. This gives a fair idea of Luke's medical background.

2. Latin Scholarship.

Latin literature and scholarship have been of fundamental importance for European culture. In their own right they are worthy objects of detailed investigation. However, from the standpoint of the NT they are of comparatively little importance. The reasons for this are many. First, no NT author gives any evidence of knowing Latin, much less of ever having read or been influenced by any Latin authors (the Latin words in the NT are a negligible factor). Second, the eastern part of the empire, in which Christianity arose and with which the NT is concerned, was saturated by Greek thought and culture. Third, Roman culture before its contact with Palestine had itself come under the spell of Greek culture. Fourth, Latin literature is from the outset inspired, derived and even copied from Greek literature, with little that is original. Thus the Roman presence in the NT, which is substantial, is invariably on the level of administration and military force (*see* Roman Administration; Roman Military). For these reasons and the fact that Latin literature is only a fraction of the size of the Greek literature, the discussion of Latin scholarship will be briefer.

2.1. The Beginnings of Latin Literature. The Roman biographer Suetonius begins his study of Latin grammarians as follows: "In early days when Rome was uncivilized and embroiled in war, with no leisure for the liberal disciplines, the study of grammar was not even pursued, much less held in esteem" (Suetonius *Gram.* 1). He then goes on to mention the first writers in Latin: the *semigraeci* Livius Andronicus (284-202 B.C.), who translated the *Odyssey* in Saturnian verse, and Ennius (239-169 B.C.), but he insists that real scholarship begins with Crates of Mallus, Pergamum's envoy to *Rome about 168 B.C. (Suetonius *Gram.* 2). Ennius, the father of Latin poetry, established the Greek hexameter in Latin *(Annales),* developed further by Lucretius, and introduced many literary genres: tragedy, comedy, satire, epigram. He was also the first to turn his attention to grammar and spelling.

Between Livius Andronicus and Ennius comes Naevius (c. 264-194 B.C.), the first to set up a Greek play in Latin. The dramatists Plautus (c. 254-184 B.C.) and Terence (195-?159 B.C.) laid under tribute for their plays such New Comedy authors as Philemon and Menander; they were in fact more translators than authors. Terence, for example, had to defend himself for occasional departures from the originals!

The visit to Rome of the head of the Pergamene school, Crates of Mallus, marks the beginning of interest in scholarship. Another early Greek visitor to Rome (155 B.C.), who whetted the Romans' appetite for learning by his famous lectures, was the head of the Platonic Academy, Carneades (Cicero *Lucullus* 137). The elder Cato (234-149 B.C.), alarmed by Greek influence on Rome, sought to prevent the spread of Greek learning (Plutarch *Cato* 22.1-23.2), but his efforts proved fruitless (cf. Horace *Ep.* 2.1.156), and in his old age he learned Greek himself and modeled his speeches after Thucydides and Demosthenes. Many of his apophthegms were merely translations from Greek (Plutarch *Cato* 2.4). Crates influenced L. Accius (170-90 B.C.) as well as Lucilius (180-103 B.C.) in matters of orthography and literary criticism. This was still the time when even histories of Rome were being written in Greek (e.g., G. Acilius, Carneades's interpreter [Dionysius of Halicarnassus 3.67.5; Livy *Per.* 53] and P. C. Scipio, son of Africanus [the Greek historian Polybius had been the tutor of the two Scipio brothers]).

Since many authors wrote under more than

one genre, their work may be discussed under more than one category.

2.2. Grammatical and Lexicographical Scholarship. The first real Roman scholar was L. Aelius Stilo Praeconinus (c. 150-74 B.C.). Around 100 he spent two years in Rhodes, during which time Dionysius Thrax resided in that city; his influence is probably to be seen in Stilo's introduction of Aristarchus's text-critical symbols in his own work. Stilo became very learned in Greek literature, and Stoic influence is perhaps discernible in his grammatical and etymological studies (Suetonius *Gram.* 3). Among his works are a critical list of Plautus's genuine plays and the works of Q. M. Numidius, as well as a glossary on etymological, historical and antiquarian matters.

Lucius Ateius of Athens came to Rome in 86 B.C. and contributed much to the study of Latin. Owing to his wide learning (he claimed to have written eight hundred works) he took, like Eratosthenes, the title of Philologus. He provided Sallust with material to write his history and advised Asinius Polio on rules for the art of composition (Suetonius *Gram.* 10).

Stilo was the teacher of M. Terentius Varro (116-27 B.C.), the most learned Roman up to this time. Varro, a universal scholar, wrote some 620 books on such subjects as *Antiquitatum Rerum Humanarum et Divinarum Libri xli,* on the relation between Trojans and Romans, and a book entitled *Aeitia,* patterned on Callimachus's book by that title. He wrote literary works on Plautus, on poetry, style and so forth. He compiled the first encyclopedic work in Latin, *Disciplinarum Libri Novem,* containing grammar, logic, rhetoric, geometry, arithmetic, astronomy, music, medicine and architecture. In the satirical genre Varro wrote his *Saturae Menippeae,* in which he followed Menippus. His *Imagines* contained some seven hundred portraits of illustrious Greeks and Romans. His grammatical writing, *De Lingua Latina,* the first extant work on grammar by a Roman, included books on etymology, analogy and anomaly and syntax. In grammar he followed Dionysius Thrax to the extent of translating the latter's definition (see 1.2.2.3 above): *grammatica est scientia eorum quae a poëtis historicis oratoribusque dicuntur ex parte maiore* ("Grammar is the science of the usual subject matter found in poets, historians and orators"). He dedicated most of this work to *Cicero, who reciprocated in the second edition of his *Academica,* in which he greatly praised Varro (Cicero *Acad.* 1.9). The debate between the Alexandrians and the Pergamene scholars over analogy and anomaly was inherited by the Romans; Varro was an analogist, like Cicero, though they allowed convention *(consuetudo);* so were also *Pliny the Elder and Quintilian. Varro's influence on Cicero, Horace, Caesar, et al. was great.

In the person of *Neo-Pythagorian P. Nigidius Figulus (98-45 B.C.) Varro had his greatest rival in learning. Through his *Commentarii Grammatici,* in which, besides grammar in general, he took up etymology and orthography, Figulus shares the honor with Varro of having shaped the terminology of Latin grammar.

During the Augustan age the greatest scholar was the librarian C. Julius Hyginus (from Spain or Alexandria), a follower of Alexander Polyhistor. Verrius Flaccus (fl. 10 B.C.), one of the most erudite scholars of the time, is known chiefly for his *De Verborum Significatu,* the first Latin lexicon. One of the greatest grammarians of the first century A.D. was Q. Remmius Palaemon (fl. A.D. 35-70), teacher of Persius and Quintilian. His *Ars Grammatica* was the first comprehensive grammar of Latin and was used by all subsequent grammarians. He was the first to distinguish four declensions of nouns (Suetonius *Gram.* 23).

During the reign of Nero, grammar was one of the safest subjects to write on, and it was to this that Pliny the Elder (A.D. 23-79) devoted himself, writing what his nephew, Pliny the Younger, calls *Dubius Sermo* (3.5.5) or Priscian *Ars Grammatica.* This may be the source for Quintilian (1.5.54—6.287). Pliny, who was an analogist, probably influenced Valerius Probus of Berytus (fl. A.D. 56-88), an "illustrious grammarian" (Aulus Gellius *Noc. Att.* 1.15.18). Pursuing text-critical work, Probus used the text-critical signs of the Alexandrians and Stilo in his recensions of Terence, Lucretius, Virgil, Horace, Persius and probably Plautus. He wrote on anomaly, tenses, nouns and verbs, and he composed other grammatical works (Suetonius *Gram.* 24). Palaemon, Pliny the Elder and Probus are responsible for the basic form of traditional Latin grammar.

2.3. Libraries in Rome. Latin letters received a great impetus by the establishment of libraries. Books found their way to Rome originally as spoils of war from Greece. Following the battle of Pydna (168 B.C.), L. Aemilius Paullus carried off the library of Pella (the first of more libraries to follow: e.g., Sulla plundered the library of Athens; the consignment from Alexandria burned down before being shipped [Dio Cassius *Hist.* 43.38; cf. Plutarch *Caesar* 49; Aulus Gellius *Noc. Att.* 7.17.3; Fraser, 1:326 and notes]). Plutarch (*Luc.* 42) speaks of Lucullus's private Greek library, whose "use was more honorable than its acquisition."

The first public library was founded by Pollio in 39 B.C. (Pliny *Nat. Hist.* 7.30; 35.2). Augustus founded two libraries, one on the Campus Martius, the other on the Palatine, which, in accordance with Greek custom, were connected with temples. Each had a Greek and a Latin section (Suetonius *Augustus* 29.3). The second library, founded in 28 B.C., whose first librarian was Hyginus (64 B.C.-A.D. 17, Suetonius *Gram.* 20), was of decisive importance for Roman scholarship. Tiberius, Vespasian and Trajan founded more libraries, until in the end their number rose to twenty-six.

2.4. Latin Literature and Literary Scholarship at Its Height. Latin literature and literary criticism reached their peak around the Augustan age, roughly from the middle of the first century B.C. to the early decades of the first century A.D. Rhetoric, poetry and prose were perfected as never before, and literary criticism became more refined.

2.4.1. Rhetoric. According to Suetonius (*Rhet.* 1), "Rhetoric was brought to our country in a similar way as grammar, but it faced greater difficulty, because, as is well known, its exercise was at times prohibited." Suetonius speaks of leading Romans, such as C. Pompeius, M. Antonius, Caesar and Nero as espousing Greek rhetoric and popularizing it. Rhetoricians flocked to the capital, many of whom lived in the miserable conditions described by Lucian of Samosata (see *Merc. Cond.*, passim, and Juvenal *Sat.* 1.1-5).

Cicero is perhaps the greatest figure in Latin literature, and in particular in rhetoric. He studied philosophy with the Epicurean Phaedrus, the Stoic Diodotus and the Academic Philon. He continued his education (79-77 B.C.) in Athens with Antiochus of Ascalon and then turned to rhetoric, first in Athens and later in Rhodes under Poseidonius. He read avidly Dicaearchos, Theophrastus and Theopompus. The beginning of his first rhetorical treatise, *De Inventione Rhetorica,* is probably indebted to Poseidonius, while later parts have borrowings from Hermagoras. He is more original in his *De Oratore* and *Brutus,* but his *Orator* seems to be inspired by Isocrates, Plato, Aristotle, Demosthenes and others. He translated several Platonic dialogues. His *De Republica* and *De Legibus* have Plato's *Res Publica* and *Leges* as prototypes, while even the dream of Scipio in *De Republica* corresponds to the vision of Er in the *Res Publica.* In his *Tuscalan Disputations* he follows Panaetius, Antiochus and probably Poseidonius. The first books of *De Officiis* are evidently based on Panaetius. In his *Consolatio,* for his daughter, he follows Crantor's "On Mourning" *(Peri Penthous).* In a letter to his friend Atticus, he admitted that the works he was writing then were mere "copies" ("*apographa sunt*"). In addition to his impressive literary output, Cicero, by his translations of Greek philosophical works (e.g., Aratus, *Epicurus, Philodemus, Chrysippus), enriched the Latin language with a large number of Greek concepts, and through it modern European languages.

From 86 to 82 B.C. dates *Rhetorica ad Herennium,* traditionally ascribed to Cicero but nowadays considered the work of an unknown person. In this work rhetoric is treated under five heads: Invention, Arrangement, Delivery, Memory and Style. This writing is a combination of various Greek systems of rhetorical theory adapted to Roman needs.

Mention may also be made of Seneca the Elder (55 B.C.-C. A.D. 40). A follower of Cicero, only parts of his work on *Oratorum Sententiae Divisiones Colores* survives. "Shrewd observation, a phenomenal memory, and an experience extending from Cicero's age into the reign of Gaius make Seneca's work a most valuable source for the literary history of the early Empire" (C. J. Fordyce, "Seneca," *OCD,* 1st and 2d eds.).

2.4.2. Poetry. Lucretius (97-53 B.C.) was an Epicurean poet-philosopher (or philosopher-poet, as he claimed). He had studied Heraclitus, Anaxagoras and Democritus; he evinces borrowings from Empedocles, possibly Poseidonius, and from Thucydides, whom he sometimes misrepresents. He imitates Hesiod and Euripides, translates Homer and lays other authors under tribute. His only work is *De Rerum Natura,* in which, in massive and majestic if somewhat rough and unfinished verse, he presents Epicurus's physical theory. He thinks of the world as finite, with a beginning and an end, and propounds the mortality of the soul and hence the unreasonableness of fearing death. He had a great appreciation for Ennius's poetry. His great feat is to have put philosophical thought in hexameter. Conscious of the poverty of Latin, he often invented new words.

In the first century B.C. Roman poetry takes on a new swing: many poets turn their attention from the classical Greek poets to the Alexandrian masters, and the attempt is made to give poetry greater technical perfection, *ars gratia artis.* The initiators of the new school, *poëtae novi,* or *neoterici* (Cicero *Att.* 7.2.1), were Lucilius and Accius. Its chief representatives were Cato (born c. 100 B.C.), Catullus (84-54 B.C.) and Calvus (82-47 B.C.), but even such works as *Culex* and *Ciris,* attributed to Virgil, exhibit Alexandrian influence. However, Alexandrian influence is evident even in poets of the older school (cf. Dihle, 2:26-40).

One of the greatest of Latin poets was Virgil (70-19 B.C.). He studied Theocritus, whom he follows in no fewer than seventeen passages of his *Eclogues* (e.g., 8.37-41 is a [mis]translation from Theocritus 11.25-26; 2.82). For his *Georgics* he borrows freely from Homer and Hesiod and even later Alexandrian poets such as Apollonius of Rhodes, Callimachus and Eratosthenes. His magnum opus, the *Aeneid,* is based in its first part on the *Odyssey* and in its second on the *Iliad.* Many of his similes are drawn from Homer and Apollonius of Rhodes. Virgil was repeatedly accused of pilfering from Homer, to which he replied "Why don't my critics try the same thefts?" Virgil is not the only plagiarist. Various degrees of plagiarism were practiced by all Romans. But so far from considering it ignoble, the Romans "made it a proud boast to have been the first to introduce a particular Greek genre into Latin poetry" (R. L. Palmer, "Plagiarism," *OCD,* 1st ed.). Perhaps they felt that as the masters of the empire, they were entitled to everything their subjects had produced or invented.

In his early *Epodes* Horace (65-8 B.C.) imitates Archilochus, while in the meter of his more mature *Odes* he imitates Alcaeus and Sappho and further shows acquaintance with Pindar. In his *Ars Poetica* he takes up the most important injunctions of Neoptolemus of Paros, and with regard to style he counsels the imitation of the Greek models. Horace also distinguished himself in the only literary genre developed by the Romans, the satire. With his better finish he improved on Lucilius (180-103 B.C.), whom he criticized for slovenliness.

Virgil and Horace became classic almost immediately and were imitated by Lucan (A.D. 39-65) and Persius (A.D. 34-62) respectively, though by the time of Quintilian and Juvenal they had become mere school textbooks. Virgil was also criticized by Hyginus, the librarian, as well as by Cornutus (born A.D. 20), the teacher of Lucan and Persius. The first critical edition of Virgil's works (as also that of Horace) was made in the latter part of the first century A.D. by the Berytian scholar M. Valerius Probus, who apparently wrote a commentary on the *Eclogues* and *Georgics.* No extant commentary on his masterpiece, the *Aeneid,* dates from our period.

Ovid (43 B.C.-A.D. 18), who had studied at Athens, produced a number of works, of which the *Heroides,* the *Ars Amatoria* and the *Metamorphoses* became famous. The first contained fictive letters of love addressed by famous women of the past to their husbands or lovers; the second described the erotic art, for which Augustus banished him to the Euxine (Black) Sea. The *Metamorphoses* were evidently drawn from two Greek books: one by Parthenius under the same title and one by Nicander. In one of the stories he gives two divergent versions, which were each preferred by different Greek authors. He shows evidence of imitating Homer, Sophocles, Euripides, Euphorion and others. This great poem has inspired European artists as well as literati such as Chaucer and Shakespeare.

2.4.3. Prose. Prose is chiefly represented by historiography. Pompeius Trogus has the honor of being the first Latin author of a universal history (9 B.C.). This was patterned on Timagenes of Alexandria and used as sources Ephorus, Timaeus, Phylarchus, Polybius and others. Sallust has already been noticed. Livy (59 B.C.-A.D. 17), the greatest historian of Augustan times, in his massive work follows Cl. Quadrigarius and Valerius Antius for Roman events but Polybius for Rome's relations with Greece (Livy *Hist.* 33.5-10 is almost an exact translation of Polybius *Hist.* 18.18-27). Later historians include Tacitus and the biographer Suetonius.

2.4.4. Literary Criticism. The beginnings of literary criticism go back to the first century B.C. The decisive influence comes from Aristotle's *Technē Rhētorikē* and *Peri Poiētikēs* as well as Theophrastus's *On Style* (lost). Volcacius Sedigitus (fl. 100 B.C.) drew up a canon of ten poets in the following order: Caecilius, Plautus, Naevius, Licinius, Atilius, Terence, Turpilius, Trabea, Luscius and Ennius (Suetonius *Vita Ter.* 5; Aulus Gellius *Noc. Att.* 15.24). Varro, like Theophrastus, recognized three types of style: the grand (*ubertas,* exemplified by Pacuvius), the plain (*gracilitas,* by Lucilius) and the moderate (*mediocritas,* by Terence) (Aulus Gellius *Noc. Att.* 6.14).

For Cicero great style must combine all the elements of excellence (Cicero *De Orat.* 3.96-97, 101). He reviewed ably the styles of such authors as Antonius, Crassus, Caesar, Hortensius, the leader of Roman Asianism (114-50 B.C.), and others. In *De Oratore* he develops a theory of the beauty of oratory based on the combination of words or on rhetorical figures and thought. He indicated certain limitations in Thucydides and Lysias and commended Demosthenes as the supreme model.

Another literary critic, Horace, in his *Satires,* criticized Lucilius's untidy style, while in his so-called *Ars Poetica* he tried to direct his countrymen away from Ciceronian and Alexandrian principles to those of classical Greece. It has been described as "the only complete example of literary criticism that we have from any Roman" (Saintsbury, 1:221). It deals with artistic unity, meter, style, genius, originality and imitation and painstaking performance. He insisted on perfect finish and was indifferent to the older poets, whom Varro and Cicero admired and Ovid appreciated. Horace's legacy was the establishment of classic norms in poetic theory (see Atkins, 2:66-103).

In a later age Petronius in his *Satyricon* (1.2.118) briefly protests against the rhetoricians' bombastic style, insisting on refined language that avoids vulgarity. Finally, with M. Cornelius Fronto (A.D. 100-166) and Aulus Gellius (A.D. 123-165) literary criticism is redirected into the furrow of archaism.

2.5. The Decline of Latin Literature in the First and Second Centuries A.D. Already by the first century A.D. Latin literature is in decline, and the explanations for this are many and varied: decay of morality (both Senecas), bad taste (Petronius), natural after a brilliant period (Velleius Paterculus), the end of republican life (Tacitus).

Tacitus (A.D. 55-120), regarded as one of the best historians of antiquity (*Annales* and *Histories),* advocated a relativity in literary standards, turning against classical rigidity. His *Dialogus de Oratoribus,* has been described as "a work of the highest originality, profundity and historic insight" (Sandys, 1:207).

By far the most important work on rhetoric ever written in Latin is Fabius Quintilianus's (c. A.D. 35-?95) *Institutio Oratoria.* This massive work is essentially a summary of Greek rhetorical principles as adapted by Romans. Evidently Quintilian draws on Palaemon (*Inst. Orat.* 1.4.1—5.54), Pliny (*Inst. Orat.* 1.5.54—6.27), Verrius Flaccus (*Inst. Orat.* 1.7.1-27), Dionysius of Halicarnassus (*Inst. Orat.* 10.1, where he admits to be citing the views of others rather than his own) and even on Theophrastus, Aristophanes and Aristarchus. He suggests a modification of classicism, a new understanding of imitation of the classics, whereby room is made for creativity. Quintilian is the culmination of Cicero's efforts to apply, in the midst of changing circumstances and rivaling influences, the highest possible standards. His system is thus mainly a restatement of Cicero's views. Quintilian's work is a complete system of rhetoric, in which the author culled what he considered best in Greek and Latin literature, backed by his own experience. The work contains discussions of grammar and language, various schools of rhetoric, the structure of speeches, the arrangement of the material, argumentation, style, figures of speech, rhythm, a recommendation for the rhetor to read Greek and Latin authors, delivery, gestures and the importance of the rhetor's character, and it even discusses the education of children. It has been hailed as a monument to Latin rhetoric.

By comparison, the younger *Seneca (4 B.C.-A.D. 65) betrays a contempt for scholarship. He was disdainful of those who studied "useless letters" and derisive of the Greeks for raising scientific literary questions. He ridiculed the *grammatici,* disparaged Didymus's learning and regarded the Alexandrian library a monument of extravagance.

Petronius (died A.D. 66), probably the *Arbiter elegantiarum* in Nero's time, wrote a partly extant picaresque novel, *Satyricon,* "the most original literary work in the history of Roman prose" (Dihle, 2:126), without a real Greek model to follow other than the Greek novel in general. It was patterned on the Menippean satire, that is, prose intermixed with verse. The main characters are of the lowest sort, their language is vulgar and obscene, and the book went unnoticed in ancient times. Persius (A.D. 34-62) satirizes professional poets, their affectations and the mania after Greek themes, preferring Roman ones.

Juvenal (c. A.D. 55-140), the greatest of Roman satirists, who like Martial, lived under humiliating conditions as a client of wealthy Romans, has left us sixteen satires in hexameter (he was the last Roman to use hexameters). Among other things, he satirized Roman ladies for preferring to speak Greek rather than Latin (Juvenal *Sat.* 6.185-87). His satirism of Domitian led to his banishment. His satires and invective often turn on the corruption of the rich and powerful.

C. Suetonius Tranquillus (c. A.D. 75-160) is our main authority on Latin scholarship. His *De Vita Caesarum* is extant; however, of his other important work on *De Viris Illustribus* on poets, orators, historians, philosophers, grammarians and rhetoricians, only fractions survive; best preserved are the brief *Lives of Grammarians.* To him, mainly, we owe our knowledge of the use of critical signs used in manuscripts.

For the second part of the second century A.D. mention may be made of the work of M. Cornelius Fronto (c. A.D. 100-166) and Aulus Gellius (c. A.D. 123-165). Fronto, a classicist, admires the earliest of Roman writers—Plautus, Ennius, Cato, Terence, Sallust—but bypasses Virgil, Horace and Tacitus. He praises Cicero but disparages Seneca. Gellius, who along with other Romans had "left Rome for Greece in search of culture" (Aulus Gellius *Noc. Att.* 1.2), spent a year or more in Athens, often as the guest of the celebrated Herodes Atticus, where in the winter he began collecting material for his famous anecdotal work, *Noctes Atticae,* in twenty books, most of which has survived. He discusses points of grammar, antiquities, lore, history, biography and textual and literary criticism. The work has preserved citations from some 275 authors otherwise lost. He is less than careful about his sources and plagiarizes others. At least a fourth of his book is devoted to Latin lexicography. This work, which exhibits interest in many scholarly fields, may here form a fitting conclusion to the present discussion of Latin scholarship.

See also ALEXANDRIAN LIBRARY; ALEXANDRIAN SCHOLARSHIP; BIBLICAL INTERPRETATION, JEWISH; BIOGRAPHY, ANCIENT; CICERO; EDUCATION: JEWISH AND GRECO-ROMAN; EPISTOLARY THEORY; GEOGRAPHICAL PERSPECTIVES IN LATE ANTIQUITY; GRAMMARIANS, HELLENISTIC GREEK; GREEK OF THE NEW TESTAMENT; HIPPOCRATIC LETTERS; HISTORIANS, HELLENISTIC; JEWISH LITERATURE: HISTORIANS AND POETS; LITERACY AND BOOK CULTURE; PAGAN SOURCES IN THE NEW TESTAMENT; PHILOSOPHY; PLINY THE ELDER; PLINY THE YOUNGER; PSEUDONYMITY AND PSEUDEPIGRAPHY; RHETORIC; ROMANCES/NOVELS, ANCIENT; SUETONIUS; TACITUS.

BIBLIOGRAPHY. The basic sources for both Greek and Latin scholarship are the ancient works themselves. The main editions are Oxford Classical Texts; Bibliotheca Teubneriana; Loeb Classical Library; The Bude Series. The greater part of ancient Greek authors is found in the CD ROM *Thesaurus Linguae Graecae* (*TLG*). The greater part of Latin authors and a great number of inscriptions and papyri are found in the Packard Humanities Institute (PHI) CD-ROM (5.3). **Greek Scholarship.** ***Texts:*** Hesychius: *Hesychii Alexandrini Lexicon,* ed. K. Latte (3 vols.; Hauniae: Munksgaard, 1953-66); Moiris: *Lexicon Atticum, in Harpocration et Moeris,* ed. I. Bekker (Berlin, 1833); Photius: *Photius Bibliothèque,* ed. R. Henry (8 vols.; Paris: Les Belles Lettres, 1959-77); idem: *Photii Lexicon,* ed. S. A. Naber (2 vols.; Leipzig, 1864-65); new ed. (in progress): *Photii patriarchae Lexicon,* ed. C. Theodoridis, A-D (Berlin: W. de Gruyter, 1982); Phrynichus: *Phrynichi Sophistae Praeparatio Sophistica,* ed. J. de Borries (Leipzig, 1911); idem: *Die Ekloge des Phrynichos,* ed. E. Fischer (Sammlung griechischer und lateinischer Grammatiker; Berlin: W. de Gruyter, 1974); Polydeuces: *Pollucis Onomasticon,* ed. E. Bethe (2 vols.; in *Lexicographi Graeci,* Stuttgart: Teubner, 1967 [1900-1931]); Suda: *Suidae Lexicon,* ed. A. Adler (4 vols.; in *Lexicographi Graeci,* Stuttgart: Teubner, 1967-71 [1928-35]). **Studies:** J. W. H. Atkins, *Literary Criticism in Antiquity* (2 vols.; Cambridge: Cambridge University Press, 1934); P. E. Easterling et al., eds., *The Cambridge History of Classical Literature,* 1: *Greek Literature,* (Cambridge: Cambridge University Press, 1985); A. D. Davies and L. Finkelstein, eds., *The Cambridge History of Judaism,* 2: *The Hellenistic Age* (Cambridge: Cambridge University Press, 1990); C. C. Caragounis, "Dionysios Halikarnasseus, the Art of Composition and the Apostle Paul," *JGRCJ* 1 (2000) 25-54; W. Christ, *Geschichte der griechischen Litteratur bis auf die Zeit Justinians* (HAW 2. Aufl.; Munich: Beck, 1890); W. Christ, W. Schmid and O. Stählin, *Geschichte der griechischen Litteratur bis auf die Zeit Justinians* (HAW 2, 1; Munich: Beck, 1959); T.

Cole, *The Origin of Rhetoric in Ancient Greece* (Baltimore: Johns Hopkins University Press, 1991); A. Dihle, *History of Greek Literature: From Homer to the Hellenistic Period* (London and New York: Routledge, 1994); P. M. Fraser, *Ptolemaic Alexandria* (3 vols.; Oxford: Clarendon Press, 1972); H. Gamble, *Books and Readers in Early Christianity* (New Haven, CT: Yale University Press, 1995); G. M. A. Grube, *The Greek and Roman Critics* (Toronto: University of Toronto Press, 1965); W. K. C. Guthrie, *A History of Greek Philosophy* (6 vols.; Cambridge: Cambridge University Press, 1962-81); ῾Ιστορία τοῦ ἑλληνικοῦ ἔθνους, ed. members of the Academy of Athens (15 vols.; Athens: Ekdotikē Athinōn, 1970-78; many articles by many authors, esp. vols. 3-6: vol. 3: Κλασσικὸς ῾Ελληνισμός" parts 1-2 (1972); vol. 4: Μέγας᾽Αλε-᾽ξανδρος ῾Ελληνιστικοὶ Χρόνοι (1973); vol. 5: ῾Ελληνιστικοὶ– Χρόνοι (1974), vol. 6: ῾Ελληνισμὸς καὶ–῾Ρώμη (1976); *Der kleine Pauli: Lexicon der Antike* (5 vols.; Stuttgart: Druckenmüller, 1964-75); *Der Neue Pauly: Encyclopädie der Antike*, ed. H. Cancik and H. Schneider, so far vols. 1-3 (A-E) (Stuttgart: Metzler, 1996-97); G. A. Kennedy, *The Art of Persuasion in Greece* (Princeton: Princeton University Press, 1963); A. Lesky, *Geschichte der griechischen Literatur* (3d ed.; Bern: Francke, 1971); idem, A *History of Greek Literature* (New York: Crowell, 1966); P. Levi, *The Pelican History of Greek Literature* (Baltimore: Penguin, 1985); *The Oxford Classical Dictionary*, ed. M. Cary et al. (Oxford: Oxford University Press, 1957 [1949]); *The Oxford Classical Dictionary*, ed. S. Hornblower and A. Spawforth (3d ed.; Oxford: Oxford University Press, 1996); *The Oxford History of the Classical World* (Oxford: Oxford University Press, 1986); *Pauly's Realencyclopädie der classischen Altertumswissenschaft*, ed. H. Wissowa et al. (Munich: Druckenmüller, 1893-1950); R. Pfeiffer, *A History of Classical Scholarship: From the Beginnings to the End of the Hellenistic Age* (Oxford: Oxford University Press, 1968); L. D. Reynolds, and N. G. Wilson, *Scribes and Scholars* (3d ed.; Oxford: Oxford University Press, 1991); G. Saintsbury, *A History of Criticism and Literary Taste in Europe from the Earliest Texts to the Present Day,* 1: *Classical and Medieval Criticism* (3 vols.; Edinburgh and London: Blackwood, 1902); J. E. Sandys, *A History of Classical Scholarship* (3 vols.; 2d ed., Cambridge: Cambridge University Press, 1906-8); S. Swain, *Hellenism and Empire: Language, Classicism and Power in the Greek World A.D. 50-250* (Oxford: Clarendon Press, 1996); H. Temporini and W. Haase, eds., *Aufstieg und Niedergang der römischen Welt,* pt. 2 (Principate), esp. vols. 16-17 (Berlin: W. de Gruyter, 1978-84), many articles are of relevance. **Latin Scholarship. Studies:** J. W. H. Atkins, *Literary Criticism in Antiquity* (2 vols.; Cambridge: Cambridge University Press, 1934; E. J. Kenney and W. V. Clausen, eds., *The Cambridge History of Classical Literature,* 2: *Latin Literature* (Cambridge: Cambridge University Press, 1982); D. L. Clark, *Rhetoric in Greco-Roman Education* (New York: Columbia University Press, 1957); D. L. Clarke, *Rhetoric at Rome* (New York: Routledge, 1996 [1953]); J. Collart, *Histoire de la Langue Latine* (3d ed.; Paris: Presses universitaires des France, 1980); G. B. Conte, *Latin Literature: A History* (Baltimore: Johns Hopkins University Press, 1994); A. Dihle, *Greek and Latin Literature of the Roman Empire: From Augustus to Justinian* (New York: Routledge, 1994); J. W. Duff, *Literary History of Rome from the Origins to the Close of the Golden Age* (3d ed.; New York: Barnes & Noble, 1953); idem, *Literary History of Rome in the Silver Age from Tiberius to Hadrian* (New York: Scribners, 1930); R. A. Kaster, *Guardians of Language: The Grammarian and Society in Late Antiquity* (Berkeley and Los Angeles: University of California Press, 1996); *Der kleine Pauli: Lexicon der Antike* (Stuttgart: Druckenmüller, 1964-75); *Der Neue Pauly: Encyclopädie der Antike,* ed. H. Cancik and H. Schneider, so far vols. 1-3 (A-E) (Stuttgart: Metzler, 1996-97); E. Norden, *Die römische Literatur* (6th ed.; Leipzig: Teubner, 1961); *The Oxford Classical Dictionary,* ed. M. Cary et al. (Oxford: Oxford University Press, 1949); *The Oxford Classical Dictionary,* ed. S. Hornblower and A. Spawforth (3d ed.; Oxford: Oxford University Press, 1996); *Pauly's Realencyclopädie der classischen Altertumswissenschaft,* ed. H. Wissowa et al. (Munich: Druckenmüller, 1893-1950); E. Rawson, *Intellectual Life in the Late Roman Republic* (London: Duckworth, 1985); L. D. Reynolds, and N. G. Wilson, *Scribes and Scholars* (3d ed.; Oxford: Oxford University Press, 1991); G. Saintsbury, *A History of Criticism and Literary Taste in Europe From the Earliest Texts to the Present Day,* 1: *Classical and Medieval Criticism* (3 vols.; Edinburgh and London: Blackwood, 1902); J. E. Sandys, *A History of Classical Scholarship* (3 vols.; 2d ed.; Cambridge: Cambridge University Press, 1906-8); M. Schanz, *Geschichte der römischen Literatur,* ed. C. Hosius and G. Krüger, 1: *Die römische Literatur in der Zeit der Republik* (4th ed.; 1927); 2: *Die römische Litera-*

tur in der Zeit der Monarchie bis auf Hadrian (1935); 3: *Die Zeit von Hadrian 117 bis auf Constantin 324* (3d ed.; 1922); H. Temporini and W. Haase, eds., *Aufstieg und Niedergang der römischen Welt,* pt. 2 (Principate), esp. vols. 16-17 (Berlin: W. de Gruyter, 1978-84), many articles are of relevance. C. C. Caragounis

SCHOOLS. *See* EDUCATION: JEWISH AND GRECO-ROMAN.

SCRIBES

In Second Temple Judaism the scribes were a class of professional exponents and teachers of the law.

1. Background
2. Scribes and Pharisees
3. Work of the Scribes
4. Scribes in the Gospels
5. Jesus and the Scribes

1. Background.

In ancient Near Eastern civilizations the highly prized skill of writing made the scribes significant members of the community, especially as political advisors, diplomats and experts in the ancient sciences and mysteries, including astrology.

In Israel's history we find that scribes began as recorders and copyists of official data (2 Kings 12:10) and formed themselves into guilds (1 Chron 2:55). They came to hold high political office (1 Kings 4:3; 2 Kings 18:18; 25:19; 1 Chron 27:32; 2 Chron 26:11; Is 22:15) and became the heirs of the *priests and Levites as interpreters of the law (2 Chron 34:13; Ezra 7:12) because of their familiarity with and understanding of the Scriptures (1 Chron 27:32).

In exilic times the scribes emerged as wise men of understanding (see Proverbs) as the Jews in a foreign land depended on them for interpreting the *Torah in a new situation. Baruch was a scribe taking down Jeremiah's dictation (Jer 36:4, 18), collecting the prophet's sayings (Jer 36:32) and acting as his representative (Jer 36:6-15).

From the fourth century B.C. Ezra, the priest and scribe, embodied all that was expected of a scribe in that period (Ezra 7:6-26; Neh 8:1-9). By about 180 B.C, when Jesus ben Sirach, a scribe who probably had a school in Jerusalem (Sir 51:23), assembled his book, the scribes were a well-developed and distinct class of high social status alongside the priesthood (Sir 38:24—39:11; *Jub.* 4:17-25). In the crisis perpetuated by Antiochus IV Epiphanes, the reputation of lay scribes rose as they were zealous for the law to the point of martyrdom (2 Macc 6:18-31), while the priestly scribes succumbed to *Hellenism.

After the fall of Jerusalem in A.D. 70, the most respected scribes settled at Jamnia as well as Lydda (*m. Roš Haš.* 1:6; 4:1-2). In *Judaism the learned were also known as elders, experts, sages and scholars. The Mishnah says that they were to be "deliberate in judgement; raise up many disciples and make a fence around the Torah" (*m. ʾAbot* 1:1).

1.1. Leading Scribes. Little of historical value is known about individual scribes before A.D. 70, the most famous pair being *Hillel and *Shammai (*m. ʾAbot* 1:1-18). Hillel came to Palestine from Babylon and, because of his poverty, hired himself out as a day laborer. His kindness and gentleness characterized his school and the leniency of his decisions (*b. Šabb.* 30b-31a; *b. Soṭa* 48b). He drew up seven hermeneutical principles in order to establish the harmony between Scripture and tradition (*t. Sanh.* 7:11).

Shammai, a native of Judea, is said to have been more stringent than Hillel in his interpretation of the law. Even though both agreed on the need to fulfill the letter of the law, the two schools met to discuss their differences (*m. Šabb.* 1:4-11).

As the regulations of the scribes were intended to be applicable throughout the Jewish community, the most respected authorities lived and worked in one place to reach common conclusions.

After the fall of Jerusalem (*see* Destruction of Jerusalem), Rabban Yohanan ben Zakkai, who lived mainly in Jamnia, was the most distinguished scribe. Another celebrated scribe, well known in the NT, was Gamaliel I, who, according to Acts 5:34-39; 22:3, taught Paul.

1.2. Lifestyle. Some scribes came from the priestly aristocracy (*m. ʾAbot* 3:2; *m. Šeqal.* 8:5). Others were ordinary priests (*m. ʾAbot* 2:8) or members of the lower orders of clergy (*b. ʿArak.* 11b). The vast majority of scribes came from every other section of society, some supporting themselves by carrying on a trade. The literature gives evidence of a commander of the temple fortress, a wine merchant, a carpenter, a leather worker, a flax comber and a day laborer being scribes. For economic reasons even the most respected rabbis undertook writing and copying of

Scripture (*b. Giṭ.* 67a).

With the need to spend time studying the law and with no set fee for giving instruction, even the most respected of these scribes could be poor and depended on gifts from their students, funds from the distribution to the poor and the temple treasury (*b. Yoma* 35b; *b. Ned.* 49b-50a). Also, it was meritorious to show *hospitality to a scribe, to give him a share of one's property or to run his business for him (*b. Ber.* 34b). Scribes were also exempt from *taxes (*m. ʾAbot* 3:5). On the other hand, some scribes were over-zealous in receiving this kindness (Josephus *J.W.* 1.29.2 §571). Others, with many pupils, were very wealthy (*b. Ketub.* 67b).

2. Scribes and Pharisees.

Along with the chief priests, these two groups are often associated in the Gospels. Some have denied that there is any relationship between them. Others have understood the scribes to be the Pharisees learned in the law or an elite amongst them. The phrase "scribes of the Pharisees" (Mk 2:16; Acts 23:9) indicates the probability that scribes were associated with various sects and associations within first-century Judaism.

3. Work of the Scribes.

In relation to their knowledge of the Scriptures the scribes occupied themselves with a number of tasks (Sir 38:24—39:11).

3.1. Interpretation and Preservation of the Law. On the basis of existing regulations and by recourse to ancient customs which had become binding as common law (Mk 7:5-8), the scribes applied the general instructions of the Torah to daily living and even extended the law to theoretical situations to build a safety fence against inadvertent breaches (*m. Hor.* 1:5). In turn, the findings of the scribes, related mainly to *festivals, prayers, cleanness and uncleanness (*see* Purity) and the temple, became common law (*m. Šabb.* 1:1—24:5; *m. Ḥag.* 1:8; *m. Ned.* 4:3). In some places writing down the tradition of the scribes is forbidden (*b. Šabb.* 115b; *b. Giṭ* 60b), so continuous study was required to maintain a working knowledge of the traditions.

3.2. Teaching the Law. Instruction usually began at an early age (Josephus, *Life* §9; *b. Giṭ.* 58a). A student was expected to give allegiance to his teacher above that of his parents and, certainly after the NT period, teachers were generally addressed as "my lord" or "master" *(rabbi)*. A student was expected to reproduce every word and expression of his teacher. In NT times teaching took place "in the temple," probably in rooms associated with the main building (cf. Mk 14:49). In other centers instruction took place in "houses of instruction" (Sir 51:23; *m. Ber.* 4:2; *m. Ter.* 11:10), which sometimes may have been the home of the scribe (*m. ʾAbot* 1:4). The scribe sat on a raised area and the pupils on rows of benches or on the floor (Acts 22:3). The scribe posed questions for the students to answer. The teacher repeated his material over and over so it could be memorized. When the student had mastered the material and was competent to make his own decisions, he was a nonordained student. When he came of age (*b. Soṭa* 22b says forty years of age), he could be received into the company of scribes as an ordained scholar.

3.3. Scribes as Lawyers. Any Jew could be asked to judge a case by a community (*b. Sanh.* 3a). But where there was a scribe he would invariably be chosen for a judicial office (Sir 38:33), and some were members of the *Sanhedrin. Aside from these major functions the scribes also attended to the following tasks.

3.4. Scribes as Theologians. Some scribes gave more attention to studying and elaborating the doctrine in the text of Scripture rather than its legal elements. While preaching was not restricted to specific people, these scribes were well qualified to speak in the *synagogues.

3.5. Scribes as Guardians of Tradition. The significance of the scribes in Jewish society was also associated with their being guardians of an esoteric tradition (Lk 11:52). They considered secrecy necessary because Scripture was silent on the reasons for many laws (*b. Sanh.* 21b), because of the offense of some stories (*m. Meg.* 4:10), because the teaching might be misused (e.g., amelioration of purity laws, *b. Ber.* 22a) and because genealogical traditions might discredit public figures (*b. Qidd.* 70b). According to the Mishnah this secret knowledge also included the story of creation and the vision of the chariot (*m. Ḥag.* 2:1; *see* Heavenly Ascent). From the description of such things in the *apocalyptic writings (*1 Enoch* 69:16-25; 2 Esdr 6:38-56) as well as direct evidence (2 Esdr 14:45-48; *As. Mos.* 1:17-18), it seems that these writings contain the theological constructions and teachings of the scribes.

3.6. Scribes as Curators of the Text. Copying Scripture was considered divine work (*b. Soṭa*

20a), and temple funds may have been used to pay for corrections in scrolls (*b. Ketub.* 106a). Even though the sacred text was known by heart, a written edition had to be set before the copyist (*b. Meg.* 18b), who would read aloud the text as he worked (*m. Meg.* 2:2). The *Qumran scriptorium may have been modelled on something similar in the Jerusalem temple.

4. Scribes in the Gospels.

"Scribe" occurs fifty-seven times in the Synoptic Gospels (and Jn 8:3 in some MSS). Twenty-one times they are mentioned with the chief priests and eighteen times with the Pharisees. The scribes are depicted as scholars and teachers of Scripture, the custodians of Jewish traditions, the major opponents of Jesus and heavily involved in his trial.

4.1. Mark. The scribes, mentioned twenty-one times, are the chief opponents of Jesus in this earliest Gospel and appear throughout the Gospel. In the first report of Jesus' teaching, his teaching with authority is contrasted with that of the scribes (Mk 2:22). Unlike the scribes, Jesus did not appeal to tradition but acted as having an authority direct from God.

Mark depicts the scribes as opposing Jesus in a number of ways. When the Pharisees are mentioned with the scribes they are questioning Jesus' understanding of the law. They ask why he contaminates himself by eating with sinners and tax collectors (Mk 2:16; *see* Taxation) and why he eats with defiled hands (Mk 7:5). The scribes also question the identity and credentials of Jesus (Mk 2:6; 3:22; 11:27) and so provide a foil over against which Mark highlights the identity, teaching and powerful authority of Jesus. On learning of Jesus cleansing the temple they seek to destroy him (Mk 11:18; 14:1, 43) and are involved in his condemnation (Mk 15:1). While he is on the cross the scribes mock Jesus (Mk 15:31). Indeed, in predicting his death, Jesus twice mentions the scribes as some who will be involved (Mk 8:31; 10:33). One scribe, however, who questions and approves Jesus' answer is said not to be far from the kingdom of God (Mk 12:28-34).

Part of Jesus' teaching is his criticism of the scribes (Mk 12:35-40) and his highlighting the new understanding of Scripture in the light of his coming (Mk 9:11-13). He says they do not understand who he is (Mk 12:35-37). The scribe is the antithesis of a disciple (Mk 3:15; 6:7; 8:29; 9:35; 10:31, 43-44) in that scribes like to go about in splendid clothes (*stolai,* cf. Mk 16:5) and, even though they do not have authority (Mk 1:22), they desire recognition and positions of honor in the synagogue and at feasts* (Mk 12:38-39). They also exploit the poor to support their religion (Mk 12:40; see 11:17-18). In showing the scribes also in conflict with the disciples (Mk 9:14), Mark may be conveying to his readers the message that they will continue to face opposition in the same areas as Jesus.

4.2. Matthew. The scribes play a more important role in Matthew than in the other Gospels. The Pharisees, chief priests, elders of the people and the scribes are brought together to represent Jewish opposition to Jesus and, in leading the people astray, they carry responsibility for the fate of Jesus (Mt 2:4; 23:1-39; 26:57; 27:19-26, 41).

One aspect of Matthew's complex presentation of the scribes is the desire to rehabilitate them, apparent in his omission of material where his sources have them portrayed negatively (e.g., Mt 12:24 par. Mk 3:22). Also, when the scribes are depicted negatively, they are always associated with another group, especially with the Pharisees (e.g., Mt 5:20; 23:2-29) but also with the chief priests (e.g., Mt 16:21; 27:41) and elders (Mt 16:21). However, Matthew's antagonism is probably only toward the scribes of the Pharisees, for he makes a distinction between the scribes of the Pharisees and other scribes (Mt 7:29 par. Mk 1:22). And, in chapter 23, where Matthew is most vicious in his attack on the scribes and Pharisees, he reverts to calling them Pharisees in verse 26 (see also Mt. 12:24 par. Mk 9:34; Mt 22:34-36 par. Mk 12:28; Mt 22:40 par. Mk 12:32-34; Mt 9:11 par. Mk 2:16).

Matthew also treats scribes positively (Mt 23:2), and the terms "scribe" and "disciple" of Jesus are interchangeable (cf. Mt 8:19 and 21), though disciples are not to use the title "rabbi" (Mt 23:8). Like the students of the traditional scribe, a disciple of Jesus is to leave his family (Mt 8:21-22), follow Jesus wherever he goes (Mt 8:19-20) and have a righteousness—set out in the Sermon on the Mount (cf. Mt 7:29)—that exceeds the pharisaic scribe (Mt 5:20). Such a Christian scribe will gain new understanding of the secrets of the kingdom of heaven as well as treasuring "old things" through the teaching of Jesus (Mt 13:11, 52), which he is to do and teach (Mt 5:19). In 23:34 Matthew seems to be warning the Christian scribe of the impending dangers of being a disciple of Jesus (cf. Mt 5:10-12).

4.3. Luke. Luke also uses *nomikoi* ("lawyers": Lk 7:30; 10:25; 11:45, 46, 52; 14:3) and *nomodidaskaloi* ("teachers of the law": Lk 5:17; Acts 5:34) for the scribes.

In Luke 11:37-54, the first of two series of criticisms, Luke softens the criticism by omitting (cf. Mt 23:23-36) references to the scribes until Luke 11:45. The second series of criticisms of the scribes, following an attack on their theology (Lk 20:41-44), is in the form of a warning to the disciples to beware of the cruelly selfish lifestyle of the scribes (Lk 20:45-47). Also, following his tradition, Luke shows the scribes antagonistic to Jesus' ministry (Lk 5:21 par. Mk 2:6; Lk 5:30 par. Mk 2:16; Lk 14:1-6; Lk 20:1 par. Mk 11:27). Furthermore, Luke shows the scribes among those attempting to destroy Jesus (Lk 19:47 par. Mk 11:18; Lk 22:2 par. Mk 14:1; Lk 22:66 par. Mk 15:1) and into the hands of whom Jesus expected to be delivered (Lk 9:22 par. Mk 8:31).

There are a number of passages where Luke removes criticism of the scribes (e.g., Lk 20:47 par. Mt 23:15; Lk 4:32 par. Mk 1:22) or softens an attack by using the term "ruler" (Lk 23:35 par. Mk 15:31), "someone" (Lk 9:57 par. Mt 8:19) or by including the Pharisees in criticism (Lk 5:21 par. Mk 2:6; Lk 5:30 par. Mk 2:16). In fact Luke only once mentions the scribes alone in a criticism of their lifestyle (Lk 20:46). This probably means that Luke does not single out the scribes as being especially antagonistic to Jesus or any more worthy of Jesus' censure than any of the other Jewish rulers. On the other hand, Luke has Jesus compliment a lawyer on his knowledge of the law (Lk 10:25).

5. Jesus and the Scribes.

Embedded in the traditions about Jesus generally held to be reliable is a contrast between the teaching and lifestyle of Jesus and the scribes. In his teaching Jesus is not only critical of the Jewish traditions (Mk 7:1-23), but also in his teaching he placed himself above, not under, the Torah (Mk 2:23-28; 10:9; cf. Deut 24:1-4). So while Jesus was addressed as a rabbi or teacher, his teaching was recognized to be authoritative in that it was charismatic rather than dependent on tradition or the Scriptures (cf. Mk 1:22). In contrast to pupils of scribes choosing their own teachers, Jesus selected his own students (Mk 1:17; cf. Jn 15:16). As with a student of a scribe, Jesus' disciples were expected to place their relationship with Jesus above all other relationships. As with some scribes Jesus is depicted as being poor and dependent on others for his support (Mt 8:20 par. Lk 9:58; Lk 8:1-3).

Numbered among the opponents of Jesus are the scribes. One reason for the scribes' disapproval of Jesus was his claim to speak and act for God (Mk 2:7). This not only provoked jealousy among the scribes but, among those including Sadducean scribes in the Sanhedrin, concern for the delicate peace with Rome being disturbed by the popular excitement Jesus caused (Mk 11:15-19). Jesus further discredited himself in the eyes of the pharisaic scribes because of his frequent association with less desirable elements of society (Mk 2:15-17).

In turn Jesus criticizes the pharisaic scribes in particular for their hypocrisy in knowing the Scriptures and how to enter the kingdom of God yet, by placing insurmountable legal burdens on people, preventing them from entering it. They also live a lifestyle which the disciples are warned not to follow (cf. Mt 23:1-36 par. Lk 20:45-47). At least those scribes who were members of the Sanhedrin shared the guilt of handing Jesus over to be crucified. Yet there is evidence that Jesus found some of the teaching of the scribes acceptable (Mk 9:11-13), and it is reported that on one occasion Jesus complimented a scribe for his understanding of Scripture (Mk 12:34).

See also PHARISEES; RABBIS; SADDUCEES; SANHEDRIN; TORAH.

BIBLIOGRAPHY. M. J. Cook, *Mark's Treatment of the Jewish Leaders* (Leiden: E. J. Brill, 1978); B. Gerhardsson, *Memory and Manuscript* (Lund: C. W. K. Gleerup, 1961); N. Hillyer, "Scribe," *NIDNTT* 3:477-82; J. Jeremias, "γραμματεύς," *TDNT* 1:740-42; G. F. Moore, *Judaism in the First Centuries of the Christian Era* (3 vols.; Cambridge: Harvard University Press, 1927-30) 1:37-47; D. E. Orton, *The Understanding Scribe* (Sheffield: Sheffield Academic Press, 1989); A. J. Saldarini, *Pharisees, Scribes and Sadducees in Palestinian Society* (Wilmington, DE: Michael Glazier, 1988); E. Schürer, *The History of the Jewish People in the Age of Jesus Christ (175 B.C.-A.D. 135)*, rev. and ed. G. Vermes, F. Millar and M. Goodman (3 vols.; Edinburgh: T & T Clark, 1973-87) vol. 2; S. Westerholm, *Jesus and Scribal Authority* (ConBNT 10; Lund: C. W. K. Gleerup, 1978).

G. H. Twelftree

SECRET OF EXISTENCE (4Q412-413, 415-421)

The *Secret of Existence*, technically known as *Sapiential Work A*, is a wisdom writing inscribed in Hebrew and extant in (apparently) seven copies found in the caves near Khirbet *Qumran. Almost entirely unknown even to scholars before access to the *Dead Sea Scrolls became general in late 1991, serious study of the *Secret of Existence* has just begun, and much about it remains unclear. Still, the work has already markedly enhanced our understanding of Israel's wisdom tradition as it developed within Second Temple Judaism.

1. Content of the *Secret of Existence*
2. Issues of Interpretation

1. Content of the *Secret of Existence*.

Somewhat in the tradition of Proverbs and the Wisdom of Ben Sira (*see* Sirach), the *Secret of Existence* has no apparent overarching organization. The writing is a farrago wherein topics are taken up, dropped, then resumed as the writer sees fit. The fact that the work is fragmentary—even factoring in all seven copies, no more than 50 percent of the original content is preserved—further hampers any attempt at summarizing the contents. In general, the *Secret of Existence* is a catechism: a senior sage instructs a junior sage about various aspects of life in this world and about ideas of how to prepare for the next. Hovering in the background, and sometimes made explicit, is the *eschatological notion of impending judgment.

One recurrent theme is that of poverty. In contrast to Proverbs, which views poverty as the unfortunate result of foolish action, in the *Secret of Existence* poverty is the assumed condition of the ideal disciple. As E. M. Cook has noted, this high view of poverty presages that of some early Christians (e.g., Lk 6:20). Cook has further noted that the genre of the *Secret of Existence*, ethical instruction under the threat of impending judgment, parallels that of the Sermon on the Mount (Mt 5—7).

Reconstruction of the *Secret of Existence* is necessarily still tentative, but the proposal of one of the official editors of the work, T. Elgvin, is well considered and reasonable. Using the twenty-three-column 4Q416 as the basis for his reconstruction, with twenty-one or twenty-two lines of text per column, Elgvin suggests the following overview of contents (columns without numbers are completely missing):

2:17-21	Arguing with a neighbor
3:1-20	The elect in relation with God and humanity; loans, property
3:21—4:3	God as provider for all creation
4:3-18	Ethics in business dealings
4:18—5:3	Life in poverty
5:3-6	Returning a deposit
5:6-8	The righteous have hope in death
5:8-15	The study of God's mysteries
5:15—6:13	Family relations: parents, wives, children
6:17—8:15	Eschatological teachings
10	God's plan for creation and history; the *Book of Hagu*
11	Purity and resisting temptation
15	The lot of the elect as the firstborn of God
20	Heritage of the elect and the ungodly
22	Farming in light of the story of Eden
23	Warning: disobedience leads to trouble and death

2. Issues of Interpretation.

A fundamental issue that requires further study is precisely which Qumran manuscripts ought to be assigned to the *Secret of Existence*. The matter is not straightforward because of three considerations: the fragmentary character of the remains, the similarity a number of Qumran wisdom writings bear to one another and the possibility of more than one recension of the *Secret of Existence*, a phenomenon well known from the **Rule of the Community*, the **Damascus Document*, the **Thanksgiving Hymns* and the **War Scroll*, among others. Elgvin argues for seven exemplars as numbered above, but he has considered whether 4Q419 ought to be included as well. Other scholars have also proposed greater inclusiveness. Cook, while tentative, has included six additional Qumran manuscripts as constituting the *Secret of Existence:* 4Q410, 4Q412-413 and 4Q419-421. A consensus has yet to be reached among Qumranologists.

A second controversial aspect of research on the *Secret of Existence* is the question of whether or not it is a sectarian writing. Elgvin has argued that the *Secret of Existence* is sectarian, by which he means a product of a putative Qumran community. His criteria for this categorization are twofold: the work's terminology and the orthography of the copies. The book does contain a phrase already known from works that are sectarian: "and according to their knowledge let them be honored, one man more than his fellow" (4Q418 55 10; Elgvin compares 1QH 18:29-30 [new numbering], overlooking another, expanded parallel at 1QS[a] 1:17-18). Also, the *Secret of Existence* mentions the mysterious *Book of Hagu,* which several sectarian writings (CD, 1QS[a]) require a sectarian leader to know. These seem to be strong sectarian connections.

Another phrase that the *Secret of Existence* uses to describe the elect, "eternal planting," is known from **1 Enoch,* the *Thanksgiving Hymns* and the *Damascus Document.* Since *1 Enoch* is not a Qumran writing, however, citing this phrase does not materially improve Elgvin's case. Other phrases and terms used by the *Secret of Existence* are similar yet not identical to the wording of sectarian texts. In short, apart from one phrase that requires some sort of literary relationship between the *Secret of Existence* and sectarian writings and the mention of an unknown book that may or may not have been sectarian, there is no concrete literary evidence in favor of Elgvin's thesis that people at Qumran wrote the work. Equally possible is the notion that the sectarians merely knew and treasured an older wisdom writing. This is the thesis of the original editor, J. Strugnell, and of H. Stegemann, who helped Strugnell in the early years of work on the text.

Elgvin's argument from orthography is weaker than the literary one. Here he has adopted the thesis of E. Tov, who has proposed that it is possible to identify works copied at Qumran on the basis of a fuller orthography and certain aspects of Hebrew morphology. Elgvin's argument is thus only as good as Tov's, and Tov's is not very good. It can be shown, for example, that copies of two of the most sectarian writings found at Qumran, the *Rule of the Community* and the *Thanksgiving Hymns,* employed by Tov's definition non-Qumran orthography. It has further been demonstrated that the scribes of the Dead Sea Scrolls were, as a rule, faithful to their *Vorlagen.* They copied what they saw without wholesale changes such as Tov's theory would require happened at some point (Lübbe). Yet another problem for Tov, and therefore for Elgvin, is that almost none of the works supposedly copied at Qumran uses only the required orthography. Rather, their orthography is mixed, Qumran and non-Qumran. This is an odd situation if the scribes really were employing a uniform standard at the site. Further, various writings in the so-called Qumran orthography have turned up at Masada; only by special pleading can this fact be explained by suggesting that people from Qumran brought the works to Masada. As F. M. Cross has suggested, Tov's fuller orthography is best understood simply as an alternate system used in the Palestine of the scrolls (Cross, 3-5). It did not attach to Qumran specifically.

Thus, though argument will doubtless continue, no strong evidence requires the connection of the *Secret of Existence* to sectarians living at Qumran. Such people may well have treasured the work, but that they wrote it cannot be demonstrated. Indeed, Strugnell and Stegemann had as their working hypothesis that the *Secret of Existence* was composed in the third century B.C., well before the rise of the sectarian movement on any theory. What seems more likely than their extremely early date is an origin in the late second century B.C., among the same circles who read but did not write the earliest Enoch literature. These same circles may have composed **Jubilees;* in any case, they treasured it also. It is attractive to think that the author or authors of the *Secret of Existence* were wisdom teachers attached to the precursor movement out of which the Teacher of Righteousness arose. The Teacher eventually founded a new movement, and it was this movement that produced the specifically sectarian writings known from Qumran. If so, the *Secret of Existence* is a writing of the second century B.C., probably incorporating earlier traditions, that came to be read by the Teacher's movement and, later, others in the first century A.D. In this way it may have been known in early Christian circles.

See also WISDOM LITERATURE AT QUMRAN.

BIBLIOGRAPHY. E. M. Cook, "The Secret of the Way Things Are," in *The Dead Sea Scrolls: A New Translation,* M. O. Wise, M. Abegg Jr. and E. M. Cook (San Francisco: HarperSanFrancisco, 1996) 378-89; F. M. Cross, "Some Notes on a Generation of Qumran Studies," in *The Madrid Qumran Conference,* ed. J. T. Barrera and L. V. Montaner (2 vols.; Leiden: E. J. Brill, 1992) 1:1-14; T. Elgvin, "Admonition Texts from Qumran Cave 4," in *Methods of Investigation of the Dead Sea Scrolls and the Khirbet Qumran Site,* ed. M. O. Wise et al. (ANYAS 722; New York: New York Academy of Sciences, 1994) 179-96; idem, "The Reconstruction of Sapiential Work A," *RevQ* 16 (1995) 559-80; D. J. Harrington, *Wisdom Texts from Qumran* (New York: Routledge, 1996) 40-59; J. Lübbe, "Certain Implications of the Scribal Process of 4QSam[a]," *RevQ* 14 (1989) 255-65; J. Strugnell, D. J. Harrington and T. Elgvin, *Qumran Cave 4.24 Sapiential Texts, Part 2* (DJD 34; Oxford: Clarendon Press, 1999); E. Tov, "The Orthography and Language of the Hebrew Scrolls Found at Qumran and the Origin of These Scrolls," *Textus* 13 (1986) 31-57; B. Z. Wacholder and M. Abegg Jr., *A Preliminary Edition of the Unpublished Dead Sea Scrolls* (3 vols.; Washington, DC: Biblical Archaeology Society, 1991-95) 2:40-173.

M. O. Wise

SECTS, JEWISH. *See* THEOLOGIES AND SECTS, JEWISH.

SELEUCIDS AND ANTIOCHIDS

The Seleucid Empire was created in the *Hellenistic period. It is important as its territory became much of the administrative landscape of what was to become the *Roman Empire, especially in Anatolia and the Near East.

1. Founding of the Seleucids
2. The Seleucids in Anatolia
3. The Seleucids and the Jews

1. Founding of the Seleucids.

The Seleucid dynasty was founded by Seleucus I Nicator (c. 358-281 B.C.), one of *Alexander the Great's generals. In 321 B.C. Seleucus acquired the former Persian satrapy of Babylonia after Alexander's death. Although he was ejected from Babylonia by Antigonus I, he regained control in 312 B.C. He was then able to initiate eastern expansion as far as the Indus. The eastern emphasis of his control is indicated by the establishment of Seleucia on the River Tigris around 305 B.C.

Following the battle of Ipsos in 301 B.C., the Seleucids gained control of northern Syria. The city of *Antioch (e.g., Acts 11) was built in 300 B.C. to serve as a further royal capital; the city itself was served by a new port, Seleucia, just to the north of the mouth of the River Orontes. This port, which was taken by the *Ptolemies on two separate occasions (under Ptolemy Euergetes and Ptolemy Philometor), is mentioned as the point of embarkation for Paul and Barnabas, who were traveling to Cyprus (Acts 13:4). The structure of Seleucid Syria, as laid out by Seleucus I, was retained when the region became the Roman province of Syria with the governor based at Antioch (*see* Roman Administration).

2. The Seleucids in Anatolia.

Lysimachus, Alexander the Great's former bodyguard, had acquired territory in Asia Minor at the end of the fourth century. However, due to court intrigues, members of his family appealed to Seleucus I to invade Asia Minor. The two forces met at the battle of Corpupedium, Lydia, in 281 B.C., when Lysimachus was killed. This gave Seleucus control of *Asia Minor.

After Seleucus's murder later that year, and the accession of his son Antiochus I, Greek cities addressed the Seleucids as "saviors" (e.g., Ilion, *OGIS* 219). The Ionian league was quick to acknowledge Antiochus's control and sought to view him as a god (*OGIS* 222).

Although parts of Seleucid territory were raided by the *Galatians, there was relative stability in the region. This was helped by the establishment by Antiochus I of a series of military colonies along the main routes to the west coast; these included Thyatira at the head of the River Caicus (Acts 16:14; Rev 2:18-29), Pisidian *Antioch (Acts 13:14; 14:21), Hierapolis (Col 4:13) and Laodicea (Col 4:13; Rev 3:14-22).

During the reign of Seleucus II (246-225 B.C.) the Anatolian territory was handed over to Antiochus Hierax, in part to gain support during continued conflict with the Ptolemies. Seleucus attempted to reclaim the territory but was defeated by a coalition of Antiochus, Mithridates II of Pontus and the Gauls (Galatians) from the region of Ancyra. As a result the Seleucids lost control of much of their former territory. This was to be reversed under Antiochus III (223-187 B.C.), who regained much of the territory from the Attalids of Pergamum. However, Seleucid expansion was to be checked by Roman forces under the command of Scipio Africanus—along with Eumenes II of Pergamum—at the battle of Magnesia ad Sipylum, Lydia, probably in January 189 B.C. This led to the peace of Apamea in 188 B.C. (Polybius *Hist.* 21.43), which effectively meant that the Seleucids gave up their empire in Asia Minor north of the Taurus mountains; they retained Pamphylia and Cilicia.

3. The Seleucids and the Jews.

Judea, which had been part of the Ptolemaic

kingdom, was acquired by Antiochus III, along with Phoenicia and the southern part of Syria (Coele Syria), during 202 to 198 B.C. Although control of the *temple initially remained with the Jews, Antiochus IV Epiphanes (175-164 B.C.)—seen through Jewish eyes as a "sinful shoot" (1 Macc 1:10)—appointed a Hellenizer, Jason-Jesus, to be high *priest, an appointment for life. As a result Greek institutions such as a *gymnasium were introduced to the city; there may even have been a move to rename *Jerusalem Antioch.

Jason was deposed and replaced by one Menelaus, who was implicated in the murder of a deposed high priest, Onias III. When Jason attempted to reclaim his post, Antiochus IV intervened while on the way back from Egypt, and the temple itself was looted and the treasures carried off to Antioch (1 Macc 1:10-25). An edict was apparently passed to the effect that throughout the Seleucid kingdom all the different peoples should give up their ancestral customs. Such a view has been challenged, given that the Seleucids were accustomed to ruling a diverse range of cultural groups within their empire. Indeed some of the desire for cultural change may have come from Jews backing Jason. This meant that the Jewish religion was suppressed and the temple in Jerusalem rededicated to a new cult of the Lord of Heaven; the cult itself may have been associated with a royal *ruler cult with Antiochus in the guise of Zeus Olympios. Such oppression directly led to the outbreak of the Maccabean revolt of 166 B.C. (*see* Hasmoneans). The death of Antiochus in 164 B.C. allowed the Jews to return to their former status under Seleucus IV.

The Hasmonean dynasty of Jewish high priests emerged from this difficult period. In particular Jonathan recovered Jerusalem. One of the last Seleucid interventions in Judea was by Antiochus VII (138-129 B.C.). His letter to Simon the priest is preserved (1 Macc 15:1-9). Although Antiochus promised to restore the fortunes of Judea, he went against his word and besieged Jerusalem; however, he was killed in an expedition against the Parthians in 129 B.C. In effect the Seleucids now lost control of Judea even though they continued to consider it their own. Rivalries between Hasmoneans, in particular John Hyrcanus and Aristobulus, led to the Roman general *Pompey's intervention in 63 B.C. and Judea's effective annexation with Syria.

The interference in Judea by the Seleucids, notably Antiochus IV, and especially his encouragement of Hellenization, can be seen as the direct influence on many of the tensions in Jewish culture and society in the NT documents.

See also DIADOCHI; HASMONEANS; HELLENISM; 1 & 2 MACCABEES; PTOLEMIES.

BIBLIOGRAPHY. M. M. Austin, *The Hellenistic World from Alexander to the Roman Conquest: A Selection of Ancient Sources in Translation* (Cambridge: Cambridge University Press, 1981); E. R. Bevan, *The House of Seleucus: A History of the Hellenistic Near East Under the Seleucid Dynasty* (London: Arnold, 1902); G. Cohen, *The Seleucid Colonies: Studies in Founding Administration and Organization* (Wiesbaden: Steiner, 1978); R. M. Errington, "Rome Against Philip and Antiochus," in *CAH* 8 (2d ed.; Cambridge: Cambridge University Press, 1989) 244-89; T. Fischer, "Hasmoneans and Seleucides: Aspects of War and Policy in the Second and First Centuries B.C.," in *Greece and Rome in Eretz Israel: Collected Essays,* ed. A. Kasher, U. Rappaport and G. Fuks (Jerusalem: Yad Izhak Ben-Zvi/Israel Exploration Society, 1990) 3-19; C. Habicht, "The Seleucids and Their Rivals," *CAH* 8 (2d ed.; Cambridge: Cambridge University Press, 1989) 324-87; H. Heinen, "The Syrian-Egyptian Wars and the new kingdoms of Asia Minor," in *CAH* 7.1 (2d ed.; Cambridge: Cambridge University Press, 1984) 412-45; A. Kuhrt and S. Sherwin-White, eds., *Hellenism in the East* (London: Duckworth, 1987); S. Mitchell, *Anatolia: Land, Men and Gods in Asia Minor,* 1: *The Celts in Anatolia and the Impact of Roman Rule* (Oxford: Clarendon Press, 1993); D. Musti, "Syria and the East," in *CAH* 7.1 (2d ed.; Cambridge: Cambridge University Press, 1984) 175-220; E. Schürer, *The History of the Jewish People in the Age of Jesus Christ (175 B.C.-A.D. 135),* rev. and ed. G. Vermes, F. Millar and M. Goodman (3 vols.; Edinburgh: T & T Clark, 1973-87) vol. 1; S. Sherwin-White and A. Kuhrt, *From Samarkhand to Sardis* (London: Duckworth, 1993); G. Shipley, *The Greek World After Alexander, 323-30 B.C.* (New York: Routledge, 2000).

D. W. J. Gill

SEMITIC INFLUENCE ON THE NEW TESTAMENT

The Semitic influence on the NT may show itself in the language, form and content of the NT. Recent studies and discoveries of texts from the Judean desert have thrown new light on the general question of Semitisms in the NT, as well as on the phenomena of bilingualism in first-century Palestine and the Aramaic of Jesus and his first followers.

1. The Nature of Semitic Influence
2. Semitisms in Greek Texts Outside the New Testament
3. The Semitic Factor in the Gospels and Acts
4. Considerations in Reconstructing the Aramaic of Jesus and His First Followers
5. The Intricacies of Ancient Bilingualism and Translation

1. The Nature of Semitic Influence.

1.1. Language. A "Semitism" (or "Semiticism") in the Greek text of the NT may be defined as an element of vocabulary, grammar, syntax, idiom or style, which (1) deviates from expected Greek usage, and in that deviation coincides with idiomatic Aramaic or Hebrew usage, or (2) although attested in Greek is relatively more frequent in the NT, possibly because it coincides with idiomatic Aramaic or Hebrew use.

1.2. Form. The Gospel tradition presents much of Jesus' teaching in literary forms akin to those characteristic of rabbinic literature. Such "forms" include miracle stories, parables, disputations, and "cases" (examples drawn from real-life situations) (see Fiebig).

1.3. Content. Distinctively Jewish material may be detected at certain points in the New Testament. This includes: (a) traditional Jewish interpretations of Scripture (Haggadah), such as the reference to "Joseph's bones" in Hebrews 11:22b; (b) matters of rabbinic law (Halakah) or custom; (c) occasional hints at political events and Jewish aspirations and slogans, known from coins, documents and reports of historians and others. The "liberation" theme in Luke is a case in point. Thus, Luke 2:36-38 (and specifically verse 38) recalls the dating formula used on many coins and documents of the First and Second Jewish Revolts against Rome: "Year X of the liberation of Israel/Jerusalem," and "Year X of the liberation of Israel at the hand of Shimeon ben Kosiba Prince of Israel" (see XḤev/Se 8, recto, upper, line 8).

Again, in Luke 24:21, Cleopas and his colleague tell the unknown stranger of their dashed hopes for Jesus of Nazareth: "We had hoped that he was the one who was about to liberate Israel." This statement encapsulates historical hope within a clear citation of a midrash identifying Moses as "the man who is about to liberate Israel" (PRE 48:82-86; see Wilcox 1992).

Features such as these serve to anchor the NT text to its historical setting and strengthen the case for the validity of any apparent "Semitism" found in the same context.

2. Semitisms in Greek Texts Outside the New Testament.

Historically, the identification and evaluation of NT Semitisms have been treated almost exclusively as a philological matter aimed at discovering their probable origins. But Semitisms are not confined to the NT. They also occur in the LXX, in other Greek versions of the Hebrew Bible and in other quasi-biblical literature. The publication of four fragmentary texts of Tobit in Aramaic and one in Hebrew from Qumran have facilitated study of the translation process. Indeed, the discoveries in the Judean desert, from Qumran, Masada, Murabbaʿat, and Naḥal Ḥever, have marked a turning point in the debate over the quest for Semitisms in the NT. Actual documents, not only religious but also political and personal, in Aramaic, Hebrew (both classical and proto-Mishnaic), Nabatean and Greek, are now available. Many of the "secular" texts have precise Roman datings and throw light on daily life in Roman-occupied Palestine in the first and early second centuries A.D., the Jewish social and cultural context within which Jesus and his movement lived and worked.

The Masada material indicates that many inhabitants of Judea were "bilingual or even trilingual," with Aramaic as the main language of the ordinary people. Hebrew was also used for everyday matters but was "dominant" in references to the priestly shares and where questions of ritual purity were involved. (Yadin and Naveh, 32-39). More interestingly, Aramaisms occur in everyday personal documents from Naḥal Ḥever, written in Greek by bilingual (or trilingual) scribes on behalf of Aramaic-speaking Jews. They date from late first to early second century A.D. and are thus very close in time to the emergent NT.

2.1. Semitism as Interference of Aramaic or Hebrew on Greek.

2.1.1. Interference of Aramaic on Greek. Two types of interference of Aramaic and Greek are clearly documented from among the texts from Naḥal Ḥever.

The first is in a deed of gift, in Greek, on papyrus, a double document dated November 9, A.D. 129, from Mahoza (XḤev/Se 64). Its Greek is so ungrammatical and unidiomatic that the editor (Cotton) found it at times understandable "only when translated back into Aramaic." Her solution was to translate it "literally, with no adaptation, into the original Aramaic."

The second is the presence of clear Aramaisms and Hebraisms in a number of Greek documents forming part of the Babatha archive (P. Yadin) and ranging in date from June 2, A.D. 110, to August or September A.D. 132 (?). Most of these Semitisms also occur in the NT and are plainly due to interference of Aramaic on the Greek. Indeed, the same document may contain both a semitized expression in one line and its correct idiomatic Greek equivalent in another. This also occurs in the NT and has been claimed there as proof that the alleged Semitisms in question were not genuine translation errors.

Further, P. Yadin 11, dated May 6, A.D. 124, actually identifies lines 29-30 as a Greek translation *(hermeneia)* of the borrower's (Aramaic) acknowledgement of debt. The original, with his signature in Aramaic, was retained by the lender.

2.1.2. Semitisms Found in the Babatha Documents. Examples of Semitisms from the Babatha documents include the following:

(a) Introduction of direct speech by *legōn, legousa* ("saying"). It is very common in the Gospels, Acts and Revelation. In the Septuagint this translates the Hebrew *lʾmr.* Its Aramaic equivalent would be *lmʾmr.* (See P. Yadin 14.25; 15.20; 24.3; 25.15, 25, 47, 60; 26.12; 35.7.)

(b) The use of *ek/ex* (= "from") in partitive expressions, representing Hebrew or Aramaic *mn* (see P. Yadin 5 b i.2; cf. Mk 14:18, *heis ex hymōn,* "one of you"; lit. "one from you"). The correct Greek idiom occurs just two verses later in Mark 14:20: *heis tōn dōdeka* ("one of the twelve"). In passing, note that the semitized form in Mark 14:20 occurs in words ascribed to Jesus.

Two NT Aramaisms found in the Greek documents from the Babatha archive also occur in the Greek version of Tobit 2:3 in Codex Sinaiticus. Only one word survives in the Aramaic of that verse, namely *ʿthnq* = Greek *estrangalētai* = "strangled." The two Aramaisms are (1) *apokritheis eipen* = *ʿnh wʾmr* = "he answered and said" (*P. Yadin* 25, lines 24-25) and (2) *heis ek tou ethnous hēmōn*" = "one of [lit. 'from'] our community."

3. The Semitic Factor in the Gospels and Acts.

3.1. The Question of "Septuagintalisms." In the quest for Semitisms in the NT we frequently meet the widely held view that the Semitisms of the Gospels and Acts are in reality "Septuagintalisms." That is, they are not true Semitisms but are due to conscious or unconscious imitation of the translation idiom of the LXX by the authors of the NT books in question. It is even argued that in Luke and Acts they have been put there deliberately by the author(s) to give the material a Jewish and/or "biblical" tone. The LXX is itself largely a set of translations from Hebrew and Aramaic, made at different times by different people (*see* Septuagint/Greek Old Testament). Its Semitisms are due to interference of Hebrew and Aramaic on Greek.

The Gospels and Acts are largely about people whose first languages were Aramaic or Hebrew, like Babatha and the author of Tobit. It is time to take them seriously. The "Septuagintalism" view is essentially based on internal evidence: we simply do not know the literary intentions of the NT authors, only what they actually wrote.

3.2. Evidence of Jesus' Spoken Aramaic. The Gospel of Mark clearly affirms that Jesus spoke Aramaic and probably Hebrew. Whether he also spoke Greek we can only surmise, but a hearing before Pilate would presumably have been conducted in Greek. Examples of Jesus' spoken Aramaic include *Talitha koum(i)* (Mk 5:41), *ephphatha* (Mk 7:34), *abba* (Mk 14:36, see also Rom 8:15; Gal 4:6), and the cry from the cross, *elōi elōi lama sabachthani* (Mk 15:34 = Tg. to Ps 22:1a; see Mt 27:46). All of these words are expressed in Greek characters and provided with Greek translations. This material, though sparse, is very precious and, taken with other examples of Aramaic speech in the NT, may throw light on the question of which dialect Jesus and his followers spoke.

Elōi Elōi lama sabachthani (Mk 15:34; cf. Mt 27:46). The most striking of these is the cry from the cross: "My God, my God, why hast thou forsaken me?" Here *sabachthan(e)i* agrees precisely with the Aramaic text of the targum to Psalm 22:1a, against the form *zaphthan(e)i* found in Codex Bezae (= *ʿazabtānî* found in the Heb original). It is all the more impressive in that it portrays Jesus in his darkest hour speaking in his mother tongue.

Talitha koum/koumi (Mk 5:41). Of these two readings *koum* is by far the better attested. The problem is (a) that the subject is feminine, and (b) *koum* represents the masculine singular imperative of *qum*, "to stand up," while *koumi* = *qûmî*, the feminine singular imperative. In Syriac and Christian Palestinian Aramaic, the *i-* of *qûmî* would be silent. Does this tell something about Jesus' spoken Aramaic, possible influence of Syriac or Christian Palestinian Aramaic, or perhaps dictational transmission of the text?

Ephphatha (Mk 7:34). Mark's Greek version of this word is *dianoichthēti*, "be opened." The *t* of the reflexive-passive prefix (*ʾt*) of the verb *ptḥ*, "to open," has become assimilated to the *p/f* of the root. This can be documented (a) as *ʾpth*, "was opened," in a Haggadah found at Genesis 49:1 in the *Fragmentary Targum* in Cod. Vat. Ebr. 440 and (b) in the formula *lʾ lmptḥ* in four first-century A.D. Aramaic ossuary inscriptions meaning either "not to open," or better, "not to be opened" (Wilcox 1984, 998-99; Fitzmyer and Harrington, nos. 67, 70, 71, 95).

3.3. Other Semitisms in the Gospels and Acts.

3.3.1. Akeldamach (Acts 1:19). The phrase *Akeldamach* in Acts 1:19 represents Aramaic *ḥql dmh* ("field/portion of blood"). Compare with this the phrase *ḥql prdš* ("a field," "an orchard/garden") in a papyrus deed of sale (XḤev/Se 9, lines 3 and 14), dated, on the basis of its script, to the end of the Herodian period. As elsewhere in XḤev/Se 9, *prdš* has its definite state in *-h*, not *-ʾ* and suits first-century Jewish Aramaic.

In the wider context, Acts 1:16-18, there is a reference to fulfillment of the Scripture "concerning Judah." Genesis 44:18 opens the section, "And Judah drew near." In *Targum Neofiti* and a Cairo Genizah fragment (D), there is a piece of Haggadah in which Judah speaks of his determination to avenge Benjamin (if he should come to harm): "For he [Benjamin] was numbered with us amongst the tribes, and received lot and inheritance [with us] in the division of the Land." Judas had forfeited his portion or lot among the Twelve, and his successor was also appointed by lot.

3.3.2. Apo mias (Lk 14:18). This phrase reflects *mn ḥdʾ* or *mḥdʾ*, idiomatic Syriac and Christian Palestinian Aramaic, meaning "suddenly," "at once."

3.3.3. Epi to auto (Acts 2:47). By itself this phrase is used in the LXX to translate the Hebrew *yḥd, yḥdw:* "together," "in the same place." That does not fit Acts 2:47. However, the full idiom in Acts 2:47 is really *prostithenai epi to auto* = Hebrew *lhwsyp lyḥd*, "to add to the Yaḥad." Compare 1QS 5:7; 8:19, where the idiom means "to join the community [the Yaḥad]." Similarly, in Acts 1:15 and 2:1, the complete idiom is *einai eis to auto* = Hebrew *lhywt lyḥd*, "to belong to the community [Yaḥad]" (cf. 1QS 5:2; 6:23; 8:12; and possibly 2:24). The Greek is thus a fairly literal translation of the Hebrew idioms (Wilcox 1965, 93-100).

3.3.4. Mark 10:11-12. The problem in this passage is that it assumes that divorce can be at the instance of either the husband or the wife, whereas the Mishnah at *Giṭin* 3:1-5 assumes that it is the prerogative of the husband. A new text from Naḥal Ḥever, XHev/Se 13, is dated 20 Sivan, year 3 of the liberation of Israel in the name of Shimʿon bar Kosibah, Prince of Israel (A.D. 134/135) and is an Aramaic deed of divorce (a "Gett") issued by the wife, Shalamzion b. Joseph *Qbsn*, to her ex-husband, Eleazar ben Hananiah. The document was issued some eighty-five years before the usual date of the codification of the Mishnah.

4. Considerations in Reconstructing the Aramaic of Jesus and His First Followers.

Several clues emerge in examination of the words of Jesus and Peter, cited in Aramaic in Mark and Acts respectively. While the basic Aramaic used seems to fit reasonably well with that of the material from Qumran, there are indications of some links with Syriac and Christian Palestinian Aramaic.

Further, in Tobit 2:1, in 4Q196 (4QpapTobit[a] ar), frag. 2 line 11, the word *šrw*, which is not listed in the Aramaic lexica, occurs. It is found in Syriac, however, with the meaning "meal," "repast," "banquet." This meaning agrees with the Greek text of Tobit in Codex Sinaiticus, which renders *šrw* by *ariston* ("dinner" or "banquet"). 4Q196 is described as "carefully written in a late semiformal Hasmonaean script" and dated to about 50 B.C. This is far earlier than we might have expected to find Syriac. Is the influence really Syriac, or were the dialect boundaries less rigid than accepted at present? This would support E. M. Cook's thesis that we should not divide Aramaic into "Eastern" and "Western" but should include a "Central" area as well.

He sees the origin of *Targum Onqelos* and *Targum Jonathan* in the Central Aramaic area, as supported by "the undoubted connection of the Peshitta [Syriac] to the targumic interpretative tradition" (Cook, 156).

A second point is that at a number of places in the NT, we find elements of Jewish midrash for which the NT material is apparently the earliest known evidence. In Acts 13:22 we have what appears to be a mixed quotation. It is usually represented as in three elements: "I found David" (Ps 89:20), "a man after my own heart" (1 Sam 13:14), "who will do all my wishes" (Is 44:28). However, the targum to 1 Samuel 13:14 replaces the phrase "a man after my own heart" with the words: "a man doing his [the Lord's] wishes" (*gbr ʿbyd rʿwtyh*). Acts 13:22 is thus the earliest known evidence for the targumic interpretation of 1 Samuel 13:14 (Wilcox 1965, 21-22). There are many more such "targumic" readings in the NT. Clearly the NT writers were not quoting the apparently late targums of Onqelos and Jonathan (*see* Rabbinic Literature: Targumim). There must have been at least an oral link between the first-century A.D. form of these traditions of Scripture interpretation and the later written forms of them in targumim and/or midrashim.

Against this background it seems wise not to be too ready to dispense with the evidence of the written targumim. It is in this area that some of the most promising discoveries are likely to be made.

Ideally we need free, spoken Aramaic, not under suspicion of being a translation and documented for the first century A.D. in Palestine. It should also be available in statistically credible quantity and range of vocabulary. J. A. Fitzmyer has argued that Qumran Aramaic along with other first-century Aramaic, such as tomb and ossuary inscriptions, is the latest Aramaic that should be used for philological comparisons of the Aramaic basis of the Gospels and Acts. Much of this material, however, does not appear to provide us with the type of free, conversational Aramaic needed for comparison with the language and style of the Gospels and Acts. *Talmud Yerushalmi and the midrashim in many ways meet the situation except for date.

Next, there is the practical problem that there are always words and idioms which we need for reconstructing the language but which are not available in Qumran Aramaic. We have seen above that some help is to hand from Syriac and Christian Palestinian Aramaic. Indeed, Casey is right when he argues that all the dialects of Aramaic are to be checked when paucity of vocabulary bars further progress. Again, despite the gaps in date, at least where midrashic material is found in the NT, it is well worth asking whether the traditional links between the midrashic material and the NT may not supply the missing words. Further, the fact that a given Aramaic word has not yet been found in texts from the period 200 B.C. to A.D. 200 does not mean that it did not exist earlier. Again, that a word or element of syntax is attested in Aramaic material from Qumran, for example, does not in itself mean that it was known to Jesus.

5. The Intricacies of Ancient Bilingualism and Translation.

The fact of genuine Semitisms in the Greek text of the NT requires consideration of the intricacies of bilingualism (and/or trilingualism) and translating. Clearly both activities are affected by the speaker's or translator's knowledge and facility in both the source language and the language in which the material is to be expressed. In XḤev/Se 64, the writer's Aramaic was no problem, but his or her Greek was minimal. The result was ungrammatical, unidiomatic and all but incomprehensible as Greek. However, rewritten *word for word* in Aramaic, the document was idiomatic and clear. Where a bilingual person or translator is either speaking or writing directly in the second ("target") language, he or she is relatively free to choose words and idioms which come naturally to mind.

But translating a (written) *text* in language "A" restricts the translator's choice of vocabulary, syntax and idiom because of the need to turn the source in language "A" into credible language "B."

The process may be further complicated if the translator is obliged, personally or by others, to put the material in language "A" into the best language "B" as he or she can, or whether, for example, the need is to produce a translation that is as nearly "word for word" as possible. The more authoritative the original material, the less free a translator will be to compose the translation idiomatically and according to sense. J. Joosten has drawn attention to the case of the Syriac Peshitta version of Matthew, where he notes that its "author" shows a tendency to represent each Greek word of that Gospel by one Syriac equivalent (Joosten, 164). Nearer to the Greek NT situation, there are intermittent Aramaisms in a number of the Greek documents from the Babatha archive (P.Yadin). From time to time, the bilingual scribe has slipped from expressing in idiomatic Greek what Babatha presumably said in Aramaic, and instead he has produced an (unidiomatic) word-for-word Greek "translation" of the original Aramaic.

M. Casey has investigated the question of bilingualism and translation techniques in connection with his project of utilizing the available first-century Aramaic to attempt a thorough reconstruction of possible source material in the Gospel of Mark (Casey, 93-110).

See also ARAMAIC LANGUAGE; ARAMAIC TARGUMIM: QUMRAN; GREEK OF THE NEW TESTAMENT; HEBREW LANGUAGE; HEBREW MATTHEW; RABBINIC LITERATURE: TARGUMIM; SEPTUAGINT/GREEK OLD TESTAMENT.

BIBLIOGRAPHY. N. Avigad and Y. Yadin, *A Genesis Apocryphon: A Scroll from the Wilderness of Judea* (Jerusalem: Magnes, 1956); M. Black, *An Aramaic Approach to the Gospels and Acts* (3d ed.; Peabody, MA: Hendrickson, 1998 [1967]); M. Broshi et al., eds., *Qumran Cave 4.19: Parabiblical Texts, Part 2* (DJD 19; Oxford: Clarendon Press, 1995); M. Casey, *Aramaic Sources of Mark's Gospel* (SNTSMS 102; Cambridge: Cambridge University Press, 1998); B. D. Chilton, *A Galilean Rabbi and His Bible: Jesus' Use of the Interpreted Scripture of His Time* (GNS 8; Wilmington, DE: Michael Glazier, 1984); E. M. Cook, "A New Pespective on the Language of Onkelos and Jonathan," in *The Aramaic Bible: Targums in their Historical Context*, ed. D. R. G. Beattie and M. J. McNamara (JSOTSup 166; Sheffield: Sheffield Academic Press, 1994) 142-56; H. M. Cotton and A. Yardeni, *Aramaic, Hebrew and Greek Documentary Texts from Nahal Hever and Other Sites, with an Appendix Containing Alleged Qumran Texts* (DJD 27; Oxford: Clarendon Press, 1998); P. Fiebig, *Der Erzählungstil der Evangelien im Lichter der rabbinischen Erzählungstils untersucht, zugleich ein Beitrag zum Streit um die "Christusmythe"* (Leipzig: Hinrichs, 1925); J. A. Fitzmyer, *Essays on the Semitic Background of the New Testament* (London: Chapman, 1971); idem, *The Genesis Apocryphon of Cave I: A Commentary* (BibO 18; Rome: Pontifical Biblical Institute, 1966); idem, *A Wandering Aramean: Collected Aramaic Essays* (SBLMS 25; Missoula, MT: Scholars Press, 1979); J. Joosten, *The Syriac Language of the Peshitta and Old Syriac Versions of Matthew: Syntactic Structure, Inner-Syriac Developments and Translation Technique* (SSLL 22; Leiden: E. J. Brill, 1996); A. Meyer, *Jesu Muttersprache: Das galiläische Aramäisch in seiner Bedeutung für die Erklärung der Reden Jesu und der Evangelien überhaupt* (Freiburg & Leipzig: Mohr Siebeck, 1896); J. P. M. van Der Ploeg and A. S. van Der Woude, with B. Jongeling, *Le Targum de Job de la grotte XI de Qumrân* (Leiden: E. J. Brill, 1971); M. Wilcox, "The Aramaic Background of the New Testament," in *The Aramaic Bible: Targums in their Historical Context*, ed. D. R. G. Beattie and M. J. McNamara (JSOTSup 166; Sheffield: Sheffield Academic Press, 1994) 363-78; idem, "Luke 2.36-38. 'Anna bat Phanuel, of the Tribe of Asher, a Prophetess. . .' A Study in Midrash in Material Special to Luke," in *The Four Gospels 1992: Festschrift Frans Neirynck*, ed. F. Van Segbroeck et al. (BETL 100; Leuven: Leuven University Press, 1992); idem, "Semitisms in the New Testament," in *ANRW* 2.25.23 (1984) 978-1029; idem, *The Semitisms of Acts* (Oxford: Clarendon Press, 1965); Y. Yadin and J. Naveh, *Masada I: The Yigael Yadin Excavations 1963-1965, Final Reports: The Aramaic and Hebrew Ostraca and Jar Inscriptions* (Jerusalem: Israel Exploration Society, The Hebrew University of Jerusalem, 1989).

M. Wilcox

SENATORIAL ORDER. *See* ROMAN SOCIAL CLASSES.

SENECA

Lucius Annaeus Seneca was a Roman moralist, politician and playwright. Born between 4 and 1 B.C. in Spain to an elite family of Italian descent, he was educated in *Rome, spent time in Egypt and achieved political prominence at an early age. Implicated in intrigue surrounding the Emperor Caligula, he was exiled to Corsica, from which he was recalled by the emperor Claudius at the encouragement of his new wife Agrippina. Seneca served as tutor of the young Nero, then as adviser during the early years of Nero's reign. Opting for retirement after Nero's behavior made his own position at court untenable, Seneca spent his final years writing philosophy. In A.D. 65 he was forced by Nero to commit suicide for his alleged participation in the Pisonian conspiracy. From the account of the Roman historian *Tacitus, it appears that Seneca modeled his suicide on that of Socrates, thus turning his death into an act of political theater celebrating the spiritual liberty of the wise man. His continuing influence on the culture of Rome is attested by the later writer Quintilian, among others.

While Seneca's prose writings include discussion of *Stoic physics (*Naturales Quaestiones*) and technical investigations of ethical issues (some of the later *Epistulae Morales*), by and large they are best considered as exhortations. They encourage the addressee, who is often a prominent political figure or a member of Seneca's family, as well as the reader to relate Stoic doctrine to the particularities of Roman life. Topics addressed include management of anger (*De Ira*), responsibilities to self and others (*De Brevitate Vitae*) and consolation on the loss of a loved one (*Ad Marciam, Ad Polybium*). Seneca's emphasis on the therapeutic and practical aspects of Stoicism has led to an undervaluing of his achievement by modern students of *philosophy, as have alleged contradictions between his teaching and his practice. Seneca's tragedies, which employ scenarios from Greek mythology, also articulate Stoic concerns and doctrine, although in a less straightforward manner than do the prose writings.

Similarities between Senecan philosophy and Christianity were early on noted by Tertullian (*De An.* 20). A forged correspondence between Seneca and Paul, already familiar to Jerome and Augustine, as well as a later legend of Seneca's conversion to Christianity, contributed to his continuing popularity among Christian writers of the Middle Ages and beyond. His brother L. Iunius Gallio Annaeanus, as proconsul of Achaia, presided over Paul's arraignment (Acts 18:12-17).

See also PHILOSOPHY; STOICISM.

BIBLIOGRAPHY. **Texts and Translations:** prose treatises, letters and plays available in the Loeb Classical Library. **Studies:** M. Colish, *The Stoic Tradition from Antiquity to the Early Middle Ages* (2 vols.; Leiden: E. J. Brill, 1985); M. Griffin, *Seneca: A Philosopher in Politics* (2d ed.; Oxford: Clarendon Press, 1992); T. Habinek, "An Aristocracy of Virtue," *YCS* 29 (1992) 187-204; M. Nussbaum, *The Therapy of Desire* (Princeton, NJ: Princeton University Press, 1994), chaps. 11, 12.

T. N. Habinek

SEPPHORIS. *See* GALILEE.

SEPTUAGINT/GREEK OLD TESTAMENT

The Septuagint is the name often and usually given to the Greek version of the OT/Hebrew Bible and a few other books, on the basis of the tradition that seventy or, more accurately, seventy-two Jewish scholars were involved in its translation. Some scholars confine the term *Septuagint* to the translation of the Pentateuch, since this was the portion translated according to the early tradition, but most include the entire OT (see Greenspoon, 156). Although the translation was the Bible of the early church and of Judaism until the late first century A.D., the Septuagint has not figured nearly so importantly in the Western church as it should have, no doubt due to the church's ultimately following the Jewish canon of the OT. However, a number of factors—including discovery of Septuagint Greek papyri, and appreciation of the role of Greek in the Greco-Roman world, among others—have maintained scholarly interest in the Septuagint.

1. Contents
2. Theories of Origin
3. Revisions and Other Greek Versions
4. Translation Technique and Relation to the Hebrew Text
5. Editions of the Septuagint
6. The Septuagint and the New Testament
7. Recent Research Initiatives and Projects

1. Contents.

The Septuagint or Old Greek version includes the twenty-four books of the Hebrew Bible (OT), plus a number of other books, not necessarily arranged in the same order in the Hebrew and Greek texts (see Kenyon, 16-17; Rost; Swete, 197-230). Even some of the Septuagint versions of the canonical twenty-four books are not the same as their Masoretic equivalent, which suggests that the earlier Hebrew versions, at least as they existed in some circles, were different from later texts. Major differences are to be seen in Jeremiah, Job and Proverbs, as well as there being additions to Daniel and Esther (see Müller, 40). Earlier scholarship thought that there was a peculiar *Alexandrian canon, which consisted of books that were part of the canon of Scriptures of the Jews of Egypt (Nairne). This canon consisted of not only the twenty-four canonical books but a number of books that were translated from Hebrew into Greek (e.g., 1 *Esdras, *Sirach [Ecclesiasticus],

*Judith, *Tobit, *Ba-ruch, Letter of Jeremiah, 1 *Maccabees, possibly the additions to Daniel; *see* Daniel, Esther and Jeremiah, Additions to) or that were originally composed in Greek (e.g., 2, 3 and 4 Maccabees, *Wisdom of Solomon, additions to Esther, *Prayer of Manasseh), although there is still dispute over the original language of a number of these books (see Müller, 13-15). This group of additional books is now usually called the OT *Apocrypha (although a few of the books above are not included in this group). Most scholars do not now believe that there was ever an Alexandrian canon that set its Scriptures apart from those of Judaism elsewhere but that the Greek Bible was in use not only throughout the Diaspora but in Palestine as well. This is now attested by the Greek OT fragments, including the *Minor Prophets Scroll,* which is one of the Judean Desert documents (see Müller, 39-40). A number of other books that seem to have been attached to this corpus in various ways and by various groups were also considered to be sacred by some Jews of the time. These consist of some of the pseudepigrapha, such as **Psalms of Solomon* and **1 Enoch,* which has been found in Greek fragmentary form, as well as 4 Esdras (= 2 Esdras of the English Apocrypha; *see* Esdras, Books of). *Psalms of Solomon* appears to have been attached to Codex Alexandrinus (according to the table of contents; see Swete, 202), and may well have been a part of the Greek Bible for some groups, although the other two listed above are more doubtful as to their scriptural status.

2. Theories of Origin.

The label "Septuagint" comes from the account in the **Letter of Aristeas* of seventy—actually seventy-two—Jewish scholars who were purportedly involved in the translation of the Jewish Bible into Greek. There are four ancient historical accounts of the origin of the Greek OT. The first is contained in the *Letter of Aristeas* (see Müller, 46-58; Jellicoe, 29-58). This document, probably written in the late second century B.C., is ostensibly written by Aristeas, a contemporary of the events reported and an official at the Egyptian Ptolemaic court. Among a myriad of other details, much of them irrelevant, he records that Demetrius of Phaleron, who was director of the *Alexandrian Library (this is a mistaken identification; see Müller, 47), was instructed by the king, Ptolemy II Philadelphus (285-246 B.C.), to gather together all of the books in the world. He noticed that the Jews' Law needed to be translated into Greek from their language for its inclusion. Gifts were sent to the temple in Jerusalem, and some exiled Jews returned to convince the high priest to send seventy-two Jewish scholars to translate the law into Greek. This they did on the island of Pharos, completing it in seventy-two days. The translation was reportedly well received by both the people and the king, and curses were placed upon any who would dare to tamper with it.

The second account of the translation of the Hebrew Bible is that of *Aristobulus, the Jewish philosopher who lived in Alexandria in 181-145 B.C. when Ptolemy VI Philometor was king (Müller, 58-61). His discussion on the translation, since it is only available to us through the work of other ancient authors, has often been questioned regarding its genuineness. Aristobulus (in Eusebius *Praep. Ev.* 13.12.1-2) claims that the Law was translated before the time of Plato and that Plato drew upon it in his thinking. It is unclear whether Aristeas used the work of Aristobulus or whether they both relied on common tradition, but Müller thinks that they both reflect a tradition in which the Egyptian king was motivated to promote the translation.

The third account is that of *Philo (Müller, 61-64). In a number of ways Philo's account in *De Vita Mosis* 2.26-44 is very similar to that of *Aristeas,* prompting the question of whether Philo is using *Aristeas* and presenting an abbreviated form of his story, or whether they are each drawing on independent tradition. In any case, Philo adds several interpretive dimensions of his own to the account. One is that Philo tends to see the translation as done in accordance with the divine will, with the result that the product was inspired. As Müller notes, "This means that the Greek Bible is not a daughter version, but a 'sister' enjoying equal rights" (Müller, 63). The second is that, as a result, the translators themselves are seen to be priests and prophets, which acts as a guarantee of their translation.

The fourth and final ancient account is that of *Josephus (Müller, 64-66). As many have noted, Josephus in his *Jewish Antiquities* 12.2.1-15 §§11-118 presents an abbreviated account of *Aristeas's* version, and in *Against Apion* 2.4 §§45-47 he includes the *Aristeas* account. The emphasis in Josephus's account is upon the accuracy of the translators' work.

Scholars have assessed the historicity of the *Aristeas* account (and those similar to it) and come to differing conclusions: from nearly factual and historical to complete and bogus fiction, with nearly every view between these extremes represented. The current position is that probably there is some basis in fact for what *Aristeas* relates—that the Law, or Pentateuch, was translated into Greek in Egypt beginning in the third century B.C. (Kenyon, 14). However, there are other parts of the account that are held to be less reliable, such as the claim that it was Palestinian Jews who performed the translation. Almost assuredly the translation of the Hebrew Bible into Greek was occasioned by the fact that the vast majority of Jews—certainly those outside of Palestine, and especially in Egypt where there was a significant number of Jews—did not have linguistic access to their Scriptures in Hebrew and required a Greek version (Müller, 38-39). The translation itself seems to reflect these realities. There is the possibility that the *Aristeas* account is given as an apologetic for a new translation meant to displace previous ones (Kahle, 212), although what may be indicated is simply that the Hebrew manuscripts were in such poor condition that it was necessary to establish a reliable text before translation could proceed (see Müller, 52). This possibility, as well as one that admits of the difficulties of creating such a translation because it would imply interpretation, is not broached by Philo or Josephus.

Although the above account is the one most widely regarded as satisfactorily explaining the basic origin of the Septuagint, there are other, modern theories that have been proposed as well (see Jellicoe, 59-73). As noted above, Kahle (209-28) thought that the *Letter of Aristeas* was written in the late second century B.C., long after Greek translations of the Hebrew Bible had been made by Jews in Egypt (not from Palestine). *Aristeas* would thus have been written in defense of a recent revision of these Greek translations in order to establish this one as the standard edition. He finds in support of this theory not only *Aristeas*'s imposing curses on those who would tamper with the text but the testimony of Ben Sira in his prologue concerning knowing the Law, Prophets and other Writings, and textual characteristics of some of the earliest manuscripts, such as P. Fouad 266, P. Rylands Greek 458, the Judean Desert Greek Bible fragments, and the *Minor Prophets Scroll.* Gaster believed that the Greek Pentateuch originated not in Egypt but in Palestine, since only an origin in Palestine would have given the translation the necessary prestige for acceptance. The Jews were by this translational act taking the initiative in confronting their religious rivals, including the *Samaritans.

Thackeray (1921, esp. 9-15) believed that the origins of the Septuagint and Jewish worship went closely together and that the latter gave rise to the former. Neither Aramaic nor Hebrew was understood in Egypt, and worship needs of these Diaspora Jews demanded a form of the Scriptures rendered into their vernacular tongue. Thackeray accepted much of the *Aristeas* tradition, such as the Pentateuch being translated first, the origin of the version in Egypt, its dating to the third century B.C. and the Hebrew scrolls being brought from Palestine. But he rejected the notion of seventy-two translators being commissioned by the king for royal purposes. Instead, he thought the task was undertaken by a very small group, perhaps five, who translated it for liturgical reasons. The Pentateuch was translated first, followed by the Prophets, and finally the Writings, although they were translated along different lines. A final theory is the transcription theory of Tychsen and Wutz (see Jellicoe, 70-73), who posited that the Hebrew text was first transliterated before it was translated.

As Jellicoe has observed in assessing these theories, some of them have been ignored (such as Gaster's), others have been pretty much discredited (such as Tychsen and Wutz's), while others have been rightly criticized (such as Kahle's) and still others have not been appreciated as fully as they should be (such as Thackeray 1921). Current Septuagint scholarship tends to treat positively the basic elements of the *Aristeas* tradition and to respond usually in the negative to the theory of Kahle. It thus accepts that the Pentateuch was translated first, in the third century B.C., followed by the Prophets and the Writings, most of which were translated by the second century (see Tov 1992, 136-37).

3. Revisions and Other Greek Versions.

Besides the translational tradition that is now identified as the Septuagint, or Old Greek version, there have been many other Greek versions of the OT. As might be expected for a text that by the turn of the era already had a lengthy history of textual transmission, there were revisions and retranslations undertaken, possibly in conjunction with revision of the Hebrew text, but probably for other reasons as well (see Tov 1992, 143). Some of the Judean Desert Septuagint documents are themselves thought to reflect such revisions. It has been accepted by many Septuagint scholars that the *Minor Prophets Scroll* reflects what is sometimes called the *kaige* recension, named after the use of this particular translational linguistic feature of the Hebrew word for "also" (see Greenspoon, 160). The *kaige* revision of expanded Daniel is also in the Septuagint (Tov 1992, 144). Other revisions have been identified with other of the early manuscripts (such as P. Ryl. Greek 458 with Lucianic features), but the nature of the revision cannot always be established (see Tov 1992, 147).

Several of the other versions of the Greek OT came about, however, as reactions to the Christian appropriation of the Jewish Bible in Greek. The Septuagint was the early Christian Bible, and Christians were quick to use various passages for apologetic purposes, such as the rendering of Isaiah 7:14 with *parthenos* ("virgin") in support of the virginal conception of Jesus. The three major Jewish or Judaistic recensions prepared in reaction to the earlier version of the Greek OT were those of Theodotion (second century A.D.), which reflects the *kaige* revision noted above and is now often referred to as the *kaige*-Theodotion recension; Aquila (early second century A.D.); and the supposedly Ebionite Christian Symmachus (late second or early third century A.D.). The Christians themselves were responsible for three revisions of the earlier Greek OT, all apparently made in the third century A.D. (see Kenyon, 22-26; Jellicoe, 100-71). These include Origen's *Hexapla*, a presentation of the Bible in six columns (the Hebrew text, a Greek transliteration, and four Greek translations) and now known only through a few later minuscule manuscripts; Lucian's Syriac or Antiochene revision, which is known in a number of minuscule manuscripts (typified by the filling of omissions, conflated readings, interpolations and additions, and word substitutions—what is also called the Byzantine or Koine text in NT textual criticism; see Metzger); and Hesychius's revision, which many scholars question as to its actual existence (see Greenspoon, 159-62).

4. Translation Technique and Relation to the Hebrew Text.

The two major questions in assessing the Septuagint as a translation are its relation to the Hebrew text and the type of translational technique used. These questions are closely related and will be handled together here, along with the related question of the kind of Greek to be found in the Septuagint (see Porter 1989, 145-47).

Thackeray was one of the first to attempt to categorize the translational techniques of the individual authors. Thackeray specifies the following categories of translation (1909, 13):

Good Koine Greek translation: Pentateuch, Joshua (part), Isaiah, and 1 Maccabees.

Indifferent Greek translation: Jeremiah (1—28), Ezekiel, the Minor Prophets, 1 and 2 Chronicles (except for the last few chapters of 2 Chron), some of Kingdoms, Psalms, Sirach and Judith.

Literal or unintelligent translation: Jeremiah (29—51), Baruch (1:1—3:8), Judges, Ruth, some of Kingdoms, Song of Solomon, Lamentations, Theodotion Daniel, 2 Esdras (possibly Theodotion), Ecclesiastes (Aquila).

Literary paraphrase: 1 Esdras, Daniel, Esther, Job, and Proverbs.

Literary and Atticistic free Greek: Wisdom, Epistle of Jeremiah, Baruch (3:9—end), 2, 3 and 4 Maccabees.

Vernacular, free Greek: Tobit (perhaps a paraphrase).

On the basis of these kinds of findings, Thackeray (1907) also thought that he could determine the number of translators involved in a particular book, especially Kingdoms. Much subsequent work has shown that Thackeray and other attempts at classification had perhaps underestimated some of the factors of the Septuagint as a translation (cf. Gehman, who posited a form of Jewish Greek used in synagogues). Brock (1972, 12, 14) has noted that the translation of the Pentateuch was a difficult task, since it was without precedent in the Hellenistic world, there being no tradition of Greek translation of oriental religious documents. This required the translators to develop their method as they proceeded, but since the translators were probably Egyptians, there is the question of whether they always understood what it was that they were translating (Barr, 15; Tov 1984). In many cases it is arguable that they did not (Lee, 18), since there are numerous oddities such as neologisms, transliterations and odd syntax. As a result, it is difficult to make the kinds of distinctions that Thackeray did, and more recent scholars are wanting to see the Septuagint as containing a mixture of literal and free translation even within a single book, as well as a historical development in the translation itself, especially from a freer to a more literal rendering as the conception of the product as "Scripture" became better recognized.

The translation is often a compromise that is not consistently literal or free (Brock 1972, 16, 18, 20-21; cf. Barr, who gives six standards for judging the ways a translation may be literal and free at the same time), and a religious text with a fair amount of "semantic tolerance" (Rabin, 9-10) in terms of its definitely being Greek in syntax and lexis, but having a distinctly Hebrew cast in certain places (Thackeray 1909, 27-28; Horrocks, 56-57). This kind of tolerance may well have prompted some of the earliest alternative translations or revisions of the Greek OT, such as those of Aquila, to some extent Symmachus and some of the Lucianic alterations, which were concerned to make the Greek text a more literal rendering of the Hebrew. Nevertheless, the Semitisms are not necessarily consistent, and the translators vary in their use of expressions, on the basis of their translational perspective (Brock, 1979, 74-79). Since many, if not most, of the users of this sacred text did not have access to the original Hebrew (in some instances, of course, there was no original Hebrew to consider), attention needs to be given to the Septuagint as a free-standing Greek religious document used in ancient worshiping communities (contra many of the studies on the language of the Septuagint, which concentrate on isolated instances of translational equivalence; see, e.g., Aejmelaus; but cf. the standard grammars and descriptions of Swete, 289-314; Thackeray; Conybeare and Stock, 25-100).

5. Editions of the Septuagint.

The primary manuscripts for establishing the editions of the Septuagint consist of a number of important Greek papyri, especially the major majuscule codices and the numerous minuscules. Since the papyri have been only fairly recently discovered and published the majuscule and minuscule manuscripts have formed the basis of editions of the Septuagint.

Like editions of the Greek NT, the first printed editions of the Greek OT were created in the Renaissance. Unlike the editions of the Greek NT, however, most of the Septuagint editions were based upon one of the major codices, thus establishing an enduring tradition of textual criticism in Septuagint studies for the creation of single-text editions (or what Tov calls diplomatic editions [1992, 140]). However, again like editions of the Greek NT, in more recent times eclectic editions of the Septuagint have been produced (what Tov somewhat misleadingly calls critical editions [1992, 140]).

The first published edition of the Septuagint was part of the Complutensian Polyglot authorized by Cardinal Ximenes de Cisnos in 1514-1521 (Alcalà, Spain). This edition utilized a number of Byzantine manuscripts reflecting the Lucianic tradition, but it also has other readings as well. This text provided the basis for a number of later Polyglot Bibles (see Metzger, 7). Most of the subsequent major editions of the Greek OT tended to follow a single majuscule codex text. For example, the Sistine Bible, published in Rome in 1586 (named after the Pope, Sixtus V, who commissioned it), utilized Codex Vaticanus as its basis (Trebolle Barrera, 305), although the editors did not apparently follow this manuscript strictly (Kenyon, 60). This edition proved very important, nevertheless, since it was the basis of Walton's Polyglot published in London in 1657 and, more importantly, the edition by Holmes and Parsons (Oxford, 1798-1827, in 5 vols.). Begun by Holmes, who finished the first volume before his death, it was completed by Parsons, and has proved to be an enduring and valuable source of information. This edition, while based upon the Sistine Bible, includes variants from 164 manuscripts and assembled the first list of minuscules, providing much useful text-critical information (see Kenyon, 49; Jellicoe, 2-3). The editions of Tischendorf are also based on the Sistine edition, but he confined himself to comparing the major codices, sometimes from inferior editions (as in Codex Vaticanus; Jellicoe, 3-5). The edition of Swete (Cambridge, 1887-94, in 3 vols.) is also based on Codex Vaticanus where this manuscript is available, but uses either Codex Sinaiticus or Codex Alexandrinus where it is not. The last of the single-text editions to mention is that by Brooke, McLean and Thackeray. Begun in 1906, and using the same principle of relying on Codex Vaticanus where possible and Codex Sinaiticus or

Codex Alexandrinus elsewhere, this edition appeared in nine parts until 1940 (3 vols. from Cambridge), but the death of the last of the editors in 1947 meant that the edition was never finally completed. The edition includes the Pentateuch, Joshua—Ruth, 1-4 Kingdoms, Chronicles, 1-2 Esdras, Esther, Judith and Tobit (Kenyon, 60-61; Jellicoe, 21-24).

Eclectic editions of the Septuagint essentially begin with the edition of Rahlfs. He followed in many ways the work of his teacher, Lagarde, who pioneered Septuagintal research into manuscript types. Lagarde claimed that all of the texts were mixed and that an attempt to arrive at the original text necessarily must involve an eclectic process of comparing and weighing evidence (see Jellicoe, 6). As a result, Rahlfs's edition of the Greek OT (Stuttgart, 1935, 2 vols., published by the Württemberg Bible Society) relied on the three major codices: Vaticanus, Sinaiticus and Alexandrinus. This means of arriving at the text in many ways resembles the principles used by Nestle in the creation of his Greek NT edition. Rahlfs prepared this edition in part as a stopgap measure while the Göttingen Septuagint Project got underway (see Jellicoe, 9-21). First edited by Rahlfs, who published an edition of the Psalter in 1931, and then by Kappler, Hahnhart and now Aejmelus, this current project is undertaking to edit eclectic texts for every book of the Septuagint, providing a very detailed critical apparatus for each volume. The publication of these volumes is sometimes accompanied by separate volumes that describe the text-critical decisions in more detail.

While there is no doubt that the Göttingen Septuagint editions marshall a phenomenal amount of text-critical information and are probably providing the most thorough analysis of these data, the question remains whether a single-text edition or an eclectic text is to be preferred. In creating a single-text edition one must recognize the incomplete or late state of some of the textual evidence (e.g., Genesis is often created out of Codex Alexandrinus for Gen 1:1—41:28, since it is lacking in Codex Vaticanus). However, along with questioning whether the Hebrew text has priority over the Greek in trying to get back to the earliest text of the OT, an assumption of most eclectic editions (see Müller, 114), one may also question the premise (from Lagarde) that all of the manuscripts of the Septuagint are mixed and have a built-in eclecticism that merits creating a hypothetical text that does not match any ancient manuscript.

6. The Septuagint and the New Testament. The importance of the Septuagint for study of the NT cannot be underestimated. Its importance lies in at least the following areas, not all of which have been fully studied:

(1) The language of the Septuagint, despite any Semitisms, is part and parcel of the Hellenistic Greek of the period in terms of its grammar and lexis, and hence it is an important body of evidence for studying the Greek of the NT and that of the Greco-Roman period (see Horrocks, 56-57, 92-93; Porter 1989, 141-56). Along with this recognition (as noted in 4 above) goes the importance of the Septuagint as an ancient translation. The insight that the Septuagint offers into translational technique in the ancient world has importance for studying the language of the NT, including the issue of the translation of the Aramaic words of Jesus into Greek (see Black).

(2) The Septuagint constituted the set of sacred writings for early Christians and many if not most Jews, even many in Palestine, in the first century. The Septuagintal papyrological finds in Egypt and Palestine bear witness to the widespread importance of the Septuagint, especially the Pentateuch, in a variety of Jewish and Christian milieux.

(3) Most important, perhaps, is the fact that the NT authors use the Septuagint form of the OT more than they do that of any other version. As Swete says, "every part of the N. T. affords evidence of a knowledge of the LXX., and that a great majority of the passages cited from the O. T. are in general agreement with the Greek version. . . . the LXX. is the principal source from which the writers of the N. T. derived their O. T. quotations" (Swete, 392). It is not surprising that recent research into Paul's use of the OT confirms the importance of the Septuagint (see Ellis; Stanley, 254-55), since he was a native Greek speaker and wrote to Greek-speaking audiences throughout the Greco-Roman Mediterranean world. Worth noting also, however, is that the Synoptic Gospels use the Greek version as well, including many quotations spoken by Jesus (*see DJG*, Old Testament in the Gospels §1, where Evans notes that this does not invalidate their possible authenticity). Again, this might not seem surprising since the Gospels are Greek

documents addressed to Christian congregations in the same world as Paul's. However, Longenecker (60-66) has noted not only that the great majority of OT quotations of Jesus are apparently from the Septuagint but that in several instances the point that Jesus makes in the Gospel account is based on the Septuagint reading (e.g., Mk 7:6-7 and Mt 15:8-9, citing Is 29:13). He notes further that in Matthew's Gospel the narrator often uses a more Semitic form of quotation while Jesus' quotations are Septuagintal, thus arguing against the narrator assimilating quotations to the Greek form for his audience. Longenecker contends that a number of explanations for this phenomenon must be taken into account, including the multilingual character of first-century Palestine. He even suggests that "it may be that in his applications of the OT, Jesus, who normally spoke in Aramaic but could also use Greek and Mishnaic Hebrew to some extent, at times engaged himself in textual selection among the various Aramaic, Hebrew and Greek versions then current, and some of the septuagintal features in the text-forms attributed to him actually arise from him" (Longenecker, 65-66; cf. Porter 2000, 126-80).

(4) There is a theological dimension to the use of the Septuagint in the NT that merits attention as well. There is the question of how the earliest Christian writers, those found in the canonical NT, interpreted their sacred writings, and in what ways this influenced later interpretation of not only the OT, but what was to become the NT (see Müller, 130-39; Longenecker, 205-20).

7. Recent Research Initiatives and Projects.
To date, when compared with scholarly work on the Hebrew OT and the Greek NT, work on the Septuagint has languished behind. Although there was significant interest in the Septuagint in the early part of the twentieth century, no doubt fueled by then-recent discoveries of Greek papyri in Egypt and the revision in perspective that this caused, and though there has continued to be steady interest in some circles (e.g., the University of Toronto has long been a center of Septuagint study in North America), there has been far less scholarly publication overall. For example, one does not find nearly so many introductions, translations or commentary series on the Septuagint as one does on the Hebrew OT or the NT.

A number of Septuagint projects are now underway, however, that will, if successful, move Septuagint study forward in these areas. The first is the French initiative entitled La Bible d'Alexandrie. This is an attempt to translate and make brief comments upon the books of the Septuagint from the standpoint of its place in the Hellenistic world. The project is headed by Marguerite Harl (for her perspective on the Septuagint, see Harl, Dorival and Munnich), and is well along, with a number of volumes published to date. The next project to mention is the New English Translation of the Septuagint (NETS), organized by the International Organization for Septuagint and Cognate Studies (IOSCS). Whereas the French project approaches the text from a Hellenistic standpoint, the NETS project emphasizes its translational nature and its derivation from the Hebrew original, sometimes using "unidiomatic" renderings of the Greek (see Greenspoon, 153). This project is supposedly nearing completion. The third and final initiative is the Septuagint Commentary Series to be published by Brill. To fill a definite lacuna in commentary literature in English, this series—for which most of the volumes have been assigned but none has yet appeared—takes an approach more like that of the French project. The text, translation and commentary are to be based on one of the major codex manuscripts, providing detailed commentary on the Greek text as a living document for its original context.

See also HEBREW BIBLE; MANUSCRIPTS, GREEK OLD TESTAMENT; OLD TESTAMENT VERSIONS, ANCIENT.

BIBLIOGRAPHY. A. Aejmelaus, *On the Trail of the Septuagint Translators: Collected Essays* (Kampen: Kok Pharos, 1993); J. Barr, *The Typology of Literalism in Ancient Biblical Translations* (NAWG I, Philologisch-historische Klasse. Mitteilungen des Septuaginta-Unternehmens 15; Göttingen: Vandenhoeck & Ruprecht, 1979); M. Black, *An Aramaic Approach to the Gospels and Acts* (3d ed.; Oxford: Clarendon Press, 1967); S. Brock, "Aspects of Translation Technique in Antiquity," *GRBS* 20 (1979) 69-87; idem, "The Phenomenon of the Septuagint," in *The Witness of Tradition*, ed. A. S. van der Woude (OtSt 17; Leiden: E. J. Brill, 1972) 11-36; C. Conybeare and S. G. Stock, *Selections from the Septuagint* (Boston: Ginn, 1905); E. E. Ellis, *Paul's Use of the Old Testament* (Grand Rapids, MI: Baker, 1981 [1957]); M. Gaster, *The Samaritans* (Schweich Lectures 1923; London: British Academy, 1925);

H. S. Gehman, "The Hebraic Character of Septuagint Greek," *VT* 1 (1951) 81-90; L. Greenspoon, "'It's All Greek to Me': Septuagint Studies since 1968," *CurR* 5 (1997) 147-74; M. Harl, G. Dorival and O. Munnich, *La Bible grecque des Septante: Du judaïsme hellénistique au Christianisme ancien* (Paris: Cerf, 1994); G. Horrocks, *Greek: A History of the Language and Its Speakers* (London: Longman, 1997); S. Jellicoe, *The Septuagint and Modern Study* (Oxford: Clarendon Press, 1968); P. E. Kahle, *The Cairo Geniza* (2d ed.; Oxford: Blackwell, 1959); F. G. Kenyon, *The Text of the Greek Bible*, rev. A. W. Adams (3d ed.; London: Duckworth, 1975); J. A. L. Lee, *A Lexical Study of the Septuagint Version of the Pentateuch* (SBLSCS 14; Chico, CA: Scholars Press, 1983); R. N. Longenecker, *Biblical Exegesis in the Apostolic Period* (Grand Rapids, MI: Eerdmans, 1975); B. M. Metzger, "The Lucianic Recension of the Greek Bible," in *Chapters in the History of New Testament Textual Criticism* (NTTS 4; Leiden: E. J. Brill, 1963) 1-41; M. Müller, *The First Bible of the Church: A Plea for the Septuagint* (JSOTSup 206; Sheffield: Sheffield Acaemic Press, 1996); A. Nairne, *The Alexandrine Gospel* (London: Longman, Green, 1917); S. E. Porter, *The Criteria for Authenticity in Historical-Jesus Research: Previous Discussion and New Proposals* (JSNTSup 191; Sheffield: Sheffield Academic Press, 2000); idem, *Verbal Aspect in the Greek of the New Testament, with Reference to Tense and Mood* (SBG 1; New York: Lang, 1989); C. Rabin, "The Translation Process and the Character of the Septuagint," *Textus* 6 (1968) 1-26; L. Rost, *Judaism Outside the Hebrew Canon: An Introduction to the Documents* (Nashville: Abingdon, 1976); C. D. Stanley, *Paul and the Language of Scripture: Citation Technique in the Pauline Epistles and Contemporary Literature* (SNTSMS 74; Cambridge: Cambridge University Press, 1992); H. B. Swete, *An Introduction to the Old Testament in Greek* (Cambridge: Cambridge University Press, 1902); H. St. J. Thackeray, *A Grammar of the Old Testament in Greek According to the Septuagint* (Cambridge: Cambridge University Press, 1909); idem, "The Greek Translators of the Four Books of Kings," *JTS* 8 (1907) 262-78; idem, *The Septuagint and Jewish Worship: A Study in Origins* (Schweich Lectures 1920; London: British Academy, 1921); E. Tov, "Did the Septuagint Translators Always Understand Their Hebrew Text?" in *De Septuaginta: Studies in Honour of J.W. Wevers on His Sixty-Fifth Birthday*, ed. A. Pietersma and C. Cox (Ontario: Benben, 1984) 53-70; idem, *Textual Criticism of the Hebrew Bible* (Minneapolis: Fortress; Assen/Maastricht: Van Gorcum, 1992); J. Trebolle Barrera, *The Jewish Bible and the Christian Bible: An Introduction to the History of the Bible* (Leiden: E. J. Brill; Grand Rapids, MI: Eerdmans, 1998). S. E. Porter

SHAME. *See* HONOR AND SHAME.

SHAMMAI, HOUSE OF

The House (or school) of Shammai apparently was the first major academy of sages. Soon after it was rivaled by the House of *Hillel. Rabbinic writings divide up first-century sages into these two houses, founded by the great teachers Shammai (first century B.C.) and Hillel (turn of the era).

Prior to A.D. 70 the rulings of the House of Shammai prevailed; afterwards the House of Hillel gained ascendancy. "These are among the Halakoth (i.e., rulings) that the sages enjoined while in the upper room of Hananiah ben Hezekia ben Gorion, the head of the House of Shammai. When they went up to visit him they voted, and they of the House of Shammai outnumbered them of the House of Hillel; and eighteen things did they decree on that day" (*m. Šabb.* 1:4; see also *m. Miqw.* 4:1). Several of these decrees are delineated in *m. Šabbat* 1:5-11.

Generally the House of Shammai ruled more stringently than did the House of Hillel, though in some instances (perhaps 20 percent) the Hillelites ruled more stringently.

> Rabbi Simeon [some MSS. read Ishmael] reports three opinions in which the House of Shammai follows the more lenient [ruling] and the House of Hillel the more stringent ruling. According to the House of Shammai the book of Ecclesiastes does not render the hands unclean. And the House of Hillel says: "It renders the hands unclean." According to the House of Shammai, sin-offering water that has fulfilled its purpose is clean; and the House of Hillel declares it unclean. The House of Shammai declares black cummin insusceptible to unclean-ness; and the House of Hillel declares it susceptible. So, too, [do they differ] concerning [whether it is liable to] tithes. (*b. ʿEd.* 5:3; on the canonical status of Ecclesiastes, see also *m. Yad.* 3:5)

One of the major differences between the Shammaites and the Hillelites concerns the manner in which one is to recite the Shema (i.e., Deut 6:4-9; 11:13-21; Num 15:37-41). "The House of Shammai says: 'In the evening all should recline when they recite [the Shema], but in the morning they should stand up, for it is written, "And when you lie down and when you rise up" (Deut 6:7).' But the House of Hillel says: 'They may recite it every one in his own way, for it is written, "And when you walk by the way" (Deut 6:7).'" Rabbi Tarfon comments that on one occasion he recited the Shema after the fashion of the House of Shammai and so put himself in danger of robbers (by reclining beside the road). His colleagues said to him, "You deserved whatever befell you in that you transgressed the words of the House of Hillel" (*m. Ber.* 1:3).

Several differences between the Houses of Shammai and Hillel are recorded in *m. Berakot* 8:1-8. For example, "The House of Shammai says: '[On a sabbath or a festival day] they say the Benediction first over the day and then over the wine.' And the House of Hillel says: 'They say the Benediction first over the wine and then over the day'" (*m. Ber.* 8:1). "The House of Shammai says: 'They wash the hands and then mix the cup.' And the House of Hillel says: 'They mix the cup and then wash the hands'" (*m. Ber.* 8:2).

Critical scholarship suspects that the Shammaites were more influential than the later *rabbinic writings admit, their authors having adopted most of the Hillelite rulings. Mystical and *eschatological traditions speculate that in the world to come the Shammaite rulings will once again dominate.

See also HILLEL, HOUSE OF; RABBINIC LITERATURE: MISHNAH AND TOSEFTA; RABBIS.

BIBLIOGRAPHY. R. Goldenberg, "Shammai, School of," *ABD* 5:1158; "Hillel and Shammai," in *DJBP*, 293; J. Neusner, *The Rabbinic Traditions About the Pharisees Before 70*, vol. 2 (Leiden: E. J. Brill, 1971); S. Safrai, "Halakha," in *The Literature of the Sages*, ed. S. Safrai (CRINT 2.3; Assen: Van Gorcum; Philadelphia: Fortress, 1987) 155-209; A. J. Saldarini, *Pharisees, Scribes and Sadducees in Palestinian Society: A Sociological Approach* (Wilmington, DE: Michael Glazier, 1988) 204-7; E. E. Urbach, *The Sages: Their Concepts and Beliefs* (Cambridge, MA: Harvard University Press, 1973; 2d ed., Jerusalem: Magnes, 1979) 576-648.

C. A. Evans

SHEM, TREATISE OF. *See* TREATISE OF SHEM.

SHIPS. *See* TRAVEL AND TRADE.

SIBYLLINE ORACLES

The sibyl is a figure of Greek and Roman legend. She is always depicted as an aged woman, uttering gloomy prophecies. Ovid (*Met.* 14.132) tells us that she was granted by Apollo that she might live as many years as there were grains of sand on the seashore, but she neglected to ask for youth, and so she remained for thousands of years a shriveled, shrunken old woman. According to Heracleides Ponticus (fourth century B.C.) she was older than Orpheus.

The legend seems to have originated in *Asia Minor, where she was claimed by the localities of Marpessus and Erythrae. The legend was brought to Italy by Greek settlers, probably about the beginning of the sixth century B.C. There the sibyl made her home in a cave at Cumae, which was made famous by Virgil, who described a consultation of the sibyl by Aeneas (Virgil *Aen.* 6). Virgil also immortalized the sibyl in the opening line of the fourth *Eclogue*, which referred to the *ultima aetas*, or final age of the Cumean (sibyl). In the Hellenistic and Roman periods there were supposed to be several sibyls. The Roman antiquarian Varro, in the first century B.C., listed ten sibyls: Persian, Libyan, Delphic, Cimmerian, Erythrean, Samian, Cumean, Hellespontian, Phrygian and Tiburtine. Other authors mention Chaldean, Egyptian and Hebrew sibyls. There is no evidence, however, that sibylline oracles were ever produced in any language other than Greek.

1. Sibylline Oracles
2. The Standard Collection of Sibylline Oracles
3. The Jewish Oracles
4. Jewish Oracles Revised by Christians
5. Christian Oracles
6. *Sibylline Oracles* 11–14
7. Enduring Influence

1. Sibylline Oracles.

Like other Greek prophecies, sibylline oracles were usually written in epic hexameters. We have only scattered examples of pagan sibylline verses. They were often predictions of war or natural disasters. There was an official collection of sibylline books in Rome, where they were consulted by the senate in times of emergency. According to legend, the sibyl offered nine books to Tarquinius Priscus, king of Rome in the early sixth century, for a price. He refused, so she burned three and repeated the offer at the same price. He refused again, so she burned three more. Finally he bought the three surviving books, and these became the core of the official collection.

About fifty consultations are reported between 496 and 100 B.C. These typically tell of some plague, famine or prodigy, and some details of a ritual prescribed by the sibylline books. Only one direct quotation survives, in the *Memorabilia* of Phlegon. This passage of seventy hexameters reports the birth of an androgyne and prescribes a long list of rituals and offerings to the gods. The Roman collection was destroyed when the temple of Jupiter was burned down in 83 B.C. When the temple was rebuilt seven years later oracles were collected from various places, especially Erythrea. When the emperor Augustus collected and destroyed some two thousand unofficial oracles in A.D. 12 he kept the sibylline books but edited even those (Suetonius *Augustus* 31.1).

Virgil's reference to a final age in the fourth *Eclogue* raises the possibility that pagan sibyls may also have been credited with extensive prophecies of the course of history and its division into periods. Such prophecies are typical of the Jewish and Christian sibylline books. No example of such a pagan sibylline oracle has survived, however, and it is possible that the extended prophecy of the course of history was a Jewish innovation in the genre.

2. The Standard Collection of Sibylline Oracles. The standard collection is made up of Jewish and Christian *pseudepigraphic writings. There are two distinct collections in the manuscripts. One group contains books 1—8; the other begins with material from books 6—8, followed by book 4. These books should be numbered 9 and 10, but since they repeat material from the first group they are omitted. The remaining books are numbered 11—14, although there are only twelve books in the collection. These oracles were collected no earlier than the sixth century A.D., but some of the oracles clearly date to the pre-Christian period. It is generally agreed that the oracles in books 3—5 are of Jewish origin. Books 1—2 and 8 contain Jewish oracles that have been incorporated into Christian compositions. Books 6 and 7 are Christian. The provenance of books 11—14 is unclear, but at least book 11 appears to be Jewish, and there is no sign of Christian authorship.

3. The Jewish Oracles.

3.1. **Sibylline Oracle** *3.* The oldest Jewish oracles are found in the third book. This is a loosely structured collection of oracles from different sources. *Sibylline Oracle* 3:1-96 seems to have been originally part of a different book. *Sibylline Oracle* 3:1-45 is different from the rest of the collection except for some fragments. They have a philosophical character and affirm the transcendence of God and denounce idolatry. *Sibylline Oracle* 3:46-92 contains three distinct oracles from the Roman period. There is also an oracle from the Roman period in *Sibylline Oracle* 3:350-80. Two anti-Macedonian oracles are found in *Sibylline Oracle* 3:381-400. *Sibylline Oracle* 3:401-88 are prophecies of various disasters, and possibly of diverse provenance. They are often attributed to the Erythrean sibyl. There is nothing Jewish or Christian in these verses, but they are very similar to other pagan sibylline oracles. They were probably incorporated into the collection to establish the sibylline character of the Jewish oracles.

The main corpus of Jewish oracles in book 3 is found in verses 97-294 and 545-808. These oracles are dated by three references to the seventh king of Egypt in *Sibylline Oracle* 3:193, 318 and 608. While seven was a sacred number and may indicate an ideal king, the number could not have been introduced with any credibility later than the reign of the seventh king of the Ptolemaic line, the Greek rulers of Egypt after the conquests of *Alexander the Great. The *Ptolemies did not bear a number as part of their title in antiquity, and so there is some ambiguity as to the identity of the seventh king, depending on whether one counts Alexander and how one counts the overlapping reigns of Ptolemies 6, 7 and 8 in the second century B.C. The most likely date of composition is in the reign of Ptolemy VI Philometor, who reigned from 180-164 B.C. and 163-145 B.C. The seventh king was still in the future when these oracles were written.

The references to the seventh king indicate the time when history will reach its climax and turning point. They do not explicitly credit the king with bringing about the change. In *Sibylline Oracle* 3:652-56, however, we are told that "God will send a king from the sun who will stop the entire earth from evil war . . . in obedience to the noble teachings of the great God." In Egyptian mythology, kings were closely associated with the sun, and this mythology was appropriated both by the Ptolemies and by anti-Ptolemaic Egyptian nationalists. (The phrase "king from the sun" is also found in the roughly contemporary anti-Ptolemaic "Potter's Oracle.") The king from the sun cannot be distinguished from "the seventh king of Egypt . . . numbered from the dynasty of the Greeks" (*Sib. Or.* 3:608). It appears then that the Jewish sibyl not only expected dramatic change in the reign of the seventh king but also looked on the Ptolemaic ruler as a virtual messiah, just as Second Isaiah had regarded Cyrus of Persia in an earlier period (cf. Is 45:1).

Ptolemy VI Philometor was especially benevolent to the Jews. The exiled high *priest Onias IV became a general in his army and was allowed to build a Jewish temple at Leontopolis. The confidence that the sibyl places in the Ptolemaic king is understandable if the author was a supporter of Onias.

Despite the sibyl's endorsement of a Ptolemaic ruler, she engages in a vigorous polemic against some aspects of Hellenistic and Egyptian culture and contrasts it unfavorably with *Judaism. Her favorite targets are homosexuality and idolatry. She urges the Greeks to send offerings to the *temple of the great God (presumably in *Jerusalem) and envisions a time when all people will send gifts to the temple and ponder the law of the great God (*Sib. Or.* 3:715-19). The interest in the temple is also intelligible if the author was a supporter of the exiled high priest. The sibyl concludes with a vision of eschatological bliss, modeled on Isaiah 11, where the wolf will lie down with the lamb (*Sib. Or.* 3:767-95).

3.2. Additions to **Sibylline Oracle** *3.* As noted already, several oracles from the Roman era were added to *Sibylline Oracle* 3. *Sibylline Oracle* 3:350-80 contains a powerful oracle against Rome, which predicts that the wealth it has taken from Asia will be returned and that a mistress will cut Rome's hair and restore peace to Asia. The mistress is most probably to be identified as Cleopatra. Other oracles, however, show a different attitude to Cleopatra. *Sibylline Oracle* 3:75-92 was written shortly after the battle of Actium and portrays Cleopatra as a widow who has brought disaster on the world. *Sibylline Oracle* 3:46-62 was also written after Actium and presupposes that Rome has gained control of Egypt. *Sibylline Oracle* 3:63-74 predicts that *Beliar will come *ek Sebastenōn*. This phrase should probably be interpreted as the line of Augustus, and Beliar should be identified as Nero, as he also is in the *Ascension of Isaiah* 4:1 ("a lawless king, the slayer of his mother").

3.3. **Sibylline Oracle** *5.* A later stage of the Egyptian sibylline tradition can be found in the fifth book of the collection, written in the early second century A.D. The tone of this book is far more bitter than that of book 3 and reflects the deteriorating circumstances of the Jewish community in Egypt. The first fifty verses introduce the book by reviewing history from Alexander to Hadrian. The next four oracles may be delimited as *Sibylline Oracle* 5:52-110, 111-178, 179-285 and 286-433. These oracles show a common pattern: (1) oracles against various nations (in *Sibylline Oracle* 5:52-110 and in 5:179-285 the oracles are mainly against Egypt; in the other oracles they are mainly against Asiatic countries); (2) the return of Nero as eschatological adversary; (3) the advent of a savior figure; (4) destruction, usually by fire.

The sibyl is even more bitter against Rome than against Egypt. Rome is denounced because of immorality, *adultery and homosexuality, but especially because of the destruction of Jerusalem (*Sib. Or.* 5:162-78). The evil of Rome is focused in the person of Nero. There was a popular legend that Nero had fled to the Parthians and would one day return. There are explicit allusions to Nero in *Sibylline Oracle* 5:137-54 and 214-27 (both passages refer to his attempt to cut through the isthmus of *Corinth) and again in *Sibylline Oracle* 5:363 ("a man who is a matricide will come from the ends of the earth"). He may also be the Persian who is said to come like hail in *Sibylline Oracle* 5:94. It should be noted that the sibyl does not envision the return of Nero from the dead, and so we cannot yet speak here of Nero redivivus. The myth of Nero redivivus is already implied in Revelation 17:11, which was probably written before the oracles in *Sibylline Oracle* 5.

The savior figure in *Sibylline Oracle* 5 is a king sent "from God" (*Sib. Or.* 5:108). In *Sibylline Oracle* 5:414 he is said to come from the expanses of heaven. In *Sibylline Oracle* 5:256 he comes "from the sky," but this is followed by a clearly Christian gloss in *Sibylline Oracle* 5:257. The notion of a king from heaven is paralleled, however, in the roughly contemporary Jewish apocalypse of

4 Ezra 14 (*see* Esdras, Books of), in which the deliverer is a man who rises from the sea and rides on the clouds. The Ptolemaic line was long defunct, and the Egyptian Jews of the early second century had no reason to expect deliverance from any Gentile ruler.

Sibylline Oracle 5 concludes with a long oracle that is mainly concerned with Egypt (*Sib. Or.* 5:434-530). The sibyl predicts the destruction of Isis and Sarapis, a prediction that may reflect the violence against Egyptian sanctuaries in the Jewish *Diaspora revolt of A.D. 115-117. Then there will be a temple to the true God in Egypt. But this too will be destroyed by marauding Ethiopians. The book ends with a battle of the stars, concluding with a starless sky. This oracle eloquently expresses the despair of Egyptian Jewry at the end of the Diaspora revolt. *Sibylline Oracle* 5 has many significant parallels to the book of Revelation, including the interest in Nero and the designation of Rome as Babylon (*Sib. Or.* 5:434).

3.4.* Sibylline Oracle *4. A different strand of Jewish sibylline tradition is found in the fourth book of the collection. Egypt receives no special attention in this book. In sharp contrast to books 3 and 5, the sibyl here declares that God does not have a house or temple (*Sib. Or.* 4:8). The place of composition is uncertain. Egypt may be ruled out. *Sibylline Oracle* 4 is sometimes located in the Jordan Valley or Syria because of the importance attached to baptism.

The core of *Sibylline Oracle* 4 is an overview of history in the guise of prophecy. Two schemata are employed: four kingdoms (cf. Dan 2, 7) and ten generations. First the Assyrians rule for six generations, then the Medes for two and the Persians for one. The Macedonians rule in the tenth generation. It would seem that this was the original climax of the oracle. The conclusion would have predicted the downfall of *Macedonia. This original oracle may or may not have been Jewish. In the present text of *Sibylline Oracle* 4, however, the fall of Macedonia is followed by the rise of Rome, although Rome is not integrated into the sequence of either generations or kingdoms. The sibyl recounts the flight of Nero to the Parthians (*Sib. Or.* 4:119), the destruction of Jerusalem (*Sib. Or.* 4:126), the eruption of Mt. Vesuvius (*Sib. Or.* 4:130) and the return of Nero ("the fugitive from Rome," *Sib. Or.* 4:138). In light of these upheavals, the sibyl calls on people to abandon violence and "wash your whole bodies in perennial rivers"—that is, to accept baptism as a sign of repentance. This oracle is therefore an important parallel to the baptism of John the Baptist. The sibyl concludes with a prediction of a coming conflagration and the bodily resurrection of the dead. Belief in resurrection was notably absent in *Sibylline Oracles* 3 and 5.

4. Jewish Oracles Revised by Christians.

4.1. Books 1 and 2. The first two books of the standard collection are one long oracle that divides history into ten generations, as does *Sibylline Oracle* 4. The first seven generations are preserved without interruption in *Sibylline Oracle* 1:1-323. Then follows a passage on the incarnation and career of Christ in *Sibylline Oracle* 1:324-400. After a transitional passage in *Sibylline Oracle* 2:1-5 the original sequence is resumed, but a considerable portion of the original oracle has been lost. There is no reference to the eighth or ninth generations, but we move directly to the tenth. The remainder of *Sibylline Oracle* 2 is an account of eschatological crises and the last judgment. There are several clearly Christian passages, while some passages could have been written by either a Jew or a Christian. It appears that an original Jewish oracle structured by ten generations has been revised by a Christian. The Christian redaction knows the fall of Jerusalem, is probably no earlier than the second century A.D. and could be significantly later. The original Jewish stratum was composed no earlier than the Roman era, since Rome is the only power singled out for destruction in the tenth generation. This oracle could be as early as the turn of the era, but since it has been so heavily altered by the Christian redactor little can be said with confidence. The Jewish oracle is thought to come from Phrygia, which is said to be the first land to emerge after the flood and to be the nurse of restored humanity.

4.2. Book 8. *Sibylline Oracle* 8 falls into two clearly distinct sections. *Sibylline Oracle* 8:1-216 is mainly concerned with political prophecies, especially against Rome. These verses are probably Jewish in origin. There are several oracles on the return of Nero, presumably from the dead. First, his return is predicted in the time of Marcus Aurelius (A.D. 161-180). There is another reference to his return in *Sibylline Oracle* 8:155, where the anonymous "man of secret birth" is said to cut through the isthmus (of Corinth, as

Nero had attempted to do). Nero is probably also the figure who will come to ravage the nation of the Hebrews (*Sib. Or.* 8:140-41). The fact that the Hebrews alone are singled out argues for Jewish origin. This oracle must have been composed in the time of Marcus Aurelius, since it predicts the return of Nero before the death of that emperor. It is primarily a powerful indictment of the greed of Rome.

The Christian stratum of this book (*Sib. Or.* 8:217-500) is taken up with christology, the Incarnation and the praises of God. It begins with an acrostic poem that spells out the words *Iēsous Christos Theou Huios Sōtēr Stauros,* Jesus Christ, Son of God, Savior, Cross. The latest date for this section is provided by Lactantius (c. A.D. 240-320), who quotes extensively from the whole book.

5. Christian Oracles.

5.1. Book 6. *Sibylline Oracle* 6 is a short (twenty-eight-verse) hymn to Christ. Nothing in the text suggests sibylline authorship or even that it is an oracle. The hymn refers to the baptism of Christ in the Jordan and mentions fire in this connection. The allusion to the Jordan is the only possible clue to geographical provenance, and that is not very compelling. The hymn was quoted by Lactantius about A.D. 300.

5.2. Book 7. *Sibylline Oracle* 7 is poorly preserved and seems to be loosely structured. There is reference to the flood in *Sibylline Oracle* 7:7-15, and Phrygia is again hailed as the first land to emerge after it. The book concludes with an eschatological passage that predicts a conflagration, eternal punishment of sinners by fire and the restoration of the earth (*Sib. Or.* 7:118-51). Much of the intervening material consists of a chaotic sequence of oracles against various places. *Sibylline Oracle* 7:40-50 refers to a rout of Rome by the Parthians, possibly at Carrhae in 53 B.C. This is followed by an oracle about Troy (*Sib. Or.* 7:51-54). Later the sibyl returns to Rome in *Sibylline Oracle* 7:108-11, but the reference is to the rise of Rome after the fall of Macedonia.

A number of unusual references in the book have *gnostic parallels (e.g., "the noble mothers of God," *Sib. Or.* 7:72-73, referring to Hope, Piety and Holiness, and the Ogdoad in *Sib. Or.* 7:140), but these references are out of context and do not make the book gnostic. Claims that it is Jewish Christian are also unfounded. Much of the interest of the book concerns its interest in rituals. *Sibylline Oracle* 7:64-75 describes the baptism of Christ; in *Sibylline Oracle* 7:76-91 sacrifice is replaced by a rite commemorating the baptism, in which water is sprinkled on fire and a dove is released toward heaven. *Sibylline Oracle* 7:85-91 prescribes a rite for accepting supplicants. The eschatology of the book resembles that of *Sibylline Oracles* 4 and 1—2. *Sibylline Oracle* 7 was cited by Lactantius, and so it was probably composed in the second century. The place of origin is uncertain.

6. *Sibylline Oracles* 11—14.

The last four books of the *Sibylline Oracles* (11—14) provide a more or less continuous outline of history from the flood down to the Arab conquest of Egypt in the seventh century, with a brief eschatological conclusion in *Sibylline Oracle* 14:351-61. The books are marked off by introductions and conclusions, but these are secondary. The text is continuous. It was probably composed over centuries, being repeatedly updated and extended. There is no sign of Christian authorship, and large parts could have been composed by a pagan. *Sibylline Oracle* 11 reviews history from the flood to Cleopatra. This book is clearly Jewish, as it eulogizes the Jewish people under the name "Assyrians" (*Sib. Or.* 11:80-103), but it lacks the religious and ethical interests of *Sibylline Oracles* 3—5. Since the review of history only extends to the time of Cleopatra, *Sibylline Oracle* 11 may have been composed around the turn of the era, but it is not certain that it was composed as a discrete unit. Egypt is the focus of much interest and was presumably the place of composition. (Egypt is said to be destroyed as punishment for its treatment of the Jews [*Sib. Or.* 11:307].) It passes negative judgment on Cleopatra (*Sib. Or.* 11:279-97) but refrains from any criticism of the Romans. This book evidently does not come from the same tradition as do *Sybilline Oracles* 3 and 5.

Sibylline Oracle 12 borrows the first eleven verses from *Sibylline Oracle* 5 but otherwise continues the review of history down to the third century. *Sibylline Oracle* 13 continues it to the middle of that century. *Sibylline Oracle* 14 is almost indecipherable, but it appears to refer to further Roman emperors and finally to the Arab conquest of Egypt. These books are of interest for the ways in which various Roman emperors were perceived in the East, but they are virtually without any religious or theological interest.

7. Enduring Influence.

The *Sibylline Oracles* were cited hundreds of times in the church fathers and were important enough to be quoted in Constantine's "Speech to the Saints." New sibylline oracles continued to be produced down to the Middle Ages. They had an important impact on millenarian thinking through Joachim of Fiore. The Tiburtine sibyl was especially popular. The sibyl is mentioned in the *Dies Irae* of Tomas a Celano. Michelangelo juxtaposed five sibyls (Persian, Eryth-rean, Delphic, Cumean and Libyan) with the OT prophets on the ceiling of the Sistine Chapel, and Raphael used four sibyls (Cumean, Persian, Phrygian and Tiburtine) to adorn the church of Santa Maria della Pace in Rome.

See also APOCALYPTIC LITERATURE; APOCALYPTICISM; PROPHETS AND PROPHECY.

BIBLIOGRAPHY. J. J. Collins, "The Growth of the Sibylline Tradition," in *ANRW* 2.20.1 (1986) 421-59; idem, "The Jewish Transformation of Sibylline Oracles," in *Seers, Sibyls and Sages in Hellenistic-Roman Judaism* (Leiden: E. J. Brill, 1997) 181-97; idem, "Sibylline Oracles," in *The Old Testament Pseudepigrapha,* ed. J. H. Charlesworth (2 vols.; Garden City, NY: Doubleday, 1983, 1985) 1:317-472; idem, *The Sibylline Oracles of Egyptian Judaism* (Missoula, MT: Scholars Press, 1974); J. Geffcken, *Die Oracula Sibyllina* (Leipzig: Hinrichs, 1902); M. Goodman, "Jewish Writings Under Gentile Pseudonyms. 1. The Sibylline Oracles," in E. Schürer, *The History of the Jewish People in the Age of Jesus Christ (175 B.C.-A.D. 135),* rev. and ed. G. Vermes, F. Millar and M. Goodman (3 vols.; Edinburgh: T & T Clark, 1973-87) 3:618-54; V. Nikiprowetzky, *La Troisième Sibylle* (Paris: Mouton, 1970); H. W. Parke, *Sibyls and Sibylline Prophecy in Classical Antiquity,* ed. B. C. McGing (London: Routledge, 1988); D. S. Potter, *Prophecy and History in the Crisis of the Roman Empire: A Historical Commentary on the Thirteenth Sibylline Oracle* (Oxford: Oxford University Press, 1990). J. J. Collins

SIBYLLINE PROPHECY. *See* PROPHETS AND PROPHECY; SIBYLLINE ORACLES.

SICARII. *See* REVOLUTIONARY MOVEMENTS, JEWISH.

SIGN PROPHETS. *See* PROPHETS AND PROPHECY; REVOLUTIONARY MOVEMENTS, JEWISH.

SIMON BAR GIORA. *See* DESTRUCTION OF JERUSALEM; REVOLUTIONARY MOVEMENTS, JEWISH.

SIMON BEN KOSIBA

The last significant Jewish freedom fighter of late antiquity, Simon ben Kosiba, also known by various sobriquets, attempted to cast off the Roman yoke in A.D. 132 but was finally defeated in 135. His defeat was a disaster for the Jewish people, ending any hope of rebuilding the *temple that had been destroyed in A.D. 70 and ending the Jewish state until its refounding in 1948. Of great interest to NT interpreters is whether or not Simon was viewed as a messianic figure and, if so, in what way.

1. Simon and the Jewish Revolt
2. The Messianism of Simon
3. Importance for Understanding the Messianism of Jesus

1. Simon and the Jewish Revolt.

Jewish, Christian and Roman sources refer to a major Jewish revolt led by one Simon ben (or bar) Koziba or Kokhba (*see* Jewish Wars with Rome). Both Koziba and Kokhba are sobriquets, the former meaning "lie" and the latter "star." Letters found at Naḥal Ḥever have revealed that Simon's name was Kosiba, with the vowels themselves supplied by a letter written in Greek. Evidently Simon was dubbed bar Kokhba, or "the son of the star," by his admirers. But after defeat, his critics, as seen especially in *rabbinic literature, referred to him as bar Koziba, or "the son of the lie."

The rebellion broke out in A.D. 132 (as papyrological, numismatic, literary and archaeological evidence suggests), not long after Hadrian completed his tour of the eastern Roman Empire (cf. Dio Cassius *Hist.* 69.12.1-2: "so long as Hadrian was close by in Egypt and again in Syria, they remained quiet . . . but when he went farther away they openly revolted"; *Seder ʾOlam Rab.* §30; Jerome *In Ezek.* 7.24; Epiphanius *Men. Pond.* 14; *Pan.* 30.12), and perdured for nearly three years, as the numismatic evidence suggests (*see* Coinage: Jewish).

Almost nothing is known of Simon ben Kosiba, the leader of the rebellion. Not until the discovery at Naḥal Ḥever of some of his correspondence were scholars able to determine his surname. The exact cause of the rebellion is not clear. Dio Cassius says it was Hadrian's refounding of *Jerusalem as Aelia Capitolina and the plan to build a temple in honor of Jupiter on the spot where the Jewish temple stood that brought on the war (Dio Cassius *Hist.* 69.12.1-2). According to the so-called *Scriptores Historiae Augustae,* which provides extracts of the lives and accomplishments of Rome's *emperors, "At this time [i.e., following Hadrian's visit to the East] also the Jews began a war, because they were forbidden to mutilate the genitals [i.e., practice circumcision]" (*Vita Hadriani* 14.2). The repeal of this ban early in the administration of Antoninus Pius (A.D. 138-161; *Digesta* 48, 8.11.1) supports this assertion, though the point is debated. Both factors may have contributed to the rebellion: imperial plans to renovate Jerusalem as a pagan city and an imperial ban that may have been interpreted as outlawing the practice of circumcision.

Although Dio says that "many outside nations" joined the Jewish rebellion (Dio Cassius *Hist.* 69.13.2), the archaeological and numismatic evidence suggests that the conflict was confined principally to parts of Judea and neighboring territory (in contrast to the first war [A.D. 66-73], which ranged throughout *Israel, and the North African war [c. A.D. 115-116], which involved much of Libya, Egypt, parts of Israel and other regions). D. Barag has pointed out that the geographical distribution of the Bar Kokhba coins suggests that Simon's forces controlled a not insignificant area, 20 to 30 kilometers north, west and east of Jerusalem, south of Jerusalem, including Bethlehem and Hebron, and the western shores of the Dead Sea as far south as Masada. Whether or not Simon controlled Jerusalem itself is disputed—the two coins found in the city may have been brought there as souvenirs by Roman soldiers. According to Appian (*Syriaca* 50.252) and Eusebius (*Hist. Eccl.* 4.5.2; 5.12.1), the Roman army had to reconquer Jerusalem. The city, which probably still lay in ruins, would have had little strategic value but would have had great symbolic value.

Dio also says that the Jewish rebels did not fight the Romans in the open but occupied places of advantage, including subterranean passages, making it necessary for the Romans to shut them up and starve them out (Dio Cassius *Hist.* 69.12.3; 69.13.3). According to rabbinic stories, Jews hid in caves, where many starved (*Lam. Rab.* 1:16 §45; *Midr. Ps.* 17.13 [on 17:14]). Jerome also passes on tradition about Jews hiding in caves during the war (Jerome *Comm. in Isa.* 2:15). The tunnels and cisterns of Masada and the Herodium, along with the relatively recent discoveries in several caves in Naḥal Ḥever of letters, shoes, clothing, cooking utensils, personal effects and human remains from the Bar Kokhba revolt confirm the general truthfulness of these stories.

Simon minted his own coins, overstriking previously minted coins, with patriotic legends that read "Simon Prince of Israel," "Year One of the Redemption of Israel," "Year Two of the Freedom of Israel" and so forth (Mildenberg; Schürer, 606). The part of his correspondence that has been recovered suggests that Simon ben Kosiba had difficulty maintaining discipline among his following. He implores his lieutenants to bring badly needed supplies and fresh recruits, while also ordering that the insubordinate be disciplined (Benoit, 155-63; Yadin 1961, 41-51; 1962, 249-55).

The Roman army finally overwhelmed Simon's forces at Betar (spelled variously; cf. Septuagint Th Josh 15:59), which is situated in the southern part of Judea. The configuration of the camp is visible, though the site has not yet been excavated. According to Dio, the losses on both sides were heavy. With regard to the Jews he says: "Fifty of their most important outposts and nine hundred and eighty-five of their most famous villages were razed to the ground. Five hundred and eighty thousand men were slain . . . and the number of those that perished by famine, disease and fire was past finding out. Thus nearly the whole of Judea was made desolate" (Dio Cassius *Hist.* 69.14.1-2; cf. Appian *Rom. Hist.* 11: *The Syrian Wars* 8 §50: "Vespasian destroyed [Jerusalem] again, and Hadrian did the same in my time"). Scholars suspect that these numbers are inflated, though their exactness makes one think that they may have been drawn from actual if greatly exaggerated reports. Dio also admits that "many Romans perished in the war" and that Hadrian found it necessary in his reports to the senate to omit the usual salutation, "I and the legions are in health" (Dio Cassius *Hist.* 69.14.3). The heaviness of Rome's losses is confirmed in Fronto's consoling letter to Marcus Aurelius Antoninus (A.D. 162), in which he reminds the grieving emperor: "under the rule of your grandfather Hadrian what a number of soldiers were killed by the Jews" (*Parthian War* 2).

The extent of the disaster is presented in

graphic and exaggerated terms in later Christian and Jewish sources. According to rabbinic legends, "Emperor Hadrian slew eighty thousand myriads of human beings at Betar" (*Lam. Rab.* 2:2 §4; *Gen. Rab.* 65:21 [on 27:22]; "eight hundred thousand," according to *y. Ta'an.* 4:5; "not a soul escaped," according to *'Abot R. Nat.* A §38). We are told that Hadrian said to Aquila: "See how I have degraded [the people of Israel], and how many of them I have slain" (*Exod. Rab.* 30:12 [on 21:1]). Elsewhere we are told that Hadrian "killed in the city of Bethar four hundred thousand myriads, or as some say, four thousand myriads" (*b. Giṭ* 57b). God will judge Rome, according to Rabbi Berekiah, because "Hadrian slew in Bethar four hundred myriads of thousands of human beings" (*Song Rab.* 2:17 §1). "How many battles did Hadrian fight? Two teachers give an answer. One said it was fifty-two and the other fifty-four" (*Lam. Rab.* 2:2 §4). The modest dimensions of Betar (Yadin 1971, 192) expose the exaggeration of these numbers. The site has not yet been excavated, but preliminary soundings have been taken (see Ussishkin).

The rabbis spared no hyperbole in describing the extent and gruesomeness of the Jewish slaughter: Rivers of blood flowed to the sea; Hadrian built a fence out of corpses from Tiberia to Seppharis; only his successor (Antoninus Pius) permitted burial; the Gentiles fertilized their vineyards with the blood of the slain; great numbers of phylacteries were found at Betar; children were wrapped in Torah scrolls and burned (*b. Giṭ* 57a, 57b-58a; *Lam. Rab.* 2:2 §4; *Seder Elijah* §28 [151]). The memory of the disaster was such that ben Kosiba's generation became known as the "generation of destruction" (*Esth. Rab.* 3:7 [on 1:9]; *Song Rab.* 1:3 §3; 8:6 §4; *Midr. Ps.* 16:4 [on 16:4], where it is identified as one of the three generations of suffering). These traditions have no historical value beyond corroborating in colorful ways the magnitude of the disaster in Judea and its enduring painful memory.

Eusebius adds: "We have seen in our own time Zion once so famous ploughed with yokes of oxen by the Romans and utterly devastated, and Jerusalem, as the oracle says [Is 1:8], deserted like a lodge" (Eusebius *Dem. Ev.* 6.13). Jerome adds a little to what has already been seen. He says that the "citizens of Judea came to such distress that they, together with their wives, their children, their gold and their silver, in which they trusted, remained in underground tunnels and deepest caves" (Jerome *Comm. in Isa.* 2:15).

2. The Messianism of Simon.

One of the most debated questions concerning Simon ben Kosiba is whether or not he was regarded by his following as the awaited Messiah (*see* Messianism). The evidence suggests that he was probably so regarded.

2.1. Rabbinic. The earliest and most important rabbinic tradition concerning the messianic recognition of Simon is found in the Palestinian Talmud: "Rabbi Simeon ben Yohai taught: 'Aqiba, my master, used to interpret "a star [*kōkhab*] goes forth from Jacob" [Num 24:17]—*Kōzeba'* goes forth from Jacob.' Rabbi Aqiba, when he saw Bar Kozeba, said: 'This is the King Messiah.' Rabbi Yohanan ben Torta said to him: 'Aqiba! Grass will grow on your cheeks and still the son of David does not come!'" (*y. Ta'an.* 4:5 [8] = *Lam. Rab.* 2:2 §4; *b. Sanh.* 93b; on messianic interpretation, cf. *y. Ned.* 3:8). Two features of this tradition are clearly secondary: (1) The reference to Simon as Kōzeba', instead of Kosiba, reflects the later, post-Aqiba negative assessment of the leader. After all, Aqiba would hardly hail the man he believed to be the fulfillment of Numbers 24:17, which in the *targums and earlier traditions (e.g., 1QM 11:4-7; 1QSb 5:27-29; CD 7:18-21; *see* War Scroll; Book of Blessings; Damascus Document) is understood in explicit messianic terms, as the "liar" who "goes forth from Jacob."

(2) The immediate rebuke by Yoḥanan ben Torta is probably artificial and represents a later correction of the famous rabbi. It is more probable that Aqiba's recognition of Simon was widely shared, at least initially. Centuries later Moses Maimonides, over against the Talmud itself, believed that Simon enjoyed widespread support among the rabbis: "Rabbi Aqiba, the greatest of the sages of the Mishna, was a supporter of King Ben Kozeba, saying of him that he was King Messiah. He and all the contemporary sages regarded him as the King Messiah, until he was killed for sins which he had committed" (*Mishneh Torah, Melakhim* 11:3, emphasis added). Later rabbinic tradition is completely legendary in nature, including another explanation for why Aqiba recognized Simon as the Messiah: "And what used Bar Koziba to do? He would catch the missiles from the enemy's catapults on one of his knees and hurl them back, killing

many of the foe. On that account Rabbi Aqiba [proclaimed him Messiah]" (*Lam. Rab.* 2:2 §4).

2.2. Christian. In his first *Apology* Justin Martyr refers to Simon by his positive sobriquet bar Kokhba:

> [The prophetic books] are also in the possession of all Jews throughout the world; but they, though they read, do not understand what is said, but count us foes and enemies; and, like yourselves, they kill and punish us whenever they have the power, as you can well believe. For in the Jewish war which lately raged, Barchochebas, the leader of the revolt of the Jews, gave orders that Christians alone should be led to cruel punishments, unless they should deny Jesus the Christ and blaspheme. (Justin Martyr *Apol. I* 31.5-6)

Eusebius, possibly dependent on Justin, similarly states that "Cochebas, prince of the Jewish sect, killed the Christians with all kinds of persecutions, when they refused to help him against the Roman troops" (Hadrian Year 17). Why did the Christians refuse to support Simon's bid for freedom? The most probable reason is that Simon was regarded as the Messiah, as both Jewish and Christian sources relate (Eusebius *Hist. Eccl.* 4.6.1–4). Therefore, Christian allegiance to Jesus as the Messiah contradicted Simon's claims and undermined his authority. Christians "alone" were dealt with severely, because among the Jews they alone regarded someone else as Israel's Messiah. This interpretation is consistent with Jerome's polemic against Simon: "That famed Bar Chochebas, the instigator of the Jewish uprising, fanned a lighted blade of straw in his mouth with puffs of breath so as to give the impression that he was spewing out flames" (Jerome *Ruf.* 3.31).

2.3. Coins and Letters. The numismatic and epistolary evidence lends a measure of support to the messianic interpretation of Simon's leadership. In both coins and letters he is called Prince of Israel *(nasi ʾyisrael).* Some of the coins depict the temple, which Simon probably hoped to rebuild, a task that the Isaiah Targum thought belonged to the Messiah (*Tg. Isa.* 53:5: "and [the Messiah] will build the sanctuary"; cf. *Tg. Zech.* 6:12-13; *Tg. Song* 1:17). The designation "prince" does not argue against a messianic identification, for the expected Messiah was often referred to in this manner in eschatological material from late antiquity (e.g., 1QM 3:15; 5:1; 1QSa 2:12, 14, 20; CD 7:19; 4Q285 4 2, 6; 5 4; 6 2; 4Q376 frag. 1 iii 1, 3). The messianic employment of the epithet *prince* may derive from Ezekiel (Ezek 34:24; 37:25; cf. *Tg. Ezek.* 34:24; 37:25, which substitutes "king" for "prince"). The absence of the self-designation as "Messiah" should hardly surprise, for a direct claim of messiahship would be viewed as highly presumptuous. One's messianic identity was to be recognized by God's people and confirmed by signs.

The most compelling datum that urges a messianic interpretation of Simon's leadership is the sobriquet bar Kokhba. Given the widespread and consistent messianic interpretation of Numbers 24:17, usage of this title strongly suggests that Simon was viewed by many of his supporters as the awaited Messiah.

3. Importance for Understanding the Messianism of Jesus.

Aqiba's recognition of Simon ben Kosiba as Messiah may shed light on the messianism of Jesus of Nazareth. According to the Babylonian Talmud, Aqiba interpreted the plural "thrones" of Daniel 7:9 as implying one throne for God and one throne for David, that is, the Messiah (*b. Sanh.* 38b; cf. *Midr. Tanḥuma* B on Lev 19:1-2 [*Qedošin* §1]). As in the tradition in the Palestinian Talmud (cited above), Aqiba is again rebuked. His interpretation is seen as a profanation of God's holy presence, for what mortal can sit beside him? Aqiba then abandons his interpretation. Again the great rabbinical authority is corrected. But on the historical level Aqiba evidently did envision a heavenly enthronement of the Messiah, which parallels closely Jesus' assertion that high priest *Caiaphas and his priestly colleagues will some day "see" Jesus as "the son of man seated at the right hand of Power, coming with the clouds of heaven" (Mk 14:62). Jesus' understanding of Daniel 7, in combination with Psalm 110:1, is similar to Aqiba's interpretation and to the interpretation held by other rabbis (cf. *b. Sanh.* 96b-97a, 98a; *Num. Rab.* 13:14 [on Num 7:13]; *Midr. Ps.* 21:5 [on Ps 21:7]; 93:1 [on Ps 93:1]).

In some exegeses Daniel 7:13 and Psalm 110:1 are combined (cf. *Midr. Ps.* 2:9 [on Ps 2:7]; 18:29 [on Ps 18:36]). Aqiba's belief that Simon ben Kosiba was the Messiah, playing on his name and the "star" passage in Numbers 24:17, shows that its messianism did not necessarily entail expectations of a supernatural figure (pace

Mildenberg, 76) but of a mortal whom God might endow with his Spirit in power and wisdom (cf. Is 11:1-5). It also shows that the christology of Mark 14:61-62 is Jewish, Palestinian, and not necessarily the product of Easter faith and *Hellenistic ideas of a supernatural being. On the contrary, there is every reason to conclude that the christology of the early church originated in Jesus himself.

See also COINAGE: JEWISH; MESSIANISM; PAPYRI, PALESTINIAN; REVOLUTIONARY MOVEMENTS, JEWISH.

BIBLIOGRAPHY. S. Applebaum, *Prolegomena to the Study of the Second Jewish Revolt (A.D. 132-135)* (BARSup 7; Oxford: British Archaeological Reports, 1976); idem, "The Second Jewish Revolt," *PEQ* 116 (1984) 35-41; D. Barag, "A Note on the Geographical Distribution of the Bar Kokhba Coins," *INJ* 4 (1980) 30-33; P. Benoit', J. T. Milik and R. de Vaux, *Les Grottes de Murabba ʿat* (DJD 2; Oxford: Clarendon Press, 1961); C. A. Evans, "Was Simon ben Kosiba Recognized as Messiah?" in *Jesus and His Contemporaries: Comparative Studies* (AGJU 25; Leiden: E. J. Brill, 1995) 183-211; J. A. Fitzmyer, "The Bar Cochba Period," in *Essays on the Semitic Background of the New Testament* (SBLSBS 5; Missoula, MT: Scholars Press, 1974) 305-54; M. Gichon, "New Insight into the Bar Kokhba War and a Reappraisal of Dio Cassius 69.12-13," *JQR* 77 (1986) 15-43; B. Isaac and A. Oppenheimer, "The Revolt of Bar Kokhba: Ideology and Modern Scholarship," *JJS* 36 (1984) 33-60; H. Mantel, "The Causes of the Bar Kokba Revolt," *JQR* 58 (1968) 224-42, 274-96; L. Mildenberg, *The Coinage of the Bar Kokhba Revolt* (Typos: Monographien zur antiken Numismatik 6; Frankfurt: Sauerländer, 1984); B. Pearson, "The Book of the Twelve, Aqiba's Messianic Interpretations and the Refuge Caves in the Second Jewish War," in *The Scrolls and the Scriptures: Qumran Fifty Years After,* ed. S. E. Porter and C. A. Evans (JSPSup 26; RILP 3; Sheffield: Sheffield Academic Press, 1997) 221-39; P. Schäfer, *Der Bar Kokhba-Aufstand: Studien zum zweiten jüdischen Krieg gegen Rom* (TSAJ 1; Tübingen: Mohr Siebeck, 1981); idem, "Rabbi Aqiva and Bar Kokhba," in *Approaches to Ancient Judaism: Essays in Religion and History,* ed. W. S. Green (Chico, CA: Scholars Press, 1980) 2:113-30; E. Schürer, *The History of the Jewish People in the Age of Jesus Christ,* rev. G. Vermes, F. Millar and M. Black (3 vols.; Edinburgh: T &. T Clark, 1973) 1:514-57, 606; D. Ussishkin, "Archaeological Soundings at Betar, Bar-Kochba's Last Stronghold," *Tel Aviv* 20 (1993) 66-97; Y. Yadin, *Bar-Kokhba: The Rediscovery of the Legendary Hero of the Last Jewish Revolt Against Imperial Rome* (London: Weidenfeld & Nicolson, 1971); idem, "Expedition D," *IEJ* 11 (1961) 41-51; 12 (1962) 249-57.

C. A. Evans

SIRACH

The Wisdom of Ben Sira, also known as Sirach or Ecclesiasticus, is a collection of sayings and lengthier instructions written by a devout Jew of the late third to early second century B.C. The author identifies wisdom with the Torah of Moses, thus anchoring his students who seek wisdom and honor firmly in the Jewish way of life at a time when commitment to Torah was no longer taken for granted among elite or upwardly mobile Jews. The author also provides guidance on a wide array of practical, domestic, social and religious topics. The collection was preserved by and widely used within the early church. It can be found in the OT canons of the Roman Catholic and Greek Orthodox churches, or in the *Apocrypha to the OT of Protestant churches.

1. Author, Date and Setting
2. Sirach and Hellenism
3. Sirach's Teaching
4. Impact on the New Testament

1. Author, Date and Setting.

1.1. Sirach and Jerusalem Before Antiochus IV. Yeshua ben (son of) Eleazar ben Sira names himself as the author of this collection (Sir 50:27) and locates himself in *Jerusalem, where it is believed the sage had a school (the "house of instruction," Sir 51:23; Di Lella; Crenshaw; Hengel). As a teacher of wisdom, his originality lies not only in the composition of new proverbs (Sir 13:26) but also in the selection, expansion and interpretation of traditional wisdom material. Ben Sira was a student, first of *Torah and the Scriptures of Israel (Sir 38:34—39:1; 39:8), then of traditional wisdom material both from native soil (although Proverbs, for example, already shows marked similarities with foreign wisdom) and from other lands (Sir 39:1-4). Ben Sira traveled extensively (Sir 34:12-13; 39:4; 51:13), acquainting himself with the wisdom traditions at least of Greece and Egypt (Sanders). One finds in Ben Sira, however, that Torah remains the measuring rod of all wisdom; if a tradition leads one away from Torah observance, it is not the road to wisdom. The famous passage on the "sage" or "scribe" (Sir 38:24—39:11) provides a window into the source of Sirach's own learning (von Rad) and no doubt his curriculum for his students: a thorough investigation of sayings and traditions, but always within the bounds of wholehearted commitment to the Torah of Moses.

The date of this collection can be determined with some certainty. In the prologue to the *Septuagint (LXX, the Greek translation), Ben Sira's grandson tells of his arrival in Egypt in the thirty-eighth year of Ptolemy VII Euergetes II, or 132 B.C. (Hengel, Di Lella). This would place his grandfather's period of flourishing in the last decades of the third and first decades of the second century B.C. The hymn in praise of the ancestors concludes with a laudatory reflection on the high priest Simon II (219-196 B.C.) but contains no references to the deposition of Onias III or the Hellenization crisis of 175-164 B.C.—a period whose harsh lessons would have reinforced his position that departure from Torah means ruin and disgrace. This places the date of the compilation between 196 and 175 B.C. (Hengel; Di Lella; Duesberg and Auvray).

Ben Sira lived and taught in a time of cultural tension. Some Jews were increasingly attracted to the Greek way of life while others were concerned to preserve the Jewish way of life or discover some viable synthesis between the two (*see* Hellenistic Judaism). First Maccabees 1:11-12 and 2 Maccabees 4:7-15 point to the role of elite Jews initiating the Hellenization of Jerusalem in 175 B.C., suggesting that pro-Hellenizing sentiments were advancing in Jerusalem in the decades leading up to the radical steps taken by Jason and Menelaus. Ben Sira sought through his teaching to turn his pupils back to a commitment to live according to Torah and to stem the tide of the growing desire to become, once again, "like the nations" (Duesberg and Auvray; Di Lella; Siebeneck).

1.2. The Translator and Textual Transmission of Ben Sira. Ben Sira wrote in Hebrew, but his work was translated by his grandson into Greek for the benefit of the Jewish community in Egypt after he had moved there in 132 B.C. Just as Ben Sira wrote so that "those who love learning might make even greater progress in living according to the Law," so his grandson publishes his translation for the sake of those who "are disposed to live according to the Law" (from the Prologue). He thus takes his grandfather's promotion of a conservative ideology into a major center of *Diaspora Judaism.

For centuries, Ben Sira's work was known to us only through this Greek translation (preserved in a number of codices of the LXX, such as Alexandrinus and Vaticanus). In the late nineteenth century, extensive portions of a Hebrew version were found in the storage room of a synagogue in Cairo. These portions have been further supplemented by finds at *Qumran and Masada (fragments dating from the turn of the era), such that two-thirds of Ben Sira is now represented in Hebrew, opening up new avenues for textual critics to work toward establishing Ben Sira's original Hebrew text. His grandson attested to the impossibility of rendering an exact translation of a text from its original to a new language, pointing in his prologue to the discrepancies between the Greek version of the Pentateuch and other Scriptures used by Diaspora Jews and the Hebrew texts in use in Palestine in the second century B.C. (a source, perhaps, of some friction between Palestinian Jews reading in Hebrew and those Jews relying on a Greek translation of Torah), "for what was originally expressed in Hebrew does not have exactly the same sense when translated into another language." Recent studies of the translation technique of Ben Sira's grandson have demonstrated that he provides an interpretation rather than a mechanical reproduction of his grandfather's original (Wright; Skehan and Di Lella). The grandson's Greek version remains the most important witness to Ben Sira's work, but the Hebrew witnesses help distinguish between the author's original words and the translator's work.

2. Sirach and Hellenism.

While Ben Sira fought against the tendency among Jewish elites to abandon their Jewish heritage in favor of Greek ways, he nevertheless shows himself to be fully a product of Hellenization in its less radical sense. The spirit of the age allowed for a freer flowing of ideas between cultures, and Ben Sira, true to this spirit, incorporated the wisdom of foreign cultures into his instruction. J. T. Sanders has carefully evaluated parallels between Ben Sira and older Greek literature, and he presents a balanced assessment of the extent of influence of the Greek classics on this Jewish author. Sirach 14:18, for example, seems to use an image from *Iliad* 6.148-49: both passages speak of humanity as a tree that is forever losing leaves (i.e., individual human beings die) to make room for new leaves. This does not imply that Ben Sira had read the *Iliad,* for it would have been easy enough for him to learn this simile from common parlance, just as so many people today may quote Shakespeare without ever having read him. Theognis, a sixth-century B.C. Greek author, may well have been on Ben Sira's reading list. Especially noteworthy are the sayings in Theognis about the character of the true friend as opposed to the fair-weather friend, and sayings about wine as a fire that shows the mettle of a person (cf. Sir 6:10, 15; 9:10; 10:6; 13:1; 31:26).

Sanders has also demonstrated Ben Sira's familiarity with Egyptian wisdom. Striking parallels exist between Ben Sira and Demotic wisdom texts with regard to the occupation of the scribe and its favorable comparison against all other occupations (e.g., artisans, engravers, smiths; cf. Sir 38:24—39:11). Similarly, shared proverbs about being a temperate eater at banquets, avoiding the gluttony or greed that would be seen as antisocial acts, testify to a broader wisdom tradition in these practical areas. In particular he appears to have learned much from the wisdom sayings of an Egyptian sage named Phibis. These two collections emphasize the dangers of gluttony and lust as causes of ruin for the fool, the merits of frugality and the need for moderation in mourning. Both also advise moderation in eating specifically for the sake of health, circumspection in approaching one's sociopolitical superiors and avoidance of the sexually promiscuous woman (while also praising the benefits of a good wife).

Such borrowing shows that Ben Sira was not closed-minded to the wisdom of non-Jews where this wisdom could coexist with commitment to Torah. What he opposed, rather, was the forsaking of the Jewish way of life in favor of the Greek way of life. This is evident in his complete identification of wisdom and the Mosaic law (von Rad; deSilva). His most extended reflection on wisdom (Sir 24:1-29) climaxes in the assertion that "all this is the book of the covenant of the Most High God, the law that Moses commanded us" (Sir 24:23 NRSV). While Proverbs claimed that the "fear of the Lord was the beginning of wisdom," Ben Sira adds that "to fear the Lord is the whole of wisdom" (Sir 1:16) and the "crown of wisdom" (Sir 1:18). He counsels his students that walking in wisdom means walking always in accordance with the Jewish Torah: "the sum of wisdom is fear of the Lord, and in all wisdom there is the doing of Torah" (Sir 19:20). God causes wisdom to dwell in Jerusalem (Sir 24:8-12): those who seek wisdom and its promised rewards must seek it first in the temple (cf. Sir 51:13-14) and the Torah; firmly anchored there, they can begin to test the wisdom of foreign peoples. Foreign wisdom that leads one away from "fear of the Lord," such as perhaps the *Epicurean teaching that, while the gods exist, they do not inquire into the affairs of human beings or hold human beings accountable (cf. Sir 16:17-23; Hengel), is to be rejected as folly.

After nearly one-and-a-half centuries of Hellenization (since the campaigns of *Alexander the Great), Jews, like other groups that had held onto their native culture, found themselves at the frontier of an emerging world culture, superior in power and, for some, superior in promise for personal achievement and enjoyment of life's pleasures. Internal desires to join with this dominant culture and Antiochus IV's ambitions to fulfill Alexander's dream of a single world united by a common culture would soon precipitate a severe crisis for Judaism. Ben Sira lives at a time when certain age groups—notably the young, who must be the more strongly admonished to honor the traditions and teachings of the older generation (Crenshaw; Hengel)—and classes—notably the elite—no longer took it as given that, being born Jewish, they would adhere to Jewish law and piety. The world was changing, and Israel was a small place in a corner of that world, continually passed back and forth from *Ptolemaic to *Seleucid control. It was a minority culture in the world of competing kingdoms that nevertheless shared a dominant culture, Hellenism. Within such a setting, Ben Sira shapes his wisdom teaching to promote adherence to the values and customs of Judaism (deSilva), combating strong tendencies to assimilate and become "like the Gentiles" (Duesberg and Auvray; Di Lella).

3. Sirach's Teaching.

3.1. Style and Sources. While Proverbs consisted mostly of discrete sayings and only a few more fully developed instructions, Ben Sira tends to expand sayings into a longer instruction (Sanders; Metzger). Where he does not develop an argument, he will frequently at least group together individual sayings that treat a shared topic. Ben Sira combines a wide array of literary forms in his collection. One finds not only the proverbs and instructions typical of wisdom literature but also a psalm of lament, a psalm of deliverance, an autobiographical poem and an encomiastic reflection on prominent figures of Israel's sacred history.

We have noted a number of non-Jewish sources for Ben Sira's work. The primary sources of his thought must be sought in the Jewish tradition in which the sage was steeped. As a diligent sage, Ben Sira occupied himself with the study of Torah (Sir 38:34; 39:8; see also the translator's prologue); in his teaching, he directs students first and last to Torah as the path of all wisdom (cf. inter alia Sir 19:20). Much of Ben Sira's wisdom may be read as an extended meditation on the precepts of Torah: care for the poor, avoidance of *adultery, honor for parents and truthfulness in speech all have a basis in the Deuteronomic law code. When Ben Sira declares that "fire and water," "life and death" have been set before his pupils, and when he urges them to choose to keep Torah (Sir 15:15-17), he echoes the similar choice set before the Hebrews in Deuteronomy 30:19. Wisdom, for him, means making the right choice in the ancient, Deuteronomic set of alternatives.

Ben Sira also occupied himself with "prophecies" (Sir 39:1; prologue). His passion for the poor, the widow and the orphan (cf. Sir 35:17-26), coupled with his declaration of God's visitation upon those who oppress such people, captures the spirit of the Hebrew prophets. Similarly, his awareness of God's sovereignty over nations and the succession of nations (Sir 10:4-5, 8) may also have arisen from his reflection upon the prophetic literature, which would include what Protestants call the Historical Books. Finally, his encomiastic survey of Israel's past includes numerous references to the prophets of Israel, even to the collection of the twelve Minor Prophets (Sir 49:10).

Finally, we may be sure that Ben Sira reflected on the Psalms in worship and in study. Not only does he imitate their form (a psalm of lament, Sir 36:1-22; a psalm of thanksgiving for deliverance, Sir 51:1-12), but also he incorporates their content and spirituality. His original psalms are replete with parallels in the canonical psalms. His reflection on God's majesty and sovereignty as revealed in the wonders of creation (Sir 42:15—43:33) recalls the appearance of the same ground for praise and awe in many psalms. Ben Sira would be particularly at home reciting the psalms that celebrate Torah as the path for instruction and for living wisely (Pss 1, 19, 119; cf. Sir 6:37; 15:1). The psalmist's declaration that "the Torah of Yahweh is perfect, reviving the soul; the commands of Yahweh are dependable, making the uneducated wise" (Ps 19:7) stands behind Ben Sira's entire curriculum.

A major source for Ben Sira remains the wisdom tradition of Israel (cf. Sir 8:8-9; 39:1-3). Proverbs especially has left a clear mark on the later tradent of that tradition. Not only does Ben Sira share common forms but also numerous topics with the older collection. Both urge the pursuit of wisdom, strong parental discipline, marital fidelity and circumspection in one's conduct around social superiors; both warn against arrogance, impropriety of speech and dishonesty in business dealings; both describe the character of the good wife and her opposite. The list could be multiplied. Ben Sira, however, intensifies the claims made in Proverbs for the rewards of pursuing wisdom (Sir 1:11-19). "Fear of the Lord," that is, caution with regard to provoking God by showing disregard for God, is no longer simply the beginning of wisdom (Prov 1:7; Sir 1:14) but also its fullness (Sir 1:16) and its crown (Sir 1:18; Skehan and Di Lella). Ben Sira is much more vocal about his commitment to the Mosaic covenant.

3.2. Wisdom and Torah. Ben Sira, like Proverbs, presents the figure of Wisdom in personified form (Sir 24:1-22; 1:4-20). Wisdom is the first of God's creation (Sir 1:4; 24:3) and God's special gift for those who revere God and God's law (Sir 1:10, 26). Unlike earlier reflection on Wisdom, Ben Sira places her home squarely in Jerusalem (Sir 24:8-12) and in effect demythologizes this personification: Lady Wisdom is none other than Torah (Sir 24:23; 19:20). This line of identification has survivals in later Jewish (*rabbinic) reflection on the eternity of Torah and on Torah as the first creation of God. While wisdom is God's gift, it is also a goal diligently to be sought by human beings, requiring labor and discipline (Sir 4:17-19; 6:23-31). The pursuit of wisdom is frequently likened to a yoke or burden, which again has survivals in the *Pharisaic and later rabbinic "yoke of Torah" (Sir 6:24-25; 51:26).

Wisdom teachers from antiquity promoted their instruction as the way to *honor, wealth, influence and a noble end. In Ben Sira's setting, abandonment of Torah was increasingly regarded as the path to greater honor for the individual as well as the nation. *Families who were willing to soften the boundaries between Jew and Gentile had already proven that this was a viable way to international prestige and economic advancement. Prominent in Ben Sira is the promotion of Torah as the sole path to honor and a good name (Sir 10:19-24; deSilva). Ben Sira condemned riches gained through transgression as a source of dishonor (Sir 11:4-6; 13:24) but commended fidelity to the Mosaic law—even if the result was poverty—as always honorable (Sir 25:10-11). Fear of the Lord is promoted throughout as one's only claim to honor (Sir 9:16; 10:22). Those who forsake the law (e.g., for the sake of advancement in the broader Hellenistic environment) will come to lasting disgrace (Sir 41:6-8; Crenshaw). Seeking what pleases God—living according to God's requirements (i.e., Torah)—is therefore promoted as the wise course of action (Sir 1:27; 2:15-17; 3:18, 20).

3.3. Wisdom and Piety. For Ben Sira, the path of wisdom was the path of piety. He himself first sought wisdom in prayer and temple services (Sir 51:13-14). Wisdom bestows her gifts on the life that is lived in the fear of God and God's law (Sir 1:14-20, 26; 32:24—33:3; 34:14-20). Wisdom cannot enter where attention to piety is lacking. Ben Sira therefore provides instructions not only on practical wisdom but also on matters of pious living.

Ben Sira warns against the dangers of transgression of Torah. "Fear of the Lord" means not presuming upon God's forgiveness and mercy but rather taking sin seriously and avoiding its path to ruin (Sir 5:1-7). The slowness of divine punishment does not mean that sin is without consequences, so one must repent swiftly and not turn again to the same sins (Sir 34:28-31). Ben Sira also cautions strongly against harboring unforgiveness against one's fellow mortals. One cannot hope for forgiveness from God if one refuses to forgive other people (Sir 27:30—28:7).

Ben Sira's celebration of Simon II officiating at the temple liturgies (Sir 50:5-21) reveals his appreciation of the beauty and marvel of liturgy. He urges his students to honor God through the giving of tithes to God's *priests (Sir 7:29-31) and encourages generous offerings to God (Sir 35:6-13). God will not, however, accept tithes from ill-gotten gains: defrauding one's fellow human being in business makes for blemished tithes. Lawful income alone makes for pleasing offerings (Sir 34:21-24). Ben Sira does not permit *piety to be divorced from ethics, and there is no room for lack of moral integrity in his religion. Indeed, moral conduct, returning a kindness, giving aid to those in need, turning a neighbor from sin and following the commandments are all counted as acceptable *sacrifices and offerings in God's sight (Sir 35:1-5). Here again one notes the strong influence of the Hebrew prophets (Is 1:11-17; 58:3-10; Jer 7:21-23; Hos 6:6).

Ben Sira's concern for the poor and marginalized runs throughout his collection. Almsgiving and works of mercy are to characterize the lives of the wise (Sir 3:30—4:10; 7:10, 3-36; 12:1-7; 29:8-13; 35:17-26). God stands ready to avenge those who are left without aid and oppressed, who cry out to God for help: the curse of the poor is powerful, for the Lord hears their cry (Sir 4:1-6; 35:17-26). Positively, generosity and care for the needy is part of God's character: those who are generous are "like children of the Most High" and are especially beloved by the God whose character they share (Sir 4:10). Investment in the poor becomes a treasure in heaven for the giver, a safeguard against calamity in the day of trouble (Sir 29:8-13).

In *prayer, the wise person seeks God's good counsel (Sir 37:15); one is to seek spiritual counsel here and not through dreams, divination and omens (Sir 34:1-8). As Ben Sira secures a place for prayer in the life of the wise person (Sir 7:10), so he also includes personal expressions of his own piety in his original psalms and praises of God. These prayers articulate a strong election theology, according to which Israel is God's own portion and the nations that dominate Israel the objects of God's wrath (Sir 36:1-3, 8-9). Gentile rulers act arrogantly, failing to honor God as God deserves (Sir 36:2, 5, 12). Ben Sira passionately hopes for the gathering of the exiles of Israel, the restoration of their inheritance and the elevation of Zion to the glory that is its due as the dwelling place of the one God (Sir 36:13, 16-19). This commitment to the particularistic destiny of Israel also reinforces the boundaries between Jew and non-Jew in a time that witnessed other Jews' attempts to erase such distinctions. The psalm of deliverance (Sir 51:1-12) bears witness to Ben Sira's reliance on God's help and not merely his own wisdom to rescue him from difficult situations: ultimately, one's surest defense is God's favor.

3.4. Wisdom and God. Wisdom for Ben Sira included theology: our created nature includes a consciousness of God, placed by God in the human heart, together with an impetus to consider creation and give praise to the Creator (Sir 17:1-12; von Rad). Ben Sira himself shows this impetus in action (Sir 42:15—43:33). The conclusion of that hymnic reflection on God through the mirror of God's marvelous creation is that God is greater than all God's creatures (Sir 43:27-28): God alone is all-seeing and all-knowing (Sir 15:18-19; 39:19-20). God is ultimately the judge of all, and it is God whom one must please in public and in private (Sir 2:15-17; 23:18-21).

Ben Sira frequently invokes God's justice. Creation itself serves the justice of God, as natural elements (such as wind, fire, hail, famine, disease and wild animals) serve to punish the ungodly (Sir 39:28-31; 40:9-10); similarly creation also serves the needs of the righteous. This is an original contribution to Jewish theodicy, one that would be developed further in *Wisdom of Solomon (Crenshaw 1975). If God does not punish sin speedily, it is not because God's justice is faulty but because mercy leads God to delay punishment and allow time for repentance (Sir 5:4; 17:15-32).

Ben Sira does not articulate a doctrine of retribution beyond death, positing rather that God's justice works upon sinners entirely during this life. God may, for example, make the last hours of the wicked so terrible that the joys of a life of sin are erased (Sir 11:26-28; Metzger). Furthermore, the reputation one left behind would enact God's justice: the pious would attain a lasting, honorable remembrance (see 3.7 below), while the name of sinners would be forever stained and disgraced (Sir 41:6-8). When pious Jews encountered the trials of the decades that followed Ben Sira's death, the doctrine of retribution and reward after death would become much more important (cf. 2 Macc 7:9, 11, 14, 23; Wis 3:1-9; 4:16—5:8; 4 Macc 9:8-9; 12:12; 13:14-17; 15:2-3; 16:25). So prominent did this view become that it found its way back into later recensions of Ben Sira's own work, beginning with his grandson's translation (Sir 7:17; 48:11; Di Lella).

3.5. Wisdom and Humanity. The lot of human beings is toil and anxiety by day, unrest by night, and calamity: what is of earth will at last return to the earth. Ben Sira derives this view of the lot of the "children of Adam" from his reflection on the primeval curse (Sir 40:1-11; cf. Gen 3:17-19). Although the first couple failed to exercise free choice correctly, humanity continues to have the power to choose obedience or disobedience. God has not decreed that any should sin, and so individuals remain responsible for their own sin (Sir 15:11-20). Living in obedience to Torah and avoiding sin is admittedly a difficult path—Ben Sira knows from his own experience that the human being is apt to stray into all manner of sin, in thought, word and deed, and requires constant vigilance (Sir 22:27—23:6). Ben Sira himself cries out to God for divine aid in discipline (Sir 23:1, 4). The passions of the flesh, particularly lust, are strong and must never be given free reign lest they drag a person to ruin (Sir 6:2-4).

Nevertheless, life holds out the promise of joy for human beings, which unfolds as people walk in the paths of God's law (Sir 40:18-27). A happy life is the goal of wisdom (Sir 30:21-25), but wisdom teaches that happiness will be found only as one shuns vice of every kind and cultivates the virtues necessary for a harmonious life with other people and a pleasing life before God. His identification of damaging vices such as arrogance (Sir 10:6-18), stubbornness (Sir 3:25-29), slander (Sir 27:22—28:26) and self-indulgence (Sir 18:30—19:3) seeks to steer his pupils away from the traps that destroy harmony and happiness. Similarly, he devotes much of his book to the promotion of the cultivation of virtues such as prudence (Sir 8:1-19), humility (Sir 3:17-24; 7:16-17; 11:1-6) and truthfulness (Sir 20:24-26) in order to lead his pupils to the lifestyle that permits the enjoyment of what blessing life has to offer (e.g., *friendship, a good *marriage, esteem in the eyes of superiors and equals alike).

3.6. Practical Wisdom. Ben Sira provides guidance on a host of practical topics, as do most collections of wisdom literature. Many of these focus on domestic life (Sir 7:18-28): the discipline and rearing of children (Sir 30:1-13; 41:5-10), safeguarding the virginity of daughters (Sir 26:10-12; 42:9-14), treatment of *slaves (Sir 33:25-33), management of property (Sir 33:20-24), caution regarding invitees (Sir 11:28-34), honor due parents (Sir 3:1-16), the selection of a wife (Sir 36:23-31) and the preservation of marital fidelity (Sir 9:1-9; 26:1-4, 13-18). Ben Sira has been justifiably criticized for his often derogatory statements about women (cf. Sir 22:3; 25:13,

19, 24; 42:14; Di Lella, McKeating). These statements, however, are reflections of a society in which women were viewed as either assets or liabilities but not as independent, equal entities. The good woman could provide a stable and well-managed home for a man (Sir 36:29-31) and was regarded as necessary for a man's well-being (McKeating), but a shameless woman (one who shows sexual initiative) is a source of danger to a man's honor, whether her father if she is unmarried or both father and husband if she is married (Sir 42:9-14).

Ben Sira also offers advice for the economic, social and political spheres. He urges his students to show integrity in business dealings, acquiring wealth only through moral means and using wealth to benefit others (Sir 14:3-10; 26:29—27:3; 31:1-11, 23-24; 34:21-27; 40:12-17). He offers guidance in proper table etiquette and conduct at a symposium (Sir 31:12-18, 25-31; 32:1-13; *see* Banquets) and cautions his students to approach social superiors with great care and circumspection (Sir 13:8-13). He has much to say about choosing, testing and keeping friends and associates and about distinguishing between reliable and fair-weather friends (Sir 6:5-17; 7:18; 9:10-16; 12:8-18; 22:19-26; 26:28—27:21; 37:1-6, 12). He even provides medical advice about temperance in eating for the sake of physical health (Sir 31:19-22; 37:27-31) and urges those who are sick to seek out the aid of physicians, preserving however a balance between seeing illness as a punishment from God, for which repentance is due, and the potential for the physician's skill (Sir 38:1-15).

3.7. Hymn to the Ancestors. The last major section preserves the famous hymn in praise of illustrious ancestors. This is a distinctive feature of Ben Sira's work, as no other surviving collection of Jewish wisdom includes a hymn celebrating the deeds not of God but of human heroes of the past (Lee). More than simply a celebration of Israel's heritage, this encomium serves to reinforce the values and motivations—most particularly, loyalty to the Mosaic covenant—promoted throughout the work. The hymn begins with an invitation to praise the distinguished people of Israel's past (Sir 44:1-2), and the examples that follow set forth the behaviors and commitments that result in a lasting, honorable remembrance. Classical *rhetorical handbooks demonstrate that praise and blame of a person's or group's conduct motivated the hearers to adopt or avoid a similar course of action.

T. R. Lee argues that the whole hymn (Sir 44:1—50:24) is an encomium celebrating the high priest Simon II. His attempt to fit the hymn into that specific genre is, however, forced, not to mention the fact that *synkrisis*—the explicit comparison of the subject of an encomium to figures of the past to demonstrate his or her equality or superiority—is absent. He is correct, however, insofar as the hymn falls properly within the broader genre of epideictic rhetoric, which is primarily concerned with strengthening the audience's commitment to certain values of particular importance for the culture (deSilva).

Ben Sira's choice of exemplars and his enumeration of their praiseworthy acts point again to Torah obedience as the path to honor and lasting distinction. Abraham enjoys "incomparable honor" (Sir 44:19) because "he kept the law of the Most High, and was taken into covenant with him; he established the covenant in his flesh, and when he was tested he was found faithful" (Sir 44:20 RSV). Fidelity to God (cf. Sir 2:10) and perseverance in the covenant (Sir 41:19) lead to a praiseworthy remembrance. Phinehas distinguishes himself through his zeal "in the fear of the Lord" (Sir 45:23). The source of his honor is his commitment to the exclusive worship of the God of Israel and the strict maintenance of boundaries between the people of God and the Gentiles (cf. Num 25:1-9). Caleb is held in high repute for his steadfastness before God's command, even if it seemed difficult: God's elevation of Caleb and Joshua above their whole generation shows that "it is good to follow the Lord" (Sir 46:10 RSV). Ben Sira hopes that his teaching will lead to the fulfillment of his prayer that "the name of those who have been honored [may] live again in their sons" (Sir 46:12 RSV). He fervently hopes that his pupils, the children of such committed ancestors, should continue in their ancestral ways—should embody the values, behaviors and commitments that marked the distinguished people of Israel's past.

This series of positive models is reinforced by brief considerations of their negative counterparts. Solomon, whose youth is marked by all the fine virtues that would make for eternal fame, mars his honor through the indiscretions of his old age—again (cf. Phinehas) centering on the transgression of boundaries between the chosen people and the Gentiles (Sir 47:19-21).

Among the kings of Judah and Israel, only David, Hezekiah and Josiah receive high praise: all the others receive lasting disgrace because "they forsook the law of the Most High; . . . they gave their power to others, and their glory to a foreign nation" (Sir 49:4-5 RSV). Forsaking Torah, they lost their sole claim to honor. This sounded a timely warning for the inhabitants of Jerusalem flirting with radical Hellenization.

4. Impact on the New Testament.

Ben Sira has had such a thorough and profound impact on the authors of the NT that a complete analysis here is impossible. As a wisdom teacher lodged in Jerusalem, Ben Sira was well placed to leave his mark on the soil on which the church would take root two centuries later. His redefinition of wisdom as fidelity to the Jewish law would have been a welcome word for the Jewish minority culture struggling to maintain its self-respect and identity. From his influence on Talmudic and other rabbinic materials (Di Lella counts eighty-two citations), one may surmise that Ben Sira's work remained a frequently consulted collection among sages and scribes throughout the intertestamental period into the first centuries of the common era.

Especially striking are parallels between Ben Sira and the sayings of Jesus preserved in Matthew and Luke. It seems certain that Jesus ben Joseph knew and valued some of the sayings of Jesus ben Sira, though one need not go so far as to posit literary dependence: Ben Sira's teaching permeated Judea sufficiently to become part of the common cultural heritage, and the presence of scores of allusions to Ben Sira in rabbinic writings suggests that Jesus may have been exposed to this teaching in the settings of local synagogue instruction.

Matthew's compilation of the Sermon on the Mount contains numerous points of connection with Ben Sira. Jesus' method of expounding on the law by extending the range of the commandments (e.g., extending the prohibition of murder to include anger and demeaning speech) appears also in Ben Sira, for whom economic oppression is also prohibited by the sixth commandment (Sir 34:26-27). Both even link obedience to the commandments of God with setting aside anger against a neighbor (Sir 28:7; cf. Mt 5:21-22). Both urge giving to the one who asks (Sir 4:4; cf. Mt 5:42) and claim that mirroring God's generosity makes one like "a child of the Most High" (Sir 4:10; cf. Mt 5:45). Both warn against "vain repetition" in prayer (Sir 7:14; cf. Mt 6:7); both address God as "Father" in prayer (Sir 23:1, 4; cf. Mt 6:9; Jas 3:9). Most arresting is Ben Sira's teaching that those who expect forgiveness from God must not harbor unforgiveness against mortals like themselves. If we expect God, whose honor is incomparably greater than ours, to forgive offenses, we must not presume to cherish grudges (Sir 28:2-5; cf. Mt 6:12, 14-15).

Ben Sira promotes almsgiving as "laying up treasures in heaven," and Jesus will also urge his followers to "distribute to the poor" so as to "have treasure in heaven" (Lk 18:22; cf. Mt 6:19-21; 19:21; Lk 12:33). Finally, Jesus' invitation to all to come to him, take up his yoke of instruction and find rest with little labor (Mt 11:28-30) brings together elements from Wisdom's invitations to do the same (Sir 6:24-28; 24:19; 51:23-27). These, and many parallels beside, suggest that Jesus took up the best of the Jewish wisdom tradition into his proclamation of the life that pleased God.

The connections between Ben Sira and the epistle of James also command attention and are all the more understandable if we place James in a Palestinian Jewish Christian setting. James's instructions concerning the dangers of the tongue build on a foundation laid by Ben Sira, who also noted that the unbridled tongue was a source of ruin (Sir 22:27; cf. Jas 3:6). Ben Sira wondered that from the same source—the mouth—could come wind to fan a fire or spit to extinguish a flame (Sir 28:12) and proceeded to urge putting a fence about one's tongue so as not to sin or err with it. James also is struck by the anomaly that the same source should put forth blessing and cursing and urges that the tongue be reserved for the former (Jas 3:9-12). James even quotes Ben Sira's proverb: "Be quick to hear, but deliberate in answering" (Sir 5:11; cf. Jas 1:19). The two authors share other concerns as well. Both point out that God is not the cause of sin or enticements to sin, which rather are lodged in human choice (Sir 15:11-20, esp. 15:12; cf. Jas 1:13-14). Both regard testing as the natural outcome of walking in God's ways and urge the acceptance of testing as an opportunity for the cultivation of steadfastness and for being proven acceptable (Sir 2:1-6; cf. Jas 1:2-4; also cf. Sir 2:5 with 1 Pet 1:7).

Finally, Ben Sira's teaching on almsgiving

has left its mark on the *Didache,* an early Christian manual for conduct and liturgy (c. A.D. 100-125). *Didache* 4.5 quotes Ben Sira's admonition: "Do not let your hand be stretched out to receive and closed when it is time to give" (Sir 4:31, NRSV) and promotes almsgiving as a "ransom for sins" (*Did.* 4.6; cf. Sir 3:30). *Didache* 1.6 also cites a proverb the second half of which preserves an admonition from Ben Sira: "Know to whom you are giving" (Sir 12:1), so as to be a good steward of charity.

See also APOCRYPHA AND PSEUDEPIGRAPHA; APOCRYPHAL AND PSEUDEPIGRAPHICAL SOURCES IN THE NEW TESTAMENT; EDUCATION: JEWISH AND GRECO-ROMAN; TORAH; WISDOM LITERATURE AT QUMRAN; WISDOM OF SOLOMON.

BIBLIOGRAPHY. P. C. Beentjes, *The Book of Ben Sira in Hebrew* (Leiden: E. J. Brill, 1997); J. Blenkinsopp, *Wisdom and Law in the Old Testament* (Oxford: Oxford University Press, 1995) 151-82; R. J. Coggins, *Sirach* (Sheffield: Sheffield Academic Press, 1998); J. L. Crenshaw, *Old Testament Wisdom* (Atlanta: John Knox, 1981) 149-73; idem, "The Problem of Theodicy in Sirach: On Human Bondage," *JBL* 94 (1975) 47-64; D. A. deSilva, "The Wisdom of Ben Sira: Honor, Shame and the Maintenance of the Values of a Minority Culture," *CBQ* 58 (1996) 433-55; A. A. Di Lella, "Conservative and Progressive Theology: Sirach and Wisdom," *CBQ* 28 (1966) 139-54; idem, "Sirach," in *The New Jerome Biblical Commentary,* ed. R. E. Brown, J. A. Fitzmyer and R. E. Murphy (Englewood Cliffs, NJ: Prentice-Hall, 1990) 496-509; idem, "Wisdom of Ben Sira," *ABD* 6:931-45; H. Duesberg and P. Auvray, *Le Livre de L'Ecclésiastique* (Paris: Editions du Cerf, 1958); M. Hengel, *Judaism and Hellenism* (2 vols.; Philadelphia: Fortress, 1974) 1:131-62; T. R. Lee, *Studies in the Form of Sirach 44—50* (SBLDS 75; Atlanta: Scholars Press, 1986); B. L. Mack, *Wisdom and the Hebrew Epic: Ben Sira's Hymn in Praise of the Fathers* (Chicago: University of Chicago Press, 1985); H. McKeating, "Jesus ben Sira's Attitude to Women," *ExpT* 85 (1973-74) 85-87; B. M. Metzger, *An Introduction to the Apocrypha* (Oxford: Oxford University Press, 1957) 77-88; G. von Rad, *Wisdom in Israel* (Nashville: Abingdon, 1972) 240-62; J. T. Sanders, *Ben Sira and Demotic Wisdom* (SBLMS 28; Chico, CA: Scholars Press, 1983); R. T. Siebeneck, "May Their Bones Return to Life!—Sirach's Praise of the Fathers," *CBQ* 21 (1959) 411-28; P. W. Skehan and A. A. Di Lella, *The Wisdom of Ben Sira* (AB 39; New York: Doubleday, 1987); J. G. Snaith, *Ecclesiasticus* (Cambridge: Cambridge University Press, 1974); C. Spicq, "L'Ecclésiastique," in *La Sainte Bible,* ed. L. Pirot and A. Clamer (Paris: Letouzey et Ané, 1946) vol. 6; B. G. Wright, *No Small Difference: Sirach's Relationship to Its Hebrew Parent Text* (SCS 26; Atlanta: Scholars Press, 1989).

D. A. deSilva

SLAVERY

Slavery is holding a person in servitude by violence, natal alienation and personal dishonor as the chattel of another. Slavery is neither simply the loss of freedom, nor the same as coerced labor nor equatable with loss of civil rights. Classical slavery means slavery in at least two different contexts: *Greece (specifically fifth- and fourth-century B.C. *Athens) and *Rome (mainly of the middle republic to the end of the Principate, 200 B.C. to A.D. 235).

1. Problems of Definition and Comparison
2. The Usefulness and Limits of the Primary Sources
3. The Sources, Number and Position of Slaves
4. Manumission

1. Problems of Definition and Comparison.

Currently no general theory allows a single definition of slavery for all cultures and times. Earlier studies took the objectivity of slavery for granted as a categorical and transcultural concept. Recent decades have seen both important advances and fierce scholarly debate, making this more controversial a subject than any other in the study of ancient literature and society.

One definition affirms Roman legal distinctions as crucial to understanding slavery as one form of dependent labor, but not the only form (Finley). Unlike peasants, helots, clients, peons or serfs, slaves are chattel that can be bought and sold. Roman jurists held that slavery was an institution of the law of nations by which, contrary to nature, a person is subjected to the power (*dominium*) of another. Slavery is remarkably the only case in the extant corpus of Roman law in which the law of nations and the law of nature are in conflict. Although Roman law, in contrast to *Aristotle, considered slavery to be against nature, this did not mean that it was considered morally wrong; the jurists clearly presumed slavery to be legitimate, proper and morally right.

An alternative definition avoids this law-oriented approach and describes slavery as a dynamic process of alienation and dishonor termed *social death* (Patterson). Social death means denying a person all dignity (as understood in that particular culture) and ties of birth in both ascending or descending generations (*see* Honor and Shame). Although they are not biologically dead, slaves in effect are socially dead to the free population.

Slavery in the Greek world of classical Athens differed markedly from slavery in Roman times. For example, Athenian freedmen were denied citizenship and thus, unlike their Roman counterparts, were excluded from political life, ineligible for all magistracies, forbidden to own land and excluded from acquiring mortgage loans; their children remained noncitzens. The term "Greco-Roman slavery" thus proves problematic. Evidence from the Greek period cannot be used as background for the Roman period of the NT authors. Additionally, ancient slavery, unlike modern, was not based on race. Racism and slavery do not necessarily go together, and neither of the two phenomena serves as the exclusive explanation for the other's existence. Comparative material from slavery in the antebellum United States South must be used with control.

2. The Usefulness and Limits of the Primary Sources.
The first task in any historical inquiry is to determine the nature of the available primary source material, and for slavery the problem is formidable. Virtually all evidence comes from the slaveholders, not the slaves themselves. Considering the ubiquity and significance of slaves in ancient daily life, there is surprisingly little discussion of them by ancient authors. Because ancient historiography concerned itself with politics, wars and great personalities, such narratives frustrate efforts to reconstruct the lives of slaves. Much of the historical material on slaves is anecdotal and mentioned only in passing, since ancient authors considered writing about the lives of individual slaves beneath the dignity of a historian. One of the longest surviving passages by a Latin historian describing an episode concerning slaves is only two pages in length; and *Tacitus includes it in his narrative only to make a rhetorical point about an attempt by the populace to influence polity (Tacitus *Ann.* 14.42-5).

Some archaeological evidence provides limited insight into the physical conditions of slave life. For example, the structural remains of excavated Roman houses reveal that the Romans did not ordinarily build separate, freestanding slave quarters; slaves typically lived in rooms within the master's walls. Other archaeological evidence includes unearthed objects relating to slavery, such as the Roman whip (*flagellum*) whose thongs had pieces of metal attached to them in order to make deep wounds into the flesh. The evidence proves the torture of ancient slaves to have been far more severe than the punishments sanctioned by the law in the slave society of Brazil, the most brutal of the modern world.

Moral exhortation literature offers additional evidence, but it has been misused in NT scholarship. One of the most sustained discussions of slavery by an ancient moralist is *Seneca's *Epistle* 47, in which he delineates the elements of the model master-slave relationship according to *Stoicism. Seneca condemns "harsh" punishment of slaves as injurious to the master's character but sees no problem with more moderate, regular disciplining of one's slaves. Such calls to kindness toward slaves were not criticisms of the institution but of its abuse by arrogant masters not abiding by Stoic ideals. These statements calling for humane treatment of slaves—analogous to modern calls against cruelty toward animals—were articulated to strengthen the institution, not to abolish it. Despite claims by some NT scholars, ancient slavery was not more humane than modern slavery (*see DPL* and *DLNTD*, Slave, Slavery).

3. The Sources, Number and Position of Slaves.
The main sources of ancient slaves were warfare, piracy, brigandage, the international slave trade, kidnapping, infant exposure, natural reproduction of the existing slave population and the punishment of criminals to the mines or gladiatorial combat. Above all else, warfare remained throughout classical antiquity an important supplier of slaves. In his campaigns in Gaul between 58 and 51 B.C. alone, Julius Caesar is reported to have shipped back to Italy nearly one million Gallic prisoners of war. Slaves by the tens of thousands poured into the markets of Sicily and peninsular Italy as early as the First Punic War (264-241 B.C.), a direct result of the annual pattern of warfare and military expansion of Rome's borders during the late republic.

Despite the inadequacy of evidence, some scholars estimate that in urban areas of Roman imperial society slaves made up one-third of the population, but others place the figure lower, within the range of 16.6 to 20 percent. We do not know for sure.

In contrast to previous scholarship, Roman historians now dispute the theory that natural reproduction, in the NT era, replaced warfare as the primary source of Rome's slaves. Although continuous expansion ceased by the time of the empire, wars and other conflicts did not. This finding challenges an idea popular among some NT scholars that under the empire slaves were treated kindly because they were raised in homes and not taken by violence in battle. Slave populations, however, rarely reproduce enough to replace themselves. Furthermore, while the slave population of the antebellum South did reproduce itself after the official closure of the Atlantic slave trade in 1809 (government census documents indicate that by 1860 slaves made up 33 percent of the Southern population), no American historian claims that having homegrown slaves caused masters to treat them kindly.

Unlike their counterparts in modern slave societies of the New World, Roman slaves were not segregated from freeborns in work or types of job performed, with the notable exception of mining operations. A few manumitted slaves enjoyed social mobility. The Latin poet Horace, for example, was the son of a freedman. Some held positions of considerable power not only over fellow slaves but also over freeborns. Imperial slaves and freedmen (belonging to the Roman emperor) were considered the most powerful of all. They were the *familia Caesaris*, the "emperor's household" (note Phil 4:22) and were assigned administrative positions. The apostle Paul met one of them, Felix, the imperial freedman of the emperor Claudius, who served as Roman procurator of Judea (Acts 24:22-27; *see* Roman Administration; Roman Governors of Palestine).

In modern slavery, slave illiteracy was often required by law; in ancient slavery, an educated slave was prized. In cities throughout the ancient Mediterranean world, slaves were trained and served as physicians, architects, craftspeople, shopkeepers, cooks, barbers, artists, thespians, magicians, *prophets (e.g., Acts 16:16-24), teachers, professional *poets and *philosophers. Some slaves could accumulate considerable wealth from their occupations.

However, most slaves were of quite modest means and worked as ordinary laborers or specialized domestics. Larger Roman households even had slaves whose sole job was to fold fancy dinner napkins. Because slaves could be found in all economic levels of society, they had no cohesion as a group and lacked anything akin to class consciousness. This analysis challenges Marxist interpretations that lump slaves into a single economic class and identify a so-called slave mode of production.

4. Manumission.

Manumission was an act that liberated a slave; the former slave was then termed a freedman or freedwoman. It was a legal procedure, not an attempt to effect political change, and so differs dramatically from emancipation, synonymous with the abolition of slavery.

It is often stated that manumission was regular in the Roman world and that this practice is unusual in the world history of slavery. Compared with classical Greece and the antebellum South this claim is true but only with strong qualification. A common misunderstanding among some NT scholars is that manumission was automatic after six years of servitude or when the slave turned thirty years of age. The only literary evidence for this claim is *Cicero (*Eighth Philippic* 32), who writes that after six years a slave could expect to be freed. But Cicero's report is more rhetoric than social description. He does not mention six years because it is a statistical minimum or average; these are the six years from Caesar's crossing of the Rubicon in January 49 to February 43, during which the Roman state was politically enslaved. Any Roman senator would understand and accept Cicero's argument even if it would never occur to him to manumit his own slaves after six years. Cicero himself did not manumit his own slave Tiro until 53 B.C., Tiro's fiftieth birthday.

Manumission in the Roman context, however, should not be exaggerated. The vast majority of slaves and especially those in agriculture were never freed. Romans saw manumission as the regular reward for their deserving urban slaves. It suited the master's interests and reinforced the institution and ideology of slavery. It is against this background that one must interpret Paul's exhortation to slaves in 1 Corinthians

7:21. By saying that believing slaves at *Corinth may take opportunities for freedom, Paul makes room in this theology for the institutionalized exercise of urban manumission.

See also FAMILY AND HOUSEHOLD; ROMAN SOCIAL CLASSES; SOCIAL VALUES AND STRUCTURES.

BIBLIOGRAPHY. K. R. Bradley, *Slavery and Society at Rome* (KTAH; Cambridge: Cambridge University Press, 1994); idem, *Slaves and Masters in the Roman Empire: A Study in Social Control* (New York: Oxford University Press, 1987); M. I. Finley, *Ancient Slavery and Modern Ideology* (New York: Viking, 1980); idem, ed., *Classical Slavery* (SASI 8; London: Frank Cass, 1987); P. Garnsey, *Ideas of Slavery from Aristotle to Augustine* (The W. B. Stanford Memorial Lectures; Cambridge: Cambridge University Press, 1996); J. A. Harrill, *The Manumission of Slaves in Early Christianity* (HUT 32; Tübingen: Mohr Siebeck, 1995); idem, "Using the Roman Jurists to Interpret Philemon," *ZNW* 90 (1999) 135-38; W. V. Harris, "Demography, Geography and the Sources of Roman Slaves," *JRS* 89 (1999) 62-75; S. R. Joshel and S. Murnaghan, eds., *Women and Slaves in Greco-Roman Culture* (London: Routledge, 1998); D. B. Martin, "Slavery and the Jewish Family," in *The Jewish Family in Antiquity,* ed. S. J. C. Cohen (BJS 289; Atlanta: Scholars Press, 1993) 113-29; O. Patterson, *Slavery and Social Death: A Comparative Study* (Cambridge, MA: Harvard University Press, 1982); S. Treggiari, *Roman Freedmen During the Late Republic* (Oxford: Clarendon Press, 1969); J. Vogt and H. Bellen, eds., *Bibliographie zur antiken Slaverei,* rev. E. Herrmann and N. Brockmeyer (new ed.; Bochum: N. Brockmeyer, 1983); A. Watson, *Roman Slave Law* (Baltimore: Johns Hopkins University Press, 1987); P. R. C. Weaver, *Familia Caesaris: A Social Study of the Emperor's Freedmen and Slaves* (Cambridge: Cambridge University Press, 1972); W. L. Westermann, *The Slave Systems of Greek and Roman Antiquity* (MAPS 40; Philadelphia: American Philosophical Society, 1955); T. E. J. Wiedemann, *Greek and Roman Slavery* (London: Routledge, 1988); idem, "The Regularity of Manumission at Rome," *CQ* n.s. 35 (1985) 162-75.

J. A. Harrill

SOCIAL BANDITS. *See* REVOLUTIONARY MOVEMENTS, JEWISH.

SOCIAL CLASSES, ROMAN. *See* ROMAN SOCIAL CLASSES.

SOCIAL MOBILITY. *See* ROMAN SOCIAL CLASSES.

SOCIAL VALUES AND STRUCTURES

The phenomenon we think of as early Christianity was shaped by and in turn helped to shape the values and structures of the societies and cultures in which it took root and grew. This article aims to identify and explain a representative selection of values and structures, awareness of which makes possible a clearer understanding of what it was like to be a Christian in the first century. Since the range of possible examples is vast and the study of what has become known as the social world of early Christianity has grown apace in the past few decades (Hanson; Elliott 1995; Malina 1996), the selection here will focus on values and structures pertinent especially to the interpretation of 1 Corinthians. More than any other NT text, this *letter reveals the extraordinarily complex mixture of Greek, Roman, Jewish and Christian elements that helped constitute early Christian existence.

1. Values
2. Structures

1. Values.

1.1. Holiness. One of the fundamental values lying behind what Paul writes in 1 Corinthians is the idea of holiness as basic to the formation of a godly community. This idea was available to him from his biblical and Jewish moral tradition (cf. Ex 19:5-6; Deut 7:6-11) and was given distinctive interpretation in contemporary groups like the *Pharisees (to whom Paul had belonged) and the *Qumran covenanters. One well-known text from Qumran, for example, expresses clearly the *priestly idea of holiness practiced by the sect and shared in certain respects by Paul:

> When these are in Israel, the Council of the Community shall be established in truth. It shall be an Everlasting Plantation, a House of Holiness for Israel, an Assembly of Supreme Holiness for Aaron. They shall be witnesses to the truth at the Judgement, and shall be the elect of Goodwill who shall atone for the Land and pay to the wicked their reward. It shall be that tried wall, that *precious corner-stone,* whose foundations shall neither rock nor sway in their place (Isa.xxviii, 16). It shall be a Most Holy Dwelling for Aaron, with everlasting knowledge of the Covenant of justice, and shall offer up sweet fragrance. It shall be a House of Per-

fection and Truth in Israel that they may establish a Covenant according to thy everlasting precepts. And they shall be an agreeable offering, atoning for the Land and determining the judgement of wickedness, and there shall be no more iniquity. (*Rule of the Community* 8:4-10; translation in Vermes, *DSSE,* 85)

In an effort to give the Corinthian Christians a stronger sense of their identity as a distinct people, members of God's new *eschatological creation, Paul also draws heavily on holiness language: "To the church of God which is at Corinth, to those sanctified [*hēgiasmenois*] in Christ Jesus, called to be saints [*hagiois*]" (1 Cor 1:2 RSV). This is the language of holiness understood as separation and obedience, but whereas in the Bible it refers primarily to the separation of *Israel from "the nations" (the Gentiles), and in the *Rule of the Community* to the separation of the righteous from the unrighteous within Israel as well as beyond it, in Paul it refers to the election and identity of a new people made up of those previously separated, Jews and Gentiles (1 Cor 12:13; cf. Gal 3:27-8; Eph 2:11-22). This ideal of holiness has a dual focus. It means that internal relations are to be governed by disciplined obedience to the will of God as revealed in Scripture and taught by the apostle. With regard to "those outside"—and without going "out of the world" (1 Cor 5:10) as the Qumran covenanters had done—it also means that believers are to live in ways that bear witness to the rule of God over all things.

This ethic of holiness helps to explain the way Paul's teaching proceeds at certain points by establishing boundaries that separate the holy from the unholy. The basic presupposition is the holiness of the temple (as at Qumran), where temple is extended metaphorically to stand for the community of God's people: "Do you not know that you are God's temple [*naos*] and that God's Spirit dwells in you? If any one destroys God's temple, God will destroy him. For God's temple is holy [*hagios*], and that temple you are" (1 Cor 3:16-17 RSV). Thus, because immorality (*porneia*) in the life of the church has a contagious, polluting effect, the polluting agent has to be expelled. Indeed, his brothers and sisters in Christ are prohibited even from eating with him (1 Cor 5:1-12). The same ethic also explains Paul's opposition to church members' recourse to the civil courts to settle internal disputes (1 Cor 6:1-11). For Paul it is a contradiction in terms, a mixture of what should not be mixed. How can "the saints" (*hoi hagioi*)—those who will judge not only "the world" but also angels (1 Cor 6:2-3) and who have been "washed," "sanctified" and "justified" (1 Cor 6:11)—take their mundane disagreements before "the unrighteous," those who are not sanctified and who will not inherit the kingdom of God?

Then there is Paul's teaching on mixed marriages. Contrary to what we might expect and to what may have been the practice of some in the church, the believing partner should not separate from the unbeliever: "For the unbelieving husband is consecrated [*hēgiastai*] through his wife, and the unbelieving wife is consecrated [*hēgiastai*] through her husband. Otherwise, your children would be unclean [*akatharta*], but as it is they are holy [*hagia*]" (1 Cor 7:14 RSV). Striking here is the way one kind of holiness rule is transcended by another on the implied grounds that the contagious power of holiness can be more powerful than the contagious power of unholiness. The believing spouse sanctifies both the unbelieving spouse and their children.

1.2. Power. The nature of the conflict reflected in 1 Corinthians will remain opaque to us without an understanding also of the ordering, display and practice of power in *Judaism and the Greco-Roman world. That power (*dynamis*) is an issue is clear: "For the word of the cross is folly to those who are perishing, but to us who are being saved it is the power of God . . . to those who are called, both Jews and Greeks, Christ the power of God and the wisdom of God" (1 Cor 1:18, 24 RSV). Against what interpretations of power and their attendant practices is Paul testifying here and elsewhere in this letter? This is a vital issue that has attracted significant scholarly attention (Holmberg; Meeks, 111-39; Marshall).

One interpretation of power that is relevant has to do with the pervasive way in which people in Greco-Roman society were valued according to certain socially recognized criteria of worth. These criteria included birth, social class, ethnic origins, gender, education, wealth, rank, physical or intellectual prowess, occupation, ritual status, rhetorical prowess, *patronage and personal achievements on behalf of the common good (Garnsey and Saller, 107-25). In a hierarchical society in which formal power was distributed unevenly and restricted primarily to the aristocracy, there was a high degree of sensitivity to the social estimation of one's public worth, prestige or honor, and this sensitivity was replicated at lower levels of society. Paul's own ironic comment assumes precisely this state of affairs: "For consider your call, brethren; not many of you were wise according to worldly standards, not many were powerful, not many were of noble birth" (1 Cor 1:26 RSV). His letter shows that this church in the Roman colony of *Corinth reflected the social competitiveness and sensitivity to status that permeated Roman society, and it did so in a quite acute and complex way by virtue of the fact that it brought together into a new society people who would normally have been social rivals or even socially segregated from each other.

This helps to explain the strong tendency toward factionalism in Corinth against which Paul has to fight so strenuously (1 Cor 1:10-31). M. M. Mitchell has shown that the dominant concern that unites 1 Corinthians is the threat of disunity in the church due to factionalism and its manifestations. This means, among other things, that what look like theological quarrels may also be quarrels between rivals for power. Thus, for example, the parties whose formation is reported in 1 Corinthians 1:11-16 are likely to have been divided by patronage rivalry at least as much as by doctrine; the wisdom referred to is likely to be about the social prestige associated with *rhetorical prowess as much as about metaphysical speculation; the boasting about (what Paul regards as) immorality in the community (1 Cor 5:6) probably has to do with the high social status of the offender at least as much as with practices arising out of incipient Gnosticism of one kind or another; the conflict between the strong and the weak over eating meat probably has as much to do with differences of wealth, status and social mobility as with fears about idolatry and apostasy (1 Cor 8:1-13); and so on (Theissen).

In terms of methodology, what this means more generally is that analysis of the theological debates in 1 Corinthians will be deficient if it fails to take into account likely concomitant sociological factors, especially those to do with power. To put it another way, theology in Corinth is not a set of arcane, disembodied ideas, remote from politics and society. Rather, it is (at least in Pauline terms) reflection on the transformation of human power relations by the inbreaking power of God revealed in the cross of Christ.

1.3. Honor and Shame. Closely related to the interpretation and exercise of power in the social world of early Christianity are the pivotal values of *honor and shame (Moxnes). Honor has been defined as "the value of a person in his or her own eyes (that is, one's claim to worth) plus that person's value in the eyes of his or her social group. Honor is a claim to worth along with the social acknowledgement of worth" (Malina 1983, 27). Generally speaking, honor takes two forms. Ascribed honor is social recognition arising from who one is by virtue of factors such as birth, wealth, class and social status. Acquired honor is social recognition on the basis of what one has done, especially one's achievements in the ongoing competition for status and reputation so characteristic of Greco-Roman society. Honor, whether ascribed or achieved, is the greatest social value in antiquity, valued more highly even than life itself. This is because a person's identity and worth arise in a social context. As C. Osiek (27) sums it up: "Without a good reputation life has no meaning."

The correlate of honor is shame (*see* Honor and Shame). This can be understood negatively as loss of honor through a refusal or withholding of social recognition. But it can also be understood positively as a proper sensitivity toward one's own honor and the honor of one's significant others, such as one's spouse, household, friends, patrons and clients. This has a gender dimension as well. In relation to the role and status of *women in a patriarchal society, shame is expressed in those patterns of deferential behavior and modesty that protect and enhance the honor of the household and the male household head (*see* Family and Household).

The importance of honor and shame in the social relations of antiquity helps to explain both what Paul says in 1 Corinthians and how he says it. For example, the competitive rivalry between factions in the church may now be understood as a quest for honor between household heads claiming the patronage of various apostolic leaders (1 Cor 1—4), something legitimate in terms of wider societal norms but in Paul's eyes contrary to the gospel of the crucified Christ that laid the foundation for transformed social values by making honorable (as a manifestation of the power of God) what was regarded normally as shameful (1 Cor 1:18-25). To put it another way, in Paul's view, the honor acquired through rivalry and boasting has been rendered shameful by the honor ascribed by God to the crucified Christ and to those apostles and others who boast only "in the Lord" (1 Cor 1:31; cf. 3:1-23).

As a corollary of this, members of the church are to see themselves and to see each other in new ways: as members of the "body of Christ" to each of whom is given "the manifestation of the Spirit" (1 Cor 12:7) and among whom differences of race, class, status and gender matter much less in view of their common identity given to them by the most powerful patron of all. That patron is God at work in Jesus the Lord bringing a new eschatological creation into being through the *Spirit. In Paul's view, what is honorable now is not the power of fine speech but the power of preaching the gospel, not self-display through the exercise of spectacular spiritual gifts but the building up of the church through the practice of love, not the flaunting of one's newfound freedom but the paradoxical surrender of freedom for the sake of the weaker brother or sister. All this represents nothing less than a reconfiguration of honor and shame in terms of the understanding of power given by revelation in the gospel of the crucified and risen Christ.

1.4. Male and Female. An important dimension of the distribution of honor and shame has to do with the perception and organization of gender relations. In the Mediterranean world generally, social space was divided up in a number of ways, one of the most important of which was the differentiation of the public domain from the private along the lines provided by the perceived differences between male and female (Barton, 225-34). It is as if the physical bodies of men and women served as a kind of map not only of the moral ordering of the social body but also of its spatial ordering. The male represents public space and what is associated with it: leadership in politics, *philosophy, *rhetoric, litigation, business, warfare and the *arena. The female represents the more circumscribed, private space of the household. This is where *women have authority that they are to exercise on behalf of the male household head in ways intended to protect his honor. This gendered ordering of social space is given eloquent expression in the writings of the Hellenized Jew *Philo of Alexandria, a contemporary of Paul:

> Marketplaces and council halls and law courts and gatherings and meetings where a large number of people are assembled and open-air life with full scope for discussion and action—all these are suitable to men both in war and peace. The women are best suited to the indoor life that never strays from the house, within which the middle door is taken by the maidens as their boundary and the outer door by those who have reached full womanhood. Organized communities are of two sorts, the greater, which we call cities, and the smaller, which we call households. Both of these have their governors; the government of the greater is assigned to men under the name of statesmanship [*politeia*], that of the less, known as household management [*oikonomia*], to women. (Philo *Spec. Leg.* 3.169-70)

In reality, the situation changed over time and was more varied from one region to another than Philo's conservative and stereotypical account suggests. There is plenty of literary and epigraphic evidence to show that women sought upward social mobility through *marriage, were active in commerce and manufacture, owned their own estates, served as patrons of local religious cults and voluntary associations, participated in syncretistic religious cults that spread from Egypt and the eastern Mediterranean and even engaged in the pursuit of philosophy (Lefkowitz and Fant; Kraemer). Nevertheless, the fact remains that the overall weight of law, custom and practice was toward distinguishing public space as predominantly male from private (domestic) space as predominantly female, with a distribution of power in a vertical direction with the male household head on top.

Against this background, a number of passages in 1 Corinthians can be seen in a new light. It is not surprising that Paul should give instruction on matters to do with male-female sexual relations (1 Cor 5—6) and rules governing Christian marriage (1 Cor 7). Given the connection in antiquity between the right ordering of the city-state (*polis*) and the right ordering of the household (*oikos*), and given Paul's determination to establish the community of Christians at Corinth as a kind of alternative *polis,* it was essential that an orderly and Christian pattern of social relations be laid down. If disorderly sexual and marital relations were a symptom of the factionalism of the church, as seems to have been the case, then the imposition of sexual discipline and marriage rules was an obvious way to build up the unity of the church.

Second, noticeable in the marriage rules is the way Paul addresses in reciprocal fashion both men and women, as in 1 Corinthians 7:3-4: "The husband should give to his wife her conjugal rights, and likewise the wife to her husband. For the wife does not rule over her own body, but the husband does; likewise the husband does not rule over his own body, but the wife does" (RSV; see also 1 Cor 7:10, 12-14, 16, 32-34). Given the overwhelmingly hierarchical ordering of male-female relations in the society of the time, this reciprocity is striking. As O. L. Yarbrough (116) puts it: "Compared with Jewish paraenesis and with most paraenetic traditions in the Greco-Roman world, Paul's careful balancing of advice to men and women is unusual." It seems legitimate to infer that not only is Paul concerned to establish a sustainable basis for order and unity in the church's life, but also that he does so in a way that incorporates distinctively Christian values, one of which is the full recognition of women alongside men as heirs of the kingdom of God.

2. Structures.

2.1. Households. In the discussion of gender (see 1.4 above), a beginning was made on a consideration of the household (Lat *familia;* Gk *oikos/oikia*). The definition of household is complex (Garnsey and Saller, 126-47). It consisted of not only husband, wife and children but also *slaves and freedmen and others living in the house (*see* Family and Household). An impressive statement about the important place of the household in the larger scheme of social relations comes in Cicero's *On Duties* 1.53-54:

> There are several levels of human society. Starting from that which is universal, the next is that of a common race, nation or language (which is what most of all holds men together). Further down comes membership of the same city; for citizens have many things in common—their town square, temples, covered walkways, roads, laws and constitution, law-courts and elections, customs and associations and the dealings and agreements that bind many people to many others. An even closer bond is that between relations: for it sets them apart from that limitless society of the human race into one that is narrow and closely-defined. Since it is a natural feature of all living beings that they have the desire to propagate, the first association is that of marriage itself; the next is that with one's children; then the household unit within which everything is shared; that is the element from which a city is made, so to speak the seed-bed of the state. (Gardner and Wiedemann, 2)

The institution of the household was probably the most significant social influence on the pattern of the early Christian groups (Malherbe, 60-91; Stowers; Banks). That the churches (*ekklēsiai*) met in private houses is typified by the formulaic greeting in 1 Corinthians 16:19: "Aquila and Prisca, together with the church in their house, send you hearty greetings in the Lord" (RSV; cf. Rom 16:5; Philem 2; Col 4:15). We also know that homes as well as *synagogues were important locations for preaching activity (Acts 20:20) and that conversion to Christianity often involved whole households, following the lead of the household head (Acts 16:15, 31-34; 18:8). Paul refers to the intermediary role played by members of Chloe's household (1 Cor 1:11) and, in a revealing aside, admits to having baptized "the household of Stephanas" (1 Cor 1:16; cf. 1 Cor 16:15-16). So it is legitimate to infer that "the church in the house of . . ." was the basic cell of the Christian movement, the nucleus of which was a single, extended household (Meeks, 75).

The implications of this for understanding 1 Corinthians are wide-ranging. First, given that "the whole church" (1 Cor 14:23) was made up of a number of separate house churches, it is likely that the rivalry and division threatening the church was a rivalry between relatively wealthy household heads who hosted churches in their houses. Second, the evident conflict and confusion over the role and authority of women (cf. 1 Cor 11:2-16; 14:33-36) and slaves (cf. 1 Cor 7:21-23; 12:12-13) may have arisen at least in part because the church in the house was a public gathering in private space and new, Christian values were impinging in unpredictable ways on members' self-understanding and role expectations. Third, the social level of the church as comparable with the social level of its constituent households—neither aristocratic nor a movement of slaves, but a broad mixture of people including a small number of relatively high status and a majority of low status—becomes clearer (cf. 1 Cor 1:26). Fourth, the fact that the meetings of the *ekklēsia* took place in a house gives us an indication of its size and internal dynamics. R. J. Banks estimates as follows: "The entertaining room in a moderately well-to-do household could hold around thirty people comfortably—perhaps half as many again in an emergency" (Banks, 35). A meeting of the "whole church" may have reached forty to forty-five people. The intensity of fellowship in such gatherings must have been strong, as also the potential for disorder: all of which, because of the household setting, was open to the critical or admiring view of outsiders (1 Cor 14:23-25).

2.2. Voluntary Associations. Alongside the household, another social pattern likely to have influenced the house churches (or at least people's perception of them) is that of the Greco-Roman voluntary *association (Lat *collegium*, Judge, 40-48; Barton and Horsley; Wilken, 31-47; Kloppenborg and Wilson). Such associations took a variety of forms and were referred to in various ways depending on their purpose, location and constituency. There were trade guilds such as the guild of silversmiths at Ephesus (Acts 19:23-41) or the proposed society (*hetaeria*) of firemen at Nicomedia (Pliny *Ep.* 10.33, 34); funerary societies (*collegia tenuiorum*), which provided conviviality in life and decent burials in death; and cult groups (*thiasoi, eranoi*) for the worship of particular deities such as Isis or Bacchus.

For example, an inscription dated A.D. 136 about a burial society in the Italian city of Lanuvium records in detail the bylaws of the society showing how the society was organized and the character of its activities. Part of the bylaws reads as follows:

> It was voted unanimously that whoever desires to enter this society shall pay an initiation fee of 100 *sesterces* and an amphora of good wine, and shall pay monthly dues of 5 *asses*. It was voted further that if anyone has not paid his dues for six consecutive months and the common lot of mankind befalls him, his claim to burial shall not be considered, even if he has provided for it in his will. It was voted further that upon the decease of a paid-up member of our body there will be due him from the treasury 300 sesterces, from which sum will be deducted a funeral fee of 50 sesterces to be distributed at the pyre [among those attending]; the obsequies, furthermore, will be performed on foot. . . . It was voted further that if any member desires to make any complaint or bring up any business, he is to bring it up at a business meeting, so that we may banquet in peace and good cheer on festive days. It was voted further that any member who moves from one place to another so as to cause a disturbance shall be fined 4 sesterces. Any member, moreover, who speaks abusively of another or causes an uproar shall be fined 12 sesterces. Any member who uses any abusive or insolent language to a *quinquennalis* at a banquet shall be fined 20 sesterces. It was voted further that on the festive days of his term of office each *quinquennalis* is to conduct worship with incense and wine and is to perform his other functions clothed in white, and that on the birthdays of Diana and Antinoüs he is to provide oil for the society in the public bath before they banquet. (Lewis and Reinhold, 274-75)

Against this background, it is fair to say that in at least some respects the Christian groups will have looked familiar to outsiders. Like the Christians, members of this burial society met regularly (monthly rather than, as with the Christians, weekly), ate food and drank wine together, honored one another by elections to office, addressed the problem of causes of disturbance in the meetings and joined together in activities of worship. Such associations, like the house churches in Corinth and elsewhere (cf. Acts 2:41-45), provided a social context for people from primarily the non-élite trades and crafts end of the social scale to participate in a common life larger than the household but smaller than the city-state. The Christians were distinctive, however, in the mixed social composition of their groups, the exclusiveness of their focus on devotion to Christ crucified and risen and the seriousness of their commitment to holiness.

2.3. Law Courts. Why does Paul proscribe civil litigation between Christians in the courts of Corinth (1 Cor 6:1-11)? His concern to maintain the holiness of the church by encouraging the development of a certain autonomy from the procedures and institutions of the world has been mentioned already. But this is not the only factor. First, there were strong precedents for establishing autonomous legal and disciplinary practices. In Judaism, there were courts that operated under the aegis of the synagogue. Paul himself was the object of synagogue disciplinary action on no fewer than five occasions (2 Cor 11:24; cf. Mt 10:17). Likewise, the sectarian community at Qumran had its own court for dealing with disputes and disciplinary procedures (Schiffman, 282-87). In the wider Greco-Roman world, there is evidence that clubs and voluntary associations also sought to keep their disciplinary problems in-house. One inscription from the Attic society of the Iobacchi, dated around A.D. 178, includes the following rules:

> And if anyone come to blows, he who has been struck shall lodge a written statement with the priest or the vice-priest, and he shall without fail convene a general meeting, and the Iobacchi shall decide the question by vote under the presidency of the priest, and the penalty shall be exclusion for a period to be determined and a fine not exceeding twenty-five silver denarii. And the same punishment shall be imposed also on one who, having been struck, fails to seek redress with the priest or the arch-bacchus but has brought a charge before the public courts. (Todd, 89)

Precedents and analogies such as these make Paul's prohibition on going to the civil court more understandable by showing that it was customary in other groups and associations of the time to settle disputes intramurally.

But more can be said, for it is likely that the way the civil courts operated was for Paul a strong deterrent, given his overwhelming desire not to exacerbate the factionalism in the church. In particular, B. W. Winter has shown that civil lawsuits were used widely as an instrument of enmity between rivals for power among the social élite and that the system as a whole was open to bribery and corruption. In the situation addressed by Paul, it appears that the power struggle between the members of the élite in the church was spilling over into disputes that where being settled in the courts. The effect was disastrous: "It should be remembered that if some had already successfully prosecuted fellow Christians, then the person who won the action would have been awarded financial compensation. This would have only aggravated the problem of strife within the Christian community as the contestants would then appear in church together. If the jury took sides, then would not the members of the church be tempted to do the same? Whether one lost or won, the effect could only be harmful to relationships in the congregation" (Winter, 115).

2.4. Patrons and Clients. Relevant to understanding the operations of the courts, voluntary associations, households and much else in Greco-Roman society is the patron-client relationship (cf. Elliott 1987; Garnsey and Saller, 148-59; *see* Patronage). From the emperor down, patron-client relations bound together in mutual obligation the empire, provinces, city-states and their respective organs and institutions. According to J. K. Chow (30-33), the patron-client relation has the following characteristics: it is an exchange relation in which the patron provides for the client in return for the client's support; it is asymmetrical, as a consequence of the greater access of the patron to scarce resources of a material or spiritual kind; it is usually a particular and informal relation in which resources are channeled to specific groups or individuals rather than bestowed universally; it is usually supralegal based on the subtleties of mutual understanding and custom; although it is a volun-tary relation, it is binding and long-range, carrying with it a strong sense of interpersonal obligation; and it is a vertical relation that binds patron and client(-groups) together in a way that tends to exclude other patrons and discourage horizontal relations between clients. An ironic testimony from Paul's contemporary the *Stoic philosopher *Seneca is suggestive of the pervasiveness of patron-client relations and the obligation entailed:

> Look at those whose prosperity men flock to behold; they are smothered by their blessings. To how many are riches a burden! From how many do eloquence and the daily straining to display their powers draw forth blood. . . . To how many does the throng of clients that crowd about them leave no freedom! In short, run through the list of all these men from the lowest to the highest—this man desires an advocate, this one answers the call, that one is on trial, that one defends him, that one gives sentence; no one asserts his claim to himself, everyone is wasted for the sake of another. Ask about the men whose names are known by heart, and you will see that these are the marks that distinguish them: A cultivates B and B cultivates C; no one is his own master. (*Brev. Vit.* 2.4, in Chow, 81)

If we look at 1 Corinthians against this background, new interpretative possibilities open up.

For example, Paul's elaborate defense of his refusal of financial support may be an attempt to win back the support of wealthy patrons in the church whose patronage he has declined (1 Cor 9:3-27). Further, his anxiety about Apollos and Cephas (1 Cor 1:12; 3:3-4; 4:6-7) may be related to the same issue, for it appears that the *benefaction he declined they accepted. Even worse, Paul had adopted the humiliating course of working with his hands to support himself (1 Cor 4:12; 9:6). The effect on Paul's authority in Corinth must have been dramatic. Paul's relations with the wealthy patrons of the church (probably those who styled themselves the strong), along with their clients and household members, were jeopardized and the unity of the church put at risk. It is likely that all the other problems Paul deals with in 1 Corinthians—going to court, slaves seeking manumission, offending the weaker brother by eating idol meat, the unequal distribution of food at the Lord's Supper, the collection for *Jerusalem, and so on—were affected in one way or another by customary expectations about patrons and clients (cf. Theissen; Marshall; Chow). But this is not surprising. For Paul, the lordship of the crucified Christ and the imperative of serving Christ as his slave implied a reordering of social relations that put him at odds with the world around him.

See also ASSOCIATIONS; BENEFACTOR; CIVIC CULTS; FAMILY AND HOUSEHOLD; GYMNASIA AND BATHS; HEAD COVERINGS; HONOR AND SHAME; HOSPITALITY; PATRONAGE; ROMAN SOCIAL CLASSES; SLAVERY; WOMEN IN GRECO-ROMAN WORLD AND JUDAISM.

BIBLIOGRAPHY. R. J. Banks, *Paul's Idea of Community* (Peabody, MA: Hendrickson, 1994); S. C. Barton, "Paul's Sense of Place: An Anthropological Approach to Community Formation in Corinth," *NTS* 32 (1986) 225-46; S. C. Barton and G. H. R. Horsley, "A Hellenistic Cult Group and the New Testament Churches," *JAC* 24 (1981) 7-41; J. K. Chow, *Patronage and Power: A Study of Social Networks in Corinth* (JSNTSup 75; Sheffield: JSOT, 1992); J. H. Elliott, "Patronage and Clientism in Early Christian Society," *Forum* 3 (1987) 39-48; idem, *Social-Scientific Criticism of the New Testament* (London: SPCK, 1995); J. F. Gardner and T. Wiedemann, eds., *The Roman Household: A Sourcebook* (London: Routledge, 1991); P. Garnsey and R. Saller, *The Roman Empire: Economy, Society and Culture* (London: Duckworth, 1987); K. C. Hanson, "Greco-Roman Studies and the Social-Scientific Study of the Bible," *Forum* 9 (1993) 63-119; B. Holmberg, *Paul and Power* (Philadelphia: Fortress, 1978); E. A. Judge, *The Social Pattern of Christian Groups in the First Century* (London: Tyndale, 1960); J. S. Kloppenborg and S. G. Wilson, *Voluntary Associations in the Greco-Roman World* (London: Routledge, 1996); R. S. Kraemer, *Her Share of the Blessings* (New York: Oxford University Press, 1992); M. R. Lefkowitz and M. B. Fant, eds., *Women's Life in Greece and Rome* (London: Duckworth, 1992); N. Lewis and M. Reinhold, eds., *Roman Civilization Sourcebook*, 2: *The Empire* (New York: Harper & Row, 1966); A. J. Malherbe, *Social Aspects of Early Christianity* (Philadelphia: Fortress, 1983); B. J. Malina, *The New Testament World: Insights from Cultural Anthropology* (London: SCM, 1983); idem, *The Social World of Jesus and the Gospels* (London: Routledge, 1996); P. Marshall, *Enmity in Corinth: Social Conventions in Paul's Relations with the Corinthians* (WUNT 2.23; Tübingen: Mohr Siebeck, 1987); W. A. Meeks, *The First Urban Christians* (New Haven, CT: Yale University Press, 1983); M. M. Mitchell, *Paul and the Rhetoric of Reconciliation* (Louisville, KY: Westminster John Knox, 1992); H. Moxnes, "Honor and Shame," *BTB* 23 (1993) 167-76; C. Osiek, *What Are They Saying About the Social Setting of the New Testament?* (New York: Paulist, 1992); L. H. Schiffman, *Reclaiming the Dead Sea Scrolls* (New York: Doubleday, 1994); S. K. Stowers, "Social Status, Public Speaking and Private Teaching: The Circumstances of Paul's Preaching Activity," *NovT* 26 (1984) 59-82; G. Theissen, *The Social Setting of Pauline Christianity* (Edinburgh: T & T Clark, 1982); M. N. Todd, *Sidelights on Greek History* (Oxford: Blackwell, 1932); R. L. Wilken, *The Christians as the Romans Saw Them* (New Haven, CT: Yale University Press, 1984); B. W. Winter, *Seek the Welfare of the City: Christians as Benefactors and Citizens* (Grand Rapids, MI: Eerdmans, 1994); O. L. Yarbrough, *Not Like the Gentiles: Marriage Rules in the Letters of Paul* (SBLDS 80; Atlanta: Scholars Press, 1985).

S. C. Barton

SOLOMON. *See* ODES OF SOLOMON; PSALMS OF SOLOMON; WISDOM OF SOLOMON.

SON OF GOD TEXT (4Q246)

The so-called *Son of God* text, 4Q246 (*olim* 4Qpseudo-Dan[d]) has sparked interest among NT interpreters because of its reference to a figure who will be called "son of God" and "son of the Most High." The text was discussed by J. T. Milik in a public lecture in 1972, was partially published by J. A. Fitzmyer in 1974 (391-94; see Fitzmyer 1979) and was finally published in full by E. Puech in 1992 and J. A. Fitzmyer in 1993 and 1994.

1. Contents of 4Q246
2. Interpretations of 4Q246
3. 4Q246 and the New Testament

1. Contents of 4Q246.
4Q246 comprises a single piece of leather, preserving two columns of Aramaic text, with nine lines in each column. With the exception of a few letters on the left-hand edge, the text of column 2 is completely preserved. However, several letters are missing on the right-hand side of column 1. The reconstructions of Puech (1992, 1994) and Fitzmyer (1993, 1994) propose anywhere from eleven to seventeen letters missing at the beginning of each line. Fitzmyer believes that he has fully restored the lost words and letters.

4Q246 evidently describes the interpretation that an unknown seer has given to a distraught king. The seer falls before the throne and then assures the king that despite serious dangers from foreign enemies (i.e., Assyria and Egypt), his son (according to the reconstruction and translation of Fitzmyer 1994, 167) "shall also be great upon the earth [and all peoples sh]all make [peace with him], and they shall all serve [him, (for)] he shall be called [son of] the [gr]eat [God], and by his name shall he be named. He shall be hailed (as) son of God, and they shall call him son of the Most High" (1:7—2:1). The vision then goes on to describe the frightening battles and carnage that lie ahead (2:1-3), "until there arises the people of God, and everyone rests from the sword. (Then) his kingdom (shall be) an everlasting kingdom, and all his ways (shall be) in truth. He shall jud[ge] the land with truth, and everyone shall make peace. The sword will cease from the land, and the provinces shall pay him homage. The great God is himself his might; he shall make war for him. Peoples he shall put in his power, and all of them he shall cast before him. His dominion (shall be) an everlasting dominion, and none of the abysses of [the earth shall prevail against it]!" (2:4—3:1).

2. Interpretations of 4Q246.
4Q246 confronts interpreters with a series of questions. The text does not make clear the identity of the king to whom the seer discloses the meaning of the dream or vision, nor does the text identify the king's son beyond the amazing epithets "son of God" and "son of the Most High" (1:9; 2:1). In a public address at Harvard University in 1972 and in a later publication, Milik (1992, 383-84) proposed that the "son of God" figure alludes to Alexander Balas, the last of the *Seleucid kings of Syria (cf. 1:6, which Milik translates "Syria," instead of the expected "Assyria"). The Greek and Latin inscriptions on coins issued by Alexander, such as *deo patre natus* ("born of divine parentage"), cohere with the epithets "son of God" and "son of the Most High." Alexander's brutal and blasphemous reign will end when the "people of God arises" (2:4). This interpretation is problematic in its identification of Assyria as Syria and in imagining a confederation between the rival powers Syria and Egypt.

Similarly, E. M. Cook has argued that 4Q246 reflects the Seleucid period, especially the Jewish struggle against Antiochus IV Epiphanes. The "son of God" is none other than a "prince of nations" (1:5), which is a significantly different reading from those of J. J. Collins, Fitzmyer and others. This prince will provoke various wars "until the people of God shall arise and all will have rest from the sword" (2:4). Line 5 should then be taken as "their kingdom," that is, the kingdom of the "people of God," not the kingdom of the evil prince who spuriously claims to be "son of God" (line 1). Cook's interpretation is based on a sequential understanding of the events described in the text, which follows a pattern and imagery typical of an older Akkadian prophetic tradition. Puech (1992, 127-31, 1994b, 556) and others see in the "son of god" figure a reference to Antiochus.

Collins (1997) responds to this interpretation, arguing that the text is closer in genre and theme to the book of Daniel (esp. 3:33; 4:31; 7:14, 27) and that the Akkadian parallels to which Cook appeals are too remote and imprecise to be relevant. Collins further observes the linguistic and thematic parallels between 4Q246 and the Aramaic paraphrasing seen in *Targum Isaiah* 10:20—11:16, as well as 1QM 1 (*see* War Scroll). Finally, he believes the events described in 4Q246 are not sequential but cyclical (see also J. Zimmermann, 182-84). 4Q246 2:4-7a describe the coming war and tribulation, followed by assurance of the coming son who will be great, make peace and be hailed as "son of God" (1:7b—2:1ab). The scenario is then repeated: The enemies of the people of God will appear as "comets," who will rule the earth for some years, trampling peoples and provinces (2:1c-3). This they will do "until the people of God arises" and peace is achieved (2:4-9).

D. Flusser believes that the "son of God" is an antichrist figure, who like the personage described in 2 Thessalonians 2:1-12 ("the man of lawlessness . . . who opposes and exalts himself against every so-called god or object of worship, so that he takes his seat in the temple of God, proclaiming himself to be God"), as well as in other texts such as **Ascension of Isaiah* 4:2-16 ("a lawless king," to whom the people will offer sacrifice), *Oracle of Hystaspes* (a king from Syria who will "call himself God and will order himself to be worshiped as the Son of God") and **Testament of Moses* 8 (a "man who rules with great power"), will pass himself off as a false messiah and persecute the people of God. Flusser's interpretation, however, is vulnerable, for it rests on a doubtful translation in 1:8 ("they will worship" instead of "they will serve") and on antichrist traditions found in Christian texts, which may not represent pre-Christian, Jewish ideas.

F. García Martínez thinks the figure is Michael the archangel, who in other texts is known as *Melchizedek, the Prince of Light. His principal support for this interpretation is found in 1QM 17:5-8, where Michael is expected to appear during the great eschatological battle and defeat the prince of the dominion of darkness. But in what sense a king can be promised an *angel for a son is not clear. M. Hengel (45) thinks the "son" is a collective for the people of God as a whole, as is the "one like a son of man" in Daniel 7:13. However, because the seer is addressing an individual (i.e., the worried king), interpreting the prophecy of the "son" as in reference to a single individual should be preferred.

Fitzmyer (1993, 1994, 1995) thinks this figure is a future Jewish king who will restore the Davidic kingship but who is not the Messiah, the future David of Jeremiah 30:9. However, the setting, involving a dream or vision that needs to be interpreted and depicts a great victory over Gentile nations, surely is suggestive of eschatology, which in turn recommends a messianic interpretation of the "son of God" figure. Would not a messianic figure, based on texts like 2 Samuel 7:13-16 and Psalm 2:2, 7, be called "son of God"? Would an epithet such as this, found in an eschatological context, not call to mind the messianic hope? Other interpreters think so.

H.-W. Kuhn (109-11), Collins (1993, 1997), Zimmermann and Puech (1994a, 34), among others, understand 4Q246 in a messianic sense. They contend that hope of a coming descendant of a Jewish king who will be hailed "son of God" and "son of the Most High" and through whom the "people of God" will enjoy peace, an everlasting kingdom, the subjugation of the Gentiles and an everlasting dominion, is surely best explained in terms of messianism. According to 1QSa 2:11-12, *Qumran expected a time "when God will have begotten the Messiah among" the community. The "first-born son" of 4Q369 may also be a messianic reference. Fitzmyer's insistence that the word *messiah* (*māšîaḥ*) must appear in a text before it can be regarded as messianic seems unnecessarily restrictive when texts like 4Q285 are taken into account. Surely the Branch of David, the Prince of the Congregation, who will slay the leader of the Kittim (i.e., the Romans) in fulfillment of Isaiah 10:34—11:1, is the Messiah. Yet the word *messiah* does not appear. One should note that in 4Q252 5:3-4 the Branch of David is expressly identified as the "Messiah of righteousness," and in 4Q161 7–10 iii 22 the Branch of David is said to "arise at the end of days." Finally, the parallels with Luke 1:32-35 seem only to confirm this messianic interpretation.

3. 4Q246 and the New Testament.

The significance of 4Q246 for NT interpretation is seen immediately in the impressive parallels with the angelic annunciation in the Lukan infancy narrative:

These parallels strongly suggest that the epithets "son of God" and "son of the Most High" carried with them messianic overtones. If they were not understood in this way, then one must wonder why Christian tradition would have applied them to Jesus as part of its christological confession.

The language of 4Q246 also calls into question the critical opinion that epithets such as "son of God" and "son of the Most High" are relatively late and non-Jewish additions to emerging christology. Here the operative assumption is that only when Christianity encountered more directly the Greco-Roman world and

Luke	4Q246
this one will be great (1:32)	your son will be great (1:7)
son of the Most High he shall be called (1:32)	son of the Most High he shall be called (2:1)
he shall be called son of God (1:35)	he shall be called son of God (2:1)
he will rule . . . forever (1:33)	his kingdom an everlasting kingdom (2:5)

its cult of the emperor (*see* Ruler Cult), who was hailed as "son of God," did Christians begin applying such language to Jesus. The discovery of 4Q246, an Aramaic text dating to one generation before Jesus, in which such language was applied to an expected victorious Jewish king, in all probability the Messiah, calls into question this older critical assumption (Hengel, 45; Zimmermann, 188).

See also MESSIANISM; PRAYER OF ENOSH (4Q369 + 4Q458); WAR OF THE MESSIAH (4Q285, 11Q14) WORKS OF THE MESSIAH (4Q521).

BIBLIOGRAPHY. J. J. Collins, "The Background of the 'Son of God' Text," *BBR* 7 (1997) 51-61; idem, "The *Son of God* Text from Qumran," in *From Jesus to John: Essays on Jesus and New Testament Christology in Honor of Marinus de Jonge,* ed. M. C. De Boer (JSNTSup 84; Sheffield: JSOT, 1993) 65-82; E. M. Cook, "4Q246," *BBR* 5 (1995) 43-66; F. M. Cross, "Notes on the Doctrine of the Two Messiahs at Qumran and the Extracanonical *Daniel Apocalypse (4Q246),*" in *Current Research and Technological Developments on the Dead Sea Scrolls: Conference on the Texts from the Judean Desert, Jerusalem, 30 April 1995,* ed. D. W. Parry and S. D. Ricks (STDJ 20; Leiden: E. J. Brill, 1996) 1-13; P. A. H. de Boer, "The Son of God in the Old Testament," *OTS* 18 (1973) 188-201; J. A. Fitzmyer, "The Aramaic 'Son of God' Document from Qumran," in *Methods of Investigation of the Dead Sea Scrolls and the Khirbet Qumran Site: Present Realities and Future Prospects,* ed. M. O. Wise et al., (ANYAS 722; New York: New York Academy of Sciences, 1994) 163-78; idem, "4Q246: The 'Son of God' Document from Qumran," *Bib* 74 (1993) 153-74; idem, "The Palestinian Background of 'Son of God' as a Title for Jesus," in *Texts and Contexts: Biblical Texts in Their Textual and Situational Contexts,* ed. T. Fornberg and D. Hellholm (L. Hartman Festschrift; Oslo: Scandinavian University Press, 1995) 567-77; idem, *A Wandering Aramean: Collected Essays* (SBLMS 25; Missoula, MT: Scholars Press, 1979) 90-93, 102-7; D. Flusser, "The Hubris of the Antichrist in a Fragment from Qumran," *Immanuel* 10 (1980) 31-37; F. García Martínez, "The Eschatological Figure of 4Q246," in *Qumran and Apocalyptic: Studies on the Aramaic Texts from Qumran,* ed. F. García Martínez (STDJ 9; Leiden: E. J. Brill, 1992) 162-79; M. Hengel, *The Son of God* (Philadelphia: Fortress, 1976); H.-W. Kuhn, "Röm 1,3f und der davidische Messias als Gottessohn in den Qumrantexten," in *Lese-Zeichen für Annelies Findeiß zum 65. Geburtstag am 15. März,* ed. C. Burchard and G. Theissen (DBAT 3; Heidelberg: Carl Winter, 1984) 103-12; S. L. Mattila, "Two Contrasting Eschatologies at Qumran (4Q246 vs 1QM)," *Bib* 75 (1994) 518-38; J. T. Milik, "Les Modèles Araméns du Livre d'Esther dans la Grotte 4 de Qumran," *RevQ* 15 (1992) 321-99, esp. 383-84; E. Puech, "Fragment d'une Apocalypse en Araméen (4Q246 = pseudo-Dan[d]) et le 'Royaume de Dieu,'" *RB* 99 (1992) 98-131; idem, "Les Manuscrits de la Mer Morte et le Nouveau Testament," *Le Monde de la Bible* 86 (1994a) 34-41; idem, "Notes sur le Fragment d'Apocalypse 4Q246—'Le Fils de Dieu,'" *RB* 101 (1994b) 533-58; J. Zimmermann, "Observations on 4Q246—The 'Son of God,'" in *Qumran-Messianism: Studies on the Messianic Expecta-tions in the Dead Sea Scrolls,* ed. J. H. Charlesworth, H. Lichtenberger and G. S. Oegema (Tübingen: Mohr Siebeck, 1998) 175-90.

C. A. Evans

SONGS OF THE SABBATH SACRIFICE (4Q400-407, 11Q17, MAS1K)

The *Songs of the Sabbath Sacrifice* is a liturgical document consisting of thirteen distinct compositions, each dated to one of the first thirteen *sabbaths of the year. Whether the cycle was specific to the first quarter of the year or was repeated for each of the other quarters of the year is debated (Newsom; Maier). The modern title is derived from the heading that introduces each of the individual compositions. Since the songs invoke angelic praise and describe the sabbath worship of *angelic beings in the heavenly temple, the composition is also known as the *Angelic Liturgy*.

1. Content and Structure
2. Purpose, Date and Provenance
3. Significance for the New Testament

1. Content and Structure.
Even though all of the ten copies of *Sabbath Songs* are fragmentary, enough remains to describe the basic structure of the individual compositions as well as the overall structure of the cycle. Each song begins with a heading and date formula (e.g., "For the Instructor. Song of the sacrifice of the first sabbath on the fourth of the first month"). Following the heading comes a call to praise, introduced by the imperative "praise," followed by a direct object (an epithet for God) and a vocative (an angelic title). The initial call to praise is expanded with one or more parallel calls to praise. The body of the song is developed differently, depending on its place in the sequence. There appears to be no standard formula for concluding a song.

The song cycle as a whole has a discernible structure, consisting of three parts, songs 1—5, songs 6—8 and songs 9—13. Each part differs in style as well as content. The first five songs describe the establishment of the angelic priesthood and its duties, as well as the praise that these heavenly *priests utter. The second song makes what appears to be the only reference to the human priesthood and worshipers. These songs are written in a parallelistic style with ordinary syntax and containing a significant number of finite verbs.

Songs 6—8 differ strikingly. Characterized by repetitious formulas in which the number seven figures prominently, the sixth and eighth songs enumerate the praises and blessings uttered by the seven chief and deputy princes respectively. The central, seventh song elaborates the initial call to praise into a series of seven increasingly elaborate calls to praise addressed to each of the seven angelic councils. After these calls to praise the song then describes the heavenly temple itself bursting into praise, concluding with a description of the chariot throne of God and the praise uttered by multiple attendant chariot thrones (*merkabot*), their cherubim and wheels (*ʿophannim*). The seventh song serves as an anticipation of the final group of songs (9—13), which progressively describe the heavenly temple and its praises, culminating in an extended description of the divine chariot throne and the angelic high priests in their priestly robes. In this third section of the cycle, nominal and participial sentences are common, as are elaborate construct chains, apparently an attempt to create a numinous style.

2. Purpose, Date and Provenance.
The purpose and function of the *Sabbath Songs* are elusive. The headings of the songs ("song of the sabbath sacrifice") might suggest that they were a liturgical accompaniment to the sacrificial act (cf. 2 Chron 29:27; Sir 50:22-28; *m. Tamid* 3:8; 7:3-4) or perhaps a praise offering that substituted for the Musaf *sacrifice of the sabbath. This function, however, depends on the assumption that the cycle was repeated quarterly, an assumption difficult to square with the preserved date headings, which refer specifically to the first and third months. Moreover, certain themes (the establishment of the priesthood in the first sabbath song, the description of the chariot throne on the twelfth sabbath, immediately after Shabuot) suggest a cycle keyed to liturgical events specific to the first quarter of the year. If the cycle was not repeated quarterly, its function should be sought not in liturgical and sacrificial praxis but in the cultivation of a communal mysticism, the experience of angelic worship in the heavenly temple (*see* Heavenly Ascent; Mysticism).

Paleographical analysis of the manuscripts suggests that the songs were composed no later than 100 B.C. How much earlier is difficult to say. If they are judged to be a composition of the sectarian Qumran community, a date between 150 and 100 B.C. would be possible. If, however, they are judged to be pre-Qumran writings, adopted and copied by the sectarian community, then they may be older. The evidence for the provenance of the text is ambiguous. The heading "For the Instructor" is the same as that which is found in the sectarian liturgical text, 1QSb (the *Rule of Blessings; see* Book of Blessings), though the expression in the *Sabbath Songs* might also be construed simply as a restrictive phrase ("for the one who is wise"). Apart from this phrase there is no technical terminology that might refer to the sect or its leaders. The solar *calendar, assumed by the *Sabbath Songs*, is common to nonsectarian texts as well as those produced by the Qumran community. Terminology regularly used for God in the *Sabbath Songs* (*'elohim*) is generally avoided in specifically sectarian texts, though the angelic context of the *Sabbath Songs* makes the comparison problematic. The fact that one of the copies of the *Sabbath Songs* was found at Masada (Mas1k) might be explained either as a copy carried there by a refugee from the Qumran community after A.D. 68 or as evidence that the composition circulated among a wider range of Jewish groups than just the Qumran community. The evidence for provenance remains too ambiguous for certainty.

3. Significance for the New Testament.

Although there is no indication of direct influence on any NT writings, the *Sabbath Songs* share common traditions with the books of Revelation, Colossians and Hebrews. Similarities with Revelation 4—5 may derive in part from a common dependence on Ezekiel 1 and 10. Certain similar stylistic features of the angelic praise, however, such as the tendency to accumulate synonyms and the existence of seven-word formulas (cf. Rev 5:12 and 4Q403 frag. 1 i 1-29) suggest common traditions independent of Ezekiel. Both the *Sabbath Songs* and Revelation depict features of the heavenly temple as animate and capable of praise (cf. Rev 9:13-14 and 4Q403 frag. 1 i 41-46). If the reference to the veneration of angels in Colossians 2:18 refers to the mystical practice of joining in common worship with angels rather than a worship of angels, then the *Sabbath Songs* may be an example of the sort of practice to which Colossians alludes. Finally, the *Sabbath Songs* may be relevant to the traditions underlying the reference to the priesthood of Melchizedek in Hebrews 7:1-3. Unfortunately, the two passages in the *Sabbath Songs* which appear to refer to Melchizedek by name are broken (4Q401 frag 1 i 11, 22), but the contexts describe a single angelic figure who is "priest in the assembly of God" and make reference to priestly ordination.

See also HEAVENLY ASCENT IN JEWISH AND PAGAN TRADITIONS; LITURGY: QUMRAN; MYSTICISM.

BIBLIOGRAPHY. D. Allison, "The Silence of Angels: Reflection on the Songs of the Sabbath Sacrifice," *RevQ* 13 (1988) 189-97; J. H. Charlesworth and C. A. Newsom, eds., *The Dead Sea Scrolls: Hebrew, Aramaic and Greek Texts with English Translations, vol. 4b: Angelic Liturgy: Songs of the Sabbath Sacrifice* (Tübingen: Mohr Siebeck; Louisville: Westminster John Knox, 1999); M. Davidson, *Angels at Qumran: A Comparative Study of 1 Enoch 1-36, 72-108 and Sectarian Writings from Qumran* (JSOTSup 11; Sheffield: Sheffield Academic Press, 1992); D. Falk, *Daily, Sabbath, and Festival Prayers in the Dead Sea Scrolls* (STDJ 27; Leiden: E. J. Brill, 1998); J. Maier, "Shire ʿOlat Hash-Shabbat. Some Observations on Their Calendrical Implications and on Their Style," in *The Madrid Proceedings of the International Congress on the Dead Sea Scrolls, Madrid, 18-21 March 1991,* ed. J. Trebolle Barrera and L. Vegas Montaner (STDJ 11; Leiden: E. J. Brill, 1992) 2:543-60; C. Newsom, "Shirot ʿOlat Hashabbat," in E. Eshel et al., *Qumran Cave 4.6: Poetical and Liturgical Texts, Part 1* (DJD XI; Oxford: Clarendon Press, 1998) 173-401 and plates xvi-xxxi; idem, *Songs of the Sabbath Sacrifice: A Critical Edition* (HSS 27; Atlanta: Scholars Press, 1985); B. Nitzan, *Qumran Prayer and Religious Poetry* (STDJ 12; Leiden: E. J. Brill, 1994); L. Schiffman, "Merkavah Speculation at Qumran: The 4Q Serek Shirot ʿOlat Ha-Shabbat," in *Mystics, Philosophers, and Politicians: Essays in Jewish Intellectual History in Honor of Alexander Altmann,* ed. J. Reinharz and D. Swetchinski (Durham, NC: Duke University Press, 1982) 15-47; A. Schwemer, "Gott als König und seine Königsherrschaft in den Sabbatliedern aus Qumran," in *Königsherrschaft Gottes und himmlischer Kult,* ed. M. Hengel and A. Schwemer (WUNT 55; Tübingen: Mohr Siebeck, 1991) 45-118; J. Strugnell, "The Angelic Liturgy at Qumran—4Q Serek Sirot ʿOlat Hassabbat," *VTSup* 7 (1960) 318-45; E. Tigchelar and F. García Martínez, "11Q Shirot ʿOlat ha-Shabbat," in F. García Martínez, E. Tigchelaar and A. S. van der Woude, *Qumran Cave 11.2: 11Q2-18, 11Q20-30* (DJD XXIII; Oxford: Clarendon Press, 1997) 259-304 and plates xxx-xxiv, liii.

C. A. Newsom

SONGS OF THE SAGE (4Q510-511). *See* LITURGY: QUMRAN.

SPORTS. *See* ATHLETICS; CIRCUSES AND GAMES.

STOICISM

Stoicism was one of the major philosophical traditions in NT times (cf. Acts 17:18) and arguably the most influential. Its aim was to teach people to attain happiness by being in control of their lives, emphasizing virtue as the only good to strive for, all other things being indifferent. Its strength lay in offering to its adherents a systematic and all-comprehensive worldview, based on a material pantheism. Students were exhorted to live in accordance with nature, which was variously identified with God, the divine principle of order, fate and providence. Despite significant differences in worldview, many early Christians were favorably impressed by the moral austerity of Stoicism.

1. History
2. Important Doctrines
3. Stoicism and Hellenistic Judaism
4. Stoicism and Early Christianity

1. History.
Stoicism was founded by Zeno of Citium (335-263 B.C.), who taught in the Stoa Poikilē ("Painted Colonnade") in Athens, from which the movement derived its name. He established the tripartite division of Stoic philosophy into logic (including theory of knowledge), physics (including metaphysics) and ethics. Zeno was succeeded as head of the Stoic school by Cleanthes of Assos (331-230 B.C.), who is best known for his religious interpretation of Stoic ideas (exemplified by his *Hymn to Zeus)* and his uncompromising ethics. The third head of the school, Chrysippus of Soli (c. 280-207 B.C.), a voluminous writer, reestablished Stoic orthodoxy and is often considered the second founder of Stoicism.

The foundation laid by these early philosophers was later adapted by so-called Middle Stoics such as Diogenes of Babylon (c. 240-152 B.C.), his student Panaetius (c. 185-109 B.C.) and the polymath Posidonius (c. 135-c. 51 B.C.) to make Stoicism more acceptable to the Roman intellectual elite and to accommodate certain *Platonic and *Aristotelian ideas. During the early empire, Stoic philosophers such as *Musonius Rufus (died before A.D. 101), *Seneca (c. 4 B.C.-A.D. 65), *Epictetus (mid-first to second century A.D.) and Marcus Aurelius (A.D. 121-180) focused almost exclusively on Stoicism as a way of life rather than a system of philosophy, although interest in the latter may still be seen in the textbook on ethics by Hierocles (early second century A.D.).

2. Important Doctrines.

2.1. Worldview and Theology. Stoic theology may be described as a monistic and materialistic pantheism, in which God permeates all of nature, from the cosmos as a whole down to the most lowly physical object (Pohlenz, 1:108). It is monistic, because of its doctrine of a single world order encompassing all that exists, including God. God, as the active principle, or reason (*logos*), acts upon the passive principle, matter, but both principles have a bodily existence (Diogenes Laertius *Vit.* 7.134). Nothing exists outside the world and its material principles; there is no spiritual world or world of ideas, such as in Platonism—hence the materialism of Stoicism. God as ordering and creative principle is physically present in all things as a fine, fiery substance, variously called the "designing fire" (*pyr technikon*) or *pneuma* ("breath" or "spirit," a fiery form of air), which gives everything its form and internal cohesion. Since he is present in the whole universe and gives everything in it the character it has, God is in a sense identical with the universe (Diogenes Laertius *Vit.* 7.137). This God as immanent ordering principle is thus very different from a transcendent Creator, outside and distinct from the world.

Since all of nature is imbued with the universal reason (*logos*), all events form part of a goal-directed rational process and a rigorous causal nexus; nothing is left to chance (Cicero *De Div.* 1.125-26; Alexander of Aphrodisias *Fat.* 191.30—192.28). Everything is providentially arranged for the good of the world system as a whole. Such a deterministic view of the world does not allow for the existence of evil—even apparently bad events such as illness, pests or natural disasters contribute to the overall well-being of the universe (Long and Sedley, 1:332-33).

Because of its rationalistic and monistic approach, Stoic theology has a monotheistic tendency, with God being identified with Zeus, the supreme god of the Greek pantheon (see Cleanthes *Hymn to Zeus* = Stobaeus *Anth.* 1.1.12). This did not entail the rejection of polytheism, however; the various gods were seen as metaphorical expressions of the God at work throughout nature. Popular myths about the gods were accepted as unsophisticated explanations of natural events, the truth of which may be uncovered by means of the allegorical method (see Cornutus *Theol. Graec.).*

2.2. Ethics. For the Stoic, happiness consists in attaining one's goal (*telos*) as a human being, which is "to live in agreement with nature" (Diogenes Laertius *Vit.* 7.87), that is, in agreement with our own rational nature, as well as in agreement with the nature of the universe of which we are part.

Virtue consists in using one's reason to make the right selections among those things that are good for us, such as health and wealth, as opposed to illness and poverty, and in trying to make these selections come true. Virtue itself, however, is the only real good that is essential for one's happiness. Our happiness does not depend on attaining positive things such as health or wealth but rather on making the right choices and attempting to put them into effect. Happiness therefore depends on what is in our power (i.e., making rational choices) and not on things beyond our power (i.e., attaining wealth or being healthy); the latter are thus "indifferent" (*adiaphora*) as regards our happiness (Diogenes Laertius *Vit.* 7.101-5).

A choice may be considered right only if it is made consciously and for the right reasons. Such a judgment is either right or wrong; there are no intermediate possibilities. Two identical actions may therefore be valued completely differently, depending on a person's motivation for performing the action. Only the truly wise person is able to make the right judgments and thus perform correct and virtuous actions, but Stoics admitted that there are very few, if any, truly wise people (Plutarch *Stoic. Repugn.* 31.1048E; Alexander of Aphrodisias *Fat.* 199.14).

Emotions such as fear or grief are false judgments about the world; rather than fearing or grieving for that which is beyond our control (such as losing a wife or a child) one should accept it as part of nature's plan and avoid giving in ("assenting") to one's emotions (Epictetus *Ench.* 5; Seneca *Ira* 2.3.1—2.4). Stoics thus advocated *apatheia* ("being without passions"; Epictetus *Diss.* 1.4.28-29; Diogenes Laertius *Vit.* 7.117) as opposed to the Aristotelian doctrine of *metriopatheia* ("moderation in passions").

Everything in nature is rationally and providentially arranged. The wise person therefore accepts his or her fate willingly without trying to resist, because it is at the same time the divine will and providence. The Stoics took pains to defend their view against the charge of determinism: according to them, even if one cannot change what providence has in store, one has the freedom to accept one's fate voluntarily or be forced to submit. This doctrine is forcefully expressed in Cleanthes' *Prayer to Zeus and Destiny:* "Lead me, Zeus and Destiny, wherever you have ordained for me. For I shall follow unflinching. But if I become bad and am unwilling, I shall follow none the less" (Epictetus *Ench.* 53; cf. Hippolytus *Refut.* 1.21).

3. Stoicism and Hellenistic Judaism.
*Philo of Alexandria (early first century A.D.), although usually considered a Middle Platonist, was nevertheless strongly influenced by Stoicism, especially by its ethics and *logos* doctrine, and used the Stoic method of allegorical exegesis extensively to interpret the Pentateuch in philosophical terms. Influence of Stoic natural theology (i.e., that the existence and actions of God are visible in nature) may also be seen in Hellenistic Jewish texts such as Wisdom of Solomon 13—14 (*see* Wisdom of Solomon).

4. Stoicism and Early Christianity.
There are significant similarities between NT and Stoic terminology (e.g., *logos, pneuma*). Paul's use of natural theology in Acts 17 and Romans 1—2, and the form and substance of the codes of household duties (Eph 5:21—6:9; Col. 3:18—4:1; 1 Pet 2:13—3:7) also indicate Stoic influence (*see* Family and Household; *DPL,* Philosophy). Many early Christian authors were attracted to the austere and demanding morality of the Stoics. A Stoic author like Seneca was appreciated as a kindred spirit by Christians like Tertullian (who calls him *saepe noster,* "often one of us"), Jerome and Augustine. This high regard led to the invention of a fictional correspondence between Seneca and Paul (Sevenster, 11-14). Evidence of Stoic influence is also visible in the natural theology of *1 Clement* 20 and in the allegorical exegesis of Clement of Alexandria and Origen.

See also EPICTETUS; MUSONIUS RUFUS; PHILOSOPHY; SENECA.

BIBLIOGRAPHY. H. von Arnim, ed., *Stoicorum Veterum Fragmenta* (4 vols.; Leipzig: Teubner, 1903-24); L. Edelstein, *The Meaning of Stoicism* (MCL 21; Cambridge, MA: Harvard University Press, 1966); M. Forschner, *Die stoische Ethik: Über den Zusammenhang von Natur-, Sprach- und Moralphilosophie im altstoischen System* (2d ed.; Darmstadt: Wissenschaftliche Buchgesellschaft, 1995); B. Inwood, *Ethics and Human Action in Early Stoicism* (Oxford: Clarendon Press, 1985); A. A. Long, *Hellenistic Philosophy: Stoics, Epicureans, Sceptics* (London: Duckworth, 1974); idem, *Stoic Studies* (Cambridge: Cambridge University Press, 1996); A. A. Long, ed., *Problems in Stoicism* (London: Athlone, 1971); A. A. Long and D. N. Sedley, *The Hellenistic Philosophers* (2 vols.; Cambridge: Cambridge University Press, 1987); M. Pohlenz, *Die Stoa: Geschichte einer geistigen Bewegung* (2 vols.; 6th & 7th eds.; Göttingen: Vandenhoeck & Ruprecht, 1990-92); M. E. Reesor, *The Nature of Man in Early Stoic Philosophy* (London: Duckworth, 1989); J. M. Rist, *Stoic Philosophy* (Cambridge: Cambridge University Press, 1969); J. M. Rist, ed., *The Stoics* (Major Thinkers; Berkeley and Los Angeles: University of California Press, 1978); F. H. Sandbach, *The Stoics* (2d ed.; Bristol: Bristol Press, 1989); J. N. Sevenster, *Paul and Seneca* (NovTSup 4; Leiden: E. J. Brill, 1961); R. W. Sharples, *Stoics, Epicureans and Sceptics: An Introduction to Hellenistic Philosophy* (New York: Routledge, 1996).

J. C. Thom

SUETONIUS

The surviving writings of Suetonius are biographical. In the lives of the early Roman emperors there are references to Judaism or Judea, especially to expulsion of Jews from Rome under Tiberius and Claudius. The latter case may have involved Jewish Christians. There is also mention of the punishment of Christians under Nero.

1. Birth and Early Career of Suetonius
2. Works of Suetonius
3. Ancient Biographical Writing
4. Suetonius's Biographies

1. Birth and Early Career of Suetonius.

Gaius Suetonius Tranquillus (c. A.D. 70-c. 130) came from an equestrian family, but his place of birth is uncertain. Discovery of a fragmentary inscription at Hippo Regius in Roman Africa in 1952 has led some scholars to regard this as Suetonius's hometown. R. Syme (780) preferred Pisaurum in northeastern Italy. But consideration should also be given to Lanuvium in Latium, probably the town of Suetonius's relative Caesennius Silvanus (so Lindsay, 463). At an early stage of his career (c. A.D. 101-103) Suetonius was about to obtain a military tribunate but requested his *patron *Pliny the Younger to transfer the posting to Silvanus (Pliny *Ep.* 3.8).

According to the Hippo inscription, Suetonius's main positions were in the civilian administration of the emperor: literary adviser (*a studiis*), public librarian (*a bibliothecis*) and correspondence secretary (*ab epistulis; see* Roman Administration). The usual arrangement of honorary inscriptions suggests that the first two offices were held under Trajan (A.D. 98-117) and the last under Hadrian (A.D. 117-138). The *Historia Augusta* reports that Hadrian "appointed successors to Septicius Clarus prefect of the praetorian guard and to Suetonius Tranquillus controller of correspondence [*epistularum magistro*] and to many others" on the ground of their excessive familiarity with the empress (*Historia Augusta: Hadrian* 11.3). This and further digressive material is inserted between summary references to Hadrian's visit to Britain (*Historia Augusta: Hadrian* 11.2; 12.1), implying a date of A.D. 122. But the unreliable author may have misplaced the information. An alternative view would see the most likely occasion for the Hippo inscription as being the visit of Hadrian to Africa in A.D. 128, when the emperor was presumably accompanied by his correspondence secretary. Dismissal of Suetonius might have occurred after return to Rome, from where Hadrian soon departed for Athens (Lindsay, 463-64; but cf. Baldwin).

2. Works of Suetonius.

The medieval Greek encyclopedia *Suda* attributes to *Trankullos* (i.e., Suetonius Tranquillus) numerous works of a scholarly or antiquarian nature; others are known by citation elsewhere. Some components of *On Famous Men* (*De Viris Illustribus*) survive; this was an example of collected *biography, containing short lives in the categories of *grammarians and *rhetoricians, *poets, orators, historians and *philosophers. The main surviving work, and pre-sumably the latest, is *On the Life of the Caesars* (*De Vita Caesarum*, or *The Twelve Caesars*). This work contains twelve lives in chronological order, beginning with Julius Caesar and proceeding through the Roman emperors from Augustus to Domitian. The work is divided into eight books, one to each of the first six figures, then one to Galba, Otho and Vitellius for A.D. 69, and one to the Flavians (Vespasian, Titus and Domitian). Even so, Julius and Augustus receive fuller treatment than do any of the others, marking the transition from republican to imperial government. The first few chapters of the first life were lost between the sixth and the ninth centuries. Hence the dedication to Septicius Clarus, reported by Johannes Lydus (Lydus *Mag.* 2.6), has also been lost. And it is unclear whether the lives were published serially or together.

3. Ancient Biographical Writing.

A. Momigliano (11) briefly defined biography as an "account of the life of a man from birth to death." Nevertheless, he was well aware that the earliest examples of Greek biographical writing do not merely present a chronological account of their subjects. In the body of his writing on Evagoras (c. 370 B.C.), Isocrates rather awkwardly combines topical and chronological treatment. A decade later Xenophon clearly divides his treatment of Agesilaus into a chronological account followed by topical presentation of his virtues. At Rome Cornelius Nepos (c. 110-24 B.C.) anticipated Suetonius in writing *On Famous Men*. These collected biographies included the categories of generals, kings, historians and probably poets and four others. Each category contained a series of foreign (mainly Greek) figures followed by an equivalent series of Romans. Contemporary with Suetonius, *Plutarch wrote in Greek a series of lives, mostly treating a pair of notable Greeks and Romans and adding a comparison.

4. Suetonius's Biographies.

Suetonius fits into the general line of development of Greek and Roman biography. Each biography contains an "account of the life of a man from birth to death." There is ample assessment of the qualities of each of his subjects. The eight books present a collection of lives of men in the same social category. The element of comparison is present but does not function in the same way as it does in Nepos or Plutarch. Since the series of lives forms a continuous chronological succession, each biography bears comparison with the next. At the same time, an "imperial ideal" (Bradley) emerges, against which each subject is individually measured. The choice of Julius and the Roman emperors as subjects is distinctively new. And the arrangement of material within each life is somewhat different from that of other biographies.

Suetonius regularly uses a tripartite structure in each life: (1) family background, youth and early career until accession to the principate; (2) assessment of the subject's performance as emperor, where both moral categories and spheres of activity may be used; (3) narrative of the subject's death, with which may be associated a description of his physical appearance, his household and his personal habits and interests. The first section is predominantly chronological, the second mainly topical; and in the third the account of death may either follow (as in *Claudius*) or precede (as in *Nero*) the other personal details. Plutarch follows a similar tripartite pattern within individual lives.

There is brief mention of Jews, Judaism or Judea in ten of the twelve lives (see Stern, chap. 94). "Among the Roman writers from the Julio-Claudian period onwards who deal with Jewish topics, Suetonius is unique for the neutrality of his tone and the accuracy of his content" (Williams, 773). All passages are of interest in reflecting aspects of the position of Judaism in the first century B.C. to the first century A.D.

Early in the central section of *Tiberius*, Suetonius aims to show how this emperor's initial pretence of moderation gives way to a tendency to tyranny. One example (from A.D. 19) is the suppression of Jewish rites in Rome, the conscription of young Jewish men to the army and the expulsion of the rest of the Jewish community "and those who followed similar practices" from the city (Suetonius *Tiberius* 36). Suetonius seems closer to the facts than do other writers who deal with the same events (Tacitus *Ann.* 2.85.5; Josephus *Ant.* 18.3.5 §§81-84; Dio Cassius *Hist.* 57.18.5a).

More problematic is another reference at *Claudius* 25.4: "He expelled from Rome the Jews, who were constantly making disturbances at the instigation of Chrestus" (*Iudaeos impulsore Chresto assidue tumultuantis Roma expulit*). The incident is one of a string of measures reported with equal brevity in order to illustrate Claudius's good administration of the empire (Suetonius *Claudius* 25.1-5). However, the complimentary nature of the catalog is undermined by the last sentence of the passage, which concludes the central section of this life. Dio Cassius also notes action taken by Claudius against the Jews (Dio Cassius *Hist.* 60.6.6), as does Orosius, the fifth-century A.D. Christian historian (Orosius *Histories* 7.6), and Acts 18:2. Each of these sources mentions only one such action under Claudius. And, according to Dio, "he did not expel them, but ordered them, while practicing their traditional life-style, not to meet together." Dio's report suggests that expulsion may have been considered but was not carried out. Suetonius gives no date. Dio mentions the matter within the first year of Claudius's reign (i.e., A.D. 41), along with other miscellaneous actions, some of which are customary rather than limited to that year. Orosius explicitly states: "Josephus reports that in the ninth year of the same (sc. emperor/reign) the Jews were expelled from the city by Claudius." Since there is no such reference in the extant works of *Josephus, Orosius's dating does not inspire confidence.

Rather than illuminating the background of Acts, Orosius may be using the probable period reflected in Acts 18:2 in order to provide a more precise setting for his Suetonius quotation. The author of Acts makes a noticeable distinction between Claudius's order "that all the Jews should depart from Rome" and the recent arrival of Aquila and Priscilla "from Italy." Paul's hosts need not have come directly from Rome immediately upon the action of Claudius. Only Suetonius mentions the "instigator Chrestus" (*impulsore Chresto*). Orosius had no doubt that Suetonius meant *Christus*. Suetonius does spell *Christiani* with *i* (Suetonius *Nero* 16.2, the only occurrence of the term). But such *e/i* variations are not uncommon for this period (cf. *Chrestiani, Christus* within a few words at Tacitus *Ann.* 15.44.2-3). Since Jesus was not alive in the reign of Claudius, Suetonius may be speaking metaphorically or misunderstanding a source. His phrase at least suggests that in some way Jewish Christians were involved. If Dio is right, an expulsion of Jews from Rome did not take place under Claudius. The restriction on Jewish assembly in Rome is likely to have been imposed early in the reign of Claudius, possibly in A.D. 41. And if Suetonius is right about the "instigator," Jewish Christians were at least partly responsible for the trouble.

At *Nero* 16.2, Suetonius reports that "the Christians, a group of people belonging to a strange and harmful cult, were afflicted with punishment" (*afflicti suppliciis Christiani, genus hominum superstitionis novae ac maleficae*). In the context, *novae* more likely refers to the nature ("strange") than the chronology of the movement ("new"). The term *maleficae* more probably indicates external effect ("harmful") than internal behavior ("evil-doing," "wicked"); compare *exitiabilis* ("destructive," Tacitus *Ann.* 15.44.3). Emendation of "afflicted" (*afflicti*) to the weaker "affected" (*affecti*) is not justified. Suetonius is heightening the language of Tacitus (*Ann.* 15.44.2-3), while retaining his designation of the Christians as a "cult" (*superstitio*).

The central section of *Nero* is formally divided between treatment of his commendable actions (Suetonius *Nero* 9—19.2) and his faults and crimes (Suetonius *Nero* 20—25, 26—39). Normally in each life Suetonius makes the emperor the subject of the main clause, and frequently of subordinate clauses, in each sentence (Louns-bury, 3750). In an unparalleled departure from this practice, Suetonius at *Nero* 16.2—17 "lists a number of 'police measures' and new regulations" (Warmington, 73), which are reported in the passive as occurring "under him" (*sub eo*). Suetonius knows that Nero personally did not deserve credit for most of these actions (see Wallace-Hadrill, 122-23). Punishment of the Christians is listed among these positive reforms. There is no specific indication of what was "strange" or "harmful" about the Christians. And Suetonius does not make any link between the Christians and the fire of Rome in A.D. 64. Nero is blamed for that, in the account that forms the climax of the portrayal of the emperor's cruelty (Suetonius *Nero* 38). But there is a congruence of vocabulary and authorial stance between *Nero* 16.2 and Tacitus (*Ann.* 15.44). Suetonius is probably alluding to the same incident of punishment of the Christians and to the same popular view, that Christians had a "hatred of the human race" (Tacitus *Ann.* 15.44.4).

Suetonius's references to Jews and Christians are all brief and incidental to his strong focus on the lives of the Caesars. "Suetonius does not explicitly state his views about Jews or Judaism" (Stern, 2:108). But, if his reporting is neutral in tone, it does include instances of suppression of Jews in Rome and in one case seems to reflect Jewish-Christian involvement. The characterization of Christians is more negative. And, while Suetonius is referring to the reign of Nero (presumably A.D. 64), the evaluative terms "strange" and "harmful" must also reflect Roman attitudes in the A.D. 120s.

See also BIOGRAPHY, ANCIENT; ROMAN EMPERORS; TACITUS.

BIBLIOGRAPHY. **Texts and Translations.** C. Suetoni Tranquilli, *Opera,* 1: *De Vita Caesarum, Libri VIII,* ed. M. Ihm (Stuttgart: Teubner, 1967 [1908]) (text); *Suetonius* (2 vols.; Cambridge, MA: Harvard University Press; 1913-14; vol. 1 rev. 1951) (translation); Suetonius, *Claudius,* ed. J. Mottershead (Bristol: Bristol Classical Press, 1986); Suetonius, *Nero,* ed. B. H. Warmington (Bristol: Bristol Classical Press, 1977); Suetonius, *Tiberius,* ed. H. Lindsay (London: Bristol Classical Press, 1995). **Studies.** B. Baldwin, "Hadrian's dismissal of Suetonius—a reasoned response," *Historia* 43

(1994) 254-56; K. R. Bradley, "The Imperial Ideal in Suetonius' 'Caesares,'" *ANRW* 2.33.5 (1991) 3701-32; idem, *Suetonius' Life of Nero: A Historical Commentary* (Collection Latomus 157; Brussels: Latomus, 1978); R. G. Lewis, "Suetonius' 'Caesares' and Their Literary Antecedents," *ANRW* 2.33.5 (1991) 3623-74; H. Lindsay, "Suetonius as *ab epistulis* to Hadrian and the Early History of the Imperial Correspondence," *Historia* 43 (1994) 454-68; R. C. Lounsbury, "*Inter quos et Sporus erat:* The Making of Suetonius' 'Nero,'" *ANRW* 2.33.5 (1991) 3748-79; A. Momigliano, *The Development of Greek Biography* (Cambridge, MA: Harvard University Press, 1971); M. Stern, *Greek and Latin Authors on Jews and Judaism* (3 vols.; Jerusalem: Israel Academy of Sciences and Humanities, 1976-84); R. Syme, *Tacitus* (2 vols.; Oxford: Clarendon Press, 1958; corrected repr. 1963, 1967); G. B. Townend, "The Hippo Inscription and the Career of Suetonius," *Historia* 10 (1961) 99-109; idem, "Suetonius and His Influence," in *Latin Biography,* ed. T. A. Dorey (Studies in Latin Literature and Its Influence; London: Routledge & Kegan Paul, 1967) 79-111; A. Wallace-Hadrill, *Suetonius: The Scholar and His Caesars* (London: Duckworth, 1983); M. H. Williams, "The Expulsion of the Jews from Rome in A.D. 19," *Latomus* 48 (1989) 765-84.

D. W. Palmer

SUPERSTITION. *See* RELIGION, PERSONAL.

SYMMACHUS. *See* SEPTUAGINT/GREEK OLD TESTAMENT.

SYNAGOGUES

The synagogue was the regular Jewish assembly for prayer and worship. Jesus is depicted as teaching and performing miracles in synagogues in *Galilee (Mt 4:23; Lk 4:15), especially in Nazareth (Mt 13:54; Mk 6:2; Lk 4:16) and in Capernaum (Mk 1:21; Lk 7:5; Jn 6:59). The synagogue in the latter city was probably built by the centurion (Lk 7:5) whose servant Jesus healed.

The synagogue continues to play an important role in the early church and is mentioned frequently in the book of Acts, occurring some nineteen times. Although Paul is depicted as visiting and preaching in synagogues routinely, he never uses the word in his epistles. The word occurs rarely in the remainder of the NT writings, appearing but once in James, in reference to Christian assembly (Jas 2:2), and twice in Revelation, in reference to a "synagogue of Satan," an assembly, perhaps Jewish (they "say that they are Jews and are not, but lie"), that opposes the Christian community (Rev 2:9; 3:9).

1. Names and Origin
2. Offices
3. Services and Other Activities
4. Remains of Buildings
5. Interior
6. The Functions of Synagogues
7. Jesus' Relation to Synagogues
8. Paul and the Hellenistic Synagogue
9. Rivalry Between Church and Synagogue

1. Names and Origin.

"Synagogue" is a word derived from the Greek *synagōgē,* which meant originally an assembly such as of the Jews meeting for worship. In the Septuagint it is used, for example, in Exodus 12:3 of the whole congregation of Israel. It came to mean local gatherings of Jews and then the building where Jewish congregations met. Especially after the *destruction of the temple in Jerusalem in A.D. 70, synagogues became the centers of both religious and communal activity wherever there was a *minyan,* or quorum of ten Jewish men. The Talmud claimed that there were eighty synagogues in Jerusalem before A.D. 70. The Pilgrim of Bordeaux (4th cent. A.D.) reported but seven remaining in his day.

The Greek word *proseuchē,* literally "prayer," was also used as a synonym for synagogues in *inscriptions, *papyri, *Philo and *Josephus. Whether the occurrence of this word in Acts 16:13 designates a synagogue or a prayer meeting at Philippi is a matter of dispute. Another Greek word used in one papyrus for a Jewish place of prayer is the term *eucheion.* In one passage Josephus (*Ant.* 16.6.2 §164) quotes the term *sabbateion* to mean "synagogue." In later Hebrew tradition the synagogue was called variously *bêt tᵉpillâ,* "house of prayer," *bêt midraš,* "house of study," and *bêt kᵉnēsset,* "house of assembly."

Though a few scholars (e.g., J. Weingreen) have stressed the preexilic roots of the synagogue, most would ascribe its rise to the postexilic period. Many would place this development in the Jewish exilic community in Mesopotamia.

The earliest possible inscriptional evidences are references to *proseuchē* in inscriptions and papyri from Ptolemaic Egypt (M. Bengel, E. Schürer), the earliest of which dates to the reign of Ptolemy III Euergetes (246-221 B.C.). This text refers to the foundation of a *proseuchē* at Schedia, some twenty miles from Alexandria. Another text from the same reign refers to a *proseuchē* at Arsinoë-Crocodilopolis in the Fayum. The existence of a synagogue at this town is also confirmed by a land survey (P. Tebt. 86). An inscription from Ptolemy VII refers to the dedication of "the pylon," the monumental gate, of a synagogue (Griffiths, 10).

Some scholars who dispute the interpretation of references to these *proseuchai* in Egypt as synagogues maintain that the synagogue as an institution developed in Palestine in the second century b.c. with the rise of the *Pharisees (J. Gutmann).

2. Offices.

Jairus, whose daughter Jesus healed (Mk 5:22, 35, 36, 38; Lk 8:49), was the head of the synagogue (Gk *archisynagōgos*). Luke 8:41 has Jairus listed as one of the *archōn tēs synagōgēs*, "leaders of the synagogue"; Matthew 9:23 refers to him simply as an *archōn*. From Luke 13:10-17 and from passages in Acts (18:1-17) we can infer that such an officer was responsible for keeping the congregation faithful to the Torah.

The relative esteem in which the "head of the synagogue" was held in Jewish society is revealed in a passage from the Talmud (*b. Pesaḥ* 49b):

> Our rabbis taught: Let a man always sell all he has and marry the daughter of a scholar. If he does not find the daughter of a scholar, let him marry the daughter of [one of] the great men of the generation. If he does not find the daughter of [one of] the great men of the generation, let him marry the daughter of a head of a synagogue. If he does not find the daughter of a head of a synagogue, let him marry the daughter of a charity treasurer. If he does not find the daughter of a charity treasurer, let him marry the daughter of an elementary school teacher, but let him not marry the daughter of an *ʿam hā ʾāreṣ* ["people of the land"] because they are detestable and of their daughters it is said, 'Cursed be he that lieth with any manner of beast' (Deut 27:21).

The word *archisynagōgos* appears in thirty Greek and Latin inscriptions. In three cases from Smyrna and Myndos in Western Turkey and from Gortyn on Crete the term is used of women. B. Brooten has argued that these and other titles (*presbytera*, "elder"; *hiereia*, "priestess") were not just honorific but referred to women leaders. One inscription to an infant as an *archisynagōgos* was certainly honorific.

A group of elders would direct the activities of the synagogue. The *archisynagōgos* was probably chosen from among them. An almoner would collect and distribute alms. The *ḥazzān*, or "attendant," was the one who took care of the Scripture scrolls. Jesus gave back the Isaiah scroll to such an attendant (Gk *hypēretē*, Lk 4:20). The *ḥazzān* also announced the beginning and the end of the sabbath by blowing the *šôpār*, or ram's horn. In later practice the *ḥazzān* was paid and lodged at the synagogue as a caretaker.

3. Services and Other Activities.

We know that the later synagogue services included such features as the recitation of the *Shemaʿ* ("Hear, O Israel," Deut 6:4-9; 11:13-21; Num 15:37-41), prayer facing Jerusalem, the "Amen" response from the congregation, the reading of excerpts from the scrolls of the Torah (Acts 15:21) and of the Prophets, translation of the Scriptures into Aramaic paraphrases, a sermon and a benediction (cf. Neh 8; *see* Liturgy: Rabbinic).

It became customary to recite while standing the *Shemoneh Esreh*, or "Eighteen Benedictions," as a prayer. Toward the end of the first century A.D. a nineteenth benediction was added, which was actually a curse against the *mînîm*, or heretics, namely, the Christians.

Any male could be called upon to pray or to read the portions from the Torah or the Prophets (*hapṭārôṭ*). On one occasion Jesus read from the scroll of the prophet Isaiah (61:1-2) in the synagogue at Nazareth. Any competent individual could also be called upon to give the sermon (cf. Acts 13:15, 42; 14:1; 17:2).

Jesus refers to the custom of the teachers of the law and the Pharisees sitting in Moses' seat (Mt 23:2). Such a seat of honor has been found at Chorazin. Stone benches along the walls were reserved for dignitaries. The general congregation may have sat on mats or carpets.

Though synagogues in the Middle Ages had segregated galleries for *women, there is no evidence for such segregation in ancient synagogues. In the NT the presence of women in the congregation is attested inasmuch as Jesus healed a crippled woman as he was teaching in a synagogue (Lk 13:10-17).

As the major community building the synagogues were not only used for services on the *sabbath, Mondays, Thursdays and festival days, but also for various community functions. Children would be taught there by the *ḥazzān*. Funds could be kept in a communal treasury at the synagogue.

Offenders could be judged before the elders in the synagogues and flogged forty stripes save one by the *ḥazzān* (Mk 13:9; 2 Cor 11:24). Apostates could be excommunicated (Jn 9:22; 12:42; 16:2).

4. Remains of Buildings.

It is estimated that we have archaeological remains for over one hundred synagogue sites from Palestine and for about twenty from the Diaspora. There are relatively few archaeological evidences for synagogues in Palestine from either the first or the second century A.D. An inscription of Theodotus from Jerusalem, which has usually been dated prior to A.D. 70, refers to the establishment of a hostel for pilgrims and may possibly be related to the synagogue of the Freedmen (i.e., former slaves, Acts 6:9). It reads as follows:

> Theodotus, son of Vettenos, the priest and *archisynagōgos*, son of a *archisynagōgos* and grandson of a *archisynagōgos*, who built the synagogue for purposes of reciting the law and studying the commandments, and the hostel, chambers and water installations to provide for the needs of itinerants from abroad, and whose father, with the elders, and Simonides, founded the synagogue.

A building (12 x 15 m) at the Herodian fortress of Masada has been identified as a first-century synagogue by Y. Yadin. It is equipped with benches and two rows of columns. The building's entrance was oriented toward Jerusalem. Yadin found an ostracon with the inscription "priestly tithe" at the site. He argues that *Herod had originally constructed the building as a synagogue for his Jewish followers. The Herodian building was later reused by the Zealots until the fall of Masada in A.D. 73 to the Romans (*see* Jewish Wars with Rome). Pits in this building served as a genizah, or storage, for discarded scriptural scrolls (Deuteronomy and Ezekiel). Nearby were *miqwāʾōt*, or stepped pools, for ritual purification.

A *triclinium* (dining room) at Herodium was transformed into a synagogue by the Zealots. The building measures 10.5 x 15 meters, with benches along the walls. A *miqwâ* is near the entrance. This building is similar in appearance to that at Masada. S. Guttman believes that a building at Gamla in the Golan heights, which he uncovered in 1976, is also a first-century A.D. synagogue.

But the alleged synagogue uncovered at Magdala in 1975 by V. Corbo and S. Loffreda has turned out to be part of a villa. No remains are visible from a first-century building excavated at Chorazin and identified by some scholars as a synagogue. The basalt synagogue which is visible at Chorazin is from a much later period. (In the Diaspora a building on the Aegean island of Delos has been identified as a synagogue dating from pre-Christian times.)

The most splendid synagogue remains in Palestine are those of the white limestone structure at Capernaum. On the basis of coins, the Franciscan excavators have dated this building to the fourth-fifth century A.D.; Israeli scholars still prefer to date it to the second or third century. In 1981 V. Corbo uncovered dark basalt walls underneath this synagogue, which he has identified as the remains of an earlier synagogue. He dug a trench within the nave and exposed a basalt wall for a length of 24 meters (78 ft). The walls are nearly four feet thick. The floor was a cobbled pavement made up of black basalt. Pottery associated with the floor establishes its date as the first century A.D. Corbo has identified this structure as the synagogue, built by the centurion, which Jesus attended (Lk 7:1-5) (see Strange and Shanks).

No certain synagogue remains from the second century have been identified except for those at Nabratein, though Roman Catholic excavators have claimed to have discovered a synagogue of "Jewish Christians" (third-fourth century) at the site of the Church of the Annunciation in Nazareth. They also identify several architectural fragments from the Franciscan monastery in Nazareth as derived from a synagogue (second-third century).

Most synagogue remains are from the Late Roman and Byzantine eras (A.D. 300-600), including about fifteen from Galilee and a similar number from the Golan Heights. The synagogues are of three architectural types: (1) Broad House, with the bema or platform on the southern long wall such as at Khirbet Shema; (2) the Basilica type, as at Capernaum and

Chorazin; (3) the Basilica with an apse at Beth Alpha.

5. Interior.

These later synagogues were elaborately decorated with symbols such as the lampstand *(mᵉnôrâ)*, palm frond and citron. They were provided with a bema or platform for the reading of the Scriptures and a niche for the display of the ark or chest *(ʾᵃrôn)* for the biblical scrolls. In 1980 E. M. and C. Meyers discovered the fragment of such an ark niche from Nabratein. This pediment is decorated with reliefs of rampant lions and a scallop shell with a hole for the chain of a perpetual lamp.

Many of the Byzantine synagogues were lavishly decorated with mosaics, including four mosaics of the zodiac at Hammath Tiberias, Beth Alpha, Naʿaran and Husifa. The mosaic at Hammath Tiberias has a central panel with Helios (sun) on his chariot and figures reflecting the four seasons at the corners.

We also have three examples of lists of the twenty-four priestly courses *(mišmārôt)*, which hung in synagogues. Most synagogue inscriptions are of donors. The third-century A.D. synagogue at Dura Europos on the Euphrates River even had paintings on its walls depicting biblical narratives.

Because of the scant remains of synagogues from first-century A.D. Palestine, some scholars have argued that Luke-Acts is anachronistic when it refers to synagogue buildings. But this is to underestimate the fragmentary nature of the archaeological evidence and to disregard not only the testimony of the NT but also of Josephus (*Vit.* 277, 280), who speaks of a *proseuchē* which was a large building at Tiberias (cf. also Josephus *J.W.* 2.14.4 §285; *Ant.* 14.10.23 §258; 19.6.3 §300). Philo's report of the anti-Semitic mob's attacks on *proseuchas* in Alexandria in A.D. 38 (Philo *Leg. Gai.* 132) clearly refers to synagogue buildings. [E. M. Yamauchi]

6. The Functions of Synagogues.

The earliest epigraphal references to synagogues come from Egypt (from the third century B.C.), where they were known generally as "places of prayer." But prayer was only one function of what might also be called a "house of learning" (Sir 51:23). Philo describes synagogues as "schools of prudence, courage, temperance, justice, piety, holiness and every virtue" (Philo *Vit. Mos.* 2.216), and he assumes that a reverent, communal reading of the Torah with exposition on the sabbath is their principal purpose (Philo *Leg. Gai.* 156). In that the latter reference is to a long-standing custom in Rome, Philo attests the common knowledge that synagogues are a well-known feature of Judaism and hardly a local peculiarity of Egypt. It is a reasonable inference that Philo's own monumental exposition of the Torah was designed to complete the process of advanced education which synagogues sometimes occasioned.

The epigraphal remains of Jews in Egypt reflect their political situation. One slab of limestone refers to the synagogue as "in honor of King Ptolemy and of Queen Berenice," which permits a dating within the reign of Ptolemy III Euergetes (246-221 B.C.; Griffiths, 4-5). Evidently, a degree of protection was claimed by such dedications (of which Griffiths gives further examples).

But to speculate from such evidence that the institution of the synagogue actually originated in Egypt is unwarranted. It has been claimed, for instance, that 1 Maccabees and 2 Maccabees contain "not a word" about the institution, so that evidence of synagogues in Palestine "is lacking before the first century BCE and perhaps even until the first CE" (Grabbe 1995, 21, 25). 1 Maccabees 3:46-54 in fact refers to a previous "place of prayer" in Mizpah, where the Israelites gathered after the desecration of the sanctuary. There they fast and do penance, read from the Torah and assemble what they can of the priestly vestments and the offerings, all the while seeking divine guidance. Mizpah, of course, is a place of sacrifice and assembly according to biblical precedent (Gen 31:44-54; Judg 20:1-3; 21:1-8; 1 Sam 7:5-16). But in 1 Maccabees it is presented as what Philo might have called a school of prudence and courage, a place where the Torah alone is guide, in terminology which corresponds well to the language of the epigraphal remains from Egypt.

What is evidenced in Egypt is an institution typical of the Judaism of the time, a gathering for accepting the guidance of the Torah with prayerful dedication. The generality of the synagogue is attested by the decree of Caesar Augustus that money for the temple tax might be stored in synagogues and that confiscation should be regarded as sacrilege (Josephus *Ant.* 16.6.2-3 §§162-66).

The range of purposes a synagogue might serve is attested by the inscription of Theodotus, which establishes that a synagogue was constructed in Jerusalem "for purposes of reciting the law and studying the commandments" as well as "to provide for the needs of itinerants from abroad" (see 4 above). The association with institutions such as the synagogues mentioned in Acts 6:9 is natural.

Unless synagogues needed to be public for some particular purpose (such as to claim political protection or to offer *hospitality) they were for the most part "located in houses with the plan and facade of private homes" (Tsafrir, 79). Only from the third century in Palestine do typical patterns of construction for synagogues become widespread, and at the same time stunning artistic embellishments are widely represented. The Dura Europos synagogue in Dura, a Syrian town on the Euphrates, represents a similar development. The third-century building, the object of a famous excavation, was the result of successive adaptations of a private dwelling (Kraabel 1995, 99). The magnificent paintings of Dura represent that same later phase, as does its prominent shrine for the Torah.

Synagogues built long after the destruction of the *temple came to take on some of the aspects of the temple. *Tosefta Megilla* 4(3):22, for example, insists that entrances for synagogues open only to the east, as in the temple. In the same vein, representations of the menorah, the lulav, the shofar and the incense shovel within synagogues reflect a consciousness of their quasi-cultic function (Dar and Mintzker, 163; Gal, 166-73).

Before the synagogue was felt to replace the temple, it had complemented it. The official function of receiving taxes for its upkeep is one example. Another is its function as a gathering of elders for the purpose of administering justice. When Paul refers to beatings in synagogues (Acts 22:19, see also 2 Cor 11:24), that corresponds to the judicial power which Mishnah also attributes to communal authorities (*m. Mak.* 3:1-14). A document from the Persian period in Babylonia (dated 511 B.C.) shows the attempt of a Jewish family to control the behavior of a daughter (Bickerman, 1:349-50); the emergence of the synagogue provided an occasion for such legal instruments. Although the implements of the temple were later associated decoratively with synagogues, the ark for the scrolls of the Law is attested as early as Caesar's edict as quoted by Josephus (*Ant.* 16.6.2 §164). The centrality of reading and interpreting the law is also conveyed in the scene of Nehemiah 8, which the rabbis of Talmud later associated with reciting the Scripture and giving its interpretation in *Aramaic (*b. Meg.* 3a; *b. Ned.* 37b; *see* Rabbinic Literature: Targumim).

The judicial function of the synagogue was not merely a punitive matter: Torah also provides for the support of the poor. Matthew 6:2 and *Tosefta Baba Batra* 8:4 in their differing ways agree that synagogues are places of charity (Safrai, 191-94). Within the first century, sites of synagogues are typically associated with miqvaot, or ritual baths (Reich, 289-97), and that association is probable in the case of the synagogue in Arsinoë-Crocodilophilus (from 113 B.C.; Kasher, 217). A particular affinity between the synagogue and the adjudication of *purity is therefore signaled by the archaeological evidence.

The functions of the synagogue must be appreciated before the accumulating archaeological data may be suitably assessed. It is a mistake of categories to expect Palestinian synagogues of the first century to be purpose-built structures, clearly labeled for the archaeologist. As long as the Jerusalem temple stood, synagogues were usually no more than large rooms, typically in the midst of other, smaller rooms (as in a private dwelling). Their purpose was the interpretation and application of the Torah, with the prayerful intent which the Torah presupposes. Some might criticize the ostentation of teachers and/ or their prayer (see Mt 6:5; 23:6; Mk 12:39; Lk 11:43; 20:46), but the centrality of prayerful teaching is a matter of record. The diverse functions of the synagogue cannot be understood simply in terms of services of worship in churches today (so McKay), but most of what we call worship took place in that setting, no doubt with less organization (and decorum) than characterizes modern liturgies.

The synagogue at Migdal (Magdala) measures 8.16 x 7.25 meters; the one at Gamla measures 19.6 x 15.1 meters (Groh, 58-59). Both feature banked seats and columns arranged around a central area. They are designed for attentive listening. Beyond that, the use of such spaces for purposes of public meeting, the collection of alms, adjudication, higher learning, disputation, local administration and hospitality would vary from place to place, depending upon the needs, resources and aspirations of the local community. Because local needs, resources and aspirations themselves can change before buildings can be altered, there is no reason to imagine all public functions took place in the same place in every community. The place of prayer in Philippi is said in Acts 16:13 to be beside a river. Local exigencies might demand outdoor meetings, as in the case of Judas Maccabeus at Mizpah. Only a simplistic obsession with monuments demands a marked, purpose-built structure for the claim to be made that those who revered the Torah read it regularly together and tried reverently to apply it.

7. Jesus' Relation to Synagogues.

The portrayal of Jesus' activity in the Gospels often corresponds to what may be known of synagogues within his period and place, although at times the presentation seems to reflect more the customs within Greek-speaking congregations in the Diaspora. Luke 4:16-21 is the most vivid example of both aspects of the representation of Jesus (Chilton 1979, 123-77).

As the text reads, Jesus simply stands and recites a text and claims it has been fulfilled. General amazement is the result (Lk 4:22), and the congregation is startled even before Jesus announces the fulfillment of Scripture (Lk 4:20). What is missing from the text is an indication that Jesus has here provided a targum, a translation of the passage into Aramaic, because in the Hellenistic Diaspora the Scriptures were simply read in Greek (*see* Septuagint/Greek Old Testament), rather than read and then translated. It has often been observed that the citation from Isaiah 61:1-2a, the principal source Jesus cites here, omits the reference to divine vengeance in Isaiah 61:2b. That might have occasioned mild surprise, but scarcely astonishment. After all, the choice of where a passage of reading should end was largely left open during the first century. The key to an understanding of what Jesus says is that it is not a simple reading of Isaiah 61:1-2, but a conflation of that passage with Isaiah 58:6, which speaks of forgiving, that is, releasing, those who are oppressed. In the underlying tradition which informed the passage, Jesus stood in the synagogue and gave a new rendering of the book of Isaiah in Aramaic, targeted on the issue of forgiveness. That motivated his omission to speak of divine vengeance.

His assertion of the new activity of God is, it has been proposed, most accurately represented in the text of the Old Syriac Gospels:

> The Spirit of the Lord is upon you,
> because of which he anointed you to preach to the poor,
> and he has sent me to preach to the captives forgiveness, and to the blind sight
> —and I will strengthen the broken with forgiveness—
> and to preach the acceptable year of the Lord.

The reading reflects the linkage between Jesus personally and the distinctive issue of his new "reading": the issue of forgiveness. That linkage, the claim of an offer of forgiveness "fulfilled" by Jesus, causes astonishment in the synagogue.

In what follows in the text of Luke, astonishment turns inexplicably to scandal (Lk 4:22-30). The experience of preachers of Jesus in synagogues nearer Luke's time is reflected, as can be seen in the similarity of the pattern of presentation in Acts 13:13-52 concerning Paul and Barnabas at Pisidian Antioch. The sequel has Paul stoned by Jews in Lystra (Acts 14:19), so that the comparability with the presentation of Jesus in Nazareth becomes all the more plain.

Nonetheless, Jesus' activity in synagogues, including his sympathetic relations with leaders of synagogues such as Jairus, is amply attested. The general pattern of teaching in synagogues (Mt 4:23; 9:35; 13:54; Mk 1:39; Lk 4:15; Jn 18:20) confirms the connection between Jesus and the targumic tradition (Chilton 1984). There is no evidence to support the contention that lectionaries of readings were fixed within the first century, and that complements the NT's picture of the freedom which Jesus and his followers enjoyed in choosing the texts that suited them. It is also striking that the question of healing is at issue in synagogues, in the idiom of disputes about keeping the sabbath (Mt 12:9-14; Mk 3:1-6; Lk 6:6-11; 13:10-17; 14:1-6) and about purity (Mk 1:21-28; Lk 4:31-37). Purity is also an implicit concern in approaching the supposed corpse of Jairus's daughter (Mt 9:18-19, 23-26; Mk 5:21-24, 35-43; Lk 8:40-42, 49-56). That issue is underlined within the tradition, as is shown by the inclusion of the story of the woman with a flow of blood (Mt 9:20-22; Mk 5:25-34; Lk 8:43-48). That Jairus would have lived adjacent to any meeting room now seems entirely plausible in light of archaeological data.

Indeed, the synagogue may have featured more prominently in Jesus' ministry than appears at first sight. Peter and Andrew are depicted as residing adjacent to a synagogue in Capernaum (Mk 1:29; cf. Lk 4:38), and they may have been leaders there. Also at Capernaum, an appeal is made to Jesus to be sympathetic to a centurion on the grounds that he had built a synagogue (Lk 7:5); Jesus' high esteem of the institution is obviously presupposed (see also Jn 6:59). Likewise, Jesus himself is assumed to be an acceptable teacher in his own home town (Mt 13:54; Mk 6:2; Lk 4:16). Jesus' pronouncement that the "leper" who approached him was clean (Mt 8:1-4; Mk 1:40-45; Lk 5:12-16) may originally have been set in a synagogue, and that is the most appropriate setting for his teaching concerning defilement (Mk 7:15; Mt 15:10-11; *see* Purity). The "house" in which Jesus is placed at the time he declared the paralytic free of both sin and disease was possibly a synagogue (Mk 2:1-12; cf. Mt 9:1-8; Lk 5:17-26); that would explain the crowd and the degree of controversy involved.

8. Paul and the Hellenistic Synagogue.

Only at a later stage in the development of the Gospels was the synagogue assumed to be a place of persecution for disciples (Mt 10:17; 23:34; Mk 13:9; Lk 12:11; 21:12). That assumption reflects hard experience, as intimated, for example, in the allusion within the source called Q to failed missions in Chorazin and Bethsaida, and even in the formerly sympathetic Capernaum (Lk 10:13-15; Mt 11:20-24; see Catchpole, 171-76).

Acts reflects something of the attempt after the resurrection by some unsympathetic leaders of synagogues to coordinate a denunciation of Jesus' followers with the help of the authorities of the temple (Acts 9:1-2; 22:19; 26:11; cf. 24:12). But the focus is so consistently upon Paul's reception in synagogues (together with Barnabas's, as Paul's companion), that it is a matter of supposition how other Christian leaders, such as Peter and James, were received in synagogues. Presumably their experience was as different from Paul's as their teaching was less radical, and James in fact cites the preaching of Moses in synagogues as a reason for non-Jewish believers to maintain a rudimentary purity (Acts 15:19-21). But Paul becomes the lens through which Acts views the institution of the synagogue.

Despite the radicalism of his message, Acts assumes that Paul is received into synagogues and that he is permitted to preach (Acts 13:13-43). The repeated opportunity permits Paul to reach non-Jewish hearers in the synagogues, which provokes jealousy among "the Jews" (Acts 13:44-52). That experience in Pisidian Antioch brings Paul and Barnabas to Iconium: some Jews and Greeks believe as a result of what they hear in a synagogue, but some people "sided with the Jews" (Acts 14:1-4). The threat of stoning (by both Gentiles and Jews) drives the apostles on to Lystra, where a similar pattern of experience results in the actual stoning of Paul because the people of Lystra are incited by antagonistic Jews from Antioch and Iconium (Acts 1:5-20).

Although much of the language of Acts suggests that there was a united Jewish front against Paul (and against Jesus before the time of Paul), the fact is that the synagogue remains Paul's customary point of entry into the communities he visits. Thessalonica (Acts 17:1-9), Berea (Acts 17:10-14), Athens (17:16-17) all hear Paul first in their synagogues. The pattern of persecution from both religious and civic leaders is represented again, and the last example shows how dispute in the synagogue could spill over into the marketplace (Acts 17:18-34).

The link between the synagogue and wider, civic debate was forged particularly by those known as Godfearers, those who acknowledged the God of Israel without accepting circumcision. As a type of believer, they are represented by the centurion Cornelius in Acts, who is converted by Peter (Acts 10:1-48). Paul is portrayed as even more effective in his ministry to them (Acts 13:16, 26). A similar group is referred to with the designation of those who "worship" God (see Acts 13:43, 50; 16:14; 17:4, 17; 18:7; the RSV often renders the usage with the adjective "devout"; *see* Proselytism and Godfearers).

But Paul's focus in Corinth continues to be the synagogue (Acts 18:1-4), and Crispus—ruler of the synagogue—is baptized with his household (Acts 18:5-11). The synagogue is Paul's introduction to Ephesus (Acts 18:19; 19:8), and it is also the place where Apollos preaches (Acts 18:26). Even the final chapter of Acts presents Paul in the company of local leaders of the Jews in Rome, gathered to hear him out, perhaps in their synagogue (Acts 28:17-22).

Paul's own letters do not use the term *synagogue,* because their concern is not with that institution. His interest is rather the definition and salvation of "Israel" (see Rom 9:6; 11:26; Gal 6:16), in which all who believe—Jew and Greek, slave and free, male and female (Gal 3:28)—are included (see Rom 4:1-25; Gal 3:6-7, 14, 27-29). The synagogue was therefore for Paul an occasion, not a limit, of operation. Even in his case, because the ultimate aim was to constitute Israel (however radically defined), the synagogue was a natural place to operate, no matter what the level of opposition to him (see 2 Cor 11:23-27). And in his case, as in the case of Christian leaders contemporaneous with him, it is difficult to imagine how the gospel could have been preached without the previous establishment of synagogues in the Mediterranean world and apart from their relative toleration of unconventional teachers.

9. Rivalry Between Church and Synagogue. Although the letter of James reflects a familiarity with the term *church (ekklēsia)* in order to refer to communities of believers (Jas 5:14), the term *synagogue (synagōgē)* also appears (Jas 2:2). The usage does not represent a formal claim to replace the most prominent institution of Judaism after A.D. 70, but the willingness to use the word itself is notable. It probably means no more than an assembly in context, but an assembly for the purpose of discerning and keeping the true "royal law" (Jas 2:8) represents an implicit challenge to other congregations that claim to uphold the Torah.

James uses negative examples to insist by way of contrast that the poor should not be treated worse than the rich (Jas 2:1-7), that the whole of the law is to be understood in the commandment to love (Jas 2:8-13), that faith apart from actions is dead (Jas 2:14-26). The principal ethical interest of the letter closes with an explicit encouragement of prayer (Jas 5:13-18), underlined—as the letter is generally—with scriptural example and allusion. The letter, in other words, is setting up the church as the true synagogue, a school of wisdom and action whose curriculum is the law correctly understood.

The irony is that the rivalry between church and synagogue was greatest when Christians most consciously adhered to their Judaic roots. The Revelation of John sets up its vision as involving the divine court (Rev 1:12-16), the very throne of God (Rev 4:1-11); the terms of reference are principally drawn from Daniel and Ezekiel. But because this vision occurs on the "Lord's day" (Rev 1:10), not during the sabbath meeting in the synagogue, any opposing institution must be a "synagogue of Satan" (Rev 2:9; 3:9). That is the inevitable alternative to the discovery of the heavenly sanctuary under the guidance of Jesus as "one like a son of man" (Rev 1:13, alluding to Dan 7:13).

These developments in the Revelation presuppose the growing antipathy of leaders of the synagogue after A.D. 70, who were increasingly influenced by the Pharisees/*rabbis. The period saw the development of the "blessing of the *mînîm*," a petition within the "Eighteen Benedictions" which cursed disloyal Jews such as the Christians. Perhaps an even greater occasion of rivalry between churches and synagogues was the decision that certain of the rituals of the temple could be conducted in the synagogue. Such a decision was made by R. Yohanan ben Zakkai at Yavneh, when he permitted the shofar, the ram's horn, to be blown at the feast of the new year in the synagogue as it once had been in the temple (*m. Roš Haš.* 4:1-4). For those who saw Jesus as the true access to the sanctuary, any transfer of the temple's function to the synagogue necessitated the replacement of that institution; from that time, the attempt to replace the institutions of Judaism within Christianity became programmatic. [B. Chilton]

See also DIASPORA JUDAISM; HOMILY, ANCIENT; JEWISH COMMUNITIES IN ASIA MINOR; JUDAISM AND THE NEW TESTAMENT; LITURGY: RABBINIC; SACRIFICE AND TEMPLE SERVICE; TEMPLE, JEWISH.

BIBLIOGRAPHY. E. J. Bickerman, "The Babylonian Captivity," in *The Cambridge History of Judaism*, ed. W. D. Davies and L. Finkelstein (Cambridge: Cambridge University Press, 1984) 1:342-58; B. Brooten, *Women Leaders in the Ancient Synagogue* (Chico, CA: Scholars Press, 1982); D. R. Catchpole, *The Quest for Q* (Edinburgh: T & T Clark, 1993); M. J. S. Chiat, *Handbook of Synagogue Architecture* (Chico, CA: Scholars Press, 1982); B. Chilton, *A Galilean Rabbi and His Bible: Jesus' Use of the Interpreted Scripture of His Time* (GNS 8; Wilmington, DE: Michael Glazier, 1984); idem, *God in Strength: Jesus' Announcement of the Kingdom* (BSem; Sheffield: JSOT, 1987 [1979]); S. Dar and Y. Mintzker, "The Synagogue of Ḥorvat Sumaqa, 1983-1993," in *Ancient Synagogues: Historical Analysis and Archaeological Discovery*, ed. D. Urman and P. V. M. Flesher (SPB

47; Leiden: E. J. Brill, 1995) 157-64; A. Finkel, *The Pharisees and the Teacher of Nazareth* (AGSU 4; Leiden: E. J. Brill, 1964); P. V. M. Flesher, "Palestinian Synagogues Before 70 C.E.: A Review of the Evidence," in *Approaches to Ancient Judaism* 6, ed. J. Neusner and E. S. Frerichs (Atlanta: Scholars Press, 1989) 67-81 [= *Ancient Synagogues: Historical Analysis and Archaeological Discovery*, ed. D. Urman and P. V. M. Flesher (SPB 47; Leiden: E. J. Brill, 1995) 27-39]; Z. Gal, "Ancient Synagogues in the Eastern Lower Galilee," in *Ancient Synagogues: Historical Analysis and Archaeological Discovery*, ed. D. Urman and P. V. M. Flesher (SPB 47; Leiden: E. J. Brill, 1995) 166-73; L. L. Grabbe, "Synagogues in Pre-70 Palestine: A Re-assessment," *JTS* 39 (1998) 401-10 [= *Ancient Synagogues: Historical Analysis and Archaeological Discovery*, ed. D. Urman and P. V. M. Flesher (SPB 47; Leiden: E. J. Brill, 1995) 17-26]; J. G. Griffiths, "Egypt and the Rise of the Synagogue," *JTS* 38 (1987) 1-15 [= *Ancient Synagogues: Historical Analysis and Archaeological Discovery*, ed. D. Urman and P. V. M. Flesher (SPB 47; Leiden: E. J. Brill, 1995) 3-16]; D. E. Groh, "The Stratigraphic Chronology of the Galilean Synagogue from the Early Roman Period Through the Early Byzantine Period (ca. 420 C.E.)," in *Ancient Synagogues: Historical Analysis and Archaeological Discovery*, ed. D. Urman and P. V. M. Flesher (SPB 47; Leiden: E. J. Brill, 1995) 51-69; S. Gutman, "The Synagogue at Gamla," in *Ancient Synagogues Revealed*, ed. L. I. Levine (Jerusalem: Israel Exploration Society, 1981) 30-34; J. Gutmann, ed., *Ancient Synagogues: The State of Research* (Chico, CA: Scholars Press, 1981); idem, ed., *The Synagogue: Studies in Origins, Archaeology and Architecture* (New York: Ktav, 1975); M. Hengel, "Proseuche und Synagoge," in *Tradition und Glaube: Festgabe für Karl Georg Kuhn*, ed. G. Jeremias, H. W. Kuhn and H. Stegemann (Göttingen: Vandenhoeck & Ruprecht, 1971) 157-84; F. Huttenmeister and G. Reeg, *Die antiken Synagogen in Israel* (2 vols.; Wiesbaden: Reichert, 1977); A. Kasher, "Synagogues as 'Houses of Prayer' and 'Holy Places' in the Jewish Communities of Hellenistic and Roman Egypt," in *Ancient Synagogues: Historical Analysis and Archaeological Discovery*, ed. D. Urman and P. V. M. Flesher (SPB 47; Leiden: E. J. Brill, 1995) 205-20; A. T. Kraabel, "The Diaspora Synagogue: Archaeological and Epigraphic Evidence Since Sukenik," in *ANRW* 2.19.1 (1979) 477-510 [= *Ancient Synagogues: Historical Analysis and Archaeological Discovery*, ed. D. Urman and P. V. M. Flesher (SPB 47; Leiden: E. J. Brill, 1995) 95-126]; L. I. Levine, *The Ancient Synagogue: The First Thousand Years* (New Haven, CT: Yale University Press, 2000); idem, *The Synagogue in Late Antiquity* (Philadelphia: American Schools of Oriental Research, 1987); idem, ed., *Ancient Synagogues Revealed* (Jerusalem: Israel Exploration Society, 1981); I. Levinskaya, "A Jewish or Gentile Prayer House? The Meaning of ΠΡΟΣΕΥΞΗ," *TynB* 41 (1990) 154-59; H. McKay, *Sabbath and Synagogue: The Question of Sabbath Worship in Ancient Israel* (RGRW 122; Leiden: E. J. Brill, 1994); E. M. Meyers, "Synagogues of Galilee," *Arch* 35.3 (1985) 51-58; L. Morris, *The New Testament and the Jewish Lectionaries* (London: Tyndale, 1964); idem, "The Saints and the Synagogue" in *Worship, Theology and Ministry in the Early Church*, ed. J. J. Wilkins and T. Paige (JSNTSup 87; Sheffield: Sheffield Academic Press, 1992); J. Neusner, *Development of a Legend: Studies on the Traditions Concerning Yoḥanan ben Zakkai* (SPB 16; Leiden: E. J. Brill, 1970); R. Reich, "The Synagogue and the Miqweh in Eretz-Israel in the Second-Temple, Mishnaic, and Talmudic Periods," in *Ancient Synagogues: Historical Analysis and Archaeological Discovery*, ed. D. Urman and P. V. M. Flesher (SPB 47; Leiden: E. J. Brill, 1995) 289-97; Z. Safrai, "The Communal Functions of the Synagogue in the Land of Israel in the Rabbinic Period," in *Ancient Synagogues: Historical Analysis and Archaeological Discovery*, ed. D. Urman and P. V. M. Flesher (SPB 47; Leiden: E. J. Brill, 1995) 181-204; E. Schürer, *The History of the Jewish People in the Age of Jesus Christ (175 B.C.-A.D. 135)*, rev. and ed. G. Vermes, F. Millar and M. Goodman (3 vols.; Edinburgh: T & T Clark, 1973-87) 2:423-54; H. Shanks, *Judaism in Stone: The Archaeology of Ancient Synagogues* (New York: Harper & Row, 1979); J. F. Strange and H. Shanks, "Synagogue Where Jesus Preached Found at Capernaum," *BAR* 9.6 (1983) 24-31; Y. Tsafrir, "On the Source of the Architectural Design of the Ancient Synagogues in the Galilee: A New Appraisal," in *Ancient Synagogues: Historical Analysis and Archaeological Discovery*, ed. D. Urman and P. V. M. Flesher (SPB 47; Leiden: E. J. Brill, 1995) 70-86; D. Urman and P. V. M. Flesher, *Ancient Synagogues: Historical Analysis and Archaeological Discovery* (SPB 47; Leiden: E. J. Brill, 1995); J. Weingreen, "The Origin of the Synagogue," *Hermathena* 98 (1964) 68-84; Y. Yadin, *Masada* (New York: Random House, 1966).

B. Chilton and E. Yamauchi

SYNCRETISM. *See* Domestic Religion and Practices.

SYRIAC BIBLE

The OT and NT in Syriac have different histories with some overlap. The translation of the OT into Syriac preceded that of the NT by at least a century or two, since the earliest Gospel text in Syriac, the Diatessaron, uses the Peshitta OT for its OT quotations rather than the Greek. The printed text of the Syriac NT is a composite, consisting of the Peshitta version for twenty-two books and probably the Philoxenian version for the other five books (2 Peter, 2 John, 3 John, Jude and Revelation). All the early versions of the Gospels (the Old Syriac, the Peshitta and the Harklean) omit the pericope concerning adultery (Jn 7:53—8:11).

1. Old Testament in Syriac
2. New Testament in Syriac

1. Old Testament in Syriac.

1.1. Old Testament Peshitta. Jews or Jewish Christians translated the OT Peshitta from the Hebrew sometime in the first two centuries A.D. at Edessa. The OT Peshitta is not monolithic: different books were translated by different translators over a period of years, as indicated by vocabulary preferences in different books (e.g., *qyāmā*ʾ versus *diyatêqē*ʾ for Hebrew *b*^{e}*rît* ["covenant"]; ʿ*ĕlātā*ʾ versus *yaqdā*ʾ *šalmā*ʾ for Hebrew ʿ*ōlâh* ["burnt offering"]). The Torah in particular reflects *rabbinic exegesis. Some scholars believe that the group started out as adherents to a form of nonrabbinic *Judaism and were subsequently converted to Christian belief.

The Peshitta is an intelligible translation of a Hebrew text into idiomatic Syriac. It stands close to the MT and offers important exegesis of the Hebrew. The role of the *Septuagint (LXX) in its formation is disputed. Some experts believe that the original translators used the LXX as a translation help; others, that revisers used it to improve the text; still others reject the notion of direct LXX influence.

A critical edition is being produced under the auspices of the Peshitta Institute of Leiden University, which supersedes all previously printed texts. The basis of this edition is MS 7a1. Peshitta scholars are in disagreement as to whether or not certain early manuscripts (e.g., 5b1 for Genesis and Exodus and 9a1 for Kings, which stand closer to the Hebrew of the MT than does 7a1) represent an earlier stage in the development of the Peshitta text than is represented by 7a1 or a later stage.

1.2. Philoxenian Version. R. G. Jenkins has demonstrated that, in his later literary works (i.e., those written after A.D. 500), Philoxenus quotes from a Syriac version different from the Peshitta and influenced by the Greek for certain OT books and that the Syrolucianic text of Isaiah (= BM Add. 17106) represents that version. Whether Philoxenus himself sponsored this version and whether it covered the whole of the OT remain open questions.

1.3. Syrohexapla. Paul of Tella produced this translation of the Greek OT at *Alexandria in A.D. 616-617. He and Thomas of Harkel (see 2.5 below) may have collaborated, since their translation techniques are similar and they worked at the same time, in the same place and under the same auspices. Representing the fifth column of Origen's Hexapla, it was a scholar's version complete with annotations, including variant readings. Its Syriac style mirrors the Greek slavishly.

1.4. Revision of Jacob of Edessa. Around A.D. 705, Jacob of Edessa revised the OT Peshitta on the basis of the Greek. He apparently used both the Syrohexapla and the Lucianic Greek tradition.

2. New Testament in Syriac.

2.1. Diatessaron of Tatian. This harmony of the Gospels produced by Tatian about A.D. 170 became the Gospel of the Syriac-speaking church from the late second century until the mid-fifth century, when it was finally suppressed through the efforts of Rabbûla, the bishop of Edessa, and Theodoret, the bishop of Cyrus in upper Syria. Ephrem (d. A.D. 373) wrote a commentary on it, which has only recently come to light in the original Syriac. Scholars are divided over whether the Diatessaron was originally composed in Greek or Syriac. One scholar has advanced the view that Tatian composed it in two languages from the beginning. The Diatessaron primarily follows the sequence of events recorded in Matthew. Tatian did meticulous work, eliminating repetitious parallels and smoothing out apparent divergences and contradictions. Besides the four Greek Gospels, Tatian apparently used a West Aramaic Gospel, as evidenced by the use of West Aramaic vocabulary (i.e., non-Syriac; e.g., *xy*ʾ ["to save" (in a religious sense)], as in Christian Palestinian

Aramaic versus OT Peshitta *prq*), preserved by both the Old Syriac and Peshitta. Further, Tatian apparently adopted the principle of using the OT Peshitta for OT quotations, rather than the Greek. The Diatessaron came to be called *ʾewangeliyōn da-mᵉḥalṭᵉṭē*ʾ ("the Gospel of the mixed") in Syriac literature, in contrast to *ʾewangeliyōn da-mᵉparrᵉšē*ʾ ("the Gospel of the separated [Evangelists]"; i.e., the four individual Gospels).

*2.2. **Old Syriac Gospels.*** Sometime in the third century, a Syriac scholar with a mediocre knowledge of Greek made an attempt to render the Greek Gospels into Syriac. He preserved much of the Diatessaron and followed it in using the OT Peshitta for OT quotations. It is represented by two manuscripts, the Curetonian and the Sinaitic.

*2.3. **New Testament Peshitta.*** Probably in the fourth century, another, more successful, attempt at rendering the Greek Gospels into Syriac was made. The translator used the four Greek Gospels and a revised text of the Diatessaron. He too followed Tatian in using the OT Peshitta for his OT quotations. The Peshitta Gospels have no direct relationship to the Old Syriac Gospels but were made independent of them. The NT Peshitta lacks 2 Peter, 2 John, 3 John, Jude and Revelation. Early manuscripts omit Luke 22:17-18.

*2.4. **Philoxenian Version.*** Philoxenus, the Monophysite bishop of Mabbug from A.D. 485 until his exile in A.D. 519, commissioned this revision of the whole of the NT for dogmatic theological reasons. The chorepiscopus Polycarp carried out the work of translation, which he completed in A.D. 508. Unfortunately for us, none of this translation has survived in itself, although J. Gwynn believed that the book of Revelation contained in the Crawford manuscript of the John Rylands Library represents this version. The later works of Philoxenus, particularly his commentaries on the Gospels, apparently preserve citations. It is widely thought that the printed texts of 2 Peter, 2 John, 3 John, Jude and Revelation found in Syriac Bibles derive from this version.

*2.5. **Harklean Version.*** In A.D. 616, Thomas of Harkel produced a revision of the Philoxenian version of the NT at the Enaton ("the ninth" ward?) of Alexandria in the monastery of the Antonians. He produced a scientific work, with annotations marked with asterisks and obeli, and marginal notes containing both variants and other items. It may have been made as a gesture of reconciliation with the Monophysite church of Egypt. It was a philologically motivated translation that attempted to mirror the Greek. The invocation of the Lord's Prayer, "Our Father who art in heaven" (*pater hēmōn ho en tois ouranois*), in Matthew 6:9 serves as a typical example of mirror translation. The Harklean version renders it as *ʾbʾ dyln haw dbšmy*ʾ. By contrast the Peshitta and Old Syriac render *ʾbwn dbšmy*ʾ. The Harklean uses the independent possessive pronoun *dyln* to mirror the Greek *hēmōn* and the demonstrative pronominal *prop haw* to represent the Greek relative pronoun *ho*. These features of translation are also found in the Syrohexapla of the OT. Some printed editions of the Syriac NT contain the Harklean version of the book of Revelation.

See also NEW TESTAMENT VERSIONS, ANCIENT; OLD TESTAMENT VERSIONS, ANCIENT.

BIBLIOGRAPHY. W. Baars, "Ein neugefundenes Bruchstück aus der syrischen Bibelrevision des Jakob von Edessa," *VT* 18 (1968) 548-54; idem, *New Syro-Hexaplaric Texts* (Leiden: E. J. Brill, 1968); S. Brock, "The Resolution of the Philoxenian/Harclean Problem," in *New Testament Textual Criticism: Its Significance for Exegesis, Essays in Honor of Bruce M. Metzger*, ed. E. J. Epp and G. D. Fee (Oxford: Clarendon Press, 1981) 325-43; P. B. Dirksen, "The Old Testament Peshitta," in *Mikra: Text, Translation, Reading and Interpretation of the Hebrew Bible in Ancient Judaism and Early Christianity*, ed. M. J. Mulder (CRINT 2.1; Assen: Van Gorcum; Philadelphia: Fortress, 1988) 255-97; idem, "Peshitta Institute Communication 22: The Peshitta and Textual Criticism of the Old Testament," *VT* 42 (1992) 376-90; R. G. Jenkins, *The Old Testament Quotations of Philoxenus of Mabbug* (CSCO 514, subsidia 84; Louvain: Peeters, 1989); J. Joosten, *The Syriac Language of the Peshitta and Old Syriac Versions of Matthew* (Studies in Semitic Languages and Linguistics 22; Leiden: E. J. Brill, 1996); A. Juckel, "Ms Vat. Syr. 268 and the Revisional Development of the Harklean Margin," *Hugoye: Journal of Syriac Studies* [http://www.acad.cua.edu/syrcom/Hugoye] 1.1 (1998); G. A. Kiraz, *Comparative Edition of the Syriac Gospels Aligning the Sinaiticus, Curetonianus, Peshitta and Harklean Versions* (4 vols.; NTTS 21; Leiden: E. J. Brill, 1996); Y. Maori, *The Peshitta Version of the Pentateuch and Early Jewish Exegesis* (Jerusalem: Magnes, 1995; Hebrew); W. L. Petersen, *Tatian's*

Diatessaron: Its Creation, Dissemination, Significance and History in Scholarship (VCSup 25; Leiden: E. J. Brill, 1994); A. Salvesen, *The Books of Samuel in the Syriac Version of Jacob of Edessa* (MPI 10; Leiden: E. J. Brill, 1999); idem, "Spirits in Jacob of Edessa's Revision of Samuel," *ARAM* 5 (1993) 481-90; M. P. Weitzman, "From Judaism to Christianity: The Syriac Version of the Hebrew Bible," in *The Jews Among Pagans and Christians in the Roman Empire,* ed. J. Lieu, J. North and T. Rajak (London and New York: Routledge, 1992) 147-73; idem, "Lexical Clues to the Composition of the Old Testament Peshitta," in *Studia Aramaica,* ed. M. J. Geller, J. C. Greenfield and M. P. Weitzman (JSSSup 4; Oxford: Oxford University Press, 1995) 217-46; idem, "Peshitta, Septuagint and Targum," in *VI Symposium Syriacum 1992 University of Cambridge, Faculty of Divinity,* ed. R. Lavenant (OCA 247; Rome: Pontificio Istituto Orientale, 1994) 51-84; idem, *The Syriac Version of the Old Testament* (UCOP 56; Cambridge: Cambridge University Press, 1999).

J. A. Lund

SYRIAC NEW TESTAMENT. *See* NEW TESTAMENT VERSIONS, ANCIENT.

T

TACITUS

Publius(?) Cornelius Tacitus was born into an equestrian family about A.D. 56, probably in Cisalpine Gaul. He was in *Rome by A.D. 75 and married Agricola's daughter in A.D. 77. By following the sequence of Roman public office he gained senatorial status; he was governor of the senatorial province of Asia in A.D. 112-113. He died sometime after he had finished writing the *Annals* (c. A.D. 120/121).

1. Works of Tacitus
2. References to Judaism or Judea
3. Reference to Christians

1. Works of Tacitus.

Early in A.D. 98 Tacitus published the *Agricola,* primarily a biography of his father-in-law but with elements of ethnography and historical monograph. Later in A.D. 98 he published the *Germania,* an ethnographic treatise describing the tribes north of the Rhine and the Danube. The authenticity of the *Dialogue on Orators* from about A.D. 101 or 102 is now widely accepted. The three speakers debate the causes of the contemporary decline in oratory at a dramatic date of A.D. 75.

From Pliny the Younger (Pliny *Ep.* 6.16, 20) it is clear that at the time of writing Tacitus had been collecting material for a historical work that included 79, presumably the lost later books of the *Histories.* This work, covering A.D. 69 to 96, was completed by about A.D. 110. It probably contained eighteen books. Only books 1—4 and 5.1-26 survive, treating A.D. 69 and part of 70.

Although at *Histories* 1.1 Tacitus forecasts a future work dealing with the reigns of Nerva (A.D. 96-98) and Trajan (A.D. 98-117), in the *Annals* he goes back to fill in the years A.D. 14 to 68. There survive only books 1—4, part of 5, 6, the second half of 11, 12—15 and the first half of 16. The narrative thus breaks off in A.D. 66 and fails to reach the starting point of the *Histories.* The arrangement of the material is annalistic, and for each year there are sections on domestic and provincial affairs.

2. References to Judaism or Judea.

There are references to Jews, Judaism or Judea in the *Histories* and the *Annals;* M. Stern (chap. 92) presents twenty-two passages. The most extensive is the ethnographic digression at the beginning of *Histories* 5, when Titus is about to conduct the final siege of Jerusalem in A.D. 70. After the digression Tacitus changes scene to Germany, and the *Histories* break off before he describes the fall of *Jerusalem, which occurred only three weeks later.

Tacitus uses digressions to provide variety and dramatic relief, to display his learning and especially to mark an important stage in his narrative (Sage, 890-91). Along with most ancient historians he also "saw personality and the individual as crucial motive forces in history" (Sage, 901). However, the portrayal of character may also be applied to racial or national groups, as with the Jewish people in *Histories* 5. Moreover, besides introductory character sketches there are also obituaries (Sage, 902). And in the *Histories* there are obituaries not only for important individuals but also for corporate entities: the city of Cremona (Tacitus *Hist.* 3.34) and the Capitol at Rome (Tacitus *Hist.* 3.71-72). The digression on the Jewish people is introduced with a reference to the death of the city of Jerusalem (Tacitus *Hist.* 5.2.1).

After a summary of the military situation in Judea (Tacitus *Hist.* 5.1), Tacitus begins his digression on the Jewish people (Tacitus *Hist.* 5.2-10) by presenting various theories of their origin (Tacitus *Hist.* 5.2-3) and an account of Jewish practices and beliefs (Tacitus *Hist.* 5.4-5). The digression is completed by a geographical survey of Judea (Tacitus *Hist.* 5.6.1—8.1) and a historical survey of the Jewish people (Tacitus *Hist.* 5.8.2—10.2). There follows an introduction to the siege of Jerusalem (Tacitus *Hist.* 5.11-13). This begins with a summary of military activity (Tacitus *Hist.* 5.11.1-2), then deals with topography (Tacitus *Hist.* 5.11.3—12.2), manpower (Tacitus *Hist.* 5.12.2-4), portents (Tacitus *Hist.* 5.13.1-2) and the circumstances of the people under siege (Tacitus *Hist.* 5.13.3), and concludes with a retrospective and prospective summary (Tacitus *Hist.* 5.13.4).

In the *Histories* Tacitus cites specific sources only twice (Tacitus *Hist.* 3.28; 3.51.2). Within *Histories* 5.1-13 he alludes to unspecified sources for each of the six theories of Jewish origins (Tacitus *Hist.* 5.2-3), for Jewish customs (Tacitus *Hist.* 5.4.3-4; 5.5.5), for Judean geography (Tacitus *Hist.* 5.6.4; 5.7.1) and for the number of those besieged in Jerusalem (Tacitus *Hist.* 5.13.3). The phrases that Tacitus uses indicate his degree of commitment to a particular theory or piece of information. And in one instance he offers his own assessment (Tacitus *Hist.* 5.7.2). Modern discussion of Tacitus's sources is speculative and inconclusive. *Pliny the Elder is one of the two named sources at *Histories* 3.28. His *Natural History* may be a source for the geographical section (Tacitus *Hist.* 5.6.1—5.8.1), and his lost general history may have supplied material for Tacitus's account of the Jewish war. Because of differences of detail and of overall attitude, *Josephus has not been regarded in recent times as a likely source for Tacitus; they may, however, have shared common sources (see Hospers-Jansen, passim; Stern, 2:1-5, 31-63; Chilver and Townend, 19-20; Sage, 893-97).

Tacitus's portrayal shows the extent of the knowledge and the attitude of a major Roman historian concerning the history and culture of the Jewish people. His discussion is systematic and well organized. Where alternative views are reported, we do not expect them all to be right. And, although many points are inaccurate or wrong, others are correct. Unlike *Josephus, Tacitus was not obliged simultaneously to defend the Jewish people and the Flavian emperors who had conquered them.

3. Reference to Christians.

The only reference to Christians in Tacitus is at *Annals* 15.44. The immediate context is the fire of Rome in A.D. 64 (Tacitus *Ann.* 15.38-45). This section serves Tacitus's wider aim of showing "how the degeneracy of the *princeps* was disastrous for Rome" (Morford, 1614; Tacitus *Ann.* 15.38.1). Despite Nero's positive measures for dealing with the fire, deliberate plans for rebuilding were suspected and the rumor persisted that Nero was responsible for the fire (Tacitus *Ann.* 15.40, 44.2). He therefore transferred the blame to the Christians (Tacitus *Ann.* 15.44.2-5). Tacitus himself does not assign responsibility for the fire to the Christians. It seems that Tacitus wishes to use the fire to present a negative impression of Nero, while he carefully avoids directly blaming Nero (see Tacitus *Ann.* 15.38.1; 38.7—39.1; 39.3; 40.2; 44.2). Despite the innuendo against Nero, Tacitus's own view must be that the fire began by chance in Nero's absence. Other writers before and after Tacitus frankly blame Nero: Pliny *Natural History* 17.1.5; [Seneca] *Octavia* 831-33; Suetonius *Nero* 38; Dio Cassius *Epitome* 62.16-18.

The "Christians" were so called by the general public (cf. Acts 11:26) and were unpopular with them because of their alleged "shameful actions" (*flagitia*) (Tacitus *Ann.* 15.44.2). The better manuscript reading is *Chrestianos.* But it is likely that this simply means "Christians," not followers of a Jewish rebel called Chrestus (cf. Suetonius *Claudius* 25.4), nor is there any allusion to the Greek adjective *chrēstos* ("good"). There is an immediate digression (Tacitus *Ann.* 15.44.3) on the "founder" (*auctor*) of the "movement" (*nomen,* lit. "name"), punished by Pilate under Tiberius. Judea is noted as the place of origin of the movement before its spread to Rome. Value judgments on the movement are emphatic in accordance with the style of Tacitus. It is a "destructive cult" (*exitiabilis superstitio*) and an "evil" (*malum*), and it is associated with "everything shocking and shameful" that flows into Rome.

Returning to the narrative (Tacitus *Ann.* 15.44.4), Tacitus reports that "those who confessed were apprehended, then, on their information, a huge multitude were joined with them not so much on the charge of arson as for hatred of the human race." What they "confessed" was that they were Christians, since Tacitus does not believe that they committed arson. With regard to the "huge multitude," the better manuscript reading is "joined with" (*coniuncti*), not "convicted" (*convicti*). The allegation of "hatred of the human race" (*odio humani generis*), previously made against Jews (including Tacitus *Hist.* 5.5.1), Tacitus now applies to Christians. He thereby indicates that Christians could plausibly be charged with arson, not on the basis of the facts but due to a prejudiced view of their general attitude. The "elaborate punishments" of the Christians in the gardens of Nero are briefly described. In conclusion, "however guilty and deserving of unprecedented and exemplary punishment they may have been, there arose a feeling of compassion for them, on the ground that they were being annihilated not in the interests of the people but to satisfy the savagery of one man" (Tacitus *Ann.* 15.44.5). Tacitus's unexpected reference to the guilt and deserved punishment of Christians is often explained on the basis that he is representing the view of those who were convinced by Nero's allegations. Alternatively, in Tacitus's view they may indeed be guilty of hatred of the human race; cf. Pliny *Epistles* 10.96.3.

If Pliny the Elder is a source for the facts of the case (Koestermann, 256), Tacitus may have drawn a number of terms from the discussion of the Christians of Bithynia Pontus in Pliny the Younger *Epistles* 10.96 (including Christ, Christians, name, punishment, cult, confess, charge). Thus Tacitus is aware of the circumstances of the origin of the Christian movement; he does not regard the Christians as responsible for the fire of Rome; and he acknowledges the public feeling of compassion for them. But he shares the general prejudice against them.

See also HISTORIANS, GRECO-ROMAN; JOSEPHUS; PLINY THE ELDER; PLINY THE YOUNGER; ROMAN EMPERORS; SUETONIUS.

BIBLIOGRAPHY. **Texts and Translations.** Cornelius Tacitus, *I.2: Ab Excessu Diui Augusti Libri XI-XVI,* ed. K. Wellesley (Leipzig: Teubner, 1986) (text of *Annals*); *The Annals of Tacitus,* ed. H. Furneaux; 2d ed., H. F. Pelham and C. D. Fisher (2 vols.; Oxford: Clarendon Press, 1896-1907) (text and commentary); Cornelius Tacitus, *II.1: Historiarum Libri,* ed. K. Wellesley (Leipzig: Teubner, 1989) (text); Tacitus, *The Histories; The Annals* (4 vols.; Cambridge, MA: Harvard University Press, 1925-37) (translation). **Studies.** G. E. F. Chilver and G. B. Townend, *A Historical Commentary on Tacitus'* Histories *IV and V* (Oxford: Clarendon Press, 1985); H. Heubner and W. Fauth, *P. Cornelius Tacitus, Die Historien, Band V: Fünftes Buch* (Heidelberg: Carl Winter, 1982) (commentary); A. M. A. Hospers-Jansen, *Tacitus over de Joden: Hist. 5, 2-13* (with an extensive summary in English) (Groningen: Wolters, 1949); E. Koestermann, *Cornelius Tacitus, Annalen, Band IV: Buch 14-16* (Heidelberg: Carl Winter, 1968) (commentary); C. S. Kraus and A. J. Woodman, *Latin Historians* (Greece and Rome New Surveys in the Classics 27; Oxford: Oxford University Press, 1997); M. Morford, "Tacitus' Historical Methods in the Neronian Books of the 'Annals,'" *ANRW* 2.33.2 (1990) 1582-1627; K. Rosen, "Der Historiker als Prophet: Tacitus und die Juden," *Gymnasium* 103 (1996) 107-26; M. M. Sage, "Tacitus' Historical Works: A Survey and Appraisal," *ANRW* 2.33.2 (1990) 851-1030, 1629-47; M. Stern, *Greek and Latin Authors on Jews and Judaism* (3 vols.; Jerusalem: Israel Academy of Sciences and Humanities, 1976-84); R. Syme, *Tacitus* (2 vols.; Oxford: Clarendon Press, 1958; corrected repr. 1963, 1967) (more recent monographs have not superseded this classic study); B. Wardy, "Jewish Religion in Pagan Literature during the Late Republic and Early Empire," *ANRW* 2.19.1 (1979) 592-644. D. W. Palmer

TALE OF BAGASRAW (PSEUDO-ESTHER) (4Q550[a-f])

The *Tale of Bagasraw* is an Aramaic literary work extant in five or, less likely, six fragmentary copies unearthed in Qumran Cave 4. (4Q550[f], formerly known as 4QAramaic N, belongs to another work, according to García Martínez.) The scholar responsible for the *editio princeps,* J. T. Milik, has argued that the *Tale of Bagasraw* served as a source for the book of Esther. Of all the books of the Hebrew Bible, Esther alone makes no appearance among the *Qumran caches—but if one of its sources does appear, then Esther's absence becomes less absolute and, for some scholars, less puzzling. Nevertheless, while acknowledging the possibility of an indirect relationship between Esther and the *Tale of Bagasraw,* scholarly consensus has stopped short of endorsing Milik's position.

1. Possible Plot of the Tale
2. Connections with Esther

1. Possible Plot of the Tale.

The *Tale of Bagasraw* has survived in such a fragmentary condition that the work's plot line is a matter of conjecture. Not only are the extant fragments broken and unconnected, such that their order is uncertain and what happens first, second and third open to debate; but also many of ond and third open to debate; but also many of the readings and even meanings of the Aramaic words are equally debatable. E. M. Cook has offered a cautious and plausible plot summary.

As with Esther, the events in the *Tale of Bagasraw* take place in the Persian court, and as with Esther the monarch at court is Xerxes. The hero is a Jew named Bagasraw (all the characters have Persian names). Bagasraw is the son of Patireza, who had been attached to the royal garmentmakers attending Xerxes' father, Darius I. In some way he was able to benefit Darius, for which reason he and his deed were inscribed in the Persian royal records. Upon becoming king and learning of the episode, Xerxes decides to bestow his favor upon Bagasraw as Patireza's son. A third character, Bagoshi, a member of the king's retinue, is friendly to Bagasraw and warns him of opposition from royal advisers jealous of the king's favor. With Bagoshi's help, Bagasraw overcomes this antagonism and receives all that the king has planned to give him. At the end, Xerxes commands those of his own time and all future generations to honor Bagasraw and his God, the Most High.

2. Connections with Esther.

In a general sense the connections of the *Tale of Bagasraw* with Esther are patent, for both belong to a genre of Jewish wisdom writings of the Second Temple period known as courtier tales. In these stories one or more Jews succeeds in the court of a foreign king, rises to prominence because of innate qualities of wisdom or character, only to suffer a fall or mortal threat through unjust persecution, and finally is vindicated. Not only Esther but also the stories of the book of Daniel (Dan 1—6) belong to this genre. Milik and others, however, have argued for a much more direct connection between the *Tale of Bagasraw* and Esther. They maintain that the author of Esther knew and used the *Tale of Bagasraw* as a source for the biblical book. The main arguments that Milik and his supporters have offered are the following.

(1) The king has the royal records read to him, as in Esther 6:1 (4Q550[a]). This is a generic if striking correspondence.

(2) One of the main characters, Patireza, bears, according to Milik, the patronymic Jair (4Q550[b] 3). According to Esther 2:5 and the *Septuagint addition A verse 1, Mordecai's father was also called Jair. Milik argues therefore that Patireza is the same person as Mordecai, Mordecai being his Hebrew name and Patireza his Persian name. (It was common for Jews in foreign settings to have both a Hebrew and a native name, as did Daniel, for example— Belteshazzar in Dan 5:12.) But Milik's argument is weak, since Mordecai is not a Hebrew name. It is Babylonian; Mordecai derives from Marduk, head of the Babylonian pantheon. Moreover, the suggestion that Patireza's father was named Jair is speculative, since only the first letter of the name can be read. Many other Hebrew names (e.g., Josiah, Joseph, Joshua) or even Persian names might be suggested in place of the Jair that Milik restores.

(3) As Mordecai is rewarded by the king in Esther 6, so also Bagasraw is rewarded in 4Q550[b]. Again, this is only a generic correspondence, natural to the tale of the Jewish courtier at the foreign court.

(4) In 4Q550[c] Milik reads the name Hama (Aramaic *Ḥ*[a]*mā*ʾ), whom he identifies as Haman in the story of Esther. Since the word in the *Tale of Bagasraw* begins with a *ḥet,* whereas the name of Haman begins with the Hebrew letter *heh* (the first being a rougher, guttural "h" sound), Milik argues that the book of Esther must have been translated into Hebrew from Greek. When the Hama of the *Tale of Bagasraw* had his name transliterated into Greek, the quality of the original consonant was lost, there being no equivalent in the Greek alphabet. Thus Milik postulates the following dubious process: first, the book of Esther was written in Aramaic, using the *Tale of Bagasraw* as a source, and the name of Hama; then Esther was translated into Greek, and the name of Hama lost its initial guttural consonant; finally, Greek Esther was rendered into Hebrew, and the name Haman was the transformed remnant of the original name. Only in this way can Milik account for the sound changes. But his whole theory is moot if, as Cook has plausibly suggested, the supposed name Hama is instead the common Aramaic verb for "to see." Where Milik and supporters render 4Q550[c] 2 as "Patireza your father, from Hama [Aramaic *min Ḥ*[a]*mā*ʾ] who arose concerning the service" (White Crawford), Cook has rendered the line, "Patireza your father. Who has seen [Aramaic *man ḥ*[a]*mâ*] that he stood over the business . . . ?" So this particular connection of the *Tale of Bagasraw* with Esther is likely to become a mere curiosity of scholarship.

(5) In 4Q550[d] i 2-3, Milik and others read the phrase "a man of Judah from the leadership of Benjamin." Mordecai is likewise said in Esther 2:5-6 to be a Benjaminite of Judah. But this is yet another problematic interpretation of the *Tale of Bagasraw*. For instead of Milik's reading and restoration of the Aramaic as *g^{e}bar y^{e}hûdāy min dabār binyām[in]*, one might equally well read and restore *g^{e}bar y^{e}hûdāy min rabr^{e}bānê m[alkâ]*, "a Jewish man from among the king's courtiers"—thus eliminating all mention of the tribe of Benjamin. Furthermore, Milik's proposal results in a lexical difficulty with the word *dabār*. The meaning Milik needs here, "leadership," is unattested in Palestinian Aramaic, being known only from Syriac; S. White Crawford's rendering "one of the leaders" (White Crawford, 32) is grammatically impossible.

(6) White Crawford, who supports the thrust of Milik's theory, has argued for another connection between the *Tale of Bagasraw* and Esther at 4Q550[d] i 4. She remarks of the Qumran text's phrase "What may I do for you (Aramaic *l^{e}kâ)*?" as follows: "[T]he 'you' is a female . . . so we have a dialogue between a female and a male. . . . There are no other scenes, to my knowledge, in biblical or Second Temple literature set at a court in which a powerful male, a king, asks his female companion what he may do for her, except the Esther story!" (White Crawford, 33). This would indeed be a remarkable parallel—if it existed. Unfortunately, White Crawford has based her assessment upon a pronominal form that is ambiguous in Qumran Aramaic. The form that follows her "you," Aramaic *antâ,* is always a masculine form (female would be antî) and resolves the ambiguity of *l^{e}kâ*. Two men are talking here; there are no women.

(7) Finally, at 4Q550[d] i 5, Milik reads/restores the name Esther. Not even White Crawford accepts this questionable interpretation of a broken context in which only the first letter of the suggested name is preserved. The proposed "s," the second letter, is a mere trace of ink that could be virtually any letter at all. We do not know from the context that a name is even in view. As White Crawford remarks, "[U]nfortunately, Esther disappears from our text" (White Crawford, 33).

In sum, the case proposed by Milik and others for a direct use of the *Tale of Bagasraw* by the author of Esther is in every instance based on problematic readings, restorations or grammatical interpretation. All that remains after an examination of the arguments is the impression of a generic relationship, and that much might be said for Esther and the stories of Daniel.

See also DANIEL, ESTHER AND JEREMIAH, ADDITIONS TO.

BIBLIOGRAPHY. E. M. Cook, "The Tale of Bagasraw," in *The Dead Sea Scrolls: A New Translation,* M. O. Wise, M. Abegg Jr. and E. M. Cook (San Francisco: HarperSanFrancisco, 1996) 437-39; R. Eisenman and M. O. Wise, *The Dead Sea Scrolls Uncovered* (Shaftesbury, Dorset, England: Element, 1992); F. García Martínez, "Las Fronteras de lo Biblico," *Scripta Theologica* 23 (1991) 774; J. T. Milik, "Les Modèles Araméens du Livre d'Esther dans la Grotte 4 de Qumran," *RevQ* 15 (1992) 321-406; S. White Crawford, "Has Every Book of the Bible Been Found Among the Dead Sea Scrolls?" *BRev* 12 (1996) 28-33, 56.

M. O. Wise

TALMUD. *See* RABBINIC LITERATURE: TALMUD.

TANAK. *See* HEBREW BIBLE.

TANHUMIM. *See* CONSOLATIONS/TANHUMIM (4Q176).

TARGUM OF JOB (QUMRAN). *See* ARAMAIC TARGUMIM: QUMRAN.

TARGUMIM. *See* ARAMAIC TARGUMIM: QUMRAN; RABBINIC LITERATURE: TARGUMIM.

TAX COLLECTORS. *See* TAXATION, GRECO-ROMAN.

TAXATION, GRECO-ROMAN

Taxation in the *Roman Empire often developed from the countries and kingdoms that had been incorporated. For example, on Sicily the corn tax was based on the tribute system established by King Hiero of Syracuse. Due to Rome's expansion, Roman *citizens in Italy had not had to make a direct contribution to the finances of the state since 167 B.C. However, the provinces were expected to make a contribution to Rome through taxation, and this included those individuals who had received Roman citizenship.

1. Direct Taxation
2. The Census
3. Indirect Taxation
4. *Publicani* and Collection

1. Direct Taxation.
Rome assessed taxes in two main forms, first on the size of the land under cultivation (*tributum soli*), second on a poll tax (*tributum capitis*). Standardizing taxation systems became possible by taking an official census.

The *tributum soli* in effect taxed the produce of the land. There is some evidence that the *tributum soli* might have included all the equipment used to cultivate the land and processing the produce. In the Greek east, cities appointed magistrates, often known as the *dekaprotoi*, to be responsible for the collection of this tax. This group of ten may have originated as a committee that had been delegated the responsibility of deciding how to pay this sum. At Lykosura in the province of Achaia, the money raised by people attending the *mysteries of the local cult went toward paying the tax (*SIG*^{3} 800). In the province of Syria, the *tributum capitis* was calculated at 1 percent.

There are some instances in which rich individuals became the *benefactors of their city or even their province by paying a lump sum for taxation. F. Millar gives the example of a priest of the province of *Macedonia paying for the whole province. At Tenos, an individual left a lump sum as a bequest so that its interest benefitted his fellow citizens (*IG* XII. v. 946).

2. The Census.
The provincial census was instituted by the emperor Augustus. In part this was to provide accurate information for the imposition of direct taxation, specifically the *tributum soli* and the *tributum capitis*. The evidence suggests that Gaul and perhaps Spain may have had a census in 27 B.C. (Dio Chrysostom *Or.* 43.22.5). Other Augustan censuses are recorded for the provinces of Lusitania and Syria. This may have included details of Roman citizens living in the provinces. The limited evidence suggests that a common pattern was that as provinces were incorporated, a census took place: this seems to have been the case for Judea, Cappadocia and Dacia. A census in the province of Syria during the *governorship of Quirinius in A.D. 6 is attested in the funerary epitaph of Quintus Aemilius Secundus (*CIL* III 6687). This may be linked to the "first enrollment" (*apographē prōtē*) mentioned by Luke (Lk 2:2). The *census* (Gk *kēnsos)* as the basis for taxation in Judea is referred to in the Gospels (Mt 22:17; Mk 12:14).

The edict for a census of A.D. 104 issued by Gaius Vibius Maximus, prefect of Egypt, is contained in a surviving papyrus (P. Lond 904 col. 2). People were instructed to return to their homes, and those unable to do so, perhaps through other responsibilities, were to register with an officer. Ulpian, writing in the early third century, gives further details about the arrangements for the census (see the section preserved in *Digest* 50.15.4). Each estate being assessed had to be defined by how much land was in cultivation, the numbers of olives and vines, the size of pasture and woodland. Individual details of *slaves also had to be registered.

The responsibility for the census may have been with individual cities. For example, a detailed inscription from Messene in the province of Achaia dates to the period A.D. 35 to 44 (*IG* V.1,1432). It seems that the *polis* was expected to pay a tax of one hundred thousand *denarii*, and the means of raising it was by imposing a tax of 8 *obols* for every *mina* of value. Aristocles, the secretary to the members of the council, who devised the calculation, was even awarded an honorific statue.

3. Indirect Taxation.
Apart from direct taxation, there were various indirect taxes, known in the imperial period as *vectigalia*. These included a tax on the movement of goods (*portoria*) that was imposed at ports or crossing points between frontiers. Rates, based on the value of the goods, could vary enormously from 25 percent on the eastern frontier (benefitting from the luxury trade with the East) to as low as 2.5 percent for Asia. Although the attempt by Nero to abolish *vectigalia* in A.D. 58 was abandoned, new legislation concerning the *portoria* was prepared, and a detailed *inscription of this period has come to light at *Ephesus (Meijr and von Nijf, no. 109). This text includes details of which ports in the province could be used for import or export. Certain exemptions from the tax were made. These included material being carried on behalf of "the people of Rome," anything carried for religious purposes and items taken for personal use on the journey.

Other indirect taxes included a sales tax, which was halved from 1 percent by Tiberius. Augustus introduced a sales tax for slaves that attracted 4 percent. When slaves received their manumission, they paid a 5 percent tax—established in the republican period—on the sum they paid to their former owner for the price of their freedom. This tax was initially collected by *publicani,* though from the reign of Claudius there is evidence to suggest that it was the responsibility of the imperial procurators. A tax on inheritance (*vicesima hereditatum*) was introduced by Augustus in A.D. 6 at a rate of 5 percent. This was introduced to pay for veterans leaving the army. Like the tax on slaves, it was initially collected by *publicani.*

4. *Publicani* and Collection.
Under the republic Rome had collected both direct and indirect taxes through *publicani.* These individuals were private contractors who undertook the service for profit. Standard forms of contract were issued by the censors as a *lex censoria.* After the republic the nature of the *publicani* changed when they were no longer engaged in supplying the army or assisting with public buildings. Ulpian, writing in the early third century, noted that *publicani* were "those who enjoy the use of what belongs to the people—hence their name—whether they pay a *vectigal* to the people or gather in *tributum* . . . and all who lease anything from the *fiscus* are rightly called *publicani.*" For example, two *publicani* in the province of Africa made a dedication to Augustan Venus (*AE* 1923, no. 22). They refer to the fact that they were responsible for "the four public taxes of Africa," presumably the *portoria,* the selling and freeing of slaves and inheritance.

During the republic some of the groups or companies of *publicani* had been quite large and thus had the power to ignore the control of the provincial governor and other Roman officials. Under the principate the oversight of the *publicani* was the role of the provincial procurator.

Income, designated in the East as *phoros,* might also be derived from land owned by the emperor or state; this income might be collected by *publicani,* as suggested from an inscription from Ephesus dating to A.D. 6/7 that refers to money *ex pecunia phorica* (*AE* 1968, 483). However, in the NT the term *phoros* (Lk 20:22; 23:2; Rom 13:6–7) might be interchangeable with *kēnsos.*

Publicani do not seem to have been popular individuals. They had various powers that could be open to abuse such as the impounding of goods that were suspected of not having been declared for taxation (*Dig. Just.* 39.4.7.1, 14, 16) and for confiscation of flocks using public pasture (*Dig. Just.* 47.8.2.20). Under Nero provincial governors were required to investigate complaints against *publicani* (Tacitus *Ann.* 51.1). In the Gospels *publicani* (Gk *telōnai*) are frequently associated with "sinners" (e.g., Lk 5:30; 7:34; 15:1; 18:11).

It appears that during the principate, and perhaps even under the late republic, cities were usually responsible for the collection of *tributum.* Under Julius Caesar, in 47 B.C., the cities of Asia rather than *publicani* became responsible for tax collection; their overall tax burden was cut at the same time (Appian *Civ. W.* 5.4; Dio Chrysostom *Or.* 42.6; Plutarch *Cases* 48; Mitchell). The same may also have been true for Judea, though at the time a client state (Josephus *Ant.* 14.10.5 §201), and other provinces in the East. In 31 B.C. Strabo (*Geog.* 10.5.3) records that his ship collected an ambassador from the island of Gyaros in the Aegean who was going to ask Augustus that the island's *phoros* be reduced from 150 *drachmae* to 100 *drachmae.* A similar reference to *phoros* exacted on a city comes in the anecdote about how in return for Apelles's painting of Aphrodite Anadyomene, which had been dedicated in the Asclepeion, the people of Kos were given a reduction of 100 talents in their taxation (Strabo *Geog.* 14.2.19).

See also ROMAN ADMINISTRATION; TAXATION, JEWISH.

BIBLIOGRAPHY. P. A. Brunt, *Roman Imperial Themes* (Oxford: Clarendon Press, 1990) chaps. 15, 17; V. Ehrenberg and A. H. M. Jones, *Documents Illustrating the Reigns of Augustus and Tiberius* (Oxford: Clarendon Press, 1976); M. Goodman, *The Roman World 44 B.C.-A.D. 180* (London: Routledge, 1997); idem, *State and Society in Roman Galilee, A.D. 132-212* (Totowa, NJ: Rowman & Allanfield, 1983); K. Hopkins, "Taxes and Trade in the Roman Empire (200 B.C.-A.D. 400)," *JRS* 70 (1980) 101-25; A. Lintott, *Imperium Romanum: Politics and Administration* (London: Routledge, 1993); F. Meijr and O. van Nijf, *Trade, Transport and Society in the Ancient World: A Sourcebook* (London: Routledge, 1992); F. Millar, *The Roman Empire and Its Neighbors* (2d ed.; London: Duckworth, 1981); S. Mitchell, *Anatolia: Land, Men and Gods in Asia Minor,* 1: *The Celts in Anatolia and the Impact of Roman Rule* (Oxford: Clarendon Press, 1993) chap. 14.

D. W. J. Gill

TAXATION, JEWISH

Jews in the time of Jesus were subject to a complex system of religious and secular taxation, the extent and burden of which is difficult to determine. The Gospels reveal the scorn directed toward those who participated especially in the Roman customs system because they were presumed to be dishonest.

1. Roman Taxation in Judea and Galilee
2. Tax Collector
3. Temple Tax

1. Roman Taxation in Judea and Galilee.
When Rome annexed Judea in 63 B.C., the high priest Hyrcanus (*see* Hasmoneans) was given responsibility to pay tribute to Rome. Julius reduced the tribute in 47 B.C. from an uncertain amount (perhaps 33 percent of the harvest as under the Seleucids) to 12.5 percent of the harvest, and he remitted taxes in the sabbatical year (Josephus *Ant.* 14.10.6 §202). Herod was required initially to pay tribute for Idumea and Samaria, but this was remitted in 30 B.C., leaving him to raise his own revenues after the Roman fashion and presumably on a Roman scale (although he did occasionally reduce taxes during crises: Josephus *Ant.* 15.10.4 §365; 16.2.4 §64). After Herod's death Rome allowed Antipas to raise tribute for Rome in *Galilee and Perea, while Judea (after the deposition of Archelaus in A.D. 6) came under direct Roman control in the form of procurators, who probably made the *Sanhedrin responsible for the collection of Roman dues (Josephus *J.W.* 2.17.1 §405).

According to the larger of Josephus's two estimates, the total revenue of Herod's territories distributed after his death was 800 talents (Josephus *J.W.* 2.6.2-3 §§92-97; in *Ant.* 17.11.4 §§318-20 it is 600 talents), which is the equivalent of 4.8 million drachmae or day wages per annum. Population estimates vary, but if we estimate 250,000 working males, we can calculate that the average man worked about three weeks per year for the state. For those who lived close to the edge of poverty—and the majority of scholars think that there were many who did—this amount would be felt as a heavy burden.

1.1. Kinds of Taxes. There were three principal kinds of duties: the land tax, or *tributum soli;* the head tax, or *tributum capitis;* and the customs system. These must be distinguished in terms of liability and quantity.

1.1.1. Land Tax. The bulk of the tribute due to Rome was collected in the form of a tax on the produce of the land. This exempted those who did not own land, although tenant farmers certainly paid indirectly in the form of rent. Owners of small plots may also have been exempt. Itinerant laborers and others, such as fishermen, were by definition exempt, but there may have been other taxes that served to distribute liability to the nonagricultural sector. Residents of Jerusalem, for example, were subject to a house tax and a city sales tax (Josephus *Ant.* 18.4.3 §90; 19.6.3 §299). The amount (usually payable in grain) required for the land tax was probably fixed by landlords or other authorities based on estimates of a percentage of the likely yield: probably about one-tenth. Since these amounts were determined in advance, the obligation for revenues lost due to bad crops or individual bankruptcy had to be absorbed by distribution within the tax district.

So little information is available concerning crop yield, population, rents and taxes that it may never be possible to calculate the burden on the average farmer. General statements in the ancient sources are not conclusive. Josephus complains about Herod's high revenues, but he specifies the charge by reference to direct appropriation of the property of nobles (Josephus *Ant.* 17.12.2 §307). In another place Josephus describes pre-war Galilee as thriving (Josephus *J.W.* 3.3.2-4 §§42-50). He makes no reference to economic causes for the war, unless this is to be deduced from his accounts of the increase in banditry (presumably due to bankruptcy) in the decade before the war. Tacitus records a request (probably granted) for reduction of taxes in A.D. 17 (Tacitus *Ann.* 2.42), but he describes the region as peaceful during the reign of Tiberius (Tacitus *Hist.* 5.9). Neither the amount nor the impact of the land tax, therefore, can be determined with precision from the extant sources. It is likely, however, that most of those in the agricultural sector lived close enough to minimal subsistence to feel almost any amount of tribute as a threatened or real burden.

1.1.2. Head Tax. Another significant portion of tribute due to Rome was collected by means of the head tax. This tax involved a periodic census (Lk 2:1-5; Acts 5:37). The amount was probably one denarius, or one day's wage, per annum (Mt 22:19-21). Liability is more difficult to assess. That males aged fourteen to sixty-five paid the tax seems consistent with Gospel accounts, but this does not preclude the possibility that men were assessed for their wives. It is also possible that, as in other parts of the empire, those who paid the land tax were exempted from the head tax.

1.1.3. Customs System. The Romans appropriated a long-standing system of tolls and duties collected at ports and at tax offices near city gates (Mk 2:11). Rates varied from 2 to 5 percent of value, but goods were subject to multiple taxation on long journeys. Rates and commissions were regulated by law, and from the time of Nero these were posted for inspection. But the complexity of the system and the assessor's power to determine value allowed for injustice. Still, given the prevalence of a village-based subsistence economy, liability was limited to those few who engaged in commercial travel through towns and cities. In these locations of large-scale exchange, tax collectors gathered—and were esteemed—like flies.

1.2. Tax Collection. The direct taxes (the land tax and the head tax) were collected by councils of Jewish leaders and their representatives on an annual basis. The indirect taxes of the customs system were "farmed": the highest bidder paid in advance to collect taxes from a district. These were Jews, not "publicans" (a technical term for members of tax-collection organizations abolished by Julius Caesar in 30 B.C.). In this tax-farming system Rome received its money in advance, and the tax farmer made his living from commissions on tolls and customs. These were the "tax collectors" *(telōnai)* of the Gospels. A "chief tax collector," such as Zacchaeus (Lk 19:1-10), was a tax farmer who supervised other collectors.

2. Tax Collector.

It is evident in the Gospels that the title itself is a term of abuse (Mt 5:46; 18:17) or a foil to the hypocrites (Lk 3:12; 7:29; 8:10-14). Elsewhere it is joined in vituperative apposition to "prostitutes" (Mt 21:31-32), and most commonly, "sinners" (e.g., Mk 2:15; Lk 15:1). This attitude was universal: the rabbis grouped tax collectors with "robbers" (*m. B. Qam.* 10:2), and Roman writers joined them with brothel-keepers (Dio Chrysostom, *Disc.* 14.14). The reasons for this scorn vary according to time, place and tax type.

2.1. Tax Farmers and Dishonesty. Some distinction was made between those who collected direct taxes and the tax farmers. The latter were constantly visible and clearly made a living from commissions. To stop people on the road and demand a portion of their goods certainly appeared to be institutionalized robbery, and the only apparent beneficiary was the tax farmer himself. Although the commission system was regulated, the power of the assessor to determine the value of some goods encouraged dishonesty. The instructions of John the Baptist to tax collectors (Lk 3:12-13) and the restitution pledge of Zacchaeus (Lk 19:8) are consistent with this tendency toward fraud.

Indeed, the practice of selling the office built into the system a disregard for the taxpayer: the highest bid translated into the most inflated assessments and the highest commissions. The fact that the tax farmer advanced the money meant that he had excessive wealth to begin with, and in an agrarian subsistence economy, usury was the most common source of such portable wealth. On this assumption, the rabbis regarded as unclean (*see* Purity) any house entered by a tax farmer (*m. Ṭehar.* 7:6). A corollary to all of this is the practical observation that an occupation that depends for success on suspicion, intrusion, harassment and force tends not to attract the most pleasant personalities. These factors combine to suggest that one did not need to be victimized to share the general view of the tax farmer as an embodiment of dishonesty.

2.2. Tax Collectors and Rome. While tax farmers were scorned primarily for their dishonesty, collectors of direct taxes were despised for their collusion with Rome. This hatred was particularly intense in Judea, which was under direct Roman control. A visiting Galilean with a reputation for association with tax collectors (Lk 7:34; 19:1-10) might well have been suspected of disloyalty, in some minds even for paying the head tax (Mk 12:13-17). It is significant that the question posed to Jesus pertains to the lawfulness, not the amount, of the tax. Its evil was not in its quantity but in its quality: to a fiercely independent people who did not understand or acknowledge military and economic security afforded by the Roman presence, taxation was a painful symbol of conquest. Jewish labor enriched a distant idolater and his local military representatives. Jesus' answer is not intended to give sanction to Roman taxation but to expose the hypocrisy of the *Pharisees, who ask the question only to force him to choose between popularity with the people and liability to secular law.

3. Temple Tax.
The half-shekel *temple tax was derived from the one-third shekel temple tax of Nehemiah 10:32-33 and was raised to a half-shekel possibly under the influence of the half-shekel atonement price of Exodus 30:11-16 (cf. 2 Chron 24:6). The fund was used for temple maintenance and *sacrifices.

3.1. Liability for the Temple Tax. Jewish males over the age of twenty (excepting *priests: *m. Šeqal.* 1:3-4), including those in the Diaspora, were subject to the temple tax. The half-shekel was the approximate equivalent of one day's wage, and it was assessed annually. None of the ancient sources, however, state that all Jews paid, and even the inference (e.g., from Josephus *Ant.* 14.7.2 §110 or *m. Šeqal.* 1:4) may represent ideology rather than history. The Essenes, for example, interpreted Exodus 30:11-16 to require only one half-shekel per lifetime (4Q159 2:6-7).

After the war, Vespasian used the temple tax as a pretense for what amounted to a war indemnity, the *didrachmon.* Liability for this tax was expanded to women, children and slaves. The tax was now compulsory, and the proceeds went to the temple of Jupiter in Rome (Josephus *J.W.* 7.6.6 §218). The fact that the Jews had used their own temple fund for the war (Josephus *J.W.* 6.6.2 §335) contributed to this connection and perhaps to a limitation (at least initially) of the tax to Pharisees throughout the empire (possibly implied in Dio Cassius *Hist.* 65.7.2). Such a situation would have exacerbated tensions between the Pharisees and other Jewish groups, including Christians.

3.2. Jesus and the Temple Tax. Matthew 17:24-27 uses the term *didrachma.* This may be an anachronistic reference to the temple tax, an attempt to speak to an issue in Matthew's community, or both. The passage does not imply that all Jews paid the tax, only that Jesus chose to do so. Indeed, the statement of Jesus that "the sons [of the king] are free" stresses voluntarism. If the passage is intended to speak to Matthew's community, it is understandable that questions of solidarity with the Jews would arise before the war, and more poignantly after the war if Pharisees were the focus of the *didrachmon.* It is less likely but also possible that by "sons of the king," Jesus is referring only to himself (and therefore only to exemption from the temple tax). But to the extent that the passage has implications for practice, it represents a conciliatory position motivated by love for the Jews.

See also TAXATION, GRECO-ROMAN.

BIBLIOGRAPHY. G. Alon, *The Jews in Their Land in the Talmudic Age* (Jerusalem, 1980); E. Bammel, "Romans 13," in *Jesus and the Politics of His Day,* ed. E. Bammel and C. F. D. Moule (Cambridge: Cambridge University Press, 1984) 365-83; F. F. Bruce, "Render to Caesar," in *Jesus and the Politics of His Day,* ed. E. Bammel and C. F. D. Moule (Cambridge: Cambridge University Press, 1984) 249-63; S. Freyne, *Galilee from Alexander the Great to Hadrian* (Notre Dame, IN: University of Notre Dame Press, 1980); D. E. Garland, "Matthew's Understanding of the Temple Tax (Matt 17:24-27)," *SBLSP* 26 (1987) 190-209; K. C. Hanson and D. E. Oakman, *Palestine in the Time of Jesus: Social Structures and Social Conflicts* (Minneapolis: Fortress, 1998) esp. 113-16; F. M. Heichelheim, "Roman Syria," in *An Economic Survey of Ancient Rome,* ed. T. Frank (Paterson, NJ: Pagenat Books, 1959); W. Horbury, "The Temple Tax," in *Jesus and the Politics of His Day,* ed. E. Bammel and C. F. D. Moule (Cambridge: Cambridge University Press, 1984) 265-86; R. A. Horsley, *Galilee: History, Politics, People* (Valley Forge, PA: Trinity Press International, 1995) esp. 137-44; idem, *Jesus and the Spiral of Violence: Popular Jewish Resistance in Roman Palestine* (San Francisco: Harper & Row, 1987) esp. 279-84; S. Mandell, "Who Paid the Temple Tax When the Jews Were Under Roman Rule?" *HTR* 77 (1984) 223-32; O. Michel, "τελώνης," *TDNT* 8:88-105; D. E. Oakman, *Jesus and the Economic Questions of His Day* (SBEC 8; Lewiston, NY: Edwin Mellen Press, 1986); P. Perkins, "Taxes in the New Testament," *JRE* 12 (1984) 182-200; E. P. Sanders, *Judaism: Practice and Belief, 63 BCE-66 CE* (Philadelphia: Trinity Press International, 1992); esp. 146-69; E. M. Smallwood, *The Jews Under Roman Rule* (Leiden: E. J. Brill, 1976); M. Stern, "The Province of Judea," in *The Jewish People in the First Century,* ed. S. Safrai and M. Stern (2 vols.; CRINT 1; Assen: Van Gorcum; Philadelphia: Fortress, 1974-76) 1:308-76; F. E. Udoh, "Tribute and Taxes in Early Roman Palestine (63 B.C.E.—70 C.E.): The Evidence from Josephus" (unpublished doctoral dissertation; Duke University, 1996). T. E. Schmidt

TEACHER OF RIGHTEOUSNESS. *See* DEAD SEA SCROLLS; MESSIANISM.

TEMPLE, JEWISH

The temple in Jerusalem was of central importance within early Judaism. The primitive communities of Christians reflected in the NT are examples of Judaic movements, and they developed distinctive policies toward the cult and the temple. Those policies clearly reflect the theological processes which brought about the emergence of early Christianity as separable from Judaism at the close of the NT period.

1. Temple Origins and Structures
2. Operation of the Second Temple
3. Attitudes Toward the Temple
4. The Attitude of Jesus Toward the Temple
5. The Temple in the Gospels
6. The Cultic Piety of the Circle of Peter
7. The Cultic Piety of the Circle of James
8. Temple Theology in Paul
9. Early Christian Assimilation of the Temple's Function
10. Theology of Definitive Replacement of the Temple

1. Temple Origins and Structures.

Before Solomon built the temple at Jerusalem, the tribes of Israel had worshiped in a number of sanctuaries, most prominently Shiloh. Shiloh was destroyed around 1050 B.C., evidently by the Philistines as a result of the battle recorded in 1 Samuel 4, when they also took from Israel the ark of the covenant. Eventually, however, the ark returned to rest in Jerusalem, and Solomon (or perhaps better David, his father—note the difference in emphasis between 1 Kings 5:17-19; 8:15-21 and 1 Chron 22:8-10; 28:3) determined to build a temple in which it might be housed. A description of the Solomonic temple appears in 1 Kings 6—7 and again, with a few variations, in the summarizing 2 Chronicles 3—4.

The description in Kings is very difficult to interpret for a number of reasons. First, the account utilizes a large number of technical terms not known elsewhere in Hebrew, some of which were distorted during scribal transmission. Second, the editor of Kings either did not have or chose to omit many details which, from an architectural perspective, are absolutely essential for any reconstruction—for example, the layout of various structures and the thickness of walls. And archaeology is no help with this matter, as virtually nothing has survived from the First Temple. Thus scholars attempting to visualize Solomon's work make do with the texts as best they can and have recourse where applicable to comparisons with other Semitic sanctuaries, especially those of Syro-Phoenicia. Not surprisingly, reconstructions differ markedly from one another, and the following discussion attempts merely to highlight those points on which there is a measure of agreement.

The Solomonic temple was a long, narrow structure oriented toward the east. It was divided into three parts: an outer vestibule *(ʾûlām)*, a large interior for worship *(hêkāl)* and a rear compartment known in Hebrew as *dᵉbîr* or *qōdeš qᵒdāšîm*, "the holy of holies." Excluding the walls, whose thickness is not given, the whole was 70 cubits long and 20 cubits wide. The interior paneling consisted of cedar imported from Lebanon. In front of the vestibule stood two bronze pillars, approximately 27 feet high; their function is uncertain, but apparently they did not support the lintel of the vestibule. Some scholars liken them to the traditional stelae *(maṣṣēbôt)* which are well known from Canaanite and Phoenician sanctuaries. The temple stood within a courtyard or inner court; later, by the mid-seventh century at the latest, there were two courts (2 Kings 21:5; Jer 36:10).

The furnishings of the temple included at first the ark of the covenant, which however was lost very early in the history of the First Temple. This stood in the *dᵉbîr*, surmounted by the cherubim. Outside the rear compartment, in the *hêkāl*, stood the golden altar of incense, the table of shewbread and ten candlesticks. Outside the temple building was the altar of bronze upon which the *sacrifices took place. To the southeast of the temple stood the "Sea" of bronze, which contained water used by the *priests for their ablutions. On either side of the temple entrance were located ten bronze basins, five to each side. Here the priests would cleanse the sacrificial victims. All of these basic cultic elements, with certain modifications, were later to be found in the Herodian temple.

It was essentially the temple of Solomon that Nebuchadnezzar destroyed in 587 B.C. when Jerusalem fell to the Babylonians. With the return from exile beginning in 538 B.C., the temple was rebuilt; apparently it was structurally very similar to the earlier version, though lacking that temple's rich adornment. Completed in 515 B.C., it is known as the temple of Zerubbabel, the governor of the period. Over the centuries that followed, this temple was damaged or, perhaps, even destroyed on various occasions; of the details little is known. In the period 200-150 B.C. we know that it suffered substantial damage at least twice. Still, it was rebuilt, and when Herod (*see* Herodian Dynasty) came to build the structure whose beauty was proverbial throughout the Roman world, practically speaking it was the temple of Zerubbabel that he tore down and replaced.

For the reconstruction of Herod's temple, we are somewhat better informed than is the case with the earlier temples. Detailed descriptions have come down in tractate *Middot* of the Mishnah and in the two major works of *Josephus, the *Jewish War* and the *Antiquities*. Tradition assigns the mishnaic tractate to Rabbi Eliezer ben Jacob, who was a young boy at the time of the First Revolt. Although his description (if it really is his) is perhaps idealizing at points, it is still useful for the task of reconstruction. Josephus's descriptions do not always agree with each other or with that of the Mishnah, but by and large these disagreements do not affect major elements of the temple structures.

Herod's work began in 20/19 B.C. and except for matters of detail and added adornment was completed within a decade. Those additional matters, however, occupied the Jews for almost all of the years between c. 10 B.C. and the outbreak of the revolt in A.D. 66, in part by design: such labor provided jobs for many who would otherwise have been unemployed.

Herod was a man of grand ambitions, and his reconstruction of the temple of the Jews reflected that aggrandizing character. He essentially doubled the foundation, or Temple Mount, that had existed from Solomon's day. To do so he lengthened the eastern wall at both ends and added new walls on the other three sides. In the process, he found it necessary to reshape the topography of Jerusalem. The middle, or Tyropoean, Valley, bordering the temple on the west, he filled in. He did the same to a small valley lying to the north of the old mount and to the upper slope of the Kidron Valley to the south. According to the Ritmeyers's recent study of the archaeological remains, the Temple Mount retaining wall measured 1,590 feet on the west, 1,035 feet on the north, 1,536 feet on the east and 912 feet on the south; it thus approximated a rhomboid equivalent in area to thirty-five football fields.

If a Jewish man and woman at the time of Jesus were to enter the temple complex from the south, they would emerge from a large plaza to ascend a broad stairway. Off to their right they would see a ritual bathhouse (it was forbidden to enter the precincts without such immersion) and the council house where the *Sanhedrin sat in session. Straight ahead would be the Double Gate and further to the right the Triple Gate. Entering through the Double Gate, they would pass directly beneath the royal stoa that surmounted the wall of the outer court. In the outer court, or Court of the Gentiles, they would now be standing in the place where the blind and lame came to Jesus (Mt 21:14), where the children greeted him (Mt 21:15) and where he drove out the merchants (Mt 21:12; cf. Mk 11:15; Lk 19:45; Jn 2:14). Surrounding this court were the pillared halls where Jesus and later the disciples taught (Mk 14:49, etc.).

Their eyes would now light upon the temple structure, rising high above them and separated by yet another stairway, a barricade and the walls of the inner courts. Entering from the outside, the first inner court would be the Court of the Women (*ʿezrat hannašîm*), where all Jews including women could advance, but which was off limits to Gentiles on pain of death. Here Anna prayed (Lk 2:37), Jesus watched the widow offer the last of her money (Mk 12:44 and par.) and, probably, the encounter with the adulterous woman has its setting (Jn 8:2-3).

The man alone could continue to advance toward the sanctuary itself, entering the Court of the Israelites. This court was open to all ritually pure Jewish men, but none others. The sacrificial altar stood here. This inner court is the narrative setting for the *Pharisee praying (Lk 18:11), for the disciples praying (Lk 24:53) and, of course, for Jesus standing before the altar (Mk 11:11). No one but priests could continue on to enter the temple building itself.

If the man were to look beyond the temple to the northwest corner of the complex, he could see the fortress called Antonia. This fortress connected to the temple's outer court by means of a stairway, so that Roman soldiers could very quickly cross if needed. They did just that, for example, at the time of the riot associated with the apostle Paul's last visit to Jerusalem (Acts 21:31-32).

Josephus relates that the entire façade of the temple was covered with gold plates. When the sun rose, the reflection was nearly blinding. On a clear day the brilliance of the temple was visible from a considerable distance outside Jerusalem. And this brilliance was not due to gold alone; the upper parts of the temple were pure white, probably marble. Once a year the priests applied whitewash to this upper section. At the very top gold spikes lined the roof. Approaching the temple, twelve steps led up to the entrance of the vestibule *(ʾûlām)*. The inner walls of this vestibule, like the facade, were gilded. Carved oak beams comprised the lintel of the portal. The vestibule rose to the full height of the inner portions of the temple but exceeded these in width by twenty-six feet on each side. This space formed two rooms wherein were housed sacrificial implements.

At the entrance to the sanctuary *(hêkāl)* hung a veil woven in Babylon, embroidered in four colors: scarlet, light brown, blue and purple. According to Josephus the veil symbolized "a panorama of the heavens, excluding the signs of the zodiac" (Josephus *J.W.* 5.5.4 §§212-14). In front of the veil was a golden lamp given by Queen Helena of Adiabene, a convert to Judaism. Two tables also stood at the entrance before the veil, one of marble and the other of gold. At the weekly changing of the priestly courses, the marble table received the new shewbread introduced into the temple, while the golden one held the old bread. Standing outside the temple and looking into the entrance, one could see into the vestibule as far as the veil and the tables holding the shewbread, but it was impossible to see further into the sanctuary.

The sanctuary and the holy of holies comprised one long room, 103 feet long, 35 feet wide and 69 feet high, and demarcated by curtains. These curtains were beautifully embroidered with lions and eagles. Entirely overlaid with gold panels, the interior of the sanctuary housed the lampstand, the shewbread table (distinct from the two tables already described that stood outside the entrance), and the altar of incense. All were made of gold. The seven branches of the lampstand symbolized the seven planets, while the twelve loaves of the shewbread, which had originally stood for the twelve tribes of Israel, had been reinterpreted so that they now represented the signs of the zodiac as well.

Only the high priest could enter the holy of holies, and that only on the Day of Atonement. In the Second Temple period the interior was devoid of all furnishings save for a small rock upon which the high priest made his annual offerings of incense and sprinkled the blood of atonement. The artisans who maintained the temple did "enter" the inner sanctum, but only in a way that was interpreted as not entering. Lowered from the roof in cages that were closed on the sides, they were unable to see their surroundings. Thus they worked blind and, technically, did not enter the room since they did not come through the entrance and saw and touched nothing.

A great deal of the intellectual and spiritual life of the city took place in the courtyards of the temple, the outermost of which, as indicated, was extremely capacious. There scholars wrote, read and instructed their students, and there political debate occurred. Surrounded by the splendors of the temple, it was only natural to feel a sort of numinous awe. That, however, was not the only or, perhaps, the most important emotion to which the temple built by Herod gave rise. [M. O. Wise]

2. Operation of the Second Temple.

The temple was the place of God's dwelling, where his "glory" (or, as was said during the rabbinic period, his "Presence" [*š*ᵉ*kînâ*]) abides. That understanding has been well established in research; the architecture of the temple in Jerusalem attests it. But the picture of the temple as a divine "house" is only helpful when it is borne in mind that the house was not only for God but for his people and his goods: the entire household was involved in sacrificial activity. *Sacrifice involved all Israel, and even those beyond the territorial limits of Israel.

Deuteronomy identifies Jerusalem as the single "place" *(hammāqôm)* where God is to be worshiped (Deut 12:5-14). Sacrifices to the Lord elsewhere are specifically prohibited (Deut 12:13, 14), and the complete destruction of the "places" of all other gods is prescribed (Deut 12:2, 3). Provisions are made for the long journeys which centralization sometimes demanded: sacrifices of the tithe may be converted into money, which is then used to purchase food and drink to eat before the Lord (Deut 14:22-27). Contrary to the prescriptions of Leviticus, the slaughter and consumption of animals outside of Jerusalem, explicitly as nonsacrificial, is permitted, provided the blood is poured out and the beast concerned is not owed as a sacrifice (Deut 12:15-28).

The strict limitation of sacrifice to Jerusalem creates the imperative of the pilgrimage. Being in the "place" is naturally an occasion for joy (Deut 12:7, 12, 18). Sacrifice in Jerusalem is the celebration and at the same time a guarantee of prosperity. Disobedience, within the Deuteronomic scheme, can only result in Israel's destruction, its scattering in the manner of the Assyrian conquest (Deut 4:25-31). But keeping the commandments ensures that the Lord will give possession of the land to his people, thrust out their enemies, and provide physical and agricultural prosperity and freedom from disease (Deut 6:17-19; 7:1-16). The dynamic heart of the promise is that Israel is holy, a people for the possession of God (Deut 7:6): the central fact that God has acquired Israel is the sole cause of their redemption from Egypt and their future prosperity in just those aspects in which Egypt had been afflicted (Deut 7:7-16). Sacrificial "rejoicing" is a way both to celebrate and to secure that blessing of God which is Israel's prosperity.

The terms of reference established by sacrifice as an act of "rejoicing" in the single, sacred "place" from which God gives Israel prosperity are precisely observed in the calendar in Deuteronomy 16. The three *feasts of Passover, Weeks and Sukkoth are carefully specified, and each—even Passover, originally a domestic meal (see Ex 12)—is made the occasion of pilgrimage. The feasts of pilgrimage are occasions on which both the map and the *calendar of Israel are routinely redrawn. Three times a year, Israel is back in the desert, redeemed from Egypt, new in their freedom, living in booths. The land which has so desperately been sought and acquired disappears from view, in order to be received again as the gift of God to his own people, complete with the prosperity and health he alone can bestow. Variety in the understanding of the worship which God requires in the single temple is evident within the Hebrew Bible itself. But the Deuteronomic prescriptions give a good indication of the prevailing rationale of cultic practice, as it was based upon the Mosaic covenant. Pluralization in definitions of Judaism was more radical by the first century (*see* Judaism).

The Sadducees probably owe their name to Zadok (the priest of David's and Solomon's time), but their loyalty to the settlement in the temple, in which the Romans effectively chose high priests, made them appear to many to be upholders of privilege. Josephus describes attempts by prophetic pretenders, and later Zealots, to disentangle the operation of the temple from collaboration with Rome (see Josephus *J.W.* 2.13.3-6 §§254-65; 7.11.1-2 §§437-46; and, on the Zealots, Josephus *J.W.* 2.20.3 §§564-65; 4.4.1 §§224-25). Even among the priesthood, nationalism was a natural outgrowth of a desire for the cultic integrity of the temple (see Josephus *J.W.* 2.20.3-4 §§562-68).

The *apocalyptic perspective within early Judaism also resulted in critical attitudes toward the temple. The book of Daniel (Dan 7—12) anticipates by visionary means an eschatological triumph, of which the principal agent is the archangel Michael (Dan 12:1-4); the temple's renewal is part of the scenario (Dan 12:11-12). Several of the documents found near *Qumran represent an apocalyptic point of view and envisage that the sect of covenanters will direct the operation of the temple in the final days (see 1QM, 1QS, CD). More recently discovered materials (**Temple Scroll*, **New Jerusalem*, **Miqṣat Ma ʿaśey ha-Torah*) attest a directly practical interest in the conduct of sacrifice in Jerusalem. Josephus reports that one of the priestly nationalists involved as a general with him in the war against Rome was John the Essene (Josephus *J.W.* 2.20.4 §567; 3.2.1 §11; 3.2.2 §19), and he relates the repute of the *Essenes for courage under Roman torture (Josephus *J.W.* 2.8.10 §§152-53). Indeed, the correspondence between Josephus's extensive description of the Essenes (Josephus *J.W.* 2.8.2-13 §§119-61) and the evidence which continues to emerge from Qumran is such as to make recent attempts to drive a wedge between the two seem even more apologetic than Josephus himself was.

The Pharisees, in their attempt to influence what the high priests did in the temple, rather than to replace those institutions definitively, appear more conservative than the Essenes and nationalistic priestly families. Josephus reports that the Pharisees made known their displeasure at Alexander Janneus by inciting a crowd to pelt him with lemons (at hand for a festal procession) at the time he should have been offering sacrifice. His response to the claim that he was unfit to hold office was to have some six thousand people killed (Josephus *Ant.* 13.13.5 §§372-73). Josephus also relates, from a later period, the teaching of the rabbis (probably Pharisees) who were implicated in dismantling the eagle Herod had erected over a gate of the temple (Josephus *J.W.* 1.33.2-4 §648-55; *Ant.* 17.6.2-4 §§149-67). That gesture was less subversive of the established authority in the cult than what earlier Pharisees had done, but Herod correctly understood that it was a deliberate challenge to his authority, and he responded with summary executions.

Paradoxically, the willingness of the Pharisees to consider the *Hasmoneans and Herodians in their priestly function, in distinction from the Essenes, involved them not only in symbolic disputes but in vocal and bloody confrontations. Alexander Janneus is reported to have executed by crucifixion eight hundred opponents, either Pharisees or those with whom the Pharisees sympathized, and to have slaughtered their families; but his wife came to an accommodation with the Pharisees which guaranteed them considerable influence (Josephus *J.W.* 1.4.6—1.5.3 §96-114). [B. Chilton]

3. Attitudes Toward the Temple.

Attitudes toward the temple at Jerusalem varied considerably from time to time and from group to group within intertestamental Judaism. In many respects the theology of the temple within this period continued along the lines already developed in the First Temple period. Thus the temple was considered to be the very dwelling place of God, in a way shared by no other place on earth. Even the prophets who had grave reservations about the cultic practices going on in their own time believed that the temple was nevertheless God's dwelling among humankind. Ezekiel, for example, who says that he saw the glory of God depart the temple because of defiling practices (Ezek 8—10), also says that God will return to live forever in a new temple (Ezek 43:1-12).

The temple was considered a sign of Israel's election from among the peoples of the earth. It stood on a site chosen by theophany (2 Sam 24:16) long before its construction; Zion was the mountain of God (Ps 68:17) and was even identified with the original location of the garden of Eden (cf. Ezek 34). Even the destruction of 587 B.C. did not disprove Israel's election; rather, God would return and once more make Jerusalem his choice (Zech 1:17). The peoples of the earth would one day stream to Jerusalem to worship, and Israel would stand at the head of the nations (cf. Is 2:1-4).

These ideas and other positive assessments of the temple continued to be believed and elaborated in the intertestamental period. But another strain of thought, also having its roots in the OT, is noticeably more prominent now: the tradition of hostility toward the temple. This tradition particularly characterizes apocalyptic thought, and—as is becoming more and more recognized—apocalyptic was the popular religion of Second Temple Judaism. This tradition of hostility toward the temple is worthy of extended consideration, since it sheds light on the Gospel tradition.

The apocalyptic tradition of aversion toward the temple at Jerusalem takes a great deal of its inspiration from the book of Ezekiel. Ezekiel 40—48 constitutes the prophet's famous vision of a new temple, a new Jerusalem and a new theocratic state. He is given a vision of a temple in heaven, whence it will be manifest in the end of days. Then the heavenly temple will descend on Zion, and God will once more take up permanent residence there. Different streams of Judaism understood this vision in different ways. As noted above, Zechariah, for example, believed that the promise was fulfilled in the temple rebuilt in his own day. But for some groups the temple of Zerubbabel was not the one promised.

This rejection of the Second Temple probably had its basis in several related perceptions. First was the fact that the temple rebuilt under Haggai and Zechariah was singularly unimpressive compared with the Solomonic version it attempted to re-create. Surely the God of all the earth would not be content to reside in such a pathetic edifice, which dimmed in comparison not only with Solomon's structure, but much the more so when compared with visions of the heavenly temple (cf. *1 Enoch* 90:28-29). Even a foremost proponent of this temple, Haggai, had to recognize this problem. He did his best to blunt the criticisms of those unimpressed with the temple of Zerubbabel (Hag 2:9; cf. Zech 14:8-11), but he was unable to silence all the critics.

A second significant reason for the rejection of the Second Temple by certain elements of the Jewish people centered on cultic practices. Already in the latter portions of Isaiah and in Ezekiel one can recognize hints of such disputes. These disagreements concerned the proper structures and procedures for the sacrificial cultus, and even the proper times for *festivals and assemblies. Note, for example, the words of Isaiah 66:3, "He who kills an ox is like one who slays a man; he who sacrifices a lamb is like one who breaks a dog's neck; he who offers a grain offering is like one who offers swine's blood . . . they have chosen their own ways, and their soul delights in their abominations" (NASB, modified). This passage is hyperbolic, of course; no one was really offering dogs or pigs. But in the author's view the priests of the temple in Jerusalem were not practicing the proper methods, and the result was the same: an illegitimate cultus. The disagreements could hardly have been more fundamental.

It would appear that during the fourth and third centuries B.C.—a period for which we have virtually no written evidence—these disagreements were to some extent resolved. Some sort of *modus vivendi* did emerge. But the problems did not simply go away. Those whose ideas were defeated naturally felt disenfranchised, and it is probably among such groups that apocalyptic ideas found their most fertile soil. In the view of these disenfranchised elements the groups regnant in the temple practiced the wrong Halakah; consequently, both the priesthood and the temple were defiled.

Again and again in the apocalyptic literature these notions recur. Thus in *1 Enoch* 83—90 (c. 150 B.C.) the writer portrays the temple of Zerubbabel as ritually impure; he says the priests tried to offer bread on the altar "but all the bread on it was polluted and impure" (*1 Enoch* 89:72-73). The Apocalypse of Weeks (now found in portions of *1 Enoch* 91 and 93; c. 200 B.C. or earlier) claims that every generation since the exile has been apostate because no one was able to discern the true cultus or "things of heaven" (*1 Enoch* 93:9). The *Testament of Levi* (first century B.C./first century A.D.) calls the priests of the former temple impure. In the last days, however, when a new priest would arise, "The heavens shall be opened, and from the glorious temple sanctification shall come upon him" (*T. Levi* 17:10). Along with many others, the author of *Jubilees* (c. 170 B.C.) despairs that the only remedy is the replacement of the sullied present structure by the eschatological version (*Jub.* 23:21).

But perhaps the strongest reason for the rejection of the present temple stemmed from a belief that it was not built to the specifications that God had provided. This belief in turn derived from a straightforward reading of the biblical accounts. The temple of Solomon, after all, was built to specifications given to him by his father David. Where had David gotten those plans? The account in Kings does not specify. This was a bothersome problem for some Second Temple Jews. The Chronicler had already offered his solution in 1 Chronicles 28:19, saying that David gave Solomon, "Everything [the whole plan detailed in 1 Chron 28:11-18] in a book from the hand of God." Thus the Chronicler believed that David must have received his temple plans from God himself and could not have relied on human artifice for so important a structure. But many Jews did not agree with the Chronicler's solution. It must be recalled that the portion of Hebrew Scripture called the Writings, among which Chronicles is numbered, was not everywhere accorded the authority given the Torah and the Prophets.

Instead, apocalyptic visionaries found another scriptural portion where God had revealed the divine plan for an earthly temple. This portion was the description of the building of the tabernacle contained in the latter chapters of the book of Exodus. Prima facie, it was inconceivable that God would have instructed Moses about every matter of the law while neglecting to describe the perfect temple. Warrant for the view that Moses had indeed seen the plan for the temple—or even the heavenly temple itself—was found in verses such as Exodus 25:9: "According to all that I am showing you, the plan of the dwelling place and the plan of all its implements, thus shall you do." For such intertestamental exegetes, the equation of "dwelling place" (*miškān*; conventionally translated "tabernacle") with the temple was self-evident. Indeed, Exodus 25:8 explicitly connected the plans which Moses was seeing with the "temple" (*miqdāš*). Accordingly, any proper temple would have to be constructed not along the lines of the Davidic/Solomonic model, but according to the plans which God had delivered once for all to his preeminent prophet, Moses. It further followed that the Davidic/Solomonic temple, the temple of Zerubbabel and the Herodian temple were all illegitimate. For the proponents of such views (which continued even after the *destruction of A.D. 70; cf. *2 Bar.* 4:2-6), the proper temple had yet to be built. The present, improper one was unacceptable to God and, accordingly, to all true worshipers.

Of course those who held that the temple should be built according to the plans God had shown Moses faced a certain difficulty: what had happened to those plans? They were not recorded in the OT. The answer that Second Temple authors devised to handle that problem was twofold: First, they said, the plans had been kept hidden until the end and were to be known only to the elect; and second, some details would require additional revelation. In accordance with such an approach several writings from the intertestamental period make claims for new temple visions.

The Qumranic text (*see* Dead Sea Scrolls) known as the **New Jerusalem* (5Q15) is one such writing. An angel appears to the anonymous seer (perhaps Ezekiel?) and takes him on a tour of the city and temple of the last days. The *New Jerusalem* takes up where Ezekiel 40—48 leaves off, providing exact dimensions for buildings associated with the sacrificial cultus. It also describes the city of that new temple, making interesting modifications on the ideas found in Ezekiel. Evidently the prophet's vision was not felt to be the last word.

The **Temple Scroll* (11QTemple), another text from Qumran, goes somewhat further. This text implicitly claims to be a new revelation to a Mo saic figure who, like that prophet, speaks with God face to face. Many details of the temple buildings appear in this text, often in the language of the tabernacle description from Exodus. That was only to be expected, since the allusions to Moses' vision of the heavenly temple occur in those portions of Exodus dealing with the tabernacle. Neither the *New Jerusalem* nor the *Temple Scroll* describe a temple precisely like that of Solomon; some of the details are decidedly different. Presumably the authors of these and similar texts must have regarded the actual temple in Jerusalem as a sort of imposter.

Still, despite all their rhetoric and even with these fundamental reasons for rejecting the Second Temple structures, one must be cautious about concluding that any groups among the Jews boycotted the temple altogether. Claims that the so-called Qumran community, for example, had deserted the temple and that its members considered themselves a new, spiritual temple, are problematic. These claims mainly depend on certain passages in the **Manual of Discipline* (the view that 4QFlor, with its reference to a *miqdaš ʾādām*, means a spiritual rather than physical temple must be rejected).

The difficulties with this particular conclusion properly require a separate exposition, but perhaps several points should be made. First, we really do not know how the authors of the *Manual of Discipline* regarded that work; some of the imagery which it uses, such as the mustering of "Israel" by hundreds and by thousands, suggests that the text describes an idealized future. If so, then the passages which many understand as rejecting the sacrificial cultus (esp. col. 9) should not automatically be taken as evidence that the group avoided the temple in the present age. Second, the *Manual of Discipline* stands in some sort of relation with the **Damascus Document* (CD), although scholars do not agree on precisely how to define that relationship. The *Damascus Covenant* certainly envisions a circumscribed participation in the temple cultus (col. 6). This fact has to be borne in mind before reaching any conclusions about the *Manual of Discipline*, especially since the latter work does not explicitly declare the temple obsolete. Third, at least one unpublished copy of the *Manual* (from Cave 4) contains a passage describing the comings and goings of the priestly courses. Such a description may imply that the authors recognized the temple's fundamental importance and could not simply reject it. Fourth, a point related to this last—the *Manual* apparently existed in various recensions. If so, it is arbitrary to decide that the Cave 1 manuscript (the only one fully published) was necessarily the one being followed at any one time—if indeed any of the versions were "followed" or were intended as anything more than idealizing literature.

Even though the present cultus be flawed, sacrifices and festivals were divinely ordained after all. Might one really entirely cease to observe them? A more prudent approach is to suggest that such groups limited their involvement with the temple to the bare necessities, while working to change the situation and to force the acceptance of their own viewpoints. [M. O. Wise]

4. The Attitude of Jesus Toward the Temple. The expulsion of traders in animals is the single point of consensus in the canonical Gospels concerning what Jesus did during his occupation of the temple. Indeed, it is the only specific point mentioned in Luke (Lk 19:45-48), which presents the sparsest account (cf. Mt 21:12-16; Mk 11:15-18; Jn 2:14-22). The expulsion of the traders is what is agreed in the Gospels (cf. *Gos. Thom.* 64) to have been the point of Jesus' ac-

PLAN OF HEROD'S TEMPLE

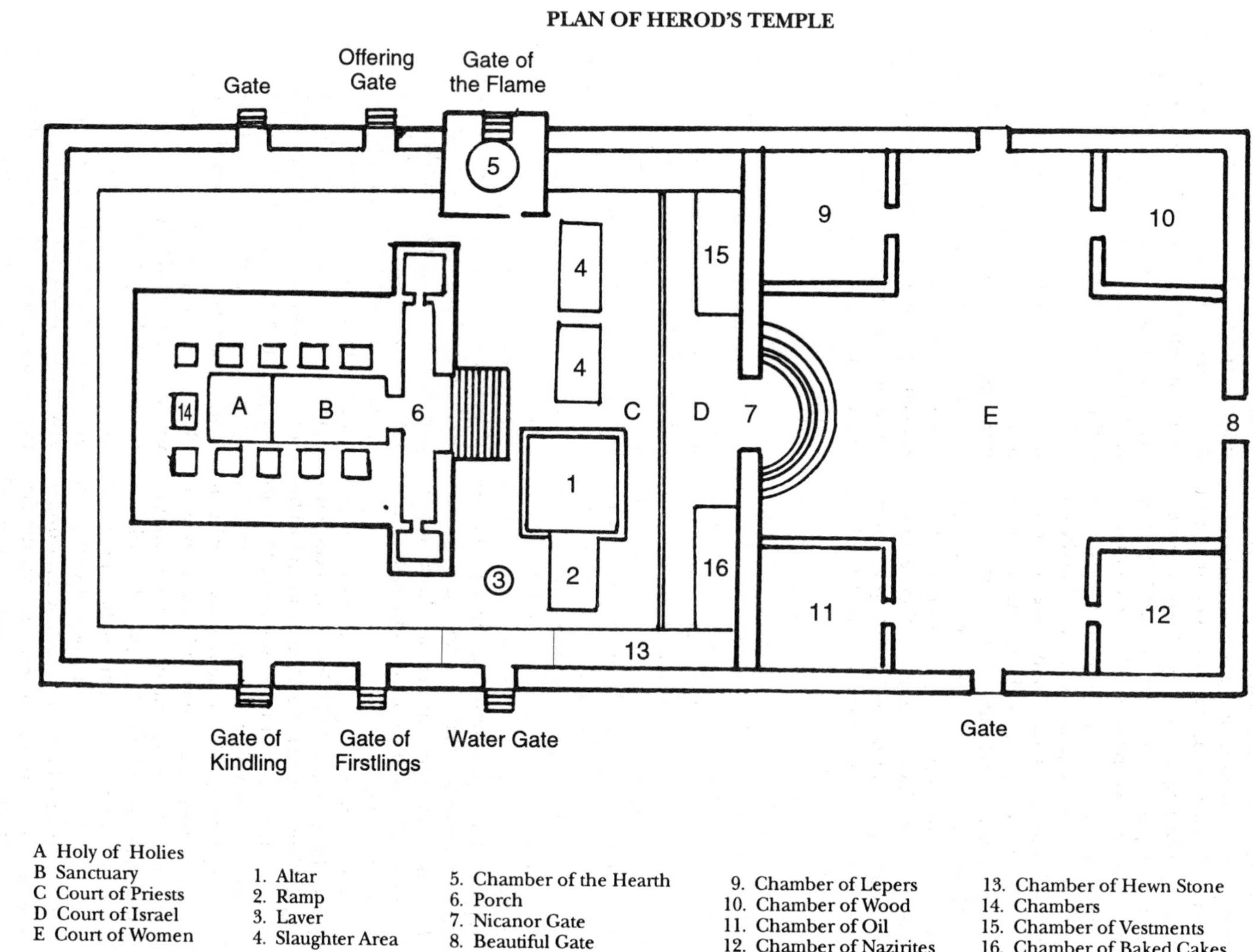
Gate
Offering Gate
Gate of the Flame
Gate of Kindling
Gate of Firstlings
Water Gate
Gate
A
B
C
D
E
1
2
3
4
4
5
6
7
8
9
10
11
12
13
14
15
16
A Holy of Holies
B Sanctuary
C Court of Priests
D Court of Israel
E Court of Women
1. Altar
2. Ramp
3. Laver
4. Slaughter Area
5. Chamber of the Hearth
6. Porch
7. Nicanor Gate
8. Beautiful Gate
9. Chamber of Lepers
10. Chamber of Wood
11. Chamber of Oil
12. Chamber of Nazirites
13. Chamber of Hewn Stone
14. Chambers
15. Chamber of Vestments
16. Chamber of Baked Cakes

tion; the action was immediately directed at neither the Romans nor the high priests and had nothing whatever to do with destroying the fabric of the edifice itself. Once it is appreciated that Jesus' maneuver in the temple was in the nature of a claim upon territory in order to eject those performing an activity of which he evidently disapproved, it is more straightforward to characterize it as an "occupation" rather than a "demonstration"; the traditional "cleansing" is obviously an apologetic designation. But the target of his activity makes good sense within the context of what we know of the activities of certain pharisaic or early rabbinic teachers.

Hillel insisted that owners should lay their hands on their offerings prior to giving them over to priests for slaughter. Another rabbi was so struck by the rectitude of Hillel's position, he had some three-thousand animals brought to the temple and gave them to those who were willing to lay hands on them in advance of sacrifice (*b. Beṣa* 20a, b). The tradition concerning Hillel envisages the opposite movement from what is represented in the tradition concerning Jesus: animals are introduced rather than their traders expelled. But the purpose of the action by Hillel's supporter is to enforce a certain understanding of correct offering. Hillel's rule requires the participation of the offerer by virtue of his ownership of what is offered. Jesus' occupation may be understood—along lines similar to those involved in the provision of animals to support Hillel's position—as an attempt to insist that the offerer's actual ownership of what is offered is a vital aspect of sacrifice. Jesus wanted Israel to offer of its own, not to purchase sacrifices in the temple.

From a period slightly later than that of Jesus, Mishnah (*Ker.* 1:7) relates a story concerning Rabban Simeon b. Gamaliel, who crafted his teaching in order to bring down the price of offerings in the temple, which he considered to be exorbitant. Hillel, Simeon and Jesus are all portrayed as interested in how animals are offered to the extent that they intervene in the court of the temple in order to influence the ordinary course of worship. Jesus can best be understood within the context of a particular dispute in which the Pharisees took part, a controversy over where action was to occur. In that the dispute was intimately involved with the issue of how animals were to be procured, it manifests a focus upon purity which is akin to that attributed to Hillel and Simeon.

The Gospels describe the southern side of the outer court as the place where Jesus expelled the traders. The exterior court was well suited for trade, since it was surrounded by porticos on the inside, following Herod's architectural preferences. But the assumption of rabbinic literature and Josephus is that the market for the sale of sacrificial beasts was not normally located in the temple at all, but in a place called Hanuth (meaning "market" in Aramaic) on the Mount of Olives, across the Kidron Valley. V. Eppstein has argued that rabbinic literature attests the innovation to which Jesus objected. It is recorded that, some forty years before the destruction of the temple, the principal council of Jerusalem was removed from the place in the temple called the Chamber of Hewn Stone to Hanuth (cf. *ʿAbod. Zar.* 8b; *Šabb.* 15a; *Sanh.* 41a). Eppstein argues that Caiaphas both expelled the *Sanhedrin and introduced the traders into the temple.

Caiaphas enjoyed a good relationship with Pilate, under whom he served for ten years and on whose departure he was removed (Josephus *Ant.* 18.4.3 §90-95). Given that he enjoyed the support of the Romans and that he was involved in disputes concerning the location of the council, the allegation of the Gospels that trade was permitted in the temple during his tenure seems plausible.

From the point of view of Pharisaism generally, trade in the southern side of the outer court would have been anathema. Purses were not permitted in the temple according to the Pharisees' teaching (*m. Ber.* 9:5). Sufficient money might be brought to put directly into the large containers for alms (cf. *m. Šeqal.* 6:1, 5; 7:1), to purchase seals redeemable for libations (cf. *m. Šeqal.* 5:4), and/or to exchange against Tyrian coinage in order to pay the annual half-shekel (cf. *m. Šeqal.* 1:3; 2:1), but the introduction of trade for animals into the temple rendered the ideal of not bringing into the temple more than would be consumed there impracticable. (References in Mt 21:12 and Mk 11:15 to people selling and buying animals within the court may even imply that serial transactions were involved.) Moreover, the installation of traders in the porticos would also have involved the removal of those teachers, pharisaic and otherwise, who taught and observed in the temple itself (cf. *m. Sanh.* 11:2; *b. Pesaḥ.* 26a).

From the point of view of the smooth conduct of sacrifice, of course, the innovation was sensible. One could know at the moment of purchase that one's sacrifice was acceptable and not run the risk of harm befalling the animal on its way to be slaughtered. It is therefore unnecessary to impute malicious motives to Caiaphas in order to understand what was going on, although it may be assumed that additional profit for the temple was also involved. But when we look at the installation of the traders from the point of view of Hillelite Pharisaism, for example, Jesus' objection becomes understandable. Hillel had taught that one's sacrifice had to be shown to be one's own, by the imposition of hands; part of the necessary preparation was not just of people to the south and beasts to the north, but the connection between the two by appropriation. Caiaphas's innovation was sensible on the understanding that sacrifice was simply a matter of offering pure, unblemished animals. But it failed in pharisaic terms and in the terms of Jesus, not only in its introduction of the necessity for commerce into the temple, but in its breach of the link between worshiper and offering in the sacrificial action. [B. Chilton]

5. The Temple in the Gospels.

In addition to the various Gospel portions which take the temple structures for their narrative setting (some of which have been noted in the temple description above), the temple plays a critical role in three particular pericopes. These are (1) the cleansing of the temple (Mk 11:15-17; Mt 21:12-13; Lk 19:45-46; Jn 2:14-17); (2) the saying attributed to Jesus concerning the destruction and rebuilding of the temple (Mk 14:57-58; 15:29-30; Mt 26:61; 27:40; Jn 2:18-22; cf. Acts 6:14; *see* Destruction of Jerusalem); and (3) the prophecy of the temple's destruction contained in the Little Apocalypse and related texts (Mk 13:2-3; Mt 24:1; Lk 21:5-6; cf. Mk 13:14; Mt 24:15; Lk 21:20). All of these passages have in common a negative attitude toward the temple. In order to gain a balanced perspective, before examining them it is important to take notice of positive attitudes toward the temple contained in the Gospels.

These positive attitudes continue one line of temple theology alluded to above. Prominently, the Gospels view the temple as the special place of God's presence (Mt 12:4; Lk 6:4). This dogma underlies the saying about swearing by the temple (Mt 23:31; cf. Mt 23:16, with a similar rationale). Jesus is depicted as saying that the temple should be a house of prayer, not of thieves—a strong affirmation of the sanctity connected with God's presence. Matthew also portrays Jesus as paying the temple tax (*see* Taxation, Jewish), if only out of tolerance rather than conviction (Mt 17:24-27).

The three negative pericopes are all problematic, and their interpretation is often a function of a particular scholar's model for understanding the historical Jesus. Furthermore, all three are currently at the vortex of Gospel scholarship. The following discussion is therefore intended as representative and suggestive rather than exhaustive.

Jesus' cleansing of the temple was an extremely dramatic, if not apocalyptic, act. At its heart is the attitude that the present cultus is corrupt—on that all agree. But is this merely the response of a prophet who acts from the righteous anger of an Isaiah or a Jeremiah in the face of improper worship, or is it more—a messianic claim? Although the cleansing plays no part in the narratives of the trial of Jesus, some (most recently and notably E. P. Sanders) have claimed that the act was that of a revolutionary and was perceived as such by the temple authorities and the Romans. Sanders can find no other reason for Jesus' arrest, trial and crucifixion. In the context of what we know about apocalyptic thinking it is undeniable that contemporaries might well have believed that Jesus was seeking to inaugurate the eschaton by his actions. In apocalyptic writings renewal of the temple is often a messianic act or is at least connected with the rise of the Messiah. And even if it were not so intended, one suspects that Jesus' act was sufficiently militant to arouse zealot feelings and thus discomfit the Romans (*see* Revolutionary Movements).

The saying about the destruction and rebuilding of the temple is, if anything, even more problematic. It is convenient to consider the so-called Little Apocalypse prediction of the temple's destruction at the same time, as the two appear to be interrelated in the Gospel traditions. According to the latter (Mk 13:1-4 and par.) Jesus predicted the destruction of A.D. 70 many years before it happened. This prediction is strikingly reminiscent of the charge made against Jesus in the trial before the Sanhedrin. There witnesses declare that they have heard

Jesus say that he will destroy the temple "made with hands" and raise upon another in three days, "made without hands." As usually understood, Mark seems to say that this charge was false and did not stand because the witnesses contradicted each other. They were, in other words, false witnesses. But it should be noted that Mark does not necessarily mean that the charge was substantively false–he says only that the witnesses disagreed in their accounts of Jesus' declaration in some unspecified manner (*houtōs*). Then in Mark 15:29 bystanders taunt Jesus with the same charge as he hangs on the cross. Were these people aware of the proceedings before the court, wanting only to repeat the false charges? Or did they perhaps believe (whether from the earlier testimony or for other reasons) that Jesus had in fact made some such statement?

The Markan account apparently wants the reader to conclude that Jesus never said that he would destroy the temple. In and of itself that conclusion would not be problematic. But on comparison with John 2:19-22 a tension arises. John places the saying in the context of the cleansing of the temple rather than in his account of Jesus' trial. The Jews ask Jesus what warrant he has for his actions, and he replies, "Destroy this temple, and in three days I will raise it up." The Johannine interpretation then follows, "But he spoke of his body." John seems to admit that Jesus did say something about destroying the temple, either advocating it or predicting it. John then seeks to deflect or at least avoid the straightforward interpretation of this tradition. If he did not have a tradition according to which Jesus said something about the temple being destroyed, his allegorical interpretation could not have arisen.

John therefore attributes a crucial saying to Jesus while Mark, as often understood, may deny that Jesus said it. Scholars have wrestled with this (apparent) contradiction without producing a consensus. If one finds some truth in a zealot model for understanding Jesus, it is felicitous to see here a messianic declaration in which Jesus clears the way for the temple of the eschaton. Such a declaration would be in keeping with the negative attitudes toward the temple, and would look forward to a new temple and, presumably, a new Jerusalem. Even if one rejects this alternative, it seems clear that the Gospel narrators, writing many years after Jesus spoke these words, found them somewhat embarrassing and in need of explanation. Perhaps that is understandable in the face of the First Revolt and the desire to distance nascent Christianity from the parent Judaism. In any event, the place of the temple traditions within the Gospels will continue to merit study. [M. O. Wise]

6. The Cultic Piety of the Circle of Peter. One of the principal reasons that make it plain that Jesus himself was loyal to the temple, even as he attempted to insist upon a distinctive view of the purity God requires within it, is that the movement which continued in his name after the crucifixion was largely centered in the temple. The picture provided in Acts is clear and consistent: under the leadership of Peter and a group of twelve, the followers of Jesus lived commonly, broke bread together regularly in their homes, and participated in the cult in the manner of devoted, nonpriestly Israelites (see Acts 1:12-26; 2:46; 3:1-26; 4:1-37).

Within Jesus' practice, meals had been occasions on which eating together had been taken as a pledge of the festivity of the kingdom of God (see Mt 8:11, 12; Lk 13:28, 29). Near the end of his life, Jesus had approved the communal wine and bread as more acceptable to God than regular sacrifice. With the words, "this is my blood" and "this is my flesh," Jesus insisted that God approved a meal in his fellowship more than the conduct of worship in the temple, where sacrificial arrangements had become too commercial (Mt 26:26, 28; Mk 14:22, 24; Lk 22:19-20; 1 Cor 11:24-25; Justin *Apol. I* 66.3).

The Petrine circle literally domesticated such meals, holding them at home and yet deliberately taking part in the worship of the temple. At the same time, Peter's group accommodated the meal of fellowship to the general, ancient and widespread practice of blessing what was consumed at meals (see *m. Ber.* 6:5-8 and *b. Ber.* 41b-45a), beginning with bread (see *b. Ber.* 46a).

Acts also places Peter in Samaria (Acts 8:14-25), Lydda (Acts 9:32-35), Joppa (Acts 9:36-43) and Caesarea (Acts 10:1-48; 12:19). Paul refers, as if as a matter of course, to Peter's presence personally in *Antioch (see Gal 2:11-14), and by the time of 1 Peter he is pictured as writing from Rome with Silvanus (see 1 Pet 5:12-13) to churches in the northeast of Asia Minor (1 Pet 1:1, 2). If, then, Jerusalem was a center for Peter in the way it was not for Jesus, it was certainly not a limit of his operations. Rather, the temple appears to have featured as the hub of a much wider network of contacts which linked Jews from abroad and even Gentiles (see Acts 10:1-48; 11:1-18, 15:1-11 with Gal 2:1-14) in common recognition of a new, eschatological fellowship defined by the teaching of Jesus. The Petrine circle took part in worship within the temple, embracing it in a way Jesus had not, and yet at the same time viewed Jesus as the source of a teaching which envisaged the participation in worship of those far outside Jerusalem. Peter's activity, centered on but not limited to Jerusalem, was motivated by the eschatological promise of Zion's place at the heart of the worshiping nations.

7. The Cultic Piety of the Circle of James.

Hegesippus—as cited by Eusebius (*Hist. Eccl.* 2.23.1-18)—characterizes James, Jesus' brother, as the person to whom immediate control of the church in Jerusalem passed. James practiced a careful and idiosyncratic purity in the interests of worship in the temple. He abstained from wine and animal flesh, did not cut his hair or beard, and forsook oil and bathing. If the report of Hegesippus is to be taken at face value, those special practices gave him access even to the sanctuary. Josephus reports he was killed in the temple c. A.D. 62 at the instigation of the high priest Ananus during the interregnum between the Roman governors Festus and Albinus (Josephus *Ant.* 20.9.1 §§197-203).

In addition to the sort of close association with the temple which could and did result in conflict with the authorities there, the circle of James is expressly claimed in Acts to have exerted authority as far away as Antioch, by means of emissaries who spoke Greek (Acts 15:13-35). The particulars of the dispute (with both Pauline and Petrine understandings of purity) will not detain us here, but it is of immediate import that James alone determines the outcome of apostolic policy. James in Acts agrees that Gentiles who turn to God are not to be encumbered with needless regulations (Acts 15:19), and yet he insists they be instructed by letter to abstain "from the pollutions of idols, and from fornication, and from what is strangled, and from blood" (Acts 15:20).

The grounds given for the Jacobean policy are that the law of Moses is commonly acknowledged (Acts 15:21); the implication is that to disregard such elemental considerations of purity as James specifies would be to dishonor Moses. Judas Barsabbas and Silas are then dispatched with Paul and Barnabas to deliver the letter in Antioch along with their personal testimony (Acts 15:22-29) and are said particularly to continue their instruction as prophets (Acts 15:32, 33). They refer to the regulations of purity as necessities (Acts 15:28), and no amount of Lukan gloss can conceal that what they insist upon is a serious challenge of Paul's position (compare 1 Cor 8, which is ignorant of the so-called decree).

James's devotion to the temple is also reflected in Acts 21. When Paul arrives in Jerusalem, James and the presbyters with him express concern at the rumor that Paul is telling Jews who live among the Gentiles not to circumcise their sons. Their advice is for Paul to demonstrate his piety by purifying himself, paying the expenses of four men under a vow, and entering the temple with them (Acts 21:17-26). The result is a disastrous misunderstanding. Paul is accused of introducing "Greeks" into the temple, a riot ensues, and Paul himself is arrested (Acts 21:27-36). James is not mentioned again in Acts, but Hegesippus's notice would suggest his devotion to the temple did not wane.

Within the Gospels certain passages reflect the exceptional devotion of James's circle to the temple. The best example is Mark 7:6-13 (and, with an inverted structure, Mt 15:3-9); although the topic of the chapter overall is purity, the issue addressed in the passage itself is the sanctity of the temple (Mk 7:6-13). The issue is spelled out in terms of a dispute concerning *qôrbān*, the Aramaic term for a cultic gift (Mk 7:11).

The dispute reflects Jesus' own stance, that what is owed to one's parents cannot be sheltered by declaring it dedicated to the temple. The crucial point of such a gambit of sheltering is that one might continue to use the property after its dedication, while what was given to a person would be transferred forthwith. The basic complaint about the practice, especially as stated in the simple epigram of Mark 7:11-12, derives from Jesus. The complaint is characteristic of him; quite aside from his occupation of the temple, he criticized commercial arrangements there (see Mt 17:24-27; Mk 12:41-44; Lk 21:1-4).

The dominical epigram has here been enveloped in a much more elaborate argument. Mark 7:6-13 is a syllogism, developed by means of scriptural terms of reference. Isaiah's complaint

(Is 29:13) frames the entire argument: the people claim to honor God, but their hearts are as far from him as their vain worship, rooted in human commandments (Mk 7:6b-7). That statement is related in Mark 7:10-12 to the tradition of *qôrbān*, taken as an invalidation of the Mosaic prescription to honor parents. The simple and unavoidable conclusion is that the tradition violates the command of God (Mk 7:8-9, 13).

The argument as it stands insists upon the integrity of the temple and the strict regulation of conduct there; it attacks opponents for too little concern for the temple, not too much. At the same time, the passage presents Jesus as maintaining a literal loyalty to the Scriptures (in their *Septuagintal form) which the Pharisees did not. Those aspects of the presentation of Jesus' saying are arguably typical of the circle of James. [B. Chilton]

8. Temple Theology in Paul.

8.1. Terminology. Paul used two different Greek words to speak of temple: *naos* and *hieron*. In terms of the Jerusalem temple, *naos* refers to the building, the place of God's dwelling, and *hieron* refers to the entire area, or precincts, including the sanctuary (Michel, 880-90). Generally speaking, *naos* was used to designate the inner courts of the temple known as the holy place and the holy of holies, whereas *hieron* designated the outer court and the temple proper.

In Paul's letters the word *naos* appears six times (1 Cor 3:16-17; 6:19; 2 Cor 6:16; Eph 2:21; 2 Thess 2:4) and *hieron* once (1 Cor 9:13). In these verses Paul maintains the distinction of definition noted above. In 1 Corinthians 9:13 Paul, addressing the issue of whether "those who proclaim the gospel should get their living by the gospel," uses the analogy of the actual physical temple. He uses the word *hieron* to indicate the place where the priests offered up animal sacrifices on the altar (1 Cor 9:13), which was situated in the outer court (see Ex 27—29, 40). When Paul refers to the abominable act of the "man of lawlessness," who usurps God's place in the temple, he uses the word *naos*—the word that designates the place of the deity's presence (1 Thess 2:4).

In all the other Pauline passages, *naos* is used metaphorically—to depict a human habitation for the divine Spirit. In one instance the sanctuary image is used to describe the individual believer's body (1 Cor 6:19); in every other instance the sanctuary depicts Christ's body, the church (1 Cor 3:16-17; 2 Cor 6:16; Eph 2:21).

8.2. Temple and the People of God.

8.2.1. 1 and 2 Corinthians. In arguing for sexual purity Paul asks the Corinthians, "Do you not know that your body is a temple [sanctuary] of the *Holy Spirit within you, which you have from God, and that you are not your own?" (1 Cor 6:19 NRSV). It is possible that some of the Corinthian believers still frequented the pagan temples and had intercourse with the temple prostitutes; in so doing, Paul argued, they became one body with a prostitute (1 Cor 6:16). But Christ has redeemed them so that they might become united to him, for "anyone united to the Lord becomes one spirit [with him]" (1 Cor 6:17). Each person who has been spiritually united to the Lord is his holy dwelling place; his or her body belongs to the Lord and must not be given to or joined with a prostitute. Those sanctified by the Lord are now his holy temple (as contrasted with a pagan temple), where he dwells by means of the Holy Spirit.

1 Corinthians 6:19 is the only Pauline passage that describes the individual believer as God's temple. Mistakenly, it is sometimes thought that 1 Corinthians 3:16-17 also speaks of the individual. According to the Greek text, it is unquestionably clear that Paul in 1 Corinthians 3:16-17 is not speaking about the individual but the local church in Corinth when he says, *ouk oidate hoti naos theou este kai to pneuma tou theou oikei en hymin* ("do you [plural] not know that you [plural] are God's temple and that the Spirit of God dwells in you [plural]?"). In the same vein, Paul in 2 Corinthians 6:16—7:1 speaks of believers corporately as "the temple of the living God" and applies to them Ezekiel's rendition of the old covenant's promise of the divine presence in Israel's midst (Ezek 37:27). Because they are inhabited by the holy God, they must live in holiness.

When the Corinthians heard Paul's analogy in 1 Corinthians of the church as God's sanctuary, they would have understood the image from their knowledge of pagan temples. But Paul probably had in mind the one temple in Jerusalem. The Gentiles had many gods with many temples in many cities; the Jews had one God with one temple in one place that he had chosen (cf. Deut 12). In the history of Israel this had helped to preserve the unity and identity of the people of God. The Corinthians needed spiritual unity, for they were fragmented due to their individual preferences (see 1 Cor 1:10-13). In the context of the letter Paul emphasizes the need for the Corinthians to see that God was producing one spiritual habitation in Corinth. God had given them many workers (such as Paul and Apollos) to lay the foundation (*themelios*; cf. Ps 118:22; Is 28:16; Eph 2:20-22) for this sanctuary (1 Cor 3:9-15); it was their responsibility to build (*oikodomeō*) with the right materials and not destroy the building with their divisiveness.

Finally, E. E. Ellis has suggested that when Paul writes in 2 Corinthians 5 of the destruction of the earthly "tent" (*skēnē*) and its replacement by a "building [*oikodomē*] from God . . . a house [*oikos*] not made with hands, eternal in heaven," he is speaking not of individual bodies but of the corporate "body" of Christ conceived as a new temple. In so doing Paul reflects the tradition of Jesus that he would destroy "this temple" and build one "not made by hands" (Mk 14:58; cf. Jn 2:19) and the early Christian tradition that God does not live in houses built by hands (Acts 7:48-49) but was now rebuilding David's "fallen tent" (Acts 15:16-18; cf. Amos 9:11-12; see Ellis).

8.2.2. Ephesians. In Ephesians 2:14-15 Christ is said to have destroyed the "dividing wall of hostility," referring to his abolishing the enmity between Jews and Gentiles and making them into one "new humanity." Commentators frequently identify the "wall" with the barrier in the temple dividing the Court of the Gentiles from the Court of Women. This barrier, beyond which no Gentile was to venture on pain of death, has been figuratively torn down in Christ.

The Ephesian passage goes on to speak of the local churches as living, organic entities which are all (corporately speaking) growing "into a holy sanctuary [*naon hagion*] in the Lord" (Eph 2:21). This interpretation depends on the textual variant, *pasa oikodomē* (supported by ℵ* B D 33 1739* and the text printed in NA[26]), which could be rendered as "every building" (i.e., every local church). The other reading, *pasa hē oikodomē* (found in ℵ[1] A C P 1739[c]), translated as "all the building" (referring to the universal church), is a scribal correction. Paul pictures each local church as providing God with a spiritual habitation in that locality (Eph 2:22) and as growing together with all the other churches into one holy, universal sanctuary for the Lord's indwelling. The several words derived from *oikos* in Ephesians 2:19-22 (*paroikoi, oikeioi, epoikodomethentēs, oikodomē, synoikodomeisthē, katoiketērion*) suggest that the "building" metaphor was closely associated with that of "temple" (cf. 1 Tim 3:15; note 2 Sam 7 where "house" is used alternately of David's home and dynasty, and the house David proposes to build for Yahweh; cf. Is 66:1; Jer 12:7; Hos 9:8, 15; Zech 9:8; 1QS 5:6; 8:5, 9; CD 3:19).

8.3. Temple and Christology. Finally, Paul seems to apply one aspect of temple imagery to Christ. In Colossians 1:19 Paul speaks of Christ as the one "in whom all the fullness was pleased to dwell," and in Colossians 2:9 he writes "in him all the fullness of deity dwells bodily." The language of God being "pleased to dwell" is used in Psalm 68:16 (LXX 67:16; cf. Deut 12:5) of Zion, the mountain where God would reside forever, and it is later appropriated to speak of divine Wisdom taking up residence in Zion (Sir 24:3-12). In the OT the glory of God which is said to "fill" the whole earth (Ps 72:19; Jer 23:24; Is 6:3) comes to "fill" his temple (Ezek 43:5). So the "fullness" of God being "pleased to dwell" in Christ suggests an application of the temple metaphor to the incarnation. [P. W. Comfort]

9. Early Christian Assimilation of the Temple's Function.

Jesus' conception at the end of his ministry was that his meals, his wine and bread, were more acceptable to God as "blood" and "flesh" than were sacrifices in the temple. In the circles of Peter and of James, as well as in other communities of primitive Christianity, a cultic understanding of the meal was preserved (and developed further). That practice led naturally to the claim that a church at worship took the place of the temple.

The theme is evident in Pauline and deutero-Pauline passages such as 1 Corinthians 3:16-17; 6:19; 2 Corinthians 6:14—7:1; Ephesians 2:19-22 (see 8 above). Comparable claims in the Dead Sea Scrolls (see, for example 1QS 9:5-6) demonstrate that the assimilation of cultic functions by a community need not imply that the temple is no longer the place of divinely mandated worship. The Essenes envisaged their place in the temple, as did James, Peter and Paul.

The assimilation of the functions of the temple, however, could develop into the expectation of its eschatological replacement. The Revelation of John represents that development clearly. The confident statement in the vision of the New

Jerusalem in Revelation 21:22, "I saw no temple" in the city, probably reflects the awareness that the edifice had been destroyed as a result of the Roman siege of Jerusalem. But the theology of the passage is its real contribution, "for its temple is the Lord God the almighty and the Lamb." Here a major theme of the Revelation, that Jesus as the Lamb of God is the object of heavenly worship (see Rev 5 and Jn 1:29), finds its climax. In time to come, Jesus is to assume all the value of the temple itself.

The theme of the eschatological replacement of the temple is also voiced in the Gospels. The most obvious case is the interpreted compendium of Jesus sayings in Mark 13 (with Mt 24—25; Lk 21:5-36), a complex of material developing an apocalyptic scenario in which the most important elements are the destruction of the temple and Jesus' coming as the triumphant Son of Man of Daniel 7.

A less obvious instance of the theme of the eschatological replacement of the temple is the way in which Jesus' occupation of the temple is presented in Mark 11:15 and Matthew 21:12, but not in Luke 19:45. Instead of simply objecting on the ground of purity to trading in the temple, Jesus is made to attack those who were changing money for the annual tax of the half-shekel. The fact of the matter is that, every year, money changing for that purpose went on publicly throughout Israel. The process commenced a full month before Passover, with a proclamation concerning the tax (*m. Šeqal.* 1:1), and exchanges were set up in the provinces ten days before they were set up in the temple (*m. Šeqal.* 1:3). Moreover, according to Josephus the tax was not even limited to those resident in the land of Israel (Josephus *J.W.* 7.6.6 §218; *Ant.* 18.9.1 §312), so that the procedure itself would not have been stopped by the sort of interruption the Gospels describe.

For reasons which have already been discussed, Jesus' occupation of the temple for the purpose of expelling vendors should be acknowledged as fully historical. The additional aspect of expelling the money changers provided warrant at a later stage for the refusal of churches to participate in the collection of the half-shekel (both in Jerusalem and abroad). John's picture (Jn 2:13-17), in which the smaller coins involved in the sale of animals were scattered, is historically plausible, but also shows (in Jn 2:17-22) how the tradition developed toward the symbol of eschatological replacement which Matthew and Mark present in narrative terms with the expulsion of the money changers.

10. Theology of Definitive Replacement of the Temple.

The Epistle to the Hebrews spells out how Jesus' replacement of the temple is not simply eschatological but already accomplished and definitive. Chapter 9 of Hebrews begins with the "first" covenant's regulations for sacrifice, involving the temple in Jerusalem. Specific mention is made of the menorah, the table and presented bread in the holy place, with the holy of holies empty but for the gold censer and the ark of the covenant (Heb 9:2-5). The reference to the censer as being in the holy of holies fixes the point in time of which the author speaks: it can only be the Day of Atonement, when the high priest made his single visit to that sanctum, censer in hand (Lev 16).

That precise moment is only specified in order to be fixed, frozen forever. For Hebrews, what was a fleeting movement in the case of the high priest was an eternal truth in the case of Jesus. The movement of ordinary priests, in and out of the holy place, the "first tabernacle" (Heb 9:6), while the high priest could only enter "the second tabernacle," the holy of holies (Heb 9:7), once a year, was designed by the Spirit of God as a parable: the way into the holy of holies could not be revealed while the first temple, the first tabernacle and its service, continued (Heb 9:8-10). That way could only be opened, after the temple was destroyed, by Christ, who became high priest and passed through "the greater and more perfect tabernacle" of his body (Heb 9:11) by the power of his own blood (Heb 9:12) so that he could find eternal redemption in the sanctuary.

Signal motifs within the Gospels are developed in the Hebrews passage. The identification of Jesus' death and the destruction of the temple, which the Gospels achieve in narrative terms, is assumed to be complete. (It is not even clear what exactly the author made of the interim between the two events.) Moreover, the passage takes it for granted that Jesus' body was a kind of "tabernacle," an instrument of sacrifice (Heb 9:11), apparently because the Gospels speak of his offering his body and his blood in the words of institution. (And John, of course, actually has Jesus refer to "the temple of his body," Jn 2:21.) "Body" and "blood" here are Jesus' self-immolating means to his purpose as high priest. The temple in Jerusalem has in Hebrews been replaced by a purely ideological construct. The true high priest has entered once for all (Heb 9:12) within the innermost recess of sanctity, so that no further sacrificial action is necessary or appropriate.

From the perspective of Hebrews there is only a short step to that of the *Epistle of Barnabas* (c. A.D. 130), where it is held that "the spiritual temple," God's word dwelling in the believer, takes the place of the temple of Jerusalem (*Barn.* 16.6-10). The physical temple was always a mistaken attempt to worship God; it was destined for destruction (*Barn.* 16.1-5). A proper, allegorical reading of such rites as the Day of Atonement (*Barn.* 7.3-11) and the red heifer (*Barn.* 8.1-7) testifies to the reality of Christ at the heart of Israel's Scripture; he is the truth behind the veil of the temple. [B. Chilton]

See also DESTRUCTION OF JERUSALEM; JERUSALEM; LITURGY: QUMRAN; LITURGY: RABBINIC; SACRIFICE AND TEMPLE SERVICE; SYNAGOGUES; TEMPLE SCROLL (11QTEMPLE); TEMPLES, GRECO-ROMAN.

BIBLIOGRAPHY. G. A. Anderson, *Sacrifices and Offerings in Ancient Israel: Studies in Their Social and Political Importance* (HSMS 41; Atlanta: Scholars Press, 1987); T. S. Beall, *Josephus' Description of the Essenes Illustrated by the Dead Sea Scrolls* (SNTSMS 58; Cambridge: Cambridge University Press, 1988); T. A. Busink, *Der Tempel von Jerusalem von Salomo bis Herodes: Eine archäologisch-historische Studie unter Berücksichtigung des westsemitischen Tempelbaus* (2 vols.; SFSMD 3; Leiden: E. J. Brill, 1970, 1980); B. Chilton, *The Temple of Jesus: His Sacrificial Program Within a Cultural History of Sacrifice* (University Park: Pennsylvania State University Press, 1992); idem, "[ὡς] φραγέλλιον ἐκ σχοινίων [John 2:15]," in *Templum Amicitiae: Essays on the Second Temple Presented to Ernst Bammel*, ed. W. Horbury (JSNTSup 48; Sheffield: Sheffield Academic Press, 1991) 330-44; J. Coppins, "The Spiritual Temple in the Pauline Letters and Its Background," *SE* 6 (1973) 53-66; J. D. G. Dunn, *The Partings of the Ways: Between Christianity and Judaism and Their Significance for the Character of Christianity* (Philadelphia: Trinity Press International, 1991); E. E. Ellis, "II Corinthians V.1-10 in Pauline Eschatology," *NTS* 6 (1959-60) 211-24; V. Eppstein, "The Historicity of the Gospel Account of the Cleansing of the Temple," *ZNW* 55 (1964) 42-58; C. A. Evans, "Jesus' Action in the Temple: Cleansing or Portent of Destruction?" *CBQ* 51 (1989) 237-70; idem, "Jesus' Action in the Temple and Evidence of Corruption in the First-Century Temple," *SBLSP* 28 (1989) 522-39; B. Gärtner, *The Temple and the Community in Qumran and the New Testament* (SNTSMS 1; Cambridge: Cambridge University Press, 1965); J. Gnilka, "2 Cor 6:14-7:1 in the Light of the Qumran Texts and the Testaments of the Twelve Patriarchs," in *Paul and Qumran: Studies in New Testament Exegesis*, ed. J. Murphy-O'Connor (London: Chapman, 1968) 48-86; R. G. Hamerton-Kelly, "The Temple and the Origins of Jewish Apocalyptic," *VT* 20 (1970) 1-15; M. Haran, *Temples and Temple-Service in Ancient Israel: An Inquiry into the Character of Cult Phenomena and the Historical Setting of the Priestly School* (London: Oxford University Press, 1978); C. T. R. Hayward, *The Jewish Temple: A Non-Biblical Sourcebook* (London and New York: Routledge, 1996); J. Jeremias, *Jesus' Promise to the Nations* (Philadelphia: Fortress, 1982) 65-70; B. A. Levine, *In the Presence of the LORD: A Study of Cult and Some Cultic Terms in Ancient Israel* (SJLA 5; Leiden: E. J. Brill, 1974); J. Maier, "The Architectural History of the Temple in Jerusalem in the Light of the Temple Scroll," in *Temple Scroll Studies*, ed. G. Brooke (JSPSup 7; Sheffield: Sheffield Academic Press, 1989) 23-62; I. H. Marshall, "Church and Temple in the New Testament," *TynB* 40 (1989) 203-22; B. Mazar and G. Cornfeld, *The Mountain of the Lord* (Garden City, NY: Doubleday, 1975); R. J. McKelvey, *The New Temple: The Church in the New Testament* (Oxford: Oxford University Press, 1969); O. Michel, "ναός" *TDNT* 4:880-90; J. Patrich, "Reconstructing the Magnificent Temple Herod Built," *BRev* 4.5 (1988) 16-29; K. and L. Ritmeyer, "Reconstructing Herod's Temple Mount in Jerusalem," *BAR* 15.6 (1989) 23-42; C. Roth, "The Cleansing of the Temple and Zechariah XIV 21," *NovT* 4 (1960) 174-81; E. P. Sanders, *Judaism: Practice and Belief 63 BCE-66 CE* (Philadelphia: Trinity Press International, 1992); idem, "The Synoptic Jesus and the Law," in *Jewish Law from Jesus to the Mishnah* (Philadelphia: Fortress, 1990) 1-96; G. Schrenk, "ἱερός κτλ," *TDNT* 3:221-47; W. R. Smith, *Lectures on the Religion of the Semites: Burnett Lectures* (London: Black, 1901 [1889]); M. Stone, "Lists of Revealed Things in the Apocalyptic Literature," in *Magnalia Dei: The Mighty Acts of God*, ed. F. M. Cross (Garden City,

NY: Doubleday, 1976) 414-52; R. de Vaux, *Ancient Israel. 2: Religious Institutions* (New York: McGraw-Hill, 1965); M. Weinfeld, *Deuteronomy and the Deuteronomic School* (Oxford: Clarendon Press, 1972); K. Wengst, *Tradition und Theologie des Barnabasbriefes* (AK 42; Berlin: Walter de Gruyter, 1971); M. O. Wise, *A Critical Study of the Temple Scroll from Qumran Cave 11* (SAOC 49; Chicago: Oriental Institute, 1990); N. T. Wright, *The New Testament and the People of God* (COQG 1; Minneapolis: Fortress, 1992); R. K. Yerkes, *Sacrifice in Greek and Roman Religions and Early Judaism: The Hale Lectures* (New York: Scribner's, 1952).

B. Chilton, P. W. Comfort and M. O. Wise

TEMPLE INSCRIPTION. *See* INSCRIPTIONS AND PAPYRI: GRECO-ROMAN.

TEMPLE SCROLL (11QTEMPLE)

The *Temple Scroll* is the longest of the *Dead Sea Scrolls; in the name of *Moses, it mandates many extrabiblical laws and the construction of a huge *temple unlike any that ever stood in Jerusalem. Since 1960 the scroll has been known to exist; in that year portions of it were first surreptitiously examined. Only in June 1967, however, was the scroll acquired for study and publication. As a consequence of the Six Day War, the Old City of Jerusalem came at that time into Israeli hands. Knowing of the scroll's whereabouts, the Israeli general and archaeologist Y. Yadin gathered a troop of soldiers and paid a visit to Kando, the Palestinian antiquities dealer in whose hands the scroll resided. Yadin found the scroll stuffed under a bed, wrapped in a shoe box and rapidly deteriorating. He immediately confiscated it. Kando was later compensated by the Israeli government in the amount of $100,000, substantially less than he might have received through sale on the open market.

Yadin always gave the ultimate provenance of the scroll as Qumran Cave 11, and scholars have accepted that idea as entirely plausible; but why Yadin thought that designation correct he never explained. Perhaps he knew more than he felt free to say. Scholars have officially designated Yadin's copy of the scroll, by far the best preserved, as 11Q19 (11QTemple[a]). Subsequently, a second, fragmentary copy of the scroll was identified, this one unquestionably from Cave 11, 11Q20 (11QTemple[b]). A third copy from that cave has also tentatively been identified, but the remains are so exiguous that certain identification is impossible (11Q21 or 11QTemple[c]). Most recently, a fourth copy of the *Temple Scroll* has emerged from Cave 4 (4Q524).

Some scholars believe that yet another fragmentary scroll from Cave 4, designated 4Q365a, represents a fifth exemplar of the *Temple Scroll*. The matter is uncertain because the fragments in question were produced by the same scribe who was responsible for a copy of a different composition, known as *Pentateuchal Paraphrase* (4Q365). The problematic fragments may therefore belong to 4Q365 itself, portions of which were then recast by the author of the *Temple Scroll* for his own purposes. In that scenario, *Pentateuchal Paraphrase* becomes a source for the *Temple Scroll*. Thus scholars have identified at least four and perhaps five copies of the work.

1. Contents and General Features of the *Temple Scroll*
2. Issues of Interpretation
3. Importance of the *Temple Scroll*

1. Contents and General Features of the *Temple Scroll*.

The *Temple Scroll* is the longest of the Dead Sea Scrolls, longer even than the famous **Isaiah Scroll* from Cave 1: comprising 66 columns, it measures more than 28 feet when it is unrolled. It lacks columns 67 on; how much longer the scroll once was, none can say, but slight portions of the lost material have survived in 4Q524. All extant copies of the work begin with a general exhortation derived from Exodus 34, Deuteronomy 7 and perhaps Deuteronomy 12, but some material is missing from the beginning. Indeed, all the early columns of the writing are badly broken or missing in every copy, but as it stands the initial exhortation did not exceed one or one and one-half columns in length. There follows a lengthy program for the construction of a central temple complex surrounded by three square courtyards. In 11Q19 this description occupies virtually all of columns 3-46, apart from a break in columns 13-29 for the insertion of a *festival calendar. Beginning in column 45—thus overlapping the building instructions—are a series of *purity laws, derived by *midrashic techniques from portions of Numbers and Leviticus. In columns 51-66, the redactor of the *Temple Scroll* presents a form of the laws of Deuteronomy 12—26, with some interesting additions and omissions, the pattern of which is a key to the scroll's purpose. The preserved portions end in the middle of a discussion on improper *marriage.

A striking aspect of the *Temple Scroll* is that its author or redactor has eliminated the name of Moses where it should appear in his biblical excerpts. This omission has the effect of rendering the biblical portions direct communication between the scroll's author and God. The work is thus one form or another of *pseudepigraphy. The author may be claiming to have found a long-lost writing from the hands of Moses—the patriarch's notes, as it were, which he later used to write the Bible—containing things that Moses chose not to reveal to the generality of his readership. Or, the author may have been even more audacious. He could be suggesting that Moses' prophetic mantel has fallen to him. Thus he becomes the "prophet like Moses" (Deut 18:15) whom certain elements of society in the late Second Temple period expected as a herald of the eschaton.

2. Issues of Interpretation.
Research on the *Temple Scroll* has focused on four basic and interrelated questions: who composed the scroll and for what purpose; how and when was it done? The answers have naturally been various. Beginning with the scroll's original editor, Yadin, most students of the text have connected it with a community thought to have inhabited the site of Khirbet *Qumran. Because of that presumed connection, they have defined the text as sectarian. Still, a sizeable minority of scholarship argues that the *Temple Scroll* is not sectarian.

Yadin presented three arguments for the sectarian origin of the scroll. First, he pointed to the laws it contains and parallels with these laws in other sectarian writings, notably the **Damascus Document*. Second, he isolated special sectarian terminology; and third, he highlighted various sorts of parallels between the *Temple Scroll* and other Dead Sea texts, including **Jubilees*.

L. Schiffman, an early opponent of the sectarian view, countered Yadin's linguistic argument with one of his own: "the basic terms and expressions of Qumran literature," he argued, "are completely absent" (Schiffman, 149). He further stressed that the underlying principles by which the *Temple Scroll* derived its laws from the Bible were different from those operative in other Qumran legal literature (*see* Legal Texts at Qumran). H. Stegemann likewise opposed the notion that a putative Qumran community composed the work. For him, they merely treasured it as an outside writing whose views were attractive. The work's laws, he noted, are "unqumranisch," unlike those of previously identified sectarian writings. Moreover, the feasts mandated by the scroll lack analogies in other Dead Sea texts, Stegemann argued; and the scroll contains no hint of a polemic against the *Hasmonean merging of high-priestly and royal functions. B. Levine was a third scholar who grouped the *Temple Scroll* with texts such as *Jubilees*, **1 Enoch* and the **Psalms Scroll* from Cave 11—texts that the Qumran sect preserved, he said, but did not write.

More recent work on the *Temple Scroll* has emphasized the work's composite character. If these views are correct, then arguments about the connection of the text to other sectarian writings from Qumran must focus on the portions of the *Temple Scroll* that can be shown, if possible, to have connections with the final redactor. Then the question becomes whether or not the redactor was a sectarian. This research tends to favor the idea that one or more members of the sectarian movement reworked earlier, nonsectarian sources to produce the *Temple Scroll*. Thus, on the matter of provenance, the situation appears to be one of both/and: the work binds together earlier, nonsectarian sources using as its glue a sectarian redaction.

As to the reasons for producing the *Temple Scroll*, Yadin argued that it was intended as a tool in the context of contemporary legal polemics. The text was thus a sort of crib sheet to aid halakic study. Stegemann agreed that the Qumran sectarians read the scroll primarily to learn how to harmonize divergent Halakoth. A few other scholars have followed suit. But more recently the question of the scroll's purpose has focused on the definition of its relationship to the Bible, Deuteronomy in particular. Redaction criticism shows that the *Temple Scroll* purposefully includes or excludes all of the laws from the Deuteronomic law (Deut 12—26). These are the laws that Deuteronomy says are to apply when the children of Israel begin to live in the land. It seems that the redactor of the *Temple Scroll* intended his work, like Deuteronomy 12—26, as a collection of laws for life in the land. And while some scholars have argued that the work is merely a reprise and supplement to the book of Deuteronomy, the fact that the redactor purposely left out some of Deuteronomy's laws argues that he intended to replace the biblical book altogether.

The notion that the *Temple Scroll* was prepared as a collection of laws for life in the promised land fits well with the ideology of the **Damascus Document* in particular. According to that work, the sectarians were presently in exile, just as Israel had been during the forty years of wandering in the desert. The typologically minded sectarians of the *Damascus Document* believed, however, that at the end of "the forty years" they would come to power. This event would mark their taking of the land just as surely as Joshua's conquest had marked the biblical precedent. Given this typological connection, it is attractive to think that the group believed that the *Temple Scroll* would take effect when the exile was over. Its laws would now be the laws one must follow, and its temple would now be built and stand in Jerusalem. The old laws of Moses, given in Deuteronomy, would largely continue in force, but some of the particulars would cease to be relevant. Those still to be in force were gathered in the *Temple Scroll*. New laws were added as well. These added laws are the place where sectarian connections exist, for the additions restate or supplement legal ideas known from multiple sectarian writings. If this line of analysis is correct, then the *Temple Scroll* was fashioned as a law for the eschaton, the latter conceived in a mundane fashion à la the prophets. The eschatological significance of the *Temple Scroll* was first argued by B. Z. Wacholder.

Suggested dates for the *Temple Scroll* have varied enormously. Stegemann has proposed the earliest option. He sees the arrival of Ezra in Jerusalem with a Persian-backed official law as the catalyst to gather together traditional materials now outlawed. Thus the work would date to the fifth or fourth century B.C. Most scholars prefer a date somewhere in the range of 150 to 60 B.C., and this assignment is most likely. It should be noted, however, that the text itself contains little, if anything, that can be dated: neither the language nor its contents lend themselves to such analysis. Moreover, if the *Temple Scroll* is a composite work, as seems likely, its constituent parts might reflect various *Sitze im Leben* and the final redaction quite another. Some scholars hold that the *Temple Scroll* was composed by the Teacher of Righteousness; if so, then its date is obviously connected to his period of activity. That connection points to the favored period noted above, 150 to 60 B.C., but the dating then depends on elements external to the text itself.

3. Importance of the *Temple Scroll*.

In addition to its importance for the understanding of many phenomena of the Dead Sea Scrolls and their readers and writers, the *Temple Scroll* is crucial to issues involved with the study of pseudepigraphy among Jews and early Christians in the period 200 B.C. to A.D. 135. Further, the work is an invaluable source for understanding Jewish legal or halakic developments during those years. Together with other Dead Sea Scrolls such as **Miqṣat Maʿaśey ha-Torah* (4QMMT) and the *Toharot* texts (*see* Purification Texts), the *Temple Scroll* represents another approach (or perhaps other approaches) to many of the legal questions considered in *rabbinic literature. Comparison of these materials is already opening up new perspectives on life and ideas of how to live in the Palestine from which emerged both Christianity and rabbinic Judaism.

See also TEMPLE, JEWISH.

BIBLIOGRAPHY. P. B. Bean, "A Theoretical Construct for the Temple of the Temple Scroll" (Ph.D. diss., University of Oregon, 1987); G. Brooke, ed., *Temple Scroll Studies* (JSPSup 7; Sheffield: JSOT, 1989); F. García Martínez, E. J. C. Tigchelaar and A. S. van der Woude, "11QTemple[b]," in *Qumran Cave 11.2: 11Q2-18, 11Q20-31* (DJD 23; Oxford: Clarendon Press, 1998) 357-409; idem, "11QTemple[c]," in idem, 411-14; B. Levine, "The Temple Scroll: Aspects of its Historical Provenance and Literary Character," *BASOR* 232 (1978) 5-23; É. Puech, "4QRouleau du Temple," in *Qumrân Grotte 4.18: Textes Hébreux (4Q521-4Q528, 4Q576-4Q579)* (DJD 25; Oxford: Clarendon Press, 1998) 85-114; E. Qimron, *The Temple Scroll: A Critical Edition with Extensive Reconstructions*, F. García Martínez Bibliography (Jerusalem: Ben-Gurion University of the Negev Press and Israel Exploration Society, 1996); L. Schiffman, "The Temple Scroll in Literary and Philological Perspective," in *Approaches to Ancient Judaism*, vol. 2, ed. W. S. Green (Chico, CA: Scholars Press, 1980) 143-58; H. Stegemann, "The Origins of the Temple Scroll," *Supplements to Vetus Testamentum* 40 (Congress Volume, Jerusalem 1986) 235-56; D. Swanson, *The Temple Scroll and the Bible* (STDJ 14; Leiden: E. J. Brill, 1995); B. Z. Wacholder, *The Dawn of Qumran: The Sectarian Torah and the Teacher of Righteousness* (Cincinnati: Hebrew Union College Press, 1983); B. Z.

Wacholder with M. Abegg Jr., "The Fragmentary Remains of 11QTorah (Temple Scroll)," *HUCA* 62 (1991) 1-116; S. White, "4QTemple?" in *Qumran Cave 4.8: Parabiblical Texts, Part 1,* ed. H. W. Attridge et al. (DJD 13; Oxford: Clarendon Press, 1994) 319-33; M. O. Wise, *A Critical Study of the Temple Scroll from Qumran Cave 11* (SAOC 49; Chicago: Oriental Institute Press, 1990); Y. Yadin, *The Temple Scroll* (3 vols.; Jerusalem: Israel Exploration Society, 1983); idem, *The Temple Scroll: Hidden Law of the Dead Sea Sect* (London: Weidenfeld & Nicolson, 1985). M. O. Wise

TEMPLE SERVICE. *See* SACRIFICE AND TEMPLE SERVICE.

TEMPLES, GRECO-ROMAN

Greek and Roman temples were largely similar, not only in form but also in function. As the monumental part of the larger sanctuary, their chief function was to house the cult statue of the deity; they did not usually serve as places for collective worship. Temples also had a variety of ancillary functions: they served as storehouses for votive offerings, banks, places of refuge and, notably, as exempla of political propaganda.

1. Greek Temples
2. Roman Temples

1. Greek Temples.

The Greek temple (*hieron, hedos*) was the residence of the deity. It was commonly the dominant feature of the larger *temenos,* the sacred precinct dedicated to a divinity. The Greek word *naos* can also denote "temple," but more often it refers to the inner room of the temple housing the image of the deity. The earliest Greek temples began to appear in the eighth century B.C., as corporate productions of the newly emergent city states (*poleis*). Originally rather simple wooden or mudbrick structures, by the sixth century they had evolved into elaborate stone, often marble, edifices. The main lineaments of the Greek temple, though not without notable variations in size and structure, remained relatively constant for centuries. Its main component was a rectangular room, the *cella,* which housed the cult image at one end. The entrance was at the other (usually eastern) end, where the walls of the *cella* extended to form a columned porch at one end or at both ends. Sometimes a smaller room, the *adyton,* was situated behind the *cella.* Most temples also featured columns surrounding the *cella,* the external colonnade, usually with six columns at each end and thirteen on either side. Larger temples included interior columns both as decoration and as a support for the roof beams and tiles. The roof was gently gabled, allowing for sculpted pediments in the more elaborate temples. Sculptured panels called metopes and sculptured friezes might also appear above the colonnade.

Urban temples would commonly be situated in the heart of a *polis,* either on the acropolis or near the *agora* ("marketplace"), though occasionally temples were located outside the city walls (*see* Cities, Greco-Roman). Some city-states also oversaw temples in the rural hinterland, either as "extraurban" or in a few cases "pan-Hellenic" sanctuaries (Marinatos and Hägg, 229-30). The former was under the direct political control of the *polis.* The latter was also overseen by a city, Olympia by Elis, for instance, but it preserved an air of neutrality. Here, even in wartime, pan-Hellenic festivals such as the Olympics would be held in the god's sanctuary for participants from all over Greece.

The chief function of the temple was to provide a monumental residence for the deity, who was present in the form of the anthropomorphic cult image. With the notable exception of the *mysteries, worshipers did not meet in the temple for the observance of collective rites, but within the temple precincts. The most important rite, the sacrifice, would be performed on the altar (*bēmos*) situated in front of the temple. The image of the god would preside from inside the cella, and participants in the sacrifice would eat outside in the temenos area, which sometimes included kitchen and dining facilities.

Worshipers were not, however, categorically excluded from the house of the god. Groups of devotees could enter periodically to cleanse the cult image or, as in the Great Panathenaea at Athens, to adorn it with a new garment. Individuals who were ritually pure were usually (with various exceptions) allowed to enter the *cella* to do homage to the deity, to offer up prayers or even to sightsee (Herodas 4.39-95; cf. Corbett).

The temple and occasionally other buildings ("treasuries") within the *temenos* served as repositories for thank offerings dedicated by individuals, groups or the state. These could include, among other things, statuary, votive images, bronze cauldrons, weapons of vanquished enemies and gold and silver plate. Because temples were theoretically inviolable, they also commonly served as banks for individuals and the state, imparting sacrosanct status to the items housed within them. This same status could be extended to individuals, and refugees were able to obtain limited asylum within the temple or its *temenos.*

A further function of the temple was political and propagandistic. In the case of the main urban sanctuaries, the *polis* would adopt a deity as its patron (i.e., Athens and Athena), who would provide protection for the city-state. The size and location of the temple would, therefore, be an indication not only of the deity's importance to the *polis* but also a barometer of the wealth and power of the city-state. In the case of Athens, for instance, the magnificence of the Parthenon with its chryselephantine statue of Athena, situated as it was upon the city's acropolis, was a direct advertisement to the magnificence, technical ability and power of Periclean Athens (Plutarch *Per.* 12-13). Within the agonistic context of the Greek city-states, a temple provided a highly visible means of competing with rival states. Extraurban temples exercised a similar function. When they were not neutral pan-Hellenic centers such as Olympia or Delphi, they could serve as a monument to the power of the sponsoring city and a rallying point for the rural populace.

In spite of the decline of the *polis* in the *Hellenistic period, Greek temple complexes continued to flourish. Hellenistic kings and the monied classes continued to provide for the maintenance of older sites as well as for the establishment of new temples and festivals. Nor did the situation appreciably change with the triumph of Rome, as can be seen, for instance, from the reference in Acts (Acts 19:23-41) to the unabated vitality of the Artemesion, the temple (*hieron*) of Artemis in *Ephesus. For the silversmith Demetrius, the temple's greatness was axiomatic; an assumption to which his occupation likewise testifies. The "silver shrines [*naous argyrous*] of Artemis" (Acts 19:24) that he fashioned were not (*pace* Koester, 130 #40) "statues of Artemis standing in a simple, small naiskos," but miniature shrines of the temple or part of the temple (Trebilco, 336-38). His trade, therefore, enabled devotees to take away with them a representation of one of the wonders of the ancient world.

2. Roman Temples.

Properly speaking, the word *templum* designates a tract of land set aside for religious purposes. Eventually, however, it came to be used loosely (as it will be here) for the building (*aedes*) housing the image of the deity. The tract of dedicated land bounded by an enclosure was the *area.* The altar (*ara*) was usually situated in front of the *aedes,* and there the sacrifices would take place. Temples tended to have a western orientation and commanded a clear view of the horizon so that the augurs could take the auspices with an unobstructed view (Varro *Ling* 7.8).

The earliest Roman temples were modeled on Etruscan prototypes (Pliny *Nat. Hist.* 35.154). By the second century B.C., however, they had become a blend of Greek and Etruscan influences (for a detailed classification, see Vitruvius *De Arch.* 3-4). Like urban Greek temples, they tended to be situated at prominent points throughout the city.

Roman temples had a variety of functions. They too housed the image of the deity and served as repositories for a broad spectrum of votive offerings and valuables (the temple of Saturnus in Rome, for example, acting as state treasury). They served as archives and even as libraries. Roman temples were also highly valued as places of assembly. The Roman senate and other official bodies conducted their meetings in temples, and legal hearings were held there. Roman religious associations (*collegia*) would commonly make use of temples as a place for assembling and dining.

Roman temples also had political and propagandistic function. In classical Greece, temple dedication was the prerogative of the state, but in Rome it was open to private individuals subject to the senate's approval. Triumphant generals would often dedicate new temples to commemorate their victories and glorify themselves (cf. Orlin). In the principate, the founding or restoration of temples was particularly associated with the emperor (*see* Roman Emperors). Augustus's establishment of the temple of Mars Ultor, "the Avenger," for instance, helped to celebrate him both as the avenger and the rightful successor to Julius Caesar. He was further able to proclaim his piety by restoring eighty-two temples in disrepair (Augustus *Res Gest.* 20, 21). Naturally, his largesse had the salutary function of making Rome a showcase of imperial power.

Temples to the genius of the emperor and to Roma had an additional function throughout the empire (*see* Ruler Cult). They were able to promote loyalty and obedience among its scattered subjects. In the same way that extraurban temples in Greece could serve as a focal point for local support, temples in the provinces promoted allegiance to Rome. One of the clearest instances of this is *Herod the Great's assiduous construction of a number of temples as part of his building program. *Josephus relates of Herod that "one can mention no suitable spot within his realm, which he left destitute of some mark of homage to Caesar. And then, after filling his own territory with temples, he let the memorials of his esteem overflow into the province and erected in numerous cities monuments to Caesar" (Josephus *J.W.* 1.21.4 §407; cf. 1.21.3 §404; *Ant.* 15.9.5 §328; 15.10.3 §363). In Rome as in Greece, therefore, temples had far more than a purely sacral importance.

See also RELIGION, GRECO-ROMAN; RELIGION, PERSONAL; RULER CULT; TEMPLE, JEWISH.

BIBLIOGRAPHY. H. Berve and G. Gruben, *Greek Temples, Theaters and Shrines* (New York: Abrams, 1963); W. Burkert, "The Meaning and Function of the Temple in Classical Greece," in *Temple in Society,* ed. M. V. Fox (Winona Lake, IN: Eisenbrauns, 1988) 27-47; J. N. Coldstream, "Greek Temples: Why and Where?" in *Greek Religion and Society,* ed. P. E. Easterling and J. V. Muir (Cambridge: Cambridge University Press, 1985) 67-97; P. E. Corbett, "Greek Temples and Greek Worshippers: The Literary and Archaeological Evidence," *Bulletin of the Institute of Classical Studies* 17 (1970) 149-58; H. Koester, ed., *Ephesos: Metropolis of Asia* (HTS 41; Valley Forge, PA: Trinity Press International, 1995); N. Marinatos and R. Hägg, eds., *Greek Sanctuaries: New Approaches* (London and New York: Routledge, 1993); E. M. Orlin, *Temples, Religion and Politics in the Roman Republic* (MnS 164; Leiden: E. J. Brill, 1997); D. W. Roller, The Building Program of Herod the Great (Berkeley and Los Angeles: University of California Press, 1998); J. E. Stambaugh, "The Functions of Roman Temples," *ANRW* 2.16.1 (1978) 554-608; R. A. Tomlinson, *Greek Sanctuaries* (London: Paul Elek, 1976); P. Trebilco, "Asia," in *The Book of Acts in Its Greco-Roman Setting,* ed. D. Gill and C. Gempf (Grand Rapids, MI: Eerdmans, 1994) 291-362.

J. R. C. Cousland

TESTAMENT OF ABRAHAM

The *Testament of Abraham,* as its name implies, is a pseudonymous writing in which Abraham's authority is claimed for a work that originated in the first or second century A.D. Study of this text is complicated by the fact that it exists in two recensions, a longer recension (A), attested by several Greek manuscripts and a Rumanian translation, and a short recension (B), also attested by several Greek manuscripts and a Rumanian translation, together with Coptic, Arabic and Ethiopic versions. It seems that the work was originally written in much the form represented by A and then rewritten in the two principal recensions together with the not-always-precise translations.

The work is charming, and its content, for its ancient readers, was no doubt instructive in its *eschatological teaching. A testament in the context of ancient Jewish literature is the deathbed declaration of a famous person. The *Testament of Abraham* offers a variation on this theme, for Abraham never makes his dying declaration. As the plot unfolds, it becomes clear that the author's interest is in the problem of human death, specifically in the universalism of eschatology.

The unfolding plot is not without comical elements. Its underlying basis is the narrative assertion that the day of Abraham's death has arrived. God sends Michael to break the news to Abraham, telling the patriarch to make his plans for departure by preparing his testament. Abraham initially refuses to listen to Michael but agrees when God offers him a ride through the sky in his chariot so that he can view the universe. One of the things that Abraham sees as he rides is certain sinners committing flagrant transgressions. Abraham righteously calls down divine punishment on these unfortunate people. God then summons the patriarch into his presence so that he can see the judgment process at firsthand and learn the discipline of mercy. Abraham interecdes for a soul whose merits and transgressions are equally balanced, and on that basis decides he must intercede for the souls he had condemned. These are brought back to life for that reason. Abraham is then escorted back to earth by Michael and again told to make his testament. Again he refuses. God finally sends Death to Abraham, who removes his soul by a cunning ruse.

It cannot be denied that here we find a theology of good works such as was caricatured by a whole tradition of Protestant scholarship on *Judaism. This idea is held in common with **2 Enoch* and **3 Baruch*. However, it is fair to say that the *Testament of Abraham* does not offer a developed or exclusivist theology of works and that what it says must be seen within a more generalized perspective. This is one in which good works are enjoined on all people, not just on Jews. Thus there is no reference in the work to the Torah or the covenant as such. The text portrays Judaism as an ethical religion in which both judgment and mercy are prominent themes.

We must also consider what has been called the work's "cosmopolitan humanity" and E. P. Sanders "the lowest-common-denominator universalism of soteriology." This works from the lack of distinction between Jew and Gentile and observes that the only specific reference to Israel is in *Testament of Abraham* 13:6 (A). The result is that every human being is held to be judged by the same standard. There is a surprising lack of any reference to the merits of the patriarchs in a text where, if anywhere, this would have been appropriate.

On the heels of this universalism, the author at least in recension A outlines what appears to be a straightforward theology of judgment. This is that if unrepented or unpunished sins outnumber merits, the soul receives a punishment. If the converse is true, the soul enters life. In the event of a hung jury, it is possible that Abraham's intercessory prayer is intended to serve as a typical instance of what prayer can achieve.

The *Testament of Abraham* is probably an idiosyncratic representative of Egyptian Judaism in the early common era. It lacks the emphasis on conversion found in **Joseph and Aseneth* and also *Philo's insistence on the concept of *Israel. For all that, it offers a comprehensible theodicy that draws attention to the need for ethical action and prescribes an appropriate remedy when things go wrong.

See also TESTAMENT OF JOB; TESTAMENT OF MOSES; TESTAMENT OF QAHAT (4Q542); TESTAMENTS OF THE TWELVE PATRIARCHS.

BIBLIOGRAPHY. M. Delcor, *Le Testament d'Abraham* (SVTP 2; Leiden: E. J. Brill, 1973); G. W. E. Nicklesburg, "Stories of Biblical and Early Post-Biblical Times," in *Jewish Writings of the Second Temple Period,* ed. M. E. Stone (CRINT 2.2; Assen: Van Gorcum; Philadelphia: Fortress, 1984) 60-64; G. W. E. Nickelsburg, ed., *Studies on the Testament of Abraham* (rev. ed.; SCS 6; Missoula, MT: Scholars Press, 1976); E. P. Sanders, "Testament of Abraham," in *The Old Testament Pseudepigrapha,* ed. J. H. Charlesworth (2 vols.; Garden City, NY: Doubleday, 1983, 1985) 1:871-902; F. Schmidt, *Le Testament Grec d'Abraham* (TSAJ 11; Tübingen: Mohr Siebeck, 1986).

J. M. Knight

TESTAMENT OF JOB

Among the lesser known books that existed in the time of Jesus and Paul, the *pseudepigraphic *Testament of Job* embellishes the biblical story of Job in such a way as to denounce idolatry and commend the virtue of patience or endurance (*hypomonē*). Following the style of classic Jewish testaments of the period, such as the **Testaments of the Twelve Patriarchs* and the **Testament of Abraham,* the work opens with a deathbed scene in which Job distributes both property and wisdom. But the book's predictable end, telling of Job's death and *ascent to heaven, comes only after regaling the reader with Job's magnanimous charities, his bravery in destroying an idol's temple, his consequent illness and phylactery-enabled recovery, his encounters with Satan (*see* Belial) in disguise and his steadfast piety in the face of an unsupportive spouse. In a text about the length of Paul's letter to the Romans, the biblical story of Job undergoes a *midrashic retelling, at times humorous and at points poetic.

The *Testament of Job* embodies a variety of interests: traditional Jewish moral exhortation, Jewish monotheistic iconoclasm, *Hellenistic *magic (Kee), a Greek psychopomp, early *merkabah* *mysticism, an interest in female *prophetic employment of *angelic dialects. The *Testament of Job* thus provides a remarkable monument to the mingled strands of variegated Hellenistic Jewish spirituality. Though some Chris-tian editing is possible, scholarly consensus views the book as an essentially or solely Jewish text datable somewhere in the first century before or after Christ.

1. Content and Structure
2. Origin and Purpose
3. Texts and Translations
4. Relation to the Septuagint
5. Backgrounds
6. New Testament Connections
7. State of Research

1. Content and Structure.

As it stands, the *Testament of Job* is framed by a brief prologue (1) presenting the deathbed scene, and an epilogue (*T. Job* 51—53) recounting the death and burial of Job. The unity of the work is questioned by the shift from first person over the bulk of the work (*T. Job* 1—45) to third person in the remaining part of the book (*T. Job* 46—53).

The main section of the book falls into a discernible structure based on Job's dealings first with an angel (*T. Job* 2—5), who warns of catastrophe yet honor if Job destroys a nearby idol shrine. Then Satan (*T. Job* 6—27) assaults Job by coming in disguise as a beggar, one like the many who were repeated beneficiaries of Job's philanthropy. Despite the losses in health, family and wealth, Job endures—accepting Satan's surrender with a line that well summarizes the moral point of the text: "Well then, my children, you also must be patient in everything that happens to you. For patience [*hypomonē*] is better than anything" (*T. Job* 27:7). Next, the three kings (upgraded from the canonical friends) and Elihu (*T. Job* 28—45) visit Job at the dump to comfort him, but only after spending three days spreading perfume to render tolerable the stench of his illness. Finally, when Job's three daughters (*T. Job* 46—50) protest the absence of any distributed inheritance for them, Job replies he has saved the best for them. Job then calls for the quasi-magical, triple-stranded cord or sash (*phylaktērion*) by which he had been cured and by which they are enabled to praise God in the language of the angels, the archons and the cherubim (*T. Job* 48—50). In the epilogue (*T. Job* 51—53) are recorded the preservation of the daughters' hymns by Nereus, brother of Job, along with the death and burial of Job.

2. Origin and Purpose.
While a few authorities (Mai; James; Spittler) have viewed the *Testament of Job* as originated or later edited by Christians, the weight of opinion views the text as a Jewish document. The abundant reference to hymns in the *Testament of Job* led some scholars (Kohler; Philonenko) to conclude a provenance with the *Therapeutae, a Jewish sectarian group in Egypt described by *Philo in *Vita Contemplativa,* a group that practiced spontaneous composition of hymns. Within Jewish circles, the document may have functioned as encouragement to those facing martyrdom (Jacobs) or as Jewish monotheistic missionary propaganda (Rahnenführer).

3. Texts and Translations.
Other than its description as an apocryphon in the sixth-century Gelasian Decree, the *Testament of Job* went unnoticed in antiquity. Reference to Job's worm-ridden illness in Tertullian (*De Pat.* 14.5), the *Visio Pauli* and the *ʾAbot de Rabbi Nathan* may have shared a common origin with the similar story in the *Testament of Job.* Though only narrowly known in the early nineteenth century, the text has come to find a secure place among collections of pseudepigrapha and in exegetical discussions (Garrett) only in the last third of the twentieth century.

The oldest known source for the *Testament of Job* appears in an incomplete and as yet unpublished fifth-century Coptic papyrus (P. Köln 3221). One complete and three partial manuscripts, dating from about the tenth century, survive in Old Church Slavonic. Four Greek manuscripts from the eleventh to the sixteenth centuries reflect three text traditions, one clearly secondary. Development of a critical text awaits publication of the Coptic text. Until then, the standard edition of the Greek text is that published by S. P. Brock in 1967.

Translations in French and Serbo-Croatian (partial) appeared in the second half of the nineteenth century. In the last third of the twentieth century, the *Testament of Job* has appeared in Dutch, English, French, German, Modern Hebrew and Spanish. Additional translations are said to be under preparation in Danish, Modern Greek and Japanese. A convenient source for an English translation appears in the first volume of J. H. Charlesworth's collection of *Old Testament Pseudepigrapha* (Spittler).

4. Relation to the Septuagint.
Though some scholars propose a Semitic origin for the *Testament of Job* (Riessler; Philonenko), no manuscript evidence survives and scholarly consensus now favors a Greek origin. Exact relationships to the *Septuagint are unclear: yet Job 1—2, 29—31, and 42 LXX provide ideas and phrases for the author of the *Testament of Job.* The Septuagintal expansion of the speech of Job's wife (Job 2:9a-e) beyond the Masoretic Text gains even further, though consistent, development in the *Testament of Job*'s considerable narrative elaboration. The *Testament of Job* shows far greater kinship with the Septuagint than with the Hebrew text, most clearly apparent in their common vocabulary. Yet the layered development of the Septuagint cautions definitive theories of dependence one direction or the other.

5. Backgrounds.
Its very form as a testament and use of a prominent biblical figure as the subject tilt the *Testament of Job* toward a Jewish environment. Yet its peculiarities also betray Hellenistic influences.

5.1. Jewish Background. Since Job's fame is remembered both in the OT and the NT (Ezek 14:14, 20; Jas 5:11; interestingly, not in Heb 11, a roll call of the enduring faithful), it comes as no surprise that he gets a testament in his name. The anti-idolatry activism of Job in the *Testament of Job,* no trait of the canonical figure, fits the well-known monotheistic apologetic of Second Temple Judaism. So do the prominent role of Satan, reference to a phylactery (though this could be an extended use of the term *charm*), the ban of foreign *marriages and especially the prominent interests in fitting burial—which are expressed for Job's children, his wife and himself. *Angels, even cherubim and archons, reflect Jewish interests as well.

5.2. Hellenistic Backgrounds. The description of a psychopomp, a descended chariot commissioned to carry off the soul of Job while his body is buried, marks a curious intrusion of non-Jewish imagery into this predominantly Jewish document. That Job's recovery was brought about by a phylactery that also had the power to endow his daughters with a capacity to shift interests heavenward and, using the language of the angels, to praise God and create hymns suggests Hellenistic *magical interests. Focus on the chariot of the psychopomp parallels esoteric Jewish speculation commonly called *merkabah* mysticism (*mrkb* is Hebrew for "chariot"), which represents not the heart of Palestinian Judaism but its more remote margins. Job's triumph over Satan gets told in the familiar imagery of Greek *athletics, used by another Jew of known Hellenistic influence (*T. Job* 27:2-5; 1 Cor 9:24-27).

6. New Testament Connections.
The single place in the NT where Job is mentioned recalls his endurance: "You have heard of the patience *[hypomonē]* of Job" (Jas 5:11). Paul's reference to Satan as an "angel of light" (2 Cor 11:14) can be compared with the master of disguise mentioned in the *Testament of Job* without suggestion of direct influence. Similarly the glossolalic use by Job's daughters of the language of the angels brings to mind Paul's reference to the "tongues of angels" (1 Cor 13:1), making it at least less likely that his reference was a linguistic creation *ex nihilo* while not requiring direct dependence.

7. State of Research.
Apart from the scant earliest modern approaches to the *Testament of Job* in the mid-nineteenth century, three periods of modern investigation into this curious and fascinating text can be identified. A fifteen-year period from 1897 to 1911 resulted in the first published texts (James; Kohler), along with the first English translation (Kohler) and the earliest extensive investigation (Spitta). Little advance occurred between the two world wars, though translations into German (Riessler, 1928) and into Modern Hebrew (Kahana, 1936-37) did appear.

With the publication of Brock's text in 1967, but anticipated by M. Philonenko's links of Qumran with the Therapeutae in 1958, a new generation of study began. The three decades from around 1960 to 1990 saw the publication of two editions of the text (Brock; Kraft), three doctoral dissertations on the *Testament of Job* (Rahnenführer; Nicholls; Spittler) and the preparation of the fresh translations into Dutch, English, French, German, Modern Hebrew and Spanish.

The final period, the decade from the late 1980s onward, mined the rich resources for women's studies. The *Testament of Job* names both Job's first and second wives, uses six separate words for female slaves, celebrates Job's care for widows and lauds the daughters for an inheritance superior to the material legacy of their brothers. At least one scholar suggests possible feminine authorship of the *Testament of Job* (Lefkowitz). Still others tap this text for its portrayal of feminine prophecy (Chesnutt, van der Horst; *see* Women).

The *Testament of Job* thus provides readers of the NT with one example of the popular Jewish literature of the first-century environment. Its role must have been not unlike that of the many thousands of Christian novels that today compete with the canonical texts for the attention of the spiritually minded.

See also APOCRYPHA AND PSEUDEPIGRAPHA; TESTAMENT OF ABRAHAM; TESTAMENT OF MOSES; TESTAMENT OF QAHAT 4Q542; TESTAMENTS OF THE TWELVE PATRIARCHS.

BIBLIOGRAPHY. C. T. Begg, "Comparing Characters: The Book of Job and the *Testament of*

Job," in *The Book of Job,* ed. W. A. M. Beuken (BETL 114; Louvain: Louvain University Press, 1994) 435-45; S. P. Brock, *Testamentum Iobi,* and J.-C. Picard, *Apocalypsis Baruchi Graece* (PsVTG 2; Leiden: E. J. Brill, 1967); R. D. Chesnutt, "Revelatory Experiences Attributed to Biblical Women in Early Jewish Literature," in *Women Like This: New Perspectives on Jewish Women in the Greco-Roman World,* ed. A.-J. Levine (EJL 1; Atlanta: Scholars Press, 1991) 107-25; S. R. Garrett, "The God of This World and the Affliction of Paul," in *Greeks, Romans and Christians,* ed. D. L. Balch, E. Ferguson and W. A. Meeks (Minneapolis: Fortress, 1990) 99-117; idem, "The Weaker Sex in the *Testament of Job,*" *JBL* 112 (1993) 55-70; P. W. van der Horst, "The Role of Women in the Testament of Job," *NedTTs* 40 (1986) 273-89; I. Jacobs, "Literary Motifs in the Testament of Job," *JJS* 21 (1970) 1-10; M. R. James, *Apocrypha Anecdota* II (TSt 5.1; Cambridge: Cambridge University Press, 1897) 104-37; A. Kahana, *Hsprym Hnṣwnym* (Tel Aviv: Masada, 1936-37) 1:515-38; H. C. Kee, "Satan, Magic and Salvation in the Testament of Job," *SBLSP* (1974) 1:53-76; K. Kohler, "The Testament of Job: An Essene Midrash on the Book of Job Reedited and Translated with Introductory and Exegetical Notes," in *Semitic Studies in Memory of A. Kohut,* ed. G. A. Kohut (Berlin: S. Calvary, 1897) 264-338; R. A. Kraft, ed., with H. Attridge, R. Spittler and J. Timbie, *The Testament of Job According to the SV Text* (Texts and Translations 5, Pseudepigrapha Series 4; Missoula, MT: Scholar's Press, 1974); M. R. Lefkowitz, "Did Ancient Women Write Novels?" in *Women Like This: New Perspectives on Jewish Women in the Greco-Roman World,* ed. A.-J. Levine (EJL 1; Atlanta: Scholars Press, 1991) 199-219; A. Mai, *Scriptorum Veterum Nova Collectio e Vaticanis Codicibus Edita* (10 vols.; Rome: Typis Vaticanis, 1953) 7:cols. 180-91; P. H. Nicholls, "The Structure and Purpose of the Testament of Job" (Ph.D. diss., Hebrew University, 1982); M. Philonenko, "Le Testament de Job: Introduction, Traduction et Notes," *Sem* 18 (1968) 1-75; D. Rahnenführer, "Das Testament des Hiob und das Neue Testament," *ZNW* 62 (1971) 68-93; P. Riessler, *Altjüdisches Schrifttum ausserhalb der Bible* (Augsburg: Filser, 1928) 1104-34; B. Schaller, "Das Testament Hiob" (JSHRZ 3.3; Gütersloh: Gerd Mohn, 1979); idem, "Das Testament Hiobs und die Septuaginta-Übersetzung des Buches Hiob," *Bib* 61 (1980) 377-406; F. Spitta, "Das Testament Hiobs und das Neue Testament," *Zur Geschichte und Literatur des Urchristentums* 3.2 (Göttingen: Vandenhoeck & Ruprecht, 1907) 132-206; R. P. Spittler, "The Testament of Job," in *The Old Testament Pseudepigrapha,* ed. J. H. Charlesworth (2 vols.; Garden City, NY: Doubleday, 1983, 1985) 1:829-68; idem, "The Testament of Job: Introduction, Translation and Notes" (Ph.D. diss., Harvard University, 1971);

R. P. Spittler

TESTAMENT OF MOSES

The *Testament of Moses* was written by an unknown Jew and received its present shape in the first decades of the common era. Purporting to represent the last words of *Moses to Joshua, the book encourages Jews to remain loyal to *Torah no matter what deprivation may result. The author provides support for such dedication by emphasizing God's providence, which assures *Israel an exalted future, and God's covenant and oath, which assure Israel's survival and the righteous Jew's vindication. While the work appears not to have left significant marks on the NT texts themselves, it provides important testimony to a strand of first-century Jewish reflection on the covenant, the role of Moses, God's providence and *eschatology.

1. Textual Transmission and Contents
2. Date and Setting
3. Genre and Purpose
4. Theology
5. Influence and Importance

1. Textual Transmission and Contents.

The *Testament of Moses* is known only from a single sixth-century Latin manuscript discovered in a library in Milan in 1861 by A. M. Ceriani. This manuscript was a palimpsest—the parchment on which *Testament of Moses* was written had been scraped and reused for another book. The ending is completely lost (perhaps as much as one-third to one-half the original document), and the condition of the text is poor in many places (Priest). There are numerous gaps in the manuscript, and many words are illegible, as would be expected in a palimpsest, so that scholars must reconstruct the text at a number of places. The textual situation is complicated by the fact that the Latin is a translation of a Greek version, which is itself a translation from the original Semitic version (probably Hebrew, but possibly Aramaic). Scholars have contended that the translators or copyists were frequently deficient in their treatment of the language they were translating. This again opens the door for translators to make many proposed emendations based on reconstructions of the underlying Greek or Hebrew (Aramaic) versions.

Ancient lists of books (e.g., Nicephorus *Stichometry*) bear witness to both an *Assumption of Moses* and a *Testament of Moses.* The two may have been joined together during the first century A.D. (Charles). Gelasius quotes *Testament of Moses* 1:14 (Gelasius *Hist. Eccl.* 2.17, 17) as part of the *Assumption* and goes on to refer to the dispute between Michael and the devil over Moses' body as also being from the *Assumption* (Charles; J. J. Collins 1984). He appears thus to have known a work that combined the *Testament* with a now entirely lost pseudepigraphon about the *Assumption.* Ceriani, following such early church usage, thought he had discovered the *Assumption of Moses,* and many scholars will refer to the *Testament* by this name. It is more probable, however, that this is an erroneous designation. The extant *Testament* expects a natural death for Moses (*T. Mos.* 1:15; 3:3; 10:12, 14), not an assumption like Enoch's or Elijah's. The *Assumption* has been lost to posterity save for brief references to its contents in, for example, Jude 9 and Gelasius.

The book opens with Moses summoning Joshua to receive his commission as Moses' successor, encouraging him to continue faithfully in the commandments, announcing God's plan from creation and giving instructions concerning the preservation of the text (*T. Mos.* 1:1-18). There follows, in the form of *ex eventu* *prophecy, the story of the conquest of Canaan, the rule of the judges, the rise of the divided monarchy, the apostasy of Israel and Judah and the exile to Babylon (*T. Mos.* 2:1—3:3). In the land of their exile, the twelve tribes repent, call upon God to remember the "covenant and oath" that God made with their ancestors and confess the accuracy of Moses' predictions (*T. Mos.* 3:4-14). An intercessor, probably Daniel, prays effectively on *Israel's behalf, and God restores them to their inheritance through the pity of the Gentile king Cyrus (*T. Mos.* 4:1-9). The restoration is followed by a second period of apostasy, which includes the Hellenizing high *priests of 175-164 B.C., the *Hasmonean house of priest-kings and the rise of *Herod the Great, all of whom are remembered unfavorably (*T. Mos.* 5:1—6:9). The most recent event remembered in this *ex eventu* prophecy is Varus's quelling of a mild rebellion in 4 B.C. The contemporary generation is ruled by godless, pleasure-seeking hypocrites (*T. Mos.* 7:1-10), whose iniquity invites the advent of the eschatological woes and final persecutions of Israel (*T. Mos.* 8:1-5). A righteous man, Taxo, and his sons fast and withdraw to a cave, resolving to die rather than transgress the Torah and assured that God will avenge the death of the innocent righteous (*T. Mos.* 9:1-7). Their show of loyalty immediately precedes divine vengeance upon the enemies of Israel and exaltation of the chosen race amid cosmic chaos (*T. Mos.* 10:1-10). The text then returns to the narrative frame, with the commissioning of Joshua and Joshua's lament at Moses' impending death (*T. Mos.* 10:11—11:19). Moses' final words assure Joshua of God's foresight and invulnerable plan for Israel, grounded upon God's covenant and oath, and assert the basic principle of Deuteronomy—those who obey Torah will flourish, but those who disobey will deprive themselves of the promised exaltation (*T. Mos.* 12:1-13). The manuscript breaks off abruptly.

2. Date and Setting.

Dates after the fall of *Jerusalem in A.D. 70 have been proposed on the basis, for example, of the references to Jerusalem as a "colony," reflecting the situation after A.D. 135, when Jerusalem was refounded as a Roman colony. Such terminology, however, need only pertain to the date of the Latin translation, which uses the updated title to translate the Greek "city." Most scholars favor a date during the Hellenization crisis of 175-164 B.C. or during the period soon after Herod's death (A.D. 7-30). Some have suggested that the work was composed during the earlier period but revised and updated for use in Herodian times.

J. Licht and G. W. E. Nickelsburg have championed the hypothesis that the *Testament* was originally written during the Hellenization crisis. These scholars point out the connections between the description of the persecution and the resolve of Taxo in chapters 8 and 9 with the events described in 1 Maccabees 1—2 and 2 Maccabees 5—7. Taxo and his sons are said to resemble closely the deaths of the Hasidim in the caves (1 Macc 2:29-38), the exhortation of Mattathias to his five sons (1 Macc 2:49-50) and the martyrdom of Eleazar and the seven brothers with their mother (2 Macc 6, 7). The vividness of these chapters suggests to them that the author was an eyewitness of the period. According to this dating, chapters 6 and possibly 7 are later interpolations meant to bring the work up to date in the Herodian period (virtually all scholars agree that the book received its present shape during A.D. 7-30). The purpose of the work, in the situation of 167-164 B.C., was to encourage a persecuted Israel that God has assured its survival and that God will soon act to avenge the deaths of the faithful and exalt Israel over its enemies (Nickelsburg).

Not all scholars are satisfied with this theory. First, that Taxo and his sons resemble so many episodes at once, and yet none of them in their particulars, suggests that the episode is derivative from the books of the Maccabees and not prior to them (J. J. Collins 1973a). Second, Nickelsburg's objection that the author could not have written in the first century A.D. and passed over the Hellenization crisis is undermined by the fact that *2 Baruch* (written in A.D. 95) does pass over these same events (J. J. Collins 1973a). These scholars argue that the work is completely understandable as originating from the Herodian period (J. J. Collins 1973a; Brandenburger; Laperrousaz).

R. H. Charles narrowed down the date of composition or at least the final redaction to A.D. 7-30 on the strength of the following observations: the Jerusalem *temple is still standing (*T. Mos.* 1:17); Herod the Great has already died (*T. Mos.* 4:6); the author knows of Varus's destruction of part of the temple (*T. Mos.* 6:8-9; cf. Josephus *J.W.* 2.3.2-3 §§47-50; 2.5.1-3 §§66-79); the author writes before Herod's heirs reign longer than Herod's thirty-four-year reign (*T. Mos.* 6:7), hence before A.D. 30. Charles sought to solve the problem of chapters 8 and 9 (which he also took to refer to the Antiochan persecution of 167-164 B.C.) by rearranging the chapters to restore chronological order. Licht has demonstrated that this is an unacceptable proposal—the eschatological vindication in chapter 10 must follow directly on the worst persecution and the readiness of Taxo and his sons to die rather than transgress the Torah. The chapters may be allowed to stand in their present order as soon as one recognizes that motifs from the Antiochan persecution are being combined with other motifs of persecution to portray the coming eschatological oppression of Israel by the "eschatological tyrant" (J. J. Collins 1973a; Reese; Laperrousaz; cf. Mk 13 and Rev 13, which also describe an end-time oppressor with images formerly attached to Antiochus IV by Daniel).

Perhaps the best approach, in the absence of certainty, is to consider that *Testament of Moses* may have had an earlier recension that served a particular purpose during the Hellenization crisis but that its present form took shape during the Herodian period in which significant elements of the earlier document were recast and significant additions made, allowing the text to speak to a new situation in which the primary concern is no longer enduring persecution but resisting corruption from within and returning to pure covenant loyalty (Priest; J. J. Collins 1973b).

Most scholars place the work's composition in Palestine, but there is much debate concerning what circles in Palestine might have produced this text. Attempts to identify a particular group have proven to be a study in the limits of scholarly certainty about the period. Charles rightly excluded Zealot circles, given the text's promotion primarily of a model of nonviolent resistance (Taxo and his sons). This point is telling against a Hasidean provenance, since they too were disposed to express their loyalty through violent resistance (their death in the caves was due not to a policy of nonviolence but to their obedience to the prohibition of warfare on the *sabbath). The figure of Taxo is antithetical to the Zealot hero Mattathias, the instigator of the Maccabean revolt (*see* Revolutionary Movements), in every way (J. J. Collins 1973a): both urge death on behalf of the Torah, but the means are diametrically opposed. Charles also rightly rejected a *Sadducean origin. The negative view of the Second Temple and the efficacy of its *sacrificial system points decisively away from a Sadducean origin, as do the descriptions of the ruling, priestly class as polluted and rapacious (*Psalms of Solomon* provides numerous parallels to the accusations found in *Testament of Moses;* Charles).

Charles lights on a *Pharisaic origin, mainly by the process of elimination of the other three sects known from *Josephus. Nothing in the document is anti-Pharisaic (vs. Laperrousaz, who sees Pharisees as the aim of the remarks in chapter 7 on the basis of *Essene and Synoptic criticisms of the Pharisees), but this may not be sufficient to warrant claiming a "Pharisaic Quietist" as the author of the work.

After the discovery of the *Dead Sea Scrolls, E.-M. Laperrousaz has reopened the argument for an Essene provenance for *Testament of Moses.* Charles's earlier objections to an Essene provenance (a supposed lack of Essene interest in the temple, in a sacrificial system and in nationalism—Charles) have indeed been rendered untenable by this discovery, which show the intense interest of *Qumran Essenes in all three. Laperrousaz sees Taxo as a type of the withdrawal into the desert for the pure keeping of Torah that characterized Qumran. He further notes the sectarian mentality of Taxo, who is aware that his ancestors are blameless with regard to Torah in the midst of an Israel that has been overcome by transgressions (*T. Mos.* 9:4)—a righteousness that gives this sectarian group its particular strength (in God's sight). The high view of determinism among Essenes described by Josephus, and the confession in the *Hymn Scroll* that justification comes by God's mercy and favor rather than by the personal righteousness of the individual, also agree with the views of the *Testament.*

There is among scholars, however, a growing awareness of the complexity of Judaism in the first century and of the possibility that we do not have a complete catalog of every sect active during that period (Priest). Moreover, Nickelsburg adds that it is not sufficient to explore "compatibility" in general between a text and what is known of a sect—we must look for the presence in the text of those distinctive emphases of the sect. It may be best not to insist that this document is either Pharisaic or Essene but rather to note what it shares in common with these sects and where it differs from or is silent about special emphases of either. We can say for certain that it arises from sectarian circles (the model of Taxo; the rejection of the institution of the Second Temple, at least under its current administration). The author looks back upon recent history quite unfavorably (the Hellenizing high priests, the Hasmonean house and Herod are all part of a period of apostasy and transgression). The circle that produced and preserved the text positions itself against militant nationalism (J. J. Collins 1973a) and advocates a return to strict observance of Torah, even withdrawal from society if such is needed to keep the law "blamelessly."

3. Genre and Purpose.

The *Testament of Moses* combines features of three distinct genres. First, it appears to be an expansion of a biblical narrative similar to **Jubilees* and the **Temple Scroll.* The book opens with a direct claim to present the words of Moses to his successor Joshua contained in Deuteronomy (*T. Mos.* 1:5), and D. J. Harrington has shown at length how *Testament* rewrites Deuteronomy 31—34. The book also shares some features in common with *apocalypses: *ex eventu* prophecy leading up to eschatological predictions; instructions to seal the book until the end time; a narrative framework for disclosure of revelation. This last aspect, however, leads us to the third genre, the testament (Kolenkow; Nickelsburg).

The testament narrates the deathbed instructions of an Israelite worthy, frequently involving some retrospect on the figure's life (which provides an example for virtuous conduct), direct exhortations and often revelations about the course of future events (or even the layout of the heavens, as in *T. Levi*). As such, this genre can frequently be expected to combine aspects of the expansion of biblical narrative (*see* Rewritten Bible) and the apocalypse. The revelation given to a great person on the deathbed carried special weight—its finality gave it an air of completeness and perfection (Kolenkow).

This particular *Testament* would have different purposes and effects in its two recensions, if the earlier one can be reconstructed with accuracy (see 1 above). In its first-century setting, the work would have, in the first instance, provided its readers with assurance. The emphases on God's covenant and oath and on God's eternal design and determination of history would remind the hearers that their collective destiny was guaranteed and that God would indeed bring to pass the full blessings of the covenant that God's prophets had promised. It would also evoke a response of covenant loyalty, even readiness to die for the sake of Torah (Laperrousaz). The opening words to Joshua also exhort the reader: "Be strong and of good courage to do with all your strength all that has been commanded, so that you may be blameless before God" (*T. Mos.* 1:10). The end-time hero, Taxo, also provides a model of praiseworthy behavior that would rouse emulation. Taxo underscores the text's call to repent and return to a single-minded commitment to Torah (Reese; Kolenkow). The way to overcome the corrupt rulers is through passive resistance, which came to characterize Jewish resistance from 4 B.C. to A.D. 48, after the failure of multiple attempts at violent uprising (Rhoads). Finally, the *Testament* may encourage intercession on behalf of Israel (Kolenkow): first Moses, then Daniel, then possibly Taxo stand in the gap, calling upon God to remember the covenant and oath. Their prayers are, the readers are assured, effective, and the prayers of those who model their lives after such loyal children of the covenant may be equally effective.

4. Theology.

While the theology of *Testament of Moses* has been called, largely, unoriginal (Laperrousaz), the work nevertheless bears witness to some important strains of thought in first-century Judaism that may provide useful background and counterpoint to NT developments.

*4.1. **God, Creation and Covenant.*** God is the God of all nations (*T. Mos.* 10:3) but remains specially the God of Israel (*T. Mos.* 3:9; 4:8). God created the world on behalf of the righteous (cf. 4 Ezra 6:55, 59; *2 Bar* 14:18) but did not reveal God's plan to the Gentiles so that they might act against God, remain in folly and convict themselves. The readers of *Testament of Moses* are privy to this divine counsel, but the Gentiles, who have no access to Moses' departing revelation, remain dangerously unenlightened (*T. Mos.* 1:18; Kolenkow). The book thus establishes a strong ideology of Israel against the Gentile nations at the outset (*T. Mos.* 1:12-13; cf. 12:4-5). The Gentiles act in darkness and ignorance—their domination now may be endured and resisted in the sure knowledge that they are storing up for themselves wrath for the day of God's visitation.

God has given to Israel a covenant and ratified it with an oath, committing God's own honor to fulfill the promises (*T. Mos.* 1:9; 3:9; 11:17; 12:13). This emphasis on God's initiative and God's determination of Israel's destiny leaves no room for a doctrine of salvation by merit (*T. Mos.* 12:7-8). The necessity of keeping Torah in order to enjoy the promised blessings does not detract from the awareness of God's gift and favor. The author dwells on God's care and fidelity toward God's covenant people in the exodus and exilic generations in order to promote the hope for God's final vindication of the present generation (Reese).

*4.2. **Moses.*** While the depiction of Moses may not be as extravagant here as in other documents from the period (Tiede), it nevertheless shows some significant developments of the presentation of Moses in the Pentateuch. Rather than fit Moses into nonbiblical paradigms of the great person, as in *Philo and Artapanus (Tiede), *Testament of Moses* develops Moses' role as "mediator," intercessor and prophet.

Moses' role as mediator (*mesites*) was ordained from the foundation of the world (1:14; 3:12). This was not a term used of Moses in the *Septuagint, but it came to be applied to him in the first century (Gal 3:19; Philo *Vit. Mos.* 3.19; cf. the depiction of Jesus as the better mediator in Heb 8:6; 9:15; 12:21; *see* Patronage). Moses acted on behalf of Israel to obtain the covenant and to maintain that covenant relationship through intercession for the people when they broke faith with God (*T. Mos.* 11:11, 14, 17). The author may understand Moses' intercessory role extending beyond his death (*T. Mos.* 12:6; Charles; Tiede). Second Maccabees 15:12-16 depicts the ongoing intercession of Jeremiah on behalf of Israel, so the possibility of viewing Moses in this way is not without parallel. If this is correct, *Testament of Moses* attests to a belief that is especially relevant for study of Hebrews, which contrasts the mediation of Jesus and Moses (among others). Finally, *Testament of Moses* lays great stress on Moses' prophetic role. Deuteronomy 31:3-6, 16-22, 29 opens the door to this view of Moses, which becomes popular in the first century (cf. 4 Ezra 14:3-6; *2 Bar* 59:4-11; 84:2-5). Moses' esteem during this period is captured well by Joshua: he is the "master of the word, faithful in all things, the divine prophet for the whole earth, the perfect teacher in the world" (*T. Mos.* 11:16).

*4.3. **Providence and Human Responsibility.*** *Testament of Moses* combines apocalyptic determinism with the covenant theology of Deuteronomy. The former asserts God's foresight, even determination, of future events, while the latter calls people to choose the path of loyalty to the covenant and preserves a more dynamic picture of cause and effect, reward and punishment, within the relationship between God and Israel. The author refuses to sacrifice one for the other and so sustains the paradox of providence and free will. The Deuteronomistic theology of history (obedience to Torah results in enjoyment of God's favor and blessings; disobedience brings punishment; *T. Mos.* 12:10-11) still provides the "guiding thread of history" (Laperrousaz). This contingent view of history is nestled, however, within God's foreordained design, expressed in the promise and oath that assure Israel's final exaltation (*T. Mos.* 3:11-12; 12:4-5). The potential inconsistency between these two affirmations is not as important to the author as the dual purpose of motivating faithful perseverance in the covenant relationship and assuring the righteous of their future, secure in God's design.

This lack of consistency has especially come to the fore in scholarly discussions of the role of Taxo and his seven sons. Licht has argued forcefully that the innocent deaths of Taxo and his sons on behalf of Torah are calculated to provoke divine vengeance for the blood of God's righteous ones and thus hasten eschatological deliverance. This would enact the promises of Deuteronomy 30:1-8 and 32:35-36, 41-43. Others, however, have difficulty harmonizing this view with the determinism of the document (Priest; Rowley). This is a tension that, as J. Priest himself noted, runs throughout this and many other books of the period. An author can affirm that God's time for intervention has been set long ago; the same author may wish to encourage the audience to respond faithfully with a view to ushering in the end, participating in its coming by their faithfulness, as it were.

Taxo may best be seen as a model for the hearers' emulation (Laperrousaz; Kolenkow). The author weaves into the eschatological scheme the heroic resolve of the individual, giving significance to the choices of the individual in the midst of apocalyptic determinism. This moves *Testament of Moses* beyond mere determinism, as it invites the audience to consider their role and responsibility toward God's covenant. Repentance (*T. Mos.* 3:10), intercession (*T. Mos.* 4:1-5), obedience to God (*T. Mos.* 1:10-11; 12:10-11) and nonviolent resistance (*T. Mos.* 9:1-7) remain the responsibility of the individual, whose resolve is nevertheless strengthened by the assurance that God has set a day in which God will vindicate and exalt the righteous.

4.4. Eschatology. While an original version of *Testament of Moses* may have depicted the persecution under Antiochus IV in chapters 8 and 9, the final form of this text uses images reminiscent of that period to portray an unprecedented period of wrath and punishment that will precede the final deliverance by God. The end-time oppression is aimed at erasing covenant loyalty, forcing Jews to blaspheme and participate in idolatry. This is the setting for Taxo's resolution—to retain their ancestral strength by not transgressing the Torah. If remaining in civilized areas meant pressure to transgress, the loyal Jew must choose to depart for the desert places even if death should be the result. C. J. Lattey sees in Taxo an early paradigm for a suffering messiah, but this is based on more speculation than most scholars can support. Taxo is rather the model for decisive action in the last days, the "model Jew, the symbol, with his sons, of the unblemished nucleus of Israel" (Licht), whose obedience to God signals that the "day of repentance" (*T. Mos.* 1:18), the day of God's visitation (cf. Mk 1:14-15), has arrived.

The vision of deliverance includes both the action of a consecrated angel (or messenger; *T. Mos.* 10:1-2) and the direct action of God (*T. Mos.* 10:3-10). This suggests to some scholars that two different sources have been utilized (Charles), but the actions of God and God's messenger are closely linked elsewhere in Jewish tradition (cf. Ex 3:2-6; Mal 3:1-2). The angelology of this work is rather subdued (Laperrousaz), mentioning only this angel and the devil, as opposed to the myriads in *1 Enoch* (*see* Enoch, Books of), Daniel or *Jubilees*. The book attests to an eschatology without a messiah, military or otherwise, which sets it apart from many other strains of thought in early Judaism (Laperrousaz).

G. Reese rightly notes that *Testament of Moses* presents an eschatological reading of Deuteronomy 32—33. God's promise to avenge the blood of his loyal servants and God's theophany on Mt. Sinai are now transposed to the end-time deliverance, accompanied by cosmic disturbances (the natural order of the sun, moon, stars, mountains and sea is unsettled). At the end, God vindicates God's honor against the idolaters and their false, rival gods. The Gentiles are debased before Israel's eyes, as Israel is exalted to the stars. It is not clear whether this is a wholly supramundane eschatology (Laperrousaz; Rowley) that relinquishes nationalistic, this-worldly hopes or just an extravagant metaphor (Priest). It remains a strictly collective dispensation of reward and punishment (Laperrousaz).

5. Influence and Importance.

5.1. Echoes in the New Testament and Other

Early Christian Literature. Jude is famous for its awareness of extrabiblical literature, but while it knows *1 Enoch* and the lost *Assumption of Moses* (Jude 9), Charles's assertion that Jude knew *Testament of Moses* appears to be unfounded. Rather, the two texts share similar language for the portrayal of enemies that is part of a broader cultural tradition of censuring rivals. The similarity between 2 Peter 2:13 and *Testament of Moses* 7:4, 8 represents more a cultural echo (the image of feasting in the daytime as a way of highlighting the depravity of one's rivals) than literary dependence (Laperrousaz).

Laperrousaz finds Acts 7:36 to be close enough to *Testament of Moses* 3:11 to signal acquaintance with *Testament of Moses* by the author of Acts. Both texts summarize the exodus experience as Moses' activity "in Egypt, at the Red Sea and in the desert for forty years." All of these elements could be derived from the Pentateuch (cf. earlier summaries in Neh 9:9-21; Pss 106:7-14; 136:10-16), but no other documents summarize the whole experience in precisely this way, suggesting that Acts knew of this terse formulation of the events. The Synoptic Apocalypse (e.g., Mt 24:19-21) also bears some striking similarities with *Testament of Moses.* Both describe the end-time oppression of God's people as unlike anything experienced previously since creation (Mt 24:21; *T. Mos.* 8:1); both also speak of cosmic disturbances (sun, moon, stars) accompanying the Day of the Lord. The first image could have been independently derived from Daniel 12:1; the second might also have been independently derived from OT descriptions of the "Day of the Lord" (cf. Is 13:10, 13; Joel 2:10, 31; 3:15-16; Mic 1:3-4), but here again the two texts show the tendency toward a common, formulaic summary of these texts, suggesting either the Synoptics' awareness of *Testament of Moses* or mutual dependence on a common tradition of the day of the Lord extracted from prophetic texts.

5.2. ***Echoes in Other Jewish Literature.*** *Testament of Moses* 3:10-13 appears to have left its mark on *2 Baruch* 84:2-5 (Charles), but other cases of direct influence have not been observed. This suggests that while apocalyptic circles may have been aware of *Testament of Moses,* it did not have anything approaching broad influence within Judaism.

5.3. ***Importance for New Testament Study.*** Despite the lack of important examples of direct dependence, *Testament of Moses* remains a useful witness to Jewish backgrounds for NT study. The portrayal of Moses as prophet, mediator and (perpetual?) intercessor is an important background for the study of Moses in Galatians and especially Hebrews. The idea of a day of repentance that precedes God's end-time action and exaltation of Israel may highlight the eschatological dimension of Jesus' call for repentance (cf. Mk 1:14-15) and his subversion of the picture of Israel's exaltation so dear to the author of *Testament of Moses.* D. M. Rhoads suggests that *Testament of Moses* opens another window into a Judaism in search of less violent forms of resistance and witness to God's kingdom (the period from 4 B.C. to A.D. 48), which provides a setting for Jesus' own message of nonviolent resistance.

Of more general interest is the book's witness to the ongoing tension between Jew and Gentile, the importance of maintaining the Jew-Gentile boundary for many Jews and the characterization of Gentiles in Jewish literature that facilitated the preservation of such boundaries. The text also bears witness to the multiple tensions that existed within the first-century Jewish community. The critique of Herodian rule, of the Jerusalem priesthood and of the adequacy of the temple in this document has significant echoes in other sects within Judaism (e.g., the Essenes), not the least of which was the early Christian movement.

See also APOCRYPHA AND PSEUDEPIGRAPHA; APOCRYPHON OF MOSES (4Q374-377); PSEUDO-MOSES APOCALYPSE (4Q388A-390).

BIBLIOGRAPHY. E. Brandenburger, *Himmelfährt Moses* (JSHRZ 5; Gütersloh: Gerd Mohn, 1976) 59-84; R. H. Charles, "The Assumption of Moses," in *The Apocrypha and Pseudepigrapha of the Old Testament,* ed. R. H. Charles (2 vols.; Oxford: Clarendon Press, 1913) 2:407-24; A. Y. Collins, "Composition and Redaction of the Testament of Moses 10," *HTR* 69 (1976) 179-86; J. J. Collins, "The Date and Provenance of the Testament of Moses," in *Studies on the Testament of Moses,* ed. G. W. E. Nickelsburg (SCS 4; Cambridge, MA: Society of Biblical Literature, 1973a) 15-32; idem, "Some Remaining Traditio-Historical Problems in the Testament of Moses," in *Studies on the Testament of Moses,* ed. G. W. E. Nickelsburg (SCS 4; Cambridge, MA: Society of Biblical Literature, 1973b) 38-43; idem, "Testaments," in *Jewish Writings of the Second Temple Period,* ed. M. E. Stone (CRINT 2.2; Assen: Van Gorcum; Philadelphia: Fortress, 1984); C. de Santo, "The

Assumption of Moses and the Christian Gospel," *Int* 16 (1962) 305-10; J. A. Goldstein, "The Testament of Moses: Its Content, Its Origin and Its Attestation in Josephus," in *Studies on the Testament of Moses,* ed. G. W. E. Nickelsburg (SCS 4; Cambridge, MA: Society of Biblical Literature, 1973) 44-52; D. J. Harrington, "Interpreting Israel's History: The Testament of Moses as a Rewriting of Deuteronomy 31—34," in *Studies on the Testament of Moses,* ed. G. W. E. Nickelsburg (SCS 4; Cambridge, MA: Society of Biblical Literature, 1973) 59-68; A. B. Kolenkow, "The Assumption of Moses as a Testament," in *Studies on the Testament of Moses,* ed. G. W. E. Nickelsburg (SCS 4; Cambridge, MA: Society of Biblical Literature, 1973) 71-77; E.-M. Laperrousaz, *Le Testament de Moïse* (Semitica 19; Paris: Librairie d'Amérique et d'Orient Adrien-Maisonneuve, 1970); C. J. Lattey, "The Messianic Expectation in 'The Assumption of Moses,'" *CBQ* 4 (1942) 9-21; J. Licht, "Taxo, or the Apocalyptic Doctrine of Vengeance," *JJS* 12 (1961) 95-103; G. W. E. Nickelsburg, "An Antiochan Date for the Testament of Moses," in *Studies on the Testament of Moses,* ed. G. W. E. Nickelsburg (SCS 4; Cambridge, MA: Society of Biblical Literature, 1973) 33-37; idem, *Resurrection, Immortality and Eternal Life in Intertestamental Judaism* (Cambridge, MA: Cambridge University Press, 1972), 43-45; J. Priest, "Some Reflections on the Assumption of Moses," *PRS* 4 (1977) 92-111; idem, "Testament of Moses (First Century A.D.): A New Translation and Introduction," in *The Old Testament Pseudepigrapha,* ed. J. H. Charlesworth (2 vols.; Garden City, NY: Doubleday, 1983, 1985) 1:919-34; G. Reese, "Die Geschichte Israels in der Auffassung des frühen Judentums" (diss., Heidelberg, 1967) 89-124; D. M. Rhoads, "The Assumption of Moses and Jewish History: 4 B.C.-A.D. 48," in *Studies on the Testament of Moses,* ed. G. W. E. Nickelsburg (SCS 4; Cambridge, MA: Society of Biblical Literature, 1973) 53-58; H. H. Rowley, *The Relevance of Apocalyptic* (London: Lutterworth, 1963) 106-10, 149-56; D. L. Tiede, "The Figure of Moses in the Testament of Moses," in *Studies on the Testament of Moses,* ed. G. W. E. Nickelsburg (SCS 4; Cambridge, MA: Society of Biblical Literature, 1973) 86-92.

D. A. deSilva

TESTAMENT OF QAHAT (4Q542)

A single Aramaic manuscript found in Qumran Cave 4 preserves part of a narration by Qahat to his sons. Although the speaker is not explicitly named, he is clearly identified by reference to "Levi my father" (4Q542 frag. 1 ii 11) and "my son Amram" (4Q542 frag. 1 ii 9). The work belongs to the genre of *pseudepigraphical last words (testaments) of the patriarchs to their sons (*see* Testaments of the Twelve Patriarchs). At least one sheet is lost from the beginning. One large fragment preserves most of one column and part of the following. It contains a blessing by Qahat on his sons "may he [God] shine his light upon you and may he make you know his great name so that you will know him" (4Q542 frag. 1 i 1-4); an admonition, warning against losing the ancestral heritage through intermarriage and assimilation (4Q542 frag. 1 i 4-7) and to hold fast to the instruction handed down by the patriarchs (4Q542 frag. 1 i 7-ii 1); instruction to his sons about the future and their role in the judgment of sinners (4Q542 frag. 1 ii 1-8); instruction specifically to Amram and his descendants about ancestral writings transmitted to Levi, thence to Qahat and now to Amram (4Q542 frag. 1 ii 9-13).

This work is above all concerned with the *priestly lineage. An adaptation of the priestly blessing is pronounced specifically on Qahat's descendants; the "great name" of God is probably the Tetragrammaton, which the high priest had to utter on the Day of Atonement. The prohibition for priests to marry foreign wives is not found in the pentateuchal restrictions on priestly marriage (cf. Lev 21:7), but this injunction echoes the Aramaic *Testament of Levi* (Bodleian Genizah fragment col. b 16-17; *T. Levi* 9:9-10; cf. 4QMMT B 75-77 [*see* Miqaṣt Maʿaśey ha-Torah]). Part of the heritage passed down through Qahat to his sons is the priesthood. The tradition that books of patriarchal wisdom were preserved by Levi's descendants is also found in the Aramaic *Testament of Levi* 88 (Cambridge Genizah fragment col. e 17-18 and 23) and **Jubilees* (45:15; Milik argued that Testament of Qahat was the source) and reflects the priestly role of preserving and teaching the Torah (Lev 10:11; Deut 17:18). Qahat reveals that his descendants will judge the wicked, but it is not clear whether this is as the righteous in the *eschatological judgment (*1 Enoch* 91 [*see* Enoch, Books of] ; cf. Dan 7; Mt 19:28; Rev 20:4) or whether it assumes the joining of royal and priestly functions as might be suggested by the application of the blessing of Judah from Genesis 49:10 to Qahat in Aramaic *Testament of Levi* 66-67 (Cambridge Genizah fragment col. c 5-7; Puech,

52, 54; see Greenfield and Stone, 219, 223-24).

In the Bible, Qahat was not a priest. He was the most important of the heads of the families descended from Levi, whose clan was responsible for transporting—but was forbidden to touch—the most holy implements of the tabernacle (Num 3—4). The priesthood was instituted beginning with his grandson Aaron (Ex 28—29; Lev 8—9). The tendency to extend the priestly lineage back to Levi is clearly expressed in the Aramaic *Testament of Levi;* Levi himself is ordained priest and clothed in the priestly vestments (Aramaic *T. Levi* 13—20 = Bodleian Genizah frag. col. b-c; cf. *Jub.* 32:1-3) and announces that Qahat is also chosen as priest (Cambridge Genizah fragment col. 5-7). As attested also in *Testament of Qahat,* Levi is instructed in the obligations of the priesthood by Abraham and Isaac, and in turn he instructs his son Qahat. It is likely that the *Testament of Levi,* the *Testament of Qahat* and the **Visions of Amram* formed an ancient cycle of Aramaic testamentary works exalting the three priestly patriarchs. In fact, Milik has suggested that these three are the writings referred to in *Apostolic Constitutions* 6:16 as "apocryphal books of the three patriarchs"—the patriarchs of the priestly tribe.

On the basis of paleography, the manuscript dates around 100 B.C. and apparent use by *Jubilees* points to composition in the first half of the second century B.C. The assumed threat to the priesthood of foreign domination and assimilation suggests that it was written as a response to the interference by foreign rulers in the appointment of high priests, beginning when Antiochus IV Epiphanes ended Zadokite succession by deposing Onias III and appointing his brother Jason (174-171 B.C.; *see* Hasmoneans). The early date points to a pre-Qumran origin (*see* Qumran).

See also TESTAMENT OF ABRAHAM; TESTAMENT OF JOB; TESTAMENT OF MOSES; TESTAMENTS OF THE TWELVE PATRIARCHS; VISIONS OF AMRAM (4Q543-548).

BIBLIOGRAPHY. K. Beyer, *Die aramäischen Texte vom Toten Meer. I* (Göttingen: Vandenhoeck & Ruprecht, 1984) 209-10; idem, *Die aramäischen Texte vom Toten Meer. II* (Göttingen: Vandenhoeck & Ruprecht, 1994) 82-85; G. Bonani et al. "Radiocarbon Dating of the Dead Sea Scrolls," *ʿAtiqot* 20 (1991) 27-32; A. Caquot, "Grandeur et Pureté du Sacerdoce: Remarques sur le Testament de Qahat (4Q542)," in *Solving Riddles and Untying Knots: Biblical, Epigraphic and Semitic Studies in Honor of Jonas C. Greenfield,* ed. Z. Zevit, S. Gittin and M. Sokoloff (Winona Lake, IN: Eisenbrauns, 1995) 39-44; E. M. Cook, "The Last Words of Kohath," in *The Dead Sea Scrolls: A New Translation,* ed. M. O. Wise, M. Abegg Jr. and E. M. Cook (San Francisco: HarperSanFrancisco, 1996) 432-33; idem, "Remarks on the Testament of Kohath from Qumran Cave 4," *JJS* 44 (1993) 205-19; R. Eisenman, "The Testament of Kohath," *BAR* (November/December 1991) 64; R. Eisenman and M. O. Wise, "Testament of Kohath," in *The Dead Sea Scrolls Uncovered* (Shaftesbury, Dorset, England: Element, 1992) 145-51; J. A. Fitzmyer and D. A. Harrington, *A Manual of Palestinian Aramaic Texts* (BibO 34; Rome: Biblical Institute Press, 1978) [no. 27] 96-97, 205; J. C. Greenfield and M. E. Stone, "Remarks on the Aramaic Testament of Levi from the Geniza," *RB* 86 (1979) 214-30; J. T. Milik, "4QVisions de ʿAmram et une Citation d'Origène," *RB* 79 (1972) 96-97 (77-97); E. Puech, "Le Testament de Qahat en Araméen de la Grotte 4 (4QTQah)," *RevQ* 15 (1991-92) 23-54; G. Vermes, "The Words of Moses," in E. Schürer, *The History of the Jewish People in the Age of Jesus Christ, (175 B.C.- A.D. 135)* rev. and ed. G. Vermes, F. Millar and M. Goodman (3 vols. Edinburgh: T & T Clark, 1973-87) 3.1:333.

D. K. Falk

TESTAMENTS OF THE TWELVE PATRIARCHS

The model for these reports of the final words and passing on of the heritage of the twelve sons of Jacob to their heirs is provided by Genesis 49 and Deuteronomy 31—32 where, respectively, Jacob and *Moses give advice and assign responsibility to their successors. In these testaments of Jacob's sons there are predictions of what is to happen in the future, including pronouncements of blessings and curses on the sons and their posterity. The recurrent features are a recall of aspects of the life of each patriarch: confession of misdeeds; exhortations to avoid sin and to exemplify virtues; instructions for burial; call for special honors to Levi and Judah, the priestly and royal leaders of the people; and predictions of the future of the covenant people, which will involve their sin, exile among the nations and ultimate restoration. Occasionally there are Christian interpolations (*T. Sim.* 6:7; 7:1-2; *T. Levi* 2:11; 4:4; 14:2; *T. Zeb.* 9:8) in the Jewish texts. There are also some cases of correspondence between the present text of the *Testaments* and fragments from the *Dead Sea Scrolls, as well as with some later Aramaic covenant texts, but the *Testaments of the Twelve Patriarchs* as a whole was written in Greek. This is evident from the use of technical Greek terms, such as measuring distances in stades (*T. Zeb.* 7:4).

1. Origins of the Testaments
2. The Structure and Features of the Testaments

1. Origins of the Testaments.
Although there is some kinship evident with Hebrew and Aramaic fragments of documents that have survived, the *Testaments* are clearly dependent on the *Septuagint for references to Scripture. This indicates that they were written after 250 B.C., when the LXX was completed. The emphasis throughout on the dual messianic roles of king and *priest—highlighting the descendants of Judah and Levi—fits well with the Maccabean period of Jewish history (167-63 B.C.), when the royal and priestly lines were linked (*see* Hasmoneans). Not surprisingly, therefore, the longest two of these testaments are those attributed to Levi and Judah. Levi is the progenitor of the priests, and it is through a descendant of Judah that God will reign eternally (*T. Reub.* 6:11-12). The assurance of the future triumph of God's purpose in the world and for his people is a major feature in these writings. There are several references in the testaments to the book of *Enoch the Righteous: *Testament of Dan* 5:6, *Testament of Judah* 18:1, *Testament of Simeon* 5:4, *Testament of Naphtali* 4 and *Testament of Joseph* 9:1. Not all these quotations are in the currently known writings attributed to Enoch.

The *Testaments* are written in fluent Greek, and the ethical concepts included are frequently stated in terms employed by *Stoic philosophy, such as the recurrent emphasis on natural law and references to reason and conscience (*T. Jud.* 20:2; *T. Reub.* 4:11). Greek words are used for which there is no Semitic equivalent, as in the designation of a burial place for Aseneth in Egypt "by the hippodrome" (*T. Jos.* 20:3). Ethical standards are likewise expressed in distinctively Greek terms that derive chiefly from the Stoic tradition. Thus, throughout the *Testaments* the law of Moses is a central feature and is to be the object of devotion (*T. Levi* 13:1-9), yet its moral requirements are perceived to be articulated through Stoic terminology and compatible with the concept of the universal law of nature.

The influence of Jewish *apocalyptic perceptions concerning evil pervades this work. The power of evil in the world is understood to be the effect of the work of *Beliar, the prince of the demons, and the final triumph of justice will come only when he and his evil spirits have been overcome by the power of God. Then the people of God will return from their dispersion throughout the world, but there will also be Gentiles who will share in the rule of God. The righteous will be raised from the dead to enjoy new life in the new *Jerusalem. The primary example of true virtue throughout the *Testaments* is Joseph.

2. The Structure and Features of the Testaments.
The typical structure of each of the *Testaments of the Twelve Patriarchs* is as follows: (1) an introduction, setting the scene; (2) a narrative of the life of the patriarch, lacking only in the *Testament of Asher;* (3) ethical exhortation; (4) prediction of the future; (5) second exhortations; and (6) the patriarch's death and burial. The content and features of each of the *Testaments* may be characterized as follows:

2.1. **Testament of Reuben.** The recurrent theme in this work is the avoidance of sexual promiscuity. Reuben is the major candidate for a negative image on this issue, since—as he confesses—his gross sin was to have had intercourse with Bilhah, his father's concubine (Gen 35:32). He urges that his offspring follow the example of Joseph, who rejected ongoing invitations from an Egyptian woman to have sex with her. Preoccupation with sex, which pervades society according to Reuben, is described by him as the "plague of Beliar" (*T. Reub.* 6:3). Instead, one should heed the injunctions of Levi, who knows the law and fosters obedience to it.

In this testament both human nature and its potential for virtue and vice are depicted in terminology that derives from the Hellenistic philosophical traditions. There are seven senses, or spirits, by which all human deeds take place, as well as seven spirits of error (*T. Reub.* 2—3): the spirit of life, by which humans are created as composite beings; the spirit of seeing, which leads to desire; hearing, which makes possible human instruction; smelling, which is linked with breathing; speech, which brings knowledge; taste, which involves food and brings strength; procreation and intercourse, which foster fondness for pleasure and are the chief cause of sin among youth. In addition, the spirit of sleep creates ecstasy of nature, as well as an image of death. Mingled with these are the spirits of error: promiscuity, insatiability, strife (in the liver and gall), flattery and trickery, arrogance, lying and injustice. The appeal is to love truth, and it will preserve those who seek it, who will gain understanding of the law.

Those who devote themselves to learning the law may gain moral integrity and will be guided by the conscience (*T. Reub.* 4:1-4), which is a fundamental Stoic concept: the knowledge of the law that pervades and orders nature is perceived through the conscience and thus is shared by all who truly and diligently seek it.

This testament is severely critical of women, for the treacherous schemes they promote (*T. Reub.* 5:1) and for their enticement of men into sexual relations (*T. Reub.* 6:1). Special honor and deference are to be offered to Levi, as the chief of the priests (*T. Reub.* 6:8). He is here seen as the one who best knows the law and offers instruction in it and who will continue to offer *sacrifices in the *temple "until the consummation of the times" (*T. Reub.* 6:8-13).

2.2. **Testament of Simeon.** This testament highlights Simeon's anger and jealousy toward Joseph, who is the model of virtue. The tension arose according to Genesis 42:18-25 when the sons of Jacob went to Egypt to obtain grain during a drought in the land of Israel. Joseph came to the aid of his brothers but insisted on holding Simeon as a hostage. He confesses his earlier hatred of Joseph, which he says was caused by the Prince of Error's having blinded his mind (*T. Sim.* 2:7).

Now he praises Joseph and warns against yielding to the spirit of envy (*T. Sim.* 3:4; 6:2), which makes the soul sad, foments wrath and conflict and murder and causes mental distraction. Simeon characterizes sexual promiscuity as "the mother of all wicked deeds" (*T. Sim.* 5:3), but Joseph was able to resist that temptation.

Instead of submission to these wicked forces, Simeon calls for one to live "in the integrity of [one's] heart," which will manifest itself in love for one's "brothers" and result in God's pouring out on the faithful "grace, glory and blessing" (*T. Sim.* 4:5). Obedience to Levi and Judah are called for (*T. Sim.* 7:1), because God will appear on the earth and will overcome the evil spirits (*T. Sim.* 6:6). What are most certainly Christian interpolations in this connection describe God's self-manifestion "as a man" in a human "body" who will "eat with human beings" and save them (*T. Sim.* 6:7).

2.3. **Testament of Levi.** Levi is taken by an angel up to the third heaven, where God is. There bloodless sacrifices are offered to deal with the sins of ignorance committed by the righteous (*T. Levi* 3:5-6). By contrast, the worship of God carried out in Shechem by the *Samaritans in their temple on Mt. Gerizim is denounced (*T. Levi* 5:3—7:4). The description of the investiture of Levi as priest (*T. Levi* 8) is followed by predictions of the establishment of three sacred offices: priest, king and prophet. From Levi's posterity will be priests, judges and scribes to interpret the law (*T. Levi* 8:17).

At Bethel Levi received detailed instructions about the role of the priest. He foresees, however, impiety and secularization of the priests, which may reflect disillusionment of pious Jews with the Maccabean rulers because of their greed and ruthless power (*T. Levi* 14—17). The designation of seventy weeks for the outworking of the divine plan of renewal reflects the chronology of the divine purpose as sketched in Daniel 9. The prediction of the killing through a priestly plot of one who will renew the law may be a Christian addition. There will be mounting corruption and defilement among the priests, until God sends the *eschatological priest to replace the present degenerate holders of that office (*T. Levi* 17). Ultimately there will come a new messianic priest to interpret the law (*T. Levi* 18), who is identified as the "Star out of Jacob" (Num 24:17), as he is in the **Rule of the Community* from *Qumran (1QS 7:18-20). He will be the instrument of universal divine blessing and of disclosure of the divine glory. Beliar, the leader of the evil powers, will be bound by him, as in Isaiah 24:22-23 (cf. the defeat of Beelzebub and Satan in the Gospel tradition [Mk 3:27; Lk 11:14-22]). The evil spirits will be trampled upon, and people must choose between obeying the law of the Lord and participating in the works of Beliar (*T. Levi* 19). The result of the work of the ultimate priest will be the renewal and purification of the whole creation (*T. Levi* 18).

2.4. **Testament of Judah.** Judah is designated as king by his father, Jacob, as a consequence of his complete obedience to his parents and his honoring of them (*T. Jud.* 1:6). He is noted for his control of wild animals (*T. Jud.* 2:1-7), but especially for his physical prowess and his effectiveness in warfare, when he defeats the Canaanites and other surrounding nations. In contrast to the self-indulgence depicted in *Testament of Judah* 10—14, there are calls for temperance, prudence, avoidance of love of money (*T. Jud.* 15—19) and for reliance on the conscience and the spirit of truth (*T. Jud.* 20). Judah's kingdom will be established by God (*T. Jud.* 22) through the Star from Jacob, who will pour out the spirit of grace. The patriarchs will be raised from the dead; there will be one people and one language (*T. Jud.* 25). Now the people must obey the whole of the law (*T. Jud.* 26).

2.5. **Testament of Issachar.** Issachar has been a model of rectitude of the heart and has lived in full obedience to the law (*T. Iss.* 3—4). God will reward such obedience with fertility and safety (*T. Iss.* 5—6), and Beliar will flee. The people should seek unity of purpose in obedience to the Lord, in recognition of the leadership of Judah and Levi, which will lead to the defeat of their enemies and their establishment in the land.

2.6. **Testament of Zebulon.** Zebulon describes his having tried to dissuade his brothers from killing Joseph (*T. Zeb.* 1—2), though this is not mentioned in Genesis 37, nor are the details of his maltreatment as here described (*T. Zeb.* 1—2). His acts of compassion and obedience to the Lord resulted in length of life and freedom from illness (*T. Zeb.* 5). He was the first to make a boat to sail on the sea and was able to provide fish for many (*T. Zeb.* 6). He urges others to follow his example of acts of compassion (*T. Zeb.* 7—8) and to achieve unity of purpose: "obey one head" (*T. Zeb.* 9:4). The Lord will come among them, but many will perform wicked works and will be rejected (*T. Zeb.* 9:9). Zebulon will rise again to serve as leader of those who remain obedient to the law of the Lord (*T. Zeb.* 10).

2.7. **Testament of Dan.** Here is offered what might be called a psychological analysis of human behavior, in which anger—though it is senseless—precludes perceiving the truth (*T. Dan* 4:1). Love the Lord and speak truth to the neighbor; otherwise Satan becomes your prince. Salvation will come through Levi and Judah (*T. Dan* 5), which will result in peace for the righteous in the new Jerusalem, where the name of God will permeate the lives of the people as they live in conformity to the law of God (*T. Dan* 6).

2.8. **Testament of Naphtali.** The order of nature in the creation of humans is described as evident in sex, senses, the body and its organs—all of which affect intelligence and attitudes (*T. Naph.* 3). This order is not to be altered by disobeying the law of God. The people's disobedience was foretold by Enoch, however, but unity will be established by God through the leadership of Levi and Judah for those who fully obey the law and benefit from the love of God and who therefore will be glorified among the Gentiles (*T. Naph.* 5—8).

2.9. **Testament of Gad.** As the result of a dispute that arose while they were together tending the flock of sheep, Gad developed anger and hatred against his brother Joseph. This led to his brothers' selling Joseph into slavery and plotting to kill him (*T. Gad* 1—2). Hatred fosters every manner of evil and leads to disobedience to the law of God. It works through Satan to bring death, in contrast to the spirit of love, which works through God's law to effect human salvation (*T. Gad* 3). Righteousness overcomes hatred, and repentance overcomes disobedience and darkness, bringing vision, knowledge and the powers of deliberation. Evident here is the impact of the abstract terminology and structuring of ethics and theory of knowledge in the Hellenistic philosophical tradition. The spirit of hatred is operated by Satan through human frailty and leads to death, while the spirit of love works through forbearance to effect deeds, words and inward thoughts that renew humankind (*T. Gad* 6—7).

2.10. **Testament of Asher.** The concept of Two Ways that are open for human thought and action (*T. Asher* 1:3-7) is anticipated in the choices that are set before Israel in the Pentateuch by Moses ("life and prosperity or death and adversity," Deut 30:15) and by Joshua (serving "the Lord" or "the gods of the ancestors," Josh 24:15). In Jeremiah 21:8 the people are offered "the way of life and the way of death" between which they must choose. These options are echoed in Sirach 15:11-17: "Before each person are life and death, and whichever one chooses will be given" (*see* Sirach). In this testament, some submit to Beliar, and all their deeds are evil (*T. Asher* 1:8-9). Many human actions are mixed, with some features good or well-intended and others evil. Being "two-faced" is to be avoided (*T. Asher* 3), although polarities pervade human life (*T. Asher* 5). Instead, truth is to be pursued with singlemindedness (*T. Asher* 6).

The sins of those who fail to achieve this goal will lead to ruin of the temple and dispersion of the covenant people, until the Most High visits the earth in order to renew it and his people (*T. Asher* 7).

2.11. **Testament of Joseph.** This work begins with an expansion of the account in Genesis 37 of his brothers' plot to be rid of him (*T. Jos.* 1) and praises God for his deliverance from this and subsequent threats to his life, as well as from the attempts of the Egyptian woman to engage him sexually (*T. Jos.* 3—9; Gen 39), which he was able to resist by virtue of his quality of self-control. Historically self-control is a central item in Stoic ethics, but here it is central in the true worship of God (*T. Jos.* 6:7) and is the basic resource by which Joseph is able to resist her ongoing efforts to force him to have sex with her. He declares that God will dwell with those who "pursue self-control and purity with patience and prayer with fasting in humility of heart" and will guard them from evil, exalt and glorify them (*T. Jos.* 10:1-3). True fear of God is displayed by those who obey the law and therefore share the love of God (*T. Jos.* 11:1).

Details are included of the plot of another Egyptian woman who claimed she wanted to free him from slavery but who wanted him for sexual relations (*T. Jos.* 12—16). The moral qualities of which Joseph boasts are a blend of "the Lord's commands" (*T. Jos.* 18:1) and Stoic virtues, such as "patient endurance," "harmony," "goodness" (*T. Jos.* 17:2-3) and "humility" (*T. Jos.* 18:3). *Testament of Joseph* 19:1-11 is found only in an Armenian text and contains more apocalyptic features than elsewhere in the *Testaments*. Verses 8-12 also appear in what is clearly a Christian interpolation, with a direct reference to "the Lamb of God who will take away the sin of the world" (cf. Jn 1:29). The animals in both versions of these added passages probably represent various rulers and leaders, as do the "ten horns" of Daniel 7:5. Unlike the biblical stories of Joseph, he is here represented as a king, whose time-bound rule is contrasted with the everlasting kingdom (*T. Jos.* 19:12). The instructions to transport Joseph's body, as well as that of Aseneth, back to Hebron in the land of Israel are to be confirmed by the presence of the Lord of light with them, while Beliar, the power of darkness, will remain with the Egyptians (*T. Jos.* 20). Mention of the hippodrome (*T. Jos.* 20:3) confirms that this work originated in the Hellenistic period.

2.12. **Testament of Benjamin.** Benjamin's special link with Joseph—both were born of Rachel, who had difficulty bearing children (Gen 30:24; 35:18)—leads him to encourage his own children to emulate the piety of Joseph. This will guard them against the wiles and actions of Beliar, from whom they are "sheltered by the fear of God" (*T. Benj.* 3:4). A Christian interpolation at 3:8 repeats the promise of the Lamb of God whose "blood of the covenant" will bring salvation for the Gentiles and for Israel, while effecting the destruction of Beliar (*T. Benj.* 3:8). The virtues that are enjoined in abstract terms—integrity, goodness, love, compassion, respect for good works, piety—reflect Stoic perspective and terminology rather than the specific injunctions of the law of Moses.

As in *Testament of Asher* 4, the mind of the good person is free of duplicity and has "one disposition, uncontaminated and pure, toward all men" (*T. Benj.* 6:5). Thus one can escape the wiles of Beliar, whose evils and the appropriate punishments for performing them come in patterns of seven, as did the punishment of Lamech (Gen 4:24). Beliar produces seven evils in the life of those who submit to him: moral corruption, destruction, oppression, captivity, want, turmoil, desolation. One whose mind is pure is able to be free of the corruptions of the earth, while the promiscuous will find no place in the kingdom of the Lord. God will provide the faithful a place in his new temple, which will exceed the glory of the historic temple (*T. Benj.* 9). Gathered there will be the twelve tribes and people from all the nations until God sends among him the eschatological prophet, as promised in Deuteronomy 18:15. A Christian interpolation describes how that prophet will be "raised up on wood," how the curtain of the temple will be torn and the Spirit of God will be poured out on all the nations (*T. Benj.* 9). Meanwhile, Benjamin exhorts his children to keep the law, awaiting the time when God will offer salvation to all the nations through the Chosen One who will bring new knowledge of God to all nations (*T. Benj.* 10—11).

See also APOCRYPHA AND PSEUDEPIGRAPHA; TESTAMENT OF ABRAHAM; TESTAMENT OF JOB; TESTAMENT OF MOSES; TESTAMENT OF QAHAT (4Q542); TESTAMENT OF SHEM.

BIBLIOGRAPHY. J. Becker, *Untersuchungen zur Entstehungsgeschichte der Testamente der Zwölf Patri-*

archen (AGAJU 8; Leiden: E. J. Brill, 1970); C. Burchard, J. Jervell and J. Thomas, *Studien zu den Testamenten der Zwölf Patriarchen* (ZNWB 36; Berlin: Töpelman, 1969); R. H. Charles, *The Greek Versions of the Testaments of the Twelve Patriarchs* (Oxford: Clarendon Press, 1908); idem, *The Testaments of the Twelve Patriarchs* (London: A & C Black, 1908); M. de Jonge, ed., *Studies on the Testaments of the Twelve Patriarchs* (SVPT 3; Leiden: E. J. Brill, 1975); idem, *Testamenta XII Patriarchum* (PsVTG 1; Leiden: E. J. Brill, 1964); idem *The Testaments of the Twelve Patriarchs: A Study of Their Text, Composition, and Origin* (Assen: Van Gorcum, 1953); M. de Jonge et al., *The Testaments of the Twelve Patriarchs: A Critical Edition of the Greek Text* (PsVTG 1.2; Leiden: E. J. Brill, 1978); H. C. Kee, "The Ethical Dimensions of the Testaments of the XII as a Clue to Provenance," *NTS* 24 (1978) 259-70; idem, "Testaments of the Twelve Patriarchs," in *The Old Testament Pseudepigrapha*, ed. J. H. Charlesworth (2 vols.; Garden City, NY: Doubleday, 1983, 1985) 1:775-828; M. Philonenko, *Les Interpolations chrétiennes des Testaments des Douze Patriarches et les manuscrits de Qumran* (CRHPR 35; Paris, 1960); M. E. Stone, *The Testament of Levi: A First Study of the Armenian Manuscripts of the Testaments of the XII Patriarchs in the Convent of St. James, Jerusalem, with Text, Critical Apparatus, Notes and Translation* (Jerusalem: St. James, 1969). H. C. Kee

TESTIMONIA (4Q175)

4QTestimonia is rare among the scrolls to have been found in the eleven caves at or near *Qumran in that it is virtually complete. It consists of one side of parchment approximately 23 cm high and 14 cm wide. There are twenty-nine lines of writing, though the last word of the twenty-ninth line drops on to a thirtieth line in the bottom left-hand corner of the text. Although the absence of stitching at either edge shows that the single column of 4QTestimonia was never part of a scroll, neither is there any writing on the reverse as can be found, for example, with the single sheets of the phylacteries from Qumran.

It has long been taken for granted that the scribe who copied 4QTestimonia was the same as the one who copied 1QS, the first cave copy of the **Rule of the Community*; such an association, which is likely, would seem to date the penning of 4QTestimonia to the beginning of the first century B.C., give or take a decade or two. Both 4QTestimonia and 1QS share the custom of representing the divine name with four dots. The association with 1QS has been implicitly important for the modern interpretation of 4QTestimonia because of the three *eschatological figures who feature in 1QS 9:11, "a prophet and the messiahs of Aaron and Israel." None of the individual texts cited in 4QTestimonia is sectarian, but the intent of the collection as a whole and the manner of its presentation would seem to be so.

1. Content and Structure
2. Historical Reference
3. 4QTestimonia and the New Testament

1. Content and Structure.

4QTestimonia contains four paragraphs, each of which seems to contain a quotation introduced by a brief formula. The paragraphs are clearly marked in the manuscript with hook-shaped marginal marks. According to their content, the first three form one section in which those favored by God are described; the fourth makes a section by itself in which those cursed by God are described. It may not be a coincidence that the four quotations appear in canonical order: Exodus, Numbers, Deuteronomy, Joshua.

The first quotation is of a text like that in the Samaritan Pentateuch for Exodus 20:21; on the basis of the Masoretic Text it seems to be a combination of Deuteronomy 5:28-29 and 18:18-19, but it is preferable to identify the text as from Exodus. The so-called Samaritan text type is known in other manuscripts found at Qumran, such as 4QpaleoExod^{m}. This does not mean that the quotation reflects *Samaritan theology, though it is clear that the Samaritan Pentateuch emphasizes the prophetic role of *Moses.

The second quotation is from Numbers 24:15-17 and is commonly perceived to have been included because of its description of the scepter understood as a reference to the princely *Messiah (cf. CD 7:19-21; 4Q266 frag. 3 iii 19-22; 4Q269 frag. 5 2-4). However, Numbers 24:15-17 seems to refer to three figures, a "man" whose "eye is penetrating," apparently Balaam, a "star" who "shall come out of Jacob," and the "scepter" from *Israel who will crush "the heads of Moab and destroy all the children of Seth." In common with much contemporary early Jewish eschatology, the princely Messiah is God's agent in the destruction of those who oppose him, but the presence of the two other figures in this text may have prompted the organizer of this small collection to provide two other texts, one of which would clarify the referent of "man," the other of which would further explain the "star." Since "man" is mentioned first, Numbers 24:15-17 was preceded by a description of the prophet who would also be associated with the law. The Numbers quotation was then followed by an extract from Deuteronomy 33:8-11, identifying the "star" with the eschatological *priest. According to CD 7:18 the star is the Interpreter of the Law.

The third quotation makes explicit the prominence of Levi and the priesthood as interpreters of the law and cultic functionaries. This prominence over the scepter and this priestly preeminence is reinforced in Aaron or his house usually being mentioned before Israel, as in 1QS 9:11. Since Moses was Aaron's brother and himself of priestly family, all three of the first set of quotations in 4QTestimonia implicitly or explicitly give prominence to the priesthood. The priestly emphasis is enhanced in the way that the image of the star is matched by the way in which Levi will cause precepts and the law to shine. This play on words is continued in the juxtaposition of blessing and curse, which is also a priestly concern: as in 1QS 2:3 there is a priestly blessing for "enlightening" followed in 1QS 2:5 by the cursing of "all the men of the lot of Belial," so in 4QTestimonia the third quotation has a prayer for the blessing of Levi (Deut 33:11), which is followed by the curse of the man who rebuilds the city, the man of *Belial.

The fourth quotation is matched precisely in 4QApocryphon of Joshua[b] (4Q379 frag. 22 ii 7-15). It is a revised and expanded form of Joshua 6:26b. There is some debate about the direction of dependence. Most scholars assume that, just as for Exodus, Numbers and Deuteronomy, 4QTestimonia is quoting from the **Apocryphon of Joshua,* which as a rewritten form of Joshua (*see* Rewritten Bible) could then be considered to have attained some form of authority for the community, as had the book of **Jubilees* (whose periodization of history the *Apocryphon* follows). A minority view suggests that the *Apocryphon of Joshua* is citing a tradition such as that which is now found also in 4QTestimonia; this is being done to make the narrative of Joshua refer directly to contemporary events and thus to show how the community's experiences are continuous with those of biblical Israel.

This fourth quotation in 4QTestimonia contains an introductory phrase that is also found in the *Apocryphon of Joshua,* a citation of the curse of Joshua 6:26 and a prophetic expansion in which the curse is applied first to "the man of Belial" and then to one or more other people. Unfortunately the precise number of people cursed cannot be ascertained because both 4QTestimonia and 4QApocryphon of Joshua[b] (4Q379) are damaged at this point. The key phrase is "the two of them being vessels of violence." Since this phrase reflects the description of Simeon and Levi in Genesis 49:5, it is more likely that the text alludes to an accursed man of Belial and his two sons rather than simply to the accursed man and one other. Because the first three quotations in 4QTestimonia refer to three positive eschatological figures, it is also likely that the fourth quotation refers to a matching wicked triumvirate.

Whereas the Masoretic Text for Joshua 6:26b refers to Jericho, neither the *Septuagint nor the version in 4QTestimonia/4QApocryphon of Joshua[b] speaks of Jericho. Perhaps the place name was added as a gloss in the proto-Masoretic text; whatever the case, 4QTestimonia explicitly refers the whole curse to illicit activity in *Jerusalem.

2. Historical Reference.
There has been ongoing debate concerning how the various figures alluded to in the text, especially the wicked threesome, should be identified (see Eshel for the various proposals). Of recent interpreters W. H. Brownlee has proposed that the accursed man and his two sons are to be identified with John Hyrcanus (ruled 134-104 B.C.) and his two sons Aristobulus (104-103 B.C.) and Alexander Janneus (103-76 B.C.), H. Burgmann has argued again for the long-standing proposal that the accursed man is Simon Maccabeus (high priest 142-135 B.C.), and H. Eshel, arguing on the basis of archaeological information from the palace at Jericho, has supported an earlier proposal that John Hyrcanus is the accursed man and his sons Aristobulus and Antigonus the two weapons of violence. Perhaps in despair J. C. Lübbe has argued that the whole document should be read eschatologically and that scholars should refrain from making historical identifications.

3. 4QTestimonia and the New Testament.
Some of the same passages as appear in

4QTestimonia feature also in the NT writings: Deuteronomy 18:15 is quoted explicitly in Acts 3:22 and 7:37; Numbers 24:17 may lie behind Matthew 2:2 and Revelation 22:16. However, there is no need to suppose that any of the NT authors relied on 4QTestimonia or a document like it for their material. The more literary parallels that emerge between the Qumran literary corpus and the NT, the more it is possible to see all kinds of minor variations between the two bodies of writing. The parallels do not suggest literary dependence so much as that the Qumran and NT authors breathed the same air of eschatological expectation and searched a limited number of suitable biblical passages to justify their messianic views. Thus, while this might undermine the exclusivity of one aspect of the NT writings, it shows us that the NT authors reflect part of their contemporary Jewish culture and that their message would have been readily understandable by many of their first readers and hearers.

The presence of a chain (*catena*) of quotations has been heralded as proof for the widely held theory that some early Christian preachers may have carried with them not whole biblical books but small scrolls on which they would have had ready access to relevant scriptural passages (testimonies; see Fitzmyer) for their own purposes. The presence of chains of quotations (*catenae*) in the NT (Rom 3:10-18; Heb 1:5-13) could show that this was a well-known literary practice in the first century A.D.

The patterned use of blessings and curses is a feature of several NT texts. Blessings and curses are found together in the Sermon on the Plain in Luke (Lk 6:20-26); blessings and woes form an inclusio in the Gospel of Matthew at the start (Mt 5:3-12) and finish (Mt 23:13-36) of Jesus' teaching. In Paul's letter to the Galatians there is thematic interplay between curse (Gal 1:8-9; 3:10-14) and blessing (Gal 3:8, 14). The juxtaposition of blessings and curses makes it plain to the reader who is included and who is excluded from the community. Thus in 4QTestimonia the reader is supposed to read the unfulfilled promise, prophecy and blessing as delimiting who will be especially favored in the last days, whereas the curses are for the enemies of the community.

See also APOCRYPHON OF JOSHUA (4Q378-379); MESSIANISM; RULE OF THE COMMUNITY/ MANUAL OF DISCIPLINE (1QS).

BIBLIOGRAPHY. G. J. Brooke, *Exegesis at Qumran: 4QFlorilegium in Its Jewish Context* (JSOTSup 29; Sheffield: JSOT, 1985) 309-19; W. H. Brownlee, "The Wicked Priest, the Man of Lies and the Righteous Teacher—the Problem of Identity," *JQR* 73 (1982-83) 1-37; H. Burgmann, *Der "Sitz im Leben" in den Josuafluch-texten in 4Q379 22 II und 4QTestimonia* (Krakow: Enigma, 1990); H. Eshel, "The Historical Background of the Pesher Interpreting Joshua's Curse on the Rebuilding of Jericho," *RevQ* 15 (1991-92) 409-20; J. A. Fitzmyer, "'4QTestimonia' and the New Testament," *TS* 18 (1957) 513-37 [= idem, *The Semitic Background of the New Testament* (Biblical Resource Series; Grand Rapids, MI: Eerdmans; Livonia: Dove, 1997) 59-89]; J. C. Lübbe, "A Reinterpretation of 4QTestimonia," *RevQ* 12 (1986) 187-97.

G. J. Brooke

TESTING AND TRIAL IN SECULAR GREEK THOUGHT

In secular Greek thought, from as early as Homer and through the NT period, the phenomenon denoted in the *Septuagint, the *pseudepigrapha and the NT and related literature by the terms *peirazein* ("to try," "to make trial of," "to put to the test," and allegedly "to tempt," "to entice" [cf. *BAGD, peirazō; see DJG,* Temptation of Jesus, §1]) and *peirasmos* ("a hard trial/ordeal," "a test" or "a testing" and perhaps "a temptation/enticement" [*BAGD, peirasmos; see DJG,* Temptation of Jesus, §1]), namely, that of probing, proving or of being put to the test for good or ill, is referred to with some frequency (Gibson, 13-15, 18). In biblical literature God, along with human beings and impersonal objects, is frequently noted as being subjected through human agency to this phenomenon (see Ex 17:7; Num 14:22; Deut 6:16; 9:22; 33:8; Pss 78:40-43; 95:8-9; Is 7:12; Wis 1:2; Jdt 8:12; Acts 5:9; 15:10; 1 Cor 10:9; Heb 3:7-9; cf., e.g., 1 Sam 17:39; Eccles 2:1; Gen 22:1-9; Deut 8:2; 1 Kings 10:1).

In Greek literature we find that while it is also spoken of with reference to impersonal objects (cf. Dioscorides *Mat. Med. Praef.* 5.12, where *peirasmos* denotes his "trial" of the efficacy of a certain drug and the Scholion on Aristophanes *Plutus* 575, where *peirazō* denotes a young bird's first "trying out" of its wings; cf. also *Anacr.* 28.12; 33.24; Apollonius of Rhodes *Arg.* 2.46; *Grk. Anth.* 9.263; 11.348; 12.213; Dionysius of Halicarnassus *Ant. Rom.* 10.12.6; 12.213; 13.4.3.2;

Herodian *Schem. Hom.* 114.2; Lucian *Podagr.* 149; 165; 279), what is denoted by *peirasmos* and *peirazō* is hardly ever conceived as something to which, through humans, divinity is subject. (Instances of this topos appear only in Herodotus *Hist.* 8.86 gamma and Aeschylus *Ag.* 1663, and there the word employed to signify such "testing" is *peiraō;* see also Apollonius of Rhodes *Arg.* 3.10, where the goddess Athena is presented as being "put to the test" by the goddess Hera, queen of Olympus.) Rather, "probing," "proving" or "being put to the test" is an event primarily aimed at or happening almost exclusively to mortals.

1. The Nature and Content of the Experience
2. Significance for New Testament Study

1. The Nature and Content of the Experience. Evidence for what this phenomenon was perceived to involve regarding human beings is to be found in certain of the works of Homer, Arrian, *Josephus, *Plutarch, Menander, Lucilius, Galen, the anonymous commentators on *Aristotle's *Art of Rhetoric* and *Nicomachean Ethics* and the scholiasts on Homer, Euripides, Apollonius of Rhodes, Aristophanes and many other classical authors, as well as in the work of Pseudo-Apollodorus, Pseudo-Callisthenes, Diodorus Siculus, Polybius, Strabo and in that of the anonymous authors of the *Vitae Aesopi,* the papyri *PSI* 927.25, P. British Museum 2208.7 *(Peirazomene), P. Oxy.* 2891, and the *Cyranides,* among others.

Listed in these works as the *peirazomenoi* (the "tested ones") are such notable figures as Odysseus (Homer *Odys.* 9.105-306; 23.1-116, 153-240), the Spartan king Kleomenes III (Plutarch *Cleom.* 7.3), certain travelers (*Cyr.* 1.21.30, Kazimakis), soldiers (Strabo *Geog.* 16.4.24), as well as various criminals (Menander *Frag.* 42.319), thralls (Homer *Odys.* 16.225-320), farmsteaders (*Vita Aesopi* 64.2), ambassadors to Philip of *Macedon from Darius (*Historia Alexandri Magni* 1.23.13 Recension beta, cf. 1.23.16; 1.26.78 Recension gamma) and such persons as judges (Josephus *J.W.* 4.5.4 §340), "the man of many friends" (Plutarch *Mor.* 230A, cf. Anonymi, *In Aristotleis Artem Rhetoricum* 98.29; sch *Hecuba* 1226.1), a Heliodorus of uncertain origin (Lucilius *Grk. Anth.* 11.183), "evil people" (Galen *Ant. Lib. ii* 14.2.6), Stoics (Anonymi *In Ethica Nichomachea Commentaria* 454.10), the Aetolians (Polybius *Hist.* 21.4.7), the children of the inhabitants of Ceylon (Diodorus Siculus *Bib. Hist.* 2.58.5), the slave/philosopher Epictetus (Arrian *Epict. Diss.* 1.9.27), the Trojan king Laomedon (Ps.-Apollodorus *Bib.* 2.5.9), and Lycaon, the king of Arcadia, and his sons (Ps.-Apollodorus *Bib.* 3.98.2).

The testimony of these texts regarding the nature and content of the phenomenon denoted by *peirasmos* and *peirazein* can be summed up in six points.

First, the phenomenon was always thought of as something rooted in and arising out of an objective encounter between an individual or a group of people and a wholly external reality. These include difficult circumstances or hardships, such as the dangers of *travel (*Cyr.* 1.21.30) and the "attacks" of scurvy and lameness in the legs (Strabo *Geog.* 16.4.24) or epilepsy (*PSI* 927.25) or the machinations both of other persons (e.g., Arrian *Epict. Diss.* 1.9.27; Diodorus Siculus *Bib. Hist.* 2.58.5) and of divine beings (Ps.-Apollodorus *Bib.* 2.5.9; 3.98.2; Menander *Frag.* 42.319). In other words, one's experience of "probing," "proving" and/or "being put to the test" was never thought of as originating subjectively, nor was it ever viewed in terms of its being an inner psychological event, that is, the rise of a desire or thought from within a person that must be expunged, resisted or overcome. Rather, it was always something known to be imposed from the outside.

Second, the phenomenon has both a passive and an active element. While the experience denoted by *peirasmos* and *peirazein* is presented as a situation that one could suddenly find oneself in or subjected to against one's will, it was also envisaged as something that one could deliberately undertake and perpetrate against another. Thus we find instances not only of mortals "being tried" or being "put to the proof," sometimes only through happenstance, but also of men (but notably never women) and gods moving intentionally and actively to subject someone to probing and testing.

Third, in these latter instances, the purpose for intentionally subjecting anyone to testing is always to establish definitively in the mind of the tester something specific about the tested party that either is previously unknown or is known but is still in need of having its certainty augmented. Furthermore, testing is perpetrated in order to answer only two sets of questions about who or what the tested party is. As is illustrated in *Odyssey* 9.105-306, the issue testing resolves is whether or not a person is cunning, brave (*eidota*) and deserving of a hero's fame; in the *Cyranides*, Strabo's *Geography* 16.4.24, Arrian's *Epicteti Dissertationes* 1.9.27, Anonymi *In Ethica Nichomachea Commentaria* 454.10 and Diodorus Siculus's *Bibliotheca Historica* 2.58.5, it is whether a person is able, as he has committed himself to do or his heritage constrains him, to bear up under tribulation. In Plutarch's *Moralia* 23a, Anonymi *Artem Rhetoricum* 98.29 and scholion *Hecuba* 1226.1, it is whether in times of misfortune (*atychia*) or tribulation (*tais thlipsesi*) the tested one is a true friend; the question dealt with and answered by means of testing concerns the nature of a person's character and the extent of his integrity. As is noted in Menander *Fragments* 42.319 and Pseudo-Apollodorus's *Bibliotheca* 2.5.9; 3.98.2, testing resolves whether a man possesses *sebia* ("piety") and honors God (*Theon sebou*); at issue is the depth of one's piety.

Fourth, the motive force behind anyone ever engaging in the testing of another seems to be limited to skepticism or distrust on the part of the agent of the experience regarding how the party to be tested thinks or acts, what his character is like, whether he is trustworthy or possesses the virtues that he, given who or what he is, should have. See, for example, Arrian's story of the testing by *Musonius Rufus of *Epictetus in *Discourses* 1.9.27. Rufus puts the professed *Stoic, who was then a *slave, to the test by lying about tortures that Epictetus's master purportedly had in store for him, because Rufus doubted that Epictetus was wont to bear punishment with equanimity (cf. Ps.-Apollodorus *Bib.* 3.98.2). Another motive is a desire to bring about the tested party's demise: see Plutarch's story of the testing of the Spartan king Kleomenes III, who suspects that the testing arises because an enemy wishes to snare him into giving away a secret that would result in the king's overthrow and death (Plutarch *Cleom.* 7.3; cf. Ps.-Apollodorus *Bib.* 2.5.9).

Fifth, the experience of being put to the test is viewed as having a fundamental pattern. It consists in finding oneself in or being brought into a forced position, that is to say, one in which avoidance of displaying the virtue one is probed for is impossible and compliance with the exigencies of the probing is absolutely necessary if one is not to be shown wanting in the test. Consider, for example, Homer's story of Odysseus's experience of being tested when confronted by Polyphemus, the Cyclops (Homer *Odys.* 9.105-289), about the whereabouts of the ship that brought Odysseus and his men to Polyphemus's island. As Homer has his hero recognize (Homer *Odys.* 9:281, *hōs fato peirazōn,* "thus he put me to the proof"), Odysseus has no choice but to show himself, as the situation demands, truly to be the man of many devices if he is to remain the one whom even the gods proclaim as the hero who never ceases "struggling for his own life and the homecoming of his companions" (cf. Homer *Odys.* 1.5).

Finally, and perhaps most significantly, nowhere do we find men's experience of being tested, probed or put to the proof and their common experience of enticement or solicitation to evil (indicated in the literature by such words as *thelgein* [cf. Homer *Odys.* 12:39ff., *epagōgon* [cf. Xenophon *Mem.* 2.5.5; Plato *Phileb.* 44C], and *goēteuma* [Plato *Phileb.* 44C]) thought of as, or assumed to be, concurrent or even the same phenomenon (on this, with further instances from the literature, see Moule, 65-75, esp. 69). When a person is subjected to testing it is always and only to see whether he will act in a particular way or whether the character he bears is well established but never to get that person to act in a particular way, especially one that is morally wrong. This is the case even in instances where hostility and the desire to see the demise of the tested person motivates the subjecting the person to testing. For it is assumed there that the person tested is already morally corrupt, not susceptible to or ripe for corruption. Indeed, it is the knowledge that if the one to be tested could be shown for what he already is, his destruction could be assured, that makes testing appropriate here.

Accordingly, in the secular Greek world, the phenomenon denoted by the terms *peirasmos* and *peirazein* was thought of as an activity designed to or having the effect of revealing something of what a person is made of. And when it is applied to men by other men or by divine beings, this phenomenon is the means by which the moral, not the intellectual or physical, condition of a man is ascertained. It seems never to have been thought of in any way other than a test of character or faithfulness.

2. Significance for New Testament Study.

The import of these observations is threefold. First, they clarify the sense in which *peirasmos* is employed at Luke 22:28; Acts 20:19; and 2 Peter 2:9 (Sinaiticus 69 al sy[h]). Against many, H. Seesemann (29 n. 35) has argued that in these instances, which speak of the *peirasmoi* endured respectively by Jesus, Paul and "those who have attained faith . . . [and are] established in the truth," the term means something more akin to danger than a test or a proving. This, he notes, is not only because "danger" "seems natural for *peirasmoi* in the pl[ural]" but because "we have other examples" of *peirasmoi* being used with this limited meaning.

The examples that Seesemann adduces to support this claim are *Cyranides* 1.21.30, where *peirasmos* is used of the "trials" which along with the "hazards" (*kindydoi*) of travel on land and sea serve to determine a traveler's mettle (*byetai de apo pasēs anagkas chalepēs kai peristaseōs, thalasiōn kindynōn kai peirasmōn en tē gē kai thalassē, kai apo daimonoōn kai pasēs nosou*) and *Syntipas* (Jernestedt and Nikitin, line 24 p. 40), a Byzantine "Arabian Nights," where *peirasmos* is used for the afflictions of life that reveal whether or not a person possesses great inner fortitude (*kai hypo peirasmōn tou kosmou stenochōroumenoi heuriskousi boētheian kai kouphismon di' euergesiōn autou*). Accordingly, instead of indicating that in Luke 22:28; Acts 20:19; and 2 Peter 2:9 (Sinaiticus* 69 al sy^h) *peirasmos* means something other than "a trial" or "a proving," the witness of usage of the term in secular Greek confirms that it must mean this.

Second, this evidence raises the question of whether Gentile readers or hearers of NT writings would have understood the use of *peirasmos* and *peirazein* in such texts as Matthew 4:1 (par. Lk 4:2; Mk 1:12); Luke 4:13; Matthew 6:13 (par. Lk 11:4); Galatians 6:1; 1 Thessalonians 3:5, James 1:13 and 1 Timothy 6:9 in terms of the notion of enticement to sin, even if, as many NT lexicons and exegetical studies of these texts claim, that this is the idea intended to be conveyed there. In the light of our observations, it seems more likely that these readers or hearers would have taken the terms as signifying only tests of faithfulness or integrity.

Third, insofar as secular Greek usage had any influence on delimiting the semantic range within which Hellenized Jewish or early Christian usage of *peirasmos* and *peirazein* took its bearings, the observations outlined above indicate that there is strong reason to doubt that in those NT texts where *peirasmos* and *peirazein* are usually construed in terms of enticement to sin, this notion ever played any part. Tendencies for lexicographers and exegetes to see that it does may therefore be the result not of a sober analysis of the linguistic data but of eisegesis and circular reasoning.

See also AFFLICTION LISTS.

BIBLIOGRAPHY. J. B. Gibson, "The Traditions of the Temptations of Jesus in Early Christianity" (D.Phil. thesis, Oxford University, 1993); V. Jernestedt and P. Nikitin, eds., *Syntipas* in *Memories de l'Academie Imperiale des Sciences de St. Petersbourg, 8me Serie, Classe des Sciences Historico-Philologique,* tome XI (1912) no. 1; D. Kaimakis, ed., *Die Kyraniden* (Musenkeim am Glan: Hain, 1976); J. Korn, *PEIRASMOS: Die Versuchung des Glaubigen in der greischischen Bible* (Stuttgart: Kohlhammer, 1937); C. F. D. Moule, "An Unsolved Problem in the Temptation Clause of the Lord's Prayer," *RTR* 33 (1974) 65-75; H. Seesemann, "*πεῖρα κτλ,*" *TDNT* 6:26-36.

J. B. Gibson

TEXTUAL CRITICISM

Textual criticism is the discipline that attempts to establish an authoritative text for a given author's work. Textual criticism involves the informed comparison of all of the known copies of a given text in order to ascertain the earliest recoverable and, if possible, the original form of the text and to trace the history of its development. Textual criticism is often thought of only in terms of NT textual criticism, but it applies to any and all of the documents from the ancient world. Textual criticism focuses usually upon literary authors, such as the classical writers (e.g., Homer, *Plato, *Aristotle, the dramatists) and the later authors such as *Philo, *Josephus and the various historians (e.g., Dio Cassius, Polybius), where there is a history of textual transmission and the original documents are no longer extant. However, there is also a need for sound principles of textual criticism to be applied to nonliterary texts, such as papyri and inscriptions (*see* Inscriptions and Papyri).

1. The Materials of Textual Criticism
2. The Methods of Textual Criticism
3. Conclusion

1. The Materials of Textual Criticism.

Textual criticism of the NT is both blessed and cursed by a wealth of materials available for study. Depending on how they are counted, there are nearly fifty-five hundred manuscripts of various sizes and shapes with various portions of the NT on them, as well as hundreds of copies of various ancient versions or translations, and quotations of the NT in the early church fathers. NT manuscripts range from the complete or nearly complete major codices, such as Codex Sinaiticus or Codex Vaticanus, to the fragmentary recently published P. Vindob. G 42417 (P^{116}), the most recently discovered and published NT papyrus manuscript with a few verses of Hebrews on it (Heb 2:9-11; 3:3-6). The original NT manuscripts were probably written on papyrus, the paper of the ancient Mediterranean world, but these are no longer extant. Instead we have copies of copies made over the course of over fourteen hundred years, as scribes copied these by hand and passed them down to others. Approximately 116 of these manuscripts are on papyrus (the number is still growing as more papyri are published), with the rest being on parchment or paper. The result of this process of copying and textual transmission is that numerous changes of various types have been introduced into these documents. Some of the changes were made intentionally to correct or improve a manuscript (or so a scribe thought), while others were unintentionally introduced through carelessness or a slip of the pen. As a result, there are no two NT manuscripts that are identical in all aspects.

Currently the earliest complete or nearly complete manuscripts of the NT date to the fourth century (Codex Sinaiticus [א 01] and Codex Vaticanus [B 03]), within four hundred years of their composition. However, there are substantial or nearly complete manuscripts of individual books of the NT, such as several of Paul's letters (excluding the beginning of Romans, 2 Thessalonians, Philemon or the Pastorals) and Hebrews, in Chester Beatty II (P. Chester Beatty II and Univ. of Michigan Inv. 6238 [P^{46}]). Of course, there are many fragments that are even earlier (such as *P. Ryl.* Greek 457 [P^{52}], a fragment of John dated to c. 125). In other words, there is a wealth of relatively early manuscript evidence for much of the NT.

Textual criticism of most classical and other ancient authors, however, is in a very different situation. F. F. Bruce (16-17) summarizes the situation for a number of ancient authors. For example, for Caesar's *Gallic Wars* there are numerous manuscripts, but the oldest is around nine hundred years later than the date of composition (58-50 B.C.). Thucydides' history is known from eight manuscripts, as well as a number of papyrus fragments, but the earliest of the manuscripts is dated to about A.D. 900, around thirteen hundred years after the date of composition, although some papyri are from the Greco-Roman era. The same is generally true of Herodotus's history. This says nothing of the authors whose works have survived only in part, such as Livy (only 35 of his 142 books of Roman history are extant) and *Tacitus (only 4.5 of the 14 books of his *Histories* survive, although with a better ratio for his *Annals,* with 10 books surviving in full and 2 in part out of 16; all of his minor works are dependent on one manuscript from the tenth century). These examples are indicative of the state of textual criticism for classical and related authors (see West, 9-10).

Textual criticism for nonliterary texts is made more difficult by the fact that for such documents as documentary papyri, there may be only the single manuscript. In many instances, this can make decipherment and establishment of the text very difficult. Sometimes the situation is aided by the fact that many documentary papyri follow particular formulas, and these formulas can be used in reconstructing the fragmentary text. The same can be true for inscriptions and other types of texts, such as official *letters. In some of these instances, the document may have been issued in multiple forms in different places for comparison (e.g., Augustus's *Res Gestae*). However, although the formulaic elements may be able to be reconstructed so that one has a sense of the shape of the document, the exact wording often cannot be known because of the specific nature of the given document.

2. The Methods of Textual Criticism.

As a result, one can imagine that on the basis of the different types of documents textual criticism can be performed in many different ways.

2.1. Stemmatic Approach. Classical textual criticism often follows what has been called a stemmatic or genealogical approach, developed in its classic form by P. Maas and recently refined by M. L. West (cf. Reynolds and Wilson, 186-213). This method involves reconstructing a family tree or stemma of surviving manuscripts, working back through the textual variants until one is able to establish an archetype (extant or nonextant) and through this to determine which is the best manuscript upon which to base the edition. The ability to do this is colored by a number of factors, such as the contamination of manuscripts. In some cases it might be possible to account for all of the variants in a stemma (called a closed recension), but in many instances this will not be possible (an open recension). Dealing with an open recension is more complex and may well result in an incomplete stemma and reliance upon other forms of tabulation of variants.

From what has been said above, one can understand both how this method is possible and why it is a desirable method in the textual criticism of classical or related texts. The limited number of manuscripts, especially those of substantial size, makes this a more manageable task and one that can thereby account for the origin and development of the variant readings. This form of textual criticism was used in NT textual criticism in the nineteenth century, before many of the earlier manuscripts were discovered or available for use, and is still used by some NT textual critics (see Colwell, 63-83). The more open the recension is, the more difficulty there is for the stemmatic method. Perhaps the inevitable criticism from some NT scholars regarding this method is that it relies on a historically based documentary method but one that cannot easily move further back in the tradition than the known documents, that is, to the nonextant autograph, so much sought in much NT textual criticism (see Holmes, 347-48, in Ehrman and Holmes). Therefore, a number of NT scholars use forms of the so-called eclectic method noted below. Nevertheless, for classical authors, as well as in instances where the textual evidence is limited (such as papyri and inscriptions), classical methods of textual criticism still have much to commend them.

2.2. Majority Text. The vast majority of manuscripts of the NT follow the Byzantine textual tradition. Two Byzantine manuscripts dating to the twelfth century, compared with a couple of others (as well as supplementing this with retranslation from Latin for a few verses), were the ones Erasmus used in preparing his edition of the Greek NT (1516). This popular edition, subsequently called the Textus Receptus, or "received text," by a printer, remained the NT text in use and the basis for most translations until late in the nineteenth century (see Porter, "Modern English Translations"). Some scholars still insist on using the Textus Receptus, but most who would still find merit in the Byzantine text type recognize that the Textus Receptus is merely one possible form of that text (see Sturz), and others have attempted to promote the majority text (for general discussion see Wallace, 297-320, in Ehrman and Holmes). Most scholars have rejected the majority text as a basis for textual criticism, since it often substitutes a counting of manuscripts for an examination of other factors, such as date, transmission and relationships. B. M. Metzger (esp. 291-92) has claimed that more than 90 percent of the extant manuscripts have a Byzantine character (Epp argues for 80 percent) but that most of these were written within the restricted confines of the Byzantine Empire and that this approach neglects the major developments in early textual transmission, including major disruptions.

2.3. Eclectic Methods. On the basis of the large numbers of manuscripts involved and the presence of widespread contamination within the manuscript tradition, the vast majority of NT textual critics practice what is called eclectic textual criticism, often developing methods elucidated by B. F. Westcott and F. J. A. Hort. The idea is that rather than confining oneself to a reconstructed stemma or relying on the reading found in the largest number of manuscripts, it is assumed that any given manuscript may or may not preserve a correct reading. Thus a process is needed to draw from all of the available resources to reconstruct what is thought to be the earliest reading and hence closest to the original text. These resources include external evidence (the manuscripts themselves, as well as sources such as the early church fathers and versions) and internal evidence (the tendencies of the scribes). On the basis of how these two factors are weighed, there are two forms of eclectic method in use: thoroughgoing eclecticism and reasoned eclecticism.

2.3.1. Thoroughgoing Eclecticism. Thoroughgoing or rigorous eclecticism is usually identified with G. D. Kilpatrick and his student J. K. Elliott (Elliott, 321-35, in Ehrman and Holmes). This form of eclectic criticism relies most heavily upon internal evidence in making text-critical decisions and does not give much weight to the external evidence, except as the manuscripts provide a collection of the possible readings to be sifted and evaluated to arrive at the correct reading. This method thus relies upon the weight of probabilities regarding scribal tendencies as a means of assessing readings. Several criticisms of this method involve the heavy reliance upon probabilities in scribal tendencies, even though the kinds of sophisticated stylistic studies of the NT that could aid in such a procedure are still relatively rudimentary and have been mostly applied to questions of authorship. Another criticism is that this method neglects the history of the textual tradition and its transmission. The result is that in some instances a relatively late variant might be accepted because it seems to fit the internal evidence, even though it may not be attested in earlier sources.

2.3.2. Reasoned Eclecticism. The vast majority of NT textual critics today practice what is called reasoned eclecticism (see Holmes, 336-60, in Ehrman and Holmes; Aland and Aland; Metzger; Epp; Epp and Fee). Reasoned eclecticism tries to strike a balance between external and internal evidence, such that the characteristics of a given variant in the light of scribal tendencies are evaluated in relation to the manuscript evidence. External evidence includes consideration of the relative dates of the manuscripts (e.g., most of the manuscripts that date from before the sixth century were unknown or unused before the late nineteenth century), their distribution geographically (readings with widespread distribution are considered better than those located in one place), the genealogical relationships that may exist between the manuscripts, and the relative quality of the manuscripts (e.g., papyri are generally thought to be of better quality than parchments, although this view must be qualified).

Internal evidence is concerned with transcriptional probabilities related to the habits and practices of scribes. The tendencies of scribes can be broken down into unintentional and intentional scribal changes. The unintentional ones include instances where letters were confused, words were divided improperly (since all of the early manuscripts were written in continuously written capital letters), the order of letter or words was switched, words were substituted, words were omitted or repeated (this often occurred in conjunction with losing one's place in a manuscript), spelling was faulty or harmonization took place unconsciously. The intentional scribal changes may well have been made with honest motives, since they often involved improving grammar and style, harmonizing Synoptic parallels, clarifying obscure points, conflating readings, adding appropriate material (such as a fuller name of Jesus) and theological changes (see Epp, 60-61).

The intentional scribal factors remain not as widely studied as the others in textual criticism, due to the more global considerations, such as style, involved. On the basis of these scribal tendencies, a number of canons or rules of textual criticism have been developed to aid in adjudicating the results of scribal analysis. On the basis of the scribal tendencies noted, these canons usually opt for the shorter, more difficult or least well harmonized reading (Epp, 62-63). The final consideration often used in this type of textual criticism is what has been called Bengel's Rule, by which is meant that in the final analysis the best reading is the one that can account for all of the other variants.

3. Conclusion.
Reasoned eclecticism has come to dominate NT textual criticism, apart from a few scholars who hold on to the majority text and a few others who utilize thoroughgoing eclecticism. The result has been so much confidence that some textual critics believe that even though we do not have any of the autographs, we have arrived at what is tantamount to the original text (see Clarke, who evaluates the ratings in the United Bible Societies' Greek New Testament and their implications). This is, however, a problematic conclusion, since it has no hope of being proved or disproved without discovering the autographs. This overconfidence also neglects the widespread disagreement regarding methods in textual criticism and the subjective nature of many of the criteria.

Two further points are to be made. The first is that this overconfidence has led some scholars to seriously question whether the original text is something that can be found through the methods currently available and whether it might not be better, in line with much classical textual criticism, to argue for the earliest establishable text. The second point follows from this. In light of this situation, it might be wise to consider not relying so heavily on an eclectic text, which is the product of modern scholarly reflection and industry, but using instead single manuscripts that date from the ancient world. For the NT this might be an edition of one of the major codices for a given book of the NT. There is much to be said for selecting and utilizing a single ancient text, since such an ancient text, despite its errors, represents a text that was used, in the case of the NT, in an ancient church context, even if it has readings that were not original.

See also LITERACY AND BOOK CULTURE; MANUSCRIPTS, GREEK NEW TESTAMENT; NEW TESTAMENT VERSIONS, ANCIENT; OLD TESTAMENT VERSIONS, ANCIENT.

BIBLIOGRAPHY. K. Aland and B. Aland, *The Text of the New Testament* (2d ed.; Grand Rapids, MI: Eerdmans, 1989); J. N. Birdsall, "The Recent History of New Testament Textual Criticism (from Westcott and Hort, 1881, to the Present)," *ANRW* 2.26.1 (1992) 99-197; F. F. Bruce, *The New Testament Documents: Are They Reliable?* (5th ed.; Downers Grove, IL: InterVarsity Press, 1960); K. D. Clarke, *Textual Optimism: A Critique of the United Bible Societies' Greek New Testament* (JSNTSup 138; Sheffield: Sheffield Academic Press, 1997); E. C. Colwell, *Studies in Methodology in Textual Criticism of the New Testament* (NTTS 9; Leiden: E. J. Brill, 1969); B. D. Ehrman and M. W. Holmes, eds., *The Text of the New Testament in Contemporary Research: Essays on the Status Quaestionis* (SD 46; Grand Rapids: Eerdmans, 1995); E. J. Epp, "Textual Criticism in Exegesis of the New Testament, with an Excursus on Canon," in *Handbook to Exegesis of the New Testament,* ed. S. E. Porter (NTTS 25; Leiden: E. J. Brill, 1997) 45-97; E. J. Epp and G. D. Fee, *Studies in the Theory and Method of New Testament Textual Criticism* (Grand Rapids, MI: Eerdmans, 1993); F. W. Hall, *A Companion to Classical Texts* (Oxford: Clarendon Press, 1913); P. Maas, *Textual Criticism* (Oxford: Clarendon Press, 1958); B. M. Metzger, *The Text of the New Testament: Its Transmission, Corruption and Restora-tion* (3d ed.; New York: Oxford University Press, 1992); A. Papathomas, "A New Testimony to the Letter to the Hebrews," *JGRCJ* 1 (2000) 18-24; S. E. Porter, "Modern Translations," in *The Oxford Illustrated History of the Bible,* ed. J. Rogerson (Oxford: Oxford University Press, forthcoming); idem, "Why So Many Holes in the Papyrological Evidence for the Greek New Testament?" in *The Bible as Book: The Transmission of the Greek Text,* ed. K. van Kampen and S. McKendrick (London: British Library Publications; Grand Haven, MI: Scriptorium, forthcoming); L. D. Reynolds and N. G. Wilson, *Scribes and Scholars: A Guide to the Transmission of Greek and Latin Literature* (2d ed.; Oxford Press: Clarendon Press, 1974); H. A. Sturz, *The Byzantine Text Type and New Testament Textual Criticism* (Nashville: Nelson, 1984); M. L. West, *Textual Criticism and Editorial Technique* (Stuttgart: Teubner, 1973); B. F. Westcott and F. J. A. Hort, *The New Testament in the Original Greek* (2 vols.; Cambridge: Macmillan, 1881).

S. E. Porter

THANKSGIVING HYMNS (1QH)

Thanksgiving Hymns (*Hodayot*) is the title given to a collection of more than thirty psalmic-type compositions. Eight copies, all of them incomplete, were preserved in the caves at *Qumran. Modeled on the biblical psalms, particularly the psalms of thanksgiving, these poems are considered among the core religious writings of the *Essenes and attest that devotional religious poetry still continued to be composed in the Second Temple period.

1. The Manuscript Evidence
2. Form and Content
3. Authorship and Unity of the Collection
4. Purpose and Use of the *Hodayot*
5. The Significance for the New Testament

1. The Manuscript Evidence.

Fifty years after the discovery of the first copies of this work, even basic questions such as where certain psalms begin and end—and hence the exact number of compositions—and the precise readings of many badly damaged sections are far from resolved.

The largest and most complete scroll containing these *Thanksgiving Hymns* (1QH^{a}) was found by the bedouin in Cave 1 at Qumran and purchased by E. Sukenik of Hebrew University in November 1947. When the scroll came to him, there were three separate damaged sheets plus more than seventy detached fragments (in recent years more than twenty more very small fragments have been identified as belonging to this scroll). Two scribes had written the manuscript; one scribe copied up until column 11, line 22 (as Sukenik arranged and numbered the columns), and another scribe took over in the middle of the line and completed the scroll; thus it is possible to determine whether even a small fragment comes from the first part or the latter part of the scroll, on the basis of the handwriting. Sukenik organized the material into eighteen columns and sixty-six unplaced small fragments and in 1954-55 published a complete *editio princeps* with plates and transcription. Since many of the psalms begin with the formula *ʾôdĕkâ* ("I give you thanks"), Sukenik called the manuscript the *Thanksgiving Scroll* (the "Scroll of the *Hodayot*").

Among the debris of Cave 1 archaeologists found two more small fragments (1Q35) that were very similar to Sukenik's manuscript in both the handwriting and the content. These were published in 1955 by J. T. Milik, who suggested that they may have originally been part of Sukenik's manuscript. However it was soon recognized that there was overlapping text, and hence this must be a second copy of the *Thanksgiving* psalms or at least a copy of part of this collection. This scroll is now designated $1QH^b$.

Six more copies of this work were identified from Cave 4 on the basis of overlapping text (4Q427-432). Five were written on animal skins and one on papyrus. These manuscripts were part of the allotment of J. Strugnell and were published by E. Schuller in 1999 in Discoveries in the Judaean Desert, volume XXIX. The new information that they supply is only beginning to be incorporated in our overall understanding of the *Hodayot*. All are very fragmentary, and much of the text must be restored from the more complete Cave 1 copy. Some sections or individual words, however, are preserved only in the Cave 4 copies, and these can serve to fill in some of the lacunae in the $1QH^a$ scroll.

The most interesting scroll is $4QH^a$ (4Q427), which includes a large fragment (frag. 7) that preserves a major segment of a psalm of which only a few scattered words had survived in $1QH^a$. There are portions of another psalm (frag. 8 i and ii) that does not appear at all in the preserved section of $1QH^a$, and the order of psalms was totally different in this copy than in $1QH^a$. Another manuscript, $4QH^e$ (4Q430), also seems to have a different order of psalms than either $1QH^a$ or $4QH^a$. $4QH^c$ (4Q429) was a small scroll with only twelve lines and very narrow columns, so that, even when complete, it would not have contained the whole collection that was found in $1QH^a$. The papyrus scroll, $4QH^f$ (4Q432) probably also only contained a portion of the psalms. This variation in the copies suggests that there were distinct subcollections of psalms (there is also evidence to this effect in the different systems of orthography in various parts of $1QH^a$). These collections were combined in a specific way in $1QH^a$ and also in $4QH^b$, which has the same order and content. But in other copies various subunits were copied separately or in a different order.

In recent years two scholars working independently, H. Stegemann and E. Puech, have reconstructed the original order of the $1QH^a$ scroll on the basis of the shapes and patterns of the damaged pieces (see Puech 1988). This reconstruction has important implications for understanding this work. For instance, the reconstruction establishes that the scroll originally contained seven sheets with four columns in each for a total of twenty-eight columns, with forty-one or forty-two lines to a column. The first three columns and the last two columns are almost entirely missing. In Sukenik's arrangement, the category of psalms that are called Hymns of the Teacher (see below) came at the beginning of the scroll, followed by the Hymns of the Community; in the reconstructed scroll, the Hymns of the Teacher come in the middle (cols. 9-17), with Hymns of the Community at the beginning (cols. 1-8) and at the end (cols. 18-28) of the scroll.

A complete reconstruction of $1QH^a$ has not yet been published. In citing references in this article, the reconstructed column and line numbers will be used and the former column and line numbers of Sukenik will be put in brackets since earlier translations and references follow this system. Recent English translations usually follow the reconstructed order but with some differences in line numbers.

2. Form and Content.

These poetic compositions are modeled to some extent on the biblical psalms, especially of the type "individual psalms of thanksgiving." Nevertheless, when the collection as a whole is studied, there is evidence of considerable diversity in both form and content rather than a strict imitation of a biblical model.

The psalms are a direct address to God in the second person. There is a first person singular speaker but, as in the biblical psalms, the "I" may be corporate, that is, the voice of the community. In a few places the speaker is the plural "we." Unlike the biblical psalms of thanksgiving, where the psalm can begin in quite different ways, these all start with a set introductory formula, either "I thank you, O Lord," or "Blessed are you, Lord." It is not clear that there is any real distinction between the two introductions, and in one case ($1QH^a$ 13:22 [5:20]) the first is erased and the second written in above the line. The psalmist then states his reason for offering praise by recounting what God has done for him: "because you have placed my soul in the bundle of the living" (1QH[a] 10:22 [2:20]); "because you have redeemed my soul from the pit" (1QH[a] 11:20 [3:19]); "for you have illumined my face by your covenant" (1QH[a] 12:6 [4:5]); "because you have dealt wondrously with dust and mightily with a creature of clay" (1QH[a] 19:6 [11:3]).

Other reasons frequently cited for giving thanks is that God has granted the psalmist knowledge of marvelous mysteries (e.g., 1QH[a] 12:28-29 [4:27-28]) and brought him into the community (the *yaḥad),* giving him fellowship with the elect on earth and the angels in heaven (e.g., 1QH[a] 11:23-24 [3:22-23]. The main body of the psalm can be quite varied in form and content. There might be an extended and elaborate development of a specific image or motif, for example, a tree planted in a garden (1QH[a] 16:5-27 [8:4-26]); a fortified city (1QH[a] 14:28-32 [6:25-29]); a woman in labor (1QH[a] 11:8-14 [3:7-13]). In some psalms, there are extended descriptions of the events to come in the *eschatological future, with particular emphasis on the destruction of *Belial and all the spirits of wickedness (1QH[a] 11:26-37 [3:25-36]; 25:3-16 [frag. 5:1-14]). As in biblical psalms of thanksgiving, there are very few petitions, although there are occasionally imperative verbs and requests to God (e.g., 1QH[a] 19:33 [11:30]; 8:29-30 [16:11-12]). There is no standard concluding formula. In the biblical psalms of thanksgiving there was often mention in the concluding section of offering *sacrifice and fulfilling vows in the temple (e.g., Pss 107:22; 116:17-18), but this element is not found in any of these texts.

All of these psalms seem very biblical because they reuse biblical phraseology and images; hundreds of allusions but rarely direct quotations have been identified, most from the Psalms, Isaiah and Deuteronomy. Yet the biblical words and phrases are reworked and reconfigured in a style that is quite different from earlier biblical poetry. Although certain standard poetic conventions are maintained, the cola tend to be much longer, with extended list-like sections, so that at times this becomes almost an elevated prose. Precisely because the language is so conventional and biblical, one of the major interpretative issues is to judge how much these psalms should be read autobiographically, even when the claim is made that they are to be attributed to the Teacher himself. Some scholars have attempted to use these psalms as sources of very specific information about details in the life of the Teacher; others have emphasized the biblical background of basic motifs such as enemies, persecution and exile and thus hesitate to draw any conclusions about the life situation of the author on this basis.

3. Authorship and Unity of the Collection. Many scholars, beginning with Sukenik, have suggested that this entire collection of psalms was a unified work and was authored by the Teacher of Righteousness. Here, it was assumed, we could find his personal devotional piety, an account of how God had given him a special revelation that he is to share with the members of his community (1QH[a] 12:28 [4:27]) and at least oblique references to his persecution and exile by the Wicked Priest (e.g., 1QH[a] 12:10-22 [4:9-10], "they have banished me from my land like a bird from the nest"; cf. 1QpHab 11:6, and *see* Habakkuk Commentary). However, a series of studies by a number of scholars in the 1960s (especially Holm-Nielsen in Denmark and the German school of Morawe, Jeremias and Kuhn) proposed that the collection is not a unity and at least two basic categories of psalms need to be distinguished.

In one group of psalms, the "I" seems highly personal. The person who speaks has an exalted position and functions as a mediator of revelation to others. There are lengthy descriptions of his sufferings and betrayal, certain repeated lexical items, highly developed imagery and extensive reliance on biblical phraseology. Six to eight psalms fall into this category, though sometimes as many as twelve are included; core exemplars include 1QH[a] 10:5-21 (2:3-19), 10:22-32 (2:20-30), 12:6—13:6 (4:5—5:4), 13:7-21 (5:5-19), 13:20—15:8 (5:20—7:5), 15:9-28 (7:6-25), 16:5—17:36 (8:4—9:36). Many scholars make the further argument that these psalms were composed by the Teacher of Righteousness and hence their designation The Hymns of the Teacher (*Lehrerliedern*); a minority opinion recognizes that these psalms form a distinct group but argues that the "I" need not be a particular individual but could be any member of the community.

In the second category, the Hymns of the Community (*Gemeindeliedern*), the "I" seems more the corporate voice of the community. These psalms are characterized by common components, especially an explicit confession of God's salvific action and justice (e.g., "I know that righteousness is yours," 1QH^a 19:20-21 [11:17-18]) and extended reflections about the sinful condition and misery of humankind, often expressed in the form of rhetorical questions (e.g., "What is one born of a woman in the midst of all your awesome works? He is a construction of dust and kneaded with water; his foundation is sinful guilt, and ignominious shame, and a source of uncleanness; a spirit of perversity rules over him," 1QH^a 5:31-33 [13:14-16]). The authorship of these psalms has not been defined with any precision. It is usually assumed that they are sectarian in origin, that is, composed by members of the Essene community. There are similarities with the **Rule of the Community* and the **War Scroll* in worldview (dualistic and deterministic) and vocabulary (words like *yaḥad*/community, *Maskil*/Instructor, Belial). As is typical of literature identified as sectarian, the divine name (the tetragrammaton) is never used. God is designated as *ʾel*, which is occasionally written in Paleo-Hebrew script in 1QH^a, or *ʾelohim* ("God") or *ʾadonai* ("Lord").

The picture is further complicated because there are some compositions that do not fit neatly into either category. One psalm (1QH^a 9:1—10:4 [1:1—2:2]) is distinctive because it contains an extended wisdom-like reflection on creation and divine determinism and concludes with an exhortation to a plural audience, "Hear, O you wise, and you who mediate on knowledge . . . O you righteous, put an end to wickedness." Another psalm, best preserved in 4Q427 frag. 7, with some smaller overlapping fragments in 4Q431 and 1QH^a 25:34—26:41, seems more liturgical in style. It contains an extended series of imperative calls to give praise, "sing, O beloved ones, rejoice . . . right forth . . . give praise, extol"; confessional statements in the first person plural, "we have known you, O God of righteousness"; and a series of summonses to "proclaim and say, Great is God/blessed is God." Toward the beginning of the psalm, the speaker describes himself in exalted language as a "beloved of the king, a companion of the holy ones" who is "with the heavenly beings" (*ʾelim*). A version of this passage, though a distinct recension, appears in another fragment that may be part of a copy of the *War Scroll* (4Q491 11 i) or perhaps is an independent composition. This is significant because it is one of the few instances where a passage appears both in the *Hodayot* and in another scroll and suggests that the author(s) of the psalms may have drawn upon existing compositions.

On chronological grounds, it is possible that some or all of the psalms were composed by the Teacher of Righteousness; all were composed in the early stages of the community's foundation. 4QH^b is the earliest copy of these hymns, and the handwriting can be dated to c. 100 to 50 B.C.; this manuscript is especially significant since it shows that the full compilation had been drawn together in a fixed order by this time. 1QH^a and 1QH^b were copied somewhat later, c. 50 to 1 B.C., and other copies are from the last quarter of the first century B.C. or the beginning of the common era.

4. Purpose and Use of the *Hodayot*.

How these psalms were used is a question that has been much debated, without any clear resolution. The length of at least a number of the compositions and the complexity of the poetry have suggested to some scholars (e.g., Nitzan) that they were more suitable for personal private meditation and/or instruction than for communal singing. There are no textual indications that they were sung on a regular basis, whether daily or for *feasts or for special liturgical services, in contrast to scrolls such as 4Q503 (*Daily Prayers*) and 4Q504 (*Words of the Luminaries*), which give clear rubrical notations. There are some rubrical-type notes, for example, in 1QH^a 20:7-14 (12:4-11) "for the *Maskil*, thanksgiving and prayer, to bow down and make supplication always"; 1QH^a 25:34 (frag. 8 10) "for the *Maskil*, a psalm," and faint traces of similar rubrics in 1QH^a 7:21 (15:8) and 5:12 (frag. 15 ia 3).

Puech has suggested that there is a fivefold division, modeled upon the five books of the Psalter, and that this is indicative of some liturgical usage. Because of the emphasis on the weak human condition and the doxological confession, elements found also in the psalm at the end of the *Rule of the Community* (1QS 10—11), it has been suggested that the Hymns of the Community may have originated in the Liturgy for Entrance into and Renewal of the Covenant (see 1QS 1:18—2:18), and perhaps secondarily came to be part of the daily "entering the Covenant of God" (1QS 10:10). There are some themes in common with the morning blessings in later rabbinic prayer (e.g., thanksgiving for knowledge; creation), but the links are general rather than specific. If there are some copies that contained only the Hymns of the Teacher, this may suggest that these particular scrolls served a special purpose; the small format of $4QH^c$ might indicate a scroll written for personal use.

Given how little we know about the shape and content of the liturgical life of the Essenes, it may not be possible to resolve the question of personal versus communal use with any certainty. Perhaps a more fruitful avenue of inquiry is that explored by C. Newsom, who concentrates not on reconstructing the original *Sitz im Leben* but rather asks how these psalms functioned rhetorically in the ongoing life of the community. Whatever their origin, given that they were copied and thus presumably used (whether communally or privately) for more than a hundred years, this poetry must have been an important factor in shaping the self-identity and worldview of the community members.

5. The Significance for the New Testament. These poems are one of most extensive collections of religious poetry of the Second Temple period. Along with the **Psalms of Solomon*, they are evidence of an ongoing and living tradition of the composition of new religious devotional poetry, modeled on traditional biblical patterns but incorporating new elements in style and content. Thus these poems provide a context for the study of the religious poetry of the NT, especially the canticles of Luke 1—2, and for NT expressions of blessings and thanksgivings; of particular note is the similar formulation of the thanksgiving in Matthew 11:25 and Luke 10:21, "I thank you, Father, Lord of heaven and earth, because you have hidden these things from the wise and intelligent and have revealed them to infants."

See also DEAD SEA SCROLLS: GENERAL INTRODUCTION; PSALMS AND HYMNS OF QUMRAN; QUMRAN: PLACE AND HISTORY.

BIBLIOGRAPHY. M. Delcor, *Les Hymnes de Qumran (Hodayot)* (Paris: Letouzey et Ané, 1962); D. Dombkowski Hopkins, "The Qumran Community and 1QHodayot: A Reassessment," *RevQ* 10 (1979-81) 323-64; S. Holm-Nielsen, *Hodayot: Psalms from Qumran* (Acta Theologica Danica 2; Aarhus: Aarhus University Press, 1960); G. Jeremias, *Der Lehrer der Gerechtigkeit* (SUNT 2: Gottingen: Vandenhoeck & Ruprecht, 1963); B. P. Kittel, *The Hymns of Qumran, Translation and Commentary* (SBLDS 50; Chico, CA: Scholars Press, 1981); H.-W. Kuhn, *Enderwartung und gegenwärtiges Heil: Untersuchungen zu den Gemeindeliedern von Qumran mit einem Anhang über Eschatologie und Gegenwart in der Verkündigung Jesu* (SUNT 4; Göttingen: Vandenhoeck & Ruprecht, 1965); J. Licht, "The Doctrine of the Thanksgiving Scroll," *IEJ* 6 (1956) 1-13, 89-101; idem, *The Thanksgiving Scroll: A Scroll from the Wilderness of Judea* (Jerusalem: Bialik, 1957; Hebrew); M. Mansoor, *The Thanksgiving Hymns* (Leiden: E. J. Brill, 1961); J. T. Milik, "1Q35. Recueil de Cantiques d'action Grâces (1QH)," in *Qumran Cave 1*, ed. D. Barthélemy and J. T. Milik (DJD 1; Oxford: Clarendon Press, 1955) 136-38; G. Morawe, *Aufbau und Abgrenzung der Loblieder von Qumran: Studies zur Gattungsgeschichtlichen Einordnung der Hodajoth* (TA 16; Berlin: Evangelische Verlagsanstalt, 1961); C. Newsom, "Kenneth Bruke Meets the Teacher of Righteousness: Rhetorical Strategies in the Hodayot and the Serek Ha-Yaḥad," in *Of Scribes and Scrolls: Studies on the Hebrew Bible, Intertestamental Judaism and Christian Origins*, ed. H. W. Attridge, J. J. Collins and T. H. Tobin (New York: University Press of America, 1990) 121-32; B. Nitzan, *Qumran Prayer and Religious Poetry* (STDJ 12; Leiden: E. J. Brill, 1994); E. Puech, *La croyance des Esséniens en la vie future: Immortalité, résurrection, vie éternelle? Histoire d'une croyance dans le Judaïsme ancien* (EB 21-22; Paris: Gabalda, 1993) 335-419; idem, "Quelques aspects de la restauration du Rouleau des Hymnes (1QH)," *JJS* 39 (1988) 38-55; E. Schuller, "4Q427-432," in *Qumran Cave 4.2: Poetical and Liturgical Texts, Part 2*, ed. E. Chason et al., in consultation with J. VanderKam and M. Brady (DJD 29; Oxford: Clarendon Press, 1999), 69-232 (edition of the 4QHodayot manuscripts); E. L. Sukenik, *The Dead Sea Scrolls of the Hebrew University* (Jerusalem: Magnes, 1954 Hebrew ed.; 1955 English ed.) (edition of 1QH manuscript).

E. M. Schuller

THEATERS

In the ancient world, theaters were among the most distinctive hallmarks of Greco-Roman society. Although they naturally had various ancillary functions, their chief purpose was to serve as the venue for the dramatic performances dedicated to Dionysus and other deities. Given these pagan religious associations, theater going was probably largely avoided by the Jews in Palestine, even if it appears to have been more generally tolerated within the *Diaspora.

Our word *theater* is derived from the Greek *theasthai,* meaning "to look at." In Greek theaters, the *theatron* ("theater") originally referred to only one part of the larger complex, namely, the area reserved for spectators. The other main parts of the theater were the *orchestra,* a flat, roughly circular area for the dancing and singing of the chorus, and the *skēnē,* a backdrop for the performers that later evolved into a discrete building. Roman theaters, by contrast, were often elaborate roofed buildings featuring an ornate *skēnē* (*scaenae frons*) of two stories or more (cf. Vitruvius *De Arch.* 5.3, 6-7 and Bieber, 189, for further distinctions between Greek and Roman theaters). In terms of their situation, Greek-style theaters would commonly be located near a sanctuary, while Roman theaters were often part of an urban complex.

1. Greek Theater
2. Roman Theater
3. Theater in Palestine
4. Theater in the Diaspora

1. Greek Theater.
The main function of the theater in classical Greece was to provide a venue for drama. Dramatic productions were performed only in the religious festivals dedicated to Dionysus, the most important being the Great (or City) Dionysia of Athens. There, famously, in the fifth century B.C., dramatic competitions (*agōnes*) were staged in his honor. Dionysus was worshiped as the patron deity of drama because of his associations with *ekstasis* ("standing outside of oneself"). He dissolved the boundaries between the self and the other, enabling the actors to assume different personae, an event symbolized by their adoption of various masks and costumes. Dionysiac ritual may also underlie all three dramatic genres—tragedy, comedy and the satyr play—but this point is disputed (Aristotle *Poet.* 4.14-21). There is no need to consider these genres in detail here (cf. Pickard-Cambridge 1962 and Easterling) except to note that, mutatis mutandis, they proved to be extraordinarily popular, influential and enduring.

Even within the fifth century B.C., theaters had begun to appear outside of *Athens, and this whole process was accelerated through the conquests of *Alexander the Great. In the Hellenistic period, the conquering Greeks built theaters for their own use, and any city with pretensions to culture would construct themselves a theater (Pausanias *Descr.* 10.4.1). As a consequence, theater and drama became ubiquitous throughout the ancient world. Yet if the religious associations between dramatic performance and Dionysus continued, drama gradually ceased to be his exclusive preserve and began to be performed in honor of other deities as well.

2. Roman Theater.
As with the Greek theater, the main function of the Roman theater was to provide a venue for drama. Our understanding of dramatic performance in Rome is somewhat limited by the paucity of extant literary sources, but there is little doubt that Greek models continued to be extraordinarily influential; Horace counsels aspiring playwrights to "work with Greek models by day, and work with them by night" (Horace *Ars Poet.* 268-69). In addition to comedy, tragedy and the satyr play, however, various other dramatic genres gradually assumed importance. Apart from the traditional Roman farces (*Atellanae*), mime and pantomime gained considerable vogue. The former was a burlesque revue of song and dance, slapstick and acrobatics that commonly featured female performers, nudity and obscene subject matter (Dio Chrysostom *Alex.* 32.4; Apuleius *Met.* 10.29-34). Pantomime, which emerged to great acclaim just before the common era, consisted of a solo dancer enacting various mythological scenes and characters to the accompaniment of instruments and a sung chorus (Lucian *Salt.*). Typically, any or all of these genres would figure in the theater shows (*ludi scaenici*) that made up one component of the religious festivals (*ludi*) of the Roman calendar year.

Apart from providing a venue for drama, theaters in the Hellenistic and Roman world served a variety of other functions. Theaters naturally doubled as complexes for other spectator events. Gymnastics, gladiatorial contests (*see* Circuses and Games), animal baiting and musical competitions could all be situated there instead of in the more customary amphitheaters. The theater also had obvious political functions. It served as a meeting point for a ruler and his subjects (Plutarch *Demetr.* 34.3), for city councils and dignitaries (Josephus *J.W.* 7.3.3 §47) and for public gatherings of various descriptions. As Acts (Acts 19:29, 31) demonstrates, it was a natural place for a mob to assemble, especially when, as in *Ephesus, the *theatron* was immediately proximate to the agora and could accommodate some twenty-four thousand people.

3. Theater in Palestine.

Given the *Hasmoneans' resistance to overt Hellenization, theaters did not appear in Syria-Palestine until the time of Herod the Great. He, as part of his Hellenizing agenda, constructed a theater and amphitheater (hippodrome?) in *Jerusalem and theaters in a variety of other urban centers (*Caesarea Maritima, Sidon and Damascus; cf. Josephus *Ant.* 15.8.1 §268; 15.9.6 §341; *J.W.* 1.21.11 §422). More theaters appeared gradually over the next two and half centuries, usually erected at a city's own expense and initiative. To date, some thirty theaters in Syria-Palestine have been discovered, mostly Roman in style, varying in capacity from about four hundred spectators (Sahr) to seven thousand (Philadelphia).

In spite of their capacity, these theaters were likely not much frequented by the local Jewish population. It was not simply that Herod's new structures were "foreign to Jewish custom," as Josephus relates (*Ant.* 15.8.1 §268). Given that dramatic productions were dedicated to Dionysus or other deities, they obviously smacked of idolatry (*y.* *ʿAbod. Zar.* 1:7; cf. Josephus *Ant.* 19.7.4 §§332-34). Images of the gods or the emperor were prominently displayed (sometimes built into the *scaenae frons*), and *prayers and sacrifices often figured as part of the proceedings. In some cases (e.g., at Sahr), the theater was used as an adjunct to the cultic practices of a temple.

A second reason for the rejection of theater would be the obscenity associated with mime. Syria was renowned for its mime performers (Polybius *Hist.* 30.26; Diodorus Siculus *Bib. Hist.* 31.16.2), so it is not unreasonable to suppose that mime was commonly featured in the theaters of Palestine, especially when both Talmuds explicitly mention mimes or clowns and buffoons (*b.* *ʿAbod Zar.* 18b; *y.* *ʿAbod Zar.* 1:7). Other *rabbinic writings reinforce this impression by directly forbidding Jewish involvement in the "customs of the nations" and by condemning the theater as the "seat of the scornful" (*ʾAbot R. Nat.* 21). Obedient Jews (including Jewish women, *Ruth Rab.* 2:22) were not to attend the theater (*Pesiq. Rab. Kah.* 15:2), and a recurring contrast is developed between the vanity of the theatergoers and the probity of those who study the Torah in the synagogue (*Eccl. Rab.* 1.7.5; 2.2.1; *Lam. Rab.* 3:5).

4. Theater in the Diaspora.

A different attitude appeared to prevail in the Diaspora, particularly in *Alexandria. As early as the second century B.C., the *Epistle of *Aristeas* (284) notably has one of the translators of the *Septuagint advise Ptolemy II to "be a spectator of entertainments which exercise restraint." More remarkable yet is the figure of Ezekiel the dramatist, our only extant Hellenistic tragedian, who was probably an Alexandrian Jew of the second century B.C. He is said to have composed "tragedies" (Eusebius *Praep. Ev.* 9.28.1), although unfortunately for us, only 269 lines remain of his one surviving play, the *Exagōgē* ("Exodus"). It recasts the Exodus story as a Greek tragedy, one that has, moreover, considerable affinities with Euripidean drama. Although both points have been disputed, in all likelihood the work was performed on stage and was intended for a Jewish and a Gentile audience. H. Jacobson (25) infers that Ezekiel wished "to elicit sympathy and respect for the Jews from his Greek audience, showing that both Greeks and Jews have similar ancestral stories of persecution, escape, and return to a homeland."

*Philo also reveals himself to be a habitué: "I have before now often seen in the theater" (Philo *Ebr.* 177; cf. *Omn. Prob. Lib.* 141), and he evidently expects his readership to be equally familiar with it (Philo *Flacc.* 38; *Leg. Gai.* 368). Rabbinic sources suggest that Jews in Egypt, like Philo, thronged to the theater (*Tanḥuma Shemot* 6) even if, like Philo, they may have protested that they favored Jewish *festivals over the theater (Philo *Agric.* 35). Evidence for the rest of the *Diaspora is limited but could suggest a similar openness: an inscription (c. A.D. 200) from a theater in Miletus appears to designate a choice block of seats in the fifth row as the "place of the Jews" (Trebilco, 159-62). While the discrepancy in attitude between the Palestinian and Diaspora Jews is marked, it may not be so pronounced as it appears. The evidence provided above indicates that the theatrical content could well have differed. A sophisticated urban center like Alexandria would have been more likely to stage classical drama than mime, while in Palestine the reverse would probably have been true.

See also ARENAS; CIRCUSES AND GAMES; GYMNASIA AND BATHS; HELLENISTIC JUDAISM.

BIBLIOGRAPHY. J. M. G. Barclay, *Jews in the Mediterranean Diaspora: From Alexander to Trajan (323 BCE to 117 CE)* (Edinburgh: T & T Clark, 1996); R. A. Batey, "Jesus and theTheatre," *NTS* 30 (1984) 563-74; R. C. Beacham, *The Roman Theatre and Its Audience* (London: Routledge, 1991); M. Bieber, *The History of the Greek and Roman Theatre* (2d ed.; Princeton, NJ: Princeton University Press, 1961); M. T. Boatwright, "Theatres in the Roman Empire," *BA* 53 (1990) 184-92; E. Csapo and W. J. Slater, eds., T*he Context of Ancient Drama* (Ann Arbor, MI: University of Michigan Press, 1995); P. E. Easterling, ed., *The Cambridge Companion to Greek Tragedy* (Cambridge: Cambridge University Press, 1997); L. Feldman, *Jew and Gentile in the Ancient World* (Princeton, NJ: Princeton University Press, 1993); E. Frézouls, "Aspects de l'histoire architecturale du théâtre Romain," *ANRW* 2.12.1 (1982) 343-441; J. R. Green, *Theatre in Ancient Greek Society* (London and New York: Routledge, 1994); H. Jacobson, *The* Exagoge *of Ezekiel* (Cambridge: Cambridge University Press, 1983); A. Pickard-Cambridge, *Dithyramb, Tragedy and Comedy* (2d ed.; Oxford: Clarendon Press, 1962); idem, *The Dramatic Festivals of Athens* (2d ed.; Oxford: Clarendon Press, 1968); A. Segal, *Theatre in Roman Palestine and Provincial Arabia* (MnS 110; Leiden: E. J. Brill, 1995); idem, "Theaters," *The Oxford Encyclopedia of Archaeology in the Near East*, ed. E. M. Meyers (New York: Oxford University Press, 1997) 5:199-203; W. J. Slater, ed., *Roman Theater and Society* (Ann Arbor: University of Michigan Press, 1996); S. Stern, *Jewish Identity in Early Rabbinic Writings* (Leiden: E. J. Brill, 1994); P. Trebilco, *Jewish Communities in Asia Minor* (SNTSMS 69; Cambridge: Cambridge University Press, 1991). J. R. C. Cousland

THEODOTION. *See* SEPTUAGINT/GREEK OLD TESTAMENT.

THEODOTUS. *See* JEWISH LITERATURE: HISTORIANS AND POETS.

THEODOTUS INSCRIPTION. *See* INSCRIPTIONS AND PAPYRI: GRECO-ROMAN.

THEOLOGIES AND SECTS, JEWISH

The beginning of understanding life in the ancient world is the realization that it worked from assumptions quite different from ours. Modern people tend to assume that theology—abstract beliefs or ideas about God and the nature of salvation—is both a distinguishable compartment of life and a criterion for distinction of one group from others. We expect in major religious traditions an authentic theological core, over against which various sects may have defined themselves. And we incline toward the assumption that individuals are free to live apart from the established practices of religion. All of these assumptions are demonstrably invalid for the study of ancient life, including *Judaism.

1. Definition and Context
2. Varieties of Judaism by Source
3. Conclusion

1. Definition and Context.

1.1. Theologies. Life in the ancient world was much more integrated than we can imagine after the French and American revolutions, with their creation of secular states. In Greek and Roman societies, virtually all public events had what we would call a religious dimension, including invocation of the divine and animal sacrifice. Service in the priesthood was part of the normal progression through civic offices in Greece and Rome and an ineluctable birthright in Judaism. From Julius Caesar's time onward, the princeps (emperor) assumed the role of high priest in Rome, and in Judea the high priest was the powerful first man of the aristocracy after the disappearance of royalty in 586 B.C. and again in 4 B.C.

In Judean society, life was just as integrated as in the rest of the Mediterranean: the laws of the land, also of expatriate Judean communities under Roman rule, were essentially the prescriptions of the *Torah. These included civil and criminal law, fully enmeshed with what we would call religious law. The ruling aristocracy of Judea was a hereditary priesthood, even as in Rome the patrician aristocracy had old priestly associations. If students in *Athens, *Rome and *Jerusalem spent much of their time in school learning the old stories of their God(s) and national heroes (*see* Education: Jewish and Greco-Roman), it is difficult for us now to extract their theology. They lived in an integrated culture.

Recognizing a degree of artificiality, it is nevertheless possible to isolate those aspects of life that had to do with one's duties toward the divine. But even here we must try to use appropriate language. The heart of one's obligations toward the deity in Mediterranean life was animal sacrifice in a public *temple. Every ancient city had its patron god as well as temples to other deities: Apollo, Athena, Artemis, Nike, Castor and Pollux, the deified emperors, and so on. Jerusalem was exceptional only in that it had but one temple, for the one God recognized by the Jews. The ancient Hebrew, Latin and Greek languages lacked exact parallels for our word *religion,* however. When the ancients spoke of these aspects of life, they tended to use words such as "piety" (Gk *eusebeia;* Lat *pietas*) or "uprightness" (Heb *ṣᵉdāqâ*), which terms could also pertain to social relations in other contexts. Thus, if we venture to speak of ancient Jewish perspectives on serving God, it must be with the understanding that such attitudes could not be disentangled from the rest of life.

Moreover, much of what we associate with religion and theology fell in the province of ancient *philosophy. Philosophers typically spoke of themselves as divinely motivated; they analyzed old texts for ethical application; and they laid out more or less rigorous programs of conduct, even diet. Not surprisingly, Jews living outside of Judea—with their weekly meetings to discuss texts and ethics, lacking temples and sacrifices—looked more like members of a worldwide philosophical school than practitioners of an ethnic piety or cult (*see* Diaspora). They were labeled philosophers by some of our earliest known outside observers. *Philo and *Josephus, the most prolific Jewish authors of the first century, adopt this category with great effect. Philo uses *philosoph-* words about 228 times but never speaks of theology (*theologia*). Josephus's entire presentation of Judaism likewise is of a philosophical culture, and he uses such word roots more than three dozen times; he uses *theologia* only three times, and two of these come in quotations of someone else (Josephus *Ag. Ap.* 1.14 §78; 1.26 §237). By the first century, then, prominent Jewish writers shared fully in the common discourse that made philosophy, not theology or religion, the place for analyzing human behavior, whether toward the God(s) or toward one's fellows.

1.2. Sects. In this context, the term *sect* also poses problems. Our modern assumptions are governed largely by the common translations of Josephus and Acts, which render their Greek term *hairesis* as "sect" (Josephus *J.W.* 2.8.1, 14 §§118, 162; Acts 5:17; 24:5), and modern sociological theory, which makes a sect something of an aberration, a group that has a strong sense of its boundaries and of its purity over against the body politic. A sect, in distinction from a party, is characterized by withdrawal from the public arena into a focus upon itself and its mission. It may be that some ancient Jewish groups were true sects, in that they would have nothing to do with more mainstream groups. But this article is not confined to such aberrant groups, and to call every group a sect would prejudice our assessment of them. In any event, the Greek term used by Josephus and Acts means only "philosophical school." So we ought not resort to the language of sects in advance.

Any generic English terms will be encumbered with some baggage. But let us proceed with a task formulated somewhat as follows: to describe the common Judaism of Judea and the eastern Mediterranean in about the first century A.D. and to sketch the main groups (whether parties, sects, voluntary associations or ad hoc clusters of followers) in and around that scheme.

2. Varieties of Judaism by Source.

2.1. Method. Reconstructing the various Jewish groups that existed two thousand years ago is no simple task. Although it might seem advisable to list the known groups and describe them, this is not historically helpful. In most cases (e.g., *Pharisees, *Sadducees, Baptists, *Essenes) we have no surviving primary sources—texts written by participants—but only the perspectives of others who mention these groups while advocating their own views. For many of the groups in question, we are also far from a scholarly consensus, so that a list of groups would entail mere summaries of the various positions that scholars have taken. In this situation, it is most economical to describe the particular instance of Judaism revealed by each text or text collection and then, where appropriate, that text's portrayal of the other groups in context.

2.2. Priestly Aristocracy. By far the most important corpus comprises the lengthy narratives by Flavius Josephus, a priest who was born a few years after Jesus' death and died about A.D. 100. Having led part of the Galilean *revolt against Rome (A.D. 66-74), he surrendered (A.D. 67) and was transported to Rome (A.D. 71), where he wrote three works. The *Jewish War,* in seven volumes, confronts the widespread postwar animosity toward the Judeans in Rome and elsewhere. Against the common assertions that the Judeans were by nature hostile to humanity, such that the revolt only expressed the national character, and that their defeat represented the defeat of their peculiar God, Josephus argues the contrary: the revolt did not arise from the collective will but from a handful of would-be tyrants who have now been duly punished; and the Judean God, far from facing defeat, has used the Romans to effect his purposes by purifying the nation. The *Antiquities* and *Life,* in twenty-one volumes, respond to requests for an outline in Greek of the Judean constitution and its underlying philosophy. He includes his own life story as a case study. The *Against Apion,* in two volumes, further develops his portrayal of the constitution through pointed refutation of slanders and polemical contrast with other constitutions.

Josephus's Judaism is that of a priest and aristocrat. He translates the old biblical system into contemporary categories by claiming for the Jews a senatorial constitution. The leading men of the nation have a bloodline that goes back two thousand years, much longer than that of any other nobility in existence. From the time of *Moses and Aaron (which he puts about two thousand years before his time), the priestly college led by the high priest has formed a senate that was regularly consulted even by Joshua (Josephus *Ant.* 5.1.2 §15; 5.1.14 §43, 5.1.16 §55). Thus the proper form of the Judean constitution is an aristocracy (*aristokratia*); monarchy, in keeping with republican sentiments in Rome, is to be avoided at all costs (Josephus *Ant.* 4.7.17 §223; 6.3.3 §36; 11.4.8 §111; 14.6.4 §91). Josephus seems truly to believe that the Jews possess what the rest of the world is seeking.

The function of the priests in this system is manifold. First and foremost, under the high priest they are the guarantors of the constitution's integrity from generation to generation. The purity of their lineage is thus a critical concern (Josephus *Ag. Ap.* 1.6-7 §§28-36). They oversee the sacrificial cult at the world-famous Jerusalem temple, but that cult is restrained in contrast to every other nation's: *sacrifices are kept to a minimum and are performed in a humane way, and the liturgy is free of wild celebration (Josephus *Ag. Ap.* 2.23 §§193-98). Equally important as the central temple institution are the judicial, exegetical and philosophical functions of the priests. Their very clothing and the temple itself symbolize the creation and the divine nature. They are the legitimate experts in, and teachers of, the national traditions, and Josephus attributes most of his own abilities—to write these histories, to represent Judaism's philosophy or to predict the future—to his priestly training (Josephus *J.W.* pref. 1 §3; 3.8.2 §352; *Ag. Ap.* 1.10 §54).

Profoundly impressed by the verifiable fulfillment of detailed predictions made by Jeremiah and Daniel, Josephus believes that God (or fate or providence) is in control of all human affairs (Josephus *Ant.* 10.11.7 §§276-81). The ancient sacred writings embody the laws of nature and encode the divine plan. In some mysterious way, human will also factors into the equation. Josephus is as vague as other philosophers about the nature of the encounter between fate and free will, but he believes that the Scriptures sort it all out (Josephus *Ant.* 16.11.8 §§395-404). He also believes in the soul's survival of death to face reward or punishment. Although he seems to cast this belief in the discourse of transmigration, he appears to envision a single rebirth after death. He assumes that God can accomplish anything but expresses skepticism about the more spectacular kinds of miracles.

Josephus does not display many of the features typically associated with *apocalypticism (see 2.4 below). In spite of his special fondness for the apocalyptic book of Daniel and his acceptance of the notion of a succession of ages under divine control, he evinces no hope for an imminent end of the age; no cosmic, anthropological or temporal dualism; no expectation of a messiah or of a decisive heavenly battle; no developed *angelology or *demonology. His philosophy of rapprochement with the world around him seems to preclude many of these themes. Yet most scholars would say that the essence of apocalypticism is the divine revelation to a human seer, and Josephus is certainly interested in special revelations of divine mysteries. He includes himself among those, in the train of his namesake Joseph(us), who are so close to the deity that they receive predictions and other disclosures.

In the course of his narratives, Josephus mentions numerous Jewish groups. In his effort to portray Judaism as a national philosophy and to isolate rebellious thinking as a deviant "fourth philosophy," he describes three traditional philosophical schools: the Pharisees, Sadducees and Essenes (Josephus *J.W.* 2.118-66; *Ant.* 18.1.1-5 §§3-22). Of these, he is most interested in the Essenes. Like his, their closeness to the deity allows them to predict the future with perfect accuracy, and he finds their Greek views of the soul and *afterlife irresistible. They revere the sun as an emblem of the deity. They lead the most exemplary, disciplined philosophical life, sharing all things in common without greed or passion, and so resemble the Pythagoreans. Spread throughout the towns of Judea, these bachelors (mainly) know the secrets of cures through their special texts. The Pharisees and Sadducees Josephus dispenses with rather quickly in these passages, asserting that the former accept immortality and fate while the latter reject both. He also notes that the Pharisees have a special body of extra-Mosaic ordinances that they hold dear, whereas the Sadducees reject these, and that the Pharisees enjoy the confidence of the people whereas the Sadducees are a small, wealthy élite (Josephus *Ant.* 13.8.6 §§297-98).

This last point brings us to the bone of contention that Josephus has with the Pharisees. While describing his beloved Judean aristocracy, he repeatedly expresses an aristocrat's frustration at the fickleness of the masses and at the demagogues who inevitably arise to capitalize on this. These demagogues appeared even in Moses' time, with Korah, who was a kind of archetype (Josephus *Ant.* 4.2.2 §§14-23). They have reappeared throughout Jewish history, cynically realizing that they are able to manipulate the masses by rhetorical persuasion. In the time of the revolt, the popular leaders fell into two groups: pseudo-prophetic visionaries and armed militants. The former included men who promised the gullible masses divine deliverance; the latter included men such as Judas the Galilean, Theudas, the Egyptian prophet, Menachem, Simon bar Giora, Eleazar ben Ya'ir, and many others (*see* Revolutionary Movements).

From *Hasmonean times to his own, Josephus also indicts the Pharisees for their ability to persuade the masses in any direction they desire, even opposing high priests and kings (Josephus *Ant.* 13.8.5, 15.5 §§288, 401-2). The wealthy and powerful Sadducees themselves must defer to the Pharisees, he says, because of the Pharisees' popular base (Josephus *Ant.* 18.1.5 §§15, 17). All of this would be well understood by a Roman audience, which had its own history of demagogues wearing the mantle of popular support.

The same conditions continue during Josephus's brilliant career as Galilean military commander: envious agitators, often in league with leading Pharisees, caused this priest-aristocrat considerable trouble, although his virtue and divine favor allowed him to triumph in the end.

Only a few popular leaders merit Josephus's approval, because of their unusual philosophical character. They are John the Baptist, whom he understands to have been a great teacher of morality (without mentioning any connection to Jesus; Josephus *Ant.* 18.5.2 §§116-19); Bannus, Josephus's own ascetic teacher for three years in the Judean wilderness (Josephus *Life* 2 §11); and perhaps Jesus and his brother James (Josephus *Ant.* 18.3.3 §§63-64; 20.9.1 §§200-1). The passage on Jesus that we have in our texts of Josephus has almost certainly been corrupted by Christian copyists. Although it is unlikely that Josephus endorsed Jesus as strongly as he now appears to do, his incidental warm comments about James a bit later on suggest that he at least spoke appreciatively of Jesus, though we cannot be certain.

Against the background of this priest-aristocrat's fairly full description of his perspective, from somewhere near the center of Judean society, we can now array the other main bodies of evidence for Jewish groups in the first century.

2.3. Wisdom Groups. Several important texts develop the philosophical tendency that we see in Josephus's Judaism. This tradition begins in the Bible itself (e.g., Proverbs, Ecclesiastes) and then takes shape with Ben Sira, about 190 B.C. Ben Sira (*see* Sirach) presents the Mosaic code as the fount of wisdom and the priests as its legitimate guardians. Nevertheless, this work seems to take a rather Sadducean and non-Josephan view of afterlife and fate. Much closer to Josephus on those issues, and also in its forthright attack on Egyptian religion, is the first-century B.C. *Wisdom of Solomon, although it goes somewhat further than Josephus in making the present life mere preparation for the afterlife. Another prominent wisdom text is *4 Maccabees, which sets out to prove a *Stoic thesis of which Josephus would approve, that the pious reason is master of the passions. Note that 4 Maccabees was traditionally thought to have been written by Josephus.

This literature reaches its apogee in Jesus'

contemporary Philo of Alexandria (c. 20 B.C.-A.D. 50). Usually considered a Middle *Platonist, Philo had thoroughly integrated his reading of the Judean sacred texts with philosophical currents of his day, though he was not an entirely consistent thinker. Philo makes much of the philosophical view of God found in the Bible. He argues that one cannot speak of God's attributes whatsoever, for he is unknowable in his real essence (*to on*). Just as one cannot look into the sun, one sees only God's works or aftereffects (Philo *Deus Imm.* 51-60; *Mut. Nom.* 7-22). Attempts to speak of God as he is are like attempts to portray God visibly, which violate the second commandment. Because of the unfathomability of the true God, one communicates with him through one or more manifestations. In Philo, these manifiestations—*Logos, Theos* and *Kyrios*—sometimes appear to be intermediate beings, sometimes only aspects of God (Philo *Mut. Nom.* 23-30).

Philo's Platonist premise that there are two ways of knowing, the naive and the profound, the superficial and the real, matches his view that there are two sorts of human beings—those who live on the level of appearances and those who live on the level of truth—and therefore also two sorts of biblical interpretation. The materially inclined will interpret the biblical text exclusively in its plain, physical sense. But the spiritual or soul-inclined will see the deeper, allegorical meaning in the text. Although some interpreters of Philo have found parallels here to Paul's allegorization and Paul's claim that spiritual circumcision renders physical circumcision unnecessary (even destructive), Philo insists that understanding the deeper meaning does not relieve one of the obligation of physical observance (Plato *Migr. Abr.* 53).

Jewish wisdom literature does not, apparently, spring from a single group. It appears to have been especially prominent in Alexandria, a major seat of philosophical study. There, some of the *synagogues (or *proseuchai*) resembled philosophical lecture halls. But it is not clear that the participants in this Jewish philosophy had any tighter group structure than was common in the conditions of the Alexandrian Jewish community. In any case, wisdom literature found a home in many other regions, including some Judean aristocratic circles.

Philo does, however, mention two particular Jewish groups that exhibit the demarcations and disciplines of schools in the proper sense. First, he discusses the Essenes of Judea, in much the same terms as Josephus does. In his most Stoic treatise, attempting to show that "every good man is free" regardless of physical circumstance, he presents the Essenes of "Palestinian Syria" as champions of the philosophical life, "athletes of virtue," because of their steadfast commitment to peace and simplicity (Philo *Omn. Prob. Lib.* 88 §13). Elsewhere, like Josephus, Philo singles out the Essenes as his best examples of lived Judaism (Philo *Hypoth.* 11.1-18). Perhaps even more purely philosophical are the second group described by Philo, the *Therapeutae, who know the secrets of curing the soul and who worship the One (*to on*) alone. Although this type of group is found throughout the world, also in Greece, Philo says, he presents the Therapeutae who live by the Mareotic Lake near Alexandria as an exemplary Jewish association. They meditate allegorically on the laws, prophetic oracles and psalms, and they observe a *sabbath.

Although the wisdom literature exhibits much variation in perspective, it shares a certain stance toward the world. It seeks to embrace all truth anywhere, claiming it for Judaism. What others describe as Fate or Zeus, or the philosophers' prime mover, is the unknowable God that the Judeans have always revered. What every reflective person would recognize as the most admirable life is lived by the Jewish Essenes and Therapeutae. Rather than standing over against world culture, as the Jews were often accused of doing by critical observers, these groups see Judaism as the highest expression of universal aspirations. This trend is present already in such early wisdom texts as the *Epistle of *Aristeas* and the fragments of Artapanus and *Aristobulus that have survived (third to second centuries B.C.). Their integration of Judaism into the world leaves little room for the several dualisms that characterize apocalypticism, and we find no messianic expectation in this literature.

2.4. Apocalypticism. Nevertheless, the many texts that scholars consider apocalyptic incorporate some important features of the wisdom tradition. As we have noted, the heart of apocalypticism is the revelation or disclosure (*apokalypsis*) of secrets by God or another heavenly being to a human seer. In Daniel, one of the chief apocalyptic prototypes, the seer and his circle, who understand the secrets of the end, are called "the wise" (Dan 9:22; 11:33-35). Some scholars consider apocalyptic a development from biblical wisdom literature. Others hold that later, second-century Jewish *Gnosticism, in which the group understands secrets not about the end of time but about hidden realities and divine affairs, represents an internalization or sublimation of apocalyptic.

In addition to the central tenet that God has revealed secrets to humanity, common features of apocalyptic thinking are a radical temporal dualism, separating the present eon of misery and oppression from the imminent arrival of God's reign, the eon to come; anthropological dualism, sharply distinguishing good persons from evil; cosmic dualism, attributing evil and suffering to a hierarchy of antagonistic spirits and all good to God, the archangels and their hosts; heavy use of symbols, including grotesque descriptions of beasts and other phenomena envisioned by the seer—evoking realties beyond human language; and coming judgment, in which evil nations and wicked individuals will finally get their comeuppance. This literature is suffused with the old prophetic theme of reversals: those who prosper and laugh now, who appear to have insurmountable power, will suffer; those who suffer now will be rewarded for their *piety. We should note that to be an apocalypse in the strict sense, a text must embody the divine revelation to the seer, but a much larger body of literature is still broadly apocalyptic in outlook, even if it is not of the genre apocalypse (*see* Apocalyptic Literature).

As in the case of wisdom literature, it is not possible to trace apocalyptic thinking and literature to a single social matrix. It used to be assumed that the producers of apocalyptic were those on or beyond the margins of political power—the disenfranchised, poor and illiterate. They would have the most obvious motive to long for the new age. But more careful examination of both the literature and the social context suggests many reasons why various groups might produce such texts of hope. For example, the group's marginalization may be largely self-imposed. These texts are often highly literate, drawing liberally from *Hellenistic and Mesopotamian myths. Some authors, such as those who produced some of the *Dead Sea Scrolls, may be priests. Although we cannot decide the issue of social class, wealth and education in a simple way, we can say that apocalyptic groups saw themselves as a righteous remnant, waiting for God to vindicate their piety against both compatriots and foreigners who had violated divine laws.

Some of the major apocalyptic texts from the period of our interest are sections of the composite work we know as *1 Enoch,* the earliest parts of which date to the third century B.C. (*see* Enoch, Books of); the **Testaments of the Twelve Patriarchs;* the **Testament of Abraham; *Jubilees; *Psalms of Solomon;* the **Testament of Moses;* 4 Ezra (*see* Esdras, Books of); and *2 Baruch* (*see* Baruch, Books of). These texts typically include predictions of future events attributed to the famous named author, which are the real author's recollections of the past. Commonly the revelation is said to have been hidden or sealed until the end of the age, the author's real time of writing.

Texts from apocalyptically minded circles are about the only places in which one finds clear messianic expectations. But surprisingly, for those who assume that ancient Jews had a single clear messianic idea, such expectations vary considerably. Only one text clearly expresses the hope for a royal son of David (*Pss. Sol.* 17). Others look for an anointed descendant of Levi or Judah or an anointed prophet. It has become clear that there was no fixed messianic idea before the emergence of *rabbinic Judaism in subsequent centuries.

2.5. Qumran Scrolls. From the wide world of apocalyptic thinking, two bodies of literature merit special attention. Both of them presuppose a close-knit sponsoring group or constellation of groups. The first of these collections is the famous Dead Sea Scrolls, which began to be discovered at Khirbet Qumran near the Dead Sea in 1947. So far, parts of about eight hundred documents in Hebrew, Aramaic and Greek have been identified. These include all of the biblical texts except Esther—about two hundred manuscripts; already known wisdom and apocalyptic texts, including Sirach, parts of *1 Enoch* and the sources of the *Testaments of the Twelve Patriarchs;* and a large cache of texts not otherwise known (exception: the **Damascus Document,* partially known but not identified since the early part of the century). This last group includes biblical commentaries, regulatory documents or rules for a community, *poetry and other liturgical texts, wisdom literature and texts of apocalyptic hope—along with a few business dealings.

It seems that at least some of these documents come from a single group, even if that group evolved over time. The origin and location of the group are contested issues, but its basic features appear in the texts. Members claim a priestly core and founder (the Righteous Teacher), and they preserve the priestly prerogative for some functions. Having established themselves in conflict with a Wicked Priest (a Hasmonean high priest?), they have developed a dualistic view of the world. Two spirits vie for the allegiance of human beings, and it is the Angel of Darkness, leader of the evil forces, who causes evil in the world. The righteous, however, scrupulously observe the divine law, avoiding the "seekers after smooth things" who have "torn down the wall" of separation (CD 1:17-18; 5:20). They are convinced that the end of the age is about to occur, and so they interpret Scripture in relation to themselves as those living in the end time. When the end comes, three anointed figures will arrive—Davidic/royal, priestly and prophetic messiahs—who will lead the sons of light in the final battle to bring in God's reign. None of these texts is an apocalypse proper, but the community's world of thought is plainly apocalyptic.

Although most scholars identify the community behind the DSS with a branch of the Essenes, largely on the basis of rough parallels in details of initiation and belief, that theory fails to explain how and why Philo and Josephus would have converted the *Qumran community into their beloved world-affirming philosopher Essenes. It is not enough to suggest that either or both authors suppressed the Essenes' dualistic and apocalyptic leanings without explaining why this is probable in view of Philo's and Josephus's general tendencies and worldviews.

2.6. Texts from Jesus' Followers. The other broadly apocalyptic group comprises some of those who followed Jesus in the generation or two following his death. Space does not permit much development of this complex issue. But scholars have recently exposed the historical error of separating all Christians (a term not attested outside of Acts in the first century) from all Jews at this early stage. It appears that many of Jesus' followers were fully observant Jews who interpreted their Judaism in light of Jesus—whether as royal Messiah, anointed teacher, Lord (in what sense exactly?), prophet, or something else.

To complicate matters, we cannot assume that such Jesus-following Jews were all Jews by birth. Paul's letters indicate that some Gentiles converted to Judaism in order to complete their following of Jesus, while some native Jews, such as Paul himself, relativized or abandoned Jewish observance because they saw life in Christ as a "new creation" (2 Cor 5:17; Gal 6:15). Attraction and conversion to non-Christian Judaism were phenomena observed by Gentile writers in the first century, especially in Rome, and it appears that for some Gentiles an initial conversion to Paul's faith served as an introduction to Jewish conversion. Finding the right labels for such people (Jewish Christians? Christian Jews? Jesus-following Jews? Jews or proselytes?) is fraught with difficulty.

The exact contours of the Jesus-following Jews' thought and practice, even the degree of their unity and disagreement, are difficult to recapture with confidence. Some may have understood Jesus as the preeminent teacher of wisdom (e.g., the NT letter of James and the *Gospel of Thomas*), whereas others may have shared Paul's preoccupation with the imminent end of the age.

Even those Christian texts that were written by Gentiles, and so cannot themselves be considered primary evidence for Jewish groups, provide important perspectives on some first-century Jewish groups, especially Jesus and his students, John the Baptist and his students, the Pharisees and the Sadducees. The self-consciously historical Luke-Acts is the most promising of these texts: the author has made a considerable effort to recover circumstances, to make important distinctions and to separate out phases of development. So a summary of Luke-Acts' perspectives on the Jewish groups is in order. Acts also mentions Judas, Theudas and the Egyptian prophet, but it does not add anything material to Josephus.

Although the author lives at a time when followers of Jesus have become distinct from Jews as a nation, he is careful enough to try to recover the situation during Jesus' lifetime. First, he gives John the Baptist considerable independence as a teacher of morality, a description that matches Josephus's account fairly well. He portrays Jesus as a prophet who had a special mission to help the sick, the sinners and the downtrodden.

The Pharisees appear in this text as three-dimensional characters (in contrast to the other

Gospels): they have broad popular support as respected teachers; they believe in the resurrection of the dead and in angels; they are preoccupied with issues of purity and legal observance and with the conventional morality that calls for keeping good company, and they have their own extrabiblical traditions; they are prosperous and self-satisfied. Jesus' tension with them is not lethal. They are scandalized by his associations but keep inviting him to their *banquets, and they respect him as a teacher; he takes every opportunity to criticize their alleged petty-mindedness and ineffectiveness, but he still regards them as fundamentally righteous, the healthy who need no physician.

The Sadducees of Luke-Acts are another story. Based in Jerusalem and associated with chief-priestly circles, they are powerful and savage in judgment. They also reject belief in resurrection and in angels. It is they, with their priestly connections and temple police, who arrest Jesus and first harass his followers.

So we have come full circle. In Josephus, we have a presentation of Judean groups from the perspective of a Jerusalem-based aristocrat who sees the priestly college led by the high priest as the only legitimate leadership. The Pharisees are respectable because of the age of their group, but they are often troublesome because of their appeal to the people. The outer circles of individual prophets and demagogues lack all credibility. In Luke we have a reconstructed perspective from the periphery, where the average people live. From that vantage point, it is the priestly center that looks dark and ominous. The Pharisees are again respected in some measure, but they are seen as ineffective. The Baptist and especially Jesus—on the edge of Josephus's horizon—are the only real hope for the common people.

*2.7. **Rabbinic Literature.*** Another body of literature appears in full form only after our period of interest, but it should be mentioned because of its great significance in scholarship on Jewish groups contemporary with the NT. By the end of the second century A.D., the *rabbinic movement was gathering considerable momentum. It produced major texts interpreting the prescriptions of the Torah for daily life and for temple observance (in a rebuilt temple?). This interpretation took the forms of commentary upon the biblical texts (*midrash halakah,* written during the late second century A.D.; *see* Rabbinic Literature: Midrash) and systematic, thematic discussions of legal observance under topical headings (*mishnah*). The Mishnah, edited by Rabbi Judah the Patriarch, would become the fundamental statement of the rabbinic movement, cited as a basis for commentary in the later Talmuds of the fifth and sixth centuries; the Mishnah was published about 200 (*see* Rabbinic Literature: Mishnah and Tosefta).

Scholarship on this early rabbinic literature has overturned old assumptions: that this material comprised simple compendia of traditional data and that it transparently represented Judaism of that period and earlier, in direct continuity with the outlook of the first-century Pharisees. Since the 1960s J. Neusner, in particular, has thoroughly recast the issues. He and others have now shown that the rabbinic movement was itself a coalition of groups that survived the great revolt (A.D. 66-73); in spite of the appearance of comprehensiveness, the Mishnah responds to a question or problem at the time of composition; it undertakes to make a coherent statement in response to that problem; and its Judaism was not recognized by many other Jews of the second and third centuries.

What the Mishnah's statement was, exactly, is much debated. Neusner, who has worked most extensively on these issues, has argued that it responds to the problem of living Judaism in the absence of the temple and in the wake of the failed revolts. Its élite scholarly contributors reinterpret Judaism along the lines of *Aristotelian philosophy: it is concerned to unify the particulars of life under a grand and meaningful scheme of sanctification, making all of life, not only the life of priests in the temple precincts, holy. The rabbis appear to recognize that their group is a minority and that "the people of the land," among others, do not share their vision.

However one resolves the problem of the Mishnah's aim, it is increasingly understood as a document of its own time and therefore not directly usable for establishing facts about Jewish groups of the first century. Although it mentions the Pharisees *(Perušim)* and Sadducees (*Ṣᵉd-dukim*), for example, these groups have limited interaction on issues of purity. The text as it stands does not give us a solid basis for historical reconstruction. Once again Neusner has tried to eke out of the early rabbinic traditions a stratification of traditions about the Pharisees, labeling those that originated before A.D. 70 and those that accreted in subsequent generations. His reconstructed pre-A.D. 70 Pharisees were a fairly small table-fellowship group concerned almost exclusively with issues of *purity. Yet this reconstruction does not sit easily with the earlier portraits of Josephus and the Gospels.

3. Conclusion.

One of the main issues debated by scholars through the last generation is the degree of unity and diversity in first-century Judaism. Reacting against an older consensus that official Judaism, dominated by the Pharisees or rabbis who had effectively supplanted a weak and functionary priesthood, was more or less universal, scholars began to focus on the diversity of Jewish groups and worldviews. Now we find what we might have anticipated: both unity and diversity. There was a common kind of Judaism centered in the temple, and the priesthood remained the recognized aristocracy of the land. Some priests, such as Josephus, were passionate spokesmen for their office and tradition. Torah observance was assumed, not on exclusively religious grounds but because it was the basic law of Jewish communities.

Nevertheless, there was a wide range of worldviews, of groups and individual perspectives, within the cultural orbit that was Judaism. Nonpriestly groups, perhaps including a share of disaffected radical priests, emerged to carry the banners of purity and/or popular demands. And every generation seems to have cultivated individual charismatic teachers, prophets and messiahs. No single spectrum is adequate for mapping out these groups and their attitudes toward Scripture and tradition; foreign powers and "this present age"; class struggles and economic issues; perennial philosophical problems of monism and dualism, fate and free will and the afterlife; militarism and pacifism; angels and demons.

The reader of the NT must always bear this diversity in mind. In the first place, it requires that we eschew simplistic claims about what the Jews as a body believed or practiced. Second, we must similarly allow the evidence of diversity among the early followers of Jesus its full weight, not assume that all Christians except the willfully aberrant held certain views in common, even if they claimed roots in Judaism. The same tensions that we see in Judaism would come to mark developing Christianity to the time of Constantine and beyond (fourth century): some Christians became more and more concerned with Jewish observance; some moved increasingly toward wisdom-based views of Jesus, resulting in Christian *Gnosticism of various stripes; and in succeeding generations there were teachers who reanimated apocalyptic hopes for the end of the age. This period also saw tensions between the growing Christian establishment (priesthood) and charismatic prophets and other leaders.

Given the observable diversity among Jewish groups, even the acceptance by some (such as Philo) of divine mediator figures, it has become a scholarly question whether all of early Christianity, even Paul's, should not be considered Jewish in some sense. Others argue that even the great diversity of Judaism had limits and that Paul fell outside of these.

Perhaps the most important observation to be made about ancient Jewish groups is that our knowledge is defective. We can summarize what we find in the texts and hypothesize about interrelationships, but the quality and quantity of the evidence do not normally permit overwhelmingly probable conclusions. For example, although we can identify wisdom-oriented groups and apocalyptic groups and can observe the logical differences in their orientations, we cannot be sure that the same people did not speak of apocalyptic in one context and wisdom about how to live in the next. Nor can we be sure that an individual Pharisee or Essene behaved in a manner somehow typical of the group or as an individual. Much remains beyond our grasp.

See also APOCALYPTICISM; DEAD SEA SCROLLS: GENERAL INTRODUCTION; DIASPORA JUDAISM; ESSENES; HELLENISTIC JUDAISM; JOSEPHUS; PHARISEES; PHILO; PRIESTS AND PRIESTHOOD, JEWISH; RABBIS; REVOLUTIONARY MOVEMENTS, JEWISH; SADDUCEES; THERAPEUTAE; TORAH.

BIBLIOGRAPHY. A. I. Baumgarten, *The Flourishing of Jewish Sects in the Maccabean Era: An Interpretation* (SJSJ 55; Leiden: E. J. Brill, 1997); J. J. Collins, *The Apocalyptic Imagination: An Introduction to the Jewish Matrix of Christianity* (New York: Crossroad, 1984); L. L. Grabbe, *Judaism from Cyrus to Hadrian* (2 vols.; Minneapolis: Fortress, 1992); R. G. Hall, *Revealed Histories: Techniques for Ancient Jewish and Christian Historiography* (JSPSup 6; Sheffield: JSOT, 1991); R. A. Horsley and J. S. Hanson, *Bandits, Prophets and Messiahs: Popular Movements at the Time of*

Jesus (San Francisco: Harper & Row, 1983); R. A. Kraft and G. W. E. Nickelsburg, eds., *Early Judaism and Its Modern Interpreters* (Philadelphia: Fortress; Atlanta: Scholars Press, 1986); S. Mason, *Josephus and the New Testament* (Peabody, MA: Hendrickson, 1992); G. F. Moore, *Judaism in the First Centuries of the Christian Era* (New York: Schocken, 1958 repr.); J. Neusner, *The Rabbinic Traditions About the Pharisees Before 70* (3 vols.; Leiden: E. J. Brill, 1971); J. Neusner, W. S. Green and E. Frerichs, eds., *Judaisms and Their Messiahs* (Cambridge: Cambridge University Press, 1987); G. W. E. Nickelsburg, *Jewish Literature Between the Bible and The Mishnah* (Philadelphia: Fortress, 1981); P. Sacchi, *Jewish Apocalyptic and Its History* (JSPSup 20; Sheffield: Sheffield Academic Press, 1990); A. J. Saldarini, *Pharisees, Scribes and Sadducees in Palestinian Society* (Wilmington, DE: Michael Glazier, 1988); E. P. Sanders, *Judaism: Practice and Belief, 63 B.C.—A.D. 66* (London: SCM; Philadelphia: Trinity Press International, 1992); E. Schürer, *The History of the Jewish People in the Age of Jesus Christ,* rev. and ed. G. Vermes, F. Millar and M. Goodman (3 vols. Edinburgh: T & T Clark, 1973-87); M. Smith, "Palestinian Judaism in the First Century," in *Israel: Its Role in Civilization,* ed. M. Davis (New York: JTSA, Harper & Bros., 1956); M. Stone and D. Satran, eds., *Emerging Judaism: Studies on the Fourth and Third Centuries B.C.* (Minneapolis: Fortress, 1989); J. Vander Kam, *The Dead Sea Scrolls Today* (London: SPCK; Grand Rapids, MI: Eerdmans, 1994); R. Williamson, *Jews in the Hellenistic World: Philo* (Cambridge: Cambridge University Press, 1989). S. Mason

THERAPEUTAE

The mysterious Therapeutae are thought to be related in some way to the *Essenes. In fact, the derivation of the name *Essene* immediately suggests this relationship. *Pliny the Elder calls the Essenes *Esseni* (*Nat. Hist.* 5.17.4). *Josephus usually calls them *Essenoi* (e.g., *Ant.* 13.5.9 §§171-72; 13.10.6 §298), but sometimes he calls them *Essaioi* (*Ant.* 15.10.4 §371), which is the form *Philo (*Omn. Prob. Lib.* 13.91; *Vit. Cont.* 1.1) and Eusebius (*Praep. Ev.* 8.11.1) use. G. Vermes (1975b, 19-29; cf. Schürer, 559-60, 593) suggests that underlying these various Latin and Greek transliterations is the Aramaic *ʾāsyāʾ* ("healer"). If so, then it is probable that the Therapeutae (Gk *therapeutai*), or "healers," were an Egyptian branch of the Essenes, which may also account for the presence of the **Damascus Document* in Egypt. Vermes also points to Josephus's statement that the Essenes were interested in health: "They display an extraordinary interest in the writings of the ancients, singling out in particular those which make for the welfare of soul and body; with the help of these, and with a view to the treatment of diseases, they make investigations into medicinal roots and the properties of stones" (*J.W.* 2.8.6 §136). According to Philo, Essenes are *therapeutai theou* (*Omn. Prob. Lib.* 12.75; cf. *Vit. Cont.* 1.2).

There are other general parallels between the Essenes and the Therapeutae (see Schürer, 591-97). Members of both groups lived communally, apart from general society. Both groups practiced asceticism and held to strict rules of membership, including probation and discipline. Both groups were well organized and hierarchical. Both groups practiced communal worship. Members of both groups practiced celibacy. Both groups were keenly interested in the study of Scripture. Both groups practiced silence, yet both groups composed *hymns. Both groups favored the use of the right hand. There are also similarities in dress. A *calendrical parallel is seen by J. M. Baumgarten (39-41), in that both groups divided the year into seven fifty-day periods.

However, there are some important differences between the Essenes and the Therapeutae. Their respective food laws and practices were at variance. The Therapeutae did not drink wine, consuming only water, and they refused to eat meat (Philo *Vit. Cont.* 9.73-74). These strictures were not observed by the Essenes, as we see in their texts (e.g., 1QS 6:5; 1QSa 2:17-20; *see* Rule of the Community) and in the archaeological evidence (i.e., the presence of animal bones in the ruins of *Qumran). The Essenes ate two daily meals; the Therapeutae fasted until sunset. Moreover, regarding the Therapeutae we hear of no rules and regulations respecting the practice of sharing property, of assigning all of one's worldly goods to the community, as was the case at Qumran. The Essenes were active; the Therapeutae were contemplative.

When Philo's exaggeration of the *philosophical characteristics of the Therapeutae is taken into account, as well as the evidence of the *Dead Sea Scrolls, the differences between the Essenes and the Therapeutae may not be very great, while it must be admitted that the similarities are numerous and striking. Recent scholarship has emphasized the importance of recognizing Philo's very selective discussion of the Therapeutae. D. M. Hay believes that Philo views their lifestyle as exemplary but may have had little sympathy for their theological views, which is why he never discusses them. If we knew more about their theology, especially their *eschatology, then the apparent differences between the Essenes and Therapeutae may be further mitigated. For these reasons, several scholars have concluded that these groups were related and perhaps had a common origin (especially if the name *Essene* comes from the Aramaic meaning "healer").

However, in a recent study J. E. Taylor and P. R. Davies interpret Philo's omissions differently. They have concluded that in all probability the Therapeutae, who came from different social, religious and economic contexts, had nothing to do with the Essenes of Judea.

Finally, Eusebius's claim that the Therapeutae described by Philo were Christians, an improbable claim in itself, may nevertheless have some probative value. It is possible that the lifestyle and philosophy of the Therapeutae contributed significantly to the development of Christian monasticism in Egypt (Richardson).

See also ESSENES; THEOLOGIES AND SECTS, JEWISH.

BIBLIOGRAPHY. J. M. Baumgarten, "4QHalakah[a] 5, the Law of Hadash and the Pentecontad Calendar," in *Studies in Qumran Law* (Leiden: E. J. Brill, 1977) 131-42 (=*JJS* 27 [1976] 36-46); R. T. Beckwith, "The Vegetarianism of the Therapeutae and the Motives for Vegetarianism in Early Jewish and Christian Circles," *RevQ* 13 (1988) 407-10; R. Bergmeier, *Die Essener-Berichte des Flavius Josephus: Quellenstudien zu den Essenertexten im Werk des jüdischen Historiographen* (Kampen: Kok Pharos, 1993) 41-47; V. Desprez, "Jewish Ascetical Groups at the Time of Christ: Qumran and the Therapeuts," *ABR* 41 (1990) 291-311; M. de. Dreuille, "The Jewish Monastic Ideal: Qumran and the Therapeuts," in *From East to West: Man in Search of the Absolute* (Bangalore: Theological Publications in India, 1979) 61-71; D. M. Hay, "Things Philo Said and Did Not Say About the Therapeutae," *SBLSP* (31 ,1992) 673-83; R. S. Kraemer, "Monastic Jewish Women in Greco-Roman Egypt: Philo Judaeus on the Therapeutrides," *Signs* 14 (1989) 342-70; V. Nikiprowetzky, "Le De Vita Contemplativa revisité," in *Sagesse et religion: Colloque de Strasbourg,* ed. J. Leclant et al. (Paris: Press Universitaires de France, 1979) 105-25; M. Petit, "Les Esséens de Philon d'Alexandrie et les Esséniens," in *The Dead Sea Scrolls: Forty Years of Research,* ed. D. Dimant and U. Rappaport (STDJ 10; Leiden: E. J. Brill, 1992) 139-55; J. Riaud, "Les Thérapeutes d'Alexandrie dans la tradition la recherche critique jusqu'aux découvertes de Qumran" *ANRW* 2.20.2 (1987) 1189-1295; G. P. Richardson, "Philo and Eusebius on Monasteries and Monasticism: The Therapeutae and Kellia," in *Origins and Method: Toward a New Understanding of Judaism and Christianity: Essays in Honor of John C. Hurd,* ed. B. H. McLean (JSNTSup 86; Sheffield: JSOT, 1993) 334-59; H. G. Schönfeld, "Zum Begriff 'Therapeutai' bei Philo von Alexandrien," *RevQ* 3 (1961) 219-40; E. Schürer, *The History of the Jewish People in the Age of Jesus Christ (175 B.D.-A.D. 135),* rev. and ed. G. Vermes, F. Millar and M. Goodman (3 vols.; Edinburgh: T & T Clark, 1973-87) 2:558-61, 591-97. M. Simon, "L'ascétisme dans les sectes juives," in *La tradizione dell'enkrateia: motivazionii ontologiche e protologiche,* ed. U. Bianchi (Rome: Edizioni dell'Ateneo, 1985) 393-426; idem, *Jewish Sects at the Time of Jesus* (Philadelphia: Fortress, 1967) 120-30; J. E. Taylor and P. R. Davies, "The So-Called Therapeutae of *De Vita Contemplativa*: Identity and Character," *HTR* 91 (1998) 3-24; G. Vermes, "Essenes and Therapeutai," in *Post-Biblical Jewish Studies* (SJLA 8; Leiden: E. J. Brill, 1975a) 30-36 [= *RevQ* 3 (1962) 495-504]; idem, "Essenes—Therapeutae—Qumran," *DUJ* 21 (1960) 97-115; idem, 'The Etymology of 'Essenes,'" in *Post-Biblical Jewish Studies* (SJLA 8; Leiden: E. J. Brill, 1975b) 8-29 [= *RevQ* 2 (1960) 427-43].

C. A. Evans

THESSALONICA

Thessalonica was the second important city Paul visited in Macedonia on his second missionary journey. He left Troas in Asia Minor after receiving the Macedonian call in a vision to "come over and help us." Paul and his traveling companions then sailed to the island of Samothrace where they spent the night and then proceeded on to Neapolis, a port on the west coast of Macedonia. From here they traveled on to Philippi where they converted a few people, and then Paul and his companions traveled on past Amphipolis and Apollonia to Thessalonica, where they founded another church.

1. Name and Location
2. Paul's Custom in Preaching
3. Diversity of Converts in Thessalonica
4. Archaeological Remains in Thessalonica

1. Name and Location.
Thessaloniki, the modern name of ancient Thessalonica, is located on the eastern coast of *Greece in the northern province of Macedonia. Built into the western slope of Mt. Khortiatis on the bay of Salonika, which is at the head of the Thermaic Gulf, Thessalonica lies in a natural amphitheater. Its upper level is crowned with a citadel and walls looking down upon the scenic harbor area. The city was founded in 316 B.C. on the site of ancient Therme by Cassander, one of the generals of *Alexander the Great, and it was named Thessalonica after Cassander's wife, the half-sister of Alexander. It became a world cultural center due to its strategic location on both the commercial sea routes and the Egnatian Way, an international highway that ran through Macedonia. When Macedonia became a province in 146 B.C., Thessalonica was made its capital. Earlier, in 168 B.C., it had been divided into four smaller districts for administrative purposes, and Thessalonica was made the capital of the second district. Amphipolis was the capital city of the first district (Acts 16:12; McRay 1991, 284), Pella of the third and Pelagonia (Herakleia Lynkestis) of the fourth.

2. Paul's Custom in Preaching.
Paul's missionary methodology involved going to cities where there were Jewish *synagogues and beginning his work among them. This is called his "custom" (Acts 17:2). His gospel was "to the Jew first and also to the Greek" (Rom 1:16). He had recently passed through Samothrace, Neapolis, Amphipolis and Apollonia without stopping to preach (Acts 16:11; 17:1). No evidence of Jewish synagogues in these cities has been found, and Paul bypassed sites that could not provide a Jewish springboard for his ministry. In Philippi he had gone on the *sabbath to the riverside, where he "supposed there was a place of prayer" (Acts 16:13, 16). In the ancient world the expression "place of prayer" frequently denoted a synagogue (Josephus *Life* §§280-93), though not necessarily a building. So when Paul and his companions left Philippi, "they passed through Amphipolis and Apollonia and came to Thessalonica, where there was a synagogue of the Jews" (Acts 17:1).

3. Diversity of Converts in Thessalonica.
Paul first visited Thessalonica on his second missionary journey (Acts 16:12), arriving in the city in A.D. 49. His ministry in the synagogue here was brief, covering a period of only three sabbath days (Acts 17:2), which could mean three weeks or possibly five weeks, including time before and after the three sabbath days. This was a period in the history of Macedonia, the early imperial age, when the process of social leveling was most intense. Paul's converts cut across the spectrum of society. Although his converts among the Jews were few, described merely as "some" by Luke (Acts 17:4), "great many" of the Godfearing Greeks were persuaded by Paul and joined him. Luke uses the word *Godfearers* for those Gentiles who have rejected paganism and accepted the one true God worshiped by Jews (*see* Proselytism and Godfearers). Although they did not become Jewish proselytes, they often attended synagogue. In *Athens, Paul argued with the Godfearers "in the synagogues" (Acts 17:17).

Among Paul's converts in Thessalonica Luke emphasized that there were a "great many" of the "leading women" (Acts 17:4). It is difficult to tell from this verse whether these leading women were Jews or Greeks. There is evidence now that *women also functioned in leadership roles in the synagogues, even holding a position among the elders. B. Brooten investigated all the known ancient inscriptions relative to the matter and found three that named women as heads of the synagogue, in exactly the same way as men. She writes: "Women synagogue heads, like their male counterparts, were active in administration and exhortation . . . perhaps they looked after the financial affairs of the synagogue . . . perhaps they exhorted their congregations, reminding them to keep the sabbath. . . . we must assume that they had a knowledge of the Torah in order to be able to teach and exhort others in it" (Brooten, 32).

Since the publication of Brooten's book, another *inscription has been found on the island of Malta, and that inscription "provides additional testimony to the likelihood that women held the office of elder in ancient Jewish synagogues" (Kraemer, 438). Six inscriptions have been found in which women bear the title *elder* (Brooten, 41). In Italy another six inscriptions have been discovered, these spanning the first six centuries, naming a woman as "mother of the synagogue." Brooten's study concludes that these women "had something to do with the administration of the synagogue" and that these inscriptions did not simply contain honorific titles (Brooten, 72).

Several men later connected with Paul's work became disciples of Jesus in Thessalonica, perhaps at this time. Aristarchus and Secundus were among them (Acts 20:4; 19:29). Aristarchus, who later accompanied Paul on his voyage to *Rome, is called "a Macedonian from Thessalonica" (Acts 27:2). Another of the men who responded to Paul's teaching and apparently hosted him during this time was named Jason (Acts 17:5-7). This Greek name was often taken by Jews whose Hebrew name was Joshua or Jeshua (Bruce, 224).

4. Archaeological Remains in Thessalonica. Almost nothing from the time of the NT is still standing in Thessalonica because the ruins are covered by the second largest city in Greece, and excavation is difficult. However, in 1917 a fire destroyed a section of the city that was afterwards reused as a bus station. The station was moved in 1962, and excavations revealed a part of a second-century forum. Work has continued in the area, and as of 1998 portions of a bathhouse and a mint from the first century have been found beneath the second-century level of the pavement on either side of an odeum, which is only partially preserved.

Archaeology has touched Thessalonica and the book of Acts in a significant way with the discovery of a number of inscriptions in Macedonia. A portion of a first-century arch was discovered at the west end of the Odos Egnatia (Egnatia Street); its inscription begins with the phrase "in the time of the Politarchs." The inscription, which is now in the British Museum, confirms not only the existence of the term *Politarch* in Macedonia in the first century but also its use for city officials. This silences critics who claimed that Acts 17:6 was mistaken in its use of this term to designate the city officials before whom Paul's followers appeared in Thessalonica. In 1960, C. Schuler published a list of thirty-two inscriptions that contain this title, nineteen of which come from Thessalonica, three of which are from the first century (Schuler, 90-100). Even more recently the word has been found in another inscription in the Thessalonica Museum and in two more from Berea and Amphipolis (McRay 1991, 295).

See also ATHENS; CORINTH; GREECE AND MACEDON; PHILIPPI.

BIBLIOGRAPHY. B. Brooten, *Women Leaders in the Ancient Synagogue* (Chico, CA: Scholars Press, 1982); F. F. Bruce, *Paul, Apostle of the Heart Set Free* (Grand Rapids, MI: Eerdmans, 1977); G. Foerster, "A Survey of Ancient Diaspora Synagogues," in *Ancient Synagogues Revealed,* ed. L. Levine (Jerusalem: Israel Exploration Society, 1981) 164-71; C. J. Hemer, *The Book of Acts in the Setting of Hellenistic History,* ed. C. H. Gempf (Tübingen: Mohr Siebeck, 1989) 444-47; R. Kraemer, "A New Inscription from Malta and the Question of Women Elders in the Diaspora Jewish Communities," *HTR* 78 (1985) 3-4; J. McRay, *Archaeology and the New Testament* (Grand Rapids, MI: Baker, 1991); idem, "The Place of Prayer: What Exactly Took Place in a Synagogue Service," *Christian History Magazine* issue 59 17.3 (1988) 24-25; R. E. Oster Jr., "Ephesus," *ABD* 2:542-49; R. Riesner, *Paul's Early Period: Chronology, Mission Strategy, Theology* (Grand Rapids, MI: Eerdmans, 1998); C. Schuler, "The Macedonian Politarchs," *CP* 55 (1960) 90-100. J. P. McRay

THEUDAS. *See* REVOLUTIONARY MOVEMENTS, JEWISH.

THREE TONGUES OF FIRE. *See* APOCRYPHON OF MOSES.

THUNDER TEXT (4Q318)

Striking testimony to the Jewish use of astrology in the NT period appears in the texts from *Qumran. Among these manuscripts are found at least four astrological works: 4Q186, a physiognomic Hebrew text inscribed in mirror writing and using a variety of scripts, including Greek; 4Q561, a second, less elaborate physiognomic work written in *Aramaic; 4QMess ar, likewise inscribed in Aramaic, which apparently predicts the birth of Noah (or perhaps that of the messiah; the point is disputed) and includes physiognomic elements; and a brontologion or "thunder text," so called because it employs thunder as an element of its scheme for divining the future. This last work has been given the official designation 4Q318 Brontologion, and it too is written in Aramaic.

1. Cultural Background and Description
2. Interpretation and Significance

1. Cultural Background and Description. Brontologia, or thunder texts, existed well before the rise of horoscopic astrology. A number came to be included in the vast Mesopotamian collection of cuneiform *omina* known as the *Enuma Anu Enlil.* The extant version of the *Enuma Anu Enlil* dates to the Neo-Assyrian period, but the existence of commentaries attempting to explain its already archaic language argues for a substantially earlier date of composition. Brontologia are largely descriptive; they concern wars, the weather, crops and domestic animals, disease, the rise and fall of great men (particularly kings) and general disturbances of all sorts. Their interest is in the nation as a whole, rather than in the fate of individuals. In the *Hellenistic period, they were elaborated far beyond their Mesopotamian predecessors. This elaboration was possible thanks to the rise of new mathematical approaches to the observation of the heavens. It is especially to Ptolemaic Egypt (*see* Hellenistic Egypt) that we owe this new, more complex class of brontologia, and it is these more elaborate thunder texts, inscribed in Greek, that afford the best parallels to 4Q318.

The first half of 4Q318 is given over to the distribution of the twelve signs of the zodiac over the days of the months. The text preserves the earliest list ever discovered of the zodiac's signs in either Hebrew or Aramaic. The underlying *calendar was a solar one, not the luni-solar calendar of rabbinic *Judaism and, presumably, the earlier *Pharisees. The week is the basic pattern for the distribution of the signs: one sign covers two days, the next another two, then another three days. A new month always begins with a new sign, and the signs of the zodiac rotate through the months such that whatever sign begins a month will also end it. Accordingly, successive months begin with successive signs of the zodiac. Yet 4Q318 begins the year with the sign of Taurus, not that of Aries, as was general throughout the Hellenistic world and in later Judaism, a point to which we shall return below.

The rationale for the thunder text's distribution of the signs of the zodiac over the days of the year emerges from a Greek parallel that explicitly states its own purpose: "the twelve signs of the zodiac for each night according to the course of the moon." The Qumran text is thus a Jewish exemplar of that class of books, widespread in antiquity, known in Greek as *selēnodromia* and in Latin as *lunaria.* These books employed the observation of the moon as an element of their divination. The statements in 4Q318 distributing the signs of the zodiac are statements of the moon's position within those signs. The text combines the sounds of thunder and the location of the moon at any given time to derive its predictions for the future.

The second half of 4Q318 is statements about the portent of thunder in relation to the moon's position. For example: "If it thunders [on a day when the moon is] in Gemini, it signifies fear and distress caused by foreigners." Little of this second half of the work has survived, but there is mention of "destruction in the royal court" and of "the Arabs"—presumably the Nabatean neighbors of Judea—and of a time when "nations will plunder one another."

2. Interpretation and Significance. As noted, Hellenistic practice, which continues to this day, was to begin the zodiac with the sign of Aries. This practice resulted from the observed phenomenon that in Hellenistic times the sun rose in Aries on the day of the vernal equinox (approximately March 21). That 4Q318 begins its zodiac with Taurus instead of Aries suggests that it was listing the signs not according to the astronomical realities of its own day but those of the time of creation. The science of the day was aware of the precession of the zodiac, whereby the signs of the zodiac slowly migrate through the heavens. Thus it was known that from about 4400 B.C. until 2200 B.C. the sun rose in Taurus on the day of the vernal equinox. By beginning with the sign of Taurus, our author may have been embracing one or another scheme of *apocalyptic chronology that sought to divide time into periods and to establish when the end of the age would come. In this respect it is notable that the chronological data of the Pentateuch imply that the world will last a total of four thousand years and that the exodus took place in the year 2666 counting from the creation. The remaining one-third of history would then culminate at about the time of Daniel, or rather at the end of his seventy week-years (490 years). There were other, similar schemes at the heart of many works composed during the last two centuries B.C. and first century A.D. Thus

4Q318 apparently conceals behind its laconic listing a definite theology.

As to its significance, the many parallels between 4Q318 and Ptolemaic Greek thunder texts suggest that the Qumran manuscript's basic framework derived from the Egyptian Diaspora. Although many of the phrases it employs have Akkadian antecedents, the elaboration of these phrases into a *selēnodromion* whose type is well known from Egypt bespeaks this western origin. The possibility is unsurprising considering the substantial Jewish presence in *Alexandria, which was itself the most important center for every kind of astrological research. Further, that this brontologion exemplifies what A. Bouché-Leclerq called the "absorption of meteorological divination by astrology" accords well with earlier understandings: the Jews came to astrology comparatively late, when it had already been refined well beyond its Mesopotamian forms. The date of 4Q318 can be specified no more narrowly than the range 100 B.C.-A.D. 70. Apart from the solar calendar that underlies it, nothing about the text is clearly sectarian, and just how sectarian the solar calendar was remains a question for further research.

See also CALENDARS, JEWISH.

BIBLIOGRAPHY. M. Albani, "Der Zodiakos in 4Q318 und die Henoch-Astronomie," *Mitteilungen und Beiträge 7, Forschungsstelle Judentum Theologische Fakultät Leipzig* (1993) 1-42; P. S. Alexander, "'Wrestling Against Wickedness in High Places': Magic in the Worldview of the Qumran Community," in *The Scrolls and the Scriptures: Qumran Fifty Years After,* ed. S. E. Porter and C. A. Evans (Sheffield: Sheffield Academic Press, 1997) 318-37; A. Bouché-Leclercq, *Histoire de la Divination dans L'antiquité* (2 vols.; New York: Arno, 1879-92 repr.); F. Cumont et al., eds., *Catologus Codicum Astrologorum Graecorum* (Brussels: In Aedibus Academiae, 1898-1953); J. C. Greenfield and M. Sokoloff (with appendices by D. Pingree and A. Yardeni), "An Astrological Text from Qumran (4Q318) and Reflections on Some Zodiacal Names," *RevQ* 16 (1995) 507-25; M. O. Wise, "Thunder in Gemini: An Aramaic Brontologion (4Q318) from Qumran," in *Thunder in Gemini and Other Essays on the History, Language and Literature of Second Temple Palestine* (Sheffield: JSOT, 1994) 13-50. M. O. Wise

TIBERIAS

The name *Tiberias* is mentioned three times in the NT, all in the Gospel of John. Two of the references (Jn 6:1; 21:1) are to the Sea of Tiberias, a large freshwater lake in *Galilee in northern Israel. The other reference is to the city of Tiberias, which is located on the western shore of the sea (Jn 6:23). John tells of boatloads of people who came from the city looking for Jesus on the north side of the sea, where he had fed the multitudes by a miracle. Thus, we must rely on information in *Josephus and the *Talmud for our knowledge of its early history. After the NT period, there is an occasional reference to the city in early Christian writers such as Epiphanius and Jerome.

1. Location
2. Founding of the City
3. Jesus and Tiberias
4. Early History and Composition

1. Location.

Tiberias is situated at the center of the western side of the pear-shaped sea, between the shore and the mountains rising sharply above it. It had the advantage of being on a major road from the Mediterranean coast to Transjordan through the Bet Netofa Valley, as well as being a scenic spot located by a lake that offered recreational and commercial activity.

Although Tiberias and Hammath, to the south of it, were once a mile apart (*y. Meg.* 2:2), they were eventually incorporated into one city as they are today. This apparently occurred in the first century A.D. (*t. ʿErub.* 7:2, 146).

The hot springs at Hammath made the location of Tiberias even more desirable. This location prompted Josephus to write that "the tetrarch Herod, inasmuch as he had gained a high place among the friends of Tiberius, had a city built, named after him Tiberias, which he established in the best region of Galilee on Lake Gennesaritis. There is a hot spring not far from it in a village called Ammanthus" (Josephus *Ant.* 18.2.3 §36). Ammanthus probably derives from the Hebrew *ḥammath,* "warm [springs]." Josephus spoke of Vespasian's camp "in front of Tiberias at Ammanthus (this name may be interpreted as 'warm baths,' being derived from a spring of warm water within the city possessing curative properties" (Josephus *J.W.* 4.1.3 §11). Josephus even refers to them as the "hot baths at Tiberias" (Josephus *Life* 85 §16).

2. Founding of the City.

Tiberias was founded by Herod Antipas, son of

Herod the Great and tetrarch of Galilee. M. Avi-Yonah dates its founding between A.D. 17 and 22 on the basis of numismatic (*see* Coinage) and other evidence, and A. Spijkerman narrows it to a span of A.D. 17 to 20 (Spijkerman, 303-4). Avi-Yonah (169) thinks the year A.D. 18 is probably most likely since Tiberius's sixtieth birthday fell in this year; it was the twentieth anniversary of his holding the *tribunica potestas,* or coregency; and if Herod Antipas began the construction authorized by Tiberius immediately after his accession as emperor in A.D. 14, he easily could have completed it and founded it officially in four years.

Tiberias was built to replace a city four miles north of Nazareth named Sepphoris, which Herod the Great had conquered in 39/38 B.C. and used as his northern headquarters until his death in 4 B.C. His son Antipas rebuilt Sepphoris to function as his headquarters until Tiberias could be completed.

Antipas was compelled to populate the city with Gentiles as well as Jews because in the course of construction tombs were discovered there that made the city unclean for religious Jews (*see* Purity). Avi-Yonah concludes, "The history of Tiberias, and especially the behavior of its population during the First Revolt, shows that the majority of the inhabitants were Jews, many well-to-do, but without religious or nationalistic fervor" (Avi-Yonah, 163; *see* Jewish Wars with Rome). The presence of a large *synagogue there also supports this view (Josephus *Life* 277 §54).

3. Jesus and Tiberias.

Since there is no explicit evidence that Jesus ever visited Tiberias, J. Finegan concludes that Jesus probably was never there. He also cites the opposition to Jesus by Antipas (Lk 13:31) as reason to think Jesus would not have gone to Tiberias (Finegan, 79). However, Finegan subsequently notes that "Jesus was not driven out of his territory by any threat from Herod" and "regarded him as crafty and weak." It should be noted that Capernaum, where Jesus lived during the three years of his ministry, was only about ten miles north of Tiberias, and he was thus not inaccessible to Herod. In fact, Joanna, the wife of Herod's steward (manager of his household or possibly a governor), was one of the women who had been healed by Jesus and who subsequently provided some financial support for Jesus (Lk 8:3).

There is no mention that Jesus was ever in Sepphoris either, which is not mentioned in the NT. But R. Batey argues that the probabilities are strong that Jesus visited and perhaps even worked as a carpenter in Sepphoris. If Jesus never visited Tiberias it could possibly have been for religious reasons, because of the uncleanness of the city (see 2 above).

4. Early History and Composition.

There is no information as to the size or population of the town during these early years. Avi-Yonah estimated the city to have been less than 1 kilometer square by the third century and to have had less than 40,000 population (Avi-Yonah, 164-65).

Herod Antipas built a palace for himself in Tiberias, which, contrary to the law of Moses (Ex 20:4) had representations of animals on it (Josephus *Life* 65 §12). It also had a roof made partly of gold, which Josephus says was later set on fire by a man named Jesus, son of Sapphias, a ringleader in the demolition of the city just prior to the revolt against Rome. He hoped to "obtain from it large spoils" (Josephus *Life* 66 §12). Tiberias had functioned as the capital until A.D. 61, when the Roman emperor Nero gave it to Herod Agrippa II (Josephus *Ant.* 20.8.4 §159).

Herod also built a stadium (Josephus *Ant.* 2.21.6 §618; *Life* 63 §330; *see* Arenas) that was used for public assemblies. When Tiberias opened its gates to Vespasian and sided with Rome against the Jewish revolt that broke out in A.D. 66, Vespasian put to death twelve hundred Jewish captives in this stadium who were elderly and considered "useless" (Josephus *J.W.* 3.10.10 §539).

On this occasion (September 67) Vespasian also sent "6,000 of the most robust" to Nero to work on the attempted construction of a canal through the isthmus near *Corinth. However, Nero eventually gave up on the mammoth project, which was not completed until 1883 (McRay, 314). The rest of the multitude of prisoners (30,400) at Tiberias, Vespasian sold, except those of whom he made a present to Agrippa, who also sold them into *slavery (Josephus *J.W.* 3.540-42).

Antipas built a synagogue, which was "a huge building, capable of accommodating a large crowd" (Josephus *Life* 54 §277) and in which people were gathered for political as well as religious assemblies. Here, Josephus says, the people of Tiberias were gathered to hear accusations against him by a delegate from Rome (Josephus *Life* 54 §§277, 280). In these references the synagogue is called, as is typical of the time, the place of prayer, a designation used by Luke in Acts 16:13, 16.

Josephus built a wall around Tiberias, except on the east side by the sea, which he later found himself attacking after his defection to the Romans (Josephus *J.W.* 3.10.1 §465; 2.20.6 §573). When Josephus used Tiberias as the headquarters of his campaign in Galilee, he set up a group of seventy older men "from the nation" as a court (perhaps patterned on the Jewish Sanhedrin) to have jurisdiction over all Galilee. (Whether the word *nation* here refers to Jews or Gentiles is not clear. It is regularly used in the NT to refer to Gentiles.) He also appointed smaller groups of seven men in each city to "adjudicate on petty disputes," reminiscent of Acts 6:1-3 (Josephus *J.W.* 2.20.5 §§570-71).

Even though the representation of human forms was forbidden by Jewish law, when Caligula replaced Antipas with Herod Agrippa in A.D. 39, Agrippa began to mint *coins in Tiberias with himself and Caligula depicted on them. Tiberias continued under Agrippa's rule until his death in A.D. 44 (Acts 12:22-23), at which time it was placed under the jurisdiction of the Roman procurators rather than Herod's son Agrippa II, because of his youth (Josephus *Ant.* 19.9.2 §§360-66; *see* Roman Administration). This lasted until A.D. 61, at which time Nero put Tiberias under the rule of Herod Agrippa II. After this, the name of Agrippa with the title of king appears on his coins.

Under the emperor Trajan (A.D. 98-117) Tiberias became an autonomous city attached to the Provincia Judea. On coins of the period Tiberias is designated as Tiberias Claudia in honor of the emperor Claudius, perhaps in gratitude for some remembered benevolence. By A.D. 170 the official Roman name of Tiberias, appearing on coins, was Tiberias Claudia in Syria-Palestina.

Tiberias was paganized by the emperor Hadrian, who put down the Second Jewish Revolt in A.D. 135, but in the second and third centuries the city became an important center of Jewish rabbinical study. Evidence of their presence can be found in the Talmud. A famous rabbinical academy was founded, and tombs of the rabbis here are still venerated. The *Mishnah, though codified in Sepphoris in 200, took its final form in Tiberias. In the fifth century A.D. the Palestinian Talmud was largely compiled in Tiberias, and in the seventh century it was the center of Masoretic work on the text of the Hebrew Bible. In the opinion of many, Tiberias became in this period "perhaps the greatest intellectual center of ancient Judaism" (Strange, 548).

In addition to excavations in 1921 and 1961 that revealed several superimposed synagogues at Tiberias, dating from the fourth to the eighth centuries, work in the 1970s in the area south of the synagogues revealed a paved road and city gate from the time of the founding of the city by Antipas. The gate consisted of two round towers, 23 feet in diameter, which projected to the south. Several courses of stone are preserved. Leading northward out of the gates the road is paved with rectangular slabs laid parallel to each other near the gate and then obliquely further north (Foerster, 1171-76).

Excavations of the city are currently underway directed by Y. Hirschfeld for the Israel Antiquities Authority (Hirschfeld 1991). Evidence of what may be an imperial villa have been found. On Mt. Berenice, above Tiberias, a Byzantine church has been found, and it is not earlier than the sixth century. It has also been shown that no palace had stood on the summit of the hill (Hirschfeld 1994b, 33).

See also ARCHAEOLOGY OF THE LAND OF ISRAEL; GALILEE.

BIBLIOGRAPHY. M. Avi-Yonah, "The Foundation of Tiberias," *IEJ* 1 (1950-51) 160-69; R. Batey, *Jesus and the Forgotten City* (Grand Rapids, MI: Baker, 1991); J. Finegan, *The Archaeology of the New Testament: The Life of Jesus and the Beginning of the Early Church* (rev ed.; Princeton, NJ: Princeton University Press, 1992) 77-80; G. Foerster, "Tiberias," *Encyclopedia of Archaeological Excavations in the Holy Land,* ed. M. Avi-Yonah (4 vols.; Jerusalem: Massada, 1978) 4:1171-77; Y. Hirschfeld, "The Anchor Church at the Summit of Mt. Berenice, Tiberias," *BA* 57 (1994a) 122-34; idem, "Tiberias: Preview of Coming Attractions," *BAR* 17 (March/April 1991) 44-51; idem, "Tiberias," *Excavations and Surveys in Israel* 14 (1994b) 33-38; 16 (1997) 35-42; J. McRay *Archaeology and the New Testament* (Grand Rapids, MI: Baker, 1991) 178; A. Spijkerman, "Some Rare Jewish Coins," *Liber Annus* 13 (1962-63) 303-4; J. Strange, "Tiberias," *ABD* 6:547-49; E. Vogel, *Bibliography of Holy Land Sites,* pt. 1 (Cincinnati:

Hebrew Union College-Jewish Institute of Religion, 1982) 34. J. R. McRay

TOBIT

Tobit is an adventure story or romance contained in the *Septuagint but not the Masoretic Text. Considered deuterocanonical by the Roman Catholic and Eastern Orthodox churches, Tobit is relegated to the *Apocrypha by Protestants. In the LXX, Tobit is placed among the historical books in the order Esdras II (Ezra-Nehemiah), Esther, *Judith and Tobit. In the Vulgate, Tobit immediately follows 1 and 2 Esdras (Ezra-Nehemiah; *see* Esdras, Books of).

1. Summary of the Book
2. Survey of Scholarship
3. Significance for the New Testament

1. Summary of the Book.

This is a fictional story about the problem of unmerited suffering. In classical literary terms, Tobit is a comedy, since it has a happy ending and treats the story with lighthearted humor. God sends an angel to deliver Tobit and Sarah from their afflictions. Even though the author informs the reader of the felicitous outcome near the beginning of the story (Tob 3:16-17), interest is sustained by melodramatic flourishes and delightful irony. The characters are arranged in a triadic pattern:

Tobit (the principal character), Tobias (Tobit's son) and Anna (Tobit's wife)

Raguel (Tobit's relative), Sarah (Raguel's daughter) and Edna (Raguel's wife)

God, Raphael (an angel sent to assist Tobit) and Asmodeus (an evil spirit who haunts Sarah)

The plot centers primarily around the trials and tribulations of pious Tobit. Ironically, this man, whose name means "goodness," suffers because of his good deeds shown to unfortunate and indigent Jews—especially those deprived of proper *burial. The author incorporates a subplot involving the harassment of beautiful Sarah, the object of lustful envy by an evil spirit. Seven grooms in succession perish on their wedding night, slain by the evil Asmodeus before they consummate their marriage to Sarah. The plights of Tobit and Sarah are mirror images of each other. We read first of Tobit's troubles leading to his petition to die because of his misery; then, of the ill-starred Sarah and her prayer for deliverance by death from an intolerable situation. Interwoven into these two plots is a third: the recovery of money deposited by Tobit from a relative in far-off Rages. The three subplots intertwine, and resolution is achieved by divine intervention in the person of an angel in disguise, Raphael, whose name means "God heals." Thus at the conclusion of this well-told story, Tobit recovers his sight, Sarah marries Tobias, and Tobias inherits both Tobit's and Raguel's wealth. In terms of the basic movements of the story, we have a joining of the two families in marriage and an exorcism of Asmodeus through the means provided by Raphael.

2. Survey of Scholarship.

2.1. Sources or Influences. A number of scholars argue that the basic plot of Tobit derives from one or more secular folktales. These have been identified as The Grateful Dead (reward for providing proper burial), The Bride of the Monster (demon-haunted woman) and The Tale of Ahiqar (*see* Ahiqar), the latter an ancient Semitic story, having a fifth-century B.C. Aramaic version, about a betrayed and ultimately vindicated courtier. Ahiqar briefly appears in our story as Tobit's nephew and benefactor (Tob 1:21-22; 14:10) but serves more as window dressing than a leading character, although final vindication is important to the plot of Tobit. Another suggestion includes an Egyptian tale called The Tractate of Khons, dealing with the exorcism of a woman. This proposal is generally linked to an Egyptian provenance for Tobit.

Many scholars draw attention to the Hebrew Bible as a major factor in the story. Some would minimize or even deny the influence of the secular folktales. The patriarchal stories of the angelic visitors (Gen 18—19), the quest for a bride (Isaac in Gen 24 and Jacob in Gen 29), the story of Joseph (Gen 37—48) and the story of Job are close at hand to provide the basic plot and substructure of Tobit. Tobit's prayer, prophesying *Israel's restoration (Tob 13:16-17), draws freely from Isaianic passages (cf. Is 54:11-14; 60:1-22). Attention has been drawn to the distinctly Deuteronomic theology of retribution underlying the basic premise of the story. Especially noteworthy are the allusions to Deuteronomy 31—32 in Tobit 12—13. In addition, two biblical prophets, Amos and Nahum, are cited (Tob 2:6 cf. Amos 8:10 and Tob 14:4 cf. Nahum 1:1; 2:8-10, 13; 3:18-19). The tales of a wise courtier in Daniel 1—6 and Esther are also germane to Tobit. Finally, there are echoes of sapiential teaching as found in the book of Proverbs (see esp. Tob 4:5-19). The influence of the Hebrew Bible is paramount in Tobit.

2.2. Literary Genre. Scholars variously characterize Tobit as a *romance, adventure story, didactic tale, novella or fairy tale. Older, conservative scholarship sought to defend the historicity of the story; few would deny its fictional character today. It is more difficult, however, to identify precisely the genre. Modern scholars tend to put several modifiers in front of their designation, suggesting the slippery nature of the task. More fruitful have been studies investigating the *rhetorical features of the work, especially *intertextuality.

2.3. Purpose. This story does more than entertain the reader. Behind the characters lurks a real and disturbing problem: the people of Israel are in exile. Tobit and Sarah represent an oppressed minority within a largely hostile culture. The author inserts three passages of moral, ethical and ritual exhortation (Tob 4:3-21; 12:6-10; 14:8-11). These function paraenetically as guidelines for correct behavior. Furthermore, the leading characters, while not perfect or famous, nonetheless serve as role models. Here are ordinary people who display extraordinary faithfulness to Torah, believing that God will ultimately vindicate and restore Israel. Through the lens of this story the anonymous author offers encouragement to Diaspora Jews. "God will again have mercy" (Tob 14:5) is the fervent conviction resonating in the climax to the story. An eloquent hymn celebrates God's certain restoration of the *temple, *Jerusalem and the Jewish people. Even the Gentiles convert to the God of Israel. Seen in this light, Tobit is fundamentally a theodicy.

2.4. Composition. The author was a pious, observant Jew. Beyond that, consensus evaporates. Identification with any particular sect seems ruled out by the probable date of writing. The book expresses the sentiments of a Jew committed to Torah and temple and concerned that Jews remain loyal to both. No consensus exists on the provenance, whether in Palestine or the *Diaspora. Perhaps a slight nod may be given to the assumed setting of the story, namely, the eastern Diaspora.

Internal evidence for dating the book consists of the following: dependence upon the Hebrew prophets, no reflection of the turbulent times of Antiochus IV (175-164 B.C.) and the Maccabean revolt (167 B.C.; *see* Jewish History: Greek Period) and no awareness of Herod's greatly expanded and beautified temple (work on this beginning in 20-19 B.C.). Since the canonization of the prophets is usually placed in the middle of the third century B.C., this would provide outside limits of 250 to 175 B.C. A few scholars push the date back into the fourth century B.C., but this is a minority position. A date in the first century B.C. is rendered unlikely by the external evidence from *Qumran—Aramaic and Hebrew fragments dating from the first century B.C.

3. Significance for the New Testament.

3.1. Life in Diaspora. Most Jews in the NT era lived in the Diaspora (cf. Acts 2:8-11). The story of Tobit portrays a Jew in the eastern Diaspora who, initially at least, is relatively well off economically. This seems to be in contrast to most of his Jewish kinsmen. The story assumes that most Jews did not enjoy economic power and status to any significant degree (Tob 2:1-3; cf. Lk 14:16-24). Furthermore, their civil and religious rights might be arbitrarily taken from them at any time (Tob 1:18-20). The picture that emerges is that most Jews lived in precarious circumstances.

This feature of Jewish life is a mirror image of the early Christian movement. NT literature incorporates the theme of Diaspora as a means of self-identity but transposes it into a different key; that is, Christians are aliens living in a foreign land, anticipating an eventual arrival at the heavenly Mt. Zion or Jerusalem (cf. Gal 4:26; 1 Cor 7:31b; Phil 3:20; 1 Pet 1:1; Jas 1:1; Heb 11:13-16; 12:22; 13:14). The issue of assimilation to the values and lifestyle of the surrounding pagan culture is a constant concern (cf. 2 Cor 6:14—7:1; Eph 4:17-24; Phil 2:15; Col 3:5-11; Tit 2:11, 12; 1 Pet 2:11; 4:1-5; Jas 4:4). The tenuous and precarious situation of these early Christian communities finds numerous expressions in the NT (cf. 1 Thess 1:6; 2:14; 3:1-5; 2 Thess 1:4-12; 1 Cor 16:13; 2 Cor 1:3-11; 4:8-12, 16-18; 6:4-10; 11:23-33; Phil 1:27-30; Col 4:5-6; Heb 10:32-39; 12:3-8, 12-13; Jas 1:1-4; 1 Pet 2:19-25; 3:9-17; 4:12-19; Rev 3—4; 6:9-11).

3.2. Angelology and Demonology. Tobit witnesses to a significant development in *angelology and *demonology during the intertestamental era. The archangel Raphael, masquerading as Azariah, plays a leading role in the story. The OT knows no such category of angelic being called an archangel—this is an intertestamental development generally traced by scholars to Persian influence. The NT mentions the angel Gabriel (Lk 1:19, 26 cf. Dan 8:6; 9:21-23), who, like Raphael, stands in the presence of God (cf. Tob 12:15) and the archangel Michael (Jude 9; cf. Dan 10:13, 21; 12:1). In the Enoch literature we learn of seven archangels who stand in the presence of God (cf. *1 Enoch* 9:1; 54:6; *2 Enoch* 8:1—10:1; *see* Enoch, Books of). That Paul accepted the tradition of archangels is implied by his passing reference to "the archangel's call" at the parousia of Christ (1 Thess 4:16). It is possible that Revelation 4:5 refers to these seven archangels as "the seven spirits of God" (cf. Rev 1:4).

Asmodeus is but one of a considerable number of demons named in intertestamental literature. The name *Asmodeus* has been connected to a Persian evil spirit called *Aesma Daeva.* The apostle Paul accepts the widespread notion of a hierarchy of angelic and demonic beings (Col 1:16; 2:15; Rom 8:38; Eph 1:21; 3:10; perhaps 1 Cor 2:8). He envisions the Christian life as a struggle against "the cosmic powers of this present darkness" (Eph 6:12; cf. 2:2; 2 Cor 4:4).

Tobit witnesses to the influence of *magic in Jewish life and culture. Raphael gives Tobias a potion that exorcises the demon Asmodeus to Egypt, a traditional haunt of magic and witchcraft. Whereas exorcism was a hallmark of Jesus' ministry and that of the apostolic church (cf. Mk 3:22 par. Mt 12:24; Lk 11:15; Mt 10:25; Jn 7:20; 8:48-52; 10:20-21; Acts 8:9-24; 13:4-12; 19:11-20), the NT warns against magic (cf. Gal 5:20 ["sorcery"]; Rev 21:8; 22:15).

3.3. Eschatology. Tobit reflects a fervent hope of national restoration (Tob 13—14), a hope widely attested in Second Temple Judaism. For many Jews, nationalism and *messianism were inseparable. Tobit, however, makes no reference to a messiah. The Gospels, by contrast, witness to a strong undercurrent of nationalistic fervor linked to a messianic figure (cf. Lk 3:15; 7:19; Jn 1:19-22; 6:15). The centerpiece of restoration in Tobit is a rebuilt Jerusalem and temple. The description of the new Jerusalem (Tob 13:15-17) echoes the language of Isaiah 54:11-12 and finds a NT counterpart in Revelation 21:9-21. In startling contrast, however, Revelation depicts the new Jerusalem as having "no temple in the city, for its temple is the Lord God Almighty and the Lamb" (Rev 21:22). Furthermore, in the NT, believers already experience in part the new Jerusalem; there is a realized *eschatology (see Gal 4:26; Heb 12:22; cf. Col 3:1-4; Eph 2:5-6).

3.4. Faith and Piety. Tobit 12:8 epitomizes Jewish *piety: *prayer, fasting and almsgiving. Strikingly, Jesus endorses precisely these three practices as essential for kingdom citizens, provided they avoid ostentation and hypocrisy (Mt 6:1-18). Furthermore, Tobit contains expressions closely parallel to Jesus' sayings in the Sermon on the Mount, such as "laying up a good treasure for yourself (Tob 4:6b; cf. Mt 6:19, 20) and a negative form of the Golden Rule (Tob 5:15; cf. Mt 7:12). A major difference, however, lies in the question of how one enters the kingdom of heaven: Jesus taught that true obedience hinges upon a personal relationship to himself (Mt 7:21-27). Though rooted in Judaism, Jesus' teaching possesses a radically new obedience (cf. Mt 5:21-48).

3.5. Paraenesis. Moral and ethical exhortation characterizes Tobit as it does NT epistolary literature. In Paul's letters several verbal parallels may be cited (cf. Tob 4:12 and 1 Cor 6:18; Tob 4:5 and 2 Cor 7:1; Tob 4:8 and 2 Cor 8:3, 12; Tob 4:7 and Gal 2:10; Tob 4:19 and Col 4:2; Tob 4:14 and Eph 5:18; Tob 4:14 and 1 Tim 4:7, 16; Tob 4:3, 4a and 1 Tim 5:4; Tob 4:5 and Tit 2:12). The point is not to argue that Paul or any other NT writer is dependent upon Tobit but rather that Christian paraenesis reflects and is indebted to a Jewish background.

See also AHIQAR; APOCRYPHA AND PSEUDEPIGRAPHA; DANIEL, ESTHER AND JEREMIAH, ADDITIONS TO; JUDITH; ROMANCES/NOVELS, ANCIENT.

BIBLIOGRAPHY. **Texts and Translations.** R. Hanhart, *Tobit* (Septuaginta 8/5; Göttingen: Vandenhoeck & Ruprecht, 1983); B. M. Metzger and R. E. Murphy, eds., *The New Oxford Annotated Bible with the Apocryphal/Deuterocanonical Books,* New Revised Standard Version (New York: Oxford University Press, 1991) AP 1-19; A. Rahlfs, *Tobit* (Septuaginta; Stuttgart: Deutsche Bibelgesellschaft, 1935, 1979); M. J. Suggs, K. D. Sakenfeld and J. R. Mueller, eds., *The Oxford Study Bible,* Revised English Bible with Apocrypha (New York: Oxford University Press, 1992) 1058-70. **Commentaries and Studies.** B. Bow and G. W. E. Nickelsburg, "Patriarchy with a Twist: Men and Women in Tobit," in *"Women Like This": New Perspectives on Jewish Women in the Greco-Roman World,* ed. A.-J. Levine (EJL 1;

Atlanta: Scholars Press, 1991) 127-43; J. Craghan, *Esther, Judith, Tobit, Jonah, Ruth,* ed. C. Stuhlmueller and M. McNamara (OTM 16; Wilmington, DE: Michael Glazier, 1982) 127-62; P. Deselaers, *Das Buch Tobit: Studien zu seiner Entstehung, Komposition und Theologie* (OBO 43; Freiburg: Universitätsverlag; Göttingen: Vandenhoeck & Ruprecht, 1982); A. Di Lella, "The Deuteronomic Background of the Farewell Discourse in Tobit 14:3-11," *CBQ* 41 (1979) 380-89; R. Doran, "Narrative Literature," in *Early Judaism and Its Modern Interpreters,* ed. R. A. Kraft and G. W. E. Nickelsburg (Atlanta: Scholars Press, 1986) 296-99; J. A. Fitzmyer, "The Aramaic and Hebrew Fragments of Tobit from Cave 4," *CBQ* 57 (1995) 655-75; idem, "Tobit," in *Qumran Cave 4.14: Parabiblical Texts,* ed. M. Broshi et al. (DJD 19; Oxford: Clarendon Press, 1996); J. M. Grintz, "Tobit, Book of," *EncJud* 1:1183-86; J. Lebram, "Die Weltreiche in der jüdischen Apokalyptik: Bermerkungen zu Tobit 14, 4-7," *ZAW* 76 (1964) 328-31; D. McCracken, "Narration and Comedy in the Book of Tobit," *SBLSP* 114 (1995) 401-18; B. M. Metzger, *An Introduction to the Apocrypha* (New York: Oxford University Press, 1957) 31-41; C. A. Moore, "Scholarly Issues in the Book of Tobit Before Qumran and After: An Assessment," *JSP* 5 (1989) 65-81; idem, "Tobit, Book of," *ABD* 6:585-94; idem, *Tobit: A New Translation with Introduction and Commentary* (AB 40A; Garden City, NY: Doubleday, 1996); G. W. E. Nickelsburg, *Jewish Literature Between the Bible and the Mishnah* (Philadelphia: Fortress, 1981) 30-35; idem, "Tobit," in *Jewish Writings of the Second Temple Period,* ed. M. E. Stone (CRINT 2.2; Assen: Van Gorcum; Philadelphia: Fortress, 1984) 40-46; M. Rabenau, *Studien zum Buch Tobit* (BZAW 220; Berlin: Walter de Gruyter, 1994); W. Soll, "Misfortune and Exile in Tobit: The Juncture of a Fairy Tale Source and Deuteronomic Theology," *CBQ* 51 (1989) 209-31; F. Zimmermann, *The Book of Tobit: An English Translation with Introduction and Commentary* (Jewish Apocryphal Literature; New York: Harper, 1958).

L. R. Helyer

TOHOROT (4Q274, 276-277). *See* LEGAL TEXTS AT QUMRAN; PURIFICATION TEXTS (4Q274-279, 281-284, 512-514).

TORAH

The Pentateuch, or Torah, as it is more popularly known, has been inextricably bound to Jewish life since the destruction of the first *temple and the exile of the Jewish people at the beginning of the sixth century B.C. This is not to minimize the significance of the Torah during the period of the first temple or even prior to it during Mosaic times. From the time it was first given, it was intended to be part and parcel of the Israelite nation (Ex 13:9), directed at *Israel (Deut 33:4, 10), and from which they were to be instructed (Ex 24:12) in how to lead their lives.

1. The Use of the Torah in Jewish Life
2. Torah: Definition
3. Torah: Its Nature and Purpose
4. Torah and Jewish Philosophy
5. Torah: The Law and Christianity

1. The Use of the Torah in Jewish Life.

1.1. Torah and Sacrifice. The institution of *sacrifice from its earliest inception, although prescribed to the last detail by the Torah itself, assumed a role of paramount importance in the life of the people in their communication with God. Starting with the sanctuary in the wilderness and continuing throughout the existence of Solomon's temple in *Jerusalem, the cultus of the altar became overemphasized to the detriment of the Torah itself, to the extent that the latter became neglected and the former abused. With the destruction of Jerusalem came the end of sacrifices, and the people of Judah found themselves in exile without this means of expiation and reconciliation with God. In spite of this gap in their spiritual life, the Jews survived as a nation since they returned to the Torah as the main purpose of their existence. With the earliest emergence of the *synagogue during the Babylonian exile, the Torah assumed the central role in Jewish life, never to be relinquished again, even through Second Temple. times, where it existed side by side with a reemerging sacrificial ritual but always looming greater in significance than the cultus.

1.2. Ezra and the Torah. The greatest moment for the reemergence of the Torah as the focal point in Jewish life occurred three-quarters of a century after the return to Judah during the time of Ezra. The reorganizer of the returned Jewish community from Babylonian exile made the Torah the nucleus of his reconstructive efforts (Neh 8:1-18). He persuaded the struggling Jewish settlement in Jerusalem to accept the Torah as its constitution for all time. Consequently, the Torah became so intricately linked to the Jewish people that the nation was able to survive the disaster of A.D. 70 and continue to remain united under the banner of Torah propagated at Yavneh and subsequently in the land of Israel, in Babylonia and in other parts of the world up to the present day.

Ezra, who was a *priest by birth and a scribe by calling, transferred the spiritual leadership of the people from the priests to the scholars who represented a nonhereditary, democratic element recruited from all classes. These scholars were the *Sopherim* (the "scribes"), and they, as well as the *rabbis who followed them, not only preserved the Torah but also gave it new life. Their activity made the Bible relevant to the needs of new generations and thus prepared it to serve as the eternal charter of humanity. These nameless scribes thus contributed in no small measure to the survival of the Jewish people. But their significance is not limited to the household of Israel. In the words of R. Gordis "the Christian world too, owes them a debt of gratitude. As founders of Rabbinic Judaism, they helped create the background from which Christianity arose, formulating many of the teachings that both religions share in common."

1.3. Torah and Synagogue. Today the Torah forms an integral part of synagogue liturgy. The practice of reading the Torah in public is quite ancient. The earliest reference to a public Torah recitation is the command to assemble the people at the end of every seven years to read the law in their hearing (Deut 31:10-13). A second mention is made during the time of Ezra, when he read the Torah to all the people (Neh 8:1-8). An early date for the introduction of regular readings is made by the rabbis (*y. Meg.* 4:1, 75a; *b. B. Qam.* 82a), who note that *Moses commanded the Israelites to read the Torah on the *sabbaths, on *festivals and on new moons, while Ezra later ordered it to be read on Mondays and Thursdays in the morning, as well as on sabbath afternoons. The custom dates back to at least the first half of the third century B.C., since the Septuagint was apparently compiled for the purpose of public reading in the synagogue.

It is, however, not unreasonable to argue that the custom reaches back as far as the sixth century B.C., when, during their Babylonian exile, the Jews conceivably assembled for *prayer. Although this prayer was not yet formulated, it could have revolved around the central part of the gathered meeting, namely, the recitation of the Torah, also not formulated as in later times. At any rate, *Josephus (*Ag. Ap.* 2.175 §362), *Philo (*Som.* 127 §498) and the NT (Acts 15:21) refer to the public Torah readings. The Mishnah (*Meg.* 3:4-6) shows that by the end of the second century A.D. there were regular Torah readings on the above-mentioned days in addition to pre-Adar Passover sabbath readings and on fast days. The Talmud (*b. Meg.* 29b) contains the earliest reference to a fixed three-year cycle of completing the reading of the Torah in Palestine.

2. Torah: Definition.

The word *Torah* is derived from the Hebrew root *yrh,* meaning "to guide" or "to teach" in the causative conjugation of the Hiphil, as in Exodus 35:34 and Leviticus 10:11. Thus the more precise meaning of the noun would be "teaching" or "doctrine" rather than "law." The Septuagint rendered the Hebrew word *Torah* by the Greek *nomos* ("law"), the Latin later following with *lex,* with the same meaning.

In Deuteronomy 4:44, "This is the Torah that Moses set before the Israelites," the word refers exclusively to the Pentateuch in contrast to the rest of the Bible. "Torah" is also used loosely to designate the entire Hebrew Bible. The term was further extended to refer to those two branches of divine revelation—the written Torah and the oral Torah, which are traditionally viewed as having been given to Moses on Mt. Sinai (*b. Yoma* 28b). The Mishnaic tractate Ethics of the Fathers (*m. ʾAbot* 1:1) opens with the statement "Moses received the Torah from Sinai." In rabbinic literature it was taught that the Torah was one of the six or seven things that God created prior to creating the world (*Gen. Rab.* 1:4; *b. Pesaḥ.* 54a). The most prestigious sage of the post Second Temple period, Rabbi Akiba, called the Torah "the instrument by which the world was created" (*m. ʾAbot* 3:14). The noun *Torah* thus designates the whole of revelation, including both commandments and statutes.

Torah constitutes a synthesis of the revealed will of God. It is the guide that assists the individual in conducting one's relationship to God himself and to one's neighbor according to the divine will. According to E. J. Gottlieb, "one of the cardinal beliefs of Judaism is the belief that the Torah, the Written Law, and also its necessary explanations, the Oral Law, were given and told to Moses by God himself, during the one hundred and twenty days that Moses spent in heaven" (Gottlieb, 110). He goes on to reason "if there is a God, who did create the world and man in it, then he could, moreover he must, have communicated with man. This creator of man had to guide man with definite and proper directives in order to enable him to reach the desired destination. In other words, the first basic principle of belief in God carries within it, and forces us to accept also, the belief in 'Torah from heaven'. If there is a God, there must be a law from God. One could hardly be without the other" (Gottlieb, 111).

3. Torah: Its Nature and Purpose.
In various passages the Torah is referred to as "the Torah of the Lord" (Ps 19:8), in others as "the Torah of Moses" (Josh 8:31). In the NT it occurs twelve times, either as "the law of Moses" or "the law given by Moses" (see 5.2 below for exact references). It is said to be given as "an inheritance to the congregation of Jacob" (Deut 33:4). Its purpose was to make Israel "a kingdom of priests" (Ex 19:6). In the *Apocrypha, the Wisdom of Ben Sira (*see* Sirach) identifies it with wisdom (Sir 6:37; 24:24-25; 39:1).

One of the very few real dogmas of rabbinic theology is that the Torah is from heaven, meaning that the Torah in its entirety was revealed by God (*m. Sanh.* 10:1). The early sage Simon the Just taught that the study of the Torah was one of three things by which the world is sustained (*m. ʾAbot* 1:2). Another sage, Rabbi Eleazar b. Shammua, said: "Were it not for the Torah, heaven and earth would not continue to exist" (*b. Pesaḥ.* 68b; *b. Ned.* 32a). God himself was said to study the Torah daily (*b. ʿAbod. Zar.* 3b).

Hillel summarized the Torah in one sentence: " What is hateful to you, do not do to your fellow being" (*b. Šabb.* 31a). The parallel to this saying is "Love your neighbor as yourself" (Lev 19:18). Rabbi Akiba's pupil Simon ben Azzai said that the fundamental principle is the verse in Genesis 5:1, which teaches that all human beings are descended from the same man and created by God in his image (*Sipra Qedoshim* 4:12; *y. Ned.* 9:3, 41c; *Gen. Rab.* 24:7).

The message of the Torah is for all humankind. Before giving the Torah to Israel, God offered it to the other nations, but they refused it; and when he did give the Torah to Israel, he revealed it in the extraterritorial wilderness and simultaneously in all the seventy languages, so that people of all nations would have a right to it (*Mekilta de Rabbi Ishmael* 5; *Sipre Deut.* 343; *b. Šabb.* 88b; *Exod. Rab.* 5:9; 27:9; *b. ʿAbod. Zar.* 3a).

4. Torah and Jewish Philosophy.
The first-century Jewish philosopher *Philo Judaeus considered the Torah the ideal law of the philosophers and Moses the perfect lawgiver and prophet. His concept of the relationship of the Torah to nature and humanity was that "the world is in harmony with the Torah and the Torah with the world."

The medieval Jewish philosopher Saadiah Gaon expounded a rationalist theory according to which the ethical and religious-intellectual beliefs imparted by the Torah are all attainable by human reason. He believed that the Torah was divisible into commandments that, in addition to being revealed, are demanded by reason (e.g., murder, fornication, theft and lying) and commandments whose authority is revealed (e.g., sabbath and dietary laws).

The Spanish Jewish philosopher-poet of a later medieval period held that Israel was created to fulfill the Torah; there would be no Torah were there no Israel. Of the Jewish philosophers who flourished in the thirteenth and fourteenth centuries, the Ralbag (= Levi ben Gershom), taught that the purpose of the Torah is to guide humanity—the masses as well as the intellectual elite—toward human perfection, that is, the acquisition of true knowledge and thereby an immortal intellect.

Abraham Isaac Kook, the first chief rabbi of Israel, whose thought was influenced by the Kabbalah, taught that the purpose of the Torah is to reveal the living light of the universe, the suprarational spiritual, to Israel and, through Israel, to all humankind. In the words of his son, Rabbi T. Y. Kook, "The soul of Israel is the Torah. Israel itself is Torah, stemming from its source of Divine existence" (Kook, 48). According to him Torah is the inner being of the community of Israel, "which finds expression in the observance of Torah, and in its learning. Israel is Torah personified" (Kook, 48).

5. Torah: The Law and Christianity.
The range of attitudes toward the Jewish law present in early Christianity exists mainly in the Pauline corpus and the book of Acts. The key conflicts over Jewish law attested in the earliest literature concern the applicability to the Chris-

tian church of circumcision and purity laws, particularly those having to do with eating.

5.1. The Early Church and the Law. P. Richardson and S. Westerholm have analyzed five different theories regarding the attitudes of the early church toward Jewish law.

According to F. C. Baur, Paulinism, or Gentile Christianity, was universalizing and would not see any further need for obedience to the particularism of Mosaic law. The earliest Christian community in Jerusalem was made up of both Hebrew and *Hellenistic Jews. The Hebrews, or Jewish Christian party, led by James, Peter and John, continued to identify with the Jewish nation and culture and to observe the Jewish law. These preached to the Jews a gospel including full observance of Torah, while the Hellenists or Gentile Christian party, spearheaded by Paul, had a more universalist view of religion, preaching to the Gentiles a gospel not including the observance of Torah. Jewish law-observant Christianity spread throughout the *Roman Empire and especially to *Rome. In Galatia, members of the Jewish Christian party were at least partly successful in convincing Gentiles that they must obey the whole Jewish law. Overwhelmingly, the Jewish Christians replaced circumcision with baptism, a move toward Christian universalism. Ritual purity laws and other aspects of Torah were progressively eliminated.

The heart of A. Ritschl's study centered around the question of the understanding of humankind's reconciliation to God by the early Christian church. The initial attitude of Christianity toward the law was set by Jesus himself. He distinguished between two types of laws: those which pertain to people's highest end and are therefore permanently and universally binding; and those which exist for the sake of people and are therefore *adiaphora* (matters of indifference). At this time there were essentially two groups within Christianity. The first group recognized faith in Jesus as the only condition for full Christianity. Within this group was the Pauline tendency accepting the apostolic decree and not requiring any further observance of the Mosaic ritual law from anyone; and also the James tendency, which expected the Gentiles to observe the apostolic decree and the ethnic Jews to observe the whole law. The second group was the Jewish Christians who did not recognize any form of Christianity except that which was based on the Jewish people.

According to H. J. Schoeps, the Ebionites were zealots for the law but in their own peculiar way. They rejected several parts of the Torah, including animal sacrifice, the temple and the Israelite monarchy. They came to the position that the law was to be judged on the basis of the life and teachings of Jesus.

According to the fourth theory, that of J. Daniélou, during the whole period of Paul's mission Jewish Christians were still the majority in the church; thus most Christians were law observant. The fall of Jerusalem and the consequent blow to Jewish nationalism changed the sociological situation, and the balance of the church changed from majority Jewish to majority Gentile with total abandonment of any Jewish legal observances by the late second century A.D.

In the fifth theory, R. Brown lists four types of Jewish/Gentile Christianity that existed in early times, each with its own attitude toward the Jewish law. One held that circumcision and obedience to the whole Mosaic law were necessary for full participation in salvation brought by Jesus. Another did not require circumcision of Gentile Christians but did require the observance of some purity laws. Still another one required neither circumcision nor observance of food regulations by Gentile Christians but were not opposed to such observances by Jewish Christians. The final one did not require circumcision or observance of food regulations and broke fundamentally with all Jewish practices.

5.2. The Law in the New Testament. The term *law* in association with Moses (i.e., that given by Moses, hence the Torah), occurs twelve times in the NT. It occurs an additional five times as just *nomos* but implying that given by Moses. Matthew 5:17 quotes Jesus as saying, "I have not come to abolish the Law . . . but to fulfill it." John 1:17 states, "The law indeed was given through Moses." The remaining passages are Luke 2:22; 24:44; John 1:45; 7:19 (2x), 23; 8:5; Acts 15:5; 25:8; 28:23; 1 Corinthians 9:8, 9; Philippians 3:4, 5 and Hebrews 10:28.

See also LAW/NOMOS IN GRECO-ROMAN WORLD; LEGAL TEXTS AT QUMRAN; RABBINIC LITERATURE: MISHNAH AND TOSEFTA; RABBINIC LITERATURE: TALMUD; RABBIS.

BIBLIOGRAPHY. R. Gordis, "The Role of Judaism in Civilization: The Bible as a Cultural Monument" in *The Jews: Their History, Culture and Religion,* vol. 2, ed. L. Finkelstein (Philadelphia: Jewish Publication Society of America, 1949)

457-96; E. J. Gottlieb, *The Inescapable Truth: A Sound Approach to Genuine Religion* (New York: Philipp Feldheim, 1971); T. Y. Kook, *Torat Eretz Yisrael: The Teachings of Harav Tzvi Yehuda HaCohen Kook* (Jerusalem: Torat Eretz Yisrael Publications, 1991); S. Pancaro, *The Law in the Fourth Gospel: The Torah and the Gospel: Moses and Jesus, Judaism and Christianity According to John* (Leiden: E. J. Brill, 1975); P. Richardson and S. Westerholm, *Law in Religious Communities in the Roman Period: The Debate over Torah and Nomos in Postbiblical Judaism and Early Christianity* (SCJ 4; Waterloo, ON: Wilfrid Laurier Press, 1991).

B. Grossfeld

TOSEFTA. *See* RABBINIC LITERATURE: MISHNAH AND TOSEFTA.

TOUBIAS THE AMMONITE. *See* ZENON PAPYRI.

TRADE. *See* TRAVEL AND TRADE.

TRAVEL AND TRADE

The Augustan objectives of an empire unhindered by chronic war and piracy, with strong ties of military and political communication and a good *coinage initiated a two-century-long period of peace—the **pax Romana* (Philo *Leg. Gai.* 47; Plutarch *Fort. Rom.* 317.B, C; *see* Roman Empire; Roman Emperors; Roman Military). This created the conditions for a general increase in travel and trade (Pliny *Nat. Hist.* 14.1.2). Persons moved with relative ease and confidence throughout the empire for a variety of reasons, many of which can be paralleled in the events and teachings of earliest Christianity—for official (Lk 2:1-7; 19:12; Acts 18:2-3; 23:23-24; 25:1-6, 13; 27:1—28:15) and business reasons (Acts 16:14; 21:2-3; 27:2, 6, 38; 28:11; Jas 4:13-15), for health reasons (Mk 3:7-10 [par. Mt 4:23-25; Lk 6:17-19]; Jn 4:46-47; Acts 9:38), on pilgrimage or to *festivals (Mt 2:1-12; Lk 2:22-38, 41-52; Jn 2:13; 5:1; 7:1-14; 12:1; Acts 2:1-11; 21:27), on holiday, to teach (Mk 1:39 [par. Mt 4:23; Lk 4:44]; Acts passim) or to be *educated (Acts 22:3) and for reasons unspecified (Acts 27:37). This period of relative peace and unprecedented freedom in travel and trade was part of that "fullness of time" (Gal 4:4) in which Christ came, and it was the helpful context for the realization of a worldwide witness to him through his disciples (Acts 1:8).

1. Travel over Land
2. Travel by Water
3. Travelogues and the New Testament Record

1. Travel over Land.

The speed at which one traveled in the ancient world was a function of the interplay of several factors: the time of year and weather conditions, the means of travel and the degree of urgency.

1.1. Time of Year and Conditions. Travelers in antiquity were much more at the mercy of the seasons than are today's travelers. Land travel was more difficult between November 11 and March 10 (Vegetius Renatus *Epit. Rei Milit.* 4.39) and potentially deadly where travelers might be caught traversing mountains or plateaus in winter conditions (Ramsay, 377). Travel could also be impeded or foreclosed by the wet season and spring runoff, which added October and the months of April and May as "doubtful times." References to exact dates and open and closed times in the ancient records, however, reflect general custom for majority traffic.

Paul appears from the NT record to have traveled after the fashion of more professional travelers such as government personnel, the military and business persons. He made extensive overland journeys that included high-elevation crossings (Acts 13:14; 14:24; 16:1; 18:23). Ministry priority rather than the avoidance of inclement weather appears to have been Paul's objective in wintering with the Corinthians (1 Cor 16:5-6). Paul's reference to danger from rivers suggests attempted crossings during the spring runoff, and the notice of hunger, thirst, going without food and being cold and ill-clad (2 Cor 11:26-27) probably indicates the rigors and toils of overland journeys (*hodoiporia*) in the doubtful or closed seasons (Murphy-O'Connor, 41) rather than the insufficient rewards of manual labor.

1.2. Means of Travel and Urgency. The most common and slowest means of travel in antiquity was by foot. Archaeological and literary evidence suggests that a normal day's journey in biblical times covered between 17 and 23 miles (Beitzel, 37). The Joppa to *Caesarea trip confirms the average rate (Acts 10:23-24, 30). Virtually all the travels of Jesus and his disciples (the Gospels), Philip's progress along the Gaza Road (Acts 8:26-30) and Paul's persecutions (Acts 9:18; 22:11) and later missions (Acts; see Acts 20:13) were pedestrian enterprises. Modern estimates of the distances one might reasonably be expected to travel in a specified time ought to reflect the reality of a largely pedestrian and probably vigorous population. This plus urgency, crisis or danger might well account for unusually long distances being covered in a relatively brief period of time (see commentary discussions of Acts 23:23, 31-32).

Travel was greatly enhanced through the use of beasts of burden. The dromedary, or one-humped camel, ideally suited to hotter climates south and east of Palestine, was used for travel Mk 10:25 par. Mt 19:24; Lk 18:25) and fighting. Its physiology allows it to go for as long as a week without water. It can carry 200 pounds plus a rider across desert and twice that much in nondesert conditions. A sustained 28 miles per day is possible; unloaded and with only its rider, distances approaching 100 miles in 13 hours are known (Cansdale, "Camel," 697).

The use of donkeys and mules was more widespread in antiquity (*NewDocs* 1:9; 2:28; Mitchell). A first-century A.D. inscription indicates the following equivalents: one mule (ox?)-driven cart = three pack mules = six donkeys. The terms of comparison relate to carrying power over a distance rather than speed, with cartloads being 625 to 950 pounds and a pack mule's load 250 pounds. Donkeys used for transport are mentioned in the NT (Mk 11:2, 4-5, 7 [par. Mt 21:2, 5; Lk 19:30, 32, 35]; Lk 13:15; 2 Pet 2:16). Luke notes wheeled transport: the Ethiopian minister's chauffeur-driven carriage (Acts 8:28-29, 38). Laden asses might make no better mileage than did a man walking, but their advantage was in a significantly increased carrying power; carts permitted a daily rate of 25 to 30 miles. The greater efficiency, however, carried a greater cost that renders unlikely Paul's resort to such conveyance.

Travel by horseback doubled or trebled the daily distances normally covered by pedestrian traffic. Horses were used chiefly by cavalrymen, hunters and dispatch riders. Daily distances of 100 to 150 miles per day could be covered, but these were exceptional and usually associated with official government business or times of crisis. Paul's hurried overnight journey under massive military escort from Jerusalem to Caesarea was on horseback (Acts 23:23-24). His route was probably that taken by Cestius Gallus and his army in October A.D. 66 (Josephus *J.W.* 2.19.1, 8-9 §§515-16, 546-55; cf. 2.12.2 §228; Hemer, 128 n. 79).

1.3. Stopping Points, Hospitality and Requisition. Great personal wealth and resources allowed a very few to travel in pomp and comfort. Imperial officials, judges, soldiers on the march, municipal magistrates and others suitably empowered could requisition the needs of land travel. This included the use of animal transport and room and board in more or less elaborate stopping stations (*mutationes, mansiones*) that local populations were required to provide and maintain. Despite regulations and compensations, the burden of requisition was often a significant flash point between agents of the Roman state and its subjects (Pliny *Ep.* 9.33; Apuleius *Met.* 9.39-40; Arrian *Epict. Diss.* 4.1.79-81; *NewDocs* 1:9; *Sel. Pap.* 2:211; *P. Lond.* 1171; Mitchell). Instances of official and unofficial requisitioning are both indicated (Mt 5:4; Mk 11:3-6 par. Mt 21:2-3; Lk 19:30-31) and implied (Acts 27:2, 6; 28:7, 10-11) in the NT.

For the ordinary traveler with no recourse to the above provisions or the next best choice of private *hospitality with family or friends, putting up at a boarding house or wayside inn (*hospitium, deversorium, caupona*) was the poor alternative. Available literary and archaeological sources attest to generally ill-kept facilities—minimal furnishings, bug-infested beds, poor food and drink, untrustworthy proprietors, shady clientele and generally loose morals (Horace *Sat.* 1.5; Petronius *Sat.* 94-97; *Acts Jn.* 60-61; Casson 1974, 176-218).

The repeated NT encouragements to *hospitality (Rom 12:13; 1 Tim 3:2; Tit 1:8; Heb 13:2; 1 Pet 4:9; 3 Jn 8) and the epistolary commendations of traveling church workers to the care and material assistance of Christian communities (Acts 18:27; Rom 16:1-2; 1 Cor 16:10-11; Col 4:10; 3 Jn 5-7) made great sense. Christian ministers were helped where hospitality was extended (Lk 9:4; 10:5-8); their ministry could be seriously impeded where it was withheld (Lk 9:5; 10:10; 3 Jn 9-10). Christian hospitality and support of churches to prisoners en route to *Rome was also a boon (Acts 27:3; 28:14; Ign. *Rom.* 5.1; Ign. *Smyrn.* 13.2). Later Christian instruction, however, called for believers carefully to discern between traveling Christian ministers and religious leeches (*Did.* 11.1—12.5).

1.4. Travel and Trade. Personal gain from business was the reason for much of the traffic of antiquity, and we have noted several NT indications of the conduct of business during the course of travel. NT indications for Paul make it clear that, far from being the primary end of travel, trade facilitated more extensive travel and more effective witness (Acts 20:33-35; 1 Cor 9; 1 Thess 4:11; 2 Thess 3:6-10). Alone in a place, Paul worked at his trade; where ministry associates were present, Paul engaged in full-time witness (Acts 18:1-5).

It seems most probable that Paul's overland journeys were undertaken by foot. Given this, the recently popular notion of a Paul who weaves tent cloth made from goat's hair or linen, whatever its other problems, seems improbable owing to the size, weight and shape of looms in antiquity. Paul the maker or repairer of tents and other leather products, carrying his bag of tools (Hock), presents a more consistent and credible picture (*see DPL,* Tentmaking).

1.5. Travel and Letters. The purpose of the public post (*cursus publicus*), as organized and developed by Augustus, was swift official communication. Outside of influence or bribery, it was not possible to send civilian correspondence by this means. The usual resort of private persons of means was to household *slaves who served as letter carriers (*grammatophoroi, tabellarii*). In the interests of a more regular and extensive flow of communication, couriers could be pooled by households. When the distances were greater, the only recourse was to travelers who might deliver letters during the course of their own business (*P. Mich.* 8.490; *Sel. Pap.* 107, 151).

We have record of official correspondence concerning Paul that goes by military carriers (Acts 23:26-30; 25:26-27). For the rest, the NT record of Christian communication indicates in-house conveyance. The determinations of the apostolic council are sent to the Gentile believers of *Antioch, Syria and Cilicia via church delegates (Acts 15:22-23). Church couriers bring *letters to Paul (1 Cor 7:1), and he in turn sends letters by trusted believers and ministry associates (Rom 16:1-2; cf. 1 Cor 16:3; Eph 6:21-22; Phil 2:25-30; Col 4:7-9; Philem 12). Whether the book of Revelation is sent on its way by a visiting Christian courier or by some other traveler we do not know. The letter destinations (Rev 2—3), however, occur in a sequence that conforms to the clockwise route a traveler would otherwise normally be inclined to take.

The same pattern can be seen in the later church. Clement sends his letter to Corinth by the hands of a deputation of three mature believers (*1 Clem.* 63.3-4; 65.1). The Christian prisoner Ignatius sends off letters from Smyrna to the Ephesians (Ign. *Eph.* 20.1), Magnesians (Ign. *Magn.* 15.1), Trallians (Ign. *Trall.* 12.1; 13.1) and the Romans (Ign. *Rom.* 10.1, 3). From Troas, letters go out to the Philadephians (Ign. *Phld.* 11.1), Smyrneans (Ign. *Smyrn.* 12.1) and Polycarp (Ign. *Pol.* 8.1). The couriers of these letters are probably the delegates of those churches who have come to see Ignatius (Ign. *Eph.* 2.1; Ign. *Magn.* 2.1; Ign. *Trall.* 1.1; Ign. *Rom.* 10.1). Because of a surprise sailing, Ignatius asks Polycarp to write further letters on his behalf and send them to churches on the road ahead of him (Ign. *Pol.* 8.1).

2. Travel by Water.

2.1. Sea of Galilee. Next to the Mediterranean, the most famous substantial body of water in the NT is the Sea of Galilee (= Gennesaret: Lk 5:1; = Tiberias: Jn 6:1; 21:1), which measures at its longest and widest 13 miles by 8 miles. The surrounding land produced grain crops as well as grapes, figs and vegetables, and there was a trade in these and other goods among the coastal populations and further abroad. Fish and the fishing industry, however, constituted its greater NT interest. Its seaport towns were the locales of much of Jesus' preaching, some of which was seaboard. The lake itself contained more than twenty species of fish in abundant supply, which were caught by methods little changed until recently (Nun). Small wonder that prominent among Jesus' first disciples were those connected with the fishing industry or that fishes and fishing figure in miracles and furnish illustrations for instruction and metaphors for mission.

The lake's geographic situation at the base of the Jordan Rift created atmospheric conditions resulting in sudden and frequent storms dangerous to watercraft. This fact is well illustrated in the notice of dangers the disciples experienced on the Sea of Galilee (Mt 8:24; Mk 4:37; Lk 8:23; Jn 6:18).

S. Wachsmann has described the 1986 excavation of an ancient vessel dug from the Galilean shore bed between the ancient sites of Gennesar and Magdala (Mt 15:39 = Tarichaea after the fish "preserving" industry there, Pliny *Nat. Hist.* 5.15; Josephus *Ant.* 20.8.4 §159; *J.W.* 2.13.2 §252; 3.10.1 §462). The ship's construction, artifacts found in situ and radio-carbon dating indicate a date somewhere between the first century B.C. and the first century A.D. Measuring 26.5 feet long, 7.5 feet wide and 4.5 feet high, this ship was outfitted for both sailing and rowing. Estimates for the ship based upon a first-century A.D. Galilee mosaic, the writings of Josephus (*J.W.* 2.21.8 §§635-37; *Life* 32 §164; 33 §§168-69) and the NT (Mark 1:20) suggest a working crew of five—four rowers and a helmsman with oar-like quarter rudder—with room for additional passengers to a maximum of perhaps fifteen. This vessel would have been of the class that transported Jesus and the disciples (Mt 14:22; Mk 4:37; 6:45; 8:14; Lk 8:22; Jn 6:16, 19).

2.2. Trade, Travel and Shipwreck.

2.2.1. The Travel Season. As noted above (1.1) for overland traffic, Mediterranean travel was also generally subject to a seasonal ebb and flow. Ancient sources indicate a safe shipping season from May 27 to September 14; the period from March 10 to May 26 and from September 14 to November 11 were risky; November 11 to March 10 was dangerous (Vegetius Renatus *Epit. Rei. Milit.* 4.39; Pliny *Nat. Hist.* 2.47.122; Tacitus *Hist.* 4.81). The dangerous season was such because of storms and also less inclement weather that rendered accurate navigation impossible. The tendency in modern discussion to speak of shipping being forbidden by custom or law, however, must be measured against ancient urgencies and official inducements.

2.2.2. Trade and Travel. While Mediterranean sea traffic saw the transport of such cargoes as foodstuffs, building materials and metals, as well as various kinds of exotica, the key commodity of the Roman Empire was grain. Of the two grains most commonly known—barley and wheat—the latter was the preferred but more vulnerable and variable-yield crop (Rickman 1980b, 261). Shortages from crop failure or interruption of transport, especially to the city of Rome, had resulted in inflation and public disorder and did threaten political stability (Dio Cassius *Hist.* 55.26.2-3; Tacitus *Ann.* 2.87; 6.13; Suetonius *Augustus* 42; *Claudius* 18). The sufficient production and regular supply of grain at stable prices was, therefore, an imperial priority. Emperors gave significant personal and financial rewards to merchants and shipbuilders as inducements to continue the transport of grain even through the winter season (Suetonius *Claudius* 18-19; Tacitus *Ann.* 12.43; 13.51; *cf.* Dio Cassius *Hist.* 60.11). This strongly indicates a free merchant rather than official maritime fleet.

A significant proportion of Rome's grain came from the vast grain reserves of the imperial province of Egypt through the port city of *Alexandria. It is consistent with the patterns of supply and transport in antiquity that the prisoner Paul's passage to Rome is booked aboard Alexandrian grain carriers clearly risking the off season (Acts 27:9; 28:11).

The Alexandrian grain carrier *Isis,* with dimensions of 180 feet long, 45 feet wide and 43.5 feet from deck to lowest point in the hold and with an estimated grain capacity of 1,228 tons, was probably one of the largest. It had three masts and a veritable army of crew members (Lucian *Nav.* 5-6, 14). The first carrier *Josephus traveled aboard must as well have been large, having besides its cargo some 600 individuals aboard (*Life* 3 §15). Paul's ship was probably not an *Isis*-class carrier. Besides cargo, it carried 276 passengers (Acts 27:38), including a relatively small crew (Acts 27:30). It may have had a two- rather than three-mast configuration. Notice of the foresail and how it was used (Acts 27:15, 40), the dual oar-like rudders that were lashed to the hull (Acts 27:40) and the dropping of four stern anchors—implying that there were more elsewhere—(Acts 27:29-30) all compare well with what we know of such ships.

2.2.3. Shipwreck. The trip from Rome to Alexandria with favoring Etesian winds took between ten and twenty days; travel against those same winds more than doubled the return journey, calling for a course along the south coast of Asia Minor, then Crete, Malta and Sicily or perhaps up along the west coast of the Peloponnesus before cutting across to Sicily. This corroborates the prisoner Paul's route by free merchant coastal trader and Alexandrian carriers (Acts 27).

Both ancient records (e.g., Josephus *Life* 3 §§14-16; Tacitus *Ann.* 15.18) and modern archaeology (Throckmorton, 60-61) confirm that maritime disasters were distressingly common. Paul's warning to the crew and owner of the first carrier (Acts 27:10) was the voice of experience (2 Cor 11:25). Peculiar challenges attached to carrying grain as a cargo in rough seas. If it was not sacked or binned in compartments, it could flow, creating sudden instabilities and pressures that threatened to breach the hull or capsize the boat. As a living cargo, it had to be kept both cool and dry. Wet grain swelled and could easily split the hull of a ship. The measures of Paul's carrier crew and passengers to undergird the ship (Acts 27:17) and progressively empty it of cargo (Acts 27:18, 38) were all attempts at preserving hull integrity.

A decision concerning the location of Paul's shipwreck (whether traditional Malta [*Melite Africana*], Mljet [*Melite Illyrica*], or Kefallinia) must be based in part upon meteorological and nautical considerations. The *Eurakylon* reading at Acts 27:14 should be preferred, indicating not a squall but the fierce *gregale* of the central Mediterranean winter that blows from the east northeast. The crew's fear of being driven southwest onto the African *Syrtis* (Acts 27:17) is consistent with this. That the ship was driven across the Adriatic (Acts 27:27) is not seriously problematic to the traditional interpretation, given the fluidity of the Adriatic's boundaries as noted in ancient descriptions. Mljet is too far north to count as a reasonable alternative. The Kefallinia theory gives no evidence that the island location was ever known in antiquity by the name *Milete*. Traditional Malta, therefore, continues to be the more probable shipwreck location (Musgrave, 19-32 for possible sites).

3. Travelogues and the New Testament Record. The NT contains accounts of a singular message and in Acts how that message was carried across the empire. In the context of recent discussion, attention has focused upon several points where Luke's narrative shifts to first person plural description of Paul's travels. Do these "we" sections of Acts (16:10-17; 20:5-15; 21:1-18; 27:1-29; 28:1-16) represent (1) the author's eyewitness report; (2) the author's use of his own or someone else's literary material; or (3) a fictional creation based upon other ancient travel accounts (Porter, 546)?

Ancient travelogues, with which Acts has been compared, note routes taken, means of transport, sailing or stopover times, winds, weather and such. V. K. Robbins has argued from his analysis of many such documents that Luke's sudden resort to first person plural description reflects a literary convention typical of sea voyage accounts. His conclusion, however, has been seriously contested. A reassessment of the supposed parallels indicates that "there are first person and third person sea voyages in ancient literature, no passage is set in first person narration simply because it is a sea voyage, and there are no convincing parallels to the shifts from third person narration to first person narration in Acts" (Praeder 1987, 210). Narrowing the focus to compare Luke-Acts only with sea voyage accounts that have prefaces after the fashion of scientific writing (*Periplus of the Erythraean Sea* 20, 57; *Voyage of Hanno* 1-3) and the historical prefatory tradition (*Episodes from the Third Syrian War;* Caesar *B. Gall.* 5.11-13; Josephus *Life* 3 §§14-16) gives no comfort to the notion of an ancient literary form used to relate sea voyages or of its relevance to Acts (Porter, 554-58).

Ancient travelogues undoubtedly furnish much valuable information that continues to illuminate many aspects of Luke's account of Paul's travels and troubles. However, in the absence of more certain comparisons for genre, there may be greater promise in an exploration of the contextual connections, patterns and literary style of the "we" passages in Acts for what they might disclose (Porter, 561-73).

See also PAX ROMANA; ROMAN EMPIRE; ROMAN MILITARY.

BIBLIOGRAPHY. B. J. Beitzel, "How to Draw Ancient Highways on Biblical Maps," *BR* 4 (1988) 36-43; H. J. Cadbury, "Lexical Notes on Luke-Acts III: Luke's Interest in Lodging," *JBL* 45 (1926) 305-22; G. S. Cansdale, "Animals of the Bible," *IBD* 1:52-68; idem, "Camel," *ZPEB* 1:695-99; L. Casson, "The Role of the State in Rome's Grain Trade," in *Ancient Trade and Society,* ed. L. Casson (Detroit: Wayne State University Press, 1984) 96-116; idem, *Ships and Seamanship in the Ancient World* (Princeton, NJ: Princeton University Press, 1971); idem, *Travel in the Ancient World* (London: George Allen & Unwin, 1974); M. P. Charlesworth, *Trade Routes and Commerce in the Roman Empire* (Cambridge: Cambridge University Press, 1924); P. Garnsey, "Grain for Rome," in *Trade in the Ancient Economy,* ed. P. Garnsey, K. Hopkins and C. R. Whittaker (London: Chatto & Windus/Hogarth, 1983) 118-30; C. J. Hemer, *The Book of Acts in the Setting of Hellenistic History,* ed. C. H. Gempf (WUNT 49; Tübingen: Mohr Siebeck, 1989); R. F. Hock, *The Social Context of Paul's Ministry: Tentmaking and Apostleship* (Philadelphia: Fortress, 1980); S. Mitchell, "Requisitioned Transport in the Roman Empire: A New Inscription from Pisidia," *JRS* 66 (1976) 106-31 and plates; J. Murphy-O'Connor, "Traveling Conditions in the First Century: On the Road and On the Sea with St. Paul," *BRev* 1 (Summer 1985) 38-47; G. H. Musgrave, *Friendly Refuge: A Study of St. Paul's Shipwreck and His Stay in Malta*

(Heathfield, UK: Heathfield Publications, 1979); M. Nun, "Cast Your Net Upon the Waters," *BAR* 19 (1993) 46-56, 70; S. E. Porter, "Excursus: The 'We' Passages," in *The Book of Acts in Its Greco-Roman Setting,* ed. D. W. J. Gill and C. H. Gempf (BAFCS 2; Grand Rapids, MI: Eerdmans, 1994) 545-74; S. M. Praeder, "Acts 27:1—28:16: Sea Voyages in Ancient Literature and the Theology of Luke-Acts," *CBQ* 46 (1984) 683-706; idem, "The Problem of First Person Narration in Acts," *NovT* 29 (1987) 193-218; W. M. Ramsay, "Roads and Travel (in the NT)," *HDB* 5 (1904) 375-402; B. M. Rapske, "Acts, Travel and Shipwreck," in *The Book of Acts in Its Greco-Roman Setting,* ed. D. W. J. Gill and C. H. Gempf (BAFCS 2; Grand Rapids, MI: Eerdmans, 1994) 1-47; G. Rickman, *The Corn Supply of Ancient Rome* (Oxford: Clarendon Press, 1980a); idem, "The Grain Trade Under the Roman Empire," in *The Seaborne Commerce of Ancient Rome: Studies in Archaeology and History,* ed. J. H. D'Arms and E. C. Kopff (Memoirs of the American Academy in Rome 36; Rome: American Academy, 1980b) 261-75; V. K. Robbins, "By Land and by Sea: The We-Passages and Ancient Sea Voyages," in *Perspectives on Luke-Acts,* ed. C. H. Talbert (Special Studies Series 5; Danville, VA: Association of Baptist Professors of Religion, 1978) 215-42; J. Smith, *The Voyage and Shipwreck of St. Paul* (Grand Rapids, MI: Baker, 1978 repr.); P. Throckmorton, ed., *History from the Sea: Shipwrecks and Archaeology* (London: Mitchell Beazley, 1987); S. Wachsmann, "The Galilee Boat: 2,000-Year-Old Hull Recovered Intact," *BAR* 14 (September/October 1988) 18-33.

B. M. Rapske

TRAVELOGUES. *See* TRAVEL AND TRADE.

TREATISE OF SHEM

The *Treatise of Shem* is preserved in only one manuscript, a fifteenth-century paper Syriac manuscript in the John Rylands University Library of Manchester. A scribe called the document the *Treatise of Shem.* Extremely cautious scholars may want to avoid the study of this manuscript, since it is preserved in no other manuscript and is not mentioned in ancient lists of antilegomena or *pseudepigrapha. The careful historian knows, however, that often an ancient work is lost or preserved in only a small fragment or merely in one quotation by an early scholar.

1. Provenance
2. Original Language
3. Date
4. Theology
5. Significance
6. Character

1. Provenance.

There is no reason to doubt that the *Treatise of Shem* was composed in Egypt. The author seems to be a Jew who attributed the work to Shem, the oldest son of Noah (cf. Gen 10:21, *Jub.* 4:33; 8:12-30; *T. Sim.* 6:5; Sir 49:16). Passover, the major Jewish *festival that commemorates the Jewish release from bondage in Egypt, is mentioned (*Tr. Shem* 1:8; 6:12). The city *Alexandria is mentioned (*Tr. Shem.* 4:3; 6:14), the river Nile is named (*Tr. Shem.* 1—8, 12) and irrigation is noted (*Tr. Shem.* 1:4; 10:18). The crops mentioned, especially wheat, barley and peas, are typical of Egypt. The seaport founded by *Alexander the Great and bearing his name is most likely the city in which or near which this Jewish pseudepigraphon was composed, since the work is replete with references to the sea, the seacoast, fishing and ships.

2. Original Language.

The extant Syriac seems to reflect a Semitic original. Many Semitisms seem original, and the personal names are defined according to the Semitic alphabet. A putative Greek original, one could argue, may be evident in some Greek loanwords (esp. *harmonia,* "well-ordered").

3. Date.

The document was most likely composed sometime after one of the greatest battles in history: when Octavian (Augustus; *see* Roman Emperors) and *Rome defeated Marc Antony and Cleopatra (and Egypt) at Actium in 31 B.C. After that date Egypt belonged to Rome, and grain was shipped from Alexandria to Ostia Antica, the ancient port of Rome.

In 34 B.C. there was a celebration in Alexandria, not in Rome as was customary; it was over Antony's defeat of the Parthians. This event appears reflected in *Treatise of Shem* 3:6-7. Also in 34 B.C. Cleopatra obtained permission to rule over Palestine; this seems preserved in *Treatise of Shem* 12:4, "And Egypt [will rule] over Palestine." Probably dating prior to 31 B.C. is the following accurate assessment: "And the king of the Romans will not remain in one place . . . a great war and misery [will occur] on all the earth, and especially in the land of Egypt" (*Tr. Shem.* 1:5-9). The battle of Actium in 31 B.C. seems to have shaped *Treatise of Shem* 6:13-17: "And the king will strive with a king and will slay him. And Alexandria will be lost. . . . And many ships will be wrecked." The reference to "the king" seems to denote a Roman emperor, hence Octavian. According to Virgil (*Fourth Eclogue* 19-22) and other ancient sources, Octavian was honored as the one who put an end to war.

4. Theology.

The document is an astrological work. It is a calendologia; that is, the author explains the quality of the year according to the astrological sign in which the year begins. One can assign to the work twelve chapters, since there are twelve signs of the zodiac. The thought proceeds counterclockwise, from Aries to Capricorn (except Pisces precedes Aquarius, probably due to a scribe's error in copying). The worst year comes at the beginning of the work with Aries, and the best year culminates with Pisces. Thus one may discern the optimism of early Jewish *apocalyptic eschatology, and there seems to be a pro-Roman bias in some verses (*Tr. Shem.* 12:9). The author reflects on the impossible having happened: Egypt with far superior armed forces was defeated by only part of the Roman army; only determinism clarified by astrology can explain such a fate. Of course, the work is full of ideas that contradict much of the theology canonized in the OT (or Tanakh); for example, rain depends on the zodiac and not God (see Amos 4:7; Zech 10:1, 1 Kings 18:1, 41-46; cf. *Jub.* 12).

5. Significance.

If the author is a contemporary of the battle of Actium, then this work is a significant reaction to a great turning point in Western culture—actually a significant nonturning point—Europe, America and the Western world are based on Roman law and customs. If Antony and Cleopatra had won the battle, then the Middle East and Egyptian law and customs might have been the basis of Western culture. Also, the evidence for astrological thinking by Jews is now confirmed to be much earlier than the Middle Ages and clearly antedates the beginnings of Christianity. We know this now for certain, thanks to the recovery of the *Treatise of Shem* and astrological writings found among the *Dead Sea Scrolls (*Horoscope* [4Q186]; *see* Thunder Text [4Q318]). Hence we have literary evidence of Jewish interest in astrology, and that helps the interpretation of astrological symbols in Matthew perhaps and Revelation. Finally, the precession of the equinoxes—the beginning of the year in spring moved from Aries to Pisces—may be also reflected in this astrological work.

6. Character.

An excerpt helps one understand this composition:

> When the year begins in Aquarius, everyone whose name contains a Lamadh or Pe [will] become sick or utterly ruined by marauders. And in the beginning of the year rain will increase. And the Nile will overflow its full rate. And Egypt [will rule] over Palestine. (*Tr. Shem* 12:1-4)

See also APOCRYPHA AND PSEUDEPIGRAPHA; CALENDARS, JEWISH; THUNDER TEXT (4Q318).

BIBLIOGRAPHY. J. H. Charlesworth, "Jewish Astrology in the Talmud, Pseudepigrapha, Dead Sea Scrolls and Early Palestinian Synagogues," *HTR* 70 (1977) 183-200; idem, "Jewish Interest in Astrology During the Hellenistic and Roman Period," *ANRW* 2.20.2 (1987) 926-56, 6 plates; idem, "Rylands Syriac MS 44 and a New Addition to the Pseudepigrapha: The Treatise of Shem," *BJRL* 60 (1978) 376-403; idem, "Treatise of Shem," in *The Old Testament Pseudepigrapha*, ed. J. H. Charlesworth (2 vols.; Garden City, NY: Doubleday, 1983, 1985) 1:473-86.

J. H. Charlesworth

TWELVE PATRIARCHS. *See* TESTAMENTS OF THE TWELVE PATRIARCHS.

U, V

UNCLEAN. *See* PURITY

URBAN CENTERS. *See* CITIES, GRECO-ROMAN

VICE AND VIRTUE LISTS

The recording of ethical lists in the *Hellenistic world extends formally from the Homeric era yet comes into full bloom among Socratic and post-Socratic moral *philosophers, notably the Stoa. Because of interaction between *Stoic and Christian discourse in the first century, vice and virtue lists serve a practical *rhetorical function as a conventional method of moral instruction in both. This is true even when the two life views diverge radically in terms of the means and the end of the moral life. In the hands of the writers of the NT, the ethical catalog constitutes an important part of early Christian paraenesis.

1. The Ethical Catalog in Antiquity
2. The Ethical Catalog as a Pedagogical Device in the Hellenistic World
3. The Ethical Catalog in Hellenistic Jewish Literature
4. The Ethical Catalog in the New Testament

1. The Ethical Catalog in Antiquity.

The grouping of ethical values into lists surfaces in diverse cultures of antiquity, from Iran and India to Egypt and Mediterranean cultures. To the extent that religion as practiced by ancient civilizations is characterized by the striving and performing of its adherents, the function of the ethical list can be seen as a natural extension. Enumerating behavior or dispositions to be emulated or avoided can serve a wide array of purposes—both polemical and nonpolemical, prescriptive and descriptive. Ethical lists in the Hellenistic world during the Homeric era occur in diverse literary and nonliterary contexts, as the work of Vögtle has demonstrated. Numerous *inscriptions, frequently at gravesites (*see* Burial) and memorials, list virtues in honor of military generals, officeholders, doctors and judges. In Hesiod, one encounters lists of transgressions of the children against parents and transgressions against the gods (Hesiod *Theog.* 77-79, 240-64). Aristophanes utilizes the ethical catalog as part of a satire in a parody of the Eleusinian mysteries (Aristophanes *Batr.* 5.145). And *Seneca employs ethical catalogs to describe, with considerable flair, his disgust with the banal trivialities of the theater as well as how fellow Romans indulge in the discovery of new vices (Seneca *Brev. Vit.* 10.4).

2. The Ethical Catalog as a Pedagogical Device in the Hellenistic World.

During the Socratic era, pre-Socratic traces of paraenetic listing blossom both in the hands of academic philosophers and on a popular level among moralists of the day. Philosophical reflection on the theoretical basis for *aretē* ("virtue") moves in the direction of its concrete and practical expression. The ethical list has an epideictic function; that is, as a form of speech it is intended to instill praise or shame (*see* Honor and Shame) in the listener or reader. The ethical list, by which the ethical life is organized, accented and stereotyped, standardizes a type of attitude or behavior and thus becomes a common feature in the paraenetic tradition.

2.1. Socratic-Platonic Schematization of Virtue. Although the virtues *andreia* ("courage"), *phronēsis/sophia* ("wisdom"), *sōphrosynē* ("prudence") and *dikaiosynē* ("justice") individually play a central role in the ethical teaching of Socrates, schematization first presses to the fore in *Plato, who is the first to designate four "cardinal" *aretai.* (Formal presentation of the cardinal virtues appears initially in Plato's *Republic,* even when similar formulations of the moral ideal predate this by more than a century—for example, in Aeschylus [*Sept. c. Theb.* 610]). Xenophon writes profusely on ethical topics—among these, order of the home, healthy relationships, the treatment of *slaves, political and military obligations—and yet is not enamored of the fourfold schema. In *Nicomachean Ethics*, *Aristotle distinguishes between ethical, political and social virtues on the one hand and intellectual virtues on the other. For the most part Aristotle resists the fourfold schema that had arisen largely out of the Pythagorean love of the number four, considered to be symbolic of life's completeness.

2.2. Stoic Schematization of Vice and Virtue. The prototypal use of ethical catalogs begins with Zeno (340-265 B.C.), founder of the Stoa, and is expanded under the Stoic teachers who follow. The early masters, notably Chrysippus (280-210 B.C.), tend to use "virtue" and "knowledge" (*epistēmē*) interchangeably, a practice that is significant for the Stoic understanding of ethical discourse. Stoic definitions of the cardinal virtues illustrate this conceptualization: justice is knowledge of what is due or right; temperance is knowledge of what to choose or not to choose; prudence is knowledge of what to do or not do in a given situation; and courage is knowledge of what should and should not be feared.

Stoic moral doctrine mirrors both a return to and an expansion of the tetradic schema that characterized Socratic and Platonic ethical teaching. Organization serves an important recall function in Stoic pedagogy. Proceeding from the four cardinal virtues, Stoic teaching derives multiple subsets of virtues. Chrysippus, for example, divides the *aretai* into two groups of cardinal (*prōtai*) and subordinate (*hypotetagmenai*) virtues, with a lengthy list of subordinates thereto attached. One of the most comprehensive catalogs of virtues comes from the Stoic Andronicus, who compiled the writings of his master Chrysippus and whose list contains no fewer than twenty *aretai* (*SVF* 3.64). All in all, the tetradic schema of organizing vice and virtue for didactic purposes occurs more frequently in earlier Stoic lists, with later teachers typically dividing cardinal traits into subsets. We encounter in Andronicus a bewildering array of variety and detail—he lists twenty-seven kinds of *epithymia* ("lust"), twenty-seven kinds of *lypē* ("sorrow"), thirteen kinds of *phobos* ("fear") and five kinds of *hēdonē* ("pleasure") (*SVF* 3.397, 401, 409, 414), although his list pales by comparison with that of *Philo, who identifies 147 vices to personify the "friends" of the *philēdonos*, the hedonist (Philo *Sacr.* 32).

The ethical list, which concretizes the moral struggle of the Stoic life view, is not merely confined to philosophical discourse. It appears as well in the poets—relatively frequently in Virgil (e.g., *Aen.* 6.732) and Horace (*Ep.* 1.1.33-40), for example—and in popular literature. The more popularized form of vice and virtue lists, while sharing a common vocabulary with Stoic philosophers, loses the tighter schematization that had characterized the scholastics. Those preaching moral uplift to the masses expand the form of the ethical catalog to include new concepts, particularly additional vices. These lists are far from the convoluted philosophical constructs that were advanced by the academic philosophers. People, upon hearing and reflecting, saw themselves in these lists—whether by vice or by virtue. Practical needs of the masses encouraged the use of ethical lists in a popular format.

As a rule, Stoic ethical catalogs do not possess a rigid hierarchy of virtues so as to suggest a moral progression leading to an ethical climax. All virtues stand in close connection to each other; all constitute a natural unity. No particular order or arrangement of virtues or vices came to typify popular usage, although paronomasia is frequently achieved through the word order. Stoic ethical lists were not intended to be all-inclusive, and the presence or absence of particular features in a list reflects the values of the author (Malherbe).

To the Stoic mind, where there exists an antithesis of one virtue, the same necessarily applies to others. For example, the health of one's soul suggests the possibility of psychological sickness. Similarly, the experience of wisdom points to folly; contentment, anxiety; brotherly kindness, enmity; and so on. Just as a virtue can be standardized, so can the corresponding vice.

The *Sitz im Leben* of the dualistic schema is generally agreed to be the propaganda of the moral philosophers. Accordingly, those heeding their advice were considered wise; those casting it aside, foolish. This dualism allows easy incorporation into Hellenistic-Jewish as well as NT literature. In many respects, a conversion to Judeo-Christian faith is conceived of in terms not unlike a conversion to the wisdom of philosophy. Consequently, the ethical list has a useful role in Hellenistic Jewish and early Christian postconversion paraenesis. The consensus of classical scholarship is that NT ethical catalogs in form and function derive from Hellenistic usage. Notwithstanding the views of D. Schroeder, who believes the NT catalogs mirror Israel's ethical dualism in the Day-of-the-Lord expectation and Deuteronomic blessings and curses, and more recently R. P. Martin, early Christian appropriation of Stoic categories in the NT is abundant, commensurate with and reflective of Stoic-Christian interaction in the first century (Zeller; Charles 1997).

An impressive array of literature provides a window into the world of ethical discourse roughly contemporary with the early Christians. By its hortatory character, molded against the backdrop of Greco-Roman culture, this served as ethical "propaganda through the living word with personal [i.e., practical] effects" (Wendland, 84). Exemplary writings that make abundant use of the ethical catalog are those of *Philo (c. 20 B.C.-A.D. 50), *Seneca (c. 4 B.C.-A.D. 65), *Epictetus (c. A.D. 50-130), *Musonius Rufus (c. A.D. 65-80), Dio Chrysostom (c. A.D. 40-120), *Plutarch (A.D. 50-120) Philostratus (late second century A.D.) and Diogenes Laertius (third century A.D.).

3. The Ethical Catalog in Hellenistic Jewish Literature.

While vice and virtue lists in the narrower sense do not appear in the OT, the tradition of ethical catalogs finds a secure place in the literature of Hellenistic *Judaism. Not infrequently these are vice catalogs that are in some way related to sins delineated in the Decalogue. Because Judaism of the intertestamental period is situated in Hellenistic culture, touch points with Stoic philosophy are frequently detected. In reading this literature one senses both polemical and nonpolemical interaction between Jewish and Stoic worldviews.

3.1. Philo. A. Vögtle's description of *Philo reflects an individual who is at home in both worlds: "By the sheer number and length of virtue and vice lists, Philo seems to have achieved the measure of the Stoic popular philosophers" (107). This impression is confirmed by a survey of Philonic literature (e.g., Philo *Sacr.* 20-27; *Leg. All.* 1.19.56; 2.23.24; *Spec. Leg.* 3.63). Philo is particularly fond of the classical fourfold schema, frequently alluding to the four cardinal passions—lust, sorrow, greed and fear (e.g., Philo *Praem. Poen.* 419; *Exsecr.* 159-60). The number four is so important to him that the four headwaters of the river flowing through Eden (Gen 2:8-14) point to four cardinal virtues (Philo *Leg. All.* 1.19.56; 2.23.24).

While Philo is anchored to the ethical teaching of the OT, he always manages to return to the Stoic emphasis on struggling against vice. From the standpoint of faith, Philo views obedience as important because it produces virtue, just as disobedience and unbelief have a downward ethical trajectory. Stoic categories and OT ethics are able to stand side by side. Philo exemplifies the extent of Stoic influence during the last two centuries B.C. and through the first century A.D. He demonstrates graphically how religious truth could be clothed in relevant literary and philosophical categories of the day, even when Philonic allegorizing may seem to have overextended itself in its attempts to reconcile Hellenistic moral philosophy and the OT.

3.2. The Wisdom of Solomon. The *Wisdom of Solomon is another relevant example of Hellenistic influence on Judaism. In this work the reader encounters the four cardinal virtues, whose tutor is said to be the wisdom of God (Wis 8:4, 7). Correlatively, serving false gods is the equivalent of ignorance (*agnoia*) and must be countered with the gnosis of God (Wis 14:22). In Wisdom of Solomon 14:25-26 a lengthy list of vices proceeds characterizes the life that is absent the knowledge of God; it manifests "blood and murder, theft and fraud, depravity, faithlessness, disorder, perjury, suppressing the good, ingratitude, soulish defilement, sexual confusion, marital disorder, adultery and licentiousness." Stoic influence in Wisdom can also be seen in the admonitions toward reflection (e.g., Wis 4:11; 12:10). The author is not concerned, however, to correct the sins he catalogs; rather, he is content merely to list the depths of depravity to which Gentiles have descended.

Although ethical lists appear in the writings of the *Qumran community, Qumran ethical teaching is molded primarily by the dualism of the righteous and unrighteous, light and darkness—characteristic Qumran theology—and less by Hellenistic literary-rhetorical patterns of vice and virtue (cf. however Wibbing and Kamlah). The **Rule of the Community* commends humility, patience, charity, goodness, understanding, intelligence, wisdom and a spirit of discernment (1QS 4:3-6) while condemning greed, wickedness and lies, haughtiness and pride, falseness and deceit, cruelty and ill temper, folly and insolence, lustful deeds and lewdness, blindness of eye and dullness of ear, stiffness of neck and heaviness of heart (1QS 4:9-11).

4. The Ethical Catalog in the New Testament.

4.1. The Logic and Language of Virtue and Vice. The use of the ethical catalog by NT writers derives from its function in Hellenistic and Jewish literature. As with Judaism, the theological motivation behind its usage is the dualism in which the righteous and unrighteous are typified. In the NT, both strands—Hellenistic form and Jewish theological assumptions—merge in the Christian paraenetic tradition (Charles 1997).

Ethical catalogs appearing in the NT take on two syntactical arrangements, as identified by A. Vögtle and S. Wibbing. They can be polysyndetic, such as the list in 1 Corinthians 6:9-10, where members are bound together rhetorically through the repetition of conjunctions in close succession ("Do not be deceived; neither fornicators nor idolators nor adulterers nor prostitutes nor sodomites nor thieves nor greedy persons nor drunkards nor revilers nor robbers will inherit the kingdom of God"); and they can be asyndetic, such as in Galatians 5:22-23a, where no connective particle is used ("But the fruit of the Spirit consists of love, joy, peace, patience, kindness, generosity, faithfulness, humility and self-control"). The lists distributed throughout the NT are fairly evenly divided between polysyndetic and asyndetic forms. D. E. Aune detects a third category, "amplified" lists, which are more discursive in form, and cites 1 Thessalonians 4:3-7 as an example.

Thirteen virtue lists appear in the NT, all but two of which are found in epistles: 2 Corinthians 6:6-8; Galatians 5:22-23; Ephesians 4:32; 5:9; Philippians 4:8; Colossians 3:12; 1 Timothy 4:12; 6:11; 2 Timothy 2:22; 3:10; James 3:17; 1 Peter 3:8; and 2 Peter 1:5-7. This listing excludes 1 Corinthians 13, which concerns the theological virtues and contains particular features of the ethical catalog. Twenty-three vice lists are found in the NT, all but two of which also occur in epistles: Matthew 15:19; Mark 7:21-22; Romans 1:29-31; 13:13; 1 Corinthians 5:10-11; 6:9-10; 2 Corinthians 6:9-10; 12:20-21; Galatians 5:19-21; Ephesians 4:31; 5:3-5; Colossians 3:5, 8; 1 Timothy 1:9-10; 2 Timothy 3:2-5; Titus 3:3; James 3:15; 1 Peter 2:1; 4:3, 15; Revelation 9:21; 21:8; 22:15 (*see DPL* and *DLNTD*, Virtues and Vices).

The Pastoral Epistles contain the densest usage of ethical lists in the NT, all of which suggest a social location of the audience not unlike that of 2 Peter, in which the foundations of morality are being called into question. S. C. Mott calls attention to the fact that adverb forms of three of the four Platonic cardinal virtues—prudence (*sōphrosynē*), uprightness (*dikaiosynē*) and piety (*eusebeia*) appear together in Titus 2:12 with the verb *paideuein* ("educate" or "train"). Seen thusly, the ethical end of salvation, at the least, manifests the goal of virtue posited by Hellenistic moral philosophy (see also the vocabulary of 2 Tim 3:16: *pros paideian tēn en dikaiosynē*, "training in righteousness"). N. J. McEleney identifies in the Pastorals the presence of five basic elements as part of a literary strategy: references to the law, a background of pagan idolatry, moral dualism, transfer of Hellenistic conceptions of vice and virtue to the Christian context and *eschatological punishment.

4.2. New Testament Vice Lists. Despite the variety found in the ethical catalogs of the NT, there appears to be an "early Christian paraenetic formula" that characterizes numerous NT vice lists. Those sharing this schema have the function of reminding the readers of what characterized their former life; thus Paul to the Corinthians: "And this is what some of you used to be" (1 Cor 6:11a; cf. Rom 13:13; Tit 3:3; 1 Pet 4:3). Furthermore, idolatry (*eidōlolatria*) and sexual impurity (*epithymia, porneia, akatharsia* or *aselgeia*) appear together frequently in NT vice lists (e.g., 1 Cor 6:9-10; Gal 5:19-21; Eph 5:5; Col 3:5; 1 Pet 4:3; Rev 21:8; 22:15). This may well correspond to the twin stereotypes of pleasure (*hēdonē*) and lust (*epithymia*) that frequently appear in pagan lists. There is reason to believe, as B. S. Easton (4-5) suggests, that the Hellenistic Jewish literary form of denouncing Gentile practice via lists of grossly depraved deeds was adopted by the NT writers, for whom it served a useful purpose.

A regularly appearing feature in the Christian paraenetic tradition is the formula *apotithēmi* ("put off") plus a list of vices. This pattern occurs in Romans 13:13; Ephesians 4:22 (again in 4:25); Colossians 3:8 and 1 Peter 2:1.

4.3. New Testament Virtue Lists. Fewer conventional formulas accompany virtue lists than vice lists in the NT. This may derive from the fact that for Christian writers righteousness rather than moral goodness per se is essential. The NT's most noteworthy listing of virtues, which has not been listed as an ethical catalog per se, is the recording of beatitudes in Matthew 5, with which none of the other NT lists share any affinity. On the whole, NT virtue lists both bear similarity to and diverge from their pagan counterparts. For example, the qualities of an elder listed in 1 Timothy 3 are reminiscent of qualities necessary of a military general; in the same vein, the lists in Philippians 4:8; Titus 1:7-8; 3:1-2 and 1 Timothy 3:2-3 diverge little from pagan usage (Easton, 11). The opposite, however, can be said of the virtue lists in Galatians 5:22-23 and 1 Timothy 6:1.

*4.4. **The Form and Function of New Testament Ethical Lists.*** Vice and virtue lists in the NT function paraenetically in different contexts. They may be used for the purpose of antithesis (e.g., Gal 5:19-23 and Jas 3:13-18), contrast (e.g., Tit 3:1-7), instruction (e.g., 2 Pet 1:5-7) or polemics (e.g., 1 Tim 1:9-10; 6:3-5; 2 Tim 3:2-5). Although these lists resist any attempts at being reduced to a single *Urkatalog* or set pattern, the rhetorical effectiveness of ethical catalogs lies in the fact that content is emphasized by means of repetition or cadence. Occasionally, though not necessarily, alliteration or assonance and inclusio enhance their descriptions. A unified structure is hard to detect, and rhetorical motivation is not always apparent, with the notable exceptions of Philippians 4:8 and 2 Peter 1:5-7. The latter, unlike other catalogs of virtue in the NT, depicts a natural progression that is rooted initially in faith and finds its climax in Christian love. The reader may assume that the progression and climax of virtues in 2 Peter 1 is mirroring a concrete situation in which there has been a fundamental ethical breakdown (Charles 1997, 44-98, 128-58). In order to address this crisis, the writer is utilizing a standard hortatory device to underscore the necessity of the moral life as proof of one's profession both to the Christian community and to the world (2 Pet 1:10; 3:11).

Given the considerable variety with which virtue catalogs appear in Jewish and early Christian literature, the repetition of particular virtues in NT and subapostolic lists may point to an additional function. The inclusion of *pistis* ("faith"), *agapē* ("love") and *hypomonē;* ("endurance") in 2 Peter 1:5; Revelation 2:19; *Barnabas* 2.2ff. and *1 Clement* 62.2 are evidence to Vögtle that virtue catalogs may have acquired in the apostolic paraenetic tradition a catechetical function (54; see also *1 Clem.* 64; *Herm. Man.* 8.9; Ign. *Eph.* 14.1). That Christian catechesis may have been preserved in such a format is not implausible; a catalogical format is faintly suggested by confessions of faith such as are found in 1 Timothy 3:16 and 2 Timothy 2:11-13. Irrespective of their precise function, for the writers of the NT virtues are no artificial mechanism. Rather, they are a natural expression of one's organic union with Christ, indeed the fruit of divine grace.

See also PHILO; PHILOSOPHY; PLATO, PLATONISM; STOICISM; WISDOM OF SOLOMON.

BIBLIOGRAPHY. D. E. Aune, *The New Testament in Its Literary Environment* (LEC 8; Philadelphia: Westminster, 1987); C. K. Barrett and C. J. Thornton, eds., *Texte zur Umwelt des Neuen Testaments* (UTB; 2d ed.; Tübingen: Mohr Siebeck, 1991); K. Berger, "Hellenistische Gattungen im Neuen Testament," *ANRW* 2.25.2 (1984) 1034-1432; J. D. Charles, "The Language and Logic of Virtue in 2 Peter 1:5-7," *BBR* 8 (1998) 55-73; idem, *Virtue Amidst Vice: The Catalog of Virtues in 2 Peter 1* (JSNTSup 150; Sheffield: Sheffield Academic Press, 1997); A. Dyroff, *Ethik der alten Stoa* (Berlin: S. Calvary, 1897); B. S. Easton, "New Testament Ethical Lists," *JBL* 51 (1932) 1-12; T. Engberg-Pedersen, *The Stoic Theory of Oikeiōsis: Moral Development and Social Interaction in Early Stoic Philosophy* (SHC 2; Aarhus: Aarhus University Press, 1990); J. T. Fitzgerald, "Virtue/Vice Lists," *ABD* 6:857-59; E. Kamlah, *Die Form der katalogischen Paränese im Neuen Testament* (WUNT 7; Tübingen: Mohr Siebeck, 1964); C. G. Kruse, "Virtues and Vices," *DNT* 1:962-63; A. Malherbe, *Moral Exhortation: A Greco-Roman Sourcebook* (LEC 4; Philadelphia: Westminster, 1986); R. P. Martin, "Virtue," *NIDNTT* 3:925-32; N. J. McEleney, "The Vice Lists of the Pastoral Epistles," *CBQ* 36 (1974) 203-19; S. C. Mott, "Greek Ethics and Christian Conversion: The Philonic Background of Titus 2:10-14 and 3:3-7," *NovT* 20 (1978) 22-48; G. Mussies, *Catalogues of Sins and Virtues Personified* (NHC 2.5; Leiden: E. J. Brill, 1981); E. Osborn, *Ethical Patterns in Early Christian Thought* (Cambridge: Cambridge University Press, 1976); D. Schroeder, "Lists, Ethical," *IDBSup* 546-47; J. Stelzenberger, *Die Beziehungen der frühchristlichen Sittenlehre zur Ethik der Stoa* (Munich: C. H. Beck, 1933); R. B. Todd, "Stoics and Their Cosmology in the First and Second Centuries A.D.," *ANRW* 2.36.3 (1989) 1365-78; H. Trüb, *Kataloge in der griechischen Dichtung* (Zurich: Buchdruckerei Winterthur, 1952); A. Vögtle, *Die Tugend- und Lasterkataloge im Neuen Testament* (NTAbh 16 4/5; Münster: Aschendorff, 1936);

H. Wendland, *Die hellenistisch-römische Kultur in ihren Beziehungen zu Judentum und Christentum* (HNT 1.2; Tübingen: Mohr Siebeck, 1907); S. Wibbing, *Die Tugend- und Lasterkataloge im Neuen Testament und ihre Traditionsgeschichte unter besonderer Berücksichtigung der Qumrantexte* (BZNW 25 (Berlin: Töpelmann, 1959); D. Zeller, *Charis bei Philon und Paulus* (SBS 142; Stuttgart: Katholisches Bibelwerk, 1990); O. Zöckler, *Die Tugendlehre des Christentums* (Gütersloh: Bertelsmann, 1904). J. D. Charles

VINEYARD TEXT (4Q500)

Not one complete sentence survives, yet this text from Qumran makes a significant contribution to our understanding of one of Jesus' best-known parables. Jesus' parable of the wicked vineyard tenants (Mk 12:1-12 par.) has occasioned much debate, especially with reference to the question of the parable's original setting and what bearing it may have on Jesus' self-understanding. Some critics have maintained that the antipriestly orientation of the parable (as seen esp. in v. 12) does not reflect the early Palestinian setting of Jesus but the later, allegorizing tendency of the church, perhaps even the Greek-speaking church (in view of the *Septuagint form of the concluding quotation of Ps 118:22-23 in vv. 10-11).

In separate publications B. D. Chilton and C. A. Evans (1984) argued that the interpretive framework of the *Aramaic paraphrase of Isaiah 5:1-7, which narrows the critical focus of Isaiah's Song of the Vineyard from the nation in general to that of the *temple establishment (as seen esp. in vv. 2 and 5), lies behind Jesus' creative introduction of the parable's tenant "farmers," who are understood to play the role of the ruling *priests.

Objections that the Aramaic paraphrase of Isaiah is too late to be of use in establishing the meaning of a parable of Jesus have been answered by 4Q500, which also presupposes an interpretive framework wherein the Lord's vineyard is understood particularly to be in reference to the temple establishment. The six extant lines read: "2 . . . your baca trees will blossom and . . . 3 . . . a wine vat [bu]ilt among stones . . . 4 . . . to the gate of the holy height . . . 5 . . . your planting and the streams of your glory . . . 6 . . . the branches of your delights . . . 7 your vine[yard . . .]" Line 3 points unmistakably to Isaiah 5:1-7 and enables the reconstruction of "vineyard" in line 7. Line 4 ("holy height") coheres with the Aramaic's "high hill" (*Tg. Isa.* 5:1), while line 5 ("streams of your glory") coheres with rabbinic interpretation of Isaiah 5:1-2 (cf. *t. Sukk.* 3:15), which also explicitly identifies the "tower" and "wine vat" of Isaiah's song as "temple" and "altar" respectively (cf. *t. Meʿil.* 1:16). These points of exegetical and thematic coherence between the Isaiah targum and rabbinic exegesis, on the one hand, and 4Q500, on the other, were first observed by J. M. Baumgarten and have been supported in subsequent research (esp. Brooke; cf. Evans 1999).

The sophisticated exegetical framework, which presupposes Aramaic Isaiah and which also coheres with Aramaic Psalm 118:22 ("the boy whom the builders rejected is worthy to become king and ruler"), is more easily explained as the creative and skillful work of Jesus rather than the later church, whose tendency was to make formal quotations of Scripture conform to the Septuagint. The parable of the wicked tenants in all probability reflects accurately Jesus' critical stance over against the ruling priests and at the same time provides important indirect evidence that Jesus viewed himself as the beloved son of the vineyard's lord, that is, as God's Son.

See also SON OF GOD TEXT (4Q246).

BIBLIOGRAPHY. J. M. Baumgarten, "4Q500 and the Ancient Exegesis of the Lord's Vineyard," *JJS* 40 (1989) 1-6; G. J. Brooke, "4Q500 1 and the Use of Scripture in the Parable of the Vineyard," *DSD* 2 (1995) 268-49; B. D. Chilton, *A Galilean Rabbi and His Bible: Jesus' Use of the Interpreted Scripture of His Time* (GNS 8; Wilmington, DE: Michael Glazier, 1984) 111-16; C. A. Evans, "Jesus and the Dead Sea Scrolls," in *The Dead Sea Scrolls After Fifty Years: A Comprehensive Assessment*, ed. P. W. Flint and J. C. VanderKam (2 vols.; Leiden: E. J. Brill, 1999) 2:573-98, esp. 588-91; idem, "On the Vineyard Parables of Isaiah 5 and Mark 12," *BZ* 28 (1984) 82-86. C. A. Evans

VIRTUES. *See* VICE AND VIRTUE LISTS.

VISIONS OF AMRAM (4Q543-548)

The *Visions of Amram* is partly preserved in five or six very fragmentary copies from Qumran Cave 4 (4Q543-548), allowing only a disjointed impression of this important composition. It receives its title from the introduction, which survives intact: "A copy of the book of the words of the visions of Amram, son of Qahat, son of Levi:

al[l that] he revealed to his sons and that he commanded them on the day of [his] dea[th], at the age of 136 which is the age of his death, [in] the year 152 of the ex[i]le of [I]srael in Egypt."

1. Content and Themes
2. Date and Composition

1. Content and Themes.
Although the content can be described as *apocalyptic, overall it belongs to the genre of patriarchal testament: Amram delivers in the first person a deathbed speech and blessing to his sons, presumably *Moses and Aaron, and his daughter, Miriam. Amram describes his journey with his father Qahat to build the tombs of the patriarchs in Hebron. For forty-one years he was separated from his wife and prevented from returning to Egypt because of a war between Egypt, Canaan and Philistia, a story also mentioned in *Jubilees* 46:10. While in Hebron he received a vision, which he recounts. He saw two angelic beings, one evil and the other good. Between them they control all of humanity, and they were disputing to whom Amram would belong. Amram learned that the first of these two spirits is called Melkiresha and rules over darkness. The other rules over light and the sons of light; it is a safe assumption that this being is called Melkizedek, who is regarded as a dominant angelic personage in the **Melchizedek* text from Qumran Cave 11. If so, *Visions of Amram* is probably the earliest known witness to Melkizedek as a heavenly figure (see van der Woude) and thus relevant as potential background to the Melchizedek tradition in Hebrews 7. Since the good angel mentions that he has three names (4Q544 frag. 3), it is plausible that the opposing leaders of the supernatural world are Michael/Prince of light/Melchizedek versus *Belial/Prince of Darkness/Melkiresha (Milik; Puech).

Visions of Amram is also similar to the *Qumran *Melchizedek* text in its conception of the end of time. All people return to their spiritual source: the sons of light are destined for light and the sons of darkness to darkness and annihilation. The priestly concern of the text is well illustrated by the elevation of Aaron from his biblical role as "mouth of Moses" to "mouth of God" and the "angel of God." Along with the **Testament of Qahat,* the *Visions of Amram* seems to have been inspired by the *Testament of Levi* (*see* Testaments of the Twelve Patriarchs), and J. T. Milik (103) argues that the three works formed an ancient trilogy of Aramaic testamentary writings about the fathers of the priestly lineage. He suggests that the three later circulated in Greek and/or Latin and were known among the early Christians: the three are referred to in *Apostolic Constitutions* (6:16) as "apocryphal books of the three patriarchs," and the *Visions of Amram* was cited by Origen and referred to in the *Apostolic Constitutions* and other Christian writings as a work about the judgment of Abraham.

Visions of Amram contains an important early attestation to the existence of a *midrashic solution to the chronology of the exile. Both the 400 years of Genesis 15:13 and the 430 years of Exodus 12:40 in the Masoretic Text are much too long for the period of stay in Egypt. The Samaritan Pentateuch and the *Septuagint calculate the 430 years as beginning with Abraham's sojourn in Canaan, and this general scheme is also assumed in *Jubilees, Testament of Levi,* *Pseudo-Philo, Galatians 3:16-17 and *Josephus. The statement at the beginning of *Visions of Amram* that Amram died aged 136 (agreeing with the Samaritan Pentateuch and the Septuagint Alexandrinus against Exodus 6:20 in the Masoretic Text, which reads 137 years) in the "year 152 of the ex[i]le of [I]srael in Egypt" must also presuppose the short exile (probably 215 years), or Moses would have been born two centuries after the death of his father.

2. Date and Composition.
The oldest copy of this work *(Visions of Amram[b])* is dated on the basis of paleography to the early *Hasmonean period (Milik), and so the work must have been produced no later than about the middle of the second century B.C. It may have been used by *Jubilees* (*Jub.* 46:6—47:9; Milik) and Jude (Jude 9; Puech). Although *Visions of Amram* displays the dualistic theology characteristic of the Qumran sect, both the early date and the apparent mention of Amram marrying his daughter Miriam to her uncle—niece marriage is forbidden in the **Damascus Document* (CD 4:7-11) suggest that it should be regarded as a pre-Qumran composition. There is no evidence that it was originally composed in Hebrew.

See also TESTAMENT OF QAHAT (4Q542); TESTAMENTS OF THE TWELVE PATRIARCHS.

BIBLIOGRAPHY. K. Beyer, *Die aramäischen Texte*

vom Toten Meer. I (Göttingen: Vandenhoeck & Ruprecht, 1984) 210-14; idem, *Die aramäischen Texte vom Toten Meer. II* (Göttingen: Vandenhoeck & Ruprecht, 1994) 85-92; idem, "Der Streit des guten und des bösen Engels um die Seele: Beobachtungen zu 4QAmr[b] und Judas 9," *JSJ* 4 (1973) 1-18; E. Cook, "The Vision of Amram," in *The Dead Sea Scrolls: A New Translation,* ed. M. O. Wise, M. Abegg Jr. and E. Cook (New York: HarperSanFrancisco, 1996) 433-36; R. Eisenman and M. O. Wise, "Testament of Amram," in *The Dead Sea Scrolls Uncovered* (Shaftesbury, Dorset, England: Element, 1992) 151-56; J. A. Fitzmyer and D. A. Harrington, *A Manual of Palestinian Aramaic Texts* (Rome: Biblical Institute Press, 1978), 90-97, nos. 22-26; F. García Martínez, "4QʿAmram BI, 14: Melki-reša) o Melki-ṣedeq?" *RevQ* 12 (1985) 111-14; P. Grelot, "Quatre centes trente ans (Ex 12,40): Notes sur les Testaments de Lévi et de ʿAmram," in *Homenaje a Juan Prado: Miscelanea de Estudios Biblicos y Hebraicos,* ed. L. Alvarez Verdes and E. J. Alonso Hernandez (Madrid: CSIC, 1975) 559-70; idem, "La Secte: B) Culture et Langues, 2) Araméen," *DBSup* 9 (1978) 801-5; P. J. Kobelski, *Melchizedek and Melchiresha*ʿ (Washington, DC: Catholic Biblical Association of America, 1981) 24-36; J. T. Milik, "Écrits préesséniens de Qumrân: d'Hénoch à Amram," in *Qumrân: Sa piété, sa théologie et son milieu,* ed. M. Delcor (Paris-Gembloux: Duculot, 1978) 91-106; idem, "4QVisions de ʿAmram et une Citation d'Origène," *RB* 79 (1972) 77-97; E. Puech, "4QVisions de ʿAmram," in *La Croyance des Esséniens en la vie future: Immortalité, résurrection, vie éternelle? Histoire d'une croyance dans le Judaïsme Ancien. II. Les données qumraniennes et classiques* (Paris: Gabalda, 1993) 531-40; P. Skehan, "Littérature de Qumrân: B) Apocryphes de l'Ancien Testament," *DBSup* 9 (1978) 822-28; G. Vermes, "The Words of Moses," in *The History of the Jewish People in the Age of Jesus Christ (175 B.C. A.D. 135),* rev. and ed. G. Vermes, F. Millar and M. Goodman (3 vols.; Edinburgh: T & T Clark, 1973-87) 3.1:334-35.

D. K. Falk

WAR SCROLL (1QM) AND RELATED TEXTS

The Qumran *War Scroll* and its related texts envision a coming battle of epic proportions and lay down the rules for preparation for this battle and for conducting the battle itself.

1. Description of the Manuscript Evidence
2. Genre
3. Contents
4. Important Issues for New Testament Background

1. Description of the Manuscript Evidence.

1.1. Cave 1. One of the most important manuscripts discovered in 1947 by the Bedouin in Qumran Cave 1 was a text that has become known as the *War Scroll* (1QM). Acquired by E. L. Sukenik of the Hebrew University and published (posthumously) in 1955, it is currently on display at the Shrine of the Book in Jerusalem. Stretching nearly nineteen columns (with a few letters of a twentieth column), and lacking only a few lines of the bottom edge and final columns, it is one of the most complete manuscripts of the nearly nine hundred to come out of the eleven caves in the cliffs at the northwest corner of the Dead Sea. It describes in some detail a war at the end of time between the "Children of Light" and the "Children of Darkness," a war whose individual battles are at times lost to the forces of evil but whose final victorious outcome is never in question.

1.2. Cave 4. Nearly five years after the first find, six additional manuscripts of the *War Scroll* (4Q491-496) were discovered among the thousands of fragments in Cave 4. Important as this second discovery was to demonstrate a link between Caves 1 and 4 and to hint at a process of development in the form of the work, the very fragmentary Cave 4 manuscripts added little of importance to the reconstruction of the Cave 1 text. However, in addition to these "copies," a significant new manuscript came to light from Cave 4 which details the events leading up to the final battle, complete with a victorious Davidic Messiah. This text, called the *War Rule* (4Q285), was first published in the popular press in the fall of 1991 and imprecisely entitled "Pierced Messiah Text," due to the mistaken impression that it contained a description of a suffering messiah. Another copy of this important manuscript also turned up in 1956 among the fragments of Cave 11, the last cave to be discovered. It may be that these two new manuscripts actually supply the missing columns at the end of the manuscript from Cave 1—the language and subject matter is virtually identical—but there is no overlapping text to make this suggestion more than conjecture.

2. Genre.

2.1. Apocalyptic. Given the general description of its contents, it is easy to understand why from the first days of examination the *War Scroll* took on the role of the Dead Sea Scroll version of the NT book of Revelation. Generically, therefore, it was often described as an example of apocalyptic literature, a type of literature which is epitomized by the book of Revelation. With a fuller understanding of the nature of apocalyptic literature there is now some doubt as to the accuracy of this description (Collins). The *War Scroll* appears to lack many of the characteristic elements that are expected in apocalyptic literature. It is wanting in heavenly interpreters and tours, which are so prominent in other examples of Jewish apocalyptic (Ezek 40:3-4; Dan 8:15-17). There are no image-rich scenes of animals, rivers, mountains and stars, which elsewhere characterize the special-effects nature of the apocalypse (Dan 8:2-14; Zech 6:1-7).

2.2. Apocalyptic Worldview. The *War Scroll* does,

however, exhibit one critical character of the apocalypse. It appears to have purposed, at least in part, to communicate a message of hope: in the face of perverse evil, the Children of Light are encouraged to persevere to the end. God was understood to be preparing to intervene and bring a permanent solution for the problem of evil. Perhaps more appropriate is the conclusion that the *War Scroll* exhibits the characteristics of an apocalyptic worldview rather than apocalyptic literature. In this, the *War Scroll* and the Dead Sea Scrolls in general prefigured the NT by understanding that (1) life on earth is influenced by supernatural beings—both good and evil, (2) God has charted the course of history in advance, and (3) there was an impending judgment to punish the wicked and reward the good (Collins).

3. Contents.

3.1. Rule. As seen in the following outline, the main purpose of the *War Scroll* was not so much to reveal what was to happen at the end of the age, as it was to inform of proper actions as the end drew near. In this, it fits more comfortably in the genre of *serek*, or "rule book," than it does apocalyptic. This type of literature was quite prevalent among the scroll caches and is perhaps best illustrated in the important *Rule of the Community* (1QS), which was also found in Cave 1. The following outline clearly reveals that the *War Scroll* could more accurately be called the *Rule of War*.

I. The Rule of Eschatological War (1:1—2:14)
II. The Rule of the Battle Trumpets (2:16—3:11)
III. The Rule of the Banners (3:13—4:17)
IV. The Rule of the Messiah's Shield (4:18—5:2)
V. The Rule for Operational Matters (5:3—9:18)
VI. Battle Liturgy (9:20—16:2)
VII. The Rule of the Seven Battles (16:3—18:8)
VIII. Victory Liturgy (18:10—19:14)

3.2. Liturgy. Although largely a "rule," sections VI and VIII reveal another important aspect pointing to an additional purpose for the *War Scroll*. These two sections provided what was lacking in the text of Deuteronomy 20, a passage quoted at 1QM 10:3-4:

> And [the priest] shall say to them, "Hear O Israel, you are going into battle today against your enemies. Do not be fainthearted, do not fear or be alarmed, do not be in awe of them. For the LORD your God is the one who goes with you to fight for you against your enemies, to save you." (Deut 20:3-4)

The notable focus on the liturgical in the Qumran community would have made an extrapolation from the "known" to the "needed" obligatory. What were the full duties of the high priest on the day of battle? Is this all he was to say before the troops? How were the troops to respond? The answers to these questions are found in the liturgical sections of the *War Scroll* (sections VI and VIII). The two verses of Deuteronomy became a seven-column script filling the gap suggested by the biblical text.

4. Important Issues for New Testament Background.

4.1. Messiah the Prince. Aside from the rather prominent role of the high priest in the extensive liturgical portions of the scroll (1QM 15:4-5, 6; 16:13; 18:5; 19:11), the expectation of another important figure is evident. Although the introduction to this significant individual is lost in the missing lines at the bottom of column 4, his shield is the topic of discussion at the top of column 5:

> and on the sh[ie]ld of the Prince of the Whole Congregation they shall write his name, the names "Israel," "Levi" and "Aaron," and the names of the twelve tribes of Israel according to their order of birth, and the names of the twelve chiefs of their tribes. (1QM 5:1-2)

His presence is also likely (although reconstructed) in the company of the high priest as they return for the victory ceremony on the day following the final battle in section VIII:

> And the chi[ef] priest shall approach there [with] his [depu]ty, his brothers [the priests] and the Levites [with the Prince] of the battle, and all the chiefs of the battle lines and [their officers . . .]. (1QM 19:12 with 4Q492 1 11)

His title according to the *War Scroll* is the Prince or Leader, a translation of the Hebrew word *nāśîʾ*. This term had clear messianic import among the Dead Sea Scrolls and is a reflection of Ezekiel 37:25:

> They shall live on the land which I gave to my servant Jacob, where your fathers lived—they and their children, and their childrens' children, forever—and David my servant

shall be their prince *[nāśî ʾ]* forever.

*4.2. **Dual Messiah.*** Thus it is likely that the *War Scroll* gives further evidence for a concept which is prevalent among the Dead Sea Scrolls, the expectation of a dual messiah: a priestly messiah descended from Aaron, and a royal messiah descended from David (CD 12:23-24; 14:19; 19:10-11; 1QS 9:11). This notion, likely originating in such OT passages as 1 Samuel 2:35 and Jeremiah 33:15-18 (see also Zech 4:12-14; 6:10-15) is very likely one of the issues the writer of Hebrews had in mind as he demonstrated that Jesus, although not a descendant of Aaron, was a better priest of the type of Melchizedek (Heb 7:1-17).

4.3. Role of Messiah the Prince. The *War Rule* (4Q285) gives further evidence which fills out the royal messianic role in eschatological battle. When this text first became available to scholars in 1991, a initial attempt at interpretation produced the translation: "and they will put to death the leader *[nāśî ʾ]* of the community." This significant suggestion was accompanied with the claim that the long-sought "suffering Messiah" figure had at last been found in Jewish literature dating before the dawn of Christianity, perhaps in reflection of Isaiah 53 (Eisenman and Wise). However, the unvocalized Hebrew of the scrolls also allows an alternate translation: "and the Prince of the community will have him put to death" (4Q285 7 4). The debate arose concerning the pronunciation of a single word; whether to read *wᵉhēmîtû* (they put [the prince] to death), or *wehᵉmîtô* ([the prince] put him to death). Ultimately the second option has gained wide acceptance as a result of several factors: (1) the immediate context, Isaiah 11 and the messianic conquest of evil; (2) the larger context, elsewhere in the manuscript (fragment 6) someone is brought before the Prince for judgment; (3) the whole scroll corpus, nowhere else in the scrolls do we find a suggestion of messianic suffering; and finally (4) grammar, the second reading is preferable according to the principles of Hebrew syntax.

The line which follows (7 5) the critical passage from 4Q285 has also been used to a bolster the theory of a suffering messiah. Eisenman and Wise translate "with woundings," a word of the same root *(ḥll)* as Isaiah 53:5, "He was pierced/ wounded." It is more likely, however, that the word should be translated as a reflection of Exodus 15:20 (and Judg 11:34), "with dancing," from the root *(ḥûl)*. The context of the victory celebration following the final battle makes the latter suggestion probable.

4.4. Eschatological Victory and Judgment. The *War Rule* thus evidences the roles of judgment and conquest which the Jewish community of the centuries before the advent of Christianity expected at the coming of the royal Messiah. The obvious confusion of the disciples as Jesus spoke of his impending death (Mt 16:21-22; Lk 9:44-45; Jn 12:16; 20:9) and his surprising statement to Nicodemus that "God did not send his Son into the world to judge" (Jn 3:17) take on a deeper significance when reconsidered in the light of the scrolls.

4.5. Dualism. The dualistic nature of Qumran thought is also evident in the *War Scroll*, given the division of humankind into the categories of "light" and "darkness." Although this appears at first glance to be a cosmic dualism, it becomes clear that the real intent is ethical, as light and darkness are best understood as metaphors for righteousness and wickedness: "[the Sons of Rig]teousness shall shine to all the ends of the world" (1QM 1:8). It is also clear that the dualism of the scrolls is not a radical dualism of equal and opposing forces, since God's fundamental purpose and authority are never in doubt: "[then the]re shall be a time of salvation for the people of God, and time of dominion for all the men of his forces, and eternal annihilation for all the forces of Belial" (1QM 1:5-6). The Dead Sea Scroll sect (Essenes) did, however, clearly understand that while God would eventually reign victorious, their present age was characterized by wickedness and was under the authority of *Belial—the Satan figure in the scrolls (see 2 Cor 6:15):

> Throughout all our generations you have made your mercies wondrous for the rem[nant of the people] during the dominion of Belial. (1QM 14:8-9, see also 1QS 1:16-18, 23-24; 2:19)

This worldview evidenced in the scrolls once again presages similar dualistic elements in the NT. The Gospel of John quotes Jesus as saying:

> Yet a little while longer the light is with you. Walk while you have the light, lest darkness overtakes you. For the one who walks in darkness does not know where he is going. While you have the light, believe in the light, so that you might become sons of light. (Jn 12:35-36, see also 3:19-20)

And Paul writes that "the god of this world has blinded the minds of the unbelieving" (2 Cor 4:4) but that Christ would win the ultimate victory (1 Cor 15:25). This ultimate victory was expected by the scroll writers as well as they read these lines near the end of the *War Scroll*:

> You have [done w]onders upon wonders with us, but from of old there has been nothing like it, for you have known our appointed time. Today [your] power has shined forth for us, [and] you[have demonstrated] to us the power of your mercies with us for an eternal redemption, to remove the dominion of the enemy that it might be no more, the power of your strength. (1QM 18:10-11)

See also APOCALYPTIC LITERATURE; DEAD SEA SCROLLS; ESCHATOLOGIES OF LATE ANTIQUITY; MESSIANISM.

BIBLIOGRAPHY. M. G. Abegg Jr., "Messianic Hope and 4Q285—A Reassessment," *JBL* 113 (1994) 81-91; J. J. Collins, *Apocalypticism in the Dead Sea Scrolls* (New York: Routledge, 1997); J. Duhaime, "Dualism," in *The Encyclopedia of the Dead Sea Scrolls*, ed. L. H. Schiffman and J. C. VanderKam (3 vols.; New York: Oxford University Press, 2000) 215-20; idem, "War Scroll," in *The Dead Sea Scrolls: Hebrew, Aramaic, and Greek Texts with English Translations, 2: Damascus Document, War Scroll, and Related Documents*, ed. J. H. Charlesworth et al. (Tübingen: Mohr Siebeck, 1995) 80–141; R. Eisenman and M. O. Wise., *The Dead Sea Scrolls Uncovered* (Rockport, MA: Element, 1992); M. Wise, M. G. Abegg Jr. and E. M. Cook, *The Dead Sea Scrolls: A New Translation* (San Francisco: HarperSanFrancisco, 1996) 150-72, 291-94; Y. Yadin, *The Scroll of the War of the Sons of Light Against the Sons of Darkness* (London: Oxford University Press, 1962).

M. G. Abegg Jr.

WEDDING. *See* MARRIAGE.

WISDOM LITERATURE AT QUMRAN

The transformation in our understanding of this literature is one of the most dramatic examples of the rapid developments and changing paradigms characteristic of *Qumran studies. Since the larger portion of the wisdom texts have come to the attention of the majority of researchers in the field only since 1990, the study of them is in its infancy.

A determination of the texts to include in a discussion of this subject is not self-evident. At least two types come under consideration. The first group of texts points to compositions that resemble the wisdom literature of the Hebrew Scriptures. The postbiblical development of this tradition reflected in works such as Ben Sira must also be considered (*see* Sirach). A more complete picture emerges if we also examine those works that make extensive use of a wide array of Hebrew terms synonymous with and including wisdom and knowledge but that do not fit into this Hebrew literary tradition on the basis of either form or content.

1. Wisdom Texts Published Prior to 1990
2. New Wisdom Texts from Qumran
3. The Significance of This Material

1. Wisdom Texts Published Prior to 1990. The abundance of wisdom terminology was evident to those researchers who read the first scrolls to come to light in 1947. However, on the basis of form or content there was no reason to connect these texts that contained terms such as *ḥokmâ* ("wisdom"), *dēʿâ* or *daʿat* ("knowledge"), *śekel* ("insight") and *bînâ* ("understanding") to the biblical wisdom traditions. These early discussions rather reflect comparisons with the evidence concerning *Gnosticism as well as hypotheses concerning the development of dualism and *apocalypticism. When J. Sanders published the *Psalms Scroll* in 1965 he noted the absence of research on the subject of wisdom at Qumran (Sanders, 69 n. 1). This was based on a perceived lack of interest in sapiential themes evident in the Qumran texts available at that time.

There are texts published prior to 1990 that reflect the direct continuation of the wisdom tradition of the Hebrew Scriptures and its successors in the Second Temple era. 1QInstruction (1Q26) and 1QMysteries (1Q27) have been identified as portions of compositions more widely attested among the Cave 4 fragments published after 1990 and hence will be discussed below. Texts such as these achieve new significance in light of the recent materials.

In 4Q184 (*Wiles of the Wicked Woman*) and 4Q185 (a sapiential work), already published in 1968, we find the primary treatment of the biblical figures of Lady Wisdom and Dame Folly at Qumran (Allegro, 82-87; Strugnell, 263-73). The wanton woman who leads the simple astray with her sexuality is found in Proverbs 2:16-19; 5:1-23; 6:23-26; 7:1-27 and 9:13-18. But the female figure described in 4Q184 has greater cosmic significance than does the seductress of Proverbs: "foundations of darkness . . . darkness of night . . . her clothes are shadows of twilight, and her ornaments are plagues of corruption . . . depths of the pit, her lodgings are beds of darkness. . . . Amid everlasting fire is her inheritance, not among those who shine brightly" (Harrington 1996b, 31-32). This representation places Dame Folly closer to the dualistic cosmological struggle between good and evil portrayed in texts such as 1QS 3—4 (*see* Rule of the Community) or as represented in the sectarian history of CD 3—5 (*see* Damascus Document) dealing with the nets of *Belial than the biblical text does. Contrast also the potential victims, described in Proverbs as the simple and unwise; in 4Q184 it is the righteous who may be led astray.

In 4Q185 Lady Wisdom finds personification similar to that in Proverbs 1—9 and Ben Sira. This composition continues the style of the wisdom instruction and paraenesis characteristic of those texts. Other features, such as the role of *angels in the adjudication of human conduct, are more compatible with viewpoints found in apocalyptic texts and other compositions from Qumran. In some instances this text moves beyond what can be found in Proverbs and Ben Sira, which would also have been compatible with viewpoints expressed in sectarian compositions found at Qumran (Tobin).

The *Psalms Scroll* (11QPsalms[a]) contains wisdom material (Sanders). The Syriac Psalm 154 (11QPs[a] 18), partially reconstructed from the Syriac text, was dubbed by Sanders a "sapiential hymn." The theme of wisdom is introduced into this psalm in line 3 of the text: "To make known the glory of the Lord is wisdom given and for recounting his many deeds is she given to man." Wisdom elements in this psalm are connected with the purpose of exhorting the righteous to bind their souls together in the praise of God. The psalm's ultimate purpose is an exhortation to teaching. Wisdom in this case is the result of revelation, received by a group referred to as *rabbîm* ("many"), *ṭôbîm* ("good"), *tāmîm* ("perfect"), *ḥasîdîm* ("pious") and many similar terms. This group is called to proclaim this wisdom to another group, the "senseless" and "foolish," so that they will not be drawn into the circles of a third group, the "wicked." While it was not necessarily composed by sectarian authors, the psalm would have been at home in those circles.

Hymn to the Creator (11QPs[a] 26:9-15) is another hymn of a sapiential nature. Within it wisdom terminology is explicitly linked with the act of creation. Of interest also is the treatment of *da ʿat* ("knowledge") as synonymous with *ḥokmâ,* the term more frequently equated with wisdom in biblical texts.

The prose section toward the end of 11QPs[a] 27:2-11 (David's Compositions) lists him as a "wise man [*ḥākām*] and a light like the light of the sun and literate [*sôpēr*]." The composition of 4,050 works is ascribed to him. As in some other texts reflective of the wisdom tradition at Qumran, they are said to be the result of revelation: "he spoke all these things through prophecy."

11QPs[a] 21:11—22:1 must also be noted. Herein is found a portion of Sirach 51:13-30, an autobiographical poem on the search for Wisdom. While both texts describe a male youth in a quest for Lady Wisdom, a figure known from Proverbs 8, Wisdom of Solomon 7, 4Q185 and elsewhere, the Hebrew text is capable of a more erotic interpretation than is the Greek. In these accounts Wisdom lets herself be found and in so doing takes over his life. Whether this is an addition to Ben Sira or part of an original Hebrew text remains a point of debate.

2. New Wisdom Texts from Qumran.
A fundamental reappraisal of our perception of wisdom in the Qumran texts is in process due to new texts that have become available to researchers since 1990. The most extensive remnants come from a work that now has been titled *Instruction, Sapiential Work A* in earlier publications. Fragments of at least seven extant copies are available: 1Q26, 4Q415-418a and 4Q423. One reconstruction proposes that the work's preface or introduction sets it within a cosmic and eschatological framework (Harrington 1996b, 40-59). This column (fragment 1) includes phrases such as "season by season," "the host of the Heavens He has established" and "[luminaries] for their portents, and signs of [their] fe[stivals]," familiar from apocalpytic and other Qumran literature. The *eschatological aspect is apparent: "From Heaven He shall pronounce judgment upon the work of wickedness, But all His faithful children will be accepted with favor by [Him. . . .] And every spirit of flesh will be destroyed(?). But the sons of Heave[n] sh[all rejoice in the day when it (sc. wickedness) is ju]dged, and (when) all iniquity shall come to an end, Until the epoch of tru[th] will be per-

fected [forever]" (Strugnell and Harrington, 83).

Cosmological interests are evident throughout the work. The type of knowledge that represents this author's central interest is captured in the term *raz nihyeh,* discussed below: "For the God of knowledge is the foundation of truth, and by the *raz nihyeh* He has laid out its foundation, And its deeds [He has prepared with all wis]dom, and with all [c]unning has He fashioned it" (4Q417 1 i 8-9; Strugnell and Harrington, 154).

The remainder of the document concentrates on the more customary wisdom theme of advice for daily living. Included are issues such as a sensitivity to the embarrassment of another; the necessity of paying back loans or surety bonds quickly; maintaining integrity in the service of others; the avoidance of selling one's soul or self for money or possessions, even if one is in poverty; not boasting about one's poverty; not violating a trust of money or property and not using poverty as an excuse for avoiding study. There are also injunctions concerning the honor due to father and mother as well as the importance of living in harmony with one's wife (Harrington 1996b, 43-45). Such instruction is similar to that found in Ben Sira and demonstrates continuity with the biblical wisdom tradition rooted in the experiences of daily living.

The volumes of sapiential texts are now available in the Discoveries in the Judaean Desert series (vols. 20 and 34). Included in volume 20 are the texts of 4Q298-305, 411-413, 420-421 and 425-426. In volume 34 are found all of the fragments of the work now titled *Instruction,* formerly known as *Sapiential Work A,* including 4Q415, 416, 417, 418, 418a, 423 and a re-edition of 1Q26. Also included are 4Q418b and 418c, the latter perhaps a fragment of another copy of *Instruction.* The majority of the texts listed below as well as *Instruction* are available in F. García Martínez or in M. O. Wise, M. G. Abegg and E. M. Cook with the Hebrew texts in B. Z. Wacholder and M. G. Abegg (see vol. 2 for the majority of these texts).

Fragments of three manuscripts of the text entitled *Mysteries* are available (1Q27, 4Q299 and 4Q300). While 4Q301 has been classified as another copy of this composition, that identification is less certain. The name is indicative of the frequency with which *raz* ("mystery") is found throughout the text and provides one tie, among others, to *Instruction.* In this composition wisdom makes it possible for humankind to "know [the difference] between g[ood and evil, and between falsehood and truth, and that they might understand the mysteries of transgression. . . .]" (4Q300 frag. 3 2//1Q27 frag. 1 i 1-2). Regrettably humankind "did not know [the *raz nihyeh,* and the former things they did not consider. And they did not know what shall befall] them. And they did not save their lives from the *raz ni[hyeh]*" (4Q300 frag. 3 3-4//1Q27 frag. 1 i 3-4). A description of God's plan for the end of time and the signs of that future era follow, reflecting an interest in eschatology that is more extensive than that interest in *Instruction.* However, this divine wisdom, rooted in the order of creation, is sealed and available only to the righteous, the only portion of humankind that God permits to see and understand it. In continuity with the biblical tradition the book of *Mysteries* does consider extensive moral advice to be wisdom.

The connection between wisdom and sectarianism is more explicit in 4Q420/421 *(Ways of Righteousness*[a, b]*).* The available fragments suggest a composite work in three sections, possibly reflecting different sources. The first section deals with the organization of the *yaḥad* and includes the exhortation, "[he shall bring all] his [wi]sdom and knowledge and understanding and good things [into the Community *(yaḥad)* of God]" (4Q421 1a i 2-3). The second section consists of a series of wisdom sayings about the righteous man, often in the form of proverbs. Herein the righteous man is exhorted to "carry the yoke of wisdom (*ʿol hokmâh*)" (4Q421 1 ii 9-10). The appearance of the term *ḥokmâ* in this fragment is significant in suggesting that the author wishes the work to be understand within the tradition based on the biblical wisdom materials. The "yoke" points to the NT wisdom text, Matthew 11:29-30, as well as to the use of the term in *m. ʾAbot* 3:5 and other *rabbinic texts. The *temple forms the center of the third section, with an emphasis on issues of purity. Allusions to 11QTemple (*see* Temple Scroll) and 4QMMT (*see* Miqsat Maʿasey ha-Torah) can be glimpsed in the fragments listing categories of persons prohibited from participation in various temple activities. Issues such as the "pure food" discussed in texts attributed to the *yaḥad* also receive mention. This text shows evidence of an intricate connection with previously published legal materials in the Qumran corpus.

Words of the Maśkîl to All Sons of Dawn (4Q298)

is written in what has been termed cryptic script, known only from the Qumran texts. What receives emphasis in the extant fragments is the necessity to "understand" for "those who seek truth. . . . [And those who k]now, have pur[s]ued [the]se things and have turn[ed . . .]" (4Q298 1-2 i 2-3). This text is addressed to the "sons of dawn," who could well be initiates who have not yet become full members of the sect, hence "sons of light." The address is introduced as the words of the *maśkîl,* referred to elsewhere in Qumran texts and discussed below. Here we find strong evidence of the sectarian origins of this wisdom composition.

The *ḥᵃkāmîm* ("wise men") are enjoined to discern a parable in 4Q302 (4QpapAdmonitory Parable), earlier classified as two separate compositions, 4Q302 and 302a. While the term *māšāl* is not found in these fragments, this rare appearance of a parable in postbiblical Jewish literature outside of the NT is important for the study of the history of the genre (*see* Rabbinic Parables). While the use of the term can refer to popular sayings or proverbs in the Hebrew Bible (1 Sam 10:12; 24:13; Ezek 12:22-23; 16:44; 18:2-3), the limited material in the fragments does not suggest a significant connection with the sapiential material already discussed. It does appear to be in the biblical tradition of parables about trees (Ezek 19:10-14; Ps 80:9-17; Dan 4:7-14, 17-18). The composition resembles an admonition based on the *rîb* (lawsuit) pattern, attested in the prophetic traditions of the Hebrew Bible and also present in texts from Qumran such as CD 2:1—4:12 and 4Q381 (*Noncanonical Psalms B*) 69 and 76—77. The admonition to the addressee, "Discern this, O wise men," and the sapiential parable suggest that the text receive consideration as part of the wisdom tradition in the Qumran texts.

Connections with NT literature are apparent in 4Q525 *(Beatitudes).* Fragment 2, column 2 contains portions of five makarisms (or beatitudes) that in some ways suggest the beatitudes of Matthew 5:3-12 and Luke 6:20-23. Both 4Q525 and the NT texts represent the development of a tradition already evident in the Hebrew Bible, mostly in the wisdom literature, and also found in other postbiblical Jewish literature. In the Hebrew texts this form is characterized by the term *ʾašrê* [*hûʾ*] . . . (happy [is the one who] . . .). In 4Q525 wisdom is equated with Torah. The person who has attained *ḥokmâ* "walks in the law of the Most High," and this accomplishment is considered to be the source of blessing. In fragment 15 evidence of the dualism familiar from other Qumran literature and apocalyptic works is manifest in its references to "eternal fire," the "venom of serpents," "darkness," "flames of death" and "flaming brimstone," apparently with regard to those who "do not attain the paths of life." Mastemah receives mention in fragment 19.

4Q424 is a set of injunctions regarding relationships with various types of persons found in a form characteristic of wisdom literature. It pays particular attention to which persons should be avoided and the attendant reasons for that advice. Many of these instructions concern legal and business relationships. The word *ḥokmâ,* characteristic of biblical wisdom, appears three times in this fragment. Issues of a moral nature are discussed. Also present in the last line of the preserved text is the term *bᵉnê ṣedeq* ("sons of righteousness"), a designation used elsewhere in the Qumran texts to specify either the Qumran sectarians or a group within that movement. These indications point to this same body of literature that will have been viewed with particular favor by the Qumran community but that should not be considered a sectarian composition.

Only two fragments of four lines from the top corners of the same column survive from a sapiential work concerning divine providence (4Q413). The form of the preserved fragment with references to wisdom and understanding places it closer to other wisdom texts discussed in this section of this article than to liturgical or worship material. As in a number of the texts just discussed we also find allusions closer to the sectarian texts: "He increased his share in the knowledge of his truth; and as he despised every wicked individual . . . [that wicked individual] would not survive." The fragment concludes with a reference to the revelation of God.

In addition to the works already discussed and those to be found in DJD 20, a number of other compositions designated as sapiential works are very fragmentary: 4Q307-308, 4Q408, 4Q410, 4Q472-476, 4Q486-487 and 4Q498 *(Sapiential Hymn).*

3. The Significance of This Material.
The literature that has become available since 1990 provides evidence of a new wisdom tradi-

tion that is not an imitation of biblical material or an expansion of the sectarian use of wisdom vocabulary noted early in the history of the study of Qumran materials. These texts are evidence of another significant wisdom tradition in Second Temple *Judaism, the study of which is only in its infancy.

This now brings us back to the sectarian literature such as the *Rule of the Community* and the **Thanksgiving Hymns* that occupied those first scholars of this library. We have a much better explanation for the preponderance of terms concerning knowledge and wisdom that are distributed freely throughout those scrolls. These compositions show evidence of being the recipients of this unique wisdom tradition. In these works, admittedly dominated by dualism and eschatology, we find an interest in creation, in the times and in the celestial bodies. In fact their dualism and eschatology are rooted in creation and the cosmos. But in these texts the speculative character of wisdom is no longer apparent. Wisdom has been placed in the service of the sect. This observation is important in the study of Christian origins.

Evidence of the central role of the *maśkîl* as a person entrusted with wisdom and responsibility for instruction is attested in a number of Qumran texts. In 1QS 3:13 the *maśkîl* is the one who "shall instruct all the sons of light and shall teach them." This line introduces 1QS 3:13—4:26, one of the crucial passages concerning the subject of dualism and wisdom. This "sage" as teacher again receives emphasis in 1QS 9:12—10:5. His knowledge is related to the Torah and to the particular practices based on the community's interpretation of it: "He shall conceal the teaching of the Law from men of falsehood but shall impart true knowledge and righteous judgment to those who have chosen the Way" (1QS 9:17-18). This figure also receives mention in wisdom texts such as *Instruction* and *Ways of Righteousness,* as well as in other sectarian texts such as 1QS, 1QSb, 1QH and CD.

This same figure is the subject of 4Q510-511 *(Songs of the Sage[a, b])* (Baillet, 215-62). Here the *maśkîl* writing in the first person is the one who "makes known [*mašmyaʿ*] the splendor of his beauty, in order to frighten and ter[rify] all the spirits of the angels of destruction" (Newsom, 381). For the sage this knowledge is the source of the authority and power necessary to gain victory within the dualistic struggle in which the *yaḥad* ("community") is engaged. This figure is not only wise but also powerful, and his knowledge is the source of power for the entire sect.

Research on the significance of this tradition for the study of Christian origins has not yet begun. The identification of a significant wisdom tradition that gradually finds a sectarian expression is an important contribution to the subject. For example, Jesus is equated with wisdom in the Gospel of Matthew (most notably Mt 11:25-30). The Qumran texts help us to understand how the writer of this Gospel could have made such a connection and how its Jewish readers could have understood it.

See also SIRACH; TORAH; WISDOM OF SOLOMON.

BIBLIOGRAPHY. J. Allegro, *Qumran Cave 4.1* (DJD 5; Oxford: Clarendon Press, 1968) 82-87; M. Baillet, *Qumran Grotte 4.3* (DJD 7; Oxford: Clarendon Press, 1982) 215-62; J. J. Collins, *Seers, Sybils and Sages in Hellenistic-Roman Judaism* (JSJSup 54; Leiden: E. J. Brill, 1997); W. D. Davies, "'Knowledge' in the Dead Sea Scrolls and Matthew 11:25-30," *HTR* 46 (1953) 113-39; C. M. Deutsch, *Lady Wisdom, Jesus and the Sages: Metaphor and Social Context in Matthew's Gospel* (Valley Forge, PA: Trinity Press International, 1996); T. Elgvin et al., *Qumran Cave 4.15: Sapiential Texts, Part 1* (DJD 20; Oxford: Clarendon Press, 1997); J. G. Gammie, "Spatial and Ethical Dualism in Jewish Wisdom and Apocalyptic Literature," *JBL* 93 (1974) 356-85; F. García Martínez, *The Dead Sea Scrolls Translated: The Qumran Texts in English* (Leiden: E. J. Brill, 1994); D. J. Harrington, "The Raz Nihyeh in a Qumran Wisdom Text (1Q 26, 4Q415-418, 423)," *RevQ* 17 (1996a) 549-53; idem, *Wisdom Texts from Qumran* (London: Routledge, 1996b); J. Kampen, "The Diverse Aspects of Wisdom in the Qumran Texts," in *The Dead Sea Scrolls After Fifty Years: A Comprehensive Assessment,* ed. P. W. Flint and J. C. VanderKam (Leiden: E. J. Brill, 1998) 1:211-43; A. Lange, *Weisheit und Prädestination: Weisheitliche Urordnung und Prädestination in den Textfunden von Qumran* (STDJ 18; Leiden: E. J. Brill, 1995); idem, "Wisdom and Predestination in the Dead Sea Scrolls," *DSD* 2 (1995) 340-54; W. L. Lipscomb with J. A. Sanders, "Wisdom at Qumran," in *Israelite Wisdom: Theological and Literary Essays in Honor of Samuel Terrien,* ed. J. G. Gammie et al. (Missoula, MT: Scholars Press, 1978) 277-85; C. A. Newsom, "The Sage in the Literature of Qumran: The Functions of the Maskil," in *The*

Sage in Israel and the Ancient Near East, ed. J. G. Gammie and L. G. Perdue (Winona Lake, IN: Eisenbrauns, 1990) 373-82; J. A. Sanders, *The Psalms Scroll of Qumran Cave 11 (11QPs*^{a}*)* (DJD 4; Oxford: Clarendon Press, 1965); J. Strugnell, "Notes en marge du Volume V des 'Discoveries in the Judaean Desert of Jordan,'" *RevQ* 7 (1970) 163-276; J. Strugnell and D. J. Harrington, with T. Elgvin, *Sapiential Texts, Part 2: Cave 4.24* (DJD 34; Oxford: Clarendon Press, 1999); S. Tanzer, "The Sages at Qumran: Wisdom in the Hodayot" (Ph.D. diss., Harvard University, 1987); T. H. Tobin, "4Q185 and Jewish Wisdom Literature," in *Of Scribes and Scrolls: Studies on the Hebrew Bible, Intertestamental Judaism and Christian Origins, Presented to John Strugnell on the Occasion of His Sixtieth Birthday,* ed. H. W. Attridge, J. J. Collins and T. H. Tobin (College Theology Society Resources in Religion 5; Lanham, MD: University Press of America, 1990) 145-52; J. C. VanderKam, L. H. Schiffman and G. J. Brooke, eds., *Dead Sea Discoveries* 4 (1997) 245-353; B. Z. Wacholder and M. G. Abegg, *A Preliminary Edition of the Unpublished Dead Sea Scrolls: The Hebrew and Aramaic Texts from Cave Four* (Washington, DC: Biblical Archaeology Society, 1992) 2:1-203; M. O. Wise, M. G. Abegg Jr. and E. M. Cook, *The Dead Sea Scrolls: A New Translation* (San Francisco: HarperCollins, 1996). J. I. Kampen

WISDOM OF BEN SIRA. *See* SIRACH.

WISDOM OF SOLOMON

The Wisdom of Solomon, a *pseudonymous work of *Alexandrian Judaism from about the turn of the era, cultivates the dedicated pursuit of a wisdom that takes as its starting point the governance of and accountability before the God of *Israel. The author assures fellow Jews that those who have forsaken *Torah, though they profit now, have chosen the path of folly: God's judgment will reveal the *honor of the righteous and the degradation of the lawless. He further encourages Jews to persist in their distinctive way of life by recalling God's care for and presence with them throughout history, especially in the exodus, and by showing the ignorance of the Gentiles who have been duped into idolatry. *Education in Torah and the Jewish wisdom tradition, he avers, provides all that Greek culture might and far more besides. The work was much read in the early church and left its imprint on the NT and the church fathers during the most formative centuries of Christian theology.

1. Author, Date and Setting
2. Structure and Contents
3. Genre and Purpose
4. Important Themes
5. Greco-Roman Philosophical Influence
6. Influence on the Early Church

1. Author, Date and Setting.
The author of Wisdom remains anonymous, choosing rather to speak in the voice of Solomon, Israel's wise person par excellence. The author was a pious Jew living in Alexandria, the famous center of learning and Hellenistic culture. This is supported in part by internal evidence: there is a marked hostility against the native Egyptians in the third part of the work (Wis 19:13-17; Winston); the author dwells on cultic practices peculiar to Egypt, such as the worship of animals or gods depicted with animal features. The strong reception of Wisdom among Alexandrian Christians provides external support for this provenance.

Theories of multiple authorship abounded in the eighteenth and nineteenth centuries (and early in the twentieth with Holmes). Supporters of this view noted that Wisdom 1—11 and 12—19 express different conceptions of God's dealing with the world (mediated through Wisdom vs. direct). These scholars also discovered striking differences in the use of certain terms, particles and types of compound words (Holmes). More recently, however, scholars have returned to single authorship, particularly because of the similar use of "unusual words and expressions throughout" (Reider), the echoes of the first part in the second half and the tight structural interweaving of the main parts of the discourse (see 2 below).

Early arguments for a Hebrew original have given way to a consensus that the book was written in Greek. The presence of Semitisms is no argument against this (Reider), and the use of the *Septuagint, familiarity with Greek *rhetorical devices (such as *sorites, accumulatio,* alliteration and assonance; see Winston), the affinity for compound words (common in Alexandrian Greek), knowledge of Greek words found only in the Greek poets (*see* Poetry, Hellenistic) and use of technical Greek *philosophical terminology are strong arguments for Wisdom being an original composition in Greek.

About the date of Wisdom there is wider debate. Scholars have placed it anywhere between 220 B.C. and A.D. 100, often insisting that it arose during "some period of persecution" (Newsome). The earliest date is set by Wisdom's clear use of the Greek translation of Isaiah, Job and Proverbs (Clarke; Reider; Holmes). The latest date is set by the evident use of the work by several NT authors (Holmes and Reider, vs. Gilbert and Grant, who express reservations concerning demonstrable dependence).

A date within the early Roman period, especially the principate, seems most likely. First, the description of the development of the ruler cult in Wisdom 14:16-20 best describes not the cult of the *Ptolemies, which was organized and promoted from the center, but the spontaneous, decentralized development of the imperial cult under Augustus (who was also Egypt's first remote ruler since *Alexander the Great; Winston). The use of thirty-five terms or constructions that do not appear in secular Greek before the first century A.D. further supports the argument for a Roman date (Winston). M. Gilbert detects a critique of the **pax Romana* in Wisdom 14:22: "though living in great strife due to ignorance, they call such great evils peace" (cf. Tacitus *Agric.* 30). Pseudo-Solomon's address to the "judges of the ends of the earth, . . . who rule over multitudes and boast of many nations" also fits the Roman imperial period better than its predecessors (Wis 6:1; Winston).

D. Winston revives the theory advanced by A. Farrar and A. T. S. Goodrick that the work comes specifically from the reign of Gaius, responding to the "desperate historical situation" of the Jews under Flaccus. It is not, however, necessary to posit a situation of open persecution in order to understand the "ferocious passion" with which the author narrates "the annihilation of the wicked" in Wisdom 5:16-23 as well as the particularly intense anti-Egyptian sentiments of the work. The Jews, for centuries under the cultural hegemony of *Hellenism, had been struggling to find ways to reaffirm their ancestral heritage in the face of a dominant majority that devalued that heritage. Such rhetoric as we find in Wisdom would have been a welcome reinforcement for Jewish commitment at any period, and the tone of hostility within the document may be intended more to promote a "we versus they" mentality in order to guard against assimilation.

2. Structure and Contents.

The contents of Wisdom fall into three major sections, and the skill with which the author has woven these together accounts for the difficulty scholars have in agreeing where one section ends and the next begins. Thus S. Holmes ends the first section at Wisdom 6:8, but J. D. Newsome at Wisdom 6:11 and Winston at Wisdom 6:21; Newsome ends the second section at Wisdom 9:18, but Winston at Wisdom 10:21 and Holmes at Wisdom 11:1. The first two parts are connected by an interlocking structure in Wisdom 6. Wisdom 6:1-11 returns to the themes of Wisdom 1:1-11 (an inclusio) with the address to the "rulers of the world" (Wis 1:1) and the assurance of God's inquiry into human ways. Wisdom 6:21, however, also looks back to Wisdom 1:1, offering a second conclusion to the section as it addresses the "monarchs over the people." Wisdom 6:12-20 introduces the theme of section two, namely, the nature, works and rewards of Wisdom. It is also difficult to discern where the third section begins. Wisdom 10:1 begins to elaborate on Wisdom 9:18, where Wisdom is credited with saving the people who received her, and thus continues the discussion of Wisdom's works; at Wisdom 11:4, Wisdom recedes into the background and God is addressed directly as the one who punishes the ungodly and delivers the righteous (a shift, however, for which the author again prepares in Wis 10:20). Any attempt to mark a definite beginning to this third section will be in some sense arbitrary, for the author effects a smooth transition from the praise of Wisdom's character and works to Wisdom's saving activity and God's saving activity. The thesis of this third section is announced in Wisdom 11:5 ("through the very things by which their enemies were punished, they themselves received benefit in their need"), and so we may for convenience mark the section's beginning here.

Wisdom opens with an invitation to the "rulers of the earth" (Wis 1:1) to pursue justice in a spirit of reverence for God. The first section contrasts vividly the fate of the "ungodly," who "made a covenant with death" by their unsound reasoning (Wis 1:16—2:1), and that of the righteous, who remain faithful to their training in the law and live with an eye to God's approval. Even though the ungodly may oppress the righteous in this life, before God's judgment seat the righteous will be exalted and the ungodly punished and put to shame. The second section presents the origin, character, deeds and rewards of Wisdom. Here the author takes on most fully the persona of Solomon, expanding on the account of Solomon's prayer for Wisdom and God's response (1 Kings 3:5-15) and on Solomon's joy and benefits from receiving Wisdom. As Wisdom's saving acts on behalf of the patriarchs are recounted, the author arrives at the recollection of the exodus and moves into the third section of his work. Within this third part are seven antitheses, contrasting God's punishment of the Egyptians with God's provision for the Israelites (Wis 11:1-14; 16:1-4; 16:5-14; 16:15-29; 17:1—18:4; 18:5-25; 19:1-9; Winston). These are intended to demonstrate the thesis found in Wisdom 11:5 (see above) and, secondarily, the thesis of Wisdom 11:16 ("one is punished by the very things by which one sins"). This demonstration includes two excurses on God's compassion (Wis 11:15—12:22) and the folly of idolatry (Wis 13—15). Part three returns to the themes of part one, especially the vivid contrast between the fate of the ungodly and of God's chosen people, and in the denunciation of "foolish" ways of thinking (from which the audience is therefore to distance itself).

3. Genre and Purpose.

Winston and J. M. Reese regard the work as a "protreptic" discourse—an exhortation to take up a particular course of action. Winston insightfully notes that the author shows that the pursuit of Wisdom is "just, lawful, expedient, honorable, pleasant, and easily practicable" (*Rhet. ad Alex.* 1421b21 on the requirements for successful exhortation; cf. Wis 6:12-14; 8:7, 10, 16, 18). Gilbert has also cogently argued that the form of Wisdom fits the form of the encomium, the speech in praise of some figure or virtue. Wisdom 1—5 briefly sums up the theme, shows the harmful results of failing to pursue the virtue being praised, criticizes those who neglect the subject of the encomium and shows the "difficult or paradoxical situations" in which such people find themselves; Wisdom 6—10 discourses on the origin, nature and deeds of the subject; Wisdom 11—19 demonstrates the benefits of pursuing this virtue through examples, and especially through *synkrisis* (the comparison with the opposite line of action). Within this section of the encomium there is room for digressions, "to fortify the resolution of the reader." Reese, though calling it protreptic, describes its function in terms more appropriate for encomium: the author writes "to glorify traditional faith and encourage Israel's future leaders to commit themselves to God's presence in history," "arousing enthusiasm for Israel's covenant-God and for its historical mission."

The observations of all three scholars may be appreciated when one considers the relatedness of "praise and counsel" in classical rhetoric (see Aristotle *Rhet.* 1.9.35-36; Quintilian *Inst. Orat.* 3.7.28). Moreover, encomia in themselves seek to encourage adherence to specific *virtues or a certain way of life by means of praise. In the case of Wisdom, Gilbert's analysis of the form is stronger, but the author enhances the general hortatory potential of the encomium with direct exhortations (frequently present in encomia: see Thucydides *Hist.* 2.43.1-4; Dio Chrysostom *Or.* 29.21; 4 Macc 18:1) to pursue wisdom and with the promises that such a way of life is easily obtained, honorable and just.

Questions of the purpose of the book are connected with the picture one forms of the audience. According to B. M. Metzger, Wisdom attempts to rekindle in apostate Jews a "genuine zeal for God and his law" (so also Winston, Reider, Clarke), provides for faithful Jews facing disappointment or persecution an "apologia that was calculated to encourage and fortify their faith and practice" (so also most scholars) and possibly addresses "thoughtful pagans" in chapters 6—9 and 13—15 on the truth of Judaism and folly of idolatry, respectively (so Clarke and Reider, who claims this "missionary" purpose for "Alexandrian-Jewish literature generally"; *see* Proselytism).

It is difficult to determine the audience envisioned by the author, but one can begin to assess the effectiveness of the work for the various proposals. The only explicit addressees in the work are Gentile rulers (Wis 1:1; 6:1, 9, 21) and God (Wis 10:20; 11:4; 15:1). It is unlikely, however, that the work would have been received kindly by either a local ruler or the emperor, given the explicit announcements of the rulers' wickedness and impending judgment. The author's delegitimation of the imperial cult would have made the work more suspect than persuasive. To the author's critique of idolatry, Metzger's "thoughtful pagans" would have said about idols the same thing Wisdom says about the bronze serpent (Wis 16:7): they certainly did not worship stone and metal but by means of such could revere the invisible deity. Also relevant here is Metzger's correct observation that the author was writing in a "high-context" environment—the readers would have to supply missing information, particularly names and episodes from the Pentateuchal narratives for much of Wisdom 10. If the author wrote to persuade Gentiles, he wrote most ineffectively.

Much more can be said for a Jewish audience (Reese). The work might open up the possibility of a return for apostates, if there remained some doubt in their mind about their choice and if they cared to read the work. Wisdom would be most effective, however, for an audience of faithful Jews. Part one assures them, in the manner of Psalms 37, 49 and 73 (Holmes), that the apostate Jews are the ones who have departed from the truth. Even if the apostates' temporal enjoyments have increased and even if they have gained the upper hand over the loyal Jews (Reider), God's court will reveal their folly and the honor of the righteous. Parts two and three encourage loyal Jews to persist in their way of life by recalling God's special relationship with them throughout history (Winston). The polemic against idolatry assures them that their way of life is the truly enlightened one, while the Gentiles and apostates, despite their pretensions, grope in darkness. The author's use of Greek philosophical terminology enhances his claim that "Judaism need not take second place to anything in Hellenism" (Clarke). Wisdom is thus surely written to encourage continued adherence to the Jewish way of life in a setting where the enticements of Hellenization and the ability of apostates to reject their heritage as of little value weigh heavily upon the Jewish consciousness.

4. Important Themes.

*4.1. **Vindication of the Righteous.*** The author takes pains to develop the unsound reasoning of the "ungodly" (Wis 2:1-20). Holmes and J. Reider have noted the similarities here with Ecclesiastes, especially in looking at this life as the "lot" or "portion" of humans and therefore making the securing of enjoyment in this life a high priority (cf. Eccl 3:22; 5:18; 9:9). Ecclesiastes, however, does not promote neglect of God or hostility toward the righteous, as do the impious in Wisdom 2. The "ungodly" whom the author has in view are, at least in part, apostate Jews (Reider; Winston; Clarke; Gilbert). The text supports this, as the "ungodly" are said to have gone against their training, sinned against the law and fallen away from God (Wis 2:12; 3:10). The opening motif of making a "covenant with death" (Wis 1:16) recalls Isaiah's description of the activity and lifestyle of the apostate rulers of Jerusalem, who had abandoned their ancestral ways and religion (Is 28:15). Their speech in Wisdom 2:1-9 has some Epicurean elements (the denial of judgment, afterlife and involvement of God in human affairs), but the ungodly take this in a direction that *Epicurus would never have endorsed.

Wisdom draws a picture of high tension not only between the loyal Jews and the Gentiles but also between loyal and apostate Jews. Despite the apparent success of the apostates in this life, however, and despite the insult and abuse that they might heap on their former coreligionists, Wisdom assures the audience that God will honor the righteous with the prize of immortality (Wis 2:21—3:9) while showering disgrace and punishment on those who have not kept to God's ways (Wis 3:10; 4:17-19). Beyond death, the apostates and all the Gentiles will confess their error and acknowledge the lasting honor of the loyal Jew. A firm belief in a judgment and reward beyond this life becomes in this period an essential part of sustaining commitment to the values of a minority culture, whether Judaism or Christianity.

*4.2. **Personification of Wisdom.*** The figure of Wisdom (derived from Prov 1:20-33; 8:22-31; Job 28:12-28) is developed to new heights of personification, even hypostatization. Like *Philo, Pseudo-Solomon speaks of wisdom as an emanation of God rather than a created being: "she is a breath of the power of God, and a pure emanation of the glory of the Almighty, . . . a reflection of eternal light, a spotless mirror of the working of God and an image of his goodness" (Wis 7:25-26). Wisdom is God's companion and agent in the creation and ongoing governance of the world (Wis 8:1; 9:9). While Reider goes too far to find in Wisdom a "throne partner" in Wisdom 6:14 and 9:4, she nevertheless affords the most intimate fellowship between God and human beings: she participates in God and, entering human souls, makes them friends of God (Wis 7:27-28). This Wisdom can be attained only through *prayer (Wis 7:7; 8:21—9:18), and while she is not here identified with the Torah as in

Ben Sira (*see* Sirach), she does teach what pleases God, and this involves keeping the commandments (Wis 6:18; 9:9).

Despite the author's interest in the special relationship between God and Israel, he defines Wisdom broadly enough to encompass also the whole realm of learning (Wis 7:17-22). That Wisdom that the one God alone can give also grants facility in all the subjects comprehended within "the curriculum in a Greek school: philosophy, physics, history, astronomy, zoology, religion, botany, medicine" (Crenshaw). Thus training in Jewish wisdom would afford one all the benefits of Greek education. This made Wisdom "the perfect bridge between the exclusive nationalist tradition of Israel and the universalist philosophical tradition which appealed so strongly to the youth of Roman Alexandria" (Winston). B. L. Mack has also shown how Pseudo-Solomon adapts the aretalogies (lists of virtues) of the popular Egyptian goddess Isis to promote the figure of Wisdom. Isis was a revealer, a savior figure (cf. Apuleius *Met.* 12), and, as Maʿat, the Egyptian goddess of wisdom, an associate of the chief deity who knows all his works. The advances made by Pseudo-Solomon concerning the figure of Wisdom as mediator between God and creation proved helpful for the early church as it wrestled with the person of the Son.

4.3. Critique of Idolatry and Gentile Rulers. In its fictive address to the "monarchs of the earth," Wisdom expressed a widely held Jewish critique of Gentile rulers. The author upbraids them because, while they had received their authority from God, they failed to honor God, disregarded the law (Torah; cf. Wis 18:4) and neglected to rule rightly and serve God's purposes (Wis 6:1-8; cf. Dan 2:37; 4:16-17, 26-27; 5:20-23; 4 Macc 12:11-12). Gentile kings are indicted as dishonorable clients of the one God and are called either to repent or face the wrath of the God whom they have disregarded. Such a critique would have encouraged those loyal Jews who felt the sting of injustice and who saw the preferential treatment awarded the apostates. The Torah-observant Jews' loyalty to the one God would assure them of vindication against their enemies when God searched out iniquity.

The author presents a lengthy argument against the legitimacy of idolatrous religion (Wis 13:1—15:19), developing criticisms from tradition (e.g., Is 44:9-20) but taking the overall polemic to a new level of sophistication. The author first reprimands those who worship natural objects such as the sun, moon and stars: while they are less blameworthy, they are still faulted for not pushing beyond fascination with created things to the adoration of the Creator (Wis 13:1-9; cf. Rom 1:19-21, 25). More reprehensible are those who worship lifeless objects—the idols that abounded in Gentile religions. The author constructs a reductio ad absurdum reminiscent of the Epistle of Jeremiah. A skilled woodcutter makes some fine utensil, uses some of the cast-off wood for a fire that heats his food and uses another scrap to fashion an idol. Pseudo-Solomon frames a series of paradoxes to show the folly of such religion: the idolater prays about an upcoming voyage to a thing that cannot move, about matters of life to a lifeless piece of wood (Wis 13:10—14:11; 15:7-17). The impropriety of idolatrous cult is poignantly expressed in Wisdom 14:11, which suggests that idolaters use the material of God's own creation to promote a cult that dishonors the Creator. Pseudo-Solomon also incorporates Euhemerus's explanation of the origin of the pagan gods in the divinization of deceased human beings (Wis 14:12-16).

Most insightful is Pseudo-Solomon's explanation of the origins of *ruler cult. He clearly recognized its origins in the desire on the part of the subject people to demonstrate their loyalty and gratitude to the distant ruler. The imperial cult represents their attempt to establish a language of diplomacy and a favorable relationship with the center of power, but Pseudo-Solomon goes on to suggest that the paraphernalia of the cult made the human origins of the king dangerously obscure. Winston insightfully suggests that Wisdom 7:1-1 and 9:5 combat this tendency, portraying a wise king emphasizing his own humble and mortal origins.

Idolatry is blameworthy not only for the affront it presents to the one God who made heaven and earth (Wis 14:21b) but also because it is the "beginning of fornication" and "corruption of life" (Wis 14:12). It is the "cause and the end of every evil," including murder, orgies, violation of marriage, theft, deceit, corruption, perjury, disloyalty, ingratitude and sexual perversion (Wis 14:22-31; cf. Rom 1:22-32). The association of Gentile religion with all things base assists the author's audience to remain steadfast in their commitment to true religion (Wis 15:1-6).

4.4. Universalism Versus Particularism. Despite

the fact that some find "an arrogant and undisguised particularism" in Wisdom, in which "God appears as a tribal god who is partial to the Jews and inimical to their enemies" (Reider), Pseudo-Solomon shows considerable interest in universalism. The matter is not as simple as Reider claims: "sinning Jews are freed from punishment, but God hates the sinning Canaanites and exterminates them for their sins." Pseudo-Solomon argues that God loves all that God has created and detests none of God's works (Wis 11:24—12:1). In this first excursus within part three, the author seeks an explanation of God's destruction of the Canaanites and punishment of the Egyptians beyond an appeal merely to God's election of Israel. The author of 2 Maccabees could write that God corrects Israel little by little so as to discipline and restore them but saves up punishment against the Gentiles to destroy them all at once (2 Macc 6:13-16), but Wisdom points to God's judging out the Canaanites "little by little" (Wis 12:10) in order to lead them to repentance. Only after this fails on account of the depth to which wickedness has taken root in the Gentiles does God finally destroy them.

There is a tension between universalism and particularism in Wisdom, since the Gentile nations are so steeped in evil that their very nature is perverse and incorrigible: nevertheless it is noteworthy to find this author attempting to weave this together with a view of God in keeping with ethical monotheism, in which punishment must never be "arbitrary or merely retributive" but rather "reformative" (Holmes). Moreover, as Winston observes, Wisdom herself is *philanthrōpos* ("benevolent, humane; Wis 1:6; 7:23), as is God, whose mercy is an example for God's people to follow (Wis 12:19). Thus even if Gentiles should persist in disregarding the righteous and rebelling against God (Wis 3:10), the righteous are called to be imitators of God's benevolence rather than their neighbors' hostility.

5. Greco-Roman Philosophical Influence. Pseudo-Solomon, while promoting loyalty to the Jewish worship of the one God, nevertheless supports his appeal with concepts taken over from Greek philosophy. Part of his appeal to his readers was this incipient synthesis of the best of the Greek tradition with the Jewish tradition. The pursuit of God-given Wisdom trains the devotee in the four cardinal virtues prized by *Stoics and *Platonists (Wis 8:7; cf. 4 Macc 1:16-18; 5:22-24). Solomon's choice of Wisdom (Wis 8:2-18) mirrors Xenophon's account of the similarly noble choice of Heracles (*Mem.* 2.1; Holmes). The author thus claims that the Jewish way of life produces the same noble virtues prized by Hellenic culture.

Pseudo-Solomon holds to the Platonic view that God created the cosmos "out of formless matter" (Wis 11:17; vs. 2 Macc 7:28, where creation is explicitly *ex nihilo*). Wisdom herself takes on the roles of the Stoic *Logos,* as mediator between God and creation in all things, and the Stoic *Pneuma,* the all-pervading force that animates all things (Wis 1:7; 7:24; 8:1; Gilbert). This latter concept is employed to express human accountability before God, for all human acts and words are exposed to Wisdom's all-pervading gaze (Wis 1:7-11). The author also uses the Stoic term *pronoia* ("providence," Wis 6:7; 14:3; 17:2) to express God's oversight and care for God's creation.

The anthropology of the book also shows striking connections with Platonic thought, beginning with the doctrine of the preexistence of souls, attested here for the first time in Jewish writing (Wis 8:19-20). The soul enters a body, which is conceived of as a "burden" to the soul, an "earthly tent" that weighs down the mind (Wis 9:15). Only God's gift of the Holy Spirit can assist the human mind in the quest for spiritual truths. Pseudo-Solomon's dependence on Plato at this point comes close to direct borrowing (cf. the remarkable similarities of word choice with Plato *Phaed.* 81 C; Holmes). Reider is wrong to attribute to Pseudo-Solomon the view that the body is "essentially evil, and that therefore an evil nature attaches to the human body (1.4)," since the point of Wisdom 1:4 is not that the body is itself evil, but that Wisdom cannot dwell in a deceitful soul or a body that is enslaved to sin (i.e., the wicked person). It can, however, dwell in the noble soul and in the body that is not an instrument of unrighteousness. Finally, the author shares the Platonic idea of the immortality of the soul, stressing that one's moral character determines one's place in the afterlife. Winston points out how Jewish writers have moved closer and closer to the Platonic position (cf. *1 Enoch* 102:5; 103:3-4; 104:6; *Jub.* 23:31; *T. Asher* 6:5-6; 4 Macc 7:19; 13:17; 16:23).

The author displays an allegorizing tendency, but not full-blown as in the Stoic treatment of the Homeric myths or Philo's handling of Torah. Thus the miracle of manna in the wilderness and the dissolution of the leftover portion teaches that "one must rise before the sun to give You thanks, and must pray to You at the dawning of the light; for the hope of an ungrateful person will melt like wintry frost" (Wis 16:27-29).

6. Influence on the Early Church.

6.1. New Testament Christology. Wisdom's depiction of the persecution of the righteous person (Wis 2:12-20) may have been read very early as a prediction of Christ's passion. Matthew himself adds to the taunt of Psalm 22:8 the rationale "for he said, 'I am the Son of God' " (Mt 27:43), the claim that the ungodly seek to test in Wisdom 2:13, 18-20. Augustine (*Civ. D.* 17.20) would go on to quote this passage explicitly as a prophecy of the crucifixion. The author of Hebrews presents the Son as the "reflection of the glory of God and exact imprint of God's nature" (Heb 1:3), thus understanding Christ's relationship to God in terms very similar to those used to describe Wisdom's relationship to God (Wis 7:26; Grant). Colossians 1:15 appears also to move in this direction, speaking of Jesus as the "image of the invisible God."

6.2. Pauline Anthropology. The most pervasive influence of Wisdom surfaces in the writings of Paul, rendering R. M. Grant's judgment that "Paul, like John, knew ideas related to Wisdom but not the book itself" highly suspect.

6.2.1. Romans. Paul's statement on the depravity of humanity on account of idolatry in Romans 1:19-32 shows strong signs of Wisdom's influence (Wis 13:1-9; 14:22-27). Both move through the same progression of thought: Gentiles ought to have been able to perceive the one God through observation of creation and so are "without excuse" (Wis 13:1-9; Rom 1:19-20); Gentiles instead turned to the worship of created things (Wis 13:2, 7; Rom 1:22-23); this ignorance of God (Wis 14:22; Rom 1:21, 25) produced all manner of wickedness, including murder, theft, deceit and sexual perversion (Wis 14:22-27; Rom 1:24, 26-31); God's just sentence remains on those who practice such deeds (Wis 14:30-31; Rom 1:32).

Paul affirms God's absolute sovereignty over the human being as God's creation in terms similar to Ben Sira 33:10-13: all are as clay in the hands of the potter, "to be given whatever he decides." Romans 9:21 shares this thought, but together with a detail from Wisdom 15:7, where the potter makes "out of the same clay both the vessels that serve clean uses and those for contrary uses." Paul shares with Wisdom the view that God's judgment is not open to criticism and his will irresistible (Rom 9:19; Wis 12:12; cf. *1 Clem.* 27.5) but also stresses that God is patient, allowing opportunity for repentance (Rom 2:4; Wis 11:23; 12:19-20; cf. Acts 17:30).

6.2.2. The Corinthian Letters. Augustine implicitly noted the connection between 2 Corinthians 5:1-4 and Wisdom 9:15 when he blended the two passages together in a paraphrase. Paul views life in the body as the soul's sojourn in an "earthly tent" (2 Cor 5:1), a "burden" that makes us groan (2 Cor 5:4). Here, even though Paul weds the images with the expectation of a new dwelling (the resurrected body), the conception of the mortal body is remarkably similar to that of Wisdom 9:15. The larger context of this verse appears also to have left its mark on 1 Corinthians 2:7-12, which, together with Wisdom 9:13, 17, announces the impossibility of the earthly mind comprehending spiritual truths or the mind of God apart from receiving the Spirit from God.

6.3. Other Resonances. A number of other texts resonate with Wisdom in intriguing ways. The description of the "armor of God" in Ephesians 6:11-17 is more closely related to Wisdom 5:17-20 than to Isaiah 59:17. Both Wisdom and Ephesians speak of God's *panoplia* ("whole armor") and add references to a shield and sword beyond the helmet and breastplate. While Ephesians is clearly aware of Isaiah's description of God's armor, it also shows signs of direct awareness of Wisdom's earlier expansion of that image. Wisdom's interpretation of the trials endured by the righteous at the hands of the ungodly as God's refining of the individual for the reward of the righteous (Wis 3:5-6) appears again in 1 Peter 1:6-7. Hebrews 8:2-5 and Wisdom 9:8 move in a similar direction in their exegesis of Exodus 25:40, both stressing that the earthly temple was but a copy of the abiding tabernacle that God "prepared from the beginning." It is likely that the author of Hebrews learned this from Pseudo-Solomon (cf. his use of Wis 7:25).

Johannine echoes of Wisdom are less evident, although Wisdom's equation of knowledge of God with "complete righteousness" and "immortality" (Wis 15:3) is similar to Jesus' definition of eternal life in John 17:3. Similarly, Jesus' equation of love of him with obedience to his commandments may recall Wisdom 6:18: "love of Wisdom is the keeping of her laws." John also depicts the helplessness of the unaided, earthly mind in the face of spiritual revelation, also in the context of receiving God's Spirit (Jn 3:10-12; cf. Wis 9:14, 16-17). Finally, just as all who receive Wisdom are made "friends of God" (Wis 7:27), so all who receive the Son are made "children of God" (Jn 1:12). Such similarities suggest that John was familiar with the ideas one finds in Wisdom, though by no means necessarily directly indebted. Revelation also shares a number of concepts with Wisdom. In both, signs precede judgment (Wis 19:13; Rev 6:12-15; 8:7—9:21; 16:1-20), God seeks to stimulate repentance before visiting destruction upon the ungodly (Wis 12:2, 10, 20; Rev 14:6-7), the ungodly steadfastly refuse to repent (Wis 12:10-11; Rev 9:20-21; 16:8-11) and natural elements play a role in helping the righteous and punishing the wicked (Wis 5:17, 20-23; 16:17; Rev 8—9; 12:16; 16:1-9, 18-20). Once more the evidence does not point to direct dependence but rather to the possibility that Revelation plays out in visionary form a number of concepts already present in the Jewish wisdom traditions.

6.4. Patristic Use. Wisdom continued to exert a pervasive influence on the early church, seen most conspicuously in the Muratorian Canon listing of the book as acceptable for liturgical use. Wisdom's teaching that death entered the world because of envy, or more particularly the *devil's envy (Wis 2:24), appears frequently (*1 Clem.* 3.4; Augustine *Trin.* 4.12.15; *In Joh.* 12.10). Augustine made much use of Wisdom 9:15, frequently interrupting his argument to reflect on the difficulty of pursuing theological reflection because this "body, which is corrupt, weighs down the soul; and the earthly dwelling depresses the mind as it meditates on many things" (cf. Augustine *In Joh.* 21.1; 23.5; 35.9; 69.2; 96.4; 124.5; *Trin.* 4.5, 10; 8.2; 17.28; 24.44). This feeds naturally into his rather negative anthropology. This human state, in which the corrupt body weighs down the soul, also explains the impossibility of coming to faith through reason alone (cf. Rom 1:20 and Wis 13:1-5, which Augustine quotes side by side in *Trin.* 15.2.3). Only the gift of the Spirit, as Wisdom 9:17 goes on to read, allows the human mind to arrive at spiritual truths (Augustine *Trin.* 3.21).

Wisdom continued to have a strong impact on the church's reflection on the person of Jesus and on the doctrine of the Trinity. Ignatius weaves phrases from Wisdom 7:29-30 and 18:14-15 into his description of Christ's manifestation (Ign. *Eph.* 19; Ign. *Magn.* 8.2). Athenagoras applies Wisdom 7:25 to the Holy Spirit (Athenagoras *Leg.* 10.4), while later Alexandrian teachers apply Wisdom 7:24—8:1 to the work of the Son, the "eternal generation" of the Son by the Father and the sharing of the Father and the Son in the same essence (*homoousios;* Origen *De Princ.* 1.2.9; also *Cont. Cels.* 3.62; 5.10; 6.63; 8.14; Grant). While Origen takes this discussion in a subordinationist direction, Augustine will show that this is by no means inherent in Wisdom, for the same texts are used by him to support the complete equality of persons in the Trinity (most forcefully in *In Joh.* 21.2; 22.10; 111.2; *Trin.* 2.5.6; 2.8.14; 3.3; 4.20.27).

See also APOCRYPHA AND PSEUDEPIGRAPHA; SIRACH; TORAH; WISDOM LITERATURE AT QUMRAN.

BIBLIOGRAPHY. E. G. Clarke, *The Wisdom of Solomon* (Cambridge: Cambridge University Press, 1973); J. L. Crenshaw, *Old Testament Wisdom* (Atlanta: John Knox, 1981) 174-80; A. A. Di Lella, "Conservative and Progressive Theology: Sirach and Wisdom," *CBQ* 28 (1966) 139-54; A. Dupont-Sommer, "Les Impies du Livre de la Sagesse Sont-ils des Épicuriens?" *RHR* 111 (1935) 90-112; M. Gilbert, "Wisdom Literature," in *Jewish Writings of the Second Temple Period,* ed. M. E. Stone (CRINT 2.2; Assen: Van Gorcum; Philadelphia: Fortress, 1984) 301-13; L. L. Grabbe, *The Wisdom of Solomon* (GAP; Sheffield: Sheffield Academic Press, 1997); R. M. Grant, *After the New Testament* (Philadelphia: Fortress, 1967) 70-82; S. Holmes, "The Wisdom of Solomon," in *The Apocrypha and Pseudepigrapha of the Old Testament in English,* ed. R. H. Charles (Oxford: Oxford University Press, 1913) 518-68; S. Lange, "The Wisdom of Solomon and Philo," *JBL* 55 (1936) 293-306; B. L. Mack, *Logos und Sophia* (Göttingen: Vandenhoeck & Ruprecht, 1973); B. M. Metzger, *An Introduction to the Apocrypha* (Oxford: Oxford University Press, 1957) 65-76; J. D. Newsome, *Greeks, Romans, Jews* (Philadelphia: Trinity Press International, 1992) 363-67; J. M. Reese, "Wisdom of Solomon," in *The Oxford Companion to the Bible,* ed. B. M. Metzger and M. D. Coogan (Oxford: Oxford University Press, 1993) 803-5; J. Reider, *The Book of Wisdom*

(New York: Harper & Brothers, 1957); R. T. Siebeneck, "The Midrash of Wisdom 10-19," *CBQ* 22 (1960) 176-82; J. P. Weisengoff, "Death and Immortality in the Book of Wisdom," *CBQ* 3 (1941) 104-33; idem, "The Impious in Wisdom 2," *CBQ* 11 (1949) 40-65; D. Winston, "Solomon, Wisdom of," *ABD* 6:120-27; idem, *The Wisdom of Solomon* (AB 43; Garden City, NY: Doubleday, 1979); A. G. Wright, "The Structure of the Book of Wisdom," *Bib* 48 (1967) 165-84.

D. A. deSilva

WISDOM PERSONIFIED. *See* WISDOM OF SOLOMON.

WIVES. *See* MARRIAGE; WOMEN IN GRECO-ROMAN WORLD AND JUDAISM.

WOMEN IN GRECO-ROMAN WORLD AND JUDAISM

In the main, history is written by for and about men, and thus the techniques and sources available for the recovery of women's history must of necessity open themselves to new avenues of research. The literary works of male authors must be augmented by *inscriptions, private *letters, legal briefs, marriage contracts, grave markers (*see* Burial), vase and wall paintings, statuary and ancient artifacts commonly used in the home life and cults of women. Their world was quite different from the military, political and economic arenas of antiquity.

Societal norms differed broadly in the NT era, so that there were marked differences in the activities, liberties, status and occupations of ancient women. We shall consider domestic and social life, *marriage and sexuality, occupations and pastimes and religious expression, beginning with Hebrew women, moving next to *Hellenistic women of the eastern Mediterranean world and finally to those of *Rome.

1. Domestic Life
2. Marriage and Sexuality
3. Occupations and Pastimes
4. Religious Expression

1. Domestic Life.

1.1. Palestinian and Diaspora Women. Within the small Palestinian house lived the family consisting of the father, mother, children, *slaves and kinsfolk. Many activities were conducted on the flat roof above the main room and the two bedrooms. Houses of more affluent families had an upper story, where there were additional living quarters. The children, both boys and girls, were tended by women in their infancy, though the Hebrew father was far more involved than was common in Greek society. The father assumed the responsibility for the training of sons, while girls were afforded limited opportunities for *education. They were schooled by their mothers in the household arts and in those parts of the law that dealt with *purity issues and the responsibilities of women. These lay heavy upon women, for the law threatened with death in childbirth those who transgressed its strictures.

Though women were usually bound to the duties of home and farm, a surprising degree of liberty is attested in biblical accounts of women who itinerated with Jesus (Lk 8:1-3). Among Jewish women not living in Palestine there seems to have been considerable latitude in practice. *Philo of Alexandria, an early contemporary of Jesus and the apostle Paul, decreed that unmarried women should go only to the door of the women's quarters whereas married women might proceed as far as the front door or even pass through the streets in a litter to *pray in the *synagogue at an hour when few others would be around. In other *Diaspora circumstances Jewish women appear to have moved about quite freely.

1.2. Greek Women. Greek women tended to be the most secluded, though lower-class women were obliged to leave their homes to draw water and to trade in the marketplace. While public places were spacious and full of light, the women's quarters were small, cramped and dark. At the height of the Golden Age (475-425 B.C.), an Athenian woman of citizen class was not supposed even to show her face at the window or door. By the first century of the common era, there were wide disparities in the freedoms and respect accorded women. Some communities and families still clung to older patterns. In Tarsus, for instance, women were more heavily veiled than elsewhere, though they were considered no less lustful.

The Greek woman was thought to have less virtue than a man and to be devoid of moral conscience. Since women could not be trusted to make responsible choices, they might be compelled to remain within their own homes. While certain philosophers propounded a far more enlightened view of women, restrictive customs were the norm in many households. In some, women neither slept nor ate nor discoursed with the men. The women's quarters were said to be hotbeds of dissension and strife. Literary evidence suggests that sequestered Greek women tended to be depressed, bitter and malicious.

The choice of whether or not a child was to be reared did not belong to the mother. Regardless of her wishes, the father made the decision whether to rear the child or to have it exposed. Daughters were far more likely to be discarded than were sons. Boys were removed from their mother's tutelage at the age of seven and entered the stimulating world of men. They might be introduced to *philosophy, literature, science, politics and sports (*see* Athletics), while girls remained confined to the women's quarters. Unequal treatment began much earlier, however, and the diet of boys contained substantially more meat than was apportioned to girls.

Conversation with males outside the family was forbidden to citizen-class women, and even communication between spouses was limited. Thus the verbal exchange between the Greek woman of Syro-Phoenicia and Jesus is all the more remarkable (Mk 9:24-28).

One of the few escapes available to women was that afforded by wine, and there is evidence that drinking began early in the morning. The custom of Roman men kissing their female relatives on the mouth grew out of a desire to ensure that the women had not been tippling. It is noteworthy that temperance in drink is a prime requisite for female church officers in the NT (1 Tim 3:11; Tit 2:3).

1.3. Roman Women. A Roman woman enjoyed far greater freedom than her Greek sisters and might engage in a broader range of activities. She was accorded deep respect and enjoyed a higher position in society. The traditional Roman matron installed on the family farm was industrious, stern, frugal and chaste. Her own conduct and that of those whom she influenced was characterized by loyalty, integrity and nobility. But military, economic and political pressures drove many families off the farms and into the larger cities. Here women found themselves living in three-story tenements, bereft of the many responsibilities and duties that had previously occupied their time. Slaves were cheap and took over even the breastfeeding and rearing of the children. Women were forced to look for new ways to occupy their time and to put meaning into their lives.

Although they might participate in many aspects of the society, Roman women were bound throughout their lives to a male protector or tutor. With some notable exceptions, a woman exchanged her tutelage from one man to another: from father to husband at marriage and to a son or guardian in the event of her husband's death. The consent of the tutor was necessary for a woman to buy or sell property, to make a will or to negotiate a divorce.

Ultimate power, known as *patria potestas,* lay in the hands of the family's father or grandfather. If we are to believe the Roman imitators of Menander, who is said to have held up a mirror to real life, wife, children and slaves would conspire together to outwit the dominant male and gain their own purposes. Against this ethos, one may better understand the biblical call for unity of purpose and direction within the family.

2. Marriage and Sexuality.

2.1. Hebrew Women. The Hebrew woman married shortly after the onset of menstruation. Betrothal was arranged by the parents and contracted in a binding agreement that could be severed only by formal *divorce. This was the major ceremonial, with the signing of contracts and exchange of gifts. The marriage was consummated several months later, when the bride was taken to the home of the bridegroom. Proof of the bride's virginity was required, and she was expected to remain chaste as a wife. The married state, rather than virginity, was prized by Jewish women, and the gift of children ardently wished. There is little evidence of unchaste behavior. Divorce was not uncommon, even among devout Jews, and the causes for its justification were a matter of lively *rabbinic debate. The school of Shammai insisted that it was possible only in cases of *adultery, while the school of Hillel maintained that there might be a myriad of reasons, such as spinning in the street, talking with a stranger, a spoiled dinner, a dog bite that did not heal or finding another woman who was more attractive. The effort to draw Jesus into the debate brought a surprising response (Mk 10:2-9).

Until the reforms of Justinian, a Jewish man might legally have more than one wife at a time, a practice that may be in view in the stipulation that an elder should be "the husband of one wife" (1 Tim 3:12). Polyandry, however, was not possible for a woman, and adultery was punished harshly.

2.2. Greek Women. The Greek woman was often married at an even younger age than her Hebrew counterpart, partly out of fear that she might cease to be a virgin if there was a delay. A disproportionately high number of grave inscriptions attest to a very heavy death rate from childbirth complications among women who were too young. For the woman who escaped the dangers of childbearing, life expectancy was about thirty-seven years.

Marriageable citizen-class women were often in short supply due to the high maternal death rate and the practice of exposing baby girls. In some of the extant literature Greek women are classified by their sexual function: courtesans for companionship, concubines for the daily pleasure of the master of the house and wives to bear legitimate children and keep the house. Wives were neglected both socially and sexually, though Solon the Law Giver had decreed that a husband should visit his wife's couch at least three times a month.

Girls exposed as infants could be reared as slaves and were useful in supplying the need for other types of sexual partners. They were trained in singing, dancing and especially flute playing. Women with these skills were in demand at dinner parties in which the legitimate wife could not appear. Those with fine minds might be given the opportunity for social and intellectual discourse with males. These courtesans, known as *hetairae* ("companions") and famed for their brilliance and wit, were attached to every school of *philosophy.

*Corinth in particular was renowned for its courtesans, some of whom grew enormously wealthy as a result of their profession. Sacred prostitutes filled the sanctuary of the patron goddess, Aphrodite, and were supposed to have a particular efficacy in their prayers. Other less religious members of the occupation plied their trade in the streets and marketplace of the thriving harbor city. Greek courtesans were much in vogue in Rome, while many a Roman prostitute adopted a Greek name in imitation of her illustrious Corinthian counterparts.

2.3. Roman Women. Roman marriages were arranged when the bride was about fourteen. She married with reluctance and sometimes had to be pulled from the arms of her mother or nurse in order to be taken to the new husband's home. The day before she had dedicated her dolls in the temple of a goddess, and her hymen was perforated on a phallic statue of the god Priapus or Mutuunus Tutuunus. This last practice was bitterly condemned by the church fathers and may be part of Paul's thinking in Romans 1:26. Although a woman might free herself from the control of a tutor by producing three children, family size was limited by the use of contraceptives (especially the drug silphium), abortion and infant exposure.

Roman prostitution was frequently of a highly sordid nature. Crowded, evil-smelling brothels known as lupanara (wolf dens) housed the lower-class prostitutes while they might still earn a living. Those too old to sell their attractions faced a bitter old age and sometimes died of starvation. Higher-class courtesans could hope for a better fate, though they too might find themselves discarded at life's end. In their prime, they might draw the ardor of politicians, statesmen or poets. From writings addressed to demimondaines by the Latin elegaic poets we gain a picture of love characterized as an obsession, illness, madness or aggression.

The love affairs described by poets, both their own and those they observed around them, were not confined to the demimonde. Many were clandestine romances with married women, and clever evasion of the jealous husband was part of the game. Adultery and divorce were common in imperial Rome, and often husband and wife did not even share the same friends.

3. Occupations and Pastimes.

3.1. Jewish Women. Within doors, the typical Jewish woman ground the meal, baked the bread, cooked, cleaned and washed the clothes, as well as spinning, weaving and sewing garments for the family. Outside the house she fetched water from the village well, gathered firewood, worked in the fields, sold produce at market and drove the animals to pasture. In the community she might serve as midwife, nurse or attendant. The position of paid mourner was an important one, especially for older women. Recently discovered documents from the time of the Bar Kokhba rebellion (*see* Jewish Wars with Rome) reveal that Babitha, twice widowed, conducted her own business affairs and managed her own property. Non-Palestinian Jewish women of doubtful orthodoxy served as fortune-tellers, *magic workers and purveyors of potions.

3.2. Greek Women. Far more is known about the occupations of Greek women. They were shepherdesses, grocers, wool workers, laundresses, scribes, hairdressers, sellers of olive oil, salt, honey and sesame seed. They sold garlands, perfume, dyes, shoes and textiles in the Women's Market. Within the households of the affluent they were wetnurses, governesses, nannies and ladies' maids. As entertainers they were flute girls, dancers, acrobats, jugglers, harpists and singers. Those with more leisure learned how to read, sometimes at the same time as their children. The works of female painters, poets and philosophers were remembered and cited. The ancient novel appears to have been developed to suit the tastes of literate, Greek-reading women, especially in *Asia Minor (*see* Literacy and Book Culture).

3.3. Roman Women. A primary source of income for the Roman woman was the textile industry, in which both Priscilla and Lydia were employed. Wool working was considered an indication of virtue, even for the most aristocratic women. The occupations of the Greek women were also pursued by their Roman counterparts. Some were independent entrepreneurs. In the taverns they were innkeepers, barmaids and waitresses. In the *theater they were actresses, musicians, gymnasts and even gladiators. Slave women performed manifold domestic tasks and frequently earned their freedom. The bloody combats of the *arena drew women of every class and provided free entertainment while instilling a relish for violence and incredible cruelty (*see* Circuses and Games). Upper-class women sought to relieve their boredom by turning to athletic, literary and academic pursuits, the theater and home games such as draughts and knuckle bones. They spent enormous amounts of slave service, time and money on their own adornment. Christianity was to offer women abundant spiritual, intellectual and emotional outlets for their energies and aspirations.

4. Religious Expression.

4.1. Jewish Rites. Attendance at Jewish rites was allowed women but not particularly encouraged, while men were carefully instructed from childhood in the faith of *Israel and expected to participate in the services. An official congregation was composed of at least ten men, but women could not qualify as constituting members. Mishnaic law forbade women from carrying their infants outside the home on the *sabbath—a restriction that must have kept many women from the synagogue, though the legislation was not necessarily enforced.

Nevertheless, the Jewish woman often was accorded by her religion a place of greater *honor and integrity than was her Gentile sister. This may have been one reason for the large number of conversions to *Judaism on the part of Gentile women. It has been argued that part of the attraction was that they, unlike the men, did not have to undergo circumcision. However, women were required to maintain a kosher household and to observe the purity laws—a challenge for any woman. It may be more valid to say that women found within Judaism a greater stability and peace than they could find in the other cults available to women. There is attestation to the leadership given to Jewish congregations, with the attribution of elder, "leader of the synagogue" and "mother of the synagogue" both in Rome and in Asia Minor (*see* Thessalonica).

4.2. Greek Religion. Traditional Greek religion had frequently denied woman legitimate participation in blood sacrifices, consulting oracles, entrance to particular temples and sometimes even in offering prayers. Women often worshiped different gods from men on different days with different modes of worship in different sanctuaries. There is evidence both in Italy and in Greece that women thronged certain temples, usually bringing rather modest offerings, though inscriptions tell of construction projects funded by wealthy women. Spindle whorls dedicated to specific goddesses have been excavated in large numbers at some shrines.

Certain cults afforded women opportunities for leadership. The Fates and Furies were served only by female officiants. Even though ordinary women might not ask their advice, the gods declared their will through women sibyls at the famed oracle sites (*see* Sibylline Oracles). By the first century A.D., there was no longer a high priest of Artemis of *Ephesus but a high priestess instead. Girls of good families participated in *civic cults such as that of the weaving and presentation of new garments each year for the sacred image of Athena, initiation rites at Brauron and processions in honor of Artemis of Ephesus.

For the lower-class and slave women there

were fewer religious options. Their manner of worship was often scorned and derided by men, and there was sometimes interference with the free practice of their religion. Several cults facilitated altered states of consciousness, whether by drugs (poppy, hempseed thrown upon hot rocks, a potent brand of wild pennyroyal and mushroom), wine, ecstasy, fasting, rhythmic movements and percussion instruments. For some women, funerals and religious occasions were the only occasions on which they might leave their homes, a welcome escape for those whose daily lives left them virtually prisoners in their own homes. Dionysus, the god of wine and madness, was viewed as lord of the loud cry and liberator of women, freeing "from shuttle and from loom." Biennial Dionysiac orgies continued until at least the second century A.D.

Particular features drew repeated comment, such as the dancing upon mountains in midwinter, tearing young animals apart (*sparagmos*) and eating the flesh while it was still raw, warm and quivering (*omphagia*), and pregnancy incurred during religious celebrations. The participants were debauched, destructive of property, promiscuous, obscene and verbally abusive. One outlet for these marginalized women was raising a loud, wild cry known as the *olulugia*. The exultant shout became an indiscriminate accoutrement in the cult of several oriental gods, and the shrill vocalizing could drown out the more serious deliberations of men (cf. 1 Cor 14:34). Women were well aware that in the sway of religion they might engage in aggression that would otherwise have been impossible in a repressive society.

4.3. Roman Religion. Aristocratic Roman women supported the worship of the traditional gods of the *Roman Empire (*see* Religion, Greco-Roman; Religion, Personal). The Vestal Virgins, dedicated to the goddess of hearth and home, were considered responsible for maintaining the welfare of Rome and held enormous prestige and power. The wife of the consul led women in the yearly worship of the Good Goddess, patroness of marriage and family life. Women assumed positions of priesthood in the worship of the Roman *emperors. Several were known as high priestesses of Asia. Often these appointments had political implications, and they were reserved for women of influential families.

Ordinary women resorted to spells, curses and magic in their efforts to contact the divine. During the terror of the Punic Wars, Roman women looked to new gods for protection. Increasingly they turned to the more exotic oriental cults. Repeatedly the records speak of the worship of Dionysus, Sabazios, Cybele the Mother of the Gods, Isis and even Demeter the Earth Mother as being introduced into the Greco-Roman world by women and restricted by government regulation. Such religions centered upon individual concerns and offered personal salvation rather than the prosperity of a city or nation. The new religion of Jesus Christ fitted admirably the needs and spiritual aspirations of women throughout the empire.

See also ADULTERY, DIVORCE; CHILDREN IN LATE ANTIQUITY; FAMILY AND HOUSEHOLD; JOSEPH AND ASENETH; JUDITH; MARIA THE JEWISH ALCHEMIST; MARRIAGE; RELIGION, GRECO-ROMAN; RELIGION, PERSONAL; ROMAN SOCIAL CLASSES; ROMANCES/NOVELS, ANCIENT; SOCIAL VALUES AND STRUCTURES.

BIBLIOGRAPHY. L. J. Archer, *Her Price Is Beyond Rubies: The Jewish Woman in Greco-Roman Palestine* (Sheffield: Sheffield Academy Press, 1990); J. P. V. D. Baldson, *Roman Women: Their Habits and History* (London: Bodley Head, 1962); B. Brooten, *Women Leaders in the Ancient Synagogue* (BJS 36; Chica, CA: Scholars Press, 1982); S. Dixon, *The Roman Mother* (Norman: University of Oklahoma Press, 1989); E. Fanham et al., *Women in the Classical World: Image and Text* (Oxford: Oxford University Press, 1994); H. P. Foley, *Reflections of Women in Antiquity* (New York: Gordon & Breach Science Publishers, 1981); S. K. Heyob, *The Cult of Isis Among Women in the Greco-Roman World* (Leiden: E. J. Brill, 1975); T. Ilan, *Jewish Women in Greco-Roman Palestine* (Peabody, MA: Hendrickson, 1996); R. S. Kraemer, *Her Share of the Blessings: Women's Religions Among Pagans, Jews and Christians in the Greco-Roman World* (New York: Oxford University Press, 1992); W. K. Lacey, *The Family in Classical Greece* (Ithaca, NY: Cornell University Press, 1968); M. R. Lefkowitz and M. B. Fant, *Women's Life in Greece and Rome: A Source Book in Translation* (Baltimore: Johns Hopkins University Press, 1993); S. B. Pomeroy, *Goddesses, Whores, Wives and Slaves: Women in Classical Antiquity* (New York: Schocken, 1975); B. Rawson, ed., *The Family in Ancient Rome: New Perspectives* (Ithaca, NY: Cornell University Press, 1986); L. Swidler, *Women in Judaism: The Status of Women in Formative Judaism* (Metuchen, NJ: Scarecrow, 1976).

C. C. Kroeger

WORDS OF MOSES (1Q22)

The opening lines of *Words of Moses* leave no doubt that this composition is intended as a rewritten Deuteronomy text (*see* Rewritten Bible). Like Deuteronomy, it begins with an introduction that situates a farewell address by *Moses to the congregation of Israel in Moab, in the fortieth year after the departure from Egypt, on the first day of the eleventh month. Unfortunately, only thirty-two small fragments of a single manuscript survive, but on the basis of J. T. Milik's skillful reconstruction the general content of the first four columns is reasonably clear.

1. Contents
2. Distinctive Characteristics

1. Contents.

In what is preserved, there are four distinct parts. (1) God summons Moses (1:1-11a) and instructs him to convocate the people; to ascend (location lost, but presumably) Mt. Nebo accompanied by Eleazar and Joshua, as becomes apparent from 1:12; to "interpret" the *Torah to the heads of the levitical families and all the priests but to "command" it to the sons of *Israel; to call the heavens and earth as witnesses that the people will abandon God and go after foreign gods, that they will "tr[ansgress every ho]ly [convocation], the sabbath of the covenant, [and the festivals] which I am commanding you today [to d]o," and that God promises to punish them in the land with the covenantal curses until they are destroyed. (2) Moses summons Eleazar and Joshua and instructs them to speak all the words of the Torah, followed by an admonition to observe God's laws (1:11b—2:5a). (3) Moses summons the people and advises them to appoint wise leaders to interpret the Torah for them, and he sternly warns them to be careful to observe the Torah (2:5b-11a). (4) Moses declares God's decrees to the people (2:11b-?). In what survives, this consists of laws concerning the sabbatical year, the Day of Atonement and probably the Feast of Weeks (frag. 41; *see* Festivals and Holy Days). The rest of the scroll is lost. It probably contained at least regulations for the other festivals and the *sabbath, as well as other laws regarded as important to the author, and may have ended with the death of Moses.

The composition can partly be explained as a condensation of Deuteronomy and expansion by harmonizing with other parts of Scripture, especially Leviticus and Numbers. For example, a speech by God to Moses only hinted at in Deuteronomy (1:3) is added; aspects from various discourses in Deuteronomy are combined into a single discourse by setting Moses' farewell speech to the nation (cf. Deut 1:3) on Mt. Nebo (cf. Deut 34:1) and transforming a warning against sinning (cf. Deut 4:25-28) into a prophecy (cf. Deut 31:14-22, 27); the *festival regulations draw heavily on Leviticus. But the reworking is more substantial and purposeful than this explanation would suggest. With heavy use of biblical phrasing, the author effectively creates a new work—albeit one that is regarded as faithful to Deuteronomy—according to a different plan that reflects the concerns of his own community.

2. Distinctive Characteristics.

Several distinctive characteristics can be perceived. First, there is a concern to emphasize the divinely mandated authority of community leaders, and particularly the priestly succession to the authority of Moses in teaching Torah. Moses speaks only what God tells him to. Eleazar and Joshua accompany Moses on the mountain and serve as mediators of the instruction. The levitical leaders and *priests receive a special interpretation of Torah from Moses by God's direction. Analogous idealization of the successors to Mosaic authority appears in *Josephus (Josephus *Ant.* 4.8.14 §218) and probably underlies certain authority structures in the sectarian scrolls (e.g., priest, overseer and judges, elders and council). Second, calendrical matters are made a central concern by adding violation of appointed times to the sin of idolatry (cf. Deut 4:25-28) as grounds for the foretold destruction (similarly *Jub.* 1:7-11) and by focusing immediately on regulations for the festivals in the legal section. Third, the Day of Atonement rituals are on behalf of the land as well as the people, a concern that is emphasized in the sectarian scrolls (e.g., **Rule of the Community* [1QS] 8:6, 10; 9:4-5; **Rule of the Congregation* [1QSa] 1:3). Fourth, the date of the Day of Atonement—the tenth day of the seventh month—seems to be identified as the date when the wilderness wanderings ended. The tendency to link festivals with events in the history of Israel is a characteristic trait of *Jubilees*.

Although such concerns are common to sectarian literature from *Qumran, there is no direct indication of sectarian origin. 1Q22 belongs broadly within a large body of texts that more or less closely rewrite Scripture. More specifically, it should be regarded as a Moses pseudepigraphon because most of the content is presented as direct discourse from Moses (*see* Pseudonymity and Pseudepigraphy). J. Strugnell suggested that it may be another copy of the **Apocryphon of Moses* B from Qumran Cave 4 (4Q375, 4Q376), but the similarities (concerning the Day of Atonement ritual) are remote and probably contradictory. Other closely related Moses pseudepigrapha include Pseudo-Moses[a-e] from Qumran Cave 4 (4Q385a, 4Q387a, 4Q388a, 4Q389, 4Q390) and **Testament of Moses*. The manuscript was not dated by the editor, but the handwriting is closest to other Qumran manuscripts dated around 100 B.C.

See also APOCRYPHAN OF MOSES (1Q29, 4Q374-377, 4Q408); MOSES; REWRITTEN BIBLE IN PSEUDEPIGRAPHA AND QUMRAN; TESTAMENT OF MOSES.

BIBLIOGRAPHY. J. Carmignac, "Dires de Moïse," in *Les textes de Qumran,* ed. J. Carmignac, É. Cothenet and H. Lignée (Paris: Letouzey et Ané, 1963) 2:247-53; idem, "Quelques détails de lecture dans . . . les Dires de Moïse," *RevQ* 4 (1963) 88-96; E. Cook, "The Words of Moses," in *The Dead Sea Scrolls: A New Translation,* ed. M. O. Wise, M. Abegg Jr. and E. Cook (New York: HarperSanFrancisco, 1996) 172-74; M. Delcor, "Qumrân: Dires de Moïse," *DBSup* 9:910-11; A. Dupont-Sommer, *The Essene Writings from Qumran* (Oxford: Blackwell, 1961) 307-10; O. Eissfeldt, *The Old Testament: An Introduction* (Oxford: Blackwell, 1965) 664-65; D. K. Falk, "Moses, Texts of," in *Encyclopedia of the Dead Sea Scrolls,* ed. L. Schiffman and J. VanderKam (New York: Oxford University Press, 2000); J. T. Milik, "Dires de Moïse," in *Qumran Cave 1,* ed. D. Barthélemy and J. T. Milik (DJD 1; Oxford: Clarendon Press, 1955) 91-97; J. Strugnell, "Moses-Pseudepigrapha at Qumran: 4Q375, 4Q376 and Similar Works," in *Archaeology and History in the Dead Sea Scrolls: The New York University Conference in Memory of Yigael Yadin,* ed. L. Schiffman (Sheffield: JSOT, 1990) 221-56; G. Vermes, "The Words of Moses," in *The History of the Jewish People in the Age of Jesus Christ (175 B.C.-A.D. 135),* rev. and ed. G. Vermes, F. Millar and M. Goodman (3 vols. Edinburgh: T & T Clark, 1973-87) 3.1:424-25.

D. K. Falk

WORDS OF THE LUMINARIES (4Q504-506). *See* LITURGY: QUMRAN.

WORKS OF THE MESSIAH. *See* MESSIANIC APOCALYPSE (4Q521).

WORSHIP, JEWISH. *See* LITURGY: QUMRAN; LITURGY: RABBINIC; SACRIFICE AND TEMPLE SERVICE.

WRITING AND LITERATURE: GRECO-ROMAN

The NT is, in fact, a collection (twenty-seven discrete documents) of Greco-Roman literary texts, although the precise categorizations of the NT texts in relationship to the larger reality of Greco-Roman literature remain an area of debate among scholars (see Aune). The NT texts are written in Hellenistic Greek, although the levels and styles of Greek vary among these texts to significant degrees.

There is little explicit self-consciousness of Greco-Roman literature among the authors of the NT texts. Acts 17:18 refers to the Epicurean and Stoic philosophical "schools." In this context, Acts' report of Paul's speech includes a citation (Acts 17:28; "some of your own poets have said") of a line from the Stoic author Aratus's poem *Phaenomena* in its proem to Zeus (line 5). This poem was the most widely read poem in the ancient world apart from the *Iliad* and the *Odyssey*. Titus 1:12 cites a Cretan prophet, usually identified with the seventh/sixth century Epimenides, whose prophetic and divine gifts were noted by Plato, Aristotle, Plutarch and Diogenes Laertius. 1 Corinthians 15:33 contains a maxim which is probably from the epigrammatic lore of Menander, a fourth/third century author of comedies. None of these data establish as fact that any NT author read directly or regularly these or similar texts; it is possible that these citations were known from anthologies and/or from general oral tradition (*see* Pagan Sources in the New Testament).

In spite of the complexities of placing the NT texts in the context of Greco-Roman literature and of the limited explicit use of such literature within the NT, the literature of the Greco-Roman period is an important and crucial resource and context for the study of the NT.

1. Writing and Reading, and Literary Production and Publication
2. Types of Greco-Roman Literature
3. Accessing Greco-Roman Literature

4. Emerging Issues for New Testament Studies

1. Writing and Reading, and Literary Production and Publication.

1.1. Writing and Reading. Although the Greco-Roman world was primarily an oral/aural culture, writing and written literature were a very significant part of the social and cultural fabric of life (*see* Literacy and Book Culture). Even the nascent church, as evidenced by the many writings in the NT and by the substantial Christian literature of the second century A.D., participated in a meaningful way in the literary culture of the Greco-Roman world (see Gamble).

It is very difficult to determine the levels of literacy in the Greco-Roman world, but it is likely that the usual level of literacy was between 10 and 20 percent of the population, with probably local variations up to 30 percent (see Harris). Probably for every five or six men who could read and write, there was one woman who was fully literate. Of course, there must have been an indeterminate number of persons who had limited degrees of literacy.

Most literate persons probably learned to read and write in the context of the *educational systems within Greco-Roman culture (see Bonner). Some (many?) nonliterate persons would have had access to some literature through both formal readers (Gk *anagnōstēs;* Lat *lector*) as well as informal readers among family and friends. Revelation 1:3 attests to the practice of public reading of written texts in group settings (presumably, this was how most of the texts of the NT were communicated to the churches which first received them).

Certainly individuals acquired collections of scrolls and books, attested as early as the fifth century B.C. Aristotle and Strato had large personal collections (see 2 Tim 3:13 for a reference to a modest personal collection of books; Lk 1:1-4; Jn 21:25 and 2 Pet 3:15-16 probably also reflect an awareness of the collection of books). The first institutional libraries appear to be those of Hellenistic monarchs. The most famous libraries of the Greco-Roman period were those at Pergamum (about 200,000 rolls) and Alexandria (about 500,000 rolls; *see* Alexandrian Library). Vitruvius, the first-century writer on architecture, mentions libraries.

1.2. Literary Production and Publication. Most writing in the Greco-Roman period, at least through the first century A.D., was done on papyrus, although the skins of sheep and goats were prepared for use in writing as well (parchment; finer skins: vellum). For literary works, papyrus sheets (or parchment pieces) were attached and made into rolls, or scrolls (see Lk 4:17 and Rev 5:1 for mention of scrolls in the NT). The standard length was probably about thirty-five feet. To some degree, the length of commercially available rolls probably determined for authors the length of individual books (see Gamble).

The development of the book, or codex (bound and written on both sides), is not completely clear; the earliest certain references appear to be in first-century A.D. authors (Martial; Quintillian). There is physical evidence for the existence of the book in the early second century A.D. (e.g., P^{52}, a papyrus book fragment of the Gospel of John). Although Christians did not invent the book form, second-century Christians apparently preferred the codex earlier and to a greater proportion than the non-Christian Greco-Roman culture (see Gamble; Roberts and Skeat).

Most literary composition was done with pen and ink. There are Greco-Roman discussions of ink in Dioscorides (*Mat. Med.* 5.117), Vitruvius (*De Arch.* 7.10) and Pliny the Elder (*Nat. Hist.* 24, 27 and 28; see 2 Jn 12 and 3 Jn 13 for references to pen and ink). Authors would have written either in their own hand or used secretaries or scribes (see Rom 16:22 for the personal attestation of a scribe by name).

Authors had few protections for the integrity and security of their literary productions. There were no commercial publishers. Authors probably moved from oral presentations and/or single copies given to friends and colleagues to the use of professional scribes for the production of multiple copies of a literary work. The production of multiple copies was probably in the first instance for a circle of friends and colleagues, before broader circulation to the general literate public. Many authors were aided in the processes of publication by wealthy friends committed to the dissemination of an author's work (*see* Patronage). There were varying levels of scribal expertise, which would affect the quality of production. There is very little evidence that multiple copies were produced by several scribes listening together to one reader; rather, most scribes made one copy at a time by copying from an exemplar (see Gamble).

Authors experienced various difficulties in the revision, production and security or protection of their work. Two personal illustrations provide considerable insight into the complexities and difficulties of stolen and altered copies, revisions and production of multiple copies: Galen *My Own Books* (8-23) and Tertullian *Against Marcion* (1.1.1-2) (see 2 Thess 2:2 for a similar concern).

There is only scattered and incidental evidence regarding the book trade in the Greco-Roman world, but it does indicate that there were active and successful booksellers (see Gamble). There were probably book dealers as early as the fourth century B.C. in Greece, but substantial evidence for a book trade does not emerge until the first century B.C. Cicero makes one reference to a bookseller. In the first and second centuries A.D. book trade is attested by Catallus, Horace, *Seneca, Martial and *Pliny the Younger.

2. Types of Greco-Roman Literature.
Modern attempts to classify Greco-Roman literature by types or genres are fraught with difficulties and are in serious danger of anachronistic or rigid misrepresentation. Yet broad categorizations are helpful for analysis and for discussion of the NT (and second-century Christian) texts in their setting in the Greco-Roman literary culture (see Aune; Dihle).

Recognizing these difficulties and noting that the boundaries between some categories are unclear and that there are social and formal levels of what might be recognized as literature, it could be said that Greco-Roman literature is comprised of at least the following types (genres or categories) of writing: poetry, including epics; plays (especially tragedies and comedies); philosophical treatises; moral treatises; history; biography (which is closely related to history); travel and geographical narratives; rhetorical treatises; scientific treatises; novels; satire; epigrams; letters or collected correspondence (although cast in "private" form, they were meant for a broader readership); and literary criticism.

The types of Greco-Roman literature that are the most significant as context and background for interpreting the texts of the NT would involve several categories (see Hornblower and Spawforth). These would include the following [with some Greco-Roman authors from section 3.3 below indicated]: moral treatises (Philodemus, Cebes, *Musonius Rufus, *Epictetus, *Plutarch, Maximus of Tyre, *Seneca [see Malherbe 1986]); history (Diodorus Siculus, Polybius, Strabo, *Tacitus, Cassius Dio, Livy; *Suetonius [see M. Grant; Mellor]); *biography (Plutarch, Diogenes Laertius, Philostatus, Suetonius [see Momigliano]); *rhetorical treatises (Dio Chrysostom, Cicero, Quintilian [see Fairweather; Kennedy]); *romances, or novels (Petronius [see Hock; Reardon]); satire (Lucian, Juvenal); and letters (Cicero [see Malherbe 1988; Stowers]). Also of some value would be the study of Greco-Roman literary criticism (see Russell; Russell and Winterbottom).

Although it would not be accurate to suggest that there was a Greco-Roman religious genre, many Greco-Roman authors, including but not limited to those of philosophical and moral treatises, wrote frequently or significantly about religious questions, many of which have importance for the study of the NT and early Christianity. Of the authors noted in 3.3 below, the most important for religious (and theological) themes would be: Cebes, Epictetus, Plutarch, Aelius Aristides, Albinus, Lucian, Maximus of Tyre and Apuleius. Of course, meaningful texts in this connection would be found in a very wide range of Greco-Roman authors (see 3.1 and 3.2 below; see especially Beard; F. C. Grant; Meyer).

It would be appropriate at this point to note those Greco-Roman authors (before the third century A.D.) who explicitly mention Jesus or the early Christians. These include: Thallos (cited only in Christian sources); Tacitus (*Ann.* 15.44); Pliny the Younger (*Ep.* 10.96); Suetonius (*Claudius* 25.4); Celsus (*True Doctrine*, in numerous passages, preserved only in Origen's *Cont. Cels.*); and Lucian (*Peregr.*, throughout; *Alex.* 25, 38).

3. Accessing Greco-Roman Literature.

3.1. Corpus Hellenisticum Novi Testamenti. As early as 1915 a group of German scholars, including G. Heinrici, A. Deissmann, E. von Dobschütz, H. Lietzmann and H. Windisch, issued an appeal to scholars to work on producing as complete a collection as possible of Hellenistic [Greco-Roman] texts parallel to the NT in the J. Wettstein tradition (see *ZNW* 21 [1922] 146-48). In 1751-1752 J. Wettstein had produced his two-volume *Novum Testamentum Graecum* (Amsterdam), which included, in addition to the text of the NT, an extensive collection of Greek and Latin (and Jewish rabbinic) texts parallel to various NT texts. The deaths of various scholars involved and two major European wars delayed this project for many years. Eventually the project became known as the Corpus Hellenisticum Novi Testamenti. Since 1961 various publications attempted to provide so-called parallels from Aelius Aristides, the Corpus Hermeticum, Dio Chrysostom, Hierocles, Lucian, Macrobius, Menander, Musonius Rufus, Philostratus, Plutarch and Seneca. There is also in process the *Neuer Wettstein* (see Strecker). A briefer and simpler "new Wettstein" is also available as the *Hellenistic Commentary to the New Testament* (see Boring). Such collections are inevitably selective and raise always the difficult questions of what constitutes legitimate and meaningful parallels (and counter-parallels).

3.2. Anthologies of Primary Sources: Selected Texts. Due to the vast amount of Greco-Roman literature available, one can appreciate and value the use of anthologies which provide, usually topically, selective primary source texts. Such anthologies usually include as well nonliterary texts (e.g., *inscriptions, private and documentary *papyri). Some anthologies collect texts on a topic for its own sake; some are directed to the relevance of such texts for the study of the NT. Most important are anthologies on history (see Austin; Bagnall and Derow; Lewis and Reinhold), philosophy (see Inwood and Gerson; Long and Sedley; Malherbe), culture and society (Shelton), religion (Beard; F. C. Grant; Meyer), ethics (Malherbe), family/household (Gardner and Wiedemann), miracles (Cotter), slavery (Wiedemann), women (Lefkowitz and Fant; Rowlandson) and epistolary theory (Malherbe).

3.3. Reading Major Greek and Latin Authors. It has been estimated that perhaps only 10 percent of ancient Greek literature has survived and that perhaps 33 percent of ancient Latin literature has survived (more Latin literature survived due, most likely, to the fact that medieval scribes knew Latin better than Greek). In spite of what has been lost, a considerable volume of Greek and Latin literature from the ancient world is available, much of it in English translations.

Virtually all surviving Greco-Roman literature is written by men. There were women writers in the ancient world (see Snyder), but relatively few. Most of the more than one hundred names of women writers known to us were poets (the most famous is Sappho, born in the seventh century B.C.); some of this work survives in fragments. In the Hellenistic period there were also some women who were writing philosophers, but their work survives only in fragments.

The two most important series of texts of ancient Greek and Latin authors are the Bibliotheca Teubneriana (the most extensive and critical text series; over 1,200 volumes) and the Loeb Classical Library (nearly five hundred volumes with text and English translation on opposite pages). Many works are also available in other series and in numerous publications apart from series.

It is difficult to identify the most significant Greek and Latin authors for the study of the NT and its context. The most important authors prior to the Hellenistic and Greco-Roman periods certainly are Homer, *Plato and *Aristotle. These authors are important both in their own right, but also for the continuing influence they had on subsequent authors, including those of our period. Although the excerpted texts collected in the Corpus Hellenisticum Novi Testamenti project and in the various anthologies of primary texts are very useful, it is important and valuable to read complete works of Greek and Roman authors in their own right for the understandings and insights that can be gained only through an encounter with the full context of authors and texts (see Dihle). The accompanying table (see Table of Greek and Roman Authors) presents what could be considered the thirty-five most important authors to read for the cultural, social, historical and conceptual background and context of the NT. To this must be added the category of Greco-Roman *romances/novels (see Hock; Reardon; *see* Romances/Novels, Ancient).

3.4. Digital Texts and Related Aids. There are various digital texts and related aids that enable one to access the Greek and Latin literary works of antiquity through various forms of word searches.

The Thesaurus Linguae Graecae (TLG) project, begun in 1972 at the University of California, Irvine, has a database of machine readable Greek text of virtually all Greek authors from Homer through A.D. 600 and beyond. This resource has over 74 million words of text available. The TLG list of Greek authors and texts included as of 1990 is availalbe in published form (see Berkowitz and Squitier).

In the late 1990s Brepols Publishers and

B. G. Teubner (now owned by Saur) in collaboration with the CETEDOC computing centre at the Universite Catholique de Louvain (at Louvain-la-Neuve) began to issue the Bibliotheca Teubneriana Latina on CD-ROM. This project will eventually include all classical Latin literature from about 300 B.C. to about A.D. 500 (and later medieval Latin literature as well).

Traditional, printed concordances to the ancient Greek and Latin literature are still valuable in many cases. Although dated, there are guides to some of these aids (see Faider; Riesenfeld and Riesenfeld).

4. Emerging Issues for New Testament Studies. Greco-Roman literature is an important and useful aspect of the background and context of the NT and of second-century Christian literature. It cannot be established that the authors of the texts of the NT were direct or regular readers of Greco-Roman literature, although given what is known, directly and indirectly, about Paul, the author of Luke-Acts, and even the authors of Hebrews and of James, it would be historically plausible that some NT authors had a degree of familiarity with some Greco-Roman literature. Of far greater importance for students of the NT are at least three issues: (1) placing the NT texts in the context of the types of Greco-Roman literature (*see* Genres of the New Testament); (2) understanding the use of Greco-Roman literary devices and forms within the texts of the NT; and (3) illuminating and contextualizing certain NT issues, ideas, themes and topics based on information contained in Greco-Roman literature.

4.1. New Testament Texts and the Types of Greco-Roman Literature. There is a considerable history in NT scholarship, especially in the twentieth century, of discussion of the genres or types of literature within the NT in relationship to the literary forms of the Greco-Roman world (see Aune; Dormeyer; *see* Genres of the New Testament).

The fundamental debate over the genre of the NT Gospels is whether to understand them in the context of Greco-Roman biographical literature or whether they should be understood as unique early church kerygmatic proclamation (see Burridge; see *DJG*, Gospel [Genre]). In all probability the Gospels belong to the Greco-Roman biographical literary tradition (see Luke 1:1-4 as one example of literary self-consciousness), but they are certainly also shaped by particular data of the Jesus tradition and the kerygmatic and didactic needs of the early church (*see* Biography, Ancient).

The discussion of the genre of Acts has been especially difficult due in large part to the perceived connection between the genre issue and that of the historical value of Acts (see Alexander, 1996; Winter and Clarke). Since Acts is a continuation of Luke and focuses to some degree on Peter and Paul, it has been seen as well as biography. The main debate, however, is whether to place Acts in the category of history or novel. It appears that the author's prologue (Luke 1:1-4) places the work within a tradition of serious writing, but it does not resolve the issue of genre (e.g., one of the "closer" parallels to Luke 1:1-4 is the prologue of Dioscorides' treatise on herbal medicines). It would probably be fair to conclude that the author and first readers of Acts perceived of the work as history, a perception supported by the content of Acts, but that Acts also reflects both Greco-Roman epic narrative and novelistic (romantic) features.

It appears to be clearly established that the many *letters of the NT (Paul's as well as those of others) reflect the Greco-Roman conventions of both private letters and also those aimed at larger and multiple audiences (see Stowers; *see DPL*, Letters, Letter Form; *DLNTD*, Letter, Letter Form). Of course, the letters, especially those of Paul, reflect distinctive concerns of the early church and what has been called a sense of apostolic (authoritative) presence (*see* Epistolary Theory; Letters, Greco-Roman).

4.2. New Testament Use of Greco-Roman Literary Devices and Forms. The texts of the NT use various forms and devices known in Greco-Roman literature, although in many cases these forms have been modified.

Probably the most important Greco-Roman literary devices used in the NT, primarily in the (Pauline) letters (but see Hebrews, too), are epistolary conventions (see O'Brien; Stowers) and various forms of rhetorical argumentation and arrangement (see Fairweather; Kennedy; Porter; *see DPL*, Rhetorical Criticism; *DLNTD*, Rhetoric, Rhetorical Criticism).

It is also likely that James is shaped in part, not only by scriptural and Jewish moral traditions, but also by Greco-Roman literary moral forms and traditions (see Johnson).

4.3. New Testament Issues Within the Contexts of Greco-Roman Literature. The old and too often acrimonious debate over the primacy of Jewish

Century	Greek Authors	Latin Authors
1st B.C.	Diodorus Siculus Polybius Philodemus	Cicero Horace Livy
1st B.C.- 1st A.D.	Strabo	Ovid
1st A.D.	Cebes (*Tablet*) Dio Chrysostom Musonius Rufus Tacitus	Manilius Martial Petronius Pliny the Elder Quintilian Seneca
1st - 2nd A.D.	Epictetus Plutarch	Suetonius
2nd A.D.	Aelius Aristides Albinus Galen Lucian Marcus Aurelius Maximus of Tyre Pausanias	Apuleius Gellius Juvenal Pliny the Younger
2nd - 3rd A.D.	Cassius Dio	
3rd A.D.	Diogenes Laertius Philostratus	

TABLE OF GREEK AND ROMAN AUTHORS

or Greco-Roman contexts for the NT should be considered as over. W. D. Davies has spoken of the "eclipse of dichotomies"; certainly much of Second Temple Judaism was influenced by Greco-Roman culture. Of course, the primary context for the NT is the Jewish one, but the significance and value of the Greco-Roman culture, and especially its literature, should not be discounted. It is not only the background of the NT that is at issue; there is also the matter of the context of the recipients and audience of the NT texts that must be considered.

Whether mediated through a Jewish context or not, certainly many of the ideas with which Paul, the author of Hebrews and the author of James deal have connections with concepts clearly attested in Greco-Roman literature (e.g., Paul: Phil 4:11-14 and Stoic-Cynic concepts of *autarkēs*; Hebrews: the Middle Platonic construction of cosmic reality; James: the moral aphorisms [see Johnson]).

Details cannot be pursued here; the guidance provided in sections 3.1 and 3.2 above is substantial. Nevertheless, a few categories and examples may suffice to indicate the importance of Greco-Roman literary texts for the study of the NT.

Many major conceptual and social issues within the NT clearly depend either in background or in communication with the recipients of the texts upon ideas and material contained in Greco-Roman literature. For example, consider the following matters: the role and status of women, church and state relationships positive and negative, slavery, miracles, the social and structural organization of early churches, various moral issues, the teachings of the "opponents" of NT authors, matters of the "trinitarian structure" of deity and more, including historical and cultural data on Greco-Romans cities mentioned in Paul, Acts and Revelation.

The Corpus Hellenisticum Novi Testamenti project (see 3.1 above) and the anthologies of selected primary texts (see 3.2 above) provide abundant material from Greco-Roman literature for consideration of its parallels and counterparallels to NT texts. Two very well-known examples would be the aphorism of 1 Timothy 6:10 and the statement about the religious nature of Athenians in Acts 17:22, both of which are attested in many Greco-Roman texts. Perhaps a few other, rarely cited examples, which represent only a fraction of what is available, gleaned from reading Greco-Roman authors (see 3.3 above), could illustrate the rich discoveries available within Greco-Roman literature: Cebes, *Tablet* 4 (and throughout) and Matthew 7:13-14 on the two ways (broad and narrow); Musonius Rufus 13 and 1 Corinthians 7 on mutual/equal consideration in marriage; Chariton's novel *Callirhoe* 6.2 and 1 Corinthians 9:25 on athletic wreaths/crowns; Pliny the Elder, *Natural History* 13.20 and Mark 14:5 on the cost and perceived value of ointments/perfumes; and Livy 34.2.9-10 and 1 Corinthians 14:34-35 on the request that wives ask their husbands at home rather than in public.

See also ALEXANDRIAN LIBRARY; ALEXANDRIAN SCHOLARSHIP; ARISTOTLE, ARISTOTELIANISM; BIOGRAPHY, ANCIENT; CICERO; CYNIC EPISTLES; EDUCATION: JEWISH AND GRECO-ROMAN; EPICTETUS; EPISTOLARY THEORY; GENRES OF THE NEW TESTAMENT; GRAMMARIANS, HELLENISTIC GREEK; HIPPOCRATIC LETTERS; INSCRIPTIONS AND PAPYRI: GRECO-ROMAN; JEWISH LITERATURE: HISTORIANS AND POETS; LETTERS, GRECO-ROMAN; LITERACY AND BOOK CULTURE; LUCIAN OF SAMOSATA; MUSONIUS RUFUS; PAGAN SOURCES IN THE NEW TESTAMENT; PLATO, PLATONISM; PLINY THE ELDER; PLINY THE YOUNGER; PLUTARCH; POETRY, HELLENISTIC; ROMANCES/NOVELS, ANCIENT; SCHOLARSHIP, GREEK AND ROMAN; SENECA; SUETONIUS; TACITUS; WRITING AND LITERATURE: JEWISH; ZENON PAPYRI.

BIBLIOGRAPHY. **Primary Source Anthologies.** M. M. Austin, *The Hellenistic World from Alexander to the Roman Conquest: A Selection of Ancient Sources in Translation* (Cambridge: Cambridge University Press, 1981); R. S. Bagnall and P. Derow, *Greek Historical Documents: The Hellenistic Period* (SBLSBS 16; Chico, CA: Scholars Press, 1981); M. Beard et al., *Religions of Rome,* 2: *A Sourcebook* (Cambridge: Cambridge University Press, 1998); W. Cotter, *Miracles in Greco-Roman Antiquity: A Sourcebook* (New York: Routledge, 1999); J. F. Gardner and T. Wiedemann, *The Roman Household: A Sourcebook* (New York: Routledge, 1991); F. C. Grant, *Ancient Roman Religion* (LR; New York: Liberal Arts Press, 1957); idem, *Hellenistic Religions: The Age of Syncretism* (LR; New York: Liberal Arts Press, 1953); B. Inwood and L. P. Gerson, *Hellenistic Philosophy: Introductory Readings* (2d ed.; Indianapolis: Hackett, 1997); M. R. Lefkowitz and M. B. Fant, *Women's Life in Greece and Rome: A Source Book in Translation* (2d ed.; Baltimore: Johns Hopkins University Press, 1992); N. Lewis and M. Reinhold, *Roman Civilization: Selected Readings* (2 vols.; RC:SS 45; New York: Columbia University Press, 1951-55); A. A. Long and D. N. Sedley, *The Hellenistic Philosophers,* 1: *Translations of the Principal Sources* (Cambridge: Cambridge University Press, 1987); A. J. Malherbe, *Ancient Epistolary Theorists* (SBLSBS 19; Atlanta: Scholars Press, 1988); idem, *The Cynic Epistles* (SBLSBS 12; Missoula, MT: Scholars Press, 1977); idem, *Moral Exhortation: A Greco-Roman Sourcebook* (LEC 4; Philadelphia: Westminster, 1986); M. W. Meyer, *The Ancient Mysteries: A Sourcebook* (San Francisco: Harper & Row, 1987); J. Rowlandson, *Women and Society in Greek and Roman Egypt: A Sourcebook* (Cambridge: Cambridge University Press, 1998); J.-A. Shelton, *As the Romans Did: A Sourcebook in Roman Social History* (2d ed.; New York: Oxford University Press, 1998); T. Wiedemann, *Greek and Roman Slavery: A Sourcebook* (Baltimore: Johns Hopkins University Press, 1981). **Studies.** L. Alexander, "Ancient Book Production and the Circulation of the Gospels," in *The Gospels for All Christians: Rethinking the Gospel Audiences,* ed. R. Bauckham (Grand Rapids, MI: Eerdmans, 1998a) 71-111; idem, "Fact, Fiction and the Genre of Acts," *NTS* 44 (1998b) 380-99; idem, "The Relevance of Greco-Roman Literature and Culture to New Testament Study," in *Hearing the New Testament: Strategies of Interpretation,* ed. J. B. Green (Grand Rapids, MI: Eerdmans, 1995) 109-26; D. E. Aune, *The New Testament in Its Literary Environment* (LEC 8; Philadelphia: Westminster, 1987); L. Berkowitz and K. A. Squitier, *Thesaurus Linguae Graecae: Canon of Greek Authors and Works* (3d ed.; New York: Oxford University Press, 1990); S. F. Bonner, *Education in Ancient Rome: From the Elder Cato to the Younger Pliny* (Berkeley and Los Angeles: University of California Press, 1977); M. E. Boring et al., eds., *Hellenistic Commentary to the New Testament* (Nashville: Abingdon, 1995); G. W. Bowersock, *Fiction as History: Nero to Julian* (SCL 58; Berkeley and Los Angeles: University of California Press, 1994); F. F. Bruce, "The New Testament and Classical Studies," *NTS* 22 (1976) 229-42; R. A. Burridge, *What Are the Gospels? A Comparison with Graeco-Roman Biography* (SNTSMS 70; Cambridge: Cambridge University Press, 1992); A. Dihle, *Greek and Latin Literature of the*

Roman Empire: From Augustus to Justinian (New York: Routledge, 1994); D. Dormeyer, *The New Testament Among the Writings of Antiquity* (BSem 55; Sheffield: Sheffield Academic Press, 1998); P. E. Easterling and B. M. W. Knox, "Books and Readers in the Greek World," in *Cambridge History of Classical Literature,* 1: *Greek Literature,* ed. P. E. Easterling and B. M. W. Knox (Cambridge: Cambridge University Press, 1985) 1-41; P. Faider, *Repertoire des index et lexiques d'auteurs latins* (CEL 3: Paris: Les Belles Lettres, 1926); J. Fairweather, "The Epistle to the Galatians and Classical Rhetoric," *TynB* 45 (1998) 1-38, 213-43; D. Feeney, *Literature and Religion at Rome: Cultures, Contexts, and Beliefs* (RLC; Cambridge: Cambridge University Press, 1998); H. Y. Gamble, *Books and Readers in the Early Church: A History of Early Christian Texts* (New Haven, CT: Yale University Press, 1995); M. Grant, *Greek and Roman Historians: Information and Misinformation* (New York: Routledge, 1995); W. V. Harris, *Ancient Literacy* (Cambridge, MA: Harvard University Press, 1989); R. F. Hock et al., *Ancient Fiction and Early Christian Narrative* (SBLSS 6; Atlanta: Scholars Press, 1998); S. Hornblower and A. Spawforth, ed., *The Oxford Classical Dictionary* (3d ed.; New York: Oxford University Press, 1996 (see especially the articles on *anagnōstēs* [reader]; books, Greek and Roman; libraries; literacy; literary criticism; papyrology, Greek and Latin; and on each individual Greek and Latin author mentioned); L. T. Johnson, *The Letter of James* (AB 37A; New York: Doubleday, 1995); G. A. Kennedy, *New Testament Interpretation Through Rhetorical Criticism* (SR; Chapel Hill: University of North Carolina Press, 1984); E. J. Kenney, "Books and Readers in the Roman World," in *Cambridge History of Classical Literature,* 2: *Latin Literature,* ed. E. J. Kenney (Cambridge: Cambridge University Press, 1982) 3-32; F. G. Kenyon, *Books and Readers in Ancient Greece and Rome* (2d ed.; Oxford: Clarendon Press, 1951); R. Mellor, *The Roman Historians* (New York: Routledge, 1999); A. Momigliano, *The Development of Greek Biography* (2d ed.; Cambridge, MA: Harvard University Press, 1993); P. T. O'Brien, *Introductory Thanksgivings in the Letters of Paul* (NovTSup 49; Leiden: E. J. Brill, 1977); S. E. Porter, ed., *Handbook of Classical Rhetoric in the Hellenistic Period 330 B.C.-A.D. 400* (Leiden: E. J. Brill, 1997); B. P. Reardon, *Collected Ancient Greek Novels* (Berkeley and Los Angeles: University of California Press, 1989); L. D. Reynolds and N. G. Wilson, *Scribes and Scholars: A Guide to the Transmission of Greek and Latin Literature* (3d ed.; New York: Oxford University Press, 1991); H. Riesenfeld and B. Riesenfeld, *Repertorium Lexicographicum Graecum: A Catalogue of Indexes and Dictionaries to Greek Authors* (Stockholm: Almquist & Wiksell, 1954); C. H. Roberts and T. C. Skeat, *The Birth of the Codex* (London: Oxford University Press for the British Academy, 1983); D. A. Russell, *Criticism in Antiquity* (2d ed.; BCP; Bristol: Bristol Classical Press, 1995); D. A. Russell and M. Winterbottom, *Ancient Literary Criticism: The Principal Texts in New Translations* (Oxford: Oxford University Press, 1972); J. M. Snyder, *The Woman and the Lyre: Women Writers in Classical Greece and Rome* (AFWL; Carbondale and Edwardsville, IL: Southern Illinois University Press, 1989); S. K. Stowers, *Letter Writing in Greco-Roman Antiquity* (LEC 5; Philadelphia: Westminster, 1986); G. Strecker et al., *Neuer Wettstein: Texte zum Neue Testament aus Griechentum und Hellenismus* (Berlin: Walter de Gruyter, 1996-); B. W. Winter and A. D. Clarke, eds., *The Book of Acts in Its Ancient Literary Setting* (BAFCS 1; Grand Rapids, MI: Eerdmans, 1993); L. B. Yaghjian, "Ancient Reading," in *The Social Sciences and New Testament Interpretation,* ed. R. L. Rohrbaugh (Peabody, MA: Hendrickson, 1997) 206-30.

D. M. Scholer

WRITING AND LITERATURE: JEWISH

The Second Temple period witnessed the production of a great wealth of literature by Jewish authors in a wide variety of genres. Much of this literary activity relates directly to the Jewish Scriptures, whether as translations of that sacred corpus or as expansions and rewritings of the biblical story (*see* Rewritten Bible). Among the bodies of literature classified as *Apocrypha and Pseudepigrapha are historical works, *apocalypses, testaments, wisdom literature and liturgical texts. Certain individual authors, such as the historian and apologist *Josephus or the philosopher *Philo, have left to posterity a prolific output. Many other lesser-known writers have contributed also to the treasury of extant historical, poetical and philosophical texts. The discovery and publication of the *Dead Sea Scrolls have made available a substantial library of texts valued and read by a Palestinian sectarian community. Finally, *rabbinic literature, though later than the Second Temple, preserves many traditions that have roots in the first centuries B.C. and A.D.

This literature provides essential information concerning the diversity of, and the struggles and the developments within, *Judaism after the prophetic period. A careful examination of the larger corpus of Jewish literature from the second century B.C. through the first century A.D. opens up the broader conversations within Judaism that shaped the minds of the founders of the church and authors of the NT texts. These offer many insights into Jesus' teachings and ministry, Paul's controversies with other Jewish voices (Christian and non-Christian) and emerging Christian theology and ethics.

1. Biblical Expansions, Additions and Versions
2. Historiography
3. Apologetic, Wisdom and Philosophical Texts
4. Apocalypses and Testaments
5. Edifying Tales and Romances
6. Qumran Literature
7. Liturgical Texts
8. Rabbinic Writings

1. Biblical Expansions, Additions and Versions. Judaism, in its various expressions, remained a religion centered around sacred texts. The need for accessible Scriptures gave rise to translations of the *Hebrew into the *Greek language, which was spoken by most Jews in the western *Diaspora. It also gave rise to the production of Aramaic versions of Scripture for use primarily in Palestine and the eastern Diaspora (*see* Aramaic Targums). The Scriptures also inspired the production of parabiblical texts—interpretive and imaginative rewritings and expansions of the biblical story, as well as additional tales based on characters or stories already present in the Scriptures. Versions and expansions provide a wealth of information concerning how Scripture was interpreted and understood during this period, as well as insights into how Scripture and parabiblical literature could be brought to bear on new situations requiring a "word from the Lord."

1.1. Additions, Rewriting and Expansions of Biblical Narratives. One of the most influential expansions of a biblical story is the collection of apocalypses (see 4.1 below) known as *1 Enoch* (*see* Enoch, Books of). Taking the story of the birth of the giants (Gen 6:1-4) as its starting point, the earlier strata of this work develop an explanation of the origins of evil and of evil spirits. Both *demonic and human workers of sin, however, stand under the judgment of God, who has already prepared the places of punishment for the wicked and reward for the righteous. The period before the flood becomes a type of the author's own age, as he looks forward to God's final judgment. This book also bears witness to a highly developed angelology (*see* Angels), including the notion of angelic intercession for humanity, and a well-defined *eschatology whose images of judgment and salvation pervade later literature. It is quoted directly by Jude and has left a strong impression upon Revelation.

The book of **Jubilees*, which appears to know *1 Enoch* 6—16 and 72—82, rewrites Genesis 1 through Exodus 12 with a distinctive interest in presenting Torah as an eternal law inscribed on heavenly tablets, obeyed by the angels and the patriarchs themselves before *Moses received the law on Mt. Sinai. Thus Abraham, Isaac and Jacob observe the feasts of Tabernacles and Firstfruits and the Day of Atonement (*see* Festivals and Holy Days: Jewish). The story of Jacob and Esau is intensified to the point that Jacob kills Esau, rather than being reconciled to him, stressing the contemporary tension between Jews and Idumeans (Edomites). Like *1 Enoch,* this book locates the origin of evil in the revolt of Satan (*see* Belial, Beliar, Devil, Satan) and his angels rather than in Adam's inherent weakness (cf. Paul and 4 Ezra). *Jubilees* looks for a return to strict Torah observance, which will precipitate a return to the enjoyment of pre-flood longevity, even to the destruction of death itself.

Although they were not particularly *Essene books, copies of both *1 Enoch* and *Jubilees* were found at *Qumran alongside rewritings of Scripture that were peculiar to the Qumran sect. The **Temple Scroll,* for example, contains a rewriting and recodification of the legal material of the Pentateuch, especially Deuteronomy (*see* Apocryphon of Moses [4Q374-377]; Words of Moses [1Q22]). These frequently reflect the particular practices of the Qumran community, thus anchoring their distinctive practices in the divine revelation of Torah. Also found at Qumran but not showing distinctively Essene interests are fragments of a **Genesis Apocryphon,* which would have provided an expanded retelling of Genesis (only stories of Noah's birth and Abraham's visit to Egypt are legible).

The *Liber Antiquitatum Biblicarum* (*see* Pseudo-

Philo) retells the biblical story from Adam to King David. The author stresses election theology as the "gospel" of the Jewish Scriptures: *Israel is God's people, chosen before creation. God's fidelity to God's people assures them of deliverance, even in times of desperation. The book also spends considerable time on the nature of leadership, connecting the quality of Israel's leaders with the fortunes of the nation (Nickelsburg). Other noteworthy rewritings or expansions include the **Life of Adam and Eve* and *1 Esdras* (a rewriting of 2 Chron 35:1—36:23 [*see* Esdras, Books of]; Ezra; Neh 7:38—8:12).

The Second Temple period also witnessed a flourishing of additions to the Jewish Scriptures, or supplements to the biblical narrative. Hebrew Esther was supplemented with a number of *prayers and other additions that brought Jewish piety and divine activity into the forefront of the narrative. The story of the famous *prophet Isaiah was supplemented with an account of the **Ascension of Isaiah,* a book that became important for the early church and that was substantially edited and expanded by Christians in order to make Isaiah an even stronger witness to Jesus as the Messiah. The Joseph cycle in Genesis inspired the composition of **Joseph and Aseneth,* the story of Joseph's betrothal to the daughter of an Egyptian *priest and her conversion to the God of Israel (*see* Apocryphon of Joseph [4Q371-372, 539]). It was most likely during this period that the tales about Daniel (Dan 1—6) were collected, along with additional tales such as Daniel's defeat of the worship of Bel and the Dragon or his discovery of the innocence of Susanna. The book of *Baruch and the Epistle of Jeremiah supplemented the testimony of the most renowned prophet of the preexilic period, Jeremiah (*see* Daniel, Esther and Jeremiah, Additions to). These two figures are enabled to speak directly to the needs of Jews in Palestine and the Diaspora, affirming the way of Torah as the only true path of wisdom, assuring the readers of the hope for repentance leading to the regathering of the exiles, destruction of the Gentile oppressors and the exaltation of Zion. The Epistle of Jeremiah offers advice on how to avoid the snares of idolatry, and rather to regard idol worship as the empty vanity that it is.

The corpus of biblical expansions and supplements bears witness to the many ways in which the Jewish Scripture could inspire its readers. Scripture could speak to readers through these imaginative retellings, these probings of difficult issues mentioned but left undeveloped in the texts (e.g., the birth of the giants), through the reflection on and narrative expansion of the virtues of the patriarchs and prophets and through the living word, which could still be channeled through such figures to new generations of faithful Jews.

1.2. Versions. The OT found in all Protestant Bibles is based on the Masoretic Text, a Hebrew text tradition with its origins in the early rabbinic period. This text, however, represents one version among many (*see* Old Testament Versions, Ancient). The Jewish Scriptures were available in Greek and Aramaic translations and a number of Hebrew versions (attested especially by the Qumran scrolls and the Samaritan Pentateuch) before the text was standardized by the rabbis (*see* Hebrew Bible). Familiarity with these different versions provides the reader with a sense of the range of possibilities for the wording of the Jewish Scriptures available to NT authors (Evans). Such research opens up the student to the streams of interpretation of Scripture already present in the first century, upon which Jesus and the authors of the NT could draw for their arguments and inspiration.

1.2.1. Greek Translations. The best known Greek version of the Jewish Scriptures is the *Septuagint (LXX). The available editions of the Septuagint represent not a single translation but a selection of available Greek translations from different periods by different hands. Every translation is an act of interpretation, but the degree of interpretative license varies greatly among the books included in the Septuagint. The Torah was translated rather closely, but some of the prophetic books amount to interpretative paraphrases of the Hebrew. The Septuagint version is not the earliest Greek translation, but it became the dominant collection by the first century A.D. and ever after in the early church. The Pentateuch may have been translated as early as 250 B.C. The **Epistle of Aristeas* preserves a story of the translation being commissioned by Ptolemy II and executed by seventy-two of the most brilliant scholars in Palestine. More likely, the translation was undertaken by *Alexandrian Jewish scholars at the request of *synagogues who needed the Scriptures in their everyday language (after Hebrew had been largely forgotten) and who needed a reliable edition of their Torah. The Prophets were translated later, as were the texts that make up the third division of the Hebrew Bible (the Writings). The Septuagint codices, however, contain many works that were not included in the Hebrew canon, with the result that the early church received more Scriptures than did emerging rabbinic Judaism. These additional books are classified by Protestants as Apocrypha.

The importance of the Septuagint is difficult to overestimate. First, it enabled closer conversation between Greek thought and the Jewish Scriptures, presenting the latter in the language and terminology of the former. For the readers of the Greek Scriptures, the connotations of the original Hebrew were frequently replaced by the connotations of the Greek terms, although the reverse process is also attested. Second, it was the Bible of the early church. Many of the NT authors relied on the Greek version for their own study and for their edification of their converts, whether Jew or Gentile. Study of the letter to the Hebrews reveals that the author frequently follows the Septuagint version of the OT. Many of his main points rest specifically on those words or phrases in which the Septuagint differs from the Masoretic Text. Psalm 40:7-9, for example, speaks of God's rejection of animal *sacrifices in favor of "digging out ears" in the psalmist for the purpose of hearing Torah and walking in obedience. The Greek text, however, speaks of God preparing a "body" for the psalmist in place of animal sacrifices. It is the Greek version that supports Hebrews' contention that the offering up of Jesus' body fulfilled the prophetic word of Scripture and instituted the new covenant of Jeremiah 31 (Heb 10:1-10). Another frequently cited example is Isaiah 7:14: in the Hebrew, a "young woman" will conceive, but the Greek translates this as a "virgin." Even Matthew, the most Jewish of the Evangelists, draws on the tradition of the Greek Scriptures as a witness to Jesus' significance.

The translation of the Torah into Greek occasioned no small tension between Palestinian Jews and Diaspora Jews. The prologue to Ben Sira (*see* Sirach) attests to the awareness of the impossibility of a precise translation, which meant that Diaspora Jews had to defend the divine authorization and the reliability of their Greek version. Several pre-Christian recensions exist that move the Septuagint version closer to the emerging proto-Masoretic text. Diaspora Jews, in conversations with Palestinian Jewish dialogue partners about the differences between their versions of the Scriptures, would invent even more extravagant proofs of the divine inspiration of the Greek version. Later rabbis, giving in to the necessity of a Greek version, commissioned reissues of the Greek Bible, the most notable being the recension of Aquila, which translate the Hebrew in a more literal, wooden fashion. The synagogue moved as a whole, however, toward *education in Hebrew and use of the Hebrew text, leaving the Greek to the early church.

1.2.2. Targumim. As Jews in Egypt required the Scriptures in their everyday language (Greek), so Jews in Palestine and in the East desired to hear the Scriptures in the vernacular, Aramaic (*see* Rabbinic Literature: Targumim). Like the translations represented in the Septuagint, these targumim (plural of targum) vary in terms of degree of paraphrase and interpretation. The use of targumim in NT studies had been contested on the ground that the earliest manuscripts date from the Middle Ages, so that the texts must postdate the NT by centuries. Discovery of fragments of Aramaic targumim at Qumran (*see* Aramaic Targums: Qumran) and at the Cairo Genizah (storeroom in a synagogue for sacred texts withdrawn from circulation), however, demonstrate that some did exist in the first century. These periphrastic translations may therefore contain traditions that could go back to the NT period and have been profitably used to explore Jesus' interpretation of the Jewish Scriptures (Evans; Chilton). There are four primary targumim to the Torah (*Onqelos, Pseudo-Jonathan, Neofiti* and the *Samaritan Targum*) and fragments of several others (4QtgLev is particularly important, since it definitely dates from the first century or before); there are also single targumim for the remainder of the Jewish Scriptures, save Ezra and Daniel (Evans).

1.2.3. Masoretic Text. The Masoretic Text, as a rabbinic standardization of the Hebrew text of the Jewish Scriptures, is rightly considered a version rather than the exact original form (Evans). It may be that other versions preserve the original reading in many specific instances and that the Masoretes revised the text to bring it in line with rabbinic interpretation or to exclude sectarian (e.g., early Christian) "misreadings" of the Scripture. Text critics must balance readings from this version against those of the Greek versions and other Hebrew text traditions in their attempt to reconstruct the original (*see* Hebrew Bible).

2. Historiography.

A number of texts are written within the genre of historiography, providing essential information about the historical, social and political developments of the period. These writings are never without bias or agendas, which, when analyzed, also are useful indicators of the ethos and conflicts of the period.

2.1. 1 and 2 Maccabees. Maccabees (*see* 1 & 2 Maccabees) tell the story of the attempts of the *Jerusalem priestly aristocracy to Hellenize Judea, the forceful repression of Judaism instigated by these apostates and supported by the Hellenistic king of Syria, Antiochus IV, and the successful rebellion against the Syrian overlords and their local lackeys by the family of Judas Maccabeus. First Maccabees goes on to chronicle the acts of Judas's brothers down to the accession to the throne and high priesthood of John Hyrcanus I, son of Simon and nephew of Judas. This book is written as a pro-Hasmonean chronicle, reminding the readership of the saving acts of this great family and of the people's willing acceptance of them as their high priests and kings in gratitude for their deliverance (*see* Hasmoneans). Enthusiasm for the Hasmonean house was clearly not unanimous, as the Qumran texts, the **Testament of Moses* and the *Psalms of Solomon show, and 1 Maccabees seeks to revive pro-Hasmonean sentiments. Second Maccabees is less concerned with the glorification of a house of heroes and more concerned with explicating the ongoing effectiveness of the Deuteronomistic covenant, according to which apostasy leads to national disaster and repentance and obedience to national well-being. Second Maccabees also provides an important early witness to the belief in the resurrection of the righteous and to the growing tendencies to speculate about angelology.

2.2. Josephus. The most familiar historian of the period is *Josephus. Much of his *Jewish Antiquities* could be classified as a rewriting of the Bible, as Josephus's historical interest reaches back to creation itself. The parts of this work that coincide with biblical narrative, therefore, can provide much insight into the interpretation of the Jewish Scriptures for the sake of a mixed readership of Jews and Gentiles. Josephus's scope reaches past the restoration of the *temple into the life of Jews in Syria, Palestine and Egypt under *Alexander the Great and his successors, the Hasmonean house and finally Roman and Herodian rule up to the outbreak of the first Jewish revolt (A.D. 66; *see* Jewish Wars with Rome). For these periods, Josephus provides an essential historical source that often preserves material not known from other documents. His *Jewish War* reviews the end of the Hasmonean dynasty and the reign of *Herod but is focused mainly on the disintegration of Roman governance of Judea and the events and aftermath of the first Jewish revolt (*see* Roman Administration; Roman Governors of Palestine). This book seeks to blame the Jewish war on certain revolutionary groups rather than the Jewish population of Judea as whole and presents a suspiciously sympathetic portrait of the Roman generals Vespasian and Titus, who became Josephus's patrons after the war. Aside from such tendencies, the book presents an essential window into the tensions in Judea and its environs during the first century and thus constitutes essential reading for all students of the NT. Josephus also left an autobiography (the *Life*), in which he defends his actions, character and historical credibility against his critics.

2.3. Other Historians. Although he is mostly remembered as a philosopher, *Philo of Alexandria has left two important historical works that provide a window into the life of Alexandrian Jews. The *Embassy to Gaius* tells of an unsuccessful attempt by Philo and his fellow delegates to gain a reasonable hearing from Gaius Caligula on the matter of the civic status of Jews in Alexandria. *Against Flaccus* provides a detailed narrative of an ethnic pogrom perpetrated upon the Jews in Alexandria during the reign of Caligula (A.D. 38-41), showing the horrors that could emerge when latent hostilities are allowed to come to open expression. Fragments of other historians also exist. As in the case of the first half of Josephus's *Antiquities,* these authors appear to have sought to present the biblical narrative in the form of historiography.

3. Apologetic, Wisdom and Philosophical Texts.

3.1. Apologetics. A number of Jewish authors wrote in order to demonstrate to their fellow Jews that Judaism was an equally noble, or even a superior, way of life as that promoted by Gentile philosophers and ethicists. Some may even have written to a Gentile audience in the hope of raising their estimation of the Torah-observant Jew. The **Epistle of Aristeas* and 4 Maccabees (*see* 3 & 4 Maccabees) have a definite, inner-directed apologetic thrust. Fourth Maccabees promotes Torah observance as effective training in all the cardinal virtues so highly prized and regarded by the Greco-Roman culture. The author uses as examples the martyrs of the Hellenization crisis in order to demonstrate that dedication to Torah makes for superior expressions of virtue than one can find among Gentiles. Particularly those commandments that separate Jews from people of other races—those laws that frequently occasion the contempt of non-Jews—are shown to lead to virtue and honor. *Aristeas* also explains the special laws of Torah as concealing philosophical and ethical principles that educated Greeks expressed elsewhere and may even have in view a Gentile readership as well as a Jewish audience. Josephus has left one overtly apologetic work—his *Against Apion,* which responds to charges leveled against Judaism by several Gentile critics. His *Jewish Antiquities* also show an apologetic thrust, stressing the antiquity and therefore legitimacy and venerability of the Jewish people and way of life.

*3.2. **Wisdom.*** The two main representatives of wisdom literature from this period are the Wisdom of Ben Sira (or *Sirach, or Ecclesiasticus) and the *Wisdom of Solomon (*see* Wisdom Literature at Qumran). The Wisdom of Ben Sira, written in Jerusalem in about 180 B.C., promotes Torah observance as the way of true wisdom and only means of attaining wisdom's rewards. It contains instruction on a wide array of topics, including teachings on prayer, forgiveness, almsgiving and the right use of wealth, that have left a strong impression on later Jewish ethical instructions and on the early church. Wisdom of Solomon, a product of Alexandrian Judaism from the turn of the era, also promotes the Jewish way of life. The author emphasizes the eternal importance of God's verdict on one's life, the rewards and nature of wisdom and the actions of God on behalf of God's people, Israel. The author takes the personification of Wisdom to its highest level and became very influential for the early church's reflection on the divinity and preexistence of Jesus. Wisdom of Solomon helps Jews remain dedicated to Torah also through a demonstration of the folly of Gentile religion, much of which is paralleled in Paul's attacks on Gentile depravity and on idolatry. It assures them that education in Jewish wisdom supplies all that Greek education had to offer and much more besides.

Epistle of Aristeas also shares much in common with wisdom literature, particularly the Greek literature featuring banquets of sages in which a topic is discussed and refined. The sentences of *Pseudo-Phocylides resemble a collection of Greek maxims, the first half of which are based on the Decalogue and Leviticus. It is interesting to find, in both of these texts, Jewish writers attributing positive evaluations of Jewish wisdom pseudonymously to Gentile authors.

*3.3. **Philosophy.*** Wisdom of Solomon and even more clearly 4 Maccabees (*see* 3 & 4 Maccabees) move among wisdom literature, apologetics and philosophy. The former incorporates numerous aspects of *Platonic and *Stoic doctrine, while the latter is cast fully as a "most philosophical" demonstration that "devout [i.e., Torah-observant] reason masters the passions," a thesis that presents a slight modification of a common philosophical topic (*see* Philosophy).

An early, important Jewish philosopher was *Aristobulus, who flourished in the middle of the second century B.C. and whose work is known from five fragments. In these fragments, he claims that Plato and Pythagoras were indebted to Moses for their philosophy, presents the Jews as philosophical monotheists, defends the *sabbath as a day of special observance by adducing passages from Homer and Hesiod and explains that the anthropomorphisms in descriptions of God and God's actions in the Jewish Scriptures are meant to be understood figuratively. He thus bears witness to numerous strands of thought that would be found in his better-known successor, Philo.

Philo of Alexandria never abandons the literal keeping of the precepts of Torah but affirms the importance of performing them with a knowledge of their spiritual meaning. His extant works provide an allegorical commentary on the Pentateuch, showing how Jewish laws teach the virtues lauded by Greek ethical philosophers and affirm basic principles such as the importance of feeding the rational contemplation of virtue rather than indulging and becoming enslaved by the lower nature. Philo also wrote topical works on such issues as providence, the eternal nature of the world and true slavery and true freedom. In all these writings, Philo shows how far a Jew could go in incorporating Greek authors and concepts into an exposition of the Jewish Scriptures and still remain a loyal, Torah-observant Jew. His writings provide important windows into a Judaism that was open to the Hellenistic philosophical environment and into the ways in which Hellenistic philosophical concepts could be mediated to the Jewish community and early church. Philo also contains certain ideas, such as the creation of two Adams in Genesis 1—2, that are instructive backgrounds for NT discussions (cf. Paul's Adam-Christ typology; Evans). Ultimately Philo's writings were preserved not by the Jewish community but by the early church, which found his allegorical exegesis of the Jewish Scriptures invaluable for reaching past the "scandal of particularity" (the laws of ethnic Israel) into a more universal message (for a Gentile church).

4. Apocalypses and Testaments.

4.1. Apocalyptic Literature. The genre of apocalypse has been defined as "revelatory literature with a narrative framework, in which a revelation is mediated by an otherworldly being to a human recipient, disclosing a transcendent reality which is both temporal, insofar as it envisages eschatological salvation, and spatial insofar as it involves another, supernatural world" (Collins, in Kraft and Nickelsburg; *see* Apocalyptic Literature; Apocalypticism). Apocalypses seek to provide the larger context (both the spatial and temporal aspects) for making sense of the author's and readers' present circumstances and arriving at the appropriate response to those circumstances. The texts combine elements of many traditions—wisdom, prophetic, mythic—as well as aspects of potentially genuine visionary experiences. Two major types have been noted: the "otherworldly journey," in which revelation is imparted through a tour and description of otherwise inaccessible regions (e.g., heaven and hell), and the "historical apocalypse," in which the angelic conversation partner describes the course of history up to and including the intervention of God. A common feature of the latter is *ex eventu* *prophecy—the narration of events that are, from the actual author's perspective, past but that are, from the perspective of the ancient worthy who purportedly received the revelation (e.g., Enoch, Moses, Ezra) still future.

First Enoch contains a number of apocalypses from a continuous tradition (*see* Enoch, Books of). The foundational part, chapters 6—36, presents an otherworldly journey to the places prepared for the punishment of the wicked and reward of the righteous, revealing an advanced angelology based on the story of the Watchers (cf. Gen 6:1-4). Other early strata (chapters 85—90; 91; 93) provide an *ex eventu* prophecy placing the audience near the time of God's breaking into the fabric of history to execute judgment. Daniel 7—12 preserve apocalyptic visions of the historical type, using beasts and other cryptic designations ("kings of north and south") to recount the history of the Greek and Hellenistic period, leading up to the repression of Judaism under Antiochus IV and the Hellenizing high priests in 175 to 164 B.C. The intervention of God and God's angels is expected imminently, at which time the righteous will receive the kingdom and the apostates and Gentiles will be punished. The Similitudes of Enoch (*1 Enoch* 37—71), composed perhaps during the first century A.D., bear witness to developments of the figure of the Danielic Son of Man and thus provide relevant material for the study of that title in the Gospels.

2 Baruch and 4 Ezra (2 Esdras 3—14) respond to the destruction of Jerusalem in A.D. 70 and to God's slowness in punishing *Rome, the immoral agent of God's chastisement (*see* Baruch, Books of; Esdras, Books of). 4 Ezra is notable for its visions of the eagle and the man from the sea, which bear striking resemblances to the visions of the first beast and the warrior Messiah in Revelation 13, 17 and 19—20. Both *2 Baruch* and 4 Ezra counsel renewed commitment to Torah as the path to God's vindication of the chastised nation, assuring readers of the nearness of God's deliverance and the certainty of the chastisement of Rome. *Testament of Levi* shows the potential for fluidity between apocalypse and testament (*see* Testaments of the Twelve Patriarchs). It contains an otherworldly journey in which Levi views the seven heavens, their inhabitants (including several distinct orders of angels) and their functions. It ends with *ex eventu* prophecy and *eschatological predictions. The text was rewritten within the early church and made into a testimony of the Jewish priesthood's rejection of its Messiah. The **Sibylline Oracles* are not apocalypses in the proper sense but are a collection of prophecies akin to the *ex eventu* prophecies of the historical apocalypses. Oracles 3 and 5 are Jewish and provide sharp criticisms of idolatry (all the more stunning since they are placed on the mouth of a pagan priestess), affirmations of the oneness of God and God's providential control of history and "predictions" of the course of history leading up to the establishment of a kingdom of righteousness (not always ahistorical—*Sib. Or.* 3 envisions this kingdom happening under a beneficent Ptolemaic monarch). Other apocalypses of note include *2 Enoch,* the *Apocryphon of Ezekiel,* the **Apocalypse of Abraham* and the **Treatise of Shem.*

4.2. Testamentary Literature. The genre of testament recalls the farewell discourses of great figures in the Scriptures (e.g., Jacob in Genesis and Moses in Deuteronomy 32—33). It is related to wisdom literature in that it concerns the passing on of ethical instructions from a father to his children. It is closely related to apocalypses by its interest in God's ordering of history, in eschatological events and in living with these factors in view. It is distinguished by casting this material within the narrative framework of a deathbed speech that incorporates a retrospect on the life of the patriarch, often as a paradigm of virtue to be imitated. The most important of these are the **Testaments of the Twelve Patriarchs,* which preserve important examples of developments in angelology, demonology, the priestly and regal functions of the Messiah, cosmology and ethics (both commendation of *virtues and admonitions against vices). The **Testament of Moses,* which may also be viewed as a rewriting of Deuteronomy 31—34, attests to the regard shown Moses as prophet, mediator and perpetual intercessor. The stance of nonviolent resistance advocated by this book stands in stark contrast to more militaristic ideologies of the period (developed on the model of Judas Maccabeus and his brother Simon; cf. 1 Macc 3; 14). The **Testament of Job* recasts the biblical book as a deathbed speech of Job, with significant variations from the biblical story. Notable is the explanation of Satan's motivation. Job provokes Satan by destroying a nearby center for idolatrous worship (witnessing thus to the understanding of idolatry as worship of demons and Satan, which is frequent in the literature of this period and in the NT) and is thereafter afflicted. Job is presented as an example of piety, generosity and patience.

5. Edifying Tales and Romances.

Instruction and theology were frequently cast in the form of edifying stories, three of which may be found in the Apocrypha. *Tobit tells the story of a Diaspora Jew and his family, illustrating God's providence, the activity of angels and demons and the efficacy of prayer and exorcism. Through Tobit's instructions to his son Tobias (Tobit 13—14 read like testamentary literature), the story promotes almsgiving and acts of charity within the Jewish community, as well as the value of kinship and endogamy. *Judith, a Palestinian work from the Maccabean period, tells of a young Jewish widow who used her charm to trap and kill a Gentile oppressor. The story affirms the importance of prayer, dietary purity and the virtue of chastity, and it illustrates God's care for God's people in times of adversity. Third Maccabees may also be classified as an edifying legend. It parallels the story of 2 Maccabees, linking the fate of Diaspora Judaism with the land of Palestine and vice versa. It affirms God's special care and closeness to Jews living in the Diaspora, separated from the promised land, and attests to the tensions among faithful Jews, apostate Jews and the dominant Gentile culture (*see* Romances/Novels, Ancient).

6. Qumran Literature.

We have already seen how rewritings of the Bible, versions, apocalypses and testaments have been found among the *Dead Sea Scrolls, but the corpus as whole merits special treatment on account of the cumulative impact the discovery has made on knowledge of Second Temple Judaism and the backgrounds of the NT. Finding the cache of the *Qumran community has made an immense contribution to *Essene studies, as well as to our understanding of the Hasmonean period, especially the resistance to the Hasmonean house, about which 1 Maccabees is understandably silent. The biblical manuscripts found at Qumran have taken OT textual criticism to a new level. A number of readings have been discovered where the Qumran texts agree with the Septuagint against the Masoretic Text, thus bearing witness to a Hebrew version other than, and potentially more original than, the MT.

The Qumran community did produce two notably unique genres of text: the rule and the *pesher.* The **Rule of the Community* and the **Damascus Document* (discovered before the turn of the twentieth century but now closely linked with Qumran) are a substantially new genre, a sort of compendium of guidelines for entering and remaining part of the community's life, which never takes root elsewhere in Judaism but becomes foundational for Christian monasticism. The *Rule* attests to a sectarian understanding of the covenant, according to which birth into Israel is meaningless and only initiation into the community brings one into God's covenant. The rule concludes with a hymn admitting the impossibility of a mere human pleasing God but celebrating God's election and justification of the sinner by God's grace—a striking witness that even the most legalistic form of Judaism was not oriented toward works righteousness. The *Rule* also organizes its ethical teaching under the "Two Ways"—the way of life of the wicked, the way of the righteous and their respective ends. This form of instruction also appears in the early church (the *Didache,* which is notably also a rule for the Christian community, and the *Epistle of Barnabas*; *see DLNTD,* Didache; Barnabas, Epistle of) These texts also speak of communal meals as foretastes of the eschatological banquet, at which the messiahs will preside, an emphasis found also in the celebration of the Lord's Supper in the early church.

The other distinctive genre is found in the pesharim, in which a few lines of the biblical text are quoted, followed by an interpretation (pesher) that applies the passage to the history of the Qumran community and its expectations for the future. The form is unique, but the principle (namely, that the Jewish Scriptures speak of the experience of the community) is shared by the early church. Pesharim have been found on parts of Habakkuk, Isaiah, Nahum, Micah, Zephaniah and Psalms 37 and 45 (*see* Habakkuk Commentary [1QpHab]).

The Qumran **War Scroll* is also a genre unto itself. Its content has much in common with apocalypses, but its form is not the same. Rather, it presents detailed instructions for the community's battle array for the eschatological war and tells of the battle and its outcome. Together with other Qumran texts, the *War* attests to the apocalypticism of the community. They held to a strict determinism and also to a radical dualism by which the "children of light" (the sect) were divided from and hostile toward the "children of darkness" (the rest of Israel and the Gentiles). This human dualism was embedded in a cosmic dualism, the war between the hosts of Michael and those of Belial, which would finally be resolved in the eschatological war. After that battle, the messiahs of Aaron and Israel would preside over the sect, which would become the new center of Israel.

The *messianism of the sect has occasioned great interest. Although the extreme claims that the main characters of the sect's history were John and Jesus ought to be rejected, the sect still preserves some important witnesses to the diversity of messianic expectation. One text, known as 4Q521, bears witness to the expectation of the "works" that the Messiah will perform—a model that is also extremely important for some early Christian communities (cf. Mt 11:2-6; Lk 7:18-23).

7. Liturgical Texts.
Numerous *prayers, psalms and other liturgical texts have been transmitted, either independently or as part of larger works. A number of these liturgical pieces appear to have been written to provide suitable prayers or responses at crucial junctures in a narrative. The Prayer of Azariah and the Song of the Three Young Men were inserted into Daniel 3: the former is a prayer of repentance and plea for God's help at the point where the three companions of Daniel are cast into the furnace, and the latter is a psalm of thanksgiving sung by the three after their deliverance (*see* Daniel, Esther and Jeremiah, Additions to). Similarly, the *Prayer of Manasseh, though not inserted into the narrative, supplies what the story of King Manasseh of Judah in 2 Chronicles 33:1-13 lacks: a record of the king's penitential prayer. This beautiful psalm, placed on the lips of the chiefest of sinners, affirms that no one is beyond God's mercy and power to forgive.

The *Psalms of Solomon are a collection of eighteen prayers, psalms of lament, wisdom psalms and psalms of thanksgiving. These look back upon the corruption and tumult of the last decades of the Hasmonean dynasty, which ended with internecine rivalry and the intervention of the Roman triumvir Pompey the Great. The Psalms view Pompey's siege of Jerusalem and entry into the holy place of the temple as a severe desecration and rejoice in God's justice (evident in the assassination of Pompey some fifteen years later). These events demonstrate for the psalmist's community the principle that departure from the law brings punishment but also that the Gentile instrument of punishment will not go free. The psalms sharply criticize a rich, exploitative priesthood, promote the way of life of the righteous, uphold God's justice, celebrate God's generosity toward all creation and affirm the value of God's corrective discipline. They also announce a messianic age under the leadership of a Son of David, the Lord Messiah, who fits the military paradigm quite well. The *Apostolic Constitutions,* a Christian document, has been found to contain numerous prayers from the *synagogue (*Hellenistic Synagogal Prayers*), which, after they have been relieved of their Christian interpolations, provide a valuable view into the piety of the early synagogue.

The Dead Sea Scrolls (see section 6 above) have brought to light many other liturgical texts: the *Hodayot* (the **Thanksgiving Scroll*), the hymn of the initiate closing the *Rule of the Community,* numerous additional psalms attributed to David, prayers, benedictions, **Songs of the Sabbath Sacrifice* and angelic liturgies all provide important windows into the worship and piety of this sect (*see* Liturgy: Qumran). Noteworthy is the sect's awareness of angels in the presence of the worshiping community, shared perhaps by some NT authors (cf. 1 Cor 11).

8. Rabbinic Writings.

Although the Mishnah, the compilation of rabbinic opinions that forms the basis for the later commentaries (the Talmuds), was not codified until about A.D. 200, rabbinic literature may also be considered a literary witness to the Second Temple period insofar as it does preserve traditions that go back to Hillel and Shammai, as well as numerous other scribes and sages from before the fall of Jerusalem (*see* Rabbinic Literature: Mishnah and Tosefta; Rabbinic Literature: Talmud). Both the Mishnah and the Tosefta, a slightly later expansion of the Mishnah, shed light on the rulership and legal procedures in Jerusalem during the period of Jesus' ministry and the second generation of the Jerusalem church. Moreover, the manner of exegesis employed by the rabbis reflects principles also known to and practiced by NT authors. Hebrews, for example, uses both the techniques of argument from the lesser to the greater (*qal wahomer*) and argument from verbal parallel (*gezera shawa*). Familiarity with rabbinic exegesis thus helps one to see the rationales at work in the arguments of certain NT authors (*see* Biblical Interpretation, Jewish). The rabbis were also known for teaching in parables and provide substantial comparative texts for the study of Jesus' parables. Finally, rabbinic literature contains many references (some rather veiled) to the ministry of Jesus: despite the negative view rabbis take of Jesus, the traditions nevertheless have been valuable as independent witnesses of his teaching and wonder-working ministry (Johnson).

Perhaps the most accessible sample of rabbinic literature is the *Pirqe 'Abot,* the Sayings of the Fathers, preserved in the fourth division of the Mishnah. This collection is more akin to wisdom sayings than the rest of the Mishnah, which preserves legal opinions about the application of various commandments to the expanding situations of everyday life. It recommends itself as a valuable introduction to the ethos of those leading minds who gave to Judaism the shape it would bear for centuries to come, particularly their regard for the role of Torah—in both its light and weighty commands—as the center of their lives and the integration of piety and ethics.

See also APOCALYPTIC LITERATURE; APOCRYPHA AND PSEUDEPIGRAPHA; BIBLICAL INTERPRETATION, JEWISH; DEAD SEA SCROLLS: GENERAL INTRODUCTION; HEBREW BIBLE; INSCRIPTIONS AND PAPYRI: JEWISH; INTERTEXTUALITY, BIBLICAL; JOSEPHUS; LITERACY AND BOOK CULTURE; MANUSCRIPTS, GREEK OLD TESTAMENT; PHILO; PSEUDONYMITY AND PSEUDEPIGRAPHY; RABBINIC LITERATURE: MIDRASHIM; RABBINIC LITERATURE: MISHNAH AND TOSEFTA; RABBINIC LITERATURE: TALMUD; RABBINIC LITERATURE: TARGUMIM; REWRITTEN BIBLE IN PSEUDEPIGRAPHA AND QUMRAN; SAMARITAN LITERATURE; SEPTUAGINT/GREEK OLD TESTAMENT.

BIBLIOGRAPHY. **Primary Texts in Translation.** L. C. L. Benton, *The Septuagint with Apocrypha: Greek and English* (Peabody, MA: Hendrickson, 1986 repr.); R. H. Charles, ed., *The Apocrypha and Pseudepigrapha of the Old Testament in English* (2 vols.; Oxford: Clarendon Press, 1913); J. H. Charlesworth, ed., *The Old Testament Pseudepigrapha* (2 vols.; Garden City, NY: Doubleday, 1983, 1985); F. H. Colson and G. H. Whitaker, *Philo* (10 vols.; LCL; Cambridge, MA: Harvard University Press, 1927-62); F. García Martínez, *The Dead Sea Scrolls Translated: The Qumran Texts in English* (2d ed.; Grand Rapids, MI: Eerdmans, 1996); B. Grossfeld, *The Targum Onqelos* (ArBib 6-9; Wilmington, DE: Michael Glazier, 1988); D.

J. Harrington, *Invitation to the Apocrypha* (Grand Rapids, MI: Eerdmans, 1999); M. Maher, *Targum Pseudo-Jonathan* (ArBib 1b; Wilmington, DE: Michael Glazier, 1992); J. Neusner, *The Mishnah: A New Translation* (New Haven, CT: Yale University Press, 1988); H. St. J. Thackeray et al., *Josephus* (10 vols.; LCL; Cambridge, MA: Harvard University Press, 1926-65); G. Vermes, *The Dead Sea Scrolls in English* (4th ed.; New York: Penguin, 1995); W. Whiston, *The Works of Josephus: New Updated Edition* (Peabody, MA: Hendrickson, 1987); C. D. Yonge, *The Works of Philo: New Updated Edition* (Peabody, MA: Hendrickson, 1993). **Secondary Literature.** J. H. Charlesworth, *The Pseudepigrapha and Modern Research, with a Supplement* (SCS 7; Chico, CA: Scholars Press, 1981); J. H. Charlesworth, ed., *The Old Testament Pseudepigrapha* (2 vols.; Garden City, NY: Doubleday, 1983, 1985); B. Chilton, *A Galilean Rabbi and His Bible: Jesus' Use of the Interpreted Scripture of His Time* (GNS 8; Wilmington, DE: Michael Glazier, 1984); D. A. deSilva, "The Dead Sea Scrolls and Early Christianity," *Sewanee Theological Review* 39 (1996) 285-302; idem, *Introduction to the Apocrypha* (Grand Rapids, MI: Baker, 2000); C. A. Evans, *Noncanonical Writings and New Testament Interpretation* (Peabody, MA: Hendrickson, 1992); C. T. Fritsch, "Apocrypha," *IDB* 1:161-66; idem, "Pseudepigrapha," *IBD* 3:960-64; L. T. Johnson, *The Real Jesus* (New York: HarperCollins, 1995); R. A. Kraft and G. W. E. Nickelsburg, eds., *Early Judaism and Its Modern Interpreters* (Philadelphia: Fortress; Atlanta: Scholars Press, 1986); B. M. Metzger, *An Introduction to the Apocrypha* (Oxford: Oxford University Press, 1957); J. D. Newsome, *Greeks, Romans, Jews* (Philadelphia: Trinity Press International, 1992); G. W. E. Nickelsburg, *Jewish Literature Between the Bible and the Mishnah* (Philadelphia: Fortress, 1981); D. S. Russell, *Between the Testaments* (Philadelphia: Fortress, 1960); idem, "Pseudepigrapha," in *The Oxford Companion to the Bible*, ed. B. M. Metzger and M. D. Coogan (Oxford: Oxford University Press, 1993) 629-31; E. Schürer, *The History of the Jewish People in the Age of Jesus Christ*, rev. and ed. G. Vermes et al. (3 vols.; Edinburgh: T & T Clark, 1973-87) 3.1; J. J. Scott Jr., *Customs and Controversies: Intertestamental Jewish Backgrounds of the New Testament* (Grand Rapids, MI: Baker, 1995); M. E. Stone, "The Dead Sea Scrolls and the Pseudepigrapha," *Dead Sea Discoveries* 3 (1996) 270-95; idem, "Pseudepigrapha," *IDBSup* 710-12; M. E. Stone, ed., *Jewish Writings of the Second Temple Period* (CRINT 2.2; Assen: Van Gorcum; Philadelphia: Fortress, 1984); J. C. VanderKam, *The Dead Sea Scrolls Today* (Grand Rapids, MI: Eerdmans, 1994).

D. A. deSilva

X, Y, Z

XENOPHON. *See* HISTORIANS, GRECO-ROMAN.

YEARS. *See* CALENDAR, JEWISH.

YOUTH. *See* CHILDREN IN LATE ANTIQUITY.

ZEALOT MOVEMENT. *See* REVOLUTIONARY MOVEMENTS, JEWISH.

ZENON PAPYRI

The Greek *papyri from Egypt preserve many documents that illuminate the life of ordinary people in the cities and towns of Egypt during the periods of Greek and Roman rule. Many of the papyri are fragmentary, in a poor state of preservation and difficult to read. And the text is often incomplete. Because of the random nature of the survival of papyri, most often individual pieces are without context. *Letters may bear the name of the sender, or his rank if he is an administrator, but frequently that is all we know about the individual, and in legal matters documents that might explain the resolution of a case presented in a petition simply have not survived. Therefore any group of documents that can be identified as belonging to, or relating to, a specific individual is of particular importance because they allow us to draw conclusions concerning the interaction of the person and his social and political milieu.

The Zenon papyri constitute a unique find and are the largest archive of documents found in Egypt. Consisting of some two thousand papyri, the archive comprises the files of Zenon, the *oikonomos* (administrator) of a vast estate given by Ptolemy II to his finance minister, Apollonios, in the third century B.C. Amongst his papers are letters, accounts, lists, receipts, memoranda and various other documents that contribute significantly to our understanding of the lifestyle and concerns of the people as well as the administrative processes that affected their lives. Fortunately, too, Zenon often wrote drafts of his letters on the back of used papyri, such as accounts, and these can sometimes be matched with the responses to them that he received. Although the majority of these papers refer to Egypt in the third century B.C., Palestine, at that time, was under Ptolemaic rule so a considerable degree of similarity in lifestyle may be supposed. Moreover, before taking up his position as administrator of Apollonios's Egyptian estate, Zenon traveled extensively in Palestine. Because the history of Palestine during the period of *Ptolemaic rule is virtually undocumented, the Zenon papyri from Palestine are of particular significance.

Although Syria, of which Palestine was part, subsequently fell under *Seleucid rule (197 B.C.) it is probable that by the late first century B.C. life in Palestine had changed little, at least for the people in the small towns and villages. The population of Syria was quite different from that of Egypt in that the majority of Egyptians were primarily peasants who did not question the power of the state whereas the Syrian population was much more diverse, made up of Phoenicians, Jews, Arabs and Idumeans, each with their own historical background and lifestyles that were different from those of the Egyptians. Outside the cites and towns in Syria there were peasants whose simple lifestyle was similar to that of the Egyptian *fellahin*. It is likely, too, that food production and diet would have been similar in both countries.

1. Zenon in Palestine
2. Trade Between Egypt and Syria
3. Food and Diet
4. Toubias the Ammonite
5. Jews in Palestine
6. Taxes

1. Zenon in Palestine.

The earliest dated texts in the archive, beginning in 259 B.C., document a journey Zenon took to Palestine on behalf of Apollonios. His journey, of almost four months' duration, took him from Stratonos Pyrgos (later Caesarea) east to *Jerusalem and Jericho and into the Ammonite territory of the sheik Toubias. He returned through the Hauran and *Galilee, reaching the coast at Ptolemais (Acre). The route of the journey can be determined, in part, from the accounts that list systematically the places in which food was purchased for the travelers. The company was made up of a number of small groups that appear in various parts of Palestine; individual members change from group to group at various times. The purpose of the journey seems to have been to establish trade with certain Palestinians, and on Zenon's return to Egypt he continued to correspond with them. Surviving in the archive are a number of letters from these associates as well as several lengthy accounts of daily rations issued to the members of the group and for the support of the large baggage train that accompanied them (*see* Travel and Trade).

2. Trade Between Egypt and Syria.
The accounts and the letters show that Zenon established trade associations between Palestine and Egypt, although, based on the surviving evidence, this trade appears somewhat one-sided, with imports from Palestine far exceeding the goods he exported from Egypt. P.Col.Zen. 2 indicates that he exported some rush mats and pickled foods. P.Cair.Zen. 1 59.012, is a document prepared for the use of the customs officials at Pelusion (the Egyptian port nearest to Syria where duties were collected on imported goods), which is a list of the cargoes of three ships belonging to Apollonios, annotated with the various customs dues and local taxes payable on each item. The goods in these consignments consisted mainly of foods, although wool, some mats and a jar of Samian earth are also listed. In addition to staples such as grain and oil, there are wines of different varieties and quality, several types of cheese, nuts, dried figs, meat (venison and goat), sea fish as well as salted and pickled fish, and honey from six different locations in Caria, Attica, Rhodes and Asia Minor, some of which must, in turn, have been imported to Syria.

3. Food and Diet.
Zenon kept detailed records of his administration of Apollonios's affairs, both during the Palestinian period and later on the estate in Egypt. Of particular interest among these records are several extensive accounts drawn up in the course of Zenon's visit to Palestine; some detail the daily distribution of food to the travelers and one, P.Lond. 7 2141, contains references to foods sent as *xenia* (gifts of friendship). Included in these foods were lobster, caviar, meat, fine wine, figs, dates and cheese; luxury foods such as these, however, were not the common fare of the ordinary people. Their simple diet can be determined by the food distribution lists (P. Lond. 7 1930, P.Cair.Zen. 1 59.004, 59.006). Each day the travelers received rations of wine, flour and fish (usually pickled or salted). Mostly these ingredients were issued to the cooks and bakers for the preparation of meals, although several persons received individual rations, particularly of wine. These meals, then, were virtually identical to the meals eaten by Jesus and his disciples as they traveled throughout Galilee (cf. Mt 15:36; Mk 6:38).

4. Toubias the Ammonite.
Several documents in the archive mention the Jewish name Toubias (Tobiah). In "the land of Toubias" members of Zenon's party were issued with flour, perhaps provided by, or purchased from Toubias (P.Lond. 7 1930. 175). He certainly provided the party with horses and donkeys that were given rations of chaff (P.Cair.Zen. 5 59.802. 2, 18), and his grooms were allocated one *chous* of wine (P.Lond. 7 1930. 49). That Toubias, a native sheikh, was a man of considerable influence, can be determined from several papyri. P.Cair.Zen. 1 59.003 is a deed of sale for a slave girl purchased by Zenon in Birta, a place in the land of Ammon. Several of the witnesses are identified as cleruchs (military settlers) serving in the troops commanded by Toubias. In all probability these cleruchs were part of a military force maintained by Ptolemy to secure the country and to protect the border. Therefore as the leader of the cleruchy, Toubias was acting as an official of the Egyptian king. Further indication of his status can be seen from two *letters he sent to Apollonios, both written on the same day. In one, he sends as gifts to Ptolemy—a known collector of strange animals—a collection of horses, dogs, white Arabian donkeys and mules. That he should send a gift to the king is not surprising, but his letter is decidedly casual.

Whereas one of his letters to Apollonios begins with the customary effusive greetings, his letter to the king (of which he encloses a copy for Apollonios) is little more than a bald statement of fact with none of the deferential language one might expect in such a letter. His only concession appears to be that he does put the king's name before his own in the opening salutation, ("To King Ptolemy from Toubias"), a courtesy he does not extend to Apollonios ("Toubias to Apollonios"). Of course, it is possible that this letter was merely an "invoice" to accompany the consignment and was not really intended for the king's eyes, but it is striking in its informality. In another letter (the one in which he sends the copy of his letter to the king) he informs Apollonios that he has sent him as a gift four young house slaves accompanied by a eunuch (perhaps their instructor). This is far more formal, beginning with formal words of greeting, but it too retains an air of informality. He writes to Apollonios as to an equal rather than deferring to him as the chief minister of Egypt.

Toubias, in fact, was from an aristocratic family whose position can be traced back from his time for at least 500 years. His ancestor, Toubias the Ammonite, is found in the book of Nehemiah opposing Nehemiah's political activity in Judah and his rebuilding Jerusalem. Clearly, when Nehemiah refers to Toubias as "the slave Toubias" (Neh 2:10, 19), the term is derogatory. He notes that Toubias is indeed a powerful man through marriage connections and that he is in regular correspondence with officials in Judah (Neh 6:17-18). Moreover he has an alliance with Eliashib, the high priest who, to Nehemiah's disgust, made available for Toubias's use a chamber in the temple of Jerusalem (Neh 13:4-8). It is of interest that the book of Nehemiah was written in the third century B.C., contemporaneously with, but unrelated to, the Zenon papyri. The earliest ancestor of Toubias can be found in Zechariah (Zech 6:10), written c. 520 B.C., and others are mentioned in Nehemiah's list of Jews returning from Babylon (Neh 7:62).

5. Jews in Palestine.

There are a number of references to Jews other than Toubias in the papyri from Palestine. Another influential village leader is Jeddous, who, like Toubias, is not cowed by the Egyptian officials. A local official named Alexandros received a request to recover a debt owed to Zenon. Alexandros, however, did not go himself, claiming he was ill, and sent Zenon's messenger, Straton, and a young man in his place. Jeddous violently drove them from the village without paying the debt. He does not appear in any other papyri, and he probably lacked the political status of Toubias, but in his letter Alexandros simply informs his superior, Oryas, of the situation without suggesting that any action should be taken against Jeddous (P.Cair.Zen. 1 59.081).

It is not always possible to determine whether or not some of the people mentioned in the texts are Jews. In the letter from Toubias to Apollonios accompanying his gift of slaves, Toubias includes descriptions of the boys as well as their names. Two are described as being circumcised, but this does not necessarily indicate that they were Jews. Their names, Audomos and Okaimos, are not specifically Semitic, and in Jeremiah 9:24-25 we learn that circumcision was practiced by a number of the peoples living in and around Palestine.

A person's name does not necessarily indicate ethnicity. In Ptolemaic Egypt parents often gave their children Greek names, and we find a very common Egyptian name, Pasis, with the epithet "the Jew" (P.Cair.Zen. 2 59.241. 2). Similarly we find a man with the Greek name Antigones also designated "the Jew" (P.Mich.Zen. 30. 5). Simon of Galilee, a worker on a camel caravan carrying grain between Palestine and Egypt, may well have been a Jew given that he is located in Palestine (P.Col.Zen. 2. 23).

6. Taxes.

There are numerous references in the Egyptian papyri of the Zenon archive which show that the Egyptians and Palestinians had much in common in their daily lives. In the NT we read of complaints about *taxes and the tax gatherers. The Zenon papyri contain references to a bewildering array of taxes and imposts. These were particularly heavy for those engaged in agriculture and included taxes on land, gardens, vineyards, the use of pastures, dikes and the maintenance of waterworks for irrigation. Add to these the taxes on animals (cattle, sheep, goats) and on their products (milk, wool, work done by animals) and a tax to pay for the payment of veterinary surgeons. In addition the sale of goods in the market was taxed as well as use of the bathhouse, brewing beer and the sale of oil. Moreover taxes had to be paid to the *temples and for the provision of guards who protected livestock and the fields during the harvest.

See also HELLENISTIC EGYPT; INSCRIPTIONS AND PAPYRI: GRECO-ROMAN INSCRIPTIONS AND PAPYRI: JEWISH; PAPYRI, PALESTINIAN; PTOLEMIES; TAXATION, GRECO-ROMAN.

BIBLIOGRAPHY. C. C. Edgar, ed., *Zenon Papyri* (P. Cair. Zen.) (5 vols.; Cairo: L'Institut Français D'Archéologie Orientale, 1925-31); idem, *Zenon Papyri in the University of Michigan Collection* (P. Mich. Zen.) (University of Michigan Studies, Humanistic Series 24; Ann Arbor, MI: University of Michigan Press, 1931); P. W. Pestman et al., eds., *A Guide to the Zenon Papyri* (P. L. Bat. 21) (2 vols.; Leiden: E. J. Brill, 1981) XI-XVIII (for an extensive bibliography of the Zenon papyri); M. Rostovtzeff, *A Large Estate in Egypt in the Third Century B.C. A Study in Economic History* (University of Wisconsin Studies in the Social Sciences and History 6; Madison, WI: University of Wisconsin Press, 1922); T. C. Skeat, ed., *Greek Papyri in the British Museum,* vol. 7: *The Zenon Archive* (P. Lond. 7) (London: British Museum Publications, 1974); V. A. Tcherikover, ed., *Corpus Papyrorum Judaicarum* (Cambridge, MA: Harvard University Press, 1957) vol. 1 (see 118 n. 4 for a bibliography of articles on Toubias); idem, Palestine Under the Ptolemies: A Contribution to the Study of the Zenon Papyri," *Mizraim* 4-5 (1937) 9-90; W. L. Westermann, C. W. Keyes, H. Liebesny, eds, *Zenon Papyri: Business Papers of the Third Century B.C. Dealing with Palestine and Egypt* (P. Col. Zen. 2) (Columbia Papyri Vol. 4; New York: Columbia University Press, 1940).

R. R. E. Cook

ZODIAC. *See* THUNDER TEXT (4Q318).

Scripture Index

Genesis
1, *2, 312, 456, 600, 734, 949, 1290*
1—2, *1295*
1—3, *1-4, 949*
1—5, *950*
1:1, *457*
1:1—41:28, *1104*
1:2, *513*
1:3, *1077*
1:9, *952*
1:26-27, *1, 792*
1:27, *2*
1:28, *199, 248*
2, *2*
2—4, *399*
2—5, *952*
2:1—41:24, *790*
2:1-2, *400*
2:2, *181, 602*
2:2-3, *1031*
2:3-7, *400*
2:4—28:9, *790*
2:7, *513, 792*
2:8-14, *1254*
2:8-18, *400*
2:17, *952*
2:19-25, *400*
2:20-21, *399*
2:24, *2, 3*
3:17-19, *304, 1121*
3:19, *931*
3:21, *468, 949*
4, *948*
4:9, *942*
4:17, *313*
4:24, *1204*
5, *602, 820*
5—11, *823*
5:1, *1243*
5:3, *359*
5:3-4, *399*
5:18-24, *399*
5:21-24, *150*
5:22, *44, 399*
5:24, *44, 70, 313, 399, 447-48, 931*
5:28—15:4, *949*
5:28-29, *950*
5:29, *412*
5:32, *459*
6, *314*
6—9, *950*
6:1-4, *62, 399, 1295*
6:1-5, *153, 154*
6:2, *399*
6:3—8:18, *950*
6:4, *581*
6:9, *399*
7:24, *180*
9:9:1, *781*
9:9:27, *781*
9:24-25, *781*
9:24-27, *950*
10, *390, 412, 581*
10:3, *390*
10:8-10, *581*
10:21, *1250*
11, *951*
11—15, *259*
11:1-9, *581*
11:4, *448*
11:6, *949*
11:8, *30*
11:17, *1037*
11:20-23, *466*
12—25, *495*
12:1-3, *838*
12:1-7, *972*
12:3, *199*
12:5, *555*
12:8—13:1, *399*
12:8—15:4, *398*
12:10, *401*
12:10-20, *495, 524*
13:17-18, *401*
14, *693, 695*
14:2, *155*
14:10, *401*
14:13, *401*
14:17, *401*
14:17-24, *524*
14:18, *400-1, 559, 694*
14:18-19, *826*
14:18-20, *400, 693-94*
14:19-20, *400*
14:21, *401*
15, *37, 450*
15:1-21, *603*
15:13, *1258*
15:18-21, *555*
16:8-9, *912*
17:1-14, *603*
17:8, *555*
17:9-14, *800*
17:10-14, *879*
17:14, *800*
18—19, *1238*
18:1-8, *524*
18:8, *707*
18:16-33, *950*
18:17-18, *385*
19:1-11, *524*
19:9-12, *400*
19:10—20:33, *399*
19:13-16, *400, 401*
19:13-19, *952*
19:17-18, *400*
19:19-20, *400*
19:21-23, *399*
19:30-38, *13*
20, *401, 524, 952*
20:7, *648*
20:9-10, *399*
20:10-16, *399*
20:12, *14*
20:12-15, *399*
20:15-18, *399*
20:18-21, *399*
20:22, *401*
20:22-23, *399*
20:28, *401*
20:31-33, *401*
20:32, *399*
21:21, *904*
21:23—22:34, *398*
22, *864, 866, 907, 948*
22:1-9, *1207*
22:1-18, *458*
22:2, *582*
22:4, *934*
22:10-12, *950*
22:12-17, *400*
22:13, *401*
24, *1238*
24:16-25, *524*
25:1-6, *582*
25:18-19, *950*
27:26-27, *628*
28:6, *950*
28:12, *450*
29, *1238*
30:14, *950*
30:24, *1204*
31:28, *628*
31:44-54, *1148*
31:47, *459*
31:55, *628*
32:11, *648*
32:22-32, *603*
32:24-32, *372*
32:25-33, *950*
32:28, *372, 554*
32:32, *372*
33:4, *628*
34, *582*
34:13-27, *948*
34:30, *582*
35:4, *1060*
35:10, *554*
35:18, *199, 1204*
35:22, *947, 952*
35:32, *1201*
37, *1203-4*
37—48, *1238*
37—50, *78*
37:35, *931*
38, *949*
38—39, *9*
38:8-10, *199*
39, *1204*
39:7, *12*
40—41, *778*
40:8, *48*
41:25, *48*
41:39, *48*
41:54, *401*
41:56-57, *401*
42:8, *952*
42:17-18, *934*
42:18-25, *1202*
42:38, *931*
43:1, *401*
44:4, *525*
44:18, *87, 1096*
46, *950*
48:22, *1060*
49, *738, 781, 1200*
49:1, *1096*
49:2-4, *950*
49:3-4, *952*
49:5, *1206*
49:5-6, *582*
49:5-7, *602*
49:8-12, *703*
49:9, *701*
49:10, *699, 702, 950, 1199*
49:20-21, *950*
50:1, *629*

Exodus
1, *949*
1—2, *524*
1—15, *582*
1:11, *305*
1:16, *457*
1:22, *457*
2:1-3, *512*
2:1-4, *512*
2:1-10, *866*
2:4, *512*
2:15, *604*
2:20, *524*
3—13, *949*
3:2-6, *1197*
3:8, *707*
3:16, *1062*
3:17, *555, 707*
3:18, *604*
4:22, *738, 820*
4:27, *628*
4:27-28, *950*
5:1, *372*
6:2—30:10, *790*
6:20, *866, 1258*
8:8, *372*
8:19, *306*
8:25-32, *372*
10, *950*
12, *373, 376, 1170, 1290*
12:1—13:10, *798*
12:1—23:19, *891*
12:2, *180*
12:3, *1145*
12:5, *1043*
12:14-20, *1043*
12:32, *907*
12:35-36, *163*
12:38, *846*
12:40, *604*
12:46, *458*
12:48, *377*
13:4, *180*
13:5, *707*
13:8, *199*
13:9, *1241*
13:11-16, *799*
13:13, *1040*
14:10, *950*
14:12-20, *950*
14:21, *952*
15, *891, 950*
15:2, *163*
15:17-18, *257*
15:18, *908*
15:22-27, *269*
16:1, *949*
16:25-30, *1031*
17:7, *1207*
17:8-13, *269*
18:7, *628*
18:13-26, *604*
19, *374, 600*
19:1, *1045*
19:5-6, *1127*
19:6, *1243*
20:2, *604*
20:3, *526, 604*
20:4, *1236*
20:4-5, *526*
20:5-6, *913*
20:8-11, *496, 802*
20:12, *355*
20:12-17, *950*
21, *950*
20:21, *1059, 1205*
20:22—23:33, *1020*
20:22-26, *604, 950*
20:26, *949*
21—22, *638*
21:1-10, *950*
21:2-11, *305*
21:15, *355*
21:32—22:13, *950*
22, *305*
22:1, *1039*
22:7, *1039*
22:9, *1039*
22:22, *305*
22:22-23, *942*
22:27, *595*
22:29-30, *1039*
23, *508*
23:10-11, *802*
23:14-17, *372, 875*
23:16, *1039*
23:19, *707, 1039*
23:20, *350*
23:21, *729*
23:29-30, *555*
24, *448, 600*
24:1-2, *150*
24:1-11, *604*
24:4-11, *143*
24:9-10, *448*
24:9-11, *150*
24:10-11, *730*
24:12, *448, 949, 1241*
25—31, *604*
25:1-2, *950*
25:8, *1172*
25:9, *1172*
25:40, *792, 1274*
27—29, *40, 1179*
28—29, *1200*
28:4-7, *196*
28:30, *65*
28:41, *698*
28:42-43, *2, 949*
29:29, *825*
29:38-46, *798*
30:7-8, *798*
30:11-16, *257, 799, 1024, 1166*
30:13-14, *1045*
30:30, *698*
31:3, *509*
31:13, *900, 913*
31:14, *900*
31:18, *949*
32, *949, 951*
32:16, *949*
32:19, *951*
33:5, *707*
33:11, *385*
33:13-18, *385*
33:14, *508*
34, *1183*
34:1, *949*
34:6, *821*
34:10-16, *557*
34:11-17, *840*
34:21, *1031-32*
34:22, *373, 1039*
34:23, *372*
34:26, *707*
34:27, *949*
34:29-35, *952*
40:13, *698*
40:13-15, *698*

Leviticus
1—7, *798*
1:3-17, *1038*
1:4, *1038*
1:9, *1038*
1:13, *1038*
1:17, *1038-39*
2:11, *373, 1039*
2:13, *1038-39*
3:1-17, *604*
4:3-12, *1039*
4:11-12, *1039*
4:13-21, *1039*
4:21, *1039*
4:22-26, *1039*
4:27-35, *1039*
5:11, *1039*
5:11-13, *1036, 1039*
5:14, *1039*
5:15, *1039*
5:16, *1039*
5:17, *1039*
5:18, *1039*
6:1-5, *1039*
6:6, *1039*
6:12-16, *1040*
6:14-18, *1039*
6:17, *373*
6:19-23, *1039*
6:24-30, *1039*
7:1-5, *1039*
7:7-8, *1039*
7:11-21, *1038*
7:19-21, *875*
7:22-27, *875*
7:26-27, *801*
7:28-36, *1038*
7:35, *698*
8—9, *1200*
10:1-3, *874, 875*
10:6-11, *875*
10:10, *9, 875*
10:11, *875, 1199, 1242*
11, *876*
11—15, *604, 801*
11:1-47, *800*
11:29, *78*
11:43, *508*
12, *601*
12:1-6, *638*
12:6-8, *199, 613, 1038*
13—14, *877*
14, *877*
14:1-8, *877*
14:9, *877*
14:10, *1039*
14:10-20, *877*
14:12-14, *1039*
14:19-20, *1038*
14:21-32, *877*
15:2-33, *873*
15:14-15, *1038*
15:25, *277*
15:29-30, *1038*
15:31, *801*
16, *90, 270, 375, 648, 1181*
16:1, *779*
16:1-2, *875*
16:3, *613*
16:5, *613*
16:6, *613*
16:9, *613*
16:11, *613*
16:12-15, *91, 258*
16:15, *613*
16:18-21, *91, 258*
16:24, *1042*
16:32, *698*
17:1-9, *875*
2, *269*
17:10-14, *801, 875*
17:11, *1037*
17:15-16, *875*
18, *734, 881*
18—20, *583, 868*
18:3, *875*
18:6-18, *13, 249*
18:8, *13*
18:9, *14*
18:11, *14*
18:16, *491*
18:21, *903*
18:24-30, *874-75*
19:1-2, *1115*
19:3, *355*
19:9-10, *639, 1032*
19:18, *458, 797, 1243*
19:33-34, *524*
19:34, *797*
20:2-5, *360*
20:10-23, *13*
20:11, *13*
20:11-12, *13*
20:11-21, *13*
20:17, *14*
20:21, *491*
20:23, *875*
20:24, *707*
21:1-4, *801*
21:1-5, *444*
21:6, *875*
21:7, *1199*
21:8, *875*
21:10-12, *801*
21:14, *875*
21:15, *875*
21:17-21, *441*
21:17-23, *1046*
21:22, *875*

21:23, *875*
22:28, *906*
23, *798, 875*
23:4-8, *1043*
23:10-15, *373*
23:15, *182*
23:15-20, *182*
23:15-22, *373*
23:17, *373*
23:21, *375*
23:22, *1032*
23:26-52, *1042*
23:39, *374*
23:39-43, *374*
23:42, *948*
24:5-9, *1041*
25, *781*
25:1-7, *802*
25:13, *694*
25:23, *555*
25:25, *876*
25:35-46, *306*
25:39-46, *257*

Numbers
1:45-46, *604*
3—4, *1200*
3:17-20, *1023*
3:32, *1063*
3:45, *604*
4:1-49, *604*
4:47-49, *950*
5—12, *891*
5:1, *891*
5:2, *648*
5:5-9, *1039*
5:11, *825*
5:11-31, *952*
5:18, *445*
6:12, *1039*
6:12-15, *10*
6:18, *443*
6:22-26, *651*
6:24-26, *1041*
7:1, *950*
11:11-29, *377*
11:16, *1063*
14:22, *1207*
15, *891*
15:31, *1051*
15:32-36, *1031*
15:37-41, *650, 951, 1107, 1146*
16:1-3, *951*
16:22, *910*
18—19, *891*
18:11-12, *799*
18:12, *182*
18:12-19, *1039*
18:13, *799*
18:15-18, *799*
18:18-19, *1038*
18:21-32, *799*
19, *261, 639, 801*
19:10-11, *710*
19:11-22, *175*
21:16-20, *164*
22—24, *509-10*
22:35, *509*
24:2, *510*
24:15-17, *258, 1205-6*
24:17, *587, 699, 702, 916, 1114-15, 1202, 1207*
25:1-9, *592, 1122*
25:1-13, *776, 891*
25:1-15, *439*
25:6-13, *1037*
25:11-13, *1063*
25:14, *78*
26:52-56, *555*
26:52—31:24, *891*
27:18-23, *1064*
28:1-8, *798*
28:3-8, *1040*
28:6, *1040*
28:8, *1040*
28:9—29:40, *798*
28:9-10, *1031, 1033*
28:16-25, *1043*
28:16-31, *798*
28:19-24, *1044*
28:26, *377*
29, *374*
29:7-11, *1042*
29:8, *1042*
29:12-38, *798*
31:8, *78*
34, *555*
35:25, *698, 1063*
35:28, *1063*
36:1-2, *950*

Deuteronomy
1—3, *79*
1:1, *912*
1:3, *1281*
4:25-28, *1281*
4:25-31, *1170*
4:44, *1242*
5:1-21, *261*
5:12, *1031*
5:12-15, *802, 1031*
5:15, *1031*
5:16, *355*
5:23, *1062*
5:28-29, *258, 1205*
5:30-31, *950, 952*
6:4, *29*
6:4-5, *458*
6:4-9, *650, 1107, 1146*
6:7, *801, 1107*
6:16, *1207*
6:17-19, *1170*
7:1-16, *1170*
7:3-4, *840*
7:5, *557*
7:6, *1170*
7:6-11, *1127*
7:7-16, *1170*
7:13, *182*
7:25, *557*
8:2, *1207*
8:5, *821*
8:8, *303*
9:10, *949*
9:22, *1207*
10:2, *949*
10:4, *949*
10:8, *825*
10:17-19, *524*
11:10-12, *555*
11:13-21, *1107, 1146*
12, *1179, 1183*
12—23, *638*
12—26, *256, 1183-84*
12:2, *1169*
12:3, *1169*
12:4-28, *143*
12:5, *1180*
12:5-14, *875, 1169*
12:7, *1170*
12:12, *1170*
12:13, *1169*
12:14, *1169*
12:15-17, *1037*
12:15-28, *875, 1169*
12:18, *1170*
12:22, *876*
12:23, *1037*
13:1, *835*
13:1-5, *65*
13:2-6, *51*
13:6-9, *356*
13:6-18, *662-63*
14:1, *444*
14:3-21, *800*
14:21, *707*
14:22-26, *799*
14:22-27, *1169*
15, *305*
15:2, *257, 306, 694*
15:12-18, *305*
16, *875*
16:1-8, *373*
16:1-17, *798*
16:2, *1043*
16:9-12, *373*
16:12, *374*
16:16-17, *372, 374*
17:8-13, *1062*
17:14-20, *638*
17:18, *1199*
18:3, *1038*
18:15, *349, 1184, 1207*
18:15-18, *351*
18:18, *939*
18:18-19, *258, 349*
18:18-22, *950*
19:15-21, *1062*
20, *1261*
20:3-4, *1261*
21:23, *907-8*
22:6-7, *707*
22:15, *686*
22:20-22, *10*
22:20-24, *10*
22:22, *9*
23:2-9, *840*
23:3, *625, 1046*
23:15, *363*
23:17, *11*
24:1-4, *1034, 1089*
25:5, *491*
26, *1040*
27—29, *565*
27—32, *349*
27:1, *1062*
27:4, *454*
27:14-26, *648*
27:18, *824*
27:21, *1146*
27:22, *14*
28—32, *62*
28:29, *824*
29:29, *150*
30:1-8, *1197*
30:11-14, *150*
30:12, *448*
30:15, *1203*
30:19, *1119*
31—32, *1200, 1238*
34, *63*
31—34, *950, 1195, 1199, 1296*
31:3-6, *1196*
31:9-13, *375*
31:14-22, *1281*
31:16-22, *1196*
31:19, *1047*
31:25, *1047*
31:27, *1281*
31:29, *1196*
32—33, *1296*
32:8, *29, 30*
32:8-9, *30*
32:14, *707*
32:17, *269, 271*
32:39, *932*
32:43, *942*
33, *378, 379*
33:4, *199, 1241, 1243*
33:8, *1207*
33:8-11, *258, 1206*
33:10, *1241*
33:11, *1206*
34, *510*
34:1, *1281*
34:9, *510, 512, 1064*

Joshua
1—21, *949*
2, *524*
4:9, *604*
4:20, *604*
5:1, *454*
6, *605*
6:26, *79, 258, 1206*
8:30-35, *454*
8:31, *1243*
10:3, *559*
11:23, *555*
13:78, *555*
15:59, *1113*
15:61-62, *884*
15:62, *884*
17:17, *604*
17:18, *604*
21, *825*
22:1-6, *604*
23:13-14, *555*
24, *948*
24:13, *555*
24:15, *1203*

Judges
1:1—2:5, *555*
1:16-36, *604*
3:5-6, *555*
3:9-10, *512*
4:17-22, *524*
4:19, *707*
5:24-31, *524*
6, *454*
6:6, *454*
6:7-10, *454*
6:25-32, *595*
6:34, *512*
8:22—9:57, *605*
9, *401*
9:8, *698*
9:8-15, *304, 910*
9:15, *698*
9:27, *374*
11, *605*
11:34, *1262*
13, *524, 866*
13:2, *682*
13:2-5, *457*
13:25, *457*
14:3, *686*
16:17, *457*
17—18, *951*
19—21, *952*
19:22-30, *524*
20:1-3, *1148*
21:1-8, *1148*
21:19, *374*

Ruth
1:1, *558*
1:9, *628*
1:14, *628*

1 Samuel
1:2, *457*
1:10-11, *199*
1:11, *457, 648*
2:1-10, *234, 457*
2:6, *932*
2:35, *1262*
3:1—4:1, *605*
4, *1167*
7:1-2, *605*
7:5-16, *1148*
7:15—8:2, *605*
8:4-22, *605*
8:11-18, *305*
9:1-2, *605*
9:6, *364*
9:9, *698*
9:16, *698*
10, *605*
10:1, *628, 698*
10:6, *512*
10:12, *1266*
13:8-15, *605*
13:14, *1097*
14:31-35, *605*
15, *605*
15:1, *698*
15:17, *698*
16:1-3, *698*
16:1-13, *605*
16:6, *698*
16:12-13, *698*
16:13, *511*
16:14, *399*
16:14-23, *270*
17:18, *707*
17:39, *1207*
18—20, *605*
18:10, *270*
19:1-6, *356*
20:4, *628*
20:31-33, *356*
21:1-6, *496, 1032*
24:6, *698*
24:10, *698*
24:13, *1266*
26:9, *698*
26:11, *698*
26:16, *698*
26:23, *698*
28:1-25, *931*

2 Samuel
1:10, *949*
1:14, *698*
1:16, *698*
5:8, *1046*
6, *605*
6:6-10, *874*
7, *379, 605, 781, 1180*
7:10-14, *257*
7:11-13, *379*
7:11-16, *379*
7:13, *605*
7:14, *380, 458, 702*
8:5-15, *267*
9—1, *605*
12:1-4, *304*
12:7, *698*
14:33, *628*
15:5, *629*
15:24, *825*
15:30, *444*
15:37, *381*
16:16-17, *381*
16:22, *13*
17:29, *707*
19:21, *698*
19:39, *629*
20:3, *13*
20:9, *629*
20:12, *444*
22:51, *698*
23:1, *698*
23:1-7, *848, 851*
24, *941*
24:16, *1171*

1 Kings
1:31, *701*
1:34, *698*
1:37, *701*
1:43, *701*
1:47, *701*
2, *605*
3:5-15, *1270*
4:3, *1086*
4:5, *381*
4:7-19, *180*
4:22-28, *305*
4:25, *304*
4:29-31, *305*
5:12, *305, 854*
5:17-19, *1167*
6, *305*
6—7, *1167*
6:1, *180*
6:38, *180*
8:2, *180, 374*
8:15-21, *1167*
9:15-22, *305*
10:1, *1207*
10:1-13, *524*
11, *606*
11:29-40, *606*
11:36, *649*
15:12, *595*
16:29—22:40, *606*
17:8-16, *458*
17:17-24, *458*
17:41, *1057*
18:1, *1251*
18:41-46, *1251*
18:42, *728*
19:15-16, *698*
19:20, *628*
21, *305, 556*
22, *150, 153, 730*
22:19, *734*
22:24, *511*

2 Kings
2, *150*
2:1, *399*
2:1-18, *449*
2:9-11, *931*
2:12, *357*
3:27, *594*
4:8-17, *524*
4:18-19, *358*
4:32-37, *458*
5:1-14, *458*
5:13, *356*
9:1-3, *698*
9:6, *698*
9:7-10, *942*
9:12, *698*
9:20, *593*
10:27, *595*
12:10, *1086*
13:11, *591*
13:14, *356*
14:9, *594*
16:1-20, *606*
16:3, *907*
17, *1053, 1058*
17:24-41, *1057*
17:25, *846*
17:29, *1058*
18:18, *1086*
20:12-13, *524*
21, *821*
21:5, *1167*
21:6, *907*
22:1—23:30, *606*
22:20, *173*
23:9, *373*
23:10, *907*
23:21-23, *373*
24:9, *591*
25:8, *377*
25:19, *1086*

1 Chronicles
1, 390
1:4-23, 412
2:55, 1086
6:1-15, 823
16, 823
21:1, 153
22:2, 1064
22:8-10, 1167
23:31, 1031
24:1-19, 916
24:7, 438
24:7-18, 181
24:7-19, 1047
27:32, 1086
27:33, 381
28:3, 1167
28:11-18, 1172
28:18, 727
28:19, 1172

2 Chronicles
3—4, 1167
3:1, 582
3:2, 182
11:15, 269
13:22, 889
17:6, 595
19:5-11, 1063
20:7, 252, 385, 496, 781
24:6, 1166
24:20-22, 653
24:27, 889
26:6, 1063
26:11, 1086
29:27, 1138
33:1-13, 1297
33:6, 822
33:11, 822
33:11-13, 821
33:12, 822
33:18-19, 821
34:1—35:27, 606
34:6, 1058
34:13, 1086
35—36, 341
35:1—36:23, 61, 1291
35:19, 822
36:9, 591, 594
36:22-23, 282

Ezra
1, 341, 342
1—10, 341
1:1-4, 282, 575
2:1—4:5, 341-42
2:1-67, 617
3, 575
3:7, 3, 575
3:10-13, 607
4, 1058
4—6, 575
4:1, 1053
4:1-3, 617
4:6-24, 341-42
4:7, 86
4:8, 448
4:8—6:18, 87
4:8-6:18, 459
4:24, 13
4:41-43, 933
5—6, 341
5:5, 1062
5:9, 1062
5:14-16, 575
6:7-8, 1062
6:9-10, 1047
6:14, 1062
6:14-18, 798
6:15, 180
6:21, 617
6:26, 842
6:39, 513
6:55, 1196
6:59, 1196
7, 332
7—10, 341-42
7:6-26, 1086
7:12, 1086
7:12-26, 87, 459
7:26-30, 50
7:26-44, 50
7:28-29, 701
7:30, 332
7:30-31, 51
7:32, 50
7:32-38, 933
7:36-43, 50
7:50, 49
7:75, 51
7:113, 49
7:117-20, 3
7:127-28, 3
8:1, 49
8:10, 707
9—10, 625, 840
9:2, 199
9:5, 1036
9:8-9, 348
9:20, 512
9:79, 556
10, 342
11:1—12:3, 701
12:31-34, 50
12:32, 50, 701
12:34, 50
13, 399
13:2-10, 700
13:3, 702
13:6, 702
13:9-11, 702
14, 512, 1110
14:3-6, 1196
14:22, 512
14:44-47, 58
14:45-48, 456
14:47, 512

Nehemiah
1—2, 575
1—7, 342
1:1, 180
2:1, 180
2:8, 117
2:10, 1302
2:16, 1062
2:19, 1302
4—6, 575
5:6-13, 306
5:7, 1062
5:11, 304
6:15, 180
6:17-18, 1302
7:2, 117
7:5-69, 617
7:38—8:12, 61, 1291
7:62, 1302
8, 341-42, 753, 1146, 1149
8—13, 607
8:1-8, 1242
8:1-9, 1086
8:1-18, 1241
8:6, 648
8:13, 342
8:14-16, 375
9, 649, 948
9:6-37, 821
9:9-21, 1198
9:30, 511
9:36, 348
10:3, 1045
10:28, 617
10:31, 802
10:32, 799
10:32-33, 1166
10:34-35, 182
10:37, 799
10:37-39, 799
11:10-18, 1047
12:10-11, 1063
13:4-8, 1302
13:15-22, 802, 1031
13:23-24, 460

Esther
1:1, 251
2:5, 1160
2:5-6, 1161
2:13, 251
2:16, 180
3, 250
4:17, 251
5:3, 376
5:6, 376
6, 1160
6:1, 1160
7:2, 376
8:1, 375
8:9, 180
8:12, 251
8:17, 844
9:15, 182
9:26-32, 182
10:3, 251

Job
1, 730, 1189
1—2, 153, 1190
1:6, 357, 582
2:1, 29
2:9, 1190
3:5, 91
3:5-9, 258
5:1, 357
6:1, 357
10:10, 707
13, 708
14:14, 932
17—42, 91, 258
20:17, 707
22:7, 524
26:3, 399
26:5, 931
27:2-5, 1191
28, 149
28:12-28, 1271
29—31, 1190
29:6, 708
30:26, 347
31:32, 524
42, 1190
42:17, 86, 92, 582

Psalms
1, 849
1—89, 848, 849-50
1—150, 849-50
1:1, 386
2:2, 698
2:7, 458, 1024, 1115
3—4, 20-21, 32, 41, 46, 55, 58, 61, 64-65, 70, 72-75, 80, 87, 90, 108, 848
6, 847
6—17, 195
9:11-12, 942
9:21, 942
16:10, 932
17, 855
18:36, 1115
18:50, 698
19:7, 1119
19:8, 1243
20:6, 698
21:7, 1115
22, 851
22:1, 458, 1095
24:4, 801
25, 1061
28:8, 698
31:5, 457-58
37, 1297
37:7-40, 257
45:1-2, 257
50, 822
51:13, 508
55:16-17, 649
55:17, 802
68:17, 1171
68:19, 448
69:21, 458
72:19, 1180
74:8, 515
74:9, 508
74:14, 51
76:2, 559
78:67, 78
80:9-17, 1266
82:2, 781
82:7, 29-30
84:9, 698
86:13, 931
87:4, 51
88:10, 931
89:4, 170
89:20, 1097
89:27, 738
89:38, 698
89:48, 931
89:51, 698
90, 848
90—150, 848-49
90:3, 931
92:13, 401
93:1, 1115
95, 162
103, 146
106:23, 170
106:37, 269, 271
110:1, 457
110:3, 1025
110:4, 695
113—118, 1043
118:22, 90, 1180
118:22-23, 1257
127:3-5, 199
132:10, 698
132:17, 698
145, 253

Proverbs
1, 152, 911
1—9, 1264
1:7, 1119
1:8, 357
1:20-33, 1271
2:16-19, 1263
3:13, 152
3:13-15, 152
4, 911
4:5, 152
4:7, 152
5:1-23, 1263
5:20, 8
5:23, 8
6:23, 821
6:23-26, 1263
6:26-35, 8
6:32-33, 519
7:1-27, 1263
7:6-23, 910
7:7-22, 152
7:13, 629
7:22-27, 8
8, 1264
8:5-6, 152
8:11, 152
8:22-31, 1271
9:5, 304
9:18, 931
10:1, 355, 911
10:20, 152
10:31, 152
11:13, 1061
12:5, 152
12:17, 152
12:18-19, 152
12:20, 152
13:24, 199, 358
14:8, 152
14:18, 152
14:29, 152
15:2, 152
15:4, 152
15:8, 649
15:33, 152
17:20, 152
17:21, 355
17:25, 355
18:12, 152
18:21, 152
20:6, 382
22:4, 152
22:10, 1061
22:14, 8
22:15, 199
22:16, 305
22:17, 911
22:22-23, 305
23:1-6, 305
23:24-25, 355
23:27, 11
24:26, 629
25:1, 911
27:6, 629
27:10, 354
27:27, 707
28:7, 355
28:22, 305
29:3, 355
29:15, 355
31:10-31, 199
31:26, 152

Ecclesiastes
2:1, 1207
2:18-21, 471
3:19-22, 471
4:1-3, 305
4:7-11, 471
8:1, 778

Song of Songs
1:2, 629
1:17, 1115
2:5, 687
3:24, 29
5:12, 708
7, 401
8:1, 628

Isaiah
1, 129
1:8, 1114
1:10-17, 305
1:11-17, 1120
1:13-15, 648
1:17, 305, 356
2:1-4, 1171
2:9, 552
2:16, 934
2:22, 552
3:10, 912
3:13-18, 130
3:21-31, 130
4:1, 1109
4:2-16, 1136
4:13, 129
5, 781, 1257
5:1-2, 1257
5:1-7, 1257
5:4-5, 942
5:17, 615
5:20, 347
6, 150, 376, 448, 727, 730, 734, 906
6—11, 130, 730
6:1-4, 728, 730
6:3, 236, 1180
6:9, 906
6:9-10, 909
6:10, 906
7:1-7, 51
7:12, 1207
7:14, 1102, 1292
7:15, 707
7:22, 707
8:11, 257, 780
9:1, 395
9:1-2, 268
9:7, 556
10:20—11:5, 780
10:20—11:16, 1135
10:34—11:1, 1136
11, 330, 514, 699-700, 1109, 1262
11:1, 700-1, 703
11:1-5, 1116
11:1-6, 699-700
11:2, 700
11:2-9, 937
11:3, 700
11:4, 700, 702
11:5, 700
11:10, 700
13:10, 1078, 1198
13:13, 1198
13:18, 438, 781
13:21, 269
14, 153
14:11, 449, 931
14:12-20, 449
14:26-27, 780
16:1-6, 942
19:18-23, 1037
20, 782
22:15, 1086
24—27, 47, 49, 153
24:7-13, 153
24:16, 615
24:17, 781
24:21-23, 153
24:22-23, 1202
24:23, 908
25—27, 409
25:1-6, 153
25:6, 146
25:6-8, 144, 908
25:8, 153, 932
26, 818
26:5-6, 153
26:14, 931
26:19, 234, 696, 932
26:19-20, 153
27:1, 153
27:10-11, 153
28:15, 1271
28:16, 704, 1180
29:13, 1105, 1179
31:4, 908
33:7, 907
34:1-7, 1037
34:14, 269
35:5-6, 696
36:11, 86
40, 863
40—55, 226, 409, 607
40:3, 23, 226, 350, 553, 554, 1022
40:3-5, 349
40:9, 908
41:8, 252, 385, 496
42:1, 170, 702,

704
43:5, 294
43:20, 170
43:21, 797
44, 85
44—46, 526
44:9-20, 1272
44:28, 1097
45:4, 170
45:14, 307
45:20, 307
45:22-25, 307
47:13-14, 262
52:7, 694, 908
52:8, 556
52:13—53:12, 458, 665, 866
53, 234, 1262
53:4, 905
53:5, 696, 905, 1262
53:9, 932
53:10, 932
11, 905
54:1-8, 851
54:11-12, 742, 744, 1240
54:11-14, 1238
54:12, 65
56—66, 42, 47, 575
56:1-8, 294, 350
56:7, 294, 350, 799
58:3-10, 1120
58:6, 350
58:6-7, 524
58:13, 1031
59:10, 824
59:17, 1274
59:20, 164
60:1-22, 851, 1238
61, 514, 694, 698
61:1, 696, 704
61:1-2, 350, 704, 1150
61:1-7, 514
61:2, 1150
62:1-8, 851
63:7-14, 508
63:14, 508
65—66, 42
65:17, 51, 54-55
66:1, 728, 1180
66:3, 1172
66:20, 801
66:22, 54, 55
66:24, 615

Jeremiah
1:13-15, 51
2:29, 912
3:18, 51
4, 250
4:6, 51
6:1, 51
6:3, 277
6:6, 277
6:14, 762
6:22, 51
7, 562
7:9-14, 10
7:11, 562
7:21-23, 1120
7:34, 562
10, 526
10:1-3, 262
10:11, 87, 459
11:20, 942
12:7, 277, 1180
14:11, 648
15:15, 942
17:19-27, 802, 1031
17:21-22, 1031
17:22, 802
20:13, 147
21:8, 1203
23:1-8, 607
23:5, 379
23:5-6, 937
23:14-15, 10
23:24, 1180
25:1-2, 149
25:11-12, 349
26:7, 149
31, 149
29—52, 151
30:9, 1136
31, 1292
31:2, 512
31:9, 738
32:12-16, 148
33:15, 379
33:15-18, 703, 1262
34, 277
36:4, 1086
36:6-15, 1086
36:10, 1167
36:18, 1086
36:32, 1086
40:5, 1058
43—44, 196
43:1-7, 148
43:6-7, 283
44:1, 283
45, 148
46:14, 283
51, 148
52:12, 377

Lamentations
4:14, 824

Ezekiel
1, 38, 53, 150, 222, 312, 448, 727, 730-32, 734, 1139
1:15-21, 1006
1:26-28, 728
1:27-28, 734
1:28, 729
2, 869
3:12-13, 730
4:14, 879
5:5, 412
7:7, 908
8:1, 149
11:19-20, 514
12:22-23, 1266
13:10, 762
14:14, 609, 1191
14:20, 1191
16:44, 1266
17:22-23, 556
18:2, 911
18:2-3, 1266
19:10-14, 1266
20:12, 1031
20:20, 1031
22:21, 711
24:7-11, 942
28, 153
31, 401
32, 153
32:21, 931
33:30-32, 149
34:24, 1115
35:15-23, 78
37, 380
37—38, 869
37:1-14, 556, 869, 932
37:23, 257, 780
37:25, 1115, 1261
37:27, 1179
38—39, 51, 409
38:6, 51
38:12, 412
38:15, 51
39:2, 51
39:17-20, 1037
40—48, 607, 732, 742, 875, 882, 1171, 1173
40:3-4, 1260
43:1-5, 869
43:5, 1180
43:6-9, 875
44:9, 875
44:10-14, 875
44:15-16, 875
44:17-18, 875
44:19, 875
44:20, 875
44:21, 875
44:22, 875
44:23, 875
48:18, 556
48:23-27, 556
48:29, 555

Daniel
1—6, 1160, 1238, 1291
1:7, 340
1:8-16, 801
2, 41, 250, 259, 330-31, 702
2:4, 86, 87, 459
2:19, 1023
2:19-23, 48
2:28-30, 1023
2:30, 48
2:37, 236, 1272
2:45, 48
2:47, 1023
3, 1297
3:5, 467
3:7, 467
3:10, 467
3:15, 467
3:23, 251
3:35, 252
3:92, 29
4, 401, 823
4—6, 454
4:1, 1203
4:3, 778
4:7-14, 1266
4:16-17, 1272
4:17-18, 1266
4:26-27, 1272
5, 1203
5:6, 1201
5:10, 649
5:11, 841
5:11-12, 48
5:12, 778, 1160
5:15, 778
5:16, 778
5:20-23, 1272
5:26, 778
6, 155, 1203
6:7, 841
6:10, 802, 1036
6:13, 802
7, 44, 154, 316, 331-32, 448, 704, 727, 734, 1115, 1181, 1199
7—8, 51
7—12, 46, 48, 154, 1170, 1295
7:5, 1204
7:9, 1115
7:9-10, 730
7:9-14, 730
7:13, 399, 458, 700, 702, 704, 1115, 1136, 1152
7:13-14, 701
7:13-27, 154
8:2-14, 1260
8:6, 1240
8:14, 615
8:15-17, 1260
9, 149, 315, 349, 351, 1202
9:1-27, 160
9:4-19, 260, 821, 950
9:7, 615
9:14, 615
9:16, 615
9:18, 615
9:21, 1036
9:21-23, 1240
9:22, 1226
9:24, 615, 870
9:24-27, 257
10, 42
10—11, 30
12, 824
10:4—11:2, 154
10:13, 30, 154, 1240
10:20, 30, 154
10:20-21, 30
10:21, 1240
11, 572
11:1, 30
11:2-4, 22
11:33-35, 1226
11:36-37, 51, 56
11:36-39, 51
11:40—12:3, 255
11:44, 738
12, 335, 824
12:1, 30, 154, 1198, 1240
12:1-3, 154, 932
12:1-4, 609, 1170
12:2, 43, 696, 824, 932, 934
12:2-3, 933
12:3, 56, 449
12:10, 49
12:11, 277
12:11-12, 1170
12:13, 251, 932
13, 251
13:32, 445
14, 251

Hosea
2:7-14, 780
4:2-3, 10
6:1-3, 931
6:2, 934
6:6, 802, 1033, 1120
9:2, 304
9:4, 304
9:8, 1180
9:15, 1180
11:1, 164, 457
13:14, 931

Joel
2:2, 55
2:10, 1198
2:13, 822
2:24-28, 144
2:31, 1198
3:15-16, 1198
3:18, 708
3:19-20, 942

Amos
2:7, 13
3:7, 554
4:7, 1251
5:6, 78
5:11, 1064
5:18-20, 55
5:21-24, 305
8:4-6, 305
8:5, 1031
8:10, 1238
9:11, 257, 380
9:11-12, 472, 1180
9:14-15, 556

Obadiah
21, 908

Jonah
1:17, 458
2:1, 934
4:2, 822

Micah
1:3-4, 1198
2:1-2, 305
4:4, 304
5:2, 937

Nahum
1:1, 1238
2:8-10, 1238
2:13, 1238
3:8-10, 870
3:18-19, 1238

Habakkuk
1—2, 779
1:5, 437-38, 541, 547-50
1:11, 780
1:13, 438
1:17, 781
2, 437
2:1, 505
2:4, 548
2:5, 438
2:6, 780
2:16, 437
3:11, 711
7:1-5, 833
7:4-5, 779, 1023
9:2-7, 277, 820
11:2-8, 181
11:4-6, 349
11:6, 1216
12:3-5, 277

Zephaniah
1:14-16, 55
1:17, 824

Haggai
1:1, 1062
1:1-13, 575
1:8, 575
2:1-7, 703
2:9, 1171

Zechariah
6, 48
1—8, 575
1:7, 180
1:17, 1171
2:6, 350
3, 614, 732, 878
3:1-2, 153
4:12-14, 1262
4:14, 703, 1062
5:1-5, 565
5:3, 614
5:3-4, 878
5:4, 614
6:1-7, 1260
6:10, 1302
6:10-15, 1262
8, 607
8:7, 294
8:19, 375
9—14, 47, 409
9:8, 1180
9:9, 614, 697, 879
10:1, 1251
10:6-10, 78
11:4-17, 614, 879
12:11, 606
13:1, 614, 878
14:8, 614, 878
14:8-11, 1171
14:9, 908
14:16, 614, 878
14:16-19, 614, 878
14:16-21, 375
14:20, 375, 614
14:20-21, 879
14:21, 614

Malachi
3:1, 350
3:1-2, 1197
3:5, 10
3:22-3, 449
4:5-6, 696

Matthew
1—2, 654
1—13, 268
1:1, 704
1:1—23:22, 463
1:1-17, 457, 866
1:13-16, 866
1:18, 400
1:18—2:23, 399
1:18-19, 400
1:19, 685
1:20, 704, 740
1:20-4, 927
1:20-21, 400
1:22, 457
1:22-23, 553-54
1:24, 72
1:25, 686
2, 979, 1016
2:1, 94, 201, 998
2:1-8, 489
2:1-10, 930
2:1-12, 202, 1245
2:2, 699, 1207
2:4, 395, 1088
2:5, 457
2:7, 928
2:12, 489
2:12-15, 927
2:13, 72, 400, 740
2:13-15, 489
2:14, 400
2:15, 164, 201, 457
2:16, 457, 489
2:17, 457
2:19, 740
2:19-20, 201
2:20-21, 557
2:20-23, 489
2:22, 964, 1016
2:23, 453, 457, 700
3, 509
3:2, 901
3:3, 553, 554
3:7, 785
3:11-12, 697
3:16, 750
3:16-17, 554
4:1, 1210
4:5, 96
4:17, 901
4:18-22, 395
4:23, 1145, 1150, 1245
4:23-25, 1245
4:24, 669
4:24-25, 267-68
5, 1256

5—7, *1090*
5:3-10, *151, 758*
5:3-12, *1207, 1266*
5:4, *1246*
5:10-12, *777, 1089*
5:11-12, *379, 521*
5:17, *458*
5:17-18, *546*
5:19, *1088*
5:20, *1088*
5:21-22, *458, 1123*
5:21-48, *1240*
5:22, *1061*
5:23-24, *798*
5:25, *395*
5:25-26, *761*
5:27-28, *458, 881*
5:28, *687*
5:29-30, *19*
5:31-32, *881*
5:31-34, *458*
5:32, *6, 249*
5:33-34, *323*
5:33-36, *1034*
5:33-37, *614, 878*
5:38-39, *458*
5:38-48, *627*
5:41, *966*
5:42, *1123*
5:43-44, *458*
5:45, *1123*
5:46, *1165*
6:1-4, *323*
6:1-18, *1240*
6:2, *800, 1149*
6:2-4, *158*
6:5, *650, 1149*
6:7, *69, 1123*
6:9, *506, 1123, 1155*
6:9-13, *306, 651*
6:11, *306*
6:12, *306, 1123*
6:13, *306, 1210*
6:14-15, *1123*
6:16-18, *626*
6:19, *1240*
6:19-21, *1123*
6:20, *1240*
7:1-2, *913*
7:4, *899*
7:12, *497, 1240*
7:13-14, *1022, 1288*
7:15, *19*
7:21-27, *1240*
7:27, *464*
7:29, *1088*
8:1-4, *1151*
8:2-4, *877*
8:4, *826*
8:5, *993*
8:5-13, *433, 458, 507*
8:6, *361*
8:11, *146, 294, 908, 1177*
8:11-12, *144*
8:11-13, *973*
8:12, *294, 785, 1177*
8:15, *262*
8:18-20, *739, 761*
8:19, *395, 1088-89*
8:19-20, *1088*
8:20, *506, 1089*
8:21-22, *175, 1088*
8:24, *1247*
8:28, *97*
8:28-34, *267*
8:34, *267*
9:1-8, *81, 1151*
9:9, *433*
9:11, *1088*
9:14-17, *626*
9:18-19, *81, 1150*
9:20-22, *1150*
9:23, *1146*
9:23-24, *714*
9:23-26, *81, 1150*
9:27-31, *81*
9:35, *1150*
9:36, *395*
10:5, *1055, 1060*
10:6, *1060*
10:9-10, *878*
10:9-11, *312*
10:11-14, *877*
10:12, *878*
10:13, *878*
10:16, *19*
10:17, *800, 1133, 1151*
10:18, *997*
10:24-25, *521*
10:25, *1240*
10:28, *934, 1029*
10:32-33, *521*
10:37, *464*
11:2-6, *697, 1297*
11:5, *81, 700, 704*
11:16-17, *714*
11:18-19, *739, 876*
11:19, *386*
11:20-24, *1151*
11:21-23, *350*
11:25, *1218*
11:25-30, *1267*
11:28-30, *69, 1123*
11:29-30, *1265*
12:1-14, *1033*
12:3-4, *496*
12:4, *464, 1176*
12:5, *1033*
12:5-7, *1034*
12:9-14, *81, 1033, 1150*
12:10-11, *1034*
12:11, *1009*
12:11-12, *1034*
12:24, *1088, 1240*
12:30, *497*
12:35, *72*
12:40, *458*
12:42, *458*
12:44-45, *507*
13:1-52, *761*
13:10, *909*
13:11, *1088*
13:12, *1000*
13:24-30, *304, 395, 934*
13:26, *304*
13:34, *935*
13:36-43, *934*
13:40, *934*
13:41, *935*
13:42-43, *934*
13:43, *449, 934*
13:45, *934*
13:45-46, *395*
13:52, *1088*
13:54, *1145, 1150-51*
13:55, *395, 490, 1003*
14:1, *491*
14:1-2, *492*
14:3, *491*
14:3-12, *490-91*
14:9, *491*
14:21, *199-200*
14:22, *1248*
14:22-33, *751, 761*
15:3-9, *1178*
15:4, *458*
15:8-9, *1105*
15:10-11, *876, 1151*
15:12-14, *777*
15:14, *785*
15:19, *761, 1255*
15:21-28, *433*
15:22, *704*
15:30-31, *81*
15:36, *464, 1301*
15:38, *199-200*
15:39, *1247*
16:1, *785*
16:6, *493, 785*
16:11-12, *785*
16:12, *493*
16:13-20, *433, 490*
16:18, *614*
16:18-19, *878*
16:19, *614*
16:21, *1088*
16:21-22, *1262*
17:1-8, *458*
17:3, *458*
17:5, *458*
17:14-29, *81*
17:24-27, *221, 799, 1045, 1166, 1176, 1178*
17:26, *306*
18:1-5, *201*
18:8, *933*
18:9, *933*
18:10, *31*
18:15-17, *249-50*
18:17, *1165*
18:23-34, *305-6*
19:3-12, *881*
19:4-6, *2*
19:4-8, *458*
19:10-12, *683*
19:16, *933*
19:21, *1123*
19:24, *899, 1246*
19:28, *316, 1023, 1199*
19:29, *933*
20:1, *304*
20:1-16, *395*
20:2, *304*
20:15, *305*
20:25-28, *521*
21:1-9, *614, 879*
21:1-11, *496*
21:2, *1246*
21:2-3, *375, 1246*
21:5, *1246*
21:8, *375*
21:9, *704*
21:10-17, *1044*
21:12, *612, 1168, 1175, 1181*
21:12-13, *350, 1176*
21:12-16, *1173*
21:13, *612*
21:14, *1168*
21:14-15, *1046*
21:15, *704, 1168*
21:31-32, *11, 395, 1165*
21:33-41, *395*
21:33-46, *395*
21:43-45, *785*
22:1-10, *144*
22:1-14, *395, 1026*
22:2-7, *686*
22:2-14, *900*
22:16, *610*
22:16-22, *433*
22:17, *1162*
22:19-21, *1164*
22:21, *996, 1028*
22:23, *610, 709*
22:23-32, *458*
22:23-33, *933*
22:34-36, *1088*
22:34-40, *395*
22:37, *899*
22:40, *1088*
22:41-45, *695*
22:42-45, *458*
23, *797*
23:1-36, *777, 1089*
23:1-39, *1088*
23:2, *800, 1088, 1146*
23:2-3, *785*
23:2-29, *1088*
23:5, *785, 802*
23:6, *800, 1149*
23:8, *354, 1088*
23:9, *357*
23:13-36, *1207*
23:15, *626, 1089*
23:16, *1176*
23:16-22, *613*
23:23, *626, 785*
23:23—28:20, *463*
23:23-36, *1089*
23:25-26, *896*
23:27, *899*
23:29-31, *653*
23:31, *1176*
23:34, *1009, 1151*
23:34-36, *614, 878*
23:35, *653*
23:37, *561*
23:37-38, *277*
24, *77, 339*
24—25, *377*
24:1, *1176*
24:1-2, *972*
24:2, *277*
24:9-10, *521*
24:15, *456, 797, 1176*
24:19-21, *1198*
24:20, *1033*
24:21, *1198*
24:22, *869*
24:23-24, *56*
24:24, *56*
24:29, *1077*
24:37-39, *399*
24:40-41, *40*
24:45-51, *395*
24:48-51, *19*
25:1-12, *900, 1026*
25:10-12, *686*
25:14-30, *395*
25:14-46, *521*
25:27, *395*
25:28, *464*
25:31-46, *52, 830*
25:36, *829*
25:43, *829*
25:59-61, *972*
26:3, *95, 179, 204, 464, 1063*
26:3-5, *376*
26:14-16, *614, 879*
26:17, *203*
26:17-20, *376*
26:17-30, *300*
26:17-35, *204*
26:23, *464*
26:25, *915*
26:26, *1177*
26:27-28, *1023*
26:28, *1177*
26:30, *232, 713-14*
26:30-34, *72, 537*
26:48-49, *629*
26:49, *915*
26:52, *627*
26:53, *992*
26:55, *1047*
26:57, *95, 179, 204, 1063-64, 1088*
26:61, *277, 1176*
26:64, *458*
26:68, *562*
27, *980, 997*
27:1, *1063*
27:1-2, *803*
27:2, *221, 803, 979*
27:2-6, *204*
27:3-10, *614, 879*
27:11-26, *803*
27:15-26, *982*
27:19, *927, 981*
27:19-26, *1088*
27:25, *867*
27:32, *995*
27:38, *395, 982*
27:39, *458*
27:40, *1176*
27:41, *1063, 1088*
27:43, *1274*
27:46, *458, 462, 1095*
27:51-53, *52*
27:62, *204*
27:63, *867*
28:2, *97*
28:2-4, *52*
28:11-12, *1063*
28:18, *582*
28:19, *232, 233*

Mark
1:1, *402*
1:2-3, *350*
1:3, *554, 1022*
1:4-5, *874*
1:4-6, *682*
1:6, *739*
1:7, *697*
1:10, *750*
1:11, *506, 704*
1:12, *1210*
1:14-15, *63, 402, 1197-98*
1:17, *1089*
1:18-20, *682*
1:20, *1248*
1:21, *1032, 1145*
1:21-28, *81, 1032, 1150*
1:22, *1088-89*
1:25, *399*
1:29, *1151*
1:31, *262*
1:32, *1032*
1:32-34, *399*
1:34, *272, 507*
1:39, *1150, 1245*
1:40-44, *877*
1:40-45, *1151*
1:44, *798, 801, 826*
2:1—3:6, *785*
2:1-12, *81, 1151*
2:4, *95*
2:6, *1088-89*
2:7, *1089*
2:10, *704*
2:11, *1165*
2:13-14, *433*
2:15, *1165*
2:15-16, *306*
2:15-17, *1089*
2:16, *1087, 1088-89*
2:18, *626*
2:19-20, *626*
2:22, *1088*
2:23-28, *1032-34, 1089*
2:25-28, *1032*
2:26, *1032*
2:27, *900, 913, 1034-35*
2:27-28, *704*
2:28, *1033*
3:1, *1032*
3:1-6, *81, 1033-34, 1150*
3:4, *1033, 1034*
3:6, *610, 785*
3:7-10, *1245*
3:10, *272*
3:11, *507*
3:12, *507*
3:13-19, *980*
3:15, *272, 1088*
3:19-30, *785*
3:22, *740, 928, 1088, 1240*
3:27, *704, 1202*
4, *913*
4:1-34, *761*
4:3, *304*
4:4-7, *304*
4:8, *1009*
4:11, *906*
4:12, *906*
4:25, *1000*
4:29, *304*
4:37, *1247-48*
5:1, *97*
5:1-20, *267*
5:7, *268, 507*
5:8, *507*
5:14, *267*
5:20, *267*
5:21-24, *81, 800, 1150*
5:22, *1146*
5:23, *399*
5:25-34, *1150*
5:29, *272*
5:35, *1146*
5:35-43, *81, 800, 1150*
5:36, *1146*
5:38, *1146*
5:41, *89, 462, 1095*
6:2, *1145, 1151*
6:3, *490*
6:4, *307, 697*
6:5, *399*
6:7, *1088*
6:8-9, *878*
6:10, *877*
6:14, *491*
6:14-16, *492*
6:15, *697*
6:17, *491*
6:17-28, *470*
6:17-29, *490-91*
6:23, *376*
6:26, *491*
6:38, *1301*
6:41, *802*
6:45, *1248*
6:45-52, *751, 761*
6:48, *196*
6:52-53, *196*
6:56, *506*
7, *71, 882*
7:1-4, *801*
7:1-5, *626*
7:1-23, *797, 1089*

7:5, *1088*
7:5-8, *785, 1087*
7:6-7, *1105*
7:6-13, *881, 1178*
7:8-9, *1179*
7:10-12, *1179*
7:11, *799*
7:11-12, *1178*
7:13, *1179*
7:14-15, *876, 881*
7:15, *1151*
7:17, *881*
7:17-19, *881*
7:20-23, *881*
7:21-22, *761, 1255*
7:25-30, *433*
7:26, *470*
7:31-37, *267*
7:32, *399*
7:34, *89, 462, 1095*
7:37, *267*
8:6-7, *802*
8:14, *1248*
8:15, *493*
8:17-18, *906*
8:21, *906*
8:22-26, *81, 490*
8:27-30, *433, 490*
8:28, *697*
8:29, *232-33, 704, 1088*
8:31, *934, 1088-89*
8:31-33, *272*
8:32-35, *399*
8:33, *155*
9:2-8, *447, 458*
9:4, *458*
9:5, *915*
9:7, *458*
9:9, *934*
9:11-13, *697, 1088-89*
9:12, *906*
9:14, *1088*
9:14-29, *81, 399*
9:20, *507*
9:24-28, *1277*
9:25, *399, 507*
9:31, *934*
9:33-37, *201*
9:34, *1088*
9:35, *1088*
9:38-39, *507*
9:40, *973*
9:43, *19, 933*
9:45, *933*
9:47, *19, 933*
9:48, *907*
10:1-12, *1034*
10:2-9, *1277*
10:2-12, *249*
10:3-9, *458*
10:6-9, *2*
10:9, *1089*
10:11-12, *1096*
10:12, *867*
10:13-16, *201*
10:17, *933*
10:25, *1246*
10:28-29, *682*
10:29-30, *307*
10:30, *777, 933*
10:31, *1088*
10:33, *934, 1088*
10:34, *76, 561, 934*
10:43-44, *1088*
10:46-52, *81*
10:47, *703*
10:48, *703*
10:51, *915*
11:1-10, *496, 614, 697, 879*
11:2, *1246*
11:2-3, *375*
11:3-6, *1246*
11:4-5, *1246*
11:7, *1246*
11:8, *375*
11:10, *375, 703*
11:11, *562, 1044, 1168*
11:15, *562, 799, 1168, 1175, 1181*
11:15-17, *612, 1044, 1176*
11:15-18, *497, 1173*
11:15-19, *1089*
11:17, *294, 562, 799*
11:18, *1088-89*
11:21, *915*
11:27, *562, 798, 1088-89*
12, *1257*
12:1, *395*
12:1-9, *305*
12:1-12, *395*
12:2, *1009*
12:10-11, *934*
12:13, *610*
12:13-17, *433, 1165*
12:14, *1162*
12:16-21, *395*
12:17, *306*
12:18, *610*
12:18-27, *458*
12:19, *491*
12:28, *1088*
12:28-31, *458*
12:28-34, *797, 1088*
12:32-34, *1088*
12:34, *1089*
12:35, *562*
12:35-37, *703, 1088*
12:35-40, *1088*
12:38-39, *1088*
12:39, *1149*
12:40, *1088*
12:41-44, *1045*
12:42, *224*
12:44, *1168*
13, *43, 51, 251, 339, 377, 1181, 1194*
13:1, *562*
13:1-4, *1176*
13:2, *277, 562*
13:2-3, *1176*
13:9, *979, 997, 1061, 1147, 1151*
13:12, *355*
13:14, *277, 278, 1176*
13:17, *562*
13:20, *869*
13:21-22, *56*
13:22, *56*
13:24, *1077*
13:24-27, *52*
13:26, *934*
13:26-27, *306*
13:27, *350*
13:34-35, *305*
14:1, *203, 1088-89*
14:1-2, *376, 798*
14:2, *562*
14:5, *1288*
14:10, *614*
14:10-11, *879*
14:11, *614*
14:12, *204*
14:12-15, *1043*
14:12-17, *376*
14:12-25, *204*
14:12-26, *300*
14:20, *1095*
14:22, *1177*
14:22-23, *802*
14:22-25, *306*
14:23-24, *1023*
14:24, *1177*
14:25, *934*
14:26, *232, 713-14*
14:26-30, *72, 537*
14:28, *934*
14:36, *506, 1095*
14:38, *277*
14:43, *1088*
14:44-45, *629*
14:45, *915*
14:48, *562*
14:49, *562, 798, 1087, 1168*
14:53, *1063-64*
14:55, *1063*
14:57-58, *1176*
14:58, *562, 934, 1180*
14:61-61, *704*
14:61-62, *1116*
14:62, *447, 934, 1115*
14:65, *562*
15, *980*
15:1, *1061, 1064, 1088-89*
15:1-15, *204, 803*
15:2-5, *434*
15:4, *562*
15:5, *562*
15:6, *562*
15:6-15, *982*
15:7, *585*
15:9, *562*
15:11-15, *471*
15:16, *1007*
15:16-32, *1004, 1007*
15:17, *1007*
15:18-19, *1007*
15:23, *1007*
15:24, *851*
15:26, *704, 982*
15:27, *585, 937, 1007*
15:29, *934, 1177*
15:29-30, *1176*
15:31, *1088-89*
15:32, *704*
15:34, *89, 458, 462, 1095*
15:39-47, *993*
15:40-41, *470*
15:42, *204*
16:1, *1032*
16:3, *97*
16:5, *1088*
16:14, *77*
16:18, *399*

Luke

1, *826, 866*
1—2, *234, 654, 1218*
1:1, *405, 548*
1:1-4, *405, 409, 599, 863, 1283, 1286*
1:5-23, *181*
1:8, *1041, 1047*
1:8-11, *798*
1:10, *650, 798, 1041*
1:11-20, *1041*
1:13, *769*
1:16-17, *696*
1:19, *1240*
1:21-22, *1041*
1:25, *199, 769*
1:26, *1240*
1:26-38, *400*
1:28, *769*
1:30, *769*
1:32, *259, 704*
1:32-35, *1136*
1:35, *400*
1:36, *72*
1:39, *1047*
1:46-55, *232-33, 769, 802*
1:58-64, *199*
1:59, *199*
1:67-79, *802*
1:68-75, *769*
1:68-79, *233*
1:69, *704*
2, *202, 1098*
2:1, *202, 976, 996, 1010*
2:1-2, *585*
2:1-3, *578*
2:1-5, *201, 1164*
2:1-7, *1245*
2:2, *202, 979, 997, 1162*
2:11, *704, 856*
2:14, *233*
2:21, *199*
2:22, *96, 1244*
2:22-24, *199, 798*
2:22-38, *1245*
2:25, *653*
2:28-32, *802*
2:29-32, *233*
2:36-38, *1094*
2:37, *798, 1168*
2:41-52, *1245*
2:46-47, *1047*
3, *509*
3:1, *95, 178, 221, 490, 803, 964, 979, 997, 1016*
3:1-2, *203*
3:2, *95, 179*
3:4, *553*
3:4-6, *554, 1022*
3:7-14, *935*
3:10-11, *761*
3:10-14, *1023*
3:12, *1165*
3:12-13, *1165*
3:14, *995*
3:15, *1240*
3:16-17, *697*
3:19-20, *376, 490-91*
3:21, *95*
3:22, *750*
3:23, *203*
3:23-27, *866*
3:23-38, *457, 866*
3:38, *1*
4, *1137*
4:13, *1210*
4:14-30, *92*
4:15, *1145, 1150*
4:15-16, *716*
4:16, *1145, 1151*
4:16-20, *433*
4:16-21, *350, 458, 554, 1150*
4:16-22, *516*
4:16-27, *800*
4:17, *167, 651, 1283*
4:18-19, *704*
4:18-27, *699*
4:20, *651, 1146, 1150*
4:22, *1150*
4:22-30, *1150*
4:24-27, *458*
4:31-37, *81, 1150*
4:32, *1089*
4:38, *1151*
4:39, *262*
4:40-41, *399*
4:41, *399*
4:44, *1245*
5:1, *1247*
5:1-11, *867*
5:12-14, *877*
5:12-16, *1151*
5:17, *785*
5:17-26, *81, 1151*
5:21, *1089*
5:27-28, *433*
5:29, *386*
5:30, *1089, 1163*
5:32, *821*
5:33-39, *626*
6:4, *1176*
6:6-11, *81, 1150*
6:15, *945*
6:17-19, *1245*
6:20, *1090*
6:20-21, *306*
6:20-23, *151, 1266*
6:20-26, *1207*
6:24-26, *935*
6:27-36, *306*
6:29-30, *627*
6:34-35, *386*
6:35, *497, 769*
6:36, *906*
6:45, *72*
7, *72*
7:1-5, *95, 967, 1147*
7:1-10, *458, 507, 1060*
7:2, *361*
7:2-9, *993*
7:5, *1145, 1151*
7:11-17, *81, 458, 740*
7:12, *174*
7:18-23, *1297*
7:19, *1240*
7:19-23, *697*
7:21, *399, 507*
7:22, *81, 700, 704*
7:29, *1165*
7:30, *1062*
7:32, *714*
7:33-35, *876*
7:34, *386, 1163, 1165*
7:36, *785*
7:38, *629*
7:41-43, *395*
7:45, *629*
8:1-3, *470, 1023, 1089, 1276*
8:1-18, *761*
8:2, *399*
8:3, *491, 1236*
8:10-14, *1165*
8:18, *1000*
8:22, *1248*
8:23, *1247*
8:26, *97*
8:26-39, *267*
8:28, *268*
8:35-36, *267*
8:39, *267*
8:40-42, *81, 1150*
8:41, *1146*
8:43-48, *1150*
8:49-56, *81, 1150*
9, *457*
9:3, *878*
9:4, *877, 1246*
9:5, *1246*
9:7-9, *376, 492*
9:10, *490*
9:18-21, *433*
9:22, *1089*
9:28-36, *458*
9:30, *458*
9:35, *458, 704*
9:37-43, *81*
9:44-45, *1262*
9:48, *770*
9:49-50, *761*
9:51-56, *1055, 1060*
9:52, *1060*
9:57, *1089*
9:58, *506, 1089*
10, *1055*
10:2, *911*
10:3, *19*
10:4, *878*
10:5, *878*
10:5-7, *877*
10:5-8, *1246*
10:6, *720, 878*
10:7, *878*
10:7-8, *878*
10:10, *1246*
10:13-15, *1151*
10:21, *399, 1218*
10:22, *770*
10:25, *1089*
10:25-37, *801, 1060*
10:27, *650*
10:30-36, *910*
10:31-32, *175, 876*
10:33, *1060*
10:34-35, *524*
11:2-4, *306, 651, 899*
11:3, *306*
11:4, *306, 1210*
11:5-8, *506*
11:9-13, *769*
11:13, *464*
11:14-22, *1202*
11:15, *1240*
11:20, *306, 704*
11:23, *497*
11:24-26, *507*
11:26, *399*
11:31, *458*
11:33, *464*
11:37, *785*
11:37-54, *1089*
11:38, *626*
11:39-44, *785*
11:40-41, *876*
11:42, *626*
11:43, *1149*
11:44, *175*
11:45, *1089*
11:47-48, *653*
11:49-51, *614, 878*
11:51, *653*
11:52, *1087*
12:1, *785*
12:4, *387*
12:5, *934*
12:11, *1151*
12:16-20, *306*
12:16-21, *69, 304, 910*
12:22-31, *306-7*
12:33, *1023, 1123*
12:35-48, *395*
12:41-48, *470*
12:42, *305*
12:42-46, *395*
12:45-46, *19*
12:57-59, *761*
13, *295*

13:1, 492, 803, 967, 1017
13:1-2, 981
13:6-9, 19
13:10-17, 1034, 1146, 1150
13:11, 399
13:13, 399
13:14, 800
13:15, 1246
13:28, 1177
13:28-29, 144, 908
13:29, 294, 1177
13:31, 785, 1236
13:31-33, 492
13:34-35, 277
14:1, 785, 802
14:1-6, 1034, 1089, 1150
14:5, 1032-34
14:12, 386
14:12-14, 306, 386
14:15-24, 146
14:16-24, 144, 395, 1239
14:18, 1096
14:28-30, 125
15:1, 1163, 1165
15:1-2, 386
15:3-7, 304
15:6, 386
15:7, 821
15:9, 386
15:11-32, 395
15:15, 19
15:19, 821
15:20, 628
15:23, 304
15:25, 714
15:29, 386
16:1-8, 305, 395
16:9, 386
16:13, 306
16:14-15, 785
16:16, 455, 458
16:18, 881
16:19-31, 305, 935
16:21, 1009
16:22-31, 400
17, 1055
17:11-19, 1060
17:14, 826
17:20-37, 339
17:26-27, 399
17:34-36, 40
18:1-8, 506
18:9-14, 306, 395, 785, 1040
18:11, 1163, 1168
18:18, 933
18:22, 1123
18:25, 1246
18:30, 933
18:35-43, 81
19:1-10, 300, 306, 395, 980, 1165
19:8, 1165
19:12, 1245
19:12-27, 305
19:28-40, 614, 879
19:30, 1246
19:30-31, 375, 1246
19:32, 1246
19:35, 1246
19:38, 375
19:39, 785
19:41-44, 562
19:43-44, 277-78
19:44, 562
19:45, 612, 1168, 1181
19:45-46, 1044, 1176
19:45-48, 1173
19:46, 612
19:47, 1063, 1089
20:1, 1089
20:19-26, 973
20:20, 979, 997
20:20-26, 433
20:22, 1163
20:27, 610
20:27-38, 933
20:34-35, 933
20:41-44, 1089
20:45-47, 1089
20:46, 1089, 1149
20:47, 785, 1089
21, 377
21:1-4, 158, 1045, 1178
21:5-6, 1176
21:5-36, 339
21:6, 277
21:12, 827, 997, 1151
21:14-15, 829
21:16, 386
21:20, 277, 1176
21:20-24, 562
21:37, 1047
22:1, 203
22:2, 1089
22:3-6, 614, 879
22:4, 1049, 1063
22:7-14, 376
22:7-31, 300
22:7-38, 204
22:17-18, 1155
22:19-20, 1177
22:20, 1023
22:24-27, 158
22:26, 307
22:28, 1209-10
22:30, 1023
22:47-48, 629
22:52, 1049, 1063
22:54, 1064
22:66, 1061-62, 1089
23, 980
23:1, 562
23:1-7, 803
23:1-25, 204
23:2, 987, 1049, 1163
23:2-4, 434
23:6-12, 204, 492, 988
23:12, 386, 492, 981-82
23:13-25, 803, 982
23:28-31, 562
23:35, 704, 1089
23:38, 982
23:46, 458
23:51, 1062
23:54, 204
24:2, 97
24:21, 1094
24:25-27, 458
24:28-35, 300
24:30-31, 146
24:39-43, 741
24:44, 378, 456, 553, 1244
24:44-45, 554
24:44-46, 554
24:46, 458
24:50-3, 447
24:51, 81
24:53, 1168

John
1:1, 457, 793
1:1-4, 761
1:1-16, 233
1:1-18, 234, 700
1:2, 793
1:3, 793
1:4-5, 1022
1:6, 793
1:9, 793
1:10, 793
1:12, 351, 1275
1:12-13, 521
1:14, 251, 740, 761, 793
1:14-18, 385
1:15, 793
1:17, 793, 1244
1:18, 793
1:19-22, 1240
1:21, 697
1:23, 554
1:28, 347
1:29, 1181, 1204
1:32, 750
1:34, 170, 262
1:38, 915
1:41, 698
1:45, 1244
1:49, 72, 915
1:51, 351
2:1-11, 724
2:2, 686
2:3, 686
2:6, 396, 626
2:13, 203, 1043, 1245
2:13—3:21, 203
2:13-17, 612, 1044, 1181
2:13-22, 497
2:14, 1168
2:14-15, 1044
2:14-17, 1176
2:14-22, 1173
2:15, 1182
2:17-22, 1181
2:18-22, 1176
2:19, 277, 934, 1180
2:19-22, 1177
2:20, 798
2:21, 876, 934
2:22, 934
2:23, 562
3, 402
3:2, 915
3:5, 351
3:10-12, 1275
3:13, 251
3:13-14, 447
3:16, 251, 351, 458
3:17, 1262
3:19, 1022
3:21, 1022
3:23, 347
3:29, 386, 686
4, 1060
4:4-26, 433
4:9, 1055, 1060
4:10, 614, 878
4:12, 457
4:14, 614, 878
4:20, 96, 1060
4:25, 698, 1060
4:31, 915
4:39, 1055
4:43-44, 761
4:46-47, 1245
4:46-53, 507
4:46-54, 433
5, 1034
5:1, 1245
5:1-5, 96
5:2, 227
5:16, 777
5:20, 386
5:24, 336
5:28-29, 935
6, 516, 737
6:1, 1235, 1247
6:15, 1240
6:15-21, 761
6:16, 1248
6:16-21, 751
6:18, 1247
6:19, 1248
6:21, 81
6:23, 1235
6:25, 915
6:40, 935
6:44, 935
6:54, 935
6:59, 1145, 1151
6:62, 447
7:1-14, 1245
7:19, 1244
7:20, 1240
7:22-23, 900, 1034
7:24, 700
7:35, 294
7:38, 453
7:40, 1009
7:53—8:11, 1154
8:2-3, 1168
8:3, 1088
8:12, 351
8:13, 785
8:22, 785
8:24, 793
8:26, 386
8:28, 793
8:44, 785, 1022
8:48-52, 1240
8:53, 400
8:58, 793
9, 1034
9:1-12, 96
9:2, 915
9:8, 395
9:16, 1034
9:22, 1147
9:30-33, 1034
10, 376
10:14, 351
10:20-21, 1240
10:22, 439
10:23, 798
10:31, 1064
11, 81
11:3, 384
11:8, 915
11:8-16, 384
11:11, 384
11:16, 384
11:19, 175
11:31, 175
11:44, 174
11:47, 1061
11:47-50, 972
11:48, 967, 1049
11:49, 95, 179
11:49-53, 204
11:55-56, 1043
12:1, 1245
12:6, 395
12:12-19, 614, 879
12:13, 375
12:16, 1262
12:20, 426
12:24, 724
12:26, 521
12:31, 156, 935
12:35-36, 1022, 1262
12:36, 1022
12:42, 1147
12:42-43, 521
12:48, 935
13:19, 793
13:20, 770
13:21-36, 300
13:33, 357
14:2, 935
14:3, 935
14:6, 770
14:17, 49, 1022
14:27, 774
14:30, 156
15:9-17, 384
15:12, 384
15:13, 384, 386
15:13-15, 384, 386
15:14, 386
15:15, 381, 383-85
15:16, 1089
15:26, 49, 1022
16:2, 1147
16:2-4, 521
16:11, 156
16:13, 49, 383, 1022
16:13-15, 386
16:14-15, 383
17:3, 1275
17:6-12, 729
18—19, 980
18:3, 994
18:4, 462
18:12, 562
18:12-24, 1049
18:13, 95, 179
18:13-14, 95, 204
18:14, 95, 179
18:20, 1150
18:24, 95, 179
18:28, 95, 179
18:28—19:16, 803
18:28-19:16, 204
18:29-38, 434
18:31, 984, 1064
18:35-36, 973
18:39—19:12, 982
19:1, 562
19:10-11, 973
19:12, 381, 761, 767, 987
19:13, 986
19:14, 204, 376
19:16, 204
19:19-22, 982
19:20, 630
19:24, 458
19:28, 458
19:31, 204, 376, 1034
19:34, 993
19:36, 458
19:40, 1009
19:42, 204
20:9, 1262
20:16, 87
20:17, 447
20:24-29, 741
21:1, 1235, 1247
21:9-14, 146
21:25, 1283

Acts
1:1, 158, 188, 405, 409, 863
1:1-12, 447
1:4-5, 561
1:5-20, 1151
1:6, 967
1:8, 411, 561, 1060, 1245
1:9, 81
1:12, 1031
1:12-26, 1177
1:13, 945
1:15, 1096
1:16-18, 1096
1:19, 87, 95, 1096
1:23-26, 928
2—4, 1047
2:1-4, 377
2:1-11, 1245
2:1-13, 182
2:2, 300
2:4, 561
2:5-11, 377
2:7, 549
2:8-11, 1239
2:9, 135
2:9-10, 563
2:9-11, 282, 565
2:10, 25, 134, 626, 1014
2:17, 549, 927
2:17-18, 561
2:17-21, 550
2:21, 550
2:29, 354
2:30, 779
2:39, 200
2:41-45, 1132
2:42, 798
2:42-47, 146
2:44-45, 307
2:44-47, 386, 1023
2:46, 798, 1026, 1177
2:46—3:1, 776
2:47, 1096
3:1, 626, 798, 1041
3:1-26, 1177
3:12, 549
3:13, 204, 803, 981
3:15-20, 550
3:18, 548
3:22, 354, 1207
3:24, 548
4, 402, 1094
4:1, 1063
4:1-2, 932
4:1-22, 1061
4:1-37, 1177
4:3, 827
4:6, 95, 179
4:9, 157
4:13, 549
4:24, 1063
4:24-30, 233
4:25-26, 379
4:26, 1063
4:27, 204, 221, 803, 981
4:32, 307
4:34-36, 770
4:34-37, 1023
4:36, 1047
4:36-37, 307
5, 901
5:1-11, 1023
5:9, 1207
5:17, 1063, 1222
5:17-42, 775
5:18-25, 827
5:21, 1061
5:24, 1049
5:26, 1049
5:27, 1061
5:27-41, 1061
5:33-39, 785
5:34, 92, 902, 1061, 1063, 1089
5:34-39, 1086
5:36, 46, 585, 834, 940
5:37, 585, 1164

5:40-41, *521*
5:42, *798*
6, *469*
6:1, *426, 469, 473*
6:1-3, *1237*
6:1-6, *468-69*
6:2, *1023*
6:5, *25, 287, 469, 626, 1023*
6:7, *35*
6:8—8:2, *1064*
6:9, *469, 1147, 1149*
6:9-15, *565*
6:12, *1061*
6:13-14, *469, 777*
6:14, *1176*
7, *469, 867, 1056*
7:2, *357*
7:2-8, *400*
7:4, *1054*
7:5, *1054*
7:12, *401*
7:22, *165*
7:31, *549*
7:32, *1054*
7:35-39, *550*
7:36, *1198*
7:37, *1054*
7:38, *602*
7:48-49, *1180*
7:51-53, *469*
7:53, *164*
7:58, *205*
8, *68, 414*
8:1, *1060*
8:1-3, *785*
8:3, *827*
8:5, *469, 1060*
8:5-6, *1055*
8:9, *1060*
8:9-24, *1055, 1240*
8:10, *729*
8:12, *469*
8:14, *1060*
8:14-25, *1177*
8:25, *1060*
8:26-30, *1245*
8:27, *965*
8:28-29, *1246*
8:32-33, *458*
8:38, *1246*
9:1-2, *1064, 1151*
9:1-9, *53*
9:1-25, *205*
9:2, *286, 827*
9:3-9, *733*
9:9-25, *669*
9:10-16, *733*
9:12, *399, 733*
9:14, *827*
9:15-16, *217, 549*
9:17, *354*
9:17-18, *399*
9:18, *1245*
9:20, *232*
9:26-30, *205*
9:29, *468-69*
9:30, *133, 469*
9:31, *1061*
9:32-35, *1177*
9:36-43, *1177*
9:37, *174*
9:38, *1245*
9:43, *1003*
10, *35*
10:1, *994*
10:1-2, *967, 993*
10:1-48, *879, 1151, 1177-78*
10:2, *361, 846*
10:7, *361*
10:7-8, *386*
10:9, *96, 650, 802*
10:9-16, *733, 879*
10:10, *734*
10:22, *846*
10:23-24, *1245*
10:24, *301, 386*
10:30, *1245*
10:36, *232*
10:38, *157*
10:43, *548*
11, *561, 1092*
11:1-3, *879*
11:1-11, *1178*
11:1-18, *879, 1178*
11:2, *550*
11:2-3, *879*
11:5, *734*
11:14, *200*
11:19, *469, 470*
11:19-26, *35*
11:19-30, *964*
11:20, *232, 468, 470*
11:25, *133*
11:25-26, *205*
11:26, *35, 205, 1158*
11:27-28, *831*
11:27-30, *35, 205*
11:28, *206*
11:28-30, *207*
12, *579, 1017*
12:1, *491*
12:1-3, *221*
12:1-19, *206, 827*
12:1-21, *381*
12:6, *491*
12:8, *828*
12:11, *491*
12:12, *1003*
12:15, *31*
12:19, *1177*
12:19-21, *491*
12:19-23, *579*
12:20-23, *206*
12:21-23, *221*
12:22-23, *1237*
12:24, *206*
12:25, *205, 206*
13, *516, 550, 964*
13—14, *563*
13—18, *294*
13:1, *469, 491*
13:1—14:28, *205*
13:1-3, *35*
13:2, *522, 549-50*
13:4, *1092*
13:4-12, *1240*
13:5, *286, 320*
13:6-12, *669*
13:7, *206, 997*
13:8, *997*
13:9, *216*
13:12, *997*
13:13, *133*
13:13-43, *1151*
13:13-52, *32, 1150*
13:14, *134, 286, 1035, 1092, 1245*
13:14-16, *320, 516*
13:14-43, *800*
13:14-52, *34*
13:15, *92, 287, 516, 565, 651, 1146*
13:15-41, *516*
13:16, *283, 566, 568, 846, 1151*
13:16-41, *516*
13:22, *1097*
13:23, *700*
13:26, *566, 846, 1151*
13:26-29, *33*
13:27, *92, 516*
13:28, *204, 803, 981*
13:33-37, *379-80*
13:34, *704*
13:38-39, *548-49*
13:40-41, *33*
13:41, *548-49*
13:42, *516, 1035, 1146*
13:43, *568, 626, 846, 1151*
13:44, *516, 1035*
13:44-45, *550*
13:44-52, *1151*
13:45, *33, 548, 565, 568*
13:46, *548, 550-51*
13:48, *33*
13:48-50, *283, 568*
13:50, *230, 283, 470, 565-66, 568, 846, 1151*
14, *964*
14:1, *283, 286, 320, 426, 566, 568, 1146*
14:1-2, *33*
14:1-4, *1151*
14:2, *283, 568*
14:2-5, *565, 568*
14:3, *205*
14:5, *283, 568*
14:5-6, *471*
14:6, *230*
14:11, *92, 134*
14:11-13, *761*
14:14, *82*
14:19, *230, 565, 568, 1150*
14:21, *33, 1092*
14:22, *777*
14:24, *134, 1245*
14:24-25, *133*
14:26, *549*
14:26-27, *550*
14:26-28, *35*
14:27, *549, 550*
14:27—15:2, *550*
14:28, *205*
15, *33, 207, 549, 561, 733, 879-80*
15:1, *550, 879-80*
15:1-2, *845*
15:1-12, *879*
15:1-29, *973*
15:1-35, *205, 469, 879*
15:2, *549-50*
15:3, *549-50*
15:4, *550*
15:4-5, *550*
15:5, *785, 880, 1244*
15:6-11, *550-51*
15:7-11, *879-80*
15:10, *880, 1207*
15:11, *880*
15:12, *550-51, 1023*
15:13-21, *377, 472*
15:13-29, *879*
15:13-35, *1178*
15:16, *380, 704*
15:16-18, *1180*
15:19, *880, 1178*
15:19-21, *1151*
15:20, *249, 758, 801, 880, 1178*
15:21, *92, 516, 800, 880, 1146, 1178, 1242*
15:22-23, *1247*
15:22-29, *880, 1178*
15:22-36, *35*
15:23, *471*
15:28, *880, 1178*
15:29, *249, 758*
15:30, *1023*
15:32, *1178*
15:32-33, *880*
15:33, *1178*
15:35—18:22, *205*
15:36-41, *35*
16, *217*
16:1, *426, 1245*
16:1-3, *564*
16:1-5, *563*
16:1-6, *33*
16:8-10, *788*
16:9, *31, 53*
16:9-10, *733, 927*
16:11, *788, 1232*
16:11—20:6, *426*
16:11-40, *788*
16:12, *787, 1232*
16:13, *285, 320, 516, 799, 800, 1145, 1150, 1232, 1237*
16:13-14, *800*
16:13-15, *470*
16:14, *131, 1003, 1092, 1151, 1245*
16:14-15, *301, 307, 788*
16:15, *200, 1003, 1131*
16:16, *800, 927, 1232, 1237*
16:16-21, *669*
16:16-24, *1126*
16:16-40, *827*
16:19, *999*
16:19-24, *788*
16:22, *829*
16:24-25, *828*
16:25, *232, 714, 829*
16:27-34, *788*
16:29, *828*
16:31, *200*
16:31-34, *1131*
16:33, *301*
16:33-34, *829*
16:34, *200, 829*
16:35-39, *977*
16:37, *217, 830*
16:37-38, *215-16*
16:37-39, *988*
16:37-40, *967*
16:39, *217, 230*
16:40, *470, 1003*
17, *99, 220, 327, 582, 1141*
17:1, *285-86, 787, 1232*
17:1-2, *320*
17:1-9, *1151*
17:1-14, *775*
17:2, *516, 716, 1035, 1146, 1232*
17:3, *232, 548*
17:4, *800, 846, 1151, 1232*
17:5, *230, 471*
17:5-7, *1233*
17:5-9, *1003*
17:6, *98, 230, 963, 1009, 1233*
17:6-9, *999*
17:7, *230*
17:9, *230*
17:10, *230, 285-86, 787*
17:10-11, *320*
17:10-14, *1151*
17:12, *800*
17:14, *230*
17:16, *122, 798*
17:17, *99, 139-40, 285-86, 758, 846, 1151, 1232*
17:17-18, *761*
17:18, *140, 326-27, 758, 1139, 1282*
17:18-34, *1151*
17:22, *759, 761, 1287*
17:22-23, *798*
17:22-31, *759*
17:23, *140, 926*
17:28, *71, 139, 281, 472, 760, 814, 1073, 1282*
17:28-29, *761*
17:30, *1274*
17:31, *654*
17:32, *326-27*
17:33—18:1, *230*
17:34, *859*
18, *206, 960*
18:1, *230*
18:1-2, *1014, 1016*
18:1-4, *1151*
18:1-5, *1247*
18:2, *206, 229-30, 285, 528, 761, 970, 1015, 1143, 1144*
18:2-3, *229, 307*
3, *1003*
18:2-3, *1003, 1245*
18:3, *829*
18:4, *229, 285, 516*
18:4-7, *286, 320*
18:5, *232*
18:5-11, *1151*
18:6, *229, 548*
18:7, *229-30, 846, 1003, 1151*
18:8, *200, 206, 230, 301, 1131*
18:9-10, *53, 230, 733*
18:11, *98, 205, 229*
18:12, *206, 230, 979, 986, 997*
18:12-17, *98, 775, 986, 988, 1099*
18:14, *230*
18:15, *307*
18:16-17, *230*
18:17, *206, 230, 287*
18:18, *228-29, 443, 1003*
18:18—19:20, *205*
18:18-19, *1003*
18:18-22, *319*
18:19, *1151*
18:19-21, *320*
18:19-26, *286*
18:20-23, *177*
18:22, *35*
18:23, *33, 225, 1245*
18:23—21:16, *205*
18:24-25, *25*
18:24-26, *229*
18:24-28, *319*
18:25, *25*
18:26, *229, 800, 1151*
18:27, *568, 1246*
18:28, *548*
19, *132, 321*
19:1, *225*
19:8, *205, 286, 320, 1151*
19:8-10, *318-19, 568*
19:9, *99, 568*
19:10, *205*
19:11-20, *1240*
19:13-16, *669*
19:13-20, *929*
19:19, *669*
19:21, *425*
19:22, *99, 205, 229-30*
19:23-41, *219, 221, 319, 1132, 1187*
19:24, *99, 122, 1187*
19:25-41, *967*
19:28, *132*
19:29, *1219, 1233*
19:29-32, *99*
19:31, *386, 961, 998, 1219*
19:33, *320*
19:35, *999*
19:38, *997*
20:1-2, *426*
20:1-6, *788*
20:3, *205*
20:4, *1233*
20:7, *146*
20:7-12, *1035*
20:9, *200*
20:12, *200*
20:13, *1245*
20:14-15, *320*
20:16, *377, 776*
20:19, *568, 1209-10*
20:20, *1131*
20:23, *827*
20:28, *1064*
20:29, *19*
20:29-30, *321*
20:31, *318*
20:33-35, *1247*
20:35, *307, 386, 472*
20:37, *628*
21, *1178*
21:2-3, *1245*
21:5, *200*
21:10-12, *831*
21:11-13, *827*
21:17—23:10, *205*
21:17-26, *776, 1178*
21:20-24, *800*
21:23-26, *798*
21:27, *615, 1245*
21:27-29, *565, 799*
21:27-30, *471, 615*
21:27-36, *775, 1178*
21:30-32, *829*
21:31, *994*
21:31-32, *615, 1168*
21:31-36, *961*

21:31-37, 980
21:32, 994
21:38, 46, 834, 940, 967, 983
21:39, 215, 287, 289, 566, 774, 1009
21:40, 87
22, 217
22—26, 980
22:1, 357
22:2, 87, 92
22:3, 92, 133, 216, 774, 785, 1086-87, 1245
22:4-5, 827
22:5, 1062, 1064
22:6-11, 53
22:11, 1245
22:17, 734
22:17-18, 733
22:17-21, 53, 733
22:19, 800, 1149, 1151
22:24-25, 829
22:25, 215, 217
22:25-29, 967, 988
22:27-29, 217, 774
22:28, 216, 987
22:30, 1061, 1064
22:30—23:10, 988
23—24, 961, 988
23:1, 1061
23:2, 207
23:6, 216, 1061, 1063
23:6-8, 933
23:7-9, 785
23:8, 610, 932, 933
23:9, 1087
23:11, 733, 927
23:12—26:32, 205
23:15, 1061, 1064
23:20, 1061
23:23, 1246
23:23—24:27, 221
23:23-24, 1245-46
23:23-26, 994
23:24, 979, 997
23:24—26:32, 207
23:26, 471, 979, 997
23:26-30, 1247
23:28, 1061
23:30-35, 988
23:31-32, 1246
23:33, 997
23:34, 960
23:35, 979
24, 238
24:1, 997, 1063
21, 984
24:2, 205, 983
24:5, 776, 1222
7, 988
24:7, 205
24:10, 982-83, 997
24:14, 548, 776
24:20, 1061
24:22, 988
24:22-27, 1126
24:23, 829
24:25, 983
24:25-26, 988
24:26, 983, 987
24:27, 97-98, 177, 207, 983
25:1, 960, 983
25:1-6, 984, 1245
25:6, 983
25:8, 1244
25:9, 177
25:9-12, 984
25:10-11, 114
25:10-12, 217
25:11, 977, 987-88
25:12, 217, 960, 996
25:13, 221, 1245
25:13—26:32, 988
25:16, 983
25:21, 996
25:25, 996
25:26, 984
25:26-27, 1247
26:2, 221
26:5, 785
26:8, 933
26:10, 827
26:11, 1151
26:12-18, 53
26:14, 87
26:19, 733
26:20, 792
26:22, 455-56, 548
26:23, 548
26:28, 221
26:29, 830
26:30, 979, 997
26:31-32, 307
26:32, 221
27, 1248
27:1, 994-95
27:1—28:16, 1250
27:1—28:31, 205
27:2, 1233, 1245-46
27:3, 386, 829, 1246
27:6, 1245-46
27:9, 1248
27:10, 1248
27:14, 1249
27:15, 1248
27:17, 1249
27:18, 1249
27:23-4, 927
27:23-24, 53, 733
27:27, 1249
27:29-30, 1248
27:30, 1248
27:37, 1245
27:38, 1245, 1248-49
27:40, 1248
28, 68
28:7, 471, 524, 1246
28:8, 399
28:10-11, 1246
28:11, 1245, 1248
28:14, 1246
28:14-16, 1016
28:17-22, 1151
28:22, 776
28:23, 456, 1244
28:28, 548
28:30, 205

Romans
1—2, 1141
1—8, 410
1:1, 186
1:3, 703
1:3-4, 232-33, 1023
1:5, 770
1:7, 186
1:9-13, 1015
1:13, 643, 1013
1:16, 294, 402, 1232
1:16—11:36, 407
1:16-17, 320
1:17, 35, 549, 1023
1:18, 54
1:18-25, 769
1:18-32, 1
1:19-21, 1272
1:19-32, 1274
1:20, 1275
1:21, 663
1:22-32, 1272
1:23, 817
1:23-25, 8
1:24, 1015
1:24-32, 881
1:25, 663, 1272
1:26, 1278
1:26-27, 761
1:28, 663, 1012
1:29-31, 757, 761, 1255
1:30, 355
1:32, 355
2, 760
2:1-5, 761
2:1-16, 757
2:4, 1274
2:9-10, 294
2:12-15, 758, 761
2:12-27, 1012
2:14-16, 1012
2:16, 55
2:17-24, 761, 769
2:17-29, 757
3, 347, 760
3:1-9, 298
3:5, 1023
3:6, 55
3:10-18, 1207
3:13-18, 233
3:20, 1023
3:21, 1012, 1023
3:21-31, 1022
3:22, 1023
3:23, 1
3:24-26, 233
3:25, 615, 665, 1043
3:28, 1023
4, 162
4:1-25, 400, 1152
4:13-16, 1012
4:13-25, 496
5, 298, 410
5:1, 298
5:1-2, 1012
5:5, 54
5:7, 384
5:8, 54
5:9-11, 298
5:12-21, 1, 54, 298, 351
5:14, 457
6:1, 298
6:1-14, 56, 770
6:2, 54
6:6, 1
6:6-7, 54
6:12-14, 54
6:15-23, 990
6:17, 768
6:19, 1015
6:22, 54
7, 760
7:1, 1012
7:1-6, 902
7:7-24, 665
7:7-25, 1, 761
7:20-24, 1012
7:23-24, 1015
7:25, 768
8:3, 613
8:5-8, 54
8:10-11, 56
8:13, 54
8:14-17, 351, 521
8:15, 990, 1095
8:15-17, 470
8:16-17, 991
8:17, 521, 777
8:18, 1, 53
8:19-20, 54
8:19-22, 1, 56
8:21, 51
8:23, 377, 990
8:29, 736
8:29-30, 172
8:32, 458, 866
8:34, 54
8:35-39, 17, 856
8:38, 1240
8:39, 54
9—11, 53
9—16, 237
9:4, 990
9:5, 55
9:6, 1152
9:19, 1274
9:20-22, 69
9:21, 1274
9:33, 233
10:3, 1023
10:4, 546, 1012
10:6, 54
10:8-9, 546
10:9, 232, 234
10:9-10, 233
11:16, 377
11:19-21, 757, 761
11:26, 164, 294, 1152
11:33-36, 233
12:1, 614, 643, 770
12:1—15:13, 407
12:1-2, 1012, 1015
12:2, 53
12:8, 771
12:13, 1246
12:14—13:7, 989
12:14-21, 989
12:17, 399
12:17-21, 627
13, 1166
13:1, 1029
13:1-4, 967
13:1-5, 627
13:1-7, 762, 774, 973, 989, 1012
13:3-4, 771, 1029
13:4, 761, 980, 1029
13:5, 1029
13:6, 1029
13:6-7, 1163
13:9-10, 770
13:13, 1255
13:13-14, 166
14, 138
14:1-3, 1015
14:2, 801
14:5-6, 802
14:6, 802
14:7-12, 56
14:10, 56
14:13-23, 880
14:14, 881
14:14-17, 1015
14:17, 908
14:17-18, 56
14:21, 1015
15:1-3, 1015
15:5-6, 712
15:12, 700
15:14, 643
15:16, 614-15, 826
15:19, 561, 788
15:19-32, 205
15:22-24, 1015
15:24, 1016
15:25-26, 561
15:25-29, 770
15:26, 425, 614
15:30, 643
15:31, 561
15:33, 774
16, 1016
16:1, 230
16:1-2, 158, 1003, 1246-47
16:3, 229-30
16:3-4, 320
16:3-5, 300, 1003
16:3-16, 407, 1009
16:5, 138, 229, 1003, 1131
16:7, 830
16:13, 354, 470
16:14, 84
16:16, 628
16:20, 54, 56, 774
16:21, 230
16:22, 230, 862, 1283
16:23, 99, 229-30, 307, 532, 770, 999, 1003
16:25-27, 232-33
16:26, 770, 993

1 Corinthians
1—3, 518
1—4, 446, 958, 1129
1:1, 230
1:2, 186, 1015, 1128
1:7-8, 57
1:10, 643
1:11, 230, 1003, 1131
1:11-16, 1129
1:12, 25, 1134
1:14, 230
1:15-16, 230
1:16, 230, 301, 1131
1:18, 1128
1:18—2:16, 761
1:18-25, 55, 1129
1:20, 53
1:24, 1128
1:26, 53, 307, 1003, 1131
1:31, 1130
2:2-5, 1006
2:6, 53
2:6-7, 53
2:8, 1240
2:11, 615
3:2, 708
3:3-4, 1134
3:4-6, 25
3:5-15, 761
3:9-17, 125
3:16-17, 761, 881, 1128, 1179-80
3:21-23, 383
3:22, 25
4:6-7, 1134
4:6-13, 17
4:7, 158
4:8-13, 1006
4:9, 114, 1006
4:9-13, 16, 324
4:12, 1134
4:14-15, 201
4:15, 356, 761-62, 770
4:20, 908
4:21, 356
5—6, 1130
5:1, 13
5:1-5, 856
5:1-12, 1128
5:4, 233
5:6, 1129
5:9, 187
5:10, 1128
5:10-11, 761, 1255
5:11, 146
6:1-8, 632
6:1-11, 988, 1128, 1132
6:2, 989
6:2-3, 1128
6:3, 56
6:9, 777
6:9-10, 57, 761, 1255
6:9-11, 908
6:11, 1128, 1255
6:12, 686
6:12-20, 740
6:16, 2
6:18, 1240
6:18-20, 881
6:19, 54, 876, 1179-80
6:19-20, 158, 761
6:20, 521
7, 1130, 1288
7:1, 229, 643, 1247
7:1-5, 720
7:3-4, 1131
7:5, 54
7:5-6, 683
7:7, 681
7:9, 687
7:10-16, 881
7:12-14, 685
7:14, 200, 685, 1128
7:15, 6
7:20-24, 1003
7:21, 366
7:21-23, 1131
7:22, 470, 990
7:22-23, 761
7:25, 643
7:25-40, 683
7:27-28, 683
7:28-40, 323
7:31, 1239
7:32-35, 324, 691
8, 138, 144, 880, 1178
8:1, 643
8:1-13, 758, 761, 1129
8:4-6, 880
8:5, 54
8:6, 232-33
8:7-13, 880
8:13, 880
9, 446
9:1, 53, 733
9:3-27, 1134
9:6, 1134
9:8, 1244
9:9, 1244
9:13, 143, 1179
9:19-23, 353, 687
9:20, 568
9:24-26, 470
9:24-27, 142, 211, 324, 665, 761, 1191
9:25, 1288
10, 145

10:4, *164-65, 867*
10:9, *1207*
10:11, *53*
10:16-22, *145*
10:18, *143*
10:20, *251*
11, *138, 1298*
11:2-10, *2*
11:2-16, *442, 447, 758, 761, 1131*
11:11, *2*
11:14-15, *445*
11:17-34, *146, 800, 1003*
11:22, *307*
11:24-25, *1177*
11:25, *615*
11:26, *232-33*
12:1, *643*
12:3, *233*
12:4-11, *54*
12:7, *1130*
12:12-13, *1131*
12:12-26, *323*
12:12-27, *761*
12:12-31, *759*
12:13, *326, 1128*
13, *758, 1255*
13:1, *1191*
13:1-4, *233*
13:5, *615*
13:11, *200*
14:6, *409*
14:7-9, *714*
14:15, *714*
14:18-19, *733*
14:20, *200*
14:23, *1131*
14:23-25, *1132*
14:25, *615*
14:26, *232, 714*
14:26-33, *409, 800*
14:33, *447, 774*
14:33-36, *1131*
14:34, *1280*
14:34-35, *1288*
15, *43*
15:3-5, *232-34*
15:4, *934*
15:8, *53*
15:19-33, *757*
15:20, *377*
15:20-22, *1*
15:20-23, *53*
15:20-28, *50, 56-57*
15:23, *377*
15:23-28, *56*
15:24, *908*
15:25, *56, 1263*
15:28, *1007*
15:29, *1007*
15:30-32, *1007*
15:31, *1006-7*
15:32, *320, 321, 762*
15:33, *70, 472, 760, 762, 1282*
15:35, *762*
15:36-38, *724*
15:44-49, *792*
15:45, *457, 792*
15:47-50, *54*
15:50, *57, 908*
15:51, *721*
15:51-52, *447*
15:51-57, *53*
15:54, *932*
16:1, *614, 643*
16:1-4, *307*
16:1-9, *205*
16:2, *614, 1035*
16:3, *561, 1247*
16:5-6, *788, 1245*
16:8, *320, 377*
16:8-9, *205, 320*
16:9, *320, 321*
16:10-11, *1246*
16:12, *25, 643*
16:13, *1239*
16:15, *230, 307*
16:15-16, *1131*
16:17, *230*
16:17-18, *770*
16:19, *229, 307, 320, 770, 1003, 1131*
16:20, *628*
16:21-24, *1009*

2 Corinthian
1:1, *1015*
1:3-4, *233*
1:3-11, *1239*
1:8, *320, 643*
1:8-11, *205*
1:14, *57*
1:22, *762*
2, *222*
2:4, *187, 1009*
2:5-6, *1023*
2:11, *54*
2:12-13, *205*
13, *1006*
2:13, *788*
2:14, *451, 993, 1004-7*
2:14—3:3, *1007*
2:14-16, *221, 760, 762, 1007*
3:4—4:6, *1*
3:6-18, *385*
3:7-18, *736*
3:18, *736*
4:4, *1240, 1263*
4:6, *1*
4:7, *17*
4:7-18, *666*
4:8-9, *17*
4:8-12, *1239*
4:10-11, *1006*
4:16-18, *1239*
4:18, *54*
5, *1180*
5:1, *1274*
5:1-4, *1274*
5:1-5, *54*
5:4, *1274*
5:9-10, *521*
5:10, *56*
5:17, *1, 51, 54-55, 351, 1227*
5:18-21, *233*
6:4, *17*
6:4-5, *568*
6:4-10, *217, 1239*
6:5, *827*
6:6-7, *17*
6:6-8, *757, 762, 1255*
6:8, *16*
6:9-10, *762*
6:14—7:1, *270, 347, 380, 1180, 1239*
6:14-7:1, *1182*
6:15, *1262*
6:16, *125, 777*
6:16—7:1, *1179*
7:1, *1240*
7:5, *788*
8—9, *205, 307*
8:1-6, *426*
8:3, *1240*
8:8-9, *158*
8:9-14, *771*
8:12, *1240*
8:13-14, *386, 770*
8:19, *768*
9:8-10, *771*
10—13, *68, 733, 757, 762*
10:4-5, *323*
10:10, *323*
11:6, *323*
11:12-15, *233*
11:14, *54, 1191*
11:19-20, *17*
11:23, *827*
11:23-25, *217*
11:23-27, *1152*
11:23-33, *774, 1239*
11:24, *568, 775, 777, 800, 1133, 1147, 1149*
11:25, *1248*
11:26, *777*
11:26-27, *1245*
11:28, *1006*
11:32, *998*
11:32-33, *206*
12, *130, 729, 733, 736*
12:1, *53*
12:1-4, *39, 151*
12:1-6, *1006*
12:1-10, *53, 733*
12:1-12, *451, 737*
12:2, *737*
12:2-4, *447-48, 733*
12:7, *54*
12:8, *733*
12:10, *17, 733*
12:14, *356*
12:20-21, *762*
13:1, *632*
13:11, *643, 774*
13:12, *628*
13:13, *232, 233*
13:14, *54*

Galatians
1, *389, 989*
1—2, *205*
1:4, *53, 351, 613*
1:6-9, *33*
1:8-9, *1207*
1:11, *643*
1:12, *53, 733*
1:14, *312*
1:17, *268*
1:18, *377*
2, *880-81*
2:1, *207, 733*
2:1-10, *207, 879*
2:1-14, *469, 1178*
2:2, *211*
2:3-10, *377*
2:4, *710*
2:9, *188, 614*
2:9-10, *990*
2:10, *307, 614, 1240*
2:11-13, *881*
2:11-14, *35, 146, 626, 1177*
2:12, *377*
2:14-21, *880*
2:16, *710, 1023*
2:21, *158, 770*
3—4, *295*
3:1, *390*
3:1-5, *770*
3:2, *711, 1023*
3:3, *665, 711*
3:5, *1023*
3:6-7, *1152*
3:6-9, *400, 880*
3:8, *1207*
3:10, *1023*
3:10-14, *1207*
3:13, *907*
3:14, *457, 1152, 1207*
3:15-29, *164*
3:16-17, *1258*
3:19, *164, 602, 1196*
3:21-26, *458*
3:24, *546, 762*
3:26, *521*
3:27-8, *1128*
3:27-29, *1152*
3:28, *326, 470, 723, 866, 1152*
4:1-11, *351*
4:4, *1245*
4:5-6, *990*
4:6, *1095*
4:6-7, *470*
4:7, *385*
4:9-10, *377*
4:10, *802*
4:19, *201*
4:21—5:1, *135*
4:21-24, *470*
4:21-31, *165*
31, *990*
4:22-26, *777*
4:22-31, *400*
4:25-26, *561*
4:26, *56, 774, 1239-40*
5:2, *845*
5:2-4, *770*
5:2-12, *879*
5:6, *845*
5:6-12, *377*
5:10, *643*
5:11, *55, 565, 775, 777*
5:12, *845*
5:13, *327*
5:13-14, *770*
5:16, *55*
5:16-17, *665*
5:16-24, *54*
5:19-21, *757, 762, 881, 1255*
5:19-23, *1256*
5:20, *1240*
5:21, *57, 908*
5:22-23, *757, 762, 1255-56*
5:25, *54*
6:1, *1210*
6:2, *770*
6:12, *565, 775, 777*
6:12-16, *377*
6:15, *1, 51, 54, 845, 880, 1227*
6:16, *880, 1152*
6:17, *643*

Ephesians
1:1, *186, 320*
1:3-14, *233*
1:4-5, *172*
1:5, *990*
1:9-10, *1*
1:10, *54*
1:14, *762*
1:17, *69, 700*
1:17-19, *172*
1:21, *1240*
2:1-10, *56*
2:5, *880*
2:5-6, *1240*
2:11-22, *1128*
2:12-19, *233*
2:13-18, *1*
2:14, *799, 980*
2:14-15, *1180*
2:19, *774, 989*
2:19-22, *762, 1180*
2:20-22, *125*
2:21, *1179*
3:1, *830*
3:1-10, *973*
3:3-4, *862*
3:6, *991*
3:10, *1240*
3:14-15, *736*
3:15, *54*
3:16-19, *172*
4:1, *830*
4:7-11, *450*
4:7-13, *830*
4:8, *1006*
4:8-10, *447*
4:17-24, *1239*
4:22, *1255*
4:22-24, *1*
4:25, *862*
4:28, *1003*
4:31, *762*
4:32, *762, 1255*
5:3-5, *881*
5:9, *762, 1255*
5:14, *234, 453*
5:16, *53*
5:18, *138, 1240*
5:19, *232, 712, 714*
5:21—6:4, *120*
5:21—6:9, *353, 687, 1141*
5:22-33, *762*
5:25, *758*
5:31, *2*
6:1-3, *355*
6:1-4, *200*
6:4, *357-58*
6:5-8, *470, 990*
6:5-9, *1003*
6:8-9, *470*
6:9, *54, 365*
6:10-17, *114*
6:11, *993*
6:11-17, *762*
6:12, *973, 1240*
6:13, *993*
6:14, *700, 993*
6:16, *993*
6:17, *700, 993*
6:19-20, *862*
6:20, *830*
6:21, *1009*
6:21-22, *862, 1247*

Philippians
1:1, *788, 990, 1023*
1:5, *990*
1:5-7, *770*
1:6, *56-57*
1:10, *57*
1:12, *643, 1006*
1:12-13, *830*
1:13, *995*
1:14, *830*
1:15, *830*
1:16, *830*
1:17, *830*
1:20-26, *323*
1:21, *762*
1:27—2:4, *519*
1:27-30, *1239*
1:29, *521, 830*
1:29-30, *830*
2, *219, 233*
2:5, *990*
2:5-11, *1, 232-33, 237-38, 521*
2:6, *72, 1009*
2:6-11, *232, 235, 447, 1009*
2:7-8, *1009*
2:9-11, *729, 736, 818, 1009*
2:10, *54*
2:15, *1239*
2:16, *57*
2:17, *762*
2:19-30, *830*
2:20, *774*
2:21, *830*
2:25-30, *788, 1006, 1247*
2:29-30, *521, 770*
3:2, *845*
3:2-11, *777*
3:5, *200, 216, 785, 876*
3:8, *785*
3:10-11, *521*
3:12, *211*
3:12-14, *665*
3:12-21, *56*
3:13-14, *759, 762*
3:20, *54, 56, 989, 1239*
3:20-21, *56*
4:2-3, *788*
4:8, *643, 757, 762, 1255, 1256*
4:9, *774*
4:10-20, *990*
4:11-12, *17*
4:11-14, *1287*
4:12, *16*
4:15, *770*
4:15-16, *205*
4:15-18, *788*
4:22, *959, 1003, 1126*

Colossians
1:12-13, *57*
1:15, *729, 1274*
1:15-17, *700*
1:15-20, *1, 225, 232-33, 235*
1:16, *54, 1240*
1:19, *1180*
1:20, *54*
1:24, *830*
2:1, *225*
2:8-14, *225*
2:9, *729, 740, 1180*
2:14, *760, 762*
2:15, *221, 760, 762, 993, 1004-5, 1240*
2:16, *602, 802, 1035*
2:16-19, *737*
2:18, *1139*
3:1, *54*
3:1-3, *56*
3:1-4, *1, 1240*
3:1-17, *225*
3:5, *1255*
3:5-6, *881*
3:5-11, *1239*
3:8, *1255*
3:9-10, *1, 736*
3:12, *762, 1255*
3:16, *232, 712, 714*
3:18—4:1, *120, 353, 687, 757-58, 762*
3:20-21, *200*
3:22-25, *470*
25, *1003*
4:2, *1240*
4:5-6, *1239*
4:7-9, *1247*
4:7-15, *830*
4:9, *320*
4:10, *827, 830, 1246*

4:11, 57
4:13, 320, 1092
4:15, 138, 1003, 1131
4:16, 67, 407, 860

1 Thessalonians
1:6, 1239
1:7-8, 425
1:8, 205
1:9-10, 53
1:10, 54
2, 367
2:1, 643
2:2, 217, 788, 830
2:4, 1179
2:4-6, 383
2:6-7, 762
2:7, 360, 708
2:11, 201, 356
2:12, 57
2:14, 1239
2:14-16, 775
2:18, 54
3:1, 205
3:1-5, 1239
3:3-4, 521
3:5, 1210
3:13, 53
4:1, 643
4:3-7, 1255
4:5, 930
4:6, 10
4:8, 54
4:9, 643
4:9-10, 521
4:9-12, 327
4:11, 1003, 1247
4:13, 643
4:13-18, 53, 56-57
4:16, 54, 450, 1240
4:16-17, 56
4:17, 447, 737
5:1, 643
5:1-4, 56
5:2, 55
5:3, 762
5:8, 762
5:11, 521
5:12, 158
5:12-13, 521
5:14, 521
5:15, 771
5:23, 53, 774
5:26, 628
5:27, 407

2 Thessalonians
1:4-5, 57
1:4-12, 1239
1:5, 777
1:5-12, 53
1:7, 54
2:1-2, 862
2:1-12, 53, 56, 339, 1136
2:2, 1284
2:3, 56
2:4, 56, 1179
2:5-12, 762
2:6-7, 867
2:7, 56
2:8, 56, 700
2:9, 56
2:9-10, 928
2:14-16, 777
3:1, 643
3:4, 643
3:6-10, 1247
3:6-13, 1003
3:16, 774

1 Timothy
1:1, 993
1:3, 320, 321
1:9-10, 757, 1255-56
1:15, 232
1:17, 232
1:18-20, 321
1:20, 211
2, 757
2:1-2, 973
2:9, 446
2:9-15, 627
2:11-15, 2
2:13-14, 1
3, 1256
3:1-7, 1023
3:2, 7, 1246
3:2-3, 1256
3:4, 200
3:4-5, 357
3:11, 1277
3:12, 200, 1277
3:15, 1180
3:16, 196, 232-35, 237
4:1, 196
4:1-4, 321
4:7, 1240
4:12, 757, 1255
4:14, 1062
4:16, 1240
5:1, 357
5:4, 200, 356, 1240
5:8, 356
5:14, 683
6:2, 158, 364
6:3-5, 1256
6:9, 1210
6:10, 761-62, 1287
6:11, 757, 762, 1255
6:12, 211, 762
6:13, 221, 803, 981
6:15, 280
6:15-16, 232

2 Timothy
1:8-10, 233
1:8-12, 830
1:16-18, 320
2:5, 211
2:8, 703
2:9, 830
2:11-12, 521
2:11-13, 232-33, 1256
2:22, 757, 762, 1255
3:1-2, 355
3:2-5, 757, 1255
3:8, 164
3:10, 1255
3:10-11, 762
3:12, 777
3:13, 1283
3:16, 1255
3:17, 862
3:20, 225
4:1, 55
4:6, 762
4:7, 211
4:7-8, 521
4:9-10, 830
4:11, 830
4:13, 828-29
4:14-15, 320
4:16, 113, 830
4:20, 99, 229-30

Titus
1:1, 990
1:3, 993
1:6, 200
1:7-8, 1256
1:7-9, 1023
1:8, 1246
1:12, 71, 472, 759, 762, 814, 1282
1:13, 762
1:13-17, 757
1:15, 880
2:3, 1277
2:5, 353, 687
2:8, 353, 687
2:10-14, 1256
2:11, 1239
2:12, 1239-40, 1255
2:15, 993
3:1-2, 1256
3:3, 762, 1255
3:4-7, 232, 233
3:7, 991
3:12, 323

Philemon
1, 300, 770, 830
1-2, 307
2, 138, 225, 1003, 1131
7, 770
9, 830
9-10, 643
9-13, 470
10, 225
12, 1247
13, 830
17, 767, 770, 990
17-19, 382
18-19, 990
19, 771, 1009
21, 643
22, 225
2, 225
22, 770
23, 827, 830
23-24, 830

Hebrews
1—8, 410
1:1-2, 458
1:2, 458
1:2-4, 729
1:3, 122, 233, 665
1:3-13, 458
1:4, 458
1:5, 458
1:5-13, 1207
1:8, 458
1:13, 457
2:2, 164, 602
2:9-11, 1211
2:10, 521
2:16, 769
2:18, 769
3—4, 557, 1035
3:3-6, 1211
3:6, 521, 665, 770
3:7—4:13, 162, 164
3:7-9, 1207
3:13, 521
3:14, 521, 665
3:19—4:2, 770
3:23-24, 696
4:9, 1035
4:14—5:14, 458
4:14-16, 769-70
4:16, 770
5:6, 704
5:10, 704
5:12-13, 708
5:13, 200, 777
5:27-41, 823
6:1-12, 708
6:4-8, 188, 519, 771
6:10, 770
6:20, 704
7, 257, 400, 496, 1258
7:1, 1055
7:1-3, 1139
7:1-10, 400
7:1-17, 704, 1262
7:1-21, 458
7:2, 401
7:3, 695
7:12, 695
7:14, 699-700
7:22, 458
8:2-5, 1274
8:5, 792
8:6, 770, 1196
8:8-13, 458
9:1-12, 377
9:2-5, 1181
9:3-4, 1054
9:6, 1181
9:6-14, 1043
9:7, 1181
9:8-10, 1181
9:11, 379, 1181
9:11-15, 665
9:12, 1181-82
9:15, 770, 1196
10:1, 792
10:1-10, 1292
10:4-10, 665
10:19-22, 770
10:24-25, 521
10:26-31, 188, 519, 521, 770
10:28, 1244
10:32, 521
10:32-34, 521
10:32-35, 775
10:32-39, 1239
10:33-34, 830
10:34, 666, 827
10:35-39, 770
11, 70, 496, 626, 1191
11:5, 70, 399, 447, 931
11:6, 665, 769
11:7, 399
11:9-10, 989
11:13-16, 1239
11:16, 666
11:17-19, 458
11:17-20, 866
11:22, 1094
11:25-26, 666
11:35, 627, 665-66
11:35-38, 775
11:37, 63, 70
12:1-2, 211, 521
12:1-4, 521, 665
12:2, 55, 665, 989
12:3-7, 775
12:3-8, 1239
12:6, 358
12:12-13, 1239
12:14-17, 188
12:18-24, 57
12:21, 1196
12:22, 1239-40
12:24, 770
12:28, 768, 770
13:1-3, 521, 770
13:2, 1246
13:3, 830
13:9, 1015
13:14, 989, 1239
13:15, 770
13:16, 770
13:20-21, 172, 408
13:22, 408
13:24, 408
13:25, 408

James
1:1, 294, 471, 1023, 1239
1:1-4, 1239
1:2-4, 1123
1:2-27, 408
1:6, 200
1:9-10, 307
1:13, 1210
1:13-14, 1123
1:19, 1123
1:19-20, 762
1:22-25, 762
1:26, 762
1:27, 356
2, 516, 760
2:1—5:12, 408
2:1-7, 307, 1152
2:1-9, 757, 762
2:1-13, 516
2:2, 1145, 1152
2:8, 307, 1152
2:8-13, 1152
2:14-26, 757, 762, 1152
2:14-27, 516
2:16, 307
2:19, 232, 233
2:21-23, 400, 866
2:23, 251, 385, 496
3:1-12, 762
3:6, 907, 1123
3:9, 1, 1123
3:9-12, 1123
3:13-18, 1256
3:15, 762, 1255
3:17, 762, 1255
4:4, 386, 1239
4:8, 801
4:12, 233
4:13-15, 1245
5:1-6, 307
5:3, 70
5:4, 307
5:11, 1191
5:13, 714
5:13-18, 1152
5:13-20, 408
5:14, 1152

1 Peter
1:1, 135, 294, 1177, 1239
1:2, 172, 1177
1:3-5, 233
1:6, 775
1:6-7, 1274
1:7, 1123
1:19, 665
2:1, 762, 1255
2:2, 200, 708
2:4-8, 125
2:5, 973
2:5-9, 826
2:6, 704
2:6-8, 232
2:9, 856, 989
2:11, 989, 1239
2:11—3:12, 757-58, 762
2:11-12, 294, 521
2:13, 967
2:13—3:7, 1141
2:13-14, 973, 989
2:13-17, 627
2:13-18, 989
2:13-25, 627
2:14, 979, 997, 1029
2:14-16, 771
2:15, 1029
2:17, 1029
2:18-21, 470
2:19-25, 1239
2:21-25, 458
3:1-6, 627
3:6, 400
3:8, 762, 1255
3:9, 627
3:9-17, 1239
3:18-22, 236, 399, 521
4:1-4, 521
4:1-5, 1239
4:3, 762, 1255
4:9, 1246
4:12-19, 775, 1239
4:13-14, 521
4:14, 700, 762
4:15, 1255
5:12-13, 1177
5:13, 967
5:14, 628

2 Peter
1, 1256
1:5, 1256
1:5-7, 757, 762, 1255-56
2:1-22, 187
2:5, 164, 399
2:9, 1209-10
2:13, 1198
2:16, 1246
2:22, 19, 762
3, 333
3:3-4, 762
3:3-13, 339
3:5-7, 762
3:10, 57
3:10-14, 57
3:11-13, 55
3:13, 51
3:15-16, 544, 1283

1 John
1:5-6, 1022
1:7, 665
2:1, 201
2:2, 232-33
2:12-14, 172
2:13, 357
2:18, 56, 201
2:21, 1022
2:22, 56, 233
2:27, 1022
2:28, 201
3:1-2, 521
3:7, 201
3:16, 384
3:18, 201
4:2, 232-33
4:3, 56, 415
4:6, 49, 1022
4:9-10, 458
4:10, 233
4:15, 232-33
5:1, 232-233
5:5, 233
5:21, 201

2 John
7, 56
12, 1283

3 John
4, 201, 357
5-7, 1246
5-8, 770
8, 1246
9-10, 1246

10, *770*
13, *1283*
15, *387*

Jude
4-16, *187*
5, *30*
9, *70, 165, 1193, 1198, 1240, 1258*
13, *762*
14, *1*
14-15, *70, 165, 399, 456*
24-25, *232-33*

Revelation
1, *1249*
1—5, *410, 737*
1:1, *45, 408-9*
1:1-3, *409*
1:3, *409, 1283*
1:4, *409*
1:4-6, *409*
1:4-8, *233*
1:6, *826*
1:7, *321*
1:9-10, *827*
1:10, *734, 1152*
1:10-11, *734*
1:12-15, *129*
1:12-16, *1152*
1:13, *1152*
1:13-15, *40*
2—3, *221, 320, 409, 1247*
2:1—3:22, *31, 186*
2:2-3, *321*
2:6, *321*
2:7, *759*
2:7—3:11, *763*
2:8-11, *132, 319*
2:9, *283, 307, 521, 563, 568, 1145, 1152*
2:10, *775*
2:12-13, *99*
2:13, *131*
2:14-15, *307*
2:18-29, *1092*
2:19, *1256*
2:20, *307*
2:26-28, *521*
3—4, *1239*
3:5, *40*
3:7, *704*
3:8, *307*
3:9, *307, 563, 1145, 1152*
3:14-22, *759, 1092*
3:17, *307*
3:19, *358*
4, *733, 736, 1182*
4—5, *238, 763, 1139*
4—6, *734*
4—22, *339*
4:1—6:17, *734*
4:1-2, *733-34*
4:1-11, *1152*
4:2, *70, 734*
4:3, *734*
4:5, *1240*
4:8, *232-33, 236*
4:9, *70*
4:10, *190*
4:11, *233, 769*
5, *760, 1181*
5:1, *70, 1283*
5:5, *700, 704*
5:5-10, *665*
5:7, *70*
5:8, *712*
5:9, *714*
5:9-10, *233, 973, 1029*
5:12, *233, 236, 714, 1139*
5:13, *70, 233*
6:9-11, *775, 1239*
6:12-15, *1275*
6:16, *70*
7:10, *70, 233*
7:12, *233*
7:15, *70*
8—9, *1275*
8—11, *40*
9:1, *70*
9:11, *87*
9:13-14, *1139*
9:20-11, *769*
9:20-21, *1275*
9:21, *1255*
11, *803*
11:15, *233*
11:17-18, *233*
12, *1161*
12—13, *251*
12:5, *447*
12:7—13:2, *1029*
12:7-9, *31, 156*
12:10-11, *521, 665*
12:10-12, *233*
12:16, *1275*
13, *26, 29, 774, 1029, 1194*
13:1-10, *56*
13:2, *1029*
13:4-6, *1029*
13:7, *1029*
13:8, *40*
13:10, *627*
13:11-14, *928*
13:11-17, *1029*
13:11-18, *56*
13:12, *1029*
13:13-14, *56*
13:13-15, *1030*
13:16-17, *307*
14:3, *233, 714*
14:6-7, *1275*
14:9-11, *769*
14:19-20, *304*
15:2, *665*
15:3, *714*
15:3-4, *233*
16:1-9, *1275*
16:1-20, *1275*
16:5-7, *233*
16:8-11, *1275*
16:12-16, *31*
16:13, *56*
16:16, *87, 606*
16:18-20, *1275*
17:1-6, *775*
17:3, *734*
17:14, *280*
17:19:16, *280*
18:3, *307*
18:9, *307*
18:11, *307*
18:15-18, *307*
18:22, *714*
19—21, *626*
19:1-2, *233*
19:3, *233*
19:4, *70*
19:5, *233*
19:6-8, *233*
19:9, *146*
19:9-17, *144*
19:10, *40*
19:11, *700*
19:11-16, *699*
19:13, *699*
19:20, *40, 56, 928*
20:1-6, *56*
20:4, *775, 1199*
20:4-6, *50, 521*
20:8, *51*
20:12, *40*
20:14, *40*
21—22, *57*
21:1, *51, 54-55, 332*
21:1-4, *57*
21:5, *51, 70*
21:8, *1255*
21:9-21, *1240*
21:10, *734*
21:19, *744*
21:19-20, *867*
21:22, *798, 1181, 1240*
21:27, *40*
22:6-21, *409*
22:8, *40*
22:15, *1255*
22:16, *700, 704, 1207*
22:17, *233*
22:19, *40*

Subject Index

abortion, 199, 681, 1278
Acco, 102-3, 107, 109, 392, 394
Achilles, 8, 12, 14, 17, 21, 122-24, 131, 363-64, 381, 384, 628, 680, 686-87, 829, 919, 1008-10
Acrocorinth, 228-29, 231
Acts of Andrew, 68-69, 189
Acts of Andrew and Matthias, 68-69
Acts of John, 68-69, 321, 714
Acts of Paul and Thecla, 33, 67-68, 189-90, 404, 410, 683, 860
Acts of Peter, 67-68, 404, 415
Acts of Peter and the Twelve Apostles, 68
Acts of Philip, 68
Acts of Pilate, 77, 858
Acts of Thomas, 67-69, 73, 416
adoption, 18, 110, 404, 407, 429, 465, 632, 769, 794, 809, 974, 990-91, 1219
adultery, 6-11, 251, 361, 445, 487, 519, 811, 1064, 1109, 1119, 1254-55, 1277-78
adulthood, 12, 179, 197-200, 248, 301, 309, 312, 354, 356-57, 360, 503, 529, 650-51, 708, 921
Aegean, 109, 130-31, 280, 325, 421, 424, 426, 467-68, 499, 871-72, 920, 1147, 1163
Aelia Capitolina, 220, 561, 624, 972, 1017, 1113
Aeneas, 44, 124, 334, 594, 1107
Aeneid, 44, 124, 310, 331, 334, 594, 772, 921, 1082
Africa, 15, 370, 412, 502, 747, 754, 819, 964, 976, 992, 998, 1014, 1078, 1142
afterlife, 15, 62, 69, 123, 175, 315, 326, 330, 334-36, 339, 344, 346, 656, 784-86, 852, 924, 930-33, 935, 1224, 1229, 1271, 1273
agora, 99, 104, 131, 139-40, 213-14, 470-71, 758, 1186, 1220
agriculture, agrarianism, 105, 126, 131, 212, 214, 299, 303-5, 309, 344-45, 368, 372, 391, 395, 470, 476, 559, 757, 759, 761, 871, 887, 894, 936, 966, 975-78, 991, 1000-1002, 1126, 1165, 1276-77
Ahiqar, 18-19, 1238
Ain Feshka, 345, 883, 887
Ain Gedi, 884
alchemy, 483, 679-80
Alexander (III) the Great, 20, 34, 102, 109, 119, 141, 154, 167, 202, 212-13, 218, 220, 267, 319, 397, 424-26, 428, 447, 464-65, 467, 473, 476, 526, 570, 617, 657, 787, 795, 819, 917, 923-24, 926, 1017, 1026, 1058, 1062, 1071, 1092, 1108, 1166, 1219, 1232, 1269, 1293
Alexander Janneus, 104, 257, 267, 440, 468, 573, 609, 619, 914, 1170-71, 1206
Alexandria, 4, 12, 22-30, 34-36, 39, 59, 75-76, 78, 82-84, 109-10, 115-18, 139, 142, 187-90, 192, 209, 212-13, 228, 242, 268-69, 275, 280-81, 284, 286-90, 292, 307, 312, 319, 321, 331, 387, 400, 412, 414-15, 436, 449, 466-67, 476-77, 481, 496, 498-99, 509, 528, 537-38, 540, 580, 582, 608, 661-62, 664, 673, 689, 694, 700, 719, 722-24, 752-53, 775, 789-91, 793, 800, 813, 815, 835, 858, 860, 865, 868, 872-873, 891, 925, 950, 956, 981, 1028, 1054, 1068, 1072-73, 1077-78, 1080-82, 1100, 1130, 1141, 1146, 1148, 1154-55, 1220, 1225, 1235, 1248, 1250, 1268, 1272, 1276, 1293-94
Alexandrian library, 500, 647, 1073, 1083
Alexandrian scholarship, 27, 1068-69
altar, 99, 104, 106, 139-40, 143, 219, 241, 341, 346, 375, 454, 468, 578, 584, 595, 637, 653, 772, 825, 845, 894, 919-21, 923, 1007, 1036-46, 1048-49, 1059, 1068, 1167-69, 1172, 1179, 1187, 1241, 1257
amphitheater, 111-12, 124, 210, 213-14, 284, 395, 470, 560, 1219-20, 1232
amulets, 72, 199, 224, 269-73, 415, 667-68, 929-30
Anacharsis, 239-40, 242
Anatolia, 32, 34, 130-36, 279, 318-19, 321, 389, 391, 422, 917, 919, 923, 1092-93, 1163
ancestors, 2, 21, 117-18, 173, 175, 438, 457, 495, 573, 582, 601-2, 608, 653, 772, 775, 867, 921, 942, 978, 1012, 1028, 1075, 1117, 1122, 1193, 1195, 1203, 1302
Andanian Mysteries, 721-22
angels of the nations, 30-31
antichrist, 56, 1136
Antiochids, 31, 348, 1092
Antiochus Epiphanes, 578, 938
Antiochus I, 35-36, 42, 51, 106, 109, 141, 213, 219, 259-60, 267, 280, 283, 439, 468, 475, 563, 572, 590, 598, 608, 618, 624-25, 658, 661, 775-76, 869-70, 942, 963, 1010, 1058, 1086, 1092-93, 1116, 1118, 1135, 1194, 1197, 1239, 1293, 1295
Antiochus II, 109, 267, 283, 563, 572, 618, 661, 963, 1010, 1092-93
Antiochus III, 109, 267, 283, 563, 572, 618, 661, 963, 1010, 1092-93
Antiochus IV, 35-36, 42, 51, 106, 141, 213, 259-60, 439, 468, 475, 572, 590, 598, 608, 624-25, 658, 775-76, 869-70, 942, 1058, 1086, 1093, 1116, 1118, 1135, 1194, 1197, 1239, 1293, 1295
Antiochus IV Epiphanes, 36, 42, 51, 106, 259, 260, 590, 598, 625, 869-70, 942, 1058, 1086, 1093, 1135
Antiochus V, 103, 223, 440, 658, 1093
Antiochus VI, 103, 223, 440, 658, 1093
Antiochus VII, 103, 223, 440, 658, 1093
Antiphon, 830, 1067
Aphrodite, 15-16, 229, 561, 762, 815, 919, 922, 1163, 1278
Apocalypse of Abraham, 37-38, 46, 385, 450, 860, 948, 1296
Apocalypse of Adam, 417, 860, 863
Apocalypse of Paul, 45, 860
Apocalypse of Peter, 45, 77, 189-90, 193, 336, 415
Apocalypse of Sedrach, 4, 339
Apocalypse of Zephaniah, 39-40, 385
apocalyptic literature, 39, 41, 47, 50-51, 55-56, 409, 450, 695, 1172, 1260
apocalypticism, 41, 42, 45-50, 52-54, 62, 130, 725, 731, 1181, 1223, 1225, 1261, 1263
apocrypha, 58-60, 66-67, 857, 912
apocrypha and pseudepigrapha, 60
Apocryphon of Jacob, 92
Apocryphon of James, 77, 184
Apocryphon of Jeremiah, 869-70
Apocryphon of Joseph, 78, 349
Apocryphon of Joshua, 79-80, 258, 1206
Apocryphon of Judah, 92
Apollo, 8, 98, 141, 219, 228, 231, 318, 722, 739, 812, 815, 831-32, 918-22, 926, 928-29, 1069, 1107, 1222
Apollonia, 103, 284, 787, 1231-32
Apollonius of Rhodes, 8, 10, 12, 524, 814, 1069-70, 1082, 1207-8
Apollonius of Tyana, 80-81, 139-40, 168, 403, 448, 739-40, 742, 1075
apologetics, 646, 704, 843
Apostolic Constitutions, 4, 236, 822, 1200, 1258, 1298
apostolic fathers, 59, 81, 517, 776
Apostrophe to Judah, 848, 851
Apostrophe to Zion, 848-49, 851
apotheosis, 447-49, 730, 923
apprentice, apprenticeship, 200, 309-10, 312
Apuleius, 8-9, 11, 209, 354, 362-64, 444, 446, 680, 684, 686-88, 708, 721, 723, 929, 995, 1219, 1246, 1272, 1284, 1287
Aqiba, 450, 679, 907, 916-17, 939, 1042, 1114-16
aqueduct, 126, 158, 176-77, 213-14, 304, 397, 560, 884, 886, 959, 976, 981, 1045
Aquila, 98, 229, 230, 285, 319-20, 528, 754, 1003, 1015-16, 1102-3, 1114, 1131, 1292
Aramaic language, 18-19, 75, 78-79, 86-93, 96, 109, 149, 153, 170-71, 179, 222-23, 227, 233, 250, 256, 258-60, 262, 266, 271-73, 283, 306, 313-14, 317-18, 341, 343, 397-99, 401, 426, 429-30, 432-34, 439, 452, 456, 459-64, 467, 469, 472, 475, 479, 535, 540-41, 543-44, 572, 576, 596, 611, 616, 630-31, 651-52, 668, 694, 696, 699, 706, 730-31, 739, 743, 745, 747, 749, 752-54, 764-66, 778, 785, 800, 822, 824, 856, 891, 898, 902-6, 908-9, 913, 949, 1023-24, 1063, 1094-98, 1101, 1104-5, 1135, 1137, 1139, 1146, 1149-50, 1154-55, 1159-61, 1175, 1178, 1192-93, 1199-1201, 1226, 1230, 1233-35, 1238-39, 1241, 1257-59, 1263, 1268, 1290-92
Christian Palestinian, 87-88, 1096-97
Galilean, 87-88, 90-91
Middle, 87, 89, 904
Official, 87-88
Samaritan, 87
Transitional, 904-5
Aramaic Apocalypse, 694
Aramaic targumim, 90, 92-93, 258, 313, 544, 1292
Aramaisms, 89, 906, 1094-95
Araspes and Panthea, 1008
archaeology, 93-94, 100-101, 108, 263, 305, 345, 421-22, 587, 808, 1057, 1167
archangels, 42, 63, 129, 154, 165, 270, 511, 609, 669, 693-94, 1136, 1170, 1226, 1239-40
Archelaus, 201, 485, 488-91, 560, 577, 585, 621, 839, 886, 938-39, 964, 979-80, 998, 1016, 1049, 1164
architecture, 103-4, 106-7, 111, 121, 124-28, 131, 173, 214, 229, 281, 286, 292, 308, 311, 396, 435, 464, 467, 515, 564, 638, 743-44, 759, 920, 975, 1000, 1011, 1080, 1147, 1169
arenas, 111-14, 121, 221, 310, 1130, 1222, 1276, 1279
Areopagus, 139-40, 423, 426, 582
Ares, 138, 244, 525, 815-16, 919, 922
Aristobulus, 116-19, 219, 263, 282, 291-92, 392, 439-41, 485-88, 573, 576, 582-85, 619-21, 699, 790-91, 820, 843-44, 979, 1093, 1100, 1206, 1225, 1294
Aristobulus II, 263, 439, 441, 485-86, 573, 576, 620, 979
Aristotle, Aristotelianism, 10, 15, 20, 28, 119-21, 144, 311, 325-26, 328, 353, 357, 361, 363-65, 380-83, 387, 403, 418-19, 425, 428, 498, 519, 525, 536, 581, 635, 642, 665, 687-89, 721, 758, 761, 768, 790, 794-95, 804-6, 812, 868, 930, 953-54, 1061, 1066-68, 1074, 1076-78, 1081-82, 1124, 1127, 1210, 1219, 1253, 1270, 1282-83, 1285
Armenia, 135, 415, 620, 918, 963-64, 971-72
Artapanus, 269, 282, 290, 292, 495, 581, 592, 1196, 1225
Artemis, 99, 122, 132, 218-19, 225, 242, 318-19, 321, 359, 759, 808, 815, 919, 922, 1187, 1222, 1279
Artemision, 132, 319
Ascension of Isaiah, 51, 63, 70, 129-30, 1109, 1136, 1291
asceticism, 67-68, 166, 236, 240, 244, 347, 416, 448, 682-83, 734, 739, 796, 807, 1015, 1224, 1230
Asclepius, 131, 228, 333, 337, 358, 483, 498-99, 721, 757, 759, 918-20, 925, 927, 929, 1013

Ashkelon, 104, 109
Asia Minor, 20-21, 31-34, 68, 83, 100, 119, 122, 130-36, 159, 213, 218-19, 225, 279, 283, 296, 319, 321, 377, 389, 391, 409, 415, 417, 421-22, 424-25, 429, 435, 444-45, 464, 470, 479, 530, 533, 540-41, 562-70, 722, 763, 810, 815, 819, 831, 847, 871-72, 918, 926, 963, 967, 977, 1029-30, 1046, 1074, 1092-93, 1107, 1163, 1177, 1221, 1231, 1248, 1279, 1301
Asiatic rhetoric, 429, 1074-76, 1083
associations, 54, 136-38, 141, 143-45, 214, 223, 288, 300-302, 306, 494, 522, 566, 762, 769, 800, 811, 901, 924, 928, 1012, 1016, 1087, 1131-33, 1187, 1218-19, 1221, 1228, 1301
Assumption of Moses, 59, 625, 1198-99
astrology, 16, 202, 262, 340, 483, 581-83, 723, 739, 831, 930, 1086, 1233-35, 1251
Athena, 99, 139, 225, 228, 424, 815-17, 864, 919-20, 922, 1187, 1208, 1222, 1279
Athens, 8, 10, 12, 14, 20-21, 26, 28, 34, 70, 80, 94-95, 99-100, 117, 119, 120, 122-23, 131-32, 139-40, 144-45, 157, 176, 205, 212-13, 219, 228, 230-31, 242-43, 279-81, 285, 295, 310-11, 318-19, 325-26, 354, 361, 384, 422-29, 443, 446-47, 466-68, 471-72, 481-82, 499-501, 503, 525, 530, 583, 617, 634-36, 647, 654, 683, 687-90, 692, 721-22, 758-59, 761, 795, 805, 812-14, 858-59, 872-73, 920, 925-26, 953, 956, 972, 1027, 1065-68, 1072-73, 1080-81, 1084-85, 1124-25, 1140, 1142, 1151, 1186-87, 1219, 1221, 1232, 1276, 1287
athletics, 131, 140-42, 144, 209-11, 213, 228, 280, 309, 324, 423, 435-36, 470, 520, 655, 665, 759, 790, 1191, 1279, 1288
Athronges, 938
Atticism, 240, 429, 655, 1075
augures, 922, 927, 1012
auspicium, 928
Azotus, 104
Baba ben Buta, 612-13, 914
Baba Qamma, 912
Babatha Archive, 11, 15, 429, 535, 540-41, 765-66, 1095, 1098
Babylonian Talmud, 612-13, 729, 889, 898, 912-13, 1051, 1053
Banias, 103, 178-79
banqueting, 116, 143-46, 157, 370, 386, 467, 492, 625, 629, 636, 900, 909-10, 919, 922, 935, 971, 1000, 1003, 1025-26, 1096, 1118, 1132, 1294, 1297
baptism, 56, 75-76, 82-83, 169, 188, 203, 232, 235-36, 301, 347, 393, 415-17, 509, 554, 723, 736, 750, 844-45, 879-80, 1007, 1110-11, 1244
Bar Kokhba, 88, 224-25, 293, 462, 471, 535, 540-41, 558, 561, 567, 580, 584, 587-88, 624, 631, 678, 765, 836, 916-17, 939, 972-73, 979, 1017, 1112, 1114-16, 1278
Bar Kokhba letters, 535
Bar Kokhba revolt, 471, 558, 580, 587, 631, 678, 973, 979, 1017
Barki Nafshi, 146-47
Baruch, 41, 44, 46, 58, 62, 69, 148-51, 251-52, 335, 513, 822, 853, 870, 1086, 1102, 1226, 1291, 1295
2 Baruch, 3, 5, 41, 44, 46, 50, 62, 149-51, 294, 335, 410, 513, 526, 556, 682, 705, 865, 1194, 1198, 1226, 1295
3 Baruch, 4, 41, 44, 46, 150-51, 335, 730, 1188
basilica, 124-25, 178, 214, 321, 396, 564, 631, 971
bath qol, 508
baths, 96, 103, 122, 126, 128, 131, 158, 213, 311, 344, 396, 436, 470, 508, 523, 641, 680-81, 723, 873, 886, 929, 971, 1000, 1002, 1042, 1132, 1149, 1235
Battle of Actium, 23, 32, 281, 477, 560, 577, 621, 787, 873, 918, 923, 969, 975, 1010, 1109, 1250-51
Beatitudes Text, 151
Beautiful Gate, 1174
Beersheba, 105
Bel and the Dragon, 69, 251, 526
belial, beliar, 154-56
benediction, 171-72, 408-9, 517, 651, 774, 822, 1146, 1298
benefactors, benefaction, 95, 157-58, 280, 287, 311, 356, 364, 382, 386, 470, 560, 565-68, 583, 641, 663, 757, 766, 768-70, 772, 962, 966, 1027, 1029, 1075, 1162, 1238
Berossus, 333, 502, 581
bet midrash, 311-12
Beth Shean, 103, 394
Beth She)arim, 394
betrothal, 7, 685, 1291
biblical interpretation, 159-62, 165, 780-82, 1054, 1225
bibliomancy, 166
bilingualism, 86, 88, 103, 109, 189, 231, 329, 468, 472, 480, 533, 671, 673, 676-77, 753, 764, 1094, 1097-98
biography, *bios*, 9, 14, 167-69, 355, 381, 383, 403-6, 471, 500, 740, 757, 789-90, 794, 809, 812, 951, 958, 1075-76, 1079, 1082, 1084, 1142-43, 1157, 1284, 1286
Bion of Borysthenes, 243
Birth of the Chosen One, 170
Bithynia, 131, 135-36, 220, 294, 777, 809, 812, 961, 963, 989, 1013, 1030, 1159
Boethusians, 493, 610, 1051
Book of Arda Viraf, 44
Book of Blessings, 171-73, 255, 731, 1021, 1138
Book of Dreams, 30, 258, 314-15
Book of the Dead, 334
Book of the Two Ways, 333
Book of Thomas, 77
Books of Jeu, 77, 415
boxing, 141, 210-11
brigands, 163, 239, 275, 485, 936-38, 945, 1009
Brontologion, 266, 1233, 1235
burial, burial practices, 4, 22, 35-36, 63, 74, 95, 97, 105, 123, 126-27, 144, 157-58, 173-75, 179, 197, 263, 284, 318, 321, 336, 359, 422, 476, 530-32, 539, 557, 563, 565, 568, 626, 654, 660, 740, 846, 887, 929-32, 943, 972, 1009, 1114, 1132, 1171, 1190-91, 1200-1201, 1238, 1276, 1278
Caesar Augustus, 8-9, 16-17, 23, 32, 34, 98-100, 111-12, 125, 133-34, 139-41, 157-58, 168, 176, 178, 201-3, 209-10, 213, 215-16, 220-21, 229, 267, 287-88, 319, 366, 368-71, 387, 389, 391-92, 412, 425, 467, 476, 480, 487-91, 524, 528, 533, 538, 560, 567, 577, 585, 598, 621, 633, 636, 641, 667, 680-81, 683-85, 688-89, 692, 771-74, 787, 795, 804, 833, 835, 918, 921-23, 959-60, 963-64, 966, 968-70, 973, 975-76, 979, 985, 991-92, 994-1000, 1010-14, 1017-18, 1027-29, 1047, 1064, 1081-82, 1085, 1108-9, 1142, 1162-63, 1187, 1211, 1247-48, 1250, 1269, 1289
Caesar's household, 959, 1126
Caesarea Maritima, 94-95, 125, 176-78, 213, 304, 470, 534, 560, 577, 621, 630, 798, 804, 979, 994, 997, 1220
Caesarea Philippi, 94, 176, 178-79, 434, 820
Caiaphas, 95, 179-80, 204, 611, 704, 1044, 1049, 1115, 1175-76
Cairo Genizah, 904-5, 1096, 1292
calendars, 34, 161, 180-83, 203-4, 210, 261-63, 315, 346, 368-71, 374-77, 533, 601-2, 609, 645, 649, 709, 809, 849, 851, 891, 920, 994, 1012, 1019, 1043, 1138, 1170, 1183, 1219, 1234-35
Caligula, Gaius, 13-14, 51, 206, 230, 284, 490, 492, 578, 598, 662, 664, 776, 778, 797, 939, 961, 968-70, 972, 996, 1011, 1028, 1098, 1237, 1293
Callimachus, 26, 628, 760-62, 813-14, 1068-71, 1080, 1082
Canatha, 266-67
canon, 58-60, 66-67, 82, 84, 160, 183-84, 187-94, 253, 341, 374, 415-16, 455-57, 461, 480, 542, 544-45, 547, 553, 607, 610, 657, 857, 860, 863, 1067, 1082, 1099-1100, 1292
Capernaum, 94-96, 127, 393-94, 396, 462, 472, 1145, 1147, 1151, 1153, 1236
Cappadocia, 131, 135, 279, 294, 488, 563, 796, 963-64, 998, 1162
captain of the temple, 1063
Carthage, 113, 191, 243, 330, 414, 425, 747, 918, 963, 965, 975, 977, 1010
Cassius Hemina, 501
catena, 195, 258, 782, 791, 828, 1207
Cave 7, Qumran, 196, 678
Cave of Treasures, 4
celibacy, 248, 263, 323, 345-46, 353, 626, 680-83, 691, 851, 1022
cella, 108, 817, 920, 923, 1186
Celts, 134-35, 389, 391, 963, 1093, 1163
census, 201-2, 216, 306, 359, 363, 536, 578, 585, 590, 596, 599, 622, 631, 662, 766, 973, 976, 980, 1126, 1162, 1164
centurions, 95, 301, 361, 386, 433, 458, 472, 879, 967, 993-95, 998, 1145, 1147, 1151
Ceres, 922
Cerinthus, 415
CETEDOC, 1286
Chaereas and Callirhoe, 382, 1008
cheirographon, 760
Cheltenham Canon, 190
chief priests, 561-62, 785, 826, 934, 945, 1027, 1049, 1063, 1087-88
children, 4, 6, 10-11, 43, 49, 54, 76, 85, 90, 120, 145, 154, 170, 195, 197-202, 215-16, 248, 255, 262, 271, 284, 289, 291, 293, 312, 322, 324, 330, 334, 338, 345, 351, 353-63, 366, 385, 393, 395, 400, 412-13, 416, 440, 457, 460, 470, 488-91, 506, 511, 514, 521, 554-56, 603, 621, 628-29, 634-35, 640, 653-54, 680-91, 693, 696-97, 707-8, 714, 722, 761, 772, 799, 815, 825, 838-39, 841, 846, 866, 869, 887, 900, 906, 936-37, 956, 971, 990-91, 994, 1001-3, 1021, 1025-26, 1046, 1074, 1083, 1090, 1114, 1120-21, 1123, 1125, 1128, 1131, 1141, 1166, 1168, 1184, 1190-91, 1196, 1204-5, 1208, 1252, 1261, 1264, 1276-79, 1296-97, 1302
chreia, 239, 243, 310, 741, 757, 761, 956
chronology, 98, 109, 119, 201-5, 207, 268-69, 341, 345-46, 474, 500, 534, 574, 581, 601, 618, 659, 715, 752, 887, 904, 1073, 1144, 1234, 1258
New Testament, 207
Pauline, 98, 206-7
chthonic spirits, 919-20
Cicero, 13-14, 16, 44, 120, 168, 198, 208-9, 215-16, 225, 241-43, 283, 285, 301, 310, 313, 325, 329, 333-34, 361, 363, 369, 380-81, 387, 411, 448, 500, 510, 522-24, 528, 535, 563, 592, 632, 634-35, 686-87, 722, 758-59, 761, 767-68, 773, 799, 828-29, 922, 928, 955, 959, 968, 973, 975, 985, 1014, 1066, 1073, 1079-84, 1126, 1131, 1140, 1284, 1287
Cilicia, 131, 133, 136, 205, 218, 563, 565, 664, 758, 760, 774, 819, 861, 963, 1013, 1092, 1247
circumcision, 135, 199, 225, 293, 377, 437, 468, 478-79, 549-50, 564, 583, 603, 619, 757, 770, 776-77, 797, 800, 802, 842, 844-45, 866, 879-80, 900, 949, 951, 1034, 1046, 1178, 1225, 1244, 1279, 1302
circuses, 111, 141, 209-11, 395
cisterns, 104-5, 107, 395, 505, 559,

743, 884, 886, 1045, 1113
cities, Greco-Roman, 212-14
citizenship, 215-18
city states, 86, 137, 157, 280, 423, 560, 598, 921, 924, 974, 1130, 1132, 1186-87
civic cults, 218-19, 299, 918, 1279
Claudius, edict of, 436, 540, 1010
Claudius, Tiberius, 13, 16, 25-26, 98, 132, 139, 142, 206-7, 215-16, 220-21, 229-30, 238-39, 284-85, 371, 425, 528, 534, 538, 540, 578-79, 641, 760, 761, 773, 959-61, 969-70, 973, 979-82, 985, 988, 993-94, 996-98, 1011, 1013-15, 1028, 1098, 1126, 1142-44, 1158, 1163, 1237, 1248
Cleanthes, 71, 231, 760-61, 814, 1140-41
1 Clement, 81, 83-84, 188, 191-93, 285, 853, 1015, 1141, 1256
2 Clement, 81, 84, 191, 853
Clementine Recognitions, 37
Cleodemus-Malchus, 581-82
client kingdoms, 979, 998
clients, 112, 157-58, 202, 272, 305-6, 381-82, 386, 389, 480, 581, 594, 632, 634, 766-71, 773, 872, 937, 938, 960, 963-64, 975, 979, 998, 1001, 1016, 1027, 1084, 1124, 1129, 1133-34, 1163, 1272
Codex Alexandrinus, 69, 470, 536, 671, 673, 676-77, 1104
Codex Bezae, 166, 671, 673, 676
Codex Claromontanus, 189
Codex Ephraemi, 676
Codex Sinaiticus, 82, 191, 470, 671, 673, 675, 678-79, 1096, 1103, 1211
Codex Vaticanus, 69, 241, 653, 671, 673, 676, 679, 1103-4, 1211
coinage, 93, 178, 220-23, 278, 440, 479, 985, 1112, 1115, 1236
coins, 95, 98, 101-2, 105, 107, 109, 132-33, 138, 178, 219-25, 229, 267, 318, 345, 381, 395-97, 433, 438, 441, 464, 468, 474, 480, 490, 567-68, 574, 587, 596, 618, 641, 759, 886-87, 939, 972, 981-82, 996, 1004, 1011, 1046, 1094, 1113, 1115, 1135, 1147, 1175, 1181, 1237, 1245
collegium, 137-38, 922, 1132
colonies, Roman, 32, 212-13, 230, 280, 283-84, 423-24, 475, 571, 574, 759, 787-88, 818, 832, 921, 961, 963, 966, 974, 994, 999, 1092, 1193
Colossae, 225-26, 320, 760
Commentary on Genesis (Qumran), 781
concubines, 11-12, 683, 688, 867, 1201, 1278
Consolations, 226-27
consuls, 98, 208, 370, 809, 819-20, 959-60, 966, 974, 976, 996-97, 1004-5, 1010, 1075, 1280
contubernium, 992
conversion, 1, 37-38, 138, 166, 205, 207, 291, 301, 323, 507, 511, 513, 548-50, 595, 625-26, 654, 685, 792, 818, 836-37, 840-46, 1006, 1014, 1099, 1131, 1189, 1227, 1253, 1279
Copper Scroll, 227, 256, 460
Coptic, 4, 39, 58, 67-68, 71-73, 77, 149, 415-17, 467, 475, 483, 535-36, 644, 666, 670-71, 677, 745-49, 1188, 1190
Corinth, 12, 15, 84, 98-100, 138-39, 146, 205-6, 211-12, 219, 227-31, 285, 301, 307-8, 319, 323, 387, 425-26, 444-45, 447, 528, 530, 534, 733, 756, 758-59, 761, 763, 771, 918, 926, 961-63, 985-86, 988-89, 991, 999, 1003-4, 1010, 1015-16, 1035, 1109-10, 1127-30, 1132, 1134, 1151, 1179-80, 1236, 1247, 1278
3 Corinthians, 67, 860
Corpus Hellenisticum Novi Testamenti, 1284, 1287
cosmology, 30, 38, 46, 49, 54-55, 58, 64, 120, 149-51, 317, 322, 333, 509, 655, 727, 731, 761, 791, 793, 806, 918, 1140, 1267, 1273, 1296
countryside, 134, 212, 218, 244, 268, 707, 811, 938, 944, 983
Court of Israel, 1046, 1174
Court of Priests, 1041, 1045-46, 1048, 1174
Court of the Gentiles, 1044, 1046, 1168, 1180
Court of Women, 396, 1045-46, 1174, 1180
courtrooms, 121, 956, 984, 987, 989
Crates, 239-41, 243-44, 358, 384, 1072-73, 1079
creed, 83, 232, 234-35, 700, 934, 1059
Cronos, 370, 815
crucifixion, 54-55, 57, 74, 77, 83-84, 113, 124, 183, 204, 235, 257, 274, 307, 335, 415, 440, 462, 492, 521, 536, 546, 561, 585, 591, 602, 609, 630, 704, 708, 803, 818, 851, 907-8, 982, 987-88, 1007, 1010, 1034, 1054, 1088-89, 1095, 1128-30, 1132, 1134, 1168, 1171, 1176-77, 1274
Cumanus, Ventidius, 238-39, 937, 980, 982
curse tablets, 666-68
curses, 1, 5, 13, 62, 76, 79, 115, 155-56, 260, 271, 349, 378, 413, 505, 565, 568, 593, 595, 639, 650, 666-69, 688, 776, 779, 781-82, 840, 907, 928-29, 951, 972, 1100-1101, 1120-21, 1123, 1146, 1200, 1206-7, 1254, 1280-81
Cynic epistles, 384
Cynics, 18, 142, 239-45, 280, 323-24, 355, 367, 383-84, 611, 681, 709, 762, 795, 1288
Cyprus, 33, 110, 115, 133, 138, 190, 205-6, 218, 279, 284-85, 414, 421-22, 424, 464, 470, 567, 580, 587, 795, 871, 963, 972, 997, 1047, 1068, 1092
Cyrenaica, 284-85, 292, 540, 567, 580, 587, 871, 964
Dagon, 107, 605
Damascus Document, 147, 152, 156, 164, 195, 246-47, 249-50, 253-54, 261-62, 265, 270, 345-46, 365, 379, 456, 495, 508, 600, 636-39, 682, 742, 779, 781, 833, 949, 1021, 1025, 1031, 1091, 1114, 1173, 1185, 1226, 1230, 1258, 1264
Daniel, additions to, 251, 1099-1100
Daphne, 8, 34, 36, 926
Daphnis and Chloe, 1008
Davidic monarchy, 49
Day of Atonement, 65, 92, 182, 257, 259, 292, 375, 648-49, 798, 825, 1036, 1042, 1051, 1169, 1181, 1199, 1281, 1290
Dead Sea Scrolls, 3, 43, 45, 57-58, 60, 64, 78, 79, 88-90, 96, 147-48, 153, 156, 160, 173, 180-81, 183, 195, 227, 246, 250, 252-53, 263, 265-66, 270, 272-73, 314-16, 332, 335-37, 343-44, 346-49, 380, 433, 437-39, 450-51, 453, 456-57, 459-60, 462-63, 484, 535, 554, 600, 603, 631, 639-40, 648-50, 697-99, 702-3, 705-7, 709, 711, 714, 719, 737-39, 745, 749-51, 753, 783, 797, 800, 803, 808, 822, 824, 831, 833, 848, 850-53, 870, 873-74, 883, 887-88, 892, 898, 900, 947-50, 952, 1024, 1026, 1036-37, 1053, 1058, 1090-92, 1134, 1137, 1139, 1161, 1173, 1180, 1185, 1195, 1200-1201, 1218, 1226, 1230-31, 1251, 1257, 1259, 1261-63, 1267-68, 1282, 1289, 1296, 1298-99
Decapolis, 107, 266-68, 274, 397, 433, 820, 1016
decurions, 214, 994, 1000-1001, 1003
deisidaimonia, 758-59, 761, 930
Demeter, 145, 225, 228, 422-23, 722, 815, 919-20, 922, 924-25, 929, 1280
Demetrius, 26, 99, 114-16, 119, 219, 221, 244, 257, 268-69, 278-80, 282, 325, 327-29, 392, 406, 440, 580-81, 592, 790, 820, 843, 872, 950, 955, 1027, 1068, 1073, 1100, 1187
demons, 48, 61, 63, 69-70, 80, 97, 153, 262, 267, 269-72, 323, 399, 416, 444, 492, 507, 669, 832, 930, 949, 981, 1223, 1229, 1239-40, 1296
Derbe, 33, 134, 205, 389-90
Descensus ad Inferos, 77
Deuteronomy Rabbah, 29, 890
devil, 42, 153, 669, 869, 941, 1290
Diadochi, 22, 278, 281, 319, 467, 570, 608, 618, 870
Dialogue of the Savior, 77, 184
Diana, 99, 132, 221, 922, 1132
Diatessaron, 75, 185, 672, 746, 1154-56
diatribe, 84, 241, 296-98, 322, 407, 516, 757, 760
Didache, 82, 85, 189-90, 193, 1022, 1124, 1297
dietary laws, 143, 564, 625-26, 665, 770, 801-2, 1243, 1279
Diodorus Siculus, 7-8, 10-15, 23, 278, 281, 302, 354, 356-57, 359, 362-63, 365, 381, 384, 441, 444, 475, 481, 501-4, 526-27, 570-71, 628, 681, 683, 686, 689, 787, 1062, 1077, 1208, 1220, 1284, 1287
Diogenes Laertius, 7, 9, 14-15, 115, 140, 168, 239-44, 297, 323, 325-26, 354-58, 363-65, 381-84, 405, 419, 465, 681, 683, 761-62, 1066, 1068, 1076, 1140-41, 1254, 1282, 1284, 1287
Diogenes of Sinope, 240, 243
Dion, 266-67, 271, 355, 923
Dionysius of Halicarnassus, 8, 330, 357, 362, 364, 381, 480, 501, 528, 634, 680, 683, 921, 1074, 1076-77, 1079, 1083
discipline, 93, 100, 110, 152, 198, 200, 211, 247, 311, 355, 358, 364, 401, 431, 500, 701, 794, 821, 851, 917, 993, 1074, 1113, 1119, 1121, 1188, 1210, 1273, 1298
dishonor, 199, 355, 518-19, 768-70, 829-30, 880, 1120, 1124-25, 1178
divination, 261, 533, 920-22, 926-28, 1120, 1234-35
divine man, 403, 656, 740-42
divorce, 6-7, 9, 21, 122, 249, 264, 353-54, 400, 446, 489, 491, 544, 632, 682, 684-85, 764, 867, 969, 1034, 1096, 1120, 1277-78
domestic architecture, 104-5, 108
domestic life, 1121
Domitian, 81, 112, 158, 210, 221, 288, 319, 321-22, 448, 596-98, 772, 778, 809, 970-71, 973, 977, 996, 998, 1011, 1084, 1142
Doq, 107, 126
Dora, 102, 397, 820
Dositheans, 1059, 1061
dowry, 80, 359, 684-85, 764-65
Dream of Scipio, 44
dreams, 44, 46, 48, 251, 259, 262, 330, 354, 399-401, 404, 447, 449-50, 489, 511-12, 582, 592-93, 628, 668, 728, 740, 778-80, 846, 866, 872, 899, 920, 926-27, 929, 941, 1039, 1081, 1118, 1120, 1135-36
dualism, 47-49, 54-55, 155-56, 290, 347, 414, 416, 694, 750, 941, 1015, 1019, 1022, 1223, 1225-26, 1229, 1253-55, 1262, 1266-67, 1297
Dura Europos, 282, 286, 371, 480, 994, 1148-49
Dyrrachium, 99
economics, 308-13
education, 308-13
Egnatian Way, 99, 963, 1232
Egypt, Roman, 25, 202, 208, 361, 473-74, 476-77, 689, 692, 1153, 1288
Egyptian religion, 290, 359, 371, 528-29, 654, 721, 919, 1224
Eleazar the Exorcist, 505, 507
Elephantine, 18, 180, 283, 475, 570, 574
Eleusinian mysteries, 334, 721-22, 724, 918, 924-25
emperor, Roman, 23, 25, 99-100, 112, 122, 132, 134-35, 139, 141, 144, 158, 166, 168, 177, 203, 206, 210, 220-21, 223, 228-30, 236,

239, 244, 267, 274-75, 280, 321, 371, 393, 396-97, 425, 447-48, 466-77, 480, 488-92, 520, 528, 533-34, 539, 563, 567, 578, 581, 586, 621, 623-24, 633, 642, 688, 699, 740, 761, 772-77, 796-97, 799, 807, 809-811, 817-18, 827, 921-23, 945, 959-61, 964, 967-73, 976-78, 980-82, 985, 987, 989, 992-93, 995-98, 1000-1004, 1007, 1011-13, 1026-30, 1047, 1074, 1098, 1108, 1111, 1113, 1126, 1133, 1137, 1142-44, 1163, 1187, 1220-22, 1236-37, 1270, 1280
emperors, 51, 56, 100, 131, 135, 178, 220, 447, 490, 534, 623, 901, 918, 922, 945, 1026, 1111, 1142-43, 1236, 1251
1 Enoch, 3, 10, 30-31, 42-44, 46, 49-51, 55-56, 58-60, 62, 69-71, 154-55, 165, 170-71, 181, 196, 258, 262, 314-18, 332, 335, 346, 349, 357, 398-400, 413, 439, 444, 448-49, 456, 496, 511, 514, 526, 556, 600, 682, 700-702, 707, 729-32, 734-35, 798, 824, 842, 860, 907, 933, 938, 949-50, 1022, 1087, 1091, 1139, 1171-72, 1184, 1197-99, 1226, 1240, 1273, 1290, 1295
  Animal Apocalypse, 46, 154, 315, 318, 600
  Apocalypse of Weeks, 50, 154, 314-15, 824, 1172
  Astronomical Book, 314-15
  Book of Watchers, 46, 50, 154-55, 258, 449
  Epistle of Enoch, 46, 50, 258, 314-15
  Similitudes, 30, 44, 46, 314, 316, 449, 514, 704, 1295
2 Enoch, 3, 7, 15, 17, 31, 41, 44, 46, 50-51, 56, 62, 314, 316-17, 335, 400, 448, 650, 693, 695, 730, 860, 1188, 1240, 1296
3 Enoch, 41, 44, 51, 314, 317, 385, 728-30, 734, 736-37, 820, 860
Ephesian Tale, 131, 1008-10
Ephesus, 80, 83, 99, 111, 114, 122, 131-32, 139, 205, 218-21, 225, 229, 281, 318-21, 359, 407, 409, 466, 470, 481, 530, 563, 567, 675, 756, 759, 788, 794, 963, 985, 997-98, 1009, 1029-30, 1066, 1068-69, 1074, 1078, 1132, 1151, 1162-63, 1187, 1220, 1233, 1279
Ephorus, 502, 1082
Epictetus, 7, 13, 16-17, 135, 142, 240, 297, 321-24, 355, 357-58, 360, 363-64, 366, 380-81, 384-85, 427, 444, 520, 523, 629, 681, 707-8, 720, 761, 773, 790, 1141, 1208-9, 1284, 1287
Epicureanism, 280, 324-27, 382, 471, 762, 790, 1081, 1118, 1271, 1282
Epistle of Aristeas, 114, 116, 282, 291, 382, 526, 753, 839, 844, 1291, 1294
Epistle of Barnabas, 81-82, 188-89, 191, 317, 1022, 1182, 1297
Epistle of Peter to Philip, 67
Epistle of the Apostles, 67, 77
Epistle of Titus, 67
Epistle to Diognetus, 81-82, 85
Epistle to the Laodiceans, 67, 860
Epistles of Anacharsis, 239-40
Epistles of Crates, 239-40, 244
Epistles of Diogenes, 239-40
Epistles of Heraclitus, 239, 241
Epistles of Paul and Seneca, 67
Epistles of Socrates, 240-41
epistolary theory and practice, 327-29, 642-44, 1009, 1285
equestrian order, 976, 996, 1001-3
eroticism, 328, 629, 851, 1082, 1264
eschatological antagonist, 51, 56
eschatology, 1, 3, 30, 37, 41-42, 44, 46-56, 63-65, 79, 144, 149, 155, 158, 171-72, 195, 226, 251, 255, 257-58, 307, 314, 330-35, 338-39, 349-51, 375, 378-79, 408, 483, 507-8, 514, 607, 609, 614, 654, 696-99, 761, 779, 791-92, 798, 821, 823-24, 833, 844, 851, 856, 861-62, 864, 867, 869, 879, 890, 908, 930, 932-35, 938-42, 1021-22, 1035, 1059-60, 1090, 1107, 1109-11, 1115, 1128, 1130, 1136, 1170, 1172, 1178, 1180-81, 1185, 1188, 1192-95, 1197-99, 1202, 1204-6, 1216, 1231, 1240, 1251, 1262, 1264-65, 1267, 1295-97
  cosmic, 330, 332
  personal, 330
  political, 330, 332
  realized, 52, 330, 336, 935
Esdras, books of, 41, 58, 61-62, 69, 149, 332, 337, 340-42, 399, 456, 512, 948, 1099-1100, 1102, 1104, 1110, 1226, 1238, 1291, 1295
2 Esdras, 41, 58, 62, 337-39, 341, 1100, 1102, 1295
Essene community, 1018
Essene Gate, 96, 100
Essenes, 61, 78, 96, 137, 246-48, 250, 263, 289, 342-48, 365, 524, 579, 585, 590, 608-9, 611, 619, 636, 682-83, 690-91, 710-11, 784, 787, 802, 807-8, 833-34, 855, 864, 876, 883, 887, 915, 941, 949, 1017-18, 1023, 1037, 1048, 1052, 1166, 1170-71, 1180, 1182, 1195, 1198, 1214, 1218, 1222, 1224-25, 1227, 1230-31, 1262
estates, 33, 104, 108, 135, 213, 303-5, 311, 325, 362-63, 394-95, 470, 476, 537, 571, 622, 688, 975, 999-1000, 1002, 1130, 1162, 1300-1301
Ethiopian Story, 1008
ethnography, 390, 500-501, 1157
Eupolemus, 269, 484, 529, 581, 592, 843
execution, 63, 111, 113-14, 122, 210, 257, 355, 444, 486, 489, 492, 548, 562, 612, 661-62, 785, 787, 805, 827-29, 907, 971, 981-82, 1051, 1171
exegesis, charismatic, 833
exile, 42, 62, 78, 122, 137, 149, 160, 180, 208, 215, 226, 241, 249, 254, 282, 293-94, 305, 313, 315, 324, 348-51, 433, 493, 524, 556-58, 560, 603, 606-7, 649, 662, 742, 798, 823, 828, 869-70, 894, 932, 950, 987, 1022, 1037, 1063, 1155, 1167, 1172, 1185, 1193, 1200, 1216, 1239, 1241-42, 1258
Ezekiel the Tragedian, 290, 449, 468, 582, 731, 790, 950
4 Ezra, 3, 41, 44, 46, 48-51, 55, 58, 62, 149, 277, 332, 337-40, 399, 448, 456, 512-13, 556, 700-702, 706-7, 842, 860, 865, 1110, 1196, 1226, 1290, 1295
fables, 310, 761, 900, 910, 956
false prophets, prophecy, 51, 56, 63, 511, 599, 629, 833-35, 862
family, 9, 14, 33, 36, 61, 76, 95, 97, 108-10, 112, 122, 126-28, 133, 143-44, 157-58, 168-69, 173-75, 179, 197, 199, 202, 212, 215, 279, 283, 299, 303-4, 306, 354-57, 359, 361-62, 382, 395, 397, 400, 403-4, 406, 423, 432-33, 438-41, 459, 471, 476, 479, 485-86, 490-91, 518, 523, 530, 539-40, 563, 571, 573, 575, 577, 579, 581, 586, 590, 597-98, 601-5, 608-11, 618-20, 628-29, 636-37, 640, 644-45, 658, 673, 677, 684-85, 687, 716, 736, 760, 765-67, 769, 776, 785, 788-89, 802, 809-10, 812, 815-16, 825-26, 839-41, 870, 893-94, 921, 960-61, 963, 968-70, 979, 990, 1000, 1002, 1011-12, 1014, 1026, 1028, 1036-39, 1045, 1047-49, 1053, 1088, 1092, 1098-99, 1142-43, 1149, 1157, 1170, 1200, 1206, 1211, 1238, 1246, 1276-81, 1283, 1285, 1293, 1296
fate, 67, 150, 188, 192, 277, 281, 331, 339, 344, 346, 354, 365, 437, 486, 561, 654, 709, 711, 759, 784, 788, 812, 875, 906, 919, 930, 969, 1017, 1050, 1088, 1140-41, 1223-24, 1229, 1234, 1251, 1269-70, 1278, 1296
Fayyum Fragment, 72, 537
Feast of Weeks, 182, 1281
Felix, 97-98, 177, 205, 207, 221, 238-39, 628, 834, 940, 944, 961, 979-85, 987-88, 997, 1003, 1126
female, 1, 8, 11-12, 67, 122, 179, 198, 221, 244, 271, 318, 359, 362-63, 440, 444, 519, 540, 589, 612, 683-84, 687, 719, 722-23, 923, 1038-39, 1067, 1130, 1152, 1161, 1189, 1191, 1219, 1263, 1277, 1279
festival calendars, 638
Festival Prayers (Qumran), 731, 1139
festivals and holy days, 111, 140-41, 143-45, 157-58, 180-82, 199, 209-10, 212, 219, 239, 256, 262, 292, 312, 324, 368-76, 470, 541, 562, 565, 592, 601-2, 638, 648-49, 651, 656, 660, 662-64, 722, 742, 798-99, 802, 892-94, 920, 944, 962, 966, 994, 996, 1004, 1009, 1019, 1035, 1042-45, 1047-48, 1059, 1065, 1107, 1147, 1173, 1183, 1186-87, 1219-20, 1242, 1250, 1281
figurines, 104, 110, 122-23, 759
First Punic War, 918
firstfruits, 43, 182, 261, 555, 638, 648, 799, 825, 931, 1036, 1039-40, 1290
flamen, 922
Florilegium, 257, 378, 456, 779
food, 143-45, 248, 288, 299, 344, 400, 469, 506, 522, 528, 565, 625-26, 636, 639, 686, 722, 794, 801, 811, 825, 828, 878, 880, 924, 945, 974, 993, 997, 1000-1003, 1020, 1035, 1037, 1040, 1132, 1134, 1169, 1201, 1230, 1244-46, 1265, 1272, 1300-1301
forensic rhetoric, 989
fortress, 104-7, 117, 124-26, 128, 252, 274-76, 323, 487, 560, 584, 587, 624, 788, 808, 970-71, 993, 1086, 1147, 1168
fortuna, 130, 930
forum, 99, 102, 111, 139-40, 213-14, 228-30, 310, 633, 788, 971, 988, 1233
Fourth Philosophy, 579, 706, 936, 941-42, 944, 946
Fragmentary Targum, 694, 904, 1096
freedmen, 136, 158, 307, 309, 598-99, 820, 959-61, 976-77, 980, 990, 997-1003, 1015, 1125-26, 1131
frescoes, 123, 282, 286, 714, 722
friendship, 33, 98, 157-58, 175, 198, 240, 244, 251, 280-81, 283, 324-26, 329, 339-40, 354, 363, 380-87, 406, 468, 471, 486, 488, 491-92, 496, 506, 510-12, 522-24, 560, 568, 578, 581, 590, 592, 595, 597, 599, 628-29, 641, 645-46, 663, 686, 761, 767-68, 770, 772, 802, 812, 816, 828-29, 861, 910, 942, 960, 964-65, 979, 986, 992, 998, 1011, 1032, 1038, 1043, 1073, 1074, 1076, 1081, 1118, 1121-22, 1129, 1190, 1208-9, 1235, 1246, 1253, 1271, 1275, 1278, 1283, 1301
Gadara, 97, 107, 244, 266-68, 275, 393, 397, 471, 479, 487, 820, 1063
Gaia, 815
Galasa, 266
Galatia, Galatians, 32-35, 52-55, 131-32, 134-36, 164, 185-87, 205, 230, 294-95, 320, 377, 389-91, 407, 410, 413, 417, 429, 469, 561, 563, 613-14, 665, 675, 710, 778, 866, 879-81, 907-8, 963-64, 966-67, 985, 989, 991, 997, 1092, 1198, 1207, 1210, 1244, 1255-56, 1258, 1289
Galilee, 15, 87, 89-91, 93, 97, 103, 107, 176, 178, 204, 268, 271, 274-75, 308, 367, 391-98, 431, 433, 440, 447, 462, 468, 470, 472, 480, 485-87, 489-93, 580, 586, 590, 595-96, 600, 617, 619, 624, 691, 749, 785, 876, 878, 903, 915-16, 934, 936-37, 939, 944-45, 964, 979, 982, 988, 1016-17, 1044, 1047, 1055-56, 1059-60, 1063-64, 1145, 1147, 1153, 1164, 1166, 1235-37, 1247-48, 1250, 1301-2
Gallio, 98, 206, 228, 230, 532-34, 960, 985-86, 988, 997, 1099

Gamala, 104, 108, 275, 396, 945
games, 111-12, 141, 198, 209-11, 214, 228, 230, 280, 324, 369-70, 391, 423, 487, 599, 668, 757, 759, 829, 918, 923, 959, 968, 970-71, 1000, 1278-79
Gaul, 135, 185, 188, 296, 490, 654, 772, 807, 810, 965, 968, 975, 995, 998, 1014, 1028, 1125, 1157, 1162
Gaza, 20, 102, 104, 109, 304, 440, 470, 487, 570, 661, 820, 1245
Gehenna, 48, 95, 314, 907, 933-34, 1060
gemara, 507, 897-98
gender roles, 680, 688-89
Genesis Apocryphon, 79, 252, 258-59, 265, 269, 273, 398-401, 495, 592, 865, 947, 949, 1098, 1290
Genesis Rabbah, 890, 892
genizah, 87, 246-47, 254, 637-38, 1147
geodesy, 1065, 1071
geographers, 131, 266
geographical perspectives, 411
geography, 27, 88, 93, 131, 133, 390, 411, 500-501, 653, 1065, 1071, 1078, 1158
Gerasa, 97, 107, 266-68, 276, 470
Gergesa, 97, 268, 393
gerousia, 287, 1061-63
Gezer, 101-2, 105, 109, 440
glass, glassware, 23, 110, 214, 304, 395, 680
Gnosticism, 5, 29, 31, 66, 68-69, 187, 191, 226, 235, 336, 414-18, 482, 484, 667, 725, 729-30, 735-37, 751, 1055-56, 1129, 1229, 1263
Golan, 102-3, 220, 1147
Gorgias, 334, 499, 953-54, 1067
Gospel of Mary, 77, 415
Gospel of Nicodemus, 71, 77
Gospel of Peter, 71, 74-75, 78, 184-85, 189, 194, 492, 672, 860
Gospel of the Ebionites, 75, 77
Gospel of the Egyptians, 71-72, 75-76, 185
Gospel of the Hebrews, 75, 184
Gospel of the Nazarenes, 75, 463
Gospels, apocryphal, 66, 72, 499, 672
governors, Roman, 176, 225, 283, 393, 534, 540, 562, 578, 585-86, 616, 633, 766, 773, 777, 798, 809, 941, 960, 978-81, 999, 1016-17, 1063, 1178
graffiti, 124
grain, 158, 182, 276, 304, 340, 372-73, 401, 476, 528, 594, 638-39, 721-22, 767, 924-25, 960, 970, 976, 997, 1001, 1025-26, 1036-42, 1044, 1046, 1049, 1164, 1172, 1202, 1247-48, 1250, 1301-2
grain offerings, 1036, 1039, 1041-42, 1046, 1049, 1172
grammar, grammarians, 32, 167, 308-9, 311-12, 329, 418-21, 431-32, 459-61, 465, 736, 739, 955, 1009, 1065, 1067, 1070-73, 1076, 1079-81, 1083-84, 1094, 1142, 1213, 1262
Great Paris Magical Papyrus, 667
Greece, 421-26
Greek Apocalypse of Ezra, 339
Greek history, 466-67
Greek language, 22, 117, 309, 311, 418, 422, 427-29, 433, 466, 469-71, 476, 478, 747, 907, 1071, 1075-76, 1290
Greek Old Testament/Septuagint, 27, 678, 1099
Greek pantheon, 280, 1140
Greek papyri, 271, 475, 1103, 1105
Greek verbal structure, 432
guilt/reparation offerings, 1036, 1039
gymnasiarch, 435
gymnasium, 2, 137, 141-42, 158, 198, 213, 243, 284, 286, 309-10, 312, 423, 435-36, 464, 468, 470, 560, 567, 573, 659-60, 789, 838, 929, 956, 1064, 1093
Habakkuk Commentary, 170, 257, 346, 349, 437, 439, 779, 1216
Hades, 39-40, 44, 77, 332, 540, 722, 815, 919, 924-25, 930, 935
Hadrian, 16, 25, 106, 136, 139, 177, 220, 230, 296, 318-19, 368-87, 397, 412, 442, 477, 482, 561, 576, 580, 587-88, 624, 661, 692, 786-88, 917, 972-73, 985, 999, 1017-18, 1085-86, 1109, 1112-15, 1142, 1144-45, 1166, 1229, 1237
haggadah, 543, 582, 589
Halakha A, 254, 638
hallel, 851
Harklean Version, 1155
haruspices, 922, 1012
harvest, harvesting, 304, 340, 368, 372-75, 377, 637, 639, 691, 872, 894, 911, 966-67, 1009, 1039-40, 1164, 1303
Hasmoneans, 61-63, 79, 102-3, 105-9, 111, 125-26, 129, 179, 222-24, 263, 267, 284-85, 305, 392, 436, 438-42, 468, 471, 479, 485-86, 493, 560, 570, 572-74, 576-77, 584-85, 588, 590, 597, 608-11, 616-17, 619-21, 625, 637, 657-58, 661, 693, 695, 699, 783-84, 800, 803, 818, 820, 826, 855, 886, 914, 938, 964, 1048-49, 1058, 1064, 1093, 1164, 1171, 1193, 1195, 1200-1201, 1220, 1224, 1227, 1258, 1293, 1296-97
head coverings, 442-46
head taxes, 962, 1164-65
healers, healing, 4, 71, 89, 131, 241, 262, 272, 343, 395, 399, 458, 462, 492, 498-99, 506-7, 589, 656, 668, 697, 703, 721, 740-41, 900, 918, 920, 927, 929, 952, 1032-34, 1078, 1150, 1230-31
hearth, 213, 299, 423, 921, 1280
heavenly ascent, 447-49
Hebraisms, 465, 1095
Hebrew
 biblical, 459, 463
 classical biblical, 459
 late biblical, 256
 Mishnaic, 87, 89, 227, 459-61, 463, 1105
Hebrew Bible, 43, 78, 92-93, 101, 120, 148, 151, 170, 180-82, 231-32, 250, 253, 256, 258, 260, 262, 338, 378, 401, 413, 452, 455, 457, 459-60, 462, 471, 480, 526, 546, 551, 554-55, 557, 604, 610, 648, 707, 730, 752-53, 756, 782, 821, 824, 838, 865, 874, 876-77, 889-91, 893, 900, 903, 905, 909, 952, 1094, 1099-1101, 1155, 1159, 1170, 1218, 1239, 1242, 1266, 1291-92
Hebrew Matthew, 463-64
Hecataeus of Miletus, 500, 1078
hekhalot, 44, 450, 732
Hellenism, 22, 61, 86, 101, 117-19, 135-36, 138, 141-43, 145, 162, 220, 238, 288, 290, 309, 313, 337, 425-26, 436, 464-67, 471-74, 477-79, 481-82, 484, 487, 502, 574, 582-83, 624, 663, 718, 838-39, 847, 902, 926, 936, 968, 1016-17, 1085-86, 1116-18, 1124, 1269, 1271
Hellenistic Egypt, 23, 145, 331, 428, 435, 443, 467, 473-77, 483-84, 685, 752, 870, 917, 1234
Hellenists, 35, 52, 236, 464-65, 468-70, 472-73, 560, 1244
Hephaestus, 139, 815, 919, 922
Hera, 8-9, 422, 815-17, 919, 922, 1208
Heraclitus, 42, 241-42, 319, 418, 681, 794, 832, 1066, 1081
Hermes, 34, 138, 220, 281, 416, 422, 482-85, 581, 722, 761, 815, 864, 919, 924, 928
Hermetic literature, 416, 482-85
Hermeticism, 416, 482-85
Herod Agrippa I, 177-78, 206-7, 221, 490, 789, 979-81, 983, 988, 1017, 1236-37
Herod Agrippa II, 178, 207, 221, 980-81, 983, 988, 1236-37
Herod Antipas, 204, 376, 393, 396-97, 468, 470, 480, 485, 488-94, 577-78, 591, 599, 621, 690, 964, 979, 982, 988, 998, 1164, 1235-37
Herod the Great, 32, 34, 94, 96, 158, 176, 178, 201, 213, 223, 305, 392, 394, 438-39, 441, 468, 480, 485, 488-91, 493-94, 496, 560, 572, 576-78, 596, 598, 620, 622, 784, 855, 973, 979, 994, 998, 1014, 1016, 1048-49, 1064, 1188, 1193-94, 1220, 1236
Herodian architecture, 126
Herodian dynasty, 493
Herodians, 223, 346, 433-34, 485, 493-94, 524, 610, 622, 1033
Herodotus, 14, 132, 225, 242, 330, 390, 392, 405, 411, 427, 500, 502-3, 523, 832, 859, 918-19, 1066, 1072, 1077, 1208, 1211
heros, 8, 21, 42, 61, 63, 122, 140, 168, 170, 213, 218, 251, 313, 363, 422, 439, 447, 494-96, 500, 522, 593-94, 602, 629, 654, 660-62, 741, 812, 831, 844, 859, 866-67, 919, 929-30, 1054, 1122, 1160, 1194-95, 1209, 1221, 1293
Hesiod, 10, 333, 354-56, 360, 423, 494, 583, 634, 655, 681, 684, 687-88, 758, 761-62, 815-16, 919, 921, 924, 930, 1066, 1068-69, 1081-82, 1252, 1294
Hestia, 423, 815, 919, 922
Hexapla, 679, 1069, 1102, 1154
Hillel, House of Hillel, 39, 496-98, 508-9, 515, 543, 611-13, 683, 700, 785, 797, 801, 841, 843, 876, 896, 898, 902, 905, 909, 912-15, 1086, 1106-7, 1175-76, 1243, 1277, 1298
Hinnom Valley, 95
Hippocrates, 239, 244, 498-99, 858, 1078
Hippocratic Letters, 498-99, 1078
historians, historiography, 7-9, 16, 25, 28, 36, 80, 84, 101, 116, 123, 201-2, 206, 284, 303, 305, 322, 330, 343, 362, 381, 383, 392-93, 397, 404-5, 414, 427, 429, 441, 454, 461, 467, 480, 494-95, 498-504, 530, 570, 574, 578, 580-81, 590-92, 663, 669, 694, 711, 713, 719, 739, 757-58, 772-73, 804, 832, 835, 837, 858-59, 967, 974-75, 1004, 1053, 1065-66, 1077, 1079-80, 1082-84, 1094, 1125-26, 1142-43, 1157-58, 1210, 1250, 1289, 1293
History of Joseph (Coptic), 77
Hodayot, 147, 336, 346, 450-51, 750, 850, 1214-15, 1217-18, 1298
holy men, 448, 471, 505-6
holy of holies, 2, 485, 732, 735, 743, 819-20, 1042-43, 1167, 1169, 1179, 1181
Holy Spirit, 129, 232, 377, 400, 464, 507-9, 513-15, 542, 561, 833, 835, 862, 867, 876, 881, 935, 957, 1061, 1179, 1273, 1275
Homer, 9-10, 12-14, 17, 21, 27, 44, 132, 143, 166, 231, 309, 312, 334, 356-57, 360, 363, 381-82, 411, 418, 420-23, 427, 435, 443-46, 466, 479, 495-96, 498, 522, 524, 535, 581, 583, 590, 593, 628, 655, 687-88, 707-8, 718, 814-16, 831, 859, 890, 919, 929-30, 953, 1066, 1069, 1071-72, 1076, 1081-82, 1085, 1207-10, 1285, 1294
Homeric religion, 816
Homeromanteion, 166
homes, private, 105, 108, 123, 128, 229, 285-86, 291, 596, 920, 1028, 1131, 1149
homily, homilies, 4, 84-85, 400, 408, 515-17, 792, 892
homoeroticism, 687
homosexuality, 14-15, 680, 1109
honestiores, 827, 1000
honor, 10-11, 32, 61, 111-12, 115, 131, 141, 157, 178, 199, 210-11, 213-14, 219, 236, 241, 280, 319, 354-55, 360-61, 364, 381-82, 386, 396-97, 423, 436, 444, 485, 487, 490, 492, 502, 518-21, 527-28, 539, 552, 556, 560, 566-67, 630, 632, 642, 653, 665, 686, 721, 744, 760, 766-71, 805, 825-27, 829, 846, 861, 876, 880, 920, 923, 925, 942, 992-94, 999-1000, 1004-5, 1027, 1029-30, 1038, 1047, 1053, 1073, 1075, 1080, 1082, 1088, 1113, 1116, 1118-23, 1129-30, 1146, 1148, 1160, 1179, 1190, 1196-97, 1202, 1219, 1237, 1252,

1265, 1268, 1271-72, 1279, 1294
horography, 500-501
horoscopes, 262
hospitality, 144, 157-58, 241, 312, 354, 471, 522-25, 571, 686, 707, 770, 788, 876, 1055, 1087, 1149, 1246
household codes, 200, 353, 361, 687, 742, 757-58, 762
households, 353-66
Huleh Valley, 103, 391
humiliores, 827, 977, 987, 1001
husbands, 2, 6-9, 13, 57, 80, 120, 229, 248, 299, 354, 360, 440, 443, 445, 487, 489-91, 493, 541, 566, 638, 682, 685, 687-90, 742, 765-66, 910, 1082, 1096, 1122, 1128, 1131, 1277-78, 1288
Hymn to Demeter, 722, 924-25
Hymn to the Creator, 848-49, 851, 1264
Hymn to Zeus, 71, 231, 759-61, 928, 1140
hymns, 68, 70, 146, 225, 231-36, 251, 255-56, 260, 264, 417, 456, 495, 508, 513, 666, 712-15, 717, 728, 749, 757, 781, 802, 811, 813-14, 818, 847, 851, 854, 858, 919, 942, 1009-10, 1020, 1111, 1117, 1122, 1190-91, 1217, 1230, 1239, 1264, 1297-98
Hyrcanus II, 223, 439-42, 485-86, 488, 573, 576-77, 620, 1063
Iconium, 33, 134, 190, 205, 230, 389-90, 471, 563, 1151
idolatry, 526, 1191
idols, idolatry, 30, 38, 61-63, 69, 99, 115, 128, 138, 228, 251, 264, 437, 446, 481, 526-29, 556, 557, 592, 606, 608, 637, 653, 777, 797, 801, 818, 840, 865, 875-76, 880-81, 910, 941, 948-49, 952, 1108-9, 1129, 1134, 1178, 1189-90, 1197, 1220, 1255, 1268, 1270-72, 1274, 1281, 1291, 1294, 1296
Ignatius, 35, 66, 76, 81-83, 85, 185-86, 283, 321, 563, 568, 777, 788, 1247, 1275
Iliad, 21, 27, 124, 140, 309, 421-22, 427, 466, 479, 498, 815, 859, 919, 928, 953, 1066, 1069, 1118, 1282
imperial eschatology, 331
imperial provinces, 425, 490, 997-98, 1016
incense, 2, 626, 777, 798, 810, 826, 875, 920, 923, 1006, 1030, 1039-45, 1051, 1132, 1149, 1167, 1169
incest, 12-14, 628, 949
India, 21-22, 68, 425, 689, 918, 1078, 1231, 1252
Indus River, 21
Infancy Gospel of Thomas, 76-77
infanticide, 198-200, 359
inheritance, 29-30, 257, 293, 351, 359, 361, 556, 604, 716, 766, 850, 875, 932, 935, 994, 1001-2, 1040, 1047, 1051, 1096, 1163, 1190-91, 1193, 1264
inspired exegesis, 43, 248
intermarriage, 476, 555, 557, 592, 638, 684, 840, 844
interpretatio graeca, 219, 299, 301, 816-17
intertextuality, 380, 541-42, 545-46, 548, 1239
Isaac, binding of, 950
Isaiah scrolls, 23, 92, 454, 551-52, 554
Isocrates, 9, 167, 354-55, 357, 382-84, 471, 502, 688, 859, 953-54, 1066-67, 1074, 1081, 1143
Isthmian Games, 141, 759, 761
Iturea, 178, 490, 619, 964, 1016
Jaffa, 104, 109, 560
Jannes and Jambres, 164, 950
Jericho, 79, 94-95, 106-8, 125-27, 129, 178, 274-75, 345, 396, 486-87, 489-90, 508, 605, 1063, 1206, 1301
Jerusalem, 559-61
Jerusalem hypothesis (DSS), 263
Jerusalem, destruction of, 37, 62, 125, 148, 150, 260, 268, 273, 275-78, 397, 497, 561, 574, 621, 653, 869, 937, 939, 1017, 1037, 1044, 1049, 1063, 1086, 1110, 1241, 1244, 1295, 1298
Jesus ben Ananias, 562, 941
jewelry, 124, 173-74, 422
Jewish communities in Asia Minor, 565-68
Jewish history, 259, 479, 490, 524, 539, 570, 573, 576, 579, 584, 657, 659, 836, 1201, 1224
Jewish sects, 96, 171, 246, 263, 326, 342-43, 346-47, 856, 1190
Jewish state, 47, 128, 570, 584, 658, 1062, 1112
Jewish wars, 95, 178, 221, 224, 267, 362, 429, 455, 539, 553, 590, 765, 773, 776, 789, 886, 937, 949, 964, 967, 970, 1011, 1017, 1112, 1115, 1158, 1236, 1293
    first revolt, 262, 264, 584-86, 623, 941, 1168, 1177, 1236
Job targumim, 258
John Hyrcanus, 79, 106, 223, 263, 438-40, 442, 468, 573, 625, 657-58, 660, 784, 1058, 1093, 1206, 1293
John of Gischala, 275-76, 586, 594, 599, 915, 946
Jonathan the Refugee, 940
Joppa, 96, 104, 275, 487, 820, 879, 1177, 1245
Jordan River, 79, 94, 97, 103, 107, 178, 252, 266, 271-73, 392, 397, 454, 490, 561, 807, 823, 834, 939-40, 1059, 1110-11, 1247, 1268
Jordan Valley, 107, 1110
Joseph and Aseneth, 291, 513, 588-89, 822, 844-45, 1008, 1189
Josephus, 590-600
    Against Apion, 583, 590, 599, 1100, 1223, 1294
    Antiquities of the Jews, 160, 597, 784
    Jewish War, 125, 128, 177-78, 221, 224, 227, 264, 267, 273-76, 278, 282, 284, 343, 393, 455, 462, 480, 504, 553, 567, 579-80, 584, 590, 596, 631, 679, 699, 764, 776, 784, 789, 799, 840, 886, 915, 949, 964, 970, 977, 992, 1011, 1053, 1057, 1064, 1112, 1116, 1168, 1222, 1236, 1278, 1293
Jubilees, 2, 30, 49-50, 58, 60, 63-64, 79, 141, 154-55, 160-61, 163-64, 181-82, 226-27, 258-59, 269, 315, 335, 391, 398, 401, 412-13, 456, 495, 511, 514, 556, 592, 600-603, 615, 638, 702, 707, 743, 820, 849, 870, 890, 947-52, 1022, 1025, 1036, 1045, 1049, 1091, 1184, 1197, 1199, 1206, 1226, 1258, 1281, 1290
Judaism and the New Testament, 603-16
Judas Aristobulus I, 440
Judas Maccabeus, 106, 438-39, 442, 468, 576, 657, 659-61, 1150
Judas the Galilean, 941, 1224
Judea, 616-24
Judith, 58, 61, 69, 445, 513, 589, 624-27, 714, 844, 854, 948, 1100, 1102, 1104, 1238, 1241, 1296
Julius Caesar, 26, 34, 140, 202, 209, 221, 223, 288, 369, 371, 441, 475, 577, 620, 787, 872, 963, 968-69, 975, 1010, 1014, 1016, 1125, 1142, 1163, 1165, 1187, 1221
Juno, 561, 817, 921-22, 994, 1011-12
Jupiter, 124, 202, 214, 221, 288, 331, 370, 524, 561, 596, 761, 799, 816-17, 919, 921-23, 925, 970, 972, 994, 1004-5, 1011, 1053, 1108, 1113, 1166
Justinian
    Code, 121, 250, 256, 366, 691, 897, 985-86, 992, 1023, 1065
    Digest, 215, 634, 826, 985-86, 991, 998, 1162
Kaddish, 651
Khirbet Qumran, 100, 250, 438, 883, 1020, 1091, 1226
Kidron, Brook, 1045
kinship, 13, 61, 133, 291, 306-7, 354, 356, 582, 603-4, 760, 794, 1190, 1201, 1296
kissing, 589, 628-29, 1277
kokhim, 126
Kypros, 107, 411-12
Lachish, 104-5, 108
Ladder of Jacob, 451, 950
lambs, 57, 144, 315, 330, 372-73, 376-77, 497, 613, 798, 877, 914, 923, 1039-43, 1047, 1109, 1172
land of Israel, 61, 86-87, 101, 294, 554-58, 742, 821, 846, 898, 1037, 1045, 1047, 1181, 1202, 1204, 1242
land tax, 1164-65
languages of Jesus, 906
laographia, 284, 662
Late Empire, 974, 977
Late Roman Republic, 974-75, 1085
Latin Infancy Gospel of Matthew, 77
Latin language, 630
Latin literature, 1079, 1081, 1083, 1285-86
Latin scholarship, 1079, 1084
laver, bronze, 1045
law courts, 310, 363, 384, 688, 800, 1062
law, legal system, Roman, 6, 9-10, 12, 198, 217, 230, 309, 356-57, 359, 361, 363, 366, 541, 565, 631-35, 683, 685, 691, 761, 765-66, 799, 984-85, 988-91, 1013, 1015, 1124, 1251
lectionaries, 88, 374, 403, 515, 672, 677, 747, 800
lectisternium, 144, 919, 922
legal texts, 253, 636, 781
legatus legionis, 961, 992
Leontopolis, 117, 126, 284, 540, 660, 798, 1037, 1109
Letter to the Philippians, 81-83, 777
letters, 327-30, 640-44
    literary, 642
    of introduction, 640
    official, 640-44
    private, 382, 407, 640, 1286
Levites, 248, 255, 557, 575, 684, 799, 801, 825, 850, 867, 875-76, 916, 1025, 1036, 1041, 1043, 1047-48, 1054, 1063, 1086, 1261
Leviticus Rabbah, 890, 892-93
lexicography, 27, 1065, 1071, 1073-75, 1084, 1210
libations, 299, 523, 762, 801, 816, 918, 921, 1175
libertini, 1002
libraries, 24-28, 45, 66, 93, 115, 131, 155, 167, 263, 281, 325, 435, 454, 476, 499, 535-36, 590, 647, 653, 667, 671, 675-76, 774, 781, 813-14, 850, 858, 872, 954, 971, 1068-73, 1080-81, 1187, 1192, 1267, 1283, 1289
Life of Adam and Eve, 4-5, 63, 156, 333, 1291
literary criticism, 27, 1065-66, 1069, 1073, 1075-76, 1079, 1081, 1083, 1284, 1289
liturgical texts, 58, 62-63, 536, 1298
liturgy, 44, 156-57, 233, 235-36, 260, 402-3, 407, 476, 648-52, 713, 715-16, 800, 802, 825, 873, 905, 1032, 1120, 1124, 1149, 1223, 1242, 1298
Lives of the Prophets, 277, 652-54
Livy, 8, 10-11, 14, 209, 357, 360-65, 369, 381, 384, 443-44, 485, 503-4, 522-25, 528, 680, 688, 708, 722, 772-73, 827, 919, 922-23, 928, 965, 985, 1004-5, 1012-14, 1073, 1079, 1082, 1211, 1284, 1287-88
loculi, 126-27
logos, 121, 232, 516, 518, 608, 722, 757, 761, 794, 954, 957, 1140-41
lower classes, 136, 477, 977, 989, 1000-1002
Lower Galilee, 1153
Lucian of Samosata, 244, 654, 721, 828-30, 832, 927, 1076, 1081
lunar month, 181, 375
Lycaonia, 134, 389, 429, 963
Lycia, 131-33, 136, 964, 998
Lystra, 33, 134, 205, 389-90, 563, 964, 1150-51
1 Maccabees, 51, 166, 343, 381, 439, 572, 581, 619, 657-61, 889, 951, 1102, 1148, 1193, 1293, 1296
2 Maccabees, 51, 69, 118, 141, 166,

284, 293, 335, 343, 435-36, 464, 471, 573, 615, 657-62, 932-33, 1117, 1148, 1193
3 Maccabees, 58, 662-63, 666, 948
4 Maccabees, 58, 615, 661, 664-66, 942-43, 1102, 1294
Maccabean martyrs, 35-36, 335, 946
Maccabean revolt, 314-15, 468, 570, 572-73, 625, 657, 659, 775, 786, 819, 1062, 1093, 1194, 1239
Macedon, Macedonians, 17, 20-22, 34, 137, 167, 205, 278-80, 330-31, 381, 413, 421, 424-25, 428, 467, 473, 476, 502, 617, 689, 787-88, 870-72, 918, 963, 1010, 1073, 1075, 1110, 1208, 1231, 1233
Macherus, 107
Magdala, 393, 396, 1147, 1149, 1247
magic, 154, 261, 271-72, 281, 382, 414-15, 483, 656, 666-69, 686, 727-28, 737, 740, 928-29, 1060, 1189, 1240, 1279-80
Majority Text, 672-74, 677, 1212
majuscules, 671-72, 675-76, 678-79, 1103
Mandeanism, 415
Manetho, 27, 502, 581, 590
Manicheanism, 416
mantic wisdom, 48
Manual of Discipline, 171-72, 254, 636, 1018-24, 1173
manumission, 115, 216, 283, 366, 539, 1001-2, 1126-27, 1134, 1162
Marc Antony, 524, 577, 787, 872, 964, 975, 1010, 1250
Maria the Jewish Alchemist, 679-80
Marisa, 101-2, 104-5, 108-9
marriage, 680-93
Mars, 99, 139-40, 202, 370, 816-17, 921-23, 925, 1011, 1187
Mars Hill, 99, 139-40
Martyrdom of Polycarp, 82-83, 85, 563, 569, 666, 777, 1030
Masada, 80, 94-95, 107-8, 125-29, 260, 262, 265, 274, 276, 343, 393, 396, 436, 461-62, 486, 534, 587, 590, 624, 630, 732, 764, 776, 808, 848-49, 852-53, 936, 939, 944-45, 1017, 1032, 1091, 1094, 1098, 1113, 1117, 1139, 1147, 1153, 1192
mashal, 913
Masoretic text, 753
Mattathias, 223, 438-39, 441-42, 468, 560, 608, 658, 660, 1193-94
Mattathias Antigonus, 223, 439, 441, 468
meals, 27, 136, 138, 143-46, 254, 286, 293, 344, 481, 613, 636, 686, 713, 716, 758, 800, 876, 880-82, 921, 1068, 1177, 1180, 1230, 1297, 1301
medicine, 27, 93, 132, 228, 241, 308, 405, 498, 499, 757, 1065, 1073, 1078-80, 1272
mekilta, 891
Mekilta de Rabbi Ishmael, 1243
Melchiresha(*, 155, 694, 1259
Melchizedek, 4, 155-56, 257, 270, 317, 400, 496, 514, 524, 581, 693-95, 704, 708, 779, 781, 826, 1055, 1136, 1139, 1258-59, 1262
Memar Marqah, 1054, 1056-57
Menahem, 179, 344, 944
Menippus, 243-44, 655, 1080
Mercury, 922, 925
merkabah mysticism, 38, 869, 1006, 1191
Messiah, 47-51, 53-55, 56, 63, 70, 266, 293, 294, 332, 338, 347, 349, 351, 376, 379, 452, 469, 514, 516, 521, 546, 549, 580, 591, 637, 695-707, 749-51, 820-21, 845, 851, 855-56, 936-37, 939, 947, 973, 1025, 1032, 1054-55, 1114-15, 1136-37, 1176, 1205, 1227, 1260-62, 1291, 1295-98
Messianic Apocalypse, 695-98
messianic banquet, 144, 1025-26
messianic expectation, 346, 937, 1025, 1225-26, 1297
messianic kingdom, 50, 56-57, 731
Messianic Rule, 254, 636, 1024-25
messianism, 49, 170, 379, 693, 697, 699-700, 703-4, 855, 856, 901, 917, 1025, 1115, 1136, 1240, 1297
  Branch of David, 699, 702-3, 1136
  Chosen One, 170, 316, 702, 704, 707, 1204
  Davidic messiah, 695
  diarchic, 703
  dual messiah, 1262
  Elect One, 170, 514, 702, 704
  priestly messiah, 79, 607, 1025
Metatron, 317, 729
Middle Platonism, 796, 806-7
midrash, 76, 87, 89-91, 195, 259, 312, 378, 398, 400, 402-3, 450, 459, 515, 543-48, 592, 639, 694, 728-29, 779-80, 865, 889-92, 898, 905, 908, 948, 951, 956, 1025, 1051, 1057, 1094, 1097, 1183, 1189, 1228, 1258
Migdal, 396, 1149
mikveh, 96, 106
military, Roman, 112, 215, 217, 275, 384, 620, 622, 966, 991-92
  auxiliaries, 994-95
  cohort, 274, 980, 992-94, 1013
  legion, 133-34, 177, 221, 361, 586-88, 624, 784, 886, 938, 960-61, 965-66, 970, 975-76, 979-80, 992-94, 996-98, 1000, 1002, 1013, 1026, 1113
  navy, 381, 994-95
milk, 143, 304, 333, 360, 555, 707-8, 1302
millennialism, 46
Minerva, 124, 561, 816-17, 921-22, 971, 994, 1011-12
Minoan Civilization, 421-22
minuscules, 671-72, 674, 677, 679, 1102-3
Miqṣat Maʿaśey Ha-Torah (4QMMT), 460, 709, 711
Mithras, Mithraism, 145, 723-25, 924-26, 994, 1011
modern linguistics, 431
Moira, 930
monogamy, 7, 9, 354, 680
morning and evening sacrifice, 1038, 1040-41
mosaics, 123, 128, 446, 564, 1148
mourning, 3, 57, 79, 87, 173-75, 377, 443-44, 629, 713, 1118
Mt. Carmel, 392
Mt. Gerizim, 22, 96, 179, 440, 581, 618-19, 625, 940, 982, 1053, 1055-58, 1202
Mt. Hermon, 102-3
Mt. Olympus, 816
Muratorian Canon, 190, 194, 860-61, 1275
museums, 24, 26-27, 115, 122-23, 139, 281, 474, 476, 530, 534, 872, 1068-69, 1071
music, 198, 233, 308-9, 311, 606-7, 711-17, 721, 851, 1048, 1065, 1068, 1080
musical instruments, 224, 467, 713-14
Musonius Rufus, 297, 322, 686, 719, 720, 1015, 1140, 1209, 1254, 1284-85, 1287
Mycenean Civilization, 421-22
mysteries, 47, 123, 145, 155, 219, 313, 317, 334, 354, 444, 513, 589, 656, 720-24, 727, 731, 779-80, 833, 925, 930, 998, 1023, 1086, 1090, 1186, 1216, 1223, 1265
  of Dionysus, 721-22
  of the Great Mother, 135, 722-23
  of Isis and Osiris, 14, 527, 722-23
  of Mithras, 722-23
mystery religions, 144-45, 371, 423, 471, 720, 723-25, 917, 924
mysticism, 44, 53, 225, 260, 314, 725-30, 732-34, 736-37, 744, 1138, 1189
Nag Hammadi, 4, 45, 66, 68, 69, 72, 76, 78, 336, 414-17, 451, 482-485, 1053
Narrative A, 738
Negev, 102, 104-5, 303, 1185
Nehemiah, 117, 167, 182, 341-42, 460, 511, 513, 571, 574-76, 593, 607, 617-18, 624, 753, 948, 1036, 1047, 1053, 1057-58, 1062, 1149, 1166, 1302
Neofiti, 87, 91, 694, 904, 1292
Neo-Pythagoreanism, 739-40, 795-96
Neptune, 922, 972
Nero, 13-15, 51, 113, 130, 134, 141, 158, 207, 216, 220-21, 230, 274-75, 283, 321-22, 393, 397, 448, 538, 586, 598, 623, 818, 828, 840, 961, 963-64, 969-73, 976-77, 982-83, 985, 996, 1007, 1010-11, 1014-17, 1063, 1080-81, 1083, 1098, 1109-11, 1142-45, 1158-59, 1162-63, 1165, 1236-37, 1288
Nerva, 288, 837, 971, 1011, 1157
New Jerusalem, New Jerusalem texts, 48, 57, 256, 74-45, 1170, 1173
New Testament manuscripts, 536, 670-74, 1211
Nicanor Gate, 1040, 1174
Nicomachean Ethics, 120, 795, 1208, 1253
nomos, 242, 243, 418, 632, 634, 1067, 1242, 1244
North Africa, 188, 190-91, 284, 424, 540, 587, 871, 918, 965, 975, 1113
novels, 7, 10, 67, 131, 359, 360, 363, 382, 403-5, 412, 622, 655, 686, 726, 929, 948, 951, 1008, 1069, 1083, 1191, 1279, 1284-86, 1288
novels, romances, 9, 12, 167, 291, 443, 471, 513, 571, 589, 683, 686, 1008-10, 1238, 1239, 1278, 1284
nursing, 198, 360, 361, 707-8, 1110, 1278
occupations, 144, 214, 304, 362, 797, 871, 921, 1000, 1001, 1118, 1126, 1276, 1279
Octavian, 134, 157, 208, 284, 425, 475, 486-87, 560, 577, 621, 787, 870, 872, 918, 964, 975, 998, 1010, 1250-51
Octavius, Gaius, 968-69
Odes of Solomon, 63, 416, 749, 751-52, 853-54, 860
Odysseus, 9, 44, 593, 816, 1071, 1209
Odyssey, 27, 121, 309, 334, 422, 427, 466, 593, 815, 919, 929, 1069, 1079, 1082, 1208, 1282
offerings, burnt, 468, 613, 1036-38, 1042, 1044, 1046-47, 1154
oil, 4, 96, 106, 143, 182, 263, 304, 340, 346, 376, 394, 397, 435, 638, 698, 702-3, 738, 798, 801, 821, 825, 871-72, 876-77, 915, 1001, 1039-42, 1044, 1132, 1178, 1301-2
Old Latin Bible, 747
olive, olive oil, 34, 360, 872, 1039, 1044, 1279
olives, olive oil, 34, 105, 133, 303-4, 360, 372, 374, 391, 394, 555, 703, 872, 1039-40, 1044, 1045, 1162, 1279
Olympian Games, 141, 423
Olympian gods, 228, 816, 919
Onqelos, 87, 90, 91, 904-5, 1097, 1292
oracle, Delphic, 832
oracles, 51, 62, 116, 130, 148, 166, 219, 259, 291, 318, 331, 333, 336, 350, 378-79, 401, 463, 509, 511, 548-49, 614, 654-56, 699, 779, 825, 831-33, 860, 878, 918, 920, 921, 926-27, 1107-12, 1114, 1225, 1279
oracular prophets, 939, 941
Ordinances, 638
ordo equester, 1000
ordo senatorius, 1000
Orestes, 635, 919, 998
Orphic cult, 816
ossuaries, 124, 127, 128, 174-75, 179-80, 539, 1096-97
otherworldly journeys, 334-36, 409, 1295
Oxyrhynchus, 237, 416, 501, 535-36, 540, 671, 717, 719
P.Berol., 72
P.Cair., 72, 672, 829, 1301-2

P.Egerton, 71, 672
P.Mert., 72
P.Oxy, 13, 72, 74, 115, 231, 359-60, 365, 381-82, 420, 535-36, 671, 678, 688, 715, 1208
P.Vindob., 71-72, 536-37, 671, 1211
pagan sacrifices, 439
paganism, 128, 145, 465-66, 469, 568, 655, 792, 994, 1232
paideia, 141, 471, 655, 1066
painting, 123, 128, 220, 309, 422, 481, 1148-49, 1163, 1276
Palestinian Talmud, 1051, 1237
Pamphylia, 32, 131-34, 390, 563, 963, 1092
pantheon, 29, 280, 817, 919, 923, 977, 1066, 1160
pantheon, Roman, 8, 816-17
Paphlagonia, 134, 279, 390, 963
Papyri Graecae Magicae, 667
papyri, documentary, 428, 474, 537, 645, 766, 1211
Papyri, Palestinian, 429, 535, 764
parables, 18, 69, 73, 84, 89, 169, 277, 304-5, 316, 385-86, 464, 512, 757, 761, 801, 876, 878, 900, 906, 909-13, 934, 935, 1026, 1040, 1060, 1094, 1181, 1257, 1266, 1298
paraenesis, 307, 354, 627, 757, 1131, 1240, 1252-53, 1264
parchment, 26, 131, 311, 474, 535-36, 640, 666, 670-71, 676, 1072, 1192, 1205, 1211, 1283
parents, 76, 175, 197-98, 200, 202, 216, 311, 325, 354-60, 362, 382-83, 519, 553, 634, 684-85, 815, 866, 919, 990, 1003, 1087, 1090, 1119, 1121, 1177-79, 1202, 1252, 1277, 1302
parentsl, 197, 200, 354, 682, 1119
Parthenia, Parthenians, 480, 486, 750, 964, 972, 1028
Passover, 118, 144, 146, 175, 182-83, 199, 201, 203, 204, 238, 253, 276, 292, 300, 306, 308, 341-42, 372-77, 462, 489, 492, 505, 602, 606, 713, 743, 798-99, 866, 939, 1037-38, 1043-44, 1047, 1059, 1170, 1181, 1242, 1250
pastimes, 634, 1276
paterfamilias, paternal authority, 197, 301, 357, 361, 687, 990-91, 1026, 1028, 1277
pax deorum, 210, 921
Pax Romana, 762, 771-75, 967, 1018, 1027
peace offerings, 1036-37, 1046
peirasmos, 1207-10
Pella, 20, 107, 244, 266-68, 776, 1068, 1073, 1081, 1232
Pentateuch, 27, 65, 91, 118, 258, 260, 290, 312, 350, 453-54, 459, 516, 583, 592, 606-7, 699, 752-53, 840, 868, 889, 903-5, 909, 950, 1038, 1053-54, 1056, 1057-59, 1099, 1101-2, 1104, 1106, 1117, 1141, 1196, 1198, 1234, 1241-42, 1258, 1290-91, 1294
Pentecost, 25, 182, 373, 377, 489-90, 649, 798, 1014, 1043
peregrini, 987, 1001, 1014
Pergamum, 25- 26, 99-100, 131, 133, 319-20, 389, 466, 498, 530, 563, 647, 858, 929, 963, 1029, 1068, 1072-73, 1079, 1092, 1283
Pergamum library, 26
persecution, 42, 44, 84, 129, 132, 192, 195, 207, 448, 470, 521, 662, 664, 775, 77-78, 839, 870, 938, 941-42, 973-74, 977-78, 991, 1011, 1014, 1072, 1151, 1160, 1193-94, 1216, 1220, 1245, 1269-70, 1274
Perseus, 21, 218, 425, 919
pesher, pesharim, 65, 162, 164, 195, 257-58, 262, 346, 378, 437-38, 456, 552, 694, 778-82, 820, 850-51, 890, 948, 1296-97
Persia, 21, 111, 135, 145, 154, 259, 297, 319, 330, 331, 334, 348, 392, 424, 425-26, 499, 502, 559, 576, 617, 689, 722, 1109
Persian apocalypticism, 41
Persian period, 102, 105, 110, 167, 475, 571, 574-75, 617, 625, 1057, 1061, 1063, 1149
Pesher Habakkuk, 437
Peshitta, 88, 746, 754-55, 853, 905, 1097-98, 1154-56
Pesiqta de Rab Kahana, 890
Pesiqta Rabbati, 890
Pharisees, 782-87
Philip II, 20, 119, 221, 308, 425, 428, 467, 787-88, 917
Philip the Tetrarch, 485, 490
Philippi, 83, 99, 178, 205, 217, 220, 228, 230, 285, 301, 426, 434, 470, 621, 759, 787-89, 961, 963, 985, 989, 999, 1145, 1150, 1231-32
Philo, 789-93
Philo the Epic Poet, 582
Philoxenian Version, 1154-55
Phrygia, 32, 134, 205, 225, 279, 283, 321, 389, 429, 563, 722, 963, 1110-11
phylacteries, 260-61, 636, 785, 802, 929, 1114, 1191, 1205
physicians, 131, 272, 311, 395, 405, 498-99, 647, 681, 790, 858, 929, 1078-79, 1122, 1126, 1228
piety, 48, 61, 63, 116, 241, 323, 339, 349, 385, 478, 495, 518, 520-21, 524, 592, 594, 602, 607-8, 625, 627, 657, 659, 759, 777, 796-97, 800, 802, 846, 862, 873, 916, 926, 930, 967, 1029, 1118, 1120, 1148, 1178, 1187, 1189, 1204, 1209, 1216, 1222, 1226, 1240, 1255, 1291, 1296, 1298
Pilate inscription, 804
Pisidia, 31-32, 34, 133-34, 136, 138, 550, 1249
Pisidian Antioch, 31-32, 34, 134, 999, 1150
Pistis Sophia, 77, 415, 749, 853-54
Plato, Platonism, 804-7
Plea for Deliverance, 270, 849, 851
plebs, 974, 1001-2
Pliny the Elder, 263, 343, 774, 807-9, 1080, 1158-59, 1230, 1283, 1287-88
Pliny the Younger, 135, 691, 719, 767, 808-9, 985, 989, 1142, 1157, 1284, 1287
Plotinus, 28, 168, 790, 795-96, 807
Plutarch, 812-13
poets, poetry, 20, 27, 62-63, 132, 139, 145, 166, 234, 239, 243, 281, 290, 309, 319, 358, 401, 419, 423-24, 429, 472, 474, 535, 580, 582-83, 607, 634, 645-47, 651, 722, 739, 750, 757, 759, 760-61, 772, 813-14, 816, 832, 854, 868, 919, 947, 969, 975, 1065-73, 1076-77, 1079-84, 1126, 1142-43, 1216-18, 1226, 1253, 1268, 1278-79, 1282, 1284-85
police, 585, 959, 961, 1013, 1030, 1144, 1228
polis, 103, 109, 136-37, 141, 212-14, 218-19, 280-81, 300, 423, 435, 468, 490, 560, 572, 598, 659-60, 808, 918, 920, 1130, 1162, 1186-87
Polybius, 330, 381, 389, 429-30, 475, 480, 500-504, 592, 758, 761, 959, 961, 967-68, 992, 1077, 1079, 1082, 1092, 1208, 1220, 1284, 1287
Polycarp, 81, 82, 83, 85, 132, 185, 321, 563, 569, 776-77, 788, 1030, 1155, 1247
polytheism, 134, 210, 312, 478, 815-16, 818, 922, 929, 1140
Pompey, 23, 34, 63, 134-35, 208, 216, 263, 267-78, 282, 285, 296, 348, 425, 441, 468, 485, 560, 570, 576-77, 580, 584-85, 610, 617, 620, 624, 802, 818-20, 855, 963-64, 968, 972, 975, 979, 995, 1010, 1014, 1016, 1073, 1093, 1297
pontifex, 922, 968, 996, 1027
pontifex maximus, 922, 996, 1027
Pontius Pilate, 95, 97, 179, 204, 221, 223, 376, 434, 472, 492, 534, 561-62, 578, 591, 596, 599, 630, 761, 767, 803-4, 840, 927, 940, 961, 972, 980-81, 984-85, 987-88, 1016-17, 1053, 1095, 1158, 1175
Pontus, 134-35, 294, 389, 415, 563, 620, 777, 809-10, 812, 963, 975, 1030, 1077, 1092, 1159
pool of Siloam, 96
Porcius Festus, 979, 983, 988, 997
porneia, 10, 249, 1128, 1255
Poseidon, 13, 141, 422, 758, 761, 815-16, 858, 919, 922
Poseidonius, 503, 665, 1073, 1077, 1081
pottery, 103-4, 107-9, 214, 394, 395, 422, 474, 530, 535, 884, 886
praefectus, 534, 959-61, 980
praetorian guard, 959, 969, 970, 993, 995-96, 1000, 1142
praetorium, 97, 176, 177, 631, 979, 992
Prayer of Enosh, 260, 820-21
Prayer of Joseph, 860
Prayer of Manasseh, 58-59, 62, 821-22, 947, 1100
Prayer of Nabonidus, 259, 822-24
prayer, personal, 648
prayers, daily, 155, 648-49, 899
prefect, 25, 113, 179, 204, 266, 534, 773, 775, 789, 804, 810, 959, 961, 964, 981, 993, 995, 997-98, 1016, 1049, 1142, 1162
pre-Republican Rome, 974
pre-Socratic, 794
Priene, 281, 286, 319, 370, 530, 533, 563-65, 569, 858, 1029
Priene Inscription, 533
priesthood, 32, 61, 172, 254, 377, 412, 449, 460, 499, 574, 579, 600, 605, 607-8, 610, 622-24, 649, 659, 693, 695, 699, 732, 757, 824, 826, 843, 875, 914, 949, 1036, 1042, 1046, 1049, 1055, 1058, 1086, 1138, 1170, 1172, 1198-1200, 1206, 1221, 1229, 1280, 1295, 1298
priestly aristocracy, 598-99, 1063, 1086, 1293
Prince of Darkness, 153, 156, 1258
Prince of Light, 49, 156, 1136
prison, imprisonment, 8, 81, 207, 215-17, 232, 275-76, 282, 285, 320-21, 324, 344, 356, 362, 395, 416, 426, 441, 470, 491, 585-86, 596, 641, 714, 760, 788, 815, 818, 821, 827-30, 863, 982, 983-84, 988, 990, 1005-6, 1016, 1125, 1246-48, 1280
proconsuls, 98, 206-7, 230, 441, 534, 620, 759, 773, 827, 936, 960, 966, 979, 988, 997-98
procurator, 98, 177, 207, 238, 266, 274, 392, 489, 539, 773, 804, 834, 939, 945, 960-61, 980, 997-98, 1016, 1049, 1064, 1126, 1163
progymnasmata, 310
proselytes, proselytizing, 10, 35, 248, 282, 286-87, 291, 469, 540, 550, 566, 625, 685, 776, 800, 836-37, 840-47, 914, 938, 973, 1014, 1046-47, 1227
prostitution, 10-12, 445, 1278
Protevangelium of James, 76-77
proverbs, 8, 18-19, 132, 262, 329, 382, 472, 512, 688, 757, 759, 780, 814, 861, 907, 909, 911-13, 956, 992, 1116, 1118-19, 1123-24, 1168, 1265-66
provincial administration, 131, 135, 807
provincial councils, 998
provocatio, 217, 987
prozbul, 497
psalm scrolls of Qumran, 847, 1048
psalmody, 232-33, 235, 712-16
Psalms of Solomon, 63, 69-70, 191, 293, 514, 556, 610, 701, 750, 820, 853-57, 860, 947, 1100, 1194, 1218, 1226, 1293, 1297
pseudepigrapha, 39, 58, 59, 60, 70, 148, 259, 484, 556, 608, 701, 749, 853, 858, 861, 898, 900, 948, 1190, 1193, 1207, 1250
pseudepigraphy, 41, 58-60, 62, 69-70, 153, 241, 253, 258, 339, 346, 496, 544, 600, 857-63, 1108, 1184-85, 1199
Pseudo-Daniel, 259, 822-24
Pseudo-Demetrius, 327-29
Pseudo-Esther, 1159
Pseudo-Eupolemus, 495, 581, 592
Pseudo-Ezekiel, 335, 349, 731, 869
Pseudo-Jonathan, 91, 904-6, 1292, 1299
Pseudo-Jubilees, 950

Pseudo-Libanius, 327-29
pseudonymity, 42, 46-47, 60, 66-67, 151, 187, 193, 244, 398, 407-8, 498, 821, 858-63, 955, 1188, 1268
Pseudo-Orpheus, 582
Pseudo-Philo, 2, 7, 9-10, 63, 79, 160, 282, 355, 359-60, 385, 398, 412, 510-12, 582, 592, 682, 690, 692, 706-7, 821, 860, 864-68, 890, 947-49, 951-53, 1258, 1290
Pseudo-Phocylides, 12, 282, 291, 582-84, 683, 868-69, 1294
Ptolemaic Egypt, 26, 440, 473, 475, 477, 870, 873, 918, 1145, 1302
Ptolemies, Ptolemaic period, 23-28, 107, 223, 280, 363, 425, 428, 473-77, 533, 560, 571, 608, 618, 662, 858, 870-73, 1058, 1068, 1072, 1092, 1108-9, 1269
Ptolemy I Soter, 22, 24, 26-27, 104, 110, 114-15, 118, 223, 259, 268-69, 280-81, 474-75, 480, 537, 570-71, 592, 618, 661, 871-72, 924, 1068, 1070, 1072, 1100, 1146, 1148, 1220, 1291, 1300
Ptolemy II Philadelphus, 24, 26-27, 110, 114-15, 118, 223, 280, 474, 480, 537, 571, 592, 618, 871-72, 924, 1068, 1070, 1100, 1146, 1148, 1220, 1291, 1300
Ptolemy III Euergetes, 24, 26, 474, 1070, 1146, 1148
Ptolemy IV Philopator, 27, 104, 268-69, 661, 1070
Ptolemy V Epiphanes, 117-18, 533, 572, 662, 872, 1070, 1072-73, 1100, 1108-9, 1117, 1146
Ptolemy VI Philometer, 117, 118, 662, 1070, 1072, 1100, 1108-9, 1117, 1146
Ptolemy VII Neos Philopator, 1070, 1072, 1117, 1146
Ptolemy VIII Euergetes II, 1070, 1072
Ptolemy IX Soter II, 1070, 1072
Ptolemy X Alexander I, 1070
Ptolemy XIII, 1070
Ptolemy XIV, 1070
public baths, 124, 214, 829
public buildings, 102-4, 108, 111, 126, 158, 212-13, 300, 423, 470, 959, 962, 969, 974, 1002
public works, 212, 476, 962, 976, 1003
publicani, 966, 980, 1163
Punic Wars, 503, 975, 995, 1125, 1280
Purification Liturgy, 648
purification offerings, 1038
Purification Texts, 873
Purim, feast of, 182, 375-77, 905
purity, 10, 39, 61, 84, 254, 334, 344, 375-76, 396, 507, 511, 513-14, 602, 605, 609-15, 620, 636-39, 648, 709, 785-86, 788, 801, 839-40, 845, 873-82, 893, 914-16, 1019, 1025, 1037, 1040, 1042, 1044, 1046-48, 1051-52, 1087, 1149, 1151, 1175, 1177-79, 1181, 1183, 1204, 1222-23, 1228-29, 1244, 1265, 1276, 1279, 1296
Purple Codex, 676
Pyrrhonism, 242
Pythagoras, Pythagoreanism, 118-19, 168, 425, 583, 739, 794-95, 806, 930, 1294
Pythian Games, 141
quadrivium, 311
Questions of Ezra, 340
Quintilian, 8, 9, 198, 329, 356, 358-60, 363, 519, 681, 683, 776, 955, 985, 1080, 1082-83, 1099, 1270, 1284, 1287
Quirinius, 202, 578, 590, 596, 599, 985, 997, 1162
Qumran, 883-88
Qumran calendar, 204, 262, 602
Qumran community, 46, 79, 92, 93, 152, 162, 170-71, 195, 204, 226, 343, 345-46, 349, 579, 600, 619, 694, 732, 850, 869, 873, 1022, 1025, 1026, 1058, 1138-39, 1173, 1184, 1227, 1254, 1266, 1290, 1296-97
rabbinic parables, 385, 909-10
rabbinic proverbs, 911-12
rabbis, 914-17
Rebukes by the Overseer, 261, 639
religion, domestic, 299-301, 921
restoration of Israel, 556, 699
resurrection, 42-44, 47-48, 50, 53-54, 56-57, 61-62, 67, 74, 77, 84, 169, 175, 232, 235, 307, 315, 326, 335-36, 344, 346-47, 351, 377, 403, 416, 438, 457, 513, 548, 554, 561, 569, 609, 653, 700, 709, 721, 723, 731, 740-41, 785, 792, 824, 869, 874, 878, 891, 931-35, 1006, 1050-53, 1110, 1151
Revelation of Ezra, 340
Reworked Pentateuch, 260
rewritten Bible, 398, 865, 947-48, 950-52
rex sacrorum, 922
rhetoric, Christian, 957
Rhetorica ad Alexandrum, 954
Rhodes, 8, 24, 110, 122, 133, 279, 281, 285, 487, 577, 629, 686-87, 773, 814, 1068-69, 1072-73, 1077-78, 1080-82, 1208, 1301
ritual purity, 36, 72, 395-96, 626, 636, 786, 801, 873, 874, 887, 1042, 1094
Roman administration, 130, 579, 622, 959
Roman army, 216, 288, 461, 645, 936, 937, 939, 963, 992, 1113, 1251
Roman calendar, 209, 368, 369
Roman cities, 212, 214, 393, 436, 580, 588, 1000, 1062
Roman colonies, 32, 131, 228, 230, 370, 445, 787, 961, 966, 984, 985, 989, 999, 1017, 1129, 1193
Roman East, 428, 429, 476, 485, 584, 630, 679, 766, 962-67, 973, 975, 999, 1028
Roman expansion, 965
Roman Republic, 212, 576, 974, 978, 991, 1010
Rosetta Stone, 475, 532-33, 539
Rule of the Community, 43, 137, 147, 155, 171, 254, 260-62, 332, 335, 345, 457, 513, 609, 636-39, 697, 742, 750, 839, 1018-26, 1090, 1128, 1205, 1217, 1230, 1254, 1267, 1281, 1296, 1298
Rule of the Congregation, 171-73, 254, 255, 261, 345, 636-37, 684, 731, 1020-21, 1024-26, 1281
Rule of War, 1261
ruler cult, 131, 158, 215, 219, 228, 283, 757, 763, 923, 966, 969-71, 994, 1026-29, 1093, 1269, 1270, 1272
sabbath, 35, 85, 119, 181-82, 199, 204, 215, 225, 229, 248, 260-63, 286-88, 292-93, 312, 320, 344, 346-47, 375, 396, 462, 478, 496-97, 516, 550, 558, 564-66, 570, 583, 601-2, 608-9, 637-38, 651, 686, 704, 716, 732, 797-800, 802, 820, 893, 895, 900-901, 913-14, 949, 972, 1014, 1021, 1031-35, 1038, 1041, 1051-52, 1065, 1107, 1138, 1146-48, 1150, 1152, 1194, 1225, 1232, 1242-43, 1279, 1281, 1294
sabbath sacrifice, 1038, 1138
sacred space, 557, 1027, 1036, 1047
sacrifices, 923, 1036-50
Sadducees, 61, 204, 246, 326, 343, 346, 348, 440, 461-62, 493, 498, 579, 585, 590, 596, 610, 637, 709-11, 784-87, 802, 849, 855, 873, 891, 902, 932-33, 941, 949, 1049-52, 1061, 1063, 1089, 1170, 1222, 1224, 1227-28
salt, 135, 760, 1038, 1043-44, 1279
Samaria, 94, 101-2, 105, 107-8, 125, 213, 239, 394, 414, 440, 479, 487-89, 560, 570, 574, 617-19, 625-26, 903, 964, 979, 982, 994, 1016, 1053, 1055-56, 1058-61, 1177
Samaritan literature, 1056
Samaritan Pentateuch, 453, 553, 1053, 1059, 1205, 1258
Samaritan, The, 889, 939, 940, 1053-54, 1056-57, 1061, 1105
Samaritans, 22, 96, 179, 207, 239, 453, 455, 489-90, 543, 618-19, 754, 803, 864, 940, 949, 982, 1017, 1052-61, 1101
Samothrace, 99, 370, 998, 1070-71, 1231
sanctuary, 21, 103, 105, 108, 131, 178, 228, 276, 293, 374, 376, 379, 423, 444, 468, 480, 557, 560, 562, 584, 604, 610, 615, 649, 653, 735, 775, 788, 825, 920, 927, 998, 1037, 1039, 1040-42, 1045, 1048, 1057-58, 1064, 1068, 1115, 1148, 1152, 1168-69, 1178-81, 1186, 1219, 1241, 1278
sanhedrin, 1061
Sapiential Work, 65, 1092, 1264-65
Sardis, 74, 131-32, 134, 136, 188, 279, 281, 283, 286, 320, 517, 540, 563-69, 838, 847, 1093
Satan, 4, 5, 10, 31, 42, 44, 48-51, 54, 63, 99, 131, 153-56, 270, 272, 350, 415, 653, 704, 851, 869, 910, 941, 943, 951, 1029, 1145, 1152, 1189-92, 1202-3, 1262, 1290, 1296
satire, 243, 655, 681, 721, 1075, 1079, 1082-83, 1252, 1284
scholarship, 5, 23, 27-28, 42, 52, 70, 74, 76, 86, 167, 201, 260, 263, 288, 297, 316, 402, 453, 469, 473, 482, 484, 504, 508, 529, 534, 538, 542-43, 598, 605, 608, 623, 647, 673, 716, 727, 735, 746-48, 778, 782, 784, 813, 818, 835-37, 861, 872, 935, 1008, 1065, 1069, 1071-73, 1076, 1079, 1083-84, 1099, 1101, 1107, 1126, 1160, 1176, 1184, 1188, 1228, 1231, 1239, 1254, 1286
scholarship, Roman, 1081
science, 20, 93, 119, 132, 423, 453, 495, 728, 739, 794, 813, 920, 930, 1071, 1078, 1080, 1234
scribes, 18, 148, 255, 262, 312, 314, 337, 395, 470, 495, 512, 537, 571, 607, 645-46, 675-76, 679, 749, 1020, 1024, 1086-89, 1098, 1117-18, 1183, 1205, 1211, 1214, 1242, 1250-51, 1283
sculpture, 122, 131
Scythopolis, 103, 107, 266-67
Second Punic War, 425, 918, 922
Second Sophistic, 132, 472, 1074-75
Secret Gospel of Mark, 71, 76
Secret of Existence, 259, 1090-91
sects, 1221-30
seers, 39-40, 57, 148, 150, 399, 510, 687, 831, 920, 1135-36, 1173, 1223, 1225-26
Seleucid rule, 109, 267, 392, 438, 560, 572, 584, 657-59, 775, 1135, 1300
Seleucids, 25, 32, 107, 154, 279-80, 348, 425, 428, 433, 440, 442, 560, 572, 574, 588, 608-9, 618-19, 660, 870, 963, 1014, 1058, 1073, 1092-93, 1164
Semitic influence, 88-89, 433, 1093
Semitisms, 38, 91, 749, 1093-98, 1103-4, 1250, 1268
senate, 23, 98, 140, 392, 425, 486, 529, 560, 584, 588, 598, 621, 629, 633-34, 722, 772, 774, 784, 809, 819-20, 831, 833, 923, 960, 965, 968-69, 971, 974-76, 979, 985-87, 993, 996, 1002, 1010, 1012-13, 1062, 1107, 1113, 1187, 1223
senatorial order, 1000, 1003
senatorial province, 425, 959, 961, 976, 1157
senatorial provinces, 425, 959, 961, 976
Seneca, 7, 8, 15-17, 114, 208, 230, 333-34, 356, 363-65, 368, 380, 383, 387, 509, 519-20, 634, 642, 664-65, 719, 758, 762, 767-69, 796, 828-30, 860, 969-70, 1015-16, 1081, 1083-84, 1098-99, 1125, 1133, 1140-42, 1158, 1252, 1254, 1284-85, 1287
Sepher Hekhalot, 314, 317
Sepphoris, 94, 224-25, 274, 391, 392-97, 433, 470, 490, 916, 1063, 1236-37
Septuagint, 28, 39, 63, 86, 92, 114, 117-18, 148, 161, 232-33, 236, 252, 262, 282, 292, 341, 413, 426, 430, 433, 437, 452, 480, 483-84,

540, 543-44, 553, 565, 582, 588-89, 592-93, 595, 613, 625, 653, 661-62, 678-79, 706, 752-55, 789, 800, 822, 850-51, 853, 868, 890, 906-7, 1053, 1095, 1099, 1100-1106, 1117, 1145, 1150, 1154, 1156, 1160, 1189-90, 1196, 1201, 1206-7, 1220, 1238, 1242, 1257-58, 1268, 1291-92, 1296, 1298
Septuagintalisms, 1095
serpents, 2, 5, 62, 721, 1266, 1270
sex, sexuality, 2, 6-12, 14, 68, 75-76, 124, 198, 249, 314, 354, 362, 382, 416, 443, 445-46, 514, 528, 583, 629, 656, 680-87, 719, 720, 722, 801, 808, 811, 851, 866-67, 873, 881, 893-94, 903, 1011, 1042, 1122, 1131, 1201-4, 1254,-55, 1263, 1272, 1274, 1276, 1278
shaman, shamanism, 44, 448
shame, 2, 7, 10, 111-12, 299, 305, 335, 443-45, 519, 704, 762, 769, 824, 829-30, 932, 1034, 1129-30, 1217, 1252, 1270
Shammai, House of Shammai, 6, 357, 497, 612, 700, 785, 797, 801, 841, 896, 898, 914-15, 1086, 1106-7, 1277, 1298
Shechem, 94, 105-6, 454, 525, 582, 602, 625, 951, 1056-58, 1060, 1202
sheep, 19, 315, 340, 370, 376, 394, 395, 612, 614, 707-8, 879, 934, 1009, 1034, 1038-40, 1043, 1044, 1060, 1203, 1283, 1302
Shelamzion Alexandra, 439-40, 619-20
Shema, 29, 199, 396, 558, 650-51, 686, 798, 801, 899, 1041, 1107, 1146-47
Shemoneh Esreh, 650-51, 1146
Shephelah, 104, 105, 588, 616
Shepherd of Hermas, 46, 66, 82, 84-85, 130, 188-89, 191, 193-94, 675
shepherd, shepherding, 30, 154, 252, 286, 315, 344, 372, 395, 654, 814, 908, 951, 1009
ships, shipping, 23, 116, 133, 176, 274, 320, 395, 424, 476, 581, 804, 816, 910, 924, 994-95, 1002, 1068, 1163, 1209, 1247-51, 1301
shipwreck, 1249
shoshbin, 386, 686
sicarii, 262, 776, 940, 944-46, 967, 983
Sicily, 243, 365, 421, 424, 443, 464, 500, 502, 805, 814, 918, 963, 967, 975, 1067, 1076, 1125, 1161, 1248
Simon bar Giora, 276, 938-39, 946
sin offerings, 1036, 1038-39, 1042
singing, 163, 232, 712-16, 811, 1041, 1075, 1217, 1278
Sipre Deuteronomy, 891, 1051
Sipre Numbers, 891, 1051
Sirach, 2, 5, 30, 49, 69, 70, 151-52, 190, 253, 258, 293, 335, 382, 455-56, 461, 495, 524, 662, 690, 696, 727, 821, 848, 851, 853-54, 890, 912, 932, 1022, 1049, 1086, 1090, 1099, 1102, 1116-18, 1124, 1203, 1224, 1226, 1243, 1263-64, 1272, 1292, 1294
Sirach, Ben Sira, 2, 58, 59, 62, 153, 162, 253, 258, 265, 461, 495, 512, 521, 607, 662, 838, 851, 890, 912, 1090, 1099, 1101, 1116-24, 1224, 1243, 1263-65, 1272, 1274, 1294
Skeptics, Skepticism, 242-43, 327, 356
slaves, slavery, 1124-27
Smyrna, 80, 83, 131, 132, 283, 318-20, 466, 563, 565, 568-69, 777, 788, 1027, 1068, 1074, 1146, 1247
snakes, 152, 833, 927, 929
social bandits, 936-37, 944, 946
social levels, 645, 1009, 1131
social mobility, 362, 478, 999, 1002-3, 1126, 1130
societas, 989-90
Socrates, 118, 167, 239, 241-42, 244, 296, 356, 402, 425, 466, 510, 635, 640, 719-20, 758, 805-6, 928, 1098
solar month, 181
Son of God, 232, 338, 694-95, 702, 705-6, 990, 1025, 1054, 1111, 1134-37, 1274
Son of God Text, 1025, 1134-35, 1137
Son of Man, 40, 43-45, 62, 70, 170, 251, 272, 316, 351, 376, 399, 458, 506, 561, 695, 702, 704, 934, 1033, 1055, 1295
songs, 79, 87, 181, 231-34, 260, 270, 376, 454, 495, 607, 625, 672, 712-14, 728, 732, 769, 829, 851, 854, 932, 1041, 1071, 1138, 1219, 1257
Songs Against Demons, 848, 851
Songs of the Sabbath Sacrifice, 260, 265, 451, 732, 737, 1032, 1037, 1137-39
Songs of the Sage, 1267
songs, spiritual, 232, 712, 714
sons of darkness, 30, 156, 609, 1019, 1258
sons of light, 30, 155-56, 347, 609, 694, 1019, 1022, 1227, 1258, 1262, 1266-67
Sophia of Jesus Christ, 72, 77, 417
Sophists, 310, 324, 499, 719, 785, 805, 859, 953, 1067, 1074, 1076
sorcery, 272, 668, 867, 928-29
Spain, 67, 205, 207, 209, 296, 424, 614, 772, 819, 965, 975-76, 992, 998, 1014, 1016, 1080, 1098, 1103, 1162
Stoics Stoicism, 28, 71, 84, 113, 120, 142, 230, 240, 242, 244, 280, 297, 311, 321-22, 324, 326-27, 333, 336, 355, 358, 360, 365, 380, 381, 383, 416, 419, 420-21, 503, 509, 592, 611, 634-35, 664-65, 681, 689-91, 719-20, 739, 758, 760-62, 790, 794-96, 806-7, 812, 814, 868, 928, 930, 1072-73, 1075, 1080-81, 1099, 1125, 1133, 1139-42, 1201-2, 1204, 1208-9, 1224-25, 1252-54, 1256, 1273, 1282, 1294
Strasbourg Coptic Fragment, 72
Suda, 322, 1068-74, 1084, 1142
Suetonius, 13-15, 26, 112-13, 206-7, 216-17, 230, 238, 285, 667, 761, 776, 818, 828-29, 833, 928, 961, 968-71, 973, 979, 981-82, 985, 998, 1011, 1014-15, 1072, 1076, 1079-84, 1108, 1142-45, 1158, 1248, 1284, 1287
Sukkoth, 374-76, 614, 878, 1170
superstition, 140, 527, 758, 814, 930, 973
surgery, 610
Symmachus, 679, 1102
symposia, 334, 405, 423, 1009, 1122
synagogues, 24, 33, 36, 60, 63, 84, 92, 95, 99, 104, 127-28, 134, 137-38, 200, 206, 216, 229-30, 233, 236, 271, 282, 284-87, 292, 312, 319-20, 357, 395-96, 402-3, 430, 450, 458, 469, 472, 478, 480-81, 495, 515-17, 521, 534, 539-40, 548-49, 562-69, 580, 649-51, 713, 716, 776, 783, 797, 799, 800, 802, 825, 838, 843, 844, 846, 890, 909-10, 915-16, 1012, 1014-15, 1032, 1035, 1047, 1087, 1088, 1102, 1117, 1123, 1131-32, 1145-52, 1220, 1225, 1232-33, 1236-37, 1241-42, 1276, 1279, 1291-92, 1298
syncretism, 295, 299, 568, 581, 606, 764, 872, 917
synedrion, 280, 392, 612, 1061-62
Syria, 25, 34-37, 67, 73, 75, 76, 82, 86, 94, 109, 130, 131, 133, 135, 139, 178-79, 185, 192, 202-3, 205, 213, 239, 266-68, 273, 279, 282-83, 319, 381, 415, 417, 422-23, 425, 433, 464, 467, 471-72, 485-87, 489-90, 492, 539, 560, 570, 571-72, 576-77, 584-85, 617-18, 620-21, 623-24, 637, 654, 664, 698, 722, 739, 749, 764, 788-89, 803, 819-20, 831, 879, 915, 917-18, 936, 938, 945, 964, 966, 968, 976-77, 979, 992, 997-98, 1010, 1013-14, 1016-17, 1028, 1063, 1092-93, 1110, 1112, 1135-36, 1154, 1162, 1166, 1220, 1225, 1247, 1293, 1300-1301
Syriac, 4, 18-19, 68, 74-75, 77, 86-88, 96, 148-49, 151, 382, 416, 467, 535, 591, 601, 653, 679, 701, 745-49, 752, 754-55, 822, 851-57, 905, 1096-98, 1102, 1150, 1154-56, 1161, 1250, 1251, 1264
Syriac Bible, 754, 905, 1154-55
Syrohexapla, 1154-55
table fellowship, 626
Tacitus, 13-14, 111, 113, 168-69, 199, 206-7, 215-7, 225, 238-39, 274, 285, 330, 354, 362-63, 365-67, 481, 485-86, 503-4, 524, 529, 534, 594, 689, 760, 761-62, 773, 775-76, 804, 808, 827-29, 832, 969-71, 973, 979-83, 985, 992, 1005, 1010, 1014-16, 1082-84, 1098, 1125, 1143-45, 1157-59, 1163-64, 1211, 1248, 1284, 1287
Taheb, 940, 1059
Tale of Bagasraw, 1159-61
Talmud, 87-89, 91, 161, 164, 200, 394, 449, 452, 456, 468, 507, 543, 612, 714, 729, 744, 803, 826, 891, 893, 897-902, 912, 957, 1057, 1063, 1114-15, 1145-46, 1149, 1235, 1237, 1242, 1251, 1298
Talmud, Babylonian, 898
Talmud, Palestinian, 898
Tanakh, 452, 1251
Targum Isaiah, 905-8
Targum Jonathan, 87, 90-91, 161, 177, 179, 249, 345, 383, 392, 439-40, 442, 468, 512, 573, 609, 611, 615, 658-59, 694, 834, 903-6, 908, 940-41, 944, 982-83, 1048, 1093, 1097-98, 1292, 1299
Targum Neofiti, 904, 1096
Targum of Job, 904
Targum Onqelos, 87, 398, 512, 1097, 1298
targumim, 3, 60, 87-93, 161, 258-59, 265, 312, 375, 398, 433, 512, 543, 611, 615, 651, 699-700, 753-54, 800, 892, 902-8, 949, 1095, 1097, 1114, 1150, 1257, 1292
taxes, collectors, 27, 212-13, 215, 222, 257, 304-6, 312, 363, 395, 440, 476, 485, 488, 490, 493, 571-72, 577, 585, 618, 662, 773, 787, 802, 871-72, 936-37, 941, 960-63, 966-67, 970, 975-76, 980, 987, 994, 1001, 1029, 1047, 1064, 1068, 1087-88, 1149, 1161-65, 1301-2
temple inscription, Jerusalem, 533
temple, Jewish, 1036-50, 1167-82
Temple Mount, 95, 96, 126, 141, 480, 560-61, 582, 1064, 1168, 1182
Temple Scroll, 64, 182, 256, 262, 266, 270, 379, 557, 636-40, 682, 743-45, 849, 947, 1032, 1045, 1170, 1173, 1182-86, 1195, 1265, 1290
temple service, 1036-37, 1040-41, 1044-45, 1058, 1120
temple tax, 221, 223, 283, 288, 292, 306-7, 481, 540, 563, 566, 799-800, 1148, 1166, 1176
temple treasury, 274, 460, 572, 618, 775, 799, 939, 1046, 1087
temples, Roman, 124, 1186-88
Templum Pacis, 774
Testament of Abraham, 4, 282, 511, 1188-89, 1226
Testament of Adam, 4
Testament of Asher, 49, 1203-4
Testament of Benjamin, 1204
Testament of Dan, 1201, 1203
Testament of Gad, 1203
Testament of Issachar, 1203
Testament of Job, 63, 156, 690-91, 730, 860, 1189-92, 1296
Testament of Joseph, 79, 1201, 1204
Testament of Judah, 277, 699, 948, 1202
Testament of Levi, 3, 30, 258, 277, 449, 730-31, 840, 1045, 1172, 1199-1200, 1202, 1205, 1258, 1295
Testament of Moses, 49, 63, 70, 293, 942, 950, 1136, 1192-99, 1226, 1282, 1293, 1296
Testament of Naphtali, 258, 1203
Testament of Our Lord, 77
Testament of Our Lord in Galilee, 77
Testament of Qahat, 92, 1199-1200, 1258

Testament of Reuben, 154, 1201
Testament of Simeon, 1201-2
Testament of Zebulon, 1203
testamentary literature, 398, 1296
Testaments of the Twelve Patriarchs, 30, 49, 154, 258, 863, 1182, 1189, 1199-1200, 1205, 1226, 1258, 1296
Testimonia, 79, 258, 1205
textual criticism, 253, 671-74, 677-79, 745, 1102, 1210-13, 1296
Textus Receptus, 673, 1212
Thanksgiving Hymns, 147, 195, 457, 508, 731, 750, 839, 851, 1090-91, 1214, 1218, 1267
theaters, 95, 97, 99, 124-25, 131, 141, 158, 176-77, 213-14, 229, 319, 395-96, 425, 435, 470, 487, 534, 560, 567, 759, 788, 804, 918, 970, 997, 999, 1000, 1003, 1016, 1099, 1218-20, 1252, 1279
theaters, Roman, 1219
Theocritus, 383, 686, 813, 814, 929, 1082
Theodotion, 679, 1102
Theodotus Inscription, 534
Theogony, 451, 467, 815-16, 919
Therapeutae, 289, 365, 682, 713, 1190-91, 1225, 1230-31
Thesaurus Linguae Graecae, 1084, 1285, 1288
Theseus, 9
Thessalonica, 98-99, 205, 228, 230, 285, 370, 426, 471, 787, 963, 985, 1151, 1231-33, 1279
Theudas, 46, 349, 585, 590, 596, 599, 834, 939-40, 1224, 1227
Tholomaus, 937
Thucydides, 405, 424, 427, 430, 500-501, 503-4, 519, 523, 590, 859, 919-20, 1066-67, 1072, 1077, 1079, 1081, 1083, 1211, 1270
Thunder Text, 261, 1234, 1251
Tiberias, 94, 275, 391, 393-96, 450, 468, 490, 534, 599, 916, 1047-48, 1235-37, 1247
Tiberius, 25, 32, 34, 98, 132, 141, 203, 220-21, 238, 289, 359, 396, 468, 490-92, 529, 538, 578, 630, 641, 688, 761, 789, 804, 829, 833, 928, 959, 964, 969, 972-73, 978, 980-82, 985, 995-96, 1000, 1011, 1014, 1016, 1081, 1085, 1142-44, 1158, 1162-64, 1235-36
Timaeus of Tauromenium, 502
Titans, 334, 722, 815-16, 818
Titus, 34, 52, 71, 111, 178, 215, 221, 233, 274-6, 283, 288, 323, 348, 371, 447, 534, 561, 586-87, 590, 596, 623, 759, 789, 807, 880, 939, 970, 971, 1005-7, 1011, 1142, 1157, 1255-56, 1282, 1293
Tobias, 571, 1238, 1240, 1296
Tobit, 3, 18-19, 58-59, 61, 69, 92, 129, 258, 270, 293, 349, 401, 456, 497, 609, 615, 625, 627, 685, 690, 742-43, 840, 853-54, 1094, 1095-96, 1100, 1102, 1104, 1238-41, 1296
tombs, 21, 74, 95, 97, 104, 105, 107, 109, 123, 126-8, 173-75, 179, 334-35, 395, 438, 443, 539, 653, 667, 680, 682, 739, 788, 870, 919, 921, 930, 943, 1097, 1236-37, 1258
Torah, 1241-45
Toubias the Ammonite, 1300-1301
towns, 23, 32, 99, 103, 106-7, 109, 125-26, 131, 139, 175-76, 178-79, 214, 225, 244, 249, 283, 304, 307, 311-12, 360, 393-94, 396, 476, 506, 558, 579, 611-12, 626, 707, 750, 795, 807-8, 810, 812, 819-20, 825, 828, 878, 915, 937, 961-62, 972, 974, 993, 995, 1001, 1008, 1021, 1047, 1056-57, 1131, 1142, 1146, 1149, 1151, 1165, 1224, 1236, 1247, 1300
trade, trading, 11, 23, 32, 105, 109-10, 115, 133, 136, 199-200, 213-14, 217, 219, 221-22, 248, 303, 307, 309, 312, 393-94, 422-24, 433, 472, 559, 572, 606, 613, 640-41, 645, 758, 766, 829, 887, 940, 971, 975, 978, 985, 1000-1002, 1045, 1086, 1125-26, 1132, 1162, 1175, 1181, 1187, 1245, 1247, 1276, 1278, 1284, 1301
Trajan, 25, 135, 142, 220, 236, 267, 268, 285, 295, 310, 397, 540, 569, 583, 584, 587-88, 767, 775, 777-78, 788, 803, 809-12, 886, 938, 971-73, 985, 989, 992, 995, 1011, 1029-30, 1081, 1142, 1157, 1221, 1237
Transjordan, 102, 107, 440, 617, 1060, 1235
travel, 68, 128, 132-33, 167, 216, 222, 228, 374, 405, 423, 523, 550, 642, 654, 828, 927, 977, 1003, 1031, 1044, 1073, 1165, 1208, 1210, 1245-49, 1284
travelogues, 1249
Treatise of Shem, 62, 860, 1250-51
trial of Jesus, 74, 1176
trials, 140, 150, 153, 339, 404, 662, 776, 810, 830, 942, 984, 986-87, 1064-65, 1121, 1210, 1238, 1274
Roman, 989, 999
tributum, 1162-64
triumph imagery, 221
triumph, Roman, 597, 1004-7
Tyros, 107
unclean, 78, 155, 175, 270-71, 490, 507, 549, 555, 710, 799, 873-76, 894, 896, 916, 1037, 1040, 1051, 1060, 1106, 1128, 1165, 1236
universalism, 471, 838, 1188-89, 1244, 1273
Unleavened Bread, feast of, 182, 372-74, 601, 798, 1043
upper classes, 136, 284, 312, 445, 480, 572, 645-46, 944-45, 977, 1000, 1003
Upper Galilee, 102, 303, 391
Uranos, 447, 815
values, 43, 111, 175, 197, 290, 301, 305, 307, 324, 339-40, 353, 358, 381, 407, 423, 432, 464, 466, 518-20, 538, 560, 588, 599, 645, 663, 687-88, 723, 726, 996, 1011, 1118, 1122, 1127, 1129, 1131, 1239, 1252-53, 1271
Varus, 393, 585, 938, 1193-94
Venus, 124, 199, 340, 922, 925, 972, 1163
Vespasian, 111, 221, 244, 274-76, 311, 371, 393, 397, 524, 534, 540, 586, 590, 596-97, 623, 699, 774, 834, 886, 915, 939, 964, 970, 995-96, 1004, 1011, 1081, 1113, 1166, 1235-36, 1293
Vesta, 370, 922-23, 1012
vestal virgin, 681
vestal virgins, 681
vices, vice lists, 2, 10, 54, 89, 155, 210, 228, 243-44, 249, 598-99, 663, 757, 761-62, 881-82, 970, 1121, 1201, 1252-55, 1296
villages, 24, 119, 134, 227, 239, 268, 318, 394-95, 397, 422-23, 433, 443, 476, 490, 506, 604, 611, 641, 686, 691, 765-66, 811, 877-78, 894, 915-16, 940, 962, 974, 1009, 1047, 1058, 1060, 1113, 1235, 1278, 1300, 1302
Vineyard Text, 1257
Virgil, 8-9, 14, 166, 310, 312, 331, 334, 354, 356-58, 360, 381, 444, 535, 594, 628-29, 631, 686-88, 708, 772, 814, 921, 923, 929, 969, 975, 1080, 1082, 1084, 1107-8, 1251, 1253
Visio Pauli, 39, 1190
Visions of Amram, 93, 155, 1200, 1257-58
voluntary associations, 136, 138, 300-301, 520, 924, 1130, 1222
Vulcan, 922
Vulgate, 58, 251, 341, 464, 747, 822, 1238
War Scroll, 30, 43, 49, 156, 250, 255, 332, 346, 349, 609, 636-37, 694, 743, 821, 839, 1025, 1114, 1217, 1260-63, 1297
water supply, 213, 582, 625, 871
weddings, 3, 11, 110, 299, 386, 685-86, 762, 900, 1026, 1049
weights, 110, 309, 480
wine, 34, 104, 108-9, 143, 182, 243, 304, 325, 335, 341, 376, 394, 396-97, 400, 636, 638, 661, 686, 694, 722-24, 777, 798, 801, 810, 866, 896, 913, 921, 1000-1001, 1007, 1030, 1036, 1038, 1040-41, 1043-44, 1065, 1086, 1107, 1118, 1132, 1177-78, 1180, 1230, 1257, 1277, 1280, 1301
wisdom literature, 63, 147, 911, 1224-25, 1263, 1265-67
Wisdom of Solomon, 2, 58, 59, 61, 69, 161, 163, 291, 333, 385, 509, 513, 556, 608, 821, 853-54, 860-61, 912, 1027, 1100, 1121, 1141, 1224, 1254, 1264, 1268, 1275, 1294
wisdom tradition, 46, 589, 757, 1263-64, 1266-68, 1275
women, 6-12, 14-15, 40, 52, 67, 120, 124, 154, 168, 197-98, 200, 222, 228, 240, 248, 263, 287, 314, 325-26, 341, 345, 350, 354, 359-62, 371, 393, 395, 416, 423, 436, 441-46, 470, 476, 541, 562, 565-66, 568, 592, 602, 606, 627-28, 632, 638, 641, 645, 651, 680, 682-91, 719, 722, 742, 75-58, 811, 825, 839, 841-42, 844, 846, 864, 866, 873, 887, 894, 925, 930, 934, 936, 982, 1003, 1008, 1021, 1025, 1032, 1036, 1041, 1048, 1051, 1082, 1121-22, 1129-31, 1146, 1161, 1166, 1168, 1191, 1202, 1208, 1220, 1232-33, 1236, 1276-80, 1285, 1287
women, Jewish, 470, 683, 690, 707, 764, 1276-77
women, Roman, 360, 444-45, 629, 689, 1277
wood offering, 182, 638, 1045
Words of Moses, 65, 259, 1259, 1281-82, 1290
Words of the Luminaries, 260, 821, 1217
works of the law, 710-11
Works of the Messiah, 695, 697
wrestling, 64, 141, 210, 372, 435
xenophobia, 523, 528
Xenophon, 9, 131, 167, 225, 303, 402, 404, 501-2, 523, 758, 761, 927-28, 1008-10, 1068, 1077-78, 1143, 1209, 1253, 1273
Yarkon, 104
Yavneh, 579, 784, 786, 896, 915-16, 1063, 1152, 1242
yelammedenu, 516-17
Yerushalmi, 613, 898, 1097
Zadokite Document, 246, 250, 639
Zadokite priests, 636, 875
zealots, 239, 945, 1176-77, 1244
Zenon papyri, 474, 571, 618, 872, 1300, 1302
Zeus, 8-9, 14, 24, 99, 103, 131, 140-41, 166, 220, 225, 302, 322-24, 355, 370, 397, 423, 447, 451, 524, 560, 619, 708, 760-62, 814-17, 831, 919, 922, 924, 926, 1004, 1068, 1093, 1140-41, 1225, 1282
zodiac, 123, 261, 450, 1148, 1169, 1234, 1251
Zoroastrianism, 41, 332

Articles Index

Adam and Eve, Literature Concerning, 1
Adultery, Divorce, 6
Affliction Lists, 16
Ahiqar, 18
Alexander the Great, 20
Alexandria, 23
Alexandrian Library, 25
Alexandrian Scholarship, 27
Angels of the Nations, 29
Antioch (Pisidia), 31
Antioch (Syria), 34
Apocalypse of Abraham, 37
Apocalypse of Zephaniah, 39
Apocalyptic Literature, 40
Apocalypticism, 45
Apocrypha and Pseudepigrapha, 58
Apocrypha of Moses (1Q29, 4Q374-377, 4Q408), 64
Apocryphal Acts and Epistles, 66
Apocryphal and Pseudepigraphical Sources in the New Testament, 69
Apocryphal Gospels, 71,
Apocryphon of Joseph (4Q371-373, 539), 78
Apocryphon of Joshua (4Q378-379), 79
Apollonius of Tyana, 80
Apostolic Fathers, 81
Aramaic Language, 86
Aramaic Targumim: Qumran, 91
Archaeology and the New Testament, 93
Archaeology of the Land of Israel, 100
Arenas, 111
Aristeas, Epistle of,114
Aristobulus, 118
Aristotle, Aristotelianism, 119
Art and Architecture: Greco-Roman, 121
Art and Architecture: Jewish, 125
Ascension of Isaiah, 129
Asia Minor, 130
Associations, 136
Athens, 139
Athletics, 140
Banquets, 143
Barki Nafshi (4Q434, 436, 437-439), 146
Baruch, Books of, 148
Beatitudes Text (4Q525), 151
Belial, Beliar, Devil, Satan, 1153
Benefactor, 157
Biblical Interpretation, Jewish, 159
Bibliomancy, 165
Biography, Ancient, 167
Birth of the Chosen One (4Q534), 170
Book of Blessings (1QSb), 171
Burial Practices, Jewish, 173
Caesarea Maritima, 176
Caesarea Philippi, 178
Caiaphas Ossuary, 179
Calendars, Jewish, 180
Canonical Formation of the New Testament, 183
Catena (4Q177), 195
Cave 7 Fragments (Qumran), 196
Children in Late Antiquity, 197
Chronology, New Testament, 201
Cicero, 208
Circuses and Games, 209
Cities, Greco-Roman, 212
Citizenship, Roman, 215
Civic Cults, 218
Coinage: Greco-Roman, 220
Coinage: Jewish, 222
Colossae, 225
Consolations/Tanhumim (4Q176), 226
Copper Scroll (3Q15), 227
Corinth, 229
Creeds and Hymns, 231
Cumanus, 238
Cynic Epistles, 239
Cynicism and Skepticism, 242
Damascus Document (CD and QD), 246
Daniel, Esther and Jeremiah, Additions to, 250
Dead Sea Scrolls: General Introduction, 252
Decapolis, 266
Demetrius, 268
Demonology, 269
Destruction of Jerusalem, 273
Diadochi, 278
Diaspora Judaism, 281
Diatribe, 296
Domestic Religion and Practices, 298
Economics of Palestine, 303
Education: Jewish and Greco-Roman, 308
Enoch, Books of, 313
Ephesus, 318
Epictetus, 321
Epicureanism, 324
Epistolary Theory, 327
Eschatologies of Late Antiquity, 330
Esdras, Books of, 337
1 Esdras, 341
Essenes, 342
Exile, 348
Family and Household, 353
Festivals and Holy Days: Greco-Roman, 368
Festivals and Holy Days: Jewish, 371
Florilegium (4Q174), 378
Friendship, 380
Galatia, Galatians, 389
Galilee, 391
Genesis Apocryphon (1QapGen), 398
Genres of the New Testament, 402
Geographical Perspectives in Late Antiquity, 411
Gnosticism, 414
Grammarians, Hellenistic Greek, 418
Greece and Macedon, 421
Greek of the New Testament, 426
Gymnasia and Baths, 433
Habakkuk Commentary (1QpHab), 437
Hasmoneans, 438
Head Coverings, 442
Heavenly Ascent in Jewish and Pagan Traditions, 447
Hebrew Bible, 452
Hebrew Language, 459
Hebrew Matthew, 463
Hellenism, 464
Hellenistic Egypt, 473
Hellenistic Judaism, 477
Hermeticism, 482
Herodian Dynasty, 485
Heroes, 494
Hillel, House of, 496
Hippocratic Letters, 498
Historians, Greco-Roman, 499
Holy Men, Jewish, 505
Holy Spirit, 507
Homily, Ancient, 515
Honor and Shame, 518
Hospitality, 522
Idolatry, Jewish Conceptions of, 526
Inscriptions and Papyri: Greco-Roman, 529
Inscriptions and Papyri: Jewish, 539
Intertextuality, Biblical, 541
Isaiah Scrolls (1QIsaiah$^{a, b}$), 551
Israel, Land of, 554
Jerusalem, 559
Jesus ben Ananias, 561
Jewish Communities in Asia Minor, 562
Jewish History: Greek Period, 570
Jewish History: Persian Period, 574
Jewish History: Roman Period, 576
Jewish Literature: Historians and Poets, 580
Jewish Wars with Rome, 584
Joseph and Aseneth, 588
Josephus: Interpretive Methods and Tendencies, 590
Josephus: Value for New Testament Study, 596
Jubilees, 600
Judaism and the New Testament, 603
Judea, 616
Judith, 624
Kissing, 628
Latin Language, 630
Law/Nomos in Greco-Roman World, 631
Legal Texts at Qumran, 636
Letters, Greco-Roman, 640
Literacy and Book Culture, 644
Liturgy: Qumran, 648
Liturgy: Rabbinic, 650
Lives of the Prophets, 652
Lucian of Samosata, 654
1 and 2 Maccabees, 657
3 and 4 Maccabees, 661
Magical Papyri, 666
Manuscripts, Greek New Testament, 670
Manuscripts, Greek Old Testament, 678
Maria the Jewish Alchemist, 679
Marriage, 680
Melchizedek, Traditions of (11QMelch), 693
Messianic Apocalypse (4Q521), 695
Messianism, 698
Milk, 707
Miqsat Ma'aśey Ha-Torah (4QMMT), 709
Music, 711
Musonius Rufus, 719
Mysteries, 720
Mysticism, 725
Narrative A (4Q458), 738
Neo-Pythagoreanism, 739
New Jerusalem Texts, 742
New Testament Versions, Ancient, 745
Odes of Solomon, 749
Old Testament Versions, Ancient, 752
Pagan Sources in the New Testament, 756
Papyri, Palestinian, 764
Patronage, 766
Pax Romana, 771
Persecution, 775
Pesharim, 778
Pharisees, 782
Philippi, 787
Philo, 789
Philosophy, 793
Piety, Jewish, 796
Pilate Inscription, 803
Plato, Platonism, 804
Pliny the Elder, 807
Pliny the Younger, 808
Plutarch, 812
Poetry, Hellenistic, 813
Polytheism, Greco-Roman, 815
Pompey, 818
Prayer of Enosh (4Q369 + 4Q458), 820
Prayer of Manasseh, 821
Prayer of Nabonidus (4Q242) and Pseudo-Daniel (4Q243-245), 822
Priests and Priesthood, Jewish, 824
Prison, Prisoner, 827
Prophets and Prophecy, 830
Proselytism and Godfearers, 835
Psalms and Hymns of Qumran, 847
Psalms of Solomon, 853
Pseudonymity and Pseudepigraphy, 857
Pseudo-Philo, 864
Pseudo-Phocylides, 868
Pseudo-Prophets (4Q385-388, 390-391), 869
Ptolemies, 870
Purification Texts (4Q274-279, 281-284, 512-514), 873
Purity, 874
Qumran: Place and History, 883
Rabbinic Literature: Midrashim, 889
Rabbinic Literature: Mishnah and Tosefta, 893
Rabbinic Literature: Talmud, 897
Rabbinic Literature: Targumim, 902

Rabbinic Parables, 909
Rabbinic Proverbs, 911
Rabbis, 914
Religion, Greco-Roman, 917
Religion, Personal, 926
Resurrection, 931
Revolutionary Movements, Jewish, 936
Rewritten Bible in Pseudepigrapha and Qumran, 947
Rhetoric, 953
Roman Administration, 959
Roman East, 962
Roman Emperors, 968
Roman Empire, 974
Roman Governors of Palestine, 978
Roman Law and Legal System, 984
Roman Military, 991
Roman Political System, 995
Roman Social Classes, 999
Roman Triumph, 1004
Romances/Novels, Ancient, 1008
Rome: Overview, 1010
Rule of the Community/Manual of Discipline (1QS), 1018
Rule of the Congregation/Messianic Rule (1QSa), 1024
Ruler Cult, 1026
Sabbath, 1031
Sacrifice and Temple Service, Jewish, 1036
Sadducees, 1050
Samaritan Literature, 1052
Samaritans, 1056
Sanhedrin, 1061
Scholarship, Greek and Roman, 1065
Scribes, 1086
Secret of Existence (4Q412-413, 415-421), 1090
Seleucids and Antiochids, 1092
Semitic Influence on the New Testament, 1093
Seneca, 1098
Septuagint/Greek Old Testament, 1099
Shammai, House of, 1106
Sibylline Oracles, 1107
Simon ben Kosiba, 1112
Sirach, 1116
Slavery, 1124
Social Values and Structures, 1127
Son of God Text (4Q246), 1134
Songs of the Sabbath Sacrifice (4Q400-407, 11Q17, Mas1k), 1137
Stoicism, 1139
Suetonius, 1142
Synagogues, 1145
Syriac Bible, 1154
Tacitus, 1157
Tale of Bagasraw (Pseudo-Esther) (4Q550^{a-f}), 1159
Taxation, Greco-Roman, 1161
Taxation, Jewish, 1163
Temple, Jewish, 1167
Temple Scroll (11QTemple), 1183
Temples, Greco-Roman, 1186
Testament of Abraham, 1188
Testament of Job, 1189
Testament of Moses, 1192
Testament of Qahat (4Q542), 1199
Testaments of the Twelve Patriarchs, 1200
Testimonia (4Q175), 1205
Testing and Trial in Secular Greek Thought, 1207
Textual Criticism, 1210
Thanksgiving Hymns (1QH), 1214
Theaters, 1218
Theologies and Sects, Jewish, 1221
Therapeutae, 1230
Thessalonica, 1231
Thunder Text (4Q318), 1233
Tiberias, 1235
Tobit, 1238
Torah, 1241
Travel and Trade, 1245
Treatise of Shem, 1250
Vice and Virtue Lists, 1252
Vineyard Text (4Q500), 1257
Visions of Amram (4Q543-548), 1257
War Scroll (1QM) and Related Texts, 1260
Wisdom Literature at Qumran, 1263
Wisdom of Solomon, 1268
Women in Greco-Roman World and Judaism, 1276
Words of Moses (1Q22), 1281
Writing and Literature: Greco-Roman, 1282
Writing and Literature: Jewish, 1289
Zenon Papyri, 1300